World War II EXTRA

An Around-the World Newspaper History from the Treaty of Versailles to the Nuremberg Trials

From the Eric C. Caren Collection

CASTLE BOOKS

Publisher's Note: Every effort has been made to contact the owners of the papers reprinted herein, and to obtain permissions where necessary, all of which are acknowledged.
In many cases, the papers are no longer in circulation or have transferred hands many times over.
We regret any inadvertent omissions.
We offer our deep appreciation for the many known and unknown publishers, reporters and photographers who worked diligently and often risked their lives to keep the home front informed.
We dedicate this book to their memory.

The materials in this book have been reproduced from old and exceedingly rare and valuable newspapers.
We believe that the articles and photographs herein are of such historic importance that an occasional lapse in the quality of reproduction is justified.

Published by Castle Books,
a division of Book Sales, Inc.
114 Northfield Avenue
Edison, NJ 08837, USA

Compiled by Eric C. Caren

ISBN 0-7858-1136-2
Printed in the United States of America

Contents

Note: Translations of foreign papers appear following the contents.

Page	Date	Publication	Headline
47	June 25, 1940	Daily Mirror (NY)	Fighting Ends In France, "Most Glorious Victory Of All Time," Says Hitler
48	June 27, 1940	Los Angeles Examiner — Extra	L.A. Nazi Agent Held By G-Men!
49	July 1, 1940	Evening Press (Island of Guernsey, U.K.)	Orders of the Commandant of the German Forces in Occupation of the Island of Guernsey. (These rules were set forth to the inhabitants to keep order.)
50	July 3, 1940	Bemidji Daily Pioneer (Bemidji, MN)	Nazis Step Up Battle For Britain
51	July 21, 1940	Baltimore American	British Repel Mass Air Raid
52	July 25, 1940	Der Danziger Dorposten Printed in German	
53	August 11, 1940	Los Angeles Examiner	Nazi Plane Rain Death Over Wide British Area
54	August 12, 1940	Los Angeles Examiner	500 Nazi Warplanes Repulsed By British!
55	August 13, 1940	Los Angeles Examiner	Total War On Britain! Invasion Due Hourly
56	August 15, 1940	The Call Bulletin (San Francisco)	Greatest Battle On! London Hit As Nazis Hurl 1000 War Planes
57	August 17, 1940	Der Danziger Dorposten Printed in German	
58-59	September 8, 1940	Sunday Chronicle (London, U.K.)	Bombs Rain Down After 'All Clear', Biggest London Raids
60	September 11, 1940	The Call Bulletin (San Francisco)	Nazis Moving To Invade Britain, Churchill Warns
61	September 12, 1940	The Times (London, U.K.)	Bomb Damage At Buckingham Palace
62	September 14, 1940	Los Angeles Examiner	Britain Invasion Attempts Revealed
63	September 27, 1940	The Call Bulletin (San Francisco)	Jap-Axis Pact Direct U.S. Threat!
64	October 3, 1940	New York Journal and American — Extra	Chamberlain Quits
	1941		
65	March 13, 1941	Evening Huronite (South Dakota)	German and British Cities Are Rocked In Violent Air Assaults
66	March 20, 1941	The Sun (Sydney, Australia)	Half A Million Cheer Americans
67	April 28, 1941	San Antonio Light (Texas)	Athens Catured By Nazis
68	May 13, 1941	Los Angeles Examiner — War Extra	Hitler Chief Deserts; Flees to Scotland!
69	May 13, 1941	The Call Bulletin (San Francisco)	Hess Faces Secret Grill By Churchill
70	May 25, 1941	Richmond Times-Dispatch	Britain's Hood, 42,100 Tons, Is Sunk By Nazi Warship Bismarck In Atlantic
71	May 27, 1941	Boston Traveler	Bismarck Sunk
72	May 27, 1941	The News-Sentinel (Fort Wayne, IN)	British Avenge Sinking Of Hood
73	June 22, 1941	The Sunday Star (Washington, DC)	Germany Declares War On Russians
74	June 30, 1941	Bangor Daily Commercial (Maine)	Nazis Seize Lwow, Minsk, Drive Half Way To Moscow
75	September 6, 1941	Pottsville Republican (Pottsville, PA)	Siege Guns Bombard, Set Leningrad Afire
76	November 14, 1941	The Williamsport Sun (Williamsport, PA)	Big British Aircraft Carrier Sunk
77	November 27, 1941	Tri-Cities Daily (Tuscumbia-Sheffield, AL)	Tobruk Garrison Fulfills Historic Mission
78	December 5, 1941	St. Paul Pioneer Press (MN)	Jap Answer Today: Break Near
79	December 7, 1941	Honolulu Star Bulletin	War! Oahu Bombed
80	December 8, 1941	Baltimore News-Post — Extra	Japs Bomb Pearl Harbor, Manila
81	December 8, 1941	Maui News (Hawaii)	U.S. Votes War! Congress Decision 470-1!
82	December 9, 1941	The Sun (NY)	Air Raid Alarms Are Sounded Here
83	December 11, 1941	Baltimore News-Post — War Extra	Germany, Italy Declare On the United States
	1942		
84	January 1, 1942	Japan Times & Advertiser (Tokyo) Japanese Propaganda Paper in English.	Brilliant War Results Revealed — Japanese celebrate Pearl Harbor bombing
85	January 2, 1942	The Chico Enterprise (Chico, CA)	Japs Capture Manila
86	January 2, 1942	Baltimore News-Post	Philippines Will Not Surrender — Stimson
87	January 4, 1942	Japan Times & Advertiser (Tokyo)	Japanese Enter Manila
88	January 4, 1942	The Japan Chronicle (Kobe, Japan)	Manila Falls
89	January 9, 1942	The Tokyo Nichi Nichi	His Majesty Reviews Army Units At Yoyogi
90	January 9, 1942	The Japan Chronicle (Kobe, Japan)	Hongkong Falls to the Japanese
91	January 31, 1942	The Call Bulletin (San Francisco)	British Quit Malaya! 'Dig In' at Singapore
92	February 13, 1942	The Tokyo Nichi Nichi	Annihilative Operations Open On Singapore I.
93	February 14, 1942	Chicago Daily News	Official Story of Dover Battle
94	February 16, 1942	Japan Times & Advertiser (Tokyo)	Premier Tojo Reports On Singapore Victory; Britain Hears Churchill In Shadow of Defeat
95	February 22, 1942	The Tokyo Nichi Nichi	Banzai! Rising Suns Fly Over City Of Lions
96	March 7, 1942	Japan Times & Advertiser — AM Edition	Nine War Heroes Revealed
97-98	March 7, 1942	Japan Times & Advertiser — Evening Edition	Japanese Forces Closing In On Naval Base At Surabaya
99	March 9, 1942	The San Francisco News	All East Indies Claimed by Japs
100	March 10, 1942	The Tokyo Nichi Nichi	Rangoon, Capital of Burma, Taken
101	March 18, 1942	Daily Telegraph (Sydney, Australia)	American Troops, Airmen Here— So Is General MacArthur
102	March 18, 1942	Los Angeles Examiner — Draft Extra	Gen. M'arthur Takes Australia Command
103	March 23, 1942	Roswell (New Mexico) Daily Record	A Broth of a Boy
104	March 26, 1942	Los Angeles Examiner	Jap Map 'Death Drive' Against Bataan Yanks

Page	Date	Publication	Headline
105	March 26, 1942	Portage Lake Mining Gazette (Houghton, MI)	Japan Reaches Out For India
106	March 28, 1942	Los Angeles Examiner	Waves Of Planes Raid Corregidor
107	March 30, 1942	Los Angeles Examiner	Bataan Drive Halted, Jap Boats Blasted!
108	April 4, 1942	The Karachi Daily (Pakistan)	The First Attack From India
109	April 10, 1942	Sitka Sentinel (Alaska)	Bataan Captured
110	April 18, 1942	The Chicago Sun	Tokyo Is Bombed, Reports Jap Radio
111	May 3, 1942	Sunday Mirror (NY)	Japs Halted Near China
112	May 7, 1942	Daily Mirror (NY)	7,000 Taken In Fall Of Corregidor
113	May 7, 1942	The Call Bulletin (San Francisco)	U.S. Sinks 7 Japan Warships In Pacific
114	May 9, 1942	Los Angeles Examiner	Jap Fleet Routed
115	May 11, 1942	Japan Times & Advertiser (Tokyo)	America Hit By Unrest Wave As Coral Sea Result Hidden: London Doubting U.S. Claims
116	May 12, 1942	The Tokyo Nichi Nichi	Myitkyina, N. Burma, Taken by Nippon Forces
117	May 13, 1942	Japan Times & Advertiser (Tokyo)	Sinking Of The Saratoga and Yorktown
118	May 18, 1942	San Francisco Chronicle	Russians Win Great Victory At Kharkov!
119	May 31, 1942	Sunday Mirror (NY)	British Take Offensive In Libya Battle
120	June 1, 1942	Watertown Public Opinion (S. Dakota)	Greatest Raid Hits Cologne
121	June 1, 1942	Daily Mirror (NY)	Record Raid: 1,250 Planes Ruin Cologne
122	June 2, 1942	The Sun (NY)	Essen Is Set Ablaze By 1036 R.A.F. Planes
123	June 4, 1942	Los Angeles Examiner — War Extra	Second Attack Made On Alaska
124	June 8, 1942	Baltimore News-Post	U.S. Victory At Midway Puts Japs On Defensive
125	June 13, 1942	The Tribune (Manila, Philippines)	Navy Controls Pacific
126	June 21, 1942	Herald American (Chicago)	First Photos - Jap Midway Rout
127	June 22, 1942	The Philadelphia Inquirer	British Surrender Tobruk To Nazis
128	June 25, 1942	New York Journal American	Churchill, FDR Decide War Plans
129	June 28, 1942	Los Angeles Examiner	Nazi Saboteurs Landed In N.Y. and Florida By Subs; 8 Seized
130	July 2, 1942	Baltimore News-Post	Tobruk 2D Dunkirk Churchill Reveals
131	July 2, 1942	Daily Mirror (NY)	Sevastopol Captured, Nazis Claim
132	July 3, 1942	Baltimore News-Post - Extra	Rommel Retreating
133	July 4, 1942	The Call Bulletin - Extra (San Francisco)	British Counter-Attack! Airmen Batter Rommel
134	July 25, 1942	The Call Bulletin (San Francisco)	Five Jap Ships Sunk
135	August 3, 1942	Illustrated Current News (New Haven, CT)	General Stilwell's Retreat From Burma
136	August 8, 1942	Germaneren (Oslo, Norway) German Occupation paper in Norwegian	
137	August 10, 1942	New York World-Telegram	U.S. Lands On Solomons
138	August 14, 1942	The Jewish News (Detroit, MI)	Britain Grants Jews Palestine Regiment
139	August 19, 1942	Los Angeles Examiner	Dieppe Attacked
140	August 25, 1942	Deutsche Ukraine-Zeitung Printed in German	
141	August 30, 1942	Deutsche Ukraine-Zeitung Printed in German	
142	September 11, 1942	Illustrated Current News (New Haven, CT)	Battle Of Midway
143	September 18, 1942	Clinton Daily Journal and Public (IL)	Battle Ranging In Streets Of Stalingrad
144	September 24, 1942	The Tribune-Telegraph (Pomeroy, OH)	'Let's Go, Young America!"
145	October 1, 1942	The Hobo News (NY)	2nd Front To Ram Axis
146	October 28, 1942	Daily Mirror (NY)	Japs Hurled Back On Guadalcanal
147	November 1, 1942	Sunday Pictorial (U.K.)	"Monty" Attacks In Egypt Once More
148	November 8, 1942	Oakland Tribune (CA)	U.S. Army Opens Second Front By Invading French West Africa
149	November 9, 1942	Los Angeles Examiner - War Extra	Yanks Win Algiers, Surrender Signed!
150	November 10, 1942	Baltimore News-Post	U.S. Troops Take Oran, Casablanca Entered
151	November 11, 1942	Baltimore News-Post	All French N. Africa Capitulates to U.S.
152	November 15, 1942	Los Angeles Examiner	Fleets Fighting for Solomons, Rickenbacker Saved At Sea
153	November 17, 1942	Baltimore News-Post	U.S. Navy In Control At Guadalcanal — Knox
154	November 25, 1942	Philadelphia Daily News	Stalingrad Siege Broken: Nazis Flee
155	November 27, 1942	Columbus Evening Dispatch (OH)	French Scuttle Fleet
156	December 11, 1942	The Jewish News (Detroit, MI)	Ghetto Jews Killed In Battle With Nazis
	1943		
157	1943	The Scrapper	A Publication For the Men and Women who Are Aiding Their Country in the Salvage for Victory Program
158	January 6, 1943	Oakland Tribune (CA)	500,000 Germans In Full Retreat
159	January 15, 1943	Illustrated Current News (New Haven, CT)	The Hornet Dies
160	January 23, 1943	Oakland Tribune (CA)	Tripoli Falls To British
161	January 27, 1943	Volkischer Beobachter (Munich) Printed in German	
162	January 27, 1943	San Francisco Chronicle - Extra	FDR Flies To Africa, Meets With Churchill
163	January 30, 1943	Deutsche Ukraine-Zeitung (Luzk, Ukraine) Printed in German	

Page	Date	Publication	Headline
164	February 9, 1943	Oakland Tribune (CA)	Shattered Japs Quit Guadalcanal
165	February 13, 1943	TAM (French Algiers) Printed in French	
166	March 9, 1943	Soviet Sahaline Printed in Russian	To Comrade Stalin—Official Order Making Stalin Marshall.
167	March 29, 1943	Baltimore News-Post	Marethline Collapses, Rommel's Army Flees
168	March 30, 1943	Coldwater Daily Reporter (Coldwater, MI)	British Forces Capture Gages and El Hamma
169	April 9, 1943	The Stars and Stripes - Africa	Yanks, British 8th Army Meet; Allies Swing North After Rommel
170	April 10, 1943	The Circuit - U.S. Edition (Sagan, Germany)	POW paper printed in German prison camp for American soldiers.
171	May 14, 1943	Tripoli Times - North Africa's First English Daily	Final African Defeat
172	June 4, 1943	Union Jack (French North Africa) — British Troop Paper	Giraud-De Gaulle Accord Complete
173	June 17, 1943	Union Jack Evening Paper / Tunis Telegraph (Tunisia)	The King In North Africa To See His Armies
174	July 2, 1943	San Francisco Chronicle	Big Air Victory! Jap Harbor Taken
175	July 10, 1943	The Stars and Stripes (Africa)	Sicily Invaded
176	July 17, 1943	The Informer (Houston, TX)	Tuskagee Flyers Get 1st Plane
177	July 26, 1943	Los Angeles Examiner	Mussolini Out! Axis Split Seen
178	July 28, 1943	Illustrated Current News (New Haven, CT)	U.S. Generals At Gela
179	August 2, 1943	Illustrated Current News (New Haven, CT)	Time Out For Laughs
180	August 21, 1943	The Noordam News "Somewhere in the Pacific"	Japs On The Run In New Guinea
181	August 23, 1943	Kingston Daily Freeman (Kingston, NY)	Hitler's Armies Leave Kharkov Stronghold
182	August 27, 1943	Illustrated Current News (New Haven, CT)	Yanks Charge Main Street
183	September 3, 1943	Daily Mirror - Extra (NY)	Allies Land In Italy
184	September 8, 1943	Boston Traveler	Italy Quits!
185	September 19, 1943	Baltimore American	Now For Hitler!
186	September 21, 1943	The Evening Star (Washington, DC)	Marshall Slated As Global Commander
187	October 13, 1943	Boston Traveler	Italy Declares War On Germany
188	November 6, 1943	The Stars and Stripes - Africa	Allies Crumble Nazi Line
189	November 10, 1943	The Stars and Stripes - Combat Edition	Reds Move Fifty Miles Beyond Kiev. Nazis Crumble Under Soviet Tanks
190	November 22, 1943	Kingston Daily Freeman (Kingston, NY)	U.S. Forces, Ashore In Two Gilbert Islands, Batter Japanese Defenses; Reds Halt Nazis
191	November 26, 1943	Illustrated Current News (New Haven, CT)	Mountbatten Inspects Guard In Chungking
192	December 1943	La France en Armes	
	December 1, 1943	Liberation	French Resistance newspapers (in French)
193	December 2, 1943	The Grand Saline Sun (TX)	Bonds Or Bondage
194	December 23, 1943	Baltimore News-Post	Death On Tarawa
195-6	December 24, 1943	Baltimore News-Post	1300 U.S. Planes Raid France, Eisenhower To Lead Invasion Of Europe
197	December 24, 1943	Los Angeles Examiner	Super-Blitz Smashes Berlin
	1944		
198	January 24, 1944	The Stars and Stripes - Mediterranean	Rome, Nazi Rear Menaced As Fifth Extends Beachhead
199	January 28, 1944	Los Angeles Examiner	Japs Slay, Torture Bataan Prisoners
200	February 4, 1944	The Stars and Stripes - Mediterranean	Ten German Divisions Trapped In The Ukraine
201	Febrary 21, 1944	Los Angeles Examiner	19 Jap Ships Sunk; 201 Planes Downed At Truk
202	March 11, 1944	Heart Mountain Sentinel (Wyoming)	Japanese Internment Camp Newspaper in English Supreme Court Considers Korematsu Case Petition
203	April 6, 1944	Panzer Voran	Tank Divison newspaper in German
204	April 11, 1944	The Stars and Stripes - Mediterranean	Russians Take Odessa, Nazi Ukraine Foothold
205	April 17, 1944	Illustrated Current News (New Haven, CT)	British Industry "Digs In" For Safety
206	April 28, 1944	Illustrated Current News (New Haven, CT)	"Commando" Kelly Greets Mother and "Clan"
207	May 18, 1944	The Call Bulletin (San Francisco)	Pass Cassino! Double Victory
208	May 27, 1944	The Guinea American (Troop paper from New Guinea)	5th Reaches "Anzio"
209	June 5, 1944	Daily Record (Boston, MA)	Rome Falls, First Photo of Yanks in Eternal City
210	June 6, 1944	The Boston Herald	Great Invasion Started
211	June 6, 1944	San Francisco Chronicle	Invasion - Allied Arnies Are Landing In North France!
212	June 7, 1944	New York World-Telegram	Beachheads Expanded
213	June 7, 1944	Revaler Zeitung Printed in German	
214	June 7, 1944	Herald Express (Los Angeles)	Allies Clear Beach; Sky Troops Battle

Page	Date	Publication	Headline
215	June 7, 1944	The Guinea American (New Guinea)	Invasion
216-7	June 12, 1944	New York World-Telegram	Crack Cherbourg Line
218-9	June 18, 1944	Yank (British Edition)	Merrill's Marauders in Burma
220	June 16, 1944	Chicago Daily News	Secret Robot Bombs Rain Fire On England
221	June 19, 1944	Reveille - The Services' Newspaper	
222	June 22, 1944	The Chicago Daily News	Rout Japan Fleet!
223	July 8, 1944	Der Rufer (SS Troop Newspaper in German)	
224	July 10, 1944	The Stars and Stripes - Mediterranean	Allies Take Caen, La Haye
225	July 10, 1944	Los Angeles Examiner - War Extra	Saipan Falls
226	July 20, 1944	Baltimore News-Post	Hitler Escapes Assassin Burned, Bruised By Bomb
227	July 20, 1944	The Chicago Daily News	Try To Kill Hitler!
228	July 21, 1944	New York Journal American	Report Revolt in Nazi Army, Yanks Land On Guam
229	August 6, 1944	Sunday Graphics (U.K.)	Big German Retreat
230	August 6, 1944	Sunday Pictorial (U.K.)	Big News! Russians Are Fighting On German Soil
231	August 23, 1944	Boston American - Victory Extra	Paris Falls
232	August 23, 1944	Los Angeles Examiner - War Extra	Yanks Head For Reich
233	August 24, 1944	The Sniper (U.S. Troop paper from France)	Paris-Marseilles Freed-Rumania Joins Allies!
234	August 25, 1944	L'aube Printed in French	
235	August 25, 1944	The Sun (NY)	DeGaulle In Paris; German Commander Surrenders Capital
236	August 26, 1944	The Chicago Sun	First Story Of Yanks In Paris: Cheers, Flags, Flowers, Bullets
237	August 27, 1944	Pariser-Zeitung Printed in German	
238	September 1, 1944	Daily Mirror (London)	We Strike Out Again
239	September 1, 1944	The Sun (NY)	Verdun Falls To Patton's Men
240	September 5, 1944	The Stars and Stripes - Mediterranean	Allied Armor Frees Brussels
241	September 6, 1944	The Stars and Stripes - Mediterranean	Yanks In Germany
242	September 7, 1944	Daily Mirror (U.K.)	Black-Out Off
243	September 10, 1944	Yank - The Army Weekly (British Edition)	Report on Joe DiMaggio in the Service
244	September 12, 1944	Daily Mirror (U.K.)	130 (Luftwaffe Planes) Shot Down
245	September 14, 1944	Baltimore News-Post	Yank 1st Army Tanks, Infantry Stream Into Reich Near Aachen
246	September 28, 1944	Daily Mirror (U.K.)	Night Retreat Ends Hell At Arnhem
247	October 15, 1944	Beachhead News (Souvenir Edition)	Founded on the Anzio Beachhead — 6th Corps Drives Through France
248	October 20, 1944	Baltimore News-Post	600-Ship Armada Took 250,000 To Philippines
249	October 21, 1944	The Stars and Stripes - Europe	MacArthur Goes Back; Aachen Falls To 1st Army
250	October 23, 1944	Brooklyn Eagle	Leyte Japs Flee To Hills; East Coast Bastion Falls
251	October 25, 1944	Baltimore News-Post - Extra	Jap Fleet Routed Roosevelt Announces
252	November 4, 1944	The Stars and Stripes - Europe	All Belgium Is Liberated
253	November 8, 1944	New York World-Telegram	Roosevelt Wins 4th Term
254	November 16, 1944	J B Printed in German	Cover Portrait of Rommel
255	November 20, 1944	Illustrated Current News (New Haven, CT)	Pass The Ammunition
256	November 27, 1944	The Stars and Stripes - Mediterranean	Alexander New MTO Chief
257	December 18, 1944	Baltimore News-Post	Nazis Drive Yanks Back In Belgium, Luxembourg
258	December 19, 1944	Baltimore News-Post	Nazi Counterattack In Belgium Rolls On
259	December 28, 1944	The Daily Sketch (London)	Bastogne Is Freed
260	December 29, 1944	New York Journal American	Smash Nazi Bulge
	1945		
261	January 11, 1945	The Call Bulletin (San Francisco)	Army to Draft All Fit Under 30, Luzon Battle On
262	January 18, 1945	The Stars and Stripes - Mediterranean	Red Army Takes Warsaw
263	February 13, 1945	The Stars and Stripes - Mediterranean	Big Three Map Victory, Insist On Unconditional Surrender
264	February 16, 1945	The Sun (NY)	1500 U.S. Planes Batter Tokyo For 9 Hours
265	February 21, 1945	The Sun (NY)	3500 U.S. Marines Casualties On Iwo
266	February 23, 1945	Baltimore News-Post	Iwo Peak Captured
267	February 25, 1945	Sunday News (Daily News, NY)	Our Flag Flies Over Suribachi
268	February 21, 1945	Illustrated Current News (New Haven, CT)	Burma and Ledo Roads Joined
269	March 1, 1945	Das Schwarze Korps (Berlin) Printed in German	
270	March 6, 1945	Chicago Daily News	Cologne Is Ours
271	March 8, 1945	Los Angeles Examiner	Patton Reaches Rhine
272	March 16, 1945	Chicago Daily News	Bitter Iwo Battle Won
273	March 20, 1945	The Call Bulletin (San Francisco)	Patton Bags 50,000 In Big Saar Smash
274	March 24, 1945	Boston Traveler	6 Allied Armies Across Rhine
275	April 1, 1945	Grapevine (26th Infantry Division) "Somewhere in Germany"	YD Whips Over Rhine
276	April 2, 1945	Los Angeles Examiner	100,000 Invade Jap Isle

Page	Date	Publication	Headline
277	April 7, 1945	Herald Express - the Saturday Pictorial (Los Angeles, CA)	Japan's Biggest Battleship Sunk
278	April 13, 1945	Philadelphia Record	Roosevelt Is Dead
279	April 20, 1945	Warm Springs Mirror (Meriwether, GA)	President Franklin Delano Roosevelt Died at the "Little White House" Thursday, April 12
280	April 24, 1945	Los Angeles Examiner	Atrocity Victims
281	April 28, 1945	The Journal (U.S. 95th Division — in Germany)	Red, Yanks Link Up
282	April 28, 1945	Times Herald (Washington, DC)	Germany Surrenders (President Truman officially denies rumor at 10pm, April 28.)
283	April 29, 1945	The Tomahawk "Somewhere In Germany"	743rd Tank Bn. Shermans Blast Nazis Since H-Hour
284	April 30, 1945	Daily Mirror	Mussolini Executed With Mistress
285	May 4, 1945	Crimen Printed in Italian	Mussolini's Corpse On Display
286	May 1, 1945	Times Herald (Washington, DC)	"Farewell, A Long Farewell To All My Greatness!" — Hitler
287-8	May 2, 1945	Los Angeles Examiner	Hitler Is Dead!
289	May 2, 1945	Baltimore News-Post	Berlin Falls
290	May 3, 1945	Il Popolo Comasco Printed in Italian	The War In Italy Is Ended
291	May 4, 1945	Baltimore News-Post	Nazis Surrender in N.W. Germany, Holland, Denmark — Eisenhower
292	May 5, 1945	Daily Mirror (U.K.)	Fighting Ends On British Front, Triumph Day for Monty's Men
293	May 5, 1945	The Montreal Daily Star (Canada)	Guns Stilled in Northwest Europe
294	May 8, 1945	The Morning Call (Paterson, NJ)	European War is Over!
295	May 9, 1945	Daily Mirror (U.K.)	Britain's Day of Rejoicing (Note Churchill in the center of the throng.)
296	May 9, 1945	Die Mitteilungen	Allied Newspaper for German Civilians Printed in German
297	May 9, 1945	Baltmore News-Post	Yanks Capture Goering
298	May 11, 1945	The Call Bulletin (San Francisco)	B-29's Deal 3 Blows To Jap Home Isles
299	May 12, 1945	Heart Mountain Sentinel (Heart Mountain, Wyoming)	Japanese-American internment camp newspaper
300	May 20, 1945	Baltimore American	Okinawa Japs Stall 4 American Divisions
301	May 25, 1945	Guerilla (Manila, Philippines)	Gestapo Chief Himmler Kills Self
302	May 29, 1945	Baltimore News-Post	Yokohama Burning After Big B-29 Raid
303	May 29, 1945	Chicago Daily News	Capture Lord Haw Haw
304	June 3, 1945	The Boston Herald	Halsey Blasts "Suicide" Bases
305	June 21, 1945	Baltimore New-Post	Nimitz Announces Victory On Okinawa
306	June 22, 1945	Los Angeles Evening Herald Express	Hitler's Super-Aryan Baby Factory (Eva Braun) Found In Germany
307	July 17, 1945	Chicago Daily News	Truman, Stalin Confer
308	August 6, 1945	Boston Traveler	Atomic Bomb Hurled At Japs
309	August 8, 1945	Baltimore News-Post	Russ Declare War On Japan
310	August 9, 1945	Oak Ridge Journal (Oak Ridge, TN)	Workers Thrill As Atomic Bomb Secret Breaks
311	August 9, 1945	Cherokee Daily Times (Cherokee, IA)	Second Atomic Bombing Hits Nagasaki
312	August 12, 1945	Nippon Times (Tokyo)	U.S. President's Speech Bare Use Of New Bomb
313	August 14, 1945	Waterloo Daily Courier (Waterloo, IA)	PEACE!
314	August 15, 1945	The China Lantern (China)	Japan Quits!
315	August 16, 1945	Daily Pacifican	MacArthur Commands Japan
316	August 16, 1945	Nippon Times (Tokyo)	Truman Issues Details Regarding Atomic Bomb
317	August 21, 1945	Nippon Times (Tokyo)	Imperial Armed Forces Ordered To Cease Fight
318	September 5, 1945	Illustrated Current News (New Haven, CT)	Japs Sign Surrender Papers
319	September 6, 1945	The Chungking Reporter (Chungking, China)	Japanese Surrender Ceremony In Nanking Postponed To Sep. 9
320	September 1, 1945	Der Ruf	German POW camp paper printed in the U.S. in German
321	September 7, 1945	Illustrated Current News (New Haven, CT)	What Atomic Bombs Did To Hiroshima and Nagasaki
322	September 11, 1945	New York Journal American	Tojo Shoots Self To Evade Arrest
323	September 17, 1945	National Herald (Chungking, China)	Disarming Of Jap Troops In S'hai To Be Completed Today
324	November 17, 1945	Tiger Rag (Bengal Air Depot)	Flying Tigers Newspaper
325	October 6, 1945	Chicago Daily News	'Belsen Beast' Admits Crimes
326	October 1, 1946	Daily Mirror (NY)	Goering To Die!

Translated Texts

Page FRENCH NEWSPAPERS

165 February 13, 1943 *TAM* Daily Journal of the French Empire (French Algiers). The Glorious Meeting – A day with General Leclerc, Hero of the Army of Chad. Photo Caption: In the service of France, a glorious Moslem soldier.

192 December 1943 *La France en Armes* France in Battle. Mobilization bulletin. We shall achieve Victory.
December 1, 1943 *Liberation* Liberation. One leader: De Gaulle. One struggle: For Liberty. Unity of the Nation. French Resistance newspapers.

234 August 25, 1944 *L'aube* The Dawn. Paris is Liberated / Long Live France! Long Live de Gaulle!
The Republic will be proclaimed at the City Hall. French and allied forces entered the city last night.

ITALIAN NEWSPAPERS

6 July 16, 1935 / *Corriere della Sera* (Milan) Daily newspaper. Fascist Italy's Unbending Policy; New Military Measures Taken for East Africa.
The Duce Orders the Mobilization of the "Sila" Division and of the V Black Shirt. 1st of February / The reconstitution of all the military formations to be sent to East. Africa; the formation of a new division, "Sila II;" the call up of aviators, engineering specialists, and automotive mechanics from the classes of 1909, 1910, and 1911; the immediate construction of ten new submarines.

290 May 3, 1945 / *Il Popolo Comasco* / The War in Italy is Over! Russians completely occupy Berlin.
The remnants of the nazi forces have been cleared from Italian territory.

285 May 4, 1945 / *Crimen* / Mussolini's Corpse On Display. *"Il Maledetto Sangue dei Traditori"* : The cursed blood of the traitors.

RUSSIAN NEWSPAPER

166 March 9, 1943 Soviet Sahaline. To Comrade Stalin—Official Order Making Stalin Marshal.
The Soviet Sakhalin: The organ of the Sakhalin Region and of the Regional Council of Deputies of Labor. Tuesday, March 9, 1943.
Next to masthead title: With great joy, the entire Soviet people greet the news about the award of the rank of Marshall of the Soviet Union to Commander in Chief Comrade Stalin. Under the leadership of the Great Stalin, onward, to victory!
To the right of photo: "To Comrade Stalin" Our dear father, friend, teacher, and leader, Joseph Stalin! Siberian women, wives, mothers, and sisters of front-line soldiers, from Stakhan collective farms and factories, engineers and technicians, doctors, teachers, artists, writers – we are gathering at the regional congress to address you with all our hearts.

GERMAN NEWSPAPERS

9 September 26, 1937 *Volkischer Beobachter* The People's Observer. September 25th The Historic Day / Germany Salutes the Duce!
The Newest Recruit: Benito Mussolini.

11 March 14, 1938 *H F am Montag* H F on Monday / Hamburg Foreign News. Headline: The Union is Announced /The Fuhrer Inducts the Austrian Military. The Vote in Austria on April 10 / The Induction into the Reich. The Austrian Military in the German Armed Forces.

13 September 29, 1938 *Münchner Illustrierte Presse* The Munich Illustrated Press. Historic World Meeting. The Fuhrer Meets Chamberlain in Godesberg.

21 September 2, 1939 *Volkischer Beobachter* The People's Observer. Hitler announces the invasion of Poland in the official Nazi party newspaper.
The Fuhrer announces the Struggle for Empire, Law, and Safety. Press Forward with the Counterattack / The Demands of the Hour.
The First Successes of Our Armed Forces. The Exact Words of the Brilliant Speech.

25 September 13, 1939 *Die Wehrmacht* (Berlin). Hitler: "I will now be nothing but the first soldier of the German Reich."

45 *Der Feuerreiter* (Cologne, Germany) NB: *Feuerreiter* is a phantom horseman who puts out fires. The Leaders of Both Nations now stand shoulder to shoulder in battle for European order. Photograph taken during the meeting of the leaders in Rome.

57 August 17, 1940 *Danziger Dorposton* The Danzig Outpost. The Strength of the Bomb Squadron in Southeast England.
Our battle group, the Bombardier Squadron, accompanied by fighter planes and destroyers, bombed the southeast coast and southern interior of England. Due to bad weather the air campaign was restricted. More than forty shot down.

136 August 8, 1942 *Germaneren* (Oslo, Norway) / German Occupation paper in Norwegian. German troops triumph in the East.

140 August 25, 1942 *Deutsche Ukraine-Zeitung* German-Ukraine Newspaper. Enemy opposition shattered at the Don crossing and in Stalingrad.
Successful battle in the Caucasus began with an attack on a strategically important Soviet military base. / The Netherlands are also protected.

141 August 30, 1942 *Deutsche Ukraine-Zeitung*. Dieppe will mark the beginning of the conquest of Paris.
OKW reveals British intentions and lies. Operation plans in our hands – evidence of a great German victory. The Fuhrer is thanked for reconstruction work in the Ukraine. / Caption over photo at bottom: The English failure at Himmel.

161 January 27, 1943 *Volkischer Beobachter* (Munich) The People's Observer. Heroic opposition in the ruins of Stalingrad. Support from our air force despite heavy artillery.

163 January 30, 1943 *Deutsche Ukraine-Zeitung* (Luzk, Ukraine) German-Ukraine Newspaper. All Strength for the Work of the Fuhrer
The 10th year of the National Socialist Revolution

203 April 6, 1944 *Panzer Voran* Front Line Panzer (Tank Divison newspaper in German). Our army destroys the place where they are trapped. The battles of our Panzer Army from March 23 to April 6, 1944. Our answer to the attack: General Hube and his squadrons in battle. German broadcasts.

213 June 7, 1944 *Revaler Zeitung* Revaler Newspaper. The Invasion has begun. Our defense is immediate. Surprise attacks fail.
Heavy battles on the coast between Le Havre and Cherbourg.

223 July 8, 1944 *Der Rufer* (SS Troop Newspaper in German) The Caller. For the troops of the Heidelager training camp.
Decision about weapons: "New and unusual ones are on the way." Hypocritical Plutocracy.

237 August 27, 1944 *Pariser-Zeitung* Paris Newspaper. German Occupation Newspaper, Paris. Confusion under French Terrorists "Street Fighting in Paris" Also in Marseilles and Toulon / the outcome in Seinebogen / The Battle on the Seine New positions.
taken. Enemy Operations thwarted.

254 November 16, 1944 *J B*. Photo Caption: Field Marshall Rommel on November 15.
"A few have fallen. The victory of the nation is secure." These words of General Field Marshall Rommel inspired the entire German people.

269 March 1, 1945 *Das Schwarze Korps* (Berlin) The Black Corps.
Newspaper of the SS of the NSDAP – Soldiers of Europe – Defend Yourselves!

296 May 9, 1945 *Die Mitteilungen* The Statement. Allied Newspaper for German Civilians. Germany Surrenders. The War in Europe Ended at Midnight on May 8th. Gratitude of the King of England / The British Prime Minister Speaks.

322 September 1, 1945 *Der Ruf* The Clarion (or The Call). German POW camp paper. Printed in the U.S. in German.
The Newspaper of German prisoners of War in the USA. Potsdam; A communication zone Germany to the conference.
Double Deathblow against Japan. The Soviet Union has declared war on Japan.

Credits and Permissions

The Montreal Gazette: May 5, 1945 (The Montreal Daily Star) Guns Stilled in Northwest Europe. The Victoria Times Colonist (British Columbia): October 14, 1939 (Victoria Daily News) 16,000 In 1st Canada Division To Go Overseas In 2 Months. The Daily Mirror (London): September 1, 1944 We Strike Out Again; September 7, 1944 Black-Out Off; September 12, 1944 130 (Luftwaffe Planes) Shot Down; September 28, 1944 Night Retreat Ends Hell At Arnheim; May 4, 1945 Fighting Ends On British Front; May 5, 1945 Triumph for Monty's Men; May 9, 1945 Britain's Day of Rejoicing; and October 1, 1938 (Daily Herald) Mr. Chamberlain Declares, "It is Peace For Our Time." The Times (London): June 5, 1940 Leaving Dunkirk: "Out of the Jaws of Death;" June 19, 1940 Parliament "Our Inflexible Resolve" –Churchill; September 12, 1940 Bomb Damage At Buckingham Palace. The Tri-Cities Daily (Tuscumbia-Sheffield, AL): November 27, 1941 Tobruk Garrison Fulfills Historic Mission. The Daily Sitka Sentinel (Sitka, AK): April 10, 1942 (Sitka Sentinel) Bataan Captured The Chico Enterprise Record (Chico, CA) January 2, 1942 (The Chico Enterprise) Japs Capture Manila The Oakland Tribune (Oakland, CA): November 8, 1942 U.S. Army Opens Second Front By Invading French West Africa; January 6, 1943 500,000 Germans In Full Retreat; January 23, 1943 Tripoli Falls To British; February 9, 1943 Shattered Japs Quit Guadalcanal. The San Francisco Chronicle: March 15, 1939 Hitler Grabs Czech Nation!; May 18, 1942 Russians Win Great Victory At Kharkov!; January 27, 1943 FDR Flies To Africa, Meets With Churchill; July 2, 1943 Big Air Victory! Jap Harbor Taken; June 6, 1944 Invasion – Allied Armies Are Landing In North France! The San Francisco Examiner: May 8, 1939 Hitler, Duce In War Pact. The Marlin Company (Illustrated Current News, New Haven, CT): August 3, 1942 General Stilwell's Retreat From Burma; September 11, 1942 Battle Of Midway; January 15, 1943 The Hornet Dies; July 28, 1943 U.S. Generals At Gela; August 2, 1943 Time Out For Laughs; August 27, 1943 Yanks Charge Main Street; November 26, 1943 Mountbatten Inspects Guard In Chungking; April 17, 1944 British Industry "Digs In" For Safety; April 28, 1944 "Commando" Kelly Greets Mother and "Clan;" November 20, 1944 Pass The Ammunition; February 21, 1945 Burma and Ledo Roads Joined; September 7, 1945 What Atomic Bombs Did To Hiroshima and Nagasaki. The Atlanta Journal & Constitution: October 4, 1938 (Atlanta Constitution) 'You are Germans Forever,' Hitler Cries As Sudetenland Acclaims Its 'Liberator.' The Honolulu Star Bulletin: December 7, 1941 War! Oahu Bombed The Maui News: December 8, 1941 U.S. Votes War! Congress Decision 470-1! The News-Sentinel (Fort Wayne, Indiana): May 27, 1941British Avenge Sinking Of Hood. The Clinton Daily & Weekly Journal (Clinton, IL): September 18, 1942 (Clinton Daily Journal and Public Record) Battle Ranging In Streets Of Stalingrad. The Cherokee Daily Times (Cherokee, IA): August 9, 1945 Second Atomic Bombing Hits Nagasaki. The Courier Waterloo (Cedar Falls, IA): August 14, 1945 (Waterloo Daily Courier) PEACE! The Boston Herald: June 6, 1944 Great Invasion Started; June 3, 1945 Halsey Blasts "Suicide" Bases; May 27, 1941(Boston Traveler) Bismarck Sunk; September 8, 1943 (Boston Traveler) Italy Quits!; October 13, 1943 (Boston Traveler) Italy Declares War On Germany; March 24, 1945 (Boston Traveler) 6 Allied Armies Across Rhine; August 6, 1945 (Boston Traveler) Atomic Bomb Hurled At Japs; September 19, 1938 (Daily Record, Boston) Britain and France Bow; November 18, 1938 (Daily Record, Boston) Nazis Prevent Jewish Exodus; June 5, 1944 (Daily Record, Boston) Rome Falls, First Photo of Yanks in Eternal City. The Daily Reporter (Coldwater, MI): March 30, 1943 Coldwater Daily Reporter, Coldwater, MI) British Forces Capture Gages and El Hamma. The Portage Lake Mining Gazette (Houghton, MI): March 26, 1942 Japan Reaches Out For India. The Bemidji Pioneer & Advertiser (Bemidji, Minnesota): July 3, 1940 Nazis Step Up Battle For Britain. The St. Paul Pioneer Press: December 5, 1941 Jap Answer Today: Break Near. The Daily Standard (Excelsior Springs, MO): April 15, 1940 British Troops In Norway. The Roswell Daily Record: March 23, 1942 A Broth of a Boy. The Star Gazette (Elmira, N.Y.): December 18, 1939 (Elmira Advertiser) Graf Spree Blown Up By Crew. The Kingston Daily Freeman (Kingston, NY): August 23, 1943 Hitler's Armies Leave Kharkov Stronghold; November 22, 1943; U.S. Forces, Ashore In Two Gilbert Islands, Batter Japanese Defenses; Reds Halt Nazis. The Brooklyn Daily Eagle: October 23, 1944, Leyte Japs Flee To Hills; East Coast Bastion Falls. The Daily News / Sunday News (N.Y.): February 25, 1945 Our Flag Flies Over Suribachi; The Associated Press (AP Photo in The Daily News Sunday News N.Y.): February 25, 1945 Our Flag Flies Over Suribachi. The New York Times Company: August 3, 1934 (The New York Herald Tribune) Hitler Becomes Germany's Absolute Dictator. The Washington Daily News, Inc. (Washington, North Carolina): April 9, 1940 Norway and Denmark Yield To Nazis. The Columbus Evening Dispatch (Columbus, OH): November 27, 1942 French Scuttle Fleet. The Portland Evening News (Portland, Maine): July 12, 1937 Jap Troops Pour Into China For War. The Philadelphia Inquirer: June 22, 1942 British Surrender Tobruk To Nazis; November 25, 1942 (Philadelphia Daily News) Stalingrad Siege Broken: Nazis Flee. The Williamsport Sun-Gazette (Williamsport, PA): November 14, 1941Big British Aircraft Carrier Sunk. The Plainsman (Huron, SD): March 13, 1941 (Evening Huronite) German and British Cities Are Rocked In Violent Air Assaults. The Watertown Public Opinion (Watertown, SD): June 1, 1942 Greatest Raid Hits Cologne. The Informer (Houston, Texas): July 17, 1943 Tuskagee Flyers Get 1st Plane. The Grand Saline Sun (Saline, Texas): December 2, 1943 Bonds Or Bondage. The San Antonio Light: April 28, 1941 Athens Captured by Nazis. The Richmond Times-Dispatch (Richmond, Virginia): May 25, 1941Britain's Hood, 42,100 Tons, Is Sunk By Nazi Warship Bismarck In Atlantic. The Washington Post Writer's Group: April 28, 1945 (The Times Herald, Washington, DC) Germany Surrenders; May 1,1945 "Farewell, A Long Farewell To All My Greatness!" — Hitler.

The Chicago Sun (Reprinted with special permission from The Chicago Sun Times, Inc. © 1999)
(1) The Chicago Sun: April 18, 1942
Column 1: Prices Soar (Cecil Dickson, Washington Bureau, Chicago Sun)
Column 2: Two More Federal Bureaus (Washington Bureau, Chicago Sun)
Column 3: Washington Recalls Envoy to Vichy (Washington Bureau, Chicago Sun)
Column 6: Six Per Cent Limit on War Profit Killed (Washington Bureau, Chicago Sun)
(2) The Chicago Sun: August 26, 1944
Column 1: Nelson May Leave WPB (Ruth Moore, Chicago Sun Washington Bureau)
Column 7-8: Kisses Shower on Americans (John Groth, Artist-War Correspondent for Parade, Special to the Chicago Sun); Pope and Churchill Confer (Special to The Chicago Sun)

Ten pages from The Chicago Daily News:
(1) The Chicago Daily News: June 17, 1940
Column 1-2: 'Britain to End Hitler's Curse': Churchill 'Will carry On World's Cause' (Helen Kirkpatrick, Special Cable to The Chicago Daily News Foreign Service. Copyright 1944, The Chicago Daily News, Inc.) Column 7-8: Peace with Honor Sought by Petain (Edgar Ansel Mowrer, Special Radio to The Chicago Daily News Foreign Service. Copyright 1944, The Chicago Daily News, Inc.)
(2) The Chicago Daily News: February 14, 1942
Column 4: Victory Time is City's Wish For Valentine (Justin McCarthy
Column 5: Witness Tells 'Final Hours' of Singapore (George Weller, Special Radio to The Chicago Daily News Foreign Service, Copyright 1942, the Chicago Daily News, Inc.) Column 6: Casey Sees Jap Ship, Bombers Beaten by U.S. (Robert J. Casey, Special Radio to The Chicago Daily News Foreign Service, Copyright 1942, the Chicago Daily News, Inc.)
(3) The Chicago Daily News: June 16, 1944
Column 2: Mission is no Adventure but Product of Cool Scientific Planning (A.T. Steele, Special Radio to The Chicago Daily News Foreign Service. Copyright 1944, The Chicago Daily News, Inc.) Columns 1-2 (bottom): U.S.Advances in Marianas; Progress Good, Says Nimitz (William McGaffin, Special Radio to The Chicago Daily News Foreign Service. Copyright 1944, The Chicago Daily News, Inc.)
Column 3: Yanks Gaining in Push to Cut Cherbourg Link (Helen Kirkpatrick, Special Cable to The Chicago Daily News Foreign Service. Copyright 1944, The Chicago Daily News, Inc). Columns 4-5: Oxie Gets Crick in Neck (Clem Lane)
Column 7: Robot Attack Fills the Bill as Nuisance (Helen Kirkpatrick, Special Cable to The Chicago Daily News Foreign Service. Copyright 1944, Chicago Daily News, Inc.)
(4) The Chicago Daily News: June 22, 1944
Column 1: One Vote Deal On for Dewey – California and Illinois 'Dickering'; Bricker Won't Quit Race (Charles N. Wheeler) Column 2: One Vote Deal On for Dewey – GOP Leaders Striving for Harmony in Party's Foreign plank (Bruce Biossat) Column 3: Planes, Cannon Pound Foe For Cherbourg Fall – (Robert J. Casey, Special Cable to The Chicago Daily News Foreign Service. Copyright 1944, The Chicago Daily News, Inc.) Column 4-6: Images – Scene of U.S. Victory (Map, Staff Artist)
(5) The Chicago Daily News: July 20, 1944
Column 1: Charges Fly as Chiefs Jockey for Number 2 Spot – Hannegan is Accused of bad Faith; Kelly Acts for Truman (Paul R. Leach) Column 2: Charges Fly as Chiefs Jockey for Number 2 Spot – Oxie Hooting Who's Who in Second Race (Clem Lane)
Column 3: Charges Fly as Chiefs Jockey for Number 2 Spot – Democratic Convention Roars to Possible End Tonight (Edwin A. Lahey)
(6) The Chicago Daily News: March 6, 1945 Cologne Is Ours
Columns 1-2: Dr. Carlson Finds K-Rations Good (Adele Hoskins)
Columns 5-8 (Bottom): Yanks Learned Their Lesson in Hate at Ardennes (Ann Stringer)
(7) The Chicago Daily News: March 16, 1945
Columns 2-4: Ruhr Road Cut Twice, Bridgehead Tough to Exploit (B.J. McQuaid, Daily News Foreign Service)
(8) The Chicago Daily News: May 29, 1945
Columns 1-2: Tokyo Raid Opens Saga of Adventure For Doolittle Vet / Jumps Onto Vesuvius, Lives in cave, Wants to Fight Japs (By William H. Stoneman, Daily News Foreign Service)
(9) The Chicago Daily News: July 17, 1945
Columns 1-6: Navy Thrusts to Tokyo Gates To Blitz Big Arms Factories (Headline)
Columns 1-2: Graft and Scandal Surround family of Duce's Mistress (Copyright 1945, by The Chicago Daily News, Inc. All Rights Reserved) Column 5-6 (Bottom): First European Vets Arrive in Philippines (By Jerry Thorp, Daily News Foreign Service) Column 6-8 (Bottom): John Q. Public Loses His White Shirt (Sue Mawer) Column 7: Russ Block Churchill's Honor Guard (Daily News Foreign Service)
(10) The Chicago Daily News: October 6, 1945
Column 1: Cubs Seek Third Win with Trim (John P. Carmichael); Columns 3-5: Series Fans Line Up for Blocks (Daily News Photo) Column 5-8 (Bottom): Only Their Ties Fit Now, Veterans Find (Norine Foley)

THE EVENING EXPRESS 45 CENTS A MONTH
Entered as second-class matter March 4, 1916, at the postoffice at Los Angeles, Calif., under the act of congress of March 3, 1879. Published daily except Sunday.

Los Angeles Evening Express

MEMBER OF ASSOCIATED PRESS

CITY EDITION
TODAY'S NEWS TODAY

VOL. XLIX, NO. 80 | Oldest Daily in Los Angeles | SATURDAY, JUNE 28, 1919 | Founded 1871 | TWO CENTS Delivered by Carrier 45 Cents a Month

TREATY SIGNED; WAR ENDS

Karr Letter Refutes Own Evidence

SENSATION SPRUNG IN NOTE TO MAYOR

A sensational affidivit was filed today by the defense in a request for a motion for a new trial for George Henderson, negro politician, found guilty of giving a bribe to Mayor Woodman.

In the affidavit which was submitted to Superior Judge Willis was embodied a letter alleged to have been written by Horace W. Karr, former newspaperman and star witness for the prosecution in the trial of both the mayor and Henderson. The letter written to Mayor Woodman is said to have been found by the city's chief executive only four days ago among his private papers.

Relates To Hackett

The letter relates to the appointment of Sergeant Hackett as the head of both the police Chinatown and purity squad.

The body of the letter refutes the greater part of the testimony given by Karr in the trial of both Mayor Woodman and Henderson. Karr testified during the trial that George Brown and George Henderson offered to raise a fund of $25,000 from denizens of the underworld as a campaign fund for Mayor Woodman.

For Police Protection

In exchange they asked that Sergeant Hackett be placed in charge of the two squads, so that they might order the granting of police protection to certain proprietors of disreputable

(CONTINUED ON PAGE 6, COL. 3)

Ratify Seven Laws of Nonpartisan League

By Associated Press

GRAND FORKS, N. D., June 28.—With less than 400 precincts to hear from of the 1938 in the state the seven nonpartisan league laws voted on last Thursday have been ratified by the voters by a majority of from 5000 to 10,000, according to present returns. The vote now stands as follows: For the laws, 42,329; against, 40,939.

Ask $500,000,000 for Waterways Systems

By Associated Press

WASHINGTON, June 28.—Expenditure of $500,000,000 during the next five years in developing a national waterways system is proposed in a bill introduced today by Representative Campbell, democrat of Pennsylvania.

Five million dollars would be spent each year for Pacific coast interior waterways.

Civilians and Service Men in Riot at Surrey

By Associated Press

LONDON, June 28 (via Montreal). Serious street fighting occurred Friday at Woking, Surrey, between Canadian and British soldiers and civilians. The Canadians came from the camp at Whitley.

LAKE STEAMER BELIEVED LOST

MILWAUKEE, Wis., June 27.—That something may have happened to the Holland, a freight and passenger boat of the Crosby line, during a gale was indicated when the coast patrol on both sides of Lake Michigan was asked to keep a sharp lookout. There are 100 passengers aboard.

Summary Today's News

PEACE TREATY

The representatives of the German government today signed the peace treaty shortly after 3 o'clock, Paris time. For the United States of America the signatures of President Wilson, Secretary of State Lansing, ex-Ambassador to France White, Colonel House and General Bliss were affixed.

Doctor Hermann Mueller, German secretary of foreign affairs, and Dr. Johannes Bell signed for the German government. The British, French and other delegations following in the order in which their several countries are named in the treaty.

Premier Clemenceau exacted of the Germans an answer to the direct question whether they were willing to sign and to "loyally execute" the provisions of the document. Their signatures preceded those of the other representatives.

* * *

China's delegates, aggrieved, withhold signature to the peace treaty having been denied opportunity to present reservations as to cession of Shantung to Japan. They had demanded the insertion of this reservation in the peace treaty itself.

President Wilson will leave immediately for the United States, leaving Secretary Lansing and Colonel House to represent him in further proceedings before the council. The peace document signed today is said to be in every respect identical with the text submitted to the Germans June 16.

FOREIGN

Gustav Noske, German minister of national defense, in view of the persistent unrest in Hamburg, has issued a proclamation threatening a ruthless suppression of disorder by any means at his command, and threatening martial law. Strikes interfering with public service will, he declares, be put down by military means.

* * *

A German plot has been uncovered whereby in the event of refusal to sign the treaty, allied armies were, in the expectation of the Germans, to be decoyed far into German territory there to be attacked by a powerful army. Jealousies appear to have upset this forlorn hope program and changed the entire course of events.

* * *

President Wilson closely following the signing of the peace treaty issued an address to Americans, urging that the treaty if carried out in good faith is to usher in a new world order. He insists that its terms are not impossible of full performance by Germany and that by living up to the conditions imposed she can regain her rightful standing in the world. He praises the treaty as the liberator of the oppressed and the creator of a new association of free government and promises the emancipation of labor from recognized injustice.

* * *

General Smuts, representing the Union of South Africa, signed the treaty but protested against certain territorial settlements as involving grave injury to Europe's industrial revival.

* * *

The Austrian peace treaty will be taken up again next Monday. The Austrians are asking a single modification to the treaty terms having to do with the liability of peoples under former Austrian rule to pay part of the war reparation from estates of private individuals who are Austrians.

NATION

New York republicans of great national prominence, headed by ex-United States Attorney General George W. Wickersham, ask the U. S. senate to promptly ratify the peace treaty as submitted.

* * *

Secretary of the Navy Daniels has ordered all naval vessels to fire a salute in recognition of the signing of the treaty of peace.

STATE

Charley Paddock, Californian and former Pasadena high school boy, has won international fame in the international athletic meet in France, winning for America the 100-meter dash in 11¼ seconds, which is within two-fifths of a second of the world record.

G. O. P. MEN FIGHT FOR LEAGUE

Special Dispatch to Evening Express

NEW YORK, June 28.—Seventy-eight republicans of national and international prominence, all residing in New York, have formally petitioned the republican senators of the United States to abandon their partisan fight against the League of Nations, demanding ratification of the peace treaty without amendment. The petition specifically refers to and upholds the League of Nations as an agency for the preservation of peace.

Distinguished among the parties signatory to this plea for prompt ratification is former United States Attorney General George W. Wickersham, who served in the Taft administration.

Mr. Wickersham declared the hope that the action taken will prove that a very considerable part of the republican party does not approve the character of opposition made by certain republican senators. They do not, he says, approve mere partisan-

(CONTINUED ON PAGE 6, COL. 2)

Forbid Tourist Travel To France This Year

By Associated Press

WASHINGTON, June 28.—Tourist travel to France from this country will not be permitted before next year, the state department announces. Business men will be permitted to send agents to any European country following the signing of the peace treaty, but restrictions as to the return trip will continue in force because of the needs of space for soldiers and civilian war department employes.

Measures to prevent undue travel to Great Britain also will be continued.

Round Trip Atlantic Flight, Is British Plan

WASHINGTON, June 28.—The British dirigible R-34 is expected to arrive in the United States July 5 or 6 on the first round trip flight across the Atlantic to be undertaken by a lighter-than-air craft.

This announcement was made here today by the British air attache, who requested that American merchant ships on the North Atlantic radio weather reports to Cape Race for both the outward and return voyages of the dirigible. The R-34 will land at Long Island and will remain only long enough to replenish its fuel and gas supplies.

French Chamber to Get Pact Text July 1

By Associated Press

PARIS, June 28.—The text of the peace treaty will be presented to the chamber of deputies July 1, by Premier Clemenceau, the Echo de Paris says. Premier Lloyd George, the newspaper says, will address the British house of commons July 1, on the peace negotiations.

Clearing-House Bank Reserve in Increase

By Associated Press

NEW YORK, June 28.—The actual condition of clearing-house banks and trust companies for the week shows that they hold $64,077,150 reserve in excess of legal requirements. This is an increase of $33,668,600 from last week.

ANOTHER DEGREE FOR WILSON

PARIS, June 27.—President Wilson has received another university degree—doctor of laws honoris causa, from the University of Geneva.

PEN PICTURE OF EXPRESS 'BEAT' WITH PEACE NEWS

A Triumph of Modern Journalism

It is 3 o'clock in the afternoon at Paris—7 o'clock in the morning at Los Angeles.

There, in the great Hall of Mirrors at Versailles, the delegates to the Peace Congress have assembled to sign the treaty with representatives of beaten Germany.

The transmission of the news was almost instantaneous, and as each signature was recorded the Associated Press report of the fact was flashed directly to the office of the Express.

In an incredibly short time after the completion of the historic event, Express extras were on the streets, so that the people of Los Angeles knew even as quickly as the people of Paris that the treaty had at last been signed.

This journalistic triumph reveals anew the supremacy of the news service the Express enjoys as the only afternoon newspaper that prints the reports of the reliable and enterprising Associated Press.

Mexican Government Stops American Oil Drilling, Is Charge

NEW YORK, June 28.—The National Association for the Protection of American Rights in Mexico has received information from private sources in Mexico that the Mexican government has sent troops to stop the drilling of wells in the properties of foreign companies in the oil fields.

The drilling work of two American companies already has been stopped by armed soldiers of the Carranza government, who surrounded the wells and under threats compelled the American drillers to stop work, the advices say.

The United States protested against the confiscation of oil lands by the Mexican government in April, 1918, the association says, and Great Britain, France and Holland joined in the protest against confiscation of oil fields owned by their nationals.

Will Hold Prisoners Till Teutons Ratify

By Associated Press

PARIS, June 28.—In the completed peace treaty signed today at Versailles, the newspapers say, were certain stipulations which it was hoped would hasten ratification of the treaty by the German national assembly.

The Journal says that the allies stipulated that the liberation of German prisoners would be dependent upon ratification of the treaty by the German assembly.

Wilson Is on Way to U. S.

By Associated Press

WASHINGTON, June 28.—President Wilson and his party will leave Paris at 9:30 tonight for Brest, to sail for home, Secretary Tumulty was notified today.

The cable from President Wilson said: "All well."

President Wilson has consented to an official reception for him on his arrival in New York. A committee of citizens, through Secretary Tumulty, had asked they be allowed to prepare an unofficial greeting. This is the first intimation of where the President would land.

Polk Congratulates President by Cable

By Associated Press

WASHINGTON, June 28.—Immediately after receiving the news of the signing of the treaty Acting Secretary Polk sent this message to the President over the special direct wire from the state department to Versailles:

"Permit me to offer my heart-felt congratulations on the completion of your great work. The American people will be ever proud of what you did as their representative for the peace of the world."

Seek Filipino for Stabbing Man During Argument Over Dog

The entire police force is today searching for Victor Ramirez, a Filipino living at 816½ Temple street, who is said to have stabbed William Cohen, a shipyard worker, living at 450 North Beaudry avenue, following an argument over a dog.

Cohen, who was treated at the receiving hospital for a stab wound in his back that pierced his kidney, was taken to the California hospital. He is not expected to live.

According to Charles Ginsberg, who conducts a bakery at 820 Temple street, where the stabbing occurred, the Filipino was sitting on the porch of his home and made some remarks about Ginsberg's dog. This was followed by threats, when Ramirez leaped from the porch with a long knife. Before Cohen could defend himself the blade was plunged into his back. Ramirez then attempted to stab Ginsberg, whom he chased for more than a block.

After the cutting affray Ramirez fled in his shirtsleeves and hatless. Ramirez has a wife and a small daughter living at the Temple street address.

Quill Pens Provided At Signing of Peace

By Associated Press

VERSAILLES, June 28.—A box of old-fashioned goose quills, sharpened by the expert pen pointer of the French foreign office, was placed on each table for the use of those peace plenipotentiaries who desired to observe the traditional formalities.

FORMAL CLOSE OF BIG STRUGGLE FOR WORLD LIBERTY IS ACHIEVED

By Associated Press

VERSAILLES, June 28 (Official report transmitted from Hall of Mirrors to State Department).—President Wilson and the American delegation completed signing the peace treaty at 3:14 o'clock, Paris time.

It also was signed by Dr. Hermann Mueller at 3:12 and Dr. Johannes Bell, for the Germans, at 3:13.

The American delegation signed in this order: Secretary Lansing, Henry White, Colonel House and General Bliss.

The other delegations, headed by the British, signed after the American plenipotentiaries in the order set forth in the treaty.

All of the plenipotentiaries having signed the treaty, M. Clemenceau declared the session closed.

((This dispatch was not timed at Versailles. It was received in Washington at 11:20 a. m.)

The Chinese plenipotentiaries did not sign and were not present.

They have written to the president of the conference stating that they would not be present and that they are awaiting instructions from their government.

Germans Are First to Sign Pact Giving Peace to World

By Associated Press

VERSAILLES, June 28.—The peace treaty was deposited on the table in the Hall of Mirrors at 2:10 o'clock this afternoon by William Martin of the French foreign office. It was enclosed in a stamped leather case.

Premier Clemenceau entered the palace at 2:20 o'clock.

A few minutes before 3 o'clock the 15 enlisted men from the American, British and French armies entered the hall amid decorous cheers.

President Wilson entered the hall of mirrors at 2:50 o'clock. All the delegates then were seated except the Chinese, who will not attend.

The Germans entered the hall at exactly 3 o'clock.

Premier Clemenceau called the session to order at 3:10 o'clock.

Premier Clemenceau put the direct question to the Germans whether

(CONTINUED ON PAGE 2, COL. 1)

WILSON URGES ACCEPTANCE OF TREATY

By Associated Press

WASHINGTON, June 28.—President Wilson in an address to the American people on the occasion of the signing of the peace treaty made a plea for the acceptance of the treaty and the covenant of the League of Nations without change or reservation. His message, given out here by Secretary Tumulty, said:

"My fellow countrymen. The treaty of peace has been signed. If it is ratified and acted upon in full and sincere execution of its terms it will furnish the charter for a new order of affairs in the world. It is a severe treaty in the duties and penalties it imposed upon Germany, but it is severe only because great wrongs done by Germany are to be righted and re-

(CONTENUED ON PAGE 6, COL. 1)

To Come to L. A. for Alleged Oregon Bandit

By Associated Press

PORTLAND, Ore., June 28.—Sheriff Anderson of Washington county will leave tonight for Los Angeles to bring back Charles Conley, alleged to have robbed the Bank of Beaverton of over $3800 on June 10.

While it is not thought that Conley will fight extradition, Sheriff Anderson is taking with him requisition papers on the governor of California. The sheriff will also take charge of the $2300 said to have been recovered at the time of Conley's arrest.

$900,000 Is Given to Fight Bomb Throwers

By Associated Press

WASHINGTON, June 28.—Two more measures aimed at anarchist, bomb throwers and other enemies of law and order were included today by the senate in the sundry civil appropriation bills. The appropriation for detection of crime was increased by $600,000, and a special fund of $300,000 for the department of labor to round up and deport alien anarchists was created.

Suffrage Is Ratified By Texas Legislature

By Associated Press

AUSTIN, Tex., June 28.—The legislature of Texas today completed ratification of the amendment to the federal constitution granting suffrage to women.

Final Treaty Draft Is Somewhat Changed

By Associated Press

WASHINGTON, June 28.—Acting Secretary Polk informed the senate foreign relations committee today that the final official draft of the League of Nations covenant showed some changes in wording from the version printed in this country.

The information was sent in response to a rquest from Chairman Lodge.

"The changes are all verbal as far as I can see," said Senator Lodge.

Hearings Refused on Iron Canyon Project

By Associated Press

WASHINGTON, June 28.—Requests of persons interested in the Iron canyon reclamation project in Northern California for an opportunity to present their views on the project to the house public lands committee in connection with hearings on Secretary Lane's plan to provide farms for soldiers and sailors, were denied by the committee.

The committee held it could not consider individual projects, as its efforts were centered on general legislation.

BERLIN BUYS CAR LINE

BERLIN, June 27.—The municipality of Greater Berlin has acquired the Metropolitan surface lines for 100,000,000 marks.

Los Angeles Examiner
CHARACTER QUALITY — AMERICA FIRST! — ENTERPRISE ACCURACY
AN AMERICAN PAPER FOR THE AMERICAN PEOPLE — THE GREAT NEWSPAPER OF THE GREAT SOUTHWEST
Reg. U.S. Pat. Off.
THE PEACH

VOL. XX—NO. 333 LOS ANGELES, FRIDAY, NOVEMBER 9, 1923 ,B PRICE FIVE CENTS

MARCH ON BERLIN!

Today

If Oxen Did It
Du Pont's Predcition
Crying Her Eyes Out
Army Happy—King Safe

By Arthur Brisbane

IN a Wild West exhibition a dozen cows are turned into the arena—"wild cows" they are called. Cowboys with lassoes and empty beer bottles are turned loose with the cows. They lasso them, throw them down, sit on them, and the cowboy that first manages to fill his beer bottle with milk, no matter how, as the cow pants and struggles, receives a special reward.

To many civilized beings that seems all right.

What should we say about a cellection of oxen if they gave a similar exhibition, only turning nursing human mothers into the arena instead of cows? We might criticize them severely for lack of delicate feeling.

MR. I. DU PONT, president of the great Du Pont Company, an da trained scientist, predicts, among other future possibilities, these:

SYNTHETIC FOOD, prepared by chemists, taking the place of eggs, butter, milk, beef, etc.

ARTIFICIAL WOOL, which which would make sheep unnecessary for their fleece, after doing away with the necessity for mutton.

Complete conquest of disease, which would mean saving untold.

Storing up the heat of the sun, which would give free or very cheap light and power.

LIGHT WITHOUT ANY HEAT. The lightning bugs understand that now, we don't.

Great reduction in hours of sleep, adding four hours a day, twenty years on the average, to a man's working life.

An interesting program, but as every scientist will tell you, it does not begin to enumerate the possibilities.

BESSIE ROGERS gets a divorce because she has been "crying her eyes out" about her husband. And she is only twenty-three.

When Napoleon III was emrepeatedly fastened to the tall column with Napoleon's statue on it, in the *Place Vendome*, verses which meant "If al the blood that thou hast spilled could be gathered in this square thou wouldst drink it without bending down."

That hurt the feelings of Napoleon III, proud of his great reputation, but it was true.

If you could gather together all the tears that women have shed, "crying their eyes out about their husbands," as Mrs. Bessie Rogers did, they would flood the whole of Chicago and overlow into the lake.

MUSSOLINI increases the pay of soldiers so that they are as well paid as civilian workers. That's an echo of old Rome. They took good care of soldiers in those ancient days that Mussolini admires and would bring back.

A contented army means a safer dictator.

The old plan was to give land to the old soldiers, and whatever they could take to the young ones. Good pay probably will do as well.

THERE are many kinds of wealth in the United States, as cotton, wheat, corn, gold, silver, iron, copper.

But the greatest crop of all is the crop of AMERICAN GIRLS, for what America IS to be, depends upon what THEY ARE.

The best posible crop news is found in the statistics of Vassar College. The college girl of today is nearly two inches taller than her sister of 1884. The modern girl wegihs more, has a larger waist measurement, and greater lunch capacity.

These statements mean stronger mothers, better babies, and therefore *a greater country.*

Most important is the waist measurement, which has increased from an average of twenty-two, to an average of twenty-five inches in young girls. Thirty inches would be better, strong muscles around the waist instead of a strong iron corset, is what women want. Look at the Venus of Milo and see the perfect type.

A WOMAN medium, quite sure that she could call spirits from the vasty deep and make them talk, is ordered by her husband not to make the tests before scientists.

He says the conditions would not be "pgsychic." Those con-

(Continued on Page 2, Part II)

MYSTERY MAN ACCUSED BY GRACE WALL

Defense Claims Slayer Left Girl With Johnson's Body to Cast Suspicion on Her

A mystery man killed Henry Willard Johnson and fled from his apartment, leaving beautiful 19-year-old Grace Wall to struggle out of the mists of intoxication and see Johnson's body on the floor, causing her to believe that she had stabbed him.

This will be the defence of Miss Wall, also known as Virginia Lavallie, who yesterday went on trial, in Superior Judge Carlos Hardy's court, charged with the murder of Johnson.

According to Attorney Stanley Visel, who outlined the "mystery man" theory, the girl's statements to the police that she had killed Johnson were made while her mind was still so befogged that she did not know what she was saying.

Miss Wall, a tall, lithe, nervous girl, helped to select the nine men and three women of the jury. Deputy District Attorney Frank Moroney and the defense counsel waived opening statements, and the first evidence was given as soon as the jury box was filled.

LISTENS INTENTLY

Wearing a brown suit, checkered with green and white stripes, and a brown hat to match her brown eyes, Miss Wall listened intently to the testimony, sometimes hiding her face in a handkerchief.

Dr. Frank R. Webb of the coroner's office testified that Johnson was killed by a knife blow that pierced his heart. A. L. Pert made the necessary identification of the body.

Mrs. Maco M. Davis, proprietor of the apartment house where Johnson lived, said that at 3 o'clock on the afternoon of August 24, Miss Wall ran to her apartment and called to her to "come quick; I have killed Johnson."

They both went into Johnson's apartment, where Miss Wall knelt tenderly beside the man, she testified, and bathed away the blood. She said she did not hear the fight or attack that Johnson is said to have made on Miss Wall. But three days later she visited the defendant in jail, and there the defendant had no recollection of what happened and said, "I must have killed him."

MOTIVE LACKING

The defense will seek to establish that she did not kill him, but merely thought so because the man was dead, and they will endeavor to show that someone else slipped into the apartment and committed the crime while she was there.

While a strong motive for the murder is said to be lacking, Deputy District Attorney Moroney and police officers on the case, say that two Spanish women came to Johnson's apartment. They assign jealousy as a possible motive.

The trial will continue this morning.

The jurors selected yesterday are: J. S. Tuley, Joseph H. Slucker, John L. Hook, Miss Anne B. Danforth, Frank Campbell, John A. Sharp, Richard Maloney, S. W. Millar, John M. Sterr, Joseph H. Douglas, Miss Reta Suhl, Mrs. Bertha Slack.

West Virginia Bank Bandits Get $5400

CLARKSBURG, W. Va., Nov. 8.—Attired in mountaineer clothing, two men held up the Lane's Bottom Bank at Camden this afternoon, grabbed $5400 in currency and rode away with a companion who had waited for the moutside in an automobile.

Young Women Try to Form Office Unions

NEW YORK, Nov. 8.

POLICEMEN yesterday dispersed a large delegation of young women who had taken up a position in front of Trinity Church on Broadway in an effort to interest the Wall Street workers in the formation of a new union of clerks and office workers.

The women were asked to "move on," police said, because their demonstration had been staged too near the site of the noonday meetings in the old church. None of the girls resisted the police order.

GIANT STEEL MILL ASSURED

$15,000,000 Corporation Buys Two-Hundred-Acre Tract in Long Beach for New Plant

The $15,000,000 steel mill for Los Angeles Harbor is now assured.

As a site for the gigantic plant, final negotiations were completed yesterday by the Pacific Coast Steel Corporation for the purchase of a 200-acre tract in Long Beach from the Los Angeles Dock & Terminal Co., for a consideration of $2,000,000.

For the last four months the steel corporation has had an option on the property, but it was not until yesterday that the board of directors definitely decided on the site.

Announcement of the huge transaction, which marks the first step in the development of one of the biggest industries in Southern California, was made public yesterday by T. T. C. Gregory of San Francisco, attorney for the Pacific Coast Steel Corporation.

With the view of deepening and widening the harbor channel past the company's property, the corporation has deposited a bond of $250,000 with city officials of Long Beach and negotiations with Government officials also are under way.

The depth of the channel is to be increased to thirty-two feet.

The erection of the first blast furnace in Southern California on the harbor property is part of the scheme of the development.

Parties representing the steel corporation locally in the transaction were R. M. Reynolds, vice president of the First National Bank; Attorney Walter M. Campbell and C. J. Curtis, president of the Los Angeles Dock & Terminal Company.

With the purchase of the 200-acre tract, it is the plan of the steel corporation to start immediately the development of the plant, whch, when fully completed, will represent an investment of $15,000,000.

Police Believe Bandit Gang Arrested in Texas

With the arrest in El Paso yesterday of three men, Pasadena police believe that the gang that robbed E. H. Evans, manager of the Elite Cafe, on Oct. 21, has been rounded up. The prisoners in Texas gave the names of Ralph Dussel, Max Zener and Lester Pullen. Last Saturday, Pasadena police arrested W. H. Wire, A. R. Stuart and R. J. Herron, who are said to have confessed to the robbery and implicated the other three.

Federal Judge Going to Fresno for Court

Federal Judge James will leave tonight for Fresno, where he will conduct a three weeks' session of the United States District Court. Tomorrow he will receive the report of the old Grand Jury and on Monday will impanel the new Grand Jury. Next week civil cases will be heard in court and on the week following liquor, narcotic and criminal cases will be called.

JURY INDICTS TWO DEPUTIES FOR FRAUD

Larimer and Blaisdell, Both of Sheriff,s Office, Must Face Fund Embezzlement Charge

Eight counts of embezzlement were returned by the County Gfand Jury yesterday against Deputy Sheriff David S. Larimer, for several years in charge of the transportation department of the Sheriff's office. Six counts were returned against Gilbert C. Blaisdel, transportation deputy sheriff. Both are charged with securing refunds on transportation tickets from the State, and thus embezzling public funds.

Judge Russ Avery, who fixed bail of $20,000 in the case of Larimer, reduced it to $10,000 at the request of Attorney John L. Richardson, who represented him, and he was released. He asked Sheriff Traeger for permission to take a leave of absence pending the trial. This request will be taken under advisement, pending suspension by the sheriff.

Blaisdel, who is also represented by Attorney Richardson, is out of the city, but sent word he would be in tomorrow to put up the bail of $5000.

Both officers say they will be able to clear up the cases in court, as they were not given the opportunity to explain their side of the case before the grand jury. They say refunds were made in cases where they bought other tickets, or paid for transportation in other ways.

Five Killed as Trains Crash Near Ironton

IRONTON, Ohio, Nov. 8.—Five persons were killed here this afternoon when a Chesapeake and Ohio passenger train, train No. 2, struck the Ironton-Ohio, Ashland bus. The five victims were unidentified. The bus was carried a considerable distance by the train and bodies were mutilated. It is believed they were from Ironton and Ashland.

Japanese Film Company Plans Incorporation

SACRAMENTO, Nov. 8.—(By International News Service.)—A Japanese motion picture concern, known as the Star Film Distributing Corporation, today filed articles of incorporation in the office of Secretary of State Frank C. Jordan. The company is capitalized at $250,000.

Philippines Will Ask Island Independence

MANILA, Nov. 8.—The Lower House of the Philippine Legislature today passed a resolution instructing the President of both the House and the Senate to petition President Coolidge to include a recommendation in favor of Philippine independence in his next message to Congress.

Public Safety Bill Passed in Australia

MELBOURNE, Australia, Nov. 8.—The public safety bill was passed by Parliament after second reading after an all night session. It was brought by disorders arising from the policemen's strike.

Dry District Goes Wet in Scotland

EDINBURGH, Nov. 8.—Out of 43 Scottish districts elections held on local option, one was converted from "dry" to "wet." Three remain "dry" and all the others voted "wet," the official returns revealed today.

BRITISH AND FRENCH MAP INTERVENTION

General Ludendorff

Ludendorff Leads Bavarians in Advance

Return of Kaiser Feared by Allies

BULLETIN

MUNICH, Nov. 8.—(Special Cable to Universal Service.) — Dictator Hitler, following the formation of the directorate and the ousting of the Bavarian Government tonight, ordered the long anticipated "march on Berlin" to begin. General Ludendorf has been made the "head" of the National army, and the Berlin government has been declared deposed by the new Bavarian authorities.

Adolph Hitler

BERLIN, Nov. 8.—(Universal Service, Special Cable.)—Revolution broke out in Bavaria tonight and the Von Knilling government, which was responsible for the appointment of Dictator Von Kahr, has fallen.

Premier Von Knilling was ousted.

Adolph Hitler, leader of the Bavarian "Fascisti," is the new dictator.

A directorate has been formed under Hitler, with General Ludendorff, General Von Lossow and Dr. Koehler.

BULLETIN

BY BASIL D. WOON
Special Cable Dispatch
Staff Correspondent Universal Service

PARIS, Nov. 8.—Persistent reports, which are wholly unconfirmable, tonight declare that France is ready to march on Frankfort, and England is prepared to occupy Bremen and Hamburg at the first sign of a Nationalist dictatorship being instituted in Germany.

In high diplomatic circles it is feared that such a dictatorship would mean the return of the Kaiser or Crown Prince, and a denunciation of the treaty of Versailles.

While French officials are mute on the subject it is learned from an unquestionable source that both Marshal Foch and the British military attache were present today at the meeting of the Council of Ambassadors.

Aux Ecoutes will say tomorrow: "When the allied control officers visit Bavaria they should be accompanied by an army division with heavy artillery and a squadron of airplanes."

Quarters opposing military measures point out that the occupation of Bavaria would mean the necessity for mobilizing at least two classes and possibly three.

Premier Poincare this afternoon telegraphed an ultimatum to the Berlin government declaring that France would view in the gravest light the establishment of a Nationalist dictatorship in Germany.

This hreat follows that of the Council of Ambassadors, whose demands that inter-allied military control be resumed in Germany was refused today by the Beriln government on the ground that German would not be able to guarantee the safety of the allied officers who would be risking death at the hands of enraged mobs.

"A German nationalist dictatorship would mean one or two things, either German revolution of a European war," says the semi-official Temps today.

Meanwhile, rumors persist that France is contemplating

(Continued on Page 2, Part II)

MISSING YOUTH FOUND IN EAST

Mystery surrounding the disappearance of George Mauser, 18-year-old student of Stanford University, was partly cleared yesterday when a telegram to George B. Mauser, wealthy business man of 1541 Ogden drive, father of the boy, announced that the young man was in Atlanta, Ga.

The telegram from the youth gave no explanation for his presence in the Southern city, and it is believed by the father that he was the victim of an attack of amnesia, following a friendly boxing bout at the university.

The young man disappeared last Saturday from the Northern city. Fellow students at the university told his father young Mauser had complained of feeling dizzy following the bout with a companion, as the result of having been struck a sharp blow with his opponent's elbow. He disappeared shortly afterwards.

Russ Celebrate Sixth Anniversary of Revolt

MOSCOW, Nov. 8.—Soldiers patrolled the streets and airplanes hovered overhead today while the Russians celebrated the sixth anniversary of the Revolution. There were no processions.

Commissar for War Leon Trotzky was sick and unable to review the troops. His place was taken by Commissar Kamenev.

L. A. WOMAN IN SMUGGLING NET

NEW YORK, Nov. 8.—(By Universal Service.)—Following the appraisers' detention and examination of more than $32,000 worth of jewels, furs and wearing apparel owned by Mrs. Abraham Meertieff of Los Angeles, Calif., who arrived on the White Star liner Majestc last Friday, attorneys for Mrs. Meertieff this afternoon agreed to pay $12,271.30 assesed by Federal officers after a lengthy consultation between Philip Elting, collector of the porte of New York, and Edward Barnes, assistant soliocitor of the legal division.

Mrs. Meertieff was represented by her attorney, Charles A. Curtin, who said that his clent was suffering from severe heart stran at the Hotel Plaza.

Formal seizure of the two necklaces valued respective at $10,000 and $6000 was made by Federal officers this afternoon. The necklaces owned by Mrs. Meertieff will be held for determination of origin. Seizure of Mrs. Meertieff's property was made last Friday by Custom Inspector Augustus Seegar, when various undeclared valuables were found on her person, including a platinum pendant, tassel-shaped, valued in this country at $1200 and a sapphire and diamond bracelet set in platinum, $1000.

Besides the jewelry Mrs. Meertieff brought ermine, persian, lamb skin and mole skin fur coats, with domestic value of $3000, and various other apparel such as gowns and wraps valued at $1262.

The Baltimore Post

Local Forecast—Increasing cloudiness, with rain or snow late tonight; highest tomorrow about 40 degrees.

SCRIPPS—HOWARD

NO. 4234 | Price Two Cents | BALTIMORE, MD., MONDAY, JANUARY 30, 1933 | Entered as second-class matter Postoffice, Baltimore

CLOSING STOCKS
NIGHT
BONDS, CURB

ADOLF HITLER NAMED GERMAN CHANCELLOR

Nazi Leader Becomes Man Of Hour in Germany

Adolf Hitler

President Von Hindenburg

GAS, PHONE COMPANIES REPORT 14 PCT. SLUMP IN 1932 NET INCOMES

Consolidated Receipts Declined $1,044,929.39 From 1931, Annual Reports Show

RATE HEARINGS THIS WEEK

Loss Considered by Commission in Asking for Reductions, P. S. C. Says

The net incomes of both the Gas & Electric Co. and the Chesapeake & Potomac Telephone Co. for 1932 dropped approximately 14 percent below the 1931 figures, according to the annual reports of the companies issued today.

The revenue for the gas company was $6,152,554 in 1932 and $7,197,483 in 1931. The telephone company's earnings were $2,836,776 in 1932, as against $3,287,265 in 1931.

The "fair valuation" of the telephone company's property during the year was given as $48,378,879. On this basis, the income represents an earning of a fraction less than 6 percent for the year.

Cite Reduced Earnings

While these reports were submitted to the Public Service Commission today, the Gas & Electric Co. filed application for approval of its purchase of the Consolidated Public Utilities Co. of Westminster, Md.

The reduced earnings of both the Gas & Electric Co. and the telephone company are cited by their officials in discussions with the commission as one of the chief reasons against any substantial reduction in either of their rates at the present time.

Gross Revenue Declines

Harold E. West, chairman of the commission, said that the figures shown in the reports were practically those which had been advanced by the utilities company officials in the rate discussions and that the decline had been taken into consideration by the commission in asking for rate reductions.

Negotiations between the Gas & Electric Co. and the commission, by which it is expected some rate reduction will be effected, will be resumed this week.

The drop in the net revenue of this company was slightly greater

(Turn to Page Two)

AUTOIST IDENTIFIED IN 'MYSTERY CRASH'

Police Name Driver in Injury To Woman

The driver of the auto which figured in an accident causing injuries to Miss Doris Roberts, first block W. Franklin St. on Friday night, has been identified as Michael Follmeyer, 3600 block Keswick Road, police said today.

Miss Roberts, suffering from cuts on the head, neck and leg, was left on the porch of the home of Dr. Chester Riland in the 2500 block Edmondson Ave., but refused treatment there. She went to Franklin Square Hospital.

The identity of the driver of the second machine figuring in the accident, which occurred at Edmondson Ave. and Pulaski St., is at present uncertain, police said. The license number of the machine, reported by a witness, did not accord with the make of the car, it was reported.

HINKLER IS REPORTED FOUND ALIVE IN ALPS

By United Press

LONDON, Jan. 30.—An unconfirmed report that Bert Hinkler, missing Australian aviator, had been found in a hut in the Alps caused indefinite postponement today of a memorial service scheduled in the City Temple for Feb. 12.

Hinkler disappeared early this month while on an attempted flight from England to Australia.

Inside The Post

GABY'S

Selections for Tomorrow

AT HIALEAH PARK

FIRST RACE—B. B. Stabie-Adrains entry, Screech, Rally Round.
SECOND—No selections.
THIRD—Dodgson, Live One, General Court.
FOURTH—The Pelican, Silk Flag, Idle Stefan.
FIFTH—Don Leon, Curacao, Ormesby.
SIXTH—BANK SHOT, Bolilee LeBruyere.
SEVENTH—Solace, Englewood, Garlic.

By Victorian

AT HIALEAH PARK

FIRST RACE—B. B. Stale-Adrians entry, Rally Round, Golden Fate.
SECOND—No selections.
THIRD—Dodgson, General Court, Eveline F.
FOURTH—Idle Stefan, The Pelican, Rapscallion.
FIFTH—Don Leon, Hibala, Curacao.
SIXTH—Bank Shot, Bolilee, Supercharge.
SEVENTH — SOLACE, Garlic, Lady Sweet.

Hialeah Park Charts

COMPILED BY UNITED PRESS

Weather Clear — Track Fast

FIRST RACE—Purse $700, claiming, 4-year-olds and up, six furlongs. Post 2:18, off 2:22 Start poor, won ridden out, place driving. Winne: b. g., 4, by Eternal-Assembly. Owned by Mrs. H. D. Cox, trained by H. D. Cox. Time, :22 4-5, :46 2-5, 1:12 1-5.

Horse	Wt.	Pos.	St.	¼	½	Str.	Fin	Jockey	Odds
Capacity	118	2	3	1^{3}	1^{5}	1^{4}	1^{4}	Gilbert	$20.40
Contribute	118	10	4	$3^{1½}$	$2^{½}$	$2^{1½}$	2^{nk}	Workman	1.05
Miss Corinne	113	8	1	8^{1}	5^{1}	$3^{½}$	3^{6}	Hanford	1.60
Hey There	118	11	2	2^{1}	3^{5}	4^{3}	4^{1}	Robertson	9.30
Claremont	118	1	7	4^{h}	4^{h}	5^{3}	5^{1}	Hathaway	25.90
Honey Locust	113	3	6	5^{nk}	6^{3}	$6^{1½}$	6^{2}	Clelland	68.90
Chokoloskee	118	6	10	9^{3}	$7^{½}$	7^{2}	7^{1}	Burke	330.90
Laura Gal	113	7	9	10^{5}	9^{2}	8^{5}	8^{2}	Snider	65.15
Battling Knight	118	9	11	11^{6}	11^{2}	9^{2}	$9^{1½}$	J. Smith	184.80
Sure Pop	118	5	12	12	12	12	10^{2}	Rausser	761.90
Sunny World	118	12	8	7^{1}	$8^{½}$	$10^{½}$	11^{4}	Riley	3,808.70
Effervesce	113	4	5	$6^{½}$	10^{4}	11^{1}	12	Bellizzi	33.45

$2 mutuels paid: Capacity, $42.80, $9.70 and $4.20; Contribute, $3.20 and $2.40; Miss Corinne, $2.60. Total mutuels..........$64.90

Capacity, displaying high speed, opened up a commanding lead the first quarter mile. He was kept under strong pressure after straightening out into the stretch, and was doing his best at the end. Contribute, vigorously ridden from the start, moved up stoutly on the stretch turn, but then faltered and just outlasted Miss Corinne. Latter broke alertly, but dropped out of contention in the early running. She closed stoutly the last three furlongs between the leaders and saved ground through the stretch to finish full of run. Hey There, prominent for a half mile, retired in the stretch run. Claremont and Honey Locust raced evenly. Battling Knight and Sure Pop were off slowly.

Scratched: Black Watch, Irene's Bob, Royal Past, Go Between, Sis Agnes, Vishnu.

SECOND—Purse $700, claiming, two-year-olds, two furlongs. Post 2:47, off 2:59½. Start poor, won ridden out, place same. Winner, ch c 2, by Mad Hatter-Shrine. Owned by Greentree Stable; trained by M. Lilly. Time, :24.

Horse	Wt.	Pos.	St.	¼	½	Str.	Fin	Jockey	Odds
xIdolatry	116	15	4	..	..	2^{h}	$1^{1½}$	Coucci	$1.95
Interruption	113	1	5	..	..	1^{h}	2^{h}	Malley	12.05
Distrust	116	4	2	..	..	3^{nk}	3^{h}	F. Smith	10.65
Sun Vestal	113	3	1	..	..	4^{1}	$4^{1½}$	Le Blanc	8.40
Jesting Queen	113	8	10	..	..	$6^{½}$	$5^{1½}$	Jones	16.85
Taunton	116	6	15	..	..	7^{1}	6^{1}	Kummer	87.40
Third Alarm	116	2	3	..	..	$5^{1½}$	7^{2}	Renick	56.25
Chief A.	116	11	13	..	..	9^{h}	8^{h}	W. Smith	2.80
xFanny	113	14	9	..	..	11^{nk}	9^{h}	Madeley	.....
Moral Miss	113	7	7	..	..	$10^{½}$	10^{h}	Clelland	30.05
Jean Via	113	10	6	..	..	8^{2}	11^{nk}	Riley	26.90
xLarrymitch	116	12	11	..	..	12^{1}	12^{h}	Richards	.....
xVoco	116	13	12	..	..	13^{2}	$13^{1½}$	Critchfield	.....
Alcorah	116	5	8	..	..	14^{2}	14^{1}	Rausser	92.15
One More Time	113	9	14	..	..	15	15	Hanford	11.55

xField.

$2 mutuels paid: Idolatry, $5.90, $3.30 and $2.50; Interruption, $9.10 and $8; Distrust, $5.70. Total mutuels..........$34.50

Idolatry, away forwardly, was hustled to front in opening furlong. He drew away steadily thereafter, but had nothing in reserve at end. Interruption, racing along the rail all the way, outlasted Distrust in final drive. Distrust, in close quarters throughout, finished with good courage. Jesting Queen, pinched back slightly after start, finished stoutly on outside. Taunton broke badly, and closed big gap. There were two jams in first sixteenth and the race was not truly run.

Scratched: May Hogan, Bulding Rose, Colonel Abe, Equilibre, Hoosier's Pride.

THIRD—

Unsettled, 105 (Meade)	$55.20	$14.80	$6.70
Black Sheep, 105 (Coucci)		$3.20	$3.10
Miss Axenstein, 105 (Obert)			$14.10
Total mutuels			$97.10

Time, 1:13 4-5. Also ran—Temple Dancer, Nutriment, Tiny Wrack, Flag Maiden, Lady Bracadale, Hill Saint, Sunny Spain, Our Moment, Three Bees.

FOURTH—

Cathop, 107 (Mills)	$6.00	$3.60	$2.90
Semaphore, 112 (Coucci)		$5.40	$4.10
Jubilate, 104 (Bellizzi)			$5.30
Total mutuels			$27.30

Time, 1:24 2-5. Also ran: Big Beau, Gift of Roses, Espinetta.

WOMAN GIVEN CHAIR FOR KILLING HUSBAND

By United Press

SUNBURY, Pa., Jan. 30.—Mrs. Mary Stancavage, 49, of Shamokin, today was sentenced to death in the electric chair after she pleaded guilty to slaying her husband, Jacob Stancavage.

Charles Keiselefski, also of Shamokin, a cripple, was sentenced to from 10 to 20 years in penitentiary when he pleaded guilty to taking part in the slaying.

NOTED LONDONER DIES ALMOST PENNILESS

By United Press

LONDON, Jan. 30.—Edgar Cohen, 80, former leader of society, finance and the turf, died almost penniless here yesterday. Cohen was said to have introduced taxicabs in London.

His intimates ranged from world celebrities to taxi drivers. During his day of wealth he entertained lavishly, his guests including Enrico Caruso and others famous in the opera and the theater.

PASTOR IS INDICTED IN ATTACK ON GIRL

By United Press

MUNCIE, Ind., Jan. 30.—The Delaware County grand jury today indicted Rev. G. Lemuel Conway, pastor of the Madison Methodist Episcopal Church, on charges of assault and battery in an attempted criminal attack on Helen Huffman, 18-year-old high school girl, in his auto.

The pastor was indicted also on a charge of assaulting William Aurand, his choir leader. The Rev. Conway surrendered immediately to Sheriff Fred W. Puckett.

WALKER AIDE WANTS TO RETURN TO GOTHAM

NEW YORK, Jan. 30.—Russell B. Sherwood, confidential agent for former Mayor James J. Walker, who fled to avoid questioning by the Seabury inquiry, is trying to make arrangements to return to New York, the World-Telegram said it had learned today "from an unquestioned source."

GAS TAX BILL PASSES HOUSE

Glass-Steagall Inflation Act Also Approved and Sent To White House

By United Press

WASHINGTON, Jan. 30.—The House today passed a resolution continuing for another year the $137,000,000 federal gasoline tax.

The levy of one cent a gallon, originally approved as a section of the revenue bill passed by the last Congress, would have expired automatically June 30. It now goes to the Senate for final action.

The House also passed and sent to President Hoover for signature a resolution extending for one year provisions of the mildly-inflationary Glass-Steagall emergency banking act.

The measure, which has been in effect nearly a year, allows reserve system banks to substitute government obligations for commercial paper as currency backing.

It also broadens the base of paper eligible for rediscount at the banks.

The bill is intended to aid in breaking the jam of frozen credits and to free surplus gold from use as currency backing.

N. C. SOLICITOR PLANS ATTEMPT TO GET LEA

Official Will Leave for Tennessee With Extradition Papers

By United Press

ASHEVILLE, N. C., Jan. 30.—Solicitor Zeb V. Nettles, of Buncombe County, said today he would "go to Nashville, Tenn., in a few days" with extradition papers for Col. Luke Lea, Nashville publisher, and his son, Luke Lea Jr., who are under conviction here for conspiracy to defraud.

Colonel Lea, former senator from Tennessee, is under sentence from six to ten years' imprisonment and his son has the choice of two to four years' imprisonment or payment of a $25,000 fine on convictions of conspiracy to defraud the Central Bank & Trust Co., of Asheville, of $1,300,000.

Their convictions have been confirmed by the U. S. Supreme Court, and their bonds of $50,000 each ordered forfeited here on their failure to appear and surrender to authorities here.

NASHVILLE, Tenn., Jan. 30.—Efforts to locate Col. Luke Lea and his son, Luke Lea Jr., here today were unsuccessful.

Hen Lays Two Eggs in One

STOCKTON, Cal.—A hen owned by Timothy Donahue, apparently convinced that the depression is over, has gone to work on a double shift to catch up on production. She laid a large egg, inside of which was another, perfectly formed egg.

FIGHT ON BEER GOES TO FLOOR

Senate Finance Committee Expects 3.05 Measure to Raise $125,000,000

By United Press

WASHINGTON, Jan. 30.—The short session beer-wine battle was shifted today to the Senate floor with formal Senate committee affirmation that proposed Volstead modification is constitutional and will raise $125,000,000 to $150,000,000 of revenue.

The Senate Finance Committee voted 12 to 5 to report the bill to the Senate. The committee left unchanged the 3.05 percent alcoholic content and the $5 per barrel tax. The report was offered to the Senate by Senator Smoot (Rep., Utah).

Beer and wine advocates will attempt to raise the prohibition issue in the Senate when the Treasury-Postoffic bill is disposd of this week. Opposd to them will be senators who desire to continue disposition of accumulating supply bills and the group which wants speedy action on the $500,000,000 La Follette-Costigan unemployment relief bill.

The Senate Judiciary Committee voted favorably on the beer-wine bill a week ago.

Treasury Secretary Mills appeared before the committee to discuss revenue features. Canon William Sheafe Chase and other prohibitionists waited outside the closed door in a vain hope of testifying.

LADY BAILEY LANDS AT BORDEAUX AIRPORT

By United Press

BORDEAUX, France, Jan. 30—Lady Bailey, English flier missing for four days while en route from North Africa to England, arrived unannounced at Bordeaux Airdrome at 2:40 p. m. today.

She left for Angouleme to spend the night. She was returning from an unsuccessful attempt to fly to South Africa, interrupted when she was forced down in the Niger River region and rescued by French fliers.

LIBBY MAY BE GIVEN TRIP OUTDOORS TODAY

By United Press

PHILADELPHIA, Jan. 30.—Libby Holman Reynolds, who has seen her baby daily for the last few days, was looking forward today to an auto ride.

She is becoming stronger, officials at the hospital said today, and is eagerly hoping the weather will permit a short trip out-of-doors.

It is expected that within three weeks Mrs. Reynolds will be able to leave the hospital.

U. S. Treasury Balance

WASHINGTON, Jan. 30. — The Treasury net balance issued today was $347,108,007.73.

Bank Clearings

Los Angeles (debits)	$15,917,039
Indianapolis	$1,319,000
Cincinnati	$5,550,264.

Bandit Robs Milkman 2nd Time in 3 Weeks

Same Man Executes Daylight Holdup Near Scene of First Robbery, Getting $150 From Earl Sommers, of Western Maryland Dairy; Got Only $30 First Time

For the second time in less than three weeks, Earl Sommers, a milk wagon driver, today was the victim of a daring daylight robbery by the same bandit.

Sommers, who was collecting for the Western Maryland Dairy, was held up in the 1900 block Vine St., the bandit taking his leather purse containing nearly $150 and running from the scene.

According to Sommers, the bandit was the same man who held him up on Jan. 9 in the 200 block N. Payson St. and got about $30, after he had saved $110 by throwing the wad of bills into an open doorway.

The milkman had just collected a small bill from Mrs. Maggie Hughes, 1900 block Vine St., when the bandit mounted the steps and pressed two guns against his side. One was an automatic and the other a revolver, according to Sommers.

'I Want it All This Time!'

"Throw 'em up!" the bandit ordered, Sommers told police. "And I want all of it this time, not part of it."

The bandit then took the leather purse, forced Sommers back into the vestibule and fled down Vine St.

Sommers described the bandit as being about 25 years of age, five feet seven inches in height, weighing 140 pounds, and wearing a brown soft hat and gray coat. He appeared to be a foreigner, probably an Italian, Sommers said.

First Holdup Recalled

The previous holdup occurred in a similar manner. Sommers was collecting from Mrs. Frank Snowden, of the 200 block N. Payson St., when the bandit entered the vestibule and ordered both to raise their hands. Sommers reached into his money bag, secured the wad of bills and threw it into the house. The bandit grabbed the bag, still containing about $30.

He then attempted to enter the house to retrieve the money, but a pet dog owned by Mrs. Snowden attacked him and caused him to flee. It was believed he had an auto parked nearby.

A half hour before the robbery in Mrs. Snowden's vestibule, Frank Ricketts, another driver for the same dairy, reported to police that a man answering the description given by Sommers had held him up. Ricketts told police that he had knocked a gun from the man's hand, and grappled with him. However, the bandit managed to retrieve his gun and escape.

15 Most Active Stocks Today

By United Press

NEW YORK, Jan. 30.—The 15 most active stocks on the New York Stock Exchange today:

	High	Low	Close	Chge.
Kreu & Toll.	1-16	1-32	1-16	+1-32
Can Pac	11⅞	10⅝	11¾	+1⅛
U S Steel	28¼	27½	27⅞	.....
Gen Mot	13¾	13¼	13⅝	+ ⅜
Ches Corp	18½	17	18⅜	+1⅛
N Y Cen	19½	18¾	19¼	+ ⅛
Paramt	1	⅞	⅞	— ⅛
Pennsy	19	18⅜	18¾	+ ⅜
Del & Hud	51¼	48½	51	+1⅞
Ches & O	29⅝	28⅞	29½	+ ½
Nat Dairy	15	14⅜	14⅞	+ ⅜
Am Can	60¾	59⅝	60⅝	+ ⅝
NYNH&H	16¾	15¾	16¾	+ ⅝
Am Tob B	61⅛	59½	61	+1
Chrysler	13½	13⅛	13⅜	.....

For news of business and finance, with complete stock, bond and Curb tables, see Pages 12 and 13.

Race Results

HAVANA

FIRST RACE—Westy's Fox, 112 (Watson), 8 to 5, 3 to 5, 1 to 3, won; Runaway Kid, 109 (J. Cavens), 2 to 1, even, second; Crossbones, 109 (Brooks), 1 to 5, third. Time 1:13. Also ran: King Cherokee, Play Choice, Mendell, Starelius, Fast Life.

SECOND—Thelma L., 115 (C. E. Allen), 3 to 1, even and 1 to 2, won; Town Limit, 112 (G. Elston), even and 1 to 2, second; Sweeping Hour, 106 (Mattioli), 4 to 5, third. Time, 1:13. Also ran: Stepping Sister, Yumuri, Thunderspeed, Marsala, Blue Mamie, Sweet One, Brown Supinet.

THIRD—Merry Green, 109 (T. Wilson), 5 to 1, 2 to 1, even, won; Logwood, 112 (May), 2 to 5, 1 to 5, second; Timekeeper, 109 (Himes), even, third. Time 1:12 2-5. Also ran: Loyola, Big Trail, Heighe Bob, Consummation, Black Darling.

FOURTH—Authority, 115 (F. Horn), even, 1 to 3 and 1 to 6, won; Yankaway, 115 (C. E. Allen), even and 2 to 5, second; Satin Shoes, 115 (Bejshak), 2 to 5, third. Time, 1:13 1-5. Also ran: Miss Boom, Tea Topics, China Bird, Check Out, Matie Hardies.

MALONE TO SPEAK AT DEFENSE PARLEY

Special to The Post

WASHINGTON, Jan. 30.—Maj. Gen. Paul B. Malone, of Baltimore, Third Corps Area commander, will be one of the principal speakers tonight at the formal opening of the annual Women's Patriotic Conference on National Defense.

More than 800 delegates, represented 38 societies, will be in attendance. Mrs. Alfred Blackburn, national president of the American Legion Auxiliary, will preside, while other speakers will be National Commander Louis A. Johnson, of the American Legion and Rear Admiral F. B. Upham.

LINDBERGH TO GET BID TO FETE MARKING HOP

PARIS, Jan. 30.—Col. Charles A. Lindbergh will be invited to the sixth anniversary celebration of his New York-Paris ftlight to be held at Le Bourget May 21, the National Aeronautic Federation decided today after consulting the Foreign Office and U. S. Ambassador Edge.

Benjamin Connor, a lawyer, one of the directors of the federation, will sail for the United States Wednesday with the invitation.

NAZI LEADER REACHES GOAL IN LONG FIGHT

Picked to Head Cabinet After Abandoning 'All or Nothing' Policy; Papen Is Aide

MOVE SURPRISES BERLIN

Government, Controlled by Fascists and Militarists, Is Sworn Into Office

By FREDERICK KUH
United Press Staff Correspondent

BERLIN, Jan. 30.—Adolf Hitler, leader of the German Fascists, came into political power in Germany today when he assumed the chancellorship in a new German cabinet.

Hitler, whose political rise as chief of the Nazis has been an amazing development of post-war politics, abandoned the "all or nothing" policy he had held toward participating in the government. He accepted Franz von Papen as his vice chancellor and Reichs Commissioner for Prussia.

Comes as Surprise

Hitler's formation of a new government to succeed that of Gen. Kurt von Schleicher took Berlin completely by surprise. Hitler conferred with party chiefs this morning, and was reported to be holding out for appointment as Reichs Commissioner for Prussia in addition to the chancellorship, which would have given him control of the regular army and the Prussian police force of 150,000 men.

Members of the new cabinet took the oath of office in the presence of President Von Hindenburg soon after formation of the government was announced.

Hitler rose to dominating power in Germany before he became a German citizen, and actually while he was a man without a country. Born an Austrian, he lost his Austrian citizenship. He did not become a German citizen until last year, when he ran for president against Von Hindenburg.

Sentenced to Jail

Hitler was granted citizenship through an appointment to a minor state office in Brunswick.

Hitler was sentenced to jail after his famous attempt at a "beer cellar putsch" failed a decade ago. His political career appeared to be ruined at the time. But he took advantage of discontent after his release to build up the Nazi organization, by fiery talks and a display of semi-military strength, into the strongest party in the Reichstag.

Herman Goering Nazi speaker of the Reichstag, was commissioned

(Turn to Page Two)

Quakes Felt in Greece

ATHENS, Jan. 30.—Strong earthquake shocks were felt today in the Chalcidici peninsula, where severe damage has been done by quakes in recent weeks.

SNOW MAROONS 2,000 AUTOISTS

Storms Along Pacific and Atlantic Coasts Cause Death And Heavy Property Loss

By United Press

SAN FRANCISCO, Jan. 30.—Storm-driven snow spread a deep blanket over inland and mountain areas of California and Nevada today, imperiling lives and causing intense suffering.

Along the coast heavy rainfall and high winds were reported. Rough seas delayed shipping and kept small craft within the harbors.

At Lake Arrowhead in the San Bernardino Mountains, a blizzard swept down to disrupt a winter sports carnival and to maroon some 500 cars, carrying about 2,000 people, on the mountain highways.

Two Japanese died in San Francisco Bay when their small boat cap-

(Turn to Page Two)

Fair Grounds Results

FIRST RACE

SPECKLE, 110 (Marshio)	$22.20	$8.40	$4.80
CATWALK, 110 (Hendricks)		$9.20	$6.60
SWEET LASSIE, 105 (Arnold)			$7.60
Total mutuels			$58.80

Time, 1:16 1-5. Also ran: Last Bid, Octavia, Whitharral, Miss Alden, Mast Man, Bright Chestnut, Almadele.

SECOND RACE

ESPINACA, 114 (Moran)	$9.80	$9.20	$3.40
BLIGHTER, 110 (O'Malley)		$31.40	$10.40
MORSUN, 110 (Richard)			$2.80
Total mutuels			$67.00

Time, 1:14 4-5. Also ran: Adrian, Rain or Shine, Jolly Pilot, Bag Smasher, The Spaniard, Silverman, Arrow.

THIRD RACE

LITTLE MARCELLEN	$32.20	$6.60	$3.60
PROMETHEUS		$4.00	$3.60
ARRAY			$6.60
Total mutuels			$56.60

MRS. ELLEN BORDEN MARRIES COMPOSER

By United Press

CAMBRIDGE, Mass., Jan. 30.—A wealthy and socially prominent Chicago couple, Mrs. Ellen Waller Borden, 47, and John Alden Carpenter, 57, composer, were married here today.

The Rev. Samuel Eliot, son of the late President Charles W. Eliot of Harvard University, officiated at the simple marriage ceremony in Elmwood, home of Prof. A. Knigsley Porter, of Harvard, and Mrs. Porter, aunt of the bride.

The brdie is a daughter of James Breckenridge Waller. She was divorced from John Borden in 1924. Carpenter's first wife, Mrs. Rue Winterbotham Carpenter, died in December, 1931.

Paint and Putty

Autoist Accused of Faking 1933 Tags

Arrested on a charge of converting 1931 auto license tags into 1933 tags by painting them blue and white and changing the final "1" to a "3" by means of putty, Samuel Weiner, 600 block E. Baltimore St., today posted $26.45 collateral for a hearing in Traffic Court on February 11.

Weiner, according to police, said he had made the bogus markers because he lacked money to buy tags and did not want to give up using his machine. He was arrested when two patrolmen saw the auto parked in Market Place near Baltimore St. last night.

WALTER LIPPMANN LOOKS AT TECHNOCRACY—THE FIRST OF A SERIES ON THE SUBJECT—TOMORROW IN THE POST

JOURNAL OF THE GERMAN LEAGUE OF NATIONS UNION

VÖLKERBUND

THE DISARMAMENT CONFERENCE

No. 73 SEPTEMBER 29, 1933 3 d.

Dr. Goebbels
On National-Socialist Germany And Her Contribution Towards World Peace

Speech to the representatives of the international press at Geneva on September 28th, 1933

It has been a painful disappointment to the German nation to note in past months that the birth of the national-socialist State and its positive repercussions on the economic and political development of the German nation have frequently been met in the world with lack of comprehension. mistrust or even hostility. The German nation realises, however, that this cannot be solely due to a lack of good will on the part of world public opinion. The problem of national-socialism is so new and its practical evolution in Germany is so unprecedented in the world that it cannot be understood or appreciated without a very close study of its problems. National-socialism is in fact a unique and unprecedented attempt to direct the destiny of a country by other methods than those that have hitherto been used and to bring about within this country a satisfactory solution of the serious crisis which has overtaken all nations of Europe. It is therefore not surprising that this attempt should be misunderstood and that this misunderstanding should extend to the attitude towards the German nation as a whole. I think, therefore, that it is my most important task briefly to explain to this audience, which is so widely representative of world public opinion, **the evolution of the national-socialist State,** its practical repercussions on home and foreign policy and thereby to bring about at least a certain amount of understanding for what has happened in Germany.

The world very largely still thinks that the national-socialist movement has seized power by force and ruthless terror in order to use this power brutally against its opponents in Germany. This conception is in contradiction to the actual course of events. Already before assuming power the national-socialist movement was by far the largest and, owing to the masses of its followers, the most influential party in parliamentary Germany. It was legally called upon to assume responsibility and it has legally consolidated its position of power in Germany. After the 30th January it was free to act according to its own judgment and without consulting the nation. It did not do so; on the contrary it consulted the nation, thus creating at the same time for its subsequent work of reconstruction the guarantees which were necessary within the democratic State. There was no question of applying terror and force. There has never before been any government in Germany which could claim to have realised such a large measure of agreement with the masses of the population as the national-socialist Government.

The elections of the 5th March, which gave this government an absolute majority, the passing of the authorisation bill in the Reichstag by an overhelming majority of two-thirds, clearly prove the legality of our action, the complete harmony between the will of the nation and that of the government as well as the undoubted concurrence of the views of the national-socialist leadership of the State with the conceptions of the German nation. What reason should there have been for us to impose our will upon the people by force and terror if this will was already in complete harmony with that of the German nation? Moreover any unbiassed visitor to Germany must admit that this process of adjusting the will has not remained stationary in the months after the last election nor moved backwards, but that, on the contrary, the whole German nation adjusts itself to an ever increasing extent to the programme of this government so that if we were to appeal again to the German nation according to democratic rules at least 75 to 85 per cent. of the German nation would freely take the side of the present government.

This must be stressed in the first place in order to create a possibility of understanding between the new authoritative Germany and the democratic world surrounding it. The nation and the government in Germany are identical. The will of the people is the will of the government and vice versa. The modern structure of the German State is a higher form of democracy in which, by virtue of the people's mandate, the government is exercised authoritatively while there is no possibility for parliamentary interference to obliterate and render ineffective the execution of the nation's will.

This applies both to home and world policy. There can be no doubt that if in the past 14 years democracy had been used to execute the mandate received from the nations authoritatively, to the benefit and happiness of the latter, Europe would now probably be in a better position than it actually is. Those, however, who say that the peoples should govern themselves completely misinterpret the principle of democracy. Nations cannot govern themselves, and they do not want to. Their sole desire is to be governed well and they are happy when they can have the conviction that their governments are working to their best ability and conscience for the benefit and welfare of the nations entrusted to them. The entire German nation is to-day filled with this happiness. Neutral observers who came to Germany full of mistrust have again and again told me after a few days' study of our internal conditions that the most striking characteristic of the German situation was the fact that the German nation as a whole was again confidently and faithfully supporting its government and that it did not only approve of the gigantic efforts made to overcome the crisis, but cooperated in them wholeheartedly; that this nation, which a few months ago had been stricken with paralysing pessimism, had recovered its optimistic outlook upon life and the confidence in its own force, and that in spite of the depression the people were going back to work with optimistic faith and that that alone should be proof enough for the fact that the German government was on the right way. Does anyone seriously believe that over 60 million people, a whole nation, which after all does not belong to the worst in the world, has been seized by a fit of madness, and does anyone really believe that a government in power could obtain the love and the sympathy of the people by force and terror. The reconstruction which we have undertaken with energy and youthful force is calculated for a long period ahead. The readjustment of economic conditions could not take place until the political elements of the crisis had been removed. It required tenacity, endurance, faith, a sense of national sacrifice. It would be doomed to failure if the government tried to carry it through without or even against the nation. If it begins to bear fruit already at this stage, this is due to the fact that in this reconstruction the will of the leaders of the State and the determination of the people are combining. The world however has every reason to deal honestly and without prejudice with this new phenomenon of State construction, whose only purpose is to get Germany out of the crisis by her own means and to relieve the world of its worries about the German situation.

This way of constructing a State is not as undemocratic as it may apear at first sight. It has found a new form of cooperation between government and nation. Under this new system the Government receives its mandate from the nation, but its execution is not controlled by a conglomeration of political parties. This mandate is a sovereign one. And to the great power which it confers upon the Government corresponds the great measure of responsibility which the government assumes. We are not governing against the nation nor without the nation. We are only the executors of the nation's will. It has been the fatal tragi-comedy of the former traditional democratic parties in Germany that although they appealed to the people, their appeal found no echo in the heart of the nation. These political parties preferred to make mistakes with the masses rather than to do the right thing against the masses. We have the courage to tell the people the truth, although it may be a bitter truth and we are happy to see that the people understands us. If true democracy means to lead the nations and to show them the way to work and peace, then I believe this true democracy has been realised in Germany against the will of the parties which represented only a distortion of the ideal of true democracy.

One of the reproaches levelled most frequently against national-socialist Germany is connected with the **treatment of Jews,** which, it is said, is contrary to the laws of humanity and will therefore meet with absolute lack of understanding in the rest of the world. Let me say a frank word on this subject considering above all the fact that public opinion in the world is deeply moved by the Jewish question and that prejudiced reports often destroy from the very outset any possibility of understanding the new Germany. I frankly admit that in the course of the national revolution in Germany incidents caused by uncontrollable elements may have occasionally occurred, but this is not decisive, particularly if one remembers that apart from these isolated incidents the German revolution, in contrast to many similar historic events, has been an act of discipline, of order and of authoritative leadership. The fact that we were opposed to Jewish predominance in Germany could well be expected to be generally known even before we assumed power. But it must be remembered that the Jews in Germany were exercising at that time a decisive influence on all intellectual life, that they were absolute and unlimited masters of the press, of literature, of the theatre and the cinema, and that in large cities, as for instance in Berlin, 75 per cent. of all members of the medical and legal professions were Jews, that they made public opinion, exercised a decisive influence on the stock exchange and were the rulers of parliament and its parties. It will be understood that in these circumstances the action undertaken to remedy this situation was just as spontaneous as it was unavoidable. Is there another nation that would have in the long run accepted without contradiction this excessive influence of the Jews on its public life? By settling the Jewish problem legally, the German Government adopted the most humane and loyal method. What we do not understand, however, is that while protests are raised against Germany's defensive action in this field, there is on the other hand an unwillingness to absorb the excess Jewish population emigrating from Germany. Moreover, it must not be overlooked that this question has been distorted precisely by those concerned in a manner which can only constitute an obstruction to its general settlement. Nothing is further from the intention of national-socialism than to exercise a cheap revenge. National-socialism would have had both the power and the possibility to do so. If it abstained from any such action it was because of its honest desire to find a real and practical solution of the Jewish problem which would no doubt produce also in this respect a final settlement. We think, however, that it is intolerable that atrocity legends spread abroad by Jewish emigrants, even involving the unprecedented allegation that members of the German Government had themselves for party reasons set the Reichstag on

THE WEATHER
Today: Probably showers, little change in temperature
Temperatures Yesterday: Max., 78; Min., 70
Detailed Report on Page 32

NEW YORK Herald Tribune

NRA MEMBER U.S. WE DO OUR PART

VOL. XCIV No. 32,037

FRIDAY, AUGUST 3, 1934

TWO CENTS In Greater New York | THREE CENTS Within 200 Miles | FOUR CENTS Elsewhere

Hitler Becomes Germany's Absolute Dictator; Hindenburg to Have National Funeral Tuesday; Army and Navy Swear Allegiance to New Ruler

Smith Quits After Charter Board Rejects His Program

Prial Balks Ex-Governor Trying to Draft Plan in Time for Submission to Voters This Fall

Commission Head Carries Out Threat

Resigns, as He Had Hinted He Would, as Soon as Meeting Ends Over His Plea to Continue

Alfred E. Smith resigned last night as a member of the Charter Revision Commission, forced out by the opposition led by Frank J. Prial, former Deputy Comptroller, to Mr. Smith's plan to formulate at last night's meeting a program for charter revision at that, meeting which could be submitted to the voters in the fall.

Mr. Smith explained that because sixty days' notice was necessary in order to submit such a proposition to the voters, action last night was imperative.

Adjournment Voted Despite Him

'Notwithstanding," said Mr. Smith after the commission had adjourned at 10:05 p. m., until Tuesday evening, "that notice was served on the commission by its counsel that nothing could be accomplished unless a program was formulated tonight, the commissione voted at 10:05 o'clock to adjourn. One big decision was made—I made that decision myself—which was to resign. Notice of my resignation will go to the Secretary of State by the first mail tomorrow morning."

The meeting of the commission was held in the County Courthouse.

Siding with Mr. Smith were Samuel Seabury, vice-chairman of the commission, and Governor Herbert H. Lehman. In Albany, a last minute appeal of Mr. Lehman to the Legislature for passage of the full program of the commission for county governmental reforms was ignored by the Republicans.

The Albany development and the attitude of the majority of the commission on borough government and city executive and administrative policy, it was believed, left Mr. Smith only two recourses, to resign or to follow the familiar strategy of many of his successful campaigns by taking the issue directly to the people.

The Bronx Chamber of Commerce met yesterday and took a stand against Mr. Smith's program for borough reform. A resolution adopted was forwarded to Mr. Smith in a letter urging "that the borough autonomy be preserved," that the "office of Borough President be retained" and that "the Borough President be selected by popular election," as now.

The Citizens Union issued a statement denying that the commission on Tuesday night had moved for a bicameral municipal assembly.

"The proposal adopted by the commission," the statement said, "does not call for a bicameral legislative body for the city, as is reported in most of the newspapers. All legislation is distinctly placed within the jurisdiction of a single-house Council alone. The Board of Estimate will have no power over any phase of what is properly termed legislation.

"It is our understanding—and this is important—that the proposed new Board of Estimate is to function only on administrative matters such as the granting of franchises and the making of contracts.

"Apparently the sole item that will come before both of the proposed bodies will be the budget. Even on this subject the board will not have concurrent power—its action may be overturned by the Council. The budget will be submitted by the Mayor to the Board of Estimate, which, in conjunction with five members of the Council, will hold public hearings. After the budget has been adopted by the Board of Estimate it will be submitted to the Council, which will have power to add, strike out or amend any item. Its actions, like all other legislative actions, will be subject only to the veto power of

(Continued on page eighteen)

Hindenburg Third Leader to Die in '34

Reichspresident Paul von Hindenburg was the third great national figure of Europe to die in the yaer 1934.

On February 17 the death of Albert, King of the Belgians, in a mountain climbing accident, shocked the world and plunged Belgium into mourning. King Albert was fifty-nine.

On July 25, only a few days ago, the assassination of Chancellor Engelbert Dollfuss of Austria occurred. His death, at the age of forty-one, and the manner of its accomplishment, threw the Continent into turmoil.

'Little Fellows' Get Johnson's Pledge of Help

Foresees Doom of Small Businesses but Holds This Is No Time to Start It

By The Associated Press

CHICAGO, Aug. 2.—General Hugh S. Johnson pledged the full powers of the N. R. A. today to maintain the present status of the small business man.

Addressing a luncheon meeting of Illinois code authorities, he foresaw a day when the evolution of mass distribution methods might eliminate small enterprises, but added: "This is no time to permit such sudden and explosive change."

He asserted that the recovery administration did not favor price fixing, and would never permit exploitation of the public by price provisions in codes. Nevertheless, the N. R. A. chief promised that such provisions would never be withheld when necessary to save an industry or maintain decent labor standards.

General Johnson spoke again tonight, delivering a radio address as a guest of the Century of Progress.

"The N. R. A. codes," General Johnson bluntly told the code authorities, "must not be used to exploit or deny its rights to labor; to exploit the public; to produce monopoly or oppress small enterprise, or to take advantage of related industries."

What fair practice codes could do, he said, was to eliminate abuses long recognized by business as destructive of legitimate profit and practice.

"In every industry there is always about a 10 per cent minority—the chiseling fringe—who just don't give a damn," General Johnson asserted. "Now the effects of competition throughout an industry are such that the practices of 10 per cent can drag down to their level the whole of that industry."

"It may be that mail order houses and filling stations sales should run all tire dealers out—that chains should eliminate all independents in every line and that employment and independent earnings there should be reduced by one-third, but this is no time to permit such sudden and explosive change.

"With between 10,000,000 and 12,-

(Continued on page eight)

President To Be Buried in Tannenberg Memorial Where He Crushed Russian Army in 1914

Hitler to Deliver Oration at Funeral

Thousands Expected at Services From All Over Germany; Nation Begins 14 Days' Mourning

NEUDECK, East Prussia, Aug. 2.—Paul Von Hindenburg, aristocrat, soldier and statesman, was honored tonight by his Fatherland in death as he had been in life.

The body of the Reichspresident lay in state in his country home where he died at 9 a. m. today (4 a. m. New York time), and a detachment of his beloved Reichswehr stood proudly on guard.

Next Tuesday a great national funeral will be held for the man who in nearly eighty-seven years served his country in three wars and for nine years stood at the head of the nation through troubled times.

Death came peacefully and without pain after weeks of suffering, through which the venerable Field Marshal maintained his usual proud and erect carriage.

Passes Away in Sleep

Last night Hindenburg, who was deeply religious, lifted his hands in prayer. Then with a look of contentment on his face and hands folded on his breast, he fell into a sleep from which he never awoke.

The huge fortress-like memorial at Tannenberg, erected near Hohenstein on the spot where Hindenburg's army turned back invading Russians twenty years ago this month, will be the scene of his funeral. His body will lie in this monument to his military prowess and his patriotism.

His family, it was announced in Berlin, yielded to a plea of the government that the final resting place of the hero be given national significance.

Hindenburg's Wishes Overruled

Hindenburg himself had expressed the wish to be buried in the Neudeck estate, which was so close to his heart in his latter years, but the family consented to the other plan.

There will be a funeral oration by Adolf Hitler. Thousands of Germans—from peasant to President—will pay their tribute.

After Hitler's oration and other services the body will be placed in one of the high projecting towers

(Continued on page two)

Late President and New 'Leader of the People and Chancellor of the Reich'

Herald Tribune photo—Acme

Paul von Hindenburg

Associated Press photo

Adolf Hitler

Roosevelt Tells Of Sorrow in Cable to Hitler

Condolences on Passing of Hindenburg His First Message to Chancellor

By The Associated Press

WASHINGTON, Aug. 2.—The death of President Paul von Hindenburg brought from official Washington today statements of regret, telegrams of sympathy and unofficial expressions of hope that his removal might not work too great a change in the course of Germany.

Officials felt Hindenburg had exercised a tremendous stabilizing influence on German affairs. On the surface, however, there was no mention of the political significance that might be attached to lodging greater power in the hands of Chancellor Adolf Hitler.

President Roosevelt telegraphed his condolences, and Secretary of State Cordell Hull issued a statement paying personal tribute to the patriotism of the war hero.

The President, in the first communication he has ever had with Hitler, said:

I learned with sincere sorrow of the death of President von Hindenburg, whose long life devoted to his country won for him

(Continued on page five)

Traffic Court in Bronx Tries 1,316 Cases in Day

Magistrate M'Gee Sets Record in 5½-Hour Session

What was believed to be a new record for speed in law enforcement was created in Bronx Traffic Court when Magistrate Leonard McGee disposed of 1,316 cases yesterday. Of this number 1,166 motorists repsonded to summonses, 100 were adjourned actions and fifty came in answer to warrants. About 10 per cent of the offenders escaped without penalties. A police drive, in which 845 tag summonses were issued for illegal parking, was responsible for the large number.

The defendants jammed the courtroom and stairs, and five patrolmen were required to keep them in order in the complaint room. A heavy traffic congestion in the vicinity of Brook Avenue and 161st Street resulted when the offenders sought to park their automobiles near the courthouse.

From the 1,166 persons answering summonses, $1,135 was collected in fines—$1 for illegal parking for a short length of time, $2 for an hour or more and $3 for all night. Seventy chose one day in jail and were released at 4 p. m.

Magistrate McGee called the court to order at 9:55 a. m. and worked until 3:15, when he took a half hour off for lunch. He finished the calendar at 4:10. The clerks worked from 8:30 a. m. until late last night.

Official German Statements

By The Associated Press

BERLIN, Aug. 2.—The text of Adolf Hitler's pronouncement to the nation today, in the form of a letter to Wilhelm Frick, Minister of the Interior; the oath of allegiance to Hitler taken by the army and navy, and the Cabinet's announcement of the change in governmental power, follow:

Hitler's Statement

The necessity for regulating the question of the chief of state, caused by the national misfortune that has overtaken our people, leads me to issue the following order:

First, the greatness of the deceased has given to the title of Reichspresident unique and non-recurring significance according to the feeling of all of us, and in what it meant to us this title is indissolubly bound up with the name of the great deceased. I therefore request that care be taken in official and unofficial communications to address me just as heretofore, as Fuehrer and Reichskanzier [Leader and Reich's Chancellor] only. This stipulation is to be observed in the future also.

Second, I desire that the vesting in my person, and thereby in the Reich's Chancellor's office as such, of the functions of the former Reichspresidency, decided upon by the Cabinet and constitutionally valid, shall receive the expressed sanction of the German people.

Steeped in the conviction that all authority of the state must proceed from the people and by them be ratified in free, secret election, I request you immediately to lay the decision of the Cabinet, with possible necessary additions, before the German people for a free plebiscite.

Army and Navy Oath

I swear by God this holy oath: That I shall be absolutely obedient to Der Fuehrer (the Leader) of the German Reich and people, Adolf Hitler, supreme head of the army, and that I will be ready as a brave soldier to give my life for this oath.

Cabinet's Declaration

The Reichs government has passed the following law, which is hereby promulgated:

The office of the Reich's President is united with that of Reich's Chancellor. In consequence thereof, powers heretofore exercised by the Reich's President are transferred to Der Fuehrer (Hitler) and the Vice-Chancellor (Franz von Papen). He (Hitler) determines who shall be his deputy.

Recluse Made 3 Million In Stock Market Deals

Pittsburgh Boarder Leaves Estate to German Relatives

PITTSBURGH, Aug. 2 (UP).—Carl Banning, who resoled his own shoes and cooked his own meals, left an estate of $3,000,000, it was revealed today. He made the money by shrewd investments in the market.

During the seventy-two years of his life, Banning had few intimate friends. To every one else he was a pitiful figure living in the back room of a downtown boarding house.

Every year the Burgomaster of Lengerich, Germany, where Banning passed the first twenty years of his life, received a check for $1,000. It was spent to give a Christmas party to the children of the town—the grandchildren of the comrades Banning knew in his youth. Most of his money was left to relatives in Germany, with provisions that the children of Lengerich shall always have their Christmas party.

Pennies From Sales Tax In Illinois $36,632,933

Revenue Makes Possible Abolition of State Property Levies

CHICAGO, Aug. 2 (AP).—Pennies of the Illinois sales tax have mounted into millions of dollars to put the state on a cash basis. At the end of its first year, state officials announced today that $36,632,933 had poured into the treasury from the 2 per cent sales tax, and acclaimed it as the "most satisfactory state tax."

The revenue, officials said, made possible elimination of all state property taxes, provided more than $18,000,000 for emergency relief, and filled in miscellaneous funds when other revenues shrank alarmingly.

"The state is on a cash basis, paying all bills and taking advantage of discounts," Knowlton L. Ames, Director of Finance, said.

France Fearful Nazi Extremists Imperil Peace

Hindenburg Death Viewed as Ending Last Vestige of Stability in Germany

From the Herald Tribune Bureau

PARIS, Aug. 2.—A feeling of profound apprehension over the future of Germany and the rest of Europe has been aroused in France by the death of President Paul von Hindenburg and the taking over of his functions by Chancellor Adolf Hitler.

The passing of the old marshal was seen here as opening an era of uncertainty that would be dangerous for the world. It was generally admitted to be an event of the greatest importance for present-day Germany, for it ended that semblance of unity and stability which Hindenburg preserved through his personal prestige.

"The marshal's death," says "Le Temps," "places Germany before the unknown, and the unknown for Germany is also the unknown for Europe." These words explain why France is in near mourning for the death of a man who once was her most feared and hated enemy.

The role of Hindenburg as the war general whom the Treaty of Versailles placed on the list of chief "criminals" in the World War has been forgotten on this twentieth anniversary of mobilization in France. Except in very extremist circles he is remembered only as President of the Reich, who alone could place a barrier in the way of National Socialist extremes.

From Nancy, where he was today at the funeral of another great soldier,

(Continued on page five)

5th Jersey Child Dies; Dysentery Germ Blamed

Intestinal Malady Identified as Flexner Type Bacillus

The intestinal malady in Jersey City which has cost the lives of five children and made twenty-nine persons seriously ill was analyzed yesterday as bacillus dysentery of the Flexner type, according to health authorities.

The fifth child, who died yesterday, was William Callahan, nineteen months old, of 102 Wayne Street, Jersey City. The child was taken sick at his home Wednesday night three hours after he had eaten some huckleberry pie. Taken to Jersey City Medical Center, the child's case was diagnosed as entero-colitis and food poisoning. Five new cases of the ailment were reported yesterday.

ccording to Dr. J. F. Von Der Lieth, Hudson County bacteriologist, a dysentery of the Flexner type is curable, although such is not often the case with young children. He said he was working on a bacteria phag for the malady which, if successful, would dissolve the germ in the child's stomach. He said efforts to trace the source of the infection, which first appeared on July 21, had been unsuccessful.

Hitler Assumes Powers of President as Soon as Field Marshal Dies, but Retains Title 'Leader'

Reich Votes Aug. 19 To Uphold Move

'Free Secret Election' Is Promised; Aids Urging Caution to Prevent Conflict With Whole World

By The Associated Press

BERLIN, Aug. 2.—Adolf Hitler in a series of lightning-like moves made himself absolute dictator of Germany today.

He concentrated in his own hands the functions of President and of Chancellor as soon as the aged President and patriot, Paul von Hindenburg, had died at Neudeck.

Then he called for and received an oath of personal allegiance from the officers and men of the entire army and navy.

After these moves, amounting to a virtual coup d'etat, the Nazi former lance corporal who succeeded a field marshal called for a plebiscite on August 19.

Plans Outlined in Letter

Although desiring the functions of the Presidency, Hitler declined tonight to accept the title, holding that "the greatness of the deceased has given to the title of Reichspresident unique and non-recurring significance."

In a letter to Wilhelm Frick, Minister of the Interior, Hitler outlined his plans to assume the office without the title, saying he desired henceforth to be known as before as "Fuehrer and Reichskanzler" (Leader and Chancellor.")

He directed that a "free secret election" be held August 19 at which the centralization of power in his hands should be ratified.

Plebiscites in Nazi Germany have come to mean rubber stamps, and the impending election promises to be no exception.

The details of the plebiscite have not been announced. Apparently it will follow the pattern of the November referendum when the ballots bore columns to answer "yes" and "no" on Germany's withdrawal from the League of Nations. Strangely, a large number of "damaged" ballots which could not be counted were cast.

The rapidity of the action which concentrated authority over 65,000,000 Germans in the hands of one man recalled the speed with which the Nazis first came to power on the morning of January 30, 1933.

Once again the Germans showed they are a disciplined people, trained to obedience. The change from a country governed, at least theoretically, by a constitution to absolute dictatorship seemed to cause no ripple. It was but another incident in Fascism's consolidation of its power.

Doubts of Reichswehr Evaporate

Dire whisperings that the Reichswehr (regular army), which worshiped the aged Hindenburg as a hero, might refuse obedience proved unfounded—as unfounded as had been reports of a general strike when Hitler became Chancellor.

By nightfall, the Propaganda Ministry announced, the entire army and navy had taken the oath, which pledge absolute obedience to Der Fuehrer (the leader).

It was administered wherever detachments happened to be or wherever ships lay at anchor or moved through the seas.

Though everything thus far has gone smoothly Hitler is known, nevertheless, to realize that a terrific task confronts him.

It was impressed on him by various advisers who visited him today—notably Wilhelm Frick and General Hermann Wilhelm Goering, Cabinet members—that the world looked on Hindenburg as the last brake on impetuous, unbridled Fascism in Germany.

Hitler's more conservative advisers urged that he must give proof to the world that under his sole leadership Germany would not embark on policies and experiments which would bring her into conflict with the whole world.

Dictator Takes no Chances

Political circles expect that Hitler will incorporate into his funeral oration for Hindenburg on Tuesday reassuring words as to the future of the Third Reich.

Some observers saw in the haste with which the new oath was administered to the army an indication that Hitler had decided to take no chances—that he believed in surprise movements executed before a possible opponent had time to think. These are the same quick, surprise tactics

Summary of Today's News

Anno 60 - N. 169 - I Ed. Mattino | Milano — Martedì, 16 Luglio 1935 — Anno XIII | Italia e Colonie, centesimi 20

CORRIERE DELLA SERA

PREZZI D'ABBONAMENTO — Italia e Colonie: ANNO L. 52.— | SEM. L. 27.— | TRIM. L. 14.50 — Estero: ANNO L. 160.— | SEM. L. 81.— | TRIM. L. 41.50

A Milano gli abbonamenti si ricevono negli uffici di via S. Margherita 16 e di via Solferino 28. I telefoni del Corriere della Sera portano i numeri 65-941, 65-942, 65-943, 65-944. 66-786, 66-695

Prezzi degli abbonamenti ai periodici per gli abbonati al "Corriere„

La Domenica del Corriere	Corriere dei Piccoli	La Lettura	Il Romanzo Mensile
Italia: An. L. 13.- Sem. L. 7.- Trim. L. 4.-	Italia: An. L. 13.- Sem. L. 7.- Trim. L. 4.-	Italia: An. L. 23.- Sem. L. 12.- Trim. L. 6.50	Italia: An. L. 18.- Sem. L. 9.50 Trim. L. 5.
Estero: „ „ 38.- „ „ 19.50 „ „ 10.-	Estero: „ „ 28.- „ „ 14.50 „ „ 7.50	Estero: „ „ 33.- „ „ 17.- „ „ 9.-	Estero: „ „ 28.- „ „ 14.50 „ „ 7.50

PREZZO DELLE INSERZIONI per mm. d'altezza (largh. una colonna): Necrologie L. 12. Pubblicità Commerciale pag. di testo L. 15; ultima L. 10. Finanziaria L. 15. Echi di Cronaca, di Spettacoli e Cronaca sportiva L. 40 la riga. Echi finanziari L. 50 la riga. Gite, viaggi, L. 40 la riga. Matrimoni e Onorificenze L. 50 la riga. Lauree, diplomi, ecc. L. 40 la riga. Pagamento anticipato. Tasse governative in più. L'Amministrazione del Corriere si riserva il diritto di rifiutare quegli ordini che a suo giudizio insindacabile ritenesse di non poter accettare.

LA INFLESSIBILE POLITICA DELL'ITALIA FASCISTA: NUOVE MISURE MILITARI PER L'AFRICA ORIENTALE

Il Duce ordina la mobilitazione della Divisione "Sila„ e della V Camicie nere "1° Febbraio„

La ricostituzione di tutte le formazioni della Milizia destinate all'Africa Orientale e la creazione della "Sila II„ - Richiamo di piloti aviatori e di specialisti del Genio e automobilisti delle classi 1909 - 10 - 12 - L'immediata costruzione di dieci nuovi sommergibili che saranno varati nei primi mesi dell'anno XIV

Il comunicato n. 8 del Ministero Stampa

ROMA 15 luglio.

IL MINISTERO PER LA STAMPA E PROPAGANDA DIRAMA IL SEGUENTE COMUNICATO N. 8:

Il ritmo accelerato della preparazione militare dell' Etiopia impone di procedere ad ulteriori misure di carattere militare.

Il Duce, ministro delle Forze armate, ha ordinato la mobilitazione della Divisione « Sila » che sarà comandata dal generale Bertini e dal vice-comandante Cerruti. E' stata simultaneamente costituita una Divisione che si chiamerà « Sila 2ª » agli ordini del generale De Michelis.

E' stata ordinata inoltre la mobilitazione di una quinta Divisione di Camicie nere, che si chiamerà « 1° Febbraio », al comando del generale Attilio Teruzzi e del vice-comandante Marghinotti.

E' in corso la ricostituzione di tutte le formazioni Camicie nere al posto di quelle destinate all'Africa orientale.

E' stato ordinato il richiamo degli specialisti dell'Arma del Genio e degli automobilisti appartenenti alle classi del 1909, 1910, 1912.

Il Ministero dell'Aeronautica ha ordinato il richiamo di altre aliquote di piloti e di specialisti.

Il Ministero della Marina ha ordinato la costruzione immediata di dieci sommergibili, che saranno varati contemporaneamente nei primi mesi dell'anno XIV.

Oltre le parole

All' orgia di discussioni, di previsioni, di informazioni tendenziose, di apprezzamenti più o meno divertevoli; all'ondata di polemiche cartacee che hanno invaso l' Europa in questi ultimi tempi semplicemente perchè l' Italia ha dimostrato di voler « far sul serio » in Africa Orientale, il Governo fascista oppone il calmo e inesorabile linguaggio dei fatti. Nuove misure militari vengono ordinate; legittime perchè necessarie; necessarie perchè da parte degli Abissini si accentuano le minacce. Gli stessi giornali stranieri più ostili alla politica italiana o altri della stessa risma abbondano in particolari sulla preparazione militare etiopica. Del resto nessuno meglio di noi conosce i sistemi tradizionali di quel Paese: guadagnar tempo insinuandosi abilmente nei dissidi fra gli Stati civili europei, e frattanto compiere la preparazione bellica; poi, all'improvviso, attaccare con forze superiori; perchè gli Abissini non si sono mai visti arrischiare una battaglia contro gli Italiani se non erano almeno cinque e più spesso otto o dieci contro uno. Ora, data la distanza che ci divide dalle nostre Colonie dell' Africa Orientale, quel sistema può offrire realmente notevoli attrattive per gli aggressori etiopici e seri rischi per noi. Da ciò il dovere categorico di preparare in tempo i mezzi coi quali rintuzzare l' improvvisa offesa. Non sarà certo la Società delle Nazioni che fermerà le orde scioane e amhara quando il Negus, dopo molte finte e ben calcolate tergiversazioni, darà loro l'ordine di muoversi contro i confini italiani. Non sarà il Gabinetto inglese con le sue tarde pressioni, di dubbia sincerità, a far sospendere la campagna aggressiva alla quale il Negus viene spinto dalle folli ambizioni e dalla puerile presunzione dei suoi consiglieri. Ciò che è accaduto ad Ualual può ritenersi, in scala dieci o cento volte maggiore. Dobbiamo esservi preparati; nessuno e nulla possono sostituire, nel momento del bisogno, i battaglioni, le batterie, le squadriglie d' aeroplani. Averle mandate in tempo, metodicamente, senza lasciarsi turbare e neppure distrarre dalla gazzarra dei vociferatori, sarà un altissimo titolo di lode per il Governo fascista, veramente benemerito della gloria e della fortuna della nostra bandiera in quei lontani paesi.

Due nuove Divisioni vengono mobilitate per l' Africa Orientale (e, come sempre, immediatamente sostituite sul territorio metropolitano): una dell'Esercito e una della Milizia. I comandanti sono noti, esperti ufficiali generali, ai quali deve farsi il più largo credito. A capo della Divisione Camicie nere «1° Febbraio » è stato chiamato dal Duce il gen. Attilio Teruzzi, capo di Stato Maggiore della Milizia: provvedimento di cui non occorre accentuare il significato morale e politico, abbastanza evidente. Il capo di Stato Maggiore delle Camicie nere, magnifica figura di combattente, di fascista, di organizzatore, prende nelle sue mani questa grande e bellissima unità, la « 1° Febbraio »: è certo che saprà farne uno strumento superbo di lotta, come del resto tutte le Camicie nere mobilitate gareggeranno in valore e in spirito di sacrificio con le granitiche Divisioni dell'Esercito, in uno spirito d'emulazione quale si può avere solo tra fratelli.

Non può passare inosservato tutto il complesso delle deliberazioni enunciate nell'8° comunicato del Ministero Stampa. Il richiamo alle armi di numerosi specialisti indica con quale larghezza di mezzi si vuole assicurare in Africa il funzionamento dei servizi, di tutti i servizi. La ricostituzione delle Divisioni mobilitate conferma una volta di più che Mussolini vuol conservare all'Esercito tutta la propria efficienza e pienezza organica. Infine la rapidissima costruzione di dieci nuovi sommergibili, in relazione con le ultime decisioni del Comitato degli ammiragli, costituisce uno dei provvedimenti che tendono a mettere sempre meglio in efficienza la nostra gloriosa Marina. Così tutte le Forze armate dello Stato e della Rivoluzione, nessuna esclusa, sono chiamate, ciascuna nel proprio campo che può essere essenziale, a garantire la sicurezza e la fortuna della Patria in questo periodo decisivo per il nostro avvenire.

E' bene che all'estero si prenda in considerazione con la dovuta urgenza questo complesso di attività militari italiane, che, mentre non hanno nulla di provocatorio e sono anzi graduate nel tempo in modo da commisurarsi strettamente ai bisogni, indicano tuttavia come il volere dell' Italia fascista si attui implacabilmente con piena indipendenza dalle remore di vario genere che vorrebbero intralciarne il cammino. Sicuri del nostro sacrosanto diritto, noi procediamo metodicamente, senza fretta ma senza sosta, sul terreno dei fatti; ritenendo anche che quanto più chiara e inequivocabile sarà la nostra azione, tanto più si affretterà il giorno in cui il nostro diritto verrà riconosciuto anche da coloro che oggi cercano di denigrarlo o affettano di disconoscerlo.

I nuovi comandanti

Roma 15 luglio.

La notizia della designazione del gen. ATTILIO TERUZZI a comandante di una Divisione di Camicie nere, destinata a partire per l'Africa Orientale, farà una simpatica impressione nel Paese. Il comandante della Divisione Camicie nere, Attilio Teruzzi, generale brigadiere dell'Esercito, nato a Milano nel 1883, è da molti anni in prima linea sulla scena della vita pubblica italiana. Dichiarata la guerra italo-turca nel 1911, Attilio Teruzzi fu tra i primi a chiedere di parteciparvi. Prese parte allo sbarco e all'occupazione di Misurata guadagnandosi, in quell'occasione, la prima medaglia di bronzo al valore. Nella seconda fase della campagna libica appartenne alla colonna Lequio che marciò sul Nalut; successivamente prese parte alla spedizione nel Fezzan, dove fu ferito e dove si guadagnò una medaglia d'argento al valor militare.

Nella grande guerra, col grado di capitano appartenne alla Brigata Barletta e quindi al 137° Fanteria; per la sua eroica condotta sul Carso e sul Monte Cimone, sul Monte Zebio e poi ancora sul Carso gli vennero conferite altre due medaglie d'argento. Col grado di maggiore ritornò poi nuovamente in Libia. Ma dal 1920, non appena rimpatriato e lasciato il servizio attivo nell'esercito, Attilio Teruzzi ha dato tutta la sua attività e tutta la sua fede alla causa fascista. Il suo passato di squadrista, di comandante di squadre d'azione, di uomo di Partito e di Governo, è noto a tutti; come nessuno ha dimenticato la sua opera brillante e ardita svolta nel governo della Cirenaica, la cui riconquista si deve in notevole parte alle sue tenaci iniziative. Dal 1929, la fiducia del Duce lo ha chiamato al delicatissimo incarico di capo di Stato Maggiore della Milizia volontaria alla quale, ampliandone e perfezionandone l'organizzazione, ha dato tutta la sua competenza di soldato e la sua fede di fascista, facendone un saldo strumento che oggi viene per la prima volta, e sotto i più lieti auspici, messo alla prova su vasta scala.

Il vice-comandante della Divisione Camicie nere « 1° Febbraio » colonnello MARIO MARGHINOTTI è nato a Caserta nel 1887. Ufficiale dal 1908, ha percorso nell'Arma di fanteria tutta la carriera. Ha fatto la campagna di Libia meritando due medaglie di bronzo, e quindi, dal 1916 al 1918, ha partecipato alla grande guerra meritando per la sua valorosa condotta a Col del Rosso, dove rimaneva ferito, alla Bainsizza e Monte Melago due medaglie d'argento al valor militare. Dopo l'armistizio tornava da maggiore in Tripolitania. Promosso per merito di guerra tenente colonnello nel maggio 1923 ebbe, fra l'altro, il comando della sottozona di Sliten (Libia) e della relativa colonna mobile nel periodo 1923-24 con funzioni politico - militari. Successivamente fu commissario del confine occidentale (Libia). Rientrato nei quadri nel 1928 fu assegnato al Comando della Scuola di Guerra.

Colonnello nel febbraio 1930, tenne per circa tre anni il comando del 40° Fanteria, e dal febbraio 1933 della Scuola allievi ufficiali di complemento di Milano.

Il generale di Divisione FRANCESCO BERTINI, comandante la Divisione « Sila », è nato a Torino nel 1878. Proveniente dall'Arma di artiglieria, durante la guerra 1915-18 fu capo di Stato Maggiore della LIV Divisione e dell' Intendenza delle Armate del Grappa e degli Altipiani, ove diede brillanti prove di capacità organizzativa. Successivamente fu assegnato allo Stato Maggiore dell'Esercito e poi addetto militare a Praga. Ha comandato l'artiglieria del Corpo d'Armata di Bologna, ed è stato ispettore di mobilitazione della Divisione di detta città. E' decorato dell'Ordine Militare di Savoia e di una medaglia d'argento al valor militare. E' stato due volte ferito durante la grande guerra.

Il generale di brigata MARIO CERRUTI, vice-comandante della Divisione « Sila » è nato a Macerata nel 1879. Nominato sottotenente nel 1899, ha percorso la carriera nell'Arma di fanteria e nel Corpo di Stato Maggiore. Durante la guerra 1915-18, cui prese parte ininterrottamente fin dall'inizio, fu capo di Stato Maggiore di grandi unità, e dal 22 novembre al 10 dicembre 1918 capo della Delegazione di Intendenza della IX Armata. Promosso generale di Brigata nel dicembre 1932, è stato ispettore di mobilitazione della Divisione militare di Gorizia e dal marzo dello scorso anno ha assunto il comando della 27 Brigata di fanteria. E' insignito della croce di guerra al valor militare.

Il generale di Brigata ATTILIO DE MICHELIS, comandante della Divisione di fanteria « Sila II », fu nominato sottotenente di fanteria nel 1903. Prese parte alla guerra di Libia e alla grande guerra quale comandante di compagnia e battaglione, distinguendosi per valore e ardire nei combattimenti del luglio e dell'ottobre 1915 sul Carso e al comando del 36° Reggimento fanteria in Val Lagarina. E' generale di Brigata dal 1932, ha comandato la 25 Brigata di fanteria (Caserta), è decorato di una medaglia d'argento e di due medaglie di bronzo al valor militare.

La partenza di 300 operai da Napoli

Napoli 15 luglio.

Il postale per il Mar Rosso *Argentina*, partendo stamane per il suo viaggio normale, ha imbarcato trecento operai specializzati diretti in Africa Orientale. E' anche partito il *Caffaro* dopo avere caricato notevoli quantità di materiali.

Nuovi concentramenti etiopici ai confini delle Colonie italiane

Il Cairo 15 luglio.

(ga.) *Il corrispondente da Addis Abeba del giornale* Ahram *telegrafa che un'atmosfera di guerra regna in tutta l'Etiopia e afferma di sapere da fonte ufficiale che il numero delle truppe abissine ammassate ai confini delle colonie italiane è stato molto aumentato. Secondo il corrispondente, il piano di guerra elaborato dal Negus consisterebbe nell'attendere l'iniziativa degli Italiani. In questo senso l'Imperatore avrebbe impartito severissimi ordini ai comandanti abissini. Vi è chi afferma però che alcuni capi militari vogliano a tutti i costi prendere l'offensiva.*

Viene confermato che il generale turco Vasiv Pascià è stato nominato consigliere militare del Negus.

Il corrispondente continua rilevando che gli ambienti dirigenti etiopici sono convinti ormai che l'Inghilterra non saprà impedire all'Italia d'impiegare le armi. D'altra parte l'annuncio della proibizione da parte del Belgio, della Cecoslovacchia e di altri Paesi dell'esportazione di armi ha prodotto profonda impressione a Addis Abeba e grande eccitazione, frammista ad avvilimento, contro tutti gli stranieri.

L'Ahram, *in un articolo sul lago Tana, ripete che all'Egitto importa l'acqua degli affluenti del Nilo Azzurro e non quella del lago Tana, il cui apporto è minimo.*

Riguardo ai diritti di passaggio del Canale di Suez e delle voci di una possibile chiusura, una personalità inglese residente in Egitto, intervistata dal Ghehad, *ha dichiarato che la chiusura del canale potrebbe verificarsi soltanto nel caso di una guerra tra l'Italia e l'Inghilterra e sempre che l'Egitto scendesse in guerra al fianco dell'Inghilterra. Poichè è chiaro che l'Inghilterra non si schiererà militarmente a fianco dell'Abissinia, il problema della chiusura del canale non ha più ragione di essere.*

Essendosi sparsa la voce di una modifica delle tariffe doganali egiziane in seguito a trattative con l'Inghilterra, tutti i giornali arabi criticano l'atteggiamento del Governo, in quanto i nuovi diritti doganali andranno a tutto vantaggio della Gran Bretagna. I giornali succitati scrivono che il Governo egiziano dedica in questi giorni la propria attività a dar soddisfazione alle richieste inglesi: tra non molto quindi l'Egitto sarà oppresso da oneri economici a tutto beneficio dell'industria tessile inglese. Negli ambienti commerciali si rileva che il sistema delle nuove tariffe preferenziali per l'Inghilterra andrebbe anche a svantaggio delle esportazioni italiane in Egitto.

Una sfilata di truppe in partenza per l'Africa Orientale

Lungo colloquio di Grandi con Hoare

Vivaci repliche inglesi a Sir Herbert Samuel

Londra 15 luglio.

Il centro dell'interesse immediato degli sforzi continui del Governo britannico per una soluzione pacifica del conflitto italo-abissino si è spostato a Parigi. Avenol è nella Capitale francese e i colloqui dell'ambasciatore britannico col Quai d'Orsay sono frequenti. Sembra oramai una cosa sicura che il Consiglio della Lega si riunisca verso il 25 di questo mese e a Londra ci si attende che l'Italia approfitti dell'occasione per denunziare ufficialmente l'Abissinia. Ma anche a Londra, ed è evidente dalla attività diplomatica che si va svolgendo, si ritiene che la decisione della Lega debba essere una decisione definitiva nei riguardi dell'Abissinia: l'Italia esige una soluzione radicale della questione. E questo lo si comprende anche a Londra dove le corrispondenze odierne da Roma alla stampa non lasciano dubbi sulle decisioni dell'Italia: è sintomatico che l'articolo del *Times* riconosca in modo esplicito i torti abissini e il buon diritto dell'Italia: non solo, ma che si proponga addirittura al Governo di prendere l'iniziativa di formulare « una proposta concreta che concilii gli scopi italiani e il lavoro della Lega ». E' evidente anche a Londra che l'Abissinia ha mancato ai suoi doveri di Nazione civile, che non ha osservato i suoi impegni dei trattati conclusi e non ha osservato neppure quelle condizioni la cui osservanza doveva permetterle di restare a far parte della Lega. Si riparla, col Covenant della Lega sempre alla mano, naturalmente, poichè la Lega va salvata a tutti i costi, secondo il punto di vista inglese, dell'art. 19 o, come ha detto il *Times*, di qualsiasi altro articolo « che conceda all'Italia qualche potere di carattere mandatario sull'Abissinia ».

Il Negus aggressivo

In verità le speranze di soluzione pacifica non sono molte, nè possono certo aiutare il lavoro anglo-francese di mediazione le dichiarazioni che il Negus ha fatto al *New York Times*, in cui si parla in tono aggressivo di negare concessioni all'Italia sia di carattere economico sia di carattere politico. L'Imperatore d'Abissinia ha dichiarato che non vuol concedere nè ferrovie nè zone di influenza all'Italia poichè, egli dice, « esse aprono la strada a una completa annessione ».

L'atteggiamento di sfida dell'Imperatore naturalmente non è commentato dagli Inglesi i quali forse, ora che cominciano a capire, vorrebbero non aver gridato tanto all'iniquità dell'azione italiana.

Tuttavia le consultazioni continuano: l'ambasciatore d'Italia Dino Grandi ha avuto anche stamane un lungo colloquio con Sir Samuel Hoare. Rimane da vedere, ed è necessario che sia così, se prima del Consiglio della Lega si possa preparare il terreno in via diplomatica, in modo da non esporsi ancora a una infruttuosa decisione societaria: ciò che conta ora è la sostanza dell'eventuale decisione e si comprende, come ha già detto Hoare, che il metodo di raggiungerla è indifferente.

Il redattore diplomatico del *Daily Telegraph* asserisce oggi che vi è una forte possibilità di una conversazione a tre anglo-franco-italiana: ma ci sembra che la data del prossimo Consiglio della Lega sia troppo vicina per una « conferenza » del genere. L'accordo, caso mai si potesse trovare con piena nostra soddisfazione, si può trovare anche per via diplomatica. Qualunque cosa accada, l'Inghilterra è ben persuasa ormai che l'Italia è decisa a risolvere radicalmente la questione abissina: i recenti provvedimenti del Duce con la nomina del gen. Dallolio a commissario per le fabbricazioni di guerra, l'intensa e perfetta preparazione italiana, le ultimissime misure precauzionali con la mobilitazione di altre due Divisioni per l'Africa Orientale, hanno ribadito il convincimento che l'Italia non può fermarsi nella sua marcia per accontentarsi di mezze soluzioni.

La piena comprensione della causa italiana si fa strada, come bisogna riconoscere, per opera di Hoare, e diventa sempre più forte il convincimento che l'Italia ha necessità di espansione.

La stampa britannica, pur se una certa sezione di essa notoriamente antitaliana continua a dare corpo alle ombre approfittando di ogni avvenimento per darvi un significato falsato ad arte, ha cambiato di tono: pur non abbandonando, come il Governo, la speranza di una soluzione pacifica, si preoccupa della Lega e delle conseguenze d'una guerra italo-abissina sulla Lega stessa. Si riconosce tuttavia che la Lega, così come è ora, necessita di riforme: il che è come riconoscere che la Lega come è non raccoglie nemmeno più la fiducia degli Inglesi.

L'Etiopia schiavista

Tanto il *Daily Mail* quanto l'*Evening News* stasera attaccano violentemente il *leader* liberale Herbert Samuel che ieri sera ha tenuto un lugubre discorso parlando di lacrime britanniche sui « poveri abissini spazzati dalle mitragliatrici italiane ». Il *leader* liberale ha parlato anche di « indignazione britannica » e di « risentimento tra il popolo britannico », ma i giornali citati lo rimbeccano violentemente dicendo chiaro e tondo che l'illustre parlamentare « parla attraverso il suo cappello ». Il *Daily Mail* parla della potenza militare italiana con le sue armi moderne, con la sua aeronautica poderosa, con l'entusiasmo e il valore dei suoi soldati e conclude:

« Che gli Italiani siano vittoriosi è certo: e vi sono anche grandi probabilità che essi vincano molto facilmente nell'eventualità d'una guerra ».

Il giornale attacca poi Herbert Samuel dicendo che « il popolo britannico non ha nessun interesse nello Stato schiavista abissino. E in questa guerra, se venisse, la solidarietà inglese è con la causa della civiltà bianca che l'Italia mantiene ben alta ».

L'*Evening News* calca stasera la dose: « A Sir Herbert Samuel — dice il giornale — e ai suoi amici liberali, non importa due pence dell'Abissinia.

« Ma essi non perdono mai un'occasione per svillaneggiare l'Italia e mettere in evidenza le loro malinconie verso un uomo che ha avuto il coraggio di eliminare il cosiddetto « negozio delle chiacchiere ». Il popolo britannico comprende benissimo che le tribù abissine sono barbare e che la schiavitù è una delle loro costumanze repugnanti. Mussolini può e vuole civilizzare l'Abissinia e noi ancora una volta gli auguriamo ogni successo. Si è detto che l'Italia non ha mai precisato le sue accuse contro l'Abissinia. Ma se è così, è perchè queste accuse sono semplicemente la denuncia evidente delle continue noie che gli Abissini hanno dato a tutti i loro vicini. Anche se l'Italia non avesse accuse specifiche da fare, le augureremmo lo stesso ogni successo perchè l'Abissinia è una macchia sul paesaggio della civiltà. »

Dopo avere detto che il compito dell'Italia è quello di soggiogare questi negri che sono ancora non controllati da bianchi e quindi ancora selvaggi e pericolosi, il giornale conclude:

« Più presto l'Italia si muove, meglio per tutti. In quanto ai nostri pacifisti litigiosi, chiediamo agli amici italiani di non misurare la loro influenza dalla forza dei loro polmoni. »

Oggi alla Camera dei Comuni il ministro degli Esteri ha dovuto rispondere a qualche interrogazione tanto sulla controversia italo-abissina quanto sull'accordo navale anglo-tedesco. Hoare ha dichiarato che « date le circostanze, una riunione del Consiglio appare inevitabile e imminente ».

Nello stesso modo evasivo Hoare ha dichiarato che il Governo sta considerando l'opportunità o meno di concedere licenze di esportazioni di armi in Abissinia. Egli ha aggiunto di sperare di poter rispondere più dettagliatamente quanto prima. Il ministro degli Esteri ha annunciato anche che il testo dell'accordo navale anglo-tedesco è stato comunicato alla Lega e sarà registrato fra breve.

Avenol a Parigi

Parigi 15 luglio.

Riferendo da Roma le informazioni sulla mobilitazione della Divisione Sila, della V di Camicie nere e di tutti gli altri apprestamenti e movimenti connessi con l'azione in Etiopia, l'*Intransigeant* nota:

« Il valore di questi provvedimenti è anche quello di annientare la voce recentemente corsa in Inghilterra di proposte italiane; esso dà anche una risposta anticipata al discorso del Negus, è insomma un avvertimento agli amici dell'Italia di non mettere troppo zelo a offrire i loro servigi, per cui non è il momento... ».

Anche il *Temps* dà ampia notizia dei movimenti militari e amministrativi che si stanno operando in Italia, compreso quello dei prefetti che mette in rapporto con l'insieme dell'azione, osservando:

« Si vede dunque che la politica interna come quella estera ora deve essere interpretata tutta in funzione del piano di espansione italiana in Etiopia ».

In un'altra corrispondenza romana lo stesso giornale rileva che tutto si svolge con la massima regolarità:

« Il movimento della macchina militare è eccellente, il popolo intero accetta la mobilitazione in corso con la massima calma. Nessuna agitazione. E' una prova non solo del patriottismo che anima gli Italiani in quest'ora storica, ma anche della loro convinzione di difendere una causa giusta ».

E' ancora a Parigi il segretario della Società delle Nazioni, Avenol, che deve essere ricevuto da Laval, occupatissimo a preparare i decreti legge finanziari. Rimane perciò per ora sospesa la riunione del Consiglio a Ginevra che il Governo inglese persiste a credere opportuna. In ogni modo pare esclusa prima della riunione del 25 luglio quella consultazione italo-franco-inglese sulla sostanza del problema, alla quale diversi giornali hanno accennato almeno come desiderio.

Sotto il titolo « Prima della guerra italo-etiopica » *Gringoire* racconta:

« L'imperatore di Etiopia è prigioniero nel suo impero. Dice: — Come volete che ne esca? Mi prenderebbero il posto. — Quando viaggia per i suoi Stati si fa sempre accompagnare da ras Sris e da ras Ailù. Fanno un terzetto inseparabile. Dormono insieme, mangiano insieme, si divertono insieme. Non che siano grandi amici; ma il Negus teme sempre che in sua assenza l'uno o l'altro faccia un colpo di Stato ».

Racconta anche questo: « Il Governo etiopico ha dei mezzi molto semplici per fare denaro. Poichè i fiumi del paese contengono oro, esso accorda delle concessioni di sfruttamento a degli stranieri. Quando la concessione è in ordine e sta per andare, l'amministrazione fa nascere complicazioni, rifiuta la mano d'opera e il concessionario, minacciato anche nella vita, non ha che il tempo di fare fagotto. Così l'imperatore possiede un certo numero di impianti che non gli sono costati molto ».

Visioni dell'Italia guerriera

COLONEL ED WINS HIALEAH 2D

THE WEATHER
Mostly cloudy, with rising temperature tonight and tomorrow. Lowest temperature tonight around 30 degrees.
Weather Report on Page 17.

MEAN TEMPERATURES

Baltimore	36	Chicago	22
Atlanta	43	Omaha	40
Boston	30	Los Angeles	57
New York	31	Salt Lake City	43
Portland, Me.	32	Seattle	48
Washington	36	New Orleans	63

THE BALTIMORE NEWS-POST
AN INDEPENDENT NEWSPAPER
The Largest Daily Circulation in the Entire South

8

VOL. CXXVIII.—NO. 106. Entered as second-class matter at Baltimore Postoffice. SATURDAY EVENING, MARCH 7, 1936 PRICE 2 CENTS

NAZI TROOPS IN RHINELAND ALLIED CHIEFS MEET IN PARIS

German troops are on the move. Under orders of Chancellor Hitler they crossed the Rhine and occupied cities in the "demilitarized" zone. Hitler scrapped the Locarno Treaty before sending his soldiers goose-stepping into the Rhineland. He declared: "Thus after three years, I believe I can consider with today the fight for German equality concluded." Picture shows part of Germany's new army on the march during war games. Picture from International News Photograph Service.

(Full Page of Pictures on Page 3)

Today

(Registered U. S. Patent Office.)

A Level Headed King.
Goodbye, Horse.
The Talmud, On Woman.
Real Value in Movies.

By Arthur Brisbane

A LEVEL-HEADED young man is the new English King. After seeing the new giant Cunarder named for his mother, walking seven miles up and down in it, he visited the slums of Glasgow, called the worst and "reddest" in England. Some ultra "Left Wing" City Councilors refused to be presented to him.

"That's perfectly all right," said the King. "Tell them I'll come and have tea with them instead."

This he did. Two thousand shipworkers cheered and called him "good old Teddy."

The King, who visited individual tenements, knocking at the doors, patting babies on the head, keeps up with the times. No English King did that before.

The automobile has conquered. After struggling vainly New York's Riding Club has folded its tent, "ceased to be." Its members in the past fifty-five years included Morgan, Carnegie, Belmont, Astor, Thomas Fortune Ryan and six Vanderbilts. For years it was hard to "get in"; then nobody wanted to join, the membership dwindled to almost nothing and now the club is as dead as the Queen of Sheba's camel.

The horse has seen his day, except on farms and as a gambling machine on the racetrack.

Mrs. Mary Beard, who feels that men do not appreciate women sufficiently, as indeed they do not, will find comfort in the writings of the Talmud. Those old rabbis spent their lives in study and observation and understood woman's value. For instance·

"Who is rich? He who has a good wife."

"If thy wife is small, bend down to take her counsel."

"Woman has better instincts in gauging the character of a stranger than a man."

"A man should be careful lest he cause a woman to weep, for 'God counts their tears.'"

Those who believe, some sincerely, that the so-called *proletariat* should or could lead the world should read the Talmud story of the snake's tail. It complained to the head:

"You always lead; I stay in the background. Why should I not lead sometimes?"

The head said:

"All right, lead."

And the tail led the way into a muddy ditch, then into a fire, next into thorns, and finally said to the head:

"YOU LEAD. I'M SICK OF IT."

The four kinds of blood with which Satan irrigated Noah's new vineyard—the blood of a lamb, a monkey, a lion and a pig—are shown in the progressive effects of drink.

There are many collections of Talmudic tales that would interest you.

Some of them appear in an article by this writer in "The March of Events" section of tomorrow's Sunday American.

Nicholas M. Schenck of the Loew Company, early in the depression, said the best thing about the moving picture industry:

"There is nothing the matter with moving pictures that GOOD pictures will not cure."

Now he demonstrates the soundness of that remark by selling easily fifteen million dollars' worth of Loew's, Inc., sinking fund debentures.

The sale, in these days of nervous bankers, of fifteen millions of debentures, not mortgage bonds, at 3½ per cent. interest rate, indicates that a

Continued on Page 4, Column 3.

Girls Jam Armory For Winter Carnival

An army of eager-eyed girls and women trooped into the Fifth Regiment Armory today to open the long-awaited Girls' Winter Carnival, presented for the first time in five years under auspices of the Playground Athletic League and The Baltimore News-Post and Sunday American.

They came on foot, in street cars—there were bus loads from Baltimore, Harford and Anne Arundel counties—to pack the Armory from floor to galleries with a throng that romped on the floor like frisky lambs, and made the place a jolly bedlam with the shouts of encouragement from the thousands of spectators.

Miss Mora Crossman, field director of the P. A. L., ordered the first "sports dish" to be served—a series of five or six big "dodgeball" games, and in a twinkling orderly competition took the place of the romping and general excitement of finding a place for lunches and discovering the whereabouts of mothers, brothers and sisters.

The total entries received number 4,500, and as soon as the first group of youngsters were finished games were to be started for girls up to seventeen, then up to twenty-one, with the evening program scheduled for those over twenty-one.

Details of events of the Girls' Winter Carnival will be found on Sports Pages.

VERY LATEST NEWS

(Race Results From Inter-State News Company, Inc.)

COLONEL ED WINS SECOND AT HIALEAH

Second—Colonel Ed, $7.10, $3.70, $2.60; Judge Leer $3.90, $2.60; Spixi, $2.50.

EXHIBITION BASEBALL

At Miami—Phila. (A), 0; Cinn. (N), 0; end 2 1-2 ins.

E. B. ROBINETTE, BANKER, DIES AT PHILA. AT 54

PHILADELPHIA, March 7.—(A. P.).—Edward B. Robinette, fifty-four, investment banker and founder of the Robinette Foundation at the University of Pennsylvania, died today. He gave $500,000 to establish the foundation for the study, treatment and prevention of cardiac and circulatory diseases.

WRIT HALTS SALE OF TVA POWER AT KNOXVILLE

WASHINGTON, March 7—(A. P.).—The Tennessee Public Service Company today was granted a temporary restraining order by the District of Columbia Supreme Court stopping sale of TVA power to Knoxville, Tenn.

AVALANCHE BURIES PAIR OF MOUNTAIN CLIMBERS

AOSTA, March 7—(U. P.).—Basilio Cuaz, twenty, and Giovanni Bertagnolo were buried alive by an avalanche near Vieille today.

Pa. Wants Guffey Coal Law Upheld

WASHINGTON, March 7—(A. P.).—Declaring that "some form of governmental regulation is indispensable to save the industry," the State of Pennsylvania urged the Supreme Court today to uphold constitutionality of the Guffey law to regulate the soft coal industry.

2 Rescued As Fire Menaces Hotel Here

A man and his wife were rescued down ladders today when flames menaced the Westminster Hotel, northeast corner of Paca and Fayette streets, driving twelve guests and employes to the street.

The blaze, which was quickly extinguished, attracted thousands of Saturday afternoon shoppers, who massed at the intersection to watch the rescue.

The fire broke out in the staircase connecting the second and third floors. Employest elephoned in an alarm.

Kenneth O'Connor, thirty-seven, and Mrs. Winnie O'Connor, twenty-four, both of New York, were asleep in their room when Mrs. O'Connor was awakened by the odor of smoke. She found escape cut off because of flames spouting up the staircase.

Rousing her husband, they called for help. Firemen sent up a ladder. Mrs. O'Connor was semi-conscious when the firemen reached her, and she was carried down the ladder to the street.

The blaze was extinguished, but damaged the second and third floors. Nathan R. Fineman, manager of the hotel, said the cause was undetermined.

RESULTS AT HIALEAH PARK

FIRST RACE—Purse $800; claiming; for three-year-olds and up; six furlongs. Off at 2.34. Time, 1.11 2-5.

M. J. Brennan, 113 (Wright)	$5.90	$4.00	$3.10
Camino Real, 108 (Kastner)		10.10	7.00
Miss Subway, 95 (Fallon)			3.80
Total mutuels			$33.90

Also Ran—Crataegus, Flag of War, Fervid, Wizard, Black Falcon, Chaumont.

What Locarno Treaty Means

By United Press.

The Locarno Treaty, regarded as the most important single diplomatic document in Europe, is in brief as follows:

1—Treaty of mutual guarantee among Germany, Belgium, France, Great Britain and Italy.

2—Two arbitration conventions, German-French and German-Belgian; also two arbitration treaties, German-Polish and German-Czechoslovakian.

3—Collective Allied note to Germany explaining implications of Article XVI.—the penal article—of the League of Nations Covenant.

The mutual guarantee treaty mentionad above provides:

1—Signatories guarantee the inviolability of the German-Belgian and German-French frontiers as filxed by the Versailles Treaty.

2—Germany, Belgium and France promise never to attack, invade or wage war against each other except in "legitimate defense" or as the result of a League obligation.

3—Germany, Belgium and France promise to settle disputes by pacific means.

4—If any party to the treaty violates Paragraph 2, regarding waging of war, each will come to the aid of the nation which the League holds to have been attacked. In case of "flagrant" violation, signatories will come at once to the defense of the nation attacked. That is, if France attacked Germany, Belgium, Great Britain and Italy would go to Germany's aid.

Allied Chiefs Confer In Paris

By Associated Press.

PARIS, March 7.—Pierre-Etienne Flandin, French Foreign Minister, told Ambassadors of three nations which signed the Locarno pact that Germany committed "a hostile act" today by sending troops into the Rhineland.

By United Press.

PARIS, March 7. — Representatives of Europe's major Powers gathered at the French Foreign Office today for an urgent conference on Germany's reoccupation of the Rhineland.

Envoys of Great Britian, Italy, Russia, Poland and represntatives for the Little Entente of Czechoslovakia, Rumania and Yugoslavia all met at the Quai D'Orsay in hasty deliberations on the problems raised by Adolf Hitler's momentous speech in the Reichstag.

SECOND PARLEY

In the evening, a second important conference of French Cabinet ministers and high army officers

Continued on Page 4, Column 6.

Temperatures

Midnight	31	7 A. M.	29
1 A. M.	30	8 A. M.	29
2 A. M.	31	9 A. M.	30
3 A. M.	30	10 A. M.	30
4 A. M.	30	11 A. M.	34
5 A. M.	30	12 Noon	35
6 A. M.	30	1 P. M.	36

NAZIS INVADE RHINELAND, HITLER SCRAPS LOCARNO

BERLIN, March 7.—Adolf Hitler, thundering to his brown-shirt Nazi Reichstag that the Locarno pact was dead, sent triumphant German troops goose-stepping into the demilitarized Rhineland today and pronounced the fight for Germany's freedom finished.

In swift, world stunning thrusts, the Reichsfuehrer offered Europe a new western demilitarized frontier on a co-operative basis, declared he was ready to sign a new non-aggression treaty and air pact with his western neighbors and expressed willingness if these things transpired, to return to the League of Nations.

Then he dissolved his standing, shouting Reichstag and called a plebiscite for March 29 to prove to the world that the German people are behind him. In these general elections Hitler and his followers expect to get a majority even greater than their previous 90 per cent.

Army Moves Swiftly

Traditional Prussian precision, orderliness and speed marked the large-scale army movements into the Rhineland zone. The movements, it was announced officially, will be completed Sunday.

In all, eighteen infantry battalions of 500 men each and thirteen artillery units of nearly 200 men each were being transferred from the interior of the country into the zone today and tonight. Most of them will be in station near the river, and the area between the Black Forest and the Rhone will have the heaviest concentrations.

Comparatively small detachments were planned for Aachen, Trier and Saarbruecken.

In addition to the ground forces, two groups of pursuit fliers were being roved in to-

Turn Over.

Showers Ending Tonight or Tuesday
Showers ending late tonight or Tuesday; slightly warmer Tuesday. Moderate east to north winds.

Portland Evening News

Portland, the Sunrise Gateway of America

Almanac For Tuesday, July 13
Sun rises 5.10 A.M. High tide 3.30 A.M.
Sun sets 8.23 P.M. High tide 4.02 P.M.
M'n rises 11.30 A.M. Low tide 9.46 A.M.
M'n sets 11.06 P.M. Low tide 10.16 P.M.
Day's Decrease, Eight Minutes.

VOL. 10, NO. 229 — PORTLAND, MAINE, MONDAY, JULY 12, 1937 — Entered as Second Class Mail Matter ★ THREE CENTS

Jap Troops Pour Into China For War

MILITIA RUSHED TO STEEL PLANT

Troops Sent To Massillon After Battle

Man Dies, 12 Hurt As Guards and Strikers Riot

Fight Lasts 2 Hours

Guardsmen Had Been Withdrawn From Factory

MASSILLON, O., (UP)—National Guardsmen were rushed back to the Republic Steel Corporation today following a pitched battle between special guards and 250 strikers and sympathizers in which one man was killed and 12 were wounded.

The fight raged for more than two hours. It ended at 1:30 A. M. (2:30 A. M. EDT) and soon afterward two truck loads of National Guardsmen arrived from Canton, which is close. by. and. resumed. their guard at the entrance to Republic's plant.

The guardsmen had been withdrawn and sent to Canton Friday after having guarded the plant for two weeks.

The dead man was identified as Sulgencio Calzada, 40, a striker. He had been shot in the head.

One of the 12 wounded—all strikers or sympathizers—was not expected to live through the night.

Page Two, 2nd Column

SOVIET FLIERS OVER ARCTIC ON HOP TO U. S.

Seek To Set New Long Distance Record

MOSCOW (UP)—Three Russian air heroes sped over the Arctic Sea on their way to the United States today, seeking to reach San Francisco or Los Angeles and break the world airplane distance record of 5,657 miles.

They started from Schelkovo airport, 20 miles from Moscow, at 3:24 A. M. (8:24 P. M. Sunday EDT) intending to fly over the North Pole and down through Canada as did their three fellow aviators who landed near Vancouver, Wash., three weeks ago.

(Page Two 2nd Column)

TOPSHAM FIRM FILES PETITION TO REORGANIZE

Pejepscot Paper Co. Seeks Relief In Court

Petitions were on file in U. C. District Court today for reorganization under Section 77-B of the National Bangruptcy Act of the

Page Two 3rd Column

With CMTC Boys At Fort McKinley

RUSS HAYES, staff photographer

Upper left, parents and friends disembarking from government steamer General R. N. Bachelder at pier, Fort McKiney Sunday afternoon; upper center, a group of members of the Diamond Island Association, left to right, Joseph P. Flagg, Mrs. Joseph P. Flagg, Miss Carroll Drew, President Walter S. Upson of the Diamond Island Association and Mrs. Upson, Edward S. Stinson; upper right, Miss Ruth P. Forbes, Captain Eugene B. Merrill, public relations officer for C.M.T.C., Mrs. Albert J. Morrison, Albert J. Morrisson, Wadsworth Owen,, Jr., George C. Owen, oldest resident of Great Diamond Island and Wadsworth Owen. Left center, Colors of C.M.T.C. pass in review; insert, Daniel W. Stubbs of Portland and Miss Eleanor Rafter of Portland caught at the camp just after the parade; center, marching straight ahead; left center, Major Keelah Bouve of the 302nd Infantry and Dr. F. H. Whipple of the Diamond Island Association review the parade; next left, Col. George B. Stebbins and two of his officers, left to right, Captain George W. Gibson, Col. Stebbins and Captain Elmer E. Ellsworth. Lower left, as the parade passed the reviewing stand; lower right, taking a cool drink of water after the parade, Nicholas Malanes, Allston, Mass., Augustus Martin, Nashua, N. H., Edward Cherowbrier, Andover, Mass., and Howard Gray of Bluehill,

Train Arrives At Tientsin With Reserves

Soldiers Rushed North From Kwantung Army

On Way To Peiping

Heavy Fighting Breaks Out Intermittently

TIENTSIN, China, (UP)—Japanese troop reinforcements began pouring into northern China from Manchukuo today, ready for a war.

The first train, bringing men from the Kwantung army—the Japanese. army. in. Asia—arrived this afternoon, on the way to Peiping, 60 miles inland, where Chinese and Japanese troops have been fighting sporadically for days.

The situatio.. which started with a clash of Chinese and Japanese troops southwest of Peiping was becoming serious. There was heavy fighting intermittently all through the early hours of Sunday.

Chinese sources asserted that a Japanese detachment tried to cross the railroad bridge over the Yingting River. Chinese held their fire until the last moment, it was asserted, then hacked to death with their big swords the leading men of the Japanese and machine gunned the rest from the bridge. There was hand to hand fighting for two hours.

Emperor Hirohito returned to the capital today from his villa at

Page Two 1st Column

200,000 PILGRIMS HEAR PONTIFF PRAY FOR PEACE

Prayer Is Broadcast To Gatherings In France

LISIEUX, France (UP) — Two hundred thousand pilgrims, gathered to see Cardinal Pacelli, Vatican secretary of State, dedicate a Basilicia to St. Therese of Lisieux, head Pope Pius yesterday pray for world peace.

The Pope spoke at his villa at Castel Gandolfo outside Rome, a bust of the saint beside him in his library, and the speech was broadcast through loud speakers here.

"The miseries and dangers and threats which oppress us from all sides are so great as to make us think again of the words of the Divine Master, 'We ought always to pray and not be faint,'" said the Pope. "Let us pray the Creator, who for that very reason is the

(Page Two 2nd Column)

COMMONS TOLD OF DANGER IN CHINA CRISIS

Eden Urges Settlement Of All Disputes

LONDON (UP)—The danger to British and other foreign interests from the current dispute in China was stressed by foreign Secretary Anthony Eden today in the House of Commons.

"The British government fully realizes the possible repercussions on British interests and international trade of the contention between China and Japan," Eden said. "If Anglo-Japanese conversations in London develop, they will give an opportunity of discussing the matter.

"It is the government's earnest desire that there should be a set-

(Page Two 1st Column)

EIGHT ESCAPE IN 5-CAR CRASH AT SCARBORO

Machines aTngle On Rain Drenched Highway

Eight persons escaped with minor injuries today when five automobiles crashed on the rain drenched Portland-Boston highway near the Scarboro marshes. All were treated at the scene of the accident by Dr. Howard M. Spario of Dunstan.

They weer Mr. and Mrs. Samuel E. Angus of 89 Clinton Street, Everett, Mass., Vincent G. Deritis, 201 Rigby Avenue, New York; Jess V. Miller, Prescott, Arizona; Curtis R. Low, West Point, New York; Barbara Noyes, 240 Cottage Road, South Portland; and Mrs. Alice Tewksbury and daughter, Bertha of 659 Stevens Avenue, Portland.

According to State Patrolman George Wood, the machine occupied by Mr. and Mrs. Samuel Angus was proceeding towards Old Orchard, followed by two other machines containing Curtis R. Low and Barbara Noyes, and Mrs. Tewksbury and her daughter.

A big roadster operated by Deritis, heading towards Portland struck the oncoming Angus machine a glancing blow after passing a parked truck. Low's car crashed into the rear end of Angus', and was in turn hit by the one driven by Mrs. Tewksbury.

Mrs. Tewksbury's version of the accident differed somewhat from that of Patrolman Wood. She said the roadster struck the Massachusetts car and continued on past her before coming to a stop. An-

(Page Two 1st Column)

BLAZING "GAS" MENACES TOWN OF HALLOWELL

Five Fire Departments Battle Flames For Hours

HALLOWELL — Blazing gasoline, leaking from one of 14 large storage tanks of the Standard Oil Company here, was extinguished after a hazardous four-hour fight yesterday during which firemen of five departments fought to save the town from destruction.

Nearby residents left their homes when it appeared that the flames would spread to the tanks.

Patrolman George Colt discovered the fire while patrolling his beat on Water Street, and rang in an alarm. Apparatus was called from Augusta, Gardiner, Lewiston and Auburn, and a supply of foamite was rushed from the Standard Oil plants in Portland and South Portland.

The blaze apparently started at a leak in the intake valves.

MEYER EXECUTED FOR SLAYING GIRL

BELLEFONTE, Pa. (UP)—Alexander T. Meyer, 20-year-old son of a wealthy coal broker, walked calmly to the electric chair in Rockview penitentiary early today, and died for the slaying of 16-year-old Helen Moyer, Modena, Pa., high school student.

Miss Moyer, an attractive, popular girl, was attacked and slain on February 11 in what Meyer's own attorney described as "one of the most brutal, gruesome murders of all time."

Lexington To Join Earhart Hunt Today

Sixty-Two Planes To Comb 360,000 Square Miles In Pacific In Three Or Four Days For Lost Fliers

HONOLULU, (UP)—Virtually all hopes of finding Amelia Earhart and Frederick J. Noonan, her navigator, lost in the Pacific since July 2, rested today with the Navy fliers aboard the carrier Lexington.

The big ship, ploughing along at half speed to conserve fuel, is expected to enter the search late today or Tuesday. There was no definite word, however, as to where the search, virtually abandoned as hopeless by the three fliers aboard the battleship Colorado, would start.

There are 62 planes and 300 fliers on the Lexington and it is estimated they can cover the entire search area of approximately 360,000 square miles in three or four days. If that fine combing of the waters around Howland Island fails to produce a trace of the missing 'round the world fliers it is presumed the Navy will abandon the hunt.

Miss Earhart and Noonan were shooting for Howland Island on a long hop from Lae, New Guinea, when they were lost. They were in the vicinity of the tiny landing station, just North of the Equator, but messaged that with their fuel running low they were unable to sight it.

The search for them and their big $80,000 plane first turned to the area North of Howland Island. Radio messages and signals, which may not have been authentic, indicated they were down in that region, but George Palmer Putnam, Miss Earhart's husband, convinced those directing the search that the area South of Howland Island was the more likely spot to find them.

JACK CURLEY, PROMOTER, IS HEART VICTIM

Noted Manager Was Interested In Wrestling

NEW YORK, (UP)—Jack Curley, 61, who promoted everything from flea circuses and one-piece bathing suits to heavyweight wrestling, died of a heart attack today at his Great Neck, Long Island, home.

Curley did what most sports experts had believed was impossible. He restored wrestling to public favor after it had been denounced as the most crooked of all off-color rackets. Under Curley's touch, wrestling flourished after 1929, and thousands paid to watch his exhibitions throughout the country.

The genial promoter, who stepped out of the field of sports on several occasions to promote a wild west circus, to manage a tour of the Vat-

Page Two, 2nd Column

N. H. MAN SLAYS WOMAN; FAILS IN SUICIDE TRY

Housekeeper Refused Proposal Of Marriage

GRAFTON CENTER, N. H., (UP)—Apparently thwarted in a suicide attempt, Samuel B. Williams, 40, Grafton road agent, today faced a possible murder charge for allegedly slaying a 32-year-old housekeeper because she spurned his proposal of marriage.

Williams shot himself twice in the head with an automatic pistol after allegedly pumping three bullets into Mrs. Gladys Newton, 32, while her three children stood by, terrified.

Hospitalized at Hanover, Williams was given a better than even chance to live. His condition was reported as critical, however.

Williams appeared late yesterday at the home of Mrs. Newton, who until Tuesday had acted as his housekeeper. He sent her children, Norma, 11, George, 9, and Mary, 7, who were playing nearby, to call their mother outdoors.

"For the last time, Gladys, are you going to come back to my house with me?" he demanded when she appeared.

"No, I won't go back," she said.

As Williams fired, the children ran into nearby woods. They emerged and ran to the house of a neighbor, Bert Lashaway ,only after Williams turned the gun on himself.

Police said that Mrs. Newton, though twice married, had been divorced only once

SCHOOLGIRL, 16, SLAIN; POLICE HUNT SUSPECT

Joseph Dumorad, 20, Is Sought In Connecticut

NEW HAVEN, Conn. (UP)—Local and state police pressed a statewide hunt today for Joseph Dumorad, 20, suspected of the brutal slaying of an attractive 16-year-old high school junior.

"He is a definite suspect," police said.

The body of the girl, Estelle Fineberg, was found battered and bruised Saturday night on the floor of Dumorad's bedroom in the house in which they both lived.

Deputy Coroner Nathan C. Sachs said she died of an intra-cranial hemorrhage caused by hammer blows on the forehead and left temple. There were evidences of strangulation also, Sachs said.

"There is a possibility the girl may have been attacked," he said.

Laboratory tests were taken, Sachs revealed, to determine whether Miss Fineberg was assaulted. Results may be available today.

ROCKLAND CHILD CRUSHED TO DEATH BY ROLLING LOG

ROCKLAND — Nine-year-old Kenneth Thomas Widdecomb, son of Mrs. Lena Widdecomb of Lime Street, was fatally injured late Saturday when a large log on the shore where he was playing rolled over and crushed him.

Süddeutsche Ausgabe
268./269. Ausg. • 50. Jahrg. • Einzelpreis für München 15 Pf., auswärts 20 Pf. Ausland m. ermäß. Porto 25 Pf., übrig. Ausl. 30 Pf., Italien Lire 1.50.

„Freiheit und Brot!"

Süddeutsche Ausgabe
München, Samstag/Sonntag, 25./26. September 1937

VÖLKISCHER BEOBACHTER

Verlag: Frz. Eher Nachf., GmbH., München 22, Thierschstr. 11. Sammelr. 22131, zw. 12 u. 14 Uhr 22134. Drahtanschr. Eherverlag - Postscheck: München 11346, Danzig 2855, Warschau 194121, Wien 79921, Prag 77303, Bern III 7205, Budapest 13532, Belgrad 68237, Bukarest 24968, Brüssel 350 75.., den Haag 211 846, Paris 190 066. Bayer. Hypoth.- u. Wechselbk., München, Fil. Kaufingerstr.; Bayer. Gemeindebank, Girozentr. München, Briennerstr. 49; Bank d. Deutschen Arbeit A. G., München; Deutsche Bank u. Disconto-Gesellschaft, Filiale München, Depositenkasse Maximilianstraße; Swiss Bank Corporation, West End Branch, 11 c Regent Street, Waterloo Place, London S. W. 1

Kampfblatt der national-sozialistischen Bewegung Großdeutschlands

Schriftleitung: München 13, Schellingstr. 39, Sammelruf 20801 - Briefanschrift: Postamt München 2 BS. Schließfach 294 - Drahtanschrift: Beobachter München -. Berliner Vertretung: Berlin SW 68, Zimmerstr. 88, Sammelruf A I (Jäger) 0022 - Erscheinungsweise wöchentlich 7 mal - Bezugspreis durch die Post RM. 2.60 einschl. 75 Pfg. Postgebühr, ausschl. 42 Pfg. Zustellung, in Orten mit eigener Geschäftsstelle RM. 3.- einschl. 55 Pfg. Botenlohn - Anzeigenabteilung: München, Thierschstraße 11 und Zweigstelle Schellingstraße 39, Ruf 22131, Anzeigenschluß 12 Uhr, 1 Tag vor Erscheinung - Anzeigenpreis laut aufliegender Preisliste 11

Der historische 25. September

Deutschland grüßt den Duce!

Gast des Volkes

Von Wilhelm Weiß

In wenigen Stunden betritt der italienische Regierungschef deutschen Boden. Zum ersten Male seit Mussolini an der Spitze der italienischen Regierung steht. Zum ersten Male seit jenem Marsch auf Rom, mit dem der Faschismus in Italien die Macht eroberte. Eroberte zu einer Zeit, in der Demokratie und Marxismus sich anschickten, sich in Deutschland häuslich einzurichten. Und während dieses Zeitalter der Demokratie im Reich noch auf Jahre hinaus in Scheinblüte stand, baute Mussolini mit seinen Faschisten im Süden Europas einen neuen autoritären Staat auf. Es war daher kein Zufall, wenn es dem Staat der Novembermänner trotz ihrer gelegentlichen Bemühungen nicht gelang, mit dem Italien Mussolinis in einen näheren politischen Kontakt zu kommen. Es hätte ja auch keinen Sinn gehabt! Denn auch Politik ist nun einmal auf die Dauer keine Angelegenheit blutleerer Berechnungen, sondern ein Vorgang, der sich an die Seele und an das Herz der Völker wendet. Das Deutschland Adolf Hitlers ist ein anderes Deutschland als jenes von 1922. Erst das nationalsozialistische Deutschland konnte dem Faschistenführer Mussolini die Brücke bauen, auf der zwei große Völker sich die Hand reichen.

Das unterscheidet den Staatsbesuch des italienischen Regierungschefs grundsätzlich von allen anderen Ministerbegegnungen oder Staatsempfängen ähnlicher Art. Denn nicht die Begegnung zweier Staatsmänner an sich ist in diesem Falle das wichtigste, sondern umgekehrt: Die Gemeinsamkeit des politischen Schicksals und die Verwandtschaft der weltanschaulichen Staatsideen bilden die Voraussetzung dafür, daß die Begegnung zwischen Benito Mussolini und Adolf Hitler mehr ist als ein äußeres politisches Ereignis. Denn etwas unterscheidet diese Septembertage in München und Berlin von allen ähnlichen Anlässen: Die innere Anteilnahme und Freude, die das italienische Volk ebensosehr wie das deutsche in diesem Augenblick beherrschen. Die beiden Völker sind es, die ihre Führer Seite an Seite sehen wollen. Zwei Männer treffen sich, die getragen sind von dem unendlichen Vertrauen der Nationen, die hinter ihnen stehen. Und wenn irgendwann der Händedruck zweier Staatsmänner die begeisterte und restlose Zustimmung ihrer Völker findet, so wird das am heutigen Tage der Fall sein.

Darin aber wird man die geschichtliche Bedeutung dieser Begegnung suchen müssen: in der bewußten Demonstration einer gemeinsamen menschheitsbewegenden Idee! Einer Idee, deren europäische Mission gerade heute sichtbarer denn je wird. Vor kaum vierzehn Tagen hat der Führer in seiner Schlußansprache auf dem Nürnberger Kongreß einen leidenschaftlichen Appell an die Kulturvölker Europas gerichtet und sie aufgefordert, sich gegen die drohende Vernichtung der europäischen Kulturwelt durch den jüdischen Bolschewismus zur Wehr zu setzen. Es gibt keine symbolhaftere Geste, um die aktuelle Bedeutung dieses Nürnberger Aufrufs zu unterstreichen, als die Zusammenkunft jener beiden europäischen Staatsmänner, die in der Bekämpfung der bolschewistischen Völkerzersetzung am energischsten und kompromißlosesten vorgegangen und demgemäß am erfolgreichsten gewesen sind. Sie konnten aber auch nur erfolgreich sein, weil sie im Kampf gegen diese Weltpest entschlossen waren, nicht allein die Machtmittel des Staates mit der in diesem Fall notwendigen Rücksichtslosigkeit einzusetzen, sondern weil hinter diesen Mitteln die Macht einer Idee stand, die jung und gesund war, und die befähigt war, Menschen zu begeistern und zu überzeugen.

Der Faschismus und der Nationalsozialismus werden in der Geschichte Europas ihre historische Rechtfertigung in dem Augenblick feierlich erhalten, in dem erwiesen ist, daß sie allein dazu fähig waren, in der europäischen Völkerfamilie eine Aufgabe zu lösen, an der die Demokratie gescheitert ist.

Der Faschismus ist ebensowenig wie der Nationalsozialismus ein etwa zufällig entstandenes Staatssystem wie irgendein anderes auch, sondern in diesen beiden großen Bewegungen hat eine geschichtliche Aufgabe von europäischem Ausmaß politische Gestalt angenommen. Darum wirkt auch der Besuch des Duce beim Führer als historisches Faktum für sich. Denn die Gemeinsamkeit des politischen Willens und des weltanschaulichen Zieles hat sich in der Geschichte noch immer als stärker und entscheidender erwiesen als die Paragraphen aller möglichen Allianzbeschlüsse.

Niemand wird daher berechtigt sein, in dieser Begegnung irgendein Moment zu suchen, das geeignet wäre, Europa zu beunruhigen. Gerade das Gegenteil trifft zu. In Nürnberg hat der Führer ein Bekenntnis zur europäischen Völkerfamilie und zur Gemeinschaft der europäischen Kulturnationen abgelegt, das nicht übersehen werden kann. Wenn daher der italienische Regierungschef im jetzigen Augenblick nach Deutschland kommt, dann zeigt er damit, daß er den Führer verstanden hat. Der Welt aber kommt zugleich symbolhaft zum Bewußtsein: Im Lager Mussolinis und Adolf Hitlers steht das junge Europa.

Aber dieses junge Europa ist ebensosehr das alte, dessen stolze Tradition es gilt, vor dem Verfall zu bewahren. Zwei Frontsoldaten des Weltkrieges sind es, die sich in der Durchführung dieser geschichtlichen Mission treffen. Aus ihrem Fronterlebnis heraus sind sie zu Schöpfern ihrer politischen Bewegungen geworden, und aus diesem gleichen Erlebnis heraus sind sie heute die treuesten Garanten für das Leben und die Sicherheit ihrer Völker. Als Soldaten der Front sind sie angetreten. Als Soldaten der Idee marschieren sie heute an der Spitze ihrer Nationen.

Foto Ghitta Carell Roma — diritti riservati

Die neueste Aufnahme Benito Mussolinis

Mussolini von Rom abgereist

Feierliche Verabschiedung durch die Faschistische Partei, die Regierung und die Wehrmacht

Rom, 24. September

Mit aller Feierlichkeit, die die Faschistische Partei dem Duce beim Antritt seiner Deutschlandreise bereiten konnte, ist der italienische Regierungschef am Freitag, mittags 12.30 Uhr, von Rom abgereist.

Vor dem Bahnhof hatten Truppenabordnungen der gesamten hauptstädtischen Garnison und große Abteilungen sämtlicher faschistischen Organisationen Roms in Uniform mit ihren Fahnen Aufstellung genommen. Zehntausende waren zusammengeströmt, um dem Duce im Augenblick des Beginns seiner Deutschlandreise ihren begeisterten Gruß zuzujubeln, den Mussolini, dessen Wagen unter den Klängen der Giovinezza angefahren war, lebhaft dankend erwiderte. Die weite Bahnhofshalle, die über und über mit italienischen Trikoloren und Hakenkreuzfahnen geschmückt war, war für die Ausfahrt des Sonderzuges von den übrigen Zügen vollkommen geräumt worden, so daß auch hier Tausende und aber Tausende zusammenkommen konnten, deren stürmischer Gruß, unterbrochen von Heilrufen auf Hitler, auch hier dem Duce noch einmal entgegenbrauste.

Auf dem Bahnhof waren sämtliche Regierungsmitglieder, die gesamte Parteihierarchie mit der Standarte, die Generalität der Garnison und eine große Anzahl höherer Offiziere der Wehrmacht und der Miliz angetreten. Unter den Klängen der Giovinezza schritt Mussolini in Begleitung von Außenminister Graf Ciano, Parteisekretär Minister Starace und dem Minister für Volksbildung, Alfieri, die Ehrenformationen der Wehrmacht und der Partei ab, um sich dann unmittelbar vor Abfahrt des Zuges in sehr herzlicher Weise von dem deutschen Geschäftsträger, Baron von Plessen, der mit sämtlichen Mitgliedern der deutschen Botschaft auf dem Bahnhof erschienen war, zu verabschieden.

Der aus acht Wagen bestehende Sonderzug setzte sich dann langsam in Bewegung, während die stürmischen Zurufe „Duce! Duce! Duce!" und das Händeklatschen kein Ende nehmen wollten.

Die Tatsache, daß der Führer bereits das Manövergelände verlassen und sich nach München begeben hat, um bei den letzten Vorbereitungen für den Empfang in der Hauptstadt der Bewegung zugegen zu sein, wird als eine ganz persönliche Geste des Führers und Reichskanzlers für seinen hohen italienischen Gast besonders hervorgehoben.

WEATHER FORECAST
Fair and warmer today; moderate southwest and west winds.
Yesterday's Temperatures: Max., 49; Min., 28.
(Details on Page 20)

THE SUN

Registered United States Patent Office

Canada's Conservatives To Hold Convention
By J. A. Stevenson —Page 11.

Vol. 202—B | PAID CIRCULATION FEBRUARY MORNING, 142,016; EVENING, 158,584 300,600 ‖ SUNDAY, ... | [BA]LTIMORE, SATURDAY, MARCH 12, 1938 | Entered as second-class matter at Baltimore Postoffice. Copyright, 1938, by The A. S. Abell Company, Publishers of The Sun. | 20 Pages | 2 Cents

HITLER SEIZES AUSTRIA

Invasion Meets No Resistance

MORGAN STALLS HEARING ON TVA BY DEFIANT IRE

Chairman Refuses To Support Charges Before Chief Executive

President Gives 3 Directors Week To Add To Statements

By J. FRED ESSARY

Washington, March 11—A stubborn, tight-lipped, angry member of the original Roosevelt Brain Trust stalled President Roosevelt's search for TVA facts today and probably has made a Congressional investigation inevitable.

It was Chairman Arthur E. Morgan, smarting under the conviction that he alone was "on trial" before the President, who refused to support any count in his savage indictment of his fellow board members.

Morgan Sees Prejudice

He refused, he said, because he was convinced that he was asked to testify before a prejudiced judge and that only Congress could make a fair and impartial finding as between him and his associates, Dr. Harcourt Morgan and David E. Lilienthal.

This impasse continued through some six hours of Presidential questioning of his three appointees. And at the end it moved Mr. Roosevelt, in effect, to demand the resignation of the TVA chairman. His concluding statement to the group was:

"All three of you gentlemen owe it to the country not to continue longer to jeopardize the public interest by personal differences and those who could not see their way clear to do so should resign."

That indicated to some minds tonight that the President was suggesting the withdrawal of all three members, but the transcript of the testimony at the hearing gave no such impression.

Hearing Is Lopsided

The President stated that he would allow the three commissioners a week in which to supplement their statements today, either orally or in writing. He did this at the request of Chairman Arthur Morgan, who intimated he might after all wish to say something more for the record.

Because of the chairman's recalcitrance as a witness—his defiance of the President, in fact—the hearing was a lopsided affair. The President meant it to be bi-lateral, he said after the hearing was over, but in this the embittered chairman thwarted him.

At first Dr. Arthur Morgan declined outright to come to Washington for the hearing. This came out in the hearing. Three communications—two from Secretary McIntyre and one from the President himself—were barely sufficient to change his mind. As it was he came bare-handed so to speak. He bore no bulky file or even a bit of vest-pocket data.

Asked To Back Charge

He had decided before arrival that he would not be drawn out; that he would invite "contempt of court" first. This came out at the very outset of the hearing. The President had made a long statement of his purposes in requiring the presence of his appointees. Dr. Morgan had been asked to substantiate his charge that the Berry marble claim had been mishandled by the board majority.

After a preliminary observation the chairman said:

"I am of theopinion that this meeting is not, and in the nature of the case, cannot be an effective or useful fact-finding occasion."

The President: Wait a minute. I don't want opinions. I have asked you a question about the Berry marble case, and I want you to confine your answers not to opinions but to facts.

Dr. Morgan: I wish to complete my statement, which will take about a minute longer.

Insists On Facts

The President: I don't want you in any statements to talk about opinions. I want you to confine yourself to facts.

Dr. Morgan: I am giving my reasons for not answering you directly and I think I must do it.

The President: Are you planning to answer the direct question?

Dr. Morgan: My statement will indicate whether I am or not. To properly substantiate the charges is not the

(Continued on Page 3, Column 8)

Figures In Austrian Crisis---Points Of Invasion

VIENNA—Dr. Arthur Seysz-Inquart, Minister of the Interior in the old Cabinet and friend of Chancellor Adolf Hitler of Germany, has been made Chancellor of Austria as a result of the Berlin ultimatum served on the Government of Chancellor Kurt Schuschnigg.

KURT SCHUSCHNIGG, *Retiring Chancellor* — GEN. WILHELM ZEHNER, *War Secretary* — WILHELM MIKLAS, *President*

VIENNA—The arrows on the map point to the three places on the German-Austrian border where troops of the Berlin Government crossed the Austrian frontier.

WHITNEY AGAIN IS ARRESTED ON LARCENY COUNT

Charged With Taking $103,000 From Yacht Club Safe Deposit Box

[By the Associated Press]

New York, March 11—Richard Whitney, whose very name had been a symbol for Wall Street probity, stood twice charged with theft tonight as the manifold investigations of the spectacular collapse of his firm opened a great fiscal scandal.

Whitney, socially impeccable, five times president of the New York Stock Exchange, the erstwhile "Morgan broker" through whom many of the orders of the mighty J. P. Morgan Company were executed, surrendered in midafternoon to John J. Bennett, Jr., Attorney General, upon a second grand larceny complaint.

The maximum penalty under that charge is ten years.

Theft From Safe Charged

His arrest had been ordered a few minutes before, after the testimony of Commodore William A. W. Stewart of the exclusive New York Yacht Club, long a friend, that Whitney, in addition to all the other derelictions charged against him, unlawfully had taken $103,000 in club bonds from a safe deposit box.

Already he was under a grand larceny indictment obtained by Thomas E. Dewey, the New York county District Attorney, for the alleged misappropriation of $105,000 from a family trust fund set up by his father-in-law for the benefit of Mrs. Whitney, her sister, Mrs. Mary Sheldon Murphy, his alma mater, Harvard University, and St. Paul's School of Concord, N. H.

Thus, near the end of the day, two prosecutors—Dewey and Bennett—already had acted against him, and the Federal Government, through Gregory Noonon, Assistant United States Attorney, was eyeing the whole case sharply.

To Decide Next Week

Noonan said he would have sufficient information by early next week to "decide whether to go before the grand jury."

While Bennett was disavowing any rivalry with Dewey for the job of bringing Whitney to trial, saying it was just a case of concurrent jurisdiction between the State and the county, Noonan remarked that any Federal indictment would not necessarily take priority.

"It's just a matter," he said, "of who catches his fish first."

Whitney appeared desperately melancholy as he turned up in Bennett's office for the quick formalities of his second arrest.

Deep Lines

There were deep lines under his eyes and mouth. He kept his lips pressed

(Continued on Page 11, Column 5)

ITALY REBUFFS FRANCE ABOUT AID TO AUSTRIA

Paris Government Regarded As Helpless To Act In Coup

[By the Associated Press]

Paris, March 11—France, without a government and rebuffed by Italy on a proposal for joint efforts to save Austria's independence, stood helpless tonight as Nazi Germany proceeded to take power in Vienna.

Foreign Office officials announced that the French and British ambassadors in Berlin had made a joint protest to the German Government over Nazi steps in Austria.

At the same time, Premier-Designate Leon Blum, confronted with a threat to the peace of Europe, let it be known he was confident of forming a National Union Government—of all parties from Communist to extreme Right.

Blum Speeds Consultations

Sources close to the Socialist leader said the Cabinet would be organized by early tomorrow and would be ready to deal with events in Austria.

Blum hurried consultations with political leaders, striving quickly to rally support. Besides the critical situation in Central Europe, he was con-

(Continued on Page 2, Column 5)

Senators Rap Entanglements In Debate On Austrian Issue

Attack Reputed Pacts As Rep. O'Connor Threatens Probe Of "Peace Organizations"

By DEWEY L. FLEMING
[Washington Bureau of The Sun]

Washington, March 11—Developments in Austria today set off sharp Senate debate on the international situation, with vigorous condemnation of existing or potential alliances between the United States and any foreign country.

Reported understandings between the United States and Great Britain for joint use of nava lbases in the Pacific—the islands of Canton and Enderbury, and at Singapore—drew specific denunciation from a group of Senators including Lewis (Dem., Ill.), Johnson (Rep., Cal.) and Clark (Dem., Missouri).

Simultaneously, the House made the $1,000,000,000 naval expansion bill its next order of business and put it in place for the start of a twelve-hour debate Monday.

Probe Of Peace Groups

As the navy bill came to the fore, Representative O'Connor (Dem., N. Y.), chairman of the Rules Committee, threatened to demand an investigation of the "so-called peace organizations" that have flooded the offices of Senators and Representatives with letters of opposition to the measure.

"Members of Congress have been swamped with communications on this measure from the so-called peace organizations," Mr. O'Connor declared. "It is evident from the character of the letters that they are in the nature of racketeering organizations.

"Certain smart boys of Washington and elsewhere appear to be playing on the emotions of church people and other good people interested in the promotion of peace. The sole purpose of these organizations, one might be led to believe, is getting people to join and pay dues.

Probe Contemplated

"The Rules Committee has been so impressed by this flood of letters that it is contemplating an investigation of this racket."

"How about an investigation to find out who has been paying the expenses of those who have been going around promoting this naval building program?" demanded Representative O'Malley (Dem., Wis.).

"If it is decided to investigation they, too, will be investigated," Mr. O'Connor answered.

Senator Lewis initiated the Senate outburst on the international situation when he called attention to the day's reports from Austria. He predicted Germany's advances into Austria would be followed by an arrangement between Germany, Italy and Japan whereby these three countries would carry out "complete possession" of the Orient.

"That complete possession," hc de-

(Continued on Page 3, Column 2)

Schuschnigg Explains Surrender To Germany

[By the Associated Press]

Vienna, March 11—Following is the text of Chancellor Kurt Schuschnigg's radio broadcast:

"Today we have been confronted with a difficult and decisive situation.

"I am authorized to report to the Austrian people on the events of the day.

"The German Government presented the Federal (Austrian) President with an ultimatum with a time limit according to which he had to appoint as Chancellor a candidate who would be proposed to him and appoint a Government according to the dictates of the German Reich.

"Otherwise German troops would march into Austria at the hour named.

"I declare before the world that reports which were spread in Austria that there have been labor disputes, that streams of blood were flowing, that the Government was not master of the situation and could not keep order, were invented from A to Z.

"The Federal President authorizes me to inform the Austrian people that we yield to force.

"Because even in this grave hour we are not minded at any price to shed German blood, we have given our armed forces an order that in case invasion is carried out they are to withdraw without resistance and await decisions on the hours which are to come.

"The President has intrusted Gen. S. Schilhawsky, inspector general of troops, with command of armed forces. Through him further instructions will be given to the armed forces.

"So, in this hour, I say good-by with the heartfelt wish that God will protect Austria."

REICH TROOPS CROSS BORDER AT 3 POINTS

Austrian Legionnaires Reported Moving From All Over Germany

[By the Associated Press]

Munich, Germany, March 11—German troops tonight crossed the frontier into Austria. They moved across the border at 10 P. M. (4 P. M., E. S. T.).

In close formation, they marched into Austrian territory at Salzburg, Kufstein and Mittenwald.

Salzburg is 156 miles west-southwest of Vienna and Mittenwald more than 100 miles further west-southwest, with Kufstein in between.

At the same time Austrian legionnaires from all over Germany were moving southward.

Troops Carry Pontoons

Earlier in the day German troops were moving toward the border carrying pontoons for making bridges and also field artillery, said motorists who encountered them on a highway south of here.

One motorist said he saw 130 military motor trucks on the road to Salzburg. Hundreds of motor-cycle troops were moving southward.

Motorized engineer detachments carried pontoons, motor boats and other material used in military crossings of wide streams. Numerous comandeered brewery trucks helped carry this material.

Going On All Night

Peasants along the highway said this had been "going on all night."

Near the border troops impressed peasants for work and commandeered horses and automobiles.

The border near alzburg is marked by the rivers Inn, Salzach and Saalach.

Evidences Of Mobilization

Evidences of mobilization were the following:

1. Able-bodied men were being called to the colors and their private cars commandeered.
2. Municipal buses and private trucks were requisitioned.
3. Owners were frankly told these

(Continued on Page 2, Column 3)

SEYSZ-INQUART NAMED HEAD OF GOVERNMENT AS SCHUSCHNIGG RESIGNS

Ultimatum From Hitler Forces Chancellor Out. Troops Ordered Not To Oppose Invading Forces

Hitler Asked By New Cabinet Head To Rush Soldiers To Vienna—Nazis Storm Headquarters Of Fatherland Front

[By the Associated Press]

Berlin, Saturday, March 12—A reliable source said today that all the members of the new Austrian Cabinet, except Chancellor Arthur Seysz-Inquart, who is in Vienna, were closeted with Chancellor Adolf Hitler.

[By the Associated Press]

Vienna, March 11—Austria capitulated to Adolf Hitler tonight.

Bowing to Germany's war power, the Government gave up its five-year fight against domination by the German Führer.

German troops, massed on the border, marched into Austria at three points. Faced with a German ultimatum demanding reorganization of the Government, the anti-Nazi Chancellor, Kurt Schuschnigg, resigned.

President Wilhelm Miklas appointed Arthur Seysz-Inquart, Austria's Nazi leader, to succeed him.

Asks Hitler To Rush Troops

Earlier, Seysz-Inquart had sent a telegram to Hitler saying that the "provisional Austrian Government" requested Germany to send troops as soon as possible to assist it in "preventing the shedding of blood."

The new Chancellor was one of five Nazi sympathizers included in the Cabinet at Hitler's order February 15. He started formation of a Cabinet which the press bureau declared would give "thorough recognition to nationalists."

Tonight's developments came after moves and counter-moves by Schuschnigg and the Nazi command. There was violence throughout Austria yesterday and today.

Austria Also Mobilizes Troops

Early today German troops mobilized near the Austrian border. Austria likewise sent troops to danger points. Schuschnigg had his regular army of 70,000, but called out 100,000 reserves and 30,000 guardsmen.

Vienna and many Austrian cities were in turmoil, with Nazis and Schuschnigg supporters clashing over a plebiscite on Austrian independence Schuschnigg had ordered for Sunday.

Nazis denounced it vehemently, claiming it was violation of Schuschnigg's agreement with Hitler at Berchtesgaden February 12.

As tension increased, Schuschnigg postponed the plebiscite indefinitely.

Moves To Avoid Bloodshed

Then Schuschnigg announced that, bowing to the German ultimatum, a new Government was being formed.

He declared that "to prevent the shedding of blood" orders had been given for Austrian troops to fall back "in case of invasion."

Before midnight the Nazi swastika flew from the Chancellery and the City Hall.

Vienna Nazis went wild.

Swastikas appeared even on flagpoles about the headquarters of the Fatherland Front, previously the only legal political party in Austria.

Minor Officials Shift To Nazis

While Schuschnigg, President Miklas and Seysz-Inquart were in conference and before appointment of the new Chancellor had

20 Pfennig

HF am Montag

Sport-Zeitung des Hamburger Fremdenblattes

Druck und Verlag von Broschek & Co., Hamburg 36, Große Bleichen 38-52 • Anzeigenpreise (Preisliste Nr. 4): Die 46 mm breite Millimeterzeile 24 Pf. • Textanzeigen: Die 70 mm breite Millimeterzeile 80 Pf. Mengennachlaß nach Staffel A der 3. Bekanntmachung des Werberates der deutschen Wirtschaft. Sonstige Preise und Bedingungen in der Anzeigenpreisliste

Achtzehnter Jahrgang • Nummer 11 — 8 — Hamburg, Montag, den 14. März 1938

Der Anschluß verkündet

Vereidigung des österreichischen Heeres auf den Führer

Volksabstimmung in Österreich am 10. April

Vereinigung mit dem Reich

Wien, 13. März

Amtlich wird mitgeteilt:

Heute ist folgendes Bundesverfassungsgesetz verlautbart worden:

Bundesverfassungsgesetz über die Wiedervereinigung Österreichs mit dem Deutschen Reich.

Auf Grund des Artikels III Absatz 2 des Bundesverfassungsgesetzes über außerordentliche Maßnahmen im Bereich der Verfassung BGB I Nr. 255/1934 hat die Bundesregierung beschlossen:

Artikel I

Österreich ist ein Land des Deutschen Reiches.

Artikel II

Sonntag, 10. April 1938, findet eine freie und geheime Volksabstimmung der über 20 Jahre alten deutschen Männer und Frauen Österreichs über die Wiedervereinigung mit dem Deutschen Reich statt.

Artikel III

Bei der Volksabstimmung entscheidet Mehrheit der abgegebenen Stimmen.

Artikel IV

Die zur Durchführung und Ergänzung dieses Bundesverfassungsgesetzes erforderlichen Vorschriften werden durch Verordnung getroffen.

Artikel V

1. Dieses Bundesverfassungsgesetz tritt am Tage seiner Kundmachung in Kraft.

2. Mit der Vollziehung dieses Bundesverfassungsgesetzes ist die Bundesregierung betraut.

Seyß-Inquart, Glaise-Horstenau, Wolff, Huber, Menghin, Jury, Neumayer, Reinthaler, Fischböck.

Das verfassungsmäßige Zustandekommen dieses Bundesverfassungsgesetzes wird beurkundet.

Seyß-Inquart, Glaise-Horstenau, Wolff, Huber, Menghin, Jury, Neumayer, Reinthaler, Fischböck.

Das Reichsgesetz

Berlin, 13. März

Reichsminister Dr. Goebbels gab Sonntag abend den Vertretern der deutschen Presse die folgenden Gesetze und Verfügungen bekannt:

Gesetz über die Wiedervereinigung Österreichs mit dem Deutschen Reich vom 13. März 1938

Die Reichsregierung hat das folgende Gesetz beschlossen, das hiermit verkündet wird:

Artikel 1.

Das von der österreichischen Bundesregierung beschlossene Bundesverfassungsgesetz über die Wiedervereinigung Österreichs mit dem Deutschen Reich vom 13. März 1938 wird hiermit deutsches Reichsgesetz.

Artikel 2.

Das derzeit in Österreich geltende Recht bleibt bis auf weiteres in Kraft bis zur Einführung des Reichsgesetzes in Österreich durch den Führer und Reichskanzler oder den von ihm hierzu ermächtigten Reichsminister.

Artikel 3.

Der Reichsminister des Innern wird ermächtigt, im Einvernehmen mit den beteiligten Reichsministern die zur Durchführung und Ergänzung dieses Gesetzes erforderlichen Rechts- und Verwaltungsvorschriften zu erlassen.

Artikel 4.

Das Gesetz tritt am Tage seiner Verkündung in Kraft.

Linz, 13. März 1938.

Der Führer und Reichskanzler.
Der Reichsminister des Innern.
Der Reichsminister des Auswärtigen.
Der Stellvertreter des Führers.

Der Minister schloß an die Bekanntgabe des Wortlauts dieser Gesetze und Verfügungen zündende Worte, in denen er die Größe der Stunde würdigte. Allen Versammelten wurde die Feierlichkeit des für das gesamte deutsche Volk historischen Augenblicks durch die Worte des Ministers in besonderem Maße bewußt.

Baldur von Schirach in Wien

Wien, 13. März

Am Sonntagvormittag ist der Jugendführer des Deutschen Reiches, Baldur von Schirach, in Wien eingetroffen.

Der Führer an den Duce

Linz, 13. März

Der Führer sandte am Sonntag an den Duce folgendes Telegramm:

„An Seine Exzellenz,
den italienischen Ministerpräsidenten und Duce des faschistischen Italiens Benito Mussolini.

Mussolini, ich werde Ihnen dieses nie vergessen!

Adolf Hitler."

Gauleiter Bürckel kommissarischer Gauleiter in Österreich

Linz, 13. März

Der Führer hat folgende Verfügung erlassen:

1. Ich erteile Gauleiter Bürckel, Saarpfalz, den Auftrag, die NSDAP in Österreich zu reorganisieren.

2. Gauleiter Bürckel ist in dieser Eigenschaft als kommissarischer Leiter der NSDAP von Österreich mit der Vorbereitung der Volksabstimmung betraut.

3. Ich habe Gauleiter Bürckel mit der Vollmacht ausgestattet, alle Maßnahmen zu ergreifen oder anzuordnen, die zur verantwortlichen Erfüllung des erteilten Auftrages erforderlich sind.

Linz, 13. März 1938.

gez. Adolf Hitler.

Der Führer am Elterngrab

d. Wien, 13. März

Adolf Hitler begann den heutigen Sonntag mit einem Besuch am Grabe seiner Eltern in Leonding, das er infolge der politischen Verhältnisse eine Reihe von Jahren nicht mehr gesehen hat. Er fuhr um 10 Uhr vom Hotel Weinzinger in Linz hinaus in das nur fünf Kilometer entfernte kleine Dorf Leonding, das am Fuß des Kürenberges unweit Eferding, also mitten im Nibelungenland liegt, denn in Eferding hat sich Kriemhild auf der Fahrt ins Ungarland mit ihren Brüdern aufgehalten. Der Führer legte am Elterngrab, das unter einem hohen Lebensbaum an der Mauer des Dorffriedhofes liegt, und wie immer reich mit Blumen geschmückt war, die unbekannte Nationalsozialisten dort niedergelegt hatten, einen Kranz nieder. Er besuchte dann die Stätten seiner frühesten Kindheit, das Elternhaus gegenüber dem Friedhof, von wo aus er mehrere Jahre täglich den weiten Weg über die Felder in die Linzer Realschule gegangen war. Er begrüßte auch die im Dorf noch ansässigen Jugendgefährten.

„Wir wollen unseren Führer sehen"

Linz, 13. März

Die Bevölkerung von Linz war am Sonntagmorgen wieder früh auf den Beinen. Die hochgestimmte Menge hat noch einen starken Zuwachs erfahren, denn aus ganz Oberösterreich und aus den übrigen Bundesländern sind Begeisterte nach Linz gekommen, um an der großen Freude des deutschen Volkes in Österreich teilhaben zu können.

In der Halle des Hotels herrscht regstes Leben und Treiben. Außer dem Gefolge des Führers harren hier die führenden Persönlichkeiten der Partei und der Behörden von Linz und die österreichische Generalität des Führers. Gegen 12 Uhr, als die Wagenkolonne des Führers vorfährt, wird es auch vor dem Hotel lebendiger. Schnell hat die Linzer Jugend den im Reich wohlbekannten Sprechchor gelernt: „Wir wollen unseren Führer sehen!" Bald wird auch ihr Verlangen gestillt. Um 12 Uhr tritt der Führer aus dem Hotel. Ein hübsches Linzer Mädchen in der Tracht ihrer Heimat, der Heimat des Führers, und ein Kind überreichen ihm einen schönen Blumenstrauß. Mit unendlicher jubelnder Begeisterung grüßen die Tausende, die seit den frühesten Morgenstunden auf dem weiten Platz vor dem Hotel und in den anliegenden Straßen ausgeharrt haben, den Führer. Dann setzt sich die Wagenkolonne in Bewegung. Der Führer tritt die Fahrt nach Leonding an, der letzten Ruhestätte seiner Eltern.

Das österreichische Bundesheer in der Deutschen Wehrmacht

Linz, 13. März

Der Führer und Oberste Befehlshaber der Wehrmacht hat verfügt:

1. Die österreichische Bundesregierung hat soeben durch Gesetz die Wiedervereinigung Österreichs mit dem Deutschen Reich beschlossen. Die deutsche Reichsregierung hat durch ein Gesetz vom heutigen Tage diesen Beschluß anerkannt.

2. Ich verfüge auf Grund dessen: Das österreichische Bundesheer tritt als Bestandteil der Deutschen Wehrmacht mit dem heutigen Tage unter meinen Befehl.

3. Mit der Befehlsführung der nunmehrigen Deutschen Wehrmacht innerhalb der österreichischen Landesgrenzen beauftrage ich den General der Infanterie v. Bock, Oberbefehlshaber der VIII. Armee.

4. Sämtliche Angehörige des österreichischen Bundesheeres sind auf mich als ihren Obersten Befehlshaber unverzüglich zu vereidigen. General der Infanterie v. Bock trifft sofort die notwendigen Anordnungen.

gez. Adolf Hitler.

Das größere Deutschland

A. H. Schneller, als erwartet werden konnte, ist der Traum einer Nation zur Wirklichkeit geworden. Österreich ist von diesem Sonntag ab, der als heiliges Datum in die deutsche Geschichte eingehen wird, ein Land des Deutschen Reiches. Durch den Willen des Volkes hüben und drüben sind die Schlagbäume einer Grenze niedergerissen, die niemals im Bewußtsein der 75 Millionen Deutschen bestand, sondern einzig durch den Willkürakt des Diktatfriedens errichtet wurde. Der deutsche Frühlingssturm, der in knappen drei Tagen über die Südmark des Reiches dahinbrauste, hat alles weggefegt, was einst vor zwanzig Jahren als ewige Fessel für das Deutschtum in Mitteleuropa gedacht war.

Mit Schauern innerer Ergriffenheit und angeweht von dem Hauche der Ewigkeit unserer völkischen Geschichte vernahmen wir Pressevertreter heute abend gegen 11 Uhr aus dem Munde des Reichspropagandaministers den lapidaren Wortlaut der Gesetze und Verfügungen, die mit der Unterschrift des Führers und Neuschöpfers des Deutschen Reiches das Ortsdatum Linz tragen. Wir spürten, wie ein Traum sich verwirklicht hat, den durch die Jahrhunderte alle aufrechten deutschen Männer als heiligstes Vermächtnis in ihrer Brust getragen haben — der Traum vom Heiligen Deutschen Reiche, das in seinen Grenzen alle Menschen birgt, deren Muttersprache das Deutsche ist. Unserem Sehnen ist Erfüllung geworden, eine Hoffnung, um die mit so viel Leid und Zwietracht gerungen wurde, hat sich in die freudige Gewißheit des Erreichten und Vollendeten gewandelt.

Auf Augenblicke umspannen unsere Gedanken ein Jahrtausend deutschen Werdens. Germanische Stämme waren es einst, die ihre Kraft und ihre Kultur in den Südosten Europas vortrugen. Dort, wo heute Wien steht, spielte eine der schönsten Episoden des Nibelungenliedes. Später hat uns jenes kerndeutsche Alpenland ein Fürstengeschlecht geschenkt, das die Kaiserwürde der Deutschen auf die höchsten Gipfel weltlicher Macht führen, aber auch in der Überfülle seiner politischen Verstrickungen zu Zeiten seine deutschen Verpflichtungen vergessen sollte. Der germanische Stamm der Österreicher war es, der gegen die Bedrohung der abendländischen Kultur durch die Türken ein unüberwindliches Bollwerk setzte. Schließlich erfüllte sich mit dem Zusammenbruch des alten Römischen Reiches deutscher Nation die Logik der Geschichte, und das Schicksalsjahr des deutschen Bruderzwistes 1866 löste im Staatlichen jene Bande des Blutes, die erst im Weltkriege wieder zur Unlöslichkeit geschmiedet werden sollten. Was im Jahre 1919 noch ein unerbittlicher Feind verhindern konnte, den Zusammenschluß der Deutschen, die zu Deutschen wollten, das ist heute im revolutionären Geschehen dreier welthistorischer Tage herrliche und überwältigende Wirklichkeit geworden.

Die Gesetze bedürfen keiner Erläuterung. Wie alles Große, was in der Welt geschieht,

Der Führer beim Betreten österreichischen Bodens
Aufn. Presse-Hoffmann

Der Führer spricht vom Balkon des Rathauses von Linz; hinter ihm der Bundeskanzler Seyß-Inquart
Aufn. Presse-Hoffmann

SHOWERS
For All New England
Slowly rising temperatures, becoming cooler at night, moderate northeast and east winds, shifting to southeast.

DAILY RECORD
BOSTON'S HOME PICTURE NEWSPAPER

FINAL

Vol. 251, No. 69 36 Pages Boston, Monday, September 19, 1938 PRICE TWO CENTS

BRITAIN AND FRANCE BOW

Sacrifice Czechs to Hitler

Story on Page 2

French Statesmen as They Arrived in London for Czech Parley

Prime Minister Neville Chamberlain of Great Britain, Foreign Minister Georges Bonnet and Premier Edouard Daladier both of France, left to right, shown at the Croyden Airdrome, where Chamberlain met the two French diplomats, who flew to England to discuss the Czechoslovakian crisis with British cabinet members. It is believed Chamberlain relayed to the Frenchmen gist of his conversation he had last week with Adolf Hitler, German Reichsfuehrer.

This Photo Was Sent to New York from London Via Radio and Rushed to Boston by Plane.

15. Jahrgang / Nr. 39
29. September 1938
Verlag Knorr & Hirth
Kommanditgesellschaft,
München

Münchner Illustrierte Presse

Preis: 20 Pfennig
Elsaß-Lothringen: 2,20 Frs., übriges Frankreich: 2,50 Frs. / Estland: 40 Cent / Holland: 20 Cent / Italien: 2 Lire / Jugoslawien: 5 Dinar / Schweiz: 40 Rappen / Tschechoslowakei: 2 Kronen

Aufnahme: Hoffmann

Welthistorische Begegnung

Der Führer und Chamberlain in Godesberg

WEATHER
RAIN
COOLER
High 1 P.M. 72 | Low 5 A.M. 58
Details on Page 10

DAILY MIRROR

Member of The BRIEF COMPLETE Associated Press

2 CENTS ★★★ FINAL

Vol. 15. No. 85 BK New York, Friday, September 30, 1938 3 Cents Outside City Limits

PEACE PACT SIGNED

See Page 3

(International Radiophoto)

An epochal picture, telephotoed from Munich to London and radioed to New York. The heads of four governments that might now have been at war, meet at a round table in the Fuehrerhaus in Munich. Left to right: Mussolini, Hitler, Daladier and Chamberlain . . . as they started their attempt to re-make the map of Europe, without shedding any blood.

(Other photos on Pages 3, 4, 20 and 21)

Daily Herald

No. 7061 SATURDAY, OCTOBER 1, 1938 ONE PENNY

MR. CHAMBERLAIN DECLARES "IT IS PEACE FOR OUR TIME"

5,000 British Troops Will Be Sent To Sudetenland

PRAGUE'S DAY OF SORROW

TO a frenzied welcome from tens of thousands of Londoners, Mr. Neville Chamberlain came home last night and announced to all the world: "I believe it is peace for our time."

GERMANS WILL MARCH AT NOON

ORDERS were given yesterday by General Brauchitsch, Chief of Staff for the German Army, to begin the march into Czechoslovakia at noon to-day (reports the British United Press).

"Our forces step into the liberated region," he said, "with the proud joy of being the bearers of German discipline and order."

The first Sudeten zone to be occupied will be the area north of Passau and Linz, in Upper Austria.

The Czech Government last night ordered evacuation to start immediately. It will be continued over the week-end.

The Premier had two agreements in his pocket:

1.—The Munich Four-Power Pact for the transfer of Sudetenland from Czechoslovakia to Germany; and

2.—An Anglo-German declaration of the "desire of our two peoples never to go to war with one another again."

Mr. Chamberlain's welcome in Downing Street was overwhelming. Women in tears cried "Thank you, thank you." Police strove in vain to hold back the throng.

"The Second Time"

From a first-floor window of No. 10 the Prime Minister spoke to the crowd.

"My good friends," he said. "This is the second time in our history that a statesman has come back from Germany to Downing Street with peace with honour. [The first was in 1878, when Disraeli returned from the Congress of Berlin.] **I believe it is peace for our time."**

Nearly 5,000 British troops will leave during the next few days for the policing of Sudetenland.

They will be battalions of the Coldstream Guards, Grenadier Guards, Scots Guards and Welsh Guards, together with two battalions of line regiments. One of these will be the Gordon Highlanders; the other had not been decided last night.

The men will travel by way of Brussels and Germany, and last night the War Office and Foreign Office were busy completing the arrangements for their transport.

The first draft of men are expected to travel to-morrow and the remainder on Monday and Tuesday.

One of the points still to be fixed is the uniform in which the men will travel.

Cabinet Meeting

A short meeting of the Cabinet was held last night, at which Mr. Chamberlain gave a brief report of the Munich negotiations.

No arrangements have been made for a further Cabinet meeting, and it is expected that the Premier will spend a quiet week-end in the country.

Parliament meets again on Monday, when it is expected the Munich agreement will be debated. Mr. Attlee, Labour's leader, and Mr. Greenwood, deputy-leader, have cancelled their week-end meetings so as to remain in close touch with the situation.

Before the House assembles, the National Council of Labour, the Executive of the Parliamentary Labour Party, and Labour M.P.s will meet.

The Prime Minister's homecoming was one long triumphal procession.

At Heston there were 10,000 people to welcome him. And there were cries of "Well done!" when Mr. Chamberlain pulled from his pocket the Anglo-German agreement and said to the crowd: "Here is a paper which bears Hitler's name upon it as well as mine."

The Premier held the document, typewritten on foolscap paper, high above his head for the crowd to see. Beneath the typescript could be seen the names "Neville Chamberlain" and "Adolf Hitler."

"I want to say," Mr. Chamberlain stated, "that the settlement of the Czechoslovak problem is only a prelude to a larger settlement in which all Europe may find peace."

"Superior Force"

From Heston the Prime Minister drove through miles of cheering streets to Buckingham Palace. Here again his reception was overwhelming. Tremendous crowds shouted "We want Chamberlain!" and sang "For he's a jolly good fellow."

The crescendo of cheering reached its climax as first the King and Queen and then Mr. and Mrs. Chamberlain stepped out on to the floodlit balcony.

INSIDE PAGES

Result of the 'HOLIDAY MUSIC PROGRAMME' COMPETITION will be announced in the "Daily Herald" on Monday. Order your copy now as there is certain to be an extra demand.

From a Window at No. 10

Mr. Chamberlain speaking from an upstairs window at No. 10 Downing Street, to the great crowd which gathered to welcome him home.

Czechs Cry "We Want To Fight"

And so to Downing Street—and more frenzied applause.

London's West End last night was filled with jubilant crowds. Traffic was at times almost at a standstill.

In contrast to all this rejoicing, Prague yesterday was a city of sorrow. Tens of thousands of people paraded the streets shouting, "We want the whole Republic! We want to fight!"

The city authorities, fearful lest Germany might seize this pretext for an invasion, ordered a "black-out" to get the crowds off the streets.

General Sirovy, the Czech Premier, broadcast a message to the nation in which he said: "We have accepted unheard-of sacrifices. . . . . Superior force has compelled us to accept. . . . . But the nation will be stronger and more united."

What They Will Lose

It is now clear that the Czechs, under the terms of the annexation, will lose

(a) The radium mines of Joachimsthal;

(b) Large seams of bituminous coal and lead deposits;

(c) Rich belts of timber;

(d) Ironworks, glassworks and breweries;

(e) The famous spas of Karlsbad, Marienbad and Franzenbad.

They will not, however, lose the famous Pilsen brewery or the great Skoda munition works.

Examination of the detailed plan (given in full on Page 7) shows great modifications by Hitler of the demands made in his Godesberg ultimatum.

Many questions which Hitler then said would be decided by Germany "unilaterally," are now to be referred to the International Commission, which held its first meeting in Berlin yesterday.

Also, Hitler will now guarantee the new Czechoslovakia if a minority agreement is reached with Poland and Hungary, and provision is made for exchange of populations.

BUT—

Poles Rush Ultimatum

BY OUR OWN CORRESPONDENT

WARSAW, Friday night.

WITHIN 24 hours of one threat of an immediate war on the Czechs being averted, Poland to-night handed a new ultimatum to Prague.

Imposing a 24-hour time limit, the ultimatum insisted on an immediate answer to the demand that all Czech territory inhabited by Poles shall be evacuated at once.

A Warsaw Foreign Office spokesman announced that the Note would reach Prague by ten o'clock to-night.

An official communiqué explained that Czechoslovakia's answer to the Polish Note, sent last Tuesday, containing a detailed plan of frontier adjustments in Teschen Silesia, reached Warsaw at 1 p.m. to-day, but had been found unsatisfactory.

The Polish Government had therefore sent another Note requesting a "clear and precise" answer and the cession of the territory.

The answer to the Note is expected by noon to-morrow.

Simultaneously with the sending of the ultimatum the threat was broadcast from all stations that failing satisfaction the Government "will resort to measures which may have the gravest consequences."

Suggestions were made that Polish troops would enter the Teschen district of Czechoslovakia to-morrow at the same time that the Germans occupied the areas ceded to them.

The official wireless broadcast a message from Teschen which declared: "The hour is approaching when Polish troops will free the Poles in Czechoslovakia with their fixed bayonets."

Reports were circulated in Warsaw to-day of alleged "incidents" on the Czech border

An urgent meeting was called, attended by General Smigly-Rydz, virtual Dictator of Poland, President Moscicki, the Premier, vice-Premier and Foreign Minister.

Colonel Beck, the Foreign Minister, then received in turn the Ambassadors of Germany, France, Italy, Britain, Rumania and the United States, and the Hungarian Minister.

The Weather
Yesterday: High, 70. Low, 52.
Today: Fair. High, 75.

THE ATLANTA CONSTITUTION

The Constitution Leads in City Home Delivered, Total City and Trading Territory Circulation

The South's Standard Newspaper
Associated Press United Press
North American Newspaper Alliance

VOL. LXXI., No. 114. ONLY MORNING NEWSPAPER PUBLISHED IN ATLANTA ATLANTA, GA., TUESDAY MORNING, OCTOBER 4, 1938. Entered at Atlanta Post Office As Second-Class Matter

Single Copies: Daily, 5c; Sunday, 10c. Daily and Sunday: Weekly 25c; Monthly $1.10

'YOU ARE GERMANS FOREVER,' HITLER CRIES AS SUDETENLAND ACCLAIMS ITS 'LIBERATOR'

JAIL-BREAK ARTIST AUBREY SMITH FREE ONCE MORE

Frequent Fugitive Escapes From Tuberculosis Ward of State Prison Hospital at Milledgeville

MAKES GETAWAY WITH 3 CONVICTS

Pal of Leland Harvey Has Long Record; Terms Once Cut by Talmadge.

By FRANK DRAKE.

Aubrey Smith, pal of Georgia's most notorious escape artist, Leland Harvey, wrote another chapter in the crazyquilt of his prison record last night by fleeing from the tubercular ward of the state prison at Milledgeville.

He was being sought by officers throughout the state last night while his pal Harvey was still safe in Alcatraz.

Reported to have escaped with him were Jess Hooberry, 34, of Memphis, Tenn., serving a 15 to 20-year sentence for kidnaping and robbery; Bonnie Oldfield, negro, 40, and J. E. Spivey, 43. All were said to have been trusties and Spivey was reported to have had a .45-caliber automatic pistol in his possession when the quartet made their escape.

Succession of Breaks.

Harvey and Smith have written a blazing page in Georgia prison history, since they started out on a career of crime that took them in and out of jails and prison camps in every section of Georgia during the past decade.

The escapades and escapes of these two men have made the front pages of newspapers all over Georgia and the nation. Smith last night added another "headline" to the long list he had accumulated before Harvey was tucked away in Alcatraz as one of the nation's "bad boys."

It was his fourth successful break for freedom but there is one blot on his record when he and Harvey attempted to escape but failed. Harvey was the champion of the two so far as escapes were concerned, for before he retired to Alcatraz at the insistence of the federal government, he had made five successful breaks, with one or more unsuccessful attempts, including a daring, gun-flaming episode on the road to Rome when Harvey tried to shoot a Floyd county deputy who was taking them both to Rome for trial on charges of robbing a $5,000 pay roll.

Talmadge's Clemency.

It was Smith and Harvey who escaped from prison a few years ago when the then Governor Talmadge, in a mellow mood, lapped off the long sentences hanging over their heads and told them "go and sin no more."

Smith was under sentences for robbery totaling 145 years and Harvey wasn't far behind with a total of 110 years.

Aubrey and Leland, who are comparatively young in years, started their career in crime about 1928.

In December, the Fulton courts

Continued in Page 2, Column 4.

In Other Pages

Escapes Guards Again

AUBREY SMITH.

PRESIDENT OF AFL LINKS LEWIS, REDS

Green in Houston Address Denounces U. S. Labor Relations Board.

HOUSTON, Texas, Oct. 3.—(AP) William Green shook his fist today and caustically accused John L. Lewis of leading an industrial union movement that Lewis labeled 14 years ago as "one of the objectives of the Communist International."

The President of the American Federation of Labor, opening its national convention, couched his keynote speech in bristling terms as he attacked the CIO chairman.

Green shouted that Lewis in 1924 gave a senate committee a statement charging Communists were attempting to gain control of the American Federation of Labor to reach an objective of "one big union."

"He is now engaged in leading a movement which has that very thing for its objective," Green said, amid shouts of the delegates, assembled in Houston's coliseum.

Clippings Produced.

Green produced a newspaper clipping describing a speech Lewis delivered last month at the Latin-American Trade Union Congress in Mexico City. Green pictured Lewis addressing a throng of "denim clad workers" waving red flags in a bull ring in Mexico City. He termed the bull ring a "fitting and appropriate place" for the speech.

Green turned to labor legislation and thundered:

"American labor will not tolerate governmental control—governmental dictation."

He branded the National Labor Relations Board "an ally of the CIO" and added "we won't stand for that."

"Word of Lewis."

He asserted the federation would ask congress to amend the Wagner labor act and then urged American employers to accept the doctrine of the American Federation of Labor. He asked employers to accord labor collective bargaining rights and urged them to pay wages as high as industry can bear.

Before stepping down from the rostrum, President Green read what he said was the words of Lewis before the senate committee in 1924.

"Let me quote," said President Green, "'Imported revolution is

Continued in Page 2, Column 5.

Labor Party Backs Governor Lehman

NEW YORK, Oct. 3.—(AP)—Governor Herbert H. Lehman, renominated by the Democrats for a fourth term, was given the nomination of the American Labor party as well tonight.

The strongly pro-New Deal party gave its indorsement to Lehman by acclamation in a shouting demonstration at its state convention.

Robert Wagner, Democratic nominee for United States senate, also received the indorsement of the labor group.

COUNCIL RESCUES DR. REED REPORT FROM 'FILE' DEATH

Councilman Couch Leads Fight To Pigeonhole Survey; Committee Is Named for New Study.

RAISES ARE VOTED FOR 20 OFFICERS

Ordinance Restricts Pasteurizing to Those Who Are Doing It at Present.

The Reed report was kept alive yesterday by city council, which refused to follow the recommendation of the ordinance and legislation committee to "file the report for future reference and information.

Instead, a committee of five, to be appointed by the mayor, was authorized to study the exhaustive report on governmental functions and to make definite recommendations at the last council meeting in December.

Couch Leads Fight.

This action followed lengthy debate on the value of the report, with Councilman J. Allen Couch, chairman of the ordinance committee, leading the attack. Couch asserted the good recommendations in the report were made years ago by city officials and said "it takes no expert" to know that the city needs such things as a new fire headquarters.

Alderman Ed Gilliam, Councilman Wilson, Councilman John A. White and others pushed through Gilliam's resolution to create a committee to study the report further.

Only Couch, Alderman G. Dan Bridges and Councilman William T. Knight voted against this procedure.

Reed Aide Listens.

Statements made on the Reed report by members of council were taken down verbatim by a court reporter, while L. R. Chubb, former assistant to Dr. Thomas H. Reed, who was employed by the Chamber of Commerce to help in putting into effect Dr. Reed's recommendations, was in the audience.

Couch presented only a brief recommendation as the ordinance committee's report. It had been planned for Alderman Roy Callaway and Couch to point out in the committee's report the recom-

Continued in Page 2, Column 3.

ATKINSON TO NAME SENATOR GEORGE AT STATE MEETING

Speaker Harris Is Expected To Renominate Governor Rivers at Democratic Convention Today

GILLIS OR ARNOLD IN LINE FOR POST

T. Grady Head and Mrs. John A. Rollison Will Make Seconding Talks.

By L. A. FARRELL.

MACON, Ga., Oct. 3.—Senator David S. Atkinson, of Savannah, chairman of the Chatham county Democratic executive committee, will place Senator George in renomination before the state Democratic convention, it was learned here tonight as the vanguard of Georgia's democracy began to arrive for the big meeting.

Seconding speeches are to be made by Revenue Commissioner T. Grady Head, of Ringgold, and Mrs. John A. Rollison, of Waycross, president of the Georgia Affiliated Women's Democratic Clubs and vice chairman of the retiring state Democratic executive committee.

A sudden shift in the convention program was determined upon tonight. Charles S. Reid, of Atlanta, retiring chairman of the state committee, who had steadfastly refused all pleas to accept re-election, probably will preside over the convention before turning the gavel over to his successor.

The new state chairman still has not been selected, although the gossip has it that the post will go either to Jim L. Gillis, of Soperton, member of the Highway Board, or State Treasurer Zack Arnold.

Should Reid preside over the convention it is understood Speaker Roy V. Harris, of the house of representatives, will place Governor Rivers in renomination.

Ex-Governor Talmadge, defeated for the senate in the Democratic primary of September 14 but who is contesting Senator George's renomination, is expected here early tomorrow. Talmadge headquarters have been set up on the seventh floor of Macon's Dempsey hotel. The offices were a beehive of activity today but the Talmadge plans still remain uncertain. Some say he will be placed in nomination and an ef-

Continued in Page 2, Column 5.

Chamberlain Talk Dubbed Threat To Strain Dictators by Arms Race

Sir Arthur Willert Says France and Britain Will Pit Vast Resources Against Those of Germany and Italy.

By SIR ARTHUR WILLERT.

(Copyright, 1938, for The Constitution and North American Newspaper Alliance, Inc.)

LONDON, Oct. 3.—(By Wireless)—The statement that Great Britain will never again disarm unilaterally, that, in fact, she will continue to build up her fighting power until other countries are prepared to talk disarmament, is regarded among diplomats here as the key passage of Prime Minister Chamberlain's speech today before the house of commons.

This passage shows that Chamberlain means to try to follow what has been called his policy of the olive branch in the mailed fist. Behind the friendly and constructive consultations which he hopes have been inaugurated with the dictators will be a spectacle of Britain and France drawing upon their economic and financial resources to do their part in the armament race, the strain of which Germany and Italy are far less able to bear.

In other words, the economic factor bulks large behind London's visions of political appeasement. It is hoped that, especially if economic conditions now improve in the democracies, the dictators may have second thoughts about self-sufficiency and find in them another reason for, wanting to do business with the democracies over disarmament and other appeasement measures.

The Anglo-American trade treaty comes into this picture. It has been in abeyance during the crisis, but there are signs now that Whitehall would like to expedite its signature. One reason for this is that, according to the time-table arranged last summer at the time of the Austrian debt settlement, negotiations for Anglo-German trade agreements are to start soon. It is felt that the spectacle of the English-speaking countries increasing their trade might strengthen the hands of important interests in Germany that want a return to freer international trading.

Another thing which, it is believed here, may incline Berlin in that direction is the prospect of losing a considerable amount of the trade that Sudetenland had been doing with the United States as a part of Czechoslovakia, owing to the fact that Germany at pres-

Continued in Page 2, Column 6.

City 'Cow Girl' Takes Ride on Bull at Fairgrounds

Constitution Staff Photo.

It wasn't raining and Miss Edith Greene, of 255 East Pace's Ferry road, N. E., was not hungry when she went to Lakewood park last night, but she carried an umbrella and was accompanied by plenty of poundage. She balanced herself on a bull from the Elm Grove Farm, Belvedere, Tenn., and added to the carnival spirit that pervaded the fair grounds. A city girl, Miss Greene found as much to interest her in the agricultural program of the day as did the farm girls who attended.

BROWN PREDICTS NO COTTON LOAN

Wallace Assistant Forecasts Department Will Reject Solons' Demands.

WASHINGTON, Oct. 3.—(AP)—Harry L. Brown, assistant secretary of agriculture, predicted today the department would reject demands of a congressional committee for increased cotton loans.

He held to his refusal to recommend a higher rate, contending such a course would serve only to "freeze" huge stocks of cotton in storage warehouses.

Brown, who came to the department from Georgia, was designated by President Roosevelt to hear the southern group's plea Saturday for either a boosted loan or an additional subsidy payment of 3 cents a pound.

Any Subsidy Plan "Absurd."

Turned down by Brown and Jesse W. Tapp, acting AAA administrator, the committee appealed by letter to Secretary Wallace.

Brown said any subsidy proposal was "absurd" because only an act of congress could authorize such payments.

Wallace was back in his office today after a speaking trip, but there was no word about a reply to the committee's letter. Brown said he had not seen the secretary.

The assistant defended the department's cotton policy against assertions that it had encouraged low prices and that the loan rate had fixed the market level.

These and similar charges were heard frequently during the two-day conference of cotton-state senators, representatives and farmers. The group was headed by Senator Smith, Democrat, South Carolina.

Supply Hurts Prices.

Brown declared the farmer and the government alike would suffer if the loan basis of 8.3 cents a pound were raised. The higher the rate, he argued, the greater would be the amount of cotton

Continued in Page 6, Column 3.

Fair Strikes Full Swing In Gay Spirit

Carnival Atmosphere Pervades Lakewood Park as Hundreds Attend.

Fair skires and a carnival spirit greeted hundreds of Atlantans yesterday as they thronged Lakewood park for the second day of the 1938 Southeastern Fair and National Livestock Show.

Gates will open at 8 o'clock this morning for "Spalding County Day," and hundreds of visitors from Griffin and surrounding towns in Spalding county will visit the grounds. A motorcade will arrive this morning, bringing many visitors.

With the Rubin and Cherry Exposition in full swing, following their arrival yesterday morning, and the various shows along the midway drawing crowds of spectators, Atlantans and Georgians found much of carnival entertainment with thrills galore on the merry-go-round, the ferris wheels

Continued in Page 6, Column 4.

RIP CHAMBERLAIN FOR NOT FIGHTING

Leaders Denounce Terms; Duff Cooper Sobs Bitter Attack in Commons.

Abstract of Chamberlain, Duff Cooper and Eden Speeches in Pages 8 and 9.

LONDON, Oct. 3.—(AP)—Prime Minister Chamberlain drove home to the somber House of Commons today his blunt belief that four men at Munich—Hitler, Mussolini, Daladier and himself—saved civilization "as we have known it."

He steadfastly backed all he had done.

Voices of dismay, humiliation and rage preceded and followed his 55-minute address explaining and justifying the accord at Munich which dismembered Czechoslovakia.

Alfred Duff Cooper, the man who until Saturday was Chamberlain's First Lord of the Admiralty, sobbed as he cried out that the

Continued in Page 8, Column 1.

Temperature Drop to 48 Degrees Is Predicted for This Morning

The mercury will plunge to 48 this morning, for Atlanta's second cold snap of the season, the weather bureau predicted last night. The day will be fair, with the temperature expected to rise to 75 degrees. Yesterday's high was 79 and the low reading was 52.

The weather will be cooler than any time since September 22, when a 48-degree reading was registered.

Meteorologist George W. Mindling again begged the public to send whatever meteorographs they may have found to the Weather Bureau in Washington, and collect a $3 reward for every one returned.

The instruments which register air pressure, temperature and humidity were attached to gas-filled balloons, and launched into a violent rainstorm from Meridian, Montgomery, Macon, Columbia and Raleigh on September 28. After rising from 10 to 20 miles, the balloons burst, and the meteorographs plummet to the ground with a valuable record of what went on up there during the height of the storm. Just what goes on has been puzzling scientists for centuries. The return of the meteorographs will therefore be very much appreciated, Mindling said.

The delicate instruments are encased in a framework of bamboo sticks to break their fall, and are decorated with red streamers to attract attention.

REJOICING CROWDS STREW FLOWERS BEFORE FUEHRER

Unsmiling Hero Follows His Army and Planes, Looks Straight Ahead as Populace Goes Wild.

STAY UP ALL NIGHT TO GREET LEADER

He Pledges That Never Again Will Territory Be Wrested From Reich.

Text of Hitler's Address in Page 8.

WITH THE GERMAN ARMY OF OCCUPATION IN SUDETENLAND, Oct. 3.—(AP)—Reichsfuehrer Hitler, hailed as liberator, rode victoriously into the Sudetenland today and proclaimed the region part of Germany with the pledge that "never again will this land be torn away from the Reich."

"Today," he said, "I may for the first time greet you as my Egerlanders. . . .

"This greeting is, however, at the same time a pledge: never again will this land be torn away from the Reich.

"Over the German, the greater German, Reich lie the sheltering German shield and the protecting German sword.

"You, yourselves, are part of this protection, and from now on will have to share your part like all other Germans. . . .

No Power on Earth—

"From now on the German people will shape its future in this community of destiny and will, and no power on earth will be able ever again to threaten this future. . . ."

He entered the Sudetenland with his soldiers, airplanes, armored cars and artillery. The populace, cheering wildly, strewed his path with flowers and shouted "We thank our Fuehrer!"

The chancellor rode in triumph for 40 miles through Zone 3 of the newly acquired territory, completing the procession at dusk, returning to Germany.

Tonight he went to Hof, not far west of Eger, to sleep in his special train. Tomorrow he will return to the Sudetenland to visit Graslitz, Bleistadt, Falkenau and Koenigsberg.

Hitler began the procession at 11:16 a. m. (4:16 a. m. Atlanta time) at Wildenau, half a mile

Continued in Page 9, Column 1.

WEATHER

GEORGIA: Generally fair, not so cool Tuesday; Wednesday, partly cloudy and slightly warmer.

OCTOBER 4, 1938.
ATLANTA—One year ago today, cloudy. High, 72; low, 68.

SUN AND MOON FOR TODAY.
Sun rises, 5:35 a. m.; sets, 5:21 p. m.
Moon rises, 2:30 p. m.; sets, 1:03 a. m.

LOCAL WEATHER REPORT.

City records:

Highest temperature	70
Lowest temperature	52
Mean temperature	61
Normal temperature	68
Precipitation in past 24 hours, ins.	.00
Total precipitation this month, ins.	.00
Deficiency since 1st of months, ins.	0.21
Total precipitation this year, ins.	27.90
Deficiency since Jan. 1, ins.	10.26

Airport records:

	6:30 a.m.	N.	6:30 p. m.
Dry temperature	51	66	61
Wet bulb	48	53	57
Relative humidity	80	40	76

Reports of Weather Bureau Stations.

STATIONS AND STATE OF WEATHER	Temp'r'ture 6:30	High	Rain 12hrs. Ins.
Atlanta, airport, clear	61	72	.00
Birmingham, clear	68	90	.00
Boston, pt cldy	52	56	.00
Buffalo, clear	48	64	.00
Charleston, clear	54	70	.00
Charlotte, clear	56	—	—
Chattanooga, clear	66	78	.00
Chicago, pt cldy	60	72	.02
Denver, pt cldy	72	80	.00
Fargo, N. D., clear	78	84	.00
Helena, pt cldy	62	64	.02
Houston, clear	78	92	.00
Jackson, Miss., pt cldy	78	92	.00
Jacksonville, clear	60	72	.00
Macon, clear	64	72	.00
Memphis, clear	74	84	.00
Miami, pt cldy	74	84	.00
Mobile, clear	68	80	.00
Montgomery, clear	70	78	.00
New Orleans, cldy	74	84	.00
Newark, N. J., clear	54	62	.00
Oakland, Cal., pt cldy	64	68	.00
Oklahoma City, clear	82	90	.00
Phoenix, clear	90	96	.00
Pittsburgh, clear	58	64	.00
Raleigh, clear	56	66	.00
St. Louis, clear	70	80	.00
Savannah, clear	56	70	.00
Washington, clear	54	66	.00

Cotton States Weather in Page 16.

CLOUDY
For all New England: Rain tonight; mild temperature; southerly winds. High tides at 7:59 a. m. and 8:29 p. m. Light autos at 4:21 p. m.

DAILY RECORD
BOSTON'S HOME PICTURE NEWSPAPER

FINAL

Vol. 251, No. 121 48 Pages Boston, Friday, November 18, 1938 ★★★★ PRICE TWO CENTS

NAZIS PREVENT JEWISH EXODUS

Story on Page 2

Here's What Happens When Mob Rule Takes Charge in Berlin

Because they were Jewish, owners of these stores in Berlin were forced to suffer this damage. Windows were smashed by the infuriated Nazi mobs as the anti-Jewish element took vengeance for the shooting of Ernst Vom Rath, German diplomatic aide, in Paris. Stores were wrecked, their contents burned and looted and synagogues were burned to the ground, while firemen stood by, "unable to do anything but check spread of flames to adjoining property." Story on Page 2 (International News Photo)

6 A.M. EXTRA

San Francisco Chronicle

THE CITY'S ONLY HOME-OWNED NEWSPAPER

FOUNDED 1865—VOL. CLIV, NO. 59 CCCC*** SAN FRANCISCO, WEDNESDAY, MARCH 15, 1939 DAILY 5 CENTS, SUNDAY 10 CENTS: DAILY AND SUNDAY PER MONTH, $1.30

COMPARATIVE TEMPERATURES

	High	Low		High	Low
San Francisco.	61	46	Denver	42	36
Los Angeles...	68	51	New York.....	46	34
Seattle	46	38	Chicago	62	34
Honolulu	76	68	New Orleans..	76	54
San Jose......	64	36	Salt Lake.....	40	28

See below for local forecast

Complete Report on Page H-5

HITLER GRABS CZECH NATION!

Prague Seized By Nazi Army

THIS WORLD TODAY

BY ROYCE BRIER

MAYBE you don't care for Herr Hitler's stage presence, but as a shut-eye he's a humdinger.

Shut-eye is back-stage for a magician. It's the better term here, because you stare at that fellow like an owl, and then you wink, and while you wink he's done it. He's the greatest alive in his line, and some of his mystifications are the equal of anything the old masters ever did. Richelieu, Metternich, Disraeli, they were all pretty good, and so was Philip II of Spain, but no whit better than this Viennese house painter.

Of course, it's an old game. What you have seen has happened at least one hundred times in the last millemnium in Europe. To shift metaphors—big fish gobble little fish. Sometimes big fish gets so big he busts. But that's the way it is in the sea.

We, in America, can't do anything but think, but we can do plenty of that. There is our memory course, reminding us Herr Hitler didn't want anything more in Europe. There was the January 30 speech, which kept the Nazis warm with exercise all during February. But it's all right. We have never been as simple as they think we are. We've always had a sneaking suspicion how things are arranged in the sea.

Czecho-Slovakia died last night. She lived 20 years, had a lot of fair-weather friends and lost them, was murdered.

The term murder is not used here invidiously, of course. You never saw a nation die more quickly, or in truth, more bloodlessly. After a week of threat from the Nazis, they abruptly found it "unbearable," as they always do. On Herr Hitler's order Slovakia, the middle area of Czechland, declared its independence of Prague, its dependence on Berlin. Meanwhile, in Carpatha-Ukraine, the eastermost area, Hungarian troops penetrated. After Munich the Hungarians and Poles attempted to join frontiers, but Hitler said nay. Yesterday there was no nay, but apparent connivance. (See below.)

But Czechland proper, Bohemia-Moravia centering on Prague, half of old Czecho-Slovakia's population, the rich quarter of its area, lived a few

Continued on Page 2, Col. 1

Anglo Bank

Thomson to Succeed Fleishhacker

Mortimer Fleshhacker resigned the presidency of the the Anglo-California National Bank yesterday, to be succeeded by William H. Thomson, executive vice president of the California Bank of Los Angeles.

Fleshhacker's resignation, accepted by directors "with the deepest regret," is to become effective March 31.

Formal assumption of his duties will be undertaken by Thomson the same day, Thomson having been made the formal proffer and accepted it at yesterday's regular meeting of the board.

Official submission of Fleishhacker's resignation confirmed his intent as published exclusively in The Chronicle March 10, coincidentally with decision of Dr. Robert Gordon Sproul to forego the post to remain president of the University of California.

Thomson's salary as head of the institution was not disclosed in the announcement of the bank's board of directors. The figure previously attributed, but never officially confirmed was between $45,000 and $50,000.

Fleishhacker's resignation message was brief.

Addressed to the board, it read:

"Gentlemen: Please accept my resignation as president of the bank to take effect March 31, 1939.

"Based on the impregnable soundness of our financial structure, I look forward with great hope to the successful future of our institution. Sincerely,

(Signed) M. FLEISHHACKER."

Appended to a copy was the following elaboration on the part of the directors:

"When Mr. Fleishhacker accepted the presidency of the bank last October, it was with the understanding that he would serve only until a successor was selected.

"Mindful of Mr. Fleishhacker's de-

Continued on Page 10, Col. 6

Justice Roberts Under Knife

WASHINGTON, March 14 (AP)—Justice Owen J. Roberts underwent today what was described by a Supreme Court attache as a "minor operation." The Justice is expected to leave the hospital within four or five days.

Weather:

The Weather Man had all the office gadgets piled in a heap—barometers, thermometers, rain gauges, humidity guessers and fog prognosticators.

"Throw all that junk down the elevator shaft," he told Anemometer, the bureau cat. "No Government apparatus is going to make a monkey out of me."

"Something wrong, boss?" asked Anemometer.

"Wrong?" bellowed the W. M. "That's the stuff that predicted the rainstorm that didn't come. I'm through with it. From now on I use my rheumatism, a wet finger, a horse hair and a divining rod. And I'll bet I come closer to it than all this Democratic junk."

And to prove it he bent over three times, found he had no rheumatism and predicted fair and mild weather for today.

Relief

F. R. Insists Bigger WPA Fund Needed

WASHINGTON, March 14 (A.P.)—President Roosevelt stirred up a tempest of congressional strife today with a sharply-worded request for an immediate, additional appropriation of $150,000,000 for WPA lest, he said, near 5,000,000 people lose the source of their livelihoods.

His appeal cut to the core of the constantly agitated issue of Government spending and led to predictions of a battle even more strenuous than that which attended the refusal of Congress, earlier in the session, to grant the very same appropriation proposed today.

In preparation for that struggle, Administration forces deposed Representative Woodrum (D., Va.), aggressive leader of the House economy bloc, as acting chairman of the subcommittee in charge of relief appropriations. He will be replaced, it was said, by Chairman Taylor (D., Colo.) of the appropriations committee, who almost immediately upon the receipt of the President's message introduced a bill to carry it out.

Full Text of Relief Message on Page 5

PROBE MOVE GAINS

As though to offset this move, the economy group rallied at once behind a proposal by Representative Cox (D., Ga.), that the appropriations committee be directed to make a thorough going investigation of WPA to determine whether it is "fish or fowl, sane or insane, good or bad."

Woodrum, denouncing the President's statements as "melodrama and emotionalism," asserted ominously that he would "still be around" when the appropriation was discussed.

Thus the principal opposition to the President's proposal came from the Democratic side of the House. For the most part, Republican members followed the lead of Representative Martin (R., Mass.), their floor leader, in saying they were "judically minded" and wanted "to see what the facts" were before coming to a decision.

ALSO MODERATE IN SENATE

In the Senate, also, the Republican leadership adopted a moderate attitude toward the President's request.

Senator McNary (R., Or.), the Republican leader, said that if the money was "actually needed for relief and not for politics" it would be forthcoming.

With this statement, he left the forthright opposition to Democrats in the chamber, and Senator Byrnes (D., S. C.) led it off with an assertion that "they'll have to show me the need for any more money."

Liner Stands by Disabled Ship

CHATHAM, Mass., March 14 (AP)—The huge Italian luxury liner Conte di Savoia reported she was "standing by" the disabled Norwegian freighter Belnor in a howling northwest storm tonight, about 700 miles east of the Virginia Capes.

"Crew is not in immediate danger," the captain radioed. "Will not proceed to New York until Captain of Belnor advises that my assistance is not necessary."

Earlier messages said the freighter's bridge had been damaged and her radio shack washed out by raging seas.

Was Hitler Foiled By Hungarians in Ruthenia Coup?

By ALBION ROSS
Foreign Editor The Chronicle

Adolf Hitler won two great victories yesterday and suffered, either through diplomatic pressure or as the result of an Hungarian coup, one defeat.

He established a military protectorate over the 6,804,000 citizens of Bohemia and Moravia, mostly Czechs, constituting a Slavic peninsula in the body of the German Reich and today his troops will be occupying the country.

He created earlier in the day a puppet state of Slovakia with 2,450,000 population, mostly Slovaks. This state gives him a headquarters squarely in the center of Eastern Europe between possibly dangerous Poland on the north and the possibly stubborn Balkan nations on the south.

He seems to have failed to create a puppet state of Ruthenia. The Hungarians blocked any intentions he may have had in that direction by a 24-hour successful ultimatum to Prague to withdraw its 20,000 troops from the province. The Hungarians invaded and last night were ten miles from the Polish border and about to realize the Polish-Hungarian ambition to have a mutual frontier.

However, there is a report that a German army is marching through Northern Slovakia to aid the Ruthenians. If so Hungary merely attempted to challenge Hitler.

Block Expansion

Much advertised purpose of the Polish-German common frontier is to block Germany's eastward expansion and form a barrier between Germany and Soviet Russia.

The little province of Ruthenia, easternmost tip of the former

Continued on Page 4, Col. 3

Dog Racing

State Tracks Banned

Attorney General Warren served warning on California's dog tracks yesterday they will have to go out of business . . . and the first target of his campaign prepared to close up shop without making a fight of it.

Because the El Cerrito track operated by John J. ("Blackjack") Jerome is the only one actually in operation at the present time, Warren directed his ultimatum at that track. He incorporated it in a letter charging that operators are violating the law and everyone who works at a dog track is being caused to violate the law.

The letter was sent yesterday afternoon.

Even before it was received by Jerome, however, it was learned that Jerome, upon its receipt, would close the El Cerrito track. He said:

"I have always believed operation to be legal. If, however, the Attorney General says it is illegal, I am not disposed to disagree with his opinion."

The El Cerrito track operated last night as usual, because, Jerome said, he had not as yet received Warren's letter.

Some 40 men, identified as Warren's deputies, were present, making bets and apparently collecting other evidence. They made no move, however, to halt the track operations.

Whether Jerome's lead would be followed by the operators of other tracks in four counties was not immediately ascertainable.

That they might was indicated by Jerome's reported intention after closing the track. This was to get behind the passage of two bills now pending in the State Legislature

Continued on Page 12, Col. 6

Inside You'll Find . . .

A Digest Of the Day In Europe

By THE FOREIGN EDITOR

Germany has announced a protectorate over the Czechs and German armies proceeded at 6 o'clock this morning to occupy Bohemia and Moravia, home of the Czech nation. Herr Hitler created an independent Slovak nation through the vote of the Slovak Diet early yesterday. Meantime Hungary was marching into Ruthenia, eastermost province of former Czecho-Slovakia.

Here are the reports and events of the day as they affected Slovakia, the Czech country and finally Ruthenia.

SLOVAKIA:

1—**Slovak Diet with 40 Deputies present voted independence of Czecho-Slovakia yesterday morning. Dr. Joseph Tiso, who fled to Hitler when Prague ousted him as Slovak Premier Saturday, told them Germany would back them. Twenty-three Deputies were absent. Tiso is elected first Premier.**

2—**Prague dissolved the federal State of Czecho - Slovakia. Prague and Slovak government exchange radio farewells promising "no bitterness."**

3—**Bratislava correspondents report Tiso has agreed to have no army except a Hlinka guard police force and to introduce a currency dependent on the German. Customs union is held probable.**

CZECHS:

1—**German newspapers filled with stories of persecution of Germans in Moravian towns, notably Brunn.**

2—**German troops cross the Czech frontier and occupy Maehrisch Ostreau, steel town in northern Moravia. Proceed to the Slovak frontier 40 miles south. Later in the day German troops reach Libotz 25 miles northwest of Prague. Another column enters Brunn in the southwestern corner of Czech territory in the Moravian valley directly north of Vienna.**

3—**President Emil Hacha reaches Berlin just before midnight with Foreign Minister Chvalkovsky. They have a three and three-quarter-hour conversation with Hitler. Reports are that Hacha offers Hitler control of Czech foreign affairs and disarmament.**

4—**In Praha Fascist bands shout "Out with the Jews" and "Heil Gajda," the Czech Fascist leader.**

5—**Prague radio announces at 4:30 in the morning German troops will start occupying Bohemia and Moravia at 6 a. m. Citizens are warned not to resist as it would bring "brutal interference."**

6—**An official German communique announces Hitler has "taken the Czech people under his protection."**

RUTHENIA

1—**Budapest yesterday morning sent an ultimatum to Prague to withdraw Czech troops from Ruthenia within 24 hours. Hungarian troops cross the frontier and capture a few villages. They are held for four hours by Czech troops. Then Czech troops are withdrawn and retreat toward Rumania.**

2—**Hungarians reach a point ten miles from the Polish frontier**

Continued on Page 4, Col. 5

Slovaks Declare Independence as Hungary Strikes

BERLIN, March 15 (Wednesday) (AP)—The German Reich of Adolf Hitler today took under its "protection" the home of the Czechs—Bohemia and Moravia—making a clean sweep of the post-war Czecho-Slovak republic.

The European democracies, Britain and France, and others who helped create the republic as a part of the World war settlement, lifted no finger.

German troops began moving into the territory of the Czechs at 6 a. m. (9 p. m. Tuesday, Pacific Time), as the Prague radio warned the stricken citizenry not to resist the advance.

Army Reaches Prague

Hitler's green-grey troops reached Kobylis Airport at outskirts of Prague at 8 a. m. Wednesday (11 p. m. Tuesday, Pacific time).

Three automobiles carrying officers previously entered the capital to contact local authorities.

Groups of several hundred solemn-faced persons gathered before loud speakers. Streets were filled with shop girls going to work and with delivery wagons on their early morning rounds. Stores opened as usual.

There was much discussion, but it was quiet. People spoke in undertones.

Jews (there are about 35,000 in Prague) and between 500 and 1000 German emigres were panic-stricken.

They sought ways of leaving what was Czecho-Slovakia but exits were closed.

They went to bed with a safe feeling in Czecho-Slovakia Monday night.

Last night they went to bed in Bohemia with an uneasy feeling. They got up this morning in a state subject to German wishes. A boundary had passed over them during the night.

Hitler promised an undisclosed degree of autonomy would be guaranteed the Czechs, although it was believed the German occupation would be permanent and would give Hitler a domain stretching far eastward toward the Russian Ukraine which he dreams of making a vassal state.

Ruthenia Opposes Hungary

The Slovak part of the federal Czecho-Slovak state, with German encouragement, yesterday declared its independence.

As a result the Cabinet at Prague resigned and President Emil Hacha hurried to Berlin for a conference with the German fuehrer.

The German communique issued early today after their historic three-hour talk ending at 4:15 a. m. (7:15 p. m. Tuesday, Pacific time), said the Czech President had "trustingly" placed the fate of his people and his country in the fuehrer's hands.

Czecho-Slovakia had been split into three parts by Slovakia's separation and the federal Czecho-Slovak state was declared officially dissolved.

The Premier of the eastern province of Carpatho-Ukraine (Ruthenia), had followed Slovakia's lead with a similar declaration—which Hungary disregarded as her troops pressed into the province and reached half-way across it toward the frontier of Poland.

Czechs, submitting to a Hungarian ultimatum, were withdrawing their troops.

The fate of Ruthenia, however, remained in doubt as Rumania was reported to have occupied some Carpatho-Ukraine villages near her frontier, Polish troops were reported reinforced along the northern frontier of the narrow mountainous corridor, and German troops were reported marching in that

Continued on Page 4, Col. 1

Arizona Slayer Seized at Church

AN AMERICAN PAPER FOR THE AMERICAN PEOPLE
AMERICA FIRST
San Francisco Examiner
Monarch of the Dailies
REG. U.S. PAT. OFF.
6 A.M. FINAL

VOL. CLXX, NO. 128 CCCC* SAN FRANCISCO, MONDAY, MAY 8, 1939 DAILY 5 CENTS, SUNDAY 10 CENTS DAILY AND SUNDAY PER MONTH, $1.30 ★

HITLER, DUCE IN WAR PACT

Fugitive Waives Extradition; Bets He Will Be Hanged

Youth Balks At Assistance From His Family

KNOXVILLE (Tenn.), May 7.—(AP)—Robert M. Burgunder Jr., handsome 22-year-old collegian, was lodged in jail here tonight to await the arrival of officers who will return him to Phoenix, Ariz., to face charges of slaying two automobile salesmen.

Burgunder was arrested as he was leaving church.

The quiet-spoken, almost shy young man refused to discuss the accusation that he killed Jack Peterson and Ellis M. Koury, auto salesmen, whose bodies were found in a lonely wash near Phoenix last Friday after they had gone on a trip to demonstrate a car.

"One wrong word right now might hang me," the suspected slayer told reporters. "I just can't discuss it except to say that I am not guilty of murder."

REFUSES HELP.

Burgunder Jr., however, did say he wants to **"face the music alone."**

"I told mother and dad to stay out of this thing and let me fight it out alone," said the collegian.

"Dad and mother have gotten me out of enough trouble and I don't want them in this mess."

Explaining that his parents were divorced, Burgunder said he sent a telegram to his father, Robert M. Burgunder Sr., former Kings County (Seattle, Wash.), prosecutor, advising him not to try to help him. The youth said he had once been to a reformatory on a robbery conviction.

Soon after he was located in jail the prisoner asked permission to send telegrams to his parents, but they were held pending approval by Arizona officers.

PERFECT CRIME AIM.

One was addressed to his father. It read:

"Stay out of this. I knew what I was doing, and will take the consequences. Stay in Seattle. (Signed) Bob."

The other to his mother, Mrs. Ruth Burgunder, Alhambra, Calif., said:

"Stay in Alhambra."

"The boy said while his father was prosecutor on the West Coast, he worked in his office," Sheriff Earl Sell related. "He told me he studied law at intervals, the work of criminals, and

(Continued on Page 9, Col. 1.)

100 M.P.H. on Safe, Super Roads Seen

Speedy Turns, No Blowouts In 1960

NEW YORK, May 7.—(AP)—A national highway system of 1960 which would permit 100-mile-an-hour speeds, turns at 50 miles an hour, and eliminate the menace of blowouts, collisions, drunks and road hogs was envisioned today by Designer Norman Bel Geddes.

Geddes disclosed his plan in outline after five years of study and recent talks with President Roosevelt and congressional highway officials.

ELABORATE PLAN.

The fundamentals of the plan are:

An integrated national highway system under one central authority instead of the present mass of roads under Federal, State and local authorities;

Complete segregation of traffic into individual lanes, separated by barriers, preventing head-on collisions and cars out of control from leaving the road;

Three required speeds—50, 75 and 100 miles an hour;

Geddes-designed intersections, taking up no more room than the present cloverleaf, but allowing left turns at 50 instead of 10 miles an hour;

Inclines only half as steep as now.

100 MILES AN HOUR.

"There is nothing morally wrong in an automobile being able to travel at the rate of 75 miles an hour," Geddes said, "and yet the fact is that road building in general is designed to prevent traveling over 40 miles an hour.

"As a matter of fact, roads can be designed and built, at practically no extra cost, that will permit automobiles to be driven over them safely at a speed of 100 miles an hour."

His fundamental concept is building roads not just "from here to there," but in accord with all the varied modern sociological requirements.

The highways of the future he said, "contrary to the accepted practice, will not be laid down using two cities as their terminal points. They will be laid down on rights-of-way in between cities, with city traffic being fed to them."

WOMAN BEATEN, ROBBED, TOSSED BY ROADSIDE

Oakland Shopkeeper Badly Injured and Sunburned From Exposure; Costly Ring Gone

Cruelly beaten, apparently by a holdup man, a 52-year-old woman was found in a delirious condition late yesterday in the flatlands near Oakland Airport.

The victim was Mrs. Lillian Kelso of 1001 104th avenue, Oakland. She was in such a critical condition that officers could not obtain a coherent story from her.

However, Inspectors Neal Plunkett and Frank Gibbs said she apparently had gone to a dance Saturday night and had been slugged on her way home. Portions of her apparel were found scattered around the swampy field in which she was discovered by two youths.

CRAWLING ON HANDS.

She was crawling on her hands and knees, a half mile north of the junction of Hegenberger road and Jones avenue, when the youths, Jack Sigmon, 16, of 2568 Sixtieth avenue, and Bill Kramer, 15, of 2852 Sixty-fourth avenue, came upon her. Although both eyes had been smashed closed, she apparently had managed to crawl more than a hundred yards.

The exposed parts of her body were severely sunburned, indicating she had been in the field several hours. The woman told police she could not remember any events since Thursday night. However, her daughter-in-law, Mrs. Victor Sonderleiter, of 6261 Robin Hood Way, said she had talked with Mrs. Kelso late Saturday, when the victim was closing the small cleaning establishment she operated and planning to attend a dance.

PURSE MISSING.

Mrs. Kelso's purse, which had contained a $1,000 diamond ring and an undetermined amount of currency, was missing.

Doctors said she was suffering from exposure, shock, a severe scalp laceration and a possible skull fracture. Bruises on the upper portion of her body indicated she might have been thrown head-first from an automobile. It could not be determined immediately whether she had been criminally attacked.

DR. SCHACHT IN MEXICO; FEARED ON OIL MISSION

U. S. Negotiations Believed Threatened by Report He Has Contract for Country's Output

WASHINGTON, May 7.—(INS)—Presence in Mexico City of the German economic wizard, Dr. Hjalmar Schacht, today brought from authoritative Washington quarters an expression of fear he may have been sent there to wreck Mexican-American oil negotiations.

The paths of Schacht and Donald R. Richberg, counsel for seventeen American oil companies, crossed at San Antonio, Tex., April 28. Richberg was en route to Saltillo, Mexico, for conferences with President Cardenas, Schacht was described by his son as on a **"sightseeing tour."**

GERMAN SALESMAN.

Since his ouster as Economics Minister and president of the Reichsbank, Schacht has become Germany's ace "traveling salesman," touring the Near and Far East in the interest of arranging economic barters.

His travels across the United States were generally unknown. The State Department's Division of American Republics, apprized of his arrival in Mexico, immediately launched inquiries through the Embassy to determine his mission.

Sources close to the Cardenas-Richberg negotiations suggested Schacht's object might be to proffer Mexico a contract for absorption by the anti-Comintern allies, Germany, Italy and Japan, of its entire export petroleum output.

Except for the axis powers, the world generally has boycotted Mexican oil since that government's expropriation of British-American oil properties, the boycott resulting in huge surpluses and production curtailment, with serious consequences to Mexican economy.

A condition of the settlement in which Cardenas and Richberg reportedly reached virtual agreement was the lifting of the boycott.

TITLE IN ABEYANCE.

Authoritative quarters said the agreement left in abeyance the question of title to the properties. The companies were to take a 40 to 50 year lease, reimburse themselves for the loss of nominal ownership out of the profits of refining and distribution, and relinquish the properties to the Mexican government unencumbered at expiration of the lease.

During the period of the lease, they were to guarantee new capital in amounts equaling that already invested for the expansion and maintenance of the oil industry.

The State Department was said on high authority to have approved the settlement, which required only a ratification by Richberg's principals and Cardenas' advisers to become effective.

Nazi-Fascist Axis Turns Into Formal Alliance; Soviet, Turks Reach Pact

Strong Peace Chain Link Forged by Action

ANKARA, May 7.—(INS)—Turkey and Soviet Russia tonight announced a new agreement almost equivalent to a military alliance, forging a new and strategically important link in the **"peace chain"** promoted by Britain and France.

On the heels of yesterday's reports that an Anglo-Turkish mutual defense pact may be unveiled tomorrow in Ankara and London, the Turkish Foreign Office issued a communique on the results of the talks conducted here last week with the visiting Soviet Foreign Vice Commissar, Vladimir Potemkin.

IDENTITY OF VIEWS.

A **"full identity of views"** was obtained in the conversations between Potemkin and Turkish Foreign Minister Sukru Saragoglu, the communique said. It added:

"The Soviet Union and Turkey have mutually determined to strengthen still further the solid bonds which link the two states and which constitute a precious pledge to the cause of peace, to which cause these two states are firmly attached."

Details of the new Turko-Soviet understanding were withheld. It was reliably understood, however, that Potemkin committed his country—possessor of the world's largest army—to spring to the aid of Turkey in the event the all-important Dardanelles are attacked, or if any other Turkish territory becomes the object of aggression.

Turkey, in exchange, was said to have promised to permit use of the Dardanelles Strait by the Soviet Black Sea fleet, the British and French navies in any common defense of Poland, Rumania, Greece and the eastern Mediterranean, provided Russia finally reaches an agreement with Britain.

ECONOMIC BARTER.

It was assumed, moreover, that Turkey and Russia agreed on methods to increase their mutual trade and economic intercourse in spite of recent economic advantages in Turkey gained by Germany.

The Ankara communique enhanced the prospect of bringing both Turkey and Russia into collaboration with the Anglo-French anti-aggression front. At the same

(Continued on Page 2, Col. 1)

New Signs Point to Nazi-Russ Treaty

By The Associated Press

BERLIN, May 7.—Talk in diplomatic circles of the possibility that Nazi Germany and Communist Russia might end their enmity raised the question today of an entirely new alignment in European politics.

Democracy appeared to be replacing Communism as Germany's official hate number one.

Diplomatic observers asserted that under subtle influence from high quarters an ideological transformation was taking place—that abuse of Bolshevism was being soft pedaled and that London, Paris and Washington soon were to be at the receiving end of the angry shafts previously hurled at Moscow.

IMPORTANT REASONS.

They said there were two important reasons for a change of front:

1—Adjustment of the controversy with Poland to the satisfaction of Germany would be easier if the long quarrel with Soviet Russia were settled.

2—There have been few surface indications of a rapprochement between Germany and Russia but there were many points of similarity in the ideology of the two nations and "force of circumstance" seemed to be drawing them together.

Poland was cited as one of these "circumstances."

These observers agreed that if Germany and Russia could come to an understanding on how to deal with the state that lies between them, a way to ironing out their own differences would be made much easier.

The decision announced in Milan of Germany and Italy to sign a political and military accord was interpreted informally here as a frank warning to Poland and her friends.

NEW NAZI ACCORD.

The implication, it was stated, seemed to be that the Rome-Berlin axis is stronger than any other political consideration in central Europe and that Italy thinks more highly of her responsibilities toward the axis than to other friendships.

In diplomatic quarters it was being said that Italy had turned on the green "go" light to Reichsfuehrer Hitler so far as the free city of Danzig and possibly other questions are concerned.

It was recalled that only a few weeks ago Italian Foreign Minister Count Galeazzo Ciano visited Warsaw for what seemed to be a most hearty discussion with Polish Foreign Minister Col. Joseph Beck.

CHOSEN GERMANY.

The impression after publication of the Milan communique was that Italy had balanced her two

(Continued on Page 4, Col. 1)

Bold Counter Blow Aimed at London and Paris

MILAN (Italy), May 7.—(INS)—Benito Mussolini and Adolf Hitler tonight enlarged their Rome-Berlin axis into an open military alliance to insure united action by Italy and Germany in the event of a European war.

This transformation, constituting the boldest counter-blow yet struck against the alleged **"encirclement"** drive led by Great Britain and France, was accomplished through the medium of a two-day meeting in Milan between Italian Foreign Minister Galeazzo Ciano and German Foreign Minister Joachim von Ribbentrop.

Together with this history-making decision, Count Ciano and Baron von Ribbentrop agreed on a **"fully satisfactory"** solution to be sought for the German-Polish crisis, involving the return of Danzig to the Reich and the granting of a German-governed route across Pomorze (Polish Corridor).

OFFICIAL COMMUNIQUE.

Promising to exert far-reaching consequences on the immediate future of Europe, the Ciano-Von Ribbentrop conversations, telephonically guided by Mussolini and Hitler, were concluded late today with issuance of a joint official communique saying:

"The present general political situation was examined. Once more a perfect identity of views between the two governments was noted.

"It was decided finally to define in a formal manner the relations between the two states of the axis through a political and military pact. In this way, Italy and Germany intend to contribute efficiently to the ensuring of peace in Europe."

In the wake of this momentous announcement, informed circles tonight predicted that efforts will shortly be launched to extend the Italo-German political-military treaty to embrace the other anti-Communist pact signatories including Japan, Hungary, Spain and possibly Yugoslavia, in order to **"encircle the democracies."**

JAPAN CAUTIOUS.

It had been hoped to include Japan at the outset in the formation of the totalitarian military alliance, but the Japanese government turned back German soundings on this subject, preferring to wait and see what Soviet Russia would do before committing itself in European affairs.

The fact that the Soviet Union today concluded what is tantamount to an alliance with Turkey may hasten an Anglo-Russian military understanding, in which event Japan might then be promptly drawn into full armed entente with Italy and Germany.

No details of the new Italo-German military agreement were given out, but it was assumed, pending further announcements, that, when finally signed, it would call for Italian army, navy and air dispositions in the Mediterranean, the Near East, the Balkans, North Africa and the Alpine frontier adjoining France, while Germany would take over the operations in Central and Eastern Europe, including the Danube and Vistula valleys and stretching west to the lowlands, the North Sea and Atlantic regions.

The Ciano-Von Ribbentrop

Have You Torn Up Your Daily Scrap Of Paper Today?

By ARTHUR "BUGS" BAER.

Offering peace suggestions these days is like trying to trap man-eating lions with bird calls.

But any sensible idea is as welcome as dawn in a haunted house.

The way we always felt about fighting is to do it and get it over with. It's about time we realized that a postponement is not a remedy.

The older this writer gets the more he resembles a diplomat. Exempt and belligerent.

Roosevelt Takes Cruise on Potomac

WASHINGTON, May 7.—(AP)—President Roosevelt took advantage of the summer weather today to slip away for an overnight cruise down the Potomac River.

He took with him as his guest Harry Hopkins, Secretary of Commerce, who has been recovering from an attack of intestinal influenza.

ROYAL PAIR IN 'DRILL'

King, Queen Don Life Preservers

ABOARD THE EMPRESS OF AUSTRALIA, May 7.—(INS)—King George VI and Queen Elizabeth, en route to Canada and the United States, today donned life preservers and engaged in "life boat drill" on the second day of their voyage across the Atlantic.

After putting the preservers around them the monarchs took positions on the promenade deck for inspection by Captain Meikle.

King George and his Queen, accompanied by their royal retinue of twenty-three, attended divine services this morning in the main dining room.

Captain Meikle conducted the services and the Queen selected the hymns.

Only 13 Days Left Until S. F. Charity Day Races

Only thirteen days to go till San Francisco's biggest horse racing event!

It's the Bay Meadows Charity Day, sponsored by the city's newspapers, to be held May 21 at the Bay Meadows track. The winners will be thousands of youngsters who will get Christmas stockings and all that go in them.

All the proceeds from the day will go to the newspapers' Christmas funds, to bring cheer to children who otherwise would have little happiness next December 25. Complete details on the Charity Day will be found on page 18.

Windsor's Radio Talk Plan Stirs British Row

By THOMAS C. WATSON
Staff Correspondent International News Service.

LONDON, May 7.—The unexpected decision of the Duke of Windsor to deliver a radio peace talk to the United States from Verdun, France, tomorrow created a stir of criticism and comment in London tonight, somewhat reminiscent of the 1936 abdication crisis.

Most of the criticism was centered around the fact that Britain's self-exiled former monarch will make his transatlantic broadcast while his brother, King George VI, and Queen Elizabeth are en route on their history-making voyage to Canada and the United States.

The surprise announcement of the Duke's scheduled radio speech was made in the United States last night by the National Broadcasting Company, only a few hours after the King and Queen sailed from Portsmouth aboard the Empress of Australia.

TIMING ASSAILED.

Lord Beaverbrook's newspaper, the Daily Express, sharply assailed the Duke's **"unhappily chosen"** time for his forthcoming talk, arguing that he should have waited at least until after the King and Queen have completed their precedent-breaking visit in the New World. Some British circles contended the Duke was taking over a duty rightfully belonging to his brother-successor—a criticism which deeply affected His Royal Highness when he heard of it in France.

Nevertheless, it was believed King George and Queen Elizabeth

(Continued on Page 4, Col. 6)

Duke Upset by London Critics

PARIS, May 7.—(INS)—The Duke of Windsor was keenly perturbed tonight when he received news from London that certain British quarters are criticizing him for agreeing to make a transatlantic radio speech to the United States tomorrow.

From reliable sources it was learned that his Royal Highness manifested worry over some British intimations that he is assuming a duty of his brother, King George VI.

But there was as yet no sign that the Duke on that account was contemplating any alteration of his plan to broadcast a ten-minute peace talk from Verdun over National Broadcasting Company facilities to America at 10 p. m. (1 p. m. San Francisco time)

THE WEATHER

Generally fair today and tomorrow; little change in temperature.

MEAN TEMPERATURES YESTERDAY

Baltimore	76	New York	64
Atlanta	74	Omaha	81
Boston	64	Portland, Me.	62
Chicago	71	Salt Lake City	79
Los Angeles	78	Seattle	62
New Orleans	82	Washington	76

THE BALTIMORE NEWS-POST

AN INDEPENDENT NEWSPAPER

The Largest Daily Circulation in the Entire South

NIGHT RACE SPECIAL

VOL. CXXXV.—NO. 102 Entered as second-class matter at Baltimore Postoffice FRIDAY EVENING, SEPTEMBER 1, 1939 PRICE 2 CENTS

HITLER OPENS WAR BOMBS POLISH CITIES

BRITAIN, FRANCE MOBILIZE AS POLAND CALLS FOR AID

Italy Again Proposes Five-Power Mediation In Nazi-Polish Dispute

LONDON, Sept. 1—(I. N. S.).—King George today signed an order in Council providing for complete mobilization of the British army and air force. The navy was mobilized completely yesterday.

PARIS, Sept. 1—(I. N. S.).—Italy today again proposed a five-Power mediation of the German-Polish conflict.

By CHARLES A. SMITH
International News Service Staff Correspondent.

LONODN, Sept. 1.—Great Britain and France will stand by their pledge to Poland and fight for her independence, the British Government announced this afternoon as the Cabinet assembled and Parliament was summoned to meet at 6 P. M. (1 P. M. E. S. T.)

An authoritative statement issued in London shortly before noon (7 A. M. E. S. T.) declared:

"If the proclamation to the Greman people by Adolf Hitler should mean, as it would seem to mean, that Germany has declared war on Poland, it can be stated on highest authority that Great Britain and France are inflexibly determined to fulfill their obligation to the Polish Government.

CALLED ULTIMATUS

"The general attitude of the British Government is that if the German Government had been sincerely desirous of settling the disputeby negotiation, they would not have adopted this procedure, which has the character of an ultimatum.

"The Polish Government, in the opinion of the British Government, ment, were fully justified in declining to submit to the treatment which the German Government endeavored to impose ⅜ upon them.

"The German account of the course of the negotiations is, of course, wholly misleading. On August 29, the eGrman Chancellor informed the British Ambassador that he expected a Polish plenipotentiary to appear in Berlin the following day with full powers to negotiate a settlement.

"He added that in the meantime he hoped to elaborate on the proposals. In other words, the Polish Government was expected to submit to the procedure imposed upon the President of Czechoslovakia and dispatch an emissary to Berlin who wasto accept terms of a character which was fully unknown to the Polish Government.

"NOT CUSTOMARY"

"The Polish Government have not unnaturally been unwilling to place themselves in this humiliating position.. It is not customary even in the case of terms being imposed upon a defeated Power to demand that negotia-

Continued on Page 2, Column 7.

France Calls All Men To Colors

PARIS, Sept. 1—(A P.).—The Cabinet decreed general mobilization and a state of siege today and called Parliament for tomorrow.

The molilization of land, sea and air forces, in quick reaction to German invasion of Poland, was ordered to take effect tomorrow.

CABINET MEETS

The state of siege was decreed throughout France and Alberia. The Cabinet's grave decisions were taken after an hour and a half meeting under President Lebrun.

While the Ministers were in session, dispatches streamed into the capital from Central Europe reporting German troops on the march into Poland and several Polish cities being bombed.

The state of siege meant military

(Continued on Page B, Column 6.)

5. [illegible] **Race entries, scratches, comment, will be found on** [illegible] **t Pages today**

Roosevelt In Plea Against Horrors

BERLIN, Sept. 1—(I. N. S.).—The United States Embassy and Consulate today decided to evacuate all American women and children in Germany. All United States citizens remaining in the couhtry were advised they would have their last opportunity to leave Berlin aboard a special train leaving the Lehrter Station tomorrow morning for Flensberg, via Hamburg. At Flensburg special busses will take them across the frontier en route to Copenhagen.

WASHINGTON, Sept. 1—(A. P.). President Roosevelt appealed to the European powers today to soften the horrors of modern warfare from the skies.

To Great Britain, France, Germany, Italy and Poland he addressed before daybreak identical messages asking each for a public pledge that it would not bombard civilian populations and unfortified cities during "the tragic conflagration with which the world is now confornted."

DAY OF CLIMAXES

Otherwise, Mr. Roosevelt said, "hundreds of thousands of innocent human beings who have no responsibility for, and who are not even remotely participating in the hostilities which have now broken out will lose their lives."

The dispatch of this message at 4.30 A. M. (E. S. T.) was the first high spot of a day that many expected would be replete with climaxes in Washington as wel las in Europe.

White House sources said today there would be no immediate action looking to invocation of the neutrality act or the calling of a special session of Congress.

The President slept but little last night. As word came that war was on, he was listening to radio reports and receiving State Department dispatches and phone calls from across the Atlantic.

One of his earliest steps was to order all naval vessels and Army posts notified of the hostilities.

Shortly after 3 A. M. Ambassador

(Continued on Page B, Column 3.)

Scratches At Narragansett

First Race — Raceaway, Stavka, Peon, Polly Girl, Jair, Petline.
Second—Sun Arbor, Grandeem, Escohigh.
Third—Glenbroom, Idle Elf.
Fourth—Disraeli.
Fifth—Zeltone, Play Pence.
Sixth—Dust to Dust, Nellie Mc. Flushing, Prince Splendor, Whooper, Secret Chatter.
Seventh—Powers Gouraud, Time to Go, Flying Orphan.
Eighth—Maewhisk, Almac.
Weather clear; track heavy.

Eyes Of World On These Leaders

ADOLF HITLER
Nazi Reichsfuehrer

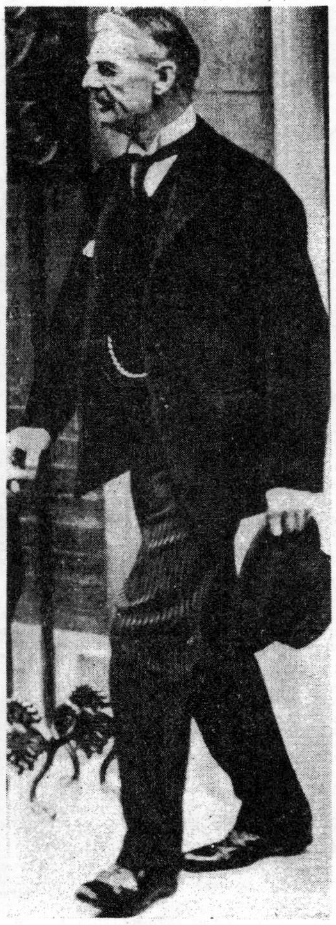

NEVILLE CHAMBERLAIN
British Prime Minister

BULLETINS

WASHINGTON, Sept. 1 — (I. N. S.). — The White House officially announced this morning the outbreak of hostilities in Europe. The White House statement said:

"The President received word at 2.50 A. M. by telephone from Ambassador Biddle in Warsaw and through Ambassador Bullitt in Paris, that Germany has invaded Poland and that four Polish cities are being bombed.

"The President directed that all Navy ships and Army commands be notified by radio at once.

"Probably a further announcement will be made by the State Department in a few hours."

Continued on Page A, Column 7.

Dickinson Cancels Speech on Morals

LANSING, Mich., Sept. 1—(A. P.).—Governor Luren D. Dickinson, refusing to permit censorship of an attack on modern day morals and dancing, has cancelled plans to deliver the speech over a Detroit radio station Sunday.

Temperatures

Midnight,	69	6 A. M.,	66
1 A. M.,	69	7 A. M.,	68
2 A. M.,	68	8 A. M.,	69
3 A. M.,	67	9 A. M.,	74
4 A. M.,	66	10 A. M.,	78
5 A. M.,	66	11 A. M.,	80

Reich Annexes Danzig; Attacks Polish Border; Blames Warsaw Army

PARIS, Sept. 1—(I. N. S.).—Poland today formally invoked the aid of France against Germany. The French Government received official notification at 10.15 A. M. (5.15 A. M. E. S. T.) that Polish territory had been invaded. France was asked to carry out her obligations under the Franco-Polish mutual assistance pact.

LONDON, Sept. 1—(A. P.).—The Polish Ambassador to London today notified Foreign Secretary Lord Halifax that Poland invoked the British-Polish mutual assistance treaty on the grounds of German aggression.

By PIERRE J. HUSS
International News Service Staff Correspondent.

BERLIN, Sept. 1.—In a fateful message to the people of Germany and the world, Reichsfuehrer Adolf Hitler informed the Reichstag today that war had broken out between Germany and Poland. He said:

"It will continue until Germany emerges victorious.

"Polish troops opened fire on our soldiers last night. Since 5.45 A. M. (11.45 A. M., E. S. T.) we have been replying with fire.

"I have ordered the air force to attack military centers.

"From now on bomb will be answered with bomb."

PLEDGE ON WOMEN, CHILDREN

He told the Reichstag as authentic military circles in Berlin stated that Warsaw and Cracow were

Turn Over.

Poland Attacked By Land And Air

PARIS, Sept. 1—(A. P.).—Hostilities between Germany and Poland have spread to the entire frontier, including that of Slovakia, Havas, French news agency, reported today from Warsaw.

Havas said Westerplatt and Puck, Polish territory near Danzig, were bombed at 6.30 A. M. (12.30 A. M., E. E. T.).

CITIES BOMBED

It said Crakow, Kattowice, Teschen and Tczew were bombed between 6.05 and 6.30 A. M. (12.05 A. M. and 12.30 A. M., E. S. T.). It reported also that three bombs were dropped on Gdynia.

The first alert signal was given in Warsaw at 6.30 A. M. and the

Continued on Page 2, Column 4.

Berliner Ausgabe

245. Ausg. / [illegible] Jahrg. / Einzelpreis 15 Pf. / Auswärts 20 Pf. Ausland mit ermäß. Porto 25 Pf. Uebriges Ausland 30 Pf.

„Freiheit und Brot!"

Berliner Ausgabe

Berlin, Sonnabend, 2. September 1939

VÖLKISCHER BEOBACHTER

Verlag: [illegible] Nachf. GmbH., Zweigniederlassung Berlin. Berlin SW 68, Zimmerstr. [illegible] Sammelruf: 11 00 22 :: Drahtanschrift: Beobachter Berlin :: Zahlungen: Postscheckkonto Berlin [illegible] Anzeigen-Schluß 18 Uhr, Sonntagsausgabe 13 Uhr, am Vortage des Erscheinens :: Gewä[illegible] Nummern unter Streifband nur gegen vorherige Einsendung von 35 Pf

Kampfblatt der national-sozialistischen Bewegung Großdeutschlands

Schriftleitung: Berlin SW 68, Zimmerstr. 88 :: Sammelruf: 11 00 22, Sprechst.: 12–13 Uhr. Drahtanschrift: „Beobachter Berlin" Münchener Schriftleitung: München 13, Schellingstr. 39, Sammelruf: 208 01 Sprechst.: 11–12 Uhr. Wiener Schriftleitung: Wien VII, Seidengasse 8–11, Sammelruf: B–39–5–40 :: Der „VB." erscheint täglich. Bezugspreis mtl. RM. 2,60, wöchtl. RM. 0,65 bei Zustellung durch Boten (nur in Berlin), bei Zustellung durch die Post RM. 2,90 zuzügl. 42 Pf. Bestellgeld.

Der Führer verkündet den Kampf für des Reiches Recht und Sicherheit

Zum Gegenangriff angetreten

dnb Berlin, 1. September.

Das Oberkommando der Wehrmacht gibt bekannt:

Auf Befehl des Führers und Obersten Befehlshabers hat die Wehrmacht den aktiven Schutz des Reiches übernommen. In Erfüllung ihres Auftrags, der polnischen Gewalt Einhalt zu gebieten, sind Truppen des deutschen Heeres heute früh über alle deutsch-polnischen Grenzen zum Gegenangriff angetreten. Gleichzeitig sind Geschwader der Luftwaffe zum Niederkämpfen militärischer Ziele in Polen gestartet. Die Kriegsmarine hat den Schutz der Ostsee übernommen.

Die ersten Erfolge unserer Wehrmacht

Berlin, 1. September.

Das Oberkommando der Wehrmacht gibt bekannt:

„Im Zuge der deutschen Kampfhandlungen aus Schlesien, Pommern und Ostpreußen wurden an allen Fronten schon heute die erwarteten Anfangserfolge erzielt.

Die von Süden über das Gebirge vorgegangenen Truppen haben die Linie Neumarkt — Sucha erreicht. Südlich Mährisch-Ostrau ist die Olsa bei Teschen überschritten. Südlich des Industriegebietes sind unsere Truppen in Höhe von Kattowitz im zügigen Vordringen. Die aus Schlesien angesetzten Truppen sind im flüssigen Vorgehen in Richtung Tschenstochau und nördlich davon.

Im Korridor nähern sich unsere Truppen der Brahe und haben die Netze bei Nakel erreicht. Dicht vor Graudenz wird gekämpft. Aus Ostpreußen vorgehende Kräfte stehen tief auf polnischem Gebiet im Kampf.

Die deutsche Luftwaffe hat heute in wiederholten kraftvollen Einsätzen die militärischen Anlagen auf zahlreichen polnischen Flugplätzen, so zB. Rahmel, Putzig, Graudenz, Posen, Plock, Lodz, Tomaszow, Radom, Ruda, Kattowitz, Krakau, Lemberg, Brest, Therespol angegriffen und zerstört.

Die Forderung der großen Stunde

Die Rede, die der Führer in der großen Stunde unseres Volkes gehalten hat, ist beendet, aber nie mehr wird sie in Deutschland verklingen, nie mehr wird es eine Generation geben in unserem Lande, die diese Rede vergessen wird.

Tief, unauslöschlich tief hat sich das Bild des Mannes im grauen Soldatenrock in unsere Seelen gesenkt, das Bild dieses Mannes, der gewaltiger ist als alle anderen, die vor ihm das deutsche Schicksal gestaltet haben; bis ins Mark haben seine mutigen, ernsten, bewegten Worte das Bewußtsein des Volkes getroffen.

Das muß ein ganz besonders armseliger Schächer sein, der selbst jetzt, nach dieser Rede, nicht weiß, daß wir alle nun anzutreten und unseren Mut und unsere Treue dem Führer darzubringen haben; diesem Führer, der vor unseren Augen in sechs Jahren Deutschland aus elender Zweitklassigkeit zu neuer Größe erlöste, der vor unseren Augen den jahrhundertealten Traum der edelsten deutschen Herzen erfüllte, der vor unseren Augen ein Großdeutsches Reich erstehen ließ, schöner, herrlicher und machtvoller, als die kühnsten und begeistertsten Streiter für Deutschland es je zu erhoffen wagten!

Das muß ein Hundsfott sein, der immer nur nahm und immer nur nehmen will und der jetzt in der großen Stunde, in der die Herzen gewogen werden, in der einmal zur Kasse gegangen werden muß, es fertigbringt, mit leeren Händen beiseitezustehen.

Mut muß unsere Gabe für Deutschland und unser Dank für den Führer sein, Mut, von dem Plutarch geschrieben hat, daß er den Anfang des Sieges bedeutet.

Mut, Treue, eiserne Manneszucht und der heilige Wille, mit jeder Faser des eigenen Daseins für unser Volk einzustehen, das ist die Verpflichtung, mit der wir uns heute wie eine Phalanx von Stahl verbinden! Feigherzigkeit sei die größte Schande!

Der Mann im grauen Soldatenrock, der geliebte Führer, der erste Soldat des deutschen Volkes, soll mit der Haltung der Nation zufrieden sein!

Job Zimmermann

Aufn.: Presse-Hoffmann

Der Wortlaut der geschichtlichen Rede

Berlin, 1. September.

In der historischen Reichstagssitzung vom 1. September hielt der Führer folgende Rede:

Abgeordnete,
Männer des Deutschen Reichstags!

Seit Monaten leiden wir alle unter der Qual eines Problems, das uns einst das Versailler Diktat beschert hat und das nunmehr in seiner Ausartung und Entartung unerträglich geworden war.

Danzig war und ist eine deutsche Stadt! Der Korridor war und ist deutsch!

Alle diese Gebiete verdanken ihre kulturelle Erschließung ausschließlich dem deutschen Volk, ohne daß in diesen östlichen Gebieten tiefste Barbarei herrschen würde.

Danzig wurde von uns getrennt! Der Korridor von Polen annektiert! Die dort lebenden deutschen Minderheiten in der qualvollsten Weise mißhandelt! Über eine Million Menschen deutschen Blutes mußten schon in den Jahren 1919/1920 ihre Heimat verlassen!

Wie immer, so habe ich auch hier versucht, auf dem Wege friedlicher Revisionsvorschläge eine Änderung des unerträglichen Zustandes herbeizuführen. Es ist eine Lüge, wenn in der Welt behauptet wird, daß wir alle unsere Revisionen nur unter Druck durchzusetzen versuchten. Fünfzehn Jahre, bevor der Nationalsozialismus zur Macht kam, hatte man Gelegenheit, auf dem Wege friedlichster Verständigung die Revision durchzuführen. Man tat es nicht! In jedem einzelnen Falle habe ich dann von mir aus nicht einmal, sondern oftmals Vorschläge zur Revision unerträglicher Zustände gemacht. Alle diese Vorschläge sind, wie Sie wissen, abgelehnt worden.

Ich brauche sie nicht im einzelnen aufzuzählen: die Vorschläge zur Rüstungsbegrenzung, ja, wenn notwendig, zur Rüstungsbeseitigung, die Vorschläge zur Beschränkung der Kriegführung, die Vorschläge zur Ausschaltung von in meinen Augen mit dem Völkerrecht schwer zu vereinbarenden Methoden der modernen Kriegführung. Sie kennen die Vorschläge, die ich über die Notwendigkeit der Wiederherstellung der deutschen Souveränität über die deutschen Reichsgebiete machte, die endlosen Versuche, die ich zu einer friedlichen Verständigung über das Problem Österreich unternahm, und später über das Problem Sudetenland, Böhmen und Mähren. **Es war alles vergeblich!**

Eines aber ist unmöglich: zu verlangen, daß ein unerträglicher Zustand auf dem Weg friedlicher Revision bereinigt wird — und dann die friedliche Revision konsequent zu verweigern!

Es ist auch unmöglich, zu behaupten, daß derjenige, der in einer solchen Lage dann dazu übergeht, von sich aus diese Revisionen vorzunehmen, gegen ein Gesetz verstößt. Das Diktat von Versailles ist für uns Deutsche kein Gesetz! (Lang anhaltende stürmische Zustimmungskundgebungen.) **Es geht nicht an, von jemand mit vorgehaltener Pistole und der Drohung des Verhungerns von Millionen Menschen eine Unterschrift zu erpressen und dann das Dokument mit dieser erpreßten Unterschrift als ein feierliches Gesetz zu proklamieren!**

So habe ich auch im Falle Danzigs und des Korridors versucht, durch friedliche Vorschläge auf dem Wege der Diskussion die Probleme zu lösen. Daß sie gelöst werden mußten, das war klar! (Tosende Beifallsstürme der Abgeordneten.) Und daß der Termin dieser Lösung für die westlichen Staaten vielleicht uninteressant sein kann, ist begreiflich. Aber uns ist dieser Termin nicht gleichgültig! Vor allem aber war er und konnte er nicht gleichgültig sein für die leidenden Opfer.

Ich habe in Besprechungen mit polnischen Staatsmännern die Gedanken, die Sie von mir hier in meiner letzten Reichstagsrede vernommen haben, erörtert. Kein Mensch kann behaupten, daß dies etwa ein ungebührliches Verfahren oder gar ein ungebührlicher Druck gewesen wäre. Ich habe dann die deutschen Vorschläge formulieren lassen, und **ich muß es noch einmal wiederholen, daß es etwas Loyaleres und Bescheideneres als diese von mir unterbreiteten Vorschläge nicht gibt.** Und ich möchte das jetzt der Welt sagen: Ich allein war überhaupt nur in der Lage, solche Vorschläge zu machen! (Nachdrückliche Zustimmungskundgebungen.) Denn ich weiß ganz genau, daß ich mich damals zur Auffassung von Millionen von Deutschen in Gegensatz ge-

Poles Beat Back Nazis

THE WEATHER
Weather Forecast on Page 2, Col. 1

The Only Newspaper in Maryland with both the Associated Press and International News Service.

THE BALTIMORE NEWS-POST
AN INDEPENDENT NEWSPAPER
The Largest Daily Circulation in the Entire South

COMPLETE MARKETS

VOL. CXXXV.—NO. 103 C Entered as second-class matter at Baltimore Postoffice MONDAY, SEPTEMBER 4, 1939 PRICE 2 CENTS

BRITISH NAVY OPENS WAR ON GERMANY

Airforce, Battle Fleet Ready As 8,000,000 Men Are Moved To Front Lines

MOSCOW, Sept. 3—(A. P.).—The official Soviet Russian broadcast tonight reported German planes bombed Warsaw eight times today.

WARSAW, Sept. 3—(I. N. S.).—Reports from the front in the German-Polish war scene announced the recapture of the frontier station at Zbazyn by Polish troops.

Polish troops were fighting fiercely in the neighborhood of Czestochowa, the "Polish Lourdes." The church was bombed by two German planes Sept. 1.

Heavy fighting also was in progress on the Silesian and East Prussian border.

German claims of having cut off the Polish Corridor "bottle neck" were vigorously denied, as were Nazi claims of the capture of Grudziadz.

It was reported that throughout Poland 1,500 civilians have been killed by German air raids.

PARIS, Sept. 3—(A. P.).—France joined Great Britain in war against Germany today.

The French Government announced officially that Germany had refused to give a "satisfactory answer" to France's ultimatum for withdrawal of Reich troops from Poland, automatically putting France at war with her historic enemy across the Rhine.

The Foreign Ministry issued a communique which said:

"Monsieur Coulondre, the Ambassador of France, was received at 12.30 P. M. (6.30 A. M. E. S. T.) by Monsieur Von Ribbentrop, Foreign Minister for the Reich.

"He asked if he was in a position to give a satisfactory reply to the communication of September 1, Monsieur De Ribbentrop replied negatively."

The communique said:

"As a result Monsieur Coulondre after recalling for the last time the heavy responsibility assumed by the Reich in engaging in hostilities against Poland without a declaration of war, and by not replying to suggestions of the French and British Governments, made known that the French Government, starting today, September 3, at 7 P. M. (1 P. M. E. S. T.) would be under obligation to fulfill engagements contracted toward Poland and which are known to the German Government."

AIRFORCE READY

While the final communique converting Europe's war of nerves into a war of arms was being issued to the press at the Foreign Ministry, Premier Daladier conferred at the War Ministry with Air Minister Guy Lachambre.

France's reborn airforce was in a state of alert to ward off any lightning attack.

Officials said Daladier probably would make a radio address to the nation tonight, similar to Prime Minister Chamberlain's broadcast to the British Empire this morning.

France and Britain watched the clock this momentous day, awaiting Germany's promised "winged lightning" war, as the world asked "what will be the strategy of this new conflict."

BATTLE FLEET LINE UP

France moved 8,000,000 men eastward. Her Navy and the giant naval forces of her British ally have been in battle positions for a week. Militarists agreed it might be some time before Britain will

Continued on Page 2, Column 7.

Latest War Bulletins

MOSCOW, Sept. 3—(A. P.).—Sources close to the Soviet Government emphasized tonight that they expected to remain neutral in a European War. They strongly hinted that in no case would their army march at the side of Germany's. At the same time these sources pointed out that they expected to lend economic aid both to Germany and her foes.

(The new Soviet Ambassador to Berlin, Alexander Schwkarzeff, was welcomed in the German capital with Nazi fanfare amid rumors that close Soviet-German relations might lead to a military pact.)

The terms of the new loan credit arranged by Germany for Russia were believed to be a determining factor in this arrangement.

The Russians, in supporting their plan to lend economic aid to both sides, asserted that during the Chinese-Japanese war and the Spanish Civil War, the United States sold munitions and other goods to both parties. So why shouldn't Russia sell to both sides, they asked?

• • •

LONDON, Sept. 3—(I. N. S.).—A Reuters dispatch from Shanghai tonight quoted reliable quarters as stating the Japanese Government has given its assurances to Great Britain that the Japanese Empire will remain neutral in the war against Germany.

• • •

PARIS, Sept. 3—(I. N. S.).—In a possible move toward winning Turkish consent to the use of the Dardenelles by the Anglo-French fleets, Foreign Minister Georges Bonnet tonight conferred at length with Turkish Ambassador Erkin.

LONDON, Sept. 3—(A. P.).—The British Admiralty tonight denied the accuracy of a report picked up by the Mutual Broadcasting System in a short wave broadcast from Paris that the $20,000,000 German liner Bremen had been captured by the British Navy. A spokesman for the Admiralty said the report was not true. No word was available, however, as to the ship's position at sea.

JERUSALEM, Sept. 3—(A. P.).—(Passed through British Censorship)—British police today lowered the Swastika

Continued on Page 5. Column 1.

LONDON, Sept. 3—(A. P.).—The First British official war communique was issued tonight.

It said that "notification that a state of war exists between Great Britain and Germany was handed to the German Charge D'Affaires at 11.15 this morning. The notification constituted a formal declaration of war."

WARSAW, Sept. 3—(A. P.).—The villa of United States Ambassador Anthony Joseph Drexel Biddle, Jr., was bombed by German planes today during a raid which Polish officials said resulted in three deaths. Biddle and members of his household were not home during the raid.

Canada, New Zealand, Australia Back England In War To Save Poland

Special Cable to International News Service

LONDON, Sept. 3—(I. N. S.)—The British Navy, largest in the world, began blockade operations against Germany and protective operations for British shipping tonight a few hours after England declared war on Germany.

The Daily Express said two coded radiograms were dispatched by the admiralty to all Naval vessels, the first placing the entire fleet on a war footing and the second commanding the Navy to "open hostilities."

OTTAWA, Sept. 3—(A. P. via Radio).—Prime Minister Mackenzie King, in a radio address today, attacked Adolf Hitler and the German Government for his "efforts to dominate the world."

He said:

"Despite her efforts to preserve the peace of Europe, the United Kingdom has become involved in war."

Canada, he said, has already answered the call to support the United Kingdom and measures will be taken to defend Canada.

The militia, naval and air service are already on active service, King said.

LONDON, Sept. 3—(I. N. S.).—Australia and New Zealand quickly responded to their sovereign's appeal by declaring themselves at war with Germany. Canada and the other dominions were expected to follow with similar declarations.

LONDON, Sept. 4.—(Monday)—(I. N. S.).—Egypt has declared war against Germany, the Dainly Express said today in a dispatch from Cairo.

By WILLIAM HILLMAN
International News Service Staff Correspondent

LONDON, Sept. 3.—Great Britain and France declared themselves at war with Germany today and immediately moved their vast land, sea and air forces into strategic positions for the first clash with Adolf Hitler's military machine.

Little more than 25 years since the beginning of the first World War, Western Europe's two democratic Powers launched what Prime Minister Neville Chamberlain described as a "fight to the finish" for the avowed purpose of ending Hitler's regime.

England first and then France proclaimed a state of war with Germany after the Nazi Fuehrer defiantly rejected Anglo-French ultimatums, which demanded immediate withdrawal of his invading forces from Poland.

Thus, the die was cast. The nightmare the world has awaited with dread for half a generation at last dawned over Europe.

Tonight the allied powers, fulfilling their treaty pledges to Poland, deployed millions of armed men and thousands of planes and ships into battle formations to strike at Hitler's mighty forces.

STRICT SECRECY

But the extent and nature of these initial moves and the numbers involved were wrapped in the strictest secrecy of a rigid censorship to prevent Hitler from thwarting any surprises in store for him.

The big question was:

"Where and how will Britain and France strike first?"

The answer awaited official announcement after the first blow has fallen.

Outbreak of the conflict that looms as history's greatest war found an estimated 5,500,000 armed men of England, France and Po-

Continued on Page 2, Column 1.

Italy To Hold Neutral Course

ROME, Sept. 3—(I. N. S.)—Italy will stay neutral in the European war arising from the German invasion of Poland, the government declared emphatically tonight.

Italian authorities insisted that no orders will be given for any military operations.

FRONTIERS OPEN

The frontiers facing France, Switzerland, Germany and Jugoslavia remained technically open, but traffic across the boundaries was virtually at a standstill.

Another two military classes, called up last week, reported at their barracks today and the Italian navy and air force remained mobilized, but the government declared these measures were merely precautionary.

SEEK ASSURANCE

It was noted, nevertheless, that Premier Mussolini himself has not yet given any definite assurance that Italian neutrality will be preserved, but observers in Rome agreed that Italy is not preparing for a military move.

Britain and France were understood to be seeking some more definite assurance from Il Duce of Italy's intentions through their ambassadors to Rome.

NO DEMONSTRATIONS

The changing of the guard at the Palazzo Venezia was called off and the square was deserted. There were no demonstrations in Rome, where the general feeling could be summed up:

"We expected England and France to enter the war since they are allied with Poland."

Special Session Of Congress Hinted

WASHINGTON, Sept. 3—(A. P.). In most quarters here today, it was considered a foregone conclusion that President Roosevelt would soon call for Congress to assemble. High officials repeatedly have indicated during the last weeks of crisis that this would be one of the first steps when it appeared definite that all hope for peace was gone.

WASHINGTON, Sept. 3—(A. P.) The White House announced today that the State and Justice Departments were drawing up a proclamation to invoke the neutrality act.

Stephen T. Early, a presidential secretary, told reporters that it had not been determined when the proclamation would be issued. He said it depended on when this government is notified officially that war has been declared.

He added, however, that "I think the government of the United States, I know the President does, assumes there is undoubtedly a state of war in existence."

AWAIT NOTIFICATION

Some delay may be encountered, Early indicated, in getting official notification to this government of the action of the British and French Governments because of the Sunday and Monday holidays.

He said that the notification would come through any channel that the British or French Governments might care to use.

An immediate effect of proclamation of the neutrality act would be to cut off British and French purchases of airplanes in this country.

While the exact status of the huge orders they have placed here is not known, it is believed that hardly more than half at the most, have been filled.

Main Provisions of U. S. Neutrality Act

WASHINGTON, Sept. 3—(A. P.). This country's Neutrality Act, when invoked by the President, puts the following restrictions into effect.

Americans are forbidden to sell, and American ships are forbidden to carry, arms and implements of war to any warring power or to any other nation for trans-shipment to a belligerent.

American ships, however, may transport any other materials anywhere they choose. Foreign ships, including those of belligerents, may come to the United States and get cargoes other than actual arms and munitions.

Americans cannot make loans to warring nations except normal, short-term commercial credits and are forbidden to collect money for them or travel on their vessels.

American merchantmen trading with belligerents cannot arm themselves for protection against attack on the high seas.

The President may close United States harbors to submarines and armed merchantmen of belligerents if such action is deemed advisable to safeguard this country's neutrality or other interests.

Eden Takes Post To Aid Britain

LONDON, Sept. 3—(I. N. S.).—Anthony Eden, former Foreign Secretary, who resigned in protest against Britain's former "appeasement" policy, tonight was appointed British Secretary for Dominions.

Earl Stanhope was named Lord President of the Council and Sir Thomas Inskip was made Lord Chancellor. Sir John Anderson was appointed Home Secretary and Minister of Home Security.

The above-named ministers will not be in the newly formed War Cabinet, but Eden will have special access to the War Cabinet, it was announced, in order to maintain contact between the War Ministry and the dominions.

Winston Churchill Cheered In London

LONDON, Sept. 3—(I. N. S.).—A crowd of Londoners in Downing street cheered Winston Churchill, First Lord of the Admiralty; Foreign Secretary Lord Halifax; War Secretary Leslie Hore-Belisha and Air Secretary Sir Kingsley Wood tonight when they left Prime Minister Neville Chamberlain's residence after a meeting of the war cabinet.

WAR NEWS IS FATAL

WASHINGTON, Sept. 3—(A. P.). The Rev. Vincent S. McDonough, S. J., former faculty moderator of athletics at Georgetown University, died of a heart attack today while listening to war news over the radio.

We Will Smash Poland---Hitler

By LOUIS LOCHNER

BERLIN, Sept. 3—(A. P.).—Adolf Hitler, in a broadcast appeal to Germany, today accused Britain of encircling Germany to further British ambitions for world domination.

In a proclamation to Germany's Eastern Army the Fuehrer announced he was leaving today to join the forces invading Poland.

VERSAILLES TREATY

Hitler declared in his broadcast that because he mobilized the German people against the Versailles Treaty, England tried to prevent Germany from obtaining needed living space.

"The British Government is mistaken about one thing," he declared. "The Germany of 1939 is no longer the Germany of 1914, and the Chancellor of the present German Reich is no longer Bethmann-Hollweg (Chancellor in 1914)."

Hitler said that except for British support Poland would not have resisted a peaceful revision of her frontiers.

"Let England understand that

Continued on Page 2, Column 6.

WAR BULLETIN EDITION

THE WEATHER
Cloudy; Probable Showers
High: 3:32 a. m., 3:56 p. m. Low
9:46 a. m., 1023 p. m.

The Times-Star EXTRA

Founded November 20, 1790

VOL. 148. NO. 208 | Entered as Second Class Matter at the Post Office at Bridgeport, Conn. | BRIDGEPORT, CONNECTICUT, MONDAY EVENING, SEPTEMBER 4, 1939 | ★★ | 8 PAGES—PRICE TWO CENTS

FRANCE OPENS ATTACK! NEARLY ALL ARE SAVED FROM TORPEDOED SHIP

FRENCH LAUNCH ATTACK BY AIR, LAND AND SEA

PARIS, Sept. 4—(AP)—The French war ministry announced today operations of "the entire ~~land and naval~~ and air forces" have begun.

The ministry's "communique No. 1"—marking the actual opening of hostilities in the French and British war against Germany—was issued at 11:30 a. m. (5:30 a. m., E. S. T.)

It said simply: "Operations have begun, involving the entire land, naval and air forces."

WESTERN FRONT

The theater of action was kept a military secret. A clue to the action, however, was given a notice in the newspaper Paris-Midi which said, "great silence is observed on military operations on the western front, but it can be assured that we are not inactive.

"The German armies are going to be forced to loosen their grip on heroic Poland whose troops at several points have passed their offensive.

Authorities started emptying Paris hospitals for military use. The first night of France's state of war with Germany had passed without word of the firing of a shot.

The communique came as the first indication that France's 8,000,000-man military machine had gone into action.

Shortly before 11 a. m., French heavy bombers flew low over the

Concluded on Page Two

LIST AMERICANS ON "ATHENIA"

WASHINGTON, Sept. 4.—(AP)—The State Department made public today the following partial list of Americans on board the S. S. Athenia when it was torpedoed:

(The department said the home addresses given were taken from passport files and might not be correct in every case): Kathryn and Margaret McGuire, Minneapolis; Hazel Casserly, Minneapolis; Charles Grant and Master Charles Grant, New York city; Mrs. Edith Bridge, Miss Constance Bridge, and Harry Bridge, Wellington, Kans.; George Cottle and Laura Cottle, Cleveland; Mr. and Mrs. Thomas Kerr, Sixteen, Mor. ; Mrs. Kate Hinds and William Hinds, Houston, Tex.; Florence Malik, New York city; Margaret Buchan, San Francisco; Rhoda Thomas, Rochester, N. Y.; Charles Prince, Sr., and Charles Prince, Jr., Kittery, Me.; Harold Etherington and Geoffry Etherington, Milwaukee; George Keli-

Concluded on Page Two

(NEA Radiophoto)
FIRST PHOTO OF DESTRUCTION by Nazis in Poland somewhere in Poland—A Polish village in flames, presumably after aerial bombardment by German planes. Photo is one of first to reach U. S.

The Second World War

— Editorial —

The declaration of war by England and France was inevitable if these two nations were to honor their pledges and have any regard for their own future. It is not Poland they are to fight for; the menace of Hitler aggression is to them almost as much as it is to Poland. They could have left Poland to her fate; they could have postponed their own day of reckoning with Nazi Germany; but they could not have escaped it. England and France have never entered a war with more justice; it is true that civilization, as we know it, is at stake in their military efforts.

For the barbarism of militarism and of a destructive ideology is on the aggressors' side. If there was any lingering doubt about this, Nazi Germany removed it yesterday with the torpedoing of the Athenia, with its 1400 passengers, including some 300 American citizens. The fact that many lives were saved in spite of the ship's sinking does not lessen the import of the tragedy. In the first World War, it took some time for barbarism to take full command. But barbarism is already top-ranking Nazi strategist in this World War.

The sinking of the Athenia, with the new World War only a few hours old, is striking testimony to the fact that this war is altogether likely to be far more terrible than anything the world has yet known.

The great tragedy is that no one was able to avoid it. But we must still seek spirit and courage to face it in all its far-reaching consequences.

Our hopes cannot but be that the forces which sank the Athenia will be speedily checked and consigned to oblivion, their destructive power stripped away from them. An immediate glimmer of hope comes in indications that the Polish army is making a stand which is not only valiant but effective. It would be a fine thing for the world to have Nazi arms proved just as deficient in a real test as is the Nazi creed itself.

EXTRA GUARDS FOR SIKORSKY'S

Until President Roosevelt makes known what the government considers "implements of war," Connecticut manufacturers will not definitely know the status of their various manufacturing enterprises.

Under the President's proclamation of neutrality, the export trade of Connecticut industries may be drastically curtailed.

At the Voight-Sikorsky division of the United Aircraft Co. plant in Stratford, three extra guards to patrol the outside plant grounds were ordered on 24 hour duty this morning.

These additional guards will augment the force which is already entrusted with protecting the inside of the plant proper.

The entire operation plan is under the supervision of inspectors from the U. S. Navy depart-

Concluded on Page Eight

REPORT MOST OF 1,347 ON LINER SAVED

LONDON, Sept. 4—(AP)—A rescue fleet, guarded by guns of British destroyers, was officially reported today to have saved all but the few persons killed by the explosion which sank the Donaldson liner Athenia, which British officials said was torpedoed by a German submarine in the open North Atlantic.

There were 1,347 passengers and crew aboard, which included United States citizens listed tentatively at 311.

Bulletins from British government agencies failed to give the number of dead. The main basis for hope was the announcement which the Athenia's master, Captain James Cooke, wirelessed: "Passengers and crew except those killed by explosion took to boats and were picked up by various ships."

This announcement was made by the ship's line (Donaldson Atlantic) and was confirmed by the admiralty.

DESTROYERS ON SCENE

Officials did not announce from what ship Capt. Cook's message was sent, nor were the names of the rescue ships made known.

It was established officially, however, that British destroyers were on the scene of the disaster, 250 miles west of Inishtrahull, Northern Ireland.

The British Ministry of Information said that of the 311 United States passengers, all fleeing the European war zones, 65 had boarded the 13,591-ton, Montreal-bound ship at Belfast, 101 at Liverpool, and 145 from Glasgow.

In the absence of a complete passenger list there was a possi-

Concluded on Page Eight

Poles Lose 1 Town But Invade Germany

WARSAW, Sept. 4—(AP)—A communique from the Polish general staff today announced withdrawal of Polish forces from Czestochowa, a town of 120,000 in southwest Poland, after a strong offensive by greatly-superior German forces using tanks and heavy artillery.

In Pomorze (Polish Corridor), severe fighting was reported around Grudziadz and elsewhere near the East Prussian frontier, with Polish defense lines holding intact.

The Communque said the Poles had recaptured Orlowo and Kack, suburbs of the port city of Gdynia, and the Polish garrison of the Westerplatte, ammunition dump in Danzig harbor, still was holding out.

A dispatch from Danzig, first received since the former free city was annexed by the Reich Friday, said the Westerplatte garrison was fighting back with machine gun fire against airplane and artillery bombardments.

Summarizing the war aloft, the Communique listed 27 German

Concluded on Page Two

Americans on Ship; Poles in Germany

SHANGHAI, Sept. 4—(AP)—A Japanese press dispatch from Amoy tonight said it was reported in Amoy that the 3,472-ton British steamer Anking had been torpedoed between Manila and Hongkong.

The world rocked with horror today as a German submarine sent a defenseless British passenger ship—with 311 Americans aboard—plunging to the bottom 200 miles off Scotland, then rejoiced as news was flashed that most of the nearly 1,400 aboard had been rescued.

The torpedo was sent crashing into the ship in direct violation, Britain charged, of the protocol in which Germany agreed to remove all passengers and guarantee their safety before attack. (Picture on Page 8.)

HITLER JOINS HIS TROOPS ON EASTERN FRONT

BERLIN, Sept. 4—(AP)—Adolf Hitler, relying on the Siegfied line of fortifications in the west to "shelter and defend" Germany against Britain and France, joined his troops on the eastern front today to direct the drive to conquer Poland and thus "burst open the ring laid around Germany."

Declaring "Germany will never again capitulate," the Fuehrer left behind him an assurance the task of subjugating Poland will take "only a few weeks," if the western army does its duty in holding off Poland's two allies.

"Then," he added, in a special message to the army facing France, "the strength of our entire ninety millions stands behind you."

TAKES COMMAND

Hitler departed to take personal command of the forces fighting on the Polish front some twelve hours after he had rejected the ultimatum presented by the British Ambassador, Sir Nevile Henderson, demanding the withdrawal of German troops from Poland.

Berlin took calmly the news of the joint declaration of war by Britain and France. A crowd of several hundred in front of the chancellery heard the announcement in silence as it was carried over loudspeakers. Newspaper extras of one page each were printed and distributed free of charge.

New war-time measures were put into effect immediately. All

FRANCE LAUNCHES ATTACK

France simultaneously launched an attack against Germany by land, sea and air. As the British fleet took battle stations to enforce a blockade of Germany, the French War Ministry announced at 7 o'clock (noon, eastern daylight saving time) that a land offensive was concentrated in the Belfort region where the Burgundy Gate cuts across the Rhine into the Reich, just north of the three-cornered border between France, Switzerland and Germany. The Burgundy Gate is a valley running northwest into the Black Forest.

Details of any planned attack to crack Hitler's vaunted west wall fortifications across from the Maginot line, were withheld. The French fleet held battle positions in the western Mediterranean.

Heavy gunfire was heard from the direction of the German border in Luxembourg, Belgium.

Concluded on Page Eight

Many Local People Still In Europe as War Rages

Anxious relatives of local people abroad today dispatched cables to various American consulates asking for information concerning the whereabouts and safety of their kin.

Some of them, in neutral countries, were planning to complete their vacation trips. Catholic youths studying in European seminaries for the priesthood are back at school, it was reported at Hartford this morning, and will remain there at least for the time being. They are in no war danger.

Other local persons were on the high seas headed for home.

Richard H. Lombard ("Good Luck"), restaurant owner here, is still in Dublin, his family here said today. They do not know of any change in his plans to return to America September 13th via the Flying Clipper.

Esther Lillian Neuss, daughter of Mr. and Mrs. Harry Neuss, of Jackman Ave., returns from a bicycle tour of Europe tomorrow aboard the Holland liner, Veendam.

According to J. Arthur Topham of Old Spring Rd., Fairfield,

Concluded on Page Eight

EMERGENCY IN U. S.

THE BALTIMORE NEWS-POST
AN INDEPENDENT NEWSPAPER
The Largest Daily Circulation in the Entire South
7 HOME FINAL
VOL. CXXXV.—NO. 108
Entered as second-class matter at Baltimore Postoffice

FRIDAY EVENING, SEPTEMBER 8, 1939
PRICE 2 CENTS

THE WEATHER

Scattered thundershowers this afternoon or early tonight. Continued warm tonight, with lowest temperatures around 70 degrees. Saturday fair and colder. Sunday fair with moderate temperatures.

Detailed Weather Report on Page 37

MEAN TEMPERATURES YESTERDAY

Baltimore	74	New York	66
Atlanta	71	Omaha	88
Boston	66	Portland, Me.	60
Chicago	88	Salt Lake City	54
Los Angeles	75	Seattle	58
New Orleans	82	Washington	75

GERMANS ENTER WARSAW

Rush Nazi Troops To West Line

Peace-Time Emergency Ordered By Roosevelt; Strengthens Army, Navy

By GEORGE DURNO
International News Service Staff Correspondent.

WASHINGTON, Sept. 8.—President Roosevelt today issued a proclamation placing the nation in a limited peace emergency for neutrality enforcement, disclosed he would strengthen the Army, Navy and Marine Corps for national defense, and clearly indicated he would call a special session of Congress.

Moving rapidly on many fronts to bulwark the United States from Europe's war, Mr. Roosevelt said that there never was a question of "whether" he would call a special sessio of Congress. However, he made clear he had not decided on a date. He expected a short session, he added.

Meanwhile, Senator Joseph Guffey (Democrat) of Pennsylvania left the White House predictin gthe extraordinary session would be called by October 1.

Limited Peace-time Emergency

The proclamation placing the country on the limited peace-time emergency—the President stressed the word peace-time over and over again—was announced at the President's regular Friday press conference.

Under the proclamation the President plans later in the day to sign four Executive orders. They will provide for increases in the Army, Navy, Marine Corps and National Guard; make immediately available to the State Department $500,000 for assistance of Americans abroad, and expand personnel of the Government's investigative agencies to combat espionage and sabotage.

The President, in reading his proclamation, stressed the fact that he was not putting the country on a war basis. He said all actions were being taken on a peace-time basis.

The President alos announced signature of a proclamation extending American neutrality to apply to South Africa, this Government having been officially notified that South Africa had declared war on Germany. The President said the Canadian proclamation was drafted but final Parliamentary action had not been taken at Ottawa.

The increases in Army, Navy and Marine Corps personnel, the President said, will be for the purpose of "filling in gaps" and will come nowhere near bringing any of the services up to their full authorized peace-time strength. The Army's

(Continued on Page A, Column 7.)

VERY LATEST NEWS

(Race Results From Stevens [illegible] Company, Inc.)

RACING RESULTS

AT NARRAGANSETT PARK

First—Wise Counsel, $16.30, $8.00, $5.50; Breadandbutter, $7.40, $5.00; Peon, $5.90.

AT AQUEDUCT

First—Tactician, 8 to 5, 1 to 2, 1 to 5; Baba, 20 to 1, 10 to 1; Transbye, 1 to 2.

SUSPEND U. S. RHODES SCHOLARSHIPS

SWARTHMORE, Pa., Sept. 8—(A. P.).—Suspension of 32 American Rhodes scholarships because of the war was announced today by Dr. Frank Aydelotte, American secretary of the Rhodes trustees.

'Will Fight To Finish,' Say Poles

BUDAPEST, Sept. 8—(A. P.).—The Warsaw radio, silent yesterday, today broadcast a statement that "the Polish army will yet start its offensive." The announcement said:

"The present retreat is for strategic reasons.

"The Poles will not capitulate. We will fight to the finish.

"The Polish air fleet is intact. The world will understand this before long."

The broadcaster appealed to all citizens to help fortify Warsaw and declared it would be defended the way Madrid was defended by the Spanish Republic.

WARSAW, Sept. 8—(A. P.)—(Havas, French News Agency, Dispatch Via Berne, Switzerland).—The Polish Army, intact after the first week of war, has withdrawn from various sectors to pre-establish defense positions along a 1,500-kilometer (931-mile) front.

Poznan Province, where Polish forces have held their original positions despite heavy German attacks, forms a huge salient between two German offensive zones.

CAVALRY ACTS

From this salient Polish cavalry and motored infantry are striking at the German flanks.

Despite the sudden German attack Polish troops have held their advance positions long enough to permit complete mobilization of

Continued on Page 2, Column 5.

U. S. Gold Imports Show Sharp Rise

WASHINGTON, Sept. 8—(I. N. S.).—A sharp rise in gold imports during the week ended September 1 was reported today by the Commerce Department with $106,000,000 of the yellow metal entering the United States, principally from Great Britain. The previous week gold inflow amounted to $65,000,000.

Byrd Aide Dies In Plane Crash

HARRISVILLE, N. H., Sept. 8—(A. P.).—George A. Thorne, Jr., of Chicago, a geologist on Rear Admiral Richard E. Byrd's first Antarctic expedition, lost his life in an airplane crash near his summer home last night even as he prepared to accompany Byrd on a new journey to the South Pole.

Torrio Turns Over $177,352.07 To U. S.

NEW YORK, Sept. 8—(I. N. S.).—Johnny Torrio, former Chicago underworld leader now serving a Federal prison term for income tax evasion, today turned over to the Government $177,352.07, the entire amount assessed for such evasion.

Athenia Survivors On Land

Nerve-wracked and apparently near exhaustion, an aged woman passenger of the torpedoed liner Athenia is shown, dressed in makeshift clothing, as she was assisted ashore at Galway, Ireland, from one of the rescue vessels that picked up survivors. International News Cablephoto. (Other pictures on Page 3.)

Steel, Motor And Aircraft Stocks Rise

NEW YORK, Sept. 8—(A. P.).—War buying continued in some directions in the nation's markets today, and subsided in others.

The buying surge in several of the commodity markets appeared to have lost vigor, and for the first time in a week, trading conditions were normal.

SHARES UP $1 TO $4

Prices in the stock market rose $1 to more than $4 a share as further large-scale buying came into steels, motors and aircrafts. Wall Street hopes of changes in the neutrality legislation to permit airplane and armament sales to belligerents appeared to have brightened.

Wheat prices at Chicago lost about 3 cents a bushel. It was noted Department of Agriculture officials said in Washington that in view of large stocks, warring nations might not be big takers of American grain for possibly a year. Livestock, corn and lard also declined.

COTTON FUTURES RISE

Large-scale buying continued in the primary textile markets, and in the morning cotton futures rose $1.50 to more than $2 a bale, but lost part of the rise after publication of the Government crop report.

The flurry in the sugar markets continued, although in the futures markets several deliveries failed to go the full ¼ of a cent a pound permitted in a single day, as they had every day recently.

Netherlands Ship Hits Mine, 29 Die

By Associated Press.

The sinking of two more ships, a British tanker and a small German freighter, today raised the known losses in the sea warfare between the Allies and Germany to ten vessels.

Neutral Netherlands suffered, too, when one of its mine-sweepers was disabled in an explosion which, survivors said, was caused when it struck a mine. Twenty-nine of the crew were killed.

NAZI'S HAVE EDGE

With the German U-boats off to a faster start than they showed in the last World War, the score on the sixth day stood 7 to 4 in favor of the Nazis. In tonnage the British and French have lost 48,128 to Germany's 14,764.

The two latest victims were the British tanker Regent Tiger, listed in Lloyd's registry as a 10,176-ton ship, and the German freighter Helfrid Bissmark, a 727-ton craft.

The loss of the British tanker was reported by Radio Marine Corporation, which picked up a radio message ..ying the steamer Jeanjadot saved the crew of 44 after the ship had been torpedoed by a submarine. The position of the sinking was not given.

7 KILLED, 7 SAVED

The Helfrid Bissmark sank in Roe Sound on the eastern side of the Danish peninsula. Seven members of her crew were killed and seven saved. The survivors believe the ship struck a mine.

At least one other British freighter and a French vessel were attacked by submarines lying in wait for prey in the Atlantic.

The sinking of the British freight-

Continued on Page 16, Column 2.

Temperatures

Midnight,	72	7 A. M.,	73
1 A. M.,	71	8 A. M.,	77
2 A. M.,	70	9 A. M.,	83
3 A. M.,	70	10 A. M.,	86
4 A. M.,	69	11 A. M.,	93
5 A. M.,	70	12 Noon,	96
6 A. M.,	71	1 P. M.,	97

Severe Earthquake In North Pacific

HARVARD, Mass., Sept. 8—(A. P.).—A "severe" earthquake, "probably in the North Pacific," was recorded today at the Harvard University seismograph station, its director, Dr. L. Don Leet, announced. Dr. Leet said the disturbance began at 7.04.47 A. M., Eastern standard time, and that recordings continued about an hour. He estimated the disturbance to be approximately 4,830 miles distant.

Six Teuton Divisions Taken From Polish Front To Aid Siegfried Defense

BERLIN, Sept. 8—(A. P.).—The German supreme high comand announcmed today that a German Army unit forced an entry into Warsaw at 5.15 P. M. (11.15 A. M., E. S. T.).

AMSTERDAM, Sept. 8—(I. N. S.—Six German divisions, totalling nearly 90,000 men, have been rushed from Poland to the Siegfried Line aboard special express trains hastily pressed into service, it was established on unimpeachable authority in Amsterdam today.

The French attack on the western front has become intensified, with 70-ton tanks brought into action to scatter land-mines for the destruction of Germany's heaviest concrete trenches.

Steady French successes were reported in dispatchs reaching Amsterdam.

PARIS, Sept. 8 — (I. N. S.). — Many German deserters from the Siegfried Line have swum across the Rhine and have been interned by French frontier guards, according to a report from Luxemburg today.

GENEVA, Sept. 8—(I. N. S.).—All villages on the German side of the Rhine between Basle and Lake Constance have now been evacuated, it was learned today. In the dpartment of Savoy near Geneva, 100 German residents were taken to concentration camps.

PARIS, Sept. 8—(I. N. S.).—Steadily improving their positions in "no man's land" between the Maginot and Siegfried lines, French forces hammered away with artillery and aircraft today. Reports from the front told of further thrusts by French troops into the soil of Germany while tanks and big guns paved the way for a major offensive.

The French are now taking up the slack in an area varying from two to 12 miles in depth, wiping out pill-boxes, machine-gun nests and hastily erected field fortifications.

COPENHAGEN, Sept. 8—(A. P.).—The thunder of guns and bombs last night and early today indicated an attack was being made on the German island of Sylt by airplanes.

The island is just off the southwest extremity of Denmark and is the site of an important German anti-aircraft defense fortification.

The humming of aircraft was heard clearly on the nearby Danish island of Roemoe.

Heavy firing by the Sylt bateries was interspersed with dull booms, suggesting exploding bombs.

PARIS, Sept. 8—(A. P.).—The French high command today reported its armies progressing across the German frontier through the wooded approaches to the Siegfried Line.

New "local advances," announced by the War Ministry's communique No. 9 this morning, were strengthening the spearheads driven into Germany's Saar basin.

Despite spirited German resistance and reinforcement of German troops on the western front, the French appeared to be pressing their attacks to relieve Poland from pressure in the east.

There the Poles were expected

Continued on Page A, Column 5.

Youngest Clipper Passenger Arrives

PORT WASHINGTON, N. Y., Sept. 8—(I. N. S.).—The distinction of being the youngest passenger ever to make a trans-Atlantic crossing in a Clipper plane belonged today to Althea Elwell, eighteen months old. The infant was not much impressed by the adventure. She slept most of the way from Foynes, Ireland, in the arms of her mother, Mrs. E. W. Elwell of New York, aboard the American Clipper.

Die Wehrmacht
HERAUSGEGEBEN VOM OBERKOMMANDO D
3. JAHRGANG · NUMMER 19 · BERLIN, 13. SEPTEMBER 1939 · EINZEL-
PREIS 25 RPF. UND BESTELLGELD · ERSCHEINT VIERZEHNTÄGLICH
„Ich will jetzt
nichts anderes sein
als der erste Soldat
des Deutschen
Reiches"

2¢

DAILY MIRROR

WEATHER FAIR, WARMER Details on Page 6.

Member of The Associated Press (Copyright, 1939, Daily Mirror, Inc.)

3 Cents Outside City Limits

2¢

Vol. 16. No. 73 New York, Saturday, September 16, 1939 FINAL EDITION ★★★

JAPS-REDS SIGN TRUCE

Story on Page 3

LATE BULLETINS

Nazis Raid Polish Ukraine

SNIATYN, Poland, Sept. 15 (UP).—A German flying column roving far in advance of the main Nazi army tonight terrified thousands of Polish war refugees, for whom all escape has been cut off, in a series of lightning raids in the Polish Ukraine.

'Lost Army' to Aid Warsaw

PARIS, Sept. 15 (UP).—The Warsaw radio announced late tonight that the "lost army" of the Polish Corridor, which broke the jaws of a German trap north of Lodz, had entered Warsaw "amid frantic acclamation" to help defend the city.

Destroy Nazi Air Base

LONDON, Sept. 16 (Saturday) (INS)—A Polish air fleet in a daring raid far behind the lines "destroyed" the principal base from which German planes took off in their repeated attacks on Warsaw, the Polish radio announced, according to a Reuter's dispatch early today.

Rumania Bars Fleeing Poles

BUCHAREST, Sept. 15 (UP).—Rumania tonight barred her frontiers to the bulk of the thousands of Polish refugees fleeing before invading German armies.

Fear Hitler May Invade Rumania

LONDON, Sept. 15 (INS).—Fear that Adolf Hitler may invade Rumania after dividing most of Poland with Russia was expressed in London tonight.

Berlin Says Moscicki Seeks Refuge

BERLIN, Sept. 15 (INS).—President Moscicki and other members of the Polish Government today appealed to Rumania for safe refuge, the official German News Agency DNB declared. Members of the government were reported in the town of Zaleszezyki, five miles from the Rumanian border.

(MORE WAR BULLETINS ON BACK PAGE)

ALLIES WIN AIR FIGHT

Story on Page 2

POLES IN RETREAT

Story on Page 3

FORECAST—Fresh to strong southwesterly winds, partly cloudy today and most of Sunday with a few light scattered showers.

Sunshine yesterday, 9 hours 12 minutes.

Victoria Daily Times

VOL. 95 NO. 88 — VICTORIA, B.C., SATURDAY, OCTOBER 14, 1939—32 PAGES — PRICE FIVE CENTS

TIDES

Oct.	Time h.m.	Ht ft	Time h.m.	Ht. ft.	Time h.m.	Ht ft.	Time h.m.	Ht ft.
14 ..	4.45	7.5	9.26	5.9	14.35	8.5	22.15	1.7
15 ..	6.04	7.6	10.10	6.6	15.02	8.5	23.00	1.7
16 ..	7.25	7.7	10.59	7.1	15.26	8.3	23.46	1.9

Sun sets, 5.28; rises Sunday, 6.32.

16,000 In 1st Canada Division To Go Overseas In 2 Months; Fear 800 Lost On Royal Oak

LATEST

3 Rhine Bridges Blown By French

By JOHN H. MARTIN

PARIS (AP)—French military advices said today the destruction by the French of three big railway bridges over the Rhine River was to forestall any attempted German surprise offensive into French Alsace.

Bridges destroyed connected Haguenau and Rastadt, Colmar and Fribourg-en-Brisgau and Mulhouse and Mulheim. Only two bridges remain across this part, both at Strasbourg, where they are incorporated in the Maginot and Siegfried lines. It was indicated at least one of these would be spared for the time being.

Halt Stalin Duce Asks Hitler

PARIS (CP) — A Havas dispatch from Rome tonight quoted well-informed Fascist sources as saying consultations are under way between Italy and Germany over the situation created by Soviet Russia's expansion.

The dispatch continued:

"It was believed in well-informed quarters that the Italian government is asking Germany to press Moscow not to go too far in its new imperialism. Russia should be content with the positions already acquired in Poland and on the Baltic states, Italy holds.

"It was also believed that Rome had drawn Germany's attention to the delicate position in which Italy has been placed.

"Italy, by diplomatic moves, has clearly supported the regrouping of the southeastern European nations which have remained outside the conflict and are resolved to defend their neutrality."

2 Million Germans Mass on Rhine

PARIS (AP) — North of the upper Rhine sector, Germans were reported in French advices to have massed enough tanks and heavy artillery between the Rhine and the Moselle to launch a large-scale offensive at any moment.

The French said the Nazi troops manning the 100-mile Rhine-Moselle front were veterans of the Polish campaign.

French officers estimated total German strength on the two main fronts, upper Rhine and Rhine-Moselle, and in close reserve, at 2,000,000 men.

No Soviet Army To Aid Germans

LONDON (CP) — The Daily Herald today printed a dispatch from Istanbul reporting that Russia has assured Turkey the Soviet Union will not fight on the side of Germany in the war. The pledge against a military alliance with the Nazis, the Herald said, was given by the Kremlin to Foreign Minister Sukru Saracoglu, in Moscow since last month negotiating an accord with Soviet leaders.

Britain Again to Buy Canadian Wheat

LONDON (CP) — The British government has temporarily halted purchases of Canadian wheat pending a solution of exchange and shipping problems which are now being discussed between the governments at London and Ottawa, according to comment by a Canadian Wheat Board spokesman today.

The spokesman added the questions at issue were merely small ones and that the position should be "cleared up within 48 hours."

Baby With Organs Outside Body Dies

SCRANTON, Pa. (AP) — A day-old boy born with several abdominal organs outside his body, died today shortly after an operation.

Dr. M. J. Noone said the baby's stomach, liver, spleen and intestines "were located outside the body during the entire period of development."

Lindbergh Speech Called 'Asinine'

WASHINGTON (CP)—Political observers predicted today that Col. Charles A. Lindbergh's suggestion that the United States should interfere with Canada's allegiance to Britain might arouse such resentment as to weaken Senate opposition to repeal of the embargo law.

Lindbergh's broadcast address was the subject of widespread comment as the Senate met in an unusual Saturday session to debate the embargo repeal bill—a measure which, it is generally agreed, would make the United States an arms reservoir for the Allies.

Few comments favorable to the noted aviator's speech were heard. "Asinine" frequently was used to describe the address.

PLANE CREW DEAD, BUT LAND SAFELY

PARIS (AP) — French observation planes took advantage of the clear weather to photograph the German lines at several points.

Both the pilot and observer of one of the planes were found dead in their seats after the craft, riddled with bullets, had landed safely behind the French lines. A camera in the plane was undamaged and contained "valuable" photographs of German positions, the French declared.

U.S. NEXT IN WAR EDITORIAL CITED

WASHINGTON (AP)—A Canadian newspaper editorial forecasting the United States will be in the war early in 1940 was exhibited in the United States Senate today by Senator Arthur Vandenberg.

It is an example of how "our friends and neighbors are being fooled," he said.

The Senator's "interesting exhibit" was a page from the Windsor Star, September 21. Holding the page aloft, he said:

"Running down through the centre of the page is an editorial stating that the American embargo will be repealed and the United States will be in the war about the middle of next January. It would be scarcely less tragic if our friends and neighbors are fooled than if we are fooled ourselves."

Attfields, Athenia Survivors, at Quebec

QUEBEC (CP) — Mrs. Lilian Attfield, Grace Attfield and Lona Attfield, 2508 Orchard Avenue, Victoria, were among a group of 69 survivors of the Athenia torpedoing who arrived here today from England, where they had been awaiting transportation home since the British liner was sunk by a submarine off the coast of Ireland September 3.

Fifty-two survivors were Canadians while the others were non-Canadian British subjects travelling to destinations in the Dominion.

Scotland Snows Under Stop-war Candidate

GLASGOW (CP) — Arthur Woodburn, Scottish secretary of the Labor Party, was returned to the House of Commons today in a by-election, decisively defeating a "stop the war" candidate.

Returns from the Clackmannan and East Stirling constituency gave Mr. Woodburn 15,645 votes to 1,060 for Andrew Stewart, pacifist.

Body of Man Found In Murder Swamp

NEWCASTLE, Pa. (AP)—An autopsy disclosed today the body of a mutilated victim found in an eerie "murder swamp" near here was that of a man and not a woman as first believed.

Toronto Pilot Missing

LONDON (CP)—Flying Officer Robert Coste, son of Frank E. Coste of Toronto, is missing, it was officially announced today in correcting a previous announcement he had been killed in active service with the Royal Air Force.

Lithuanians Vote Pact

KAUNAS (CP-Havas) — The Lithuanian senate today unanimously ratified the new mutual assistance treaty with the Soviet union.

Winter Training For Canadians In English Camps

By FRANK FLAHERTY

OTTAWA (CP)—Canada's first overseas division probably will proceed to England within the next two months to complete its training there and receive service equipment.

Like the first contingent in the first Great War, the probability is the division of about 16,000 men will spend the winter, or a large part of it, in England.

LACK WINTER CAMPS

Lack of facilities for concentrating a large body of troops in Canada under winter conditions makes the final training of the division in Canada impracticable. Although there are a number of large military training grounds in Canada, none of them have sufficient all-weather buildings to house a division, although they can accommodate considerable numbers of troops during the summer when tents may be used.

Valcartier, Que., Petawawa, Niagara-on-the-Lake and camp Borden in Ontario and Dundurn, Sask., would be suitable for summer training. Before another year passes it is expected one or more of these camps will be made into a winter establishment, but the task of erecting huts, installing service works and heating systems for upward of 15,000 men requires time.

The division is composed of some of the crack units of the Canadian nonpermanent and permanent active militia. Practically all units selected have now been recruited up to wartime strength and are receiving training by units at their local headquarters.

In England the troops may be trained in brigades and perhaps receive divisional training.

NEW BATTLE DRESS

By the time the division sails the troops will be completely equipped with the new battle dress uniform of blouse, loose-fitting trousers and gaiters. The infantry units may take rifles with them, but generaly speaking equipment will be obtained in England, and the men will take only their clothing and personal kit.

Machine guns, field guns, anti-tank guns and transport will all be provided after the division reaches the United Kingdom.

Major-General A. G. L. Mcnaughton will command the first overseas division and probably the entire Canadian overseas force if and when other units are sent.

Appointment of brigade commanders and headquarters' staff officers is receiving consideration by defence authorities, and announcements will be made in due course.

The infantry battalions, artillery batteries and other units are already organized under their own commanding officers.

ALL PROVINCES SHARE

All sections of Canada are represented in the division. One infantry brigade consists of units from western Canada, another of units from Ontario and the third of units from Quebec and the Maritime Provinces.

One artillery brigade is entirely made up of permanent force batteries, a second of nonpermanent batteries from Quebec and the Maritime Provinces and the third of nonpermanent western batteries.

The division consists of a squadron of mechanized cavalry, three brigades of artillery, each containing four batteries, three brigades of infantry, each containing three rifle battalions and a machine gun battalion; four companies of engineers, three companies of signallers and the serving units.

The latter include an ammunition company, a petrol company, divisional supply column, three field ambulances, field hygiene section for sanitation, provost or policing company from the Royal Canadian Mounted Police, division postal unit and the employment platoon of labor troops.

Just 25 years ago today the First Canadian Continent landed at Plymouth, England, for the first Great War. It consisted of 30,000 men and from it the first four Canadian divisions to serve in France and Belgium was organized.

The first contingent spent 16 weeks on Salisbury Plain, England, in training before the first division left for France in February, 1915.

The troops were under canvas for part of their stay in England, but huts were built on the plain and eventually the whole contingent had roofs over their heads.

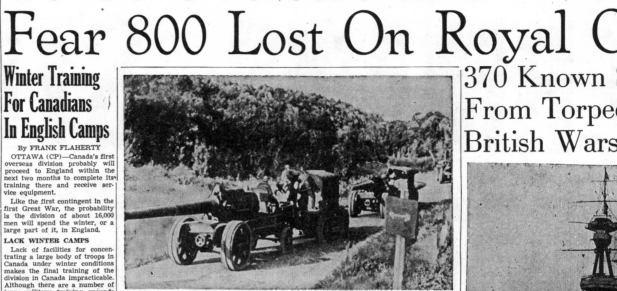

TO THE FRONT—Heavy French guns, drawn by tractors, roll along a country road in France en route to the western front. (Acme telephoto.)

Air Mission Reaches Canada

QUEBEC (CP)—Headed by Lord Riverdale, an eight-man British mission arrived here today to discuss with Dominion authorities methods for Empire air-strength co-ordination.

A communique said that "one of the primary objects of the discussions will . . . be to concert measures for enabling each member of the Commonwealth to take over that part of the common task which by reasons of its industrial capacity, its manpower and its geographical position, it is best suited to undertake."

Australian and New Zealand missions will reach Ottawa "at an early date."

With Lord Riverdale were Air Marshal Sir C. L. Courtney; J. B. Abraham, permanent assistant secretary of the British Air Ministry; Group Captain A. Gray, Group Captain L. N. Hollinghurst, Group Captain J. M. Robb; F. R. Howard, mission secretary, and J. R. Smyth of Air Ministry's financial division.

Second Pay Day For Boys in Khaki

Today was the second pay day of the war for Canadian troops.

Paymasters of the various units this morning came to town and went to the banks to get the right number of bills and change. Each man is paid in cash.

The men lined up in small groups and marched to the paymaster's office, where they received their pay, which amounts to $1.30 a day for a private, and more according to the rank. From this amount so much was deducted for wives and dependents.

This evening the boys in khaki who can get leave, will come to town to spend their pay, before returning to camp to await another pay-day in two weeks.

BRITISH DESTROYER DROPS A DEPTH CHARGE—This gripping picture illustrates the devastating force of a depth charge, the main weapon used by the British navy in combating the menace of German U-boats. When a sub is located the destroyers dash in like hornets and "lay their eggs." The depth charges are timed to explode at a certain depth which give the destroyers a chance to get clear. The depth charge increases the water pressure on a submarine to such an extent that rivets are started, instruments thrown out of kilter and, in some instances, the hull is opened up so extensively that the craft plunges instantly to the bottom.

MECHANIZED WAR—A trainload of tractors being checked over by workmen "somewhere in France," as they start their journey to the battle front. (Acme telephoto.)

370 Known Saved From Torpedoed British Warship

H.M.S. ROYAL OAK

LONDON (AP) — The Admiralty announced this afternoon that approximately 370 men thus far had been saved from the sunken battleship Royal Oak. The warship's complement it said, was approximately 1,200 men.

This left 830 missing, far in excess of the loss of 515 men September 17 when the aircraft carrier Courageous was torpedoed by a German submarine.

First announcement by the Admiralty expressed belief the heavily-armored warship was the victim of "U-boat action."

A second Admiralty communique issued this afternoon said:

"The secretary of the Admiralty announces that so far as is presently known the number of survivors from H.M.S. Royal Oak is approximately 370.

"As already stated, lists of survivors will be published as soon as the names have been received. The complement of the ship was approximately 1,200. The above figures include both officers and men."

During the first six weeks of the last war no battleship was sunk, although the navy lost three cruisers, two destroyers and a mine-sweeping gunboat.

The announcement of Britain's second big loss of the war came just a few hours after the Admiralty had told how British guns had sent three German submarines to the bottom of the sea. Responsible British naval sources amplified the government's "Friday the 13th" announcement describing two of the three U-boats as of the enemy's largest ocean-going type.

SAFELY BROUGHT ASHORE

The first list of Royal Oak survivors made public by the Admiralty contained 15 names, including a lieutenant and three lower grade officers. All already had been brought ashore. None were gravely injured. The list: A. M. Seymour, Cook G. R. Stares, Marine J. W. Woods, Leading Seaman A. Harmer, Ordinary Seaman E. Smith, Ordinary Seaman Chrichton, Ordinary Seaman R. Martin, Roy E. W. Scovell, Chief Stoker C. Hine, Stoker H. P. Cleverly, Paymaster Cadet M. Holligan, Warrant Engineer G Dunstone, Petty Officer P. Higgins, Petty Officer E. A. Rowland, Able Seaman G. B. McCable.

It was indicated several days might elapse before the complete list of survivors could be compiled.

CAPT. BENN COMMANDED

The August, 1939, naval list showed the Royal Oak was commanded by Captain W. G. Benn. Before she was recommissioned during the summer at Portsmouth the Royal Oak was with the second battle squadron of the British Home Fleet. Her displacement was 29,150 tons.

The keel of the Royal Oak was laid down at Devenport in January, 1914, and she was completed in May, 1916, at a cost of £2,468,-269—somewhat below the average for four other battleships of her class, the Royal Sovereign, Resolution, Ramillies and Revenge. All had been fitted as flagships.

The Royal Oak was 620 feet long over all and was capable of a speed of about 22 knots. "Jane's Fighting Ships," a compendium of the world's warcraft, says the ship mounted eight 15-inch guns and 12 six-inch guns with four submerged torpedo tubes. She carried one catapult for aircraft. The lighter armament of the Royal Oak included eight four-inch anti-aircraft guns, four three-pounders and one 12-pounder.

BULGES ON HULL

The defensive armament of the Royal Oak included deep bulges extending almost to the gun batteries. Bulges are armored air spaces designed to explode torpedoes without fatal damage.

Vessels of her class were fitted with special internal protection, and, with the protective bulges, the defence against underwater attack had been considered strong.

Whether the new blow at the British navy marked the start of the "total war" threatened by Adolf Hitler following Prime Minister Chamberlain's rejection of German terms for peace remained to be seen.

The landing of 158,000 British soldiers in France, and British successes against German submarines had led London observers to declare Britain was ready for Hitler's next move — whether in warfare or diplomacy.

The press also generally agreed that Britain could play a waiting game and ultimately crush the Nazi military machine at the "strategic" moment.

WAR EXTRA

Complete Markets

Los Angeles Examiner

CHARACTER QUALITY — AMERICA FIRST! — ENTERPRISE ACCURACY

AN AMERICAN PAPER FOR THE AMERICAN PEOPLE — THE GREAT NEWSPAPER OF THE GREAT SOUTHWEST

Reg. U.S. Pat. Off.

COMPLETE RACES

VOL. XXXVI—NO. 310 CC LOS ANGELES, TUESDAY, OCTOBER 17, 1939 Two Sections—Part I—FIVE CENTS

GERMANS STRIKE!

Invade France; Bomb Scotland, Warships

In Nazi Jail?

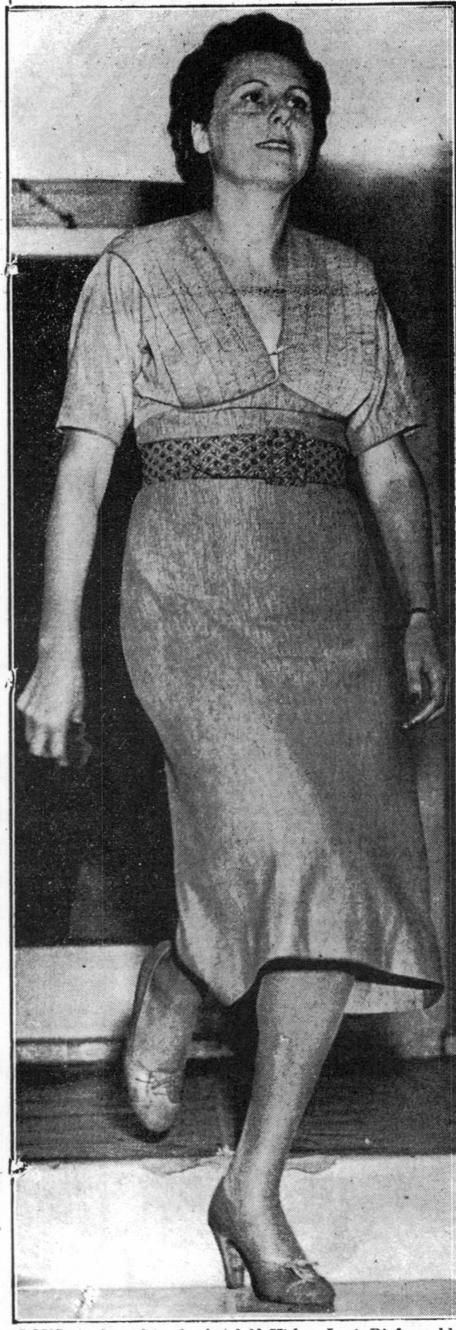

LONG A close friend of Adolf Hitler, Leni Riefenstahl, German actress and film producer, was reported under arrest by Nazis yesterday. (The story is on Page B.)

—Los Angeles Examiner photo.

NAZIS BATTLE THEIR WAY TO FRENCH TOWN

Though Thrown Back, Still Keep Precarious Hold on Allied Soil for First Time During War

PARIS, Oct. 16.—(AP)—Waves of Nazi troops in field gray today launched a long-awaited attack in force against French positions on the northern flank of the Western Front, drove the French out of German territory at one point and although thrown back still held a precarious foothold on French soil for the first time since the European war began.

A French communique acknowledged tonight the Germans

(Continued on Page A, Cols. 7-8)

Berlin Exults Over U-Boat Victories

LONDON, Oct. 16.—(INS)—Fishermen returning to Oslo today reported that three British warships and an airplane attacked and sank a German warship Saturday in an engagement off the west coast of Norway, according to a Reuters dispatch from the Norwegian capital.

BERLIN, Oct. 16.—(AP)—Adolf Hitler appeared tonight to have determined on a policy of sinking or disabling one British warship

(Continued on Page A, Column 6)

Olson Frees Billings

SAN FRANCISCO, Oct. 16.—(AP)—Governor Culbert L. Olson late today commuted the sentence of Warren K. Billings to time served, following receipt of word from California Chief Justice William H. Waste that a majority of the court approved the action.

Billings was convicted September 21, 1916, of first degree murder in connection with the Preparedness Day bombing on Mar-

(Continued on Page 6, Column 4)

British Ship Reported Hit

AMID REPORTS yesterday of major air and sea engagements between German and Allied forces, the Nazi high command announced in Berlin the same submarine which sank British battleship Royal Oak last week had torpedoed the Repulse (above), putting it out of commission. London naval quarters ridiculed reports the battle cruiser had been badly damaged by a Nazi sub. The Repulse had 32,000-ton displacement.

—Wide World photo.

Planes Attack Firth of Forth

LONDON, Oct. 17 (Tuesday).—(AP)—The admiralty announced early today two naval officers and 13 men were killed in the German air raid on the Firth of Forth, Monday.

In addition to the 15 killed, the casualties included 12 men seriously injured, the admiralty said.

LONDON, Oct. 16.—(AP)—Nazi bombers, making their first raid on the crowded shipping and industrial area about Edinburgh and the Firth of Forth, today damaged the cruiser Southampton and caused 35 casualties aboard her and two other warships. At least three bombers were shot down.

A joint air ministry and admiralty communique which described the raid said 12 or 14 Nazi raiders made up the attacking squadron. Three of the four casualties were brought down by Royal Air Force fighters, it added.

The communique said the bow of the 9100-ton cruiser Southampton was slightly damaged by a glancing bomb.

Bomb splinters caused three casualties aboard the Southampton, seven aboard the 10,000-ton cruiser Edinburgh and 25 aboard the destroyer Mohawk.

The communique said the Southampton was the first Brit-

(Continued on Page A, Cols. 1-2)

Streamliner Wreck Suspect Held

EXTRA

Complete Markets

CHARACTER — QUALITY — AMERICA FIRST! — ENTERPRISE — ACCURACY

Los Angeles Examiner

AN AMERICAN PAPER FOR THE AMERICAN PEOPLE — THE GREAT NEWSPAPER OF THE GREAT SOUTHWEST

Reg. U.S. Pat. Off.

VOL. XXXVI—NO. 311 P LOS ANGELES, WEDNESDAY, OCTOBER 18, 1939 Two Sections—Part I—FIVE CENTS

NAZI BOMBERS RENEW ATTACKS ON BRITAIN!

Iron Duke Hit; Sky Raiders Sweep Coast

LONDON, Oct. 17.—(AP)—German warplanes struck twice today at the Scapa Flow lair of Britain's fleet, hitting and damaging the training ship Iron Duke, and ranged over the east coast of England and Scotland in widespread scouting raids.

Four German planes were reported shot down, bringing their losses to eight in two days.

The attacks followed yesterday's raid on the Edinburgh and Firth of Forth area in which three British naval vessels were slightly damaged, 16 sailors and officers killed and 45 injured.

In the first attack today, at 10:30 a. m. (1:30 a. m. P.S.T.), four German planes damaged the training ship Iron Duke, Admiral Jellicoe's flagship in the World War.

SCENE OF SURRENDER

Scapa Flow was the scene of one of the most dramatic incidents in naval history when the German high seas fleet was scuttled there June 21, 1919, by German sailors who opened the seacocks rather than let the British have the surrendered ships intact.

One of the four planes was said by the British to have been shot down in this first attack, and another damaged.

The second attack was from 12:30 to 2:30 p. m. (3:30 to 5:30 a. m. P.S.T.) and was by "two formations of six and four aircraft," the admiralty said.

No damage was done and one German plane destroyed, the admiralty reported.

SHOOT DOWN TWO

An official announcement accounted for the other two German planes reported shot down by saying that "subsequent to reports of enemy activity on the east coast today two enemy aircraft were later observed on the northeast coast and were attacked by Royal airforce fighters. Both were shot down by our fighters and fell into the sea."

(DNB, German official news agency, admitted the loss of but one German plane. This plane was shot down, DNB said, in the Scapa Flow raid in which a "British battleship" was bombed. The Germans said they had shot down a British pursuit plane in the raid.)

The admiralty said there were no casualties in either raid.

German aviation also was ac-

(Continued on Page A, Cols. 1-2)

German 'Eggs' Laid on Navy Base

DESTRUCTION IN the form of German bombs cascaded from the skies over the British Isles for the second time within 48 hours when a squadron of Nazi bombers attacked the huge naval base at Scapa Flow yesterday. London officials reported one of the German planes was shot down. Here are German soldiers loading bombs in truck.
—Picture from International News Photograph Service.

Hitler Drives to End British Rule of Seas

THE HAGUE, The Netherlands, Oct. 17.—(INS)—Firing by German anti-aircraft guns at Emden on Dutch frontier patrol planes today explained reports of an Allied air raid on the German port, according to information here. No Dutch planes were damaged, but some projectiles exploded over Dutch territory. The Netherlands protested to Germany.

BERLIN, Oct. 17.—(AP)—German raids on the important British naval base at Scapa Flow—by warplane today and by submarine Saturday—were described by German officialdom tonight as part of a lightning campaign to break British resistance.

News of the air attack on Scapa Flow came while the public still was celebrating yesterday's air raid on the Firth of Forth and the submarine assault at Scapa Flow which resulted in the sinking of the 29,150-ton battleship Royal Oak Saturday.

"England no longer is mistreses of the seas," newspapers said.

According to DNB, official German news agency, German air raiders in an attack on the British harbor of Scapa Flow today bombed a British battleship, shot down a British plane and escaped from heavy fire with the loss of one machine.

ATTACK SUCCESSFUL

The DNB announcement read:

"On October 17 German airforce units advanced to Scapa Flow. Vessels of the British battle fleet lying in the harbor were attacked with success. Among others a battleship was struck by bombs of heavy and medium caliber.

"In the air battle which followed one enemy pursuit plane was shot down by our bombers. Despite the heavy enemy antiaircraft fire all German planes, with the exception of one machine, managed to return undamaged to their home harbors."

The German press reflected official views that the lightning campaign against the British fleet was Germany's reply to the refusal of the Allies to make peace on Adolf Hitler's terms.

"After a week or 10 days of this uninterrupted attacking

(Continued on Page A, Cols. 6-7)

French Claim 2000 Nazis Casualties

PARIS, Oct. 17.—(INS)—Germany's offensive on the Western Front cost the Reich 2000 dead and wounded, French military circles believed tonight. French casualties were described as negligible in comparison.

PARIS, Oct. 17.—(AP)—The French general staff reported tonight there were "sharp infantry engagements at certain points" and "local activity on the whole (Western) Front," although the fighting failed to bring any change in positions.

The communique added that "a German merchant ship has been captured by our Atlantic patrol," but gave no details.

Reference to infantry fighting was taken by military observers to mean that small groups of both French and German troops were continuing activity of purely localized character following the French repulse of two German attacks yesterday.

Premier Daladier and General Maurice Gustave Gamelin conferred at the war ministry during the afternoon.

The general staff's assertion

(Continued on Page A, Cols. 1-2)

British Battleship Damaged by Bombs

DAMAGED BY bombs dropped on the famous Scapa Flow naval base yesterday was the British battleship Iron Duke (above), veteran of Jutland naval battle of World War days. The Iron Duke, which has been converted into a training ship, was flagship of the British commander, Admiral Jellicoe, in the last conflict. Much of her armament was removed when she was taken off the battle line and placed in training service. There were no casualties aboard the Iron Duke, it was reported.

Streamliner Suspect Held Here

Said by railroad detectives and Federal agents to have been in the vicinity of Elko, Nev., August 12 at the time of the disastrous wreck of the Union Pacific streamliner City of San Francisco, Olin Graves, 29-year-old laborer, was being held for observation in Lincoln Heights jail yesterday.

It was learned exclusively by the Examiner that G-men were comparing samples of Graves' hair with hair found on one of two men's coats discovered by detectives at the scene of the rail tragedy.

ARRESTED IN L. A.

The suspect was arrested October 14 by Los Angeles officers, and admitted walking from a hospital in Yuma, Ariz., and another in Salinas, Calif., where he had been under observation.

He has been questioned repeatedly by special agents of the Southern Pacific Railway, and it was understood he had located himself in the vicinity of the wreck scene on the day that the crack Union Pacific streamliner

(Continued on Page B, Column 5)

2¢

DAILY MIRROR

Member of The Associated Press

(Copyright, 1939 Daily Mirror, Inc.)

WEATHER INCREASING CLOUDINESS.

3 Cents Outside City Limits

2¢

Vol. 16. No. 120 C New York, Friday, November 10, 1939 COMPLETE SPORTS

NEW DEATH THREAT TO HITLER

Story and Late Bulletins on Back Page

Hundreds Arrested In Nazi Bombing Roundup

Story on Page 2

Here is where Hitler beat a time bomb by minutes! Terrific force of the explosion is seen in this radioed picture of the Munich beer hall turned shambles. Note how the ceiling was ripped open. The bomb apparently was planted in an attic above the beer hall. Crumbled masonry and plaster is piled high on the floor. Pillar at right is stripped thin!

(A. P. Radiophoto)

(More blast photos on Back Page)

20,000 Russians Trapped, Finn Commander Reports

Good Morning

There's Another Sea Battle Today ... in Alley Oop. Read About It, Page 6.

Elmira Advertiser

The Weather

U. S. Official Forecast

Cloudy, Slightly Colder Today; Snow or Rain Tonight or Tuesday; Colder Tuesday.

VOL. LXXXVII—No. 299 | ELMIRA, N. Y., MONDAY MORNING, DECEMBER 18, 1939 | THREE CENTS

GRAF SPEE BLOWN UP BY CREW

Hitler Order Dooms Raider; Blasts Send Ship to Bottom Outside Port; Crew Escapes

Montevideo (AP)—Proud and powerful marauder of the high seas, the Nazi pocket battleship Admiral Graf Spee was blown up and sunk Sunday night to save her from defeat and destruction at the point of British naval guns.

Capt. Hans Langsdorff and "every member of the crew" which went out to scuttle the Graf Spee were reported by officials to have reached safety aboard other boats before the 10,000-ton war monster, her hull shattered and her wreckage aflame from the explosions of internal mines, sank in 25 feet of water three miles from shore, within sight of the city.

The German freighter Tacoma, carrying two or three hundred members of the crew, anchored in Montevideo harbor late Sunday night. The captain immediately was arrested for violating a port-closing order earlier in the day, and Uruguayan authorities said they would intern all Graf Spee crewmen who remained in Uruguayan waters. The remainder of the crew—about 1,000 men—were reported en route to Buenos Aires aboard tugs and launches and will surrender to the Argentine Government.

Captain Langsdorff and other ship's officers also were reported headed for Buenos Aires aboard a Graf Spee launch.

Langsdorff, last to leave his ship, sent a bitter wireless ashore from the bridge before he gave the order to abandon ship, protesting that Uruguay's refusal to let the Graf Spee remain in the harbor later than this evening "leaves me no alternative than to sink my ship near the coast and save my crew."

The alternatives he refused were to resume the battle with the British warships outside the harbor from which he fled last Wednesday or to let his ship be interned for the rest of the war.

The pocket battleship, which had sunk at least nine British freighters in far-ranging raids, was blown up less than two hours after she had steamed slowly away from he anchorage and headed south out of Montevideo harbor.

All Montevideo saw or heard her blown up, just as the sun was dipping beneath the horizon. She was on the bottom within three minutes after the blast thundered across the harbor.

Captain Langsdorff and the other ship's officers were reported to have escaped by ship's launch. Other members of the crew tumbled over the side into a small fleet of rescue tugs and barges and pulled away to safety. Later they were taken aboard the German freighter Tacoma, which had followed the Graf Spee out of Montevideo.

As a sunset haze drifted in from the sea, about to hide the Graf Spee both from shore and from the British warships waiting below the horizon, the first powerful blast shattered the battleship, sending flame and smoke leaping into the air.

Two other explosions then rumbled across the water.

For a moment the thousands on shore thought a second naval battle had begun. But as they watched, the Graf Spee settled and sank in 25 feet of water, her superstructure showing above the surface.

A little more than half an hour later, as a pillar of fire and jet black smoke plumed upward from the wreckage, a second series of blasts ripped even this away and it sank from view.

The Graf Spee first moved out of the harbor limits as though headed directly for the British blockaders. Then, when three miles offshore, she went hard to starboard and headed south.

Watchers, among them myself, saw the Tacoma follow the same course.

The warship moved slowly for a time, then appeared to anchor as a pair of tugs from Buenos Aires drew up to her side, one of them drawing a barge.

Through a telescope I saw supplies being loaded onto the barge.

Within a few minutes, sailors aboard the Graf Spee climbed from the warship into the smaller boats.

Occupants of a nearby pilot boat said that as the boats drew away Captain Langsdorf, last to leave the Graf Spee, carried a light cable attached to a mine deep in the ship's hull.

The small boats were nearly a mile away when the first explosion shook the warship.

The captain himself operated the first mine, occupants of the pilot boat declared:

Official sources said Germany had made a formal protest to Uruguay because of its refusal to let the Graf Spee stay here longer.

Uruguayan naval and port authorities started an immediate investigation of the explosions which scuttled the Graf Spee. They occurred well within the River Platte waters over which this country claims jurisdiction.

However, patrol boats sent to the scene were unable to get close because of the heavy layers of burning oil on the water and the thick smoke.

The Graf Spee had gone to her self-chosen grave with the Nazi swastika flying proudly from her mast and her depleted crew standing by to abandon ship.

Forced out of her neutral anchorage by a Uruguayan time limit, she sailed at 6 p. m. (4:30 p. m. EST), hovered off shore for a time, and was scuttled at 7:28 p. m. (5:57 p. m. EST) just at sundown.

Captain Langsdorf, in a statement issued through the German Legation here after the scuttling, said the refusal of the Uruguayan government to give him ample time to make the Graf Spee "navigable" left him no alternative but to sink the Graf Spee and save the crew from British warship guns.

At least three British cruisers and, presumably, the French battleship Dunkerque, remained well outside the harbor, invisible from port, during Sunday night's brief drama.

Five British planes dipped over the Graf Spee as she maneuvered toward her grave but made no hostile maneuvers.

The 10,000-ton pocket battleship ended her career after participating in the first great sea battle of the war off Uruguayan shores four days ago, in which she lost 36 dead and inflicted a death toll of 72 men on her three British antagonists, the cruisers Exeter, Achilles and Ajax.

About 40 minutes after the Graf Spee was scuttled, a series of fresh explosions swept the wreck, apparently as flames reached munitions and fuel untouched by the first blast.

Continued on Page 3

When The Associated Press uses the word "Flash," it means something. Six minutes after the Graf Spee was blown up, the news of it arrived in The Advertiser office. The AP flash follows:

FLASH!

Montevideo — Graf Spee exploded sinking.

RB601PES

The "RB601PES" following the flash is wire code for 6:01 p. m. Eastern Standard.

Spee Believed Sunk to Hide Naval Secrets

By the Associated Press

The big question raised Sunday night by one of the war's most dramatic episodes, the "suicide" of the Graf Spee, was why destruction was chosen in preference to internment.

Aside from speculation that Adolf Hitler may have desired just such drama to fire Germany's realization of his desperate determination, there seemed to be one far more practical answer.

Interned or captured, her plans and specifications would immediately have become the objective of scores of foreign agents. She had been through the only major engagement between really modern sea fighters. Undoubtedly, weaknesses in her armament and design were disclosed, particularly the one-shell disablement of the tower which controlled the fire of her major weapons, the 11-inch guns.

With her two sister ships, the Deutschland and the Admiral Scheer, the objects of an intense search by France and Britain, the Spee's captain probably made sure that the charges which were to end her brief but spectacular career were so placed as to wipe out all clues to her major details.

That, at any rate, seemed the best answer in the absence of any factual statement.

Trapped Ship Sunk On Hitler's Orders, Berlin Reports

Berlin (AP)—Adolf Hitler, as supreme commander of Germany's armed forces, gave the order to blow up and destroy the raiding pocket battleship, Admiral Graf Spee, it was announced early today by DNB, official German news agency.

The German public early today still did not know the Graf Spee had been scuttled. The DNB communique was issued after morning papers had appeared and the government-controlled radio was closed for the night.

DNB's announcement said:

"The Fuehrer and supreme commander ordered Capt. Hans Langsdorff to destroy the warship by blowing her up, as the time required to reestablish the seaworthiness of the ship was declined by the Uruguayan government."

THE NAZI POCKET BATTLESHIP, ADMIRAL GRAF SPEE, at right, as she looked just before leaving Montevideo harbor on her fatal voyage Sunday afternoon. It was the irony of war that the ship at left happened to be the French liner Formose, which the Graf Spee was chasing when set upon by three British cruisers and driven to cover. Another Graf Spee picture on Page 12.

U.S. Blamed In Red Ouster

Moscow (AP)—The United States Sunday was accused by the Communist Party newspaper Pravda of influencing Latin American states to support expulsion of Soviet Russia from the League of Nations.

Soviet newspapers also charged Britain with juggling League machinery to oust Russia but declared the expulsion gave the Soviet Union "a free hand."

Pravda said the League Assembly sessions were held "behind closed doors but in the presence of an American 'observer,' Mr. Edgar, in the role of school supervisor. He was silent but watched carefully over the behavior of Latin American diplomats.

11 Policemen Accused

New York (AP)—A 151-page presentment demanding disciplinary action against 10 police lieutenants and a sergeant in connection with the Brooklyn bail bond racket investigation has been handed up, Special Asst. Atty. Gen. John Harlan Amen announced Sunday.

Police Commissioner Lewis J. Valentine immediately suspended the police officers without pay and ordered departmental trials.

Amen said the presentment, sealed until Valentine had been informed, was only a beginning of his probe of conditions which he said involved all 29 Brooklyn precincts. He said he would deliver more evidence of a similar nature to the extraordinary grand jury.

CCC Urged As Relief Cut

Albany (AP)—The state, pressing its drive to reduce costs of home relief, urged local welfare officials Sunday to help fill New York's January quota of boys for the Civilian Conservation Corps.

The request came from Social Welfare Commissioner David C. Adie, who viewed the CCC as "an aid to the boys themselves, to their families and to the relief costs in this state."

New York has a quota of 6,400 boys for the CCC enrollment from Jan. 1 to 20.

Divorcee, 14, Wed To Farmhand, 21

Houston, Mo. (AP) — The marriage of Ray Johnson, 21, farmer, and Jennie Lucille Stanton, 14, was disclosed Saturday by Justice of the Peace L. R. Haney.

It was the bride's second marriage. She was granted a divorce from Robert Vestal, 17, at the November term of Circuit Court. Houston is in the heart of the Missouri Ozarks country.

NOTED ARCHITECT DIES

New Haven, Conn., (AP)—William Edwards Parsons, nationally known architect and associate professor of architecture at Yale University, died Sunday at his home. He was 67.

Gannett Hits Plan To Transfer FCA Control

Washington (AP)—E. T. Benson, secretary of the National Cooperative Council, said Sunday that his group and other farm organizations would appeal to Congress to override any order giving Secretary Wallace complete control of the Farm Credit Administration.

He added that these groups were prepared to carry the issue to the voters in the 1940 presidential campaign "if necessary."

Some officials of the Department of Agriculture have predicted that control of the FCA would be transferred to Wallace after President Roosevelt returns to Washington from a weekend visit to Hyde Park.

Frank Gannett, Rochester, who led a fight against legislation conferring broad powers of government reorganization upon the President, entered the FCA controversy Sunday, declaring the transfer would "impair the financial integrity" of the loan agency.

In a telegram to Mr. Roosevelt, the publisher said, in part:

"Can you be aware of the shocking immorality and injustice of the purpose of the Secretary of Agriculture to destroy the independence and to impair the financial integrity of the Farm Loan Credit Administration as announced by your secretary, Mr. Early, at his press conference on Thursday?

"By misuse of the powers vested in you by the Executive Reorganization Bill, the farm credit system created 20 years ago, largely financed and directed by the farmers themselves, by democratic processes, will become a political football."

Gannett added that last April when President Roosevelt transferred the FCA to the Agriculture Department, Mr. Wallace declared he would exercise only broad supervision. Congress thus did not exercise its power to block the transfer, Gannett said, because it trusted "the pledged word of a Cabinet member."

2 Executed For Slaying

Bellefonte, Pa. (AP)—Two Philadelphia Negroes, one-time bootblacks, died quietly in Pennsylvania's electric chair early today for killing a watchman with a cuspidor during an attempted robery.

They were James Fuller, 25, and Fletcher Legrand, 22. They pleaded guilty to the murder of John Heyworth, a 70-year-old watchman in a Philadelphia store. Heyworth was killed when he was struck on the head with a cuspidor during an attempted robbery on the store.

Heywood Broun's Condition Better

New York (AP)—The condition of Heywood Broun, columnist and president of the American Newspaper Guild, who is ill with pneumonia, was somewhat better Sunday.

"Mr. Broun has maintained the slight improvement registered Saturday evening," it was announced at the Columbia-Presbyterian Medical Center, where he has been placed in an oxygen room. "His temperature is 102. He is still seriously ill."

INDIAN'S ESTATE SETTLED

Muskogee, Okla. (AP) — Five years of litigation over the estate of Jackson Barnett, known as "world's richest Indian," apparently was ended Sunday as Federal Judge Robert L. Williams held the legal heirs to 33 restricted Creek Indians and a white woman.

British Balk Air Attack; Raid on Nazi Bases Fails; Fronts Quiet; Ship Sunk

London (AP)—The Air Ministry announced Sunday night that German aircraft appeared over several points of the East British coast during the late afternoon and anti-aircraft guns opened fire.

British fighters went up and chased the German planes back out to sea, the Air Ministry communique said.

No air raid warnings were sounded.

There was anti-aircraft fire for a short time in the Humber district.

Berlin (AP) — British bombing planes in continued attempts to cripple Germany's air arm again raided the island bases of Norderney and Sylt, off the Northwest German coast, a high command communique reported Sunday.

"British bombers on night of Dec. 16-17 attempted to attack the islands of Norderney and Sylt," the communique said. "A small number of bombs fell in the sea."

It was the second British air attack on the Island in four days.

German airplanes carried out scouting flights over the North Sea, the communique also reported.

"The air force carried through reconnaissance flights over the North Sea.

"On the West Front, no fighting worth mention."

London (AP)—The 487-ton British steamer Serenity has been sunk and her eight crewmen saved by lifeboat off the Northeast British coast, it was disclosed Sunday night. Details were not available.

London (AP) — The Japanese freighter Sanyo Maru was released Sunday after a 24-hour stay at a British contraband control base, thereby failing to become a test case on Britain's blockade of German exports.

The 976-ton vessel left Rotterdam Saturday with German machinery and potash and was detained by the British for examination.

On her release it was explained the Japanese government had given an assurance that all goods of German origin on board had been paid for before Nov. 27, when the order in council decreeing the blockade was issued.

CIO Asks Changes in Labor Act

Washington (AP)—The Congress of Industrial Organizations, abandoning its previous stand against any change in the National Labor Relations Act, called on Congress Sunday for three amendments.

Its proposal was contained in a legislative program drafted by a committee headed by the CIO chief, John L. Lewis.

It asked for an amendment to prevent the National Labor Relations Board from "carving up any industrial units" established by the CIO.

The two other amendments were intended to strengthen enforcement of the act. One would provide criminal penalties for employers convicted of violating the act. Under present law, the board can enforce its orders only by procuring a court order and then having an employer cited for contempt of court if the order is ignored.

The other amendment would prohibit the government from awarding contracts to employers who had violated the Labor Relations Law.

Missing Boy Found Dead

Denville, N. J. (AP)—The body of 4-year-old Eugene Bauman, object of New Jersey's biggest hunt since the Lindbergh baby kidnaping, was found Sunday wedged in between the pilings of an Indian Lake boathouse about a half mile from his home.

A State Trooper and two Madison Boy Scouts, discovered the body shortly after noon, 48 hours after the youngster had disappeared from his home last Friday.

Police Chief Harry B. Jenkins said the boy had drowned, and that an autopsy would be performed.

Reds Asked Bremen Leave, Says Master

Berlin (AP)—Commodore Adolf Ahrens, master of the 20 million dollar German liner Bremen, intimated Sunday that the vessel was moved from her neutral haven at Murmansk, Russia, at the request of the Russians after their Finnish invasion.

Welcomed to Berlin in tribute to his feat of navigating her from Murmansk to her home port of Bremerhaven, he said the huge boat practically had blocked the Murmansk harbor and the Russians wanted the space.

3 HURT AT FIRE

Perth Amboy, N. J. (AP)—Police Chief James Murray was struck by a falling ladder and two firemen were overcome by smoke Sunday while fighting a blaze which wrecked a millinery shop and a dress store in the heart of the city's business district.

$5 COIN BRINGS $1,000

New York (AP)—A $5 gold coin minted by a private firm in California in 1851 was sold at auction for $1,000 Saturday. Identity of the buyer was not disclosed.

Woman Slays Infant Son

Philadelphia (AP)—A 35-year-old children's governess confessed Sunday, Detective Capt. James Ryan said, that she killed her 20-month-old son, dismembered the body with a saw and dumped the torso along a shadowy street where it was found Saturday night.

The child's head, arms and legs were found in the woman's room at a boarding house, packed neatly in a small traveling bag, the detective said. He quoted her as saying she planned to dispose of the limbs piece by piece.

Ryan said the woman, whom he identified as Tilly Irelan, told him she killed her son because he interfered with her work and kept her from attending parties.

Sirovich, Drama Critics' Foe, Dies

New York (AP)—Rep. William Sirovich (D-NY), 57, physician and playwright, died of a heart attack Sunday while bathing in his home at 539 E. Sixth St.

He had been a member of Congress since 1926, representing the 14th District, on the city's East Side.

Sirovich's post as Patents Committee chairman involved him in a controversy with George Jean Nathan and other dramatic critics in 1932, when he held a hearing on the advisability of a law to make drama criticism a criminal offense on the ground that an unfavorable review would be financially damaging to a play.

Labor Board Probe Will 'Clear Air,' Says Healey

Washington (AP)—An administration supporter who voted against the House investigation of the Labor Relations Board, predicted Sunday that the inquiry would help "clear up the atmosphere around this whole situation."

The view was expressed by Rep. Healey (D-Mass.), a member of the investigating committee, in reviewing the first week of the committee's public hearings.

While asserting that any discussion of amending the Wagner Labor Relations Act at this time would be "premature," the New Englander declared that the extent to which the committee was going into the administration of that law gave assurance that when the inquiry was over "if anything needs to be done, we will know all about it."

Meanwhile, on Capitol Hill, Edmund M. Toland, committee counsel and his staff drove ahead with preparation of cases to be presented today and Tuesday. The committee plans to recess Tuesday until after Congress convenes in January.

Toland said Philip G. Phillips, the board's regional director at Cincinnati, was scheduled to testify today.

The attorney disclosed that in view of the plan to suspend the hearings until next month, he had temporarily excused a number of witnesses.

In that connection, Toland emphasized that members of what one witness called the board's "goon squad" would be summoned for questioning.

Three Nabbed As Kidnapers

Pittsburgh (AP) — The Federal Bureau of Investigation announced Sunday night three Connellsville, Pa. youths charged with kidnaping and robbing a Connellsville store manager will be returned to Fayette County for prosecution.

The three, William Jones, Floyd Goodwin and Charles Pegg, all 19, were arrested by FBI agents at El Paso, Tex., as they crossed the border from Mexico.

They were charged with holding up and kidnaping James Campbell, manager of a Connellsville grocery last Dec. 3, and taking $500 in cash and $1,000 in checks from the store safe and $40 from Campbell.

24 Arrested In Blackmail

New York (AP)—Twenty-four men have been arrested in a cleanup of a large blackmail ring reported to have extorted one million dollars from hundreds of socially prominent victims during the last two years, police disclosed Sunday.

News of the blackmail syndicate, hidden by authorities during more than a year's investigation, came out with the docketing for trial today of Charles Farcier, alias Carl Thomas, 28; Salvatore Andinoici, 27, and Edward Sheehan, alias Edward Shine, 59. More than 30 were indicted and many have pleaded guilty.

Strikes Power Line, Army Pilot Unhurt

Cumberland (AP)—Lieut. J. J. Vander Zee of the Army's 94th Pursuit Squadron, Selfridge Field, Mich., struck a power line while landing an Army pursuit plane late Sunday, but escaped injury. One wheel, the left wing and the tail assembly of the plane were damaged.

Invaders Claim Gains on 2 Fronts

Stockholm (AP)—General Vallenius, commander of the Finnish troops on the Salla and Petsamo fronts, told Swedish correspondents Sunday night that two Russian forces, each of about 10,000 men, were surrounded in the vicinities of Suomussalmi and Tolvajarvi.

There has been fierce fighting reported for days in this region. Tolvajarvi, close to the Russian border and about 45 miles north of Lake Ladoga, and Suomussalmi, about 200 miles on to the north, were points at which the Russians attempted to penetrate Central Finland.

General Vallenius was quoted also as saying the Finnish Army command was convinced that the Russian tanks which recently attacked Salmijarvi, on the Norwegian border in the Petsamo sector, had crossed the Norwegian border and used a road over Norwegian territory.

The Finns said their roads were tightly guarded but this attack came unexpectedly from a flank. Norwegian authorities who could be reached for comment said they had received no information about such a crossing into their territory.

Moscow (AP)—The advance of Red Army troops to a point over 80 miles within Central Finland was announced Sunday in a communique issued by Soviet Russian commanders.

The communique, also covering Saturday's activity in the Soviet-Russian conflict in Northern Finland, stated that Soviet troops had progressed almost 50 miles along the road south of Petsamo, Arctic coastal town.

Helsinki, (AP)—Destruction of three Soviet "land battleships"—30-ton tanks—was reported Sunday night by a Finnish Army communique which said three other tanks and a motorized column had been smashed by field batteries on the shores of Lake Ladoga.

The communique, reporting bitter fighting, declared 30 Russian tanks had been sent to the scrap heap in the past two days.

Fighting was particularly intense north of Lake Ladoga, where the Red Army has attempted to outflank Finland's "Mannerheim Line," but the Finnish Army declared all the attacks had been repulsed.

Success on other fronts also was reported by the communique, which said:

"On the Karelian Isthmus the enemy attacked many times at the Taipale River supported by extremely heavy artillery fire. All the attacks were repulsed.

"In the course of battle Dec. 15 and 16, 30 enemy tanks were destroyed.

"Enemy attempts to cross Suvanto Lake also were repulsed.

"On the Western Karelian Isthmus there was artillery fire and local attacks. All were repulsed. Three 30-ton tanks were destroyed. Enemy attacks continued in sectors directly north of Lake Ladoga. The attacks were repulsed.

"In the vicinity of Limola two enemy battalions were dispersed. In the vicinity of Tolvajarvi our own advance slowly continued. Fierce fighting took place all day in the area of Aeglaejarvi.

"Certain batteries along Ladoga destroyed three tanks and an enemy motorized column.

"At sea there was only patrol activity. In the air enemy aircraft was active chiefly over Petsamo and over Northern Lapland lesser bombing raids were undertaken. Our own air forces were quite active during the day bombing, among other things, an enemy tank detachment near the firing line."

Battle reports encouraging to Finland came from the frigid Northern Front where Russian forces were said to have faltered before the fortifications of Salmijarvi, near the Norwegian frontier.

Finnish troops were making a determined stand there in Arctic darkness with the temperature 13 degrees below zero.

THE ARCTIC LEAGUE . . .

Realized $2,319.20 from Sunday's broadcast. But nearly $5,000 remains to be raised to reach the goal. Don't pass up your chance to help this great cause.

WEATHER—
Generally fair and slightly cooler. Wednesday fair and slightly warmer in interior.

WASHINGTON DAILY NEWS

FOUNDED 1909—31ST YEAR | NO. 202. EIGHT PAGES TODAY | WASHINGTON, NORTH CAROLINA | TUESDAY AFTERNOON, APRIL 9, 1940 | PRICE FIVE CENTS; DAILY EXCEPT SUNDAY

NORWAY AND DENMARK YIELD TO NAZIS

Nazis Demand Border Nations Danube River Allow Police Patrol

AVERT RECURRENCE BLASTING ATTEMPTS

Demand That Yugoslavia, Hungary, Bulgaria And Rumania Accept German River Police Along Entire Length Of Danube River To Thwart Efforts Cripple German Transportation.

Belgrade, Apr. 9.—(AP)— The German government, it was learned on high authority today, has demanded that Yugoslavia, Hungary, Bulgaria and Rumania accept German river police along the entire length of the Danube river to secure this vital supply route for Germany.

The demand was made after the German press accused Britain of plotting to dynamite the narrow Danube canal through the "iron gate" to cripple Germany's transportation of oil, foodstuffs and raw materials from southeastern Europe.

Rumanian police seized British barges loaded with dynamite. The British said that the explosives were to have blown up British and French vessels in the event Germany invaded Rumania.

It was learned that Hungaria, Yugoslavia and Rumania previously had tentatively rejected the German demands. Then they were made a second time.

Diplomatic quarters here freely expressed the belief that the German news agency here as well as the Berlin foreign office has seized upon the rest of seizure of the British explosives as the basis for the renewed demands for a German police patrol of the Danube.

These sources also believed the demand was a possible forerunner of a German move into southeastern Europe to obtain Rumania's oil.

THIRD TERMERS REACH SHOWDOWN ILLINOIS VOTES

Illinois And Nebraska Give Two More Farm Tests Popularity

(By The Associated Press)

Illinois and Nebraska provided two more farm belt tests today of the popularity of the Roosevelt third term movement and of Thomas E. Dewey's campaign for the presidential nomination.

Dewey, who won Wisconsin's 24 Republican delegates last week over Senator Arthur Vandenburg, was matched against the same opponent in the Nebraska primary. He had no party opposition in Illinois.

The Democratic situation was the reverse. President Roosevelt who has given no hints as to whether he would accept another nomination, was unopposed in Nebraska.

In Illinois, however, the third term forces reached a showdown with supporters of Vice-President Garner. Two-fold interest centered on the Illinois voting for 50 national convention delegates.

The Kelly-Nash Democratic organization was out to roll up a big vote for President Roosevelt, on the theory that an overwhelming victory would lead to his early nomination. . . .

Garner men, on the other hand, pinned hopes on a showing formidable enough to curb third term talk. In Nebraska 14 delegates were at stake in each party.

Festival Workers To Attend Meeting

Lee (Togo) Wynne, general Festival chairman, has issued a call urging all workers for the Tulip Festival to meet with him and Mrs. William Rumley in the assembly room of the Washington Golf and Country Club on Wednesday evening, April 10, at 8:15 o'clock.

The chairman emphasizes the importance of this meeting, which is to draw last minute plans for the festival and includes the following workers: city and county school officials, presidents of all clubs assisting in festival plans, ministers of the respective city churches, press representatives and all others assigned to various phases of the festival.

COOPER TO SPEAK IN HYDE COUNTY

Tom Cooper, gubernatorial candidate and mayor of Wilmington, will speak at the Hyde county courthouse in Swan Quarter tomorrow at 12 o'clock.

Following the address at Swan Quarter he will go to Engelhard where he will speak at 2 o'clock. He also plans to visit Fairfield after Engelhard.

Colorful Goldsboro Corps To Take Part In Festival Parade

The Goldsboro Junior Drum and Bugle Corps, under the direction of J. Robert Moore and the W. P. A., will be here on Friday, April 19, to lend their color to the Fourth Annual Tulip Festival.

The corps, which is composed of Scouts, Sons of the Legion and other youth groups, will give a special exhibition drill Friday afternoon, between the hours of three and six, in addition to their participating in the parade.

The colorful group is divided into three sections, gold, white and blue, the uniforms being these colors. Along with them come three tumbling teams and six drum majors.

They have attended 21 festivals and were invited to the premier showing of "Gone With the Wind" but were unable to attend.

Italians Rushing Arms Production

Rome, April 9.—(AP)—Gen. Umberto Favagrossa, Italy's commissioner general for war manufacturers, informed Premier Mussolini yesterday that more than 700,000 workers now are employed in the manufacture of war materials.

General Favagrossa said 929 auxiliary factories now are controlled by the war manufacturers' board.

HUNGRY NAZIS

HOT SERVICE—Food and coffee brought up through German wire, back of Nazi Westwall, in special metal containers to troops on front lines. These German soldiers are wearing specially camouflaged helmets.

Appeal United States Citizens To Keep Calm

So Say Senators In Discussing Latest Dramatic Moves By European Warring Nations; "Maintain Our Poise And Equilibrium"—Senator McNary

Washington, Apr. 9.—(AP)— Germany's advance into Denmark and Norway prompted several Senators today to appeal for the United States to take this latest dramatic war development calmly.

While Senator Pepper (D.-Fla.) declared that "it brings the shadow of the war and conquest by force nearer the shores of every peaceful country in the world, including our own," Senator Norris (Ind.-Neb.) said that "this affair is none of our business and we should keep out of it."

Norris described the march into Scandinavia as "the same old process—take whatever you have the power to take."

Senator McNary of Oregon, the Republican leader, declared, "The United States must keep calm. No matter how distressing the news is from Europe, we must keep our heads and must not be swept into hysteria."

"If we maintain our poise and equilibrium they will help us to withstand these recurrent shocks from Europe."

"The invasion of Denmark and Norway," said Senator Brown, (D.-Mich.) "is condemned by all thinking people. It makes the situation more serious. I see no reason, however, why our government should act. This is a time for calm contemplation. I think the long view of the situation will show that Germany has made her task much more difficult because she has added enemies and stifled any sympathy for her anywhere in the world.

Reverses Option And Slices Bill

Washington, Apr. 9.—(AP)— The Senate appropriations committee reversed the option of its sub-committee and sliced $55,000,000 from proposed waterway projects of the War Department civil functions bill.

Holding its approval of total expenditures to $223,362,517, the full committee struck out $30,000,000 for flood control projects and $25,000,000 for rivers and harbors works, inserted in the appropriation measure by the sub-committee.

It accepted a $15,000,000 item the sub-committee put in the bill to start a third set of Panama Canal locks.

Tempo Of State Campaign Should Quicken Next Week

The Daily News Bureau,
Sir Walter Hotel.

(By HENRY AVERILL)

Raleigh, Apr. 9.—The tempo of the currently sluggish state campaign should quicken after this week, when all local races will have been closed and the local politicians will know just where they stand with regard to the situation at home.

Saturday of this week is the deadline for filing notice of candidacy in the legislative and local contests all over the State, and when once these lists are closed, it is quite probable that more attention will be paid to the statewide campaign.

This is true for more than one reason. In the first place, the quickening of interest in local contests will almost surely carry hand in hand with it a corresponding quickening of general interest in things political.

Then it is equally sure that such candidates for local office as find themselves without opposition will be free to begin stirring things up for the state candidates of their choice. They will be free of the fear that they might stir up a hornet's nest and bring opposition to themselves by taking active part in some other race.

And, finally, even the local candidates who have opposition will know the full extent of it and will be able to do a bit of trading, trafficking and lining up of factional support for themselves in return for support of statewide candidates.

This year there will be many local contests, although of course each county will have to select a legislative candidate for the House, at least. Other battles will be mostly confined to county commissioners, some few registers of deeds, and here and there a heated race for the judgeship or solicitorship of some county or recorder's court.

NOW AND THEN

John G. Bragaw

We are not supposed to find the Bible amusing, and of all the books in the Bible that called Ecclesiastes is the last one in which we should expect to find humor. It was not intended for humor when it was written, but one portion of one verse toward the end of the book is amusing. For the man who wrote Ecclesiastes complained that "of making many books there is no end."

It is amusing as we look back today and think of how few books there were in the days of The Preacher, when it took perhaps as long to make one book as it takes now to turn out several millions volumes. If The Preacher thought the making of books in his day was a burden, think how he would feel if he should sit down today and look over just one issue of The Bookman, or the Sunday Herald-Tribune or the Sunday New York Times' Book Review. Or even the News and Observer.

But even before The Preacher voiced his cynicism, some Egyptian writer had lamented the fact that "everybody wants to write a book."

I wonder sometimes how men and women who make a profession of reviewing and criticising books can stand the strain. I should think they would be exhausted, reading one book after another, and then discouraged when they realize that they cannot touch even one small fraction of the books that are turned out week after week and month after month and year after year.

It is not that I am against books. I like books. I used to like to read them when circumstances permitted. Some books I love. When a lady asked me the other day if I remembered "Scottish Chiefs" I wanted to embrace her, for the mention of the name brought back one of the most delicious thrills of my youth. That is the trouble with reading. It is Scottish Chiefs and Ben Hur and Lorna Doone and Westward Ho! and The Cloister and The Hearth and The Count of Monte Cristo and Les Miserables and Hypatia and the John Esten Cooke and the Captain Charles King books—those are what I think of when books are mentioned, and I feel so dreadfully out of date, what with no acquaintance with anything that has come out in the past fifteen years.

When I look over a book catalogue, or one of those book pages, or a list of best sellers I feel so utterly inadequate. I think to myself, "Well, now, I just WILL read some of those best sellers that everybody is talking about," —and then a few weeks later when I look at the best sellers I find an entirely new set, and those that were in the list a few weeks before are back numbers, and mostly forgotten, and I say, "well, I WILL read............" and know full well that I will not.

Some on centuries ago invented the phrase, "the writers' itch," and some on else said later that it was a disease that could be cured only by the scratch of a pen.

And it was Oliver Wendell Holmes, who certainly had no reason to be ashamed of being called a writer, who penned a rhyme on the subject of that ailment:

If all the trees in all the woods
were men,
And each and every blade of grass
a pen;
If every leaf on every shrub and
tree
Turned to a sheet of foolscap;
every sea
Were changed to ink, and all the
earth's living tribes
Had nothing else to do but act as
scribes,
And for ten thousand ages, day
and night,
The human race should write, and
write, and write,
Till all the pens and papers were
used up,
And the huge inkstand were an
empty cup,
Still would the scribblers clustered round its brink
Call for more pens, more paper
and more ink.

Neutrals Offer Only 'Slight Resistance' As Nazis Occupy Oslo And Copenhagen In Lightning Thrust By Land, Sea And Air

BRITISH NAVY MOVES NORTHERN CONFLICT

Naval Units Already Engaged With Germans At Points Along Norwegian Coast; Chamberlain Charges Germany Premeditated Invasion Norway And Denmark.

London, Apr. 9.—(AP) — Britain's powerful navy is moving into the northern conflict to aid Norway against German invasion, Prime Minister Chamberlain told the House of Commons today in a brief, lustily cheered speech.

Chamberlain charged that Germany had premeditated the invasion of Norway and Denmark and he pledged the "full aid" of Britain and France to Norway.

"Powerful units of the navy are at sea," Chamberlain told the House, explaining that details must necessarily be kept secret.

Reports reached London by way of Paris, that Allied naval forces already were engaged with the Germans at various points along the Norwegion coast in a heavy storm.

Chamberlain said that the German plan for invasion of Norway and Denmark were "made and put into operation long before yesterday's mine laying."

"Otherwise some of the troops which have landed in Norway already would not have been there," Chamberlain declared.

He said that the British government had "at once assured the Norwegian government that in view of the invasion, his majesty's government had decided forthwith to extend their full aid to Norway and will fight the war in full association with them.

"This fresh, rash and cruel act of aggression will rebound to Germany's disadvantage and contribute to her ultimate defeat," he said.

BOARD TO MEET

The Official Board of the Christian Church will hold its regular monthly meeting tonight in the pastor's study at seven-thirty o'clock.

Oslo Surrenders German Forces

Stockholm, Apr. 9.—(AP)— The city of Oslo, capital of Norway, surrendered to German forces at 4 p. m. (10 a. m. E.S.T.) today.

Dispatches reaching Stockholm, said that the Norwegian police chief had resigned and that he was replaced by German officials.

North of Oslo, Norwegian aircraft was reported to have shot down two German planes.

The Norwegian government moved to the lake village of Hamar, north of Oslo.

The Norwegian army was reported to be guarding a defense line between Oslo and Hamma to protect the new capital and protect the mobilization of inland towns.

Fully half of the population was reported to have left Oslo before the city surrendered to German troops. The Germans were landed from warships along the city's harbor.

The Swedish Parliament was called into session for 8 p. m. (2 p. m. E.S.T.) tonight.

Late News Flashes

New York, Apr. 9.—(AP)— A squadron of British bombing planes which invaded northwestern Germany this morning was repulsed by German pursuit ships, said an official German broadcast picked up by N. B. C.

The announcement said several British planes were shot down.

London, Apr. 9.—(AP)— Rome radio reports intercepted in London today said communication between Germany and Hungary had been severed.

London, Apr. 9.—(AP)—The Supreme War Council of the Allies met today at Number 10 Downing street with Premier Paul Reynaud and Defense Minister Edouard Daladier representing France.

London, Apr. 9.—(AP) — A British source said tonight that it understands a naval action is progress somewhere near the coast of Norway between British and German forces.

The British press association said "there is reason to believe that good news may be forthcoming within 12 to 24 hours, but later asked its subscribers to delete this last sentence.

Tarboro, Apr. 9.—(AP)— A wire from Bill Terry, manager of the New York Giants, this morning advised Carl Hubbel will definitely pitch in tomorrow afternoon's game with Cleveland, here.

London, Apr. 9.—(AP)— The British foreign office was said authoritatively tonight to have he-established communication with Norway and to have been informed that the Norwegian government was in good heart and bent on resistance.

The German radio was said to have announced that Howard Smith, British minister to Copenhagen and his staff, had been

(Continued on Page Eight)

Occupation Of Most Important Objectives In Norway By German Troops Is Proceeding Rapidly; Dispatch From Copenhagen Says Danish Government Has Accepted The German Protection "With A Protest"; Germans Say Movement Was To Counteract British Aggression Against Neutrality Norway And Denmark By Mine Laying.

Berlin, April 9.—(AP)—Germany invaded Norway and Denmark by land, sea and air today.

Germany announced she has extended "armed protection" to these states "to counteract British aggression" against their neutrality.

By this afternoon, German armed forces had occupied Copenhagen, capital of Denmark, which did not resist, and Oslo, the capital of Norway, where Norwegian troops put up what the Germans called "slight local resistance."

This afternoon the German high command said that "occupation of the most important objectives in all Norway by German troops is proceeding rapidly."

"At most points," said the afternoon communique, "slight local resistance by Norwegian troops has ceased."

"A dispatch from Copenhagen by the official German news agency said that the Danish government had accepted the German protection "with a protest" in view of the circumstances and conditions of the protection.

Germany gave the signal to march northward less than 24 hours after British warships steamed into Norway's territorial waters to sow free mine fields to cut off German iron ore shipments from Sweden through Norwegian coastal waters.

In order to counteract British aggression under way against the neutrality of Denmark and Norway, said an official communique, German armed forces have assumed the armed protection of these states.

"For this reason strong German forces of all army units entered and landed this morning in these two countries. x x x.

For months England and France have attempted to make a new battlefield out of Scandinavia.

In a blistering statement delivered personally to assembled press representatives of many nations, Foreign Minister von Ribbentrop charged the western powers with plotting to extend the war to the north and declared that the Reich had "assumed responsibility" for protecting Scandinavian neutrality.

As he spoke the Nazi high command broadcast a proclamation assuring Norway and Denmark that Germany has no designs on their independence and urging them to accept as friends the German troops already pouring over their frontiers by land and sea.

HARRISON RITES TOMORROW AT 2

Death Comes Yesterday To Well Known Local Man

Clyde Harrison, Sr., one of this city's best known and highly regarded citizens, passed away yesterday afternoon at 4:15 at the Tayloe Hospital where he had been a patient for the past nine days. Mr. Harrison had been in declining health for the past two yaears and Saturday a week ago entered the hospital where he underwent a major operation. He apparently withstood the surgical nicely until Wednesday morning, when he developed pneumonia, gradually sinking until the end yesterday afternoon.

Mr. Harrison was born near Plymouth, May 15, 1882, a son of the late Joseph and Virginia Frances Harrison. In 1904 he came to Washington and for a number of years was associated in the grocery business with the late M. T. Archbell. Later he became proprietor of that establishment which he operated until becomnig affiliated with S. R. Fowle and Son where he served his last active working years.

In 1910 he married Miss Olive C. Wicks, of Norfolk, and since that time he and Mrs. Harrison and family had resided in Washington. Mr. Harrison was an active and devoted member of the First Christian Church and for a number of years served as deacon. He was a member of the Red Men of which he was a past district deputy, the Odd Fellows and the Junior Order and in each was a leading member.

Mr. Harrison was well known and a host of friends who admired him for his kindly nature and many friendly gestures, a man who loved his home and had always taken an active interest in civic matters.

Surviving are his widow, two sons, Clyde Harrison, Jr., and Richard Leigh Harrison, of this city; one daughter, Mrs. F. W. McClintock, of Miami, Florida; two brothers, A. F. Harrison, of Norfolk, and H. C. Harrison of

(Continued on Page Eight)

ATTENTION TAU TRIBE

A special meeting has been called for Wednesday afternoon April 10, at 1 p. m. at the hall for the purpose of attending the funeral of Brother A. C. Harrison. Be sure and wear Fez. By order of the Sachem Theodore Hodges.

A. C. Cutler, Chief of Records.

Kugler Elected To Head Softball; 5 Teams Entered

John Kugler was elected temporary president of the Washington Softball League at a meeting of softball players and managers held in the City Hall last night. Plans for the coming season were formulated.

A committee of C. C. Duke, John Wilkinson and S. H. Purdue was appointed to draw up a set of by-laws and constitution to be presented at the next meeting. It was also decided that the affairs of the league would be administered by a board of directors consisting of five members. The board will be selected at the next meeting.

Five teams have signified their intention of entering the race this year, which promises to overshadow last year in action as well as standard of playing.

The teams entering the league are: Lawyers, Clerks, Firechiefs, Hustlers and Battery. All teams are to be equipped with full uniform and all new uniforms purchased are to be of the baseball type.

It was suggested to the schedule committee that each team play three games each week if possible.

The next meeting of the league was set for some time during the latter part of next week.

There are still openings in the league for more teams, anyone wishing to enter a team is asked to see John Kugler before the next meeting.

J. W. McGiffin Newspaper Co
223 Dwight Bldg.

Published at the Nation's Health Capital—Home of the Ten Famous Mineral Waters

The Daily Standard

The World's Greatest Newspaper—for Excelsior Springs and the Clay-Ray Area

EXCELSIOR SPRINGS, MO. ★ ★ ★ MONDAY EVENING, APRIL 15, 1940 ★ ★ ★ VOL. 52—NO. 90

World News . . .

—Today's Headline Events In a Nutshell for Our Busy Readers.

WEATHER

Occasional light showers and cooler tonight and Tuesday.

TEMPERATURES:

7 a. m.	66
9 a. m.	72
12 noon	79
3 p. m.	79

BRITISH TROOPS IN NORWAY

STEAMER FLASHES U-BOAT ATTACK

New York—The British steamship Craig, 3,638 tons, sent first an SOS call onnouncing a submarine was approaching it 750 miles east of New York, and then an SOS message indicating an attack, Mackay Radio reported today. The first message, picked up by Mackay from the Camperdown, Nova Scotia, station, had been sent by the ship at 4:55 a. m. The SOS was picked up at 6:10 a. m. The Craig's position was well outside the American neutrality zone. The Craig carried a crew of 34.

GERMANS DRIVEN OUT OF NARVIK, PAPER ASSERTS

Stockholm—The Swedish newspaper Dagens Nyheter reported from Lulea, Sweden, today that the northern Norwegian port of Narvik had been occupied by British forces. The newspaper said the British had landed after a heavy bombardment from British warships had driven German forces of occupation into the hills. Germans who fled into the hills were reported to have encountered heavy fire from Norwegian troops holding positions back from the coast.

ITALIAN SHIPS STIR BALKANS

London—Balkan diplomats have received reports that Italy has quietly concentrated a fleet in its Dodecanese Islands off the Turkish coast at the eastern end of the Mediterranean, about 400 miles from the Suez Canal. According to the reports, the fleet was concentrated while Germany was invading Scandinavia and in the belief of diplomats it was part of an agreed "axis" which would tend to retain the Allies and Turkey from moving against Germany in the Balkins while Adolf Hitler was trying to secure domination of Scandinavia.

GERMANS DENY BRITISH TROOPS LANDED.

Berlin.—Official sources stated today no British troops had landed in parts of Norway occupied by German forces. Authorized sources pointed out, however, that the Norwegian coastline is 1,200 miles long and irregular. Therefore, it was stated, it was possible British troops had lande' at some points not yet occupied by the Germans. These sources said the British had not landed at Narvik. They said the British fleet still was blockading Narvik but there had been no air attacks there today.

SENATOR TAFT IN TOPEKA MAY 18.

Topeka.—Sen. Robert Taft, of Ohio, will speak in Topeka Saturday night, May 18, Walter Fees, chairman of the Republican State Committee said today. Frank Gannett, Rochester, N. Y. publisher, will speak at Lawrence May 2.

THIRD VICTIM OF ACID BURNS.

Joplin, Mo.—Wid Sawyer, 46, who was burned by acid at the Atlas Powder Company's TNT plant near here last week, died today. Two other men were burned fatally by the acid. Roman Deller, of Carthage, who also was burned, is recovering. Sawyer lived at Scotland, near Carthage.

LIFER FLEES PRISON MILL.

Jefferson City.—Bill Goodwin, life-term murderer, escaped late last night or early today from the state prison sawmill at Tebbetts. Goodwin, 52, was sentenced from Dunklin county in 1931. Guards reported he was at the swamill at the 9 p.m. checkup last night, but was missing when the roll was called again at 5 a.m. today.

War Bulletins

By UNITED PRESS

PLEDGE TO NORWAY

PARIS—France, in full accord with her Allies, will give Norway "the most complete and most efficacious aid in all fields by all means in her power," President Albert Lebrun said today in a message to King Haakon of Norway.

★ ★ ★

DENIAL ON SCHEER

LONDON—The Swedish radio said today the German legation at Stockholm denied the German pocket battleship Admiral Scheer had been struck by a torpedo from a British submarine. The Admiral Scheer was "absolutely undamaged," the legation said.

★ ★ ★

DOWN NAZI PLANE

STOCKHOLM—Swedish antiaircraft guns shot down a German plane at Uddevala, on the west coast, yesterday, killing all but one member of the crew, it was announced officially. The survivor, seriously injured, was sent to a hospital. The number of men in the plane was not known, as the craft burst into flames.

Keynote For Harmony At State Demo Meet

CLAY COUNTY GROUP "IN THE FIGHT"

Although no direct word has been received here today from the Clay county delegation of Democrats at the state convention, it is known that the local group, preponderantly pro-Stark in feeling, is "in there fighting" for the Governor's place on the "big eight."

A strong undercurrent of discord lurked beneath the outward calm at the convention this morning, dispatches stated, with some delegates on the warpath to bar Stark as a delegate-at-large at the national convention.

The Stark-Clark feeling broke the surface at the Fishing River township meeting here, and in many other local communities, and the ripples have grown into a sizeable wave.

State Administration Has "Given Missouri Clean Competent, Satisfactory Regime," Says Judge Taylor Smith, Temporary Chairman.

ST. LOUIS, April 15—(U.P.)—A keynote for harmony "above all cliques and beyond all personalities" was struck today by Circuit Judge Taylor Smith of Farmington in an address prepared for delivery after his election as temporary chairman of the state Democratic convention.

Judge Smith said "we pledge ourselves to keep our Democratic party progressive; never to allow it to become reactionary."

"We look back upon the accomplishments of the last seven years as a period of tremendous progress —a progress not measured by mergers and ticker tape, but by the common welfare and the common good," he said.

As if seeking to dispell the factional strife that has rocked the party, Smith opened with this statement:

"We have entered this hall as Democrats—not as Democrats for this or Democrats for that—but as a united Democracy, under the full and controlling belief that the traditions and the policies of the Democratic party are above all cliques and beyond all personalities, that their preservation is more important than that of any office, or any official."

He praised President Roosevelt as representing "the triumph of the principles of democracy over the hosts of privilege and shameful reaction." The Republicans, he said, can agree on nothing except opposition to Democrats.

He said the state administration, "following in the footsteps of the national administration," had given Missouri a "clean, competent and satisfactory regime."

Indirectly touching the cleanup of the machine in Kansas City, he added:

"The state administration has brought renewed assurance to its citizens that they are safe from the depredations of organized crime; that those who abuse the democratic progresses will be punished, and that honest government can be had through tne exercise of their rights as voters and free citizens."

CO. FINANCIAL REPORT TO BE PRINTED SOON

Daily Standard Bids Low for Voluminous Statement Required Annually By Law; To Provide Supplements for All Papers.

LIBERTY, April 15—(Special)—The publication of the annual financial report, required by law, was ordered published in The Daily Standard at Excelsior Springs, after bids were opened this morning by the Clay County Court.

The Standard's bid, which was under the amount allowed by law, was low for the publication. Its bid also provides for publication of supplements containing the statement, for insertion in all newspapers in Clay county, at no additional cost to the court.

It was pointed out that this feature of the bid will take the statement to all taxpayers in the county, which is the intent of the law requiring publication of same.

Copy for the financial statement, a manuscript of many pages, was received by The Standard today. Work of setting the report in type, a sizeable task, will begin right away and it will be published as soon as mechanically possible.

Washington Raises Pay of Councilmen

WASHINGTON, Mo., April 15—(U.P.)—The old city council bowed to its successor with an ordinance increasing the pay of city councilmen from $2 per meeting to $3.50. It was the first change in council pay for 40 years.

Peggy Lee Hash Rites at Kearney

KEARNEY (Special)—Funeral services for Peggy Lee Hash, two-year-old daughter of Mr. and Mrs. Loma Hash, were conducted at the Kearney Christian church Wednesday. She died Monday at a Kansas City hospital. Burial was in Fairview cemetery here.

Surviving are her parents and a sister, Betty Hash; two brothers, John and Bobby Hash; grandparents, Mr. and Mrs. Robert Hash and Mr. and Mrs. O. E. Thomas; and great grandmother, Mrs. E. A. Thomas, all of Kearney.

Kansas City Scouts Enjoy Week-end Camp Trip Here

A group of 22 Boy Scouts of Troop No. 3 of Kansas City enjoyed a week-end camp outing at the Scout Cabin on top of Siloam Mountain here.

The boys arrived here Saturday afternoon and left late yesterday afternoon. They attended services in uniform at St. Luke's Episcopal church yesterday morning and enjoyed a swimming party at the mineral water pool in the Hall of Waters yesterday afternoon.

This troop has quite a colorful history. It is the third oldest troop, in point of continued registration, in Kansas City and the fourth oldest troop in the state of Missouri. The troop was organized on July 12, 1916 at St. George's Episcopal church.

The Rev. Edward M. Blum, pastor of the St. Luke's church here and scoutmaster of the local troop, joined this troop and was later its scoutmaster.

The troop is now under the direction of Scoutmaster Robert Brancamp and Assistant Scoutmaster Miles Blum, a brother of the Rev. Blum. Both men were scouts in the troop under Rev. Blum.

Rev. Blum said the troop enjoyed the outing and plans to come here again this summer for a longer stay.

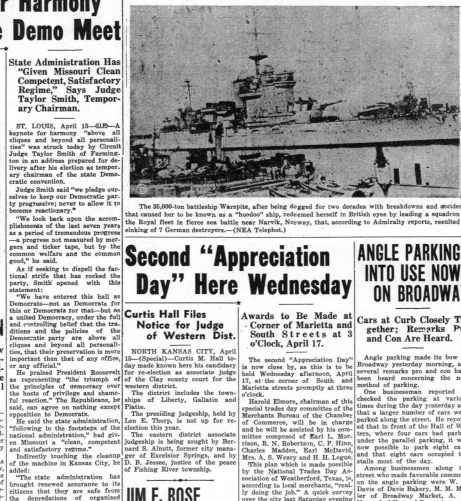

BRITISH "HOODOO" SHIP REDEEMS HERSELF

The 35,000-ton battleship Warspite, after being dogged for two decades with breakdowns and accidents that caused her to be known as a "hoodoo" ship, redeemed herself in British eyes by leading a squadron of the Royal fleet in fierce sea battle near Narvik, Norway, that, according to Admiralty reports, resulted in sinking of 7 German destroyers.—(NEA Telephot.)

Second "Appreciation Day" Here Wednesday

Awards to Be Made at Corner of Marietta and South Streets at 3 o'Clock, April 17.

The second "Appreciation Day" is now close by, as this is to be held Wednesday afternoon, April 17, at the corner of South and Marietta streets promptly at three o'clock.

Harold Elmore, chairman of this special trades day committee of the Merchants Bureau of the Chamber of Commerce, will be in charge and he will be assisted by his committee composed of Earl L. Morrison, R. N. Robertson, C. P. Hinn, Charles Madden, Earl McDavid, Mrs. A. S. Weary and H. H. Logue.

This plan which is made possible by the National Trades Day Association of Weatherford, Texas, is, according to local merchants, "really doing the job." A quick survey over the city last Saturday evening indicated that a larger buying crowd was in the city than for quite some time. Parking space was at a definite premium, it is reported.

Tickets will be accepted at the award corner up until ten minutes before the program begins, C. P. Hinn, general chairman of the merchants bureau, advises.

Curtis Hall Files Notice for Judge of Western Dist.

NORTH KANSAS CITY, April 15—(Special)—Curtis M. Hall today made known here his candidacy for re-election as associate judge of the Clay county court for the western district.

The district includes the townships of Liberty, Gallatin and Platte.

The presiding judgeship, held by Len E. Thorp, is not up for re-election this year.

The eastern district associate judgeship is being sought by Bernard S. Alnutt, former city manager of Excelsior Springs, and by D. B. Jessee, justice of the peace of Fishing River township.

JIM E. ROSE IS NEW AGENT AT BUS DEPOT

Succeeds Jack Potts Who Is Now Traveling Passenger Agent of Kansas City Division of Union Pacific Stages.

Jim E. Rose comes here tomorrow to take charge of the local Union Bus Depot as passenger agent, succeeding Jack Potts, who was transferred to the position of traveling passenger agent of the Kansas City division for Union Pacific Stages.

Mr. Rose has been employed by the Union Pacific Stages for the past 13 years.

He and Mrs. Rose will make their home here soon. They have a son, Bill Rose, who is also in the bus business, as passenger agent at Raton, New Mexico.

R. B. "Bob" McKown will continue at the local bus depot as assistant agent.

The Interstate Bus Lines, a branch of the Union Pacific Stages, runs seven buses daily to and from Kansas City.

Mrs. Carder Loses 3 Diamond Rings

LIBERTY (Special) — Mrs. O. John Carder, of Hessel-Carder Funeral Home, laid her three diamond rings down in the ladies' rest room of the court house Saturday.

She failed to pick them up—and, evidently, some one else did. No trace of the rings had been reported today.

INTER-CIVIC CLUB COUNCIL MEETS TUES.

Urge Representatives of All Member Groups to Be Present for Session at Hall of Waters.

Members of the Inter-Civic Club Council which organization includes representatives from more than thirty groups in the city, have been notified of a regular meeting of this council for tomorrow night at five o'clock in the assembly room of the Hall of Waters. Robert Lightstone is the chairman of this group.

The purpose of this organization is to develop community cooperation, also exchange ideas and clear activity dates which have a definite public interest. The council was formed more than a year ago and has been holding regular monthly meetings since that time.

The meeting tomorrow night will be devoted to the regular business of the council as outlined above.

Chairman Lightstone asks that representatives of all member organizations make a special effort to attend. The meeting will be short but important, he adds. A recent member added to the council is the Junior Council.

ANGLE PARKING INTO USE NOW ON BROADWAY

Cars at Curb Closely Together; Remarks Pro and Con Are Heard.

Angle parking made its bow on Broadway yesterday morning, and several remarks pro and con have been heard concerning the new method of parking.

One businessman reported he checked the parking at various times during the day yesterday and that a larger number of cars were parked along the street. He reported that in front of the Hall of Waters, where four cars had parked under the parallel parking, it was now possible to park eight cars, and that eight cars occupied the stalls most of the day.

Among businessmen along the street who made favorable comment on the angle parking were W. K. Davis of Davis Bakery, M. M. Miller of Broadway Market, A. M. Howard of Howard Drug store, and A. C. Weien of Weien-Logue drugs.

It is believed the new angle parking will provide parking facilities for about 75 per cent more cars than the parallel plan. This added space, the supporters point out, will give more parking facilities for visitors and shoppers.

Although the new parking plan takes part of the open traffic space of the street, there is still sufficient room for two cars to pass—allowing single parallel parking on the north side of the street.

However, the narrower driving space will necessitate lower speeds of driving along the streets—but it is also understood this "cutting down the speed" has been a problem of the police department for some time.

As this is at present only an experimental plan, the lines were only partially marked out.

Methodists to Hear Bishop Broomfield at Supper Tuesday

In keeping with a state-wide program, Excelsior Springs Methodists will assemble at the church at 7 o'clock Tuesday evening for a "covered dish supper."

Later in the evening by means of radio and a state-wide hookup they will hear a message from Bishop J. C. Broomfield, of St. Louis, the Presiding Bishop in the Missouri Area.

All local Methodists and friends are urged to be present to join in this state-wide radio audience of 225,000 Methodists who will be assembled in their respective churches on that evening.

The special broadcasts may be heard in this area over the following stations: KFEQ, St. Joseph at 8:30 p. m.; KCMO, 8:45 P. M.; and KFRU, in Columbia at 8:45 P. M.

Allied Planes Bomb German-Held Ports; 17 Nazi Ships Sunk

Norwegian Defense Positions Only 30 to 50 Miles North of Oslo; a Quick Thrust By British Would Isolate German Troops in Northern Part of Peninsula.

BULLETIN

PARIS, April 15—(U.P.)—British military circles said today it was officially reported Allied forces had landed on Lofoten Island near Narvik. No details were offered, but it is understood the landing of troops has materially strengthened the Norwegians' position.

★ ★ ★

BY UNITED PRESS

Great Britain landed armed forces on a new battlefield in Norway today—six hectic days after Germany's thrust into Scandinavia—and Europe nervously watched for signs that Adolf Hitler might move again toward a new front in Sweden or the Balkans.

British fighting men—probably a combined army and marine force—set foot on Norwegian soil at "several places," the official London statement said.

The move had been expected several days. Meantime, R. A. F. planes bombarded German-held Norwegian ports. British warships blasted German ships wherever they could be brought to action. Allied submarines and mine-layers sought to sever the vital German sea routes through the Kattegat and Skagerrak to Norway.

London did not specify where British forces landed under navy and aerial protection. But speculation centered on five points—Narvik, in the Far North, Trondheim, Bergen, Mansos and Andalsnes, near Alesund.

A landing at Trondheim would be most important strategically. Here Norway is a scant 50 miles wide. A quick British thrust to the Swedish border would cut Norway in two and isolate German garrisons to the north. It also would aid the Norwegians in consolidating and holding their rough, hastily thrown up defense lines to the south.

Rail and Highway Links

The southern center of Norwegian resistance is about 150 miles southeast of Trondheim and linked to Trondheim by direct rail and motor highway connections. The Norwegian defense positions are from 30 to 50 miles north of Oslo, the Norwegian capital.

Most of the Norwegian troops apparently are near Skarnes and Kongsvinger on the Glomen River northeast of Oslo and close to the Swedish border and around Hamar and Elvenrum, about 25 miles due north of the Skarnes-Kongsvinger front. Another smaller force is near Eidsvold, from which they were dislodged by the Germans. This Skarnes-Hamar-Eidsvold front forms a rough triangle protecting the railroad to Trondheim.

A British landing at Trondheim would be important also in a nutcracker operation against the Germans to the north. About 25,000 Norwegian troops are concentrated in the Far North near Narvik. British landings at Trondheim and Narvik probably would enable them to operate with the Norwegians in pinching off the northern German forces.

Nazis Claim Gains

Berlin, however, reported German troops were improving and maintaining their position in Norway. They claimed to have put 27 British warships out of action, sunk or damaged, up to Sunday and to have shot down 24 British planes. The toll reportedly included seven British submarines.

On the sea front the British admiralty said British submarines had sunk 15 German ships and scored at least one hit on the German pocket battleship Admiral Scheer. Two more German transports were sunk, the British asserted.

★ ★ ★

LONDON (U.P.) — The admiralty and the war office, in a 10-word communique said today British forces had landed at several points in Norway.

Meet Force With Force Says F.D.R.

WASHINGTON, April 15.—(U.P.) —President Roosevelt declared today the 21 American republics must be prepared "to meet force with force" if their system of peaceful relations is challenged.

The President spoke before the governing board of the Pan-American Union in commemoration of the union's fiftieth anniversary, and radio carried his voice to most of the world.

He said he prays that the Western Hemisphere never shall have to resort to force for its defense. But should strong measures be necessary, he said he was convinced the Americas would be "wholly successful" in defending their way of life because "the inner strength of a group of free people is irresistible when they are prepared to act."

Mr. Roosevelt made no direct reference to the extension of the war to Norway and Denmark. He condemned that invasion in a statement Saturday.

Emphasizes Preparedness.

The President emphasized the necessity of adequate preparedness if the Americas are to live in peace. He said preparedness is important because in his conception the "whole world now is struggling to find the basis of its life in coming centuries."

"The cooperative peace of the Western Hemisphere was not created by wishing; and it will require more than words to maintain it," he said.

"In this association of nations, whoever touches any one of us touches all of us. We have only asked that the world go with us in the path of peace. But we shall be able to keep that way open only if we are prepared to meet force with force if challenge is ever made."

Diplomats representing the other 20 American republics, which with the United States comprise the Pan-American Union, and representatives of other nations, too, heard Mr. Roosevelt declare "universal and stable peace remains a dream."

"Can Have No Illusions."

"War, more horrible and destruc-

(See "Meet Force,' 'page 6)

WAR EXTRA

COMPLETE RACES

Complete Markets

Los Angeles Examiner

CHARACTER · QUALITY · AMERICA FIRST! · ENTERPRISE · ACCURACY

AN AMERICAN PAPER FOR THE AMERICAN PEOPLE · THE GREAT NEWSPAPER OF THE GREAT SOUTHWEST

Reg. U.S.Pat.Off.

VOL. XXXVII—NO. 141 CC LOS ANGELES, TUESDAY, APRIL 30, 1940 Two Sections—Part 1—FIVE CENTS

FIVE NAZI THRUSTS MENACE ALLIED ARMY!

ALLIED FORCES attempting landing on Norway's rocky coast have been subjected to fierce bombing attacks by German warplanes. Here is Examiner Staff Artist Howard Burke's conception of a Nazi raid on British transports and supply ships such as took place off Trondheim. The Germans claimed a British cruiser was struck

Rail Objective of Lightning Norway Push

NEW YORK, April 29.—(INS)—The National Broadcasting Company's short-wave listening post tonight picked up a Berlin radio broadcast quoting the German high command as claiming Allied troops north of Trondheim have been pushed back toward their landing places and are therefore isolated.

STOCKHOLM, April 29.—(AP)—Germany's lightning legions struck in a five-forked attack—four from the south and one from the north—against Allied positions along vital railway lines in central Norway tonight.

The Allies were described as strategically placed, however, with machine gun nests and light artillery defeding their positions.

Up the Gulbrandsdalen, a valley lying northwest-southeast across Norway, the Germans were reported in Norwegian dispatches reaching here to have occupied Kvam, 35 miles southeast of the British-held railway junction of Dombaas.

Farther east, where the Osterdalen (eastern valley) roughly parallels the Gudbrandsdalen, a German column smashed northwestward from the region of Alvdal to the vicinity of Hjerkinn, where they came upon strong Allied positions. Fighting was reported in progress there, with the British battling to defend the railway which links their forces at Dombaas and Storen to the northward.

FIGHTING IN SNOW

Norwegian troops were reported fighting a third German contingent tonight at Kvikne, on the snowy highway about two-thirds of the way from Tynset to Ulsberg. This battle began last night and was reported still in

(Continued on Page A, Cols. 7-8)

Nazi Air Force Blasts British

BERLIN, April 29.—(AP)—A British attempt to squeeze the German-held port of Trondheim in a 200-mile pincers movement has backfired into a German push from five directions on Allied forces in central Norway, an authoritative source here indicated tonight.

These sources said the Allied attempt to clamp twin holds on Trondheim from Andalsnes, 100 miles south of Trondheim, and from Namsos, an equal distance north of the port, had been converted into a five-ply German movement on Andalsnes.

It was said there is a prospect that the British troops who came ashore at Andalsnes soon will be in difficulties.

The strength of the British landing party at Andalsnes is not known here, but has been

(Continued on Page A, Column 2)

LONDON, April 29.—(AP)—Damaging attacks by low-flying German bombers on the Allied troop-landing bases of Molde and Andalsnes emphasized in British minds tonight the belief that control of the air will be the decisive factor in the major battle which slowly is developing in central Norway.

Aware that German planes also are harrying British lines of communication and protecting the German columns moving swiftly from the south toward the garrison in Trondheim, London was gloomy after a week of indifferent news from the north.

Meanwhile, however, Britain appeared determined to plug any possible gaps on the diplomatic and economic fronts.

The most welcome item of news in this connection was the disclosure that Foreign Secre-

NAZIS STOPPED By Belgians And Dutch

WAR EXTRA

CHURCHILL PRIME MINISTER

WAR FLASHES

HOLLAND VOWS DETERMINATION TO FIGHT

LONDON, May 10 (INS).—Holland's firm determination to resist the Nazi invasion was announced in an official broadcast by the Dutch radio today.

7 KILLED, 61 HURT IN BRUSSELS RAIDS

BRUSSELS, May 10 (INS).—Thirty-seven persons were killed and 61 wounded in German air raids on Brussels today, a checkup revealed tonight. Five German bombing planes were brought down by Belgian anti-aircraft batteries and three others by fighting planes.

BRITISH TANKS ROAR INTO BELGIUM

ON THE FRANCO-BELGIAN FRONT, May 10 (INS).—British tanks, armored cars, motorcycles and transports roared across the French border into Belgium in a never-ending stream tonight. It was estimated that the vanguard already was many miles inside the Belgian territory.

ALLIES, GERMANS CLASH IN BELGIUM

NEW YORK, May 10 (INS).—The French shortwave radio in Paris at 4:55 p. m. today (EDT) announced that "allied and German troops have established contact in Belgian territory. The French broadcast was received in New York by Columbia broadcasting system.

OTHER NEWS—

HOUSE CUTS S. F. FAIR CASH TO $200,000

The House today approved a rerolution for continued participation in the S. F. Exposition, and sent it to the Senate for concurrence, but reduced the $300,000 appropriation proposed by the latter group to $200,000,A. P. reported from Washington.

5TH RACE, PIMLICO—Zayin, won, 20.60, 10.80, 3.40; Run By, 2d, 15.80, 4.70; Ringie, 3d, 2.20. T., 1:45 2-5.

7TH RACE, JAMAICA—Fencing, won, 16.30, 9.20, 4; Miss Selection, 2d, 7.90, 3.90; Good Flavor, 3d, 2.60. T., 1:47 2-5.

U. S. War Policy Unchanged: F. R.

WASHINGTON, May 10 (AP).—President Roosevelt today expressed "full sympathy" with Queen Wilhelmina's proclamation that Germany violated a "solemn promise" by invading Holland, but said there was no change in the United States neutral status.

As if to emphasize his opinion of the German invasion of Belgium, the Netherlands and Luxembourg, the President told reporters who jammed his office they could put these words in direct quotations:

"FLAMING PROTEST"

"I think I can say I am in full sympathy with the very excellent statement that was given out, the proclamation by the queen of the Netherlands, and let it go at that. It is worth reading.

In her proclamation read to the Dutch people over the radio, the queen also addressed a "flaming protest against this unexampled violation of good faith and what is considered decent between civilized countries."

There was not much else he could say about the situation abroad, Mr. Roosevelt asserted in response to other questions. It spoke for itself, he said.

Then a reporter asked whether the chief executive "would care to say at this time what you think the chances

Continued on Page 6, Col. 1

Stocks Fall, Wheat Up: Pound Hits New Low

Stocks on the San Francisco and New York exchanges were under heavy selling pressure today, while, wheat, corn, rubber, tin and several other commodities went abruptly higher on the German thrust into the low countries. Volume in New York was 2,086,240 shares.

The British pound sterling slumped to a historic low in San Francisco and New York, down 30 cents in terms of the dollar at one time. Later it recovered about 10 cents.

Losses in the security markets ranged from $1 to around $5 in the leading shares. Pulp and paper stocks were under the most pressure in San Francisco.

Wheat futures in Chicago, up 5 cents a bushel at the start, closed with gains of 3 to 4⅛ cents a bushel. Corn jumped around 2 cents and rye about 3 cents a bushel.

Speed of U. S. 'Red' Army Amazes Commanders

LEESVILLE, La., May 10 (AP). Still amazed at the speed of their own divisions, commanders of the "red" army of Texas sought today to drive an irresistible wedge toward Alexandria, La., in mock war games.

The immediate problem was to push as near the city as possible before the enemy "blues" could gather up their slowly forming forces for the organization of a defense line.

FINAL NIGHT EDITION — WEATHER: FAIR Details on Page 18

THE CALL BULLETIN — SAN FRANCISCO — AN INDEPENDENT NEWSPAPER

85TH YEAR — CALL AND POST. VOL. 147. NO. 92 / THE CALL-BULLETIN. VOL. 167. NO. 92 — FRIDAY, MAY 10, 1940 — 5c DAILY 90c a Month

British Shift Chiefs

NAZIS CLAIM BIG GAINS IN DRIVE

3 Cities, Spans Taken in Holland, Belgium, Reports Berlin

BERLIN, May 10 (AP).—The Berlin radio announced tonight that German troops had taken Maastricht, Holland, and Malmedy, Belgium.

The Nazis crossed the Maas River with a few men on the west Dutch-German frontier at several points, the announcement said.

Previously, the capture of The Hague had been announced.

WARPLANES DESTROYED

An official announcement tonight said almost 100 "enemy" airplanes either had been shot down in aerial battles or destroyed on the ground.

Seven German airplanes were reported missing, in addition to two known to have made forced landings, it said.

Maastricht is almost due west of Aachen, and Malmedy is on a line due west of Coblenz.

GERMANS REACH YSEL

"German troops reached the Ysel River (east of Arnheim) early in the afternoon Friday, and crossed the Maas River on Dutch territory in several places," the radio said.

"Maastricht and bridges over the Albert canal west of the city are in German hands."

(The Albert canal comprises part of Belgium's great defense system.)

"Malmedy has been taken. Farther south, the troops moving forward through Luxembourg have crossed the Belgian frontier."

Belgian airports at Brussels and Antwerp also were raided and bombed by strong German units, the announcement said.

PLANES LAND TROOPS

The air force landed numerous German troop units in Holland

Continued on Page A, Col. 7

At a Glance

LOW COUNTRIES—"Low countries," Belgium, Holland, Luxembourg, with aid of British and French forces, reported stopping invading Nazi legions "cold"; German radio announces seizure of The Hague, Netherlands capital; seizure denied.

BRUSSELS—King Leopold III replays father's 1914 role, leading Belgian troops in stand against Nazi invaders; Germans bomb Brussels; general mobilization ordered. Belgium's crack little army halts German advance.

BERLIN—Hitler goes to western front, tells troops: "The hour has come! The fight beginning today decides the fate of the German nation for the next 1,000 years."

PARIS—French-British army moves rapidly across Belgian border to meet German onslaught; military spokesman says "most gigantic battle of all time" may be imminent.

THE HAGUE—Attempt to capture Queen Wilhelmina fails; Netherlands opens canal system gates, has army of 400,000 ready, downs seventy German warplanes, attacks chine gun German parachute "suicide" squads; capture of Hague by Germans denied.

LONDON—Chamberlain resigned today and Winston Churchill becomes prime minister.

WASHINGTON—President Roosevelt called White House conference to draft new neutrality regulations.

TOKYO — Rumor that Japanese fleet en route to Dutch East Indies current in Tokyo. American fleet reported to have taken up positions at Manila, Philippines.

Jap Fleet Reported On Way to Indies

International reaction to the Nazi invasion of the Netherlands, as focused on the fate of the Dutch East Indies, follows in brief:

1—Martial law declared in Batavia, Java. Nineteen German vessels reported seized.

2—Rumors heard in Tokyo that Japanese navy vessels already en route to Dutch East Indies.

3—Japanese foreign office spokesman said in Tokyo that Japan is following policy of "strict non-involvement."

4—U. S. fleet, at Pearl Harbor, ordered to leave Monday and Tuesday for maneuvers at Lahaina Roads, straits southeast of Honolulu, retaining bulk of fleet indefinitely in mid-Pacific.

5—In Washington, Secretary of the Navy Edison kept in contact with fleet commander, as navy high command silent on future plans; freely predicted drastic steps would be taken to prevent seizure of Indies.

6—Offered German guarantees reported from Amsterdam that Holland would retain her possessions "in Europe and overseas" if no resistance to invasion; otherwise "complete destruction" threatened.

TOKYO, May 10 (INS).—A rumor spread in Tokyo tonight that the Japanese fleet is en route to the Dutch East Indies. Officials refused to comment.

The foreign office would not discuss the possible effects of the German invasion of Holland on the Dutch East Indies.

FLEET REPORT

Tokyo also heard a report that the United States fleet has taken

Continued on Page C, Column 5

American League

At Philadelphia—	R. H. E.
Wash'ton. 000 130 0	
Philadel.. 200 210 0	

Krakauskas, Haynes, Masterson and Ferrell; Dean and Hayes.

At Cleveland—	R. H. E.
St. Louis ..100 1	
Cleveland .000 0	

Kennedy and Swift.
Milnar and Hemsley.

At Detroit—	R. H. E.
Chicago ...000 000	
Detroit ...000 003	

Rigney and Turner.
Newsom and Sullivan.

At New York—	R. H. E.
Boston 000 000 2	
New York .020 000 0	

Harris, Wilson, De Sautels, Peacock; Chandler and Rosar.

National League

At Brooklyn—	R.	H.	E.
New York .300 001 030—	7	12	2
Brooklyn ..200 000 000—	2	5	0

Gumbert and Danning.
Wyatt, Ferrell and Franks.

At Chicago—	R. H. E.
Pittsburgh .010 00	
Chicago ...010 02	

Brown and Davis.
Lee and Todd.

COALITION CABINET LOOMS

Chamberlain Resigns; Laborites Agree to Join New Regime

LONDON, May 10 (AP).—Winston Churchill, belligerent first lord of the admiralty and long time target of Adolf Hitler's wrath, tonight became Britain's man of destiny, succeeding Neville Chamberlain as prime minister as war surged over western Europe.

CHAMBERLAIN QUITS

The government announced "the Right Honorable Neville Chamberlain resigned the office of prime minister and first lord of the treasury this evening and the Right Honorable Winston Churchill accepted his majesty's invitation to fill the position.

"The prime minister desires that all ministers should remain at their posts and discharge their functions with full freedom and responsibility while the necessary arrangements for the formation of a new administration are made."

Chamberlain, the apostle of appeasement, who saw his policy fail and when war came expressed the hope he could carry on long enough to see Hitlerism destroyed, had been in office since May 28, 1937.

Churchill, whose mother was an American, has been Chamberlain's First Lord of the Admiralty since the outbreak of the European war and has been given more and more of the burden of the war effort to carry.

HELD POST BEFORE

Churchill, 65 years old and the man to whom Britain has entrusted an increasing burden of carrying on the war, appeared on the threshold of the last high office hitherto withheld from him in Britain's government.

Summoned by Chamberlain on the day war was declared on Germany, Churchill resumed the post of first lord of the admiralty, which he held in the world war.

Later, he became head of the committee of service ministers and then, in Chamberlain's latest effort to stave off defeat, he was named defensive chief, in direct charge of all British war strategy.

LLOYD GEORGE CONSIDERED

The finger of destiny also pointed to David Lloyd George, world war prime minister, for reports today said he would be willing to serve under Churchill as minister without portfolio.

Labor leaders already had an-

Continued on Page D, Column 5

Fierce Plane Battles Over 4 Countries

AMSTERDAM, May 10 (AP). — The commander in chief of the Netherlands forces declared tonight Germany's surprise attack on Holland a failure.

By Associated Press

Allied and German advance guards clashed tonight along the French-Luxembourg frontier as "the most gigantic battle of all time" appeared imminent following Adolf Hitler's triple thrust into the little low countries—Belgium, Holland and Luxembourg—aimed apparently at getting a base for an attack on England.

Winston Churchill, long a target of Hitler's wrath, became the new prime minister of England, succeeding Neville Chamberlain, as the British planes bombed German airports.

Hitler in Command at Front

Hitler, in personal command of Nazi troops on the western front, proclamed the start of a titanic fight "to decide the fate of the German nation for the next 1,000 years.

Britain and France themselves were raided by the German air force in bombing forays over both countries.

From Rotterdam came reports that German troops invading the city had been hurled back, and that the Dutch defenders were making a gallant stand.

A reported attempt to capture Queen Wilhelmina by German parachute troops was foiled.

Beriln said German troops captured The Hague, Netherlands capital. Nazis also claimed to have captured the Dutch city of Maastricht, and the Belgium city of Malmedy.

Belgians Stop Germans

The German high command and the Berlin radio boasted that Nazi invaders had broken resistance everywhere. The radio asserted that 100 enemy planes had been shot down in aerial conflict or bombed to bits.

Winston Churchill was appointed British prime minister today as Chamberlain resigned. British planes in France reported successful bombing of German troops.

Hitler sped to the front and took personal charge of invasion campaign.

The Belgian foreign ministry announced that the Nazi invaders had been stopped cold a few hundred yards inside the frontier. The German thrust, it was said, crumpled against the Belgian "demolition zone."

Allied troops went to the defense of the imperiled small nations, which are able to muster a combined military strength of 1,000,000 men.

Holland opened her flood gates and dikes, blew up bridges and threw her army into action, holding the Germans near Arnheim.

Nazi bombers blasted Antwerp and Brussels and the French cities of Nancy, Lille and Calais, and Chilham, in England, also were bombed.

Berlin said Luxembourg had been overrun in the early hours of the pre-dawn invasion, and the Berlin radio asserted Nazi troops had occupied The Hague.

70 German Planes Downed

However, dispatches received four hours later directly from Amsterdam, thirty miles from The Hague, did not mention its fall.

The Dutch said at least seventy German planes had been shot down, four armored trains destroyed and that German parachute troops had been swiftly surrounded and captured.

In London, the ministry of home security issued a gen-

Continued on Page A, Column 1

7TH WAR EXTRA

HOLLAND SURRENDERS

Rotterdam Bombed Into Submission

Sedan Captured by Nazis

Dutch Chief Orders Army 'Cease Firing'

By Associated Press

LONDON, May 15 (Wednesday)—An official announcement early today said "a state of war between Germany and The Netherlands continues," although the Dutch commander-in-chief has ordered his men to stop fighting.

By Associated Press

AMSTERDAM, May 14.—Gen. Henri Gerard Winkleman, commander-in-chief of the Dutch armies, tonight ordered all Dutch troops except those in the far southwestern province of Zeeland to cease fighting.

The order came after Rotterdam had been bombarded during the afternoon and after Utrecht, in the words of Winkleman, was faced "with complete annihilation."

Rotterdam is the western seaport, which the Germans reached after circling below the water-line defenses of western Holland; Utrecht is in the center of the main water line.

The proclamation said General Winkelman had been left in supreme command by Queen Wilhelmina, now in England, and that he was authorized to make whatever military decision was necessary.

"In order to save the civilian population and prevent further bloodshed, I think I am entitled to order the troops concerned to stop fighting," the general's announcement said.

The commander told his troops to "maintain order until the arrival" of the Germans, and that "order and quiet must be strictly observed."

"Fighting in Zeeland goes on," he said.

In a proclamation read to her people early in the afternoon, Queen Wilhelmina declared she had gone to England with her family and the government "to avoid government capitulation."

She pointed out that there is Dutch territory in the East and West Indies, as well as in Europe.

"Where the aggressor rules," the Queen urged, "the local authorities must do all that can be useful for the population and, in the first place, collaborate to maintain order and calm."

In conclusion she said:

"The Netherlands will one day,

(CONTINUED ON PAGE TWELVE)

Belgians Deny Fall Of Liege

By Associated Press

PARIS, May 14.—Havas, French news agency, reported from Brussels that German parachutists were landing this morning in the Belgian capital, but were pounced on by the inhabitants as fast as they touched ground.

One parachutist, who landed a few yards from the Belga News Agency, was lynched by the crowd after he tried to make use of his firearms, Havas said.

By United Press

PARIS, May 14.—The Paris newspaper L'Intransigeant reported from Brussels today that the Belgian city of Namur, southwest of Liege, was in flames after an intensive German aerial bombardment. The newspaper said that the Germans had been bombing Liege for the past 12 hours.

By Associated Press

BRUSSELS, May 14.—Premier Hubert Pierlot told the nation tonight that Belgium's defenders had made "certain modification of defense positions according to order" but that there had been no German "break through" despite smashing assaults in many sectors.

"The situation is normal," the premier assured his people in a radio broadcast.

In the fortified area of Liege, he declared Belgian guns were inflicting tremendous losses on wave upon wave of attacking Germans.

(CONTINUED ON PAGE FOURTEEN)

(Sports on B-8 to B-11.)

(Eastern Baseball Scores see Page B-8.)

7 STAR COMPLETE SPORTS ★★★★★★★

Only Los Angeles Newspaper With All Leading News Services—Associated Press, International News, United Press, Dow-Jones

LOS ANGELES EVENING HERALD AND Express

The Evening Herald and Express Grows Just Like Los Angeles

HERALD-EXPRESS PHONE Richmond 4141

RACE RESULTS NIGHT FINAL

VOL. LXX | TUESDAY, MAY 14, 1940 | Two Sections Section A | NO. 42

F. D. R. READY TO ASK BIG ARMS FUND

By United Press

WASHINGTON, May 14.—Gen. John J. Pershing, commander of the American Expeditionary Force during the World War, declared late today that the United States faces practically the same condition now as in 1917 and must immediately step up its defense program.

By Associated Press

WASHINGTON, May 14.—President Roosevelt asserted today that the important thing at this time was the national defense and that the method of supplying the millions of dollars to perfect defenses was a secondary consideration.

Mr. Roosevelt declared at a press conference that he might send to Congress tomorrow a message requesting additional funds to build up the nation's military and naval establishments, but he suggested no specific amount. He did add that

(CONTINUED ON PAGE FIFTEEN)

Herald-Express Special Features

War Today

Dutch Quit as Huge Armies Collide Head-on Along Meuse

(For map of today's war see Page A-3.)

By Associated Press

The Netherlands command capitulated last (Tuesday) night to the smashing force of German arms, while battling Belgium was at least one-third over-run and the Nazi war machine burst into France and attacked the Allies in one of history's greatest battles in the celebrated Sedan sector—scene of French defeat at German hands in the War of 1870.

The Netherlands commander-in-chief ordered all Dutch troops except those in the little southwestern province of Zeeland to cease fighting.

Gen. Henri Gerard Winkelman said he ordered arms laid down "to save the civilian population and prevent further bloodshed." He said the western seaport of Rotterdam had been bombarded again and that Utrecht, on the main water line, faced annihilation.

In their last struggling gasp, the Dutch set fire to vast petroleum stores in Amsterdam to prevent their falling into German hands.

The apparent acknowledgement of The Netherlands' defeat came as giant artillery thundered along the Siegfried

(CONTINUED ON PAGE EIGHT)

BULLETINS

Belgian Royal Tots to Go to England

By United Press

LONDON, May 14.—Princess Josephine Charlotte and Princes Baudouin and Albert, children of King Leopold III of Belgium, are expected to arrive in England shortly, it was reported reliably tonight.

Nazi Report 2 Cruisers Sunk

By International News Service

BERLIN, May 14.—It was officially announced tonight that German bombing planes sank two Allied cruisers and one destroyer in fighting off the Dutch coast. Another cruiser was said to be severely damaged and burning. Two transports, one a 25,000-ton vessel and the other of 8000 tons, were struck and set afire in the attack, it was claimed. They were said to have been burning for several hours.

Warn Dutch Not to Destroy Food

By International News Service

BERLIN, May 14.—The German radio tonight warned the Dutch people not to destroy food supplies which might fall into the hands of German invaders. The broadcast, in the Dutch tongue, specifically warned the Dutch not to heed the advice of British agents who are said to be urging them to burn all food stores.

(CONTINUED ON PAGE THIRTEEN)

ROTTERDAM GIVES UP, SAY NAZIS

By United Press

BERLIN, May 14.—News of the surrender of Rotterdam was broadcast by all German radio stations tonight. The announcement was followed by the song, "We Are Sailing Against England."

By PRESTON GROVER
Associated Press Staff Correspondent

BERLIN, May 14.—Germany reported Dutch resistance officially given up after surrender of the great seaport of Rotterdam tonight, while in Belgium the Reich's thunderous war machine smoothed a bloody path along World War battlefields.

Announcing the fall of Rotterdam, the German high command said the capituation had preserved it from complete destruction by dive bombers and armored forces.

"After the capitulation of Rotterdam, and in view of the imminent threat to the Dutch capital, the Dutch commander has given up his hopeless resistance and given his troops the order to cease fighting," said a supplementary communique.

DNB, official German news

(CONTINUED ON PAGE THIRTEEN)

Weather

Night, Morning Fog to Keep L. A. Cool

"Fair, with night and morning fog . . ."

Such is the weather Angelenos will continue to have through today, tonight and tomorrow, according to Meteorlogist L. H. Daingerfield.

His forecast included "little change in temperature" and "moderate southwest to northwest wind."

Light rain fell along the Oregon coast but none was in sight for this region, Daingerfield said.

The temperature rose today to 80 degrees,

Thousands of Hitler, Allied Planes in Fight

By International News Service

LONDON, May 14.—Using all available planes, the Royal Air Force launched a slashing air offensive against German armies engaged in a fresh Belgian thrust around a corner of the Maginot Line tonight, according to a Reuter dispatch from somewhere in France. German air raids were carried out on northeastern France throughout the day, with many civilian casualties in isolated villages, the dispatch said.

By HENRY C. CASSIDY
Associated Press Staff Correspondent

PARIS, May 14.—The columns of Germany smashed into France today down the historic Meuse valley, tried and trampled path of invasion, and collided in tremendous battle with the French army around Sedan.

Sedan, where Napoleon III gave up his sword to the king of Prussia and the second empire fell in the war of 1870, was emptied by the French.

The Germans, hurtling 60 miles from their own border, through Luxembourg and Belgium, engaged the French (here five words were censored) in a vast new conflict which is being called "the greatest battle of all times in all countries."

Both sides flung tanks, planes, guns and men into furious fighting, for their armies were involved in a life or death struggle.

On the whole front, French dispatches estimated, the Germans are employing between 6000 and 7000 planes.

The main front extends for 100 miles, along the Meuse from the Belgian citadel of Liege through Namur and Dinant, Belgium, to the French fortresses around Sedan (part of France's northern defenses known as "the little Maginot line").

Two German armored divisions, followed by masses of infantry on foot and artillery hauled by tractors, reached the

(CONTINUED ON PAGE TWELVE)

British Claim Nazi Air Losses 4 to 1

By Associated Press

LONDON, May 14.—Lord Beaverbrook, famed newspaper publisher, tonight was appointed Minister for Aircraft Production. Other cabinet appointments announced tonight were Sir John Reith former Minister of Information, to be Minister of Transport, and Dr. Hugh Dalton, Laborite, Minister of Economic Warfare.

By Associated Press

LONDON, May 14.—British fighting pilots were officially announced tonight to have "inflicted on the enemy at least four times the losses they have suffered themselves today."

A communique said that "throughout yesterday and last night our bomber aircraft continued to attack the enemy's road and rail approaches to the Dutch and Belgian battlefields," inflicting considerable damage.

"Vigorous attacks were made on enemy columns along roads in

(CONTINUED ON PAGE ELEVEN)

THE BALTIMORE NEWS-POST
AN INDEPENDENT NEWSPAPER
The Largest Daily Circulation in the Entire South
VOL. CXXXVII.—NO. 26
Entered as second-class matter at Baltimore Postoffice.

TUESDAY EVENING, JUNE 4, 1940
PRICE 3 CENTS
7 HOME FINAL

THE WEATHER

Clear to partly cloudy and continued warm tonight. Wednesday partly cloudy and continued warm.

Detailed Weather Report on Page 30

MEAN TEMPERATURES YESTERDAY

Baltimore	76	Chicago	77
Atlanta	73	Omaha	78
Boston	75	Los Angeles	66
Jacksonville	74	San Antonio	80
New York	74	Salt Lake City	62
Miami	79	Seattle	60
Portland, Maine	65	Tampa	75
Washington	74	New Orleans	78

Asks 68 New Warships For U. S.

335,000 RESCUED CHURCHILL REPORTS

Says Britain Will Keep Fighting

LONDON, June 4—(A. P.).—Prime Minister Churchill, speaking in Commons today, said Britain will carry this war to victory "if necessary for years—if necessary alone," despite the "colossal" defeat in Flanders. "We shall go on to the end," the Prime Minister said. "We shall fight in France. We shall fight on the seas and oceans. We shall fight with growing confidence and growing strength in the air.

"We shall defend our island whatever the cost may be. We shall fight on the beaches. We shall fight on the landing grounds. We shall fight in the fields and streets and in the hills.

"We shall never surrender and even if, which I do not for a moment believe, this island or even a part of it is subjugated and starving, then our empire across seas, armed and guarded by the British fleet, will carry on the struggle until, in God's good name, the New World in all its strength and might sets forth to the rescue and liberation of the Old."

He said the Allies had suffered "a colossal military disaster," that the French Army had been weakened and Belgium lost.

The deliverance of the troops from Dunkerque, he said, was largely due to the work of the Royal Air Force, guarding the 220 light warships and 620 other vessels employed in the work.

Partial text of Prime Minister Churchill's speech will be found on Page 3.

Churchill declared that all the Channel ports now are in German hands and warned Britain that "we must expect another blow to be struck almost immediately at us or at the French."

He said 30,000 men in the B. E. F. had been killed, wounded or are missing, but added proudly that 335,000 Allied troops had been saved from annihilation or capture.

PROMISES OFFENSIVE

Churchill disclosed that the R. A. F. used "part of the main metropolitan fighter strength" assigned to guard London to strike at German bombers and their protecting fighters who were harassing the movement of the troops across the channel.

He told the cheering House that Britain "shall not be content with a defensive war" and said the nation would never surrender and never give up the struggle against German tyranny. He said:

"We will reconstitute and build

Continued on Page 2, Column 1.

IN THE NEWS

WHEN your columnist was new in the newspaper business—indeed new in any business—and as a matter of fact new in life and experience—he was editing the San Francisco Examiner.

There was a very clever, smart writing, smooth talking reporter on the paper who was not new.

He was up to all the tricks of the trade, and there were more tricks in those days than there are now.

At least the tricks were not so well known, and worked more successfully.

One day there was a big bank robbery in San Francisco, and the robbers fled into the interior and hid themselves somewhere.

The police of the city and the constabulary of the State were searching for the fugitives.

The papers were full of news of the pursuit, and speculation as to the whereabouts of the robbers.

YOUR youthful and innocent editor was concentrating his faculties on the situation, when the glib reporter walked into the sanctum.

The reporter was surrounded with an air of mystery.

He said that he had some secret information, the source of which he was not at liberty to reveal, but which he felt sure would enable him to locate the criminals.

All he needed was a few days' time at his own disposal, and a hundred dollars of expense money.

The finances were arranged. The reporter disappeared. Nothing was heard for three days.

Then a telegram was receievd. It read:

"Am on the trail. Send another hundred."

The communication was not entirely satisfactory, but the other hundred was forwarded.

Then another telegram arrived:

"Have a wonderful clue leading right to the hiding place. Send a hundred."

Details sort of seemed to be lacking, but the hundred was dispatched.

FINALLY a third telegram arrived:

"Have fine idea for trapping the whole bunch. Send a hundred."

The hundred was reluctantly relinquished this time, and a note accompanied it saying that the office expected less expenditure and more expedition. Days elapsed.

Some of the office force began to fear that the reporter might have been ambushed by the robbers.

Others were afraid that he had not been.

At last a telegram arrived. It read:

"Plan failed. Have another clue. Am still chasing the robbers. Send a hundred."

The reply said:

"Stop chasing the robbers and chase another job. You're through."

Even an innocent gets wise some time.

CONGRESS, in these days of the New Deal, is a little bit like that innocent editor of long ago.

Mr. Roosevelt, with all respect, is a little bit like that eager and persuasive reporter.

Says Mr. Roosevelt—I have a grand idea for accomplishing this or that or the other. Please appropriate a billion dollars.

Whereupon Congress enthusiastically appropriates the billion.

Nothing is accomplished, but pretty soon Mr. Roosevelt has another wonderful idea which requires another billion.

Great ideas follow each other in quick "concussion," as the fellow said, and billion-dollar appropriations are flying through the air like the golden leaves of autumn.

Seven billion dollars has been appropriated for preparedness, and we have no preparedness.

Sixty billion dollars have been appropriated in eight years for Government expenses and dole and W. P. A. and Farm Relief, and every kind of boon and boondoggling.

What is the result?

Government expenses are still mounting, the deficit is still growing, the debt limit has been reached and raised, the taxes have been enlarged, unemployment is still increasing, farm parity payments are greater than ever before, prosperity is still around the corner—and even the corner is receding farther and

Continued on Page A, Column 7.

Nazis Enter Dunkerque, Capture Fort; Set For Big Land Offensive

BERLIN, June 4—(I. N. S.).—The German Propaganda Ministry admitted today that Allied planes had bombed the outskirts of Munich. A spokesman said:

"Some Allied planes penetrating Southwestern Germany penetrated the outskirts of Munich, but did not reach the city proper. Damage and casualties are not known at present."

BERLIN, June 4—(A. P.).—Nazi troops have entered Dunkerque and captured one of its forts, the German High Command reported today, as the Nazi airforce, back from an "experimental" bombing of the Paris region, waited orders to strike again—in conjunction with a great land offensive which most Germans expect to start in the West any day.

Puncture of the Allied rear guard defending the withdrawal from the German pocket in Flanders was achieved in hard fighting, the High Command acknowledged.

Four hundred Allied warplanes were destroyed in hangars and on the ground in addition to 79 shot down by Nazi fliers yesterday, its communique declared, acknowledging that "nine of our own machines are missing."

NEARING THE END

The high command said the fighting for Dunkerque, the Allies' exit from the German trap in Flanders, was nearing its end.

Nazi troops, it said, penetrated the city and took Fort Louis after hand-to-hand fighting.

French troops, it acknowledged, still are resisting from house to house to protect the debarkation of remnants of the Allied forces withdrawing from Northern France.

The Nazi bombing forays yesterday surprised the base of the French air force around Paris. The communique said:

"They succeeded in eliminating the enemy air defense and, in attacks at high and low altitudes, they obtained the strongest effect on ports and industrial establishments of the French air force.

NUMEROUS FIRES

"Numerous fires and explosions were observed.

"In air fights 104 airplanes were shot down and between 300 and 400 machines were destroyed in sheds and on the ground.

"Our anti-aircraft shot down 21 machines on June 3.

"Despite these extraordinary successes only nine of our machines are missing."

The high command said Allied planes repeated night raids last night in Holland, Western and Southern Germany with success "just as small as hitherto."

SEEKS U. S. NEUTRALITY

While getting set for the next blow, Germany took extraordinary steps in an effort to convince the United States that she has no desire to see the Western Hemisphere involved in the war, and that she is taking unusual measures to avoid even accidental affront to America.

The Foreign Office formally

Continued on Page 2, Column 6.

8 Face Paris Death Penalty

PARIS, June 4—(A. P.).—Eight persons charged with espionage—one of them a woman—face the possibility of the death penalty at a secret military tribunal trial opening today. In another spy case, Marcel Veiry was sentenced today to death by a military tribunal at Bescanon, near the Swiss border. Veiry's home was Geneva.

Leopold Tells Roosevelt Of Capitulation

By LOUIS P. LOCHNER

WITH THE GERMAN ARMY, June 4—(A. P.).—John Cudahy, United States Ambassador to Belgium, disclosed today that President Roosevelt, from a personal letter written him by King Leopold III. of the Belgians, knows the inside story of the King's capitulation to the Germans.

Cudahy visited Leopold Sunday for two hours at the castle assigned him by the German Army.

Here the defeated King handed Cudahy the letter for President Roosevelt in which the monarch told his side of the story.

Cudahy declined to comment on the letter or the status of King Leopold. The American Ambassador is out of touch with the world, living on an island as it were. He has contact with neither Washington nor Berlin.

Still, he sticks to his post for he feels he has big work to do with the Red Cross.

Realizing that Leopold's dramatic

Continued on Page A, Column 1.

SIR ARNOLD MISSING

LONDON, June 4—(A. P.).—Sir Arnold Wilson, a member of Parliament serving as a machine-gunner with the Royal Air Force, was reported missing today.

Roosevelt Asks Funds To Start Work On 68 New Naval Vessels

WASHINGTON, June 4—(A. P.).—President Roosevelt asked Congress today for funds to start 68 new naval vessels in submitting a defense request for $1,277,741,170 for both the Army and Navy. The vessels included three aircraft carriers, 13 cruisers, 22 submarines and 30 destroyers.

WASHINGTON, June 4—(A. P.).—Secretary Hull announced today that "I heartily approve" a resolution declaring the United States would not recognize or acquiesce in transfer of any Western Hemisphere region from one non-American Power to another.

The Secretary of State made the statement in a letter to Chairman Bloom (Democrat) of New York, of the House Foreign Affairs Committee. Bloom made the letter public after the committee had discussed the resolution for two hours without taking action. Said Hull:

"The proposed resolution is based squarely upon the idea of full respect for established sovereignties. It would not interfere in any way with continuance of equality of commerce and trade for all nations of the world in their relations with the countries of the American continents."

U. S. DISAPPROVES

The resolution in effect would declare that the United States officially disapproved any change in the status of Western Hemisphere nations or depencies as a result of the European war.

Hull said that this Government "must necessarily insist" that possessions of European nations in the Western Hemisphere shall not become the "subject of barter or conquest between rival European powers or be made the scene of the settlement of European difficulties."

The House Committee was called together to approve the bill quickly today. Even befort it met Repre-

Continued on Page A, Column 3.

Duce Backs New War Measures

NEW YORK, June 4—(A. P.).—The Italian Line today began placing advertisements listing a revised schedule of sailings from New York to Italy. The Rex, largest ship in the Italian merchant marine, is scheduled to leave New York June 22 and other sailings were listed for June 29, July 6 and July 13.

ROME, June 4—(A. P.).—Speculation on the date of Italy's plunge into war ranged today from the end of this week to the end of June as Premier Mussolini's Cabinet stamped an okay on undisclosed plans for war.

One source close to the Government said no move to step into the conflict was likely in the immediate future.

But Italy made ready.

In an anxiously awaited 90-minute session, with Il Duce presiding, the ministers moved to extend war preparations to Italy's African empire, to strengthen the navy and tighten discipline in the war industries.

But Italy's position as a nonbelligerent ally of Germany remained unchanged by the meeting, to which the world had looked for days for a clue to Il Duce's next move.

The measure dealing with war industries provided punishment for infractions of discipline which would interfere with output.

The Cabinet voted additional funds for warship construction, but the amount was not disclosed.

Provision also was made for the admission of more student officers to the Royal Naval Academy.

Regulations restricting the em-

Continued on Page 2, Column 3.

IN THE NEWS-POST TODAY

Allies Leave Only Ruins For Nazis

BERLIN, June 4—(I. N. S.).—The huge fortress at Dunkerque was captured by the German Army after a hard battle with the Allied troops, the German high command announced today. Forty thousand Allied prisoners were captured, the high command said.

PARIS, June 4—(A. P.).—Fires were started by incendiary bombs in the French port of Le Havre as Germans repeated their air raids there last night and this morning.

PARIS, June 4—(A. P.).—Allied forces entrenched in shell-battered Dunkerque have destroyed all war material which cannot be removed, a semi-official news agency reported today. The report added:

All other ports along the French-Belgian coast, the agency added, had been "rendered unusuable" before the departure of the Allied troops.

The entrance to Nieuport harbor was cited as an example. Here

Continued on Page 2, Column 8.

Temperatures

Midnight,	73	7 A. M.,	74
1 A. M.,	73	8 A. M.,	80
2 A. M.,	72	9 A. M.,	85
3 A. M.,	72	10 A. M.,	88
4 A. M.,	71	11 A. M.,	89
5 A. M.,	70	12 Noon,	90
6 A. M.,	70	1 P. M.,	91

VERY LATEST NEWS

(Race Results from Howard Sports Daily, Inc.)

GERMANS REPORT RHONE VALLEY AIR RAID

BERN, Switzerland, June 4—(A. P.).—German warplanes were reported today to have repeated their air raids on the Rhone Valley in Southern France.

AT BELMONT

First—Black One, $6.90, $3.40, $3.00; Take Wing, $3.50 $3.50; Sea Fever, $10.20.

AT SUFFOLK DOWNS

First—Kleig Light, $20.00, $5.20, $3.60; Izarra, $3.20, $2.60; Machillinda, $3.40.

LEAVING DUNKIRK: "OUT OF THE JAWS OF DEATH"

THE EMBARCATION FROM THE DUNES.—The remarkable achievement in bringing nearly 335,000 British and French troops away from Dunkirk under conditions of appalling difficulty was described by Mr. Churchill yesterday. Various aspects of the embarcation are illustrated on this page, and some of the pictures indicate clearly the hazardous nature of the work involved. That above was taken specially for *The Times* from a British destroyer engaged in the work of rescue, and shows troops on the sands at Bray Dunes waiting to be taken away.

BOARDING A DESTROYER.—Troops of the British Expeditionary Force on the pier at Dunkirk just about to board a destroyer.

REACHING A DESTROYER.—Whalers drawn by a motor-boat reaching a destroyer. The other picture, specially taken for *The Times* from a destroyer, is of remarkable interest. It shows troops making their way along the pier at Dunkirk to embark, and some troops on board with a machine-gun ready for any attack from the air.

WAITING ON THE DUNES.—British troops on a beach near Dunkirk forming into long winding queues ready to take their turn to board small boats which took them to larger vessels. The marvellous work of all three Services and, indeed, every one engaged in the embarcation was described by the Prime Minister.

BROADCASTING

A SYMPHONY CONCERT

The last of the B.B.C. Symphony Orchestra's summer concerts conducted by Sir Adrian Boult, which will include Beethoven's "Eroica," will be broadcast to-night at 8 o'clock. Listeners to the Forces programme at 5.20 will hear on records some favourite songs of Miss Florrie Ford as a tribute to her memory.

HOME SERVICE

(767kc.) (391.1m.) and (668kc.) (449.1m.).

6.45 a.m., News in Norwegian. **7**, Time; News. **7.15**, Donald Thorne (organ). **7.30**, Physical exercises. **7.50**, Interlude. **7.55**, A thought for to-day. **8**, Time; News. **8.15**, Harold Bradbury (tenor) and Vivian Joseph (cello). **8.45**, B.B.C. Salon Orchestra. **9.15**, Orchestral Concert. **9.55**, At Home To-day. **10.15**, Time; Daily Service. **10.30**, Records. **11**, Schools: Music and Movement for juniors (ages 7-9). **11.20**, Current Affairs (ages 13 and over). **11.40**, For Home listening (ages 7-12). **12**, Town and Country: a Northern Notebook. **12.20**, Orchestral Concert. **1**, Time; News. **1.15**, Sandy Macpherson (organ). **1.35**, Boulevard Players. **2**, Schools: Music-Making (ages 9-15). **2.15**, Interlude. **2.20**, Biology (ages 11-15). **2.35**, Interlude. **2.40**, Junior English (ages 9-12). **3**, B.B.C. Theatre Orchestra. **3.30**, Smetana: Quartet in E minor, played by the Stratton String Quartet. **4**, Shades of the Past: A radio comedy by E. Eynon Evans. **4.30**, Jack Payne with his Band. **5**, News and a studio service in Welsh. **5.20**, Children's Hour. **6**, Time; News. **6.15**, Accent on Rhythm, presented by James Moody with Three in Harmony. **6.30**, News in Norwegian. **6.45**, The World Goes By. **7.15**, Announcements. **7.30**, Danger—Men still at work. **8**, Symphony Concert, Part 2—from the closing programme of a series of summer concerts: the B.B.C. Symphony Orchestra, conductor, Sir Adrian Boult. **9**, Time: News. **9.20**, To-night's Talk. **9.35**, B.B.C. Military Band. **10**, Radio Party Night at a South-Coast hotel. **10.30**, A Gaelic musical programme. **11**, Ambrose and his Orchestra. **11.40**, John Amadio (flute) and John Ticehurst (harpsichord). **12**, Time; News. **12.20-12.30 a.m.**, News in Norwegian.

PROGRAMME FOR THE FORCES

11 a.m. to 10 p.m. (804kc.) (373.1m.); 10 p.m. to 11 p.m. (877kc.) (342.1m.)

6.15 a.m., Gramophone. **7**, News. **7.15**, Donald Thorne (organ). **7.30**, Gramophone. **10.58**, Bow Bells. **11**, Time: followed by Tom Jenkins (organ). **11.30**, The Coventry Hippodrome Orchestra. **12**, Variety. **12.30**, Melody and Co. (a recording). **1**, Time; Foreign Languages Bulletin. **1.15**, Home Service. **1.35**, The Central Band of the Royal Air Force. **2.15**, Records. **3**, Home Service. **3.30**, Records. **4.10**, Six Folk Songs arranged by Holst. **4.30**, Home Service. **5**, Time; Brain-Teasers: North Wales v. the rest. **5.20**, Down at the Old Bull and Bush: A tribute to the memory of Florrie Forde—records of some of her favourite songs. **5.40**, Parlez-vous Français? Bill and Bob Somewhere in France. **6**, Foreign Languages Bulletin. **6.30**, What's Yours? Winifred Davey and Ruby Taylor (piano). **6.45**, Home Service. **7.15**, Top of the Bill. Claude Dampier, assisted by Billie Carlyle. **7.30**, Home Service. **8**, For the Australian Forces. **8.20**, Variety. **9**, Foreign Languages Bulletin. **9.15**, What's On To-morrow? **9.20** Harry Jacobson (piano). **9.30**, A Reading by Eric Gillett. **9.35**, Home Service. **10**, Time; Home Service. **10.30**, Records. **11 p.m.-12.20 a.m.**, Home Service.

NEWS IN ENGLISH FROM ABROAD

Note.—Times of transmission are B.S.T., and are p.m. unless otherwise indicated.

Radio-Paris (1,648m.), 10.15. **Rome** (420.8m.) and **Milan** (368.6m.), 7.28 and 12.30 a.m. **Budapest** (549.5m.), 11.10. **Bucharest** (364.5m.), 10.55. **L'Ile de France** (249.2m.), 6.45, 9.15, and 10.45. **Moscow** (1,744m.), 11. **Schenectady** (19.56m.), and (31.48m.), 9.55. **Ankara** (19.74m.), 1.15.

THE ESTATE MARKET

NOTTINGHAM LAND

Next Monday in Nottingham Messrs. John D. Wood and Co. (Berkeley Square) and Messrs. Bernard Thorpe and Partners (Westminster) will offer Bestwood Lodge and 3,485 acres. Portions that are let produce £3,340 a year. If Bestwood is not sold as a whole the lots will include 15 large farms, 900 acres within Nottingham City boundary, and a vast quantity of matured timber.

In less than a week after instructions Messrs. James Styles and Whitlock have sold Pipers, a sixteenth-century house at Whitchurch, near Aylesbury. "Maister" John Shorne, rector of the parish in 1290, was credited with a saintly power of curing ague, which, according to the "Fantaisie of Idolatrie," quoted by Foxe, "he jugeleth with a bote." Shorne's shrine was a place of pilgrimage, and Heywood mentions him in a sixteenth-century poem as being commemorated at Canterbury, and another old rhyming allusion shows that Shorne "conjured the Devil into a boot." In 1478 the shrine was moved to Windsor.

Mr. S. R. J. Gorringe (Clifford Street) has bought for a client The Dower House and 38 acres at Heythrop, Messrs. James Styles and Whitlock acting for the vendor.

AUCTIONS TO-DAY

REAL ESTATE, REVERSIONS, &c.

Auctioneers	Place of Sale
Messrs. E. Owers	The Mart
Spencer and Kent	Dulwich

FURNITURE, WORKS OF ART, &c.

Auctioneers	Place of Sale
H. Butcher and Co.	Leicester
Christie, Manson and Woods	King Street, S.W.
Sotheby and Co.	New Bond Street
Robinson and Foster ..	King Street, S.W.

ST. JOHN AMBULANCE BRIGADE

The annual report of the St. John Ambulance Brigade for the year 1939, just issued by the Brigade Chief Commissioner, Major-General Sir John Duncan, shows that the number of members of the Brigade rose during the year to 121,308, an increase of 31,563. The number of new brigade units formed was 298, making a total of 2,831 units.

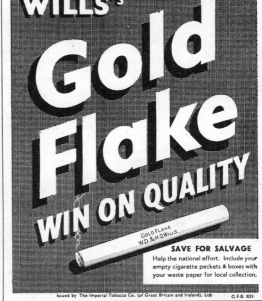

THE TIMES CROSSWORD PUZZLE No. 3,209

ACROSS

1 Stable selection, originally (two words) (7, 6).
8, 9 The Knight of Lyonesse with a mixed drink becomes a famous novel (two words) (8, 6).
10 Vessel with a cargo of timber often grilled (6).
11 Score, Sir (anag.) (8).
12 "A supremely ridiculous person" (S.O.E.D.) (6).
14, 16 The Grantly girls (two words) (8, 8).
18 Coypu's coat (6).
20 Evidently not a panacea (8).
23 Shylock took much interest in them (6).
24 Less valuable than wisdom (6).
25 Content's approved? Not in his case (8).
26 Norman stronghold, but by no means a ruin (three words) (4, 2, 7).

DOWN

1 He gets it clear afterwards, but in the wrong order (9).
2 Not for those who desire a "place in the sun" (7).
3 The perfume of lace (5).
4 A sum on account (5).
5 "Thou foster-child of Silence and slow Time, Sylvan ——" (Keats) (9).
6 Do fanciers? (7).
7 Kirkwood, perhaps (5).
13 An announcement may be made by means of it (9).
14 Depart this way (3).
15 A kind of timber flotation (9).
17 Rumpus (7).
19 "While you sat and played ——s, stately at the clavichord" (Browning) (7).
21 It's exactly the sound (5).
22 This bird should have no difficulty in picking things up (5).
23 Tennyson's echoes were three times (5).

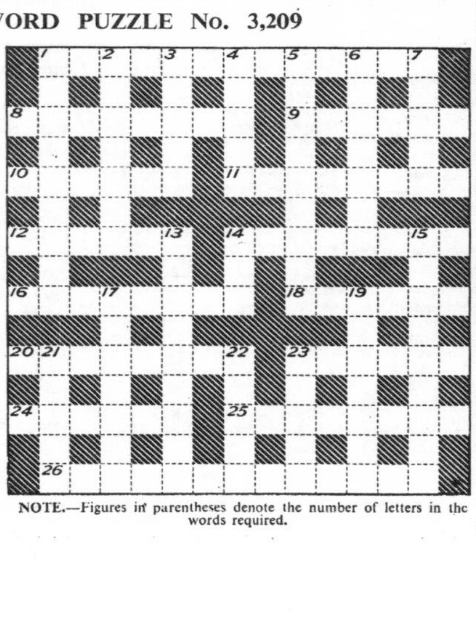

NOTE.—Figures in parentheses denote the number of letters in the words required.

SOLUTION OF PUZZLE No. 3,208

COMRADES IN ARMS.—French troops from the Army commanded by General Prioux, who fought gallantly in the region of Dunkirk, seen on their arrival at a British port yesterday.

THE BALTIMORE NEWS-POST
AN INDEPENDENT NEWSPAPER
The Largest Daily Circulation in the Entire South

VOL. CXXXVII.—NO. 26 · Entered as second-class matter at Baltimore Postoffice. · WEDNESDAY, JUNE 5, 1940 · PRICE 3 CENTS

THE WEATHER
Showers to partly cloudy today; clear tomorrow.

The Only Newspaper in Maryland with both the Associated Press and International News Service.

COMPLETE MARKETS

Broadcast From Hitler's Camp Hails Flanders Victory

BERLIN, June 4—(I. N. S.).—The Berlin radio tonight carried a broadcast from Adolf Hitler's headquarters stating the battle of Flanders has been completed. The German High Command termed the action which started on May 10 as constituting the "greatest military victory of all time."

CHURCHILL HINTS BRITISH OFFENSIVE

BERN, Switzerland, June 4—A. P.).—The Swiss high command announced today that "two or three" German planes were believed to have been shot down by fighters in an air battle over the Swiss Jura mountains in which one Swiss plane was brought down and its pilot killed.

BERLIN, June 4—(A. P.).—Ominous suggestions of new German operations—perhaps a thrust toward Paris from the Somme front—were heard tonight along with claims that the Nazis had captured Dunkerque and 40,000 prisoners and destroyed between 400 and 500 French war planes yesterday around Paris.

The announcement of the fall of Dunkerque—the last Allied stronghold in the north and the Channel port through which their fleeing armies had streamed for days in the historic retreat from Flanders—was accompanied by the jubilant observation that now the entire French and Belgian Channel coast clear down to the Somme estuary was in German control.

(The French said they had abandoned Dunkerque.)

It was the smashing end of a campaign which the Germans claimed brought them nearly 400,000 prisoners, sent the British Expeditionary Force back to Dover and broke off the spear point of the Allied defense by the destruction of massed mechanized forces

A preliminary tabulation had declared 330,000 prisoners were taken before the fall of Dunkerque.

But even more portentious than this substantial end to the long and bloody battle of Flanders was the High Command declaration that yesterday's raids over the Paris area had "succeeded in eliminating the enemy air defense," and that 104 French planes had been shot down in the skies and between 300 and 400 destroyed in sheds and on the ground.

RAID MERE "OVERTURE"

It is a familiar German strategy to insure air control before beginning any vast ground movement

Continued on Page 2, Column 6.

PARIS, June 4—(A. P.).—French war planes today carried out "retaliatory" raids on air fields and industrial areas in Munich and Frankfurt, it was officially stated tonight. British planes bombed stations and refineries in the Ruhr, it was said. Official statements declared that 25 German planes were brought down during yesterday's Nazi air raid on Paris.

LONDON, June 4—(A. P.).—Winston Churchill today gave the British Commons and people the measure of defeat and the epic of rescue for the Allied armies in Flanders and, with blunt imagery, held out hope of help from "the new world," or America, if Britain is broken by invasion.

With the plainest language, the Prime Minister, in a long war statement to the House of Commons, pledged the nation to fight on "alone if necessary," even from her Empire outposts, and declared the British Government would never content itself with a defensive war on Germany.

The heaviest blows are yet to come from the conquerors of the lowlands, he warned. They may come, he said, "almost immediately."

Point by point Churchill told the story of the German Army sweep—like a "sharp scythe"—around the Allied forces of Flanders; how the Belgian surrender isolated them and how a lost garrison of 4,000 men spurned an ultimatum to capitulate and fought to the death in Calais.

335,000 RESCUED

He gave the British losses in Flanders as more than 30,000 dead, wounded or missing; he estimated the Allied rescued, by the heroic work of an armada of a thousand boats, big and little, as more than 335,000.

A week ago, he and other "good judges" thought only 20,000 or 30,000 men could be saved from the German Army, its gun and its bombers, he said.

With the Flanders battle and the rescue ended, Belgium and her army lost and the continent's channel ports in the invader's hands, Churchill told the Commons:

"There is always a chance of invasion. We shall defend our island whatever the cost may be. We shall fight on the beaches, the landing grounds, in the fields, in the streets and on the hills."

"We shall never surrender.

LOOKS TO 'NEW WORLD'

"And even if, which I do not for a moment believe, this island or a large part of it were subjugated and starving, then our empire beyond the seas, armed and guarded by the British fleet, will carry on its struggle until, in God's good time, the new world with all its power and might sets forth to the liberation and the rescue of the old."

He solemnly warned the British against over-evaluating the brilli-

Continued on Page 2, Column 1.

British Planes Raid German Arms Plants

LONDON, June 4—(A. P.).—Attacks by Royal Air Force bombers on munitions works at Mannheim, Germany, and on German troops advancing into Dunkerque and Nazi batteries shelling the port last night were announced today by the Air Ministry.

In the Mannheim region, it was said, hundreds of incendiary bombs were dropped and at many points in the industrial Ruhr Valley fuel plants, oil tanks and munitions works were successfully bombed.

WIDE AREA COVERED

The captain of the last British air craft over one area said that when he arrived on the scene the whole place was "a mass of flames."

The German area covered by the raiders, the ministry said, "extended from Emmerich in the north to Frankfort in the south," including "industrial targets and communication centers."

Strong opposition was encountered from "guns of light and heavy caliber, all working in close co-operation with searchlights."

REFINERIES ATTACKED

In Germany, it said, refineries, oil tanks, supply depots and freight yards in the Ruhr Valley, in Rhenish Prussia and in the neighborhood of Frankfort were among the military objectives attacked.

German air bases were attacked also in northwest Germany and Holland, it said.

Roosevelt Asks 68 New Warships

WASHINGTON, June 4—(A. P.). The Senate approved legislation today authorizing expansion of the naval air force to 10,000 planes, manned by 16,000 pilots, and providing for the establishment of a defensive ring of naval air bases around the United States.

WASHINGTON, June 4—(A. P.). Congressional tax leaders were reported authoritatively today to be considering a boost in the pending tax bill to more than $1,000,000,000. One method proposed was broadening the income-tax base and increasing the rates on incomes below $60,000.

The pending tax bill, estimated to raise $656,000,000, would increase income taxes by a flat 10 per cent. and would boost most excise taxes.

WASHINGTON, June 4—(A. P.). President Roosevelt asked Congress today for funds to start 68 new naval vessels in submitting a

Continued on Page A, Column 4.

Allies Leave 'Wrecked' Dunkerque

PARIS, June 4—(A. P.).—Fires were started by incendiary bombs in the French port of Le Havre as Germans repeated their air raids there last night and this morning.

PARIS, June 4—(A. P.).—The French Admiralty announced tonight that the last Allied naval and army units had abandoned Dunkerque, leaving the city entirely to the Germans after destroying all supplies.

It admitted that seven French destroyers and a supply ship were lost carrying out the embarkation

Continued on Page 2, Column 8.

Temperatures

Midnight,	73	9 A. M.,	85
1 A. M.,	73	10 A. M.,	88
2 A. M.,	72	11 A. M.,	89
3 A. M.,	72	12 Noon,	90
4 A. M.,	71	1 P. M.,	92
5 A. M.,	70	2 P. M.,	94
6 A. M.,	70	3 P. M.,	89
7 A. M.,	74	4 P. M.,	89
8 A. M.,	80	5 P. M.,	86

Youths March In Spain, Cry For Gibraltar

MADRID, June 4—(I. N. S.).—Anti-Allied sentiment in Spain took another spurt today following large student demonstrations in Barcelona.

The students marched through the streets shouting:

"Gibraltar is Spanish!"

Other demonstrations occurred in other sections of the country.

Wilson Wins Iowa GOP Primary Race

DES MOINES, Ia., June 4—(A. P.).—On the basis of unofficial returns, Gov. George A. Wilson today had won renomination over two opponents in the Republican party's largest Iowa primary turnout in the last six years.

STILL ON SHERIFF'S FARM

SPARTA, N. C., June 4—(A. P.). Sheriff Dewitt Bryan found a large moonshine still in operation on his own farm.

"I was never so surprised in all my life," said the sheriff.

London-Portugal Air Service Begun

LONDON, June 4—(A. P.).—Twice weekly air-mail and passenger service from London to Lisbon, Portugal, was begun today by British Overseas Airways to connect with Pan-American Airway's flights to New York.

LOWER DANUBE FLOODS

BUCHAREST, June 4—(A. P.).—The lower Danube flooded today with heavy loss of life. Homes were swept away and villages inundated.

Delaware Results

FIRST—Five furlongs. Off at 2.06½. Time, 1.01 3-5.

aBright Arc, 116 (J. Wagner)	$11.20	$5.30	$3.90
Cherriko, 113 (A. Shelhamer)		14.70	10.10
Cut Off, 118 (R. Donoso)			7.60

Also Ran—Canterlin, Weatherite, Pops Sister, Rodalma, Merwick, Rose B., aAbbots Maid, Goober Lad and Buckle Up.
aSalubria Stable and H. P. Metcalf entry.

SECOND—Six furlongs. Off at 2.40½. Time, 1.15 1-5.

Circus Wings, 108 (E. Smith)	$24.70	$10.50	$5.50

Continued on Page 27, Column 3.

$975,650,000 For WPA Is Approved

WASHINGTON, June 4—(A. P.). A $975,650,000 fund for the WPA was approved today by a Senate Appropriations Subcommittee after it had attached provisions for training thousands of CCC youths in noncombatant national defense activities.

English Baronet Killed In Action

LONDON, June 4—(A. P.).—Sir Marmaduke Blennerhasset, thirty-seven-year-old Lieutenant of the Royal Naval Volunteer Reserve, has been killed in action, it was announced today. A nine-day-old son succeeds to the baronetcy.

Leopold Asserts Allies Failed Him

BRUSSELS, June 4—(I. N. S.).—Described as "heartbroken" over criticism in the United States of his surrender, King Leopold of Belgium sent an emissary to American correspondents in Brussels today to describe the events leading up to his capitulation.

The full story, according to the version given out in this capital, which is now under German control, is as follows:

On May 10 King Leopold presided at a war council meeting at which British Commander Lord Gort, French General Betolle and Belgian Commander-in-Chief Gen.

Continued on Page A, Column 1.

IN THE NEWS

WHEN your columnist was new in the newspaper business—indeed new in any business—and as a matter of fact new in life and experience—he was editing the San Francisco Examiner.

There was a very clever, smart writing, smooth talking reporter on the paper who was not new.

He was up to all the tricks of the trade, and there were more tricks in those days than there are now.

At least the tricks were not so well known, and worked more successfully.

One day there was a big bank robbery in San Francisco, and the robbers fled into the interior and hid themselves somewhere.

The police of the city and the constabulary of the State were searching for the fugitives.

The papers were full of news of the pursuit, and speculation as to the whereabouts of the robbers.

YOUR youthful and innocent editor was concentrating his faculties on the situation, when the glib reporter walked into the sanctum.

The reporter was surrounded with an air of mystery.

He said that he had some secret information, the source of which he was not at liberty to reveal, but which he felt sure would enable him to locate the criminals.

All he needed was a few days' time at his own disposal, and a hundred dollars of expense money.

The finances were arranged. The reporter disappeared. Nothing was heard for three days.

Then a telegram was receievd. It read:

"Am on the trail. Send another hundred."

The communication was not entirely satisfactory, but the other hundred was forwarded.

Then another telegram arrived:

"Have a wonderful clue leading right to the hiding place. Send a hundred."

Details sort of seemed to be lacking, but the hundred was dispatched.

FINALLY a third telegram arrived:

"Have fine idea for trapping the whole bunch. Send a hundred."

The hundred was reluctantly relinquished this time, and a note accompanied it saying that the office expected less expenditure and more expedition. Days elapsed.

Some of the office force began to fear that the reporter might have been ambushed by the robbers.

Others were afraid that he had not been.

At last a telegram arrived. It read:

"Plan failed. Have another clue. Am still chasing the robbers. Send a hundred."

The reply said:

"Stop chasing the robbers and chase another job. You're through."

Even an innocent gets wise some time.

CONGRESS, in these days of the New Deal, is a little bit like that innocent editor of long ago.

Mr. Roosevelt, with all respect, is a little bit like that eager and persuasive reporter.

Says Mr. Roosevelt—I have a grand idea for accomplishing this or that or the other. Please appropriate a billion dollars.

Whereupon Congress enthusiastically appropriates the billion.

Nothing is accomplished, but pretty soon Mr. Roosevelt has another wonderful idea which requires another billion.

Great ideas follow each other in quick "concussion," as the fellow said, and billion-dollar appropriations are flying through the air like the golden leaves of autumn.

Seven billion dollars has been appropriated for preparedness, and we have no preparedness.

Sixty billion dollars have been appropriated in eight years for Government expenses and dole and W. P. A. and Farm Relief, and every kind of boon and boondoggling.

What is the result?

Government expenses are still mounting, the deficit is still growing, the debt limit has been reached and raised, the taxes have been enlarged, unemployment is still increasing, farm parity payments are greater than ever before, prosperity is still around the corner—and even the corner is receding farther and

Continued on Page A, Column 7.

THE BALTIMORE NEWS-POST
AN INDEPENDENT NEWSPAPER
The Largest Daily Circulation in the Entire South
VOL. CXXXVII.—NO. 27
Entered as second-class matter at Baltimore Postoffice.

WEDNESDAY EVENING, JUNE 5, 1940
PRICE 3 CENTS
NIGHT
Wall St. Opening

HITLER OPENS NEW OFFENSIVE

Launches Army Against French On 200-Mile Front

BERLIN, June 5—(A. P.).—Adolf Hitler at dawn today sent his armies of the west plunging against France on the Somme-Aisne line to teach an "historic lesson" to the Allies, as the Fuehrer said, and speed "the bloom of a new and better world." Said Hitler's high command: "In the early morning hours today new attack operations began from the present defense front in France."

This second phase of Germany's "total war" in the west—following closely upon the Allied disaster in Flanders—transformed a nearly 200-mile section of Northern France, from the Channel coast to the shattered junction of the Maginot Line with its northern extension, into one great field of raging combat.

The high command said that Allied attacks at either extreme of the Somme-Aisne line, near Abbeville on the coast, and south of Longwy, near the junction of the French, Belgian and Luxembourg frontiers, had been repulsed.

The daily communique said:

"Near Abbeville an enemy attack using strong artillery and tanks was repelled.

"Similarly, an attack on our fighting vanguard south of Longwy foundered with heavy losses for the enemy."

The communique said that German airmen "successfully attacked enemy concentrations south of Abbeville" and mentioned yesterday's aerial assault on the French port city of Le Havre, now perhaps the most vital contact between Great Britain and France.

LE HAVRE PORT ATTACKED

The port facilities at Le Havre, said the high command, were attacked by fighting and power-diving bomber units of the air arm.

Occupation of the Netherlands, Luxembourg, Belgium and about 10,000 square miles of Northern France since the "total war" was launched May 10 had freed Nazi legions for what Germans hope may be the final phase of the war.

'PLUTOCRATIC RULERS'

Hitler today proclaimed his "boundless" confidence in German armed forces and asserted that German victory would answer "the plutocratic rulers of England and France," who, the Fuehrer said, have pledged each other to avoid with all means the bloom of a new and better world . . . Hitler declared:

"Our victory will be their historic lesson."

HEAVY FIGHTING

Authorized spokesmen were reserved about the new offensive. They intimated it might be several days before details are forthcoming. This has been the high command's policy.

That heavy fighting was under

Continued on Page 2, Column 1.

Nazis Launch Big Paris Drive

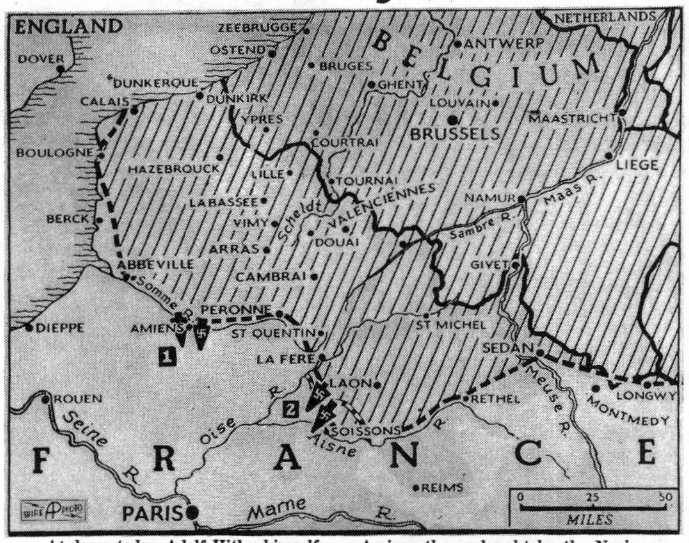

At dawn today Adolf Hitler himself, from his Western Front headquarters, touched off the long-awaited German drive on Paris. The drive began with a furious artillery barrage along French lines on the Somme-Aisne front. Then came an aerial and land attack along 125 miles of the Somme-Aisne front, from the English Channel to Laon. (1) At Amiens the onslaught by the Nazis was particularly heavy. (2) Another heavy blow was directed toward Paris in the Laon-Soissons area. The latter city is but 58 miles from the French capital. Concentration of heavy attack at these points indicates possible formation of twin Nazi columns, to be used in a "pincers" movement on Paris.

IN THE NEWS

Of course this great and once rich, this extensive and potentially powerful United States of America ought to be armed and prepared against possible hostile attack.

What is more, the next time it becomes properly prepared to defend itself against invasion and to dominate all approaches along the open highway of the sea, it should STAY PREPARED.

As everybody now knows, we were fully prepared for defense in 1922.

We had disbanded our armies in 1918. We had no further use for them.

But we possessed the greatest and finest Navy in the world and we had every use and need for that supreme Navy.

We had and have two lengthy coasts to protect—in fact, three coasts if we consider the Gulf of Mexico on the south.

This great Gulf Coast is not to be lightly regarded or disregarded. It embraces the shores of Florida, Alabama, Mississippi, Louisiana and Texas, and the extremely important eastern or rather northern entrance to the Panama canal.

Control of the Gulf of Mexico also includes protection of the mouth of the Mississippi, a waterway leading to the vital heart of the interior of the country—and together with its immense tributaries, the Ohio and Missouri rivers, contacting by navigable waters many of the most important interior States of the Union.

As FOR our West Coast, we were and are always subject to possible attack there by Japan or Russia—more likely by Japan, of course, but in present day complications possibly by Russia—or conceivably by both Japan and Russia.

We have the rich coasts of California and Oregon and Washington to protect on this Pacific side of the continent.

We also have the wholly unprotected shores of Alaska and the Aleutian Islands, which, while not of commensurate value, are nevertheless American territory.

They deserve full protection not only on that account but because of their very real danger as bases for hostile attack on the rest of the country should they fall into enemy hands.

These Northwestern shores are only a few miles from Siberian territory and indeed only a few more miles from Japan.

We have no adequate defenses on the Pacific Coast of any kind.

We have in the Pacific no sufficient bases for sea warfare except Hawaii.

The Philippines, which would offer the most effective menace to the home bases and the communications of any Oriental power conducting an offensive against the United States, are practically unfortified, unprotected and unprepared.

In fact, it is part of the suicidal policy of our Government to surrender these islands within a few years, ostensibly to the natives but actually to Japan.

On the East Coast we have as a more or less perpetual danger the constantly recurring wars in Europe.

There is practically never a time when the ambitions of Germany or Austria or Russia or France or Italy do not lead to an attempt to dominate Europe.

In this conflict England is frequently enmeshed.

The danger is consequently real on all three coasts if conflict reaches our shores.

And the need for a great Navy, —a two-coast Navy — a three-coast Navy—is conspicuously apparent.

After the World War we had such a supreme Navy.

In 1922 we scuttled a large and important part of it.

About twenty-five per cent. of our Navy was destroyed.

We agreed to scrap some 750,000 tons of ships, including many of our best and latest battleships.

We also agreed by treaty not to construct any new capital ships—a provision of the Treaty of London which we kept and which the other contracting parties to the treaty did not keep.

The cost of the twenty-six battleships which we destroyed was four hundred million dollars, and the scrapped vessels included some of the best and newest battleships in the fleet.

PERHAPS the best way to secure an accurate estimate of what destruction actually oc-

Continued on Page 4, Column 1.

German Offensive Along Aisne-Somme, Reports Paris; Centers In Amiens

PARIS, June 5—(A. P.).—An air raid alarm sounded in the West Central region of France at 2 P. M. today (8 A. M., E. S. T.). There was no immediate word of any air attacks, however.

PARIS, June 5—(A. P.).—Supported by heavy artillery and dive-bombing planes, Germany launched a great offensive against France's newly fortified Somme-Aisne front today on a 125-mile front extending eastward from the English Channel. The new battle began with a violent artillery bombardment of the French lines.

Under cover of the barrage, masses of infantry moved forward to the attack as the Nazi air force roared overhead, bombing and strafing.

The heaviest attacks were launched in the region of Amiens and along the Ailette Canal below the World War battle ground of Chemin Des Dames.

There were no immediate reports on the progress of the fighting. Semi-official French sources said merely:

"The battle is continuing. Actually there are no details."

The attack came in blitzkrieg fashion less than 24 hours after the fall of Dunkerque, which signalized the end of the great battle in Flanders and left the Germans in complete control of Holland, Belgium and some 10,000 square miles of northern France.

First reports indicated the German offensive, apparently aimed directly at Paris, was confined entirely to the Somme-Aisne front, which the French have been hastening to fortify.

East of Laon, on the eastern flank of the new battle line, and along the Maginot Line no unusual activity was reported.

CENTER AT AMIENS

The Amiens sector, where one phase of the battle appeared to be

Continued on Page 2, Column 7.

Temperatures

1 A. M., 76	7 A. M., 75
2 A. M., 75	8 A. M., 76
3 A. M., 74	9 A. M., 81
4 A. M., 74	10 A. M., 84
5 A. M., 71	11 A. M., 86
6 A. M., 71	

Americas Next, Wallace Warns

WASHINGTON, June 5—(A. P.). A secret statement from the Army high command on "Fifth Column" activities in several Latin-American countries kept hemisphere defense problems to the fore today in the crush of preparedness considerations.

There was added emphasis on the subject in the declaration of a Cabinet member, Secretary Wallace, that "the dictator nations have definite designs" on the New Yorld. Wallace said:

"If England and France are conquered the Americas will be the next objective."

CLOSED MEETING

Reasons for the Army's manifest concern over conditions in some parts of the Western Hemisphere were outlined yesterday in a closed

Continued on Page 4, Column 4.

RACE ENTRIES, COMMENT WILL BE FOUND ON PAGES 22-24.

Harley St. Heart Surgeon Killed

LONDON, June 5 — (A. P.).—Laurence O'Shaughnessy, a noted Harley street heart surgeon, has been killed in Flanders, where he served with the Royal Army Medical Corps, it was announced today.

JUMP REPORTED SAFE

NEW YORK, June 5—(A. P.).—Lawrence A. Jump, driver for the American Voluntter Ambulance Corps in Europe, who was reported missing recently, is safe in a German prison camp at Stuttgart, the Avac said today.

Troops Disperse Rome Students

LAUSANNE, Switzerland, June 5 (A. P.).—The Swiss Army today closed the southern Valais Canton, covering the St. Bernard and Simplon passes in the Alps and bordering on what might be a battleground between France and Italy, to all civilians not living in the zone or not equipped with special army passes.

ROME, June 5—(A. P.).—Fascist students attempted to organize new anti-Allied demonstrations today as Italy marked time on the edge of war, but were disbanded by police in the vicinity of the British Consulate.

The youths, many of whom had just completed their examinations in the early closing of schools, formed a procession in the downtown streets.

TROOPS AT CONSULATE

After they were dispersed, troops were stationed at doorways near

Continued on Page 2, Column 6.

British Air Force Being Expanded

LONDON, June 5—(A. P.).—Sir Archibald Sinclair, Minister of Air, told the House of Commons today that the flying and training organization of the Royal Air Force was being expanded "on a considerable scale" to meet "all further requirements."

Hitler's Message To People, Army

BERLIN, June 5—(A. P.).—Adolf Hitler announced from his headquarters on the Western front today that his armies again were on the march.

He declared in a special message to the people ordering an eight-day nation-wide celebration of the German victory in the Battle of Flanders:

"This morning German divisions and air squadrons began anew the march for continuation of the fight for the liberty and future of our people."

ORDER OF THE DAY

At the same time, in the order of the day to his army, Hitler said:

"Soldiers, beginning today the West front is ready to march again.

"Numerous new divisions are assisting you who for the first time will see the defeat of an opponent."

The Fuehrer asked that homes be decorated for eight days and that church bells ring for three days.

TEXT OF ORDER

The text of the order of the day follows:

"Soldiers of the West front:

"Dunkerque has fallen. Forty

Continued on Page 2, Column 3.

THE WEATHER

Mostly cloudy and continued moderately warm with local thunderstorms tonight and Thursday afternoon. Lowest temperature tonight about 65 degrees. Moderate variable winds, mostly southwest.

MEAN TEMPERATURES

Baltimore	82	Chicago	77
Atlanta	75	Omaha	76
Boston	65	Los Angeles	64
Jacksonville	74	San Antonio	78
New York	79	Salt Lake City	64
Miami	80	Seattle	58
Portland, Maine	63	Tampa	78
Washington	77	New Orleans	79

New York World-Telegram

Copyright, 1940, by New York World-Telegram Corporation. All rights reserved.

Local Forecast: Occasional light local showers tonight; tomorrow partly cloudy and warmer, thunder storms in late afternoon.

SCRIPPS-HOWARD

VOL. 72.—NO. 292.—IN TWO SECTIONS—SECTION ONE | NEW YORK, MONDAY, JUNE 10, 1940. | Entered as second-class matter, Post Office, New York, N. Y.

CLOSING WALL ST. PRICES

Real Estate, Page 28

PRICE THREE CENTS

ITALY DECLARES WAR

'We Need U.S. Horsepower, Not Manpower'---Reynaud

By WILLIAM PHILIP SIMMS,
Scripps-Howard Foreign Editor.

PARIS, June 10.—"Tell America," Premier Reynaud said to me in an exclusive interview today, "that in our fight to save the world from a return to the dark ages we shall not falter.

"Tell her that, whatever may be the immediate outcome of the hurricane of fire and steel now raging, we shall not stop until those who would make robots of all mankind have been driven back from the lands they have invaded.

"But tell her also that we need her help—not her manpower, but her horsepower, motorized equipment, planes and other products of her tremendous industrial organization—all she can possibly offer us.

Wm. Philip Simms

"And tell her finally, as I have just told the people of my own country, that the stake is immense and the time is short."

The interview took place in the Premier's own office—within sound of enemy's guns. M. Reynaud, not only Prime Minister, but Minister of National Defense and Foreign Minister as well, has in his hands more power than France has entrusted to any man since Clemenceau, Premier in the first World War. His is, indeed, a "battle Cabinet."

"You may ask," M. Reynaud went on, "why the Allies were not so well equipped for war as the Germans when the Nazi attack began last September.

"The answer is quite simple. As democracies, we had stressed peace, just as the Nazis had stressed war. We believe in—and, despite everything, continued to work toward—peace, just as surely as Hitler believed in and worked toward war. (Four words censored.)

"Even while he was dictating that Germany's entire national energy must be devoted to creating a machine to make war, we on this side of the frontier spent most of our time, energy and money on an attempt to raise the standard of living of the masses. And those like myself, who said we must also obtain tanks and armored motorized divisions for national defense, even if listened to were not heeded.

"Democracies, like it or not, must learn that it is necessary for them to be always prepared to defend themselves. Nor can they afford to forget that decisions as to the size of their fighting forces are not solely theirs to make. Such decisions depend upon the strength of their potential enemies.

"Disagreeable as it is for civilized people to have to face, there are still large sections of the earth where brute force is the only thing that counts. The peace-minded democracies must not lose sight of that fact, for if they do they will be wiped off the map, one by one.

"In America's early days, when your pioneers were carving a great new nation out of a wilderness they carried their muskets and powder-horns when they went to the fields to plow. And they kept their powder dry. They had to do that to survive.

"Today the pioneer democracies are confronted by a somewhat analagous situation. The international forests are still full of savages whose only law is the law of the jungle.

"Democracies owe it as a duty to themselves, and to the hard-

(Continued on Page Two.)

Duce's Troops Invade at Riviera

By REYNOLDS PACKARD,
United Press Staff Correspondent.

ROME, June 10.—Premier Mussolini took Italy into the European War today on the side of Germany.

The declaration of war against Great Britain and France was announced by the Premier in a speech from Venice Palace balcony to a wildly cheering crowd at 7 p. m. (1 p. m., New York time).

[Italian forces marched into French territory through the Riviera at approximately 6:30 p. m. today (11:30 a. m., New York time), reporters were told by authorized sources at a conference at the Berlin Foreign Office called by Foreign Minister von Ribbentrop, the Associated Press said].

Premier Mussolini.

[Information concerning the Italian invasion of France was given out before a statement by von Ribbentrop].

[The Foreign Minister declared all Germany was "filled with jubilant enthusiasm" over Italy's intervention and said Nazi and Fascist forces would fight shoulder-to-shoulder until 'the rulers of England and France are ready to respect the vital rights of both our nations."]

"The hour of destiny has arrived for our Fatherland," Mussolini said. "We are going to war against the decrepit democracies . . . to break the chains that tie us in the Mediterranean."

The Premier, speaking in a strained, powerful voice to perhaps 80,000 persons in the Venice Palace Square and side streets and to millions throughout Italy and the world, said there was but one watchword for Fascists:

"It is to win!"

"We salute the Fuehrer of Germany," he added. "Fascist Italy is on her feet and prepared to strike."

The Premier, who once said that Italy had 10,000,000 bayonets ready for action, declared that "this gigantic struggle is a logical part in our revolution."

"This revolution," hecontinued, "asserts itself

(Continued on Page Three.)

'A Long Period of Peace'

The text of Premier Mussolini's address, as translated and transcribed by N. B. C., follows:

Combatants on land, sea and in the air, Blackshirts of the Revolution and of the Legion, men and women of Italy, of the Empire and of the Kingdom of Albania, listen:

An hour signed by destiny is ticking on the skies of our country. An hour of the irrevocable decisions, a declaration of war, has already been given to the Ambassadors of Great Britain and France.

We shall descend on the fields against the plutocratic democracies and the reactionary democracies of the west—who in all times have always obstructed the march of the Italian people. Some facts of more recent history can be assumed in these words, promises, menaces, threats against us by 52 states. Our conscience is absolutely quiet. With us the whole world is a testament that Italy has done

(Continued on Page Two.)

Fresh British Divisions Rush to French Front

Fighting 'More and More Violent'---Nazis Cross The Seine at 2 Points

Fresh British divisions were hurled into the fighting line on the Somme-Oise-Aisne front today as the French High Command reported that the Battle of France, now in its sixth day, "continues more and more violently," with the Germans only 25 to 30 miles from Paris.

In Paris it was admitted that the enemy had slashed through the defense lines along the Seine, the Oise and the Aisne and that advanced units were operating south of Beauvais, directly north of the capital.

The most savage fighting took place on a flat plain near Fere-en-Tardenois, about 10 miles south of the Aisne, where 150,000 Germans supported by heavy tanks, pushed across the river and advanced slowly across a battlefield covered with their own dead, French sources said.

Advices from Paris indicated that the capital had been

(Continued on Page Three.)

Nazis Push Spearhead 25-30 Mi. from Paris

By RALPH HEINZER,
United Press Staff Correspondent.

PARIS, June 10.—Germany, throwing 1,500,000,000 men and 4000 tanks into the Battle of France, today was reported to have broken through defense lines of the Seine, the Oise and the Aisne, moved on toward the Marne and thrust a spearhead within 25 to 30 miles of Paris.

German tank columns were operating south of Beauvais, apparently within 25 or 30 miles of Paris. Beauvais itself is only a little more than 35 miles from the capital.

Other tank units were reported to have smashed through Normandil and the departments of Seine Inferieure and Eure, just northwest of Paris.

Attacking Plateau.

In the east heavy German columns were attacking on the Tardenois plateau, southeast of Soissons, threatening to flank both important cities of Soissons and Reims.

All along the front reports indicated that French positions were in danger of being flanked or taken from the rear due to slash-

(Continued on Page Two.)

Wall Street At a Glance

The stock market took Italy's declaration of war in good style today. Weak earlier in the day, the general run of issues staged a good recovery following the Mussolini speech which carried prices well up from their lows. Trading was light

Pound sterling dropped around 25 cents. Commodities moved downward early and then rallied.

Paris Bourse Closed Down

And Government May Move South

By the Associated Press.

PARIS, June 10.—Trading was suspended on the Bourse today and there were indications that the government might move from the capital.

[Reuters, British news agency, reported that Paris had been placed in a state of defense. The agency said the permanent staffs of ministers were removed yesterday and today to the provinces.]

Premier Reynaud cancelled a Cabinet meeting scheduled for tonight in Paris, but this morning the Ministries still were functioning here.

Some important files and papers of the government have already been moved out of the city.

The usual morning military press conference at the War Ministry was omitted today, and only orderlies remained at the ministry.

In the last war the government moved to Bordeaux for a few

(Continued on Page Two.)

City Saved 56 Million

William Fellowes Morgan, Jr., Commissioner of Markets, reported to the Mayor today that his department saved the consumers of the city $56,000,000 by co-ordinating distribution and preventing excessive profits in 1939. The Department made a net profit of $377,117 during the year, Mr. Morgan said.

American Home Bombed

By the United Press

CHUNGKING, China, June 10.—The home of A. B. Bassi, American advisor to the Chinese Ministry of Communications, was destroyed in a Japanese bombing raid May 28, it was disclosed today.

Postponed Games

American League.

Tigers vs. Yankees, rain.
Indians vs. Red Sox, rain.

Roosevelt to Talk To Nation Tonight

By the Associated Press.

WASHINGTON, June 10.—Italy's entry into the war was expected to bring from President Roosevelt in an address at Charlottesville, Va., tonight a new appraisal of the place of "democracy" in a growing world conflict.

This hint was given by Stephen Early, presidential secretary, who told reporters Mr. Roosevelt had received word of Premier Mussolini's declaration of war against Britain and France in a telephone call from Ambassador William C. Bullitt in Paris at 12:53 p. m. New York time.

Mr. Roosevelt had awaited Mussolini's scheduled address which became a declaration of war, before whipping into final form his speech at the university's commencement excercises.

While there was obvious concern among employees at the White House over Italy's decision to join Germany, the only immediate result was cancellation of a projected presidential visit to Hyde Park, after the Virginia speech.

'Putnam Plan' Solves Problem Of Defense Jobs

Mechanics Trained Fast by Springfield, Mass., as Specialists

By ALLAN KELLER
World-Telegram Staff Writer.

SPRINGFIELD, Mass., June 10.—This community has succeeded in shattering the bottleneck caused by a shortage of skilled mechanics and machinists and thereby offers to the nation a pattern for a wholesale attack on the crucial stoppage that threatens the whole national rearmament and defense program.

It is a solution born of expediency and Yankee ingenuity. It is based on close co-operation between the city government, industry and the unemployed. Mayor Roger L. Putnam, architect of the plan, calls it a double-barreled attack on unemployment and industrial labor shortage.

The Springfield plan, or the Putnam plan, in its briefest form,

(Continued on Page Five.)

Cobber Kain Dies In Plane Crash

By the Associated Press.

LONDON, June 10.—Britain's first air ace of the war, Flying Officer E. J. (Cobber) Kain, unofficially credited with more than 40 German planes shot down in action, has been killed, it was disclosed today.

His death resulted from a flying accident while on duty, not in action.

A New Zealander, Kain had recently been named to head a group of British pilots "with a bag of 20 or more" enemy planes on roving commissions.

Kain, who was 22 years old, was the first British airman to win distinction in France in the present war.

While on leave in England last April Kain announced his engagement to Joyce Phillips, 23-year-old actress.

Admiralty Admits Loss Of Aircraft Carrier Glorious

By the United Press.

LONDON, June 10.—The Admiralty today announced one of the most severe losses of the war—The presumed sinking of the 22,500-ton aircraft carrier, Glorious, and an escort of two destroyers, the transport Orama, and the tanker Oil Pioneer—a total of 50,706 tons of shipping.

[The German High Command asserted yesterday that the Glorious and its escort vessels had been sunk in naval action off Norway in which the German battleships Gneisenau and Scharnhorst participated.]

The Admiralty, which yesterday said merely it had been advised of "operations" in the Norwegian area, today said that "as no further information has been received regarding the naval operations in connection with the withdrawal of our forces referred to in yesterday's Admiralty communique and as up to the present it has not been found possible to establish communications with certain ships," they must be presumed lost.

Norway Planes Held

By the Associated Press.

LONDON, June 10.—An exchange telegraph agency dispatch from Helsinki today said seven Norwegian military planes had landed at Salmajaervi and Petsamo. The planes and crews were interned, the dispatch said.

Antiaircraft Fires During Night at Paris

PARIS, June 10.—Heavy antiaircraft fire started at 7 a. m. today (2 a. m. New York time) after intermittent activity throughut yesterday and the early hours of this morning.

[It was reported that German planes had bombed the southern suburbs of Paris yesterday, but the United Press Paris Bureau said that according to the best information available there had been no bombing yesterday closer than the Oise Valley, 20 miles away.]

House Unit Approves National Guard Plan

By the United Press.

WASHINGTON, June 10.—The House Military Affairs Committee today voted, 16 to 8, to approve a bill authorizing President Roosevelt to order out the National Guard in event of an emergency prior to the next Congress.

But it limited him to using the guard in the continental United States, its possessions and the Canal Zone.

The committee also reported a bill authorizing an increase in the strength of the regular army to 400,000.

Defenses at Canal Found Inadequate

The American people today are united in determination to provide this country with impregnable defenses.

But what must we defend? And how? What is the condition of our present defenses? What steps are necessary to improve them? Charles T. Lucey and Lee G. Miller, of the Scripps-Howard Newspapers' Washington staff, have been seeking the answers to these and other questions concerning an all-important subject.

Today, in the first article of a series, they begin their report to readers of this newspaper.

By CHARLES T. LUCEY and LEE G. MILLER,
Scripps-Howard Staff Writers.

WASHINGTON, June 10.—The Panama Canal, keystone of the sea power which forms the first and strongest line of America's defense, is no longer impregnable.

That stark admission is implicit in the great sums now being expended on improvement of its defenses. Some of those improvements will take years to complete.

It is the swift advance in two techniques of war—aviation and the Trojan horse—that has challenged the supposed invulnerability of this 40-mile chain of locks, lakes and ditches linking the Pacific and the Caribbean.

General George C. Marshall, Chief of Staff of the Army, warned a House committee the other day—in advocating Presidential power to send the National Guard outside the United States if need be—that subversive influences afoot in Latin America were dangerous to this

(Continued on Page Four.)

World-Telegram Index

The Weather

(Official United States Forecast.)

New York and Metropolitan Area—Occasional light local showers tonight; tomorrow partly cloudy and warmer; thunderstorms in late afternoon; diminishing easterly wind.

Lowest temperature expected tonight, 60.

New Jersey—Cloudy with occasional light rains tonight; tomorrow partly cloudy and warmer, followed by local showers.

Connecticut—Cloudy with occasional rains tonight; tomorrow partly cloudy and slightly warmer followed by local showers.

TODAY'S READINGS.

	Temp.	Hum.		Temp.	Hum.
Midnight	65	..	8 a. m.	58	90
1 a. m.	63	..	9 a. m.	58	92
2 a. m.	61	..	10 a. m.	60	89
3 a. m.	59	..	11 a. m.	59	85
4 a. m.	58	..	Noon	58	86
5 a. m.	58	..	1 p. m.	59	91
6 a. m.	59	94	2 p. M.	59	90
7 a. m.	58	95			

High and low a year ago, 84—66

Additional weather data on page 2.

WAR EXTRA

CHARACTER QUALITY — AMERICA FIRST! — ENTERPRISE ACCURACY

Los Angeles Examiner

AN AMERICAN PAPER FOR THE AMERICAN PEOPLE — THE GREAT NEWSPAPER OF THE GREAT SOUTHWEST

Reg. U.S. Pat. Off.

CALIFORNIA FORECAST
Los Angeles and Vicinity—Fair Friday and Saturday, with some morning cloudiness; no change in temperature; moderate west and northwest winds.

TEMPERATURES

	H.	L.		H.	L.
Los Angeles	81	56	New York...	92	68
San Francisco	64	52	Boston	90	61
San Diego...	72	59	Chicago	78	56
Seattle	70	57	Detroit	80	67
Portland	75	61	Washington .	79	60
Omaha	83	61	Atlanta	90	68

VOL. XXXVII—NO. 186 CCC LOS ANGELES, FRIDAY, JUNE 14, 1940 For Complete Weather Forecasts See Page 12, Part I Two Sections—Part 1—FIVE CENTS

NAZIS TAKE PARIS

REYNAUD BEGS U. S. FOR HELP; TURKS, BULGARIANS BATTLE

IN THE NEWS

YOU MAY not approve of the American citizen who goes abroad to fight for some alien theory or some foreign land.

You might not have applauded the action of those misguided American youths who went to Spain to fight for Communism.

You might not have understood their amazing willingness to surrender their solid American advantages and opportunities for the unsound principles of red radicalism.

But at least you realized that they had some commendable quality.

They were willing to make material sacrifices for their spiritual convictions.

Say what you would, and say it as sincerely and as severely as you pleased, yet there was in your heart some reserve of admiration.

These mistaken enthusiasts were yielding THEIR OWN LIVES in support of THEIR OWN IDEALS.

Gentle reader, you undoubtedly are a very true and loyal American.

You require from yourself the first and best of your devotion for your own dear country.

You measure others by their loyalty to their native land.

You set that high standard as the test of their patriotic merit and devotion.

But you certainly have respect for a man who is willing to give up his life for a cause—be it your cause or his cause—be it a righteous cause or even a mistaken cause.

Those Americans who wish to go to France to fight for the success of France have your respect and your honest admiration.

You may not wish your country to be involved in the unending wars of Europe, but if individual Americans, out of spiritual conviction, want to sacrifice their own lives for other ideals than ours, the act is heroic.

It compels our respect. It challenges our admiration.

But what do you think of the American who prospers in this land, and prospers from it, but owes no obligation to it or to another?

He does not want to go abroad to fight in foreign lands. He does not want to risk there or here his own thick hide.

He does not wish to make personal sacrifice of blood, or even of comfort.

Yet he is willing to send somebody else abroad to do the fighting—eager to entrust someone else [illegible] the duty of suffering an[illegible] while he—tender heart [illegible]pathetic soul—sits en[illegible] his easy chair and r[illegible]e casualty lists in the ne[illegible].

[illegible] all respect the views of a m[illegible]who is willing to back them [illegible] with his life.

We [illegible]all go down to the ship and [illegible] the departure of the man [illegible] is willing to prove the sincerity of his sentiments by sacrifice.

But what can we say or think of the m[illegible] who wants to send our child[illegible] to be immolated as burnt offerings on the fiery altars of war, while he reposes in security by his own fireside?

Must mothers feed their babes to Moloch to satisfy his safe sentiments?

Americans are inspired by ideals. They are not aroused by sordid and selfish advocacies. They are not led by laggards.

Senator Rush D. Holt, Democrat of West Virginia, says of these vicarious heroes:

"If the danger is what they say, and the cause is what they preach, they should have the courage to offer THEIR lives."

Certainly it is no evidence of courage, or even of sincerity, to offer, no matter how liberally, the lives of others.

THE poll of Congress by the Hearst papers on the best coordinated plan for the defense of the United States has developed interesting suggestions.

The decision, however, will undoubtedly be made by the President.

Almost everything in government is decided by the President nowadays.

To use preparedness phraseology, the President is the drill sergeant. The Congress is but the company of raw recruits going through the manual at arms under his sharp commands.

"Hay-foot, straw-foot" up and down the halls of Congress go the obedient rookies.

There are a few stragglers, but most of the congressmen have learned the drill well enough to respond promptly, keep step per[illegible] and obey absolutely.

[illegible] the way it must be in [illegible]ar, boys. What is inde-

(Continued on Page 2, Cols. 7-8)

HOUSE PASSES BILL TO DEPORT HARRY BRIDGES

Roll Call Vote of 330 to 42 Follows Bitter Debate in Ouster of Labor Chieftain

By Lee Rashall
Staff Correspondent International News Service

WASHINGTON, June 13.—The House today passed a bill calling for immediate deportation of Harry Bridges, alien West Coast C. I. O. maritime labor leader.

It was the first time that Congress acted upon any bill to deport a single individual. The measure was approved by a roll call vote of 330 to 42.

Tumultuous debate preceded the vote. During its course Bridges was subjected to bitter bi-partisan attacks as a "most dangerous enemy of national defense," and a "wrecker" of the American merchant marine. Eleven members of the House rose on the floor to oppose the bill.

WIRE-TAPPING O. K.'D

Meanwhile the House judiciary committee approved unanimously a bill to permit the Department of Justice to use wire-tapping in its investigation of fifth column (traitors and spies) activities.

Sponsored by Representative Cellar (Democrat) New York, the measure would give the department the right to listen in on telephone conversations of anyone suspected of sabotage, espionage or any activity seeking to hamper the preparedness program.

The Bridges deportation bill was sponsored by Representative Allen (Democrat), Louisiana, who declared this nation "is now serving notice on all enemies within our borders that we will not tolerate them"—the bill was sent to the Senate, where its disposition was questionable. If passed there, a Supreme Court

(Continued on Page 10, Cols. 1-2)

Breakfast - Food Cannon U. S. Idea of Preparedness

BY ARTHUR "BUGS" BAER

Give Henry Ford the contract for a million planes but don't let Hank make the parachutes.

They belong in the dry goods department. And when it comes to the rustle of silk Henry is a bit tone deaf.

Our military preparedness in the last 20 years consisted mostly of shooting breakfast-food out of guns.

But we get hot slow and we cool off slow like the handle on the coffee-pot of a dude ranch.

French Premier Seeks Quick Aid; Hitler Tells Aims

America Virtually Asked by Paris to Declare War on Germany

PARIS, June 13.—(INS)—Premier Paul Reynaud, in a dramatic "last supreme appeal" to President Roosevelt tonight, virtually called on the United States for a declaration of war on Nazi Germany and "fresh squadrons of planes from overseas," lest France perish.

"This is the last time he can help," Reynaud broadcast over the radio in an anguished speech filled with emotional mingling of hope and despair.

Even as he spoke the hard-pressed French armies suffered new reverses in the raging battle around Paris.

WEAPONS NOT ENOUGH

He especially urged dispatch of airplanes, but going far beyond his earlier appeals, Reynaud hinted that material aid was not enough.

"Each time I asked the President of the United States to increase all forms of aid permitted by American law, he did so generously and was approved by his people," said the Premier.

"But today we are beyond that point. . . . There is no longer time for half-hearted measures.

"Will the American people still hesitate to declare themselves against Nazi Germany?"

The translation of the text of French Premier Reynaud's second and "final" appeal to

(Continued on Page A, Column 6)

Fuehrer Sets Out Attitude Toward Americas in Interview

By Karl H. von Wiegand
Chief Foreign Correspondent of the Hearst Newspapers and for 28 years outstanding American political observer in Europe and the Far East

WITH THE GERMAN ARMIES NEARING PARIS, June 13.—"The Americas to Americans, Europe to the Europeans."

This reciprocal basic Monroe Doctrine, mutually observed, declared Adolf Hitler to me today, not only would insure peace for all times between the old and the new worlds, but would be a most ideal foundation for peace throughout the whole world.

In caustic language, with scorn and indignation, he denounced "the lies" that he has or ever had in "dream or thought" played with the faintest idea of interfering in the Western Hemisphere by any manner or means.

CALLS FEARS "CHILDISH"

He characterized America's fears of him or Germany as most flattering but "childish and grotesque," and the whole idea of the possibility of the invasion of the United States from Europe by sea, air or the "mythical fifth column" as "stupid and fantastic."

With his great German war machine, whose amazing perfection of organization, strength, strategical and tactical leadership has startled the world, now on the edge of Paris, Hitler told me he had no intention of attacking the beautiful French capital

(Continued on Page 4, Cols. 1-3)

FLOOD CONTROL EXPANDED

More Funds Urged for Los Angeles

WASHINGTON, June 13.—(AP)—The Bureau of Army Engineers recommended to Congress today an expansion program to cost $185,000,000 for flood control in California, in the Los Angeles and San Gabriel River basins, and on Ballona Creek.

An expenditure of $82,541,000 had been authorized earlier. Of the additional amount, $22,500,000 would be provided by local interests, which would be required to furnish land for rights-of-way and bear the cost of relocating highways and bridges.

The expanded project involves construction of the Lopez and Whittier flood control basins, various main stream channels, debris basins at the mouths of the canyons and improvement of tributary channels.

Of the additional money recommended, $71,843,000 would be spent on the Los Angeles basin; $74,125,000 on the San Gabriel basin; $21,739,000 for Rio Hondo, and $18,276,000 on the Ballona basin.

ALLIED WAR COUNCIL VOWS FIGHT TO END

Great British Force Will Rush to Aid of France; Masses of Nazis Pour Over Seine

PARIS, June 13.—(INS)—The Allied Supreme War Council tonight decided to fight "to the end," even though huge masses of German troops are "pouring" across the Seine towards the Paris suburb of Versailles and the exhausted French army is outnumbered three to one in men and material.

British assistance in great force is to be rushed immediately to bulwark the retreating French troops, it was announced after the emergency supreme council meeting, attended by Prime Minister Churchill and Premier Reynaud.

Shortly after the French high command decided to abandon Paris to the on-pressing Germans rather than see its beauties blasted and charred, Reich mechanized divisions rolled below the Seine so swiftly in a three-forked advance that it appeared a major break-through southwest of Paris had been effected.

With his troops so tired they were unable to reorganize effective resistance at this stage, Premier Reynaud sent a "last supreme" appeal to President Roosevelt for aid.

TOURS, FRANCE, June 13.—(AP)—Invading Nazis pressed down on both sides of Paris tonight, hourly threatening to engulf the city.

Some of their vast number struck toward the rich Loire valley and the grand routes leading

(Continued on Page A, Cols. 1-2)

Pill Substitutes for Vaccination in Scarlet Fever

NEW YORK, June 13.—(AP)—A pill which immunizes against scarlet fever was announced to the American Medical Association today.

These pills are a substitute for vaccination and are taken with a drink of water.

They were developed by Dr. George F. Dick and Gladys Henry Dick, who devised the scarlet fever vaccine.

The pills have been tried on 102 persons, the Dicks reported. They are taken daily for two or three weeks. Of these test cases, 94 per cent were immunized and the rest had transient scarletine rashes.

Bullitt Shifts Rule of Capital to Berlin

Turkey Signs Nazi Pact

Officials Say Trade Treaty Has O. K. of Allies

ISTANBUL, June 14 (Friday).—(INS)—Clashes between Turkish and Bulgarian soldiers in which an estimated 200 were killed or wounded, were reported today by travelers returning from Adrianople.

The clashes occurred Tuesday night, it was reported. The casualties were principally wounded, and the deaths few, it was said.

ANKARA, June 13.—(AP)—Turkey signed a pact with Germany today for the exchange of 14,000,000 American dollars' worth of tobacco for spare machinery parts, but Turkish officials said the treaty had the approval of their Allies, Britain and France, and represented no lessening of the alliance.

The Allies, it was said, do not object to Turkish tobacco going to Germany, nor to Turkey getting machines and parts from

(Continued on Page 2, Column 5)

Allies Act to Spare French City Needless Ruin, Will Fight to End; Nazis Gain on 3 Fronts

WASHINGTON, June 14 (Friday).—(AP)—The German army is "inside the gates of Paris," Ambassador William C. Bullitt informed the State Department early today.

"Transfer of the city has been made by Ambassador Bullitt" . . .

That announcement in German over the Paris Mondial shortwave broadcasting station, transmitting on the 31-meter band, was picked up in Los Angeles at 8:58 p. m. last night by S. F. Henkel, 6320 Fountain avenue.

Henkel in reporting the apparent fall of Paris to the Examiner said his receiver was tuned in on the Paris station for an hour and 10 minutes and nothing was heard but the French carrier wave.

The silence, which followed the partial playing of a phonograph record of the "Marseillaise," was broken by the German announcement.

Paris was saved from destruction last night by France's decision not to defend the capital and by Germany's acceptance of the city as an "open town" as Nazi troops marched into the suburbs.

France, however, can be saved only through immediate, active American aid to the Allies, Premier Reynaud declared in a radio address to his countrymen, whom he informed that he was making a dramatic "last supreme appeal" to President Roosevelt for full military assistance.

The war situation in Europe yesterday developed as follows:

1. France and Britain, after a conference of the Allied Supreme Council, decided to fight to the end.
2. Approximately 2,000,000 Nazi troops, many of them fresh, pressed in upon Paris from three sides

DUEL PLAN ROCKS ARGENTINE

Cabinet Aide Quits to Battle Senator

BUENOS AIRES, June 13.—(AP)—President Ortiz tonight accepted the resignation of one of his cabinet members who was arranging to duel a senator in a Fascist-Democratic quarrel.

At the same time a lightning raid by police on hidden quarters of a semi-Fascist youth organization where the sympathizers with strong one-man regimes were reported accumulating bombs, emphasized Argentina's growing sensitiveness to "fifth column" (spies and traitors) activities within her borders.

The threatened duel grew out of a heated senate session debating behind closed doors a government bill to strengthen neutrality through close press control.

Jorge Eduardo Coll, minister of justice and public education, and Senator Matias Sanchez Sorondo,, an avowed admirer of totalitarian regimes in Europe, were reported to have engaged in argument and a challenge to duel, presumably at dawn tomorrow, resulted.

Dueling is illegal in Argentina.

U. S. PLANES PRAISED

SOMEWHERE IN FRANCE, June 13.—(AP)—"American bombers recently arrived have proved extremely effective," a French war office spokesman said tonight, "but if they are to influence the final issue there must be many more."

WAR EXTRA

COMPLETE RACES

Complete Markets

Los Angeles Examiner

CHARACTER QUALITY AMERICA FIRST! ENTERPRISE ACCURACY

AN AMERICAN PAPER FOR THE AMERICAN PEOPLE — THE GREAT NEWSPAPER OF THE GREAT SOUTHWEST

Reg. U.S. Pat. Off.

VOL. XXXVII—NO. 190 | CC | LOS ANGELES, TUESDAY, JUNE 18, 1940 | Two Sections—Part I—FIVE CENTS

FATE OF FRANCE IN HITLER'S HANDS

British Fight On; Dictators Meet Today

LONDON, June 17.—(AP)—Great Britain flung into Nazi Germany's teeth tonight the defiant decision to fight on alone—"unconquerable"—from the little island seat of the world-wide empire.

Prime Minister Winston Churchill, in a two-minute radio address, said the fight would go on "until the curse of Hitler is lifted from the brows of mankind."

CHAMPIONS OF WORLD

He told his people that they now have become "the sole champions in arms to defend the world cause."

Speaking for the British Empire, he declared:

"We shall do our best to be worthy of this high honor."

He spoke as sorely-afflicted France asked her Nazi conqueror for peace, a development which made it plainer than ever that England herself is menaced by the triple threat of blockade, bombardment and direct invasion from Hitler's legions.

"What has happened in France," Churchill said, "makes no difference to Britain's *'faith and purpose.'*"

WILL DEFEND HOME

He continued:

"We shall defend our island home and with the British Empire around us we shall fight on, unconquerable until the curse of Hitler is lifted from the brows of mankind.

"We are sure that in the end all will come right.

"The news from France is very bad, and I grieve for the gallant French people who have fallen into this terrible misfortune.

"Nothing will alter our feeling toward them or our faith that the genius of France will rise again."

The talk was made at the request of the British press that Churchill give a message to the

(Continued on Page A, Cols. 4-5)

ROME, June 17.—(AP)—Premier Mussolini left blacked-out Rome tonight on a dimly lighted train to confer with Adolf Hitler at Munich tomorrow on the joint peace terms they will put before France.

Secrecy surrounded the departure of the private train and few saw the Premier leave.

Before taking the train, Mussolini had a long conference with Marshal Pietro Badoglio, chief of the general staff of Italian armed forces.

ACCOMPANIED BY CIANO

On the train with Mussolini was his son-in-law and foreign minister, Count Galeazzo Ciano, who will be at Mussolini's side when he meets Hitler.

Such a meeting by the two war lords would come exactly three months after their secret 2½-hour talk in Brenner Pass, on the German-Italian border, which preceded Germany's britzkrieg on Scandinavia and Western Europe.

(In Berlin, there was speculation that Hitler and Mussolini might meet at Versailles, seat of treaties ending the war of 1870 triumphantly for Germany and the World War, when the Reich was beaten.)

JUBILATION IN ITALY

The mention of Munich as the meeting place of the dictators recalled that it was there in September, 1938, that Hitler and Mussolini, with Neville Chamberlain, then British prime minister, and Edouard Daladier, then French premier, arranged the settlement which eventually doomed Czechoslovakia.

Word that the French were suing for peace with Germany caused a flash of jubilation throughout Italy. Thousands of Italians took it as a sign that the war—which they entered at the call of Mussolini just a week ago—soon would be over.

At the same time the Italian high command reported aerial assaults of Allied naval bases

(Continued on Page A, Column 3)

They Map Peace Terms Today

TO CONSIDER the French suit for peace, offered "with a broken heart" by aged Premier Henri Petain, Benito Mussolini sped out of Rome yesterday for a conference with his axis partner, Adolf Hitler. Fearing the worst, but praying for best, Petain addressed his battered nation, announcing he had asked for "peace with honor."
—Wide World photo.

BRITAIN WILL FIGHT UNTIL HITLER FALLS—CHURCHILL

LONDON, June 17.—(AP)—The text of Prime Minister Winston Churchill's radio broadcast today follows:

The news from France is very bad, and I grieve for the gallant people who have fallen into this terrible misfortune.

Nothing will alter our feelings toward them or our faith that the genius of France will rise again. What has happened in France makes no difference to British faith and purpose.

We have become the sole champions now in arms to defend the world cause and we shall do our best to be worthy of this high honor.

We shall defend our island home and with the British Empire around us we shall fight on unconquerable until the curse of Hitler is lifted from the brows of mankind. We are sure that in the end all will come right.

Franco Asked to Arrange for Peace Parleys

MADRID, June 17.—(AP)—Spain's leader, General Francisco Franco, has been invited to act as intermediary in French-German armistice negotiations and also to send delegates to any subsequent peace discussions, usually reliable sources said tonight.

BORDEAUX, June 17.—(AP)—The armies of France fought on tonight along the whole confused front after their government asked Adolf Hitler for terms of peace and received no immediate reply.

With what strength of men and munitions was left after 12 days of ceaseless retreat against heavy odds, the exhausted French still defiantly demanded "an honorable peace" as the condition of surrender.

VIOLENT FIGHTING

A French night communique said the fighting still was violent, that French resistance continued, and that there had been no letup in the fierce Nazi onslaught south and east from the River Loire.

Military spokesman admitted, however, that the front was disorganized and that the Germans had split the French forces into four ribbons.

Hardest fighting was reported in the vicinity of Orleans, along the Loire River, 75 miles south of Paris.

(The Germans said they had taken Orleans and crossed the Loire.)

"SAME BRAVERY"

The French communique told of desperate resistance all along the middle Loire, but said German spearheads still stabbed deeper into France in the region of Dijon and Autun, east of the Loire, 150 to 175 miles southeast of Paris.

The French admitted German mechanized units had pushed into the Departments of Doubs and Jura west of the Swiss frontier.

"At all points of contact," the communique said, "our troops still are fighting with the same

(Continued on Page A, Column 2)

BERLIN, June 17.—(AP)—Adolf Hitler and his axis partner, Premier Mussolini, will meet, probably tomorrow somewhere in western Europe, to decide the fate of prostrate France and dictate terms to the republic, which lay crushed tonight under the German military machine.

Mussolini was speeding northward from Rome to an unannounced destination for what promised to be a history-making conference with Hitler. Decisions influencing the French destiny possibly for generations were expected.

(Rome dispatches said Mussolini's destination was Munich, scene of the 1938 partitioning of Czechoslovakia by the four powers—Britain, Germany, Italy and France—but the reference to "somewhere in Western Europe" was taken to mean the fate of France might be decided at Versailles, where World War victors dictated peace to Germany.)

RESISTANCE BROKEN

Meanwhile, the crumbling of French military resistance went on apace. The mighty French fortress at Metz fell before German onslaughts this afternoon, the German high command reported.

In the east, France virtually was wide open to tremendous blows which Germany's unexhausted forces were in position to strike.

The position of France seemed dark and from a military point of view there remained only faint glimmers of desperate hope.

The request for terms by Marshal Henri Philippe Petain, France's new premier, appeared to be a mere formality and the prospects were he and France would be obliged to accept what-

Parliament

"OUR INFLEXIBLE RESOLVE"

MR. CHURCHILL'S CONFIDENCE IN FINAL VICTORY

PLEDGES TO FRANCE REAFFIRMED

HOUSE OF LORDS

TUESDAY, JUNE 18

The LORD CHANCELLOR took his seat on the Woolsack at 4 o'clock.

The Saint Mary Magdalene Hospital (Newcastle-upon-Tyne) and the Christchurch Corporation Bill were read the third time and passed.

WITH BRITAIN "TO THE END"

DOMINION ASSURANCES

VISCOUNT CALDECOTE, Secretary of State for Dominion Affairs, in reply to LORD ADDISON, made a statement on the international situation. He said that the resolve of his Majesty's Government stood rock-like. (Hear, hear.) As long as the resolution of our Ally abided the British Empire was shoulder to shoulder with them. If, on the other hand, we stood alone to defend the right, the future of our own homes and land, as well as of the nations that had been soiled and ravaged by the German invasion, then he hoped our courage would match our pride in a great hour. (Cheers.)

It was a dark hour for France, and the sufferings of the French people had been immense. They had been tortured beyond endurance. Whether they ceased to fight or not, we were persuaded that the French authorities would do all in their power to remove every hinderance to the continuance of the struggle by their Ally. Our course was plain. The foe had to break the spirit of our Imperial race or he must fail. The centre of our resistance now lay in these islands. Our power to defend them, and in defending them to defend the Empire, would decide this struggle. We might feel confidence in our own strength to resist invasion.

EXPULSION OF FEAR

Invasion from the air was a new factor, of which we had to take the most serious account. No doubt we had to face in this country an ordeal by fire which would call up all our native resources and endurance and fortitude. Fear was a traitor that must be expelled from our councils. The greatest qualities of our race would now be called upon to play their part. Of our armies, it was unnecessary to speak of their gallantry. Many of them lately back from France, where they had a searching and testing experience, were anxious for only one thing, and that was to achieve by their valour on other fields, or the same fields, the victory of their country.

He had left to the last mention of one great and unfailing source of confidence. The Dominions had made a magnificent contribution to our strength. (Cheers.) We had received many a message from each of them. If he quoted two of them they would not misunderstand him; they were but examples which might be multiplied over and over again. He referred to one which had been received by Mr. Churchill from the Prime Minister of the smallest of our Dominions—New Zealand:—

> If his Majesty's Government in the United Kingdom decide to fight on, we pledge this Dominion to remain with them to the end, and we are confident this policy is unchangeable in the Dominion. At the same time, we again pledge New Zealand to every form of assistance within our power and with the sole desire to render the maximum help we will gladly and sympathetically consider any suggestions of any kind and at any time which his Majesty's Government may desire to make.

From the youngest of our Dominions—the Union of South Africa—the Prime Minister had sent a telegram to himself (Lord Caldecote) in which he said:—

> Whatever the difficulties and trials ahead and however long the road to victory may be, we hope to follow it to the end in company with our Commonwealth, friends, and Allies. (Hear, hear.)

From Canada and Australia messages of equal resolve to stay with us, fight with us, endure with us, and win with us had been received. (Cheers.)

LORD ADDISON ON TWO LESSONS

LORD ADDISON said that we reverenced the historic sacrifices of France, and it was a great comfort to all of us to read in the statement this morning that they regarded their honour above all things, and would accept no degrading peace. But it did mean that not for the first time we stood alone—for the time being. He was quite sure there was not a man or woman in the land whose resolution was abated. Indeed, there was no one who had not more resolve than ever.

We had stood in a similar position before, and seen the conquest of liberty in Europe ultimately turned back by Britain. At that time we did not have the great Dominions for our support, and, indeed, at that time we did not have the promise of priceless materials from the peoples across the Atlantic.

There were two plain lessons for all of us. We could not fight mechanical arms unless we had superior equipment, and we could obtain it. There was no man or woman in the country who was other than longing to help. Their longing was a demand for leadership, and he was sure that from the Prime Minister they would have efficient leadership. We might confidently look for that leadership in the great Service which was our first line of defence—never broken. With this leadership there was no limit to the self-sacrifice and service we were prepared to render.

GRIEF FOR FRANCE

The MARQUESS of CREWE said the news from France came as a deep grief to us all, most of all to those who loved France and who had some knowledge of the country and who had spent years there and enjoyed many French friendships. We could all be united in our great admiration for the valour and endurance which the French soldiers had shown against overwhelming odds, and it seemed that, so far as they could, they were continuing to show those qualities.

It was useless to speak of the past. There was no more futile way of encountering misfortune than to spend time in discussion on who was most to blame. Instead, we should devote energy and thought in deciding how the faults could be repaired. To consider now the responsibility for the fact that Germany had achieved that vast mechanical superiority which had been the one secret of her success would be idle. We must think of the present and of the future.

Their lordships were all heartened by the staunchness of the Prime Minister's broadcast, and the whole spirit of that was introduced in the statement of Lord Caldecote. The messages from the Dominions might have been repeated over and over again and in a similar form from many of the great Colonies. Therefore, we were able to feel that though these events might have set the end much farther off, yet the end was equally sure. (Hear, hear.)

The Confirmation of Executors (War Service) (Scotland) Bill passed through Committee. The Indian and Colonial Divorce Jurisdiction Bill was read the third time and passed.

Their lordships rose at 18 minutes before 5 o'clock.

HOUSE OF COMMONS

TUESDAY, JUNE 18

The SPEAKER took the Chair at a quarter to 3 o'clock.

The Gosport Water Bill and the Monmouthshire and South Wales Employers' Mutual Indemnity Society Limited Bill were read a second time.

A new writ was ordered for the election of a member for the Bournemouth Division, in the room of Lord Croft, raised to the peerage.

PETROL SUPPLIES

In reply to Mr. LEVY (Elland, U.) and Mr. LEACH (Bradford, Cent., Lab.), Mr. G. LLOYD, Secretary for Petroleum (Birmingham, Ladywood, U.), said:—The House will be glad to know that as a result of action taken by the Government before and since the war, our supplies of petrol are at present very satisfactory. Substantial economies in the civil consumption of petrol have already been made by rationing, and this automatically secures a corresponding economy in lubricating oil. I have recently issued a new Rationing Order designed to check abuses in the use of petrol, and I am proceeding with the appointment of inspectors to aid in this purpose. In view of these facts, I do not propose at this moment to make a further general reduction in petrol allowances, but I would emphasize that it is vital that all petrol users should cooperate to the full in the strict observance of the Rationing Order.

Replying further, Mr. LLOYD said that it was not an abuse to use the limited amount of petrol allowed in the basic ration for purposes of reasonable recreation. (Hear, hear.) It was an abuse to use petrol obtained on a supplementary allowance for purposes for which it was not given. In regard to that he had powers. He intended to use them, and prosecutions would be taken in appropriate cases.

GERMANS IN EIRE

Mr. SHAKESPEARE, Under-Secretary, Dominion Affairs (Norwich, L. Nat.), in reply to MAJOR BRAITHWAITE (Buckrose, U.), said he understood that none of the engineers of German origin who assisted in building the Shannon Power Scheme now remained in Eire. He also understood that the official staff of the German Legation in Dublin was composed of six persons, together with three typists.

CIVILIAN CASUALTIES AT DUNKIRK

SIR A. BAILLIE (Tonbridge, U.) asked the number of civilians killed and wounded, respectively, in aiding the Royal Navy to remove men of the British Expeditionary Force and French Army from Dunkirk.

SIR V. WARRENDER, Parliamentary Secretary, Admiralty (Grantham, U.).—I regret that 125 civilians were killed and 81 wounded in this operation. Of these, four killed and two wounded were civilian volunteers, and the remainder regular merchant seamen. I should like to take this opportunity of expressing once more the profound admiration of the Royal Navy and the Admiralty for the spirit and courage of these men. I am sure that the House will wish me to express the deepest sympathy with the relatives of those who lost their lives or were wounded. (Hear, hear.)

Sir K. Wood's appeal for interest-free loans will be found on page 6.

NEW MEMBER

Mr. C. KAY, who has been elected as Labour member for Bow and Bromley in the room of the late Mr. G. Lansbury, took the oath and his seat. He was introduced by SIR C. EDWARDS, Joint Parliamentary Secretary to the Treasury (Bedwellty, Lab.) and Mr. GROVES (Stratford, Lab.).

MR. CHURCHILL'S SPEECH

HEROIC FRENCH RESISTANCE

On the motion for the adjournment,

Mr. CHURCHILL, Prime Minister (Epping, U.), said: I spoke the other day of the colossal military disaster which occurred when the French High Command failed to withdraw the Northern Armies from Belgium at the moment when they knew that the French front was decisively broken at Sedan and on the Meuse. This delay entailed the loss of 15 or 16 French divisions and threw out of action for the critical period the whole of the British Expeditionary Force. Our Army and 120,000 French troops were indeed rescued by the British Navy from Dunkirk, but only with the loss of their cannon, vehicles, and modern equipment. This loss inevitably took some weeks to repair, and in the first two of those weeks the battle in France has been lost.

When we consider the heroic resistance made by the French Army against heavy odds in this battle, and the enormous losses inflicted upon the enemy and the evident exhaustion of the enemy, it may well be thought that these 25 divisions of the best trained and best equipped troops might have turned the scale. However, General Weygand had to fight without them.

Only three British divisions, or their equivalent, were able to stand in the line with their French comrades. They have suffered severely, but they have fought well. (Cheers.) We sent every man we could to France as fast as we could re-equip and transport their formation. I am not reciting these facts for the purpose of recrimination. That I judge to be utterly futile and even harmful. We cannot afford it. I recite them in order to explain why it was we did not have, as we could have had, between 12 and 14 British divisions fighting in the line in this great battle instead of only three.

LOOKING TO THE FUTURE

Now I put all this aside. I put it on the shelf, from which the historians, when they have time, will select their documents to tell that story. We have to think of the future and not of the past. This also applies in a small way to our own affairs at home. There are many who would hold an inquest in the House of Commons on the conduct of the Governments and of the Parliaments—for they are in it too—during the years which led up to this catastrophe. They seek to indict those who were responsible for the guidance of our affairs. (Opposition cheers.) This also would be a foolish and pernicious process. There are too many in it.

Let each man search his conscience, and search his speeches as I frequently search mine. Of this I am quite sure that if we opened a quarrel between the past and the present we shall find that we have lost the future. Therefore, I cannot accept the drawing of any distinctions between members of the present Government. It was formed at a moment of crisis in order to unite all the parties and all sections of opinion. It has received the almost unanimous support of both Houses of Parliament. Its members are going to stand together, and, subject to the authority of the House of Commons, we are going to govern the country, and fight the war. (Cheers.)

It is absolutely necessary at a time like this that every Minister who tries, each day, to do his duty, shall be respected, and their subordinates must know that their chiefs are not threatened men, men who are here to-day and gone to-morrow, but that their directions must be punctually and faithfully obeyed. Without this concentrated power we cannot face what lies before us.

I should not think it would be very advantageous for the House to prolong this debate this afternoon under the conditions of public stress. Many facts are not clear that will be clear in a short time. We are to have a secret session on Thursday and I should think that would be a better opportunity for the many earnest expressions of opinion which members will desire to make and for the House to discuss our vital matters as I have said before without having everything read the next morning by our dangerous foes.

BRITISH EMPIRE TO FIGHT ON

The military events which have happened during the past fortnight have not come to me with any sense of surprise. Indeed, I indicated a fortnight ago, as clearly as I could, to the House that the worst possibilities were open, and I made it perfectly clear then that whatever happened in France would make no difference to the resolve of Britain and the British Empire to fight on if necessary for years, if necessary alone.

During the last few days we have successfully brought off the great majority of the troops we had on the lines of communication in France—a very large number, scores of thousands, and seven-eighths of the troops we have sent to France since the beginning of the war; that is to say, about 350,000 out of 400,000 men are safely back in this country. Others are still fighting with the French, and fighting with considerable success in their local encounters with the enemy.

We have also brought back a great mass of stores, rifles, and munitions of all kinds which have been accumulating in France during the last nine months. We have, therefore, in this island to-day a very large and powerful military force. This force includes all our best-trained and finest troops, and includes scores of thousands of those who have already measured their quality against the Germans and found themselves at no disadvantage. (Cheers.)

OUR ISLAND GARRISON

1,250,000 IN ARMS

We have under arms at the present time in this island over 1,250,000 men. Behind these we have the Local Defence Volunteers numbering 500,000, only a portion of whom, however, are yet armed with rifles or other firearms. We have incorporated into our defence forces every man for whom we have a weapon. We expect a very large addition to our weapons in the near future, and, in preparation for this, we intend to call up, drill, and train further large numbers at once. Those who are not called up or who are employed upon the vast business of munitions production in all its branches—and it runs through every kind of grade—they serve their country best by remaining at their ordinary work until they are required.

We also have Dominions armies here. The Canadians had actually landed in France, but have now been safely withdrawn, much disappointed—(laughter and cheers)—but in perfect order with all their artillery and equipment. (Cheers.) These very high-class forces from the Dominions will now take part in the defence of the Mother Country. (Cheers.)

Lest the account which I have given of these very large forces should raise the question why they did not take part in the great battle in France, I must make it clear that apart from the divisions training and organizing at home only 12 divisions were equipped to fight upon a scale which justified their being sent abroad. This was fully up to the number which the French had been led to expect would be available in France at the ninth month of the war.

The rest of our forces at home have a fighting value for home defence which will, of course, steadily increase every week that passes. Thus the invasion of Great Britain would at this time require the transportation across the sea of hostile armies upon a very large scale, and after they had been so transported they would have to be continually maintained with all the mass of munitions and supplies which are required for continuous battle, as continuous battle it would be. (Cheers.)

SEABORNE INVASION DIFFICULT

Here we come to the Navy. (Cheers.) After all we have a Navy. (Cheers.) Some people seem to forget that. We must remind them. (Cheers.) For the last 30 years I have been concerned in discussions about the possibilities of oversea invasion, and I took the responsibility on behalf of the Admiralty at the beginning of the last War of allowing all Regular troops to be sent out of the country, although our territorials had only just been called up and were quite untrained. Therefore, this island was for several months practically denuded of fighting troops. The Admiralty had confidence at that time in their ability to prevent a mass invasion, even though at that time the Germans had a magnificent battle fleet in the proportion of 10 to 16, even though they were capable of fighting a general engagement every day and any day, whereas now they only have a couple of heavy ships worth speaking of.

We are also told that the Italian Navy is to come to gain sea superiority in these waters. If that is seriously intended I can only say that we shall be delighted to offer Signor Mussolini a free and safeguarded passage through the Straits of Gibraltar in order that he may play the part which he aspires to do. (Laughter.) There is general curiosity in the British Fleet to find out whether the Italians are up to the level they were at in the last War, or whether they have fallen off at all. (Laughter.) Therefore, it seems to me that so far as seaborne invasion on a great scale is concerned we are far more capable of meeting it to-day than we were at many periods in the last War, and during the early months of this war, before our other troops were trained and while the B.E.F. was already abroad and still abroad. (Cheers.)

The Navy have never pretended to be able to prevent raids by bodies of 5,000 or 10,000 men, flung suddenly across and thrown ashore at several points on the coast some dark night or foggy morning. The efficacy of sea power, especially under modern conditions, depends upon the invading force being of large size. It has to be of large size, in view of our military strength, to be of any use. If it is of large size then the Navy have something they can find and meet and as it were bite on. (Cheers.)

SEA SUPERIORITY

Now we must remember that even five divisions, however lightly equipped, would require 200 to 250 ships, and with modern air reconnaissance and photography it would not be easy to collect such an armada, marshal it, and conduct it across the sea, without any powerful naval forces to escort it and with the very great possibility that it would be intercepted long before it reached the coast and the men all drowned in the sea, or at the worst blown to pieces with their equipment while they were trying to land. We also have a great system of minefields, recently strongly reinforced, through which we alone know the channel. If the enemy tries to sweep passages through these minefields it will be the task of the Navy to destroy the minesweepers and any other forces employed to protect them. There should be no difficulty in this owing to our great superiority at sea.

Those are the regular well-tested, well-proved arguments on which we have relied during many years in peace and war. But the question is whether there are any new methods by which those solid assurances can be circumvented. (Hear, hear.) Odd as it may seem, some attention has been given to this by the Admiralty—(laughter)—whose prime duty and responsibility it is to destroy any large seaborne expedition before it reaches, or at the moment when it reaches, these shores.

It would not be useful to go into details. It might even suggest ideas to other people which they have not thought of, and they would not be likely to give us any of their ideas in exchange. (Laughter and cheers.) All I will say is that untiring vigilance and mind-searching must be devoted to the subject, because the enemy is crafty and cunning, and full of novel treacheries and stratagems. (Hear, hear.) The House may be assured that the utmost ingenuity is being displayed and imagination is being evoked from large numbers of competent officers well trained in tactics and thoroughly up to date to measure and counterwork novel possibilities, of which many are suggested, some very absurd and some by no means utterly irrational.

BRITISH AIR STRENGTH

"THE IMPENDING STRUGGLE"

Some people will ask why, then, was it that the British Navy was not able to prevent the movement of a large army from Germany into Norway across the Skagerrak. But the conditions in the Channel and in the North Sea are in no way like those which prevail in the Skagerrak. (Cheers.) In the Skagerrak, because of the distance, we could give no air support to our surface ships, and consequently, lying as we did close to the enemy's main air power in those waters, we were compelled to use only our submarines. We could not enforce the decisive blockade or interruption which is possible from surface vessels. Our submarines took a heavy toll, but could not by themselves prevent the invasion of Norway. In the Channel and in the North Sea, on the other hand, our superior naval surface forces, aided by our submarines, will operate with close and effective air assistance. (Cheers.)

This brings me naturally to the great question of invasion from the air, and of the impending struggle between the British and German air forces. It seems quite clear that no invasion on a scale beyond the capacity of our air forces to crush completely is likely to take place from the air until our Air Force has been definitely overpowered. (Cheers.) In the meantime there may be raids by parachute troops and attempted descents of airborne soldiers. We should be able to give those gentry a warm reception, both in the air and if they reach the ground in any condition to continue the dispute. (Cheers.)

But the great question is, Can we break Hitler's air weapon? Now, of course, it is a very great pity that we have not got an air force at least equal to that of the most powerful enemy within striking distance of these shores. (Hear, hear.) But we have a very powerful Air Force, which has proved itself far superior in quality, both in men and in many types of machine, to what we have met so far in the numerous fierce air battles which have been fought. (Cheers.)

THE DUNKIRK BATTLE

In France, where we were at a considerable disadvantage and lost many machines on the ground in the aerodromes, we were accustomed to inflict losses of as much as two to two-and-a-half to one. In the fighting over Dunkirk, which was a sort of no man's land, we undoubtedly beat the German air force, which gave us the mastery locally in the air, and we inflicted losses of three or four to one. Anyone who looks at the photographs which were published a week or so ago of the re-embarcation showing the masses of troops assembled on the beach and forming an ideal target for hours at a time, must realize that this re-embarcation would not have been possible unless the enemy had resigned all hope of recovering air superiority at that point.

In the defence of this island the advantages to the defenders will be very great. We hope to improve on the rate of three or four to one which was realized at Dunkirk, and in addition all our injured machines and their crews which get down safely—and there are surprisingly a very great many injured machines and men who get down safely in modern air fighting—all of these fall in an attack upon these islands on friendly soil and live to fight another day, whereas all injured enemy machines and their complements will be total losses as far as the war is concerned. (Cheers.)

During the great battle in France we gave very powerful and continuous aid to the French Army both by fighters and bombers, but in spite of every kind of pressure we never would allow the entire metropolitan strength of the Air Force in fighters to be consumed. This decision was taken and it was right because the fortunes of the battle in France could not have been decisively affected even if we had thrown in our entire fighter force.

EXPLOITS OF FIGHTER PILOTS

The battle was lost by the unfortunate strategical opening and by the extraordinary and unforeseen power of the armoured columns and by the great preponderance of the German Army in numbers. Our fighter air force might easily have been exhausted as a mere accident in that great struggle, and we should have found ourselves at the present time in a very serious plight.

But as it is I am happy to inform the House that our fighter air strength is stronger at the present time, relatively to the Germans, who have suffered terrible losses, than it has ever been—(cheers)—and consequently we believe ourselves to possess the capacity to continue the war in the air under better conditions than we have ever experienced before. (Cheers.) I look forward confidently to the exploits of our fighter pilots who will have the glory of saving their native land, their island home, and all they love from the most deadly of all attacks.

There remains the danger of bombing attacks which will certainly be made very soon upon us by the bomber forces of the enemy. It is true that the German bomber force is superior in numbers to ours, but we have a very large bomber force also which we shall use to strike at military targets in Germany without intermission. (Cheers.)

THE ORDEAL AHEAD

QUALITIES OF BRITISH RACE

I do not at all underrate the severity of the ordeal which lies before us, but I believe our countrymen will show themselves capable of standing up to it like the brave men of Barcelona—(cheers)—and will be able to stand up to it, and carry on in spite of it, at least as well as any other people in the world. Much will depend upon this, and every man and every woman will have the chance to show the finest qualities of their race and render the highest service to their cause. For all of us at this time, whatever our sphere, our station, our occupation, our duty, it will be a help to remember the famous lines:—

> He nothing common did or mean,
> Upon that memorable scene.

I have thought it right on this occasion to give the House and the country some indication of the solid practical grounds upon which we base our inflexible resolve to continue the war—(hear, hear)—and I can assure them that our professional advisers of the three Services unitedly advised that we should do so, and that there are good and reasonable hopes of final victory. (Cheers.) We have also fully informed and consulted all the self-governing Dominions, and I have received from their Prime Ministers—Mr. Mackenzie King, Mr. Menzies, Mr. Fraser, and General Smuts—messages couched in the most moving terms in which they endorse our decision and declare themselves ready to share our fortunes and to persevere to the end. (Cheers.)

BLOCKADE POWER INCREASED

We may now ask ourselves—in what way has our position worsened since the beginning of the war? It is worsened by the fact that the Germans have conquered a large part of the coastline of Western Europe, and many small countries have been overrun by them. This aggravates the possibilities of air attack, and adds to our naval preoccupations. It in no way diminishes, but on the contrary definitely increases, the power of our long-distance blockade. (Hear, hear.) Should military resistance come to an end in France, which is not yet certain—(cheers)—though it will in any case be greatly diminished, the Germans can concentrate their forces, both military and industrial, upon us. But for the reasons I have given to the House, these will not be found so easy to apply.

If invasion becomes more imminent, we, being relieved from the task of maintaining a large army in France, have far larger and more efficient forces here to meet it. If Hitler can bring under his despotic control the industries of the countries he has conquered, this will add greatly to his already vast armament output.

On the other hand, this will not happen immediately, and we are now assured of the immense, continuous, and increasing support in supplies and munitions of all kinds from the United States—(cheers)—and especially of the aeroplanes and pilots from the Dominions and across the oceans, who will come from regions which are beyond the reach of enemy bombers. I do not see how any of these factors can operate to our detriment, on balance, before the winter comes, and the winter will impose a strain upon the Nazi régime, with almost all Europe writhing and starving under its heel, which, for all their ruthlessness, will run them very hard.

DEFENCE IMPROVED

We must not forget that from the moment when we declared war on September 3 it was always possible for Germany to turn all her Air Force upon this country, together with any other devices of invasion she might conceive, and that France could do little or nothing to prevent her doing so. We have, therefore, lived under this danger, in principle and in a slightly modified form, during all these months. In the meanwhile, however, we have enormously improved our methods of defence, and we have learned what we had no right to assume at the beginning—namely, the individual superiority of our aircraft and pilots.

Therefore, in casting up this dread balance-sheet, contemplating our dangers with a disillusioned mind, I see great reason for intense vigilance and exertion, but none whatever for panic or despair. (Loud cheers.) During the first four years of the last War the Allies experienced, as Mr. Lloyd George will remember, nothing but disaster and disappointment, and yet at the end their moral was higher than that of the Germans, who had moved from one aggressive triumph to another. During that War we repeatedly asked ourselves the question, "How are we going to win?" and no one was able ever to answer it with much precision, until at the end, quite suddenly, quite unexpectedly, our terrible foe collapsed before us and we were so glutted with victory that in our folly we cast it away. (Loud cheers.)

"THIS WAS THEIR FINEST HOUR"

BATTLE OF BRITAIN TO BEGIN

We do not yet know what will happen in France, or whether France's resistance will be prolonged, both in France and in the French Empire oversea. The French Government will be throwing away great opportunities and casting away their future if they do not continue the war in accordance with their treaty obligations, from which we have not felt able to release them. (Hear, hear.)

The House will have read the historic declaration in which, at the desire of many Frenchmen and of our own hearts, we have proclaimed our willingness to conclude, at the darkest hour in French history, a union of common citizenship. (Cheers.) However matters may go in France, or with the French Government, or with another French Government, we in this island and in the British Empire will never lose our sense of comradeship with the French people. If we are now called upon to endure what they have suffered we shall emulate their courage and, if final victory rewards our toils, they shall share the gains—(hear, hear)—aye, and freedom shall be restored to all. We abate nothing of our just demands—Czechs, Poles, Norwegians, Dutch, Belgians, all who have joined their causes to our own, shall be restored. (Cheers.)

What General Weygand called the Battle of France is over. I expect that the Battle of Britain is about to begin. Upon this battle depends the survival of Christian civilization. (Hear, hear.) Upon it depends our own British life, and the long continuity of our institutions and our Empire. The whole fury and might of the enemy must very soon be turned on us. Hitler knows that he will have to break us in this island or lose the war.

If we can stand up to him all Europe may be free, and the life of the world may move forward into broad, sunlit uplands; but if we fail then the whole world, including the United States—(hear, hear)—and all that we have known and cared for, will sink into the abyss of a new dark age, made more sinister and perhaps more prolonged by the lights of a perverted science. Let us therefore address ourselves to our duty, so bear ourselves that if the British Commonwealth and Empire lasts for a thousand years men will still say, "This was their finest hour." (Loud and prolonged cheers.)

A UNITED NATION

Mr. LEES SMITH (Keighley, Lab.) said that Labour members, from their experience of the mass of the people, could say that never in their lives had the country been more united than it was to-day—(hear, hear)—in support of the Prime Minister's assertion that we should carry on right to the end. One sentence could summarize what they felt—"Whatever the country is asked for in the months, and, if necessary, the years, to come, the Prime Minister may be confident that the people will rise to their responsibilities." (Cheers.)

SIR P. HARRIS (Bethnal Green, S.W., L.) congratulated the Prime Minister on his brave speech and the great leadership he had given to his country. The nation was behind him. (Cheers.)

SIR H. O'NEILL (Antrim, U.) said he took it that in view of the serious matters the Prime Minister had raised to-day the secret session on Thursday would be devoted to the general question of the present grave situation of the war.

Mr. CHURCHILL said the debate on Thursday would be on the adjournment, and members could have the regular freedom. But home defence was the focus of it, and he was not aware that the larger topics he had mentioned to-day displaced that.

COLONEL WEDGWOOD (Newcastle-under-Lyme, Lab.) said that the Prime Minister's speech would be of inestimable benefit in restoring the sanity and courage of the country. (Cries of "There is no lack of sanity and courage.") Anxiety in the country would be removed if the people realized that something was genuinely being done to remove the risks of casual raids. Everybody was anxious to do something, and it was distressing to the man in the street when he was so anxious to bear his part to find that the War Office did not need his services. They wanted an assurance that the Local Defence Force was not a mere step-child of the War Office.

MR. LLOYD GEORGE'S VIEW

Mr. LLOYD GEORGE (Caernarvon Boroughs, L.) said that it would be very good to have a useful discussion on the very broad and momentous questions which had been raised by the Prime Minister. There was real anxiety that they should be discussed under conditions where there would be no report, but where the House of Commons would be able, without any fetters at all, to discuss the whole broad issue.

He assured the Prime Minister that there was no desire merely to waste time upon recriminations about the past. (Hear, hear.) But there ought to be a very frank discussion as to where we stood now. There were many members who had suggestions to make; he would like to make a few himself. (Hear, hear.) They might be valuable or not, but if they were it would be valuable to the enemy to know them. He hoped the Prime Minister would not consider it a breach of faith if anybody should traverse the all-important question of defence and raise general issues.

Mr. CHURCHILL.—The debate will be under the ordinary rules of order. In a debate on the adjournment anything can be raised. I should certainly not regard that as a breach of faith. The Ministers themselves will be focusing their minds on these questions.

Mr. LLOYD GEORGE said that was what he meant. We had come to a tremendous crisis—so far as we were concerned the greatest crisis in the war. Parliament was responsible to the nation, and the nation expected their representatives to discuss the very issues they were discussing in their own circles everywhere, and they trusted Parliament to see that these issues were raised and faced. Then if members got satisfactory replies they would be able, each in his own sphere, to assure the country that everything humanly possible was being done.

Mr. J. MORGAN (Doncaster, Lab.) said, amid cheers in which Mr. Churchill joined, that the House ought at least to wish Sir Stafford Cripps "Good luck!" in the important job he had been given by the Government, because there were signs that whatever might be immediately confronting us potentially there was the same fate destined for another great Power.

The motion was withdrawn.

EVACUATION IN SCOTLAND

The House went into Committee of Supply on the estimates for the Scottish Office, SIR D. HERBERT, Chairman of Committees (Watford, U.), in the Chair.

On a vote for £2,395,500 for the salaries and expenses of the Department of Health in Scotland,

Mr. E. BROWN, Secretary of State for Scotland (Leith, L.), said that by the building of additional hospitals and the conversion of other buildings 25,000 casualty beds were now ready in Scotland, and another 6,000 would be ready in a few weeks.

The advantages of the policy of dispersal in the Scottish evacuation scheme were demonstrated by the fact that whereas in the sending areas the average population was 14,000 a square mile the population in the receiving areas was only 100 a square mile. Of 100,000 children who were evacuated in September, 20,000 were still in the receiving areas. New plans which could be put into operation if the need arose contemplated the evacuation of half the schoolchildren who were still left in the sending areas.

In the course of the debate, Mr. McKIE (Galloway, U.) said it was desirable that those responsible for administering the Home Department in Scotland should be fully aware of the activities of certain individuals in lonely parts of Scotland. They were not too friendly disposed towards the present policy of the Government. He knew of certain persons living in his constituency. One was the Marquess of Tavistock, who was a tenant of his. Questions had been asked about him in the House of Commons, and not very satisfactory answers were given. In view of the fact that we were engaged in a life and death conflict and of the Prime Minister's words of warning to-day, the Home Department in Scotland should take this matter into very serious reckoning. He had received seven or eight letters from this individual during the eight months we had been at war.

AN HON. MEMBER.—Does he pay his rent?

Mr. McKIE said that he had asked to get off it early in September, because he thought that owing to the increased taxation he would not be able to pay it.

Mr. WESTWOOD, Under-Secretary for Scotland (Stirling and Falkirk, Lab.), replied, and the debate was adjourned.

The House resumed, and the Marriage (Scotland) (Emergency Provisions) Bill passed through Committee and was read the third time.

The House adjourned at two minutes past 9 o'clock.

PARLIAMENTARY NOTICES

HOUSE OF LORDS

At 4

Viscount Samuel, motion on the food situation.

HOUSE OF COMMONS

At 2.45

Finance Bill, Report and third reading.

COMMITTEE

HOUSE OF LORDS, Select Committee: Newcastle-upon-Tyne and Gateshead Gas and Mid-Wessex Water, Room 3, at 11.

HOME COMMERCIAL MARKETS

TIN AGAIN LOWER

LONDON, June 18.—TIN.—The East reported sales of 325 tons at £275 per ton, c.i.f., a fall of £27 10s. per ton. The French announcement was not known during yesterday's official market, but this and the collapse in prices in the Straits were reflected here at the opening, though there was no particular pressure to sell. Buying interest, however, was limited and prices weakened, though the close was about steady, with standard cash £21 10s. to £21 5s. and three months £21 to £21 5s. per ton lower. Sales amounted to 225 tons. Cash to-day sold at £264, cash at £266 to £264, June £266 to £264, August at £267 10s. to £265, September at £265, and three months at £268 to £265 to £265 5s. Settlement price, £264. Official closing quotations:—Standard, cash, £264 to £264 10s. (previous, £285 10s. to £285 15s.); three months, £265 10s. to £265 15s. (£286 10s. to £287). There was a firmer tone in the after hours market, when August sold at £265 10s. to £267 10s., September at £266 10s. to £267 10s., and three months at £266 10s. to £268. Sales, 100 tons. English common tin, £264 15s. per ton, ex Liverpool, and Straits tin in warehouse here nominally at £284 10s. per ton.

TINPLATES.—Home delivery, 24s. 9d., basis I.C., 14 by 20, f.o.t. makers' works; high-speed canning plates, 9d., basis extra; subject to any new prices ruling at the time of delivery. Export, 30s. to 31s., basis f.o.b. South Wales. ALUMINIUM.—Ingots and bars for home delivery, £110 per ton. ANTIMONY.—English regulus, £106 to £107, and Chinese regulus, £98 to £99 per ton, ex warehouse; Chinese for shipment nominal at £82 to £86 per ton, c.i.f. WOLFRAM.—Empire, 50s. per unit, f.o.b. NICKEL for home delivery, £190 to £195 per ton. PLATINUM.—Refined quoted at £9 10s. per oz. QUICKSILVER on the spot firmer at £53 18s. 6d. to £55 per flask, ex warehouse, London.—*Comtelburo*.

GRAIN AND FARM PRODUCE

LONDON (Baltic Exchange), June 18.—WHEAT.—In sympathy with option prices in North America and the continued absence of buying interest, f.o.b. offers of Canadian were further reduced 4½d. per qr. Australian was unchanged, but Argentine shippers held for 3d. advance. No. 1 Northern Manitoba, Montreal, August 1-15, 29s. 10½d.; August 16-31, 30s. 1½d.; No. 2 Northern Manitoba, Montreal, August 1-15, 29s. 1½d.; August 16-31, 29s. 4½d.; No. 3 Northern Manitoba, Montreal, August 1-15, 28s. 1½d.; Australian, in bulk, June, 26s. 9d.; Baril, 62lb., June, 28s.; and Baruso, 62lb., June, 27s. 6d. per 480lb., f.o.b. MAIZE remained in limited demand. Yellow La Plata was about 3d. higher, June-July shipment being quoted at 12s. 6d. and July-August at 12s. 9d. African sorts were unaltered, No. 2 white flat, July-August, 18s. 3d. and No. 6 yellow round, July-August, at 18s. 6d. per 480lb., f.o.b. BARLEY unchanged. No. 1 Australian Chevalier, June-July, 29s. 6d.; and No. 2, 28s. per 448lb., f.o.b.

POTATOES (the Borough).—Supplies of new potatoes were plentiful and prices continue to droop; Jersey sold at 18s. and English at 18s. to 20s. per cwt., ex market, while the prescribed maximum wholesale price under the Order is 25s. 4d. per cwt. until June 29. Old crop potatoes were scarce and firm, with best siltland King Edward quoted at 8s. 6d. to 9s., skirtland King Edward 8s., and Majestic and Doone Star 7s. 6d. to 8s. per cwt., ex market.—*Comtelburo*.

FRUIT AND VEGETABLES (Covent Garden).—Trade generally was poor. Apples, Australian, 16s. to 25s. per box; English cooking, 9s. to 11s. per bushel. Pears, Australian, 21s. to 25s. per case. Grapes, South African, white, also black, 10s. to 15s. per box. Bananas, Jamaica, and Brazilian, 14s. to 15s. per case. Strawberries, 4½d. to 1s. 3d. per lb. Cherries, English, 6d. to 7d. per lb. Gooseberries, 4d. to 4½d. per lb. Grapefruit, Jaffa and Trinidad, 38s. to 45s. per case. Oranges, South African, 18s. to 24s. 6d.; Brazilian, 19s. to 24s. 6d. per box. Lemons, Messina, 50s. to 60s. per case. Brazils, 60s. to 65s. per cwt. Tomatoes, English, 7s. to 9s. per 12lb. Cucumbers, 6d. to 8d. each. Asparagus, English, 8d. to 1s. 4d. per round, 1s. 4d. to 2s. 6d. per fan. Lettuce, English, 1s. to 2s. per crate. Mushrooms, 1s. to 1s. 4d. per lb. Rhubarb, 1s. 6d. to 2s. 6d. per dozen. Cabbage, 4s. to 5s. per crate. Spinach, 3s. to 4s. per crate. Turnips, 3s. to 5s. per bag. Parsnips, 3s. to 5s. per half-bag. Carrots, 10s. to 12s. per half-bag. Onions, 15s. to 16s. per bag. New potatoes, Teneriffe, Cyprus, and Moroccan, 14s. to 16s.; Jersey, 16s. to 18s. per cwt. Peas, English, 7s. to 8s. per bag.—*Comtelburo*.

COTTON

LIVERPOOL, June 18.—Conditions on the spot market were quieter. Quotations of American were reduced 22 points; middling 7.33d. American and others 22 points lower; middling 7.43d. Brazilian and Peruvian declined 22 points; North fair 6.98d., and g.f. Tanguis 7.93d. Egyptian 31 to 34 points down; f.g.f. Giza 7, 10.05d., and f.g.f. Upper 10.23d. African reduced 23 points; Mid West 7.03d., and g.f. East 8.43d. East Indian 5 to 15 points lower; fine Broach 6.33d., and Central Province 6.04d. per lb.

American futures closed quiet, 7 points higher to unchanged, with Oct. and following months nominal. New York 11 a.m. prices.—July, 10.35; Oct., 9.28; Dec., 9.14; March, 8.89.

Amer. Futures	To-day			Prev. day		
Delivery—	Hghst.	L'west	Closing	Hghst.	L'west	Closing
June	—	—	7.10	—	—	7.03
July	7.10	7.06	7.10	7.34	7.00	7.03
August ..	—	—	7.01	6.96	6.96	6.97
September	6.93	6.92	6.92	—	—	6.92
October	6.86	6.86	6.86*	—	—	6.86
November	—	—	6.79*	—	—	6.79
December	—	—	6.76*	—	—	6.76
January	—	—	6.74*	6.83	6.74	6.74
February	—	—	6.71*	—	—	6.71
March	—	—	6.69*	6.77	6.77	6.69
April ..	—	—	6.66*	—	—	6.66
May	—	—	6.64*	6.76	6.64	6.64
June	—	—	6.61*	—	—	6.61

* Nominal.

The American and other growths' contract finished nominally 7 points higher to unchanged. June, 7.00; July-Aug., 6.91; Sept.-Oct., 6.76; Nov.-Dec., 6.66; Jan.-Feb., 6.61; March-April, 6.56; May-June, 6.51.

In Egyptian futures the Giza 7 contract closed very steady at 48 to 49 points advance. June to Sept., 9.81; Oct. and Nov., 9.84; Dec. and Jan., 9.85; Feb., 9.87; March and April, 9.89; May and June, 9.91. The Upper contract closed steady at a rise of 50 to 45 points. June to Sept., 9.85; Oct. and Nov., 9.65; Dec. to April, 9.63; May and June, 9.65.

Prices for control.—American, July, 7.09; Egyptian, Giza 7, July, 9.50; Upper, July, 9.60.—*Comtelburo*.

MANCHESTER, June 18.—The cloth market was quieter to-day than for a long time. Many oversea buyers have not been showing much interest in cotton goods recently, but the French move for an armistice has virtually killed enterprise for the time being, even though cotton prices were remarkably steady.

COLONIAL AND FOREIGN PRODUCE

LONDON, June 18.—SUGAR.—Prices of British refined sorts were unchanged.

COCOA.—The market was nominal.

SPICES.—Prices were mostly nominal.

SHELLAC.—The market was nominal and unquoted. Calcutta advices dated June 18:—Spot, June, and July quoted Rs.20, value.

RUBBER.—The market for plantation grades opened nominal, but subsequently there was a small business and near deliveries showed a decline of a 1d. per lb. Smoked sheet, spot, sold from 1s. 2½d. to 1s. 1½d. per lb. and buyers; July from 1s. 2¼d. to 1s. 1¼d. and buyers; Aug. from 1s. 1¼d. to 1s. 1⅛d. to 1s. 1¼d. and sellers; Oct.-Dec. from 1s. 0½d. to 11¾d. to 1s. and sellers; Jan.-March quoted 11½d., value. Para grades were unchanged; hard fine, spot, quoted 1s. 3½d. per lb. At the committee meeting of the Rubber Trade Association held at 4 p.m. on June 17, it was decided that the Emergency Committee has power to stop all dealings at a moment's notice pending a committee meeting being called to fix maximum and minimum prices if considered necessary. The Committee considers that in present circumstances no new speculative commitments should be undertaken except in liquidation of existing contracts.

JUTE.—Calcutta advices dated June 18:—Firsts, June and July, Rs.56, sellers; lightnings, June and July, Rs.46 8a., sellers.

HESSIANS AND TWILLS were unsettled. 10oz., Aug., quoted 27s. 1d.; 8oz., Aug., 20s. 4d., sellers, c.i.f., per 100 yards. Liverpool twills, Aug., 66s. 6d.; B., Aug., 59s. 6d., sellers, c.i.f., per 100 bags.—*Comtelburo*.

WINNIPEG GRAIN

WINNIPEG, June 18.—WHEAT opened steady and unchanged. United States interests absorbed hedging on reports of showers in the West. There was no export business, but the close was steady, unchanged to ¼c. up. July, 71½c. per bushel; Oct., 74½c.; Dec., 75¾c. Carlot receipts:—No. 1 Northern, 743; No. 2, 210; No. 3, 13; No. 4, 2; other grades, 33. Total, 1,001. OATS barely steady, ⅛c. to ½c. lower. July, 30c.; Oct., 27⅞c.; Dec., 27c. RYE easy, 1⅛c. down. July, 45¼c.; Oct., 43½c.; Dec., 43¾c. BARLEY barely steady, ½c. down. July, 34¼c.; Oct., 34⅝c.; Dec., 35½c. LINSEED easy, 10c. down. July, 138½c.; Oct., 141½c.

The Canadian visible supply of wheat this week is 279,784,000 bushels, against 279,919,000 last week and 110,213,000 in the same week last year.

AMERICAN MARKETS

STEADY CLOSE IN STOCKS

NEW YORK, June 18.—The prospects of heavy spending for defence, augmented by British demands, were the principal prop in the stock market. Of the 707 stocks traded in the turnover of 720,000 shares 408 were higher, while 145 were lower and 154 remained unchanged. Oils were restrained by the cut in the price of Pennsylvania crude oil. Early gains were reduced, but the close was steady and mostly fractions to a point higher.

Dow Jones averages:—Twenty railroad stocks, 25.63 (previous, 25.04); 30 industrials, 123.21 (122.80); 15 utilities, 20.79 (20.60).

Moody's commodity price index (December 31, 1931 = 100):—To-day, 156.6; previous, 156; month ago, 154.4; year ago, 142.2.

The daily average production of crude oil last week was 3,816,200 barrels, against 3,816,900 the previous week.

Call money, 1 per cent.; outside rate, 1 per cent. Prime paper, ½ to ¾ per cent. Open market discount rates, ½ to 7-16 per cent. for 90-day bank bills and ⅝ to 9-16 per cent. for six-month bills.

Sterling exchange opened 2½ points lower at $3.64 and declined to $3.61 during the morning. The rate subsequently recovered to $3.63½, then reacted to $3.61, but finally rallied and closed 4½ points down (compared with the previous close) at $3.61½.

EXCHANGE	Method of Quoting	Parity	June 18	June 17
		$	$	$
MONTREAL on— London, cables	£1	4.86⅔	4.52½	4.56⅛
NEW YORK on— London, demand	£1	—	—	—
Cables.. ..	£1	4.86⅔	3.62¾	3.66½
Montreal, cables	$100	100	80.000	80.250
Paris, cables ..	100f.	—	—	—
Rome, cables ..	100lr.	8.93	5.05*	5.05*
Amsterd'm, cables	100fl.	68.06	—	—
Oslo, cables ..	100kr.	26.80	—	—
Stockholm, cables	100kr.	26.80	23.85	23.85
Copenh'g'n, cables	100kr.	26.80	—	—
Berlin, cables ..	100mk.	40.30	40.10*	40.10*
Brussels, cables ..	100bel.	23.54	—	—
Zurich, cables ..	100f.	—	22.42½	22.42
Barcelona, cables	100pes.	19.30	9.25*	9.25*
Budapest, cables	100pen.	26.81	—	—
Belgrade, cables	100din.	1.76	—	—
Athens, cables ..	100dr.	1.29½	—	0.70
		Cents	Cents	Cents
B. Aires, mkt. rate	—	—	22.10	22.00
Official buying	—	—	29.78	29.78
Rio, cables	1 mil.	11.86	5.10	5.10
Yokohama, cables	1 yen	59.83	23.48	23.48
Shanghai, cables	$1	—	6.05	6.05

* Nominal.

Silver was unchanged at 34¾c.—*Reuter*.

NEW YORK, June 18.—WHEAT steady, unchanged to ⅜c. up. No. 1 Northern Manitoba, c.i.f. New York, 83c. per bushel; No. 2 Manitoba, c.i.f. New York, 81c.; No. 2 hard winter, c.i.f. New York, 97¾c.; No. 2 red winter, 96¼c. MAIZE steady, ⅝c. up. Western No. 2 mixed, 77⅛c. OATS barely steady, ¾c. down. No. 2 white (per 36lb.), c.i.f. New York, 45⅛c. RYE steady, ⅜c. lower. No. 2, f.o.b. New York, 60¼c. BARLEY barely steady, ⅝c. down. No. 2, New York, all growths, Federal inspected, 55⅞c. FLOUR unchanged. Spring clears, $4.35 to $4.45; Kansas, straights, $4.45; Minneapolis patents, $4.65; bakers' clears, $4.40; rye flour, $5.45 to $5.70, all per 196lb. Sales for export, 3,000 barrels.

COFFEE on spot unchanged. Rio No. 7, 5⅜c.; Santos No. 4, 7⅛c. per lb. Futures closed irregular, with Rio unchanged to 6 points up and Santos 9 to 6 points down. Rio No. 7:—July, 3.97c.; Sept., 4.04c.; Dec., 4.08c.; March, 4.25c. Sales, 1,000 bags. Santos No. 4:—July; 5.81c.; Sept., 5.97c.; Dec., 6.18c.; March, 6.30c.; May, 6.40c. Sales, 27,000 bags.

COCOA.—Spot 4⅞c. per lb. Futures closed very steady, 7 to 4 points higher. July, 4.81c.; Sept., 4.91c.; Oct., 4.93c.; Dec., 5.01c.; Jan., 5.04c.; March, 5.11c.; May, 5.19c. Sales, 190 lots.

SUGAR on spot unchanged at 2.68c. per lb. In futures the old contract closed irregular and 1 point higher, while the new contract finished barely steady, unchanged to 2 points lower. Old contract:—July, 1.78c.; Sept., 1.86c.; Nov., 1.91c. Sales, 76 lots. New contract:—July and Sept., 1.08c.; Dec., 1.10½c.; March, 1.13c.; May, 1.14½c.; July, 1.17c.; Sept., 1.19c. Sales, 60 lots.

COTTON on spot closed 14 points higher at 11.03c. per lb. (nominal). Futures opened steady, with the old contract 4 points lower in July, and the new contract 5 to 3 points down. After easing in sympathy with Bombay the market rallied sharply on the firmness of the stock market and on short covering in July. The close was steady, with the old contract 14 points up and the new contract 14 to 10 points higher.

Futures	New Contract: To-day				Previous	
	Highest	Lowest	Clos'g	Range	Clos'g	Range
July ..	—	—	10.44	10.44	10.31	10.31
August ..	—	—	10.19	10.19	10.06	10.06
Sept. ..	—	—	9.34	9.34	9.22	9.22
Oct. ..	9.42	9.17	9.34	9.35	9.22	9.22
Nov. ..	—	—	9.28	9.28	9.15	9.15
Dec. ..	9.28	9.05	9.22	9.22	9.09	9.09
Jan. ..	—	—	9.11	9.11	8.97	8.97
Feb. ..	—	—	9.02	9.02	8.90	8.90
March ..	9.00	8.80	8.94	8.94	8.83	8.83
April ..	—	—	8.86	8.86	8.76	8.76
May ..	8.85	8.66	8.79	8.79	8.69	8.69

COPPER steady. Lake, spot, delivered consuming points in Middle West, unchanged at 11.50c. per lb. (producers' price); electrolytic, f.a.s., New York, prompt, 25 down at 11.25c. (outside market). TIN.—Straits weak. Spot, New York, 52c. per lb. (previous, 56c.); 30 days, 51c. (55c.); 90 days, 50c. (54.25c.).

Tin futures (Straits) weak, 3.87½c. to 3.50c. down. July, 50.75c. to 51.50c.; Sept., Dec., 49.75c.; March, 49.25c. Standard copper futures easy, 18 to 15 down. July, 10c. to 10.04c.; Sept., Oct., 10.05c.; Dec., March, 10.05c. to 10.10c.

LEAD unchanged. Spot, New York, 5c. per lb.; East St. Louis, 4.85c. SPELTER unchanged. Spot, East St. Louis, 6.25c.

HIDES 7 to 4 down. June, 10.09c. per lb.; Sept., 10.15c.; Dec., 10.34c.; March, 10.56c. Sales, 129 lots.

RUBBER.—No. 1 contract closed steady, 30 to 39 points down. July, 21.50c. per lb.; Sept., 19.12c.; Oct., 18.49c.; Dec., 17.89c.; Jan., 17.74c.; March, 17.54c.; May, 17.47c. Sales, 103 lots. The outside market was steady. First latex thin crêpe, spot, 21⅝c., buyers; smoked ribbed sheet, spot, 22c. buyers, 22¼c. sellers; July-Sept., 20⅝c., buyers; Oct.-Dec., 18¼c. buyers, 18½c. sellers.

COTTON OIL 1 down to 3 up. July, 5.96c. per lb.; Sept., 6.09c.; Oct., 6.10c.; Dec., 6.15c. Sales, 70 lots.

TALLOW steady. Spot, extra, loose, 4c. per lb.; special extra, 3⅞c.; in tierces, 4¼c. Futures steady. July, 4c., nominal; Sept., 4.10c., nominal; Oct., 4.20c. bid.

PETROLEUM.—Mid-continent crude (36deg. Baume at well, per barrel), 102c. Pennsylvania crude (barrel at well), lower price, 112c., representing Corning crude; higher price, 225c., representing Bradford and Alleghany.

SHELLAC, T.N., 13½c. TURPENTINE, spot, 31¼c.

SAVANNAH, June 18.—TURPENTINE, spot, 26¼c. per gallon. ROSIN, grade F, $3.95; K, $4.02½; W.W., $5.65 per 280lb.

DULUTH, June 18.—LINSEED steady, unchanged. July and Sept., 165c.

CHICAGO, June 18.—After firmness on unwanted rains in the South-west, grains reacted on reports minimizing rust development in Kansas. The proposed inter-Hemisphere cartel to dispose of surpluses was a constructive factor. WHEAT opened ¾c. to 1⅜c. up and closed steady, ½c. to ⅛c. up. July, 77¾c. per bushel; Sept., 78⅛c. to 78¼c.; Dec., 78¾c. to 79c. MAIZE opened ⅜c. to ¾c. up and closed very steady, ⅝c. to ½c. up. July, 61½c.; Sept., 59¾c.; Dec., 57c. OATS barely steady, ¾c. to ¼c. lower. July, 30⅝c.; Sept., 29¼c.; Dec., 29⅞c. RYE barely steady, ⅜c. to ½c. down. July, 41c.; Sept., 42¾c.; Dec., 45c. LARD.—Spot unchanged. Prime Western steam, loose, $4.65 per 100lb. Futures steady, unchanged to 2½c. up. July, $5.47½; Sept., $5.65; Oct., $5.75; Dec., $5.92½.

	Bacon, fat backs (12-14lb.) (per 100lb.)	Dry salted bellies: Spot	July	Hogs: Light	Heavy
To-day ..	6.87½	6.00	6.00	4.60-5.10	4.75-5.05
Previous ..	6.87½	6.00	6.00	4.60-5.20	4.80-5.10

Hog receipts—	Western	Chicago
To-day	95,000	23,000
Previous	81,000	18,000
Same day last year	69,000	18,000

Receipts of hogs at 15 principal Western centres, including Chicago, since March 1 total 5,874,000, against 4,791,000 for the same season last year.—*Reuter*.

ARGENTINE GRAIN

BUENOS AIRES, June 18 (4 p.m.).—WHEAT steady, unchanged. June, 8.45; July, 8.55; Aug., 8.67. MAIZE steady, unchanged. June, 4.08; July, 4.20; Aug., 4.29. OATS steady, unchanged. June, 4.98. LINSEED steady, unchanged. June, 15.11; July, 15.25; Aug., 15.45. Prices in pesos per 100 kilos, delivery Buenos Aires.—*Reuter*.

NEW YORK STOCK PRICES

RAILS	Eng. Eqv.§	Closing Bids June 18	June 17	RAILS	Eng. Eqv.§	Closing Bids June 18	June 17	RAILS	Eng. Eqv.§	Closing Bids June 18	June 17
At. Coast ..	14 9/16	11¾	11⅛	Ches.& Ohio	44⅛	35⅝	34½	N. Pacific ..	7⅛	5¾	5½
Bal. & Ohio	4 7/16	3⅝	3⅜	G. N., Pfd.	26	21	20⅝	Pennsylvania	22⅝	18¼	17½
Do., Prefd.	5 11/16	4⅝	4⅜	Illinois Cent.	9⅛	7⅜	7⅛	S. Rly. ..	13⅝	11	10¼
Can. Pac. ..	3 11/16	3	2¾	N.Y.,C.St.L.	15 5/16	12⅜	12	Do., Prefd.	22¾	18⅜	17⅜
INDUSTRIALS											
Amer. Loco.	16⅛	13	13	Gillette ..	5 1/16	4⅛	4	Patino M...	8 1/16	6½	6¾
Amer. Metal	18¼	14¾	15	Glidden Co.	14⅞	12	12*	Remgt'n Rd.	8 11/16	7	6⅝
Am. R. Mls.	14¼	11½	11½	G'rich B.F.	16¼	13⅛	12¾	Reynolds S.	9	7¼	7¼
Am. Smelt.	47 11/16	38⅝	38½	Good. Tire	19 11/16	15⅞	15¾	Sears Roebk.	87½	70⅝	69¾
Amer. Tele.	193	156⅛	155¾	Hud. Motors	4 7/16	3⅝	3½	Shell Un. ..	9⅞	8	8⅛
Amer. Water	9⅞	8	8	Int. M. Mar.	7 7/16	6	6	Socony Vac.	10⅝	8⅝	8½
Anaconda ..	26⅝	21½	21⅝	Int. Nickel..	29 7/16	23¾	22¾	Stand. Bds.	7⅛	5¾	5½
Arm. of Il.	5 9/16	4½	4⅝	Int. P. & P.	16	12⅞	13	Std. G. & E.	1 11/16	1⅜	1⅜
Atl. Refin...	25 13/16	20¾	21⅛	Int. Tel. (F.)	4⅛	3⅜	3⅛	Std.O.of Ind.	28⅝	23⅛	23
Barnsd. Cpn.	9⅝	7¾	8	Lehigh P.C.	19 3/16	15½	16⅛	Std.O.ofN.J.	43⅜	35	36⅜
BoeingAircft	17 1/16	13¾	77½	Lib. O. Ford	40⅞	33	33	Stone & W.	8 11/16	7	7⅛
Briggs Man.	20 7/16	16½	16⅞*	Lig. My. B.	116 15/16	94¼	93½	Studebaker	8 11/16	7	6⅞
Budd Man.	4 5/16	3½	3⅝	Lockh'd Air	32⅝	26⅜	27⅛	Tim. D. Axle	28⅜	22⅞	22½
Budd Wheel	5 11/16	4⅝	4¼	Lorillard, P.	25 1/16	20¼	19½	Tim. R. Brg.	51⅛	41⅛	40
Cel. of Am.	30½	24⅝	24¾	Mack Tcks.	25⅜	20½	20	Tri-Cont. ..	2	1⅝	1⅜
Col. Gas ..	6 13/16	5⅝	5⅝	Nash Kelvin.	5¼	4¼	4	20 Cent.-Fox	8 9/16	6⅞	6¼
Com. Solvts.	11 9/16	9⅜	9⅛	Nat. Biscuit	22⅝	18¼	18¼	Utd. Corp.	2⅜	1⅞	1⅞
Com.& Sthn.	1¼	1	1	Nat. C'h R.	13 15/16	11¼	11	Utd. Drug...	4 15/16	4	4⅛
Cont. Can.	50½	40¾	38	Nat. Dairy	16⅞	13⅝	13½	Utd. Gas Im.	13½	10⅞	11
Crown Cork	28½	23	22⅛	Nat. Dists.	23 9/16	19	18¼	U.S. Leather	5 9/16	4½	4⅛
Cruc. Steel	37 13/16	30⅝	30¾	Nat. P. & L.	8 11/16	7	6⅞	U.S.SteelPfd	137½	111	111
Curtiss-W...	9 7/16	7⅝	7¾	Otis Steel ..	10½	8½	8¾	Warner Bros	2 15/16	2⅜	2⅜
East. Kodak	159 3/16	128½	132½	Owens-Il. G.	58¼	47	46	Wgh'se El.	111½	90	91¼
Elec. P. & L.	5 9/16	4½	4½	Pac.Gas& E.	34⅜	27¾	27¼	Woolworth	39 1/16	31½	31½
Gen. Motors	54½	44	43⅞	Parm't Pict.	6½	5¼	5⅛	Yngst.S.&T.	40 1/16	32⅜	33
CURB EXCHANGE											
Braz. Tract.	4	3¼	3¼	E. Bd. & Sh.	6 1/16	4⅞	5¼	Penn. Corp.	1 11/16	1⅜	1⅝
BONDS	English Eqv.§	Last Sales June 18	June 17	BONDS	English Eqv.§	Last Sales June 18	June 17	BONDS	English Eqv.§	Last Sales June 18	June 17
U.S., 2⅞%, '55-60 ..	132¼	106 25/32	106⅝	Braz.Fdg.'51	32 3/16	26	24½	Denm. 4½%	29¾	24	24½
Arg. 4%, '72	81½	65¾	66	Do., 6½%	—	—	9¾	Jap. 6½% '54	109 1/16	88	89
Aust. 5%, '57	50 13/16	41	41½	Canada, 5%, '42-52 ..	109 1/16	88	88	S.P. Coffee 7%, '31-40	29¾	24	23½
Belg. 7%, '55	—	—	48	Chile, 6%, '26-60	—	—	—	Tokio, 5½%	74 15/16	60½	60½

* Ex dividend. § At $4.03½. In Bond quotations no allowance is made for accrued interest.—*Reuter*.

A
16. Jahrgang · Nr. 25
Erscheint wöchentlich

Der Feuerreiter

Köln, 22. Juni 1940
Einzelpreis 20 Pf.

Verlag Hans Struth
Köln · Hochhaus

Die Führer der beiden Nationen

die nun Schulter an Schulter im Kampf um die europäische Ordnung stehen.

Aufgenommen beim Besuch des Führers in Rom.

Presse-Hoffmann

WAR EXTRA

COMPLETE RACES

Complete BASEBALL

CHARACTER QUALITY — AMERICA FIRST! — ENTERPRISE ACCURACY

Los Angeles Examiner

AN AMERICAN PAPER FOR THE AMERICAN PEOPLE — THE GREAT NEWSPAPER OF THE GREAT SOUTHWEST

Reg. U.S. Pat. Off.

VOL. XXXVII—NO. 196 CC LOS ANGELES, MONDAY, JUNE 24, 1940 Two Sections—Part I—FIVE CENTS

NAZI PEACE TERMS TOLD

To Occupy Half of France, Intern Fleet; Britain Breaks With Premier Petain

Exile Leaders Will Continue as London Ally

LONDON, June 23.—(INS)—Great Britain tonight broke off relations with the French government of Premier Marshal Petain in Bordeaux.

Because of the armistice with Germany, it was announced, Britain will recognize a "provisional" French exile government now being formed to carry on the war.

Formation of a "French national committee" was announced in a broadcast over the official British radio by General Charles Degaulle, undersecretary of war in the former French cabinet of Paul Reynaud.

SAY PLEDGE BROKEN

Charging France broke a solemn pledge in making a separate peace with Germany, an official statement said:

"His Majesty's government finds the terms of the armistice just made, in contravention of the agreements solemnly made between the Allied governments, reduce the Bordeaux government to a state of complete subjection and deprive it of all liberty and the right to represent free French citizens.

"His Majesty's government therefore now declares it can no longer regard the Bordeaux government as the government of an independent country.

"His Majesty's government has taken note of the proposal to form a provisional French national committee, fully rep-

(Continued on Page A., Cols. 1-2)

Italy Peace Aims Given to French

ROME, June 23.—(AP)—Italy handed her armistice terms to France tonight at a closely-guarded meeting in a villa near Rome and the plenipotentiaries of the two warring nations immediately began their solemn parleys on a truce to end France's fight against the Rome-Berlin axis.

A brief official announcement said the Italian peace delegates had given their armistice conditions to the four French representatives at 7:30 p. m. (9:30 a. m., P. S. T.) in a country place 12 miles from the Italian capital.

The meeting of the two groups, a short while after the French arrived in German planes from Munich, lacked the show surrounding the French-German conferences at Compiegne Forest, France, which ended in the signing of the French-German armistice yesterday.

PEACE LIKELY AT DAWN

Fighting will not cease in France, however, until six hours after Germany has been notified that Italy and France have reached an agreement.

(In Bordeaux, temporary French capital, reliable sources said the Italian reply might be received during the night and the cease fire order given around dawn Monday.)

Some political circles said the Italians failed to inject the drama any symbolism of the Compiegne meeting into the Rome deliberations because the Italians had not been forced to sign an armistice with the French in 1918 as did the Germans.

Italy was France's ally in 1918.

DUCE NOT AT MEETING

Premier Mussolini was not at the meeting. His foreign minister and son-in-law, Count Ciano, headed the Italian group.

During the French stay, the delegates will be lodged in three different villas in the Rome area.

Besides Count Ciano, other Italian plenipotentiaries were:

Marshal Pietro Badoglio, chief of the general staff of the armed forces.

Admiral Domenico Cavagnari, chief of staff of the navy.

General Francisco Pricolo, chief of the air force.

General Mario Roatta, assistant chief of staff of the army.

The same delegates who signed

(Continued on Page A, Cols. 6-7)

French Area Demanded by Axis

MAP SHOWS French territory axis will occupy under armistice terms. Germany holds all France north of a line from Geneva through Lyon to Angers and the entire west coast. Italy will take over entire Mediterranean coast. The shaded portion represents the occupied area. The French government will be allowed to have Paris as capital.

U. S. Political Campaign Expected to Spur Axis Into Seeking Death Blow on England

By Karl H. von Wiegand
Chief foreign correspondent of the Hearst Newspapers and for 28 years outstanding American political observer in Europe and the Far East.
(Special Wireless Dispatch to the Los Angeles Examiner)

ROME, June 23.—With the close of the Republican and Democratic national conventions and their presidential nominations, there will begin a mad, dramatic and bloody German and Italian drive to force a decisive end to the war with England by or before our November election.

That election will be a whip and spur to Hitler and Mussolini in dynamics of force and speed to bring England to serious thought concerning a peace which promises to find terrific expression across the Channel and perhaps reprisals in Germany.

INTERVENTION FEAR

Rightly or wrongly, the fact is, that in Berlin and Rome, in the Fuehrer's headquarters in France and in the royal imperial Italian general headquarters, the impression is deep that Roosevelt's nomination and election would bring active American intervention much nearer after November, if England holds on till then.

Since it is fully realized any effort whatever to influence the course of the election in the United States would indeed be a boomerang, it is planned to mobilize and concentrate directly on all possible means to assure that "this phase of the war" be finished by autumn.

France is practically eliminated and the war against England centers strategically and tactically with operations on the two main sectors—on England itself and on the empire's communications in the eastern Mediterranean.

Once offering guarantees to all and sundry on the continent,

(Continued on Page 4, Column 4)

Reich Armies to Take Over All West Coast

GENEVA, June 23.—(AP)—Fascist sources here said tonight the whole Mediterranean coast of France would be occupied by Italian troops by agreement with Germany and that after the war a semi-independent buffer state will be formed of Nice, Savoy and part of Dauphine.

LONDON, June 23.—(AP)—Complete disarmament, surrender and internment of the French navy, and German occupation of half of France are the price of France's armistice with Germany, an authoritative British source disclosed tonight.

With the final terms of peace yet to be worked out, such an armistice would give Adolf Hitler new guns, new tanks, new ships, new planes—and a broad coastline from which to launch long-threatened invasion of England.

Unimportant Amendments

The British informant said German occupational armies would take the whole western coast of France, and hold all France north of a line from Geneva, Switzerland, through Lyons, on the Loire River.

That is almost exactly the territory already seized in the steady German advance.

The French proposed "certain relatively unimportant amendments" to the armistice terms, some of them accepted and some rejected, the British informant said.

Other provisions of the armistice, he said, included:

That French armed forces be demobilized and disarmed, only a small force being permitted in the unoccupied portion of France;

Merchant Ships Detained

That France pay for the territorial occupation;

That no French forces leave French soil;

That no materials be converted to help Britain;

That Germany may demand surrender in good condition of all artillery, tanks, aircraft and munitions;

That no merchant shipping leave French harbors, and that ships outside France be recalled;

That the French government facilitate transport of merchandise between Germany and Italy;

That a part of the French fleet to be

DAILY MIRROR
Member of The Associated Press
2¢ 2¢
WEATHER CLOUDY, SHOWERS (Details on Page 6.)
Copyright, 1940. Daily Mirror, Inc.
3 Cents Outside City Limits
Vol. 17. No. 2 C New York, Tuesday, June 25, 1940 FINAL EDITION★★★

FIGHTING ENDS IN FRANCE

'Most Glorious Victory Of All Time,' Says Hitler

PETAIN GOVERNMENT SIGNS TRUCE IN ITALY

Story on Page 3—Late Bulletins on Back Page

Dewey Put in Nomination; GOP Cheers

EXTRA

Complete Markets

Los Angeles Examiner

CHARACTER QUALITY — AMERICA FIRST! — ENTERPRISE ACCURACY

AN AMERICAN PAPER FOR THE AMERICAN PEOPLE — THE GREAT NEWSPAPER OF THE GREAT SOUTHWEST

Reg. U.S. Pat. Off.

(Telephone RIchmond 1212)

VOL. XXXVII—NO. 199 P LOS ANGELES, THURSDAY, JUNE 27, 1940 Two Sections—Part I—FIVE CENTS

L. A. NAZI AGENT HELD BY G-MEN!

G. O. P. Adopts Militant 'Shun War' Platform

By W. W. Chaplin
International News Service Correspondent

PHILADELPHIA, June 26.—The Republican National Convention tonight unanimously adopted a militant "keep us out of war" platform, pledging national defense so strong that no aggressor country would dare invade America, and branding the New Deal a party leading the way toward war.

Adoption of the 3500-word platform clearly defined the major issue in the coming presidential campaign as national defense to guard against war and paved the way for the Republican candidate, still to be nominated, to go to the people on a peace-or-war program.

After stating that the Republican policy stands for peace and preparedness, the platform adds:

"We accordingly fasten upon the New Deal full responsibility for our unpreparedness and for the consequent danger of involvement in war."

SPIRIT IN PLATFORM

The platform was adopted by acclamation after Delegate C. Wayland Brooks of Chicago rose to place in the record the fact that the Illinois delegation had battled in vain for inclusion of a pledge that no American boy would ever again "spill a drop of blood on foreign soil." He said the delegation was satisfied, however, that the spirit of that pledge was in the platform, and the convenion shouted approval.

The platform pledged the Republican Party to a program of "Americanism, preparedness and peace," but favored all possible aid "under existing laws" to countries fighting for liberty or whose liberty is threatened.

NATIONAL DEFENSE

The plank on national defense, given leading position in the G. O. P. platform, began with the statement:

"The Republican Party is

(Continued on Page 2, Column 5)

By Damon Runyon
Staff Writer International News Service

CONVENTION HALL, PHILADELPHIA, June 26.—Thomas E. Dewey's name is first before the Republican National Convention as a candidate for the presidential nomination, through a fine speech delivered by his old friend, John Lord O'Brian of Buffalo.

It is greeted by a demonstration consisting of much cheering and a ragged march through the aisles of men and women delegates from all over the country, bearing their state standards and making all the noise possible.

16 STANDARDS MISSING

But, ominously for Dewey, as some see the situation, the standards of 16 states, several with big delegations, are missing from the march. New York itself—Dewey's home state—is only partially represented. An attempt by the followers of Wendell Willkie to start a demonstration for their man before the formal nominating speeches are called for proves somewhat abortive and winds up in some boos from other delegates.

The attempt starts when Indiana, in a preliminary roll call, announces that it intends placing Willkie in nomination, though the delegation itself is reported split. Willkie at this time remains 2-to-1 favorite in the betting with Dewey and Taft quoted at 3 to 1, and the others anywhere from 8 to 100 to 1, the latter being the favorite sons who are merely courtesy nominations. Dewey is still claiming over 400 votes on the first ballot, but his opponents dispute this claim.

Presentation of Dewey's name for the nomination follows the unanimous adoption of the platform, which does not quite declare strongly enough against the United States becoming involved in war to suit some of the delegates from Illinois whose protest is voiced in the most brilliant speech of the conven-

(Continued on Page 2, Cols. 7-8)

'Peace and Preparedness'

A PARTY PLATFORM which bitterly attacked President's foreign policy, pledged freedom from entanglement in European conflict and carried a strong preparedness plank was given the Republican convention yesterday. Chairman H. K. Hyde of the party's resolutions committee is pictured delivering the platform to gathering.
—Associated Press Wirephoto.

$25,000 Bail Set; Details Kept Mystery

Believed to presage exposure of a gigantic foreign agent system in Southern California, Herbert Hoehne, German agent, was arrested by Federal operatives yesterday and was ordered held under $25,000 bail.

The tall, blond, powerfully built Nazi was seized on a technical charge of failure to register with the Secretary of State as an agent of a foreign power, the German Reich, in accordance with a law recently enacted to combat "Fifth Column" (traitors and spies) movements.

DETAILS GUARDED

Circumstances of the arrest, which was made by Department of Justice agents under Arthur Cornelius, head of the Federal Bureau of Investigation office in Los Angeles, was closely guarded.

Hoehne was arraigned before United States Commissioner David B. Head. Through an interpreter, he denied participation in either espionage or subversive activity.

Observers pointed to the unusually heavy bail fixed by Commissioner Head as an indication of the importance of the arrest.

AIRCRAFT CAPITAL

It likewise was pointed out that Southern California is the world aircraft capital, and that hundreds of military planes are being built here not only for the United States, but for Great Britain.

There was every hint of sensational developments as Hoehne was held under heavy guard by the Federal agents.

It was learned that an investigation was under way into his possible connection with members of the German-American Bund and other organizations sympathetic to the Nazis and said to harbor "fifth columnists."

British Raid Nazi Continent Base

LONDON, June 27 (Thursday).—(AP)—Planes, believed German bombers making their sixth raid on Britain in nine days, were reported over eastern England early today.

LONDON, June 26.—(AP)—An audacious British raid on the German-held continental coastline was disclosed today amidst suggestions Britain is starting a campaign of harassment to prevent the Nazis from making full use of those areas for a major attack on England.

Heavily armed shock troops, supported by fleet and Royal Air Force units, stormed German positions at undisclosed points along the coast.

They landed men who came away with "much useful information," an official announcement said.

The success of the foray, which took place yesterday, was attributed by military observers to its element of surprise.

These sources said significantly, however, that "further" raids might be equally successful.

"The party," said one naval observer, "may have attacked one of the numerous submarine bases which the Germans have

(Continued on Page A, Cols. 3-4)

Evening Press

No. 10,972 REGISTERED AT THE G.P.O. AS A NEWSPAPER. POSTAGE 1d. GUERNSEY, MONDAY, JULY 1, 1940 TELEPHONE 1400 (FIVE LINES) GRATIS

ORDERS OF THE COMMANDANT OF THE GERMAN FORCES IN OCCUPATION OF THE ISLAND OF GUERNSEY

(1)—ALL INHABITANTS MUST BE INDOORS BY 11 P.M. AND MUST NOT LEAVE THEIR HOMES BEFORE 6 A.M.

(2)—WE WILL RESPECT THE POPULATION IN GUERNSEY; BUT, SHOULD ANYONE ATTEMPT TO CAUSE THE LEAST TROUBLE, SERIOUS MEASURES WILL BE TAKEN AND THE TOWN WILL BE BOMBED.

(3)—ALL ORDERS GIVEN BY THE MILITARY AUTHORITY ARE TO BE STRICTLY OBEYED.

(4)—ALL SPIRITS MUST BE LOCKED UP IMMEDIATELY, AND NO SPIRITS MAY BE SUPPLIED, OBTAINED OR CONSUMED HENCEFORTH. THIS PROHIBITION DOES NOT APPLY TO STOCKS IN PRIVATE HOUSES.

(5)—NO PERSON SHALL ENTER THE AERODROME AT LA VILLIAZE.

(6)—ALL RIFLES, AIRGUNS, PISTOLS, REVOLVERS, DAGGERS, SPORTING GUNS, AND ALL OTHER WEAPONS WHATSOEVER, EXCEPT SOUVENIRS, MUST, TOGETHER WITH ALL AMMUNITION, BE DELIVERED AT THE ROYAL HOTEL BY 12 NOON TO-DAY, JULY 1.

(7)—ALL BRITISH SAILORS, AIRMEN AND SOLDIERS ON LEAVE IN THIS ISLAND MUST REPORT AT THE POLICE STATION AT 9 A.M. TO-DAY, AND MUST THEN REPORT AT THE ROYAL HOTEL.

(8)—NO BOAT OR VESSEL OF ANY DESCRIPTION, INCLUDING ANY FISHING BOAT, SHALL LEAVE THE HARBOURS OR ANY OTHER PLACE WHERE THE SAME IS MOORED, WITHOUT AN ORDER FROM THE MILITARY AUTHORITY, TO BE OBTAINED AT THE ROYAL HOTEL. ALL BOATS ARRIVING FROM JERSEY, FROM SARK OR FROM HERM, OR ELSEWHERE, MUST REMAIN IN HARBOUR UNTIL PERMITTED BY THE MILITARY TO LEAVE.

THE CREWS WILL REMAIN ON BOARD. THE MASTER WILL REPORT TO THE HARBOURMASTER, ST. PETER-PORT, AND WILL OBEY HIS INSTRUCTIONS.

(9)—THE SALE OF MOTOR SPIRIT IS PROHIBITED, EXCEPT FOR USE ON ESSENTIAL SERVICES, SUCH AS DOCTORS' VEHICLES, THE DELIVERY OF FOODSTUFFS, AND SANITARY SERVICES WHERE SUCH VEHICLES ARE IN POSSESSION OF A PERMIT FROM THE MILITARY AUTHORITY TO OBTAIN SUPPLIES.

THESE VEHICLES MUST BE BROUGHT TO THE ROYAL HOTEL BY 12 NOON TO-DAY TO RECEIVE THE NECESSARY PERMISSION.

THE USE OF CARS FOR PRIVATE PURPOSES IS FORBIDDEN.

(10)—THE BLACK-OUT REGULATIONS ALREADY IN FORCE MUST BE OBSERVED AS BEFORE.

(11)—BANKS AND SHOPS WILL BE OPEN AS USUAL.

(Signed) THE GERMAN COMMANDANT OF THE ISLAND OF GUERNSEY

JULY 1, 1940.

BEMIDJI DAILY PIONEER

WEATHER

Minnesota: Fair tonight and Thursday; somewhat warmer Thursday and in north and west portions tonight.

VOLUME XXXVIII; NUMBER 63. BEMIDJI, MINN., WEDNESDAY EVENING, JULY 3, 1940. PRICE FIVE CENTS

Nazis Step Up Battle For Britain

CITY PROMISED BIG FOURTH OF JULY PROGRAM

American Legion Sponsoring All-Day Celebration For Entire Community

AFTERNOON-EVENING EVENTS AT FAIR GROUNDS

Street Parade at 10:30 A.M. to be First Major Event on Independence Day

One of the biggest and best Fourth of July celebrations ever sponsored in this community by the Ralph Gracie post of the American Legion has been arranged for Thursday, July 4, and with favorable weather it is expected that thousands of visitors from surrounding communities will be attracted to Bemidji to join in the celebration of Independence Day.

Starting at 9:30 a.m. when races are staged for boys and girls of all ages on the lake side of the Bemidji armory, a full day's program has been arranged, including a grand street parade at 10:30 a.m., a full afternoon's entertainment program at the fair grounds starting at 2 o'clock and an evening show, also at the fair grounds, which will be highlighted by a gorgeous display of fireworks.

Bemidji business houses are to be closed the entire day so that the entire community may join in the celebration. Heading the general committee in charge of arrangements for the annual observance are Dr. A. Dannenberg, C. W. Richards, Otto Thelander and George Phillipson as co-chairmen, with various other Legionnaires comprising separate committees for various phases of the day's activities.

To keep the youngsters entertained while waiting for the 10:30 parade, races will be staged near the armory starting at 9:30 a.m., with cash prizes to be awarded the winners. There will be a 40-yard dash for boys of 10 or under, a 40-yard dash for girls of 10 or under, a 60-yard dash for boys 11 to 12 inclusive, a 60-yard dash for girls 11 to 12 inclusive, an 80-yard dash for boys 13 or over, an 80-yard dash for girls 13 or over, an 80-yard free-for-all dash for boys, an 80-yard free-for-all dash for girls and a 60-yard free-for-all dash for girls.

Parade participants are to assemble at the Sports Arena at 10 a.m. to prepare for the start of the parade at 10:30 sharp. The parade will form on America avenue in front of the arena, heading south. Participating in the procession through the main business district will be bands, drum corps, marching organizations of various kinds, CCC units and floats, commercial floats of various kinds, decorated floats, decorated cars, bicycles

(Continued on Page 3)

PACKARD MOTOR CO. MAY MAKE AIRPLANE ENGINES

Tentative Agreement Reached to Make Motors for U. S. and Great Britain

Washington, July 3—(AP)—The national defense commission announced today that the Packard Motor Company had agreed tentatively to undertake a contract for 9,000 aircraft engines—3,000 for the United States and 6,000 for Great Britain.

William S. Knudsen, in charge of defense production, said the agreement was subject to approval of the Packard directors. Henry Ford refused the order, saying he would work only for the United States.

Meanwhile, a supplementary defense program which may run into additional billions of dollars was talked over at a conference between President Roosevelt and key men in the defense setup.

White House officials were unable to suggest what amount the program might reach or in what manner or when it would be submitted to Congress.

There have been indications that the supplementary program was intended to build up the army in such equipment as guns, tanks and planes.

The navy awarded contracts today to the Newport News, Va., Shipbuilding and Drydock Company for three aircraft carriers to cost $45,662,000 each and two cruisers to cost $19,272,500 each. They are the last of the 92 combatant vessels for which Congress had provided funds.

The airplane motors in the Packard transactions are of Rolls Royce design, hitherto made only for Britain.

M. M. Gilman, Packard president, said his company's Detroit plant would be tooled and prepared to begin actual production ten months from

(Continued on Page 3)

July 4, 1940

WATER SPORTS DAY ARRANGED

Outstanding Features Will Be Presented Here on July 12 Before Canoe Race Opens

A Water Sports Day in honor of the Bemidji to Minneapolis Aquatennial Canoe Derby entries will be held here on July 12 and from all indications will be one of the most outstanding summer attractions ever held in the city.

An afternoon program to be staged on the lake near the armory, featuring sprints by the Derby entries, will be followed in the evening by an Aquatennial dance that is packed with features.

During the afternoon there will be events for speed boats and outboard motors, a program staged by the local Boy Scout troops, including canoe tilting; bait casting; life saving demonstration; race for junior canoeists under 18 and as a final event the sprint in which the majority of those entered in the Aquatennial derby will take part.

The evening dance is to be staged at Shorecrest with a local orchestra. One of the features of this event will be the staging of a regional contest at which the Aquatrot, the official dance of the Aquatennial, will be presented. A dancing team from Minneapolis will be present to give a demonstration and to assist in the judging. Diagrams of the basic steps of the new dance will be received in

(Continued on Page 2)

SIX BOYS AND GIRLS ARE KILLED IN TRAIN CRASH

Chicago, July 3—(AP)—Three girls and their three boy companions, all 'teen aged, were killed instantly by a train at a grade crossing near suburban Maywood last night as they sped to a hospital for medical assistance.

The six young victims were attending a roadhouse party when one of the girls complained of an attack of appendicitis. Her companions decided to take her to a hospital in an automobile.

Witnesses said the driver ignored signal lights and bells and swerved around a line of cars stopped for the oncoming Soo Line passenger train. The body of one boy was thrown clear but the other victims were crushed in the wreckage as the locomotive carried the car 1,800 feet.

The victims were Lorraine O'Leary, 19, Lorraine Norris, 17, and Catherine Clark, 19 all of Oak Park, Ill., and Francis Frehe, 19, the driver, Joseph Santo, 19, and John Brennan, 18 all of Chicago.

TORNADIC WINDS CAUSE MUCH DAMAGE IN TEXAS

Taylor, Tex., July 3—(AP)— Tornadic winds wrecked three school houses, damaged scores of buildings and laid waste crops in this section last night. No loss of life was reported.

School houses at Horndale, San Gabriel and Delmond were crushed.

Almost an inch of rain fell here in less than 30 minutes, bringing precipitation to almost eight inches in five days.

HITLER DRAWS CAREFUL PLANS

German Dictator Would Leave England No Way of Escape From Destruction

By Dewitt MacKenzie
(AP Foreign Affairs Writer)

Herr Hitler is rapidly drawing his lines in a manner calculated to leave no way of escape from destruction open to Britain.

The second of the three grave threats against the life of England—wholesale bombing, starvation by blockade and invasion — has now shown itself in the heavy losses inflicted on British merchantmen recently by both Nazi and Fascist U-boats.

Ships totaling more than 88,000 tons—many undoubtedly laden with precious food and war supplies—were sent to the bottom in the week ending June 23. The German high command also claimed that 299,000 tons of Allied shipping had been sunk by Nazi air forces since June 5.

Meanwhile the rain of death from the air has increased over England in ever widening circles which finally have touched virtually all parts of the United Kingdom. It's easy for German pilots to reach England these days from the many new bases along the continental coast opposite the little island.

We may expect the bombing and torpedoing to swell rapidly from now on, preparing the way for actual invasion.

Thus far there has been no indication of the precise plan which Hitler proposes to follow. Quite likely he will be governed by circumstances. It is patent, however, that he is getting set, from Norway right down the coast to Brest in France, so that the invasion can be put in motion if and when the time seems right.

As a matter of fact, the coordinated starvation-blockade and bombing campaign might be sufficiently devastating—if the British defense proved ineffective—thus relieving him of the

(Continued on Page 2)

ARMY AND NAVY ORDERS PLACED

More Than One Billion Dollars Worth of Defense Contracts Signed in Past Month

Washington, July 3 —(AP)— The army and navy put their pens to more than $1,000,000,000 worth of defense contracts during the last month, a recapitulation showed today.

The contracts — covering items from beans to bombers, solder to submarines — represent, for the most part, the first big block of expenditure commitments in the $4,500,000,000 cash program voted by Congress for the fiscal year which began July 1.

Reports of this progres game as the senate naval cammittee scheduled consideration of the unprecedented $4,000,000,000 navy expansion bill which would authorize a 70 per cent jump in fleet strength. The house already has approved the measure.

In compiling the billion dollar contract record, the navy led the way with orders for 87 vessels at a cost of $910,279,000. The sum represents hull construction and machinery only. At least $250,000, 000 more will be required to complete equipment of the ships.

The awarding of the navy contracts put under way all the 11 per cent fleet expansion voted earlier this month, with the exception of two cruisers and three aircartf carriers.

Although a large part of the contracts represent funds contained in the $4,500,000,000, appropriations for the new fiscal year, some — notably those for final equipment of warships — were made under authorizations for which money will be voted during the next several years.

Other defense devlopmnts:

(Continued on page 2)

KNOX NOMINATION WINS APPROVAL OF COMMITTEE

Washington, July 3—(AP)—The Senate naval affairs committee approved, nine to five, today the nomination of Col. Frank Knox, Chicago Republican, to be secretary of the navy.

This action cleared the way for Senate consideration, probably early next week, of the Knox appointment and of the nomination of Henry L. Stimson, also a Republican, to be secretary of war.

The naval committee vote came after Knox had been questioned at length about, and had denied specifically, a report that he favored sending United States soldiers to fight in Europe. Stimson's nomination was approved yesterday by the Senate military affairs committee.

Third Wave of Air Raids Is Staged This Afternoon

RUMANIA SEEKS MEANS TO STOP FURTHER LOSS

Mourning Ceremonies Today Mark End of Five Days of Grief Over Reverses

INTERNAL STRIFE ALSO WORRYING KING CAROL

Great Economic Loss Involved in Ceding of Bessarabia and North Bucovina to Reds

By Robert St. John

Bucharest, July 3—(AP)— Rumania, torn by strife within and territorial demands without, held mourning ceremonies today to mark the end of a five day period in which she lost one-sixth of her total area and one-fifth of her population.

Refugees from areas ceded under ultimatum to Soviet Russia participated in the observance.

While Rumanians wept over the loss of Bessarabia and Northern Bucovina anti-Jewish demonstrations spread throughout the shaken Balkan kingdom and King Carol II met with his ministers to devise means of saving his country from further loss of territory, prestige and unity.

Great economic loss was involved especially since the agriculturally rich province of Bessarabia was nearing, at the moment of the Soviet occupation, a bumper harvest of wheat and corn.

It is estimated that 300,000 homeless men, women and children fled into old Rumania ahead of the Red army advance.

On the other hand, at least 100,000 Jews in old Rumania were reported to have migrated into Bessarabia after the Soviet occupation began.

The country showed its grief with squares of black cloth thrown over the yellow portion of its red, yellow and blue flags.

King Carol was reported in close contact with the German Minister, Johann Fabricius.

It was reported that Soviet Russia had protested sharply mean-time against the "tone" of yesterday's announcement of Foreign Minister Constantine Argetoniau that "Bessarabia and Bucovina are and will remain Rumanian."

The status of German-Soviet relations was a topic of speculation in diplomatic circles.

It was reported that a German general arrived today to confer with a military mission already in Bucharest.

A German delegate who went to Bessarabia to look after the interests

(Continued on Page 5)

HIGHWAY CHIEF APPEALS TO AUTOMOBILE DRIVERS

Careful Driving Is Urged to Save Lives Over Fourth of July and Week-End

Citing the July safety proclamation issued by Governor Stassen and recalling that over last year's July 4th holiday week end traffic accidents alone claimed eight dead and 260 injured in the state, M. J. Hoffman, state highway commissioner, today appealed to every motorist and pedestrian in Minnesota to do his part to maintain safety on the highways.

He pointed out that half the drivers involved in these traffic tragedies last year were in violation of the law, and urged, as a means to accident prevention, strict adherence to traffic laws, supplemented by extraordinary caution and alertness on crowded highways.

"Governor Stassen has appealed to every man, woman and child to cooperate in efforts to reduce the state's annual July toll of preventable accidents," Commissioner Hoffman said. "It is significant that the largest single factor contributing to that toll seems to lie in the field of traffic.

"Despite the fact that last year Minnesota won national honors both for traffic accident prevention and for pedestrian safety, the fact remains that during the Fourth-of-July holiday week end 185 major traffic accidents, in which 307 drivers were involved, caused eight deaths and 260 personal injuries.

"Approximately half of all the drivers involved were violating the law. Nearly 12 per cent of them had been

(Continued on page 2)

Two Daylight Raids Follow Up Usual Night Attack as War Takes on New Fury

ALLEGED "WIN THE WAR" PLANS BARED BY NAZIS

German News Agency Holds Allies Planned to Drag Most of Europe Into Conflict

(By the Associated Press)

German bombers rained incendiary bombs over England late today in the third wave of raids in 24 hours.

The Nazi planes struck twice in broad daylight in an apparently intensified new schedule of attack to spread terror and destruction among Britain's densely-populated millions before launching the projected invasion of the island kingdom.

In the afternoon assault, German bombers set fire to a big building in southeast England, while others touched off alarms in the northeast.

Nazi U-boats also increased attacks on British shipping.

In Washington, meanwhile, the national defense commission announced that the Packard Motor Company has tentatively agreed to build 9,000 aircraft engines—3,000 for the United States and 6,000 for Britain.

In Berlin, the official German news agency, DNB, published alleged Allied "win the war" plans for dragging most of Europe into the 10-months-old conflict.

DNB asserted documents captured in France disclosed an Allied program for entangling Rumania, Turkey, Greece, Yugoslavia and Scandinavia to gain wide-spread new battlefronts against Germany.

The Nazi high command said German planes attacked a convoy off the English channel coast and sank 18,000 tons of British shipping. German submarines, the high command reported, torpedoed another 39,000 tons.

German sky raiders, displaying new boldness in a daylight sortie instead

(Continued on Page 2)

LATE NEWS

Bucharest, July 3.—(AP)—A declaration in Berlin disclaiming any assurances of German support to Rumania left a grave question here tonight as to this nation's future policy in the event of further frontier attacks.

Tokyo, July 3. (AP)—Great Britain has refused the Japanese demand that the arms route through British Burma to the Chinese forces of Generalissimo Chiang Kai-Shek be closed, it was reliably reported tonight.

Manila, July 3.—(AP)—More than 1600 British women and children fleeing the British crown colony of Hongkong in a precautionary evacuation because of unsettled conditions in the Orient, reached a haven of safety here today.

Istanbul, July 3.—(AP)—The Turkish government denied today reports that Soviet Russia had demanded of Turkey concessions concerning the Dardanelles.

Rome, July 3.—(AP)—The Italian armistice commission entrusted with carrying out the terms of the truce with France has begun work with headquarters at Turin, it was disclosed today. General Pietro Pinto, commander of the First army, heads the commission.

TWISTING RING IN BULL'S NOSE SAVES FARMER'S LIFE

Montevideo, Minn., July 3—(AP)—The strength an injured 63-year-old farmer exerted with two fingers in a ring in a bull's nose meant the difference between life and death.

Knocked down and pummeled in the back, Fred Falk of Clearfield, the farmer, got two fingers through the ring and twisted so hard the huge animal was forced to the ground.

Falk sustained broken ribs and severe bruises and could not flee. He called for help and subdued the beast for ten minutes while members of the family came to his aid.

The aged man, known for his strength, twisted so hard on the steel ring that blood gushed from the bull's nose. His hand was severely bruised by the exertion.

GERMAN FLIERS LASH AGAIN AT BRITISH ISLES

Daylight Raid Is Staged Today in Following Up Night Raid Which Killed 12 Persons

OVER HUNDRED INJURED IN SCATTERED SECTIONS

Heavy Losses Claimed by Nazis on British Merchant Fleet in Past Few Weeks

(By The Associated Press)

London, July 3.—The German air force, piling attack upon attack in its war of nerves and bombs, lashed at the British Isles again today—in broad daylight—but the British counted the 24th raiding plane destroyed in a half-month of defense against big scale raids.

German planes spanned south coast defenses this morning and dropped bombs at several points, following up a night assault which killed 12 persons and injured 123, officials said. This was the greatest casualty list of German raids thus far on British soil.

Indicating the persistence of the Germans attacking from the south, a joint air ministry-home security ministry communique, issued shortly afternoon, said anti-aircraft defenses were still in action.

The noon communique said simply: "Several enemy aircraft crossed the south coast this morning and have dropped bombs at a number of points. Anti-aircraft defenses are in action."

The heaviest of the night raids came at three northeastern coastal towns.

British fighter planes took off this morning after an enemy plane was seen flying toward the southeast over the south coast.

The invader fired machine-gun bursts off the coast, strafed soldiers near the beach and dropped incendiary bombs.

At least 10 of the dead and many of the injured were reported in one town where a lone raider dropped high explosive bombs on thickly inhabited areas.

In a section embracing four or five streets, firemen and air raid precaution squads worked in relays throughout the night digging for trapped victims.

Shattered glass coated the streets for more than a quarter of a mile.

Eight persons were injured—two seriously—when bombs fell in another northeast town and in the outskirts of another. One woman running for refuge died of a heart attack.

The Nazi raiders dropped bombs "at

(Continued on Page 2)

CANOE DERBY ENTRIES TO CLOSE SATURDAY MIDNIGHT

Twenty 2-Man Teams Entered for River Contest to Start From Bemidji July 13

Entry of ten more teams in the 450-mile Aquatennial Paul Bunyan Canoe Derby is expected before the closing of entries at midnight Saturday, July 6, John Scheefe, chairman, announced today.

Twenty two-man teams have entered and received official derby numbers. The race, the most gruelling canoe contest in the northwoods since 1928, will start July 13 in Bemidji and end in Minneapolis July 20, the day the nine-day Aquatennial opens. Overnight stops will be made at Grand Rapids, Palisade, Aitkin, Brainerd, Little Falls, St. Cloud and Anoka.

The northwoods' most vaunted paddlers, including woodsmen with a life-time's experience as well as Indian guides and trappers, will provide stiff competition for the $500 first prize and the $600 in other prizes. Additional entries must be mailed to Aquatennial headquarters, Builders Exchange, Minneapolis, by midnight Saturday.

Teams entered are Louis Boorom and Art Hamilton, Detroit Lakes, guides, number 1; William D. Smith, crane operator, and Fred Otis, truck driver, both of Minneapolis, number 2; Robert Ed, commercial artist, and Donald Lind, printer, both of Minneapolis, number 3.

Jesse Goodin, once world champion log roller, and LeRoy Goodin, his brother, also a log roller, both of Minneapolis, number 4; Al E. Neue, Minneapolis, painter, and Al D. Eberly,

(Continued on Page 3)

MARYLAND FORECAST
Baltimore and Vicinity: Generally fair and continued warm today and tomorrow; gentle winds, mostly southwest.
WEATHER REPORT ON PAGE S-9
MEAN TEMPERATURES YESTERDAY

Baltimore	89	New York	84
Atlanta	82	Omaha	87
Boston	74	Portland, Maine	70
Chicago	82	Salt Lake City	78
Jacksonville	81	San Antonio	84
Los Angeles	67	Seattle	68
Miami	82	Tampa	84
New Orleans	82	Washington	86

CHARACTER QUALITY AMERICA FIRST! ENTERPRISE ACCURACY
Baltimore American
AN AMERICAN PAPER FOR THE AMERICAN PEOPLE
The Largest Sunday Circulation in the Entire South

FINAL EDITION
PRICE 10 CENTS
Have the Baltimore Sunday American Served by Carrier.

Est. 1773 Vol. CCLXVI. ★ SUNDAY, JULY 21, 1940 Entered as second-class matter at Baltimore Postoffice. LExington 0100

BRITISH REPEL MASS AIR RAID
R. A. F. BOMBS GERMAN BASES

MERCURY HITS 99.6 HERE; 1 MAN PERISHES

Four Overcome on Hottest Day of Summer; Many Seek Relief in Park at Night

Rounding into mid-season form, the mercury yesterday scorched upwards till it barely missed the century mark and set a new high for this summer.

Ninety-nine degrees at 3 P. M., was the official reading.

This was the highest since September 8 of last year when an even 100 degrees was scored. Highest this year up till yesterday was 94 degrees, reached June 4, July 11 and last Friday.

And last night, like Friday night, was hot—87 degrees at 10 P. M., was the official figure.

The heat caused one death by drowning as a man took an early dip yesterday in an effort to get relief from a night which had been oppressive.

MAN OVERCOME.

Four persons were overcome, one at breakfast.

Thousands of people last night sought a breath of air in the parks, many improvising beds on the grassy slopes.

Other thousands made an exodus for the near-by beaches.

RECORD CROWD.

Fort Smallwood, municipally controlled waterfront park, reported the biggest Saturday crowd of the season—some 3,500 ashore and in the water, with more arriving during the afternoon.

Other shores and beaches reported increased popularity.

Maryland's Ocean City was the magnet for many Baltimoreans and other Marylanders who jammed the highways.

Rail and highway traffic to other coast resorts was also reported heavy.

The hot weather helped the steamer lines, too.

And, of course, the resort proprietors, who have been rather down on their luck by reason of the unseasonably cool weather earlier, were picking up heart.

That this was a week-end increased that exodus, but did not exactly speed it. Traffic was too heavy for that.

At 3 P. M. yesterday the thermometer at Logan Field registered 99.6 degrees.

Then it began to decline, to the accompaniment of westerly breezes. Half hour later it was down over a point.

By 5 P. M. it was slightly more frigid at 96 degrees.

SEES LITTLE HOPE.

Weatherman John R. Weeks held out little hope of an early break in the temperature and a break for the populace.

The best he could do was to envision possibility of widely scattered local thunder showers this afternoon.

MID-WEST SWELTERS.

Mr. Weeks explained that the torrid conditions here are due to a heat wave which is blanketing the mid-West.

Temperatures in Kansas, Nebraska and other States, he pointed out consolingly, are ranging from 100 to 105 degrees.

The drowning victim was John Gorski, 3800 block Leo street, Fairfield, who decided to cool off with a swim in Stony Creek.

Anne Arundel county police were told he dived off Stony Creek bridge into 35 feet of water, swam around for a few minutes, then sank.

The rescue squad of Orchard Beach fire department recovered the body and spent two hours in a futile effort at revival.

MAN OVERCOME.

The man who collapsed at breakfast was Irvin Levin, thirty-seven, 2200 block Callow avenue, who was having his morning meal in a Frederick avenue lunch room.

A municipal ambulance took him to Franklin Square Hospital, where he was treated for heat prostration.

Turn to Page 4, Column 2.

Duke Romance On Rocks

RENO dispatches yesterday reported that Mrs. Priscilla St. George Duke (above), wife of Angier Biddle Duke, had arrived there and was planning to seek a divorce. Duke is heir to part of the huge tobacco fortune amassed by the late Benjamin N. Duke and is a nephew of the U. S. Ambassador to Poland, Anthony Drexel Biddle, Jr. Mrs. Duke, whose sporting dogs have won high honors at Baltimore shows, is widely known in society circles here. —Picture from International News Photograph Service.

Bullitt Back, Finds Petain Is No Fascist

NEW YORK, July 20—(I. N. S.).—Since the Nazis conquered France, they have cut off all confidential diplomatic communication between that country and the United States, U. S. Ambassador William C. Bullitt revealed today as he arrived on the Dixie Clipper.

Consequently, said Bullitt, he had to come home and tell his story directly to President Roosevelt and Secretary of State Hull to be certain other ears would not be listening.

NO FASCIST, HE SAYS.

In a 20-minute interview, the first he ever gave on any of his trips here from the Paris Embassy, Bullitt told how he narrowly escaped death in the first Nazi bombing of Paris and said of the present French Government of 84-year-old Marshal Petain:

"I don't know that you are right to call it Fascist.

PETAIN RESPECTED.

"There is plenty of food in some parts of France, none in others.

"Transportation of food faces enormous difficulties.

"But Petain, who is universally respected in France and I think the whole world, is rapidly bringing order out of desperate disorder, he is a very fine, straightforward gentleman.

"The people are standing up wonderfully. About the future, I don't want to say. I have to see the President and Secretary Hull and tell them first."

WON'T GO INTO MISTAKES.

Bullitt would not say why he thought France collapsed, as it did in 43 days, but did assert:

"I hope everyone realizes the French people still have all the same magnificent qualities they've always had. The soldier of 1940

Turn to Page 2, Column 6.

Hunt Boy

Blimps Aid Search For Child in Jersey

BEACHWOOD, N. J., July 20—(I. N. S.).—More than 400 searchers, aided by two navy blimps, beat through woodlands surrounding Beachwood today for Craig Bender, three, who has been missing since Thursday evening.

Mayor Jarue said:

"We've done everything possible, but we're not giving up the search."

The boy's father advanced the theory the boy who, many believed had wandered into the woods from his parents' home, might have been hit by a motorist and taken far from the accident scene.

Willkie Is Backed By Alfalfa Bill

OKLAHOMA CITY, July 20—(A. P.).—William H. "Alfalfa Bill" Murray, who once sought the Democratic nomination for President, pledged his support to Wendell Willkie today in a telegram to the Republican nominee. He wired Willkie:

"I pledge you my support for President and for a Congress to assist you, for I will not vote for any man for a third term."

U. S. TO HAVE MIGHTIEST WORLD NAVY

Roosevelt Signs Expansion Bill Calling For 200 More Ships at Cost of 4 Billions

WASHINGTON, July 20—(I. N. S.).—The White House today announced that President Roosevelt has signed the Vinson naval expansion bill authorizing this nation to construct the mightiest navy in the world's history.

It would permit a 70 per cent. expansion in the present U. S. naval strength, at an estimated ultimate cost of more than $4,000,000,000.

200 MORE SHIPS.

In terms of ships it would authorize the construction of 200 additional fighting vessels.

In terms of tonnage the new law would authorize an expansion to 3,049,480 tons. The present authorized tonnage is 1,325,000.

SECOND BILL SIGNED.

The law is the second of its kind to be passed and signed by the President since Congress convened last January.

An earlier bill, also authored by Chairman Carl Vinson of the House Naval Affairs Committee, authorized an 11 per cent. expansion of the fleet.

1,000-MILE GUARD.

The Armada, according to testimony in hearings on the bill, would enable this nation to meet and overcome simultaneous attack in both the Atlantic and Pacific oceans, and to keep actual naval combat 1,000 miles from the continental shores.

But the number of proposed vessels, by separate classification, remains a naval secret. Tonnage increases are:

Battleships, 385,000; cruisers, 420,000 destroyers, 250,000; submarines, 70,000; and aircraft carriers 200,000.

701 SHIPS.

The resulting Navy would number 701 vessels, including the strongest line of 35 capital dreadnaughts in the world, 20 aircraft carriers, 88 cruisers, 378 destroyers and 180 submarines.

Before signing the bill Mr. Roosevelt had requested Congress to provide $83,000,000 in funds to enable prompt beginning on the program.

U. S. Ship's Waiter Cited For Bravery

NEW YORK, July 20—(I. N. S.). Ernst Schlorb of Springfield, Ill., first class waiter aboard the U. S. liner Washington, has been presented a medal and bonus in recognition of his action on the liner when it was challenged by a submarine off Portugal on June 11.

All members of the crew were cited by H. A. McCarthy, vice-president of the line, when the Washington arrived here this week.

Ohio 'Favorite Son,' Mulcahy, 75, Dies

AKRON, Ohio, July 20—(I. N. S.). Cornelius Mulcahy, seventy-five, Akron, Ohio's second choice "favorite son" candidate for the Democratic Presidential nomination this year, was dead today. A heart attack several weeks ago forced him to abandon plans to attend the convention, the first he missed since 1920. Burial will be in Belfast, N. Y., Monday.

10 U. S. Destroyers At N. Y. Anchorage

NEW YORK, July 20—(I. N. S.). A flotilla of ten United States destroyers dropped anchor in the Hudson river today with 315 midshipmen aboard eager for a week-end of shore leave after six weeks' training at sea.

Nazis Lash At English Coast, 12 Invader Planes Shot Down

Nazis Put Peace Rejection Blame On Roosevelt

Surprise Hint

BERLIN, July 21—Sunday)—(I. N. S.).—German morning newspapers today blamed President Roosevelt for Britain's rejection of Chancellor Hitler's peace appeal.

Mr. Roosevelt, according to an editorial in the Deutsche Allgemeine Zeitung, "stiffened Britain's back." The paper said:

"The White House has aroused dangerous illusions in the groundless belief that the United States will share Britain's fate."

'CHURCHILL CLIQUE.'

Germany refused to regard the attitude of the "Churchill clique" in Britain as representative of the British people's stand.

While awaiting the "true" British reaction, Germany claimed a fresh series of successful attacks on British shipping and military centers.

Said the Lokalanzeiger:

"The British war party continues its agitation. There is no chance for reason."

And the D. A. Z. added:

"Churchill wants a war of destruction."

'GREATEST SURPRISES.'

German circles, meanwhile, hinted at the "greatest surprises" in store for Britain if the British people do not over-ride their "plutocratic ruling clique" and signify acceptance of Chancellor Hitler's peace bid.

Although the Fuehrer alone will choose the time when the heralded onslaught on Britain is launched, the talk was that it would be a matter of "days, not weeks" before the "greatest blitzkrieg by land, sea and air any country has ever witnessed" descends upon the British Isles.

There were indications, however, that Hitler is disposed to wait at least a little while in order to let his Reichstag "last appeal to reason in England" soak into the British consciousness.

'HASTY, IMPUDENT.'

Nazi quarters dismissed the British press and radio reactions to the Fuehrer's speech as being "hasty, impudent" expressions of the Winston Churchill Government not truly reflecting the desires of the British masses.

The war against Britain was carried further with German air assaults on English and Scottish airdromes, harbors, power plants,

Turn to Page 2, Column 1

War At A Glance

LONDON—Germans intensify air raids on British shipping, at least 12 Nazi bombers downed; Britain seen shifting partly to offensive plans while waiting Nazi invasion.

BERLIN—Morning press blames Roosevelt for Britain's rejection of Hitler's peace appeal.

ROME—Informed Fascist weekly declares landing of German troops in Britain is "logically a question of days."

BUCHAREST—Lean Rumanian wheat forecasts reflect poor crop throughout Southeast Europe, probably diminished exports to Germany.

NEW YORK—Ambassador W. C. Bullitt back from France, says Petain is no Fascist.

ALEXANDRIA—Crews of British French warships cheer as British men o' war bring in 545 rescued men from Italian cruiser.

Ex-Sen. Reed Joins Anti-3d Term Group

Special to the Sunday American

WASHINGTON, July 20.—Two moves were started today to line-up anti-third term Democrats against President Roosevelt in the coming election.

Former Senator James A. Reed, of Missouri, who led the revolt of Jeffersonian Democrats against the New Deal in 1936, sent out a call for a meeting of 1940 revolters in Chicago next Thursday.

O'CONNOR OFFERS AID.

Former Congressman John J. O'Connor, of New York, who was a victim of Roosevelt's purge in 1938, offered to make his Andrew Jackson Democratic party the nucleus of the anti-third term movement.

In Chicago, where O'Connor's offer was announced, it was said that August 15 had been set as tentative date for a St. Louis meeting of representative anti-third termers in the Democratic ranks.

SEE FIVE MILLIONS JOINING.

Leaders in the plans for the St. Louis gathering said they believe at least 5,000,000 Democrats will join hands with them.

Reed's entrance in the fight against Roosevelt was made known by Senator Burke, Nebraska Democrat and the first major Democratic figure in Washington to pledge his support to Wendell L. Willkie, Republican Presidential nominee, because of his antagonism to a third term.

MEETING PROPOSED.

Burke's office released a telegram from Reed inviting the Senator to meet with Reed and other members of the "Jeffersonian Executive Committee" at Chicago's Hotel Stevens on Thursday.

Burke's staff said he had not decided whether to accept the bid.

Reed called a similar meeting in 1936 when Alf M. Landon was the Republican nominee for President. The Jeffersonian Democrats have organizations in several States, notably California and South Carolina.

SAM JONES HITS WALLACE.

In New Orleans, Gov. Sam Jones of Louisiana declared he was "100 per cent." against Secretary of Agriculture Wallace, Democratic candidate for Vice-President.

John Caffrey, a Louisiana delegate to the Democratic National Convention, announced simultaneously he would vote for Willkie.

SUGAR PLANTERS REVOLT.

South Louisiana sugar planters are revolting en masse against Wallace and will support Willkie and Senator Charles L. McNary of Oregon, G. O. P. candidate for Vice-President, according to Charles A. Farwell, official of the American Sugar Cane League.

Recalling that the 1936 Democratic platform called 3 cents too low a price for raw sugar, Farwell pointed out the price today is 6.62 cents.

In a 1934 speech in Louisiana, Wallace was said to have branded the sugar producing industry "inefficient," which has not been forgotten by the sugar men.

CONVENTION CHIEFS SWITCH.

Word coming from Chicago was that a number of leaders at the National convention had pledged themselves to join the anti-third term movement.

The summons for the organization of an independent Democratic party will go out in the next few days.

The sole purpose is to block the President's attempt to stay in the White House 12 years and to provide a vehicle for the protest vote of Democrats unwilling to be forced under the Republican banner.

DEFECTIONS DISCLOSED.

A series of conferences held in Chicago following the renomination of the President on Wednesday disclosed defections in the ranks of practically every State delegation.

Among those where opposition to the third term was outspoken were:

New York, every New England State except Connecticut, Maryland, Virginia, West Virginia, Indiana, Ohio, Michigan and all the north and northwestern States.

"SOLID SOUTH" IN DANGER.

In such States as Connecticut, where the nomination of the Presi-

Turn to Page 2, Column 7.

W. R. Hearst's Lemmings Article Brought Up Again

Special Cable to The Sunday American

LONDON, July 20.—In an editorial the London Daily Sketch today refers to a recent article by William Randolph Hearst in his "In The News" column, citing to Hitler the lesson of the little Lemmings which always perished when they tried to cross the sea.

Mr. Hearst's article, which warned Hitler not to try to invade England, was cabled in full to London. It was widely published and commented on editorially in leading newspapers throughout the British Empire.

The Daily Sketch sees in Hitler's latest "peace plea" a disposition to heed Mr. Hearst's advice.

In today's editorial the Daily Sketch says:

"Some time ago Mr. William Randolph Hearst offered some advice to Hitler. Mr. Hearst told the Fuehrer that he had not command of the sea, that he was not likely to get it, and that, therefore, now was the time for Hitler to offer peace.

"The Fuehrer seems to a certain extent to have taken that advice to heart. . . .

"Mr. Hearst has taken away a good deal of the effect of Hitler's speech by suggesting in advance the reason why it should be made.

"Hitler hasn't command of the sea."

3 Lives Taken By Train Wreck

CARTERSVILLE, Ga., July 20—(A. P.).—At least three persons were killed in a freight-train wreck near here today and 20 or more persons were reported injured when gasoline tank cars exploded and sprayed their contents over spectators.

Raiders Attack British Shipping, Inland Centers

Counterblows

By THOMAS C. WATSON
International News Service Staff Correspondent.

LONDON, July 20.—At least 12 German warplanes were shot down today during one of the most violent and widespread series of air raids Great Britain has yet withstood, the Air Ministry announced late tonight.

While swarms of Nazi raiders attacked British shipping and inland centers to meet with fierce resistance, heavy British aerial counterblows against Germany's giant Emden naval base and other vital spots struck at the roots of the invasion machinery Adolf Hitler has assembled.

5 BRITISH PLANES LOST.

Britain admitted loss of five planes, including three counter-attacking bombers and two fighters defending British soil and waters.

The day's Nazi raids, which lashed at nearly the entire coastal region of the main British Isle from dawn until past nightfall, were climaxed this evening with a spectacular air battle involving nearly 100 planes off England's southeast shore.

GERMANS DRIVEN AWAY.

The battle was provoked when a flock of Stukas (dive-bombers) repeatedly hammered at a British naval convoy with high-explosive bombs.

Anti-aircraft guns of British warships and shore batteries roared as British fighters streaked into the sky and, after a series of dogfights, drove away the German air fleet.

None of the merchant vessels or warships were hit by bombs.

In addition to the dozen German planes shot down during the day, the air ministry said several others were so severely damaged that it is doubtful they were able to reach their home bases.

The British forces were answering with bombs and bullets Adolf Hitler's "peace or perish" ultimatum.

Seaplane bases and airdromes in Northwestern German and Northern Dutch coastal areas were subjected to heavy attack by Royal Air Force bombing squadrons.

The big northwestern Nazi naval

Turn to Page 2, Column 1

Wallace to Confer With Roosevelt

DES MOINES, Iowa, July 20—(I. N. S.).—Secretary of Agriculture Henry A. Wallace, Democratic Vice-Presidential nominee, was back in his home town of Des Moines, Iowa, today for a short rest.

He said he will discuss campaign plans with his running mate, President Roosevelt, in Washington Thursday.

Bainbridge's Death Is Called Suicide

HOLLYWOOD, July 20—(I. N. S.).—Barton Leon Bainbridge, estranged husband of Screen Actress Evelyn Keyes, today was listed by police as a suicide.

Separated for little more than a month from his wife, who played Suellen in "Gone With The Wind," Bainbridge was said by friends to have been despondent.

MRS. DAISY CLISBY DIES

KENNEBUNKPORT, Maine, July 20—(A. P.).—Mrs. Daisy I. Clisby, of Mobile, Ala., and New York, for many years president of the United Daughters of the Confederacy of Alabama, died here today.

Einzelverkaufspreis 15 Rpf.

Der Danziger Vorposten

Amtliches Organ der NSDAP und Verkündungsblatt des Reichsstatthalters und seiner Behörden

Verlagsanschrift: Danzig, Elisabethkirchengasse Nr. 11/12. — Fernruf Nr. 217 14- und 217 15 — Postschließfach Nr. 331. Postscheck: Danzig Nr. 2075. Bank Sparkasse der Stadt Danzig, Bank der Deutschen Arbeit. — Schriftleitung: Danzig, Ketterhagergasse Nr. 11/12. — Fernruf Nr. 225 51.

Nr. 202 — Donnerstag, den 25. Juli 1940 — 10. Jahrg.

Erscheinungsweise 7 mal wöchentlich morgens. Bezugspreis monatlich RM 2,50 (einschließlich Zustellgebühren). Bezugspreis bei Abholung RM 2,30. Durch die Post RM 2,50 (einschließlich Postzeitungsgebühr), zuzüglich Zustellgebühr RM —,42. Anzeigenpreis und Nachlässe nach der Preisliste 3.

Begeisterter Empfang unserer Feldtruppen in Danzig

Mit stürmischem Jubel empfing Danzigs Bevölkerung ein heimkehrendes Infanterieregiment

Heimkehr der Sieger

Die Stunde des gestrigen Tages, in der die Soldaten unseres heimgekehrten Infanterieregimentes an Generalleutnant Bock vorübermarschierten und Gauleiter Forster sie im Namen der Bevölkerung Danzigs grüßte, ist für uns alle mehr gewesen als nur ein militärisches Schauspiel schlechthin. In dieser Stunde, in der wir den heimkehrenden Frontkämpfern ins Angesicht schauen durften, ist uns der ganze Wandel der Zeit noch einmal in voller Deutlichkeit bewußt geworden.

Von den Zehntausenden, die die Marschstraßen umsäumten und mit stürmischem Jubel ihrer Begeisterung und ihrer Dankbarkeit Ausdruck gaben, haben nicht wenige den Vater, den Mann, den Bruder in den Reihen der Soldaten gefunden und nicht wenigen hat neben dem Stolz auch die Trauer das Herz bewegt, weil einer der Ihren in diesen Reihen mitmarschierte, als sie damals auszogen, um Frankreich zu schlagen — einer, der heute fern im Westen unter einem schlichten Holzkreuz ruht, der für Deutschland gestorben und darum unsterblich ist.

Dieses Erlebnis der stolzen Freude und der stolzen Trauer, das mit einer solchen Heimkehr nun einmal verbunden ist, haben nicht nur die Danziger gestern gehabt. Viele Städte des Reiches haben in diesen Tagen ihre heimgekehrten Feldtruppen begrüßen dürfen und überall sind Freude und Schmerz die Elemente des Erlebnisses der Heimat gewesen. Dieser Vergleich zwischen Danzig und anderen Städten des Reiches soll damit nicht weniger besagen, als daß Danzig nun wirklich auch in jeder Phase seiner Existenz zum Reich gehört. Denn es gibt ja keine größere Gemeinsamkeit als die der Freude und des Schmerzes. Nun hat auch Danzig, das zwei Jahrzehnte abseits stehen mußte, seinen Anteil am Schicksal des deutschen Volkes bis zur letzten Folgerung auf sich genommen. Nun sind seine Söhne mit hinausmarschiert auf die Schlachtfelder, auf denen sich Deutschlands europäische Sendung erfüllte, sind Kämpfer und Sieger gewesen und haben ihr Blut hingegeben. Es steht manch ein Kreuz im französischen Land, unter dem ein Danziger ruht.

Dieses Blutopfer, das Danzig ohne Zaudern in freudiger Bereitschaft dem Großdeutschen Reich gebracht hat, ist die herrlichste Krönung seiner Heimkehr geworden.

In diesem Bewußtsein ist die Feierstunde des Einzugs heimkehrender Feldtruppen in Danzig zu einem außerordentlichen Ereignis geworden, an dem die gesamte Bevölkerung den lebendigsten Anteil genommen hat. Das militärische Schauspiel der Parade vor dem Kommandierenden General ist zur erneuten leidenschaftlichen Bestätigung des großdeutschen Bewußtseins in Danzig geworden.

Noch ist der Krieg nicht zu Ende. Die ungeheure militärische Leistung der Schlacht in Frankreich steht den Soldaten im Angesicht geschrieben. Keiner von ihnen aber weiß, welche Aufgaben noch an ihn herantreten werden.

Wer den jungen Soldaten auf ihrem Zug durch Danzigs Straßen in die Augen schauen konte, der hat gesehen, daß das Gesetz des Krieges sie in seiner ganzen Gewalt erfaßt hat, der hat aber auch die ungeheure Bereitschaft gesehen, mit der diese jungen Soldaten sich auf jeden Platz stellen werden, den der Führer ihnen weist. Der letzte große Kampf steht uns noch bevor. Einmal werden diese Soldaten wieder durch die Stadt marschieren, dann werden die Glocken unserer Kirchen Frieden läuten und der Marsch unserer Soldaten in die Heimat wird der Marsch in ein neues Europa sein.

str.

Der Vorbeimarsch vor dem stellv. Kommandierenden General, Generalleutnant Bock

Links Gauleiter und Reichsstatthalter Forster, rechts Generalmajor Eberhard — Photos Sönnke

Generalleutnant Bock begrüßt verwundete Soldaten und Weltkriegsteilnehmer

Die Feldküche auf dem Wallplatz sorgte für das leibliche Wohl der Soldaten

CHARACTER QUALITY — AMERICA FIRST! — ENTERPRISE ACCURACY
Los Angeles Examiner
Reg. U.S.Pat.Off.
AN AMERICAN PAPER FOR THE AMERICAN PEOPLE — THE GREAT NEWSPAPER OF THE GREAT SOUTHWEST
Giant of Journalism

VOL. XXXVII—NO. 244 A LOS ANGELES, SUNDAY, AUGUST 11, 1940 Eight Sections—Part I—TEN CENTS

NAZI PLANES RAIN DEATH OVER WIDE BRITISH AREA

LEGIONNAIRES JAM SAN DIEGO FOR CONCLAVE

50,000 Expected at Opening of State Convention Today; Parade Highlight of Meet

By Walter Naughton

SAN DIEGO, Aug. 10.—Overseas caps are the present leading style in headgear here as thousands of American Legionnaires from all sections of the state gather for their 21st annnual convention.

San Diego fairly swarms with the ex-service men and women today as the convention officially opens to continue through next Wednesday. Estimates by Department Commander William S. Dunn, Convention Chairman Harry F. Foster and others tonight were that at least 50,000 of the state's 67,000 Legionnaires and 27,000 Auxiliary members will attend.

Parking spaces, both for people and automobiles, is at a premium tonight with all downtown hotels and many in outlying sections crammed to capacity. So heavy is the attendance that the housing committee has been forced to line up space in private homes for some of the late comers.

OPEN REGISTRATIONS

Registration opened at 10 a. m. this morning at the U. S. Grant Hotel, Legion headquarters, the El Cortez headquarters for the Auxiliary and other centrally located places. By noon more than 5000, including most of the 2000 convention delegates, had registered. At registration headquarters the visitors learned the locations of the reunions banquets of the various World War divisional and regimental organizations. Approximately 150 of these reunions have been arranged to take place between now and next Tuesday night at 11 p. m. when most of them will be held.

Approximately 100,000 San Diegans and residents of near-by towns tonight will watch the annual illuminated parade of the '40 et 8,' Legion play and honor unit. The colorful replicas of French box cars will be the main feature of the show as the voyaguers, attired in French smocks and poilu overseas caps, stage their fun parade. After that the annual "Grand Wreck" of the 40 et 8 will be held in Eagle Hall.

Special Legion church services will be held in all San Diego houses of worship tomorrow morning. About 11 a. m. tomorrow the Legionnaires will start for Tia Juana and Agua Caliente for a "Day in Mexico." It will be Legion Day at the Agua Caliente racetrack with the American Legion Handicap as the feature of the 12-race program.

SERVICE TOMORROW

The opening memorial services will be held tomorrow night at 7 p. m. in Balboa Park with the public invited. No admission will be charged and a crowd of 15,000 is expected to attend. The me-

(Continued on Page 3, Cols. 1-3)

6-YEAR-OLD MOTHER AND BABY SON

HERE IS THE WORLD'S YOUNGEST MOTHER, Line Medina, 5, shown here with her son, aged 15 months. Line herself was born in Lima, Peru, and has been the center of much controversy among doctors and scientists ever since her child was born. She is coming to America and will be in Chicago, September 23, date of her sixth birthday. The Peruvian government has made Line and her son state wards.

—Photo copyright by Richard S. Kaplan and released by International News Photograph Service.

Early Resignation Seen for Cudahy

Remarks Lead to Diplomat's Recall and Censure

WASHINGTON, Aug. 10.—Expectations of an early resignation by John Cudahy, United States Ambassador to Belgium, accompanied official censure and a presidential "request" the diplomat return for "consultation."

The State Department, in a public statement, declared his remarks asserting German soldiers behaved "better than United States soldiers would have done" in the occupation of conquered territories and that Belgium faced near-famine conditions by mid-September unless it received American food supplies were made in "violation of standing instructions."

Cudahy's assertion about food conditions in Belgium was widely interpreted as a hint that American food should be allowed through British blockade.

Senate Conscription Fight Grows Hotter

WASHINGTON, Aug. 10.—With battle lines drawn tighter, the Senate faces bitter debate Monday when the conscription bill again is tackled—with increasing insistence from Administration quarters that it be passed.

"Imminent" danger of an attack by Japan was cited by Senator Sheppard (Democrat), Texas, chairman of the Senate military affairs committee, as a warning against further delaying passage of the measure which would conscript 12,000,000 Americans between the ages of 21 and 31 years.

Senator Holman prefaced Sheppard's remarks with a statement that he had learned "from authoritative military sources of imminent peril of an invasion" along the entire Pacific Coast, including Alaska.

The debate which is expected to get under way Monday will prove to be the most controversial issue placed before the Congress since rejection of President Roosevelt's plan for expansion of the United States Supreme Court. it is believed here.

CHALLENGES BILL

Senator McNary (Republican), Oregon, minority Senate leader and vice presidential candidate, has challenged Senator Sheppard to prove that the Administration's conscription bill combines the principle of voluntary enlistment, as has been claimed by its supporters, and has further intimated that conscription may become a leading issue in the 1940 campaign.

Senator Vandenberg (Republican), Michigan, who has consistently maintained that the voluntary enlistment system has not been given a fair trial, asked the Senate:

"What is there about the experience of the Army and War

(Continued on Page 3, Col. 3)

Willkie Acceptance to Give Platform

Home Town Banners Out for G. O. P. Candidate

By Stanford E. Stanton

ELWOOD, Ind., Aug. 10.—Shining like a bright new penny, Elwood is waiting impatiently for the Big Day.

Next Saturday, Wendell L. Willkie, standing on the steps of the Elwood High School, formally will accept the Republican nomination for President.

Nothing like it has happened to Elwood in the 100 years of its existence.

At a minimum, 100,000 persons from all parts of the United States will pour into Elwood for the day. The crowd may reach 300,000. Estimates vary, but Elwood is ready, regardless.

CITY PLANS WELCOME

Mayor George O. Bonham, Homer E. Capehart, Indiana-born industrialists, and every one of

(Continued on Page 8, Col. 4)

Mines Sown by RAF Planes Sink German Warship, 11 Vessels

Lloyd George Says:

Battle of England Still Delayed

But War for British Empire Now in Full Swing, He Asserts

By David Lloyd George

Prime Minister of Great Britain during the World War.

(Copyright, 1940, By United Feature Snydicate, Inc. Reproduction in whole or in part phobhibited.)

LONDON, Aug. 10.—The Battle of Britain has not begun in real earnest. The battle for the British Empire has undoubtedly started. As to the struggle for conquest of these islands, the Nazis have not yet hurled against them any offensive of such size or magnitude as could, by any possibility, end in their subjugation.

LLOYD GEORGE

They have bombed our coastal towns, they have penetrated sometimes into our interior, but not with sufficient aerial forces to indicate any immediate design of wholesale destruction of factories, workshops, railway junctions or even ports.

Their onslaught on our shipping has been of a more serious and determined character both from the air and from under waters. On land no considerable damage has been inflicted upon our means of production or upon our population. Although losses to our shipping have been more substantial, they have not yet reached dimensions which are alarming. German broadcast estimates, I am convinced after careful inquiry, are utterly fantastic.

It is quite clear the Germans, either in the air or at sea, in their deadly struggle with their last and toughest enemy have not yet put forth their whole effort. There is a general impression they have something worse in reserve than anything yet attempted.

(Continued on Page 9, Cols. 1-4)

Britain Withdraws Troops From China

LONDON, Aug. 10.—Announcement here that all British regular troops were being withdrawn from China has added uncertainty to an already delicate position in which Great Britain finds herself in the simmering Far East.

Reports here made it known that the troop movement is by no means subsequent to any Japanese pressure, but merely a military contingency. This was in answer to Japanese officials who were reported as highly pleased with the turn of events, indicating satisfaction with what they might have called a "moral victory."

The British war office announcement said the withdrawn troops will be transferred for "service elsewhere," but did not specify where they would be sent. It was thought likely they may be dispatched to reinforce Britain's menaced far eastern bases at Hongkong and Singapore.

WASHINGTON, Aug. 10.—(AP)—The United States will adhere to its own position in China despite the withdrawal of British troops from the northern part of that country.

Reich Bombers Blast at Coast Defense Blimps

LONDON, Aug. 10.—(AP)—German bombing planes attacked "many districts" of Britain during the night, causing casualties "some of which were fatal," the government announced.

LONDON, Aug. 10.—Following the terrific aerial bombardment carried out over the British coast last Thursday and Friday, Germany widened even more the scope of her aerial "blitzkrieg." While earlier Reich attacks had been for the most part localized on convoy shipping in the English Channel, the new offensive from the skies hammered at sections of the Welsh and Scottish coasts, as well as the renewal of raids on the coastal defense system of balloons.

This was considered a reply to the mine barrage laid by British bombers in German-held harbors, which brought disaster to Reich shipping. It was already reliably learned that at least 12 German ships had been sunk by these newly sown mines, including a warship.

Renewing the mounting air struggle, increasing numbers of German raiders hurtled across the English Channel and North Sea during last night and this morning, bringing into play hundreds of anti-aircraft guns, searchlight beams and British night-fighting planes.

RAID ON BALLOONS

Southeast England was the scene of the first of the new raids which included many attempts to shatter balloon-cable networks shielding important ports and the machine-gunning of streets. Then, as midnight came and passed, Nazi squadrons and individual raiders were reported successively over southwest, northeast and northwest England, Wales, southeast Scotland and in industrial midlands.

Three high-explosive bombs landed in the residential district of one southwest coastal town, wrecking numerous houses, but

Hurricane Pounds South-East Coast

Complete SPORTS

CHARACTER · QUALITY · AMERICA FIRST! · ENTERPRISE · ACCURACY

Los Angeles Examiner

AN AMERICAN PAPER FOR THE AMERICAN PEOPLE · THE GREAT NEWSPAPER OF THE GREAT SOUTHWEST

Reg. U.S. Pat. Off.

(Telephone RIchmond 1212)

EXTRA

VOL. XXXVII—NO. 245 | LOS ANGELES, MONDAY, AUGUST 12, 1940 | CC | Two Sections—Part I—FIVE CENTS

500 NAZI WARPLANES REPULSED BY BRITISH!

10,000 Legionnaires in Mighty Parade Today

CITIZEN GROUP OPENS SCHOOL INVESTIGATION

Committee, Aroused by Youths' Suicides, Starts Thorough Quiz Into Conditions Today

Stirred by two suicides within a year and many reports of atrocious brutalities, a citizens' committee today will open a comprehensive investigation of conditions at the Whittier State School for Boys.

Disregarding the "white wash" report on the school issued Saturday by Dr. Aaron J. Rosanoff, state director of institutions, the committee will seek to determine:

1. What prompted Edward Leiva, 16, and Benny Moreno, 13, to hang themselves in the "lost privilege" cottage within a year.
2. Whether cruel and unusual punishment is used by guards, as related by at least 15 former inmates of the institution.
3. Whether the "lost privilege" cottage is a "necessary evil," as asserted by Dr. Rosanoff, or a torture chamber.
4. Whether the entire system of "rehabilitation" at the school has degenerated into a sadistic form of juvenile punishment.

IGNORE REPORT

That Dr. Rosanoff's report will have no bearing on the committee's investigation was made clear yesterday by Superior Judge Ben Lindsey, chairman of the committee, when he announced:

"We ask that every person having important information on conditions at the Whittier State School for Boys report in the Assembly Hall on the ground floor of the State Building at 10 o'clock Monday morning."

The hearing, he reiterated, will be an open one—in contrast to Dr. Rosanoff's "private" investigation—and all former inmates, and all parents of present or former inmates, who know anything of mistreatment of the boys are urged to appear and testify.

Appointed by Governor Olson,

(Continued on Page 2, Column 1)

50,000 TAKE POSSESSION OF SAN DIEGO

Stage Completely Set for First Session; Conventioneers Full of Praises of City as Host

(Full page of American Legion convention pictures on Page B.)

By Walter Naughton

SAN DIEGO, Aug. 11.—California's Legionnaires, 50,000 strong, now have complete possession of San Diego as they go into full stride for their 22nd annual department convention.

With the Legion, the Auxiliary, Sons of the Legion, Junior Auxiliary, forty et 8 and eight et 40, honor and play units of the Legion and Auxiliary, and other organizations holding its state convention here in this fine border city which Mr. Balboa found for United States of America couple of centuries back is today a gigantic camp of ex-service men and women, their sons and daughters and their friends.

Amid the noise of the drum and bugle outfits, the bands, the miniature cannons and firecrackers of the forty et 8'ers as they parade through the streets and hotel lobbies you can hear continuous shouts of praise for San Diego as a city that really knows how to put on a convention. Is fact, many of the boys, and gals, would vote right now to make this the permanent convention city, if possible.

WEATHER COOPERATES

Everything has been perfect and figures to continue that way, and, best of all, the weather man has kept his word and today again has presented us with a nice cool 74 and the ever welcome breeze from the Coronado Islands. And don't think for a minute that these Legionnaires, now of an average age of 47 years, don't like it cool and pleasant, especially when there is some parading and other roadwork to be taken care of.

The stage is set for the first big day of the convention tomorrow with the opening session in

(Continued on Page 4, Column 1)

Boys Give Their Chief a Lift

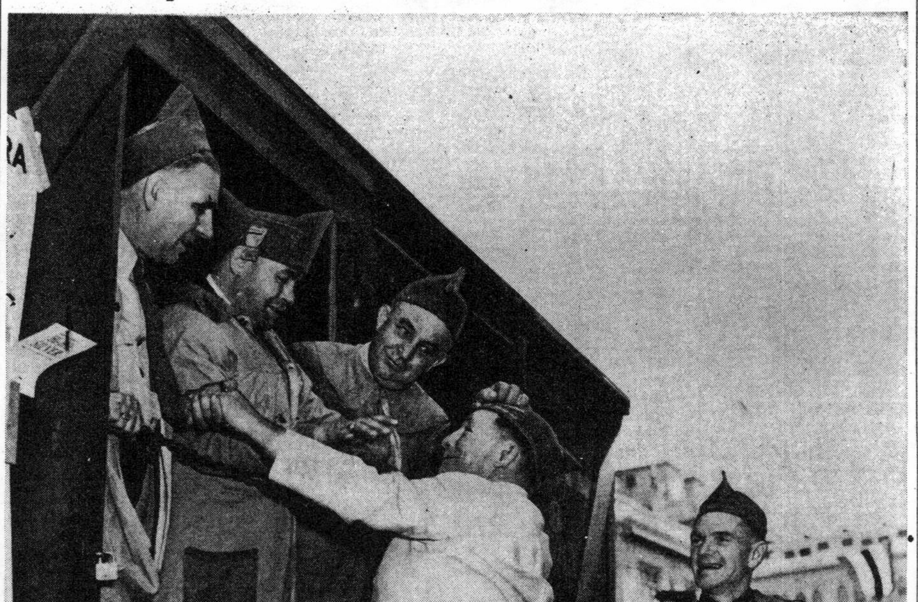

LOGAN E. RUGGLES of San Diego, department commander of Forty et Eight of California, gets a hand up from Walter Kingerey, while Hugh Rawlings gives him a hand from car. Herb Allen looks on from extreme right.
—Los Angeles Examiner photo.

164 Airships Reported Lost in Big Battle

BERLIN, Aug. 11.—(INS)—Germany tonight claimed an overwhelming victory in history's biggest air-sea battle in which 89 British planes were declared to have been shot down, three British merchant ships sunk and four other vessels, including one destroyer, seriously crippled by direct bomb hits.

The German high command admitted the loss of only 17 bombing and fighting planes in the titanic melee that raged over the length and breadth of the English Channel from dawn until after dusk, with British warships and coastal anti-aircraft batteries joining in.

(London estimated at least 75 German raiders had been shot down by nightfall, thus making a total of no less than 164 planes on both sides claimed to have been destroyed. The British admitted loss of only 19 planes. They estimated some 500 German planes

(Continued on Page A, Cols. 3-4)

LONDON, Aug. 11.—(INS)—German raiders tonight renewed their onslaughts on southern Britain. Hostile planes appeared after nightfall over Wales and southeast and southwest England. A short time later other Nazi bombers were reported over northeastern England.

By Thomas C. Watson
Staff Correspondent International News Service

LONDON, Aug. 11.—Cyclonic attacks by some 500 German warplanes against Britain's most vital southern ports and naval stations, as well as convoyed ships in the English Channel, were declared tonight to have been hammered back into broken retreat with an estimated 75 of the raiders shot down.

In a day of continuous, unprecedented battle that roared over

(Continued on Page A, Column 1)

Wind and Seas Devastate South

CHARLESTON, S. C., Aug. 11.—(A. P.)—The Charleston Weather Bureau announced late this afternoon that "the worst is over" as a hurricane that reached a velocity of 75 miles an hour apparently began losing force as it moved inland. There were no known casualties.

SAVANNAH, Ga., Aug. 11.—(INS)—A raging hurricane pounded the South Carolina and Georgia coast tonight, spreading destruction over a wide area.

Communication facilities through most of the area were disrupted by winds with velocities estimated from 60 to 80 miles an hour.

Although fears were expressed for the safety of many persons in low-lying regions along the coast, no immediate reports of loss of life were received.

With trees uprooted, windows shattered, signs blown down and buildings damaged, Savannah bore some resemblance to European cities smashed by the blitzkrieg. The city was without lights and communication facili-

(Continued on Page A, Column 2)

Arizona Bars Communist Party From Ballot

PHOENIX, Ariz., Aug. 12.—(AP)—The Secretary of State's office banned the Communist Party from the September 10 primary and November general elections today.

As formal notification of the action was dispatched by registered mail to Morris Graham, executive secretary of the party in Arizona, Governor Bob Jones expressed "100 per cent approval."

Dan Garvey, Assistant Secretary of State, who wrote the letter in the absence of his chief, Harry M. Moore, said the only way the Communists can get on the ballot now is to bring mandamus actions against the secretary's office and the 14 County Boards of Supervisors.

Garvey's letter said:

"This is to inform you that in accordance with the opinion rendered by the Attorney General of the State of Arizona, the Communist Party is denied the privilege of a ballot in this state at the primary election to be held September 10, 1940, or a place on the ballot at the general election to be held in November, 1940.

The Attorney General's opinion said that a Communist could not qualify to hold office in Arizona "because his avowed purpose and object and his duty to his organization require that he do everything possible to overthrow the Constitution of the United States by force," and the oath of office requires that he uphold it.

Petitions seeking a place on the ballot and bearing 436 names were received by the Secretary of State's office Saturday, a short time before the Attorney General ruled that the secretary could deny the party a position on the ballot.

Garvey said a mandamus action would be welcome "because it would bring the Communists out into the light so everyone could learn what their principles are."

The Communists, through Graham, issued a statement last night denying that it believes in "force and violence," and stating that it had abided by the law in circulating petitions for a ballot position.

"We are a legal party composed of loyal Americans," the statement said. "We are ready at any time to lay down our lives in defense of our country, but will not and do not believe that American blood should be shed for Wall Street profits."

CHARLESTON, W. Va., Aug. 12.—(AP)—Circuit Judge Julian F. Bouchelle granted the American Legion a temporary injunction today restraining Secretary of State W. S. O'Brien from placing the Communist Party ticket on the state's November 5 election ballot.

CHARACTER QUALITY — AMERICA FIRST! — ENTERPRISE ACCURACY

Los Angeles Examiner

Reg. U.S. Pat. Off.

AN AMERICAN PAPER FOR THE AMERICAN PEOPLE — THE GREAT NEWSPAPER OF THE GREAT SOUTHWEST

(Telephone RIchmond 1212)

EXTRA

VOL. XXXVII—NO. 246 | Complete U. S. Weather Bureau Forecast On Page 7, Part II. | LOS ANGELES, TUESDAY, AUGUST 13, 1940 | CCC | Two Sections—Part I—FIVE CENTS

TOTAL WAR ON BRITAIN! INVASION DUE HOURLY

IN THE NEWS

IN THIS so-called and so-considered popular government of ours the one thing which is most difficult to secure is a definite and determining expression of the popular will on national issues.

There is no Federal constitutional provision for referenda on issues, and of course platform declarations amount to nothing.

The pledges of platforms and the promises of candidates have no legal or even moral binding force.

These purely political commitments are more or less disregarded by all parties and entirely disregarded by the Democratic Party which should, if it were true to its name, be peculiarly representative of the popular will.

Everyone knows that our esteemed President (now incumbent) has not, only repudiated his pre-election pledges, but has consistently, or rather inconsistently, done exactly the opposite of what he promised.

Everyone knows that there is no legal authority to make even the decision of a national election on an accepted issue in any degree definite and conclusive.

President Wilson ran for re-election on the slogan, "He kept us out of war." Yet his first important act after his election was to put us into war.

It is certainly, therefore, a conspicuous fact that we have not through the written Constitution or through practice any positive method of determining the will of the people, and of making that will prevail.

This is a fundamental fault in a democracy. Indeed, a governmental system without a definite method of determining and enforcing the public will cannot properly be called a democracy.

Even the expression of popular desire and judgment through letters to Congressmen is resented by the executive departments, and this modest expression by correspondence of the sympathies and wishes of the public is denounced as lobbying and an improper effort to influence the action of the legislators.

However, influencing the action of legislators by appointment of the legislators' friends and dependents, and by the expenditure of public monies in their districts, and by purges of opponents of the Administration is not regarded as lobbying or as anything criticizable.

Consequently, the drift in our country is more and more in the direction of authoritarian government and of concentration of power in the hands of the executive.

It would therefore be exceedingly wise, if popular Government is to be retained, to institute by constitutional amendment a means of referring important issues to the decision of the people.

What more important issues than the issue of war or of conscription for war?

Senator Holt in a communication to this column on Saturday last said in reference to the Burke-Wadsworth conscription bill:

"It is probably one of the most important pieces of legislation that ever faced America, because it is an entirely new innovation not only to our military system and our economic system but to our every day life."

Senator Holt is right in this statement.

There can be no question of the importance of this legislation.

There can be no question that this Government of ours is a government supposedly "of the people, by the people, for the people."

Yet no constitutional means exist to have the people register their opinions in regard to this vital innovation.

The nearest thing approaching a referendum is the vast amount of mail pouring in to members of Congress urging defeat of the Burke-Wadsworth conscription bill.

Since the entire lower House and one-third of the Senate is up for election this year, the protest of the public against the bill may be heeded.

But even then there is still no means of imposing the will of the people upon the new House of Congress or upon the Senate after the election.

There is no unavoidable, inescapable mandate compelling compliance with the popular will provided for in the Constitution of the United States.

Even Germany's constitution of Weimar provides for submission of an administration program to the people, and further provides that a two-thirds vote of the people constitutes a man-

(Continued on Page 2, Cols. 4-5)

W. J. FARRELL STATE'S NEW LEGION CHIEF

Petaluma Man Given Honor by Acclamation; Meetings Adjourned During Parade

(Full Page of American Legion Convention Pictures on Page 9)

By Walter Naughton

SAN DIEGO, Aug. 12.—On the sturdy shoulders of William J. (Bill) Farrell of Petaluma rests the responsibility of leadership of California's 67,000 American Legionnaires for the next year.

Farrell, 50-year-old, bald headed and an ex-infantryman who sells automobiles to the citizens of Petaluma, took over the state's highest Legion post at this morning's opening convention session in Ford Bowl, Balboa Park, when no other candidate was nominated for department commander.

This meant Farrell's election by acclamation as the successor to outgoing Commander William S. (Bill) Dunn, Imperial County's famed druggist.

Enlivened by the keynote address of Legionnaire-Attorney General Earl Warren; a scathing criticism of Harry Bridges by Past Department Commander Archie Closson of Lodi; the welcoming address of Mayor Percy J. Benbough of San Diego and

(Continued on Page 8, Cols. 1-2)

Whittier Horror Told Under Oath

Beatings, Starvation, Tortures Bared by Lindsey Committee

Sworn testimony of brutalities—beatings, "duck walking," starving—and a host of other cruel forms of punishment at Whittier State School for Boys, yesterday was publicly presented to the Lindsey investigating committee.

The tales heard by the three-member committee, appointed by Governor Olson, to make a sweeping investigation of the conditions at the school as a result of the suicides of Edward Leiva, 16, and Benny Moreno, 14, rivaled in truth the Oliver Twist fiction stories of Charles Dickens.

One after another of the witnesses gave graphic and sensational evidence to the committee members, while Dr. Aaron J. Rosanoff, head of the Department of Institutions and author of a "whitewash report" of his investigation of his own department, and School Superintendent E. J. Milne, sat in silence.

DAY'S DEVELOPMENTS

Highlights of the day's developments follow:

1. Mrs. Olive Davis of Altadena, mother of eight children, including a son, Harold, now at Preston, revealed how her boy had been beaten against the wall by a guard who formerly handled insane patients at Norwalk State Hospital, and furnished the com-

(Continued on Page 6, Cols. 1-2)

St. Barbara Fire Perils 20 Men

Racing down the mountain slope to within eight miles of the city, the Santa Barbara forest fire was burning furiously out of control yesterday as nearly 1000 men fought desperately to stem the onrushing tide of flames.

With 3500 acres ravaged by the blaze, damage was estimated unofficially late in the day at more than $250,000.

All 35 cabins in the Painted Caves summer resort in the

(Continued on Page 16, Cols. 2-4)

Big Douglas Bomber Burns; Flyer Killed

(Picture on Page 3)

Trapped in the hurtling plane while two companions parachuted to safety, a test flyer was carried to a flaming death yesterday when a big Douglas bomber crashed and burned near the Culver City airport.

Victim of the test-flight crash was John W. Park, 25, Douglas flight engineer. Those who landed by parachute were Robert Brush, test pilot, and Paul Dennis, also a flight engineer.

Company officials said cause of the crash could not be immediately determined, but that Government agencies and the corporation would make a searching investigation, including the possibility of sabotage.

The plane, a DB-7 attack bomber of the type being built for Britain, had left the Municipal airport on a routine test hop not long before the crash.

Witnesses said they saw the ship circling at about 1500 feet when it went into a steep glide and seemed to go out of control. Robert Bower, civilian pilot flying near by, said he saw parts of the cowling and other parts flying off.

One of the flyers leaped from the plane at 500 feet and the other at 300 feet, but Park apparently became wedged in the door and was killed when the craft struck in a bean field 100 yards from the airport with terrific force and burst into flames.

Brush and Dennis were reported not to have been injured in landing, but were whisked away by Douglas officials, who threw a cordon of guards around the wreckage.

Park, who was married recently, lived at 2208 Montana street, Santa Monica. He was the son of Dr. W. S. Park of Las Vegas, Nev.

Brush lives at 12169 Greenock lane, West Los Angeles, and Dennis at 3117 Crest drive, Manhattan Beach.

It's Precedential Year! 3rd Term Issue Isn't New

BY ARTHUR "BUGS" BAER

Just to remind you that this third-term business is nothing new, some of our more established debutantes can remember way back to 1876. That's the year the House of Representatives adopted an anti-third term resolution.

And 52 years later, in 1928, the United States Senate adopted a similar resolution blistering the paint on third-term aspirations.

So you can see that the House and the Senate can agree on certain subjects, but not in the same year.

We could go further and carry you back to Thomas Jefferson and George Washington. But as the song only carries you back to old Virginny, we will stop there.

That precedent is as solid as a stone barn. And we predict that once again this will be a precedential year.

PAY BOOST TO WOO DRAFT FOES PLANNED

Amendment Giving $30 a Month Agreed To; Norris Calls Conscription Dictatorship Road

By Stanley Carroll

Staff Correspondent International News Service

WASHINGTON, Aug. 12.—Confronted with powerful "anti-conscription" forces, Senate Administration leaders tonight agreed to support an amendment to the compulsory military training bill which would increase Army pay for enlisted men from $21 to $30 a month.

The concession, made privately, came after polls showed that the final vote on the conscription measure would be extremely close and that the outcome would hinge upon a handful of Senators who, as yet, are undecided on the issue.

This "deal," which may become an important factor in the outcome of the bitter controversy over conscription of the nation's young men, came as Senator Norris (Independent-Republican) Nebraska, warned the Senate that the bill to compel registration of 12,000,000 men between the ages of 21 and 31 might bring the country to the borderline of "dictatorship."

As Norris was condemning the conscription bill on the floor of the Senate, the House military

(Continued on Page 4, Cols. 4-5)

Marriage No Guarantee of Draft Escape

WASHINGTON, Aug. 12.—(AP)—Young men who take their best girls' hands and rush to the marriage license bureau to become husbands before Uncle Sam can draft them for military duty, have no assurance they won't be called for a year's active training under terms of the Burke-Wadsworth conscription bill now before the Senate.

The measure contains no specific exemption for married men. They will be required to register for service, just as any other male citizen from 21 through 30 years of age, if it becomes law.

The President is authorized, however, to defer the training "of those men in a status with respect to persons dependent upon them for support which renders their deferment advisable." The measure contains no definition of "dependents."

Nazi Channel Guns Reported in Action

Blitz Raids Softening Foe's Morale, Say Germans; Claim 71 Pilots Down

BERLIN, Aug. 12.—(INS)—Destructive aerial blows against Britain's air force, naval bases and air fields during the last two days have softened English defenses to the point where invasion is but a matter of hours, unofficial but authoritative sources said tonight.

Seventy-one British warplanes were claimed to have been shot down in today's aerial blitzkrieg on the British Isles, bringing the total destroyed to 160 within the last 48 hours. Ninety-three were reported shot down in Sunday's battles.

The extent of the damage wrought to Royal Air Force squadrons in the two days of uninterrupted battering has brought the first serious cracks in the British personnel's morale, according to authentic German sources.

NAVAL BASE BOMBED

Returning Nazi pilots were quoted as having declared that British pilots today avoided combat, instead of seeking to engage the Reich's warplanes as they did in Sunday's great aerial duels. A revised German estimate said 93 British planes were destroyed in these battles.

Summarizing today's widespread attacks, official quarters

(Continued on Page 2, Cols. 4-6)

500 Hitler Planes Hammer England Between Dover, Portsmouth

LONDON, Aug. 13—(Tuesday)—(AP)—Adolf Hitler's long-threatened aerial blitzkrieg on Britain burst into a full-throated roar of destruction today as Nazi warplanes struck at every corner of England.

They thus carried into the third consecutive day a ferocious assault which began with flights of 400 or more planes, leaped to 500 or more yesterday, and reached undisclosed numbers this morning.

There were indications that the onslaught may now be backed by cannon fire from the Continent and possibly aided by Italian airmen.

PATTERN UNVARIED

The pattern of attack remained unvaried, as it has since extensive raids first began June 18, but the scope was tremendous.

From northeast, northwest, southeast, southwest — from every direction—came reports of damage were confined to civilian structures as the novelty "scream" bombs hurtled down.

British fighters, anti-aircraft gunners and searchlight crews teamed up to make the sky a deadly jungle for the invaders.

The raids this morning and last night followed up those of

400 Italians Killed in Albania

British Report Bloody Toll as 8000 Revolt

NEW YORK, Aug. 12.—(AP)—At least 400 Italian soldiers have been killed in an Albanian uprising which has been in progress since Friday, the British wireless reported in a broadcast heard tonight by N. B. C.

The report followed an Italian broadcast denying previous British news agency reports of disorders.

The British announcement said that nearly 5000 Albanians were under arms in the Milidatti district and another 3000 in the Mati area, birthplace of the exiled King Zog.

It said three Italian warships took troops to the Albanian port of Durazzo yesterday as the fighting spread. The Albanians are distributing leaflets urging all their men of military age to flee to the mountains to avoid conscription by the Italian army, the British reported.

Exchange Telegraph, British news agency, reported Sunday and today that Albanians were battling Italian troops to avoid conscription of men, food and livestock.

King Zog, his beautiful half-American Queen Geraldine, their infant son, Skander, and Zog's three sisters were reported July 15 to be in London and hoping to come to the United States.

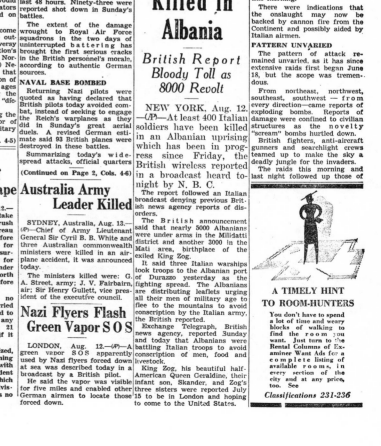

Australia Army Leader Killed

SYDNEY, Australia, Aug. 13.—(AP)—Chief of Army Lieutenant General Sir Cyril B. B. White and three Australian commonwealth ministers were killed in an airplane accident, it was announced today.

The ministers killed were: G. A. Street, army; J. V. Fairbairn, air; Sir Henry Gullett, vice president of the executive council.

Nazi Flyers Flash Green Vapor S O S

LONDON, Aug. 12.—(AP)—A green vapor SOS apparently used by Nazi flyers forced down at sea was described today in a broadcast by a British pilot.

He said the vapor was visible for five miles and enabled other German airmen to locate those forced down.

FINAL NIGHT EDITION

WEATHER: FAIR Details on Page 16

THE CALL BULLETIN — SAN FRANCISCO — AN INDEPENDENT NEWSPAPER

EXTRA

85TH YEAR CALL AND POST. VOL. 148. NO. 18 THE CALL-BULLETIN. VOL. 168. NO. 18 — SAN FRANCISCO, THURSDAY, AUGUST 15, 1940 — 5c DAILY 90c a Month

GREATEST BATTLE ON! LONDON HIT AS NAZIS HURL 1,000 WAR PLANES

Guard Call Bill Passed By House

Proposal to Restrict Use of Reservists Voted Down

WASHINGTON, Aug. 15 (AP).—Legislation authorizing President Roosevelt to order 396,000 National Guardsmen and organized army reservists itno active service was passed today by the House.

The vote was 342 to 33.

The bill ,wihch would permit use of reserves and guard in the Western Hemisphere, American possessions or Philippine Islands, now goes back to the Senate for consideration of House amendments.

RESTRICTION REJECTED

Passage came after the members had defeated, 210 to 110, an amendment by Representative Miller (R., Conn.) to limit use of the reservists to the continental United States and its island possessions, the Philippine Islands, the Panama Canal Zone and Alaska.

The measure would empower the President, until June 30, 1942, to call up for a one year training period 227,000 national guardsmen, 116,000 reserve officers, 38,000 enlisted reserves, 3,700 retired officers and 12,000 retired enlisted men.

DOWNEY PROPOSAL

Guardsmen with dependents would be permitted to resign within twenty days after they were ordered to active duty or to receive such allowance for dependents **"as may be prescribed by the President."**

Senator Downey, Democrat of California, proposed today that the Burke-Wadsworth compulsory military service bill include provision for construction of a national system of super high-

Continued on Page 9, Column 2

SUB SINKS GRECIAN WARSHIP

Rome, Athens Phones Cut; Relations Grow More Tense

ATHENS, Aug. 15 (AP).—The 2,115-ton Greek cruiser Helle was sent burning today to the bottom of the Aegean Sea—sunk, said the government, by an unidentified submarine—and a few hours later telephonic communication with Rome was cut off and a strict censorship imposed on all outgoing calls.

Premier John Metaxas, already making preparations regarded by foreign observers here as designed to set up Greek defenses against a possible Italian attack from Italian Albania, summoned his military and naval chiefs into urgent conference.

SITUATION GRAVE

These maneuvers reflected the increasing gravity of Greece's position, which for days had been precarious because of her reported rejection of German and Italian demands she end her friendship with Britain.

That friendship has been based on a British pledge to support Greek independence and territory in case of attack.

(Editor's Note: Budapest reported Italian troops concentrated on Greek border, with danger of clash between Bulgaria and Greece.)

The government issued an order tonight forbidding all Greek ships to leave port.

VESSEL AT ANCHOR

The Helle, small as it was, was substantially half of this small pro-British kingdom's **"first line"** navy. It was one of Greece's two vessels which were above the destroyer category, the other being the 9,450-ton cruiser Averoff.

The vessel went down as she lay at anchor about half a mile

Continued on Page 8, Col. 2

Ruins Left in England by Raiders

This is how a Nazi bomber left someone's home in England. According to the censor-approved caption of this cabled photo, the crushed house is in the Midlands district. The air raid shelter in background was unharmed. —Associated Press Wirephoto.

Mystery Ship Off U. S. Coast

WASHINGTON, Aug. 15 (INS).—Coast guard headquarters today ordered an amphibian to fly out over the course of the Norwegian freighter Thermopylae, reportedly being followed by a "mystery ship" in the Atlantic, 375 miles east-southeast of New York.

NEW YORK, Aug. 15 (AP).—The Norwegian freighter Thermopylae, 6,655 tons, radioed today that she was being **"tracked by a mystery ship"** at a position well within the neutrality zone set up by the twenty-one American republics.

The ship's first message intercepted by Mackay Radio indicated a submarine attack. Later the ship said **"no distress, but please inform my position."**

10 Insurance Firms Taken Over by State

State Insurance Commissioner Anthony Caminetti Jr. seized control today of ten California mutual life and disability insurance companies with $59,000,000 of insurance in force for more than 100,000 policyholders.

Two of the companies, the Mount Moriah Life Insurance, with 7,500 policyholders, and the Physicians Life Insurance, with 1,000 policyholders, are San Francisco firms. Seven of the others are Los Angeles companies.

SEIZED FIRMS LISTED

The remaining company has headquarters at Santa Barbara.

In addition to the San Francisco firms, companies taken over were the Benjamin Franklin Life Assurance Company, the Great States Life Insurance Company, Guaranty Life Insurance Company, Master Life Insurance Company, National Guaranty Life Company, Southwestern Life Insurance Company, State Mutual Life Insurance Company and the Sunset Mutual Life Insurance Company.

It was explained that the insurance commissioner did not intend to liquidate any of the companies, as all had sufficient assets to meet claims.

The order to take the compa-

Continued on Page Five, Col. Two

Churchill Report Stirs Row

LONDON, Aug. 15 (AP).—Stormy debate was precipitated in the House of Commons and one member asked the speaker's protection against what he called Prime Minister Churchill's **"gross and lying innuendo"** today in a discussion of the government's secret anti-fifth column committee, which has caused many rumors in Britain.

Refusing to discuss in detail the work of the mysterious committee set up under Lord Swinton to combat espionage and fifth-columnists, Churchill warned that **"the danger of invasion has by no means passed away"** although **"we are much stronger than we were in May."**

SECRECY QUESTIONED

After the prime minister had declared that fifth column activity danger was being diminished **"to its proper proportions"** by the committee, Austin Hopkinson, independent, declared he could not understand **"why so much mystery has been made about this."**

Churchill sharply replied that if the member "had paid half the attention to the full and very respectable statement I have just made, as he did when

Continued on Page 8, Column 7

Test at Hand, Britons Fear

Berlin Boasts Vital Areas Bombed

BERLIN, Aug. 15 (AP).—**German planes were reported over London tonight in a surge that carried them past the thickly netted defense of** coast and vital docks up the Thames estuary to the very citadel of Britain's power. The German radio said thirty-six British planes were shot down during the flight of the invaders, while only four German planes are missing.

D. N. B., the official German news agency, reporting a great onslaught against all Britain's vital centers, as well as her coasts from northeast to soutnwest, said the German planes reached London at 5 p. m. despite intense antiaircraft fire.

NO WORD OF BOMBING

D. N. B. said there was no word as to whether London was bombed.

(But from London came word that the Nazi raiders had attacked the famous airport of Croydon, only 10 miles from Piccadilly.)

The German agency said the bombers reached Tilbury, noted for its huge docks only 13 miles east of London on the Thames, and **"calmly followed their course, dropping bombs with deadly accuracy on important objectives."**

Intense fire was encountered at Sheerness, Chatham and Rochester, where navy yards and arsenals are situated, the agency related, and clouds of anti-aircraft fire were observed over London itself.

ARMS PLANTS BOMBED

In other raids the huge rambling armament works of Vickers, Armstrongiat, Hebburn and the port of Newcastle, in northeastern England, were reported set upon by a rain of bombs.

The German radio announced that up to 8:15 p. m. 20 British planes had been downed, nine of them over central England and near Newcastle.

It said one German squadron bombed the Driffield Airdrome in Yorkshire. Twelve British Spitfires were reported attacked, with numerous hits on the defenders against none on the raiders.

OPERATIONS CONTINUE

Several air bases and harbors in central England were among the objectives reported raided.

"Operations of the German

Continued on Page Eight, Col. Six

Raiders Blast Factories, Docks And Airdromes; One Wave Spread 30 Miles Wide

LONDON, Aug. 15 (AP).—A thousand Nazi warplanes—perhaps even thousands—loosed upon Britain today the mightiest aerial offensive ever known, and tonight German bombs fell in South London at the great Croydon Airdrome, only eight miles from Charing Cross.

There were an undetermined number of street casualties in the suburb of some 200,000 population in which Croydon airdrome is located. A bus passing the airport was damaged by bomb splinters.

They struck in Scotland; they struck in vital munitions areas of northeast England; they smashed at the long southern coast all the way from the Thames Estuary—leading to London—to Lands End, the far eastern frontier of the islands.

(Editor's Note: Germany's official news agency, DNB, said Nazi airmen were sweeping the lower Thames—on the path which might be used for a cross-channel troop invasion—threatening all British military plants with destruction.)

Plane Caught in Trap

LONDON, Aug. 15 (AP).—A German bomber was reported caught today in a British "plane trap," wrecked and all its occupants killed.

Details concerning the "trap" were not immediately available beyond the assertion that it was erected by the transport ministry for the military authorities.

Of Incredible Fury

It was an attack of such incredible fury as to make the ceaseless assaults of three days seem but mere preliminaries.

A single Nazi armada was reported so big it covered a strip thirty miles wide.

Every indication was the hour of the great test had come at last.

The royal air force, defending this kingdom from such a blow as never was struck before, loosed every turreted gun in its fighter force and crippled airplanes fell steadily on English soil.

The air ministry declared tonight that ninety-one German planes were known to have been shot down, against an acknowledge British loss of nineteen.

Everything Bombed

The German strategy was simple: While German fighters took on the British Hurricane and Spitfire patrols miles above the ground—from 12,000 to 15,000 feet up—the Nazi bombers snaked across the coast in close formation.

The objectives of this unprecedented raid were every-

Continued on Page A, Column 1

Call-Bulletin Today

Radio—Page 13

Green Flash Section

Special Features

MORE MEN BATTLE 10,000 ACRE FIRE

MISSOULA, Mont., Aug. 15 (AP).—New crews were sent into the Nez Perce national forest of northern Idaho today to battle the spread of a 10,000 acre forest fire southwestward into yellow pine stands.

EX-SAN MATEO SHERIFF ASKS PROBATION

UKIAH, Aug. 15 (AP).—Robert Chatham, 67, one-time San Mateo County sheriff, asked for probation today when he appeared in court for sentencing on a drunk driving conviction. The case was referred to the probation office for a report Aug. 23.

SCALISE ADMITS FALSE STATEMENTS

NEW YORK, Aug. 15 (AP).—Counsel for George Scalise acknowledged today that the former president of the Building Service Employes' International Union (AFL) made false statements in obtaining $60,087 of union funds, but asserted he would prove that Scalise was entitled to the money.

5TH RACE, WASHINGTON—Valdina Babe, won, 19.20, 9, 5.80; Valdina Joe, 2d, 7.40, 5.20; Rahanee, 3d, 5.40. T., 1:38 3-5.

Einzelverkaufspreis 15 Rpf.

Der Danziger Vorposten

Amtliches Organ der NSDAP und Verkündungsblatt des Reichsstatthalters und seiner Behörden

Verlagsanschrift: Danzig, Elisabethkirchengasse Nr. 11/12. — Fernruf Sammel-Nr. 225 51. — Postschließfach Nr. 331. — Postscheck: Danzig Nr. 2075. — Bank: Sparkasse der Stadt Danzig, Bank der Deutschen Arbeit. — Schriftleitung: Danzig, Elisabethkirchengasse Nr. 11/12.

Nr. 225 — Sonnabend, den 17. August 1940 — 10. Jahrg.

Erscheinungsweise 7 mal wöchentlich morgens. Bezugspreis monatlich RM 2,50 (einschließlich Zustellgebühren). Bezugspreis bei Abholung RM 2.30. Durch die Post RM 2,50 (einschl. 33,6 Rpf Postzeitungsgebühr), zuzügl. Zustellgebühr RM —,42. Anzeigenpreis und Nachlässe nach der Preisliste 3.

Starke Stuka-Geschwader über Südost-England

Unsere Kampf- und Sturzkampfgeschwader, begleitet von Jägern und Zerstörern, bombardierten die Südostküste und den Süden Englands • Wichtige Rüstungswerke in massierten Angriffen zerstört • Luftkampfhandlungen durch schlechtes Wetter eingeschränkt • Über 40 Abschüsse

Berlin, 16. August.

Am Freitag haben unsere Fliegerverbände wieder verschiedene Angriffe auf militärische Ziele im Süden und Südosten Englands durchgeführt, Flugplätze in der Gegend von Portsmouth sowie Flugplätze und Sperrballone in der Grafschaft Kent erfolgreich angegriffen. Auf den Flugplätzen wurden mehrere Hallen getroffen, einige in Brand gesetzt, Unterkünfte und sonstige Gebäude schwer beschädigt. Mehrere Flugzeuge wurden am Boden vernichtet, eine Anzahl Sperrballone in der Luft abgeschossen. Insgesamt wurden die Luftkampfhandlungen über England durch die Wetterlage eingeschränkt.

An verschiedenen Stellen fanden kleinere Luftkämpfe statt, bei denen, nach bisher vorliegenden Meldungen, über 40 feindliche Flugzeuge abgeschossen wurden. Von eigenen Verlusten wurden bisher 15 Flugzeuge gemeldet.

Deutsche Aufklärungsflugzeuge überflogen heute im Laufe des Tages die Ziele der letzten nächtlichen Bombenangriffe, um Einzelheiten über den Umfang der Zerstörungen, die in der Dunkelheit der Nacht nicht festgestellt werden können, zu fotografieren.

Seit den Mittagsstunden sind wieder die deutschen Kampf- und Sturzkampfgeschwader, begleitet von Jägern und Zerstörern, zum Fluge gegen England unterwegs. Soeben wird gemeldet, daß u. a. 30 deutsche Stukas einen Angriff auf die Südostküste Englands durchführten.

*

Wie schon im OKW-Bericht bekanntgegeben, hat die Luftwaffe auch in der Nacht vom 15. zum 16. 8. wichtige militärische Ziele in England mit Bomben angegriffen. Wir erfahren hierzu noch, daß auch die Staatswerft von Chatham das Ziel der deutschen Bombenangriffe war. Die an der Themsemündung gelegenen Docks und Werftanlagen wurden erfolgreich bombardiert. In Birmingham-Longbridge wurden Bomben auf „The Austin Co. Ltd.", eine Auto- und Motorenfabrik abgeworfen. Diese Fabrik baut während des Krieges die bekannten Bristol-Flugmotoren. In Brought bei Hull wurden die „Blackburn Aircraft-Werke" mit zahlreiche Bomben belegt. In dieser Flugzeugfabrik werden u. a. die englischen Stukas gebaut, mit denen die britische Luftwaffe versuchen will, den berühmten deutschen Stukas Konkurrenz zu machen. Alle britischen Versuche in dieser Richtung sind bisher mißlungen.

Karte von Portsmouth und Umgebung

Mindestens 143 Flugzeuge vernichtet

Die Bilanz der Kämpfe am Donnerstag in Fortsetzung der wuchtigen Luftangriffe auf England 21 Sperrballone abgeschossen

Berlin, 16. August.

Das Oberkommando der Wehrmacht gibt bekannt:

Am 15. August und in der Nacht zum 16. August setzte die Luftwaffe ihre Angriffe auf Seehäfen, Anlagen der Rüstungsindustrie, Flugplätze und Ballonsperren weiter fort. Die Hafenanlagen von Portland, Scarborough, Bridlington und Middlesborough, Flugzeug- und Motorenwerke in Birmingham und Brought bei Hull, sowie Hallen und Unterkünfte auf mehreren Flugplätzen in Süd-, Südost- und Mittelengland wurden schwer beschädigt. Dabei kam es zu heftigen Luftkämpfen, in deren Verlauf Major Galland seinen 20. Luftsieg errang. Mehrere britische Häfen wurden vermint.

Die Nachtangriffe britischer Flugzeuge gegen Westdeutschland richteten keinen nennenswerten Schaden an.

Die Gesamtverluste des Gegners am 15. 8. betrugen mindestens 143 Flugzeuge, von denen 106 im Luftkampf, der Rest am Boden zerstört oder durch Flakartillerie abgeschossen wurde. Außerdem gelang der Abschuß von 21 Sperrballonen. 32 deutsche Flugzeuge kehrten nicht zurück, jedoch konnte unser Seenotdienst neun deutsche und einen britischen Flieger im Kanal retten.

Ein Unterseeboot versenkte zwei bewaffnete Handelsschiffe mit zusammen 14 000 BRT.

Einige Minenräumboote schossen von 10 angreifenden feindlichen Spitfire-Flugzeugen vier ab.

Erneute Einflüge über die Schweiz

Der italienische Wehrmachtsbericht • Offensive im Britisch-Somali noch in voller Entwicklung

Rom, 16. August.

Der italienische Wehrmachtsbericht vom Freitag hat folgenden Wortlaut:

Das Hauptquartier der italienischen Wehrmacht gibt bekannt:

In Britisch-Somaliland sind unsere Offensivoperationen noch in voller Entwicklung. Ein feindliches Flugzeug ist in Flammen über Zeila abgeschossen worden. Zwei feindliche Einflüge über die Flugplätze von Colbolcia und Massana haben leichten Schaden verursacht. Es gab vier Tote und 12 Verwundete unter den Italienern und Eingeborenen.

Im Laufe einer Luftaktion gegen Wagir sind zwei feindliche Flugzeuge am Boden zerstört worden. Ein englischer Flieger ist im Luftkampf abgeschossen worden.

Formationen unserer Bomber, die von Jagdflugzeugen begleitet waren, haben den Flughafen von Holfu (Malta) bombardiert, ihre Ziele getroffen und Brände verursacht. Die feindlichen Jagdflugzeuge haben sich nach einem kurzen Angriffsversuch auf unsere Formationen zurückgezogen. Ein feindliches Flugzeug ist abgeschossen worden. Alle unsere Flugzeuge sind zurückgekehrt.

In Nordafrika haben unsere Flugzeuge die Bahn Fuca-Matruk bombardiert.

In den frühen Morgenstunden ist von über die Schweiz kommenden feindlichen Flugzeugen ein neuerlicher Angriff auf norditalienische Ortschaften durchgeführt worden, wobei Bomben abgeworfen wurden, von denen einige auf die Bauerndörfer Merate und Olgiate fielen und zwei Tote sowie fünf Verletzte zur Folge hatten. Es wurde nur geringer Materialschaden verursacht. Ein feindliches Flugzeug ist von unserer Flak in Turin getroffen worden und bei Cerescele d'Alba abgestürzt. Die aus fünf Mann bestehende Besatzung ist teils umgekommen, teils gefangengenommen worden.

Die pausenlosen deutschen Luftangriffe

gegen England haben bereits zu wesentlichen Ergebnissen geführt. Es haben sich im Laufe der Kämpfe Entwicklungen ergeben, die für eine Beurteilung der zweiten Phase dieses unmittelbaren Kampfes gegen England charakteristisch sind. So hat seit Beginn der Kämpfe die Ausdehnung der deutschen Operationen und damit die Ausdehnung des großen Feldes der Luftschlacht ständig zugenommen und eine entscheidende Erweiterung erfahren. Während die ersten Angriffe am 8. August sich noch auf einzelne Gebiete an der englischen Südküste beschränkten, wurde am 11. und 12. August bereits der ganze Raum über Südengland in einer Ausdehnung von rund 500 Klm. zum Felde der Luftschlacht. Bis zum 15. August hat sich dieses Schlachtfeld über Mittel- und Ostengland erweitert und sich damit im Raum vervielfacht. Die neuesten Luftangriffe haben das ganze englische Gebiet von Wales bis Schottland betroffen, wobei sich die Hauptkämpfe über Mittel- und Ostengland abgespielt haben. Diese Ausdehnung ist ein Kennzeichen dafür, daß der Kampf planmäßig erweitert und gesteigert wird. Es ist den Engländern nicht gelungen, den deutschen Kampfflugzeugen und Jägern den Einflug bis tief nach England hin zu sperren, obwohl diese Einflüge am Tage stattfanden. Weder die englischen Flugzeugsperren, noch die Ballonsperren haben die deutschen Kampfflugzeuge daran hindern können die ihnen gesteckten Ziele zu erreichen und anzugreifen. Auch die englischen Jäger haben den Luftraum über England nicht sperren können. Nach den vorliegenden Ergebnissen der letzten Tage scheint die englische Flak-Abwehr planlos zu werden, die Gegenwirkung von britischen Jagdflugzeugen unregelmäßig einzusetzen und nachzulassen. Entweder haben die englischen Jagdgeschwader bereits empfindliche Verluste erlitten oder die britische Luftwaffe ist infolge der Ausdehnung des Schlachtfeldes gezwungen, sich zu verzetteln. Und diese Erfolge bereits jetzt, wo es sich erst um eine verstärkte „bewaffnete Aufklärung" handelt, zu der britische Zeitungen und Londoner Rundfunk behaupten, daß mehrere tausend deutsche Flugzeuge eingesetzt seien — nach einer aus Neuyork kommenden Nachricht sollten sogar 16 000 Flugzeuge über England kämpfen —, während es sich in Wahrheit nur um Bruchteile dieser Zahlen handeln dürfte. Diese übertriebenen englischen Angaben über die Zahl der deutschen Flugzeuge sollen offenbar die an zahlreichen Stellen entstandenen schweren Schäden und das Versagen der britischen Abwehr begründen. Doch wird niemand daran zweifeln, daß Deutschland in der Lage ist, mit weit mehr Flugzeugen als bisher die Schlacht fortzuführen. Was das bedeutet, kann man ermessen an den bisherigen Erfolgen, wurden doch in der Zeit vom 8. bis 15. August rund 550 feindliche Flugzeuge vernichtet.

Die Versorgung der besetzten Gebiete

macht der englischen Publizistik offenbar Sorgen. Sie hegt diese Sorgen aber nur, um gegen Deutschland hetzen zu können. Sollten nämlich ernsthafte englische Sorgen zu diesem Thema bestehen, so wäre dem sehr schnell abzuhelfen, indem England die völkerrechtswidrige Blockade der angeblich notleidenden Gebiete aufhebt. Wir haben wiederholt zu diesem Thema Stellung genommen und dabei auch sogenannte „neutrale" Stimmen, die völlig auf englischem Geleis liefen, zurückgewiesen, die gleichsam Deutschland mit der Verantwortung für die Versorgung der besetzten Gebiete belasten wollten und dabei sogar Deutschland die Absicht unterstellten, es wolle z. B. Frankreich bewußt aushungern. Deutschland, das angesichts der mutwilligen Zerstörung der Lebensmitteldepots durch den Gegner, namentlich in der ersten Zeit, die notleidende Bevölkerung der besetzten Gebiete aus eigenen Beständen ernährt hatte, soll heute fälschlich beschuldigt werden, die Besatzungstruppen völlig aus dem Lande leben zu lassen, wozu es übrigens auf Grund der Haager Landkriegsordnung ausdrücklich berechtigt wäre. Besonders erstaunt wird man aber über die Behauptung sein, daß das Reich aus seinen Beständen die Verpflegung der in seinen militärischen Bereich gelangten Gebiete zu übernehmen habe. Diese Auffassung weist mit Nachdruck die „Deutsche diplomatisch-politische Korrespondenz" zurück. Das Organ der Wilhelmstraße erklärt, daß die Abschnürung der Zivilbevölkerung eines Landes von dem Bezug von Lebensmitteln schon in sich eine Völkerrechtswidrigkeit sei. Es könne deshalb niemals eine Verpflichtung Deutschlands bestehen, für die Verpflegung der betreffenden Gebiete zu sorgen, sondern diese Länder hätten das Recht, — und darum gehe es — sich aus den neutralen Ländern die Nahrung durch Kauf oder in Form von Unterstützungen zu beschaffen, die für die Bedürfnisse der Bevölkerung notwendig sei. Wenn gewisse Hilfeleistungen an die polnische Zivilbevölkerung ermöglicht worden seien, und nun plötzlich Maßnahmen ähnlicher Art für die anderen besetzten Gebiete ausgeschlossen sein sollen, so sei dies nur ein Beweis dafür, daß die Verletzung des Völkerrechts der britischen Kriegführung keinerlei Skrupel bereite.

Griechischer Kreuzer torpediert

Athen, 16. August.

Am Fest Mariä Himmelfahrt, 15. August, wurde nach einer Mitteilung der Agence d'Athenes der auf der Reede des Hafens der Insel Tinos liegende Kreuzer Helli von einem U-Boot unbekannter Nationalität torpediert.

Englische Lügen um den griechischen Kreuzer „Helli"

Rom, 16. August.

Zur Versenkung des griechischen Kreuzers „Helli" weist man von zuständiger italienischer Seite auf das entschiedenste die von englischer Seite sofort verbreitete Version zurück, wonach das griechische Kriegsschiff von einem italienischen U-Boot versenkt worden sei.

Man betont, daß nach Berichten, die von italienischen U-Boots-Kommandanten eingeholt wurden, die Torpedierung durch kein italienisches U-Boot vorgenommen wurde und fügt hinzu, daß außerdem kein italienisches U-Boot in der genannten Zone sich befindet. Die Tatsache, daß England unmittelbar nach der Versenkung diese Version verbreitet habe, lasse ohne weiteres den Schluß zu, daß der Coup von London ausgehe, wo man offenbar einen neuen „Athenia"-Fall konstruieren wolle. Außerdem bezwecke das englische Manöver die wegen der Ermordung des albanischen Patrioten Hoggia zwischen Italien und Griechenland eingetretene Spannung zu verschärfen und überhaupt durch derartige Unterstellungen den Balkan in Unruhe zu versetzen.

Schweden und die Genfer Liga

Stockholm, 16. August.

Der schwedische Außenminister Günther gab am Freitag vor den beiden Kammern des schwedischen Reichstages eine Erklärung über die außenpolitische Lage ab, in der er u. a. ausführte, daß hinsichtlich der schwedischen Außenpolitik keine prinzipiellen Veränderungen eingetreten seien.

Zur Stellung Schwedens gegenüber der Genfer Liga betonte der Außenminister, daß der bisherige schwedische Gesandte in Bern, der kürzlich nach Rom versetzt worden sei, der zuständige Vertreter Schwedens bei der Liga gewesen sei. Ein neuer Vertreter bei der Liga sei nicht ernannt worden, und was die schwedischen Beiträge für den Völkerbund für das Jahr 1940 betreffe, so sehe die schwedische Regierung keine Veranlassung, diese Summe zu zahlen, da die Genfer Liga öffentlich ihre Funktion beinahe völlig aufgegeben habe.

Sunday Chronicle
and Sunday Referee

SUNDAY CHRONICLE Founded 1885
SUNDAY REFEREE Founded 1877

LATE LONDON EDITION

Broadcasting—Back Page

c LONDON: SEPTEMBER 8, 1940 TWOPENCE

Hitler throws everything in—and admits losses

BIGGEST LONDON RAIDS

'Revenge' attacks by 500 planes: 21 down • Crowds see battles over City streets

"WE HAVE HAD TO PAY WITH GREAT SACRIFICES"

—German Communique

LONDON bore its most terrific aerial attacks yesterday when a raid soon after dark followed quickly on a tea-time raid in which 500 German planes took part.

Wave after wave of them roared over the central area, to be met by a terrific anti-aircraft barrage and flight after flight of British fighters.

Late last night the Air Ministry announced that 21 enemy craft—16 of them bombers—were shot down by our fighters. Five of our machines had been lost.

The German radio, announcing last night that the attack was in "reprisal for the night attack on Berlin by the Royal Air Force," admitted that the results achieved were gained only at the cost of "great sacrifices."

As the first wave of the raiders roared over the Central London area, shopping crowds, despite the sirens call to shelter, lingered to watch the opening of the battle high above.

They saw the pinpoint gleams as British fighters, twisting and turning in their grapple with the attackers, caught the flash of the evening sun.

Over another district they saw the blue sky fill with the fleecy bursts of anti-aircraft fire. Buildings shook as the barrage roared.

Then came the thump of bombs from several quarters.

The Air Ministry communiqué admitted damage and fires, saying:

"Late this afternoon enemy aircraft in large numbers crossed the coast of Kent and approached the London area. They were heavily engaged by our fighters and A.A. guns, but a number of them succeeded in penetrating to the industrial area of East London.

Factories fired

As a result of these attacks fires were caused among industrial targets in this area. Damage was done to the lighting and other public services and some dislocation of communication was caused. Attacks have also been directed against the docks. Information as to casualties is not yet available.

"BOMBS WERE ALSO DROPPED ON AN INDUSTRIAL INSTALLATION ON THE NORTH BANK OF THE THAMES ESTUARY, CAUSING FIRES.

In the night attack a variety theatre and a store were hit.

A fire broke out in one area at a factory which was struck by a bomb; an off-licence and a furniture store were also damaged.

A TRAIN WAS HIT, AND THERE WERE SOME CASUALTIES.

About 500 people assembling for a greyhound meeting had remarkable escapes when bombs fell.

A spectator said: "There must have been fifty bombers accompanied by fighters.

"Three bombs fell first—one outside the grounds, one behind the stand, and then came one bang on the track.

"When the other two fell people immediately rushed for cover, so when the third fell on the track they were not so exposed as they would otherwise have been.

"It was fortunate, because afterwards pieces of bomb were found under the back seats of the stand. Some women fainted afterwards.

"We saw two enemy planes shot down. The occupants baled out and came down by parachute."

Four thousand people at a football match had a grandstand view of one fierce air battle. They were so engrossed that they forgot the risks of falling shrapnel and cheered when they saw the first plane belching smoke and flames.

"I counted at least twelve machines," a spectator said. "They dropped bombs in the distance before being caught in a fierce A.A. barrage which drove them into our fighter formations.

"A parachute dropped from one of the German machines.

"WAVES OF BOMBERS SWEPT IN FROM ALL DIRECTIONS. THE CRUMP OF BOMBS, THE STACCATO BARK OF A.A. FIRE, AND THE

(*Continued in Columns 3 and 4.*)

To-day's Call to Prayer

WHEREVER the English language is spoken in the world, the people, led by the King and Queen, will be at prayer to-day.

Special services will be held and sermons preached in every Christian church throughout the British Empire and the United States.

THIS IS THE FIRST TIME IN HISTORY THAT THE WHOLE WORLD HAS BEEN GIRDLED WITH A PRAYER-CHAIN OF WHICH THE CHIEF LINK IS THE BRITISH CROWN.

It is expected that the whole of ordinary civil life will pause in order to join the King at prayer. The only exception will be the workers on war production.

LONE RAIDERS BROKE LULL

WHINE OF OUR FIGHTERS PROVIDED A DRAMATIC SOUND BACKGROUND TO THE THRILLING SPECTACLE.

"Palls of smoke—some from shot-down bombers—began to drift up into the blue sky.

"Fighters met the second wave of the enemy before they reached the central London area.

"Our Spitfires chased the stragglers, and it seemed that several of them were winged and in difficulties before they passed out of sight making for home."

Chased by fighters

Until this dramatic resumption of the blitzkrieg South-East England had had only one alarm.

That was when 30 Messerschmitts 109 fighters, converted into light dive-bombers, made a half-hearted attack on an aerodrome.

ONE TASTE OF THE A.A. BARRAGE WAS ENOUGH FOR THEM. THEY TURNED AND FLED.

Elsewhere there was sporadic activity as enemy planes in small numbers were met by Spitfires and Hurricanes.

An Air Ministry and Ministry of Home Security joint communiqué issued during the afternoon said:

"Enemy attacks on this country during the morning have been on a reduced scale. An aerodrome in Kent was unsuccessfully attacked, but a bomb which fell in the neighbourhood caused some casualties, details of which are not yet available.

"An attack was also made on a cathedral town in the West country, when a school and other buildings near the cathedral were damaged, but no casualties have been reported.

"Reports up to midday show that two enemy aircraft, one a bomber and the other a fighter-bomber, have been shot down this morning by our fighters, without loss to themselves.

Picture and fires by R.A.F.

THIS is what R.A.F. Wellington bombers did to Asmara aerodrome—Italian base in East Africa. And they stayed to get this picture of the fires they had started.

—AND R.A.F.'s BIGGEST ON BERLIN

Power station hit in Nazi capital

THE R.A.F.'s biggest raid on Berlin for which the Germans say their raids on London yesterday were a "reprisal," was described in an Air Ministry communique last night:

The raid on Berlin, stated the communiqué, began soon after eleven and went on until one o'clock in the morning (Saturday morning).

Our raiders flew through an intense barrage from light and heavy A.A. batteries.

One section of bombers visited the West Power Station, which had already been damaged in previous attacks.

At Spandau, in the north-west of the city, B.M.W. aero engine works was located and set on fire, although so difficult were the conditions that one bomb aimer, bombing through a gap in the clouds, barely had time to release the stick of high explosives before the ground was again blotted out.

The Salzhof oil reservoir near the banks of the Tegel See was apparently badly damaged, for several particularly violent explosions followed the bursting of the bombs.

Forest Fires

Meanwhile, attacks on military objectives concealed in the Black Forest were renewed. After the bombers had scattered incendiaries over new areas, a fierce fire was started, a deep red glow from which could be seen fifty miles away.

As the flames roared through the pine forests there came a series of explosions.

At the northern end of the forest the flames destroyed stocks of material hidden in the trees, and in the middle the flames, spreading westwards, approached the Rhine to the east of Strasburg.

The railway sidings at Krefeld, Hamm, Soest, Mannheim, and Ehrang were bombed with success.

Our bombers continued their counter-attacks on the enemy gun emplacements and aerodromes near the French Channel coast. They followed each other at brief intervals between nine and ten o'clock on Friday night, and dropped high explosives and incendiaries on the German long range guns at Cape Gris Nez.

"Fires at once broke out among the emplacements.

"As the aircraft re-crossed the English coast on the way home there was a big explosion from the direction of the gun emplacements.

Arrested!

GAMELIN REYNAUD DALADIER

GENERAL GAMELIN and the two former French Prime Ministers, M. Daladier and M. Reynaud, have been arrested, says the German News Agency.

They are interned in a chateau near Riom, where the trial of French ex-Ministers is to take place.

The news agency, quoting a Vichy report, says their arrest is a preventive measure based on the law recently passed by the Cabinet for maintaining public security.

Under this law people dangerous to the State may be arrested "for the duration."

U.S. asked to buy raiders

TWO Messerschmitt fighters, both in perfect condition, are being offered for sale in America—by Britain!

They are a Messerschmitt 109 and a Messerschmitt 110 that were shot down by R.A.F. fighters.

The Ministry of Aircraft Production (reports B.U.P.) is asking £31,250 for each of them, cash down, but in the event of competition the planes will go to the highest bidders.

More children reach Canada

MORE children, sent by the Children's Overseas Reception Board, have arrived safely in Canada, it was announced yesterday.

Fighting in Indo-China

FIGHTING has broken out on the borders of French Indo-China between French forces and units of Chiang Kai-shek's Army according to reports received in Vichy to-day.

The despatches assert that units of Chiang's Army violated the frontier on Thursday. French covering units met the Chinese advancing along the frontier at Red River and repulsed them after a fierce fight in which one French soldier was killed and ten wounded.—British United Press.

LATE NEWS

"WELL DONE," SAYS GERMAN PILOT.

German bomber seen to crash about three miles from a Kent town last night. Two German airmen baled out and landed in the town. The first persons to reach them were two women. Comment of one airman was, "Well done, Spitfires."

BLACK-OUT TIME

London — 8-1-5.55 a.m.

BOMBS RAIN DOWN AFTER 'ALL CLEAR'

Military Target— German Version

2 Hit Homes of Workers

ACCORDING to the official German News Agency yesterday, the attacks on London on Friday night "were particularly successful."

If the killing of a few women and children, the shattering of humble workers' homes means "success" to Goering's vaunted Air Force, the Agency is right.

The Elephant and Castle district, dense huddle of workers' houses and tenements, was the focal point of the Germans' night attack.

Road and rail delays slight

Its only "military objective" is the crossroads—the Clapham Junction of the tramway system of South London.

High explosive and incendiary bombs were rained on the area by raiders gliding down with engines ticking over after an "all-clear" had been sounded.

Two heavy bombs fell on a large tenement block. One hit a corner of the building and extensively damaged the upper floors.

The other fell into the central courtyard, shattering windows and doors on every floor.

Had the bombs fallen a minute or two later, the casualties would have been heavy. But the residents, leaving their shelttrs after hearing "raiders passed," had not reached the two top floors.

ONLY ONE PERSON WAS KILLED.

In a street nearby another big bomb wrecked two or three houses. Demolition squads were digging in the debris yesterday for victims. Several people are believed to be buried there.

Four men and women and two children were killed by a third bomb in this district.

Patients were all evacuated

Road and rail services were affected for some hours. 'Buses were diverted to skirt the danger zone and trams were stopped at points outside, but by 9 a.m. yesterday were working normally. There were full services on all railways by 7.20 a.m.

Four bombs which fell within thirty yards of each other caused seven deaths in another South London district. In one house an elderly couple stayed in their back bedroom when the warning sounded, but a daughter, with her child, took refuge in an Anderson shelter in the garden.

The house was demolished by a direct hit. The old couple were killed. Their daughter and grandchild were unhurt.

The body of a man was found in a garden five houses away.

One house near by was left standing when a bomb demolished a house on one side and two on the other side of it.

In one of the wrecked houses, Mr. and Mrs. Leonard Mosley, with their two boys, aged 3 and 5, were in the front room when the bomb dropped. Mother and sons were killed outright, Mr. Mosley was rescued by neighbours, suffering only severe shock.

In another, Mrs. E. Walker, a widow, took refuge with her 21-years-old married daughter under the staircase.

ONLY THE STAIRCASE REMAINED INTACT AFTER THE EXPLOSION, AND MOTHER AND DAUGHTER WALKED OUT UNAIDED TO THE STREET.

A neighbour said: "We live a few doors away, and our house was shaken by the blast.

"When the all-clear sounded I ran out into the garden and shouted, 'Who's got it?' A man in a house which was hit shouted back through a hole in the wall, 'It's us. The unlucky thirteen.'"

The number of the house was thirteen, but no one in it was injured.

The "objective"

In another South London district, high-explosive bomb severely damaged an isolation hospital.

There were no casualties, for some time ago all patients were evacuated, and the building had been left in charge of a small emergency nursing staff.

The bomb wrecked part of the hospital's laundry, and made a huge crater in the yard of the adjoining ambulance garage.

Great lumps of concrete from the yard flew in all directions, making holes in several roofs nearby.

Here is what the German News Agency had to say about all this terrorism.

"The railways of the southern suburbs of London were so heavily bombed that transport was completely stopped.

"Hundreds of thousands of City workers were unable to return to their homes after the "All Clear" had been sounded in the late afternoon and were caught in town at the time of the third alarm."

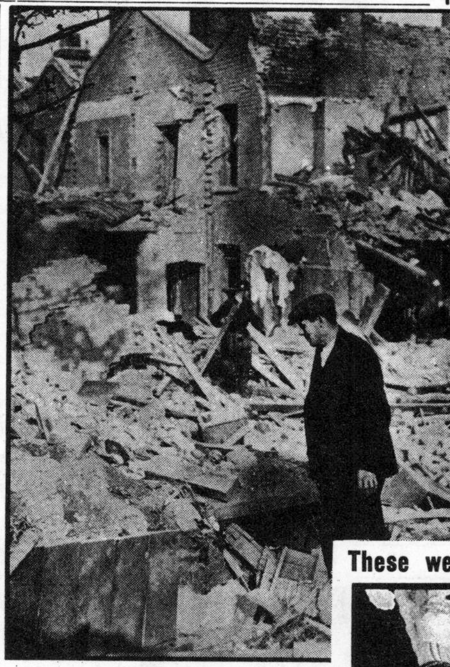

JOAN, Violet and their father, Mr. Ratingky, saved themselves—and the family pet rabbit—when a German bomber blew their home to bits. They were in their Anderson shelter and when they came out they saw the wreckage (above). Five minutes earlier that rubble had been a happy and comfortable British home.

Raids on London

HOSPITAL HIT: IT WAS 'EMPTY'

These were saved

R.A.F. Bombers Swoop in Waves on Berlin

POLICE H.Q. WRECKED

WAVES OF R.A.F. BOMBERS SWOOPED ON BERLIN EARLY YESTERDAY, BOMBING SMALL ARMS WORKS AT SPANDAU, A SUBURB OF THE CAPITAL, AS WELL AS TARGETS IN THE CENTRAL DISTRICT.

The population went to shelter when the sirens sounded at 12.15 a.m. and stayed there until 3 a.m. while the bombers swept over the city from the north-west.

They admit we got there

Although Nazi officials claimed that the raiders were "quickly broken up and driven back," they admit that many high explosive and incendiary bombs were dropped by those which got through.

They declared that a balloon barrage, put up as a surprise for the attackers, kept the bombers high and made accurate aiming difficult.

American reporters cabled yesterday that the raids were the most severe that Berlin has yet suffered.

Despite Nazi denials, they say that many heavy bombs fell in the centre of the city—all close to military targets—and dozens of fires were started.

The Berlin correspondent of the Swedish newspaper, "Dagens Nyheter," says that the crash of the A.A. barrage was frightening. Shell splinters rained all over the city throughout the alarm period, he reports.

Berlin yesterday admitted that a police barracks facing the Tiergarten, the city's Hyde Park, was hit by a heavy bomb.

THERE WERE SEVERAL CASUALTIES, IT WAS STATED.

The official German News Agency alleges that the working class district of Wedding "was the target of a senseless attack."

Fires were started in this area, and several buildings were wrecked by high explosives, the agency says. Several civilians were killed, and a number injured.

Another flight of bombers attacked Magdeburg, arms, aircraft building and oil storage centre, west of Berlin.

Here, too, the Germans admit several killed and more injured.

They say that a searchlight post, destroyed by high explosive, was the only military target hit.

While these two spectacular raids were in progress, bombing forces were carrying out the R.A.F.'s "routine schedule" of nightly bombing in the Ruhr, the Rhineland and aerodromes in occupied France, Holland and Belgium.

Until late last evening the Germans would release no news of these attacks.

Air War Costs Germany 4,000 Airmen

HITLER'S AIR-KRIEG AGAINST THIS COUNTRY HAS COST HIM MORE THAN 4,000 AIRMEN IN LESS THAN THREE MONTHS.

These losses are out of all proportion to ours. For instance, last week, up to Friday, 800 German airmen were shot down by us while we lost only 57 British pilots.

Official statistics show that from June 17 to Sept. 6 we have brought down, by our fighters and anti-aircraft guns, 1,688 German aircraft of all types. Of these 686 were bombers and 408 were fighter-bombers up to the end of August.

Although we lost 143 fighter machines during last week up to Friday, 86 of our pilots baled out and were saved.

That is where the German wastage in trained personnel press so heavily upon them, for no matter how many of their airmen bale out, they fall into our hands as prisoners.

A great deal of sleep is lost by people who keep listening for the sounds of planes, and in the majority of cases it is only the sound of our own aircraft overhead.

Voice Aids Red Cross

DOROTHY THOMPSON, "Sunday Chronicle" contributor, summed up Hitler and gave a grand tribute to British ideals in a recent broadcast to Canada.

That broadcast has now been recorded by "His Master's Voice."

Profits from the sale of the record go to the British Red Cross, and Miss Thompson has insisted that her copyright and other fees shall also be devoted to the cause.

Miss Thompson's articles will be resumed in the "Sunday Chronicle" next Sunday.

We have, we shall

"We have proved to Hitler that he cannot defeat us. Now we must prove that we can defeat him."—Mr. E. Shinwell, M.P. (Labour, Seaham) speaking at Huddersfield last night.

The Barber had afternoon off

By H. W. SEAMAN

"MAKE it quick," said I to the barber. "I'm tired."

"All right, sir," said he, tucking the towel under my chin. "I don't feel too bright myself."

"I have been up half the night," I said.

"Would you like to know what I was doing last night?" the barber asked.

"I am too tired to tell you what I was doing, so you tell me," I replied. "But make it quick, please."

"Well, sir," said he, "I am usually on A.R.P. duty from 7 to 11. Yesterday was my afternoon off, so I thought I'd get a bit of gardening done. But I had hardly got home when the siren went, so I put my tin hat on and went on duty for a couple of hours. Then I had my tea.

"I was just about finishing my tea when the siren went again, so out I went again. It turned out to be one of those long warnings, and every now and then it got exciting.

Air-Raid Baby

"There were two houses blown up, and three more set on fire, so I helped the firemen for a while. I also helped the First Aid people with three hospital cases.

"And then, to top the lot, a woman gave birth to a baby when the old Hun was still overhead.

"It was five o'clock in the morning when the All Clear went. It was half-past five when I hit the hay, and I had to be here at eight. But I did get a little sleep."

Dumb Insolence

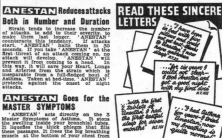

WITH typical Prussian arrogance this German pilot, shot down and captured, strolls with his hands in his pockets to the car waiting to take him to an internment camp. Where are our sergeant-majors?

'Big Chief' Gracie

GRACIE FIELDS is having a grand time in Canada. Well away from the wail of sirens and the thud of bombs, Gracie puts on her war-paint for a garden party at Calgary.

ARROWS OF LIGHT AID BOMBERS

GERMAN agents in Britain are using reflector arrows to guide attacking planes to their objectives at night.

The guides are glass or polished steel plates, which are placed, usually on grassland, in arrow formation.

When the invading planes drop flares their bright light is reflected by the plates, which then appear like illuminated arrows pointing to the target to be bombed.

Several cases of the discovery of arrows are already being investigated.

"If any member of the public finds one he should leave it where it is and contact the police at once," an official told the "Sunday Chronicle" yesterday.

Save Your Broom

Because of the great shortage of broom handles, and the poor prospect of additional supplies becoming available in the near future, housewives are advised to keep and re-use their present broom handles.

DON'T STAY AWAKE FOR THE SIRENS

AFTER more than a month of night air raids, people in raided districts can be sorted into three classes.

Those who find the loss of a few hours' sleep does not hurt them; those who sleep through air raids; those who worry because they cannot sleep.

Here are some hints by the "Sunday Chronicle" Medical Correspondent for those who cannot sleep.

Stay in bed

Go to bed downstairs if possible, preferably in a basement room. Do not stay up after your usual bedtime because a warning has sounded or because you expect one.

Have warm outdoor clothes and a gas-mask handy.. If you hear bombs or gunfire, resist the temptation to get up and see what is happening.

Stay in bed. Do not turn on the light if you can help it. Do not read, for that would keep you awake. So would a cup of tea. Just lie and rest in the dark.

Most people can get along with much less sleep than they are accustomed to get, or think they need.

Buckingham Palace Bombed EXTRA

NAZIS MOVING TO INVADE BRITAIN, CHURCHILL WARNS

FINAL NIGHT EDITION WEATHER: PARTLY CLOUDY Details on Page 20

THE CALL BULLETIN — SAN FRANCISCO — AN INDEPENDENT NEWSPAPER

85TH YEAR CALL AND POST, VOL. 148, NO. 41 THE CALL-BULLETIN, VOL. 168, NO. 41 WEDNESDAY, SEPTEMBER 11, 1940 5c DAILY 90c a Month

Yankees Lead League

Di Maggio, Dahlgren Star as N. Y. Wins Contest, 3 to 1

The world champion New York Yankees mastered young Master Bobby Feller and the Cleveland Indians today at Cleveland and rose to first place in the American League for the first time since the race took shape last May. The score was 3 to 1.

The Yanks' league lead may be shortlived—they have another game to play with the Indians this afternoon—but between games they were definitely on top of the league, holding a slight edge over the Indians and Detroit, whose game with Boston was still incomplete.

Detroit led the Sox, 4 to 3, in the fourth inning of their game in Detroit. Freddie Hutchinson, former Seattle star, started on the mound for the Tigers, but was replaced by Gorsica in the third inning.

JOE DOUBLES

Former coast leaguers turned the trick for the Yankees today.

Joe Di Maggio doubled and Babe Dahlgren singled him home for the first run and Di Maggio singled in another tally later on.

Ernie Bonham, former Oaklander called down from Newark recently, outpitched Feller, who allowed but five hits in eight frames.

DOWNS INDIANS

Bonham never allowed a hit after the third inning and not an Indian among the last eighteen to face him reached first base.

(Box Scores, Details on Sports.)

King, Queen Take To Raid Shelter

LONDON, Sept. 11 (INS).—King George and Queen Elizabeth took to an air raid shelter during an alarm in a southeast district of London today.

The alarm interrupted their majesties' tour of a severely bombed area. Police served the king and queen with tea while the alarm was in progress and they continued the tour when the "all clear" sounded.

The alarm was believed due to passage of German reconnaissance aircraft attempting to take pictures.

King George and Queen Elizabeth look at the damage made by a Nazi bomb of a corner of Buckingham palace. This photo, cabled from London today, shows the queen, in light dress and hat, and the king, in naval uniform, standing on the edge of a crater fifteen feet deep blasted in the ground by the delayed action bomb. Soldiers and attaches are in the crater. The wreckage at right is part of a glass-walled swimming pool, just under the queen's sitting room. (Other bombing pictures on Page B, Page 1, Second Section.) —Associated Press Wirephoto.

Royal Pair See Damage

Berlin, London Suffer Heavy Raid Damage

Premier Sees Crisis Near For England

LONDON, Sept. 11 (AP).—Prime Minister Winston Churchill broadcast a warning to his fortress nation today that Adolf Hitler's long projected attempt at invasion appears to be at hand and that the next week may be the most critical in England's history.

The Germans already are moving self-propelled barges and convoys of larger ships from northern ports to the whole French coast, he said, slipping along, from port to port, under the protection of German coastal batteries. The attack, he warned, may be made on England, Scotland and even Ireland, with forces concentrated as far north as Norway.

WIDESPREAD BOMBINGS

Even as he spoke widespread bombing attacks by British planes on concentrations of barges along the German held French, Belgian and Dutch coasts, such as might be used for an invasion of Britain, were reported tonight by the air ministry.

Britain is ready, Churchill said, praising the air force, the navy and the land army.

"This is the time for every one to stand, to hold firm, as they are doing," Churchill said.

Then as he spoke of "these cruel, wanton, indiscriminate bombings of London," as a "part of Hitler's invasion plan," the prime minister continued:

"KINDLES A FIRE"

"What he has done is to kindle a fire in British hearts, here and all over the world, which will glow long after all trace of the conflagration he has caused in London have been removed."

(Text of Churchill's speech on Page B.)

Historic Sites At 2 Capitals Attacked

LONDON, Sept. 11 (AP).—German warplanes charged repeatedly at London's defenses and fought desperate battles with Britain's airmen today as the greatest air war in history was disclosed to have destroyed a part of Britain's Buckingham Palace and damaged Germany's Reichstag building and Brandenburg Gate, historic structures of the two capitals.

The air ministry said British dive bombers also repeatedly hit with "great precision" the famous Potsdam railway station in Berlin.

(This was denied by the Berlin radio.)

(As retaliation Berlin sources announced Germany would send 10,000 tons planeloads of bombs daily to the London area for the next few days.)

A formation of probably 125 German planes encountered savage resistance from British fighters and the heaviest anti-aircraft fire yet heard in London in one of the five daylight thrusts today at this capital.

Signs of an approaching crisis in the greatest air war in history developed as German warplanes made repeated, determined thrusts at London.

Other developments included:

TIME BOMB HITS PALACE

A time bomb was disclosed to have blown out a corner of the royal residence, Buckingham Palace, on Tuesday, injuring no one.

(Editor's Note: International News Service reported today that long-range German guns hammered the southeast coast of England late this afternoon, firing from emplacements just behind newly-observed concen-

Continued on Page A, Col. One

Draft Bill Hits Reds, Bund

By WILLIAM S. NEAL
Staff Correspondent International News

WASHINGTON, Sept. 11 (INS). The Senate-House conference on the conscription bill today approved a provision declaring it the sense of Congress that members of the communist party and German-American Bund be barred from jobs vacated by drafters.

In taking this action, the conferees eliminated another provision which was inserted in the House bill, calling for a ban on jobs to aliens.

PROVISION REVEALED

The new provision read:

"It is the expressed policy of this Congress that whenever a vacancy is caused in the employment rolls of any business or industry by reason of induction into the service of the United States of an employe pursuant to the provisions of this act, that such vacancy shall not be filled by any person who is a member of the communist party or German-American Bund."

Members said they eliminated the alien ban because the bill provides for draft of aliens who have declared their intention of becoming citizens.

"I think we should get an agreement tonight," said Senator Sheppard (D.), Tex., chairman of the conference.

COMPROMISE SEEN

A compromise on age limits was considered, while it was indicated strongly that the Fish amendment, opposed by the administration and condemned by Republican Presidential Nominee Wendell Willkie, would be scrapped.

Although the Senate voted to

Continued on Page 7, Column 6

NINE TRAPPED MINERS RESCUED

PARK CITY, Utah, Sept. 11 (AP).—Nine men, trapped more than 12 hours by collapse of a "chute set" in a meatls mine here, were rescued uninjured today.

HOUSE VOTES CITIZENSHIP BAN ON REDS, NAZIS

WASHINGTON, Sept. 11 (AP).—Without hearing a word of opposition the House passed and sent to the Senate today legislation which sponsors said would bar Communists, Nazis and Fascists from naturalization as United States citizens.

AT BOSTON (Nat., 2d Gm.)—Cincinnati 3, Boston 1; final.

AT DETROIT (Am.)—Boston 5, Detroit 7; 5th in.

AT CLEVELAND (Am., 2d Gm.)—N. Y. 2, Cleveland 0; 1st in.

5TH RACE, HAWTHORNE—Doorbell, won, 3.80, 2.80, 2.20; Philyra, 2d, 4.60, 3.40; Last Rose, 3d, 3. T., 1:40.

6TH RACE, NARRAGANSETT—Zacatine, won, 14, 6.60, 4.40; R. Marlboro, 2d, 4.70, 3.50; Misty Quest, 3d, 4.70. T., 1:12 3-5.

7TH RACE, AQUEDUCT—Third Try, won, 15.80, 7.90, 5.40; Fire Marshal, 2d, 7.20, 5.10; Granduce, 3d, 5.10. T., 2:06 1-5.

Span Purchase Bonds Sold

SACRAMENTO, Sept. 11 (AP). The state virtually completed the purchase of the Carquinez and Antioch toll bridges today with the sale of $6,433,999 of revenue bonds at a price so low officials estimated the two structures could be made toll free late in 1947.

Kaiser & Co. and Sargent, Taylor & Co., both of San Francisco, submitted a joint bid which gave a premium of slightly in excess of $500,000 and the California Toll Bridge Authority quickly authorized its acceptance.

Actual taking over of the two structures and the Martinez, Benicia ferry, also involved in the deal, will be completed Monday.

Not only will tolls be discontinued approximately six months prior to the time provided for under private ownership of the structures, officials said, but tolls will be lowered Monday to 30 cents for passenger automobiles.

Japanese Typhoon Kills 22, Destroys 50 Houses

TOKYO, Sept. 11 (AP).—A typhoon which swept today over Kyushu, southwestern island of Japan proper, killed at least 22 persons, destroyed 50 houses, disrupted communications and damaged crops.

British Bomb Reichstag

BERLIN, Sept. 11 (AP).—British demolition and incendiary bombs struck the heart of the German Reich today in the R. A. F.'s most spectacular Berlin attack and forced evacuation of several streets lest bomb-weakened buildings collapse.

Promising retaliation, Nazi quarters in Berlin asserted that 10,000 plane loads of bombs will be rained daily on the London area in the next few days, striking from French coastal bases in a massive "all out" assault.

The British raiders dropped bombs that hit the Reichstag (Parliament) building, the Academy of Arts next to the United States embassy, and also damaged famous Brandenburg Gate in Unter Den Linden. The high command said also that two hospitals were hit in the center of the city.

FIVE KILLED

(London claimed today that the Potsdam railway station in Berlin was also bombed and damaged, but the official German radio denied the report.)

Officially the civilian toll of the attack was five killed.

"In the diplomatic section a number of streets had to be evacuated temporarily because of danger of houses collapsing," the daily communique reported.

Only quick action by air raid precautions workers prevented "numerous incendiary bombs from causing bigger damage," the communique went on.

The high command acknowledged British bombs were dropped in northern France, Belgium and elsewhere in northern Germany, but insisted they **"caused but little damage."**

PLANE REPORTED DOWN

"Some enemy planes succeeded in penetrating Berlin, unloading bombs," said the communique. "At numerous places in residential and business sections fires started."

One British plane was reported brought down by anti-aircraft guns, with pursuit planes getting another. German naval artillery on the channel coast was said to have shot down four British planes.

The Germans acknowledged loss of but three of their own planes in the preceding twenty-four hours of action against England and chalked up these successes:

Most of the big Thameshaven oil tanks were burned out and destroyed.

A large formation of German bombers today attacked giant oil storage tanks at the Victoria dock, on the Thames, on London's eastern outskirts, and caused huge fires.

FIRES RAGING

Other attacks left raging fires along London's Millwall docks, the West Indian docks and in the Kensington residential section in the west end.

The official German wireless in a broadcast today said that 54 British planes were shot down in fighting over Britain this afternoon. Eighteen German planes are missing, the radio said.

Bombing and sinking of an

Continued on Page A, Col. Six

BOMB DAMAGE AT BUCKINGHAM PALACE

BUCKINGHAM PALACE has suffered from one of the many bombs which have fallen in all parts of the London area. The above picture was taken when the King and Queen were inspecting the crater and débris left by the bomb, one of the delayed action type, which narrowly missed the main building and did substantial damage to one wing.

ON THE SIDE OF ALLAH

AN INDIAN SOLDIER'S VIEW OF THE WAR

We publish by permission the following letter written to an English correspondent by an Indian officer, Major Mahommed Akbar Khan, on what the "average Muslim soldier" thinks of the war:—

Since February, 1940 [writes Major Mahommed Akbar Khan], I have had the unique privilege of not only renewing contacts with my old friends whom I have known from my childhood but also of meeting countless friends of my revered father. Throughout these contacts the ever-recurring question that was asked me has been, "What does the average Muslim soldier think of this war, or, for that matter, what does the average Indian think of this gigantic conflict?"

Since it is almost impossible to answer this very complex question to the satisfaction of all I thought I might put my answer in writing and that in the simplest and most direct way I can, not as a politician, which I am not, but as a soldier by birth and by choice. I hope, therefore, that my observations will be taken as such.

Any student of the Holy Quran is familiar with the great Prophet Mohammed's injunctions regarding war and the participation in war. It is written in the Holy Quran 2, 190:—"And fight in the way of Allah with those who fight with you, and be not aggressive, surely Allah does not love the aggressor." (Translation from The Religion of Islam, p. 554.)

Islam leaves the reader no doubts as to when, where, and why he should take up arms. It is needless for me to go into any lengthy enumeration of these points. For my purpose it is sufficient to give the following four clear-cut objects of such an effort:—

1. To preserve peace and order.
2. To safeguard life and property.
3. To secure religious freedom.
4. To take up the cause of the oppressed where the basic essentials of life as understood by Muslims are threatened with annihilation. "Allah will help him who will help His cause."

The Prime Minister's declaration in the House of Commons the other day when he termed our present struggle as a crusade, a crusade in which are involved many of the priceless values of life which man has achieved through countless ages, expresses views identical with those of the Muslims when they talk of "Jihad."

The Nazis in their intolerance of everything, including religion, have become "pagan" and more dangerous than any pagans the world has ever known. A pagan would blush with shame if ever identified with what the world has known and seen of the Nazis so far. Any student of comparative religion will be aware of the fact that the Muslims accept Christ as a prophet of Allah, as they also do the Hebrew prophets. In fact they are all "people of the Book." Now the Nazis have no room for the people of the Book or for any other people save those who subscribe to their fiendish ways and their philosophy of terror and destruction. A Muslim is fully aware of his debt of gratitude to the prophets who had preceded his own. Nazism threatens the destruction of all foundations, including his own. Therefore, it is perfectly obvious to a Muslim where his position is in this conflict. The Holy Prophet states:—"He is noblest who serves mankind."

One of the main reasons which went to sanctify war to a Muslim was "self defence." A Muslim now knows that he has to fight Nazism in self-defence. War for its own sake or for domination over others has never been a Jihad to a Muslim. What have Hitler and Mussolini done but trample under foot peoples and nations that have only desired peace and freedom. It is only a Nazi who could be made to believe that a small people like Czecho-Slovakia could threaten Germany with annihilation. The reasons given by Mussolini for his adventure into Abyssinia and Albania are equally false and crude.

In view of what Hitler and Mussolini have already done to helpless and inoffensive peoples a Muslim is fully aware of the fact that he must take up arms against the aggressor according to the Prophet's injunctions, even though he knows in the background of his thinking that, if he fails to do this, his turn will be next.

"An aggressor is Allah's enemy."

Therefore, in the final analysis a Muslim has no other choice but to take an active part in a course in which his own existence is now threatened. This is what we call in Islam Fi Sabil Allah, which means fighting on the side of Allah.

A RECORD OF WAR SAVINGS

WHAT THE REGIONS ARE DOING

The September number of "War Savings," the Journal of the National War Savings Movement, contains among interesting features reproductions of some of the attractive posters shown by school-children at the recent exhibition in London, of which a notice appeared in *The Times*. This exhibition has been taken to Leeds for the War Weapons Week—the beginning of a provincial tour.

In an article on what the Regions are doing, reference is made to the campaign in the coastal districts. Bournemouth leads the whole country with the highest rate of saving, and Newcastle-on-Tyne stands third in the list. The figures for Dover show that air-raids are treated as a tonic to War Savings. There, as all round the coast, the Savings Groups maintain full service to their members, says the writer, who adds:—"I saw two South Coast groups formed while raids were in progress."

"War Savings" also contains an interview on the Press with Mr. Fred Champion, Editorial Director of the National Savings Committee.

NEW SERVICE IN BOMBED AREAS

Lord Trent, Regional Commissioner for the North Midlands, is to appoint a special officer to take immediate charge of people whose houses have been destroyed or seriously damaged in air raids. This Administrative Incident Officer, as he will be known, will establish a temporary post indicated by a blue and white flag at the scene of the damage, and he will wear a blue and white armlet. Instead of each householder being interviewed by a number of officials the new officer only will obtain a list of their total requirements.

THE KING AND QUEEN IN POLICE SHELTER

WARNING DURING TOUR OF BOMBED AREA

The King and Queen, who were accompanied by Sir John Anderson, Home Secretary and Minister of Home Security, were in the street yesterday when the alarm signal was given and took shelter beneath a police station. They were on a tour of inspection of the damage which had been done during recent air raids in the outer suburbs of South-East London.

When the alarm was sounded a police car piloted the car in which were the Kin gand Queen to a police station which had narrowly escaped the raiders' bombs, for the adjoining police court had been demolished on Saturday night. Their Majesties were taken to a room beneath the station fitted up as a shelter, where there were already gathered court officials, policemen in uniform, the canteen staff, and some of the A.R.P. workers who had been working on the demolition of the police court. When the King and Queen entered the dimly-lit shelter the people assembled there could hardly believe their eyes, and after the initial surprise gave them a hearty cheer. The King and Queen were given chairs, and the King lighted a cigarette.

TEA FROM THE CANTEEN

One of the canteen workers began preparations to provide the unexpected visitors with tea and biscuits, but before she could do so the siren was heard again. The King said that though the "all clear" had sounded he intended to wait for his tea. It was served to the King and Queen in thick china cups bearing the mark of the police canteen. The Queen declared that the tea was delicious and commented on the speed with which it had been made. While she was in the shelter the Queen spoke to a youngster in A.R.P. overalls who had been helping to clear away the remains of the court house. He told her that he was a builder, and the Queen replied that in his latest occupation, clearing away the remains of the court house, he had been working the wrong way round.

During their tour of this district the King and Queen saw a number of places where bombs had been dropped and expressed their sympathy with some of the people who had lost relatives or homes during the indiscriminate bombing of the last few days. At one place, where a bomb had fallen in the middle of a block of workers' flats, they were cheered by a small crowd which afterwards sang, "There'll always be an England."

BOOKS FOR PRISONERS OF WAR

EXTENSION OF RED CROSS SCHEME

The Red Cross and St. John War Organization, which has already in operation an educational book scheme for British prisoners of war and interned civilians as part of its Prisoners of War Department, under Lord Clarendon, has decided to assume responsibility for supplying books, other than educational books, and also games. The War Organization has invited Lord Gorell to organize and take charge of this extension of its work. The organization has no wish to minimise the excellence and importance of the activities of the various voluntary agencies and committees, which have been carrying out individual parts of this work during the past year, and full cooperation will be maintained with these; but to prevent overlapping it is regarded as essential that a single central section of the Prisoners of War Department of the War Organization should now be brought into being to deal with the work as a whole. Offers of help, especially from educationists, authors, and publishers will be gratefully considered: these should be sent to Lord Gorell, Education, Books and Games Section, Prisoners of War Department, Red Cross and St. John War Organization, St. James's Palace, London, S.W.1.

BRITISH PAINTING SINCE WHISTLER

The opening of the second version of the exhibition, "British Painting Since Whistler," together with the Retrospective Exhibition of the Drawings of Augustus John, has been postponed. The new opening date will be announced later. The private view had been announced for September 17, and the public opening for September 18.

THE TIMES CROSSWORD PUZZLE No. 3,294

ACROSS

1 Airs for the allotment (two words) (10, 5).
7 No idle vet, he learned to speak to horses (two words) (6, 8).
10 Jeering whistles (7).
11 A call from the itinerant vendor? (two words) (5, 2).
12 As between Jameson and ourselves there is a difference of opinion as to the meaning of the word (4).
13 Athletic description of a bale-out (two words) (4, 4).
17 Instrument for a private reception (8).
18 Hollow warning (4).
20 A Truck Act expert one might think (7).
23 Asleep (7).
24 Cook's ingratiating way with a rosette (two words) (8, 6).
25 A self-definition of Henley's (four words) (7, 2, 2, 4).

DOWN

2 One who makes fast the ship alone? (9).
3 It is used with a mortar-board, but not at school (6).
4 Creature wrapped in a towel (5).
5 A bird might find it difficult to pay this way (two words) (6, 2).
6 Willy is divorced apparently, perforce (5).
8 Chits I'd written in verse (7).
9 A discovery in Sandwich? (two words) (4, 4).
10 Though the oyster has it, it isn't necessarily bad (two words) (4, 4).
14 The expression of a canicide, perhaps (7).
15 "Celebrated, cultivated, underrated nobleman" (two words) (5, 4).
16 Capital place for a pierrot (8).
19 Not where a brother would go for fish and chips (6).
21 Concealed by the Zulu surprised in his sleep (5).
22 But the monarch has a crown overhead not an umbrella (5).

SOLUTION OF PUZZLE No. 3,293

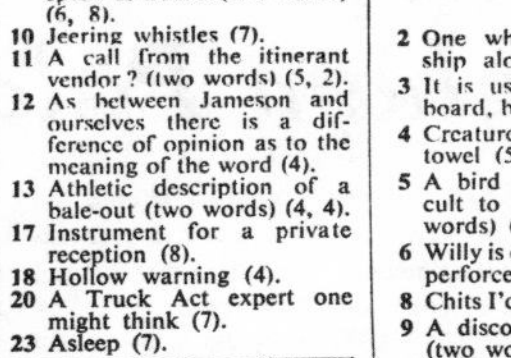

NOTE.—Figures in parentheses denote the number of letters in the words required.

THE ESTATE MARKET

LORD DARESBURY'S GROUND-RENTS

The late Lord Daresbury's freehold ground rents of £822 a year on property in Warrington, were sold, at a local auction, by Messrs. Herbert Johnson and Son (Warrington).

The average price realized was just under 20 years' purchase, the 42 lots changing hands for a total of £16,114. The sale was necessary to provide money wherewith to pay Death Duties. Bidders concentrated on the business in hand despite the sounding of sirens during the auction.

Offers by Messrs. Hampton and Sons (Arlington Street) include a choice freehold of five acres, near Henley-on-Thames. A picture of the house appeared in *The Times* yesterday (p. 10) and the list gave concise details of many Wimbledon Common residences to be let or sold, as well as Surrey and Chiltern Hills freeholds.

A total of £34,350 was obtained by Messrs. Ford, Howes and Williams (Bristol) at an auction, in Bristol, of the late Mrs. R. G. Burden's estate. Stonehill Farm, 98 acres at Hanham, near Bristol, realized £6,500; 174 acres of open land at Abbots Leigh, near Clifton, £7,000; and Wallscourt Farm, 397 acres at Stoke Gifford, five miles from Bristol, £14,200.

The date of the auction of Sharpham, a South Devon property of 1,276 acres, has been fixed for September 24 at Totnes. Messrs. John D. Wood and Co. (Berkeley Square) cooperating with Messrs. Rendells (Chagford) will deal with the Georgian mansion and park, and the varied and valuable components of this Dart valley freehold, in many lots. There are six farms of from 40 to 340 acres, small holdings, 37 cottages, licensed premises, and 80 acres of timber of the type now so much needed.

AUCTIONS TO-DAY

FURNITURE, WORKS OF ART, MISCELLANEA

Auctioneers	Place of Sale
Jackson Stops and Staff	Elmleigh, Dallington, Northampton
Messrs. Giddys	Hillside, Sunningdale
Robinson and Foster	King Street, S.W.
W. & F. C. Bonham & Sons	New Burlington Street, W.

From THE TIMES of 1840

SATURDAY, SEPTEMBER 12, 1840. Price 5d.

The account from which this narrative is taken [of the death of Richard II from a blow with a poleaxe on the back of the head] is that of the *Fabian Chronicle*, and Fabian did not write until the reign of Henry VI. Froissart, who was, however, too partial to King Henry [IV], does not relate the death of King Richard in this manner, and Walsingham, a partisan of the house of Lancaster, says King Richard starved himself. It is a remarkable fact that the skull of this monarch was found unbroken when his tomb in Westminster Abbey was opened and the body examined. This would seem to refute the common opinion of the manner of his death.

⁂ From a column review of the third volume of "Lives of the Queens of England," by Agnes Strickland.

* * *

If they referred to the pages of English history they would find that this country generally enjoyed the greatest prosperity when under the dominion of a lady. Such was the case in the reign of Queen Elizabeth, and such he trusted and confidently believed would be the case in the reign of Victoria.

⁂ With these prophetic words Mr. Robert Allen, barrister of the Oxford circuit, proposed the loyal toast at a dinner of the Birmingham Licensed Victuallers' Protection Society, which is reported at some length.

Cons. 87½ to 87.

The Lord Chancellor has appointed Mr. George Trevor Kelway to be the Registrar of Pembroke Dock, Narberth, and Haverfordwest County Courts and District Registrar in the High Court of Justice in Haverfordwest as from September 9.

BROADCASTING

HOME SERVICE

1,013kc. (296.2m.); 767kc. (391.1m.); and 668kc. (449.1m.)

6.45 a.m., News in Norwegian. 7. Time; News. 7.15. Records. 7.30. Exercises for women. 7.45. Records. 7.55. A thought for to-day. 8. Time; News. 8.15. The Kitchen Front, by Ambrose Heath. 8.20. Lloyd Thomas (organ). 8.40. Peggy Mayle (piano). 9.10. Records. 9.35. Watson Forbes (viola) and Myers Foggin (piano). 10.5. School News Commentary and Interlude. 10.15. Time; Daily Service. 10.30. Jack Leon and his Orchestra. 11. For the Schools: The Music Shop. 11.20. Intermediate French. 11.40. Senior Geography. 12. The Northcountrywoman (21). 12.20. Sheffield Transport Department Band.

1. Time; News. 1.15. B.B.C. Orchestra (Section C); conductor, Sir Adrian Boult. 1.55. Calling All Women. 2. For the Schools: Nature Study. 2.15. Music. 2.20. Physical training. 2.35. Music. 2.40. British History. 3. Sandy Macpherson (organ). 3.30. Jack the Giant-Killer: A moral folk-tale, written and produced by Francis Dillon. 4. Rhythm on Reeds. 4.15. Talking It Over. 4.30. Modern British songs and piano music—George Parker (baritone) and Berkeley Mason (piano). 5. News in Welsh. 5.20. Children's Hour.

6. Time; News; and Announcements. 6.30. News in Norwegian. 6.45. Learning to Fly; broadcast from an R.A.F. Training Centre. 7.5. B.B.C. Orchestra (Section B). 7.40. Has the Christian Way Failed? by Professor T. E. Jessop. 8. Hippodrome Memories (Part 2)—from 1927 to 1940. 9. Time; News. 9.20. War Commentary, by General Sir Hugh Elles. 9.35. Everybody's Scrapbook, presented by Leslie Baily and Francis Worsley. 10.15. Service: address by Rev. Anthony Otter. 10.35. Anthology—Sound the Pibroch. 10.45. Old Scottish Airs and Dances. 11.15. Van Straten and his Music. 11.53. And So To Bed; presented by M. H. Allen. 12. Time; News. 12.20-12.30 a.m., News in Norwegian.

PROGRAMME FOR THE FORCES

6.15 a.m. to 10 p.m. (804kc.) (373.1m.); 10 p.m. to 12.20 a.m. (877kc.) (342.1m.)

6.15 a.m., News in French. 6.30-8. Records: News at 7. 10.30. Home Service. 11. Programme summary, followed by Harold Hunt (organ). 11.30. Records. 12. Welsh Airs. 12.15. News in French. 12.30. The World Goes By (recording).

1. News in Dutch. 1.15. B.B.C. Theatre Chorus. 1.30. Claydon Quintet. 2. Time; Time Dances On, presented by Vernon Harris; with Jan van der Gucht, Marjorie Westbury, George Melachrino, Anne Lenner; Revue Chorus and B.B.C. Variety Orchestra. 2.40. Records. 3. Home Service. 3.30. Avalon Quartet. 3.45. Band of the Royal Tank Regiment. 4.15. Charles Ernesco and his Quintet, with Mervyn Saunders. 4.45. Canadian Variety (recorded). 5.15. Programme for Anti-Aircraft and Balloon Barrage personnel.

6. News in Dutch and French. 6.30. Geraldo and his Orchestra. 7. Twentieth-Century Drawing Room, produced by David Miller; with Edna Hatzfeld and Mark Strong, Gwen Catley and Carl Carlisle; devized and written by Mark Strong and Carl Carlisle. 7.15. Programme in Dutch. 7.30. Parish Mag.; from a village in Westmorland. 7.50. Join and Sing, with some troops. 8.15. News in French. 8.30. French programme. 9. News in German. 9.15. The Adventures of Alonzo Mactavish, by Peter Cheyney (No. 9). 9.30. Big Bill Campbell and his Canadian Cowboys in Rocky Mountain Rhythm. 10. Time; Tudor Sextet. 10.30. White and Woodman (songs at the piano), and Al Durrant's Swing Quintet. 10.45 p.m.-12.20 a.m., Home Service.

SATURDA

UNKN

[Na]zi Bombs Rip Center of London

Complete BASEBALL

CHARACTER QUALITY · AMERICA FIRST! · ENTERPRISE ACCURACY

Los Angeles Examiner

AN AMERICAN PAPER FOR THE AMERICAN PEOPLE · THE GREAT NEWSPAPER OF THE GREAT SOUTHWEST

Reg. U.S. Pat. Off.

(Telephone RIchmond 1212)

VOL. XXXVII—NO. 278 P LOS ANGELES, SATURDAY, SEPTEMBER 14, 1940 Two Sections—Part I—FIVE CENTS

WAR EXTRA

BRITAIN INVASION ATTEMPTS REVEALED

BRITISH HOUSE OF LORDS HIT IN NEW RAIDS

Downing St., Palace, Whitehall Targets in New Onslaught; Admiralty Building Struck

LONDON, Sept. 13.—(AP)—German raiders bombed the very seats of Britain's monarchy and Britain's government today and returned tonight in their seventh consecutive heavy nightly assault to dump more bombs and do mighty battle in the skies with London's reinforced anti-aircraft batteries.

They opened the night attack at 9 p. m. (12 noon, P. S. T.), and hours later they still shuttled high over the city, while below the thundering artillery raised a red dome of bursting shells all over the metropolitan area.

Nowhere was the action so violent as in the center of the city. Both explosive and fire bombs came hurtling down.

Shell splinters from the defenders' fire drummed loudly upon the rooftops.

The day's attack was centered upon the greatest symbols of the empire.

Buckingham Palace was hit by explosive bombs; Downing street, the home of Prime Minister Winston Churchill, and the length of Whitehall, the avenue of the kingdom's government, by fire bombs.

KING, QUEEN ESCAPE

King George VI and Queen Elizabeth, themselves, were in the palace air raid shelter but escaped injury when five bombs fell.

Authorities disclosed tonight that an incendiary bomb—quickly smothered—had hit the House of Lords, noble chamber of Parliment, in the south wing of the Houses of Parliament. They did not say exactly when this happened. But today, fire bombs were dropped on Downing street, where Prime Minister Winston Churchill lives, and elswhere in the Whitehall area, where almost all of the government's business is transacted.

They nicked a wing of the admiralty from which the operations of the world's greatest navy are directed. Other bombs were loosed upon a world famous square, and very near the Victoria Memorial Post in front of Buckingham Palace, and in more

(Continued on Page A, Column 3)

Here's Regent Street After an Air Raid

FAMOUS REGENT street, fashionable shopping area not far from Piccadilly Circus, looked like this yesterday after numerous German bombs, crashing into the heart of London, blasted the windows out of stores, hammered masonry into powder. Photo cabled yesterday from London.

British King, Queen Escape Injuries as Nazis Attack Buckingham Palace

BERLIN, Sept. 14 (Saturday).—(AP)—An authorized spokesman said today that German bombs dropped "in the vicinity of Buckingham Palace" yesterday were aimed at oil storage tanks.

Another German squadron, the spokesman said, bombed Erith on the railway between London and Gravesend on the Thames Estuary, attempting to hit pulp and paper mills. One German plane was reported missing.

LONDON, Sept. 13.—(AP)—The King and Queen of England were bombed in Buckingham Palace today by a twin-engined German raider participating in the longest daylight attack on London of this total war.

King George VI and his cheerful Scottish Queen were not hurt, nor were they cowed.

After the raid, they climbed out of palace air raid shelters, surveying the damage that five bombs had wrought to royal chapel, inner quadrangle and roadway, and then the King told a thankful war cabinet and people:

"Like so many other people, we now have had a personal experience of German barbarity, which only strengthens the resolution of all of us to fight through to final victory." Then, with the Queen, he departed for another tour of London's bombed slums.

The little princesses, Elizabeth and Margaret Rose, were not in the palace—(it is understood they have been kept away from London throughout the war)—but their mother and father stayed on beneath the royal

(Continued on Page A, Column 6)

Many Drowned in Channel as Efforts Fail

LONDON, Sept. 13.—(AP)—The British censor passed tonight for publication in Britain the story of Dr. Charles F. Bove to the effect that the Germans had tried and failed to invade England several times, but there was no immediate comment from officials.

JERSEY CITY, N. J., Sept. 13.—(AP)—An American surgeon returning home after spending nearly a quarter century in France said today that the German army already had made several unsuccessful attempts to invade England from the shores of conquered France.

Basing his statement on personal observation and information from "many French sourc es," Dr. Charles F. Bove, 52, head surgeon of the American Hospital in Paris, declared on his arrival from Lisbon on the American export liner Excambion that "the Germans have tried the invasion several times at different points and each time they failed."

HUNDREDS OF BODIES

He reported having seen "hundreds of German bodies in the waters near Cherbourg, France."

The Germans, he said, were constantly practicing for invasion all along the French coast—the practice including maneuvers in which Nazi soldiers in full uniform jumped from vessels and swam long distances with all their equipment.

Other passengers would not comment on the reported invasion attempt, but Dr. Bove's statement bore out similar reports received recently in New York in letters from two French officials.

LIKENED TO SUICIDE

These letters told of a German attempt to land troops on the wes coast of England that proved "othing short of suicide."

The Excambion, which carried 173 passengers, including 83 Americans, came *by* way of Bermuda, where British censors confiscated 420 bags of mail and placed aboard for return to New York 560 sacks previously taken from other ships.

It also brought $3,000,000 in gold from the Bank of Lisbon for the U. S. Federal Reserve Bank.

SEEK U. S. ENTRY

Dr. Bove said that when he left Paris there were 350 Americans in and around the city, "most of them hoping the United States would enter the war."

Declaring the Germans were taking "everything they could" out of France he said they "relieved" him of $100,000 in personal property, his automobile and his horse.

He reported "at least 300,000 German women and children in occupied France," whom he said were being fed by the French. General feeling in France was that Germany would occupy the entire French nation, he added.

R. A. F. Bombers Strike At Nazi 'Lifelines'

By Michael Wilson

Staff Correspondent International News Service

LONDON, Sept. 13.—A concentrated British aerial drive to paralyze the railroad network feeding troops and supplies to Germany's blitzkrieg "springboards" along the European coast was revealed tonight as a major part of the Royal Air Force counter-offensive.

While British bombers dealt fresh destruction to dozens of widely scattered Nazi bases, an air ministry communique disclosed that numerous rail junctions, depots and distributing centers behind the continental coast of the English Channel were particular targets of tons of demolition and fire bombs.

KEY POINTS RAIDED

These key points in the pattern of lines along which Germany is moving men and material for the expected invasion of Britain included Osnabruck, Schwerpe, Hamm, Ehrang and Brussels. Against all of them the R. A. F. leveled furious assaults.

At the same time, British bombing squadrons blasted anew today at the German invasion takeoff platforms themselves. Violent raids lashed these ports, emplacements and ship concentrations along the northern coast of France.

Planes of the British coastal command in a daylight attack Thursday were revealed to have flown down the French coast as far as Le Havre, where they bombed German shipping. They

(Continued on Page A, Column 6)

TRIBE FANS K. O. DETROIT STAR

Football Cartoon in Color
SWINESKIN GULCH
In Today's Sports Section

FINAL NIGHT EDITION — WEATHER: FAIR Details on Page 2

THE CALL BULLETIN — SAN FRANCISCO — AN INDEPENDENT NEWSPAPER

EXTRA

85TH YEAR CALL AND POST. VOL. 148, NO. 55 THE CALL-BULLETIN. VOL. 168, NO. 55 — SAN FRANCISCO, FRIDAY, SEPTEMBER 27, 1940 — 5c DAILY 90c a Month

JAP-AXIS PACT DIRECT U. S. THREAT!

★ ★ ★ ★ ★ ★ ★ ★ ★ ★

122 Nazi Planes Downed

YOUTH HITS TEBBETTS; FELLER PITCHES

Greenberg Pelted by Tomatoes; Rookie on Mound for Tigers

MUNICIPAL STADIUM, CLEVELAND, Sept. 27 (AP). Riotous scenes marred the opening innings of the vital game between Detroit and Cleveland here today, climaxing in the second game when Catcher Birdie Tebbetts of the Tigers, standing in the bullpen, was struck by an object thrown by a fan from the upper stand.

The thrower, a youngster, was taken away by police, while Tebbetts, after a few minutes, was able to go to the dressing room under his own power.

CROWD WARNED

A big ladies' day crowd in the left stands previously had pelted Hank Greenberg of Detroit with tomatoes, bringing a warning from Umpire Summers that the Detroit club would be removed from the field if the throwing continued.

Manager Oscar Vitt of Cleveland appealed to the crowd to settle down and let the game continue.

NEED ONE GAME

Witt, the disputed leader of the Indians, sent Bobby Feller, 27-game winner, in to pitch. Del Baker, Tiger manager, used Floyd Giebell, a rookie who beat the Athletices last week in his only major league appearance.

The Tigers need one game to put Cleveland out of the pennant race, two to keep away from a tie with the Yankees if the latter sweep their remaining four games.

Neither team scored in the first three innings.

FOURTH INNING BREAK

First break of the game came to the rampaging Tigers in the fourth inning. Feller walked Gehringer and fanned Greenberg. Then York rammed out his 33d home run of the year.

Giebell held the Indians scoreless and to three hits in four innings.

The scoreboard showed the Yankees trailing the Athletics, 6 to 0, in the eighth inning, good news for the Tigers. One defeat would put the Yankees out of the flag race.

Details in Sports)

Vincent Astor Wed To Eastern Beauty

Mary Cushing, who became the bride of Vincent Astor, the nation's "No. 1 matrimonial catch." She is the sister of Mrs. "Betsey" Cushing Roosevelt, former wife of the President's son, James. —International News Sound Photo.

Ex-Mrs. Roosevelt's Sister Millionaire's Bride

By MAURY PAUL

NEW YORK, Sept. 27.—Vincent Astor, the U. S. A.'s No. 1 "matrimonial catch" and largest single owner of New York real estate, conferred his name on tall, slim and beautiful Mary Cushing at noon today.

"CRUISE OF ROMANCE"

While there have been rumors Mr. Astor would make Miss Cushing his bride, news of today's wedding at East Hampton, L. I., will come as a complete surprise to society—plans for the ceremony having been kept secret until almost the moment Mr. Astor arrived at Heatherdune, the ocean front villa where the bride's mother, Mrs. Harvey Cushing of New Haven, Conn., has passed the summer.

All week, the 265 foot Astor yacht Nourmahal lay anchored in the Hudson River, off Seventy-ninth street. Late yesterday afternoon Mr. Astor, his mother, Lady Ribblesdale (the former Mrs. John Jacob Astor) and William Rhinelander Stewart Jr., whose friendship with the head

Continued on Page 3, Column 1

F D R to Inspect Defense Units in Maryland Area

WASHINGTON, Sept. 27 (AP). President Roosevelt announced today he would make an inspection Monday of defense units in Maryland, including the army's proving ground at Aberdeen, the chemical warfare plant near Aberdeen, the Martin bombing plane factory in the northeast section of Baltimore and Camp Meade, Md.

The chief executive will leave tomorrow evening, after dedicating the terminal building of the new Washington airport.

KIDNAPER INDICTED IN RUSH

Indicates 'Guilty' Plea; 'What Else Can I Do?' He Asks

Just a week after he kidnaped Marc de Tristan Jr.—almost to the hour—Wilhelm Jakob Muhlenbroich, 40, was indicted today by the San Mateo County grand jury for violation of California's "Little Lindbergh act."

As the grand jury went into session to consider the indcament Muhlenbroich, nervous and showing his first sign of regret for his act, indicated that he would plead guilty to a charge of kidnaping.

"What else can I do?" he shrugged.

NURSE, CAPTOR TESTIFY

Before returning the indictment, the jury heard testimony from Marc's nurse, Mary Foley, who was injured in a struggle with the kidnaper when he snatched the child from her at noon last Friday; Hillsborough police, Federal Bureau of Investigation agents, Cecil Wetsel, who made the heroic capture of Muhlenbroich, and others.

District Attorney Gilbert Ferrell revealed, following the grand jury meeting, that Miss Foley had identified Muhlenbroich as the kidnaper yesterday in the county jail in Redwood City, picking him from among a group of five other prisoners.

Wetsel also visited the jail to see Muhlenbroich before appearing before the grand jury, and a curious scene resulted, the sheriff's office said. Deputies reported that the captor and the captured solemnly shook hands.

LIFE TERM PENALTY

The indictment specifically charged:

"Wilhelm Jakob Muhlenbroich did willfully, unlawfully and feloniously sieze, abduct, kidnap and carry away and conceal and hold and detain one Marc de Tristan Jr., with the intent to hold and detain said

Continued on Page 3, Column 7

Missing U. S. Bomber, 4 Men Found at Yakima

DAYTON, O., Sept. 27 (AP).—A Douglas bomber, reported missing with four men aboard, landed safely last night at Yakima, Wash., it was announced today by Wright Field officials.

RAF Hits Hard at Channel

German Invasion Bases Are Fired; Berlin in Counter Attack

LONDON, Sept. 27 (AP). German warplanes attacked all England by the howling hundreds today in one of the mightiest aerial offensives yet launched in the long battle for Britain, and late in the afternoon 122 of the raiders had been officially declared shot down.

The defense thus was operating with a fury not seen in nearly two weeks.

CROWDS CHEER

Great air battles were fought in the sight of observers in southwest London during one raid when black anti-aircraft bursts pitted the skies from a furious barrage, and cheers broke from crowds when plumes of smoke told of hits on some of the 100 planes.

A communique said 25 British planes were lost in today's fighting, but that ten of the pilots were safe.

(Other sources reported that nearly 500 German planes took part in the London attack today.)

British and German long-range artillery also fought a duel across the 22-mile Dover Strait, the German shells rocking the Dover area with two shells every two minutes, and the British fire increasing in intensity after half an hour.

ATTACK ON KIEL

The air ministry declared **"particularly heavy damage"** was inflicted on the channel ports, including Ostend, Calais, Boulogne and Le Havre, last night.

In addition, Kiel, the German naval base and terminus of the vital Kiel canal, and other **"mili-**

Continued on Page 13, Column 1

U. S. STANDS ON ASIATIC POLICIES

Hull Says Axis Move No Surprise; Doesn't Affect Diplomacy

WASHINGTON, Sept. 27 (AP).—Secretary Hull said today that Japan's alliance with the German-Italian axis merely made clear **"a relationship which has long existed in effect"** and which the United States had taken into account in determining its own policies.

Hull made this comment in a brief formal statement to a press conference. Previously President Roosevelt had told reporters he could not say anything about the pact signed today in Berlin because he had received nothing official on it.

HIS STATEMENT

Hull's statement follows:

"The reported agreement of alliance does not, in the view of the government of the United States, substantially alter a situation which has existed for several years.

"Announcement of the alliance merely makes clear to all a relationship which has long existed in effect and to which this government has repeatedly called attention.

"That such an agreement has been in process of conclusion has been well known for some time, and that fact has been fully taken into account by the government of the United States in the determining of this country's policies."

NO ELABORATION

Hull refused to elaborate in any way on this statement, asserting that he did not desire to be cross-examined.

The secretary said that he had

Continued on Page 4, Column 1

'First' Vote at 96!

Politics Finally Stir Pioneer

SANTA ROSA, Sept. 27 (INS). Mrs. Lavonia J. Finley, 96 year old Sonoma County pioneer who came to California from Missouri in her girlhood, said today she will cast her first vote for a President in the November election.

"When I was young," said Mrs. Finley, "women didn't take much interest in politics. They left that to the men, as I have done. Now I want to vote for a President before I die."

Registered as a Democrat, Mrs. Finley will not go to the polls, she said, because of frail health, but will cast an absentee voter's ballot.

3-Way Treaty Aims to Split Europe, Asia

Latest developments in the crisis in the Orient included:

1. Berlin announces signing of military and economic pact by axis partners with Japan, sounding warning to United States to keep out of the war.

2. Official quarters in Washington indicated there would be no softening of U. S. attitude against disturbance of status quo in Pacific despite pact.

3. Japan's Foreign Minister Matsuoka infers new pact may call for momentous decisions.

4. Virginio Gayda, Italian spokesman, calls pact warning to U. S. to keep hands off European war.

(Radio Photo Berlin Treaty Group, Page 13.)

By LOUIS P. LOCHNER
Associated Press Staff Correspondent

BERLIN, Sept. 27.—Germany, Italy and Japan welded a new totalitarian bloc today with a one-for-all and all-for-one pledge of aid against any new enemy entering either the European or China war—an implicit warning to the United States.

With Adolf Hitler as an onlooker, the Rome-Berlin foreign ministers and the Japanese ambassador to Berlin signed a solemn ten year military and economic treaty declaring the readiness of the three governments to join their 250,000,000 people as world scale battle comrades.

Advance preparations for such an eventuality were written into the treaty by an immediate undertaking for joint technical consultations by representatives of the three powers.

Influence Spheres Divided

The three powers formally divided spheres of world influence, Japan being recognized as the leader in founding a "new order in greater east Asia" and Germany and Italy for "establishment of a new order in Europe."

An authorized spokesman said the "war mongers" against whom Foreign Minister Joachim von Ribbentrop declared the pact is aimed included "a certain group" in the United States.

But spokesmen refused to make clear the scope of the treaty with respect to Asia—whether it included the Philippines, French Indo-China, Australia and eastern Siberia.

The three powers affirmed that the terms in no way affect the political status of any one of them as regards Soviet Russia. Germany, with her Russian non-aggression pact, is the closest of the three to the U. S. S. R.

The pact brings together the original membership of the anti-comintern accord, but goes infinitely further than the old agreement to exchange information for curbing activities of international communists.

United Front to Attackers

As for their world front, the Tokyo-Berlin-Rome signatories pledged **"to assist one another with all political, economic and military means when one of the three contracting powers is attacked by a power not at present in-**

Continued on Page A, Col. One

RUSSIA SOURCES REGARD JAP-AXIS PACT 'DANGEROUS'

LONDON, Sept. 27 (AP).—Informed Russian sources declared tonight that the Soviet Union's position in the light of the new German-Italian-Japanese military pact is "dangerous and very grave."

FIRST FLEET GROUP BACK FROM HAWAII TONIGHT

SAN DIEGO, Sept. 27 (AP).—The navy indicated today that the first contingent of the U. S. fleet, which departed last April 1 for annual maneuvers in the midpacific, would return from Hawaii during the night to bases in San Diego and San Pedro.

FIRE BREAKS OUT AT GEARY ST. CAFE

A Two alarm fire broke out this afternoon in Will King's Koffee Kup restaurant at 5424 Geary boulevard.

AT PHILADELPHIA (Am.)—New York 2, Phils 6; final.

AT CHICAGO (Am.)—St. Louis 3, Chicago 3; 9th in.

AT CLEVELAND (m.)—Detroit 2, Cleveland 0; 5th in.

6TH RACE, NARRAGANSETT—Erin's Sun, won, 156.20, 31.60, 13.50; Somali, 2d, 4.50, 3.20; Miss L. P., 3d, 3.50. T., 1:55.

Call-Bulletin Today

CHARACTER · QUALITY · New York · ENTERPRISE · ACCURACY
Journal AND American
AN AMERICAN PAPER FOR THE AMERICAN PEOPLE

CITY EDITION

EXTRA

No. 19,282—DAILY | In Two Sections —Section One | THURSDAY, OCTOBER 3, 1940 | Copyright, 1940, by King Features Syndicate, Inc. | DAILY 3 Cents | SATURDAY 5 Cents | SUNDAY 10 Cents

CHAMBERLAIN QUITS!

Churchill Shakes Up Cabinet for 'Total War'

Rush Hour in London Subway, as Bombers Roar Outside

1—These photos, better than others more dramatic, bring home picture of modern war to New York's army of straphangers. In London, as night comes on, the city's residents don't go to bed, but flock to subway stations to elude flaming cargoes of death hurled out of skies by Nazi raiders. Here is typical London "subway rush," with persons of all classes lounging about before dropping off to sleep. International News Photograph Service.

2—Another London subway scene, taken while bombs burst in the air outside. Picture passed by British censor, and received here today by Air Clipper, shows family group on London subway platform, calmly going about their card game during raid. Later they'll stretch out and drop off to sleep, emerging in the morning after the "all clear." International News Photograph Service. Other war pictures on Page 1, 2d Section.

IN THE NEWS

FRIENDS and fellow citizens, our good President in Washington, at the rate he is going, is likely to get us into war not only with Italy and Germany and Japan, but possibly with Spain in the next few months.

The democracies of this world are not being very far-sighted.

They are picking fights with warlike nations which are prepared for any kind of conflict while they themselves (the democracies) are largely unprepared.

It might even have been hasty for England to declare war on Germany until she herself was sufficiently prepared for war.

It might be still more ill considered and precipitate for the United States, while lamentably unprepared, to provoke war with Italy and Germany and Japan and Spain.

If it is our desire to aid England it is doubtful if we are aiding her by involving ourselves in war.

In fact, we may be to a large degree depriving her of the aid we are now giving.

IT IS OBVIOUS that if we shall get into war with Japan we will have to strengthen our Navy instead of weakening it, and we will have to employ our Navy on the West Coast to the neglect of the East Coast.

What applies to our naval defense applies also to our air defense, and also largely to our land defenses.

We cannot ship planes to England if we are going to need them to defend New York and Boston, San Francisco and Los Angeles.

We cannot supply arms and ordnance to England if we are compelled to use all we can build or buy to protect such vital and critical locations of our own as the Panama Canal, and our transcontinental roads and railways.

We would also have to consider the protection of our essential ports and harbors, of our factories and air fields with modern planes and modern guns.

We will need all the tanks and mechanized divisions that we can organize together with the guns to make them effective.

We will need an army of much more than a million.

We will need a NATION IN ARMS, and will at last be forced to adopt the Swiss system or some similar UNIVERSAL military training.

THEN if we actually get ourselves into such a great war we may not be able to depend entirely on defensive measures.

We may be compelled by the rules of major strategy to take the offensive at times.

That would then necessarily mean sending our boys to fight on the foreign soils of Europe and Asia and Africa and South America.

The Associated Press reports Captain Rickenbacker as saying, in an address to the Evansville Civic Clubs:

"If Britain lasts through the Winter we will be in the war by April,—although I am against it.

"But forces too strong to halt are in motion. We are in it now."

Captain Rickenbacker may be right.

We may be in the war now,—but assuredly NOT in it as much as we will be if we are not thoughtful and careful,—not as much as we will be if we invite trouble in Europe, trouble in Asia, trouble with Italy, Germany, Japan and Spain,—and naturally some resultant trouble in America.

SPAIN may not be important from a naval and military point of view but she is certainly important as an influence in Latin America.

To invite her hostility would be to nullify everything Mr. Hull has been trying to accomplish in friendly union of the South American republics with the United States.

The Republic of Panama is an instance of what might result generally in case Spain joins the axis powers and shall come to consider the United States as an enemy.

The Republic of Panama is not

Continued on Page 2. Column 7.

Detroit 8 to 5 Favorite in 2d Game

THE LINEUPS:

DETROIT (A. L.)	CINCINNATI (N. L.)
Bartell, ss	Werber, 3b
McCosky, cf	M.McCormick, cf
Gehringer, 2b	Goodman, rf
Greenberg, lf	F. McCormick, 1b
York, 1b	Ripple, lf
Campbell, rf	Wilson, c
Higgins, 3b	Joost, 2b
Sullivan, c	Myers, ss
Rowe, p	Walters, p

Umpires—Ormsby (A. L.), plate; Ballanfant (N. L.), first base; Basil (A. L.), second base; Klem (N. L.), third base.

Weather Forecast—Fair, little change in temperature.

Time of game—1:30 p. m., New York Time.

By Sid Mercer

CINCINNATI, Oct. 3.—Detroit, with Lynwood "Schoolboy" Rowe on the mound is an 8to 5 bet to defeat Cincinnati's Bucky Walters i nthe second game of the World Series this afternoon, and a 2 to 1 favorite to win the classic.

Cincinnati fans are pessimistic. Their big ace, Paul Derringer, failed miserably in the series

Continued on Page 19, Column 4.

Willkie Flays Defense Delay

By WALTER KIERNAN,
International News Service Staff Correspondent.

WILLKIE TRAIN EN ROUTE TO PITTSBURGH, Oct. 3.—With the finest show he has yet experienced behind him, Wendell Willkie headed toward Pittsburgh today to make nine street corner speeches and a major speech in Forbes Field.

After touring the State of Michigan, warm toward his cause in some parts and hostile in others, Willkie arrived in Cleveland last night to encounter the most enthusiastic audiences he has found since the beginning of his campaign.

The Lake City, which in 1932 and 1936 voted for President Roosevelt and voted Republican in 1938, met Willkie at Union Terminal with as many persons as could crowd into the building.

It lined the streets with an estimated 150,000 and poured 21,000 more—a capacity crowd—into the public auditorium to hear Willkie warn of the dangers to the United States in the Italian-German-Japanese mutual assistance pact and declare the New Deal is "playing politics with preparedness."

Congress-at-large George Bender, who formerly was in show business, stage-managed the auditorium show.

With the assistance of Rep. Joe Martin, chairman of the National Republican Committee, Governor Bricker, Mayor Burton and Rep. Charles Halleck of Indiana, Ben-

Continued on Page 4. Column 4.

Egypt Forces On Alert for Suez Drive

LONDON, Oct. 3.—On the alert throughout the entire Empire, Britain was consolidating her forces in Egypt today against reported preparations for a large-scale Italian-German attack to seize the Suez Canal.

Apparently authentic information that Hitler is rushing strategists and troops to assume control of the Italian drive into Egypt was bolstered by the almost complete absence of Nazi Stuka dive bombers from raids on Britain.

DEFENDERS DOUBLED.

It was assumed these strafers had been shifted south—to Africa. Of significance also were reports that foot and motorized Nazi troops have been moving through Italy to the African theatre of combat to reinforce Marshal Rodolfo Graziani's desert divisions.

There were reliable signs that Britain has just about doubled her defenders and defense implements in Egypt. The Italians are building fortifications in the vicinity of Sidi Barrani, their spearhead point 60 miles into Egypt, and seem also to be active near Fort Giaghbub, 150 miles south of Sollum.

Nazi Convoy, Oil Bases Blasted

LONDON, Oct. 3 (By International News Service).—Renewed attacks on Germany's continental invasion bases and vital oil storage plants and communications within the Reich itself by strong forces of Royal Aair force bombers were officially announced today.

Following up the fierce counter-thrust of other British bombers which early Wednesday finished long night raids on Berlin as well as dozens of military targets along the French coast and within Germany, the fresh swarms of RAF warplanes took off just as Nazi airmen began their night attacks on Britain.

Shortly before the new nightly assault on the Reich's invasion centers, British dive bombers and shore batteries hd blasted a Nazi

Continued on Page 2, Column 1.

Roper Seriously Ill Of Pneumonia Attack

WASHINGTON, Oct. 3.—Daniel C. Roper, former New Deal Secretary of Commerce and Minister to Canada, is seriously ill with pneumonia.

New British PostFormed

By CHARLES A. SMITH,
International News Service Staff Correspondent.

LONDON, Oct. 3.—Bowing at last to demands that he quit the British Government, Neville Chamberlain, who preceded Winston Churchill as Prime Minister ,resigned today as Lord President of the Council.

Simultaneously a major cabinet reshuffle was announced.

Official announcement of Chamberlain's resignation climaxed recurring demands that he leave the cabinet because of his former appeasement policies.

Heretofore, however, Churchill had steadfastly defended

Continued on Page 2, Column 3.

THE WEATHER

Continued cool with occasional rain. Clearing later.

Sun rises, 5:54 a. m.; sun sets, 5:36 p. m. High tide Governors Island, 9:18 a. m. and 9:43 p. m.

HOURLY TEMPERATURES

8 p. m.	58	2 a. m.	57
9 p. m.	58	3 a. m.	57
10 p. m.	58	4 a. m.	56
11 p. m.	58	5 a. m.	56
Midnight	58	6 a. m.	56
1 a. m.	57	7 a. m.	56

(Complete Weather Table on Page 24)

TODAY'S INDEX

55 Years of Service to CENTRAL SOUTH DAKOTA

EVENING HURONITE

LEADING FARM DAILY OF THE NORTHERN GREAT PLAINS

The Weather
Huron and Vicinity: Fair tonight; Friday partly cloudy to cloudy; not much change in temperature.
South Dakota: Fair, increasing cloudiness tonight, Friday partly cloudy, light snow west and extreme north, colder northwest.

VOLUME LVI — HURON, SOUTH DAKOTA, THURSDAY, MARCH 13, 1941 — ★ ★ ★ — SINGLE COPY 5c

German And British Cities Are Rocked In Violent Air Assaults

$3,446,585,144 Asked For Two-Ocean Navy Program

Project Would Give U. S. Greatest Fleet In History

$1,515,000,000 Of Appropriation Would Go For Ship Building; Superiority Of Axis Is Cited

WASHINGTON, Mar. 13—(AP)—A $3,446,585,144 appropriation bill to carry forward the two-ocean navy construction program was presented to the House today along with a warning from the navy's high command that the critical world situation "may continue to grow worse for some time to come."

Recommending the huge outlay for the year starting July 1, the appropriations committee told the House that the fleet expansion program called for "collateral expenses of staggering proportions" and $5,553,976,000 additional will have to be appropriated during the fiscal years 1943-46, to complete the current shipbuilding program.

A total of 729 ships of all types and categories is now under construction or contracted for and, when completed, will give the United States the most powerful navy in the world history.

A fund of $1,515,000,000, the largest single item in the bill, is for shipbuilding.

Other large items include $434,550,000 for the naval aircraft program, aimed at procurement of 7,129 planes which were ordered last year, and the maintenance and operation of aircraft and air stations; $443,000,000 for maintenance and operation of the existing fleet; $475,000,000 for pay, subsistence and training of personnel and $321,342,960 for expansion or establishment of naval shore bases.

For the first time, the committee wrote into the navy bill a provision to prohibit payment of any of the funds to persons advocating overthrow of the government by force or who belong to organizations advocating such tactics.

The navy high command urged that completion of the two-ocean navy be rushed because of the potential superior strength of the combined Axis fleets.

Secretary Knox told the House appropriations committee during testimony made public today that the German, Italian and Japanese fleets comprised 1,835,000 tons on Jan. 1, compared with this country's 1,250,000 tons. Acquisition of the French fleet would swell the Axis strength further.

Asserting that major units of the two-ocean fleet now under construction would not be completed until 1946-47, Knox said that in the meantime the United States was confronted with these two possible developments:

"The defeat of Great Britain in the near future, leaving us to face the united strength of the Axis powers on a two-ocean front."

" x x x the possibility of Japan becoming an active participant as a belligerent in the Far East on the side of the Axis.

"It is obviously to our interest to prevent either of these possibilities from becoming realities as it is probable they would result in the United States becoming involved in a war." The policy of aiding Britain, he added, was a major step toward meeting the problem.

Admiral Harold R. Stark, chief of naval operations, reminded the committee that while "no one can predict with accuracy the turn of events," requests undoubtedly arise in excess of the $3,358,732,186 sought to carry on the huge naval expansion program during the year starting July 1.

The two appeared before the committee personally February 3. Their testimony, and that of others, was turned over to Congress today with the committee's report on the bill.

The bill carries funds to increase the enlisted strength of the navy from 232,000 to 258,000, although the average is expected to be about 245,000 men for the year. The committee said that the number of Marine Corps reserves on active duty will be increased by 5,475 by July 1, raising the corps' total enlisted strength to 50,566.

CALAIS IS BOMBED BY BRITISH FIGHTERS

LONDON, Mar. 13—(AP)—British fighters and bombers attacked a German occupied airdrome at Calais this afternoon, the air ministry announced tonight

Roosevelt Signs Lend-Lease Bill To Aid Britain

President Roosevelt signing the Lend-Lease bill in his White House office after the House had completed final action on historic bill with an hour's debate. Congress started hearings on the Lend-Lease program today following President Roosevelt's request yesterday for $7,000,000,000 to set the program in operation.—(NEA Telephoto.)

Hitler Sees Smashing Nazi Victory; Il Duce Warns His Army Generals

Fuehrer Makes Prediction At Ceremonial Feting Anniversary Of Austrian Union

LINZ, Germany, Mar. 13—(AP)—A prediction by Adolf Hitler that the war will end with a tremendous Nazi victory insuring plans for "a greater Germany" sounded the keynote for ceremonies today commemorating the third anniversary of the union of his native Austria with the Reich.

The Fuehrer made the prediction in an unheralded speech as he arrived here last night to take part in the celebration. (There was no indication whether Hitler planned to continue on to Vienna, Austrian capital).

Recalling the "tremendous success" Germany achieved in the war of 1870, Hitler declared "the end of today's struggle will not differ a hair's breadth."

"The hour of our final victory will come," he said, "whereupon we will develop very thoroughly the plans we have made.

"Then we will work harder and more and more to give the

See HITLER—Page 10

Failure Of Italian Offensive Brings Order To "Do Something"

ATHENS, Mar. 13— (AP) —Dispatches from the Albanian front today said that the large scale offensive presumably ordered by Premier Mussolini himself from field headquarters had failed before powerful Greek resistance.

An earlier report said that Mussolini had given his generals until Saturday to "do something."

The Italians, dispatches from the front, said, have been unable to gain a single inch of ground and in the last six days their losses unofficially have been placed at more than 10,000, including 2,000 dead. These figures do not cover the prisoners listed by the Greeks.

A Greek spokesman said captured Italian officers reported Premier Mussolini has been in Albania almost a week to bolster the morale of his troops and himself had ordered the recent ferocious series of attacks on the central front, attacks which the Greeks reported smashed over a 12-mile sector in four days of bloody fighting.

The captives, the spokesman added, said Mussolini had told "his gen-

See MUSSOLINI—Page 10

Call 141 Men For April Draft

South Dakota Youths To Be Inducted At Omaha And Fort Snelling

RAPID CITY, Mar. 13.—(AP)—The first April selective service call for 141 men was announced today by Col. E. A. Beckwith, state selective service director.

Under the call two South Dakotans will be inducted at Omaha April 8, and 50 at Fort Snelling, Minn., and 80 at Omaha April 9.

Since it is now the policy to induct men at 10 day intervals, Col. Beckwith said he expected two more April calls will be received.

He also announced the induction station at Sioux Falls will be closed April 1, and thereafter all South Dakotans inducted for one year of military training will be sent to either Fort Snelling or Omaha induction stations.

Coal Mine Blast Claims Four Lives

REVLOC, Pa., Mar. 13.—(AP)—Four men were killed early today by an explosion in the Monroe Coal Mining Company's mine.

State Mine Inspector William Lamont tentatively attributed the explosion to an accumulation of gas.

The World Today

(By the Asssociated Press)

RAF bombers pound Berlin, Hamburg, Bremen in war's heaviest raids on Germany; 16 killed, 37 wounded in Nazi capital; British unleash new type planes, may be U. S.-built bombers; Germans report 10,000 bombs rained on Liverpool in "super-coventry" assault.

Greeks say big-scale Italian offensive personally directed by Mussolini has failed, report Fascist attacks smashed in four days of bloody fighting, with 10,000 Italian casualties, 2,000 dead; Rome asserts Greek drive repulsed with heavy losses.

Ask Creation Of Mediation Board

WASHINGTON, Mar. 13—(AP)—President Roosevelt received today from Secretary Perkins and defense directors Knudsen and Hillman a specific recommendation for a mediation board to handle labor problems related to the defense program.

No details on what they had suggested were announced but Miss Perkins told reporters that the idea of a mediation board was taking "definite" shape.

5 Percent Income Tax Is Talked

Congressional Experts Scan Means Of Paying For British Aid Program

WASHINGTON, Mar. 13—(AP)—Congresional fiscal experts, casting about for new revenue sources to help pay for the $7,000,000,000 British aid program, were reported considering today the possibility of imposing a 5 per cent tax on the weekly pay of most of the nation's workers.

If such a 5 per cent "earned income" tax, should be levied, that amount would be deducted for the government each week from the pay envelopes of a large proportion of jobholders. Thus a worker now receiving $40 weekly would get, instead, $38 and a tax receipt for $2. Small wage earners—possibly those receiving $25 weekly or less—would be exempt.

It was emphasized that this proposal was merely in the discussion stage and might never mature. Responsible individuals estimated that such a levy would raise $3,500,000,000 yearly.

Acknowledging that the proposal might arouse a storm of protest from wage earners, advocates said it would have to be accompanied by increases in taxes upon incomes from investments, rentals and other sources so that there could be no discrimination.

It would entail, they pointed out also, a reversal of previous admin-

See INCOME TAX—Page 2

Congress Digs Into Lend-Lease Work; Hearings Secret

Speed Is Keynote As Committee Pushes For Vote By Early Next Week; Longer Work Week May Be Asked

WASHINGTON, Mar. 13—(AP)—With speed the keynote, Congress started work today on the biggest peacetime appropriation bill in the nation's history—President Roosevelt's request for $7,000,000,000 to produce "the tools of defense" for Britain, Greece and China.

The measure started its legislative journey before an 11-man House appropriations subcommittee which has passed on the bulk of this country's multi-billion dollar defense plans since the collapse of France last spring.

One informed legislator said that the size of President Roosevelt's request had a definite purpose—"to demonstrate that Uncle Sam means business." He reported that originally the plans were to ask only about half the present amount in cash and the other half in authorizations. Subsequently, however, it was decided to seek the full $7,000,000,000 in cash, he said, because of the psychological effect that it might have on the Axis powers.

Secretary Hull was the first on the list of high administration officials called to appear before the House appropriations subcommittee for brief, secret testimony. Rep. Woodrum, Democrat, Virginia, the acting chairman, said the state department head would be followed by Secretaries Morgenthau; Stimson; Knox; Gen. George C. Marshall, army chief of staff; Admiral Harold P. Stark, chief of naval operations and William S. Knudsen, defense production chief.

Woodrum said he planned to close the hearings Saturday, if possible, so as to bring the bill to the House floor for debate early next week. He anticipated little disposition to trim the British-aid fund, despite its huge size, once it reaches the floor.

Discussing plans for the hearing, he said:

"We will go into the international picture briefly with Secretary Hull, and will try to find out from the army and navy people what weapons and other items of equipment they may be able to spare."

The details would be carefully guarded, Woodrum said, and little will be made public at least until such disclosures would have no military significance.

There was talk that President Roosevelt might make some dramatic effort to accelerate the nation's industrial machinery and get faster production for the aid program.

It was suggested the chief executive might appeal for such a speedup in a "fireside chat" or that he might call for lengthening of the work week in some industries. Defense chiefs have said all along, however, that "bottleneck" industries already are on a 24-hour basis.

Senator Nye, Republican, North Dakota, who opposed enactment of the British aid law, demanded today that administration leaders

See CONGRESS—Page 2

The War Today

Germany Pictures Uncle Sam As Rat In New And Weak Propaganda Move

MacKenzie Doubts Whether Germans Or Their Axis Partners Actually Believe Accusations Hurled Over Radio

By DEWITT MACKENZIE

Nazidom, speaking through the government-controlled radio, charges that Uncle Sam is a double-dealer in the matter of aid for Britain and "intent only upon the speediest acquisition of a maximum number of British possessions."

That is so far from the fact that I doubt whether the Germans or their partners in the triple alliance, Italy and Japan, really believe Uncle Sam is such a rat as to double-cross a friend and then knife him in the back for gain. It isn't even a very smart piece of propaganda, but more in the class of thumbing one's nose to express resentment.

Still, the allegation is a reminder that self-analysis is always good. Just what is our feeling as we start to pour our resources out for the Anglo-Allies?

I have talked with people of all classes in many parts of the country since the war began, and have no doubt that America is impelled by high and unselfish motives. If the security of our country and ways of life is foremost in our minds, that is natural. But beyond this my definite impression is that the majority of Americans in supporting aid for Britain are honestly anxious to help preserve the security and ways of life of other countries who are victims of aggression.

Uncle Sam hasn't arrived at his present pitch of determination, however, without long and grave thought. It was the same with the Allies, for that matter.

When I was in England in Aug-

See MACKENZIE—Page 6

New-Type Planes Are Used By RAF In Sweeping Raids

Tremendous Fires Are Reported Started In Berlin, Hamburg And Bremen; Britain Has New Air Raid Defense

LONDON, Mar. 13—(AP)—Swarming over the continent from Boulogne to Berlin and from the low countries to Norway, the RAF has launched its greatest offensive of the war. The British declared they had been freed of worry over plane replacements by passage of the United States' aid to Britain bill.

British planes sped across the English Channel this afternoon to follow up "very successful" raids yesterday and last night on Berlin, industrial plants at Bremen, naval shipbuilding yards at Hamburg, airdromes in Norway and the Netherlands, docks at Boulogne and shipping at Ijmuiden, the Netherlands, and at Ostend Belgium.

With new and more powerful bombers thrown into the assault, a well-placed source declared today that as a result of passage of the British aid bill, "we are now able to launch a really offensive war."

Britain, he added, is in a position to open up with everything she has because she does not have to worry now about where she is to get more war equipment or how she is going to pay for it.

"We were not able to risk exhausting our reserves before because we had quite frankly reached the point where we just didn't have the money for replacing on a cash-and-carry basis," the informant added. "It kept us penuriously defensive."

His assertion was borne out further by the fact that, within 48 hours after President Roosevelt signed the bill, the British also counter- punched German night attackers with hordes of new night fighters, heavier barrages and secret weapons described only as "other devices."

Big flights of American-made consolidated and four-motored Boeing bombers to help British Short Stirlings and Avro-Manchesters with heavy long-range bombing, a well-placed source said, would enable the British to spread their attacking area.

This spread, he asserted, besides increasing the effectiveness of the raids, is expected also to force the Germans to disperse their anti-aircraft defenses, givng the RAF a better break.

Britain's night fighters are using new weapons in defensive warfare and her barrages are operated on a shotgun system of concentrating a pattern of shells in heavy coordinating fire.

There also is a new balloon barrage described as "lethal."

The British bomber offensive against Germany's home front was viewed by observers as increasing the chances of British middle East forces.

Tremendous fires and explosions were declared by the air ministry to have been started at Berlin, Hamburg and Bremen and a German destroyer was reported torpedoed in the Skagerrak, arm of the North Sea between Norway and Denmark.

Matching the massive offensive operations, informed sources said Britain now was prepared also to fill the skies over England with night fighters to fend off the Luftwaffe's destructive dusk-to-dawn assaults.

The effectiveness of the reinforced defense set-up was demonstrated by a one-night record last night when at least nine German bombers were shot down in a "large scale" attack on the Merseyside, important shipping area concentrated at Liverpool. It was estimated that about 200 German planes were over England last night.

Further proof was offered in the declaration that the ratio of one raider downed out of 30 heretofore had been reduced now to a one-to-20 ratio.

Informed sources said that when this proportion reached one out of ten the night bomber menace would be whipped.

A communique appeared to hint at a new defensive weapon in stating that the German bombers were harassed by fighters, anti-aircraft

See LONDON—Page 2

Germans Claim Destruction "Worse Than That At Coventry" In Liverpool; Report Sea Victories

BERLIN, Mar. 13.—(AP)—Destruction "exceeding that at Coventry" was reported by German sources today to have been wrought in a vast night raid on Liverpool, in which they said several hundred planes dropped bombs for hours.

This attack was carried out as the British Royal Air Force, also taking advantage of improving weather, made its first assaults on Berlin in 82 nights.

Sixteen persons were killed and 37 injured in Berlin, informed persons said, and other damage was inflicted at Bremen and Hamburg, two of Germany's chief ports.

The high command said the attack on the Liverpool area was carried out by several hundred planes in waves, and DNB, official news agency, said returning crewmen declared the devastation was worse than at Coventry, the midlands industrial town which was virtually razed the night of Nov. 14.

"Hell broke loose on the Mersey," one pilot reported, describing an "ocean of flames" visible 25-minutes flight away from the scene. Another observer declared 10,000 explosive and incendiary bombs were dropped, many ships in the harbor were damaged, and huge losses were inflicted especially among grain elevators and storehouses.

Thirteen British planes were said by the high command to have been shot down, ten of them in the attacks on Berlin, Hamburg and Bremen.

"Only residence sections, hospitals and a church" were listed as damaged. Military and industrial objectives escaped for the most part, it was declared. The many fires were extinguished quickly and night fighters and anti-aircraft guns often forced the British to dump their bombs prematurely, the Germans said.

In other actions, the high command reported:

The sinking of a British destroyer by a Nazi speedboat off the English southeast coast.

The hitting of three big merchantmen and the sinking of another in attacks by reconnaissance planes on convoys off the British east coast.

Daylight attacks on industrial and military objectives in Scotland and south England.

The German air force "effectively fought" British transport columns in North Africa.

Another raid was made on Malta, in cooperation with Italian fliers.

A United States embassy attache said the building of the United States consulate general at Hamburg was hit in the British raid there, but no one was injured.

At Bremen, DNB said, three persons were killed and three slightly injured and only slight damage was done. Only minor damage was done to Hamburg's industrial centers, the agency added.

The high command admitted losing six of its own planes.

Plane Output Is Lower In February

WASHINGTON, Mar. 13.—(AP)—Airplane manufacturers delivered 972 planes during February, a decrease of 64 from the January total.

William S. Knudsen, director of the office of production management, announced the figures today and said that of the February deliveries 879 planes went to the British and to the United States Army and Navy. He did not disclose how many the American armed services received, nor how many of the planes were combat craft and how many were other types.

The decline in production was attributed by OPM officials to the smaller number of working days in February than in January

LATE FINAL EXTRA

NET WEEKLY SALES LARGER THAN THOSE OF ANY OTHER NEWSPAPER IN AUSTRALIA
SAVE THIS PAPER FOR THE SALVAGE COMMISSIONER
THE SUN
ABOVE ALL "FOR AUSTRALIA"
No. 9737 (Registered at the General Post Office, Sydney, for transmission by post as a newspaper) SYDNEY: THURSDAY, MARCH 20, 1941 PRICE 2d Phone: BO 333

Don't Waste Water

FORECAST
Showery, Finer To-morrow.

HALF A MILLION CHEER AMERICANS

City Gives Wildest Welcome In History

AMAZING SCENES ON MARCH

Streets Rocked With Thunder Of Cheers

In an amazing outburst of enthusiasm, Sydney let itself go to-day to give the men of the United States Squadron the wildest welcome in our history. Police estimated the excited crowd at half a million.

Officers and men marched in triumphal progress through the city, above and about them a mad flurry of flying papers and confetti, and a many-hued jungle of streamers.

The city had seen nothing like it and the Americans stepped out to a never-ceasing thunder of cheers. Nobody believed that Sydney could cheer like this.

The people crowded on every ledge, on every parapet, at every window. Hats and handkerchiefs waved in the gleams of sunlight.

To the visitors themselves it was a revelation. They had expected nothing like it; and their amazement and appreciation were sincere.

When "Old Glory" appeared at the top of Martin Place, surmounting a moving forest of white caps, the cheering throng, caught up in a surge of genuine emotion, nearly bore down the police barriers by sheer weight.

Sun-tanned American officers who led the march were taken aback and gazed in wide-eyed wonder at the scene ahead. A lacery of paper streamers of every hue in the prism had spread itself as a bright, giant cobweb right across Martin Place.

Through its strands swirled a rising storm of colored papers. Every window, on floor after floor of banks and insurance offices, erupted papers. Down from the roofs and parapets cascaded more paper.

Tumultuous Welcome In Martin-place

Cheering crowds, colorful streamers and showers of confetti greeted the men of the American squadron as they marched through Sydney streets to-day. This contingent is swinging along through Martin-place.

Police Barriers Groaned

At this appropriate moment a flood of sunshine for the first time for the day poured down through a break in the murk.

It lighted up a Martin Place such as none of us had seen before and the Americans strode on into a glowing furnace of color.

They marched into a ravine of people, that rocked and swayed to the thunder of cheers, athrob with excitement.

Small flags sprouted in great banks of red, white and blue—colors common to a Dominion at war and a great Republic at peace.

Police barriers never before groaned under such a press of people. This sea of heads flung its spray on to windowsills and parapets.

Typists and girl clerks framed in 5000 windows screamed a shrill soprano welcome to the marching naval men.

And the sailors, steering through a blizzard of flying paper, acknowledged the welcome by flinging kisses to the girls.

An immense host had poured into the city to do honor to the Americans. It not only choked the available area along the line of march, but jammed itself solidly into every side street from which it was possible to see only the flash of a white cap or the occasional glint of a bayonet.

Thousands saw none of the marchers but they cheered with merry abandon all the same.

Thousands more gained only a blurred impression of a restive trooper's horse standing on its hind legs near the Rural Bank, a silken flag bearing U.S. in letters of gold and band music drifting in the breeze

So it was that, when the marchers passed one point, there was a wild scamper of thousands to catch up with the march in George-street.

Fully 30,000 men, women and children burst into deserted Pitt-street with this object in view, only to be halted by a phalanx in Market-street a block deep.

There were no vantage points to be had at noon, either on ground level, on a verandah awning, or at windows.

Swinging along eight deep, the Americans strode the path of a Roman conqueror. Flowers were hurled at them. Megaphones blared at them. Streamers enmeshed them. Petals and confetti bespangled their caps and caught in their hair.

Set Standard For Ever

Sydney set itself to disprove the accusation by Senator Foll that Australians were not "cheer-conscious," and the amazing spectacle of Martin-place to-day must have given our American visitors an idea that we are the most emotional people in the world.

The warmth of the welcome indicated that in the hearts of that great crowd the Anglo-American understanding was complete, and that these sailors were accepted not as interesting foreigners, but as friends and brothers, long separated by ancient differences, but now home again.

Even if the House Guards were to march in all their pride through Sydney, they could not have had a more spectacular or heartfelt greeting. It was a revelation—even to those who remember the delirium of Armistice Day, 1918.

And, after that, the next time our own boys come back from their victories in far seas, Sydney should be able to stage a welcome worthy of it.

Each officed vied with its rivals in maintaining the paper and streamer barrage.

Girls in the Commonwealth Bank alone flung down three hundredweight of confetti on the marching men. They ransacked suburban gardens to furnish a shower of petals. They mobilised 1500 rolls of colored streamers to add to the rapidly growing web. From every window they waved special pennants.

Typists and clerks of the Department of the Interior had torn up countless newspapers. They [illegible] this paper storm from the eleventh floor.

For a minute or two it almost blotted out the Police Band and the first five ranks of Americans.

"We want to make the boys feel at home," chirruped the girls in the lower windows.

But if the visitors thought that the paper blizzard would abate when they turned into George-street, they were mistaken.

It swept down with equal violence from the windows of the retail stores. Gusts of confetti blew into their faces, and a new streamer network stretched from kerb to kerb.

As in Martin-place, the smiling sailors were greeted by incessant crackles of cheering, and the applause was none the less sincere for the representatives of the R.A.N., the Army and the Air Force in the march.

One of the big problems of the police was to defend the rear of the march. Motor cycle police were in position, but the shouting and cheering crowds surged close behind them, and threatened at every street corner to take a short cut and break int, the ranks of the R.A.A.F. trainees.

Constables and special plainclothes police had to push the crowd back behind the barriers, and at the corners had to link hands, forming a cordon for a few minutes to save the marchers from being engulfed.

The Governor-General (Lord Gowrie), surrounded by members of the War Cabinet and representatives of Australia's fighting services, took the salute from Rear-Admiral Newton, Commander of the American unit, amid a whirling shower of confetti.

Though brief, the ceremony was impressive. The crowd was silent as Rear-Admiral Newton left his men at attention on the roadway and walked forward to greet Lord Gowrie.

As Lord Gowrie took the salute, a storm of cheering burst from the dense crowd which packed the surrounding streets.

Smiling, Rear-Admiral Newton shook hands with Lord Gowrie, the State Governor (Lord Wakehurst), and Cabinet members, and Army, Navy, and Air Force chiefs.

After a brief conversation, the Lord Mayor (Ald. Crick), invited the party inside the Town Hall.

Men of the American ships then began to file through the red-carpeted entrance.

Wave after wave of cheering followed them into the Town Hall for the official luncheon.

The official party of welcome included Major-General J. D. Richardson, Air-Commodore A. W. Anderson, Rear-Admiral Sir Ragnar Colvin, and Lieut.-Commander Best, the Acting Prime Minister (Mr. Fadden), Minister for Supply (Senator McBride), Minister for External Affairs (Sir Frederick Stewart), Minister for Commerce (Sir Earle Page).

SQUADRON SAILED UNDER SEALED ORDERS

Cruise A Surprise For Admiral

"The American Navy is one hundred per cent. behind President Roosevelt's foreign policy," said Rear-Admiral John H. Newton, in an exclusive interview to-day aboard his flagship, U.S.S. Chicago.

"It's your guess as much as mine whether this visit to Australia and New Zealand has anything to do with that policy.

"The visit came as a complete surprise to us," he said.

"We left Pearl Harbor under sealed orders, and it was not until we were at sea that we knew that the squadron was to split up—some to go to New Zealand, others to come to Australia."

The Admiral smiled amiably throughout the interview, his face, tanned deep brown by two decades in the tropical Pacific, running into tiny furrows as his smile deepened.

Only when he was asked to comment on the situation did he become grave.

"I'd rather not comment on the situation in the Pacific," he said. "I probably think the same as you."

"I have never previously visited Australia," he said. "I almost did so in 1906, but missed the ship I was to join in Manila, the U.S.S. Baltimore, by 24 hours.

"That was just after I had joined the U.S. Navy from the Naval Academy at Annapolis, which I entered in 1901, and from which I graduated in 1905. I was with the U.S. Asiatic Fleet until 1908."

Rear-Admiral Newton was 36 years of age when the United States entered the Great War in 1917. He was in command of the Fifth Destroyer Flotilla in the North Sea, and after the Armistice, was transferred to the Mediterranean and Adriatic.

Rear-Admiral Newton left the U.S.A. in May, 1939, in command of a division of heavy cruisers.

Seven weeks ago he was appointed Commander Cruisers, Scouting Force. This force comprises 18 heavy vessels of the latest design.

STOP-PRESS

PAKENHAM RACES

Pakenham Handicap.—Quiamo 1, Windbeau 2, Smoke Screen 3. Scratched: Suliman, Decurio.

No Isolationists On Ship

He hopes to celebrate his 60th birthday this year with Mrs. Newton, who is in Honololu. An only son is in the United States Navy.

"I certainly did not expect, when I was with my family in Hawaii a fortnight ago, that I would be in Sydney to-day," he said.

"We left after the Lend or Lease Bill was enacted by Congress, but before President Roosevelt's fine speech of a few days ago.

"I think everybody aboard these ships is 100 per cent. behind President Roosevelt and what he says.

"His speech, which, of course, we heard by radio, was a remarkably good one, and just what you would expect him to say.

"Naturally, what President Roosevelt says goes with us. The President is also the Navy's Commander-in-Chief.

"There are no Isolationists in these ships."

Rear-Admiral Newton revealed that the sealed orders received after his departure from Pearl Harbor did not go any further than Brisbane. The squadron will depart during the week-end for Queensland.

"I've not the least idea where we'll be going after we leave Brisbane," he said.

SAN ANTONIO
THE LIGHT
AN INDEPENDENT TEXAS NEWSPAPER
Member of the Associated Press ★ A Constructive Force in the Community

STATE EDITION

VOL. LXI—NO. 99. Published by The Light Publishing Company. San Antonio, Texas. MONDAY, APRIL 28, 1941. FOURTEEN PAGES. PRICE FIVE CENTS.

ATHENS CAPTURED BY NAZIS

Churchill Sees Spread of War

IN THE NEWS

232 Madison Avenue,
New York,
April 15, 1941.

MR. W. R. HEARST,
San Simeon, Calif.

My Dear Mr. Hearst:

Please allow me to thank you for the fearless work you are doing in informing our people as to the growth and danger of communism in America.

There can be no doubt as to the fact. Twenty years ago I made a prolonged personal inquiry into what was then the beginning of this menace. I found it already growing on the Pacific coast, where alien agents had traveled from Russia via Siberia, and spreading east with alarming rapidity. Since then I have had a brief glimpse of the devastation which is Russia, and also some experience of its skillful propaganda work here.

The open intention is to overthrow our form of government by fomenting discontent, thus leading eventually to revolution and civil war. It is not necessary to add that a country thus torn by internal struggle will be helpless to defend itself from outside attack.

It is this situation which you are fighting, without fear and without prejudice. And I sincerely hope that you will continue to arouse our people to their danger.

Cordially yours,
MARY ROBERTS RINEHART.

Camara de Commercio Mexicana
Mexican Chamber of Commerce,
Los Angeles, Calif.,
April 22, 1941.

MR. W. R. HEARST,
Los Angeles Examiner,
Los Angeles, Calif.

Dear Mr. Hearst:

Your very timely and generous endeavor to publicize and promote material aid for the affected people of Colima, Mexico, from the terrifying cause of the recent earthquake will be long remembered and greatly appreciated by every Mexican citizen here and in Mexico.

We of the Mexican chamber of commerce, will immediately launch a campaign for this great cause, and hope to be able to contribute and collaborate with the authorities directly in charge of these donations, so that this help may reach its needy destination as soon as possible.

Your mention of this fact in your widely read columns may serve to aid us in the necessary contributions; also, humanitarily inclined people living in the East Los Angeles district may find it more convenient to make their donations at the above mentioned address. Our offices are opened from 1 a. m. to 4:30 p. m. every day.

Yours very truly,
Mexican Chamber of Commerce of Los Angeles, Calif.,
F. I. BELENDEZ, President,
A. FLORES, Secretary.

April 14, 1941.

DEAR Mr. Hearst:

All of us long at times to get away from it all—especially during these dark days of lost ideals and false aims. Mankind seems to have gotten out of touch with God. An almost too ruthless reality rules the world. Here's how I feel about it:

LET'S GO!

If I could take this heart of mine
Away, so far away,
From all the worries that combine
To make it ache today!

If I could take this weary soul,
So sick of human guile,
To some far desert island
Where 'twould learn again to smile!

Away from clanging telephones—
From headlines, full of gore—
Away from screaming radios
With news about the war!

Maybe my long lost dreams await
In some forgotten bay?
I know that I'll find peace of mind
When my heart sails away.
—Nick Kenny.

MR. W. R. HEARST,
San Simeon, Calif.

Dear Sir:

Congratulations, sir, on your Easter peace proposal. Your Pittsburgh editorial conveying the Easter peace message of Pope Pius was an inspiration to all true Christian Americans.

Will you not continue to hammer away at this peace offensive?

Cannot all American forces against war including our anti-war committees, the Catholic and other churches be united in

(Continued On Page 2, Col. 1)

EXTENSION OF U. S. PATROL PRAISED

America, Britain Will Win Battle of Atlantic and War, is Prediction.

LONDON, April 27.—(AP)—The "tremendous decision" of the United States to patrol the "wide waters of the Western hemisphere" was hailed by Prime Minister Winston Churchill tonight as vital to the battle which Britain must win to survive—the battle of the Atlantic.

"No far-seeing men can doubt," he declared, "that the eventual and total defeat of Hitler and Mussolini (whom he called a whipped jackal) is certain in view of the respective and declared resolves of the British and American democracies."

In a grim 30-minute review of the entire war situation, broadcast to the empire and to America, Churchill acknowledged the German victories in Yugoslavia and Greece and predicted.

WAR SPREAD SEEN.

"We must now expect the war in the Mediterranean, on the sea and in the desert, and above all, in the air, to become very fierce, varied and widespread * * *

"War may spread to Spain and Morocco, to Turkey and Russia. The Germans may lay their hands upon the granaries of the Ukraine or the oil wells of the Caucasus, but there is one thing which is certain: Hitler cannot find safety from avenging justice in the Middle East or the Far East."

Instead, Churchill said, "to win this war he (Hitler) must defeat this island or cut the lifelines between us and the United States.

For this reason, the prime minister asserted, it was with "indescribable relief" that he learned of the United States patrol decision.

CITES U. S. DANGER.

The battle of the Atlantic still will be "long and hard", said Churchill, but the United States is responding to his plea of 10 weeks ago for the "tools" of war, and the battle "has entered upon a more grim but at the same time a far more favorable phase".

He stated Americans were "taxing themselves heavily" and had turned a large part of their "gigantic" industry to making the munitions which Britain needs.

"I could not believe that they would allow the high purposes to which they set themselves to be frustrated and the products of their skill and labor sunk to the bottom of the sea," he said, remarking that the president and congress of the United States had pledged aid to Britain "because they know their own interests and safety would be endangered if we were destroyed."

SMALL GREEK FORCE.

The prime minister gave only a short exposition of the situation in Greece and North Africa, but disclosed the army with which Gen. Sir Archibald P. Wavell defeated the Italians in Libya at no time exceeded two divisions, or about 30,000 men.

When Greece called for aid against the Germans, it was a point of honor for Britain to send it, Churchill said, despite the small size of the imperial army in Africa.

Flood Damage In S. A. Looms

With 3.37 inches of rain falling in San Antonio since Friday morning in a steady downpour, the San Antonio fire department placed its forces to watching Olmos dam and the San Antonio river late Sunday afternoon for possible danger.

The river stood within seven feet of the bridge at the police station at 4 p. m. Sunday. Shortly before Fire Chief Butler ordered the Olmos gates closed and 11 feet of water had backed up behind the dam within one hour and a half.

"Unless heavy rains fall during the night, we have everything under control," he said. Flood waters above the dam can be held in check, but with creeks rising within the city, heavy rains might bring on a serious situation in certain parts of the town, he said.

Since midnight Saturday until 4:30 p. m. Sunday, the rainfall had amounted to 1.97 inches. Cars stalled in flooded streets.

Coal Mediation Efforts Failure

WASHINGTON, April 27.—(AP)—The defense mediation board's efforts to settle the coal mine stoppage collapsed today and board officials said that it planned no further action.

W. H. Davis, chairman of the panel which considered the dispute, said it had recommended unanimously that President Roosevelt's proposal for reopening the mines be accepted.

This recommendation was accepted by the United Mine Workers (CIO) and the Northern bituminous coal operators, Davis added, but rejected by the Southern operators.

Henderson Fights Lumber Rate Hike

WASHINGTON, April 27.—(INS) In the first action of its kind, Federal Price Control Administrator Leon Henderson Saturday night disclosed he had filed a brief with the interstate commerce commission opposing a proposed increase by steamship companies of rates for transporting lumber from the Pacific to the Atlantic coasts.

Henderson charged the rate increases would be harmful to the defense program.

MINERS LOSE LIVES

SALINA, Kan., April 27.—(AP)—Overcome by mine gas, three men lost their lives today in a shaft at salt mine works near Kanopolis, Kan.

MORE TROOPS REACH ENGLAND

A BRITISH PORT, April 27.—(AP) Thousands of Canadian fighting men and the largest force of Canadian-trained imperial fliers yet to reach the United Kingdom have arrived from Canada to take their posts in the war against Germany.

Arrival of the heavily-guarded convoy was announced after the troops have taken trains to their new stations and the convoy was dispersed.

The soldiers said the crossing was "quiet and dull."

Canadians, New Zealanders, Australians, Britons and a scattering of Americans were included in the air force detail in the convoy.

Axis Triumphs in Africa Claimed

ROME, April 27.—(AP)—The axis powers reported fresh triumphs today on the North African front of their vast pincer movement aimed from two sides of the Eastern Mediterranean at Suez.

The Italian high command announced axis land and air forces repulsed British tank and infantry assaults at Tobruk, Libyan port 80 miles west of the Egyptian frontier. ... British tanks and several armored cars were declared destroyed.

British advance units, the German high command claimed, were thrown back to the south in the Fort Capuzoz-Salum area along the Egyptian-Libyan border.

The British acknowledged axis units crossed the Egyptian frontier at several points. They claimed, however, that the Tobruk situation remained unchanged.

The Italians listed more than 400 casualties, including 101 dead, in last Tuesday's British naval and air assault on Tripoli, main port of entry for axis forces in North Africa.

NON-DEFENSE SPENDING FOUGHT

Roosevelt Backs Solons Against Increase In Farm Payments.

WASHINGTON, April 27.—(AP)—The White House was reported today to have urged house conferees to stand pat against a $238,000,000 increase in farm "parity" payments voted by the senate.

This action was accepted at the capitol as indicating the administration was prepared to give strong backing to a suggestion by Secretary of the Treasury Morgenthau that congress scale down non-defense expenditures by $1,000,000,000.

He proposed cuts in expenditures on farm benefits, the Civilian Conservation corps and the National Youth administration.

House Majority Leader McCormack of Massachusetts said he was opposed to the "parity" payment increase, but Senate Democratic Leader Barkley of Kentucky said it was "obvious we can't save a billion there", adding he did not know where congress could cut ordinary expenditures very much.

At the same time, Senate Republican Leader McNary of Oregon said he had assured representatives of farm organizations there would be strong Republican support to maintain the "parity" figure at the $450,000,000 level voted by the senate.

Parity payments are designed to raise farm purchasing to the level of pre-World war days.

The house approved an outlay of $251,000,000 for this purpose and committees of both houses planned to meet this week to compose their differences.

400-M.P.H. Plane Produced for RAF

LONDON, April 27.—(INS)—A new fighter plane claimed to be the most formidable in the world and known as the Hawker Typhoon is now in full production for the R. A. F., it was revealed Saturday.

The Hawker Typhoon develops a speed of more than 400 miles per hour with its new and secret "sabre" engine of 2400 horsepower. Its fire-power is said to be greater than that possessed by any other fighter plane.

Jones County Asks Quick-Freeze Unit

AUSTIN, April 27.—Jones county has put in its first bid for the newly-invented University of Texas quick-freezing process, officials here disclosed today.

Following last week's announcement of a new process which streamlines food-frosting, a letter was received from the Jones County Observer—West Texas weekly newspaper—offering to help sponsor a quick-freeze plant in that area, W. R. Woolrich, engineering dean here, said.

6-Inch Rain Hits Crops in Nueces

ROBSTOWN, April 27. — Much damage to spring cotton, feed and onion crops in the Robstown-Nueces county area was observed late Saturday after a six-inch rain fell within a few hours after noon. Roads and field throughout the area were inundated.

Ethiopia Waits Return of King

LONDON, April 27.—(AP)—British dispatches tonight said Addis Ababa is decorated in green, gold and red gunting, the national colors, in preparation for the forthcoming return to his capital of Emperor Haile Selassie.

U. S. Strengthens Atlantic Patrol

WASHINGTON, April 27.—(AP)—Disclosure patrol operations of the Atlantic fleet have been greatly extended indicated today the United States has concentrated a large number of small war vessels along the Eastern seaboard in recent months.

Craft in patrol work include destroyers, submarine chasers, the heavier types of reconditioned yachts, mine-layers and mine-sweepers and, functioning in conjunction with these, long-range airplanes.

The navy has been building such craft in increasing quantities, and in informed quarters here it was believed most of them have gone to the Atlantic rather than the Pacific fleet.

PATROL LINE EXTENDED

When the neutrality patrol was first set up in the fall of 1939, the Atlantic squadron, numbered about 125 vessels. Informed opinion now is that i includes more than 200, and that most of these are operating in waters off New England and Canada where run Britain's principal supply routes from this country.

The first neutrality patrol area in the North Atlantic extended from a point south of Canada's vital port of Halifax out about 125 miles to the sixtieth degree of latitude and south along that longitude to near the northern coast of South America. The area was less than half that now believed to be under surveillance.

Establishment of American defenses in Greenland of itself extended United States naval lines across a whole new section of the Atlantic.

DENIES CONVOYING

President Roosevelt's Friday press conference report the patrol would operate as far out in the Atlantic as necessary to protect American defenses was interpreted as indicating the original outer limit of operations may have been moved eastward to the approximate mid-way point to Europe.

Roosevelt denied emphatically any convoying was being done by United States ships.

Authorities professed to see in the move, however, a maneuver of considerable benefit to Britain since her navy would be relieved of the necessity of convoying in the Western Atlantic to the extent that those waters are made safe for her ships.

30,000 U. S. Plane Increase Asked

WASHINGTON, April 27.—(AP)—Initial funds for expansion of the nation's airplane production capacity from the present goal of 50,000 planes a year to an ultimate goal of 80,000 were said by informed persons today to be part of a $6,574,605,468 army supply bill scheduled for consideration by a congressional committee Monday.

It was reported the measures carrying funds to finance the growing land forces for the year starting July 1, would include money for the purchase of a substantial number of additional airplanes for the army.

A major portion of them are expected to be heavy, long-range bombers—the "backbone" of aerial striking power. At present, the army is working toward a goal of 21,000 planes.

The army has entered into a $24,000,000 contract with the Glenn L. Martin company of Baltimore for construction of one new heavy bomber plant and expansion of its existing units.

Well-posted sources said President Roosevelt had earmarked $1,500,000,000 of the $7,000,000,000 lend-lease fund for plant expansions to include two bomber plants, five airplane engine plants, and about 30 additional ordnance plants of various types, including those for the manufacture of tanks, guns and ammunition.

RAF's Big Bombs Shatter Hamburg

LONDON, April 27.—(AP)—The RAF dumped cargoes of Britain's powerful new bombs on Hamburg, Germany's biggest port and second city, last night in a raid which one pilot said left a half-mile area "a huge, heaving mass like a volcanic eruption".

The air ministry said an assault almost as violent was made on the big German shipbuilding yards at Bremerhaven, and that other RAF units pounded Emden and Cuxhaven in Germany, Le Havre, France, and Ijmuiden, the Netherlands.

One participating pilot brought back this account:

"I had with me one of the powerful bombs, and after it burst I could see a circle of red and on the rim of it, quite a distance from the center, I saw buildings going up in the air.

"Although I have been on 31 raids I have never seen anything to match the effect of this bomb."

Other pilots said the big bombs caused raging fires elsewhere in Hamburg, sending huge clouds of black smoke billowing upward.

The air ministry said German night fighters tried to intercept the RAF bombers but presented no great obstacle.

GERMAN FLEET IN GREEK AREA

BERLIN, April 27.—(AP)—Units of the German fleet are in the Mediterranean harrassing British efforts to deliver the expeditionary force out of Greece, DNB, German news agency, reported tonight.

The fleet apparently was co-operating with the Nazi air force, which, it said, has sunk 11 ships in the last two days and damaged a greater number, including large passenger liners.

German sources earlier reported that units of the Nazi fleet co-operated with the army in occupying islands off Greece and Turkey.

6000 Bomb-dead In Belgrade

BUDAPEST, Hungary, April 27.—(AP) — Travelers from Belgrade, bomb-ravaged capital of Yugoslavia, report 6000 dead have been buried and the city is returning to normal.

German military authorities are organizing a new city administration and ruins of buildings are being razed.

The travelers report Jews and Serb war prisoners are being put to work clearing the wreckage.

The food situation in Belgrade was described as critical.

Rockefeller for Arms Carrying

NEW YORK, April 27. — (AP) — John D. Rockefeller Jr., declared today it was his firm conviction that the people of the United States and all the Americas "should stand by the British empire to the limit and at any cost".

Calling for the American people to stand solidly behind President Roosevelt and to see that quantities of war munitions sufficient to win victory were "laid down at Britain's door", Rockefeller said the issue being fought was freedom versus slavery and added:

"I would rather die fighting the brutal, barbarous, inhuman force represented by Hitlerism than live in a world which is dominated by that force."

His views were given in a letter to Arthur Hays Sulzberger, publisher of the New York Times.

Rockefeller asserted it was not enough merely to fabricate munitions of war and to supply needed foodstuffs—that these were all "valueless unless laid down at Britain's door".

The financier-philanthropist, asserting "every hour is precious", said a united determination on the part of both labor and capital was necessary to keep industry running at top speed and to eliminate "all strikes, lockouts, labor disputes and stoppages of every character".

INJURED

FRITZ KREISLER
When he played in S. A.

Fritz Kreisler Hurt By Truck

NEW YORK, April 27.—(AP)—Fritz Kreisler, 66, violinist and composer, was still semi-conscious today 27 hours after he was struck by a delivery truck, but physicians at Roosevelt hospital expressed belief he was "improving."

A bulletin said:

"Not much change. We are of the opinion he is improving."

Hospital authorities added, when asked if the violinist was conscious, "he's not really conscious yet."

Hospital authorities said the virtuoso was suffering from a skull fracture and possible internal injuries.

Police said the violinist, 66, was crossing the street against traffic lights when he walked into the side of a moving truck.

Kreisler lives in New York.

U. S. Convoying of British Aid Urged

NEW YORK, April 27.—(AP)—Lewis W. Douglas, chairman of the national policy board of the Committee to Defend America By Aiding the Allies, tonight declared himself in favor of convoying American supplies to Great Britain.

Characterizing the loss of Allied merchant shipping as "alarming, even ominous", Douglas admitted convoying would involve great risk.

But, he added, the risks are "incalculably less than by indolently, fearfully, cravenly waiting until we shall stand without a friend on earth, in desperate solitude".

U. S. SOLDIERS SAIL

NEW YORK, April 27.—(AP)—The U. S. army transport Leonard Wood sailed today for Newfoundland.

PURSUIT OF RETREATING BRITISH PUSHED

Occupation of Capital Comes After Three Weeks of War.

VICHY, France, April 27.—(AP)—Diplomatic circles here expressed belief today Germany's next thrust would be towards the Russian Ukraine—Europe's breadbasket.

BERLIN, April 27. —(AP)— Adolf Hitler's legions swept into the Peloponnesus, last tip of unoccupied Greek territory, in pursuit of remnants of defeated Greek and British forces today after planting the swastika atop the Acropolis at Athens.

They were driving at a quick finish to the conquest of the kingdom of the sturdy Hellenes.

Beating down desperately resisting allied rearguards, the spearhead of Nazi armored forces rolled triumphantly into Athens just three weeks and four hours after launching their Balkan blitzkrieg against Greece and already vanquished Yugoslavia.

Immediately the swastika was hoisted over the oblong rocky mass of the Acropolis, crumbling fortress stronghold of ancient Athens.

EIGHTH TO FALL

This was accomplished the occupation of the eighth European capital to fall to German arms after opposition.

There was no indication here whether fighting occurred inside Athens or whether it was necessary to shell the city. It was assumed by Germans here it was undamaged.

Correspondents of D. N. B., German official news agency, said Greek civilians received the Nazis in silence.

German parachutists and S. S. Elite Hitler bodyguard already had stormed across water barriers into the two north corners of the Peloponnesus in what appeared to be a fast-developing pincers movement to snap off the last trace of resistance in the lower peninsula.

MANY CAPTURED

In the northwest corner of the Peloponnesus Hitler's specially-trained S. S. body guard drove across the narrows between the gulfs of Patron and Corinth. Then they fought their way into Patras, much-bombed chief seaport on the western coast of Greece.

Many British were declared captured in the Peloponnesus.

In the north eastern corner of the Poloponnesus daring parachute troops yesterday came into action for the first time in the Balkan campaign, apparently to circumvent the obstacle presented by the narrow, four-mile long canal across the isthmus of Corinth.

The city of Corinth was taken by these forces, the Germans announced.

While the Germans pressed hard on the heels of the withdrawing allies, Stuka dive-bombers made it hot for the British escaping by sea.

SECOND DUNKERQUE

The high command announced one British cruiser was sunk, two cruisers damaged, four transports totalling 22,000 tons and a merchantman of 5000 tons sunk and 20 other ships totalling 155,000 tons damaged in Greek waters yesterday and today.

Additional accounts, said three merchant ships aggregating 27,000 tons were sunk and two others damaged by the luftwaffe pouncing relentlessly on the embarking British expeditionary force yesterday.

In continued assaults on Britain proper, the luftwaffe was reported to have blasted Liverpool heavily overnight.

British night raiders dropped fire and explosive bombs on various towns with Hamburg bearing the brunt of the attack.

With Franz Von Papen, ambassador to Turkey, in Berlin, the press directed attention to the importance of the capture of the Greek island of Lemnos, which stands athwart the Aegean entrance to the Turkish Dardanelles.

The presence of the German forces there undoubtedly will be a strong talking point in an effort to bring Turkey into line when Von Papen returns to Ankara.

WAR EXTRA

COMPLETE RACES

Complete Markets

Los Angeles Examiner

CHARACTER QUALITY AMERICA FIRST! ENTERPRISE ACCURACY

AN AMERICAN PAPER FOR THE AMERICAN PEOPLE — THE GREAT NEWSPAPER OF THE GREAT SOUTHWEST

Reg. U.S. Pat. Off.

Examiner Telephone RIchmond 1212 — Examiner Building, 1111 S. Broadway

VOL. XXXVIII—NO. 153 — LOS ANGELES, TUESDAY, MAY 13, 1941 — CC — Two Sections—Part I—FIVE CENTS

HITLER CHIEF DESERTS; FLIES TO SCOTLAND!

Amazing Story

FOUND BY the Examiner in heavily guarded hideaway, Violet Wells, key figure in San Bernardino triple slayings, yesterday told amazing story. (Story on Page 4.) —Los Angeles Examiner photo.

SENATE GROUP APPROVES SHIP SEIZURE BILL

No Major Changes Made in Measure; Slashes in Auto, Furnace Production Hinted

WASHINGTON, May 12.—(AP)—Empowering President Roosevelt to take over foreign ships in American ports and use them in the defense or aid-to-Britain program was approved without major changes today by the Senate commerce committee.

Meanwhile, as officials worked on oher aspects of the defense and aid plans, it became apparent that many sacrifices by American consumers were in prospect. For one thing, William L. Batt of the office for production management forecast that the nation's entire aluminum supply would be devoted to military needs by 1942.

Other defense officials said that a second 20 per cent cut in automobile production was a "distinct possibility" although "s'till in the pure speculation stage" and that if a sharp upswing occurred in defense demands, the manufacture of furnaces, refrigerators and other household goods might also be curtailed.

AMENDMENT LOSES

Before the Senate committee akayed the House-approved ship-seizure bill, 11 to 4, it defeated a move by Senators Vandenberg (Republican), Michigan, and Clark (Democrat), Missouri, to prohibit transfer of any Axis Ships to Britain.

This amendment lost, 1 0to 6, but its sponsors gave notice that they would press for its adoption on the Senate floor when the measure comes up for debate. Senators Johnson (Republican), California, and Burton (Republican), Ohio, joined Vandenburg and Clark in voting against the bill as a whole.

Those voting for it were reported by committee members to be Senators Bailey, Caraway, Overton, Bilbo, Radcliffe, Pepper, Lee, Hill and Mead, Democrats, and Senators McNary and Barbour, Republicans.

Incidentally, the committee heard from Chairman Emory S. Land of the Maritime Commission that his report of last week that only eight of the ships sailing from American ports for Britain had been sunk in the first three months of this year did not include vessels which

(Continued on Page 2, Cols 2-3)

Number 3 Nazi Deserts

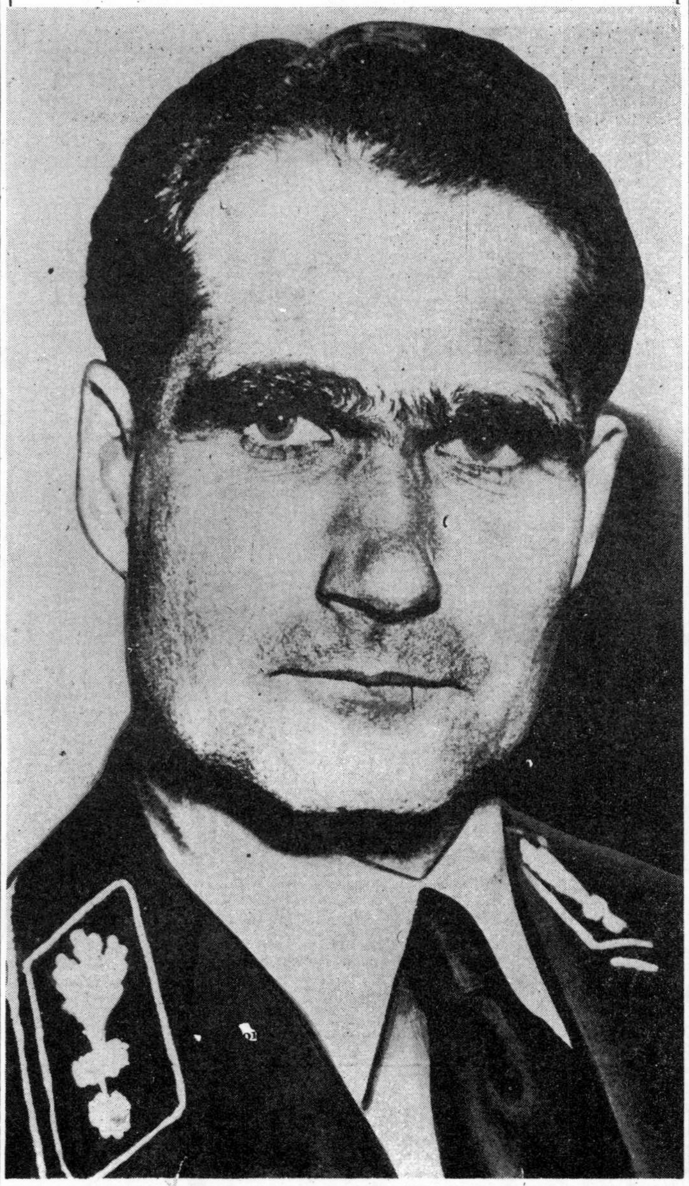

WITH STRONG indications that he had staged an "escape" from Germnay, Rudolf Hess (above), No. 3 man in Nazi regime, parachuted to British soil from a German warplane, it was revealed yesterday. Nazis charged he had lost his mind. Wide World photo.

Number 3 Nazi Uses Plane to Escape Purge

LONDON, Tuesday, May 13.—(AP)—The ministry of information announced today that the man who landed from a German fighter plane in Scotland had been identified as Rudolf Hess—"beyond all possible doubt."

BERLIN, May 13 (Tuesday).—(AP)—Authorized quarters repeated an official German statement early today that Rudolf Hess, No. 3 Nazi leader, was missing on a forbidden airplane flight and, suggesting he was suffering from "hallucinations," insisted nothing was known of London's official report that he had landed in Scotland.

By Thomas C. Watson
Staff Correspondent International News Service

LONDON, May 13 (Tuesday).—Rudolf Hess, second only to Adolf Hitler in command of Germany's ruling Nazi Party, has been taken a prisoner of war in Scotland, it was disclosed early today, after he landed by parachute from a warplane which he had piloted alone in a dramatic escape from the Reich.

Bearing pictures of himself and papers to prove his identity, the "crown prince" of the Nazi political hegemony came to earth Saturday evening on the verdant banks of storied Loch Lomond, breaking his ankle as he reached the refuge of "enemy" soil, which he apparently had deliberately sought.

A humble Scottish farm laborer "captured" the high-ranking German official whose history-making solo flight was made—in secret defiance of Chancellor Hitler's personal command—in order evidently to surrender himself to Great Britain and escape a possible "blood purge."

IDENTITY POSITIVELY VERIFIED

Today Hess was under heavy guard in a military hospital at Glasgow as the British government announced his identity had been established "beyond all possible doubt."

The 45-year-old "Fuehrer-to-be" was writhing in agony, his parachute wrapped around him, when the farm worker came upon him just before nightfall Saturday. The farmer pulled him clear of the tangled 'chute and helped him to a near-by two-room farm cottage from where he telephoned the police of his "find."

Neither the farmer nor the police dreamed that their prisoner was one of Germany's highest chieftains when they turned him over to a British army patrol.

DELIBERATELY FLEW TO BRITAIN

That Hess deliberately flew to Britain to surrender himself and thus gain haven from his rivals in the Nazi Party hierarchy was amply indicated by the photographs and documents he brought with him on his almost incredible flight of some 800 airline miles from Augsburg, southwest Germany, to the Glasgow district of nor[illegible] west Scotland.

His big, broad-shouldered frame w[illegible]ttired in a G[illegible] man officer's uniform as he bumped to [illegible]

HESS FACES SECRET GRILL BY CHURCHILL

FINAL NIGHT EDITION R

WEATHER: SHOWERS Details on Page 22

THE CALL BULLETIN
SAN FRANCISCO
AN INDEPENDENT NEWSPAPER

86TH YEAR CALL AND POST, VOL. 149, NO. 93 THE CALL-BULLETIN, VOL. 169, NO. 93

SAN FRANCISCO, TUESDAY, MAY 13, 1941

5c DAILY

Germans Tried To Block Flight

Bullet Holes In Crashed Plane Indicate Hitler Ordered Aide Shot Down

Today's developments in Hess' arrival in England included:

1. Prime Minister Churchill and other high officials to grill Hess on Hitler's secret war plans at "hide-out."
2. British authorities hail Hess' capture as "more important" than winning great battle; physicians declare hostage "healthy and sane"; leaders warn of Hitler "trap."
3. Hitler addresses all Reich leaders and district chiefs at special meeting in Berlin.
4. German authorities attribute Hess' flight to insanity and mental derangement; adjutants of Hess arrested.

By EARL REEVES
Staff Correspondent International News Service

LONDON, May 13 (INS).—A desperate effort by outraged Nazis to halt the flight to Glasgow of Nazi Party Leader Hess was revealed in London today while British officials sought to wrest from his knowledge and memory the key to victory over Germany.

As Hess—an apparent fugitive from a Nazi system he had come to hate—was whisked to a secret hideaway for a grilling by Britain's highest officials, Prime Minister Churchill and Foreign Secretary Anthony Eden, disclosure was made that the tail of his Messerschmitt 110 had been riddled by more than twenty bullets.

Hint Flight From Purge

British fighters sighted Hess' plane when it wheeled in over the North Sea after Hitler's No. 3 man had put 700 miles of land and ocean between him and the Nazi Reich he helped to create.

But for reasons not yet explained they refrained from attacking the plane and let Hess continue until he finally bailed out in a parachute on the estate of the Flying Duke of Hamilton, landing in a field with an injured ankle.

Belief was expressed Hess' machine was spared mainly because he came in over an unimportant area industrially just as the bulk of Royal Air Force fighters were busy with hundreds of German planes launching Saturday night's terrific attack on London.

Examination of pictures made of the bullet holes indicated they were made by a ground machine gun as well as rifles. The holes were widespread and clean cut instead of the rips made by aerial machine guns.

It was assumed therefore that Nazi machine gunners at Augsburg, learning at the last minute of Hess' fantastic plan to fly to sanctuary in Britain, possibly from a new Hitler purge, had attempted to stop him.

Officials pointed to announcements in Berlin to the effect that letters and papers left behind by Hess revealed his "deranged" plan to fly to Britain and endeavor single handed to bring about "Anglo-German understanding."

Map Marked With Route

The British were inclined to scoff at this story, and virtually every person in a position to talk emphasized the likelihood that Hess' flight was just that—an escape from some peril or some forthcoming development concerning which the world has not yet been enlightened.

Editor's Note: Two homeguardsmen who took Hess into custody Saturday night near Glasgow were quoted by the Associated Press as saying Hess told them he flew to Britain with an extra gasoline tank and a map marked with the route "Augsburg to Scotland" marked in blue pencil.

(Hess was quoted as saying he fitted the extra gasoline tank to the plane to make certain he had enough fuel for the 800-mile trip and dumped the extra gasoline when he crossed the Scottish coast.)

Churchill to Quiz Hess

It was pointed out, however, that if these papers were found at the last minute, orders might have been flashed from the Wilhelmstrasse to Augsburg to stop Hess at all costs, with the result that his own machine gunners, who once idolized him as a pillar and king-pin of the Third Reich, turned their weapons against him.

Meanwhile, Churchill disappointed the House of Commons when pressed for a statement this afternoon.

Addressing the members, meeting in a makeshift cham-

Continued on Page A, Column 1

F. R. HELP IN STRIKE HERE URGED

C. of C. Asks Immediate Action in Shipyard Tieup

Branding the tieup of 11 bay region shipyards and repair plants as a "body blow at the national defense program," the San Francisco Chamber of Commerce, in a telegram to President Roosevelt, today urged immediate action by the chief executive toward resumption of work.

HAAS SIGNS WIRE

As 1,700 A. F. L. and C. I. O. machinists remained on strike at the plants here and in the East Bay, with resultant idleness for more than 10.000 workers for the second day, this wire was dispatched to the President over the signature of Walter A. Haas, president:

"Machinist strikes in San Francisco Bay shipyards tying up $500,000,000 naval contracts and $165,000,000 maritime commission contracts are a body blow at national defense program and a flagrant violation of spirit and purpose of the recently negotiated coastwide shipbuilding pact which outlawed strikes and lockouts in Pacific Coast shipyards.

'URGE YOU ACT'

"The very security of the nation demands that, regardless of the issue, all men return to work immediately pending negotiations and settlement of the differences. We urge that you act to re-establish this vital national defense work immediately."

At the same time, Joseph Keenan, special A. F. L. representative of the United States Office of Production Management, whose

Continued on Page 2, Column 4

Former E. Bay Auditor To Face Embezzle Charge

Extradition was waived today by Edward E. Grow, 34, former employe of the Contra Costa County auditing office arrested by FBI agents at Seattle on a two year old charge of embezzlinig $4,000, Sheriff John A. Miller, Martinez, reported.

Rudolf Hess, who parachuted from his Messerschmitt plane over Scotland, is the center of this photograph made recently in Berlin. At the extreme left is Franz von Papen, German ambassador to Turkey. The German officer at the right is unidentified.
—Associated Press Wirephotos.

Pepper Asks U. S. Convoy All Ships

WASHINGTON, May 13 (AP).—With a Senate showdown approaching on the convoy question, Senator Pepper (D., Fla.) urged today that the United States undertake to help to assure the safe delivery of all supplies to Britain, regardless of the country from which they were shipped.

DAWES BACKS HOOVER

Meanwhile, in Chicago, Charles G. Dawes, Vice President in the Coolidge administration, said:

"I strongly endorse the advice of former President Herbert Hoover against using American warships as war convoys and against participating in the war in any manner."

But capital circles wondered just what Secretary Knox meant when he said:

"It is very possible . . . that convoys are not the answer after all. Perhaps we have to develop a new defense to assure the arrival of our goods on the other side."

The statement was made by Knox in an extemporaneous speech after he had declared, **"We cannot half fight the battle . . . we are committed to all the support (to Britain)) necessary to produce a victory."**

"PUBLIC FOR CONVOYS"

Pepper, who has been demanding "affirmative action" by this country against the axis, told reporters:

"Public opinion has reached the point where, if convoys are necessary to deliver the goods, the people will support them.

"The question of convoys is far broader than just getting

Continued on Page 9, Column 6

White Sox Down Red Sox, 3-2

The Chicago White Sox moved into the American League second spot today when they downed Boston, 3 to 2, at Boston.

Rigney hurled for the White Sox, allowing the Red Sox four scattered hits, while the winners pounded Wagner for seven bingles.

American League

At BOSTON—		R.	H.	E.
Chicago	002 000 100—	3	7	1
Boston	000 100 001—	2	4	1

Rigney and Tresh.
Wagner, Fleming and Pytlak.

At Pittsburgh—		R.	H.	E.
Phila'phia.	010 001 0			
Pittsburgh	020 310 0			

Grissom and Warren, Davis.
Sewell and Baker.

At Chicago—		R.	H.	E.
Boston	000 0			
Chicago	300 0			

Tobin, Johnson, Earley and Berres, Masi.
Olsen, Mooty and McCullough.

At Cincinnati—		R.	H.	E.
Brooklyn	012 01			
Cincinnati	000 20			

Casey and Owen.
Walters and Lombardi.

National League

At NEW YORK:		R.	H.	E.
Cleveland	010 000 0			
New York	.000 001 0			

Feller and Hemsley.
Russo and Dickey.

At WASHINGTON:		R.	H.	E.
Detroit	...013			
Wash'ton	.000			

Newsom and Tebbetts.
Hudson and Early.

At PHILADELPHIA:		R.	H.	E.
St. Louis	..000 300			
Philadel.	..201 110			

Kennedy, Trotter, Caster and Grube. Swift.
Knott and Hayes.

Hitler in Parley With Nazi Chiefs

By PIERRE J. HUSS
Staff Correspondent International News

BERLIN, May 13 (INS).—Reichsfuehrer Adolf Hitler tonight summoned all German gauleiters (local leaders) and delivered a brief address.

Marshall Hermann Wilhelm Goering and other dignitaries flanked Hitler on the platform.

OVATION FOR HITLER

Announcing the session, which came soon after the Rudolf Hess sensation, the Nazi party headquarters said:

"The fuehrer addressed the assembly, whereafter he was given a tremendous ovation, thus demonstrating Germany's determination to win the war."

A "fixed obsession"—that by personal contact with British friends he could bring about an Anglo-German understanding—was blamed today for Deputy Nazi Leader Hess' astonishing flight to Scotland.

The offical German radio gave this explanation for Hess' action in the first definite German admission Hitler's number 3 Nazi actually is a prisoner of war in British hands.

SINGLE-HANDED PEACE

The broadcaster gave the impression that Hess for some time had been obsessed with the idea of swinging a single-handed peace that would benefit Nazi Germany and at the same time end war in the world.

"A check of Herr Hess' documents," the broadcast said, "revealed he apparently was obsessed with the conviction that personal contact with Britishers known to him personally would result in an Anglo-German understanding.

"It is known Hess recently followed the advice of certain astrologers and magicians whose responsibility in the tragedy will be examined."

The official correspondence

Continued on Page A, Col. Six

SUCH WEATHER!

By Ray Sonde
(The Mechanical Weather Gadget)

Being the sort of a gadget who likes his stimulants strong and his weather weak, I am happy to report that the storm center causing all this disturbance is losing strength pretty fast.

Up here at 53,000 feet, where I can't even get a good strong cup of coffee, I can see more showers in prospect for today and tonight, but clearing tomorrow and then some fine, fair May weather. So I passed this lowdown to Forecaster E. H. Jones.

Labor Candidate Victor in Minneapolis Mayor Race

MINNEAPOLIS, May 13 (AP). Mayor George E. Leach, who has served six 2-year terms in the last 20 years, conceded defeat today in yesterday's city primary election. He ran third in a field of five in which a labor-endorsed candidate was first.

AT NEW YORK (Am)—Cleveland 2, New York 1; final. 10 ins.
AT PHILADELPHIA (Am)—St. Louis 3, Phils 7, final.
AT WASHINGTON (Am)—Detroit 4, Washington 3; 5th inn.
AT CINCINNATI (Nat)—Brooklyn 4, Cincinnati 3; final.

AT ST. LOUIS (Nat)—New York 0, St. Louis 2; 3d inn.
AT PITTSBURGH (Nat)—Phils, 3, Pittsburgh *; final.
AT CHICAGO (Nat)—Boston 3, Chicago 4; 7th inn.

6TH RACE, SUFFOLK—Bell Tower, won, 5.80, 5.60, 4.20; Silver Tower, 2d, 5.60, 4.20; Prima Donna, 3d, 4.40. T., 1:39.

7TH RACE, BELMONT—Bonzar, won, 13.10, 4, 3; Yawl, 2d, 3.10, 2.40; Bright Gray, 3d, 3.60. T., 1:46.

7TH RACE, SUFFOLK—Miss Gallant, won, 5.60, 3.40, 3; Dizzy B, 2d, 14.20, 7.80; Maecaro, 3d, 10.20. T., 1:46.

(Earlier Race Results Will Be Found on Page 18)

Call-Bulletin Today

Virginia Forecast—
Fair Today and Monday, Warmer Monday.
(See Report on Page 7)

Richmond Times-Dispatch

The 1940 Census—
Reports during the last years the United States amounted to over a trillion (1,000 billion) board feet.
Virginia Population 1930 1940
SUSSEX County 13,100 12,485

91st Year Volume 91 Number 146 ...1903, at the Post Office ... as Second Class Matter. Richmond, Virginia, Sunday, May 25, 1941 Dial 3-4242 Calls The Times-Dispatch Ten Cents

Britain's Hood, 42,100 Tons, Is Sunk By Nazi Warship Bismarck in Atlantic

H. M. S. Hood, 42,100 Ton British Battle Cruiser, Long Considered the World's Most Powerful Warship

Big Vessel Explodes As Magazine Is Hit; 1,300 Men Are Lost

LONDON, (AP)—The 42,100-ton battlecruiser Hood, largest warship in the world, was blown to bits in the waters between Greenland and Iceland yesterday by the new German battleship Bismarck during a battle of grave historic import between the behemoths of the British and German navies.

The admiralty, in announcing this largest single naval loss the British navy has suffered since the war began, attributed it to an unlucky hit in a munitions magazine and expressed fear that more than 1,300 men had been killed.

The 35,000-ton Bismarck received damage and last night was fleeing, pursued by the remaining British warships, the announcement said.

The German high command, which first disclosed the destruction of the Hood in a special communique, placed the scene off Iceland and said the Bismarck and all the other German forces emerged from the battle virtually unscathed and continued their Atlantic operations. A British battleship was forced to withdraw, the Germans said.

Greenland, protection of which has been assumed by the United States, and Iceland, now under British occupation, are separated by a 250-mile stretch of water, the Strait of Denmark. It was apparently somewhere near the mouth of this strait, on the edge of the Western Hemisphere, that the battle occurred.

London Issues Communique

The brief British communique shocked the empire during celebration of the 122d anniversary of Queen Victoria's birth. It said:

"British naval forces intercepted early this morning off the coast of Greenland German naval forces, including the battleship Bismarck.

"The enemy were attacked, and during the ensuing action H. M. S. Hood (Captain R. Kerr) wearing the flag of Vice-Admiral L. E. Holland, received an unlucky hit in a magazine and blew up.

"The Bismarck has received damage and the pursuit of the enemy continues.

"It is feared there will be few survivors from H. M. S. Hood."

That was all.

Speculation Arises

Speculation immediately arose whether the Tirpitz, sister ship of the Bismarck and known to have been completed about the same time this year, also was in the Western Atlantic battle.

It was assumed that probably both these battleships and other German vessels—two more battleships may have been completed recently—slipped past the British blockade along the Norwegian coast on a raiding mission.

Apparently they went at once to the Greenland-Iceland area, for German authorities claimed yesterday that their submarines had sunk nine British ships near Greenland, and authoritative British quarters hinted on Friday that German raiders were near American shores.

The Hood's loss was tragically ironic in tha ther completion in 1920 was delayed for the installation of special armor to protect her vitals as a result of the lessons learned in the 1916 battle of Jutland.

Cost of $30,000,000

In that battle, at least two British capital ships were destroyed by exploded magazines.

Built at an original cost of more than £6,000,000 (normally $30,000,000), the Hood was reinforced heavily in a two-year overhaul in 1929-30.

She was rated a battlecruiser—one of three in the British Navy—because she was of battleship size and armament but was more lightly armored in the interests of speed.

In trials she turned up 32 knots, compared with an estimated 30-knot speed for the Bismarck. The 1930 additions to her armor, however, undoubtedly cut the Hood down a few knots. Her armor weighed 13,800 tons, or about one-third the total displacement, but still was regarded as less protection than modern battleships wear.

In gun-power, Hood and Bismarck were almost equal, each

Continued on Page 5, Column 5

Admiral Hood Died In Magazine Explosion

By The Associated Press

The British battlecruiser Hood was destroyed in the identical manner that Vice-Admiral Horace Hood died.

He was killed in the Battle of Jutland, May 31, 1916, when a shell from the German battleship Derfflinger hit the magazines of his battlecruiser Invincible, blowing the British vessel to bits and taking more than 1,000 lives.

The Hood was the third British warship of that name, in honor of the British admiral, Sir Samuel Hood of the eighteenth century.

Admiral Horace Hood was his lineal descendant.

Hood Victory, Gains in Crete Exalt Nazis

BERLIN, (AP)—The German high command proudly announced yesterday a Nazi penetration into Crete and the destruction of the British battle cruiser Hood.

Although the command's communique was the first official German disclosure of the attack which began on Crete on Tuesday, it was the sinking of the powerful British warship which most excited the imagination of Germans.

The German battleship Bismarck, newly-completed 35,000-ton pride of the new German fleet was matching guns with an enemy for the first time when it encountered the 42,100-ton Hood off Iceland yesterday and destroyed that largest of warships with a shot into an ammunition magazine.

Graf Spee Recalled

This outweighed the activities in Crete in the sentiment of more German commentators, especially because loss of the German pocket battleship Admiral Graf Spee in December, 1939, has rankled here ever since.

The National Zeitung of Essen said the sinking of the Hood "knocked out the last pillow from the illusoroy structure of British hopes for victory."

It called the Hood "the greatest warship of the world, pride of the English fleet, swagger piece of British naval strength, and most powerful bulwark of English sea prestige."

It said that "the German fleet unit remained as victor on the battlefield and continues its operations in the battle of the Atlantic." (The British Admiralty said the damaged Bismarck was being chased by other British ships.)

First Big Battle

It was stressed here that this was "the first meeting of heavy naval forces on both sides which fought through to the end."

[The Admiral Graf Spee took refuge in Montevideo, Uruguay, in December, 1939, after a running fight with three British cruisers, and later was blown up at Hitler's order rather than go out to meet the waiting British.]

The initial announcement concerning Crete was an unemotional one.

The western portion of Crete is firmly in the hands of German troops, the high command told German citizens, who up to late afternoon knew of the fighting there only through rumor and by confusing reports of foreign radio stations to which they are forbidden to listen.

Operations continue "according

Continued on Page 5, Column 4

Price Asks Air Lookout BeOrganized

Elliott to Head Volunteer Group

Governor Price yesterday directed the State Defense Council to take immediate steps to enroll 18,000 volunteers in a Virginia Aircraft Warning Service and designated Captain W. Glenn Elliott of Richmond as State organizer.

Captain Elliott, assigned to the general staff of Brigadier-General E. E. Goodwyn, commanding the Virginia Protective Force, presented details of the proposed aircraft warning service to the executive committee of the Defense Council at a meeting yesterday. Organization of the service would be one of the first steps in making operative the Civil Defense Program in the State.

The committee also heard plans for an experimental airplane landing strip adjacent to U. S. Route 17 and State Route 2, near Fredericksburg, a possible forerunner of some 400 similar strips in the United States. The area would be used as an emergency landing field and for parking space for Army motor convoys. The committee took under advisement the matter of indorsing the plans.

1,139 Observation Posts

Plans for the Aircraft Warning Service, prepared by Captain Elliott with the assistance of Army authorities during the last several months, call for the establishment of 1,139 observation posts to care for the entire State. There would be 111 organizers appointed to handle the task of selecting 1,139 chief observers, who in turn will appoint 15 observers to man local observation posts on a 24-hour a day basis.

The chief observer would be responsible for the operation of the post and he also will select the exact location within the area designated as his territory. Each observation post would be equipped with telephone service. Chief observers will be instructed not to make public the exact location of their stations.

Reports from listening posts would be made to "filter centers" to be located in Richmond and Roanoke, and these centers would report to State headquarters at Norfolk. Several hundred volunteers would be needed for the filter centers and State headquarters.

All Volunteer Workers

Governor Price said the entire organization would be manned with volunteer workers. There will be no paid jobs, nor will listening posts be rented. Except in rare instances, existing telephone facilities would be used.

Captain Elliott was expected to designate 111 organizers within the next two or three days. He said yesterday that plans for organizing are complete.

Organizers will be supplied with forms for chief observers to fill out, giving details concerning their vision, hearing, clarity of speech, education, experience and references which can be checked as to their character and loyalty. Chief observers will have similar forms filled out for their volunteer observers.

Women May Enroll

Captain Elliott said plans approved yesterday require the majority of volunteers to be men capable of service out-of-doors at any season of the year, but the plan does not preclude the enrollment of women volunteers, if they are qualified for the type of service desired.

While organized under the direction of the Virginia Defense Council, General James A. Anderson stated that regional defense councils will be assigned su-

Continued on Page 8, Column 4

Dovell Urges State Budget Postaudit

Moore Board Hears C. of C. Proposals

Speaker Ashton Dovell told the Moore Reorganization Commission yesterday that the General Assembly's greatest needs were a postaudit of the State budget and better legislative drafting service.

He expressed the hope that the commission would compare the cost of all ad interim boards, councils and commissions with the cost of more frequent legislative sessions.

The speaker, who recently withdrew from the race for the Democratic nomination for Governor, said he had kept quiet for 16 months while some legislators and some sections of the press blamed him for a big part in the defeat of the Governor's reorganization proposals in 1940. He said he was glad to see some of his critics admitting there was some justification for the defeat.

"Golden Opportunity"

He urged the commission to recommend a prescription "which will be taken," instead of offering a report embracing so much that it would merely become an addition to the State archives. He added that there was a "golden opportunity" to correlate conservation activities, and asserted North Carolina had outstripped Virginia in this respect.

Mr. Dovell spoke after the commission had heard J. Vaughan Gary, chairman, and Dr. James E. Pate of the College of William and Mary, research adviser, discuss in detail the reorganization proposals of the committee on taxation and government of the Virginia State Chamber of Commerce, made public just before the convening of the 1940 legislative session. Governor Price based his reorganization proposals, to a considerable extent, on the committee's recommendations.

In response to an inquiry from Junius P. Fishburn, Roanoke member of the Moore Commission, Mr. Gary said he thought the most important reorganization proposals offering the opportunity of enactment at the next session were the consolidation into three departments of the various agencies and divisions in the fields of finance, conservation and public welfare. Mr. Fishburn said a war psychology might make a thorough reorganization of the government impossible at the next session of the Assembly.

Mr. Gary explained that the State chamber did not contem-

Continued on Page 12, Column 3

U. S. Defense Output, Gaining Steadily, Insufficient at Year's End, Knudsen Says

WASHINGTON, (AP)—America's great defense drive was a year old yesterday, with William S. Knudsen, the director of production, asserting that airplane deliveries had increased 400 per cent in that period, 1,625 new industrial projects had been started and $15,200,000,000 worth of orders placed.

With the nation's factories now swinging into mass production of planes, tanks and guns, it was apparent too that the defense program was also taking on new directions and objectives. And just where it goes from this point may be indicated by President Roosevelt in a long-awaited fireside chat Tuesday night.

What he plans to say is, of course, a closely guarded secret, but millions will be at their radios listening intently for any indication of his views on the convoy issue, civilian defense and the question of repealing the neutrality act, a proposal that has had strong support from two members of his cabinet—Secretaries Knox and Stimson.

Nutrition Conference Set

One of the newest developments of the program is scheduled for Monday, however, a national nutrition conference for defense to be held under the direction of Paul V. McNutt, the Federal security administrator. Some 400 delegates are expected to attend the three day session. Among the questions to be discussed are:

How much responsibility should the Government assume and what should be the national economic policy with respect to nutrition? How best can the related problems of undernutrition and farm surpluses be solved? How can America send Britain the food she needs and, at the same time, give American families an adequate diet?

Another new development is the creation of the Office of Home Defense under Mayor Fiorello H. LaGuardia, mayor of New York City. Its task will be to train civilians in the protection of life, property and strategic points such as bridges and industrial plants in the event of any war emergency.

Must Promote Morale

In addition, the officials of the agency are to be charged with responsibility for promoting the national morale, advising on any schemes for the organized use of civilians in defense measures, and supervising the co-ordination of State and Federal home defense units.

Developments yesterday related to defense and the foreign situation included:

Senator Gillette (D., Iowa) said he had received reports that American companies had supplied war materials to Axis powers in "scores and scores of instances." He urged a congressional investigation.

It was learned that the United

Continued on Page 7, Column 5

Early Says President To Displease Foes

WASHINGTON, (AP)—President Roosevelt's restatement of the nation's foreign policy in a radio address Tuesday night, a White House official said yesterday, will "not be pleasing to opponents of democracy either at home or abroad."

Press Secretary Stephen Early made the statement when asked by reporters what the President would say.

R.A.F. Rejoins Crete Battle, Bags 14 Craft

Bombers Are Equipped As Distance Fighters

CAIRO, (SUNDAY)—(AP)—The R. A. F. was back in the Battle of Crete early today and big bombers, fitted out as long-range fighters, flew from Egyptian desert airdromes to engage and smash the German air-borne forces which are fighting to widen their hold on the Malemi sector in the west of the island.

In one day these makeshift fighters, plus regular bombers, accounted for 14 big troop transports, the R. A. F. announced—on Malemi Airdrome and on the beaches of Western Crete.

Confronted with overwhelming German air superiority at the beginning of the Nazi invasion on Tuesday, the R. A. F. withdrew from Crete then, but disclosed on Friday the action of the big bombers and fighters.

Distance Is Difficulty

Equipping some of the bombers as fighters was necessary because Crete is out of range of ordinary fighters operating from such distant bases, 450 or more miles from Malemi.

These planes, operating entirely from the mainland, made no attempt to land on Crete. Their assault followed up bombings of airports in Greece and a base on the Island of Melos, which the Germans are using as hopping-off places.

The announcement led to speculation whether some of the American-built Douglas DB-7 bombers were being diverted from the Middle East. The DB-7 is called the "Boston" when it is used as a light bomber in day operations and the "Havoc" when fitted for long-range night fighting.

Havocs Praised

The Havocs, whose range is 2,400 miles, have been highly effective in raids on occupied territory in Western Europe.

The Mediterranean fleet also is known to be supplied with American-built Grumman Martlet fighters, with a range of 1,100 miles. They probably are seeing action at Crete, too, if the fleet is using aircraft carriers near by.

In addition to the American-made craft, the British Middle East forces also are understood to have Blenheim IV models which have a 1,900-mile range and are usable as day bombers or fighters.

The Germans have managed to bring in some artillery and mortars in their effort to enlarge their foothold at Malemi, British sources acknowledged, and are continuing to fly in reinforcements.

The R. A. F., however, said large numbers of Junkers 52 troop transports were attacked on Friday on the beach and airdrome at

Continued on Page 4, Column 2

Hull Requested To Negotiate For Martinique

Peaceful Acquisition Of Bases Sought

WASHINGTON, (AP)—Senator Mead (D., N. Y.) urged Secretary Hull yesterday to undertake "friendly negotiations" with the Vichy government for the establishment of American defense bases on the island of Martinique and other French possessions in this hemisphere.

"Should this effort prove futile and should it be the judgment of our Government that the interests of this hemisphere are in jeopardy," Mead added in a letter to Hull, "Seizure by force should be accomplished without delay."

Acquisition of French island possessions has been advocated by other senators, among them Clark (D., Mo.), and Reynolds (D., N. C.), who have been critical of present administration foreign policy.

Pepper for Negotiations

Senator Pepper (D., Fla.) who proposed a week ago that the United States seize French islands in this hemisphere, agreed with Mead that negotiations for bases should be undertaken first.

"While we could take Martinique and other French possessions without difficulty," Pepper said, "we should try first to negotiate for bases and then see what happens."

Mead expressed belief that friendly negotiations initiated by this country would "invite the sympathy and support of a large portion of the French population."

"If a proposal to negotiate were rejected by the Vichy government," he told Hull, "such a rejection could hardly be interpreted as anything else than an action taken as a result of extreme pressure from the contemporary continental conqueror."

Methods Suggested

The New York senator suggested three methods by which the Vichy government might lease Western Hemisphere bases to the United States:

"1. By cancellation of a por-

Continued on Page 7, Column 1

Fight to Halt Plane Suicide Fatal to Two

WICHITA, Kas., (AP)—A suicide-intent flying student and his would-be rescuer crashed to their deaths yesterday after a dramatic struggle in the air for control of a pitching training plane.

Dead were William D. Woodward, 20, and John K. Blanpied, 21.

Coroner Lang P. Bowman said three notes found in Woodward's automobile indicated the youth intended to crash. One was addressed to a girl friend.

John Knightly, employee of the flying school who witnessed the takeoff and crash, told this story.

Woodward arrived at the school early yesterday and taxied out a two-seat, dual-control trainer of a type heavier than he was qualified to fly.

Climbed Onto Wing

Blanpied, also a student pilot and employed as a ground mechanic at the school, ran across the field and climbed onto a wing of the advancing craft. He reached into the cockpit and cut the switch, but Woodward threw the ignition on again and managed to get the plane into the air.

Again Blanpied cut the switch, and again Woodward caught up the sputtering motor.

Then as the rocking plane alternately lost and gained altitude, Blanpied climbed into the unoccupied front cockpit, gesturing and shouting.

He reached back, struggled with Woodward, but the latter put the plane into a dive.

The ship crashed in a meadow near the airport, strewing wreckage over an area of 150 yards. It did not burn. Both bodies were mangled.

The coroner said he planned no inquest if the notes found in Woodward's car were proved authentic. He added the youth's father, an oil man, had identified the handwriting as that of his son.

Former Film Actor Killed

HOLLYWOOD, (AP)—Leopoldine Konstantin, one-time Viennese actress, said yesterday British authorities had informed her that her son, Alexander Strakosch, former Hollywood actor, had been killed in a London air raid.

Eire Fears North Ireland Conscription

De Valera Calls Dail To Discuss Situation

DUBLIN, (AP)—Opposing British military conscription in the six counties of Northern Ireland which remain under the English crown, Prime Minister Eamon de Valera yesterday called the Irish Parliament, the Dail Eireann, into special session tomorrow to discuss the explosive situation.

The Northern Irish at present serve in Britain's armed forces only on a volunteer basis, but Prime Minister John Miller Andrews of Northern Ireland, who has urged conscription there, was in London yesterday with several of his cabinet ministers to discuss the situation with British Prime Minister Churchill.

Churchill has promised a statement at the next session of the House of Commons.

Eire Is Anxious

De Valera has expressed fears that conscription of the Northern Irish would bring the war closer to neutral Eire. Observers expected him to make a statement to the Dail on the economic and defense problems of Eire as well as on the military service question.

Reports from Belfast, capital of Northern Ireland, told of an anti-conscription movement already started there by nationalists, who favor unification of the six northern counties with the 26 counties of independent Eire.

In language similar to a 1917 resolution on the same subject, they proposed the following pledge:

"Denying the right of the Churchill government to enforce compulsory service in Ireland, we pledge ourselves solemnly to one another to resist conscription by the most effective means at our disposal, consistent with the law of God."

Joseph Cardinal Macrory, Catholic primate of all Ireland, summed up the situation in this fashion:

"We are convinced that any such attempt (at conscription)

Contined on Page 5, Column 8

Richmond Called On to Make Sacrifice for U. S. Defense

Two cities in the United States, one of them Richmond, have been called on by national defense officials to make a specific contribution to the nation's defense program, but details of the plan have not yet been made public.

The State Defense Council, it was announced yesterday, has received the call from Washington. The matter has been turned over to the Richmond-Hopewell-Petersburg Regional Defense Council for execution.

While defense leaders here indicate they were not ready to let much be known about the Washington appeal, they did say that it would mark Richmond's first definite contribution—something of a sacrifice—to America's defense efforts.

Full information on the entire plan will be announced Tuesday afternoon, according to regional council headquarters.

In addition to Richmond City proper, the appeal will affect Henrico and Manchester Magisterial District of Chesterfield County.

Commenting on the forthcoming announcement, Dr. Douglas S. Freeman, chairman of the State Defense Council, said the special call from Washington will entail definite sacrifices from the people of the affected area.

"No other community in the United States, save one, is being requested simultaneously for this service," he declared. The metropolitan area is honored and challenged. Your Council of Defense asks that every family in this district be prepared for the announcement Tuesday."

On the Inside

FIVE SECTIONS—88 PAGES

BISMARCK SUNK

WALL ST. STATE ST. COMPLETE

Boston Traveler

New England's Largest Evening Circulation — Complete Associated Press and United Press Wire Services

EST. 1825 — 116th YEAR — NO. 275 TUESDAY, MAY 27, 1941 44 PAGES 2 CENTS

(AP Photo)

SUNK BY BRITISH—The 35,000-ton German battleship Bismarck, which was sent to the bottom by British naval units. (The above photo was released by Berlin.)

Ruth's Husband Aids Erring Wife on Stand

Greets Her with Friendly Smile; Father Sobs as He Tells Story

By WILLIAM G. SCHOFIELD AND CHARLES ASHLEY

Kenneth A. Steadman, with a broad smile of greeting for the wife accused of murdering her illicit-love partner, stepped into superior court today and testified that the mother of his child threatened suicide more than a month before the body of Robert G. Emery, 26, was found in her West End apartment.

DEFENDS ERRING WIFE

Coming to the defense of his erring wife, Ruth, 27, the tall, young Pittsburgh insurance man gave testimony adding to Mrs. Steadman's defense, which claims that Emery died in a suicide pact and not in a strangulation murder.

Steadman's appearance followed closely the appearance of Francis J. Stanwood, father of the defendant, and the outbreak of sobs from father and daughter that accompanied the gray-haired man's testimony.

QUICK PLAY OF EMOTIONS

Steadman, slender and soft-spoken, was called shortly before the noon recess and his entrance into the court produced a quick by-play of emotions, between himself and his wife.

Before entering the court, he had not faced his wife since before the date of Emery's death, last Jan. 21.

As he strode down the aisle, Ruth turned in her prisoner's pen and watched his approach. She caught his glance, and flashed him a tentative, half-cmile—as though uncertain of its reception.

Steadman answered with a broad, friendly smile that brought an immediate response from his wife. Her face lighted up.

"Hi, Ruth," he said, amiably, as he passed her seat.

MURMURS HER ANSWER

Her answer was a soft-spoken murmur, accompanied by a look of greater animation and confidence than she had shown since the trial began.

He was questioned by Flynn.

DRAMATIC HIGHLIGHT

In the most dramatic moments of the trial to date, Stanwood was called to the stand by defense counsel Edward F. Flynn and stalked down the courtroom aisle, glancing neither right nor left as he passed the prisoner's pen where his daughter is awaiting the end of her trial.

On the stand, he told of ordering Emery to "get the hell out"—and he told of the moment when his daughter, Ruth, threw her arms around his neck before going with Emery to the West End apartment where the killing took place.

The 27-year-old defendant, who had appeared more smiling and self-composed than at any time during her trial, abruptly lost her poise as her father was called to the courtroom.

RUTH'S CALM BREAKS

She went rigid and shook her head violently when his name was called.

As Stanwood strode into the courtroom, she lost her poise completely.

She leaned from the prisoner's pen with a passionate plea, as he walked by.

"Dad," she cried. "Please don't—don't!"

Stanwood passed her without a glance, and took the stand.

Within a few moments after start-

(Continued on Page Twenty)

Four Escape As House Falls

Condemned Chelsea Building Crashes

Four persons missed death by a matter of seconds today when a 3½-story brick building, 32-34 Walnut street, Chelsea, against which condemnation proceedings had been started, split in two and one-half of the structure collapsed, raining tons of brick and rubble on an adjoining house.

Isaac Cohen, 50, Chelsea contractor, pushed Mrs. Lena Kitiver, 48, of 28 Walnut street, and Abe Sadetsky, a carpenter who had been building a new porch on the Kitiver home, into the house a split second before the porch was buried under a crashing cascade of bricks.

LEFT BEFORE COLLAPSE

George Valdman, 48, last remaining occupant of 34, the part of the building which remained standing, had been moving his furniture out of the house. He was ordered to the street by Sergt. Valentine Elmore of the Chelsea police a moment before the collapse came.

The building, which originally contained four tenements, had shown so many signs of impending

(Continued on Page Nine)

Strike Stops Elevators In Woolworth Building

NEW YORK, May 27 (AP)—A strike of elevator operators in the 60-story, 792-foot Woolworth building, sixth tallest in New York, halted up-and-down traffic at lunch time today.

The Manhattan local of the Building Service Employes' International Union (AFL) said 139 elevator and maintenance men were called out because, it charged, the building owners had refused to reach an agreement with the union and were not meeting the prevailing rate of $29.50 a week for operators.

Traveler Index

Conscription Off in Ulster

British Government Relents After Talks

LONDON, May 27 (AP)—Prime Minister Winston Churchill yielded today to Irish pressure and told the House of Commons that enforcement of conscription in Northern Ireland would be "more trouble than it is worth."

"We have made a number of inquiries," he said, "in various directions with the result that we have come to the conclusion that at the present time, although there would be no dispute about our rights or our merits, it (conscription) would be more trouble than it is worth to enforce such a policy."

The House cheered Churchill and cried "No" when Sir Hugh O'Neill asked if it would not make "a rather bad impression throughout the Empire that once again the government has burked this issue because of pressure from Southern Ireland."

Churchill explained simply that "we thought it better."

O'Neill asked if the government of Northern Ireland thought conscription "could and ought to be applied" and Churchill said "Yes."

RACE RESULTS
AT SUFFOLK DOWNS

FIRST RACE

Cuckoo (Bodiou)	12.40	6.40	3.40
Allmar (Sisto)	—	5.00	3.60
Legion (Hettinger)	—	—	3.60

Time—1:40 1-5. Florian 2nd, Henryeis Pick, Bonnie Buzz, Jim Blazes, Travis L., Nopolosa Rojo, Blackmail, The Loom and Lovick also ran.

SECOND RACE

Village Belle (Smith)	7.80	4.60	3.40
Balmorhea (SConza)	—	13.60	8.00
Moo (Atkinson)	—	—	7.00

Time—1:13 3-5. Unimond, Delicto, Ohio's Choice, Back Number, Cove Spring, Mate Watch, Hendersonian and Miss High Hat also ran.

DAILY DOUBLE PAID $53.60

Rain Hampers Youth Search

Maine Woods Hide Two Lost 48 Hours

KOKADJO, Me., May 27 (AP)—Continued rain added today to the perils of Paul Atkinson, 12, and Melvin Davis, 11, lost in the Kokadjo wilderness since Sunday, as new posses joined Legionnaires in the search for the youths.

Piscataquis county commissioners and Red Cross officials headed a posse of approximately 100 men assembled during the morning hours. Food and other supplies were gathered to meet needs of the searchers.

Rain fell throughout the night turning many of the woods roads into quagmires, impeding the advance of the searching parties. Much of the terrain in the lake-dotted region is swampland.

Aerial Torpedoes, Naval Shell Fire Avenge the Hood

FDR EXTENDS TALK TO TELL U. S. POLICIES

President Will Remove All Doubt In Fireside Chat at 10:30 Tonight

By LYLE C. WILSON

WASHINGTON, May 27 (UP)—White House Secretary Stephen Early indicated today that President Roosevelt will outline American foreign policy in detail in his fireside chat tonight. The speech will be extended 15 minutes longer than previously anticipated, to 45 minutes.

TO DISPEL ALL DOUBT

"On the speech," Early said, "I think you can say that by Wednesday morning there will no longer be any doubt as to what the national policy of this government is."

Early asked radio networks, which previously had granted the President 30 minutes for tonight's address, to give him an additional 15 minutes. He explained that as the speech was being completed, the President found that he could not compress what he wants to say into half an hour.

Accordingly, Early said, the speech will run almost 45 minutes—which would make its wordage approximately 4000 to 4500 words.

CANCELS ALL ENGAGEMENTS

The President cancelled all engagements today, including his 4 P. M. press conference, to concentrate on final preparation of the address, which all evidence indicates may be historically decisive.

Early's disclosures come as Con-

(Continued on Page Fifteen)

FDR Asks 3 Billion For Planes

By MACK JOHNSON

WASHINGTON, May 27 (UP)—President Roosevelt today asked Congress for $3,319,000,000 in new appropriations to provide more planes for the army and navy.

The request, made in a letter to Speaker Sam Rayburn, Tex., asked for $2,790,000,000 for planes for the army and $529,000,000 for naval planes.

The request reflected an imminent tremendous expansion of aircraft production schedules, but gave no details as to number and type of planes to be produced.

It was understood the army request included an item for several thousand heavy bombers.

Bridges Warns Of Nazi Victory

Tells Advertisers 'We in America Could Lose Shirts by Remote Control'

Other stories, and pictures, of the convention of the Advertising Federation of America pages 2, 3, 4, 5 and 6.

By BOB SIBLEY

If Hitler armies roll over England, Germany will control the commerce of the world, even if Hitler does not carry out his threat to visit his might directly upon America, U. S. Senator H. Styles Bridges declared here today, scoffing at the theory that today's war was merely another of Europe's recurring conflicts. And England cannot stand alone, he warned.

GUEST AT LUNCHEON

The Republican senator from New Hampshire was speaker at the luncheon session of the New England Newspaper Advertising Executives Association at the Parker House, held in conjunction with the 27th annual convention of the Advertising Federation of America, with many other group meetings at the Statler, Copley-Plaza and elsewhere.

If Germany controls world commerce, "the farmers of America would be forced to compete with the vassal regions of Europe, Asia, Africa and South America," Senator Bridges declared.

"There are those," he said, "who persist in the belief that this is merely another of Europe's periodic wars . . . that no matter what the outcome . . . life as we know it will continue wiithout interruption.

"To such beliefs neither my mind nor my conscience will allow me to subscribe.

"Hitler has said that even the

(Continued on Page Two)

39 from Torpedoed Boat Rescued by Coast Guard

WASHINGTON, May 27 (AP)—The coast guard announced today the cutter General Greene had picked up 39 survivors of a torpedoed merchant ship somewhere in the Atlantic today.

Officials refused to give the exact location of the rescue, the name or nationality of the sunken ship or to say whether the sinking occurred in the western hemisphere.

The survivors, rescued from two lifeboats, were quoted as saying that three other lifeboats containing about 60 more men were still to be accounted for. The General Greene was searching for them in heavy fog.

The ship was torpedoed yesterday. The only hint of its location was the fact that the Greene spotted the lifeboats about 4 A. M. (EST) today while on ice patrol in the north Atlantic. This patrol usually is off Greenland.

FORT DE FRANCE, Martinique, May 27 (UP)—The 8379-ton French freight and passenger steamer Winnipeg was captured by a "foreign warship" off the south coast of Martinique last night, the central information service of Martinique announced today.

U. S. Treasury Balance

WASHINGTON, May 27—Balance today, $1,985,574,142.

Customs receipts, $32,623,298.

American-Made Airplane Discovers Fleeing Ship, Calls British to the Kill

Pictures and Stories on Bismarck Sinking—Pages 17, 18, 19, 36, 37

By NED RUSSELL

LONDON, May 27 (UP)—British aerial torpedoes and shellfire sank the new German battleship Bismarck in the Atlantic at 11 A. M. (5 A. M., Boston time), today. The Royal Navy thus exacted vengeance for the Bismarck's sinking, 72 hours ago, of Britain's pride, the world's largest warship, the 42,100-ton Hood.

His eyes gleaming with excitement, Prime Minister Winston Churchill personally announced the end of the Bismarck.

TRAPPED ON RUN FOR PROTECTION

Churchill made the announcement in the House of Commons and personally told the story of how British sea and naval power finally had closed in on the great German battleship and brought her to her end.

The Bismarck went to her death in the Atlantic as she ran for the protection of the Nazi-held French coast.

German communiques located the scene of the action 400 sea miles west of Brest, some 2000 miles from Denmark straits, between Greenland and Iceland, where the epic encounter started Saturday morning with the sinking of the Hood.

U. S. MADE PLANE CALLS AVENGERS

An American-made airplane signalled the word that brought British torpedo planes and warships racing to end the Bismarck's crowded, brief career.

The plane, a consolidated four-motored flying boat, sighted Bismarck about noon yesterday and crackled out an urgent wireless warning, advising the Royal Navy of her position and that she was racing for the French coast.

Charging across the sea came units of the Royal Navy, the ancient aircraft carrier Ark Royal—often "sunk" in Nazi communiques but still in action—apparently well up in front.

SWOOP ON BISMARCK

Within flying range of the Bismarck, the Ark Royal released a covey of swordfish torpedo planes. The aerial destroyers which have wrought such great destruction against the Italian fleet in the Mediterranean.

The planes swooped down on the Bismarck, her speed probably already somewhat reduced from torpedo hits and minor shell damage suffered in Saturday's curtain-raiser action.

Planes vs. Warships

Maj. A. P. deSeversky, international authority on aircraft, compares the merits of aircraft and battleships in a thrilling article on Page 29 of today's Boston Traveler.

This time the torpedoes went to a vital spot. One well-aimed shot apparently smashed into the Bis-

(Continued on Page Eighteen)

6 Warships Lost In Cretan Battle

German Claim of 25 Is Refuted; Nazi Dead in Fighting Now 18,000

[By the Associated Press]

CAIRO, Egypt, May 27—Britain's Mediterranean fleet has lost two cruisers and four destroyers in the raging week-end battle of Crete, but has balked German efforts to land sea-borne troops, and the epic struggle on land now "hangs in the balance," the British announced today.

1016 OF CREWS SAVED

(In London the admiralty announced that it had accounted for 60 officers and 956 men from the ships lost. It said there was good reason to believe that others will be reported later.)

Besides the sunken ships high official quarters said that two battleships and several other cruisers had been damaged, but said "there is no question whatever of our naval position in the eastern Mediterranean."

The allied garrison on Crete was said to be receiving reinforcements while it was admitted that the Germans still were parachuting down troops in swarms.

With these reinforcements, the Middle East command said the Germans had been able to broaden their major foothold at Malemi airport, west of Canea, the Crete capital. The imperial forces were forced back to new positions.

The British asserted heavy losses still were being inflicted on the Germans in fierce hand-to-hand fighting and Greek sources placed the number of Nazi dead at 18,000. Of these, these said 5000 were drowned in attempts to land by sea.

LIST OF LOST WARSHIPS

The British announced that the warships lost—all victims of Axis planes—were the cruisers Glouces-

(Continued on Page Two)

THE WEATHER

U. S. Official Forecast

SHOWERS TONIGHT AND TOMORROW

Sunrise 5:13, Sunset 8:10

Moon sets 9:20 P. M.

High tide 12:33 A. M., 1:03 P. M.

Weather Map, Report on Page

Variable Cloudiness And Continued Warm; Thundershowers Likely Wednesday Afternoon.

The News-Sentinel

The News-Sentinel Is Home Owned, Home Edited and Home Read.

News—Established 1874
Sentinel—Established 1833

FORT WAYNE, INDIANA, TUESDAY, MAY 27, 1941.

36 PAGES—PRICE 3 CENTS

British Avenge Sinking Of Hood

$200,000 For New Homes Here Given Approval By FHA

Firm Formed By Greater Fort Wayne Development Corp. Outlines Project.

Residences Planned In Industrial Area

Harvester Park, Shady Brook Additions Chosen For Building Project.

A line of credit for $200,000 has been approved by the Federal Housing Administration to the Harvester Park Housing Corporation, an affiliate of the Greater Fort Wayne Development Corporation, for building a substantial number of new homes here to meet the need created by this city's part in the national defense program.

Word of the action of the FHA in Washington was received here by A. H. Schaaf, secretary and general manager of the Development Corporation, from R. Earl Peters, State FHA director, at Indianapolis. The line of credit was given under the new title six of the FHA which provides for insuring mortgages of homes in areas designated as vital to the defense program. This city has been designated as such an area.

Mr. Schaaf said the new homes, which will cost from $3,000 to $4,000 each, are to be erected in Harvester Park Addition and Shady Brook Addition. These residential additions are in the near vicinity of this city's industrial area in the southeast section of the city.

Final Plans Not Made.

Final details have not been ironed out concerning the residential building project, but it is anticipated that it will be started in the near future. Mr. Schaaf said that although he cannot say how many homes are to be built, a substantial number are planned. All of the sum approved by the FHA is to be spent for this purpose.

Mr. Schaaf said directors of the Development Corporation have been working for several months on the housing program and recently formed the Harvester Park Housing Corporation to carry it out.

Homes For Defense Workers.

Directors of the corporation felt the organization should do its part in aiding Fort Wayne to meet its increased housing needs because of the expansion of the many local industries due to the defense program and particularly to supply homes for defense workers who are to be employed by the new Studebaker Corporation airplane gear factory under construction on New Haven Avenue Extended, Mr. Schaaf said. The Studebaker plant is expected to be in operation next Fall.

Although several Fort Wayne builders are considering plans for projects under the FHA title for building homes in defense areas, the line of credit given the Harvester Park Housing Corporation is the first approval granted here under the act. Other projects are expected to be approved soon as the city will need several hundred additional residential units, according to realtors and builders.

The Weather

Tuesday, May 27, 1941.

Fort Wayne and vicinity: Variable cloudiness and continued warm tonight; Wednesday variable cloudiness with a few scattered thundershowers likely in afternoon and continued warm; moderate to fresh south to west winds.

WARM

Indiana: Fair to partly cloudy and continued warm tonight and Wednesday; a few scattered thundershowers Wednesday afternoon in extreme north.

Lower Michigan: Considerable cloudiness, occasional showers and thunderstorms Wednesday and in north and central portions tonight; not much change in temperature.

Ohio: Generally fair and continued warm except for local thundershowers and not quite so warm in extreme north portion tonight; Wednesday generally fair and continued warm in south and scattered thundershowers and not so warm in north portion.

Extended weather forecast for the period from 7:30 p.m. May 27 to 7:30 p.m. May 31. (Central daylight time):

Region of the Great Lakes: The temperature will average above normal except near normal Lake Superior region. Much above normal lower lakes at beginning of period, becoming cooler by end of period. Precipitation will average heavy with rather frequent showers.

Upper Mississippi Valley and Indiana: The temperature will average above normal except near normal Minnesota, much above Illinois and Indiana. The precipitation will average heavy, except moderate south and Central Illinois and Indiana in the form of frequent showers.

Local weather data for the 24 hours ending at 12 noon.

Central Standard Time

Temperatures at—

1 p.m.	83	1 a.m.	72
2 p.m.	84	2 a.m.	72
3 p.m.	84	3 a.m.	72
4 p.m.	84	4 a.m.	71
5 p.m.	83	5 a.m.	70
6 p.m.	80	6 a.m.	72
7 p.m.	74	7 a.m.	74
8 p.m.	73	8 a.m.	77
9 p.m.	72	9 a.m.	80
10 p.m.	72	10 a.m.	82
11 p.m.	71	11 a.m.	85
Midnight	72	Noon	87

Extremes of temperature:
Highest during the 24 hours 87.
Highest on this date last year 66.
Lowest during the 24 hours 70.
Lowest on this date last year 52.
Highest since the first of the month 91 on the 22nd.
Lowest since the first of the month 36 on the 11th.
Relative humidity at—
6:30 p.m. 33; 6:30 a.m. 70; 12 noon 43.
Barometer, reduced to sea-level (inches):
6:30 p.m. 29.94; 6:30 a.m. 30.02.
Precipitation (inches):
Total for the 24 hours 0.
Total since the first of the month 1.82.
The stage of the Maumee River at 7 a.m. was 0.6 feet.

Six British Vessels Lost Near Crete

London Admits Two Cruisers, Four Destroyers Sent To Bottom.

CAIRO, Egypt, May 27.—(A.P.)—Britain's Mediterannean fleet has lost two cruisers and four destroyers in the raging week-old battle of Crete but has balked German efforts to land sea-borne troops and the epic struggle on land now "hangs in the balance," the British announced today.

Besides the sunken ships high official quarters said that two battleships and several other cruisers had been damaged.

The Allied garrison on Crete was said to be receiving reinforcements while it was admitted that the Germans still were parachuting down troops in swarms.
Middle East command said the Ger-
With these reinforcements, the mans had been able to broaden their major foothold at Malemi airport, west of Canea, the Crete capital. The imperial forces were forced back to new positions.

The British asserted heavy losses still were being inflicted on the Germans in fierce hand-to-hand fighting and Greek sources placed the number of Nazi dead at 18,000. Of these, these said 5,000 were drowned in attempts to land by sea.

Germany's air-borne soldiers on Crete, "after the occupation of several localities and successful fights, continue their advance according to schedule." the German high command announced.

(Dive-bombers, with effective attacks on British positions, troop concentrations and field camps, aided the land forces, the communique said.)

British fighter planes shot down five troop-laden German planes at Malemi airdrome near Canea yesterday and destroyed several other Nazi planes, the RAF Middle East command announced today.

SITUATION GRAVE

British Say Issue In Crete Hangs In Balance.

LONDON, May 27.—(I.N.S.)—The situation in Crete is grave and the issue "hangs in the balance," Prime Minister Winston Churchill told the House of Commons today.

"Fighting has been most bitter and severe," he said, "although the enemy's losses up to the present have been much heavier than our own.

"We have been unable to prevent the further descent of air-borne troops. The weight of the enemy's attack has grown from day to day.

"The battle has swayed backwards and forwards with indescribable fury around Canea, Retimo and Heraclion (Candia). Reinforcements of men and supplies continue to reach General Freyberg (B. C. Freyberg, British commander in Crete).

"At the moment, the issue hangs in the balance. Our navy has prevented landing of sea-borne expeditions, and

(Continued on Page 4, Column 5)

Pride Of German Navy Is Sunk

The Bismarck.

Delay Likely In Induction Of Youths

July 1 Registrants Not To Be Called Until Older Class Exhausted.

WASHINGTON, May 27.—(U.P.)—Selective service officials today planned to dust off the historic World War draft "goldfish bowl" again for a second peace-time national lottery in mid-July to determine order numbers for new 21-year-old registrants.

Affected by the proposed drawing will be men who have become 21 since last October 16 and who, under a proclamation issued by President Roosevelt yesterday, must register for selective service on July 1. It was estimated that between 1,250,000 and 1,300,000 men are involved. Officials said present plans, subject to change after further study, provide for classification of the new registrants at the bottom of the list of men 21 to 35 who registered last October 16 and whose order numbers were drawn in the first peacetime lottery last October 29.

Unless the Army requests a big allotment of men under 30 or 26, it was said, the new registrants will not be called up for induction until the list of eligible men in the initial registration has been exhausted. The July 1 registration will be handled by local draft boards. Officials said plans for it were made well in advance of Mr. Roosevelt's proclamation, and that "we are all set." The October registration, involving approximately 16,000,000 men, was handled mostly by school teachers and other volunteer workers. No date for the proposed lottery was fixed. Selective service headquarters said it probably would be held within two weeks after registration.

Railroad Pier Burns With Loss Of One Life

JERSEY CITY, N. J., May 27.—(I.N.S.)—The captain of a railroad car float was burned to death today and 25 cars and two barges were destroyed when fire swept an 1820-foot Jersey City pier of the Pennsylvania Railroad.

For a time, the fire threatened large quantities of defense construction materials nearby.

South Bend Extends Daylight Saving Time

SOUTH BEND, Ind., May 27.—(A.P.)—South Bend today is on a six-month schedule of daylight saving time. The city council last night extended the period to the last Sunday in October. Previously the city always reverted to standard time the last Sunday in September. The period commences the last Sunday in April.

Five Escape From Indiana Prison Farm

Honor Prisoners Make Getaway; Sleepy Guard Is Dismissed.

MICHIGAN CITY, Ind., May 27.—(I.N.S.)—Escape of five convicts within two days was disclosed by State Prison officials today coincident with the dismissal of a dormitory guard who admitted that he fell asleep at his post.

Three trusties stole a prison truck and fled from the Summit Honor Farm 10 miles south of here early this morning, while a search still was in progress for two convicts who escaped from the same farm yesterday.

Those who escaped today were Leonard L. Goheen, 36, sentenced from Kokomo in 1938 to one to five years for petit larceny; Menlo Williams, 33, sentenced from Bedford in 1939 to one to 10 years for vehicle taking, and Arthur Smith, 32, Negro, sentenced from Marion in February of 1940 to two years for second degree burglary.

Prison officials said the trio apparently pushed a ton and a half truck away from the institution grounds and then started the motor. They were missed at the 4:30 a.m. checkup, having last been seen at 2:45 a.m. by a dormitory officer.

Authorities said the guard, who admitted he fell asleep after the 2:45 a.m. check, was dismissed, but they declined to reveal his name.

Frederick Coy, 30, serving one to five years for passing a fraudulent check in Greene County, and Ernest Van Cleave, 34, serving from one to 10 years for vehicle taking in Putnam County, escaped from the Summit Honor Farm yesterday.

Coy, who came to the prison June 18, 1940, would have been eligible for a parole on June 18, 1941. Van Cleave was sentenced April 22, 1941.

Must Repay Bonuses

NEW YORK, May 27.—(I.N.S.)—George W. Hill, president of the American Tobacco Company, and four vice-presidents of the firm, today were under a New York State supreme court order to return to the company $2,018,033.44 paid to them in bonuses.

The other officers of the company affected by the decision are George W. Hill Jr., son of the president, Paul M. Hahn, Vincent Riggio, and Charles P. Neiley. It was understood that attorneys for the men will make an appeal from the decision.

Britain Wants United States To Get Into The War At Once

WASHINGTON, May 27.—(I.N.S.)—Great Britain, is was learned today, wants the United States to enter the war at once.

Britain's leaders have made this clear to representatives of the American Government. The British desire for American entry into the conflict has been expressed informally but nonetheless frankly.

American officials are being given the impression that Britain may not be able to hold out beyond this year unless the United States enters the war.

The British not only want the assistance of the United States Navy, but an American air force as well.

Britain's leaders want the United States Navy to assume a substantial share of the burden of protecting by all necessary means the shipment of war supplies across the Atlantic.

By "all necessary means," the British are understood to refer not only to convoys, which is considered by them defensive action, but also to the establishment of a safe sea lane across the Atlantic which would be kept free of German submarines, raiders and long-range bombers.

The British now take the position that the convoy work which their navy is called upon to perform alone is putting too great a strain on the fleet. They want to be relieved of some of that work so that they can detach stronger units of the British fleet to search for German naval squadrons and surface raiders on the high seas as well as to reinforce their Mediterranean fleet.

The British also believe American entry into the war would have a tremendous psychological effect on the German people; would bring Turkey into the war on the side of the democracies and would serve to speed up this country's defense program.

They believe that the advantages to be derived from American entry into the conflict would be worth the risk of Japan's entry into the war under the terms of its alliance with the Axis powers.

This view is by no means shared by American diplomatic experts, who would prefer to give Japan an opportunity to back out of its pledge to the Axis by letting Germany or Italy resort to the first aggressive action against this country.

The British also take the position that they now need American crews to man the warplanes that are being sent over. They claim the British pilots are not familiar with the mechanical equipment of the American machines and that valuable time is lost getting them acquainted with the planes.

Britain, authoritative quarters disclosed, already has persuaded American aircraft companies to start sending American mechanics over with the new planes. The number of American mechanics that have gone over is not known, but they are expected to increase as time goes on.

Although Britain's leaders now are, in private conversations, speaking quite frankly of the urgent need for American entry into the war, there are no indications that President Roosevelt has been "sold" on the idea. Secretary of the Navy Knox and Secretary of War Stimson are known to favor American entry as soon as possible, but other leading members of the Administration are believed to be opposed to any such move unless the United States is attacked first by the Axis powers.

Roosevelt Is Asked Not To Get Into War

Letter From Congressmen To Be Delivered Before Broadcast Tonight.

The address of President Roosevelt, beginning at 9:30 CDT tonight, will be broadcast by CBS, MBS and both networks of NBC.

WASHINGTON, May 27.—(I.N.S.)—Headed by Senator Wheeler (D), Mont., the congressional non-interventionists meet today—in anticipation of President Roosevelt's fireside chat—to draft a formal request that he "take no steps to put this country into war" unless approved by Congress.

At the same time, the so-called anti-war group will inform the President that they propose to conduct a national referendum "on the issue of peace or war."

The national referendum program, coupled with the request that Congress be given an opportunity to pass on all momentous questions pertaining to the emergency, will be forwarded to the White House before the President delivers his address tonight.

The letter to the President will be given final approval at a meeting in the office of Wheeler. Senate and House non-interventionists will attend. A tentative draft of the letter which has not yet been approved by the group says:

"We hope in your radio address to the Nation you will give renewed assurance that you will take no step to put this country into war without the approval of the people through their congressional representatives, in the constitutional American way."

Informing the President of the intended referendum the letter adds:

"The members of the Senate and the House of Representatives who indorse this letter realize the tremendous responsibility of your high office and are mindful of your desire to translate public opinion into constructive action on the basis of what is best for America.

"There can be no other yardstick when confronted with the momentous decision of war or peace, which transcends all party lines and threatens the national life and destiny of America. . . .

Dangers Seen.

"We undertake this program because we have lately seen the dangers involved in taking a nation into war—particularly an undeclared war—when the will of the people is divided or unknown."

The letter also says that "the American people have had no opportunity to vote on this greatest of all issues," and that "we, therefore, propose to conduct without delay a national referendum on the issue of peace or war."

The letter seeks to assure the President that the question relating to the issue of peace or war "will be worded in the clearest and briefest language so that there can be no misunderstanding."

"The returns will be audited insuring a reliable result," it continued. "In addition we shall ask or challenge all the daily newspapers

(Continued on Page 4, Column 5)

News And Feature Index

Great German Battleship Bismarck Sent To Bottom In Naval-Aerial Battle

Pride Of Hitler's Fleet Destroyed After Being Crippled By Planes.

Went Down Fighting, Says Berlin

Accompanying Nazi Cruiser Prince Eugen Is Still Being Sought.

LONDON, May 27.—(I.N.S.)—Hunted down by every available ship and plane of Britain's avenging Navy, the 35,000-ton German battleship Bismarck was demolished and sent to the bottom of the Atlantic today in retribution for sinking of the British battle-cruiser Hood.

The Bismarck, launched on February 14, 1939, at Hamburg with the blessings of Reichsfuehrer Adolf Hitler himself, was crippled by aerial torpedoes.

Her propellors smashed, her gear out of control, the Bismarck was circling aimlessly at some unspecified spot in the trackless North Atlantic when the "coup de grace" was administered.

The Bismarck sank in broad daylight at 11 a.m.

Officially announcing the victory, First Lord of the Admiralty A. V. Alexander said:

"Aircraft from the Ark Royal put two torpedoes into the Bismarck last night and joined the Royal Navy in putting the finishing touches this morning . . .

"We suffered severe fighting in the Mediterranean last week.

(The Admiralty admitted loss of two cruisers and four destroyers.)

"This has been one of the greatest and most epic battles of the war. Many officers and men made the greatest sacrifice.

"We must put more in all the time if we are to get more out of final victory."

Immediately belief was that credit for the smashing British victory would go to Royal Air Force planes of the coastal command. In any case, they obviously played a major role in sinking one of the best and one of the newest ships of Hitler's admittedly redoubtable fleet.

Pending further details by the Admiralty, it was not known whether the Bismarck struck her flag or went down with guns blazing.

(Berlin announced that the Bismarck fought until the last.)

If the former was the case, naval officials said, some or all of the crew may have been rescued. Otherwise at least a thousand men lost their lives.

Bombers Could Not Aid.

Scene of the sinking was well out of range of any German bomber assistance from French air bases, leading to belief it was in the open Atlantic, well south of Denmark Strait between Greenland and Iceland.

Lloyds of London followed tradition by ringing the famed Lutine bell to announce the victory. This capital—bombed to bits in places and sagged down by disaster to the Hood—suddenly took on a Mardi Gras atmosphere. Toasts were drunk in cafes and restaurants. Even the magistrates at famed Old Bailey halted court proceeding to announce the event. Virtually all newspapers carried this headline:

"Our navy gloriously avenges the Hood!"

The 35,000-ton Nazi dreadnaught, which on Saturday fought and destroyed the British battle cruiser Hood in a brief engagement off Greenland, was hammered to the bottom by British forces that swarmed to the kill in one of the greatest naval hunts in all history.

A brief Admiralty announcement gave no details of how or where the Bismarck was destroyed or whether its officers and men were rescued. The communique merely said:

"The German battleship Bismarck has been sunk by our naval forces.

"Details of the operations will be announced as soon as possible."

(Authoritative German sources revealed that a British torpedo had hit the Bismarck's propellors, rendering the giant ship impossible to maneuver. They said the battleship was a "virtually motionless target" but that it was fighting desperately for its life against two large British battleships in a dramatic struggle.)

Britons reading the Admiralty announcement broke into spontaneous cheers. For it meant that the loss of the Hood and its 1,300 officers and men—and the blow to British naval prestige and dominance in the Atlantic—had been avenged.

The news spread like wildfire through London.

London Rejoices.

The tidings raced from lip to lip through the capital and then spread through the nation via an official British radio broadcast. Everywhere there were scenes of intense jubilation.

London authorities immediately pointed out that the Bismarck was the newest and most powerful battleship in the world—but not new or powerful enough to escape the armada that Britain sent against it. Its destruction means Britain's task in ruling the Atlantic Ocean has been simplified to a considerable degree, they said.

According to authoritative London circles, the death struggle of the giant Nazi warship began yesterday afternoon when aircraft operating from the aircraft carrier Ark Royal

(Continued on Page 4, Column 3)

Lone Veteran Of Civil War To Be In Memorial Day Parade

Richard Foss, 95, Is Only Survivor Of Army Of Blue In County.

ALTHOUGH Bass-Lawton Post of the Grand Army of the Republic passed out of existence with the death several months ago of John T. Young, commander and last surviving member, Fort Wayne's annual Memorial Day parade Friday morning is to include a veteran of the Civil War.

Richard Foss, 95, who served in the Sixteenth Pennsylvania Cavalry under General Sheridan, expects to represent the almost faded line of blue in the parade. Arrangements for his participation in the procession as an honorary member were made by Henry W. Lawton Camp No. 35, United Spanish War Veterans. The Spanish-American War veterans will provide a car to transport Mr. Foss in the parade, and he has agreed to participate if his health permits.

Mr. Foss came to Fort Wayne in May, 1940, from Washington, D. C., and resides with a niece, Mrs. A. O. Buchman, 2610 Smith Street. He joined the Sixteenth Pennsylvania Cavalry in 1863 and served in the Union Army for two and a half years. Mr. Foss was shot in the wrist during the war and although the doctors succeeded in saving his arm he was left handicapped for life with a crooked wrist.

Native Of Pennsylvania.

The aged veteran was born December 4, 1845, at South Huntington in West Moreland County, Pennsylvania. He is a former member of the GAR post at St. Cloud, Fla., where he formerly spent the Winters.

Richard Foss.

His many years have left Mr. Foss hard of hearing and his eyesight is dimmed by cataracts although he can distinguish objects. His mind is alert and he can take walks with assistance, Mr. Buchman said.

This will be the first year in history of the Memorial Day observance here that a GAR member will not participate in the parade and program. Mr. Foss is believed to be the only surviving Civil War veteran now residing in Allen County.

C. Of C. Opens New Program Counsel Series

Business, Industrial, Professional Leaders Attend First Of 12 Meetings.

The first of a series of 12 new program discussion meetings preliminary to a reorganization campaign to be held by the Fort Wayne Chamber of Commerce June 12 to 19 were held today at the Chamber of Commerce Building. Commercial, industrial and professional leaders of the city attended the meetings and offered suggestions on how to improve the program and work of the Chamber of Commerce.

Henry J. Herbst, president of the Chamber of Commerce and chairman of the new program survey, presided at the first meeting at 10:30 a.m. Donnelly P. McDonald presided at the second meeting of the series at noon. Two other sessions were to be held during the afternoon. Four additional meetings are to be held on each Wednesday and Thursday.

Mr. Herbst, in opening the initial meeting, asserted that no solicitations are to be made at the discussion meetings but that they are being held to

(Continued on Page 4, Column 6)

County School Head Will Be Named June 2

Kelro Whiteman's Term Expires Aug. 15; Republican Successor Likely.

Appointment of a new superintendent of county schools is scheduled for Monday, June 2, at 10 a.m. at a special meeting of the Allen County Board of Education, comprised of the 20 township trustees.

The term of Kelro Whiteman, Democratic incumbent, expires August 15, but the law stipulates that the appointment be made by June 1. Inasmuch as the date falls on Sunday, however, a successor will be named on the following day.

Whiteman's chances of succeeding himself, according to Republican members of the board, are slim as the proverbial snowball in July, despite the fact that there are as many Democratic township trustees as there are Republican. For serving as chairman at the closed session and empowered to vote in case of a tie will be County Auditor John A. Brewer, a Republican. The meeting will be held in Brewer's office.

Candidates Listed.

Republican township trustees held

(Continued on Page 4, Column 7)

Anti-War Sentiment Growing Rapidly, Senator Nye Declares

A GROUND SWELL of sentiment against American participation in an European war is growing rapidly, and even now is threatening to engulf interventionists in Washington.

There are not enough pro-war votes in the Senate to get a declaration of war, and the position of the House is questionable.

America, with a 45-billion-dollar debt on the books to start with, cannot finance another war.

These are the firm beliefs of Senator Gerald P. Nye, expressed in an interview Monday afternoon, prior to his address in the Shrine Auditorium, Monday night. The address was sponsored by the Fort Wayne chapter of the America First Committee.

Senator Nye, a distant cousin of the famed Hoosier humorist, Bill Nye, has been 17 years in the Senate, and the change of sentiment in that body is apparent, he thinks, to one who watches closely.

"Today, it would be impossible to get a declaration of war in the Senate, and it is doubtful in the House," Senator Nye believes.

Pressure Is Terrific.

"My own mail is running four or five to one against intervention, and the pressure on President Roosevelt from sane Americans has been so terrific that he has postponed his widely advertised fireside chat three times.

"And don't let anyone tell you he doesn't read the mail that pours into the White House. He takes a lot of it to bed with him. He is undergoing a terrible mental strain, torn between his own tendency to meddle in Europe's wars, and the growing opposition of the electorate."

Replying to a query as to how long America could finance another war, he said, "We can't finance one at all. With the domestic debt already piled up, another war would be our complete undoing."

In his address at the Shrine, which was heard by a cheering crowd of more than 2,000 persons, the Senator declared that "after twenty years of swearing, 'Never again,' Americans have recently been on the verge of allowing themselves to be led by war-mad hypnotists into the disaster of another European conflict."

"We have issued ourselves an invitation once more to take part in someone else's war," he declared, "and for what? In 1918 we went into the First World War with lofty ideals of making the world safe for democracy, and for bringing our way of life to foreign lands. We know now that every cause for which our soldiers fought and died only two decades ago, was lost.

The Senator, whose reputation has been built largely on his ability to tear an issue apart, ripped into what he called the "pure, naked madness" of President Roosevelt's promise to

(Continued on Page 4, Column 1)

Senator Wheeler Will Reply To Roosevelt

Senator Burton K. Wheeler will reply Wednesday night to the fireside chat to be made tonight by President Roosevelt. Senator Wheeler's talk will be delivered in the Cadle Tabernacle, Indianapolis, under auspices of the America First Committee of that city.

The talk is scheduled for 8 p.m. (CST).

Weather Forecast
From the United States Weather Bureau report. Full Details on Page A-2.
Generally fair, continued warm today and tomorrow. Temperatures yesterday—Highest, 96; lowest, 70.

The Sunday Star

WITH DAILY EVENING EDITION

Subscriber or Newsstand Copy
If Sold by Newsboy, Please Notify Star, NA. 5000

No. 1,891—No. 35,481. WASHINGTON, D. C., JUNE 22, 1941—126 PAGES. (AP) Means Associated Press. TEN CENTS

GERMANY DECLARES WAR ON RUSSIANS; HITLER ASSAILS SOVIET AS ARMIES MOVE

Wave on Wave Of R.A.F. Planes Pound Nazis

Ports of Channel Blasted 11th Day Of Offensive

BACKGROUND—
Germany entered the war in 1939 with vast superiority over Britain in aircraft, and in the big air battles over Britain last September British fighter planes were credited with saving England from quick defeat. British plane production has been so stepped up in last year that Germany's margin of supremacy, reduced by heavy losses in the numerous battles she has fought, has been sharply curtailed.

BULLETIN.

LONDON, June 22 (AP).—R. A. F. bombers attacked Western Germany last night, an authoritative source said. It was the 11th consecutive night of these attacks.

By the Associated Press.

LONDON, Sunday, June 22.—The R. A. F. last night carried out an unceasing bombardment of Channel ports and Northern France, capping a smashing daylight offensive in which masses of planes, 150 to the wave, were used to batter the Luftwaffe and its bases.

The roar of explosions was heard on the Kentist coast from the setting in of darkness until dawn as British bombers pounded away at targets which have been battered and rent for the eleventh day by Britain's heaviest and newest bombs.

Attacking with a force which observers on the coast said was as great as that which Germany sent against this country in the battle of England last fall, the British reported 28 German planes shot down in the fierce air fights which developed in the series of tran-channel raids yesterday.

For these victories, the British said, they paid a toll of five R. A. F. machines.

Tonight's attacks seemed to strike much deeper into the occupied territory than is usual, besides hitting the coast.

In return, the Germans appeared up to a late hour to have directed no extensive thrust at this country. But the British said two night bombers of the German airforce had been brought down.

In the "greatest day" of the battle of Britain last September 15 Germany sent over two waves of 150 and two of 100, and British claimed a total bag of 185.

Around midnight tonight the R. A. F. was at it again, giving the Nazi-held Channel bases a blasting that made the ground tremble along the English Kent coast on this side.

(The Rome radio announced tonight that the R. A. F. for the 11th consecutive night had hammered Western Germany "causing some losses in civilian life and domestic dwellings." The broadcast was picked up in New York by N. B. C.)

"It was the fighter command's most successful day of operations since the battle of Britain last year and two of the largest sweeps yet made over enemy territory since our fighters resumed the offensive," the Air Ministry said.

Striking Demonstration.

The attacks which continued through the full light of the year's longest day and on into the long twilight, were described by United States Army and Navy air observers as "the most striking dem-

(See RAIDS, Page A-5.)

Germans Charge Soviet Had Secret British Treaty

By the Associated Press.

NEW YORK, June 22—The German radio announced early this morning that within the next 24 hours representatives of the international press will be given documentary proof that the Soviet Union came to a secret understanding with Great Britain behind Germany's back, N. B. C. reported.

Ancient Damascus Falls to British And Free French

Allies March Into Moslem Capital After Two Weeks' Siege

BACKGROUND—
British and Free French invaded Syria and Lebanon two weeks ago in preventive move against anticipated German use of French-mandated territories for attacks on Suez Canal. Spearheads drove into Syria from Palestine, Trans-Jordan and Iraq, but progress nowhere has been rapid.

By the Associated Press.

CAIRO, June 21.—The ancient capital city of Damascus, a city of 4,000 years of war-spotted history, fell today to the British and Free French Armies on the 14th day of their invasion of French-mandated Syria, the British Near East command announced tonight.

The Allied forces marched into the ancient Moslem capital just 24 hours after they began to shell it with big guns. This bombardment was launched after French High Commissioner Gen. Henri Dentz had refused a British ultimatum to withdraw his defending troops.

(The German radio reported that British artillery had destroyed Mezze, western suburb of Damascus, with artillery fire prior to fall of the capital. A French dispatch from Beirut, Syria, indicated that the capital itself may not have been defended. This dispatch said French troops withdrew from the city, after which it was occupied by the British.

(The French, in dispatches from Beirut, admitted they had been forced to withdraw from the capital to positions to the north, where it was said the Vichy troops were taking up new defense positions.

(The British radio also said French forces were retreating northwestward toward Beirut. The radio said this meant the main body of French in the mandate would be concentrated in front of that coastal city and that the main battle for Syria might take place there.

(Just before the fall of Damascus, the French admitted the British had almost surrounded the city and were holding positions from only a mile to 6 miles outside its gates.)

Gen. Charles de Gaulle told Reuters, British news agency, his Free French forces entered the city at 3 p.m.

Allies Delayed Attack.

The British and Free French forces which entered Damascus had smashed their way to within 10 miles of the city in the first three days of their peneration of Syria, but stiff resistance and an avowed British reluctance to carry the fighting into the capital itself made further progress slow.

The fall of Damascus, believed to be the oldest inhabited city in the world, came almost two weeks after Syria's frontiers were first crossed on the opening day of the campaign June 8.

The attacking forces apparently closed in hard in their final thrusts from both the south and west, with hard fighting today just outside Damascus. The city, with its narrow streets, plaster and wood buildings and 200 mosques, was reported shelled prior to its fall.

The British and Free French ran into their first strong resistance in the drive on Damascus 10 days ago at the town of Kissoue, 10 miles to the south. Thence they made their way northward only slowly, while

(See SYRIA, Page A-3.)

Reich's Move Is Sensation In Capital

Senator Pepper Urges Quick Lease-Lend Aid to Russia

By the Associated Press.

Germany's move against Russia created a sensation in diplomatic quarters here last night and caught Government officials unprepared for a development of such far-reaching significance.

President Roosevelt had retired early, before Adolf Hitler's proclamation was read over the German radio, and White House aides said that so far as they knew, he was not awakened for the news.

Secretary of State Hull was advised immediately, but he and other State Department officials remained at home since the department so far lacked any official reports on the sudden development. In view of slow communications, it was expected that direct word from American diplomats abroad would not reach here for several hours.

Despite widespread rumors of Russian-German tension for several days, Hitler's decision to turn his armies eastward came as a distinct surprise at this time.

Chairman George of the Senate Foreign Relations Committee said the move "will give the United States time to meet all its commitments, including aid to Great Britain and the building up of our own defense."

Pepper Urges Aid to Russia.

Senator Pepper, Democrat, of Florida, a committee member, remarked that "the President should declare tomorrow morning that Russia will be a recipient of the lease-lend program."

Senator Pepper asserted that Hitler's move made it plain that "he is going to get rid of every country which threatens him, so he can advance against England and the United States later on."

"When you are in a fight," he added, "you can't be too choosy about a fellow who steps in and helps you out."

"Hitler again is demonstrating," Senator George observed, "that he will not let any country run counter to his interests.

"Hitler wants to be certain of two points—that he will have Russian war material and will close his eastern door against attack and that he may be able to obtain some propaganda advantage from an attack against the Soviet."

"Finns' Only Enemy Hunger."

The only diplomat to comment last night was Hjalmar Procope, the Finnish Minister, who said that "Finland's only enemy is hunger." He issued the following statement:

"I have had no information from Helsinki about the general situation. Finland is in the midst of international troubles for the moment. In a statement made by President Risto Ryti to an American newspaperman yesterday he emphasized that Finland's only enemy is hunger.

"Finland is an independent and sovereign state. She is ready to fight for freedom, but her firm and sincere wish is to keep friendly relations with all nations. We Finns

(See REACTION, Page A-12.)

Senator Harrison Weaker; Family Fears End Near

By the Associated Press.

Senator Harrison, Democrat, of Mississippi grew steadily weaker last night and his family feared the end was drawing near.

His physician, Dr. Sterling Ruffin, said yesterday after an afternoon call on his patient that Senator Harrison was not as well as Friday and tha this condition was "grave."

The 59-year-old Senator Harrison, President pro tempore of the Senate and chairman of its powerful Finance Committee, underwent an operation for an intestinal obstruction Monday.

Navy Diver Fails to Reach O-9 At Record Depth of 370 Feet

Pressure Forces Crocker to Surface, Navy Renews Attempts During Night

By the Associated Press.

PORTSMOUTH, N. H., June 21.—The first two attempts by Navy divers to reach the pressure-crushed submarine O-9 failed today, and the probability grew that the craft and her 33 dead had found a permanent grave 440 feet below the surface of the Atlantic.

The second effort resulted in a descent of 370 feet—the deepest working dive ever made in the North Atlantic—but the tremendous pressure at that depth, said the Navy laconically, forced "difficulty in breathing."

Earlier, Frank Knox, Secretary of the Navy, returned from the scene to report that "at that depth it is highly improbable that a salvage attempt would be undertaken."

He said "some form of service" would be held over the spot where the 23-year-old submarine rested upon a muddy clay bank, if it was decided she could not be raised.

Died as Heroes.

Obviously moved, Knox expressed a reluctance to speak publicly at any length.

"Those poor fellows are dead out there," he explained. "They are just as much heroes as if they had died in action."

George Crocker, 30-year-old native of Seattle, Wash., made the first two diving attempts today, and even after he finally had been hauled up, Rear Admiral Richard Edwards, commander of the submarines in the Atlantic fleet, announced the diving efforts would continue.

In a brief message from the sub-

(See SUBMARINE, Page A-3.)

Army Air Force Made Autonomous Under Unified Command

New Organization Seen As Answer to Moves For Independence

By GOULD LINCOLN.

Creation of the "Army Air Forces," designed to bring about "autonomy of the air arm rather than segregated independence," was announced yesterday by Secretary of War Stimson in letters addressed to the chairmen of the Senate and House Military Affairs Committees.

The Army air arm remains under the jurisdiction of the War Department in the new setup. Secretary Stimson in his letters insisted that the new organization provided in his order, would be more effective and better suited to present needs than an independent air force under a new department of aviation as provided in pending bills.

The Army Air Forces will be organized into the Headquarters Army Air Forces, the Air Force Combat Command and the Air Corps. The chief of the Army Air Forces—uniting the whole air arm into a co-ordinated whole—will be Maj. Gen. Henry H. Arnold, who is deputy chief of staff for air.

The Air Force Combat Command will be commanded by Lt. Gen.

(See AIR FORCE, Page A-12.)

U. S. Assumes Control Of Rubber Imports; Civilian Use to Be Cut

20 Pct. Reduction in Next Six Months Ordered; Ceiling for Tire Prices

BACKGROUND—
The Government warned Friday that rubber uses soon would be cut to the bone because of defense needs, although officials emphasized no present shortage exists. Rubber for America comes by ship from the Netherlands Indies and British Malaya. Since the European war's beginning, officials and private chemical firms have worked on development of synthetic rubber and the Agriculture Department has encouraged development of Latin American rubber plantations, in order to bring the United States nearer the source of supply.

By the Associated Press.

The Government, extending far-reaching control over all manufacturing use of rubber, yesterday suspended private imports from the Far East and ordered civilian consumption cut 20 per cent in the next six months.

At the same time, it acted to guard against sharp rises in automobile tire prices by announcing that a "ceiling" would be established within a few days that would provide, in effect, that prices may not exceed those charged on June 16.

Federal Loan Administrator Jones announced that effective June 23 the Rubber Reserve Co., a Government corporation, would become the sole buyer for crude rubber exported

(See RUBBER, Page A-14.)

Government Asks Gifts Of Discarded Aluminum

By the Associated Press.

Housewives throughout the Nation were asked by the Government yesterday to contribute their discarded aluminum pots and pans to the defense program. A Nation-wide drive for collection of such aluminum probably will be conducted for one week in July.

The Office of Production Management decided on the campaign after it had conducted tests in Madison, Wis., and Richmond, Va., which brought in approximately 80,000 pounds. The aluminum collected will be sold by the O. P. M. and the funds probably will be used in the civilian defense program.

Police Will Attempt To Find 'Overlooked' Strieff Case Clue

Keck Says Investigators, Baffled, Must Now Retrace Their Steps

(Picture on Page B-1.)

Stymied by collapsing clues and unable to discover a single lead from almost a week's investigation, police disclosed last night they would start all over again on the trail of the murderer of Jessie Elizabeth Strieff.

Going over the ground a second time, police hope to find something they might have overlooked in their search.

Capt. Ira E. Keck, acting chief of detectives, told reporters last night police have checked everything that might be expected to furnish a clue to the murder. His supersquad of investigators, he said, had checked almost every basement and trash can between the slain girl's apartment at 2110 Nineteenth street N.W. and the garage behind 1717 Q street, where her body was found. In addition, every one in the neighborhood has been questioned.

"We'll just have to go back over the whole thing again on the chance we missed something," he declared.

Questioned and Released.

Latest in the long line of suspects to be questioned and released was a young Government employe who came to police headquarters voluntarily last night. His only connection with the case was that he lives in the same block in which the girl's body was found and he owned a number of photographs described by police as "arty."

His landlady had said he was away from his room all last Sunday, the day Miss Strieff met her death.

Questioning at headquarters established the fact that the young man and a friend had driven to Mount Vernon before the rain Sunday and from there had gone to Glen Echo, returning home at about 9 p.m.

A possible clue disclosed by police last night brought an unknown man into the case. Capt. Keck told reporters he had been told that a man had taken Miss Strieff on a date three months ago. This man, according to the story told Capt. Keck, had driven the 23-year-old War Department employe to a vacant house where his attentions annoyed her.

Never Went Out Again.

Miss Strieff, Capt. Keck said he had been told, had immediately demanded to be taken home and the man complied. She never went out with the man again, Capt. Keck said.

The detective chief explained that the information had come to him from a friend of Miss Strieff, to whom the girl had told the story. She had not told the friend the name of the man.

This is the first man to be mentioned in connection with Miss Strieff besides her fiance, with whom she had spent almost every evening for some months, according to friends.

Capt. Keck, however, is inclined to discount the theory that Miss Strieff was criminally attacked and murdered by any one she knew. In his opinion, she was either pulled into a hallway or cellar on her way to or from the store where she had gone to buy butter, or she stepped into a car or taxicab to escape the downpour which must have caught her somewhere along the way.

"I think the murderer was just a fiend and the storm played a big part in it. He was just lucky that nobody saw him." Capt. Keck declared. "He certainly didn't plan this. He just took a chance and he's gotten away with it up to now."

He also is convinced on two other

(See MURDER, Page A-3.)

Finns and Rumanians Already on March in Gigantic Offensive

Goebbels Reads Denunciation Of Treaty; Work of OGPU In Reich Is Attacked

BULLETIN.

BERLIN, June 22 (AP).—German troops are smashing their way into Soviet Russia in a defensive war, Foreign Minister Joachim von Ribbentrop said today in a note addressed to the Soviet government.

By the Associated Press.

German armies marched on Soviet Russia along a 1,500-mile front from Norway to Rumania today after a sudden declaration of war by Adolf Hitler which burst asunder the devious partnership that was a prelude to the European war.

Hitler ordered the Nazi troops to invade Russia after assailing the Soviet bitterly in a proclamation broadcast to the world at dawn (10:30 p.m., Saturday, Washington time).

The London radio immediately announced a declaration had been issued in Moscow stating the U. S. S. R. and Great Britain were in full accord on the international situation.

The Italian Army was said by the Rome radio to be standing by ready to aid Germany in the struggle.

A dispatch telephoned from Berlin to New York said German troops massed in East Prussia, along with soldiers from Finland and Norway in the north and Rumania in the south, were on the march.

Finland and Rumania Join Germany.

Later it was announced in Berlin that Finland and Rumania had joined Germany in the fight.

The announcement said that mobilized on Germany's side were the forces of Field Marshal Baron Carl Gustav Mannerheim of Finland and Chief of State Gen. Ion Antonescu of Rumania.

East Prussia and Norway were mentioned specifically as points from which the high-powered German Army was moving.

The German radio declaration of war called the movement "the greatest march the world has ever seen."

That actual contact had not yet been established was intimated, however, by the German radio in a subsequent news bulletin picked up here by N. B. C. It said the German troops along the border were "moving into their last-minute positions."

Turkey reacted immediately on the war declaration, the Rome radio said, asserting that President Ismet Inonu had left Ankara for Istanbul to hold an important session of the Turkish cabinet and meet foreign representatives.

War Under Way, Hitler Announces.

Hitler, who at the moment his men marched into Poland on September 1, 1939, boasted by radio that his back was secure by reason of his pact with Russia seven days earlier, chose a similar method to tell the world that the deal was off, and that the war between national and international Socialism was actually under way.

Hitler's scorching denunciation of Russia was read over the radio by his propaganda minister, Dr. Paul Joseph Goebbels.

Foreign Minister Joachim Von Ribbentrop followed with the actual declaration of war.

Hitler and Von Ribbentrop both had strongly suggested that Finland and Rumania, each with an old grudge against land-grabbing Russia and both newly friendly with Germany, were sending their men to march beside the Germans against the Russian borders.

Hitler accused the Russians of a tremendous double-cross, of having signed in bad faith the German-Russian non-aggression pact of August 23, 1939. He himself, Hitler asserted, had entered into that pact with sore misgivings, but had to do it because of Britain's policy of encircling Germany.

Charges Underhand Means.

He accused the Soviet Union—despite the welcome gift by Germany of half of Poland—of having ever since tried by underhand means to cut Germany's throat.

Bitterly he excoriated Russia for the Finnish and Baltic land grabs, the slicing up of Rumania. He blamed the Communist diplomats for playing England's game and stirring up the Yugoslav coup d'etat of March 27 and the Rumanian Iron Guard revolt of last January.

Von Ribbentrop added to the list of charges, declaring Russian diplomats had been guilty of espionage against Germany and that Russia long had conducted a campaign of sabotage against the Reich.

The Axis victory in the Balkans momentarily foiled the deep-laid Communist scheme, Hitler said, of involving Germany in a long war and then, with English aid and American supplies, throttling the Reich.

At last, he said, the moment has come when Germany can tolerate no more.

No Precedent, Declares Goebbels.

The shrill-voiced Goebbels concluded with these stern words of his master:

"The march of the German armies has no precedent. Together with the Finns we stand from Narvik to the Carpathians. At the Danube and on the shores of the Black Sea under Antonescu German and Rumanian soldiers are united. The task is to safeguard Europe and thus save all.

"I have, therefore, today decided to give the fate of the German people and the Reich and of Europe again into the hands of our soldiers."

Hitler, like Napoleon before him, had turned to the East.

Hitler was back on one of the tracks he so long ago outlined for himself in "Mein Kampf"—enmity for Russia and for Communism. But he still was at war with Britain—a situation he professed in "Mein Kampf" to abhor.

Britain was apparently less surprised than the the United States by the German step which her wishful thinkers had so long forecast and which so often in the past had proved to be but a figment of unhappy imagination.

The only word that British sources could give was that apparently Hitler was convinced he could not quickly beat Britain and that he had decided to mop up Russia so as to gain a vast new

(Continued on Page A-5, Column 2.)

Body of Fourth Victim In Gun Affray Found

By the Associated Press.

LAS VEGAS, Nev., June 21.—Officers found the body of 21-year-old Galen Gilmore on a desert road today and listed him as the fourth victim of gunfire in a domestic quadrangle.

James Clark, police investigator, said W. J. Tyler, 24, a railroad brakeman, killed his wife, Evelyn, 21; Gilmore, and Charles J. Decker, 34, also a brakeman.

Tyler, sitting at a bar, killed himself yesterday as officers entered with drawn guns to arrest him for killing Mr. Decker. A few minutes later they found the body of Mrs. Tyler in Gilmore's automobile.

$500,000 U. S. Arms Loan Granted to Costa Rica

By the Associated Press.

SAN JOSE, Costa Rica, June 21.—An official announcement tonight said the United States Government had granted Costa Rica a $500,000 credit to acquire war material, chiefly for anti-aircraft guns.

Phone Lines Interrupted

BUDAPEST, June 21 (AP).—Telephone communications between Budapest and Berlin have been interrupted for the past four days.

Mr. X Decided He Was for America First, So U. S. Didn't Get His Private Plane

Mr. X was for America first, and so the Government didn't get his private plane, which it wanted "in order to meet an immediate and urgent military requirement." He is the only man in the United States who refused to turn in his Lockheed Lodestar Model 18.

President Roosevelt, without identifying the man, told Congress the story yesterday by releasing five telegrams between Mr. X, Secretary of Commerce Jones and Arthur Whiteside, chairman of the Commercial Aircraft Priority Committee, O. P. M. Here they are:

Telegram April 27 from Mr. Whiteside to the man whose name was withheld:

"In order to meet an immediate and urgent military requirement requests are being made to all private owners of Lockheed model 18 airplanes, irrespective of the use to which those airplanes are now put, to make them available to fill this requirement. I have been asked to determine whether or not you will voluntarily turn back your model 18 to the manufacturer at the earliest possible date, but not later than May 2, either for cash reimbursement or replacement at an indefinite future date. A prompt telegraphic response is requested. You are reminded that such delivery for military purposes would call for no publicity."

Telegram May 8 to the same man from Mr. Jones:

"All plane owners requested to transfer transport type planes to the Government for emergency needs have responded except you. I do not want to believe that you are less patriotic than others, but notwithstanding repeated attempts to reach you we have had no reply from you. We have tried to reach you at Pyramid Lake, Nev.; Glenbrook, Nev.; Sea Island, Ga.; Santa Barbara, Calif.; Medford, Oreg., and through your secretary to advise us where you could be reached by telegram, telephone, radio or airplane courier."

Telegram May 12 received by Mr. Jones:

"Just returned from camping trip and found your wires. Do not consider my type plane essential for England's defense and being more interested in America first desire to keep it conserved for America's possible secondary defense. Therefore, refuse to turn this ship over and will protest any seizure. If any time

(See MR. X, Page A-4.)

Weather
Tonight—Fair
Tomorrow-Warmer
Full Report—Page 2

Bangor Daily Commercial

Late Evening Edition 3c

The Evening Home Paper of Eastern and Northern Maine

VOLUME 69 BANGOR, MAINE, MONDAY EVENING, JUNE 30, 1941 ESTABLISHED 1872

Nazis Seize Lwow, Minsk, Drive Half Way to Moscow

Stubborn Resistance With Two Shortcut Drives Foiled Is Russian Claim; Panzer Force Is Reported Trapped

By The Associated Press

Moscow, June 30—Now under attack in strategic sectors of the whole of a 2,000-mile front with Germany and her Allies, the Red Army reported today a stubborn resistance to the invaders in the areas of Murmansk, Dvinsk, Minsk and Luck, the repulse of two attempted shortcut drives toward Leningrad and aerial entrapment of a Panzer force.

The last 24 hours brought an extension of the active front through a German attack across the extreme north of the Finnish border toward the Russian Arctic port of Murmansk and repeated assaults on Russia's Karelian Isthmus frontier with Finland, north of Leningrad.

(Continued on Page Seven)

PANZER PUNCH ON THE EASTERN FRONT—A German soldier pops up through the turret of his tank and hurls a hand grenade toward a Russian Army hideout, according to the Nazi censor-approved caption. Name of the town in flames was not given.

France And Reds In Break

Vichy Severs Relations, 200 Russians Held

Vichy, Unoccupied France, June 30—(AP)—France severed relations with Soviet Russia today and it was learned that at least 200 persons accredited to Russian diplomatic and consular services have been held for questioning.

Russian men and women who were held were concentrated in the Stadium outside Vichy where only yesterday Chief of State Marshal Petain gave a flag to the French youth labor camps.

All Roads to and From Vichy Guarded

For 24 hours before the decision to break relations with Moscow, all roads leading to and from Vichy were heavily guarded.

As soon as the break became known, the Russians informed the

(Continued on Page Seven)

Big Pocket Being Formed Around Russian Troops In Smolensk Region; Russian Division Also Encircled

Berlin, June 30—(AP)—German troops were reported today to have captured Minsk and to be almost half way along the 450-mile road from Minsk to Moscow.

A Germany military spokesman asserted Minsk was in German hands shortly after the high command reported capture of Lwow, on the lower Polish front, and Libau, Latvian port on the Baltic Sea.

The spokesman intimated German troops were in sight of Smolensk, 200 miles east of Minsk. A big pocket was being formed around Russian troops in the Smolensk region, he said.

DIVISION ENCIRCLED

The High Command bulletin on the capture of the Latvian port was preceded by a report that a Soviet Russian division near the Baltic coast had been encircled in a new German northward push in Lithuania and Latvia.

"The ring is so narrow and tight," around the Red Army forces on the Baltic front, DNB, official German news agency, said, "that destruction of the Bolshevist units is certain."

The agency also said several hundred Russian tanks and 42 cannon were destroyed or captured by German forces at Rawa Ruska, just inside Sovietized Poland about

(Continued on Page 2; Column 2)

Bangor Plans For Draft Registrants

All Reaching 21 Years Since Previous Registration to Report Tomorrow; Sheriff Named Jail Registrar

Bangor's two draft boards were today making final preparations for the registration tomorrow, July 1, of all young men who have become 21 years of age since the previous draft registration. It is estmated that some 750,000 will register at the 6400 draft boards throughout the country.

Draft Board No. 1

Bangor Draft Board No. 1 expects to register between 150 and 200 and Board No. 2, about 150. The hours of registration will be from 7 a. m. to 9 p. m. Eastern Standard Time, or 8 a. m. to 10 p.

(Continued on Page Seven)

"Bottleneck" Blamed On Army, Navy

Fail to Let Contracts Fast Enough, Says Michigan Governor

Boston, June 30—(AP)—The Army and Navy were blamed for "the real defense bottleneck" by Governor Murray D. Van Wagoner of Michigan today because of failure to let contracts "fast enough or large enough."

With co-operative action as their keynote, Governor Van Wagoner, Governor Herbert H. Lehman of New York and Governor Frank M.

(Continued on Page Seven)

Japs Pondering Attitude In War

Tokyo, June 30—(AP)— Two extraordinary conferences of the government with high generals and admirals were held today in continuation of Japan's efforts to decide a course in the Russian-German war.

While the cabinet talked with the military and naval high commands, Emperor Hirohito received reports from key ministers. Navy Minister Admiral Koshiro Oikawa reported to the throne on the naval situation, and Foreign Minister Yosuke Matsuoka was with the Emperor for two hours to outline the diplocatic picture.

New pressure was exerted by Nationalist groups which have favored full cooperation with Germany and Italy.

Auburn City Head Succeeds Somerville

David Walton Named Unemployment Compensation Comm. Chairman

Augusta, June 30—(AP)—David Walton, Auburn's city manager and former chairman of the Maine State Liquor Commission, today was named by Governor Sumner Sewall as chairman of the State Unemployment Commission.

Walton was appointed to fill the unexpired term of Clifford A. Somerville of Portland whose resignation was announced Saturday by the Governor. Walton will serve the unexpired term of Somerville which would have ended in December, 1942.

(Continued on Page 2; Column 4)

Dispute Ties Up Billions In Appropriations

Congress' Leaders Expects Bills to Pass Tonight, However

Washington, June 30—(AP)—A dispute over $35,000,000 tied up a pair of billion-dollar appropriation bills today, but Congressional leaders expressed confidence both measures would go to President Roosevelt before the fiscal year ends at midnigh.t

The bills involved were the $935,905,000 relief bill and the

(Continued on Page 2; Column 6)

Finds Stomach of Mrs. Joss Missing

"Impossible" to Determine How Much Morphine In Slain Woman's Body, Says Dr. Julius Gottlieb

by JOHN P. RODERICK

Bath, June 30—(AP)—Because the stomach was missing when he examined the exhumed body of Dr. Luverne Harris Joss, it was "impossible," Dr. Julius Gottlieb asserted today, to say how much morphine was in the 38-year-old woman's body after she had been slain in her Richmond home March 27.

Stomach "Disposed Of"

The Lewiston pathologist, a witness for the state in its attempt to convict Dr. Merrill E. Joss, 34, of wife-murder, testified that an analysis of liver and kidney tissue revealed evidence of only one-tenth of a grain of morphine. "The amount found was very small," he said.

(Continued on Page 2; Column 1)

Bandsmen Of 152nd Home On Furlough

Guardsmen Arrive In Bangor From Blanding This Morning

Proudly carrying new laurels added to an already distinguished record, the Regimental Band of the 152nd Field Artillery, Maine National Guard, arrived in Bangor early this morning on a 12-day furlough from Camp Blanding, Fla.

Back July 13

The band, intact but for two members and Warrant Officer Francis G. Shaw, is scheduled to be back at the Southern training site by taps on July 13.

The two band members who did not make the journey, enjoyed their furloughs during the past

(Continued on Page 2, Column 4)

German Planes Bomb New York

London, June 30—(AP)—German planes bombed New York last night but there wasn't much damage. It's a little village in Lincolnshire.

29 Arrested In Huge Spy Suspect Hunt

Many Engaged In Defense Work, 22 Born In Germany

New York, June 30—(AP)—Swiftly and secretly during the weekend the nation wound up the greatest spy suspect hunt in its history with the arrest of 26 men and three women on espionage charges.

Agents of the Federal Bureau of Investigation entered homes and taverns in four states to seize 24 suspects. FBI Chief J. Edgar Hoover announced yesterday, while five others already were in custody on other charges.

(Continued on Page 2; Column 4)

Cannon Roar Along 600-Mile Finnish Front

Finland Ends Policy Of Passive Resistance To Russia

Helsinki, Finland, June 30—(AP)—Cannon roared along the entire 600-mile Finnish-Soviet Russian frontier Sunday as the Finns ended their declared policy of passive resistance to the U. S. S. R.

"After all," a Finnish army spokesman declared, "Finns are not the kind to sit with hands folded while their land is laid waste and women and children massacred."

Field Marshal Baron Carl Gustaf Mannerheim, venerated military leader of the Finns, signalied end of the passive resistance policy of the first week of the Russian-German war by issuing a midnight order of the day calling on Finns to follow him in a "holy war" against the Russians.

"Follow me this last time—when Karelians rise again and a new day dawns for Finland," he appealed.

(Continued on Page 2; Column 5)

Molotov-Steinhardt Confer

Moscow, June 30—(AP)—U. S. Ambassador Laurence A. Steinhardt conferred with Foreign Commissar Vyacheslav Molotov for more than an hour yesterday, it was learned in diplomatic quarters today. The nature of their talk was not made public.

Army to Call Up 50,000 Monthly

Big Percentage During Next Six Months to Come From 750,000 Men Of 21 Who Register Tomorrow

Washington, June 30—(AP)—The army probably will call up about 50,000 selective service trainees a month during the last half of this year, and a big percentage of them will come from the ranks of the 750,000 men of 21 who must register tomorrow.

Army Welcomes Younger Men

Selective Service Headquarters, it was learned today, has worked out a system of interspersing the newest registrants in the list of those who enrolled last October.

The effect will be to make many of tomorrow's young registrants quickly available for military service—a welcome result to the Army High Command which regards men just turned 21 as ideal soldiering material.

As final arrangements were completed for the second Selective Service registration, selectees already in training received a good official indication that their tour of service woud not be extended beyond the year fixed by law.

The temporary White House at Hyde Park, N. Y., released an executive order by President Roosevelt yesterday, which fixed 900,00 as the number of trainees

(Continued on Page 2; Column 3)

Bangor Man Heads State Association

Leslie J. Bowler New President of Maine Registry of Deeds Unit

Leslie J. Bowler of Bangor, register of deeds, was elected president of the Maine State Register of Deeds Association at the annual meeting held at Lakewood on Saturday. Eleven of the 16 counties were represented and officials brought members of their famlies. Business sesssions were held forenoon and afternoon and the party enjoyed the performance at the theater.

(Continued on Page Seven)

Digest of Today's Financial Markets at 2 P. M.

STOCK EXCHANGE

Stocks remained practically unchanged. Trading extremely light in one of the dullest sessions of the year.

CURB EXCHANGE

Stocks were quiet and steady today in an exceptionally dull market.

BONDS

Second and medium grade domestic loans in general were slightly easier on the day. U. S. Govts and foreign bonds firm.

Foreign Market by Dow-Jones News

London market quiet and firm.

Furnished by Hornblower & Weeks

EVENING
POTTSVILLE REPUBLICAN

VOL. CXIII—NO. 112 | Published Week-day Afternoons. Mail $9 Yearly. Carrier 3c Copy. | POTTSVILLE, PA., SATURDAY EVENING, SEPTEMBER 6, 1941 | Entered 2d Class Mail Pottsville, Pa., P. O. under Act Mar. 3, 1874 | THREE CENTS

SIEGE GUNS BOMBARD, SET LENINGRAD AFIRE

Big Tax Bill Passes Senate By 67 to 5 Vote

Exemptions of Married Persons Reduced to $1500 And Single to $750; Goes Back to House

WASHINGTON, Sept. 6, (AP)—Jubilant over the Senate's 67 to five approval of the record $3,583,900,000 tax bill late yesterday, administration lieutenants strove today to hurry along the adjustments of differences between that measure and similar legislation passed by the House.

The bill, which would bring an estimated 4,911,000 additional persons under the income tax structure and thus raise an extra $303,000,000 of revenue, was rushed thru the Senate in only three days.

Both proponents and opponents said the measure was only a step toward paying the nation's huge defense bills. The House Ways and Means Committee has estimated that all federal expenditures would exceed $22,000,000,000 during the next fiscal year, which begins on July 1.

Chairman George (D-Ga) of the Senate Finance Committee, predicted the total federal income would approach $15,000,000,000.

To win fast Senate approval of the tax measure, leaders had to make two important concessions.

1. They dropped a finance committee amendment, estimated to raise $50,000,000 a year, which would have prevented husbands and wives in community property states from dividing income for tax purposes. Such property division usually results in lower total tax liabilities for married couples.

2. They promised pension advocates that the Finance Committee would consider promptly a proposal to give $30-a-month pensions to all persons over 60. The pension plan had been offered as a rider to the tax bill.

Democratic Leader Barkley and Chairman George, worried because each day's delay in enacting the tax measure costs the Treasury about $3,000,000 in uncollected "nuisance"

(Continued on Page Seven)

—VVV—

CRAMP'S BEGINS SHIP BUILDING

"Clyde of America" Lays Kiel of Navy Cruiser Wilkes-Barre

PHILADELPHIA, Sept. 6 (AP)—Keel-laying of the 10,000-ton navy cruiser Wilkes-Barre today was the signal for official reopening of century-old Cramp's Shipyard, famed builder of a major portion of Uncle Sam's civil and world war fleets.

Reclaimed from rust and desolation after 14 years of idleness, the giant plant has been turned into a modern warship for defense and already is well launched on a $110,000,000 government building program to help equip America's two-ocean navy.

Industrial heart of the city's Kensington community, the yard's revival prompted arrangements for a huge celebration topped by a parade of 10,000 after the keel laying (12:30 p. m.) and keynote speech by Admiral Harold R. Stark, chief of naval operations and native of Wilkes-Barre, Pa., for which the new warship is named.

Launching its new era on a rising tide of ships which again has made the Delaware the "Clyde of America," Cramp's is going about its work with the same urgency that it turned out surf-boats for Winfield Scott's Mexican Expedition, iron-clads in '64, and gray, waspish destroyer in a deadly stream during '17 and '18.

Real awakening of the slumbering plant to meet 1941 naval needs occurred 11 months ago for Cramp's thousands of workers and since have been launched two naval auxiliary craft along with start of work on the Miami, sister ship to the Wilkes-Barre.

WORKING TIME

At The Collieries

The following is the working time as furnished by the companies' offices:

WORKING MONDAY

Miscellaneous: Buck Run, Repplier, Oak Hill, Pine Hill, Primrose Coal Co., Frackville, Salem Hill, William Penn, Raven Run, East Bear Ridge, Packer 5, Continental, Morea, New Boston, St. Clair, Bell, Reevesdale Stripping a double shift, Delano, Park Colliery, Hammond, Westwood, Williamstown.

L. N. C. Corp.: Tamaqua, Greenwood, Coaldale, Lansford.

Locust Coal Co.: Sections 2 and 4 and Weston Breaker.

Edison Coal Co.: Nesquehoning.

P. & R. C. & I. Co.: Alaska, Reliance, Locust Gap, Potts, Locust Summit (full breaker two shifts).

On The Railroads

Reading, 6 7 5, Reading Division Enginemen—T. J. Horan, J. F. Carr, Shamokin Division Engineman—Edward Jones, E. Heberling. Reading Division Firemen—J. Dando, J. Kreichbaum, E. Eifert, R. Merton. Shamokin Division Firemen—T. Monahan, M. E. Glasser. Brakemen—F. P. Spleen, F. McKeone, J. G. Lynaugh.

Penna. Extra Enginemen—W. J. Yost. Extra Firemen—J. Schrader, H. Fisher, R. L. Kelce. Brakemen—P. Nace. Vacancies—none.

—VVV—

Al Maurer really wants to be a "big" Dictator. He's even trying to control Minersville with candidate Al Kellar for Chief Burgess. VOTE FOR HASENAUER!

PAVED ALL BACK STREETS, ALLEYS

City Highway Costs Cut From $62,000 to $29,000

By James A. Lynaugh

It is reassuring to Pottsville folks to have councilmen in office who are thoroughly familiar with all the intricate details of our municipal affairs. That is where

JAMES LYNAUGH

James A. Lynaugh fits into this picture. He is a lifelong resident, a volunteer fireman for 50 years, a former member of borough council, active always in all the affairs of Pottsville.

Mr. Lynaugh is an expert road builder. He was formerly in the contracting business, so that the word expert means something in this case. He retired from private contracting about three years ago.

When the Penna. Turnpike was being built he was engaged as a special inspector and he saw to it that Penna. got a good job. That job is about finished. He has not determined upon his future activities.

While most street officials make special efforts to pave main streets where everyone can see them and praise them, Jim's ambition has been to see that every back street and alley of the city is paved. He has largely accomplished that ambition. He will be able to give to every resident a paved street in front of his home inside of another year. There is probably no city in Penna that can make such boast.

As head of the highway department he has saved about $30,000 a year to the taxpayers. When he went in office the highway budget was $62,000. Last year it was $29,000. He says the people pay too much taxes and if he can bring them down he will do so and the way to bring them down is to cut expenses.

(Continued on Page Seven)

—VVV—

ADMITS STREET ATTACK ON GIRLS

Former Orchestra Leader Caused Reign of Fear in Central Penna.

LOCK HAVEN, Pa., Sept. 6 (AP)—Major Charles C. Keller of the State Police said today a 21-year-old Belefonte electrician and former orchestra leader had involved himself in attacks on eight Central Pennsylvania girls within the past few months after 24 hours of questioning by a staff of seven veteran detectives.

Keller said District Attorney Musser Gettig of Centre County, where six of the attacks occurred, and District Attorney Burritt Haag of Clinton County, where two others took place, were planning to charge the youth with aggravated assault and battery some time today.

Hagg said the young musician first made statements admitting two Lock Haven attacks, the first of which occurred Thursday night and led to his immediate apprehension.

The Thursday night attack was on Miss Ruth Andrews, 19, who was felled from behind, as were the other girls who were assaulted on darkened streets of Lock Haven, Bellefonte, State College and Howard.

Passersby who noted the youth in flight aided in his capture Hagg said.

Sheriff D. Edward Grenoble of Clinton County reported the youth had admitted the others in Centre County a few hours later.

The wave of street sluggings of unescorted girls began shortly after the Central Pennsylvania communities were shocked by the slayings of Rachel Taylor, Penn State co-ed, and Fay Gates, pretty office clerk, who resided in secluded Spook Hollow, near Bellefonte.

Richard Millinder, a neighbor of Miss Gates, was sentenced to life for her slaying. The Taylor murder never has been solved.

Major Keller said the youth was questioned in connection with the Taylor murder, along with additional street attacks in the area, which totaled 16 altogether. Some of the assaults never were brought to public light.

—VVV—

Al Maurer had better watch himself or Leidich will doublecross him like he did the Republicans when he was defeated in his third term try for Controller. VOTE FOR HASENAUER!

Claim Sub That Attacked Greer A Nazi and Sunk

No Official Confirmation; May Be Challenge to U. S. Policy of Freedom Of Seas

WASHINGTON, Sept. 6, (AP)—An effort to fix officially the nationality of the submarine which attacked the U. S. Destroyer Greer was indicated today as the American government's next step toward clarifying the incident preliminary to possible stern diplomatic action.

Although Washington authorities were tight-lipped on the question of nationality, word came from Reykjavik, Iceland, where the Greer put in with her cargo of mail yesterday, that the submarine had been described there as a German vessel.

Authors of this description which passed both Reykjavik and London censors were not given, but the implication was clear that the destroyer's officers might have gathered some evidence bearing on the vital matter.

Such evidence, if found conclusive here, would settle one of the two principal uncertainties still involved in the incident and, through diplomatic protests, might lead to clarification of the other one—whether the attack constituted a deliberate attempt to sink an American warship in what would amount to a challenge to this country's declared policy of keeping hostile craft out of the sea lanes to Iceland.

—VVV—

4 SOLDIERS HURT ON NAGLE TRAIL

Four soldiers attached to the Third Cavalry at Fort Myer, Va., enroute to their homes in Wilkes-Barre and Nuremberg were injured when their atuo crashed into the side of the Beckville arch on the Gordon Nagle trail shortly after last midnight.

They missed their route at the Nagle trail intersection in Cressona, and drove beyond the arch before they realized their mistake. It was while coming back through the arch enroute again to Cressona that the accident occurred.

John G. Hudock, of Wilkes-Barre was the most seriously hurt, sustaining severe lacerations of the scalp and a cut ear. Anthony Lastkowsky of Freeland, suffered from shock; John Slovik, of Nuremburg from a laceration of the scalp and of the eye, and Roy Boehmer, of Nuremburg, contusions of the left shoulder. All were treated at the Pottsville Hospital.

The atuo was damaged to the extent of $50. Pottsville motor police investigated.

—VVV—

Ravine

WOODEN BRIDGE IS WASHED AWAY

High Water Damaged Bridge Much Used As A Short Cut

The wooden bridge crossing at Swatara near Lorberry Junction has been partly washed away by high water and is roped off to traffic and travel. This bridge was washed away and again rebuilt 35 years ago and is on a short piece of road leading from route 125, and is very much needed as a short cut from said route to Lorberry. Rausch Creek and especially to the Oak Ridge Coal Co. breaker near by. This bridge should by all means be rebuilt for the benefit of the public.

CLAUDE A. LORD

THIS IS THE MAN WHO:

—Gave Pottsville a business administration.
—Put the city on the map.
—Increased the efficiency without increasing the cost.
—Raised $42,000 in the Industrial Drive.
—Was a member of the committee who collected $500,000 for new industries.
—Declared a Third Thanksgiving Day to lay the cornerstone of the Aetna Steel Plant.
—Gave 2,300 pairs of shoes to poor children.
—Helped to sell thousands of tons of coal to the Government and others.
—Gave 1,000 chickens to the poor last Thanksgiving.
—Was responsible for the 104th Cavalry parading in Pottsville.
—Organized the first Defense Council in the United States.
—Gives 500 free ambulance calls annually.
—Organized and direced "Club Americana."
—Raised $1,900 for the Pottsville soldiers' fund.
—Sponsored the Pottsville Aluminum Drive.
—Conducts Good Will Tours for under-privileged children annually.
—Takes 125 children to the movies every other Saturday all year.
—Conducted a drive to buy two pony cycles for the play grounds.
—Assisted, by bringing new industries here, in creating more than a $25,000 increase in the weekly payrolls.
—Aided the business men to increase their business.
—As one of the Pottsville Council members, secured the Centre Street Boulevard Lighting.
—Promoted the Pottsville Soap Box Derby for two seasons.
—As one of the Present Council members, lowered the bonded indebtedness of the city.
—Devotes his life to Pottsville.
—Loves his fellow-men.
—Should be re-elected.

This article was suggested by friends of Claude A. Lord who believe that since he will not speak of his good deeds, some one should do it for him, and they urge you to ask the recipients of these kindnesses what they think of Mayor Lord.

TUSCARORA

Mrs. Norman Brachman and Mrs. Laura Liddle, of Tuscarora, visited Mrs. Carria Boran, a patient in the Pottsville Hospital.

Mr. and Mrs. Dick Hahn and son, Joey, Mr. and Mrs. Jack Starr and son, Jackie, were Lansford callers.

Joe Kenney spent several days in Atlantic City, N. J.

Mrs. Alex Satoris, Tamaqua, spent several days with her sister, Mrs. Steve Lehotta.

Mr. and Mrs. Steve Geguzis, Newark, N. J., visited at the home of Mr. and Mrs. John Lehotta.

Norman Stutzman is visiting relatives in Phila.

Mrs. Norman Stutzman, Eleanor Belsak and Mary Chinchar, were Tamaqua visitors.

Ladies Aid Meeting

The Reformed Ladies Aid held their monthly meeting in the social room of the church. A delicious roast beef dinner was enjoyed before the business session. Members who were present were: Mrs. Allen Schneck, Miss Ida Stout, Rev. and Mrs. H. C. Correll, Mrs. Alice Hesser, Mrs. Emma Young, Mrs. Clara Kramer, Mrs. Mabel Lengle, Mrs. Emma Brown, Mrs. Wm. Dewalt, Mrs. James Lehr, Mrs. John Leffler, Mrs. Chas. Lengle, Mrs. Elmer Lengle, Mrs. Abel M. Kintzel, Mrs. Raymond Christ, Mrs. Ray Lengle, Mrs. Mark Haldeman, Mrs. Grace Stauffenberg.

Harvest Home Services

The annual Harvest Home Services in St. Paul's Reformed at Ravine and St. Peter's Reformed, Pinegrove, will be observed Sunday, Sept. 14th.

Personals

Clara Zimmerman and Harry Entzweiler motored to Indiana where they spent five pleasant days among relatives and friends.

Mr. and Mrs. Chas. Umbenhauer, Mardell Zimmerman, Mr. and Mrs. Harry Boyer, daughter Betty, visited relatives at Manheim.

Mr. and Mrs. Ralph Bohr, Mr. and Mrs. John Oden of Coshocton, Ohio, Ruth Anna Aungst, of Jonestown, Samuel Bohr, of Pinegrove, Mr. and Mrs. John Bohr of Lickdale, Mrs. Elvena Bohr of Suedberg, were visitors at the home of Mr. and Mrs. Raymond Christ.

—VVV—

TREASURY BALANCE

The treasury [illegible] Saturday was $2654,107,085.03.

—VVV—

People in [illegible] say Leidich won't even [illegible] and Leidich seems to know it. [illegible]

WILLIAMSTOWN

Mr. and Mrs. Chester Bear, of Enola, visited her father, Thomas Warlow.

Mrs. Sara Robison and Hazle Walkingshaw are spending some time in New York.

Mr. and Mrs. Elmer Umholtz and daughter, Matilda, of Wiconisco, spent a day at the home of Mary D. Hess on Market street.

Mr. and Mrs. Joseph McAuliff were Pottsville visitors.

Margaret Watkins of Harrisburg, visited her parents, Mr. and Mrs. Harrison Watkins.

Nellie Williams of Harrisburg visited her sister, Mr. and Mrs. Ray Smeltzer.

Mr. and Mrs. George Uhler spent a day at Hershey.

Mr. and Mrs. Joseph Warlow and daughter, of Detroit, Mich., was home for several days.

Robert Thomas and wife returned home after spending his vacation of two weeks in Canada.

Her Birthday Today

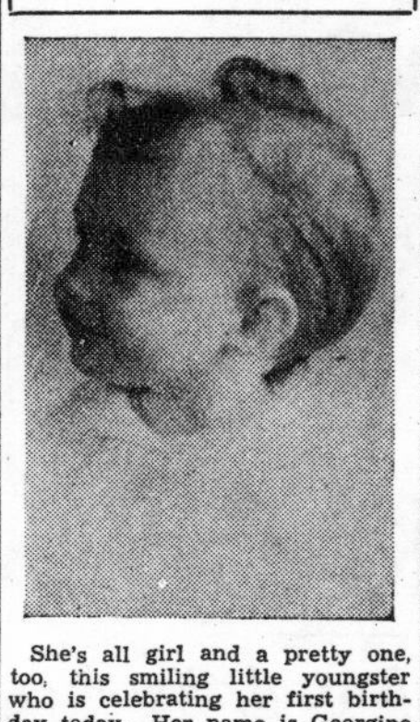

She's all girl and a pretty one, too, this smiling little youngster who is celebrating her first birthday today. Her name is Georgine Elizabeth and she is the apple of the eye of her grandad who is a local contractor and builder. Georgine is blonde and blue eyed and has a most delightful habit of wrinkling up her nose when she smiles in a way that is just too cute for words. Her dad is a carpenter, and works for his father. That enough clues? On page four is identified the baby whose picture appeared Sept. 3.

—VVV—

MINER, 18, DIES IN ROCK FALL

Peter Smalley, 18, of Black Heath Victim of Coal Hole Accident Late Friday

Struck by a fall of rock in a bootleg coal hole in which he and his father and brother were working, Peter Smalley, 18, of Black Heath, near Minersville, was instantly killed Friday afternoon shortly before 4 o'clock.

Deputy Coroner Allen Keller of Minersville said the youth died of a fractured skull.

According to Keller, Peter, his father George and another brother were working in the coal hole near Primrose and had fired a shot. Peter went down and with a pick was pulling out the loose coal when the fall occurred.

He is survived by his parents, Mr. and Mrs. George Smalley and the following brothers and sisters, Andrew of Bridgeport, Pa.; Mary, wife of John Kardisco, of New York; Eva, wife of Pete Krupa, of Conshohocken; John, Lillian, Joseph and Nicholas at home.

Funeral arrangements are in charge of Hahn, Minersville. The funeral will be held Monday from his late residence in Primrose with mass being celebrated in St. Nicholas Greek Catholic Church, Minersville.

—VVV—

Y. M. C. A. ACTIVITIES

An important meeting of the staff of the Pottsville Y. M. C. A. will be held Sunday at the summer camp. It will be attended by General Secretary J. L. Hastie, Don Felix, Chas. Faust, Ralph Krecker, Jos. Rutter and A. J. Zimmerman. A dinner will be extended the general campaign chairman and committee chairmen, who officiated during the recent U. S. O. drive, which will be held at the Necho Allen Hotel, next Monday, at 6:30 p. m. It will be in the nature of appreciation and victory gathering.

The bowling alleys are being resurfaced for use starting next week. The Men's League have called a meeting of captains to plan the new season's schedule, next Friday, at 7 p. m., at the Y. M. C. A.

—VVV—

vote for Burt J. Hasenauer. He served four years as Deputy under the late Gordon Nagle. VOTE FOR HASENAUER!

RED MISSION COMPLETES FLIGHT TO U. S.—Ending a flight from Moscow, this plane, one of two carrying 47 Russians enroute to Washington, D. C., on a technical mission to study U. S. plane production, alighted on Lake Washington, Seattle. Note the Red Star marking.

Street Paving Torn Up In Odessa for Barricades, Expect an Early Decision

The German invasion of Russia, finishing its eleventh week today, was a story of three cities—Leningrad, Kiev and Odessa—each defended by all the steel and sinew the Soviet Union could bring to bear against the close-drawn peril of conquest.

For all three the climax seemed approaching.

The German High Command, with a brevity that has grown typical of late, said only: "Operations of attack in the East are progressing favorably."

The Russians, admitting the steady force of assault, said that soldier and citizen armies were grimly defending each of the great cities.

Paving Blocks Barricade

Odessa, the Black Sea port whose history dates back to early Grecian days, was reinforced by sailors from the Red fleet and still stood encircled but defiant atop the 150-foot bluffs that make it a natural fortress.

The Russian government newspaper, Izvestia, said 82,000 civilian volunteers had riped up the cobblestone paving to complete breastworks for a street-to-street defense if necessary.

Kiev, the mother of Russian cities and capital of the Ukraine, continued to stave off a semi-circle of German assaults which have endangered it for weeks.

Cossacks Harrass Nazis

Wild Cossack cavalrymen, skilled with carbine and sabre in the military style of an earlier day, were credited by the Russians with wreaking continual havoc behind the German lines, lessening the fury of the modern mechanized thrusts of the Nazis.

But it was at Leningrad on the north, separated from Odessa by the width of a continent, that the battle raged with greatest heat and least respite.

The Russians said counter-attacks had hurled the Germans back a mile or more, and the Germans claimed to be no nearer than 20 miles from the city.

Fires in Leningrad

But already it has been under direct artillery fire for more than 24 hours, and the Finnish forces [illegible] down from the north [illegible] they could see great fires raging in the city which Peter the Great es-

(Continued on Page 6)

—VVV—

ICELAND IS STRONGLY HELD

Turned into Gibraltar of North and Is Strongly Manned

(Editor's Note: Drew Middleton, of the London Associated Press Bureau, who covered the BEF in France and reported subsequent war developments in Britain, has arrived in Iceland. He tells in this dispatch of the military activities on the North Atlantic island.)

By DREW MIDDLETON

REYKJAVIK, Iceland, Sept. 6, (AP)—Within a few short months this Atlantic Ocean island has been turned into a United States-British Gibraltar of the North.

Iceland bristles today with guns,

(Continued on Page Seven)

—VVV—

FIRE IN READING FOUNDRY PLANT

READING, Sept. 6 (AP)—A general alarm of fire early today caused damage estimated at more than $10,000 to the plant of the Reading Foundry & Supply Company in the heart of the city.

All fire companies were called out to fight the blaze which authorities said started in the core shop of the block-long plant.

Ruling out the possibility of sabotage, officials of the company, which manufactures radiators, boilers, pipes and heating equipment, said they had some defense orders but that they were not working on any "important" contracts for the government. Most of the damage, these officials said, was in a large building used mainly for storage purposes and the fire did not reach the foundry, machine shop and shipping departments.

—VVV—

TRUCKS BADLY DAMAGED BUT DRIVERS UNHURT

Two trucks were damaged to the extent of $750 but the drivers escaped unhurt in a crash on the Morea road just outside the Frackville borough limits Friday afternoon. One truck, driven by John Litwinchuk, of 361 Ash street, Girardville, was making a left turn off the highway, Frackville, motor police said, when his truck was in a collision with another driven in the opposite direction by Elbert T. Stegmeire of 7 Market street, Tamaqua. No arrests were made.

—VVV—

If you vote for Walter, it's a vote for Houck. If you vote for Leidich, it's a vote for Houck, too. VOTE FOR HASENAUER!

GERMANS ADMIT ATTACK ON GREER

BERLIN, Sept. 6(AP)—A German Communique declared today in connection with the case of the U. S. Destroyer Greer that Nazi U-boat fired two torpedoes at a destroyer in water declared to be within the German blockade zone, but asserted the action was in self-defense against attacks.

It asserted that the destroyer was violating neutrality and that the u-boat's action was justifiable.

The incident, it declared, proved that President Roosevelt had given shooting orders to the United States Navy and was now trying to provoke incidents to force the American people into war.

—VVV—

Nazis Cleared From Zone in 3-Day Battle

MOSCOW, Sept. 6, (AP)—Russian forces, pressing counter-attacks on the approaches to Leningrad were reported today to have driven the Germans out of an entire zone along a vital railway after a three-day battle.

The Russian counter-blows still were smashing at the Germans, the report said.

It did not specifically locate the area claimed to have been cleared of the invaders but designated it as the zone between railway stations "F" and village "N."

Thick autumn fog hung over the north western sector where heavy artillery of both sides are dueling in the bitter struggle over Russia's second largest city.

A Red Star dispatch said 30 German planes, flying despite the fog, attempted to bomb military objectives outside Leningrad but that 15 were downed and the others fled. Two of those fleeing were said to have been destroyed trying to reach their base.

At the opposite end of the battlefront the Red army's defense ring around besieged Odessa was declared to have withstood a heavy assault and the press reported the Nazis stalled and set back outside of Kiev after two major attacks in the past month.

Along the entire battlefront fighting is raging without let-up, the Soviet mid-day communique declared as the war neared the end of its 11th week.

—VVV—

REPUBLICAN 598,747 LEAD

HARRISBURG, Sept. 6, (AP)—The Republican Party enters next Tuesday's Primary election with a lead in registration of 597,747 over the Democrats, despite a drop of more than a quarter million in the total number of Pennsylvania voters enrolled.

Last year the Republican lead over the Democrats was 621,583.

The figure from county election boards, final except in Luzerne and Lackawanna Counties, where the books still were open today, showed this political division:

Republicans—2,632,077.
Democrats—2,034,330.
Others—62,758.

American Recruits Drowned

GLASGOW, Sept. 6 (AP)—Four American recruits for the RAF were drowned and two injured when the boat in which they were crossing the Atlantic was torpedoed, it was disclosed here today.

—VVV—

The old folks well remember how Ray Leidich forgot them when he voted against the Old Age Pension. VOTE FOR HASENAUER!

WEATHER

Eastern Penna., N. J., and Dela.: Fair tonight and Sunday; slightly cooler tonight.

A. M.						TODAY						P. M.
1	3	5	7	9	11		1	3	5	7	9	11
60	62	62	63	69	75							

A. M.						YESTERDAY						P. M.
1	3	5	7	9	11		1	3	5	7	9	11
65	66	68	70	72	78		85	86	85	80	85	68

—Go to the Polls Next TUESDAY and VOTE HASENAUER—

POLITICAL NEWS ON PAGE NINE

Weather Forecast
(From U.S. Weather Bureau)

EASTERN PENNA. — Mostly cloudy and not so cold tonight, with few light showers in north portion late tonight and Saturday morning, followed by partly cloudy and not so warm Saturday afternoon.

THE WILLIAMSPORT SUN

Associated Press — Newspaper Enterprise Association — United Press

VOL. 72, NO. 116. WILLIAMSPORT, PA., FRIDAY EVENING, NOV. 14, 1941 28 PAGES

Daily Entered as Second Class Matter, Post Office, Williamsport

Traffic Record Since Jan. 1
Checked at 2 p.m. for previous 24 hours

CITY	1941	Past 24 Hrs.	1940
Accidents	549	0	469
Dead	4	0	7
Injured	204	0	229
COUNTY	**1941**		**1940**
Accidents	271	0	289
Dead	13	0	11
Injured	252	0	271

Totals: 1941—A., 820; D., 17; Inj., 456.
1940—A., 758; D., 18; Inj., 500.

BIG BRITISH AIRCRAFT CARRIER SUNK

ARK ROYAL VICTIM OF TORPEDO, LOSS OF LIFE UNKNOWN

Giant Craft Sinks East of Gibraltar While Being Towed Early This Morning After Submarine Attack Late Yesterday—Undisclosed Number of Crew of 1,600 Men Had Remained Aboard in Struggle to Save Ship.

LONDON—(AP)—The three-year-old, $16,000,000 aircraft carrier Ark Royal was torpedoed late yesterday east of Gibraltar, probably by an Italian submarine, and sank early today despite a desperate effort to bring the listing giant to port.

She carried down with her an undisclosed number of her crew of about 1,600 men who remained aboard in the struggle to save the ship.

"A very large number of the ship's company was taken off," the Admiralty said, and indications were that personnel losses were "fortunately not heavy."

Not in Action When Torpedoed

The story of the sinking, pieced together from the Admiralty's brief announcement and word in authoritative quarters was that the Ark Royal was not in action when she was torpedoed and that she was en route to Gibraltar.

The strong suggestion was that an Italian submarine was the victor, although there was no positive identification.

Many of the company remained aboard after the hit or hits and helped to keep the Ark Royal afloat, in tow, during the hours of darkness as she listed further and further. Many worked to the very end. She finally rolled under the sea short of Gibraltar and safety.

Third of Class Lost

The loss was belated fulfillment of many a German claim, since the beginning of the war, that the carrier had been sunk.

The concise communique said that the 22,000-ton floating airfield sank somewhere on some undisclosed date while in tow after having been torpedoed.

She was the third aircraft carrier lost by Britain in the war and the newest of them all.

The Admiralty communique identified the submarine only as a "U-boat" which while originally a German designation might apply also to an Italian submarine.

Worst Blow Since Hood

The vessel was under the command of Capt. L. E. H. Maund, but whether the commander was among the "fortunately not heavy" casualties was not made public. The carrier's normal complement was 1,575 men.

His wife in London said, "so far I have had no news as to whether my husband is safe. I am getting in touch with the Admiralty, but I do not think they have any further information."

Loss of the Ark Royal was the greatest single blow suffered by the British navy since the avenged sinking of the battle cruiser, Hood, by the German battleship, Bismarck, between Greeland and Iceland last May 24.

The loss of the Ark Royal left the British, however, with more aircraft carriers than they had at the start of the conflict—seven in commission and two scheduled for completion in 1942, as indicated by the naval manual, Jane's Fighting Ships.

Those believed in operation include the Eagle, 22,600 tons, a converted battleship, the 23,000-ton Il-

(Cont. on Page 10, Col. 3, this Sec.)

NO WORD OF LOST PLANE WITH ENVOYS

TEHERAN, Iran—(AP)—The Soviet embassy said this evening that it still had no news of the plane in which U.S. Ambassador Laurence A. Steinhardt, Russian Ambassador Maxim Litvinoff and about a dozen others are reported missing en route here from Kuibyshev, Russia.

The British legation here reported that an American woman journalist, Alice Moats, and an American magazine writer, Quentin Reynolds, were among the passengers.

The Russian embassy said it had received up to nightfall no reports from either South Russian or North Iranian airfields along the route.

COUNTY BOARD NO. 1 TO SEND EIGHT DEC. 8

Eight draftees from Lycoming County Draft Board No. 1, Montoursville, will be inducted into the U.S. Army Dec. 8. The men have been notified to report to Fort George Meade on that date. They will leave Williamsport by train.

Dorsey Lee Burkhart, 335 Mulberry Street, Montoursville, has been named leader of the group.

Others are: Dyle James Miller, Williamsport R.D.1; Robert Bruce Willits, 438 Wilson Street, Jersey Shore; Wilbur Glenn Mills, Hughesville R.D.1; Eugene Alexander Bubb, 131 South Second Street, Hughesville; Kenneth Leroy Deppen, 320 South Main Street, Hughesville; LaRue Kimble Lundy, Williamsport R.D.1; Donald Ward Everett, 409 Broad Street, Montoursville.

LITTLE CHANGE IN OFFICIAL BALLOT COUNT

Totals of the official count including the military vote were announced today by county commissioners acting as County Board of Elections. The official figures vary but little from the unofficial newspaper totals.

Results follow:

City Council—Smith 3,572; Heiser 3,533; Henninger 6,677; Shay 6,313.

School Director — Sutliff 3,714; Harer 4,708; Mosser 6,537; Furst 5,969; Bowman 6,142.

Judge Supreme Court — Carr 8,896; Parker 12,923.

Judge Superior Court—Musmanno 8,485; Kenworthey 13,074.

Judge Common Pleas — Katzmaier 8,549; Larrabee 14,913.

Coroner—Brandon 16,645.

Jury Commissioner — Levering 8,936; Heim 13,259.

Health, Welfare Day

FRIDAY, NOV. 14

This is "Health and Welfare Day" in Civilian Defense Week.

"Health and Welfare Day" takes as its theme the fact that the ability of a nation to defend itself depends as much upon the health and stamina of its men, women and children at home as upon the caliber of the armed forces and their equipment.

It stresses the fact that there is a job for everyone in building a strong, healthy community and in keeping America "fit for defense."

TELEPHONE CO. SEEKS RIGHT TO INCREASE RATES

About 2,400 Subscribers To Be Affected by Change on Jan. 1.

MUNCY—The West Branch Telephone Company, with headquarter offices in Muncy, has filed new tariff rates with the Public Utility Commission raising monthly rates from $3 to $3.50 for one-party lines and making corresponding increases for other services.

The new rates will go into effect Jan. 1, 1942 and about 2,400 telephone subscribers will be affected, it was learned from Ralph A. Decker, manager, today.

An Associated Press dispatch from Harrisburg this morning states that the Public Utility Commission considered today a new tariff of this firm, increasing business party rates 50 cents monthly and similar residential service 25 cents a month.

The West Branch Company furnishes service in Hughesville, Montgomery, Picture Rocks, Stone Church and Muncy, Lycoming County; Turbotville and Watsontown, Northumberland County, and adjacent sections of Lycoming, Northumberland and Union Counties.

Lines of the West Branch Telephone Company connect with the Bell Telephone system.

Extensive Shipments Of Trout for County To Be Distributed

Extensive shipments of trout for stocking in Lycoming County streams are scheduled for receipt during the latter part of this month, according to W. H. Corson, chairman of the fish committee of the Consolidated Sportsmen of Lycoming County, and Carl Bidelspacher, fish warden.

Arrangements have been made to have the trucks met at designated points by regional representatives of the sportsmen's association and all persons interested in the stocking are asked to report at these points to those in charge.

The schedule follows:

Nov. 20—Loyalsockville, 11 a.m., brown and brook trout for Wallis Run and Little Bear Creek, Clyde Maley in charge.

Nov. 20—Waterville, 11 a.m., rainbow trout for Little Pine Creek, L. Huff, Charles Wentzel and Homer Love in charge.

Nov. 20—Cogan Station, 11 a.m.,

(Cont. on Page 12, Col. 2, this Sec.)

Scraps Neutrality Act

SOVIET GAIN IN BIG DRIVE IS REPORTED

Red Armies Claimed to Have Forced Nazis Out Of 20 Villages

COUNTER OFFENSIVE ON KALININ SECTOR

Tank-Led German Shock Troops Hurled Back in Front of Tula

By ASSOCIATED PRESS

Russia's armies before Moscow, pressing a tempestuous counter-offensive, were reported today to have driven the Germans out of 20 villages in the past 24 hours in the Kalinin sector, while on the northern front, the Soviet radio said Red troops had scored a break through the Nazi siege ring outside Leningrad.

Repulse German Tanks

Tass, the Soviet news agency, reported also that tank-led German shock troops had been thrown back from the outskirts of Tula, 100 miles south of Moscow, after a bloody two-week battle.

"The Germans were here yesterday. Today only their corpses are here," Tass said.

The news agency said the Germans hurled 15 consecutive tank attacks at the little village of Rodezhesny, on the southern outskirts of Tula, and gained a temporary foothold before being smashed back with heavy casualties.

Amid these successes, the London Admiralty acknowledged the loss of the 22,000-ton aircraft carrier Ark Royal which the Germans have repeatedly claimed as sunk.

Take Turn for Worse

In the Far East crisis, relations between Japan and Russia took a turn for the worse as Moscow replied to Tokyo's protest over the sinking of the Japaneses liner, Kehi

(Cont. on Page 10, Col. 8, this Sec.)

DISTRICT SNOW REMOVAL PLANS NOW COMPLETED

Highway Department Officials Report Crews Ready for Storms.

Fully mechanized and manned, the State Highway Department snow removal machinery is being geared up for the first heavy snow of the approaching season.

The equipment lined up for the assault against the Winter elements embraces 851,820 feet of snow fence, 150 department owned or rented snow removing units, and thousands of tons of cinders for the eight-county Williamsport District.

Close to 600 men have been called in past years to cope with severe storms and this year stand ready to keep program highways in this Central Pennsylvania area open.

The snow removal program for this district extends over 1,219 miles of state road and 503 miles of what are termed rural highways, making a total of 1,722 miles on the program.

Highway officials explained these roads receive first attention and

(Cont. on Page 10, Col. 6, this Sec.)

BOARD EXAMINER HERE TO CONDUCT HEARINGS

Two cases were scheduled before an examiner of State Liquor Control Board at the Court House today. Mrs. Margaret Belcofski, Mt. Carmel, is making application for a new license. Joseph Pachick, Kulpmont, was ordered before the examiner for an alleged violation.

Bankers Meet Here Tonight

Group 4, Pennsylvania Bankers' Association, will hold a dinner meeting at The Lycoming this evening at 6.30 o'clock when R. R. Williams, statistician of the Federal Reserve Bank, Philadelphia, will speak.

$380,000 HERE IN CHRISTMAS SAVING FUNDS

Local Banks Preparing to Release Checks Early Next Month.

Almost 11,000 persons in Williamsport, South Williamsport and Montoursville, will share this year in the disbursement of $380,000 in Christmas savings accounts, local bank officials announced today.

Checks are being prepared now for the annual disbursement and are expected to go into the mail early in December.

Last payments in the various clubs are due on Saturday and it is expected that the books will be closed shortly after Nov. 15 to permit completion of the clerical work in time for December mailing.

The bank spokesman said today that greater interest has been shown during this year by depositors in the Christmas accounts, and a larger percentage of them is paid up to date than has been true in some previous years. One or two institutions said their disbursements for 1941 will be the largest in their history.

Engineer Dies Of Injuries in Sunday Wreck

KENTON, O. — (AP)—Engineer Rolla E. Shuler, of Fort Wayne, Ind., died today, the 13th fatality in Sunday night's Pennsylvania passenger train wreck at nearby Dunkirk. About 40 were injured.

Shuler was piloting the "Pennsylvanian" at 60-70 miles an hour when it struck a half-ton cylinder head blown from a passing freight train. The train was derailed and wrecked a signal control tower.

The engineer suffered a badly crushed arm and head injuries. An infection which developed in the arm was reported as largely responsible for his death.

Shay Expense Account

Philip Shay, successful candidate for City Council, filed an account with county commissioners Thursday showing expenditures of $289.42 in his campaign.

STATES U.S. WON'T ORDER CLOSED SHOP

Says Government Will Never Compel Minority to Join Union

ASKS C.I.O. CHIEFS CONTINUE EFFORTS

Question of Averting Strike in Captive Mines Issue at Session

WASHINGTON—(AP)—President Roosevelt, asking the C.I.O. United Mine Workers and steel company heads to continue negotiations to avert a strike in the captive mines, told them today that "the government will never compel" the minority non-union miners affected by the dispute to join the union.

Makes Clear Statement

"I tell you frankly," he said, "that the government of the United States will not order, nor will Congress pass legislation ordering, a so-called closed shop."

The union is asking a union shop in the mines, which supply coal to steel mills busy on defense orders. Such an arrangement would require that all employes become members of the union after a probationary period.

The closed shop provides that the employer may not hire any man who is not a union member.

The President asked the mine leaders and the steel representatives to give him a report on an agreement to continue production by Monday, or at least a progress report.

A spokesman for the mine workers announced soon afterward that they would accede to the request for three days of direct negotiation on the dispute.

The Chief Executive released a statement which declared unequivocably that the cessation of production of coal would "create a further danger to American defense" and that it was the "indisputable obligation of the President" to see that "necessary coal production be continued and not stopped."

With no element of threat, the Chief Executive disclosed that he

(Cont. on Page 12, Col. 1, this Sec.)

U.S. Ships to Get Freedom Of the Seas

House Vote of 212 to 194 to Adopt Senate Revision of Act Climaxes Hard-Fought Legislative Battle. Action Comes After Dramatic, Last-Minute Appeal From the President. Sweet Victory for Administration.

WASHINGTON — (AP) — American merchantmen regained complete freedom of the seas today by act of Congress, and with it the right to mount guns and shoot if attacked.

The House finished the legislative job in a suspense-packed, historic session yesterday by scrapping the neutrality act amendments which since 1939 have prohibited American shipping from entering the combat zones or belligerent harbors.

The vote was 212 to 194—no tremendous majority but a very sweet victory to administration leaders who had been haunted by visions of a photo finish where two or three votes could mean defeat.

Climax of Hard Fight

The final roll call climaxed the hardest battle yet waged to uphold President Roosevelt's hand in a matter affecting foreign policy. And it came after the tense House heard a dramatic, last-minute appeal from the President.

By its vote the House joined the Senate in broadening the original House ship-arming bill to end all neutrality act restrictions on the movement of vessels flying the Stars and Stripes.

Just as soon as the legislation was approved, Speaker Rayburn quickly affixed his signature, and the strokes of his pen began the official scratching of the neutrality act bans from the statute books.

Raises Technicality

There remained the formality of adding the signature of Vice President Wallace before the measure could go to the White House for the final name: Franklin D. Roosevelt. However, an objection by Senator McNary (R-Ore), the minority leader, made it necessary for Wallace to wait until the Senate reconvenes Monday before signing.

Nevertheless, there was abundant evidence that the technicality of the brief, three-day delay would

(Cont. on Page 10, Col. 1, this Sec.)

Berlin Declares Presentation of Facts Was False

BERLIN—(AP)—Authorized German sources declared today that Congress voted on the basis of a false presentation of facts by President Roosevelt and Secretary Hull in revising the United States neutrality act.

They expressed satisfaction that the congressional majority did not reach one-half of the entire House.

The next days will show what a dangerous path Congress has trodden, they added.

CABLE CHANGE PUTS TRAFFIC LIGHT IN ORDER

Blinker System at Fourth And Hepburn Restored To Operation.

With a makeshift cable a threatened 10-day blackout of the Fourth and Hepburn Street traffic lights has been cut to five days.

The signals were in operation today with the aid of a four-strand aerial cable strung from the Third Street circuit. Chief of Police John G. Good indicated the arrangement may be somewhat permanent.

Last Monday, city electricians found a wire serving the broken down lights was grounded. Inquiry about a new cable immediately brought the response it could not be delivered in less than 10 days or two weeks.

Although the same breakdown can occur at any one of the intersections at any time, there still has been no reported move on the part of city authorities to replace the entire system to make it conform to state standards which go in effect in another 46 days.

The Fly Wins

The larva of a small fly of the North Carolina mountains, platyurs fultoni, reverses roles and spins a web that captures spiders. Perhaps there is some other interesting fact about insect and animal life that you want to know? If so, just write your question plainly and send to The Sun Service Bureau, 1013 Thirteenth Street, Washington, D.C. Sign your name and address and enclose a three cent stamp for return postage.

U.S. Navy Mother Seeks Citizenship

—By Sun Staff Photographer.

Already having pledged allegiance to the U.S.A. by offering her four sons to the navy, Mrs. Mary Madeline Pattarino, 211 West Jefferson Street, now seeks formal papers for citizenship.

Although a resident of this country for 30 years, and mother of an American-born family, Mrs. Pattarino had never acquired citizenship papers. She is shown here taking the preliminary step, making petition to Arthur J. Hodge, naturalization examiner for U.S. Government.

Proud of her sons, Mrs. Pattarino speaks caressingly of her "Tony, Mike, Jerry and Charlie." Mike is bound for Iceland, according to word received by his mother. Two others are on the high seas, and a fourth, Tony, is in Coast Guard service at Brooklyn, N.Y.

AP LEASED WIRE

The Associated Press' full leased wire brings to the readers of this newspaper best and latest coverage of state, national and worldwide news. No other paper can offer Muscle Shoals' citizens a parallel service.

The Tri-Cities Daily

Dedicated To The Interest Of The People Of The Muscle Shoals District

LOCAL COVERAGE

No other public... regardless... resources or m... pic pages, bring you news of Muscle Shoals... nearly so well as can this news paper. Speed, accuracy of detail and an understanding interest in local problems are part and parcel of our service.

VOLUME XXXV | The Associated Press | TUSCUMBIA—SHEFFIELD, THURSDAY AFTERNOON, NOVEMBER 27, 1941 | N. E. A. Service | NUMBER 199

Tobruk Garrison Fulfills Heroic Mission

The War Today

By DEWITT MacKENZIE

The appointment of William C. Bullitt as special presidential observer in the Near East served to emphasize the vast and growing importance of this war-theater which, in conjunction with the Russian front, may provide the decisive field of the war for land operations.

If and when the Allies deliver the coup de grace to the Germans, it likely will be achieved in the main by forces striking at eastern Germany from Russian soil. Through the Near and Middle East will pour troops and resources to back this victory drive.

Should the time come when the British call on the United States for an expeditionary land force—and to my mind that need occasion no surprise—in all probability the necessity will arise from this Middle Eastern zone upon which hangs so much. For that reason alone it is essential that this country have such first-hand information as can only be secured by American observers like Bullitt.

To look at this situation from another angle, the only way Hitler can win the war as the cards now lie is to smash Russia and break down through the Caucasus and into this selfsame Middle Eastern zone. That would in effect shatter the British naval blockade which is strangling him, and would provide him with fresh military bases from which he might pour out defeat against the Allies.

Thus we see how vital is the outcome of the greatest desert battle of all time which is now raging across the hot wastes of Libya. Look at it through Hitler's eyes or from the Allied viewpoint and the answer is the same—that battle must be won or a mirage of disaster may rise up out of the inhospitable sands.

Recognition of this is seen in the unceasing fierceness of the struggle which centers in the Rezegh region south of the port of Tobruk. The great battle of the tanks, which finally died down from pure exhaustion and losses among these land destroyers on both sides, has for the moment given way to old fashioned infantry fighting with cold steel, though more tanks are being rushed into the conflict from reserve.

The battle is still too young for prophecy. Both Berlin and London are cautious and non-committal; only Rome exemplifies the perfect optimist in its claims. However, two important facts give us a certain amount of guidance, though it isn't conclusive:

1. The Allies appear to retain the initiative, despite the powerful Nazi defense and counter-stroke under the fine leadership which one would expect to find in any German command.

2. The outcome of the battle is likely to turn on supplies and reinforcements, and here the Allies would seem to have a great advantage.

The Germans are rushing everything they can by air to the support of General Rommel, but with a British fleet of warships guarding the coast of Libya it would appear that the help which can be sent to him is likely to fall far short of his needs. The British, on the other hand, reportedly have ample supplies and reserves which can be rushed across the desert—indeed, are being brought into the fighting.

Thus, while Rommel has been doing a soldierly job in handling his forces in the face of a heavy surprise attack, the chances would seem to be against him. However, no battle has been won until the last shot is fired, and on that basis it would be rash to get categorical.

Just as this last sentence was written a bulletin arrived from Cairo to announce that New Zealand troops have made junction with British forces which have been fighting their way out of besieged Tobruk. This may be taken as added indication that things aren't going at all badly for the Allies.

U. S. TO PURCHASE ALL OF ARGENTINA'S TUNGSTEN NOW

BUENOS AIRES, (AP)—A three-year agreement under which Argentina will sell her entire production of tungsten to the United States has been concluded, an authorized source announced today.

The agreed price is $21 a ton. (Tungsten ore, or wolframite, most of which comes from China, has been selling at $24 to $26 a ton in New York.)

Tungsten is essential for the production of steels used in manufacture of munitions.

NEGRO TEACHERS TO MEET

Lauderdale county negro teachers are asked to meet at the Slater school, Florence, Saturday, Dec. 6, at 10 a.m., it was announced today by W. Herschel Walker, superintendent.

AT THEATRES TODAY

PRINCESS—Vivien Leigh and Laurence Olivier in "That Hamilton Woman!" Also March of Time presents, "Main Street—U. S. A."

RITZ—Don Ameche and Mary Martin in "Kiss the Boys Goodbye."

STRAND—Greer Garson and Walter Pidgeon in "Blossoms in the Dust," in Technicolor.

MAJESTIC—Alice Faye and Don Ameche in "That Night in Rio," in Technicolor.

PRICE CONTROL BILL IS FACING MORE THREATS

Farm, GOP Blocs Are Opposed; Broader Plans Defeated

WASHINGTON, (AP)—Victorious over a much broader substitute proposal, the administration-backed price control bill found new difficulties ahead today as House groups lined up for an attempt to force the legislation back to committee for additional study and perhaps drastic revision.

There was a temporary lull in the actual battle, for the House was celebrating the second Thanksgiving day with a recess. This postponed until Friday a vote on whether the measure should carry a clause empowering the government to buy and sell commodities to keep their prices stable. The administration favors such a provision.

The pending bill weathered its first test yesterday by a margin of 218-to-63, when the House crushed an attempt to substitute stringent control of all prices, rents and wages for the administration plan of imposing price ceilings on only those commodities whose prices got out of line.

But important opposition was brewing on two important points. The Republicans were dead set against a proposal to license dealers handling regulated commodities, and representatives of farm states did not favor the omission of wage control. This double dissatisfaction evoked speculation on the possibility of a coalition drive for recommittal.

Apparently in recognition of this, majority leader McCormack (D-Mass) took the floor late in yesterday's debate to caution the farm bloc that the measure was "eminently fair to agriculture" and that recommittal probably would mean a bill "far more drastic."

The possibility remained, however, that the farm group would attempt to tack on a wage control amendment on the grounds that ceilings over commodities automatically would put a roof on the income of agriculture producers.

For the present, House attention focused on the "buy and sell" clause demanded by the administration, a provision which gained the support of the banking committee after a long and bitter dispute among its members over the potential effect upon private business.

"This proposition is un-American and vicious," protested Rep. Crawford (R-Mich). "It would put the government into business against every producer and every merchandiser in the country."

POLIO FATAL TO WEISENBERGER

Florence Youth Dies This Morning At Birmingham

Robert C. Weisenberger, aged 16, son of Mr. and Mrs. Harry Weisenberger, Florence, passed away at 9:10 o'clock this morning in a Birmingham hospital after an illness of some three months, diagnosed by physicians as infantile paralysis.

Since his illness, which began Sept. 9, young Weisenberger had put up a terrific struggle with this disease and was placed in an iron lung where he remained the greater part of his illness in the Coffee Memorial hospital. He was carried to Birmingham Tuesday in an ambulance from Brown-Service.

Deceased was a prominent member of the younger set in the Tri-Cities and would have been a junior in high school had he been able to attend this term. He was a member of the Coffee High school band and active in other youthful activities in this district.

The body was being brought to Florence this afternoon by Brown-Service who will announce funeral arrangements later.

BIRMINGHAM, (AP)—Robert C. Weisenberger, 16-year-old Florence high school student, died in a county hospital here today.

He was brought here from Florence several days ago, suffering from infantile paralysis.

MASONS TO ASSEMBLE

MONTGOMERY, (AP)—More than 1,200 Masons are expected to assemble here Dec. 1-3 for annual sessions of the grand Masonic bodies of Alabama. The grand chapter of Royal Arch Masons will begin its annual meeting at 7:30 p. m. Dec. 1; the grand council of Royal and select Masters will assemble Dec. 2, at 2 p. m., and the grand lodge, A. F. and A. M., will begin sessions Dec. 2 at 8 p. m.

AVERAGE PRICE HIGHER

NEW ORLEANS, (AP)—The average price of middling 15-16ths inch cotton today at nine designated Southern spot markets was 7 points higher at 16.27 cents a pound; average for the past 30 market days 16.30; middling 7-8ths inch average 16.35.

Refugees Both

Hanna Pillarska, 4, and friend arrive in New York aboard Excambion from France.

POLICE ARREST TWO YOUTHS IN LOVELESS DEATH

Discovery Of His Car In Kentucky Leads To Solution Of The Crime

APPALACHIA, Va., (AP) — Police Magistrate T. F. Jones said two young men were picked up in a hotel before dawn today in connection with the slaying of Ward Loveless, 51, Washington, D. C., tax attorney whose shot and battered body was found stuffed into a china closet at his Leesburg, Va., home Monday.

Jones said Kentucky state troopers and Virginia authorities, acting on information furnished by a Taxi driver, traced the men to the Houston hotel here and found them asleep. One of the men had several bandages on his head, Jones said.

Loveless' green Ford coupe was found at Cumberland, Ky., just across the Virginia state line, last night and a search was begun for two youths who were reported to have driven it there.

The taxi driver, Jones said, informed authorities he had driven two boys from Cumberland to Appalachia last night and officers searched the town until the two were found.

The magistrate added that the boys seemed concerned principally with the manner in which the police managed to trail them. They were returned to Kentucky, he added.

Patrolman Jimmy Johnson of Cumberland quoted the boys as admitting robbing and beating Loveless but denied knowing the capitol lawyer was dead. Johnson said both boys admitted "some shots were fired," during a scuffle.

The patrolman said Cumberland police were tipped off to the two boys by an aunt of Hoback who read of the Loveless killing and noticed that the automobile bore the same license tags as those listed for Loveless' automobile in the newspaper story.

Johnson said Cumberland police

(Continued on Page Two)

CHILD FALLS IN WELL, DROWNS

Tragedy Occurs Wednesday Afternoon In Tenn.

William Don Gatlin, two and one-half year old son of Mrs. Edith Howard Gatlin, Anderson, was found drowned in a well at the home of his grandparents, Mr. and Mrs. Coy Gatlin, Minor Hill, Tenn., about 2:30 o'clock Wednesday afternoon after he had been missing from the spot where he was playing with several other children for about 45 minutes.

The child, it is presumed, climbed upon the top of the well and fell in and had been dead about 40 minutes when the body was found.

Survivors are his mother, Mrs. Edith Howard Gatlin, Anderson; his father, William Gatlin, Detroit, Mich.; the maternal grandparents, Mr. and Mrs. W. D. Howard, Anderson; and the parental grandparents.

Funeral services will be held Friday morning at 11 o'clock at the Church of Christ, Anderson. Interment will follow in the Mitchell cemetery, near Anderson, Brown-Service directing.

GARDINER WARRING GETS ANOTHER FEDERAL AWARD

WASHINGTON, (AP)—The War Department has awarded the following contracts:

Gardiner - Warring Co., Inc., Florence, wool drawers $60,439.

King and Boozer, Anniston, Ala., prefabricated buildings and insulating boards, $64,846.

U. S. Pipe and Foundry Co., Birmingham, shells, $90,687.

ISSUE OF WAR OR PEACE PUT UP TO NIPPON

Parleys Fail To Find Any Middle Ground For Settlement

WASHINGTON, (AP)—Japanese envoys reported after a White House conference today that they had had a "very friendly" conversation with President Roosevelt.

They were silent, however, as to whether negotiations looking to solution of Japanese-American problems would be resumed.

The White House meeting followed the action of Secretary of State Hull last night in putting the question of peace or war in the Pacific squarely up to the Japanese government.

Saburo Kurusu, special envoy, told reporters however, that he had no orders to return to Japan. He added he would not say now whether he would see Hull in the next few days.

Hull participated in the White House conference, as did Admiral Kichisaburo Nomura, the Japanese ambassador. The conference lasted 45 minutes.

Replying to a barrage of questions, Kurusu said, "we had a very friendly conversation." He added that he and the ambassador had been invited to the White House.

Asked whether the United States proposals handed to him last night provided a basis for further negotiations, Ambassador Nomura said he had not heard from Tokyo and therefore could not answer that.

By LLOYD LEHBRAS

WASHINGTON, (AP)—The United States put the issue of peace or war in the Pacific squarely up to the Japanese government today.

It was for Japan to accept or reject the formula of basic principles which the United States considered essential to the maintenance of peace and security in the Far East.

And those basic principles, in their application, would be diametrically opposed to the often stated policies which Tokyo officials have proclaimed for "the greater East Asia co-prosperity sphere" that Japan envisions.

Relations between the United States and Japan reached this critical juncture late yesterday after

(Continued on Page Two)

MASSIVE NAZI ATTACK THREAT TO RED DEFENSE

Situation Of Soviet Troops Admittedly "Aggravated" In One Sector Of Front

MOSCOW, (AP)—Massive German attacks near Volokolamsk, 65 miles northwest of Moscow, endangered outer Russian defenses to the capital today.

The newspaper Izvestia admitted the situation of Soviet troops in this sector was "aggravated."

Resistance to the expanding German drive was continuing, however, Izvestia said. In the last 10 days the Germans have failed to turn the flanks protecting Moscow although they have driven closer, Pravda, the Communist party organ, added.

Izvestia described the German offensive near Volokolamsk, one of the many spearheads aimed at Moscow, as "enormous."

In one action, the Germans threw six tank and five infantry divisions into the drive against the Soviet lines, Izvestia reported. The Germans sought to encircle the Russians and push them back into a lake, the newspaper added, "but Soviet resistance thwarted this plan."

In one sector 33 German tanks and about three infantry battalions were destroyed. One Soviet regiment broke out of the encircling ring and killed at least 350 Germans, according to Izvestia.

"The result of the enormous German offensive was less heavy than expected," it concluded.

NEW BUILDING PERMITS ISSUED

Largest Is Office Structure By Dr. W. R. Trapp

Permits for erection of six new structures, including one office building and five dwellings, have been issued in recent days by Chief Floyd A. McCorkle, Tuscumbia building inspector, to a total of $14,450.

Largest of these jobs is a brick and tile office, to be erected by Dr. W. R. Trapp on East Fifth street at a cost of about $9,000; work on the foundations for this building is going forward.

O. B. Clark obtained permits for erection of three four-room frame dwellings, at 503 and 505 East Ninth street, and 509 East Eleventh street, each to cost about $1,000.

Roy Sparks obtained a permit for a four-room frame house at 208½ West Fourth street, to cost about $750, and Ed Abernathy is erecting a five-room frame residence at 709 East Ninth, to cost approximately $800.

Nazis Crack Moscow Defense Arc

Winter on the frigid Moscow front has failed to keep Nazis from launching smashing new offensives. Map shows how three breaks in a Russian defense arc of men and machines imperil the Soviet capital eight weeks after Germans opened big drive here.

CHURCHILL GETS 326 TO 2 VOTE OF CONFIDENCE

Germany Believed Shaping Peace Offensive Through Anti-Comintern Front

LONDON, (AP)—The Churchill government, bolstered today by a new vote of confidence, voiced belief that Germany, seeking respite from the war in Russia, was shaping a peace offensive through the expanded anti-comintern pact.

But in the same breath, the government, speaking through foreign secretary Anthony Eden, served notice that the German move would not affect by "one jot" the determination of Britain and her allies to carry the war to a victorious conclusion.

The House of Commons overwhelmingly squelched a move by the four-man independent labor party to unseat the Churchill government today and, in debate, covered virtually every phase of government operations, including conduct of the war.

The independent laborites moved to amend the House's traditional reply to the message from King George VI which opened the present session of Parliament on Nov. 12. They proposed to insert a note of regret that the king's speech contained no definite proposal for cleaning up the economic system.

While the motion was foredoomed to failure, the debate afforded John McGovern, one of the independent laborites, an opportunity to charge, among other things, that the United States was "prepared to use British bodies to blast her way into the markets of the continent."

The amendment was defeated 326 to 2. (Apparently two of the independent laborites had been called on to act as tellers as in the past.) The House then unanimously adopted the Commons' reply to the King's speech, embracing formal approval of government policies as outlined by the King as well as an expression of confidence in Prime Minister Churchill and his cabinet heads of the armed services.

REVIVAL IS ARRANGED

The Church of the Nazarene, East Florence, will hold a revival meeting beginning Monday and continuing throughout the week, with the Rev. E. D. Simpson, district superintendent of the Alabama district of the Church of the Nazarene, preaching. Services will be held each evening at 7 o'clock. Mrs. Simpson will accompany the Rev. Simpson and will assist in singing for which she is well known. The Rev. J. D. Reid, pastor, invites everyone to attend and hear these splendid persons.

HOLD MOLOTOV'S SON

BERLIN, (AP)—German authorities today introduced to about 100 foreign correspondents a young Russian infantry private who, speaking through an interpreter, asserted that he was the only son of Vyacheslaff Molotoff, Soviet Russia's foreign commissar.

The World Today

(By The Associated Press)

Junction between Libyan offensive and Tobruk garrison announced; British claim recapture of Rezegh and Italians recapture of Sidi Omar in Turbulent battle of Libya; British say their stronger reserves may prove decisive in mechanized struggle.

Germans hammer at flanks of Moscow defenses, apparently trying to circle behind anchors of defense line; Moscow admits situation in Volokolamsk sector, northwest of capital, has been "aggravated" in past 24 hours.

Hull statement apparently ends seven-month-long Japanese-American negotiations, leaving the peace of the Pacific up to Japan's acceptance or rejection of the United States' position.

First detachment of United States Marines quits Shanghai.

British and German air forces exchange overnight raids.

SPECIAL BOARD ASKS COMPANIES TO BARE STAND

Reports Published That 2 Steel Firms Unwilling To Accept Decision

(By The Associated Press)

The special arbitration board named by President Roosevelt to settle the union shop issue in captive coal mines of the nation's major steel companies today asked the companies whether they would accept the board's findings as final after reports were published that two steel firms had not agreed to accept them.

Dr. John R. Steelman, board chairman and public representative, telegraphed executives of nine steel companies asking them to reaffirm or clarify their position with respect to the case and to say if they wished to appear before the board.

Published reports said Republic Steel Corporation and the National Steel Corporation had not agreed to abide by the arbitration board's future decision.

In general, the labor situation seemed improved. A jurisdictional strike of 8,500 AFL machinists in the St. Louis area was ended and another special presidential fact-finding board held a preliminary meeting with Mr. Roosevelt before opening new hearings in Washington on a threatened nationwide strike by railroad employes.

Wayne L. Morse, dean of the Oregon University Law school, board chairman, would not say what the members discussed with the President. Last Tuesday in announcing

(Continued on Page Two)

WILLIAM PENNINGTON, II, IS NOW A FLYING CADET

William Pennington, II, son of Mrs. Hazel Ann Lewellen Pennington, Florence, is now a member of the first class of cadets in the new air corps replacement center (air crew) at Kelly Field, Tex. Pennington formerly attended the school of chemical engineering at Washington University, St. Louis, Mo.

At the replacement center he will go through five weeks of preliminary training before being sent to a primary flying school where he will start his flight training. This five weeks course will give him a thorough military background for becoming an officer in the United States army upon graduation from an advanced flying school 30 weeks later.

Upon completion of the course Cadet Pennington will enter one of the 18 primary schools located in the Gulf Coast air corps training area, prepared to concentrate more fully on flying itself than was possible in the past.

Conglomerate Heroes Strike Through And Join With Offensive

Reward Of Seven Months Under German And Italian Siege Is Heralded By The Middle East Communique Today

(By The Associated Press)

The Tobruk garrison, a conglomerate of British imperial troops and their Polish and Czech allies, has fulfilled its mission as a flank threat to the Axis in Libya by striking through to a junction with the main British offensive on that turbulent front, the British Middle East command announced today.

This was the reward of seven months under German and Italian siege.

The Tobruk force came out of its shell and bombarded fortifications on Nov. 18, when the main British drive was launched from the Egyptian border.

The Germans and Italians sought to contain the garrison but, pointed by tanks brought by sea to the besieged port, the men of Tobruk thrust relentlessly through a land mine belt and siege intrenchments to capture Duda yesterday, and juncture with the New Zealanders was effected there early today.

This was achieved after the New Zealanders recaptured Rezegh Tuesday night, according to the Middle East communique.

German troops hammering at Moscow's arc of defenses have taken 14 villages "after desperate hand-to-hand fighting," Berlin war dispatches said today.

The specific locations of these gains were not given.

The British reported the recapture of Rezegh today and the Italians that of Sidi Omar in sharply divergent counter-claims of success in the turbulent Libyan battle of armored armies whipped to new fury by reinforcements for both sides.

An authoritative British source said New Zealand forces had retaken Rezegh, to date the pivotal point of the new battle of Libya.

The captors of Rezegh, it was said, were the same troops which took Bardia—which, the Italian high command reiterated today, is firmly in Fascist hands.

That was the chief contradiction between the British and Axis reports, which also claimed successes in the new flare-up of the Libyan battle on which may depend ultimate control of the whole North African coast.

Axis forces, the Italian war bulletin asserted, have retaken Sidi Omar, near the Egyptian-Libyan frontier, and have repulsed British sorties from Tobruk.

The British were said to have taken Rezegh in the first thrust of their campaign, now in its 10th day, then lost it to the Germans and retaken it again last night.

According to the Italian communique, fighting has been resumed in that sector.

On reserves already thrown into the fight to replace depleted machines on both sides and on others still withheld may hinge the ultimate decision of the costly desert struggle.

In this, British in Cairo expressed belief the advantage was theirs. They said the Axis probably had exhausted most of its reserve strength with little chance of getting new tanks or armored cars across the Mediterranean.

In Russia, the German high command said, the Red army has lost heavily near and north of Rostov-on-Don, at the southern end of the long eastern front, and has been frustrated in a new attempt to break out of the Leningrad siege ring in the north.

Advices to Pravda, the organ of the Communist party, acknowledged that the Germans had made new

(Continued on Page Five)

SEVEN-MONTHS TOBRUK SIEGE APPEARS OVER

Relief Column Joins Hands With Heroic Garrison, Report

CAIRO, (AP)—The seven-months siege of Tobruk, one of history's most dramatic, appeared ended today as the British command announced that a relief column which had recaptured the bloody battleground of Rezegh en route had joined hands this morning with the Tobruk garrison.

New Zealand forces supported by tanks smashed northward to meet a column from the conglomerate Tobruk defenders this morning, a communique said.

The great tank and infantry battle swirled through its tenth day with both sides throwing in new reserves. The main battle still apparently was about Rezegh, 10 miles south of Tobruk, but was spreading far to the east into Egypt, where the British fought to wipe out an Axis column which drove across the frontier yesterday.

British officers said the junction with the Tobruk force meant the British eighth army had won the first round but they predicted heavy fighting still to come.

They admitted that although British advance elements had joined hands there remained pockets of Axis resistance between the main British forces.

The main British objective, it was stated, remained the destruction of the Axis armored forces and this was being achieved steadily. Therefore the recapture of Rezegh was minimized.

Here is the official British account of the relief of Tobruk:

"During the night of Nov. 25-26 New Zealand forces supported by British tank formations recaptured Rezegh and occupied Eir Bir El Hamed in the face of heavy opposition.

"Stiff fighting continued in that area throughout yesterday and it was not until early this morning that elements of the relieving forces

(Continued On Page Five)

DIXON SEEKING SCHOOL FINANCE DATA IN STATE

Orders State Examiners To Check Condition Of All Sixty-Seven Counties

MONTGOMERY, (AP)—Governor Dixon, whom organized educational forces are urging to call a special session of the legislature, has ordered state examiners of accounts to give him immediately reports on school finances in each of the 67 counties.

The governor said he anticipated a report sometime next week, and it was learned elsewhere 68 examiners are busy assembling data to show amounts received by schools in the three years of the Dixon administration, the year previous, and the comparative length of terms and teachers' salaries.

Educators have been pressing for a special session to appropriate to schools a surplus of $1,783,000 accumulated over the last fiscal year in the special educational trust fund.

A 1935 law directing that any surplus in this fund be used for lowering property taxes recently was held unconstitutional by the Supreme Court.

Governor Dixon repeatedly has insisted he would call a special session only in event of grave emergency, but the Alabama education association, working through county superintendents, recently obtained a pledge from a majority of legislators they would vote against anything but release of the surplus should they be called.

All delegations visiting the governor thus far have been told: "I'll give serious consideration to your case." Otherwise, there has been no comment.

KIWANIANS MEET FRIDAY

The Florence Kiwanis club will hold its weekly meeting Friday noon at Basil's cafe when Horace Springer, who is in charge of program arrangements, will present a musical program. All members are expected to be present.

TUSCUMBIANS ASKED NOT BURN LEAVES IN STREETS

Tuscumbia residents were asked today by officials, to desist from burning of leaves and other trash in the gutters, where heat is ruining the asphalt with which the streets are paved.

Mayor John C. Geise pointed out that, when damage to public property of this nature is done, it is just as much a loss to the individual as to the city; should the streets have to be repaved, it will be at cost of the home-owner.

City ordinances, too, it was pointed out, prohibit such actions, and unless residents change their habits, the city will be forced to prosecute the law violators.

HOLLIMAN IS ASSIGNED

Donald T. Holliman, Florence, who has been stationed at Fort McPherson, Ga., has been assigned to the air corps, Wichita Falls, Tex.

THE WEATHER

ALABAMA: Fair, frost in south portion, temperature 32 to 36 in interior of south portion and 38 to 40 on the coast tonight; Friday fair, slowly rising temperature. Light to gentle variable winds on the coast.

TENNESSEE: Continued fair with moderate temperatures tonight and Friday.

Maximum temperature for 24-hour period ending at 6:30 a. m., 62 degrees; minimum, 29. Pickwick lake stage, 8.33 feet, rise of .07 foot.

Minnesota Weather
Rain or snow, colder.

Hour	1	2	3	4	5	6	7
Temp.	55	56	56	55	53	52	51
Hour	8	9	10	11	12	1	2
Temp.	50	50	49	49	49	49	49

Detected weather report on Page 21.

St. Paul Pioneer Press

Oldest and Largest Morning Newspaper in Minnesota

What's NEW in Hollywood? What new pictures are in production? Read the "SHOW" Section of the SUNDAY PIONEER PRESS for all the latest interesting developments from the Film Capital.

88TH YEAR—NO. 339 | 24 PAGES | ST. PAUL, MINN., FRIDAY, DECEMBER 5, 1941. | Telephone CEdar 5011 | C | 3 Cents In Twin City Area, 5 Cents Elsewhere

JAPS ANSWER TODAY; BREAK NEAR

AN OLD FRATERNITY CUSTOM—
14 Redheads Keep Luncheon Date

Fourteen redheads — count them—were guests of the Phi Gamma Delta fraternity at a date luncheon Thursday noon in the fraternity house, 1129 University ave. S. E., Minneapolis. Entertaining henna-hued girls on the University of Minnesota campus is an annual project of Phi Gamma Delta.

Oleo Ruling Stirs War on Bureaus

Sentiment Growing To Nip Authority

By L. D. PARLIN

Encouragement of the oleomargarine business by the federal government through allegedly unfair means is developing a feeling among Midwest farm leaders that they may have to launch a congressional battle to shear off some of the vast powers wielded by government "bureaucrats".

Minnesotans who returned from a series of dairy state conferences in Chicago this week report that sentiment is growing for an all-out move to take away from the Federal Social Security division the right to build up "imitation butter" sales at the expense of the Midwest farm population.

Many dairy leaders believe that a federal employe, such as Paul V. McNutt, social security director, should not have power to take actions which may jeopardize the future of one of the nation's greatest farm industries—butter production.

State Senator Oscar Swenson of Nicollet, one of the national leaders in the fight against government encouragement of artificially colored and flavored oleomargarine, declared there was much discussion along this line in Chicago.

McNutt took the side of

(Please Turn to Page 9, Col. 2)

Wars on Spies

Unlike his famous father, William Jennings Bryan Jr. has not won fame as an orator but he is serving his country as collector of customs for the Port of Los Angeles. The son of the "Great Commoner" aided the cause of defense by preventing alien spies masquerade as fishermen and he helped to stem the flood of propaganda pouring into the United States. Story on Page 12.

National Union O.K.'s Plant Hiring

St. Paul Plasterers' Unit Cleared of Charges

Charges that the St. Paul local of the Plasterers and Cement Finishers union "sold" jobs at the St. Paul Ammunition plant are "absolutely without foundation in fact", an international union official announced Thursday following a four-day investigation.

Brought about through charges of a Minneapolis Cement Finishers union agent, the investigation backfired on the Minneapolis local since the St. Paul union was given a clean bill of health by the international.

"The international union recognizes the jurisdiction of the St. Paul local," Harold J. Olsen, international vice president of the union, declared after completing the investigation which he made at the insistence of T. E. Hendrickson, Minneapolis business agent.

"I told the Minneapolis agent," he added, "that he could not expect the Minneapolis wage scale to prevail on the New Brighton job and that his demands that Minneapolis mechanics be paid $1.50 per hour on straight time plus transportation were unreasonable demands."

"I have investigated the charges of the Minneapolis busi-

(Please Turn to Page 2, Col. 4)

Green, Murray Flay Smith Bill

Wallace Refers It To Labor Committee

By WALTER RIDDER
Pioneer Press Staff Writer

WASHINGTON — While spokesmen for organized labor bitterly condemned the measure, the Smith bill regulating unions and strikes was referred Thursday to the Senate education and labor committee by Vice President Wallace.

Attempts had been made to steer the bill away from the New Deal labor committee by referring it to the judiciary committee, but Wallace said he had "come to the consideration that there is no basis whatever for reference to the Senate judiciary committee".

The attitude of labor spokesmen toward the bill, passed Wednesday by the House, 252-136, strengthened Senate feeling that the measure is too drastic. William Green, president of the AFL, called it "America's first move toward totalitarianism".

Green lashed particularly at the sections which bar sympathy or jurisdictional strikes and which prohibit strikes on the closed shop issue. He said the right to strike is one of democracy's basic freedoms and it "cannot be abridged or restricted by law without exposing all our freedoms to danger of destruction".

At the same time, Philip Murray, president of the CIO declared the Smith bill and other anti-labor legislation now before Congress, "undermine and eliminate the basic rights and privileges of the American people".

Capital circles believe the Smith bill will be considerably modified by the Senate. It is regarded as highly possible that

(Please Turn to Page 6, Col. 3)

Nazis Ask French Bases; Denied Fleet

Petain Said to Refuse to Strike At British Blockade

By UNITED PRESS

Germany has made the long-expected demand for French naval and air bases in Africa, arguing that they must be protected against possible American or British invasion, according to reliable reports from Europe Thursday night.

There were conflicting views as to whether France complied, but the best indications were that she had rejected another demand for the use of her powerful fleet.

The crisis has been brought to a head by the British campaign in Libya. German and Italian armies there are cut off from all but air-borne supplies, due to the British blockade of the Mediterranean

France could possibly save the day for the Axis powers by turning over Tunisian ports for supply bases and using her fleet to break the blockade. The question of whether France will do so is the key to the whole African situation.

Reports circulated in London that at the conference in St. Florentin, south of Paris, on Monday, Reichs Marshal Goering obtained permission from French Marshal Petain for the Germans to occupy all naval and air bases in French North Africa.

In return, Germany agreed, according to these reports, not to touch the French fleet, to liberate some French war prisoners and to reduce the "occupation costs", which have drained from three to four hun-

(Please Turn to Page 3, Col. 3)

London-Like Fog Blankets East Coast

By THE ASSOCIATED PRESS

Another London - like fog turned Eastern coastal, lake and river valley areas into a ghost world of dim, hazy lights and shadowy figures again Thursday night, virtually halting all marine and air traffic and reducing highway traffic to a snail's pace for the second consecutive night.

At LaGuardia airport in New York City, all air travel was canceled indefinitely and experienced observers said the gray blanket was worse than that of the preceding day and night.

The blinking lights of Manhattan's skyscrapers grew dimmer and dimmer as the fog lowered, seemingly clipping off one floor after another.

WAVES TO HIS CHILDREN—
Killed Seconds Later

A Minneapolis fireman waved a greeting to his four little girls Wednesday as he sped past his home, perched on top of a fire truck.

Seconds later he fell from the truck as it rounded a corner at Sixth and Plymouth, a block away. He died in General hospital of a fractured skull.

The fireman, Arthur Tyczncski, 50 years old, was responding to a minor blaze at 1728 Second st., N.

His children returned to play just before their father fell and did not witness the accident. The fire station is a block from Tyczncski's home.

Other men on the truck said that Tyczncki had inhaled smoke earlier in the day while fighting a three-alarm fire on Lowry ave.

Reds Push Nazis Back at Kharkov Following Attack

FROM LATE DISPATCHES

Russian armies broke a new German offensive in the Upper Donets basin, scored new successes at each end of the Moscow defense arc and continued pursuit of beaten Nazi forces on the Azov coast Thursday—but a powerful German thrust at Moscow from the southwest admittedly drove a panzer wedge into Red defense lines and forced a Soviet withdrawal.

In Libya, British imperial troops repaired damages and maneuvered for new battle positions, with Axis armored divisions strongly situated except for supplies and the outcome of the desert campaign by no means certain.

A "Free Yugoslav" army in the Serbian mountains was reported, without confirmation, to have so developed this "third front" that it was engaging seven full German divisions (105,000 men) in battle and had captured the important towns of Cacak and Uzice.

German spokesmen insisted that their forces in Russia had established a strong defense line between Rostov and Tagan g on the Azov coast and were repelling attacking troops.

German news dispatches said the Nazis had called upon their Italian and Slovak allies in an effort to halt the powerful and relentless tank, infantry and cavalry charges of the Red army. However, the Nazi spokesman ridiculed Soviet reports that the Reds had reached Taganrog, 40 miles west of Rostov.

Soviet defenders of the Kharkov segment of the southern front said they absorbed the impact of a big German attack, apparently designed to ease the plight of Nazis routed from Rostov, then counter-attacked so strongly that the Germans were pushed back from original positions.

While a correlated strengthening of Field Marshal von Kleist's resistance on the road back from Rostov toward Mariupol, 100 miles to the west, was noted, Soviet informants said that the great Red push still is rolling generally unchecked.

Some dispatches asserted that whether or not any important German forces manage eventually to get out alive, Von Kleist already has irrevocably lost a great engagement, especially in the vast numbers of tanks and cars captured by the pursuing Reds.

At Kalinin, 95 miles north of Moscow, a Soviet offensive was said to have driven the Germans back, recapturing a vital town. On the Tula sector, 110 miles south of Moscow, Russian cavalry was said to have driven the Germans southward at Stalinogorsk. An artillery duel was raging at Tula itself.

The admitted Soviet setback southwest of Moscow was in the Mozhaisk-Maloyaroslavets region. In a powerful breakthrough attempt the Germans hurled 100 tanks against the Red lines and followed them with masses of motorized storm troops.

Nazis Kill 36 Nazis

WITH THE RAF IN THE WESTERN DESERT — (AP) — Thirty-six German prisoners were killed and 60 wounded early Thursday when German planes bombed freight cars carrying them to the Nile valley from the Libyan battlefront.

The attack was made in the darkness.

Husband Killed As Wife Waits

Man, 79, Struck by Car on University Ave.

Because Mrs Evelyn Williams always greeted her husband when he came home from work each night, she did not leave their house Thursday night to investigate the sound of a siren at University and Milton, a half-block away.

"I didn't want to see a fire and miss John's arrival," she said.

But there was no fire at University and Milton and John Williams did not come home.

He was killed almost instantly when struck by an auto at the intersection. It was the ambulance siren Mrs Williams heard.

The driver, Vernon Kolstad, 22 years old, of 60 W. Summit, told police he failed to see Williams as the latter crossed University ave. on foot.

Police reported that Williams, 79 years old, apparently had just alighted from a west-bound University ave. street car, waited until it had passed and then crossed the avenue.

Married 23 years, Mr and Mrs Williams, whose home is at 917 Aurora ave., had no children.

Hull's Terms for Peace Denounced

Reply to Both F. R. and Secretary Expected; Tokyo Diplomats in Mexico Rush to Return Home

Washington—(AP)—Foreboding statements at Tokyo and significant developments here Thursday night indicated an imminent major break in the Far Eastern crisis—upon which may hang the question of peace or war.

An official of the Japanese embassy announced that its diplomats will carry to the State department today Tokyo's answer to President Roosevelt's pointed demand for an explanation of large-scale Japanese troop movements which seem to threaten an invasion of Thailand.

Perhaps, the same official said, they will take with them the long-awaited reply to the memorandum in which Secretary Hull last week restated America's unalterable opposition to Japanese aggression.

Meanwhile, Domei, authoritative Japanese agency, circulated a dispatch saying the Hull declaration of principles cannot stand as a basis for continued negotiations looking toward maintenance of peace in the Pacific.

It quoted "observers" as its authority for this assertion. However, its close ties with the Tokyo government are well known, and the dispatch was widely regarded as an accurate forecast of what Japan will say in answer to Hull.

Domei's dispatch was preceded, moreover, by a series of pessimistic statements from government leaders and Japanese newspapers. The latter were said to have expressed "shocked surprise and extreme pessimism" at statements by Hull. These statements, they thought, indicated an unbridgable gap between Washington and Tokyo.

The gloomy expectation of portentous developments here was further increased by a dispatch from Mexico City which told of the Japanese diplomatic staff there making hurried preparations for a return to Japan. Their activities were reportedly prompted by the arrival of a courier from Washington bringing confidential reports of the progress of the American-Japanese negotiations.

The Japanese minister to Mexico and the legation's second secretary applied at the United States consulate for transit visas which would permit them and their families to board ship at Los Angeles. A number of Japanese residents of the Mexican capital were reported trying to dispose quickly of their Mexican properties in the belief, it was said, that Mexico would inevitably be drawn into any war between the United States and Japan.

Washington has been awaiting a reply to Hull's memorandum for more than a week. Tokyo has been formulating its answer in a long and deliberative series of cabinet meetings.

Domei's statement Thursday quoting reliable observers said:

"Such a document cannot serve as a basic datum in Japanese-American negotiations henceforth.

"Japanese-American conversations have taken place twice since the United States handed over to Japan the document in question, and the United States government has sent the Japanese inquiries pertaining to certain questions.

"But there is no tangible evi-

(Please Turn to Page 2, Col. 1)

Army and Navy Investigate Leak

Check on AEF Story In Chicago Tribune

WASHINGTON —(AP)— The War and Navy departments launched investigations Thursday to determine how a Chicago Tribune reporter obtained copies of highly confidential correspondence between the White House and the departments.

The Tribune published these documents Thursday morning and interpreted them as meaning an American Expeditionary Force of five million men is contemplated for an offensive against Germany by July 1, 1943.

This interpretation promptly was brought into House debate on an $8,243,839,031 supplemental defense bill, and was disputed by Representative Cannon (D., Mo.), in charge of th bill, and Representative Tab (R., N. Y.), senior minority member of the appropriations committee.

The White House, the W… and Navy departments all carefully refrained from saying what may or may not have been said in confidential exchanges between the President and his defense advisers. But al emphasized, somewhat grimly that inquiries are underway determine the source or sour of the story written by Ch…

(Please Turn to Page 4, Col

Labor Parliamentarians Fussed When Non-Union Man Pickets Bar

A union picket, who turned out to be a non-union picket, had union parliamentarians scratching their heads Thursday afternoon on the sidewalk in front of Wally's bar, 391 Robert st.

The picket himself got so fussed that he expressed complete willingness to turn in his banner and drop the whole thing.

The ball got rolling when a couple of beer drivers accosted the picket, stationed in front of Wally's by AFL Teamsters union, and asked to see his credentials.

"I haven't got any credentials, because I'm not a union man," the picket answered.

The beer drivers were stopped cold on that one, so they decided to call headquarters of the Brewery Workers union. One beer driver kept an eye on the picket, so he wouldn't get away, while the other phoned.

Headquarters of the Brewery Workers union opined that it was irregular of the Teamsters union to pick a non-union man to do their picketing, but that there's no law against it.

Police broke up the sidewalk forum which followed, and the picket, muttering about the "grief" connected with his job, resumed his picketing.

Several other taverns over the city were picketed Thursday by AFL Teamsters who are seeking to force beer and soft drink drivers to give up their affiliation with the Brewery Workers union, which has been suspended by the AFL, and join a new local set up under the AFL Teamsters International.

Teamsters union spokesmen claimed that many of the taverns Thursday either refused beer deliveries or, after accepting deliveries, ordered the breweries to come and take back the beer.

In the event that a tavern accepted beer from drivers still affiliated with the Brewery Workers union, Teamsters union representatives stationed a picket outside the tavern and threatened to cut off milk and bread deliveries to the place.

Joseph Obergfell, secretary-treasurer of the Brewery Workers International union, Thursday night pledged a "finish fight" against what he termed the "strong-arm" attempt of the AFL Teamsters union to gain control of brewery truck drivers in St. Paul and Minneapolis.

Obergfell, who was the principal speaker at a mass meeting of more than 600 Brewery Workers union members in Ramsey hall in the Auditorium, revealed that legal steps to enjoin the AFL union from "forcing Brewery Workers members and their employers to break their legitimate contracts" will be taken in Hennepin county district court Monday.

He said legal action in St. Paul might be delayed for the present because "there have been no overt acts as yet".

Faces Gleam and Tummies Bulge At Early Christmas for 250 Boys

(Picture on Page 13)

Remember back in the days when you were a kid—those boyish wishes you had?

Meet a real football player.

Eat all the ice cream your stomach could hold.

Talk to Santa Claus personally.

Those wishes were satisfied Thursday night for some 250 Twin Cities underprivileged boys of all ages who celebrated their Christmas early as guests of the University of Minnesota's 26 academic fraternities.

For the kids it was three hours of a swell time.

Look at the things there were to do and see and eat.

Bundled into cars, the youngsters were driven off to the various fraternity houses for dinner. There was no end of good things to eat. Roast turkey, chicken, mashed potatoes and gravy, lots of dressing and ice cream and cake.

The kids ate and ate and ate until their tummies were full and their belts too tight. And for once in their lives, as one little fellow put it:

"I couldn't look at another dish of ice cream. I didn't think that could happen."

After dinner they sang a lot of songs and received presents. The best was yet to come.

Leaving the fraternity houses they assembled at Tenth ave. S. E. and University and marched in a torchlight parade to Coffman Memorial Union for a special Christmas party.

There they met University of Minnesota football players, got the lowdown on the football season by seeing motion pictures of the games, and took in a wrestling exhibition.

And then—just like he does in the books—Santa Claus stomped in, carrying a big bundle of presents with him. Only it wasn't Santa Claus, but one of his best representatives, Bill Daley, Gopher grid star.

After more presents had been handed out, the kids ate popcorn, sang a few songs and then went home, reluctantly, but in high spirits.

The world, Thursday night, was a happy peace.

Honolulu Star-Bulletin 1st EXTRA

Evening Bulletin, Est. 1882, No. 11278
Hawaiian Star, Vol. XLVIII, No. 15359

8 PAGES—HONOLULU, TERRITORY OF HAWAII, U. S. A., SUNDAY, DECEMBER 7, 1941—8 PAGES

★ PRICE FIVE CENTS

WAR!

(Associated Press by Transpacific Telephone)

SAN FRANCISCO, Dec. 7.—President Roosevelt announced this morning that Japanese planes had attacked Manila and Pearl Harbor.

OAHU BOMBED BY JAPANESE PLANES

SIX KNOWN DEAD, 21 INJURED, AT EMERGENCY HOSPITAL

Attack Made On Island's Defense Areas

By UNITED PRESS

WASHINGTON, Dec. 7. —Text of a White House announcement detai ling the attack on the Hawaiian islands is:

"The Japanese attacked Pearl Harbor from the air and all naval and military activities on the island of Oahu, principal American base in the Hawaiian islands."

Oahu was attacked at 7:55 this morning by Japanese planes.

The Rising Sun, emblem of Japan, was seen on plane wing tips.

Wave after wave of bombers streamed through the clouded morning sky from the southwest and flung their missiles on a city resting in peaceful Sabbath calm.

According to an unconfirmed report received at the governor's office, the Japanese force that attacked Oahu reached island waters aboard two small airplane carriers.

It was also reported that at the governor's office either an attempt had been made to bomb the USS Lexington, or that it had been bombed.

CITY IN UPROAR

Within 10 minutes the city was in an uproar. As bombs fell in many parts of the city, and in defense areas the defenders of the islands went into quick action.

Army intelligence officers at Ft. Shafter announced officially shortly after 9 a. m. the fact of the bombardment by an enemy but long previous army and navy had taken immediate measures in defense.

"Oahu is under a sporadic air raid," the announcement said.

"Civilians are ordered to stay off the streets until further notice."

CIVILIANS ORDERED OFF STREETS

The army has ordered that all civilians stay off the streets and highways and not use telephones.

Evidence that the Japanese attack has registered some hits was shown by three billowing pillars of smoke in the Pearl Harbor and Hickam field area.

All navy personnel and civilian defense workers, with the exception of women, have been ordered to duty at Pearl Harbor.

The Pearl Harbor highway was immediately a mass of racing cars.

A trickling stream of injured people began pouring into the city emergency hospital a few minutes after the bombardment started.

Thousands of telephone calls almost swamped the Mutual Telephone Co., which put extra operators on duty.

At The Star-Bulletin office the phone calls deluged the single operator and it was impossible for this newspaper, for sometime, to handle the flood of calls. Here also an emergency operator was called.

HOUR OF ATTACK—7:55 A. M.

An official army report from department headquarters, made public shortly before 11, is that the first attack was at 7:55 a. m.

Witnesses said they saw at least 50 airplanes over Pearl Harbor.

The attack centered in the Pearl Harbor, Army authorities said:

"The rising sun was seen on the wing tips of the airplanes."

Although martial law has not been declared officially, the city of Honolulu was operating under M-Day conditions.

It is reliably reported that enemy objectives under attack were Wheeler field, Hickam field, Kaneohe bay and naval air station and Pearl Harbor.

Some enemy planes were reported short shot down.

The body of the pilot was seen in a plane burning at Wahiawa.

Oahu appeared to be taking calmly after the first uproar of queries.

ANTIAIRCRAFT GUNS IN ACTION

First indication of the raid came shodtly before 8 this morning when antiaircraft guns around Pearl Habor began sending up a thunderous barrage.

At the same time a vast cloud of black smoke arose from the naval base and also from Hickam field where flames could be seen.

BOMB NEAR GOVERNOR'S MANSION

Shortly before 9:30 a bomb fell near Washington Place, the residence of the governor. Governor Poindexter and Secretary Charles M. Hite were there.

It was reported that the bomb killed an unidentified Chinese man across the street in front of the Schuman Carriage Co. where windows were broken.

C. E. Daniels, a welder, found a fragment of shell or bomb at South and Queen Sts. which he brought into the City Hall. This fragrent weighed about a pound.

At 10:05 a. m. today Governor Poindexter telephoned to The Star-Bulletin announcing he has declared a state of emergency for the entire territory.

He announced that Edouard L. Doty, executive secretary of t he major disaster council, has been appointed director under the M-Day law's provisions.

Governor Poindexter urged all residents of Honolulu to remain off the street, and the people of the territory to remain calm.

Mr. Doty reported that all major disaster council wardens and medical units were on duty within a half hour of the time the alarm was given.

Workers employed at Pearl Harbor were ordered at 10:10 a. m. not to report at Pearl Harbor.

The mayor's major disaster council was to meet at the city hall at about 10:30 this morning.

At least two Japanese planes were reported at Hawaiian department headquarters to have been shot down.

One of the planes was shot down at Ft. Kamehameha and the other back of the Wa-

Turn to Page 2, Column 1

Hundreds See City Bombed

Hundreds of Honolulans who hurried to the top of Punchbowl soon after bombs began to fall, saw spread out before them the whole panaroma of surprise attack and defense.

Far off over Pearl Harbor the white sky was polka-dotted with anti-aircraft smoke.

Rolling away from the navy base were billowing clouds of ugly black smoke. Sometimes a burst of flame reddened the black sources of the smoke.

Out from the silver-surfaced mouth of the harbor a flotilla of destroyers streamed to battle, smoke pouring from their stacks.

Turn to Page 2, Column 3

Schools Closed

All schools on Oahu, both public and private, will remain closed until further notice, Edouard L. Doty, territorial director of civilian defense, announced at 11 a. m. today. This does not apply elsewhere in the territory.

Names of Dead and Injured

The city emergency hospital reported at 10:30 a list of 6 killed and 21 injured.

The complete list will be carried later. Here is a partial list:

Peter Lopes, 34, of 2641 Kamanaiki St., was reported at 9:30 a. m. to be in serious condition from wounds in the upper abdomen.

Bernice Gouveia, 12, 2708 Kalihi St., is suffering from a mangled thigh, lacerations on the right leg and left arm.

A Portuguese girl, unidentified, 10 years old, died on arrival from puncture wounds.

Another victim who died on arrival was Frank Ohashi, 29, 2705 Kamanaiki St., from puncture wounds in the chest.

Cecelia Broadly, 38, Moanalua gardens, was released from the hospital after treatment for lacerations.

Three were reported injured and one reported killed from the bomb that fell at Fort and School Sts.

Editorial

HAWAII MEETS THE CRISIS

Honolulu and Hawaii will meet the emergency of war today as Honolulu and Hawaii have met emergencies in the past—coolly, calmly and with immediate and complete support of the officials, officers and troops who are in charge.

Governor Poindexter and the army and navy leaders have called upon the public to remain calm; for civilians who have no essential business on the streets to stay off; and for every man and woman to do his duty.

That request, coupled with the measures promptly taken to meet the situation that has suddenly and terribly developed, will be needed.

Hawaii will do its part—as a loyal American territory.

In this crisis, every difference of race, creed and color will be submerged in the one desire and determination to play the part that Americans always play in crisis.

BULLETIN

Additional Star-Bulletin extras today will cover the latest developments in this war move.

JAPAN DECLARES WAR ON U. S. AND BRITAIN

TOKYO, Monday, Dec. 8---(A. P.)---Japanese Imperial Headquarters announced at 6 A. M. today that Japan had entered a state of war with the United Staes and Briain in the Western Pacific as from dawn today.

EXTRA THE BALTIMORE NEWS-POST EXTRA
AN INDEPENDENT NEWSPAPER
The Largest Evening Circulation in the Entire South
VOL. CXL.—NO. 28 Entered as second-class matter at Baltimore Postoffice. MONDAY, DECEMBER 8, 1941 PRICE 3 CENTS

JAPS BOMB PEARL HARBOR, MANILA

By Associated Press.

The war that Adolf Hitler started in September, 1939, exploded into a world conflict today as Japanese bombers, striking without warning, attacked the United States' great Pearl Harbor Naval Base at Honolulu and bases at Manila, the Philippines.

War Flames Over Pacific With Japanese Bombing U. S. Outposts

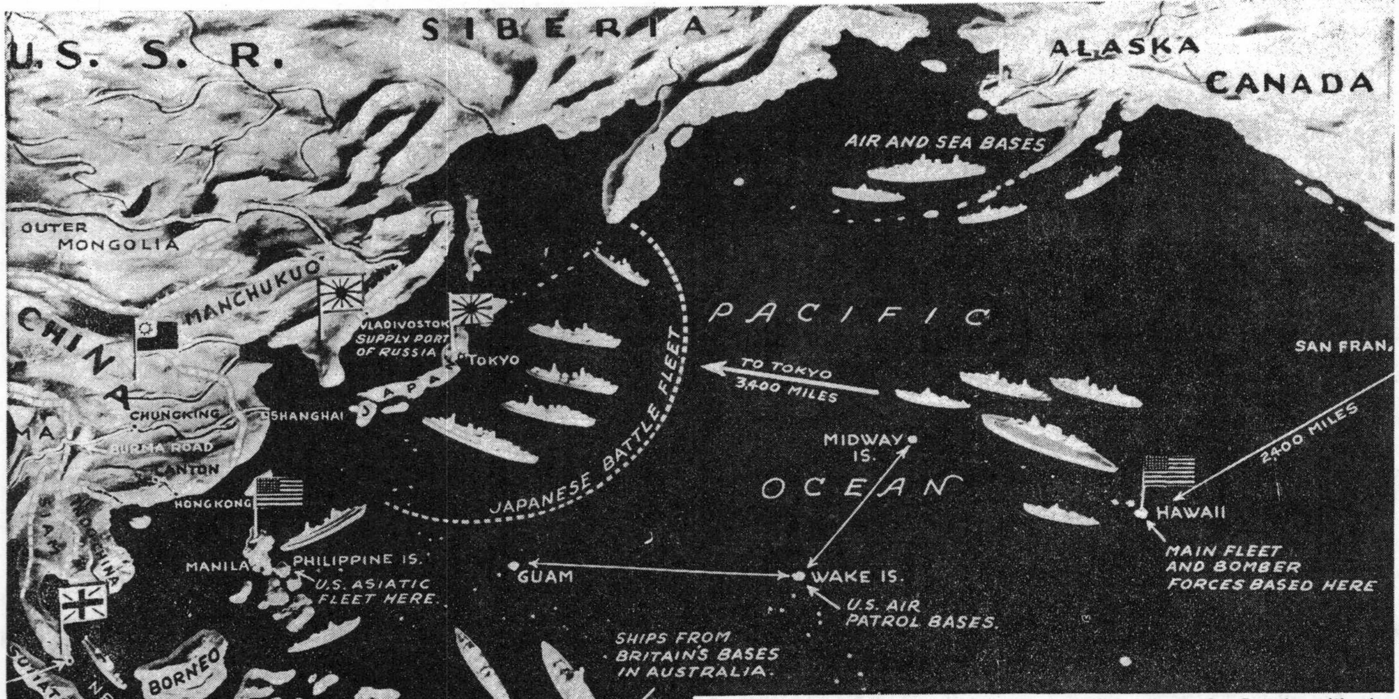

With the bombing of American Pacific outposts at Pearl Harbor and Honolulu in Hawaii and Manila in the Philippine Islands the Far Eastern situation has exploded with the United States at war and the conflict which started in Europe threatening to engulf the entire world. The Pacific is scaled down in the map to the size of a large lake to show more clearly the disposition on naval, land and air forces involved. A glance is sufficient to see that Japan's position is unenviable and to indicate the encirclement by bases of the United States, Great Britain, Russia and China, which the amazingly bold bombing attack from the air was intended to check. Working in concert the four Powers would have a ring of steel around the Island Kingdom which experts believe the military might of Japan would have a hard time breaking.

A bulletin from Honolulu said a naval engagement was in progress off that famed island playground, with at least one black aircraft carrier in action against Pearl Harbor's defenses.

The British radio also reported that a "foreign warship" had begun bombarding Pearl Harbor.

Aerial doffights raged in the skies over Honolulu itself as American warplanes rose to give battle to the Japanese invaders.

In Washington the White House announced that a U. S. Army transport, carrying lumber rather than troops, had ben torpedoed 1,300 miles west of San Francisco—thereby placing Japanese naval action well east of Hawaii, toward the United States mainland.

A N. B. C. broadcast from Honolulu said the Japanese attack had inflicted untold damage on the U. S. naval base at Pearl Harbor and on the city itself.

Several Japanese planes were reported shot down.

As the Japanese airplanes today attacked American defense bases at Hawaii and Manila, and President Roosevelt ordered the Army and Navy to carry out undisclosed orders prepared for the defense of the United States.

The White House said that Japan had attacked America's vital outposts in the Pacific—Hawaii and Manila—at 3.20 P. M. (E. E. T.) and that so far as was known the attacks were still in progress.

Announcing the President's action for the protection of American territory, Presidential Secretary Stephen Early declared that so far as is known now the attacks were "made wholly without warning—when both nations were at peace—and were delivered within an hour or so of the time that the Japanese ambassadors had gone to the State Department to hand to the Secretary of State Japan's reply to the Secretary's memorandum of the 26th.

Promptly, Navy officers said that long prepared counter measures against Japanese surprise attacks had been ordered into operation and were "working smoothly."

There was a disposition in some quarters here to wonder whether the attacks had not been ordered by the Japanese military authorities because they feared the President's direct negotiations with the Emperor might lead to an about-face in Japanese policy and the consequent loss of face by the present ruling factions in Japan.

4TH WAR EXTRA

AIR RAID INSTRUCTIONS

AIR RAID SIGNAL: two one-minute blasts of mill whistles, one minute apart.

ALL CLEAR: two three-second blasts at one-half minute intervals, repeated for three minutes.

REMEMBER that the long blasts mean an air raid, and the short ones all clear.

Persons in frame houses, if time permits, should go outside under cover such as trees, etc., and remain motionless. If on roads, they should take to cover in ditches, depressions or shadows. If in automobiles, they should stop and take cover.

If flares drop, persons should remain motionless and refrain from looking up as the face reflects light.

U.S. VOTES WAR!

All 'Americas' Join In Fight

CONGRESS DECISION 470 TO 1!

MAUI NEWS

41ST YEAR—No. 5592 — MAUI NEWS, MONDAY, DECEMBER 8, 1941 — PRICE FIVE CENTS

18 Countries Line Up With U. S. In Struggle

In less than one hour after President Roosevelt had issued his momentous message to congress at noon today, the house and senate joined in a vote for a declaration of war that fell short of unanimity by a single nay. The vote in the two houses was 470 to 1. And all the Americas, Great Britain, China and the Dutch East Indies joined their forces with the United States in the great war of the Pacific.

Britain's parliament, in fact, "beat the United States" to a formal vote by a few minutes after Prime Minister Churchill had appeared in person and demanded that the British house support his pledged word of a month ago that Britain would declare war on Japan within hours of an attack upon United States territory.

The South American republics were unanimous in their support of the United States, Argentina being the only country not having declared war at 4 p.m. today. The latter's ambassador to Washington, however, informed President Roosevelet that his cuntry would abide by Article XV of the Havana agreement which constitutes a pledge of war aid in the event of an attack upon the Western Hemisphere. Argentina voted the Hawaii attack as an invasion of this hemisphere today.

ROUND UP NATIONALS

Central American nations likewise joined the United States in an active participation in the war and immediately started a roundup of all totalitarian nationals.

Cuba moved to permit its congress to vote a war declaration Tuesday and Mexico, by special decree of the president of that country set Tuesday as the day for a formal declaration.

Meanwhile Mexico interned all nationals, handed the Japanese ambassador his passports and froze Japanese credits totalling $30,000,000.

Most of the declarations in the American republics were enthusiastically adopted with full aid pledged to the United States and her allies including the use of all harbors, ports and airports.

In congress the senate immediately settled jdown to a rapid cojnsideration of the Connally resolution declaring a state of war between the United States and Japan. Without debate and without speeches, the senators unanimously adopted the resolution by 82-0 and rushed it to the house.

In the house, brief, one-minute speeches preceeded the formal vote with Minority Leader Joe Martin pledging his own and his party's full support of the nation's war president. Rep. Luther A. Johnson declared the attack to be a "dastardly act of treachery, characteristic of totalitarian powers."

Rep. Jeannette Rankin of Wyoming, only member of congress to cast a negative vote, vainly attempted to gain the floor during the brief one-sided debate but Speaker Sam Rayburn, turning his head deliberately away from her, refused to give her recognition. The vote quickly followed Johnson's final speech.

In the house the vote was 388 to 1.

(Continued from Page One)

Malulani Asks Aid

In order to relieve congestion at Malulani Hospital during an emergency, a call is made for volunteers to take care of one or more of the indigent aged men in their homes, temporarily or preferably permanently. 35 beds may be made available in this way. Volunteers phone Dr. R. J. McArthur at 958 or 5405.

In a hushed presidential chamber, with leaders of both parties surrounding him, President Roosevelt signed the bill and posed for newspaper photographers at 4:10 p.m., just four hours and ten minutes after Mr. Roosevelt had addressed the joint session.

THE WAR SITUATION

From Washington came official reports of the progress of the war after a silence of almost 12 hours.

In the opening phases of the Battle of Hawaii the United States lost one out-moded battleship which capsized in Pearl Harbor after Japan's Sunday bombing attack and one destroyer which was blown up by dive bombers. Several smaller craft were disabled and put out of action and a relatively large number of defending planes were lost.

American casualties in the Hawaii attack were listed at 3,000 according to official reports to Washington, including 1,500 dead and 1,500 injured. These figures, while from official sources, are incomplete at this writing. A large percentage of the casualties on Oahu were army and navy personnel.

Admiral Stark, chief of operations, in a report to the secretary of the navy, declared that the United States navy is entirely "adequate" to meet the situation in the Pacific and said that it was growing stronger daily.

From the White House came a pronouncement that heavy reinforcements in planes and fighting equipment were being rushed to Hawaii to be thrown into the battle against the Japanese invaders.

Soviet Ambassador Maxim Litvinoff arrived in Washington Sunday and was immediately received by President Roosevelt, at which time he presented his credentials. After conferring for sometime with the president he told reportehs that of course the principal topic of conversation was the Japanese situation. zzzzz

It was also announced officially in Washington that Manila had been subjected to a terrific bombardment.

The White House also announced that an undetermined number of Japanese submarines had been destroyed but could give no figures on Japan's losses in larger ships and aircraft. The navy department announced that the fight was proceeding on a wide area in the Pacific, including the waters and air surrounding Hawaii, Guam, Wake and the Philippines but could give no details as to the nature of the battle except to say that it was intense in all sectors.

From Honolulu came reports that repairs to damaged air fields and hangers were being rushed and that the defending planes would increase in numbers today and tonight as a result of the refitting of the fields.

PRESIDENT CHARGES JAPAN

President Roosevelt authorized a statement on the situation charging that "Germany obviously pushed Japan into the war to end our lend-lease program. As usual the wish is father to the thought!"

It was pointed out by the White House spokeman that Tokyo's news broadcasts over the past 24 hours,

(Continued on Page Two)

Thailand Battle Still Indecisive, British And Dutch Retaliate

Conflicting reports on the situation involving Thailand were heard over the radio today. While Japan claimed the capitulation of Thai, Washington officially denied the report and stated that fighting was continuing througout the country and along its borders. Japan's squeeze, however, created a serious situation there, Washington admitted.

While Japan gained the first victory in her blitz attack in the Far East, British and Dutch forces were beginning to regain an advantage in counter-offensives on land, in the air and on the sea.

Japanese transports were attacked successfully by British in the Malaya sector and two out of a flotilla of 15 were destroyed by gun fire and dive bombers. While Japan fought alone against the combined A-B-C-D forces, grave doubt was expressed in the Far East that Germany would be able to render any assistance to her aggressor partner.

MARINES AR ETAKEN

Believed to be the first American prsioners of war were approximately 200 United States Marines who were still stationed in China when Japan suddenly struck Sunday. They have been interned for the duration.

British RAF planes conducted an all-day bombing raid on Japanese transports off the Malay peninsula and sent at least three more to the bottom during the late hours of the day.

In the Singapore area the British were struggling to break the spearhead of the Japanese attack with fighting being described as "furious."

British troops were subjected to a terrific bombardment 20 miles Northeast of Penang and the Japanese were reported to be attempting a landing in British North Borneo without success as yet. Japanese troopships were forced to retire by plane fire after a warm engagement, reports from Manila stated.

In Thai, 63 were killed and 160 wounded when Japanese landed under cover of a heavy aerial bombardment.

British denied serious damage in the region of the power-

HEAVY DAMAGE DENIED

ful Singapore base. While the British still held Hongkong, the area was being vigorously defended, British broadcast reported.

Encouraging reports on Dutch air and naval strength were revealed today. More than 1,000 fighting planes are in service in the Dutch East Indies with a majority of the craft being of American make. The DEI navy is likewise strong in submarines. There are several aircraft carriers in service in the Far East.

In the African campaign the British claimed that one-third of the German forces had been destroyed or captured and that the situation was well in hand.

Only comment out of Berlin today was an admission that Rostov, on the Eastern front could not be taken before the first of the year. Berlin made no comment on the Japanese declaration of war, nor on the Libyan situation.

...EDITORIAL...

KEEP YOUR HEADS COOL AND YOUR FEET ON THE GROUND

For 24 hours the United States has been in a state of war with Japan, and Oahu—which means all Hawaii—has been in a state of seige. Thus far Maui and Mauians have come through the ordeal in admirable fashion. A calm has prevailed throughout the many communities and the people have endeavored to carry on normal pursuits so far as this has been possible.

There is, however, a dark spectre moving ominously through the towns and villages of the Island against which all residents must be constantly alert.

This is Dame Rumor, sometimes innocent, but oftentimes a malignant, premeditated falsehood calculated to create panic and hysteria.

Already we have met rumor in her many forms. Only a few hours ago there ran through the Island a so-called report that the Lurline had been sunk at sea; another that Japanese planes had been sighted over Spreckelsville, that parachutists had been seen in Makawao.

None of these reports have the slightest foundation of truth insofar as can be learned by the authorities.

(Continued on Page Two)

General Short Now Military Governor Of The Territory

Lieut.-General Walter C. Short has been designated as military governor of Hawaii and the Territory has been under martial law since Sunday night, Colonel Charles B. Lyman, commandiug Maui district, announced this morning.

Colonel Lyman is in full command of the Maui district, which includes Molokai and Lanai and has appointed Chief George F. Larsen Jr., as acting provost marshall.

"In martial law there is nothing to alarm the good citizens," Colonel Lyman said in announcing the military setup. "It is the strong arm of the military interposed between him and anarchy and between his home and the horrors of invasion. Success demands the united exertions of the entire Territory, and the direction by a single hand of all defensive means available. Nothing will be omitted which will contribute to this success."

The following orders have been issued by Colonel Lyman for the cnduct of life in the Maui district during the duration of the war:

1. All schools closed until further notice. notice. Public schools may be opened at an early date, but all foreign language schools closed indefinitely.

2. No public assemblies, either indoors or outdoors, may be held without permit of the Acting Provost Marshall Larsen, and no permits will be issued except for daylight hours only. Church and other religious meetings may be held without permit in daylight hours only, provided they are open to the public at all times, and held in their regularly established meeting places.

3. No communication by any means with the enemy will be tolerated.

4. Telephone communications are restricted to matters of urgent necessity only, and no conversations will be tolerated relative to discussion of the present military situation on Maui or elsewhere. All calls to be as brief as possible. Any person violating this rule will be subject to summary action, and possible removal of his telephone.

5. All radio transmitters, except authorized Army, Navy, and Police, and such persons acting under direct orders of official agencies, are ordered to remain silent, and all portable transmission apparatus is ordered delivered to the Acting Provost Marshall immediately.

6. All owners or keepers of carrier pigeons are to report to Chief Larsen the location and number of pigeons iin their possession, and

(Continued on Page Two)

SPORTING FINAL
★★★★★★
BID AND ASKED PRICES

The Sun

Copyright, 1941, by The New York Sun, Inc.

SPORTING FINAL
Sport Results on Page 40
7th EDITION —LATE— RACING

Partly cloudy tonight and tomorrow; colder; strong northwest winds, diminishing tomorrow.
Temperatures—Minimum, 34; Maximum, 42.
(Detailed weather report on page 32.)

VOL. CIX—NO. 84—DAILY. Entered as Second Class Matter Post Office, New York, N. Y. NEW YORK, TUESDAY, DECEMBER 9, 1941. THREE CENTS

AIR RAID ALARMS ARE SOUNDED HERE

RAID SIREN STIRS SMALL EXCITEMENT

Sun Staff Photo.

Close to City Hall the Fire Department cart seen here set off its siren at full pitch today for the first air raid alarm ever sounded in New York city but the thin stream of pedestrians walked on calmly and no crowd gathered.

ALL CLEAR AT 2:41 FOLLOWS REPORT HOSTILE AIRCRAFT WERE APPROACHING

Schools Evacuated, Police Put on Emergency, Mitchel Field Planes Rise---Alert Rouses Whole East Coast---Officials Disagree on Whether Warning Was a Rehearsal.

Air raid warnings wailed and wailed again in New York's streets this afternoon, while fighter planes from Mitchel Field roared through the air, children streamed out of dismissed schools and thousands stared skywward.

The alarms, the first at 1:30 o'clock, came a little more than an hour after first reports that hostile war planes had been sighted 200 miles off the Virginia coast, headed toward the city. With the report, the whole Eastern coast went on the alert.

There were two alerts in New York. After the warning at 1:30, an "all clear" was barked by sirens at 1:45. At 2:04 a second warning was sounded and the second "all clear" did not come until 2:41. There was some evidence that the second warning was more or less inadvertent, but that remained one of the minor confusions of the public's confusing experience.

Several hours after the first rumors of the hostile air fleet, no planes had been sighted. At 4 o'clock it appeared that there was confusion, amounting to sharp difference of opinion in official sources, as to whether a real raid had threatened or the "raid" was only a rehearsal for days which may come.

In New York, for example, Major-Gen. Herbert A. Dargue, commander of the First Air Force, said that he did not "think" the series of warnings was a rehearsal. This bore out the apparent opinion of subordinate army officers at air fields, who gave every indication of believing the danger real.

Gen. Dargue Is Cryptic.

Gen. Dargue said, on being told of other statements that the alarm was only a test, said:

"We can't explore the mechanics of our alarm system. Remember the number of alarms over London without any bombs being dropped. I will not disclose the source of this alarm."

In Boston, which was under an alert for more than an hour, J. W. Farley, executive director of the Massachusetts Committee of Public Safety, told the news service:

"The Army and Navy now inform us that this was a dress rehearsal. All phases of the test were met satisfactorily."

The first report that possibly hostile planes had been sighted went to Mitchel Field around noon.

Within minutes, planes of the interceptor command base at Mitchel Field were in the air and manned anti-aircraft guns pointed upward angrily. Excitement

Continued on Page 27.

Air Raid Warning Signals

Official air raid warnings will be sounded by fire apparatus. One long blast of their whistles followed by one short, sounded continuously for five minutes is the signal that enemy aircraft may be expected. The all-clear signal is a series of short blasts from the whistles.

Hull Warns of Nazi Surprise

He Says U. S. Must Guard Against New Coup—Berlin Talks of Shooting War.

Washington, Dec. 9 (A. P.).—Secretary of State Hull indicated today that this country should be on guard against a sudden German move supporting Japan in fulfillment of the Axis tri-partite pact.

[The Berlin radio declared today that "America now faces a two-front war, a shooting war in the Atlantic and a rapid-fire war in the Pacific, and America is unprepared." The broadcast was heard in New York by NBC.]

In reply to a press conference question of whether he thought such a German move would be like the Sunday morning attack on Honolulu by Japan, Mr. Hull said that the United States always should be on guard against surprise moves, especially when international desperadoes were prowling around the world.

Any preliminary military move of the character of the Pearl Harbor attack, he said, would only arouse the American people to resist with all the speed and all the might that this nation can exert.

With specific reference to Japan's air and submarine attack on Pearl Harbor, Mr. Hull said that if the national effort to which he referred were put forward, no American need fear the outcome of the attack which he said was so outrageously and treacherously undertaken by Japan.

Predicts Early Declaration.

An NBC broadcast from Stockholm, Sweden, predicted today that Germany would declare war on the United States within a few hours. The broadcast was by

Continued on Page 23.

Roman Boys Parade In Gesture for Japs

Rome, Dec. 9 (A. P.).—Several score schoolboys paraded in the streets with Italian flags today in a demonstration of friendship toward Japan in her war with the United States.

King of Rumania Received by Pope

Vatican City, Dec. 9 (A. P.).—King Michael of Rumania and his mother, Queen Helen, visited the Vatican Museum today following a private audience with Pope Pius XII on their arrival from Florence on a sight-seeing trip yesterday.

BLACKOUT READY AT WHITE HOUSE

Washington, Dec. 9 (A. P.).—Preparations have been completed for blacking out the White House.

Just what steps were taken was not disclosed, but officials said that arrangements had been made to black out the Executive Mansion upon orders from the proper authorities.

San Francisco Warned Again

Police Report Planes Coming In From Sea—U. S. Flyers Hunting Carrier in Pacific.

San Francisco, Dec. 9 (A. P.).—The police radio broadcast a warning at 11:59 A. M. today that "planes had been sighted approaching from sea." The same warning was issued by the Oakland police at noon.

The "all clear" signal was flashed nine minutes later.

Thirty-odd enemy planes ranged last night from San Jose at the south tip of the bay to the huge naval yard at Mare Island, the Fourth Army Interceptor Command reported.

The flight caused the first blackout in San Francisco's history. Two other blackouts followed in the darkness of early morning, but army authorities did not disclose whether enemy planes again appeared.

Army interceptor planes followed the first of the enemy squadrons, but were unable to determine where they finally went. The navy then took up a search for a plane carrier, presumably lurking off California's coast, and possibly 500 or 600 miles at sea.

"I don't think there's any doubt that the planes came from a carrier," said Lieut.-Gen. John L. DeWitt, in command of the Fourth Army and the Western Defense Command.

San Francisco learned of the presence of enemy planes after hours of confused and conflicting

Continued on Page 21.

Japanese Say Troop Landing Has Been Made in Philippines

Army Spokesman at Shanghai Declares No Losses Were Suffered—Manila Has 2 Night Air Raid Alarms.

Berlin, Dec. 9 (A. P.).—DNB, the German official news agency, in a dispatch from Shanghai today quoted the Japanese army spokesman as saying that Japanese troops had landed in the Philippines.

The spokesman asserted that the landing was effected without losses, and told of successful landings without casualties also on Britain's Malay Peninsula and in Thailand (Siam), according to DNB. This was a cause for satisfaction, he said, since stubborn resistance had been expected because "British airplanes had sighted the Japanese convoy prematurely."

Two Alarms in Manila.

Manila, Dec. 9 (A. P.).—Manila had two air alarms tonight, the second coming at 9:50 P. M. (8:50 A. M., New York time).

The first alarm came at 7:41 P. M. (6:41 A. M.). At that time enemy planes were reported over the Manila Bay area.

[The presence of Japanese raiders over Manila was learned from radio reports in New York earlier today.]

The Philippines, target of re-Philippine Islands, target of repeated and widespread Japanese air raids, faced a new threat meanwhile as reports reached here that Japanese troops had seized Lubang Island about fifty miles off the entrance to Manila Bay.

Adding to the anxiety over this situation was the fear that the Japanese might effect a landing

Continued on Page 25.

In The Sun Today

BULLETINS

Report Tokio Bombed.

Ford Wilkins, CBS correspondent in Manila, reported today at 9:12 A. M., Eastern standard time (10:12 P. M. Manila time), that there had been unverified reports of bombings of the Japanese island of Formosa and the cities of Tokio and Kobe. The latest announcement of Japanese defense headquarters in Tokio, as picked up by the Associated Press from a Domei broadcast, said there had been no air attack on Japanese territory up to this morning.

Brazil Acts to Curb Japanese.

Rio de Janeiro, Brazil, Dec. 9 (A. P.).—All police reserves were ordered to duty immediately today in Sao Paulo State, which contains the greater part of Brazil's 170,000 Japanese residents.

Chinese at War With Axis.

The British radio said late today that the Chungking Government of Chiang Kai-shek had declared war on Japan, Germany and Italy. NBC heard the London broadcast.

Warning Blasts of City's First Air Raid Siren Seem to Baffle Rather Than Alarm Crowds

The warning blasts of the siren of a fire engine that tore around blocks surrounding City Hall Park two separate times between 1 and 2 P. M. today seemed to baffle New Yorkers, created some confusion and caused a few untoward incidents. But, typically American, a lot of the people were joking a few moments after the blasts had ceased.

When the first series of blasts began, people on the street looked around uncertainly — at each other, and at the sky, which was clear except for clouds.

Hundreds of persons in office buildings came to the windows and looked up and down their streets to see where the sounds were coming from. From their expressions it was obvious that they, too, wanted to know the reason for the sounds.

In the streets, little groups of people gathered around newsstands and silently stared at headlines which proclaimed that enemy planes had been reported two hours out over the Atlantic Ocean.

Vehicular traffic seemed unaffected, but pedestrian traffic was largely at a standstill.

On the corner of Broadway and Reade street a barber wearing the coat of his trade got into an argument with a pedestrian over whether the staccato blasts of the fire engine at Chambers street and Broadway, a block away, was an alarm or an all-clear. The barber was authoritatively advising all to take cover. The belligerent pedestrian told the barber to go back to his shop.

In short order the argument was on the verge of fisticuffs and a crowd had gathered to see developments no matter whether the signal was an all-clear or an alarm. It turned out to be an all-clear and the simmering tempers cooled.

Wisecracks were plentiful among the fun-loving New Yorkers who could not bring themselves to believe that an air raid

Continued on Page 27.

WAR EXTRA

THE WEATHER

Fair today and tonight. Colder today, with the highest temperature near 40 degrees. Increasing cloudiness Friday with slowly rising temperature.

MEAN TEMPERATURES YESTERDAY

Baltimore	42	New York	37
Atlanta	48	Omaha	15
Boston	38	Portland, Maine	34
Chicago	16	Salt Lake City	32
Jacksonville	57	San Antonio	51
Los Angeles	58	Seattle	42
Miami	70	Tampa	62
New Orleans	54	Washington	42

THE BALTIMORE NEWS-POST

AN INDEPENDENT NEWSPAPER

The Largest Evening Circulation in the Entire South

NIGHT RACE SPECIAL

VOL. CXL.—NO. 32 — Entered as second-class matter at Baltimore Postoffice. — THURSDAY EVENING, DECEMBER 11, 1941 — PRICE 3 CENTS

GERMANY, ITALY DECLARE WAR ON UNITED STATES

NEW YORK, Dec. 11---(A. P.).---Declarations of war on the United States were announced today on behalf of both Nazi Germany and Fascist Italy by Premier Mussolini. Il Duce declared in a speech heard by **N. B. C., "This is another day of great moment in history, marking a new course in the history of the Continent.**

"Fascist Italy and National Socialist Germany have allied themselves with Japan in a war against the United States of America."

Cheers swelled from the crowd before the moment Il Duce appeared on the balcony

WASHINGTON, Dec. 11—(I. N. S.).—President Roosevelt today was expected to call another joint session of Congress to give a speedy answer to the German and Italian declaration of war against the United States.

at th Palazzo Venezia in Rome at 7.51 A. M. (Eastern standard time).

He began speaking at once and made the fateful declaration in the first few minutes of his speech.

He told the cheering crowds:

"We shall bring you victory."

In a radio broadcast of the fateful speech, heard in both New York and London, Mussolini declared that thus 250,000,000 men of tripartite pact nations were joined in a military alliance pledged to achieve a common victory. He said:

"I want to tell you that it is an honor to fight together with the Japanese—with the courageous soldiers of the Far East . . .

"Italian men and women, once again I tell you in this great hour: We shall be victorious."

He held that the Axis was not the instigator of the spread of he field of war. He asserted:

"Neither the Axis nor Japan wanted extension of the hostilities.

"Only one man wanted it . . ."

This man, Mussolini declared:

"Is a democratic despot who has committed a series of provocations."

Mussolini said:

"This man has, against the will of his people, prepared for war day by day with diabolic hypocrisy."

This was Mussolini's fateful message:

This is another day of solemn decision in Italy's his-

(Turn Over.)

U. S., Filipino Troops Mopping Up Jap Army, Parachutists In Luzon

MANILA, Dec. 11—(6.15 P. M., local time, 5.15 A. M., E. S. T.)—(A. P.).—Japanese parachute troops were reported today to have landed at an airport six miles from Llagan, in Isabela Province 80 miles south of Aparri, and the Filipino constabulary was organizing to repel them.

MANILA, Dec. 11—(4.45 P. M., local time, 3.45 A. M., E. S. T.)—(A. P.).—Japanese forces which landed on the coasts of Luzon Island are being disposed of and mopped up by United States and Philippines troops, A. U. S. Army spokesman declared today, saying:

"The situation is completely in hand."

LAND ACTION

On land, the spokesman said, there have been no major developments since yesterday with the exception of light attacks by Japanese ground troops in the vicinity of Lingayen, a port on the gulf of Lingayen on the western coast of Luzon. A Philippine army division stopped this thrust, he said.

(BACKGROUND NOTE: The mention of Lingayen placed the Japanese land forces near Manila on Luzon than at any time thus far. Previous action on Luzon has centered north of Virgan, about 200 miles north of Manila. However, the Japanese have been reported on Lubang island, 50 miles off the entrance to Manila Bay.)

Meanwhile, United States and Filipino troops were battling the Japanese, who landed along the 160-mile coastline between Virgan and Aparri.

The Philippine Army received reports that the Japanese had been checked at Aparri, on the northern tip of the island 250 miles from Manila.

FIERCE RAIDS

The Cavite naval base and Manila itself counted probably heavy casualties from fierce Japanese daylight raids yesterday.

Conservative press reports said at least 30 persons were killed and 300 wounded during the afternoon raids by 71 planes on six major objectives in this area.

Other reports said 37 were killed

Continued on Page 2, Column 5.

RACE ENTRIES, COMMENTS WILL BE FOUND ON PAGES 40-43-44

Japan Battleship Hit, Set Ablaze By U. S. Bomber

MANILA, Dec. 11—(U. P.).—An Army communique announced today that a United States vombing plane had set fire to a 29,000-ton Japanese battleship and asserted that the situation was completely in hand in the fight against a Japanese attempt to invade the Philippines.

The battleship, first major Japanese casualty, burst into flames after three direct bomb hits off the northern coast of Luzon Island and was left blazing fiercely.

BOMBS AT SIDE

Besides the direct hits, the American bombing plane dropped two bombs close to its sides.

The ship was said to be of the 29,000-ton Hiranuma class.

(BACKGROUND NOTE: The authoritative Jane's fighting ships lists no battleship of that name or class. There are, however, two battleships of the Kongo class, the Haruna and Karisima, in active service. These are of 29,330 tons each. Two other ships of this class, Kongo and Hiei, are used as training ships. Ships of the Kongo class were completed just before and during the last war. All have been extensively refitted in view of developments in naval design and some have been completely rebuilt as modern ships of the line. Japan has two 29,330-ton battleships in addition, Huso and Yamasiro, and two 29,990-ton battleships, Ise and Hyuga.)

OFFICIAL COMMUNIQUE

The Army communique said:

"One of our Army bombers late yesterday attacked a Japanese battleship of the Hiranuma 29,000-ton class, a capital ship, 10 miles northeast of Northern Luzon and scored three direct hits and two very close alongside.

"When the bomber left the battleship was blazing fiercely."

Temperatures

12 Midn't,	33	6 A. M.,	28
1 A. M.,	31	7 A. M.,	28
2 A. M.,	29	8 A. M.,	29
3 A. M.,	29	9 A. M.,	31
4 A. M.,	29	10 A. M.,	33
5 A. M.,	28	11 A. M.,	35

BULLETIN

LONDON, Dec. 11—(A. P.).—The Berlin radio today quoted the Japanese as saying the American aircraft carrier Lexington had been sunk off Malaya. German broadcasts heard elsewhere said the Lexington was reported sunk off Hawaii. The report is not confirmed anywhere. The 33,000-ton Lexington, completed in December, 1927, at a cost of more than $45,000,000, was built to carry a maximum of 90 warplanes and a normal crew of 2,122, including flying personnel.

(Picture on Page 3)

Cecil Brown Tells:

How Japs Sank Wales, Repulse

NEW YORK, Dec. 11—(U. P.).—The first eye-witness account of the sinking of the British capital ships, Prince of Wales and Repulse, was received by the Columbia Broadcasting System today from its Singapore correspondent, Cecil Brown.

Brown was aboard the Repulse.

TELLS HIS STORY

His account follows:

"I was aboard the battle cruiser Repulse when she was sent to the bottom under the fiercest Japanese attack in the South China sea far off the Malaya coast.

"As I was swimming in thick oil water I also saw the Prince of Wales go to the bottom a half mile away in the greatest British naval loss of this war.

"Like hundreds of others I jumped 20 feet into the water when

Continued on Page 4, Column 1.

Hawaii Put Under Military Control

By RICHARD HALLER
International News Service Staff Correspondent.

HONOLULU, Dec. 11.—After dealing severely with the relatively few blackout violators, military authorities of Hawaii today announced the populace generally is well behaved and co-operative in the severe defense preparation.

While the Pearl Harbor naval base and the city of Honolulu continued to clear up debris from the heavy Japanese bombing attacks of Sunday, which started the war, the Hawaiian Islands were proclaimed under martial law.

Lieut. Gen. Walter C. Short, commanding the Hawaiian Department for the U. S. Army and new Military Governor of the islands, co-operated with Civil Governor J. B. Poindexter in smoothing out the new regime.

GOVERNOR'S REPORT

After announcing that no hostile attacks had been reported on the islands since Sunday, General Short said:

"The military government of Hawaii is functioning smoothly. Last

Continued on Page 2, Column 6.

MORNING EDITION

Japan Times & Advertiser

No. 15,353 | (THE 17th YEAR of SHOWA) | TOKYO, THURSDAY, JANUARY 1, 1942 | 第三種郵便物認可 昭和十五年十二月二十七日 | Price 15 Sen

Brilliant War Results Revealed

— (News on Page 2) —

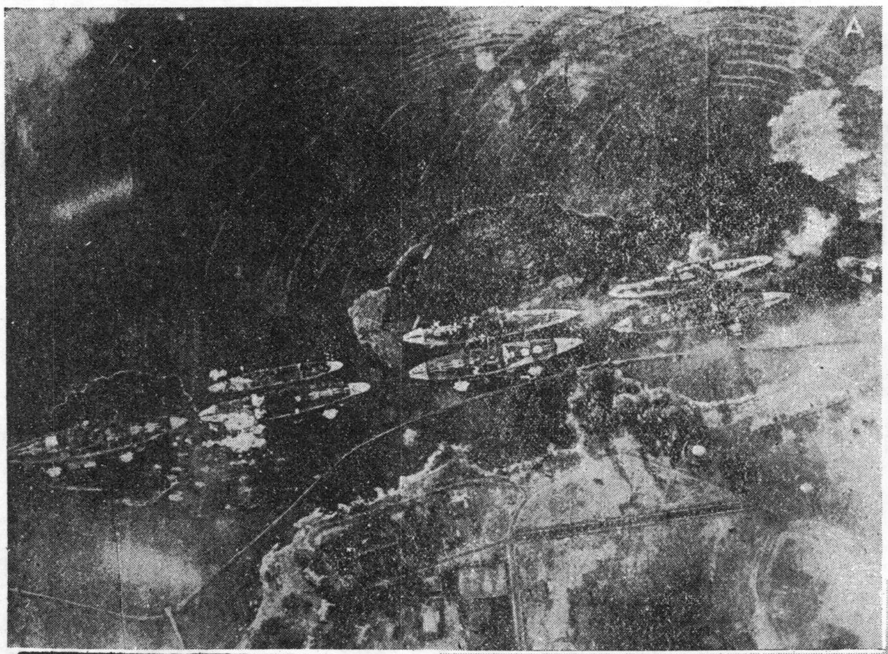

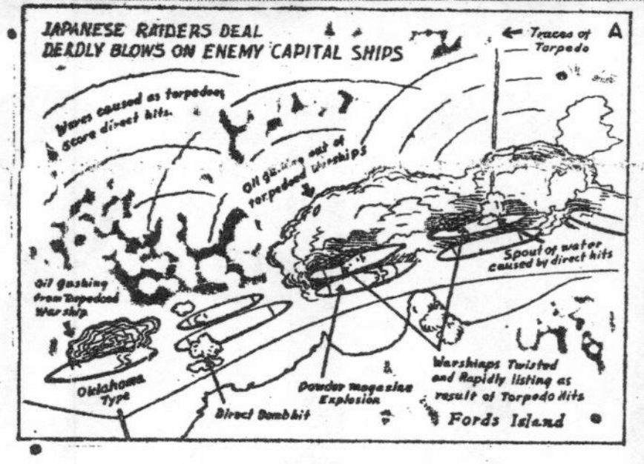

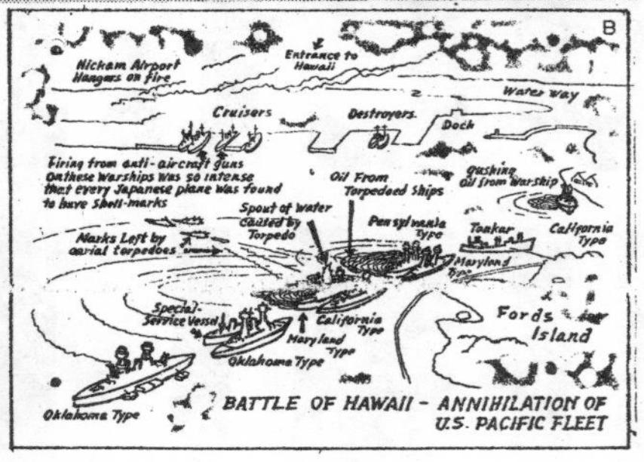

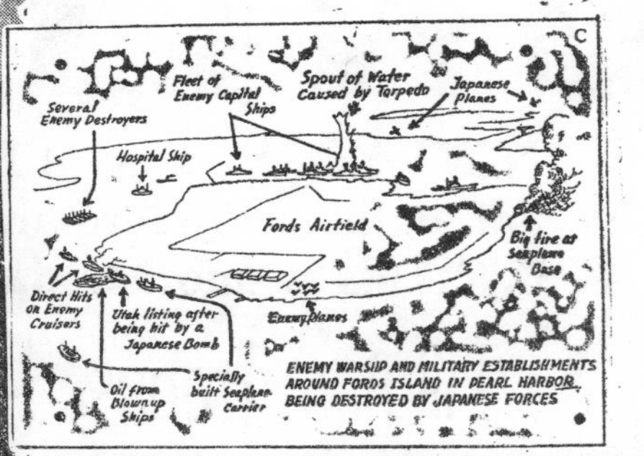

On December 8, 1941 occurred the greatest victory in naval history and the greatest catastrophe also. Japanese naval planes blasted to atoms the U.S. Pacific Fleet doxing in Pearl Harbor upon the declaration of war against America and Britain by the Japanese Empire. Suddenly appearing from nowhere like ghosts flying, planes of the Imperial Japanese Navy droned their way over sleeping Pearl Harbor and nearby Honolulu, capital of the Hawaiian Islands to unleash their destruction. On that memorable day, to be exact, morning of Sunday, December 8, the pride of the U.S. Navy, the Pacific Fleet was knocked out. Losses suffered by the enemy was incalculably high, so terrifying that the enemy authorities did not make it public for fear of repercussions. On the other hand Japanese naval officials claimed the destruction of two battleships and some cruisers; this announcement was a modest one for the Japanese Navy men did not wish to make claims until confirmation was made. Subsequent findings, however, proved that what the Japanese naval aces dropped and pelted the defense facilities had caused the annihilation of the U.S. Pacific Fleet. Thus in one day was reduced to a third-rate naval Power the might of the U.S. Navy. In these pictures above which were all permitted by courtesy of the Imperial Japanese Navy, the story of the cataclysm that visited the U.S. Pacific Fleet in Hawaii is told. (A) Capital ships of the U.S. Navy are photographed being exposed to intense Japanese bombings. (B) Another view of the ships previous to their doom. (C) Fords Island which is also an airbase is shown. The spout of water in the picture proves how accurate and deadly were the aim of the Japanese fliers. (D) A rousing Banzai is given naval fliers who are about to take off from a certain warship in Hawaiian waters to blow the enemy into bits. (E) Wheeler Field, about 15 miles from Pearl Harbor, got a taste of Japanese bombings. Heavy dense smoke signifies that the barracks has been turned into a funeral pyre.

U. S. TO SPEND $5,000,000 HERE

—Weather—
Yesterday's Rainfall
Nichols Hardware Records
Rainfall last 48 hours .... .00
Rain to date 13.56
Temperature
2:30 p. m. today 42

THE CHICO ENTERPRISE

ASSOCIATED PRESS AUTOMATIC PRINTER LEASED WIRE SERVICE; FULL NEA FEATURES

73RD YEAR—NO. 214 THE CHICO ENTERPRISE, FRIDAY EVENING, JANUARY 2, 1942 60 CENTS A MONTH—8 PAGES

This Date
HISTORIC EVENT:
January 2, 1776, U. S. flag first raised.

Paid Circulation December '41
AVERAGE 3464
NO FREE DISTRIBUTION

JAPS CAPTURE MANILA

Philippine Capital and Cavite Base Fall to Nipponese Island Invaders

British, African Troops Capture Port of Bardia; Release 1000 Prisoners

LONDON, Jan. 2—(AP)—The British announced the capture of the North African port of Bardia today.

CAIRO, Jan. 2—(AP)—British and South African troops have captured Bardia and released 1000 British prisoners who were held there by the Libyan port's Axis garrison, it was announced today.

The announcement came in a special GHQ communique, which said the Britons were released when Bardia's citadel was taken.

Capture of the port, near the Libyan-Egyptian frontier and some 300 miles east of the main British spearhead now engaging the bulk of axis African forces at Agedabia, came after an intensive attack lasting several days in which the South Africans were supported by British tanks and artillery and the RAF.

In addition to releasing the British prisoners, the capture of Bardia also resulted in the seizure of more than 1000 German and Italian troops.

"The number of enemy prisoners taken is not yet known," said the special communique, "but our casualties are reported to be light."

"An earlier middle east communique had reported that:

"Owing largely to weather conditions our own and enemy activity in the Agedabia area yesterday was on a reduced scale," the middle east command's communique said.

"Meanwhile operations in the Bardia area are developing satisfactorily and the number of prisoners has now risen to over 1000."

The drive at Bardia was being aided by intensive RAF bombing and low-flying machine-gun attacks.

The communique also said enemy shipping and supply columns, west of Agedabia, were heavily attacked from the air.

Cold Wave in Valley Continues

SAN FRANCISCO, Jan. 2.—(AP)—The weather bureau warned today temperatures would range between 25 and 30 degrees again tonight in interior valleys of California.

SAN FRANCISCO, Jan. 2.—(AP)—Freezing temperatures in northern California and near zero weather through most of Nevada were forecast for today in a continuation of the cold wave which has brought a touch of snow to the usually mild San Francisco region.

The weather bureau, in a warning to agriculturists, said minimum readings of 20 degrees could be expected in the Sacramento and Livermore Valleys, of 25 degrees elsewhere in th interior farming country and of 32 on the coast.

New Year's dawn found heights surrounding San Francisco bay whitened with snow, and thermometers, here dipped to 40 degrees, lowest of the season. East Bay Oakland registered 32.

58 Killed in Mine Explosion

BURSLEM, Staffordshire, England, Jan. 2.—(AP)—Six more bodies of the 58 men and boys killed in an explosion in the Sneyd Colliery, 2,400 feet underground, were recovered today. Twelve bodies had been brought to the surface earlier.

Workers said it would be several days before the wreckage is cleared and the other bodies raised.

One official said he thought every man was killed instantly in the blast, Britain's worst mine disaster since 1938.

WAR BULLETINS

TOKYO, Jan. 2—(Official Broadcast Recorded by AP)—The Japanese cabinet directed today that the eighth of every month be celebrated as a national holiday in commemoration of the start of the war with the United States and Britain.

ABOARD THE FLAGSHIP QUEEN ELIZABETH OF THE MEDITERRANEAN FLEET, Jan. 2, — (AP) — The British destroyer squadron smashed Nazi attempts "to keep Bardia going by sinking one Italian and two German submarines, Admiral Sir Andrew Browne Cunningham said today.

VICHY, Unoccupied France, Jan. 2 — (AP) — Marshal Philippe Petain, French chief of staff, has sent New Year's greetings to President Rosevelt and Pope Pius XII.

CANBERRA, Jan. 2—(AP)—The Australian Associated Press said today it was learned authoritatively that General Sir Archibald Wavell, British commander for India and Burma, would be placed in command of land, sea and air forces in the Pacific.

TOKYO, Jan. 2—(Official Broadcast Recorded by AP)—Japanese reconnaissance planes were said today to have returned safely from a flight "in the direction of Australia" on an undisclosed mission.

LONDON, Jan. 2—(AP)—A British spokesman declared today that British and American fleets cannot be expected to operate effectively in the south Pacific until they can obtain adequate air support.

Help on Way To British Army In Far East

SINGAPORE, Jan. 2.—(AP)—General Sir Henry R. Pownall, new commander in chief of British forces in the Far East, declared today "considerable help is on the way" to Malaya where Japanese forces struck closer to Singapore in fresh landings on the west coast below the big tin town of Ipoh.

His statement, published in the Malay newspaepr Kuala Lumpur did not disclose the nature of the help, but said "it is intended to fight for every inch of ground down the Malay peninsula."

Fighting already had closed in to approximately 190 miles from Singapore on the east coast, in the Kuantan region, and 275 miles on the west coast in lower Perak province.

It was in lower Perak the new Japanese forces were landed and engaged by British defense forces, a communique said.

First Pearl Harbor Wounded Arrive in U. S.

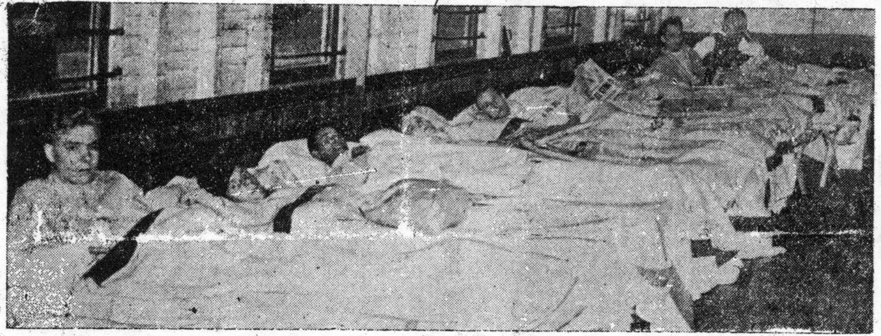

Here is the first picture of war wounded from Hawaii as they reached the mainland—U. S. sailors, victims of Japan's attack on Pearl Harbor. In a line of stretchers, they are waiting their transfer to hospitals. (Passed by U. S. Navy Censor).

26 Nations Sign Solidarity Pact Against Axis

WASHINGTON, Jan. 2 — (AP) — Twenty-six nations of the new and old worlds have formally pledged themselves, the White House announced today, to employ their full resources against the Axis powers and to enter into no separate armistice or peace.

The announcement of the pact was made simultaneously here and in the capitals of the other countries concerned.

The others are:

The United Kingdom of Great Britain and Northern Ireland, Russia, China, Australia, Belgium Canada, Costa Rica, Cuba, Czechoslovakia, the Dominican Republic, El Salvador, Greece, Guate-

(Continued on page 8, column 6)

Seen or Heard This Forenoon

By Enterprise Reporters

MARGARET OSBORN nursing bad cold.

RALPH COOPER rushing into the fire house to check the water meter, stops long enough to fill his pipe and light it.

PETER BAY and his little dog on daily walk through city plaza.

SHIRLEY COX swathed in warm gloves.

CUSICK MALLOY interested in JUDGE MORGAN'S court procedure.

MRS. W. E. KOCHER helping out with the vehicle license renewal annual rush.

GARDNER GUILL checking postal receipts for his department.

Christmas street decorations being tucked away for another 12 months.

Dear Cynthia

What is the cold wave doing?

What all cold waves do, wet or dry—covering us with gooseskin.

Air Base $5,000,000 Project; Expect Allotment in Week

Between $3,000,000 and $4,000,000 will be allocated for the Chico airbase in about one week, according to a special dispatch released today by Col. R. C. Hunter, of the United States army engineers' office in Sacramento, through an Associated Press announcement to the Chico Enterprise.

According to Colonel Hunter, who is supervising construction at the local airport, the Chico basic air corps training school and repair depot will "ultimately be a $5,000,000 project."

"Plans and specifications are completed and we are now working on the job," according to Colonel Hunter.

Chico was chosen as the site to replace Moffett Field training school last August 27 and was originally designated as a $2,500,000 school. Present war exigencies have doubled the original sum to be invested here and in addition to an army air corps training school the local airport will also become a sub repair depot.

Close to 3000 officers and men will be headquartered at the Chico airport beginning April 15 and an additional 350 engineers and mechanics will be assigned to the repair depot.

Barracks are to be constructed for the single men while married men and officers will be expected to find quarters in Chico.

Chamber of commerce officials and members of the city council have been cooperating with army officials since August in an effort to ascertain housing, transportation,

(CONTINUED ON PAGE 4, COLUMN 3)

U. S. Fleet Units Join Dutch in East Indies

BATAVIA, N. E. I., Jan. 2.—(AP) Units of the United States fleet have joined the Dutch navy in defense of the widespread East Indies Archipelago.

The official disclosure came in today's communique from the Dutch high command, which reported that "one of the warships belonging to the American forces which are cooperating with the Netherlands navy in the defense of these regions" had been attacked—without suffering "serious damage"—by Japanese planes in the northern part of the islands.

An official communique said that in the same area Japanese aircraft also attacked two U. S. planes. The American planes were not damaged.

In their "continued attempts to terrorize the population," the high command added, three Japanese planes bombed the east coast of Sumatra, yesterday.

Aneta, N. E. I., news agency, which released the communique, said the Japanese attack took place at Labcean Bilik, a small settlement "entirely devoid of all military objectives." (Labcean Bilik is 145 miles southeast, down the Sumatra coast, from Medan, where more than 30 persons were reported killed in a Japanese air attack Sunday.)

The communique said other Japanese planes bombed and machine-gunned Amcerang, on the island of Celebes, where their targets appeared to be copra warehouses, and Bobo in New Guinea, where one adult and two children were reported killed and two adults and 12 children injured, four of them seriously.

The toll of an air raid December 29, on Sorong, North New Guinea, was set officially at three persons killed and six wounded.

BUTTER AND EGGS

SAN FRANCISCO, Jan. 2.—(AP)—Butter, eggs, cheese and poultry unchanged.

Butte County's Tire Allotment Is Announced

SACRAMENTO, Jan. 2.—(AP)—County allocations of tires and tubes for January under the war time rationing program were announced by the council of defense office today.

The office of price administration in Washington gave the state of California a quota of 8995 tires and 7529 tubes for passenger cars and motorcycles, and 18,669 tires tnd 15,607 tubes for light trucks and busses.

The county quotas effective December 30, were determined by the federal agency and for Butte county is as follows:

Passenger cars: Tires 57, tubes 48.

Light trucks: Tires 201; tubes 168.

ANNOUNCEMENT SOON

WASHINGTON, Jan. 2.— (AP) — President Roosevelt told a press conference today the White House expected to have some kind of announcement late in the afternoon, but he gave no clue to its nature.

Defense Forces Retreat To Corregidor Fortress For 'Last Stand' Battle

WASHINGTON, Jan. 2—(AP)—Manila and the nearby naval base of Cavite fell to the Japanese today.

(A Tokyo dispatch said that General MacArthur's forces had fallen back to Corregidor Fortress.)

Both places, the war and navy departments said, had been evacuated of military and naval supplies and equipment before advance units of the enemy arrived.

"The loss of Manila, while serious, has not lessened the resistance to the Japanese attacks," the war department said.

At Manila all military installations were removed or destroyed when the capital of the Philippines was declared an open city, and all troops, both Filipino and United States, were removed, the war department said.

The navy said all equipment, records and stores not destroyed by Japanese bombers had been removed from Cavite, but that the naval hospitl personnel remained to care for the wounded.

The advanced units of the Japanese entered Manila at 3 p. m. (1 a. m., E. S. T.) the war department said.

$25,000,000 Loss

The navy had more than $25,000,000 worth of property and supplies on hand in the Philippines in June this year, most of it centered around Cavite.

This total does not consider how much material had been sent there from June 30 to the opening of hostilities December 7. Neither did it include the value of planes and ships and other fighting equipment.

American-Filipino troops were said to be occupying strong positions north of the city and were holding Manila bay fortifications to prevent use of the harbor by the enemy.

Japanese air activity was reported to be somewhat less intense than for several days.

Fight Continues

Meanwhile heavy fighting con-

(Continued on page 6, column 1)

DOMESTIC NEWS PARAGRAPHS A.P. LEASED WIRE

KILLED BY AUTO

SAN FRANCISCO, Jan. 2.—(AP)—John Lighti, 68, of San Francisco, was struck and killed by an automobile at a street intersection yesterday and Police Officer Ed Watda arrested Thomas McDonough, 25, of Redwood City, driver of the car.

LAUDS DEFENSE

WASHINGTON, Jan. 2.—(AP) President Roosevelt expressed his appreciation again today of "the courageous defense of their homeland as now, being exhibited by the Filipino pepole" and said he had no doubt "that those residnig in the United States will also serve with equal credit."

TWO TO ONE

HOLLYWOOD, Jan. 2.— (AP) — Paced by three Westmore Brothers and two of the Bennett sisters, the film colony had 100 marriages and only 50 divorces in 1941.

GUARD DROWNED

SAN FRANCISCO, Jan. 2.—(AP) Private Donald Teff, 24, an army guard, drowned today in an unexplained fall from a wharf which he was patrolling.

URGES SANITY

WASHINGTON, Jan. 2.—(AP)—President Roosevelt urged all private employers today to adopt a "sane policy" regarding employment of aliens and foreign-born citizens. He said in a formal state-

(Continued on Page 3, Column 5)

Screen Actor Now Officer

MOFFETT FIELD, Jan. 2.—(AP)—It used to be James Stewart, screen actor, then Corporal Stewart, but today it's Second Lieut. Stewart, U. S. A.

After studying war department extension courses for several months, the motion picture star was commissioned a second lieut. yesterday without ceremony.

Lieut. E. L. Reid, personnel officer at this army post, bestowed the commission and said Lieut. Stewart would be assigned to the west coast air training center.

U. S. TROOPS AIDED BY FLEET IN JAPANESE BATTLE

THE WEATHER

Light to moderate rain with slowly rising temperatures tonight.

The Only Newspaper in Maryland with the Associated Press, United Press and International News with moderate humidity today.

THE BALTIMORE NEWS-POST

AN INDEPENDENT NEWSPAPER

The Largest Evening Circulation in the Entire South

COMPLETE MARKETS

VOL. CXL.—NO. 50 Entered as second-class matter at Baltimore Postoffice. FRIDAY, JANUARY 2, 1942 PRICE 3 CENTS

PHILIPPINES WILL NOT SURRENDER—STIMSON

IN THE NEWS

THE President of the United States has asked the American people to make the first day of 1942 a national day of prayer.

He was moved to do this by the fact that the country is at war, and it will be a year of heavy blows and sore trials.

He was mindful of the further fact that Americans habitually preface their great undertakings with prayer.

Let us certainly pray for victory.

Let us surely pray for peace.

But let us also pray that what is achieved by our enterprise always reflects an earnest desire and intention that God's way be sought and God's will be done.

That is the spirit in which America was conceived and had its beginning.

A nation capable of prayer in that spirit will survive hard years and bitter wars, and will endure forever.

Americans must never lose their faith in prayer.

For prayer is much more than words.

PRAYER is the companion of and the condition of clean, honest, wholesome thought and deed.

Prayer is the essential ingredient of all the good things we do, the patience and forbearance we have for the shortcomings of the weak among us, the tolerance and justice we demand as the inviolable rights of all among us.

Prayer is inseparable from brotherhood, affection and love; indispensable to charity, mercy and compassion.

Prayer is the natural and instinctive refuge of Americans, not simply in adversity, not merely for strength and success, but in eager and earnest quest for understanding and truth.

Mr. Roosevelt was well aware that no word of his was necessary to obtain individual performance of this duty.

But he believed, and he was right, that the tasks in which we are now joined as a nation require a NATIONAL demonstration of faith.

We need strength for these tasks, far beyond the strength of mere arms and purpose.

And Americans do well to turn for that strength, as their President suggests, to the deep religious faith in which their fathers confidently sought it and amply found it.

"We are confident in our devotion to country, in our love of freedom, in our inheritance of courage," said the President.

"But our strength, as the strength of all men everywhere, is of greater avail as God upholds us."

Let us be humble in our prayers, said Mr. Roosevelt, *"Asking forgiveness for our shortcomings of the past."*

Let us be determined and of high resolve in our prayers, he said, in *"consecration to the tasks of the present."*

AND having thus given evidence of humility and of devotion, he counselled, we are justified in prayers *"asking God's help in days to come."*

As Americans, we have a firm belief that it was God's special purpose that our coun-

Continued on Page 4, Column 1.

Admiral Nimitz Says U. S. Fleet Is Aiding In Fight Near Hawaii, Philippines

PEARL HARBOR, Hawaii, Jan. 1—(I. N. S.).—The United States Pacific fleet is "active" in the waters between Hawaii and the Philippines, Admiral Chester W. Nimitz, new commander in chief of American warships in this area, announced today.

The admiral, for obvious reasons of security and strategy, would give no details.

But in taking over command from Admiral Husband E. Kimmel, Nimitz said the Pacific fleet in the waters between these islands and the besieged Philippines was active "in assistance of our forces there."

PEARL HARBOR, Hawaii, Jan. 1—(A. P.).—Admiral Chester W. Nimitz, new commander of the United States Pacific fleet, warns that Japanese submarines operating off the West Coast of the United States might attempt to shell coastal cities.

Speaking to reporters aboard a big new submarine yesterday just three hours after he assumed command, Admiral Nimitz said:

"It's relatively safe and simple for a submarine to arise to the surface near a port and throw a few shells into a city.

SAYS ATTACK POSSIBLE

"It is not beyond the bounds of possibility that Japanese submarines operating off the West Coast of the United States may attempt to lay their shells into cities before they leave."

The ocean, he added, is "too big to prevent it entirely."

A reporter asked the significance of submarine shelling of three points in the Hawaiian Islands the night of December 30.

Admiral Nimitz replied that

Continued on Page 2, Column 3.

Stork, New Year In Photo Finish

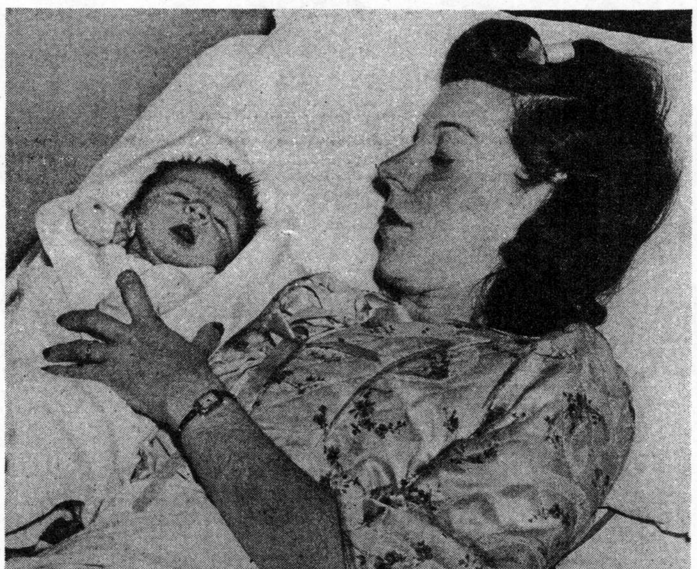

Ho-hum! Being the first New Year's baby born in Baltimore is very trying to a girl my age. The center of attention at Franklin Square Hospital, Mrs. James M. Kuntz (above) and baby had first claim on the stork after the whistles blew at midnight. Thirty seconds later the baby was born. The parents live at 5310 Gwynn Oak avenue.

Cold Wave Hits 41 Below Zero

PORTLAND, Ore., Jan. 1—(U. P.).—A cold wave that sent temperatures to as much as 41 degrees below zero swept the Northwest today. The weather bureau withheld all weather data for the area west of the 120th Meridian, but announced that Butte, Montana, reported the low point.

'We Shall Recover Country'—Petain

LONDON, Jan. 1—(A. P.).—Marshal Petain told the French nation tonight that he hoped for a relaxation of Germany's armistice terms "so that France's dignity can be restored." He complained that many officials of his Vichy regime were not giving to the state the support that was due it.

VICHY, Unoccupied France, Jan. 1.—(A. P.).—Marshal Petain asked Germany today to bear in mind that France is the only great Power remaining outside a conflict which has put "the planet in flames," but that France "recognizes her duty toward Europe."

He said that the new French constitution soon would be ready, but that it could only be promulgated from Paris "after liberation of the occupied territory." He said:

"Frenchmen . . . We must do our best to regain our dignity. United, we shall recover our country."

HOUR OF TRIAL

Speaking of the French Empire, he specially mentioned Indo-China (now the base of much of Japan's military power in the Far East)

Continued on Page 2, Column 7.

MacArthur's Forces Hurl Back Nipponese In Major Battle Near Manila

WASHINGTON, Jan. 1—(U. P.).—Army officials have received word from Gen. Douglas MacArthur that all wounded in the Philippines have been evacuated to Australia.

NORTH HOLLYWOOD, Cal., Jan. 1—(I. N. S.). An apparently unofficial Tokyo broadcast picked up by N. B. C.'s listening post today declared that the Japanese are about 30 miles from Manila on the "southern front."

By JOHN HENRY
International News Service Staff Correspondent.

WASHINGTON, Jan. 1.—The American flag still flies today at Manila as Gen. Douglas MacArthur's staunch defenders hurled back Japanese forces in severe fighting north of the city in what the War Department described as a "major battle."

Secretary of War Stimson said the American forces are inflicting "heavy losses" on the invaders and announced there will be no surrender of the Philippines.

The combined American and Philippine forces have been consolidated and "are continuing to resist the Japanese advance," according to a communique made public by Stimson.

The Secretary told reporters at a press conference that there is no thought of capitulation in the minds of officials or by General MacArthur.

He said MacArthur has not been advised, nor instructed to abandon the Philippines nor even leave the islands.

CONFIDENT OF VICTORY

The Secretary told newspapermen that he is "confident that America can and will defeat Japan in the end, but not by looking through rose-colored spectacles."

The communique covered operations up until 9.30 A. M. (E. S. T.) today, the War Department said.

(BACKGROUND NOTE: Tokyo got a deferment from one quarter today. Secretary of War Stimson was asked by reporters whether the War Department was planning to carry out Gen. Douglas MacArthur's recommendation that there be reprisals for the bombing of Manila. Stimson said:

("We have a lo-- way to go before considering that. We have other things to consider now.")

While the Japanese hordes were locked in mortal combat in their drive toward the Philippine capital Nippon's submarines, the War Department reported, shelled three islands in the Hawaiian group.

The communique said that Hilo, on the Island of Hawaii, the harbor of Kahului on Maui Island and Lihue on Kauai Island were shelled by the enemy. There were no casualties in the attacks and the dam-

Continued on Page 2, Column 7.

Lauds Defense Of Philippines

WASHINGTON, Jan. 1—(I. N. S.).—Defense of the Philippines was described as "masterly" by Secretary of War Henry L. Stimson today in a press conference.

At the same time he cautioned the nation that the Japanese armed forces are tough, well disciplined and well equipped.

He denied reports that the Japs are a mob of badly trained soldiers.

He said:

"The cold truth is that the Japanese are well equipped, well disciplined and in China have shown excellence of their staff work."

The Secretary then added "that nothing has occurred to make any of us think that General MacArthur's defense has been anything but masterly."

The Secretary disclosed that the Japanese, although greatly outnumbering General MacArthur's forces, have suffered "big losses."

Racing Results At Tropical Park

FIRST RACE—Mile and three-sixteenths. Off at 10.03½. Time, 2.00 2-5.

Geneva Cross, 110 (C. McTague)	$8.80	$4.20	$3.80
Portsmouth, 111 (B. Cruickshank)		4.80	3.90
Brave Action, 110 (R. Watson)			7.90
Total mutuels			$33.40

Also Ran—Chigre, Iron Bar, Laura Lyon, Dogo, Room Service, Nico, Sickle Bill, Mobcap, Crimson Glory.

SECOND—Six furlongs. Off 10.30 ½. Time, 1.12 2-5.

Penobscot Bay, 116 (A. Schmidl)	$6.40	$3.80	$3.10
Leib Light, 116 (P. Roberts)		4.90	3.10
Tee Midge, 111 (W. Day)			2.80
Total mutuels			$24.10

Also Ran—Steuben, False Play, Here Now, Arthur J. and China.

Daily Double—Geneva Cross, Penobscot Bay, $52.80 for $2

THIRD—Six furlongs. Off 10.58½. Time, 1.11 2-5.

Night Tide, 113 (C. Durando)	$37.70	$14.90	$5.90
Anopheles, 113 (K. McCombs)		6.60	4.30
Not Yet, 106 (C. McCreary)			2.90
Total mutuels			$72.30

Also Ran—Wise Hobby, Circus Wings, Classic Beauty, Truda, Time Please, Argos, Rugged Rock, Our Chuckle and Castigada.

FOURTH—The Horned Frogs; six furlongs. Off at 11.30½. Time, 1.11.

Balmy Spring, 116 (T. Meloche)	$8.10	$4.50	$3.90
Cuckoo Man, 113 (W. Day)		4.00	3.10
Weisenheimer, 113 (L. Haskell)			7.00

Also Ran—Double B, Singing Heels, Night Lady, Uncle Walter, Catapult, Range Dust, Commencement, Star of Padula and Highscope.

FIFTH—Mile and 70 yards. Off at 11.54½. Time, 1.42 2-5.

Eternal Peace, 111 (W. Day)	$7.30	$3.30	$3.00
Wood Robin, 116 (McTague)		3.20	2.80
Horn, 111 (A. Schmidl)			4.10

Also Ran—Bay Ridge, Ask Me, El Toreador, Isle De Pine, Whiscendent, Clip Clop, Flashalong and Jack K.

SIXTH—The Orange Bowl Handicap. One mile and a sixteenth. Off at 12.20½. Time, 1.44 2-5.

Total Eclipse, 110 (Keiper)	$17.20	$5.70	$3.70
Benefactor, 113 (Atkinson)		3.40	2.70
The Chief, 115 (Stout)			3.10

Also Ran—Troise Pistoles, Blue Warrior, Tex Hygro and Jezebel.

SEVENTH—Mile and an eighth. Off at 12.47½. Time, 1.51 4-5.

Flying Legion, 113 (McCreary)	$7.30	$4.00	$2.90
Grand Central, 105 (C. Rogers)		6.20	4.00
Oversight, 113 (K. McCombs)			4.00

Also Ran—Tedder, Gallant Play, Sandy Boot, Dear Yankee.

EIGHTH—One mile and three-sixteenths. Off at 1.15. Time, 2.00.

Memory Book, 113 (S. Young)	$5.20	$3.90	$3.00
Catomar, 100 (J. Brennan)		5.80	4.50
Ebony Boy, 113 (H. Krovitz)			7.00

Also Ran — Dick Bray, Fire Marshal, Conrad Mann, Who Reigh, Placer Inn and My Bobby.

U. S. May Commandeer Private Cars

THE WEATHER
Clear and rather cold today.
The Only Newspaper in Maryland with the Associated Press, United Press and International News Service.

THE BALTIMORE NEWS-POST
AN INDEPENDENT NEWSPAPER
The Largest Evening Circulation in the Entire South

COMPLETE MARKETS

VOL. CXL.—NO. 51 | Entered as second-class matter at Baltimore Postoffice. | SATURDAY, JANUARY 3, 1942 | PRICE 3 CENTS

IN THE NEWS

WINSTON CHURCHILL, Prime Minister of England, made a magnificent speech before the United States Congress.

He extolled the United States for sending its war equipment to England.

He besought the continued protection of England.

He gloried in the conquest of the Libyan sand hills by England and exulted in the restoration of the Abyssinian Haile Selassie to his ancestral throne by England.

Mr. Churchill's address was most eloquent, and it may truthfully be said in praise of democracies that they do unerringly select their very best talkers for the conduct of their wars.

HOWEVER, it might interest Mr. Churchill to know that the average American does not care one tinker's dam about Haile Selassie and his Abyssinian throne, and does not think that it makes a lot of difference in the eventual issue of this war who owns the sand dunes of the Libyan desert.

The people of the United States want to give all possible aid to the people of the BRITISH EMPIRE,—not merely to England.

The English-speaking people of the world include the people of Canada and of Australia and of New Zealand and of South Africa and of the United States.

Let us not forget the United States—although we have forgotten it very largely.

And it would be particularly appropriate at this time to remember also Australia and New Zealand.

They are English-speaking people, too, and at this crucial moment are much more in need of immediate aid than is England.

AUSTRALIA and New Zealand and the Australian Archipelago, and incidentally and not unimportantly, Canada and the United States, where the greatest bodies of English-speaking peoples abide, are menaced by Oriental invasion.

England is completely safe from any invasion of any kind.

When she prudently withdrew her armies from Europe to protect herself and concentrated them in England, and then surrounded that tight little island with a considerable part of her mighty fleet, nobody could reach her to invade her, and nobody could invade her if he reached her.

Planes could annoy her but not destroy her.

Troops could not cross the Channel.

No armies could find a footing to land.

The hosts who attempted invasion would be repelled from the shores and submerged in the seas.

You knew that, thoughtful reader, and your columnist knew it and wrote *"The Lemmings."*

And the eloquent Mr. Churchill knew it and so did the disappointed and defeated Mr. Hitler.

MR. CHURCHILL thinks that if Germany had tried to invade England in 1940, disaster might have been England's lot.

No, Mr. Churchill.

The greatest naval disaster in history would have been

Continued on Page 5, Column 1.

JAPS TAKE MANILA

Naval Base At Cavite Falls

WASHINGTON, Jan. 2---(A. P.).---Manila and the nearby naval base of Cavite fell to the Japanese today. Both places, the War and Navy Departments said, had been evacuated of military and naval supplies and equipment before advance units of the enemy arrived. The War Department said:

"The loss of Manila, while serious, has not lessened the resistance to the Japanese attacks."

At Manila all military installations were removed or destroyed when the capital of the Philippines was declared an open city.

All troops, both Filipino and United States, were removed, the War Department said.

The Navy said all equipment, records and stores not destroyed by Japanese bombers had been re-

TOKYO, Jan. 2—(Official broadcast recorded by A. P.).—The Japanese declared today that part of Gen. Douglas MacArthur's forces were attempting to cross Manila bay to the fortress island of Corregidor and other American and Philippine troops were cut off on the Batal peninsula, north of Corregidor.

Japanese bombers were said to have attacked repeatedly as the American troops attempted to cross the bay to the heavily armed island.

(BACKGROUND NOTE: Tokyo radio claimed that Gen. Douglas MacArthur had been reported wounded by shrapnel near Manila.)

moved from Cavite, but that the naval hospital personnel remained to care for the wounded.

The advanced units of the Japanese entered Manila at 3 P. M. (1 A. M., E. S. T.), the War Department said.

Japanese air activity was reported to be somewhat less intense than for several days.

American-Filipino troops were said to be occupying strong positions north of the city and were holding Manila Bay fortifications to prevent use of the harbor by the enemy.

(BACKGROUND NOTE: The Navy had more than $25,000,000 worth of property and supplies on hand in the Philippines in June this year, most of it centered around Cavite.

(This total does not consider how much material had been sent there from June 30 to the opening of hostilities December 7. Neither did it include the value of p[illegible] and ships and other fighting eq[illegible]ment.)

Meanwhile heavy fighting continued on the ground in the past

Continued on Page 2, Column 1.

GENERAL VIEW OF CAPTURED CAPITAL WITH SOME DISTRICTS AND BUILDINGS LOCATED

26 Nations Sign Axis Death Pact

WASHINGTON, Jan. 2—(A. P.).—Twenty-six nations have formally pledged themselves, the White House announced today, to employ their full resources against the Axis powers, and to enter into no separate armistice or peace.

The announcement of the pact was made simultaneously here and in the capitals of the other countries concerned.

The others are:

The United Kingdom of Great Britain and Northern Ireland, Russia, China, Australia, Belgium, Canada, Costa Rica, Cuba, Czechoslovakia, the Dominican Republic, El Salvador, Greece, Guatemala, Haiti, Honduras, India, Luxembourg, the Netherlands, New Zealand, Nicaragua, Norway, Panama, Poland, South Africa and Yugoslavia.

President Roosevelt signed for the United States and Prime Minister Winston Churchill for Great Britain.

FORMALLY PLEDGED

The countries formally declared:

"(1) Each government pledges itself to employ its full resources, military or economic, against those members of the Tripartite Pact and its adherents with which such government is at war.

"(2) Each government pledges itself to co-operate with the governments signatory hereto and not to make a separate armistice or peace with the enemies."

The brief statement of international unity of purpose said also that other nations may adhere to it in the event they are rendering or may render material assistance "in the struggle for victory over Hitlerism."

Saturday Made Navy Work Day

CHARLESTON, S. C., Jan. 2—(A. P.).—Rear Admiral W. H. Allen, commandant of the Sixth and Seventh Naval districts, today ordered that Saturdays be observed as full work days by all naval activities throughout the district and that 24-hour watches be established on all posts.

Group Approves Price Control Bill

WASHINGTON, Jan. 2—(A. P.). A broad-termed war-time price control measure was approved today by a Senate Banking sub-committee after listening to a lengthy dispute between Price Administrator Leon Henderson and Secretary of Agriculture Wickard over who should control farm prices.

Chairman Brown (Democrat) of Michigan said the Senate group avoided a direct decision on this dispute by giving President Roosevelt authority to shift powers among existing Government agencies.

New Russ Planes To Fight Germans

LONDON, Jan. 2—(A. P.).—The Moscow radio said today that Soviet plans called for production of new types of airplanes, including three fighters, to combat the Germans in 1942.

Nation May Take Over Private Cars

WASHINGTON, Jan. 2—(A. P.). Price Administrator Leon Henderson said today that the Government might eventually have to buy or commandeer private automobiles when available stocks of new cars—estimated at a maximum of 650,000 units—are exhausted.

In face of present conditions, he told a press conference, "I can't see any passenger car production for the duration" other than about 200,000 units which the automobile industry will be allowed to complete before production finally is halted about January 31.

Automobile rationing will begin about January 15.

Asked whether the Government might therefore be forced into commandeering, Henderson said that this was a "hot" question which had not yet been answered even in England and Germany and that it was one of several "gloomy prospects" faced by the United States.

U. S. May Export Cars To South America

WASHINGTON, Jan. 2—(A. P.). Leon Henderson said today the United States "likely" would export automobiles to South American countries out of the present available supply. He said:

"We try to regard the people of South American countries much the same as our own civilian population. The automobiles will be going for necessary purposes down there, the same as here."

Under a rationing plan, the Administrator said, steps will be taken to prevent United States automobiles from falling into the hands of Japanese or other Axis nationals in South America.

Henderson said that by exporting cars to Latin America from existing stocks the United States would be "making it up to them for failing to deliver the automobiles sooner." This failure, he said, resulted from a lack of transportation facilities.

SOLDIER DROWNS

SAN FRANCISCO, Jan. 2 — (A. P.).—Private Donald Teff, twenty-four, an Army guard, drowned today in an unexplained fall from a wharf which he was patrolling.

Chinese Battling To Halt Jap Gains

CHUNGKING, China, Jan. 2—(A. P.).—Japanese occupation of the northern suburbs of Changsha, Hunan Province capital and silk center, was acknowledged by the Chinese today as fighting in a shifting, no-quarter battle for possession of the city raged without a pause.

(BACKGROUND NOTE: German correspondents at Shanghai reported today that Japanese forces entered Changsha, Hunan province capital, at noon yesterday after breaking through five divisions of Chinese defending the city.)

Japanese troops, supported by aircraft, forced their way across the Liuyang river into the suburbs yesterday, the Chinese Central News Agency reported.

ATTACK CITY

Simultaneously Japanese war planes attacked the heart of the city, unloading explosives from a low level and machine-gunning the streets.

Other Hunan province towns, including the important railway junction of Hengyang, about 100 miles south of Changsha, also were bombed.

The main battle for Changsha was in progress on the plains just northeast of the city of 300,000 population.

CASUALTIES HEAVY

Casualties on both sides were said to be enormous.

HEAD OFFICE
65, NANIWA-MACHI, KOBE
Tel.: Sann. 3970 & 3971
OSAKA AGENCY:
MANSHIN-SHA
Dojima Kami 3-chome, Kita-ku
Tel.: Kita 218 & 219
KYOTO AGENCY:
Manshin-sha Karasumaru Rokujyo
Tel.: Shimo 4730

The Japan Chronicle

With which is Incorporated the "Hiogo News"
Established in 1868.

毎日一回發行
日曜及祭日翌日休刊

明治廿五年三月十五日
第三種郵便物認可

SUBSCRIPTION RATES
DAILY EDITION
Japanese Empire and China (except Hongkong) 15 sen per copy, ¥3.50 per month, ¥38 per annum. Post Free.
Abroad: 25 sen per copy or ¥64 per annum. Post Free.
WEEKLY EDITION
Japanese Empire and China (except Hongkong) 40 sen per copy, ¥18 per annum. Post Free
Abroad: ¥13 per six month, ¥25 per annum. Post Free.

No. 15,506 | 17th YEAR OF SHOWA, KOBE, SUNDAY, JANUARY 4, 1942 | Four Pages. 15 sen | [Registered as a Newspaper.]

MANILA FALLS

Complete Occupation On Friday Afternoon

OPERATIONS IN BATANG CONTINUE

IMPERIAL FORCES NOW WITHIN 200 MILES OF FORMIDABLE BRITISH NAVAL BASE OF SINGAPORE

FURIOUS ALL-NIGHT RAID STAGED

The Army Section of the Imperial Headquarters announced yesterday at 4.45 p.m., that the Japanese attacking forces completely occupied Manila on Friday afternoon. It further said that Japanese forces are continuing their attacks on the enemy who is still offering resistance in Batang peninsula.

The Army Section of the Imperial Headquarters announced yesterday at 9 a.m. that Imperial Army units have been entering the city of Manila since the afternoon of the previous day.

The Japanese Army Air Corps attacked enemy transports in the Malacca Straits and sank one 2,000-ton ship and severely damaged one 3,000-ton vessel, and also sank one torpedo-boat and disabled three torpedo-boats, it was announced by the Army Department of the Imperial Headquarters at 5.15 p.m. Friday. The announcement follows:

"The Army Air Force which has been active in the Malay sector obtained the following results on January 1st:

"1. The Japanese Air Corps attacked enemy transports in the Malacca Straits, and sank one 2,000-ton ship and severely damaged a 3,000-ton vessel. Discovering a group of speed torpedo-boats running northward, our planes made a daring diving attack, and sank one of them and disabled three.

"2. Upon discovering a Martin 139-W type plane flying over a certain spot, our planes shot it down."

KUANTAN CAPTURED

Kuantan on the eastern coast of the Malay Peninsula, where the British battleships Prince of Wales and Repulse were sunk by the Imperial Japanese Navy Air Corps on December 10th was occupied by the Japanese Army Force on the morning of December 31st according to a communiqué issued by the Army Section of the Imperial Headquarters at 3 p.m. on New Year's Day. The official announcement follows:

"Kuantan, key point in the eastern district of the Malay Peninsula, was occupied at 10.20 a.m. December 31st by Japanese Army units which are now marching along the eastern coast of the peninsula."

The Army units which placed Kuantan under their occupation effected a successful landing on Kota Bharu on the east coast immediately following the outbreak of the Greater East Asia War in the face of severe enemy resistance. Since then the Army units have been continuing their southward march along the east coast sweeping the enemy and surmounting great topographical disadvantages. Finally, the brave soldiers of Yamato occupied Kuantan. Kuantan is located about midway between Kota Bharu and Singapore.

WAR RESULTS LISTED

The Army Section of the Imperial Headquarters at 6 p.m. January 1st issued the following announcement:

"The Imperial Army Air Corps in the Malay and Philippine areas is now offering close co-operation to the Imperial ground forces which have been making swift advance for the past several days. They also gained the following war results:

In the Malay area:

(Continued on Page 4)

Domei] Lisbon, Jan. 2.

According to a Reuter message received here from Washington, the U.S. War Department today officially admitted that Japanese forces have entered Manila.

The War Department's announcement follows: :

"Japanese forces entered Manila at 2 o'clock this afternoon." (5 p.m. Japan time).

Fierce Attack On Corregidor

Domei] Undisclosed base in P.I. Jan. 3.

The fortified island of Corregidor, at the mouth of Manila Bay, is now being subjected to a fierce attack by Japanese army and navy forces.

With the fall of Manila imminent, the United States forces in the Philippines, concentrating their transports off Manila Bay, are attempting to retreat, according to Japanese reconnaisance reports.

Given Full Protection

Asahi] Shanghai, Jan. 2.

According to a Havas dispatch from Washington intercepted here, the U.S. War Department announced today that Police in Manila have been instructed to accord all Japanese national residing in Manila full protection, in accordance with international law against likely riots. The announcement adds that the protection offered complies with the request made by the Japanese Consul-General and is applicable to all Japanese residents on the island of Luzon counting some 3.000 in all.

200 Miles From Singapore

Domei] Lisbon, Jan. 1.

Japanese troops smashing southward in a victorious march towards Singapore are now within 200 miles of the formidable British naval base, a Singapore broadcast intercepted this morning declared.

British forces defending the Malay Peninsula are no match for the superior Japanese troops and are simply fighting in an attempt to delay the inevitable fall of the "Gibraltar of the Far East."

The Singapore broadcast declared that the populace of the island celebrated New Year eve in dug-outs, due to the heavy Japanese raids against military objectives in Singapore.

Japanese dive bombers are admitted to have greatly hindered the transport of supplies by their intense attacks on communications lines.

All Night Raid

A Domei telegram from Saigon says that according to a radio broadcast from Singapore, Japanese air units heavily bombed Singapore from Friday evening till yesterday morning.

Withdrawn From Sarawak

Domei] Saigon, Jan. 2.

The British General Headquarters at Singapore today announced that the bulk of the British forces has been successfully withdrawn from Sarawak, it is reported here in an Arip report.

Evacuates to Australia?

Asahi] Shanghai, Jan. 2.

A San Francisco flash reports without official confirmation that the Philippine Commonwealth Government has evacuated to Port Darwin, Australia.

HAWAIIAN PORTS BOMBARDED

Asahi] Stockholm, Jan. 2.

A Washington dispatch intercepted here reports that according to a U.S. War Department announcement issued yesterday, a fleet of Japanese submarines bombarded Hilo, port in Hawaii, Kahului port in Maui, and the Lihue dstrict of Kauai, all in the Hawaiian archipelago recently, but damages were slight.

The City of Changsha in Hunan Pro-vince, which Imperial forces re-entered on Friday.

LUFTWAFFE POUNDS FEODOSIA

HEAVY LOSSES INFLICTED ON RED FORCES WHICH EFFECTED LANDING

Domei] Berlin, Jan. 1.

Strong formations of the Luftwaffe yesterday attacked Red Army forces which had landed at the Crimean port of Feodosia, as well as the Soviet supply route across the Black Sea, and inflicted heavy losses on the Red troops in men and materials, the German High Command announced today.

JAPANESE FORCES RE-ENTER CHANGSHA

Asahi] Hankow, Jan. 2.

The Japanese Army headquarters in Central China announced at 10 a.m. today that the Japanese Army in Central China, which started activity to restrain the Chungking Army in the districts further inland of Canton, by way of co-operating with the Japanese forces attacking Hongkong, entered Changsha again today at 5 p.m.

Other formations of the German air force, operating in the central sector of the Soviet-German war front, continued their systematic raids on Soviet ground forces, bombing and setting military targets on fire and destroying or disrupting railway communications, the communiqué said.

The communiqué added that German planes also destroyed on the ground a large number of Soviet planes in the vicinity of Lake Ilmen.

On the North African front, German and Italian troops have made further progress in the Agedabia sector, destroying the past few days a total of 48 British tanks and many armoured cars.

Three British planes were shot down by Axis aircraft in aerial battle, according to the communiqué.

German aircraft effectively bombed air ports on the island of Malta by day and and night, the communiqué concluded.

ALL U.S. RESERVISTS TO BE MOBILIZED

Asahi] Buenos Aires, Jan. 2.

A Washington flash reports that the U.S. War Department, having decided to mobilize all reservists by February 1st. instructed all regional commanders to convene in Washington at once to make arrangement for the forthcoming mobilization.

The flash adds that all young men of 18 and 19 years of age will also be mobilized for compulsory military service.

CEILING FOR U.S. INCOMES?

DRASTIC MEASURES INEVITABLE TO MEET HUGE DEFENCE SPENDING

Domei] Buenos Aires, Jan. 1.

The United States' Administration is considering extensively increased taxation raising the revenue of $5,000,000,000 to $10,000,000,000 during the 1942 fiscal year to meet the colossal draft budget of $57,800,000,000 which will be laid on the table in the 77th Congress beginning on Saturday, January 3rd, it is reported here.

The report quoted Mr. Henry Morgenthau, Jr., Secretary of the United States Treasury, to the effect that the new increased taxation, though it aims at no radical change in the American social life, will unavoidably disturb individual household finance to some extent.

In view, however, of the fact that this large increase in taxation is still short of filling the vast Government's expenditure of nearly $5,000,000,000 in the monthly average or $60,000,000,000 in the average annual total, the Administration may have recourse to other no less drastic measures, including the creation of a ceiling for individual annual incomes at between $15,000 to $20,000 or at $25,000, with some extremists even claiming that the Government may absorb any individual incomes exceeding the ceiling.

The Treasury Department of the United States is also reported to be considering a wage cut, obliging the managing class to pay to the Government the amount equal to 15 per cent of the wages for labour which the former is using.

ROOSEVELT SIGNS ALASKAN DEFENCE BILL

Asahi] Shanghai, Jan. 2.

According to Washington information quoted in a Lisbon flash intercepted here, President Roosevelt has just signed the much-mooted Alaskan Defence Bill, which is designed to strengthen the defences of all public utility projects of Alaska against a possible attack by Japanese forces.

CHILE DECLARES NEUTRALITY

According to a Domei telegram from Santiago, the Chilean Government declared neutrality yesterday in the Greater East Asia War. Thus, three big South American countries—Brazil, the Argentine and Chile—have declared themselves neutral, despite the United States' desperate efforts to induce them to declare war upon Japan.

IMPERIAL EDICT OBSERVANCE DAY

TO BE OBSERVED ON EIGHTH OF EVERY MONTH UNTIL OBJECT OF GREATER EAST ASIA WAR COMPLETELY ACHIEVED

CABINET ISSUES OFFICIAL NOTICE

What is called the Imperial Edict Observance Day has been inaugurated, in accordance with a decision reached at the first Cabinet meeting of the year held on Friday. This Day will be observed on the eighth of every month until the object of the Greater East Asia War is completely achieved. The Ko-A Hokobi or Asia Development Day, which has hitherto been observed on the first of each month, will be abolished in the sense of being incorporated in the new Imperial Edict Observance Day.

In this connection. an official notice was issued by the Cabinet on Friday in the name of General Tojo, the Premier. On December 8th, 1941, the Imperial Edict was issued declaring war on the United States and Britain, and in this Edict His Majesty the Emperor clearly indicated the righteous cause of the Japanese Empire and the course which the nation should follow, the official notice says. The future prosperity of the Japanese Empire and the future rise of East Asia hinges on the issue of the present war, it goes on, and the entire nation is firmly resolved to do everything possible to aid the grand Imperial undertaking by bearing up under all sorts of hardships which it may encounter.

[illegible] day which every sub[illegible] is, indeed, the [illegible] not forget through [illegible] life. This is the day in which the g[illegible]l mission of establishing a new order was imposed on the Japanese nation. Since January, 1942, until the object of the Greater East Asia War is completely attained, therefore, the eighth of each month will be observed as Imperial Edict Observance Day. This Day should be looked upon by the entire nation as the source of its constant practice of the Imperial Injunctions and all should redouble their efforts to discharge their respective duties faithfully in consonance with the Imperial wishes so as to contribute towards the accomplishment of the final object of the Greater East Asia War, it is urged.

On the newly created Imperial Edict Observance Day, the first of which will be observed on the eighth of this month, a ceremony will be held at all Government and public offices, schools, companies, factories, etc. at which the Imperial Edict declaring war upon the United States and Britain will be read. The hour of ceremony is left to these institutions to be fixed properly in accordance with their peculiar circumstances.

At shrines, temples and churches, services will be held praying for Japan's victory in the Greater East Asia War.

The national flag will be displayed on this Day over every door.

All people must make redoubled efforts on this Day in the discharge of their respective duties. The idea of making the Day a holiday must be positively discouraged.

Other items of the national movement which may be carried out on the Day will be fixed by the Imperial Rule Assistance Association.

IF 8TH FALLS ON SUNDAY

If the Day happens to be Sunday, it is not necessary for Government and public offices, schools, companies, factories, etc., which rest from work on Sundays, to hold their ceremonies. Their officials, students and employes should observe the Day at home in a manner befitting the occasion.

Lieut.-General Ando, Vice-President of the Imperial Rule Assistance Association is quoted as saying that it was on September 1st, 1939, that the Ko-A Hokobi or Asia Development Day was first observed. Since then the Day has been observed 29 times as the day of the source of vigour for the practice of the new life. The Vice-President of the Imperial Rule Assistance Association refers appreciatively to the hearty co-operation which the entire nation has given his Association in the observance of the Day.

The newly created Imperial Edict Observance Day, he says, is the day on which the 100,000,000 people of the Japanese Empire commemorate their inspiration and determination. It is the day on which they renew their avowals of devotion to their respective duties and aid to the Imperial rule. The high morale of the nation is to be further elevated and a healthy and powerful national movement is to be developed more vigorously.

The Imperial Rule Assistance Association will be the central organ to fix details for the observance of the new Imperial Edict Observance Day, and the Vice-President of the Association expressed the hope that the entire nation will put forth the same earnest efforts as they exerted on the past Ko-A Hokobi for the observance of the new Day.

YEAR'S FIRST CABINET MEETING

The initial Cabinet meeting was held at the Premier's official residence on the 2nd at 10.30 a.m., Premier General Tojo and all the other members of the Cabinet being present.

New Year greetings for a victorious year were exchanged and all members present pledged to exert all efforts to bring about a complete victory in the greater East Asia War.

The meeting rose [illegible] 30 p.m.

FLYING FORTRESSES EASY PREY

ARMY FLYER TELLS HOW ONE WAS SHOT DOWN IN DOG-FIGHT

Asahi] Somewhere in P.I., Jan. 1.

According to Sub Lieutenant Teiso Kanemaru, an Army flyer who has just returned to his base following fourteen days of being marooned on a friendly island, Boeing B-17 bombers, better known as "Flying Fortresses" are but easy victims of Japanese airmen if ever engaged in an encounter. He speaks with the voice of experience for it has been revealed that just prior to going amiss on the day the Japanese forces effected the first landing on Luzon, he engaged a "Flying Fortress" in a dog-fight and shot it down. His account follows:—

"My plane and two others were assigned to collaborate with the sea surface forces in the landing of Japanese forces on Luzon. As we were patrolling the air we sighted a Boeing B-17 bomber flying at an altitude of approximately 7,500 metres. We zoomed at once and machine-gunned the bomber from the rear twice at a distance of about 80 metres. One of its four motors broke out in flames, but the remaining three were apparently intact. The plane then started to flee. At an altitude of about 3,000 metres, we again engaged the plane, this time causing the further left motor to start smoking, and soon afterwards the plane went into a tail-spin.

"We machine-gunned the bomber again at an altitude of about 1,000 metres. The "Flying Fortress" after that last volley of bullets went completely out of control. It soon spun its way down to explode in the crash. It was exactly at 12.51 p.m.

"We sighted another "Flying Fortress" soon afterwards, but I was compelled to leave it for the others to attack, due to motor trouble and loss of gasoline through bullet holes in the tanks received during the encounter with the first "Fortress." I managed to land on a lonely island on the way back to the home base at about 1.40 p.m. Fortunately I had two days' rations on hand, but putting it aside for an emergency, I tried to live on fruits and other available natural foodstuffs. On the fifth day, I encountered five Filipinos who offered shelter and food. I lived with them until spotted by comrade naval planes on December 20th at about 1.40 p.m., after fourteen days of marooned life. The rescue party arrived the next day.

U.S. FREIGHTER SUNK IN N.E.I. WATERS

Asahi] Shanghai, Jan. 2.

The Netherlands East Indies authorities today officially admitted that an American freighter on January 1st was attacked and sunk by a formation of Japanese planes in N.E.I. waters, adding that forty-eight of those aboard have been saved by a passenger plane which was rushed to the scene from Batavia.

We Also Publish
In Nipponese
The Osaka Mainichi
The Tokyo Nichi Nichi
With Combined Circulation
Of 3,500,000 Daily

Sunday Mainichi, Braille Mainichi, Economist, Year Book, Home Life, Mainichi Children's Daily, Tonichi Children's Daily, 'Dai Nippon Seinen', Chinese Mainichi

A National Newspaper For International Readers
The Osaka Mainichi &
The Tokyo Nichi Nichi

Turkish Income Tax

Domei

BERLIN, Jan. 6.—In an effort to minimize the effects of the rising cost of living on minor employees, the Turkish Government will reduce income taxes on monthly incomes below 90 Turkish pounds, it was announced in Ankara today, according to a dispatch received by the German news agency from the Turkish capital.

No. 6824 B 毎日一回發行 月曜日休刊 昭和十七年一月九日發行 FRIDAY, JANUARY 9, 1942 大正十一年四月十日第三種郵便物認可 PRICE: 7 Sen

His Majesty Reviews Army Units At Yoyogi

Crack Nippon Units Are Closing In On Strategic Stronghold In Selangor

SINGAPORE COMMUNIQUE ADMITS RETREAT

Nippon Attack Being Concentrated On Enemy Position Forming Advance Defense Of Kuala Lumpur; Malay Operations Progressing

Domei

MALAYAN FRONT, Jan. 8.—Crack Japanese troops entered a certain city forming a position directly in front of the greatest vantage point in Selangor state on January 7 at 1.30 p.m.

The enemy's main strength is engaged in the defense of the greatest vantage point in Selangor state.

With the penetration of the city by the Nippon corps, the war situation on Malaya has made a sudden turn and various Nippon detachments are continuing to make rapid progress through the mountainous region south of a certain place.

From Our Staff Correspondent

MALAYAN FRONT, Jan. 8.—The Japanese contingents which entered Selangor state have already advanced to a certain river, having made rapid progress southward between January 6 and 7.

The vanguards of some units already are very close to the enemy position right in front of Kuala Lumpur.

Another Nippon force, on the other hand, crossed a certain river and stormed the western area. The force has already completed preparations for charging into the enemy's key point.

From Our Staff Correspondent

SHANGHAI, Jan. 7.—The British High Command in Singapore issued a communique, stating that the defending British forces have retreated to the northwest of Kuala Selangor as a result of the ever-increasing pressure exerted by the Nippon forces, according to a report from Singapore received here today.

Decisive Kuala Lumpur Battle Nears

Fall Of Federal Capital Will Sound Death Knell Of Singapore Fortifications; Foe Reinforced

From Our Staff Correspondent

MALAYAN FRONT, Jan. 8.—What is believed to be the decisive battle on the Malayan front is looming with Kuala Lumpur, the federal capital, as the center, the fall of which would sound the death knell for what is claimed to be the impregnable Singapore fortifications.

Victory or defeat in the impending battle is expected to be decided within a week or so.

Just one month has elapsed since the outbreak of the Greater East Asia War on December 8, during which brief period the Nippon forces have occupied the greater part of British Malaya.

In view of the strategic importance of Kuala Lumpur, the enemy forces, which are continuing to retreat, are expected to put up a hard fight. New enemy reinforcements are being concentrated in the area.

In that sense, the impending battle of Kuala Lumpur is expected to determine the future course of military operations in Malaya.

Now that the Nippon troops have penetrated into Selangor state and completed the sieging position, it is believed that the battle of the Kuala Lumpur region is expected to continue only for a week or so, however stubbornly the enemy forces may resist.

It is the consensus of opinion of British officers taken as war prisoners and the leaders of the people of the region who have seen the rapid progress of Nippon forces that Nippon contingents will before long occupy Singapore and complete the occupation of all British Malaya.

S'pore Comes Within Attacking Range Of Battleplanes

From Our Staff Correspondent

BERLIN, Jan. 7.—With the Japanese occupation of Kuantan and its airfield, Singapore has come within attacking radius of Japanese battleplanes, according to a Singapore war report issued on January 7.

The information added that the British forces were further compelled to retreat between Ipoh and Kuala Lumpur as the Nippon contingents came attacking after crossing the Tengi marshes.

Britons Withdrawing

From Our Staff Correspondent

BUENOS AIRES, Jan. 7.—Wholesale withdrawal of the British forces in Malay peninsula was today reported in a Singapore communique.

The British today revealed that British forces were swiftly withdrawing from Pahang state. The retreat was said to be proceeding according to plan.

Driving forward with armored cars, Nippon troops were admitted to have effected an important break-through in the British lines at one point. Nippon troops were said to be pouring through the break-through, pressing closely on the British defenders.

Domei

MALAYAN FRONT, Jan. 7.—With the enemy defending the eastern coast of Malaya fleeing southward following the fall of Kuantan, the most important enemy point on the eastern coast, no enemy troops were seen in the regions north of the Pahang river 60 kilometers south of Kuantan on January 6.

Wavell In Surabaya

From Our Staff Correspondent

SOMEWHERE ABROAD, Jan. 7.—Reports from Batavia today stated that General Sir Archibald Wavell, new commander-in-chief of the allied Anglo-American forces in the southwestern Pacific, has established his headquarters at Surabaya.

For Reorganization

British Oriental Fleet Commander Leaves Singapore

Domei

BUENOS AIRES, Jan. 7.—Sir Geoffrey Layton, commander-in-chief of the British Oriental Fleet, has left the British naval base to reorganize Britain's naval forces "in order that the allies may attain naval supremacy in East Asia as soon as possible," it was announced in Singapore, according to a report reaching here.

Meanwhile, observers here recalled that British sea power in the South Pacific was utterly smashed on December 10 when Japanese warplanes swooped down on the battleships Prince of Wales and Repulse and sent the two British warships to the bottom.

Australia Dissatisfied

From Our Staff Correspondent

BERLIN, Jan. 6.—The London Daily Mail today published a letter from an Australian, expressing deep dissatisfaction with British aid to Australia, according to a Stockholm dispatch.

The Australian declared that if Britain does not provide immediate and considerable assistance, he would not be surprised if Australia eventually turned to the United States for cooperation, leaving Britain entirely to her own devices.

Shigemitsu Leaves Moji

MOJI, Jan. 7.—Mamoru Shigemitsu, new Ambassador to the National Government of China, accompanied by Counselor Shigenori Tashiro and others, sailed from here for his post this morning seen off by many leading officials and citizens.

Riding Immediately Behind His Majesty Is General Shigeru Hasunuma, Chief Aide-de-Camp To His Majesty. General Kotaro Nakamura, Commander Of The Troops To Be Reviewed, Is Shown On The Left End.

Military Administration Is Accepted To Maintain Peace, Order In Manila

VARGAS IS RECOGNIZED AS MAYOR

Agreement Reached Between New Mayor And Nippon Army Representatives; Lives And Property Protected; Freedom Of Faith Assured

Domei

MANILA, Jan. 7.—The Imperial Expeditionary Army in the Philippines today at 4.30 p.m. issued a communique, regarding an agreement reached with Dr. Jorge B. Vargas, new mayor of Manila, with reference to military administration in order to maintain peace and order in post-occupation Manila.

The communique reads:

Representatives of the Imperial Army met Dr. Jorge B. Vargas, mayor of Manila, at its headquarters today (January 7), in the course of which the highest commander of the Imperial Army formally proclaimed the occupation of Manila and the establishment of military administration in the city, effective January 3, 1942.

To Restore Public Utilities To Normalcy

The highest commander requested Mayor Vargas to comply with the following terms:

1. To maintain peace and order in Greater Manila and to restore to normalcy such public utilities as transportation, communications, gas, power, city water, hospital, and fire-fighting facilities.

2. To control the conveyance of commodities to and from Greater Manila, to control the movements of commodities therein, and to see that the Imperial Army and citizens are supplied with commodities.

3. To curb hostile and illicit actions of alien enemy nationals and those who resort to hostilities or entertain hostile designs against the Empire of Nippon.

4. To recognize the right of the Imperial Army to requisition necessary labor and to use necessary facilities.

5. To see that all officials, public servants, and citizens in Greater Manila surrender their firearms. (This does not include those who are permitted by the Army authorities

(Continued on Page 2)

Corregidor Bombing Is Continued

Domei

LISBON, Jan. 7.—The U.S. War Department in an announcement made in Washington today, maintained that the United States and Philippine forces on Luzon are resisting fierce bombing and machine-gun assaults launched by Japanese warplanes.

Japanese aerial assaults also were admitted to have been carried out for several hours yesterday against Corregidor island at the entrance to Manila bay and Bataan peninsula.

RAF Bombs Dropped On Bangkok Hospital

Missiles Also Blindly Hit Bank; Fires Started; Population Calm

Domei

BANGKOK, Jan. 8.—Two British bombers, taking advantage of a bright moon, raided this city early today at 4.10 a.m., but meeting an intense barrage from the anti-air units of the Imperial Army, dropped bombs and incendiary shells at several places where there were no military facilities and fled in panic.

Enemy bombs fell on the Thai hospital, French church, French Indo-China bank, and the streets of Chinatown and started conflagrations at three places, as well as killing and injuring several Thai and Indian residents.

Under a strict blackout, the citizens conducted themselves coolly throughout the raid and put out the fires within an hour. However, the people are highly indignant that the British should have bombed only the residential districts.

Churchill For Home

Is Scheduled To Arrive At London On Friday Aboard Cruiser

From Our Staff Correspondent

SHANGHAI, Jan. 7.—British Prime Minister Winston Churchill left the United States secretly on January 4 aboard a British cruiser and is scheduled to arrive in London on Friday, January 9, according to a report received here from well-informed quarters.

It is also believed here that Churchill, after the conference with President Roosevelt, went to Halifax by plane on January 4, from where he proceeded to a certain naval base by automobile, although his movements are wrapped in the usual secrecy.

20,000 IN NEW YEAR EVENT

500 Planes Stage Grand Air Pageant While 150 Tanks And Other Ground Units March Past

His Majesty the Emperor as the Supreme Commander of the Imperial Army reviewed approximately 20,000 officers and men in the annual New Year military parade at Yoyogi, Tokyo, on Thursday morning, January 8. Approximately 80,000 citizens were permitted to watch the event, which was rendered especially significant by the outbreak of the Greater East Asia War.

His Majesty in the service uniform of the Supreme Commander of the Army and wearing insignias of the Grand Order and the First Order of the Golden Kite, motored from the Imperial Palace at 9.35 a.m., General Shigeru Hasunuma, Chief Aide-de-Camp, being permitted to share the tonneau of the Imperial limousine.

The limousine was followed by other motorcars carrying Imperial Household Minister Tsuneo Matsudaira, Admiral Saburo Hyakutake, Grand Chamberlain; Tomiji Jo, chief of the general affairs section of the bureau of Imperial Mausoleums, in charge of the Imperial journey, and other high Court dignitaries.

The Imperial party arrived at the Yoyogi parade ground amid the playing of Kimigayo by the military band, and amid the most reverent bows of Princes of the Blood, various Imperial appointees, foreign military attaches, and Government officials of the shinnin and chokunin ranks at 9.57 a.m. His Majesty then entered the Imperial pavilion.

Review Begins At 10.02 A.M.

At 10.02 a.m. the review began.

His Majesty, led by an Imperial ensign borne by Sergeant-Major Hideo Kobayashi and guided by Colonel Akira Yokoyama, Aide-de-Camp, rode past the assembled troops on the Imperial charger Shirayuki.

Accompanying His Majesty on horseback were the Princes of the Blood; General Kotaro Nakamura, commander of the troops to be reviewed; General Hideki Tojo, Premier and War Minister; and the military attaches of Thailand, France, Rumania, Germany, Italy, Manchoukuo, the U.S.S.R., and China.

As the Imperial charger approached them, all stood at attention. His Majesty graciously acknowledged their attention with a salute.

At 10.21 a.m. His Majesty on horseback stood in front of the field stand. Amid the playing of the Review March by the band, all troops commanded by General Nakamura marched past His Majesty, who acknowledged the march-past with a salute.

Approximately 150 tanks marched past His Majesty, while 500 Army planes commanded by Lieut.-General Abe zoomed overhead in formation. This was followed by the march-past of artillery corps, special mechanized corps, cavalry, and transport corps.

The New Year parade ended at 11.15 a.m.

Amid the playing of Kimigayo by the band and the most reverent bow of the throng, His Majesty left for the Imperial Palace at 11.20 a.m.

H.I.H. Prince Kuninaga Kaya, as a company leader of the East Nippon 8th corps, and H.I.H. Prince Captain Takahiko Asaka, as a battalion commander of the East Nippon 6th corps, participated in the military review.

Review In Osaka

The New Year's military review in Osaka was held on the Midosuji boulevard Thursday morning, January 8, beginning at 11 a.m., Commander Fujii of the Central Nippon Army reviewing the troops.

Favored with fair weather, huge throngs of people turned out to witness the grand event, including many students and pupils.

After receiving the report of the number of officers and men participating in the review from Commander Seki of the Osaka Division, Commander Fujii inspected the troops.

Later he reviewed the march-past of the infantry, cavalry, artillery and other mechanized corps of the Osaka district.

6 Spitfire Planes Downed In Duel As Nippon Fliers Raid Rangoon

IMPERIAL GENERAL HEADQUARTERS, Jan. 8. (4.20 p.m.)—The Imperial Army air force daily raiding Malaya and Burma has achieved great results.

1. **Burma raid:** Powerful air units of the Army, raiding Galadon air base near Rangoon on January 4, shot down all of the six Spitfire planes engaged in air combat. All planes returned safely to the base. From January 4 to 6, inclusive, Army planes in repeated raids on those bases either at dawn or at night, blew up facilities and hangars, besides causing fires at many places.

2. **Singapore raid:** Since December 29, Army planes have raided Singapore almost every night, showering bombs on Tenger, Sembawang, and Karang air bases in the suburbs, inflicting great damage on enemy facilities.

Rangoon Raided

Domei

LISBON, Jan. 8.—The Imperial Air Force again raided the northern part of Rangoon today at 12.30 a.m. (Burma time), according to a dispatch from that city.

From Our Staff Correspondent

SOMEWHERE ABROAD, Jan. 7.—According to Australian reports, Japanese planes carried out today a third attack upon Australian territory when two long-range Japanese bombers attacked Australian defense positions near Rabaul on the northern tip of New Britain island.

From Our Staff Correspondent

SOMEWHERE ABROAD, Jan. 7.—Rangoon was bombed last night for the third straight night by Japanese planes, according to British reports from East Asia.

Domei

LISBON, Jan. 6.—Nippon forces advancing from Victoria Point, strategic area on the Malay-Burma border, have occupied a region between Victoria Point and an undisclosed sector, a report from London admitted today.

Shanghai Banks

Establishments Of Hostile States Closed

From Our Staff Correspondent

SHANGHAI, Jan. 8.—The Nippon Army and Navy authorities here yesterday summoned the managers of foreign banks of countries hostile to Nippon such as Britain, America, the Netherlands, and Belgium and notified them to close their offices immediately.

Simultaneously, the Nippon authorities ordered six Nippon banks, namely, the Yokohama Specie Bank, the Mitsui Bank, the Mitsubishi Bank, the Sumitomo Bank, the Bank of Taiwan, and the Bank of Chosen, to take over the business of the above foreign banks for the time being to properly settle their accounts.

Thus, these foreign banks will close their offices from January 8. However, they will be allowed to pay back a small amount at one time to their depositors under the supervision of the Japanese banks from January 12 in order to prevent possible panic in monetary circles here.

HEAD OFFICE
65, NANIWA-MACHI, KOBE
Tel.: Sann. 3970 & 3971
OSAKA AGENCY:
MANSHIN-SHA
Dojima Kami 3-chome, Kita-ku
Tel.: Kita 218 & 219
KYOTO AGENCY:
Manshin-sha Karasumaru Rokujyo
Tel.: Shimo 4730
ADVERTISEMENT TARIFF:
Per column inch—3.50 one day; ¥5.50 two days; ¥7.50 three days; ¥12.00 six days.

The Japan Chronicle

With which is Incorporated the "Hiogo News"
Established in 1868.

毎日一回發行
日曜及祭日翌日休刊

明治廿五年三月十五日
第三種郵便物認可

SUBSCRIPTION RATES
DAILY EDITION
Japanese Empire and China (except Hongkong) 15 sen per copy, ¥3.50 per month, ¥38 per annum. Post Free.
Abroad: 25 sen per copy or ¥64 per annum. Post Free.
WEEKLY EDITION
Japanese Empire and China (except Hongkong) 40 sen per copy, ¥18 per annum. Post Free
Abroad: ¥13 per six month, ¥25 per annum. Post Free.

No. 15,510 — 17th YEAR OF SHOWA, KOBE, FRIDAY, JANUARY 9, 1942 — Four Pages. 15 sen — [Registered as a Newspaper.]

The Formal Occupation of Hongkong. Imperial Army and Navy forces staged a triumphant entry into the former British Crown Colony on Sunday, December 28th, last year. Picture shows Army and Navy commanders on horseback leading the procession. (Passed By Army & Navy Censors).

Some of the Japanese planes which zoomed over Hongkong during the formal occupation ceremony which was staged last month. (Passed By Army & Navy Censors).

SELANGOR DEFENCE LINE CRUMBLING

JAPANESE LAUNCH BIG OFFENSIVE

GENERAL DRIVE BY POWERFUL MECHANIZED FORCE: BRITISH FC[illegible]D TO STAGE WHOLESALE RETREAT

FIERCE RAIDS ON CORREGIDOR CONTINUE

The Army Section of the Imperial Headquarters announced yesterday at 4.20 p.m., that air units of the Imperial Army are repeating daring raids on many points in Malaya and Burma every day with telling effect. Regarding air raids in Burma, the announcement says that on the afternoon of January 4th, powerful army air units raided the Lingaradon aerodrome and the suburbs of Rangoon. They fought an air combat with six enemy Spitfire fighters and soon shot down all of them, after which all Japanese planes returned to their base safely.

From January 5th to the following day, the announcement further says, Japanese army air units repeatedly raided all aerodromes in Burma either before dawn or under cover of night, and set afire various establishments, hangars and other buildings of these aerodromes.

Concerning raids on Singapore, the statement says that since December 29th Japanese army air units have repeatedly launched night raids on the Tenga, the Karan and the Senbawan aerodromes around Singapore and blew up hangars and other establishments of these aerodromes, inflicting very heavy damage on them.

Asahi] Shanghai, Jan. 8.
According to a Singapore flash intercepted here, Japanese forces, enlisting the collaboration of powerful motorized and tank units, opened up a general drive on the British defence line in Selangor Province early yesterday morning, the offensive being concentrated on the Malacca Strait to the south-west of Kuala Lumpur. British forces all along the line have been compelled to retreat southwards, the report added.

Meanwhile, another flash reports that air raid sirens were sounded in Singapore all night long on Thursday, with the entire city remaining in a complete black-out.

Domei] Somewhere in Mayala, Jan. 8.
Imperial forces operating in western Malaya have opened up a general offensive against the enemy defence line extending 40 kilometres in Selangor Province and by 1 p.m. on Wednesday, January 6th, not only penetrated the enemy line at a certain point and advanced beyond a certain river, but on the way captured an undisclosed base and moreover laid siege on another. The complete collapse of the Selangor defence line is but a question of time, and when it falls, the Imperial forces will be placed in a most advantageous position to administer the final blow to an undisclosed enemy base.

Domei] Somewhere in Malaya, Jan. 8.
The Imperial forces on Wednesday at 1 p.m. successfully entered a certain city in Selangor Province, considered the most important defence fortification point in this sector, while units operating in the mountaineous regions are reported to be advancing with very little opposition.

Asahi] Shanghai, Jan. 8.
Washington authorities announced today that Japanese forces in the Philippines have resumed intensive operations in all sectors, particularly in their attack on Corregidor Island and the Bataan Peninsula fortifications, aided by powerful units of warplanes, it is reported here by a Reuter dispatch from Washington.

Domei] Stockholm, Jan. 8.
According to a Washington dispatch intercepted here, the U.S. War Department announced on Wednesday that Corregidor Island was subjected to an air raid by Japanese air units lasting seven hours and that fortifications in Bataan Peninsula were also heavily bombed and machine-gunned by Japanese warplanes. The announcement added, however, that the American-Philippine Army is bravely resisting despite the handicaps and also that the extent of damages inflicted is unavailable.

Domei] Lisbon, Jan. 7.
The U.S. War Department, in an announcement made in Washington today, maintained that United States and Philippine forces on Luzon are fiercely resisting bombing and machine-gun assaults launched by Japanese warplanes. Japanese aerial assaults are admitted to have been carried out for several hours yesterday against Corregidor island at the entrance to Manila Bay and Bataan peninsula.

INCREASED AERIAL ACTIVITY IN BURMA

Domei] Shanghai, Jan. 8.
Havas dispatch from Rangoon yesterday disclosed that the activities of the Japanese air forces in Burma are being intensified from day to day. Meanwhile, the Rangoon branch of the British Broadcasting Corp. reports that the city of Rangoon was fiercely bombed three times on Tuesday, by the Japanese air forces and suffered heavy damage.

Domei] Shanghai, Jan. 8.
A Havas dispatch from Rangoon dated January 7th reports that Japanese air units [illegible] Burma, while a B.B.C. broadcast intercepted here states that Rangoon was raided three times on Wednesday night, January 6th.

Asahi] Shanghai, Jan. 8.
According to a Rangoon dispatch intercepted here, Mulmein air base, to the south-east of Rangoon, and military objectives in its vicinity were heavily bombed by Japanese air units at 3.40 a.m. on Wednesday, January 6th.

Domei] Lisbon, Jan. 8.
According to a Rangoon dispatch intercepted here, Japanese air units again bombed the northern part of Rangoon at 12.30 a.m. (Rangoon time) today.

ANOTHER RAID ON RABAUL

Domei] Lisbon, Jan. 7.
Japanese air units smashing at vital British military objectives in the Bismarck archipelago, last night and early this morning launched their third aerial assault against New Britain island raining bombs on aerodromes at Rabaul, on the northern tip of the island, a report received here from Melbourne, Australia, revealed today.

Domei] Lisbon, Jan. 7.
A Melbourne flash intercepted here reports that Japanese air units last night bombed the Bismarck Islands, particularly the Rabaul air base on New Britain Island, for the third time, inflicting irreparable damages.

BRITISH BOMB THAI HOSPITAL

Domei] Bankok, Jan. 8.
Two British bombers raided Bangkok for the first time this morning at 4.10 o'clock but were driven off by heavy anti-aircraft gunfire. No military objectives were bombed but the Thai Hospital, a Buddhist temple, and a few houses in the Chinese quarter were hit. Three fires broke out but they were extinguished within an hour, thanks to the collaboration of the civilians. It is believed that a few Indians and Chinese were killed, but casualities in any event were very slight.

ALLIED HQS. TO BE IN N.E.I.

Domei] Lisbon, Jan. 7.
Netherlands East Indies officials announced yesterday that headquarters for the joint Allied High Command, headed by General Sir Archibald Wavell, Supreme Commander-in-Chief of the Allied Forces in the South Pacific, will be established somewhere in the Netherlands East Indies, according to a Havas report received here from Batavia today.

The new Allied headquarters will begin activities starting next week, the report said. The exact place where the joint Allied headquarters will be established was not disclosed, however.

New C.-In-C. For British Fleet In Malayan Waters

Asahi] Shanghai, Jan. 8.
According to an official announcement made by the Singapore authorities on

(Continued on Page 2)

LITTLE ACTION ON LIBYAN FRONT

Domei] Rome, Jan. 7.
Despite unfavourable weather condition in North Africa, Italian aircraft unit yesterday carried out short-range fligh over Cyrenaica, Libya, successfully bomb ing British mechanized columns, the Hig Command anoounced today.

Italian and German aircraft aga raided yesterday the British naval and a base at Malta. the communiqué said.

Intense British artillery fire is said have been directed against Axis posse sions in the Sollum and Halfaya zon in Libya. Nothing of importance

[...]ke time-out for a rest. (Passed By Army Censor).

ALL-ROUND INCREASE IN TAXES

WILL BOOST GOV'T REVENUE ¥1,100 MILLION PER NORMAL YEAR: NEW LEVIES ON GAS, ELECTRICITY CONSUMPTION

TOTAL EXEMPTION CLAUSE

The Government has decided to introduce an all-round heavy increase in taxes, particularly direct taxes, to take effect from the next fiscal year (April 1942—March 1943), in order to cope with the abruptly inflated finances resulting from the outbreak of the Greater East Asia War.

At the extraordinary Cabinet meeting held on the 7th, the question of increased taxation was taken up and after a detailed explanation by Mr. Okinori Kaya, the Finance Minister, the matter was duly approved.

It is, of course, the intention of the Government to augment the State's revenue, thereby strengthening Japan's financial position under war conditions, by the proposed increased taxation, but, at the same time, it is aimed to prevent abnormal financial inflation.

Simultaneously, three new taxes are to be introduced, i.e., on advertisements, electric and gas consumption and parimutuels.

It is estimated that the Government's extra revenue arising from the increased taxation will amount to over ¥900,000,000 for the first fiscal year and no less than ¥1,100,000,000 thereafter per normal year.

It is further explained that the Government hopes to realize an extra revenue of over ¥2,000,000,000 through the various emergency financial measures adopted since the fall last year, inclusive of the additional profits accruing to the sale of tobacco on a monopoly basis which has been enacted since last Autumn (¥140,000,000 for a normal year), the increased indirect taxes (¥630,000,000 for a normal year), the increased railway freight and passenger fares (already decided upon), and the proposed increased taxation referred to above.

While on the one hand the Government is contemplating imposing very high rates of taxes in general, the authorities are, on the other, giving serious consideration to the question of reducing the burden of the people so that the Greater East Asia War can be brought to a satisfactory conclusion. For instance, in the event of calamities say through enemy air-raids, etc. taking place during the course of the war, the Government is prepared to either reduce or wholly exempt the collection of income taxes, business taxes, etc, from affected persons and similar treatment will also be accorded to those companies which have been forced to liquidate due to prevailing war conditions.

Below are particulars of the proposed increase in taxes:—

I. INCOME TAXES:

a) CLASSIFIED TAXES

1) There will be approximately a 60 per cent increase in classified income taxes. The untaxable limit will be somewhat lowered.

2) The amount of exemption from taxes in favour of those householders who have large families to support, will be enlarged as also in respect of inheritance taxes.

3) New classified income taxes will be instituted on profits derived from dealings in stocks and shares on the futures market.

b) COMPREHENSIVE TAXES

1) There will be an increase of about 30 per cent in the aggregate amount of taxes. The rate of tax on optional comprehensive tax to be increased from the present rate of 15 per cent to 25 per cent.

2) Surtax on incomes derived from dividends (No. 3 of Art. 33 of Income Tax) to be abolished.

II. TAX ON JURIDICAL PERSON:

To be increased from the present rate of 18 per cent to about 25 per cent.

III. TAX ON SPECIAL JURIDICAL PERSON:

To be increased from 6 per cent to abuot 12½ per cent.

IV. EXTRAORDINARY PROFITS TAXES:

1) In respect of juridical person, the rates to be increased to about 35–75 per cent (presently 25–65 per cent).

2) In regard to individuals, the rate to be increased from the present figure

(Continued on Page 2)

INCREASED POSTAL CHARGES

CABINET BRAWS UP REVISIONS FO[illegible] DIET [illegible]

5 SEN FOR ORDINARY MAIL

As another step towards increasing the national revenue, it was decided at the regular Cabinet meeting on Wednesday, Jasuary 7th, to partially increase postal charges and accordingly a bill will be presented to the forthcoming session of the Diet for approval.

The proposed changes as reported by the vernaculars are as fololws:—

1) The initial postage rate of 4 sen on ordinary first class mail matter and also on sealed letter cards of second class mail category will be raised to 5 sen.

2) The existing rates for post cards and prepaid return postal cards, which come under second class mail matter, shall be left unchanged.

3) The surcharge of ½ sen for every 60 grammes currently charged on newspapers, magazines and other third class mail matters shall be changed to 1 sen per 100 grammes.

4) The existing surcharge of 3 sen on every 120 grammes or any additional weight charged on photographs, printed matter and other fourth class mail matter shall be changed to 4 sen per 100 grammes.

5) The existing surcharge of 1 sen per 120 grammes charged on seeds and other agricultural products, which come under the fifth class mail matter category shall be changed to 1 sen per 100 grammes.

A.E.F. FOR NORTH IRELAND?

BRITAIN SAID PREPARING FOR LANDING AT ULSTER

Domei] Berne, Jan. 7.
Faced with the constant threat of a German invasion, Great Britain has been preparing for the landing of U.S. expeditionary forces and aircraft and receiving warships at Ulster, in North Ireland, where American engineers and experts have been working for months to establish a base, according to an *Exchange Telegraph* report received here from London today.

United States Senator Robert Taft, Ohio Republican, has declared that the occupation of Ulster by the Americans would allow Britain to send 50,000 men to other fronts, the reports said.

Meanwhile, according to reports received here from New York, Mr. Wendell Willkie, 1940 Republican candidate for the U.S. presidency, has revealed that additional American bases would be established in Scotland.

MacArthur Holding!

EXTRA

BRITISH QUIT MALAYA! 'DIG IN' AT SINGAPORE

BLUE STREAK EDITION — SATURDAY PICTORIAL

We're In It— Let's Win It!

THE CALL BULLETIN — SAN FRANCISCO — AN INDEPENDENT NEWSPAPER

87TH YEAR — CALL AND POST, VOL. 151, NO. 5 THE CALL-BULLETIN, VOL. 171, NO. 5 — SAN FRANCISCO, SATURDAY, JANUARY 31, 1942 — 5c DAILY

Allies Evacuate Moulmein Area

Associated Press Far East War Summary

SINGAPORE, Jan. 31 (AP).—Britain suffered two grave reverses in the far Pacific today as imperial defenders of Malay fell back onto Singapore Island, and far to the north, British troops evacuated strategic Moulmein, across the bay from Rangoon, Burma.

Simultaneously, Japan struck a new barb into the fabulous Indies as sea-borne Japanese troops landed on Amboina Island, site of a big Dutch naval base. A furious battle was reported in progress.

Burma, gateway to the vast treasure house of India, is also vital to China as the "backdoor" of the Burma road, life-line of China's war supplies.

HEAVY JAP LOSSES

"Our troops have withdrawn over the Salween River after removing all stores and equipment," a British bulletin said, adding that heavy casualties had been inflicted on the Japanese.

The Salween River empties into the Gulf of Martaban at Moulmein, 100 miles east across the gulf from Rangoon.

Japanese dispatches said Moulmein had been left virtually a "ghost city."

CAUSEWAY CUT

With the collapse of British resistance on the Malay peninsula, Singapore authorities destroyed the causeway to the mainland and called on every man to battle Japan's siege armies "until help can come."

Thrown back 350 miles in two months of bloody jungle fighting, the outnumbered Australian, British and Indian imperial troops retired to the $400,000,000 island fortress under cover of darkness, it was announced officially.

SIEGE BEGUN

"The Battle of Malaya has come to an end and the Battle of Singapore has started," Lieutenant General A. E. Percival,

Continued on Page A, Column 1

State Acts To Close New Areas To Aliens

Supplementing action by the federal government, the state of California took swift, definite steps today to safeguard its vital defense areas from a Pearl Harbor fate.

At the same time, twenty-seven new zones, from which all enemy aliens will be barred, were being readied for announcement today by Attorney General Francis Biddle in Washington.

NEW AREAS CLOSED

These will be in addition to the two previously announced, closing the San Francisco waterfront from China Basin to the Presidio and the Los Angeles waterfront, aircraft factory and oil refinery areas to Japanese, German and Italian aliens after February 24.

The new restricted areas, which will be closed to enemy aliens on and after February 15, will be in less populated districts but will be protective measures for important military or industrial establishments, it was reported.

DULLEA ACTS

To render the state's 93,000 Japanese, both alien and American-born alike, incapable of sabotaging war establishments or of engaging in espionage, a series of actions were being taken, to apply with equal force to alien Germans and Italians.

In San Francisco, Police Chief Dullea, co-ordinator of civilian defense, made full United States citizenship a requisite for service in such defense and ordered enemy aliens, about 200 of them,

Continued on Page 4, Column 2

S. F. To Get 700,000 Gas Masks

As protection against one of the grimmest phases of an enemy attack, San Francisco was assured today of enough gas masks for its entire civilian population.

The assurance came from Chief of Police Charles Dullea, the city's civilian defense co-ordinator, who said 700,000 gas masks were included in a vast list of civilian defense material requested from Washington, D. C., headquarters.

SEEN AS PRECAUTION

"We're dressing up our civilians as a precautionary measure," Chief Dullea said. "Every soldier has a gas mask here—it's part of their regulation garb."

Included in the supplies for which Dullea is asking are 50,000 safety hats for civilian defense

Continued on Page 4, Column 1

U. S. BOMBERS REACHING DUTCH EAST INDIES

MELBOURNE, Jan. 31 (INS).—American bombers and fighters are arriving in the Netherlands East Indies in a "steadily increasing flow" Rear Admiral Costa, director of N. E. I. purchasing commission in Australia, said today. (Earlier details on Far East column 7, this page.)

RUSS RACING TOWARD DNIEPROPETROVSK

VICHY, Jan. 31 (INS).—Reports from Stockholm said today Russians are nearing the bend of the Dnieper River with one Russian column having reached the railway twelve miles southwest of Lozovaya and another racing within thirty-seven miles of Dniepropetrovsk. (Earlier details column 5, this page.)

2,300 SERBS EXECUTED IN NAZI REPRISAL: MOSCOW

LONDON, Jan. 31 (AP).—Reuters said it heard the Moscow radio declare today that 2,300 Serbs had been shrot in German-dominated Yugoslavia in reprisal for the death of 23 Germans.

British Retreat In Libya--Page 3

Russ Retake 46 Towns--Page 3

YANKS TAKE PRISONERS IN LUZON

Jap Infiltration Move Blocked; Front Called 'Quiet'

WASHINGTON, Jan. 31 (AP).—General Douglas MacArthur reported today his American-Filipino defenders of the Batan Peninsula in the Philippines had frustrated determined enemy attempts at infiltration through the lines in the past 24 hours.

The War Department said in a morning communique that some Japanese prisoners were taken.

SPORADIC FIGHTING

Fighting on the peninsula, where fresh enemy troops have been arriving amid apparent Japanese preparations for resumption of a large scale offensive, was said in the communique to have been only sporadic in nature. Virtually no hostile air activity was noted.

The communique, No. 86 of the war, based on reports received up to 9:30 a. m., Eastern Standard Time, said:

"1. PHILIPPINE THEATER:

"There was sporadic fighting on the Batan peninsula during the past 24 hours. Determined enemy attempts at infiltration through our lines were frustrated. Some Japanese prisoners were taken.

"Practically no hostile air activity was noted.

"2. There is nothing to report from other areas."

SEES OFFENSIVE

Contemptuously ignoring a demand for surrender, the general

Continued on Page A, Col. 7

TODAY'S BLOW for LIBERTY

Learn to knit and help keep the boys in the service warm.

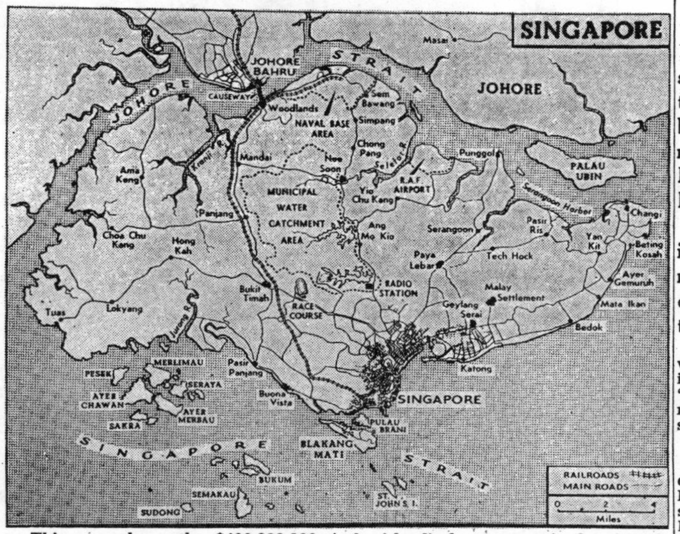

This map shows the $400,000,000 Singapore Island fortress outnumbered Australian, British and Indian imperial troops retired to under cover of darkness, The island is 14 miles wide and 27 miles long. The causeway separating the island from Johore province was breached by retreating forces. Hugging the island's lower coast is the city of Singapore, with a population of 600,000. Across Singapore Strait, a few miles away, are the northern most islands of the Dutch Indies. In an air raid yesterday 90 were reported killed and 246 wounded as the Japanese started bombing the island. —Associated Press Map by Wirephoto.

Retread Molds On Priority

WASHINGTON, Jan. 31 (AP). The War Production Board, it was learned today, has prohibited manufacturers of tire retreading and recapping machinery from filling any further orders except those accompanied by preference rating certificates.

The orders were issued by J. S. Knowlson, director of the WPB industry operations division, as a result of complaints from small tire dealers that large companies had bought up all available retreading and recapping molds.

Knowlson said the supplies had been distributed in such an uneven manner that many sections of the country were unable to meet their requirements for such machinery.

In addition to halting deliveries, Knowlson directed the manufacturers to submit by next Monday a list of all orders on their books, including customers' names, shipping addresses and types of equipment ordered.

The WPB will issue formal orders soon establishing a distribution system designed to assure equitable distribution of available supplie.

Italy Trains Halt, Malta Blitz Seen

Associated Press Europe War Summary

NEW YORK, Jan. 31 (AP).—A hint of possible axis maneuvers to challenge British control of the Mediterranean on an unprecedented scale was contained in a third-hand report today that passenger train service will be sharply curtailed in Italy tomorrow.

PLANES MASS IN ITALY

The report came through Exchange Telegraph, a British news agency, from Zurich, Switzerland, and quoted Rome dispatches.

Restrictions on civilian railway traffic have frequently attended large troop movements within the lands dominated by Adolf Hitler. British intelligence work already has disclosed an unusual concentration of German planes in southern Italy.

BLITZ FOR MALTA

Mobilization aimed at knocking Malta out of the war would be a logical development of axis strategy following the surprise successes of Field Marshal General Erwin Rommel in recapturing Bengasi and driving back the British from other newly won Libyan bases.

Malta, a fortified island lying between Sicily and the Tripolitanian coast, has been subjected to daily air raids for weeks.

On the Russian front, recapture of 46 more villages and towns was reported by the Red army in its drive against German winter lines in the center and south.

WARN OF RED VICTORY

The Germans, while officially dismissing Nazi withdrawals as inconsequential adaptations to arctic fighting conditions, broadcast warnings from Berlin to western Europeans on "what a Russian conquest would mean."

Call-Bulletin Today

Special Features

("G" Indicates Green Flash Section)

Ivory Coast King Joins Free French

LONDON, Jan. 31 (AP).—De Gaullist headquarters announced a new ally today—Koadio Adiomani, king of 200,000 natives inhabiting the Bondoukou district of the Ivory Coast, part of Vichy-controlled French West Africa.

An announcement said he had joined Free French forces with thousands of his subjects.

Rainstorm Saves Far East Convoy

LONDON, Jan. 31 (AP).—A report received by the army said today that a heavy rainstorm recently saved a large allied convoy which since has arrived at Singapore carrying planes, troops and materials.

"Sixty Japanese planes," the report said, "appeared menacingly and it looked as if just as they were ready to swoop down the heaviest rainstorm in weeks broke and the ships were blotted out."

(In San Francisco, the CBS listening post picked up a broadcast in which Australian army authorities revealed that a large convoy bound for Singapore was saved by a tropical rainstorm just as 60 enemy planes were about to attack.)

Tokyo has officially announced that six allied transports had been sunk and five others set on fire or heavily damaged Tuesday and Wednesday in aerial attacks on the Sumatra port of Padang. The dispatch said two ships of 400 tons each and four small vessels were sunk, while one 10,000 ton ship, three ships of 6,000 tons each and one of 2,000 tons were set afire or damaged.

Fourth of Copenhagen Burned, Says Rome Radio

LONDON, Jan. 31 (AP).—The Rome radio, quoting dispatches from Stockholm, said today that a quarter of Copenhagen, the capital of German-occupied Denmark, had been destroyed by fire.

(The dispatch did not bring out whether the fire was started accidentally, by incendiarism or attacks of British bombers which have been raiding Danish military objectives.)

We Also Publish
In Nipponese
The Osaka Mainichi
The Tokyo Nichi Nichi
With Combined Circulation
Of 3,500,000 Daily

Sunday Mainichi, Braille Mainichi, Economist, Year Book, Home Life, Mainichi Children's Daily, Tonichi Children's Daily, 'Dai Nippon Seinen', Chinese Mainichi

A National Newspaper For International Readers

The Osaka Mainichi &

The Tokyo Nichi Nichi

Army Planes Active

Domei

AIR BASE, Feb. 10.—Continuing to bomb British troops holding positions in front of the main force of the Nippon Army units in Burma, the Nippon Army air corps today inflicted serious losses on the British.

The air squadron also blasted enemy trains and motorcars at an undisclosed point.

No. 6854 B 毎日一回發行 月曜日休刊 昭和十七年二月十三日發行 FRIDAY, FEBRUARY 13, 1942 大正十一年四月十日第三種郵便物認可 PRICE: 7 Sen

Annihilative Operations Open On Singapore I.

Navy Planes Blast Batavia; Banjermassin Is Taken

20 FOE PLANES DOWNED

DEI Capital Is Raided; Army Units On Dutch Borneo Advance From Tanangrogot

IMPERIAL GENERAL HEADQUARTERS, Feb. 12. (6.15 p.m.):

The Imperial Navy air arm carried out an extensive raid on Batavia, the capital of the Dutch East Indies, on February 9, and attacking Tjililitan, Kamajolantjon, and Tandjoengpriok airfields, shot down 20 enemy planes and blasted various enemy military establishments.

IMPERIAL GENERAL HEADQUARTERS, Feb. 12. (6 p.m.):

The Imperial Army units in the Dutch Borneo area, advancing 400 kilometers over a hazardous route after landing at Tanangrogot, completely occupied Banjermassin, a key point on the southern coast of Borneo island on February 10 at noon.

Macassar On Celebes Falls

IMPERIAL GENERAL HEADQUARTERS, Feb. 12. (7.45 p.m.):

The Imperial Navy special landing party completely captured Macassar, a key point at the southern end of Celebes island, and Gasmata, on the southern coast of New Britain, on February 9.

British Learn Bitter Lesson

London Paper Says Britons Realize Japanese Are Strong Enough; Powerful Army Necessary

From Our Staff Correspondent

BUENOS AIRES, Feb. 11.—"Britain has realized fully that Japan is strong enough," said the London Evening News today, it was reported here. "In order to resist a strong army, Britain must also have a strong army. This is the lesson learnt from the downfall of Singapore," the paper said.

Fall Is 12-Month Setback To Allies

From Our Staff Correspondent

LISBON, Feb. 11.—"The fall of Singapore will mean a 12-month setback to the allied cause," said the N.B.C. broadcast this morning, after admitting that the defense of Singapore is hopeless.

The radio added that the British are wrecking and blasting all installations of the naval base and fortresses at Singapore which might be of any use to the Nippon forces.

This report is viewed here as an affirmation that the city's defense already has been given up.

Incomparable Victory, Lauds German Radio

From Our Staff Correspondent

BERLIN, Feb. 11.—The fall of Singapore is an incomparable victory, the German radio stresses, and the Japanese will be proud of the conquest of the allegedly impregnable bulwark forming a stepping-stone to India.

The victory coincides with the anniversary of the founding of the Nippon Empire.

The most important and powerful sea-fortress has been conquered from land by ingenious strategy, simultaneously creating an ideal protection for the flanks in Borneo and Celebes on one side and menacing Burma on the other side.

Kimigayo Played

From Our Staff Correspondent

BERLIN, Feb. 11.—The German radio, after a special report on the Nipponese entry into Singapore, played the Japanese anthem and broadcast a historic review of the Japanese Empire from the earliest beginning of the Imperial Family.

All newspapers published the report of the Nippon entry into Singapore on the front page with bannerlines and commentaries.

FDR Appeals To Boy Scouts Over Radio

From Our Staff Correspondent

BUENOS AIRES, Feb. 11.—Regarding the downfall of Singapore, President Roosevelt of the United States spoke over the radio as follows:

"The United States is going to be a realist regarding the results of this war, which is daily becoming more serious, but we receive sorrowful news with coolness.

"Now all the American people are sure to recognize fully, whether they like it or not, that the entire world is now in the throes of war. The United States must do her best to prevent enemy invasion and to deal as much damage to the rivals as possible. While preventing enemy attack, the United States must also complete her preparations."

Roosevelt spoke through the radio demanding all members of the Boy Scouts to become soldiers and sailors when they are grown up for the defense of the United States and for the sake of democracy.

Power To Wavell

From Our Staff Correspondent

STOCKHOLM, Feb. 11.—After the fall of Singapore, the British Command in the southwestern Pacific will be left entirely in the hands of General Sir Archibald Wavell, according to the decision arrived at in London Wednesday at the first meeting of the newly organized Pacific War Council.

Chiang To Meet Gandhi

From Our Staff Correspondent

BERLIN, Feb. 11.—Chiang Kai-shek is expected to meet Mahatma Gandhi this week-end and Jawaharlal Nehru next week, as well as Abal Kalam, President of the Indian National Congress, a Reuters report from Delhi relayed by Stockholm announced.

Bombay Shocked

From Our Staff Correspondent

BUENOS AIRES, Feb. 10.—A Bombay dispatch reveals that the British authorities there, shocked by the imminent fall of Singapore, have ordered greater precaution against air-raids. Important districts of the city are to blacked out every night from 1 a.m. to daybreak.

Diet Program Today

House of Peers: Plenary session, 10 a.m.

House of Representatives: Plenary session, 1 p.m.

Joy Over Victories Of Imperial Forces

National Primary School Children Cheering In Front Of The Imperial Palace After Learning Of The Occupation Of A Part Of Singapore By The Imperial Forces.

Martaban Captured

IMPERIAL GENERAL HEADQUARTERS, Feb. 12. (6 p.m.)—The Imperial Army units in the Burma area completely occupied Martaban on the right bank of the Salween river on February 10 at 1 p.m., crushing enemy resistance.

Bataan's American-Filipino Troops Will Have To Retreat: Washington

From Our Staff Correspondent

SHANGHAI, Feb. 11.—The United States War Department issued a war communique announcing that the situation on the Bataan peninsular front is becoming increasingly unfavorable to the American troops, according to a telegram received here from Washington.

The contents of the communique follows:

1 According to a report from General Douglas MacArthur, commander-in-chief of the United forces in East Asia, powerful Nippon units are continuously being landed in the region of the Bataan peninsular front. With reinforcements arriving, intense attacks are being continued. The situation at the front is becoming increasingly unfavorable to the American troops.

2 According to a report from the commander-in-chief of the American forces in the Hawaiian region, the United States transport Royal Frank was sunk by a Nippon submarine off the Hawaiian islands on January 28.

Regarding the military situation on Bataan peninsula, informed military quarters at Washington regard the withdrawal of the American-Filipino troops from the Philippines as inevitable in the near future due to the recently increased attacks by the Japanese forces on various points on the peninsula, particularly on Corregidor fortress.

Premier To Clarify Ideals Of East Asia Before Lower House

Diet Members To Present Resolution Of Thanks To Servicemen

A detailed program for the establishment of the Greater East Asia Co-prosperity Sphere in accord with the recent developments of the Greater East Asia War will be announced by Premier General Hideki Tojo in the plenary meeting of the House of Representatives on February 13, it is learned.

In the session, the Lower House will hear emergency reports on military operations for the capture of Singapore and the proceedings of the Naval Battle off Java from War Minister General Tojo and Navy Minister Admiral Shigetaro Shimada.

A resolution expressing the Lower House's appreciation of the efforts on the part of the armed forces will thereafter be presented jointly by various factions of the House. After approval, the resolution will be sent to the officers and men on the front.

Following the expected announcement by the Premier, the House will further unanimously approve another resolution expressing its appreciation of the efforts on the part of the crew members of mobilized vessels and the temporary employees of the armed forces.

In addition, the revised Immovable Property Registration Law and four other measures will be adopted following reports on them by the chairmen of inquiry committees.

The Lower House will continue to sit in a plenary meeting on February 14 in which the statement of accounts for the 1940-41 fiscal year and other measures will be approved.

Completing its agenda of the present 79th regular Diet session, the House will enter an actual recess on February 14 until March 25.

Adm. Hart Resigns

Is Succeeded By Helfrich, DEI Navy Chief

From Our Staff Correspondent

BUENOS AIRES, Feb. 11.—Admiral Thomas Hart, commander-in-chief of the allied naval forces, today resigned because of ill-health, according to a report from Washington. It is said that his resignation has been accepted by the United States Government.

Adm. Hart

The report added that he was succeeded by Admiral Helfrich, Secretary of Navy of the Dutch East Indies.

Commands In Malaya

Lieut.-General Tomoyuki Yamashita

Stockholm Astonished

By Eiichi Kohgo
Staff Correspondent

STOCKHOLM, Feb. 11.—We were celebrating Kigen-setsu at Charge d'Affaires Koda's when we got the news that the Japanese had penetrated a part of Singapore.

Of course this was expected, but our rejoicing was very great and now we are waiting for the city's complete occupation. The people of Stockholm, of course, were astonished by the quick and brave Japanese action, while German and Italian circles are also rejoicing.

The German Minister here expressed congratulations to Mr. Koda this morning.

FORTRESSES REDUCED 1 BY 1

Enemy's Mainstay Faces Destruction Near Reservoir; Nippon Units Devastating Foe Positions

Imperial General Headquarters, Feb. 12. (12.20 p.m.):

Penetrating deep into enemy positions in the city of Singapore yesterday, February 11, from Bukit Timah, the Imperial Army units now besieging the British stronghold have sealed its fate. Meanwhile, powerful units have been reducing one enemy position after another by means of land and air bombardments.

Today, February 12, since dawn, the Imperial Army has been inflicting an annihilative blow on the main enemy force near the reservoir on Singapore island.

Domei

SINGAPORE FRONT, Feb. 12.—Fresh Imperial troops sweeping like a tidal wave from the vicinity of Johore causeway toward the south are co-operating closely with the troops charging into Singapore by applying strong pressure from the north. The troops now are fiercely attacking the enemy on the heights near the reservoir.

Fierce Street Fighting Developing

Foe Commander Disregards Humane Nippon Offer; Imperial Units Resume General Drive

From Our Staff Correspondent

SINGAPORE FRONT, Feb. 12.—Under the personal direction of Lieut.-General Tomoyuki Yamashita, highest commander, the Imperial Army units on the Singapore front resumed the general drive against the enemy today shortly after 10 a.m., determined not to spare one man of the hostile force. Fierce street fighting has since ensued.

The Army units which had penetrated the northwestern corner of the city yesterday evening, temporarily suspended the general assault pending the enemy attitude toward the Nippon proposal for surrender.

The enemy commander, apparently unmindful of the welfare of Singapore's citizens, disregarded the humane proposal. This left General Yamashita no choice but to order the annihilation of the enemy remnants.

Nippon's Humane Offer Turned Down

From Our Staff Correspondent

SINGAPORE ISLAND, Feb. 12. (10.10 a.m.)—Lieut.-General Tomoyuki Yamashita, highest commander of the Imperial Army in Malaya, prior to launching the general drive against Singapore harbor today at 10 a.m., issued a proclamation to the citizens of Singapore by means of handbills which were dropped from aloft.

The proclamation read:

"The British Army, disregarding the humane proposal of the Imperial Army, apparently wishes to continue resistance at the sacrifice of the welfare of the citizens. The citizens of Singapore are hereby advised to seek shelter in places of greater safety and to await the entry of the Imperial Army, which is prepared to extend a helping hand.

Bukit Mandai Fort Is Captured

By Shoichi Matsuda, Staff Correspondent

SINGAPORE ISLAND, Feb. 12.—Part of the units of the Imperial Army which had been advancing south along the main highway on the island after landing on the sector east of the Johore causeway captured Bukit Mandai fort yesterday afternoon.

Charging Fiercely Through Enemy Lines

By Shoichi Matsuda, Staff Correspondent

SINGAPORE FRONT, Feb. 12.—In the center and northern and southern ends of the city of Singapore, a fierce struggle unto death is raging as the Imperial troops, boldly accepting the challenge offered by the resisting British troops, are charging fiercely through the enemy lines.

After surrounding the enemy positions on Bukit Timah, the Imperial troops have swept into the city of Singapore from the southern sector in one fierce wave, but they have found the enemy's resistance in the city more stubborn than they had expected.

The Hanawa, Kobayashi, Watanabe, and Miyamoto detachments, advancing southward over the Bukit Timah highway, charged into the city on February 11 at 8.30 p.m. from the southwestern end of the race course.

Another unit advancing swiftly along the central railway line reached a point west of the city, when the enemy resisting from the formidable positions on Monks Hill and in Fort Canning, as well as in the vicinity of the central railway station, blazed away with their artillery and machine-guns to obstruct the advance of the Imperial troops.

Domei

BERLIN, Feb. 11.—Fierce street warfare is raging between the Nippon troops which charged into the city of Singapore today at noon, and the British troops defending the city, according to a Reuters dispatch intercepted here today.

The British troops, who had entrenched themselves in the city in order to stop the Nippon units advancing from the west, have destroyed the city's naval and military facilities in order to prevent their use by the Nippon forces, the report further stated.

25,000 British, Indian Troops Trapped

From Our Staff Correspondent

SINGAPORE FRONT, Feb. 11.—Under the ceaselelss bombardment of the Imperial Army air force, the 25,000 British and Indian troops on Singapore island have lost all their routes of retreat and have no other alternative but to be annihilated or to be taken prisoner.

The intense bombardment of the Singapore waterfront by squadrons of the Army air force was further in-

(Continued on Page 2)

First Photos of Navy Blitz on Jap Bases

SEE THE BACK PAGE

THE CHICAGO DAILY NEWS

67TH YEAR—38. REG. U. S. PAT. OFF. COPYRIGHT 1942 BY THE CHICAGO DAILY NEWS, INC. SATURDAY, FEBRUARY 14, 1942—THIRTY PAGES. [the magazine "This Week," 4 pages of Comics and 4 pages of PHOTOGRAVURE.] Telephone DEArborn 1111. FIVE CENTS

RED STREAK

OFFICIAL STORY OF DOVER BATTLE

RACE RESULTS
AT HIALEAH PARK, FLA.

1—Big Talk, 10.40, 4.60, 3.30; Kopla, 3.90, 2.60; All Good, 3.30.
2—Milk Flip, 6.50, 3.70, 3.00; Sentinel, 3.00, 2.40; Count Haste, 3.10.
Daily double—Big Talk and Milk Flip—paid 90.00.
3—Exploration, 37.20, 12.50, 7.00; Bally Boy, 4.00, 3.20; Greedan, 4.00.
4—Bright Willie, 8.40, 3.70, 2.80; Sir War, 5.70, 3.20; Incoming, 4.70.
5—Daily Delivery, 7.10, 4.00, 2.90; Speed to Spare, 4.40, 3.10; C. Basis, 3.30
6—Transient, 10.60, 3.50, 2.90; Sweet Willow, 3.30, 2.80; The Swallow, 3.40
7—Dit, 5.00, 2.90, 2.30; Johnnie J., 6.90, 3.40; Big Ben, 2.90.
8—Dogo, 11.10, 4.60, 3.40; Navarin, 3.30, 2.90; Brown Bomb, 3.80.

HERE ARE RULES FOR SIGNING IN DRAFT MONDAY

Heavy Penalties Provided For Failure to Comply; Defense Workers Aided.

OPERATE 40 PHONES

Selective Service officials announced that 40 telephone inquiry stations will be in operation today, tomorrow and Monday to answer questions regarding the draft registration for defense workers today and tomorrow and for the general male public Monday. It was suggested that inquiries be confined to the one question of where to register, letting other questions go until later to avoid overloading the lines. The number to call is Dearborn 3050. But read your newspaper first, the officials said.

(A list telling you where to register and a ward map appear on page 21.)

All men between 20 and 45, not previously registered and not in the Army, Navy, Marine Corps or Coast Guard or other excepted grouping, must register for military service Monday. Heavy penalties are provided for those who fail to comply.

Selective Service officials have set up a series of registration offices throughout Chicago and Cook County and every unregistered male who was 20 on or before Dec. 31 and will not be 45 on or before Monday should go to the office nearest his home between 7 a. m. and 9 p. m. and answer the nine questions on his registration card. The questions merely establish the identity of the registrant.

The registrant will receive, at the time of registering, a "certificate of registration" from the registrar. He should carry this with him at all times.

Follow Former Practices.

The details of questionnaires, classification, appeal and induction will follow the practice established in the first two drafts. The new order numbers will be integrated with the present numbers so that some of Monday's registrants may be called for service within the next couple of months.

Today and tomorrow special arrangements are being made to register defense workers in advance of Monday's general enrollment, so that they will not lose time from essential production through being obliged to register Monday.

Local board offices will be open for this purpose. The registration offices proper—the list of which has been printed in The Daily News yesterday and today—will be open only Monday. Local board offices are listed in the telephone directory under "United States of America—Selective Service System."

Aliens must register, or get out of the country in three months, unless they are accredited diplomatic or other representatives. Persons confined in hospitals will be registered by a clerk who will make the rounds of the wards. Men bedridden at home must notify their local boards, which will send a clerk to them.

Travelers must register at the local board wherever they happen to be and the board will forward their cards to their home boards. Other persons prevented from registering by unalterable circumstances, such as those too ill to be questioned, must register as soon as possible afterward.

Visitors to Register Here.

Chicago, as the great convention center of the country, will have some 5,000 visitors here for meetings Monday, it was estimated today. There will be meetings of several medical groups, leather goods manufacturers, motor manufacturers, and other organizations. For their convenience, registration offices have been set up in hotels.

Illinois will register approximately 610,000 men at 361 draft boards and registration offices, most of which are in public school buildings, with 20,000 volunteer registrars helping in the task. Some 9,000,000 men will be registered by 6,443 boards throughout the nation.

Steffey Gets Life Term in Four Attacks

(Picture on page 3.)

David Reese Steffey III, 18-year-old dabbler in moral philosophies, today was sentenced to life imprisonment for four of his confessed criminal attacks on women.

In a dramatic and despairing denunciation of the sentence, Steffey waved his arm at Judge Julius H. Miner and exclaimed, "You might as well shoot me!"

He refused further comment and was led away to a cell in the County Jail. Meanwhile, his mother collapsed, weeping on the shoulder of her husband.

"When will he be eligible for parole?" the elder Steffey asked Judge Miner, as he worked his way before the bench. He was told: "In 20 years."

'Won't Have Chance,' Cries Dad.

"Why that's destruction — complete destruction!" the father cried. "He won't have a chance."

As she left the courtroom, Mrs. Steffey's emotions reached the breaking point and she turned to scream at the courtroom spectators, who numbered some 15 or 20 women, half of them teen-age girls:

"I hope these women are satisfied. Some day they'll have sons of their own, and then they'll know. They are to blame. They are the ones who spoiled my son's life."

In his lengthy written opinion, Judge Miner referred sympathetically to the father and mother "who have reared him so tenderly until he became uncontrollable."

"But what about the fine mothers he desecrated and the innocent young girls he violated?" he asked. "The court pities also the husbands and fathers of these unfortunate victims who had the fortitude and courage to bring this culprit to justice."

Young Steffey had sat up attentively as Judge Miner began to read the opinion in which he traced the youth's criminal tendencies to his abandonment of religion. Before the court had finished reading the first paragraph, however, the blond defendant slouched in his seat and half covered his eyes, seemingly indifferent.

'Cruel, Wicked' Conduct.

"Under the defendant's plea, the court can only measure the degree of guilt and impose sentence commensurate with his many crimes," the opinion said. "Neither the parents of the defendant nor his lawyer would want his release. There can be no question that his conduct was cruel, wicked and inhuman, the most dastardly acts in the annals of crime. It was difficult for the court to listen to the atrocities, tortures and perversions inflicted upon the complaining witnesses without feeling that savagery has returned in its ugliest form.

"In mitigation of these heinous crimes, the defense tried to show the mental condition of the boy, not that he is legally insane, but that he is a sort of intellectual freak—brilliant in some respects and peculiar in others.

"The psychiatrists term is schizophrenia, a split personality, but they all agree that the defendant is legally sane. Under the plea of guilty, the court must so treat the defendant."

Likens Steffey to Anarchist.

Judge Miner then went into a discourse on Steffey's philosophy, declaring that he had "willfully and deliberately rejected the law of God and the law of the land and become a law unto himself." He likened him to an anarchist, saying that he understood fully the seriousness and consequence of his acts.

"His conduct was exemplary, as long as he retained his religious view and influences," the court went on. "His criminal tendencies and inclinations are traceable directly to his newly acquired atheistic convictions. Not that every atheist is a criminal, but in this court's experience every criminal is estranged from the church."

Judge Miner granted a stay of mittimus for 60 days, to allow Steffey's parents and his attorney, Benjamin Ehrlich, to consult with him and make arrangements for treatment, if found necessary, at the penitentiary. The court said Dr. Harry Hoffman, state alienist, would be asked to examine him.

DISINTEGRATED JAP BASES IN SMASH

The anti-aircraft guns aboard a United States cruiser are shown in action off the Wotje Atoll in this first picture of the United States Navy's devastating attack on Japan's Marshall and Gilbert Islands in the Pacific. Note the helmeted gun crews at their stations and the companion vessel in the background. [Associated Press Wirephoto from Pathe News.]

COURT ORDERS FULL SERVICE ON SHORE LINE

Federal Judge Michael L. Igoe today ordered resumption of full through service on the North Shore electric line to end a situation he called "silly, sickening and unpatriotic."

"I am going to instruct these receivers," the judge said today at a hearing on the North Shore's "switch-out," "that this service must go back into operation Monday morning.

"If it does not, there will be action by this court to see why it does not."

H. M. Lytle, vice-president of the Rapid Transit Lines, said the first North Shore train scheduled to use the Rapid Transit tracks Monday morning will be a northbound local due to leave Roosevelt road at 2:31 a. m., and to reach Howard street at 2:56.

Barred from Chicago.

North Shore trains have been barred from Chicago since Feb. 1, when employees of the elevated lines, over whose tracks the North Shore operated in the city, refused to switch the North Shore trains into the elevated system.

They charged that employees of the railroad brotherhoods had been raiding their membership by persuading North Shore employees to drop out of the Amalgamated Association of Street, Electric Railway and Motor Coach Employees, to which both North Shore and elevated employees belong, and join one or the other of the railroad craft unions.

Riders Must Transfer.

As a result, passengers on the North Shore have to transfer to or from elevated trains at Linden avenue, Wilmette, and at Howard street.

The dispute between the unions has produced bad feeling among the men, the unions said, and many offensive remarks are batted around the locker rooms, while trainmen make faces at tower operators as they rattle by.

That was what Judge Igoe got wind of today.

"To me," he said, after explaining that he has always been friendly to labor, "this is a silly and sickening situation.

"More than that, it is an unpatriotic situation."

WEATHER INDICATIONS

(United States Weather Bureau Forecast.) Feb. 14, 1942.

For Chicago and vicinity—Little change in temperature this afternoon; occasional light snow and slightly warmer tonight; gentle to moderate winds.

Temperatures beginning with 6 p. m. yesterday:

6 p. m.	34	9 a. m.	28
8 p. m.	33	10 a. m.	30
10 p. m.	31	11 a. m.	32
12 midnight	30	12 noon	32
2 a. m.	30	1 p. m.	33
4 a. m.	30	2 p. m.	33
6 a. m.	29	3 p. m.	33
7 a. m.	29	4 p. m.	33
8 a. m.	28	5 p. m.	33

Sunrise today, 7:47; sunset today, 6:22; moonset, 6:57 p. m. tomorrow.

(Today's weather chart on page 25.)

Victory Time Is City's Wish For Valentine

(Picture on page 3.)

BY JUSTIN M'CARTHY.

The first thing to do is find a pair of lovebirds. They know all about St. Valentine's Day.

"What is the latest thing in valentines?" you ask the lovebirds who are cooing at each other in a bird store on Madison street.

"Don't be a stupid cupid," gurgles Mr. Lovebird. "Haven't you heard what Kitty Carlisle, the singer, suggested?

Double-Barreled Message.

"She suggests this year's valentines be double-barreled messages of affection to your sweetheart and Uncle Sam. You buy defense stamps, which you call Victory Valentines. Cupid shoots a dart at your sweetheart and Uncle Sam shoots some Japs."

"Dear Gen. MacArthur:
The Japs are yellow.
Your men are true red, white and blue.
Here are 500 planes for you."

The patriotic motif is all over the place.

"Sure I use lipstick, soldier, but not to keep chaps like you off my lips," is one valentine greeting that smacks of lots of love.

Ending with a Punch.

On State street you find that while the girls get sentimental cards, candy and flowers for their valentines, the stores suggest neckties for the men. They have a familiar appearance, too. They look like a re-order of the ones that were there at Christmas time.

This is a funny St. Valentine's Day. The Loop seems almost empty because there are so few automobiles. Well, might as well end with a greeting to the guy that's responsible for the tire shortage.

"Dear Hirohito:
Roses are red, violets are bluer.
Why don't you go jump in the Pacific?"

ARTILLERY DUELS MARK FIGHTING IN PHILIPPINES

Washington, Feb. 14. — (AP)— Heavy artillery dueling on the Bataan Peninsula in the Philippines and resumption of Japanese siege firing on the Corregidor fortifications were reported today by the War Department.

War communique No. 106 said:

"1. Philippine theater:

"Operations in Bataan during the last 24 hours included heavy artillery dueling and aggressive infantry skirmishes. In some sections of the front enemy troops are entrenching their positions.

"Enemy artillery fire from the Cavite shore was again directed against our harbor defenses. No material damage resulted.

"The enemy was active in the air on all parts of our front.

"2. There is nothing to report from other areas."

WITNESS TELLS 'FINAL HOURS' OF SINGAPORE

BY GEORGE WELLER.
SPECIAL RADIO.
To The Chicago Daily News Foreign Service.
Copyright, 1942, The Chicago Daily News, Inc.

Batavia, Feb. 14.—Singapore under a thick pall of smoke from vast oil tanks and burning naval stocks, with Japanese artillery spreading a curtain barrage through the island's suburban hills and Japanese bombers pouring endless cargoes of explosives upon British troops from disdainfully low altitudes: Such was the picture of the final hours brought here today by the first officers released from the mid-island battle.

(The Singapore radio said tonight that the reservoirs on Singapore Island are still in British hands, but Singapore communiques indicated that at least part of these central basins were in Japanese hands. Associated Press dispatches from London said British guns were taking a "terrible toll" of Japaneses invaders, while United Press reported a Tokyo broadcast as saying that Japanese forces had captured official buildings in Singapore City.)

Among these officers was Col. Ian Stewart, the first D.S.O of the Malayan campaign and leader of the hard-struck Argyll Sutherland regiment, a thin and physically frail Scotsman.

I found Stewart a few moments after he arrived in this intensely blacked-out city and obtained partly from him and partly from his companions the story of how the Japs sent tanks by the scores, by night, down the main road from the Johore causeway.

An expert at jungle fighting, Col. Stewart received orders from General Headquarters—which, incidentally, the Argylls were guarding—to leave for Java before dawn on Thursday. The orders came after four days and nights of almost continuous fighting, from Sunday night, when the Japs first crossed the straits successfully, to Thursday morning, when their artillery was throwing shells to within a few hundred yards of the water front, already afire with repeated bombardment.

En route, the ship carrying the colonel and a pair of staff officers, was attacked by bombers and suffered continuous attacks for four hours before entering the gantlet of the Bangka Straits, where raids are the fiercest. About 160 bombs were dropped in about 15 runs over the ship by several flights of a total of approximately 50 bombers flying at approximately 10,000 feet altitude. Few took effect.

Singapore's restricted shoreline could not be supported to a suf-

(Continued on page 2, column 3.)

Nazis Rule Death for Aid To Americans in France

Vichy, Feb. 14.—(AP)—Nazi authorities decreed the death penalty tonight for anyone aiding Americans or citizens of other countries at war with Germany to hide from occupation authorities.

CASEY SEES JAP SHIP, BOMBERS BEATEN BY U. S.

Americans Try in Vain to Save Stricken Enemy Crew.

(This is the second installment of Robert J. Casey's thrilling eye-witness account of the U. S. Navy's devastating attack on Japan's Marshall and Gilbert Islands Feb. 1, in which five warships, 11 other major vessels, 38 warplanes and huge military stores were wiped out. In it Mr. Casey describes a heroic, but futile, battle by a Japanese patrol boat and the destroyer on which he sailed with the fleet and then relates an air attack on the American ships by big Tokyo bombers.)

BY ROBERT J. CASEY.
SPECIAL RADIO.
To The Chicago Daily News Foreign Service.
Copyright, 1942, The Chicago Daily News, Inc.

With the Pacific Fleet at Sea.—(Delayed.)—The officer on the signal bridge took a last look at the stretch of blue water where one unidentified Japanese, accompanied by a lot of other unidentified Japanese, just had died. He laid down his glasses.

"If Japan ever gets around to putting up a statue for that guy," he said, "I'll contribute and so will the rest of the United States Navy."

"Peace to his ashes," commented the marine sergeant at the five-inch gun. "He had what it took."

After that nobody said anything much because the main battery had begun to fire, and waves and currents of sound were shaking the ship and beating in one's ear. But none needed to say anything.

The fleet, as you know, had come to this dangerous corner before sunrise after an audacious drive at high speed through the submarine zone which had been looked on as the main defense of this region. It had spread out for the elimination of the Japanese bases in the Gilbert and Marshall Islands squarely on schedule.

Unit Steams Slowly.

Our unit had slipped over to the edge of possible minefields and steamed slowly, momentarily awaiting bombing planes—bombing planes and light enough to shoot by. The gunnery officer stood looking now at his stop watch, now at the moon, yellow and blatant, and presently at the shadowy line forming on the starboard horizon. The cloudy sky in the east became streaked with banks of solid white, dimming to black in the north where the sea was still hazy and mysterious.

The bombers came. We couldn't see them but the red glare of bursting bombs flashed unsteadily against the dark sky over the atoll. After awhile the thumping, unreal noise of explosions came back to us. The gunnery officer took an-

(Continued on page 2, column 6.)

IN THE DAILY NEWS TODAY

Jap Chutists Invade Coast Of Sumatra

BULLETIN.

Washington, Feb. 14.—(AP)—The War Department reported today an attack by 12 heavy American bombers on enemy shipping in the Macassar area in the Netherlands East Indies during which, it was believed, at least one large Japanese ship was hit. All the planes, which were of the long-range four-engine type, returned safely to their bases.

Batavia, Feb. 14.—(AP)—Striking close to the heart of the Dutch East Indies, Japan attacked the northeast coast of Sumatra today with air-borne troops that landed from more than 100 planes near Palembang, important oil port, 250 miles from Batavia. Dutch defenders were declared officially to be more than holding their own and killing parachutists by the dozens.

(As the danger thus came closer to the heart of the Dutch islands, the Australian radio reported that Australian and other British Imperial troops had landed at Batavia and "are taking up positions for the defense" of the key island.)

The Japanese also were reported to be pressing down closer to Java from the north and the Dutch command said there were unofficial reports that Bandjermasin, capital of South Borneo, had been occupied by the invaders.

Dutch Destroy Equipment.

The Dutch already had carried out careful destruction at the town on the South Borneo coast just across the Java Sea from Batavia and the big Soerabaja naval station.

The attack on Palembang was described officially as the first confirmed Japanese use of parachutists in five weeks of operations against Netherlands Indies territory. It also was the first land operation on the 1,000-mile-long island.

Guarded by Fighters.

The first of the Japanese-dropped onto Sumatra near Palembang in the morning, followed by more and more as troop-carrying planes soared over guarded by fighters, the war bulletin said.

Although troops were dropped at three places in the Palembang area, the communique said "Palembang itself is not threatend" and "there are no indications that parachutists dropped close to or entered the town."

AUSTRALIAN FLIERS BLAST JAPS AT NEW BRITAIN PORT

Melbourne, Feb. 14. — (AP) — Australian warplanes again attacked Japanese invasion forces yesterday at Gasmata, New Britain, bombing shipping in the harbor and blasting grounded enemy planes, a communique announced today.

Japanese fighters attempted to intercept the raiders and ground batteries put up a heavy barrage, but all the Australian planes returned safely, the announcement said.

SUMATRA AIRDROME RAIDED; 9 PLANES DESTROYED: TOKYO

Tokyo—(From Japanese Broadcasts), Feb. 14.—(AP)—A Domei dispatch from "a Japanese air base in Malaya" said today that Japanese warplanes raided Palembang airdrome in Sumatra twice yesterday and that they shot down or destroyed on the ground nine aircraft.

The War Today

PACIFIC AREA.

Singapore.

Reservoirs on Singapore Island still remain in British hands as defenders counterattack to establish a new line, while artillery guns keep Japs from using the Johore Causeway.

Philippines.

Heavy artillery dueling and infantry skirmishes mark fighting on Bataan Peninsula as Japs resume siege firing on the Corregidor Fortress.

Dutch East Indies.

One hundred Jap planes land chutists near Palembang, important oil port in Sumatra.

Burma.

Fighting slackens, indicating apparent collapse of second Jap attempt to crack Salween River line in Paan area.

EUROPEAN AREA.

German-Russian Front.

Red Army forces, driving west of the Moscow-Leningrad line, storm fortifications built by Nazis for stand until spring.

AFRICAN AREA.

Libyan Front.

A German motorized column has been driven back in Libya in the Ain E Gazala area, Cairo reports.

BRITISH DESCRIBE FUTILE EFFORT TO STOP NAZI FLEET

Bravery of Britons in Face of Superior Forces and Bad Weather Told.

London, Feb. 14.—(AP)—The Admiralty issued this press statement tonight concerning the Dover Strait engagement with the German naval squadron):

Further details can now be given of the navy's part in intercepting and damaging the enemy force in channel battle.

The enemy was first identified and reported at the western entrance to Dover Straits at 11:35. The first striking force of six Swordfish aircraft was at once ordered to take off from a shore airdrome to attack.

(The German radio said tonight no damage was suffered by any German warships in the Channel battle with the British Thursday except for the loss of a patrol boat and damage to a torpedo boat, the Associated Press reported.

(The prize German battleships Scharnhorst and Gneisenau and the heavy cruiser Prinz Eugen were declared last night to have reached home berths safely in their dash for freedom from Brest.)

This striking force was led by Lt. Comdr. E. Esmonde, D. S. O

Lt. Comdr. Esmonde and th crews of his Swordfish knew very well that the task of attacking the Scharnhorst and Gneisenau and Prinz Eugen was very different from attacking even a very heavily armed ship on the high seas.

Ships Hugging Coast.

The German ships were hugging the coast of enemy territory very closely. They were covered by an umbrella of hundreds of short based fighters, all of them having more than twice the speed and maneuverability than the Swordfish carrying torpedo.

Moreover, enemy ships were passing in succession past airdromes and landing grounds from which fighter escorts could be reinforced at a moment's notice. If the crews of the Swordfish ever thought of the odds against them the thought certainly did not deter them.

They knew they were flying aircraft very vulnerable to fighters they were bound to meet. They knew they were about to attack a naval squadron which was capable of putting up a tremendous volume of anti-aircraft fire, but they knew also the task was to press home the attack and score hits with torpedoes on the enemy.

Outcome Yet Uncertain.

They had to contend with bad weather as well as the enemy, but they found targets and pressed home their attacks. Exactly what happened in the closing stages of the attack is not yet certain but conditions were such that it was almost impossible for anybody to observe with certainty whether or not the enemy ships were hit.

Fighters of the R. A. F., engaging enemy aircraft high overhead, reported explosions and flashes which they considered to be one certain and two possible hits with torpedoes.

Crews of the fighters speak of having seen the Swordfish dive down almost to sea level, and press home their attacks regardless of all opposition. But not one of those six Swordfish came back. Only five men from the crews were subsequently saved by our light craft.

Torpedo Boats Speed Out.

Meanwhile, all available motor torpedo boats in the Dover area had put to sea at full speed despite the fact that the weather was by no means suitable for these small, fast craft.

It was nearly half past 12 when the first of the motor torpedo boats sighted the first of the enemy heavy ships. The enemy's main units were heavily screened by destroyers and E-boats.

As our motor torpedo boats went into attack they were engaged by very heavy fire and they also were engaged by German aircraft who dived on them continually, firing machine guns and cannons. The motor torpedo boats held on until it was obvious unless they fired through their torpedoes at once, their opportunity would be gone. Thus they carried out their attacks and fired their torpedoes, refusing to be deterred by enemy aircraft or enemy shell fire or by the fact

(Continued on page 3, column 2.)

EVENING EDITION

Japan Times & Advertiser

Incorporating
The JAPAN CHRONICLE and The JAPAN MAIL

EVENING EDITION

No. 15,399 (THE 17th YEAR of SHOWA) TOKYO, MONDAY, FEBRUARY 16, 1942 Price 8 Sen

PREMIER TOJO REPORTS ON SINGAPORE VICTORY; BRITAIN HEARS CHURCHILL IN SHADOW OF DEFEAT

Fall of Vaunted Stronghold Admitted in Tragic Announcement — More Dangers Are Warned

ALL MALAYA NOW IN JAPANESE HANDS

Domei

LISBON, February 15.—Over a world-wide broadcast, Prime Minister Winston Churchill admitted tonight that Singapore had fallen, it was revealed here today from London.

The Prime Minister tragically declared, "I speak to you all under the shadow of heavy and far-reaching military defeat."

Indicating that the end of British reverses has not yet come, he continued, "Other dangers gather about us."

"Singapore has fallen," it was dejectedly announced, and the Prime Minister added, "All of Malaya has now been over-run by the enemy."

Didn't Stand Chance

LONDON, February 15.—(Special)—Prime Minister Winston Churchill made the startling announcement that Singapore had fallen to the Japanese in a speech which was at first scheduled to be a survey of the war situation to date.

Speaking without his usual confident air, Churchill announced the loss sardonically by declaring, "Tonight I speak to our friends in Australia and New Zealand, and to those in India and Burma. I speak to our loyal friends and allies, the United States and Russia, and also to our gallant allies, the Dutch and the Chinese. I speak to you all under the shadow of a great military defeat for the British. SINGAPORE HAS FALLEN. All of Malaya has now been taken by the enemy."

Warning that no one must under-rate the power and the weight of the Japanese Armed Forces which have proved themselves in the air, on the sea, and man to man on land, Churchill admitted that Britain did not have the slightest chance against the Japanese even if she had been prepared.

In an attempt to appease the Australians, the Dutch, and the rest of her allies in the southwest Pacific who have been scoring her for not sending more reinforcements, Churchill explained that Britain was barely able to keep her head above the water at home, by fighting in the Atlantic, the Mediterranean, and North Africa, as well as sending as much aid as possible to Russia. "Not a plane, tank, ship, or anti-aircraft gun has stood idle", he said.

The Prime Minister reminded Britons that they were not alone in this great struggle as they had been in the summer of 1940 when the whole world thought that England was through. He urged them to display their poise and determination in this hour of misfortune and show the world that they can meet reverses with dignity and renewed strength.

Surrender Announced

Domei

STOCKHOLM, February 15.—According to a Reuter News Agency report received here tonight, the

British Government officially has announced that Singapore has surrendered and is now in Japanese hands.

Last Base Falls

Domei

SINGAPORE, February 15.—Singapore, the last and most formidable of the Allied three great bases in East Asia surrendered tonight.

Lieutenant-General Tomoyuki Yamashita, Commander-in-Chief of the Japanese Expeditionary Forces in Malaya, representing the victors, and Lieutenant-General Robert Percival, Commander-in-Chief of the British forces representing the vanquished, signed documents at 7:50 p.m. tonight which wrote finis to the Malay phase of the Pacific War. Hostilities ceased along the entire Malay front at 10 p.m.

With the surrender, ragged Tommies, and Anzacs stumbling with fatigue after being continually driven before the relentless Japanese juggernaut enjoyed their first real rest in a month and a half since the Japanese machine began hitting its stride down the paved highway from Ipoh on January 31.

The surrender papers were signed in the prosaic background of the Ford Motor Plant at the foot of Bukit Timah heights. The British sued for cessation of hostilities at 2:30 p.m. today when they found themselves surrounded in Singapore city and the central section of the island—helpless to defend themselves against the rain of bombs and shells.

The peace mission of four British officers headed by Major Wilde of

(Continued on Page 2)

LONDON STUPEFIED BY SINGAPORE FALL

Thought Fortress Would Hold Out Longer Than 7 Days Before Surrendering

NO FAITH IN OWN TROOPS

Doubts if Britain Can Repulse Anticipated Nazi Offensives—Berlin Hails Victory

Special to the Yomiuri

STOCKHOLM, February 15.—Londoners are stupefied with the news of the surrender of Singapore, according to reports reaching here. Of course, since the landing of the Japanese Forces on Singapore Island on February 9, the British people seemed to have given up any hope of saving the island and they are now in blank dismay as the great fortress of Singapore had surrendered to the Japanese Forces so soon

Hongkong stood the Japanese onrush for seven days and thus, the people generally believed that Singapore would at least stand any attack more than 15 days. Consequently, in the meanwhile, they believed the majority of the British troops in Singapore would be able to withdraw to the Netherlands East Indies, but they are dumbfounded Singapore had surrendered after only seven days' resistance.

In the light of this feat, the proud British people have finally lost all confidence in the fighting strength of their own troops. Particularly the clumsiness that was shown by the British troops in preventing the landing of the Japanese Forces on Singapore had disappointed the British public.

This, together with the passage of the German fleet through the Straits of Dover, is making the people doubt whether the Germans could be prevented from landing on England or whether the defense of England would be assured.

Berlin Celebrates Fall

Special to the Yomiuri

BERLIN, February 15.—The fall of Singapore was broadcast in Germany today, following the playing of the Japanese anthem, Kimigayo. Not only Japanese residents but also the German public in general are celebrating the surrender of Singapore.

Toward the end of last year, the German people were depressed as Soviet forces commenced strong resistance but with the news of the fall of Singapore, they regained their confidence and bright prospect. The city of Berlin is full of joyous sentiment. Last year, the Japanese were surprised by German lightning advances, but now, the Germans are astonished by the rapid Japanese drive on all fronts.

The success of the Japanese operations in East Asia will give courage and confidence to Germany in her spring offensives.

Quick Capture Amazes

Special to the Yomiuri

BUENOS AIRES, February 15.—When Japanese Forces landed on Singapore, the people here believed that the fall of that great British fortress island would be a question of time, but they never expected that it would fall within one week.

The surprise of the United States is astounding, as the fall of Singapore

(Continued on Page 2)

East Asia Cultural and Economic Aspects, In Hand With Singapore Victory, Stressed

Spokesman Hori Touches on Comparatively Neglected Subjects in Special Statement Issued to Foreign Correspondents

The political and military significance of the fall of Singapore needs no elaboration, said Tomokazu Hori, Spokesman of the Board of Information, at the regular meeting of foreign correspondents in Tokyo, Monday, and went on to describe the economic and cultural phases of the present war which have been comparatively neglected both at home and abroad. Mr. Hori stressed the fact that the establishment of the Greater East Asia Construction Council is a sure promise of an epoch-making reconstruction in this part of the world. His statement in full follows:

"Premier Tojo has just announced at the Diet a general outline of Japan's policy in prosecuting the present War of Greater East Asia. I need not, I believe, elaborate on the political and military significance of the fall of Singapore. Suffice it to say that the occupation of Singapore spells the doom of British imperialism in East Asia. What I want to say at this time is the phase of the present War which is likely to be forgotten by the general public both at home and abroad.

"The War which Japan is now prosecuting against the United States and the British Empire is not merely to crush those two powerful opponents in a military sense but to realize a new order in this part of the world. Even during the China Affair, Japan has exerted extraordinary effort to increase her productive capacity in economic and industrial fields especially in heavy industries, replenishing necessary equipments. This is testified by the fact, although I cannot give the exact figures under the circumstances which are obvious to you, that Japan's industrial productive capacity has witnessed a remarkable expansion so much so that she is now more than able to carry on the present War with the United States and British Empire to a successful end.

"In financial matters also, there has been a phenomenal growth of our country's strength during these war years as shown by the fact that huge budgets have been made to work without any appreciable hitch. As for the development of the natural resources, thanks to the close economic cooperation between Japan, Manchoukuo and China, it has made such progress that the inexhaustible natural resources of both Manchoukuo and occupied territories in China have been steadily developed to the benefit of not only Japan but the peoples of those countries concerned. The deserted mines and factories in China have been revived to produce necessary materials and goods, while a considerable number of industrial plants have already been restored to the Chinese in accordance with the Basic Treaty concluded sometime ago between the Japanese Government and the National Government at Nanking. Not only that, Japan has extended whole-hearted support to the latter Government to realize peace, order and economic prosperity in the regions under the latter's political jurisdiction. Even in the British Concessions in China, peace has been consistently maintained with their inhabitants contented in their daily life. The prevailing peace in the International Settlement in Shanghai attests to Japan's policy directed toward the recovery of peaceful economic life of the people concerned.

"Our relations with French Indo-China is an outstanding example of Japan's peaceful intention. Trade between Japan and French Indo-China has grown considerably in volume with their amicable intercourse increasing in warmth.

"As regards Thailand, our ally, her cordial cooperation with Japan has been

(Continued on Page 2)

BOARD ISSUES PLANS FOR VICTORY PARADE

Nation to Celebrate Fall of Singapore at Hibiya Park on Entry Day—Tojo to Broadcast

With the fall of Singapore into the Japanese hands as a result of the British forces' unconditional surrender as officially announced by the Imperial Headquarters a 10:10 p.m. on Sunday, the whole nation will celebrate the Imperial Forces' victories so far achieved from the start of the War of Greater East Asia.

In this connection, the Board of Information made public its first victory celebration program and the instructions to be followed by the nation on that occasion. The program follows:

1. The national flag will be hoisted by every household from the day of fall to the day of the Imperial Forces' formal entry into the city of Singapore.

2. At noon on the day of the formal entry, the whole nation will pray in appreciation of the Imperial Forces' glorious war achievements. Meanwhile, Premier General Hideki Tojo will deliver an address on the nationwide radio hookup. Subsequently, the people will join the Premier

(Continued on Page 2)

JAPANESE PREPARED FOR 100 YEARS WAR

Colonel Ohira Asserts People Will Not Give Up Fight Till Enemies Crushed

"Japan is firmly determined to fight, in close collaboration with Germany and Italy, even a 100-year war to crush the United States of America and Great Britain," declared Colonel Hideo Ohira, chief of the Army Press Section of the Imperial Headquarters in his address made Saturday at the party held in celebration of the Japanese victory in Singapore.

The party was sponsored jointly by the Tokyo Municipality and the Japan-Germany-Italy Friendship Society at the Kyoritsu Kodo, Kanda. His address, in gist, follows:

"With the outbreak of the War of Greater East Asia on December 8 of last year, Imperial Forces took over enemy concessions on the continent,

(Continued on Page 2)

DIET CALLED TO HEAR REPORT ON SINGAPORE

War and Navy Ministers Make Detailed Talk—Thanks to Forces Voted

The plenary session of the House of Peers was urgently called at 10 a.m. this morning, following the surrender of Singapore on Sunday at which War Minister General Hideki Tojo and Navy Minister Admiral Shigetaro Shimada submitted reports on the historic fall of Singapore.

Following the reports by the War and Navy Ministers, Prince Kuniyuki Tokugawa, representing all parties in the House, proposed a motion for expressing thanks to the Army and Navy for the successful campaign in Malaya and Singapore. When the motion was unanimously approved by the House, the War and Navy Minister expressed appreciation for the manifestation of thanks by the House of Peers.

Then, Premier Tojo delivered his historical address to the House.

The House of Representatives will also meet in a plenary session at 1 p.m. this afternoon. After hearing the reports by War Minister General Tojo and Navy Minister Admiral Shimada on the fall of Singapore, the House will also pass a motion for expressing thanks to the Army and Navy, proposed by Matajiro Koizumi, representing all parties.

SINKING OF NORMANDIE RAPPED BY U.S. PUBLIC

Lampoons Navy and Government for Rotten Labor Policy —Press Wants Truth

Domei

STOCKHOLM, February 15.—The recent burning and sinking of the gigantic French luxury liner, Normandie, at New York during its conversion into an army transport has brought serious repercussions in the United States, according to a New York report received here today.

The incredible lack of discipline on the part of the workers and United States naval authorities has resulted in a steady stream of violent criticism of the United States Government's "rotten labor policy," the report stated.

The American press, as a result of the sinking, has begun a campaign demanding that the Government give the public the truth of the actual situation confronting the Democracies, it was said.

Song of Triumph Sweeps Over Malaya As Anglo-Chinese Oppression Is Ended

The 2,200,000 Malays in the Malay Peninsula are singing a song of triumph, says the Yomiuri. The fall of Singapore marks the end of British and Chinese oppression in Malaya, and the starting line whence they can embark on a new life as free people of East Asia.

Ever since the Japanese Forces entered Malaya, the people there have been touched by the kindly attitude of the Japanese. On one occasion the Japanese soldiers helped the Malays obtain necessary provisions which the Chinese had hidden in cellars underground, and which they refused to sell to the Malays.

There was a Malay bandit called Malay Mousey who was noted for his hostility toward the British. The British authorities had driven him to take shelter in the hills, but when the Japanese troops approached, Malay Mousey led all his gallant rogues to the camp of the Japanese commander, and begged to be allowed to join the Japanese troops.

On another occasion, a Malay driver of a truck loaded with British prisoners passed a Japanese car. The Malay driver waved his hand at the driver of the Japanese car, shouting out, "Finis to the British troops! Long live the Japanese. Long live the Malays."

With the fall of Singapore the temporary shelters erected by the Malay refugees from Singapore in the rubber plantations of Johore have become unnecessary, and the Malays are ecstatic with joy. The somber gloom of the rubber estates is gay with the scarlet-colored sarongs of the Malay woman dancing with joy.

A Yomiuri correspondent asked them why they were so glad. They replied that they were happy because they would able to eat fish again!

The Japanese fishermen in Singapore had monopolized the fishing trade of Malaya, and Japanese fisheries supplied almost all of the fish that the Malays used to eat. Before the war the British authorities had placed severe restrictions on the Japanese fishermen, and this not only caused the fishery trade to suffer, but also caused a dearth in the fish market. The Malays, who are fish eaters, suffered the most. But now that the Japanese are masters of Singapore, they will be able to eat fish again! That was why they were dancing with joy.

Even a slight incident like this illustrates the great principle of mutual benefit in the Greater East Asia Co-Prosperity Sphere, concludes the Yomiuri.

FALL OF SINGAPORE IS COUP ON BRITAIN

Capture of Island Tantamount To Loss of Australia, India, Kiwao Okumura Says

SOUTHERN TIES AGE-OLD

Malayan Name Pahang Derived From Japanese Prince's Ship Called Bahan

The long expected fall of Singapore has come at last and in the very month of the founding of the Japanese Empire, Kiwao Okumura, Vice-President of the Board of Information, stated in a radio speech Sunday night, in a voice which resounded with the glorious victory of the Japanese Empire Forces in Singapore. He pointed out that the loss of Singapore not only marks the withdrawal of Britain from East Asia but also the loss of Australia and India. His speech follows:

The long-expected fall of Singapore has come at last, and in the very month of the founding of the Japanese Empire. Since the declaration of war against the United States and Britain on December 8 last year, the three great bases of British and American imperialism in East Asia, Hongkong, Manila, and now Singapore, have fallen one after the other under the onslaughts of the Japanese.

These brilliant victories, achieved within the short period of 70 days, together with the victories of the German and Italian troops in Europe, mark the success of the Axis Powers all over the world, and guarantee the establishment of the New Order on a firm and lasting basis.

The unique position of Singapore gave it the command of the trade routes to and from the East, but its development as a free port and as a naval base began from the time the British occupied it at the beginning of the nineteenth century. In the eighteenth century, the British had succeeded in conquering the whole of India. In 1786 they occupied the island of Penang. The Vice-Governor of Bencoolen, in Sumatra, at that time was Sir Stamford Raffles. Raffles bought the island of Singapore from the Sultan of Johore at a very cheap price and the British have held Singapore for 120 years since.

Singapore gave the British command of India, China and Australia. The Russian menace had been held at bay by Japan, and as Japan increased in strength, Britain attempted to strangle this country by surrounding her with an economic blockade.

At the Washington Conference, America and Britain forced Japan to accept a minimum standard of armament, whilst American fortifications at Guam and in the Philippines, and British fortifications in the island of Singapore, went on uninterrupted.

The colossal sum of £15,000,000 was raised for the construction of the Singapore Naval Base. When it was completed in 1938 it rivalled Gibraltar, Pearl Harbor, and Heligoland as one of the world's four greatest naval bases, and became the pivot of the A.B.C.D. ring against Japan.

Singapore was important to the British Empire and to the United States not only because of its military strength, but also because of its great

(Continued on Page 2)

Singapore Fall Is Death Knell to Britain; Japan's Ultimate Win, Says Masanori Ito

"The British loss of Singapore means the end of the British Empire, just as it means the ultimate victory of the Japanese in the Greater East Asia War," declared Masanori Ito, Japan's famous Navy commentator, in an interview with the Yomiuri on Sunday.

"Admiral Sir John Jellicoe declared that the defense of the British Empire in East Asia would be perfected by the construction of a great naval base in Singapore sufficient in scale to accommodate a fleet not smaller than the whole Japanese Navy," continues the well-known commentator.

"Jellicoe knew that Singapore would not only assure the safety of Australia, India, Malaya, the East Indies, and other British possessions in the southwestern Pacific, but also that it would form a base for further British operations in this area. Singapore, thus formed the heart of the British Empire. The fate of the Empire rested on the Seletar Naval Base.

"The work on the construction of the naval base began in 1920, but four years later the work was stopped when the MacDonald Government came into power. The work was discontinued on the grounds that Singapore was too far from the homeland, and that it would take too much time to send troops from England in case of war. There was also an undercurrent of fear that Japan would regard the base as a threat against her, and come on the offensive.

"However, all opposition was swept aside and the construction was resumed in 1926. The base was finally completed in 1938.

"The size of the base may be judged from the fact that it can accommodate the entire Japanese Navy and still have room to spare. The base enabled the British to regard French Indo-China as being within their sphere of influence and formed a strategic center of military operations in case of war.

"Moreover, the British boasted that from this base, British submarines could extend their operations as far as the Sea of Japan and that it would enable them to destroy entirely the Japanese merchant fleet.

"Now that the world's most important naval base has fallen into our hands, it means that the fate of Australia, India, Burma, the East Indies has also fallen into our hands.

"Calcutta, Sourabaya and Port Darwin, the bases in the second line of defense, are of no earthly use for the connecting link of Singapore has been cut.

"Already the British have been forced to stand at bay at their last base, Calcutta. It can be safely asserted that there can be no doubt that the British will soon be driven from even this last base."

Leader Explains Significance of New Success —Determination for Future Is Fully Pledged

OPEN ARMS ARE EXTENDED TO INDIA

Explaining the significance of the fall of Singapore and the future policy of Japan, Premier General Hideki Tojo, in his much-awaited report to the Diet this morning, expressed his determination to execute the Greater East Asia War until all the objectives of the nation have been attained.

Reiterating his promises made to the peoples of East Asia he called on all the nations in the area to awaken to the real aims of Japan in order that the benefits of our victories might be fully enjoyed by them.

The Premier's speech follows, in full:

Swift Successes Told

"As has been already announced by the Imperial Headquarters, the Imperial Forces have occupied Singapore yesterday, February 15.

The Army and Navy authorities will make their report concerning the circumstances of the actual fighting. However, I am glad to state my views and conviction at this opportunity.

"At the outset of the War, following the issuance of the gracious Imperial Rescript, our Forces immediately crushed the main body of the American-British fleet; and in 18 days they brought Hongkong to submission; in 26 days they occupied Manila, and in 70 days they brought about the fall of Singapore. Thus the important bases of of the United States and Britain for their encroachment on East Asia for many years past have all fallen into the hands of the Imperial Forces. Such strategic points as Borneo, Celebes, and New Britain have also all been occupied by our forces, and, moreover, the main body of the Dutch East Indies fleet has been annihilated. The Imperial Army and Navy are now carrying out operations in a vast area, the largeness of whose scale is unparalleled in the history of mankind.

"These brilliant victories are solely due to the August Virtue of His Majesty the Emperor under which the officers and men of the Imperial Forces are bravely and energetically carrying on their campaign. To the spirits of those who have offered their lives for the defense of the Empire, with no concern for their homes and their own lives; to those officers and men who are sick or wounded in remote strange lands; to those who are strenuously fighting on land, sea, and in the air by defying extraordinary difficulties and dangers; and to those fellow countrymen who have sent their husbands, sons, and brothers to the front enabling the latter to exert themselves without worry and who are looking after their homes or helping them and are doing their best in the service behind the guns by enduring all difficulties—to all of them I wish to render my profound appreciation.

Co-Existence and Co-Prosperity

"As I have already stated on various occasions, the object of the War of Greater East Asia has its origin in the great ideal which inspired the founding of our Empire. It aims at securely establishing a new order of co-existence and co-prosperity on ethical principles, with our Empire as its nucleus, by making each country and people in Greater East Asia have its proper place. It is completely different in its essential character from the attitude of the United States and Britain toward East Asia.

"Singapore and other strategic points, which have hitherto been the bases of the United States and Britain for the invasion and domination of East Asia, are resurrecting with the boundless hope and glory as bases for the construction of the New Order and defense for the peoples of Greater East Asia. Hongkong, the Philippines, and the Malay Peninsula are already starting on the road for such new construction with steady strides.

"On this epochal occasion I wish to reiterate once more the real intentions of Japan to the peoples and countries concerned.

"The Imperial Forces are steadily carrying out offensive operations in the region of Burma also with its strategic points falling one after another into their hands. But the true intention of Japan in marching into Burma is to crush British military bases as well as to cut off the route for American and British aid to the Chiang Kai-shek regime: It is farthest from the thought of Japan to regard the Burmese people as her enemy. Therefore, if the Burmese people take full cognizance of the actual situation of Britain, operate with Japan by shaking off the shackles of the British rule of many years past, Japan will gladly extend them its positive cooperation for the establishment of Burma for the Burmese, the long-cherished aspiration of the Burma people.

Chance for India

"It is a golden opportunity for India having, as it does, several thousand years of history and splendid cultural tradition, to rid herself of the ruthless despotism of Britain and participate in the construction of the Greater East Asia Co-Prosperity Sphere. Japan expects that India will re-

News in Pictures

The Osaka Mainichi &
The Tokyo Nichi Nichi

Exclusive Features

8 SUNDAY, FEBRUARY 22, 1942 大正十一年四月十日第三種郵便物認可

Banzai! Rising Suns Fly Over 'City Of Lions'

Shouts of Banzai reverberate on the southern front as Nippon troops victoriously enter Singapore (now renamed Shonan city) after the unconditional surrender of the British forces on February 15. Reproduced here are the latest photographs rushed from the tropical front.

1. Imperial Army units entering Shonan city from the vicinity of burning Empire Dock (Taken by a staff cameraman).

2. General Count Hisaichi Terauchi, commander-in-chief of the Imperial Army forces in the southern region, riding on horseback at a certain place (Taken by a staff cameraman).

3. Crossing the Johore strait before enemy gunfire.

4. Banzai!—At the Empire Dock. Blakang Mati island is seen in the distance (Taken by a staff cameraman).

5. Nippon tanks battling their way at Bukit Timah on Singapore island prior to the fall of the city.

6. Lieut.-General Tomoyuki Yamashita, highest commander of the Imperial Army forces in Malaya, watching Singapore city just prior to its fall.

7. Indian soldiers following their surrender take a rest before the statue of Sir Stamford Raffles in front of the Victoria Memorial Hall.

8. A portion of the destroyed floating dock in Seletar naval base (now renamed Shonan naval base) can be seen above water (Approved by the Navy Office. No. 565.)

MORNING EDITION

Japan Times & Advertiser

Incorporating
The JAPAN CHRONICLE and The JAPAN MAIL

MORNING EDITION

No. 15,418 (THE 17th YEAR of SHOWA) TOKYO, SATURDAY, MARCH 7, 1942 第三種郵便物認可 昭和十五年十二月二十七日 Price 15 Sen

NINE WAR HEROES REVEALED

Meet Gallant Death Aboard Special Attack Flotilla at Hawaii

Nation Pays Respects for Men Who Sacrificed Their Lives for The Emperor

UNDERGO STRICT TRAINING

"Five vessels of the Japanese Special Attack Flotilla have not returned yet." These words were contained in the last paragraph of the famous Imperial Headquarters announcement on the Battle of Hawaii—the paragraph which threw, and is still throwing the whole Japanese nation into a crucible of indescribable excitement. The great task of annihilating the United States Pacific Fleet was thus accomplished.

Whenever the Battle of Hawaii is on the lips of the Japanese, their thoughts never fail to dwell on the special attacking corps which, it was announced, "has not returned yet." The entire Japanese nation has been praying for the safety of these brave men.

Now, it has been revealed that these daring death-defying heroes will never return. This announcement was contained in the Imperial Headquarters communique issued Friday which for the first time made public the exploits of this brave Attack Flotilla. Words fail to express the sentiments of Japanese toward these nine heroes who gave up their lives in such a death-defying manner for His Majesty the Emperor and the great cause which Japan has taken up arms to achieve. The entire nation prostrates itself in paying the deepest respects for their souls.

Created by Iwasa

The strategy for the attack by the special submarines was created and drafted by Commander Naoji Iwasa and several officers who actually participated. The men who also participated in this history-making event were specially selected from among those who had pledged to share the fate of their seniors at any moment. They, therefore, did not act under orders. These officers and sailors worked as one, in perfect unity. The plan was audacity itself and when first presented caused the higher Navy officers moments of doubt. Finally, however, Admiral Isoroku Yamamoto, Commander-in-Chief of the Combined Fleet, decided to approve, being convinced that this method promised sure success. Admiral Yamamoto must have been struck deeply by the daring officers' and men's enthusiastic determination when he granted his permission.

All officers and men then carefully made last minute preparation in order to see that no mishap occurred. Technicians and factory operatives who were interested in the enterprise indirectly also offered their wholehearted cooperation. All went on in absolute secrecy. Preparations and training as well as manufacture and experiments were conducted with unbending energy and unflinching efforts throughout day and night. Theirs really was a training of gods, not human beings, and this was responsible for the great success they reaped in the Battle of Hawaii. The men and officers never expected to return to their base, as they were all well aware of the great difficulty they would experience in passing through the narrow channel of Pearl Harbor in the face of intensive enemy attacks. Each and every member of the submarines' crew were determined to die but not until they had achieved their objective. They never made the slightest mention of their undertaking to parents, brothers, or close friends. During several months before the outbreak of the War of Greater East Asia they were steeped in training.

The time finally came for them to meet death. The five vessels manned by the nine brave crew dashed full-speed ahead toward the enemy base. After fully carrying out their mission, which included a forceful daylight attack, night raid in the moonlight, and other daring actions, all shared the fate of their vessels. While their comrade airmen were engaged in fierce bombing and discharging torpedoes, these special submarines approached enemy warships so closely that it has never been known in the annals of the world's history of warfare and after remaining submerged for long spells, came up and attacked objectives at night.

The instant sinking of the warship Arizona by them at night was so spectacular that it was clearly seen by the Japanese Forces located far off Hawaii then. After successfully discharging their torpedoes in Pearl Harbor, they sent out wireless messages telling their comrade forces that "the attack was a success" and then they all shared the fate of their submarines in complacency.

Unparalled in History

Such examples of bravery and loyalty in action have never been seen anywhere else in the world. The tradition of the Japanese Navy officers and men engaged in submarine warfare has been handed down from the late Lieutenant Tsutomu Sakuma, who during the initial period of submarine technique nearly 40 years ago, shared the fate of a submarine in the Inland Sea of Seto. The great results of the Battle of Hawaii were brought to a more brilliant relief by the exploits of the Special Attack Flotilla. A new history of Greater East Asia thus has been unfolded by these nine war gods.

The life careers of these nine heroes follows:

Commander Naoji Iwasa was born in 1915, at Maebashi City, Gumma Prefecture. This war god is survived by his father Naokichi, 75 years old, mother Teru, aged 68, and two brothers Takemotsu, 53, and Goro, 40. He was graduated from the Naval Academy in 1938. It was in October, 1941, that he was promoted to the rank of lieutenant after serving aboard the warships Hiei, Maya and Kashima. His rank was posthumously elevated two grades to commander, because of his illustrious services.

The late Commander Iwasa was a man with a keen sense of responsiility and was highly respected by his juniors and friends for his strict character which resembled an ancient warrior and patriot. He was commander of the Flotilla attacking Pearl Harbor. Before the outbreak of the war he was confident of overawing the enemy.

Lieutenant-Commander Shigemi Furuno was born in 1918 at Oga village, Fukuoka Prefecture. He is survived by his parents and five brothers. He entered the Naval Academy following graduation from the Tochiku Middle School in that prefecture. It was in 1939 when he graduated from the Academy. He served aboard the warships Yakumo and Ise and later was transferred to the submarine service. He was promoted to first-lieutenant in October last year shortly before the outbreak of the War and was posthumously elevated to Lieutenant-Commander on his meritorious services at Pearl Harbor. He was a judo expert and a typical navy officer. When he went home last September to look after his aged parents, his father scolded him for

(Continued on Page 2)

ANNOUNCEMENT
By Navy Ministry
3 P.M. MARCH 6, 1942

The outstanding achievements attained by the Special Attack Flotilla of special submarines in the sea battle in Hawaii on December 8, 1941, have been honored in a citation by the Commander-in-Chief of the Combined Fleet, which the Navy Minister has submitted to His Imperial Majesty the Emperor.

The citation dated February 11, 1942, reads:

"At the start of the war on December 8, 1941, the Special Attack Flotilla, in concert with the Naval Air Force, struck the main body of the American Pacific Fleet in the Hawaiian naval base as the spearhead of the Japanese Naval Force and attained splendid achievements. The outstanding military service of the Special Attack Flotilla is hereby specially mentioned, having enhanced as it did both at home and abroad the reputation of the loyalty of the members of the Imperial Navy, as well as the morale of the entire service."

ADMIRAL ISOROKU YAMAMOTO
Commander-in-Chief of the Combined Fleet

The nine members of the gallant death-defying Special Attack Flotilla which achieved such brilliant results in the Battle of Hawaii: (1) Commander Naoji Iwasa, (2) Lieutenant-Commander Shigemi Furuno, (3) Lieutenant-Commander Masaji Yokoyama, (4) Lieutenant Akira Hiro-o, (5) Special Second Sub-Lieutenant Naokichi Sasaki, (6) Special Second Sub-Lieutenant Shigenori Yokoyama, (7) Chief Warrant Officer Kiyoshi Inagaki, (8) Chief Warrant Officer Sadamu Uyeda, (9) Chief Warrant Officer Yoshio Katayama.

Superb Technique and Incomparable Loyal Spirit of Imperial Navy Hailed

SANK ARIZONA INSTANTLY

The heroic action of the Special Attack Flotilla which surprised the entire world at the outset of the War of Greater East Asia in the Battle of Hawaii was revealed in a detailed announcement made by the Imperial Headquarters at 3 p.m. Friday. The announcement which describes the gallantry of the nine naval heroes follows:

"Regarding the unparalleled heroic raid on Pearl Harbor by the Special Attack Flotilla, a public announcement has previously been made. The plan of the attack that astounded the peoples of the whole world owed its conception to First-Lieutenant Iwasa and several other officers. Several months ago, these officers secretly applied to the Commander-in-Chief of the Combined Fleet through their respective officers in command with their plan to be put into execution in case an emergency should arise, expressing their desire to perform thereby their duty of loyally serving the Sovereign and the State.

"The Commander-in-Chief, finding after careful study and consideration, that there was a definite possibility of success of the plan and that a way could be found for taking in the men and vessels after the battle, acceded to the enthusiastic desires of the applicants.

Very Best in Navy

"The non-commissioned officers, who participated in this heroic exploit, are also the very best of the excellent men in the Imperial Navy. They are the men in whom the participating officers had always full trust and who had wished to be with their commanding officers in life and death. It was unnecessary, therefore, to recruit applicants especially for carrying out the plan. In an utterly calm and unconcerned manner, applications were presented by their respective commanding officers stating that they desired to have these non-commissioned officers to participate as members of the Special Attack Flotilla and the Commander-in-Chief ordered their participation as they had desired.

"Since then, with strict secrecy maintained even within the service, tacticians and engineers and even workers in complete unity of purpose, devoted themselves day and night without rest or sleep to the construction and experiment or preparatory training with the result that the work was successfully completed in a brief period of time amidst the tense situation preceding the opening of the present war. As it has been confirmed from the above, we may well be proud of the superb technique of the Imperial Navy as well as the incomparable loyal spirit of the officers and men who participated in the attack and the zeal of those who were concerned with the technical and constructive aspects of the project.

"In the execution of the plan, all possible measures were, of course, adopted to assure the taking in of the vessels and crews. However, it is not hard to imagine the difficulty for the vessels to return by weaving between the debris of the sunken enemy ships lying on the sea bottom and passing through narrow channels in withdrawing from the severe counter-attacks, for the enemy's vigilance would be even more strict after they have attacked his main force. It is, therefore, quite natural that as officers and non-commissioned officers of the Imperial Navy they should have made necessary preparations for self-destruction in case of an emergency.

Enters Pearl Harbor

"With absolute faith in the divine help under the august virtue of His Majesty the Emperor, the Special Attack Flotilla set out on a certain day of a certain month on its glorious expedition. It sped its way toward Pearl Harbor, and passing through the enemy's vigilant guardlines and complicated channels, all vessels of the Flotilla penetrated into the harbor, each taking its pre-assigned position. They attacked the enemy in broad daylight or made a surprise attack by night, carrying out a thrilling exploit without precedent in history; and after performing their duties the crews shared the fate with their vessels.

"In particular, the instantaneous sinking of a battleship of the Arizona class as the result of a night assault by the Special Attack Flotilla was clearly observed by the Japanese Naval Force far away from the Hawaiian naval base. At 4:31 p.m., December 8 (9:01 p.m. of December 7, Hawaii time), just two minutes after the moon-rise, a tremendous explosion occurred in Pearl Harbor, sending fiery columns high up into the air, together with the scattering red hot iron splinters. In a few minutes, the fiery columns disappeared, whereupon the enemy anti-aircraft batteries went into action, apparently mistaking the raid of the Special Attack Flotilla for that of Japanese Aerial Force. At 6:11 p.m., the same day (10:41 p.m., Hawaii time), a wireless message from one of the Special Attack Flotilla was received, announcing its successful mission.

"The vessels of Special Attack Flotilla are regarded as having either blown themselves up or having been sunk by the enemy after 7:14 p.m., the same day, when the wireless communication from the Flotilla ceased.

"During its daylight attack, there is not the slightest doubt that the Special Attack Flotilla attained supreme results amidst the confusion reigning in Pearl Harbor where the enemy failed to identify the Special Attack Flotilla, though the enemy fleet may have barely witnessed its movements. At present, however, it is difficult to distinguish the results attained by the Special Attack Flotilla from those of the air force.

No Vessel Returned

"The Flotilla was instructed to rejoin the fleet, following the conclusion of its attack, but no vessel of the Flotilla returned. We cannot but conclude that the Flotilla attacked the enemy warships at an unprecedentedly close range, against the rain of bombs and air-torpedoes dropped by the Japanese Air Force, or remained submerged during the daytime and came up to the surface with the moonrise to concentrate attacks on those enemy capital ships which they confirmed had suffered comparatively little damage from the daytime attacks. All the crews meanwhile were entirely devoted to attaining the maximum results of attack with the idea of rejoining the fleet being entirely left out of their consideration, as they were above the question of life or death.

"The offensive spirit, inspired by an unswerving devotion to His Majesty the Emperor is true to the best tradition of the Imperial Navy, having no parallel in the world: it adorns the opening page of the annals of the current War."

FOUR-DAY AIR ATTACKS BY NAVY NET 73 PLANES WITH NO LOSSES

In their large-scale bombing raids on Broome, a key point on the northwestern coast of Australia, Wyndam, another important base on the north coast of Australia, and other enemy airfields lying east of eastern Java, which were carried out for four days in succession from March 1 to March 4, Japanese Naval Air Units accounted for no fewer than 73 enemy planes, with no loss of plane on their own side. When the raid was made on Broome airfield on March 3, six 4-motored PB2Y and thirteen 4-motored PBY hydroplanes, three 4-motored bombers, five 2-motored bombers and one transport plane were just about to take off for Java to reinforce the enemy air force there. The Japanese raiders swooped down upon them and destroyed all of these 28 planes at one fell sweep.

In their raid on Wyndam airfield, Japanese Naval Air Units machine-gunned one enemy transport plane and one hangar and set them on fire.

On March 4, 18 enemy planes were either shot down or destroyed on the ground at Bandoeng, and on March 1 and 2, many enemy airfields in the Sunda islands were raided and a large number of enemy planes were destroyed, besides causing fires in many places.

BROOME AND WYNDAM DESCRIBED

Broome is a town on Boebuck Bay on the northwestern coast of Australia. It is well-known as a base of pearl-fishing ships. A large number of Japanese engaged in pearl-fishing live there, their number at one time reaching 1,000. The town reminds one strongly of a Japanese town. It has a population of about 3,000, the majority of whom are aliens. The chief exports from this port are pearl, wool and skin and hide. It has a civilian airfield.

Wyndam is a trading port on the north coast of Australia which is known for the exportation of cattle and frozen meat. It has big canneries, which are capable of producing some 200 tons of tinned beef a day. There is a regular shipping service between this port and Port Darwin and other Australian ports.

GERMAN FORCES REPULSE SOVIET PUSH IN DONETZ

Nazi Troops Inflict Heavy Losses on Stalin's Men in Fierce Battle

D.N.B.

BERLIN, March 5.—The Soviet attacks in the Donetz sector were again repulsed, the High Command stated on Thursday night. On Wednesday in this sector numerous Soviet attacks were driven back with heavy losses inflicted on the attacker.

On Thursday fresh attacks were launched in which about one Russian division participated, supported by strong artillery fire. Despite the employment of tanks they did not succeed, however. A village which they temporarily occupied was retaken in a determined German counter-attack, supported by dive bombers. In a sector of the same front German Alpine troops penetrated the enemy lines as well as enemy troop concentrations, dispersing two Soviet regiments and capturing or destroying six guns as well as other arms and war materials. The enemy left some 500 dead on the battlefield.

Soviet Claims Refuted

Competent military circles state emphatically that the Soviet reports about the alleged encirclement of German troop formations on the Eastern front are without foundation whatsoever. Neither the 16th German Army nor any German division, as was claimed by the Soviet Army Command recently, have been encircled on the Eastern front, it is stressed.

Minami Leaves Keijo

General Jiro Minami, Governor-General of Chosen, at 11:30 a.m. Friday left Keijo for Tokyo, where he will consult with the Government on affairs under his jurisdiction, reports Domei.

Foreign News Spotlight
Exclusive Flashes

BRITISH GIRLS TO REGISTER FOR LABOR SERVICES

The shortage of manpower has compelled Great Britain to call up its young women for services in its vital war industries. A British Government spokesman announced on Thursday that all girls between the ages of 15 and 17 years must register immediately with the authorities for eventual labor service. Adding that girls of 18 will also be required to register, he said that they will be placed in industries immediately. It is expected that 35,000 young women of this age class will be mobilized under this plan.

AUSTRALIA PREPARES FOR JAPANESE ATTACK

Women and children were being evacuated from possible danger zones, and steps were being taken to release all available manpower for national services, as Australia prepared for a possible landing attempt by the Japanese, according to reports from Melbourne.

The Government announced on Thursday that kindergartens in northern and western Australia will be closed in order to encourage women and children to evacuate from those areas which have been specified as possible danger zones. Simultaneously, it was revealed that all shop window displays will hereafter be prohibited in these areas, as they constitute a prime danger in the event of an air raid. Many merchants have already removed the plate glass in their show windows, the report said.

MADAGASCAR PREPARED TO MEET AGGRESSION

One Desire Is to Remain Solely French, Declares Governor General

D.N.B.

VICHY, March 5.—"Madagascar wants only one thing, namely to remain French," declared Governor General Anne of Madagascar in a broadcast from Tananarivo after returning from a tour of inspection through the South of Madagascar. He declared that he had learned from foreign Press reports about speculations, made with regard to the future role Madagascar would play in the world conflict. On his inspection trip he learned, however, that everyone on the island was quietly doing his work and endeavoring to overcome the difficulties, resulting from insufficient communications, and that he therefore wished to emphasize once more that Madagascar had only the one aim—to remain French.

For the attainment of this aim no assistance was required from any other nation, not even temporary assistance, he stressed. In conclusion, the Governor declared that animated by this will to remain French and relying on her own strength for every defense, Madagascar was prepared to meet aggression, no matter from which side it might come.

Premier Invites Sato

Premier General Hideki Tojo on Friday gave a luncheon at his official residence in honor of Naotake Sato, newly appointed Japanese Ambassador to Moscow.

ENEMY SOLDIERS IN BANDOENG, BATAVIA COMPLETELY ISOLATED

Domei

LISBON, March 5.—An overwhelmingly strong Japanese Force today succeeded in landing at an unspecified point on the west coast of Java Island, and Batavia and Bandoeng, former and wartime capitals of the Netherlands East Indies, respectively, now have been completely isolated and cordoned off, a British Broadcasting Corporation radio broadcast heard here discloses. The fall of key traffic point southwest of Rembeng into Japanese hands completely has paralyzed communications between Surabaya, Batavia and Bandoeng, the radio said. The radio also revealed that Japanese aircraft working in cooperation with Japanese troops, today carried out four successive raids on Bandoeng with good results.

JAPANESE OCCUPY MORE PLACES IN SUMATRA

Domei

A JAPANESE BASE, March 6.—As Japanese Forces continued to enlarge their area of occupation in southern Sumatra with little or no resistance from the enemy, field dispatches indicate that from 60 to 70 per cent of the rich oil fields of southern Sumatra have passed undamaged into Japanese hands. These oil fields include wells in the Palembang area, Lahat, which was captured on February 22, and Benkulen on the Indian Ocean coast which was occupied on February 24. Five hundred more enemy troops have been pursued into Suralangun in the foothill region of Barisa mountains and have been wiped out by Japanese mopping-up contingents on February 28, according to late field dispatches.

ARMY AIR UNITS DESTROY 13 PLANES

Domei

JAPANESE BASE ON SHONAN ISLAND, March 5.—Keeping up aerial activities in cooperation with Japanese Army ground forces, the Japanese Army Air Force yesterday afternoon either shot down or destroyed 13 enemy planes on Java Island,

(Continued on Page 2)

EVENING EDITION

Japan Times & Advertiser

Incorporating
The JAPAN CHRONICLE and The JAPAN MAIL

EVENING EDITION

No. 15,418 (THE 17th YEAR of SHOWA) TOKYO, SATURDAY, MARCH 7, 1942 Price 8 Sen

NAVAL LEADERS EXTOL ACTION OF SPECIAL ATTACK FLOTILLA; HISTORIC BACKGROUND IS TOLD

Heroism in Former Wars, Sakuma Incident Are Reviewed

YAMAMOTO IS MOVED

Extolling to the skies the glorious achievements of the nine gallant members of the death-defying Special Attack Flotilla, great admirals of the Imperial Navy, including Admiral Isoroku Yamamoto, Commander-in-Chief of the Combined Fleet, told about the historical background which underlies the history-making special undersea craft attack at Pearl Harbor, one reviewing the activities of the torpedo-boat squadrons during the Sino-Japanese War, another looking back upon the achievements of blockading squadrons at Port Arthur in the Russo-Japanese War and a third, recollecting the heroic death of the late Commander Tsutomu Sakuma, who shared the fate of a submarine 40 years ago in the Inland Sea of Seto.

Admiral Yamamoto, who must be somewhere on the Pacific at present, recently sent a letter to a certain Admiral at home in which he says.

"The time is not yet ripe enough for me to dwell upon the particulars of the activities of the Special Attack Flotilla that penetrated into Pearl Harbor. It is clear, however, that those submarines have sunk at least one enemy warship.

Moved to Tears

"In the light of the fact that the young participants in the attack including some, who graduated from the Naval Academy only a year ago have scored such brilliant results, I have been shown that the young should never be thought of lightly merely because they are young. I confess that I was moved to tears at the gallant acts of these officers and men."

The letter according to the Asahi, shows how Admiral Yamamoto, who has granted a citation to these warriors in the capacity of the Commander-in-Chief of the Combined Fleet, was moved at their gallant acts also as a man.

Alluding to the death-defying attack of the Second and the Third Torpedo-Boat Squadrons, which succeeded in sinking three leading warships of the Chinese navy at the time of the Sino-Japanese War, Baron Admiral Kantaro Suzuki, retired, ex-Supreme War Counselor, attributed the achievements of the Special Attack Flotilla to the traditional fighting spirit of the Imperial Navy.

"At daybreak on February 5, 1895, 30 torpedo-boats of the Second and the Third Squadrons, approached through the mouth of the Wei-hai-wei Port to the main ships of the Chinese navy consisting of the Teien, Raien and Ien through the mouth of the Wei-hai-wei Port, where those ships had taken shelter after being pursued by the Japanese Fleet.

"Torpedoes in those days had only short shooting range and consequently, the torpedo-boats had to approach close to the targets before they could release the torpedoes. The members of the crew could, of course, entertain no hope whatever of returning alive.

Sneaked Into Port

"The squadrons rushed to the enemy warships undergoing a terrific bombardment from the Chinese scout-vessels. They succeeded in immediately sinking the Teien and one transport, but our forces also suffered great loss, one torpedo-boat being sunk by the enemy fire and another running on a rock. Before dawn the following day, the First Squadron sneaked into the port and sunk the remaining two warships.

"At that time, I was a Lieutenant and the chief of the Third Squadron. The activities of the sea battle in Wei-hai-wei Port was then called a "death-defying strategy." This was the time when the traditional death-defying spirit of the Imperial Navy was clearly manifested for the first time.

"This spirit was enhanced for the second time during the Russo-Japanese War when our torpedo-boats attacked and sunk the Russian warship, Sebastopoli.

"At midnight of a certain snowy day in December 1904, one of the torpedo-boat squadrons approached within 40 meters of the enemy ship and sunk it immediately.

"In the historic sea battle in the Japan Sea on May 27, 1905, many of our destroyers drew so near to the enemy fleet that they had to cross the line of the enemy fleet to the opposite side and fire after taking careful aim from a proper distance.

"In my opinion, the achievements of the Special Attack Flotilla at Pearl Harbor is to be considered the florescence of the traditional spirit of our Navy, which has long been cultivated

(Continued on Page 2)

His Majesty Cables Condolence Message To Monarch at Rome

His Majesty the Emperor graciously dispatched on Friday, a telegram of condolence to King Vittorio Emanuele III of Italy upon the recent death of Duke of Aosta, former Viceroy of Ethiopia, and late Commander of the Italian Forces in East Africa.

HIRAIDE EXPRESSES PRAISE IN AIR TALK

Superhuman Feat Lauded to Skies by Spokesman of Navy in Statement

INSPIRATION IS RENEWED

Traditional Spirit of Sea Arm Remains Unchanged — Mothers Remembered

Expressing his highest praise for the superhuman feat of the nine guardian Gods of the country, who penetrated deep into Pearl Harbor and wrought havoc with the enemy fleet, thus fulfilling their weighty mission successfully at the supreme sacrifice, Captain Hideo Hiraide, Navy spokesman of the Imperial Headquarters, issued a long statement through the JOAK microphone on Friday night.

The gist of his speech follows:

"One hundred million people of Japan cannot help but renew their inspiration in recollecting the great services rendered by the nine national heroes, particularly at a time when their third anniversary of death is close at hand.

"I should like to picture, with the aid of some of the information received from the American side, their activities within the waters of the formidable enemy naval base.

Entered Pearl Harbor

"The narrow entrance to Pearl Harbor is virtually impossible to pass as the strip of water is screened in order to prevent submarines from entering the port, while the neighboring water is infested with innumerable mines, not to mention the most up-to-date facilities in detecting the approach of enemy craft and the strong batteries on both sides of the entrance. The nine men, nevertheless, successfully surmounted these difficulties and entered into the harbor.

"During the day, members of the Special Attack Flotilla spent the monotonous hours playing with the wooden toys which they took along, or probably, writing the diary which they knew very well would be their last.

"Thus, waiting deep in the waters of Pearl Harbor until the dead of night, they started carefully toward the interior, dodging many obstructions in the narrow path inside the port, and commenced their operations as the aerial bombardment started.

"Through their periscopes, they probably noticed the fierce attack on the enemy warships by the Imperial Navy Air Units while some, their periscopes spied by the enemy, were obliged to submerge before ascertaining the result of their torpedo attack as the enemy destroyer moved toward their direction for a counter-attack.

"By this time, the aerial attacks of the Imperial Forces were greatly intensified, actually presenting a Dante's Inferno in front of their very eyes as the thunderous explosions, violent flashes and scraps of flying steel mingled with the screaming enemy figures grasping the air as they fell on the decks of the sinking vessels continued in rapid succession.

Down to Davey Jone's Locket

"With remarkable coolness, unthinkable to be that of a man facing a certain death, the captain of one special submarine, at the terrific report of an explosion, brought his craft on the water surface and ascertained the tragic end of the enemy warships on which he fired with deadly accuracy. This was seen by the Japanese Forces standing by in a distance outside the harbor, who reported that simultaneously with the sound of a terrific explosion, a column of water belched skyward, setting the enemy ship ablaze and sending it to the bottom a few seconds later.

"Early on the morning of December 8, or at 10:41 p.m. Hawaiian Time, the Special Attack Flotilla sent out a wireless message to the effect that the attack was a success and then the members, nine in all, shared the fate of their submarines in complacency.

Throne Hears Reports

"The highest honor justly due them has been conferred upon the nine members of the Special Attack Flotilla when their daring feat and sublime spirit of fealty and patriotism probably unparalleled in history was graciously heard by His Majesty the

(Continued on Page 2)

Blow That Will Live Forever in Navy Annals

One by one, the prides of the U.S. Navy crumple amid smoke and flame under the furious baptism of bombs and torpedoes unleashed by our intrepid air and submarine units. The above is a vivid reproduction of the memorable daylight attack on the American fleet in Pearl Harbor launched by our Navy Forces on December 8, 1941, as depicted by Takeshi Matsuzoe. (Censored by Navy Ministry. No. 571)

DISSENSION GROWING IN CHUNGKING CIRCLE

Leaders Seen at Odds Over Foreign Policy as Allied Setbacks Continue

Domei

HONGKONG, March 6.—Reflecting the confusion caused by successive Allied setbacks in the Pacific, High Chungking leaders are seriously split over questions of foreign policy, according to reliable reports received here today.

Advocates of "wait and see," including General Ho Ying-chin, War Minister, Chan Ki and Tai Tien-chu, are bitterly opposed to the pro-Anglo-American clique led by Dr. H. H. Kung which is clamoring for closer cooperation with Britain and the United States.

Further dissension is apparent between the pro-Soviet faction headed by General Feng Yue-hsiang, Sun Fo and other Kuomintang diehards, such as Chen Kuo-fu, it was said.

The dispatches further revealed that Chungking leaders are extremely pessimistic regarding successful Allied resistance in India, despite professing agreement with Generalissimo Chiang Kai-shek's policy of aiding Britain's attempt to hold India.

N. China Enemy Wiped Out

Domei

NANKING, March 6.—The last remaining Chungking strongholds in North China virtually have been destroyed as a result of the mopping-up campaign begun early in February, it was revealed by the Japanese Army Headquarters here today in reviewing the week of February 27 and March 5.

Twenty thousand Chungking troops belonging to the 51st Army, the newly organized 4th Division and the 11th Division have been cut to pieces in strongly manned permanent fortifications in the mountains of Shantung Province.

The headquarters also announced that 35,000 troops under General Sun Liang-cheng, which lately have been showing signs of making trouble, were routed March 2 in western Shantung Province.

To Start New Tanna Bore

The Railways Ministry Thursday announced that boring will begin from March 20 on the new Tanna tunnel near Atami hot springs, which is one of the stiffest obstacles to the completion of the projected Tokyo-Shimonoseki high-speed railway line. The new trunk line will be the only wide-gauge railway in Japan, and the bullet train will make the run of more than 1,000 kilometers in less than nine hours.

Consulate at Tayeh

Domei

NANKING, March 5.—A branch of the Japanese Consulate-General at Hankow was established on Wednesday at Tayeh, in eastern Hunan Province, in view of the increasing number of Japanese working in iron mines in the Tayeh district, it was announced here today.

Bushido Spirit Fully Shown By 9 Gallant Navy Warriors

Calm Fortitude in Face of Certain Death Seen In Letters, Poems and Spoken Words Of Intrepid Heroes

The nine war heroes, who astounded the entire world with their heroic action in the Special Attack Flotilla at the outset of the War of Greater East Asia during the Battle of Hawaii, have left behind them letters, poems, and spoken words in the memory of their friends, which show that to the last they were filled with the indomitable spirit of self-sacrifice, which makes the impossible possible, and the unattainable attainable.

Through the medium of their letters and the reports of their friends, they indicate their Bushido spirit during their last moments, just before they launched out on their death-defying expedition from which they were never to return.

Commander Naoji Iwasa, before departing with the Special Attack Flotilla for the Battle of Hawaii, wrote a letter to his former commander, a Captain of the Imperial Navy, in which is the following clause: "In the event of my failing to carry out my duty, you will know that the fault will lie entirely with me."

There is no better illustration of the Sakuma spirit, that courageous spirit of responsibility, which has been handed down through the ages in the Imperial Navy ever since the submarine commanded by Commander Tsutomu Sakuma met with its disastrous fate in the Inland Sea of Japan.

Part of the letter follows:

Happy to Get Assignment

"I am overwhelmed at the wonderful opportunity thus offered to me, and I am determined to sacrifice my life for the achievement of the noble duty entrusted to me.

"I am very grateful to you for your kind and diligent efforts to train a foolish and clumsy man like me into a first-rate warrior, and I take this opportunity to apologize most sincerely for my failure to come up to your expectations.

"Our country is threatened by a grave peril and for the preservation of the Yamato race, it has become necessary to take this final step and launch out into the offensive.

"The honor of dealing the first blow has been granted to your humble servant, this insignificant officer, and I know no greater glory. Here is the opportunity of putting into actual practice the teachings you have so graciously wasted on me.

"In the event of my failing to carry out my duty, you will know that the fault will lie entirely with me.

"Thank you very much for all your help and teaching while I was still alive. Praying for the perpetuance of your military fortunes, I remain, Naoji Iwasa."

Lieutenant-Commander Masaji Yokoyama left the following note:

"The opportunity for sacrificing my life in the service of my country at the time of her greatest need has at last descended upon me and I know no greater glory. Long Live His Majesty the Emperor! I respectfully shout thus three times.

His Farewell Message

"I take this opportunity to tender my heartfelt thanks to my parents and relatives, to the teachers of my alma mater, to the instructors of the Imperial Navy, to my superior officers, and to those who have been before me for all the trouble they have taken over me.

"I tender my heartiest sympathies to the bereaved family of Warrant Officer Sadamu Uyeda, who is with me.

"Finally, I am deeply grieved that I have been unable to repay even the minutest fraction of the debt of gratitude that I owe to His Imperial Majesty, and I am heartily ashamed of my unworthy self. First-Lieutenant Masaji Yokoyama."

Real Poet

Besides the above, Lieutenant-Commander Yokoyama's notebook contains the following poem:

Peace reigns in my heart.
Of victory I am assured.
We meet the enemy fleet
At the entrance to Pearl Harbor.
What a fierce battle below.
And what a bright moon above!

Lieutenant-Commander Shigemi Furuno sent his father a "Waka," a Japanese poem of 31 syllables:

The young cherry blossoms
Drop from the tree
At the height of their glory
Without regret.
Thus shall I overcome
The submarine-nets
And mine-laden seas.
And scatter my bones like a broken pearl
In Pearl Harbor.
The morning sky is bright
With the joy of our meeting
At the Yasukuni Shrine.

Lieutenant Akira Hiro-o has left nothing except some official records, but according to his comrades, he was always talking of the anticipated victory of the Japanese Forces, and before his departure with the Special Attack Flotilla he was full of spirit.

"The ice-cream sold at Honolulu is specially fine," the Lieutenant said. "I will bring you some when I come back." His comrades burst out laughing at this.

Looked Forward for Action

The Lieutenant continued, "I shall take my revolver and my sword. When we land at Honolulu, I should like to engage in some hot action with these. Of course, I prefer to have two revolvers, but I shall have to be content with only one."

"Are you going in your working outfit?" asked one of his comrades.

"No," said the Lieutenant. "I shall go fully armed, but since it is very hot, I shall be lightly dressed."

(Continued on Page 2)

U-BOATS CONTINUING DRIVES ON ATLANTIC

12 More Ships Added to Mounting Toll—Moscow Raided First Time This Year

Domei

BERLIN, March 6.—German submarines operating off North and Central America in the Atlantic have sunk an additional 12 enemy ships, totaling 82,500 tons, including seven large tankers and one large United States destroyer, and damaged with torpedo hits two other vessels, the High Command announced today.

German aircraft continued attacks against Sebastopol in the Crimea, and Moscow, blasting buildings of military importance in the center of the Soviet capital, the communique said.

Other German aircraft formations were said to have sunk a 3,000-ton freighter in waters around England and to have blasted barracks in southern England and supply plants at Portland.

In the central and northern sectors of the eastern front, Germans forces, with the cooperation of the Luftwaffe, were reported to have repulsed all Soviet attacks despite the setting in of the cold spell and heavy frosts.

Referring to North Africa, the communique said German aircraft yesterday raided British air bases and railway facilities in the Fuka and El Daba areas in Egypt.

German aircraft blasted with heavy caliber bombs British airfields and submarine bases on the island of Malta yesterday, the communique stated.

German naval long-range batteries stationed along the French coast, today shelled a British convoy, which was attempting to steam through the English Channel, forcing it to return to Dover.

First Moscow Raid

Domei

LISBON, March 6.—According to a London dispatch received here today, a Moscow radio broadcast intercepted in the British capital has announced that German aircraft for the first time this year, last night bombed Moscow, raining bombs on a number of key-points within the Soviet capital and causing great damage.

A number of casualties have been sustained in the raid, the Moscow radio declared.

Limp Into Gibraltar

Domei

ALGECIRAS, Southern Spain, March 6.—A British destroyer and a submarine, both badly damaged, have arrived at Gibraltar, it was learned here today.

Both vessels were said to have landed an undisclosed number of dead and wounded.

It is believed here that the two warships were attacked somewhere in the Mediterranean by Axis planes and managed to limp into Gibraltar for repairs.

Italians Repulse Attack

Domei

ROME, March 6.—On the southern Libyan front, Italian Sahara units yes-

(Continued on Page 2)

JAPANESE FORCES CLOSING IN ON NAVAL BASE AT SURABAYA; DJAMBI AND RIMAU OCCUPIED

Capture of Batavia Is Hailed by Spain; Naval Power Seen

Domei

MADRID, March 6.—News of the Japanese conquest of Batavia has aroused both admiration and joy in Spain. Meantime, all journals played up the fact that the lightning speed with which the Japanese have struck at enemy objectives have clearly proved the superiority of the Japanese Navy over that of the united nations.

OFFICIAL AID ASKED IN BOOSTING HEALTH

Welfare Minister Outlines Policy For Physical Improvement of Nation

GOVERNORS HEAR HONJO

Kishi Stresses Need of Intensifying General Mobilization Structure

Welfare Minister Surgeon Lieutenant-General Dr. Chikahiko Koizumi, and Commerce and Industry Minister Nobusuke Kishi addressed the fourth-day session of the Governors' Conference on Friday.

The session was called to order at 9 a.m. and Welfare Minister Koizumi was the first speaker.

Pointing out the urgent policy of improving the health of the people, the Welfare Minister particularly drew the attention of the governors to the improvement of the health of children, who are to develop as future soldiers and industrial workers. The problem of extending medical service to all remote parts of the country was also discussed by the Minister.

General Shigeru Honjo, President of the Military Relief Board, next told the governors the increasing necessity of looking after the welfare of wounded soldiers and the families of war heroes.

He requested the prefectural heads to give utmost attention to adopt proper measures for their relief and welfare, as the living conditions of wounded soldiers and bereaved families would greatly influence the general life of the people.

In the afternoon session, Commerce and Industry Minister Kishi in his address stressed the necessity of intensifying the general mobilization structure.

"We must be prepared for a long war, and must be determined to execute the war to establish the Greater East Asia," he said. "While we are making military operations, it is our duty to speedily carry out constructive works. For effecting this economic construction, the national wartime structure has to be intensified.

"First, the Government organized various control associations and there are now 12 associations.

"Second, there will be required more labor and materials for producing war materials and increasing production for the economic control has to be further strengthened. The national productive capacity has to be expanded by adjusting the supply of labor and materials, and reorganizing rationally the industrial structure of the country.

"As regards trade, it is natural that the former trade policy has to be changed, as the nation's foreign trade now consists of dealing with the countries within the East Asia Co-Prosperity Sphere since the outbreak of the present war. Thus, by trade means the smooth exchange of goods with Manchoukuo, China, French Indo-China and Thailand.

"Concerning the southern occupied territories, the Government as a temporary measure is undertaking the purchase of their products and the sale of our goods.

"Lastly, the low-price policy will be further maintained, although it is not meant to peg prices at the present figures. Prices will be adjusted according to the amount and cost of production.

"In this respect, I wish to request your cooperation in executing the Government policy so that all measures will be smoothly carried out for the attainment of our final object."

The Governors' Conference will end today, and in the last day's session, the attending governors will be instructed on affairs under the jurisdiction of the Communications, Overseas and Agriculture and Forestry Ministries.

Bahrein Ruler Chosen

Domei

BERLIN, March 5.—Sheik Salman al Khalifa, eldest son of the late Sheik of Bahrein, island in the Persian Gulf, has been elected ruler of Bahrein, the German News Agency reported from Amsterdam today.

Full Offensive Flung in Java Sector by Imperial Troops

OIL CENTERS SEIZED

Domei

LISBON, March 6.—Japanese Forces are pressing hard on Surabaya, and already have reached a point close to the great Dutch naval base, it was reported here from Bandoeng today.

The Japanese are throwing the full weight of their land, sea and air forces against all fronts in Java and Netherlands military authorities gloomily have admitted that the war situation in the Dutch East Indies has reached a critical point, Bandoeng dispatches declared.

Djambi Occupied

Domei

WITH JAPANESE FORCES IN SUMATRA, March 6.—Japanese Forces occupied Djambi, 200 kilometers northwest of Palembang Wednesday after crushing stiff enemy resistance.

Djambi and Rimau, which also was occupied by Japanese Forces are important oil centers.

Moving to West Indies

Domei

LISBON, March 6.—With Batavia in Japanese hands and Bandoeng, wartime Dutch colonial capital, in imminent danger of falling before a direct Japanese offensive, Netherlands East Indies authorities are planning removal of all Government offices and leading commercial concerns to the Dutch West Indies where they will be under American protection, a dispatch from Bandoeng revealed today.

Colony Lost Forever

Domei

SHANGHAI, March 6.—Commenting on the Japanese attack against the Netherlands East Indies, Lieutenent-Colonel Kunio Akiyama, Japanese Army Spokesman, at his press conference this afternoon, declared that the Dutch Asiatic colony has been torn away from Holland forever.

Lieutenant-Colonel Akiyama emphasized, "We don't think for a moment that the islands will be restored to the Netherlands."

The Spokesman said Holland is powerless and it is "inconceivable that she will be able to regain the Indies single-handed."

Lieutenant-Colonel Akiyama then pointed out that in view of the strategic importace of Java, "we may now say the Japanese have crossed the fence of the Indian Ocean."

"We now can go anywhere," he said, adding, "Australia virtually is defenseless—naked, we may say and with a long coastline, she is extremely vulnerable."

Lieutenant-Colonel Akiyama then cited that both the Netherlands East Indies and Australia sent aid for the defense of Malaya from their scanty air forces which now is one of the causes for their inability to defend themselves.

Pointing out the irony of the Australian aid the spokesman asked, "what percentage of Australian assistance is Britain returning to Australia?'

Lieutenant-Colonel Akiyama warned that Australia may be attacked by the Japanese "if Australia does not relinquish its belligerency," adding significantly that we can launch operations without reinforcements."

U.S. SEA SERVICE HALTED

McCormack Line Discontinues South American Calls

Transocean

LISBON, March 5.—The South American shipping service will be discontinued by the McCormack Line, it was announced in New York City.

The ships of the so-called "Good Neighbor Fleet" will remain temporarily in New York at the disposal of the United States Government. This sudden announcement will have a serious effect upon the passenger traffic between the American continents, shipping circles fear.

NAVY CHIEFS EXTOL INTREPID WAR DEED

(Continued From Page 1)

and trained through frequent emergencies."

Admiral Nobumasa Suetsugu, retired, ex-Commander-in-Chief of the Combined Fleet stated to the following effect:

Truly War Gods

"Those officers and men, who participated in the battle at Pearl Harbor on board five special undersea-craft are indeed worthy of the name of War Gods.

"It is said that those heroes had before their start uttered not a word of boast as to their prospective exploits nor were they excited at the time of their ephocal mission. They went on their expedition as if on an excursion, sheerly disregarding life or death.

"The Commander-in-Chief on the other hand, is said to have allowed them to try the epoch-making enterprise only after deliberate consideration and investigation testified the possibility of their returning back safely after the battle.

"The participants thought nothing of their lives and the Commander thought of every possible means of saving their lives. What a beautiful and heart-rending manifestation of the more than cordial relationship between the seniors and juniors of the Japanese Navy!

"I hear that those nine warriors had prepared for self-destruction presupposing the impossibility of safe return. This kind of heroic resolution must have appealed to the hearts of Gods and enabled them to achieve so magnificent a result."

Reason Japanese Navy Strong

Describing the unique spiritual force and superior "spirit of attack," which is characteristic of the Japanese Navy and which made possible the gigantic successes achieved on December 8, 1941 in the attack of Pearl Harbor, Admiral Sankichi Takahashi, retired, and Admiral Ryokitsu Arima, retired, in a press interview on Friday said the spirit of loyalty and patriotism multiplied by the spirit of transcending life and death, is the driving force of the officers and men of the Japanese Navy, reports Domei.

"Ever since Captain Sakuma's submarine disaster off the coast of Shinminato, Yamaguchi Prefecture in 1910, there has developed a unique spirit held only by the officers and men of the Japanese submarine service," Admiral Takahashi pointed out.

"This spirit of the crew of the submarines is something apart from the so-called "Spirit of the Wild Eagles," Admiral Takahashi said, adding, "airplanes soar in the skies, and every deed undertaken, dangerous and death-defying though it may be, is glorious and spectacular.

"Contrary to this, submarines have a most quiet and unpretentious mission. The officers and men have to go through long, tedious hardships, with a spirit of profound endurance which needs the height of courage.

"Let us imagine a submarine disaster. Gradually the air becomes thinner and thinner; slowly and steadily the water rises, and death can be felt coming closer and closer every minute.

"It would be much easier to die a sudden death, but that is not permissible in the submarine. Every one must stand by his post to the very last, and I feel sure that the Japanese officers and men are the only ones who can do this.

Classmate of Sakuma

"The well-known First-Lieutenant Sakuma, who was Captain of Submarine No. 6, which went down off the coast of Shin-minato while maneuvering, was my classmate in the Naval Academy. He and his 12 men stood at their posts until death, which was later discovered, and, in the note which the Captain left behind he said he hoped this disaster would not affect the morale of the Navy.

"This spirit," emphasized Admiral Takahashi," remains in the heart of the Japanese Navy, and it has been fostered and developed, culminating in a superior spiritual attitude which can be called 'the soul of the submarine.'

"This soul of the submarine," described the Admiral, explained in a few words, is 'daringness amid prudence.' and this spirit is what made possible the successes of the Special Attack Flotilla.

"At the time of the first World War," he continued "Japanese submarines were way behind those of other countries in every aspect. But after the war, Japan bought seven U-boats from Germany and carried out intensive efforts in developing the ships.

"And now," Admiral Takahashi concluded, "after only 20 years, Japanese submarines compare favorably with any in the world."

Traditional Spirit Unchanged

Declaring that the traditional spirit of the Japanese Navy has remained unchanged since the blockade of Port Arthur at the time of the Russo-Japanese War, Admiral Arima, who took command of the blockade said, "It is that calm, composed and courageous spirit which those men of the Special Attack Flotilla held to the last that characterizes the Japanese Navy and which was seen at the time of the blockade of Port Arthur.

"These men," he continued, "did what they knew was their duty, not caring about praise or commendation, and they were happy to give their lives for the cause of the country.

"It is true that although the spirit manifested by the young men only in their twenties is the same traditional spirit brought down since the Russo-Japanese War." Admiral Arima said, adding, however, "the technique with which the attack of Pearl Harbor was carried out is far superior to that of the blockade of Port Arthur.

"Indeed, at this time I bow my head in reverence to the loyal, patriotic and courageous young men of today, who have upheld the tradition of the Navy and who have shown the world the strength and might of the Japanese Navy."

The Attack on Pearl Harbor

"Thunderous explosions, violent flashes, scraps of steel hurled high into the air and an American battleship of the Arizona type was no more." Thus eye-witnesses described the sinking of this warship which occurred at 4:33 p.m. on December 8, 1941, in Pearl Harbor. With the issuance of the Imperial Headquarters communique on Friday, the whole nation now knows full details of the gallant exploits of the death-defying Special Attack Flotilla which caused such havoc in the Battle of Hawaii. In the painting above, Takeshi Matsuzoe, famous artist, vividly reproduces the attack on Pearl Harbor. (Censored by Navy Ministry No. 571)

JAPANESE PRESS COMMENTS

Saturday, March 7

HOCHI—Nine War Heroes
MIYAKO—Heroes in Sea Battle
ASAHI—Batavia Completely Occupied
CHUGAI—British Appeasement Policy Toward India

Nine War Heroes

HOCHI

The outstanding achievements attained by a special attack flotilla of our submarines in the surprise attack on Pearl Habor on December 8 last year fully displayed and enhanced the matchless offensive spirit and tradition of the Imperial Navy. It not only deeply impressed the Japanese people on the home front, but their heroic achievements at the very outset of the war astounded the peoples of the entire world and dealt a fatal blow to the United States Navy. On the occasion of the citation by the Commander-in-Chief of the Combined Fleet, Admiral Isoroku Yamamoto, for the heroic attack, the Imperial Headquarters revealed in detail the peerless heroic action of the special attack flotilla.

According to the announcement, the plan of the attack, which astounded the world, owed its conception to Commander Naoji Iwasa and several other officers who desired to perform their duties loyally, serving the Sovereign and the State by putting the plan into execution in case of an emergency. The non-commissioned officers who took part in the plan were, according to the announcement, men in whom the officers had always full trust and who had wished to be with their commanding officers in life and in death. Keeping strict secrecy, even within the service, tacticians and engineers in complete unity of purpose devoted themselves day and night without rest or sleep to the construction of the undersea craft and preparatory training. The painstaking efforts in this preparatory period by these heroes are more than enough to stir the timid into activity.

As they set out on the glorious expedition the special attack flotilla sped on its way toward Pearl Harbor, and passing through the enemy's vigilantly guarded and complicated channels, staged daring attacks in broad daylight and under the cover of darkness. Thus, they dealt an annihilating blow to the United States Pacific Fleet at the very outset of the war of Greater East Asia. All the crews were entirely devoted to attaining maximum results from the attack with hopes of rejoining the fleet being entirely left out of consideration. Heroic deeds such as placing oneself above the question of life and death can only be performed by the officers and men of the Imperial Forces who are always willing to sacrifice themselves for the Sovereign and the State.

Behind the glorious victories achieved by the Imperial Forces, there are always a great number of loyal and gallant officers and men. The people on the home front must renew their resolution again for the successful execution of the War of Greater East Asia.

Heroes in Sea Battle

MIYAKO

The activity by a special attack flotilla of special submarines in the Battle of Hawaii which astounded the whole world was revealed in detail by the Imperial Headquarters Friday, together with the names of the heroes who willingly sacrificed their lives. The entire world has been anxious to know the plan, structure, and formation of the attack flotilla. The announcement revealed that it was a perfect example of the unity and the traditional loyal spirit of the Imperial Navy as well as its superb tactics and technique.

Despite instructions to rejoin the fleet after execution of attack, the crews were entirely devoted to the attainment of maximum results, and they gave no consideration to rejoining the fleet. After confirming the instant sinking of a battleship of the Arizona type and communicating this feat to the fleet by wireless, they are believed to have either been sunk by the enemy or to have smashed themsolves up. This heroic action is nothing but the fullest manifestation of the offensive spirit of the Imperial Navy which disgards the question of life and death from the very beginning. We have nothing but words of appreciation for the loyal and heroic action of these youthful heroes who successfully fulfilled their difficult tasks.

His Imperial Majesty the Emperor, fully recognizing the heroic deeds of these nine officers and non-commissioned officers, was pleased to promote them by two ranks, and a special citation was given them by the Commander-in-Chief of the Combined Fleet, Admiral Isoroku Yamamoto, in honor of their outstanding achievements. As long as our Empire exists, the spirit manifested by this special attack flotilla will live in the hearts of the Japanese people, whom we believe will display it in the future whenever necessary.

Batavia Completely Occupied

ASAHI

Pressing the enemy in the Greater East Asia Sea area back to Java Island and seizing the control of the sea and air in that region, the Imperial Forces successfully made landings on March 1 at three different points, on Java Island. Although the occupation of the entire island has since then been regarded as a matter of time, the Imperial Forces, fighting speedily and gallantly, completed on March 5 the capture of Batavia. For this, we cannot help renewing our thanks and appreciation.

Batavia is known as the political and economic center of the Netherlands East Indies, and the significance of its occupation is comparable with that of Kuala Lumpur in the Malay Peninsula. Although the Netherlands East Indies Government was removed somewhere else before our occupation of Batavia, the enemy's political structure in Java Island has been virtually destroyed and the fate of Java Island is now completely sealed. While carrying out mopping-up operations of the enemy remnants on the one hand, the Imperial Forces will endeavor to the construct a new order in the island in cooperation with the inhabitants there.

Although there is some difference between the operations in the Malay Peninsula and those in Java Island, as the Imperial Forces took complete control of the entire Malay Peninsula 20 days after the occupation of Kuala Lumpur by penetrating into Johore Bharu at the southern extremity of the peninsula, the Imperial Forces operating in Java Island will, without a doubt, sweep through the distance of 700 kilometers between Batavia and Surabaya in a short period. Coupled with clever and speedy tactics, the occupation of Batavia will undoubtedly accelerate the campaign of the Imperial Forces in the island. This, needless to say, will make the strategic position of the Empire toward the Indian Ocean and Australia more solid and unshakable than ever.

British Appeasement Policy Toward India

CHUGAI SHOGYO

Desertion of the Netherlands East Indies by Britain on the pretext of defending India and Burma which clearly reveals the true colors of that country is nothing surprising for us. Declaring that they would put up stiff resistance, with the Netherlands East Indies as the last base of operations in the southwestern Pacific Ocean, the British made Australia and the East Indies rely firmly on them. As the situation developed unfavorably for the Allied forces, the British left the command of the Netherlands East Indies in the hands of the Dutch military authorities and transferred General Archibald Wavell, Commander-in-Chief of the Allied forces in the southwestern Pacific region, to India. No matter how indignant they are toward the British, the East Indies authorities have nobody to blame but themselves, as such a predicament was caused simply by the lack of their foresightedness as well as their over-reliance on other nations. We can never forgive the outrageous attitude of the British but the prevailing situation did not allow them to remain calm for Burma and India were exposed to imminent danger. Thus they were compelled to take such a faithless attitude.

With the complete occupation of Burma by the Imperial Forces imminent, India cannot remain calm and peaceful. If the war is extended to India, it is obvious that the independence movement in that country will be intensified. In view of this situation, the British Government, while maintaining a suppressive policy on the one hand, has been trying to appease India as much as possible on the other. Thus, in order to make India join the anti-Axis front, the British Government even asked Chiang Kai-shek to visit India and confer with Indian leaders. It is, however, quite dubious whether India will accept Britain's persuasion at this moment or not. Britain will undoubtedly try hard to win the cooperation of India. But if India joins hands with Britain the golden opportunity for its independence will be lost forever. Thus it would be only proper and natural that India has neither accepted Chiang Kai-shek's persuasion nor joined hands with Britain despite various flattering proposals.

It is quite obvious that the recent visit of Chiang Kai-shek was made at the request of the British Government. If India forms a joint front with the Chungking regime, needless to say it will become a battlefield, and the chance for its long-cherished independence will perhaps be gone forever. Although the political situation in India appears to be quite complicated, it was after all, caused by the cunning colonial policy of the British Government. Leaving India in confusion and internal discord, Britain deftly utilized such a situation in its favor. The Indian people must realize that they are at the crossroads of success and failure for their country. This is no time to hesitate for if they do, the Indians will miss the opportunity for independence which is in their hands now.

Hiraide Expresses Praise in Air Talk

(Continued From Page 1)

Emperor.

"Just before they set out for their never-to-return mission, the members had a moment of gaiety with their comrades. joking and laughing as if they were starting on a short pleasure trip.

"One of the members, known for his love for sake, was encouraged by his companion who, after wishing for his success and his safe return, offered him any amount of sake when he came back from his mission. This man, however, did not accept the offer of drink although he was grinning good naturedly at the well intended remark of his comrade.

"Thus, the youthful heroes, who are now deified as War Gods, left for their suicide trip in the best of spirits.

"It was found later that though each member wrote down words of thanks to the superior officers and comrades for their guidance and friendship and kept a detailed record of their official duties in order, not many wills were found among them.

"What I wish to state here with special emphasis is the great maternal influence, which played a vital role in developing such a self-sacrificing spirit as manifested by these nine men.

"Each member of the Special Attack Flotilla was well known for his filial piety and most of the members considered it their happiest moment to return home and spend a day with their mothers whenever they were given vacations.

Lauds Japanese Mothers

"Consequently, the efforts of their mothers in leading these men to the right path and sacrifice themselves to help build up such a spirit is indeed worthy of the highest praise. If it were not for the pains and hardships of the Japanese mothers behind the scene, the rearing of such outstanding characters as the nine War Gods is quite beyond possibility.

"There is a world of difference between the actions of these men and those of the American and British soldiers, who take to their heels whenever they come across a superior opponent or hesitate to undertake a task if there is a least risk of danger. Behind such men lies the egoism and epicurism of American and British mothers.

No Comparison With Yankees

"For one example, the chief reason for the American sailors in joining the navy is to see the world at the country's expense, draw an extraordinarily high pay and to make it their pleasure to call at various ports of the world for enjoyment purposes. These were made clear by statements issued by the soldiers captured by the Japanese Forces during the current hostilities.

"The whole world is just spell-bound at the great and marvellous accomplishments of our forces at all fronts achieved since the outbreak of the War of Greater East Asia.

"I feel certain that they will envy the Japanese Nation when they find that behind such spectacular successes, there is the stout determination such as demonstrated by the members of the Special Attack Flotilla in the heart of each and every Japanese subject.

"The nine members of the submarines, apart from being the Gods of War, are also the Gods of Peace Construction. The thing that is to follow the War of Greater East Asia is the establishment of lasting peace in the world.

"The present hostilities is not the War of Destruction but that of construction and when such a time comes when Japan undertakes the holy task of constructing a New Order, I feel confident that the spirit of these guarding Gods of the country will guide the way."

TOLL OF RAID BY RAF ON PARIS ANNOUNCED

Greatest Crime in History Between Formerly Allied States, Says Berlin

Domei

PARIS, March 6.—The total number of persons killed during the British air raid on Paris has now reached 700, it was revealed here today.

Meantime, countless numbers of persons who have been rescued from under the debris are said to be in a "pitiful" condition as the result of their narrow escape from death.

Berlin Scores Crime

D.N.B.

BERLIN, March 5.—Concerning the bombing of Paris by the R.A.F., the Wilhelmstrasse emphasizes: "The sympathies of the German people are with the French people." It points out that regardless of any political or legal problems, the people of Germany express profound sympathy for the French citizens who have to bury either wife, father, mother or child as a victim of the indiscriminate British attack.

Dakar, Oran and Paris are being characterized by the Wilhelmstrasse as stages of the British policy toward an ally who collapsed under the burden of the war incited by Britain, and whose capital has now been bombed "like any Kaffir village that rose up in protest against British taxes." It is declared, furthermore, that against Paris, probably were employed those airmen which refused to participate in the battle in the Pacific, in Africa or other dangerous spots, preferring the much less risky job of bombing Paris.

"The bombing of Paris will go down in history as the greatest crime ever committed between formerly politically befriended and allied States," these quarters declared.

Height of Shamelessness

As the height of shamelessness, Berlin quarters characterize the announcement, made in London solely in the French language, in which the King of England and the British Government expressed their deep-felt sympathy for the victims of the British bombing. The King of England, obviously affected by this monstrous bombing, held it his duty to express such words of hypocrisy. The world, however, is deeply shaken by what has happened in Paris—shaken in view of the fact that British politicians who formerly claimed to love Paris like a woman, now, for no reason whatsoever and in an absolutely senseless manner militarily, sent bombing planes to Paris and let hundreds of French civilians be murdered.

The freedom, proclaimed by the pamphlets which the British dropped simultaneously with their bombs, is described by Berlin quarters to be apparently the freedom of a graveyard that England wants to donate to the French people.

Sumner Welles statement in which the U.S. Under-Secretary of State declared that he had been personally informed of this impending attack is regarded as most remarkable in Berlin, since this had been stated by the representative of a State which, at least formally, is still maintaining diplomatic relations with Vichy. "Like everyone in history," Wilhelmstrasse quarters stressed, "also this crime will fall back on the perpetrators and neither we nor the French people will ever forget the bombing of Paris."

Two Planes Downed

It has been confirmed in Berlin that German A.A.-guns were being employed in the defense of Paris and during the attack two British planes were shot down. It is stated, however, that up to now the A.A. artillery at Paris was not as strong as that in Berlin because a British air attack on the capital of the former ally of England was thought hardly probable. With regard to the big number of casualties, it is pointed out in Berlin that the raid was made in the clear moonlight and that also parachute torches had been employed which must have afforded the British airmen fairly good visibility. Moreover, owing to the lack of adequate A.A.-defenses, the British airmen could descend to an altitude from which they must have been able to hit the points they intended to hit.

The question whether the German High Command will undertake retaliatory measures has been left open. It is stressed in this connection that the German High Command is interested not in the bombing of cities as such but in the destruction of enemy troop concentrations and the bombing of important war objectives.

U-Boats Continuing Drives on Atlantic

(Continued From Page 1)

terday repulsed enemy attacks, the High Command announced today.

Meantime, Axis air formations continued to carry out attacks against enemy objectives and in cooperation with land forces in southern Libya, forced the enemy to withdraw.

One British plane was said to have been shot down during the encounters yesterday.

Bushido Spirit Shown By 9 Navy Warriors

(Continued From Page 1)

"We wish you luck," said the others, "and we will wait for your return."

"Thank you very much. I shall do my best. But what's all this? Lunch, cider, chocolate,—well, well, I feel like I'm going on a hike, not a battle. Ha, Ha."

A Hero at 22

Lieutenant Hiro-o was only 22 years old. In his diary is the following entry:

My parents and relatives do not know that I am out here. They think I am having a holiday, for that was the impression I gave them when I parted from them. All of you, forgive me please. I am going to die for my country, for the sake of the nation, and perhaps in later days you will recognize this, and say, Ah, the blighter has done it after all.

Promised to Sink Battleship

Special Second Sub-Lieutenant Shigenori Yokoyama held the following conversation with his comrades before his departure:

"I'm sorry to have troubled you for such a long time," said Yokoyama, taking out some beans and offering them to his comrades, "I shall sink a battleship for you."

"Best of luck," said the others, "But mind you, it must be a battleship, not a destroyer, or a cruiser."

"Sure," nodded Yokoyama.

"Not even a submarine," pursued his comrades.

"Of course, of course," said Yokoyama. "The Commander always aims at a battleship."

"When you come back, let's all drink like the devil," suggested one of his friends.

But Yokoyama left without making any promise about it.

Special Second Sub-Lieutenant Naokichi Sasaki, after receiving his orders and instructions about the projected operations of the Special Attack Flotilla, went up on deck with his comrades.

Determined to Die

Lighting a cigarette, he said to them, "When I received my orders, I was so overwhelmed that my whole body was trembling. I had half-expected it, but the determination to die in performing my duty was formed the moment I heard the orders. Now that my objective is clear, I know what to do, and I shall do my best."

Chief Warrant Officer Yoshio Katayama was told by his comrades just before he left that it would be all up with him if he was discovered and attacked with depth-charges.

"In that case," said Katayama, "I shall rush full speed at the enemy ship, and burst a hole in its bottom. What do you think of this verse,

Before the God of War I heard
Tomorrow's cry of dismay
From the lips of President Roosevelt.?"

Chief Warrant Officer Sadamu Uyeda was a scholar, and among his articles were the "Moji Kuzushikata Jiten" and the "Shosei no Michi."

Chief Warrant Officer Kiyoshi Inagaki's last words were, "I shall fight to the last. When we meet again, it shall be at the Yasukuni Shrine."

Japan Times & Advertiser
Published by
The Japan Times, Limited
TOSHI GO. President and Editor

TOKYO OFFICE:
1, Ichome, Uchisaiwai-cho, Kojimachi-ku, Central P.O. Box 144, 357, 358.
Telephone: Ginza (57) 303, 403, 5857 5858, 5859, 7003.
Telegraphic Address: "Times Tokyoyubin" Furikae No. Tokyo 64848.

BRANCH OFFICES:
OSAKA, Dojima Bldg., Tel. Kita 1770.
YOKOHAMA, 157 Yamashita-cho, Tel. Honkyoku (2) 5240.
KOBE, 65 Naniwa-machi, Kobe-ku; Tel. Sannomiya 3970-71.

SUBSCRIPTION RATES:
One month, ¥5.00; six months, ¥28.00; one year, ¥55.00. Postage free to all parts of the Japanese Empire, Manchoukuo and China. For foreign countries, including postage, six months, ¥42.40, one year, ¥83.80. All subscriptions are payable in advance.

MOSTLY TANKERS SUNK

80 Ships, Totaling 532,900 Tons, Destroyed by U-Boats in January

Transocean

BERLIN, February 21.—More than half of the 80 vessels, aggregating 532,900 tons, which have been sunk by German submarines off the North American Atlantic coast since the beginning of January are tankers, of which there is a particular shortage in Britain as well as in the United States, according to competent Berlin military quarters.

The significance of the U-boats' successes is illustrated most vividly by comparing the figures with the official announcement made by the United States Shipping Board before the United States entered the war, stating that during the first nine months of 1941 the United States completed the construction of 65 commercial vessels displacing a total of 522,000 tons.

Office: .... 1, 1-chome, Uchisaiwai-cho, Kojimachi-ku, Tokyo
Publisher and Printer: .... MASAO TAKAHASHI

The San Francisco News

"The White Newspaper—Easy to Read and Worth Reading."

SCRIPPS-HOWARD

Vol. 40 Entered as second-class matter. San Francisco, Cal., Postoffice. SAN FRANCISCO, MONDAY, MARCH 9, 1942 No. 58

EXTRA FINAL

ALL EAST INDIES CLAIMED BY JAPS

We Must Go On Offense, Author Says

Lewis Mumford Warns Americans That War May Be Lost Unless Everyone Starts to Fight It Immediately

See editorial, "Suppose We Begin to Fight," Page 14.

BY KAY WAHL

Start now, this minute.

If you want your country and the democracies to win this war, you must start to fight it.

You—and you. Aggressively, not defensively. Now, and not tomorrow.

LEWIS MUMFORD.

With the voice of a prophet without honor until Dec. 7, Lewis Mumford gave this call to arms today, to every San Franciscan, to every Californian, to every American.

It was a very deceptive interview. It was Mr. Mumford, author of "Culture of Cities," here to speak for the San Francisco Housing & Planning Association on "What Kind of World Are We Planning For?"

But it was Mr. Mumford, author of "Men Must Act," written in 1938 after Munich, who paced the floor of his St. Francis Hotel room filled with the urgency of his belief.

"If you are living the same life you were living before Pearl Harbor," he said, "before the fall of France—we will not win this war!

Not Doing Well Enough

"We are in a perilous state. Every one is talking about our orderly progress in production for 1944 and '46—for an occasion which will take place this spring.

"Just this morning there was a report by Knudsen that we were progressing reasonably well — no one should say that. We are not doing well enough!

"Every little effort by our heroic forces in the East is treated as a great victory—when actually they are only holding on by their teeth. We haven't got the guts to blast ourselves. We are living a delusion, a fantasy."

Mr. Mumford, who in 1935 and in 1938, before as well as after Munich, gave himself a reputation for lunacy, even with his friends, by asserting as often as he could make himself be heard, that we must fight the Fascist powers, not wait until they fought us, declared he is in complete agreement with Lieut. Col. W. F. Kernan's book, "Defense Will Not Win the War."

"The Axis powers have been telling us for 10 years what they were going to do to us," he said. "When we kept saying we would not fight them until they attacked us, that was an invitation.'

Must Change Attitude

We must all change our attitude, he insists, with a vehemence that sounds almost desperate, this attitude that is a "disease, a corruption, that extends from the top down."

"There should be bands playing, marching soldiers in the street. You, or you, or any one, could have a band playing in the street by noon—don't wait for some one to tell you what to do—go to some rich man and say, 'Your money won't be any good when it's over, unless we win—let's have a band playing!'

"We are like a man with a low temperature, boasting that he hasn't a fever—in some diseases, a low temperature leads to death. And there should be no promises of what we will do afterward—like a world union, or social justice. We should have those things now, and then we'll know we mean it."

He is horrified by talk of evacuation of California. "We should not even consider the possibility," he said. "But if the Japanese should have a force strong enough to invade, there is only one thing to do—we should stand here with our women and children and fight them, with our bare hands if necessary. We should emulate London and Moscow, not Vichy.

"We cannot defend this country, except by attacking. Defenses crumble away, the defensive attitude cannot match in production the aggressive attitude."

WAR REGISTRY OF WOMEN URGED

By United Press

NEW YORK, March 9.—The National Industrial Conference Board said today that a nationwide registry of women would be necessary to determine the number available and qualified for war industry jobs.

The percentage of women now in war work is "only a fraction" of the number at the peak of production during the first World War, the board, an independent research group, said.

If the employment ratio of the last war is duplicated this year, it said, the number of women employes will rise from the present 500,000 to 3,500,000.

AUSSIES BOMB 2 POINTS IN NEW GUINEA

Continent Prepares For Attack; Dutch Governor Arrives

By United Press

MELBOURNE, Australia, March 9.—Australia—counting heavily on American and other Allied aid—mobilized maximum fighting strength and battered Japanese invaders of New Guinea with bombing planes today in expectation of an imminent enemy offensive from the north.

Japanese troops, landed at Salamaua and Lae on the north coast of New Guinea, are 425 miles from the Australian continent. Conquest of the island would bring the enemy within 100 miles of Australia, across Torres Strait.

The small Australian home defense corps withdrew before the invasion troops to the hills of the interior after destroying all military and supply installations, Government communiques said.

Aussie Airmen Attack

The Australian forces had prepared fully for demolition, and before the Japanese got ashore, the defenders were out of the towns and in the open country where they might hope to continue resistance.

As soon as the news of the invasion had reached the Government, Australian planes raced out to the attack.

They were so prompt they apparently caught the Japanese by surprise. They dived down on warships and transports, through a rain of anti-aircraft shells, to bomb and machine gun. It was believed heavy casualties were inflicted on the invaders.

By the time Japanese fighter planes arrived to challenge them it

(Turn to Page 6, Column 1)

Diary of the War

MONDAY, MARCH 9, 1942

Bad News

Japan's offensive engulfs Java and Rangoon and sweeps toward Australia with seizure of two bases in New Guinea.

Tokio Radio claims "the entire Dutch East Indies have surrendered to the Japanese"; that Java capitulated with Nipponese capture of Bandoeng and the Dutch naval base of Soerabaya; that 93,000 Dutch and 5000 Americans, British and Australians laid down their arms. ((Unconfirmed by Allies.)

Japanese Armies tighten an invasion grip on New Guinea, threatening a coming attack on the Australian Continent. Using strong air and sea armadas, Nipponese land at Salamaua and Lae on north New Guinea's Gulf of Huon, only 180 miles from Port Moresby, which lies only 100 miles from the northern tip of Australia. New raid made on Port Moresby by 10 enemy bombers.

Australians are warned the enemy may be expected to strike as quickly as possible toward Port Darwin, Broome and Wyndham airbases and north Queensland. Australian Cabinet in emergency session.

British admit withdrawing troops from Rangoon, Burma's capital, which Japanese claim to have occupied. Enemy claims severe defeat inflicted on British at Pegu railroad junction. Tokio estimates British losses in Burma at nine divisions—about 125,000 men.

Tokio claims destruction of 219 Allied ships up to last week and 52 vessels, totaling 210,000 tons, since Wednesday.

Good News

General Douglas MacArthur's strong defense in Bataan is reported by the War Department to have resulted in Japan sending her most famous general of this war—Tomoyuki Yamashita, conqueror of Singapore—to the Philippines to attempt to knock out the American and Filipino defenders.

He succeeds General Masaharu Homma, who is reported to have committed hara-kiri because of his failure to defeat General MacArthur. (Tokio denies the suicide.)

Allied forces claim to be fighting on in Java, where large war stores had been hidden for guerrilla war. Netherlands Government officials in London declare "there will be no surrender in Java in any circumstances whatever."

Java's Lieut. Gov. Hubertus Van Mook arrives in Australia, thus showing determination of the Dutch to organize further resistance.

In Burma American flyers are still battling Japanese air forces. Britain braces against the Japanese sweep toward the gateway to India by a change of command that puts General Harold R. L. G. Alexander in charge of Allied forces in Burma.

Australian planes sweep over New Guinea's Gulf of Huon, blasting at enemy invasion forces.

In Russia, Red Army reports virtually destroying the German 48th Infantry Division at Sychevka, important railroad center between Rzhev and Vyazma. Sychevka, 40 miles south of Rzhev, is captured by Russians.

Russians reportedly have five million equipped men in reserve to meet Hitler's expected spring offensive; Germans (according to Swiss reports) have so far lost 1,500,000 men.

The Royal Air Force, renewing attacks on factories working for the German war machine in Occupied France, blast the industrial suburb of Poissy, 17 miles north of Paris, and raid the German industrial city of Essen.

MAKE THE BAD NEWS GOOD NEWS. BUY DEFENSE BONDS AND STAMPS TODAY!

NAZI DIVISION IS 'ANNIHILATED'

By United Press

MOSCOW, March 9.—Russian forces have "almost completely destroyed" Germany's 48th Infantry Division in a bloody, two-day battle for Sychevka, strategic rail city midway between Rzhev and Vyazma, dispatches said today.

Sychevka is 40 miles south of Rzhev on the railroad connecting that city with Vyazma, and its capture created a new Soviet threat against the German garrisons in both of the larger cities.

The destroyed 48th division consisted mostly of Poles, who deserted to the Russians in large numbers when the fighting began.

Soviet forces pressing westward from Yukhnov on the central front are continuing to force German troops to retire despite stubborn resistance, dispatches said.

By United Press

BERLIN, March 9 (German Broadcast Recorded by United Press in New York).—German troops scored local successes on the eastern front while repulsing unsuccessful Russian attacks, a high command communique from Adolf Hitler's headquarters said today.

It said the German Air Force scored hits on 36 Russian transport trains in the Valdai region, northwest of Moscow. Sixty-two Soviet tanks were said to have been destroyed from March 6-8.

(Other Soviet gains—Page 3.)

'Free Sunday' Shipyard Move Signed by 5000 Workers

The ball is rolling.

The shipyard workers who want to do an extra shift, gratis, for Uncle Sam "because we know better than anybody that we've got to get more bottoms" are still signing up.

Five thousand men, it was announced today, have enrolled in their own "Beat the Japs" program, a plan for a volunteered Sunday's work which Bethlehem shipyard workers started last week as their own way of demonstrating a determined hardworking morale.

The new total was reached as last night's shift added fully 1000 signatures to the lined sheets of paper, circulating among the hulls: "We, the undersigned, would like to donate our services without pay, of a Sunday, for Uncle Sam."

Their "inspiring spirit" was lauded today by Will L. Merryman, general manager of the San Francisco Chamber of Commerce, as he flew to Washington to consult with Donald M. Nelson, War Production Board head, on shipyard and other production facilities here.

Workers in other Bay Area plants share the attitude of the Bethlehem men, he declared.

Twelve hundred plants in the Bay Area, with machine shops, chemical works, foundries and other vital defense facilities—but no defense contracts—are the reason for Mr. Merryman's consultation with Mr. Nelson. He's going to see how these 1200 plants can be put to work for the nation.

(Read Arthur Caylor on Page 13).

SURPRISE CHINESE ATTACK

CHUNGKING, March 9.—A dispatch from southern Kiangsu Province today said Chinese forces on the Kiangsu-Chekiang border had made a surprise attack on Japanese positions and inflicted heavy casualties on the enemy.

LAST-MINUTE NEWS

JOHNSON, GRADY NAMED TO U. S. INDIA MISSION

WASHINGTON.—The State Department announced today that Louis Johnson, former assistant secretary of war, will head the United States advisory mission which will assist in the war effort in India. Henry F. Grady of San Francisco, president of the American President Lines, will handle general economic surveys.

WASHINGTON.—The House today tentatively approved a reduction from $10,000 to $1000 in the maximum amount of soil conservation payments which may be made to any individual or corporation in the fiscal year 1943.

'U-Boats Hi-Jack Fishing Vessels'

By United Press

ATLANTA, Ga., March 9.—Enemy submarines off the Georgia coast have "held up" shrimp fishing boats in "one or two instances" and taken their supplies of oil and gasoline, State Wildlife Comsr. Zack Cravey said today.

Cravey said he had no details, "but there has been a slump in fishing."

A Note on Leaner-Backers

The American is a leaner-backer. He leans back in his chair, and at the same time he leans back mentally.

He likes to listen to the other fellow's story. "Now, mebbe there's something TO what I've just heard," he reacts; refusing to believe that the "other fellow" might be thoroughly dishonest and completely a scoundrel.

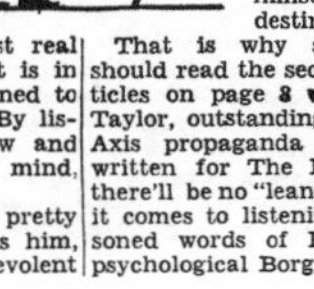

That's because the American is the most real democrat in the world. It is in this way that he has learned to govern his own country. By listening to the other fellow and then making up his own mind, by cracky.

All of this makes him a pretty lovable guy. But it makes him, too, a sucker for those malevolent political propagandists who possess a genius for building up half truths—and one-quarter and one-eighth truths—into whole truths.

It makes him, in short, unfair game in wartime for the enemy's army of psychologists—highly skilled and infinitely cunning propagandists trained to twist the American's mind—to confuse him, leave him unsure of himself and of his destiny.

That is why all Americans should read the second of two articles on page 8 which Edmond Taylor, outstanding authority on Axis propaganda methods, has written for The News. . . . So there'll be no "leaning back" when it comes to listening to the poisoned words of Herr Goebbels' psychological Borgias.

Rangoon Too

BURMA CAPITAL WITHDRAWAL IS ADMITTED

Rail Line Broken; Command Is Changed; Ruin Left in City

By United Press

LONDON, March 9.—British forces have been withdrawn from the smoke-blanketed Burmese capital of Rangoon, General Sir Archibald Wavell's headquarters at New Delhi, India, admitted tonight, following an afternoon announcement that London still was in communication with Rangoon.

A terse War Office communique announced that General Harold R. L. G. Alexander had been named commander in chief on the Burma front under the supreme command of General Sir Archibald Wavell, effective last Thursday.

General Alexander succeeds General Thomas J. Hutton.

Rangoon Fall Claimed

(Tokio propaganda broadcasts yesterday said that Rangoon had been taken by the Japanese after a severe battle at Pegu, north of the capital, where 4000 Australian and Indian troops were encircled and pounded until their lines were broken. Japanese claimed occupation of four military airdromes near Rangoon and "undisputed mastery" of the air throughout Burma.)

Reports from Rangoon said that the skies were filled with smoke from fires lighted by saboteurs in addition to the destruction by British fires done to prevent important installations from falling into enemy hands.

"The place to fight the Japanese may or may not be Rangoon," the British commentator said.

"The fight in Burma has been and will be very hard," he declared.

Rail Line Broken

The commentator refused to disclose the sector in which the main British forces had been disposed but said that so far as was known the center of fighting was still around Pegu, 50 miles above Rangoon. He admitted that successful enemy infiltration there would threaten the main Rangoon-Prome road.

The Japanese had broken the Rangoon-Mandalay railway line to the Burma Road by taking Payagi, 10 miles north of Pegu, and Pyinbon, eight miles above Payagi.

(Rangoon afire—Page 6.)

Baby Smothers

Efforts of a fire department inhalator crew yesterday failed to save the life of seven-months old Donald Canciamilla after he had been found unconscious in his crib. Mrs. Carmel Canciamilla, the infant's mother, reported to police she had found him unconscious, blankets tightly wrapped around his head.

TRY AGAIN

GEN. TOMOYUKI YAMASHITA.
He'll try to do the job.

GEN. MASAHARU HOMMA.
Failed to crush MacArthur.

ACE GENERAL IN M'ARTHUR DRIVE

By United Press

WASHINGTON, March 9.—Japan's most famous general of this war has been sent to the Philippines for the evident purpose of leading a new attempt to knock out General Douglas MacArthur's American and Filipino forces.

The War Department announced today that General Tomoyuki Yamashita, the conqueror of Singapore, has succeeded General Masaharu Homma, who is reported to have committed suicide because of his failure to defeat MacArthur.

General Yamashita has arrived at headquarters north of the Bataan battlefront to take over the task in which General Homma failed despite the vast numerical superiority of his forces.

Hara-Kiri Reported

Announcement of the shifting of Yamashita to the Philippines was regarded as further corroborative evidence in support of what General MacArthur on Sunday described as "persistent" reports that Homma had ended his life in the tradition of hara-kiri.

Military observers believed that with the hard-hitting Yamashita in command of the 200,000 or more invading troops a new offensive against General MacArthur's forces was anticipated.

Some quarters believed that the new commander-in-chief in the Philippines might be bringing with him reinforcements which had been used at Singapore or the Indies.

Lull on the Front

Battled to a standstill for two months and then thrown back, Homma is reported to have committed hara-kiri about Feb. 26 in the same suite of rooms in the Manila hotel that had been occupied by General MacArthur. (Tokio radio denied the suicide report.)

A lull has hung over the Bataan battlefront for the past 24 hours, today's War Department communique said, perhaps while Yamashita reorganizes his forces for an effort to repeat his Malayan-Singapore triumph.

Yamashita (pronounced Yah-mahsh-tah) has established his field headquarters at San Fernando in Pampanga province, about 25 miles northeast of the Battan battlefront and 18 miles north of Manila Bay.

(Yamashita's career—Page 6.)

'98,000 ALLIES AND JAVA ARE SURRENDERED'

'Soerabaya Falls'; But Dutch Report Fight to Continue

By United Press

TOKIO, March 9 (Broadcast Recorded by United Press in San Francisco).—Radio Tokio today claimed "the entire Dutch East Indies have surrendered to the Japanese."

It was claimed that all of Java had been surrendered unconditionally after battles at Soerabaya and Bandoeng, and that defense forces of 93,000 Dutch and 5000 Americans, British and Australians laid down their arms today.

The same broadcast said the great Dutch naval base of Soerabaya fell at 3:15 p. m. yesterday.

"Coming within a few hours of Japan's celebration of Army Day, the collapse of the Dutch command came as a pleasant surprise to the Japanese nation," the broadcast said.

It was disclosed the commander of the Japanese forces in the Dutch East Indies is Lieut. Gen. Itoshi Inomura.

DUTCH CLAIM TO BE STILL FIGHTING IN JAVA

LONDON, March 9.—Allied forces fought on in the Java mountains today.

Denying Axis claims that Dutch resistance in Java has ended, authoritative Netherlands Government sources said: "There will be no surrender in Java in any circumstances whatever.

"We have decided to defend Java to the death of the last man," the Dutch official Army spokesman here said. "I do not believe we will surrender regardless of what happens."

The Dutch and a handful of other Allied troops have strong positions in the mountains, where large war stores had been hidden, and it was believed that they might wage guerrilla war against the enemy much as General Douglas MacArthur has done in the Philippines.

The Dutch spokesman estimated that in Java the Japanese had about 11 divisions or up to 220,000 men.

He cited lack of Allied air support as the principal reason for Japanese successes in Java, combined with heavy Dutch naval losses.

(Allied drive demanded, Page 6.)

F. R. Talk May Hit Farm Bloc

By United Press

WASHINGTON, March 9.—The House may vote today on the farm bloc's demand for parity prices in the sale of Government-owned farm surpluses.

And this evening—at 6:55 (Pacific Time) — President Roosevelt will make a five-minute speech over major radio networks on the ninth anniversary of the New Deal's farm program. (KGO, KPO and KQW will carry the address.)

If the Administration suffers another defeat in the House on the farm issues, it was considered likely that Mr. Roosevelt might take the opportunity tonight to carry his fight with the farm bloc to farmers and the country at large.

Inside The News

AIR RAID WARDENS: KEEP UP YOUR HANDBOOK, SAVE THIRD IN SERIES OF DEFENSE NOTES, PAGE 2

Publishers Of
The Osaka Mainichi
The Tokyo Nichi Nichi
In Nipponese
With Combined Circulation
Of 3,500,000 Daily

Sunday Mainichi, Economist, Jikyoku Joho, Children's Daily, Dai Nippon Seinen, Seikatsu Kagaku, Greater East Asia War Graphic, Home Life, Chinese Mainichi, Braille Mainichi, Fujin Nippon, Year Book

A National Newspaper For International Readers

The Osaka Mainichi &

The Tokyo Nichi Nichi

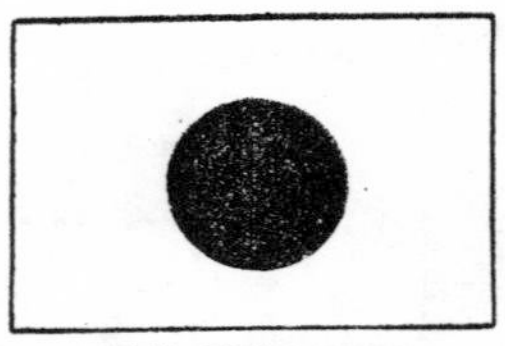

Fall Of Rangoon
Army Day

No. 6875 B 毎日一回發行 月曜日休刊 昭和十七年三月十日發行 TUESDAY, MARCH 10, 1942 大正十一年四月十日第三種郵便物認可 PRICE: 7 Sen

Rangoon, Capital Of Burma, Taken

Nippon Military Administration Is Proclaimed In Java

PROCLAMATION IN BATAVIA

Administration Of DEI Is Taken Over By Japanese Army Authorities; Local Officials Are Told

Domei

BATAVIA, Mar. 8.—The Nippon forces in the Dutch East Indies region, deciding to take over the D.E.I. administration simultaneously with the recent occupation of Batavia, issued a proclamation on March 7 at 2 p.m., formally announcing the enforcement of military administration.

The proclamation was read by the chief of the military administration department of the Nippon forces before a member of the D.E.I. Council, the mayor of Batavia, the Indonesian Resident of Batavia province, and the Resident of Meester Cornelis province.

Collapse Of Java Defense Imminent

From Our Staff Correspondent

AIR BASE, Mar. 8.—The iron ring around Bandoeng, Java, is being increasingly tightened from three directions by the Nippon forces.

The last day of the Dutch East Indies troops on the island is fast approaching. The collapse of their resistance is regarded as a question of time.

Surabaya Under Direct Artillery Fire Of Nippon Forces

From Our Staff Correspondent

LISBON, Mar. 7.—A Reuters dispatch from Java today revealed that Surabaya, chief naval base in Java, was now under direct Japanese artillery fire.

Northern Defenses Of Bandoeng Broken

From Our Staff Correspondent

LISBON, Mar. 7.—The Dutch East Indies Aneta news agency today reported that the Nippon forces in Java have broken the northern defenses of Bandoeng and were now about 10 miles from the center of the city.

Japanese Unit In Sight Of Bandoeng

From Our Staff Correspondent

JAVA FRONT, Mar. 7.—Succeeding in breaking through the enemy position in the mountainous region at a short distance from Bandoeng by means of a severe night attack on March 6, a certain Nippon unit advancing on Bandoeng from the north occupied a certain pass which commands the view of Bandoeng.

Previously, the contingent, assisted by heavy bombing on the enemy position by Nippon warplanes, definitely defeated stubborn resistance put up by a large number of enemy troops in that area.

Assuming an absolutely superior position to the routed enemy troops, the Nippon detachment, in cooperation with the Nippon Army air corps, is about to annihilate the enemy troops at one blow.

'End Of Java'

Domei

LISBON, Mar. 8.—Assembling all reports received here from London, local circles are led to believe that the British have already recognized the end of organized allied resistance on the island of Java and that there is no need to wait for any announcement.

The hour, 7.45 p.m. on March 7, when the Bandoeng radio station made its tragic farewell address, is taken to be the time when the resistance ceased.

The B.B.C. broadcasting station itself admitted the loss of Java in its broadcast at 2 p.m. (London time) today. However, in order to distract the attention of the public from this sad defeat, the broadcast feverishly hinted at the supposed activities on other fronts. The broadcast was as follows:

"The battle of Java has ended with the defeat of the D.E.I. forces, but in the Sumatra, Borneo, Celebes, and Timor sectors, the allied forces are still continuing fierce resistance."

'All Hope Gone'

Domei

BUENOS AIRES, Mar. 8.—American correspondents who fled from Java have reported to their respective journals in the United States that the United States Navy failed completely in operations off Java, the Nacion reports here today.

The Nacion's correspondent in Washington also reported that depression and gloom was deeper in the United States as continued reports from the Great East Asia War front contain nothing but news of Japanese successes.

The American public, the journal reported, has given up all hope for the Philippines and Java.

Java Radio Silenced

From Our Staff Correspondent

BUENOS AIRES, Mar. 8.—Complete silence descended upon all means of communication between the Dutch East Indies and the allied world today.

The last two words of any kind reaching the Western Hemisphere were heard by a listening post of the Radio Corporation of America late Saturday night, according to information available here today.

The reported words of farewell were: "Goodbye until better times. Long live the Queen."

The Associated Press said that there were many secret radio stations in Java with transmission power just strong enough to be heard in Australia. These too, however, were utterly silent today and obliged the allied world to listen to Nippon overseas broadcasts for information.

Port Darwin Raided

Bombing Attack Concentrated On Military Facilities

From Our Staff Correspondent

LISBON, Mar. 8.—The Australian radio today reported that Nippon planes carried out bombing attacks on Port Darwin on Saturday, March 7, dropping bombs aimed at military establishments and equipment.

Pt. Moresby Again Bombed

From Our Staff Correspondent

LISBON, Mar. 7.—The Nippon air force carried out a bombing attack on Port Moresby shortly after noon today, it was reported from Canberra.

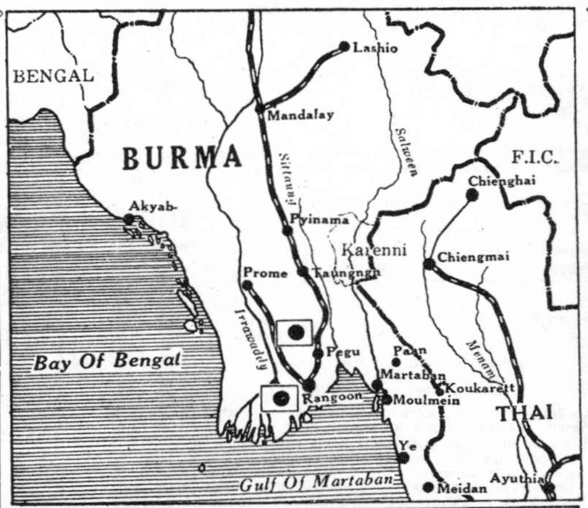

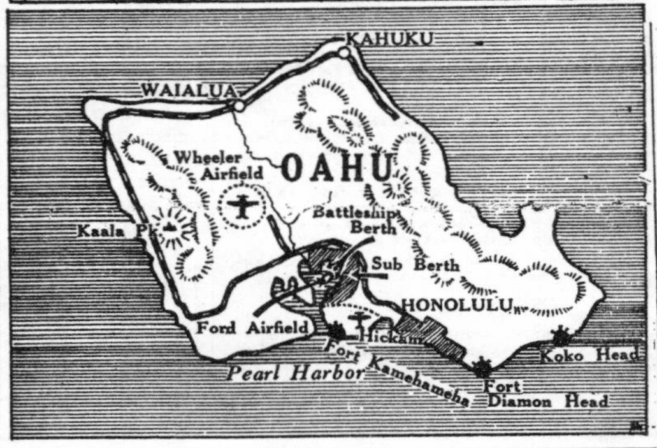

Jambi Taken; Southern Sumatra Controlled

IMPERIAL GENERAL HEADQUARTERS, Mar. 8 (at 5.15 p.m.).

Occupying Jambi, strategic point in central Sumatra on March 4 at 5 p.m., the Nippon Army units in the Sumatra region secured the oilfields in the district south of Jambi.

The contingent further defeating the routed enemy troops in the vicinity of Moeratebo, completed pacification operations in the whole of south Sumatra on March 5.

On Burma Front

Lieut.-General Iida

Russians Repulsed

From Our Staff Correspondent

BERLIN, Mar. 8.—The German High Command today announced that in the fierce fighting which occurred in the Lake Ilmen sector, the German Army, strongly supported by tank corps, and the air force, threw back the repeated attacks launched by the Russians, who left 800 dead against the German losses of 40 lives.

Malta Destruction Continues

From Our Staff Correspondent

LISBON, Mar. 7.—The British Air Ministry in London today announced that Axis planes continued their destruction raids on Malta both in daylight and at night on the Valetta base.

Paris Again Bombed

From Our Staff Correspondent

LISBON, Mar. 8.—Royal Air Force bombers last night again attacked a Paris factory eight miles from the center of the city, according to a London announcement.

No details of the actual damage were available.

JAPANESE ENTER RANGOON

Main Force Of Enemy Is Destroyed In Vicinity Of Pegu, Rangoon; Entry On Mar. 7 And 8

IMPERIAL GENERAL HEADQUARTERS, Mar. 9. (11.05 a.m.):

Defeating the main enemy force in the vicinity of Pegu and Rangoon, the Nippon Army units in the Burma region completely occupied Pegu on the afternoon of March 7 and Rangoon on March 8 at 10 a.m.

The Nippon Army corps in the Burma region, occupying Martaban on February 10, continued a brave advance in accordance with undisclosed strategy while defeating enemy troops at various points.

Crushing one division of the enemy offering stubborn resistance in the region of the Bilin river during the period from February 16 to 19, the Nippon contingents in hot pursuit of the routed enemy troops annihilated them in a sector east of the Sittang river.

Crossing the river before enemy gunfire beginning on March 2 at night, the Nippon forces launched operations for the capture of Rangoon.

The occupation of Rangoon means the completion of the main object of the military operations in the Burma area.

Lieut.-Gen. Iida Is Highest Commander

IMPERIAL GENERAL HEADQUARTERS, Mar. 9. (11.20 a.m.):

Lieut.-General Shojiro Iida is the highest commander of the Nippon forces in the Burma region.

Rangoon-Mandalay Railway Cut

From Our Staff Correspondent

BUENOS AIRES, Mar. 1.—The San Francisco radio admitted last night that Nippon units succeeding in crossing the Sittang river had cut the Rangoon-Mandalay railway line in the vicintiy of Pegu.

Burma Route Absolutely Nullified

By Staff Writer

The Imperial Army units advancing from the Thai-Burmese border captured Rangoon, the capital of Burma and the greatest concentration center in the so-called Chiang-aiding Burma Route, on Sunday, March 8, or 51 days after they opened the Burma drive on January 17.

The fall of Rangoon not only has completely intercepted the Burma Route, but will prove a direct menace to India, Britain's priceless treasure vault in Asia. This will just about make it impossible for the allied Chungking and British forces to establish and maintain effective liaison.

Furthermore, the fall of Rangoon has revived the high hopes of the Burmese in releasing themselves from the age-old shackles of British oppression. They realize more keenly than ever before that they now stand a rare opportunity of regaining their independence under the paternal guidance of Nippon.

Jungles Penetrated

Since they crossed the Thai border into Burma on January 17, the Imperial Army units penetrated the dense jungles of the Shan states, some of which tower 1,800 meters above sea level. Two days later they captured Tavoy, a key point facing the Gulf of Martaban.

Advancing steadily, they captured Moulmein on January 31. Moulmein is Burma's third largest city, situated on the mouth of the Salween river which empties into the Gulf of Martaban. On February 16 they crossed the Beeling river, whence they crushed the Anglo-Chungking forces.

On February 23 and 24 they succeeded in crossing the Sittang river against enemy gunfire. This river is one of the tributaries of the Irrawaddy river, and formed the last flank of the Rangoon defense lines.

On February 27 they intercepted the Rangoon-Mandalay railway near Pegu, whence they closed definitely in on the Burmese capital, eventually capturing it on March 8.

The Imperial Army deserves all the more credit because of the adverse conditions under which the Burmese campaign was carried out. They had to traverse wide expanses of jungles infested with ferocious beasts and venomous snakes.

Either on elephants' backs or on their own shoulders, the officers and men carried arms and supplies across roadless stretches and across the steep canyon in the upper reaches of the Salween river, whose whirlpools defy passage by launches and barges.

Malicious Propaganda Of Enemies Is Blasted In Statement By Tokyo

Refuting all groundless and malicious Anglo-American propaganda intended to harm the traditional "Bushido" spirit of Nippon, the spokesman of the Board of Information released a written statement at 6 p.m., on Monday, March 9.

The text of the official statement is as follows:

Confronted by the hopeless military situation resulting from its successive major defeats in the field of battle with the consequent loss of face before the world, the Anglo-American camp is now resorting to the only remaining method of resistance, namely propaganda mainly by the press and radio.

Reuters News Agency circulated on February 25 a report that the Japanese authorities are maltreating prisoners of war and that the discipline of the Japanese soldiers is so lax that they are maltreating or otherwise abusing women and girls or killing innocent persons in the occupied territories.

We can well gather that a story of this kind is apt to fall easy on the ears of uninformed peoples of Great Britain and the United States whose eyes are biased by their Governments' policy of hiding the truth of the defeats of their forces on land, sea and in the air wherever the latter come in contact with the Japanese.

We would simply ignore such a mendacious propaganda as unworthy of any serious attention, if we were not to cherish the good name of the Imperial Japanese forces.

For the sake of Truth, we want, therefore, to take this opportunity to state briefly regarding the actual treatment of prisoners by the Japanese authorities in Nippon and the occupied territories and the conduct of Japanese soldiers toward the inhabitants in the war zones.

It is the maxim of "Bushido" to honor and to be merciful to opponents who are brave on the battlefield as well as to fight loyally and courageously regardless of life or death. This principle has always been the guiding spirit of the Japanese fighting services.

It is a matter of historic record that, during the Sino-Japanese War of 1897-1898, the commander-in-chief of the Japanese Fleet, Admiral Yukyo Ito, sent gracious gifts to the spirit of the Chinese commander-in-chief, Admiral Ting Ju-chang, who ended his life with poison after surrendering to the Japanese in Weihaiwei.

When the Russian General Stoessel, commander of the brave Russian garrison at Port Arthur (Ryojun), surrendered after a series of bloody fights in the Russo-Japanese War of 1904-1905, General Maresuke Nogi offered the Russian General and his staff officers the rare privilege of wearing their swords thereby expressing his respect, as a soldier, for the bravery of the erstwhile opponents.

The same magnanimity is manifested by the Japanese military and naval authorities to prisoners in the present War of Greater East Asia, notwithstanding the contrary stories spread by the enemy propaganda machine.

Cases Are Cited

Let us cite at random some of the numerous cases of actual treatment afforded the war prisoners in their own words. Captain Jose Rasa, a Filipino Army officer, who was taken prisoner in the northern Bataan peninsula on January 15, stated:

"I was told by Americans that Japanese are cruel like beasts and devils, but I have found with my own eyes that they are quite well disciplined as well as kind-hearted. The well-kept peace and order under Japanese occupation affords a marked contrast to the indescribable scene of vandalism left by American troops."

At the outset of the war, the British troops seized about 400,000 bags of rice stored in the warehouses of merchants in Kowloon and requisitioned all rice and wheat of the citizens and carried them away to the British Army warehouse in Hongkong, causing untold difficulties to those civilians.

In their retreat from Kowloon, the British destroyed the city's water system and electric power plant to the consternation of the civilian population. It was upon the entry of the Japanese troops that the people of Kowloon breathed the sigh of relief. The city is now in the midst of peaceful reconstruction under the leadership of the peace maintenance committee in hearty cooperation with the Japanese.

What Americans Say

Let us now listen to what the American, Australian and New Zealand prisoners have to say regarding their treatment by the Japanese. The Japan Broadcasting Corporation recently offered its radio service to hundreds of these prisoners, who were so eager to tell their folks at home concerning their present condition and treatment.

Here are some of the messages:

Lieutenant Commander Tilden T. Moe of the American Navy, taken in Guam, said: "I have arrived safely in Nippon and am being well provided for. Please do not worry about me. The Japanese are treating all of us with kindness and considera-

(Continued on Page 2)

Empire Will Observe 1st Army Day Since Outbreak Of Asia War Today

The first Army Day since the opening of the Greater East Asia War will be observed today, in the midst of the swift and brilliant achievements being attained by the Imperial forces on all fronts.

This year's celebration is the 37th since the establishment of Army Day in 1906 in commemoration of the signal victory of the battle of Mukden.

In greeting this memorable day, we must renew the sense of profound gratitude to the loyal officers and men who have been offering their utmost, surmounting all difficulties, for the cause of the country. We must also pay high respects to those who have sacrificed their lives for the realization of the lofty ideal of the Empire.

Simultaneously, we must renew the determination to push forward the Greater East Asia War until the final victory is achieved.

On the eve of Army Day, Premier General Hideki Tojo, concurrently War Minister, in the latter capacity, issued a verbal statement, expressing his profound appreciation of the officers and men, who are fighting with courage and vigor overcoming adverse elements over a wide area, and urging the 100-million people of the Empire to arouse themselves and to withstand all difficulties in order to attain the final victory.

Daily and Sunday Telegraph Net Weekly Sales Largest in Australia

HIGH TIDES: 10.12 a.m. (4ft. 8in.); 10.32 p.m. (4ft. 7in.).

Daily Telegraph AND DAILY NEWS

FINAL EDITION

Vol. VI. No. 309 (New Series) Telephone: M2406 SYDNEY, WEDNESDAY, MARCH 18, 1942 Registered at the G.P.O., Sydney for transmission by post as a newspaper. Price, 2d

AMERICAN TROOPS, AIRMEN HERE —SO IS GENERAL MacARTHUR!

To Take Supreme Command

The B.B.C. announced early today:

"General Douglas MacArthur today arrived in Australia to assume supreme command of the United Nations' forces in the South-West Pacific, including the Philippines.

"Considerable numbers of both air and ground troops of the American Army are now in Australia.

"First official announcement of the arrival of these U.S. forces was made in Washington by U.S. War Secretary Mr. Stimson.

"No information is available about the strength of American units or of their exact location.

"We knew unofficially, of course, that U.S. troops were in Australia."

No comment on this announcement was sent yesterday from Washington, nor was any statement made from Canberra.

Philippines Chief Here At Request Of Commonwealth

News of General MacArthur's arrival in Australia was released early today.

A U.S. War Department communique issued in Washington and broadcast by the B.B.C. said:

"General MacArthur will be supreme commander in the Anzac area, including the Philippines, at the request of the Australian Government.

"General MacArthur was accompanied by his Chief of Staff (Major-General R. J. Sutherland), Major-General Harold H. George, of the U.S. Army Air Corps, and several staff officers.

"His wife and sons are with him."

GENERAL MACARTHUR.

Led Gallant Stand

The communique added: "On February 22, President Roosevelt directed General MacArthur to transfer his headquarters from the Philippines to Australia.

"General MacArthur asked for a delay, to enable him to finalise arrangements to hand over his Philippines command.

"This delay was authorised by the President."

The B.B.C. said that the appointment followed the announcement by the U.S. Secretary for War (Mr. Stimson) that American forces had arrived in Australia.

Held Bataan

The B.B.C. added: "General MacArthur's stubborn resistance to the Japanese on Bataan Peninsula has caught the imagination of the whole free world.

"Since the fall of Manila his small forces have held Bataan and the fortress of Manila Bay against huge odds.

"His forces have wiped out whole regiments of Japanese troops.

"General MacArthur was the youngest Chief-of-Staff the United States Army ever had.

"He was appointed to command the forces in the Philippines on July 22 last year.

"He has 13 decorations for gallantry under fire."

General MacArthur is 62, having been born in Arkansas, on January 26, 1880.

His American and Filipino forces have held out against enormous odds for 14 weeks, since the Japanese invaded the Philippines on December 9.

At his first time under fire, when he was a 23-year-old lieutenant, his peaked hat was shot from his head in an action in the Philippines.

Many Ordeals

A U.S. sergeant said to him: "The rest of your life is now on velvet."

In the 39 years since then General MacArthur has come through many dangerous ordeals.

When bombs were whistling down near Manila early in December, an orderly tried to "shoo" him into a dug-out.

MacArthur replied: "Give me a cigarette, Eddie," and went on watching.

MacArthur has been a soldier all his life, has served in two wars, and served three times in the Philippines.

He was the youngest of division commanders before he left for France during the last war with the famous Rainbow Division.

He was continually being cited for heroism—and getting himself wounded because of his passion for not wanting to die in bed.

General MacArthur has proved his brilliance as a staff officer, and his mettle and leadership under fire.

He is a man who wears his hat at the most rakish tilt permissible by regulations, and lets nothing interfere with his profession of being a soldier.

He is said to be the sort of man who can do more with what he has than anyone expects.

His father—Lieutenant-General MacArthur—was military governor of the Philippines 40 years ago.

Time, American news-magazine, gives this description of General MacArthur when he was organising the Philippines Army before the Pacific war:—

"He would stride back and forth across the room purpling the air with oratory, punctuated by invocations of God and the flag, pounding his fist in his palm, swinging his arms in great sweeping gestures.

Great Leader

"Nights he paced his apartment atop the Manila Hotel so vigorously that people in the rooms below complained."

"Early in the Philippines fighting, after he had worked day and night, he said to his sweating staff: 'Well, slaves, I'm going home to eat.'

"Wherever MacArthur goes, he travels as if draped in the American flag itself, and preceded by a guard of honor.

"But while civilian critics used to consider MacArthur a swash-buckling, colorful, impeccably-dressed soldier, with a penchant for oratory, most of his Army contemporaries thought him a strict disciplinarian, a magnificent leader of men in action, a first-class fighting man."

Hero worship of General MacArthur has become widespread throughout the United States, making him Public Hero No. 1.

Some American newspapers even suggested him as the next President of the United States.

U.S. SUBMARINE SINKS JAPS

WASHINGTON, Tuesday (A.A.P.).—A United States submarine has sunk two more enemy ships in Far Eastern waters, states a Washington communique.

They were a freighter sunk in Japanese waters and a 3000-ton tanker sunk off the Philippines.

HOW ANZACS ARE MADE

NEW YORK, Tuesday (A.A.P.).—"The Making of an Anzac" is the principal article in this month's National Geographic Magazine.

The article, written by Howell Walker, is beautifully illustrated with photographs of Australia and New Zealand.

"These two countries of the South Seas—one of vast plains and sunshine, the other of verdant valleys and rugged mountains—have cradled the Anzacs," Walker writes.

"The Anzac is the Storm Trooper par excellence of the Democracies.

"He is the straight product of a free land, where living is healthy, but tough.

"Looking at an Anzac in his homeland, it seems perfectly natural that he should depart for the other side of the world, with bronzed skin, cheeky grin and all, to get into the fight.

"A quality of deep insight somewhere in these regions of 'go-as-you-please' inspires men to protect their shores thousands of miles away."

Australia Can Expect American Naval Help

Australia can expect American naval help, says the United Press' Washington correspondent.

Naval reinforcements will be sent, or are already on their way, to Australia, he says.

"Washington experts declare that the naval situation in the South-West Pacific is far from hopeless," the correspondent adds.

"But they emphasise that, because of Allied losses in the Java Sea battle, the burden of Australia's defence for the moment falls on land and air forces."

The correspondent adds that Washington military experts admit that the setback to the Allied Fleet in the Java Sea battle has "gravely complicated" Allied plans for the defence of India and Australia.

In this battle, from February 27 to March 1, the Australian cruiser Perth and the sloop Yarra, with four other Allied cruisers and seven destroyers, were lost.

Mark Sullivan, New York Herald-Tribune columnist, says that the Java Sea losses increase greatly the likelihood that Japan will move towards Australia with all force and speed.

Japan's Chance Now

"To move towards Australia is to move towards us," Sullivan adds.

"Japan wants, needs Australia, and can hardly ever have a better chance to take it than now.

"Every day Japan waits before pouncing on Australia is a day lost.

"It is desperately urgent that our people recognise what the Japanese seizure of Australia would mean."

The New York Times says that a Japanese victory over Australia can be won only through Australia's lack of air power in light and heavy bombers.

"These we can send, and are sending," the paper adds.

"The coming battle for Australia will be decided by the rate at which help is kept moving through the South-west Pacific.

"Although Allied air attacks on enemy bases in New Guinea and New Britain have increased noticeably, it is too soon to say how successful they have been.

Blows Predicted

"Japan has not yet gathered her strength to strike at Australia, but there is little doubt that she will strike with all her power.

"Japan's naval victory in the Java Sea destroyed the only fleet which could menace her communication lines in the area she has conquered.

"Japan is free to convoy landing forces anywhere she likes on Australia's west and north coast, so the blows, wherever they fall, must be countered from the air.

"There Japan may find herself at a disadvantage. That is why she is striving so desperately to establish air bases immediately north of Australia.

"The Japanese are hardly likely to try a frontal march across the Great Australian Desert.

"Their most probable strategy will be to conquer the continent, port by port, and leave the interior to the future, as they did in Borneo.

"But distances in Australia are enormous. Except in the north, invasion can be supported by air only by plane-carriers.

"These are not enough. They can be blown out of the water by land-based planes."

William Simms, foreign editor of the Scripps Howard newspaper chain, writes:

"Unless Japan can maintain her record for quick knock-outs—until she has conquered Australia, China, India, Siberia, and Hawaii—her doom is certain.

"As long as the United Nations have at their disposal any one of these five bases they have a foothold from which to launch an offensive which only the most inexcusable bungling can prevent from getting under way sooner or later.

"To remove Australia from the United Nations' line-up would be a colossal blunder."

Defence Tactics

The American Press Service, which has a world-wide organisation, in an article on Australia distributed to its subscribers, says:

"It is difficult to picture any static position of defence for Australia—if such tactics are still anywhere possible in modern warfare.

"What is indicated is 'defence' by wide, flanking manoeuvres, counter-strokes against lengthened enemy lines of communication by land, sea, and air.

"First of all it will be a battle for the approaches, then, when and if beach-heads are secured by the foe, fighting for the defence of vital cores of the war effort and the national life.

"Loss of territory will not defeat Australia.

"The Battle of Australia promises above all to be a struggle for roads, airways, and railways, with distance the foe to both invader and invaded.

"But the advantage undoubtedly is with the defence."

Little We Can Do, Says England

LONDON, Tuesday (A.A.P.)—Commenting on the threatened Japanese invasion of Australia, the Daily Mail says:—

"Australia is in imminent peril, but there is little we can do.

"Time presses, and we are so far away. Our hands are full.

"Australia's problem is the same that has been faced by every Allied country facing invasion, including Great Britain.

"The problem is to hold out until supplies and reinforcements become available on such a scale to enable an offensive to be launched."

Fall Of Kharkov Reported

Jap Claims Discounted

The Federal Government yesterday described Tokio reports that Japanese forces were preparing to land on Thursday Island as "groundless."

Berlin radio, elaborating this Tokio claim, said that Japanese naval forces had arrived in Torres Strait to cover "the landing."

The Federal Government knows nothing of any clash north of Moresby between Japanese and Australian troops.

Tokio alleges such a clash has occurred.

Moresby, on the southern coast of New Guinea, is 180 miles south of Japanese-held Salamoa.

Berlin radio claims that a battle is progressing in the centre of New Guinea, and that the situation there "has reached a decisive stage."

Moresby Still Intact

It was officially stated in Canberra yesterday that Moresby is still intact.

If there had been any major military action in the area, the Federal Government would have been officially advised by now.

Japanese troops could be north of Moresby only if they landed from troopships, it was pointed out. It is considered impossible for them to have reached that area by crossing the unexplored mountain country from their base at Salamoa.

The Prime Minister (Mr. Curtin) yesterday denied reports circulated on Monday that there had been fresh landings by Japanese in the New Guinea or Papua areas.

The Army Minister (Mr. Forde) described as "ridiculous and without foundation" rumors that Cairns had been declared an open town.

Darwin Casualties

Two service men were killed and 11 wounded in the Japanese raid on Darwin on Monday, states a war communique issued yesterday by Mr. Curtin.

The only other casualty was an aborigine, who was wounded.

Mr. Curtin said the Darwin raid was directed at R.A.A.F. objectives, and was carried out by two formations, each of seven bombers.

About 100 bombs were dropped, mostly of the anti-personnel type.

There was some damage to buildings, but no aircraft were destroyed.

The Japanese planes operated from a height of about 15,000 feet.

No attack was made on Darwin township.

The renewed bombing of Darwin is featured in New York morning papers.

The New York Times' Canberra correspondent warns Americans that the small scale of recent enemy raids suggests that the Japanese forces menacing Australia are waiting for air reinforcements.

A Washington communique reveals that it was an American pilot flying a P40 fighter plane who rammed a Japanese Navy Zero fighter near Thursday Island on Saturday.

The American did this to save a companion who was being chased by Japanese. Both his plane and the rammed Jap plane were destroyed.

The communique states that nine U.S. P40 fighters encountered a large flight of enemy bombers escorted by fighters.

Though greatly outnumbered, the American planes attacked the Japanese formation.

In addition to the rammed Jap plane, another enemy fighter and one enemy bomber were destroyed. Eight American planes returned to their base undamaged.

On Friday a United States Flying Fortress, on reconnaissance, heavily bombed the Japanese-held aerodrome at Vunkanau (near Rabaul, capital of New Britain).

Bombs On Runways

Bombs were dropped on runways, causing considerable damage, states a Washington message.

A direct hit was scored on parked aircraft, destroying at least two planes.

British Official Wireless, quoting a message from Port Moresby says it now seems clear that the Japanese drive against Australia will be made by way of New Guinea.

NAZIS FIRE CITY BEFORE RETREAT

Daily Telegraph Service and A.A.P.

LONDON, Tuesday.—A Stockholm report says the Russians have recaptured Kharkov, which fell to the Germans on October 28, 1941.

"Germans set fire to the city, and those who managed to escape were put to flight by the Russians," the report adds.

There is no confirmation from European sources of Kharkov's recapture.

Kharkov, giant industrial city in the northern Ukraine, is 410 miles south of Moscow.

The Red Army newspaper, Red Star, said two days ago its fall was near.

An all-out German drive to capture the besieged city of Leningrad is imminent, states the New York Times' Stockholm correspondent.

Leningrad, second Russian city, with a population of 3,191,304, is in the 206th day of siege.

"The German drive against Leningrad will possibly be based on Viborg (70 miles north-west of Leningrad, on the Gulf of Finland)," the New York Times' correspondent adds.

This will mean an assault on Leningrad from the rear, as the German siege lines are now south and east of the city.

"The drive has been planned principally because of the prestige which would result from its success.

"Huge German troop concentrations are reported to be based on Viborg.

"Another significant move is the departure from Oslo (Norwegian capital) to Helsinki (Finnish capital, 140 miles west of Viborg) of Hitler's famous Panzer strategist Field-Marshal Siegmund Wilhelm List.

"Field-Marshal List had been in Oslo supervising the arrival of tanks and other mechanised material.

"These shipments, which took place last month, are the first of their kind to be shipped to Norway by the Nazis since the campaign ended there in May, 1940."

Latest reports from the Russian fronts:—

NORTHERN: Moscow radio states that the 16th German Army, encircled at Staraya Russa (140 miles south-south-east of Leningrad), has lost an important defence point on its southern sector.

Trapped and surrounded by Russian forces for 19 days, only about 40,000 of the original 96,000 men of the 16th Army are thought to be alive.

CENTRAL: The Daily Express' Stockholm correspondent says that units of the Red Army cut the vital Viazma-Smolensk railway yesterday morning.

This railway is the German "life-line" in the assault on Moscow.

The cutting of the railway also completes the encirclement of Viazma (130 miles west-south-west of Moscow), closest German stronghold to Moscow.

A Swedish correspondent in Moscow says the Russians have captured a place, P—probably Pysjovka, 10 miles east of Viazma.

CRIMEA: Moscow radio reports that the Soviet cruiser Krasni Kavkaz (8030 tons) recently attacked a German-occupied island in the Black Sea.

"After the cruiser had bombarded the fortifications, a landing party raided the island," the radio adds.

"The operation was carried out in darkness, and the Germans were completely surprised."

A Swedish correspondent in Moscow says the Germans in the Donetz Basin lost 20,000 troops in one day.

Russians Want Second Front, P. 3, Cols. 1 and 2.

VICHY'S WISHFUL THINKING

Daily Telegraph Service

LONDON, Tuesday.—Vichy radio's version today of the B.B.C. announcement of the arrival of U.S. troops in Australia was:

"The B.B.C. reports that Japanese reinforcements have been landed in Australia."

DRAFT EXTRA

CHARACTER QUALITY — AMERICA FIRST! — ENTERPRISE ACCURACY

Los Angeles Examiner

AN AMERICAN PAPER FOR THE AMERICAN PEOPLE — THE GREAT NEWSPAPER OF THE GREAT SOUTHWEST

Reg. U.S. Pat. Off.
Examiner Telephone Richmond 1212 — Examiner Building, 1111 S. Broadway

VOL. XXXIX—NO. 97 — LOS ANGELES, WEDNESDAY, MARCH 18, 1942 — P — Two Sections—Part I—FIVE CENTS

GEN. M'ARTHUR TAKES AUSTRALIA COMMAND

3485 First Number in Draft Lottery

Hershey Hints Plan to Draft Factory Labor

WASHINGTON, March 17.—(AP)—Number 3485 bobbed up tonight as the first drawn in the new war's first draft lottery intended, said Brigadier General Lewis B. Hershey, selective service chief, to add "millions to that pool of men who stand ready for selection for the necessary tasks, whatever they may be."

Hershey stressed that some of the 9,000,000 men involved in the lottery might be drafted to man factories while their comrades manned guns.

The first number was drawn by Secretary of War Stimson from among 7000 slips encased in opaque green St. Patrick's Day capsules. It meant that among the men who registered February 1, those holding that serial number would be the first in their districts to be called for possible service.

Navy Secretary Knox drew the second number, 2850, and the third, 4301, was pulled out by Representative May (Democrat), Kentucky of the House Military Committee.

The capsules, first of all, were dumped into a mixing device, a glass walled cylinder so arranged that by turning a crank the capsules would tumble over and over one another and be thoroughly mixed. Fifteen minutes before drawing began an Army officer stood turning the cylinder over and over.

The brief opening ceremonies found General Hershey referring to the possibility that men might be drafted to man the factories.

"Modern war, mechanized war—yes, total war—demands a great variety of tasks from the citizens of a nation," he said.

"Men are selected to fly airplanes; they may be selected

(Continued on Page 3, Cols. 1-2)

LIST OF DRAW

WASHINGTON, March 17.—(AP)—The order in which an estimated 9,000,000 men will be called for classification for possible military service was determined tonight by the first war-time draft lottery conducted by the Selective Service System. In 7000 capsules were the serial numbers assigned to those who registered with their local draft boards February 16. One by one these capsules were drawn from a large gold-fish bowl. The order in which a number was drawn determined the order in which the holders of those numbers will be called before local boards for classification.

The serial numbers assigned to February 16 registrants were preceded by a "T" to denote the third registration since the Selective Service law was enacted. In the following tabulation the "T" is omitted for the sake of simplicity. The order numbers to be assigned on the basis of tonight's lottery will begin at 10,000 and run to 17,000 to prevent possible confusion with order numbers given registrants in the two preceding peacetime lotteries. Again in the interest of simplicity the extra digits required to begin at 10,001 are omitted in the tabulation, but any registration may determine his final order number immediately by adding 10,000 to the number opposite his serial number below:

Order No. 1 to 50

3485	2850	4301	441	3743
3417	5298	6724	4618	4002
4205	6339	6941	3340	2986
6481	5004	3070	1817	4024
1103	4912	1790	1584	6330
176	4894	1577	1156	4304
6957	5931	4722	3475	2309
3382	5539	4906	2203	5446
3735	6319	606	5030	359
5255	4353	3203	129	4560

(Continued on Page 3, Cols. 7-8)

GRIM, DETERMINED General Douglas MacArthur, nation's foremost warrior, has arrived in Australia from the Philippines. He will be supreme commander of United Nations' forces in southwest Pacific. General MacArthur's inspiring leadership has won the nation's heart.

—Associated Press Wirephoto.

Jubilant Allies Predict Great Offensive Soon

WASHINGTON, March 17.—(AP)—The dramatic transfer of General Douglas MacArthur, hero of Bataan, to supreme command of United Nations forces in the Southwest Pacific gave a lift to Allied morale tonight and stirred hopes of early offensive blows against the Japanese foe.

MacArthur, only Allied general who has fought a major Japanese drive to a standstill, arrived in Australia today by plane, the War Department disclosed. His gallant defense of the Philippines already an epic, the fighting general was shifted to his new command with its vastly greater responsibilities and wider opportunities, by the orders of President Roosevelt and at the request of the Australian government.

Jubilant members of Congress labelled the news the best of the war to date, and from abroad came expressions of British and Australian satisfaction.

"He's the best man for the job," the Australians said.

OFFENSIVE PREDICTED

Following the War Department's disclosure that American ground troops and air force units have arrived in Australia "in considerable numbers," the assignment of MacArthur to the supreme command there gave impetus to the growing hope of a major offensive against the Japanese, who as yet have hesitated to risk a direct attack on Australia.

Arriving at an undisclosed destination in Australia, MacArthur was accompanied by his wife and small son, and by several members of his staff. Among the latter were Major General Richard K. Sutherland, MacArthur's chief of staff, and Brigadier General Harold H. George, of the air forces.

The Philippines remain a part of MacArthur's command in his new job, but direct command of the American and Filipino troops still fighting the battle of Bataan and harassing the invaders elsewhere in the archipelago, passes to Major General Jonathan M. Wainwright, senior officer remaining in Bataan.

(In a late afternoon communique the War Department reported

MacArthur Gone, Japs Attack; Same Results

WASHINGTON, March 17.—(AP)—A sudden renewal of Japanese attacks against American forces in the Philippines was reported today by the War Department, which said that all of the enemy assaults were unsuccessful.

A raid on the defending lines in Bataan was "easily repulsed" by Major General Jonathan M. Wainwright's troops, a department communique reported, and a bombardment of harbor defenses by enemy batteries on the Cavite shore of Manila Bay caused only slight damage. A Japanese destroyer shelled the port of Cebu, but caused no damage.

A BROTH OF A BOY

Meet Paddy Finucane who's brought down more than 50 enemy planes and whose exploits have made him a symbol of the R.A.F.

By John Cahill

FOR reasons that are obvious in view of the complicated nature of modern war in the air and the need for truly scientific teamwork among pilots, gunners, navigators and the hard-working but unsung men on the ground, the aerial High Commands of both Great Britain and the United States are doing their utmost to discourage publicity for individual heroes.

There are exceptions, of course, such as our own Lieutenant Colin Kelly of imperishable fame who gave his life in sinking the first Japanese battleship to go down in this war. And in England, there is "Paddy" Finucane of the R. A. F., whose exploits just could not be hidden under a bushel basket.

There is no resentment among the thousands of other pilots and bombardiers in the R. A. F. that Finucane has come to be something of a symbol for modest greatness in this war which is being fought so largely in the air. Paddy just happens to be a magnificent flier, with a sense of timing, vision and a sure trigger finger that makes it bad news indeed for any Germans who happen to get in his way. His unofficial total of enemy planes shot down is well over fifty. He has the Distinguished Service Order and the Distinguished Flying Cross with double bar, both conferred personally by King George VI himself.

But there is something more than uncannily accurate firing and indomitable courage that propelled Paddy out of the anonymity of the R. A. F.

In the first place, Flight Lieutenant Brendan (no one calls him by his given name) Finucane is a middle-class Irishman, Dublin-born. In the second, he flies with an Australian squadron, and there are no more picturesque fighters on the face of the earth than the warbirds from down under. Among them there is no "officer class," no "old school-tie" hugger-muggery. They are the same breed who marched against the Italians in Libya singing "We're off to see the Wizard, the wonderful Wizard of Oz."

They come, too, from that same fighting line of true democrats who not so long ago were reviewed by a new Australian commanding general who, contrary to all Australian custom, sported a monocle. It was really to correct a slight eye defect, but it so amused the Aussies that on the very next review, each of them turned out with a half-crown piece—just monocle size—screwed in front of an eye.

The general proved he too was a true Australian. He looked up and down the solid line of khaki mockery, saw the smile playing about each lip beneath the silver coins, and drew the monocle from his own eye. Without saying a word, he tossed it six feet into the air and then almost miraculously caught it again—in perfect position in his eye-socket.

"All right, boys," he called out. "Let's see if any one of you can do that."

The answer was a resounding cheer and, as a single man, the Australians put their money back into their pockets Never again was that general or his monocle held up to ridicule.

Anyway, Paddy Finucane has won the hearts of men like these. To the Aussies he is a natural, and his broad

Just back from a sweep, Dublin-born Lieutenant Brendan ("Paddy") Finucane is about to step from the cockpit of his shamrock-decorated Spitfire. Early in the war Paddy promised himself that before he had reached his twenty-first birthday, he'd bring down 21 enemy planes—and he kept the pledge. Since then he's kept right on and today his record has passed the fifty mark.

Here a Spitfire, similar to that flown by Paddy Finucane, takes to the air. Paddy's mechanic and rigger look upon him with worshipful admiration and no Spitfire in the R. A. F. is more carefully tended and nursed than his; no holes from enemy bullets more quickly and expertly patched than those which his show after almost every sortie.

To an R. A. F. pilot there's no more beautiful sight in the world than a squadron of Spitfires in flight—unless it's the sight of a Messerschmitt hurtling down in flames. Paddy flies with an Australian squadron and of his fellow fliers, says: "They're the most loyal and the gamest crowd I've ever known. Many times they've saved my bacon . . ."

Here Paddy Finucane is shown leaving Buckingham Palace with a friend immediately after having received a bar to his Distinguished Service Order. Paddy has also received the Distinguished Flying Cross with double bar.

Irish brogue and his own delight in mimicking the accents and habits of upper-class Englishmen makes them roar with laughter. To his mechanic and his rigger, Finucane is close to a god and no Spitfire in the whole R.A.F. is more carefully tended and nursed than his. The shamrock painted on its side glows always in pristine green glory and no hole from an enemy bullet is more quickly and expertly patched than those which show up after almost every sortie on Finucane's plane.

One of the Australians who flies with Paddy puts his successes down solely to extraordinary vision and a hair-trigger mind.

The pilot then went on to tell how during a recent dog-fight a German plane dived into an opaque cloud. Finucane was on his tail. A few seconds later, Paddy's plane zoomed out of the cloud at 350 miles an hour and at the same second the Nazi ship came screeching down in flames.

Within the limits of the aforementioned essential teamwork, all good fighting pilots have certain routines which they like the best and which hold out most promise of success. Paddy likes to get a German slightly below him and in his direct line of fire and no Nazi yet has proved sufficiently quick on the draw to faze him. The Irishman has an honest admiration for the Polish fliers in the R. A. F. who are the most daring of all, but he doesn't want to emulate their method. The Poles like to get the enemy head-on, at point-blank range and identical level. They figure that if the Germans get a telling shot in first, they can always ram the enemy plane before the fight is over and get their man even if it means certain death for themselves.

Paddy wants to live and is looking forward to settling down in Australia.

Finucane's Distinguished Service Order ribbon was sewn on his tunic by a hospital nurse last November while he was laid up with a broken foot—his only injury in the course of unbroken active service since Dunkirk, and it happened when he jumped over a wall in a blackout and fell 20 feet into a hidden areaway.

The incident happened at a "wake"—one of the innovations he introduced into his squadron at its command base. Every time the officer pilots settle their mess bill, each drops a couple of extra shillings into a pot to be used for whiskey at appropriate ceremonies the next time one of their number "goes missing." On this occasion, a particularly close friend had failed to return from a sweep over Northern France and he was posted as dead. There was only ten dollars or so in the kitty, which precluded any vast amount of drinking, so when Paddy spied the wall he rather figured that if the missing man was there he would enjoy seeing someone jump over it. Paddy did and broke his foot. The missing pilot, incidentally, later turned up as a prisoner of war in Germany, so the party was more or less wasted.

In the R. A. F. Paddy is regarded as successor to the amazing Douglas Bader (above) whose exploits, until capture, were on every British tongue.

The exploits and personality of this 21-year-old Irishman attracted so much attention that while he was in the hospital the British Air Ministry unbent sufficiently to allow him to be interviewed. It was generally recognized that Paddy was accepted by the R.A.F. as the logical successor to the amazing Douglas Bader as Britain's Number One fighter pilot. Bader was a prisoner of war in Germany, under lock and key after a daring attempt to escape with the aid of two aluminum legs dropped to him by parachute to replace those damaged in his own crack-up. Paddy's chief memory seemed to be a terrific dogfight over France when his squadron tackled 100 Messerschmitts, tangling with 30 of them for half an hour.

"It was quite a scrap," he said. "One of my pilots shot down one, while the other three destroyed two between them. I got two. The first blew up after a full burst of fire in its belly.

"I've been on about 50 sweeps across enemy territory," he went on. "Most of my victories have been over France. I've never been shot down — knock wood—and only once have I been badly shot up.

"I hope this doesn't sound too Irish. Really, I must thank the pilots of my section for all this. They're Australians, you know, and the most loyal and gamest crowd I've ever known. They've saved my bacon many times when I've been attacked from behind while concentrating on a Messerschmitt out front. They've followed me through thick and thin."

More than 50 times Paddy has swept over enemy territory and each time an enemy plane, flaming to earth like some whirling torch, has been the result. "I've never been shot down myself," says Paddy—knocking wood.

The Australians confirmed their willingness to tag along after Paddy "through hell and high water." He was asked if he knew the meaning of fear.

"Don't think I don't have that funny feeling in my tummy just before taking off," he confessed.

"But it goes soon enough. Once you're in the air, everything's fine. Your brain works fast and, if the enemy's met, it seems to work like a clockwork motor—accepting this, rejecting that; sizing up this, remembering that. You haven't time to feel anything, really. But your nerves may be on edge, not from fear but from excitement, from the intensity of mental effort.

"I've come back from a sweep with the shirt of my tunic wet through with perspiration. Our chaps sometimes find they can't sleep after shows over France and Germany. You come back and find it's the hardest thing in the world to remember what happened.

"It isn't just a blank though. Maybe you have a clear impression of three or four incidents which stand out like illuminated lantern slides in your mind's eye—perhaps the picture of two Messerschmitts belting down on your tail out of the sun and already within firing range. Perhaps there's another picture of your cannon shells striking in the belly of a Messerschmitt and spraying debris all over the place. But for the life of you, you can't remember just what you really did.

"Later, when you've turned in and sleep steals over you, a tiny link in the forgotten chain of events comes back to you. Instantly, you are fully awake, and the whole story of the operation pieces itself together.

"You lie there—sleep driven away. You lie there and re-live every moment of the combat, congratulating yourself on this thing, blaming yourself for that. And then, if you're lucky, you get back to sleep."

"Don't think I don't get that funny feeling in my tummy just before taking off," confesses Paddy. But once "up there" . . . ah, that's different!

U.S. Hammers Island Bases

WAR EXTRA

CHARACTER QUALITY AMERICA FIRST! ENTERPRISE ACCURACY

Los Angeles Examiner

AN AMERICAN PAPER FOR THE AMERICAN PEOPLE — THE GREAT NEWSPAPER OF THE GREAT SOUTHWEST

Reg. U.S. Pat. Off.
Examiner Telephone Richmond 1212 — Examiner Building, 1111 S. Broadway

VOL. XXXIX—NO. 105 — LOS ANGELES, THURSDAY, MARCH 26, 1942 — CC — Two Sections—Part I—FIVE CENTS

JAPS MAP 'DEATH DRIVE' AGAINST BATAAN YANKS

BERLE SIGHTS FALL OF NAZIS THIS SUMMER

Germany Makes No Provision for 1943 Production, Says State Department Aide

NEW YORK, March 25.—(AP)—A. A. Berle, Assistant Secretary of State, predicted tonight that the summer of 1942 would make it plain that "the Nazi rulers of Germany have lost the war and have decreed their own ruin."

In an address prepared for a Greek Independence Day dinner here, Berle asserted:

"We now have information from sources inside of Germany making it clear that the Germans themselves know that there can be but one end. The German people know, as we know, that no provision has been made by the Nazi government for the year 1943.

"They know that the machines they need to produce the tools of war are no longer repaired. They know that the skilled workmen and the young engineers who must do the production of tomorrow have been and are being sent, half trained, to the slaughter on the fighting fronts in Russia. They know that the battalions which go out, do not come back—save as a collection of shattered wrecks.

"They know, indeed, that the men who have gone to the Russian front are frequently not allowed to come back to Germany, lest the German people learn what has befallen."

GREEKS AID FALL

Berle traced the predicted collapse of the German war effort to the resistance of Greece in 1941, which, he said, "made possible the reinforcement of the eastern Mediterranean," and "de-

(Continued on Page 12, Cols. 2-3)

Death Trial—and a Reunion

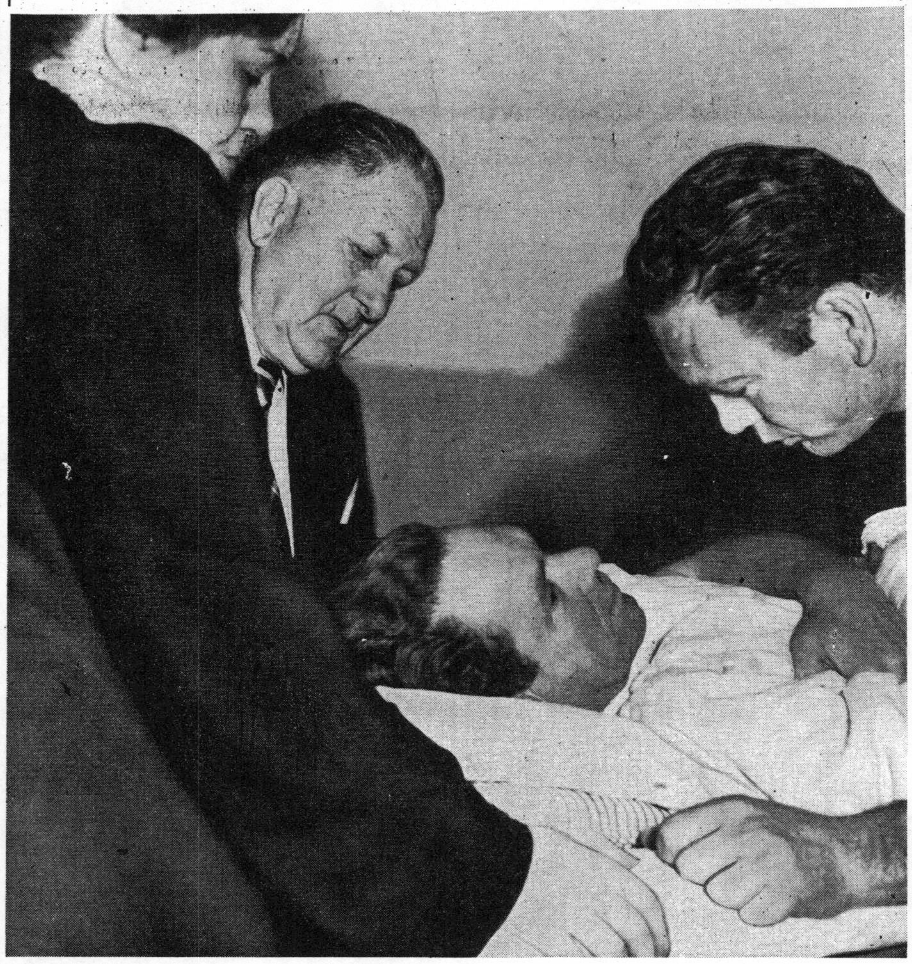

WOUNDED, POLICE said, during his participation in holdup in which officer and bandit were killed, Lyle Gilbert (on stretcher) is shown at preliminary hearing yesterday. With him are his brother, Max, another defendant; Vernon Gilbert, father (rear), and Rosalind Bates, his attorney. (The story will be found on Page 3.)
—Los Angeles Examiner photo.

NAVY WIPES OUT JAP WAKE, MARCUS BASES

Tokyo Blacks Out in Fear as Raid Strikes Only 1000 Miles Away; 2 Planes Lost

(Page of Pictures—Page 24)

WASHINGTON, March 25.—(AP)—Striking powerfully at the flank of Japanese supply lines into the southwest Pacific, an American task force raiding within 1000 miles of Yokohama has virtually wiped out enemy installations on Marcus and Wake Islands, the Navy announced today.

Although the operation thrust ships and planes of the Pacific fleet deep into enemy territory only light opposition was encountered and the total American losses were but two aircraft.

TOKYO BLACKED OUT

Advices from Pearl Harbor said the raids threw such a scare into Tokyo that that city's lights were blacked out for several nights.

The action, conducted by Vice Admiral William F. Halsey, 59, who was awarded the Distinguished Service medal for similar attacks on the Marshall and Gilbert Islands January 31, was hailed by naval authorities here as an eminently successful operation weakening the protection which the Japanese are able to afford their vital routes of supply.

A Navy communique said the attack on Wake, which the Japanese captured from defending Marines December 23, was carried out February 24, by both ships and planes and wrecked defenses which "the enemy has worked feverishly to strengthen." A few prisoners were taken there.

Shells from cruisers and destroyers and 219 aerial bombs sank two enemy patrol boats, demolished two four-engined

(Continued on Page 2, Cols. 1-2)

Bombers Again Hit Manila Bay and Corregidor

WASHINGTON, March 25.—(AP)—The Japanese were believed today to be reinforcing their already numerically superior forces on the island of Luzon preliminary to another drive to wipe out the American-Filipino resistance on the Bataan Peninsula.

"Continued enemy ground activity in Bataan indicates the arrival of Japanese reinforcements," a war communique said, adding that Nippon flyers were also continuing hammering blows at defense positions.

Twenty-seven bombers, accompanied by smaller craft, the War Department said, blasted at harbor defenses on Manila Bay and "our front lines and rear installations in Bataan." There were no reports of the damage, or that any of the attacking planes had been shot down.

Renewal of aggressive Japanese operations against the outposts held by General Jonathan M. Wainwright on Bataan and in Manila Bay called attention again to the importance of these positions in the war patterns of both sides.

Observers here point out that there are only two places of great strategic importance on the islands—Davao, which the Japanese hold, and Manila Bay. Ironically, the Japanese have their most complete occupation on Luzon—the richest and most highly developed island of the entire archipelago—and yet Bataan and the tiny island fortresses of Mills (Corregidor), Drum, Frank and Hughes deny them control of the bay.

When a United Nations counter-offensive is launched, observers explained, the ability to use Manila Bay as a naval supply, repair and operating base could be all-important to Japan since Manila lies some 1800 miles nearer the Indies-Australia front than Japan proper.

In all, the Japanese occupy considerably less than one-half the Philippine territory.

Off the southern tip of Luzon, they hold the Island of Masbate, and opposite the entrance to Manila Bay, the small Island of Lubang. Southeast of Lubang they have occupied the Port of Calapan and a small coastal strip on the north shore of Mindoro, across the narrow Verde Island passage from Batangas Province, Luzon.

Southward, there is a group of large islands still free of the Japanese except for an occasional shelling of their ports by enemy naval ships. Panay, Negros, and Cebu, heavily populated, important producers of rice and other agricultural products and centers of native fishing industries, are in this group. So are the large islands of Leyte and Samar, but these, while containing valuable resources of timber, are sparsely inhabited and to a great extent still unexplored.

DAVAO FELL EASILY

Below these lies Mindanao, southernmost of the large islands and roughly the same size as Luzon. Here the Japanese hold approximately as much territory as the American-Philippine forces still retain in Luzon. A large Japanese settlement existed at Davao long before the war began, and the enemy moved into that important south coast with ease early in the war.

Except for a limited coastal area along Davao Gulf, however, plus a small area at the port of Zamboanga on the southwestern tip of Mindanao, the Japanese have not moved into this large island, and attempts to extend their hold on it are certain to meet stiff resistance from the warlike Moros who inhabit it.

Even the enemy's Zamboanga and Davao footholds are not free from attack. Yesterday Allied forces, presumably bands of Moros, were reported to have inflicted heavy losses on the Japanese in an attack on a motor column near Zamboanga. Today the War Department announced successful skirmishes with the enemy near Digos on Davao Gulf.

Southwest from Mindanao the islands of Sulu Archipelago form a chain to Borneo, and only the central island of Jolo in this group has been occupied by the Japanese.

Portage Lake Mining Gazette

VOL. LXXXIV, No. 39 — HOUGHTON, LAKE SUPERIOR, MICH., MARCH 26, 1942 — TERMS $2.00 PER YEAR

JAPAN REACHES OUT FOR INDIA

U. S. Navy Blasts Wake and Marcus Island Bases

RAIDS THROW SCARE INTO TOKYO CITY

Attacks Disclose Both Islands Are Inadequately Manned by Japanese.

SINK ENEMY BOATS

BY JOHN M. HIGHTOWER

WASHINGTON, March 25 (AP)—Striking powerfully at the flank of Japanese supply lines into the southwest Pacific, an American task force raiding within 1,000 miles of Yokohama has virtually wiped out enemy installations on Marcus and Wake islands, the Navy announced today.

Although the operation thrust ships and planes of the Pacific fleet deep into enemy territory only light opposition was encountered and the total American losses were but two aircraft.

RAIDS SCARE TOKYO

Advices from Pearl Harbor said the raids threw such a scare into Tokyo that that city's lights were blacked out for several nights.

The action, conducted by Vice Admiral William F. Halsey, 59, who was awarded the distinguished service medal for similar attacks on the Marshall and Gilbert islands January 31, was hailed by naval authorities here as an eminently successful operation weakening the protection which the Japanese are able to afford their vital routes of supply.

A navy communique said the attack on Wake, which the Japanese captured from defending Marines December 23, was carried out February 24, by both ships and planes and wrecked defenses which "the enemy has worked feverishly to strengthen." A few prisoners were taken there, presumably rescued from the water.

Shells from cruisers and destroyers and 219 aerial bombs sank two enemy patrol boats, demolished two four-engined seaplanes—a third was shot down—tore great craters in aircraft runways, and damaged defense batteries. One of the American aircraft was lost at Wake.

BOMB MARCUS ISLAND

A week after the Wake bombardment, powerful units of the task force, including an aircraft carrier, swept within aerial range of Marcus island before dawn on March 4. Bombing squadrons soared into the darkness and away to their objective. Over the island they released flares which floated groundward, brilliantly illuminating the targets.

The enemy went into action with heavy anti-aircraft fire but had neither aircraft nor ships to aid his defense. The United States squadrons dropped 96 bombs which wrecked hangars, ammunitions, fuel and gasoline storages and a radio station, and considerably damaged an air field the Japanese were building. The second American plane was lost here, shot down by anti-aircraft fire.

The Navy communique reporting on the raids was issued simultaneously

(Continued on Page 9.)

Henry Ford Offers Lindbergh Job in Willow Run Plant

DETROIT, March 25 (AP)—If the War department approves, Charles A. Lindbergh, whose help Henry Ford once said he would like to have for mass production of airplanes, will go to work in Ford's new Willow Run bomber plant.

Harry Bennett, Ford personnel director, said tonight the famous trans-Atlantic flier had accepted Ford's invitation to devote his engineering abilities to Ford's vast armament program and only permission of the War department is needed to complete the arrangement.

"Lindbergh said that he wants very much to work here and will do so if it is all right with the War department," Bennett said.

What Lindbergh's precise duties might be in the big Willow Run plant were not disclosed. Some productive activity already is under way in the factory some 20 miles west of here. Ford sources have said that in full activity it would turn out at least one of great four-motored aerial battle ft an hour.

THE WEATHER

Lower Michigan: Showers and somewhat warmer Thursday and Thursday evening; fresh to moderately strong winds.

Upper Michigan: Rain and little change in temperature Thursday and Thursday evening; strong winds.

Temperature in Houghton yesterday—maximum, 39.8.. minimum, 33.5.

Light British Warships Rout Powerful Italian Battle Fleet Off Malta

(Editor's Note: One of the most sensational naval engagements of the war, the rout by light British warships of a strong Italian naval force in the Mediterranean and the torpedoing and firing of a 35,000-ton Italian battleship, is described in eye-witness detail in the following dispatch by Preston Grover, Associated Press war correspondent, who risked death to deliver his story.)

BY PRESTON GROVER

ALEXANDRIA, March 25 (AP)—We feinted and bluffed, dodged in and out of smoke screens, fired our guns—although it was sometimes like shooting peas at a barn—took time out for tea in the midst of battle, and got our convoy safely to Malta after a naval engagement in which valor triumphed over might as it seldom does, even in the most romantic of fiction.

After it was all over the captain of the cruiser which I was aboard added this statement to the brief report of the admiral:

"Our admiral has fought one of the most brilliant actions against greatly superior forces ever successfully brought off."

And so it was. As the battle began I never thought I would get out alive to tell of it.

CHARGE HEAD-ON

Our light squadron of British cruisers and destroyers sailed head-on into an overwhelmingly powerful Italian fleet in the central Mediterranean, three times drove it away from the convoy and ultimately delivered our supplies to the beleaguered little island of Malta.

It was a battle which will go down in naval annals, for not in the recollection of any officer present had such a prolonged fight been won by so small a force against such great odds.

I saw the battle with another American correspondent, Richard Mowrer of the Chicago Daily News. I was aboard one of the cruisers which charged straight into the enemy's teeth, cuffed him off, rained shells upon and around him and finally pulled the convoy to safety right out of what had appeared to be certain destruction, not only to the freighters but to the bulk of our thin-walled fighting vessels.

The battle occurred Sunday, beginning in the early afternoon and ending only after dark when the Italian fleet withdrew, puzzled, whipped and wounded.

In the Italian fleet were one battleship of the Littorio class with 15-inch guns, two eight-inch cruisers of the Trento class, four six-inch cruisers of the Condottieri class and a screen of destroyers.

Against them we had a six-inch cruiser and anti-aircraft cruisers whose heaviest guns were five-and-a-quarter-inch and 16 destroyers. There wasn't a single gun in the British

(Continued on Page 2.)

JAPS BOMB PORT MORESBY WEAKLY

Curtin Sees Turning Point in War on Australia.

MELBOURNE, Australia, March 25 (AP)—The Japanese bombed Port Moresby weakly and warily from the respectful altitude of 25,000 feet today, while Prime Minister Curtin told the Australian house of representatives that the turning point of the war might well be the general Allied recognition of Australia's high importance.

It was the 19th raid on Port Moresby, principal city of the island of New Guinea and obviously regarded by the Japanese as the key to any invasion of northern Australia.

BOMBS FALL INTO SEA

Only three bombers and four fighters participated. Most of their 16 bombs fell into the sea, an Australian communique said, crediting accurate anti-aircraft fire with keeping the Japanese too high for effective aim.

In his address to the house in Canberra, Prime Minister Curtin expressed confidence that Port Moresby not only would be held but would serve as a base from which to hit back at the outstretched Japanese.

Turning to the broader picture of war strategy, Curtin said that the Australian opinion on the importance of the southwest Pacific had been strengthened by the "calamitous trend of events" at Singapore and that Allied recognition of that view "may well indicate a turning point in the war provided it is followed by swift and resolute action."

AN ACTIVE PARTNER

In this connection, he said the Australian government had given authority of "the highest order" to the American general, Douglas MacArthur, and Australia "has now become a much more active partner in the operational direction of the war."

Found Guilty of Draft Violation

GRAND RAPIDS, Mich., March 25 (AP)—Douglas M. Galbreath, 24-year-old conscientious objector from Schoolcraft, today was convicted by Federal Judge Fred M. Raymond of violating the selective service act.

Galbreath, a member of a religious sect, was charged with failure to report to Camp Stronach, a detention area for conscientious objectors near Manistee. He will be sentenced Saturday.

During the trial the court ruled that evidence considered by a draft board in determining a registrant's classification is not admissible as evidence in a criminal acton brought against the registrant.

Nazi Planes Raid Southwest Englan

LONDON, Thursday, March 26 (AP) German raiders heading inland roa over the southeast English coast ea today in the face of a terrific anti-ai craft barrage.

Coastal observers said the grou fire was the fiercest in more than year, and the drone of planes conti ued for a long time indicating that t Germans were in considerabl strength..

Some bombs were d... in the coastal area, but no ... damage was reported.

JAPS HAMMER AT BATAAN DEFENDERS

Enemy Reinforcements Arrive But U. S. Hold Ground.

WASHINGTON, March 25 (AP)—The Japanese were believed today to be reinforcing their already numerically-superior forces on the island of Luzon preliminary to another drive to wipe out the American-Filipino resistance on the Bataan peninsula.

"Continued enemy ground activity in Bataan indicates the arrival of Japanese reinforcements," a war communique said, adding that Nippon fliers were also continuing hammering blows at defense positions.

Twenty-seven bombers accompanied by smaller craft, the War department said, blasted at harbor defenses on Manila Bay and "our front lines and rear installations in Bataan." There were no reports of the damage or that any of the attacking planes had been shot down.

The renewal of aggressive Japanese operations against the outposts held by General Jonathan M. Wainwright on Bataan and in Manila Bay called attention again to the importance of these positions in the war patterns of both sides.

Observers here point out that there are only two places of great strategic importance on the islands—Davao which the Japanese hold, and Manila Bay. Ironically, the Japanese have their most complete occupation of Luzon—the richest and most highly developed island of the entire archipelago—and yet Bataan and the tiny island fortresses of Mills (Corregidor), Drum, Frank and Hughes deny them control of the bay.

Report Increase in Sale of Auto Licenses in 1942

LANSING, March 25 (AP) — Gus T. Hartman, deputy secretary of state, said today more motor vehicles have been licenced in Michigan to date than on the corresponding date of last year, but that car and tire rationing probably would hold the full year's revenues below the 1941 totals.

A survey, complete as of March 17, showed 39,000 more vehicles were licensed up to that date of the license year, as compared with the total in the 1941 license year.

The figures: 1,034,954 full year 1942 licenses with revenue of $12,846,464; 1,017,822 full year 1941 licenses with revenues of $12,591,688; 524,252 1942 half year licenses with revenues of $3,863,450; 502,408 1941 half year licenses for $3,669,683.

In all of last year 1,877,967 vehicles were licensed, revenues totaling $23,936,573.

BIDDLE RAPS ARNOLD FOR LABOR STAND

Anti-Trust Chief's Comment Unfortunate at This Time, He Says.

OTHER REACTIONS

WASHINGTON, March 25 (AP)—Attorney General Biddle rapped the knuckles of Assistant Attorney General Thurman Arnold today for accusing organized labor of "injuring and destroying" independent business and of holding farmers and consumers "at its mercy."

In response to questions at a press conference he said he thought Arnold's "comment was pretty unfortunate at this time" and that it did not represent the views of the justice department.

Arnold, head of the anti-trust division, made his remarks last Saturday during a hearing before the House Judiciary committee.

OTHER REACTIONS

Biddle's reaction was one of several developments in Washington today bearing on the labor situation. Another was a charge by Senator Thomas (D-Utah), chairman of the Senate Labor committee, that the Chamber of Commerce of the United States had instituted a write-to-congress campaign which would disturb labor management-harmony.

Such a campaign, he said, would disrupt a voluntary agreement between employers and unions covering the forty-hour week. On March 20, he said, the chamber asked its local organizations to become "aggressive" in bringing opinion to bear upon congress.

Three members of a five-member panel recommended to the War Labor Board that it deny a union shop for 25,000 workers of the International Harvester company, but grant a 4½ cents an hour pay increase retroactive to Jan. 15. The dissenters were John Brophy of the CIO and Richard Gray of the AFL, who held the wage increase inadequate and said only a full union shop would satisfy the workers.

PROBE EXCESSIVE WAGES

Another development was a disclosure on capitol hill that some time ago two Oakland, Calif., wood caulkers claimed $160 each for eight hours work on a naval auxiliary.

Rear Admiral Ray Spear, chief of the Navy's bureau of supplies and accounts, told the story of the caulkers in recent testimony before the House naval committee.

They contended that union regulations fixed 150 feet of caulking on deck, or 100 feet on the hull, as an eight-hour day's work. But they had caulked 550 feet each outside the ship and 375 feet on deck.

On that basis they figured they had worked 64 hours each, and since the work was done on Saturday that they were entitled to double pay, or a total of $160 each. They were paid $50 each pending a ruling.

The union announced removal today of all limitations on the amount of work permitted to be done in one day.

General MacArthur Awarded Congressional Medal of Honor

WASHINGTON, March 25 (AP)—The award of the congressional medal of honor to General Douglas MacArthur for conspicuous gallantry and intrepidity in action against the invading Japanese forces in the Philippines was announced today by the War department.

In a radiogram to Major General ichard K. Sutherland, MacArthur's ief of staff, President Roosevelt dicted Nelson I. Johnson, United ates minister to Australia, to present e medal in his name to MacArthur.

The citation awarding the medal, the hest decoration for valor which the my can bestow on a soldier, said:

"General Douglas MacArthur, commanding general, United States army forces in the Far East. For conspicuous leadership in preparing the Philippine islands to resist conquest, for gallantry and intrepidity above and beyond the call of duty in action against invading Japanese forces, and for the heroic conduct of defensive and offensive operations on the Bataan peninsula. He mobilized, trained and led an army which has received world acclaim for its gallant defense against a tremendous superiority of enemy forces in men and arms.

"His utter disregard of personal danger under heavy fire and aerial bombardment, his calm judgment in each crisis, inspired his troops, galvanized the spirit of resistance of Filipino people, and confirmed the faith of the American people in their armed forces."

RUNS RAILROAD FOR U. S.

J. W. Barriger (right), federal manager of the vital 239 mile Toledo, Peoria and Western railroad, and George Voelkner, an assistant, arrive in Peoria to supervise government operation of the property which was ordered seized by President Roosevelt. (NEA Telephoto.)

Arms Production Effort Speeds Up Employment

BY DAVID J. WILKIE
(Wide World Automotive Editor)

DETROIT, March 25 — The things that make for mass production in the automobile industry are being coordinated to the war implement output effort more rapidly than even the most optimistic of the former car manufacturers anticipated when they began converting their plants and equipment.

This means, say sources closest to the company heads, that by June 1 something like half a million men who last year made automobiles will be producing vital war weapons. Previous estimates had placed this point of progress around the middle or end of July.

ONLY HALF WAY POINT

So far as employment is concerned that will be only the half way point in the motorcar industry's 1942 war effort, for fully double the highest number previously employed in car manufacture are expected to be needed by the year-end.

The accelerated production, of course, has cut sharply into the unemployment total throughout the industry. Early predictions were that the cessation of passenger car production and subsequent plant conversion would mean idleness for something like 300,000 persons. Authoritative sources assert the aggregate at no time exceeded 225,000 and that this number has dwindled much more rapidly than had been expected.

By way of explanation the company heads point to the progress that was made in re-tooling for war production throughout last year while civilian output still was under way and to the enormous orders that were placed with the industry immediately following Pear Harbor.

WORK LONG SHIFTS

Many companies of course have had workers in certain departments on a 10-hour seven-day basis rather than on three shifts. This has been necessary to dispose of the great volume of preliminary machine work essential to mass production.

As a regular routine, however, the 10-hour day has not been satisfactory from the management standpoint. Company executives assert the longer work week with its overtime for Saturday and Sunday developed a growing percentage of absenteeism, with a consequent dislocation of work schedules.

Generally the company heads believe the unemployment situation created by the switch to 100 per cent war weapon production has been little more serious than that normally occasioned by the change-over from one model automobile to another.

At the same time it is the second lay-off within approximately six months for many of the workers, several weeks of idleness having developed in connection with the switch last August from 1941 to 1942 model passenger cars.

SYNTHETIC RUBBER PATENTS RELEASED

All Formulas Thrown Open to American Industry.

WASHINGTON, March 25 (AP) — A vast store of patents—complete with the "know-how" for using them—was thrown open to American industry today through the settlement of a Justice department complaint that Standard Oil company (New Jersey) combined illegally with the German dye trust to restrain trade the world over.

Of prime interest among the thousands of patents released for free licensing until the end of the war were those concerned with both German and American-developed methods for producing synthetic rubber and gasoline. Numerous other important chemical processes are involved, however.

OFFICIALS PAY FINES

The day's action included the filing of a criminal information alleging violation of the Sherman anti-trust law, a plea of nolo contendere by the defendants, a civil complaint identical with the information, and a consent decree agreeing to terminate the practices complained of and freeing the patents.

Standard Oil, six subsidiaries and three top officials were fined a total of $50,000 in the federal district court at Newark, N.J., where the filings took place.

I. G. Farbenindustrie Aktiengesellschaft, the German dye trust, was named a co-conspirator but not a defendant. The alleged conspiracy involved the companies known as the world's largest selers of chemicals and of petroleum products. I. G. is Germany's largest corporation while Standard is this country's largest industrial company.

PATENTS RELEASED

Standard issued a statement that it had agreed to the consent decree and nolo contendere pleas because "to obtain vindication by trying the issues in the courts would involve months of time and energy of most of its officers and many of its employes."

The consent decree calls for making available without royalty all patents relating to synthetic rubber and gasoline and all I. G. patents controlled by Standard along with the knowledge and experience needed to use the patents. A charge covering the cost may be made for this knowledge.

LOCK BILL APPROVED

WASHINGTON, March 25 (AP)—The Senate approved without debate today a $9,300,000 appropriation for construction of a lock and auxiliary works at Sault Ste. Marie on St. Mary's river. The appropriation was contained in the bill for civil functions of the War department, which now goes back to the House, which previously had approved a smaller total for all functions.

Hitler, King Boris Hold Conversation

BERN, Switzerland, March 25 (AP)—Adolf Hitler and King Boris of Bulgaria were reported tonight to have had a long talk somewhere on the eastern front regarding Bulgaria's future role in Axis plans.

At the same time growing friction between Rumania and Hungary lent support to the belief that Hitler again was playing his Balkan junior partners against each other in an effort to gain more armed support for his spring campaign in Russia.

What Hitler asked of King Boris naturally was not revealed, but the Berlin correspondent of the Zurich newspaper Die Tat sent a long dispatch entitled "Germany, Bulgaria, and Turkey," indicating that the latter neutral country was the main conversational pivot.

The only possible hint of German intentions given in Die Tat's analysis of the Hitler-Boris conversations was that "Berlin circles" said Turkey was being menaced by Russia.

TYPEWRITERS RELEASED

WASHINGTON, March 25 (AP) — More than 100,000 new typewriters, chiefly portables, will be released for rationing April 13, Acting Price Administrator John E. Hamm announced today.

ENEMY TAKES ISLANDS IN BENGAL BAY

Nipponese Forces Outflank Chinese-British Army in Central Burma.

PINCERS ON INDIA

BY WILLIAM SMITH WHITE
(Associated Press War Editor)

The Allied position in the far western Paciifc theatre was sharply worsened last (Wednesday) night, the Japanese having got in position to menace eastern India and the Allied sea routes by occupying the principal Andaman islands in the Bay of Bengal while their land forces were creeping up toward the central Burma oil fields.

This, it appeared more and more likely, was to be the next arena of major decision, for the Australian front was quiet save for ineffectual enemy bombing of Port Moresby on New Guinea above the mainland.

A significant feature of both raids—which had a fear repercussion that caused Tokyo to black out for several nights—was the fact that few enemy planes or ships were found in the areas.

The fall of the Andamans on India's flank was not unexpected, since they had been untenable since the loss of extreme southern Burma and were not and could not be effectively defended, but it raised some unpleasant spectres.

The islands lie only 800 miles northeast of the British naval base on Ceylon island, which is just off the southern Indian mainland, and would provide points of attack on both Madras and Calcutta, the latter a prospectively vital port of entry for supplies to China.

NEW DELHI, India 25 (AP)—Japan reached out for India by sea tonight, occupying the Andaman islands in the Bay of Bengal, barely 500 miles off the United Nations' Ceylon-to-Calcutta supply route, and struck by land toward the riches of central Burma in heavy fighting which partly outflanked the British-Chinese positions at Toungoo.

The government of India disclosed the seizure of the Andaman group, first actual Indian territory to go to the enemy, in a communique which said the blow was struck two days ago, March 23, and was not opposed. The small British-Indian defense forces had been withdrawn "some days previously."

POPULATION REMOVED

Much of the population and some of the convicts in the penal settlement on the islands also were removed, the communique said.

The position of the Andamans had been defenseless since the Japanese occupied Malaya, Rangoon and the lower Burmese delta. At their nearest point, the 204 islands lie about 120 miles from the Burmese mainland, Cape Negrais.

Their real significance, however, lies in the fact that they afford excellent anchorages—Port Blair and others—and air bases for combined sea and air attacks on Calcutta, Ceylon and the vital ship lanes in between.

The Andamans are but 590 miles from the mouth of the Hugli, most important of the mouths of the Ganges and not much farther from Calcutta itself.

PINCERS ON INDIA

Accounts of the occupation, which the Japanese had yet to announce, gave no details as to the size of the occupying force, but there was, apparently, little or nothing to halt its expansion.

Actually it was part of a giant sea-land pincers on India, at a time when Britain is feverishly endeavoring to organize its military defense and to soothe its troubled politics through the mission of Sir Stafford Cripps.

The invaders' land arm of the scissors was closing slowly today on the eastern road to Mandalay.

Air action was heavy in the Burmese theater, with mounting losses on both sides. Japanese bombers with fighter escorts made heavy attacks on the remaining RAF airdromes, one coastal landing ground having been bombed yesterday.

Bill Designed to Help Small Plants

WASHINGTON, March 25 (AP)—The Senate banking committee today approved legislation designed to help thousands of small plants and industries share in war production and authorized a $100,000,000 fund for the program.

The final draft of the much-amended measure calls for creation of a "smaller war plants corporation" and represents one of the few legislative defeats that Secretary of Commerce Jones has suffered at hands of a congressional committee.

Members of the Senate banking committee and the special Senate committee on small business said that Jones sought to control the new agency but that the banking committee rejected his proposed amendments.

Russ Open New Nazi Front

CHARACTER · QUALITY · AMERICA FIRST! · ENTERPRISE · ACCURACY
Los Angeles Examiner
AN AMERICAN PAPER FOR THE AMERICAN PEOPLE · THE GREAT NEWSPAPER OF THE GREAT SOUTHWEST
Reg. U.S. Pat. Off.
Examiner Telephone Richmond 1212 · Examiner Building, 1111 S. Broadway

WAR EXTRA

VOL. XXXIX—NO. 107 · LOS ANGELES, SATURDAY, MARCH 28, 1942 · P · Two Sections—Part I—FIVE CENTS

WAVES OF PLANES RAID CORREGIDOR

RUSS TROOPS LANDED ON ARCTIC COAST

Force Disembarks Behind Nazis With Air, Fleet Aid to Clear Murmansk Seaway

MOSCOW, March 27.—(AP)—A Russian seaborne force has landed behind the German lines on the Murmansk coast under the protecting guns of the Red fleet in a surprise Arctic offensive to clear the Allied northern supply lanes and menace the Nazi-Finnish northern flank, it was announced tonight.

The Red air force was in cooperative action with the sea and land troops—this, it is apparent, was the significance of the great German-Russian air battle over Murmansk earlier in the week, in which the Russians shot down 11 out of 66 Nazi planes.

Meager accounts of the action, broadcast by the Moscow radio, said the Russian landings—(presumably on the Rybachi Peninsula northwest of Murmansk)—caused vast confusion among the German troops who have holed up there all winter.

NAZI TRANSPORTS SUNK

The radio itself said the Nazis were trying to meet the new offensive with heavy air attacks.

Small Soviet submarines, operating in adjacent waters, were reported to have sunk at least 10 German transports in operations connected with the Russian troop move.

The action was described as "a purely Russian operation."

The landing had deep implica-

(Continued on Page 5, Cols. 1-2)

Doctor Jailed in Hollywood Attack Case

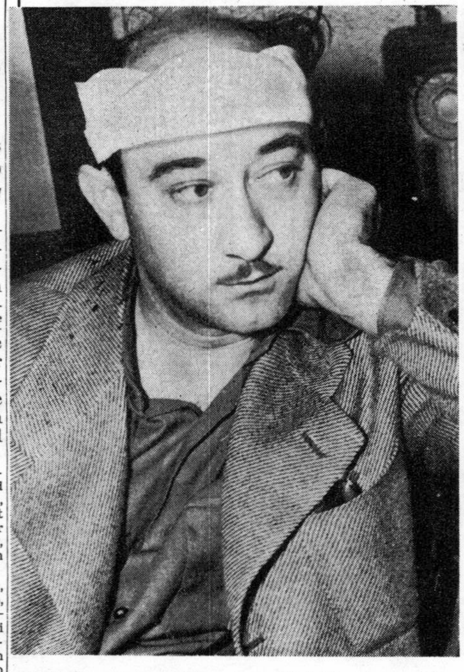

IN JAIL yesterday while police sifted the charges of a woman patient was Dr. William H. Kanner (above), who was beaten severely by the woman's enraged husband.
—Los Angeles Examiner photo.

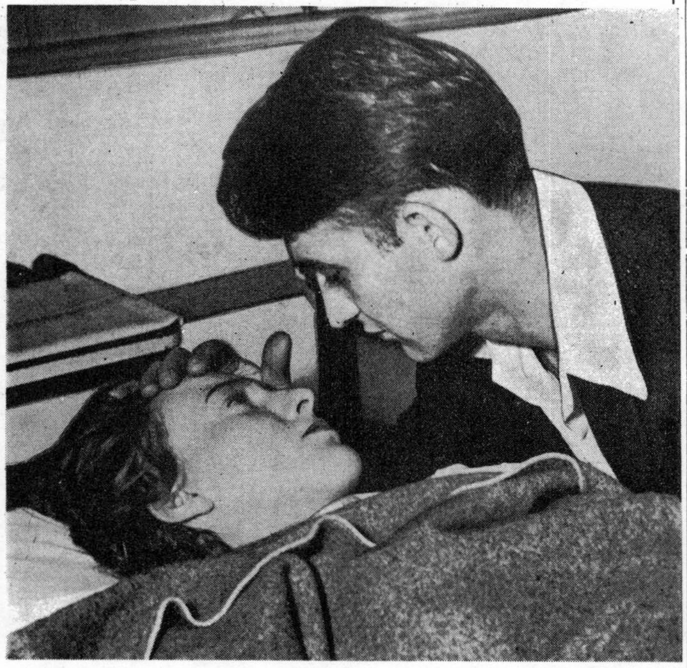

PICTURED IN hospital yesterday as she was comforted by her husband, Delmar, Mrs. Louise Marshall told police she had been attacked by a studio official at a Hollywood party, and that she became a patient of Dr. W. Kanner. (Story Page 3.)
—Los Angeles Examiner photo.

ARMY PILOTS IN SUB PATROL PUT UNDER NAVY

By Edward E. Bomar

WASHINGTON, March 27.—(AP)—The command of Army planes hunting U-boats off the Atlantic and Pacific Coasts was turned over to the Navy by an order announced today as a new move to increase the effectiveness of the war on submarines.

The order, issued Wednesday by General George C. Marshall, Army chief of staff, and Admiral Ernest J. King, Fleet commander in chief, was disclosed by the War and Navy Departments, which asserted in identical communiques that cooperation already was "close and effective" in other respects.

The Army air units were made subject to orders of naval commanders of the "sea frontiers" to end any uncertainty over control of the weapons used in the anti-submarine campaign.

The Atlantic "sea frontier," extending from the Canadian border to the Caribbean, is commanded by Rear Admiral Adolphus Andrews, who was relieved of shore administrative duties 10 days ago to devote his full attention to the anti-submarine war.

The newest action toward unity of command closely followed a

(Continued on Page 2, Cols. 4-5)

Jap Raid Starts at Dawn, Ends at Midnight

WASHINGTON, March 27.—(AP)—The straight shooting of American and Philippine anti-aircraft gunners, who already have downed at least seven enemy bombers this week, appeared today to have frustrated a dawn-to-midnight assault on Corregidor by successive waves of Japanese planes.

A report to the War Department from Lieutenant General Jonathan M. Wainwright, commanding in the Philippines, indicated that the defenders' fire kept the enemy aircraft high enough to destroy the accuracy of their attack. Most of the bombs fell in Manila Bay, said a department communique, and those which struck the fortified island caused little damage.

TREMENDOUS HEIGHT

Since the defending forces are without air strength which could intercept the formations of enemy bombers, only anti-aircraft guns can counter the attacks. Japanese bombing on other fronts in the Pacific has shown a high degree of accuracy, and observers said the guns of Corregidor must have kept the enemy at a tremendous height to have interfered with their aim at an island four miles long. Captain Colin Kelly sank the battleship Haruna with a direct hit from an altitude of more than 20,000 feet.

Several of the attacking planes were believed to have been hit, but verification was impossible.

Early Thursday the Japs began the attack, heaviest since they resumed aerial bombardment of the fortificatitons last Tuesday, and kept hammering at Corregidor with seven successive waves of bombers.

Except for a short lull at sunset, the assault was maintained until midnight, although decreasing in intensity in the late afternoon and night, and it was resumed early today.

While this attack was in progress, sharp fighting between patrols also occurred along the front lines in Bataan, and one American-Filipino patrol carried out a successful raid on a strong enemy position.

Japanese dive bombers engaged in unsuccessful operations against the rear of Wainwright's lines, and he reported that movements of troops and trucks behind the enemy's lines led him to expect an increase in the Japanese pressure in Bataan.

The War Department said President Manuel Quezon had transferred the government of the Philippine commonwealth to Australia in order to continue the close cooperation with General Douglas MacArthur which

(Continued on Page 2, Cols. 1-2)

Meet Gen. Wainwright in Sunday's Examiner

4 PAGES OF PHOTOS OF HEROIC DEFENDERS OF BATAAN IN PICTORIAL REVIEW

S.P. Main Line Sabotaged

WAR EXTRA

Los Angeles Examiner

CHARACTER · QUALITY · AMERICA FIRST! · ENTERPRISE · ACCURACY

AN AMERICAN PAPER FOR THE AMERICAN PEOPLE · THE GREAT NEWSPAPER OF THE GREAT SOUTHWEST

Reg. U.S. Pat. Off.
Examiner Telephone RIchmond 1212 · Examiner Building, 1111 S. Broadway

VOL. XXXIX—NO. 109 · LOS ANGELES, MONDAY, MARCH 30, 1942 · P · Two Sections—Part I—FIVE CENTS

BATAAN DRIVE HALTED, JAP BOATS BLASTED!

Sees Mother Slain

MRS. ANNA FERGUSON, who was killed yesterday, allegedly by her estranged mate, Frederick Ferguson, shown with her daughter by another marriage, Colleen DeGroat. The child was not harmed. (Story on Page 3).

CRIPPS TELLS OF DOMINION PLAN FOR INDIA

Britain Ready to Grant Same Terms as Other Lands of Empire When War Ends

NEW DELHI, India, March 29.—(AP)—Sir Stafford Cripps announced today that the British war cabinet's plan of freedom for invasion-threatened India proposes creation after the war of a new Indian union which would be a dominion within the British Empire but which would have the power to secede.

During the interim Britain would continue to direct and control defense of the vast empire and its 390,000,000 people, now in bombing range from Japanese planes in Burma and the Andaman Islands, but Sir Stafford declared that Britain looked to the Indian people to fully mobilize their man power and war resources under the impetus of their dawning independence.

CONCESSION TO MOSLEMS

Turning to the troublesome problem of India's many discordant minorities, Sir Stafford said states or provinces which did not accede to the new constitution could agree upon a separate constitution which Britain

(Continued on Page 10, Col. 4)

Japanese Must Report to Army Command Today

Attention, Japanese!

Two thousand members of the families of Japanese volunteers who already have gone to Manzanar are scheduled to leave Wednesday or Thursday for the Army reception camp in the Owens River Valley.

A responsible member of each adult family group affected MUST report before 5 p. m. today at the Western Defense Command Civil Control Station, 707 South Spring street, to be informed of arrangements for their removal.

This is an official order issued by Colonel Karl R. Bendetsen, assistant chief of staff for civil affairs, Western Defense Command.

Busby Berkeley, Claire James Wed

ACTRESS CLAIRE JAMES yesterday became the bride of Director Busby Berkeley. They met in Phoenix, flew to Las Vegas for the ceremony and then returned to Los Angeles. They had been engaged for some time.

By Louella O. Parsons
Motion Picture Editor International News Service

Spring and Cupid worked overtime yesterday in Las Vegas, where Claire James became the bride of the well-known director, Busby Berkeley, and Linda Brent married Stephen Cornell, young actor.

The ceremonies, of course, were separate, and at the time Judge Mahlon Brown united Berkeley and his bride, Mr. and

(Continued on Page 3, Column 3)

TWO BRIDGES SOAKED WITH OIL, BURNED

Traffic Blocked on Vital Artery in Imperial Valley; Signal Saves Crack Train

Saboteurs set fire to two Southern Pacific main line bridges in Imperial Valley early yesterday, halting passenger and freight traffic on one of the nation's principal western defense transportation arteries.

The trestles, each 100 feet long

(Continued on Page 4, Column 8)

Yanks Hurl Enemy Back; Shell Ships

WASHINGTON, March 29.—(AP)—American-Filipino forces have hurled back a new Japanese attack on the Bataan Peninsula front with "heavy losses" to the enemy, the War Department reported today, while artillery fire from the island fortress smashed a concentration of small, hostile boats off Patungan Beach.

Heavy bombing attacks on Corregidor and the Bataan rear positions accompanied what the department said was a "heavy" attack on the right center of the American-Filipino line. Military observers here tonight thought the apparently synchronized activities of the enemy might be the forerunner of a long-expected offensive.

A war communique said American-Filipino land casualties were "relatively light" and the bombing damage slight.

The small boats, presumably an invasion fleet, had been assembled by the enemy almost opposite Carabao Island, site of Fort Frank, farthest outlying American fortification, and about 10 miles due south of Corregidor. A similar concentration of barges and small boats was hammered to pieces several weeks ago by the big guns of the fortresses.

FIFTH DAY OF BOMBING

The Corregidor attack marked the fifth successive day that Japanese airmen have bombed this rocky island fortress, but antiaircraft fire from Fort Mills, the War Department said, kept the planes at "extremely high altitudes and as a result the bombing was inaccurate."

To date, eight Japanese bombers have been bagged by Fort Mills' gunners.

The communique, number 167, based on reports received until 1 p. m. Eastern War Time, said:

"1. Philippine theater:

"The enemy launched a heavy attack on the right center of our line in Bataan late

Mighty MacArthur! See Page 2

"Mighty MacArthur, Pride of the U. S. Army"!

That is the title of the new adventure strip which starts in today's Examiner.

The life story of brave General Douglas MacArthur is told in pictures filled with the dramatic action that has characterized the hero's career.

Born on an Army post in the Indian-fighting country . . . top man at West Point . . . valiant junior officer in the Philippines . . . brilliant commander with the A. E. F. . . . chief of staff of the Army . . . stumbling block for the Japanese hordes at Bataan. . . .

Those are but a few of the highlights in the life of the mighty MacArthur . . . as it is depicted from inspiring fact in the exciting historical panel which begins in the Examiner today, and will appear daily except Sunday.

Tel: No. 2955 — Editor:—Dr. Tarachand J. Lalvani. — Reg. No. S. 739

Karachi Daily Voices THE NEW SPIRIT IN SIND Without Fe r or Favour.

THE KARACHI DAILY

The People's Paper: Nett Sales Exceed That Of Any Other English Daily In

Rates Of Subscription.

Months	Local	Mofussil
1	0-14-0	1-4-0
3	2-8-0	3-12-0
6	4-12-0	7-0-0
12	9-4-0	13-12-0

VOL. 6 No. 1753 | KARACHI, SATURDAY, APRIL 4 1942 | HALF ANNA

The First Attack From India

American Flying Fortresses Go Into Action

Enemy Shipping Attacked At Port Blair

—:oOo:—

NEW DELHI, Saturday.

THE United States Air Forces stationed in India have now gone into action against the enemy.

A Communique issued by the Headquarters of the United States Air Forces in India states that American Flying Fortresses of the U. S Air Force made their first attack from India on April 2.

Intense Anti-Aircraft Fire

Led by Major General Lew Brereton, a squadron of heavy bombers attacked the enemy shipping at Port Blair setting fire to one Japanese cruiser and one troopship and probably damaging two other ships.

Enemy pursuit was encountered and also intense anti-aircraft fire, but no damage was sustained. All our planes returned safely.—U P.

Kasturbha Having High Fever

Gandhiji Wanted In Wardha

NEW DELHI, Saturday.

IT is understood Gandhiji will leave for Wardha this evening. It is gathered that Mrs. Kasturbha Gandhi is having high fever and Gandhiji is wanted in Wardha—U.P.

Sir Bhutto's Term Extended

Karachi Daily Staff Reporter

KARACHI, Sat.

THE latest Sind Government Gazette announces that the Governor of Bombay is pleased, with the previous concurrence of the Governor of Sind, to extend the tenure of office of Sir Shah Nawaz Khan Ghulam Murtaza Khan Bhutto, Kt., C.I.E., O.B.E., Member of the Public Service Commission for the Provinces of Bombay and Sind, for a further period of five years from the 31st day of March 1942.

Azad-Pandit-Wavell Meeting At Six

NEW DELHI, Saturday.

THE Meeting of Maulana Azad and Pandit Jawaharlal Nehru with General Wavell and Sir Stafford Cripps will take place this evening at 6 p.m.—U.P.

NEW DELHI, Saturday.

THE Hindu Mahasabha has fixed the 10th May as the All-India Anti-Pakistan Day.—

PAKISTAN----"MISCALLED SELF-DETERMINATION"

—:oOo:—

Important Resolution Of Hindu Mahasabha

—:oOo:—

NEW DELHI, Saturday.

THE Working Committee of the All-India Hindu Mahasabha, which met last evening, adopted a resolution expressing the view that if the scheme of Sir Stafford Cripps involving Pakistan, "miscalled self-determination", was allowed to stand it would confirm the original view of the Hindu Mahasabha that Britain was fighting the war not for liberty or democracy but for self-aggrandisement only.

Warning To British Government:

By the resolution, the Hindu Mahasabha warns the British Government that the effect of these proposals cannot but affect the war effort adversely inasmuch as they are bound to create an apprehension in the minds of Hindus that even a British victory would be followed by nothing but vivisection of their motherland. The Mahasabha declares its irrevocable determination to resist the scheme at all costs and with all possible means.

The Hindu Mahasabha also declares that if any party directly or indirectly encourages in implementing the scheme, it would be regarded as enemy of the country by all those who stand for unity and integrity of Hindustan.

Sons Of Bharatmata

The Mahasabha calls upon all the sons of the Bharatmata to present a united national front against vivisection of India.

The Working Committee of the Hindu Mahasabha has congratulated all those parties, particularly the Sikh Party, who have taken a courageous stand in opposing uncompromisingly "this most dangerous scheme". It has resolved that an All-Party Anti-Pakistan Conference be held in Amritsar under the joint auspices of the Hindu Mahasabha and Akali Dals, as agreed between the leaders of the two organisations.

The Committee unanimously ratified the memorandum submitted to Sir Stafford Cripps in reply to his proposals.—U.P.

Development Of Delhi University

Karachi Daily Correspondent

NEW DELHI, Saturday.

PROPOSALS relating to the development of the Delhi University and the Central Advisory Board of Education, educational concessions to the children of soldiers who take part in the present war, and the provision of certain hot weather amenities for offices and residences in New Delhi, were approved by the Standing Finance Committee at its meeting held in New Delhi on March 31, 1942.

Jinnah-Wavell Meeting Next Week

NEW DELHI, Saturday.

IT is understood that a meeting has been arranged between Mr. M. A. Jinnah, President, All-India Muslim League, and General Sir Archibald Wavell, Commander-in-Chief of India early next week.

Men Of Wardha

—oOo—

(Karachi Daily Correspondent)

LAHORE, Saturday.

"GANDHI in the shoes of Petain"; "Men of Wardha act like Men of Vichy".

THESE banner headlines are inscribed on big posters displayed all over the city of Lahore by the Punjab Radical Democratic Party.

THEY accuse Mr. Gandhi of being in league with the Fascist forces by denouncing the "scorched earth" policy in the columns of "Harijan". Mr. Gandhi, it is alleged, is thus sapping the manhood of Indians and fostering among them a spirit of defeatism.

"CAN any progressive and self-respecting nation brook the spiritual alliance of its leader with devilish Fascism"? it is asked. The posters end with slogans: "Down with Nazi Germany and her aggressive allies; Down with Fascist India; Long live Free India."

Muslim Wadero's Regard For Hindus

(Karachi Daily Correspondent)

NAWABSHAH, Friday.

THAT there is plenty of ground for believing that, given opportunity, sincere workers can bring about Hindu-Muslim unity in Sind in no time, is evidenced by the fact that there undoubtedly exist among the majority as well as the minority community many persons who have more than enough regard for the safety of life and property of either community and instances have not been wanting to prove it.

The latest instance in that regard comes from village Gahi Mahesar wherein Wadero Sher Mohmed of that village on being informed of two Hindus, Karmoomal and Aratmal, having been waylaid and robbed by a party of 3 persons of their horses and other property while procceeding from Mehar to Kazi Araf, forthwith gathered a few men and hastened in pursuit of the culprits whom he succeeded in overtaking in a jungle near Syed jo-Goth where the culprits were finally secured along with the property and handed over to the police who also soon arrived there.

Sitka Sentinel

THE GEM OF THE PACIFIC --- SITKA ON BEAUTIFUL BARANOF ISLAND

10c A Copy

...E III Member of Associated Press SITKA, ALASKA TERRITORY FRIDAY, APRIL 10, 1942 NUMBER 18

BATAAN CAPTURED

CORREGIDOR STILL HOLDING

Flag Still Flies Over Beleaguered Fortress

Washington — April 10 (AP) General Wainwright reported to the President from Corregidor that "Our flag on the beleaguered island fortress still flies." Shortly before, however, the War Depart ment reported the fighting on the Bataan Peninsula had apparently ceased.

President Roosevelt, talking at a press conference, said, "Of course we all feel badly about Bataan."

There was no further news on this, he said, except that he had received what he called a grand message from General Wainwright in answer to one he had dispatch ed to the General.

Neither message was released in full and Roosevelt read only a single sentence of Wainwright's communication, "The flag is still flying over Corregidor."

The communique said General

(continued on back page)

Take Offensive In South Pacific

Melbourne — The United States and Australia have taken the of fensive in the air but have as yet been unable to lay the ground work for a total counter drive, it was stressed officially, while the Japanese consolidated further gains in their arc of bases facing this continent.

In actual warfare, 7 Jap bomb ers with fighter escorts raided the stragetic New Guiena harbor of Port Moresby for the 25 time.

The enemy was believed to have lost at least one bomber. First reports of the 20 minute raid mentioned no damage or casual ties.

The attackers once more en countered Allied interceptor planes and the defending airmen pitched the resistance note struck by Lieut. General Brett, Air Chief deputy Commander under General MacArthur in the South Pacific, who said, "We've taken the of fensive against the Japanese in the air and will continue to in crease it."

New City Officials In Monday Night

Monday evening the City Coun cil will meet at the Public Utili ties office for the last meeting of the retiring council. They will clear unfinished business from the table and then U. S. Commission er W. W. Knight will swear in the new members.

Those who will take office are William Hanlon as mayor; Will iam Beach, John Hollywood, Har ry Hagen and John Loidhamer as councilmen; Theodore Kettleson and Harold E. Schaeffer as mem bers of the Public Utilities Board and Mrs. C. G. Stuart as member of the School Board.

J. J. Conway is the retiring mayor; A. B. Holt and Charles Wortman leave the council; Neill Anderson from the Utilities Board and John Hollywood from the School Board.

The new mayor and council are expected to make their per manent appointments at the re gular meeting of the Council on Tuesday evening.

A. G. Shoup, 61, Ex-Mayor Dies

San Jose, Calif. — Arthur G. Shoup, 61, once Deputy Marshal and United States Attorney for Alaska and once Mayor of Sitka, died after a lengthy illness.

He came here from Alaska to practice law in 1926 and was Uni ted States Commissioner until re recently.

Shoup was Marshall from 1902 until 1910; was admitted to the bar in 1913; was a member of the Legislature from 1913 to 19-15; in Sitka was Mayor for three terms and then became United States Attorney in 1921.

He leaves a widow and three children.

So Much With So Little; MacArthur Lauds Bataan

Melbourne — General Douglas MacArthur said of the defenders of Bataan, "No Army ever will do so much with so little.

"The Bataan force went out as it would have wished, fighting to the end of it's flickering, forlorn hope.

"Nothing became it more than the last hour of trial and agony.

"To the weeping mothers of it's dead, I can only say the sacrifice and halo of Jesus of Nazareth de cended upon their sons. He had taken them unto Himself."

Jap Cruiser Sunk By Torpedo Boat

Washington — The War De partment reported an American torpedo boat sank a Jap cruiser off Cebu, in the central Philip pines.

The cruiser reported sunk was one of a fleet of five warships and ten transports, the War De partment said, which apparently comprised the invaders fleet land ing troops at Cebu.

Blackout Rules

PARTIAL BLACKOUT — 6:00 P. M. to 3:30 A. M.

No unnecessary lights (i.e. porch lights, etc.) should be showing at any time. Blinds should be drawn wherever the lights are in use. Homes and business houses must not be left with unattended lights.

COMPLETE BLACKOUT — 3:30 A. M. to 6:00 A. M.

Absolutely no lights must be showing during this period.

AIRRAID ALARM or BLACKOUT SIGNAL

Continuous Blast of ALL Sirens and Cold Storage Whistle

ALL CLEAR SIGNAL — 1 Short Blast of the Above

Violators Will Be Prosecuted

Physically Exhausted Heroes Capitulate

Washington, April 9 (AP) — Overwhelming Japanese forces in the Philippines, the War Depart ment communique said today, made advances which indicated the probability that the "defense of Bataan was overcome" despite the heroic counter attack attempt of the physically exhausted de fenders.

Informed quarters here ex pressed the growing belief that the stubborn resistance of the American and Filipino troops, who have held part of the penin sula since early in January again st all Japanese attacks, had vir tually ceased.

Army men expressed doubt that any number of surviving troops could be evacuated under fire across the two miles of open water between the southern tip of the peninsula and the island

(continued on back page)

Restrict Building In Federal Order

Washington — The War Pro duction Board prohibited the new contruction of nonessential resi dences, roads and commercial buildings and also indicated that these projects now under way might be prohibited if the mater ials being used were needed in the war program.

The order, effective April 9th, specifically bans any residential construction of $500.00 or more other than maintenance and re pairs, without government permis sion.

It also bars agriculture constru ction, such as barns, etc., if the cost is over $1,000; other types are limited to $5,000.

This applies to both private & public construction, with exemp tions which include army and government jobs, the replacement of recent fire or similar losses & houses under $6,000 which come under the recent order regarding the specified critical defense areas such as Seattle.

Women May Be Registered Next

Washington — President Roose velt disclosed that in connection with the studies of the mobiliza tion of man power for war indus tries, the Government was con sidering the voluntary registration of all women from 18 to 65.

Probably within a week, the President asserted some decision would be reached as to how to go about channeling the man power into war jobs.

One difficulty in registering women, he asserted at a press con ference, was inherent in the num ber of persons who would come forward to enroll.

This would create mechanical difficulties, he said, remarking that the preparation of cards alone was a tremendous job.

Enemy Active In Indian Oecan

London — Britian's first air craft carrier, the 23 year old "Hermes" was sunk in Japan's unabated effort to beat down the sea and air shield against the in vasion of India; but the enemy's total claims of victory are too extravagant, the British Admir alty said in a communique.

Japanese planes, either bomb ers or torpedo craft, sank the ten thousand ton "Hermes" about 10 miles off Ceylon, the pivot of British strength in the tip of India, to the western side of the broad Bay of Bengal.

The Japanese claimed even greater successes. A Japanese naval communique said that be sides the "Hermes", a 9,100 ton cruiser of the Birmingham class and a 7,500 ton cruiser of the Emerald class were sunk yester day off the Trincomalee Naval Station in Ceylon.

The London Admiralty counter ed saying "the Japanese claim to have sunk these cruisers off Trincomalee is known to be quite untrue."

The Weather
Warmer, but remaining cool near lake; moderate winds. Details on page 12.

THE CHICAGO SUN

FINAL

VOL. 1—No. 136 COPYRIGHT, 1942, BY THE CHICAGO SUN TRADE MARK REGISTERED. Tel. ANDover 4800 SATURDAY, APRIL 18, 1942 30 Pages TWO CENTS IN CHICAGO AND SUBURBS ELSEWHERE THREE CENTS

TOKYO IS BOMBED, REPORTS JAP RADIO

Prices Soar; Henderson Under Fire

C. I. O. Blames OPA Chief as Fight on Inflation Bogs Down

By Cecil B. Dickson.
Washington Bureau of The Chicago Sun.

Washington, April 17. — Anti-inflation machinery of the government has bogged down.

Prices are still soaring despite administration efforts to keep them under control.

Drastic measures, including over-all wage and price ceilings, have been proposed to President Roosevelt.

Decision on what steps to take has been delayed because of differences of opinion among the Chief Executive's advisers and the influence of powerful labor and farm groups.

Cabinet Weighs Problem.

President Roosevelt and his war labor cabinet discussed the problem yesterday, but there was no agreement.

President Philip Murray of the C. I. O., a member of the labor cabinet, in blaming the government for the situation today, demanded that wage freezing be ruled out. He warned that it was unnecessary and "profoundly dangerous."

Declaring that the cost of living had increased 12 per cent in the last 12 months, Murray submitted a four-point program to bolster the government's machinery.

Fair Prices Sought.

It provides for:

1. An immediate and vigorous determination and enforcement of fair retail prices for food, clothing and rent.
2. Immediate rationing to divide available consumer goods fairly and to control expenditures for necessary consumer goods.
3. Progressive taxation to absorb all unreasonable war profits; no general sales tax or payroll withholding levy.
4. Stabilization of wages by the present machinery for collective bargaining and the War Labor Board.

"Labor is unalterably opposed to wage freezing," Murray said.

Henderson Urges Freezing.

Henderson has urged the President to freeze wages and set price ceilings.

The Federal Reserve Board

See FIGHT ON on Page 4.

The House ways and means committee concluded hearings Friday on the new tax bill and prepared to draft a measure to provide not much more than the $7,600,000,000 Treasury figures. Details on Page 25.

WHERE IT IS

RAF Bombs Strike Near Hitler Villa

Map on Page 4.

London, Saturday, April 18.—(UP)—Heavy British bombers flew deep into Germany yesterday to bomb an important arms factory at Augsburg in Bavaria, not far from Hitler's mountain retreat at Berchtesgaden, it reliably reported early today.

[Augsburg is an important arms center. The main Messerschmitt airplane factory is located there. It is believed that this plant was the target of the Royal Air Force formation.]

This flight, which carried the British more than 500 miles from their bases into Germany, was probably the most audacious aerial venture yet undertaken. According to early reports, the British bombers made the flight without fighter escorts, arriving about dusk. Augsburg, which is also an important machinery, textiles and chemical center, was bombed once before by the R. A. F. in August, 1940, in a night attack. The city is 35 miles from Munich, birthplace of the Nazi Party.

Raids on France Continue.

British planes pounded northern France again in continuation of an offensive that has sent 1,800 fighters and bombers over that area in the last six days and caused the Germans to divert 1,500,000 soldiers and civilians to air-raid duty in western Germany alone.

The total number of R. A. F. planes sent to France for the week is expected to reach 2,000 tomorrow when, it was said, the day fighters go out again to pound factories and airdromes along the occupied channel coast.

The figure includes only those planes making daylight sweeps and not those which have been pounding Germany and the occupied countries nightly.

British Losses Reach 54.

One British bomber and two fighters were lost today and, plus two bombers lost in raids Thursday night, it ran the total losses for the week to 54 planes. An American Eagle squadron pilot shot down a German dive-bomber today and another bomber was bagged during the night, bringing the German losses for the same period to 21 planes.

An air ministry communique said that a shell-filling factory at Marquise, near Boulogne, France, was attacked today by Hurricane fighter-bombers. American-built Boston (Douglas) bombers attacked targets in Calais, Rouen and Cherbourg, hitting the main railway line to Calais, a power-station, shipyards and fuel tanks.

Mrs. Harry Whitney Dies in New York

New York, Saturday, April 18.—(UP)—Mrs. Harry Payne Whitney, sculptress and art patron, died at 2:50 a. m. today at New York Hospital of heart complications after an illness of 10 days.

Mrs. Whitney, the former Gertrude Vanderbilt, was the aunt of Gloria Vanderbilt di Cicco, to whom she served as guardian for several years after winning her custody in 1934 in a court battle with her sister-in-law, Mrs. Gloria Morgan Vanderbilt.

MODERN SECTION OF TOKYO from the air. Jap radio reported last night that the city was bombed by "Allied planes" and that schools and hospitals were hit. The radio denied, however, that the attackers had reached this area. This section of the city, built of steel and stone, looks much like modern Western cities. But the Jap capital also has thousands of houses made of wood, bamboo and paper.
BRITISH COMBINE PHOTO.

Big Naval Base At Yokohama Also Hit: Berlin

Tokyo, Saturday, April 18.— (Japanese Broadcast Recorded by United Press)—United Nations warplanes attacked metropolitan Tokyo shortly after noon today and dropped bombs on homes, a school and a hospital, inflicting slight damage.

It was the first enemy air raid on Tokyo since the outbreak of war in the Pacific.

The London radio said the Japanese news agency Domei reported that the Tokyo-Yokohama area was attacked. Yokohama is the site of a huge Japanese naval base.

[The raiders first appeared over the Tokyo-Yokohama area at 12:30 p. m. (9:30 p. m. yesterday, Chicago time), converging from several directions, the official German news agency DNB reported from Tokyo.]

Military authorities from the Eastern Army headquarters said Japanese pursuit planes shot down nine of the attacking planes.

An air raid warning sounded and traffic in the streets was cleared immediately. Every person took his appointed station.

'Telling Damage' Admitted Early

[In its original announcement, Tokyo radio said the hostile planes caused "telling damage" to cultural establishments and residential districts.]

[The War Department in Washington said early today that it had "no confirmation, official or unofficial," of the raid.]

The Japanese radio, in a report from Eastern Army headquarters, said the enemy planes "failed to make an appearance over the heart of the city as they batted (sic) about, releasing a few bombs on the outskirts of the city.

"Japanese interceptor planes immediately took chase. The hostile planes were seen winging at high speed but were made easy prey of the Japanese pursuit planes.

"Ironically enough (said Tokyo radio), the bombs dropped struck several homes, while other reports indicated that a school and a hospital were hit.

We're Indignant, Say Japs

"Military authorities disclosed that none of the military establishments were made targets of the raid.

"First official reports of the raid emanating from the Eastern Army headquarters revealed that nine enemy planes had been shot down.

"The damages have been confirmed as slight as the mounting indignation over the indiscriminate bombing is being felt among the people."

[This version of the enemy bombing of Tokyo was given by the Japanese radio at 10:30 p. m., Chicago time, nearly an hour and a half after the Tokyo announcer first interrupted a musical program to give a "news flash" that United Nation planes had bombed Tokyo for the first time.]

"Metropolitan Tokyo," said the Japanese radio in its statement, "experienced its first taste of an enemy air invasion shortly past noon today when a small unit of unidentified planes appeared shortly after the air raid warning."

The original English-language announcement of the air raid said:

"Enemy bombers appeared over Tokyo for the first time since the outbreak of the current war of Greater East Asia. The bombing inflicted telling damages on schools and hospitals. The raid occurred several minutes past noon today. The invading planes failed to cause any damage to military establishments.

Casualties Unknown.

"The casualties in the schools and hospitals are as yet not known. The inhuman attack on these cultural establishments and the residential districts is causing widespread indignation among the populace."

[The Columbia Broadcasting System's listening station in San Francisco heard Tokyo radio give a Japanese-language broadcast that the enemy planes were "repulsed" by a heavy barrage "from our defense guns" and that losses were light.]

[Thursday night the Tokyo radio issued a strange "denial" of a report attributed to Reuter that three American airplanes bombed Tokyo. No such report was carried by

See TOKYO BOMBED Page 4.

U. S. Recalls Vichy Envoy

On Alert for Blow Against Free French

By Thomas F. Reynolds.
Washington Bureau of The Chicago Sun.

Washington, April 17. — The United States today called Ambassador William D. Leahy home from Vichy and reportedly began preparations to prevent any naval or military surprise attempt by the Berlin-dominated Vichy government of Pierre Laval.

The United Nations, including the United States, were dangerously close to shooting war with Vichy because of the possibility that Laval, acting on orders from Berlin, might attempt to launch the powerful French navy against strategically important territories now held by the Free French.

President Roosevelt, Acting Secretary of State Sumner Welles, and Army and Navy chieftains, it was understood, were keeping one objective paramount—that no matter what adventure Laval forces upon France, the United States must not be caught napping.

Mr. Roosevelt ordered Leahy home from Vichy officially for "consultation."

Although French circles remained silent, it was considered certain that Gaston Henry-Haye, Vichy's ambassador here, quickly would be called back to France in retaliation for the United States move.

Welles offered an ominous hint that momentous decisions and

See LEAHY RECALL on Page 2.

Malaria, Not Japanese, Defeated Bataan Yanks

20,000 of 36,000 American Troops Ill With Fever in Final Fighting

By Frank Hewlett.
Copyright 1942, by the United Press.

Melbourne, Australia, April 17.—In the last desperate showdown, the Battle of Bataan ended because the quinine pills ran out.

I saw the last scenes of the drama and this is the story.

Ten thousand of our troops lay in two field hospitals, most of them ill with malaria. Another 10,000 were confined to camps with lighter cases of malaria.

(There were 36,800 troops in all on Bataan, according to War Department figures. Thus more than half were incapacitated in the final phase of the battle.)

There was plenty of ammunition when I saw American and Filipino soldiers in their last stand. When the end came they blew up a million rounds of .30 caliber ammunition.

No Quinine to Fight Malaria.

There was courage in plenty to pit against the Japanese. But there was no quinine to fight the deadliest enemy—malaria.

It was malaria and dysentery—not Japanese tanks or dive bombers or bayonets—that told the final story.

I broke through the Japanese blockade by a route that cannot be disclosed. After Bataan fell, and after we had undergone ruthless, steady bombardment on the rocky little fortress of Corregidor, I reached Australia this week with the American bomber squadron that had attacked four Japanese bases in the Philippines.

Fever Became Rampant.

Even before he left the Philippines a month ago, Gen. MacArthur expressed concern over the quinine shortage, saying, "We have been lucky from the health standpoint but it may be a different story soon—with the exhaustion of the quinine supply and the rainy season coming on."

As long as there was enough quinine for all, there was little disease.

See MALARIA on Page 2.

Burma Fall Near; Oil Wells Fired

British Put Torch To Petroleum Field

Additional story and map on page 2.

New Delhi, April 17.—(UP)—The Indian Navy has evacuated 40,000 Indians from Burma and hard-pressed British troops have put the torch to the Yenang-Yaung oil fields in the face of a Japanese drive that threatens all central Burma, it was announced tonight.

[A dispatch from the London Bureau of The Chicago Sun said that the British and Chinese were withdrawing for a last stand together at Mandalay and that all Burma seems falling into Japan's grip.]

Abandoning the key Irrawaddy River town of Magwe, the British were reported to have destroyed 6,000 of the 8,000 wells in the Yenang-Yaung field 17 miles to the north, last important United Nations petroleum source in the Far East.

The Indians were evacuated from Burmese ports, an official announcement said, indicating that the United Nations still hold considerable sway over the west coast of the colony despite Axis reports of a landing at the main port of Akyab and an advance along the northwest shore toward the Indian border 75 miles away. Besides Akyab, the British apparently still

See BURMA on page 2.

THE WORLD AT WAR

The Tokyo radio announced officially early today that Allied bombers had attacked the city. The broadcast said severe damage had been caused to schools and hospitals, but that military installations were not hit. [Page 1.]

* * *

Forty thousand Indians have been evacuated from Burma, according to a New Delhi communique. Reports from Chungking and London indicated that the position of British and Chinese troops in central Burma was desperate. The British announced destruction of 6,000 oil wells in their retreat from the Irrawaddy valley. [Page 1.]

* * *

Malaria, not Japanese guns, brought about the defeat of American-Filipino forces on Bataan, Frank Hewlett, United Press correspondent evacuated from Corregidor, revealed in the first story of the defenders' last days. [Page 1.]

* * *

While Japanese planes continued to bomb Corregidor, American batteries on the island fortress silenced three batteries of enemy artillery on Bataan peninsula and Cavite shores. Fierce fighting was reported on the island of Panay, where 8,000 Jap troops have landed. [Page 2.]

* * *

The announcement of General Douglas MacArthur's staff will be made tomorrow, naming the members of the high command in the southwest Pacific. Meanwhile in Washington, Secretary of War Stimson denied that there were any obstacles in the path of MacArthur's assumption of command in Australia. Stimson indicated that an Allied offensive is ready. [Page 3.]

* * *

British heavy bombers on a 1,000-mile round trip deep into Germany bombed an important factory, believed to be the Messerschmitt airplane plant, at Augsburg in Bavaria. The factory was attacked in a daring daylight raid as the R. A. F. continued its offensive for the sixth day. [Page 1.]

* * *

With the resignation of the Petain cabinet, the way was cleared for Pierre Laval to announce his new collaborationist cabinet, rumored to include Gen. Henri Dentz, Syrian high commissioner who fought the British in the Middle East, and Dr. Alexis Carrel, Nobel prize-winner. [Page 2.]

Two More Federal Bureaus Will Be Transferred to Chicago

Washington Bureau of The Chicago Sun.

Washington, April 17. — Two more federal agencies were ordered to move to Chicago today by the Bureau of the Budget and another announced tentative plans to establish an important pivotal regional office in that city.

Budget Director Harold Smith announced that officials of the Federal Deposit Insurance Corporation have agreed to orders transferring a substantial portion of its Washington setup to Chicago.

More than half of the 500 employees of FDIC now in the capital will occupy new offices in the Field Building in Chicago by June 15, it was announced.

The annual pay roll of the 250 or more employees affected will total well in excess of a half million dollars.

At the same time the Budget Bureau Director disclosed that it has been decided to establish a major portion of the newly created Alien Property Custodian's office in the Field Building.

The National Housing Administration, although its plans are now in a tentative stage, announced it will in all probability place one of its 10 important regional offices in Chicago. This will be part of NHA's program to decentralize administration of the billion dollar War Housing Program and place

See BUREAUS on Page 4.

Six Pct. Limit on War Profit Killed by Congress Conferees

Washington Bureau of The Chicago Sun.

Washington, April 17.—House and Senate conferees on the $19,000,000,000 sixth supplemental national defense bill today agreed upon a formula for profit control which may remove the necessity for further action.

The conferees, representing the appropriations committees of both houses, decided to drop from the bill that part of the Senate amendment which limited profits on war contracts to 6 per cent. They agreed upon the section which gives to the secretaries of the Army and Navy authority to renegotiate any contract which appears to promise excessive profits to the contractor.

One member of the conference committee, who felt that the language of the bill regarding profit limits was "rather vague," said that the House and Senate members in executive session expressed the opinion that the new tax bill would take care of excessive profits through the excess profits tax. The House Ways and Means Committee completed hearings today on the tax bill.

The defense bill conferees also slashed a $19,000,000 appropriation for forest fire protection to $5,000,000. Their agreement represented a compromise between the $2,000,000 voted by the House and the highest figure, approved by the Senate.

The conferees agreed that the money should be spent for equipment to be used in combatting forest fires, and that men to handle the equipment should be supplied by the forest service, CCC camps, state and local communities and paid by the federal government.

5¢
6 Cents in Canada

SUNDAY MIRROR
Member of the Associated Press
Buy WAR Bonds
WEATHER PARTLY CLOUDY (Details on Page 2)
(Copyright, 1942, Daily Mirror, Inc.)
FINAL EDITION
Vol. 11. No. 18 C New York, Sunday, May 3, 1942
84 Pages and Sixteen Pages of Comics Including 20 Page Magazine

5¢
6 Cents in Canada

JAPS HALTED NEAR CHINA

CLAIM CAPTURE OF MANDALAY

Story on Page 3

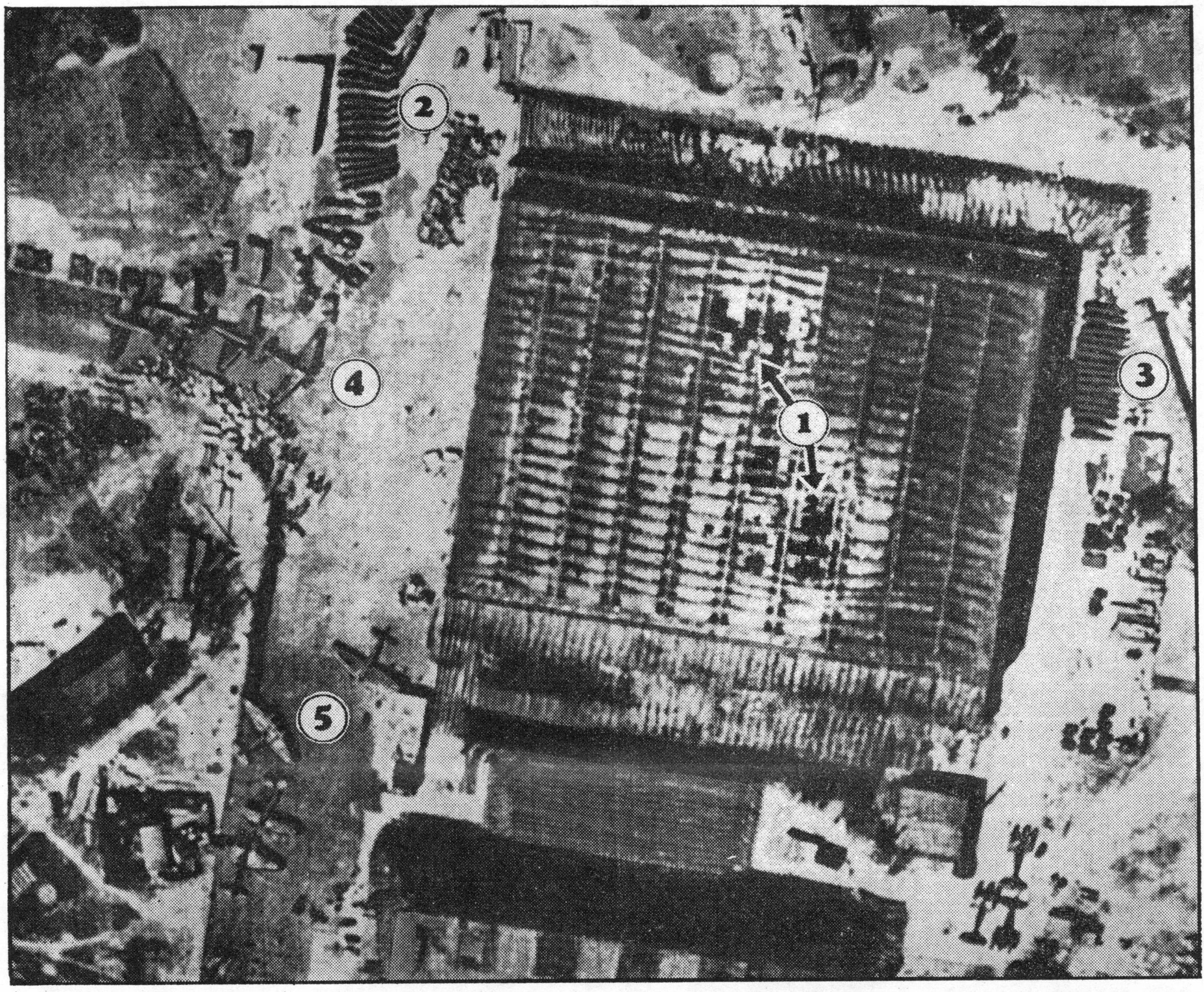

Rostock Plant Blasted By RAF

An RAF observation plane made this photo of a factory in Rostock, German Baltic port, after last week's terrific raiding of its four nights in succession. (1) is the Heinkel plane plant, with double arrows pointing to bomb holes. (2) and (3) are plane fuselages which British reconnaisance indicate were dragged out damaged but salvageable. (4) and (5) are nearly-finished Heinkels, also salvaged. British Air Ministry asserts the plant will have no further production for many months.
(International Cablephoto)

Begin TERROR on the Island, Exciting New Thriller. Page 28

2¢

DAILY MIRROR

Buy WAR Bonds

Member of the Associated Press

WEATHER MILD (Details on Page 2)

(Copyright, 1942, Daily Mirror, Inc.)

3 Cents Outside City Limits

2¢

Vol. 18. No. 273 C New York, Thursday, May 7, 1942 COMPLETE SPORTS

7,000 TAKEN IN FALL OF CORREGIDOR

Story on Page 3

Last Photo From Fort Until We Return

Simultaneously with the news of Corregidor's capture, this latest photo was released for publication. It was made from Corregidor looking toward the heights of Batan across the narrow waters. It was from those heights that the enemy's big guns bombarded the courageous defenders, overcome more by hunger, disease and lack of ammunition than by the foe they had stood off in a ceaseless 27-day siege. Superstructure of a sunken ship (circle) protrudes from the strait.

(U. S. Marine Corps Photo from International)

WAR EXTRA

7TH SPORT .:. NIGHT FINAL

87TH YEAR

THE CALL BULLETIN

SAN FRANCISCO

AN INDEPENDENT NEWSPAPER

CALL AND POST. VOL. 151. NO. 87
THE CALL-BULLETIN. VOL. 171. NO. 87

SAN FRANCISCO, THURSDAY, MAY 7, 1942

5c DAILY

U. S. Loses 11,575 at Corregidor

WASHINGTON, May 7 (AP).—The War Department announced today that approximately 11,574 soldiers, sailors, marines and civilians presumably were captured by the Japanese on Corregidor and the other Manila Bay forts.

The estimate was based on reports received up to April 15, a communique said, and did not take into consideration casualties which might have been suffered in the last three weeks.

The total included 2,275 naval personnel, 1,570 marines, 3,734 American soldiers, 1,280 Philippine scouts, 1,446 soldiers of the Philippine Commonwealth Army, and 1,269 casuals including civilians and individuals not otherwise classified.

The communique was issued at a press conference by the undersecretary of war, Robert P. Patterson, who said that Lieutenant General Jonathan M. Wainwright, commanding the American-Filipino forces, presumably was among those captured.

U. S. SINKS 7 JAPAN WARSHIPS IN PACIFIC

S. F. CARMEN READY FOR WALKOUT

WLB Told City Refuses New Pact For $1 Pay Increase

Municipal Railway carmen will strike Monday unless their demands are met before that time, and the War Labor Board in Washington has been so informed, William McRobbie, president Municipal Carmen's Local 518, said today.

WLB ASKED TO ACT

In a telegram to the WLB, McRobbie declared:

"I wish to advise you that Carmen's Local 518 is involved in a wage dispute which the employer refuses to adjust.

"Due to the increase in the cost of living, we will be forced to strike to get our wages.

"This will upset transportation to the shipyards and other vital defense industries. Due to this fact, we are asking you to take jurisdiction over this

Continued on Page 2, Column 5

Hint Ban on Sunday Driving

WASHINGTON, May 7 (AP).—Robert P. Patterson, undersecretary of war, described the rubber shortage today as "so acute" that the time had come to stop "Sunday trips, visits to Cousin Joe and petting parties" while Congress head charges that the rubber shortage was a "myth."

And, in another quarter Congress also was told that though War Production Board officials had stated synthetic rubber could be produced most simply and speedily from alcohol, only 10 per cent of the program to produce 800,000 tons yearly had been allocated to a company with the alcohol process.

EXTRA TIRES PLAN

Undersecretary Patterson revealed that the government has plans to purchase extra tires on a voluntary basis from the public, but not to requisition the fifth, or spare, tire at this time.

LT. BULKELEY, NAVAL HERO, IN S. F.

Four naval officers fresh from spine-tingling heroic exploits with their torpedo boat squadron in Philippine waters arrived in San Francisco today by way of Australia.

SQUADRON'S VICTORIES

Heading them was one of the United States Navy's outstanding heroes of this war, famed Lieutenant John D. Bulkeley, 30, of Long Island City, N. Y., who revealed that his squadron of fast and deadly surface boats had accounted for seven Japanese ships—one a 6,000-ton light cruiser—and four big seaplanes.

The quartet, after a brief stopover here, was to take a plane for Washington, D. C., en route to New York and further orders.

ON ORDERS

"When our usefulness was at an end," Lieutenant Bulkeley

Cont'd on Page B, Column One

Heydrich New GestapoChief For France

VICHY, May 7 (INS).—Reinhard Heydrich, assistant chief of the German Gestapo and "protector" of Czecho-Slovakia, has arrived in France, presumably to take over punitive measures against dissident elements, it was learned today.

Heydrich will establish a new police director for the entire occupied area who will hold the rank of SS brigade leader.

Report Food Situation In Germany Getting Worse

LONDON, May 7 (AP).—The food situation in Germany and the occupied countries is grave now and is growing progressively worse, the ministry of economic welfare said last night.

HUNGARY, BRAZIL BREAK

RIO DE JANEIRO, May 7 (AP).—The government announced today that Hungary and Brazil have broken relations.

REPORT 400 NAZIS IN MUTINY EXECUTED

LONDON, May 7 (INS).—A Tass New Agency dispatch from Moscow today said 400 German soldiers had mutinied after a heavy defeat on the Bryansk front annd all were executed.

AT PITTSBURGH (N) (2d Game)—New York 1, Pitts 1; 4th. Koslo & Danning; Heintzelman & Lopez.

4TH PIMLICO—Pet, won, 9, 4.20, 3.10; Belle D'Amour, 2d, 3.10, 2.40; Cousin Nan, 3d, 3.60. T., 1:47 4-5.

5TH PIMLICO—Star Copy, won, 10.90, 5.90, 3.50; Steel Beam, 2d, 5.30, 2.80; Spiral Pass, 3d, 2.40. T., 1:13 4-5.

5TH NARRAGANSETT—Snarleow, won, 11, 4.60, 3; Little Suzanne, 2d, 5.10, 3.30; El Osuna, 3d, 2.80. T., 1:13 4-5.

5TH JAMAICA—War Melody, won, 7.10, 4.20, 3.10; Hubbub, 2d, 10.90, 4.60; Anytime, 3d, 2.70. T., 1:13 3-5.

6TH JAMAICA—Hypocrite, won, 6.60, 3.10, 2.40; Argonne Woods, 2d, 2.40, 2.10; Trimly, 3d, 3.30. T., 1:47.

(Earlier Races Will Be Found on Page 18)

Senate O. K.'s Funds for Huge Submarine Fleet

WASHINGTON, May 7 (AP).—The Senate completed congressional action today on legislation authorizing an increase of 200,000 tons of new submarines.

8 Canadian Fliers Die In Newfoundland Crash

ST. JOHN'S, Newfoundland, May 7 (AP).—Eight members of the Royal Canadian Air Force were killed last night in a flying accident at Torbay, ten miles north of here. Details were not disclosed.

Call-Bulletin Today

Special Features

("G" indicates Green Flash Section)

British Take Navy Base on Madagascar

VICHY, Unoccupied France, May 7 (AP).—The French government announced tonight that the Madagascar naval base of Diego Suarez had capitulated to the British, but declared that the Vichy forces would continue the fight to hold the rest of the island.

LONDON, May 7 (AP).—Strong British land and naval forces have captured the Diego Suarez naval base and surrounding territory on the strategic north tip of the French island of Madagascar at a cost of something more than 1,000 men, it was announced today.

48 HOUR BATTLE

Occupation of that key point on the Indian Ocean supply routes, to prevent its falling into axis hands, was accomplished 48 hours after British commandos, marines and soldiers landed at dawn Tuesday, but only after one assault had been thrown back Wednesday morning by hard fighting colonial troops and seamen loyal to the Vichy French regime.

STRONG FORCES

Prime Minister Churchill, reporting the action to the House of Commons, declared the coup had been planned for three months and that "in order to prevent bloodshed so far as possible, very strong forces of all arms were employed."

The French said the British force included 23 warships, of which five were of heavy tonnage—signifying battleships or large cruisers.

BASE CAPTURED

The war office, the admiralty, the ministry of information and Churchill contributed to details of the quick conquest, which began with a landing on the northwest side of the island at Courrier Bay and progressed eastward to the successive capture of the vil-

Continued on Page A, Column 1

Two Coast Academies In Senate Bill

WASHINGTON, May 7 (INS)—Republican Senate Minority Leader McNary of Oregon introduced a bill today which would authorize establishment of a United States military academy and a United States naval academy on the Pacific Coast.

The academies would be situated either in California, Oregon or Washington, according to the determination of the secretaries of war and navy.

British Admit Loss of Cruiser in Arctic Fight

LONDON, May 7 (AP).—The loss of the 10,000-ton cruiser Edinburgh and four convoyed merchantmen in a running sea fight along the storm-tossed Arctic supply line to Soviet Russia was announced today by the admiralty, which declared that 90 per cent of the convoy got through safely, despite plane, warship and U-boat attacks.

NAZI LOSSES

The attacks, severest from April 2 through May 2, cost the Germans one destroyer sunk, another damaged severely, at least two dive bombers destroyed and others perhaps crippled, the admiralty said.

Two British convoys were targets of the air, sea and undersea assaults. One, laden with war supplies, was said to have got through 90 per cent intact, with a loss of three ships. The other, headed home, lost one ship in ballast.

BY OWN FORCES

The admiralty said the Edinburgh, completed in 1939, was struck by torpedoes and "later had to be sunk by our own forces, as towing was no longer practicable in the weather conditions prevailing."

The fight apparently was the same reported three days ago by the German high command, which said a 10,000 ton British cruiser had been sunk. This German version said six convoyed ships, totaling 37,500 tons, also were sent to the bottom in a furious running battle, which lasted for several days.

FLIERS RAIN BOMBS ON WARSHIPS

ALLIED HEADQUARTERS, Australia, May 7 (AP).—An ominous increase in Japanese naval activity around New Britain and the Solomon Islands was reported today, with the allied bomber command swifly countering with high explosives this developing threat to the all-important American-Australian supply routes.

JAPS ATTACKED

A headquarters communique, noting the strengthening of the Japanese in those two north-northeastern groups where they already have established footholds, said the Japanese potential invasion armada massing near Bougainville, in the Solomons, 300 miles east of New Britain, were "attacked successfully" yesterday.

The Solomon Islands are about 850 miles from Australia.

No details were given, but a communique said allied warplanes rained explosives on the enemy fleet.

JAP MOVE SEEN

Obviously headquarters was alive to these implications of any strengthening of the invader's forces in those areas: A direct assault on Australia or an encircling move to seize the screen of islands east of this continent.

These developments emphasized the continued danger menacing Australia, although headquarters reported diminishing Japanese air pressure on Port Moresby, vital Allied outpost on the south shore of New Guinea.

Observers expressed belief that the lessening of aerial attacks on Port Moresby was direct evidence of the hard blows dealt Japanese airdromes at Lae, on the northwest coast of New Guinea, and Rabaul, New Britain.

INVASION PERIL

An Air Corps spokesman warned, however, that the danger of further southward penetration by the Japanese had not been removed, although their timetable may have been upset.

Allied headquarters did not elaborate on its statement concerning increased Japanese naval activity around New Britain and there was no indication of the size of the units involved.

Soldier Electrocuted

NEWPORT, Ore., May 7 (AP). The accidental electrocution of Private First Class John L. Langdon, Long Island, N. Y., yesterday was reported here.

BULLETIN

WASHINGTON, May 7 (INS).—The Navy announced today that United States Pacific fleet units in a naval engagement with Japanese forces in the Southwest Pacific had sunk seven Japanese warships and damaged two others.

At the same time the Navy announced that its submarines operating in the Far East had sunk a medium-sized cargo ship, one medium sized tanker and one small cargo ship.

The action, near the Solomon Islands, was carried out with the loss of but three American planes, a communique said.

At the same time, it was announced that United States submarines on patrol in the western Pacific had sunk three enemy ships.

These various sinkings and damagings raised to more than 230 the number of Japanese vessels destroyed or damaged by the United States forces to date.

The following damage was sustained by the Japanese:

One light cruiser, two destroyers, four gunboats and one supply vessel were sunk.

One 9,000-ton seaplane tender, one light cruiser, one cargo vessel and one transport were badly damaged.

Six planes were destroyed.

No details of what apparently was a great naval engagement involving Japanese forces striking at the flank of the American supply line to Australia were given in the Navy report, except as to results and the fact that it occurred May 4.

SURFACE UNITS

The communique began by saying simply that "very excellent news has been received."

Naval authoritiees declared that employment of the term "naval engagement" left no doubt that this was an action involving American and Japanese surface units as well as airplanes, the first on any considerable scale since the battle of Java Sea in which the Japanese emerged victorious.

The Navy Department issued the following communique:

"SOUTHWEST PACIFIC:

"1. Very excellent news has been received. A naval engagement between United States and Japanese forces on May 4 resulted in the following damage to the enemy:

"(a) One light cruiser, two destroyers, four gunboats and one supply vessel were sunk.

"(b) One 9,00-ton seaplane tender, one light cruiser, one cargo vessel and one transport were badly damaged.

"(c) Six planes were destroyed.

"2. This highly successful action took place in the vicinity of the Solomon Islands, and was accomplished with the loss of but three planes.

"FAR EAST:

"3. United States sumbarines on patrol in the Far East have sunk the following enemy vessels: One medium-sized cargo ship, one medium-sized tanker and one small cargo ship.

"4. The above actions have not been announced in any previous Navy Department communique.

"There is nothing to report from other areas."

Anti-Trust Lawyers Probing Alcohol Firms

WASHINGTON, May 7 (AP).—Assistant Attorney General Thurman Arnold testified today that government anti-trust lawyers were investigating the concentration of "production of industrial alcohol in a few companies."

Arnold, appearing before a Senate agriculture committee hearing, said he was not yet ready to bring any judicial action or make any charges public.

National League

At PITTSBURGH—

(First Game)

		R.	H.	E.
N.York	000 010 000 00—	1	5	0
Pittsbg.	000 001 000 01—	2	12	0

Carpenter and Danning.
Wilkie and Phelps.

Battle Halts in 6th Day

WAR EXTRA

CHARACTER · QUALITY · AMERICA FIRST! · ENTERPRISE · ACCURACY

Los Angeles Examiner

AN AMERICAN PAPER FOR THE AMERICAN PEOPLE · THE GREAT NEWSPAPER OF THE GREAT SOUTHWEST

Reg. U.S.Pat.Off.
Examiner Telephone Richmond 1212 — Examiner Building, 1111 S. Broadway

VOL. XXXIX—NO. 149 — LOS ANGELES, SATURDAY, MAY 9, 1942 — CC — Two Sections—Part I—FIVE CENTS

JAP FLEET ROUTED

This Type of Nip Craft Sunk

FOE DEATH, SHIP LOSS HUGE

They're Torpedo Boat Heroes of the War

PERSONALLY AWARDED the Silver Star by General Douglas MacArthur, Ensign Anthony B. Akers, Westwood, yesterday described torpedo boat raids. (Story, Page 7.)

—Los Angeles Examiner photo.

HERO'S HOMECOMING! Lieut. John D. Bulkeley, Navy torpedo boat hero, sees new son for first time. Bulkeley's wife (left) and mother introduce them. Daughter Joan waits dejectedly for her turn in limelight. He's a New Yorker. (Page 7.)

17 Jap Ships Knocked Out, Says Navy

WASHINGTON, May 8.—(AP)—A thunderous Allied-Japanese naval battle that started among the islands northeast of Australia five days ago and was continuing tonight has cost the enemy 11 ships, including nine warships, the Navy Department announced tonight.

In addition to the sinking of these vessels, six other Jap craft, including four warships, have been damaged.

The figures were given in a communique which scrupulously avoided claiming a victory for American and Allied sea and air forces in the gigantic conflict but inferentially indicated that their losses might be inconsiderable in comparison with those of Japan.

"Details of losses and damage to our forces are not fully known at present, but no credence should be given to claims that have been or may be put out by Tokyo," the Navy said.

NO DETAILS GIVEN

The communique fixed the scene of the running battle as being in the Coral Sea southward of the Bismarck Archipelago. That would put it somewhere between 500 and 1000 miles east of the northeast coast of Australia and means that the Japanese force has been within range of shore-based aircraft from the continent.

No details of how the Japanese ships were sunk, whether

(Continued on Page 3, Cols. 3-4)

Waves of Dive Bombers Blast Enemy Carriers

LONDON, May 9 (Saturday)—(AP)—Reuters in a dispatch from Sydney today said a vast Japanese invasion fleet off northeastern Australia has been smashed.

Remnants of the Japanese invasion fleet are on the run, the dispatch said.

Reuters said its dispatch was based on reports from an advanced Allied base.

The toll of Japanese sea losses, the Reuters dispatch said, rose to 18 ships sunk and four damaged, including the certain destruction of two aircraft carriers, one cruiser, six or seven destroyers and other vessels.

UNITED NATIONS HEADQUARTERS IN AUSTRALIA, May 9 (Saturday)—(INS)—The great southwest Pacific sea battle between United Nations and Japanese naval forces has "ceased temporarily," it was announced early today.

There was no immediate enlargement of the brief announcement.

LONDON, May 8.—(INS)—The Japanese navy has suffered its "greatest defeat" of the war in the Pacific, the news agency Reuter declared tonight in a dispatch from Australia, quoting reports from an advanced United Nations base regarding the battle of the Coral Sea.

United States dive bombers opened the engagement when they caught the enemy armada south of the Solomon Islands and definitely sank two Japanese aircraft carriers, one cruiser and seven destroyers and damaged "many other" vessels, Reuter's said.

This dispatch was the first to state that two enemy aircraft carriers were known to have been sunk and that as many as seven Japanese destroyers had been sent to the bottom.

Official United Nations announcements hitherto had said only that one aircraft carrier was certainly sunk and a second so gravely damaged that it is believed a total loss, while only two Japanese destroyers had been listed as sunk so far in the great engagement.

Describing the first phases of the battle, the Reuter dispatch quoted reports from the advanced United Nations base as stating:

"After waves of dive bombers attacked, one enemy aircraft carrier rolled over and sank immediately.

"The second was bombed and attacked with torpe-

(Continued on Page 2, Cols. 2-4)

EVENING EDITION

Japan Times & Advertiser

Incorporating
The JAPAN CHRONICLE and The JAPAN MAIL

EVENING EDITION

No. 15,483 (THE 17th YEAR of SHOWA) TOKYO, MONDAY, MAY 11, 1942 第三種郵便物認可 昭和十五年十二月二十七日 Price 8 Sen

AMERICA HIT BY UNREST WAVE AS CORAL SEA RESULT HIDDEN; LONDON DOUBTING U.S. CLAIMS

Expert Quarters Discern Heavy Naval Loss Behind Silence

BRITAIN ASKS TRUTH

Special to the Yomiuri

STOCKHOLM, May 9.—The Battle of the Coral Sea, which suddenly arrested the attention of the whole world, is now history, but the American and British authorities concerned have not yet announced the results of the encounter.

Since the official announcements hitherto have always been incorrect and uninforming, the American nation at present is feeling great doubt and unrest.

According to a Washington dispatch, American naval expert quarters, judging from the announcements made by the Japanese Naval authorities, voice frankly the following views under the assumption that the announcements of the serious losses having been suffered by the American-British combined fleet are reliable:

"So far, the American naval authorities have not made clear, with reliable announcements, the results of the Battle of the Coral Sea. But judging from the fact that the Japanese Naval authorities have already published detailed reports of the battle, we warn that the nation at this moment should refrain from cherishing optimistic views of the situation without swallowing merely the facts such as have already been made public by the American naval authorities.

"Seeing the developments and the scope of the battle, we shall have to naturally expect, as an inevitable fact, that the Anglo-American combined fleet in the latest sea battle has suffered a great failure after losing several warships and two aircraft carriers."

Optimism Warned

Special to the Yomiuri

BUENOS AIRES, May 9.—U.S. Secretary of the Navy, Colonel Frank Knox, in a press conference today made a statement which seemingly confirms the Japanese announcement of the war results achieved in the Battle of the Coral Sea, according to a Washington dispatch. Secretary Knox said:

"Detailed reports of the Battle of the Coral Sea have not yet been received, and the naval authorities are refraining from comments on the results of the battle. Accordingly, the nation is strictly warned not to cherish optimistic views of the situation until detailed reports of the battle results are announced."

U.S. Claims Doubted

Special to the Yomiuri

STOCKHOLM, May 9.—With regard to the results of the Battle of the Coral Sea, the British authorities are still maintaining silence on the ground that details are not yet to hand.

However, military critics are holding the view that in the light of the splendid war results achieved by the Japanese Navy, parallel with those of the Army, since the commencement of the present war, the prowess of the Japanese "Invincible Navy" must be unconditionally recognized.

They, furthermore, declare that the previous official announcements of the Japanese side have always been quick and accurate and the present attitude of Japan is befitting a great nation in issuing the glorious war results of the Japanese Navy, followed quickly by the clarification of the loss of the Japanese side.

Judging by these facts, these circles assert that the heavy loss of the Allied navy must be considered certain. On this assumption, the military critics are making various comments.

Faith in Japan's Reports

Meantime, Patrick Laski, commentator for the BBC, in his radio broadcast today, stated that announcement of facts as facts will prove advantageous in ultimately bringing about victory to the Allied countries, stressing that the United States should understand this. Thus, blasting the American propaganda reports, he supported the practice of the Japanese side in announcing the truth.

"The American and English newspapers have been dazzled by the small success in Madagascar, and are purposely inattentive to the fact of the war fronts of Burma and Australia being placed in a serious situation.

"The victory in Madagascar is a matter of course because the operation there is like that of wrenching the arms of a baby. On the contrary, the enemy strength confronting the Allied forces in Burma and Australia is overwhelmingly superior in number and quality, so that success or otherwise in these two directions is so important as to decide the fate

(Continued on Page 2)

His Majesty's Proxies Leave Capital to Tour Kansai, Kyushu Areas

Eikei Koide, Chamberlain and proxy for His Majesty the Emperor, left Tokyo at 9 a.m. Sunday on an 11-day inspection tour of the Kansai district to observe conditions of the people there, reports Domei. Mr. Koide will inspect seven places in Osaka Prefecture, 10 places in Hyogo Prefecture, 16 places in Kyoto and 15 places in Shiga Prefecture before returning to the capital on May 21. Meanwhile, Aimasa Irie, another Chamberlain and Imperial proxy, left for the Kyushu district on a similar mission. He is scheduled to return here May 20.

SPOKESMAN SCORES ALLIED PROPAGANDA

Anglo-U.S. Powers Resort to Lies Concealing Losses in Coral Sea Battle

The Battle of the Coral Sea offered another opportunity to the Anglo-American camp for making another of their malicious propaganda reports, which, however, are so obviously fictitious that they fail to deceive all intelligent people, declared Jun Tsuchiya, acting spokesman of the Board of Information in the absence of Tomokazu Hori, at the regular meeting of foreign correspondents, Monday.

"The Anglo-American camp is making malicious propaganda regarding the results of the Battle of the Coral Sea," said Mr. Tsuchiya; "but the fictitious nature of their claims is self-evident when one examines the contents of their official communique."

The speaker pointed out that in sharp contrast to the Imperial Headquarters communiques the announcements of the Anglo-American camp are incomprehensibly mysterious, for they fail to mention even the names of the class of ships they claim either to have sunk or damaged.

"The truth will soon be out even in the United States and Britain," declared Mr. Tsuchiya, "as has been the case with the sea battles off Surabaya and Batavia, and in the Java Sea, if one but watches the war development consequent upon the recent sea battle."

Aussie Premier Worried

The speaker then reminded the correspondents that the general consternation on the part of the Anglo-American camp was revealed by the Australian Prime Minister, John Curtin, when he said in the House of Commons on May 8 that "the events that are taking place today are of crucial importance to the whole conduct of the war in this theater." In addition, the B.B.C. radio station had reported that the American Government officials "are much concerned" with the battle.

"These are nothing but an admission of the defeat 'of crucial importance' to the future conduct of the war on the part of the enemy Allies," continued Mr. Tsuchiya, "with which the Anglo-American officials 'are much concerned'.

"It is quite peculiar that the United States Navy Department says their losses will be made public when such information will be without value to the enemy, especially so since the Anglo-American high command must be fully aware of the fact that their combined fleet fought in the Coral Sea with the very enemy fleet that already has first hand information of great value regarding the battle."

In reply to a question if the battle was still going on, the speaker said that the battle of the Coral Sea was over.

THAI STUDENTS FOR HOME

After Graduating at Universities Here Leave for Bangkok May 8

Eleven Thai students who have been studying at various seats of learning in Japan for the past few years sailed from Kobe for Bangkok on Friday, May 8.

The group of Thai students, among whom were five girls, recently graduated from well-known universities such as Rikkyo, Hosei, Tokyo University of Commerce and others. Among the girl students were graduates of St. Luke's and Gyokusei nursing schools.

The students were Thongchai Sarikavaja, Prayad Svatizuto, Vuthi Sujadam, Sanid Bandhu Bisalputra Boon Srisavardi, Thian Uneklab, the Misses Thanom Suey Samang Chamnong Chayananda, Ladda Miyakawa, Sangad Montrikul and Aroon Laddapudra.

For Offense and Defense of East Asia Skies

The might of the Imperial Army Air Force now resounds through the world, bringing terror to our enemies and a grateful sense of security to those who dwell under its protective wings. Sweeping away all Allied resistance from the skyways in this part of the world, these slim, silvery warriors of the air continue their grim activities to hasten the coming of an era of happiness and prosperity. (Censored by War Ministry)

PRESSURE BY ALLIES FORCED IRAN'S MOVE

Japanese Envoy, in Hailar, Says Nation Is Hot-Bed of Enemy Propaganda

The people of Iran, though their Government recently cut off diplomatic relations with Japan, remained very friendly toward Japanese residents. This manifestation of true friendship has already revealed that the country's daring move was forced under British pressure, declared Hikotaro Ichikawa, Japanese Minister to Iran when he arrived at Hailar, Sunday, en route to Japan after his withdrawal from Teheran.

"I intended to return via Kuibishev, but however, in accordance with the request of the Soviet Government, I followed the route across the Caspian Sea. From Pahalevi on the southwestern coast of the Caspian Sea, I sailed to Krasnovodsk from where I entrained on a special train. After crossing Central Asia, reached Manchuli in due time." the Minister revealed to the press.

"Iran has been under martial law since August 25, last year, when the advance into the country of British and Soviet troops was reported. These troops have under their control all the communication facilities in the country.

"The British-Soviet-Iranese Alliance was apparently forced upon Iran by two other countries. All Axis countries, simultaneously with the Anglo-Soviet advance, withdrew their diplomatic representatives from Iran, leaving Japan as the only pro-Axis country holding its legation in Teheran. The Iranian breakage of diplomatic relations with the Axis and pro-Axis countries was made with the will of Britain rather than that of Iran itself.

"Teheran is now the center of all fabricated news provided by Britain and the United States. The inhabitants, however, are not so easily fooled for their version is usually proved false by the official reports from Japan radiocast in English and French.

"Germany and Italy broadcast news to Iran in the Persian language. The Iranians are very friendly toward Japanese residents, and deeply regretted our departure when we withdrew from Teheran."

Lieutenant-Colonel Kazuo Murasawa, military attache to the Japanese Legation at Teheran, who accompanied Minister Ichikawa, remarked on the Iranian situation viewed from the military angle, as follows:

"Generally speaking, Iran now has the Soviet forces in the north and the British in the south. The two groups of troops are each supposed to have 50,000 to 60,000 officers and men. There are only a few Soviet and British soldiers stationed in Teheran at present.

"As far as I could learn, there was no indication of the alleged move of the Soviet troops over to the coast of the Persian Gulf. Neither was there any sign of a tense situation on the Iran-Turkish border.

"To all appearances, Turkey will maintain its strict neutrality."

21 Allied Vessels Sunk

D.N.B.

FUEHRER'S HEADQUARTERS, May 10.—Twenty-one more enemy vessels totaling 118,000 tons were sunk by German submarines in American waters, the Caribbean Sea and the Gulf of Mexico, according to an announcement of the German High Command.

Wainright's Surrender to Japanese Army Is Termed 'Most Pathetic' Ever Witnessed

Describing the historic scene of the surrender of Lieutenant-General Jonathan Wainright, Commander-in-Chief of the United States forces in the Philippines, the Nichi Nichi correspondent on Corregidor Island reports that the surrender of the commander of the enemy forces on Wednesday, May 6, was one of the most pathetic scenes ever witnessed by the Japanese expeditionary forces in the Philippine Islands.

When requested by the commander of the advance Japanese Forces on Corregidor Island to return to his former position to fight out the battle to the end, Lieutenant-General Wainright stated, according to the correspondent, that he realized that his troops were no match for the Japanese Forces, and that he had surrendered with the idea of not returning to his former position.

Requested to issue an order for all the American and Philippine forces in the Philippines to surrender upon this occasion, the Commander-in-Chief of the enemy forces declared that due to the fact that the combined forces were scattered too widely over the many islands, his order would not be obeyed.

However, according to the correspondent, Lieutenant-General Wainright said that the entire forces on the Corregidor Island as well as on Caballo Island would surrender according to his orders.

When the commander of the Japanese Forces stated that he was unable to discuss the question of the surrender of the enemy with one who was unable to issue a command to the entire forces, Brigader-General Louis Peep, Chief of Staff, implored the Japanese Forces to respond to the surrender of the United States forces, the Nichi Nichi report stated.

Moved by these words of the enemy chief-of-staff the commander of the Japanese advanced forces accepted the surrender of the United States forces on Corregidor, and thus, all the chief officers of the United States forces in the last enemy fortress in the Philippines were taken prisoner by the Japanese landing forces, the correspondent reported.

NEW ASIA

Big Progress Noted

Asahi Service

SHONANTO, May 10.—Colonel Watanabe, who attended the conference of military administrators in North Sumatra, held recently at Medan, returned to Shonanto today, and made the following observation concerning the conditions in North Sumatra.

"It was my first visit to North Sumatra, but I was impressed by the progress already made there. The administration of Sumatra aims at the speedy establishment of peace and order, and the development of natural resources. Peace and order have already been recovered with the subjugation of remnants of the enemy forces, and all inhabitants are happily engaged in the routine of their daily activity.

As regards natural resources, an investigation party has recently come from Japan, and a detailed study into the forest and mineral resources is now being conducted. Not only are the present conditions of the natural resources as well as the damages caused to them by war being investigated, but also the question of transporting them to Japan and other markets is being studied. So far the results of the investigation have been very successful.

"With the reopening of various industries and the revival of the transportation system, the industrial development of North Sumatra is progressing satisfactorily. Formerly the Netherlands Government devoted much of its attention to the development activities of Japan, and it is often said that it did not pay any attention to Sumatra.

Huge Port Constructed

"It has become clear, however, that the Netherlands Government did make a program of developing districts around Sudan, Badan and Tobah. Since the first World War, the Netherlands Government constructed a port on the Sabang islands, equipping it to rival Singapore. The port is of such a gigantic scale as to surprise any visitor.

"Furthermore, the Netherlands Government made a thorough in-

(Continued on Page 2)

ENVOY OSHIMA HONORED BY COLOGNE UNIVERSITY

Japanese Ambassador Made Honorary Senator of Institution for Cultural Efforts

D.N.B.

COLOGNE, May 10.—Japanese Ambassador to Berlin, Lieutenant-General Hiroshi Oshima, was made an honorary Senator of the University of Cologne by the dean and Senate of the institution in recognition of his assistance in stimulating the exchange of German scientific and spiritual goods with Japan, at the ceremony held at the University of Cologne today.

The Ambassador accompanied by Embassy Counselor Sakuma arrived at Cologne on Sunday and was welcomed at the station by District Leader State Counselor Grohe.

At the function, Dr. Winkelkemper, Lord Mayor of Cologne, praised Ambassador Oshima as a friend of the German nation and as one of the leading men in the great struggle of the nations of the Tripartite Powers.

Subsequently, he was followed by Professor Dr. Berin, dean of the University of Cologne, who in his speech reminded the audience that a livery exchange of research workers and scientists had existed for many years between Germany and Japan mentioning in this connection, the Japan-German Society established at his university.

The Ambassador, thanking for the cordial reception and the great honor bestowed on him, declared that it will bind him to further support the scientific and cultural cooperation between Japan and Germany.

"I look upon this distinction not only as an honor concerning me but also as an expression of the high esteem felt by the German people for allied Japan," he stated. "Both nations are united by close ties regarding their common aim and by their cooperation, I am sure victory will doubtless be attached to our banners."

Following the Ambassador's speech, Counselor Sakuma delivered a lecture about Japanese spirit and Japan's victories.

ALLIED FALSEHOOD SCORED BY GERMANS

Cowardly Attack on Madagascar Shows Up Allies in Their True Colors

Domei

BERLIN, May 8.—Commenting on Prime Minister Winston Churchill's disclosure in the House of Commons that British forces had plans of occupying Madagascar even three months ago, political circles here point out that the Prime Minister's statement exposes Anglo-American misrepresentations while revealing their plans of occupying French Colonial territories in the Western Hemisphere.

British-American efforts to justify the action in Madagascar by terming it a counter-measure for Pierre Laval's ascendancy are revealed as nothing but falsehoods by the British Prime Minister's declaration, these circles claim.

Since Japanese operations were concentrated on the Dutch East Indies three months ago, they harbored no threats on Madagascar in the Indian Ocean, these circles point out, asserting that Prime Minister Churchill's declaration, therefore, directly reveals British-American invasion plans on the French territory regardless of outside events.

The excuse given by Prime Minister Churchill on this occasion, that the recent British action was but a natural measure taken in the interests of France's revival, indicates that Great Britain will occupy other French territories under the same pretext.

The United States maintains the same attitude, these circles continued, pointing out that recent American actions in occupying St. Pierre and Miquelon islands off Newfoundland, the recognition of the de Gaullist regime and the establishment of a United States consulate in Brazzaville in French Equatorial Africa give full testimony to its stand.

Meanwhile, the British and American press are unanimous in reporting that the French possession of Martinique has become an immediate problem while Dakar, on the extreme western end of Africa, and Oran in Algeria, once more have become the centers of British-American interest, these quarters concluded.

Hits Treacherous Act

D.N.B.

BERLIN, May 8.—Severely criticising the treacherous British attack on French colonial territory, the German newspaper Diplomatisch-Politische Korrespondenz declares that the "honor of arms" such as it is understood by decent nations, seems to have been altogether lost in London and Washington. This, the paper asserts, is undoubtedly because of the Jewish mentality of the leading personages in Britain and America.

Continuing its attack, the journal declares:

The renewed British attack on French colonial territory, Madagascar this time, which they undertook with Roosevelt's approval has called forth in the United States a number of proud and boastful utterances. While the American commander of the so-called invincible island fortress of Corregidor had to hoist up the white flag not even half a year after the war with Japan had broken out, American

(Continued on Page 2)

CHITTAGONG AIRFIELD STRUCK IN FIRST AIR ATTACK BY ARMY; 7 PLANES, FACILITIES SMASHED

Thai Mission Ends Sojourn in Tokyo; Big Send-Off Given

The Thai Congratulation Mission headed by Lieutenant-General Phya Phahol Pholphaynha Sena left Tokyo at 9 a.m. today for Kyoto and home. The road from the Imperial Hotel to Tokyo Station was lined by pupils of national schools, middle schools and girls' high schools, who waved Japanese and Thai flags to express the goodwill of the people toward Thailand. At the station, Premier General Hideki Tojo, General Gen Sugiyama, Chief of General Staff, Admiral Osami Nagano, Chief of Naval General Staff, Navy Minister Admiral Shigetaro Shimada and other officials of the Government bid farewell to the members of the Thai mission.

U.S. LAUNCHES TALK ON MARTINIQUE ISLE

State Department Issues Statement on Negotiations With Governor-General

Special to the Yomiuri

BUENOS AIRES, May 10.—The State Department of the United States Government issued a statement, on May 9, that Admiral John Hoover, Commander of the American Fleet in the Caribbean Sea, and an official of the State Department have been dispatched to French Martinique to negotiate with the French authority there regarding the future of the island.

The communique said, in substance, as follows:

"The United States Government has dispatched Admiral Hoover and an official of the State Department to Martinique where they are now negotiating with the French Governor-General. Admiral Hoover is authorized to confer with the French authorities concerning: (1) the sovereignty of Martinique Island which is to remain in the hands of France, and (2) the authority of the French Governor-General of Martinique which will be respected and his power recognized as French sovereignty in the waters around the island.

"When the agreement is concluded, France will guarantee to the United States that the island will never be used by the Axis Powers and that it will take no action aiding the Axis in any form, while the United States will promise to give economic aid to the French territory in the Caribbean Sea."

Political observers in Washington say, however, that the statement of the State Department demands that in return for the protection of Martinique, the United States troops be allowed to be stationed there.

The French airplane carrier Bearn, 22,146 tons, and 3,000 officers and men now at Martinique will be placed under the protection of the United States, it is reported.

The United States Government seems to think that the American demand will be approved as the island has no power to reject it. However, after all, what the United States intends to do with Martinique is similar to what the British had done to Madagascar.

Laval Holds Conference

D.N.B.

VICHY, May 10.—Informed circles report that Premier Laval has held a conference with his closest collaborators on the Martinique situation.

According to reports from Amer-

(Continued on Page 2)

MINISTER KEN HARADA PRESENTS CREDENTIALS

Japanese Envoy to Vatican to Be Given Treatment Accorded to Ambassadors

Domei

ROME, May 9.—Ken Harada, the first Japanese Minister to the Vatican, presented his credentials to Pope Pius XII this morning when he was received in audience by the Pope.

Following the presentation of his credentials, the Japanese Minister informally had an interview with the Pope.

Mr. Harada then paid a courtesy call on Cardinal Luigi Maglione, Secretary of State, who later proceeded to the lodgings of the Japanese Minister to make a return call.

Meanwhile, it is learned that the Holy See has decided to accord Mr. Harada the treatment of an ambassador.

Japanese Raiders Gain Good Results in Bad Weather

BURMA HOPES GONE

Asahi Service

A CERTAIN BASE ON BURMA FRONT, May 9.—Kitajima, Narazaki and Kato units of the Army Air Force made their first air raid on the airfield at Chittagong, in the eastern part of India, flying from a distant base on May 8, and obtained glorious results.

The weather was unfavorable on that day, but our air units attacked the Chittagong airfield and destroyed four large planes and three small planes on the ground by bombing and machine-gunning. Also the fuel storage house and other facilities of the airfield were bombed and burnt up. All the planes safely returned to their base.

Chittagong is located 250 kilometers, northwest of Akyab, and is an important port on Bengal Bay. The Chittagong airfield, which was one of the main air bases of the enemy, was entirely destroyed by the first air raid.

India Port Again Hit

Special to the Asahi

STOCKHOLM, May 9.—Japanese Air Forces raided the port of Chittagong on Bengal Bay on May 8, and bombed and machine-gunned facilities on the ground, according to a Reuter report from New Delhi. The Japanese Forces again raided the port on May 9.

Burma Situation Bad

D.N.B.

AMSTERDAM, May 10.—The situation in Burma is bad, stated Cyril Raigh in the British broadcast. China has been attacked from the "backdoor" and the Burmese oil has been taken away from the Allies and their supply to Burma has been cut off. By the Japanese operations in Burma the Allies are deprived of their last opportunity of throwing Chiang Kai-shek's troops into battle and of employing American planes for operations against the Japanese from Chinese bases.

Defense Plan Laid

Asahi Service

BANGKOK, May 9.—With the speedy advance of the Japanese Forces in Burma, the Viceroy of India, Marquis of Linlithgow is now occupied in defending India and it is reported that on May 8, he issued an order to all provinces to the following effect:

"A defense commander is to be appointed in each province under the supervision of the provincial governor and each village will appoint an officer, who will be responsible for local defense. In this way, the organization of the defense of the entire villages of India will be established."

However, as the people are already drifting away from British influence, it is regarded doubtful how far this order of organizing a village defense system will be carried out and it is feared that under the existing conditions, the order might become only a dead letter.

Daring Epic Recounted

Special to the Asahi

AN UNDISCLOSED BASE IN BURMA, May 10.—Another page was added to the annals of the invincible Japanese Air Force, when the heart-gripping story was recently disclosed concerning the almost superhuman act and the tragic death of the late Flight Lieutenant Kanekichi Yamamoto, who, after diving into an airdrome in Rangoon tried to fly out in an enemy fighting plane.

According to the account, as the Japanese Forces entered Rangoon, the local Indians and Burmese excitedly told the Japanese soldiers about the superhuman valor of a Japanese flying officer, who died a gallant death at the airdrome in the city.

Subsequently, the commander of the Imperial Air Force wished to search for the place where the officer's plane fell, but since it was urgent for the air units to immediately commence advancing toward Mandalay in cooperation with the Army forces, the plan was temporarily held in abeyance.

After Mandalay was occupied and the campaign came to an end, the commander of the Yoshioka air unit dispatched his men to Rangoon to have the corpse of the fallen hero duly buried. Arriving in Rangoon, the men found ruins of a Japanese warplane in one corner of the airdrome. The number of the plane

(Continued on Page 2)

Publishers Of
The Osaka Mainichi
The Tokyo Nichi Nichi
In Nipponese
With Combined Circulation
Of 3,500,000 Daily

Sunday Mainichi, Economist, Jikyoku Joho, Children's Daily, Dai Nippon Seinen, Seikatsu Kagaku, Greater East Asia War Graphic, Home Life, Chinese Mainichi, Braille Mainichi, Fujin Nippon, Year Book

A National Newspaper For International Readers

The Osaka Mainichi &

The Tokyo Nichi Nichi

Diplomats At Barcelona

From Our Staff Correspondent

LISBON, May 10.—The first group of Axis diplomats from South America arrived at Barcelona, Spain, en route to Lisbon on Friday, May 8, according to reports received here today.

No. 6928 B 毎日一回發行 月曜日休刊 昭和十七年五月十二日發行 TUESDAY, MAY 12, 1942 大正十一年四月十日第三種郵便物認可 PRICE: 7 Sen

Myitkyina, N. Burma, Taken By Nippon Forces

Chittagong In Bengal Province, India, Is Air-Raided For 1st Time, Report

NIPPON PLANES MAKE 3 SUCCESSIVE ATTACKS

British Air Base At Strategic Communications Center Of Burma-India Traffic Subjected To Attack; Is Also Important Trade Harbor

From Our Staff Correspondent

LISBON, May 9.—A British communique from New Delhi today announced that Chittagong in Bengal province, 120 kilometers northeast of the Burma frontier, had its first air-raid yesterday.

Japanese planes yesterday afternoon made two heavy attacks on the base, which were followed by another raid this morning, the communique announced.

CHITTAGONG

Chittagong, town and port of British India, is situated on the right bank of the Karnaphuli river, about 19 kilometers from its mouth. It is the terminus of the Assam-Bengal railway and a port of call for steamers. Its population in 1921 was 36,030. Tea is brought here from Assam for export to Europe. Mineral oil from Burma is also brought here to be put into tins and distributed by railway. Other exports are jute, raw cotton, rice, and hides.

Chittagong has been a rear base for the British air force in recent years.

Special Committee

Group Of 33 Organized To Study Measures Re Political Power

A special committee of 33 was organized in order to study concrete measures for organizing the political power of the nation at the first general meeting of the preparatory committee for gathering political power to assist the Imperial Rule held on May 8 at 2 p.m. at the Dai Toa Kaikan, Tokyo.

The meeting, held with Masatsune Ogura in the chair, was attended by 63 out of 72 members of the preparatory committee.

Views were expressed by Mannosuke Yamaoka, Yoshito Takagi, Ichiro Kiyose, Tatsunosuke Yamazaki, Jun-ichiro Kobayashi, Baron Iwakusu Ida, Viscount Masatoshi Okochi, and Torataro Ushizuka.

Tadahiko Okada submitted a motion that a special committee be established by the naming of the chairman in order to study concrete measures. Approved by the assembly, Chairman Ogura named 33 men to form the special committee.

The 33 members are:

Lieut.-General Kisaburo Ando, Baron Iwakusu Ida, Tadaatsu Ishiguro, Baron Michitomo Iwakura, Sotaro Ishiwata, Torataro Ushizuka, Ryusaku Endo, Tadahiko Okada, Tadao Oasa, Kozo Ota, Dr. Masataka Ota, Viscount Nagakage Okabe, Masanori Katsu, Shotatsu Kimura, Dr. Ichiro Kiyose, General Kuniaki Koiso, Fumio Goto, Vice-Admiral Takuo Godo, Admiral Nobumasa Suetsugu, Kotaro Sengoku, Lieut.-General Yoshito Takagi, Masao Taki, Tokichi Tanaka, Ryutaro Nagai, Seinosuke Hashimoto, Colonel Kingoro Hashimoto, Aiichiro Fujiyama, Inosuke Furuno, Yonezo Maeda, Tatsunosuke Yamazaki, Dr. Mannosuke Yamaoka, Sukenari Yokoyama, and Dr. Hiroshi Shimomura.

Principle Is Decided

Yokusan Political Power To Respect Constitution

The platform and the rules of a new organization for the gathering of Yokusan political power were drawn up in the meeting of the subcommittee of the Yokusan Political Power Gathering Preparatory Council at the Dai Toa Kaikan on May 10 at 2 p.m.

In the subcommittee meeting, statements made in the session of the special committee on May 9 were adjusted. After discussing the contents of the platform and the rules, the conferees agreed on their principle as follows:

"For the purpose of the successful execution of the Greater East Asia War and the establishment of the Greater East Asia Co-prosperity Sphere, Yokusan political power will be gathered in strict observance of the stipulations of the Constitution and close connection with the Taisei Yokusan Kai."

Those present in the subcommittee meeting included Kozo Ota, Masao Taki, Tadao Oasa, Tatsunosuke Yamazaki, and Ichiro Kiyose as members of the subcommittee, as well as Fumio Goto, Sukenari Yokoyama, Seinosuke Hashimoto, and Masataka Ota.

Count Kaneko Worse

HAYAMA, May 11.—Anxiety is still prevailing over the condition of Count Kentaro Kaneko, who is now having difficulty in breathing and appears to be unconscious.

At 6 a.m. today, his temperature was announced as 36.8° C., pulse 84, and respiration 29.

It was further announced at noon that his temperature was 36.3° C., pulse 90, and respiration 30. He ate 100 grams of oatmeal and one egg.

HAYAMA, May 10.—The condition of Count Kentaro Kaneko is growing worse and his strength is weakening.

At 9 a.m. today, his temperature was announced as 36.6° C., pulse 98, and respiration 30. He ate a little oatmeal. The Count's pulse is irregular and he hiccoughs occasionally.

Foreign Minister Shigenori Togo visited the Count at his bedside in the afternoon.

Vice-Ministers' Parley

The regular Vice-Ministers' conference was held in the Premier's official residence on May 11, at 8 a.m., and a report was given by Chief Secretary Naoki Hoshino to the effect that the coalescing of the nation's new political power is progressing smoothly.

Subsequently there was an explanation on latest developments surrounding the hostile and neutral nations' actions in connection with the Greater East Asia War from Vice-Director Kiwao Okumura of the Board of Information. The highlights were as follows:

The wartime system of the United States is at last being materialized in earnest. Discontent against the present Government in Britain is rapidly rising. Russia frankly recognizes the victories of the Imperial forces in the present war.

Then Lieut.-General Heitaro Kimura, War Vice-Minister, reported that the United States and Britain are conspiring in various ways to transform the present war into a racial war and requested the conferees to guard against this machination.

After asking, furthermore, for the close attention of the people against careless statements, the meeting was closed at 9 a.m.

Governors, Mayors Of New Philippines To Hold 2-Day Talk

MANILA IS SITE

Great Significance Seen; Central Policy Will Be Clarified

Domei

MANILA, May 9.—The first conference of provincial governors and mayors of the new Philippines under Nippon occupation, which is comparable with a gubernatorial conference in Nippon, will be convened in Manila on May 18 and 19.

It is believed that the administrative policy of the central authorities will be clarified and various important problems will be discussed at the conference, such as pacification, food supply, and welfare of the inhabitants.

With the enforcement of various measures for meeting the new stage of hostilities following the fall of Corregidor, the forthcoming conference is regarded to be of great significance.

At present the provincial governors and mayors of the Philippines under Nippon occupation are executing administrative affairs with the approval of the Nippon military commander.

Sumatra Administrators

Domei

SHONAN CITY, May 10.—With the steady restoration of peace and order on Sumatra, the Japanese administrators of various provinces of the island were announced today following their formal appointment. The new administrators include:

Lieut.-Colonel Shigeta Kawase, administrator of Atjeh province.

Colonel Kunisuke Kurokawa, Oostkust province.

Colonel Nobuyoshi Masaki, Tapanoeli province.

Colonel Saburo Fujiyama, Westkust province.

Lieut.-Colonel Takeo Kojima, Benkoelen province.

Colonel Masanao Matsuki, Palembang province.

¥10-Million Donated

From Our Staff Correspondent

HSINKING, May 6.—Governor Yoshisuke Aikawa of the Manchuria Industrial Development Corporation visited Premier Chang Ching-hui at his official residence today at 3 p.m. to donate ¥10-million toward expenses in connection with the cemmoration project of the 10th anniversary of the founding of Manchoukuo.

The contribution was based on the resolution passed by the shareholders of the corporation at their general meeting held at Tokyo on February 17.

Whole Bismarck Archipelago Placed Under Command Of Nipponese Fleet

Pt. Moresby Blasted

Domei

LISBON, May 10.—The Japanese air force on Friday, May 8, carried out a bombing raid on Port Moresby, causing heavy damage to an airfield, according to Melbourne report received here today.

Kiian, Nancheng Bombed

Domei

SHANGHAI, May 11.—Imperial air units bombed Kiian, Nancheng, and Yushan in Kiangsi province yesterday and caused great damages, according to a dispatch from Chungking intercepted here.

SAILORS LAND AT LORENGAU

Enemy Remnants In Dampier Strait Region Are Mopped Up; New Britain Island Is Under Complete Control

By Naval Reporter Miyamura

ABOARD A WARSHIP, May 9.—A special landing corps of the Imperial Navy operating in the southern Pacific succeeded in landing without bloodshed on Lorengau, the principal town of Manus island in the Admiralty group, on April 8 at 4.30 a.m.

Navy units operating in New Guinea waters mopped up enemy remnants in Dampier strait between New Britain and southeastern New Guinea, which enabled them to place the entire island of New Britain under control.

Imperial Navy units which had been operating in the waters north of Australia since capturing Rabaul, New Britain, and Kawieng, New Ireland, on January 23, have now assumed complete command of the Bismarck archipelago, extending over an area 500 nautical miles east to west and 360 nautical miles north to south.

ADMIRALTY ISLANDS

The Admiralty islands are among the most important groups in the Bismarck archipelago, studded over a wide area between New Ireland and New Guinea. Manus is the chief island of the group, and Lorengau the principal town.

The Australian Navy had a seaplane base at Lorengau which served as a relaying station for flying boats reconnoitering the neighboring seas until the Imperial Navy captured Rabaul.

After Rabaul and Kawieng had been captured, Wild Eagles of the Imperial Navy frequently raided key points on the Admiralty islands, destroying military establishments.

By the time the special naval landing corps captured Manus island the citizens of enemy nations had fled. The Navy found the local telegraph station, barracks, magazines, and fuel depots in a dilapidated state due to air attacks carried out late in January.

In pre-war days several Japanese were engaged in cultivating coconut trees and truck gardening in the Admiralty islands. They were apparently taken away and interned somewhere after the outbreak of the war.

USA Demands Martinique Governor Not To Permit Use Of Island By Axis

— Washington Dispatches Admiral Hoover —

From Our Staff Correspondent

BUENOS AIRES, May 9.—According to latest reports from Washington, U.S. State Department announced that Admiral Hoover, commander-in-chief of the American naval forces in the Caribbean, today arrived in Martinique, French island in the Caribbean, to demand a guarantee of Admiral Robert, French governor of Martinique, that the island will not be handed to any of the Axis powers or be utilized by them.

Dismantling Of Carrier, 2 Warships Demanded

From Our Staff Correspondent

LISBON, May 10.—Taking an increasing high-handed attitude toward France, the United States demanded the immediate dismantling of the aircraft carrier Bearn, the minelaying cruiser Emile Berti, and the cruiser Jeanne d'Arc, three French warships anchored at Martinique, French island in the Caribbean, according to a Reuters dispatch received here today.

Previously, the U.S. State Department announced at Washington that America requests assurances from the French governor of Martinique that the island will not be handed over to the Axis powers or be utilized by them.

The State Department them refrained from indicating the measures to be taken by the United States in the event France rejects the American request.

Domei

LISBON, May 11.—A four-point demand from President Roosevelt was presented to the governor of Martinique by Admiral Hoover, commander-in-chief of the American naval forces in the Caribbean, according to information received here from Washington.

The contents of the demand follow:

1. French authorities in all of French islands in the Caribbean must withdraw from the jurisdiction of the Laval regime.

2. The United States will freeze all funds and property, estimated at U.S. $250-million and belonging to French residents throughout the Caribbean, until the end of the war.

3. The French fleet anchored at Martinique and Guadeloupe shall not be used by the Vichy government although the warships are recognized as French property unless they start action.

4. Among those resident in the French islands in the Caribbean, those objecting to the above agreement are free to return to France.

Status To Stay Unchanged

From Our Staff Correspondent

BUENOS AIRES, May 10.—Regarding the question of Martinique island, the U.S. State Department today issued a statement affirming that the status of Martinique will not be changed in any way by the United States unless absolutely necessary.

It is believed in Washington that Admiral Robert will continue as the governor of Martinique provided he gives assurances that he will not give aid to the Axis.

It is recalled that three big French warships including the 22,000-ton aircraft carrier Bearn are anchored at Martinique.

1st Step To Occupation?

By Staff Writer

The United States has always threatened France with the occupa-

(Continued on Page 2)

TO LUKIANG EAST BANK

Remnants Are Defeated Everywhere, Announces Imperial GHQ Communique

GRACIOUS RESCRIPT GRANTED

IMPERIAL GENERAL HEADQUARTERS, May 11 (5.30 p.m.)—His Majesty the Emperor, Supreme Commander of the Imperial Army and Navy, inviting Army and Navy chief staff officers today, granted an Imperial Rescript to the commander-in-chief of the Nippon Expeditionary Forces in the southern region and the commander-in-chief of the Combined Fleet.

The Rescript read to the following effect:

* * *

The Army and Navy units operating in Burma and the Indian Ocean, making extended advance to distant regions or conquering mountainous regions in defiance of scorching heat, have rapidly and efficiently annihilated the enemies, severed the supply routes to China or destroyed the enemy naval and air corps everywhere.

We are highly gratified by their achievements.

IMPERIAL GENERAL HEADQUARTERS, May 11. (5.20 p.m.):

The Imperial Army corps in the Burma region, annihilating the remnants of the defeated enemies everywhere, advanced to the eastern bank of the Lukiang river, Yunnan province, on May 6 and completely occupied Myitkyina on May 8.

Collective War Results In Burma

Total Of 554 Planes Shot Down, Destroyed; 333 Tanks, Armored Cars Blasted

IMPERIAL GENERAL HEADQUARTERS, May 11. (6.40 p.m.):

Imperial Army air force operating in the Burma region, during the five months since the outbreak of the Greater East Asia War, obtained the following collective war results:

1. Attacks on the enemy airfields, 126 times.
2. Planes shot down or destroyed, 554.
3. Motorcars and trucks destroyed, 1,213.
4. Tanks and armored cars destroyed, 333
5. Rolling-stock destroyed, 1,543; trains destroyed, 115.
6. Vessels sunk, 92.
7. Enemy military establishments smashed, 666 places.

Troops Advance Beyond Myitkyina To North

Domei

BURMA FRONT, May 10.—The Imperial Army units which captured Myitkyina, the terminus of the Burma railway, have further advanced to the north of the city and intercepted the enemy path of retreat along the Irrawaddy to the northern Burma border.

Many hostile nationals who had not fled in time have been captured in the city by the Imperial Army and are being placed under surveillance.

Since the advance upon Myitkyina was made with lighting swiftness, humerous enemy automobiles are seen scattered along the highway between Bhamo and Myitkyina.

Enemies' False Claims Self-Evident; War Developments Will Prove Truth

Making a comparative study of the Anglo-American announcements on the recent Coral Sea Battle with those of the Imperial General Headquarters, Jun Tsuchiya, acting spokesman of the Board of Information, declared at his conference with foreign correspondents on Monday, May 11, that the fictitious nature of the enemies' claims is "self-evident when one examines the contents of their official communique."

As usual, Mr. Tsuchiya asserted, the Anglo-American camp is issuing fallacious propaganda reports vis-a-vis the results of the battle and their announcements are incomprehensively mysterious in sharp contrast with Nippon's, failing to mention even the names of the class of ships they claim either to have sunk or damaged.

Continuing, the acting spokesman said: "The truth will soon be out, even in the United States and Britain, as has been the case with the sea battles of Surabaya and Batavia and the Java Sea, if one but watches the war development consequent upon the recent sea battle.

"In fact, general construction on the part of the Anglo-American camp is revealed by Australian Prime Minister John Curtin, when he said in the House of Representatives on May 8 that 'the events that are taking place today are of crucial importance to the whole conduct of the war in this theater,' while the B.B.C. reported that the United States Government 'is much concerned' over the battle.

"These are nothing but admissions of the defeat of crucial importance' to the future conduct of the war on the part of the enemy allies over which the Anglo-American officials are 'much concerned.'"

It is quite peculiar, Mr. Tsuchiya observed, that the United States Navy Department says that the allied losses will be made public when such information will be without value to the enemy, especially so since the Anglo-American High Command must be fully aware of the fact that their combined fleet fought in the Coral Sea with the very enemy fleet that already has first-hand information of great value regarding the battle.

24 Warcraft Taken

From Our Staff Correspondent

CORREGIDOR, May 9.—A Nippon Army unit, which engaged in the guarding of the troops landing before enemy fire at Corregidor, captured a total of 24 enemy warcraft and other vessels.

The Nippon Army unit used fishing boats, tugboats, and other vessels of less than 50 tons which were captured in Manila bay, as well as guns and shells also captured from the enemy.

As the Nippon units came to the waterway between Bataan peninsula and Corregidor on the night of May 5, it came across two enemy submarines and four patrol ships and succeeded in repulsing them after a daring battle.

Chasing some of the enemy vessels which had fled to San Jose port, the corps captured a total of 24 vessels, including a 3,000-ton military transport, gunboats, patrol ships, and speedboats.

EVENING EDITION

Japan Times & Advertiser

Incorporating
The JAPAN CHRONICLE and The JAPAN MAIL

EVENING EDITION

No. 15,485 (THE 17th YEAR of SHOWA) TOKYO, WEDNESDAY, MAY 13, 1942 第三種郵便物認可 昭和十五年十二月二十七日 Price 8 Sen

VITAL PART PLAYED IN CORAL SEA FIGHT BY THE AIR TORPEDO

Former Commander-In-Chief of Combined Fleet Lauds Historic Encounter

PRAISES NAVAL ORDNANCE

Australia Now Has Been Isolated, Faces Serious Situation, Says Admiral Takahashi

The destructive power of our air torpedoes as shown by our naval air units in the Battle of the Coral Sea was lauded yesterday by Admiral Sankichi Takahashi, former Commander-in-Chief of the Combined Fleet, in an interview with the Asahi. The retired Admiral also paid high tribute to the ordnance officers who produced the effective torpedoes and explosives, saying that the honor conferred on the naval air units by His Majesty the Emperor on Tuesday must have been meant to be shared also by these ordnance officers.

Admiral Takahashi said:

"The formidable power displayed by the air units of the Combined Fleet must be said to be simply amazing. Some time ago our air units attacked and sank the 'unsinkable' Prince of Wales and the Repulse. Thus they showed that the British warships were no match for the Japanese Naval Air Arm. And the war results just achieved by the Japanese Navy Air Units have conclusively proved that British or American men-of-war can in no way whatever offer effective resistance to the Japanese.

Cannot Face Japan

"America and Britain this time, if not in the past, must have clearly realized how futile it would be for them to bring their naval forces to the East. Generally speaking, it is the height of their folly to bring to this part of the world one or two capital ships singly at a time. But if they bring over their capital ships in a mass, that would prove more to our fancy. Before the death-defying tactics and the intensive offensive spirit of Japanese airplanes the power of resistance offered by the British and American fleets will prove nil.

"America and Britain have ascribed the Pearl Harbor debacle to 'a surprise attack.' Their fatal reverses suffered in the sea battle fought off the coast of Malaya have been regarded by them as being attributable to the fact that they failed to take their air units with them. Thus they consoled themselves only in a very pitiable manner. But now with their aircraft carriers defiantly escorting them they have been given a crushing blow, which leaves them no room for making excuses.

Possess Destructive Power

"The technique displayed by the Japanese Naval airmen is simply amazing, as every sensible observer may have realized. But the Japanese Naval airmen at the same time showed how excellent were our torpedoes and how overwhelming their destructive power as compared with those of other countries. In this manner they reminded us of the extraordinary painstaking efforts made by our naval ordnance officers in the production of these weapons.

"The present Imperial Rescript has been granted to the air units, it is true. But by the granting of the same Rescript His Imperial Majesty, I could perhaps have reason to believe, has been graciously pleased also to indicate the August appreciation of the efforts contributed by those naval ordnance officers in the making of the torpedoes and other explosives. This gracious Imperial Will thus shown touches our hearts ever so profoundly.

"It is already many years since air-torpedo tactics were first adopted by the Imperial Navy. About the time when I was Commander-in-Chief of the Combined Fleet the tactics already had attained some notable progress. Since the outbreak of the China Affair in 1937 the Combined Fleet has directed its particular care to training. This has enabled them to achieve striking progress in the employment of the tactics, which have shone in their latest great war achievement.

Battle Was Fierce

"Our side also in the Coral Sea Battle has suffered certain sacrifices in the shape of some unreturned airplanes and a small-type aircraft carrier which has been sunk. This would make one readily realize how hard and fierce was the latest naval engagement. To the loyal spirits of the war heroes who sacrificed themselves for the achievement of those glorious results go our profound respects and gratitude.

"By all this Australia has now been isolated. Its suffering and tribulation being experienced over the development is imagined to be quite serious. The fact that two of the enemy aircraft carriers have been sent to the bottom at a single stroke signifies a great effective achievement, viewed from the standpoint of the air defense of the Japanese mainland. For this signal achievement I am heartily thankful as a member of the nation."

British Practise Using Gas Bombs in Warfare For Offensive Purposes

D.N.B.

STOCKHOLM, May 12.—The London press continues to deal with gas warfare, reports the Nya Dagligt Allehanda. According to the British press, there existed huge dumps of gas bombs and gas cylinders in Britain and, for the past 12 months the British forces have practised an offensive in gas warfare.

CREW LIVES 10 DAYS AS MODERN CRUSOES

Three Members of Ill-Fated Bomber Land on Barren, Uninhabited Island

Eating sea weeds, octopus and oysters, and without shelter, three warriors of the Imperial Naval Air Force lived the life of modern Robinson Crusoes for 10 days until they were rescued by a fishing boat, states an Asahi correspondent in his report dispatched from a certain base in the south under date of Tuesday.

They are first lieutenant Giichi Shimizu and sub-lieutenants Yoshiaki Sonoda and Kohei Nakayama of a bomber which was forced down on the sea near Ubin Island. Leaving the sinking plane they managed to reach the island and lived there without proper food and shelter. Their narrative reported by the correspondent follows:

"The dusk was gathering fast in the tropical sky and the clouds hovered low. The wireless apparatus got out of order and we had no means of establishing connection with comrade planes and our base. We wandered like orphans in the sky. Finally our fuel ran short. We had to seek a landing place in the dark. We were flying over the sea.

"We sighted in the gathering darkness a black dot, which on nearing was found to be an islet surrounded by cliffs in all directions. It was impossible to find a landing place and we had no alternative but to land on the sea 500 meters from the isle.

"Leaving our sinking plane we swam and swam for the isle against the current. We managed to reach the coral isle 100 meters wide and 500 meters long. On the isle, however, not a single plant was to be found, it was literally a no-man's island.

"In a sunken place we found, we had to spend a night with empty stomachs. From the following morning a life of Robinson Crusoe was started on that no-man's isle.

"Nothing to eat was found on the ground. In coral-reefs we gathered sea-weeds, which we devoured to our hearts' content. We drank water filtered through a cloth flag.

"Night came again and we had no shelter and materials to build a shelter. Trembling in the cold we slept under the starlit sky. On the following morning we gathered oysters and octopus and ate them raw.

"The third night was rainy and we could not sleep a wink because of cold. In this manner each day passed and we became weaker and weaker. There seemed to be no hope of being rescued.

"However, fortunately we were discovered by a fishing boat which happened to come near the isle and were brought to our base where our comrade fliers were anxious about our fate."

AUSTRALIA'S DEFENSES NOT FULLY MOBILIZED

Crisis Seen Looming After Allied Loss in Coral Sea, Says Forde

D.N.B.

AMSTERDAM, May 12.—The Australian Minister of War, Francis M. Forde, according to a British report from the Allied Headquarters in Australia, declared that Australia's defense had been considerably improved during the last months but that Australia was not yet fully mobilized.

He stressed that everything should be done by Australia to accelerate the supply of aircraft equipment and ammunition to Australia since it was likely that, after the recent allied loss in the Battle of the Coral Sea, Australia might be confronted with a sudden crisis.

The Australian author, Collins, declared over the British wireless that the former days of comfort and ease had vanished from his life and that life in Britain had become as uninteresting as in Australia since the war had hit Britain harder than any other country on account of its having lived too well for such a long time.

The rationing of foodstuffs in Britain was becoming more rigorous from month to month and he had almost forgotten what an orange looked like.

Sinking of the Saratoga and Yorktown

In the Battle of the Coral Sea, the American-British combined fleet was thoroughly destroyed, and the Pacific is now practically made safe from the Allies' major naval operation. To commemorate the great naval battle, Ken Matsuzoye, noted painter of marine pictures, has painted an imaginary picture of the last moment of the United States aircraft carriers, Saratoga and Yorktown, and presented it to the Navy Ministry on May 12. In the foreground is shown the Saratoga fast sinking under the heavy bombing by the Japanese warplanes, planes on her deck already spilled into the raging waves, while behind is depicted the Yorktown, which is also rapidly sinking down to Davy Jones Locker.

AUSTRALIA SHOULD FOLLOW JAPANESE

Ex-Consul-General Wakamatsu Analyzes Fighting Resources Of That Country

Australia, now bereft of all aid from the United States and Britain, will have nothing to depend on, other than its complete acceptance of the Japan-sponsored principle of the Greater East Asia Co-Prosperity Sphere to the utter abandonment of a "White Australia," according to Torao Wakamatsu, former Consul-General to Sydney.

"Japan's victory in the battle of the Coral Sea was a historic achievement," Mr. Wakamatsu said in high spirits at his Tokyo residence on Tuesday to the visiting reporter from the Miyako Shimbun. Then at the request of the newspaperman, the ex-Consul-General talked on Australia and the plight in which the vast country has just been placed, as follows:

"It is plain that Australia is now standing out in the cold as the result of the successful operations of the Japanese Navy in the Coral Sea. This miserable state, however, is the outcome of Australia's own foolish policy of following, up to now at least, what has been dictated by the United States and Britain.

"Since that country found its reliance on Britain gradually becoming impossible because of the Imperial Forces' success in cutting the traffic routes between that country and other British territories, Australia has been left with no other means for his subsistence than to look toward the United States for assistance. There was no alternative for Australia so long as that country foolishly remained opposed to the principle of a Greater East Asia as sponsored by Japan.

On Hunt for Bases

"This state of affairs in Australia, on the other hand, afforded a good opportunity for the United States which was desperately on the hunt for some bases in that region for the continuance of its futile resistance against Japan after the Philippines and the Netherlands East Indies fell into the hands of the Japanese.

Under the circumstances, the United States sent aid to Australia, so much so that Britain became jealous about it. Then came the brilliant success of the Japanese Navy in the Coral Sea which shattered the Australian hopes of obtaining succour from the United States.

"The United States, of course, will try to stage guerrilla naval warfare with the aim of maintaining its contact with Australia, but they, even if realized to some extent, will soon be annihilated by our invincible Navy. What can Australia do then to hold her own, except by faithfully accepting the principle of the Greater East Asia? Let's see if Australia has its own resources to resist Japan.

"Firstly, it is quite plain that Australia has not enough armed forces to resist our country with any hopes of maintaining prolonged warfare

(Continued on Page 2)

Imperial Naval Party Finds Lone Grave Of Japanese Made by Fak-Fak Savages

The adventurous Japanese have established themselves far and wide throughout the world. A grave of a Japanese has been found even at Fak-fak in southern New Guinea, where the weird booming of the drums of a barbaric tribe can still be heard, reports a member of the Navy Information Corps from Fak-fak.

"Soon after occupying Fak-fak without bloodshed on April 1," he said, "the Naval Landing Party found in a corner of this village a grave of a Japanese colonist.

"This village is surrounded by dense forests and rocky mountains, and although it is said to be one of the few ports in southern New Guinea, it has a population of only 1,000.

"Except for the Dutch boat that calls once a month for the copra that is abundant here, it has hardly any intercourse with the outside world. It is even said that the gruesome drumming of the Kaya-kayas, a totally uncivilized, man-eating tribe, can be heard from the rugged mountain behind the village.

Finds Grave

"Among the bushes on this barbaric land was found a tombstone, which indicated that the grave belonged to Tomizo Nishikado, of Shiomisaki, Wakayama Prefecture, who died in October, 1930 at the age of 67.

"According to our native guide, Tomizo had lived here for 20 years as the only Japanese. He ran a grocery store and was loved and respected by the natives as their father.

"'This grave was made,' the guide said, 'by his two sons, who returned to Japan after their father's death, and also by the inhabitants of the village who helped them in the construction of the grave'. So saying he reverently placed on the grave a spray of wild flowers.

"Tomizo Nishikado must now be rejoicing over the landing of the Imperial Navy from his resting place."

INDO-CHINA RESOURCES SHOULD BE DEVELOPED

Member of Investigation Party, Uchida, Stresses Fact on Return to Capital

The need to develop natural resources in French Indo-China as part of the economic program for the Greater East Asia Co-Prosperity Sphere was stressed by Goro Uchida, leading member of the Japanese investigation party to the French colony, who returned to the capital on Tuesday, reports Domei.

Other members of the party are also en route back here from French Indo-China after completing their actual work on the spot since September last year.

Interviewed by Domei, Mr. Uchida declared that the party will report to the Government on the results of its investigations as well as measures to develop the natural resources in the French colony.

"Natural resources in French Indo-China are more promising than formerly believed," he said.

He expressed his thanks for the active cooperation of the French authorities in the actual work by the party, stating that they were so kind as to send French experts to the spot to facilitate the party's investigations.

COUNT KANEKO NOT BETTER

Condition of Statesman Turns Slightly Worse

The condition of Count Kentaro Kaneko, member of the Privy Council, who has been confined to bed at his villa in Hayama since May 2 became slightly worse, reports Domei.

At 9 p.m. on Tuesday, his temperature stood at 36.9 degrees, while the respiration was 36 and the pulse 96.

STATUE TO BE ERECTED FOR DR. SUN IN SHANGHAI

Fumio Asakura Will Be Sculptor —To Be Unveiled on Patriot's Birthday

A huge bronze statue, of Dr. Sun Yat-sen, father of the Chinese Republic, will be erected this autumn in the square in front of the Municipal Government building in Shanghai, the Hochi reported on Tuesday, reports Domei.

The statue of the great Chinese leader and patriot will be built by Fumio Asakura, one of Japan's greatest sculptors, and will be unveiled on October 12 the birthday of Dr. Sun.

The statue which will be the largest of its kind in Asia, will be 36 feet high and will stand on a huge granite slab of 180 square feet.

The statue will be of Dr. Sun when he was about 60 years of age as he died at 61, and will portray him in Chinese costume.

SURABAYA PORT REPAIRS ARE ALMOST COMPLETED

Reconstruction Was Started in Early April—1,000 Natives Help

Domei

SURABAYA, May 12.—Ninety per cent of the shipbuilding and harbor facilities of this port city, which had been destroyed by the Dutch troops prior to its capture on March 8 by the Japanese Forces, have been repaired, thanks to the efforts of the Japanese naval experts as well as the Indonesian workers.

Reconstruction work was started by the Japanese early in April, participated in by about 1,000 Indonesian workers.

ALLIES MUST FIGHT TO APPEASE PUBLIC

U.S., Britain Forced to Continue Guerrilla Tactics, Says Vice-Admiral Hamada

Despite successive fatal blows dealt to their naval forces, the United States and Britain will be forced to continue their naval guerrilla warfare out of consideration of public opinion, although it is clear for them that such tactics will lead necessarily to miserable consequences. Thus declared Vice-Admiral Yoshijiro Hamada, retired, in his article entitled, "Naval Warfare in the Pacific in the Future" which appeared in the Yomiuri on Wednesday.

His article in gist follows:

As a result of the loss of the United States Pacific Fleet; the Prince of Wales and the Repulse, the main force of the British East Asiatic Fleet and capital ships in several sea battles fought since the outbreak of the War of Greater East Asia, their East Asia operations were completely overthrown

Thus, the United States and Britain have no alternative but to postpone their large-scale offensives against the Axis Powers until the repletion of their armaments. This is clearly shown in President Roosevelt's message delivered in Congress on January 6. In his message President Roosevelt said: "The intensified offensive will be launched at a proper time. By that time this country must exceed the Axis Powers overwhelmingly in the production of arms."

Namely, the United States and Britain intend to win the current war through "time" and "materials". Thus, we are waiting until our armaments are replenished. Yet, hostilities will be continued.

The enemy wanted to postpone the hostilities, however, this country would not allow them to do so. The United States deserted Singapore, Hongkong, Guam, Wake and the Philippines, with folded arms but, however, Australia is not a country which they can desert politically, even though they may run the risk strategically.

In this area, the enemy will be forced to fight us, whether they like it or not. If the United States and Great Britain had not taken any measures for the rescue of Java Island, their allies would not have placed confidence in them. This is the reason why the battles off Surabaya and Batavia took place.

To extend their hands for the rescue of Australia, the battle in the Coral Sea was fought with the result that they were again dealt a fatal blow.

The enemy would desire to suspend hostilities to foster their warring strength. But out of consideration for the public opinion demanding offensive operations against the Axis Powers, the United States and, British navies must do something to satisfy the public. As a result, naval

(Continued on Page 2)

GERMAN OFFENSIVE STARTS ALONG ENTIRE DONETZ FRONT; FIERCE BATTLE SAID RAGING

British Armed Forces Suffer Huge Casualties In Two Years of War

Domei

LISBON, May 12.—Major Clement R. Attlee, British Deputy Prime Minister, and Secretary of State for the Dominions, has announced in the House of Commons that the British Army and Navy sustained a total of 183,550 casualties in the two years from September 3, 1939 to September 2, 1941, according to a Reuter's dispatch from London today. The report added that the announced casualties included 48,973 killed, 46,363 injured and 29,756 missing, as well as 58,458 taken prisoners.

2 Million Men Reported To Be Moving Steadily Against Russians

RESISTANCE STRONG

Asahi Service

STOCKHOLM, May 12.—German-Rumanian forces have commenced large scale offensive against the Soviet troops in the Kertch Peninsula on May 8 under the strong protection of the air force, it is reported by Reuter.

Meanwhile, the Berne correspondent of the New York Times reports that the German forces have started an offensive on the entire Donetz front with 2,000,000 men, according to the Reuter report from New York.

In the engagement it is reported that about 24 mechanized German divisions with 1,000 to 2,000 airplanes have opened offensive activities on the entire front extending 400 kilometers from Dniepropetrovsk in the north to the Kertch Peninsula in the south, and are steadily advancing.

The report further said that in the Leningrad sector, the Reich forces have also commenced positive operation.

Fierce Battle Raging

D.N.B.

BERLIN, May 12.—According to an announcement of the High Command, German and Rumanian troops, supported by strong formations of the Luftwaffe, have started an offensive on the peninsula of Kertch on May 8. The battle has been raging in full intensity since that date.

The local evening papers published lengthy comments on the new German offensive on the Kertch Peninsula. The Deutsche Allgemeine Zeitung writes that the enemy had the possibility of filling up his formations and that the present Soviet formations were in number far superior to the German forces.

The paper points out that at this point the Soviets had their Black Sea fleet at their disposal and that they were in possession of bases for the supply of their troops across the Black Sea. During the winter period they, moreover, had been able to extend their fortifications on the peninsula.

For military as well as for psychological reasons considerable resistance was to be reckoned with, writes the paper, since the Soviets would certainly be anxious to deny that the initiative in this front sector had been taken over by the Germans.

Churchill Is Flayed

The "Berliner Boersenzeitung" stresses that this fresh German and Rumanian attack on the Kertch Peninsula constituted a characteristic illustration of Churchill's boastful statements in the House of Commons. As late as the evening of May 10 Churchill declared arrogantly that he knew nothing of preparations for a German offensive in the East. Either, the paper stated, his Soviet ally had kept secret from him these German preparations or Churchill had deceived his people also in this point of his speech.

3 British Destroyers Sunk

D.N.B.

BERLIN, May 12.—The British news service officially confirmed the sinking of three British destroyers in the Mediterranean in the vicinity of the Island of Crete by the Luftwaffe.

The names of the destroyers are given as Lively, Jackal and the Kipling.

The Lively had a displacement of 1,920-tons, carried eight torpedo tubes and six 12 centimeter guns. She was capable of a speed of 36.5 knots.

The Jackal and the Kipling displaced each 1,690-tons carrying six torpedo tubes and six 12 centimeter guns each.

It is emphasized in Berlin military quarters that the sinking of these British destroyers constituted a particular success of the German air force, since the destruction of this British destroyer formation meant another serious blow to the British shipping routes from Port Said and Alexandria to Malta and Gibraltar.

At the same time, the German submarines operating in the Mediterranean under the most difficult conditions have been greatly relieved.

With the inclusion of these three destroyers Britain, since the outbreak of the war, has lost a total of 72 destroyers while during the World War she only lost 66.

Java's Rail Resumed

Domei

SURABAYA, May 12.—All railway services in Java have been restored to normalcy with the single exception of the Batavia-Merak railway, it was revealed here today.

15 TANKS CAPTURED IN YUNNAN SECTOR

Other War Trophies Include Six Armored Cars and 1,200 Automobiles

Domei

YUNNAN FRONT, May 12.—In addition to large amounts of aid-Chungking materials seized in Yunnan Province, Japanese troops have captured a sizeable quantity of arms and ammunition at various places along the Burma route.

A total of 15 tanks, six armored cars, 1,200 automobiles, 20 light machine-guns, 100 small arms, one mountain gun, 200 rounds of mountain-gun shells and 3,000 hand grenades has fallen into Japanese hands.

Red Remnants Routed

Domei

CENTRAL HOPEI FRONT, May 12.—Crack units of the Japanese Expeditionary Forces in North China have routed Chinese remnants under Yu Chuen-shin, which were encircled by the Japanese iron ring, it has been revealed.

On the other hand, the Chinese remnants encircled by the Japanese near Hukiachih-chen in Hopei Province left 100 dead on the battlefields following fierce actions.

During the engagements the Japanese Forces gained a large quantity of arms and ammunition.

To Crush Supply Base

Domei

CENTRAL HOPEI FRONT, May 12.—The current Japanese campaign in the Central Hopei Province primarily aims at the overthrowing of the supply base in that area for the Communist troops in the Tahan Mountain Range in western Hopei Province, the spokesman of the press section of the Japanese Expeditionary Forces in North China declared in a statement issued at 3 p.m. today.

Pointing out that the Communist forces which are at present resisting the Japanese Forces have been infesting the plains in Central Hopei Province and sending materials to other Red troops in western Hopei, the spokesman said that extirpation of the Communist elements from Central Hopei will largely promote the reconstruction of North China.

He added that the central Hopei plains promise large cotton crops.

Wan Kawnhawng Falls

Domei

BURMA FRONT, May 12.—Wan Kawnhawng, strategic town in eastern Burma, fell into Japanese hands last Sunday, after spirited Japanese drives along the Loilem-Keng Tung road in pursuit of the main body of the Chungking Sixth Army and part of the Fifth Army, it was revealed here today.

Enemy positions near Wan Laihka, on the Mong Pawn River, last Saturday, and Wan Kawnhawng was occupied the following day, thereby cutting the last road for the Chungking troops to escape toward the Keng Tung sector.

Rangoon Hails Native Son

The citizens of Rangoon were recently overjoyed when Superior Private Tatsuo Ota, the son of a Japanese father and Burmese mother, who had lived for a long time there, entered his native city, Rangoon, reports a Yomiuri correspondent somewhere on the foremost front in Burma. The report follows:

"Mandalay, where the combined British and Chungking forces put up a desperate resistance, has fallen. The Japanese troops are entering the city with Rising Sun flags at the head of the ranks." So broadcast the Tokyo Broadcasting Station in clear and crisp Burmese over Rangoon several days ago. The citizens of Rangoon listened to the broadcast with intense joy.

The announcer was a Burmese woman who had been married to a Japanese named Yoichiro Ota. Mr. Ota, who had long been in Rangoon,

(Continued on Page 2)

San Francisco Chronicle

THE CITY'S ONLY HOME-OWNED NEWSPAPER

FINAL
Morning Edition

FOUNDED 1865—VOL. CLIV, NO. 123 CCCC**** SAN FRANCISCO, MONDAY, MAY 18, 1942 DAILY 5 CENTS, SUNDAY 12 CENTS: DAILY AND SUNDAY PER MONTH. $1.40

RUSSIANS WIN GREAT VICTORY AT KHARKOV!

War in Russia

Red Army Advances 30 Miles, Takes 300 Towns Near Kharkov

Soviet Says Resistance Definitely Broken, Nazi Units in Wild Flight

By HENRY C. CASSIDY
Associated Press Staff Writer

MOSCOW, May 18—The Russian offensive on the Kharkov front has resulted in a Soviet advance of from 20 to 60 kilometers (from 12.4 to 37 miles) and the recapture of 300 populated places, the government announced in a special communique today (Monday).

The smashing Red armies have inflicted a terrific toll upon the Germans, killing about 12,000 Nazi soldiers and officers during the week's onslaught in this area, the announcement said.

"The offensive continues," the bulletin concluded.

More than 1200 prisoners have been taken, the announcement said, and a great amount of Nazi war material has fallen to the Red army. Four hundred German tanks have been destroyed.

The special announcement followed official advices from the front telling of headlong flight of broken German forces before Kharkov, key to the all-important Ukraine.

German resistance in the Kharkov sector has been "definitely broken," it was stated.

The special announcement summarized action before Kharkov since the opening of the Soviet offensive there May 12 and pronounced the first week's operations a resounding success for the Red Army.

THE TEXT OF THE COMMUNIQUE

It said:

"On May 12 our troops, launching an offensive in the Kharkov region, broke through the German defense line and having repulsed a counter-attack of large enemy tank formations and armored troops, are pressing forward westward.

"From May 12 to May 16 our units advanced to a depth of 20 to 60 kilometers and liberated more than 300 inhabited localities.

"During the same period, according to incomplete figures our troops captured the following trophies from the enemy: 365 guns, 25 tanks, 188 mortars, 379 machine-guns, 46,413 shells and 89 cases of shells.

"Other trophies were: 23,384 mines, about 1,000,000 cartridges, 13,000 hand grenades, 90 trucks, 29 radio stations, and 38 artillery provision and supply dumps.

"More than 1200 prisoners were taken.

"During the same period we destroyed 400 German tanks, 210 guns, 33 mortars, 217 machineguns, about 700 trucks, more than 100 supply carts, 12 dumps of various kinds and 147 planes.

"About 12,000 German soldiers

Continued on Page 3, Col. 1

WILSON TO SIGN DRAFT BILL TODAY . . . Senate Passes Measure 65 to 8 . . . GERMANS BURNING PATH FOR RETREAT . . . JAPANESE GUNBOATS JOIN ALLIES IN HUNT FOR TEUTONIC SHARKS . . . ALSACE AND LORRAINE DECLARE FOR RETURN TO FRANCE . . . STEINHART WILL GIVES $240,000 FOR AQUARIUM

Weather Man

"Flash!" said Anemometer, the Weather Bureau cat. "G'evening-mr.andmrs.northamericaandallthe shipsatsealetsgotopress. Flash!"

"What do you think you're doing?" said the Weather Man, eyeing the cat with disgust. The cat preened himself in front of the mirror.

"I'm understudy for Walter Winchell at the Navy Relief Show tomorrow night," he said.

"Why all this interest in Navy Relief?" said the W. M.

"My relief money goes to ships' cats," said Anemometer. And he continued to practice muttering under his breath. "Flash! Flash! Flash!"

The Red Army's storm planes, often flying at from 50 to 100 feet over the German lines, are reported pounding tanks and scattering Nazi troops. In this Associated Press Radiophoto, received from Moscow yesterday, Red planes attack a German tank column. Note the explosions and burning tanks.

The Military Digest: Chinese Claim Three Burma Victories; New Jap Drive Threatens

By PETER D. WHITNEY

The German claim to have captured the city of Kerch is at last becoming true. The Soviet communique admits fighting has reached districts of the city. The Germans announce their air forces are fiercely attacking Red Army units being evacuated across the Kerchenski straits to the Taman peninsula. Some 68,000 prisoners are claimed by the Berlin radio.

On the other hand, the Timoshenko offensive in the Kharkov area progresses with such weight that it very likely will snatch from Adolf Hitler the fruits of his victory farther south.

Red Star, Red Army newspaper, says the citizens of Krasnograd must hear the "sounds of spring," the heavy Soviet cannonade which presumably announces the armies of liberation. Krasnograd, 55 miles southwest of Kharkov, is along the railway from Soviet-held Lozovaya to Poltava, a rail junction subsidiary in importance only to Kharkov itself. Timoshenko, studying the chessboard of the Ukraine at his headquarters, knows that the capture of Poltava would make him master of the strategic situation from Kiev to the Crimea.

Western Front

Sir Stafford Crips told his Bristol constituents the governments of the U. S. and Britain are "as keen and anxious" for a second front against the Nazis as the people; "the only difference is that you can talk freely about it; whereas we cannot."

The RAF resumed its daylight raids against Boulogne docks, but met the most formidable German fighter offensive of 1942. Result: an air battle reminiscent of the battle of Britain, or Dunkerque.

War Against Japan

Chungking commentators were claiming three separate victories in Burma, where the Japs have not yet mustered sufficient force or courage to cross the Salween river. From the south, however, there were indications the Japanese were going to bring to life an entire new front along the Thai and Indo-China borders with China's Yunnan.

For one thing, the Japs were admitted to have advanced from Thailand, captured the important hill city of Kengtung in the Shan states of Burma, and thence to have been hurled back by the Chinese. For another, the AVG, which has established itself on new airdromes, made a fierce assault on Jap trains and trucks at Laokay, near the Chinese border in Indo-China.

Laokay, ever since the Chinese destroyed their part of the railroad that used to run from Hanoi to Kunming, has been the railhead of this once-important line, and a logical place for Japanese supply and troop concentrations.

Tokyo radio declared a task force composed of the two crack U. S. aircraft carriers Hornet and Enterprise, with cruisers and destroyers, had been sighted by Japanese air reconnaissance 500 miles east of the Solomon islands, but sharply altered its course.

If this was true, there is likely to be a battle today or tomorrow. Tokyo identified the two carriers as above because she had mendaciously claimed the sinking of their sister ship, Yorktown, in the Battle of the Coral Sea.

The Japs again raided Port Moresby with Zero fighter planes. One of the nine was shot down; two others damaged.

In China proper, Japan was carrying on heavy air raids in connection with her offensive against secret Chinese bases in coastal Chekiang province.

Lew Ayres Will Join the Army Today

WYETH, Or., May 17 (AP)—Lew Ayres, the Hollywood film actor, will leave the conscientious objectors' camp here tomorrow to enter the Army.

Ayres, who insisted he still held unwavering objections to arms-bearing, said he had received notice to report to the draft board at Hood River, Or., and would be assigned later to a medical corps.

Harold Herschner, draft board chairman, said at Hood River that Ayres would be inducted like any other man entering the Army.

Ayres probably will take the 13-week basic training period and be assigned to a medical unit.

Japs profess to have unearthed a traitor in their Diet, son of the last liberal Premier—who was murdered by fanatics — see Foreign News Fronts on Page 2.

RAF Meets Surprising Resistance

By J. WES GALLAGHER
Associated Press Staff Writer

LONDON, May 17—The German Air Force in occupied France suddenly put up its first real opposition to British fighters in several weeks today and sought in day-long battles to smash one of the biggest RAF cross-channel sweeps of the year.

At least nine Nazi planes and eight British were reported destroyed.

(The Berlin radio broadcast a German High Command announcement saying the German planes shot down 15 planes without any Nazi losses.)

Observers described the morning RAF bombardment as "one of the heaviest and most continuous series of explosions since the days of Dunkerque."

Reichsmarshal Goering's air force for the first time in a week threw its full-scale fighter strength into the attempts to smash back the British attack, reversing sharply the recent German policy of conserving strength while trying to pick off stragglers.

Goering was reported to have been in Paris recently and it was not definitely know whether he had gone back to Germany. It was possible that one of the objects of his trip to occupied France was to bolster aerial resistance, with the results shown in today's heavy fighting.

Boston (Douglas) bombers, roaring under an umbrella of Spitfire and Hurricane fighters, smashed at Boulogne's much-bombed docks.

Flight Lieutenant Carroll Warren McColpin of Buffalo, N. Y., of the Third American Eagle squadron, shot down one of the two Nazi fighters destroyed in the

Continued on Page 2, Col. 7

Dewey Backed Over Willkie

HAMILTON, N. Y., May 17 (U.P.)—New York's Young Republican Clubs indorsed former New York District Attorney Thomas E. Dewey for the Republican gubernatorial nomination today.

The indorsement, which came at a special session behind closed doors, was considered a victory for Dewey over Wendell L. Willkie, who won the 1940 Presidential nomination from the New York "gang buster." It was reported that the resolution was not unanimously approved.

INSIDE EUROPE

Five of America's top correspondents, just arrived in Lisbon from Axis internment camps discuss Italy, Germany, Axis Europe and possible phases of the war this summer.

See Page 4

Millions in Pay Yielded By Ship Labor

By the Associated Press

CHICAGO, May 17—Representatives of the Nation's shipyard workers agreed today to relinquish an estimated $75,000,000 to $100,000,000 in wage increases today, in the first major demonstration of labor's acquiescence to President Roosevelt's anti-inflation program.

A wage stabilization agreement covering some 550,000 workers in the Nation's private shipyards was adopted today, providing:

1—Wage increases of 8 per cent which will total from $125,000,000 to $150,000,000 in the next 12 months, instead of the $225,000,000 to which "cost of living" clauses in existing contracts entitled the men.

2—Investment of wage increases in U. S. savings bonds "which will not be cashed except in case of extreme emergency."

3—Uniform wages in the shipbuilding industry throughout the Nation and abolishment of a differential in the Gulf Coast zone.

4—Elimination of Saturday and Sunday as "premium days," requiring double pay. Under the agreement the men will work a five-day, 40-hour week with time and a half for any sixth day and double time for any seventh day in one week.

The agreement was reached today after three weeks of negotiations

Continued on Page 5, Col. 1

Mexicans Stone German Factory

MONTERREY, Mexico. May 17 (AP)—A crowd of workers protesting the German sinking of the Mexican tanker Potrero Del Llano stoned a German-owned soap factory yesterday, breaking windows and firing shots into the air.

Prices: Ceilings Go Into Effect Today and Cost of Living Will Drop About 1½%

By Associated Press

WASHINGTON, May 17—The cost of living is due to take a drop of about 1½ per cent tomorrow when a Government ceiling becomes effective on retail prices of virtually everything Americans eat, use or wear.

That doesn't mean you will find marked reductions in prices if you walk into a store tomorrow. A ceiling went into effect a week ago on wholesale prices and most retailers already have brought their prices into line. Many items have not risen above the ceiling.

But economists figure the ceiling—a prohibition against charging a higher price for covered items than the highest charged in March—will mean a saving to the average home budget of about 1½ per cent, compared with costs in the last 30 or 40 days.

For millions of consumers the ceiling is intended to be a lid on the cost of living for the duration of the war.

Most drastic economic restraint ever imposed in the United States, it pegs the cost of thousands of articles. Only exceptions important to the average family are a limited list of food commodities, such as eggs and poultry, butter, flour, mutton and lamb.

All canned and bottled goods, clothing, milk, bread, household sundries, furniture and tobacco are affected.

Terming the universal ceiling "The citizen's charter of security against rising living costs," Price Administrator Leon Henderson urged consumers to acquaint themselves thoroughly with these facts:

All commodities sold at retail, except those specifically excluded from the price regulations, are price-controlled.

The maximum prices are the highest charged by each individual seller during March, 1942.

This means that different stores will have different maximum prices for the same article—just as they did in March. And you may still shop around for the best bargain.

There is nothing in the regulations to prevent a retailer from reducing his prices. No price, however, may exceed the ceiling.

Important groups of commodities have been designated "cost-of-living" items and the ceiling prices on them must be posted by every retailer, beginning tomorrow. However, the fact that no "ceiling price" is publicly shown does not mean that an item is exempt from control; whether the price is posted or not, the item is covered unless specifically exempt.

Automatically, as the ceiling prices become effective, each retailer becomes a licensee of the Government, although he will have no physical evidence of this licensing until after a national registration of all retail outlets, scheduled soon. If, after an OPA warning, a retailer continues to violate the price ceiling, he may have his license to do business taken away and become liable to fine or imprisonment.

Henderson urged, however, that consumers co-operate with merchants and "be tolerant of misunderstandings and honest mistakes over the next few weeks."

"OPA is proceeding," he said, "on the assumption that every American is fully aware of the importance of price control and that every retailer will take it as a matter of duty to his country to abide by the letter and the spirit of the regulation."

Births Break All State Records

California's birth rate during 1941 broke all State records with a total of 125,050 births, the Department of Public Health announced yesterday. There were 111,840 births during 1940.

Los Angeles county topped the State with 48,735 births in 1941, against 42,865 the preceding year. San Francisco came next with 9812, compared to 8810 in 1940.

Dominicans Elect Ex-President

CIUDAD TRUJILLO, Dominican Republic, May 17 (AP)—Gen. Rafael L. Trujillo, former president of the Dominican republic, has been re-elected to the office without opposition.

Malta Bags Five Axis Planes

CAIRO. May 17 (AP)—Five more Axis aircraft have been shot down in raids on Malta, the RAF Middle East communique said today and three RAF craft lost in the same fighting.

5¢
6 Cents in Canada

SUNDAY MIRROR
Member of the Associated Press
Buy WAR Bonds

WEATHER Continued Warm. (Details on Page 2)
(Copyright, 1942, Daily Mirror, Inc.)
FINAL EDITION ★★

Vol. 11. No. 22 C New York, Sunday, May 31, 1942 80 Pages
Including 20 Page Magazine and Sixteen Pages of Comics

5¢
6 Cents in Canada

BRITISH TAKE OFFENSIVE IN LIBYA BATTLE

Story on Page 3

(Mirror Photo)

Heroes' Tribute

Veterans of Foreign Wars carry their colors past the grand stand at 89th St. and Riverside Drive in annual Memorial Day march commemorating the nation's war dead. More than 650,000 spectators lined the parade course to watch 26,000 marchers, including four G. A. R. veterans.

(Story on Page 2, Other Photos on Pages 2, 22 and 23.)

WATERTOWN PUBLIC OPINION

VOL. LVIII | ASSOCIATED PRESS | WATERTOWN, S. D., MONDAY, JUNE 1, 1942 | LEASED WIRE SERVICE | NUMBER 128

GREATEST RAID HITS COLOGNE

Hundreds Here For Start Of State Fire School

Parade Opens 5-Day Convention; Many Contests

Governor Bushfield Shares Afternoon Program With Goehring

Hundreds of South Dakota firemen were gathered in Watertown Monday for their annual five-day school, which includes contests, entertainment events and business meetings as well as sessions of instruction each day.

A parade of firemen and bands, here for the convention, opened the school Monday afternoon after the morning was spent on registration. Prizes were offered to the fire department with the most men in line and the largest bands.

In the parade were Peck's Watertown band, bands from Estelline, Henry and Florence; and groups of firemen from ten South Dakota towns. The parade was led by massed flags and a car carrying Governor Harlan J. Bushfield, Mayor George Beier and firemen association officials.

Governor Harlan J. Bushfield was to be the main speaker at the opening session of the school. He was to share the program with Sam Goehring, Avon, president of the Firemen association; Mayor George Beier and Penn Thompson, secretary of the Watertown Chamber of Commerce, who were to give the addresses of welcome, and George K. Burt, state fire marshal.

A question and discussion period was to conclude this afternoon's session, with Harry K. Rogers of the Western Acturial bureau at Chicago, in charge.

Band Concert Tonight

A massed band concert is scheduled for 7 o'clock tonight to be followed by a dance. The concert will be held on the court house lawn if the weather permits. Otherwise it will be in the city auditorium. The dance will be held in the auditorium.

Flags lined the Watertown streets today to welcome the visiting firemen who have never met in this part of the state before.

National defense is being stressed at the fire school this year with such topics as "First Aid and Gas Masks" and "Salvage" taking a prominent place on the program. All sessions of the school are open to the general public.

$1,750 In Prizes

Contests among the fire departments of the state will be among the highlights of the convention. Prizes totalling $1,750 have been offered in the events, the first of which—a three man 150 foot hose carrying contest with a $40 purse—will be held Tuesday afternoon at 3 o'clock in front of the municipal auditorium.

Tuesday's program will include also three instruction sessions beginning at 8:30 and 10:30 a. m. and 1:30 p. m., and a Dutch Lunch served by the Watertown fire department at 6 p. m.

Officers of the state association will be elected at the annual business meeting at 7:30 o'clock Thursday evening. Friday morning, the last day of the school, will be devoted to contests.

Present officers of the state association are: Sam Goehring, Avon, president; H. W. Hanigan, Pierre, vice president; I. D. Lee, Madison, treasurer; Mike Sullivan, Parkston, secretary; Ted Wagner, Rapid City; Gaile Villier, Hudson; and L. J. Bingham, Hot Springs, directors. John Muller of HotSprings is an honorary member of the board of directors; and George K. Burt, Pierre, is an ex-officio member.

Tuesday Program

Tuesday's program follows:

8:30 to 9:00 a. m. — Address, A Challenge to your Courage—Walter G. Rundin.

(Continued On Page 2)
(See Convention)

Boy Is Drowned In Creek Near Mitchell

MITCHELL—(AP)—Ivan Olson, 14-year old son of Mr. and Mrs. Lambert Olson, farmers living northeast of Mitchell, was drowned in Rock creek near their farm home Sunday. Ivan and two younger boys had gone to the creek earlier. The lad went into the ordinarily placid stream of water to retrieve his hat and was unable to crawl out. The younger boys ran for help and the body was recovered about two hours later.

Today In Congress

(By The Associated Press)

Senate
Routine Session.
House
Considers $140,000,000 bill to construct Florida pipe line and barge canal.
Saturday
Senate and House
In recess.

Weekend Rains Boost May Moisture

THE WEATHER

(By The Associated Press)

SOUTH DAKOTA —Showers and thunderstorms this afternoon and tonight; no important change in temperature.

MINNESOTA—Not much change in temperature today and tonight except cooler extreme southeast portion tonight; scattered showers and thunderstorms southeast portion today.

NORTH DAKOTA—Showers and light thunderstorms this afternoon and tonight; warmer west this afternoon.

TEMPERATURES

Temperatures and precipitation for 24 hour period ending 7 a. m. today:

	High	Low	Prec.
Watertown	61	63	...
Aberdeen	60	52	...
Sioux Falls	66	54	.51
Pierre	64	54	...
Brookings	62	55	...
Spearfish	62	45	...
Philip	64	53	...
Chadron, Neb.	69	52	...
Ashley, N. D.	63	50	...
Sioux City, Ia.	80	62	.32

State Offers Checks To Show Douglas Payoff

$500 Declared Paid State Treasurer In $200,000 Deal

ABERDEEN—(AP)— The state introduced checks Monday which it contends substantiate Phill T. Burns' testimony that he gave State Treasurer W. G. Douglas $500 payoff of a $200,000 cement plant bond sale.

The exhibits were introduced while William H. Paulsen, Minneapolis auditor, was on the stand.

Paulsen, now an employe of the Northern Pump company but formerly with the Harris Upton company branch office at Minneapolis, identifide the instruments. One was a $500 check made out by Burns, Aberdeen bond broker, and the other a cashier's draft Paulsen testified he issued to Burns in exchange for the other check.

Burns, who stepped down from the stand while Paulsen testified, had declared the Burns company profits from the $200,000 sale were $1,688.92. He said he drew $500 from the company with which to pay Douglas, then in Minneapolis.

Alters Testimony On Wife

Burns altered previous tesctimony that his wife saw him give Douglas the $500.

"Just state the circumstances," the state's counsel asked him.

"Well,'' he said, "the only way to state it, my wife had seen Mr. Douglas accept money on two or three occasions and she saw one payoff in May, 1941.''

"Where was it?"

"In the Nicollet hotel."

Burns said he discovered his wife was not present when a "payoff" was made in the $200,000 deal after he had testified in preliminary hearing early in May.

The state also asked Burns to step down from the witness chair while State Auditor W. W. Warner identified expense vouchers and a state draft made out to Douglas in connection with the sale of $70,000 soldiers' bonus bonds.

Collected For Trip Twice

Burns had testified that he paid Douglas 'expenses into Minneapolis so he could sign the bonds and make them negotiable. The state contends Douglas collected also from the state.

Relating the soldiers' bonus bond deal, Burns said that after the deal was completed the Northwestern National Bank of Minneapolis objected to paying the postage and insurance costs of mailing to Pierre and the Burns company offered to assume that obligation.

"I volunteered to pay the mailing costs," Burns said, "but Douglas said he wanted to see some baseball games that were in the twin cities at that time and he would go into Minneapolis to sign the bonds, if the Burns company paid the expenses."

Letter Introduced

The state introduced a carbon of a letter from Douglas to Burns and also an itemized expense statement for $51.10, which Burns had said he received from Douglas.

Also presented in evidence were a letter Burns said he wrote Douglas that time and a check. The letter said "I hope the baseball games were good."

Burns said his company's profit was $220.50 and he received a draft from the state for that amount.

"Is that the only transaction in which you were paid by a treasurer's check?'' Prosecutor E. D. Barron asked him.

"That was the only time."

(Continued On Page 2)
(See State Officials)

Restoration Of Communication Reveals Damage

Friday Night Rain 1.82 Inches Here--Total Above Six

Sunshine and warm weather were in demand in northeastern South Dakota Monday as June started with a mist and cool temperature, after a month of rain and destructive wind storms.

May brought Watertown more than six inches of rainfall, over two inches above the average May figure of 3.72. Exact amount of May prescipitation here was unavailable because war censorship restrictions ban reporting of rainfalls of less than .10 of an inch.

Reported precipitation for the month of May here was 5.21 inches. In addition to this amount rainfall during the last four days of April totalled 2.47, making a total of 8.38 inches of rain in a little over one month.

Heavy Rain Friday

A heavy downpour of rain struck Watertown Friday night, flooding streets in low parts of the city. Total precipitation during the Friday night storm was reported at 1.82 inches at the airport weather station.

The Friday night storm followed by a little more than 12 hours a destructive wind, hail and rain storm which caused an estimated million dollars damage to farm and town buildings in Hamlin and Clark counties.

Restoration of communications between the storm area and Watertown brought reports of widespread damage in southern Clark county as well as in Hamlin county.

Vienna Buildings Damaged

Scarecely a building in the Vienna vicinity escaped broken windows, and south and west of Clark, the rain came in deluges, many residents of that area reporting that furnishings were practically ruined by the rain that poured in through smashed windows. One woman said she found her living room curtains up on the eavespouts, and another reported that she hasn't even found part of hers yet.

Rye was most seriously damaged in the storm-swept area. Other small grains were hard hit, but it is believed that it will grow up again. Heavy poultry losses were reported over a wide area.

On the Walter Hallberg farm, sheep were reported killed, and extensive damage was done to the house, which had been newly decorated. After the storm, leaves from trees and bits of glass were beaten into the new wall paper, and rugs and furniture were watersoaked.

Barns were blown down on the Emil Larson and Pete Mitchell farms, and an addition to a barn was partially damaged on the Clarence Day farm. The Frank Glines farm near Vienna was hard hit, almost every building except the house being wrecked.

Many Windows Broken

Smashed windows from hail was the most commonly reported damage. On the Peter Trevithick farm 56

(Continued On Page 2)
(See Storm Damage)

State Salvage Board Named

PIERRE —(AP)— Governor Harlan J. Bushfield has appointed members to a salvage section of the bureau of industrial conservation under the state defense council following appointment of York Sampson of Sioux Falls as executive secretary to the group.

Sampson's committee is to work with industrial committees already organized by South Dakota business men.

The committee includes Carl A. Quarnberg, Rapid City, chairman. He is president of the Greater South Dakota Assocation which had set up district salvage groups.

Cikibek Edward A. Beckwith, Rapid City, chairman of the state defense council; Claude A. Hamilton, Sioux Falls, American Legion commander; J. W. Stonebarger, Watertown, manager of International Harvester company, to represent business; Adolph S. Anderson, Sioux Falls, representing Boy Scouts; Mrs. C. E. Robbins, Pierre, representing Girl Scouts; Richard M. Pease, Huron, secretary of Associated Retailers; Miss Harriett Folds, Sioux Falls, for the Business and Professional Women's Clubs; Alfred Barnes, Huron, chairman of the South Dakota U. S. Department of Agriculture war board, and Mrs. J. C. Lepler, Watertown, president of South Dakota Parent-Teachers Association.

Price Of Wool Drops 7 Cents On Import Order

NEW YORK —(AP)— Wool tops futures lost as much as 6 and 7 cents a pound Monday in an early flurry of liquidation that followed the report President Roosevelt had authorized purchase abroad and duty-free import of materials needed for war purposes.

Trade sources estimated contracts covering more than 300,000 pounds of wool tops changed hands by noon.

The March delivery reacted 7.3 cents to $1.20 a pound, December lost 6.5 cents to $1.19½, and other deliveries showed losses of 1.8 to 5 cents a pound.

Cotton futures, weak from the opening, declined as much as $1 a bale as traders considered the possibility of heavier imports from South America under the presidential authorization.

While a ceiling of $1.39 a pound had been placed on wool tops, prices have ranged well under that figure recently.

BASEBALL MEETING CALLED

Members of the Park & Grant baseball team have been asked to meet Tuesday evening at 7:30 o'clock at the Maple Leaf Cafe.

The announcement was made by Jack Lang, manager of the Park & Grant team.

Barrymore Funeral To Be Held Tuesday

LOS ANGELES —(AP)— Brief and simple funeral services will be held for John Barrymore Tuesday with only 33 persons invited, among them two of the actor's four former wives, Elaine Barrie and Dolores Costello.

Father John O'Donnell of the Immaculate Heart church, who received Barrymore back in to the Catholic faith shortly before his death last Friday night, will officiate at requiem mass. The body will be placed in the family crypt.

Japs' Midget Subs Sunk In Sydney Raid

(By The Associated Press)

A parried thrust into Sydney harbor by a force of Japan's midget submarines, successful Allied air raids on Japanese island bases facing Australia and valiant Chinese efforts to check Japan's Chekiang province offensive were reported today from the Far Pacific war.

Following the Sydney attack, General MacArthur conferred for four hours with Prime Minister Curtin at Melbourne and the Prime Minister's happiness was so evident that some observers speculated that the submarines mothership had been damaged or captured.

It could be assumed that the appearance of the little raiders at Sydney had touched off an intense search for their base.

Submarines, apparently of the two man type which the Japanese had used fruitlessly at Pearl Harbor, ran into thundering shellfire and depth charges in the Australian harbor Sunday night and three of them probably were destroyed.

The only achievement of the suicide raiders, believed similar to the midget undersea craft which figured in the attack on Pearl harbor last Dec. 7, was the sinking of an old steamer used as a ferry.

The raid, however, carried the war to southern Australia for the first time and gave the residents of Sydney—the largest city in this broad continent—an exciting night punctuated by the sounds of heavy gunfire.

Spotted At 11 P. M.

The submarines were spotted first at about 11 P. M. and two sudden gunshots from Allied defense batter-

(Continued On Page 2)
(See Japs)

THE WAR TODAY----

Growing Allied Air Power Seen In Cologne Raid, Libyan Action

BY DEWITT MACKENZIE
(Wide World War Analyst)

The Allies very definitely are getting ahead with their job of tapping Herr Hitler to learn the measure of his girth.

Latest and most impressive proof of this rests in the revelation of air power in the record British bombing raid by some 1,250 warplanes which laid waste a large area of the ancient Rhenish city of Cologne—a really terrifying exhibition.

That is, to use the language of British Premier Churchill, "a hearald of what Germany will receive, city by city." This statement acquires added significance through the announcement Monday in London by Lieut. General Henry Arnold, head of the United States air forces, that he has practically completed conferences with British leaders to develop "the maximum impact of our combined air strength" on Germany.

Overwhelming Air Power Coming

In short, the curtain has been drawn aside to give us a glimpse of an Allied air fleet which is rapidly developing into a force that nothing on earth will be able to withstand. We shall in due course be able to blast Hitler's Germany off the map, to make way for another Reich which will fit into the new world order.

Still, we shouldn't let this spectacular event obscure the momentous development on the Russian front. The struggle for the main gateway to the golden Caucasus, upon which the outcome of the war depends to such large degree, appears to have reached the lull which may be said to mark the end of the first stage of this armageddon, with the advantage resting on the Allied side.

True, the Hitlerites have suffered no overwhelming defeat along the great Kharkov-Rostov sector which

(Continued On Page 2)
(See War Today)

Seven Dead, Others Injured As Huge Wave Sweeps Lake Erie

CLEVELAND —(AP)— The Lake Erie shore counted seven dead Monday from the sudden sweep of a water wall, described at one point as 15 to 20 feet high, which plundged against night fishing parties in a 60-mile stretch of the lakefront.

At least seven others were injured and hospitalized.

A sudden shift in wind direction was the major cause of the huge wave the Cleveland weather bureau reported.

The wall of water struck about 2:15 A. M. Sunday as all-night fishermen were bent on their holiday weekend sport.

John Austin, of Wooster, O., said "There was a slight swell followed by a strong undertow. The next thing I knew a wall of water about 15 or 20 feet crashed down on us, overturning our boat."

The disaster recalled the loss of five lives in a similar tragedy in Lake Michigan, near Holland, Mich., on July 13, 1938. Another huge wave, followed by a giant undertow, swept eleven bathers to death in Lake Erie near Brant, south of Buffalo, N. Y., on Aug. 8, 1926.

Powerful Blow From Air Heralds Allied Offensive, Now Near

Destruction Most Of Germany's Fifth Largest City In 90 Minutes Declared Sample Of Anglo American Plan To Blast Reich, City By City, Out Of War

By CLYDE A. FARNSWORTH
Associated Press War Editor

A superlative aerial campaign to weaken Germany for a knockout invasion from the west, perhaps this summer, has been launched with tremendous success by the British amid prospects of direct and imminent American aid to multiply the destructive effort.

At least temporary stalemate in the broad sense in the battle of Russia on Germany's east, reverses for the cause of the United Nations in China and the uneasy balance between belligerents in the Australian war zone could not dim the glowing offensive spirit among the United Nations.

* * * *

Reports from the Libyan front, indicating a decisive land victory for the British, fanned this spirit.

Axis armored forces, erstwhile attackers, were said now to have gone on the defensive ,trying to escape British entrapment.

Invasion of Italy?

There may be a sharp relationship between the turn of warfare on that north African front and the 6,000,000 pounds of bombs dropped by the RAF in the 90-minute raid on the Rhineland Saturday night.

For a knockout of Axis forces in Libya might open the way to invasion of Italy—a second European front against Hitler.

As an additional blow to the Axis on the hot sandy Libyan battle-zone, General Ludwig Crewell, immediate commander of the German Afrika Korps under Marshal Erwin Rommell, had been taken prisoner.

A diary found in his possession showed that Cruewell had conferred with Adolf Hitler a week before Rommell's present drive started.

A light reconnaissance plane bearing the General over British lines had been knocked down yesterday by anti-aircraft fire. The pilot was killed.

And so the offensive spirit glowed among the Allies against Hitlerism though no one could say that dark days were ended.

It burned with the brightness of the incendiary bombs with which more than 1,000 planes touched off the Saturday night heolocaust at Cologne, Germany's fifth city, in the greatest air operation of history. At least 1,250 planes, counting the bombers' supporting aircraft, participated in this mission of destruction to the Rhineland.

Lieut. Gen. Henry H. Arnold, head of the United States air forces, in enthusiastic congratulation of the RAF command, said that "our air forces hope very soon to fly and fight beside them (the RAF) in these decisive blows against our common enemy."

London Conferences Near End

Air Marshal A. T. Harris, chief of the RAF bomber command, responded, "we, too, look forward to the time now so near when the United States army air force, which already so gallantly and effectively share their (the RAF's) burden in the far east and elsewhere, commence operation at our side in this theater of war."

Significantly, Arnold, who is in London with Lieut. Gen. Brehon Somervell, chief of the United States army supply service, and rear Admiral John H. Towers, chief of the United States navy bureau of aeronautics, announced he had "practically completed" talks with the British on developing "the mavimum impact of our combined air strength.''

'My visit has, I hope, hastened the day when our air arm shall join in an air offensive against the enemy which he cannot meet, defeat or survive," Arnold said.

"It is obvious that no offensive against Nazi-occupied Europe can succeed without air superiority, and we mean to have it."

He called the RAF's Cologne attack "a wonderful show" and said that the sooner American air forces take their place at the side of the RAF "the better it will be ...No combat planes are being kept back in the United States beyond the absolute minimum required for practical training."

On the land fronts of the European-African war this was the apparent situation Monday:

Libya

The bulk of Marshal Erwin Rommel's two German tank divisions, main bulwark of his Afrika korps, was at-

(Continued On Page 2)
(See Cologne)

Great Allied Air Offensive Planned

By DREW MIDDLETON

LONDON —(AP)— The hour of joint United States-British mass aerial assaults to blast the Reich out of the war, city by city, was declared officially Monday to be nearer at hand and the Germans were advised to look to the still smouldering ruins of devastated Cologne for a glimpse of the future.

With plain words, the generals who would give the word to go made it clear that "the Yanks are coming;" that the British-American partnership of power in the air will repeat and may even dwarf the RAF's terrific Saturday night 1,000-bomber attack which loosed on the war-plants of Cologne the greatest weight of steel and explosive ever borne on wings.

Day of Great Offensive Near

Lieut. Gen. Henry H. Arnold, head of the United States air forces, said his conferences in London were nearly completed and had "hastened the day when our air arm shall join in an air offensive against the enemy which he cannot meet, defeat or survive."

Reuters, in a dispatch datelined "on the German frontier," said hundreds of thousands of homeless people were being removed from the Rhineland following upon the attack on Cologne.

Wealthy Germans were reported anxiously trying to transfer to safer districts.

Replying to General Arnold's congratulations on the Cologne raid, Air Marshal A. T. Harris, chief of the RAF bomber command, said:

"We are supremely confident that with their aid our common enemies—faced with certain devastation of their own land—will have cause to bitterly rue the day on which they forced our two countries into war."

Stung by the fury of the attack on the fifth greatest city in all the Reich, German fliers struck back Sunday night at Britain's ancient cathedral town of Canterbury, sending over 25 planes in three waves.

Several historic buildings were wrecked (the fate of Canterbury cathedral itself was not disclosed), but casualties were reported unofficially as light.

Weather Curtails New Attacks

Despite weather unfavorable to a repetition of mass attacks Sunday night the British again sent hurricanes and Boston bombers over the channel in forays against airdromes and rail lines in northern France and Holland, and other flights winged east by daylight to continue the battering.

Of such magnitude was the Cologne raid that only a masterwork of organization, with the bombers swarming over their targets at six-second intervals, made it possible.

Its paralyzing might was told in astronomical figures:

Of Three-fourths of Cologne afire and under a three-mile-high pall of smoke.

Of more than 1,000 bombers roaring over their German targets in Cologne, and elsewhere in the Rhineland and the Ruhr valley in a 90-minute procession of death and destruction;

(Continued On Page Two)
(See Smashing Raid)

McLaughlin Man For Lieutenant Governor

McLAUGHLIN—(AP)—State Senator E. Y. Berry, attorney and publisher here, announced Monday he was a candidate for republican nomination for lieutenant governor at the party's convention in Pierre next Monday.

Berry, a two-term senator, was sponsor of the defeated homestead tax exemption bill the last session. He is third vice president of the State Bar Association, editor of the South Dakota Bar Journal and publisher of the McLaughlin Messenger.

He is director of the South Dakota Reclamation Association and was appointed by Governor Bushfield to represent South Dakota on the Missouri river states water conservation committee. He has been Corson county judge four terms.

Nazis Shoot 82 For Attack On Heydrich

LONDON—(AP)—Nazi firing squads in Prague Sunday added 20 more persons to the list of those executed in reprisal for the attempted assassination of Reichs-protector Reinhard Heydrich last Wednesday.

The executions brought to 82 the number of those reported shot since the attack.

British Gain Upper Hand in Libya

Story on Page 2

2¢

DAILY MIRROR

Member of the Associated Press

Buy WAR Bonds

WEATHER MILD. (Details on Page 2)

(Copyright, 1942, Daily Mirror, Inc.)

3 Cents Outside City Limits

Vol. 18. No. 294 R New. York, Monday, June 1, 1942

COMPLETE SPORTS

2¢

RECORD RAID: 1250 PLANES RUIN COLOGNE

RAF Rains 3000 Tons of Bombs

Story on Page 3

Fire Guts Hudson Boathouse

Flames spurting from an oil cook-stove started this two-alarm fire aboard the Waverly Club boathouse, tied up at the W. 157th St. pier in the Hudson River. No lives were lost. Club members estimated damage to their clubhouse and rowing equipment at about $10,000. Several shells, worth $1,000 each, were destroyed.

(Mirror Photo)

SPORTS EDITION
WALL STREET CLOSING
BID AND ASKED PRICES

The Sun

Copyright, 1942, by The New York Sun, Inc.

SPORTS EDITION
Sport Results on Page 22
LATEST RACING RESULTS

Intermittent light rains with light or moderate winds, without much change in temperature. Temperatures—Minimum, 56; Maximum, 59. (Detailed weather report on page 28.)

VOL. CIX—NO. 231—DAILY. Entered as Second Class Matter Post Office, New York, N. Y. NEW YORK, TUESDAY, JUNE 2, 1942. THREE CENTS

ESSEN IS SET ABLAZE BY 1036 R.A.F. PLANES

STANDARD OIL (N. J.) RUBBER ACTS RATIFIED

Gerard Leads Stockholders in Vote of Confidence in Farish Regime.

PERSONAL GAINS DENIED

Four Officers and a Director Reply to Question at Stormy Meeting.

Flemington, N. J., June 2 (A. P.).—President W. H. Farish, three other officers and a director of the Standard Oil Company (New Jersey) swore before the annual meeting of the stockholders today that the five had never received any personal gain from the company association with I. G. Farbenindustrie.

"I swear under oath I never received any compensation or recompense from any sources whatsoever, including the Germans," Mr. Farish said.

His statement was in answer to a question by Philip Blumenthal, representing Mrs. Elizabeth Booling of New York, holder of 300 shares of Standard stock.

The stockholders vociferously gave a vote of confidence to Mr. Farish and his associates.

Mr. Blumenthal told Mr. Farish that Mrs. Booling was not impressed by his statement made at the stockholders meeting in answer to Assistant Attorney-General Thurman Arnold's charges leveled at Standard Oil. Mrs. Booling had asked whether Standard directors had received any pecuniary return from the German trust.

Letter to Truman Read.

William Ross of Brooklyn said the question was a direct insult to Standard Oil officials."

"I agree it is an insult," Mr.

Continued on Page 12.

JUSTICE BLACK FINED

Pays $5 for Driving Car Against One-way Rule.

Washington, June 2 (A. P.).—Driving in the wrong direction on Rock Creek Parkway, which is one-way into Washington in the morning and one-way toward Maryland in the afternoon, cost Supreme Court Justice Hugo L. Black $5.

Park Policeman J. W. Macon gave him the traffic ticket.

At his Alexandria home Justice Black laughed off the incident today, saying that he sent his $5 to the Traffic Bureau and adding:

"He was a nice officer and treated me nicely."

ALTERNATE-DAY MILK DELIVERY PLAN IS HALTED

Disputants Honor Request by WLB for Making No Change Now.

BOARD WILL DECIDE ISSUE

Metropolitan District, Including Jersey, Is Affected—New Scheme Was Due Tomorrow.

The "every other day" plan for delivery of milk in the metropolitan area, which was to have started tomorrow, has been postponed indefinitely by the distributors at the request of the National War Labor Board, the distributors announced today.

A statement to this effect was issued by the New York-New Jersey Metropolitan Milk Industry War Conservation Committee after a session at the Hotel New Yorker.

The postponement followed shortly after Mayor LaGuardia in a broadcast from the City Hall had urged the War Labor Board to formulate a program not only for the milk controversy but for all other situations which might affect thousands of people throughout the country as result of strikes or threatened strikes.

The Mayor also urged the milk companies to share part of the differential between delivered milk prices and prices of milk in stores as "salary" for men working for milk drivers who might lose their jobs through the skip-delivery system.

Text of the Statement.

Meanwhile members of the distributors group adjourned to the office of the impartial vice-chairman of the milk industry, Alfred L. Bernheim, at 295 Madison avenue, where they were going into conference with representatives of the Milk Drivers Union—a section of the International Brotherhood of Teamsters and Chauffeurs.

Some milk drivers, through their union, had opposed the

Continued on Page 12.

2 Killed, 56 Injured In Trinidad Train Wreck

Port of Spain, Trinidad, June 2 (A. P.).—The engineer and fireman were killed and fifty-six passengers injured, thirteen seriously, when a Port of Spain-San Fernando train was derailed Sunday.

TO SUN READERS

The New York Sun, complying with the order of the Office of Defense Transportation to restrict deliveries for the wartime conservation of gasoline and rubber, has cut the number of its editions from seven to four daily. This curtailed schedule was started yesterday. School news will be carried in the first edition, which is now called the Night Edition. Sun readers will help in the conservation program by buying their Sun from the same Sun dealer daily. Thus, the dealer can plan for a sufficient number of papers without requiring extra deliveries. You will make sure of getting your copy of The Sun when you want it, and delivery miles will be saved. The Sun thanks its readers for their co-operation.

In The Sun Today

HUGE NAZI MUNITIONS WORKS HIT BY R. A. F. BOMBERS

A pre-war view of part of the vast Krupp works, chief target of a heavy raid on Essen last night.

LEND-LEASE PACT WITH CHINA READY

Signatures to Be Affixed in Washington Today.

Washington, June 2 (A. P.).—The White House announced today that a lend-lease agreement with China would be signed at the State Department this afternoon.

It is patterned after an agreement with Great Britain which provides that major adjustments of the lend-lease ledgers will be delayed, probably until a post-war accounting, and that the nations shall collaborate after the war in the field of economic rehabilitation.

Presidential Secretary Stephen Early asserted that President Roosevelt had concluded negotiations which had been underway with China for some time, permitting the signing of the agreement by Secretary Hull.

A similar master agreement also has been submitted to Soviet Russia officials.

PULLMAN HEAD HEARD

Testifies Company Builds for Any Customer.

Philadelphia, June 2 (A. P.).—Charles A. Liddle, president of the Pullman-Standard Car Manufacturing Company, testified today that the firm would sell any kind of a car which it is able to build to any person, firm or corporation which is ready, willing and able to buy.

Called as a defense witness at a hearing on the Government's anti-trust charges against the Pullman companies and thirty-one officers, Mr. Liddle said that Pullman-Standard never refused to manufacture or sell any kind of a car where the buyer was ready, except as the company may have been limited in capacity.

John F. Deasy, operating vice-president of the Pennsylvania Railroad, testified that the public ultimately would pay increased transportation charges if railroads operated their own sleeping car service instead of leasing it.

Hungary Prepares For Rumanian Struggle

The Moscow radio said today that railway traffic between Hungary and Rumania has ceased, and that Hungary is openly fortifying her border with Rumania. The broadcast was heard in New York by CBS.

British in Libya Mopping Up Trapped Tanks As Rommel's Army Is Divided in Desert War

Portion of His Force Behind Defense Line Hit by Land and Air, but London Hears of Renewed Axis Thrust.

Cairo, June 2 (A. P.).—German armored forces, the cream of Field Marshal Erwin Rommel's Africa Corps, which were trapped east of the Ain el Gazala-Bir Hacheim line are being ceaselessly harried and destroyed by British troops and planes and are being mopped up, the British commander announced today.

"Latest reports show the enemy may have withdrawn some of his tanks through the gaps" in the line, a communique by Gen. Sir Claude Auchinleck said but "a large number of his tanks and many transport vehicles, however remain on the wrong side of this barrier."

[A Reuters dispatch from Cairo to London tonight reported that a considerable Axis force of all arms again was thrusting east behind the Ain El Gazala-Bir Hacheim Line.]

"It is still difficult to give a firm estimate of the number of vehicles and tanks knocked out or disabled," the communique said, but it was said the Axis losses had been very great.

Unable to Surprise.

In a summary of the seven-day campaign Gen. Auchinleck said that the enemy failed to surprise when he attacked with two German armored and one light divisions and two Italian armored and motorized divisions, with the objective of taking Tobruk.

He disclosed that Axis forces attempted to land from the sea behind the British lines, but the enemy was driven off by the navy.

Gen. Auchinleck's statement said in part:

"From captured documents it was clear that Rommel's object was to defeat our armored forces and capture Tobruk.

"The main ingredients of his plan were: First, to capture our defended locality at Bir Hacheim held by our gallant Allies, the

Continued on Page 6.

King George Receives American Generals

London, June 2 (A. P.).—Lieut.-Gen. Brehon B. Somervell, commanding general of the United States Army Service of Supply, and Major-Gen. James E. Chaney, commander of the A. E. F., in Britain, were received today by King George in Buckingham Palace.

QUEZON DECLARES FAITH IN AMERICA

Tells House Nothing Will Daunt Filipino Spirit.

Washington, June 2 (A. P.).—President Quezon of the Philippines told the House today that neither death, ruin nor destruction had daunted the spirit of the Filipinos "nor lessened our faith in America."

Mr. Quezon, speaking to a well-filled and hushed House, quoted President Roosevelt as having told him: "I give to the people of the Philippines my solemn pledge that their freedom will be redeemed and their independence established and protected."

As the members applauded loudly, the slender statesman, who only recently came to this country, said: "I hope that the pledge of the President of the United States will be considered as a pledge by every one of you."

MADAGASCAR FIGHTS

Vichy Reports End of Lull on Big Island.

Vichy, June 2 (A. P.).—Reports reaching Vichy today said that active hostilities between the French and British on Madagascar appear to have been resumed, ending the lull which followed the British capture of Diego Suarez.

These accounts said that there was increased air activity on both sides. It was said that the bulk of the island and most of its ports still are in Vichy French hands and are very difficult to reach because of mountainous terrain.

GERMANS ATTACK IN KHARKOV ZONE

Reported Retaking Town Eight Miles From City.

London, June 2 (A. P.).—A Reuters dispatch from Stockholm declared today the Germans had started a new drive to recover ground lost to Marshal Semeon Timoshenko before Kharkov and already had regained Tamilovska, eight miles northeast of the city.

Russians Attacking, Too.

Moscow, June 2 (A. P.).—The Red Army struck strongly at German lines at two points northwest of Moscow in conformity with the Soviet tactics of keeping the enemy back on his heels and preventing him from undertaking his own offensive, front line reports said today. The dispatches said the Russians attacked both in the Kalinin sector and in another northwest area, improving their positions there and drawing the Germans into counter-attacks.

No essential change in general positions on the Russo-German front was reported, however.

On Kalinin Front.

The Red Star said that the Russians fought their way into an inhabited point on the Kalinin front, which extends northwest and west of Kalinin toward the Valdai hills and Rzhev and Veliki Luki. A factory which was part of the German armament system was reported captured and street battles for fortifications in the suburbs were said to be in progress.

In another battle the Germans were said to have launched six counter-attacks and lost more than 1,000 dead in an effort to

Continued on Page 6.

Berlin Says Russians Lost Army Commander

Berlin, (From German Broadcasts), June 2 (A. P.).—The German High Command said today that Major-Gen. Gorodajansky, commander of the Russian Sixth Army in the battle of Kharkov, had been killed. The Sixth Army was one of three which the Germans said last week were annihilated.

KRUPP INDUSTRIES HIT IN GREAT RUHR RAID

Churchill Says 35 Bombers Were Lost—Air Squadrons Swarm Over France by Daylight After Night Attack on Reich.

London, June 2 (A. P.).—The R. A. F. turned the lethal, devastating might of 1,036 R. A. F. planes loose on Germany last night, almost all of them on the region of the Nazi arsenal city of Essen, Prime Minister Churchill announced today.

The second of the crushing raids which the R. A. F. has made against the sources of Adolf Hitler's military strength in three days struck at the home of the huge Krupp munitions works, and Mr. Churchill promised that more of even greater severity would follow "when we are joined, as we soon shall be, by the air force of the United States."

The Essen raid came after a pause of but one night, when bad weather held the R. A. F.'s great bomb-carrying armada grounded after the mammoth attack by considerably more than 1,000 British bombers on Cologne.

Reports from Folkestone, England, late today stated that great forces of R. A. F. planes had roared across the channel in forays which southeast coast observers called one of the biggest daylight operations of the war. Hour after hour many squadrons headed for various targets in northern France. Planes returning early in the evening created a great din.

Again, British losses were relatively slight for an air offensive of such magnitude. Mr. Churchill said thirty-five bombers had failed to return.

Numerous Fires Started.

He told the House of Commons that the raiders had sown numerous and widespread fires last night and that the two raids introduced "a new phase in the British air offensive against Germany" which will put the enemy to "an ordeal the like of which never has been experienced in any country in continuity, severity or magnitude." He cautioned the British, however, not to expect all future raids to be "above the four-figure scale" in number of planes, adding that "methods of attack will be continually varied according to circumstances."

The Air Ministry's disclosure that aircraft of the bomber, fighter, coastal and army co-operation commands attacked

Continued on Page 3.

SUMMARY TRIAL SET

Paris Food Rioters to Face Special Court.

Vichy, June 2 (A. P.).—A special Cabinet meeting called by Chief of Government Pierre Laval decided today to turn over persons arrested in a food riot in Paris last Sunday to a tribunal of state which is authorized to expedite trial and pass sentences of death.

Laval called the meeting after returning from Paris. Marshal Petain presided over the deliberations.

Two policemen were killed and three were wounded in the Sunday disturbance in which a food store was looted.

Battleship Maine To Be Built in Basin

Bath, Me., June 2 (A. P.).—The new battleship Maine will be built in a basin rather than on ways.

Senator Brewster of Maine said yesterday that the Navy had decided to try the new technic in construction of a capital ship because of its proved efficiency at the Todd-Bath iron yard in South Portland, where eleven British freighters have been floated from three huge drydock-like basins in the first use of the system by the American shipbuilding industry.

The War on All Fronts

(1006th Day)

By MARTIAL.

(This roundup of the war news covers the situation on all fronts up to press time today, June 2, 1942. It is based on information reaching The New York Sun from all its news sources.)

The Royal Air Force gave strong indication that its Cologne raid was but the first of a series when more than a thousand British planes visited the Krupp Works at Essen, Germany, last night. The raid would have been made Sunday night but for bad weather, it was hinted in London.

In Libya it appeared that although Field Marshal Rommel's forces have been defeated, efforts completely to trap his two mechanized divisions have not yet been successful. The situation in Russia is comparatively quiet, while Japanese armies are again trying to open the Canton-Hankow Railway in China.

Gen. MacArthur's planes have again raided Japanese invasion bases in the southwest Pacific. Aside from continued submarine sinkings in the Atlantic, the war news is generally good.

EUROPEAN FRONT.

As Cologne was digging itself out of the utter ruin caused by more than a thousand R. A. F. bombers coming in at six second intervals, the city of Essen was getting the same dose last night. The vital Krupp munitions works are located there, and the number of planes involved guarantees tremendous damage. In the meantime other German cities must play the macabre game of trying to figure whether they'll be next.

LIBYAN FRONT.

Field Marshal Rommel's panzer corps has halted its retreat today. The battle continues.

FAR EASTERN FRONT.

1. Rabaul, New Britain, and Lae and Salamaua, New Guinea, were raided by Allied planes yesterday. Thirty Japanese planes raided Port Moresby, and nine were felled or damaged.

2. The spearhead of a Japanese army of 50,000 men has pushed north along the Canton-Hankow Railroad in an effort to cut the only major communications line between Central and South China.

WAR EXTRA

LATE SPORTS

CHARACTER · QUALITY · AMERICA FIRST! · ENTERPRISE · ACCURACY

Los Angeles Examiner

AN AMERICAN PAPER FOR THE AMERICAN PEOPLE · THE GREAT NEWSPAPER OF THE GREAT SOUTHWEST

Reg. U.S. Pat. Off.
Examiner Telephone RIchmond 1212 · Examiner Building, 1111 S. Broadway

VOL. XXXIX—NO. 175 · LOS ANGELES, THURSDAY, JUNE 4, 1942 · PCC · Two Sections—Part I—FIVE CENTS

SECOND ATTACK MADE ON ALASKA

JAPANESE PLANES yesterday attacked the American naval base at Dutch Harbor, pictured above. Details of damage were not revealed and it was believed, since fighter planes participated, that the attack, first ever made on the North American continent, started from a carrier. The raid, which came a 6 a. m. there, 9 o'clock Pacific War Time, is believed to have been Japan's face-saving effort to answer the American raid on Tokyo. Dutch Harbor is on Unalaska, largest of the Aleutian Islands, 2000 miles from San Francisco.
—Associated Press Wirephoto.

Casualties, Damage Reported as Light

WASHINGTON, June 3.—(AP)—The Navy announced tonight that Japanese planes had made a second attack on Dutch Harbor six hours after four bombers and about 15 fighters had made the initial foray. (About 3 p. m., P. W. T.)

(Page of Pictures on Page 26.)

WASHINGTON, June 3.—(AP)—Japanese planes struck at Dutch Harbor, American Naval base in the Aleutian Islands, today, but were apparently beaten off in short order.

There were but few casualties, the Navy announced, and while some warehouses were set on fire, no serious damage resulted. Four bombers and 15 fighter planes made up the attacking force.

Officials had long expected an assault in the Alaskan area principally as a face-saving device after Brigadier General Jimmy Doolittle's raid on Tokyo and other Japanese cities, and the station was described as prepared to meet it.

"Japan was expected to try to retaliate for the raid by our American fliers," said Chairman Connolly (Democrat), Texas, of the Senate Foreign Relations Committee, "it was apparently part of their face-saving process."

But whether it was merely a nuisance raid or the start of an offensive designed to knock out the North Pacific bases from which American planes may strike at the Japanese mainland could not be determined from officials here pending the release of further information.

At Seattle, Rear Admiral C. S. Freeman, commander of the 13th Naval District, said:

"This attack was not a surprise and the station was prepared to meet it. Further reports may be expected from the

How Doolittle 'Colognized' Tokyo Told in Pictorial Review

Three smashing picture pages in next Sunday's Pictorial Review reveal intimate glimpses of the hard-hitting heroes of the Shangri-La to Tokyo tour

THE WEATHER

Somewhat cooler, somewhat lower humidity, moderate winds and no rain tonight.

Read The Baltimore News-Post for complete, accurate war coverage. It is the only Baltimore newspaper possessing the three great wire services—
ASSOCIATED PRESS
INTERNATIONAL NEWS SERVICE
UNITED PRESS

THE BALTIMORE NEWS-POST
AN INDEPENDENT NEWSPAPER
The Largest Evening Circulation in the Entire South

7 HOME FINAL

VOL. CXLI.—NO. 30 Entered as second-class matter at Baltimore Postoffice. MONDAY EVENING, JUNE 8, 1942 PRICE 3 CENTS

U. S. VICTORY AT MIDWAY PUTS JAPS ON DEFENSIVE

Arnold Says Tokyo Lost 4 Planes For Each One By U. S.

Air Force Head Declares 'Raids Like Those On Cologne Just Starters'

MOUNT PLEASANT, Iowa, June 8—(A. P.).—Lieut. Gen. H. H. Arnold, commander of the United States Army Air Force, declared here today:

"For every one of our planes shot down, the Japs have lost four."

In an address prepared for the one hundredth annual commencement of Iowa Wesleyan College, at which he received an honorary doctor of laws degree, the General said:

"The day of reckoning is not as far off as some people think.

MORE RAIDS DUE

"I am telling Tokyo that we have thousands more Colin Kellys and Butch O'Hares and Jimmy Doolittles on the way. This is just the dawn of a day of wrath."

The General, who recently returned from Europe, said:

"I did not fly to London to go on the defensive.

"Raids like those on Cologne and Essen were just starters to those which are to follow where U. S. and R. A. F. fighters and bombers ride the skies as a team . . .

"The Axis knows that the next six months will spell victory or defeat for their forces. For the Axis it is now or never.

SHIPS, FIGHTERS BEST

"The flying fortress has no peer in its field today.

"Our B-25C medium bombers can go farther, faster and carry more bombs than the best ships of our enemies . . .

"The United States has the best young pilots in the world and they are proving their superiority in combat in the air."

By the end of this year, the General said, the Army air force will have "over 60,000 officers and close to a million men. By June of next year, if it becomes necessary, we will double that."

Keep 'Em Fleeing, New Slogan At Pearl Harbor

PEARL HARBOR, June 8—(I. N. S.).—The defenders of Pearl Harbor have a new slogan today:

"eKeep 'em fleeing."

It was contributed by Lieutenant General Henry H. Arnold, chief of the United States Army Air Force, in a message to Lieutenant General Delos Emmons, military commandant for Hawaii, in connection with the battle of Midway.

He said:

"The gratitude and admiration of every American are with us in this triumphant hour.

"Keep up the good work and keep 'em fleeing."

U. S. Plane Output 5,000 Per Month

By WILLIAM S. NEAL
International News Service Staff Correspondent.

WASHINGTON, June 8.—Senator Elmer Thomas (Democrat) of Oklahoma today disclosed that American airplane production has soared to nearly 5,000 planes a month.

A spokesman for the industry reported United States output will soon exceed that of Germany, Japan, Italy and the occupied countries.

INCREASES VAST

While Army and Navy officials decline to reveal the exact production, the figure given by Thomas, chairman of the Senate Appropriations Military Subcommittee, is the highest yet.

That American plane production will soon top efforts of the combined enemy was revealed by Col. John H. Jouett, president of the Aeronautical Chamber of Commerce of America.

In a special progress report Colonel Jouett also announced that plane output has increased nearly 85 per cent. in the six months since Pearl Harbor.

In addition, Colonel Jouett stated many striking advances in manu-

Continued on Page 2, Column 1.

Quit Coastal Area, British Tell French

LONDON, June 8—(A. P.).—Reuters said in a dispatch datelined "at the French frontier" today that Otto Abetz, the German Ambassador, had acknowledged in conversations in Paris that 11,000 to 12,000 persons were killed in the R. A. F.'s bombardment of Cologne and that 180,000 persons had been ordered evacuated.

LONDON, June 6—(A. P.).—The British radio broadcast instructions to the French people today to evacuate a broad coastal area from the Belgian to the Spanish border, which strip the Germans have designated as a prohibited military zone.

"Operations of capital importance," for the liberation of France will start in due time, said the broadcast.

"It has been shown on several occasions that the presence of the civilian population on the scene of active operations hinders the action of troops, and particularly of friendly troops, in a very grave manner."

The warning continued:

"The coastal regions of Occupied France are likely to become more and more a theatre of war operations. They will inevitably bring with them the gravest dangers for the civil population."

Yale Gets $630,000 Gift From Alumnus

NEW HAVEN, Conn., June 8—(U. P.).—Yale University announced today receipt of a $630,000 gift from John A. Hoober, York, Pa., president of the Alumni Association. Hoober was graduated from Yale Law School in 1891.

Rubber Inquiry Appoints Simpson To Counsel Post

WASHINGTON, June 8—(I. N. S.).—Elliott E. Simpson, New York independent rubber dealer who charged before various Congressional committees that major rubber companies are dominating the war program, today was appointed counsel to a special House subcommittee to investigate the rubber situation.

Representative Andrew L. Somers (Democrat) of New York, chairman of the House Coinage Committee, made the appointment in the wake of Simpson's charges of monopoly in the rubber production field and his claim that the rubber shortage is a "myth." Somers said:

"The charges are of such a serious character that our committee authorized the appointment of a special seven-member subcommittee to investigate the whole rubber situation.

"The shocking revelations presented to the committee proved conclusively that the big four rubber companies have gained control of the rubber program."

Simpson is a director of L. Drexsage Company and P. A. Maguire & Co., Inc., New York, and an associate in a number of other rubber firms.

4 Gals. Of Gas To Average Driver

WASHINGTON, June 8—(A. P.).—East Coast motorists will get an average basic ration of nearly four gallons of gasoline a week under the regular coupon-book system starting next month, Joel Dean, OPA fuel rationing administrator said today. Under present temporary program, non-essential drivers are allowed about three gallons weekly.

Dean told reporters the additional ration would be permitted because of tighter controls made possible under the new plan.

Considerably fewer "B" coupons will be issued, Dean explained, since motorists will be required to prove need for supplemental allowances.

MUST SHOW NECESSITY

They must show to the satisfaction of local rationing boards that use of their cars is required in their businesses, that they have formed transportation "pools" of not less than four persons, or that no other means of transportation is available to them.

The East Coast plan, expected to serve as a model if nation-wide rationing is instituted, is based on an allowance of 2,800 miles of driving a year for the average "non-essential" motorist.

Basic "A" books will be issued to every passenger-car driver who registers. These will contain 48 coupons, each good for four gallons of gasoline.

BOOKS TO BE DATED

The "B" books, containing 16 coupons, will be issued on evidence of need and will be used in addition to the basic "A" book.

Each "B" book, however, will be dated, depending upon the local ration board's estimate of the applicant's gasoline requirements.

Thus, one "B" book could be used only for three months, while another would be good for a year.

A third "C" book, containing 96 coupons, likewise will be "tailored" to fit absolute requirements.

On the basis of the motorist's proved mileage requirements, the local board will tear out coupons if necessary to cut the "C" book down to the driver's needs.

All commercial vehicles, including trucks, taxicabs, buses and Government-operated automobiles, will receive "S" books—likewise "tailored" to fit.

All "C" books will be reviewed and reissued every three months; "S" books will be reviewed and reissued every four months.

War At A Glance

WASHINGTON—

U. S. wrests initiative from Japan in the battle of the Pacific.

AUSTRALIA—

Japanese submarines shell two cities.

LONDON—

R. A. F. continues operations, London radio urges French in German-held coastal region to move inland.

MOSCOW—

Sevastopol still holds after seven months' siege by Germans.

British Blast Channel Ports

LONDON, June 8—(A. P.).—Hundreds of fighting planes and fighter-bombers from the scores of airfields of Britain swept in a series of thrusts over Hitler's Channel ports and defenses today, continuing the regular daylight offensive which has accompanied the R. A. F.'s heavy bombing drive.

British warplanes attacked targets in Northern France and Holland last night and damaged a German ship off the Frisian Islands, the Air Ministry announced.

But bad weather over the Continent kept the R. A. F. from following up its Saturday night assault on Emden with another massed raid on Germany.

All the planes which participated in the overnight operations returned safely to their bases, a communique said.

Fighter command planes which carried out the sweeps over France were reported to have bombed a railway yard near Caen and shot up a train at Montdidier, 21 miles southeast of Amiens. A lone Boston bomber also attacked the German airdrome at Leeuwarden, Holland, 70 miles from Amsterdam.

BULLETIN

WASHINGTON, June 8—(A. P.).—President Roosevelt approached a decision today on the issueof drafting youths eighteen and nineteen years old for the nation's fighting services, calling in Major Gen. Lewis B. Hershey, Selective Service director, to talk over the problem.

Mr. Roosevelt has taken no position publicly on the question of drafting youths in this ago group, who are now exempt from Selective Service. Hershey has pointed out that in every major war the country has called on youths of eighteen and nineteen to augment its armed services.

Temperatures

12 P. M.,	73	6 A. M.,	72
1 A. M.,	74	7 A. M.,	73
2 A. M.,	73	8 A. M.,	74
3 A. M.,	73	9 A. M.,	75
4 A. M.,	72	10 A. M.,	76
5 A. M.,	72	11 A. M.,	77

Enemy Fleet Withdraws After Running Into Trap; Contact With Foe Lost

WASHINGTON, June 8—(A. P.).—Desperate new Japanese efforts to break the growing might of America's air and sea power in the Pacific were predicted in informed quarters here today as the only course left open to the enemy, now clearly on the defensive.

Subsequent to the United States victory in the battle that started with the repulse of a huge attacking force at Midway Island last week, authorities said that the Japs must either initiate new operations somewhere along the sweeping defense line that runs from Alaska to Australia or else by inactivity admit their eventual complete defeat even before the grand offensive of the United Nations starts rolling in the Pacific.

ARMADA WITHDRAWS

Meanwhile the armada of battleships and aircraft carriers, cuisers and destroyers which steamed into what appears to have been a trap at Midway apparently had withdrawn.

Admiral Chester W. Nimitz, commander of the Pacific fleet, said, in a communique from Pearl Harbor, that contact with the enemy fleet was lost sometime Saturday night.

In Washington, Admiral Ernest J. King, commander in chief of the United States fleet, declared at a press conference that the battle just ending might decide the course of the war in the Pacific, depending on the extent of damage inflicted on the enemy.

BULK OF SEAPOWER

Without relating statistics, Admiral King said that the Japanese had thrown the bulk of their seapower into the effort to take Midway, but that the Army and Navy had been prepared for just such an attempt.

Land-based aircraft "played a big part" in repelling the attack, King said, and he used that fact to give a clue to the limits beyond which the pursuit of the routed enemy would not be continued.

It would not be "well advised," he explained, for the American forces to rush into any territory where the Japanese could bring their land-based bombers and fighter planes into action.

'KEY TO PACIFIC'

The gravity of the action at Midway for the United States was emphasized by King with the assertion

Continued on Page 2, Column 1.

Jap, U. S. Losses In Big Naval Battle

PEARL HARBOR, June 8—(A. P.).—Japan lost at least 16 and possibly more warships and transports sunk or damaged in its disastrous attempt to seize Midway island.

American losses were one destroyer sunk and one aircraft carrier hit.

The box score of the first great hostile fleet invasion in American waters of the Eastern Pacific:

JAPANESE LOSSES

	Sunk	Damaged
Aircraft Carriers	2	1 (or 2)
Battleships	x	3
Cruisers	x	4 (possibly 6)
Destroyers	1	x
Transports	x	3
	—	—
Totals	3 (or 4)	11 (or 14)

AMERICAN LOSSES

	Sunk	Damaged
Destroyers	1	x
Aircraft Carriers	x	1

THE WEATHER
Yesterday's Max.: 32.7 C. or 90.9 F. at 1:35 P. M. Min.: 25 C. or 77 F. at 7:05 A. M.

The Tribune

5 Centavos
4 Pages

YEAR XVIII — MANILA, PHILIPPINES, SATURDAY, JUNE 13, 1942 — NUMBER 74

NAVY CONTROLS PACIFIC

Fake Drug Makers Face Prosecution

Laboratory Owner, Son Held By Constabulary

Several charges will be filed against Simon Umali, 65, owner of the Star Pharmaceutical Laboratory and Drug Co., and his son, Jose, in connection with their arrest for the manufacture of fake quinine, sulfanilamide and other tablets.

Arrested last Thursday noon at 394 Lardizabal, Sampaloc, where the laboratory is located, Umali and his son are still detained at headquarters of the metropolitan constabulary.

Police findings disclosed that the Umalis had already sold P10,000 worth of fake quinine and other tablets, which upon analysis by the Institute of Hygiene were found to be made of not the real drugs but merely starch and talc.

Umali and his son have reimbursed half of the money to purchasers who had been swindled into buying the fake medicinal tablets.

Among the charges likely to be preferred against the Umalis are for mislabelling, unfair competition in connection with Act No. 46, violation of the pure food and drugs act, and for estafa.

Also found by the police when they raided the Star Pharmaceutical Laboratory were fake container labels for sodium bicarbonate tablets purporting to have been manufactured for the "United Naval Stores—New York." The police have also detained a local printer who has admitted

(Continued on page 4)

Slot Machine Operators Held

Two Chinese were the masterminds of a syndicate operating the slot machines racket in the city which has been busted by the police.

Arrested a few days ago, the two were charged with violating the gambling law. The city fiscal's office, however, dropped the charges, after giving them a stern warning and after they agreed to remove all their machines from restaurants, grocery stores, nightclubs, sari sari stores and other business establishments.

Police investigation also established that minor operators owned other slot machines in the city. Both these parties and the owners of places where the machines were set up were likewise ordered to remove them.

Sold More Than ₱10,000 Worth Of Fake Tablets

SIMON UMALI — JOSE UMALI

Who were arrested by the police who raided their laboratory in Sampaloc where they were allegedly manufacturing fake medical goods.

Indian Leaders Are for Freedom

TOKYO, June 12 (Domei).—Though some divergence of views exists among Indian leaders, as to the best ways and means to attain Indian independence, India's leaders as well as masses appear solidly united on one point, namely, British withdrawal from India constitutes the prerequisite to Indian independence, the Niti Niti reported from Buenos Aires quoting Bombay dispatches.

The journal cited that Pandit Jawaharlal Nehru, leader of the Indian National Congress party, recently boldly declared, that Britain not only the enemy of the Axis but also India's. The paper said that Nehru's statement evoked great sensation among the Indian people as an indication that Nehru and Mahatma Gandhi have come closer in their views that "Britain must go."

The Niti Niti added that considerable significance as to India's policy vis-a-vis the United States is seen in Nehru's remark, though the United States is regarded as India's friend and India must not unduly estimate America's position.

Meanwhile, the Niti Niti reported from Saigon quoting New Delhi dispatches that the Duke of Gloucester, younger brother of King George VI, yesterday unexpectedly arrived in Karachi by plane ostensibly to make an effort to appease the Indian people following the dismal failure of the Cripps mission to India. It will be recalled that the Duke of Gloucester has been making a tour of the Middle East as proxy of King George.

TOKYO, June 12 (Domei).—Spokesman Tomokazu Hori of the cabinet board of information, commenting on the arrival

(Continued on page 4)

Japanese Storm Into Kienchang

Town Is Completely Occupied—Linhsien Also Falls

CANTON, June 12 (Domei).—It was learned today that Nanking troops belonging to the 30th division of the Chinese National Government have been actively participating in the recently opened Japanese offensive in southern China against Chungkingers.

CHEKIANG FRONT, June 12 (Domei).—Japanese forces advancing southward in pursuit of enemy troops escaping from Chuchow stormed into the headquarters of the 67th division at Chienho 20 kilometers southwest of Chuchow.

KIANGSI FRONT, June 12 (Domei).—Hard on the heels of the retreating enemy, Japanese troops operating on the 60-kilometer wide front crossed the Chekiang-Kiangsi border into eastern Kiangsi last evening after capturing Changshan, 35 kilometers west of Chuchow, and Kiangshan, 37 kilometers southwest of the same point, field reports revealed.

KIANGSI FRONT, June 12 (Domei).—Driving forward in

(Continued on page 4)

Retailers Split Into Buying Units

To effect an equitable distribution of cigarettes and matches, the Filipino retailers' associations in Greater Manila are being split into several buying units to which a limited number of members have been assigned.

The existence of only one association in a district in Manila was found to be inadequate to serve efficiently and satisfactorily its increasing members as well as to handle the correspondingly big volume of buying orders.

The division of each association into several units, it is believed, will do away with the alleged irregularities believed to have been committed by the management in the distribution of cigarettes and matches to members which later, it is said, has led to the prevailing and unavoidable high selling prices of these two controlled goods.

(Continued on page 4)

SOLDIERS STUDYING MALAYAN DIALECTS

TOKYO, June 12 (Domei).—With the knowledge of native dialects absolutely necessary to facilitate the construction of the Greater East Asia Co-Prosperity Sphere, the Japanese army in the southern regions recently started a short course in Malayan language with more than ten representatives from each army unit attending the studies, the "Niti Niti" reported from Rangoon. A graduate course in Malayan language will soon be organized.

Upon graduation each language student will become a teacher of the Malayan language in his own unit. It was learned that soldiers taking this course will be prohibited from speaking one word of Japanese during the course which will last two months.

In the future it is expected that there will be many Japanese soldiers who can speak Malayan as well as the natives.

U. S. Denials Suspicious Is London View

STOCKHOLM, June 12 (Domei).—The United States denial of Japanese occupation of Aleutian island bases was greeted with suspicion in London, while keen interest centered on Admiral Ernest King's statement that "something is going on" in that area, according to a report from London.

A London observer declared last if it is correct that Japanese forces have occupied Aleutian island bases it would be her most sensational strike since Singapore as the Aleutian islands may be utilized as a springboard from Japan to the American continent.

This observer stressed that Japan is already holding Singapore and Soerabaja besides strategic bases elsewhere and if she could establish naval bases in the Aleutian islands, Japan would be in a position to threaten the western shores of Canada and the United States.

Warns Against Reprisal Raids

LISBON, June 10 (Domei)—Reflecting the apprehension prevailing in the United States despite the propaganda of Washington authorities that the Allied nations are winning victories, New York reports disclosed that Major General Follett Brandley, commander of the U.S. First Army Air Force, last Wednesday warned residents of the eastern cities to expect reprisal raids on account of the Allied bombing of Germany.

LISBON, June 10 (Domei)—Reflecting the consternation in the United States on account of the heavy losses of American merchantmen due to Axis submarine activities, Washington reports revealed that Navy Secretary Frank Knox held a closed session Wednesday for two hours on plans for combatting the submarine menace with the subcommittee of the special Senate committee investigating national defense.

Secretary Knox reportedly said that it would take time and much planning in order to correct the submarine menace and that all

(Continued on page 4)

PHARMACY TESTS ARE SET FOR JULY

With authority from the director-general of the military administration, the Board of Pharmaceutical Examiners will conduct pharmacist examinations at the School of Nursing, Philippine General Hospital, on July 7, 9 and 11, 1942, (theoretical) and July 15, 1942 and following days (practical).

Many Enemy Capital Ships Destroyed

Naval Authority Praises Superior Strategy of Japan

TOKYO, June 12 (Domei)—A decisive battle between contending capital ship forces has been conspicuous by its absence in the War of Greater East Asia, and yet the control of the Pacific has been firmly secured by the Japanese Navy, Retired Rear Admiral Gonkiti Nakazima commented in an interview with the Asahi. Rear Admiral Nakasima is a noted authority on naval strategy and the history of naval warfare.

Paying a glowing tribute to Admiral Isoroku Yamamoto, commander-in-chief of the Japanese Combined Fleet, Rear Admiral Nakazima observed that the Japanese Navy has destroyed the enemy capital ships separately, one by one, without engaging them in decisive battle. He attributes Japan's marvelous successes not only to superior strategy but also to the superiority of Japanese auxiliary vessels and the Japanese air arm in equipment and fighting power which enabled the Japanese to disperse the enemy naval strength by separate attacks without giving the latter any chance to concentrate in full force.

Commenting on the naval battle off Midway, Rear Admiral Nakasima said that the Japanese fleet took a bold action, contrary to common sense strategy which deprecates an attempt to attack an enemy fleet covered by a landbased airforce, simply be-

(Continued on page 4)

39 Pass Tests For Accountants

Thirty-nine passed the certified public accountant examination given by the board of accountancy last December, according to an announcement yesterday by the bureau of civil service.

The highest rating was obtained by Eliseo S. Yanga, who received a grade of 87.17 per cent. The complete list of those who passed is as follows:

Eliseo S. Yanga, 87.17; Benedicto C. Lagman, 86.83; Perfecto Palma, 86.17; Leonardo T. Sicat, 86.05; David L. Francisco, 85.83; Conrado S. Reyes, 85.83; Melchor M. Dimayuga, 85.17; Wenceslao P. Zafra, 84.33; Manuel Miranda, 84.33; Mariano M. Ornum, 84.25; Celeste D. de Rivera, 84.17; Cesar F. Bocaling, 83.67; Marcos Ahido, 81.45; Francisco Testa, 81; Amado S. Manas, 81; Gaudencio Poblete,

(Continued on page 4)

Bureau Willing to Help In Manufacture of Flour

To satisfy a brisk demand for cassava flour at present processed in the bureau of plant and animal industry and eventually to step up the local manufacture of starch and flour on commercial scale, Dr. Gregorio San Agustin of the bureau has announced that his office at 692 San Andres street, Malate, will accept from interested parties, gaplek (dried cassava meat) for manufacture into flour at the rate of eleven centavos per kilo of flour turned out.

The bureau of plant and animal industry operates two initial grinding machines and one bolting or refining machine, besides a number of slicers and graters, solely for the purpose of processing cassava tubers raised at its nearby agricultural experiment stations and, when they can be spared without detriment to the normal functions of his bureau, they can be employed for processing gaplek from private parties.

The director said that if the people can be induced to prepare their cassava tubers into

(Continued on page 4)

Early Collections Show Goal Of Red Cross Will Be Reached

Collections during the first week of the drive of the Philippine Red Cross for relief funds have met with previous expectations, and it is expected that the goal set will be reached at the end of the campaign on July 11.

At the opening meeting, Mayor Leon Guinto of Greater Manila promised the full support of the government of the city and municipalities under his jurisdiction, and made suggestions as to how best the campaign may be conducted to make it a success. He was seconded by other representatives of the various branches of the government.

The bankers' group pledged P15,000 for each of the Philippine banks now in operation and this, it was announced that the advance gift committee quota has been exceeded.

In the next meeting, a report of the general progress of the first week of the campaign will be available. However, the campaign management is eager to have all campaigners and government and private group representatives cooperating to be present so that a thorough check-up of results and further coor-

(Continued on page 4)

THE WEATHER

CHICAGO AND VICINITY—Not much change in temperature today and this evening, except cooler near the lake this afternoon; gentle winds.

ILLINOIS—Not much change in temperature today and this evening; scattered thunderstorms in south portion this afternoon and evening.

INDIANA—Scattered showers and thunderstorms in east portion today and in extreme southwest portion this evening; no decided change in temperature.

WISCONSIN—No decided change in temperature today and this evening.

CHICAGO Herald American SUNDAY

Registered in U. S. Patent Office.

C 7

FINAL COMPLETE

62ND YEAR No. 11. —41

CHICAGO—SUNDAY—JUNE 21—1942

DAILY, 3 Cents | SATURDAY, 5 Cents | SUNDAY 10 Cents

FIRST PHOTOS—JAP MIDWAY ROUT

A MASS OF TWISTED STEEL, JAP HEAVY CRUISER IS SHOWN AFTER MIDWAY BATTLE. OTHER PHOTOS ON PAGE 14. (A.P. Wirephoto from the U. S. navy.)

AXIS MINE SINKS SHIP OFF U. S.

Weizmann Here, Bares Palestine's War Production

Zionist Leader Tells Growing Factory and Farm Output

BY MEYER ZOLOTAREFF.

Palestine, once a poverty-stricken country, is now producing an increasing volume of food and industrial goods for the armies of the near and Middle East, Dr. Chaim Weizmann, president of the Jewish Agency for Palestine and of the World Zionist Organization, declared here yesterday.

This was made possible, he aded, because of the faith and tenacity of the Jewish people in Palestine who have rebuilt an ancient land from desert waste and have brought new hope not only to the despoiled Jewries of Europe but to all men eager to found a more secure world order in the days to follow the war.

The noted Jewish leader, who flew here from London to discuss with the American govern-

Continued on Page 4, Column 2.

Map Drive for U.S. Prisoners

SAN FRANCISCO, June 20.—(INS)—The San Francisco Press Club today offered to sponsor a nation-wide drive to furnish food, cigarets and other comforts for American prisoners in the Philippines.

Urging the federal government to make arrangements for transportation, the club dispatched telegrams to President Roosevelt and Secretary of State Cordell Hull, promising to sponsor the relief campaign nationally "if properly constituted administrative authorities take steps about neutral participation in the effort." The telegram added:

"We have been told that the time for this is not yet ready. Likewise, we have been told that Australia has made arrangements for her prisoners of Hong Kong and South Sea battles. Let international law prescribe the way and we will do the rest."

The club's action followed a dinner meeting of working newspaper men at which members heard an address by an army officer who was one of the last to leave Bataan before it fell to the Japanese.

Report Pope Gains Over Mild Illness

BERN, June 20.—(AP)—Pope Pius XII, who has been reported mildly ill, has improved considerably and the "crisis" can now be considered past, the Italian news agency Stefani reported today.

War Newsreel Man, Now Marine, Weds

SAN DIEGO, Cal., June 20.—(AP)—Capt. Arthur Menken, U. S. marine corps, former news reel war correspondent, and Carol Littig, San Diego, were married today at the naval air station.

U. S. BUSINESS SUBSIDY URGED BY HENDERSON

BY LEE CARSON,
International News Service Staff Correspondent.

WASHINGTON, June 20.—(INS)—Price Administrator Leon Henderson today staked claim as a contestant for Secretary of the Interior Harold Ickes' self-imposed title of "most unpopular man in the United States."

Since clamping down on the home front, Henderson admitted he has made remarkable headway in becoming the nation's favorite villain. This doubtful progress, the price administrator said, is no surprise to him. Fixing prices and rationing folks never made any man "belle of the ball."

Commenting on whispers that he will quit as chief of the wartime price control and rationing administration, Henderson declared:

"Over a period of years I've had one working agreement with my boss—that is, when I reach the end of my usefulness I'll say good-by. I think I'll leave it up to him on my resignation."

The one exception of this rule of letting "the boss" hand down his walking papers, the OPA chief said, was his decision to make a deal with Congress "if necessary." He will "get out," Henderson promised, if Congress agrees to approve government subsidy of businesses and industries.

The OPA, he explained, "very badly needs" the power to subsidize industry and business as an aid in maintaining price ceilings. He added:

"Our job is not to force producers to operate at a loss." The subsidy power is badly needed. In England they allot $1,000,000,000

Continued on Page 6, Column 4.

Men of 33d Go to War Fronts

Take it from a fightin' soldier: the boys of Illinois' Thirty-third Division are proving themselves tough hombres on the fighting fronts of the world.

The authority for that statement is no less than Maj. Gen. Frank C. Mahin, a "soldier's soldier," who succeeded Maj. Gen. Samuel T. Lawton in command of the division at Camp Forrest.

HALF SENT ELSEWHERE.

Deftly rolling a cigaret—he scorns the tailor-mades—Gen. Mahin told members of the old Thirty-third, in reunion at the Morrison Hotel last night, that "more than 50 per cent of the original personnel of the division have left Camp Forrest."

He wouldn't say what percentage have reached combat fronts, but the impression was that a lot of them have. He mentioned one regiment of artillery in New Caledonia. News dispatches have told of Illinois boys in Ireland and Australia.

DRAFTEES FILL RANKS.

Gen. Mahin, who was born in Clinton, Ia., across the river from Illinois, said the ranks of the division at Camp Forrest have been filled up by drafted men. Many of the old members have gone out as nucleus of new divisions.

All the artillery now at Camp Forrest, he said, will leave June 24 for Fort Sill, Okla., for firing practice. They will be accompanied by the 139th Infantry.

(News of Thirty-third Division veterans' meeting on Page 11.)

Three Die, 6 Hurt in Kansas Storm

WICHITA, Kas., June 20.—(AP)—Three persons were killed and at least six injured tonight in a storm that dipped through a farming community two miles northeast of nearby Mulvane. The dead were identified as Mrs. Pearl Rivers, her son, Charles, and her daughter, Virgolina. Mrs. Rivers' husband, C. W. Rivers, was missing.

Greece's King Visits West Point

NEW YORK, June 20.—(INS)—King George II of Greece went to West Point today to see America's future generals on parade.

O. K. PAYROLL DEDUCTION FOR INCOME TAX

WASHINGTON, June 20.—(A.P.)—The House ways and means committee killed sales tax proposals today, and then quickly adopted a formula for collecting a part of each employed individual's income taxes from his regular pay checks, beginning in January.

With the decisions the committee virtually completed a tentative draft of new tax legislation intended to add at least $6,640,000,000 to federal revenue. Final action sending the bill to the House is expected to be taken next week.

The treasury had asked for $8,700,000,000, which Secretary Morgenthau said was the least Congress should raise. Advocates of a sales tax had argued that a 5 per cent retail sales levy, with government and state purchases exempted, would produce $2,500,000,000.

At the end of the meeting today Chairman Doughton (D.) of North Carolina announced a sales tax would not be considered in this bill.

Representatives McKeough (D.) of Illinois and Healey (D.) of Massachusetts, who led the fight against such a levy, contended it would fall disproportionately heavy on those with low incomes.

By a 10-to-9 vote, the committee agreed tentatively to the pay-as-you-go system of collecting individual income taxes. It is de-

Continued on Page 10. Column 3.

British Beat Back Axis Thrusts Near Egyptian Frontier

Hammer at Flank of Foe Massing for Tobruk Siege

NEW YORK, June 20.—(INS)—Axis troops probably have entered the town of Bardia, the British radio said tonight, quoting one of its observers in the Libyan desert. The broadcast was heard by CBS. Bardia is only five miles from the Egyptian border.

BY GEORGE LAIT,
International News Service Staff Correspondent.

CAIRO, June 20.—After turning back two Axis columns that approached within thirty miles of the Egyptian frontier, British armored patrols tonight dealt piston-like blows at the rear and flank of enemy siege forces massing for an anticipated assault on isolated Tobruk.

Lieut. Gen. Ritchie's forward units, thrusting west from a new British defense line paralleling the Egyptian border, sought to break up—or at least delay—an enemy blow at Tobruk or another eastward push on Bardia, Libyan coastal town five miles from Egypt's border.

Reports from the desert late tonight indicated the possibility that British evacuation of Bardia might have begun, placing the town in a "no man's land." This,

Continued on Page 4, Column 3.

Action on All War Fronts

BY FOREIGN NEWS EDITOR.

Berlin — A purge of all anti-social elements—those who disagree with the Nazis—was launched in Austria and Vienna, and soon will be effective in Germany proper, the German news agency DNB announced. Hitler's recently acquired power of sole judge will rule all cases. It also was rumored the Nazis have pressed Vichy for 1,000,000 tons of French shipping now in the Mediterranean.

London—The RAF renewed daylight attacks on German ports and French cities after a night bombing raid on the port of Emden. British marines were reported to have sunk three Jap ships in the Straits of Malacca, off Malaya.

Libya—Two axis armored thrusts at the Egyptian border were turned back and besieged Tobruk prepared to fight off heavy axis attacks. The British radio said axis troops probably had entered Bardia, ten miles from Egypt.

Moscow—The Nazis smashed savagely at Sevastopol, where Red forces are mowing down waves of axis infantry and blasting tank attacks to hold the Crimean port. There were reports of a Russ offensive opening in the Smolensk area near Moscow, but Soviet spokesmen were silent.

Washington—President Roosevelt and Prime Minister Churchill continued their secret talks of a second front and aid to Britain in Libya. The navy announced enemy mines in Atlantic coastal waters had sunk an American ship and damaged another.

SECOND CRAFT DAMAGED BY NEW SEA PERIL

WASHINGTON, June 20.—(AP).—The Navy Department announced today that the sinking of one merchant ship and damaging of another off the Virginia coast recently resulted from striking enemy mines.

The ships referred to were the two which thousands of seaside vacationists on the Virginia shore saw blasted early this week, the department said.

Originally the boats had been listed as victims of submarine attacks.

The navy said the mines apparently were laid by an enemy submarine operating "under the cover of darkness, when detection is extremely difficult."

There was no indication in the statement of the extent of such activity that might have been undertaken.

The statement follows:

"Careful investigation of the circumstances surrounding the sinking of one merchant vessel and damage to another off the Virginia coast has definitely convinced the Navy Department that these casualties were the result of the vessels striking enemy mines, and were not caused by submarine attacks, as previously believed.

"Undoubtedly, these mines were laid by an enemy submarine under the cover of darkness, when detection is extremely difficult."

(Other U-boat war details on Page 2.)

REICH OCCUPATION ARMY

U. S. Orders Medals for Troops

NEW YORK, June 20.—(INS)—The United States army is preparing for the day when there will be an American occupation force in Nazi Germany.

Manufacturers of medallions and decorations have been asked by the quartermaster's department at Philadelphia to bid on between 500,000 and 1,000,000 decorations for soldiers of the army occupying Germany after the war, it was learned tonight. Bids on some 3,000,000 other decorations also were asked.

The number of ribbons involved indicates the army occupying the reich after World War II will be several times larger than that sent into Germany after the last war.

Another cheerful note: all decorations are to be delivered within six months under contracts enjoying A-1 priority ratings.

PRICELESS RUBBER

Boy Asks Special Place for It

WALTHAM, Mass., June 20.—(INS)—A 12-year-old boy walked into a filling station today carrying two bags of rubber articles.

He handed one to the operator, watched him weigh it and took his payment. Then he gave him the second with a note and walked quickly away. The note read:

"The President's friend:

"These little rubber boots and beach sandals belonged to my little brother, who died ten years ago. He was only 3 then. I don't remember him very well, as I was only a year old at the time.

"My mother has often said that all the money in the world could not buy these things, but now she is giving them for the scrap rubber drive. Because they were so highly thought of by my mother, I don't want you to throw them in with the other old rubber. Sort of keep them in a special little place of their own.

"Very truly yours,

"PETER NORTON."

Col. Boyd Wagner's Sister to Be Bride

PITTSBURGH, June 20.—(INS)—Attractive Phyliss Wagner, of Johnstown, Pa., sister of the famous army air corps hero, Lieut. Col. Boyd ("Buzz") Wagner, came to Pittsburgh today to marry A. Dean Gilbert, Johnstown post office employe.

The Philadelphia Inquirer

PUBLIC LEDGER

An Independent Newspaper for All the People

FINAL CITY EDITION

CIRCULATION: May Average: Daily 444,703, Sunday 1,251,755 — a b d e f g h — MONDAY MORNING, JUNE 22, 1942 — Copyright, 1942, by The Philadelphia Inquirer Co. VOL. 226, No. 173 — Second Largest 3c Morning Circulation in America — THREE CENTS

British Surrender Tobruch to Nazis, 25,000 Troops Captured in 'Disaster;' Army Planes Bomb Japs in Aleutians

Today

Russians Confident
A Burning Faith
Tales of Heroism
Industry Winning
Quotas Exceeded

—By Maurice Hindus—

SOMEWHERE IN AZERBAIJAN, U. S. S. R., June 21.

THE most impressive thing about the Russian people is their overwhelming faith in victory.

The outside world, particularly America, can hardly apprehend how universa' and impassioned is this faith. Soldiers and civilians, adults and children, city folk and peasants are as imbued with it as they are with rightness of the cause for which they are fighting.

Even before Foreign Commissar Vyacheslav M. Molotov's visit to London and Washington, when the second front was only a subject of debate in the English-speaking countries and of speculation and suspicion—very deep suspicion—in many a Russian mind, the average Russian had not the least doubt of ultimate triumph.

"We'll lick the infernal Fritzes," said a stocky, dark-skinned blacksmith in a village bazaar, "even if we have to fight them all alone."

When I asked why he thought so, he grunted and pursed his lips as though in resentment. Then, as if remembering I was a foreigner, freshly arrived in Russia, his demeanor suddenly changed and he said:

"When Leningrad was surrounded last winter, 30,000 Komsomol (Young Communist) girls went out to fight the enemy. Do you understand what it means?"

With true Russian expansiveness he proceeded to narrate at length the deeds of heroism of soldiers and civilians, of women and even of children, during the dark days when the Germans were battering at the gates of Moscow and Leningrad.

To him that alone was a symbol of invincibility and a guarantee of victory.

Nor is he alone in this conviction. Hardly a Russian I have met in the few days I have been here has failed to start the conversation with a gush of talk about the heroism of the people, not only last winter but all the time.

Last night a Russian woman whose home I was visiting and whose husband perished in the war showed me several items in the day's papers which speak for themselves.

Up north beyond the Arctic Circle, at a railroad station, an incendiary bomb started a fire.

Nearby were several oil tanks, and to prevent the fire from engulfing the tanks a young girl named Petrova threw herself in her clothes on the rising flames and put them out.

"Luckily," said the woman, "she was unhurt. But she might have caught fire and burned to death. Yet, she didn't think of that. She was thinking only of saving the oil tanks."

Another item in the daily paper concerned the dramatic exploit of five sailors on the Sevastopol front. They fought until two of them were dead and the others were out of ammunition except for anti-tank grenades. They stuck the grenades in their belts, threw themselves under the advancing German tanks and blew them up.

"With their lives," said the woman "the dear ones broke up a tank attack." Slowly, devoutly, she read the names of the five sailors: Nikolai Filshenko, Vasilo Tsibulko, Yuri Pashin, Ivan Krasnoselski, Daneel Odintsov, and then added: "We have millions like them, millions, and we'll win."

The heroic deeds of soldiers and civilians have fired not only the imagination and the fighting spirit but the faith of the Russian people.

All the greater is this faith now because of Molotov's agreements with London and Washington, especially with London, and even more because of the astounding achievements of Russian industry.

The headlines in the daily press all over the country are devoted not to action at the front but to industrial successes. There is scarcely a factory but is exceeding the planned quota of output. This is particularly true of ammunition factories.

One shop in Kuznetsk, the gigantic steel plant deep in the heart of Siberia, has exceeded its May quotas by .568 tons of steel. In flaming headlines the press tells the public that from this amount of steel will be made eight tanks, 12 machine guns, 5000 minethrowers, 6000 automatics, 34,000 grenades.

Most significant is the report from factories that had to be moved eastward. Three such factories, engaged in the manufacture of tank engines and other tank parts, already are yielding

Continued on Page 4, Column 2

GAS 'FAMINE' FAILS TO HALT AUTO TRAVEL

Traffic Heaviest Of Rationing Era; Dealers Expect New Supply Today

Illustrated on Page 14

Exhaustion of Philadelphia's gasoline supply by mid-afternoon failed yesterday to check the greatest outpouring of automobile traffic since fuel rationing began.

By 3 P. M. there wasn't a drop of gasoline to be bought in the metropolitan area but the motorized rush to the countryside and seashore rolled on in full force.

NEW SUPPLY AWAITED

Only 20 percent of the city's 3400 filling stations are open for business on Sundays, but those which were open yesterday rapidly sold out their last few gallons for the 10-day quota period which ended at midnight.

A relative abundance of the fuel is expected in pumps this morning, when deliveries of the dealers' new 10-day supplies get under way and stations which were closed yesterday reopen.

THOUSANDS 'STOCKED UP'

Such traffic barometers as the Delaware River Bridge's toll records showed that highway travel yesterday was the heaviest of any Sunday since gasoline rationing began May 15.

Observers laid this paradox to the fact that thousands of car owners have stocked up with gasoline since the Office of Price Administration

Continued on Page 6, Column 1

Policeman, Shot Twice, Gets His Man

A paroled criminal was critically wounded and a policeman was shot twice in the arm early yesterday in the climax of two running gun battles which aroused scores of residents in Moorestown, N. J., as shots echoed over the streets.

Although struck twice by bullets from the fugitive's revolver, Patrolman Frank Walters, 27-year-old Army reservist, finally managed to turn the criminal's gun on him and made the capture.

PRISONER SHOT IN SKULL

The prisoner, Earl Chester, 37, Negro, of Lombard st. near 15th, was shot at the base of the skull and is in Burlington County Hospital. Police said that his criminal record

Continued on Page 11, Column 3

TOKIO CRUISER HIT, TRANSPORT SUNK AT KISKA

Enemy Advances Under Arctic Fog; Tents, Temporary Quarters Blasted

Map on Page 2

By JOHN M. McCULLOUGH

Inquirer Washington Bureau

WASHINGTON, June 21.—One Japanese transport has been sunk and another cruiser damaged by Army bombers in their attacks on enemy occupation forces in the harbor of Kiska Island, 585 miles southwest of the United States Naval Base at Dutch Harbor, Unalaska, the Navy Department reported in a communique today.

For the first time in the 18-day-old, fog-shrouded "Battle of the Aleutians," the communique admitted the Japanese have occupied Kiska Island, in the Rat group.

TENTS ERECTED

Naval reconnaissance planes, which reported the Army bombing successes, likewise brought back word that "tents and minor temporary structures" have been erected by the enemy on Kiska.

So far as official Navy Department reports are concerned, the toll wrought against Japanese shipping since the opening of the North Pacific theatre, coincidentally with the ill-fated enemy advance against Midway, stands thus:

Sunk: One transport.

Damaged: Four cruisers, one destroyer, one gunboat and one transport.

SILENT ON 5TH CRUISER

Thus far, neither the Navy nor the War Department has officially confirmed the sinking of a cruiser and the torpedoing by Army B-26 medium bombers of a Japanese aircraft carrier—information which was conveyed to Glenn L. Martin, builder of the B-26, in a telegram from Lieutenant General Henry H. Arnold, commanding general of the Army Air Forces.

Arnold's telegram was made public on June 15, at almost the same time the Navy reported the first combat successes since the relatively light Japanese bombing attack on Dutch Harbor itself on June 3.

MAY BE ON OTHER ISLES

At the time, it was impossible to ascertain from official sources whether the cruiser which General Arnold's telegram reported as sunk was one of the three reported damaged by the Navy's communique of the same day. Nor has any clarification been proffered since, through the unofficial inference is that such is the case.

On the basis of today's communique, it now appears the Japanese have occupation forces on Attu,

Continued on Page 2, Column 6

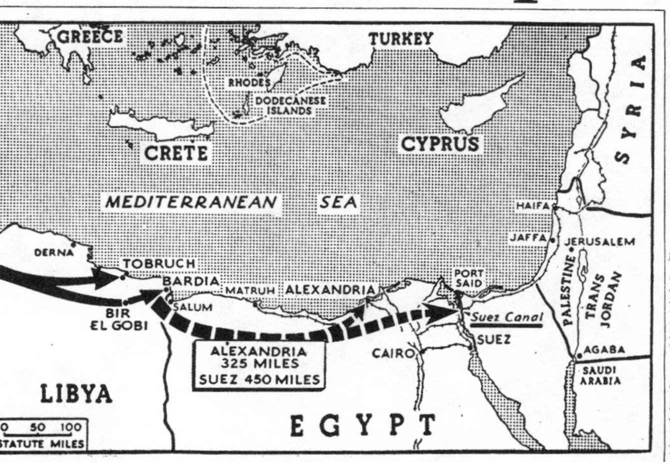

(A. P. Wirephoto)

AXIS LIBYAN VICTORIES PAVE WAY FOR DRIVE INTO EGYPT

London yesterday admitted the disastrous loss of Tobruch, Bardia and Bir el Gobi (solid arrows), in eastern Libya, paving the way for Axis thrust into Egypt toward Alexandria, Cairo and the Suez Canal (broken arrows). Alexandria is only 325 miles from the Axis spearhead, and Suez but 425 miles.

ENEMY SUB SHELLS VANCOUVER ISLAND, CAUSES NO DAMAGE

Canadian Radio Station 110 Miles From U. S. Is Target

VICTORIA, B. C., June 21 (A. P.).—An enemy submarine, presumably Japanese, shelled the Canadian Government radio station at remote, sparsely populated Estevan Point, on the west coast of Vancouver Island, for about half an hour last night, but failed to hit the building, it was announced tonight.

It was the first attack on Canadian soil since the war began.

"The shells landed on the beach and on the rocks well beyond the station," Lieutenant General Kenneth Stuart, chief of the Canadian General Staff, said tonight. "A few windows in the radio office were broken by the concussion."

POPULATION OF 33

Estevan is an isolated settlement of 33 persons midway up the rocky island coast. The radio station is on a promontory jutting six miles out into the Pacific and is protected by a rocky reef extending along the offshore waters.

Most of the residents are white employees of the radio station and of a lighthouse there.

The attack, first disclosed officially by Defense Minister J. L. Ralston in a brief announcement at Ottawa, occurred at 10.35 P. M. Saturday Pacific Time (1.35 A. M. Sunday, E. W. T.).

Estevan Point is situated about midway on the western coast of Vancouver Island, approximately 110 miles from the nearest point on the United States frontier.

RECALL CALIFORNIA ATTACK

The submarine shelling recalled the attack near Santa Barbara, Calif., last Feb. 22, when an underwater craft appeared off the town of Goleta and fired two dozen shells at an oil refinery near the shore.

(The States of Washington and Oregon ordered their coastlines dimmed out as the result of the Vancouver Island shelling. The action was suggested by the 13th U. S. Naval District commandant.)

Town Fined by Nazis For Slurs On Hitler

NEW YORK, June 21 (A. P.).—The little town of Grevenmacher in Luxembourg was fined 250,000 marks by German authorities because an extraordinary number of anti-Hitler slogans were chalked on the walls, a British broadcast heard there said today.

The Germans announced the fine in a German-controlled Luxembourg newspaper.

Stalin's Son Wins Medal for Bravery

MOSCOW, June 21 (U. P.).—Vol Vassilov Josefovieh Stalin, the Russian Premier's second son, was one of 25 Soviet aviators awarded the Order of the Red Banner "for exemplary execution of fighting tasks with courage and bravery," it was announced today.

Log of Battle Tells Grim Midway Story

Illustrated on Page 14.

(The Battle of Midway extended from June 3 to June 6, inclusive, but the day which decided the outcome was Thursday, June 4, when major Japanese forces were put to flight. Following are excerpts from the Associated Press correspondent's log of that day.)

By WENDELL WEBB

WITH THE PACIFIC FLEET, June 4 (Delayed) (A. P.).—Talk was quiet at breakfast—it looked like there was a big day ahead.

We knew the Japanese had bombed Dutch Harbor yesterday in what might have been a feint to draw our forces north. We also had heard that Army bombers last night attacked a major Japanese concentration west and north of Midway Island.

It was 8.18 (ship's time) when the unearthly clatter of general quarters sounded. A headlong rush for battle stations followed with cries of "Let's go get 'em!" There was plenty of enthusiasm, and the pre-battle tenseness was gone.

8.20. Everyone is at his station.

Continued on Page 2, Column 3

War Summary

Monday, June 22, 1942

EUROPE-AFRICA

Tobruch, last and most important British base in Libya, fell suddenly yesterday before an overwhelming Axis dive bombing and tank assault. Some 25,000 British troops were captured in the disaster.

The loss of Libya not only paved the way for an Axis drive into Egypt and on toward the Suez Canal and the Near East oil fields, but also was regarded as imperiling Allied plans for a second front in Europe, due to the necessity of rushing reinforcements to Egypt.

The other arm of the gigantic Axis pincers gained in Russia as the Reds admitted the Nazis had driven a wedge into the Sevastopol defense lines and had turned the southern flank at the Crimean fort. However, the Russians said they had wiped out 100,000 Axis troops in the battle.

PACIFIC FRONT

U. S. Army bombers hit a Japanese cruiser, sank a transport and blasted Jap forces encamped on Kiska Island, in the Aleutians, where the enemy was revealed to have consolidated his earlier advance.

An enemy submarine—presumably Japanese—shelled a Dominion radio station on the western Canadian island of Vancouver, but there was no damage. Vancouver Island is 110 miles north of Seattle.

NAZIS DRIVE WEDGE IN SEVASTOPOL LINE, LOSE 100,000 MEN

Reds Also Admit South Flank Turned, But Hold in North

By HENRY C. CASSIDY

MOSCOW, June 22 (Monday) (A. P.).—Beginning the second year of the war against the Axis with "no surrender" resistance along the entire 2000-mile front, Russia acknowledged officially today that the enemy had succeeded in driving a wedge into the defenses of Sevastopol although "at the cost of tremendous sacrifices."

The price paid by the Axis was indicated in newspaper dispatches reporting that at least seven Axis divisions—five German and two Rumanian—totaling up to 100,000 men have been wiped out in the bitter battle for the Crimean port.

TURN SOUTHERN FLANK

"During the course of June 21, on the Sevastopol sector, our troops repelled constant fierce attacks of German Fascist troops," the Soviet Bureau of Information announced in the first communique of the new year of war.

"The enemy at the cost of tremendous sacrifices succeeded in driving a wedge in our defenses."

Earlier newspaper dispatches from the roaring battle front said the Germans, by dint of superior numbers and repeated attacks, forced the Red

Continued on Page 3, Column 7

Canadian Favored As 2d Front Chief

MONTREAL, (Monday) June 22 (A. P.).—The Gazette, in a dispatch from its Washington correspondent, L. S. B. Shapiro, says today that Lieutenant-General A. G. L. McNaughton, commander of the Canadian Corps overseas, "is heavily favored to assume supreme command of all United Nations forces charged with opening the second front in Europe, probably during 1942."

The dispatch quotes a military source as confirming that "without question the British War Office favors General McNaughton above all others," and that "President Roosevelt and General George C. Marshall, United States chief of staff, were so deeply impressed by the Canadian commander on his visit here last winter that they are most likely to support the choice of the British War Office."

King Peter Lands In Washington

WASHINGTON, June 21 (A. P.).—King Peter II of Jugoslavia arrived in Washington by plane this afternoon, the State Department announced, accompanied by the Jugoslavian Foreign Minister M. Nitchich.

The 18-year-old monarch will leave tomorrow "for a few days in the country," the announcement said, and will travel incognito until Wednesday, when he returns to the capital to begin his official program. King Peter came here from England.

Air-Tank Assault Ends '2d Siege' Of Port in a Day

CAIRO, Egypt, June 21 (A. P.).—The "second siege" of Tobruch ended abruptly today in a short overpowering assault which toppled that key supply harbor into Axis hands and advanced German Marshal Erwin Rommel's armored hosts to the borders of menaced Egypt.

Captured in the overwhelming rush, said German and Italian communiques, were 25,000 British soldiers and several generals—almost a duplication of the number of Italians taken prisoner when the port surrendered to the British on Jan. 22, 1941.

MOST OF NEW EQUIPMENT LOST

It was possible, too, that most of the equipment convoyed to Tobruch by the British Navy at great cost only a few days ago had fallen into Axis hands, for the enemy announcements claimed the capture of vast stores.

With this thorn removed from the side of the Axis coastal flank, the Germans claimed to have rushed on and seized Bir el Gobi, a desert track-crossing 40 miles southeast which has been much fought-over, and Bardia, only eight miles from the Egyptian border.

Observers did not doubt these claims, for it was not believed these places were strongly held.

AXIS FORCE NEARS EGYPTIAN BORDER

(An Axis armored force, followed by infantry in some strength, has passed through Bardia and through the ruins of Fort Capuzzo, former Italian stronghold just inside the Libyan border, according to Richard Dimbleby, correspondent in Libya for the British Broadcasting Corp. He said the Axis had not yet launched any attack against Imperial positions on the Egyptian frontier.)

There was no ready explanation of the stunning blow that the British had suffered, but it was feared they had lost a large proportion of their tanks and were unable to give battle to the Axis armored columns or they would not have surrendered so readily the fortress to which they clung through thick and thin in a siege last year.

KEY PORT ON ALLIED SUPPLY ROUTE

Tobruch, the best deep harbor between Alexandria and Tripoli and thus a key point in the vital problem of supply in the desert, had been British since January, 1941, when the British seized it from the Italians in the first Libyan offensive.

It was cut off on April 12 when the Germans led the Axis rebound, but for eight months the British held on despite terrific dive bombings and artillery bombardments and despite a high cost in ships which supplied the garrison.

At length, on Dec. 10, 1941, the siege was lifted when the British began their second offensive.

TERRIFIC DIVE BOMBING ATTACK

It was cut off again three days ago by Axis armored forces which surged past to the coast.

The only available accounts of the last attack said the Germans began a terrific dive bombing attack yesterday, then

Continued on Page 3, Column 1

Loss of Libya Perils Allied 2d Front Plans

By J. WES GALLAGHER

LONDON, June 22 (Monday) (A. P.).—Britain's crushing defeat in North Africa approached disastrous proportions today, imperiling Allied plans for a second front, as German Marshal Erwin Rommel's African Corps turned toward Egypt and Suez after capturing the great fortress of Tobruch.

Military experts expressed the belief that the United States and Britain must now divert supplies and men to stave off an Axis drive for the Suez Canal, regarded in serious danger. The diversion would be at the expense of the European theatre.

OFFICIALLY CONFIRMED

The fall of Tobruch was officially confirmed by the British early today. Confirmation of the Axis claim that 25,000 British prisoners were captured there was not forthcoming immediately, but it seemed plausible here.

Bardia and Bir el Gobi, which the Axis claimed to have occupied, were undefended.

The fact that Tobruch fell after only two days of assault was a clear indication of Rommel's great strik-

Continued on Page 3, Column 3

Laval on Air Today To Explain Axis Tie

BERN, Switzerland, June 21 (A. P.).—Pierre Laval, French chief of government, will broadcast an address to the French nation at 8 P. M. (2 P. M., E. W. T.) tomorrow in which he is expected to explain his program of sending laborers to Germany and probably define his views on the whole question of collaboration with the Axis.

U. S. WEATHER FORECAST

Eastern Pennsylvania and New Jersey: Somewhat cooler in south portions today.

Sun rises 5.31 A.M. Sets 8.32 P.M.
Moon rises 1.54 P.M. Sets 1.22 A.M.

Other Weather Reports on Page 2

IN TODAY'S INQUIRER

Rommel 110 Miles in Egypt

Read the New York Journal-American for complete, accurate war coverage. It is the only New York evening newspaper possessing the three great wire services—ASSOCIATED PRESS, INTERNATIONAL NEWS SERVICE, UNITED PRESS.

NEW YORK Journal-American
AN AMERICAN PAPER FOR THE AMERICAN PEOPLE

In Two Sections—Section One

No. 19,903—DAILY | THURSDAY, JUNE 25, 1942 | DAILY 3 Cents | SATURDAY 5 Cents | SUNDAY 10 Cents

7TH SPORTS RACING
SPORTS COMPLETE

AS PACIFIC WAR COUNCIL MET TODAY

These members of the United Nations Pacific War Council are pictured today at White House meeting after which it was announced that a "victory plan" had been drafted. They are (left to right) front row, seated, Prime Minister Winston Churchill and President Roosevelt; back row, Foreign Minister Dr. Eelco Van Kleffens of The Netherlands government-in-exile; Sir Owen Dixon, Australian Minister to the United States; Leighton McCarthy, Canadian Minister; Prime Minister W. L. MacKenzie King of Canada; Lord Halifax, British Ambassador, and Foreign Minister T. V. Soong of China.

International News Photo.

CHURCHILL, FDR DECIDE WAR PLANS

Late Racing and Baseball Results on Page 22

Rommel Drives 110 Miles In Egypt

LONDON, June 25 (INS).—Gen. Field Marshal Erwin Rommel is "throwing everything he has" into a smash against Marsa Matruh, 110 miles inside the Egyptian frontier, northern anchor of the new British defense line, the London Daily Express said today.

Rommel's forces, said to include between 500 and 600 tanks, supported by approximately 10,000 vehicles, several hundred mobile guns and motorized infantry, were said to be advancing on Marsa Matruh at the present time.

By GEORGE LAIT,
International News Service Staff Correspondent

CAIRO, June 25.—Units of German Gen. Field Marshal Erwin Rommel's Afrika Korps have driven more than 60 miles inside Egypt to a point southeast of Sidi Barrani on the Mediterranean coast, the British Middle East High Command disclosed today.

It was revealed at the same time that Lieut. Gen. Neil M. Ritchie had withdrawn his British Eighth Army from fortified positions on the Libyan-Egyptian frontier running south from Solum to Sidi Omar.

The Axis penetration into Egypt and the advance toward Sidi Barrani was affected during the night.

British Wellington bombers and

Continued on Page 6, Column 3.

U. S. Appoints Second Front Commander

WASHINGTON, June 25 (UP).—Establishment of a "European theatre of operations for United States forces" — presumably a prelude to eventual opening of a second European front by the United Nations—was announced by the War Department today.

Designated as commander of the new war theatre was Maj. Gen. Dwight D. Eisenhower, 51-year-old strategist and until now assistant chief of staff in charge of the Army's operations division.

In army parlance, a "theatre of operations" normally means an area of actual or prospective combat, as distinguished from a training area. The American forces in Northern Ireland and England thus far have been engaged in training.

Establishment of the European operations theatre follows close after formal announcement that the need for creation of a second European front was agreed on in the recent conferences here between President Roosevelt and other American officials and

Continued on Page 6, Column 1.

Br-r-r-r-razil!

MANAOS, Brazil, June 25 (UP).—South America's record cold wave struck this tropical, Amazon River zone today and the mercury dropped to 42 degrees. This city lies only about three degrees south of the equator.

Council Told Of Strategy

By KINGSBURY SMITH,
International News Service Staff Correspondent.

WASHINGTON, June 25.—While Congress echoed to sharp criticism of Prime Minister Churchill's conduct of the British phase of the war, members of the Pacific War Council today emerged from a two-hour conference at the White House with hopeful expressions and the disclosure that President Roosevelt and Churchill have drafted a victory plan.

New Zealand Minister Walter Nash told newspapermen that the President and the Prime Minister outlined to the council "a job they definitely have got in hand which ultimately will give us the results we want."

Nash also predicted that the Axis forces of German General Field Marshal Rommell are going to get a surprise if they attempt to move much further into Egypt.

The meeting of the war conference was preceded by a session between Congressional leaders and the President and Churchill at which some members, including Sen. Tom Connally (D.-Tex.), blunt-spoken chairman of the Senate Foreign Relations Committee, asked critical questions concerning the British conduct of the war and the reverses in Libya.

This was followed by a speech in the Senate by Sen. Ellender (D.-La.), in which he criticised Churchill at length and declared that both the American and British people are "nauseated and disgusted" over the maintenance of a large army on the British Isles while defeats are being suffered elsewhere.

Representatives of all the Pacific powers gathered for the council session.

Chinese Foreign Minister T. V. Soong said he had made an urgent appeal to the Pacific War Council for increased aerial support to the embattled armies of China.

Asked if he felt that the council members appreciated the importance of the Pacific situation, Soong replied:

"I have no doubt of it."

However, there was good reason to believe that both the President and Churchill made it clear that stopping Hitler in Europe this year must be the major objective of the United Nations.

Foreign Minister Van Kleffans of the Netherlands was extremely optimistic on leaving the White House meeting.

At the meeting with Congressional leaders, Churchill, in response to questions of a critical nature, assured the assembled members of the Senate and House that Egypt and the Suez Canal will be held and that the Libya reverses will be rectified.

Payroll Levy Cut To 5% Asked

International News Service Staff Correspondent

WASHINGTON, June 25.—The House Ways and Means Committee, Secretary of Treasury Morgenthau disclosed today, is studying a proposal to apply a 5 per cent payroll levy to collect personal income taxes, instead of the 10 per cent figure which had been "tentatively" approved by the committee.

Morgenthau also stated that he had suggested to Committee Chairman Doughton (D., N. C.), a plan under which individuals would be given the option of paying their 1942 taxes monthly, beginning Feb. 1, 1943, instead of quarterly as at present.

As explained by the Treasury, the 5 per cent withholding tax on wages, salaries, interest and dividends would apply after Jan. 1, 1943, and would be used only to meet 1943 tax payments which fall due on March 15, 1944.

Woman Killed by Train

A woman identified as Nina Fulco, 27, of 78 W. 21st st., Bayonne, N. J., was killed when she fell or jumped into the path of a freight train at the 22nd st. station in Bayonne.

1st Dutch Harbor Battle Story Told

Picture in today's Pictorial Review
(MAP ON PAGE 2.)

SEATTLE, June 25 (AP).—In the first dramatic eye-witness report of what happened at Dutch Harbor, evacuees and seamen told upon arrival of a transport here how the Japanese air attack at 5:45 a. m. on June 3 caught civilians by surprise.

They also told how the gallant gunners on their ship and ashore laid a deadly screen of anti-aircraft fire about the raiding planes.

While Army and Navy men operated the anti-aircraft guns, some of the ship's crew snatched up rifles and blazed away at the dive bombers. The transport had a cargo of explosives for Dutch Harbor in her hold.

Lifting of the military restrictions disclosed that the commander of the Dutch Harbor naval base issued a commendation for courageous duty under fire by the Army transport's crew and the gunners.

How many Jap planes were downed has never been announced officially. Reports brought by the witnesses to the raids failed to clarify the point.

[The official Navy announcement at the time of the raid reported four bombers and 15 fighter planes over the base in the morning of June 3, with an unreported number of planes returning six hours later. The Navy reported damage was not extensive although some warehouses were set afire, and casualties were not great.]

Mayor John W. Fletcher of Unalaska (Dutch Harbor is in Unalaska Bay) said application

Continued on Page 2, Column 1.

Joe Louis in Cavalry

FORT RILEY, Kansas, June 25 (AP). — Corp. Joe Louis Barrow was assigned today to a horse troop at this cavalry replacement training center.

Two Navy Patrol Ships Sunk

WASHINGTON, June 25 (INS).—The Navy announced today that Axis submarines in the Atlantic have sunk two armed U. S. patrol boats resulting in the loss of 20 crew members.

A Navy Department communique said:

"Atlantic Area—Two small anti-submarine patrol craft have been lost off the Atlantic coast during the current month as the result of enemy submarine attacks.

"The USS Gannet, a sea-going tug, used to service patrol planes, was torpedoed and sunk. Sixteen members of the crew were lost.

"The YP-389, a small fishing craft, which had been taken over by the Navy and armed for anti-submarine patrol duty, was sunk by gun fire. Four members of the crew were lost.

Both commanders of the small patrol craft were rescued. They were Lieut. Francis Edward Nuessle, 31, of Bismarck, N. D., commander of the 840-ton Gannet, and Lieut. Roderick Johnstone Philips, 43, commander of the smaller craft, whose home address is 115 E. 37th st., New York

AVG Fliers Sink Four Jap Ships

CHUNGKING, June 25 (AP).—With a force of its fighting planes doubling as bombers, the American Volunteer Group has attacked Hankow, Japan's major inland base in occupied China, and sunk one Japanese warship and three transports in the broad Yangtze there.

An AVG communique today said other vessels probably were damaged and military establishments were blown up on Tuesday in the Flying Tigers' debut over Hankow, which is in Hupeh Province and is China's greatest interior city.

Coupled with this blow and others in which Chinese airmen also figured were reports that Chinese troops, long without adequate air support, had pushed the Japanese 12 miles back from recaptured Kweiki, in the long, harrowing battle for the Chekiang-Kiangsi railway.

This was reported to have widened the remaining Chinese-held gap on the important rail line to more than 60 miles in place of the bare 50 to which the defenders had been reduced by eastward and westward drives of the enemy.

THE WEATHER

Moderately warm.

Sun rises, 5:25 a. m.; sun sets, 8:32 p. m. High tide Governors Island, 6:57 a. m.; 6:36 p. m.

HOURLY TEMPERATURES

8 a. m.	62	12 Noon	69
9 a. m.	64	1 p. m.	69
10 a. m.	66	2 p. m.	69
11 a. m.	67	3 p. m.	73

(Complete Weather Table on Page 18)

TODAY'S INDEX

The New York Journal-American has the largest circulation of any evening newspaper in America.

Three Pages of Pictures and Text

What Doolittle Hit—And What He Saw!

Next Sunday in the JOURNAL-AMERICAN

CHARACTER QUALITY AMERICA FIRST! ENTERPRISE ACCURACY
Los Angeles Examiner
AN AMERICAN PAPER FOR THE AMERICAN PEOPLE — THE GREAT NEWSPAPER OF THE GREAT SOUTHWEST
Reg. U.S. Pat. Off.
Examiner Telephone Richmond 1212 — Giant of Journalism — Examiner Building, 1111 S. Broadway
VOL. XXXIX—NO. 199 — CCC — LOS ANGELES, SUNDAY, JUNE 28, 1942 — Seven Sections—Part 1 — 10 Cents in 100-mile zone — 12 Cents beyond 100 miles

Remember PEARL HARBOR

NAZI SABOTEURS LANDED IN N. Y. AND FLORIDA BY SUBS; 8 SEIZED

War Plants, Rivers, Rails on Bomb List; 2 Spies From L. A.

All Former U. S. Residents, 2 American Citizens; Had $150,000 for Payoffs

NEW YORK, June 27.—(AP)—Eight German experts in sabotage, landed from submarines on the American coast with money and explosives for a two-year campaign of terror against American war industry, have been captured by the Federal Bureau of Investigation, J. Edgar Hoover announced tonight.

All are former U. S. residents, (including several from Los Angeles); several are former German-American Bundsmen and two are citizens of the United States. One was once a member of the Michigan National Guard.

Details of Landing Bared

A group of four men, graduates of school for sabotage in Berlin, came ashore on Long Island east of New York City the night of June 13 and the other four at Ponte Vedra Beach near Jacksonville, Fla., three nights later, Hoover said.

The New York group landed from a submarine which stood 500 yards offshore and dispatched them in a rubber boat. Once ashore the quartet of wreckers buried their Nazi uniforms in the sand of Amagansett Bay together with their TNT, fuses, time clock firing devices for delayed action bombs and other equipment for sabotage. Donning civilian clothing

(Continued on Page 15, Column 1)

Planned to Wreck U. S. War Industries

GEORGE JOHN DASCH — HEINRICH HARM HEINCK — RICHARD "DICK" QUIRIN — ERNEST PETER BURGER — EDWARD JOHN KERLINE — WERNER THIEL

(Background stories of these men and their associates on Page 14)

L. A. ACCLAIMS WAR HEROES IN PARADE TODAY

America at war—thousands of men on the march, tanks and mechanized cavalry deploying swiftly, airplanes filling the sky. . . .

And in six months' time, even from the first minute a Jap bomb dropped on Pearl Harbor, America has these potent elements of military might on the move.

ALL SEATS FREE

It's all free today and it's first come first served!

It's War Heroes Day today at the Memorial Coliseum with 105,000 free seats, parade, 22 bands and special events.

COLISEUM SCHEDULE
Doors open 12 noon.
Band concert, 1 p. m.
Parade starts 1:30 p. m.
Entertainment and events, 3:30 p. m.

And it also has its heroes, dating back from that fatal minute, and thousands of other heroes in the making—at home and on the five continents.

In the first celebration of its kind in Los Angeles, all the Southland today—War Heroes Day—may witness the war machine of Uncle Sam's in its various units and also pay a homage to 16 of the United Nations' decorated heroes and other men who in time will prove themselves equally as brave.

A small-scale review of the nation's might will be seen in a two-hour military parade.

And the 16 Americans and British heroes, for whom the occasion is being held, will be seen and heard giving brief accounts

(Continued on Page 8, Cols. 3-4)

People Want Facts About Aleutians

THE LATE Will Rogers used to say that all he knew was what he read in the papers.

If he were alive today and, in common with the rest of the American people, restricted in what he knew about the war to what he read in the papers, he would probably say he did not know very much.

He particularly would know very little about the dangerous situation in the Aleutians, and would be very anxious to know more—as we all are.

The situation in the Aleutians is more than dangerous.

We know the Japanese have successfully occupied two islands in the Aleutian chain, one of them having what is described as one of the best harbors in the world.

Since, as an American naval officer is reported to have said, the Japanese do not send a boy to do a man's job, it is assumed they are consolidating their positions there with a view to further occupations.

The further occupations envisioned, of course, concern Dutch Harbor, and the principal American bases in Alaska, with progressive encroachment on the North American mainland.

THE American people naturally and confidently take it for granted that the Japanese will be intensively resisted in these enterprises, and will not attain their objectives.

But the people only know about these matters what they read in the papers, and the papers print only what the Government gives and permits them to print—which in the case of the Aleutian incident has not been very much or very reliable.

On June 10, a week after Dutch Harbor was bombed, when the Japanese announced occupations in the Aleutians, our official Navy spokesman said **"none of our inhabited islands or rocks are troubled with uninvited visitors up to this time."**

And of course that is what the papers printed and what the people knew about the situation, and ALL they knew.

But, on June 12, when the American Navy De-

(Continued on Page 2, Cols. 7-8)

BRITISH ARMY REINFORCED TO HALT ROMMEL

CAIRO, June 27.—(AP)—The British eighth army stood reinforced at full strength tonight 15 miles west of Matruh against a powerful Axis striking force spearheaded by three mechanized divisions aiming at Alexandria, 165 miles away, and the Suez Canal beyond.

The Allied desert army was in position on a chosen line 115 miles inside Egypt, and military men said that when the imminently expected German onslaught comes, the veterans will defend Egypt inch by inch.

150 MILES FROM NILE

With the enemy within 150 miles of the lush Nile Valley where 98 per cent of the Egyptians live, there was no doubt the situation was serious but the Eighth Army—smarting from its bad defeat in Libya—was described as determined that the enemy shall not pass.

Marshal Erwin Rommel, the Axis commander, has thrown everything he has into his Egyptian invasion, military men said, but before he can reach the Nile he must smash through the 40-mile desert stretch between the Mediterranean and the great Quattara depression—a great inland sea of sand through which a modern army cannot move.

Rommel had advanced 15 miles overnight but he definitely had been slowed.

Throughout the day and night, the Allied air force which includes some of the United States Army's mighty B-24 bombers,

(Continued on Page 6, Column 4)

FDR, Churchill to Strike Hitler

Worst Nazi Blows Fail in Crimea

By Henry C. Cassidy

MOSCOW, June 28 (Sunday).—(AP)—The valiant defenders of Sevastopol smashed attack after attack by storming Nazi forces which tried without success to advance all day yesterday in bitter fighting over stacks of their Axis dead, the Russians reported early today.

The siege of the Crimean port roared into its 24th day with no indication of a German break into the vast defenses of Sevastopol.

On the Kharkov front it was the same story, military dispatches said.

There Marshal Timoshenko's forces were credited with halting the eight-day-old German drive, and in one sector threw the Germans back in slashing tank counterattacks.

MAKE NO HEADWAY

The Germans were unable to make any headway whatever, the frontline accounts said, despite the extravagant use of massed air attacks in an effort to enlarge their gains.

These accounts were pointed up by the midnight communique, which told of the continued

(Continued on Page 15, column 5)

Leaders Agree Upon Blow to Aid Russ; New Sub War

WASHINGTON, June 27.—(AP)—President Roosevelt and Prime Minister Churchill today jointly promised a stroke at Germany which will divert Nazi troops from the Russian front and said the outlook for victory had improved in the last six months.

With Churchill safely back in London, they issued a statement which in addition called transportation the present "major problem" of the United Nations. But it noted that while the U-boat toll in the Atlantic is heavy, ship production was increasing and said new steps against the submarines were planned by the British and American navies.

The statement made no specific mention of a "second front," but nevertheless included a paragraph which provoked an intensive whirl of speculation on that subject.

WILL DIVERT GERMANY

"While exact plans, for obvious reasons, cannot be disclosed," the statement said, "it can be said that the coming operations which were discussed in detail at our Washington conferences, between ourselves and our respective military advisers, will divert German strength from the attack on Russia."

Many observers concluded that the millions of Americans and English troops mobilized in the British Isles were to be thrown into an invasion of the Nazi-held continent. Since the project had

Honors Given Men Who Bombed Japan With 20-Cent 'Sight'

TOKYO RAIDERS get flying crosses at Bolling Field, D. C., from Lieut. Gen. Henry H. Arnold (arrow). Col. Arthur Innis hands him medal. Brig. Gen. James H. Doolittle is on Arnold's left. (Story Page 5.)

ROMMEL HALTED, CLAIM

THE WEATHER
Light rain and mild temperature today. Somewhat cooler tonight. Gentle winds.
Detailed Weather Report on Page 30

Read The Baltimore News-Post for complete, accurate war coverage. It is the only Baltimore newspaper possessing the three great wire services—
ASSOCIATED PRESS
INTERNATIONAL NEWS SERVICE
UNITED PRESS

THE BALTIMORE NEWS-POST
AN INDEPENDENT NEWSPAPER
The Largest Evening Circulation in the Entire South

HOME FINAL 7

VOL. CXLI.—NO. 51 | Entered as second-class matter at Baltimore Postoffice. | THURSDAY EVENING, JULY 2, 1942 | PRICE 3 CENTS

TOBRUK 2D DUNKIRK CHURCHILL REVEALS

Admits Allies Lost 50,000 Men

Reds Refuse To Surrender At Sevastopol As Troops Fight Hand To Hand In City

MOSCOW, July 2—(A. P.).—The Red Army reported at noon today that bitter fighting was continuing in Sevastopol, and dispatches telegraphed yesterday to the army newspaper Red Star said German assault troops had carried the battle into the city itself.

Red Star's accounts pictured heavily superior numbers of Nazi forces rolling slowly forward against staunch defenders of the Crimean base.

IGNORE NAZI CLAIMS

The situation in the last Soviet stronghold in the Crimea was described as "extremely tense and difficult."

(BACKGROUND NOTE: Two successive Russian communiques have ignored German claims of having captured Sevastopol.)

The latest information came in dispatches from Sevastopol yesterday to the army newspaper, Red Star.

Red Star's correspondent telegraphed:

"The enemy continues to move forward slowly to the outskirts of the city in a number of sectors.

"In some places the enemy succeeded in carrying the battle directly into Sevastopol city."

The dispatch ended:

"Nevertheless the glorious defenders of Sevastopol continue their stubborn resistance to the enemy."

With hand to hand fighting going on and the Germans numerically 10 to 15 times superior, at some points Red Army troops and Black sea fleet sailors were reported to be refusing to surrender.

REPULSED 5 ATTACKS

One company which repulsed five attacks by two enemy battalions retreated only when the Germans sent in a third, fresh battalion.

An artillery battery was cited also for firing constantly until it was outflanked and surrounded. Then it broke its way through the enemy encirclement and resumed fighting.

(BACKGROUND NOTE: In Berlin the German High Command declared that total Nazi losses on the Russian front from June 22, 1941, to last June 21—the first year of invasion — were 271,621 officers, non-commissioned officers and men killed and 65,730 men missing.)

U. S. War Cost In Year: $25,953,665,954 Expended; Record

WASHINGTON, July 2—(A. P.).—Secretary Morgenthau announced today the Treasury spent a record total of $25,953,665,954 for cash war expenses during the fiscal year which ended Tuesday night.

In a year-end statement, he said:

"In the fiscal year just closed we expended approximately 25 per cent. of the national income for the war effort. In the fiscal year 1943 the contemplated war expenditures will represent approximately 55 per cent. of the national income."

REFERS TO ESTIMATE

He referred to a Budget Bureau estimate that war costs in the new fiscal year just beginning will cost the Treasury $67,000,000,000. He He continued:

"The rate of expenditure for war purposes has risen rapidly, month by month reflecting the steady expansion of our war production.

EXPENDITURE CITED

"In June, 1941, we spent on national defense $832,000,000, or approximately 10 per cent. of the estimated national income for that month. In June, 1942, we had succeeded in increasing war production so that war expenditures had risen nearly five-fold to $3,823,000,000, or about 40 per cent. of that month's estimated national income."

Adding in non-war and other expenses of the Government total Treasury expenditures were at the unprecedented figure of $32,491,307,397 for the fiscal year.

Revenues, also a record, aggregated $12,799,061,621, leaving an unequalled deficit of $19,692,245,776.

Seek Death Penalty For 8 Saboteurs

WASHINGTON, July 2—(A.P.).—The death penalty will be sought when eight men go on trial before a special commission next week charged with rowing ashore from German submarines for the purpose of blowing up American military installations.

As tentatively developed during a series of conferences between War and Justice Department officials, plans for the trial of the alleged saboteurs rounded up by the F. B. I. after they landed in Florida and on Long Island called for appointment by President Roosevelt of a seven-member military commission to pass judgment.

The trial will be closed and will be held in Washington or at one of the nearby Government reservations. The defendants will have counsel.

While there are few precedents to guide the procedure, it was expected the trial would follow the general pattern of a court-martial.

Congress In Battle Over Adjournment

WASHINGTON, July 2—(I.N.S.). Congress today headed into a battle over whether it will adjourn for a month while the war is raging.

Democratic leaders of the Senate and House called for an outright adjournment after the lower chamber passes the tax bill, probably about July 20.

Republican Senate Leader McNary, however, demanded Congress merely recess for three days at a time with an assurance that no business would be transacted. By doing this, he contended, Congress could assemble more quickly in case of an emergency.

Odell Waller Dies In Electric Chair

RICHMOND, Va., July 2—(A. P.). Odell Waller, Negro sharecropper, was electrocuted at the Virginia State Penitentiary today for the murder of Oscar Davis, his white employer, on July 15, 1940.

Temperatures

12 Midn't,	73	7 A. M.,	70
1 A. M.,	73	8 A. M.,	70
2 A. M.,	73	9 A. M.,	71
3 A. M.,	72	10 A. M.,	73
4 A. M.,	70	11 A. M.,	75
5 A. M.,	69	12 Noon,	78
6 A. M.,	70	1 P. M.,	79

Axis Armored Forces Stopped Seventy Miles From Alexandria Base

By GEORGE LAIT
International News Service Staff Correspondent.

CAIRO, July 2.—The headlong eastward drive through Egypt by Axis mechanized forces was halted today 70 miles west of Alexandria after the Germans and Italians were smashed back by the British defenders.

The British Middle East High Command announced that its forces based on El Alamein had repulsed heavy attacks by Axis armored units.

It was disclosed that the German and Italian mechanized units during the course of day-long battling yesterday made a temporary break in the defense line of the British Eighth Army but subsequently were driven back.

BATTLES CONTINUE

The British communique said that fierce battles continued throughout yesterday and that the results were "not unfavorable" to the defending forces.

(BACKGROUND NOTE: The Italian High Command claimed in a communique broadcast from Rome that Axis forces had captured El Alamein yesterday. A Berlin radio broadcast of a German News Agency dispatch asserted that the Germans had broken through the El Alamein positions and were "pursuing the Eighth Army which is retreating toward the Nile delta."

(The break-through referred to by both Rome and Berlin probably is the same mentioned by the British. The Axis says nothing, however, about the fact that the Germans and Italians later were driven back.)

'DEFENDED LOCALITY'

El Alamein, within 70 miles of the British Eastern Mediterranean naval base of Alexandria, was not mentioned directly in the communique as the point of break-through but reference was made to a "defended locality."

The Middle East High Command said:

"Our forces at El Alamein repulsed enemy attacks.

"Yesterday fighting continued throughout the day. The results were not unfavorable to us.

DRIVEN OUT

"One attack by enemy tanks effected a temporary break in a defended locality but the enemy later was driven out."

The desert wastes of Northern Egypt resounded with the roar of artillery and the clatter of tanks as the British and Axis forces clashed in the greatest mechanized battle in the history of North Africa, upon which depends the fate of Alexandria and the Suez Canal.

4th Celebrations Here Called Off

The cancellation of all Fourth of July celebrations scheduled in the Baltimore parks and in the Stadium was announced today by Richard M. Baker, a member of the Park Board.

Mr. Baker said this action was taken as a result of a War Department warning of the danger of hostile sabotage and token air raids designed to paralyze civilian populations during the celebration of the national holiday.

TWO AFFAIRS CANCELED

Among the largest celebrations canceled was the annual display of fireworks in Baltimore Stadium, sponsored by the Greater Northeast Baltimore Association, and the fireworks display that was to have been held in Patterson Park by the Exchange Club of Highlandtown.

Mr. Baker said approximately 15 celebrations of various kinds that had been scheduled for the public parks will not be held, and added:

"Numerous other celebrations scheduled for Baltimore and outlying sections where fireworks were to have been featured will undoubtedly be called off."

HOLDING MEETING TODAY

Major General Milton A. Reckord, commanding general of the Third Corps Area, is holding a staff meeting today at which the scope of the War Department's directive will be interpreted.

J. Howard Holzer, entertainment chairman of the Greater Northeast Baltimore Association's Fourth of

Continued on Page 2, Column 6.

Churchill Declares Aid Is Due In Egypt; Tells Of U. S. Ships

LONDON, July 2—(A. P.).—Prime Minister Churchill told the House of Commons today that "very considerable" reinforcements have reached or "are approaching" the British Army in Egypt and "I do not consider the struggle in any way decided."

He also declared the United States "is building this year four times as much gross tonnage of ships as Britain is building" and will build eight to ten times more in 1943."

Allied Fliers Raid 6 Jap Bases

UNITED NATIONS HEADQUARTERS IN AUSTRALIA, July 2—(I. N. S.).—Fanning out of a line more than 2,500 miles long, from Celebes to the Solomon Islands, the Allied Air Force carried out raids on six Japanese bases north of Australia, Gen. Douglas MacArthur's headquarters announced today.

The combined raids constituted the heaviest assault in the United Nations' program of softening up the enemy's strongholds in preparation for an early offensive to drive the Japanese from the islands fringing Australia.

The targets ranged from Kendari on the southeast tip of Celebes to Tulagi on Florida Island in the Solomon group. Intervening enemy bases which were attacked and heavily damaged included Dilli, on Portuguese Timor, Lae and Salamaua on New Guinea and Bougainville in the Solomon Islands.

In nearly every instance the enemy was taken by surprise and offered little resistance. Coming on the heels of Sunday night's surprise Commando raid on Salamaua, the far-flung attacks were regarded as highly significant and an indication that General MacArthur would increase the intensity and range of the "softening-up" attacks on enemy bases.

IN THE NEWS-POST TODAY

Cites 'Mortal Peril' To British Empire, Warns Commons Of Long War

BULLETIN

LONDON, July 2—(A. P.).—The House of Commons voted confidence in Winston Churchill's direction of the war today by a vote of 475 to 25.

LONDON, July 2—(A. P.).—Prime Minister Churchill met his critics today with a blunt admission of near-disaster in the Mediterranean and Middle East area which, he said, had brought "a recession of our hopes and prospects . . . unequaled since the fall of France."

By LEO V. DOLAN
International News Service Staff Correspondent.

LONDON, July 2.—The British Empire is in "mortal peril" and the present gravity of the situation is unequaled since the fall of France, Prime Minister Winston Churchill told the House of Commons today.

Replying to a series of attacks upon his conduct of the war, the Prime Minister reprecated the current debate as a "time waster" and castigated his critics as "muck-rakers."

He said:

"It is most difficult to concentrate my thoughts upon this debate and withdraw them from the tremendous and most critical battle now raging in Egypt.

"GRAVE IMPORTANCE"

"At any moment we may receive news of grave importance."

Churchill made no attempt to disguise the seriousness of Britain's position in Egypt, where Gen. Sir Claude Auchinleck and the British Eighth Army are attempting to hold back the Nazis from the Nile.

He said:

"At the moment we are in presence of a recession of our hopes and prospects in the Middle East and the Mediterranean unequaled since the fall of France."

Already, Churchill revealed, Britain has lost upward of 50,000 men in Libya, plus a great mass of materiel, "large quantities of which have fallen into enemy hands."

Most of the 50,000, Churchill said, were taken prisoners.

On the night before the fall of Tobruk, Churchill revealed, Auchinleck cabled to London to the effect that the Libyan seaport was adequately garrisoned and supplied for a 90-day siege.

FALLS WITHIN 24 HOURS

Despite this the town fell within 24 hours.

This the Prime Minister did not attempt to explain, but he said:

"If General Auchinleck was wrong, we were wrong too, and I am most ready, on behalf of the Government, to take my full share of responsibility."

Churchill put the seal of official confirmation upon what everyone else in Britain and the United States had suspected—that the loss

Continued on Page 2, Column 1.

War At A Glance

LONDON—
Churchill admits near-disaster unequaled since fall of France.

CAIRO—
Axis troops halted 70 miles west of Alexandria.

MOSCOW—
Germans carry battle into city of Sevastopol.

CHUNGKING—
Chinese fliers blast Jap positions.

AUSTRALIA—
Allied airmen raid six Nipponese bases.

FBI Arrests 12 Bundists In Navy Yard, Yorkville Raids

Story on Page 2

2¢

DAILY MIRROR

Member of the Associated Press

Buy WAR Bonds

WEATHER SLIGHTLY COOLER (Details on Page 2)

(Copyright, 1942, Daily Mirror, Inc.)

3 Cents Outside City Limits

Vol. 19. No. 8 C New York, Thursday, July 2, 1942 COMPLETE SPORTS

2¢

SEVASTOPOL CAPTURED, NAZIS CLAIM

Story on Page 2

HUGE BATTLE RAGING 62 MILES FROM NILE

Story on Page 3

THE WEATHER
Moderate temperatures today and tonight, with gentle to moderate winds and no rain.

Read The Baltimore News-Post for complete, accurate war coverage. It is the only Baltimore newspaper possessing the three great wire services—
ASSOCIATED PRESS
INTERNATIONAL NEWS SERVICE
UNITED PRESS

THE BALTIMORE NEWS-POST
AN INDEPENDENT NEWSPAPER
The Largest Evening Circulation in the Entire South

EXTRA
NIGHT EDITION

VOL. CXLI.—NO. 52 | Entered as second-class matter at Baltimore Postoffice. | FRIDAY EVENING, JULY 3, 1942 | PRICE 3 CENTS

ROMMEL RETREATING FIERCE BRITISH ATTACK SMASHES AXIS DRIVE

Military Board Maps Trial Of 8 Saboteurs; Hunt Canal Spy Aides

Latest developments on the anti-sabotage front:

WASHINGTON—Army to organize more than 200,000 private plant guards into anti-sabotage patrols; arrangements being made to try eight saboteurs before military commission empowered to decree death.

CANAL ZONE—Seek accomplices of 20 already taken into custody; huge spy ring smashed.

DETROIT—German-born Max Stephan convicted of treason in aiding fleeing German war prisoner.

Map Plans To Try Eight Saboteurs

By JACK VINCENT
International News Service Staff Correspondent.

WASHINGTON, July 3. — The Army planned to organize more than 200,000 private plant guards into anti-sabotage patrols today as arrangements were made under personal direction of President Roosevelt to bring the first eight Nazi saboteurs caught to trial before a military commission empowered to send them before a firing squad.

Roosevelt, in a proclamation, ordered the trial of the eight men to start July 8.

They were captured by the

Continued on Page 2, Column 1.

Accomplices Of Canal Spy Ring Hunted

CARIBBEAN DEFENSE HEADQUARTERS, Canal Zone, July 3—(I. N. S.). — Intelligence officers charged with protecting the Panama Canal against sabotage and ferreting out subversive activities in the Canal Zone pressed their search today for accomplices who may have escaped the net of United States officials who smashed a spy ring known to have consisted of at least 20 persons.

Lieut. Gen. Frank Andrews, commander of the Caribbean area, warned that enemies of the United States undoubtedly have others in the field to continue the operations

Continued on Page 2, Column 1.

Bremen Blasted By 300 Planes

LONDON, July 3—(I. N. S.).—Lethal explosives from British bombing planes crashed down upon the great German port and naval base of Bremen for the fifth time within a month last night when the Royal Air Force hammered Northwest Germany, the Air Ministry announced today.

The attacking force was described by the Air Ministry as "powerful," but the actual number of the planes participating was not revealed.

Many large fires were started in the target areas, it was said.

13 PLANES MISSING

The official communique said that 13 of the British bombers failed to return from the attack, which was carried out under weather conditions described as "good."

The German radio acknowledged that "a town in Northwest Germany" had been bombed during the night but said the raid was "without effect."

FORCE OF 300

The loss of 13 British planes would indicate that a force of at least 300, and possibly more, took part in the Bremen raid. This is based on proportionate percentage losses during previous large-scale R. A. F. assaults.

A total of 52 craft were lost when more than 1,000 planes attacked the "queen city" of the Reich exactly a week ago.

Gas Shortage Criticized As 'Mess'

By JAMES L. KILGALLEN
International News Service Staff Correspondent.

NEW YORK, July 3.—The gasoline shortage in the Eastern seaboard area today gave Fourth of July week-end motorists a sharp headache and evoked bitter criticism in some quarters.

Sol A. Herzog, counsel for the Eastern States Gasoline Dealers' Conference, representing approximately 65,000 of the 85,000 dealers in the rationed area, described the situation as "a terrific mess."

Thousands of motorists, unable to buy gas at filling stations, gave up the idea of making week-end trips to beach resorts or to the mountains.

GAS QUOTA MIRAGE

The July gas quota, estimated to keep tanks reasonably filled for 10 days, proved a mirage and motorists who thronged filling stations drove off with small allotments or none at all.

Automobiles waited in line as much as three blocks long. The motorists had the optimistic—but erroneous—idea that they would be taken care of under the new July quotas to filling stations. This quota was to be 50 per cent. of the normal sales of last July.

But the harried motorists could obtain only three to six gallons, or

Continued on Page 2, Column 3.

Fire, Explosion Wreck War Plant

PHILADELPHIA, July 3—(A. P.). Fire followed by explosions heard several miles away destroyed the war production plant of Hagin Frith & Sons today in suburban Abington township. Night shift employes were at lunch shortly after midnight when the blaze started in the acre-square plant, Hagin Frith, the owner, said. No one was injured.

Sub Victim Off Florida Coast

Under a towering inverted pyramid of heavy black smoke a tank ship ends its career off the coast of Florida. The ship was torpedoed by Axis submarine. The photo was made from an Army plane shortly after the attack. Picture from International News Photograph Service.

War At A Glance

CAIRO—
British communique says Axis attacks on El Alamein sector in Egypt repulsed; British counter-attack forces enemy to fall back.

MOSCOW—
Reds continue fighting in Sevastopol.

LONDON—
R. A. F. again bombs Bremen port.

AUSTRALIA—
Allied planes blast Japanese base at Dili on Timor Island.

Temperatures

12 Midn'ht,	71	6 A. M.,	68
1 A. M.,	70	7 A. M.	67
2 A. M.,	70	8 A. M.,	70
3 A. M.,	69	9 A. M.,	73
4 A. M.,	69	10 A. M.,	75
5 A. M.,	68	11 A. M.,	78

Scratches At Delaware

First Race—Toy-Quay, Cheater.
Second—Alsace, Gayest Nell, Tripod, Mouette, Thespian, Pointing.
Sixth—Accord, Hadawin, Glanceabout.
Seventh—Giboir, Leonardtown, Silver Play, Whistling Dick, Gendarme, Kimesha.
Eighth—Slugger, Black Boo, Toast, My Elsie, Penny Arcade, Dingmans.
Track slow.

THE NEWS-POST
Will Be Published
TOMORROW—JULY 4

Enemy Suffers Heavy Losses, Allied Positions Intact, Cairo Declares

By GEORGE LAIT
International News Service Staff Correspondent.

CAIRO, July 3.—The British Eighth Army in Egypt gained the upper hand over the Axis today and sent the mechanized German and Italian forces reeling in retreat west of El Alamein.

The Axis armored columns were smashed back after having advanced to within 70 miles of the British Eastern Mediterranean naval base at Alexandria.

The Middle East High Command announced:

"A general attack on El Alamein July 2 was repulsed.

"The enemy suffered losses and withdrew to the west.

"The British positions remain intact."

The headlong eastward drive of the German and Italian armored units was brought to an abrupt halt when the British defense line based on El Alamein held firm in the face of two strong Axis assaults.

The British countered with a flanking movement that threatened to crush the Axis legions. Part of the Eighth Army was sent around the Axis southern flank to pound the enemy from the rear.

SURPRISE MANEUVER

The surprise British maneuver was effected just as German General Field Marshal Erwin Rommel, the wily "desert fox," commander of Hitler's Afrika Korps, began a

Continued on Page 2, Column 7.

Reds Still Fight In Sevastopol

BERLIN (From German Broadvactc), July 3—(A. P.). German and other Axis troops have broken through the Russian front on a width of nearly 300 kilometers (about 185 miles), the German High Command announced today.

The communique said 50,000 prisoners had been taken at Sevastopol.

MOSCOW, July 3—(I. N. S.).—Russian defense forces still are battling Nazi siege forces in the streets of Sevastopol, the Red Army High Command declared today.

At the same time it was disclosed that German armies, apparently hoping to find a weak point somewhere along the extensive Russian defense line, had launched a new offensive northeast of Kharkov.

Soviet troops in the Crimea offered stubborn resistance to Nazi attempts to gain uncontested control of the Sevastopol naval base.

ON OUTSKIRTS

The German besiegers, according to the Soviet High Command, also were engaged by Russian forces on the outskirts of Sevastopol.

(BACKGROUND NOTE: Hitler's headquarters on the Russian front claimed that Sevastopol had been captured Wednesday.)

The noon communique said that heavy battling was in progress on the Kursk front.

30-MILE FRONT

The new offensive north of Kharkov, where the Germans have sought in vain to smash through for a new drive to the southeast on the Caucasus oil fields, broke out over a 30-mile front approximately 40 miles above the industrial capital of the Ukraine.

The attack was launched between Bielgorod and Volchansk.

Large-scale tank battles continued to rage on the Kursk front, 115 miles north of Kharkov, where the German armies were thrown back to the original positions after a futiles attempt to pierce the Soviet line.

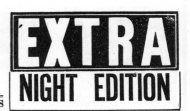

BRITISH COUNTER-ATTACK! AIRMEN BATTER ROMMEL

EXTRA

'No Holds Barred' In Desert War

BLUE STREAK EDITION R SATURDAY PICTORIAL

THE CALL BULLETIN

SAN FRANCISCO — AN INDEPENDENT NEWSPAPER

87TH YEAR CALL AND POST, VOL. 151, NO. 137 THE CALL-BULLETIN, VOL. 171, NO. 137 SATURDAY, JULY 4, 1942 5c DAILY

Blasted by Axis fire, the errand of mercy of a British ambulance came to a sudden halt on the Egyptian desert. Smoke at right comes from the blasted ambulance while the wounded driver is being assisted to safety by the crew of a second ambulance. The battle is still raging on. —Associated Press Wirephoto.

S. F. Celebrating First Wartime Fourth at Work

Grave and resolute, San Francisco joined the nation today in the first Fourth of July celebration of the war.

Independence Day took on new meaning as the festive sputter of fireworks gave way to the clang of shipyards, tools, and the gaiety of former years was replaced by an aroused spirit of wartime determination.

The tramp of marching feet and the blare of martial music mingled at trim ranks of service men formed for the city's spectacular morning parade.

Thousands of participants from

Continued on Page A, Col. Six

SENATE COMMITTEE APPROVES FARM FUNDS

WASHINGTON, July 4 (AP).—A Senate appropriations subcommittee today approved a resolution to continue funds for the Department of Agriculture through the month of July on the basis of appropriations for June. (Hint farm bill may die. Pg. 2.)

24,000 NAZIS REPORTED KILLED IN OREL AREA

MOSCOW, July 4 (AP).—Soviet guerrillas, using every kind of weapon from squirrel rifle to bomb, have killed 24,000 Germans in the Orel region southwest of Moscow, Tass reported today. (Russ repulse Nazis. Col. 6, this page.)

3 FRENCHMEN GET LIFE FOR BREAD TICKET THEFTS

VICHY, Unoccupied France, July 4 (AP).—Three Frenchmen were condemned to life imprisonment at hard labor today for the theft of 800 sheets of bread tickets from a ration card distribution center at Tours.

Baseball Schedule

NATIONAL LEAGUE	AMERICAN LEAGUE
Boston at New York.	New York at Boston.
Brooklyn at Philadelphia.	Philadelphia at Washington.
Cincinnati at Pittsburgh.	Detroit at Cleveland.
Chicago at St. Louis.	St. Louis at Chicago.
(All Doubleheaders)	(All Doubleheaders)

WILD CHASE JAILS BOY DRIVER

A 15 year old San Francisco boy was captured early today after a 15 minute chase in which police fired five shots at his speeding automobile, and was lodged in the juvenile home on a charge of auto theft.

SPOTTED BY POLICE

The boy, John Balsells, 305 Monterey boulevard, was spotted on Twenty-second street near Mission in a car previously reported stolen by Syl Moise, 1783 Thirty-third avenue, according to Radio Car Officers Nick Crivello and Frank Gregg.

The officers said they chased the car across town on Army, Sanchez and Duncan streets, and finally forced it to the curb at Duncan and Dolores streets.

SHOOT IN CHASE

The shots were fired during the wild race, which at times reached a speed of sixty-five miles an hour, they said.

Young Balsells leaped from his car as the officers drew alongside, fled into a vacant lot and surrendered as they closed in on him with guns drawn.

Heat Kills 22 Persons In Oregon

PORTLAND, Ore., July 4 (AP). Twenty-two persons died of heat prostration in Oregon late this week as soaring temperatures held the state in a record shattering grip.

Fifteen of the deaths were reported yesterday, six Thursday and one Wednesday.

Hospitals treated scores of others who were overcome. Most of the victims were in their 60's and 70's, although one was only 45 years old.

Earlier in the week, drownings claimed three lives as streams and lakes were sought by persons trying to minimize the effect of the heat.

Puerto Rico Statehood Move Made By Tugwell

WASHINGTON, July 4 (AP).—A White House secretary said today that President Roosevelt had approved a suggestion of Governor Rexford Guy Tugwell a study be undertaken on proposed legislation to give Puerto Rico the right to elect its own governor.

This would be a step toward ultimate statehood or independence.

Yanks Join A.E.F. Raid

Blast German War Centers In Holland

LONDON, July 4 (AP).—The United States air forces and the R. A. F. made a joint raid this morning on three air fields in Holland, the air ministry announced.

The Fourth of July attack was described officially as the first United States Army Air Force participation in R. A. F. bomber command operations from the British Isles.

The airfields raided were at Hamstede and Alkmaar, where bombs hit hangars, administration buildings and dispersal points, and at Valkenburg which was heavily machine-gunned.

VESSELS ATTACKED

Patrol vessels off the Dutch coast also were attacked.

The communique follows:

"Today, July 4, for the first time United States Army air forces have taken part in offensive operations in conjunction with the bomber command.

"In the early morning 12 Boston bombers, six of which were manned by American crews, raided enemy airdromes in Holland.

"The attacks were pressed home from very low level in the face of intense FLAK. . . . .

"At Hamstede and Alkmaar bombs were seen to burst on hangars, administrative buildings and dispersal points. The Valkenburg Airfield was heavily machine-gunned and an enemy fighter on the ground set on fire.

THREE PLANES LOST

"Enemy control vessels off the Dutch coast also were attacked.

"Three aircraft (two manned by American crews) are missing."

It was indicated the Americans borrowed their planes from the R. A. F. for this inaugural of their assaults upon German positions in western Europe.

The text of an earlier communique, No. 1 of the U. S. Army headquarters in Europe, issued through the ministry of information, said:

"In joint operation with R. A. F. light bombers, six American air crews attacked targets in German occupied territory today.

"Two American planes are missing.

"The American crews flew A-20A type aircraft (Douglas Bostons) in a daylight, minimum altitude attack."

RUSS CLAIM REPULSE OF NAZIS

By HENRY C. CASSIDY
Associated Press Staff Correspondent

MOSCOW, July 4 (AP).—A Russian counter-attack in the Kursk sector, at the junction of the central and southern Russian fronts, has thrown the Germans back across a strategically important stream, front line dispatches said today.

15,000 NAZIS KILLED

Hitler lost 15,000 men in dead alone in this titantic battle yesterday which paralleled in savagry anything yet seen in the bloody struggle, the official Tass news agency reported, quoting Izvestia, the government newspaper.

Colliding with greatly strengthened red army troops, the Germans were badly battered in this encounter while east of Kursk the pressure of their tank assaults was slackened.

(A Nazi communique asserted that Axis troops attacking in the Kharkov and Kursk sectors, 120 miles apart, "have beaten the enemy along the whole of the front," and that German troops "are advancing speedily toward the Don" after what was described as a gigantic breakthrough in the Ukraine. The Don

Continued on Page A, Col. Three

Southpaws Hurl Here Today

SEALS STADIUM, July 4.—Two left-handers were slated to face each other in the first game of today's Independence Day double-header here between the Seals and Portland.

Tom Seats, Seal southpaw, was nominated to face Sid Cohen. In the second game, Bob Joyce, Seal right-hander, and Ad Liska were the starting choices. The lineups:

PORTLAND	SEALS
Martinez, 2b	Trower, ss
Brown, ss	Holder, cf
Thompson, cf	Hodgin, rf
Amaral, rf	Jennings, 3b
Norbert, lf	Lewis, rf
Barton, 1b	Fain, 1b
Owen, 3b	Perry, 2b
Mayer, c	Ogrodowski, c
Cohen, p	Seats, p
Liska, p	Joyce, p

Allies Check Egypt Drive

By HARRY CROCKETT
Associated Press Staff Correspondent

CAIRO, July 4 (AP).—A determined British counter-attack, launched under an umbrella of "unprecedented" air force co-operation, has checked, at least temporarily, Field Marshal Erwin Rommel's thrust toward Alexandria and the Nile Valley, a British headquarters communique said today.

"Our forces attacked the enemy who was attempting to thrust eastward yesterday in the El Alamein area," the communique declared.

"Allied air activity is on an unprecedented scale for the Middle East area.

"Our troops captured forty guns and several hundred prisoners and put a number of enemy tanks out of action. Twenty-eight enemy planes were destroyed."

AMERICANS IN FORCE

(A vague Italian dispatch, relayed through Stockholm to London, said "several thousand excellently equipped American troops" were fighting at El Alamein, but there was no confirmation from any other source. New York received an unconfirmed report that 900 more American-made tanks had joined the Egyption battle.)

Some of the fiercest fighting of the campaign took place as the reinforced imperial forces moved in to halt a new drive eastward by Rommel's forces, the communique added. Earlier, Rommel had been reported "digging in" west of El Alamein, located sixty-five miles west of Alexandria.

Enemy planes raided the Suez Canal area last night and alarms sounded in Cairo and other areas. The Egyptian interior minister said that a few bombs were dropped. There were three casualties, one fatal.

(A London military commentator described the British counter-attack as "successful" and added, "Things could be very much worse.")

HUGE AIR BATTLE

Apparently the full weight of the British, American and South African air forces was thrown into the El Alamein action and the communique indicated that a tremendous air battle ensued.

A commentator's summary of the last three days of fighting showed that the German onslaughts were steadily diminishing in numerical strength, if not in vigor.

(International News Service reported from Cairo that great reinforcements of American "General Grant" tanks have arrived in Egypt and are being rushed to the battlefront by

Spirit of 4th Rules World, F.D.R. Says

WASHINGTON, July 4 (AP).—President Roosevelt declared today that the spirit of democratic freedom symbolized in America's Independence Day had spread over the entire globe.

The Fourth of July, he said, was being celebrated this year "not in the fireworks of make-believe, but in the death dealing reality of tanks and planes and guns and ships."

WAR WORK GOES ON

In a formal statement, the chief executive said the day also was being observed by running the war production assembly lines without interruption.

"Not to waste one hour," he said, "not to stop one shot, not to hold back one blow—that is the way to mark our great national holiday in this year of 1942."

MESSAGE BY HULL

Secretary of State Hull said in a Fourth of July message that "the spirit of liberty and freedom" which inspired the founding and development of this nation "is the spirit that will win this war."

This spirit, Hull added, should be "revitalized and cultivated to the fullest extent by all of the United Nations and their peoples."

(Text of President Roosevelt's Statement on Page A.)

Call-Bulletin Today

Special Features

("G" Indicates Green Flash)

FIVE JAP SHIPS SUNK

Periscope Photo Jap Destroyer Sinking!

7TH SPORT .:. NIGHT FINAL SATURDAY PICTORIAL

THE CALL SAN FRANCISCO BULLETIN

AN INDEPENDENT NEWSPAPER

CALL AND POST, VOL. 151, NO. 155
THE CALL-BULLETIN, VOL. 171, NO. 155

SAN FRANCISCO, SATURDAY, JULY 25, 1942 5c DAILY

EXTRA

Doom of a Japanese warship is seen through a United States Navy submarine periscope in this unique picture taken by a Navy photographer. The Navy identifies the ship as a large Japanese destroyer in its death throes. The picture was made aboard the ship which launched two torpedoes into the destroyer and is the first combat action photo taken through the periscope of an American submarine. At the right note the sailors (circled) on conning tower of the sinking ship. Note the rising sun insignia atop the forward gun turret. Marks on the left and line are periscope etchings. The warship was mostly under water at the time this remarkable photo was taken. The area was not disclosed.
—Associated Press Wirephoto From United States Navy.

Subs Get Warship, Tanker, 3 Others

Sixth Cargo Ship Is Damaged, Probably Lost, Says U. S.

By HUGO SPECK
Staff Correspondent International News

WASHINGTON, July 25 (INS).—Continuing its daring undersea campaign against Japanese shipping, the Navy announced today that American submarines have sunk five additional Nipponese vessels including a modern Jap destroyer and damaged one cargo ship in the Far East.

TOTAL NOW 223

The Navy's 100th communique brought to 223 the total of Japanese ships sunk and damaged by all types of action in the Pacific.

In addition to the destroyer, the latest Navy action sent to the bottom of the Pacific one medium sized tanker and three cargo ships, while a medium sized cargo vessel was reported damaged and believed sunk.

SUBS SINK 55

American subs thus have definitely sunk 55 Japanese ships since the Nipponese launched their sneak attack on Pearl Harbor December 7. A total of 15 other Jap ships are listed as probably sunk, while 14 additional have been damaged by American submarine action, giving America's undersea craft a total bag of 84 enemy ships.

ALEUTIAN SUCCESSES

Previous to today's report on far eastern waters, the latest submarine successes had been reported from the Aleutians, where American subs sent six destroyers to the bottom.

Thirty-eight Japanese destroyers now have been sunk or damaged in all types of action in the Pacific. Twenty-three of these were sunk, seven probably sunk and eight damaged.

Against the total Japanese losses of 223 ships put out of action, the United States has had twenty-eight ships sunk and nine demolished to prevent capture and nine damaged for a total of forty-six.

(For Navy communique, see Page A.)

132 MORE ALIEN HOMES RAIDED IN MICHIGAN

DETROIT, July 25 (INS).—Arresting one war plant worker, and ordering several other persons to report for questioning, the FBI today raided the homes of 132 German and Italian aliens in Detroit and other cities in western Michigan. (Earlier FBI raid stories on Page 3.)

12,000,000 U. S. ARMY SEEN

LONDON, July 25 (INS).—An American army of 12 million men is a distinct possibility, the Daily Sketch declared today in a dispatch from its New York correspondent. But this ns a development of the comparatively distant future, the dispatch said.

CHUNGKING BOMBED, VICHY REPORTS

LONDON, July 25 (INS).—The Exchange Telegraph Company said today that the Vichy radio broadcast a report that the Chinese capital of Chungking had been bombed for 3 hour Friday.

5TH RACE, ARLINGTON—Signator, won, 11.40, 6.60, 4.40; Best Seller, 2d, 3.80, 3; Smacked, 3d, 4. T., 1:22 2-5.

6TH RACE, EMPIRE—Over, won, 20.50, 7.70, 3.30; Rise Above It, 2d, 5.20, 2d, 5.20, 3; Bell D'Amour, 3d, 2.40. T., 1:53.

8TH RACE, ROCKINGHAM—Vulcanus, won, 6.40, 3.40, 2.80; Panther Creek, 2d, 2.80, 2.20; Betty's Broom, 3d, 3. T., 1:48.

AT CLEVELAND (A)—Washington 10, Cleveland 6; Final.

FBI Warns German Saboteurs at Large

By JACK VINCENT
Staff Correspondent International News Service

WASHINGTON, July 25 (INS).—A nation-wide hunt was launched by the FBI today for three expert German saboteurs who are known to have attended the sabotage school in the Reich in which the eight Nazi agents now on trial in Washington were schooled in their plot for destruction of vital war industries in the United States.

At the same time, it was disclosed the German high command had planned to set up a permanent German sabotage organization, with headquarters in Chicago.

J. Edgar Hoover, director of the FBI, not only asked all police agencies of the nation to be on the watch for the saboteurs, but

Continued on Page 3, Column 4

Call-Bulletin Today

Special Features

"G" Indicates Green Flash)

Ex-Internee Tells Of Manila Life

(Here is the story of Jennifer White, wife of the Associated Press correspondent at Peiping, China. She was caught by the war in Manila while en route home. She is now in Lourenco Marques on her way to the United States.)

By JENNIFER WHITE

LOURENCO MARQUES, Portuguese East Africa, July 23 (Delayed) (AP).—The Japanese guards at Manila's internment camp frequently asked us:

"How can you Americans be so happy here?"

Apparently they were unable to understand how 3,200 civilian internees were able to work

Continued on Page 2, Column 2

2,000 German Tanks Rip Rostov Defenses

By JAMES E. BROWN
Staff Correspondent International News

MOSCOW, July 25 (INS).—Six hundred thousand German troops, aided by 2,000 tanks and the entire Nazi air force stationed on the Russian front, hammered at the gate of Rostov today and broke through one sector of the Soviet defenses.

Russian defenders reeled and then rallied before Rostov against the German might tonight in a determined stand to the "last drop of blood" while other Nazi vanguards had forced a tentative crossing of the Don 120 miles upstream and reached the midsection of the river perilously close to Stalingrad.

(A Vichy radio asserted that tremendous explosion which disintegrated blocks of houses were hindering German occupation of Rostov.

(The heat from innumerable fires was said to be terrific. Buildings on principal streets were said to be in ruins.)

(Meanwhile, Berlin said German detachments have thrust forward from Rostov to capture Apsaitskaya, wiping out all Russians on the northern bank of the Don River.)

The steel and concrete Rostov forts which have been strengthening for eight months were pierced at points on the north side of the Don, but the Russians were said to have slowed the tempo of the powerful German onslaught.

The battle for Stalingrad—the immediate German objective—was begun when the Germans crossed the Don River in the Tsimlyansk area. The one railroad connecting Stalingrad with the northern Caucasus is only 25 miles beyond and already is under heavy aerial bombardment.

The German strategy probably is to cut the railroad at Kotelnikov and move northward toward Sarept and southward toward Zimovniki.

(The German radio announced today that Nazi troops had captured Novocherkassk, 20 miles northeast of Rostov.)

The appalling extent of Nazi casualties was disclosed in an of-

Entered as second-class matter April 15, 1931, at the post office at New Haven, Connecticut, under the act of March 3, 1879

ILLUSTRATED CURRENT NEWS

Published Monday, Wednesday and Friday by Illustrated Current News, Inc., New Haven, Conn. Subscription Annually, $20.80

August 3, 1942—No. 4512

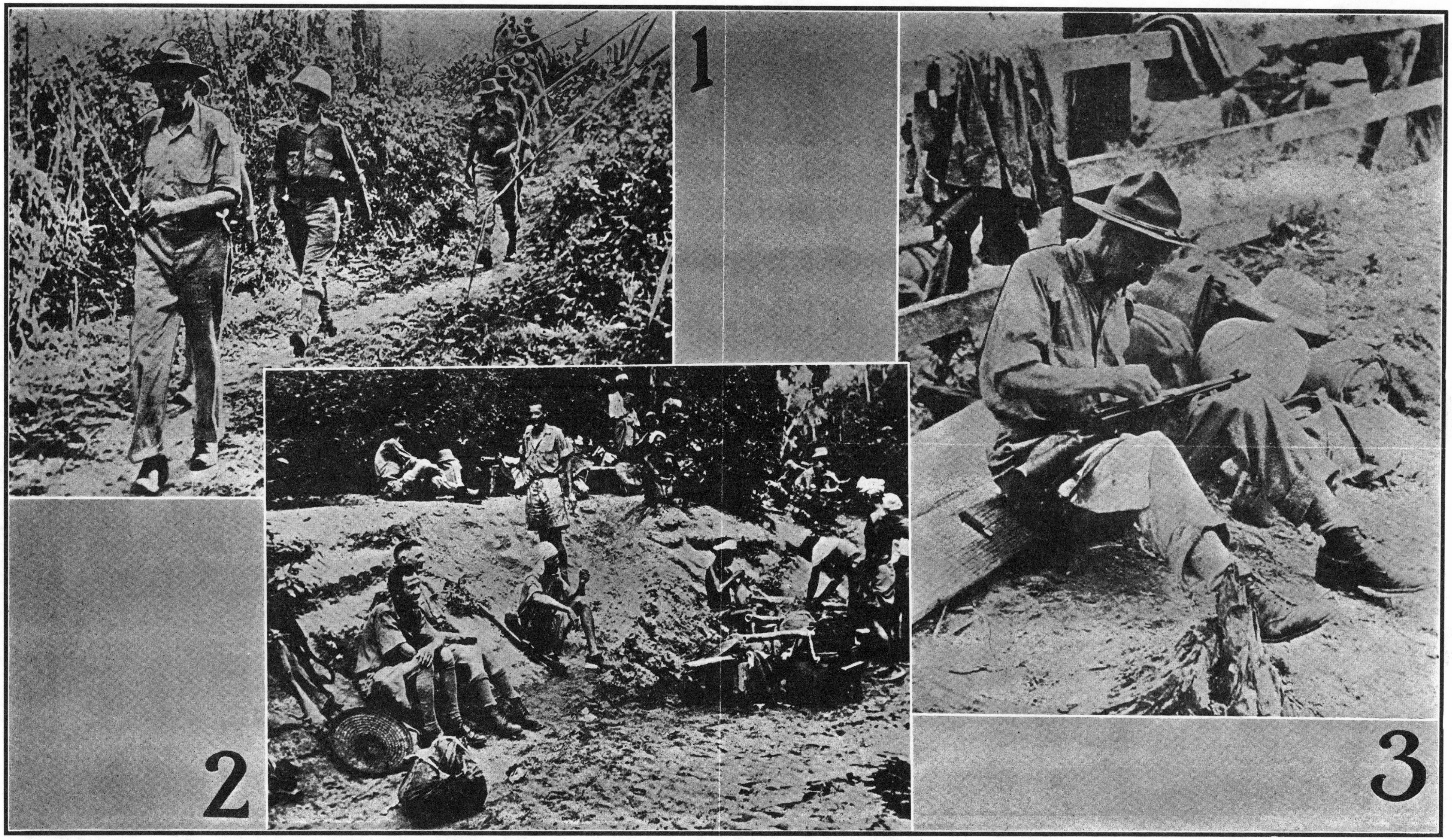

GENERAL STILWELL'S RETREAT FROM BURMA

Burma—The general, who marched at the head of the column the entire way of the epic 140-mile trek, leading the group through the Burma jungle. (2) American enlisted men, officers, British and Burmese, shown during rest period. (3) The general, puffing away on a cigarette, works on a tommy gun.

LØSSALG 25 ØRE

Oslo. 8. august 1942.
1. årg. — Nr. 2.

Germaneren

KAMPORGAN FOR GERMANSKE ᛋᛋ NORGE

Vår største triumf

av Halldis Neegård Østbye.

Frihetstanken har vært et bærende prinsipp for de germanske folk.

Og et *germansk folkefellesskap* må derfor nødvendigvis bygge på et felleskap mellem frie germanske folk.

Å virkeliggjøre denne tanke midt i krigens ragnarok vil naturligvis by på mange vanskeligheter og sette store krav til forkynnerne av denne idé.

Det er klart at det er tungt for et germansk folk med én så fanatisk frihetstrang som det norske, at det er kommet i et okkupert og beseiret lands ydmygende stilling. Og det gjelder således her et kameratslig samarbeide mellom germanerne, hvorav den ene part er seierherren, og den annen i virkeligheten militært beseiret.

Det stiller svære krav til begge parter.

Men saken vilde enno ikke ha vært så komplisert hvis *alle* nordmenn hadde vært klar over tingenes virkelige sammenheng og lagt godviljen til — og ikke store deler av folket var slått med blinnhet uten å kunne eller ville forstå det som er skjedd, og skjer. Vi norske nasjonalsocialister er derved kommet i en særlig vanskelig stilling. På den ene side de villedte landsmenn som turer fram i sin tross og galskap, på den annen side okkupasjonsmaktens representanter, hvis tålmodighet settes på den allerstørste prøve ved jøssingenes dårskap.

Det er en *grunnfeil* hvis man dømmer det norske folk ut fra det man ser i dag. Det befinner seg i en meget farlig psykose, det er *sykt, det er ikke seg selv.* De fleste av våre tyske frender, som er i Norge idag, de kjenner ikke nordmennene så å si i *normal* tilstand. De ser *vrangsiden,* av et folk som ellers er både godmodig og omgjengelig, med en høi moral.

Men intet folk i hele verden hadde kunnet tåle en slik daglig giftinnsprøitning som den det norske folk mottok fra aprildagene inntil radioapparatene ble inndradd, og det ryktesvineri som i mellomtiden er blitt så fullkomment organisert. Så meget verre måtte virkningene bli i et folk som allerede fra 1905 ble offer for en systematisk pro-britisk propaganda, og etter bolsjevikrevolusjonen i 1917 innsprøitet med den kommunistiske gift, kanskje mere enn noe annet nordisk folk. I tillegg hertil kommer så den alminnelige demoralisasjon som gjerne følger i krigens spor.

Mere enn 60 av Moskvas og Vestmaktenes mere eller mindre fordekte organisasjoner arbeidet i dette lille folket på å gjennemsyre det med falske unordiske idéer og tanker. Gjennom tusener av skjulte kanaler fløt strømmen inn over Norge fra de jødiske centra. Alle nordiske retts-, æres- og moralbegreper ble systematisk satt på hodet, hele vårt kulturgrunnlags bærende prinsipper systematisk forhånet og latterliggjort.

Når det på toppen av denne årelange forgiftning inntrer en akutt krise som aprildagene 1940, taper folket fullstendig likevekten og vi ser det sørgelige bilde som hver dag presenteres for våre øyne av jøssingene.

Det er imidlertid helt galt å dømme det norske folk ut fra denne tilstand. Nordmennene er i sannhet et ekte germansk folk, nå som før, men ulykken var at det *politisk* var uvitende, og systematisk ble holdt i uvitenhet om tidens strømninger. Naivitet, blåøiethet, og også trassighet er i virkeligheten germanske egenskaper, som nok har ført germanene ut i store ulykker, men de er på en måte også grunnlaget for noen av deres beste og mest tiltalende egenskaper: at de er ærekjære, likefremme, renhårige og går like på målet istedenfor å sno seg fram fyllt av mistenksomhet og mistro til alle kanter, som de slue og bereknende jøder.

Men det er en farlig svakhet, forsåvidt som det gir jødene og deres medhjelpere et lett spill.

Alle våre store seere og diktere har profetert om store og skjulte evner hos det norske folket — rike evner som under det politiske vanstyre og den hundreårige avhengighet av fremmede levet under overflaten og bare delvis kom fram i dagen.

Det er også en av Vidkun Quislings største fortjenester at han har gitt det norske folket troen på slike evner og på rike muligheter for Norge i den nye verden, som fødes.

En slik åndelig ekspansjon som den vi har opplevet i Norge med århundreskiftets store diktere og kunstnere er det vel få folk forundt å oppvise maken til, i forhold til folketallet. Men med parlamentarismens og demokratiets gjennombrudd, etterfulgt av den marxistiske oppløsningeprosess etter 1917, havnet vi i en internasjonal sump som hemmet de nasjonale krefters utfoldelse og førte mange rike begavelser på avveie.

Det er derfor ingen grunn til å tro at de store evner som ligger i det norske folket plutselig skulde være ebbet ut med jøssing-epoken.

Jøssing-syken er et forbigående fenomen.

Det er bare spørsmål om *tid,* om utholdenheten hos dem som er bærerne av den nasjonale reisning — og den nødvendige forståelse og overbærenhet hos vårt tyske broderfolk — og naturligvis først og sist så avhenger alt av aksemaktenes endelige seir over bolsjevismen og dens forbundsfeller.

Å virkeliggjøre den germanske tanke i Norden stiller derfor de allerstørste krav til oss alle.

Det kan overhodet ikke herske tvil om at Norge nettopp som selvstendig stat og nordmennene som et fritt folk kan yde store og kanskje avgjørende bidrag til berikelse av den germanske kulturverden.

Adolf Hitler har forstått dette og dømmer ikke det norske folket ut fra den oppløsningstilstand det befinner seg i idag. Nettopp derfor har han gitt Norge sjansen til igjen — under Vidkun Quislings førerskap — å bli en fri stat. Også innen de øvrige germanske folk vil det føles som en triumf for den germanske tanken at dette skjer. Derved viser Tyskland at det handler germansk, at det tenker og handler *stort,* som det sømmer seg et seirende germansk folk.

Og på de norske nasjonalsocialisters skuldre hviler det tunge ansvar for at det germanske brorskap virkeliggjøres i vårt land, i nordisk og norsk ånd.

Villedte, og motstandere over hele verden har sine øyne rettet mot Norge. Det betraktes som prøvestenen på den germanske tankes virkeliggjørelse.

Et lite land som Norge er i det hele tatt kommet til å spille en forunderlig dominerende rolle i dette verdensoppgjør. Først på grunn av sin strategiske beliggenhet midt i krysset av stormaktsinteressene, dernest på grunn av den så å si «ideologiske» rolle det er kommet til å spille.

Et gjenreist og suverent Norge vil være det største slag for jøssinbolsjevikene i alle land, og den største triumf for den germanske tanken.

Halldis Neegård Østbye.

På vakt.

New York World-Telegram

Copyright, 1942, by New York World-Telegram Corporation. All rights reserved.

Local Forecast: Thundershowers this afternoon and evening.

7TH SPORTS
LATEST RACING
Final Stock Tables
PRICE THREE CENTS

SCRIPPS—HOWARD VOL. 75—NO. 34— IN TWO SECTIONS—SECTION ONE. NEW YORK, MONDAY, AUGUST 10, 1942. Entered as second class matter Post Office, New York, N. Y.

U. S. LANDS ON SOLOMONS

Big AEF Lands in Britain

Growing Yank Forces Alarm Nazis

By EDWARD BEATTIE,
United Press Staff Correspondent.

HEADQUARTERS, UNITED STATES GROUND FORCES, Somewhere in England, Aug. 10.—A large contingent of United States troops landed at a British port today to bolster the forces that Maj. Gen. Mark W. Clark is preparing for the day the second front invasion starts.

General Clark, a proponent of offensive warfare, is commander of United States ground forces in the European theater and he already has told newspapermen that American troops didn't come to Britain to "sit on their rear sides and be on the defensive."

Expanding Camp.

The camp here has been turned over to the United States in every detail, and it is being expanded so rapidly that General Clark soon will be using a plane to get around it. As the General said, he already is "humping" to find places for the Americans arriving, and those landed today will add to his problem.

The men who came off the transports were superbly equipped and apparently glad to be here. For hours tenders plied between the docks and the transports with soldiers and baggage, and a Scots band greeted them with stirring Sousa marches.

Nazi Train Is Wrecked.

Preparations for a second front at some future date weren't confined to Britain, however. In Holland, where Gen. Friedrich Christiansen, chief of German occupation forces, recently completed a survey of his ground defenses, search was being made for men who Friday wrecked a military train, reportedly the 40th so destroyed in recent months.

In Paris it was reported that Grand Marshal Eric Raeder had completed inspection of German naval bases along the occupied coast, and other reports were that the Norwegian puppet Premier Vidkun Quisling had gone running to Adolf Hitler again because of invasion fears coupled with internal dissession.

In the sprawling camp where U. S. forces are getting their final physical tune-ups under General Clark and his chief of staff, Col. Lowell Rook, of Walla Walla, Wash, the invasion slogan is "The Sooner the Better!"

Joint Action With RAF Is Planned

By the Associated Press.

LONDON, Aug. 10.—Maj. Gen. Carl Spaatz, commander of the United States army air forces in Britain, declared today that the American air force was ready to begin attacks against Germany "within the immediate future."

"The American air forces and the Royal Air Force have worked in such full co-operation that we are proceeding ahead of the actual schedule," he said.

"Within the immediate future operations in accordance with plans that have been in the making between the Royal Air Force and the American Air Forces will commence."

Declaring his gratification at the helpfulness of "our British ally," General Spaatz added:

"Our enemy at the appointed time will feel the might of a thoroughly co-ordinated British-American air force."

Waldman Leads Bayside Acers

Mrs. Atkinson High Among the Women

By LARRY ROBINSON,
World-Telegram Sports Writer.

BAYSIDE LINKS, L. I., Aug. 10.—The first contingent of ace golfers of the 11th annual World-Telegram hole-in-one tournament was sighting with keen eye on the special greens today here, firing shot after shot within the birdie circles.

But the three to four-foot area from the cup was the nearest they came to the mark at which they are shooting—a repeat ace.

The leader at the end of the morning shooting was Frank J. Waldman, a member of the Oceanside Golf Club, with a four-foot, three-inch shot. Waldman charged into the lead amid a flurry of accurate shots when five of six players pierced the magic scoring ring.

He is a member of the same club that produced two winners—Jack Hagen, with his five-inch-shot that won in 1938, and Dr. Matthew Feinman, winner of the all-section prize (as was Hagen) in 1939.

Second to Waldman at the noon hour was Jerry Zolan, pro at the Orchard Hills C. C. in Jersey, who came over from the Garden state to have his five tries. Zolan made them count before an appreciative gallery, putting his best of five shots 4 feet 6 inches from the pin. That

(Continued on Page Sixteen.)

Bennett, Mead Called Pawns In Big Game

Real Stake Is Control Of State Delegation At 1944 Convention

By THOMAS L. STOKES,
Scripps-Howard Staff Writer.

New York offers the four-star, super-de-luxe political show of this otherwise rather dull election season with a performance which is by way of being a sequel to the 1940 third-term battle and, at the same time, the curtain raiser for the 1944 Presidential campaign.

What is becoming known as "the private Roosevelt-Farley war" is in many ways a strange and disturbing spectacle. At least it seems so to many ordinary citizens who read the headlines daily and watch ships plow silently out to sea, heavy with cargo for battle fronts all over the world.

It all came about because President Roosevelt elected to move boldly into his home state and seek to dictate the nomination of a Democratic candidate for Governor, thus attempting to upset, at the 11th hour, the well-laid plans of his one-time friend, James A. Farley, the man who directed two of his campaigns for the Presidency, and who as state party leader claims a voice in the mateer himself.

Merely Pawns.

The two contestants for the nomination—Senator Mead, whom the President shoved into the race against that genial gentleman's own best impulses, and Mr. Farley's candidate, Attorney General John J. Bennett, Jr.—are merely submissive pawns in the much bigger game.

While the immediate prize is a

(Continued on Page Two.)

Blast Scare Halts Traffic in Tunnel

Patrolman Charles Huber, on switchboard duty at the W. 54th St. station early today, heard a heavy voice grate in his ear over the telephone, "In half an hour the Lincoln Tunnel will be blown up."

A moment later a small army of police descended on the tunnel, stopped all traffic and made a quick search. Traffic was then resumed and a thorough search lasting an hour and a half was made. Nothing was found.

Nevertheless the tunnel guard was doubled. The Queens Midtown and Holland tunnels were also searched, just in case, but with the same result.

Jail 5 Hawaii Japs For Slowdown

By the United Press.

HONOLULU, Aug. 10.—Five Japanese workers at Hickam Field began prison sentences today because they ridiculed conscientious workers and tried to get them to work less hard. Maj. Samuel E. Murrell of Provost Court sentenced one to a year in jail, and the others to nine months.

Prosecution witnesses said the workers had been told they were "suckers" for working so hard. However, this was denied vigorously by one of the defendants, Schichi Tao, who received the one-year sentence.

"If we sat down," said Tao, "we were tired—not loafing."

Nazi Drive for Oil Cracks Red Lines

Panzer Tide Breaks Through Northern Caucasus Defenses

By HENRY SHAPIRO,
United Press Staff Correspondent.

MOSCOW, Aug. 10.—German panzer forces have smashed Russian defenses in the Kropotkin area of the northern Caucasus and are streaming toward Armavir and the oil fields of Maikop, dispatches from the Caucasian front said today.

[Russian defenses in the foothills of the Caucasus, which guard the Maikop oil fields, also were reported crumbling by the Associated Press out of Moscow.]

[German motorized forces have occupied Pyatigorsk, in the Caucasus foothills 110 miles southeast of Armavir, said German broadcasts today, as reported by the Associated Press.]

Cossacks Take Big Toll.

Don and Kuban Cossack cavalrymen killed at least 7000 in two actions—1000 Rumanians and 6000 Germans.

Having broken through around Kropotkin, the Germans were pushing along paved highways, graveled roads and across sun-baked steppes toward Armavir, to join other German forces fighting in that area. It is 45 miles to the southeast from Kropotkin to Armavir.

[The German High Command claimed last night that Maikop had been stormed and captured, as well as Krasnodar, 60 miles to the northwest.]

A Soviet communique reported that in the Armavir area Soviet units fell back to new defense positions. Tense fighting continued, it said, with enemy groups which had broken through on a neighboring sector (perhaps Kropotkin).

Nazi Wedges Held.

The communique indicated that German wedges, driven deep into Russian defenses around Kletskaya and Kotelnikovski, 75 miles

(Continued on Page Seven.)

Tojo Holds Hirohito Virtual Prisoner

The following dispatch is by the former United Press manager in Japan, filed at Rio de Janeiro while en route to the United States after six months' internment near Tokyo.

By ROBERT BELLAIRE.
Copyright 1942 by United Press.

RIO DE JANEIRO, Aug. 10.—Gen. Hediki Tojo, the war lord Premier of Japan, is striving to establish himself as undisputed dictator over the Japanese people and has made Emperor Hirohito a virtual prisoner in the Imperial Palace, denied even access to the daily newspapers.

Tojo, who bears the nickname The Razor because of his cunning, realizes that he is unpopular among the masses and he travels with a strong bodyguard in fear of assassination.

Wants To Be Shogun.

He is trying to build up personal popularity for himself as a means of achieving his ambition of becoming Japan's first Shogun — possessor of power eclipsing even that of the Emperor—since the 1867 revolution swept away the Tokugawa Shogunate that had ruled for 264 years.

Like Hitler, who undermined Von Hindenburg and Mussolini, who usurped Victor Emanuel's power, Tojo wants to become "the people's choice"—even over Hirohito. He is the first Premier in recent decades who has made such open attempts to win over the people.

His picture appears almost daily in the newspapers, showing him kissing babies, talking with young students and even assisting old women across the street.

Wears Civilian Clothes.

All of Tojo's recent speeches emphasized that while he is the

(Continued on Page Seven.)

Courtmartial Tries Texan in England

By the Associated Press.

SOMEWHERE IN BRITAIN, Aug. 10.—Private Travis P. Hammond, 25, of Texas, the first American soldier of the second AEF to be tried by general court-martial in Britain, pleaded innocent today to a charge of assaulting an English girl, 16.

If convicted he is liable to a death sentence or life imprisonment.

Isolationism Issue In 3 Other States

By the United Press.

Isolationism before Pearl Harbor will be an issue in primaries in Idaho, Nebraska and Ohio tomorrow.

Nebraska—Representative Coffee (D.) is seeking the Democratic Senatorial nomination, opposed by Foster May, a radio announcer, and four others. Mr. Coffee is a pre-Pearl Harbor isolationist, and that is the issue.

Ohio—Representative Sweeney (D.) is opposed by renomination of Michael Feigham, who charges Mr. Sweeney with isolationism.

Idaho—Senator Thomas (R.) and Representatives White (D.) and Dworshak (R.) are being opposed for renomination on their pre-Pearl Harbor voting records.

The Weather

(Official United States Forecast.)

New York and Metropolitan Area: Moderately warm this afternoon; local thundershowers with moderate winds this afternoon and before midnight tonight; not as warm tonight as last night.

New Jersey: Scattered thundershowers likely this afternoon or this evening; rather warm tonight.

Connecticut: Little change in temperature tonight.

Highest and lowest temperature a year ago, 82-69.

TODAY'S READINGS.

	Temp.	Hum.		Temp.	Hum.
Midnight	67	..	8 a. m.	68	88
1 a. m.	67	..	9 a. m.	70	87
2 a. m.	67	..	10 a. m.	72	82
3 a. m.	66	..	11 a. m.	72	86
4 a. m.	67	..	12 Noon	71	84
5 a. m.	67		1 p. m.	70	92
6 a. m.	67	90	2 p. m.	76	83
7 a. m.	67	90	3 p. m.	73	87

Starting Today

With home sewing on the increase as a patriotic and smart activity, the World-Telegram will publish sketches and descriptions of dresses and needlecraft for which patterns may be purchased. This new feature appears daily on the women's page.

Police in India Fire on Mobs As Riots Grow

Disorders Spread To Many Cities After Gandhi Arrest

By JOHN R. MORRIS,
United Press Staff Correspondent.

BOMBAY, Aug. 11.—Police, reinforced by troops, were forced to fire on rioters in this city at least 10 times today, while disorders, strikes and mass demonstrations demanding the British quit India and grant independence spread throughout the country.

A critical situation caused by mob violence, attacks on street cars and the burning of busses was reported growing steadily worse in the northern districts of this city.

A government communique said eight persons were killed and 169 wounded, including 27 police, in riots on Sunday.

There were more casualties today, but details were withheld. Unofficially deaths over the week end were put at a dozen at least.

Curfew Lengthened.

The police guarded all suburban railway stations in Bombay today and the curfew order was widened to include the hours 7:30 p. m. to 6 a. m.

[The Associated Press reported government grain shops were burned, trains and automobiles were stoned and that workers left their jobs in 18 mills. Schools also were closed by strikes.]

Disorders and arrests extended to Poona, Lucknow, Calcutta and many other cities and towns, with the greatest mass demonstrations clogging the streets of Delhi, seat of the British Viceroy.

[At Lucknow, said the Associated Press, police fired also on a crowd of striking university students who were trying to form a parade. Thirteen were arrested.]

Gandhi Letter Posted.

The Bombay correspondent of the Calcutta Hindustan-Standard said a letter written by Mohandas K. Gandhi, making a last, friendly appeal for the British to accept the Congress party independence demand, was being posted today at Bombay.

The British government, how-

(Continued on Page Seven.)

Bank Burglars Get $20,000 in Woodridge

By the Associated Press.

WOODBRIDGE, N. J., Aug. 10.—Thieves broke into the night depository of the Woodbridge National Bank during the week end and, while the amount stolen still was undetermined, the Federal Bureau of Investigation estimated today it might total $20,000 to $25,000.

E. E. Conroy, assistant director of the FBI, said in Newark that first reports were that a window in the bank building, usually barred, was undergoing repairs and the thieves evidently had taken advantage of the bars' temporary removal.

EXTRA!

BULLETIN.

By the United Press.

WASHINGTON, Aug .10.—Admiral Ernest J. King, Commander-in-Chief of the U. S. Fleet, announced today that American forces have effected landings on the Solomon Islands. The enemy has counterattacked with "rapidity and vigor."

He reported that at least one of our cruisers was sunk.

Two U. S. cruisers, two destroyers and a transport were damaged.

The Admiral said information as to the extent of damage inflicted on the enemy was incomplete, but that a large number of Japanese planes had been destroyed and surface units put out of action.

By the United Press.

GENERAL MacARTHUR'S HEADQUARTERS, Australia, Aug. 11 (Tuesday).—The Battle of the Solomon Islands entered its fifth day today with American and Australian air forces steadily pounding enemy bases and supply lines to break up movement of Japanese reinforcements.

There has been no official hint of progress other than a statement that stiff resistance had been encountered.

This caused some faint concern here, but it generally was suggested that the Allied forces already had made their bid for a foothold in the Tulagi-Guadalcanal area of the Solomons and—since Tokyo admitted the fight still

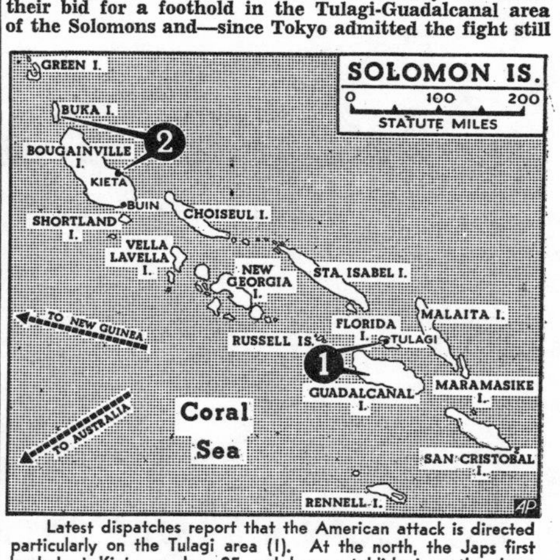

Latest dispatches report that the American attack is directed particularly on the Tulagi area (1). At the north, the Japs first landed at Kieta on Jan. 25 and have established another base at Buka (2). A. P. Map.

was in progress—probably had succeeded in the first phase of operations.

Despite strictest military secrecy, official sources warned against any premature conclusion that Allied invasion forces had landed attack units to move against the Tulagi and Guadalcanal bases.

[The Associated Press said there were unelaborated reports that Allied land forces were in action.]

It was pointed out that Admiral Chester Nimitz would not have undertaken so big an expedition without being assured that he had adequate forces to overcome whatever resistance the enemy could offer, but the Allied commanders necessarily must preserve wireless silence.

Reliable sources said it was not impossible that the Japanese learned of the invasion drive in time to rush reinforcements from Rabaul, which Allied planes have been heavily bombing for three

(Continued on Page Seven.)

Held in Laundry Row

Edward Brown, 22, 351 W. 128th St., was in jail today in default of $10,000 bail for shooting at Wong Lee, 35, a laundryman of 316 W. 127th St., who refused to give him his laundry without a ticket. Police said in Felony Court yesterday that Brown fired two shots at Lee after the latter had refused to give up the shirt.

Kearny Ships in Battle, Knox Tells Workers

Special to the World-Telegram.

KEARNY, N. J., Aug. 10.—The intimate relationship of the men behind the lathes and the men behind the guns was dramatically illustrated here today when Navy Secretary Frank Knox disclosed that warships built at the Federal Shipbuilding and Dry Dock Co. were attacking Japs in the Solomon Islands while he spoke.

To tumultous yells and cheers from 6500 federal workers and executives, he said:

"Right now, while I talk to you, elements of the Navy, supported by Army and Marine Corps men, are carrying on a battle in the Southwest Pacific. The men in the battle are using some of the ships you made here. That is the close relationship between you and those men. You sustain the men that carry on the battle."

Presents 'E' Award.

Mr. Knox presented the new Army-Navy "E" production award to the federal yard, and proudly, L. H. Korndorf, president, raised the half red and blue burgee with its gold oak leaves on a small flagpole at the speakers' stand.

Mr. Knox, in his brief speech, emphasized the unity of the Army and Navy as expressed in the unified commands of various Army generals and Navy admirals over both Army and Navy elements throughout the world.

Mr. Korndorf disclosed that Federal turned out more ships in the first half of this year than in all 1941, now building, he said, "at almost three times the rate of last year."

J. P. Morgan Attends.

"And we have established new records in construction of destroyers," he added.

Among the spectators was J. P. Morgan, a stockholder in United States Steel, which owns the Federal yards, who sat beside Mr. Knox.

"He came to see what the boys in the yard are doing," an executive explained.

The War Today

SOUTH PACIFIC—The Battle of Solomon Islands goes into fifth day with relentless aerial pounding of Jap bases and hints of land activity, but all details withheld.

SOVIET RUSSIA—Nazi Panzer forces smash through Russian defenses in Kropotkin area and stream toward Armavir and the Maikop oil fields; Germans claim capture of Maikop and Krasnodar, 60 miles northwest, as well as Pyatigorsk, 110 miles southeast of Armavir.

INDIA—Troops reinforce police as disorders and strikes spread; Gandhi and his wife under arrest.

CHINA—U. S. fliers bomb Haiphong, Indo-China, in surprise raid, blasting ships and harbor area.

EGYPT—Allied bombers attack Benghazi.

ENGLAND — Grounded two nights by bad weather, RAF attacks Osnabruck, Germany, railroad and factory center.

Hanover, N. J., Fights Army Condemnation

Special to the World-Telegram.

FORT DIX, N. J., Aug. 10.—The township committee of New Hanover today were preparing a resolution to the State Legislature protesting against an army proposal to take over part of the town and add it to the Fort Dix reservation.

Pointville, which used to be no more than a crossroads stopping place and now has about 50 establishments doing a soldier trade, is the section the army wants. Condemnation proceedings were filed in Trenton last Friday to the surprise of the town, according to Walter H. Oldrey, chairman of the township committee, who said the army didn't need the land because it already had full trespass rights.

"Everybody in Pointville"—that being about 500 souls—"is all steamed up about it," Mr. Oldrey said, adding that he didn't suppose their protests would do them any good.

Sees 'Two-Way' Gambling Traffic

Special to the World-Telegram.

YONKERS, Aug. 10.—Movement of gamblers between Yonkers and New York City is two-way traffic, Mayor Benjamin F. Barnes of Yonkers said today in commenting on a statement attributed to Police Commissioner Valentine of New York that he had ordered police to watch for gamblers who may be moving to New York.

"If Commissioner Valentine has to watch out for gamblers from Yonkers, we have to watch for those from New York," said Mayor Barnes. "New York gamblers come in here, hire an apartment and then jump out when we try to get them."

World-Telegram Index

A Salute to Mr. Elmer of IRT

By ED WALLACE,
World-Telegram Staff Writer.

In these times of mechanical ferocity, when the engines of might are clanking together in fatal immensity, one is prone to overlook the work of Frank Elmer, long associated with the IRT.

Mr. Elmer is the trusted employee who, when the subway trains come walloping into his station, pulls the lever which makes the steel platform extension slide out. It is Mr. Elmer alone, gentle rider, who keeps you from stepping through.

At this job men spend their days in pervading dust and tumbling noise to become the unstrung heroes of the subway. Men do not seek this job.

Mr. Elmer, however, seems peculiarly fitted for this trying chore. He is rounding out three and a half years on the downtown platform handle at Brooklyn Bridge station and still smiling. Not so with Sam Cucolo, late of the Third Ave. elevated. Mr. Cucolo, operating the uptown platform, said it was the worst job in all the ramifications of rapid transportation.

"The perfect place to blow your top," said Mr. Cucolo solemnly, but his words were smothered by an incoming train. He pulled down the handle.

"I say it's the perfect place to blow your top!" Mr. Cucolo shouted again as the train pulled out. "Yeah, top! A man can't stand it long."

Mr. Cucolo hastily explained that he was merely sitting in while the regular uptown man was out getting a drink of water. He wanted no part of it as a job. He didn't want to become identified with it.

Back on the downtown side with Mr. Elmer was like another world, however. He smiled and laughed easily, wiped his brow and laughed again. Each incoming train was like a new adventure.

(Continued on Page Seven.)

For Victory Buy U. S. Defense Savings Stamps And Bonds

THE JEWISH NEWS

A Weekly Review of Jewish Events

For Victory Buy U. S. Defense Savings Stamps And Bonds

VOL. I—NO. 21 2114 Penobscot Bldg. RA. 7956 Detroit, Michigan, August 14, 1942 34 22 $3.00 Per Year; Single Copy 10c

Britain Grants Jews Palestine Regiment

—Page 3

Sincerity of Vichy's 'Protest' is Doubted

"The free world neither understands nor approves Vichy's treatment of an unhappy people," N. Y. Herald-Tribune asserts in evaluating Petain's attempt to temper the Nazi persecution of Jews.

—Page 2

Ellsberg Acclaimed for Salvage Achievement

U. S. Navy officer's accomplishment in Eritrea called "one of greatest mass salvage operations in naval history."

—Page 11

United Hebrew Schools Start Sessions Monday

Classes commence at nine branches upon conclusion of vacation period . . . Morning sessions in force until reopening of public schools.

—Page 3

Rep. Sweeney Loses Election and Law Suit

Rabble-rouser denied appeal in libel suit on anti-Semitic question . . . Decisively defeated for renomination in Ohio Primaries.

—Page 6

Joint Distribution Committee Spent $9,285,000 to Provide Help for Million Needy Jews

—Page 2

Jewish Children's Bureau Appeals To Mothers for Foster Homes

—Page 16

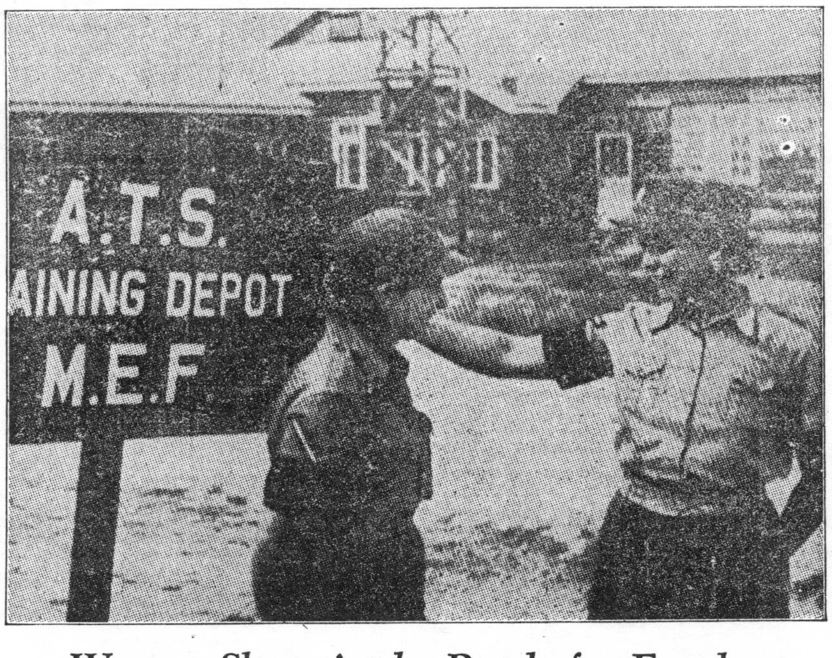

Women Share in the Battle for Freedom

The Palestine Regiment to fight against the Axis includes women as well as men.

To relieve men for active fighting, Jewish girls in the Palestine Auxiliary Territorial Service (PATS) are now working in the Military Police Force. The photograph shows two of the girl volunteers at their training depot.

TO KEEP AN OPEN BIBLE

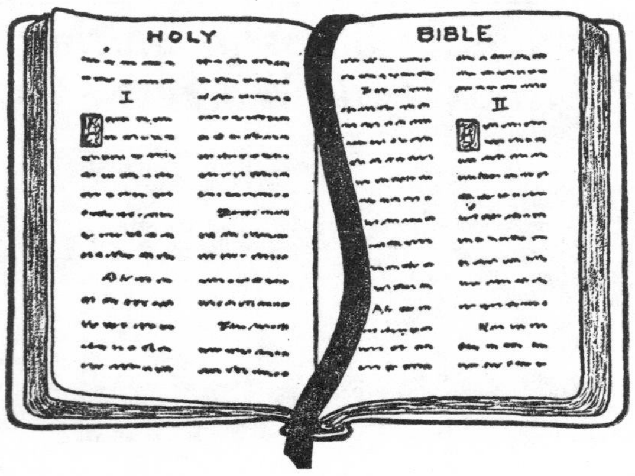

The War Against Paganism

Nazism and Fascism spell the end of religion and the triumph of paganism. This is a war to defend the basic principles of all faiths against the threats that come from the Axis. To keep the Bible open for mankind—

BUY WAR BONDS

★ IN THIS ISSUE ★

CHARACTER QUALITY — AMERICA FIRST! — ENTERPRISE ACCURACY

Los Angeles Examiner

AN AMERICAN PAPER FOR THE AMERICAN PEOPLE — THE GREAT NEWSPAPER OF THE GREAT SOUTHWEST

Reg. U. S. Pat. Off.
Examiner Telephone Richmond 1212 — Examiner Building, 1111 S. Broadway

Remember PEARL HARBOR

VOL. XXXIX—NO. 251 — CCC — LOS ANGELES, WEDNESDAY, AUGUST 19, 1942 — Two Sections—Part I—FIVE CENTS

COMMANDOS RAIDING FRANCE
SECOND FRONT MOVE IN EGYPT

U. S. Planes Hunt Nip Fleet as Navy Showdown Looms

Sea Control Vital to Continuance of Solomons Offensive

GENERAL MacARTHUR'S HEADQUARTERS, Australia, Aug. 19 (Wednesday).—(AP)—Allied reconnaissance planes today were reported to be searching the Pacific front as strong units of U. S. Vice Admiral Robert Lee Ghormley's combined Fleet deployed in anticipation of a naval showdown as a sequel to the Solomon Islands invasion.

Aside from reconnaissance flights no activity was officially announced. One of the reconnaissance planes, however, dropped a number of bombs in airdrome dispersal areas at Kavieng, New Ireland, north of the Solomons battle arena.

Dispatches from Allied naval headquarters in the South Pacific area laid the greatest stress on forthcoming operations at sea now that the U. S. landing forces are firmly established in the Guadalcanal-Tulagi area of the Solomons.

TURNING POINT HINTED

These advices, necessarily unofficial, suggested that the big sea battles still brewing in the waters of the Solomon chain would prove the turning point in the fight for the barrier bases north of Australia—New Britain, New Ireland, New Guinea and others even more distant.

One correspondent at the Allied South Pacific headquarters, writing for the Melbourne Herald, put the position this way:

1. The Allies must keep the sea supply lanes to the Solomons open to maintain their hold there.

2. The Japanese are not liable to yield the Solomons until they are decisively defeated at sea, for once these islands are all in American hands, Japanese tenure of New Britain and Papuan (New Guinea) ports will become increasingly precarious.

3. Therefore the enemy may either try to overpower the American naval units in the

(Continued on Page 4, Cols. 5-6)

Sen. Wallgren Says: Command in Alaska Must Be Unified

Congress Investigator Puzzled by Split in Army, Navy Duty

ANCHORAGE, Alaska, Aug. 17 (Delayed)—(AP)—Senator Mon C. Wallgren (Democrat), Washington, member of a military affairs subcommittee inspecting Alaskan defenses, said today he believed the territory's most urgent military need was a unified command.

Wallgren, together with three other members of the committee, Chairman A. B. Chandler (Democrat), Kentucky; Senators Harold Burton (Republican), Ohio, and Rufus Holman (Republican), Oregon, and Consultant George Malone, is here as guest of Major General Simon B. Buckner.

After visiting various posts and talking to commanders of pilots and ground troops as well as to civilians, Wallgren declared himself confused by the division of duties between the Army and Navy in the job of ousting the Japanese from the Aleutian Islands.

(Japanese using seaplanes in Aleutians as rocky ground fails to give air bases. Page 4.)

AFL, CIO Peace Parleys Postponed

WASHINGTON, Aug. 18.—(INS)—After a conference between Philip Murray, C. I. O. president, and Harry C. Bates, A. F. of L. representative, it was announced today that peace conferences between the two rival labor organizations had been postponed until "late September."

Pacific Exchange Ship Due Aug. 25

WASHINGTON, Aug. 18.—(AP)—The State Department announced tonight that the liner Gripsholm, with 1451 American and other nationals from the western Pacific area, is expected to arrive at New York August 25.

TENNEY FLAYS GOVERNOR ON STATE GUARD

Failure to Call Special Term of Legislature on Project Hit; Legion Fight on Reds Recited

By Walter Naughton

"Governor Olson had it within his power to call a special session of the Legislature which would have enacted laws providing for an adequate State Guard. He did not do so.

"Should the Governor, even now, reconvene the Legislature our Legion program for an adequate State Guard would find favor with the Assembly and Senate. A poll of the majority has established this."

Legionnaire Jack B. Tenney of Inglewood, department legislative chairman, made that statement yesterday as he rendered his report for the year to delegates of the 24th annual state convention of the American Legion in Philharmonic Auditorium.

FURTHER CHARGES

Tenney further asserted:

That William Bauer, former secretary of the German-American Bund in San Diego, is an inspector in the City Engineer's office there;

That Mrs. Don Healey, wife of Don Healey, former state central committeeman of the Communist Party in California, was photographed holding a Communist Party banner, and that Mrs. Healey is now a Deputy Labor Commissioner in San Francisco.

Tenney named Sylvester Andriano, president of Draft Board No. 100 in San Francisco, and said:

"Andriano is connected with most of the suspected societies of Fascist leanings in San Francisco and has been decorated three times by Mussolini's government and is an officer of the Crown of Italy."

Tenney said that politics played a major part in the first state legislature session which brought out the "present, inadequate State Guard Act." He said that legislators were ready to return and correct the situation, but that Governor Olson has steadfastly refused to call them into session.

"The Legion went on record demanding an adequate State Guard long before Pearl Har-

(Continued on Page 5, Cols. 2-3)

John G. Winant Victim of 'Flu

LONDON, Aug. 18.—(AP)—United States Ambassador John G. Winant has been ill with influenza for several days and has conducted urgent embassy business from his home, an embassy spokesman said today.

Churchill, Stalin Map 2nd Front

WINSTON CHURCHILL, British Prime Minister, and Josef Stalin, Russian Premier, exchange smiles in Moscow meeting as they talk over plans for second front. Roosevelt envoys were present at meeting.
—Associated Press wirephoto by radio from Moscow.

County Basic Tax Cut 11.38 Cents

Levy for 1942-43 to Be $1.3489 on Each $100 Assessed Valuation

County Supervisors slashed 11.38 cents yesterday from the basic county tax rate.

The new rate, for 1942-43, will be $1.3489 on each $100 of assessed valuation.

Last year's rate was $1.4627.

An increase of 131 million dollars in countywide taxable assessed valuations, most of the increase due to expanding war industries, accounted for 5 cents of the tax rate cut, and the remainder was credited to county budgetary economies.

Slightly more than one-half of the money raised by the new tax rate will go to county-supported institutions and charities.

FLOOD TAX PROPOSAL

The tax levy will raise $34,013,176 of a gross county governmental cost of $77,819,308 for the fiscal year now under way. The gross requirements will be reduced $34,013,176 by miscellaneous revenues estimated to be $34,122,546; unsecured tax collections totaling $3,318,591, and a budgeted surplus of $6,364,995.

Led by Supervisor John Anson Ford, a majority of the Supervisors balked at the proposal of a $.1985 county flood control district tax rate. Last year's flood control tax (additional to the basic county tax rate) was $.22 on each $100 of assessed valuation.

Ford insisted that the flood control tax rate could be cut to $.17 and the Supervisors ordered a resurvey of flood control costs to eliminate items that may be considered unnecessary.

While property taxes comprised 60 per cent of the overall tax load in 1932-33, today it is only 21 per cent of the total.

L. A. Speeds Dim-Out as Zero Hour 12 Tonight

With the Army dim-out orders effective one minute after midnight tonight, police and civilian defense authorities yesterday were confident Los Angeles will be "100 per cent perfect in compliance."

This was based on the showing made Tuesday night and on the promise of merchants, theaters, hotels and other establishments throughout the city that their outdoor lights would be dimmed-out.

The Downtown Business Men's Association said its members were cooperating in the voluntary effort to dim-out Los Angeles' skyglow 24 hours in advance of the effective time of the order issued by Lieutenant General John L. DeWitt of the Western Defense Command.

DOUSING LIGHTS

In Hollywood, Police Lieutenant William H. Wingard reported that of 350 outdoor signs on Hollywood boulevard between Argyle and La Brea avenues, 302 were out Tuesday night. S. D. Mandle, Hollywood Chamber of Commerce secretary, reported the balance probably would be doused last night.

George Watters, director of the Amusement Industries Committee of the Civilian Defense Council, and Rodney Pantages, alternate director, said theaters gradually have been dimming lights since last Wednesday and they anticipated almost total compliance by last evening.

The dim-out order affects all outdoor signs, marquees and other lighting fixtures permitting light to flow upward, thus creating a skyglow visible at sea and silhouetting ships that are made targets for enemy submarines.

In a ruling vitally important to motion picture studios, the Office of Civilian Defense held film production is an "industry" rather than "commercial" enterprise, thus enabling night filming and set construction outdoors under controlled lighting.

Meanwhile, thousands of placards were being posted by police, Automobile Club of Southern California engineers and air raid wardens throughout the dim-out area, with special notices posted in the "visible from the sea" sections instructing motorists to dim their car lights.

Businessmen in doubt about whether they are complying properly with the order were asked to contact lighting experts of the City Defense Council.

The Office of Civilian Defense pointed out that violators of the dim-out order may be excluded from the Western Defense Command territory—California, Oregon, Washington, Idaho, Montana, Utah, Nevada and Arizona.

Cuban Break With Spain, Vichy Hinted

HAVANA, Aug. 18.—(AP)—Dr. Jose Manuel Cortina, retiring secretary of state, said today the government was studying "a firm line of conduct concerning diplomatic relations with certain countries which are openly friendly to the Axis powers," a statement that caused speculation on the possibility of a Cuban break with Spain and Vichy France.

Dieppe Attacked; British Army Shift Hints Offensive

AEF in Egypt; Auchinleck May Head New Action to Aid Russia

LONDON, Aug. 19 (Wednesday).—(AP)—The Commandos made a raid on the Dieppe area of occupied France early today, British headquarters announced.

The bulletin said the operation still was in progress.

Meanwhile, it added, the French people were being advised by radio that the raid was not a full-fledged invasion.

A major shift in the British commands in the Middle East, landing of the largest American convoy of troops and equipment to reach Egypt, and another terrific "softening" air raid on one of Germany's main rail centers brought a new surge of second front speculation yesterday.

Widespread conviction that the new Allied strategy decided upon in the Churchill-Stalin talks in Moscow would be felt first in the Middle East received support with the British announcement that General Sir Harold R. L. G. Alexander, hero of Dunkirk and an officer whose slogan is "offensives and more offensives," has been made supreme commander in the Egyptian-Lybian battle zone.

Spotlight on Auchinleck

But the spotlight of the second front command was on General Sir Claude Auchinleck, who was left without an assignment when he was replaced by Alexander. Auchinleck or "the Auk" as he is known, is one of Britain's topflight fighting generals and took command of the British forces in the field himself and halted Nazi Marshal Rommel when he threatened recently to drive through Egypt to the Suez.

Military experts in London felt that the "Auk" was the man to head a second front as he has had invasion experience.

On the other hand, the London Daily Herald declared editorially that in its opinion "Auchinleck was dismissed from the Middle East command because of the Libyan collapse earlier this summer."

Cairo revealed that Prime Minister Churchill visited the Libyan battlefields, met Allied leaders as American troops poured into that sector. Medium American bombers also appeared in the air, indicating new airforce arrivals.

Cairo, meanwhile, was a hotbed of rumors. Most popular of these was that Churchill discussed the feasibility of a third front in the Western desert to relieve pressure against the Soviets.

By James E. Brown
Staff Correspondent International News Service

MOSCOW, Aug. 19.—(Wednesday)—Russia admitted today that her troops were forced to withdraw northwest of Stalingrad and that Nazi armored hordes were plunging into the heart of the Caucasus Mountains.

Simultaneously, the Soviet air force dealt a destructive blow at the air forces supporting the German offensive. A squadron of Russian bombers, it was announced, raided a base for long-range Nazi bombers, far behind the southern front line. Sixty grounded German bombers were declared to have been knocked out, including 30 destroyed and 30 crippled.

A Soviet announcement declared that Adolf Hitler has lost 1,250,000 officers and men, including 480,000 killed, in the past three months as against 606,000 Russian officers and men dead, wounded and missing in the same period.

Asserting that Germany had hurled some 1,380,000 reinforcements of "extra man power" from all parts of Europe as well as all of the Reich's "main re-

Reynolds Admits He and Heiress Wife Expect Baby

WASHINGTON, Aug. 18.—(AP)—Senator Reynolds (Democrat), North Carolina, acknowledged today a report that he and Mrs. Reynolds were expecting the birth of a child "sometime in the fall."

Asked about the report, Reynolds said, "well, that's one thing I can't deny."

Mrs. Reynolds, the former Evalyn Washington McLean, and the North Carolina Senator, chairman of the Senate military committee, were married in October, 1941. A daughter of Mrs. Evalyn W. McLean, prominent Washington social leader, she is the Senator's fifth wife. Mrs. Reynolds is 20, the Senator 57.

DRAFT DEFERMENTS HIT

Employers' Requests to Be Ignored

SACRAMENTO, Aug. 18.—(AP)—Effective immediately, draft boards in California will no longer grant induction deferments to men seeking commissions in the armed forces or to men whose temporary services are requested by their employers, it was announced today by Lieutenant Colonel K. H. Leitch, state selective service director.

All local draft boards have been notified of the new policy, Colonel Leitch said.

It has been the policy in the past to grant stays in induction to meet the convenience of employers or to permit men to seek armed service commissions, he said.

But "recent delivery failures have increased materially," Colonel Leitch said, necessitating the change in procedure.

Married Men to Be Inducted Soon

BOSTON, Aug. 18.—(INS)—The selective service system will soon start inducting married men with and without dependents to fill the Army's growing ranks, Ted Luther, its public relations director, disclosed today.

Speaking before the Army and Navy Legion of Valor, he declared the Army had already mobilized most of the nation's 1-A men and that draft boards are about to reclassify the man power reservoir under 45 years in 1-B and 3-A classifications.

War Output Hits $13,600,000 Daily

DETROIT, Aug. 18.—(INS)—America's automotive industry is producing armaments for this country and her allies at the rate of $13,600,000 worth a day, the Automotive Council for War Production said tonight.

The pace exceeds by 20 per cent the average annual rate of peak civilian production, according to Alvin Macauley, president of the council.

'Longies' May Be Given Shortcut to Popularity

NEW YORK, Aug. 18.—(INS)—A return to old-fashioned long underwear was recommended today by C. E. A. Winslow, professor of public health of Yale Medical School.

Professor Winslow said proper dress would permit comfortable living this winter in room temperatures 5 to 15 degrees below normal.

He urged "dictators" of women's fashions to glamorize ski suits for home, office and factory wear as they would hide feminine "longies."

MEXICO POSTS CANAL GUARD

Camacho Garrisons Vital Pacific Isles

MEXICO CITY, Aug. 18.—(INS)—Acting under orders from President Manuel Avila Camacho, the Mexican navy today established garrisons on the strategic islands of Guadalupe and the Revillagigedo group, which guard the approach to the Panama Canal along Mexico's west coast.

Guadalupe lies 253 miles off the coast of Lower California, while San Benedicto, nearest of the Revillagigedo Islands, is 285 miles out in the Pacific from Manzanillo. Other islands in the Revillagigedo group, once a hangout for pirates, are Rojo Partido, Clarion and Socorro.

The United States Navy kept a watchful eye on these islands, all Mexico-owned, before the Mexican government acted.

In the hands of an enemy these islands could be used as a threat to the Canal as well as bases to harass West Coast shipping.

Preis: 2 Karbowanez
Im Reich: 20 Rpf.

Deutsche Ukraine-Zeitung

Postverlagsort: Luzk — Verlag und Schriftleitung: Luzk/Wolhynien — Ruf: Luzk 104 und 105 — Postsendungen durch Deutsche Dienstpost Ukraine — Bankkonto: Wirtschaftsbank Luzk Nr. 28; im Reich: Postscheckkonto Berlin Nr. 800 der Dresdner Bank mit Vermerk „Für Deutsche Ukraine-Zeitung".

1. Jahrg. Dienstag, 25. August 1942 Nr. 184

Die Deutsche Ukraine-Zeitung erscheint täglich morgens, mit Ausnahme montags. Bezugspreis: in der Ukraine monatl. 30 Kar, im Reich: monatl. RM 3,— zuzügl. Zustellgebühr. Bestellungen können im Reich bei jeder Postanstalt, in der Ukraine bei den Deutschen Dienstpostämtern oder beim Verlag aufgegeben werden

Donübergang bei Stalingrad Feindverteidigung durchbrochen

Der Angriff gegen den strategisch wichtigen Stützpunkt der Sowjets hat begonnen
Erfolgreiche Kämpfe in den Bergen des Kaukasus

duz Berlin, 24. August

Das Oberkommando der Wehrmacht bricht in seinem heutigen Bericht das seit Tagen währende Schweigen über den Fortgang der Operationen im Raum von Stalingrad, indem es mitteilt: „Nordwestlich Stalingrad erzwangen deutsche Infanteriedivisionen und Schnelle Truppen, von der Luftwaffe hervorragend unterstützt, den Uebergang über den Don und durchbrachen im Vorstoß nach Osten stark ausgebaute feindliche Verteidigungsstellungen."

*

Die nachrichtliche Zurückhaltung, die das deutsche Oberkommando in letzter Zeit gegenüber den Ereignissen im Kampfraum von Stalingrad wahrte, findet heute eine bemerkenswerte Erklärung mit der Mitteilung, daß der Angriff der verbündeten Streitkräfte gegen den strategisch wichtigen sowjetischen Stützpunkt begonnen hat und sich erfolgreich weiterentwickelt. In dem Kampf um den Verteidigungsraum von Stalingrad ist also eine neue Phase eingetreten, die vor allem dadurch gekennzeichnet ist, daß es deutschen Infanteriedivisionen und Schnellen Truppen gelungen ist, den Don nordwestlich der Stadt kämpfend zu überschreiten und die Schlacht damit in den Raum außerhalb des großen Donbogens getragen ist. An dieser neuen Angriffsfront, an der die sowjetischen Verteidigungsstellungen durchbrochen wurden, dringt der Angriff erfolgreich weiter vorwärts.

Die Entwicklung, die zu dieser neuen erfolgverheißenden Kampflage geführt hat, ist durch drei zusammenhängende und planvoll durchgeführte Operationen gelenkt und bestimmt worden.

Erstens: Vor Wochen bereits haben verbündete Streitkräfte, die aus dem Raum zwischen Don und Sal nach Osten vorgestoßen waren, den südlichen Verteidigungsraum von Stalingrad in zum Teil harten Kämpfen erreicht und trotz stärksten sowjetischen Widerstandes ihre Positionen behauptet und fortschreitend verbessert.

Zweitens: An zweiter Stelle erfolgte in Durchführung des planvollen deutschen Angriffs die Säuberung des Donbogens von den dort in mehreren Brückenköpfen hartnäckig kämpfenden Sowjets, die den Auftrag hatten, die verbündeten Streitkräfte um jeden Preis aus dem innersten Winkel des Donbogens fernzuhalten.

Drittens: Mit der Säuberung des Donbogens war schließlich die letzte Voraussetzung geschaffen, um nun auch von Nordwesten her den Angriff über den Don in die Landbrücke zwischen Don und Wolga hineinzutragen. Die jetzt erfolgte Ueberwindung des Donlaufes darf als eine hervorragende Waffentat bezeichnet werden, die es der deutschen Führung ermöglicht hat, den Angriff gegen die strategisch so bedeutsame Stellung am Wolgaknie einzuleiten.

Man gewinnt aus den Mitteilungen das Bild eines zangenartigen Angriffs, der von Süden und Nordwesten her gegen Stalingrad gerichtet ist. Naturgemäß leisten die Sowjets an diesem Angelpunkt ihrer Front zwischen Don und Wolga einen erbitterten Widerstand, der die Erhaltung einer strategischen Position bezweckt, die räumlich, rüstungswirtschaftlich und verkehrsmäßig von einzigartiger Bedeutung ist.

Die Bolschewisten sind sich über die Folgen des deutschen Vordringens in diesen Räumen durchaus im klaren, denn sie versuchen weiterhin, die deutschen Operationen im Kaukasus durch Gegenangriffe zu durchkreuzen. Nach Abwehr der Gegenstöße stießen die deutschen Truppen dem zurückweichenden Feind aber nach und kämpften sich trotz aller Geländeschwierigkeiten und Minensperren weiter nach Süden vor. Auch im eigentlichen Gebirge, wo das von Urwäldern bedeckte Kampfgelände und die tief eingeschnittenen mit zahlreichen Sperren versehenen Täler die Verteidigung des Feindes begünstigen, gewann der deutsche Angriff nach heftigen der deutsche Angriff nach heftigen, aber erfolgreichen Kämpfen weiter an Boden.

Amerikanische Zeitungen plaudern aus

Churchills Invasionsabsi chten eindeutig enthüllt

Eigener Auslandsdienst

bd Lissabon, 24. August

Den besten Beweis dafür, daß der anglo-amerikanische Landungsversuch bei Dieppe die von den Sowjets so ungeduldig geforderte zweite Front schaffen sollte, liefern die sensationellen Ueberschriften der großen amerikanischen Zeitungen, die jetzt in Lissabon eingetroffen sind. In den ersten Stunden des so kläglich gescheiterten Abenteuers von Dieppe, als man in London offenbar noch an einen Erfolg des Unternehmens glaubte, ließ die britische Zensurpresse Telegramme nach Amerika passieren, die das erwachende New York in einen hysterischen Taumel versetzte. Die New Yorker Straßen waren überfüllt von heftig diskutierenden Menschengruppen, und die Zeitungen brachten in sensationeller Aufmachung Extrablätter heraus, die den Verkäufern aus den Händen gerissen wurden.

Außerordentlich bezeichnend ist die Tatsache, daß die vielspaltigen Balkenüberschriften den Eindruck zu erwecken suchten, als ob hauptsächlich die Nordamerikaner und weniger die Engländer den erlösenden Vorstoß durchgeführt hätten. So schrieb die „New York Post" in riesiger Aufmachung: „Wir landen in Frankreich" und das „New York Weld Telegram" jubelte: „Unsere Truppen stürmen die französische Küste". Die „New York Sun" brachte eine die halbe erste Seite bedeckende Ueberschrift: „Unsere Truppen landen in Frankreich zusammen mit britischen Kommandos". Das „Journal American" erklärte begeistert: „Amerika und England fallen in Frankreich ein". Mit diesen sehr eindeutigen Ueberschriften also hat die New Yorker Presse die Meldungen über den Invasionsversuch veröffentlicht, von dem die britischen Agitationsakrobaten nachträglich der Welt einreden wollten, daß es sich nur um eine größere Uebung gehandelt habe. Die Ueberschriften der amerikanischen Presse am 19. August sprechen eine so deutliche Sprache, daß die alliierten Hoffnungen eindeutig enthüllt werden.

Dr. Thierack Reichsjustizminister

Aufbau einer nationalsozialistischen Rechtspflege durch den Führer angeordnet

Berlin 24. August

Amtlich wird mitgeteilt:

Der Führer hat sich in Anbetracht der besonderen Bedeutung, die den Aufgaben der Rechtspflege während des Krieges zukommt, entschlossen, den seit dem Ableben des Reichsministers Dr. Gürtner unbesetzt gebliebenen Posten des Reichsministers der Justiz wieder zu besetzen. Der Führer hat daher den Präsidenten des Volksgerichtshofes, Staatsminister a. D. Dr. Thierack, der nach der Machtergreifung bis zur Verreichlichung der Justiz sächsischer Justizminister war, zum Reichsminister der Justiz ernannt.

Gleichzeitig hat der Führer den mit der Führung der Geschäfte des Reichsjustizministers beauftragten Staatssekretär Professor Dr. Schlegelberger von diesem Auftrag entbunden und ihn auf seinen Antrag in den Ruhestand versetzt. Der Führer hat dem Staatssekretär Dr. Schlegelberger in einem Handschreiben seinen Dank für die dem Deutschen Reich in jahrzehntelanger aufopferungsvoller Arbeit geleisteten hervorragenden Dienste ausgesprochen, ihn hierauf ferner zur persönlichen Abmeldung im Führerhauptquartier empfangen. Zum Staatssekretär im Reichsjustizministerium hat der Führer den Präsidenten des Hanseatischen Oberlandesgerichts in Hamburg, Senator Dr. Rothenberger, zum Präsidenten des Volksgerichtshofes den Staatssekretär im Reichsjustizministerium Dr. Freisler ernannt.

Ferner wird amtlich mitgeteilt: Der Führer hat dem neu ernannten Reichsminister der Justiz Dr. Thierack durch nachstehenden Erlaß besondere Vollmachten erteilt: „Zur Erfüllung der Aufgaben des Großdeutschen Reiches ist neue starke Rechtspflege erforderlich. Ich beauftrage und ermächtige daher den Reichsminister der Justiz, nach meinen Richtlinien und Weisungen im Einvernehmen mit dem Reichsminister und Chef der Reichskanzlei und dem Leiter der Parteikanzlei eine nationalsozialistische Rechtspflege aufzubauen und alle dafür erforderlichen Maßnahmen zu treffen. Er kann hierbei vom bestehenden Recht abweichen."

Die Reichspressestelle der NSDAP. gibt dazu bekannt:

Der bisherige Führer des Nationalsozialistischen Rechtswahrerbundes, Präsident der Akademie für Deutsches Recht und Leiter des Reichsrechtsamtes der NSDAP., Dr. Frank, hat den Führer gebeten, ihn von diesen Aemtern zu entbinden, um sich ganz seinen Aufgaben als Generalgouverneur widmen zu können. Der Führer hat dieser Bitte entsprochen und zum Präsidenten der Akademie für Deutsches Recht sowie zum Leiter des Nationalsozialistischen Rechtswahrerbundes den neuernannten Reichsminister der Justiz, Dr. Thierack, berufen. Das Reichsrechtsamt der NSDAP., die Gau- und Kreisrechtsämter hat der Führer aufgelöst und die bisherigen Leiter der Gau- und Kreisrechtsämter in die Gau- und Kreisstabsämter eingegliedert. Die NS-Rechtsberatungsstellen führen im Rahmen dieser Aemter ihre Tätigkeit weiter.

In den Gewässern westlich Afrikas

In letzter Zeit war in den Meldungen des OKW oft die Rede davon, daß deutsche U-Boote feindliche Handelsschiffe in den Gewässern westlich Afrikas versenkten. Dieser Hinweis zeigt, daß die deutschen U-Boote an allen Stellen eingesetzt sind, an denen der Gegner besonders hart getroffen werden kann. Bei den alliierten Schiffen, die im Einsatzraum westlich Afrikas versenkt werden, handelt es sich regelmäßig um Schiffe, die entweder Lebensmittel für England oder Kriegsmaterial für die entlegenen Kriegsschauplätze des britischen Empire transportieren. Hier an der westafrikanischen Küste schneiden sich der Seeweg von der britischen Insel nach Australien, Indien und den Fronten des Nahen Ostens und der Weg der amerikanischen Kriegsmaterialtransporte nach den westafrikanischen Häfen.

Gerade der letzte Weg sollte im Rahmen der alliierten Kriegspläne besondere Bedeutung erlangen. Seit der Plan, von Aegypten aus durch eine Ueberrennung Libyens und die Eroberung der gesamten nordafrikanischen Gebiete einen Anschluß Aegyptens an die westafrikanischen Häfen zu erreichen, gescheitert und der Seeweg um die Südspitze Afrikas herum durch das Rote Meer nach Aegypten immer unsicherer geworden ist, rückten die Pläne der Alliierten, eine direkte Verbindung von Westafrika aus quer durch den Kontinent nach dem Nil-Land zu schaffen, immer mehr in den Vordergrund. Schon früher wurde eine ständige Luftverbindung von Amerika über den Atlantik durch das Innere des afrikanischen Kontinents nach Aegypten geschaffen. Diese Verbindung beginnt in Natal (Brasilien), führt über Bathurst, Freetown, Khartum nach Kairo, um dort Anschluß an die Linie nach Bagdad zu gewinnen. Auf diesem Weg wurden Kampfflugzeuge zur ägyptischen Front, zum Iran und zur Kaukasus-Front befördert.

Entsprechend dieser Luftverbindung ging man daran, auch eine Landverbindung zwischen der westafrikanischen Westküste zum Roten Meer und zum Indischen Ozean zu schaffen. Als Ausgangshäfen sollten vor allem Bathurst, Freetown, Monrovia, Lagos, Duala, Pointe Noire und Libreville dienen. Die nördliche Linie soll von Duala nach Khartum führen, wo sie Anschluß an die Eisenbahnlinie nach Kairo erhält, die südliche nach Juba am Weißen Nil, mit Abzweigungen nach Khartum und Mombassa in Nordafrika.

Es ist nicht schwer zu erkennen, daß es sich bei diesen Plänen mehr um Phantasien handelt als um praktische Projekte, deren Durchführung von großem Nutzen für den Gegner sein könnte. In einem Aufsatz hat Konteradmiral Gadow mit Recht darauf hingewiesen, daß auf dieser Straße 1500 Kraftwagen unterwegs sein müßten, um die Ladung eines einzigen mittelgroßen Dampfers über die 3000 bis 4000 Kilometer betragende Entfernung zu befördern. Dazu kommen Schwierigkeiten, die sich vor allen Dingen aus der Bereitstellung des Treibstoffes und der Beanspruchung des Wagenmaterials ergeben.

Was aber für die Beurteilung des strategischen Wertes dieser Route von größter Bedeutung ist, ist die Tatsache, daß das Material, das auf ihr transportiert werden soll, zuerst einmal von den amerikanischen Verladehäfen zu See nach Westafrika über eine Entfernung von annähernd 10 000 Kilometer gebracht werden muß. Hier nun zeigt sich die Bedeutung der Schiffsversenkungen im westlichen Atlantik, durch die die Pläne unserer Gegner, eine direkte Verbindung zu den Fronten im Nahen Osten zu erhalten, noch gewagter erscheinen, als sie es ohnedies sind. Es ist daher der Gedanke nicht von der Hand zu weisen, daß der Plan dieser Verbindung durch den afrikanischen Kontinent, nicht nur der Erwägung entspringt, einen Ersatzweg für die gefährdete Seeverbindung um Südafrika herum, sondern gegebenenfalls auch einen Rückzugsweg aus der Orientstellung zu haben. Darauf deutet hin, daß, wie Gadow ausführt, England bereits eine Auffangstellung für die Armee Aegyptens am Südende des Suezkanals vorbereitet, der sie dem interkontinentalen Weg nach Westafrika näher bringt. duz.

Zwischen Don und Wolga

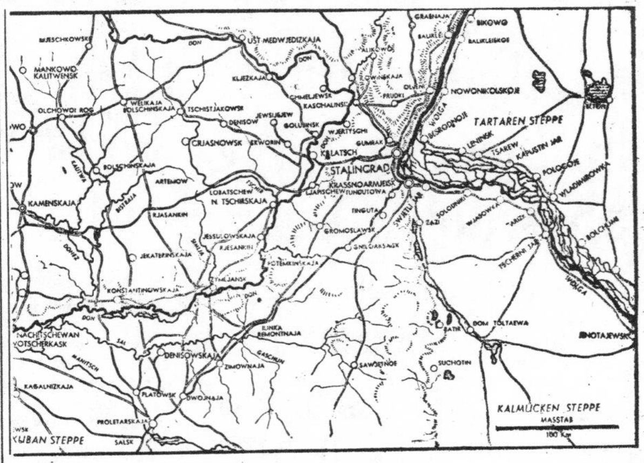

Karte: Penkala

Das alliierte Oberkommando

Ein kaum lösbares Problem für unsere Gegner

Auch im Weltkrieg konnten sich die Alliierten erst in den Stunden höchster Gefahr entschließen, ihre Armeen unter ein einheitliches Kommando zu stellen. Als die deutschen Truppen im März 1918 über Montidier hinaus auf Amiens vorstießen und sich westlich von Villers Bretonneux das Loch zwischen der französischen und der britischen Armee gebildet hatte, einigten sich Clemenceau und Lloyd George endlich auf die Person des Marschalls Foch als Oberkommandierenden. Der amerikanische General Pershing aber trat in diese Kombination nur mit so vielen schriftlich garantierten Vorbehalten ein, daß er praktisch selbständig blieb. Auch die französisch-englische Zusammenarbeit erfolgte unter größten Schwierigkeiten. In Erinnerung an diese unerquicklichen Vorgänge schreibt Foch denn auch in seinen Memoiren, er wünsche keinem französischen Offizier jemals wieder ein alliiertes Oberkommando führen zu müssen.

Die zweite Probe auf das Exempel wurde in diesem Kriege gemacht und ging auch diesmal nicht auf. In der Stunde der Krise, nach den Kämpfen an der Somme und Schelde, marschierte General Gort entgegen den Befehlen des Oberkommandierenden Gamelin nach Dünkirchen, überließ die Franzosen und Belgier ihrem Schicksal und rettete von seiner Armee, was zu retten war, nach England.

Heute stellt sich das Problem eines einheitlichen Oberkommandos in mehrfacher und recht komplizierter Form. Wenn es nach der Meinung des kleinen Mannes in den Vereinigten Staaten ginge, wäre die Sache freilich sehr einfach. Dann würde das Weiße Haus zum Hauptquartier der Alliierten erklärt und der Krieg an allen Fronten von dieser Stelle aus geführt. Aber Stalin hat es wiederholt kategorisch abgelehnt, sich in dem sogenannten alliierten Kriegsrat von Washington vertreten zu lassen. Zwischen dem sowjetischen Generalstab und denen der übrigen Alliierten besteht überhaupt keine direkte Verbindung. Jeder Gedankenaustausch geht über die Militärattachés oder Botschaften durch den diplomatischen Kanal, wie in Friedenszeiten. Die wenigen englischen und nordamerikanischen Offiziere in Moskau und Kuybischew dürfen die Front nicht besuchen und keine anderen Informationen nach Hause schicken, als die ihnen von den sie begleitenden und überwachenden GPU-Offizieren gegeben werden.

Um General Wavell in Indien ist es sehr ruhig geworden, und wenn er sich nicht selbst ab und zu vor das Mikrophon stellte, würde kaum noch jemand von ihm sprechen. In den Vereinigten Staaten hat er, der erste vom alliierten Kriegsrat ernannte Oberkommandierende für die pazifische Kriegszone, seit seiner Flucht von Java nach Delhi jeden Kredit verloren. Das gleiche gilt für General Stilwell, der nach der Katastrophe von Burma in Indien erschien, während die von ihm befehligte chinesische Armee kämpfend nach Yünnan zurückwich. Auch die Vorschußlorbeeren für General Mac Arthur, Wavells Nachfolger als Oberkommandierender in der pazifischen Kriegszone, beginnen schon zu welken. Allzu oft hat er Offensiven angekündigt und dann nichts unternommen. Aber in den breiten Massen der Vereinigten Staaten ist er immer noch ziemlich populär. Der große Generalanzeiger von New York, die „Daily News", klagt beinahe täglich Roosevelt an, ihm deshalb kein aktiveres Kommando zu übertragen, weil er auf Mac Arthurs Volkstümlichkeit eifersüchtig sei.

Die aus den Vereinigten Staaten eintreffenden Vorschläge zu dem Thema des einheitlichen Oberkommandos wollen diese Zusammenfassung der Armeen dann erfolgen lassen, wenn die Kriegsorganisationen Englands und der Vereinigten Staaten miteinander verschmolzen worden sind. Sie möchten also zunächst einen gesunden Untergrund schaffen, auf dem sich eine einheitliche Wehrmacht mit einem einheitlichen Kommando bewegen kann. Vorläufig haben die beiden Länder aber noch verschiedene Wehrmachtorganisationen, verschiedene Waffen und verschiedene Ausbildungsformen. Die britischen Truppen in Aegypten mußten monatelang mit den amerikanischen Panzern vertraut gemacht werden, bis sie sie in der Schlacht benutzen konnten. Diese Unterschiede zu beseitigen, ist deshalb beinahe unmöglich, weil England und die Vereinigten Staaten nun einmal verschiedene Staatsformen haben, die jede für sich in ihrer Art ihre Kriegs- und Rüstungsanstrengungen macht.

In den vergangenen Monaten wurde versucht, durch kombinierte Agenturen beide Länder besser aufeinander abzustimmen. In Washington wie in London sind Kriegsräte ins Leben gerufen worden, die beide aber so gut wie nicht miteinander verkehren. Der von Roosevelt geleitete Washingtoner Rat hat einen kombinierten Generalstab zur Seite, dem für die Vereinigten Staaten General Marshall und Admiral King, für England Feldmarschall Dill, Admiral Cunningham, Luftmarschall Evill und Generalleutnant McReady angehören. In England besteht etwas Derartiges nicht. Zwischen den auf britischem Boden stehenden Teilen der amerikanischen Armee und der englischen Armee wird der Verkehr über Verbindungsoffiziere aufrechterhalten. Ueberhaupt ist England in diesem System deutlich an die zweite Stelle gerückt, denn alle wichtigen Agen-

Auch die Niederlande sind gesichert

Für den Fall, daß es den Briten einfiele, das „Unternehmen Dieppe" an der niederländischen Küste zu wiederholen, ist auch dort von der deutschen Wehrmacht alle Vorsorge getroffen worden, um ihnen den gebührenden Empfang zu bereiten.
PK-Aufn.: Kriegsber. Müller (PBZ)

Preis: 2 Karbowanez
Im Reich: 20 Rpf.

Deutsche Ukraine-Zeitung

Postverlagsort: Luzk — Verlag und Schriftleitung: Luzk/Wolhynien — Ruf: Luzk 104 und 105 — Postsendungen durch Deutsche Dienstpost Ukraine — Bankkonto: Wirtschaftsbank Luzk Nr. 28; im Reich: Postscheckkonto Berlin Nr. 800 der Dresdner Bank mit Vermerk „Für Deutsche Ukraine-Zeitung".

1. Jahrg. Sonntag, 30. August 1942 Nr. 189

Die Deutsche Ukraine-Zeitung erscheint täglich morgens, mit Ausnahme montags. Bezugspreis: in der Ukraine monatl. 30 Kar, im Reich: monatl. RM 3,— zuzügl. Zustellgebühr. Bestellungen können im Reich bei jeder Postanstalt, in der Ukraine bei den Deutschen Dienstpostämtern oder beim Verlag aufgegeben werden

Dieppe sollte der Auftakt zur Eroberung von Paris werden

Der Abschlußbericht des OKW enthüllt die britischen Absichten und Lügen — Operationspläne in unserer Hand — Beweise für die Größe des deutschen Sieges

Führerhauptquartier, 29. August

Das Oberkommando der Wehrmacht veröffentlicht über den englischen Landungsversuch bei Dieppe am 19. August 1942 einen amtlichen Bericht, in dem es heißt:

„Die dem Oberkommando der Wehrmacht vorliegenden Berichte von Heer, Kriegsmarine und Luftwaffe, erbeutete Befehle und Gefangenenaussagen ergeben nunmehr ein vollständiges Bild über die schwere Niederlage, die der Feind bei seinem Versuch zur Errichtung der zweiten Front bei Dieppe erlitten hat. Die Absichten des Feindes sind durch die Ergebnisse der eigenen Aufklärung und durch den erbeuteten Operationsbefehl von nicht weniger als 21 eng bedruckten Schreibmaschinenseiten eindeutig geklärt. Sie beweisen, daß es dem Feind nicht darauf ankam, einzelne Objekte nach Art der Kommandoangriffe zu zerstören, sondern daß schon der ersten Welle die Aufgabe gestellt war, Stadt und Hafen Dieppe einzunehmen und einen tiefen Brückenkopf zu bilden, dessen Umfang durch den als Angriffsziel genannten Ort Arques la Bataille, sieben Kilometer von der Küste entfernt, gekennzeichnet ist.

Für die Beurteilung des Wertes dieses Brückenkopfes sind folgende Feststellungen wichtig:

Dieppe ist der der französischen Hauptstadt nächstgelegene Hafenplatz. Seine Hafenanlagen erlauben die Ausladung von Panzern und schwerem Gerät und damit das Anlanden der weiteren Angriffswellen. Der Besitz eines tiefen Brückenkopfes bei Dieppe schafft die Voraussetzung, um die Küstenverteidigung zwischen Somme und Seine aufzurollen und durch die Einnahme von Abbéville und Le Havre weitere leistungsfähige Häfen zu gewinnen

Weitgesteckte operative Ziele

Zur Durchführung dieser Absichten war in der ersten Welle die 2 Kanadische Division in einer Breite von etwa 25 Kilometer zur Landung an sechs verschiedenen Stellen angesetzt Diese Truppen bestanden aus ausgesuchten, hochwertigen, seit Monaten für die Landungskämpfe besonders ausgebildeten Kräften die in der Hauptsache allerdings nicht Engländer, sondern Kanadier umfaßten. Hinter dieser ersten Welle standen — neben zahlreichen anderen im Seegebiet zwischen Dieppe und Portsmouth erkannten Gruppen von Landungsbooten, Transportern und leichten Seestreitkräften bis zur Kreuzergröße — eine schwimmende Reserve von sechs großen, auch mit Panzern vollbeladenen Transportern und drei Frachtern. Weiter nördlich befand sich eine starke Gruppe — wohl das Gros der Landungsstreitkräfte — mit 26 Transportern in See, auf deren Decks dichtgedrängt Truppen standen. An Luftstreitkräften hatte der Feind über 100 Kampfflugzeuge, darunter zahlreiche viermotorige, und mindestens 1000 Jäger vorwiegend zum Angriff auf die deutsche Küstenverteidigung eingesetzt. Dieser starke, wenn auch in der Hauptsache den Verbündeten zugefallene Kräfteeinsatz beweist besser als alle nachträglichen amtlichen und nichtamtlichen Täuschungsversuche, daß mit der Landung weitgesteckte operative Ziele verfolgt werden sollten

Unterstrichen wird diese Tatsache noch durch die Erklärung des Vorsitzenden des amerikanischen Senatsausschusses für militärische Angelegenheiten, der nach United Preß noch am 20. August der Hoffnung Ausdruck gab, daß der gemeinsame Kommandoangriff sich zur zweiten Front entwickeln und ausdehnen würde. Die gelandeten Kräfte wären stark genug dazu, und das Kampfgelände wäre für Landungsoperationen äußerst günstig.

Der Hafen als erstes Ziel

Die aufgefundenen Befehle geben auch noch in anderer Hinsicht wertvolle Aufschlüsse Damit sie nicht in unsere Hand fielen, durften nur die beiden Brigadestäbe die Befehle zu dem Unternehmen mitführen. Durch die Gefangennahme eines Brigadestabes kam aber der Operationsbefehl in unseren Besitz. Die ersten Ziele sollten in der Zerstörung einzelner Küstenbatterien bestehen, die Küstengewässer und Strand beherrschen, um dann, unterstützt von den Geschützen zahlreicher Marineeinheiten, am Strand auszuladen, den Hafen und die Stadt in Besitz zu nehmen. Plündern in jeder Form war strengstens verboten. Die Begründung dafür in dem Operationsplan lautete, daß „die deutschen Besatzungstruppen einen hohen Standard individuellen Anstandes entwickelt haben" und danach auch die Landungstruppe durch die Einwohner beurteilt würde. Zur Ueberwachung dieser Anordnung, die ebenfalls auf die Absicht eines längeren Verbleibens an Land schließen läßt, war eigens ein Gendarmerieoffizier mit Hilfskräften vorgesehen. Trotzdem glaubte man, daß die französische Bevölkerung von den landenden Truppen

(Fortsetzung auf Seite 2)

Der Führer dankt für die Aufbauarbeit

Programmatische Rede des Reichskommissars über die deutsche Aufgabe in der Ukraine

Rowno, 29. August.

Der Reichskommissar, Gauleiter Erich Koch, hielt auf der Dienstbesprechung der Hauptabteilungsleiter von Ernährung und Landwirtschaft, der Generalbezirke und der Wirtschaftskommandos eine programmatische Rede, in der er in großen Zügen die grundsätzlichen Probleme, die das Reichskommissariat Ukraine berühren, darlegte und die Wege zu ihrer Lösung wies.

Zu Beginn seiner Rede überbrachte der Gauleiter den Dank des Führers an den Landesbauernführer Körner und seine Mitarbeiter für die bisher geleistete Arbeit. Dann führte der Reichskommissar u. a. folgendes aus: Die Ukraine und der Aufbau des Landes seien reale und nüchterne Angelegenheiten und forderten deshalb auch einen klaren politischen Standort, von dem aus die Probleme erfaßt und gelöst werden müßten. Eingedenk des Opfers, das unsere Soldaten hier gebracht haben, dürfe es keinen Platz für irgendwelche phantastischen Pläne geben. Nur eine Aufgabe überrage alle anderen: die Voraussetzungen zu schaffen, daß der Endsieg erfochten werde und daß dem deutschen Volk, das die größte Last des europäischen Befreiungskrieges trage, die erforderliche materielle Grundlage erhalten bleibe.

Dieser schwere und ehrenvolle Auftrag des Führers müsse ohne Rücksicht auf menschliche Schwächen und sachliche Schwierigkeiten durchgeführt werden.

Unter dem Beifall der Anwesenden führte der Gauleiter aus: „Wir schaffen durch unsere Arbeit, durch unsere Energie und durch Einsatz unseres nationalsozialistischen Glaubens — eines Glaubens, der Berge versetzen kann — die Mengen Getreide und Nahrungsmittel, die der Führer für Deutschland braucht!" Ein Unmöglich dürfe es für den nicht geben, der vor dem Urteil der Geschichte bestehen wolle. Rücksichtsloser Einsatz von oben und unten sei geboten, denn die Verpflichtung gegenüber den gefallenen deutschen Soldaten, den Opfern des deutschen Volkes und der europäischen Gemeinschaft sei riesengroß. Deshalb gehe es hier nicht allein nur um die große Politik, sondern auch um die persönliche Haltung jedes einzelnen Deutschen, der zugleich Repräsentant der Nation sei. Den großen politischen Aufgaben, die im Blickfeld der künftigen Entwicklung des Großdeutschen Reiches und des neuen Europas eine Lösung erheischten, müßten alle anderen Fragen der Wirtschaft und der Kultur untergeordnet werden. Die Ukraine werde als Kornkammer Europas darin ihren realen und unabdingbaren Platz finden. Die Arbeit in diesem Gebiet müsse ausschließlich unter diesem entscheidenden Gesichtspunkte erfolgen. Weiterhin betonte der Gauleiter, daß jede besondere Leistung durch ein Prämiensystem ihre verdiente Belohnung finden werde.

Der Gauleiter zeichnete zum Schluß die politische und strategische Lage Großdeutschlands und seiner Verbündeten auf. Er würdigte hierbei die einmalige Leistung der deutschen Wehrmacht und der verbündeten Armeen sowie die letzten großen Schlachtenerfolge im Osten, Westen, in Afrika und im Pazifik. Mit nochmaligem Dank und dem Hinweis, daß nur Arbeit und Opfer den Endsieg verbürgten, schloß der Reichskommissar seine eindrucksvolle Ansprache. Landesbauernführer Körner, der Leiter der Tagung, richtete Begrüßungs- und Dankesworte an den Gauleiter.

Das Eichenlaub für einen Jagdflieger

Berlin, 29. August

Der Führer hat Hauptmann Brändle, Gruppenkommandeur in einem Jagdgeschwader, das Eichenlaub zum Ritterkreuz des Eisernen Kreuzes verliehen und ihm folgendes Schreiben übermittelt: „In dankbarer Würdigung Ihres heldenhaften Einsatzes im Kampf für die Zukunft unseres Volkes verleihe ich Ihnen als 114. Soldaten der deutschen Wehrmacht das Eichenlaub zum Ritterkreuz des Eisernen Kreuzes." Hauptmann Brändle hat sich mit rund hundert Abschüssen in die Liste unserer erfolgreichsten Jagdflieger eingetragen.

36 englische Bomber als Verlust einer Nacht

Berlin, 29. August.

Wie von militärischer Seite mitgeteilt wird, haben an den militärisch wirkungslosen Störflügen britischer Bombenflugzeuge in der Nacht zum Sonnabend über Südwest- und Süddeutschland etwa 230 bis 250 britische Flugzeuge teilgenommen. Die Briten stießen wiederum auf eine außerordentlich wirkungsvolle Abwehr durch Flakartillerie und Nachtjäger. Die im OKW-Bericht genannte Zahl der Abschüsse hat sich von 32 auf 36 erhöht.

Erkenntnisse in Moskau

Ueber die Stimmung, die in der Moskauer Bevölkerung nach der Abreise Churchills herrscht, äußert sich der dortige Korrespondent der englischen Wochenzeitschrift „New Statesman and Nation" in ausgesprochen resignierter Weise, die in offenkundigem Widerspruch steht zu dem Triumphgeschrei, das die angloamerikanische Agitation über die „belebende Wirkung" anstimmte, die durch die „epochemachende Begegnung" zwischen Churchill und Stalin angeblich auf die Kriegführung der Sowjetunion wie der vereinigten Nationen überhaupt ausgelöst worden sein sollte. Churchill und seine Reisegesellschaft hätten Moskau verlassen, so stellt der Journalist fest, aber auch nicht die geringste Spur von ihrer Anwesenheit sei heute in der Stimmung der Sowjetbevölkerung noch anzutreffen. Diese sei tatsächlich um kein Haar zuversichtlicher, als vor den Verbrüderungsschwüren im Kreml, durch die hoch und heilig versichert wurde, daß man bis zum Tode an der Seite der Sowjetunion ausharren wolle. Alle diese Versprechungen und Stimmungsmache hätten die Sowjetbevölkerung gar nicht interessiert, denn diese sei allzusehr mit der militärischen Lage beschäftigt. Man vergegenwärtige sich in Moskau, so stellt der Korrespondent der englischen Zeitschrift fest, daß Deutschland fast alle europäischen wirtschaftlichen Hilfsquellen kontrolliere, während die Sowjetunion Tag für Tag mehr Rohstoffgebiete verliere und zudem von ihren Alliierten im Stich gelassen werde.

Bezeichnend für die Aufmerksamkeit, die man Churchill in Moskau widmete, sei beispielsweise auch die Tatsache gewesen, daß der „Rote Stern" es nicht für nötig befunden habe, der ersten Reise eines britischen Premierministers nach Moskau einen Leitartikel zu widmen. Daß die Moskauer Reise Churchills ein „epochemachendes Ereignis" gewesen sei, habe die Sowjetpresse nie anerkannt, übrigens auch die in Moskau lebenden Amerikaner nicht, in deren Kreisen unmittelbar nach Schluß der Konferenz unden entsprechenden Gefühlen Luft gemacht worden sei. Was das „Bankett" im Kreml betrifft, so sei die Atmosphäre dort, wie man erfahre, sehr „muffig" gewesen, und die äußerlich zur Schau getragene joviale Unterhaltung habe deutlich Zeichen innerer Hohlheit getragen. Offensichtlich habe Churchill in Moskau es eben mit Leuten zu tun gehabt, auf die seine Natur keinen großen Eindruck machte.

Der Korrespondent kommt dann nochmals auf die agitatorische Bedeutung zu sprechen, die das „berühmte" Londoner Kommuniqué anläßlich des Besuches Molotows zur Folge gehabt hatte und in dem der Sowjetunion klipp und klar eine bindende Zusage gegeben wurde, noch im Laufe dieses Jahres die zweite Front zu schaffen. Dieses Versprechen sei von der Sowjetbevölkerung sozusagen als bare Münze hingenommen worden. Wenn die Engländer jetzt damit begonnen hätten, diese Zusicherung wegzuargumentieren, so empfänden die Sowjets das als eine unwürdige Haarspalterei angesichts der fürchterlichen Leiden, die die Sowjetunion durchmachen müsse. Die Umstände seien noch umso erschwerender, als auf britischer Seite nicht der geringste Versuch gemacht worden sei, die Bedeutung dieses Versprechens ins richtige Licht zu rücken, als die Sowjetpresse über das englische Versprechen jubelte und der Bevölkerung sozusagen als eine Tatsache vor Augen führte.

Kurzum, wenn England eine wahre zweite Front im Jahre 1942 nicht zustande bringe, dann ginge das Molotow-Kommuniqué als eine der katastrophalsten Betrügereien in die Weltgeschichte ein. Für die Wirkung aller dieser Dinge auf die Sowjetbevölkerung sei, so führt der Korrespondent in seinem Bericht weiter aus, jedenfalls die Feststellung eines einfachen Soldaten der Sowjet-Armee von der Front kennzeichnend, der sagte: „Jede Nation Europas, die sich auf Englands Hilfe verlassen hat, ist bisher noch im Stich gelassen worden. In wenigen Wochen hat sie sogar zu bestehen aufgehört. Die Sowjetunion kämpft jetzt seit 14 Monaten allein gegen Deutschland, und England klagt immer noch, es sei mit seinen Vorbereitungen zum Kampfe leider noch nicht fertig!" id.

Die englische Niederlage am Himmel

Die Kamera des Kriegsberichters hat die Luftkämpfe am Himmel über Dieppe eingefangen, bei denen die Briten 127 Flugzeuge verloren haben. PK-Aufn.: Kriegsber. Eichen (PBZ)

Rückzugsstraßen der Sowjets

Waffen und Fahrzeuge aller Art bedecken die Rückzugsstraßen der Sowjets, deren Heeresberichte dieses Chaos als „planmäßige Räumung" bezeichnen. PK-Aufn.: Kriegsber. Wittmack (HH)

Die Lehre des 19. August

Zum deutschen Abschlußbericht über Dieppe

Mit einer verdächtigen Schnelligkeit haben die amtlichen britischen Stellen, der Rundfunk und die Zeitungen, das Thema des Invasionsversuchs bei Dieppe von ihrem Programm abgesetzt. Noch während die letzten — wie eine englische Zeitung schrieb — „rußgeschwärzten Soldaten" nach ihrer Rückkehr an Land gingen, versuchte man in London, die Aufmerksamkeit des Volkes auf andere Schauplätze und Entwicklungen des Krieges zu lenken. Wenige Tage nach dem Scheitern des Churchillschen Versuches, eine zweite Front zu errichten, war die Diskussion, die sonst aus Anlaß irgendeiner von England unternommenen Aktion wochenlang die Gemüter bewegte, verstummt. Seitdem stehen die Erörterungen im Zeichen der Frage, was England alles zu tun gedenkt, um die gefährdete Nahoststellung zu sichern. Ohne Zweifel sind gerade hier in diesem Raum die Sorgen unserer Gegner infolge der militärischen Entwicklung an der Kaukasusfront und der Ungewißheit über die Absichten Rommels außerordentlich gewachsen. Die plötzliche starke Hervorkehrung dieses Themas ist indessen besonders unter dem Gesichtspunkt interessant, daß die Engländer das größte Interesse daran hatten, die Ereignisse an der Kanalküste so rasch wie möglich vergessen zu machen, die zu einer katastrophalen Niederlage führten, deren Bedeutung sich keineswegs darin erschöpft, daß das Unternehmen von Dieppe eine schwere militärische Schlappe darstellt, sondern daß es auch schwerwiegende psychologische Folgen für die Einschätzung britischer Aktionsmöglichkeiten überhaupt hat. Die Tatsache allein, daß das englische Informationsministerium wenige Tage nach der Aktion nichts mehr zu sagen hatte, war ein klarer Beweis für das Ausmaß der Enttäuschung, die der britischen Führung durch das Fehlschlagen des Unternehmens bereitet wurde. Denn hätten die Engländer auch nur einen kleinen Teilerfolg errungen, so hätten sie es sich nicht entgehen lassen, noch wochenlang von diesem Erfolg zu zehren und ihn agitatorisch auszunützen. So aber blieb nur der Weg, das Unternehmen zu bagatellisieren, indem man aus der geplanten Invasion einen Erkundungsvorstoß mit begrenzter Zielsetzung machte, der, wie es echt englisch hieß, „ermutigende Ergebnisse" gezeitigt habe, dessen Ziel aber ja gar nicht die Landung gewesen sei.

Die Berichte, die von englischer Seite aus, noch während die Operationen im Gange waren, herausgegeben wurden — in einem Zeitpunkt also, in dem man in London noch glaubte, auf einen Erfolg rechnen zu können —, waren bereits ein deutlicher Beweis dafür, welche großen Absichten man verfolgte und mit welchem für die weitere Kriegführung geradezu entscheidenden Erfolg man rechnete. Aus der ganzen Anlage des Unternehmens, dem Aufmarsch starker Flotteneinheiten, zahlreicher Transporter und starker Luftwaffenverbände war zu schließen, daß der Zweck des Unternehmens in nichts mehr und nichts weniger bestand als darin, nun endlich die seit Monaten geforderte zweite Front zu errichten, die einmal die Sowjets entlasten und zum anderen der Welt beweisen sollte, daß England und Amerika zu entscheidenden Aktionen fähig seien. Der Vorsitzende des amerikanischen Senatsausschusses für militärische Angelegenheiten hat dies, als das Unternehmen bereits gescheitert war, ausdrücklich bestätigt, indem er darauf hinwies, es sei zu hoffen, daß der gemeinsame Angriff sich zur zweiten Front entwickeln und ausdehnen könne. Von deutscher Seite wurden schon damals die Hintergründe des Churchillschen Abenteuers gekennzeichnet. Der englische Premierminister handelte unter dem Druck Moskaus, das am 22. Juni ein befristetes Ultimatum auf die Errichtung der zweiten Front gestellt hatte. Bei seinem Besuch im Kreml ist es Churchill dann nicht gelungen, den bolschewistischen Bundesgenossen davon zu überzeugen, daß eine Invasion ein zu großes Risiko in sich schließe. Wir wissen zwar nicht, welcher Art die Drohungen Stalins für den Fall, daß Churchill der sowjetischen Forderung nicht nachkommen sollte, waren. Sicher aber ist, daß Churchill lieber bereit war, das Risiko einzugehen, als

Entered as second-class matter April 15, 1931, at the post office at New Haven, Connecticut, under the act of March 3, 1879

ILLUSTRATED CURRENT NEWS

Published Monday, Wednesday and Friday by Illustrated Current News, Inc., New Haven, Conn. Subscription Annually, $20.80

Sept. 11, 1942—No. 4529

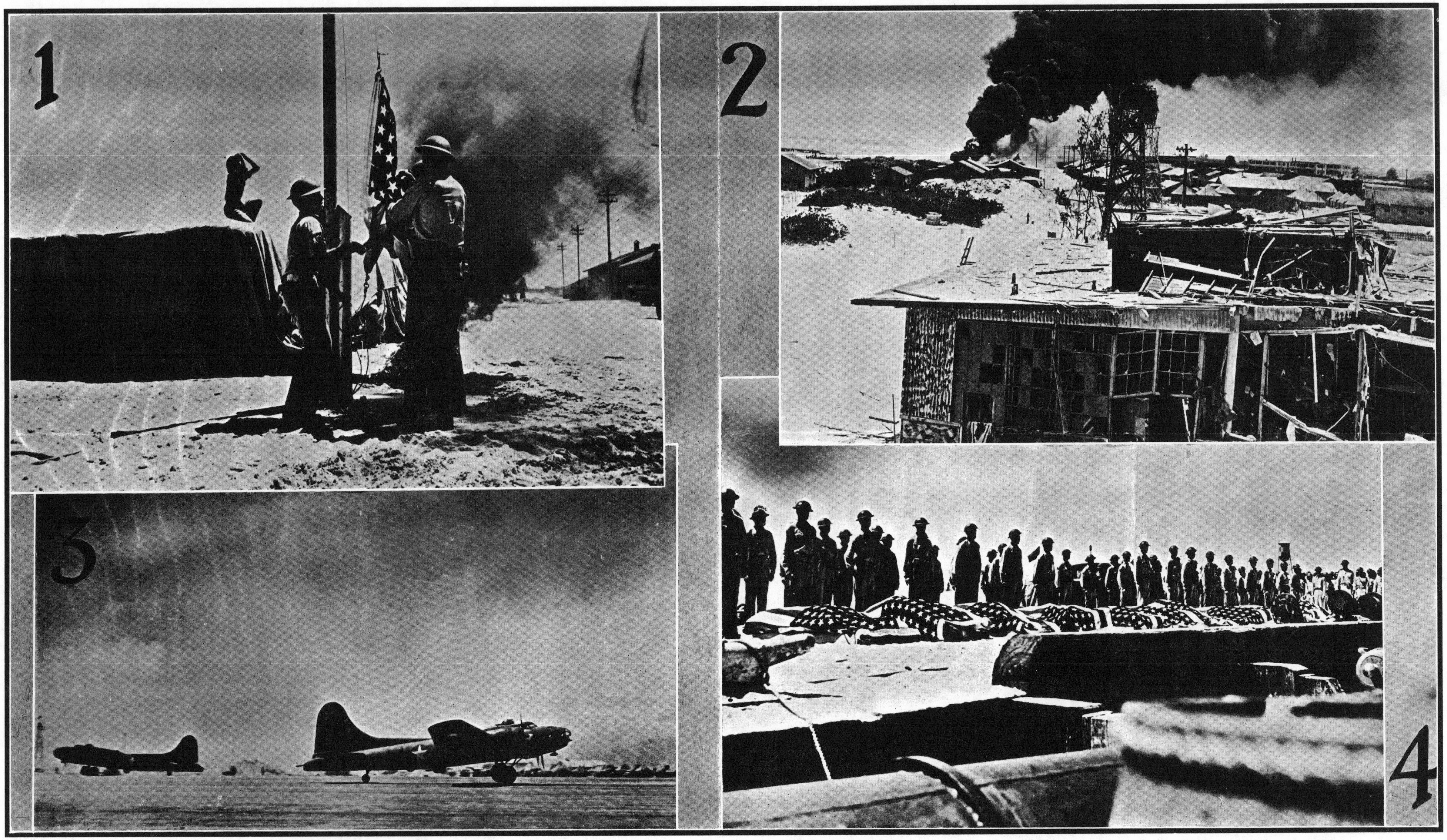

THE BATTLE OF MIDWAY

Midway Island, U. S. — Scenes of battle in which Japanese raiders were beaten off by U. S. forces when they attempted invasion of U. S. Pacific base. (1) Flag raised under fire. (2) Damage done by attackers before they were forced to give up. (3) U. S. Flying Fortresses headed for battle. (4) Services for those who were killed in battle.

THE JOURNAL AND PUBLIC IS INDEPENDENT IN POLITICS, RELIGION AND BUSINESS. A PAPER FOR THE PEOPLE WHO THINK AND ACT ACCORDINGLY. NOW IS THE TIME TO SUBSCRIBE

CLINTON DAILY JOURNAL AND PUBLIC

THIRTY-FIFTH YEAR | CLINTON, ILLINOIS, FRIDAY, SEPTEMBER 18, 1942 | No. 171

BATTLE RAGING IN STREETS OF STALINGRAD

AMERICAN FORCES SLOW JAPANESE IN SOLOMONS; BLAST ENEMY IN ALEUTIANS

Washington, Sept. 17—(UP)—American forces have delivered new setbacks to the Japanese at both ends of the far-flung Pacific battle line, slowing the enemy drive to recapture the Solomon Islands and inflicting shattering blows on ships, planes, shore facilities and men in the Aleutian Islands.

Eight enemy ships were blasted by American planes at Kiska Island in the Aleutians, two of them being sunk.

From Guadalcanal came the cheering news that Navy and Marine Corps dive bombers have damaged two Japanese cruisers while Marine land forces not only are holding their positions on that main American base in the Solomons but have diminished the initial ferocity of the Japanese counter-attacks which started last Saturday.

Those reports on developments in the Pacific war theater were issued last night in two naval communiques.

Jap Base Hit Hard

The communique on two attacks on the enemy in the Aleutians was the first mention of that fog-shrouded area since August 22. But it told of a large-scale attack by fighter-escorted American Army heavy bombers to Kiska which must have left much of that main enemy base in the island chain off Alaska destroyed.

In addition to the enemy ships sunk and damaged, 500 troops were killed or wounded, six planes were destroyed and fire was set to storehouses and supply dumps ashore.

Not a single American plane was lost during the attack as a result of enemy action, the Navy reported. Admiral Chester W. Nimitz reported in Pearl Harbor, however, that two pilots of P-38 fighters were killed when their planes collided.

Also significant was the apparent feebleness of the Japanese defenses at Kiska. The Navy made no mention of enemy resistance to the "strafing attack" on September 4. Of the low altitude bombing and strafing attack on September 14 during which most of the damage was inflicted, the Navy said this:

"The enemy attempted to repel this attack with planes and weak anti-aircraft resistance."

Senator To Press For Draft Of Men 18 And 19 Years Old

Washington, Sept. 17—(UP)—Despite flat opposition by the Senate military affairs committee, Senator Chan Gurney, R., S. D., said today he would press for immediate action on his bill to draft 18 and 19-year-old men.

The committee yesterday refused to hold hearings on the bill until the war department reports. Democratic Senators said privately that it would not be made until the administration gives the department the green light.

"Hitler and the Japs aren't waiting for the elections," Gurney commented.

"Men experienced in the arts of war say that young men make the best and most effective fighting men, and that we need 18 and 19-year-old fighters. For the salvation of the country, let the young men fight."

Air Raid Wardens to Meet—Ralph Moreland has called a meeting to organize assistant wardens in his district, at the city hall Friday night at 7:30 o'clock. They will also receive instructions on the blackout which is soon to be held here.

FOOD SALE

By C. P. church of Dewitt at Rundle's Market, Saturday. Chickens, eggs, and bakery goods.

Mrs. Ruth Denison, Weldon, shopped here yesterday.

Pensions For State Employees Discussed

Springfield, Ill., Sept. 17—(UP)—The state budgetary commission today began consideration of a plea for pensions for approximately 28,000 state workers.

The proposal was urged at a commission meeting yesterday by representatives of the Employes' Retirement Association of Illinois.

The plan would cost the state $1,000,000 a year, the commission said. Before a decision on the matter, the group will consult with the Civic Federation and the Taxpayers' Federation of Illinois to learn their views on state employes' pensions.

Commission members pointed out that even without such additions to the budget, the state faces a serious problem in maintaining revenues to defray present expenses. Possibility that the sales tax may be removed from food by a constitutional amendment this November is a further threat to revenues, they added.

Farm Machinery Being Rationed

Washington, Sept. 17—(UP)—The agriculture department today began rationing new farm machinery and equipment in order to stretch limited supplies to meet critical needs and assure the "greatest possible contribution toward meeting the goals of our food-for-freedom program."

The rationing program was started on a temporary plan ordered by Secretary of Agriculture Claude R. Wickard and covering sales of machinery and equipment during the remainder of 1942. A permanent plan for 1943 will be announced when details have been worked out.

The power to ration farm supplies was delegated to Wickard by the office of price administration, which previously had been authorized by the war production board to ration farm machinery or turn the power over to someone else.

NAZIS BATTER INTO OUTSKIRTS OF STALINGRAD

Red Army To Fight To Last Defender At Volga City

(By M. S. Handler)
(United Press Staff Correspondent)

Moscow, Sept. 17—(UP)—A powerful Nazi army, described as "fighting like devils," battered into the northwest outskirts of Stalingrad today, but the Red army made plain its intention to fight house by house, street by street and pillbox by pillbox to the last defender before relinquishing the Volga river city.

The assault on the northwest outskirts of Stalingrad carried the Nazis to within 9 to 12 miles of the center of the city. It was reported that out of a total German assault army of possibly 1,000,000 men some 450,000 troops were hammering at the narrow northwest front.

Despite the slow Nazi advance into Stalingrad, the Red army organ, Red Star, published an illuminating dispatch on "the internal defense of invested cities" which made plain its intention to fight for Stalingrad to the last.

The dispatch said that "even a completely destroyed city can and must fight to the last."

"Destruction of a city by aerial bombardment," it said, "paralyzes its peacetime existence but does not impair its fighting ability.

"A defense can be organized amidst the ruins which no force can conquer. All the ruined houses must be transformed into machinegun nests.

"The experience of Tula, Sevastopol and Leningrad provides that if the defense of inhabited points is properly organized they can be held as long as the defenders want to hold—even when completely surrounded.

"We must fight for each city and town to the last. We must die rather than surrender a single house or pillbox."

Armistice Move In Madagascar Has Broken Down

Vichy, Sept. 17—(UP)—Madagascar will be defended to the utmost against British military invasion, the French government said today in a communique which said that armistice negotiations had broken down.

"Governor General Armand Annet reports from Madagascar that armistice negotiations have broken down and fighting continues," the announcement said. "Madagascar will be defended to the final limit."

The ministry claimed that the British covered only 100 miles during the first week's operations, and that fighting was taking place today 120 miles from Tananarive, the capital.

Fires Set At Tobruk Described By Yank

London, Sept. 17—(UP)—The Libyan port of Tobruk looked like a "monster orchid" from fires started by British forces in Sunday night's sea-borne raid, an American flier was quoted by the air ministry today.

The flier, an unidentified major from Lafayette, Ind., said he was with the American squadron which bombed Benghazi Sunday night.

"Coming back, when we were about 10 miles short of Tobruk, we could see there was plenty going on there," the air ministry quoted him. "As we got nearer I saw a really enormous red fire on the north side of the harbor.

"It looked for all the world like a monster orchid, glowing and pulsating. Coils of oil smoke were squirming up from it. It must have been a big naval fuel tank.

"We passed about 40 miles off Tobruk. The ack-ack and searchlights were in pretty poor shape by then—the former was erratic and the lights were twittering all over the place. We got a grand view 50 miles after we passed the harbor. A bit of the show was still going on."

F. D. R. ORDER ON FARM PRICES INTERPRETED

Congressional Leaders Find President Doesn't Want New Formula

Washington, Sept. 17—(UP)—President Roosevelt told Congressional leaders today that he does not want a new farm price parity formula written into pending anti-inflation legislation, as some members of the Congressional farm bloc had interpreted the wishes expressed in his Labor Day message on the cost of living.

After a full-dress conference among the President and his Congressional and government leaders, Senate Majority Leader Alben W. Barkley, Ky., said the President had cleared up a "perfectly honest misunderstanding" on a phrase of his message which led to introduction in the House of legislation that would have established a new and higher parity base.

Barkley said the misunderstanding came from a line in Mr. Roosevelt's message which said that calculation of parity should include the cost of production, including "the cost of labor."

A "great many people," Barkley said, thought the President meant the "cost of farm labor," but that actually the chief executive "meant the cost of labor going into the things the farmer buys—which is already in the parity formula."

Barkley said the President's message "tended to suggest that in addition to the present parity formula, the cost of farm labor should be added."

The misunderstanding, he said, arose in "perfectly good faith."

Laval Strikes Back At Catholic Church

On the French Frontier, Sept. 17—(UP)— French Premier Pierre Laval has struck back at the Catholic church for opposing Jewish persecution in France by interning one of its leaders and warning to the clergy to "handle religion—I'll handle the government," it was disclosed today.

It was learned that Laval had ordered Father Chaillet, of the staff of Cardinal Gerlier, Archbishop of Lyons, interned in "fixed residence" at Privas in the Department of Ardeche in southern France. Father Chaillet is president of the "Christian Amity" group which preaches tolerance for depressed groups in Europe.

Cardinal Gerlier has been active in letters of protest to Marshal Philippe Petain over the round-up and deportation of Jews in France.

AIR WARDENS NOTICE

Air raid wardens and block captains of the southeast sector, under the direction of Ralph Moreland, are asked to meet tonight in the City hall at 7:30 o'clock. Wardens and captains of other sectors, who have missed their meetings, should attend tonight.

JAP BATTLESHIP FLOTILLA SENT TO SOLOMONS

Nipponese May Decide To Risk Major Naval Battle With U. S.

Chungking, Sept. 17—Usually reliable sources received reports today that Japan has dispatched a battleship flotilla to the Solomons and may decide to risk a major naval battle with United States forces in the south Pacific.

These unconfirmed reports said four of Japan's six available dreadnaughts have been assigned to the battle in the south Pacific where the Japanese are attempting to recapture American positions in the Solomons.

Authentic reports that Emperor Hirohito conferred with Premier Hideki Tojo's war cabinet on highly important issues caused reliable Chinese quarters to suggest again today that a Japanese assault on Siberia was impending.

Many military men here contended, however, that Japan will not attack Siberia until "favorable developments" in the Solomons are guaranteed.

It was reported here that, of Japan's estimated 11 original battleships, one was sunk, one seriously damaged, and three damaged at the battle of Midway and still undergoing repairs in drydock.

Chinese sources expressed the opinion that Japan may risk a naval showdown for two reasons:

1. Allied retention of the Solomons and power in Australia probably will mean future landings in New Britain, making Japanese bases at Salamaua, Lae and Buna untenable and providing bases for attacks on Japanese supply lines. Allied air domination in the area would help protect shorter pushes toward the Philippines.

2. Japanese may believe that large portions of the United States forces are not operating now in the Pacific, thereby giving the Japanese navy a superiority not obtainable later.

Rural Travel Has Dropped Considerably

Springfield, Ill., Sept. 17—(UP)—The state highway research bureau has reported a 22 per cent drop in Illinois' rural primary highway traffic for August as compared with the same month in 1941.

August normally is the peak traffic month, the bureau said, but volume this year was only 98.5 per cent of that during an average 1941 month.

NOTICE

My office will be closed until September 21.

DR. V. E. WILLIS

RED ARMY TO FIGHT FOR EVERY FOOT OF GROUND IN CITY; URGE SECOND FRONT

Axis Shipping Off Benghazi Bombed

Cairo, Sept. 17—(UP)—Allied heavy bombers Wednesday carried out a daylight attack on Axis shipping off Benghazi, a joint communique announced today.

"Hits were claimed on two vessels, one of which was set on fire," the communique said.

Royal Air Force heavy and medium bombers, striking at German Field Marshal Erwin Rommel's supply lines, have raided the strategic Axis-held ports at Tobruk and Crete again, it was disclosed.

The British planes, following up Sunday night's commando-like raid on Tobruk, raided there again Monday, it was announced. They started five fires in the fuel installations northwest of the city and another along Tobruk's south shore. Further attacks were made against the harbor jetties.

Urge Switch To Coal Burners In Oil-Rationed States

Washington, Sept. 17—(UP)—Millions of persons in oil-rationed states face the prospect of "uncomfortably cold homes this winter" unless they immediately convert their oil-burning furnaces to coal burners and insulate their homes to cut down on fuel consumption.

Those unable to convert their oil burners will have to keep the temperatures of their homes down to 65 degrees.

That warning was issued last night by Price Administrator Leon Henderson. Areas affected are the 30 eastern and midwestern states where 96,890,000 persons — almost three-fourths of the nation's population—live and in which fuel oil will be strictly rationed to offset a transportation shortage.

Brother Dies—Perry C. Sandidge, 53, of Bloomington, brother of Mrs. Ed Hale of Farmer City, died in St. Joseph's hospital, Bloomington, Tuesday night after a five weeks illness.

Willkie Arrives In Kuibyshev With American Views

(By Harrison Salisbury)
(United Press Staff Correspondent)

The battle for Stalingrad raged in the streets of the Volga city Thursday with the Red army making plain its determination to fight for every foot of ground so long as any defender remains alive.

The great struggle had repercussions from London to Chungking with increasing Soviet pressure for second front aid and Chinese speculation that Japan may seize the opportunity to attack Siberia.

There was no indication that the urgent and forceful Soviet declarations of the necessity of Allied intervention in western Europe to relax pressure in the east had changed the secret war plans of Britain and the United States.

Arrival of Wendell L. Willkie in Kuibyshev brought the possibility that the Soviet position might be restated to him. Willkie is in a position to present to the Russians the American views on the critical issue.

Nazis Inside Suburbs

The most dangerous Nazi penetration of Stalingrad appeared to be in the northwestern quarter of the city where Moscow conceded the Nazis were inside the city's outskirts. A force estimated at 450,000 Germans and Rumanians were blasting forward but apparently making only slow progress.

A Red Star dispatch made plain the Soviet high command's intention to defend every street and building of Stalingrad, even if the city should be isolated. Red Star advanced the military opinion that successful defense of a city such as Stalingrad could be carried out indefinitely so long as the defenders' determination holds out.

The British occupation of Madagascar reached its final phase with an armistice expected to be negotiated shortly by Vichy French representatives.

Myron Taylor, President Roosevelt's special representative to the Vatican, passed through Madrid en route back to his post, setting off speculation in Axis circles as to the possibility of American diplomatic maneuvers.

The Royal Air Force aimed another heavy blow at Germany's war industries, attacking the Ruhr area in strength that apparently was not far short of the 1,000 plane mark.

Mr. and Mrs. Clarence Mayall and children have returned to their home in Chicago after a visit with his parents, Mr. and Mrs. Homer Mayall, at Maroa, and his brother, Ralph, who is stationed at Fort Riley, Kansas.

Mrs. Mace Welch, Dewitt, was a Clinton shopper yesterday.

ALLIED OFFENSIVE BLOW FROM WEST URGED QUICKLY BY SOVIET GOVERNMENT

London, Sept. 17—(UP)—The epochal battle of Stalingrad has sharply revived the question of the timing and direction of the coming Allied offensive blow from the west and has brought out as sharply Soviet fears that delay will not only vastly prolong the war but change the course of history.

The net result of the recent weeks of Allied discussions and Prime Minister Winston Churchill's visit to Moscow may now be summed up clearly:

Premier Josef Stalin wants an iron-clad agreement to launch an Anglo-American offensive in Europe on the greatest possible scale immediately, but the British and Americans—without rejecting a 1942 invasion—failed to reach an agreement in line with the Russian desire or an adequate substitute for it.

Reds Think Now Is the Time

This does not prevent an Allied offensive on France tomorrow morning and it also means there will be no weakening of co-operation in supplying war materials to Moscow. But it leaves no doubt of the Soviet view that the time has come for the Allies to defy any difficulties and face the longest struggle to come to their aid.

It has been pointed out that the Russians and the British and Americans have lived in an atmosphere of mutual suspicion since the Bolshevik revolution. But the present struggle has gone far to eliminate the Russian distrust as Anglo-American war supplies arrived to bolster the Red army, which aroused Allied admiration and evoked praise from the former severe critics of the Soviet Union—such as Churchill.

Churchill's visit to Moscow was regarded as taking this a step further. Personal relationships among London, Washington, and Moscow are most important.

However, from the Russian viewpoint, the question arises whether the Soviet people's view has been affected as a result of the delayed second front.

It has been emphasized that the second front has nothing to do with the Russians' unweakening determination to fight on to victory, but it might outweigh and erase the progress already made toward mutual trust on the global battle fields and collaboration in the post-war world.

JAPS EXERT HEAVY PRESSURE ON ALLIED TROOPS 32 MILES NORTH OF PORT MORESBY

(By Don Caswell)
(United Press Staff Correspondent)

Gen. MacArthur's Headquarters, Australia, Sept. 17—(UP)—Japanese forces driving through the towering Owen Stanley mountains of New Guinea are exerting heavy pressure on Allied troops only 32 air miles north of Port Moresby, Gen. Douglas MacArthur announced today.

Serious fighting was in progress on the south slope of the 7,000-foot range, MacArthur said in a communique.

A headquarters spokesman said the general combat zone was north of the village of Ioribaiwa, and hostilities involved parts of the main strength of both the Allied and enemy forces.

"The skirmishing now involves more than patrols," he said. "The fighting is see-sawing back and forth and the patrols of both sides have been reinforced."

The Japanese were using light mountain artillery and relying on infiltration tactics similar to those they have employed throughout the entire jungle campaign in New Guinea.

Air Force in Support

Allied air forces were supporting the ground troops in attacks on the Japanese lines and communications in the Stanley range and in wide sweeps north and east of New Guinea.

MacArthur sent an armed reconnaissance air unit over the mountains again to the Japanese main base at Buna, on New Guinea's north shore, where enemy barges on the beach were bombed. Results were not observed.

Allied air units raided dispersal areas in a night attack at Rabaul, on the northeastern tip of New Britain, but pilots were not certain of the results.

Medium bombers, flying 600 miles northeast of Port Moresby, started fires in the dispersal areas of the island of Buka, northernmost of the Solomons adjacent to Bougainville Island.

No Allied planes were lost in the widespread activity, MacArthur reported.

Observers believed that although the Buna raid was another direct attack on the main source of supplies for the enemy drive on Moresby, the raids on Rabaul and Buka might have been associated with the hostilities in the Solomon Islands, where the Japanese had been attempting to land fresh troops.

100 YEARS OF SERVICE TO MEIGS COUNTY

The Tribune-Telegraph

YOUR DUTY— BUY WAR BONDS AND STAMPS

VOL. II—NO. 189 | POMEROY, OHIO, THURSDAY, SEPTEMBER 24, 1942 | Editorial Office—Phone 236

MEIGS COUNTIANS LOOK FOR VITAL "SCRAP"

Middleport Council Holds Meeting; DeWees Remains as Chief of Police

Middleport—It's Chief of Police Fred DeWees again, after an opinion from Solicitor Edgar Ervin that since the officer's resignation following the adjournment of Middleport Council, Monday, Sept. 14, had been placed in the hands of Mayor C. O. Fisher, and before the next meeting of council, which was last night, the withdrawal of the resignation was requested by DeWees, the resignation and withdrawal did not exist as far as council was concerned.

In the meantime, Mayor Fisher, declaring "an emergency", appointed Jack Bartrum as Acting Chief of Police, which position he has held for the past 10 days, and it was the concensus of opinion that Bartrum would occupy the position. A uniform was ordered, but since Solicitor Ervin's opinion, and the rejection of council for a third officer DeWees has the job and Bartrum the uniform.

After an appearance of Co-ordinator of Civilian Defense Charles McMaster and committee at the council meeting last night, a resolution stating that $600 was needed for adequate civilian defense expenses was passed. The resolution, which will be sent to the State Office of Civilian Defense, also to the County Budget Committee stated that because of the strategic importance of Middleport, where the junction of two railroads occur, where a manufacturing unit in defense orders is located, it's proximity to the Pomeroy-Mason bridge, also the W. V. O. W., at Pt. Pleasant, considerably more than the $100 allotment of the original $1415 apportioned to the county, should be given to the village. The council and officials pledged their support of the local defense council, and to the Co-ordinator, Charles McMaster, who declared that no further steps could be taken until adequate financial support was forthcoming.

McDaniel Funeral Services Held

Middleport—Funeral services for George McDaniel, age 68, were held this (Thursday) afternoon at the Methodist church in Heights, W. Va. Mr. McDaniel, ill only a short time died from heart attack early Tuesday morning. He is survived by his wife, Mrs. Mary McDaniel, a daughter, Mrs. Detner Roush, Pomeroy, and a son Everett McDaniel N. Second Ave. Sisters and a brother, including Mrs. H. S. Mourning, and seven grandchildren, also survive. Interment was made at Lone Oak Cemetery.

LIBRARY BOARD MEETS

The Pomeroy Library Board met recently. The following report for August was pesented: circulation 2058; books added 13;; new members registered 17; attendance 958.

The matter of a librarian to replace Miss Virginia Ramsey was discussed.

The book committee will meet on Friday of this week to order new books for the library.

New books that have been added recently are: Until the day break by Bromfield; Drivin' woman by Chevalier; The just and unjust by Cozzens; The amazing story of repeal by Dobyns; Du Pont, one hunyears by Dutton; Castle on the hill by Goudge; Staff nurse by Hancock; The Gay sisters by Longstreet; The uninvited by Macarde; Cross Creek by Rawlings; Surgeon in charge by Seifert.

Middleport P. T. A. Extends Greetings To 42-43 Members

Middleport—Mrs. Karl Owen, new president of the Parent-Teacher Association extended greetings to parents and teachers attending the first meeting of the calendar year, held Monday night in the high school auditorium. She also conducted the business meeting.

The Rev. James Redmon, pastor of the Church of Christ, was the speaker of the evening. He was introduced by program chairman, Mrs. Pearl Reynolds The Rev. Mr. Redmon had as his subject, "Training Up the Child".

The meeting was opened with a prayer by the Rev. H. A Rothrock, with group singing following, under the leadership of Miss Lois Cecil, public school music teacher Reports of the secretary, treasurer were heard, alss the report of the successful pre-school roundup, given by the chairman, Mrs. M. L. French. New teachers were introduced by Supt. L. W. McComas. The new teachers are Miss Patience Brandle, Miss Virginia Hamm and M. H. Fowler, all members of the high school faculty. It was decided that the president or an alternate be sent to the state congress, which will be held in Akron. It was also voted to award the room having the largest attendance each month with one dollar The award for this month went to the kindergarten.

Mrs. Owen announced these standing committees: Program, Mrs. Pearl Reynolds, Miss Lois Cecil, Gordon Harris; Health, Mrs. Harold Chase, Mrs. Harley Devol, Mrs. L. E. Triplett, Mrs. Alfred Roush, Mrs. Kenneth Byers; Membership, Mrs. Edgar Allensworth, Mrs. Kauff, Mrs. Nora Mills, Mrs. Willis Anthony Mrs. George Childs, Mrs. Harold Chase, Mrs. Maggie Pickens, Mrs. William Britton, Mrs. James Murray, Mrs. Dale Mourning, Mrs. John Dillard, Mrs. Max Roller, Mrs. Paul Smart, Mrs Glen Lambert, Mrs. Lewis Sauer, Mrs. Home Rice, Mrs. Charles McElhinney, Mrs. H. A. Rothrock Mrs. Bruce Lloyd Mrs. Don Davis Mrs. William Bradford Mrs. Homer Glaze. Magazine chairman is Mrs. William Britton; publicity chairman Mrs. George Schaaf; chairman of room mothers Mrs. Sidney Russell; safety chairman Mrs. Leo Kennedy; hospitality committee, Mrs. Cedric Clark, Miss Patience Brandle, Miss Virginia Hamm, Mrs. C. O. Fisher and Mrs O. P. Klein. County Council reresentatives, Mrs. Lewis Sauer, Mrs. L. D. Diles, Mrs. John Dillard, alternates, Mrs. William Bradford, Mrs. Noah Haskins.

Mrs. O. L. Roush led the business discussion of the Band Booster meeting, which was held immediately following the P. T. A. meeting. Following the routine reports, Gordon Harris, instrumental instructor and bandmaster gave an account of the expenditures of the summer which included the purchase of 15 leather music books, instruction books for the Junior Band, drum heads and reeds for use as needed through the season, a baton and new trousers for the drum major, and a down payment on five complete band uniforms.

Projects for making money were discussed, and the first date—Thursday, Oct. 13th was set for a community dinner to be served in the high school, proceeds to go to the band. Mrs. Ed Tewksbary, Mrs. M. L. French, Mrs. Cedric Clark were named on the committee Mrs. C. H. Wise, Jr., Mrs. D. A. Miller and Mrs George Childs were assigned on the ticket committee It was decided to have a Band Tag Day and Mrs. Paul Smart was appointed chairman of the Tag Day committee. Volunteer workers who will make the "tags", have been asked to meet at Mrs. Smart's home, Thursday afternoon, October 1.

Soldier Ends Life With Rifle At Langsville

Max Gorby, age 29, a soldier on furlough from Camp Funston, Kas., ended his life Monday evening near his home at Langsville with a small calibre rifle which he told his moter he was taking from their home to hunt squirrels. The body was found Tuesday morning by Dan C. Gorby after a search had been started by members of the family.

Gorby had been stationed at the Kansas camp with the Ninth Division for some time and was engaged in bridge work, according to members of his family, who could give no reason for his suicide. He was unmarried.

Surviving are his mother, Mrs. Ellsworth Gorby, at whose home he had been visiting for several days, a brother Roy at home, a brother Wade who is with the Army in England, and two sisters, Mrs. Herbert Huber, of Doanville, Ill., and Mrs. Herbert Nelson, of Union Furnace. Funeral arrangements are being completed today.

Mrs. Weiss, 67, Dies at Clinic

Mrs. Lorena Weiss, 67, of Mason, died in the Mason Clinic Monday morning at 6:00 o'clock. She had been ill quite a long time and had just been removed from her home to the clinic Saturday night.

John Weiss, her husband, preceded her in death only two months ago.

Survivors are two daughters, Lorena and Hilda Weiss at home.

Funeral services were held at the Methodist Church Wednesday afternoon at 2:00 o'clock with Rev. W. L. Gearhart officiating. Interment took place in the Adamsville cemetery by Foglesong Funeral Home.

Meigs Countians Repair Property

A total of 19 families in Meigs County, Ohio, made property repairs or started on the road to home ownership under the National Housing Act in the year 1941, it was reported here today by A. L. Guckert, Federal Housing Administration Distict Director for the Cental District of Ohio.

Included in this total were 18 Property Improvement Loans insured under Title I amounting to $7,346 and 1 small home mortgage accepted for insurance by FHA amounting to $4,000.

Despite certain necessary restrictions in the supply of materials necessary for home improvement, authorities have no intention of hindering the normal upkeep of America's eighty billion dollar investment in property.

FHA's Property Improvement program was recently further libealized by Congessional action in an effort to revive additional living quarters for war workers thru conversion of existing structures. Under the changes, several rooms suitable for rooming or housekeeping privileges may be remodeled. An attic or second story may be remodeled into an apartment. A structure not now a dwelling may be remodeled into a one or multi-family house.

Loans up to $2,500 are available from qualified lending institutions under the FHA plan for necessary maintenance and repair work on homes. These loans are not limited to war production areas. Loans above $2,500 and up to $5,000 are available from the same sources for the conversion of existing structures into living quarters for war workers in designated war poduction aeas.

Salvage Committee is Appointed For Meigs Scrap Metal Drive

Ben F. Turner, Pomeroy, was named chairman of the Meigs County scrap metal drive, in Monday night's launch for salvaging scrap. Mr. Turner, a World War veteran, has taken active parts in vaious activities and is a leader in the Meigs Chapter Disabled American Veterans.

The meeting was opened by George Carson, county chairman, who forcifully called attention to the urgent need of scrap metal in the war effort. Mr. Carson introduced Harold Hilligas, co-chairman for the county; Ben Turner, Pomeroy chairman; J. H. Grate, Middleport chairman; Willis McMurray, industrial committee chairman, and Frank Ferneau, assistant executive secretary for the salvage drive in Ohio.

Mr. Ferneau, principal speaker, stated that 80 per cent of the scrap metal is found on farms and 20 per cent in villages and towns. He stressed the importance of saving kitchen fats, due to the fact that the United States has no source of supply from imports and the supply is nearing exhaustion. Fats supply glycerin, 10 per cent of which is used in medicine and the remainedr in powder for explosives. He offered as a though for every participant in the drive: "Brave men shall not die because I have failed"

Harold Hilligas, co-chairman, also told of details of the plan for the scrap drive. First plans were made at a meeting on Sept. 8 attended by Hilligas, Herbert Shields, C. E. Blakeslee and Vaughan Crites. At the Monday night meeting the township and village chairmen will be announced as soon as all have been contacted and have accepted the posts.

It is planned that all farm people shall be contacted by Oct. Each farm family will be given a form to fill out and return to the solicitor. Persons supplying scrap metal will be paid for the metal, receiving a receipt on delivery. The receipt will be redeemed by check through the township trustees.

Oct. 5 to 11 will be the fin week of the drive, with the period from Oct. 12 to 15 set aside for a clean-up.

"LET'S GO, YOUNG AMERICA!"
SAVE, SERVE, CONSERVE....
WAR STAMPS
RAY BAILEY
SCHOOLS AT WAR PROGRAM

Contract Ended With Marietta Navy Yards

Stressing the fact that the Navy Department's decision was "not influenced by any feeling that the Marietta Company could not build the ships" and that "we know they can build ships and good one," Capt. N. L. Rawlings, of the Bureau of Ships, Washington, D. C., announced definitely Monday afternoon that the Navy Department had terminated and would eventually cancel contracts with the Marietta Manufacturing Co., for the construction of facilities to build ships and for the construction of the ships themselves.

Repeating what had been published last week about the sudden shut-down of the 80 per cent-completed shipyards, Captain Rawlings said that the move was necessitated by "strategic considerations" and "minor re-adjustments of the ship-building program" be cause "a number of ships are no longer required" and "a reduction to that extent has been authorized."

6 Other Shipyards

The particular type of ship planned for the new Point Pleasant shipyards was also being constructed at six other shipyards, Captain Rawlings said The country has more capacity to build ships than it has materials with which to build them, he went on, and primarily for the purpose of determining what activities must be reduced that yards were surveyed to ascertain which should be stopped.

The Department was influenced by the status of the shipyards as far as facilities were concerned by:

First, ship construction underway; second, labor now employed; third, labor eventually to be employed; fourth, the effects on any other work undertaken by the Department.

"The Department, taking these things into consideration, determined that the Marietta contracts should be canceled in their entirety," the Captain asserted.

Proposed To Lesser Extent

"The Marietta would have cost more than any other especially in critical materials," he went on, "and by canceling the Department saved more money than by canceling any of the others. The work on the ships themselves at the Marietta ad progressed to a lesser extent than in any other shipyard, with one exception, and in that one exception the prospects were considerably in excess of the Marietta overa period of time.

"The Navy Department doesn't like to do this," the officer told two reporters in a conference in Lieut. Commander O. S. Montesi's office at the new shipyard, "because it disturbs its program as well as the program in the community and is troublesome to labor as well as to management, but when the need for ships disappears, such a situation must be accepted. The Marietta works for the War Department, too, of course, and that Department made representations to us because of the double program and asked for relief. The cancellation will be advantageous to the War Department.....

"In arriving at this decision, the Navy Department was not influenced by any feeling that the Marietta Company could not build ships, for we know that they can build ships and good ones. There is no reason to believe that we made any mistakes in contracting with the Marietta insofar as its ability to build ships is concerned.

"As to a determnation of what disposition will be made of the buildings nearly completed here," Captain Rawlings stated, "if the Navy Department finds that it can make no use of them at all for storage purposes, they will be transferred to some other government agency, and they can be completed elatively easily and inexpensively"

In answer to a question, the Captain repeated that the transfer would be made, if deemed advisable to some "other government agency."

The work of finishing the fabrication of parts already started will be completed, Captain Rawlings said, and they will be moved out to other shipyards in as large pieces as can be handled. "We will not discontinue subcontract work for several months," he said, "and it will be carried on to the fullest extent here and elsewhere that the Marietta has subcontracts.

The officer predicted that this work would be finished in two or three months at the new Point Pleasant shipyard.

L. M. Caruthers, fireman on N. Y. C. R. R. died in a Charleston hospital Thursday morning No details.

Embryo Hold-up Is Nipped In The Proverbial Bud

Middleport—Two would-be hold-up artists hurriedly left the scene of the crime, Sunday night, when told by George "Shorty" Hackett, that the owner of the service station lived across the street and had a "forty-five". The youths had stopped at the Chase station and had inquired the way to Wheeling. When Shorty, son of Mr. and Mrs. George Hackett and freshman at Middleport High School was pointing out the route on a road map, he was hit over the head, and temporarily lost consciousness. Upon regaining his senses, he warned them of the proximity of the owner, and the two young men took to their heels. Local officer, H. B. Higgins, Sheriff George Bearhs and state highway patrolmen joined in the search for the pair. The attempted holdup occurred about 9:30 p. m

Egg Production Is Important

Meigs county egg producers are playing an important part in producing Food for Victory, according to records submitted to the Meigs County Extension Service. Five Meigs county egg producers during the month of August averaged as high or higher egg production than the State Standard of 12 eggs per hen.

Topping the list was Warren Pickens of Reedsville, with an average of 17 eggs per hen. James A. Welsh, Harrisonville; V. S. Greenler, R. No. 1, Harrisonville; Charles Grueser, Pomeroy and John Holliday, Dexter, were the other producers to produce at the rate of better than 12 eggs per hen.

These records are part of a state program to assist egg producers in keeping records and improving production methods. Any producers in the county may secure Profitable Egg Production record calendars through the office of C. E. Blakeslee, county agent. These records include the most up-to-date information needed to help farmeres adjust their feeding and management programs to meet war conditions.

Middleport—Local volunteer firemen were called to the John Kincaid home on N. Fourth Ave., early Sunday evening, after their radio "blew up". Slight damage was reported.

ATTENTION SUBSCRIBERS

Subscribers are receiving past bills on subscriptions this week. In order to straighten our files because of the change in publication we would appreciate your cooperation in calling to our attention any mistakes that are made on your bill.

We have no other way of knowing these mistakes without your help and we sincerely hope we cause no ill feeling among our faithful readers because of it. Thank you.

The Tribune-Telegraph.

Two Middleportt Persons Injured

Middleport—Two prominent citizens received painful injuries, which might well have proven fatal, the past week. Mrs. Garen Stansbury, president of the Southeast District of the Ohio Association of Garden Clubs sustained torn ligaments in her hand and arm and other body injuries, when she fell down a flight of steps at her home on Grant St. The Stansburys only recently returned to their former home to live after having spent several months in their apartment in the former Boggess property, next door.

Mayor C. O. Fisher, while returning from a business visit to Chillicothe, received head and leg injuries when the light truck he was driving skidded on the wet highway. Turning over several times, the truck landed right side up, with the mayor still in the driver's seat. The truck was only slightly damaged.

Mayor Endorses Annual Drive

Hearty endorsement of the annual For-Get-Me-Not Drive of the local Meigs Chapter No. 53, Disabled American Veterans, to be conducted in Pomeroy on Argonne Day, Saturday, Sept. 26, has been extended by His Honor M. D. Hartley of Pomeroy, in a statement reading as follows:

Twenty-four years ago, our gallant soldiers started the last big offensive of the World War in the Meuse-Argonne Forest, which led to VICTORY and the Armistice on Nov. 11, 1918. It is therefore fitting that the Disabled survivors of that conflict should designate their annual drive for public support as Argonne Day.

"May their present barrage of ForGet-Me-Nots find their marks with our fellow citizens just as effectively as did their barrage of bullets for our citizens 24 years ago.

"The service, which the Disabled American Veterans are thereby enabled to render for their less fortunate comrades, has been and will be, of incalculable value to this community.

"I trust that every civic-minded citizen will wear a little blue flower of remembrance on For-Get-Me-Not Day, next Saturday.

M. D. Hartley, Mayor
City of Pomeroy, Ohio.

Home Destroyed In Naylors Run

The home of Jimmie Meier in Naylors Run, was destroyed by fire Wednesday afternoon, about 1:15.

Mr. Meier, who lived alone, was not at home at the time and the cause of the conflagration is not known.. Several witnesses deplored the fact that because of the lack of water pressure, the home nor any of its contents were saved.

NOTICE

The bankrupt proceedings published in the Athens Messenger was for the Meigs Publishing Company and in no way pertains to the present owners of the Tribune-Teelegraph.

TRIBUNE-TELEGRAPH

Notice To Landlords

Every landlord is required to file a registration statement with the Area Rent Office at Gallipolis, O., giving information about the rent charge and other basic facts.

Registration date commences on September 17, 1942, and all registration forms must be in the area Rent Office by the first day of October, 1942. Registration blanks may be obtained at the following places:

United States Unemployment Office at Pt. Pleasant, W. Virginia.

United States Unemployment Office at Pomeroy, Ohio, located in the City Building.

Fire Department, in the City Building, at Gallipolis, Ohio.

United States Post Office at Ripley, W. Virginia.—Perry J. Bailes, Area Rent Director.

Pledge Made To Uncover Needed Scrap

"Brave Men Shall Not Die Because I Faltered". This is the motto of the Meigs County scrap iron drive which opened last night with a meeting of 75 workers from all parts of the county. George E. Carson and Harold Hilligas, Chairman and Co-chairman respectively, were in charge of the meeting.

Frank Ferneau, Assistant Executive Secretary, Salvage Section, War Production oard for the State of Ohio stated that the United States needs seventeen million tons from July 1st to January 1st of the past year. Ohio has a quota of 2,632,000 tons.

On the same basis of 180 pounds per person, Meigs Counties quota for the present six months period is 2200 tons of scrap metal.

Mr. Ferneau emphasized the need for this metal at once so that soldiers on the far-flung battle fronts of the war will be supplied with arms and ammunition. Approximately one half of the metal that is used is to be scrap iron. Every farm and home in Meigs County can help provide the scrap iron and steel necessary in this war.

One old flat iron will help make two steel h elmets or 30 hand grenades. An old lawn mower is the equivalent of six 3-inch shells. One old set of golf clubs equals one .30 caliber machine gun. An old disc equals 210 automatic light carbons. One tractor equals 10 37 m. m. tank guns

Plans outlined last night are for township chairman to secure additional men and women and make a detailed campaign of every farm and home in their township, asking that the scrap iron on that farm be collected and either delivered to a junk depot or piled in a pile for collection later by salvage trucks. All contacts in the county will be made on or before October 3rd. The reports of these contacts will be turned in to the township chairman and then to the County Chairman and trucks will be routed out the week of October 5th to 10th to pick up all scrap.

J. W. McMurray of Pomeroy has been named as industrial County Chairman and he will direct the program designed to secure all the scrap metal in and around industrial plants, coal mines and other such areas.

Township Chairman who have been selected are: Bedford, Weber Thoma; Columbia, H. B. Pickett; Chester, George Genheimer; Lebanon, Fagan Price; Letart, Ernest Shank; Olive, C. E. Humphrey; Orange, Merl Tuttle; Rutland, Bert Vance; Salem, Gerald Grate; Salisbury, Norman Heilman; Sutton, Pernon Nease; Scipio, J. E. Cotterill.

Town and Village Chairmen are Ben Turner, Pomeroy; William Grate, Middleport; Fred Shumway, Syracuse; Marcus Roush, Tom Porter, Rutland; C. N. Jones, E. R. Hayes, Chester; J. S. Davis, Tuppers Plains; Edna Stewart, Lucy Kibble, Reedsville; Dorsal Reibel, Long Bottom; Ben Price, Portland; Ray Hayman, Letart Falls, Charles Hayman, Freeland Norris, Hayman Hardware, Curt Carnahan, Racine; C. C. Caton, Salem Center; Harold Pickering, Harrisonville; Floyd A. Miller, Langsville; Sid Vale, Dyesville.

Scrap depots are: Ward Gas Station, Langsville; Vance and Son, Danville; C. C. Caton, Salem Center; Howard Weyand, Point Rock; W. R. Amos, Dexter; Chase Gas Station, Harrisonville; Townsend Store, Pageville; Burson Store, Burlingham; Barnhill Service Station, Tuppers Plains, Barnett Store, Reedsville; R. L. Larkins, Long ottom; Ben Price, Portland; Chapman Merchandise Company, Apple Grove; Allen Service Station, Letart Falls; H. D Sayre, Racine; Alvin ailey, Bashan; C. A. Swick, Rutland; Standard Oil Station, Middleport.

WAR STAMP SALES IN POMEROY SCHOOLS

Stamp sale Wednesday, Sept. 23: Total $128.75.

Sugar Run School	$28.35
Central School	27.00
Junior High School	42.50
Senior High School	30.90
	$128.75

War Stamps sold to date—$236.65

Helen Stanley Dies At Mason

Helen May Stanley, 16, died at her home in Mason, Monday at 11:00 o'clock, after an illness of long duration.

She was a daughter of Mr. and Mrs. Roy Stanley who survive, along with a brother Charles, 4, and Ray, 14.

Funeral services were held this afternoon at 2:00 o'clock at the West Columbia United Brethren Church, with interment in the Suncrest cemetery by Foglesong.

10c A LITTLE FUN TO MATCH THE SORROW

PUBLISHED 1st AND 15th OF EVERY MONTH AT 44 WEST 17th ST., N. Y. C.

THE HOBO NEWS

2ND FRONT TO RAM AXIS

BONEHEAD

Extra! *Extra!*

Hitler Takes Castor Oil!

BULLETIN

LONDON, England.—It was officially announced today by Teuters agency that the German army had taken Castor Oil.

The British war office announced that they seriously doubt the ability of the Germans to hold it. Latest dispatches declare that the strain of the rear is tremendous and internal disturbances or a sudden shift are expected hourly.

The British Admiralty expressed the belief that a flood of protest would ensue.

The British forces in the district have caught them on the run several times some miles from La Trene while the Germans were trying to evacuate along the lines.

Several flank movements have been undertaken, while the action at times resembles a gas attack.

An attack is expected in the region of the Alimentary Canal.

The Nazis have tried valiantly to suppress the report but it has leaked out and the allies have got wind of it.

Perhaps the Germans now realize the value of "a scrap of paper."

THE HOBO NEWS
ISSUED SEMI-MONTHLY at 44 W. 17th St., N. Y.
PATRICK MULKERN, Publisher
New York, N. Y.
Price $2.00 per year
Vol. 2 OCT. 1, 1942 No. 30

ALLIED PRINTING TRADES UNION LABEL COUNCIL NEW YORK 77

2¢

DAILY MIRROR

Member of The Associated Press

WEATHER CONTINUED COLD (Details on Page 2) (Copyright, 1942, Daily Mirror, Inc.)

MEN OF ACTION JOIN THE NAVY

3 Cents Outside City Limits

2¢

Vol. 19. No. 109 C New York, Wednesday, October 28, 1942 COMPLETE SPORTS

JAPS HURLED BACK ON GUADALCANAL

Story and Late Bulletins on Back Page

Dead Japs Attest to Marines' Bitter Defense

The bodies of dozens of Japs lie strewn on a Guadalcanal Island beach after U. S. Marines had stoutly repulsed the enemies' attempt to land reinforcements. The Leatherneck conquerors examine the fallen foe, whom their sharpshooting had removed from the Solomons' battle. The number of bodies bears witness to the Japs' ruthless determination to retake the island, all-important to air control of the South Pacific supply lines.

(Other photos on pages 22 and 23)

(Official U. S. Marine Corps Photo from News of Day Newsreel. Supplied by International).

Sunday Pictorial

November 1
TWOPENCE
No. 1,442

GIRLS! HAVE A LAUGH WITH US
It's on Page 12

'MONTY' ATTACKS IN EGYPT ONCE MORE

Last Night's Latest: Back Page

THIS latest battle-line picture—sent by radio last night from Cairo—brings to the people of Britain a vivid glimpse of the Eighth Army's ferocious battle to destroy Rommel.

It shows, dimly silhouetted in the swirl of battle smoke and desert sand, British soldiers, with bayonets fixed, dashing up to capture the crew of a disabled enemy tank.

It shows, too, more graphically than words could, what war in the desert is really like.

Rommel has lost many tanks and their crews in scenes like this in the last eight days.

Our Campaigns Are Winning!

FIVE MORE WAR WIDOWS GET A SQUARE DEAL: PAGE 10

DELIVERY SERVICE
Call your Tribune boy dealer by telephone, if you miss your paper. If you cannot reach him, telephone TE-6000 and everything possible will be done to correct your service.

Oakland Tribune

EXCLUSIVE ASSOCIATED PRESS... WIREPHOTO... WIDE WORLD... UNITED PRESS

LAST EDITION

VOL. CXXXVII— 15c SUNDAY CCCC OAKLAND, CALIFORNIA, SUNDAY, NOVEMBER 8, 1942 5c DAILY NO. 131

U.S. ARMY OPENS SECOND FRONT BY INVADING FRENCH WEST AFRICA

Youth Draft Delay to Hit Married Men

Induction of 200,000 Husbands May Be Needed to Fill Quota

By JACK BELL

WASHINGTON, Nov. 7. — (AP) — Congressional delay in enacting the 'teen-age draft bill will cause the induction of 200,000 married men into the armed forces in December who otherwise might not have been called until late next Spring if at all, informed legislators said today.

This was an over-all figure for the country as a whole. The effect will vary with each locality, depending on the supply of unmarried men still available to each draft board.

Chairman Reynolds (D., N.C.) of the Senate Military Committee said that even if the measure is finally passed next week and it is signed immediately by President Roosevelt, actual induction of 18 and 19-year-old youths probably would not start until about January 1.

Confirming this estimate, Senator Gurney (R., S.D.) attributed the result to delay caused by congressional controversy over a Senate amendment requiring a year's military training after induction before 18 and 19-year-old selectees could be sent into combat abroad.

OBJECTS TO CHANGE

The War Department has objected strenuously to this restriction and has bent every effort to convince House members they ought to vote to eliminate it. The matter will come to a test in the House Monday on a motion of Representative Rankin (D., Miss.) to accept this and other Senate amendments including a provision directing draft boards to defer irreplaceable agricultural workers.

Selective service officials said it would take from 30 to 40 days after the bill becomes law to "process" the 18 and 19-year-old selectees and actually begin to get them into the Army.

Those who have become 18 since the last registration may be asked to register shortly and there has been talk of installing an automatic system under which each youth would be required to report to his local draft board for registration within five days after his 18th birthday.

TO CALL MARRIED MEN

testified before the Senate Military Committee October 15 that if the draft age were lowered from 20 to 18 immediately, selective service could begin calling 18 and 19-year-olds in December.

Hershey said that in order to increase the Army to 7,500,000 by the end of 1943, it would be necessary to call about 200,000 selectees a month beginning in December.

He estimated that 800,000 to 900,000 youths 18 and 19 would be available for these calls, counting out those in that age class already enlisted and those likely to be rejected as unfit. For that reason he said he believed he could delay calling married men, except those inducted in November, until April or later if the younger men were made available at once.

AMERICANS DRIVE NEAR BUNA BASE

GENERAL MacARTHUR'S HEADQUARTERS, Nov. 8 (Sunday)—(AP)—American combat troops are in action near Buna, vital Jap base on the north New Guinea coast, General Douglas MacArthur disclosed today.

Simultaneously, General MacArthur disclosed that the Allies have occupied Goodenough Island to the northeast of New Guinea, off Collingwood Bay, in an obvious flanking movement.

(The United Press said it was alsoalso revealed that U.S. Infantry has been in active service in New Guinea since September.)

BASE FOR DRIVE

It was from Buna, in mid-Summer, that the Japanese began a drive across tortuous trails of the Owen Stanley Mountains which carried to within 32 miles of Port Moresby, Allied base on the south coast, before it was stalled. Late in September the Allies began encircling and infiltration movements which rolled the Japs back and yesterday's communique had mentioned bitter fighting at Oivi, which is 55 miles south of Buna.

"American ground troops in force, transported by air from Australia during the last month, have penetrated central and northern Papua to the vicinity of Buna," a communique stated.

"The Allied forces now control all of Papua except the beach head in the Buna-Gona area."

FROM MILNE BAY

The surprising development came as a thrust around the eastern end of New Guinea from Milne Bay where Jap troops landed in July, only to be pinned against the sea and slain or forced to their ships.

"Units from Milne Bay," the communique said, "have now completed clearing remnants of hostile forces from the islands to the North and have occupied adjacent strategic points."

While this disclosure was being made, Australian ground forces still were meeting fierce resistance at Oivi, where the retreating Japs are making a stand. Today's communique said the Australians maintained constant pressure and were resorting to their hitherto successful tactics of local encircling movements in efforts to dislodge the defenders.

Brest Blasted By U.S. Bombers

LONDON, Nov. 7.—(AP)—United States heavy bombers smashed at the big German submarine base at Brest in a daylight attack today, and reports from France and Switzerland indicated that the R.A.F. had its big bombers out again tonight for a new attack on Northern Italy.

The raid on Brest was made by Flying Fortresses and Liberators (Consolidated B-24), accompanied by R.A.F. fighters. A communique said bombs were seen striking the targets—the docks and submarine pens—but no details of the damage were given.

All the bombers returned safely, despite heavy anti-aircraft fire. One German fighter was shot down and one Allied fighter was reported missing.

Sunday Tribune Index

Allies Advance Beyond Matruh

100,000 Axis Soldiers Captured or Trapped As Empire Army Sweeps Toward Libya Border; Rommel Panzer Stand Smashed

By the Associated Press

CAIRO, Egypt, Nov. 7.—Approximately 100,000 men of Marshal Rommel's Axis Army of 140,000 were reported captured or pinned down in pockets far behind the swiftly moving African front today as the British Eighth Army swept on toward the Libyan border after smashing the German armor in its second attempted stand.

Disregarding the thousands of foot soldiers left in the dusky backwash of the battle front, Lieut. Gen. Bernard L. Montgomery's British and American tanks tore into the disorganized flanks of their main prize—the battered remnants of the German armored devisions—west of Matruh, in an effort to eliminate them entirely. They already had caught up with this fleeing force once and sent it into headlong harassed retreat a second time.

Montgomery spurred his men on to swifter pursuit of the enemy with the admonition that the "battle just won is only the beginning of our task." The British object apparently was to carry Rommel's men constantly so they could not rest or regroup their shattered forces.

American fliers have shot down 45 enemy planes against a loss of six of their own in the Middle East since October 1, Maj. Gen. Lewis H. Brereton's headquarters announced tonight.

In addition, the announcement said, the Yanks have seriously damaged an uncalculated number of tons of enemy shipping and knocked out a number of tanks and other motor vehicles.

The announcement covered the period from October 1 to November 5.

5188 Japs Are Killed

Known Enemy Losses In Solomons Since August Revealed

By JOHN M. HIGHTOWER

WASHINGTON, Nov. 7.—(AP)—American soldiers and Marines, and their supporting air and naval forces, have killed at least 5188 Japanese in the Guadalcanal-Tulagi area of the Solomon Islands since the invasion began three months ago today.

Comparable American losses can be estimated at about one-fifth of the Japanese total, or 1000 men, on the basis of a remark by Secretary Knox yesterday that enemy casualties were more than five times as great as ours.

The total of Japanese dead was announced by the Navy in a communique which also reported that 369 enemy planes had been destroyed in the South Pacific during the single month of October. Including these, the total of Jap planes destroyed since the beginning of the Solomons campaign as reported in Navy communiques stands at 529.

Yanks Drive Forward To Trap Jap Force

Pictures On Page 10-D

By JOHN M. HIGHTOWER

WASHINGTON, Nov. 7.—(AP)—Army troops have advanced to the eastward of main American positions on Guadalcanal Island, the Navy announced today, in a move to slash off the eastern arm of a Japanese pincer operation.

The advance, made against light enemy resistance, placed the Army forces not more than four miles inland and roughly parallel to the north coast of Guadalcanal where the Japs have set up around Kaoli point a beachhead from which to strike against the American east flank.

(United Press said the United States forces advanced several miles.)

If successful, this latest American action, following up earlier attacks on Japan's Koli Point forces, could well have the effect of confining the enemy within a small area from which he could neither advance toward the American held air-field along the coast nor strike it from the rear by moving through the jungles.

CROSS RIVER

A Navy communique giving the latest reports of developments on the Solomon Islands battleground said that the Army advance was made Friday, Guadalcanal time, and carried the troops across the Malimbiu River.

Fighting on the American western flank, where the main opposing forces had been hotly engaged all week, appeared to have decreased somewhat in intensity after the American offensive which began November 1 and two nights of Japanese counter-attacks.

CONTINUOUS BOMBING

On these night actions, the communique said that "during the night of November 5-6 United States Marines repulsed light attacks against our western flank in the vicinity of Point Cruz."

In the air, United States planes were reported bombing and strafing enemy troops and supplies without permitting the Japs any breathing spell whatever.

EYEWITNESS AT LANDING TELLS OF NEW A.E.F.

By WES GALLAGHER

ALLIED HEADQUARTERS IN NORTH AFRICA, Nov. 8, (Sunday)—(AP)—American soldiers, Marines and sailors from one of the greatest Naval armadas ever put into a single military operation swarmed ashore today on the Vichy-controlled North Africa shore before dawn, striking to break Hitler's hold on the Mediterranean.

Tall, decisive Lieut.-Gen. Dwight D. (Ike) Eisenhower, supreme commander of the huge forces involved in the operation, worked throughout the night directing the first great American blow at the Axis.

Included in the forces were crack combat troops, rangers (air borne units) and the cream of America's airmen.

British Naval and Air Force units supported the American landing forces, who were preceded by a snowstorm of leaflets and a radio barrage promising the French the United States had no intention of seizing French possessions and only sought to prevent Axis infiltration.

LONGEST HAUL

It undoubtedly was the longest overwater military operation ever attempted, with hundreds of ships in great convoys coming thousands of miles under the protection of British and American sea and air might.

I came on one of these big convoys.

Fighting-fit American soldiers and airmen, who did not know their destination until a few hours before scrambling into assault barges, crowded the ships to the very funnels, guarded by aircraft carriers, racing cruisers and destroyers.

ARRIVE ON TIME

Our big convoy arrived at its destination with the split-second timing of a subway train, despite storms for many days at sea and danger from planes and submarines.

The entire operation was carried out with the delicate synchronization of an expensive watch, justifying the months of careful planning by Eisenhower and his British-American supreme command.

HUGE FLEET STEAMS FOR AFRICA ZONE

By E. C. DANIEL

LONDON, Nov. 8. (Sunday)—(AP)—Possibly the greatest invasion armanda assembled in Europe since the start of the war undertook the invasion of French North Africa today in the first large scale action in the European theater in which the United States has participated.

A force of 24 warships, transports and freighters, followed by the great battleship Rodney and a heavy air escort, was reported by the German news agency D.N.B. to have left Gibraltar Thursday night.

Later, Rome said, another big convoy of troops and supplies entered the Mediterranean under escort of seven destroyers and numerous speed boats and was reinforced at Gibraltar by two cruisers and an aircraft carrier.

A possibility that as many as four aircraft carriers accompanied the attack fleet was seen in Axis reports. German broadcasts said the Furious, the Argus and another unidentified "flattop" had been observed in the harbor at Gibraltar and a later Vichy report said four carriers were seen there.

In addition to the vessels which set out eastward into the Mediterranean, D.N.B. said, at least 100 other ships waited at Gibraltar.

Among the 125 originally there, the German reports said, were six cruisers, one auxiliary cruiser, 26 to 28 destroyers, four submarines and one monitor. To transport men, equipment and supplies there were two transports, one of them large, and possibly 40 merchantmen and 12 tankers. The remainder of the vessels were not identified.

VICHY, Nov. 7.—(U.P.)—An Allied naval squadron of 63 units was reported tonight to have steamed eastward through the Mediterranean Parallel with the French African coast and was said now to be near the Straits of Sicily.

F. R. Message to French People

WASHINGTON, Nov. 7.—(AP)—The text of the address broadcast by President Roosevelt, in French, to the French people follows:

"My friends, who suffer day and night, under the crushing yoke of the Nazis, I speak to you as one who was with your Army and Navy in France in 1918.

"I have held all my life the deepest friendship for the French people—for the entire French people. I retain and cherish the friendship of hundreds of French people in France and outside of France. I know your farms, your villages, and your cities.

I KNOW YOUR PEOPLE

"I know your soldiers, professors, and workmen. I know what a precious heritage of the French people are your homes, your culture, and the principles of democracy in France. I salute again and reiterate my faith in liberty, equality and fraternity. No two Nations exist which are more united by historic and mutually friendly ties than the people of France and the United States.

"Americans, with the assistance of the United Nations, are striving for their own safe future as well as the restoration of the ideals, the liberties, and the democracy of all those who have lived under the Tricolor.

"We come among you to repulse the cruel invaders who would remove forever your rights of self-government, your rights to religious freedom, and your rights to live your own lives in peace and security.

SOLELY AGAINST FOE

"We come among you solely to defeat and rout your enemies. Have faith in our words. We do not want to cause you any harm.

"We assure you that once the menace of Germany and Italy is removed from you, we shall quit your territory at once.

"I am appealing to your realism, to your self interest and national ideas.

"Do not obstruct, I beg of you, this great purpose.

"Help us where you are able, my friends, and we shall see again the glorious day when liberty and peace shall reign again on earth.

"Vive la France eternelle!"

American Troops Land In Force to Trap Axis

President Roosevelt and General Eisenhower Appeal to French People for Co-operation

By the Associated Press

WASHINGTON, Nov. 7.—Powerful American expeditionary forces are landing on the Atlantic and Mediterranean coasts of the French colonies in Africa in the first big-scale offensive of the war under the Star Spangled Banner.

An announcement of the action, obviously aimed at winning complete domination of the Dark Continent and reopening the Mediterranean Sea for the United Nations in conjunction with the victorious British drive westward from Egypt, was made in a simultaneous announcement tonight by President Roosevelt and a communique from the War Department.

The White House statement said the purpose of the move was two-fold:

1. To forestall an Axis invasion there which "would constitute a direct threat to America across the comparatively narrow sea from Western Africa."

2. To provide "an effective second front assistance to our heroic Allies in Russia."

Thus the Axis had an emphatic answer to its attempts to "fish for information" by broadcasting accounts of heavy Allied troop convoys escorted by warships mustering at the Rock of Gibraltar in recent days.

The troops apparently were some of those which have been concentrated in the British Isles for some time, itching for action as they went through the final stages of their battle training, for they were commanded by Lieut. Gen. Dwight D. Eisenhower, commander-in-chief in the European theater, whose headquarters had been in Britain.

General Eisenhower Broadcasts Assurance That Americans Come Only as Friends

General Eisenhower broadcast a message to the people of French North Africa on behalf of the President, assuring them that "we come among you solely to destroy your enemies and not to harm you" and issued a proclamation instructing them how to co-operate.

To signify co-operation, the General directed that they fly the French Tricolor and the American flag, one above the other, or two tricolors by day and shine a searchlight vertically into the sky by night. He also directed French naval and aviation units to remain idle.

Eisenhower's message indicated that the troops were pouring ashore in Morocco, which has both Atlantic and Mediterranean shores, and the remainder of French North Africa which comprises Algeria and Tunis on the Mediterranean.

Landings also presumably were being made in the French West African colonies, including Senegal, whose capital of Dakar lies only 1870 miles across the South Atlantic from the bulge of Brazil.

The announcement gave no details of the composition of the troops and their equipment, for obvious military reasons, but said that they were equipped with "adequate weapons of warfare," and that they would "in the immediate future, be reinforced by a considerable number of divisions of the British Army."

There was no doubt that the expeditions were made in heavy force with tanks, artillery and all the accoutrements of modern warfare for this new and promising phase of the conflict. The offensive far surpassed in weight the American invasion of the Solomon Islands in the South Pacific, undertaken just three months ago today.

Announcement of Landings Timed to Coincide With Debarkation of Troops

Announcement of the landings was timed to coincide with the actual debarkation of the troops on their destinations at 9 p.m., Eastern War time (3 a.m. Sunday, West African time), and was made only after a reassuring message from President Roosevelt's own lips had been broadcast to the French people, asking for their aid to rout their own enemies.

The landing, the announcement said, was being assisted by the British Navy and air forces, and "it will, in the immediate future be reinforced by a considerable number of divisions of the British Army."

White House Secretary Stephen Early called newspapermen to a special press conference to make the formal announcement. He said it was issued in the name of President Roosevelt, with simultaneous communiques coming from the War Department and in London.

The announcement said the landing was to prevent an enemy invasion, which, if successful, would "constitute a direct threat to America" across the comparatively narrow sea from Western Africa.

"This combined Allied force," the announcement said, "under American command in conjunction with the British campaign in Egypt is designed to prevent an occupation by the Axis armies of any part of Northern or Western Africa, and to deny to the aggressor nations a starting point from which to launch an attack against the Atlantic Coast of the Americas."

The formal White House statement also said the landing "provides an effective second front assistance to our heroic allies in Russia."

Simultaneously with the official Presidential statement, the White House made

Continued Page 6, Col. 1

WAR EXTRA

Los Angeles Examiner
CHARACTER · QUALITY · AMERICA FIRST! · ENTERPRISE · ACCURACY
AN AMERICAN PAPER FOR THE AMERICAN PEOPLE · THE GREAT NEWSPAPER OF THE GREAT SOUTHWEST
Reg. U. S. Pat. Off.
Examiner Telephone Richmond 1212 — Examiner Building, 1111 S. Broadway
9 A.M. FINAL
VOL. XXXIX—NO. 333 — LOS ANGELES, MONDAY, NOVEMBER 9, 1942 — Two Sections—Part I—FIVE CENTS

YANKS WIN ALGIERS, SURRENDER SIGNED!

PLANES SMASH JAP SOLOMONS NAVAL THRUST

GENERAL DOUGLAS MACARTHUR'S HEADQUARTERS IN AUSTRALIA, Nov. 9 (Monday).—(INS)—Allied bombers raided a Japanese airdrome and installations on New Britain, northeast of Australia, a communique announced today.

In addition, an Allied bomber unit plastered Japanese coastal shipping at Koepang, Timor, north of Australia.

Coastal installations on Maklo Island, at the southwest tip of New Britain, were damaged by a flight of B-25's.

Medium bombers destroyed the Japanese wireless station and bombed enemy planes and an airdrome at Gasmata.

By H. K. Reynolds
Staff Correspondent International News Service

WASHINGTON, Nov. 8.—The Navy Department announced tonight American planes have smashed a new Japanese naval thrust at the Solomon Islands as United States troops on Guadalcanal gained new ground east of Henderson Airfield.

Attacking a Japanese naval task force 150 miles north of Guadalcanal, American bombers damaged and probably sunk the leading cruiser, and badly damaged one of the 10 destroyers engaged in the operation.

With the cruiser gone, it was believed the Japanese ships retired to their bases in the northwest Solomons.

This action took place on November 7 (Solomons time). On the same day, United States motor torpedo boats attacked two Japanese destroyers off Lunga Point, the northern extremity of American position on Guadalcanal.

DESTROYER IN DOUBT

One of the destroyers, the Navy said, is believed to have been sunk.

Japanese naval losses in the Solomon Islands have thus been increased to 80 ships sunk or damaged.

The Japanese also lost 12 more planes in the sea-air action north of Guadalcanal, making a total of 541 of the enemy's bombing and fighting planes destroyed by American forces since they moved into the southeastern Solomons at the beginning of August.

United States Army troops, after crossing the Malimbiu River, continued their advance eastward of Henderson Field.

They reached the Metapono

(Continued on Page 5, Cols. 6-8)

Vichy Breaks Relations With U.S.

By Wade Werner

WASHINGTON, Nov. 8.—(AP)—The Vichy regime of France severed diplomatic relations with the United States today as Chief of State Petain rejected a call from President Roosevelt for cooperation in the African drive against the Axis.

First news of the rupture came from Vichy itself when pro-Nazi Pierre Laval, chief of government, handed formal notice to S. Pinkney Tuck, United States charge d'affaires.

No official word of the action had been received at the State Department here. It was understood, however, that the official American attitude toward a formal rupture would be one of indifference.

After news of the break by Vichy and after the French radio had reported Petain reproaching Roosevelt for the military move against the African colonies, the White House disclosed the President had sent a personal message to Petain aside from the appeal and explanation Roosevelt addressed to the French people by radio.

APPEAL TO FRANCE

"As an old friend of France and the people of France," the President expressed to Petain his "anger and sympathy" over the suffering inflicted on France by the Germans and declared the ultimate aim of the African campaign was "the liberation of France and its empire from the Axis yoke."

He explained that he was calling on French authorities in North Africa for "cooperation in repelling Axis threats" and reaffirmed that America sought no territories for itself.

Petain replied that he learned of the American "aggression" with "bewilderment and sadness" and that Roosevelt in his message "invoked a pretext which nothing justifies."

Secretary of State Hull, in an unusual Sunday afternoon press conference, had declared earlier that diplomatic relations had been maintained with the collaborationist Frenchmen at Vichy chiefly to pave the way and prepare the background for the current military operations.

That purpose now has been

(Continued on Page 4, Cols. 2-3)

SIX ITALIAN DIVISIONS IN BRITISH HANDS

By W. P. Saphire
Staff Correspondent International News Service

CAIRO, Nov. 8.—All six Italian infantry divisions of the routed Axis Afrika corps have now fallen into British hands with their entire equipment and most of the remnants of the German tank units have fled out of Egypt into Libya, it was revealed tonight.

The debacle wrought upon Field Marshal Erwin Rommel's once-vaunted legions was almost complete as the Eighth Army swept beyond Sidi Barrani and surrounded and smashed the enemy's rear-guard detachments just east of Halfaya (Hellfire) Pass on the Libyan border.

Nothing was left to Rommel except a shrunken body of troops numbering less than 20,000, and scarcely more than a handful of tanks and other vehicles. Total obliteration of this skeleton force was regarded as merely a matter of a few days, if not hours.

ABANDONED BY NAZIS

Abandoned by their German Allies, the six Italian infantry divisions, comprising some 90,000 troops, were taken over by the British after they had been trapped for several days by the Eighth Army tide that surged around their positions and far beyond. Hungry, thirsty and tired, they were rounded up, together with their complete material.

Latest unofficial estimates in Cairo, meanwhile, said the Eighth Army has now destroyed or captured 500 Axis tanks and 1000 field guns since the spectacular offensive was launched in the Egyptian desert 16 days ago.

After occupying the Egyptian coastal town of Mersa Matruh, British troops pressed their hot pursuit of the smashed German remnants to and beyond Sidi Barrani, within 70 miles of the Libyan frontier. Field dispatches said Nazi rear-guard units had attempted a stand before Halfaya Pass, but were encircled and beaten.

Nevertheless, the bulk of Rommel's remnants appeared to have reached and crossed the Libyan border, 240 miles west of the former El Alamein battlefront, in a desperate effort to escape annihilation.

Indications were that swift-

(Continued on Page 3, Col. 3)

Drive on North Africa Spreads; French Fleet Battles Invasion

California Trained

MAJOR GENERAL George Smith Patton Jr., commander of United States Army troops which landed in West Africa, is seen here taking compass reading beside his starred tank during tank maneuvers in Southern California desert last summer. (Story on Page 6.)
—Los Angeles Examiner photo.

Outstanding developments yesterday in the opening of the second front in North Africa were:

French Surrender Algiers to Invading Americans.
Big U. S.-French Naval Battle Off Morocco.
Vichy Breaks Diplomatic Relations With America.
Revolt Against French Is Reported in Morocco.
Oran, in Western Algeria, Flanked, About to Fall.
Casablanca Bombarded by U. S. Warships.
U. S. Troops Still Landing at Numerous Points.

ALLIED HEADQUARTERS IN NORTH AFRICA, Nov. 9 (Monday, 2 a. m.).—(AP)—American combat forces led by Major General Charles W. Ryder have wrested one of the key points in the western Mediterranean from Axis domination with the swift occupation of the port of Algiers despite strong opposition from Vichy's naval units.

The famous city fell just 12 hours after a lightning assault. The port is the only one within easy reach of German air bases in Sardinia and Sicily, but the synchronized arrival of American fighter planes on Algiers airfields within a few seconds after their capture made it sure that any raiding Nazi bombers would get a hot reception.

A covering force of American fighters permitted use of the port for unloading troops which completed the occupation.

Oran, some 250 miles west of Algiers and the heart of Admiral Jean Darlan's German-inspired resistance, continued to offer strenuous opposition, particularly by navy-controlled coastal batteries.

In between the two key ports American landings encountered only the lightest resistance. The troops were welcomed by the population and made deep penetrations.

By Associated Press

LONDON, Nov. 8.—The city of Algiers on the south coast of the Mediterranean Sea surrendered to U. S. troops tonight as a mighty American Expeditionary Force occupied French African colonies.

Resistance at Algiers, important French naval base, was broken by Rangers who stormed ashore in the face of fire from coastal batteries, by swarms of American planes and by a powerful naval force which lay off the harbor.

The capitulation, approved by Admiral Darlan, came at 7 p. m., Greenwich time (12 noon P. W. T.), and American soldiers tonight were patrolling the streets of the ancient city. The fate of Darlan, who for a time at least might have been a prisoner, was not clear.

At the end of the day United States forces dominated many miles of the Mediterranean coast facing the Axis.

Americans seized and were soon operating from

BULLETINS

VICHY, Nov. 9.—(From French Broadcasts).—(AP)—A French communique reported today fierce fighting was proceeding in French Morocco and said naval engagements were in progress off Casablanca.

Another broadcast report from the Vichy radio said the formal armistice convention for Algiers was signed at 10 a. m. today (3 a. m. Pacific War Time.)

It said Lieutenant General Dwight D. Eisenhower, A. E. F. commander, signed for the United States and General Voeldz, commander of the 19th French Army Corps, signed for France.

Yanks Speedy

ALLIED HEADQUARTERS IN NORTH AFRICA, Nov. 9 (Monday).—(INS)—Advances by American forces in northwest Africa are proceeding faster than it was originally planned, it was announced today in a communique.

United States air forces are getting fighter planes onto captured air fields even faster than the Germans were able to do at the height of their assault on Norway, it was said.

The air units are thereby strengthening greatly the hand of American ground forces, it was added.

Rome Alarmed

LONDON, Nov. 9 (Monday).—(INS)—A warning to Vichy France that it must maintain resistance in French North Africa was broadcast over the Rome ra-

(Continued on Page B, Column 7)

Gen. Doolittle Commands Africa Invasion Air Forces

By Michael Chinigo
Staff Correspondent International News Service

WASHINGTON, Nov. 8.—The American Navy tonight was in complete control of contested Atlantic and Mediterranean waters off French North Africa as Lieutenant General Dwight D. Eisenhower catapulted fresh forces into the fray that the War Department said was everywhere "proceeding according to plan."

Youthful Lieutenant General Dwight D. Eisenhower was officially disclosed to have been named commander in chief of the combined British-American Expeditionary Forces attacking the northwest and western humps of the African continent as a preliminary maneuver to an all-out assault against the European continent.

Subsequently it was announced that America's top-ranking tacticians, led by Brigadier General James H. Doolittle of Tokyo-raid fame, had been attached to Eisenhower's "invasion" staff.

The War Department's complete roster enumerated:

1. Commander in Chief: Lieutenant General Dwight D. Eisenhower.
2. Deputy Commander in Chief: Major General Mark W. Clark.
3. U. S. Naval Commander: Admiral H. K. Hewitt.
4. Commander of American forces landing on the west coast of Africa: Major General George S. Patton.
5. Commander of American

(Continued on Page B, Cols. 3-5)

THE WEATHER
Showers and scattered thunderstorms this afternoon, ending early tonight; much colder this afternoon and tonight, fresh to strong winds.
Detailed Weather Report on Page 26

Read The Baltimore News-Post for complete, accurate war coverage. It is the only Baltimore newspaper possessing the three great wire services—
UNITED PRESS
INTERNATIONAL NEWS SERVICE
ASSOCIATED PRESS

THE BALTIMORE NEWS-POST
AN INDEPENDENT NEWSPAPER
The Largest Evening Circulation in the Entire South

WALL ST. CLOSE 9

VOL. CXLII.—NO. 5 Entered as second-class matter at Baltimore Postoffice. TUESDAY EVENING, NOVEMBER 10, 1942 PRICE 3 CENTS

U. S. TROOPS TAKE ORAN CASABLANCA ENTERED

U. S. Troops On Way To Libya

LONDON, Nov. 10—(A. P.).—Oran, French naval port on the Mediterranean coast of Africa, has fallen to an American tank attack, and Casablanca, on the Atlantic, apparently was nearing the last stages of its resistance.

Without pausing, the Americans were said to be striking out toward Libya—their first thrust aimed directly at expelling the Axis from North Africa.

The occupation of Oran within a few hours after American tanks launched an all-out assault was announced in Communique No. 4 from Allied headquarters.

FRENCH ENDING FIGHT

It said that, with Oran in American hands and Algiers already having surrendered, French resistance on the Mediterranean coast was virtually ended.

The occupation of Oran capped a day of whirlwind developments in which aged Marshal Petain himself shouldered the burden of commanding France's shattered defenses and the Germans were reported to have sent Field Marshal Erwin von Witzleben to North Africa to direct the Vichy forces in the field.

Casablanca apparently still was resisting, but strong landing forces were enclosing it ashore and United States naval forces had smashed most of its sea defenses.

BEACHHEADS SEIZED

Allied headquarters said that the beachheads at Safi, Fedala and Mehdia, flanking Casablanca, "are in our hands" and that the new 35,000-ton French battleship Jean Bart was burning in Casablanca harbor.

Wes Gallacher, Associated Press correspondent with the expedition, said the eJan Bart had been hit by American warships which had wiped out light forces of French destroyers hampering the landings and were bombarding the Casablanca harbor.

So rapid was the American campaign's progress, still only in its third day, that it outstripped the expedition's communication system's ability to report it.

An Allied headquarters spokesman here, however, declared the

Continued on Page 2, Column 1.

Laval Rule In France Totters

LONDON, Nov. 10—(U. P.).—Pierre Laval today appeared to face the possible collapse of his regime, but was bolstered somewhat by the feeble assumption of military command by Marshal Henri Philippe Petain.

Quarters closely in touch with the French situation believed the United States operations in French North Africa spelled the almost inevitable finish of the Vichy regime, either immediately or as the British-American offensive begins to take final shape.

There were indications that Admiral Jean Francois Darlan, whose supreme command of the French armed forces was assumed by Petain, might bo over to the Allies and take with him such military leaders as Gen. Alphonse Juin, commander of the Vichy forces in North Africa, and even possibly Auguste Nogues, Vichy resident-general in Morocco.

Charles St. Bus Route Dropped

Suspension of bus lines A and G in Baltimore after December 28 to save rubber and equipment was ordered today by the Office of Defense Transportation in Washington.

The A route is the Charles street-University Parkway line and the G route is known as the East Fayette street line.

ODT officials in Washington said suspension of the lines would release 32 buses for use elsewhere. It was asserted that the lines involved operate either on the same streets used by trolleys or parallel to trolley lines or in easy access to other means of transportation.

Route A, extending 3.5 miles, links downtown Baltimore with railroad connections, the University section and outlying residential sections.

Route G, 3.62 miles long, parallels the Sparrows Point line except for short distances at either end, the ODT announcement declared, and in the downtown area is closely linked with other available means of transportation.

Mrs. Roosevelt In Northern Ireland

BELFAST, Northern Ireland, Nov. 10—(U. P.).—Mrs. Franklin D. Roosevelt has arrived in Northern Ireland, Prime Minister John M. Andrews disclosed today. He said:

"We of Ulster are delighted and honored in having among us so distinguished a lady and the bearer of so great a name.

"Between the American troops and the people of Ulster the friendliest relations exist. We have all been thrilled by the quality of the American fighting force, first in Africa, and we are confident that the comradeship of the two nations in arms will lead to still closer cooperation dealing with world problems when the war has passed into history."

SHIP SURVIVORS LAND

A BRITISH WEST INDIAN PORT, Nov. 10—(U. P.).—Forty-nine survivors of a torpedoed ship have been landed here after spending several days at sea, authorities announced today.

VERY LATEST NEWS

(Race Results From Howard Sports Daily, Inc.)

COUNT FLEET WINS SIXTH RACE AT PIMLICO

Fifth—Layaway, $8.30, $3.80, $2.80; Natomas, $3.40, $2.60; Brown Saxon, $3.60.
Sixth—Count Fleet, $2.20, $2.10, out; Uncle Billies, $2.60 out; Rough Doc, out.

AT BELMONT PARK

Fifth—Coronal, $9.10, $5, $3.20; Tweedy, $9.90, $4.20; Vali, $2.70.

AT ROCKINGHAM

Fourth—Flying West, $8.80, $4.40, $2.80; Bell Bottom, $8.60, $5.00; Dainty Ford, $3.40.
Fifth — Colors Up, $4.40, $3.00, $2.60; Paille, $3.40, $2.60; On the Line, $4.20.

AT CHURCHILL DOWNS

Third—Modwena, $5.00, $3.20, $3.20; Bolo Ella, $5.80, $4.20; Love Song, $6.60.

NEW YORK STOCK EXCHANGE TOTAL SALES

NEW YORK, Nov. 10—(A. P.).—Total sales on the New York Stock Exchange today were 772,220 shares.

Africa War Bulletins

MADRID, Nov. 10—(U. P.).—Reports from La Linea today said that the British aircraft carrier Furious, six destroyers and a convoy of 22 large merchantmen had arrived at Gibraltar from the Atlantic and were anchored in the bay. The convoy wa sprotected by 14 American bombers, the report said.

Thirty American and British fighter planes piloted by U. S. fliers were said to have taken off from Gibraltar and flown in both easterly and westerly directions.

The battleship Nelson was anchored at the Rock along with some cruisers and several destroyers, according to the report. Gibraltar was described as the scene of extensive preparations.

WASHINGTON, Nov. 10—(I. N. S.).—The War Department announced today that U. S. naval forces "to a large degree" have overcome resistance by French naval units off the coast of Casablanca and have set the French battleship Jean Bart on fire. At the same time, the War Department said that land operaions at Algiers have ceased during the armistice negotiation.

BERLIN, Nov. 10 (By Official German Wireless) —(I. N. S.).—French Chief of State Marshal Henri Phillipe Petain today repeated his order to French troops in North Africa to resist the Anglo-American invaders. His lates order said:

"In a message to Admiral Darlan and other military commanders in North Africa, I gave the order to defend yourselves against aggressors. I maintain my order."

New Guinea Japs Now Surrounded

WASHINGTON, Nov. 10—(A. P.).—Carrying the fight to the enemy, American and Allied troops have encircled one Japanese position on New Guinea and apparently are holding the upper hand on Guadalcanal Island in the embattled Solomons.

The western jaw of a vise which the Japanese had hoped to squeeze upon Henderson airfield—control spot of the Solomons has been stationary for two days.

This was interpreted as evidence that soldiers and marines have halted the original Japanese threat against the airfield from that quarter.

To the east American troops are pushing forward in a drive to encircle the enemy beachhead at Koli Point, where reinforcements for the original invasion force were landed.

The Americans advanced four miles east of the beachhead Saturday, Guadalcanal time, the Navy said, apparently isolating that eastern jaw of the vise.

Meantime in New Guinea Allied

Continued on Page 2, Column 8.

Daily Double (Damon Burgoo Maid) Paid $17.90

PIMLICO CHARTS

Copyright, 1942, by Triangle Publications, Inc. (Daily Racing Form.)

TRACK FAST.

FIRST RACE—SIX FURLONGS. CHUTE. FOR THREE-YEAR-OLDS AND UP. Maidens. Claiming. Purse $1,000. Value to winner $700, second $150, third $100, fourth $50. Went to post at 1.21½. Off at once. Start good from gate. Won driving, place same. Winner ch g 3, by Sun Briar-Dinah Victory. Owned by T. D. TAGGART. Trained by H. WELLS. Time 22 2-5, 46 2-5, 1.14 1-5.

	Wt.	Post	St.	¼	½	Str.	Fin.	Jockeys	Odds
Damon	117	6	3	3h	2¹	2²	1n	F. Zufelt	.75
Cavalcadia	114	1	5	1¹	1h	1h	2³	L. Ensor	20.60
Tripod	114	5	7	5h	5²	5³	3¹	T. Luther	8.80
Helen Mowlee	114	11	4	4²	4³	4¹½	4²½	R. Sisto	97.60
aTinto	114	2	2	2¹	3¹½	3½	5¹	W. Eads	3.20
Alsace	112	8	6	7³	7⁶	6²	6¹½	J. Tammaro	11.10
Samuel D	120	7	11	11²	10²	9⁴	7h	W. Dufford	100.95
Meysah	114	10	1	6²	6½	7³	8³	J. Harrell	90.30
Little Tyke	120	12	9	9²	8³	8²	9¹	M. Berg	64.30
Night Bird II	120	9	12	12	12	11h	10³	P. Keiper	148.80
Lucky Cloud	120	3	10	10²	11²	10½	11¹²	H. Claggett	34.70
aJohn's Last	114	4	8	8⁴	9½	12	12	C. Rollins	3.20

aO. S. Jennings and L. Alagia entry.

$2 Mutuels Paid—Damon, $3.50 straight, $3.20 place, $2.60 show. Cavalcadia, $11.60 place, $7.60 show. Tripod, $4.50 show. Total mutuels $33.00

Damon well ridden and factor from the start, moved forward when ready, stumbled when challenging for the lead, impeded Cavalcadia slightly when recovering and came on to reach the lead and began drawing away at the end. Cavalcadia opened

Continued on Page 26, Column 4.

French Fleet Is Eliminated

LONDON, Nov. 10—(A. P.).—Reuters reported tonight that United States troops, supported by tanks, have entered the outskirts of Casablanca.

ALLIED HEADQUARTERS IN NORTH AFRICA, Nov. 10—(5 P. M.)—(U. P.).—Lieut. Gen. Dwight Eisenhower announced late today that American troops had occupied Oran, last major Algerian center of French resistance and had left the 35,000-ton French battleship Jean Bart a blazing hulk in a blow which crushed French naval resistance at Casablanca.

When French destroyers at Casablanca put up strong resistance against American naval units protecting U. S. troop landings there, Rear Admiral H. K. Hewitt, commander of U. S. Naval forces for the operation, threw in the whole weight of his battle fleet against the French ships.

Hewitt employed dive bombers, as well as naval units and the entire flotilla of French destroyers and lighter craft was wiped out, and the 35,000-ton French battleship Jean Bart was left a burning hluk.

(A Vichy broadcast said that American troops marched into Oran at 9 A. M., and that United States headquarters had been established in the center of the city this afternoon. Only mild skirmishing occurred inside Oran and all was quiet after 3 P. M., Vichy said.)

The French offered naval resistance at Oran as well as Casablanca and Admiral Sir Andrew Browne Cunningham replied in kind.

He beat off the French with naval gunfire and aircraft bombings while American troops advanced into Oran with tanks and infantry.

The American attack was a pincers movement from east to west.

Another American force drove east to meet a strong French counter-attack in the vicinity of St. Cloud and Lamacta, about 10 miles northeast of Oran.

(A communique issued in London simultaneously with Eisenhower's announcement said that the cities of Safi, Fedala and Mahdia in Morocco were in American hands.)

The full power of the American

Continued on Page 2, Column 6.

Unit Drops Teen Age Rider

WASHINGTON, Nov. 10—(A. P.). A joint Senate-House committee agreed today on a 'teen-age draft bill eliminating a Senate provision requiring a year's military training before eighteen and nineteen year old selectees could be sent into forign combat.

The conference agreement came after the House had rejected by an overwhelming vote yesterday a motion by Representative Rankin (Democrat) of Mississippi to instruct its conferees to accept the training amendment.

SEE SPEEDY APPROVAL

Elimination of this provision cleared the way for expected speedy final approval by Congress of the legislation which would lower the draft age from the present minimum of twenty to eighteen.

In approving the compromise, which must be acted upon by both Houses before it can be sent to President Roosevelt for his consideration, the joint committee agreed to accept a Senate amendment directing local Selective Service boards to defer calling essential farm workers into the armed forces.

Representative Short (Republican) of Missouri, one of the House conferees, said that Majority Leader McCormack and Minority Leader Martin had said the measure might be taken up in the House today by unanimous consent.

EXPLAINS ACTION

Senator Gurney (Republican) of South Dakota, author of the Senate's teen-age draft bill, explained the conference action to newspaper men. When they thanked him, Gurney smiled and said:

"I hope the rest of the country feels like saying *'Thank you,'* too. I know this will help in the conduct of the war."

The conference committee's action was reported to have been unanimous.

U. S. Progress In Africa Revealed

WASHINGTON, Nov. 10—(I. N. S.).—The War Department today issued this communique:

("North Africa.

("1—Land operations at Algiers have ceased during the armistice negotiations. Our troops received a friendly welcome in the city and co-operation of French workers and the general population has been good. Royal Air Force fighters are giving air cover over Algiers bay.

("2—American troops have captured Oran, supported by the Royal Navy and the United States Army Twelfth Air Force and naval aircraft.

("3—United States naval forces have overcome to a large degree the resistance by French naval units along the coast in the Casablanca area. The French battleship, Jean Bart, is burning in port. Naval aircraft continued to support Army forces on shore. Safi, Fedala and Mehdia are in our hands.")

Draftee Furlough Time Will Vary

WASHINGTON, Nov. 10 — (A. P.).—The effective date for shortening the post-induction furlough for selectees from two weeks to one week will vary in the nine Army service commands, National Selective Service Headquarters said today, but the new policy will be adopted throughout the country "during the month of November."

Temperatures

12 Midn't.	55	8 A. M.	58
1 A. M.	54	9 A. M.	58
2 A. M.	55	10 A. M.	60
3 A. M.	55	11 A. M.	63
4 A. M.	56	12 Noon	65
5 A. M.	56	1 P. M.	67
6 A. M.	57	2 P. M.	68
7 A. M.	58	3 P. M.	70

Africa At A Glance

By Associated Press.

United States Progress In French North Africa:

American vanguards are reported moving toward Libya.

Oran, chief French port and naval base, has been entered by a tank-led United States column.

Casablanca, rejecting an offered armistice, is being pounded from the sea and enclosed by land encirclement.

More United States landings are reported in Southern Morocco.

The Crumbling Of Vichy Resistance:

Admiral Jean Darlan is a prisoner of the Americans at Algiers.

Marshal Petain himself has assumed Darlan's command of all Vichy French forces.

The Rout Of Rommel:

Britain's Army of the Nile is smashing at Axis rear guards making their last stand on Egyptian soil.

THE WEATHER

Colder tonight, with lowest temperature around 28 degrees in the northern and westerr. suburbs and 34 degrees in the center of the city.
Detailed Weather Report on Page 41

Read The Baltimore News-Post for complete, accurate war coverage. It is the only Baltimore newspaper possessing the three great wire services—

UNITED PRESS
INTERNATIONAL NEWS SERVICE
ASSOCIATED PRESS

THE BALTIMORE NEWS-POST

AN INDEPENDENT NEWSPAPER

The Largest Evening Circulation in the Entire South

9

VOL. CXLII.—NO. 6 | Entered as second-class matter at Baltimore Postoffice. | WEDNESDAY EVENING, NOVEMBER 11, 1942 | PRICE 3 CENTS

ALL FRENCH N. AFRICA CAPITULATES TO U. S.

Occupation Of France Widens

LONDON, Nov. 11—(A. P.).—Goaded by the American coup in Africa, Adolf Hitler scrapped his armistice with France today, sent his gray-clad columns racing south toward Toulon and Marseille, and launched parachutists and air-borne infantry into French Tunisia. The Mediterranean took its grim place as the great new front of the war.

The wedge-shaped French protectorate of Tunisia, through which President Roosevelt asked passage for American forces from Algeria to Libya, was the first contested prize.

German broadcasts, perhaps seeking an excuse for Axis troop action, said Tunis, the capital city, "has been attacked by United States troops since Wednesday morning," and declared that the garrison there was resisting.

The Mediterranean took its grim place as the great new front of the war.

The wedge-shaped French protectorate of Tunisia, through which President Roosevelt asked passage for American forces from Algeria to Libya, was the first contested prize.

SAYS TUNIS ATTACKED

German broadcasts, perhaps seeking an excuse for Axis troop action, said Tunis, the capital city, "has been attacked by United States troops since Wednesday morning," and declared that the garrison there was resisting.

Axis forces already were there. An Allied headquarters spokesman said Nazi combat planes and airborne soldiers had been moved into Tunisia "for some little time." B. B. C. said Italian marines had occupied the Tunisian port of Bizerte and other reports told of German parachutist landings.

Lieut. Gen. Dwight D. Eisenhower's powerful A. E. F. was racing for a clean-up in Algeria and French Morocco.

French defenders of the key Atlantic port of Casablanca were reported to have asked for an armistice today after their defenses were shelled from the sea, dive-bombed from the air and assaulted by armored columns from the land.

From Algiers other American columns were reported striking southwest toward Tunisia and Libya, but a spokesman at the Allied headquarters said he did not know whether American or British troops were in Tunisia.

German and Italian troops alike moved into southern France while Marshal Petain, the hero of Verdun and the tired old man of Vichy, protested sadly and in vain.

Hitler sought to undercut whatever resistance the French might yet offer.

POSES AS FRIEND

In a lengthy message to Petain he posed as France's friend. In a message to Frenchmen he cast himself in the role of their guardian against American attack upon Corsica and the French south coast.

He said:

"The German Government has known for 24 hours that plans of these operations (in North Africa) provide that the next attack will be made aaginst Corsica, in order

Continued on Page 2, Column 1.

Temperatures

Midnight,	48	8 A. M.,	41
1 A. M.,	47	9 A. M.,	42
2 A. M.,	46	10 A. M.,	44
3 A. M.,	45	11 A. M.,	46
4 A. M.,	44	12 Noon,	44
5 A. M.,	43	1 P. M.,	45
6 A. M.,	42	2 P. M.,	46
7 A. M.,	41	3 P. M.,	47

VERY LATEST NEWS

(Race Results From Howard Sports Daily, Inc.)

SIR ALFRED WINS FIFTH RACE AT PIMLICO

Fifth — Sir Alfred, $11.70, $3.50, Out; Bushwhacker, $2.40, Out; Caduceus, Out.

AT BELMONT PARK

Fourth—Hopeville, $4.40, $2.70, $2.30; Rackatack, $6, $3.10; Miss Daunt, $3.10.

AT ROCKINGHAM

Fourth — Stimuli, $10.60, $7.20, $5.40; Malinda B., $10.40, $7.60; Skeeter, $5.80.

AT CHURCHILL DOWNS

Second — Okabena, $70.60, $13.80, $4.80; Count Fearless, $3.60, $2.80; Lazy Tongs, $2.40.

Third — Lady Sponsor, $6.60, $3.00, $2.80; Warrigan, $4.80, $4.60; Kantar Run, $11.00.

EXECUTE 3 SWISS SOLDIERS FOR ESPIONAGE

BERN, Switzerland, Nov. 11—(A. P.).—Three Swiss soldiers were executed today for espionage, the first executions in Switzerland since the outbreak of the war.

AFRICA WAR BULLETINS

LONDON, Nov. 11—(A. P.).—The Admiralty issued a communique today to deny reports on the German radio that the demilitarized French naval squadron at Alexandria had been taken over by the British Navy. The report is "entirely without foundation," the Admiralty said. A British informant said it would take months to get the French ships ready for action, even if the French crews were willing to man them.

ON THE FRENCH FRONTIER, Nov. 11—(A. P.). Marshal Petain bitterly accused Adolf Hitler of breaking the 1940 French-German armistice by sending German troops into the former unoccupied zone today and Vichy reports said the aged Chief of State had set France free to defend herself against this latest Axis aggression.

"I protest solemnly against decisions incompatible with the armistice agreement," the eighty-six-year-old Marshal said in reply to Hitler's announcement that he was sending his armies swarming across Southern France on the pretext of heading off an Allied assault.

Bluntly, Petain charged the Nazi Fuehrer with "suppressing the first assumptions and principles of the armistice" signed by conquered France on June 24, 1940, in Compiegne Forest.

AT THE FRENCH FRONTIER, Nov. 11—(A. P.). Advices from Vichy said today unconfirmed reports were circulating there that France's fleet had left Toulon and was believed to be somewhere off Corsica en route to join forces with the United Nations.

HUESCA, Spain, Nov. 11—(A. P.).—German troops reached the French-Spanish frontier today north of Cancanfranc, a small Spanish town in Huesca Province, at a pass in the towering Pyrenees mountains.

ALLIED HEADQUARTERS IN NORTH AFRICA, Nov. 11—(U. P.).—Reports to Allied headquarters today said that about 400 American prisoners who were in French hands have been released.

VICHY (From French Broadcasts), Nov. 11—(A. P.). Italian troops arrived at Nice, on the French Riviera, this afternoon and an advance detachment continued to the west.

LONDON, Nov. 11—(U. P.).—Prime Minister Winston Churchill revealed today that an American column had occupied Bougie, Algeria, 120 miles east of Algiers, about one-third of the distance to the French naval base of Bizerte.

WASHINGTON, Nov. 11—(A. P.).—Secretary of State Hull today denounced the German invasion of unoccupied France as an act in complete harmony with Hitler's regime of lawlessness and utter disregard of solemn obligations.

18 Draft Approved By Senate

By WILLIAM S. NEAL
International News Service Staff Correspondent.

WASHINGTON, Nov. 11.—Swift Senate approval of the eighteen-nineteen draft bill conference report tomorrow was indicated today when sponsors of the one-year training amendment virtually abandoned opposition to the measure.

Some Senators who attended a conference called by Senator O'Daniel (Democrat) of Texas, author of the amendment prohibiting sending of youths under twenty into combat until they had received a year's training, predicted that approval would be unanimous. Senator Chavez said:

"I think the conference report will be adopted without opposition. I know that several of us in the meeting expressed that opinion. The record has been made and there is no use stirring up an argument."

Senator McKellar (Democrat) of Tennessee added:

"The House has gone so far that it looks as if we might go along."

O'Daniel, who called the conference, declined to make a statement.

EARLY SIGNING DUE

The bill may reach President Roosevelt in time for signature late tomorrow, so that Selective Service can set into motion machinery to bring 'teen age youths in the Army and thus check the rising average age of combat divisions.

The original plan of Gen. George C. Marshall, chief of staff, called for induction of eighteen-and nineteen-year-old youths during December, January and February.

Despite delay in passage of the legislation, Selective Service officials indicated induction can start next month.

TRAINING AMENDMENT

The Senate originally added to the bill the amendment of Senator O'Daniel (Democrat) of Texas, requiring the year's training, but leaders predicted that the upper chamber would bow to insistence of the Army that it be relieved of "hamstringing" amendments.

Senator Norris (Independent) of Nebraska, who started the one-year training fight, said that the fact that conferees retained the Tydings amendment requiring deferment of essential agricultural workers, will make final approval easier.

The Baltimore News-Post today is printed in
3 Sections
Be sure you get the complete newspaper.

Daily Double (Henry's Imp / Hornbeam) Paid $165.70

PIMLICO CHARTS

Copyright, 1942, by Triangle Publications, Inc. (Daily Racing Form.)
TRACK SLOW.

FIRST RACE—SIX FURLONGS. CHUTE. FOR THREE-YEAR-OLDS AND UP. Maidens. Special weights. Purse $1,000. Value to winner $700, second $150, third $100, fourth $50. Went to post at 1.26. Off at 1.26½. Start good from gate. Won driving, place same. Winner ch f 3, by St. Henry-Impulse. Owned by J. MADDOCK. Trained by C. BUTLER. Time 23 4-5, 49, 1.17.

	Wt.	Post	St.	¼	½	Str.	Fin.	Jockeys	Odds
Henry's Imp	112	3	7	6³	5½	3¹½	1ⁿ	W. Eads	$7.15
Cornelia Jane	113½	8	5	3¹	2²	1½	2ⁿᵒ	J. Pannell	31.00
Earth	107	2	6	5½	3½	2½	3⁴	J. Tammaro	9.60
Fairy Bay	113	5	4	2ʰ	4¹½	4¹	4²	C. Rollins	99.60
Setting Sun	115	10	10	7¹½	7²	7¹⁵	5¹	L. Ensor	16.75
Zacamay	107	6	2	1¹	1ʰ	5²	6ʰ	H. Trent	1.55
Hemsley	118	1	1	4½	6²	6²	7⁶	W. Balzaretti	45.00
High Welcome	115	7	8	9½	9²	8¹	8¹	J. Harrell	9.05
Annadace	110	4	11	11	10²	10⁵	9¹½	W. Mann	103.10
Smug	115	9	9	8⁶	8⁶	9¹½	10²	H. Mora	2.85
Little Tyke	118	11	3	10²	11	11	11	W. Rudert	57.45

$2 Mutuels Paid—Henry's Imp, $16.30 straight, $8.10 place, $6.20 show. Cornelia Jane, $18.60 place, $9.50 show. Earth, $6.60 show. Total mutuels....$65.30

Henry's Imp worked his way forward steadily, was sent to the outside for the drive and wore down the leaders in the last stages. Cornelia Jane factor from the start, came to the inside entering the stretch and finished strongly. Earth was never far back, raced forward when ready and tired. Fairy Bay was unable to keep up. Setting Sun lost much ground. Zacamay had good speed and stopped in the drive. Smug appeared to not like the track

Continued on Page 37, Column 4.

Troops Push To Tunisia

By WES GALLAGHER, U. S. Correspondent with the A. E. F. in Africa.

ALLIED HEADQUARTERS IN FRENCH NORTH AFRICA, Nov. 11—(A.P.).—American Expeditionary Forces under Lieut. Gen. Dwight D. Eisenhower completed their lightning occupation of a huge sweep of the Atlantic and Mediterranean coast line today when all French North Africa capitulated. Hostilities ceased in Morocco and Algeria at 7 A. M. (3 A. M., Eastern war time), but American and British forces sped, without pause, eastward from their now-secure base of Algiers toward Tunisia and

ALLIED HEADQUARTERS IN FRENCH NORTH AFRICA, Nov. 11—(A. P.).—Admiral Jean Darlan, former French chief of all defense forces, who has been negotiating secretly for days with U. S. Maj. Gen. Mark W. Clark, today ordered the cessation of hostilities in all French North Africa.

occupied Bougie, 200 miles from the Tunisian border.

(There were strong indications that a clash with Axis forces in this buffer wedge of Vichy territory was shaping up.)

Cessation of hostilities in Morocco after just three days of the campaign meant the fall of Casablanca. General Eisenhower already had disclosed that American troops were in Rabat, the Moroccan capital.

The disclosure was made when General Eisenhower ordered Maj. Gen. George S. Patton, the American commander on the Moroccan front, to place a wreath on the tomb of Marshal Louis Lyautey, founder of the French empire, at Rabat.

Commemorating the 1918 Armistice anniversary, the Allied supreme commander offered a "solemn assurance" that the African empire would remain French.

Casablanca Asks For Armistice

LONDON, Nov. 11—(A. P.).—The Allied occupation of French Northwest Africa was near completion today with the request of the French commander at Casablanca for an armistice, but German air-borne troops and warplanes were reported to have landed in Tunisia, the buffer protectorate between Algeria and Libya.

The Vichy radio announced that Admiral Michelier, the French commander at the Moroccan port of Casablanca, had been compelled to ask an armistice because "after three days of fierce fighting all means of resistance are exhausted."

THREE CHIEF CENTERS

Collapse of the fight there followed the surrender of Algiers on Sunday and the entrance of American troops into Oran yesterday. These were the three chief centers of resistance in Algiers and Morocco.

It was not known whether any British or American forces had yet succeeded in reaching Tunisia, said the Allied spokesman who an-

Continued on Page 2, Column 4.

Front In Europe—Churchill

LONDON, Nov. 11—(A. P.).—A second front in Europe was promised by Prime Minister Churchill today addressing Commons as the Germans overran all of France.

He declared:

"An attack will be made in due course across the Channel or the North sea."

Of the epochal events changing the whole military and political complexion of the war on two continents, even as he spoke, Churchill declared:

"Today news reaches us that Hitler has decided to overrun all of France, thus breaking the armistice to which the Vichy Government had kept such pitiful and perverted fidelity at the horrible cost even of sacrificing their ships and sailors in firing on American rescue ships.

STRUCK DOWN

"They have been struck down by their German task masters . . .

"Here is the moment when all Frenchmen should sink personal views and rivalries and think, as General DeGaulle is thinking, only of the liberation of their native land."

Churchill periodically gave reports of the progress of the war in North Africa—he told Commons the news of Casablanca's capitulation had come just as he entered the chamber—and made this prediction:

"The House may be sure that many things are going to happen in the next few days and I should be merely presuming if I attempted to give a digested opinion on the situation which will develop in North Africa, in France or in Italy, except that we shall shortly have far greater facilities for bombing Italy."

CITES PREPARATIONS

Of an invasion of Northern Europe, he said:

"Such an attack requires an im-

Continued on Page 2, Column 7.

—For Salvage Information
(1) Iron and Steel
(2) Kitchen Fats
(3) Tin Cans
Call PLaza 6877

War At A Glance

By Associated Press.

France:

Hitler scraps 1940 armistice, marches into former unoccupied French zone; Mussolini sends troops into Southern France.

Petain protests, reported to have set France free to defend herself. Unconfirmed reports say French fleet left Toulon to join United Nations.

Africa:

All French North Africa, including Morocco, capitulates to the American expedition.

Germans land air-borne troops in Tunisia, next door to American-occupied Algeria. Vichy says Italian marines occupy Bizerte, Tunisian naval base.

British Eighth Army engages Rommel's rear units at Buqbuq, 30 miles inside Egypt, after driving Axis main body into Libya.

Maas' Report on Pacific Spurs Demand for Probe—See Page 5

CHARACTER · QUALITY · AMERICA FIRST! · ENTERPRISE · ACCURACY

Los Angeles Examiner

AN AMERICAN PAPER FOR THE AMERICAN PEOPLE · THE GREAT NEWSPAPER OF THE GREAT SOUTHWEST

Reg. U.S. Pat. Off.

Examiner Telephone Richmond 1212 · Giant of Journalism · Examiner Building, 1111 S. Broadway

VOL. XXXIX—NO. 339 · CCC · LOS ANGELES, SUNDAY, NOVEMBER 15, 1942 · Seven Sections—Part One · 10 Cents in 100-mile zone · 15 Cents beyond 100 miles

FLEETS FIGHTING FOR SOLOMONS

RICKENBACKER SAVED AT SEA

PINCERS PERIL AXIS IN AFRICA

SECT. BERLE URGES REVOLT BY ITALIANS

Promise of Liberation Sent to Underground Forces Now Planning Upheaval

By Seymour Berkson

Managing Editor of International News Service, formerly stationed in Italy as chief of the Rome Bureau of International News Service

NEW YORK, Nov. 14.—(INS)—In the most forthright official bid of its kind ever offered to the people of Italy, Assistant Secretary of State A. A. Berle Jr., tonight called on the Italians to overthrow the Fascist regime now, pledging both military and economic aid in the liberation of their country.

The diplomat's historic declaration of American policy, delivered by him before a meeting of leaders in the free Italian movement, headed by the former Italian Foreign Minister Count Carlo Sforza, was later broadcast to Italy in the Italian language over the shortwave facilities of the Office of War Information.

MESSAGE FROM ITALY.

That his words were destined to be picked up and circulated by members of a powerful anti-Fascist movement already operating inside Italy was indicated when Luigi Antonini, chairman of the meeting and president of the Italian-American labor council, revealed the existence of the underground and read a message just received in America from its leaders. The message disclosed that mounting hate in Italy for the Mussolini regime is reaching the explosion stage.

Setting the stage for the eventual organization of a new free government in Italy, which would ally itself with the United Nations, Berle declared the "march of freedom has begun in the Mediterranean" and urging all Italian patriots to rise up now and "join the struggle against the Nazi and Fascist tyranny."

"The armies of the United Nations stand within gunshot of the Italian shore," Berle pointed out, citing the remark-

(Continued on Page 8, Column 2)

Barbara Bennett Missing 26 Hours; Widespread Hunt

Barbara Bennett, ex-film actress and sister of Film Stars Constance and Joan Bennett, last night became the object of a widespread search after she had been missing for 26 hours.

Her husband, Addison Randall, film actor, said that she disappeared shortly after 5:30 p. m. Friday at which time she was preparing to go to a dinner party in Beverly Hills.

Miss Bennett, the former wife of Morton Downey, the singer, recently lost custody of their five children by a court decision in Connecticut.

Since then, according to Randall, who said he was going to seek the aid of law enforcement agencies in trying to locate her, she had been despondent and for a few days [illegible] from a collapse.

Ace Found on Raft With 2 Flyers 600 Miles Off Samoa

CAPTAIN EDDIE RICKENBACKER, missing since October 21 in flight over Pacific, who with two companions has been rescued from raft north of Samoan Islands.

—Associated Press wirephoto

By Lee Carson

Staff Correspondent International News Service

WASHINGTON, Nov. 14.—Captain "Eddie" V. Rickenbacker, flying ace of World War I and death-defying pioneer of the airlines, has come through hell and high water of the South Pacific to serve again in his country's behalf.

After 23 days of clinging to life aboard a small rubber life-raft, the dauntless "Rick" was said by the Navy today to have been rescued by a Catalina flying boat 600 miles north of the Samoan Islands. While details were lacking on Rickenbacker's amazing "return from the dead" it presumably occurred during yesterday's traditional day of bad luck, Friday the 13th.

Forced into the sea at an unknown point in the

(Continued on Page 3, Cols. 1-2)

Troy Blasts Oregon, 40-0; Bruins Draw Bye; Irish Lose

Scoring at will with tremendous bursts of power, University of Southern California's Trojans yesterday blasted the Oregon Webfoots, 40-0, before 40,000 fans at the Coliseum.

Troy scored five touchdowns in the first half and added one more late in the fourth quarter against the team which last week administered the Bruins their first Pacific Coast Conference defeat, 14-7.

The Bruins drew a bye yesterday.

Other coast games saw Stanford smother Oregon State, 49-13; Washington State eke out a 7-0 win over Idaho; California conquer Montana, 13-0, and St. Mary's Preflight School held to a surprising 0-0 tie by Washington at Seattle.

The Navy had been established a heavy favorite over the Huskies.

A big third quarter enabled Michigan to overpower Notre Dame, 32-20, while Georgia Tech scored its eighth straight victory at the expense of Alabama, 7-0.

(Details in Sports)

PARATROOPS LEAD ALLIED TUNIS DRIVE

French Under General Giraud Battle Airborne Reserves Rushed Across Sea by Nazis

Yesterday's developments in the Allied offensive in Africa are summarized as follows:

1. Allied forces, preceded by hundreds of paratroops, are reported to have entered Tunisia.

2. French in Tunis reported fighting Germans.

3. Malta planes bomb Nazi airfield at Tunis.

4. Vichy announces suppression of small revolt by General Lattre de Tassigny.

5. Admiral Darlan acting in conjunction with Lieutenant General Eisenhower for defense of North Africa.

6. British Eighth Army in Libya occupies Gazala, 40 miles west of Tobruk.

By William Wade

Staff Correspondent International News Service

LONDON, Nov. 15 (Sunday).—Allied troops, preceded by hundreds of parachutists, were reported driving swiftly into Tunisia from the west today, while from the east the British Eighth Army

LONDON, Nov. 14.—(INS)—General Henri Honore Giraud, famous French war hero who is organizing an anti-Axis army in North Africa, has taken direct command of French troops in Tunisia that are fighting the Germans in that protectorate, it was reported tonight. The report was carried by the Fighting French News Agency.

dashed some hundred miles beyond Tobruk in a giant nutcracker advance against the last Axis positions in Africa.

Supported by incessant Allied air attacks that wreaked destruction on tenuous German footholds in Tunisia and fleeing Nazi skeleton forces deep in Libya, the two jaws of the American-British pincers drew closer to each other, squeezing the

(Continued on Page 12, Cols. 3-4)

Latin-American Pictures Appear in Today's Paper

Viva Mexico — Viva Guatemala — Viva Estados Unidos. Long live Mexico — Long Live Guatemala—Long Live United States. That there is solidarity in purpose and action in wartime among our good neighbors is graphically shown in a thrilling five-page picture section in today's Pictorial Review with the Examiner.

Marching men of Mexico . . . their President Avila Camacho . . . Guatemala's great military leaders . . . President Ubico . . . native scenes . . . all are shown in a glorious procession of pictures. Don't miss it.

Japs Say 6 Cruisers Sunk; Admit Own Battleship Hit

Stop Japan NOW—Save Civilization

UNLESS Japan is defeated, and defeated soon, Japanese military and naval power will dominate the world.

This warning was spoken in New York City a few days ago by no less an authority than Joseph C. Grew, who was our Ambassador at Tokyo at the time of the Pearl Harbor attack.

Mr. Grew made his ominous statement at the annual meeting of the Academy of Political Science, which was also addressed by General George C. Marshall, Army chief of staff, and Admiral Ernest J. King, commander in chief of the United States Fleet.

"The new Japan, born in the conquests of 1942," Mr. Grew said, "is a new terrible power, not known before in the world. . . .

"If Japan could defeat indomitable China, organize her present holdings and consolidate her position, Japan—not Germany, not Britain, not Russia, not ourselves, but Japan—could become the strongest power in the world."

MR. GREW described the vast and densely populated territories which Japan has seized as having every material thing a great power needs—food, rubber, oil, coal, iron, electric power and labor.

"All she needs," he added, "is TIME. She has EVERYTHING ELSE needed for victory."

Inevitably, therefore, Mr. Grew asserted, we face irretrievable defeat if we **"let this slave empire become entrenched"** and the actual situation is now so desperate that for us **"to lose A SINGLE DAY is as bad as losing a ship."**

Representative Melvin J. Maas, ranking Republican member of the House naval affairs committee, who has seen service with the Marines in the Solomon Islands, has CONFIRMED what Mr. Grew says.

IN A radio broadcast, Mr. Maas told the American people:

"If Japan wins this war—and she HAS WON IT unless we can carry the war to her and drive the Japs back to their original islands and deprive them of their fantastic new empire—THE END OF WESTERN CIVILIZATION IS HERE."

Apparently Congress is being startled into action by Representative Maas, who—as Senator Vandenberg remarked—**"cannot be dismissed as an armchair strategist."**

The Republican leader, Representative Joseph Martin, has recommended that Congress act to retrieve our perilous position in the Pacific war.

With one of its own members bringing dire news out of the South Seas, substantiating the previous warnings of our recent Ambassador to Japan, Congress should indeed act with utmost dispatch if it is going to act at all.

Tokyo Claims Three Allied Transports Set Afire

TOKYO, Nov. 14.—(From Japanese Broadcasts).—(AP)—Japanese imperial headquarters announced today that two Japanese destroyers had been sunk and a battleship damaged in a fierce, still-continuing battle off Guadalcanal in which, it said, Allied losses were six cruisers and a destroyer sunk and two cruisers and three destroyers heavily damaged.

The Japanese also listed three Allied transports as set afire and 19 planes shot down and said more than 10 of their own aircraft were missing.

(There has been no confirmation from any source for any part of this Japanese statement, either of their own or Allied losses or even for a major new sea-air battle.)

Powerful Japanese air and naval forces launched the attack Thursday, Imperial headquarters said, and by night had penetrated deep into the Allied naval lines and "destroyed more than half of the entire enemy naval craft and transports there."

U.S. to Broadcast Frost Warnings

POMONA, Nov. 15.—Wartime secrecy on weather predictions will be lifted enough for United States Weather Bureau frost warning forecasts to be broadcast to California's citrus growers from Pomona beginning tomorrow night.

Every night until February 15 the warnings will be broadcast over radio station KFI at 8 o'clock.

Areas to be covered run from the Sacramento Valley to Imperial Valley.

U. S. Holding Facts Secret; Yanks Close In on Buna

GENERAL MACARTHUR'S HEADQUARTERS, Australia, Nov. 15 (Sunday).—(AP)—Australians who fought across the Owen Stanley Mountains and Americans flown to the battle scene in aerial transports are closing in on the Jap-held coast base of Buna, in northeast New Guinea, the high command reported today.

By H. K. Reynolds

Staff Correspondent International News Service

WASHINGTON, Nov. 14.—A great naval battle raged tonight in the South Pacific as the United States Fleet fought off determined Japanese efforts to recapture the southeastern Solomon Islands.

The battle, described in a Navy Department communique as a "series of engagements," began last Wednesday night, Washington time, and is continuing in full fury.

Both the American and Japanese forces, the Navy said, have suffered losses, but no details will be reported while the fighting is still in progress.

TOKYO CLAIM UNCONFIRMED

There was no confirmation in Washington of Tokyo claims that six United Nations cruisers and one destroyer have been sunk, and that two other cruisers and three destroyers were damaged.

The Japanese radio admitted that two of their destroyers have been sunk and at least one of their battleships damaged.

Navy communique No. 192, issued at noon, E.W.T., said:

"South Pacific: (All dates are east longitude.)

"A series of naval engagements, which commenced on the night of November 12-13

Rules Issued for Girls, 16, to Work in War Factories

WASHINGTON, Nov. 14.—(AP)—The Labor Department opened the gates of war plants today to girls 16 and 17 years old.

Secretary of Labor Perkins, under authority of the Walsh-Healey Public Contracts Act which permits her to exempt employers from the 18-year age limit for women on Federal contracts, dropped the age requirement to 16 to permit more girls to take their places on the production lines.

She acted at the request of the War and Navy Departments and the Maritime Commission which found that continuation of the 18-year limit would "impair seriously the conduct of Government business by retarding essential production and interfering with the successful prosecution of the war in which the United States is engaged and which requires the complete utilization of the human and national resources of the nation."

THE WEATHER
Warmer today and tonight, with gentle to moderate winds, increasing humidity and no rain.

Read The Baltimore News-Post for complete, accurate war coverage. It is the only Baltimore newspaper possessing the three great wire services—
UNITED PRESS
INTERNATIONAL NEWS SERVICE
ASSOCIATED PRESS

THE BALTIMORE NEWS-POST
AN INDEPENDENT NEWSPAPER
The Largest Evening Circulation in the Entire South

NIGHT
Wall St. Opening

VOL. CXLII.—NO. 11 | Entered as second-class matter at Baltimore Postoffice. | TUESDAY EVENING, NOVEMBER 17, 1942 | PRICE 3 CENTS

U. S. NAVY IN CONTROL AT GUADALCANAL--KNOX

JAP FLEET SMASHED IN 3 DAY BATTLE, 23 SHIPS SUNK

U. S., British In Move To Trap Axis Forces At Tunis And Bizerte

LONDON, Nov. 17—(U. P.).—Allied forces are thrusting into Southern Tunisia in a drive intended to trap the Axis forces at Tunis and Bizerte and take the United States and British armies to the Gulf of Gabes, only 100 miles from the Libyan border, British dispatches reported today.

Lieut. Gen. Kenneth A. N. Anderson, with the British First Army and strong American Army support, including mobile units, was reported to be pushing a powerful force from the Tebessa area of Algeria, near the Tunisian border, toward Gabes, on the gulf of the same name on the Southeastern Tunisian coast 190 miles from Tripoli, capital of Libya.

157 MILES

It is 157 miles from Tebessa to Gabes. In a march on that route, the Allied armies would follow two narrow gauge railroads which would aid them in moving supplies.

Axis forces landed by air and sea to defend Northern Tunisia would be left isolated, to be disposed of at will, and the sole German hope would be to defend the narrow coastal corridor between Gabes and the Libyan frontier.

The main Allied army would be free to strike direct for Libya to meet the forces of Field Marshal Erwin Rommel, fleeing westward before the British Eighth Army under Gen. Sir Bernard Montgomery.

NEW FORCE

The German - dominated Vichy radio reported that a new and powerful Allied naval force, including two battleships, two aircraft carriers, four cruisers and nine destroyers had left Gibraltar for the Mediterranean and that 36 merchantmen, five transports and two

Continued on Page 2, Column 7.

East Faces Gallon Cut In Gas Coupon

WASHINGTON, Nov. 17—(A. P.).—A Congressional drive to postpone the nation-wide rationing of gasoline, now scheduled to start on December 1, was reported by its backers today to have gained strength in influential quarters.

By PHILLIPS J. PECK
International News Service Staff Correspondent.

WASHINGTON, Nov. 17.—East Coast motorists today faced a one-gallon cut in the value of their gasoline ration coupons.

The Office of Price Administration reportedly has decided definitely to reduce the coupon value from four to three gallons in order to save 80,000 barrels of petroleum products daily.

At its regular meeting a week ago the War Production Board agreed to accept Oil Co-Ordinator Ickes' recommendation for a reduction of 139,000 barrels daily in the consumption of petroleum and petroleum products along the Atlantic seaboard.

NEEDED FOR OFFENSIVE

The new military offensive in North Africa brought about the necessity for curtailing civilian use of petroleum along the Atlantic coast.

OPA Chief Leon Henderson was delegated by the WPB to determine how the 139,000-barrel saving could be made and reportedly decided first on cutting the gasoline consumption. The balance is expected to be made up by cutting fuel oil for homes and non-essential industries.

It was learned, however, that OPA officials have encountered considerable difficulty in determining what are non-essential industries.

FUEL OIL CUT LOOMS

Officials found many industries, the bulk of whose production was unessential, which were producing some war materials.

The allotment of fuel oil for residential heating probably will be cut to allow only 60-degree heat, generally, although special provisions are expected to be made for homes where there are small children or where there is illness,

Halsey Is A Tough Man Running A Tough Job

'Pudge' Hits Fast, And Where The Foe Least Expects It

WASHINGTON, Nov. 17—(A.P.). United States naval forces which smashed the Japanese fleet in the Solomons were led by one of the toughest men we have afloat.

Vice-Admiral William Frederick Halsey, Jr., commander of United States naval forces in the Southern Pacific, symbolizes America's answer to the boast of Admiral Isoroku Yamamoto that he would dictate peace in the White House.

Admiral Yamamoto now has other things than peace to think about. One of them is how to stop "Pudge" Halsey.

The naval record shows that Halsey had Tokyo's number even before the war began. On November 28, ten days before Pearl Harbor, a carrier task force set out for Wake Island to deliver planes under absolute war conditions. Tokyo was making fancy passes at Thailand (Siam) in those days, you remember.

WASN'T FOOLED

Halsey wasn't fooled. His orders to the carrier force were to blow any Jap ship out of the water and shoot any planes out of the sky.

Halsey is, among other things, one of our most air-minded admirals. He learned to fly at fifty-two.

He knows he still can learn and that the more you learn the better you fight.

He is, furthermore, our most experienced carrier task-force commander, and, to Tokyo's misfortune, most of this experience has

Continued on Page 2, Column 7.

VICE ADMIRAL WILLIAM F. HALSEY

Temperatures

12 Midn't,	48	5 A. M.,	45
1 A. M.,	47	6 A. M.,	45
2 A. M.,	46	7 A. M.,	43
3 A. M.,	45	8 A. M.,	42
4 A. M.,	45	9 A. M.,	45

—For Salvage Information
(1) Iron and Steel
(2) Kitchen Fats
(3) Tin Cans
Call PLaza 6877

Scratches At Bowie

First Race—Mango, Sumpin, Scouting, Grey Squire, Publist, Fly Whisk.
Second—Park Bench.
Third—Milk Flip, White Front, Brooklandville, Italian Harry, Sky Soldier, Mischief Afoot.
Fourth—One Link, Misty Lady, At Bat, Lei Ilima.
Fifth—Briarlass, Gold Regnant, Orlene.
Seventh—Caumsett.
Eighth—Son Altesse, Peace Day, Wheat, Justice Nap, Noptown Lass, Circus Wings.
Track fast.

Results Of Naval Battle

Japanese losses in the Solomons naval battle were:

SUNK—One battleship, three heavy cruisers, two light cruisers, five dsetroyers, eight transports.
DESTROYED—Four cargo transports.
DAMAGED—One battleship, six destroyers.

American losses were:

SUNK—Two light cruisers, six destroyers.

20,000 To 40,000 Enemy Troops Lost; Cost To U. S. 2 Cruisers, 6 Destroyers

WASHINGTON, Nov. 17—(A. P.).—Secretary of Navy Knox said today that the United States clearly had won Round Two of the battle for the Solomon Islands, but that it "must not be forgotten" that there may be a Round Three.

The Secretary called last week's American naval victory —which cost the Japanese 11 warships and 12 other vessels sunk and seven ships damaged—a major action, but not a decisive one."

Knox said in response to a press conference question:

"We have at this moment naval supremacy around Guadalcanal."

WASHINGTON, Nov. 17—(A. P.).—The United States Navy dominated the battle-quickened waters of the Solomon Islands today after crushing a mighty Japanese armada in an epic struggle which might well have broken the back of the enemy fleet.

In a savage three-day conflict that sent the foe's battered naval remnants into hiding, 23 Nipponese ships were sunk, seven were damaged and possibly 20,000 to 40,000 Japanese troops were lost in the swirl of sunken transports.

First details of the battle that raged from November 13 to 15 were released by the Navy last night.

MAY BOOST TOLL

Further reports may boost the staggering toll taken of enemy ships, but already the victory was hailed by naval officers unofficially as the greatest of the war thus far, and perhaps of modern times.

The partial reports listed the sinking of a Japanese battleship, three heavy cruisers, two light cruisers, five destroyers, eight crowded transports and four cargo ships. The American losses were given as two light cruisers and six destroyers.

Thus, in eleven months of war, Associated Press records show that 365 Japanese ships have been sent to the bottom of the Pacific as against 84 American vessels, including those at Pearl Harbor.

AT CLOSE RANGE

Much of the running sea fight was fought at close range and in darkness. So furious was the action that at one time two of three large Japanese units that converged for an attack on prized Guadalcanal Island "seemed confused," the Navy said, and "were firing at each other."

Admiral Chester W. Nimitz, commander in chief of the Pacific fleet,

Continued on Page 2, Column 1.

D. C. View:

Naval Power In U. S. Favor Now

WASHINGTON, Nov. 17—(U. P.).—The smashing American naval victory in the Solomons has gouged another gaping hole in the Japanese fleet and probably left the United States holding the balance of naval power in the Southwest Pacific.

The final returns are not in. But preliminary reports of 23 Japanese ships, including a battleship, sunk, seven more damaged, and between 20,000 and 40,000 Japanese troops killed gave Americans their greatest naval victory in history.

TWO NEW HEROES

They also have at least two new naval heroes — Vice-Admiral William F. Halsey, Jr., who directed the attack against numerically superior forces and sent the Japanese reeling back to their base, and Rear Admiral Dauiel J. Callaghan, former Presidential naval aide, who was killed in action during a furious night naval engagement that apparently broke the back of the main enemy offensive.

Numerically, the Japanese were

Continued on Page 2, Column 6.

Adventure calls men of 18-19

There's plenty of action and adventure waiting for men between 18 and 19 years old who enlist in the United States Army.

Shooting zeros out of the sky or winging a junkers with antiaircraft guns may appeal to you, or perhaps some other branch of the service which appeals to men seeking adventure while defending their country.—See page 4.

She'll fly over Tokio

PHILADELPHIA DAILY NEWS
THE PEOPLE'S PICTORIAL

Entered as Second-Class Matter Daily, Except Sunday, at the Postoffice at Philadelphia, Pa., Under the Act of March 3, 1879.

2 Cents in City Limits; 3 Cents Elsewhere. 50c a Month by Mail in U. S. A. 52 Issues with Candid Editions $1.

RITtenhouse 5200—Bell RACE 2443—Keystone

3 ★ ★ ★ EDITION

WEATHER
Continued quite cold today.

(OCTOBER CIRCULATION 130,034 COPIES DAILY)

★ Philadelphia, Wednesday, November 25, 1942 VOL. XVIII—No. 205

STALINGRAD SIEGE BROKEN; NAZIS FLEE

Story on Page 3

ENEMY shell burst less than 20 yards away [illegible]ed soldiers sweep in on a village in the northern Cacausas. Nazis now face major military disaster in Stalingrad sector as Russian offensive steamrollers them out.—(Int.)

FIVE JAPANESE tanks lie smashed and harmless on sand spit across mouth of Matanikau river in Guadalcanal, following foray against U. S. Marine positions on right bank of the river. An additional four tanks were knocked out.—(Official U. S. Marine Photo from International Soundphoto)

FOR VICTORY BUY UNITED STATES WAR BONDS AND STAMPS

WEATHER
Continued cold tonight.
Today's low, 20 at 10 a. m.

Columbus Evening Dispatch
OHIO'S GREATEST HOME DAILY

Associated Press News, Features, And Wirephotos
International News Service

VOL. 72, NO. 150. ** Telephone—MAin 1234 COLUMBUS, OHIO, FRIDAY, NOVEMBER 27, 1942 (Entered at Columbus, Ohio, Post Office as Second-Class Matter) 30 PAGES PRICE 3 CENTS

FRENCH SCUTTLE FLEET

Vessels Sunk As Hitler Seizes Toulon

BRIEF RESISTANCE CRUSHED TOO LATE TO SAVE WARSHIPS

Italian and German Troops Move In As Hitler Again Scraps Pledge Made to France.

(By The Associated Press)

Defiant French seamen were reported to have scuttled the entire French naval squadron of 62 warships at Toulon today as Adolf Hitler, ruthlessly crushing the last of France's free homeland under the Nazi boot, seized the big French naval base after overcoming resistance.

A Vichy broadcast said German troops marched into Toulon at 4 o'clock this morning.

"By orders of Admiral De La Borde, vessels of the French squadron at Toulon scuttled themselves," the broadcast said.

"At 10 a. m., there was not one vessel afloat."

The German high command said merely that "part" of the squadron had been sent to the bottom by their French crews as Axis troops moved in to thwart an alleged plot for the fleet to escape to the Allies.

Thus Hitler trampled another solemn pledge into the dust, putting all France in the same category of conquered nations as Norway, Belgium, Holland, Greece and Yugoslavia.

The last thin veil of "collaboration" between Vichy and Berlin was ripped aside to the crackle of gunfire by stout-hearted French troops who fought briefly but long enough to permit the scuttling of French warships in Toulon harbor.

Sixty-two French warships, including three battleships, are based at Toulon.

DNB, the official German news agency, said Hitler himself gave the order which sent German troops marching into the base last night.

A German communique said the coup was effected "to

Warships lie at anchor in the French naval base at Toulon, where Warships lie at anchor in the French naval base at Toulon, where the French fleet is reported to have been scuttled.—(AP) Wirephoto.

protect this region against further violation by the British and American aggressors" following the Anglo-American offensive in North Africa.

Toulon lies across the Mediterranean from Tunisia, where U. S. Army and British troops were now driving a wedge between Axis-held Tunis and Bizerte.

The German high command said Hitler and Premier Mussolini ordered the occupation "to prevent the French Mediterranean fleet from putting to sea as planned" and that in addition "unsure contingents of the French army" would be demobilized.

A Vichy broadcast said Hitler had ordered the immediate demobilization off all French naval and army forces and had placed Field Marshal Gerd von Rundstedt in supreme command in France.

The broadcast quoted Hitler's letter to old Marshal Philippe Petain as saying:

"On Nov. 12, 1942, orders were given by French authorities to the defenses at Toulon not to open fire in the event of an Anglo-American landing in this town. Existence of this order has been proved."

The Communique said German and Italian troops "nipped in the bud the resistance of elements instigated by Anglo-Saxon influence which flared up at isolated points and in a few hours carried our their allotted tasks.

"Part of the French fleet has scuttled itself in spite of the counter-order of the French (Vichy) government."

Besides the 26,000-ton battleships Strasbourg and Dunkerque and the 22,000-ton battleship Provence, these war vessels are believed to have ben lying in Toulon:

Four havy cruisers, each of 10,000 tons; three light, 7600-ton cruisers, a 10,000-ton seaplane tender, 25 destroyers and 26 submarines, sloops and auxiliaries.

President Is Firm On Date Of Gas Ration

Orders Plan Effective Dec. 1 Despite Protests.

'ABSOLUTE NECESSITY'

Farmers, War Workers To Get Needs, Jeffers Says.

WASHINGTON, NOV. 27.—(AP).—Farmers and war workers will be allowed necessary gasoline to meet their needs, Rubber Administrator William M. Jeffers told senate investigators today in reiterating that immediate nationwide rationing was "an absolute necessity."

Jeffers went to Capitol Hill backed by President Roosevelt's order of yesterday that nationwide gasoline rationing should go into effect Dec. 1 to conserve rubber, despite protests from congress members.

Testifying before the special senate defense investigating committee, Jeffers disclosed he had asked Price Administrator Leon Henderson and Transportation Director Joseph Eastman to make changes in the rationing program for farmers and war workers.

"I suggested to Mr. Eastman that farmers and stockmen generally have a very necessary use for trucks and that pending iron-

Widespread rumors that the government would "freeze" the sale of gasoline some time prior to the start of rationing next Tuesday could not be confirmed in any quarters Friday. So far as The Dispatch could learn, there was no basis for the rumors.

The rumors resulted in a rush to filling stations on the part of motorists seeking to fill their tanks before the start of rationing.

ing out of local difficulties they should be given to understand that they are to continue their normal operations until such time as their individual needs are determined.

Up to Boards

In the case of war workers, he said in a memorandum that rationing boards should be governed by recommendations of management-labor boards set up to determine individual needs of the men.

"If there are any disputes," he asserted, they will be resolved in such a way as "to preclude the possibility of there being any difficulty in people generally going about their activities without interference, until the matter can be straghtened out."

With no new rubber available, Jeffers testified, "we face the absolute necessity of the rationing program, which will enable us to continue essential driving through the fall of 1943 and spring of 1944."

Jeffers said the production of synthetic rubber was clouded by "ifs" including a big "if" in regard to "the success of the pro-

Continued on Page SIX, Column TWO

LONG-SEPARATED BROTHERS REUNITED IN NAVY

Assigned To Adjoining Bunks, Sailors Become Friends, Learn of Relationship

Series of Strange Coincidences Brings Boys Together in Fiction-like Manner

Two long-separated brothers, one a Columbus lad, who were parted when one one was four and the other two years of age, have been reunited at Norfolk Navy Yard, Va., after a series of the kind of coincidences that no novelist could use without being labeled fantastic.

In 1927, when he was four years old, Charles Woods, next to the youngest in a family of eight rphaned children in Barbersville, Ky., was adopted by Mr. and Mrs. J. B. West, who gave the boy their name and treated him as a son.

Two years later, the Wests and their adopted child moved to Columbus. Charles lost all contact with his brothers and sisters, including Garrett, the youngest.

On Sept. 24 occurred the first strange coincidence that was to bring these two boys back together. Charles West, who had been Charles Woods, was sworn in as a navy recruit at the Columbus naval office. At almost the same minute that Charles was taking his oath of allegiance, Garrett, his younger brother, was joining the navy in Louisville, Ky.

Both lads were sent to Great Lakes naval training station. With thousands o' rookie seamen there, making the chances of their meeting slim, the wheel of fortune spun again. The two brothers were assigned to the same company and to adjoining bunks.

Although neither was aware of his relationship with the other, the neophyte sailors took a liking to each other. They found they had similar interests and liked many of the same things. They became good friends.

Upon completion of their "boot" training, the two were sent to Norfolk navy yard, arriving Nov. 7. They slept in

When this picture was taken at Norfolk navy yard a few weeks ago, Charles West (second from left in bottom row) and Garrett Woods, (third from left, bottom row) didn't know they were really brothers. They made this discovery just in time to have an especially good excuse to celebrate Thanksgiving day.

the same barracks and the friendship continued to ripen.

It was last Saturday when Charles, who is now 19, asked 17-year-old Garrett: "Do you know what my real name is?"

"It's West, isn't it?" Garrett replied.

"No," said Charles, "it's Woods, the same as yours."

"You're kidding," scoffed Garrett.

"No, that's really my name," Charles replied. "My foster-father told me about a year and a half ago that he adopted me in Kentucky when I was four years old and that my name was Charles Woods."

Sensing a possible relationship, the two began firing excited questions at each other. Charles revealed that he had established contact with a twin sister in Artemius, Ky., who had sent him a picture of herself a year or so ago. He described her to Garrett.

"Fhy, she's my sister, too," cried the younger lad.

The amazing truth struck them simultaneously.

"We're brothers!"

Charles lost no time in telephoning the good news to his foster-father, who lives at 2156 Dartmouth avenue. Mr. West was so elated by the news of the discovery of the lad's long-lost brother that he promised to come to Portsmouth, Va., at once to congratulate the boys in person.

The two sailors were granted leave and Mr. West brought them back to Columbus with with him, where Thanksgiving Thursday took on a new significance around the West household.

"We certainly have something special to be thankful for this year," the youths declared. "We hope we can stay together as long as we're in the navy."

Mr. and Mrs. J. B. West (left) of 2156 Dartmouth avenue now have two "sons" instead of one. Their adopted boy, Charles, discovered recently that his buddy at Norfolk navy yard was really his brother, Garrett Woods, (right) from whom he'd been separated for 15 years.

Separated since early childhood, these two sailors with the cheerful grins, who had been buddies during training in the navy, discovered about a week ago that they were brothers. Charles West, age 19, (left) whose name was Woods before adoption, and Garrett Woods, age 17, spent Thursday with the former's foster-parents, Mr. and Mrs. J. B. West, 2156 Dartmouth avenue.

Young Assailants Sought In Murder Of Railroad Engineer

W. C. Conkle Fatally Shot During Holdup on St. Clair Viaduct.

A long series of beatings, strong-armed robberies and shootings in Columbus was climaxed early Thursday with the brutal murder of William C. Conkle, age 42, a Pennsylvania railroad engineer ,and police Friday were still without a clue as to the identity of the two youths sought in the killing.

The victim, bound for his home at 525 St. Clair avenue, was shot in the back and left to die on the St. Clair avenue viaduct by two colored youths who were surprised in the act of rifling his pockets by Morgan R. Swain, 152 Lechner avenue, a clerk from the railroad dispatcher's office, who told police the pair fled when he approached.

It was believed that a short struggle occurred before Mr. Conkle was shot. The victim's

Continued on Page SIX, Column FOUR

Fatally wounded by two youthful bandits, William C. Conkle, 42-year-old engineer, is pictured here with his fiancee, Miss Evelyn Bodkins, 468 St. Clair avenue.

Allied Spearhead Is 15 Miles From Tunis

(By The Associated Press)

LONDON, NOV. 27.—Allied spearheads were reported today to have lanced to a point 15 miles from Tunis and to have clashed with Axis forces at Mateur, a communications junction 25 miles south of Bizerte, in an effort to drive a wedge between the fortified capital and the naval base of Tunisia.

Both developments were announced in a Berlin radio broadcast.

The position of the task force striking at Tunis was not stated, but an Allied commique earlier announced that British First army troops, striking northeastward, had captured Majez El Bab, 30 miles southwest of Tunis, over stiff resistance and were "advancing successfully."

Mateur lies athwart the railway line and one of two highways between Tunis and Bizerte, in which Htler has concentrated the ma- majority of German and Italian troops in Tunisa. London commentators estimate their numbers

Continued on Page SIX, Column THREE

Nazi Lifelines Periled By Russian Offensive

MOSCOW, NOV. 27.—(AP).—Danger deepened hourly for Hitler's battered spearhead at Stalingrad today, the latest battle dispatches indicated, as fresh strength poured into the aggressive Red army garrison over a newly won land route and fast-wheeling field columns cut across the besiegers' lifelines to the west.

A confused war of movement swirled across the broad steppes west of Stalingrad and it was impossible to define battle lines clearly, but overnight dispatches said that in some places the Red offensive gained such momentum that fleeing Germans were frustrated in efforts to burn warplanes on fields overwhelmed too swiftly to permit takeoffs.

Dozens of planes were reported captured undamaged at one airdrome in a sector described only as hilly.

Overnight reports pushed to 115,600 the number of Axis soldiers said to have been killed or captured in the nine-day-old drive, with possibly another 150,000 wounded.

The German radio not only ac-

Continued on Page SIX, Column EIGHT

BUY WAR STAMPS

Mercury Hits New Low; Cold Will Continue

A "trace" of snow accompanied a new seasonal low to the city, Friday, according to the weather bureau. A few snowflakes fell during the middle of the morning. The minimum of 20 was reached at 10 a. m., and the forecast is for continued cold weather Friday night. Thursday's high temperature was 48 at 7 a. m.

News In Brief

WASHINGTON—Canadian merchant vessel sunk by enemy submarine in Caribbean in early November.

WASHINGTON—Quota of 85,000 new adult bicycles established for rationing in December.

PONTIAC, MICH.—City bus drivers strike in wage dispute.

WINDSOR, ONT.—Workers at three plants of Ford Motor Co. remain on strike.

Two Local Youths Killed in Action

Navy department messages revealed Friday that two more Columbus sailors had been killed in action and that a third had been wounded.

Casualties were John G. Fisher, jr., 26-year-old son of Mr. and Mrs. John G. Fisher, sr., 417 Welch avenue, and John Catalogna, son of Mr. and Mrs. C. J. Catalogna, 475 East Rich street. Francis N. Holmes formerly of 192 East Beck street and son of Mrs. Iva Mae Holmes of Battle Creek, Mich., was reported wounded.

A petty officer first class and electrician's mate first class, Fisher was fatally burned when the U. S. Destroyer Meredith was lost in the battle of the Solomons, his parents were advised Thanksgiving morning. He was a graduate of South high school. Four sisters and a brother also survive. He had been in the navy six years.

Second Class Seaman Catalogna previously had been reported missing in action, word of his death reaching his parents this week.

A water-tender second class, Holmes enlisted in the navy following his graduation from South high school four years ago.

Ickes Tipped As Labor Secretary

NEW YORK, NOV. 27.—(AP).—The New York Times and the New York Herald Tribune said today reports were current in Washington of a major cabinet reorganization which would assign Harold L. Ickes as secretary of labor to consolidate control of war man power and procurement under civilian jurisdiction.

An executive order to accomplish the revision had been delayed, the paper said.

The reported shuffle would involve naming Ickes, secretary of the interior, to the labor post held by Frances Perkins and would place under Ickes' control the man power jurisdiction now belonging to Paul V. McNutt, war man power commissioner and federal security administrator.

McNutt, the reports said, would be made secretary of the interior and Miss Perkins would administer the federal security agency. The United States employment service, the machinery of selective service and the series of federal training programs would be placed under Ickes as head of a revitalized labor department.

You Will Find---

IN SUNDAY'S DISPATCH

Camera glimpses of thrilling plays in Ohio State's game with the Iowa Seahawks come to you Sunday in a full page of action pictures in the big Sports section, together with a full page of Wirephotos of other big games all over the country.

Ohio had its birth as a state just 140 years ago this Sunday. A magazine article takes you back to those pioneer days to review a dramatic chapter in our state history.

In another article, an Ohio woman who taught in a girls' school in Greece relates the soul-stirring story of that country's courage under the tribulations of Nazi conquest.

Written by the author of the famous "Thin Man" stories, the most thrilling mystery yarn of the year appears in one of the Sunday magazine sections. Be sure to look for the first of three installments of Dashiell Hammett's "Dead Yellow Woman." Don't miss this super-duper thriller-chiller.

And there are many other interesting features that you will want to read this Sunday, besides 16 pages of the world's best comics and the complete news.

If you are not a regular subscriber to The Sunday Dispatch, tell your Dispatch carrier to leave you a copy, Sunday morning, or have your newsdealer reserve you one, or phone MAin 1234 and have it home delivered.

For Victory Buy U. S. War Savings Stamps And Bonds

THE JEWISH NEWS

A Weekly Review of Jewish Events

For Victory Buy U. S. War Savings Bonds And Stamps

VOL. 2—NO. 8 | 2114 Penobscot Bldg. | RA. 7956 | Detroit, Michigan, December 11, 1942 | 34 22 | $3.00 Per Year; Single Copy, 10c

Ghetto Jews Killed In Battle With Nazis

JDC Spends $7,250,000 Aiding Victims of Axis

Relief, emigration assistance, educational and reconstructive help was given to 795,000 refugees during last year, 28th annual report reveals; organization helped 7,700 persons escape from Europe to America and Palestine . . . Three United Jewish Appeal agencies spent $18,053,000 in 12 months.

—Page 2

Welfare Council Calls War Emergency Parley

Federation and Welfare Fund Group advances date of 10th annual General Assembly in Cleveland, to Jan. 16-18, because of urgency of war-time problems. Meetings will be restricted to working sessions at which 187 cities will be represented . . . James Marshall of New York is chairman of program committee.

—Page 2

Police and Gestapo Massacre Victims Fighting Deportation In Barricaded Polish Towns

—Page 7

War Honor Roll of Detroit's Jews Serving in the U. S. Armed Forces

—Pages 13-16

Jews and Non-Jews Give Support To Strong Palestine Home Appeal

—Page 2

Spirit of Maccabees Lives Again in Ranks of Jewish Servicemen

The Hanukah festival, which comes to a close today, finds the Jewish people throughout the world encouraged by the Maccabean valor our men in the service of the United Nations are displaying on all fronts.

The above photographs show groups of Palestinian Jewish fighters in action on the Egyptian desert, crossing a bridge "somewhere in the Middle East," in battle position with machine guns and on the march to meet the common enemy. The lower right photograph shows a group of Polish and Jewish Boy Scouts fraternizing in Tel Aviv. There are now 47,000 Palestinian Jews serving with the British combatant forces.

THE SCRAPPER

PUBLICATION AND DISTRIBUTION APPROVED
IN PRINCIPLE BY
WAR PRODUCTION BOARD

EDITORIAL OFFICE
ROOM 3303A—350 FIFTH AVE.
NEW YORK, N. Y.

SUBSCRIPTION OFFICE
420 DE SOTO AVENUE
ST. LOUIS, MO.

A PUBLICATION FOR THE MEN AND WOMEN WHO ARE AIDING THEIR COUNTRY IN THE SALVAGE FOR VICTORY PROGRAM No. 10

WPB IN SOS FOR MORE FATS

Every Kitchen Is an Arsenal

MADE FROM WASTE FATS
1 LB. WASTE FAT FIRES 4 ANTI-AIRCRAFT SHELLS
MACKENZIE

(Mat No. 278)

At 92 He Wins Illinois Prize With 17,000-lb. Collection

MINONK, Ill.—They don't grow old in Illinois, and A. H. Parks, who is only 92, tipped his hat down over his forehead, gave his pants a hitch, and stepped into Minonk's scrap drive, wherein to the amazement of gaping youngsters, he topped the list with 17,000 pounds collected.

Having lived through three wars—he was eleven years old when the Civil War began—he has learned to take them in his stride. And his stride was long in scrap collecting. His biggest contribution was a 31-year-old 14,000-pound Flour City tractor. Mr. Parks, a former implement dealer, donated it to local salvage officials with the comment: "We hope to give our enemies a good job of thrashing."

They gave a prize to the biggest contributor in Minonk, and Mr. Parks calmly took it.

Now, Whose Move Is It?

NEW BEDFORD, Mass.—A truck, manned by Boy Scouts conducting a salvage drive here recently, blocked a bus in a residential neighborhood. "Will you kids move that truck?" the driver leaned out to shout. "I've got a lot of people on this bus who want to get home." "Mister," yelled back one of the Scouts, "I've got two brothers overseas. They want to get home, too."

Village of 812 Gets 150 Tons

ISSAQUAH, Wash.—This town of 812 citizens collected 300,000 pounds of scrap, or nearly 370 pounds per person, in a recent campaign sponsored by the Kiwanis Club.

A committee divided the town and surrounding countryside into districts. Business and professional men began a telephone campaign, making a personal plea for scrap. Boy Scouts visited the homes which could not be reached otherwise.

On collection day 20 trucks were used and 175 volunteers responded. Business establishments closed. The bank, which could not legally close, sent representatives to aid. Boy Scouts were dismissed from school. When the drive ended the workers were treated to ice cream.

Every Housewife Urged to Act Now

WASHINGTON—The need for waste fats to make explosives for our fighting forces has grown so critical that the War Production Board is sending this SOS to every housewife in America:

"WPB requests fat collections be increased immediately to maximum amount possible."

The lives of American soldiers, sailors and marines depend upon the speedy response to this SOS.

Admittedly, the collection of waste fat has been "spotty," but that fault has been remedied by approval of a new OPA amendment designed as a step toward completion of collection facilities. This amendment allows shipping and collections costs to be added to the ceiling price paid for waste fat.

Instructions Issued

Following approval of the amendment, R. K. White, Chief of the General Salvage Section of WPB, issued the following instructions:

"All State Executive Secretaries should immediately complete facilities to collect waste fats from meat dealers, or arrange for direct shipment from one designated meat dealer in each area to a rendering plant."

In his bulletin, White pointed out that "EVERY HOUSEWIFE, regardless of size or location of the community in which she lives, is being asked via radio, newspapers and motion pictures to save waste fats. Meat Dealers and operators of Frozen Food lockers also are urged constantly to buy these waste fats from the housewife.

"Obviously, the dealer cannot continue to buy waste fats if no regular method of sale and ship-

(Continued on page 7)

Rosenwald Appeals To Retail Meat Men

WASHINGTON — Lessing J. Rosenwald, Director of WPB's Conservation Division, appealed to all independent, cooperative and chain groups in the retail meat trade for increased effort in the collection of waste fats in the following telegram:

"War Production Board requests fat collections be increased immediately to maximum amount possible. Therefore, we ask again your valuable cooperation. The American Meat Institute is making distribution to retail dealers of the new Waste Fat and Grease store display material. Will you see that your members and affiliates cooperate by putting up the new display material immediately."

Fellow Scrappers! We Need Your Help

Fill out this blank and return it to us at once. The paper is designed to help you in your salvage efforts and you can help us by letting us know if we are doing the job, and how we can do it better. Your cooperation in promptly returning this blank will be greatly appreciated.

The SCRAPPER
Room 3303A—350 Fifth Avenue
New York, N. Y.

The SCRAPPER is useful in my salvage efforts. Yes ☐ No ☐

I would like to make the following suggestions for improving the paper:

....

....

....

....

SIGNED ....

AFFILIATION ....

ADDRESS ....

500,000 GERMANS IN FULL RETREAT

Oakland Tribune

EXCLUSIVE ASSOCIATED PRESS... WIREPHOTO... WIDE WORLD... UNITED PRESS

HOME EDITION

VOL. CXXXVIII | 5c DAILY | OAKLAND, CALIFORNIA, WEDNESDAY, JANUARY 6, 1943 | 15c SUNDAY | NO. 6

FLYING FORTS DEVASTATE SOUSSE

★ ★ ★ ★ ★ ★ ★ ★ ★ ★ ★

U.S. Labor Official Seeks Machinist Strike Peace

Parley Today With Marine Board, Navy

U.S. Department of Labor representatives today continued San Francisco conferences looking toward adjustment of the controversy which has resulted in approximately 30 of the 200 C.I.O. machinists remaining away from duty at the General Engineering & Drydock Company shipyard at Alameda.

Following initial meetings with union officials yesterday, Robert F. Amis, of the department's Wages and Hours Bureau, said he would endeavor to contact all interested parties and at the conclusion of conferences would issue a complete statement.

It is believed that sessions will be held today with employers and representatives of the Army, Navy and Maritime Commission, but no official comment was forthcoming. Some sources reported the Navy, which had not been appraised of the initial conference arranged by the Washington authorities, is now "fully cognizant" of the presence of the two men.

NO UNION STATEMENT

James P. Smith, business representative of the local union, was not available for comment, nor was any statement issued by Harry Hook and E. F. Dillon, business representatives of San Francisco Local 68 of the A.F.L. Machinists' Union. The three men, together with James Thimmes, representing C.I.O. Steel Workers, were the first to meet with Amis, Charles Reynolds, of the labor department's solicitor's office and R. J. Manguno, administrative assistant of the Shipbuilding and Ship Repair Stabilization Committee.

Union spokesmen had no comment on a report that they had avoided attending a conference called on New Year's Day by Vice-Adm. John W. Greenslade, commandant of the 12th Naval District; Lieut. Gen. John L. DeWitt, commander of the Western Defense Command, and Maj. Gen. Frederick

Continued Page 2, Col. 1

TRUCE CALLED ON LABOR LEGISLATION

By WESLEY E. ROBBINS

SACRAMENTO, Jan. 6.—A truce in labor legislation which may shorten the days of the 55th session of the California Legislature and eliminate hard fought battles which have widened the rift between organized labor and employers today became a possibility.

At a conference called late yesterday by Senator William P. Rich and Speaker of the Assembly Charles Lyon, representatives of industry, employing groups and agriculture sat down with union labor leaders. Out of the conference is expected to come an attempt to confine legislation introduced at this session to minor adjustments of existing laws to meet wartime needs.

The proposal has the approval of Governor Earl Warren, according to reports made to the conference

Continued Page 4, Col. 1

Alameda Names City Manager

ALAMEDA, Jan. 6.—Don C. McMillan, 44, city manager of Ventura for several years, was appointed city manager of Alameda last night by the City Council.

The appointment will be effective February 1. McMillan's salary will be $500 a month.

Last week the council named George Sperbeck, city engineer, to serve as acting city manager until a permanent appointment could be made to fill the vacancy left by the departure of Charles R. Schwanenberg, who now is city manager of Oakland.

City officials said here that McMillan's record of service at Ventura has been outstanding. During the depression, they related, he managed to raise the salary of city employees and, at the same time, reduce city expenditures.

Fights Ahead As Congress Opens Today

More Congressional News on Page 4

WASHINGTON, Jan. 6.—(AP)—The 78th Congress of a Nation of free people convenes today, consecrated to victory at arms to preserve that freedom, but sharply divided on home-front policy and uncertain of the scope and detail of the peace to follow the war.

The first session opens on a note of self-assertion, with House Speaker Rayburn (D., Tex.) reportedly telling a Democratic caucus that Congress no longer would yield to "bureaucrats" and that the Congress "must reassert itself."

And while harmony in the Administration party hung in the balance, Republicans likewise blasted at "bureaucracy" and "waste," and called for many changes in wartime Government operations—all pointing to rough and possibly bitter days ahead in Washington.

President Roosevelt, in an address that may vie in importance with his messages asking war on the Axis, will appear before a joint session of the Senate and House tomorrow to report on the state of the Union.

SPEECH EAGERLY AWAITED

Some leaders expect him to deal not only with the progress of the conflict, and domestic problems, but to give some clue to his ideas on the peace to follow, in the writing of which this Congress may take a place in world history.

Congressional leaders were expected to confer with Roosevelt today on the text of his message, and it was understood some would urge him to skip any proposals for Social Security revision or expansion, contending that such propositions in wartime might cause "an unnecessary fight that might disrupt the entire congressional program."

Gavels fall in both Houses at noon (Eastern wartime) today, and the separate chambers will proceed immediately to matters of organization, including election of the House speaker.

G.O.P. MAKE GAINS

Reflecting the Republican resurgence at the polls last November will be the swearing-in of new members — seven Republicans and two Democrats in the Senate; 67 Republicans, 41 Democrats and one Farm-Laborite, in the House. The November elections almost wiped out the Democratic majority in the House, but in the Senate the Democrats are more comfortably fixed.

In pre-session caucuses yesterday, Sam Rayburn of Texas was nominated by the Democrats for the speakership, and the Republicans put forward their floor leader, Joseph W. Martin Jr., of Massachusetts. The bald, soft-spoken, businesslike Rayburn appeared certain to retain the chair, as the Democrats still hold 222 House seats to 208 for the Republicans.

The majority party re-elected John W. McCormack of Massachusetts as its floor leader. Senate Democrats will caucus Thursday and

Continued Page 2, Col. 6

British Take Important Hill

CAIRO, Jan. 6.—(AP)—Heavy bombers of the United States Army's Ninth Air Force pounded the Eastern Tunisian harbor of Sousse again yesterday in a daylight attack without the loss of a plane, an American communique announced today.

"All the bombs fell within the target," the communique said. "Bursts were observed on commercial phosphate plants and the southern quays."

A British communique, apparently referring to the same attack, said that "hits were scored on quays and buildings" by Allied bombers.

Long-range fighters, it was reported, shot down a German bomber off Lampedusa Island, between Malta and the Tunisian coast. Only one plane was lost in these and other operations, the communique reported.

British commandos and regular soldiers in a swift down attack threw the Germans out of a strong position in the hills a few miles west of Mateur, which is 20 miles southwest of the Tunisian naval base of Bizerte, Reuters said today in a dispatch from North Africa.

The date of the attack was not given, but apparently it occurred either Monday or yesterday.

After a night-long downpour, it reported, the British advanced quickly over bare hillsides and, supported by artillery and fighter-bombers, occupied the position in three hours.

This success was stated to have been achieved against some of the best German forces in Tunisia. The Germans had been digging in there for weeks. How much they valued the position was indicated by advices that they launched an immediate counter-attack.

Parachute troops took part in the British attack, it was added.

A month ago the British tried a similar assault but were beaten back, mainly because they lacked air support. This lack was remedied in the new attack.

Clark Heads U.S. 5th Army

ALLIED HEADQUARTERS IN NORTH AFRICA, Jan. 6.—(AP)—Lieut. Gen. Mark W. Clark, 46, the tall American officer who made a daring landing on the hostile shore of North Africa from a submarine for a secret meeting with French officers before the Allied occupation, has been placed in command of the newly activated U.S. Fifth Army, now preparing with its British and French allies to drive Axis forces from Tunisia.

The announcement that General Clark, formerly deputy commander-in-chief to Lieut. Gen. Dwight D. Eisenhower in North Africa, had assumed his command came as most of the long Tunisian front lay quiet in the mud of Winter rains.

(A Reuters dispatch from the Tunisian front, said that crack troops of the British First Army, including commandos and parachutists, had driven the Germans from a strong position in the hills a few miles west of Mateur, about 20 miles southwest of Bizerte.)

As the U.S. Fifth Army came into being under General Clark, it was learned that a detachment of Canadian officers and non-commissioned officers had arrived in North Africa to gain battle experience with the British First Army under Lieut. Gen. K. A. N. Anderson.

(The announcement of the activation of the U.S. Fifth Army indicates that a force of at least two or three divisions has been organized and made ready to take its place besides the British First Army and the French forces fighting in Tunisia as an independent entity. American troops have of course been engaged in the fighting since the beginning of the occupation.)

Tunis and Tripoli Nazis Near Merger

By EDWARD W. BEATTIE

LONDON, Jan. 6.—(U.P.)—The battles of Tunisia and Tripolitania are gradually merging today, and the forces of Marshal Erwin Rommel and Lieut. Gen. Walther Nehring are so close together they are drawing on the same pool of supplies and men.

Mud restricted operations on the northern sector in Tunisia, but on the southern sector, where the Germans had suffered heavy losses in futile efforts to turn the Allied right flank, heavy fighting is reported raging.

The Nazis' radio Vichy broadcast

Continued Page 2, Col. 5

Chain Store Head Dies

WILKES BARRE, Pa., Jan. 6.—(AP)—Charles Anson Bond, 70, founder of a men's clothing store chain bearing his name and former mayor of Columbus, O., died here last night.

YANKS SINK 9 JAP SHIPS AT RABAUL

MELBOURNE, Jan. 6.—(AP)—Heavy bombers of the Allied air forces under Gen. Douglas MacArthur's command have smashed again at massed enemy shipping in Rabaul harbor, leaving eight vessels afire or sinking and destroying a ninth with a direct hit by a half-ton bomb, it was officially announced today

Probably a tenth vessel was destroyed, an Allied headquarters communique reported on the heels of warnings that the Japanese were gathering a new war fleet in the southwest Pacific.

In all, 50,000 tons of shipping suffered under the newest blows of the bombers which have been making Rabaul, capital of New Britain Island, the objective of concentrated attacks ever since the Solomon Islands campaign opened. The direct hit was on a destroyer tender. Alongside her was a destroyer which might have been damaged. The eight other ships were merchant vessels.

One bomber was reported lost on the flight but six Japanese planes were downed among a flight of about two dozen that tried to intercept the attack.

EXTENSIVE BOMBINGS

The communique also noted anew bombings of Lae, Salamaua and Madang, in northeastern New Guinea; Gasmata airdrome in southern New Britain, and on Timor Island, northwest of Australia. Airdromes at Lae, Madang and on Timor were the targets.

One air force unit also pounded the Japanese ground forces holding the spit of beach at Sananada Point, north of Buna, as Allied tank, artillery and infantry closed in, the headquarters report said.

The air forces began intensive bombardment of the Japanese beach position two days ago, dropping 11,000 pounds of the missiles on the Japs in their first sortie, William

Continued Page 2, Col. 8

Bowling Alley Fire Kills Six

CHICAGO, Jan. 6.—(AP)—Six persons were killed and more than 100 injured in a fire and explosion in a bowling alley on the far South Side shortly before last midnight. Many of the 200 patrons who escaped to the street were blown through doors by the force of the blast.

The sixth body, that of Joseph R. Bingham, 41, was recovered from the ruins today more than eight hours after the blaze started. Fire Marshal Anthony Mullaney estimated the damage at $150,000.

One of the bodies was identified as William Gutrich, 19, son of a policeman who had been reported missing. Ferdinand Gutrich, the father, was assigned to the Gresham police station. The fire was at 9354 South Ashland Avenue, in the Gresham district.

The other dead were identified as Thomas Podzimek, 30; Carl Peter Deddo, 28; Anthony Erris, 29, and Phillip Gardner, about 50.

In the Little Company of Mary

Continuel Page 2, Col. 7

Lowell, Former Head Of Harvard, Is Dead

BOSTON, Jan. 6.—(AP)—A. Lawrence Lowell, 86, president emeritus of Harvard University, died today at his Boston home.

The elderly educator, who presided over the destinies of the three centuries-old university for three decades, died after a brief illness.

His family said funeral services would be held at the Harvard Memorial Church in Cambridge, at 11 a.m. Saturday.

Caucasus, Don Armies Routed

LONDON, Jan. 6.—(U.P.)—Soviet troops have captured the crest of Mamayev Nurgan, the most vital defense point of the German troops encircled in the Stalingrad region, radio Moscow said today.

By HENRY C. CASSIDY

MOSCOW, Jan. 6.—(AP)—The German Army was reported in full retreat in the Caucasus today, blowing up bridges and mining roads in a desperate effort to check the surging advance of Russian forces driving hard at its heels.

Red Star, organ of the Soviet Army, said Russian forces, which already had stormed and won the important towns of Mozdok, Nalchik, Prokhladnenski, Kotlyarevskaya and Maiskoye, continued their sweeping advance along a wide front, winning back a large number of additional towns.

The entire Province of North Ossetia, lying between Ordzhonikidze and Nalchik, had been won back under the Red banner by Soviet forces operating along the west bank of the Terek River, while other Russian troops rolled the Germans back to the north, Red Star asserted.

(Reuters, British news agency, estimated in London that more than a half-million of Adof Hitler's finest troops were in full retreat in the Caucasus and the Middle Don.)

RUSS MOVE FORWARD

To the north, along the lower don, the Russians were reported fighting forward after overrunning the important Nazi bridgehead town of Tsimlyansk and thus driving a second spearhead within 125 miles of Rostov, whose fall might doom the entire German force in the Caucasus.

The first spearhead was thrust earlier southwest of Kamensk to a point about 100 miles northwest of the great Don mouth port of Rostov.

Red Star said the main line of German fortificaitons at the eastern end of tthe Caucasus front was shattered Monday when the Russians stormed the approaches to Nalchik and occupied the city after a terrific street battle.

Soviet troops were said to have pursued the Germans northward from this sector across a western branch of the Terek River. In a 12-mile final thrust yesterday, Red Star said, the Russians drove into and captured the town of Prokhladnenski, 30 miles northeast of Nalchik.

VITAL RAIL JUNCTION

Prokhladnenski is the juncture where the trunk line Caucasus railroad from Rostov to the Baku oilfields meets a branch line running south to Ordzhonikidze.

Still other forces rolled the Germans back to the west at an accelerated rate, with tanks and infantry overwhelming enemy centers of resistance, the Army newspaper reported.

Don Cossack guardists, swinging their sabers in mounted action and then dismounting for action with modern automatic weapons, were reported playing an epic part in the Caucasus campaign.

Izvestia, the Government newspaper, said the cavalry raided German flanks, slashed through to the rear and stormed enemy defenses in attacks leading to the recapture of Mozdok on Monday.

Izvestia said the Germans hurled tanks against the horsemen, but the Cossacks withstood the counter-attacks, outmaneuvered the heavy machines, and charged on over the Nazi positions.

The fall of Tsimlyansk was announced in a triumphant special Russian communique which de-

Continued Page 2, Col. 4

Doctors Act In Food Crisis

Bay area residents will have to take still another notch in their belts as far as rationed food products are concerned, wholesalers announced today.

In San Francisco the City Health Department revealed a plan whereby grocers will honor doctor's "prescriptions" for supplies in which there are shortages, for babies, mothers and the sick. Already heavy whipping cream for diabetics has been given on a doctor's orders, and physicians are writing canned milk prescriptions for infants and hospitals.

Demanding that the Government repeal as "unessential" provisions of the Baking Industry War Order forbidding sale of sliced bread, West Coast bakers asserted the prospective Federal regulations would result in no savings because sliciing bread in bakeries is an automatic and mechanized step in production. They contended that such a law would result in waste of "a great quantity of critical materials," since housewives would have to purchase bread knives.

ASK POSTPONEMENT

At the same time, bakers asked that the effective date of food distribution be postponed from January 18 to March 1.

The vital question of "where and when do I get butter," remained unanswered except by Food Administrator Claude R. Wickard's statement that he would follow up his drastic cuts in civilian supplies of the commodity as well as canned citrus fruits.

Officials admitted that shortages of some foods have reached the point where something drastic must be done soon to meet complaints arriving from virtually all areas, but they emphasized that local shortages generally are the result of poor distribution.

Wickard's latest food orders—os. 2 and 3—were designed to assure adequate supplies of butter and canned citrus fruit for American armed forces and other United Nations.

CIVILIAN BUTTER CUT

He directed butter manufacturers to set aside for war uses at least 30 per cent of all creamery butter stocks—a move expected to lower average annual civilian butter consumption

Continued Page 2, Col. 2

MacArthur's Work Praised by Marshall

ALLIED HEADQUARTERS IN AUSTRALIA, Jan. 6.—(AP)—Gen. Douglas MacArthur has received from General George Marshall, Army chief-of-staff, this message of congratulations:

"We are stimulated and encouraged by the news of completing of the enemy's destruction in the Buna sector (of New Guinea).

"I know the terrific difficulties under which you have operated and the handicaps under which you initiated and staged your campaign. My thanks and congratulations to you and all concerned."

R.A.F. Commander in Egypt Dies in Crash

CAIRO, Jan. 6.—(AP)—Air Vice-Marshal Wilfred McClaughry, commanding the Royal Air Force in Egypt, was among 11 persons killed Monday in an airplane crash, it was disclosed today. Lady Tedder was killed in the same crash. Her death was disclosed yesterday.

Today's Index—Weather Talk

By EARLE ENNIS

Colonel Washington Dilly of the Dilly Weather Bureau reported for work in fine fettle. He had won at poker, the night before, he had slept well, and when he started for the office he got a seat in a bus for the first time in two weeks.

"Now, let's see," he remarked. "Shall we have frost or clouds? Hm—guess we'll bear in mind the economic phase of the situation and have frost."

"Why frost?" asked Casey, the cat.

The Colonel chuckled.

"Because, my little whiskered nincumpoop," he said, "clouds come higher . . .!"

And shutting his door softly he tip-toed over to his desk and so to work.

Statesman Succumbs

LONDON, Jan. 6.—(AP)—Pangeran Adipati Ario Soejono, minister without portfolio in the Netherlands Government and first native of the East Indies to be named a member of the cabinet, died here last night.

CONGRESS OPENING WORRIES ENGLAND, FEAR U.S. WILL BECOME WORLD HERMIT

LONDON, Jan. 6.—(AP)—London newspapers displayed anxiety today over the opening of the new Congress in the United States.

Headlines read:

Daily Mirror: "Will U.S. again become a world hermit?"

Daily Mail: "Roosevelt's foes today start Congress battle to cut down his power."

Daily Express: "The next 60 days—don't lose faith in America."

Daily Telegraph: "This U.S. Congress will strive to influence policy-bias which will challenge not the war effort but 'New Deal' planning."

Entered as second-class matter April 15, 1931, at the post office at New Haven, Connecticut, under the act of March 3, 1879

Published Monday, Wednesday and Friday by Illustrated Current News, Inc., New Haven, Conn. Subscription Annually, $20.80

Jan. 15, 1943—No. 4583

THE HORNET DIES

The 20,000-ton aircraft carrier Hornet lies dead in the waters of the Pacific with a destroyer trying to tow her to safety. Attacked by Jap bombers (arrow indicates bomb hole) and torpedo planes, she was seriously crippled. A second attack rendered her so impotent she was sunk by U. S. ships.

ARMY JOINS HUNT FOR TWO NAVY PLANES, 25 ABOARD

The only way to be sure you get all of the vital news is to have The Tribune delivered to your home, by carrier, every day. PHONE TEMPLEBAR 6000, NOW!

Oakland Tribune
EXCLUSIVE ASSOCIATED PRESS... WIREPHOTO... WIDE WORLD... UNITED PRESS

FINAL NIGHT

VOL. CXXXVIII | 5c DAILY | OAKLAND, CALIFORNIA, SATURDAY, JANUARY 23, 1943 | 15c SUNDAY | NO. 23

TRIPOLI FALLS TO BRITISH

★ ★

Russ Bombard Donets Citadel, Gain On Kursk

New Downpour Soaks Bay Area

Soggy and battered by almost a week of gale-proportion storms, the Bay region and most of California dripped today under the first impact of another windy downpour that the U.S. Weather Bureau warned would strike today and tomorrow.

Storm warnings, hoisted yesterday afternoon at the direction of the Weather Bureau, still were flying today in the area between Point Arguello, Santa Barbara County, and Point Arena, Mendocino County.

The Weather Bureau permitted the announcement today that by 4:30 a.m. Thursday the rainfall in Oakland was nearly five inches over normal. At that time, the seasonal fall stood at 12:94 inches as against a normal of 7.7. A total of 4.34 inches fell in the 24-hour period up to Thursday morning. At this time last year, only 10.47 inches had fallen.

RIVERS RUN HIGH

Rivers throughout California were continuing to run at high levels today, though most danger of floods had passed. Several hundred acres of lowlands in the valleys were under water yesterday, but the rivers had crested and it appeared there might not be widespread damage.

Most of the damage in the cities was caused by the winds, which reached gale velocity at times, uprooting trees, tearing roofs off homes and business buildings and causing automobile accidents. At Cragmont Avenue and Bret Harte Road, in Berkeley, a high-tension wire was blown down and a tide that followed broke a gas main. The "hot" wire ignited the gas, but firemen turned off the current and extinguished the flames before they had done any damage.

On the Bay Bridge, so many automobiles were delayed during the night by the whipping rain that patrolmen were unable to supply tow fast enough.

MAIN WASHED OUT

At Pleasanton, the roots of a falling tree broke open a water main and service was interrupted for several hours. One hundred feet of Alameda gas main was washed out in Niles Canyon early yesterday, cutting off the fuel for 60 homes and the California Pottery Company. Emergency crews repaired the damage and had the gas flowing again by evening.

Alameda Creek had reached flood stage near Alvarado and hundreds of acres of farm land were under water, but agricultural directors said that it would help rather than harm the farmers. They said the water would be particularly good for the big cauliflower crop and would help graze lands, orchards and plants newly set out.

One family near Niles was forced to flee before the rising waters. They reported at least $3000 damage to garlic, spinach and tomato plants. The flood there was caused, authorities said, by the removal of

Continued Page 3, Col. 3

WHERE TO FIND IT

MARSHALL MAY HEAD ALLIED EUROPE DRIVE

By REUEL S. MOORE

WASHINGTON, Jan. 23.—(U.P.)—London's broadcast warning that France will become a war zone, the collapse of Axis defenses at Tripoli, and continued Russian successes are viewed here today as building toward major developments for offensive action in Western Europe.

Allied strategists are believed to be working out plans to time them to best advantage with Russia's blows in the east.

A supreme inter-Allied commander for Africa and Western Europe—who ultimately would direct the conquest of Europe—is proposed. The name of Gen. George C. Marshall, U.S. chief of staff, long has been mentioned in speculation over the possible creation of such a post.

FOUR-POWER COUNCIL

There is increasing interest in reports current both here and in London that a four-power war council—of the United States, Britain, Russia and China—may be formed to integrate world-wide operations.

Sen. Elbert Thomas (D., Utah), member of the Senate Foreign Relations Committee, hoped the reports are true.

"I have long urged closer co-operation between the United Nations — continuous conversations among them with no break at all," he said. "The sooner we get started on joint United Nations action and get it right out in the open, the sooner the United Nations will be able to work together effectively both in war and peace."

POSSIBLE DEVELOPMENTS

The range of specific possible developments was outlined in well-informed circles as including:

1—Aerial offensive against the "under-belly" of the Axis, the European Mediterranean Coast. This seemed implied in London's radio-cast warning. Similar warnings were given the French in Northern France. Apparently the Allied commanders are confident their multiplying resources and the deterioration of the enemy will render such attacks possible and advantageous.

2—Land action against Western Europe after the conquest of Tunisia, which still will require much hard fighting. But the pincers is closing on Axis forces in Tunisia and on Marshal Erwin Rommel's Armies fleeing into Tunisia from Tripolitania. The full force of Allied strength in Tunisia has not been tried against the Axis, owing to adverse weather, and the tempo of events there may accelerate rapidly.

POLITICAL TURBULENCE

3—Settlement of the North African political turbulence, which was viewed as a prerequisite to consolidation of that area.

4—Junction in Tunisia of Allied forces from the Middle East and North Africa which will bring two theaters of war together.

The British Eighth Army under Lieut. Gen. B. L. Montgomery, which has chased Rommel across Libya toward the North African theater, ranks parallel in importance with the British First Army under Lieut. Gen. Mark W. Clark, both of which are under the supreme command of U.S. Lieut. Gen. Dwight D. Eisenhower.

One solution would be to place the Eighth Army under Eisenhower, instead of under Gen. Sir Harold R. L. G. Alexander, British commander in chief in the Middle East. Alexander also commands forces in Egypt, Syria, Iran and Iraq, including the British Ninth and Tenth Armies.

Nazis Blasted In R.A.F. Raid

LONDON, Jan. 23.—(AP)—For the second night British bombers were reported today to have stabbed at western Germany, which embraces the great industrial Ruhr Valley and such important centers as Duesseldorf, Essen, Duisburg, Cologne and Frankfurt.

First news of the raid came from the Berlin radio, which said scattered bombings had caused civilian casualties and some property damage.

The R.A.F. had been over Germany on 12 previous nights this month, including the heavy attacks on Berlin last Saturday and Sunday.

German planes struck back by bombing several places in northeastern and southern England last night, but the raids were not on a heavy scale and while damage was done casualties were reported light.

A number of German raiders, gliding in above the clouds, bombed and machine-gunned a village in south England this morning, causing considerable damage. There were casualties, including some killed, it was reported.

Yesterday swarms of British, American and Allied planes made extensive sweeps over northern France and Belgium, ranging from Ghent to the Cherbourg Peninsula. Seven German fighters were reported destroyed while four Allied bombers and six fighters were listed as missing.

Targets included oil installations at Terneuzen, near Ghent, and German airfields in the vicinity of Maupertus, Abbeville, St. Omer and Cherbourg.

1,000,000 Pacific Mi. Flown by Squadron

MELBOURNE, Jan. 23.—(AP)—One American Flying Fortress squadron operating in the southwest Pacific has flown more than 1,000,000 miles on 630 missions in the last six months, during which it, has destroyed 33 Japanese fighters in combat and more than 20 aground, sunk a heavy cruiser, and sent two merchant ships and a transport to the bottom.

The disclosure was made in Sydney today by Sergeant Pilot Mervyn Bell of the Royal Australian Air Force, co-pilot of one of the planes in the squadron.

Bell was enthusiastic about his American flying mates, declaring: "The Yanks are the greatest team I've ever been with."

Salisbury Rites Set

ALTADENA, Jan. 23.—(AP)—The body of O. J. Salisbury, prominent Utah and Southern California businessman who died yesterday, will be sent to Salt Lake City for burial. Survivors include the widow, Marian; a daughter, Mrs. Gage H. Irving of Pasadena, and two sons, O. J. Salisbury Jr., now in South America, and Donald M. Salisbury, Stanford University student.

Papua Japs Wiped Out; 4 Ships Sunk

By VERN HAUGLAND

SOMEWHERE IN NEW GUINEA, Jan. 23.—(AP)—Organized Japanese resistance in Papua ended at 2:05 p.m., local time, yesterday when the last two remaining pockets of an enemy which once numbered 15,000 were wiped out by victorious American and Australian forces.

The last to fall was a group of Japs on the coast northwest of Sanananda. Attacked in the early morning by Australians, enemy resisted bitterly but withdrew a short distance. Artillery and mortars softened the new defense and an afternoon attack crumpled the enemy.

The Americans subjected the few remaining Japs to well-organized mortar and artillery battering starting at mid-morning. Shortly after mid-day, the Americans reported the Japs cleaned out.

Fourteen Jap stragglers were killed south of Gona. As far as is known, the only remaining Japanese in Papua are isolated soldiers wandering hopelessly in the swamps. These are being hunted down.

RADIO SET TAKEN

The Australians captured a big wireless transmitting set near Sanananda on January 20. Examination showed it was in perfect condition, capable of reaching Tokyo. Evidently the Japs were surprised and hadn't had time to destroy it.

The Americans yesterday captured three Jap field ammunition dumps, 122 mortar trucks and much other equipment. Today they captured large quantities of rifles, light, medium and heavy machineguns, mortars, grenades and technical equipment, especially signalling devices and two anti-aircraft guns.

Mopping up operations were carried out chiefly by companies commanded by Captains Jack Vanduvn of Eugene, Ore., Robert Hamilton of Bozeman, Mont., Ed Reams of Billings, Mont., and Lieut. John G. Boyd (home town unavailable).

Capt. Reams, himself, accounted for nine Japs with a Garand rifle.

The folks back home would have had to see the conditions under which the main attack started in order to believe it.

IN SEA OF MUD

In the bivouac area, men camped in a sea of mud after a nightlong rain judged at 10 to 11 inches—almost one-tenth this area's total annual rainfall.

Yesterday's action was the culmination of an offensive which opened January 16 with a successful American push around the right flank of the Jap perimeter which enabled them to cut off any enemy retreat.

Captain Reams was modest about his personal exploits. The 6-foot, 220-pound giant said most of his victims were "playing possum or were already wounded by artillery or mortar bursts."

But from others in his company it was learned that he led his outfit into action, several times getting so far out in front that the platoon

Continued Page 3, Col. 6

Nazis Yield On 3 Fronts, Lose Materiel

By HENRY SHAPIRO

MOSCOW, Jan. 23.—(U.P.)—Red Army artillery opened a bombardment of Voroshilovgrad today while storm troops drove on that rich Donets Basin war industry and mining city from lines only 10 miles away.

On the southern front, the Russians advanced on Tikhoretsk, on the main Rostov-Caucasus railroad, after taking Salsk, junction point and greatest German air base in the entire region, 75 miles to the north-east.

In the Caucasus, the Russians were within 70 miles of Maikop, oil fields center in the Black Sea area, after capturing Mikoyan Shakhar, where the Germans had made their deepest penetration in the mountains, and freeing the towering peak of Mt. Elborus, 18,471 feet high, whose scaling the Germans had so proudly announced.

(The Moscow rado, heard in London, reported that advance Russian troops had entered the region of Kursk, on the main Kharkov-Moscow railroad through the Ukraine, where they had last been reported 85 miles from the city.)

GAIN ON THREE FRONTS

The noon communique reported fresh gains on all three major fronts.

Several new towns and villages were claimed on the Voroshilovgrad front, including five taken by a single unit. A number of inhabited places were taken on the southern or Salsk front, the noon communique said, and "dozens" in the north Caucasus in addition to several of the Voronezh front where the Russians are advancing on Kursk.

In the capture of Voroshilovgrad, one of the great objectives of their Winter offensive, in sight, the Russians reported that on the Voronezh (Kursk) front they captured several inhabited places during the night, including a village in which they killed 200 Germans, took 150 prisoners and captured five field guns, 18 machine guns and war and food dumps, and another where 220 Hungarians, surrounded, downed arms and surrendered.

DRIVE FOR FOCAL POINT

The Red Army reached within 10 miles of Voroshilovgrad, on the east, when it took the big rail junction town of Kondrashevskaya yesterday. They were closing in also on the northeast and north, driving for a focal point of the German defensive-offensive system in southern Russia.

The Russians also took Novoaidar, 31 miles above Voroshilovgrad, and Evzug, farther to the north.

As they closed in on Voroshilovgrad today, the Russians defeated the one counter-attack which the Germans essayed, routing 2000 men supported by tanks. The Germans lost eight tanks. In another sector 200 Germans were killed and three tanks destroyed.

On the Sask front, the Russians were advancing down the Stalingrad-Tikhoretsk railroad on Belaya, Glina, 40 miles southwest of Salsk and 40 miles northeast of Tikhoretsk.

SMASHING OF DUCE'S EMPIRE COMPLETED

By ALFRED E. WALL

LONDON, Jan. 23.—(AP)—The conquering British Eighth Army wrested Tripoli from the Axis today and the conquest of Premier Mussolini's African Empire, which Prime Minister Churchill pledged in 1940 would be torn "to shreds and tatters," was all but complete.

Rear guards "left" behind by Marshal Erwin Rommel to slow the pursuit of his main forces into Tunisia were overwhelmed and the British took possession of the burning city at 5 a.m., officials announced in Cairo.

The Italian high command communique broadcast later by the Rome radio said Axis troops evacuated the city and moved westward last night after fierce fighting. It said motorized elements battled yesterday south of the city, around which a wing of the Eighth Army was swung to speed the chase.

EMPIRE DESTROYED

Berlin likewise officially acknowledged the loss of Tripoli.

British War Secretary Sir James Grigg, skipping the pending mop-up of the western reaches of Libya, said that the fall of Tripoli "completes the destruction of the Italian Empire in Africa."

"Both the Russian and British Armies have had their dark days of retreats," he said. "For both we believe the tide is now firmly turned."

In the destruction of the Italian Empire the British "have had the ungrudging help of American supplies and the American Air Forces in the latest stage, but nevertheless it has been overwhelmingly our show," the war secretary said.

BRITISH PRESS ON

Having dealt a shattering psychological as well as military blow to the Axis, the British pressed forward without pause toward Tunisia on the heels of Rommel's remaining troops, estimated to number 63,000.

In an effort to chop off rear elements of Axis troops before they could reach the Mareth line, 85 miles inside the Tunisian border, some of General Montgomery's forces were believed to have cut across the coastal plain through El Azizia, 20 miles southwest of Tripoli.

While the occupation of Tripoli was being accomplished, flights of British and American bombers and fighters were ranging far ahead into Tunisia in destructive attacks on Rommel's material and manpower.

While the retiring Germans and Italians undoubtedly demolished many installations in Tripoli's fine harbor, adding to the destruction wrought by Allied bombers, London military sources said the port probably could be made useful in short order.

BENGASI REPAIRED

Bengasi, they pointed out, was reported "totally destroyed" several times in the course of the war in Libya, but each time was repaired quickly by the troops capturing it.

The captured capital of Tripoli-

Continued Page 3, Col. 1

Ocean, Inland Area Searched

A widespread search by planes, ships and ground parties was pressed throughout the West along the ocean shores today for two missing Navy planes, one of them a big four-motored ship flying in from Pearl Harbor.

Nine crewmen and 10 naval officers were aboard the larger plane, which last reported itself over San Francisco Bay Thursday morning at 7:14 o'clock and then dropped out of sight.

The other plane, a twin-engined craft carrying mail and cargo, had three officers and three enlisted men aboard. It has been overdue since 5:40 p.m. Thursday on a flight from Winslow, Ariz., to San Pedro. The plane last was reported by radio when it was 26 miles out of Winslow.

Vice-Adm. John Wills Greenslade ordered every available surface vessel and plane into the search for the four-motored plane, sending them over every mile of the area from Monterey Bay north to Eureka. The Army joined the Navy and pressed its search as far inland as the foothills of the Sierra.

IDENTITIES WITHHELD

The Navy declined to reveal the identities of the missing officers and fliers on either plane.

Its announcement that the ships were missing came only a few hours after an Army board of inquiry started an investigation of a crash in Dutch Guiana on January 15, which cost the lives of nine crew members and 26 passengers. Maj. Eric Knight, author, and prominent Army and State Department officials were killed.

The disappearance of the big seaplane from Pearl Harbor was announced late yesterday in Washington, and Admiral Greenslade, commander of the Western Sea Frontier, issued the following statement last night:

"Upon being notified by the authorities that an aircraft was overdue, bound from Pearl Harbor to San Francisco, he (Admiral Greenslade) immediately instituted a search by surface craft and aircraft to endeavor to cover all possible areas wherein the ship could have landed.

WIDESPREAD SEARCH

"Surface craft available and all aircraft under the Western Sea Frontier, ably assisted by Army authorities, are searching from Monterey Bay to Eureka, and 225 miles to the west of San Francisco.

"In addition, the Army has searched the same general area up to the foothills of the Sierra Nevada. This search, up to the time of this release, has not located the missing ship.

"The surface search will be continued. Additional air searches will be carried out when weather conditions are favorable.

"The surface and aircraft of the Northwestern Sea Frontier are co-operating in this search."

All of the searchers were handicapped by the gale that has lashed the Pacific Coast this week, with rain and fog here and snow in the north. Both planes may have crashed into the ocean, though the search for the San Pedro-bound plane is being concentrated today in the San Francisco Mountains of Arizona.

Ranchers in Coconino County reported to Sheriff Perry Francis at Flagstaff they had heard a plane over the mountains shortly after the transport left Winslow. Francis and R. H. Hussey, supervisor of the Coconino National Forest, planned to lead a searching party of 15 men on skis and snowshoes into the mountains today.

Flynn Probe Nears Test

By JACK BELL

WASHINGTON, Jan. 23.—(AP)—A senatorial controversy over the qualifications of Edward J. Flynn, minister-designate to Australia, appeared today to be nearing a test vote as the Foreign Relations Committee sought to wind up public hearings with testimony from Mayor F. H. LaGuardia of New York City.

LaGuardia was scheduled as an afternoon witness in an unusual Saturday session which Chairman Connally (D., Texas) said he hoped would end the presentation of testimony on Republican charges that Flynn is unfit to hold the diplomatic post.

Connally made it plain, however, that if Flynn, former National Democratic Committee chairman, wants to testify again in his own behalf, he may. Otherwise, the committee planned to take advantage of the week-end recess to study the testimony preparatory to a vote early next week on President Roosevelt's nomination of Flynn.

FLYNN DENIES KNOWLEDGE

LaGuardia was called to testify primarily on charges made against Flynn by previous witnesses that he knew a courtyard in his Putnam County, N.Y., country estate was being paved with New York City materials and labor.

Flynn has denied that he had any knowledge at the time that the work was being done by Bronx Borough laborers. The committee called Robert L. Moran, former Bronx commissioner of public works, to the stand as the first witness of the day to testify what part he played in the transaction.

Earlier the committee heard from Assistant Secretary of State A. A. Berle Jr. and from District Attorney Samuel Foley of the Bronx.

REVIEWS FISCAL AFFAIRS

Berle said he did not take part in any discussions at the State Department relative to Flynn's appointment to Australia and generally confined his testimony to a review of financial affairs in the office of the chamberlain of New York City—a post held by Flynn from 1925 to 1929, and assumed by Berle in 1934.

Foley told the committee that a Grand Jury which he guided in the investigation of the paving block case found no evidence that Flynn knew the work was being done with city-owned materials and city labor.

The day's last witness was Daniel A. Daly, foreman of the Grand Jury in the paving block investigation. He appeared to answer a charge by Senator Bridges (R., N.H.) that he was given a Federal job shortly after what the senator called the Flynn "whitewash."

Daly testified he was an experienced steel man and was appointed an Army-Navy expediter in New York on his own merit and with no weight given his service on the jury.

'Japs Tough—Not Super,' Avers Vandergrift

AN ADVANCE SOUTH PACIFIC BASE, Jan. 23.—(AP)—Ten Japs have been killed on Guadalcanal for every American soldier lost, and their air losses in the Solomons have been seven to our one, Maj. Gen. A. A. Vandergrift of the U.S. Marine Corps said today.

"The Jap is a good fighting man, and anyone who says differently is mistaken," he said in a brief interview. "But he is no superman by any means, and he can be killed the same as anyone else."

General Vandergrift conferred with Adm. William F. Halsey, commander of the South Pacific fleet. He has been relieved of his command on Guadalcanal after months of the hardest fighting in the fighting Marines' history.

"At the present moment," General Vandergrift said, "I feel Guadalcanal is secure to us."

Without citing figure, he said he saw American troops were taking a terrific toll of Japanese in the Solomons fighting aside from many thousands of the enemy aboard troopships which have been sunk attempting to land in the area.

General Vandergrift has turned over his command to Maj. Gen. Alexander Patch, who had been commanding an advance base since March.

"The situation is in good hands,"

Süddeutsche Ausgabe

27. Ausg. 56. Jahrg. Einzelpreis für München 15 Rpf., auswärts 20 Rpf. Frankreich Frs. 2.—, Italien Lire 1.50, Schweiz 30 Rappen

„Freiheit und Brot!"

Süddeutsche Ausgabe

München, Mittwoch, 27. Januar 1943

VÖLKISCHER BEOBACHTER

Verlag: Frz. Eher Nachf., G. m. b. H., München 22, Thierschstraße 11—17. Sammelruf 2 21 31, nach 17 Uhr 2 21 34, Drahtanschrift: Eherverlag — Postscheck: München 113 46, Prag 773 03, Preßburg 58 60, Bern III 72 05, Budapest 135 32, Belgrad 682 37, Bukarest 249 68, Brüssel 350 797, den Haag 211 846, Bayerische Hypotheken- und Wechselbank, München, Filiale Kaufingerstraße, Bayerische Gemeindebank, Girozentrale München, Brienner Straße 49, Bank der Deutschen Arbeit AG., München, Deutsche Bank, Filiale München, Depositenkasse Maximilianstraße, Reichsbankgirokonto, Kreditanstalt der Deutschen, Prag, Kommerzialbank Krakau, Slovenska Banka, Bratislava

Kampfblatt der nationalsozialistischen Bewegung Großdeutschlands

Schriftltg.: München 13, Schellingstr. 39, Sammelruf 2 08 01 - Briefanschrift: München 2 BS. Schließfach 294 - Drahtanschrift: Beobachter München - Berliner Schriftleitung: Berlin SW 68, Zimmerstraße 8, Ruf 11 00 22 - Wiener Schriftleitung: Wien VII, Seidengasse 3—11, Ruf B-3 95 40 - Erscheinungsweise wöchentlich 7 mal - Bezugspreis durch die Post RM. 2.60 einschl. 75 Pf. Postgebühr, ausschließlich 42 Pf. Zustellung in Orten mit Agenturen RM. 3.— einschl. Zustellgeld - Anzeigenabteilung: München 22, Thierschstr. 11—17 und Zweigstelle Schellingstr. 39, Ruf 2 21 31, Anzeigenschluß 12 Uhr, 1 Tag vor Erscheinen - Gewünschte Einzelnummern sind nur gegen vorherige Einsendung von 30 Pf. lieferbar

Bürgerliche Hemmungen?

Die verbissene Erbitterung des Kampfes an der Ostfront, der im Ringen um Stalingrad jetzt seinen geschichtlich symbolischen Ausdruck und in seiner Härte zugleich auch einen unvorstellbaren Höhepunkt gefunden hat, ist einmalig, wie der Zusammenprall zweier totaler Revolutionen, des Nationalsozialismus und des Bolschewismus überhaupt. Was die Sowjets uns durch ihre brutale Despotie und ihren Primitivitätskult voraushaben, ist die totale Mobilisation ihrer Massen für den Krieg. Sie wurde von diesem Sklavensystem schon seit zwei Jahrzehnten vorbereitet und durchgeführt und im Jahre 1940 mit der Militarisierung der gesamten Wirtschaft vollendet. Der Nihilismus der Sowjetjuden ermöglichte dabei die radikalsten Methoden. Kulturelle, traditionsgebundene oder menschliche Rücksichten gab es für den Bolschewismus nie und bürgerliche Hemmungen schon gar nicht. Er kannte nur ein Ziel: Weltrevolution, und das hieß zuerst einmal Vernichtungskrieg gegen die starken und freien Völker, alles, was in seinem Bereiche bürgerlich war, hat er mit Stumpf und Stiel schon längst ausgerottet, und er würde als Triumphator in Europa mit sadistischer Lust bei uns ebenso verfahren. Das mögen sich die stets vor Augen halten, die heute noch immer glauben, in diesem Kriege mehr oder weniger unbeteiligte Zuschauer spielen zu können. Die nationalsozialistische Revolution hat als schöpferische Revolution nicht das Ziel, die bürgerliche Welt zu ermorden, sondern sie zu wandeln und zu überwinden. Sie hat die Starken aufgerufen, um die Schwachen mitzureißen und zu erziehen. Sie muß sich deshalb heute noch mit jenen bürgerlichen Hemmungen im eigenen Volk und in Europa beschäftigen, die ihre Toleranz und ihren Edelmut bis heute nicht verstanden und deshalb auch nicht verdient haben. Jetzt gilt es auch bei uns, die totale Mobilisation vollends durchzuführen. Dabei können uns keinerlei Rücksichten auf bürgerliche Hemmungen mehr beeinträchtigen. Irgendwelche Ichsüchte, falscher Ehrgeiz, Vornehmheit, Bequemlichkeit und andere bürgerliche Götzen haben bei uns jetzt keinen Platz mehr. Mit unserer Fahne ist der Sieg. k. n.

Der Tennô empfing den scheidenden deutschen Botschafter Ott

Tokio, 26. Januar

Zu Ehren des scheidenden deutschen Botschafters Eugen Ott gaben der Tennô und die Kaiserin einen Empfang, an dem u. a. Prinz Takamatsu und Außenminister Tani teilnahmen. Der Tennô und die Kaiserin sprachen bei dieser Gelegenheit Botschafter Ott herzliche Worte der Anerkennung für die hervorragenden Verdienste aus, die er sich während seiner Tätigkeit in Tokio durch die Verstärkung der Beziehungen zwischen Japan und Deutschland erworben hat.

Glückwunsch des Reichsmarschalls an Eichenlaubträger Major Günzel

Berlin, 26. Januar

Der Reichsmarschall des Großdeutschen Reiches und Oberbefehlshaber der Luftwaffe sandte anläßlich der Verleihung des Eichenlaubes zum Ritterkreuz des Eisernen Kreuzes an Major Reinhard Günzel, den erfolgreichen Kommandeur in einem Kampfgeschwader, folgendes Glückwunschschreiben:

„Lieber Günzel! Der Führer hat Ihre überragenden Kampfleistungen, vor allem bei Angriffen auf die feindliche Versorgung, durch Verleihung des Eichenlaubes zum Ritterkreuz des Eisernen Kreuzes gewürdigt. Ich freue mich, daß wieder einer meiner kühnen Kampfflieger eine solche Anerkennung fand, und ich beglückwünsche Sie zu der hohen Tapferkeitsauszeichnung. Mit meinem Dank für Ihre hervorragende Bewährung auch als Verbandsführer übermittle ich Ihnen meine besten Wünsche für neue große Erfolge.

Göring,
Reichsmarschall des Großdeutschen Reiches und Oberbefehlshaber der Luftwaffe."

Immer wieder die Juden!

Japan droht mit drastischen Maßnahmen

Tokio, 26. Januar

Die japanische Militärverwaltung in Manila richtete eine ernste Warnung an die auf den Philippinen lebenden Juden. Als Folge der nachsichtigen und großzügigen Haltung der japanischen Behörden hätten die Juden, wie es heißt, versucht, Vorteile für sich zu gewinnen und sich nicht nur des Schwarzhandels sowie Preistreibereien schuldig gemacht, sondern versuchte Spionage zuschulden kommen lassen. Die Behörden würden künftig solche Vergehen mit drastischen Mitteln beantworten.

Heroischer Widerstand auf den Ruinen Stalingrads

Unterstützung durch unsere Luftwaffe unter schwersten Einsatzbedingungen

Aus dem Führerhauptquartier, 26. Jan.

Das Oberkommando der Wehrmacht gibt bekannt:

Der Ansturm der Sowjets gegen weite Teile der Ostfront nahm gestern an Heftigkeit wieder zu. In schweren Abwehrkämpfen gegen vielfach überlegenen Feind behaupteten sich die deutschen Armeen gegen alle Durchbruchs- und Umfassungsversuche.

In Stalingrad haben sich die Verteidiger, bei denen sich neben den rumänischen Divisionen auch ein kleiner kroatischer Verband befindet, im südlichen und mittleren Teil der Stadtruinen auf einen Raum zusammengeschlossen. Sie leisten dort unter Führung ihrer Generale weiterhin heroischen Widerstand, von der Luftwaffe unter schwersten Einsatzbedingungen nach Kräften unterstützt.

Im Kuban- und Manytschgebiet wurden feindliche Angriffe in harten Kämpfen abgewiesen, die Bewegungen zu den befohlenen Frontverkürzungen verlaufen im übrigen planmäßig. Panzertruppen und motorisierte Verbände setzten zwischen Manytsch und Don ihren Angriff mit Erfolg fort. Der Feind wurde weiter nach Nordosten zurückgeworfen. Im Don- und Donezgebiet dauern die erbitterten Abwehrkämpfe an.

Südwestlich Woronesch griff der Feind mit neu herangeführten Kräften in breiter Front erneut an. Er wurde im wesentlichen blutig abgewiesen. Die Kämpfe sind noch im Gange. Örtliche Angriffe der Sowjets bei Rschew und südwestlich Welikije Luki scheiterten. Auch südlich des Ladogasees brachen erneute mit Panzern vorgetragene feindliche Angriffe nach erbitterten Kämpfen zusammen.

In Nordafrika Spähtrupptätigkeit.

In Tunesien scheiterten Versuche des Feindes, in den Vortagen verlorene Stellungen zurückzuerobern. Seine Verluste in der Zeit vom 18. bis 24. Januar 1943 betrugen viertausend Gefangene, 21 Panzerkampfwagen, 70 Geschütze, zweihundert Kraftfahrzeuge, über einhundert Maschinengewehre und zahlreiches anderes Kriegsmaterial.

An der holländischen Küste verlor der Feind bei einem militärisch wirkungslosen Tagesangriff vier Bombenflugzeuge. Schnelle deutsche Kampfflugzeuge griffen am Tage eine Ortschaft an der Südküste Englands mit gutem Erfolg an.

Vor Ehrfurcht schweigen

Sofia, 26. Januar

Das Regierungsblatt „Dnes" kommentiert die Kämpfe an der Ostfront. Das größte Heldenepos, so unterstreicht es, das die menschliche Geschichte kenne, schreiben die Kämpfer von Stalingrad. Alle Bemühungen, in der Vergangenheit solche Tapferkeit und Aufopferungsbereitschaft zu finden, bleiben erfolglos, da der Heldenmut der deutschen Bataillone nicht seinesgleichen habe und alle bisherigen Heldentaten der Weltgeschichte in den Schatten stelle.

Das Blatt erklärt, daß die Vorstellung dieser Kämpfe in ihren wirklichen Ausmaßen nie zu ermessen sei. Jedes Wort sei zu blaß, um dieses Maß an Tapferkeit, Mut und Pflichtbewußtsein zu schildern. Dort sei alles so groß, so erhaben und so ruhmreich, daß jeder anständige Mensch vor Ehrfurcht und Bewunderung schweigen werde. Ein Volk, das solche tapfere Söhne habe und dessen Heldentaten so zahlreich seien, müsse die Gewißheit des Endsieges in sich tragen. Dieses Heldentum könne nicht umsonst in die Geschichte eingehen, sondern es werde in der Zukunft seine Früchte tragen für das Wohl der gesamten Menschheit.

Sowjets stoßen immer wieder südlich des Ladogasees vor

Berlin, 26. Januar

Nach dem Scheitern aller bisherigen Durchbruchsversuche flauten südöstlich des Ilmensees die Kämpfe immer mehr zu örtlichen Geplänkeln zwischen Sicherungspostierungen ab. Nur an einer Stelle griffen die Bolschewisten an. Die vordringenden Panzer wurden jedoch durch Sturmgeschütze erfaßt und sechs von ihnen zerschossen. Damit scheiterte auch dieser Vorstoß am raschen Einsatz der schweren Waffen, die auch während der vorangegangenen Abwehrkämpfe so oft die Entscheidung brachten, wenn die Bolschewisten mit großer Übermacht Einbrüche zu erzwingen versuchten. Als sie zum Beispiel gegen den Abschnitt einer Grenadierkompanie mit zahlreichen Panzern und starken Infanterieverbänden anrannten, zerschoß ein einziges Sturmgeschütz elf der Panzerkampfwagen, davon die ersten acht schon im Vorfeld, den letzten aber erst 12 Meter vor dem Kompaniegefechtsstand. An dem einen Geschütz zerbrach die ganze Panzerwelle und an den Grenadieren der Ansturm der sowjetischen Bataillone. An anderer Stelle spannten sich in kritischer Lage unsere Panzerjäger vor ihre schwere Panzerabwehrkanone und schafften sie mühsam im Mannschaftszug durch die tiefverschneiten Wälder und Sümpfe zur Hauptkampflinie. Von dort aus schoß die Pak kurz hintereinander sieben feindliche Paks zusammen und schlug damit dem feindlichen Stoßkeil die Spitze weg, so daß die folgende Infanterie glatt abgewiesen werden konnte.

Was den Bolschewisten am Ilmensee mißlang, versuchten sie jetzt südlich des Ladogasees. Immer wieder brechen sie seit Tagen mit starken Kräften vor, die sie durch massierte Artillerie und zahlreiche Schlachtflugzeuge unterstützen. Fortgesetzt kommt es zu harten Kämpfen, aber unsere Grenadiere halten ihre Stellung, wenn auch manchmal zur Bereinigung örtlicher Einbrüche erbittert gerungen werden muß. Auch am 24. Januar erfolgten die feindlichen Vorstöße ununterbrochen, wobei es den Bolschewisten gelang, während der Nacht zweimal in die deutschen Stellungen einzubrechen. Der Feind konnte seinen Vorteil aber nicht ausnutzen. Noch vor Morgengrauen waren beide Stellen abgeriegelt und die eine im Gegenstoß bereits wieder bereinigt.

Während der heftigen Kämpfe südlich des Ladogasees verstärkten die Bolschewisten gleichzeitig ihre Späh- und Stoßtrupptätigkeit gegen die deutschen Stellungen am Wolchow. In der letzten Woche verging keine Nacht, ohne daß die Sowjets mehrfach mit ungewöhnlich starken Spähtrupps erschienen, um unsere Hauptkampflinie zu beunruhigen und durch Überfälle die dort eingesetzten Kräfte zu fesseln. Die Bolschewisten wurden aber jedesmal durch die Posten rechtzeitig erkannt und von den alarmierten Grabenbesatzungen zurückgetrieben. Allein im Gefechtsabschnitt zweier schlesischer Jäg.-Regimenter haben unsere Jäger seit Beginn der Kämpfe südlich des Ladogasees 29 starke Erkundungsvorstöße der Sowjets ohne eigene Ausfälle blutig abgeschlagen.

Unsere Panzergrenadiere

In den harten Kämpfen südöstlich Toropez rannten die Bolschewisten tagelang gegen die Stellungen einer niedersächsischen Panzergrenadierkompanie an und brachen in unsere Gräben ein. Der Kompanieführer, ein junger Oberleutnant, riß seine Panzergrenadiere zum Gegenstoß vor, stieß in erbittertem Ringen über das Angriffsziel hinaus und brachte 150 Gefangene ein. Die Bolschewisten verloren bei diesen Kämpfen über 300 Tote. Am nächsten Tage griffen unsere Grenadiere einen befestigten Ort an dem feindlichen Hauptversorgungsweg an. Trotz zahlenmäßiger Überlegenheit der Verteidiger stürmten unsere Panzergrenadiere die zäh verteidigte Ortschaft, erbeuteten zahlreiche Geschütze und fügten den Bolschewisten schwerste Verluste zu. Der Feind mußte allein über 800 Tote auf dem Kampffeld zurücklassen.

Italiens Flotte versenkte bisher 322 Schiffe

Rom, 26. Januar

Die italienische Flotte hat in den 30 Monaten der Kriegführung vom Juni 1940 bis zum 31. Dezember 1942 der feindlichen Kriegs- und Versorgungsschiffahrt folgende Verluste zugefügt:

Versenkt wurden 132 feindliche Kriegsschiffe, darunter vier Schlachtschiffe, 18 Kreuzer, 30 Torpedojäger, 80 U-Boote mit 270 000 Tonnen Gesamttonnage, ferner 190 Handelsdampfer und Tankdampfer mit eine Gesamttonnage von 1,3 Millionen Tonnen. Insgesamt hat damit die italienische Flotte 322 feindliche Schiffe versenkt.

Andrang in der Reparaturwerkstätte Gibraltar

Rom, 26. Januar

Ein schwer beschädigter englischer Kreuzer konnte erst nach 14tägiger Wartezeit im Hafen von Gibraltar in ein Trockendock gebracht werden, wie „Messagero" aus Algeciras meldet. Die Verzögerung ist auf die Überfüllung des Hafens und der Docks mit reparaturbedürftigen Schiffen zurückzuführen. Eine größere Anzahl von Zerstörern und anderen kleinen Einheiten liegt schon seit Wochen im Hafen von Gibraltar vor Anker. Diese Schiffe können aber erst in Reparatur genommen werden, wenn die größeren und schwerer beschädigten Einheiten ausgebessert sind.

Im Südatlantik torpediert

Von unserem Berichterstatter

Stockholm, 26. Januar

Das USA.-Marinedepartement gab am Montag bekannt, daß ein britisches Handelsschiff Anfang Januar im Südatlantik vor der Ostküste Südamerikas von einem feindlichen Unterseeboot torpediert und versenkt wurde.

Mit MG. und Giftgas gegen die hungernden Inder

Von unserem Berichterstatter

Rom, 26. Januar

Über die heilige Hindustadt Nasic, die kaum 150 Kilometer von Bombay entfernt liegt, wurde von den Engländern wegen anhaltender Massenrevolten der Belagerungszustand verhängt, außerdem wurde von 18 Uhr abends bis 8 Uhr früh ein Ausgehverbot angeordnet, wie die italienische Presse aus Schanghai meldet. Tausende von Hindus, von Hunger geplagt, demonstrierten seit Tagen in den Straßen von Nasic, plünderten die Lebensmittelgeschäfte und stürmten die staatlichen Büros. Die Polizei war gegen die Revolte machtlos, die schließlich so anwuchs, daß die ganze Stadt innerhalb von drei Tagen in die Gewalt der Aufständischen kam. Diese bildeten sogar einen provisorischen Gemeinderat. Erst als größere Truppenverstärkungen in Nasic eintrafen, die mit Maschinengewehren und Giftgas gegen die Aufständischen vorgingen, wurden die Hindus überwältigt.

Die Zahl der toten Eingeborenen übersteigt hundert, die der Verwundeten 2000, bei den britischen Truppen und bei der englischen Polizei wurden 10 Tote und etwa 150 Verwundete gezählt.

USA.-Militär schießt auf Iraner

Stockholm, 26. Januar

Wie „Dagsposten" berichtet, kam es nach Meldungen aus Teheran im Raum von Meschhed in Iran zu neuen Zwischenfällen infolge des Nahrungsmittelmangels. Eine größere Volksmenge wandte sich gegen eine Kaserne, worauf nordamerikanische Truppen auf die Kundgeber schossen. Eine Anzahl von Personen wurde verhaftet. Mehrere Personen sind verwundet worden.

Tiefangriffe gegen Hafen der englischen Südküste

Berlin, 26. Januar

Schnelle deutsche Kampfflugzeuge starteten am Vormittag des 25. Januar zu einem überraschenden Tiefangriff gegen einen Hafen der englischen Südküste und warfen ihre Bomben auf nebeneinanderliegende englische Kriegsfahrzeuge, von denen vier durch Volltreffer versenkt wurden. Beim Abflug nahmen die deutschen Flieger feuernde Flakartillerie in der Umgebung des Angriffszieles unter Bordwaffenfeuer und brachten die Geschütze zum Schweigen. Der deutsche Verband kehrte von diesem Vorstoß ohne eigene Verluste zurück.

Jagderfolge unserer Luftwaffe im Norden der Ostfront

Versuche der Sowjets im nördlichen Abschnitt der Ostfront, durch rücksichtslosen Einsatz ihrer fliegenden Verbände die Erdkämpfe entscheidend zu beeinflussen, wurde auch in den letzten beiden Tagen wieder durch die schlagkräftige Abwehr unserer Jagdflieger vereitelt. Wie schon gemeldet, schossen Jagdverbände am 24. Januar 21 feindliche Flugzeuge allein im Gebiet nördlich des Ilmensees ab. Bei diesen Luftkämpfen erzielte der Träger des Eichenlaubs mit Schwertern zum Ritterkreuz des Eisernen Kreuzes, Hauptmann Philipp, seinen 163. Luftsieg, während der Eichenlaubträger Leutnant Beiswenger mit zwei Abschüssen seinen 129. Luftsieg errang. Im Laufe des Montagvormittags waren wieder zwei hervorragend bewährte Jagdflieger des unter Führung von Major Trautloft stehenden Jagdgeschwaders im nördlichen Abschnitt der Ostfront besonders erfolgreich. Die Eichenlaubträger Major Hahn und Leutnant Stotz versprengten einen starken unter Jagdschutz anfliegenden Bomberverband und schossen aus ihm innerhalb von vier Minuten sieben Sowjetflugzeuge heraus. Infolge der ungestümen Angriffe der deutschen Jagdfliegerrotte warf der feindliche Flugzeugverband seine Bombenlast ungezielt ins Feld und brach nach diesen schweren Verlusten seinen Angriffsversuch ab. Major Hahn erzielte damit in den Luftkämpfen der letzten Tage seinen 91. bis 97. Luftsieg, während sein Rottenkamerad, Leutnant Stotz, mit den Abschüssen am Montag die stolze Zahl von 144 Luftsiegen erreichte.

*

Im mittleren Abschnitt der Ostfront führten deutsche Sturzkampfflugzeuge wirksame Angriffe gegen feindlichen Bahnverkehr im Raum von Welikije Luki durch. Dabei faßten sie einen Panzerzug, der bis dicht an die Front vorgefahren war, um in die Artilleriekämpfe einzugreifen. Die aus geringer Höhe abgeworfenen Bomben rissen den Zug auseinander.

Alle Kräfte für den Krieg

Die Leistungsreserven der deutschen Kriegswirtschaft

„Eine Vollbeschäftigung in der kapitalistischen Wirtschaft (und der mit ihr wesensgleichen bolschewistischen) ist eben etwas anderes als eine vollbeschäftigte nationalsozialistische Wirtschaft." Dieser Satz aus der Rede des Reichswirtschaftsministers, über die wir an anderer Stelle berichten, scheint uns den Mittelpunkt zu bilden. Denn er kennzeichnet einerseits die Schwierigkeiten, deren Vorhandensein Reichsminister Funk in der englischen und USA.-Wirtschaft aufzeigt, und andererseits die großen Möglichkeiten, die die deutsche Volkswirtschaft birgt.

Das Zeitalter des englischen Manchestertums und der britischen Herrschaftsstellung auf den Weltmärkten ist zu Ende, denn nach den Angaben des Reichsministers sind die englischen weltwirtschaftlichen Machtpositionen weggeschmolzen. Während die Goldbestände und Dollarguthaben Englands bei Ausbruch des Krieges 5 Milliarden Dollar betragen haben, sind die Goldbestände Englands im Jahre 1942 auf schätzungsweise 50 Millionen Dollar zusammengeschrumpft. Die gesamten englischen Kapitalanlagen im Auslande sind von 5 Milliarden auf 2,6 Milliarden zusammengefallen. Und wenn England seine Gläubigerstellung gegenüber Indien und Kanada verloren hat, und anstatt dessen Kanada bereits Gläubiger Englands geworden ist, so liegt hierin mehr als eine Umkehr auf finanzkapitalistischem Gebiete, weil damit auch die Machtstellung Englands unterhöhlt worden ist.

> *„Das Gebet wird in Erfüllung gehen: „Herrgott, gib uns die Kraft, daß wir uns die Freiheit erhalten, unserem Volk, unseren Kindern und unseren Kindeskindern!"*
>
> Der Führer am 30. Januar 1942.

Anstrengungen, ihre Produktion zu rationalisieren, haben die USA. und England wohl gemacht. Aber die Rationalisierung konnte doch nur die Fortsetzung jener Rationalisierung sein, wie sie dort vor dem Kriege schon betrieben wurde, und damit jenes Rationalisierungsprozesses, der sich „im Kraftfeld der freien Konkurrenz und unter dem beherrschenden Gesichtspunkt der Rentabilität vollzog", und, wie der Reichsminister sagt: „Die ganze Problematik dieser Rationalisierung zeigt sich ja gerade jetzt in den ungeheuren Schwierigkeiten der amerikanischen Kriegsproduktion."

Gegenüber dem Niedergang der englischen Wirtschaftsmacht steht der gewaltige Anstieg der deutschen Produktion und die Entwicklung jener Produktionsmethoden, die nicht allein auf den Krieg beschränkt sind, sondern auch nach dem Kriege ihre Fruchtbarkeit in der Volkswirtschaft des deutschen Sozialismus beweisen werden. Gegenüber der Rationalisierung auf der Feindseite, deren Problematik sich jetzt „in den ungeheuren Schwierigkeiten der amerikanischen Kriegsproduktion" offenbart, steht die staatlich gelenkte deutsche Kriegswirtschaft, die „den gestaltenden Kräften der Rationalisierung einen vollständig anders gearteten Ausgangspunkt" gibt.

Während des Krieges ist die deutsche Volkswirtschaft entscheidend umgestaltet worden. Dahinter steht eine gewaltige Führerleistung, wie sie aufgebracht wurde von dem Verantwortlichen für den Vierjahresplan, Reichsmarschall Göring, dem Reichswirtschaftsminister Funk, und dem Reichsminister für Bewaffnung und Munition Speer. Nur im nationalsozialistischen Staate war eine derart enge, sich ergänzende Zusammenarbeit möglich. Hier gibt es nicht jene Diskrepanzen, von denen aus den USA. berichtet wird. Und nur im nationalsozialistischen Reiche ist als Frucht einer langen Erziehung jene Wirtschaftsgesinnung vorzufinden, die die Grundlage der Autorität und Verantwortung darstellt. Aus der Rede des Wirtschaftsministers tritt der Aufbau der Kräfte, die uns unsere Kriegsproduktion ermöglicht haben, klar zutage. Den ersten Rang nimmt die nationalsozialistische Gesinnung ein. Aus ihr ist erwachsen sowohl die große geistige Leistung der Führungsstellen, wie auch die Mitarbeit der Wirtschaftler, wie der Arbeitswille des gesamten deutschen Volkes.

Weil dem so ist, vermag die gelenkte Wirtschaft im autoritären Staate des Nationalsozialismus Leistungsreserven in einem Umfange zu mobilisieren, wie dies

San Francisco Chronicle EXTRA

THE CITY'S ONLY HOME-OWNED NEWSPAPER

FOUNDED 1865—VOL. CLVI, NO. 12 CCCCAAB SAN FRANCISCO, WEDNESDAY, JANUARY 27, 1943 DAILY 5 CENTS, SUNDAY 15 CENTS: PER MONTH $1.50 DAILY AND SUNDAY

FDR FLIES TO AFRICA, MEETS WITH CHURCHILL

'43 Offensive is All Set--Its Aim Is Unconditional Axis Surrender

THIS WORLD TODAY

By ROYCE BRIER

HE was a little, stocky man and he had a curious pitching, shuffling gait. He looked sleepy often, had strange periods of torpor, and he was a steady drinker. He didn't have much to say, and what he said seldom had a ring to it, though he lived in a ringing time.

Nobody thought he would amount to much. His chosen career had ended in middle-aged disgrace. He had sunk to anonymity and frustration. But there was some granite somewhere in his soul. This may have had something to do with it, yet nobody to this day quite understands how he emerged from hundreds with more promise in them, and came to command the first, small bumbling army of farm boys thrusting blindly south into the wilderness to put down the great rebellion.

He moved into Tennessee, and after an initial success to the Cumberland River with about 22,000 men. It was winter and there were bitter snowstorms. A great many other commanders were wiring around that they couldn't fight in such weather, couldn't move their big guns. But this commander said nothing. He just besieged Fort Donelson. The fort was commanded by General Simon Bolivar Buckner, the father of Major General Simon Bolivar Buckner Jr., now commanding our forces in Alaska.

The Confederate proposed a commission for surrender of his 15,000 men. Grant wrote: "No terms other than an unconditional and immediate surrender can be accepted. I propose to move immediately on your works."

Buckner then submitted to unconditional surrender.

Fighter It was the first victory. The North went wild, and the little, stocky man with the sleepy exterior and some granite in his soul went on to glory. For, you see, he was a fighter. He was a hell of a fighter, and not much else (even the famous words may have been conceived by Rawlins, his chief of staff), but not much else was needed right then. Or, if much else was needed, still, it was no good without fighters. In the end all his antagonists in the field had to submit to unconditional surrender.

So it is quite fitting that in this time of trial 81 years later almost to a day, we revive that granite-souled phrase, and no-

Continued on Page 4, Col. 1

—A. P. Wirephoto

PRESIDENT ROOSEVELT
He with the "jaunty-angled cigarette"

The 'Unconditional Surrender Meeting'

Allied Leaders Meet for 10 Days In Casablanca; De Gaulle, Giraud Also There; Stalin in Close Touch

U. S. and British War Staffs Attend; Chiang Kai-shek Is Pledged Full Aid; President Inspects AEF in the Field

By WES GALLAGHER
Associated Press Staff Writer

CASABLANCA, French Morocco, Jan. 26—President Roosevelt and Prime Minister Churchill, in the most unprecedented and momentous meeting of the century, have reached "complete agreement" on war plans for 1943, designed to bring about the "unconditional surrender" of Germany, Italy and Japan, it was disclosed today.

Defying every tradition, the President of the United States flew across 5000 miles of the Atlantic ocean for a 10-day meeting with Winston Churchill, which saw the leaders of the two nations bring General De Gaulle and General Henri Honore Giraud together for the first time since the fall of France. De Gaulle and Giraud met in a little villa outside this city.

Virtually the entire war staffs of both nations participated in day and night discussions, which ended Sunday afternoon with a press conference before a group of war correspondents flown secretly from Allied headquarters half-

Continued on Page A, Col. 5

—A. P. Wirephoto

PRIME MINISTER CHURCHILL
He with the "inevitable cigar"

The War In Russia

Only 12,000 Left Of Nazi Army At Stalingrad

By the Associated Press

LONDON, Wednesday, Jan. 27—The Russians announced last night the substantial liquidation of the 50,000 Axis troops that had survived in the Stalingrad trap, the bloodiest defeat ever suffered by one of Hitler's armies and one which had resulted in capture or death for more than 200,000 German and mercenary troops.

"The troops of the (upper) Don front, continuing their offensive against German Fascist troops encircled in the area of Stalingrad, have broken through numerous and powerful enemy fortifications after fierce battles and have in the main completed the liquidation of the German Fascist grouping," the Soviet Command proclaimed in a special communique.

Only 12,000 of this lost army remained in action, Moscow added, and that force was split in two and isolated. Moreover, the three big railroads fanning out from Stalin-

Continued on Page 4, Col. 4

The Index

'Reunion in Vallejo'

Assembly Asks OPA to Provide Larger Rental Inspection Staff

By MILTON SILVERMAN
Chronicle Staff Writer
Copyright, 1943, by The San Francisco Chronicle Publishing Co.

The State Assembly joined with California Congressmen yesterday in demanding a clean-up of the Vallejo rent-gouging scandal.

Moving swiftly into action the Assembly voted unanimously for a resolution asking the Federal Government to supply more OPA inspectors in the Vallejo district.

Thousands of cases of rent-gouging have been reported, involving many naval heroes and their families. In no other city, The Chronicle disclosed, have they suffered such acute victimizing.

In Washington, Congressmen demanded criminal prosecution for landlords gouging these service families with illegal rents.

Representative John Z. Anderson told Associated Press he had wired Rear Admiral W. L. Friedell, commandant of the Mare Island Navy Yard, for full details.

Anderson, a member of the House Naval Affairs Committee, said he had received reports that military men were being subjected to high rentals by Vallejo landlords.

"If such is the case," he told reporters, "the situation is most reprehensible and should be corrected immediately. But we will await further information before taking action."

Representative J. Leroy Johnson of the House Military Affairs Committee declared landlords should be prosecuted if they had violated rent rules.

FAIR TREATMENT FOR ALL SERVICEMEN

"We want to see every member of the military forces dealt with decently," he declared. "There should be no pumping up of rent rates, and certainly no gouging of men in our armed forces."

The State Legislature began its clampdown on gouging when the Assembly passed the Crowley resolution by a vote of 67 to 0.

Introduced by Assemblyman Ernest Crowley of Fairfield, the resolution called for an increased number of OPA administrators in the Vallejo area and a lightening of building restrictions.

The present staff of inspectors in Vallejo, he declared, is insufficient to check complaints of excessive food prices and rentals.

"There are fair landlords and fair restaurant operators in Vallejo, and there are those who are taking advantage," he claimed. "Justice would be better attained with the assignment of a sufficient staff of investigators."

NEARLY 400 LEGAL CASES NOW ON FILE

Even law-abiding landlords would be aided if more OPA men could be assigned there, he added. There are between 300 and 400 cases where landlords are seeking legal adjustments from Federal officials. The understaffed OPA office has been unable to hear these cases promptly.

"The same conditions are true in other cities, such as San Diego and Seattle," Crowley declared, "where there has been a large population influx due to war conditions."

Federal housing officials mean-

Continued on Page 14, Col. 2

Inside . . .

The Day's Military Digest

Nazis Are Massacred by Own Strategy

By PETER D. WHITNEY

The Russians yesterday announced the liquidation of the German Sixth Army, cream of the Wehrmacht, which in September stormed so proudly up to the gates of Stalingrad on the Volga. Moscow's special communique, declaring that all but 12,000 of about 220,000 Germans have been killed or captured, adds:

"The history of wars has never known the encirclement and annihilation of such large numbers of regular troops saturated to the limit with modern military equipment," And indeed, it is a bitter irony that the proud German army, whose commanders are forever aspiring to achieve encirclement-and-annihilation battles ("another Cannae," or "another Tannenberg"), should have had one of the greatest inflicted on it.

This is the blow at German morale which Propaganda Minister Goebbels has been preparing to ward off for 10 days. Yesterday Captain Sertorius, a military expert of the German radio, said that the Sixth Army was still resisting, but that every man in it "probably has forfeited his life . . . part of them only continue fighting with bayonet and rifle butt."

The German communique yesterday contained two other interesting hints, first as to "renewed" Russian attacks south of Voronezh, and second as to German counterattacks between the Don and Manych rivers, about 45 miles due east of Rostov. These counterattacks are doubtless covering the retreat from the Caucasus, and if they continue to be successful they will prevent the Russians from realizing their hope of an enormous entrapment.

War in Africa

Heavy rains have again all but washed out the Tunisian fighting, though American and French patrols made contact with the Germans in the Ousseltia valley, where a distinctly threatening thrust had developed last week. The German communique, describing Monday's fighting, declares that Allied attempts to recapture positions lost the day before had failed, and claims 4000 prisoners in six days.

The Eighth Army, whose headquarters announcements still come from Cairo 1500 miles away, announced occupation of Zauia, 30 miles beyond Tripoli, on Monday. There is no certainty yet whether Rommel is going to try a stand on the Mareth line, but it is expected.

War Against Japan

A large Jap air armada was driven off before it could bomb our positions on Guadalcanal Monday, while U. S. troops were consolidating their hold on Kokumbona, once Jap headquarters, and the stretch of beach on which the enemy used to land his troops.

General MacArthur's communique announced scattered light raids on the principal Jap bases north of New Guinea.

De Gaulle-Giraud Talk

The 'Exchanges of Views' Will Continue; Differences Remain

LONDON, Wednesday, Jan. 27 (AP)—The lack of concrete details in the announced agreement between Generals Charles De Gaulle and Henri Giraud at Casablanca was taken in political circles here today as meaning the meeting had failed to bridge the fundamental differences between them, but the French National Committee announced the "exchanges of views" would be continued.

In a statement issued after a meeting with De Gaulle on his return, the committee said it had been decided at the Casablanca conference that "the necessary liaisons should be established immediately."

The conversations took into account the "new situation" in French North and West Africa, the committee said, and then it added:

"Exchanges of views on this subject will be continued. Complete union of empire and armed forces in conjunction with the movement of resistance in France, to be accomplished under conditions consonant with the will and dignity of the French people, remains the immutable aim of General de Gaulle and the National Committee."

Since there was no evidence of achievement either of political fusion or a working military agreement at Casablanca, political sources said it appeared each group would retain its separate status, working together as Allies beneath the broad umbrella of British-American sponsorship, but without any coincidence of political views.

De Gaulle will continue to direct the Fighting French and preside at his National Council, and Giraud will remain head of the North African forces and civil administration, they said.

It was understood on good authority that De Gaulle and Giraud will exchange representatives, each having practically the status of an Ambassador to create a liaison.

It was considered likely that General Georges Catroux, who is the best diplomat of the Fighting French, would be sent to North Africa as De Gaulle's representative.

De Gaulle was understood to have made a full report on the North African conference to the

Continued on Page C, Col. 1

Peace Without Hatred Urged

TUCSON, Ariz., Jan. 26 (U.P.)—An approach to the peace table without rancor or passion was advocated here today by Frank O. Lowden, former Governor of Illinois, as the only possible means to an enduring peace after the Allied victory in this war.

Lowden celebrated his 82nd birthday here today. He was a contender in the 1920 Presidential race.

Peru Breaks With Vichy

LIMA, Peru., Jan. 26 (U.P.)—Peru has broken off diplomatic relations with Vichy France, it was officially announced late today.

Was There More to It?

Rumors Hint at Italian and Finn Delegates

By C. R. CUNNINGHAM
United Press Staff Writer

ALGIERS, Jan. 26—There was a growing conviction tonight among correspondents who attended the Roosevelt-Churchill press conference in Casablanca that the 10-day meeting was not devoted entirely to the "unconditional surrender" pronouncement contained in the official communique.

There was a welter of rumors in Casablanca. Rumors had it that Italian, Spanish and even Finnish and Turkish delegates had representatives at the meeting. Rumors were that those representatives were invited not necessarily to join the United Nations but to become convinced of the might of the Allies. Then they could make their choice.

None of these rumors were authoritative, but it was not believed that President Roosevelt would have dared risk a 6000-mile airplane ride for a "heart-to-heart" talk with Prime Minister Churchill or to review events of 1942 and discuss coming events of 1943. The combined Allied staffs could have done that without the presence of either the President or Prime Minister.

During the Roosevelt-Churchill press conference correspondents were not given the opportunity to ask the President or Prime Minister questions. Immediately after it, we were rushed to a conference room, where Allied staffs had held daily meetings. We were given a few hours in which to write our stories and next day came back to Allied North African headquarters.

British Execute 'Refugee' Spy

LONDON, Jan. 26 (AP)—Franciscus Johannes Winter, a 40-year-old German spy who came to Britain in the guise of a refugee, was executed today in Wandsworth Prison, the Home Office announced.

Preis: 2 Karbowanez
Im Reich: 20 Rpf.

Deutsche Ukraine-Zeitung

Postverlag: Luzk — Verlag und Schriftleitung: Luzk/Ukraine — Ruf: Luzk 104 und 105 — Postsendungen durch Deutsche Dienstpost Ukraine — Bankkonto: Wirtschaftsbank Luzk Nr 28; im Reich: Postscheckkonto Berlin Nr 800 der Dresdner Bank mit Vermerk „Für Deutsche Ukraine-Zeitung"

2. Jahrg. Sonnabend, 30. Januar 1943 Nr. 25

Die Deutsche Ukraine-Zeitung erscheint täglich morgens, mit Ausnahme montags. Bezugspreis: in der Ukraine monatl. 30 Kar, im Reich monatl. RM 3,— zuzügl. Zustellgebühr. Bestellungen können im Reich bei jeder Postanstalt, in der Ukraine bei den Deutschen Dienstpostämtern oder beim Verlag aufgegeben werden

Alle Kraft für das Werk des Führers

Der 10. Jahrestag der nationalsozialistischen Revolution im Zeichen eherner Entschlossenheit

Es hat vor zehn Jahren, am 30. Januar 1933, als der Führer die Macht übernahm, wenige gegeben, die erkannten, daß damit nicht nur in der Entwicklung des deutschen Volkes und Reiches eine entscheidende Wende begonnen hatte, sondern dieser Tag auch der Ausgangspunkt einer neuen Epoche der Weltgeschichte war. Heute, da wir uns in einem gigantischen Ringen um die Freiheit unseres Vaterlandes und die Sicherung der Errungenschaften der nationalsozialistischen Revolution befinden, wissen wir zwar im einzelnen noch nicht, was am Ende des damals begonnenen Wandlungsprozesses stehen wird, wohl aber ist die tiefe und weltweite Wirkung, die von jenem Tag ausging, auch denjenigen offenbar, die sich lange gegen die Einsicht in die schöpferische Kraft der deutschen Erneuerung gesträubt haben.

Die Zeit ist nicht dazu angetan, rückwärts zu schauen. Unser ganzes Denken und unsere Arbeit sind gerade in diesen Tagen, in denen das deutsche Volk in der härtesten Bewährungsprobe seiner Geschichte steht, ausgerichtet auf die Forderungen, die diese Schicksalsstunde an uns alle stellt. Wenn wir dennoch am Geburtstag unseres neuen Staates den Blick zurückwerfen auf die hinter uns liegenden zehn Jahre, so deshalb, weil sich uns in dieser Ueberschau der letzte und tiefste Sinn unseres Ringens in diesem Krieg am deutlichsten offenbart. Denn was war diese kurze Zeitspanne für unser Volk anderes als die große Stunde seiner wechselvollen, an Höhen und Tiefen so reichen Geschichte, in der es immer wieder um die seinem Wesen und seiner Bestimmung entsprechende staatliche Form und die seinen Leistungen und Größe gemäße Stellung gerungen hat, ohne je, wie andere Völker, das Ziel ganz zu erreichen! „Ein Tag kann eine Perle sein, und ein Jahrhundert nichts." Gilt dieses Wort Gottfried Kellers nicht für die Entwicklung unseres Volkes und Reiches in dem Jahrzehnt 1933 bis 1943, wenn man sie an unserem tausendjährigen volklichen und staatlichen Werden mißt? Wir haben auf dem Weg unserer Volk- und Reichwerdung glanzvolle Höhepunkte erlebt, aber kaum je haben sich deutsches Wesen und deutsche Kraft so entfaltet, wie in der Erneuerung, die der Not und dem Elend nach 1918 folgte. Zum erstenmal ist die deutsche Sehnsucht nach dem großen und freien Reich aller Deutschen in einer Form und in einer Idee erfüllt worden, die Dauer verspricht. Was nur wenige für möglich gehalten haben, hat der Führer verwirklicht: Nachdem die Geschichte endgültig ihr Urteil gesprochen zu haben schien, ist das Reich neu erstanden, hat die Idee des Nationalsozialismus vom ganzen Volke Besitz ergriffen, war der Neubau des Staates auf dem dauerhaften Fundament wahrer Volksgemeinschaft errichtet worden — ein Wunder, wenn man sich vergegenwärtigt, daß dieser Aufbruch nicht mit den Mitteln äußerer Macht geschah, sondern aus der inneren Kraft der deutschen Seele. Darin liegt die erste gewaltige Tat des Schöpfers unseres neuen Reiches, dessen Werk nicht das Ergebnis irgendeiner zufälligen politischen Ideologie oder geschichtlicher Bedingtheiten, noch eines Machtkampfes mit anderen Völkern war, sondern die Frucht einer inneren Erneuerung, des Bewußtwerdens deutscher Sendung.

Das andere, nicht nur für uns, sondern für ganz Europa Entscheidende der Revolution des Jahres 1933 aber ist dies: Die Idee, welche die Sehnsucht der Deutschen nach dem Reich erfüllte, mußte in der geschichtlichen Situation, in der sie zum Siege gelangte, nicht weniger revolutionierend auf die Ordnung wirken, die die imperialistischen Mächte geschaffen hatten, um ihre Herrschaft über den Kontinent und in der Welt aufrechtzuerhalten. Die Verwirklichung des Großdeutschen Reiches setzte voraus, daß jener Zustand beseitigt wurde, der in allen Jahrhunderten die Ursache für die Friedlosigkeit zwischen den Völkern Europas gewesen war, der Zustand, in der dem größten Volk im Herzen des Kontinents die Rolle des Entrechteten zugedacht war. Die mit Spannung geladene europäische Völker- und Staatenordnung neu zu gestalten, das war die universale Bestimmung, die die nationalsozialistische Revolution als geschichtsbildende Kraft in sich trug. Wieder war damit, wie schon so oft, die „deutsche Frage" aufgeworfen, die fruchtbar nur gelöst werden konnte, wenn die Siegermächte von Versailles sich der Einsicht nicht verschlossen, daß es einen dauerhaften Frieden ohne oder gar gegen das Reich niemals geben könne.

Vor dieser Entscheidung standen die Mächte 1939, nachdem das Reich in einer einzigartigen inneren Aufbauarbeit und dem erfolgreichen Kampf um die Durchsetzung seiner Lebensrechte seine schöpferische Kraft zur Neugestaltung bewiesen hatte, ohne auch nur im geringsten die Interessen der Staaten berührt zu haben. die sich dem deutschen Aufstieg entgegenstellten. Es ist eine der infamsten Lügen, wenn unsere Gegner behaupten, sie hätten uns deshalb den Krieg erklärt, weil das nationalsozialistische Reich sich den Kontinent unterwerfen wollte und nach der Weltmacht strebte. Worum es ihnen ging, war auch dieses Mal wieder das egoistische Ziel, das größte europäische Volk niederzuhalten, die Durchsetzung jenes natürlichen Rechts zu verhindern, auf das jede Nation Anspruch hat.

Deutschland war aus eigener Macht, aus der inneren Kraft seiner Seele wieder stark geworden, das „heilige Herz der Völker" hatte wieder zu schlagen begonnen. Dieses neue Reich zeigte durch den Fleiß und die Tatkraft seines Volkes der sterbenden Welt des Liberalismus, daß es einen Ausweg aus dem chaotischen Zustand gab, dem das Zeitalter des Liberalismus entgegenstrebte. In friedlicher Aufbauarbeit schuf es die Voraussetzungen für den Wohlstand des Volkes, während die reichen Staaten ihren inneren Problemen unfähig gegenüberstanden, gab es mit seinen Leistungen ein leuchtendes Beispiel dafür, was ein Volk zu vollbringen vermag. So trieb seine Gegner der Neid und die Angst vor der deutschen Tüchtigkeit, ihr Egoismus, der auf Kosten anderer ein sorgenfreies Leben führen, niemals aber ein Opfer bringen will, zum Verbrechen, die Völker wieder in den Krieg zu stürzen. Was sie auf friedlichem Wege nicht durchsetzen konnten, die neue Unterwerfung Deutschlands unter ihre Herrschaft, hofften sie nun noch einmal mit dem Schwert zu erreichen.

Es bedarf heute keiner Erörterung mehr darüber, daß unsere Gegner, wenn sie auch ahnen mochten, daß ihnen im nationalsozialistischen Deutschland ein anderer Partner gegenübertrat als vor 25 Jahren, das Wesen der neuen Kräfte verkannten, die in den vergangenen zwei Jahrzehnten sich nicht nur in Deutschland, sondern auch in anderen Staaten durchgesetzt hatten. Die Entwicklung des Krieges von der deutsch-polnischen Auseinandersetzung zum Weltkrieg zwischen den Plutokratien demokratischer und bolschewistischer Prägung und den jungen nationalen Kräften hat es in immer stärkerem Maße offenkundig gemacht, daß dieser Krieg zur Entscheidung dieses Jahrhunderts schlechthin geworden ist, daß es in ihm längst nicht mehr nur um rein machtpolitische Veränderungen geht, sondern um letzte Prinzipien politischer, wirtschaftlicher und geistiger Neuordnung. In der Geschichte walten zwar nicht die Gesetze der Natur, es herrschen hier viel weniger Logik und Zwangsläufigkeit, als man gemeinhin anzunehmen geneigt ist. Aber wenn wir uns heute den Prozeß in den hinter uns liegenden zehn Jahren vergegenwärtigen, dann sehen wir doch eine unerbittliche, schicksalhafte Gesetzmäßigkeit, vor der es kein Entrinnen gibt und die uns die blutige Auseinandersetzung bis zur endgültigen Entscheidung als logische Folge aus dem Ringen der geschichtlichen Triebkräfte seit dem ersten Weltkrieg erscheinen läßt. Es ist müßig, die Frage zu erörtern, ob eine friedliche Lösung möglich gewesen wäre. Unsere Gegner wollten sie nicht. Damit war der Kampf mit den Waffen unabwendbar, den zu vermeiden der Führer zu den größten Opfern bereit war, während unsere Gegner keinen Fußbreit ihre egoistischen Interessen, ihres Reichtums und ihrer Vorherrschaft preisgeben wollten.

So hat uns das Schicksal vor die größte Bewährungsprobe gestellt, die ein Volk je zu bestehen hatte, sind wir in einen Kampf getrieben worden, in dem es um Sein oder Nichtsein geht. Indem die Plutokratien sich mit dem Bolschewismus verbündeten, haben sie der Welt gezeigt, daß sie lieber das Chaos wollen, als die Anerkennung unseres Rechtes, unserer Freiheit und Größe. Wir brauchen keine moralische Rechtfertigung für den Kampf, den wir führen. Das Schicksal selbst hat uns aufgerufen, unsere geschichtliche Aufgabe, die wir nicht nur unserem Volk, sondern dem ganzen Abendland gegenüber haben, zu erfüllen. Wir ringen für die Größe und Sicherheit des Reiches wie für den Bestand der europäischen Völkerordnung und der abendländischen Kultur gegen die zerstörenden Kräfte des Bolschewismus und des Liberalismus. Wir sind Kämpfer für das neue Zeitalter, das im Zeichen der schöpferischen Kraft einer Revolution steht, die, aus den Tiefen völkischen Lebens emporgewachsen, gerade noch in letzter Stunde ihre Macht entfalten konnte, um Europa vor der Zerstörung zu retten.

Die Kämpfe, die unsere Soldaten an den Fronten zu bestehen haben, geben uns das Maß für die ungeheure Schwere der Auseinandersetzung, in der wir erleben, daß alles Große nur aus Opfern entsteht. In dieser Lage vergessen wir keinen Augenblick, daß dieser Krieg nichts anderes ist als die entscheidende Phase der Revolution, die uns vor zehn Jahren ein neues Gesetz unseres volklichen und staatlichen Lebens gab, daß wir mit ihm erfüllen, was damals begonnen wurde, als die Tat des Führers Volk und Reich aus Not und Elend rettete. So gibt uns gerade der Rückblick auf die hinter uns liegenden zehn Jahre die Erkenntnis, wofür wir kämpfen und welche gewaltige Aufgabe wir zu erfüllen haben. Eine gerade Linie führt von dem Tag der Machtergreifung zu den gewaltigen Schlachten dieses Krieges. Nun, da die Zeit der Bewährung gekommen ist, kann kein anderes Gesetz für uns gelten als das, das über der Revolution stand: sich einzusetzen für die Idee, die unsere Freiheit verheißt.

An diesem Tag sind alle unsere Gedanken bei den heldenmütigen Kämpfern, die draußen an der Front Tag für Tag das leuchtende Beispiel der Treue und Opferbereitschaft geben, ohne die es kein würdiges Leben für ein Volk gibt. Und unsere Gedanken sind bei dem Manne, der Deutschland wieder stark und groß machte und unser Volk wieder zu seiner Bestimmung als führende Nation Europas hinführte. Ihm zu folgen, wohin der Weg auch führe, alles auf uns zu nehmen, was die Schwere der Zeit von uns erfordert, uns noch mehr einzusetzen als bisher, damit wir den Endsieg erringen, sei unser Bekenntnis.

Dr. Karl Weidenbach.

Bekenntnis

Festigkeit zeigt sich im Widerstand gegen das Unglück. Nur Feiglinge beugen sich unter das Joch, tragen geduldig ihre Ketten und erdulden ruhig die Unterdrückung. Niemals könnte ich mich zu solcher Schmach entschließen, denn die Haupttugenden der Germanen waren Tapferkeit und die Treue, mit der sie ihre Verpflichtungen erfüllten.

Nur sehr fleißige Arbeit, beständige Aufmerksamkeit und viele kleine Einzelheiten bringen bei uns die großen Dinge hervor. Unsere Verbündete sind: Die Tapferkeit und die Ausdauer, und die Truppen sind die Säulen des Staates. Wenn man sie nicht mit beständiger Aufmerksamkeit in Ordnung und in gebotener Vortrefflichkeit erhält, droht dem Staat der Untergang, und der erste Sturm wirft ihn um. In einer Armee muß alles auf das vollkommenste gebracht werden, und man muß sehen, daß alles, was geschieht, das Werk eines einzigen Mannes ist.

Die Disziplin bildet die Seele der Heere. So lange sie herrscht, ist sie die Stütze der Reiche. Man darf sich niemals einbilden, alles getan zu haben, wenn noch etwas zu tun übrig bleibt. Denn alles, was möglich ist, kann geschehen. Mir tut jeder Tag meines Lebens leid, den ich nicht fleißigem Streben gewidmet habe.

Das Leben ist nur lebenswert, wenn es von Ehre und Achtungswürdigkeit begleitet ist. Der Tod ist der Bedrückung und Schande vorzuziehen. Wenn das Vaterland das Recht hat, das Leben von uns zu fordern, mit wieviel mehr Grund kann es beanspruchen, daß unsere Tätigkeit ihm nützlich werde.

Die Menschen sollen niemals an ihren alleinigen Vorteil denken. Dächte jeder so, gäbe es keine menschliche Gesellschaft mehr, denn anstatt eigene Vorteile zugunsten des Gemeinwohls aufzugeben, würde man das Gemeinwohl dem persönlichen Eigennutz opfern.

Es gibt Umstände, wo man mit den Waffen die Freiheit der Völker verteidigen muß, die ungerecht bedrückt werden sollen, wo man durch Gewalt erringen muß, was die Ungerechtigkeit der Menschen der Güte verweigert. In solchen Fällen bewahrheitet sich das, was wie ein Widerspruch klingt: daß erst ein guter Krieg einen guten Frieden gibt und sichert.

Im Kriege besonders erkennt man den Wert der Tatkraft und der Wachsamkeit. Jeder lasse sich durch zwei Prinzipien leiten: das eine ist die Ehre, das andere das Interesse des Staates. Die Gesetze, die diese Prinzipien mir vorschreiben, sind erstens: niemals eine Handlung zu begehen, deretwegen ich erröten müßte, wenn ich darüber meinem Volke Rechenschaft legen sollte; und zweitens: für das Wohl und den Ruhm meines Vaterlandes den letzten Blutstropfen zu opfern.

Wahrhaftig das große Rad der Ereignisse Europas zu drehen, ist eine rauhe Arbeit. Ich beschwöre Dich, erhebe Dich über alle Ereignisse, denke an das Vaterland und bedenke, daß es unsere erste Pflicht ist, es zu verteidigen. Wenn Du erfährst, daß einem von uns ein Unglück zugestoßen ist, so frage, ob er im Kampf gefallen ist. Es gibt für uns nur Tod oder Sieg.

Friedrich der Große

EXTRA

The only way to be sure you get all of the vital news is to have The Tribune delivered to your home, by carrier, every day. PHONE TEMPLEBAR 6000, NOW!

Oakland Tribune

EXCLUSIVE ASSOCIATED PRESS . . . WIREPHOTO . . . WIDE WORLD . . . UNITED PRESS

HOME EDITION

VOL. CXXXVIII | DAILY | OAKLAND, CALIFORNIA, TUESDAY, FEBRUARY 9, 1943 | 15c SUNDAY | NO. 40

SHATTERED JAPS QUIT GUADALCANAL

Huge Allied Offensive in Tunisia Looms

By WILLIAM B. DICKINSON

LONDON, Feb. 9.—(U.P.)—Neutral dispatches reported "hectic preparations" for a big Allied offensive in Tunisia today.

The Allies, dispatches from Algiers, via Madrid, said, were expected to strike from the west at the moment Lieut.-Gen. Bernard L. Montgomery's British Eighth Army resumes its pursuit in force of the Afrika Korps.

Montgomery's Army, with heavy artillery and tanks, was reported poised along the Tripolitanian-Tunisian frontier, with forward elements probing enemy positions eight miles from the Mareth line, inside Tunisia.

Still, only light land engagements were reported, and it was believed that the Allied nutcracker was being held for better weather or until its preparations were absolutely complete.

MESSINA IS RAIDED

The Middle Eastern command reported only Eighth Army patrol activity and artillery exchanges in the northern sector yesterday in today's communique. Allied planes from the Middle East "heavily attacked" the train ferry terminus at Messina, Sicily, in daylight yesterday.

Observers had emphasized that the Allies could not take chances on a bobble, that their final offensive had to throw the Germans and Italians into the sea.

The Germans' Radio Paris said Lieut.-Gen. Dwight Eisenhower was concentrating his forces, probably for a drive to the Tunisia East coast to cut off the retreat of the Afrika Korps.

SOFTENING UP FOE

The thundering blows being landed by Allied airpower on Sicily, Sardinia, Southern Italy and Axis bases in Tunisia were softening up the enemy for the final onslaught.

The Germans had rushed squadrons of the Messerschmitt 109-G—their newest and best high altitude fighter—to the African theater in a desperate effort to keep from being knocked out of the skies.

To counteract the Messerschmitt 109-G's, the Allies were believed sending Spitfire 9's, faster and more heavily armed than the Messerschmitts.

The French announced that they had taken an "important height" in the region of the Kebir River Valley, presumably in the Pont du Fahs sector, 27 miles southwest of Tunis.

'FIGHTING'S FUN'

Capt. James E. (Jimmy) Peck, Berkeley, hero of the R.A.F. and United States Army Air Corps, came home grinning yesterday. —Tribune photo.

Berkeley Ace Home to Rest

BERKELEY, Feb. 9.—The fighting kid, Capt. Jimmy Peck Jr., who at 21 has bagged six German planes without suffering a scratch, came home yesterday to take a breather.

"Fighting's fun," he said. "It's like a game, something like skeet shooting. I just want to rest a wihle, and then go back, with a good American plane under me."

Looking like any high school or college boy, Jimmy, rejected by the U.S. Army Air Forces in 1941, arrived yesterday on his first visit home in 20 months.

He had stopped in Los Angeles to visit his mother, Mrs. James E. Peck, who is ill there, and a sister, Mrs. George Uhl, wife of the Los Angeles city health director.

But on hand to meet him were his father, who is chief field engineer for Bethlehem Alameda Shipyards, and a sister, Mrs. Bernard Shapiro, 2433 B Waring Street.

Continued Page 5, Col. 3

DUTCH MAN U.S. PLANES, NEARLY WIPE OUT JAP TOWN IN AROE ISLANDS

ALLIED HEADQUARTERS IN AUSTRALIA, Feb. 9.—(AP)—Dutch fliers, manning American Billy Mitchell bombers, blasted and burned three-quarters of the Japanese-occupied town and harbor of Dobo in the Aroe Islands about 500 miles north of Darwin, Australia, yesterday, an Allied communique said today.

Photographs showed that three-quarters of the town was in ruins after the raid, the communique said. Two waves of planes attacked the Japanese base and the fires were visible for 40 miles, it was reported. The Aroe Islands are in the Arafura Sea between northern Australia and the western end of New Guinea.

Other Allied bombers raided the Japanese-held Kahili airdrome at Buin in the Solomon Islands, started huge fires visible for 60 miles, set fire to several large aircraft and destroyed a 2000-ton ship lying off shore, the communique said. Explosions from an ammunition dump near the beach rocked one of the Allied planes flying at a height of 9300 feet, it was reported.

In the ground fighting on New Guinea, an enemy pocket of resistance east of the Wau Airdrome, 35 miles southwest of Salamaua, was reported wiped out. Allied aircraft strafed and bombed Japanese targets in this area from a low altitude.

Other Japanese-occupied positions at Babo in Dutch New Guinea, Gasmata in New Britain and Finschhafen and Lae in northern New Guinea also were attacked.

Russ Drive on In 3 Sectors

By EDDY GILMORE

MOSCOW, Feb. 9.—(AP)—The Red Army smashed anew at sagging German lines in three sectors today after storming into Kursk, an enemy anchor point on the Moscow-to-Crimea rail line, and destroying the German Kursk Army, commanded by General Schneider.

Front line dispatches and communiques told of the Red Army sweeping in on the German citadel from several directions to overwhelm a garrison that had held Kursk since November 11, 1941.

One story said the Russians found Kursk to be "an enormous cemetery."

Advance units pursued the Germans west and south of Kursk.

Kharkov, another important German bastion on the same rail line 125 miles south of Kursk, was menaced by similar encirclement tactics. Kharkov has been in German hands since October, 1941.

Col. Gen. N. F. Vatutin's mobile units and ski troopers pressed on from Kramatorsk southward into the Donets Basin and toward the Sea of Azov.

NAZI COUNTER-ATTACK

About Rostov the Germans were counter-attacking in an attempt to hold that city, said the first news dispatches from that Don River port since the Russians drove to within three miles of it.

East of Rostov the Soviet troops took a large unidentified place.

The Germans had hoped that their lines before Kursk would hold near Schchigri and Tim. When they were smashed last week, anxiety mounted within the garrison.

The Red Army troops then took the station of Zorino, cut the railway at Kursk-Lgov and stormed into the village of Lebiazhie. The Kursk Army's advanced posts were knocked back, the Russians said, and at dawn yesterday the Russians reached the suburbs.

The first heavy thrust at Kursk was delivered from the northeast. Ditches and ravines in that section offered a considerable problem and the Germans pushed reserves into the area, including a motorcycle battalion and several infantry battalions which reached the garrisons from Lvov before the railway was severed.

STORM INTO CITY

The Russians, however, drove into the Yamskoy district, broke into the Street of the Young Pioneers, fought their way into Gorsy Street, the main artery, then stormed across the Tuskar River into the heart of the city after fierce battles, the dispatches said.

The far side of the Tuskar River is an elevated bank and the Red Army troops had to scale it under heavy machine-gun and mortar fire.

Pravda said that the Russian soldiers used bayonets, and even rifle butts, to batter the garrison into submission.

Another Soviet column, meantime, broke through from the southeast and crossed the River Seim, occupied the railway station and advanced into Proletarian Square.

One last counter-attack by the Germans was beaten down.

"Part of the Kursk Army was exterminated," Pravda said, "and part was captured."

The city was reported to have been virtually demolished, with a prized museum and picture gallery destroyed and numerous fine buildings burned.

Food Drive Here Starts

Steps toward alleviation of the general food shortage problem for the Bay area and California as a whole were under way today, with Gov. Earl Warren expected to order either a legislative investigation or separate inquiry into the meat situation.

The Governor's direct appeal yesterday to Secretary of Agriculture Claude R. Wickard and Price Administrator Prentiss Brown was made as those two officials announced they will attend a special meeting tomorrow of the California House delegation to discuss meat relief.

TRANSPORTATION LACKING

Other developments today were:

1—Dan C. McKinney, secretary of the California Cattlemen's Association, branded as "absolutely false and without foundation" charges that livestock producers are on a "sit-down" strike and withholding meat animals from the market to obtain "exorbitant" prices.

2—An intensified Pacific Coast meat shortage threatened by a 40 per cent drop in Northern California trucks available to haul livestock to market, was predicted in a stockman's committee report to the Office of Defense Transportation in San Francisco.

3—The Office of Price Administration in Washington announced that it soon will establish Nationwide ceilings on the prices farmers receive for fluid milk in an effort to avert further retail milk price increases.

MEETING TOMORROW

4—This announcement was counterbalanced when Bay region dairy farmers and milk distributors, meeting in San Francisco, urged another half-cent per quart boost in the retail milk price as necessary to offset rising production costs.

5—A warning that "black market" meat likely is diseased and that consumers should protect themselves against uninspected meat was issued by Dr. C. U. Duckworth, chief of the State Division of Animal Industry.

6—The Home Food Advisory

Continued Page 2, Col. 5

'More Go, Less Stop' in Traffic Signals Sought to Save Gas, Tires and Time

WASHINGTON, Feb. 9.—(AP)—The Government sought today to put more "go" and less "stop" in traffic signals in order to save tires, gasoline and time.

Joseph B. Eastman, defense transportation director, asked all State and municipal authorities to adjust traffic control methods to keep pace "with changing conditions."

Suggestions, based on a report by 20-odd traffic experts, included:

Elimination of unnecessary signals.

Shortened signal cycles, generally 35 to 50 seconds.

A system of primary transportation routes, to which preferred traffic control treatment would be given in each municipality.

EVACUATION ANNOUNCED BY TOKYO

NEW YORK, Feb. 9.—(AP)—Japanese Imperial headquarters announced today withdrawal of Japanese forces from Guadalcanal Island in the Solomons "after their missions had been fulfilled," the Berlin radio reported in a dispatch datelined Tokyo.

The broadcast said the Japanese also announced evacuation of the Buna area in New Guinea, apparently an admission, nearly three weeks delayed, of the destruction of the Jap Army in Papua by General MacArthur's American and Australian forces.

The announcement put Japanese losses in the two theaters at 16,734 dead. The Associated Press recorded the Berlin broadcast. Reuters, in London, heard the same announcement on the Tokyo radio, while the OWI reported it also was broadcast from Tokyo on a beam for Latin America.

'MISSION FULFILLED'

"Withdrawal of Japanese troops from Buna on the northeast coast of New Guinea and from the Solomon Island of Guadalcanal after their missions had been fulfilled was announced Tuesday night by the Imperial Japanese headquarters," the Berlin broadcast said.

"The announcement declares that thanks to a strong vanguard situated at Buna, which repulsed repeated enemy attacks, strong bases were able to be established on New Guinea and in the Solomon Islands which now permit new strategy.

"After this objective was reached, Buna was evacuated by the end of January.

"For the same reason troops stationed on Guadalcanal, who since last August had repelled strong attacks of forces the enemy landed there, were moved to other places at the beginning of February, having likewise fulfilled their task.

"As far as is known, in these operations since August of last year 25,000 enemy troops were wiped out, more than 240 enemy airplanes were shot down or destroyed, and more than 30 guns and 25 tanks were put out of commission.

16,734 PERISH

"Japanese losses in dead amounted to 16,734 either killed in action or died of wounds and illness. In addition, 139 Japanese airplanes were lost."

A Navy communique said Sunday that American forces "have established a strong position at Titi, one-half mile west of Marovovo on the northwest coast of Guadalcanal Island" and that "patrol operations are progressing satisfactorily."

This advance, apparently carried out in a 40 to 50 mile flanking move overland, put the Americans within about five miles of the enemy headquarters on Cape Esperance, where Japanese resistance centered.

All Resistance Ceases On Island, Says Knox

By JOHN M. HIGHTOWER

WASHINGTON, Feb. 9.—(A.P.)—The Japanese have evacuated Guadalcanal Island in the Solomons, Secretary of the Navy Knox said today in labeling as "true" an enemy admission to that effect. He added that all resistance to American fighting men there "has apparently ceased.

Thus for the first time in the war the tenacious Japanese have been forced to give up an important position completely and, in Knox's words, the way now opens for blows by the United States against "some of the most important bases of the Japanese." There may be a few enemy groups left on Guadalcanal, he said, but they are too feeble to prevent use of the strategic South Pacific island for a further offensive. Gone is the Japanese hope for a stronghold there from which to harry the shipping lanes to Australia.

This jungle island was the scene of six months of bitter fighting under some of the worst conditions in which troops have ever striven. Captain Eddie Rickenbacker, a visitor, called it "mud and corruption" in hell-holes of discomfort, danger and disease.

Japs Admit Buna Evacuation

Belatedly, the Japanese also said they have evacuated Buna in New Guinea. Here some three weeks ago the Americans and Australians reported final annihilation of a 15,000-man Japanese force. This victory climaxed another jungle campaign in which, first, the Japanese were stopped en route to the important Allied post of Port Moresby, then driven back over rugged mountains to the sea.

The Navy secretary talked to a press conference shortly after the Berlin radio announced the Japanese withdrawal.

Knox noted that no such broadcast, as the story stated, had been received directly from Tokyo, but said:

"I don't think there's any doubt about the truth of that report."

Naval Clashes Cover Withdrawal, Belief

He expressed the opinion that it was possible that widespread recent sea and air activity in the Solomons might have been "a demonstration to cover their withdrawal" in discussing the reported retreat of the Japanese from the highly strategic Solomons Island, on which is located Henderson Field.

This apparent end of a six months' campaign to gain control of the island, Knox said, has denied to the enemy a base from which to raid American lines of communication to Australia.

"The story of the Southwest Pacific would have been a vastly different story for the last three or four months had we not established our position in the Solomons," Knox said.

He reported that he was without any further information of sea and air engagements in the Solomons area and said he assumed that "the same preliminary plays are still going on down there," just as they have been since around January 29.

He readily agreed with questioners, however, that the enemy might be planning some new blow, as naval spokesmen had heretofore indicated was the case.

Knox opened his press conference with a statement recalling that when he returned from Guadalcanal last week he made an estimate of the situation to the effect that "significant Japanese resistance had collapsed."

He then read an Associated Press bulletin from New York reporting that the Berlin radio had broadcast an official Tokyo statement that Buna on New Guinea and Guadalcanal had been evacuated.

Late Information Confirms Report

Knox added that it might easily be possible that recent enemy activities which had been considered here to be reinforcements "probably were attempts to evacuate the island," but he cautioned that this, too, merely was speculative and "we must await confirmation."

Later he said, in response to questioning, "We have some information that the Japs have been evacuating the island."

Churchill 'Stops Show'

LONDON, Feb. 3.—(AP)—Prime Minister Churchill told the House of Commons today that he would soon make a statement on the war situation, including a reference to the creation of a United Nations war council. He spoke in answer to a question.

The Prime Minister, who returned Sunday from his trip to North Africa and the Middle East, stopped the show in Commons.

He entered unobtrusively during the question period and started toward his seat on the Treasury bench. One of the ministers was replying to an interpellation when Churchill appeared.

An explosion of cheering and applause burst on all sides and continued until the Prime Minister was seated. He was smiling broadly.

QUERIED ON RUSSIA

Asked by Laborite Emanuel Shinwell to make a statement on supplies to Russia, Churchill declared: "I am glad to take this opportunity of declaring that we have been and are now doing and will continue to do our utmost."

He described Lord Beaverbrook's demand last week for more aid to Russia as "what one might call a process of emphatic stimulation."

Responding to further questions, Churchill said he would also discuss the import and shipping situation in his forthcoming statement.

He acknowledged that Britain was "dipping into" her food reserves, but said he was "not unduly anxious about the situation" from a long-term viewpoint.

'FOOD SITUATION O.K.'

"I think we are going to be able to get through pretty well on the lines we are now running in the way of food," Churchill said.

Churchill gave King George a first hand account of his trip when they had lunch at Buckingham Palace today.

WHERE TO FIND IT

YW. 22.388

Au service de la France

Un glorieux soldat musulman

DIRECTEUR GENERAL : PIERRE ARGENCE
DIRECTEUR des SERVICES D'AFRIQUE du NORD : CLAUDE CHATELUS
REDACTEUR en CHEF : MARCEL SAUVAGE
L'abonnement d'un an 149 francs à verser au compte de Chèques Postaux TAM, 47, rue Michelet, Alger. C/c 144.19 - Tél. 367.50

TAM

3f L'HEBDOMADAIRE DE L'EMPIRE
REDACTION - ADMINISTRATION - PUBLICITE
47, rue Michelet - Alger - Téléphone : 367.50
2e Année - N° 28 - 13 FEVRIER 1943

Le glorieux rendez-vous

Une journée avec le général LECLERC le héros de l'Armée du Tchad

De notre correspondant de guerre **Claude CHATELUS**

« JE peux vous emmener à Rhadamés où le Général Leclerc se trouvera demain. Vous vous ferez tout petit dans la queue du bombardier. »

« Bien, mon Général, et... merci ».

Le lendemain, le Général Delay, commandant du Front Est Saharien, part à la rencontre du Général Leclerc. La situation militaire nécessite une prise de contact entre les deux chefs, la première. J'ai l'honneur d'être témoin de cette entrevue.

Les deux Douglas, réguliers comme des horloges, se suivent. Armés de neuf mitrailleuses, ces bombardiers ont fière allure et la cabine ouverte du radio-mitrailleur est un observatoire idéal pour admirer le sol qui défile à quatre cent kilomètres à l'heure.

Ouargla a déjà disparu. Seul un fil noir nous relie encore à la capitale des Oasis. Il est tendu sur le sable comme sur une peau de chamois froissée par une main divine. C'est la piste rectiligne que nous survolerons jusqu'au bordj de Fort-Lallemand et qui continuera vers Fort-Flatters.

Fort Lallemand est un puits qu'il a fallu défendre. Un bordj est sorti de terre, sentinelle avancée qui, autrefois, annonçait les mouvements des dissidents remontant sur Ouargla.

Nous piquons sur Rhadamés, direction Sud - Sud-Est. Au dessous de nous une mer de sable blond légèrement ondulée.

Puis, les belles lignes soufflées font place à des mamelons pointus, à facettes, que le soleil et l'ombre marquent de tâches claires et foncées. Ils s'alignent à l'infini comme d'innombrables fourmilières. Quelques taches, blanches, galeuses, gènent l'œil qui s'était habitué à cet or poudreux.

Subitement, plus de sable. Comme tracée au crayon, rectiligne, cette ligne de démarcation surprend. Une immensité gris noir, sale. Le plateau à découvert laisse apparaître les roches. Seules, des tables de pierres coupent la monotonie du terrain : surface noire, parois de sable.

Voici le bordj de Mariksène où nos troupes ont soutenu pendant sept heures et demie deux assauts italiens. La Compagnie Saharienne Portée, ayant reçu l'ordre de ne pas reculer a défendu le bordj, appuyée par les pelotons du Goum d'El Oued, et a fièrement « tenu » malgré la supériorité écrasante de l'ennemi et son artillerie meurtrière. Des morts, de nombreux blessés ont payé de leur sang cette terre française.

Fort-Saint, réoccupé par nos troupes, paresse sous le soleil.

L'avion tourne sur Rhadamés. Des palmiers, bien sur, puisque c'est une oasis, mais en nombre restreint.

L'aérodrome s'annonce par un immense cercle de chaux ou le nom italien « Gadames » aligne ses lettres blanches.

Les troupes sont là : Méharistes alignés sur un rang, à la verticale, les troupes motorisées sur le terrain, un seul avion avec les cocardes tricolores et la croix de Lorraine.

Le Général Leclerc est sur le terrain.

Nous atterrissons.

Les clairons sonnent « Le Rappel ».

Le Commandant de la Colonne du Tchad approche. Serrement de mains. C'est le premier contact de deux chefs français sur une terre étrangère.

— « Je suis heureux, dit le Général Delay, de vous rencontrer sur cette terre française pour la première fois et de vous apporter les félicitations chaleureuses des camarades de l'armée d'Afrique ».

Le Général Leclerc paraît moins jeune que je ne pensais.

« Il a quarante trois ans seulement, me dit le Colonel Delange ».

Son visage émacié est bruni par la marche dans le désert. Ses sourcils brûlés par le soleil ont des reflets roux. Une petite moustache courte et tombante lui donne le type de « chez nous ». Son regard est clair, profond, un peu triste ; le regard d'un homme qui a surmonté des obstacles immenses et dont la tâche n'est pas terminée. Tout son être semble encore tendu par l'effort qu'il a fourni.

Il porte le manteau kaki cintré, sans martingale, cher aux officiers de « la Coloniale ». Son képi est recouvert de tissu de chèche et deux grosses étoiles mates le distinguent de la coiffure des légionnaires. Une canne recourbée pend à son bras et paraît être le compagnon inséparable.

Et c'est la revue des troupes : légionnaires kaki aux épaulettes rouges ; nègres géants droits comme des I défilant autour du drapeau qu'ils amènent du Tchad ; pelotons méharistes, officiers en tête, qui, du haut de leurs chameaux, passent fiers et distants.

(*Suite en page 6*)

Le général G. MARSHALL

chef de l'armée la mieux équipée du monde

DERRIERE l'organisation et l'expansion de l'armée américaine qui occupe des postes de combat sur tous les fronts de guerre, il y a la personnalité et la volonté du Général Georges Marshall.

En moins de trois ans, il vient de remanier et de créer une force ultra-moderne.

Le Général MARSHALL, chef d'Etat-Major général de l'Armée américaine, photographié à son bureau de travail à Washington. Les quatre étoiles qui parent ses épaules sont les signes distinctifs du grade le plus élevé de l'armée. YW. 22.206

EN PAGE 3 NOTRE REPORTAGE PHOTOGRAPHIQUE

Dans le courant de l'été 1939, le président Roosevelt le fir passer par dessus vingt généraux de brigade et quatorze généraux de division, pour le nommer chef d'état-major général de l'armée.

Depuis le jour de sa nomination, il a toujours eu carte blanche pour agir comme il l'entendait.

Il faut avouer qu'il en a profité.

Le corps des officiers a été radicalement transformé par un procédé d'élimination et de remplacement. Les éléments inactifs et incompétents furent éliminés et placés dans des postes administratifs. Des officiers âgés mais qui avaient une valeur se mirent à étudier la formation des chars, les moteurs et les avions.

On rogna sur le temps d'entraînement de chaque soldat. On supprima six mois des dix-huit qu'on avait de tout temps jugés indispensables pour former une recrue.

On créa des cours d'entraînement, de signalisation, de transport de divisions blindées, et de génie.

Ainsi lorsque le général Mac Arthur eut besoin d'établir des communications et des liaisons, en Australie, lorsqu'il lui fallut construire des avant postes nouveaux ou faire réparer ses chars de combat, il fit appel à ces unités de spécialistes.

Tout cela fut fait suivant les grandes lignes tracées par le Général Mac Arthur, le Général Graig, précurseur de Marshall.

La simple réorganisation du Département de la guerre à Washington a permis au Général Marshall d'économiser 90 % de son temps au point de vue administratif.

Le Chef de son Intendance, le Commandant des Forces de l'Air, ou celui des Forces de terre résolvent neuf sur dix des problèmes qui lui sont journellement soumis et décident avec une très grande liberté dans leur domaine propre.

Le général Marshall est d'une franchise redoutable mais spirituel et fort agile d'esprit. Sa mémoire excellente et il ne permet pas à celle de ses collaborateurs d'être défaillante.

On conte l'histoire de ce jeune lieutenant qui n'étant pas d'accord avec son chef fit valoir son point de vue, entra en discussion fougueuse avec le général, s'emballa, se fâcha, et finalement convainquit le général amusé.

J'aime aussi les tactiques orthodoxes. Un officier s'était engagé, à la tête de sa section, sur une fausse route. En manœuvre ce n'est pas grave, mais en guerre...

Le général, au lieu de réprimander son subordonné, profita, au contraire, de la présence de cette unité pour modifier ses plans et employer les hommes sur place, au lieu de les forcer à refaire de longs kilomètres.

Il se couche à n'importe quelle heure, mais préfère être au lit dès huit heures du soir, car il est, tout au long de la nuit, réveillé constamment par des coups de téléphone, des appels, et des demandes du département de la guerre.

Cet ancien as de foot-ball a actuellement un dada... : le cheval.

Son heure de promenade matinale est sacrée, il en revient de bonne humeur, l'esprit ouvert, l'œil vif et pétillant, à sept heures du matin prêt à affronter la journée qui commence.

Renée Pierre GOSSET.

Nos interviews

Le plus batailleur des amiraux des temps modernes

Sir Andrew CUNNINGHAM

Grand amiral de la flotte britannique

nous dit...

par Marie-Louise PERREUX

NON, je ne suis pas de ceux qui pensent qu'il faille se laisser attaquer par l'ennemi. Je suis pour l'offensive, avant tout.

Et ce sont les premiers mots que me répond l'amiral, lorsque je lui parle de la tactique qui lui est si particulière.

L'AMIRAL CUNNINGHAM. YW. 22.474

Il est là, devant moi, le plus fameux marin des temps actuels, celui qui semble avoir pris comme devise les paroles célèbres de Danton : « De l'audace, encore de l'audace, toujours de l'audace. »

Il est de taille moyenne, bien pris dans son uniforme sobre, qu'éclairent discrètement les rubans de ses nombreuses décorations. Son visage hâlé est comme pétri d'énergie. Ses yeux clairs pétillent d'intelligence, de vivacité, d'esprit et de malice. Ses façons sont celles d'un homme uniquement fait pour l'action. Il parle net et va droit au but.

— On prétend, amiral, que vous êtes toujours à guetter sur le pont de votre navire ?

— Pensez-vous, je vais sur le pont uniquement parce que c'est l'endroit où on est le plus en sécurité...

Cette réponse de froid humour le caractérise admirablement.

Se battre pour lui est tellement naturel, qu'il pense que ce n'est même pas la peine d'en parler. Quant au danger... cela fait trop partie de sa vie pour qu'il n'y soit étrangement familiarisé.

— Voyez-vous, dans la guerre moderne, continue l'amiral, il s'agit avant tout de dépister l'ennemi. Or, du moment que nous avons la possibilité de le faire et de repérer les sous-marins, il faut toujours attaquer, attaquer aussitôt avant que l'adversaire ne le fasse.

— Votre grande expérience des petits bateaux de guerre, je veux dire à faible tonnage, que vous avez commandés de préférence, vous sert-elle actuellement ?

— Oui, cela m'a appris à avoir des réactions immédiates et vives, à ne jamais être surpris.

— Croyez-vous que l'aviation doive travailler en union étroite avec la marine ?

— Leur union est, à mon avis, indispensable. Les avions doivent surtout dépister les sous-marins et protéger ainsi les navires de surface.

— L'aviation a-t-elle joué un rôle de premier plan dans la fameuse bataille de Matapan où la marine anglaise se montra si efficace et où une partie de la flotte italienne fut engloutie, ce qui vous valut un télégramme personnel de félicitations du roi?

— Un rôle considérable, évidemment... J'avais à Toranto un bateau porte-avions et, de surcroît, l'aide de la Royal Air Force a été splendide.

— Combien un porte-avions peut-il aligner d'appareils ?

— Cela dépend, de quarante à cent parfois.

— D'après un thème, très en faveur en Allemagne, l'aviation et les sous-marins doivent, seuls, gagner la guerre. Qu'en pensez-vous ?

— C'est faux. Les grosses unités sont indispensables. Je ne parle pas seulement des cargos, des bateaux de la marine marchande qui, modestement, sans gloire, font du si bon travail et transportent armements, matériel et vivres, mais encore des cuirassés, torpilleurs et beaucoup d'autres bateaux. Ils sont nécessaires pour défendre les convois qu'ils accompagnent comme pour attaquer l'ennemi.

— Etant donné le rôle primordial de la marine en cette guerre, une grande partie de l'effort des Alliés a donc été orientée vers la fabrication intensive des navires ?

— Oui, c'est pourquoi, malgré les lourdes pertes que nous avons subies, le tonnage actuel de notre marine est bien supérieur à celui que nous avions au début de la guerre.

— Les femmes qui, en Angleterre, jouent actuellement un rôle si actif au point de vue militaire, sont-elles acceptées dans la marine ?

— Oui, dans les Women Royal Naval Service, en abrégé « Wrens ». Elles ne naviguent pas, mais elles rendent dans les ports et dans tous les bureaux de grands services. Ici, il y en a une trentaine et je les apprécie beaucoup.

— L'Angleterre possède-t-elle une infanterie de marine importante ?

— Oui, des hommes, à la fois marins et soldats, capables de se battre à terre comme d'excellents fantassins.

— Ils auraient pu se battre au désert. Connaissez-vous le Sahara ?

— Non, je connais le désert de Libye seulement.

— Ne trouvez-vous pas qu'il y a une grande ressemblance entre le désert et la mer ?

— C'est exact, c'est pourquoi ceux qui aiment la mer, aiment également l'océan des sables.

— Puis-je vous demander, enfin, amiral, ce que vous pensez de la guerre, c'est-à-dire du point où elle en est ?

— Il me semble qu'elle va d'une façon très satisfaisante, lentement mais sûrement. Dans un temps raisonnable, peut-être plus tôt qu'on ne le pense, l'ennemi sera complètement chassé de l'Afrique du Nord. M. Churchill a dit que, des côtes africaines, ce serait plus facile d'atteindre le sud de l'Axe qui est la partie la plus vulnérable et je crois que nous suivrons son conseil. En attendant, il n'y a qu'une chose qui compte : « S'unir dans l'effort ».

L'amiral se lève sur ces mots. Il est connu pour n'être pas disert et déteste la publicité. Je gage que cette interview qu'il voulut bien donner à TAM, pour aussi brève qu'elle soit, n'aurait pas été accordée si elle avait pu être considérée comme un simple reportage et non comme un hommage rendu par l'amiral de la flotte à la marine britannique qui participe si grandement, si vaillamment à la libération des peuples.

(En page 3. La carrière de Sir Andrew Cunningham.)

En page 6
RHAT et RHADAMES
VICTOIRES FRANÇAISES

L'entrée des Britanniques à Tripoli

Une rangée de chars britanniques sur la place principale de TRIPOLI. A l'arrière plan, le port.
(en page 3 notre reportage photographique). YW. 22.473

ПРОЛЕТАРИИ ВСЕХ СТРАН, СОЕДИНЯЙТЕСЬ!

СОВЕТСКИЙ САХАЛИН

ОРГАН САХАЛИНСКОГО ОБКОМА ВКП(б) И ОБЛАСТНОГО СОВЕТА ДЕПУТАТОВ ТРУДЯЩИХСЯ

№ 56 (5271) | ВТОРНИК, 9 марта 1943 года | Год изд. XVIII

Весь советский народ с большой радостью встретил весть о присвоении Верховному Главнокомандующему товарищу Сталину военного звания Маршала Советского Союза.

Под водительством Великого Сталина вперед, к победе!

УКАЗ

ПРЕЗИДИУМА ВЕРХОВНОГО СОВЕТА СССР

О ПРИСВОЕНИИ ВЕРХОВНОМУ ГЛАВНОКОМАНДУЮЩЕМУ ВООРУЖЕННЫМИ СИЛАМИ СССР СТАЛИНУ И. В. ВОЕННОГО ЗВАНИЯ МАРШАЛА СОВЕТСКОГО СОЮЗА

Верховному Главнокомандующему вооруженными силами СССР **Сталину** Иосифу Виссарионовичу присвоить военное звание Маршала Советского Союза.

Председатель Президиума Верховного Совета СССР М. КАЛИНИН

Секретарь Президиума Верховного Совета СССР А. ГОРКИН

Москва, Кремль.
6 марта 1943 года.

ПОД ВОДИТЕЛЬСТВОМ СТАЛИНА МЫ РАЗГРОМИМ ВРАГА

ГОРЬКИЙ, 7 марта. (ТАСС). Весть о присвоении Верховному Главнокомандующему вооруженными силами СССР военного звания Маршала Советского Союза встречена трудящимися города Горького с большой радостью. На заводах «Красное Сормово», «Красный якорь» и других предприятиях состоялись беседы.

— Под руководством товарища Сталина наши войска разгромили врага на ряде участков советско-германского фронта, — говорит инженер автозавода имени Молотова тов. Чернов, — товарищ Сталин указал Красной Армии и всему советскому народу пути окончательного разгрома немецко-фашистских захватчиков. Имя товарища Сталина является выражением воли советского народа к победе. Вот почему Указ Президиума Верховного Совета мы, автозаводцы, восприняли с большим удовлетворением, с горячим желанием работать еще лучше.

Москва, Кремль

товарищу СТАЛИНУ

Дорогой наш отец, друг, учитель и вождь, Иосиф Виссарионович!

Женщины-сибирячки, жены, матери и сестры фронтовиков, стахановки колхозов, заводов и транспорта, инженеры и техники, врачи, учительницы, артистки, писательницы, собравшиеся на областной с'езд, обращаются к Вам с искренним, горячим письмом, от всей души желая Вам долго здравствовать на славу и благо нашего народа.

В этом письме мы хотим рассказать Вам, товарищ Сталин, как сибирячки борются за победу над врагом, как мы хотим в этом году отметить свой день 8 марта.

В дни великой отечественной войны, в дни смертельной опасности, нависшей над нашей родиной, мы с огромной силой почувствовали как дорога нам родная земля, наша Советская власть, наша партия, открывшая путь к счастливой, свободной жизни.

Нелегко нам было расставаться со своими сыновьями, мужьями, отцами и братьями, отправляя их на фронт, на смертный бой с врагом. Но у советских женщин есть чувство более высокое, чем материнская любовь и привязанность жены к мужу — это чувство любви к священной родине, чувство неугасимой ненависти к врагу.

Провожая близких и родных, мы дали им наказ: с честью выполнить свой долг перед страной — разгромить и уничтожить врага, изгнать его из пределов нашей родины. И мы горды сознанием того, что наши мужья и сыновья, наши отцы и братья не посрамили славы русского оружия, показали, как умеют драться с врагом воины-сибиряки.

Силу мощных ударов сибирских дивизий фашисты крепко почувствовали под Москвой, под Калининым, под Сталинградом и на других фронтах отечественной войны.

Мы, сибирячки, гордимся и тем, что в рядах Красной Армии мужественно и бесстрашно дерутся наши сестры и дочери, многие из которых отмечены высокими правительственными наградами.

Чтобы всеми силами помогать фронту, Красной Армии в разгроме ненавистного врага, посягнувшего на честь и свободу нашей родины, мы, женщины, оставшиеся в тылу, встали к станкам, овладели мужскими профессиями, сели за руль трактора, за штурвал комбайна, взялись за топор лесоруба, спустились в шахты, рудники, вышли на берега наших рек и озер рыбачить.

Блестящие победы, одержанные за последние три месяца нашими доблестными бойцами на фронте, влили в нас новые силы, укрепили нашу уверенность в близком разгроме врага.

Но мы твердо помним, товарищ Сталин, Ваше указание, что борьба с немецкими захватчиками еще не кончена, что она только разгорается, что глупо было бы полагать, что немцы покинут без боя хотя бы километр нашей земли. Поэтому мы готовы с еще большим напряжением, не покладая рук, трудиться, чтобы огромные неиссякаемые богатства Сибири направить на помощь фронту.

Перед тем, как собраться на областной с'езд, мы на своих собраниях в колхозах, на предприятиях и в учреждениях, на сельских и городских, районных конференциях обсудили и приняли на себя новые дополнительные обязательства:

добиться нового под'ема выработки каждой женщиной в промышленности, на транспорте, на рыбных и лесных промыслах, чтобы дать фронту дополнительное вооружение и продовольствие;

вовлечь в промышленность и на транспорт новые сотни и тысячи женщин, организовать силами женской общественности присмотр за детьми, чтобы многосемейные матери могли работать на предприятиях и в колхозах;

женщины — инженеры и техники, высококвалифицированные работницы на предприятиях беруться организовать индивидуальное обучение вновь поступивших на предприятия;

принять шефство над общежитиями подростков и учащихся ремесленных училищ, эвакуированных из прифронтовой полосы, помочь им починкой одежды, стиркой белья, улучшением их быта;

женщины-колхозницы и работницы МТС совхозов обязуются подготовку к весеннему севу и весенний сев провести по-фронтовому, чтобы вырастить высокий урожай, урожай победы:

для ускорения сроков сева каждая колхозница берется приучить к ярму корову личного пользования, каждая колхозница соберет верхушки клубней картофеля, семена овощей в помощь эвакуированным семьям военнослужащих для их индивидуальных огородов;

на каждый колхозный двор вырастить не менее 3 птиц — кур, гусей или уток для Красной Армии, для бойцов, находящихся на излечении в госпиталях;

каждая колхозница обязуется засеять на своем приусадебном участке не менее одной сотой гектара картофелем и махоркой и весь урожай внести в фонд Красной Армии;

мы приложим все силы к тому, чтобы вырастить и воспитать наших детей и сирот мужественными патриотами нашей родины, беззаветно преданными великому делу Ленина—Сталина. Постараемся, чтобы дети сибиряков были достойны своих отцов-героев отечественной войны.

Собравшись на областной с'езд женщин-стахановок, мы решили по-новому, по-фронтовому, отметить в этом году Международный Коммунистический Женский День — 8 марта — работать в этот день так, как не работали ни в один день за все время войны, и весь заработок этого дня внести на постройку боевой эскадрильи «Сибирячки—фронту».

Участницы с'езда сегодня уже внесли на постройку эскадрильи 42.000 рублей наличными и 13.000 рублей облигациями госзаймов.

Пусть день 8 марта станет фронтовым днем в тылу! Пусть он будет днем усиленной помощи нашей героической Красной Армии, днем дальнейшего роста наших вкладов в сталинский фонд победы!

Все силы на разгром врага, все для фронта — таков будет наш ответ на всех участках работы, где бы ни находилась женщина-сибирячка.

Мы обращаемся ко всем женщинам Новосибирской области, ко всем женщинам Советского Союза с призывом последовать нашему примеру.

Во имя нашей родины, ее чести и независимости, во имя счастья наших детей будем еще напряженнее трудиться для полного разгрома врага и изгнания его из пределов нашей родины!

Смерть немецким оккупантам!

Да здравствует наша доблестная Красная Армия!

Да здравствует великая партия Ленина—Сталина!

Да здравствует наш вождь, наш учитель, наша надежда — Великий Сталин!

Президиум первого областного с'езда женщин-стахановок Новосибирской области.

В ПОСЛЕДНИЙ ЧАС

Наши войска заняли город Гжатск

В результате двукратного штурма наши войска овладели городом **Гжатск**. Захваченные трофеи подсчитываются.

Совинформбюро.

THE WEATHER
Not quite so cold tonight and Tuesday morning, with lowest temperature around 28 degrees in the suburbs and 32 in the city.
Detailed Weather Report on Page 25

Read The Baltimore News-Post for complete, accurate war coverage. It is the only Baltimore newspaper possessing the three great wire services—
ASSOCIATED PRESS
INTERNATIONAL NEWS SERVICE
UNITED PRESS

THE BALTIMORE NEWS-POST
AN INDEPENDENT NEWSPAPER
The Largest Evening Circulation in the Entire South
VOL. CXLII.—NO. 123 | Entered as second-class matter at Baltimore Postoffice. | MONDAY EVENING, MARCH 29, 1943 | PRICE 3 CENTS
HOME FINAL 7

MARETH LINE COLLAPSES ROMMEL'S ARMY FLEES

British Batter 25-Mile Front Allies Now 20 Miles From Gabes

ALLIED HEADQUARTERS IN NORTH AFRICA, March 29—(A. P.).—Field Marshal Erwin Rommel's Mareth Line defenses have collapsed under the pounding of the British Eighth Army and his forces are retreating northward with heavy losses, it was announced today. Scattered pockets of resistance were left behind, but Gen. Sir Bernard L. Montgomery's infantrymen were reported mopping them up, one by one, as Allied squadrons joined ground forces in powerful attacks along the Axis escape corridor.

The Mareth Line broke on a 25-mile front at three points, ranging from 20 to 30 miles from the Axis supply port of Gabes.

Beset by powerful forces forward and the desert flanking coumn at El Hamma in his rear, Rommel yielded Mareth, Matmata and Toujane at the northern end of the Mareth fortifications yesterday and dispatches said that every strong point of that 40-mile-long Little Maginot Line was now in Allied hands.

They were wrested from the enemy in some of the fiercest combats of the war—combats in which more than 6,000 German and Italian soldiers were captured. Thousands of tons of bombs had been loosed upon the line by day and by night to supplement continual heavy artillery barrages.

FIELDS PLOWED UP

Dispatches from Cairo said it was officially announced that Axis air fields protecting Gabes were being plowed up, which would be a sure sign that Rommel intended to abandon that area to the Allies.

(BACKGROUND NOTE: Since air protection would be necessary for a Dunkerque escape by Rommel's army through Gabes, any further withdrawal probably would mean he intended to attempt a fighting retreat for 200 miles or more up the coast to a junction with the command of Col. Gen. Jurgen von Arnim in the Tunis-Bizerte region.)

Threatening his escape corridor for a stretch of 100 miles were the United States troops of Lieut. Gen. George S. Patton, Jr., pushing toward the coast from newly captured Fondouk, Maknassy and El Guetar.

YANKS SMASH AHEAD

Field dispatches said American infantrymen smashed forward before dawn Sunday in an attack from El Guetaria Pass toward the last important high ground between them and the Gulf of Gabes. First reports told of the capture of 30 prisoners and said the chief opposition was from Italian mortars.

"The attack, which was launched on the afternoon of March 26 on the enemy's strong position of El Hamma, has forced the enemy to withdraw from the Mareth area."

The southern front developments were coupled with Allied

Continued on Page 2, Column 1.

Axis In Retreat

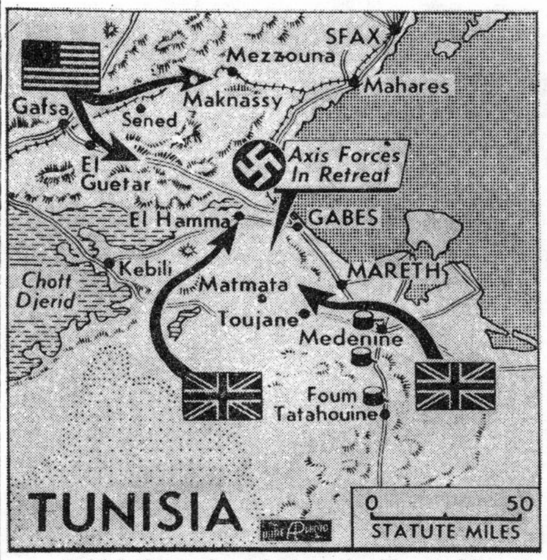

British forces have broken the Mareth Line of fortifications, it was announced today, and Axis troops are retreating northward toward Gabes under aerial pounding. British have taken Mareth, Matmata and Toujane, and another British column to the northwest has reached El Hamma. Arrows show Allied drives, with Americans pressing eastward above the Axis bottleneck at Gabes.

Unified Command Needed In Pacific, Officers Tell Faris

By BARRY FARIS
Editor-In-Chief of International News Service.

NEW YORK, March 29.—A moot question throughout the Pacific and Australia today is: "Why not a unified command?"

American Army and Navy leaders, talking off the record, make no effort to hide their belief that the Japanese cannot be defeated until the entire Pacific and Australian war effort is placed under the control of one leader.

SENTIMENT SHARED

This same feeling is strongly held among high officials in the Australian Government and among Australian military leaders.

With the Japanese daily concentrating more and more strength in the islands to the north of Australia, the men who are taking an active part in the Allied war effort in that area are growing more concerned over the divided command that today exists in the South Pacific and Australia.

This question also seems to be uppermost in the minds of many of our Army and Naval leaders in this country. Since returning from the South Pacific I have met and talked to many. Repeatedly I have been asked whether, when out in that area, I saw any indications or heard any reports that the commands in the Pacific may be unified and placed under the control of one leader.

SERVICES CO-OPERATING

Publicly both Army and naval officers all through the Pacific and Australia tell you that the Army and Navy are co-operating beautifully. I saw nothing while in that area that would not substantiate that belief. Nevertheless, talking privately and off the record these same officers tell you that our maximum efforts cannot be achieved until the "whole show," as they call it, is being directed by one leader.

One high officer told me:

"We cannot really go to town out here until the entire effort is being directed from one headquarters. These Japs, as you know, are being directed by one over-all authority who can move against us at any place he chooses with fleet, air force and ground troops.

"With our present set-up we have to counter and move at present around Australia from General MacArthur's headquarters. If the enemy attacks somewhere east of General MacArthur's area the move to stop him must come either from Admiral Halsey or Admiral Nimitz.

SHOULD HAVE CONTROL

"It is true that back in Washington there is a central directing force. This is as it should be, but in addition the field commander should have control of the entire area as very often there is no time for an exchange of messages with other commands or with Washington before action has to be taken. To put it simply the captain in the field should be empowered to bring into play all the forces we have in this area whenever the occasion demands quick action."

The Allied war effort in the Pacific today up to a line 700 miles east of Australia is being directed by Admiral Chester W. Nimitz, commander in chief of the Pacific fleet. The Army in the Hawaiian Islands is led by Major Gen. Delos C. Emmons, who comes under Admiral Nimitz's command.

HARMON HEADS ARMY

In the South Pacific area Admiral William F. Halsey is in charge, under the direction of Admiral Nimitz. The Army forces in the South Pacific are led by Major Gen. Millard F. Harmon, who comes under Admiral Halsey's command.

Beginning at the line 700 miles east of Australia—and the line extends from the South Pacific all the way to Russia—Gen. Douglas MacArthur commands all the Al-

Continued on Page 4, Column 3.

Chinese Seize Town On Yangtze

CHUNGKING, March 28—(A. P.).—The Chinese High Command announced today that Chinese forces in Hupeh Province had recaptured a town on the south bank of the Yangtze river and encircled Japanese troops at a number of other points in a series of successes which once more exposed Japanese communications to the base of Ichang to Chinese attacks.

Temperatures

12 Midn't,	37	7 A. M.,	29
1 A. M.,	36	8 A. M.,	30
2 A. M.,	34	9 A. M.,	32
3 A. M.,	33	10 A. M.,	35
4 A. M.,	32	11 A. M.,	38
5 A. M.,	31	12 Noon,	40
6 A. M.,	30	1 P. M.,	42

Jefferson Test Semi-Finals Due To Open Tonight

By ALDINE R. BIRD

The spirit that moved Thomas Jefferson to write America's immortal Declaration of Independence will be rekindled tonight as more than a score of the best orators of Maryland high schools meet in the semi-finals of the Jefferson Oratorical Contest in quest of honor and award.

Having spent a fortnight in reviewing every phase of his life, his contributions to democracy and his ideals which today are the American ways of life, the students will seek to win a place in the State-wide finals, set for Friday night.

IN TWO SECTIONS

Tonight's eliminations will be divided into two sections, and a committee of judges will sit in judgment and select some of the best speakers for the finals.

One section will be staged in the Central Young Men's Christian Association, and the other in the

Continued on Page 18, Column 7.

Meat Rationing Begins; City's Supply Reported Lowest In Many Weeks

Red ration stamps were exchangeable for meat in Baltimore today—if you could find the meat.

A spokesman for one major packer here said meat supplies were at a new low today, so low that "you wouldn't need a toothpick to move them."

Week-end livestock shipments into this area were reported 50 per cent. below normal. This fact, with last week's buying spree in the face of rationing, left the city more nearly meatless than at any time during the current shortage, dealers reported.

OPA CHECKING STORES

To determine just how much meat is available to consumers the State Office of Price Administration today began a store-by-store check of supplies in the hands of retailers.

Leo McCormick, OPA director for Maryland, said his office would sek relief if it were found that the area faces serious hardship. He added that special surveys are being made in the neighborhoods of war industries to discover whether stores serving the workers and cafeterias within the plants have an adequate supply. He declared:

Continued on Page 2, Column 7.

Army And Navy Map Drive On Japanese

WASHINGTON, March 29—(A. P.).—A group of high ranking Army and Navy officers from Pacific war theatres has just completed a series of conferences in Washington on plans for future campaigns against the Japanese.

In making this announcement today, the War Department said the United States joint chiefs of staffs called the meetings to acquaint commanding officers in the Pacific combat zones with the strategy approved at the Casablanca conference of President Roosevelt and Prime Minister Churchill in January.

None of the decisions was disclosed.

Heading the group of 15 officers were Lieut. Gen. Delos C. Emmons, commanding Army forces in Hawaii; Lieut. Gen. George C. Kenney, commander of Allied air forces in the Southwest Pacific, and Lieut. Gen. Millard F. Harmon, commanding Army forces in the South Pacific.

The announcement said the officers would be return to their overseas stations in the near future.

Crash Kills 23; Two From U. S.

MELBOURNE, Australia, March 29—(A. P.).—The Government announced today that two United States Army officers were among 23 persons killed in the crash of a Royal Australian Air Force transport plane near Brisbane Saturday. The plane crashed into heavy timber soon after the take-off.

R. A. F. Batters Big U-Boat Base

By JOHN E. LEE
International News Service Staff Correspondent.

LONDON, March 29.—A heavy concentrated attack was made last night by the Royal Air Force against the Nazi U-boat base of St. Nazaire, it was announced today.

Two British bombers were lost in the raid.

3 STRAIGHT NIGHTS

It was the third consecutive night bombardment of a large enemy objective on the continent and followed by less than 24 hours the greatest R. A. F. raid on Berlin.

Parts of the Nazi capital were reported still ablaze as the British planes struck out anew against the Germans.

When it was first disclosed that the R. A. F. again was in operation the Germans, still quaking under the battering Berlin assault, jubilantly announced that the Reich was unscathed last night. A Berlin broadcast said:

"The enemy made no excursions over the Reich last night."

While the British were blasting the large submarine base on the coast of France, the Nazi radio said, German planes were attacking the East Anglian industrial city of Norwich, 114 miles northeast of London.

BOMBERS SOAR AGAIN

Observers along the coast of England reported that a force of Britain's huge bombers equal in size to that which scourged Berlin Saturday had swept toward the continent during the night. The

Continued on Page 2, Column 1.

Neutrality Of Spain Assured

LONDON, March 29—(U. P.).—Diplomatic sources said today that Spain had received assurances from both the Axis and Allies that neither will violate her neutrality.

Report Allied Raid On Norway

STOCKHOLM, Barch 29—(U. P.).—The Berlin correspondent of Allehanda today quoted the German military spokesman as saying that 18 British planes had been shot down off Norway, during what appeared to be a big raid somewhere in Norway.

LONDON, March 29—(U. P.).—Official sources said today that there was no information available in London regarding reports of a British raid on Norway.

Daniels Is New Roosevelt Aide

WASHINGTON, March 29—(A. P.).—The appointment of Jonathan Daniels, Raleigh, N. C., newspaper man, as an Administrative assistant to President Roosevelt was announced today by the White House. He is the son of Josephus Daniels, who, as Secretary of Navy, was President Roosevelt's "boss" during the last World War. Mr. Roosevelt then was Assistant Navy Secretary.

War At A Glance

AFRICA—British smash through Mareth Line on 25-mile front, now only 22 miles from Gabes; American forces advance again.

GERMANY—R. A. F. blasts St. Nazaire after big raid on Berlin; shakeup in German foreign office near.

PACIFIC — American Navy smashes Japs in battle off Kiska; Allied planes batter Jap bases in South Pacific.

RUSSIA—Reds take two more towns.

BULLETINS

LONDON, March 29—(I. N. S.).— Gestapo Chief Henrich Himmler has proclaimed a virtual state of siege in all Germany, a Geneva dispatch to the Tass (Soviet) news agency said today.

LONDON, March 29—(A. P.).—Flying Officer Warren Whitewright Duncan Pearl, twenty-two-year-old son of Colonel and Mrs. Warren Pearl of the United States Embassy in London, has been killed while flying with the R.A.F.

LONDON, March 29—(U. P.).—The Tass News Agency reported from Berne today that Marshal Hermann Goering recently replaced the SS men guarding his residence with non-commissioned officers of the German air force.

STOCKHOLM, March 29—(I. N. S.).—Bogus food ration cards were dropped on Berlin in Saturday night's heavy raid, a Berlin dispatch to the Newspaper Dagens Nyheter reported today. It was stated that Nazi authorities threatened that any persons using the cards will be severely punished or put to death.

NEWS-POST

WEATHER
WARMER

KNOWLEDGE ONCE GAINED CASTS A LIGHT BEYOND ITS OWN IMMEDIATE BOUNDARIES.—Tyndall

Coldwater Daily Reporter

EVENING HOURS
READING HOURS
Your Ad. in Reporter
Read at Home Fireside.

ESTABLISHED DEC. 16, 1895 — COLDWATER, MICHIGAN, TUESDAY, MARCH 30, 1943 — PRICE FOUR CENTS

BRITISH FORCES CAPTURE GABES AND EL HAMMA

RAF Bombers Give Berlin Another Pounding

BELIEVE RAID HEAVIER THAN PREVIOUS ONE

Smaller Formations Raid Ruhr District; 33 Planes Missing

London, March 30.—(UP)—British four-engined bombers battered Berlin with hundreds of tons of demolition and fire bombs last night while the German capital was still smouldering from its heaviest raid of the war only 48 hours earlier.

Twenty-one bombers were lost, an indication that the raiding force may have numbered nearly 400 planes. If confirmed, this would mean that more than 1,000 tons of bombs were cascaded on Berlin in a raid exceeding in weight even that of Saturday night when between 900 and 1,000 tons were dropped.

Smaller, but still substantial, formations were blasting at the same time the industrial city of Bochum and other points in Germany's Ruhr valley wth a loss of 12 planes.

An Air Ministry communique said preliminary reports indicated that the heavy attack on Berlin was "successful."

Foe Acknowledges Raid

The raids carried the resumed Anglo-American pre-invasion aerial offensive through its fourth night and followed the second straight day of raids on the German-occupied Dutch port of Rotterdam, where shipping was hit. Other daylight raids yesterday were directed at industrial targets in Holland and the railways yards at Abbeville in north France.

The German radio acknowledged that British bombers dropped high explosive and fire bombs on Berlin during a two-hour air raid alarm last night, but mentioned damage only to residential quarters and said civilians were killed and injured.

The alarm was sounded at 1:30 a. m. Berlin time and the bombers met a "gigantic anti-aircraft barrage" and swarms of night fighters, the broadcast said.

It was the 60th raid of the war on Berlin and the seveuth this year. Bochum, an important railroad junction, has been attacked only once previously, on the night of Sept. 6, 1940.

The loss of 33 bombers in last night's widespread operations was the largest since 52 failed to return from an attack on the German port of Bremen the night of June 25, 1942.

Germans Retaliate

German planes once again sent weak forces against Britain, both during the night and in daylight today. A few bombs fell harmlessly in the east Anglian coastal area last night and four hit-and-run Focke-Wulf fighter bombers swept in low over a southwest coastal town this morning, scattering their bombs. One daylight raider was shot down.

The increasing damage being wrought by the British night raiders in Germany has prompted the Reich government to make all able-bodied citizens liable for call for emergency air raid precautions duties.

"Call-ups by police of individual persons for air raid protection self-aid are therefore no longer necessary and will not take place in the future," A DNB dispatch broadcast over radio Berlin said. "All persons available in a house may be detailed for tasks for self-aid under direct orders of local air raid protection chiefs."

Meantime, the Air Ministry announced that the British Thunderbolt raid on Munich, home of the Nazi party, on March 9 burned the

(Continued On Page Six)

Plan to Request Jury Trial For Their Son

Ionia, Mich., March 30—(U.P.)—The parents of Donald Temelco, 17-year-old Ionia high school student charged with first degree murder, indicated today they would seek a jury trial for their son despite his reported confession to the slaying of Clara Johnson, 18-year-old war plant worker.

Mr. and Mrs. Riste Temelco said an attorney had been retained and that the case would be carried through its various preliminary steps to a circuit court trial.

Temelco declined to enter a plea and demanded an examination when arraigned before Justice William Heath yesterday. The hearing was set for April 10.

U. S. Fighter Planes Fire Jap Destroyer

Washington, March 30.—(U.P.)—Low strafing American fighter planes set a Japanese destroyer afire after making a damaging attack on the enemy's seaplane base on Faisi island in the Solomons, the Navy announced today.

Five to seven Japanese planes were set ablaze by a group of Lockheed Lighting and Vought Corsair fighter group came across a Japanese destroyer off Alu island, near Faisi, and left the craft burning. come in over their quarry, that So low did the American airmen three feet of the wing of one plane was sheared off by the destroyer's mast.

All U. S. planes returned from the attack.

HOUSE REJECTS AMENDMENT TO RUML TAX PLAN

Oppose Skipping Tax On Only First $25,000 Of Income For 1942

Washington, March 30. — (U.P.) — The House today unanimously voted down an amendment to the Carlson-Ruml skip-a-year income tax plan proposed on behalf of Rep. Clare Boothe Luce, R., Conn., which would have forgiven taxes on only the first $25,000 of 1942 income.

Mrs. Luce's plan would have forgiven all taxes owed on 1942 income of $25,000 or less. Taxes due on amounts of 1942 income above that would have been spread over a period of five years.

The Carlson-Ruml bill as now written would forgive all income taxes owed on 1942 income.

Rejection First Action

Rejection of Mrs. Luce's plan was the first action as the House moved into the actual voting stage in its deliberations on the confused tax picture.

The eventual outcome appeared greatly in doubt, and it may be some days before final action is taken.

The Ruml plan was formally placed before the House by Rep. Frank Carlson, R., Kas., as a substitute for the Ways and Means committee bill which provides no forgiveness at all but would start a 20 per cent withholding tax on wages and salaries on July 1.

Mrs. Luce was out of town because of the death of a friend. Her amendment was offered on her behalf by Rep. Bertrand W. Gearhart, R., Calif., the only republican member of the Ways and Means group who is opposed to the Ruml plan. It was defeated by a voice vote in which not a single

(Continued On Page Six)

FARMER GIVES UP TO PASTOR

Surrenders On Charge Of Murder After Day's Siege at Farm Home

Lexington, Ky., March 30.—(U.P.)—Frank Hopkins, wounded farmer, surrendered to a Lexington minister on a murder charge today after barricading himself in his home for nearly 24 hours, threatening to kill his wife and four children if any attempt were made to arrest him.

Hopkins, 45, who withstood a constant siege of his farm shack since he shot and killed Andrew Pierson, 50, at mid-morning yesterday, gave up to the Rev. Dr. J. Archer Gray and was taken to the Good Samaritan hospital in a critical condition from loss of blood.

Hopkins' wife and children were unharmed. They remained in their home under guard of state militiamen. A crowd of several thousand persons who remained on the floodlighted scene throughout the night, was not allowed to leave immediately.

Wounded in Shoulder

The farmer was wounded in the right shoulder during the fight with Pierson, a wealthy contractor and tobacco grower. Pierson had shot Hopkins with a small rifle after accusing him of thefts from his barn near Hopkins' home.

Hopkins fled to his home. When officers arrived, he said he would "see my wife and children dead before I will give up."

Sheriff J. Porter Land and County Patrol Chief J. W. McSord called for 40 militiamen and tried to persuade Hopkins to surrender. At nightfall, they trained searchlights on the shack.

Hopkins called for Gray last night, but still refused to give up. The minister entered his home this morning, however, and the farmer agreed to go to a hospital.

ACTION IN TUNISIA --- BOMBERS ATTACK AMERICAN PATROL

THIS REMARKABLE PHOTO, one of the finest actual battle pictures to come out of the war, shows an American patrol, caught in an open field, somewhere in Tunisia, by Axis bombing planes. Two heroic members of the Army Medical Corps are seen bandaging the leg of one of two men who have been hit by bomb fragments while bombs burst nearby. Photographer deserves a medal, too. (International).

SOVIETS SMASH NAZI DEFENSES

Capture Three Towns Near Smolensk; Hurl Back Foe in Donets

Moscow, March 30.—(U.P.)—Soviet troops smashed into a network of German fortifications northeast of Smolensk and captured three hamlets today while forces on the Kharkov front hurled back renewed enemy attempts to force the upper Donets.

Nearly 300 German officers and men were killed in the fighting that led to the capture of the three towns south of Bely on the Smolensk front, the Soviet mid-day communique said. Three guns, a mortar battery and a supply dump were captured.

Elsewhere on the muddy defense perimeter of Smolensk, the mid-day communique reported only patrol activity with one Soviet unit being credited with killing 200 enemy infantrymen, destroying an artillery battery and capturing assorted war material.

Three Other Towns Fall

Three other towns on the Smolensk front fell to the Russians yesterday, the Monday midnight communique reported. The Soviets wedged themselves into the German defenses, then, with another force which had swept around to the enemy's rear, annihilated the greater part of the German garrison. German counter-attacks were repulsed.

Along the middle reaches of the upper Donets, the Russians threw back German tommy gunners attacking their positions on one sector of the Kharkov front and broke up a large enemy infantry concentration with artillery fire in an-

(Continued On Page Six)

Leave Docks to Open Great Lakes Season

Chicago, March 30.—(U.P.)—The Great Lakes shipping season was opened today when two Inland Steel company vessels, the Joseph Block and the N. F. Leopold, left south Chicago docks for Port Inland, Mich.

The freighters, each with a capacity of 10,000 tons, will take on a load of limestone there. Inland officials said they could not estimate how long the round trip would take since the length of the journey is dependant on weather conditions.

Two other boats were expected to leave later in the week, they said. These are the L. E. Block and the P. D. Block. They will go to Escanaba, Mich., to pick up loads of iron ore.

Inland officials said the season was being opened approximately a week later than last year.

TELLS HOW YANKS REPELLED THREE THRUSTS BY ENEMIES

With American forces, near Maknassy, Tunisia, March 29.—(Delayed)—(U.P.)—Germans and Italians suffered heavy losses today in three successive attacks against Americans in the Maknassy pass sector and fighting still was in progress at dusk.

The Americans suffered light losses in fighting off the first two attacks, which were described as "heavy."

German troops fought desperately with the aid of Italians in an atempt close Maknassy pass against the Americans, whose push toward the sea is intended to menace the northward route of communications for Marshal Erwin Rommel's Afrika Korps.

Attack Vital Hill

(Madrid dispatches reported that Rommel had set up headquarters in the El Djem sector, on a narrow gauge railroad some 40 miles north of Sfax, and was launching Axis counter-attacks in an effort to keep his retreat corridor open.)

The Axis attacks were directed against a vital hill position whch the Americans hold directly north of the town of Maknassy.

The attacks aganst the American infantry positions were met at 5:30 a. m. with the first light of dawn, shortly before noon and at 4 p. m. each was heavier than the one before it.

The Axis artillery and mortar fire was accurate, and the explosives could be seen landing amid the American positions in advance of the infantry attack. They failed to break the American defense.

Each succeeding wave of infantry was hurled back, and at dusk the American still were holding their hill position.

Progress Is Steady

Farther south, Amercan infantry advanced slowly against stubborn air, artillery and infantry resistance.

In the area of El Guettar the American progress was steady in heavy fighting. The Americans had one more hill to conquer before there was any immediate likelihood of cutting off the Axis forces on the Kebili road.

Judging from the trend of the fighting beyond El Guettar and Maknassy, it seemed likely that the junction of the American forces and the British Eighth army would be effected soon.

American fighter pilots scored nine victories in combat and damaged several more Axis planes without losing a single machine.

DRAFT BOARDS TO RECLASSIFY

Men Still Left In Non-Deferrable Jobs To Be Affected

Lansing, March 30.—(U.P.)—Michigan selective service boards will commence April 1 reclassifying men still left in non-deferable jobs, Major Wilbur J. Myers, of state selective service headquarters announced today.

Men now classifieid in 3A may be reclassified as 1A's available for immediate military call if working in a job classified as non-essential, regardless of dependency status, it was stated.

Local boards may grant postponements in induction where evidence indicates sickness of the registrant or immediate family, physical disqualifications, reasonable vacation, or compelling circumstances which show that a registrant would be exposed to undue hardship in a change of employment.

Each registrant reclassified is to be given an automatic 30-day stay of induction if they give local boards proof they have registered with the U. S. Employment Service

(Continued On Page Four)

Two Million Cases Of Canned Foods to Be Released Soon

Washington, March 30.—(U.P.)—The Department of Agriculture announced today that more than 2,000,000 cases of canned fruits and vegetables will be released soon by the Food Distribution Administration to augment civilian supplies.

The food will include canned tomatoes, pears, plums, apples and peaches, and smaller quantities of other foods. These stocks, most of which were purchased from the 1941 pack, have been held to meet emergency war needs.

The department also announced the transfer of about 12,000,000 cases of canned fruits, juices and vegetables—principally canned corn and peas—by the Army to the Food Distribution Administration. These supplies will be released later by the FDA in meeting emergency food situations. FDA officials said that changing conditions, either in war strategy or in the shipping or storage situation, occasionally make possible such releases of government stocks into civilian channels. They said that government requirements must include reasonable reserves to meet emergencies that develop.

Total taxes collected by the states in 1940 ranged from New York's high of $587 million to Neveda's low of $4 1-2 million.

EDEN TO LEAVE CAPITAL TODAY

British Secretary to Visit Ottawa; Honored By Hull at Dinner

Washington, March 30. — (U.P.) — British Foreign Secretary Anthony Eden leaves for Ottawa today after more than two weeks of conferences with President Roosevelt and other American officials.

Authoritative sources said the talks had been extremely helpful in laying the groundwork for post-war planning, and in giving an opportunity for personal contact between the men who will be preparing on both sides of the Atlantic for a secure peace.

The conferees made no binding decisions or commitments.

Eden was honored last night at a dinner for 40 guests given by Secretary of State Cordell Hull. The dinner brought together the foreign ministers or ambassadors of all the four great powers of the future—the United States, Great Britain, China and the Soviet Union.

Eden, in the only formal address of his American visit, at Annapolis last week stressed the necessity of collaboration among those four powers if a lasting peace is to be attained.

The ministers of Canada, Australia, South Africa and New Zea-

(Continued On Page Four)

LATE NEWS BULLETINS

Algiers, March 30— (U.P.) —Gen. Georges Catroux, Fighting French delegate conferring here with Gen. Henri Honore Giraud, said today that a union of all French elements will be achieved.

Stockholm, March 30— (U.P.) — Ruthless Nazi rule, accompanied by the usual firing squad method of dealing with recalcitrants, has started a wave of strong anti-German resistance in Lithuania, according to reliable reports reaching Sweden today.

Stockholm, March 30—(U.P.)—The Germans clamped a tight censorship on reports of the British air raid on Berlin last night, giving the impression that it was more effective than official Nazi accounts admitted.

New York, March 30—(U.P.)—The New York World Telegram said today that it had learned from a close associate of Mayor F. H. LaGuardia that the mayor "probably will enter the Army on Friday as a brigadier general."

Patient in Ambulance Gives Up Cot to Aide

Adrian, Mich., March 30.—(U.P.)—Franklin Lennox, funeral director's assistant, was attending William K. Porter as an ambulance sped the victim from the scene of an automobile accident.

Suddenly the rear door flew open and Lennox was pitched onto the pavement. Porter called to the driver. He stopped and went back for the attendant, who lay unconscious on the road.

Porter gave up his bed and watched over Lennox as the ambulance completed its journey to Emma L. Bixby hospital.

REPORT ALLIES PREPARING FOR INVASION SOON

Massing Gigantic Land, Sea and Air Striking Forces For Big Push

London, March 30—(U.P.)—Britain, the United States and Canada are massing gigantic land, sea and air striking forces for invasion of Europe to follow quickly on the Axis rout from Tunisia, allied observers said today.

The main allied landings, they believed, may be made in Norway and Greece, with possible diversionary thrusts across the English Channel and North sea into France, Belgium and Holland and across the Mediterranean into Italy.

Prime Minister Winston Churchill already has disclosed that the allies are preparing to launch "invasions"—and it was noteworthy that he used the word in the plural—this year. Men and war machines are pouring into Britain from North America in endless streams and a similar constant flow is probably also being maintained to North Africa, the base for any invasion of South Europe.

Threat to Nazi Bases

The attacks, if they are made through Norway and Greece, probably would constitute a great pincers movement directed at Germany herself. Any landing in Norway would be a potential threat to the great German naval bases of Wilhelmshaven and Kiel and might force Axis warships to abandon the Baltic to avoid being bottled up there, thus giving Soviet warships free rein.

Should the allies invade Greece, they would find guerrilla forces waiting to join them in the march through Jugoslavia and other occupied countries to Berlin.

The Germans have shown ample evidence of their concern over im-

(Continued On Page Three)

CONCEALED OLD PRISON RECORD

Disclosure Made When Van Dyke Justice of Peace is Arraigned

Detroit, March 30—(U.P.)—A prison record which Justice of the Peace John C. Munro had concealed successfully for 12 years was disclosed today when the Van Dyke court official was arraigned on charges of assault and battery.

Taken before Recorder's Judge Joseph A. Gillis to answer charges brought by Mrs. Lela May Blanchard, a soldier's wife, Mruno was identified as having served two years in Southern Michigan prison for involuntary manslaughter in 1929.

Munro denied he possessed a criminal record during an investigation a year and a half ago of alleged laxity in his courtroom. But today, after hearing results of a fingerprint check, he admitted serving the prison term.

Pleads Innocent

The defendant pleaded innocent, however, to Mrs. Blanchard's charges that he struck her when she resisted improper advances in a tavern last March 19. He was released under $1,000 bond pending trial next Tuesday.

Police records disclosed that Munro was sentenced to 2 1-2 to 15 years on the manslaughter charge in October, 1929, in connection with the traffic death of Frank James, Detroit. He was paroled in November, 1931.

He also has been convicted for assault and battery and three times for minor traffic violations, the records disclosed.

Munro, Van Dyke justice since April, 1940, was under fire in 1941 for allegedly failing to report to state authorities a reckless driving conviction against Cyril De Vriendt, Van Dyke contractor. De Vriendt later struck down and killed two baby sisters, and now is serving a seven year manslaughter term.

AFRIKA KORPS CONTINUES TO FLEE RAPIDLY

Yankee Columns Make Headway in Drives to Trap Rommel's Army

Allied Headquarters, North Africa, March 30.— (UP) — The British Eighth army seized the key Tunisian towns of Gabes and El Hamma and drove Marshal Erwin Rommel's forces northward today under furious aerial bombardment while American columns in central Tunisia edged forward in bitter battles.

Led by highlanders and New Zealanders under the veteran Gen. Sir Bernard Freyberg, the Eighth army advance units which broke the Mareth line defenses had Rommel "on the move" north of Gabes on the 84-mile road toward Sfax despite stiff rear guard opposition.

At the same time, an American column east of El Guettar in the Gafsa sector made progress in hard fighting against the Germans who are trying to protect Rommel's northward communication lines. A second American column at Maknassy pass beat off two enemy counter-attacks with heavy losses. Both battles continued with severe fighting in progress as the allied air force dared dust storms and haze to lash at the enemy positions and at retreating columns.

First Army Slowed Down

In northernmost Tunisia, the British First army and Moroccan native troops were slowed down in their push eastward from the Djebel Abiod sector toward Bizerte but continued to make progress over difficult ground on both flanks.

Almost 9,000 prisoners have been taken by the allied forcecs on various fronts in the past 10 days, including 8,000 in the southern area.

While the Eighth army vanguard passed through Gabes and continued to press northward in contact with the enemy, the Americans and French again thrust eastward from the Gafsa sector toward the coast, advancing under heavy enemy mortar fire toward the junction of the Kebili-Gabes road in the "hot corner" foothills southeast of Djebel Berda.

United Press Correspondent Phil Ault, accompanying this spearhead, reported that the American infantry was about 12 miles southeast of El Guettar and 58 miles northwest of Gabes and still advancing slowly.

The allied forces in the Gafsa area, where two columns narrowing Rommel's escape corridor are now within about 50 miles of the coast, have taken 200 prisoners in local attacks, the communique said.

Pressure was maintained by allied units on other northern sectors and in the far north the British First army, aided by French Moroccan troops, continued to advance "in difficult mountainous country and against strong enemy opposition," according to the communique. More than 700 prisoners were taken on the northernmost sector in two days, it added, as the British north of Djebel Abiod continued to make progress in the general direction of Bizerte, the great north coast naval base.

Get Air Support

The allied operations were given strong air support, especially in attacks by fighter bombers and light bombers on the Axis forces north of Gabes, where many vehicles were destroyed. Allied bombers also renewed their blasting of Rommel's line of retirement in the Sousse and Sfax areas.

(In London, Prime Minister Winston Churchill told the House of Commons that "another severe defeat" had been inflicted on the Axis, that the enemy had suffered "very serious" losses in men and material and that his panzer divisions in particular are remarkably mauled and enfeebled. But he warned that heavy fighting lies ahead.)

Montgomery's veteran desert troops lost no time in crashing northward to Gabes—and beyond—after breaking the Mareth line by a bold encircling movement through supposedly impassable desert lands to El Hamma.

Ned Russell, United Press correspondent with the Eighth army at El Hamma, reported that a lightning attack by British troops and a moonlight clash with German armor helped to break enemy resistance.

Coming Auctions

April 3—Harry Davis, city household goods sale.

THE STARS AND STRIPES
AFRICA
Vol. 1 - No. 18 - Friday, April 9, 1943
U. S. Army Newspaper
Two Francs

Yanks, British 8th Army Meet; Allies Swing North After Rommel

British And American Recon Patrols Merge Amid Desert Wastes

Sgt. Joe Randall Of State Center, Iowa Greets Sgt. A. W. Acland Of London, "Hello, You Bloody Limey!"

By MILTON LEHMAN
(*Stars and Stripes Staff Writer*)

WITH THE AMERICAN FORCES IN SOUTHERN TUNISIA, April 7—"Hello, you bloody Limey!"

That was the affectionate hello given by Sgt. Joseph A. Randall, State Center, Iowa, to Sgt. A. W. Acland, of Maida-Vale, London, as the reconnaissance patrols of the British 8th Army and American armored forces headed eastward, met in the historic juncture of the two armies, on the macadam road, 42 miles from Gabes amid desert wastes.

"Very glad to see you," answered Acland, with typical British restraint.

And these two enlisted men—the helmeted, grinning American and the freckled-faced, red-haired Britisher with a blue beret and a turtle-necked sweater — stepped forward and shook hands for the first formal contact uniting British forces which pursued Rommel for 1,500 miles and the Americans who slapped back the Germans 140 miles from Kasserine Pass in six weeks. This is Acland's story of the meeting for which soldiers on both sides have been eagerly looking forward to for weeks:

"At first we thought you were Jerries because of your helmets. We had been having trouble with Jerry all the night before and all this morning we had been picking up Italian prisoners.

"We were seriously considering opening fire on you, especially when we saw the big gun sticking out of your armored lorries. Then we got the idea that it was you. We remembered that everybody was saying yesterday that we would meet the Yanks today and when you fellows started running out of your vehicles, we recognized you.

"Then everything happened at once. We were in a big stretch of wasteland with bare mountains in the middle of nothing. There were five armored cars on your side—your halftracks with 75 mm. guns—and we had three armored dingos, or scout cars, each holding two persons.

"One Yank hollered, 'Christ, what's this' when he saw everybody ahead of him start throwing their arms around each other. All of us were chuckling and laughing. I'm a British Army photographer so I was already busy taking pictures of the scene.

We met at exactly 1525. I looked at my watch to note the time.

(*Continued on Page 8*)

EISENHOWER TO ALEXANDER:

'A Magnificent Fight'

Following the juncture of the American and British 8th Army in southern Tunisia, Gen. Dwight D. Eisenhower, Commander-in-Chief of the Allied Forces, sent the following message to his Deputy Commander-in-Chief, Gen. Sir Harold R. L. G. Alexander, who 's in charge of the Tunisian campaign:

"I hope that you and all ranks serving under you will accept my personal congratulations and those of the entire Allied Headquarters on your recent successful operations which have joined up the victorious Eighth Army with the British, French and American forces that have been carrying on through four months a magnificent fight in Central Tunisia under most unfavorable conditions. While everyone of us fully appreciates that great difficulties and bitter fighting still lie ahead of you, and that beyond this campaign lie still greater hardships and sacrifices, still you and your 18th Army Group, and the Navy and the Air Force are now in position to exact the full price from the enemy confronting us in Africa. You may be sure that the whole democratic world is applauding your successes against forces that have outraged our concepts of freedom and human rights. Good luck!

(Signed) DWIGHT D. EISENHOWER

Historic Union Crowns Drives By Both Forces

French Contact Mair U. S. Positions East Of El Guettar

(*By a Staff Writer*)

WITH AMERICAN FORCES IN SOUTHERN TUNISIA, April 7—An American armored column, after rolling 20 miles on the heels of the retreating enemy east of El Guettar met forward units of the British 8th Army on the Gafsa-Gabes road in an historic union today and immediately swung north together to finish the job of chasing the Axis from Africa.

While the advance patrols of the two armies met at 1525 about half-way between Gafsa and Gabes, the formal juncture of the two armies in force came 30 miles northwest of Gabes at 1610. Extended patrol tentacles of both armies also met at other points and it appeared a matter for future historical debate just when two forces met and merged.

With Rommel pulling out his legions overnight, the road to Gabes was clear sailing today for American tanks. While the Germans rushed to the north for shelter and to prepare new positions, the only enemy the American force met along the macadam Gabes-Gafsa road were large groups of Italians left behind as rear guards. With nothing left to guard and no heart in the fight, many of the Italian groups came down from the hills to the road to surrender to the Americans. Most of them seemed relieved that their fight was over.

PRISONERS POCKETED

The juncture of the two armies left a vast pocket of enemy troops east of Gafsa and another pocket of prisoners developed when the French army under General Boisseau contacted main American infantry positions east of El Guettar near Djebel Berda.

The French troops brought 70 Italian prisoners along with them whom they had captured on the way.

With the Germans retreating to the north, the road to Gabes was open to Allied traffic and the road from Gabes to Sfax seemed next in line.

The historic juncture of the two armies was no surprise to the men here. We had been expecting it for days, but what held up the meeting was the large number of mines left behind and the fact that the Nazis had concentrated a strong striking force of troops and tanks in the sector separating the two forces.

The British break-through to the north involved the taking of high ground in front of a well fortified Wadi. Once that barrier was broken, there was little but a long flat plain behind. In its move

(*Continued on Page 2*)

Prisoner Hans Insists Nazis Will Win—Soon!

By RICHARD BRUNER
(*Stars and Stripes Staff Writer*)

NEAR THE TUNISIAN FRONT—There's a German youngster named Hans with an American bullet in his belly in a prisoner of war camp up here. He's only 20 years old, and about the nearest thing he has to a God is his former leader, Field Marshal Erwin Rommel. He thinks Hitler is all right, too.

The same icy stare which seems a part of all Nazi troops was frozen on Hans's face as Pfc. Ralph Safdieh, an MP from Brooklyn, and I approached his hospital cot. Safdieh was to act as interpreter, but that turned out to be unnecessary. Hans had studied English in his home town, Berlin, and spoke it well.

Hans was bitter towards the war in Russia. "The Russians," he muttered, "don't fight fair. They fight just like animals. The soldiers of the Reich fighting in Russia," he said, "are anxious to come to Tunisia and fight the British and Americans because," he insisted, "we put up a fair fight.

Hans assured us that the Allied prisoners of war received excellent treatment in German camps and he was enthusiastic about the work of the American doctors. "They are very good," he admitted.

He grappled for the pack of American cigarettes as we handed them to him and his eyes sparkled as we promised to let him have some American magazines. "I'd like to go to a prison camp in America," he exclaimed. "I'm tired of North Africa." Hans has been with Rommel a year.

We brought the only smile of the day to his stern face when we asked him if he had a girl-friend back home. He nodded and said his girl understood what the war meant to both of them and would wait for him to return victorious.

We didn't have the heart to tell him she would have quite a wait

(*Continued on Page 2*)

"Doughnuteers" Popular Visitors At Front Airbase

Airmen Slick Up In Sunday' Best For Red Cross Girls

By RED MUELLER
(*Correspondent for Newsweek*)

AN AMERICAN AIRBASE IN TUNISIA—You could tell right away something was up.

A month ago, you hobnobbed with a bunch of dirty, bearded, mud-stained fighter pilots and bomber crews, full of frontline battle talk seasoned with plenty of four-letter words, and looking forward to chow time as their chief diversion from the strain of constant war duty.

Now, from brass hats to the lowest dogface, these guys were clean-shaven or industriously trimming beards and mustaches; wearing shirts and ties under spotless uniforms, and flashing brilliantly shined shoes. Even their language was toned down to a kind of sedate parlor talk.

Were Generals Eisenhower or Doolittle expected to visit the field? The answer was a surprised "Oh no."

DOUGHNUTEERS

Neither was Archbishop Spellman due nor had American nurses moved into the neighborhood, the fellows were quick to assure you. As they continued to refuse the desert and tea with sheepish and guilty grins, and you'd just about decided they were all goldbricking their way into the nearest rest home, the object of their attendance hove into sight. It looked like a cross between a station wagon and a nightmare by Rube Goldberg. But what stepped out on both sides and began unloading more Goldberg contraptions were strictly refugees from Hollywood.

Both wore smartly tailored, grey uniforms, pert hats, silk stockings and black shoes, and on each shoulder was a little, white badge marked "Red Cross." One of them, a sedate beauty, could have doubled for Greer Garson, and the other was a statuesque blonde in the best Ziegfield tradition. We began to understand.

If you could get near the former and ask why she left films she'd say you're very nice to say such sweet things but she is only Peggy

(*Continued on Page 2*)

NEWS FROM HOME

Chicago's Subway Roars In Dry Run; White House Cancels Its Egg Rolling, And Marriage Booms, Among Other Things

Subway Born

CHICAGO — The long-awaited, much-disputed Chicago subway has finally come to life, although it will be some time before it will be ready for the cash customers. All that happened this week was that a newly-painted, specially decorated, eight-car train, carrying mostly officials, sped through the new underground in a special dry run.

Coincident with the birth of the new subway was the death of "Burma Road," the name Chicagoans called the torn-up streets through which the underground runs. For years now the citizens here have become accustomed to traffic jams, trip-ups and extended detours caused by the ripped-up streets.

The subway, a modest affair as far as big cities go, was built to relieve the traffic problem in the famous "Loop" area which, up until now, has had to accommodate buses, trolleys and an elevated railroad. The subway runs north and south on State Street.

Cupid In Khaki

NEW YORK — Marriages last year reached an estimated record-breaking total of 1,800,000, of which two-thirds had servicemen as bridegrooms. This is 11 percent more than in 1941 and 83 percent more than in 1932.

The greatest increases took place in the Far West where San Diego, Cal., scored a 159 percent jump to lead the United States. San Antonio led the Southwest with a 62 percent rise.

One magazine attributed the marital boom to the lower draft age, the increase in the armed forces and the war production rise bringing greater employment.

Easter Casualty

WASHINGTON—The traditional Easter egg-rolling ceremonies on the White House lawn have been cancelled again this year. The Department of Agriculture asked that Easter eggs this year be used only for eating and hatching. The Department is also trying to discourage Easter purchases of baby chicks and ducks as pets.

Women MD's In Army

WASHINGTON — Women doctors will soon have direct commission in the Army and Navy, if

(*Continued on Page 3*)

It's An Order

Propaganda Chief Dr. Paul Joseph Goebbels told German women this week that they would be expected to do their all for the total Nazi war effort. At the same time he told the girls that it was their duty to make themselves as attractive as possible for husbands, fiances or friends at home on furlough.

"The more that young girls fulfill their duties willingly, joyfully and without compulsion the better it will be for the nation," he said. was broken, there was little but a long flat plain behind. In its move

U. S. EDITION
NUMBER 1
MONDAY, APRIL 10

THE CIRCUIT

SOUTH COMPOUND

GEPRÜFT 41

STALAG LUFT III
SAGAN, GERMANY
MONDAY, APRIL 10

RELIGIOUS SERVICE HELD IN THEATRE

PASTORS TEACH ETHICS, PHILOSOPHY AND PSYCHOLOGY

Religion is a vital part of Kriegie life. Both Protestant and Roman Catholic services are held each Sunday in the camp theatre.

Padre Murdo MacDonald, a Scottish pastor captured while serving with the British paratroops in Africa, is "unofficial" chaplain for the south compound. Protestant services are under his leadership as well as a discussion group and Bible Study class. The Padre also teaches a session in psychology and philosophy.

Father Goudreau, a French Canadian priest taken from the sinking "Zambeyi" in the early part of the war whiale enroute to missionary work in Africa, cares for the spiritual needs of the Roman Catholic officers and men. He divides his time between this and another camp. In addition Father Goudreau conducts a weekly ethics class.

Services have recently been enhanced by the addition of an altar cross and floral pieces, the contributions of Don Stine, Alameda, Calif., and J.M. Diffley, Birmingham.

OTHER CAMP PUBLICATIONS HAVE SHORT DURATIONS

The CIRCUIT had not been long in publication when the American spirit of competition prompted the appearance of two other news sheets, "The Shaft," and "The New Yorker," the latter fashioned on the U.S. publication of the same title. Their run was brief but brilliant.

"The Shaft" was printed by hand and appeared weekly. The cartoons and prose of Joseph Boyle, Ten Eyck, N.J., assisted by Norman Retchin, Barrington, Ill., provided more humor than the conservative news coverage of The CIRCUIT.

Del Ray of Buffalo, N.Y. fathered "The New Yorker," writing and typing two entire issues.

EDITORIAL

Through these composite publications we endeavor to bring you greetings from a community of Americans, and in the pages to set the temper of our existence.

Introspection suffers with intimacy, and it is not our wish to decry our position any further than to offer a smile for worried next-of-kin and a tolerant smirk on super sanquine bestowers of "country club" tags.

Suffice it to say that speakers, musicians, writers, artists, actors, men who were none of these but are learning to be - all are using these days to build a world of mind that embraces tolerance and ability to work together.

We hope to make the "home" editions a periodical function and thus send ourselves factually to you.

By means of this simple expedient, we say - and in the echo are unspoken hopes - "Hello," American style.

FOUR FILMS SHOWN SINCE SEPTEMBER

GERMAN "GINGER ROGERS" STARS IN TWO MUSICALS

Four motion pictures have been provided for prisoners since the opening of the south compound last September.

Marika Rökk, "Germany's Ginger Rogers" starred in two musical comedies provided by the Reich.

The American pictures were "Shall We Dance"" starring Fred Astaire and Ginger Rogers, and the Katharine Hepburn Cary Grant comedy, "Bringing Up Baby."

E.F. Schrupp, Young America Minn. acts as interpreter of the German movies for a none too spellbound audience.

OUT OF THE MAILBAG

Fremont, Neb. - "Do you have enough money or do you want me to send some in a money order?"

H.H. Van Anda

Chicago - "Your copy of the new Sears Roebuck catalogue has possibly already reached you.

"It isn't always possible for a member of our Army to reach a shopping center, but with our catalogue it is a simple matter."

Captain J.W. Swanson

KRIEGIE LYRICAL NEEDS SUPPLIED IN VARIED FORMS

SING-SONGS PAVE WAY FOR CHORUS AND SWING BANDS

Music ranks high in entertainment value for all POW's. It is supplied in many and various forms.

Before the organization of the bands and chorus, sing-songs, led by Tex Newton, accompanied by a few guitars, were held in the open air, indoors during colder weather.

Four YMCA phonographs, a set of records with each, passing from room to room, serve fourteen barracks.

A larger audience heard recordings upon delivery of an amplifying system shared with neighboring camps.

Norm Simpson and Oran Highley organized a chorus of forty who presented a Christmas program, and had a large part in the musical revue.

Band instruments serve double duty. They are used alike by the Luftbandsters, under the direction of Major Hal Diamond and a junior jazz band called the Swinging Troubadours, led by Tex Ellis.

CURRENT EVENTS ROOM SOURCE OF WORLD NEWS

Kriegies rely for their news on the German newspapers and a Reich loud speaker recently installed on the cook-house wall. Additionally, a paper in English published by the Germans for American POW's, brings summaries of foreign news plus sports items and local news from the States.

As only a small portion of prisoners can read German, most important articles from the papers are translated into English and posted beside explanatory maps in the "gen" -news-room in the theatre building.

The majority of the work in keeping news up to date falls to Edward McMillan, Philadelphia, J.H. Embach, Phoenix, Ariz. and A.J. Schmidt, Vineland, N.J.

CAMP ORGAN MAKES DEBUT OCT. 6, 1943

BULLETIN STYLE, THE CIRCUIT APPEARS THREE TIMES WEEKLY

The need of an organ to disseminate camp news and collect a somewhat meager store of "home" information was answered October 6, 1943 by the CIRCUIT, south camp's tri weekly.

Typed in form imitative of U.S. dailies and with lettered in heads, the single issue is posted on the cook-house wall, by custom the lager bulletin board.

Motivating force behind the CIRCUIT has been and is Ollie Chiesl of Chicago. Through him, as well as another Chicagoan Capt. Deadman, and L.J. Hawley, Berkeley, Calif., has the compound's only newspaper assumed the task of reporting, criticizing, reminding - in brief, aiding readers to find an optimum basis for adjustment.

Post-war reproduction of our CIRCUIT issues is planned.

Departments of theatre, sports, literary, and band are managed by Joe Klaas, Seattle, R.M. Rahner, N.Y., Sam Dorrance, Brooklyn, and Sgt.Graves, Council Bluffs, Ia. Deadman covers the military situation with lucid comments reared of years service with the "Times'" foreign desk.

Essential art work is in the facile hands of Ben Smotherman, Fort Worth, Frank Meyers, Cleveland, Ed Allen, Houston, and L.F. Hamaker, Santa Ana, Calif. Smotherman's "Penny", a cartoon depicting adventures of a girl correspondent in the ETO, appears during the week, while Meyers' droll "Looie" cavorts on the weekly Sunday comic page along with "Hercules, the Pup," by Allen. Cpl. Gilker, New York City has contributed skillful portraits and landscape sketches.

Invaluable in repertorial capacities are Robert Katz, Honnesdale, Pa., Joe Hudson, Little Rock, Ark., C. L. Farnhart, Lebanon, Ohio, Charles Goldschmid, N.Y.C., George Vasil, Spokane, Wash., C.C. Dartt, Oneonta, N.Y., L.C. Brown, Albuquerque, N.M. and W.L. Barker, Indianapolis. Among the latters' jobs is the collecting of mail items used in "Out of the Mailbag."

American POW's in Germany refer to themselves as Kriegies.

It's an abbreviation of the German, "Kriegsgefangener," war prisoner, which the Americans and British found too hard to pronounce.

S T A F F

S.A.O., Stalag Luft III	Col. Alkire, San Francisco, Cal.
S.A.O., South Camp	Col. Goodrich, Augusta, Ga.
Executive	Lt.Col. Clark, San Antonio, Texas.
Adjutant	Lt.Col. McNickle, Doland, S.D.
Education, Entertainment	Lt.Col. Klocko, Miami Beach, Fla.
Theatre	Major Houston, Dundalk, Md.
Music	Major Diamond, Van Nuys, Calif.
Kitchen	Capt. Shuck, Lewiston, Pa.
Papers	Capt. Frost, Oak Park, Ill.
Mail	Capt. Carmichael, Maryville, Mo.
Sanitation	Capt. Smithwick, Palm Sprgs., Cal.
Chaplain	Capt. MadDonald, Portree, Scotland.
Medical	Capt. Daniel, Spokane, Wash.
Parcels	Capt. Williams, Marietta, Ohio.
Interpreter	Lt. Schrupp, Young America, Minn.

PENNY

By Ben Smotherman

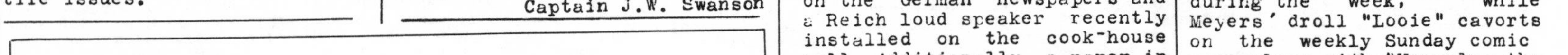
MISS PENNY, THE BOYS AND I WERE WONDERING IF YOU WOULD PICK THE BEST COSTUME AT OUR BALL TONIGHT! WOULD YOU OBLIGE US?
CERTAINLY, BILL! I'LL EVEN KISS THE WINNER!
So that night.....
WE'RE READY FOR YOU TO JUDGE US, MISS PENNY!
!
WELL, BOYS, IT LOOKS LIKE AN ALL-AROUND TIE! LICK YOUR LIPS....AND THE LINE FORMS ON THE RIGHT!
Ben Smotherman

TRIPOLI TIMES

No. 93. FRIDAY, MAY 14, 1943. **NORTH AFRICA'S FIRST ENGLISH DAILY** PRICE TWO LIRE

FINAL AFRICAN DEFEAT

OUR BOOTY NOW IS:

150,000 AXIS PRISONERS | 1200 GUNS - 250 TANKS
VON ARNIM CAPTURED | THOUSANDS OF VEHICLES

The war in Africa has ended. The dramatic finale was written when the British 6 Armoured Division joined up with Eighth Army, and the German Commander-in-Chief of the Axis Forces, Gen. Von Arnim was taken prisoner together with 11 other Generals.

The 150,000 prisoners taken means the smashing of 11 German divisions and 26 Italian divisions. 110,000 of the prisoners were German.

Mr. Atlee, Deputy Prime Minister, gave the news to the House of Commons yesterday and said «North Africa is ours. It is no longer a place to be defended but is one of our forward bases. In the fullness of time, Hitler, just like his generals, under the blows of the United Nations will be forced to accept unconditional surrender. »

FRENCH REVENGE

The French Commander had the satisfaction of receiving the surrender of the German division which made the break-through at Sedan in 1940.

German soldiers surrendering made the « V » sign, which Goebbels had tried to make a sign of Axis liberation.

The large number of prisoners taken in North Africa has completely reversed the holdings of the enemy nations. Before the end of the African campaign, there were 90,000 British prisoners in German hands and 30,000 Germans in British hands. Now the British hold 140,000 Germans.

Among the quantity of material which the Axis could not destroy before the collapse was a dump of 4,000,000 litres of petrol, 250 tanks were captured and many thousands of motor vehicles.

From the United Nations' new base the attack has already begun. R.A.F. planes have maintained a continuous attack on the Pantellaria islands and on Sicily. Allied planes are bombing those points again and again.

BOATS INTERCEPTED

The Navy brought in some of the Axis prisoners. They found them endeavouring to reach Pantellaria or Sicily in small boats. 156 were taken on their way to the islands.

The R.A.F. has also attacked shipping in the Aegean sea and off the west coast of Greece. They sank one small sailing vessel and damaged at least five others.

Leaflets were showered over Marsala by Allied planes and they bore only one sentence: « If you want this bombing to stop, demand peace; demostrate in the streets your desire for peace. »

FRONT DESPATCH

P.R. 2 Eighth Army H.Q., Wednesday

Organised resistance by the Axis Army of Africa ceased last night. The commander in chief of the enemy's forces, General Von Arnim is in our hands. He and his staff were captured by an Eighth Army formation, the 4th Indian Division, near St. Marie Du Zit ten miles north east of Zaghouan.

Brisk fighting in which gunners played a leading role went on all yesterday morning on the Eighth Army front where the remnants of the German 90th Light Lorried infantry and the 164 Divisions, and of the Italian Pistoia and Young Fascists made their last stand with varying degrees of determination.

Meanwhile First Army units were attacking down the coastal sector from Bou Ficha and by afternoon the iron circle had been closed around the doomed foe. Their progress was assisted by our light bombers which plastered the enemy's positions on three successive raids.

« CEASE FIRE » HITCH

Declaring that he would only surrender to the Eighth Army —General Messe the enemy commander requested an interview with Gen. Freyberg V.C. and a meeting was arranged.

Owing to a misunderstanding this did not take place but by late afternoon all the enemy divisions had ceased fire except the 164 on the Western flank.

This formation even launched a local counter-attack against our French Allies opposite them but the attempt was squashed by the fire of our guns.

This morning they were still in position but their resistance may be regarded as a token one designed to secure for this « Baby » of the German desert army the honour of being the last to surrender. The 164 Division came from Crete in time for the battle of Alamein where they suffered severe losses. They also had heavy casualties at El Hamma.

In the hilly country east of Zaghouan isolated parties of the enemy are being rounded up and every where else the process of tidying up is in full swing.

The total of prisoners is definotely over the 150,000 mark. It is worthy of note that this figure exceeds the catastrophe of Stalingrad where 90,000 of the enemy were taken prisoner by the Russians.

A final count of the material captured has not yet been made, but a provisional total of 1,200 guns, including 150 88 mm and 200 tanks have been taken since our final offensive opened on May 6.

Von Armin who has surrendered to 8th Army came to Africa from Russia.

He was a noted Anglophobe and only recently he sent out an order which stated that a legend had sprung up that the British were fair opponents. This pernicious propaganda, declared Von Arnim, must be stamped out and the German troops will show up the Englishman for what he is. Officers are responsible to see that this instruction is carried through.

His family has a long military record and he is not the first Von Arnim to be a general.

The official German war communique announces that an A.A. Division of the Luftwaffe, commanded by Major-General Neuffer, destroyed 37 tanks with their last shells.

CEASE FIRE

By Tripoli Times War Correspondent Richard Elley

Enfidaville, Thursday.

At 9.15 this morning came the final « Cease Fire » order to Eighth Army units. It marked not only the end of the North African campaign but the end of the pathetic attempts by the enemy remnants to hold the last stretch of the North African coasts, a stretch—seven or eight miles between Bou Ficha and Enfidaville—flat and marshy, dominated by hills in which the enemy troops were almost surrounded. Across it runs the coast road and to the seawards there is a biggish lake.

In the olive groves on the Bou Ficha side, Eighth Army's self-propelling guns of the 11th R.H.A. and 25 pounders nad 7.2 gun howitzers of the 1st Army were pounding away. Standing near them, I could see the shells bursting among the enemy positions on the hillside. Every few minutes a shell hit the stretch of coast road which was under enemy observation and on rare occasions one whistled through the olive trees. But that was all his artillery was able to do.

Now and again a dribble of surrendering Germans and Italians appeared from the direction of the hills.

SURRENDER OR—

It was rather boring but the wireless set in the tank, hidden among the trees kept us informed of what was going on. At 3 o'clock the radio told us that the commander of the Italian 1st Army had asked for surrender with the honours of war. From Eighth Army he was told there would be no surrender except unconditional surrender. He was warned that the shelling would continue and the bombers would be over soon. Twenty minutes later over came the bombers in three waves of 18.

As the dust and smoke cleared away, after three bomb loads had been dropped, I looked at the hills with my field glasses. All along appeared white flags; it was all over bar the shouting. Tanks moved out from the olive grove across the marsh and a carrier patrol went out along the seaward side of the lake to make a contact which makes unbroken the Allied control of the coast from Spanish Morocco to Turkey.

As the tanks moved on without any attempt being made to fire in their direction, bigger batches of prisoners came in. They were all cheerful, especially men of the 90 Light, who claimed their unit was the last to hold out, and that they had fired to the last round. Prisoners in one batch found old friends in other batches and greeted them with hugs and handshakes.

Three hours after the bombers had done their work I was able to drive my car along the coast road and straight through to Enfidaville.

This morning I walked through some of the last positions the Germans had held. Fortifications and dug-outs were strong and neatly finished, but the ground showed how thorough had been our barrage and bombing. There was little left in the way of enemy equipment. They had destroyed most of it before surrendering.

In a village on the hillside some Arabs asked if the « boom-boom » was finished and whether they could bring their families back. They were probably the last Arabs to have their homes disturbed by Axis forces and now they too can return to a peaceful life.

P. R. 2

CHURCHILL TO BROADCAST

The Prime Minister will make a world broadcast at 9 p.m. Central European time.

FOR DIAMONDS READ KNOBS

Field Marshal Rommel has been decorated with the highest German military award, « Pour Le Merite », with diamonds on. He thus becomes the second German General to be honoured in a moment of catastrophe.

Paulus of the Sixth German Army was promoted to Field Marshal the day before he surrendered at Stalingrad.

It is hoped that more and more German Commanders will be similiarly honoured.

CAPE BON-FIRE

By Paul Bewsher of the « Daily Mail »

With the Western Desert Air Force, Thursday.

« Nobody told them the war is over. That's the trouble. We know it, but they don't know it. »

A young pilot summed up the situation aptly with these few words as he reported the strange scene in the last pocket of enemy resistance north of Enfidaville.

He had just been flying round to see what was happening in the swiftly changing situation.

He gave me a vivid picture of the last fighting hours of the trapped remnants of the once vaunted Afrika Korps.

« There were columns of transports driving up and down the roads in both directions », he said, « but they didn't seem to realise that wherever they went they were just driving into the bag. I suppose they didn't understand the situation and were trying to find some way out. »

Other pilots described how the whole area was covered with fires and explosions as the cornered army blew up dumps and stores.

HUGE FIRES

« Great pillars of dust and smoke and debris were shooting up into the air and billowing out into mushroom heads », they said. « Black oily columns of smoke were curling up all over the place from dozens of fires.

« Just by the coast an ammunition dump was blazing and continual explosions were flashing out amidst the flames. But way down in the south our guns were still busily shelling their lines which they were still holding in the hills.»

« The whole of the sunlit finger of the Cape Bon peninsula pointing out into the blue Mediterranean was smoking as if it were dotted with volcanoes.

« A Cape Bonfire » remarked another pilot.

That same night the pilots, together with all the men, of a South African squadron were watching the film « Desert Victory », recalling many events which they had studied in the air at the time and faithfully reported.

For them, at this swift ending of the whole compaign, it had a very special significance.

As they walked back to their tents there was still the heavy thump and rumbling of guns from the Enfidaville front where the trapped remnants of an overwhelmed army were putting up a hopeless and useless resistance in the mountains — for no reason at all.

As that pilot put it, « Nobody told them the war is over. That's the trouble.

DEPTH CHARGES are being used to clear the entrance to Bizerta Harbour which the Germans blocked by sinking 22 vessels, including two submarines. Here is a charge being lowered to a diver down below, who will place it in position.

UNION JACK

THE NEWSPAPER FOR THE BRITISH FIGHTING FORCES

No. 34 | Friday, June 4, 1943 | One Franc

Giraud - De Gaulle Accord Complete

To Fight Together Till Victory

From UNION JACK Reporter Ronald Haines

COMPLETE accord has now been reached in the discussions between General Giraud and General de Gaulle about how the French war effort is to be conducted under a unified control.

The newly-formed Executive Committee which is to be the French sovereign power until France is liberated last night issued a stirring appeal to all Frenchmen.

Presidency of the new Committee is shared equally by General Giraud and General de Gaulle. The members already elected are General Catroux, General Georges, M. Massigli, M. Andre Philip, and M. Monnet. Others will be added later.

New Governor-General

General Catroux also becomes the new Governor-General of Algeria in succession to M. Marcel Peyrouton, who offered his resignation to both the Free French leaders.

The full text of the Document of Agreement is:

«The Committee thus constituted is the central French power. The Committee conducts the French war effort in all its forms, and in all places. In consequence it exercises a French sovereignty over all territories outside of those enemy-controlled, and administers and ensures the defence of all French interests in the world. It takes authority over the territories and over our land, sea and air forces which up to now were under the control either of the French National Committee or of the Civil and Military High Command.

Every measure necessary to realise the fusion into one organisation of the administrations controlled by these two French bodies will be taken without delay by the Committee.

Until Victory

According to the text of the letters exchanged between General Giraud and General de Gaulle, the Committee will hand over its powers to the provisional government, which will be constituted according to the laws of the French Republic as soon as the liberation of France will permit it, and not later than at the time of the total liberation of France.

The Committee will pursue the fight in close co-operation with all the Allies with a view to bringing about the complete liberation of all French and Allied territories and until total victory over all enemy powers has been achieved.

The Committee takes a solemn oath to re-establish all French liberties, the laws of the French Republic and the Republican form of government destroying at the same time the arbitrary power and personal leadership which is to-day inflicted upon the country.

The Committee is the servant of the French people. The war effort, the resistance and the trials of the French people, as well as the necessary revival of the French Nation, require the union of all national energies

The Committee calls upon all Frenchmen to follow its guidance so that France will be able to find again through victory its liberties, its greatness, and its traditional place among the great Allied Nations and to bring at the peace conference its contribution to the council of United Nations which will then determine the conditions of Europe and the world.

Apart from the discussions about the membership and powers of the Committee there have been other important developments in the past two days.

Admiral Muselier, who has commanded the Free French naval forces under the control of the Free French National Committee in London, has been appointed as deputy to General Giraud, the military and civil C.-in-C. in North Africa, with the special task of ensuring order in Algiers and district.

General Weiss, who formerly commanded the French air forces in Tunisia, has placed himself at General de Gaulle's disposal.

M. MARCEL PEYROUTON: designation accepted.

REVIEW OF WAR PENSIONS

SIR Walter Womersley the Pensions Minister is making a detailed survey of war pensions. When it is finished, the House of Commons will have a full debate on the subject.

Mr. Clement Attlee the Deputy Prime Minister, made this promise in the House of Commons yesterday.

Full Debate

A Conservative member asked if Sir Walter would consider the position of the widows and children of men who had been receiving War Service Grants while they were alive. He suggested that 18/- a week might be given in these cases.

Sir Walter said in reply that this was one of the questions that he was examining in a full survey of pensions on which he was engaged at the moment.

Mr. Attlee then said that the House would be given the opportunity of a full debate when the survey was concluded.

Asked by Mr. Walter Greenwood if the Government would put Sir Walter's conclusions in a White Paper, Mr. Attlee replied that this would be considered.

Axis Failure At Sea

General Franco's Chief Executive Officer in the Spanish Government said in Madrid that the Axis with its submarines had been unable to achieve «negative domination of the sea.»

He said that the United Nations dominate the seas, despite their losses. From the first day of war, Britain's fleet had completely blocked Axis ocean traffic, and if the Axis had been a maritime power, it would already have perished.

U-Boats' Worst Month: Page 4

ISLAND FORT SHELLED FOR THIRD DAY

THE island of Pantellaria, spring board island for any invasion of Italy, has been shelled by Allied warships for the third day running, said yesterday's Italian communique.

The Allied communique from North Africa made no mention of this. It merely stated that the island had been attacked by medium and fighter-bombers in the last 24 hours.

Pantellaria, which lies about half-way between Tunis and Sicily, was shelled from the sea for the first time three weeks ago.

The port was heavily hit on the night of May 30-31. There was no resistance, and we suffered neither casualties nor damage.

On the afternoon of June 1, barracks and artillery emplacements were also shelled. This time shore batteries did reply, but again we did not suffer any casualties.

In Washington, Mr. Henry L. Stimson, War Secretary, said: «The Axis bases on Pantellaria, Sicily and Sardinia have been neutralised and Allied shipping is now moving almost unmolested from one end of the Mediterranean to the other.»

Allied Naval forces operating off Cape Spartivento, southernmost tip of Sardinia, on Tuesday night, caused havoc among ships of an Axis convoy.

The enemy lost a merchant vessel which blew up; an accompanying merchant ship sunk by direct fire, a destroyer set ablaze before it was beached by the crew, and a torpedo boat, which was sunk.

Keep in the Picture

Vast Air Fight in Kuban

AIR battles as fierce as any yet seen in the Russian campaign are being fought out over Novorossisk and the Kuban peninsula.

Reuter's Moscow correspondent reports several full-scale battles between hundreds of planes, and says that the mountains near the Black Sea coast and estuary of the Kuban River are strewn with the bodies of German pilots.

Five hundred German planes raided Kursk to try and wreck the rail junction where the [illegible] plies from Voronezh. Of these 123 German planes were shot down for the loss of 30 Russian.

On land the Germans admit heavy defensive fighting in the Kuban sector. Moscow gives no details of these operations.

In the province of Kalinin, north-west of Moscow, the Red Army was forced to give ground under a sharp German attack, but counter-attacked in force and drove the enemy back to his original positions. The Germans lost 2,000 dead.

China

MORE progress is reported in the Chinese counter-offensive along the Yangtse River. The Chinese have captured two towns in the neighbourhood of Ichang and now hold strategic points on both sides of the river.

Ichang is the forward base from which the Japanese recently set out to make a drive towards Chungking, 300 miles away. Now the invader finds himself in danger of being cut off from his rear base at Hankow.

American bombers and fighters of General Stilwell's force are supporting the Chinese attack.

Film Star Lost In Shot Down Plane

LESLIE HOWARD, the film actor, is among 17 people missing in a British air liner reported overdue and presumed lost between Lisbon and Britain. The last message from the plane said that it was being attacked by enemy aircraft.

The plane belonged to British Overseas Airways Corporation, and carried 13 passengers and four crew. Other passengers were a South African journalist, Kenneth Stonehouse, and his wife, and at least one other woman and two children. The crew were Dutch.

Unofficial reports say that the attacking aircraft was a German reconnaissance plane, and that the air liner was shot down into the Bay of Biscay on Tuesday morning. Leslie Howard had won wide celebrity in recent years by his brilliant performances in «Pygmalion,» «Pimpernel Smith,» and «49th Parallel.» He had recently begun work on a film about the A.T.S He was 49.

U.S. STRIKERS WARNED

PRESIDENT ROOSEVELT has ordered the 400,000 U.S. miners now on strike, to go back to work on Monday, it was announced in Washington late last night.

He has also ordered Mr. Harold Ickes, Secretary for the Interior to have the mines opened.

Mr. John L. Lewis, the miners' leader, has accused the Labour Board of acting illegally in suspending all negotiations on the men's claim for two dollars a day more pay, while the strike goes on.

Accusation

The men went on strike three days ago after a truce to permit of negotiation on their claim. They say that the Labour Board which was carrying on the negotiations was not impartial.

An anti-strike bill is being considered by the House of Representatives. A number of amendments have been proposed, but a vote may be reached to-day.

The first United States war factory has ceased production because of lack of coal. This is the American Windowglass Company, which makes glass for aircraft.

The important Packard factory, now making Rolls-Royce engines for aircraft, also stopped work. But here the workers object to the upgrading of some negro employees. It was stated last night that the workers had decided to go back.

ANY QUESTIONS?

A new B.B.C. programme, in which experts will answer questions on any subject sent in by listeners starts on June 17.

The experts will include Dr. Julian Huxley and Geoffrey Crowther. The programme time is 1730-1745 hours, G.M.T. It will be broadcast in the Overseas Service.

Soldiers in North Africa are invited to send questions. They should be addressed to:

Soldiers' Questions, B.B.C., London.

Union Jack Evening Paper

TUNIS TELEGRAPH

No. 17
THURSDAY JUNE 17 1943
Price : 1 franc

FIRST BRITISH PAPER IN TUNISIA

THE KING IS IN NORTH AFRICA TO SEE HIS ARMIES

HIS Majesty the King is in North Africa to visit the men of his victorious forces. He arrived at Algiers on Saturday morning last in the same Liberator bomber that brought Mr. Winston Churchill here a few weeks ago.

One of the King's first acts was to confer on General Eisenhower the Grand Cross of the Order of the Bath.

This is the second time since war began that the King has left England to visit his troops fighting abroad. His first trip was to France in the early months of the war.

He had made up his mind for a long time to visit his men in North Africa, but the details of his historic flight were only settled on Tuesday of last week, when Mr. Churchill lunched at Buckingham Palace, after his first reception since his return

On Friday last, the Captain of the King's Flight, Group Capt. Fielden, saw the King and told him the final weather expectations.

The King later left Windsor Castle by car.

The Liberator flew in company with one carrying Sir James Grigg, Minister for War, and Sir Archibald Sinclair, Secretary of State for Air. Others in the Royal party were the King's Private Secretary and the Master of the Household.

The plane landed at the busiest airport in North Africa.

Here, General Eisenhower, Admiral Sir Andrew Cunningham, Air Chief Marshall Sir Arthur Tedder, and the British Resident Minister in Algiers, Mr. Harold McMillan, were waiting to receive him.

Soldiers rubbed their eyes

In a few minutes, almost before the hundreds of R.A.F. men on the field knew that he had landed, the King was speeding away in General Eisenhower's car.

The secret of his presence in North Africa could not be kept for long. Little groups of soldiers in Arab villages and cross-roads rubbed their eyes as he drove past.

On Saturday the King dined with General Eisenhower and spent the night in Algiers.

On Sunday he appeared in the white uniform of an Admiral of the Fleet and attended a religious service in the port chapel at Algiers. Behind him were rows of men from every type of ship in the Mediterranean Fleet.

Later, he visited a convalescent home in the pine woods, where men from all the services were recuperating from wounds. The men were running, bathing and swimming on the beach. The King went out on to a verandah of a villa that is being used as part of the home.

In a few seconds, the men realised who it was and came tumbling out of the sea. They gathered below the verandah and sang « God Save the King ».

Then the King came down on to the beach. He was completely surrounded and talked for some time with the men, shaking hands with them. They sang « For he's a Jolly Good Fellow ».

Afterwards the King said: « That was the most delightful experience of my visit so far. It reminded me of my seaside camps for boys before the war ».

The next day, the Royal aircraft took off again taking the King to see General Mark Clarke, commander of the American 5th Army. He lunched in the open air eating roast beef and sweet corn out of American mess tins.

Afterwards he inspected an American combat team with jeeps, guns and tanks.

In the evening he saw them at battle drill, live ammunition being used in a realistic assault on a dummy village.

He laid a memorial wreath on an American cemetery before departing.

He has since toured the battlefields and visited some of his ships.

Before he left for Africa the King appointed five Councils of State to act for him in his absence.

Sicily's turn for non-stop raids

THE air attack on Sicily, the next in Mussolini's chain of island defences, is growing every day. Day and night for the last two days, Allied bombers and fighters from North Africa and Malta have been over the island.

Aerodromes have been heavily plastered. After night raids on four of the main airfields, heavy bombers carried on the attack at dawn.

The defending fighter aircraft struggled hard to protect their home bases, but they could not stop the bombers from doing great damage at five airfields. In these raids, 16 Axis planes were destroyed. We lost seven.

It has been disclosed that Mussolini personally ordered the garrison of Pantelleria to surrender after a report from the island that the Allies bombing could be endured no longer.

Brigadier General Achille Maffei, Fascist leader of the garrison, said that Admiral Gino Pavesi, the governor and commander, sent a message to Mussolini that they had been without food or water for three days.

Mussolini replied that they should surrender for the sake of the civil population, and Admiral Cavesi signed an armistice.

There were not many casualties among civilians through our bombing, as, after the first two raids they left their homes to shelter.

The Allied High Command have closed the Syrian Turkish frontier to prevent leakage of information to German intelligence agents on Turkish soil.

The Germans, who recently expelled the Turkish Consul at Salonika, have now demanded the removal of the Turkish Consul at Mydilene.

V. C. FOR LEADER OF RUTHLESS ATTACK

THE KING has approved the award of the Victoria Cross to Captain Tupper of the Indian Army Second Rifles for his ruthless determination in a silent raid on an enemy position at Oued el Zay last April.

Capt. Tupper and his company had to break through and secure the only vantage point from which the enemy's main position could be seized.

The first contact with the enemy was made at the foot of a crossway winding up a narrow cleft, completely guarded by enemy machine guns. After crossing the cleft, our men had to get into a small arena into which mortar and shell fire were being poured.

Using cutlasses and bayonets, Capt. Tupper and his company killed all the garrison of the outerlying post, and then Capt. Tupper led his men through a storm of hand grenades and machine gun fire, to deal with a number of machine gun nests.

He and two riflemen got to the top of a crest and covered the advance of the rest of the company.

The official description says that this objective was an essential feature covering the advance of the brigade.

LABOUR'S 'NO' TO COMMUNISTS

THE LABOUR PARTY has refused the application of the Communist Party for affiliation by a majority of nearly three to one at the annual conference.

Mr. Herbert Morrison, Home Secretary referred to the suggestion that the Comintern would be re-created.

«That may be so,» he said «but I do not think it is so.»

« Indeed, I think there are strong reasons, from the point of view of Mr. Stalin, one of the world's greatest men; why he should have taken this step.

THE REST OF THE NEWS

General de Gaulle, General Catroux and M. Monnet have had further discussions on the re-organisation of the French Army.

* * *

German and Italian troops have carried out defence exercises on a large scale in the south of France. Feverish activity is reported and Nice, Cannes and Marseilles are said to be strongly fortified.

* * *

Reports from Sydney say that the internal situation in Japan is critical and had obliged Tojo, the Prime Minister to call a meeting of the Diet. The morale of the workers leaves much to be desired and production is not what it should be.

* * *

The body of a woman found in the debris of a Japanese bomber, shot down by an American fighter plane at Hang Yang, is thought to have been that of the radio operator.

* * *

The Germans have ordered the evacuation of Rheims and have given the inhabitants only a few hours notice to go, says Ankara Radio.

GERMANS DRIVEN BACK AT OREL

THE main land fighting in Russia continues to be in the area east of Orel. Fierce fighting has raged round one of the towns the Russians have captured.

But, at the end of the day, the Germans gave up their assaults. They had lost 400 dead.

The Red Air Force is making its main attacks against German targets in the Donetz area. Railway stations, trains and supply stores have been bombed.

In a surprise raid on a northern port, Russian dive bombers sank a German transport and damaged harbour installations.

Polish patriots have executed 12 German officials in Poland. All are members of the S. S.

Nazis Worry

Air Marshal Goering has ordered Marshal Kesselring, Commandant of the Southern Air Force to transfer his H. Q. from Sicily to the Italian mainland.

EXTRA!

San Francisco Chronicle

THE CITY'S ONLY HOME-OWNED NEWSPAPER

FOUNDED 1865—VOL. CLVI, NO. 168 CCCA SAN FRANCISCO, FRIDAY, JULY 2, 1943 DAILY 5 CENTS, SUNDAY 15 CENTS: DAILY AND SUNDAY PER MONTH, $1.50

Chronicle Home Delivery Service

Federal war regulations to conserve rubber prohibit all special deliveries. If for any reason you do not receive your Chronicle, kindly telephone GArfield 1112 or your local Chronicle Dealer before 10 a. m. so the delivery may be checked. We appreciate your co-operation in this emergency.

BIG AIR VICTORY! JAP HARBOR TAKEN

THIS WORLD TODAY

By ROYCE BRIER

THREE or four years ago there lived in one of the hilly suburban counties of the Bay region a high school kid of 19 years.

This kid was a hot number, no fooling. The old man had a nice Cadillac job, but the kid didn't get his hands on it often. He didn't feel at home in it, anyway.

His transportation was a 1931 flivver. It cost him $50, plus $150 to hop it up. The paint job was bad but the rubber was good. This was before the day of the love-stripe, so the tonneau had the usual wisecracks bordering on the risque daubed here and there.

He went to school after a fashion, but he also worked in a gas station some of the time. This would seem to fill the day, but no. Sometime during most days you would see him in the driveway working on the flivver. It would be in 200 different parts scattered around the grass. So it wasn't transportation at all in daytime, only potential transportation. After dinner it never failed to become transportation.

He maintained a steady 65, except right in town, when he cut her down to 50. He never hit a telephone pole, but nicked one occasionally. He would never even hit you, if you didn't get startled and swing into him. He got a ticket a week, without observable effect.

In daytime he depended on his open cut-out, and at night on his lights as warning. You would hear him roaring up the hill at night with a load of boys and girls. Sometimes he would be surprised on a curve. Then he would cut into the bank, take a load of dirt on his running board, and continue for his destination. Up to 1941 he always made it.

Remember, this was a few years ago, and the kid is gone now. He has other work. He was a great kid, and although a little older, he's still a great kid. No other people on earth—the Germans, the Russians, the Japanese, the English—had him, or had anything like him. He was never seen anywhere until about 1920.

Only America thereafter built up two or three millions of him, for only America had what created him—gasoline, car, roads. Or maybe he helped to create them. At any rate, he added to the synthesis an immortal longing for freedom in space, and this kept him fussing with car-

Continued on Page 5, Col. 1

House Hits At NYA

Senate Fund Amendment Is Rejected

By the United Press

WASHINGTON, July 1—The House today by a vote of 197 to 176 insisted on liquidation of the National Youth Administration when it rejected a Senate amendment to the labor-Federal security appropration bill to give NYA $48,000,000 in the new fiscal year beginning today. The House proposed to provide NYA with only $3,000,000 to finance its liquidation by January 1.

This and other actions left the appropriations deadlock unchanged. Four Government departments and 18 war agencies found themselves without funds because of the log-jam at the Capitol.

VACATION DELAYED

Congress' vacation was delayed to await an expected veto of the bill that would halt the Administration's rollback of food prices.

The Senate re-affirmed its demand that the Federal crop insurance program be continued by a 53 to 21 vote and sent back to conference the $875,000,000 agriculture appropriation bill.

Conferees on the $127,889,141 Interior Department supply bill broke up for the day in disagreement, with Senate conferees insisting on $22,000,000 for Western irrigation projects which they declared would produce food for the war effort within two years.

Shortly before acting on the NYA fund, the House voted 169 to 11 to insist on the provision it wrote into the labor-Federal security bill to prohibit the National Labor Relations Board from entering jurisdictional disputes in plants where contracts already are in existence.

AGREES TO EASE BAN

It agreed, however, to ease its ban to the extent of ordering that before employer-union contracts become effective, notices of their proposed signing must be posted for three months to give other unions

Continued on Page 5, Col. 3

Strikes Halt Stockton Buses

STOCKTON, July 1 (AP)—Service on the city's bus lines, used by 17,000 persons, halted today as bus drivers failed to appear for work.

The 40 drivers, members of the AFL Amalgamated Association, recently asked for a pay raise from 80 cents an hour to $1. The privately-owned company, Stockton city lines, offered 90 cents, subject to approval of the War Labor Board.

The contract between the union and the line expired at midnight.

—(AP) Wirephoto

Dodges Death

Max Stephan (above), convicted traitor, escaped the gallows by a few hours yesterday, when President Roosevelt commuted a death sentence to life imprisonment. Stephan was scheduled to die this morning at Milan, Mich. See story on Page 5.

Jury Orders Probe of S. F. Smoke Death

A Coroner's jury yesterday recommended further investigation in the death of Mrs. Pearle Ann Gillette, 41, whose body was found in a smoke-filled bedroom at 4550 California street on June 13.

Her husband, Lieutenant Jasper Gillette, 42, of the Marine Corps, testified he found his wife's body when he returned to their apartment after a tour of night spots with two other women.

He admitted, under questioning by the coroner, Dr. John L. Kingston, that he and his wife had quarreled before he left home on the afternoon preceding discovery of her body.

The jury's verdict declared:

"Death was causedby asphyxia in a manner unknown to the jury and we recommend further investigation in this case."

Inspectors Frank Ahern and Al Carrasso of the police homicide squad announced they would continue the investigation.

No charge was placed against Lieutenant Gillette.

THE FIRST THEORY

When the woman's body was discovered, it was believed she had been suffocated by fumes from a fire caused possibly by a smouldering cigarette.

Evidence introduced at the coroner's inquest indicated her death was not due to the fire and that the sleeping tablets found in her room were not of sufficient potency to cause death. She had suffered

Continued on Page 5, Col. 5

The False Alert

Army and OCD Probes Mixup In East Bay

United States Army and Alameda county civilian defense officials launched an investigation yesterday afternoon into an air raid warning which awoke half a million residents of the East Bay, snarled traffic, stopped automobiles, street cars and commuter trains, cost thousands of man hours of war plant production, made thousands late to work on both sides of the bay—and turned out to be a false alarm.

The question to be solved by the investigating officials was:

"Who did it?"

The alarm alerted Alameda county and the adjoining parts of Costra Costa county for 48 minutes.

There was no alarm in San Francisco nor elsewhere in the Bay Area.

That in itself constituted one of the puzzles to be solved; the other element was whether or not an honest mistake had been made.

THE SEQUENCE BEGINS

The sequence of events began shortly after 6 o'clock yesterday morning and the story was pieced together from statements by Captain of Inspectors Hugo Radbruch of the Alameda County District Attorney's office, Assistant District Attorney Robert Hunter; Mrs. Marcella Cohen, Civilian Defense control center operator; J. A. Szizek, acting chief co-ordinator for the Oakland Defense Council; City Manager Chester Fisk, and from an official Fourth Army communique.

It went like this:

Mrs. Cohen was on duty shortly after 6 a. m. when the control bell sounded and the "red" alert button on the San Francisco circuit lighted on the switchboard.

According to customary procedure,

Continued on Page 2, Col. 3

Veronica Lake Injured in Fall

HOLLYWOOD, July 1 (AP)—Film Actress Veronica Lake, an expectant mother, was taken to Good Samaritan Hospital early today suffering from the effects of a fall at her studio yesterday.

Hospital attendants reported her condition was favorable. She fell when she tripped over a cable, the studio said.

The Index

U. S. Destroys 65 Jap Planes

Allied Forces Capture New Guinea Port; U. S. Transport Sunk After Landing Troops

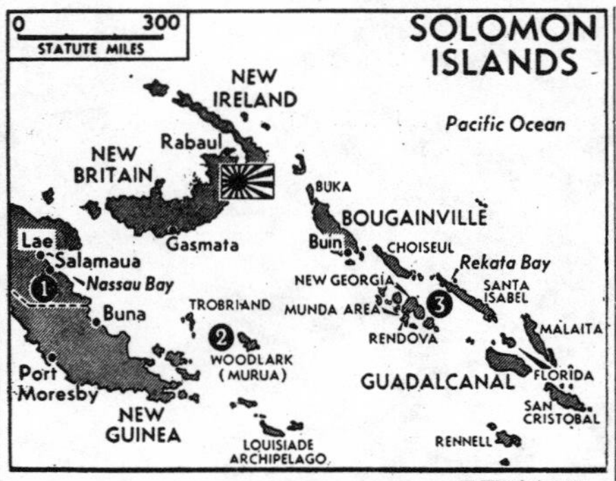

—(AP) Wirephoto map

NEW ALLIED OFFENSIVE IN THE PACIFIC—In a wide-spread attack Allied forces have landed at Nassau Bay (1), on Trobriand and Woodlark islands (2) and at Rendova and New Georgia islands (3). With General MacArthur in supreme command of the land, sea and air forces, the offensive is apparently aimed at the Jap base of Rabaul on New Britain (Jap flag symbol). It's the first big push against the Japs since the Allied landings in the South Solomons last year.

U. S. Batters Palermo

Heavy Bombers Pound Depots, Rake Airfields

By the Associated Press

ALLIED HEADQUARTERS IN NORTH AFRICA, July 1—American Flying Fortresses, encountering little opposition, smashed the main Sicilian port of Palermo yesterday in an unrelenting aerial prelude to trans-Mediterranean amphibious operations, expected to be the greatest in history.

Escorted by P-38 Lightnings, the American heavy bombers spread new debris amid the island capital's storage depots and barracks and raked four airfields, a communique said today.

Prime Minister Churchill's forecast of heavy fighting in this area before fall did not surprise anyone here—soldier or civilian. Both Allied and Axis leaders know that invasion thrusts across the Mediterranean—when they come—will be and must be the greatest ever undertaken.

The Axis leaders also must know

Continued on Page 2, Col. 4

Friend Richardson Has Heart Attack

Former Governor Friend W. Richardson is "seriously, but not critically" ill in Merritt Hospital, Oakland, his family announced yesterday.

He suffered a heart attack several days ago at his home, 878 Arlington avenue, Berkeley, and was removed promptly to the hospital.

War on The U-Boats

Their Score Is Lower as Ours Goes Up

By the Associated Press

Hitler's U-boat fleets, punished by Allied planes and surface craft recently as never before, were reported in official German broadcasts yesterday to have sunk only 20 British and American merchantmen, totaling 107,000 tons, in June.

And, British naval observers said, Germany is now losing at least one U-boat, built by slow and costly precision methods, for every mass-produced Allied freighter sunk by the undersea craft.

A CONSERVATIVE ESTIMATE

An estimate of 20 U-boats destroyed during the month probably would be conservative, Malcolm MacDonald, British High Commissioner to Canada, announced Tuesday that at least 14 of the underseas raiders were killed in the previous 14 days and Prime Minister Churchill disclosed in his Guildhall speech on Wednesday that the Allies' average

Continued on Page 2, Col. 5

Col. Roosevelt Arrives in N. Y.

NEW YORK, July 1 (AP)—Lieutenant Colonel James Roosevelt, U. S. M. C., accompanied by his wife and his mother, Mrs. Eleanor Roosevelt, arrived by plane from Washington today.

Reporting 'I'm really feeling fine," the President's son said he would spend the rest of his sick leave at the family home at Hyde Park, N. Y.

Stimson Says Battle Is Going Well on All Fronts, Warns of Stiff Fight Ahead

By the Associated Press

WASHINGTON, July 1—Powerful American sea and air forces beat off Japan's first aerial counterattack on the Solomons prong of the South Pacific offensive, the Navy announced today, while troops ashore on New Georgia island captured Viru Harbor, only 30 nautical miles southeast of the enemy's Munda airbase.

At last 65 Japanse planes were destroyed in a violent all-day battle off Rendova Island two days ago when American troops were first being discharged there in a flanking move on Munday, five miles away. This was more than half the estimated total of 110 enemy fighters, level bombers, dive bombers and torpedo planes, which took part in the successive assaults.

A Navy communique said that 17 United States aircraft were reported missing and that the 7712-ton transport McCawley, formerly the Grace liner Santa Barbara, was damaged in the air attack and later sunk by a Japanese submarine. The troops she carried to the area already had been put ashore, and available information indicated there was no loss of life in the sinking.

In the New Guinea area, where General Douglas MacArthur is personally directing operations, the Western prong of the drive aimed at the big enemy base of Rabaul apparently was continuing to develop in the direction of Salamaua, Japanese outpost protecting the flank of Rabaul.

Great Drive Is Going Very Well

Generally the overall progress of this greatest offensive of the Pacific war, under the overall direction of MacArthur, was officially described as going along very well.

MacArthur's headquarters in Australia announced today that Lieutenant General Walter Krueger, whose arrival in Australia to command the Sixth U. S. Army was disclosed last February, is in charge of "certain phases of operations" in the joint land, sea and air operation against Nassau bay in Eastern New Guinea and the Trobbian dand Woodlark Islands off the north coast of Papua.

Secretary of War Stimson summed up the results of two days of co-ordinated attacks on the New Guinea and Solomons fronts, 500 miles apart, by telling a press conference that "reports are incomplete but satisfactory progress apparently already has been made."

(In London, Reuters said that a special night bulletin from Allied Headquarters in the Southwest Pacific announced that operations against the Japanese were "proceeding successfully under constant cover of Allied fighter planes." It was added that naval torpedo boats were playing a big part in the new campaign.)

"We've Reached Japan's Outer Defenses"

'Our forces have reache dthe outer defenses of Japan," Stimson said, "and strong enemy reaction may be expected."

Clearly indicating the scope of the operation and the great striking power of the units involved, Stimson spoke of the drive as a "co-ordinate dattack of land, sea, and air forces." He said it was planned in Washington several weeks ago.

What the Japanese fleet would do continued to be one of the major questions of speculation in Washington. In view of what Stimson said, it seemed possible he anticipated that the

Continued on Page 3, Col. 4

The Weather Man

"I'm glad I'm on a milk diet," said Anemometer, the bureau cat.

"Howzat?" asked the Weather Man.

"The price of liquor's going up again. People'll drink more."

"How? They won't be able to afford it."

"That's the trouble. It's what they can't afford that people buy most of."

"Maybe that's why cafes are so crowded," grumbled the W. M. over today's DIM-OUT WARNING: Sun sets at 8:36.

IN OTHER WORDS, THE MORE PRICES GO UP, THE MORE LIQUOR GOES DOWN

THE STARS AND STRIPES
AFRICA

Vol. 1, No. 31, Saturday, July 10, 1943 — U. S. Army Newspaper — Two Francs

SICILY INVADED

Allied Forces Begin Landing Operations On Axis Island

Sicily—New Allied Battlefield

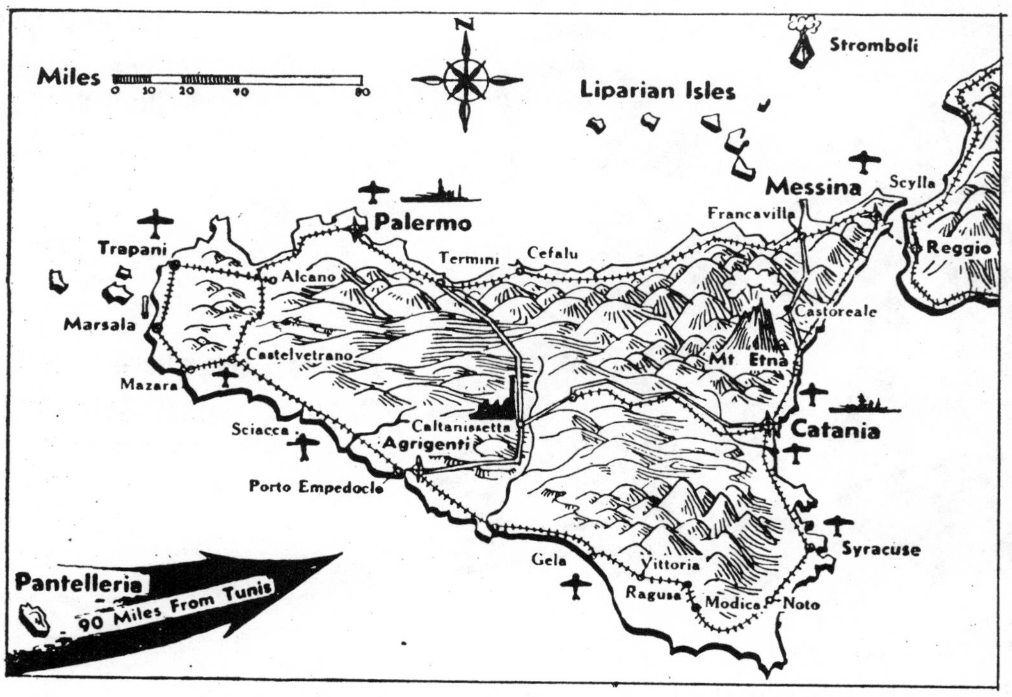

Il Duce's On The Spot; Pleads For Support

Tells People Invasion Must Be Resisted To Last Man

Axis sentries from Greece to Norway walked the rim of the European Fortress with one eye to sea and the other turned nervously inland last week as invasion tension and internal dissension, especially in weak-sister Italy, mounted to fever pitch.

At Rome, Mussolini frantically tried to jack up Italian resistance to an invasion threat and break down a growing mass indifference to Fascism; in Greece, the Germans met an outbreak of strikes, demonstrations and guerrilla activity that forced them to declare a "state of revolution" in the country; in Holland, the Swiss reported huge numbers of German troops arriving at the Dutch coast, and in France, key coastal cities of the Mediterranean and along the southern Atlantic were ordered evacuated.

Il Duce and his faltering Fascists took the spotlight, when Radio Rome Wednesday broadcast 13 days late an amazing speech delivered by Mussolini June 24 before the Fascist Party Directorate.

A strange mixture of rebuke and flattery, Mussolini's address was the most revealing to come from any totalitarian leader in the present war. He admitted that growing labor unrest, with strikes at Milan and Turin, necessitated more stringent labor compulsion. He acknowledged black markets and the failure of Party economic measures. But mostly he pleaded for a return by the Italian people to a faith in the party itself.

"The Fascist Party is still the party of the masses," he declared. "A nation of 46 millions needs be led by several thousand political leaders, helped by hundreds of thousands of collaborators inspired by the same faith. The figures concerning the numerical forces of the Party are really imposing.

"Of course there are negative and opposing elements to the Party," he admitted, "but we control all that and they will never be in a position to extirpate the regime. Where the laws in effect

(Continued on Page 8)

Air Arm Batters Island All Week

ALLIED FORCE HEADQUARTERS, July 9—Hundreds of bombing, strafing planes of the Northwest African Air Forces have kept Sicily reeling all week with unending blows at the island's air, transport and communication installations.

Stinging day and night raids have been made on the triangular island by first-line American bombers—Flying Fortresses, Mitchells, Marauders, Bostons and Baltimores—working with British night-bombing Wellington s and fighters — Lightnings, Warhawks and Spitfires.

While heavy and medium bombers were setting down tons of explosives on Sicilian targets, fight-

(Continued on Page 8)

Think It's Hot Now? Wait Till Next Month

By Cpl. JOHN M. WILLIG
(Stars and Stripes Staff Writer)

The weatherman at AFHQ, wiping his face determinedly with a sweaty old handkerchief, remarked with frayed humor that being not in Africa was all a matter of humidity, just like in New York or Wabash, Ind.

"If you think you were hot this week with the temperature mostly hitting the 100-degree mark or around there, what are you going to do in late July and August, when the temperature shoots up tc 112 along the coast and as much as 120 degrees inland?" he asked coolly.

He had to agree, though, that even the natives complained about the heat wave during the week and admitted it was a bit out of order. At Algiers, soldiers sweated as the mercury climbed to 96 degrees. Souk Ahras reported a high of 100 degrees in the shade and Constantine sweltered under a record-breaking 108 degrees on Tuesday. Farther west, the mercury dallied around the 100-degree mark, with Oran getting a 97 and Oujda a 98.

Some small comfort was forthcoming when the weatherman took that old saw about heat and humidity apart.

Actually, you won't be as hot in

(Continued on Page 8)

Radios Warn French People To Wait For Right Moment

SPECIAL COMMUNIQUE

ALLIED FORCE HEADQUARTERS, July 10—This special communique was issued here at 6 AM today:

ALLIED FORCES UNDER COMMAND OF GENERAL EISENHOWER, BEGAN LANDING OPERATIONS ON SICILY EARLY THIS MORNING. THE LANDINGS WERE PRECEDED BY ALLIED AIR ATTACK. ALLIED NAVAL FORCES ESCORTED THE ASSAULT FORCES AND BOMBARDED THE COAST DEFENSES DURING THE ASSAULT.

Simultaneously with announcement of the invasion of Sicily, Allied radio stations throughout the world broadcast a warning to the people of metropolitan France and underground workers instructing them to remain calm lest they give themselves away by premature action. The warning came from Gen. Dwight D. Eisenhower, Allied Force commander, and read:

"The United Nations Armed Forces have today launched an offensive against Sicily. It is the first stage in the liberation of the European continent. There will be others. I call on the French people to remain calm, *not* to allow themselves to be deceived by the false rumors which the enemy might circulate. The Allied radio will keep you informed on military development. I count on your sang-froid and on your sense of discipline. Do *not* be rash for the enemy is watching. Keep on listening to the Allied radio and never heed rumors. Verify carefully the news you receive. By remaining calm and by *not* exposing yourselves to reprisals through premature action you will be helping us effectively.

"When the hour of action strikes we will let you know. Till then help us by following our instructions. That is to say: keep calm, conserve your strength. We repeat: when the hour of action strikes we will let you know."

No details of the size of the attacking Allied Forces were given, and it was too early to say what kind of opposition the Allied Forces met on the initial operations. There could be little doubt, however, that the enemy would put up the stiffest opposition for such a strategic island.

As the zero hour for Sicily approached, the bombers and strafing planes of the Northwest African Air Force had the island staggering with day and night attacks that went on for a week.

Sicily's air defense had taken a terrific pounding. The relentless aerial offensive had smashed at airports and transportation centers. All the ports around the triangular island were singled out and shellacked by light, medium and heavy bombers. Varying the all-out onslaught were the fighters

(Continued on Page 8)

REV. A. A. LUCAS, NAACP BLAMED FOR DETROIT RIOT

(See Cols. 7-8)

Tuskegee Flyers Get 1st Plane

CITY EDITION

The Informer
TEXAS AND FREEMAN

50th YEAR 1893 - 1943

VOL. 48—No. 87 HOUSTON, TEXAS., SATURDAY, JULY 17, 1943 PRICE: 10 Cents

Fatally Stabbed By Wife

HOUSTON.—21-year-old Winston King died in Jefferson Davis hospital early Saturday morning in spite of doctors fight to save his life. The man was brought back to the hospital after he became worse from a stab wound received at the hands of his common-law wife during an altercation in a late Friday night argument at 1912 Jensen Drive.

Taken to Jefferson Davis hospital in a Ross-Stripling ambulance, King was treated for a stab wound in the chest and then told to go home.

Early Saturday morning the man began to complain about his chest and became so much worse that the people of the house were forced to take him back to the hospital. When King arrived at the hospital and attendants saw the condition of the man, a corps of doctors was called in and the fight to save King's life began. Despite the frantic efforts of the doctors, King died a few minutes after he was placed under treatment.

According to witnesses, King and his wife had become involved in an argument after he had returned home rather late. The common-law couple argued for some time and blows were passed between them. Mrs. King, according to witnesses, secured her knife and stabbed King one time in the chest. Mrs. King was not arrested until King died at 10 a. m. the morning following the stabbing. She was filed on for a charge of murder in Judge Reagan's court.

300 FHA Houses To Be Erected

Houston.—The local housing agency confirmed today the report that the War Housing program has authorized 300 private housing units for Negroes in the rental bracket from $31.00 to $39.99 per month in this area. They are to be built by private capital under FHA mortgage insurance in close proximity to war industries.

The Clinton Park Construction company, which has built the largest number of such houses in the past, announced not long ago that it probably would not do any building now because of the difficulty of getting help and the scarcity of material. But inasmuch as the authorization is made, it is expected that some private company will take advantage of the opportunity to build more Negro units.

Incidentally ,the War Housing Center, which has charge of the rental part of the work after construction, requested that announcement be made that there is still a shortage of rent houses, and if anybody has any for rent they should please call that office: Charter 4-1835.

TWO MEN REPORTED MISSING IN SICILIAN BATTLE, ONE THOUGHT SAFE; LIEUT. HALL MAKES HISTORY

By OLLIE STEWART

(Copyright by the Afro-American and Informer Chain of Newspapers. Reproduction in whole or in part strictly prohibited.)

Censored from Stewart. Advanced Air Base, North Africa—They are giving their all over here for somebody over there. No maybe so about it this time, Lt. Charles Hall, Princeton, Ind., Friday, July 2, in P-40 Warhawk shot a German plane out of the sky and watched it crash on the ground to become the first pilot in my fighter squadron to chalk up certain victory, it was announced officially a few hours later. Two other enemy ships were damaged and probably destroyed in the same encounter by Lts. Charles B. Ryden of New York and Walter Lawson, Newtown, Va. Two men from the unit are missing but one is thought to be safe.

The action occurred in Sicily during an early morning bomber escort mission, and Hall's victim was a FW 190, one of three who jumped him on the way home. He fought off the trio for several minutes, losing altitude and rapidly running out of ammunition after many bursts from his sizzling guns. Finally Perry crossed his sights and Hall blasted away. Down went ship and pilot in a crazy spin, belching smoke from both sides to crash and burst into flames.

It was the most vicious dogfight our boys have run into and white pilots from neighboring squadrons who took part in the mission have

(See STEWART, Page 8, Col. 5)

CHAMP WEIGHS THE BABY

Chicago, Ill.—Home on furlough from Fort Riley, Kan sas, Sergeant JOE LOUIS, heavyweight champion of the world, puts his five-month-old daughter, Jacqueline, on the scales and finds that she is "just seventeen pounds ringside." Mrs. Louis beams approval. Joe can croon a lullaby, change a didy or fix a bottle as smoothly as he can throw a right hook.—INP Photo

Reporter Calls Meet Fighting Conference

By T. JOHN WOOD

DETROIT.—(ANP) — The Name of Rev. A. A. Lucas, pastor of Good Hope Baptist church, Houston, figured prominently in an open dispute between Walter White, executive secretary of the NAACP, and A. M. Smith, feature writer for the Detroit Daily News (white) after the News reporter last week alleged that the NAACP Emergency conference here early last month stirred up discontent which resulted in the recent race riot.

Rev. Lucas' name entered into the controversy after Walter White had protested to an article in which Smith stated that the conference "sowed seeds of violence in the hearts of youths, both Negro and white" and that these "seeds fell into the kind of soil in which violence and crime breed."

Smith, in his article, which was the first of a series on crime and juvenile delinquency, alleged that the June 3 to 6 conference was a "fighting" conference and as a result, many Negro and white youth, imbued with this fighting spirit, took part in the June 21 race war.

'Quotes' Rev. A. A. Lucas

Protesting the article and the accusation against the NAACP, White declared that the conference did not play any part in causing the riot. In defense of his statement, Smith then quoted the Rev. Lucas as having said, "Down in our state of Texas we don't ask; we fight for what we want—and get it." Smith declared, in answer to White that this was "one of the fightingest speeches I have ever heard."

In a further attempt to link the N.A.A.C.P. conference with the causes of the riot, Smith wrote "let it be recalled that nearly 50 per cent of those arrested in connection with the riots were under the age

(See RIOT, Page 8, Col. 4)

REV. A. A. LUCAS

Officer Says Race Soldiers Shot Up Town

GRENADA, Miss.—Several minor racial clashes injuring a number of whites and Negroes were reported this week at Duck Hill, a small town near here. According to information received from a reliable source, race friction followed an accusation by an unnamed white woman that she had been raped by nine Negro soldiers.

It was learned from authoritative

(See OFFICER, Page 8, Col. 8)

War Is Everywhere; Martin Finds No Actual Battle-Line

By FLETCHER P. MARTIN
Informer Chain and Louisville Defender War Correspondent

SOMEWHERE IN AUSTRALIA.—During this long trek northward to the battle zones, many Negro troops have been encountered. Although miles behind the battle lines, it is their task to get the supplies northward. Technically they are behind the lines, but theoretically it has been proven that the battle line as such is non-existent; war is everywhere.

Decontamination Unit

In this area is located a Negro decontamination unit, perhaps the first of its kind in the U. S. Army. The purpose of the unit as described to this correspondent and a Yank field correspondent is to move in, if the enemy uses poison gas, and decontaminate the area so the gas will do a minimum of harm. S-Sgt. F. J. Corbett, Rocky Mount, North Carolina, supply sergeant, gave this information.

In one of the smaller, but neat camps the men talked freely about their work. They are chosen men, picked out for their unusually high IQ. ratings and today they have a crack outfit which has won citations for efficiency on maneuvers and several have toured Australia giving demonstrations to Australian and American soldiers, and to civilian defense workers.

These men wear a gas-proof suit that covers the body entirely and has a window in the front for seeing purposes. The suits look very much like those worn by deep sea divers. They can work for hours in gassed areas. Special tank trucks equipped with hose and spray guns speed the men to an area in the event of an attack. If the truck can't get through, portable cylinders of decontam-

(See MARTIN, Page 8, Col. 5)

MRS. JULIA C. HESTER

MRS. JULIA C. HESTER, a deservnig civic minded Christian woman who has spent her life trying to promote the welfare of her community, was honored recently when the board of directors of the new community center to be located in fifth ward unanimously voted to name the project Julia C. Hester House in recognition of this beloved Houston citizen.

THIS IS FREEDOM CALLING

By H. A. BULLOCK

THE NEGRO PROBLEM IS DIFFERENT—

Recent Fourth of July celebrations, filled with the idea that all men are created equal and have certain inalienable rights, reawakened our consciousness of the Christian sense of fair play that must have been in the minds of the creators of the Declaration of Independence. Those men who wrote this document during the era of 1776 lived a very simple life. There was very little sense of class difference among them and the peole whom they represented.

Since all of them were either immigrants or chilldren of immigrants, they thought of themselves as belonging to one national society in which the privileges of each one were as great as those of the other. Such Negroes as were here were accepted as slaves —beasts of burden—and were not thought of as human beings even when the constitution was framed. There was no race problem as we now know it. American society was thought of as an organization of whites, and American democracy got started with the under-

(See FREEDOM, Page 8, Col. 6)

Fifth Ward Community Center Named Julia C. Hester House For Houstonian

HOUSTON—The Board of Directors of the new Community Center to be located in the Fifth Ward voted enthusiatically and unanimously to name the project JULIA C. HESTER HOUSE in recognition of one of Houston's most beloved citizens.

Mrs. Hester a Worthy Citizen

Julia C. Hester was loved and respected by thousands throughout the city and state. She was a deserving, civic minded Christian woman who spent her life trying to promote the welfare of humanity. She came to Houston in 1893 and gave efficient service as a teacher in the public schools. Mrs. Hester was aware of the problems of

(See COMMUNITY, Page 8, Col. 5)

North Side Air Raid Drill Is Only Partially Successful

Lack of Service Reveals Need of Cooperation

With everything in readiness, and with every warden at his post at the appointed time, 8:30 p. m., Monday, July 11, the North Side air raid demonstration which took place on Quitman street between Jensen Drive and Stevens street got off to a good start. The stage was set for eight kinds of service to be demonstrated; but in the course of the thirty minutes failure of some of these to show up revealed a sore lack of cooperation and a definite need on the part of the Negroes.

The sector warden, W. J. Jensen (white), and the senior warden, John B. Gillon had done their part by having everything in readiness, and by furnishing all equipment,

(See DRILL, Page 8, Col. 3)

Man's Body Found In Front Of Estranged Wife's House

HOUSTON.—The body of James Allen Freeman, 28, of 1703 Napoleon, was found early Wednesday morning lying in a ditch in front of the home of his wife, Mrs. Hattie Freeman at 2609 Bell by a passerby. His death according to the coroner's report was due to heart failure.

Word began to spread around the community that Freeman had met with foul play when several people who viewed the body as it lay in the ditch, claimed that they saw blood over the man's face. Police were summoned to make an investigation and several people including his wife were questioned.

Judge Ragan, who held an inquest of the death of Freeman refused to render a verdict until an autospy of the dead man was held. The body was taken to Jefferson Davis hospital where doctors revealed that Freeman had died of heart failure.

In a statement to a reporter, Mrs. Freeman stated that she and her husband had been separated about three months and that in the meantime he often came around to see and talk to her. She stated that he had been to see her earlier in the week.

According to the police records an open knife was found near the body of the dead man. When questioned about this by the reporter, Mrs. Freeman said that it was customary for him to carry his knife open whenever he traveled dark streets at night. Mrs. Freeman also said that the reason that the people got excited about seeing blood on his face was due to the fact that he had shaved that night and "whenever he shaves he cut bumps on his chin." It was the results of seeing the dried blood resulting from his recent shave that caused the alarm that he had met with foul play.

According to the dead man's wife, he had been suffering from heart trouble for some time and during the five years they were married

(See BODY FOUND, Page 8, Col. 7)

Local CIO Hearing Before NLRB Scheduled July 23

By CARTER WESLEY

HOUSTON. — It seems that the local CIO is bent upon cramming achievements and victories down the throats of its tranducers until it chokes them to death. The latest cramming is the hearing before the NLRB, scheduled for July 23, to go into the matter of general raises for all of the men.

The chief issue is that after the WLB fixed and set the amount of raise that could be gotten, the Independent union, which was then functioning for the men at Hughes Tool, entered an agreement with the company to forego any right to contend for the amount the WLB had fixed as the maximum in consideration of a five-cent raise. The CIO is contending that the negotiators of the Independent union voluntarily gave away money that rightly belonged to the men from the date of the Little Steel freezing of rates until the present, and that the men need the money with the cost of living going up as it is.

Independent Sides with Company

The peculiar thing about this new movement is that the Independent union has intervened in the hearing on the side of the company Now from the layman's standpoint it looks almost as if the Independent union men are fighting themselves, when they take any step to preclude an adjustment upward of wages of all of the men at Hughes Tool. Why would they intervene against the contention of the CIO, which is now the bargaining power, even if they were mistaken, or if they are now accused of being mistaken? One will have to imagine that the Independent union negotiators are mighty mad

(See NLRB, Page 8, Col. 2)

FEPC Reports Findings In Detroit Riot; Senators Ask Probe

Haas Gives Causes Of Riot; Plans To Take Action Soon

WASHINGTON—(ANP)—Besides eliminating axis agents and the Ku Klux Klan as the procateurs in the Detroit riotings, Msgr. Francis J. Haas, chairman of the Fair Employment Practice committee, had a good deal to say about the causes of rioting, and actually gave indication that the committee might conceivably attempt to reach out and do something about it. At least, this thought is gaining currency.

There are several things which stand out like sore thumbs in the press conference Fr. Haas held last week which might give validity to this thinking.

Haas' Report

In his prepared statement, the chairman said: "The objective (of the committee) is to further the prosecution of the war, worker morale, and national unity." Further down he adds: The committee is conscious that this sound objective must be pursued where wartime crowding in houses, buses and recreation grounds have bred irritation among decent people . . ."

When asked directly, Fr. Haas said that the observation of conprimary purposes of his visit, and that he planned to prepare a memorandum on his findings. The question as to whom the memorandum would be for brought a nudge from an assistant.

Causes of Riot

He reiterated his belief that housing, recreation and city transportation are basic causes for friction, and that a recurrence of the tragedy can be prevented if the underlying causes are eliminated."

At another point in the confer-

(See PLANS, Page 8, Col. 7)

Pastor's Plea For New Riot Trials Denied

DETROIT.—(ANP) — Presiding Judge Donald M. Van Zile of recorders court last week denied a request made by the Rev. Horace A. White that new trials be granted more than 100 persons convicted for participation in the June 21 rioting here. Rev. White's request suggested that the judges, in sentencing those brought to trial during the riot, probably sent to prison innocent bystanders, and that the judges were probably frightened.

In denying the request, Judge Van Zile declared, "It is impossible to make any such blanket order as the Rev. White suggests. At no time has there been, or will there be, any change in the regular and orderly procedure which has always been followed in this court. This procedure cannot be carried at the request of any citizen or organization."

Riot Rumors Cause Jitters Among People Of Indiana Town

EVANSVILLE, Ind.—(ANP)—Soldiers, war workers, and others of the civilian population were gripped with the jitters the past week-end as sinister rumors of race war were circulated throughout the city. The fear sensation heightened with the noticeable absence from streets and boulevards of the usual overflow of soldiers from nearby Camp Breckenridge.

An "out of bounds" order issuing from the fifth corps area headquarters at Fort Hayes in Columbus, Ohio, resulted in the huddling of soldiers on leave into jeeps and trucks bound for Camp Breckenridge and the paratroop base on the outskirts of town.

Dame rumor began her work at a local war plant Friday when it was revealed that former white employees of the concern had telephoned a message to Negro employees that a contingnt of white paratroopers was planning to descend upon the city Saturday and start a riot. The soldiers were said to be moved to revenge for the alleged stabbing of a paratroop officer by three Negro youths several days ago.

Rumor piled upon rumor until it was almost accepted as a fact that the officer had died from his wounds and the paratroopers had stolen several machine guns. The whole situation created a tenseness that threatened to break out into open violence. That there was some basis for apprehension was seen in an order from the police department requiring Derbyville business men to close their stores early and civilians to remain off the streets.

Late Friday steel-helmeted mili-

(See RUMORS, Page 8, Col. 7)

NY Judge Warns Against Riots

NEW YORK. — (ANP) — Determined that insofar as the courts are concerned, there will be no riots in New York City, Judge Jonah J. Goldstein, one of the outstanding jurists in this area, in impanelling two general session grand juries for the July term, Wednesday, directed that "as a matter of great public concern" they be on their guard to prevent race riots here in New York such as occurred in Detroit.

"Rioting, particularly race-rioting of the type we have seen breaking out these days, is merely the surface manifestation of deep and underlying causes," he told the 46 grand jurors. "Mob passion does not reach a pitch sufficient to result in the taking of human life and destruction of property unless there are deep-seated causes.

"Discrimination on the basis of

(See JUDGE, Page 8, Col. 8)

Los Angeles Examiner

CHARACTER · QUALITY · AMERICA FIRST! · ENTERPRISE · ACCURACY

AN AMERICAN PAPER FOR THE AMERICAN PEOPLE · THE GREAT NEWSPAPER OF THE GREAT SOUTHWEST

Reg. U. S. Pat. Off.

Examiner Telephone RIchmond 1212 · Examiner Building, 1111 S. Broadway

VOL. XL—NO. 227 · LOS ANGELES, MONDAY, JULY 26, 1943 · CCC · Two Sections—Part I—FIVE CENTS

MUSSOLINI OUT! AXIS SPLIT SEEN

Its Different Picture Now

BENITO MUSSOLINI, left, ousted Italian Premier, shown with King Vittorio Emanuele during army maneuvers at an earlier time. The King has now assumed personal command of the nation's military forces.
—Associated Press wirephoto.

U. S. Adopts 'Wait and See' Policy; Peace With Honor Plea Expected

By Frederic Tuttle
Staff Correspondent International News Service

WASHINGTON, July 25.—Authoritative diplomatic sources in Washington tonight regarded the resignation of Premier Mussolini as the beginning of the end for Italy in the war.

The State Department adopted a "wait and see" policy as the Rome radio announced that Il Duce had turned over the reins of the government to Marshal Pietro Badoglio, with King Vittorio Emanuele assuming supreme command of Italy's armed forces.

Badoglio's assertion that the "war will continue" was believed to mean that the Italian troops will resist the Allied invasion until their new government can obtain the "peace with honor" terms suggested by President Roosevelt and British Prime Minister Churchill.

The upset of the Fascist regime came less than a week after the 500-plane American raid on Rome which knocked out railroad yards and industrial installations.

It followed by only a short period the ultimatum of the President and the Prime Minister to the Italian people to quit the war or suffer the consequences.

The resignation of Mussolini is connected directly with the successful Allied invasion of Sicily, which now is almost completely in American and British hands with Italian troops surrendering by the tens of thousands.

Responsible quarters took the view that Adolf Hitler must have informed Mussolini in their latest meeting at the time that Rome was bombed that southern Italy could not be defended.

They said that the German

(Continued on Page A, Column 4)

Italian King Names Badoglio Premier as Duce Deposed

By Thomas C. Watson
Staff Correspondent International News Service

LONDON, July 26 (Monday.)—Benito Mussolini was deposed from his Fascist dictatorship Sunday in a momentous upheaval that placed his long-time personal foe, Marshal Pietro Badoglio, and King Vittorio Emanuele III in command of the Italian government and armed forces, presaging Italy's early removal from the war.

In proclamations containing not one mention of either Germany or Fascism, the King and the marshal sought to rally the Italian people around their leadership and professed a desire to continue fighting, but spok significantly of the "grave wounds" already suffered by Italy.

The ouster of Mussolini just four days before his 60th birthday, was announced by the Rome radio late Sunday night and was immediately interpreted in the most competent London quarters as a sign that the European Axis has been rent asunder.

'Biggest Axis Bombshell of War'

One diplomatic commentator called it the "biggest Axis bombshell of the war" and added:

"One of the two pillars of the European Axis has been blown sky-high."

Whether or not Mussolini had been banished from Rome or even imprisoned remained to be seen. His ouster was widely interpreted as indicating a serious split between Italy and Germany.

The British radio early today seized the occasion to appeal to the Italian armed forces to kick the Germans out of their country and surrender to the Allies forthwith as the only way of saving Italy while General Dwight D. Eisenhower's armies are swiftly approaching the Italian mainland via Sicily.

A Reuter's Stockholm dispatch today quoted Swedish dispatches from Berlin as saying Nazi quarters had hinted that the replacement of Mussolini may be followed by "changes in Italo-German relations."

King's Manifesto Read Over Radio

This intimation of a possible break-up of the European Axis was said to have appeared in a dispatch from the German capital to the Stockholm paper Social Demokraten. The message, according to Reuters, said Mussolini's "resignation" was "no surprise" to Germany, but quoted a spokesman for the foreign office in Berlin as saying:

"We can say nothing."

The monarch called upon all Italians to "bow before the grave wounds that have rent our fatherland" to to rally behind Italy's "old institutions" as the "way to recovery."

Badoglio, Italy's foremost soldier and hero of several wars until Mussolini shelved him in 1941, declared that the "war con-

(Continued on Page A, Cols. 1-3)

Named Prime Minister

MARSHAL PIETRO BADOGLIO, newly appointed Premier of Italy, shown in typical attitude. He has a brilliant military record and is known for his loyalty to the King.
—Associated Press wirephoto.

Mussolini Ouster Fails to Halt Battering of Axis

While the ouster of Mussolini as ruler of Italy took precedence over all other war developments yesterday the armies of the Allies—on the ground and in the air—continued battering the Axis.

These were the developments:

EASTERN EUROPE— Following the record-smashing R. A. F. raid on Hamburg Saturday night, when more than 2600 tons of bombs were dropped, American bombers today battered four key points in Germany. One of the points was Hamburg. (Story on Page 2.)

MEDITERRANEAN THEATER— Allied armies continued their sweep across Sicily as the Axis defenders prepared for what is expected to be the "last battle of Sicily" on the Mt. Etna-Catania line. Meanwhile the Allied air arm battered key points in Italy, including Bologna and Leghorn. (Stories on Page 2.)

SOUTH PACIFIC THEATER— Allied bombers yesterday delivered the heaviest air blow on Munda, a communique from General MacAthur announced. More than 200 planes dropped more than 186 tons of bombs. (Story on Page 2.)

Entered as second-class matter April 15, 1931, at the post office at New Haven, Connecticut, under the act of March 3, 1879

ILLUSTRATED CURRENT NEWS

Published Monday, Wednesday and Friday by Illustrated Current News, Inc., New Haven, Conn. Subscription Annually, $20.80

July 28, 1943—No. 4666

U. S. GENERALS AT GELA

Gela, Sicily—Lt. Gen. George S. Patton, Jr., (right) calls attention to a point of interest to Brig. Gen. Theodore Roosevelt (left) as they pass along the streets of this captured town.

News Note—It is Expected That Italy Will Soon Surrender.

Entered as second-class matter April 15, 1931, at the post office at New Haven, Connecticut, under the act of March 3, 1879

ILLUSTRATED CURRENT NEWS

Published Monday, Wednesday and Friday by Illustrated Current News, Inc., New Haven, Conn. Subscription Annually, $20.80

Aug. 2, 1943—No. 4668

TIME OUT FOR LAUGHS

England — The roar of American laughter is louder than the usual roar of bomber motors as Bob Hope gives forth with the jokes at a U. S. airfield in Great Britain. There isn't a sober face in this great crowd of American air force personnel who surround the comedian.

News Note: Mussolini Reported In Jail Near Rome.

THE NOORDAM NEWS

Vol VII No. 1 — Somewhere on the Pacific — 21 August 1943

JAPS ON RUN IN NEW GUINEA

ITALY POUNDED AGAIN

ALLIED HEADQUARTERS IN NORTH AFRICA Allied aviators are now slashing at Italy's interior lifelines--her railroads. Thursday the communications center of Foggia was blasted in saturation block-buster raids while American naval forces were siezing the Aeolian Islands north of Sicily, stepping stones to the mainland. Thirty-eight enemy fighters were downed at Foggia as the Axis made a desperate effort to protect the railway city.

******

MORALE LOW IN ITALY

LONDON: Observers believe that the Allies may strike at other European objectives without waiting to polish off Italy. Meantime, Italy's morale appears to be growing steadily worse. King Victor Emanuel issued a proclamation last night to the people of Sicily which was silent about any intention to continue the war. The King told the Sicilians that although they are "cut off" from the rest of Italy and have for the present nothing but sorrow they should have faith "in a better future".

******

JAPANESE THWARTED IN SOLOMONS

GENL MACARTHUR'S HQ IN AUSTRALIA: The Japanese have made another attemp to run the American blockade of enemy bases in the Central Solomon Islands, but this effort was thwarted.

WITHDRAW FROM POSITIONS BEFORE SALAMAUA

SOUTHWEST PACIFIC THEATRE; The Japanese are on the run in the battle for the important base of Salamaua in New Guinea. General Douglas MacArthur's headquarters says the Japanese suddenly gave up positions before Salamaua from which they had long held off Americans and Australians. On Friday, the enemy withdrew from three towns close to the base. The day before, the allies had driven to within three miles of the Salamaua airdrome, by capturing Bobdurbi Ridge on the Francisco River. Possession of the Salamaua field would put the allies within fighting plane distance of Japanese bases on New Britain.

******

BASEBALL SCORES

Thursday

American League

New York	2	Cleveland	1
Detroit	10	Boston	0
St. Louis	3	Phila.	0

National League

Brooklyn	9	Chicago	2
Phila.	6	St. Louis	5

Friday

American League

New York	10	Cleveland	5
Detroit	1	Boston	0

National League

Brooklyn	6	Chicago	3
New York	3	Pitts.	2

Your buddy would like to read this paper too......Pass it along.......

Weather Outlook
Tonight,
Warmer
Temperatures today: Max., 81; Min., 59
Detailed Report on Last Page

The Kingston Daily Freeman

First in News
Local, National, Foreign
Ulster County's Leading
Advertising Medium

VOL. LXXII.—No. 259 CITY OF KINGSTON, N. Y., MONDAY EVENING, AUGUST 23, 1943. PRICE FIVE CENTS.

Hitler's Armies Leave Kharkov Stronghold; Allied Planes Destroy Salerno Rail Center

Conference Decides on Air Routes

Arrival of T. V. Soong Suggests Allies Are to Build Air Power in China

Japs Will Know

Japanese Will Learn What Nazis Know of Allied Bombings

By DOUGLAS B. CORNELL

Quebec, Aug. 23 (AP) — The belated arrival of Chinese Foreign Minister T. V. Soong at the Quebec war councils suggested today that decisions had been made to build up air squadrons in the eastern bulge of China to bomb enemy life lines in the China Sea and the Japanese mainland itself.

Soong flew in from Washington late yesterday, at the request of President Roosevelt. Presidential Secretary Stephen Early emphasized that his discussions with the Chief Executive and Prime Minister Churchill of Britain "will have to do with the plans for the war on Japan."

That fact gave support to the idea that Allied strategy perfected here calls for powerful aerial thrusts at the Japanese from bases in Eastern China.

Pure logic, and these additional facts, also weighed in favor of an agreement to wreck the enemy supply route in the China Sea and give Japan a sample of the destruction already heaped on ports and industrial cities of Germany:

President Roosevelt has proclaimed publicly the determination of the Allies to send up aerial armadas from China to scourge the Japanese.

China is known to have asked that the bomber force now operating in her eastern zone be increased perhaps 10 times for exactly that purpose.

A resurvey of air transport facilities operating out of India is said to have shown that it would be possible to supply and service three to four times the number of bombers presently in Eastern China. Moreover, the end of the Sicilian campaign, may release additional transport planes for the India-China ferry route.

If the war is to be brought to bear on Japan itself, which must be done eventually in any event, she is most vulnerable to attacks from the west, where heavy bombers can make the round trip from China.

The blasting of Japanese shipping out of the China Sea would soften the enemy's resistance all around her defense perimeter and help cripple war industries at home; the China Sea route is used not only to supply Burma, the Netherlands East Indies and even more advanced Japanese army outposts, but also to bring back to Japan the raw materials of warfare acquired in these conquered regions.

Secretary of the Navy Knox, whose main interest is in the Pacific war theatres, where navy men for the most part are in command, arrives today on the scen of the Quebec conference.

Soong was brought to Quebec for a purpose, and obviously he would not have been invited to participate in discussions with Roosevelt and Churchill on the next to the last day of the conference if they merely had bad news for him or if any far-reaching decisions on the conduct of the war in the Pacific remained on the agenda.

Reds Give Views

Pravda Says Anglo Isles Should Be Main Base for Invasion

Moscow, Aug. 23 (AP)—Pravda, the Communist newspaper, said today that the British Isles should be "the main base for invasion of the continent."

"A crushing blow upon Germany is almost impossible to conceive without utilizing the enormous strategic advantage of the British Isles." Pravda asserted.

Invasion from England, the newspaper added, could be supported by a strong aerial fighter force as well as Army and Navy bombers. It estimated 20 times fewer ships would be required to land and supply forces in western Europe than would be needed for an invasion from the Mediterranean.

Japanese Lose Last Foothold in North America

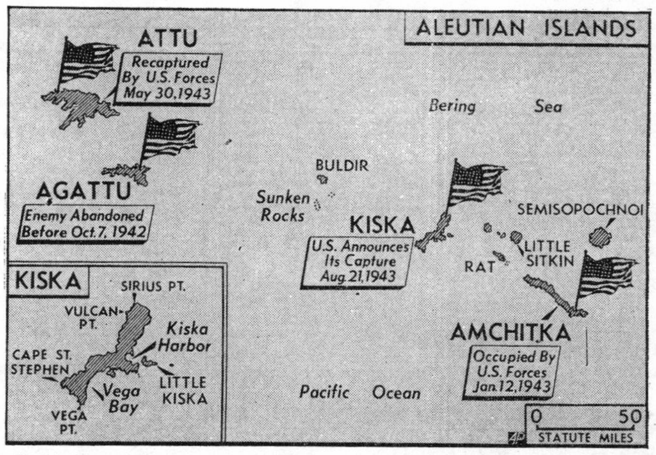

Here is the step-by-step story of American control over island bases of Attu, Agattu, and Kiska, once Japanese bases in the Aleutians. Amchitka was never occupied by the Japs before it became a U. S. base.

Science Has Done Miraculous Job in Sicilian Campaign

Medicos Were Within Gun Range and Showed Steady Nerves in Doing Work

By DON WHITEHEAD

Allied Headquarters in North Africa, Aug. 23 (AP)—Medical science moved up with range of the guns of the enemy during the Sicilian campaign to perform miracles of surgery which undoubtedly saved many lives.

Along the dusty mountain roads field medicos set up tented hospitals—often with their own artillery roaring about their ears and frequently with enemy shells bursting nearby.

It took steady nerves to stand in those shelters and operate on wounded men. Teams of skilled surgeons, however, showed it could be done, and thus a new technique of "front line surgery" was perfected by the U. S. Seventh Army.

Army authorities say it worked —at peak efficiency."

This new phase of medical care for battle casualties resulted from a modification of the original casualty evacuation setup. Under the original setup the wounded were transported by ambulance to operating stations five or six miles behind the front, and no matter how carefully or rapidly they were evacuated were subject to a certain degree of shock.

The "front line surgery setup" made it possible for them to receive expert attention within one or two miles of the enemy guns, and the minutes saved resulted in saving a proportionate number of lives.

"The establishment of these complete operating units," said Col. Edward D. Churchill of Boston, Mass., surgical consultant with the surgeons office for the North Africa theatre, "did away with the shock and lapse of time we formerly had to deal with."

Each operating unit was equipped with modern sterilizers, tables, instruments and batteries of lights, and functioned independently.

The front line stations gave treatment for severe shock, compound fractures, abdominal and chest wounds, head wounds, performed amputations and handled cases of gangrene and uncontrollable hemorrahage.

A large share of the credit for their success of course, goes to the first aid men working with the troops in the lines and the litter bearers who brought the wounded out under enemy fire. Much of this evacuation work had to be done at night.

Too much praise, however, cannot be given the surgeons who worked under the most trying conditions in their front line stations.

One day four German planes dived to bomb and strafe a vehicle stalled near one of these units. Clouds of dust and smoke rolled over the operating tent.

When the attack was over, I was among those who rushed over to see what damage had been done to the hospital. We found that shrapnel had sliced holes in the tent, but inside the surgeons were going camly about their work as though nothing had happened.

Frank Walker Will Meet With New York Democrats

Postmaster General Will Discuss Nomination of Men to Take Up Candidacy

New York, Aug. 23 (AP)—Frank C. Walker, postmaster general and National Democratic chairman, will meet here today with New York Democratic leaders to discuss nomination of a candidate for lieutenant governor but no announcement was made as to the identity of the group invited to the meeting.

State Democratic Chairman James A. Farley, however, had not been asked up to last night. He has called a conference of state leaders for tonight in an effort to decide upon a candidate to be submitted to tomorrow's state committee session here.

The entrance of Walker into the state scene was said by State committee members to indicate that he and other high-ranking party leaders regard the coming election to name a successor to the late Thomas W. Wallace as a barometer for the 1944 presidential race.

Political observers also looked upon Walker's visit here as pointing to personal interest by President Roosevelt in his home state's election this year.

The latest name put forward for consideration as the Democratic candidate is that of former Lieutenant Governor M. William Bray, of Utica, now State Public Service Commissioner.

Other mentioned for the nomination include Lithgow Osborne of Auburn, former State Conservation Commissioner now assistant to former Governor Herbert H. Lehman, director of Foreign Relief and Rehabilitation; and Owen D. Young, chairman of the General Electric Company.

Mayor Joseph J. Kelly of Buffalo; William H. Morgan, Cortland County Democratic chairman; Mayor Vincent Corrou of Utica; State Senator John J. Dunnigan of The Bronx; Brooklyn Borough President John Cashmore; Assemblyman Irwin Steingut and Representative Matthew J. Merritt.

Meanwhile, Democratic leaders kept in mind the American Labor Party's nomination Saturday of Joseph V. O'Leary as its candidate for lieutenant governor. The A.L.P. voted a resolution permitting withdrawal of O'Leary if either the Democrats or Republicans named a candidate deemed favorable to labor by A.L.P. leaders.

Republicans have not yet decided upon a candidate for lieutenant governor and will nominate tomorrow in Albany. Leading candidates for the G.O.P. nomination are Secretary of State Thomas J. Curran, New York county chairman, and State Senator Joe R. Hanley of Perry, Wyoming county, now acting lieutenant governor.

Dewey Will Speak

Buffalo, N. Y., Aug. 23 (AP)—Governor Thomas E. Dewey will be the principal speaker tonight at a dinner climaxing a three-day celebration of incorporation of the Federation of Orthodox Greek Catholic Churches primary jurisdictions in North America. Articles incorporating the federation were signed Saturday under authority of a law signed by Gov. Dewey on March 25.

Landing Gear on Plane Stuck While Over City Sunday

Pilot Searches for Landing Field here as Transport Loses Its Altitude While Over City

Sunday morning a large transport plane circled low over Kingston several times and apparently made attempts to land at the Kingston Airport but the pilot was unable to set the big ship down because of the wires which run near the port. After circling the city at a low altitude several times the plane set off in a westerly direction and it is reported that it later landed at Wurtsboro. Sheriff Anderson sent men from the sheriff's office to the field in case the plane landed.

During its visit to the city the plane flew several times low over the Wiltwyck golf course but made no attempt to land there. It was reported that the pilot was having trouble with one of the motors and apparently sought to make an emergency landing, although when the plane circled over town shortly after 11 o'clock there was no apparent difficulty noticeable to observers on the ground.

Local police also reported the plane to the Kingston observation post when calls were received at headquarters.

At the Kingston Aircraft Warning Service Center atop the Governor Clinton Hotel, the plane was spotted as it dropped down. There it was stated the plane was en route toward New York city when its landing gear became stuck. The pilot attempted to lower the landing gear and circled the city several times while working on the landing gear. During that time the plane lost altitude as the

(Continued on Page Two)

Governor Dewey Says State Labor Has Kept Its Pledge Not to Strike

Buffalo, N. Y., Aug. 23 (AP) — Governor Thomas E. Dewey told the 80th annual convention of the State Federation of Labor today "there have been no industrial strikes of any moment" in New York state since Pearl Harbor and added "labor in this state has kept its no-strike pledge."

In an address prepared for delivery before the opening convention session, Governor Dewey said "teamwork" was responsible for the lack of labor conflict.

Recalling his election last fall when he became the first Republican named to the governorship in 20 years, Dewey said that with the change "there was not one second's interruption of the public service or the production of goods, services and food for the war."

"In this critical year we have had no contest between the executive and the legislative branches of the state government," he added. "We have had no squabbling between department heads in the public prints, or, * * * in private. In order that the nation might fight better abroad we made certain that in this state there should be no fighting at home."

Federal regulations governing hours, wages and conditions of employment in large measure have superseded the functions of collective bargaining, Dewey continued, adding "in time of total war such an abridgement of our rights is probably inescapable."

"But it is a condition which can only be justified by the sacrifices of war," he declared. "We are fighting to make sure that such totalitarian conditions cannot exist in time of peace."

"The hard-won rights of labor which have been abridged by wartime controls are as fundamental as freedom of speech and freedom of the press. Like these other rights, they must be restored intact to a people who have temporarily yielded them in the cause of freedom. * * *"

Allied Siege Guns Pound Salamaua From 2 Miles

Kiska Seizure Clears Way for Attack on Japan; Heavy Blows May Fall

(By The Associated Press)

Allied siege guns blasted the Japanese stronghold at Salamaua in New Guinea today as enemy troops retreated deeper into their last circle of defenses, and dispatches from Gen. Douglas Mac Arthur's headquarters said the fall of the big air base appeared almost within sight.

From newly captured ridge positions, American and Australian gunners turned their fire on the enemy at a range of only two miles, and Allied troops moved up all along the semi-circular front.

Meanwhile, United Nations military chiefs agreed that the bloodless conquest of Kiska in the Aleutians had placed the Allies on the shortest route to Toyko.

"The Jap is on the run," said Lieut.-Gen. John L. DeWitt, commander of the western defense command.

"The Jap navy is in hiding, dispersed. The reoccupation of Kiska has cleared our shortest highway to the Japanese empire."

Similar expressions broadly hinting that the Allies may be poised to strike heavy blows against Japan came from Vice-Admiral Thomas C. Kinkaid, commander in the North Pacific, and Maj.-Gen. William C. Butler, commander of the 11th Army Air Force.

"We have completed our northern road to Japan," Admiral Kinkaid said.

"Our chain or air and naval bases will protect our surface vessels and shipping units two-thirds of the way to Toyko."

Gen. Butler declared the way was now open for the operation of a multiple-jawed pincer closing on the enemy in the Pacific.

In Quebec, scene of momentous deliberations by President Roosevelt and Prime Minister Churchill, the arrival of Chinese Foreign Minister T. V. Soong was seen as heralding a new Allied campaign to bomb Japan's lifelines in the China Sea and the Japanese mainland itself.

Dispatches from Quebec said newly-perfected Allied strategy would apparently call for powerful aerial thrusts at the Japanese from bases in Eastern China, and Presidential Secretary Stephen Early emphasized that Soong's discussions with Mr. Roosevelt and Mr. Churchill could center on "plans for the war on Japan."

While Salamaua tottered, American jungle fighters in the Solomons cleaned out a Japanese pocket of resistance on Baanga Isle, seizing field guns with which the enemy had been shelling Munda airfield on nearby New Georgia Island.

A Toyko broadcast, unconfirmed by Allied sources, asserted that Japanese troops defending Kolombangara Island, a few miles north of New Georgia, "foiled landing attempts by United States forces at dawn yesterday."

The broadcast said the landing attempt was made by about 15 barges and torpedo boats.

Carriers In Mediterranean

London, Aug. 23 (AP) — The Vichy radio, broadcasting a dispatch from Algeciras, Spain, said today that five aircraft carriers entered Gibraltar late yesterday and that four of them headed into the Mediterranean during the night. The broadcast was recorded by The Associated Press.

Several Hundred Cars Stalled Here In Gas Shortage

Vacationists Abandon Cars and Return by Bus or Train; No Gas Sign Hanging Out

Many people who came to Ulster county and adjacent summer resort sections of the Catskills by car found it impossible to secure gasoline enough to get back home during the past week-end and many boarding houses today reported that guests who were compelled to get back to business had abandoned their cars and returned by bus or train. Other guests who were fortunate enough to get an extension of their vacation remained to await a supply of gasoline to get them back home.

It was estimated that several hundred cars were stalled in this area at boarding houses while others who ventured out on a chance of getting gasoline on the road were forced to abandon their cars when gas ran out and proceed home as best they could.

A very serious gasoline shortage developed during the past week in this area when August quotas, cut 25 per cent, became exhausted and the demand went up as vacationists with "vacation permits" thronged to the area by car.

At the Nevele Country Club in Ellenville, Ben Slutsky said guests had abandoned about 25 cars when their tanks went dry and returned to the city by any available means of transportation. Many of them doubled up with more fortunate drivers and in some cases where drivers of two cars had insufficient gas to operate both cars the gas was transferred to one car and the return journey made in one car while the other car was left to be driven back later.

In practically all sections of the county the "no gas" sign was out over the week-end and where stations had a small amount of gas it

(Continued on Page Two)

Local Men Are Fined in Catskill

Charged by Police With Being Common Gamblers

The Etna Club, located on Bronson street, Catskill, was raided Saturday afternoon by State Troopers working out of the Albany office, and racing sheets, racing board, and other equipment was seized together with what cash was found in the building.

The place, it is charged, was operated by the Ruzzo Brothers, and they and five employes were placed under arrest and arraigned before Police Justice John T. Whittaker in Catskill on a charge of being common gamblers. The justice imposed fines of $50 each which were paid.

According to the authorities the Etna Club was known as a horse room, where bets could be placed on the races.

The raiders were led by Inspector Edward O. Hageman and Lieut. H. A. Keator of Troop G at Albany, and eight State Troopers.

The amount in cash seized was reported to be $1,200.

As the State Troopers took over the club all of the customers were lined up and their names requested. The names were checked by the troopers requiring each customer to produce his draft registration card.

Some of the customers, it was said, gave fictious names which were quickly checked when they were forced to produce their draft cards. After taking the names of all the customers, which included 30 women, they were allowed to leave.

Seven Arrested

The seven men arrested in the raid, according to the State Troopers barracks at West Coxsackie, were:

Victor Ruzzo of 670 Broadway, Kingston.

Guerino Ruzzo of 670 Broadway, Kingston.

Eugene Robert Harrison of the Saulpaugh Hotel, Catskill, formerly of 190 Clinton avenue, Kingston.

George Henry Schoonmaker of 116 Hudson avenue, Poughkeepsie.

Amedo Cercone of 622 Broadway, Kingston.

Floyd Eaton Goodrich of Athens.

William Joseph Macarelli of 44 Grandview avenue, Catskill.

Appointed

Andrei A. Gromyko (above) has been appointed Russian ambassador to the United States, relieving Maxim Litvinoff the Moscow radio announced. Gromyko has been serving as counselor of the Soviet embassy in Washington, D. C.

Litvinoff Recall Has No Bearing on Quebec's Sessions

However, Speculation Is That Russia Is Not Pleased at Lack of European Front

By JOHN M. HIGHTOWER

Quebec, Aug. 23 (AP)—As nearly as it could be accomplished without a fortright official statement, the recall of Maxim Litvinoff as Soviet ambassador to Washington was divorced today from proceedings of the British-American war conference here.

Moscow's purpose in making known at this time that Litvinoff would not return to the United States remained obscure in the absence of an explanation from the Russian capital, but the understanding of American officialdom regarding the incident was made clear by an authority closely associated with the Quebec conference.

His statement was that the replacement of Litvinoff by Andrei A. Gromyko, embassy counsellor and charge d'affaires in Washington, was not connected in any way with the conference. The fact that Litvinoff would not go back to Washington had been known to officials in the American capital for weeks, it was brought out, but the matter was one for Russian, not American, announcement.

In relation to the Quebec meeting and the fact that Russia has no representation here, the same authority said that again he could see no significance.

The questioning was occasioned by speculation here, as well as in dispatches from London, that Russia was replacing Litvinoff as a gesture of disapproval with the work of British-American leaders and also as a means of emphasizing her repeated demands for an invasion of western Europe.

The real purposes of Litvinoff's withdrawal, of course, could merely be guessed at. The possibilities mentioned in discussion here, outside the second front speculation, were mainly concerned with the theory that he was needed for some other assignment.

Moscow broadcast the announcement of Litvinoff's recall early yesterday and newspapers there published a brief notice on the back pages. Indication was given of a new assignment for Litvinoff, but he retained the title of Vice Commissar for Foreign Affairs.

Treasury Receipts

Washington, Aug. 23 (AP)—The position of the treasury August 20: Receipts, $86,327,110.24; expenditures, $333,088,881.62; net balance, $8,004,538,660.77; working balance included, $7,241,853,700.08; customs receipts for month, $25,564,565.36; receipts fiscal year (July 1), $4,137,205,823.94; expenditures fiscal year, $12,239,451,364.66; excess of expenditures, $8,102,245,540.72; total debt, $147,497,137,401.70; increase over previous day, $59,010,876.04; gold assets, $22,291,966,599.78.

2,000th Plane Completed

Long Beach, Calif., Aug. 23 (AP) —The army today let the Douglas Aircraft Company make a proud announcement—it has completed its 2,000th military cargo and troop transport plane. Production of the twin-engined craft has increased so rapidly, said a company statement, that a day's output now equals a week's output of a few months ago.

3rd Bitter Setback In Few Weeks

Fourth Time the 'Soviet Pittsburgh' Changed Hands, Twice Nazis Seized It

Battle of Italy

Italian Newspapers Say Germany Is Blocking Withdrawal

By ROGER GREENE
(Associated Press War Editor)

Adolf Hitler's armies were announced to have evacuated the great Ukraine stronghold at Kharkov before dawn today, fleeing through a 13-mile-wide escape gap toward the Dnieper river in a retreat marking their third bitter setback in recent weeks.

Previously, Belgorod and Orel had fallen to the triumphant Red armies.

D.N.B., the official German news agency, gave this account of the withdrawal:

"In the course of last night German troops have evacuated Kharkov after having destroyed all vital installations in the town and without being pressed by the enemy.

"Since the town has changed hands several times in the course of the fighting, it does not represent any longer a valuable center of traffic and supply.

"German positions are being considerably shortened and improved by the evacuation."

It was the fourth time the city, Russia's third largest and known as the "Soviet Pittsburgh," had changed hands. Twice the Germans had seized it, and twice the Russians have stormed back to regain it.

Other events at-a-glance:

Battle of Italy — Allied warplanes virtually destroy Italian rail center at Salerno, shoot down 28 Axis aircraft, big-scale Allied raids devastate rail network in Naples area, set stage for isolation of southern Italy.

Italian newspapers for first time openly admit German pressure blocks Italy's withdrawal from war; Swiss reports say German troops flooding into Italy through Brenner Pass.

European air war — R.A.F. bombers return to assault on Germany, pound chemical works at Leverkusen near Cologne; German radio says raiders also hit Duesseldorf in Rhineland.

Quebec — Roosevelt-Churchill war council nears end; experts forecast Allied campaign to bomb Japanese lifelines in China Sea and Nipponese mainland itself.

The Nazi evacuation of Kharkov, 400 miles south of Moscow and 260 miles east of the Ukraine capital at Kiev, was announced in a Berlin overseas broadcast, but the Germans at home were told that "there is nothing new."

Subsequently, however, the German high command acknowledged the loss of Kharkov in a broadcast for domestic consumption, but asserted that the city "today is only a heap of ruins" and that it was evacuated "in the course of planned detaching movements."

The big steel center, heart of a bristling system of hedgehog defenses, served the Germans as their mightiest base in all southern Russia and was the springboard of the German 1942 summer offensive that swept to the gates of Stalingrad.

Berlin's acknowledgement that

(Continued on Page Two)

115 Cars Smashed

Medium Bombers Hit Rail Yards; Heavy Bombers Are Active

New Delhi, Aug. 23 (AP)—United States B-25 Mitchell medium bombers smashed more than 115 freight cars—a record number—in raids on railroad yards at Sagaing, Mandalay, and Ywataung yesterday, while heavy bombers hit Japanese installations at Monywa, a Tenth Airforce communique said today.

Damage also was reported after forays in the Meiktila area, along the Chindwin river north of Alon, at Pakokku and against the Pagoda Point landing grounds south of Rangoon.

All aircraft and crews returned safely.

Entered as second-class matter April 15, 1931, at the post office at New Haven, Connecticut, under the act of March 3, 1879

ILLUSTRATED CURRENT NEWS

Published Monday, Wednesday and Friday by Illustrated Current News, Inc., New Haven, Conn. Subscription Annually, $20.80

Aug. 27, 1943—No. 4679

YANKS CHARGE MAIN STREET

Messina, Sicily—An American infantry patrol is shown hustling down a main street here, as the last Axis outpost on the island fell to Allied invaders. The building (left foreground) is the Bank of Sicily. This photo was radioed from Algiers.

News Note — Invasion Plan Ready As Parley Ends In Quebec.

2¢ **DAILY MIRROR** 2¢
Member of the Associated Press
BUY WAR BONDS 10% EVERY PAY DAY
WEATHER COOL (Details on Page 2)
3 Cents Outside City Limits
Vol. 20. No. 62 RRRR NEW YORK, FRIDAY, SEPTEMBER 3, 1943 FINAL 6 A.M.★★★★

EXTRA

ALLIES LAND IN ITALY

ALLIED HQ., North Africa, Friday, Sept. 3 (AP). — Allied troops stormed across the narrow Strait of Messina today to land in Italy and launch the long-heralded invasion of the European Continent.

A brief announcement from allied headquarters disclosed that allied troops had set foot on the continent and revealed the invasion force was spearheaded by the crack British 8th Army, veterans of smashing victories over the Axis in North Africa.

The landings were preceded by days of violent aerial bombardment which knocked out Axis railway communications between southern and northern Italy and reduced Axis positions on the toe of the Italian boot to a shambles.

Canadian troops were included in the attacking forces, Allied headquarters disclosed.

The new blow was struck about dawn today.

Invasion of the continent came quickly on the heels of the cleanup of the Sicilian campaign, begun at dawn July 10 and brought to a victorious conclusion 38 days later with all Axis troops either killed, routed or prisoners.

A special communique, announcing the mainland landings said:

"Allied forces of General Eisenhower continue their advance. British and Canadian troops of the Eighth Army, supported by allied sea and air power attacked across the Strait of Messina early today and landed on the mainland of Italy."

As in the Sicilian landings, powerful Allied air fleets gave protection to the landing troops.

Both American and British fliers took part in the air cover that accompanied the landing.

By moving across the Strait of Messina from the eastern shore of Sicily, the Allied forces had only a few miles of water to cross. The strait at its narrowest point at the extreme northeastern corner of Sicily is only a little over two miles wide and can be crossed by fast boat in about 20 minutes.

The announcement of the landing was issued here shortly after 7 a. m. (1 a. m., Eastern War Time.)

It was recalled that Canadian troops had been withdrawn from

(Continued on Back Page)

BLUE STREAK EDITION
Boston Traveler
New England's Largest Evening Circulation Complete Associated Press and United Press Wire Services
EST. 1825 — 119th YEAR — NO. 55 WEDNESDAY, SEPTEMBER 8, 1943 • 36 PAGES 3 CENTS

VICTORY EXTRA

ITALY QUITS!

Surrender Is Unconditional

Eisenhower Grants Armistice

ALLIED HEADQUARTERS IN NORTH AFRICA, Sept. 8 (AP)—Gen. Dwight D. Eisenhower today announced the unconditional surrender of Italy in the greatest victory for Allied arms in four years of war.

Gen. Eisenhower announced he had granted a military armistice---approved by Russia, as well as Britain and the United States---to the war-sick, tottering junior Axis partner being chewed by invasion.

A MOTHER REJOICES—Mrs. Lucia Martini of Prince street, North End, had a special reason for jubilation over Italy's surrender. As indicated by th eservice flag, she has two sons in uniform. At her left is a picture of one.

EUROPEAN FORTRESS CRACKED

Hitler's "European Fortress" was cracked, the way was opened for new offensives, the course of World War II immeasurably shortened.

Surrender of Italian armed forces "unconditionally" was made by the government of Marshal Pietro Badoglio, successor of Benito Mussolini, the architect of Fascism.

Thus the Casablanca "unconditional surrender" ultimatum received its first application.

MILITARY ARMISTICE GRANTED

Announcing the brilliant news, Eisenhower who led the Allied triumph in Tunisia and Sicily as well, declared:

"The Italian government has surrendered its armed forces unconditionally, the terms of which have been approved by the governments of the United Kingdom, the United States and the Union

(Continued on Page Twenty-three)

No Manpower Shortage Seen In This Area

Capital Official Reports on Check

Mobilization of Greater Boston's essential workers in a 48-hour minimum work week, announced in an address last night by Leo J. Kowal, Boston director of the War Manpower Commission, was qualified somewhat today by Kowal's superior, Regional Director Joseph A. Smith, who added a "probably," but Kowal insisted "the date has been set."

In Washington, William Haber of the staff of Paul V. McNutt, national head of WMC, said that Kowal had made a recommendation that Boston be named a critical labor area Oct. 1. but that there had been no final decision on whether the recommendation will be approved. The decision, he said, is due later this month.

Later, Haber reported that a further check showed no indication from the WMC's current labor analysis that Boston will be placed in Group 1, or area of acute labor shortage.

Haber aded that there was not even an indication that Boston should be placed in Group 2, or stringent labor area where acute labor shortage may occur within six months. On the basis of Kowal's recommendation, a change to Group 2 may be considered later this month, if latest analysis then warrants it, Haber suggested.

Smith issued a formal statement in which he said: "In the event that recruitments do not meet labor needs in Boston it will probably be necessary to extend the 48-hour

(Continued on Page Two)

U. S. Treasury Balance

WASHINGTON, Sept. 8—Balance today, $5,574,959,463.
Customs receipts, $6,025,074.

Traveler Index

OTHER NEWS AND PICTURES ON ITALIAN SURRENDER ON PAGES 4, 10, 21 AND 23.

Boston Jubilant Over Surrender Of Italians

Boston was a pandemonium of loudspeaker announcements, chiming bells and fire engine whistles as word reached the city of the unconditional surrender of Italy.

Mayor Tobin, in Wianno with his family, hurriedly telephoned John J. Walsh, executive director of the Boston Committee on Public Safety, ordering him to make the announcement over the 29-station air raid alarm system throughout the city.

DAY OF JUBILATION

Meanwhile, City Council President Thomas J. Hannon, as acting mayor in Tobin's absence, requested Fire Chief Samuel J. Pope to have fire apparatus at all stations driven out into the streets and the bells rung and sirens sounded.

Said Hannon: "I proclaim this a day of public jubilation in Boston. The unconditional surrender of Italy means the saving of tens of thousands of American lives."

The loud-speaker announcements consisted of the ringing of chimes, followed by the announcement of the surrender, repeated three times, then a verse of "Columbia, the Gem of the Ocean," the announcement again, and, finally, a verse of "God Bless America."

CHAPEL BELLS RING

Pedestrians throughout the city gathered in little knots, looking toward the buildings from the top of which the announcement was coming. Principal stations for the air-raid system are the courthouse at Pemberton square, the United Shoe Machinery Corporation building, the New England Mutual building, the Christian Science Monitor building and the Sears - Roebuck plant.

The bells of King's Chapel, at Tremont and School streets, were one of the first to start ringing out the good news.

Bars and taverns were scenes of happy, back-slapping, convivial confusion. Total strangers embraced. Newsboys were paid nickels and

(Continued on Page Twenty-three)

Italian Morale Broken by Bombs

By RICHARD G. MASSOCK
(Chief of the former Rome bureau of the Associated Press)

WASHINGTON, Sept. 8 (AP)—An Italian people broken in morale by bombs and defeats on land, sea and in the air, capitulated to Allied might today to lop off the weakest Axis partner but leaves for the moment unanswered:

How much of Italian soil will the Nazi forces of Hitler attempt to hold? What of the future of the Balkans?

Italy's capitulation, announced from North Africa by Gen. Dwight D. Eisenhower, probably shortened

Continued on Page Twenty-three

Italian Bulletins

LONDON, Sept 8 (UP)—The Exchange Telegraph agency quoted "reliable information" from Ankara today that Benito Mussolini is seriously ill with cancer and surgical intervention my be necessary. Mussolini has been reported variously in a Roman villa and on an island off Sardinia in government custody.

LONDON, (AP)—The German International Information Bureau reported today that tho big convoys totalling 200 freighters and transports were moving off Italy and that their presence "suggests American troops are aboard to carry through yet another landing." The dispatch said "considerable American and British shipping movements" had been observed north of Sicily and west of northern Calabria.

(Continued on Page Twenty-three)

'War' Shares Break In Stock Market

NEW YORK, Sept. 8 (AP)—War shares declined generally today from 25 cents to as much as $2 a share in the Stock Exchange after the announcement of Italy's capitulation, but a number of the so-called "peace stocks" rose almost as sharply.

The Italian news brought a considerable amount of liquidation in speculative commodity markets, no-

(Continued on Page Twenty-three)

RACE RESULTS
(On Page Twenty-Nine)

The Weather

U. S. Official Forecast
RAIN AND COOLER TONIGHT
Temperature at 3:30 P. M. 69
Sun rises 6:16; Sun sets 7:07
High tide 6:06 A. M., 6:29 P. M.
Dimout 8:07 P. M., 5:40 A. M.

Stars to Entertain 14,000 Store Employes at Garden

WASHINGTON, Sept. 8—President Roosevelt will open the third war loan drive with a 10-minute address tonight about 9:40 (EWT). The President will speak during an hour's program which begins at 9 P. M.

Stars of the footlights and the microphone will entertain 14,000 Boston retail store employes tonight at a "night before" rally in Boston Garden, launching the Third War Loan Bond Drive.

The guests, for whom admission is free, will have the seriousness of speeches on the bond drive lightened by the appearance of stars like Walter O'Keefe, who will be master of ceremonies; Philip Morris' "John-

(Continued on Page Twenty-three)

Welles Won't Talk But Shows Delight

BAR HARBOR, Me., Sept. 8 (UP)—Undersecretary of State Sumner Welles, who has been vacationing here for two weeks, said today when told of the unconditional surrender of Italy:

"I have made it a point while here to make no comment of any sort on any subject."

But he added, with a chuckle, "You can well imagine my feelings—they're probably much like yours."

NOW FOR HITLER!

Adolf Hitler was at top of his career when this picture was taken in 1937. His speeches were carried by radio all over the world and Americans listened eagerly to every word. Now Adolf isn't talking much.

AMERICA FIRST!

Baltimore American

AN AMERICAN PAPER FOR THE AMERICAN PEOPLE

The Largest Sunday Circulation in the Entire South

Entered as second-class matter at Baltimore Postoffice.

Est. 1773 Vol. CCLXX SUNDAY, SEPTEMBER 19, 1943 PRICE 15 CENTS

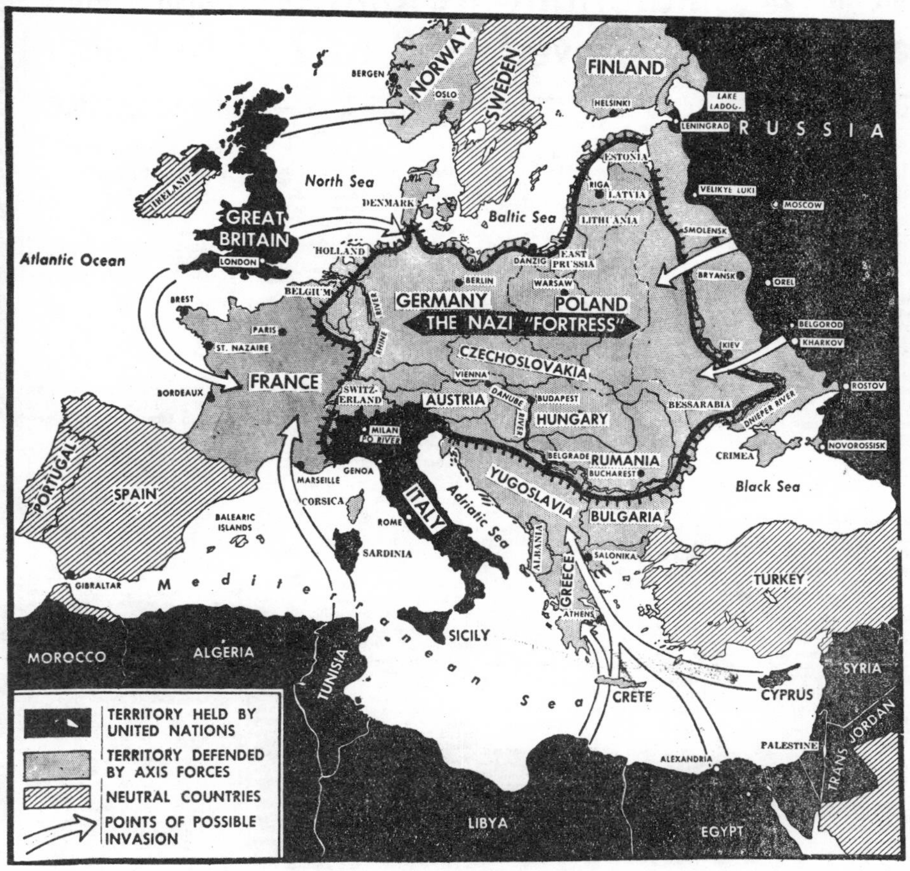

MAP shows how Allies may drive into Germany.

26 Days Left For You To Mail A Christmas Gift Overseas

By FLORENCE WESSELS
(Universal Service.)

NEW YORK, Sept. 18.—Only 26 days left in which to get off those Christmas gifts for our boys overseas!

That applies whether you are playing September Santa Claus to a service man in your own family or whether, like many thousands of other big-hearted Americans, you are "adopting" some soldier for Christmas Day under the nation-wide plan initiated by the William Randolph Hearst newspapers.

It's pretty bad to be in a far-off land on Christmas Day and to see other fellows opening their gifts around you—and to have none to open of your ownn.

But under the Hearst newspapers' "Goodfellows-Gifts for Soldiers" plan that doesn't need to happen.

FOLLOW DIRECTIONS.

Just follow directions, given elsewhere, on obtaining the name of some "forgotten soldier" in your neighborhood. Then make out your gift list, do your shopping, prepare your parcel according to postal regulations, and mail it. And, above all, mail it early—before October 15—sooner, if possible!

It was at first thought that most of those joining in the Hearst gift program would be people who have no soldiers or sailors of their own to remember. But experience has shown that many are not only sending Christmas gifts to their own friends and loved ones, but are finding time to look after still another service man.

For instance, there's Mrs. Emma Van Coutren of 143 East Thirty-ninth street, New York city. Smiling, plucky Mrs. Van Coutren has seven sons and three daughters in service. Four of the sons and one of the daughters, a WAC, are overseas.

"ADOPTS" ANOTHER.

Well—Mrs. Van Coutren not only has shopped and mailed already for all the members of her overseas family, but is now busy preparing another parcel for a soldier she never saw!

She subscribes enthusiastically to the Hearst newspapers program, saying:

"I know just how one of my boys or girls would feel if he or she was forgotten on Christmas Day. And I don't want any American boy to go through that.

"I'm sure all the mothers in America will be grateful to Mr. Hearst and his newspapers for sponsoring this wonderful and thoughtful Christmas undertaking on behalf of our boys overseas."

Many Army wives are sending Xmas parcels under the "goodfellow" program. This, of course, is in addition to sending big parcels to their husbands, and **sending them early**, if the husband happens to be overseas.

Glenn Killam, fifteen-month-old son of Capt. Fred G. Killam, is the "goodfellow" in the Killam home at 610 Victory boulevard, Staten Island, N. Y.

Of course, his pretty mother had to do the Xmas wrapping and mailing for him, but it was plain Glenn's heart was in the task. After all, his Daddy's a soldier.

Something new in the way of Christmas seals was thought up by "Goodfellows" Kay Guier and Marci Flynn, dancers at Billy Rose's Diamond Horseshoe, famed New York niterie.

SIGNED WITH KISS.

Kay, after getting the address of a soldier from her Hearst newspaper, bought a large assortment of presents—including a patent pillow for fox-hole sleepers that can be worn in the helmet when not in use—and then signed her Christmas card with a beeyootiful lipstick kiss.

That's going to give some far-off soldier an extra Christmas thrill this December 25.

Remember: The last day the post office will accept Christmas

Continued on Page 2, Column 2.

Dog Forestalls Anti-Cruelty Unit

CHICAGO—(A. P.).—Sisters of St. Vincent's Orphanage noticed a mournful chow keeping vigil at the entrance. It was still there the next morning, and the nuns offered food. The dog refused.

That went on for three days and three nights, during which the sisters sought the dog's owner. Finally they called the anti-cruelty society.

Just before the agents arrived the dog sniffed the air and left.

Slights Alderman In Share-Mayor Plan

HARTFORD, Conn.—(A. P.).—A "share-the-mayor's-chair" program on a record-breaking scale has been launched by Mayor Dennis P. O'Conor, now on vacation.

For every day of this week he named a different alderman acting mayor—all except Alderman Allen L. Hopkins.

He will serve next Sunday and Monday—both holidays.

Holy Land Wives Bring High Price

JERUSALEM, Sept. 11 — (U. P.).—Prosperity has brought its own problems to sections of the native population in the Holy Land, and the latest baffling poser for young and matrimonially minded people is the high price of wives.

The time-honored custom of fathers getting dowries for their daughters, instead of dowering their daughters upon marriage, has assumed the aspect of a "boom."

No longer is the Moslem pater familias with an abundance of daughters to be pitied as an ineffective son-maker; he is envied by fathers of boys.

The more marriageable daughters a Palestinian father has, the bigger his fortune is likely to become.

One villager in the vicinity of Gaza, where Delilah sheared Samson's locks to facilitate the Philistine blitzkreig, is just reported to have paid £1,000 for a bride.

The pre-boom dowry was never above £50-60; in fact, a pedigreed cow used to be more expensive than a wife.

There is even a "black market" in brides among the Bedouin tribes, adds the report.

Once a willing helpmate was obtained from her father for £15; now price is £250.

Many of the semi-nomads cannot afford to marry.

Hitler Comes Next In Allied Sweep

Special to the Sunday American.

LONDON, Sept. 18.—With Mussolini erased from the international picture and Italy out of the war the Allies are concentrating all their forces of ground units, warships and airplanes in a mighty effort to break down German morale and bring about the collapse of Adolf Hitler.

"Now for Hitler!" or "Hitler's next!" is what one hears from the man on the street in London today.

The average Londoner is convinced that the surrender of Italy marks the beginning of the end for the Axis, although there is no feeling here that the war will be over next week, or next month or even next year.

The landing of mighty British and American forces in Italy has caused a widespread feeling of satisfaction here among a public which recalls that it was only a little more than three years ago that Mussolini stabbed France in the back when she was reeling under German assaults.

SHOE ON OTHER FOOT.

Now the shoe is on the other foot and Italy, beaten to her knees, is assisting the Allies to administer the knockout blow to her former ally—if Germany could have been called an ally rather than a master.

Italy is becoming a base of Allied operations against Germany as swiftly as ships and planes can ferry men and material across the Mediterranean.

While the next great move of the Allies is naturally a military secret, it is believed in some quarters here that the British and American forces will strike through the Brenner Pass at Austria.

This was forecast when Allied bombers in force attacked the pass and pulverized the railroad lines there over which Benito Mussolini and Adolf Hitler travelled to their frequent conferences in which they plotted their next moves against Europe.

NATIVE WELCOME.

If the Allies manage to crash the Brenner Pass under the safety of an umbrella of fighting planes it is believed in some quarters here that they might be welcomed by the natives as deliverers almost as heartily as they were greeted by the Sicilians.

In this connection it is pointed out that many Austrians, almost a majority in fact, never welcomed the compulsory anschluss forced upon them by Hitler, even

Continued on Page 2, Column 1.

Motorists Cagey On Destinations

BATON ROUGE, La.—(A. P.). A traffic survey conducted by the State highway department turned out the wrong way.

Motorists, stopped and asked how far they intended going and why—data sought for plans for post-war road-building, all played dumb, mumbled vaguely or deliberately gave wrong answers.

They thought it was the Government checking up for gas rationing travel violations. Only after a couple of weeks spent explaining its innocent purpose in newspaper and radio announcements was the highway department able to convince the motorists. This time the department's questioners got the right answers.

'A Rose By Any Other Name—'

SANTA FE, N. M.—(A. P.).—Since the fall of Mussolini, Artist Will Shuster has renamed the three-visaged figure of Zozobra—"Old Man Gloom"—which will be burned at the stake in Santa Fe's famed fiesta next month.

Shuster first called it "Zozobra Hirohitmus."

Now he has changed it to "Zozobra Hirohittlepuss."

Weather Man Pays Heavily For Error

ALBANY, Ore.—(A. P.).—Seth T. French glanced at the clear skies and decided not to throw a canvas over the temporarily unshingled roof of his bedroom.

Hours later he was awakened by a heavy downpour in his face.

French is local weather observer.

TROUBLES OF EUROPE'S NEWEST BOY KING

Born in Nation Seething with Revolt, Child Monarch of Bulgaria, Must Live Under Constant Guard

SEE NEXT SUNDAY'S BALTIMORE AMERICAN

Uncle Sam Is Using 95 Per Cent of His Income to Fight the War; Back Him With War Bonds

Weather Report
Rain tonight and continued cool.
Temperatures today—Highest, 65, at 3:30 p.m.; lowest, 61, at 7 a.m. Yesterday—Highest, 65, at 1:20 p.m.; lowest, 55, at 4 a.m. Full report on page A-22.
United States Weather Bureau Report.
Closing N. Y. Markets—Sales, Page A-23.

The Evening Star

WITH SUNDAY MORNING EDITION

NIGHT FINAL
LATEST NEWS AND SPORTS
CLOSING MARKETS
(AP) Means Associated Press.

91st YEAR. No. 36,302. WASHINGTON, D. C., TUESDAY, SEPTEMBER 21, 1943—FORTY-FOUR PAGES. Washington and Suburbs THREE CENTS. Elsewhere FIVE CENTS

MARSHALL SLATED AS GLOBAL COMMANDER

Churchill Promises Mass Invasion of Europe's Coast From West

No Time Lost Needlessly in Italy, He Says

Escape of Mussolini Laid to Failure of Guards to Act

(Partial Text, Page A-8.)

By the Associated Press.

LONDON, Sept. 21.—Prime Minister Churchill declared today that the second front will be thrown open "at the right time" and "a mass invasion of the continent from the west will begin."

Calling the Mediterranean battlefield the "third front," the Prime Minister told the House of Commons that the second front "already exists potentially" and "already is rapidly gathering weight. * * * The second front exists and is a main preoccupation already with the enemy."

"It has not yet been thrown into play," he continued. "That time is coming.

"At what we and our American Allies judge to be the right time this front will be thrown open and a mass invasion of the continent from the west will begin."

"The House may be absolutely certain," said the Prime Minister, "that the present government will never be swayed or overborne by an uninstructed agitation, however natural, or pressure, however well meant, in matters of this kind.

"It will not be forced or cajoled into undertaking vast operations against our better judgment in order to gain political unanimity or a cheer from any quarter."

Gives Full Picture.

Surveying the whole sweep of the war with serene confidence, Mr. Churchill also declared:

1. Not a moment was lost needlessly in the operations against Italy, and, except for the failure of Italian guards to do their assigned duty, Benito Mussolini would have been shot when Hitler's agents rescued him at Gran Sasso.

2. American forces have landed on the Island of Sardinia to assist Italian troops who drove the German garrison over to Corsica, now being occupied by French units.

3. A tripartite conference of representatives of the United States, Britain and Russia will take place "at an early date" and no question will be barred from discussion. Any differences will be set aside for a conference of President Roosevelt, Premier Stalin and the Prime Minister himself.

4. The Allies are prepared to place large armies in Italy and to deploy a weighty and active fighting front against the enemy on whatever line he chooses, to resist and to maintain against him with increasing weight and vigor if need be through the fall and winter.

5. A French army of 300,000 to 400,000 is being steadily organized and the battleship Richelieu will soon take its place in the French fleet.

Urges Lasting Association.

Speaking of the prospect of a

(Continued on Page A-8, Column 1)

Fulbright Resolution Approved, 360 to 29

By the Associated Press.

In an historic stand on foreign policy, the House overwhelmingly passed today the Fulbright resolution, placing Congress on record in favor of United States postwar collaboration with other nations to maintain a "just and lasting" peace.

The first congressional pledge of its kind was made on a rollcall vote of 360 to 29, or more than the two-thirds' vote required for approval. The measure goes now to the Senate, where it will be considered by the Foreign Relations Committee along with several other resolutions similar in purpose but different in language and scope.

In sharp contrast to the narrow division in the strength of interventionists and non-interventionists during pre-Pearl Harbor legislative fights, the topheavy vote reflected a mounting congressional demand for American participation in world councils in peacetime as well as in war.

During two days of debate that sentiment was reflected in speeches

(See POSTWAR, Page A-8.)

Nazi Winter Defense Line Smashed by Red Army Thrust

Stalin Announces Great Victory in Order of the Day

By the Associated Press.

LONDON, Sept. 21.—The whole German Desna River winter defense line collapsed today under a terrific Red Army onslaught which broke the Nazi stand along the entire west bank and took by storm the important bastion town of Chernigov, 30 miles from the Dnieper River and 77 miles northeast of Kiev, Marshal Stalin announced in an order of the day.

The successful forcing of the Desna, described by Stalin as a "skillful outflanking maneuver," followed three days of violent fighting, the Premier's announcement said.

The order of the day, broadcast by Moscow and recorded by the Associated Press, said as the result of Chernigov's fall, "the Germans' defenses prepared on the western bank of the River Desna have been overcome by our troops along the whole length of the river and the plan of the Germans to stem the advance of our troops on the line of the River Desna must be considered to have failed."

Cut Escape Route.

An earlier Moscow communique announced that Red Army forces had slashed across the Kiev-Chernigov highway on the middle Dnieper and cut the main Crimean escape railway between Zaporozhe and Dniepropetrovsk. Other Russian troops stormed on from captured Velizh, 65 miles northwest of Smolensk, to outflank that German central-front anchor.

The earlier Moscow communique disclosed an amazing list of triumphs marked up by the Russian troops, including the start of a great wheeling movement pointed toward Cherkasy, key rail center on the Dnieper southeast of Kiev, in an attempt to entrap the hundreds of thousands of German troops reported massed in the river bend.

More than 1,130 towns and villages fell before the slashing Soviet advances, the Russian war bulletin said. The broadcast version was recorded here by the Soviet monitor. Tremendous piles of war equipment, including strings of fully loaded troop and materiel trains, tanks, armored cars, guns and ammunition were reported ta-

(See RUSSIA, Page A-22.)

War Bond Sale Here Reaches 59 Per Cent Of Campaign Goal

District Subscribes $55,700,000, City Committee Says

Washington's Third War Loan purchases have reached $55,700,000, or 59.2 per cent of the city's $94,000,000 quota, the District War Finance Committee announced today. The figures include sales made yesterday.

The Treasury reported $10,745,000,000 of its $15,000,000,000 goal had been subscribed, but nationally and locally the task was becoming more difficult. It was explained that the "big money" is already in the till, and that millions of individuals would have to be enlisted in the "Back the Attack" army.

A breakdown of District sales was expected late today from the Richmond Federal Reserve Bank. While awaiting official tabulations, District leaders said the figures probably would reveal the same lag here in Series E bond sales that has been experienced nationally.

Virginia purchases through yesterday amounted to $91,851,782. The Old Dominion's quota is $153,000,000.

How to spur individual purchases remained the principal stumbling block. Treasury and District officials called for renewed emphasis on the "door-knocker" campaign. By siphoning small sums from millions of individuals, inflationary trends can be halted, officials stressed.

Meanwhile, Gov. O'Conor of Maryland, who put up a barrel of Chesapeake oysters against a cornfed Nebraska hog that Maryland's sales would exceed Nebraska's, told Gov. Dwight Griswold to be ready to deliver the porker. Maryland's feat in being the first State to oversubscribe its quota elicited a congratulatory telegram to Gov. O'Conor from Treasury Secretary Morgenthau.

"Please relay this message to your workers who are demonstrating their ability to 'Back the Attack' in

(See WAR BONDS, Page A-2.)

Late Bulletins

23 Guilty of Treason

BERN, Switzerland (AP).—A Swiss military court today sentenced 23 persons on charges of treason committed between November, 1941, and October, 1942. One defendant was given a life sentence, the others terms of from several months to 15 years.

Suspects Refuse Plea

DETROIT (AP).—Mrs. Emma Leonhardt and Mrs. Marianne Von Moltke, indicted by a Federal grand jury last week with six other persons on charges of conspiracy under the Espionage Act, stood mute on arraignment this afternoon before Judge Edward J. Moinet and were ordered held under bond of $50,000 each. Mrs. Leonhardt's husband, Carl Leonhardt, has pleaded guilty.

ODT Asks Curb on Sale Of Football Tickets

By the Associated Press.

The Office of Defense Transportation today called on all school, college and other football teams to restrict sales of tickets to residents of the area in which the game is to be played.

The already heavy overload on intercity transportation systems was given as the reason.

ODT also asked that football teams use coach accommodations in trains and refrain from making reservations until the day before departure.

French Capture Entire Western Side of Corsica

Venice Is Bombed by Allies; 5th Army Occupies Eboli

BULLETIN.

By the Associated Press.

ALLIED HEADQUARTERS IN NORTH AFRICA, Sept. 21.—A French communique announced tonight that "the whole western side of Corsica is now liberated" from the Germans and that advance troops are in possession of St. Florient in the north.

By the Associated Press.

ALLIED HEADQUARTERS IN NORTH AFRICA, Sept. 21.—American Liberators threw new weight into the conquest of Italy by bombarding the historic port of Venice as French troops and native guerrillas proceeded today to mopping up German resistance on Corsica and the United States 5th Army registered new gains in the Salerno beachhead.

Slowly and steadily pressing the Germans backward, the 5th Army stormed and took the key town of Eboli, 16 miles inland, which had served the enemy as a communications center during last week's heavy fighting about Salerno.

Lt. Gen. Mark W. Clark's soldiers also battered their way to Montecorvino, 9 miles inland, in a sustained push, an official source disclosed.

Nazis Seek to Avoid Trap.

A military spokesman also announced that the Germans are swinging the lower end of a line which formerly inclosed the Salerno bridgehead to the north and east to avoid being trapped by the continued rapid advance of the British 8th Army.

(The Oslo radio reported that the Italian port of Naples was being shelled by Allied artillery.

(The broadcast was recorded in London by the Associated Press.)

The German's retreat already has taken the bulk of their forces north of the Sele River.

The Nazis are using infantry supported by small groups of tanks to fight a delaying action in the Eboli area and the 5th Army also was reported encounteringg elaborate minefields and demolitions in its slow but continued advance north of Salerno.

The enemy possesses excellent defensive positions in the hill country north and northeast of Salerno, the spokesman said, and the progress of the Allied troops is necessarily slow in such terrain.

German prisoners were quoted in official reports from the front as giv-

(See ITALY, Page A-9.)

Stanton Park Group Asks Curfew for Juveniles

The Commissioners today were asked by Stanton Park community leaders to establish a 9 p.m. curfew for all children under 16 "not in the company of their parents or guardians or not carrying a note of special permission from them."

The proposed restriction is necessary, said Mrs. Frank Caruso, chairman of the Stanton Park Community League, and Mrs. Louise Ramirez, chairman of the Committee for Civic Improvements, to "prevent delinquency on the part of youth and in order to allow workers their proper rest."

Curfew action was requested along with the making of improvements, such as increased police protection, adequate housing, sufficient garbage and trash collections, a day center for children of colored working mothers, another Boys' Club, smoke and soot control and more frequent alley cleaning.

Nazis Reported Making Naples 'City of Horror'

By the Associated Press.

WITH THE 5th ARMY IN ITALY, Sept. 21.—The Germans have turned Naples into a city of horror, killing thousands of Italian civilians and looting, burning and destroying, it was reported today by persons who filtered through the battle lines into Allied-held territory.

Civilians said the town already was without water or any means of lighting the houses. A little food was brought down from orchards and farms in the mountains, but the organization for distributing it has broken down completely under the harsh German restrictions regarding the curfew.

It means death to go out of houses at night looking for food and water, the Italians said. German soldiers patrolling the streets do not challenge or ask for identification. They shoot first.

Asked an estimate of how many Italians had been killed in that manner in the last two weeks, the people who arrived in this area said "thousands."

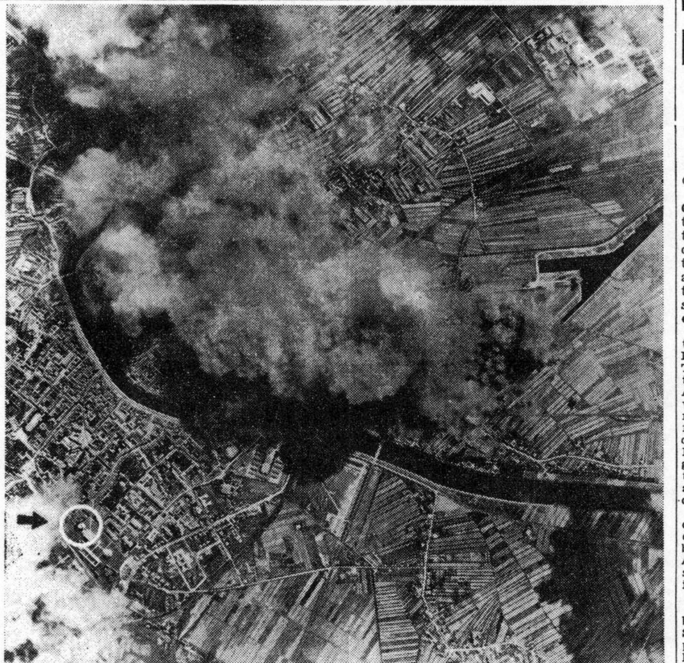

UNITED STATES BOMBERS AVOID LEANING TOWER OF PISA—Smoke rises from hits made by United States bombers of the Northwest African Air Force on the railway marshalling yards at Pisa, Italy, on the Arno River, 165 miles northwest of Rome. The famous Leaning Tower is shown in circle at lower left, unharmed and well outside the bombing range.
—Army Air Forces Photo.

Landings on Dodecanese Isles Are Confirmed by British

Announcement Follows RAF's Revelation It Has Seized Airdrome on Coo

By the Associated Press.

CAIRO, Sept. 21 — British forces have landed on the Aegean Islands of Coo, Lero and Samos off the coast of Turkey, it was announced officially today.

The confirmation of Allied activity on Coo and Lero in the Italian Dodecanese group and the Greek island of Samos immediately to the north followed an RAF communique announcing that the RAF had seized the Coo airdrome and is now operating from there. There have been reports for several days of landings in the area.

Coo (Cos) is 50 miles northwest of German-occupied Rhodes, largest island capital of the Dodecanese group in the Aegean Sea. It is about 5 miles from Turkey. The Italian personnel of Coo is co-operating in the occupation, the communique said.

"During the past few days, several enemy air attacks have been beaten off," the communique continued, adding that in the last few days a Heinkel 111 and a JU-88 had been shot down, "while attempting to attack the island."

It gives the Allies an airbase in the very center of the Dodecanese group and on the north side of the Nazi Mediterranean outpost of Crete.

A few days ago it was announced

(See DODECANESE, Page A-22.)

Senate Unit Demands Inspections Reports After Gallinger Visit

Call on Commissioners For Full Information Within 36 Hours

The rapidly developing Senate inquiry into the care of patients at Gallinger Hospital today resulted in an unannounced visit by two Senators to the institution and a demand that the Commissioners furnish the Senate investigators with information on their own inspections of the hospital "within 36 hours."

These developments followed a disclosure by Chairman McCarran of the Senate District Committee last night that Controller General Lindsay Warren had complained of irregularities in the management of the institution.

Senator Holman, Republican, of Oregon, and Senator Buck, Republican, of Delaware, accompanied by R. A. Selig, secretary to Senator Bone, Democrat, of Washington, said they found evidence of patients cooking in their rooms at the municipal hospital when they made their unannounced visit today.

The congressional group, escorted by Dr. P. S. Rossiter, chief of the medical staff, in the absence of Dr.

(See GALLINGER, Page A-22.)

Man in Plane Killed In Fall; Craft Soars On

By the Associated Press.

SELINGSGROVE, Pa., Sept. 21.—A man fell from an airplane and was killed today and the plane continued westward without slowing down.

The body landed in a field near the farm of Arthur Brouse, five miles west of here.

Coroner Charles W. Strouse went to the scene.

Truman Voices Doubt Army Needs 630,000 More Men This Year

Will Vote Against Wheeler Bill to Defer Prewar Fathers

By J. A. O'LEARY.

Chairman Truman of the Senate War Investigating Committee today questioned the Army's need for 630,000 more men this year but announced he would not vote for the Wheeler bill to defer prewar fathers until after January 1.

Although consideration of the bill has been postponed until Friday, Senator Truman took the floor to deplore the calling of draftees sooner than they are needed, and also declared the drafting of fathers "is not warranted as a mere scheme to force a shift of manpower."

Majority Leader Barkley said Minority Leader McNary and Senator Wheeler, Democrat, of Montana had agreed to the delay to permit members to study the voluminous testimony taken before the Military Affairs Committee.

Bernard M. Baruch, presidential adviser who recently completed a study of West Coast labor shortages, is scheduled to testify at 2 p.m. tomorrow as the final witness in the committee's hearing on the bill.

Calls It WMC Problem.

Senator Truman told Senator Wheeler, however, that he would not support the draft deferment bill, because he believes the problem is an administrative one that should be worked out by the War Manpower Commission.

"But I do question whether we need 5,000,000 men in the Army this month in continental United States, and whether the Army needs this year an additional 630,000 men, so that even if we achive our hoped-for goal of 4,750,000 men abroad by the end of 1944, we shall still

(Continued on Page A-9, Col. 5.)

Big Allied Offensives To Be Started Shortly, Marshall Tells Legion

America Will Attack With 'Power and Force' to Assure Early Victory

By the Associated Press.

OMAHA, Nebr., Sept. 21.—Great offensives in which the full strength of America's armed forces will be hurled against the enemy in Asia and Europe are "just about to begin," Gen. George C. Marshall said today.

President Roosevelt, in a message read before the Legion convention, called for "an increased rather than lessened effort" in "many phases of the national program," and pointed to civilian defense as "an example of this sort of latent need." The message was read by National Commander Roane Waring.

Addressing the American Legion convention, Gen. Marshall said there appeared to be some public misunderstanding of the recent Allied success, a tendency to believe that the final steps of the war were being taken.

On the contrary, he said, the last year and a half has been spent lergely in preparation for operations of the large forces still to go into action, in establishing bases for future campaigns.

Ready to Hit Hard.

"Now at last we are ready to carry the war to the enemy," Gen. Marshall said, "all overseas, thank God, with a power and force that we

(See LEGIONNAIRES, Page A-9.)

Wife of Officer Here Murdered in Detroit

Discovered in Basement With Throat Slashed

(Picture on Page A-5.)

By the Associated Press.

DETROIT, Sept. 21.—Police hunted today for the knife-wielding slayer of Mrs. Mary Gallian, pretty 18-year-old bride of an Army officer.

Mrs. Gallian's body was found yesterday in the basement of her mother-in-law's home, a pink underslip knotted around her neck and her throat slashed. A blood-stained butcher knife and two rags, apparently used to mop up the blood on the floor, were found near the body.

Police said they believed that Mrs. Gallian, surprised while washing clothes in a basement laundry tub, was strangled and then her throat was cut.

Mrs. Violet Richards discovered the body of her daughter-in-law, married only a year to Second Lt. James Gallian, stationed with a military police unit at Washington, when she returned home from work at the Hudson Naval Arsenal. Mrs. Gallian, the daughter of Mr. and Mrs. Ernest Lee Mash of Corsicana, Tex., had been living with her mother-in-law for about six weeks.

General Chosen By Allied Chiefs In Quebec Talks

Appointment Awaits Approval of War Cabinet in London

By KIRKE L. SIMPSON.
(Copyright, 1943, by the Associated Press)

The blunt fact about Gen. George C. Marshal, is that he is tentatively slated to become virtual global commander-in-chief of all Anglo-American forces in the field, ground, sea and air, and put into execution the pattern of victory East and West shaped at the Quebec Conference.

Just when an announcement to that effect will be forthcoming from London or Washington is uncertain. This writer can say, however, that the nomination of the American Army Chief of Staff for the task was perhaps the major decision reached at Quebec. If it meets the final approval of the London war cabinet as expected, it will put Gen. Marshall at the head of a super-global field command with authority to co-ordinate aggressive action on all fronts under the Quebec strategic directives.

It will recognize, also, that in successive inter-Allied military conferences, from Washington to Casablanca to Washington to Quebec, the American Chief of Staff was the outstanding contributor to the fashioning of the strategic plans for victory.

Won Respect of British.

Rumors that Gen. Marshall is to be eased out of his present Chief of Staff assignment because of the pressure of interests opposed to him, presumably British, are in direct conflict with the facts. The Chief of Staff has won the admiration and respect of all the British officials with whom he has come in contact, including Prime Minister Churchill.

The unprecedented scope of his contemplated ultimate command, giving Gen. Marshall presumptive authortiy even over Gen. Dwight D. Eisenhower in the Mediterranean theater, Gen. Douglas MacArthur in the Southwestern Pacific and Admiral Lord Mountbatten in Southeastern Asia, might stir debate in Britain. It is understood to be wholly acceptable to Canada, however, and as far as known to French forces in the Mediterranean.

One thing is absolutely certain, Gen. Marshall stands so high in President Roosevelt's estimation both personally and for his professional attainments that the White House would veto any change in his present assignment that Gen. Marshall himself opposed, that was not a definite recognition of his abilities and—perhaps most of all—that Mr. Roosevelt did not regard as an important contribution to victory over the Axis.

"Smash Germany First."

The primary and dominating element of Allied war plans still is to smash Germany first, then turn the full weight of ever increasing Anglo-American armed power on Japan. For that reason Gen. Marshall is expected to assume command of the "direct attack across the English channel on Germany in France and the Low Countries" for which Mr. Churchill told Parliament today the present Mediterranian campaign was "an essential preliminary."

"Our toughest job is to reach Berlin and Marshall is the toughest soldier we (the Allies) have got to do it," a high-placed Government official told this writer today.

It also was indicated that in Gen. Marshall the Anglo-American Joint Chiefs of Staff saw the only officer of either nation to whose supreme

(See MARSHALL, Page A-9.)

Baltimore Thieves Steal Ration Board's Ton Safe

By the Associated Press.

BALTIMORE, Sept. 21.—Thieves carried away a 1-ton safe last night from War Price and Rationing Board. The loot included ration books and certificates for gasoline, tires, fuel oil, stoves and food.

John T. Busby, board chairman, said the safe contained only coupon books estimated as a one-day's supply since the bulk of coupons were kept in a bank and removed only as needed.

Spanish Writers See Salerno as Big Nazi Defeat

By the Associated Press.

MADRID, Sept. 21.—Spanish correspondents in Berlin said today that the Salerno campaign in Italy had been a "military and propagandistic defeat" for Germany and made these other statements and predictions, remarkable both for their content and origin:

The German Ukrainian administrative government already is evacuating Kiev.

The "threat of evacuation hangs over Smolensk," and a Russian penetration there would force the Germans to lift the siege of Leningrad.

Advices from the French border said the landing of French Commandos in Corsica had led to spontaneous and widespread increase in sabotage of German communications in France.

Army Conference Slated Here With Labor-Industry Leaders

Undersecretary of War Patterson today invited 200 leading American industrial and labor leaders to a conference at the Pentagon Building next Monday and Tuesday for a review of the war to date and an estimate of what the Nation will need in men and machines before victory is won.

"As our troops begin large-csale operations on the continent of Europe we are calling together the representatives of those on whom we depend for the instruments of war, so that they may know precisely the military job that lies ahead," Mr. Patterson said.

The Army's guests will visit the War bond show at the Monument Grounds and witness an exhibition by engineering and air force personnel at Fort Belvoir next Tuesday.

The labor delegation will be headed by William Green, president of the American Federation of Labor, and Philip Murray, president of the Congress of Industrial Organizations.

Many of the others invited are War Department contractors. The Monday session will be opened by Mr. Patterson and Gen. George C. Marshall, Army chief of staff, will outline military operations in all combat zones. Strategy will be explained by Lt. Gen. Joseph T. McNarney, deputy chief of staff.

Eyewitness accounts will be given of the bombing raids over Germany, amphibious landings in Sicily and the organization of overseas bases.

A report on what American equipment is doing in the field will be given by Lt. Gen. William S. Knudson, Army director of production.

Guide for Readers

ITALY DECLARES WAR ON GERMANY

BLUE STREAK EDITION
Boston Traveler
New England's Largest Evening Circulation
Complete Associated Press and United Press Wire Services
EST. 1825—119th YEAR—NO. 84—WED., OCT. 13, 1943 *44 PAGES 3 CENTS

Churchill Raps U. S. Politicians In War Rows

LONDON, Oct. 13 (UP)—Prime Minister Churchill inferentially rebuked American politicians today for indulging in political rows in the midst of the war.

BloodiestFighting Ahead, Warning By Churchill

By J. EDWARD MURRAY

LONDON, Oct. 13 (UP)—Prime Minister Winston Churchill warned today that the bloodiest fighting of the war lies ahead of the British people, barring an unexpected German collapse "which we would be absolute fools to count upon."

REJECTS MINE SUGGESTIONS

Opening the second day of a debate in Commons on the government's coal policy, Churchill bluntly rejected suggestions that the drafting of miners be halted and that coal men be released from the armed forces to work in the pits.

"In the advent of the bloodiest fightnig of the war, so far as this people are concerned, I am not prepared to weaken the field forces or the reserves of trained manpower lying behind them beyond a limited

(Continued on Page Twenty-two)

CITES "SOME COUNTRIES"

He told Commons that in "some countries which I should not venture to name" the soldiers abroad and the politicians at home were fighting "with equal vigor."

BEARS ON SENATORS' TRIP

His remarks coincided with the political controversy touched off by charges of five U. S. senators on their return from the world's fighting fronts.

"As soon as the war is ended," he said, "the (British) soldiers will leave off fighting and the politicians will begin. Perhaps that is rather a pity, but at any rate it isn't so bad as what goes on in some countries which I shouldn't venture to name where the soldiers are fighting abroad and the politicians are fighting at home with equal vigor."

Laughter swept the house.

The London Daily Mail in an editorial today recommended that the slogan, "Careless talk costs lives," be brought to the attention of the five American senators.

The Daily Mail said they "apparently are busy throwing large-sized spanners into the delicate machin-

(Continued on Page Twenty-two)

YES, IT'S BOSTON COMMON—And the only indication that it isn't a suburban field is the State House in the background. Jim Roache and a team are harrowing the Boston Victory Garden plot after 1943 crops have been cleared in anticipation of new yields next year.

Badoglio Denounces Robbery and Violence

By RICHARD D. McMILLAN

ALLIED HEADQUARTERS, Algiers, Oct. 13 (UP)—Italy declared war today on Germany, its one-time ally, and was granted the status of a co-belligerent by the United Nations.

APPEAL TO ITALIANS

The declaration, made in a proclamation by Premier Pietro Badoglio, came 35 days after Italy signed the armistice that removed her from the ranks of nations giving military assistance to Germany.

"Italians! There will not be peace in Italy as long as a single German remains on Italian soil," Badoglio said in his proclamation.

(In Washington it was announced that President Roosevelt, Prime Minister Winston

(Continued on Page Ten)

Senate Group Favors World Role for U. S.

La Follette Dissents On Postwar Plan

WASHINGTON, Oct. 13 (AP)—A Senate foreign relations sub-committee approved 7 to 1 today a post-war foreign policy declaration which would pledge the United States to "join with free and sovereign nations in the establishment and maintenance of international authority with power to prevent aggression and to preserve the peace of the world."

LA FOLLETTE OPPOSES

The resolution, voted over the opposition of Senator LaFollette (Prog., Wis.), goes to the full committee next week. Chairman Connally (D., Tex.) predicted the full committee would approve it soon and expressed the opinion that the Senate also would concur.

LaFollette's opposition to the meas-

(Continued on Page Twenty-two)

Anglo-U. S.-Russ Texts on Italy

WASHINGTON, Oct. 13 (AP)—The text of a joint statement by President Roosevelt, Prime Minister Churchill and Premier Joseph Stalin on the declaration of war by Italy against Germany follows:

BECOMES CO-BELLIGERENT

The governments of Great Britain, the United States and the Soviet

(Continued on Page Ten)

Allies Stage 10-Mile Drive In Italy

Town Commanding Key Highway Taken

By DONALD COE

ALLIED HEADQUARTERS, Algiers, Oct. 13 (UP)—Allied troops, driving 10 miles beyond the broken Calore River line, have captured the central Italian town of San Croce di Sannio, from which they command the arterial trans-peninsula highway between Naples and Termoli, it was announced officially today.

ALLIES FORGE AHEAD

American and British forces battered forward all along the [illegible] toward the Naples-Termoli, [illegible] bringing most of it within gun rang and capturing several towns.

The new gains carried the Allie well through the Calore defense—an eastward extension of the Volturno River line in the West coas

(Continued on Page Seventeen)

Man Gets 5 Life Terms

Albert Murray, 22, Sentenced Here On 5 Charges of Armed Robbery

Five life sentences, the most severe in the memory of veteran court attaches, were meted out today to 22-year-old Albert Murray, former East Weymouth "neglected child," when he pleaded guilty in Suffolk superior criminal court to five charges of armed robbery.

PLEADS GUILTY

Murray's sentencing, by Judge Allan G. Buttrick, came just before the court was to resume his trial along with four other defendants on charges of armed robbery.

Counsel for Murray asked the court's permission to enter a guilty plea and Judge Buttrick gave his consent. Then, when Murray answered the clerk's charge with a

(Continued on Page Twenty-two)

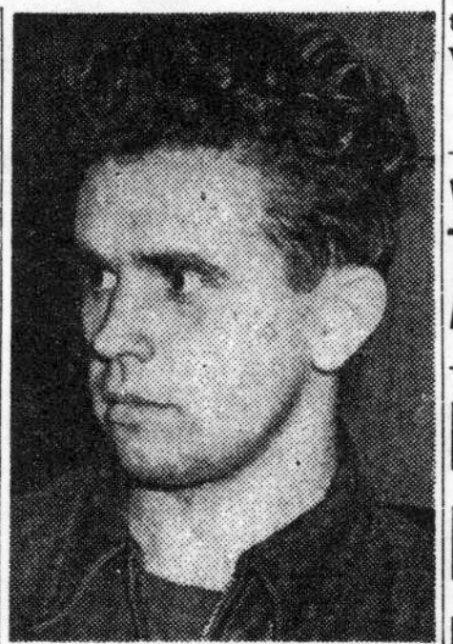

ALBERT J. MURRAY

'Youngsters' In Top Jobs Hit in Report

'Real Bottleneck,' Say Congressmen

WASHINGTON, Oct. 13 (AP)—A Congressional committee charged today that "inexperienced youngsters" holding some of the top personnel jobs in Washington "constitute a real bottleneck" to the government's war effort.

The youthful executives lack "the experience and tact" necessary in "top-notch management officials,"

(Continued on Page Twenty-four)

Delay Proposed On Lewis Issue

Watts Assails A. L. Head's Ideas As 'Subversive'

Robert J. Watt, the Lawrence labor leader who became international representative of the American Federation of Labor, today clipped the words "subversive ideology" to the speech given here in a stormy session of the American Federation of Labor convention by Warren Atherton, new commander-in-chief of the American Legion.

STRIKERS "BLACK SHEEP"

Speaking before the Rotary Club, also at the Hotel Statler this noon, Watt asserted that he views "with concern anyone who tries to array class against class under the guise of patriotism" in an address in which he pointed to labor's excellent war production record, dismissed the strikes which have occurred as the

(Continued on Page Seven)

Executive Council Action Urged

By SARA WHITE

John L. Lewis' journey back home into the American Federation of Labor seemed stalled this noon when the resolutions committee recommended that the AFL supreme hierarchy, the executive council, be empowered to negotiate terms and admit Lewis and his 500,000 miners later.

Likelihood of an entire year's delay arose shortly after, when Harvey W. Brown, powerful president of the Machinists, rebelled against the growing habit of defaulting to the executive council and argued for reconsideration of the Lewis application by the authorized delegates themselves in next year's convention.

WORDS TEMPERED

"We have waited for five years . . . So let us not be moved at this convention to act hastily because the United Mine Workers of America decided five months ago to come

(Continued on Page Fifteen)

Traveler Index

A. L. Ripley, Banker, Dies

Merchants National Chairman Began Banking Career in 1888

ALFRED L. RIPLEY

Alfred L. Ripley, chairman of the board and former president of the Merchants National Bank of Boston, whose banking career spanned more than half a century, died today at his home in Andover. He would have been 85 years old next month.

Mr. Ripley was born at Hartford, Nov. 6, 1858, son of George and Mary E. (Aiken) Ripley. He attended Phillips Academy at Andover and was graduated from Yale in 1878, later receiving his master's and doctor of laws degree there. He studied at Dartmouth and the Universities of Berlin and Bonn.

CAREER BEGAN IN 1888

He entered the banking business in 1888 with the Hide and Leather Bank in Boston, and remained with the organization when it was merged with the State National Bank, of which his father was president.

After a merger with the Merchants National Bank, Mr. Ripley became vice-president, and was president from 1917 until his resignation in 1929, when he was made

(Continued on Page Twelve)

Late News

WASHINGTON (AP)—Secretary Ickes says bituminous coal stocks dropped 597,000 tons the first nine months of 1943, compared with a 19,949,000 tons increase the corresponding 1942 period. Estimated bituminous production the week ended Oct. 2 was 12,080,000 tons, compared with 12,100,000 tons the previous week, and anthracite 1,283,000 tons, compared with 1,299,000.

NEW LONDON (AP)—Virtually waterless since Monday, New London residents enjoyed the return of water service today as repairs were completed on five leaks in the city mains.

(Continued on Page Twenty-five)

U. S. Treasury Balance

WASHINGTON, Oct. 13—Balance today, $18,688,760,255.

Customs receipts, $11,861,500.

Oct. 12—Balance today, $18,718,619,881.

Customs receipts, $10,257,672.

Bears Steal Family's Rations

THE FORKS, Me., Oct. 13 (UP)—By rigid self-denial Mr. and Mrs. Guy Berry managed to save up enough ration coupons to lay away six pounds of butter, six pounds of salt pork and five pounds of bacon for the winter.

Today they reported to the OPA that three bears had broken into their storehouse and consumed the entire supplies.

With Gil Hammond Overseas

Fliers Play the Numbers

Pravda Blasts Russian-Nazi Peace Rumors

Assails U. S. Papers Publishing Them

BULLETIN (Latest)

LONDON, Oct. 13 (UP)—The Berlin radio reported today that Russia had launched a great new offensive on a 200-mile central front and signs inercased that the Red Army was squaring off for an attempt to wrest the Crimea from Nazi hands.

MOSCOW, Oct. 13 (UP)—The newspaper Pravda today denounced rumors of a possible separate Russian-German peace when the Red Army reaches the Soviet frontier and of Russian intentions to enter Berlin first in order to dictate the post-war organization of Europe.

"PROVOCATIVE CAMPAIGN"

Pravda, official organ of the Communist party, condemned what is

(Continued on Page Twelve)

First Shows Half Required Raid Done, Second Means: 'Go Home

By GIL HAMMOND
Traveler War Correspondent

A U. S. BOMBER STATION, England, Oct. 13—In all Army centers there is a special magic in the numbers "7" and "11" often spoken in regard to the requirements of young children for additional footwear. But at Flying Fortress stations there are two other numbers of special and glorious significance.

Mustn't put a name to them, but it's not so important to know their exact sum, it's what they stand for. So, let's call them "sockteven" and "umptyzing." You couldn't do any arithmetic with those even in Japanese.

Old Anaxagoras himself never squeezed as much juice out of numbers as Fortress men get out of these. For "sockteven" means you're over the hump. You've gone on more than half the raids required for your rest and furlough.

"Umptyzing" means you've made your point and can go home with the marbles. You've earned your lay-off from combat. About three-quarters of the umptyzing men are furloughed back to the states. The rest relax on this side. Some never play their innings out and that's what gives the score its meaning.

There are pilots and gunners and radiomen without nerves

(Continued on Page Twenty-three)

Leopard Kills Keeper In Cleveland Zoo

CLEVELAND, Oct. 13 (AP)—Bozo, a male spotted leopard, killed 62-year-old Keeper John Thomas at the Cleveland Zoo today.

Thomas was found lying in the cage, his jugular vein severed. Attendants drove the leopard into another cage and discovered the keeper was dead.

"We are at a loss to understand how it could have happened," declared Fletcher Reynolds, zoo director.

Big Anglo-American Fleet Leaves Gibraltar Harbor

MADRID, Oct. 13 (UP)—Odvices from La Linea said an impressive Anglo-American fleet, including the British battleship King George V, two British aircraft carriers and a United States battleship moved out of Gibraltar harbor into the Mediterranean today.

The U. S. battleship was not identified in the information reaching here from the border town near the naval base.

The aircraft carriers were said to be the Illustrious and Formidable, both of 23,000 tons. They were accompanied by four British and three American destroyers.

The vessels left behind 35 merchantmen of various tonnages, including nine damaged ships. Two Italian tankers were said to be among the ships at Gibraltar.

RACE RESULTS AT ROCKINGHAM PARK

FIRST RACE—Track fast

Norsweep (Trent)	5.00	3.40	2.40
Tyrone (McMullen)	—	9.20	5.40
Wessex (Williams)	—	—	4.20

Time—1:14 3-5. Auletta, Camp Brill, Silt, Paper Cutter, Hy Gay, Diamond Back, Beau Brannon, Buckets, Noahvale also ran.

(Continued on Page Thirty-four)

The Weather

U. S. Official Forecast

SLIGHTLY WARMER TONIGHT

Full Report on Page 2

Temperature at 3:30 P. M. 68

Sun rises 6:54; Sun sets 6:06

High tide 11:38 A. M., 12:04 P. M.

DIMOUT 6:36 P. M., 6:26 A. M.

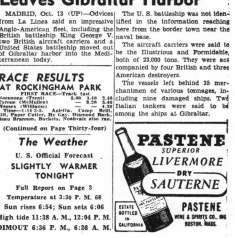

THE STARS AND STRIPES
AFRICA
Vol. 1, No. 48, Saturday, November 6, 1943
For U.S. Armed Forces
TWO FRANCS

Allies Crumble Nazi Line; NAAF Socks Austrian Plant

Entire Ukraine East Of Dnieper Cleared Of Nazis

Tremendous Victories Shut Off Escape By Land From Crimea

LONDON — The entire Ukraine east of the Dnieper River—except a small bridgehead across the river from Nikopol—has been liberated from the Wehrmacht, the Soviet communique announced yesterday after the capture of Aleshki, at the mouth of the stream opposite Kherson.

The victory at the Dnieper's estuary gave new splendor to a jubiliant week in Moscow. The signing of the Allied declaration there Monday showed that the Soviet Union had come of age politically. The tremendous victories in the southern Ukraine in which they cleared the Germans from the east bank of the Dnieper and sealed off the Crimea gave notice to the world in general and Adolf Hitler in particular that the Red Army had taken the eastern front war in its own hands and would probably direct its further course.

BIG HOLIDAY

And tomorrow Russia will celebrate the outstanding holiday on the Soviet calendar, the revolution of Nov. 7, 1917, when Nikolai Lenin came into power as the first head of the Union of Soviet Socialist Republics. Under Lenin's taciturn successor, Marshal Joseph Stalin, the Russian people have fought a hard war against the German invaders. The 26th anniversary of the revolution is the first since the war began on which the people of Moscow could look at their newspapers and be sure that victory lay ahead.

Every day during the past week brought added indications—if any were needed after this summer's victories—that the Germans were just about through in Russia. The proud Wehrmacht that had battered its way across the steppes of the Ukraine and into Stalingrad has lost every inch of land east of the Dnieper except the small bridgehead around Nikopol on the lower arm of the bend, a bridgehead that grew smaller every hour.

ESCAPE BARRED

Crushing the German defenses south of Melitopol last week, the Red Army quickly advanced down the railroad to the Crimea and Saturday captured Genichesk at the western approach to the Crimea. The Russians sped across the Nogaisk steppes, seizing Perekop Monday night and cutting

(Continued on Page 14)

Bombers Cripple Big Genoa Port As Weather Lifts

ALLIED FORCE HEADQUARTERS, Nov. 5—Heavy bombers of the NAAF this week gave the Germans an inkling of what to expect all winter from Mediterranean-based Allied planes when Flying Forts and Liberators in an historic raid practically destroyed the Messerschmitt factory at Wiener Neustadt in southern Austria. At least half the defending force of 100 fighters was shot down during the attack, officially described as one of the most destructive ever made from this theater. Allied losses were six bombers.

GENOA SMASHED

Good flying weather brought more Allied planes into the Italian skies than at any time since the Salerno landings. Heavy and medium bombers and fighters provided total air support for attacking Allied armies by pulverizing enemy positions in the battle area and communication and supply points far behind the lines.

Forts and Liberators crippled Italy's chief seaport of Genoa in two giant raids, the first from this theater. Then, systematically moving westward, heavy bombers shattered the Mediterranean rail line from Genoa up the coast to southern France. Medium and fighter bombers closed a highly successful week with return engagements to Axis targets in the Balkans.

15TH ACTIVE

Opening its career with the Wiener Neustadt mission, the new 15th U.S. Air Force crossed the Brenner Pass for the third NAAF raid on the sprawling plant that turned out one-quarter of the single-engine fighters for the Luftwaffe. When they roared away from their targets—marking the northernmost point ever reached from this theater—the factory was so shattered that production is expected to cease for some time. They did not leave unscathed, however, and enemy fighters engaged them in savage dogfights which filled the sky with swarming planes.

Over Italy, the battle against enemy communications reached a new high yesterday when 15th Air Force Fortresses joined their smaller brethren in raids that lasted throughout the day and continued last night. Railroad lines and shipping along both coasts were hit, and in central Italy, par-

(Continued on Page 16)

Marks Anniversary

GENERAL DWIGHT D. EISENHOWER

To commemorate the first anniversary of the Allied landings in North Africa on Nov. 8, 1942, General Dwight D. Eisenhower, Allied Commander in Chief, is sending out two congratulatory messages. One is addressed to American military and civil forces in the North African theater, and the other is addressed to the British naval, military and air leaders with the request that congratulations from General Eisenhower be passed on to all British forces.

Following is the text of the anniversary message from General Eisenhower to all men and women of the American Military and Civil Forces in the North African theater:

"We have reached the first anniversary of initial British-American landings in this theater.

"You came here to take part in a crusade to eliminate ruthless aggression from the earth and to guarantee to yourselves and to your children security against the threat of domination by arrogant despotism.

"During the year just past, you have written a memorable chapter in the history of American arms, a chapter in which are recorded deeds of valor, of sacrifice, of endurance and of unswerving loyalty. You have worked effectively and in friendly cooperation with the Armies, Navies and Air Forces of our Allies and have established in a foreign land a reputation for decency and dignity in conduct. Hour by hour your efforts are contributing toward the ultimate defeat of mighty military machines that hoped to conquer the world. You are just as surely the protectors and supporters of American democracy as your forefathers were its founders.

"From my heart I thank each of you for the services you have so well performed, in the air, on the sea, in the front lines and in our ports and bases.

"All of us salute with reverence the memory of the comrades we have lost, as we earnestly pray that Almighty God will bring comfort to their loved ones.

"But we must now look forward, because for us there can be no thought of turning back until our task has been fully accomplished.

"We are on the mainland of Europe, carrying the battle, daily, closer to the vitals of the enemy. More Americans and more of our Allies will continue to follow steadily into the fight. All of us will work together as one. With the gallant and powerful Russian Army pounding the European enemy on the East and with growing forces seeking out and penetrating weak spots in his defenses from all other directions, his utter defeat — even if not yet definitely in sight—is certain. Victory will likewise be ours in the far off Pacific, where Allied Forces are already on the offensive and where unconquerable China, awaiting the time when the full power of the Allies may come to her assistance, continues to defy one of the most powerful and vicious of our enemies.

"The heart of America supports our every endeavor. Reports of sporadic troubles on the home front are occasioned by the ill-considered actions of a relatively few individuals. Let us always re-

(Continued on Page 14)

Fall Of Isernia Puts Wehrmacht Back Over Plains

ALLIED FORCE HEADQUARTERS, Nov. 5—Two-thirds of the powerful German defense line 90 miles below Rome crumbled this week before triumphant Allied troops who climbed mountains 2,000 to 5,000 feet high to dislodge the enemy from strongly entrenched positions. Having completely occupied the towering ranges blocking the road to Rome, British and American units began to drive the Wehrmacht back across the plains of central Italy.

ISERNIA KEY

The German collapse was accelerated yesterday by the fall of Isernia, key pivot point controlling the only coast-to-coast highway below Rome. Defending forces abandoned the town after previous heavy fighting failed to stem the advancing 8th Army. After Isernia's capture British and American troops fanned out over the surrounding roads.

Americans on the right flank of the 5th Army secured domination of the upper reaches of the Volturno and were on the outskirts of the important town of Venafro, whose fall was expected momentarily. On the west coast British and American units were approaching the Garigliano River, with the retreating enemy constantly harassed by dive-bombing Allied planes.

WEAKEN IN EAST

Even in the east, where the Germans have been holding out most successfully, their position was growing weaker. General Sir Bernard L. Montgomery's men threw additional bridgeheads over the Trigno River and beat off successive counterattacks. On the extreme east coast, the British finally broke through intensified opposition and captured San Salvo above the river. The Germans were now in danger of having their strong mountain positions north of the Trigno outflanked by the 8th Army.

The breakthrough on the lower portion of the enemy line assures the 8th Army rapid control of the

(Continued on Page 16)

Elections Good Or Bad— Depending On Party

By T-Sgt. JOHN M. WILLIG
(Stars and Stripes Staff Writer)

NEW YORK—The biggest excitement on the political homefront blew in this week with the local off-year elections on Tuesday, and professional politicians immediately dusted off their crystal balls for a look into the future—the future being the 1944 national elections.

National Republican and Democratic leaders divided sharply on the significance of the Republican victories. House Republican Leader, Joseph W. Martin, Jr., underscored his party's victories in New York, New Jersey and especially in Kentucky as a definite indication of things to come in the 1944 presidential election, while Democratic National Chairman, Frank C. Walker, said he saw "no national political trends whatsoever" in the results. He further pointed out that "the administration did not take an active part in a single contest."

For the Republicans, the victory of State Senator Joe Hanley for New York's Lieutenant Governorship and the unexpected victory of Judge Simeon Willis in nosing out Democratic candidate J. Lyter Donaldson for the governorship of Kentucky were the portents to which the GOP called attention. Senator Hanley's election was hailed by Republicans as a vote of confidence in Governor Dewey's administration. Some observers said that the outcome in New York was especially pleasing to those Republicans who would prefer Governor Dewey to Wendell L. Willkie as the party's 1944 national nominee.

The experts dug down for some statistics in the GOP record books

(Continued on Page 14)

Allies Bash Japs On Bougainville

ALLIED SOUTH PACIFIC HEADQUARTERS — One of the most impressive Allied land, sea and air operations of the South Pacific was unfolded this week to crack the Japanese eastern defense bastion on Bougainville Island.

Biggest thrust of the northern Solomon Islands attack, begun last week with landings on islands flanking Bougainville on the south, came Monday when U.S. Marines forced a landing at Empress Augusta Bay, midway down the west coast of Bougainville.

But the greatest immediate blow to the enemy in this action was struck by the Allied naval task force which brought the ground troops in. Attacked by at least 12 Japanese warships shortly after the Marines had landed, American naval vessels sank four enemy destroyers and one cruiser. The Japanese later admitted the loss of the cruiser and two of the destroyers. None of our vessels was lost.

While the Marines on Bougainville fought inland in an attempt to cut off the estimated 25,000 Japanese trapped in the south of the island, the enemy, 260 miles northward in New Britain's Rabaul Harbor, already was massing

(Continued on Page 16)

FIFTH ARMY
THE STARS AND STRIPES
COMBAT EDITION

VOL. I, NO. XIX "BE ALERT AND LIVE" Italy, 10 November, 1943

Reds Move Fifty Miles Beyond Kiev; Nazis Crumble Under Soviet Tanks

Eighth Overlooks Sangro

FIFTH ARMY HQ., Nov. 9—While the troops of the Fifth Army improved their positions in the vicinity of Venafro today, the men of the Eighth Army continued their advance up the Adriatic coast.

Today's communique reads: "In the Eighth Army area our troops are meeting with many demolitions but advances were made all along the army front. In the north we reached positions overlooking the River Sangro. Heavy rains hampered Fifth Army operations. Our troops made limited advances and improved positions previously gained."

The Fifth Army made some gains but face strongly held positions on Monte Maggiore.

Gen. Mark Clark's men sent the Jerries a-running as they were forming for a counter-attack west of Galluccio. The attack was broken up before it got started.

The Eighth Army continues its push forward rapidly along the eastern coast. In moving up to the Sangro River the British troops took Torigo and Paglieta. Further inland Torrebruna was captured and near the center of the Italian front Pescoaianciano is in our hands.

Both the Fifth and Eighth Armies are in contact, except in the central Appenines, with what prisoners have spoken freely of as the German winter line. This line is described by the prisoners as running generally around the Garigliano and Sangro Rivers and is backed by high ground to the north of the rivers and the Appenine massifs in the center. The line is organized to considerable depth in some places, according to a staff officer at 15th Army Group headquarters.

Arab Protest Made

CAIRO, Nov. 9—The Arab League has addressed a sharp protest to Cordell Hull, U. S. Secretary of State, against recent messages sent by Wendell Willkie and Thomas Dewey to a meeting of Jewish dealers in which Jewish immigration to Palestine was supported.

The protest read: "Arab Union points out that these messages ignore the rights of Arab peoples to whom alone Palestine belongs and constitute a flagrant injustice. The statements are incompatible with the Atlantic Charter, with the "Four Freedoms' of United Nations policy, and with the Palestine White Book."

Nazis Abandon Tanks

MOSCOW, Nov. 9—The Red Army reports that many German tanks are being found on the battlefield, abandoned and in perfect condition.

The explanaiton, says Moscow, lies in the enormous number of Nazi tanks destroyed in the past 12 months, with the consequent death of trained crews.

The Red Army claims to have destroyed 25,000 German tanks in a year's time. Now, says Moscow Hitler is forced to use less well-trained men in his armored units, and when the fighting gets hot and complicated, they run for—not knowing how to handle their machines in tight spots.

Slav Patriots Active

YUGOSLAVIA, Nov. 9—The communique of the Yugoslav National Army of Liberation reported that on the peninsula of Pelyesac in Dalmatia partisan troops have pushed back German troops in a western direction.

In Croatia attempts of the Germans to penetrate from Ogulin into liberated territory have been repelled. In the province of Zagorye, north of Zagreb, several German garrisons were hard-hit by attacking patriots.

New Gains Made Within Crimea

MOSCOW, Nov. 9 — Russian motorized spearheads are 55 miles beyond Kiev, which they took only three days ago. They drive disordered Germans before them like straw in the wind.

Northwest of Kiev the Reds are approaching Marianovka, on the railroad running southwest towrads Berdichev. That city, which is southwest of Kiev, they are also nearing. These are tank thrusts that are pushing a sharp salient into the German line, and threaten a break-through that would be disastrous for the Nazis.

At these points the Russians are some 200 miles to the west of the German troops fighting at KrivoiRog in the Dnieper Bend, and a giant flanking move upon those troops looms as a possibility.

Southeast of Kiev there is fighting around the Pereyaslav bridgehead, and this, following the taking of Fastov, is subject to an encircling movement which would catch another German force in another Russian vice.

The Germans are trying desperately to re-group their shattered units in the region of the sharpest thrust from Kiev. They constantly throw in picked panzer outfits, only to find them crushed by the overwhelming weight of Russian tank forces.

Meanwhile, at other points up and down

(Continued on Page 4)

Threat of Railway Strike Darkens Home Front; Vote Taken After Wage Increase Denial

WASHINGTON, Nov. 9—The prospect of a strike by millions of American railway workers, with all the bleak implications thereof, confronts the Federal Government.

Union spokesmen rejected a wage increase of four cents hourly which was recommended by a special board created by President Roosevelt to consider the railwaymen's demand for a substantial increase.

A strike ballot is now being taken. Should the railway workers carry out their threat and strike it means a complete tie-up of the country's railway systems, with the possibility of the government taking them over.

The crisis is in many ways greater than that of the coal strike. A tie-up in transportation would be a crippling blow to America's war program. It is not considered likely that the railwaymen will refuse to work.

Mrs. Roosevelt commented today that the War Labor Board's approval of the wage increase for the United Mine Workers would inevitably lead other workers to make similar demands.

She pointed out that, "Although the 'Little Steel Formula' has been effective in the past, no formula can hold a stabilization line that is only partially set."

Weather Outlook
Tonight
Clear, colder
Temperatures today: Max., 34; Min., 29
Detailed Report on Last Page

The Kingston Daily Freeman

First in News
Local, National, Foreign
Ulster County's Leading
Advertising Medium

VOL. LXXIII—No. 31 | CITY OF KINGSTON, N. Y., MONDAY EVENING, NOVEMBER 22, 1943. | PRICE FIVE CENTS

U. S. Forces, Ashore in Two Gilbert Islands, Batter Japanese Defenses; Reds Halt Nazis

Bid Is Made To Remove La Guardia

Midtown Civic League Resolution Says Mayor Is Lax; Curran Sees Confidence Move

Patrolman Speaks

Bronx Policeman Says Mayor Doesn't Work With Department

New York, Nov. 22 (AP)—A demand that Mayor F. H. LaGuardia be removed from office because his actions and testimony in regard to crime in Brooklyn's- Bedford Stuyvesant section "clearly indicate misfeasance" was before Governor Thomas E. Dewey today.

A resolution directed to the governor calling for LaGuardia's ouster was adopted yesterday at a mass meeting sponsored by the Midtown Civic League, shortly after the mayor had defended himself against charges of laxity in crime prevention during his weekly radio broadcast.

The mayor last week ordered a detailed police investigation of the Brooklyn area, known as "Little Harlem," after a Kings County Grand Jury held that LaGuardia was responsible for "a deplorable state of lawlessness" in the section.

Highlight of the mass meeting, attended by about 500 including some negroes, was a speech by David Liebman, 28, a Bronx patrolman, who declared that LaGuardia was "not cooperating at all with the police department."

Liebman, who said he a graduate of the University of Alabama and interested in juvenile delinquency and sociology, declared that crime conditions similar to those in Brooklyn existed in the Bronx. He stated: "If we had more policemen, we would be able to do a better job."

On his radio broadcast over station WNYC, LaGuardia made no specfic mention of Brooklyn but said "at no time did law and order ever get beyond the control of the police department and it is not getting beyond the control of the police department at this time."

Curran Speaks

New York, Nov. 22 (AP)—Mayor F. H. LaGuardia's analysis of the recent elections, says Secretary of State Thomas J. Curran, "was made for the purpose of trying to restore the shattered confidence of all the despairing cohorts of the New Deal.

Curran made the assertion yesterday over city-owned station WNYC in reply to LaGuardia who two weeks ago said on this weekly broadcast that the Republican state victory was not a New Deal defeat and that the Republicans were to blame for the election of Thomas A. Aurelio to the Supreme Court.

In answering LaGuardia's contention that Republican backing of a third nominee aided Aurelio's election, Curran said that his party did not endorse Matthew M. Levy, Democratic and American Labor Party candidate, because:

"We believed him unqualified

(Continued on Page Three)

Study Is Ordered

Ickes Demands Contracts Be Re-examined for Canol Oil Project

Washington, Nov. 22 (AP)—Petroleum Administrator Harold L. Ickes today demanded a re-examination of contracts for the U. S. financed $130,000,000 Canol oil project in Canada which he said the War Department undertook without prior consultation with his office.

Ickes told the Senate's Truman committee that in return for "enormous investments and risks which we alone have assumed," the nation should be accorded "a permanent peace-time share of the oil and products to be produced upon terms commensurate with the magnitude of the contribution which this government has made."

The project consists of experimental drilling, a pipeline from Fort Norman to White Horse, Canada, an oil refinery at White Horse, and roads and other facilities being built by a Canadian oil company.

Cars Collide, Injuring Five

Freeman Photo

Sunday afternoon at 4:59 o'clock automobiles driven by Sidney Pearson and Thomas Edwards collided at the intersection of Linderman and Washington avenues, resulting in serious injury to five occupants of the cars. Photo taken from Linderman avenue looking south, shows the Pearson car back of a tree, and the Edwards car on left.

Saugerties Man, 21, Suffers Skull Fracture in Accident

Four Others Are Injured in Collision of Cars at Intersection on Sunday

Five people were injured, one seriously, when automobiles driven by Thomas Edwards, 48, of 60 Lafayette avenue, and Sidney Pearson, 21, of Route 2, Box 393, Saugerties, collided at the intersection of Linderman and Washington avenues, at 4:59 o'clock Sunday afternoon.

The injured:

Sidney Pearson, possible skull fracture and fractured ribs. Condition serious.

Edward Miles, Bergenfield, N. J., laceration of neck, condition fairly good.

Thomas Edwards, laceration and possible skull fracture. Condition apparently fair.

Breir Ducker, 22, Route 2, Saugerties, left elbow, leg and hip, and possible head injury. Condition apparently fair.

The four persons above are in the Kingston Hospital.

Lorraine Blaum, 14, of Guttenberg, N. J., injury to knee. She was not hospitalized.

The police department received a telephone call that there had been a serious automobile crash at the street intersection and asking that an ambulance be sent. The Conner ambulance responded.

Officers Joseph Fallon and Joseph Myers in one of the radio cars were sent to the scene and directed traffic and assisted the injured.

According to the police report Mr. Edwards was driving south on Washington avenue, while Mr. Pearson was proceeding west on Linderman avenue, when the two automobiles crashed together. The cars were so badly damaged they had to be towed away.

Of the five persons injured, Pearson is reported as the most critical, and at the hospital today his condition was reported as still serious.

Mr. Edwards was driving the automobile of his brother, John F. Edwards of 186 Main street.

The police are making an investigation of the crash, and will endeavor to obtain statements from the drivers of the cars when they have recovered sufficiently to be able to talk.

Stone Refuses Any Part in Selection

Under Terms of Bill He Might Have to Pick Vote Decider

Washington, Nov. 22 (AP)—Chief Justice Harlan F. Stone said in a letter read to the Senate today by Senator Vandenberg (R.-Mich.) that he would decline to take part in appointing any member to a proposed war ballot commission which would administer absentee voting by the armed forces.

Under terms of the pending servicemen's vote bill, the chief justice could be requested by the President to appoint an associate justice of the Supreme Court or a Circuit Court judge to serve as an umpire and cast the deciding vote in case of a deadlock on the proposed four-member bipartisan commission.

Vandenberg told Senator Green (D.-R. I.), co-author of the measure with Senator Lucas (D.-Ill.), that the chief justice's objections to following this procedure made it necessary to rewrite "the very heart and center of the bill," designed to permit service personnel to vote in next year's general election.

Earlier in the day a Republican Senate caucus left the way open for individual attempts to change the bill on the floor, but the party members did not commit themselves jointly to any specific amendments.

Much of the discussion in the closed meeting involved a suggestion to eliminate the proposal for a judge to pass on contested decisions. Some members want the commission confined to two members of each major party with a requirement that at least three members agree on any question.

Senator Connally (D.-Tex.), introduced an element of Democratic opposition with a challenge to the constitutionality of the whole plan.

Treasury Receipts

Washington, Nov. 22 (AP)—The position of the treasury November 19: Receipts $93,714,244.11. Expenditures $365,568,827.57. Net balance $16,315,835,803.56. Working balance included $15,553,113,-912.06. Customs receipts for the month $22,006,741.10. Receipts fiscal year (July 1) $13,764,780,-237.39. Expenditures fiscal year $35,154,147,951.27. Excess of expenditures $21,389,357,713.88. Total debt $169,810,539,265.49. Increase over previous day $29,868,-566.65. Gold assets $22,080,798,-523.66.

Goldstein's Assistant

Albany, N. Y., Nov. 22 (AP)—George R. Loveys, Elsmere, former state editor of the Associated Press, holds a $7,500 post as executive assistant to Attorney General Nathaniel L. Goldstein. Loveys, 34, who was appointed yesterday, served as publicity director for Lieut. Governor-elect Joe R. Hanley. He resigned from the Associated Press in September.

Lonergan Pleads Innocent

New York, Nov. 22 (AP)—Wayne Lonergan, 25-year-old R.C.A.F. cadet, pleaded innocent today to an indictment charging him with first degree murder in the slaying of his wife, Patricia, a month ago. The plea, routine because a defendant may not plead guilty to first degree murder, was taken speedily before General Sessions Judge George L. Donnellan. Lonergan did not speak during the procedure. His Chief Counsel Edward V. Broderick, entered the plea and an associate counsel sought and received 10 days in which to file motions. Broderick told reporters later that no arrangements had been made to have a psychiatric examination of the defendant.

Deaths in Congress Halt Showdown on Subsidy Program

Representative Steagall Is Heart Victim, While Ditter Is Killed in Crackup

Washington, Nov. 22 (AP)—Two sudden deaths among the House membership today delayed for at least a day a showdown vote on the administration's consumer-subsidy program, and removed from the scene one of the leading figures in the bitter subsidy dispute.

Shortly after the House arranged to suspend business for 24 hours in respect to Representative Ditter (R.Pa.), a powerful figure in his party's counsels, killed yesterday in a navy plane crash, Representative Steagall (D.-Ala.), frequently an administration stalwart, but recently lined up against the White House subsidy plans, died suddenly in a Washington hospital.

Steagall, who was stricken with a heart attack, had as chairman of the banking committee wielded powerful influence in this dispute, playing an important role in lining up farm state opposition to consumer-subsidies.

His death automatically elevated Representative Spence (D.-Ky.) to the chairmanship of the banking committee.

Spence has taken the position that "subsidies should be sustained under the present circumstances in view of Congress' instruction to the President to hold the line."

While the two deaths will delay the House decision in the controversy, it was not expected to affect the outcome. Even the most optimistic of President Roosevelt's stalwarts on Capitol Hill have con-

(Continued on Page Three)

Fourth Big Battle for Changsha Is Likely; Japs Push Two Salients

Chungking, Nov. 22 (AP)—A fourth great battle for Changsha, capital of Hunan province in Central China, loomed as a possibility today as the Japanese extended two strong spearheads toward Changteh, west of Tungting Lake, and were reported to be strengthening their Yochow base east of the lake.

Changteh, 100 miles southwest of the Yangtze river port of Ichang and 25 miles west of the lake, would provide the Japanese with a potential springboard for a thrust at Changsha, which is 100 miles to the southeast.

Brig. Gen. Edgar Glenn, chief of staff of the U.S. 14th Air Force, describing the Tungting Lake sector as "area No. 1 in importance," said that "we are giving all support possible to the Chinese troops trying to repel the advance on Changteh, which is the corridor of approach to Chungking."

He said the Japanese were within 10 miles of Changteh.

The Japanese hurled repeated bomber-supported attacks against the Chinese near Izeli, at the junction of the Link and Liu rivers, 30 miles northwest of Changteh, but the Chinese were striking back vigorously. Another Japanese spearhead was thrusting southward immediately west of the lake in a move which threatened Changteh's communications.

American airmen, supporting Chinese ground forces, bombed Japanese installations at Tzeli on Saturday, starting many fires, it was announced. Warehouses and barracks on Nampang Island off the China coast also were bombed by formations of B-25s.

A comunique from headquarters of the U.S. 14th Air Force today disclosed that American medium bombers had swept out over the China Sea, sinking a Japanese gunboat and a freighter and damaging five other cargo vessels.

U. S. Mitchell bombers also attacked wharves and warehouses at the former treaty port of Swatow, the bulletin said. All planes returned safely from the two forays.

Poles Says Reds Face Bitter Resistance Unless They Enter Poland as Ally of Country

Reestablishment of Diplomatic Relations With Poles in Exile at London Will Be Gauge of Friendliness of Soviet Government

Washington, Nov. 22 (AP).—Polish sources that can not be otherwise identified declared today that the Russian army must enter Poland as an ally, and not as a conqueror, or else face desperate resistance by the Poles themselves.

Determination to fight back unless the Soviets reestablish diplomatic relations with the London Polish-government-in-exile was voiced in responsible quarters here as Red troops plunged closer to the old Polish frontier, established in 1921.

Despite a recent statement by Constantin Oumansky, Soviet ambassador to Mexico City, indicating that Russia still recognizes the western boundary drawn with the Germans in 1939, the Poles maintain that only the pre-war frontier is valid.

The Polish position as stated by an authoritative source who requested anonymity pending clarification of the stand to be taken by the Allied high command is:

If military necessity requires Soviet occupation of Polish territory, there must be an understanding between the two governments based on the resumption of normal diplomatic relations and on the principle of sovereign equality.

(The Russians severed their relations with the exiled Polish government early this year after the latter had requested an international Red Cross investigation of reports that the Russians had killed thousands of Polish officers near Smolensk.)

The policy taken by the Russians when they occupy Poland will be considered a test case of the four power Moscow declaration. It was pointed out that when the Red troops reach Poland, it will be the first time in this war that territory of one member of the United Nations is occupied by another.

The Soviet Union should guarantee administration of liberated territories by the London government-in-exile.

If such an agreement is not reached, the Poles anticipate an attempt to Sovietize Poland through the Union of Polish patriots, headed by Wanda Wasilewska in Moscow, or deportation to Russia of underground leaders.

A suggestion on the conduct of the occupation previously sent by the Poles to the Anglo-American-Russian conference at Moscow was that after relations were reestablished, the Allies should set up a council on central Europe similar to the council on Italy.

O.P.A. Cites Savings

Washington, Nov. 22 (AP)—The O. P. A. said today that if it were not for its controls, the nation's rent bills would be $1,000,000,000 higher this year. Basing this estimated saving on the results of a survey in 39 war production centers, the agency stated that despite the slice, landlords are better off than they were in 1939 and 1940. "Actual figures taken from the books of landlords throughout the country show that the rate of net operating income for apartment houses during six months of rent control was 34 per cent greater than in 1939," said O. P. A. "The increase for landlords of small structures over the same period was 36 per cent."

Italian Lessons Given

New York, Nov. 22 (AP)—Lessons in Italian are appearing in the Naples edition of Stars and Stripes, army newspaper. Don Hollenbeck, N. B. C. reporter, radioed today that the soldiers are practicing their syntax and pronunciation with pungent observations to the local citizenry, such as: "Yes. I have no fiancee." "In civilian life in America, I was an honest millionaire."

Eighteen Die in Crash

Washington, Nov. 22 (AP)—The deaths of 18 persons in the crash of a U. S. Naval transport plane 30 miles east of Rio de Janeiro were announced by the navy last night. The victims included 16 navy officers and men, an American civilian engineer and a Brazilian. The accident occurred last Friday. The announcement here said the transport burned after falling but the cause of the crash was not known.

Postwar Projects

Albany, N. Y., Nov. 22 (AP) — New York localities planning 1,-287 additional postwar public works projects will receive $802,-146 of state money to help finance plans and specifications. The Postwar Public Works Planning Commission said yesterday New York city has been allowed $418,-230 for 750 projects, while upstate communities have been allowed $383,916 for 537 proposed constructions.

Tax Commission Proposes Overhaul Of Business Levy

Corporation Statutes Now Tend to Discourage Manufacturing, Cut State Income

Albany, N. Y., Nov. 22 (AP)—The first major pattern for a modernized state tax structure sought by Governor Dewey was ready today for his scrutiny.

The State Tax Commission sent him a report urging a complete overhaul of corporation tax statutes which, it said, curtail state revenue, discourage manufacturing and cause "unjust" tax discrimination among business corporations.

The governor, in his first message to the Legislature last January, recommended quarterly payment of personal income tax, more liberal exemptions and reductions from that levy and other changes to "adjust our tax laws to the human needs of our citizens." Then, asserting "our entire tax system needs further improvement," he announced appointment of a committee to study the whole tax structure.

Subsequently the State Tax Commission, headed by Rollin Browne, began a separate study with the assistance of several tax lawyers, accountants, and state officials.

Taxation for the privilege of doing business in New York state, the commission reported today, is "distributed unequally, and therefore unsoundly and unwisely, among corporate taxpayers generally."

Chief recommendations would:

Establish a flexible tax schedule applicable to corporations, investment trusts or holding corporations instead of what the commission termed present "arbitrary" division of the three into "rigid" classifications.

Adopt a new formula for computing business income within and outside the state, in place of a system which the commission said now discourages manufacturing and either under-taxes or over-taxes many corporations.

Require current payment of franchise taxes from the time a corporation organizes in the state or begins doing business here.

Present law, the report said, permits a corporation to "organize or start doing business in the state shortly after any November 1 and continue for nearly two years, without becoming liable for any tax based on income."

In recommending a flexible tax schedule, the commission explained business corporations now pay six per cent and investment trusts 4½ per cent on that part of their income allocated to New York, and holding corporations are taxed one mill on that portion of their capital allocated to this state.

To tax corporations to the exact extent that they come under one of the three classifications, the commission proposed:

A tax on the portion allocated

(Continued on Page 12)

Sergeant Gleason Receives Award

Flatbush Road Soldier Gets Silver Star Medal for Gallantry

SGT. JOHN GLEASON

Mrs. John Gleason of the Flatbush road recently received a citation and the Silver Star Medal awarded to her husband, Sgt. John Gleason, who is now stationed in Sicily. The Silver Star Medal was awarded to Sergeant Gleason for gallantry in action.

The text of the citation follows: "On 21 July, 1943, the reconnaissance platoon of which Sergeant Gleason is a member was advancing on Castelvetrano, Sicily. On several occasions when hostile positions were encountered, Sergeant Gleason volunteered to take a scout car forward in order to draw enemy fire, thus revealing the strength and disposition of the hostile force and expediting the attack by the platoon and supporting elements. While moving forward in the face of enemy fire, Sergeant Gleason's vehicle was struck many times by small arms fire and shell fragments from artillery. Sergeant Gleason's coolness and courage not only made the rapid advance of the platoon possible, but served as a splendid example to members of his organization."

While in Sicily Sergeant Gleason has met John Dolan and George Diehl of Kingston and Thomas Brady from Eddyville. They are in the same outfit.

Famed Organist Dies

New York, Nov. 22 (AP)—Pietro Yon, 57, famed organist and musical director of St. Patrick's Cathedral and honorary organist of the Vatican, died early today at Huntington, N. Y., the Rt. Rev. Msgr. Joseph Flannelly of the cathedral announced. Yon suffered a stroke April 8. He succumbed in his sleep at 6:15 a. m. (E. W. T.) at the estate of his son's father-in-law, Ricardo San Vero.

Construction Drops

Albany, N. Y., Nov. 22 (AP)—Employment in New York's construction industries dropped 6.8 per cent from mid-September to mid-October, while payrolls shrank 5.3 per cent and man-hours, 7.8 per cent. Records from 103 cities and villages showed 3,170 building permits issued in October, covering construction estimated at $4,-718,404 or about $1,500,000 below the preceding month.

Fleet, Air Support Is Given Men

Mac Arthur's Pincers on New Guinea Put Rabaul in Greater Danger

Allies Gain

Forces in Italy Push Ahead on Eastern Flank

By RICHARD McMURRAY
(Associated Press War Editor)

American forces invading Makin and Tarawa in the Gilbert Islands battered dug-in Japanese defenses on those central Pacific stepping stones today with the support of battleships, carriers and sky fleets in fighting which Tokyo described as heavy.

The offensive opened at dawn Saturday and its outcome must be decided swiftly because the islands are too tiny for large land forces and too bare to provide much cover. Resistance on Tarawa, main enemy base in the Gilberts which Japan seized from Britain two years ago, was strong. Opposition on Makin, a seaplane base, was moderate.

Admiral Chester Nimitz's drive complemented the continuing offensive of General MacArthur and Admiral Halsey in the Southwest Pacific. On Bougainville in the Solomons, U. S. forces enlarged and consolidated their bridgehead at Empress Augusta Bay. On New Guinea, the Australians lashed at the Japanese with tanks within a mile of Sattleberg. Both prongs of MacArthur's pincers threatened the great base of Rabaul on New Britain, the southern end of which was pulverized with a record load of 138 tons of bombs dumped on Gasmata. Japanese opposition on land and in the air increased.

Forces engaged in the Pacific were but a tiny fraction of those locked in violent combat in Russia, where the Red Army with massed artillery was opposing serious German assaults against their Kiev bulge, 60 miles west of the Ukrainian capital. The Russians said the Germans had been halted since their recapture of Zhitomir, but the Nazis claimed to have driven within 40 miles of Kiev. The Russians called the situation serious.

The Russians mounted a new offensive thrust against Krivoi Rog, inside the Dnieper Bend, to divert German power. Moscow said that Nazi resistance collapsed south of Kremenchug and that other Soviet columns were gaining southwest of Dnepropetrovsk and in the Rechitsa area of White Russia. Berlin reported a new Russian landing in the Crimea south of Kerch.

Slogging through heavy rains in central Italy, the British Eighth Army captured Vastogirardi and San Pietro Avellana, three and a half miles short of the highway junction of Castel Di Sangro. Large Canadian forces arrived to swell the Allied armies. Week-end advances in the center have shortened the battle line by 20 miles.

Allied planes attacked Albania and Civitavecchia, north of Rome. In Yugoslavia, the Partisans said they drove the Germans from two villages in Bosnia and smashed a

(Continued on Page Three)

O.P.A. Gives Rule

Registration Consolidation for Industrial Users Will Be in Effect

Washington, Nov. 22 (AP)—The Office of Price Administration today announced a consolidation of registration procedure for obtaining rationed foods for industrial use.

Under the new arrangement, all industrial users will register with O.P.A. between December 19 and January 5. They will use a single form and make application for food allotments under all rationing programs at one time. Previously, three registrations were necessary under the sugar, processed foods and meats-fats programs.

Simultaneously, O.P.A. announced that applications for industrial food allotments for the remainder of 1943 must be filed before December 15 to facilitate the new registration.

Entered as second-class matter April 15, 1931, at the post office at New Haven, Connecticut, under the act of March 3, 1879

ILLUSTRATED CURRENT NEWS

Published Monday, Wednesday and Friday by Illustrated Current News, Inc., New Haven, Conn. Subscription Annually, $20.80

Nov. 26, 1943—No. 4718

MOUNTBATTEN INSPECTS GUARD IN CHUNGKING

Admiral Lord Louis Mountbatten, Allied commander in southeast Asia, (in front group), and General Ho Ying Chin with other senior officers, inspect the Guard of Honor at the Chungking airfield after Lord Mountbatten's arrival at the Chinese wartime capital. Mountbatten is now in India.

News Note: British Bombers Smash At Berlin Again.

LA FRANCE EN ARMES

DECEMBRE 1943
N° 1

Le Général Smutts bavarde sur l'avenir de la France..

COMBATTONS pour la rétablir dans son intégrité et sa grandeur.

BULLETIN DES OFFICIERS DU CADRE DE RESERVE DES FRANCS-TIREURS ET PARTISANS FRANCAIS.

MOBILISATION

"La Victoire sera gagnée; elle le sera, je le jure, avec les armes de la France".

Ces paroles, dont nous avons fait un mot d'ordre ont été prononcées par le Général de Gaulle en juin 1940. Depuis, en Tripolitaine et en Algérie, en Tunisie, sur toutes les mers du monde, en l'air sur l'Allemagne et sur le front de l'Est, dans les rues de nos villes françaises, dans nos montagnes et dans nos forêts avec les francs-tireurs et les réfractaires, notre drapeau a été à l'honneur.

Et voici qu'en France, au bout de la résistance, s'annonce la lutte armée qui mène à la Victoire.

La puissante armée allemande qui occupe et opprime notre pays chancelle sous les coups de nos Alliés Anglais, Américains et Soviétiques. Les Nations-Unies reconnaissent notre gouvernement légitime. Officiers de tout âge et de tous grades, nous attendons avec impatience le moment de reprendre les armes. Ce moment vient.

En Corse, un peuple entier levé à l'appel du Comité d'Alger pour l'Insurrection Nationale, encadré par des organisations militaires, appuyé par des troupes régulières a, dans une courte et brillante campagne, jeté à la mer l'envahisseur allemand.

La libération de la Corse est oeuvre française. Le prestige de la France dans le monde a grandi.

Il n'est Français, il n'est surtout soldat français qui ne veuille prendre exemple sur la Corse.

Question de dignité nationale, certes: nous avons ressenti doublement comme Français et comme Soldats la honte de la trahison militaire et de l'humiliation nationale. Nous avons le devoir et le droit de la laver nous-mêmes, à la française.

Mais aussi, souci des intérêts et de l'avenir de la Patrie. Cette Patrie a été moquée, bafouée, compissée par tous les roquets de l'anti-France depuis trois ans. Notre action peut aider notre gouvernement à conserver le prestige et l'autorité dont il a besoin aujourd'hui dans les consultations inter-nationales et dont il aura besoin demain à la Conférence de la Paix.

Un homme d'état, parlant en son nom personnel, a cru pouvoir, dans un discours récent, prédire l'avenir historique de l'Europe. Cet avenir qui se fait chaque jour dans la lutte, c'est la solidité de toutes nos alliances, c'est le combat et le sacrifice des Français qui l'assureront.

Obéissant aux autorités légitimes fidèles à leurs alliances, agissant en plein accord avec les Armées Alliées, les Français se doivent d'être au premier rang dans la bataille pour la libération.

C'est la mobilisation.

Echappez à l'ennemi qui tentera de vous interner.

Organisez-vous en petits groupes de trois ou quatre amis.

Perfectionnez vos connaissances techniques.

Informez le Commandement Français.

La France compte sur vous.
Vos chefs vous appellent.
Vous répondrez présent pour que

VIVE LA FRANCE.

LA FRANCE EN ARMES.

N° 40 ORGANE DES MOUVEMENTS UNIS DE RÉSISTANCE Edition Z. S. 1er Décembre 1943

LIBÉRATION

Un seul chef : DE GAULLE ; une seule lutte : POUR NOS LIBERTÉS

« Notre seul but est de rendre la parole au peuple Français » DE GAULLE

Le continent n'était qu'un vaste cachot privé de toute communication avec cette noble Angleterre, asile généreux de la pensée, illustre refuge de la dignité de l'espèce humaine. Tout à coup deux extrémités de la terre, deux grands peuples se sont répondus, et les flammes de Moscou ont été l'aurore de la liberté du monde.

Benjamin CONSTANT,
(Introduction à l'esprit de conquête)

UNION DE LA NATION

Dans un numero de juillet dernier, qui a valu à LIBERATION l'honneur d'être largement cité et attaqué par le Cri du Peuple, journal allemand paraissant à Paris sous la direction du traître Jacques Doriot, nous demandions en particulier, " pourquoi M. Couve de Murville de longue date le représentant autorisé de la synarchie française" et " M. Jean Monnet, délégué accrédité des intérêts capitalistes américains " appartenaient au Comité de la Liberation nationale d'Alger.

Des amis, sur les sentiments desquels il ne pouvait y avoir de confusion, se scandalisèrent de ce franc-parler. Il faut, nous disaient-ils, faires des sacrifices à la nécessité de l'Union. Certes, répondions-nous, mais union signifie d'abord égalité. Jamais nous n'admettrons que, sous pretexte d'union, trois puis antes nations, même patriotes, aient une voix au moins égale à celle de 10 000 ouvriers clandestinement syndiqués et risquant chaque jour leur vie dans la lutte contre l'ennemi. Jamais nous n'accepterons que quelques dizaines de généraux, honteusement vichyssois et quelques douzaines de hauts fonctionnaires, résolument réactionnaires, se fassent plus facilement entendre que des milliers et des millions de patriotes organisés ou non. Nous disions : " Union, oui, mais chacun à sa place et les combattants d'abord."

Emmanuel d'ASTIER
Fondateur de LIBÉRATION
Commissaire à l'Intérieur du C.F.L.N.

«Bernard» nous avait dit «au revoir», il y a moins d'un mois. Avant son depart, ses amis n'ignorant pas que toutes les polices françaises et allemandes possedaient son signalement, lui avaient conseillé un deguisement pour le trajet en chemin de fer à travers la France. Bernard, docile, - car il ne fallait pas qu'il se fasse prendre, il fallait comme les autres fois, qu'il revienne - avait essayé : comme les autres fois, il avait echoué. Il restait le nez, la silhouette interminable, les épaules un peu voûtées, l'ardeur soudaine du regard quand il fallait attaquer ou se défendre. Un chapeau sur la tête de Bernard, prend toujours les mêmes bosses, une houppelande quelconque toujours les mêmes plis.

Pendant l'été 1940, Emmanuel d'Astier de la Vigerie qui faisait l'apprentissage de la clandestinité et ignorait encore la nécessité des pseudonymes, conspirait pour former un «gang de terroristes». La dernière colonne exterminerait les traitres ! Un peu plus tard ce fut la rencontre avec quelques camarades qui se cachent encore sous leurs pseudonymes, et ce fut LIBERATION.

Que venait faire cet «aristocrate» dans le mouvement populaire de Résistance ?

Il le créait, il l'animait. Cet «aristocrate» fut le premier à publier dans le numéro 3 de LIBERATION, qu'avec ses camarades il distribuait lui-même, l'appel du dirigeant le plus autorisé du mouvement syndicaliste invitant la classe ouvrière à reprendre la lutte.

Bernard ne reviendra pas. Il reviendra avec la victoire. Nous savons que c'est a contre-cœur qu'il nous a abandonnes, que ce n'est pas sans un difficile débat de conscience, qu'il a assumé la périlleuse responsabilité que lui offrait le général de Gaulle. Il a accepté pour nous.

Tous les camarades, militants des M.U.R. qui se sont d'abord groupés dans LIBERATION, forment le vœu que «notre Bernard» puise dans leur volonté toute la force dont il a besoin.

Notre droit à parler ainsi, le courage des militants qui font circuler notre journal le garantissait et nous n'avions à connaître d'autre censure que celle de notre raison. Nous savions que notre voix, unie à celles de tous nos camarades, avait son écho à Londres et à Alger. Nous savions aussi que Charles de Gaulle n'ignorait pas que, par notre plume, s'exprimait la pensée de la France tout court. Nous savions enfin que si, pour certains nous pouvions paraître jouer les enfants terribles, pour ceux qui avaient la redoutable mission de résoudre le cas Giraud et le cas des transfuges de Vichy, notre attitude était une aide certaine et même indispensable.

Les évènements qui ont marqué les premiers mois de la collaboration de Gaulle-Giraud (élimination de Peyrouton, Boisson et *tutti-quanti*), nous ont été agréables, mais et nous l'avons dit, ils ne nous ont pas donné satisfaction. Nous n'avons pas dit cependant à quel point ils étaient loin de nous donner satisfaction. Nous savions le général de Gaulle engagé sur la bonne voie ; tôt ou tard le dénouement devait se produire et celui-ci dépendait pour une bonne part d'une situation internationale délicate sur laquelle, mal informés, nous ne pouvions risquer des jugements trop catégoriques.

Que se passait-il ?

Nous avons raconté en son temps l'Histoire de ces 76 generaux chenus et decorés et de leur croisade pour délivrer le Marechal. Mais nous n'avions pas dit que cette armée Giraud n'était pas autre chose que le refuge et le conservatoire des légionnaires, S.O.L., doriotistes et autres traitres vichyssois. Nous n'avions pas dit que dans les Etats-Majors si abondamment pourvus de cette armée, où l'exemple de Franco faisait l'objet d'études assidues, on rencontrait par exemple un certain commandant Boisson qui n'était autre que le gouverneur général limogé, le criminel de Dakar qui fit tirer sur les Français libres.

Protégés par le général Giraud et son entourage, partout, dans les confortables fauteuils de l'administration, on rencontrait à Alger les fascistes de Vichy, un peu revus mais nullement corrigés. On voyait ces hommes, fraichement lavés de la politique de Montoire et ne s'étant pas donnés le temps de redresser l'échine, prêts aux concessions les plus humiliantes et nullement accessibles à ce sentiment de rage qui a animé tous les véritables patriotes à l'annonce de l'exclusion de la France de la Conférence de Moscou et du Comité européen.

Tout cela on le soupçonnait. Plusieurs de nos camarades, qui, il y a quelques semaines, participaient encore à notre action, l'ont vu de leurs propres yeux, convoqués à Alger pour siéger au Conseil Consultatif provisoire.

Les représentants de la Résistance ont posé des questions : «Pourquoi, ont-ils demandé, le général Giraud n'a-t-il jamais publiquement désavoué le maréchal Petain? Pourquoi Pucheu n'a-t-il pas encore été fusillé ? Pourquoi... ?

Un vent de panique souffla sur Alger-Vichy. On parlait de fusiller ! Le général de Gaulle avait-il à ce point renié sa particule pour avoir commis l'inqualifiable légèreté de convoquer ces garçons mal appris ? On n'osa pas trop dire — mais on le pensait - que Pucheu était, lui, un garçon bien élevé. " Mais, répondait-on, la voix un peu tremblante, pour fusiller, il faut juger, il faut un tribunal, il faut un dossier. " En France, répondit la voix du peuple, nous n'avons pas besoin de tribunal, pour fusiller les traitres. Le tribunal, il est tout constitué : Pucheu relève du Conseil de Guerre. Quant au dossier, il est tout prêt il porte sur sa couverture, un seul mot "Châteaubriand", et il contient la liste des otages livrés à l'ennemi. De plus, ajoutaient les représentants à Alger de la Resistance, prenez garde : si vous pretendez revenir en France avec vos Ministres et hauts fonctionnaires vichyssois, **nous les tuerons.**

Ainsi, le dénouement d'une crise trop prolongée, fut-il précipité.

Nous ne dirons pas que ce dénouement donne entièrement satisfaction au peuple français. Nous pensons cependant qu'il est

BONDS OR BONDAGE?

"We cannot all have all we want, if our Soldiers and Sailors have all they need".
—Franklin D. Roosevelt

Which Do You Prefer?

Do we prefer the bonds of slavery or the kind that pays interest? The bonds of slavery pay no dividends. We must loan our money to keep our bombers going over Berlin and then over the land of The Rising Sun. Yes, we are reading a lot now about our losses on the battlefield . . . yes, and day by day our losses will increase to a figure we cannot now imagine. We may not be fit for military service but we can perform a yoeman service by investing every dollar . . . . yes every dime . . . in the kind of bonds that pays good interest. We may have done our bit . . . NOW WE WILL DO OUR BEST. THE AXIS STOPS AT NOTHING. We must not stop at 10 per cent.

THIS CHRISTMAS WILL NOT BE A NORMAL ONE

There was a pioneer Christmas in America . . . when a lonely little band of Pilgrams knew fear, cold and hunger. There was a Revolutionary Christmas . . . . when a nation struggling to be born almost perished at Valley Forge. There was a Christmas in years of civil strife and bloodshed . . . when brother fought against brother, friend against friend. There was a Christmas when the first World War looked heartbreakingly unsure. THESE TIMES, TOO SHALL PASS AWAY.

We Americans will live to know a day when boys and girls can love and marry and not be torn apart . . . when mothers can tuck their children into bed without an anxious look to the sky . . . . when America will not only be the land we know and love, but a land of richer promise than man has ever dreamed.

We advance several reasons why this will not be a normal Christmas: Our loved ones are scattered to every battlefront . . . . The gifts we would like to give are not to be found . . .

That Christmas dinner will not taste the same with a vacant chair, formerly occupied by the one whom you loved so dearly and one from whom you have had no news since the big drive into enemy territory . . . No, he will not be here for this Christmas, but his love will warm your family hearth. There will also be little boys and girls whose father has gone to fight for the principles we love and cherish. To these little boys and girls we would say that your father won't be home this Christmas to help you play with those pretty little toys that Santa brought . . . He has gone to make all the rest of your Christmas celebrations with him happy and enjoyable to both you and your dad.

When he left you didn't understand . . . Well, sonny you have only loaned your father to America . . . The America you, too, will grow up to love. Your dad has taken up arms against evil and all it stands for . . . He wants to do this job once and for all . . . He is going to prove that all men are created with certain inalienable rights, among which are Life, Liberty and Pursuit of Happiness. And sonny your father won't be home until he has wiped out every threat to these rights. You see, Sonny, we here in America were caught off guard . . . We had been too confident . . . We thought every body was as peace loving as we were . . . There were too many who thought we could play ostrich . . . Hide our heads and become invisible to everyone around us.

But Sonny these people were surprised on December 7, 1941, despite the fact that our Great Commander-in-Chief, Franklin D. Roosevelt had warned of the approaching calamity. Your father is not fighting a rich man's war as some might tell you . . . He is fighting for you and all other little boys and girls whether rich, deaf or dumb, black or white. You see, your father is the kind of a guy that believes in equality for all and special privileges to none, and believing so strong in these principles he is willing to give his life that you, his beloved son, might live as he has lived—FREE. He believes in Democracy . . . He believes in Democracy because it is like Christianity—they both must be followed to be proven.

Even though we were unarmed, unmanned, and unprepared for war, yet when war came, our men in arms, our men and women in the production lines showed the world that a Democracy could do in months what it took years for the aggressor nations to accomplish. Yes, Democracy works in war as in peace. Democracy is the only way to overcome the slavery of want, the slavery of ignorance, the slavery of discrimination, whether it be of creed, class or color.

To any little boy or girl whose father has gone to war, we say that your father will be home much sooner if we, here at home, will do our part . . . That is, give them something to fight with. You would be very unhappy to know that your father was sent in line of battle with nothing but his bare fits wouldn't you? You wouldn't like it much if you knew that your father, the one for whom you would give your life, was dodging bullets and sleeping in foxholes, while around you were some people who were griping because they are inconvenienced a little here at home. No, my little ones you wouldn't like this and we don't blame you and if you do hear of people like this, you write their name down or get mother to and daddy will take care of them when he comes home.

Your dad is going to have plenty of help in this war and millions more are being trained to make this one of the most over-whelming victories in the history of mankind. Millions more of us stay here in America to feed and supply the many that are helping your father.

HOW SALT WORKER'S UNION IS HELPING YOUR FATHER OR HUSBAND OR SON

Salt is classified as one of the 34 essential food items so necessary in winning this war. We load as well as produce this item by the carloads every day except Sunday. We fill government orders by the score and we have cooperated with our employer in filling these orders. As an example, our employer asked us if we would work Armistice Day and Thanksgiving Day, two holidays we always celebrate by resting. Our employer informed us that he had a number of government orders unfilled. We accepted his invitation to work and we were more than willing to do so—and we knew we were NOT TO RECEIVE double time for our services, but merely to perform a patriotic service toward the war effort, and God willing we will continue to do so.

To our more than 60 of our members in the armed services, we want to say to you that we will not let you down by work stoppages or in any other manner and to each of you in the service we wish for you a very Merry Christmas and may God share with us an early victory in 1944 and God bless all of you and your beloved families.

SALT WORKERS UNION NO. 18952

GENE CARROLL, President

THURSDAY, DECEMBER 23, 1943

The Lessons Of Tarawa

THE combined land, naval and air forces under Gen. Douglas MacArthur have achieved brilliant success in establishing beach heads on the island of New Britain, with laudable and welcome economy of men and equipment.

The economy in American lives reflects the thorough preparation for the assault to be credited to General MacArthur and his staff and is in sharp contrast with the recent experience of other commanders on Tarawa which while successful was extremely costly.

The results achieved by General MacArthur and the methods he employs are commended to the other American commanders in the Pacific, for their study and emulation.

The American people have had a vigorous defense of the Tarawa action—that is, the planning and strategic direction of it—from Secretary of the Navy Knox, who cites the heavy bomb tonnage hurled against the island as evidence of thoroughness.

But the American people have had ANOTHER story from Tarawa, by Sergt. Jim Lucas, trained combat correspondent of the United States Marine Corps.

Sergeant Lucas landed with the marines at Tarawa.

"Before we started," he reported, "it was great fun. We grinned and chortled . . . naval and air bombardment was to all but destroy the island."

The naval and air bombardment was indeed impressive, as he said.

"But something suddenly appeared to have gone wrong . . . the pounding continued. There was little doubt there were still living and fighting Japs on the island."

The rest of the story is a matter of gruesome record. The island was not reduced by bombardment, and the marines went through a withering fire to take it.

What the American people have not learned yet, and want to know, is WHAT WENT WRONG.

As the Chicago Tribune has since said editorially:

"The question in everybody's mind is whether the loss of more than a thousand killed and more than 2,500 wounded was a NEEDLESSLY high price to pay.

"It is clear that the planning of the operation was deficient and defective. The strength of the defense was miscalculated. The preliminary bombardment by planes and ships' guns was insufficient."

In contrast with the frightful and frightening experience at Tarawa is the long series of masterfully planned and executed defensive and offensive operations in the Pacific areas commanded by Gen. Douglas MacArthur.

In fact, the Tribune suggests:

"The only commander in the field who has shown real capacity is General MacArthur. Although he has been treated as a stepchild and denied the support he needs, he has yet been able to achieve remarkable results through the soundness of his strategy and his tactics.

"His planning has frequently been brilliant and has always been careful, with the result that he has achieved his goals without devastating battle losses."

Doubtless there should be better CO-ORDINATION between the American Army and Navy in this war.

In the Pacific theater of war, the two services as a matter of fact should be under ONE HEAD.

And of course that one head should be GENERAL MacARTHUR.

Divided authority in the Pacific theater is only causing indecision and friction, fanned by the effort of politicians in Washington to minimize the achievements of General MacArthur in rescuing Australia from the Japanese and steadily advancing toward the recovery of the Philippines.

General MacArthur has demonstrated his great and unquestioned capacity for sole command in the Pacific war. Why let the jittery New Deal politicians and the envious Washington brass-hats obstruct him?

Let The Army Take Over

REPRESENTATIVE CLAIR ENGLE of California, urging a "house cleaning" of the War Relocation Authority by Congress, has sharply admonished his colleagues that the familiar bureaucratic trick of changing administrators will not accomplish the purpose.

As he said, the eventual removal of War Relocation Director Dillon S. Myer is assured by full establishment of the fact, and general recognition of it, that Mr. Myer has made a thorough mess of his administration and lacks the confidence of both the Congress and the public.

Mr. Myer should certainly be removed.

But it would not improve the character or change the policies of the War Relocation Authority if a process of bureaucratic juggling simply elevated another director of the same stripe to his place.

That is the "out" the New Deal Administration habitually, and too often successfully, seeks from its own inefficiency and ineptness.

Whenever an agency of the New Deal finds itself in difficulty with the people or Congress it merely goes through the MOTIONS of reform.

If it is compelled to remove an agency head to meet the wishes of the people or Congress he usually shows up in another field of the vast New Deal bureaucracy—often with more authority and a better hold on the public purse than before.

In extreme cases, if the clearing of its own political skirts warrants it, the offending administrator may even be abandoned as a scapegoat.

But the offending bureaucratic agency itself is never willingly abandoned or made to change its character or policies—however the people and Congress may object to it and demand its reform or elimination.

It would not correct the incompetent and futile record of the War Relocation Authority to have Director Myer removed, and then compensated with another and perhaps better and more profitable and powerful New Deal bureaucratic assignment.

Nor would it correct the situation to have Mr. Myer made the "fall guy" for the New Deal Administration.

Another social experimenter in the place of Mr. Myer would continue the objectionable policies of Mr. Myer and make the same mistakes and wind up with the same mess on his hands.

The War Relocation Authority should be ABOLISHED rather than merely put through the wringer of pretended reform.

Its functions should be taken over by the United States Army, which understands the character of the Japanese enemy better than any civilian or political agency can possibly know it.

The Army could be relied upon to refrain from conducting social experiments with the Japanese.

The Army, with the alert and intelligent co-operation of the Federal Bureau of Investigation, dealt vigorously and promptly and adequately with the Japanese problem in this country at the start of the Pacific war.

The Army well knew that a large portion of the Japanese residents of the country were here for the PURPOSE of sabotage and espionage.

It, therefore, moved them OUT of the West Coast combat and mobilization and embarkation and production areas where they had their best opportunities to conduct sabotage and espionage.

It moved them ALL out. It did not attempt the wholly IMPOSSIBLE task of determining which of the Japanese were loyal or disloyal. It refused to take any CHANCES and accordingly there has not been any Japanese sabotage and espionage.

The only real trouble the country has had with the Japanese has developed AFTER the War Relocation Authority took over jurisdiction from the Army.

Let the Army take the responsibility BACK and instantly there will not BE any Japanese problem in the country.

For answer to those who argue that such a course would lead to reprisals against American prisoners in Japan or Japanese-occupied lands, let us not be childish. The American Army never has treated its wards with either brutality or injustice and never will—a fact which the Spanish representatives of the Japanese Government can be depended upon to ascertain and report to Tokyo.

But since when has the Japanese Government refrained from brutality and injustice against prisoners for the reason that we have so refrained?

A Good Deal In Waste Paper

TO DISPOSE of waste paper was a problem up to a few months ago.

Now it has become a valuable patriotic service to save waste paper and help get it into the hands of the War Production Board.

Waste paper is needed urgently for hundreds of uses, all connected with the armed services' material requirements.

Mr. Nelson of the WPB, asking for the paper, turned wisely to two agencies that have never failed him in the various scrap drives: The newspapers and the school children.

The newspapers are publicizing, explaining and stimulating the salvage; school children are doing the field work. Both are doing a bang-up job with enthusiasm and efficiency.

It is generally overlooked that scrap drives, notably that for waste paper, have beneficial by-products to all householders. Piles of old papers, stored or forgotten, are definite fire hazards, clutter up space and form ideal breeding places for disease carriers. To get rid of them has always been a disagreeable chore.

But, since the newspapers and school children got busy, the problem has disappeared, safety and cleanliness have increased. And, above all, the drive has been an educational activity for the youngsters and another opportunity for the community to share like good neighbors in a patriotic effort.

In spite of the fine work so far performed there are still big stocks of unwanted paper lying about. Let every citizen ransack his premises, call his active young friends, and donate what is useless to him but valuable to the country.

It is hard to imagine a better deal all around.

Text For Today "And then will I profess unto them, I never knew you: depart from me, ye that work iniquity."—St. Matthew, vii., 23.

Suggested by the Rev. John E. Holt, pastor Highland Methodist Church.

Death On Tarawa

(This graphic eyewitness account of the bloody conquest of Tarawa was written by Master Technical Sergeant Jim G. Lucas, Tulsa, Okla., the first Marine Corps combat correspondent to land on that little Gilbert Island.)

TARAWA, Nov. 23 (Delayed)—(A. P.).—Five minutes ago we wrested this strategic Gilbert Island outpost and its all-important air strip from the Japanese who seized it from a few missionaries and natives weeks after they had attacked Pearl Harbor.

It has been the bitterest, costliest, most sustained fighting on any front. It has cost us the lives of hundreds of United States marines. (Official reports listed 1,026 Americans killed.) But we have wiped out a force of 4,000 Imperial Japanese marines—we expected to find only 2,000, mostly dead.

Before we started it was great fun. We grinned and chortled. We said, "There won't be a Jap alive when we get ashore."

That was the plan. Naval and air bombardment was to all but destroy the island. The few living Japs were to be so shellshocked there would be no opposition. I recalled Major Mills' instructions:

"We don't intend to neutralize the island. We don't intend to destroy it. We will annihilate it."

As dawn broke, Tarawa was completely enveloped in smoke and flame. Japanese gun emplacements — eight inchers—continued to reply. Our battleships looked like sullen, defiant bulldogs as they ignored them and continued to pound the shore.

At dawn our planes came in. We could see them disappear into the smoke and flame. We could hear the sputter of their machine guns. We could see the debris raised by their bombs. It was wonderful.

But something suddenly appeared to have gone wrong. We learned—hour has been delayed thirty-one, then forty-five minutes. The pounding continued. There was little doubt there were still living—and fighting Japs on the island.

Our assault waves were in the water, ready to hit the beach. We were in the second wave, due to hit after the first men reached shore. Without warning, an eight-inch shell hit and exploded ten yards off our side. We dived behind a hatch, laughing at each other as we came out. A second shell hit five yards off, killing a sailor and spraying our deck with shrapnel and salt water. We upped anchor and steamed out of range.

Fifteen minutes later we climbed into our tank lighter, sharing it with many other marines, a truck and a trailer.

"We have landed against heavy opposition," came the first word from shore. "Casualties severe."

As we pulled toward the beach we were met with enemy shell fire. A boat on our starboard side received a direct hit. Five men were killed. We pulled alongside and dragged in the survivors. There was no chance to salvage their equipment. Swiftly we moved out of range.

At 1 P. M. we started in again, moving toward the pier which appeared undamaged. We were stopped by machine-gun fire. Corporal Raymond Matjasic, twenty-three, of Cleveland, one of our combat photographers, who had been seated in the cab of the truck, fell to the floor. The truck's windshield was knocked out.

At 3 P. M. we tried again. Shells tore the water on all sides. Two more boats went down, and more marines died. We backed out again, unable to pick up the survivors. Many of them swam to us, and were later moved back to their transports. Many of the wounded drowned.

At midnight the control boat appeared out of the darkness. We were to try again.

We inched toward the dock, partially wrecked by our own shelling. The hulk of a Japanese merchantman loomed to the right. Two direct hits from our destroyers had put it out of action. On the lookout for snipers, we covered it with our machine guns.

When we reached the dock, snipers in the wrecked ship opened up, but they were firing over our heads. We climbed on the dock and more snipers fired. We hit the deck.

We were uncertain where to go. The Jap lines were only fifty yards past the end of the pier, and there was no command post. Matjasic and I discarded our typewriter, our packs and our field glasses and started to the shore.

The last seventy-five yards of the pier was white coral grit. There was a brilliant moon—at home I would have called it beautiful. We swore at it viciously. We were perfect targets.

Crouched, we sprinted down the pier, silhouetted against the coral. Snipers opened up, and six men fell, screaming in agony. We lay like logs.

"We can't stay here," someone said up the line, "they'll shell hell out of us and we'll all be gone."

"Advance slowly. Five feet between each man. They won't get us all that way."

We started, three more marines fell, and we hit the ground. Inch by inch we moved up. Each ten yards cost us the lives of more marines. Each time I expected to get mine. Finally we were within fifteen yards of the beach. Ahead were shadows.

"Throw away everything, including your camera," I told Matjasic. "We'll come back and get it if we can. We're making a run for it."

A sergeant beside me cracked:

"Take your rifle. You'll probably never get to use it, but you might."

I grinned. Ray and I ran for the shadows. It was an anti-climax. Not a shot was fired at us.

On the beach the fire was still hot. We ducked behind the wreckage of a Japanese steam roller, which appeared to be between us and the enemy. I found a shovel and began frantically to dig. Within five minutes we had our first foxhole on Tarawa. It turned out to be the safest spot on the island.

There we spent the night. It was 4 A. M. when we got to lie down.

At dawn we found our position precarious. Our own men were on the left of us, the Japs not more than fifty yards on the right. We were in no-man's land.

At 6 A. M. a fight began over our foxhole. Scores of bullets nicked off the big steam roller, while we burrowed deeper.

Shortly before noon the Japs were driven back, and we came out of hiding.

Our cruisers and destroyers resumed their shelling of the Jap half of the island, knocking out the last remaining big guns. The concussion was terrific, for the shells were landing not more than 100 yards away. Our planes came in strafing. At least 150 planes made at least seventy-five sorties over the area during the day.

I waded and swam through a small bay to reach the opposite shore, but was unable to find anyone. Virtually every one I knew was reported dead or missing.

Far down the beach (not more than fifty yards, but it took me two hours to cover it), I saw a marine with a camera. Painfully I crawled to him, for my body was one mass of bruises.

He was a stranger.

"Where'd you get it?" I asked.

"From Lucas," he replied.

"Where is Lucas?" I asked.

"Over there," he replied. "Dead."

"I'm Lucas," I told him.

From his description I decided he meant Sergt. Ernest J. Diet, thirty-six, Hammond, La. Later I found a body I thought was that of our sergeant-photographer. I was almost hysterical when Diet showed up 24 hours later. He learned finally that it was someone else's camera, and that he had found some of my papers. But, meanwhile, he had officially reported me killed in action.

I left my foxhole at noon, went 100 yards and returned at 6 P. M. It was that tough.

The night was hellish. More men came in, and more were killed on the pier.

We had had enough experience with the enemy's infiltration tactics. We had orders to shoot any man who came toward us. During the night we learned that guards on the pier killed a Jap who had sneaked in with a drum of gasoline, intending to set the pier afire. It would have been the end for us, for the pier was loaded with high explosives. At dawn the enemy sent its first bombers. There were only two of them, and five men were killed.

We awoke to one of the strangest sights in history. We badly needed replacements. Men were being landed 500 yards from shore in the surf at low tide and were wading in past enemy machine-gun emplacements. Many men fell before they reached shore. In the afternoon marines were still staggering ashore, carrying the limp forms of buddies between them.

The heaviest fire came from a Jap snipers' nest in the beached enemy merchant ship. Assault waves were held up while our dive bombers went to work on it, dropping high explosives in its hulk. And yet, when the next boats came in, machine-gun fire continued from the blazing ship! We settled the matter by sending aboard men to wipe out the snipers in hand-to-hand combat, and to hold it as an outpost.

Shortly before noon the Japs opened up on us with mortars. One landed near enough to tear the top off our steam roller, and to deafen me for two days. A marine who occupied the foxhole next to ours was killed by shrapnel. We dug deeper.

By now, however, the Japs were being forced steadily back. We were able to move about. Snipers continued, but we ignored them. One was killed in a cocoanut tree fifty feet away.

Still our naval and air poundings continued. On the third day the heaviest fighting took place in a cleared space around the air strip. One of our tanks lumbered into the clearing. A Jap broke from the bush and tried to throw a grenade in its tracks. He was shot down.

Suddenly there was firing at our rear. Seven Japs had been found in the ruins of a dugout less than ten feet from the command post from which our officers were directing the operations. They were wiped out.

I went with Chief Pharmacist's Mate Roy J. Barnhill, thirty-three, Salt City, to the front where our men were blasting out a Jap pillbox. Last night Barnhill went back of the Jap lines to pick up six wounded marines. A Japanese sentry tossed two hand grenades in their direction. Both were duds.

I returned to the beach to find snipers again sweeping the pier where ammunition was being unloaded. They fired from the wreckage of one of our boats fifty yards away. I ducked into the water on the opposite side, and found five husky military policemen herding a convoy of Japanese prisoners toward the beach in water up to their waists and up to the Japs' shoulders. Three dead marines were in the water. The MP's herded the Japs out to a waiting landing barge. As the frightened prisoners climbed aboard they were subjected to murderous fire from their own snipers. Three were killed.

I got back in time to be in on the battle that broke Japanese resistance on Tarawa. Several hundred Japs had been holed up for two days in a bomb-proof shelter at the end of the airstrip, holding up our advance.

Private First Class Robert Harper, twenty-two, Houston, Texas, and Sergt. John Rybin, twenty-five, Laurel, Mont., dashed forward with their flame throwers while automatic riflemen covered them. At the entrance of the bomb shelter, Harper threw his flame on a Jap machine-gun nest, charring three enemy marines beyond recognition. He poured on more fire. There were screams inside the shelter, and the marines rushed forward to capture their objective.

Harper returned to our post.

"They were all huddled in there scared to death," he said. "I turned on the heat and that was all."

From this point on our advance was rapid. Following our advancing troops I came upon one position we had held less than five minutes and counted 27 Japanese who had committed hara-kiri by strapping their feet to the triggers of their rifles, placing the muzzle in their chests and pulling the trigger with a kick.

During the night the Japs made a final desperate bayonet charge. They killed two of our flame throwers but were repulsed.

And this morning the island was secured. For the first time we were able to sit up without ducking. There were a few desultory sniper shots, but no one noticed them.

Staff Sergeant George Stutsman, Natchez, Miss., brings us two cartons of cigarets and a carton of matches. We get a five-gallon keg of water—a real luxury. It rains briefly and we stand in the open, soap and shower ourselves off.

This is civilization.

1,300 U. S. PLANES RAID FRANCE

2 RAIL UNIONS CALL OFF STRIKE

THE WEATHER

Fair and not quite so cold tonight. Saturday increasing cloudiness and rising temperature.

Detailed Weather Report on Page 18

Read The Baltimore News-Post for complete, accurate war coverage. It is the only Baltimore newspaper possessing the three great wire services—

ASSOCIATED PRESS
INTERNATIONAL NEWS SERVICE
UNITED PRESS

THE BALTIMORE NEWS-POST

AN INDEPENDENT NEWSPAPER

The Largest Evening Circulation in the Entire South

10

VOL. CXLIV.—NO. 43 | Entered as second-class matter at Baltimore Postoffice. | FRIDAY EVENING, DECEMBER 24, 1943 | PRICE 3 CENTS

EISENHOWER TO LEAD INVASION OF EUROPE

1,300 Yank Planes Blast Rocket Coast

LONDON, Dec. 24—(U. P.).—More than 1,300 American warplanes, including the largest force of Flying Fortresses and Liberators ever hurled against a single target, teamed up with a huge Allied bombing fleet today to devastate German military installations along the invasion coast of France.

The entire weight of the mighty Allied bombardment — probably the greatest aerial blow of the entire war—fell upon the Pas de Calais area of the French Channel coast, directly across the narrow Dover straits.

The attack opened only a few hours after a big formation of R. A. F. heavy bombers battered Berlin with more than 1,000 tons of high explosives and incendiaries.

Apparently dooming German hopes for a raid-free Christmas, the R. A. F.'s four-engined bombers resumed their offensive to blast the Nazi capital off the map after a week's respite, and the Air Ministry announced that huge fires were left burning with smoke rising to a great height.

RAID AACHEN

The air armada, taking advantage of one of the longest nights of the year, delayed its take-off until midnight in an attempt to catch the German defenses off guard and only 17 bombers were lost in the raid and in subsidiary attacks on central and western Germany.

A German DNB news agency

Continued on Page 2, Column 8.

Pope In Yule Plea For Peace

LONDON, Dec. 24—(U. P.).—Pope Pius XII. appealed to the leaders of the warring nations today to conclude a just peace that will preserve the rights of all states, but warned somberly that the conflict is growing more widespread and savage and that there is little hope for its sudden end.

"The horrible pages of past history fade away in comparison with the bloody disaster happening today," he said in a broadcast over the Vatican radio.

The present is witnessing a "moral decadence which is burying all humanitarian sentiments, but in the midst of this dark night, the Light of Bethlehem must shine," he said.

"Only Christ alone can alleviate the dark entiments . . . only Christ can alleviate the tortures of humanity."

FIFTH WAR CHRISTMAS

The Pope aid the world for the fifth time was preparing to celebrate Christmas in a "tense atmosphere of death and hatred."

He said the Church would do all it could to alleviate the pains of "all suffering humanity," calling on all Christians to take comfort from their faith.

The Pope said he realized that death, anxiety for war prisoners and fears for deported persons

Continued on Page 2, Column 3.

Temperatures

Midnight 20	9 A. M., 17
1 A. M., 19	10 A. M., 19
2 A. M., 18	11 A. M., 21
3 A. M., 17	12 Noon, 24
4 A. M., 16	1 P. M., 26
5 A. M., 16	2 P. M., 28
6 A. M., 15	3 P. M., 29
7 A. M., 16	4 P. M., 30
8 A. M., 16	5 P. M., 30

Two Railroad Unions Call Off Strike

WASHINGTON, Dec. 24 — (A. P.).—Chiefs of the brotherhoods of railroad trainmen and the locomotive engineers announced at the White House today they were calling off the strike set for December 30 as far as their two unions are concerned.

They said they were acting in view of President Roosevelt's proposal to arbitrate the whole wage dispute, involving both operating and non-operating brotherhoods.

FOLLOWS CONFERENCE

A. F. Whitney, president of the trainmen, and Alvanley Johnston, head of the locomotive engineers, made the announcement to newsmen after conferring with War Mobilization Director James F. Byrnes and Economic Stabilization Chief Fred M. Vinson.

Whitney said action to withdraw their strike call, to be taken this afternoon and tomorrow morning, was decided on despite the fact that the three other operating unions had declined to go along with the President's arbitration proposal.

The unions which have refused arbitration are the firemen and enginemen, the conductors and switchmen.

Asked whether the two unions agreeing to arbitrate could keep

Continued on Page 2, Column 4.

Hamburg Raiders To Face Trial

LONDON, Dec. 24—(U. P.).—Nazi broadcasts suggested today that British and American fliers who raided Nurnberg and Hamburg would be the first Allied prisoners tried by Germany as "war criminals" in retaliation for the hanging of three German officers after the Kharkov war guilt trial in Russia.

The controlled Oslo radio warned that future "Anglo-American terror pilots who drop bombs purposely on residential districts of German towns will receive appropriate punishment."

"Then they and their relatives can thank their own Governments," the Oslo broadcast said.

A Paris broadcast heard by the London Daily Mail listening post reported flatly that airmen who participated in attacks on the arms and transportation center of Nurnberg would be the first to be placed on trial on charges of violating international law in bombing "women and children."

Radio Berlin ignored Nurnberg, however, and instead, emphasized that Anglo-American airmen who attacked Hamburg would be arraigned with civilian women and children as witnesses against them.

"German judges will examine witnesses—both pilots and mothers and children of Hamburg—cooly and objectively," the Berlin broadcast said.

British and American planes all but blasted Hamburg, Germany's second city, off the map with 9,000 tons of bombs July 24-August 2.

INVASION COMMANDER—President Roosevelt today announced the appointment of Gen. Dwight D. Eisenhower (above) as commander of invasion forces in the forthcoming Allied drive into Europe. International News Photo.

Roosevelt Forecasts Great New Offensives; Sees 'Bad News' For Japs

Montgomery To Lead British Forces Under U. S. Commander

LONDON, Dec. 24—(A. P.).—General Sir Henry Maitland Wilson tonight was designated Allied commander in the Mediterranean area, succeeding Gen. Dwight D. Eisenhower, who becomes chief of Allied second front forces. The appointment of Wilson, who has been commander in chief of British forces in the Middle East, was announced at No. 10 Downing street.

Gen. Sir Harold Alexander, who in speculation had been mentioned most prominently as Eisenhower's successor, will be commander in chief of Allied Armies in Italy.

Gen. Sir Bernard L. Montgomery will be commander in chief of the British group of armies under Eisenhower.

Lieut. Gen. Carl A. Spaatz will command the American strategic bombing force operating against Germany.

HYDE PARK, N. Y., Dec. 24—(A. P.).—President Roosevelt forecast today great new offensives, led by Gen. Dwight D. Eisenhower, to complete the "encirclement" of Germany, and declared that there would be "plenty of bad news for the Japs in the not too far distant future."

In a Christmas Eve broadcast to the nation and to the armed forces overseas, the President reported on his recent conferences at Cairo and Teheran and declared:

"The war is now reaching that stage where we shall have to look forward to large casualty lists—dead, wounded and missing."

He said that when he addressed the new Congress he would disclose further details of the conferences and as a possible indication that he would comment then on home front controversies said, "I shall also have a great deal to say about certain conditions here at home."

AGREE ON FORCE

The President also declared:

(1) That Russia, Britain, China and America were agreed that:

"If force is necessary to keep international peace, international force will be applied—for as long as it may be necessary."

(2) That he, Prime Minister Churchill and Marshall Stalin had agreed that Germany must be stripped of her military might, but that:

"The United Nations have no intention to enslave the German people."

(3) That as a result of a "false reasoning" by some persons at home that the war would be over quickly he thought he detected "an effort to resume or even encourage an outbreak of partisan thinking and talking."

PRAISES MARSHALL

The President's announcement of Eisenhower's appointment to lead the new combined attack "from other points of the compass" came two days after the Associated Press, in a London dispatch, said that General Eisenhower was leading the field for the job of Allied commander in chief for the western invasion.

The President praised the work of Gen. George C. Marshall, chief of staff, who it was once rumored would lead the western invasion, and of Admiral Ernest J. King, commander in chief of the fleet. The President said:

"Upon them falls the great responsibility of planning the strategy of determining when and where we shall fight."

He said he, Churchill and Premier Josef Stalin of Russia, in three days of intense and consistently amicable discussions at Teheran, had "agreed on every point concerned with the launching of a gigantic attack upon Germany."

(BACKGROUND NOTE: A dispatch from a British port today said further reinforcements for the Canadian Army overseas have arrived safely in a convoy from Canada.

The President added:

"The Russian Army will con-

Continued on Page 2, Column 5.

VERY LATEST NEWS

(Race Results From Howard Sports Daily, Inc.)

RACING RESULTS

AT FAIR GROUNDS

hird—Rover, $3.80, $3.20, $2.40; Late Issue, $17.40, $5.20; Mere Markette, $3.00.

ourth—Granny Reigh, $9.40, $4.60, $2.80; Valdina Czar $6.00, $5.00; Napoo, $3.00.

RED ARMY CAPTURES 60 POPULATED PLACES

LONDON, Dec. 24—(A.P.).—The Red army stormed s way into Gorodok today and captured more than 60 ther large populated places, Moscow announced.

21 BELOW GRIPS NEW ENGLAND

BOSTON, Dec. 24.—(A. P.). — Bitter cold ranging own to 21 degrees below zero gripped all New England day.

POLISH SUBMARINE SINKS ENEMY SUPPLY SHIP

LONDON, Dec. 24—(U. P.).—A Polish naval comunique said today that the submarine Sokol sank a 500-ton enemy supply ship and five smaller vessels reently in the Mediterranean.

TROPICAL PARK RESULTS

FIRST RACE—Six furlongs. Off 2.04. Time, 1.12 1-5.

Air Beauty, 111 (A. Skoronski)	$13.70	5.50	$4.60
Son Islam, 116 (E. Arcaro)		4.50	3.30
Balmy Spring, 116 (G. Hettinger)			4.90
Total mutuels			$36.50

Also Ran—Valdina Pledge, Velvet Heels, Ask Me, Vinal Haven, Admiral Jim.

SECOND—Mile and 70 yards. (Off 2.32.) Time 1.46 2-5.

Miss Reward, 113 (A. Skoronski)	$15.90	$7.30	$4.70
Whippett, 111 (W. Gerlock)		15.60	8.80
General War, 116 (A Snider)			8.00
Total mutuels			$60.30

Also Ran—Cee Raf, Cherbourg, Santa Marie, Big Raid, Piccany.

Daily Double—Air Beauty and Miss Reward paid $64.80

THIRD—One mile and a sixteenth. Off at 3.01½. Time, 1.46 2-5.

Precision, 115 (J. Layton)	$16.40	$9.00	$6.80
Neddie Lass, 105 (R. Permane)		6.00	5.00
Valdina Joe, 116 (J. Martin)			10.90
Total mutuels			$54.10

Also Ran—Valdina Bishop, Scarlette II., Bitter Ender, Knock Knock, Michigan Sun, Wood Robin and Fettacairn.

FOURTH—Six furlongs. Off 3.32 ½. Time, 1.12.

Reztips, 116 (L. Haskell)	$3.60	$2.90	$2.40
Hill Sun, 114 (J. Brennan)		6.70	3.20
Star Blen, 114 (P. Roberts)			3.20

Also Ran—Counsellor, Flying Silver, Polymelior.

FIFTH—Six furlongs (chute). Off at 4.11. Time, 1.13 4-5.

Robins Crown, 116 (L. Haskell)	$30.20	$11.90	$6.50
Night Bomber, 118 (C. Bierman)		4.60	3.30
Class Book, 110 (G. McMullen)			6.50

Also Ran—Payable, Over the Dam, Oaking, Cling, Sunamit, Black Africa, Our Damsel and Cavallena.

SIXTH—Six furlongs (chute). Off at 4.39½. Time, 1.11 3-5.

Dream Parade, 116 (T. Atkinson)	$9.40	$4.20	$3.20
Free Air, 108 (R. Permane)		3.50	3.40
Blue Pom, 116 (A. Snider)			4.60

Also Ran—Dartaway, Soverton, Scotch Abbot, Cherry Crush, For Granted.

Gifts Cheer Vets In Md. Hospitals

(Picture on Page 3.)

Hundreds of heavily laden boxes, emblematic of the kindliness and generosity of a patriotic Maryland public, were distributed today among the wounded and ill veterans of World War II., guaranteeing to them as happy a Christmas as possible.

To these men Santa Claus was to be found in The Baltimore News-Post and Sunday American, which jointly conducted with the Variety Club a campaign to solicit gifts and funds to make their Christmas a truly merry one.

The gifts, many of them from families which had packed them with loving care, and filled their bundles to overflowing with carefully selected presents, were taken by Army truck to four big hospitals in this territory yesterday.

PUBLIC RESPONSE

The distribution was the culmination of a solicitation of public support which resulted in thousands of gifts and many cash donations being sent to the club from a generous public.

Mr. and Mrs. Edward J. Perotka distributed presents to the veterans of World I. and World War II. at the Fort Howard Veterans' Hospital.

Some of the veterans of the present war entered the hospital today. Several others were being discharged to go to their homes.

The presents were distributed as the veterans gathered around a Christmas tree. Gifts were car-

Continued on Page 2, Column 4.

NEWS-POST

CHRISTMAS SCHEDULE

The Baltimore News-Post will not be published tomorrow, Christmas Day.

The first edition of the Baltimore Sunday American will be on sale Christmas night after 7 o'clock.

As Another
Wartime Christmas Dawns
LET'S SPEED THE VICTORY!
As another war year approaches, let us all buckle on the armor of battle —and buckle down to the job of winning. Here are ways in which we at home are called to duty . . . to end the war sooner and bring loved ones home to us more surely:
★ SAVE A FIGHTING MAN'S LIFE...by donating a pint of blood to the Red Cross.
★ BUY WAR BONDS REGULARLY... to help pay for the equipment for Victory.
★ SAVE FAT FOR AMMUNITION . . . every ounce is vitally needed, now as never before.
Free State Brewery Is Honored To Repeat Its Pledge Of A Year Ago:
FOR THE DURATION...IN HUMBLE GRATITUDE AND RESPECT...WE SHALL PAY TO OUR EMPLOYEES IN THE ARMED FORCES 40% OF THEIR FORMER SALARIES
Free State Brewery
BALTIMORE, MARYLAND

CHARACTER QUALITY AMERICA FIRST! ENTERPRISE ACCURACY
Los Angeles Examiner
AN AMERICAN PAPER FOR THE AMERICAN PEOPLE — THE GREAT NEWSPAPER OF THE GREAT SOUTHWEST
Reg. U.S. Pat. Off.
Examiner Telephone Richmond 1212 — Examiner Building, 1111 S. Broadway
FINAL 9AM
VOL. XLI—NO. 13 — LOS ANGELES, FRIDAY, DECEMBER 24, 1943 — S — Two Sections—Part I—FIVE CENTS

SUPER-BLITZ SMASHES BERLIN

GERMAN ROCKET GUNS IN ACTION

Hurry Your Yule Cash for Gifts to Vets in Hospitals

Only 2 Days Remain for Contributions to Examiner Xmas Fund

It's Christmas Eve, but there still is time for you to remember the war wounded in Southern California military hospitals.

Two days still remain—today and tomorrow—and in those two days you can help some plucky soldier, sailor or Marine fighting his way back, to receive a gift on Christmas.

If you can, bring your cash donations to the Examiner personally.

Or, if you can't do that send it by someone or mail your contribution special delivery to the Examiner War Wounded Christmas Fund, Los Angeles Examiner, Los Angeles 54, California.

Back from world battle fronts, thousands of badly wounded fighting men are trying to get well. Far from home, many of them, their thoughts will be pretty lonely Christmas Day.

THEY NEED CASH

You can help remove these pangs of loneliness and the thoughts of home folk far away by your contribution of cash.

For this selfsame cash will be delivered tomorrow by Examiner representatives in all Southland military hospitals in which these suffering, wounded heroes of World War II are confined.

Cash is the thing they need and cash you can supply. The Examiner will see that it is rushed to the men who have fought so bravely for America's cause.

And it will be a warm Christmas, a jolly Christmas to these men, knowing that the people of Southern California think enough of them to see that they are not forgotten at Christmas time.

It's you that is not forgetting them. They fought for you and now they are fighting for themselves—fighting to recover from severe injuries.

Don't let them fight alone. Your gift will help them to fight that much more. It will give them spirit—the spirit of knowing that someone else cares besides themselves and their families.

Bring your contribution personally to the Examiner. Do it today.

Do it on Christmas Eve.

Honor Roll

In behalf of the Examiner War Wounded Christmas Fund, the Examiner acknowledges the following contributions:

Previously contributed	$43,001.08
Yesterday's contributions:	
Arthur H. Samish	250.00
Shell Oil Company	$ 200.00
Studio Utility Employees	100.00
A. S. Vinnell Company	100.00
Bar of Music	100.00
Anonymous, Ocean Park	50.00
Harry Clunan and Dutch Dickson	50.00
Frank H. Plaisted	50.00
Anonymous, Pasadena	50.00
Mrs. Bertha R. Vasquez and Anselmo Vasquez	50.00
Anonymous	50.00
Harry Jameson	50.00
Jennie Marie Peterson	50.00
Frances Marion	50.00
Employees of Consolidated Film Co.	46.00
Employees of James Graham Co.: Curtis McCallum, H. O. McCallum, Cal Morris, Dale F. Miller, Edna Enger, Frank Enger, Jackie Taylor, Leo Norris, Mrs. R. Foster, Kenneth I. Draper, C. D. Kelly, Calvin O. Borvell, C. L. Petry, W. A. Long, Glen M. Bartlett, Stephen Berdan, Francis Neaderhiser, J. Elizalde, A. C. Cazares, W. O. Dorsey, Joe Antista, John Meals, Lee Traynor, A. W. Merriher, W. D. Merriher, Ross Munro, I. J. Lavergne, Melissa Warner, Helen Baker, A. E. Olson and C. E. Hite	44.50
Examiner Display Advertising Dept. Employees	27.00
Jos. A. Rodifer Co.	25.00
Monash Milstein	25.00
Nellie Kersting, Glendale	25.00
Club Eleanora Duse	25.00
Mrs. Geo. A. McKee, Oxnard	25.00
Culbertson Chevrolet Co., Huntington Beach	25.00
Employees of Dorsey Mfg. Co.	25.00
C. & H. Machine Co., employees	19.50
Night crew, Cine Grill, Hollywood Roosevelt Hotel	19.00
Nite Life Cafe (Pete and John, Jack, Gus, Myrtle and Mary)	18.00
Mrs. Eugene Vigo	15.00
Peerless Machine Co.	15.00
Sadie Turner, Beverly Hills	15.00
Ed Rice	10.00
Dr. A. Zimmerman	10.00
Mr. and Mrs. N. Novak, Indio	10.00
Mrs. E. S. Reynolds, Pasadena	10.00
A Friend	10.00
William Gillir, Pico	10.00
Mary A. Paul	10.00
Roland Ramgren, Torrance	10.00
Mr. and Mrs. R. C. Crawford, 2201 La Mesa drive, Santa Monica	10.00
A. J. Hansel	10.00
Ralph, Jessie and Danny Bush	10.00
Minnie Lee Reeves	10.00
Bob Weinberg, U. S. Navy	10.00
Denny Weinberg, Downey	10.00
Mr. and Mrs. Marvin Schoen	10.00
A. L. Tilton, Artesia	10.00
W. N. and Hulon Wigington, El Centro	10.00
Winifred Blackburn	10.00
"Big Swede," Whittier	10.00

(Continued on Page 10, Cols. 1-6)

Pope Pius Will Broadcast Annual Yule Message Today

LONDON, Dec. 23.—(AP)—Pope Pius XII will broadcast his annual Christmas message to the world at 12:15 p. m. (4:15 a. m., P. W. T.) tomorrow. The address is expected to last about half an hour.

The Vatican radio said today there will be no public Christmas Eve mass, as originally planned, because of the 6 p. m. Rome curfew imposed by the Germans.

The Pontiff will celebrate mass in private at 5 p. m. (9 a. m., P. W. T.) however, and the Vatican radio said this service would be broadcast.

FDR MOVES TO TAKE OVER RAILROADS

Attorney General Instructed to Prepare Government Action to Avoid Lines Tieup Dec. 30.

By Horace M. Coats
Staff Correspondent International News Service

WASHINGTON, Dec. 23.—A White House spokesman announced tonight that President Roosevelt has directed Attorney General Biddle to begin preparation of the legal documents necessary for the Government to take over the nation's railroads.

The announcement followed a flat rejection on the part of three of the Big Five operating brotherhoods of President Roosevelt's offer to arbitrate their wage difficulties with the carriers.

TIEUP SLATED

The 350,000 members of the operating unions and one million 100 thousand nonoperating rail workers had set 6 a. m., December 30, as the date for a nationwide tieup of wartime rail transportation.

The Presidential action came shortly after a conference between Mr. Roosevelt and 12 chiefs of the nonoperating unions in which his offer to arbitrate was repeated for the wage increase demands of the nonoperating workers.

THREE REFUSE

Two of the Big Five brotherhoods—the Order of Railway Trainmen and the Brotherhood of Locomotive Engineers—brought the rail crisis to a climax when they broke ranks and joined with the carriers in accepting the President's offer personally to arbitrate the wage controversy.

These two unions represent approximately 230,000 of the 350,000 operating workers.

The other three brotherhoods, however flatly refused to go along with the Engineers and the Trainmen and with the carriers in the proposal to permit the President to settle their difficulties.

The White House announced later that no date for taking over the railroads has been fixed.

Text of a formal statement issued at the White House follows:

"The President tonight directed the attorney general to prepare the necessary documents for the taking over of the railroads by the United States Government.

"At a conference called this afternoon by the President he told the representatives of the carriers and the brotherhoods that the war could not wait—that he would not wait."

(Pacific-Electric railmen plan to strike if nationwide rail strike is made effective December 30. Page 13.)

Churchill Makes Steady Progress

LONDON, Dec. 23.—(INS)—Prime Minister Winston Churchill continues to make steady progress in his recovery from pneumonia, a bulletin issued at No. 10 Downing Street said today.

LATEST NEWS BULLETINS

New Nazi Weapons Duel Across Channel

LONDON, Dec. 24 (Friday).—(AP)—The Germans declared today they used their rocket gun for the first time last night in a channel duel between a German convoy and British long-range batteries, Royal Navy motor torpedo boats, and R. A. F. fighter-bombers.

The Berlin broadcast said merely that rocket guns went into action, without stating whether they were emplaced on land in France, or fitted to vessels of the convoy escort.

This was the first Nazi announcement of the use of rocket guns—which might be the "secret weapon" the Germans have threatened to use to shell England and possibly London.

Ox-Bow Incident Voted Best Film

NEW YORK, Dec. 23.—(AP)—The National Board of Review of Motion Pictures today named 20th Century Fox's "The Ox-Bow Incident" the best film drama of 1943 in its 18th annual selection of the 10 best pictures of the year.

The board chose the British-made "Desert Victory" as the best documentary and Warner Brothers' "Watch On The Rhine" as the most popular of the year.

The best 10 were named in the following order: "The Ox-Bow Incident," "Watch On The Rhine," "Air Force," "Holy Matrimony," "The Hard Way," "Casablanca," "Lassie Come Home," "Bataan," "The Moon Is Down," and "The Next Of Kin."

For outstanding direction, the board selected William Wellman, director of "The Ox-Bow Incident," and Paul Lukas for outstanding acting in "Watch On The Rhine."

Partisan Government Labeled 'Imposters'

LONDON, Dec. 24 (Friday).—(INS)—A Cairo dispatch to the London Daily Miror today quoted a spokesman for King Peter's Yugoslav government as declaring the partisan government of Field Marshal Josip Broz (Tito) is composed of a group of "imposters."

Replying to the action of Tito's council in stripping King Peter's government of its rights, the spokesman was quoted as stating:

"We cannot spend time in answering imposters who brazenly attack our monarchy and our legal government."

'Mystery Man' Returns to U. S.

MIAMI, Dec. 23.—(INS)—Charles E. Bedaux, the international "mystery" man, who was arrested by Allied authorities in North Africa last January on the charge that he traded with the enemy, tonight was disclosed to have secretly returned to the United States aboard a military plane.

Bedaux, a former close friend of the Duke and Duchess of Windsor, was permitted to go to a downtown Miami hotel following his arrival last night but, while now at liberty, was said to be technically under official observation pending determination of his status Friday.

Market Operator Slain by Gunmen

SAN DIEGO, Dec. 23.—(AP)—John Yoklavich, 50, Pacific Beach market operator was shot and killed in his home tonight by one of two young gunmen who forced their way in the house, Lieutenant Ed Dieckmann, homicide bureau chief, reported.

Dieckmann said the youths apparently knew that Yoklavich brought his day's receipts home with him. When Yoklavich refused their demands to give them money, one of the thugs shot him, Dieckmann said. The two gunmen escaped.

New Bolivia Regime Recognized by Ecuador

NEW YORK, Dec. 23.—(INS)—The Swiss radio at Bern quoted a DNB report today that the Equadorean minister to La Paz "informed the new government of Bolivia of its recognition by the government of Ecuador."

The Swiss broadcast, recorded by CBS, said the DNB report came from Buenos Aires, and pointed out that Ecuador is the first country to recognize the new government, if the report is confirmed.

NEW TACTICS USED BY RAF IN BIG RAID

Huge British Bomber Armada Waits Until After Midnight to Take Off for Assault

By Leo V. Dolan
Staff Correspondent International News Service

LONDON, Dec. 24.—A great striking force of Royal Air Force heavy bombers delivered another smashing raid on Berlin before dawn today—an attack believed to have been one of "super-blitz" proportions.

The air ministry officially disclosed that the Nazi capital had been the target of the night assault, but details were not immediately disclosed.

However, the Nazi agency, DNB, quoted by Reuter, described the raid as "another terror attack," saying:

"Early in the morning hours of Christmas Eve the R. A. F. made another terror attack on Berlin. Workers' quarters were especially hard hit. German fighter formations and anti-aircraft batteries downed a considerable number of four-engined bombers."

The British raiders did not leave their home bases until shortly after midnight, but at an early hour this morning the authoritative British Press Association announced that large formations of heavy R. A. F. bombers were seen soaring out over the North Sea headed for Germany.

The fact that the attackers did not leave Britain until that late hour suggested that the Allied Bomber Command may have altered its tactics from those employed in previous hammer-blows at the Nazi capital.

In virtually all previous night attacks on Berlin and other distant targets in the Reich, the Allied bombers have left their British bases at or shortly after dusk, and often returned home before midnight, their mission completed.

One possible reason for the new tactic was suggested—that by starting at a later hour long-range Allied fighters would be able to meet the returning bombers in the early light of dawn and shelter them from the attacks of Nazi interceptors which on raids in the past have harried the returning raiders almost the entire length of the homeward flight in the darkness.

By Howard Berry
Staff Correspondent International News Service

LONDON, Dec. 23.—Swarming hundreds of fighter-supported Allied medium and light bombers blasted the "rocket gun" coastal region of northern France for the fourth straight day today and American Thunderbolt fighter-bombers wrecked the Gilzerjan Airdrome in Holland.

An air ministry communique said tonight that R. A. F., Dominions and other Allied medium and light bombers, maintaining a steady battering of Germany's supposed "secret weapon" areas,

(Continued on Page 2, Cols. 2-3)

Japs Mass 20 Ships to Reinforce Troops on Marshall Isles

Nazis Plan to 'Try' Allied Flyers

Broadcast Intention to Retaliate for Russ Hangings

By William Wade
Staff Correspondent International News Service

LONDON, Dec. 24 (Friday).—Germany announced early today that captured American and British airmen in the Reich will be placed on "trial" before Nazi military tribunals as alleged "war criminals" in connection with the bombings of German cities.

Claiming that Russia's recent Kharkov trial of three Germans who were hanged for perpetrating mass murders had established a "precedent," the new Nazi threat of reprisals against Allied airmen was made in a statement attributed to the German foreign office. The official announcement was broadcast by the German overseas agency in a wireless transmission picked up in London.

The German statement declared that the Kharkov trial was in line with a "decision" allegedly reached at Teheran by President Roosevelt, Prime Minister Churchill and Premier Stalin sanctioning Allied trials of "individual soldiers" for war crimes.

ANNOUNCED BY RADIO

The new Berlin announcement was broadcast first by the Oslo radio and then from Paris Wednesday night. Transocean confirmed early today that its source was the German foreign office.

The Paris broadcast stated that the first Anglo-American prisoners of war scheduled to be "tried" for "violations of international law" will be airmen who participated in the raids on the Bavarian city of Nuremberg, Nazi party rallying center.

(FCC monitors quoted the German radio as declaring that "cooly and objectively, German judges will examine witnesses—both British and American pilots, and mothers and children of Hamburg. In public trial the British and American pilots will be able to state what their orders were, and in what manner they were carried out.")

The Oslo broadcast came some 24 hours after the Wilhelmstrasse (German foreign office) had made its first statement on the subject Tuesday. At that

(Continued on Page 2, Cols. 1-2)

U. S. Raiders Battle Nine Zeros, Strafe Installations of Foe on Omieji

By Clinton Green
Staff Correspondent International News Service

PEARL HARBOR, Dec. 23.—The greatest concentration of Japanese shipping spotted in the bomb-blasted Marshalls since an American carrier task force pounded the strategic islands on December 4 was reported today by Seventh U. S. Army Air Force headquarters.

Crew members of Army and Navy Liberator bombers which pummelled the Kwajalein and Roi islands, part of the Kwapalein atoll, Tuesday afternoon said more than 20 Jap ships were berthed in Kwajalein Lagoon.

The report, the most definite indication yet that the Japs are reinforcing the Marshalls, did not say if any of the ships were attacked.

The raiders, according to the headquarters announcement, survived a scrap with nine Zeros without suffering any damage. It was not announced whether any of the Zeros were shot down.

The preceding day, a formation of Navy Hellcat fighters and Army and Navy Dauntless light bombers bombed and strafed installations on Omieji Island, in the Jaluit atoll, damaging a medium-sized merchantman and a smaller vessel in the lagoon.

One American plane was shot down by anti-aircraft fire, said the announcement, adding that no Jap planes rose to intercept the raiders.

Earlier the same day, two enemy planes bombed American-held Tarawa, in the Gilberts, from high altitude, damaging one American plane on the ground.

By Joseph A. Bors
Staff Correspondent International News Service

WASHINGTON, Dec. 23.—A concentration of 20 Japanese ships in the enemy's Marshall Islands was reported today by the Navy following two more aerial assaults against those important Jap islands in the central Pacific.

It was the first mention of such a large enemy ship concentration in the Marshalls since American airmen began blasting

GENERAL MacARTHUR'S HEADQUARTER'S, New Guinea, Dc. 24 (Friday).—(INS)—General Douglas MacArthur today sent the following Christmas message to "all men and women in the armed forces" of the Southwest Pacific area:

"On this Christmas Day anniversary of the birth of our Lord Jesus Christ, I pray that the merciful God may preserve and bless each one of you."

THE STARS AND STRIPES
MEDITERRANEAN

Vol. 1, No. 59, Monday, January 24, 1944 ITALY EDITION TWO LIRE

Rome, Nazi Rear Menaced As Fifth Extends Beachhead

Landing Covered By Air Support Over Wide Area

Constant Patrol Eased Way For Assault Troops

ALLIED FORCE HEADQUARTERS, Jan. 23—Allied Air Forces of the Mediterranean, in their busiest day since the Salerno landings, flew 1,300 sorties yesterday in their contribution to the land-sea-air operation that brought American and British soldiers within the shadow of ancient Rome. The role of the Air Forces was three-fold: to protect the convoy bearing the assault troops, to cover the landings and beachhead, to paralyze the movement of German reinforcements into the new combat area.

At least 600 fighters and fighter bombers of the Tactical Air Force kept up constant patrols over the 5th Army beachhead. In contrast, the Germans were able to put up no more than 100 light aircraft over the whole of land and sea areas involved—and these planes concentrated most of their efforts against Allied shipping.

German bombers, with fighter escort, attempted to break through six times throughout the day, and on at least one occasion succeeded. But several times their hit-and-run dashes were intercepted and in one formation of more than 20 FW-190s six were shot down by a P-40 squadron of the famed 79th Fighter Group. One P-40 was downed in this mass dogfight but the pilot is safe.

This was the same P-40 squadron, now commanded by Capt. George Lee, Norwood, Mass., which destroyed 17 enemy planes in one day in fighting over Cape Bon last June.

Two other German planes were shot down over the beachhead area yesterday, for the loss of one Allied aircraft, making a total count for the day of 14 to 9.

Light, medium and even heavy bombers throughout the day struck at key road junctions over which the Germans might send rein-

(Continued on page 3)

Democratic Group Urges FDR To Run

WASHINGTON, Jan. 23 — The Democratic National Committee unanimously adopted a resolution yesterday "earnestly soliciting" President Franklin D. Roosevelt "to continue as our great world humanitarian leader."

At the same session the committee selected Chicago as the site of the 1944 Presidential convention, the date of which will be decided later. This gave the Great Lakes both major party conventions, the Republicans having chosen Chicago a few days ago.

Pilots Found Invasion 'Nothing Like Salerno'

By Sgt. JACK FOISIE
(Stars and Stripes Staff Writer)

AN ADVANCED AIR BASE, Jan. 23—I flew over the vicinity of the newly-won Allied beachhead at Nettuno today and then deep into German territory to bomb Frosinone, key junction town on the road to Rome.

This is what I saw from the plexiglass nose of the American A-20 Boston bomber:

The Allied invasion fleet, extended in a long line, three or four ships abreast, from the beach out many miles into the mist.

To us, at 10,000 feet, they were but dark slivers on a calm sea, but reports said that landings were progressing rapidly, thanks to an untroubled sea.

Time and time again the pilots, upon returning to their advanced fighter strips, said almost the identical words:

"Certainly nothing like Salerno," or "A soft touch compared to Sicily."

While over the beachhead I did not observe any naval firing whatsoever. This was at three o'clock in the afternoon. Early morning patrols had reported some naval firing but few returns from the enemy.

Further inland I could see vehicular movement on the road. They must have been ours, for P-40s, A-36s and P-38s were over the territory constantly, going down to the deck to investigate any suspicious activity. And around the beachhead they found none, although inland German traffic was moving at a hurried pace but without panic.

It was our mission to bomb the town of Frosinone, to tumble the buildings into the street and block the main artery. Each plane carried six 250-pound demolition bombs for the job — and there were a lot of planes.

This was all part of the overall coordination of air and ground in this new amphibious assault: the plan, in essence, called for the fighters to protect the convoy and landings, while the fighter-bombers and bombers cut the main routes of communications to forestall enemy reinforcements converging on the assault force until it had time to establish itself and gain positions.

How well the air has been able to do the job will be told in the fighting of the next few days.

The full strength of the 47th Bomb Group, commanded by Col Malcolm Green, San Francisco.

(Continued on page 3)

Troops Amazed By Quick Success

By Sgt. MILT LEHMAN
(Stars and Stripes Staff Writer)

WITH THE 5TH ARMY AMPHIBIOUS FORCES, Jan. 22 — (Delayed) — By-passing many weary miles of the road to Rome, a great Allied amphibious force landed at 0200 hours this morning on the beaches south of the Eternal City.

Troops who went ashore on one sector of the beach were amazed at the handful of Germans defending the coast line. Not one artillery shell was fired against them. Most of the defenders of the German positions fled our approach and of the few who elected to fight, one oberlieutenant now lies dead, and in our stockade are four drunken Jerries picked up driving a Volkswagon wildly in the face of the Allied landing.

The only signs of war in the moonless early morning were our own fire and our patrol boats moving on the beaches ahead of the first waves. As the landing boats came in on the flat sandy beaches, troops moved quickly ashore troubled only by very light mine fields which were soon neutralized.

Dawn revealed hundreds of landing craft bobbing peacefully off the beaches south of Rome while our fighter-bombers shuttled overhead in large formations. At 0845 hours, 12 Focke-Wulfs screamed out of the sky and dropped bombs

(Continued on page 4)

Enemy Mentions Place Of Landing

LONDON, Jan. 23—Although the landing place of the 5th Army's amphibious force which hit the west coast of Italy Saturday was not mentioned in Allied reports, a German report heard in Switzerland said:

"The Anglo-Americans succeeded under cover of darkness to form bridgeheads between Nettuno and the Tiber estuary south of Rome and to occupy the harbor of Nettuno. More detailed reports are not available on the heavy fighting in progress there since the early morning hours."

Nettuno is about 30 miles southeast of Rome.

Swiss reports based on diplomatic advices out of Rome said that the road out of the Italian capital to the north was filled with the official cars of German and fascist officials fleeing because of the Allied forces closing in from the south. These reports added that the headquarters of the German quartermaster corps had been moved north and the communications center for the German high command had been pulled back.

Two Seaside Towns Fall; Enemy Resistance Weak

ALLIED FORCE HEADQUARTERS, Jan. 23—American and British troops have deepened and widened the substantial beachhead they seized south of Rome early Saturday, it was officially announced today. At a late hour tonight no Allied sources had defined the extent or location of the area occupied by the invading forces, except to state that it was deep in the rear of the German lines.

Newspaper correspondents reported from the beachhead that Allied troops immediately captured two seaside towns, largest of which was taken with only two casualties. One of the towns taken was described as a watering place which had been shattered by past Allied bombings. The beachhead was said to be several miles wide and several miles deep.

There was reason to believe that the 5th Army's amphibious move had caught the German high command completely off guard, but there was nevertheless little disposition to regard this lack of opposition as anything but momentary. One correspondent with the 5th Army said that casualties among the landing troops were light and were caused principally by exploding mines. Observers said that both naval and military losses were unbelievably small. Lt. Gen. Mark W. Clark, who made a dawn to dusk tour of his Army's landing areas, was said to have been pleased with the progress of the operation.

American and British forces, spearheaded by Rangers and Commandos were believed well on their way to their first objectives. Correspondents said that only small, scattered detachments of Germans were met and these were quickly knocked out. Long range German artillery was shelling ineffectively and a few sneak attacks made on the beaches by the Luftwaffe met with little success.

Allied military commentators admitted that the bold 5th Army plan had succeeded beyond expectations so far, but warned that the net result of the operation will not be known for several days. It was emphasized that the Allied stab into the enemy flank carries with it such a threat to German communications that heavy counter-attacks may be expected at any moment.

Timed with the landings behind the enemy's lines were heavy Allied attacks which raged over much of the original 5th Army combat zone. In the face of withering fire from German screaming-meemies, machine gun and artillery fire, Yank infantrymen crossed over the Rapido River in the area of San Angelo. Unlike the operation on the beaches south of Rome, the enemy's resistance here was bitter and deadly. Every approach to the river had been carefully surveyed and zeroed and heavy preparatory artillery fire by the Americans did not wipe out the defenses. Although costly, the attack doubtless pinned down the Nazi defenses in the Cassino sector and contributed to the ease with which the landings further north were made.

Intense fighting also took place

(Continued on page 4)

Bitter Fighting Rages On Rapido

WITH THE 5TH ARMY, Jan. 23 — The first phase of a bitter battle in which American elements tried to establish a bridgehead across the Rapido River against a thick wall of German opposition has come to an end. The action, in which heavy losses were suffered on both sides, was described by a high-ranking American officer as "The Battle of Guts." Certainly it was one of the most hellish struggles in the Italian campaign.

The Americans crossed the river early Friday morning, and before the men had penetrated 400 yards across the flatlands fronting the German Gustav Line they were met by a withering crossfire of enemy machine guns and mortars. Before dark on Saturday evening the enemy had staged two fierce, well-coordinated counterattacks.

Men who participated in this Rapido River assault received credit in high Army quarters today for having contributed a large share to the success of amphibious operations now being carried on by Allied troops south of Rome. A high officer said:

"This battle has been, in effect, the second landing of the division. These men came in at Salerno. Their efforts to establish this bridgehead, and their efforts to

(Continued on page 4)

Biddle Is Named Eisenhower Aide

WASHINGTON, Jan. 23 — Anthony J. Drexel Biddle resigned today as U.S. ambassador-minister to various Allied governments-in-exile in London and was sworn in as a lieutenant colonel on the staff of General Dwight D. Eisenhower. Lt. Col. Biddle will serve as Gen. Eisenhower's liaison officer to the governments of occupied countries.

In accepting the resignation, President Roosevelt wrote Biddle that the period is approaching "when these governments must look forward to the re-establishment of their countries." He said it was therefore "right and proper" that Biddle serve as liaison officer between them and our armies.

Los Angeles Examiner

CHARACTER · QUALITY · AMERICA FIRST! · ENTERPRISE · ACCURACY

AN AMERICAN PAPER FOR THE AMERICAN PEOPLE · THE GREAT NEWSPAPER OF THE GREAT SOUTHWEST

Reg.U.S.Pat.Off.

Examiner Telephone RIchmond 1212 · Examiner Building, 1111 S. Broadway

FINAL 9AM

VOL. XLI—NO. 48 · LOS ANGELES, FRIDAY, JANUARY 28, 1944 · S · Two Sections—Part I—FIVE CENTS

JAPS SLAY, TORTURE BATAAN PRISONERS

THE 'MARCH OF DEATH'

HORROR MARCH— Hands over their heads and guarded by grinning Japs with bayonets, heroic survivors of bloody Bataan, gaunt, hungry and deathly tired by those last ghastly days, start on the "March of Death," the calculated Jap brutality that ended in the peace of death for hundreds of American soldiers. For scorching hot days they were without food, without water, without rest. This is a Japanese photo.

—International News photo.

Yanks Starved, Beheaded, Buried Alive by Captors

Brutality and Butchery After Surrender Told by Army and Navy; 2200 Americans Die in Two Months at One Camp

WASHINGTON, Jan. 27.—(AP)—A horror story scarcely paralleled in the annals of modern war—how the Japanese starved, tortured and in some cases wantonly murdered the gallant defenders of Bataan—was told by the Army and Navy tonight.

Documented by sworn statements of officers who escaped from prison camps, the joint announcement described a cold-blooded campaign of savagery carried out after the 36,000 Americans and Filipinos on Bataan and Corregidor were overwhelmed by superior numbers.

The 4000-word account began by telling of thousands of deaths in Japanese camps (2200 Americans died in two months in one camp) and then recited that:

When the Americans and Filipinos first were taken prisoner, those found with Japanese money or tokens were beheaded. Survivors were beaten along a "march of death" from the scene.

Twelve thousand men were kept penned in a 100-yard-square area without food for a week. There was a 12-hour wait to fill canteens at the one water spigot.

A widely used torture was the "sun treatment." Captives were made to sit in the boiling sun all day without cover and with little water.

Six men—three Americans and three Filipinos—ill from mistreatment, were buried while still alive.

More Prisoners Die Than Reported by Japs

Men "literally were worked to death." It was not unusual for 20 per cent of a work detail to die and "in one instance, 75 per cent were killed that way."

Three officers who attempted to escape had their hands tied behind them, then their hands were pulled upward by ropes attached to an overhead purchase so they had to remain standing and bent forward to ease the pressure on their arms. They were left thus for two days and periodically beaten with a two-by-four. One officer was then beheaded and the other two were shot.

Lesser brutalities, indignities and humiliations were innumerable . . . the Japs gave three chickens and 50 eggs to 500 men, then broadcast to the world that their prisoners were fed on chickens and eggs . . . American Flags were habitually and designedly used as rags in kitchens.

From reports made by a naval officer and two Army officers who escaped from the Philippines after almost a year as prisoners, the two departments assembled the story, including the report that several times as many American prisoners in the hands of the Japanese have died—mostly of starvation, forced hard labor and general brutality—as the Japanese have ever reported.

"At one prison camp, Camp O'Donnell, about 2200 American prisoners died in April and May, 1942," said the report. "In the camp at Cabanatuan, about 3000 Americans had died up to the end of October, 1942. Still heavier mortality occurred among the Filipino prisoners of war at Camp O'Donnell."

The calculated campaign of brutality began against the battle-spent, hungry Ameri-

Penal Reform Urged by Warren

SACRAMENTO, Jan. 27.—(AP) — Governor Warren won the first round in a legislative fight over his proposal to reorganize the state prison system tonight when the Senate governmental efficiency committee recommended his plan.

The committee action was by voice vote with only Senator Thomas F. Keating, San Rafael Democrat, expressing opposition.

By Carl Greenberg
Los Angeles Examiner Staff Correspondent

EXAMINER BUREAU, SACRAMENTO, Jan. 27.—California legislators, meeting today in special session, heard Governor Earl Warren

(Continued on Page 14, Cols. 1-2)

Bricker Says Politics Perils Soldiers' Vote

By George Rothwell Brown
(Special to the Los Angeles Examiner)

PITTSBURGH, Jan. 27.—Governor John W. Bricker of Ohio charged here tonight that politics in Washington threatens to deprive eight or nine millions of Americans in the armed services of their voting privileges in the coming presidential campaign.

He placed the blame for delay in passing soldiers vote legislation on Congress and the Administration.

Standing squarely behind Senator Robert A. Taft of Ohio, and other Republicans in Congress, the Governor denied President Roosevelt's charge of "fraud" in the bill which would retain supervision of elections in the states.

Making his first political appearance in an Eastern state since announcing his candidacy for the Republican nomination for President, Governor Bricker spoke tonight as the McKinley Day orator

(Continued on Page 9, Cols. 1-3)

Dyess' Widow Tells Hero's Suffering

Fighting to keep back tears, a slender girl dressed in black yesterday told of her hero husband and his escape from a Jap prison camp, only to die later in a plane crash in Burbank.

She was Mrs. Marajen Stevick Dyess, widow of Lieutenant Colonel William E. Dyess, whose story on Jap atrocities to American prisoners of war, disclosed last night, has jarred the nation.

Colonel Dyess, at 27 years of age, died December 22, 1943, when his P-38 fighter plunged to earth after developing engine trouble.

He was attached at the time

(Continued on Page A, Cols. 7-8)

Have You Bought YOUR Extra War Bond to Back the Attack?

THE STARS AND STRIPES
MEDITERRANEAN

Vol. 1, No. 69, Friday, February 4, 1944 ITALY EDITION TWO LIRE

U.S. Forces Seize Two Strongholds In The Marshalls

No Ship Losses, Casualties Low, Nimitz Reports

WASHINGTON, Feb. 3—The Marines have won control of Roi and Namur Islands in the northern part of the 70-mile-long Kwajalein atoll and Army infantrymen are rapidly driving back the Japanese garrison on Kwajalein Island itself, according to the latest Navy communique on the Marshall Islands fighting.

As more details come out of the new battle zone, it would appear that the Japanese had been stunned by the immense sea-air-land striking power of the U.S. forces. The enemy was beaten almost before he could start to fight. Admiral Chester W. Nimitz, commander in chief of the Pacific fleet, declared:

"We have suffered no naval losses and casualties are very moderate."

Admiral Nimitz' Pearl Harbor headquarters reported that troops of the 7th Infantry Division encountered considerable rifle and machine gun fire but their biggest obstacle proved to be the huge fires started by the earlier pounding by their own warships and aircraft.

The landing on Kwajalein was made after the most intense bombardment in the history of the Pacific war. For three days and nights American warships, including new 16-inch-gun battleships, blasted the island, concentrating their fire on the narrow 600 yards of the eastern beach. Bomber fleets roared overhead dropping all sizes of bombs, even blockbusters. In addition, infantrymen quickly occupied eight nearby islets and set up land artillery which added to the great stream of firepower pouring into the

(Continued on page 4)

Sofia Lies In Ruin, MAAF Reveals

MEDITERRANEAN ALLIED AIR FORCES HEADQUARTERS, Feb. 3—Every major target in the Bulgarian capital of Sofia has been either destroyed or damaged by Allied airmen, a special communique today disclosed.

MAAF Headquarters said reconnaissance photographs just taken show that the heart of the capital's industrial center is blasted out, railway stations and yards are a mass of twisted rubble and the rail shops are gutted. Secondary targets like the police station and barracks have also felt the weight of Allied bombs.

Another victim of Allied bombing is the ball bearing works at Villa Perosa, near Turin in northwestern Italy. Photos show that 50 to 60 percent of the vital war goods factory was knocked out and it is thought doubtful that any part of the works can be put back in working order. Of seven shops in the main factory one was obliterated while five others were badly damaged.

Ten German Divisions Trapped In The Ukraine

NEW LANDINGS IN PACIFIC

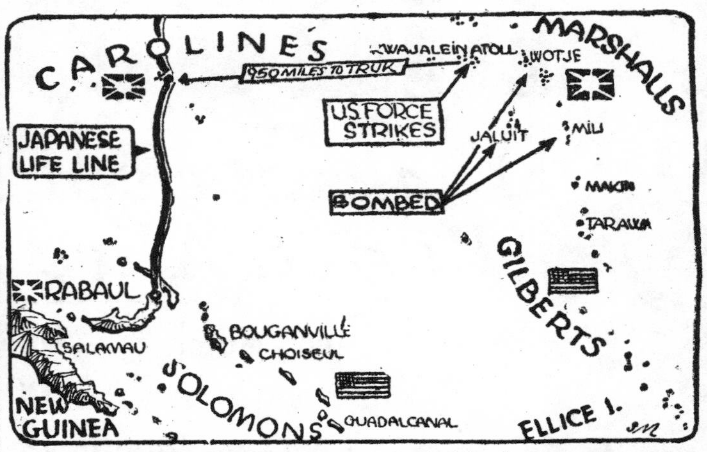

AMERICAN FORCES moved on to fresh island conquests in the Pacific when they made successful landings in the Marshall group, held by Japan since World War I.

Raymond Clapper Killed While Covering Invasion

Raymond Clapper, Washington columnist and political commentator, was killed in an airplane accident while covering the invasion of the Marshall Islands, the Navy Department announced from Washington tonight. He was 51 years old.

Clapper was one of the most respected newspapermen in the nation's capital, and his influence was so widespread that it was said no Congressman or high government official dared to miss his newspaper column. He recently went into the radio field, and his broadcasts increased his audience still more.

Clapper was primarily an observer of the political scene in Washington, and he understood its workings as few others did. His commentaries were always well-tempered and sane, and all shades of political opinion read him.

It was only during the past year that Clapper went overseas. He visited Great Britain, flew up to Sweden, and down to North Africa. In Algiers he was a welcome visitor at The Stars and Stripes office, and he wrote an article for this newspaper on his impressions of Sweden. His latest trip took him to the South Pacific, where he interviewed General Douglas MacArthur.

Clapper was the type of reporter who went wherever the news took him, and his death adds another name to the long list of newspapermen killed in this war.

Clapper started in as a reporter for the Kansas City (Mo.) Star in 1916. In 1919 he began working for United Press, and headed various city bureaus until he took over the Washington office, where he was chief political writer. He has written a regular column for Scripps-Howard since then.

P.O.W. Deaths Rise

WASHINGTON, Feb. 3 — The War Department today released the names of 62 more U.S. soldiers who have died of disease in Jap prison camps since the fall of Bataan and Corregidor.

The total of such deaths, which Secretary of State Cordell Hull this week flatly attributed to slave labor, inadequate food, clothing and medical care, has now reached 1,617.

1,100 U.S. Planes Bomb Nazi Port

LONDON, Feb. 3—More than 1,100 U.S. bombers and fighters swept over 400 miles of the North Sea today to carry out a saturation raid on the great German base at Wilhemshaven, home of the German North Sea Fleet and center of Nazi U-boat construction.

The Air Ministry tonight disclosed few details of the daylight assault beyond saying that the main force was made up of four-engined bombers. American fighters capable of making the 800-mile round trip escorted the heavies.

Wilhelmshaven has been the target for several previous attacks by the 8th Air Force planes. On Nov. 3, last year, 400 bombers pounded the city's naval facilities in what was then the heaviest daylight assault of the war. The German port was also the target of the first heavy daylight bombing by American planes on Jan. 27, 1943.

While the heavies were pounding Wilhelmshaven, Marauders of the 8th Air Force, escorted by RAF and Dominion fighters, were out again over northern France, their seventh attack on invasion coast targets in six days.

Defeat Is One Of Worst Since Stalingrad Rout

LONDON, Feb. 3—In one of the greatest Russian victories since the battle of Stalingrad, two great Soviet armies have thundered forward to encircle ten German divisions deep in the Dnieper River bend.

Marshal Josef Stalin tonight described how, in five days of bitter fighting, the two Russian armies burst through strongly fortified German defenses from opposite directions and made contact in the heart of the Dnieper bend. Soldiers of General Ivan Koniev crashed toward the west from the region north of Kirovograd while the troops of General Nikolai Vatutin simultaneously pounded through the German forces in an easterly direction from the great Kiev Bulge. A large part of Hitler's forces in the Ukraine have thus been trapped.

Marshal Stalin addressed his Order of the Day to the two generals, telling how they had thrown a steel ring around nine Nazi infantry divisions and one tank division, which now faces annihilation. The Russian commander in chief stated that the crushing offensives of the two armies had developed on fronts 100 to 110 miles wide, moving forward 30 to 45 miles to meet. In the course of their tremendous drives, the two forces liberated more than 300 Ukrainian cities and towns, including Smela, big railroad city about ten miles south of Cherkassy and the Dnieper River, and Zvenigorodka, Shkola and Kanev. Citizens of Moscow hailed the great victory of their armies with the firing of 20 salvoes from 224 guns.

The Soviet offensive snapped off the huge German salient which abutted onto the middle Dnieper at the town of Kanev, northwest of Cherkassy. Troops of the two Ukraine armies linked up in the Zvenigorodka-Shkola area, in the center of the river bend country, and thereby closed the circle surrounding all of the German forces north of the Soviet columns.

Meanwhile, Red Army soldiers of General Leonid Govorov, who have already cleared the Germans from 10,000 square miles in the Leningrad region, have surged across the Estonian border and captured the town of Krivayaluka, a mile inside the frontier.

Moscow announced that Soviet troops were already besieging Narva, ten miles inside the border.

What started out 14 days ago as the battle to free Leningrad has developed into a campaign to liberate Estonia and Latvia. General Govorov's sensational northern victories have extended over an area 150 miles in width, extending from the Volkhov River on the east to the Narva River and Lake Peipus on the west, and 60 miles in depth. The Germans have been forced into headlong

(Continued on page 4)

LONDON, Feb. 3 — Today's German communique announced the evacuation of Rovno and Luck, two important railroad towns and Nazi base section headquarters just west of the Pripet Marshes. Rovno and Luck are respectively 30 and 60 miles within the pre-1939 Polish border. They abandoned, the communique said, in the course of "bitter battles."

Street Fighting Rages In Cassino

By Sgt. RALPH G. MARTIN
(Stars and Stripes Staff Writer)

ON THE 5TH ARMY FRONT, Feb. 3—American troops and tanks were bitterly streetfighting reinforced Germans in the northern suburbs of Cassino today, while the southern half of the town received an intense artillery pounding.

After strongly counterattacking in the hills several miles north of the town and successfully holding back the American push there, the Nazis have decided to make a last stand in Cassino itself. As they did at San Vittore, they have converted every house into a fortress, and every piece of cover into a gun position, thus making the entire town a highly organized defensive position. In addition they have brought in more troops and tanks and anti-tank guns and self-propelled 75s.

Fifth Army troops pushing in slowly from the north of town have been subject to terrific artillery fire from German 88s placed in the high ground directly under the town's landmark, which is the monastery, sticking 1,500 feet up on the north side of the hill. To clean out the town completely, the infantry must first mop up the gun position and all these gun positions have been deeply dug in under thick layers of concrete and steel plates and even railroad ties.

The artillery has been doing an all-out over here in the past few

(Continued on page 4)

Groundhog Spotted ... Result's Secret

WITH THE 5TH ARMY AMPHIBIOUS FORCES, Feb. 2 (delayed by the Adolf Hitler anti-groundhog division)—The groundhog put on his steel helmet and came out of his foxhole today to take a look at his shadow.

"Nothing can stop my early rising for a looksee, not even war," muttered the rodent, ducking as a shell whistled over his head. The groundhog then leveled his bazooka at a tank that came thundering toward him.

Nothing has been heard from him since, so whether the groundhog did or did not see his shadow is still a secret, equals British most secret.

CHARACTER QUALITY AMERICA FIRST! ENTERPRISE ACCURACY
Los Angeles Examiner
AN AMERICAN PAPER FOR THE AMERICAN PEOPLE — THE GREAT NEWSPAPER OF THE GREAT SOUTHWEST
Reg. U.S. Pat. Off.
Examiner Telephone Richmond 1212 — Examiner Building, 1111 S. Broadway
VOL. XLI—NO. 72 — LOS ANGELES, MONDAY, FEBRUARY 21, 1944 — CCC — Two Sections—Part I—FIVE CENTS

19 JAP SHIPS SUNK; 201 PLANES DOWNED AT TRUK

U. S. INFLUENCE SEEN IN RUSS FINN TERMS

Observers Say Stalin May Offer 'Reasonable' Peace Under Pressure From America

STOCKHOLM, Feb. 20.—Well-informed observers said today that under American pressure Marshal Stalin may be induced to offer Finland a "reasonable" peace instead of the severe terms believed to have formed the basis of Moscow's latest demands on the Finns.

Meanwhile, Dr. Juho K. Passikivi, Finnish statesman and negotiator of the 1940 peace between Finland and the U. S. S. R., was expected to return soon to Helsinki with the latest Soviet conditions for peace which he has received during his stay in Stockholm.

The following conditions are being mentioned as likely to form the basis of the new Moscow bid for peace:

(1) Restoration of the 1941 frontier, with the Arctic port of Petsamo going to Russia.

> **Karl H. von Wiegand, dean of American war correspondents, reveals the Soviet plan to engulf Finland.—Page 4.**

(2) The question of the Gulf of Finland port of Hangoe left open. The Finns are said to be determined not to give any concessions regarding Hangoe, rejecting even the temporary Soviet occupation of any part of Finland proper.

Other observers stress the fact that whereas Russian propaganda, via the Moscow radio and Washington Embassy, indicates the Soviet Union intends to try to give Finland a "severe" peace, Stalin himself is not necessarily committed to what his government-controlled radio and press or even his embassies say.

The former Finnish Social Minister Fagerholm, writing in the Vecko Journalen, declared:

"It all depends on what the peace conditions look like, if they are unreasonable, humiliating or violate our independence and right to govern our own country, the world will see

(Continued on Page 5, Cols. 4-5)

Hail Deluges L. A., Floods Stall Cars, Traffic Snowbound

HAIL BROADWAY!—This picture, taken at 11th and Broadway looking south, presents a bleak wintry scene as a result of a freakish hail storm that struck downtown Los Angeles after downpour of rain. The ruts made by cars show the depth to which the hail covered the street.
—Los Angeles Examiner photo.

British Destroyer Janus Lost in Action

LONDON, Feb. 20.—(AP)—The admiralty tonight announced the Loss of the destroyer Janus, one of the veteran British warships of the Mediterranean war. The communique gave no details.

Lightning Hits Power Lines, Storm Rainfall 4.80 Inches

"Unusual" was the right word for the weather yesterday.

Two inches of hail whitened a large area of Southern California, the deepest white since a two-inch snowfall on January, 1932. Storm rainfall, practically all of it within 24 hours, had reached 4.80 inches at 6:30 last night.

Not only automobiles were stalled by flooded streets, but more than 30 yellow streetcars stood helpless over Los Angeles, their armatures watersoaked.

Lightning struck Jack F. Carlin, Pacific Electric supervisor, as he was directing streetcar traffic at Fifth and Flower streets. He was treated at Georgia Street Receiving Hospital.

RAID SIREN SCREAMS

An air raid siren at Slauson avenue and Compton boulevard was shorted and screamed for 30 minutes.

Police at the Los Angeles 77th street station were forced to use candlelight and police of Lynwood were operating by flashlight because of power failure caused by lightning.

Hail-coated rails and deep water caused yellow streetcars to travel at a snail's pace down Broadway and a "lake" at Fifth and Flower streets forced diversion of the "U," "P" and "3" cars from 4:45 to 5:40 p. m.

Lightning knocked out an Edison power line across the main Pacific Electric lines just below Compton, tying up all cars between Los Angeles and Long

(Continued on Page 3, Cols. 1-3)

Inn Owner Found Slain With Four Aces in Hand

WAUKEGAN, Ill., Feb. 20.—(INS)—The bizarre murder of a roadhouse owner, found dead behind his own bar and with four aces from a deck of cards clutched in his hand, confronted police officials of Lake County tonight.

The victim of the mysterious slaying was Anthony Rubaitis, for 10 years proprietor of the Clover Inn on Green Bay road three miles west of Waukegan.

He was found by a party of three young couples who entered the roadhouse for drinks. A blast from a shotgun, fired at close range, had shattered the victim's chest.

In addition to the four aces clutched in the dead man's hand, a king and a queen from the pack lay on the floor near him. The rest of the deck was on the bar beside an untouched drink.

Police immediately ruled out robbery as a motive, pointing out that there was a valuable diamond ring on one of Rudaitis' fingers. In his pockets were a valuable watch and a roll of bills. And the cash register, containing approximately $100, was untouched.

2000 YANK PLANES BLAST REICH PLANTS

War's Heaviest Daylight Blow Delivered Against Leipzig, Brunswick and Other Centers

By Howard Berry
Staff Correspondent International News Service

LONDON, Feb. 21.—(Monday.)—A record armada of some 2000 American fortresses, Liberators and fighters struck the war's heaviest daylight blow against five great fighter-manufacturing centers in the heart of Germany yesterday in a bid for air domination during the coming invasion of western Europe.

Among the vital targets pounded, United States headquarters announced today, were Leipzig, hit less than 12 hours earlier by a powerful R. A. F. fleet; Oschersleben, big Focke-Wulf manufacturing center 80 miles southwest of Berlin; Brunswick, Messerschmitt and rocket-firing fighter center 120 miles west of the Reich capital; Bernberg, 42 miles northwest of Leipzig, and Gotha, 75 miles southwest of Leipzig.

HIT FIGHTER OUTPUT

(General Henry H. Arnold United States Air Force chief announced in Washington that 2000 planes carried out the assaults and estimated they deprived Germany of 25 per cent of her fighter production capacity.

(General Arnold also revealed that among the targets hit and not mentioned in the United States Air Force communique was Halberstadt, site of a big Junkers plant 32 miles southeast of Brunswick.)

Sixty-one Nazi planes that attempted to break up the raids were blasted out of the skies by escort fighters, while the number of enemy planes downed by bomber gunners has not yet been tabulated, a communique announced.

(General Arnold said "more than 100" enemy planes were downed by American fighters.)

Despite the fact the largest number of heavy bombers ever dispatched had to penetrate an area where 60 per cent of the Nazi fighter strength is massed, only 22 big bombers failed to re-

(Continued on Page 6, Cols. 2-3)

Nazis Driven Back by U. S. Tank Force

ALLIED HEADQUARTERS, NAPLES, Feb. 20.—(AP)—American armored columns smashed into the German flank today, and have driven two miles toward Carroceto in a fierce counterattack sprung after invasion beachhead forces had blunted an all-out, reckless onslaught by nine Nazi divisions on the American beachhead at Anzio.

The tide of battle has turned, and "the beachhead was never more secure than today"—the date reportedly set by the Germans for its extinction—Associated Press Correspondent Daniel De Luce said in a front dispatch written at 12:30 p. m. today.

GERMANS RELAX

The mauled Germans relaxed the initiative, he declared, and the U. S. armored thrusts, biting into the eastern flank of the Nazi salient, gained "as much as three kilometers (two miles) in the direction of Carroceto." These blows by tanks and infantry began at 6:30 a. m. Saturday, and continued today.

Thus the ground lost below Carroceto to the intense German charges was being recovered, and De Luce said the Germans may have lost so heavily "that another attack cannot be mounted on a similar scale."

More than 500 prisoners have been taken in the last 24 hours, he added, and "German aggressive spirit faded in some spots along the front." German at-

(Continued on Page 6, Cols. 5-7)

Army Planes Pound Jap Base at Kusaie in Caroline Islands

WASHINGTON, Feb. 20.—(AP)—Army bombing planes struck at Kusaie, in the Caroline Islands, on Friday, while Army and Navy planes teamed up for an attack on four atolls in the Marshall Islands, the Navy reported tonight.

Army Liberators from the Seventh Air Force bombed docks and shipping at Kusaie, Japanese stronghold in the eastern Carolines, and sank one small ship.

Army Warhawks and Navy Ventura and Liberator bombing planes pounded ground installations, an air fields and a radio station in the Marshall Island raids, the Navy said in an announcement released in Washington and Pearl Harbor simultaneously.

The atolls hit in the Marshalls were not identified, in line with the Navy policy of keeping the Japanese high command in the dark on operations in the Marshalls. None of our planes were lost in the attacks.

2 Light Cruisers, Three Destroyers Bagged by Yanks

Air and Sea Armada Blasts Navy Base; U. S. Loses Seventeen Aircraft

By Richard V. Haller
Staff Correspondent International News Service

PEARL HARBOR, Feb. 20.—Twenty-six Japanese ships, including fourteen warships or auxiliaries, and more than 250 enemy planes were destroyed or damaged by the powerful United States sea and air armada that smashed with stunning surprise at Truk last week.

Nineteen ships, including 11 warships or auxiliaries, were sunk and seven others "probably sunk." At least 201 Jap planes were destroyed and "more than" 50 others damaged.

Magnitude of the American victory in the blow against Japan's formidable base in the Carolines was disclosed in a communique from Admiral Chester W. Nimitz which declared in its opening paragraph:

The Pacific Fleet has returned at Truk the visit by the Japanese fleet at Pearl Harbor on December 7, 1941, and effected a partial settlement of the debt."

Navy, Planes in Two-Day Action

Admiral Nimitz revealed the attack, carried out by United States Naval forces and several hundred carrier-borne planes, was a two-day action prosecuted last Wednesday and Thursday.

Sunk in the Pearl Harbor-avenging assault were:

Two light cruisers.
Three destroyers.
One ammunition ship.
One seaplane tender.
Two oilers.
Two gunboats.
Eight cargo ships.

Listed as heavily damaged and probably sunk were the following enemy ships:

One cruiser or large destroyer.
Two oilers.
Four cargo ships.

127 Enemy Planes Shot Down

Of the 201 enemy planes reported destroyed, 127 were shot down in flames. Fifty additional enemy aircraft were damaged on the ground.

In addition to the staggering toll of enemy ships and planes exacted as partial payment for the treacherous sneak attack on Pearl Harbor, the shore installations and airdrome runways of the enemy's so-called "Pearl Harbor" of Truk were "thoroughly bombed and strafed," Admiral Nimitz said.

The cost of this avenging blow, which is but one of a series now being dealt the Japs in the Central

HEART MOUNTAIN SENTINEL

VOL. III No. 11 | Heart Mountain, Wyoming | Saturday, March 11, 1944 | 2 Cents Within City 5 Cents Elsewhere

Our Cards on the Table

——o——

An Editorial

The American public is entitled to know, despite what reflections might be cast upon us as a race, that selective service in relocation centers is going well regardless of the unfavorable publicity coming upon us from several directions. At some centers small but vociferous groups have been taken into custody by federal officials for failure to respond to their calls for pre-induction physical examinations.

This is as it should be.

We hope that the FBI and the office of the U.S. District Attorney will treat any draft evaders at Heart Mountain in the same manner—and quickly.

At the same time these deluded youths have our deepest sympathy because in most cases they themselves are not entirely guilty for their failure to realize their responsibilities. This situation is due to a number of factors.

Chief among these factors is the influence of some issei. We frankly believe some of our parents are skating on thin ice in their relations with their adopted country and their native Japan. Unfortunately, they prefer to do no ill toward either nation, thus keeping clear their records. After the war, if there is nothing against them in either country there is no reason for their not being able to re-establish relations between the two countries. Anyone thinking that trade relations between the two warring nations will not be restored after the war is denying precedence and reality. Commerce is the basis of peace.

(Continued on page 4)

Many Young Nisei Are Content In Being 'Quislings' to Selves

By JOHN KITASAKO

"Say, you know, our mess hall coffee's getting better," someone remarked, to which his friend said, "No, it isn't. You're just getting used to it."

Our "coffee" of life is not getting better. We cannot say that our manners have improved in camp, or that our thinking has been stimulated, or our attitude made more wholesome, or our sense of values sharpened.

We don't notice it because we're getting used to it. If we think or act bad often enough, the mere fact of repetition will deaden our sensitivity to evil.

Our attitude and behavior are sabotaged by the aimlessness and abandon with which we go through our daily paces of living. It is easy to become "quislings" unto ourselves and sell out our moral and spiritual values for momentary pleasures as an avenue of escape from the boredom of confinement. It is easy to have our character standard lowered.

These are days when we can ill-afford to lower the bars on our code of ethics, for these are days when we are faced with the necessity of meeting and solving great problems and making wise decisions.

In this vale of problems and decisions, when we are being tested to see whether or not we have the right stuff, we are on our own. The right solutions to problems will be found and the correct decisions will be made by those of us who have clung to a sound, healthy way of life, and who have not become diseased by the sordid and demoralizing aspects of camp life.

"To every man there openeth, A high way and a low, And every man decideth, Which way his soul shall go,"—John Oxenham said. Which road shall we take, the way to growth and happiness, or the way to deterioration and misery?

Last winter when the ground was a gorgeous sea of mud, two girls were looking out of their barrack window. One girl said, "For Pete sakes, what a holy mess of mud!" The other girl, casting her eyes toward the majestic, snow-covered mountains beyond, said, "Aren't those mountains beautiful, so peaceful and strong!"

Two girls looking out of the

(Continued on page 6)

Supreme Court Considers Korematsu Case Petition

Nisei Braves Sniper's Bullets To Save Wounded Major's Life

The major was lying in the rain on a rocky hillside between Cassino and the abbey of Mount Cassino.

Every one knew he was badly hurt, but between him and the nearest man was 18 yards of open ground under fire of German snipers and a German tank which was on the road to the abbey, according to a recent Associated Press dispatch from the 5th Army in Italy.

The major had gone forward with one of the most advanced units attacking a castle above Cassino and had gone too far over the lip of a gully. Snipers pinned him down there. His head and the upper part of his body were protected by a little rock shelter he had piled up, but his legs protruded and he was hit several times on his legs so that he was helpless—unable even to try a desperate dash to safety.

The nearest man happened to be Sgt. Gary Hisaoka from Hilo, Hawaii, who came into the army directly from the University of Hawaii.

"Hisaoka began digging a shallow trench toward the major, hoping that he would be able to slide thru it and drag the major to safety," Froning related.

Hisaoka had a trench about eight yards long when he suddenly threw down his shovel. There was still 10 yards to go.

"Hell, I'm going now," the sergeant said. "It's getting late and I won't get there 'til night at this rate."

Hisaoka crouched down, slid out to the end of his trench,

(Continued on page 6)

Trail Blazer May Get DSC

Crawling thru the muddy mine field on hands and knees, and removing fuses from mines with his bare hands after his mine detection equipment had failed, Tech. Sgt. Calvin K. Shinogaki, an American of Japanese descent, blazed a trail of safety for his company during a night attack on the Cassino front, according to an Associated Press dispatch from the 5th Army in Italy.

Shinogaki's company had advanced only a short distance when mines began to go off. The men were floundering in knee-deep mud. Sgt. Shinogaki got down on his hands and knees and began to crawl. Soon he whispered over his shoulder, "Okay," and tossed a defused mine to one side. Three times in the next 50 yards the column lay panting in the mud while Shinogaki neutralized the death traps planted by the Germans. The column then worked its way out of the flat to a stone wall.

Shinogaki has been recommended for the legion of merit and the distinguished service cross.

Legion Pledges Respect to Nisei Fighting for U.S.

"The American Legion has pledged its confidence in and its full support of our army and navy. Numerous persons of Japanese ancestry are now serving with the armed forces of our country on the battlefronts, and according to all reports, are serving valiantly and well.

"We salute all men and women who love this country enough to fight and, if need be, die for it. Every person good enough to fight for us is entitled to our respect and equal protection under the constitution." — Commander William P. Haughton, in the California Legionnaire.

63 Draftees Take Physicals At Ft. Warren

BULLETIN

FORT WARREN, Wyo.—Nine of the selectees of the three groups called for pre-induction physical examinations from Heart Mountain this week have been accepted it was learned late Friday.

The group leaving Heart Mountain Wednesday had six acceptables, including Masao Higashiuchi, Mason Funabiki, John Okumura, John Miyamoto, Motomu Nakasako and Albert Tanouye.

Frank Shiraki was held over from the Tuesday group while Sam Fujishin and Joe Kiyan passed. Of the Monday group only Yosh Tanaka passed. All others were rejected.

* * *

Sixty-three draftees were ordered to report for pre-induction physical examinations at Fort Warren this week. The total called from Heart Mountain since the reinstitution of selective service last January is 79 with the next group scheduled to report about March 22.

There was a small number among those called who failed to appear at the assembling point in Powell, according to Douglas M. Todd, acting pro-

(Continued on page 5)

Inductees Free To Visit Center

Evacuees who have passed their pre-induction physical examinations may return to relocation centers from seasonal or indefinite leave to spend part or all that time before their induction into the armed forces with their parents or relatives, according to a directive issued by National WRA Director Dillon S. Myer this week.

"It will not be the policy of the War Relocation authority to consider them to be visitors and require payment for food and lodging during the period of such residence," the notice stated.

Such inductees are advised to present to the relocation officer a certificate of fitness indicating their acceptance for service in the armed forces which will be certified for their return to the center.

ACLU Acts As Sponsor In Action

With the filing of a petition to review the opinion of the ninth circuit court of appeals, the constitutionality of the military evacuation orders excluding from the Pacific coast American citizens of Japanese ancestry and directing their internment now awaits decision by the Supreme Court of the United States. The petition was filed by Fred Korematsu.

The Korematsu case was sponsored and is being carried through the courts by the northern California branch of the American Civil Liberties union. Supporting the appeal, in a brief filed as a friend of the court, is the national office of the ACLU.

When the case was tried before the ninth circuit court of appeals, that court summarily upheld the evacuation orders relying upon the Supreme Court views expressed in the Gordon Hirabayashi case. However, it was pointed out that in the Hirabayashi case, the Supreme Court merely upheld the curfew orders, issued by Gen. John L. DeWitt, and expressly avoided passing on the legality of the exclusion orders.

In the circuit court, Judge William Denman criticized the action of the other judges of that court for not considering and passing upon the issues in that case, and for relying solely upon the Supreme Court's general language in the Hirabayashi decision.

In the brief filed by the northern California ACLU it is held that Korematsu was unconstitutionally deprived of substantially all his rights of citizenship in the absence of crime on his part without due process of law by both the act of congress which makes it a crime to violate a military order, and the military orders themselves as applied to him.

The brief concludes:

"This petition presents constitutional issues of a novel nature and great gravity.

"The final determination of these questions is a matter of national concern and, to a degree, is a matter of international concern. The rights of national citizenship of the petitioner and 70,000 American citizens and native-born children, who have been unfortunate enough . . . to have had ancestors, who, for a period of time, were nationals of Japan, directly depend upon the final determination of the issues involved herein. Indirectly the rights and liberties of all native-born and naturalized citizens likewise depend on the final settlement of these issues."

Panzer voran
Sonder-Ausgabe
Frontzeitung einer Panzerarmee im Osten

Eine Armee sprengt ihren Einschließungsring

Die Kämpfe unserer Panzerarmee vom 23. März bis 6. April 1944

Im Verlauf von mehreren Großangriffen der Sowjets gegen die Nachbarabschnitte einer unter dem Oberbefehl des Generals der Panzertruppe H u b e stehende Panzerarmee, war diese am 23. März von fünf feindlichen Panzerarmeen beiderseits umfaßt und von ihren Verbindungen nördlich des Dnjestr abgeschnitten worden. Nur der Weg nach Süden über den Dnjestr war zunächst noch offen. Als am 25. März durch ein weit vorgestoßenes Panzerkorps die Stadt Kamenez-Podolsk genommen wurde, lag Gefahr vor, daß auch dieser Weg versperrt und die Armee von allen Seiten eingeschlossen wurde. Die Sowjets planten eine Schlacht, die an die Vernichtungsschlachten von Cannae, Sedan und Tannenberg erinnern sollte.

Am 23. März aber traf der entscheidende Führerbefehl ein: Die Panzerarmee bricht nach Westen durch und stellt die Verbindung mit den deutschen Truppen im Raum von Tarnopol her.

Die Schwierigkeiten bei Durchführung dieses Befehls waren ungeheuer: Zahlenmäßig überlegener Gegner ringsum, unzureichende eigene Versorgung, schwieriges Gelände, Schnee, Regen und andauerndes Tauwetter hatten alle Wege in Morast verwandelt. Fünf tiefe Flußabschnitte, unter ihnen Zbrucz und Sereth als schwierigste, waren zu überwinden. Durch tiefzerklüftete Täler mußten Brückenköpfe gebildet und mittelgebirgsähnliche Höhenunterschiede überwunden werden.

Der Gegner aber, der die Kraft der eingeschlossenen Armee weit unterschätzte, hatte sich in seinen Zielen in echt sowjetischer Ueberheblichkeit übernommen. So sehr war er sich seines Sieges gewiß, daß er mit einer operativen Kräftegruppe in unserer tiefen rechten Flanke

seine Operationen nach Süden in Rumänien fortsetzte und von der Einschließungsfront im Westen ebenfalls Kräfte auf das südliche Dnjestr-Ufer abzog. Am 29. März begann der Angriff in Richtung auf den Zbrucz, während im Osten unter schrittweiser Aufgabe des Geländes verbissene Nachhutkämpfe, im Norden unter eisernem Festhalten der eigenen Linie harte Abwehrkämpfe geführt werden mußten. Wie eine Sturzflut brachen die deutschen Panzerdivisionen auf den zwischen Zbrucz und Sereth stehenden, völlig überraschten Feind. Geländeschwierigkeiten wurden in geschickter Ausnutzung aller kleinen Hilfsmittel, die die Truppe im Osten nun nach jahrelanger Kriegführung beherrscht, überwunden. Zahlreiche Angriffe sowjetischer Schlachtflieger mußten durchgestanden werden. Aber dann ging der Angriff zügig vorwärts. Unsere Panzer-Divisionen kesselten ihrerseits bei Kamenez-Podolsk eine sowjetische Panzerarmee ein und fügten ihr schwerste Verluste zu. Die Angriffsgruppe erzwang den Uebergang über den Zbrucz bei Okopy und Skala und bildete Brükkenköpfe. Der Feind versuchte vergeblich, unsere Ost- und Nordfront einzudrücken und durch überholende Verfolgung im Norden zwischen Zbrucz und Sereth zu einer neuen Umfassung zu kommen. In harten Kämpfen wurde jedoch dem Feind ein Angriffsverband nach dem anderen zerschlagen und unter dem Schirm der tapferen Verteidiger unserer Ost- und Nordfront marschierte die gesamte deutsche Panzerarmee, — nachdem am 2. und 3. April der Sereth im kühnen Panzerangriff bezwungen — bis zum 6. April hinter den Sereth. Am gleichen Tage trafen sich die Angriffsspitzen der Panzerarmee mit den von Westen her vorstoßenden Kräften der Waffen-ϟϟ. Fast schien es, daß ein hereinbrechender Schneesturm in noch nicht gekannter Stärke uns den Erfolg in letzter Minute streitig machen wollte. In ungeheuerlichen Schneeverwehungen blieben unsere Marschkolonnen im Gefecht oder auf ihren Marschstraßen im Schnee stecken. Aber die unbändige Energie unserer Truppe meisterte auch diese Naturgewalt und brachte in den folgenden Tagen die Marschbewegung wieder in Fluß.

Der aufopfernde Einsatz der Luftwaffe war für das Gelingen dieses Kampfes entscheidend. Oftmals im Schneesturm und Nebel landeten die Ju's neben ihren kämpfenden Kameraden in vorderster Linie und brachten nach Ueberwindung von vielen Schwierigkeiten Munition und Betriebsstoff, so daß die Versorgung der Panzerarmee nie abriß. Besonders waren die Soldaten über das Herausfliegen der tapferen Verwundeten dankbar. Es war ein stolzer Erfolg der Versorgungsführung, daß alle Verwundeten herausgeflogen oder in die Freiheit zurückgebracht werden konnten.

Alle Waffengattungen haben mit der Waffe in der Hand ihr Letztes hergegeben.

Gewiß waren die Kämpfe in den ersten schweren Tagen, als sich der entlastende Stoß nach Westen noch nicht bemerkbar machte, mit dem Gefühl eines Rückschlages verbunden. Aber dies wurde bald durch den Kampfgeist der Truppe überwunden. Und als ein besonderes Erlebnis knüpfte sich vom hohen Truppenführer bis zum jungen Grenadier ein unzerreißbares Band der Kameradschaft. Unter den besonderen Umständen dieser Schlacht trat die Einheit von Führung und Truppe, von Offizier und Mann sichtbar in Erscheinung.

Als der Weg nach Westen frei war, harrte der Kämpfer von Kamenez-Podolsk noch ein besonders starkes Erlebnis. Hinter ihnen lag die Oede der sowjetischen Steppe mit ihren durch die bolschewistische Erziehung abgestumpften Menschen in ihren armseligen Lehmhütten, ihren wenigen kalten und nüchternen Zweckbauten. Vor ihnen breitete sich ein Landschaftsbild aus, das die ersten Spuren der Heimat aufwies: Höhen und Täler abwechslungsreich gegliedert, freundliche Häuser, mit offenen Menschengesichtern, Dörfern mit Kirchen und gepflegten Friedhöfen. Dieser offensichtliche Unterschied hat wohl jeden von uns zum Nachdenken gebracht und ihm eine neue Klarheit gegeben, warum dieser unerbittliche Kampf notwendig ist.

Zum Abschluß der Kämpfe konnte die Armee das stolze Ergebnis melden, daß 358 feindliche Panzer, 279 Geschütze, 42 Sturmgeschütze, 314 Pak, 1085 MG. und zahlreiches anderes Kriegsmaterial erbeutet oder vernichtet wurde.

Durch das tapfere Durchkämpfen unserer Armee nach Westen wurden die weitreichenden Pläne der Sowjets während ihrer Frühjahrsoffensive vereitelt. Nicht mit dem Gefühl der verhinderten Niederlage, sondern mit der stolzen Gewißheit, allen Gewalten zum Trotz einen Erfolg abgerungen zu haben, kommen unsere Soldaten aus der großen Durchbruchsschlacht nördlich des Dnjestr zurück. Die ganze Armee hat die lebendige Gewißheit: „Es gibt keine aussichtslosen verzweifelten Lagen, es gibt nur verzweifelte Menschen, und zu denen gehört kein braver Soldat."

Unsere Antwort war der Angriff

General Hube über die Kämpfe seiner Kräftegruppe – Sendung des deutschen Rundfunks

Der deutsche Rundfunk sandte aus Anlaß des erfolgreichen Abschlusses der Operationen eine zusammenfassende Uebersicht von General der Panzertruppe H u b e über die vierzehntägigen Kämpfe im Raum von Kamenez-Podolsk. Die Uebersicht hat folgenden Wortlaut:

„Die Bolschewisten bezeichneten Ende März unsere Lage als völlig aussichtslos. Am 31. März richteten sie die Aufforderung an meine Truppe, sich bis zum 2. April zu ergeben, widrigenfalls würden alle erschossen. Jeder weitere Widerstand sei zwecklos, weil ein dreifacher Ring sie umschließe.

Unsere Antwort war der Angriff. Wir traten an und schlugen zu, schlossen eine russische Panzerarmee völlig ein, überrannten starke sowjetische Infanterieverbände und schnitten eine weitere Panzerarmee von ihren Verbindungen ab. Der feindliche Führungswille war gebrochen, der Operationsplan der Bolschewisten zerschlagen. Unter schwierigsten Wetter- und Geländeverhältnissen kämpften meine Soldaten. Anfang April fegten noch einmal Schneestürme über Felder und Hänge; die Schneeverwehungen behinderten unsere Bewegungen.

Während im Osten geschickt und wendig geführte Nachhutkämpfe stattfanden, griffen unsere Panzer und Panzergrenadiere im Westen fortlaufend an, um den Weg zur Verbindung mit der übrigen deutschen Front zu bahnen. An der Nord- und zeitweise auch Südfront mußten dagegen erbitterte Abwehrkämpfe durchgestanden werden, die das Eindrücken unserer Flanken verhinderten. Zahlreiche tief zerklüftete Abschnitte, dabei die wichtigen Flußtäler des Zbrucz und Sereth mußten im Angriff überwunden werden. 110 km wurden im Angriff nach Westen durch meine selbständig kämpfende Kräftegruppe zurückgelegt.

Grenadiere, Pioniere, Panzerschützen und Artilleristen erwiesen erneut in diesem erbitterten Ringen gegen die an Menschen und Material weit überlegenen Bolschewisten ihren überragenden Kampfwert. Nicht vergessen sei die Nachrichtentruppe, die dafür sorgte, daß die Fäden, die Führung und Truppe verbinden, keinen Augenblick abrissen. Durch die Transport- und Kampfverbände der Luftwaffe fanden wir in unserer schwierigen Versorgungslage kameradschaftlichste Unterstützung. Die wichtigen Versorgungsgüter Kraftstoff und Munition flogen sie herein und brachten unter schwierigsten Verhältnissen in aufopferungsvoller Kameradschaft unsere Verwundeten zurück.

Die Anforderungen, die ich in diesem Kampf gegen Feindmassen, Schlamm und Schnee an Führung und Truppe stellen mußte, sind ungeheuer. Wieder einmal erwies der deutsche Soldat, daß sein Kampfwille eine scheinbar aussichtslose Lage immer noch in einen großen Erfolg zu verwandeln vermag. Der Feind verlor 223 Panzer, 190 Geschütze und Pak, 29 Sturmgeschütze und zahlreiches weitere Kriegsmaterial (die abschließende Zählung ergab 358 Panzer und 42 Sturmgeschütze).

Am 6. April reichten sich unsere Angriffsspitzen mit den entgegenkommenden Kameraden der Waffen-ϟϟ die Hand. Die angeblich von einem dreifachen Ring eingeschlossenen Verbände stehen nach wie vor bereit, dem Feind weiter so harte Schläge zu versetzen, wie in dieser großen Durchbruchsschlacht nördlich des Dnjestr."

Verantwortlicher Hauptschriftleiter:
Leutnant Wilhelm Schaub
Feldpostnummer 12 600

THE STARS AND STRIPES
MEDITERRANEAN

Vol. 1, No. 126, Tuesday, April 11, 1944 ITALY EDITION TWO LIRE

Russians Take Odessa, Nazi Ukraine Foothold

Plane Plants Struck Hard By Bombers

Americans Sweep France, Belgium In Day Bombings

LONDON, April 10 — Luftwaffe production centers were targets for the third successive day for British-based American bombers today when strong formations of fighter-escorted 8th AAF Flying Fortresses and Liberators swept over France and Belgium.

Up to 750 U.S. four-motored bombers took part in today's missions to two aircraft repair plants and an airdrome near Brussels in Belgium, an aircraft plant at Bourges in central France, and "military objectives" in the Pas de Calais region of northern France.

The American daylight raids came just over 12 hours after moonlight assaults by RAF heavy bombers on railway targets at Villeneuve, a few miles southwest of Paris, and at Lille in northeastern France, near the Belgian border. Mosquitoes bombed Mannheim and other undisclosed objectives in western Germany. The air ministry also reported a very extensive minelaying operation, "at great range." The RAF lost 11 planes in the night's operations.

Approximately 800 Fortresses and Liberators, with a 1,000-plane fighter escort, made yesterday's mass attacks on German aircraft factories on the Baltic coast and deep into Poland and East Prussia. The AAF reported that 20 Germans fighters were shot down, in addition to a number of grounded aircraft destroyed, and that 34 U.S. bombers and 24 fighters were lost.

Berle Asks Axis Air Ban

LONDON, April 10 — Germany and Japan should be excluded from any international air plan, United States Assistant Secretary of State Adolph Berle said today following a five-day talk on postwar world-wide civil flying agreements with a special British committee headed by Lord Beaverbrook.

Admitting that concessions would have to be made by both the Americans and British, Mr. Berle said:

"We are agreed that while the quality of competition between the two countries in the air is desirable, it must never be permitted to color international relations, to interfere with the common interest of national security or to promote problems which will engender bitter relations."

Merchantmen Hit In Mediterranean

WASHINGTON, April 10 — The Liberty ships Peter Skene Ogden and George Cleve were put out of commission by enemy torpedoes in the Mediterranean a few weeks ago, the War Shipping Administration announced this weekend. The ships were said to have been hit during an attack on an Allied convoy.

Spies Stalemated, Says FBI Chief

WASHINGTON, April 10 — Crafty German military intelligence leaders have been stalemated in their persistent efforts to rebuild the spy rings which flourished in the U.S. before G-men smashed them early in the war, J. Edgar Hoover, Federal Bureau of Investigation, disclosed this week.

Mr. Hoover said that the Germans had been unable to establish a single successful spy ring although they have attempted to slip in operatives who posed as concentration camp refugees and, in one case, murdered an entire Jewish family to give a secret agent an excuse to enter the U.S. He did not elaborate on the incident.

Guns Active In Cassino

ADVANCED ALLIED HEADQUARTERS, April 10—New Zealand guns boomed out Saturday evening three miles south of Cassino, breaking the quiet that lasted during the day and partially destroying two enemy strongpoints at San Angelo in Teodice, today's communique announced. Cassino itself sweated out some heavy German shelling the same night.

The German propaganda campaign that has now spread to all parts of the front continued as another batch of leaflets was dropped three miles north of Cassino. Contents are still undisclosed, but presumably the Nazis were trying to make the most out of their Cassino stand.

The Anzio beachhead was described officially as quieter than usual, with some patrol activity and a brief air attack reported. Another remote control baby tank — now known as Goliaths — was knocked out by rifle fire north of Sessano, in the same sector where three others had been previously destroyed and another damaged.

Action flared up in the lower Garigliano Valley where 21 enemy tanks or self-propelled guns lumbered into view at dusk Saturday

(Continued on Page 4)

Hull Drops Broad Hint To Neutrals

WASHINGTON, April 10—Neutrals were warned to stop aiding the Axis countries by Secretary of State Cordell Hull in a radio address late Sunday night (Monday, Mediterranean time) which was a broad outline of U.S. foreign policy.

While Mr. Hull mentioned no neutrals by name, observers recalled that the U.S. has recently protested the policy of Argentina, Eire and Spain. The Secretary of State declared that the Allies would not try to force any neutral to join our side but emphasized: "We can no longer acquiesce in those nations drawing from the resources of the Allied world when at the same time they contribute to the death of (Allied) troops whose sacrifice contributes to the salvation of neutrals.

Over-all Allied foreign policy, Mr. Hull stated, had three main goals: (1) Creation of a stable Europe; (2) abolition of Fascism; (3) creation of democratic institutions.

Genuine agreement among Britain, Russia, China and the U.S. was the only method of attaining these objectives, Mr. Hull said. "This," he declared, "is fundamental. However difficult the road may be, there is no hope of turning victory into enduring peace unless the real

(Continued on Page 4)

Giraud May Refuse

ALGIERS, April 10—It was considered likely today that General Henri Giraud had turned down, at least tentatively, his recent nomination as inspector general of the French Army.

General Giraud, who was relieved last week as commander in chief of the French Army when General deGaulle assumed the post, was understood to have referred to the inspector general position as "only honorific."

Partisans Join Russians, Battle Retreating Nazis

LONDON, April 10—Imminent Russian invasion of Czechoslovakia links the partisans of Central Europe battling with increased violence against retreating German forces of occupation according to various European sources today. An underground Polish army is said to have already gone into direct action in cooperation with Red Army troops battling into the provinces of Wilna and Wolhynia.

Czech partisans in Ruthenia, at the far eastern tip of Czechoslovakia, are striking Hitler's forces in the back, as the First Czech Brigade in the van of Marshal Zhukov's Russian army climbs the Carpathians range.

Adolf Hitler, according to Turkish news sources, has met with his political and military leaders at Berchtesgaden, seeking ways to evade defeat in the Balkans or to counteract the critical effect of such a defeat on the morale of the German at home.

Neutral observers in Ankara declared that the great battle for the Balkans was on. They foresaw a final German stand for Central Europe made on a south-by-southeast line running from the Carpathians, on the Czech border through Rumania—specifically to Foscani and the Serets River, to Galatz and the Black sea, near the mouths of the Danube. This line would involve the surrender of Bucharest and Ploesti to the Russians.

In preparation, a Reuter's man in Moscow said, the German war room staff for the Russian southern front has been moved backward to the Rumanian capital, Bucharest.

Meanwhile, the exiled Czech government of Edouard Benes, confident of an irresistible Russian advance, declares itself ready to take over civil administration of the nation, in accordance with plans approved in Moscow when Dr. Benes talked with Premier Joseph Stalin last December.

WARNS

CORDELL HULL

Bombers Hit New Guinea

WASHINGTON, April 10—Allied heavy bombers, sweeping down the north coast of New Guinea, have again attacked Jap bases at Hollandia, Wewak and Hansa Bay, it was reported today from Allied Southwest Pacific headquarters.

In the third raid in seven days, the badly battered enemy air installations at Hollandia received more than 150 tons of bombs which destroyed many buildings in the township, damaged the jetty and two small freighters and started fires in fuel and supply dumps. Bivouac and supply areas were also set afire at Wewak and Hansa Bay. No Jap fighters were met on any of these attacks.

Allied aircraft also continued to hammer at the enemy Bismark Archipelago bases of Rabaul, New Britain, and Kavieng on New Ireland. Solomons-based medium and light bombers hit Rabaul with 75 tons of explosives, while torpedo and dive-bombers dropped 30 tons of bombs on Kavieng.

An International News Service dispatch reported that the Allied Southwest Pacific aerial offensive has been launched from 5th AAF airfields in Kumai Valley, New Guinea. Captured last September, the base was rebuilt and supplied from materials brought in by air. From it has come the principal air support for Allied ground force penetration of the Bismark Archipelago and the striking power for the New Guinea offensive.

Partisans Smash 2 Nazis Thrust

LONDON, April 10 — Marshal Tito's Partisan forces smashed two large-scale Nazi attacks, one in the Jajace sector of western Bosnia and the other in northwestern Yugoslavia, not far from the Italian frontier.

The German breakthrough attempt in the north was spearheaded by a considerable force of home-grown Fascists.

Black Sea Base In Enemy Hands Since Oct. 1941

LONDON, April 10—Odessa, the great Black Sea port and last foothold of the Germans in the Ukraine, has fallen to the Red Army. Tonight, in an Order of the Day addressed to General Rodion Malinovsky, commander of the Third Ukrainian Army, Marshal Stalin officially announced the news and called for an extraordinary salute of 24 salvoes from 324 guns in Moscow and 12 salvoes from 120 guns of the Soviet Black Sea fleet.

Marshal Stalin described Odessa as an "important economic and political center of our country" and attributed its liberation to a "clever and unexpected maneuver by motorized units, infantry and cavalry and a frontal attack."

The Germans had earlier asserted that they had successfully evacuated the city, but military observers here felt it was an attempt to minimize a heavy defeat.

A city of 600,000 when German and Rumanian troops captured it Oct. 16, 1941, after a 69-day siege, Odessa is the third largest city in the Ukraine and, according to the Russians, constituted a vital stronghold for the Germans in the defense of the central regions of Rumania.

The fall of Odessa was seen to imperil even further the German garrison in the Crimea of which there has been little official news with the exception of occasional Nazi reports of fighting on the Kerch peninsula.

Elsewhere along the whole front from Odessa to the Carpathians the Russian armies were reported advancing victoriously. The two-way offensive in Rumania by the

(Continued on Page 4)

Muggy Skies Halt Planes

MAAF HEADQUARTERS, April 10—Air action yesterday was limited to attacks by Tactical fighter bombers on German communications north of Rome and installations near the battle area. All other bombers were grounded because of bad weather.

Warhawks ranged over the railroad north of Rome to Lake Bracciano, scoring hits on the tracks at various points near the lake. Other Warhawks and P-47 Thunderbolts bombed motor transports near the beachhead and on the Cassino front. A-36 Invaders struck German-held towns between the Garigliano and the beachhead, including Terracina, on the coast between Minturno and Anzio, and Littoria, east of the beachhead.

Kittyhawks attacked the railways at Spoleto and Terni.

Purge In Italy

LONDON, April 10 — A German news agency over the weekend said that 17 more Italian officials have been fired from their government jobs at Milan. The sackings were said to be in line with a plan to purge weaklings from the Fascist set-up.

Entered as second-class matter April 15, 1931, at the post office at New Haven, Connecticut, under act of March 3, 1879

ILLUSTRATED CURRENT NEWS

Published Monday, Wednesday and Friday by Illustrated Current News, Inc., New Haven, Conn. Subscription Annually, $20.80

April 17, 1944—No. 4779

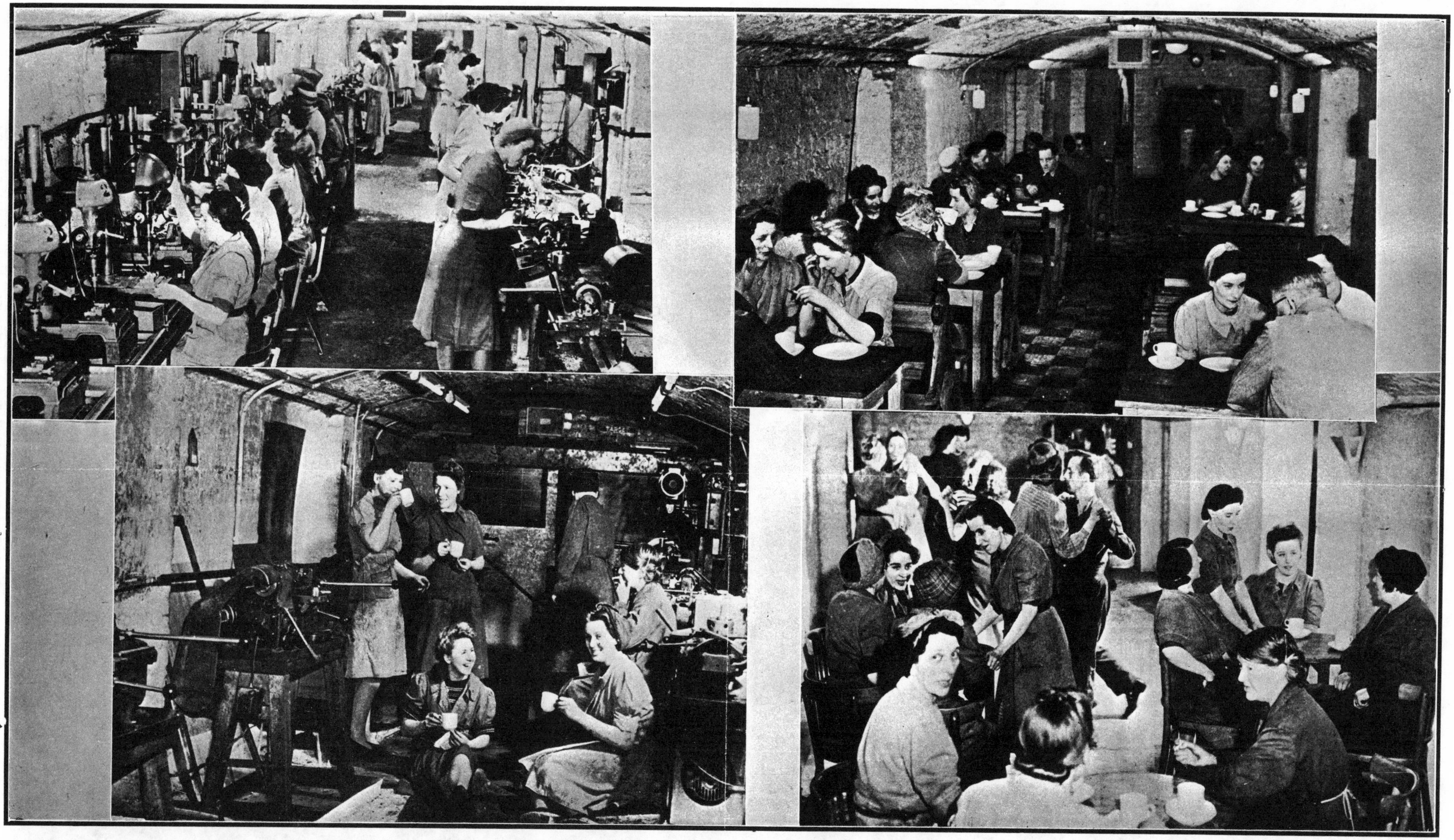

BRITISH INDUSTRY "DIGS IN" FOR SAFETY

Pictures from "somewhere in England" show how one manufacturer conducts "business as usual" in 20 underground tunnels, safe from Nazi bombs. Top row: Work-shop and lunch room. Bottom row: Rest period and a "spot o' tea", and the workers' sub-cellar night club.

News Note: OWI says 2,000,000 more women are needed in jobs.

Entered as second-class matter April 15, 1931, at the post office at New Haven, Connecticut, under act of March 3, 1879

ILLUSTRATED CURRENT NEWS

Published Monday, Wednesday and Friday by Illustrated Current News, Inc., New Haven, Conn. Subscription Annually, $20.80

April 28, 1944—No. 4784

"COMMANDO" KELLY GREETS MOTHER AND "CLAN"

The Kellys were out in mass formation when the family met Tech. Sgt. "Commando" Kelly in Pittsburgh on visit home by the Congressional Medal of Honor winner who, single-handed, destroyed 40 of Hitler's "invincibles" on the Italian front. L. to R., (all Kellys): George, Danny, Charles, Eddie, Mrs. Kelly, Jimmy, Eugene and Frank. John is behind the "Commando".

News Note: U. S. Units Near Hollandia Air Fields.

PASS CASSINO! DOUBLE VICTORY

FINAL NIGHT EDITION R WEATHER: FAIR Details on Page 5

THE CALL BULLETIN
SAN FRANCISCO
AN INDEPENDENT NEWSPAPER

89TH YEAR CALL AND POST, VOL. 155, NO. 93 THE CALL-BULLETIN, VOL. 175, NO. 93 THURSDAY, MAY 18, 1944 5c DAILY

TAKE BURMA AIRFIELD

Yanks In Formia, Peril Road to Rome

LONDON, May 18 (INS).—Formations of the Allied Fifth and Eighth armies have joined in the Liri Valley and are continuing their advance, the Algiers radio reported tonight.

ALLIED HEADQUARTERS, NAPLES, May 18 (AP).—The British Eighth Army has captured the fortress ruins of Cassino and the battered Benedictine monastery, and American troops twenty-five miles to the southwest have seized the coastal city of Formia, southern anchor of the Hitler line, in a stunning double victory, the Allied command announced today.

Gustav Line No More

"The Gustav line now has ceased to exist," the announcement declared.

The double victory toppled strongpoints at both ends of the fiercely-fought Nazi line in Italy.

Already U. S. and French troops were driving into the trackless Aurunci Mountains above Formia, where the Germans have based their second defense—the Hitler line—along natural obstacles. This drive was reported winning positions for a possible break-through into the coastal plain beyond—the plain leading to the Anzio beachhead.

British troops slammed into Cassino—which had withstood siege since January—while Poles seized Monastery Hill. A substantial portion of the elite German First Parachute Division—the Green Devils—was wiped out in the two strongholds, a special announcement declared.

Both Cassino and the dominating height of Monastery Hill were captured this morning. Other important objectives have been seized by American troops pushing westward on the Fifth Army front, headquarters said, but these were not identified.

Big Casualties Avoided

The German defenders of Cassino were encircled by tactics that avoided heavy casualties that would have resulted from frontal assaults such as were beaten back two months ago.

A special Allied announcement declared:

"The enemy has been completely outmaneuvered by the Allied armies in Italy following the original breach of the Gustav line by the Fifth Army on May 14, and the subsequent rapid advance of French and American troops through the mountains.

"Troops of the Eighth Army have fought their way forward in the Liri valley and during the last 24 hours developed a decisive pincer movement which cut highway 6 (from Cassino to Rome) and so prevented the withdrawal of the enemy."

Earlier headquarters disclosed Polish troops had seized Hill 593, northern hinge of both the Gustav and Hitler lines.

American troops struck within two miles of Itri—Appian way

Yank Fliers Saved Under Truk Guns

Among 22 Navy fliers saved in daring sea rescue by U. S. submarine Tang under noses of Japs at Truk were these nine crowded on wings and in fuselage of plane, a two-man craft which had landed in Truk lagoon to rescue them, was damaged and unable to fly. Submarine was under command of Lieutenant Commander Richard O'Kane of San Rafael. (Other photos of rescue on Page 1, Green Flash section.)
—Associated Press Photo From Navy.

Machinists In New Row Over Layoffs

A new labor-employer controversy involving San Francisco machinists flared today as members of Machinists Lodge 1327 met here to protest the newly ordered elimination of the graveyard shift at Hammond Aircraft Company's plant No. 1.

SEEK DELAY

The union members were considering a motion to "strenuously protest" the move and seek a two week delay in the proposed layoff "to find out just why the shift is being discontinued."

Anthony Ballerini, business agent of the local, told the members he had been informed by the company that the shift would be discontinued, beginning Sunday, "because they have been ordered to cut back production."

A union member, describing himself as the father of three sons in the Air Forces, declared:

"I can't see why there should be any letup in plane production, when General Arnold is so eagerly calling for it."

DECLINE COMMENT

Hammond officials confirmed Ballerini's announcement of the shift discontinuation, but declined comment pending issuance of a formal statement.

Meantime members of Machinists' Lodge No. 68, at odds with the War Labor Board in a long-standing row over their ban on overtime work beyond 48 hours a week, shrouded in secrecy their response to the WLB's order that the ban be lifted.

From a meeting of union members held here last night came reports that:

1. The union voted to ignore the WLB demand, claiming lifting of the overtime ban would constitute "complete surrender of union strength."

2. That the overtime question wasn't even put to a vote of the membership.

Business Agent Ed Dillon of the union—who less than two weeks ago was summoned to Washington to explain another defiance of the federal government by his local—flatly refused to make public how—or if—his members voted.

The WLB in demanding that the overtime prohibition be lifted, pointed out that war work was hampered seriously by the ban and that the government did not seek to force any individual to work overtime hours against his will.

STILWELL'S MEN PERIL KEY CITY

SOUTHEAST ASIA HEADQUARTERS, KANDY, Ceylon, May 18 (AP).—In a surprise attack climaxing a spectacular forced march over rugged ter-rain, American and Chinese forces yesterday captured the Myitkyina airdrome and now are besieging Myitkyina city, major Japanese base and largest city in northern Burma, Allied headquarters announced today.

Capture of Myitkyina is essential to the success of Lieutenant General Joseph W. Stilwell's drive to link the new Ledo highway with the old Burma road, thus opening a direct overland supply route into China. It appeared likely that Myitkyina would fall into his hands before the coming monsoon season bogs down major operations.

PLAY IMPORTANT PART

Brigadier General Frank D. Merrill's jungle-wise American Marauders played an important role in the capture of Myitkyina airdrome.

The airfield was taken in good condition, enabling gliders and transport planes to land there almost immediately with American engineers and Chinese reinforcements.

(International News Service reported that General Merrill's radio message to General Stilwell was "cafeteria lunch"—the prearranged code signal announcing seizure of the airfield.)

Myitkyina is one of the two main Japanese bases in northern Burma and one of the immediate major objectives of Stilwell's offensive.

MENACING MOGAUNG

Mogaung, the enemy's other principal base in northern Burma, situated about 40 miles west and slightly south of Myitkyina, is menaced by a second Stilwell column moving down from the north along the Mogaung valley.

Fall of the airdrome climaxed a forced march of 20 days by three columns of Chinese and Americans under direct command of Merrill, which pushed forward over rough, tortuous ground from the Dumon hills on the eastern side of the Mogaung valley, a communique said.

One of the greatest tests of stamina occurred when Merrill's men scaled a 50 degree grade on a 6,100 foot mountain northwest of Myitkyina, cutting steps through the undergrowth and advancing virtually on all fours.

(Chinese relieve pressure on Loyang, Page 3.)

Yanks Bomb Ploesti, Belgrade Rail Yards

ALLIED HEADQUARTERS, Naples, May 18 (AP).—U. S. heavy bombers struck into the Balkans today, bombing Ploesti, in Romania, and Belgrade and Nis, in Yugoslavia.

Ploesti, the Romanian oil center, was last bombed May 5. Today's attack was by Flying Fortresses and Liberators, escorted by Lightnings, Thunderbolts and Mustangs, which helped fight off a number of enemy aircraft.

The rail yards at Belgrade and Nis were targets, with the air crews reporting good results. Weather prevented observation of the results at Ploesti, however.

(The United Nations radio at Algiers said today's attacks were made by 500 to 750 heavy bombers, which with fighter escort made up a force of probably 1,500 planes.)

With English Channel skies overcast and dark banks of rain clouds hovering over the French coast, there was no indication of major aerial activity from British bases. Britain had a raidless night and apparently the R. A. F.'s night bombers were grounded.

Claim Allied Raid Killed 60 Clerics

ALLIED HEADQUARTERS IN AUSTRALIA, May 18 (AP).—A Roman Catholic bishop and 59 other missionaries were killed outright or died later of injuries, when Allied planes strafed a Japanese prison ship off the New Guinea coast, it was asserted here today by a Dutch priest, Father Willem van Baar, superior in Australia of the Society of the Divine Word. His report was quoted in an official Netherlands and Netherlands Indies New Agency bulletin.

Big League Games

AMERICAN LEAGUE

Chicago at New York.
St. Louis at Boston.
Detroit at Philadelphia.
Cleveland at Washington.

NATIONAL LEAGUE

New York at Chicago.
New York at Chicago, postponed.
Philadelphia at Cincinnati.
Boston at St. Louis.

Speed New Plan To Unify Trolleys

Negotiations under which a "semi-consolidation" of the Municipal and Market Street railways might be effected before the city actually takes title to the latter line were under way here today.

Officials responsible for the unification of the two systems, decisively approved by the voters at Tuesday's election, said they were trying to work out means by which trackage on Market street might be interchanged and some of the Market Street line's idle equipment renovated before completion of the purchase.

Marshall Dill, president of the Public Utilities Commission, scheduled a conference for today with Samuel Kahn, Market Street Railway president, "to talk over the legal problems involved and see what we can do."

While unofficial opinions from the city legal staff indicated no money could be spent on the old Market Street cars and buses until the city held title to them, there were strong indications efforts might be made to "get around" the legal obstacles and get at least some of the carriers into operation right away.

One unofficial suggestion understood to be under consideration at City Hall was an arrangement whereby the Market Street line itself would repair some of the cars "on the city's account," to be repaid for the work upon settlement of the purchase contract.

Another proposal was an informal dollar-a-year lease arrangement under which the city might take immediate possession

Continued on Page 5, Column 2

Airport Projects Halt Opposed By Congress Bloc

WASHINGTON, May 18 (AP). Members of Congress from 17 states, aroused over an Army order halting construction of airports in their states, organized a committee today to take immediate steps toward resumption of the work.

Charles B. Donaldson, director of airports for the Civil Aeronautics Administration, told the group that Army officials apparently had interpreted a presidential request for a resurvey of the projects, numbering 28, to mean that they should all be deferred.

U. S. Sub Rescues 22 Navy Fliers

By JOHN R. HENRY
Staff Correspondent International News

PEARL HARBOR, May 18 (INS).—Twenty-two Navy airmen, plucked from death's door by a United States submarine, gave heartfelt thanks today to the captain of the underseas craft, Lieutenant Commander Richard Hetherington O'Kane of San Rafael, Cal., who dared Japanese shore batteries on a thrilling rescue mission during the mighty carrier assault against the Jap bastion at Truk April 29 and 30.

O'Kane, captain of the U.S.S. Tang, swept under the very noses of the Japs and braved the dangers of jagged coral reefs to pick up the wingless airmen who were downed at sea.

The Tang, one of the fleet's newest submersibles, came in from patrol with her innards

Continued on Page 3, Col. 2

War Risk Insurance Rate in Atlantic Cut

LONDON, May 18 (AP).—The war risk insurance rate for cargo on voyages between the United Kingdom or Eire and the Pacific coast of North or Central America has been cut from 3¼ to 3 per cent, it was announced today.

He Sings; Jury Convicts Him

Songwriter LeRoy Jeffries, 25, of 178 Grant avenue, awaited sentence on an attempted rape charge today after singing his summation to a juvenile court jury.

Jeffries, accused of an attempted attack upon a 13 year old girl, spurned legal counsel and decided to serve as his own attorney. As the case drew to a close, he obtained from Judge Theresa Meikle permission to deliver his musical argument in the form of "a song I composed today."

The piece was all about Old Glory and "justice for one and all."

Judge Meikle said it was "very fine." She said she thought the jury "enjoyed it very much."

But even the part about "guarantees your liber-tee" didn't move the jury, which came back in thirty minutes and delivered an unmusical, prose announcement:

"Guilty!"

Jeffries didn't give up.

"I wrote another song last night to show the jury my philosophy," he told the judge.

Judge Meikle had heard enough. No more songs, she decreed.

Ironically, it was one of Jeffries' songs which led to his arrest, testimony in the case showed. The girl victim identified her attacker by remembering Jeffries' name printed on a song he proudly displayed to her.

Call-Bulletin Today

Special Features

("G" indicates Green Flash Section)

U. S. BOMBERS HIT WAKE

PEARL HARBOR, May 18.—Striking hard at Japanese positions on Wake Island and throughout the mandated islands, American planes sank a big tanker and a cargo ship, bombed air fields and battered enemy positions Tuesday. Nauru, Truk, Ponape and Marshall Islands were hit.

YANKEE GUNS POUND GAETA

WITH THE AMERICAN FIFTH ARMY IN MARANOLA, Italy, May 18.—American big guns began battering the coastal city of Gaeta, the Germans' artillery powerhouse, today as swift-moving Fifth Army troops to the north kept the enemy's Intri-Pico escape road under fire.

STIMSON WARNS OF NAZI TRICKS

WASHINGTON, May 18 (INS).—The nation was warned today by Secretary of War Stimson to be on guard against Nazi propaganda "tricks" designed to confuse the Allies about the coming invasion of Europe.

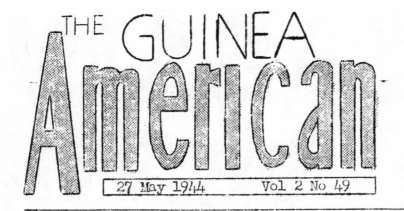

THE GUINEA American

27 May 1944 Vol 2 No 49

Elsewhere:
CHUNGKING: Chinese troops are racing to besieged Loyangh.
RUSSIA: Small sea action only.
TURKEY: Lend-lease aid stopped by United States and Britain.

5TH REACHES "ANZIO"

NAPLES, 26 May--American and French troops of the 5th Army shook hands with American and British troops of the Anzio beachhead on Thursday, the 14th day of the new Italian offensive.

Other results announced by Army News Service and British Broadcasting Corp:

1. Northeast of beachhead: Lt. Gen. Mark Clark is leading Anzio forces against the struggling foe.
2. East of beachhead: Canadian forces are hounding the Nazis.
3. Cisterna, new "little Cassino", has been pierced by tanks and infantry.
4. Taken in the drive: Terracina, Pontecorvo, Aquina.
5. Destroyed on this 14th day: 500 Nazi vehicles.

Other news: The meeting of the two Allied groups makes solid a 60-mile front...Cisterna, new name in the news, is called "the anchor of the enemies' right wing South of Rome." In its center, hand-to-hand fighting is taking place. And Nazi snipers are active in this rail, river and road junction...Pontecorvo was first bypassed, then frontally assaulted and taken.

In the air: Allied planes, dawn to dusk, attacked the already cut Appian Way...230 enemy vehicles were demolished on the Via Casilina. Total to date: 800...Communications from Rome up to and including Florence were slammed in 2,300 sorties, which also took in railyards...Raids 200 miles inside southern France were made...

New news: 5th Army has just run into anti-tank guns...More planes have struck Vienna and points in Yugoslavia...Canadians have crossed a big river.

news briefs

KANDY, Ceylon, 26 May--The 7th day of the "Battle of Myitkyina": American and Chinese troops repelled a heavy counter-attack...The Allies hold one-third of the base...Despite bad weather one Allied column fought to a position commanding a road junction leading to Myitkyina, Mogaung and Ft. Hertz.

LONDON, 26 May--The 40th consecutive day of pre-invasion bombing: 6,000 Allied planes hit Belgium, France, with 8,000 tons, pounding 15 airfields, 21 freight yards. RAF also slammed Berlin. On Saturday, the 8th and 9th Air Forces made up the American team which conducted the "first combined assault" on Hitler's Europe.

PACIFIC, 26 May--U.S. carrier-based planes hit the Marcus Islands (1,200 miles southeast of Tokyo, 150 tons, gun positions, supply dumps) on Saturday and the Wake Islands (700 miles from Marcus, 110 tons) on Tuesday in a total of 700 sorties in 7 sweeps. On Wakde mainland the Allies have reached the enemy-held airfield at Sarmi, 6 miles across the Torre River. Elsewhere: Ponape (23rd time), Kuriles (twice lightly), Biak (supply, camp areas), Rabaul (48 tons, airdromes), Bougainville (scattered targets), Marshalls, Solomons, Carolines, bombed. Also, Wewak (100 tons). ANS

WEATHER
FAIR AND
WARMER
Report on Page 21

DAILY RECORD

THE RECORD-AMERICAN HAS THE GREATEST CIRCULATION IN NEW ENGLAND

Vol. 262, No. 134 36 Pages Boston, Monday, June 5, 1944 Entered as second class matter at Boston Postoffice 3 CENTS

LEGAL EDITION

ROME FALLS

STORY ON PAGE 2

First Photo of Yanks in Eternal City

Allied troops, riding on the rear of this tank and in other vehicles, are shown here as they passed this sign on Route 6 showing they had just entered on the edge of Rome, as they drove forward and pushed the Germans out of the Italian capital. City was completely mopped up of Nazis, who fled across Tiber river. This U. S. Army Signal Corps photo was radioed from Rome yesterday.

Warmer Today
Boston and vicinity—Considerable cloudiness, warmer today. Cooler tonight. High tides—11:50 A. M., 12:01 P. M. Low tides—5:41 A. M., 5:52 P. M. Sunrise—5:07 A. M. Sunset—8:18 P. M. Full report Page 5.

THE BOSTON HERALD

6 A. M. EXTRA

VOL. CLXXXXVI, NO. 158 | (Copyright, 1944) Boston Herald-Traveler Corporation | BOSTON, TUESDAY, JUNE 6, 1944—TWENTY PAGES | ★★★★★★ | THREE CENTS

GREAT INVASION STARTED

Gen. Eisenhower Bares Landings in France By Both Sea, Air from Le Havre North; Fierce Fight at Caen, Dunkerque Rocked

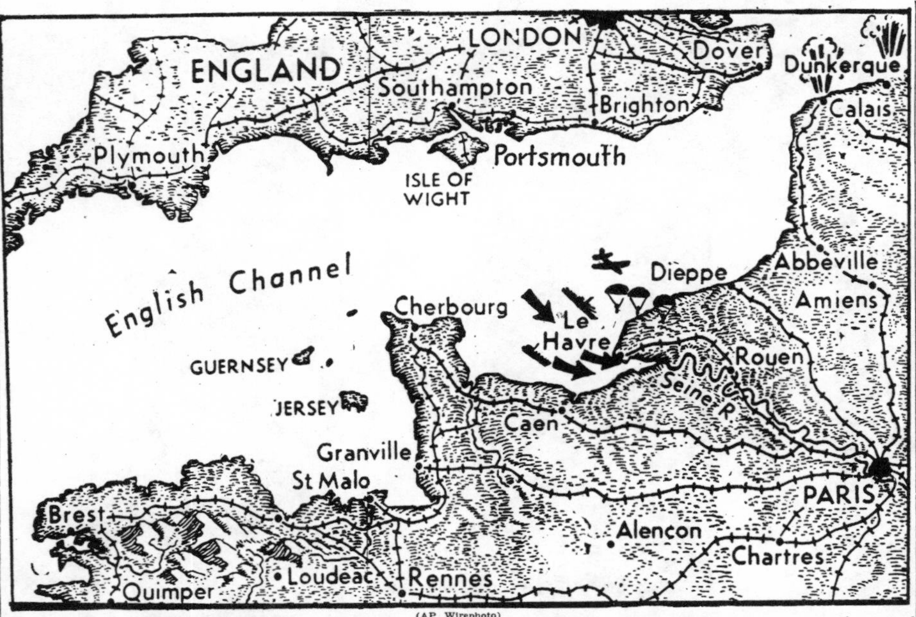

(AP Wirephoto)

WHERE GERMANS REPORT START OF ALLIED INVASION—Le Havre, where German radio services reported start of land-air invasion at 1 A. M. Eastern War Time Today, is 100 miles across the channel from Portsmouth, England. Bombings of Calais and Dieppe were announced along with terrific naval bombardment of Le Havre. Berlin said shock troops and German naval forces had engaged Allied landing forces.

Bulletins

ALLIED ARMY REINFORCED, NAZIS SAY

LONDON, June 6 (AP)—The German news Agency DNB said in a broadcast shortly before 10 A. M. (4 A. M. EWT) that Anglo-American troops had been reinforced at dawn at the mouth of the Seine river in the Le Havre area.

NEW YORK, June 6 (AP)—The London radio, in a Dutch language broadcast recorded by NBC, warned European underground workers today to report to their leaders with all speed and to "be prepared for anything."

"Keep away from military installations," the broadcast said. "Underground members report to your trusted leaders. Act with speed. Be prepared for anything. There is bombardment in the port of Le Havre."

LONDON, June 6 (AP)—The Germans news agency DNB commentator, Capt. Ludwig Sertorius, declared in a broadcast early today that the "great contest between the Reich and the Anglo-Americans has begun."

LONDON, June 6 (AP)—The Berlin radio said today that

(Continued on Page Three)

Paratroops Hit Nazis In Pre-Dawn Assaults

SUPREME HEADQUARTERS, ALLIED EXPEDITIONARY FORCE, June 6 (AP) — American, British and Canadian troops landed in northern France this morning, launching the greatest overseas military operation in history with word from their supreme commander, Gen. Dwight D. Eisenhower, that "we will accept nothing except full victory" over the German masters of the Continent.

The invasion, which Eisenhower called "a great crusade," was announced at 7:32 A. M. Greenwich mean time (3:32 A. M., Eastern War Time) in this one-sentence communique No. 1:

Under the command of Gen. Eisenhower Allied naval forces supported by strong air forces began landing Allied armies this morning on the northern coast of France.

The Germans said the landings extended between Le Havre and Cherbourg along the south side of the bay of the Seine and along the northern Normandy coast.

Parachute troops descended in Normandy, Berlin said.

Berlin first announced the landings in a series of flashes that began about 6:30 A. M. (12:30 A. M. Eastern War Time).

The Allied communique was read over a trans-Atlantic hook-up direct from Gen. Eisenhower's headquarters at 3:32 E. W. T., designated "Communique No. 1."

A second announcement by Shaef (supreme headquarters Allied expeditionary force) said that "it is announced that Gen. Sir Bernard L. Montgomery is in command of the Army group carrying out the assault. This Army group includes British, Canadian, and U. S. forces."

(Continued on Page Two)

BOMBING HITS 90-HOUR MARK

Pre-Invasion Raids Rake Atlantic Wall

By DREW MIDDLETON
[Boston Herald-N. Y. Times Cable]

LONDON, June 5—The main weight of the pre-invasion Allied air offensive again fell on targets along the invasion coast of northern France and on enemy communications behind the Atlantic Wall today. More than 500 Liberators and Fortresses of the Eighth Air Force blasted German military installations around Boulogne, Calais and in Pas de Calais generally in the day's largest operation.

Tonight RAF heavy bombers took up where United States daylight raiders left off and were pounding the coast well past the consecutive 90-hour mark.

Despite indifferent weather over northwestern Europe, Marauders and Thunderbolts of the Ninth Air Force carried out a number of

(Continued on Page Seven)

Roosevelt Sees Fall Of Rome First Step

'One up, Two to Go'; Long Road Ahead

Roosevelt text, Page Six

By CHARLES W. HURD
[Boston Herald-N. Y. Times Dispatch]

WASHINGTON, June 5—President Roosevelt tonight hailed the capture of Rome, first of the three major Axis capitals to fall, as a great achievement on the road toward total conquest of the Axis. Rome, he said, marked "one up and two to go" on the roads that lead also to Berlin and Tokio.

He cautioned that the struggle with the Nazis would be tough and costly and that the day of Germany's surrender "lies some distance ahead."

The President spoke for a quarter-hour on the radio, as had been announced yesterday, but his speech was notable for its lack of heroics.

(Continued on Page Six)

F. H. FAY DIES AT 71

Noted Engineer Long On Planning Board

Frederic H. Fay, 71, a member of the Boston planning board 20 years and senior member of the civil engineering firm of Fay, Spofford and Thorndike, died last night at Charlesgate Hospital. His home was at 227 Savin Hill avenue, Dorchester.

Mr. Fay was a consulting engineer for many federal, state, municipal and private construction projects, including the $25,000,000 Army Base at South Boston in 1918-1919.

He entered the city's service as a draftsman for the Boston bridge works in 1894, was in charge of bridge design and construction in the city engineer's office from 1895 to 1910, and from then until 1914 was division engineer in charge of the city bridge and ferry division. He resigned in 1914 to form the private engineering firm with Prof.

(Continued on Page Thirteen)

Today's Index
Page 4

SMALL U. S. CARRIER LOST

British, U. S. Subs Sink 47 Axis Ships

WASHINGTON, June 5 (AP)—The Navy, in new accountings of the war at sea, reported today the loss of a U. S. escort carrier and the sinking of 16 more Japanese merchant ships by American submarines.

The small aircraft carrier Block Island was sunk by enemy action in the Atlantic last month with "light" casualties, the Navy said in a communique. She was the 158th Navy ship lost during the war, and the first American aircraft carrier announced lost in the Atlantic.

In another communique, the Navy gave a fortnightly report on its submarine warfare against the Japanese. The 16 enemy merchant ships reported in today's announcement lifted the total of Japanese ships sunk by American submersibles to 589.

The announcement about the Block Island did not say how she went down—whether by submarine attack, gunfire, aerial bombs or mines.

LONDON, June 5 (AP)—British

(Continued on Page Eight)

NAZIS ANNOUNCE D-DAY—PLAY MUSIC

LONDON, Tuesday, June 6 (AP) — The German-controlled Calais radio came on the air today with the following announcement in English:

"This is D-Day. We shall now bring music for the (Allied) invasion forces."

Allies Cross Tiber In Pursuit of Nazis

ROME, June 5 (AP)—Allied armor and motorized infantry roared through the Eternal City today—not pausing to sight-see—crossed the Tiber, and proceeded with the grim task of destroying two battered German armies fleeing to the north.

Flashing forces of Allied fighter-bombers spearheaded the pursuit, jamming the escape highways northward with burning enemy transport and littering the fields with dead and wounded Nazis.

The enemy was tired, disorganized and bewildered by the slashing character of the Allied assault, which in 25 days had inflicted a major catastrophe on German forces in Italy and liberated Rome almost without damage to the historic city.

Joining the relentless program of destruction, 500 American heavy bombers blasted rail yards at five points in northern Italy between Venice and Rimini along which

(Continued on Page Four)

INVASION EXTRA!

Chronicle Home Delivery Service

Federal war regulations to conserve rubber prohibit all special deliveries. If for any reason you do not receive your Chronicle, kindly telephone GArfield 1112 or your local Chronicle dealer before 10 a. m. so the delivery may be checked. We appreciate your co-operation in this emergency.

San Francisco Chronicle

THE CITY'S ONLY HOME-OWNED NEWSPAPER

COMPARATIVE TEMPERATURES

	High	Low		High	Low
San Francisco	67	53	Chicago	86	73
Oakland	72	51	New Orleans	92	72
Sacramento	92	56	New York	67	51
Los Angeles	83	58	Salt Lake City	75	46
Seattle	73	46	Washington	72	58

Forecast: Fair

FOUNDED 1865—VOL. CLVIII, NO. 143 CCCCAAB SAN FRANCISCO, TUESDAY, JUNE 6, 1944 DAILY 5 CENTS, SUNDAY 15 CENTS: DAILY AND SUNDAY PER MONTH, $1.50

INVASION!

ALLIED ARMIES ARE LANDING IN NORTH FRANCE!

Communique No. 1 By Eisenhower

Montgomery Commanding Yanks, Britons, Canadians

By the Associated Press

SUPREME HEADQUARTERS, Allied Expeditionary Force, June 6 —Gen. Dwight D. Eisenhower's headquarters announced today:

"Under the command of Gen. Eisenhower Allied naval forces supported by strong air forces began landing Allied armies this morning on the northern coast of France."

The Germans said the landings extended between Le Havre and Cherbourg along the south side of the Bay of the Seine and along the Northern Normandy coast.

Parachute troops descended in Normandy, Berlin said.

Berlin first announced the landings in a series of flashes that began about 6:30 a. m. (9:30 p. m. Monday, PwT).

(Earlier stories received before confirmation, appear on

Continued on Page 2, Col. 1

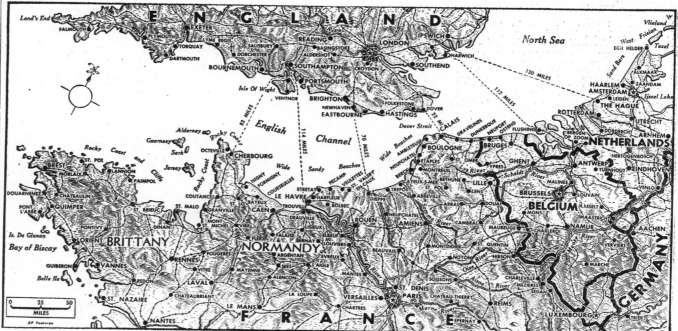

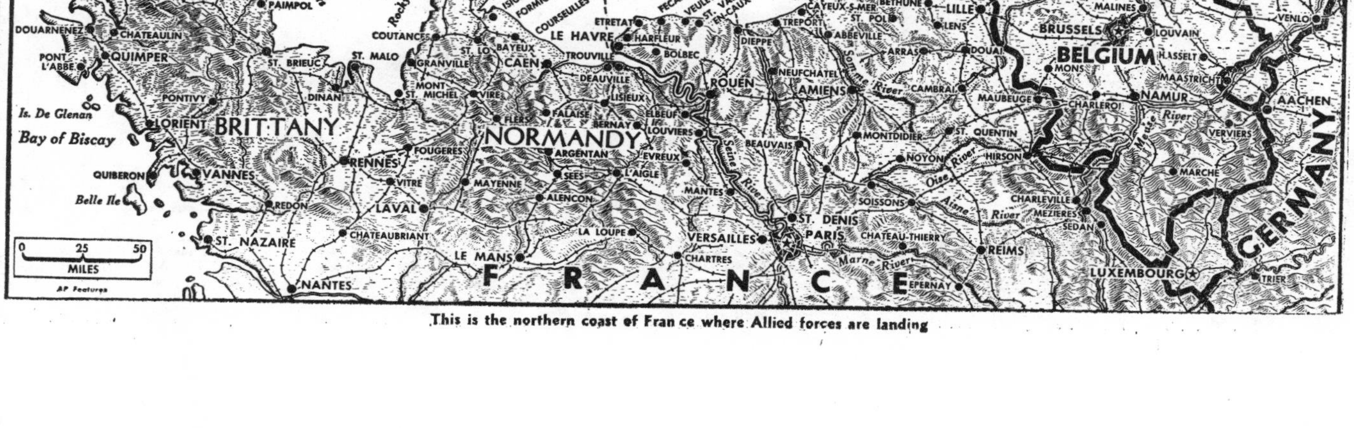

This is the northern coast of France where Allied forces are landing

SCRIPPS—HOWARD

New York World-Telegram

NIGHT
LATEST NEWS
Five Cents

Local Forecast: Partly cloudy today, moderately warm, highest temperature 78 degrees. Tonight, fair, rather cool.

VOL. 76—NO. 286—IN TWO SECTIONS—SECTION ONE. NEW YORK, WEDNESDAY, JUNE 7, 1944 Entered as second class matter Post Office, New York, N. Y.

BEACHHEADS EXPANDED

Troops Pour In by Air; Fighting Heavy; Nazis Launch Attack; We Push Ahead

By VIRGIL PINKLEY, *United Press War Correspondent*

ALLIED SUPREME HQ., LONDON, June 7.—Five great waves of aerial troop carriers, including a skytrain 50 miles long, poured reinforcements into the Allied beachheads in Normandy during the night and the invasion forces were reported pushing inland today against increasingly fierce German resistance.

American, British and Canadian assault forces firmly held pockets of undisclosed size and location along a 60-mile stretch of the northwest coast of France between Cherbourg and the Seine and were tightening their grip on them and expanding them in heavy fighting.

[Wes Gallagher, Associated Press war correspondent, said the fresh Allied troops from the huge sky glider train seized key positions on Cherbourg Peninsula and reinforced Allied soldiers fighting against Nazi tank counterattacks.

[Three waves of U. S. Ninth Air Force gliders strung out in a 50-mile-long train across the Channel brought "a steady stream of men, equipment and supplies" to troops smashing inland.

SOME TOWNS CAPTURED.

[Front dispatches said airborne forces had seized bridges and roads, and linked up with troops landed from the sea at several points. Some towns already have been captured.] Thunderbolt pilots returning from a flight over the invasion area said Allied tanks were rolling into the outskirts of a town which was in flames.

A spokesman at Gen. Dwight D. Eisenhower's headquarters said the fighting was very heavy in some sectors of the Normandy invasion zone, and Berlin claimed that German reserves had massed around the Allied lines during the night and now were attacking with "terrific ferocity."

[Berlin radio, meanwhile, declared that "a second daylight invasion attempt at Pas-de-Calais was opposed this morning by German long-range artillery," according to an Associated Press report. The heavily bombed Pas-de-Calais area lies across the narrowest stretch of the Channel from Dover on the English coasct, and is northeast of the Cherbourg peninsula. There was no Allied confirmation.]

Communique No. 3 of Allied Supreme Headquarters announced that "satisfactory progress has been made" and reinforcements were moving steadily into the first Allied pockets carved out of the Nazi Atlantic Wall, which was penetrated in the first few hours of the invasion.

BULLDOZERS CLEAR FIELD.

(A Blue Network correspondent who witnessed the landings said the Allies had capture da 50-mile stretch of the coast to a depth of 12 or more miles, while a British broadcast heard by the same network asserted that Allied Bulldozers were clearing an RAF airfield on the occupied coast.)

The first three waves of United States Ninth Air Force gliders were towed by C-47 cargo planes in a 50-mile train last night and delivered thousands of men to the Cherbourg Peninsula of Normandy.

The German Transocean News Agency said that the Allied airborne forces had occupied a circular area between Valognes and Carentan on the east side of the Normany peninsula and opened a corridor to the coast.

Two more such waves followed in the wake of the mighty aerial procession. Landing at positions designated in advance, the gliders both fed men and supplies into consolidated positions and seized new footholds.

For good reasons the Allies were not telling anyone much about the invasion. If they did, it would become a godsend to the German High Command, which still does not know whether more landings are coming and if so whether they will overshadow the current fighting.

NO SPECIFIC WORD.

There still was no specific word fixing the extent of the Allies successes beyond Prime Minister Winston Churchill's word yesterday that fighting was going on in the town of Caen, nine and a half miles inland.

British tanks and infantry were revealed to have taken a 25-mile stretch of the Normandy coast and pushed inland nearly three and a half miles to cut a coast road vital to the Nazi movement of reserves.

Berlin acknowledged that the Allies had established one beachhead—possibly the one credited to the British

(Continued on Page Two.)

BULLETINS!

By the Associated Press.

WITH THE NINTH AIR FORCE, June 7.—Twelve C-47 troop carriers and 12 gliders were reported missing today from overnight reinforcing operations beyond the beachheads in Normandy. This was the first specific report of losses from air-borne operations since the invasion began.

By the Associated Press.

The British Broadcasting Co. said today that Allied tanks were moving up toward Caen, some nine miles southwest of Le Havre, where Allied troops—presumably airborne forces—previously were reported engaged in heavy fighting. The broadcast was recorded by the Blue Network.

By the Associated Press.

LONDON, June 7.—The German International Information Bureau broadcast today that German naval forces surprised and attacked three Allied destroyers in the mouth of the Seine at 3:38 a. m., setting one afire. There was no Allied confirmation.

Clouds Lift Over Channel

By the United Press.

LONDON, June 7.—The weather was dull over the Straits of Dover today with occasional breaks in the clouds.

Visibility was good.

A fresh westerly wind was blowing at 11 a. m., and the sea was carrying waves about three feet high.

Cloud banks which have prevailed over the French coast for the last few days were reported lifting.

Invasion Closeups

From the Air—

Curtains of Flak Thrown Up by Foe

By HOWARD COWAN,
Associated Press War Writer.

AT A NINTH U. S. ARMY AIR FORCE TROOP CARRIER BASE, June 7.—The Allied expeditionary air force had just completed another airborne landing behind enemy lines in Nazi-occupied France, but unlike the first operation this was no milk run.

I know. I flew in the leading ship of a group commanded by a crackerjack pilot from my home town, Lt. Col. John Ueale of Shawnee, Okla. He is the brother of Billy Neale, who is in the automobile supply business with Champ Johnson. That army borrowed him from the Pennsylvania Central Airline, of which he is vice president and chief pilot.

When we came back to England the metal hide of our powerful twin-engined C-47 was messed up like a bride's first entry into a can of early June peas. The radio and electrical systems were damaged, but nobody was hurt.

We were lucky. Some came with dead and wounded aboard. Some didn't come home. The Germans were ready this time. Hundreds of planes had been in ahead of us, and it seemed we flew down an avenue lined with machineguns and fountains on both sides.

Colorful Tracers Arcs.

Red and green tracers overlapped in huge arcs that reminded you of an old-fashioned grape arbor. Flares from flak bursts made you jump, but they were far off and they were so far off there was no noise and didn't seem to matter much—at least not like the 20-millimeter shell which sawed through the fuselage next to my window and then went off like an indoor firecracker explosion.

This may sound as if I was scared. Well, I was. It was the first time any of us had been under fire.

Beside Col. Neale others in the crew were co-pilot Capt. Bob Creamer, Tulsa, Okla.; Navigator Lt. Charles F. Chester, Santa Barbara, Cal.; Lt. Eugene A. Waterfill, Lawrenceburg, Ky.; Sgt. Norman Sabloff, 101 Eaton Pl., East Orange, N. J., and crew chief Sgt. Dennis Halpeska, Victoria, Texas.

The pilot of a big force of gliders was Lt. Joe Herriage, Bonham, Texas, and flight officer Howard M. David, Hollywood, Cal., his assistant.

No Cook's Tour.

I had an invitation to fly on the invasion opening paratroop operation but I explained it would be pretty dark and there would not be much to see and write about. I

(Continued on Page Eleven.)

From the Sea—

Offshore Reporter Watches Landing

By TOM YARBROUGH,
Associated Press Correspondent Representing the Combined American Press.

ABOARD BRITISH DESTROYER COTTESMORE, Off the North coast of France, June 6 (Delayed).—This little ship with four hot guns is going back to England now after spending 12 incredible hours in the front ranks phase of the Allied invasion of France—an operation that came off ten times as smoothly as anyone aboard expected.

From where we sat—about a mile and a half off shore—it seemed too easy and too smooth to be true. The men of this ship, through several tense and expectant months, had come to refer to this thing (the invasion) as the blood bath, and not altogether facetiously.

Sitting in Front Row.

But it was not a blood bath at all.

They thank God—several of them told me so—that it went as well as it did this first day, though they know full well the hardest part is yet to come. It's still almost incredible, though, that this force of men and ships spent 12 hours within easy shooting distance of Hitler's Europe and did not encounter a single German plane or ship.

It was like seeing a play in which some of the leading actors failed to show up. With strong binoculars, standing on the bridge, I saw thousands of men and machines tumble safely across beaches bristling with ugly spikes driven into the sand at crazy angles and topped with mines—beaches smoking from terrible plastering of bombs and naval shells. The glasses brought the scenes up close in spectacular detail.

This account deals primarily with only one sector of the beach assaulted by men from the United Kingdom and covered by the British Navy and embraces only the things we could see and which were reported to us from the shore immediately ahead.

Here are the salient highlights of what occurred around us—one of four small Hunt class destroyers in the front row center of one of the two major assault forces.

First Landing Seen.

At 7:29 this morning, 27-year-old Royal Navy Lt. William D. O'Brien, his keen blue eyes fixed on the beach, said, "The first vehicles are touching down. This is H-Hour now."

Opposition was so weak generally—thanks to the seemingly complete tactical surprise—that this ship and others were still asking for targets when no more targets were available. One enemy shell exploded within about 50 feet of us, but caused no damage.

Landing troops moved across the beaches and advanced about 300 yards inland before noon, pushing ahead with tanks over green, tree-lined fields sloping up from the shore. Our sector included little Normandy towns with Caen farther back from the coast area immediately east of the Cherbourg peninsula.

No Sign of Germans.

We could see our own men moving along, but couldn't make out figures of Germans or Frenchmen anywhere. It looked as if civilians had been moved out long before. Windows of many buildings were bricked up.

The weather seemed shaky at first, but went through some changes in our favor. In an operation involving so many ships—more than 4000—some collisions seemed inevitable in even the best weather, but we had considerable northwest wind at certain stages and still heard of no collision.

Reds Prepare Offensive on Eastern Front

Red Star Declares Attack Will Bolster Invasion in West

By the Associated Press.

MOSCOW, June 7.—Russia is prepared to throw the great weight of the Red army into the growing offensive against Germany, Red Star, the Soviet army newspaper, said today.

"A strong, mounting attack of all the armies of the United Nations will be fully developed," Red Star said.

The great armies which at Tehran gave solemn promises not to make a separate peace are beginning to move forward for a meeting in Berlin, the newspaper added.

Muscovites got up early this morning to read the freshest invasion bulletins, despite one of the wildest nights of celebration during the war. Outside the windows the radio blared forth the latest details, and the Soviet press, in an unprecedented display, turned over whole pages to the momentous military operations Russia had long awaited.

All newspapers published a picture of Gen. Dwight D. Eisenhower, the supreme commander of the Allied Expeditionary Force.

Invasion Termed Jap Death Knell

By the United Press.

CHUNGKING, June 7.—War Minister Ho Ying-chin said today the opening of the Western Front was a death knell for the Jap aggressors and "their fate is as good as sealed."

He predicted Europe would be liberated in the "very near future," after which the Allies can concentrate their entire strength to liquidate Japan.

Major Gen. Demoted, Sent Home for D-Day Tip

By the Associated Press.

SUPREME HQ., ALLIED EXPEDITIONARY FORCE, June 7.—One of America's best known major generals was demoted to lieutenant colonel and sent home for indicating in advance the time of D-Day.

The supreme command allowed this information to be cabled abroad today after holding it up several weeks for security reasons.

The major general was one of the commanders in the American Air Force, the announcement said. An army man of long standing, he swiftly felt the supreme command axe after talking indiscreetly at a London cocktail party, the announcement added.

The conversation was said to have taken place almost two months ago when the invasion was expected almost daily. The general was reported to have said in the presence of several persons: "On my honor the invasion will take place before June 15."

His action was reported to security police by a woman guest and Gen. Eisenhower immediately ordered him reduced to the permanent rank of lieutenant colonel and sent home after an investigation.

His name was not given.

The Weather

New York and Metropolitan Area: Partly cloudy today, moderately warm, highest temperature 78 degrees. Tonight fair, rather cool, lowest 60 in the city and 55 in the suburbs. Tomorrow fair, moderate temperature. Dry air and moderate winds today through tomorrow.

New Jersey: Somewhat cloudy with moderate temperature today; fair and cooler tonight. Tomorrow fair, warmer in afternoon.

TODAY'S READINGS.

	Temp.	Hum.		Temp.	Hum.
Midnight	70	..	5 a. m.	67	..
1 a. m.	70	..	6 a. m.	65	63
2 a. m.	69	..	7 a. m.	63	60
3 a. m.	69	..	8 a. m.	64	60
4 a. m.	68	..	9 a. m.	66	55

High and low a year ago, 70-57.

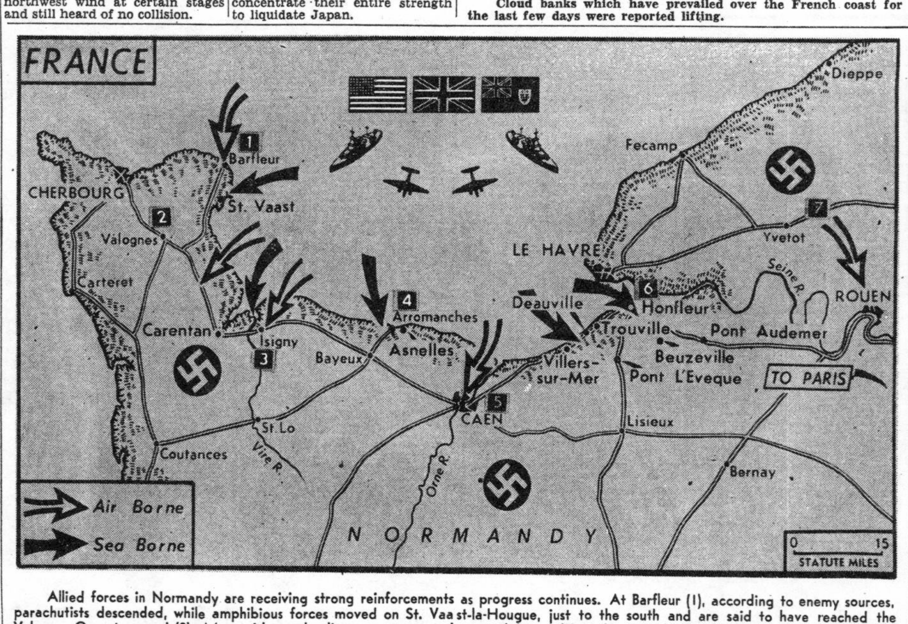

Allied forces in Normandy are receiving strong reinforcements as progress continues. At Barfleur (1), according to enemy sources, parachutists descended, while amphibious forces moved on St. Vaast-la-Hougue, just to the south and are said to have reached the Valognes-Carentan road (2). More airborne landings were reported around Isigny (3) and troops landed near Arromanches (4). The Germans still speak of the Caen (5) area as the main battle site and report invaders have gone in at Honfleur (6). No more definite information of previously reported paratroop landings around Rouen (7) has been announced. U. S. and British troops have occupied a 50-mile stretch of coast and advanced at some places 12 miles, according to a report from London. A. P. Map.

World-Telegram Index

REVALER ZEITUNG

Postverlagsort im Reiche: Tilsit. Zu abonnieren bei allen Postanstalten. Erscheint täglich, ausser Montag. Banken: Notenbank Ostland, Reval; in Berlin: Postscheckkonto Nr. 800 der Dresdner Bank mit dem Vermerk für „Revaler Zeitung"

Verlag u. Schriftleitung: Reval, Langstrasse 40/42 (Pikk 40/42). Anschrift für Post mit dem Vermerk: „Durch Deutsche Dienstpost im Ostland"

Abonnementspreis Mk. 2.50 einschl. Zustellgebühr. Einzelpreis 10 Pf. — im Reiche: Monatsbezug Mk. 3.36 einschl. Zustellgebühr. Einzelpreis 20 Pf. Fernsprecher: Verlag und Schriftleitung: 47720; Anzeigen, Vertrieb und Drucksachen: 47720

Reval, Nr. 131 — Mittwoch, 7. Juni 1944 — Jahrgang 3

Die Invasion hat begonnen

Sofortiges Einsetzen der Abwehr — Überraschungsmoment misslungen — Schwere Kämpfe an der Küste zwischen Le Havre und Cherbourg

Reval, 6. Juni

Niemand in der Welt gibt sich einem Zweifel darüber hin, dass die nunmehr von den Anglo-Amerikanern begonnene Invasion in der Mitte der französischen Westküste ein Wagnis allerersten Ranges darstellt. Somit ist der Feind zu der grossen entscheidenden Schlacht dieses Krieges angetreten, die er lange zu vermeiden gehofft hatte, die aber von der allgemeinen politischen Entwicklung gebieterisch gefordert wurde. Dementsprechend haben sich Engländer und Nordamerikaner zu diesem Waffengang in jeder erdenklichen Form gerüstet und nicht nur eine Millionenzahl von Truppen bereitgestellt, sondern auch alle modernen technischen Hilfsmittel bis in die kleinsten Feinheiten hinein in monatelanger Vorarbeit ausgenutzt. Die deutschen Vorbereitungen für die Entscheidungsschlacht sind nicht minder umfangreich, denn das gesamte Kriegsgeschehen seit dem Herbst 1942 stand in Europa im Zeichen der vom Oberkommando der Wehrmacht erwarteten Entscheidung im Westen. Wir haben an der Ostfront weite Strecken Landes aufgegeben, wir haben in Italien nur mit hinhaltendem Widerstand gekämpft, Rom geräumt und der Heimat musste das Ausharren gegenüber einem herausfordernden Bombenterror zugemutet werden. Dennoch haben sich die Überlegungen der deutschen Führung, die die vorhandenen Streitkräfte nicht verzetteln wollte, als richtig erwiesen. Der Tag, um dessen willen wir den Talgang dieses Krieges mit allen seinen Erniedrigungen bewusst beschritten haben, ist angebrochen. Wir können jetzt das Bewusstsein aussprechen, dass die beste Wehrmacht der Welt ausgerüstet mit den hervorragendsten Erfindungen Deutschlands wohl durchtrainiert und mit dem Kriegshandwerk in jeder Beziehung vertraut, dem landenden Feind gegenübertritt.

Noch fehlen verständlicherweise Einzelheiten über die ersten Kampfhandlungen, die zur Zeit mit den abgesetzten Fallschirmjäger, Luftlandetruppen und Seelandetruppen im Gange sind. Dennoch scheint das Riesengebiet zwischen Cherbourg und le Havre das Hauptangriffsziel der ersten Invasionsphase zu sein. Dieses Gebiet war, wie ein Blick auf die Karte lehrt, für Invasionsversuche von England nach Frankreich geradezu einladend. Eine breite geschützte Bucht, die bequeme Einfahrt in den ozeanischen Hafen le Havre und die Nähe der französischen Hauptstadt Paris müssen für den Angreifer ein verlockendes Ziel darstellen. Ausserdem bietet die breite Front der südenglischen Hafenstädte eine angenehme Rückendeckung. Wahrscheinlich wird deshalb der Feind versuchen, erst einmal an der Südengland zugekehrten französischen Küste, an der auch das durch einen unrühmlichen Invasionsversuch bekanntgewordene Dieppe liegt, möglichst viele Stützpunkte zu errichten, über die er dann das Gros der Invasionstruppen nach Frankreich hineinschleusen kann. In diesem ersten Abschnitt der Landungsschlacht befinden wir uns im Augenblick, und die zur Zeit zwischen Cherbourg und le Havre tobenden heftigen Kämpfe sind der Abwehr der feindlichen Stützpunktbildung gewidmet.

War das Oberkommando der Wehrmacht in der Lage, die militärische und politische Entwicklung dieses Krieges so genau vorauszusagen, dann ist auch anzunehmen, dass es die taktischen Absichten der sowohl im Leben [illegible] im Kriege nicht besonders fantasievollen Engländer durchschaut hat. Dann allerdings dürfte der Küstenstreifen zwischen Cherbourg und le Havre zu den stärksten Befestigungswerken des Atlantikwalles gerechnet werden müssen. Auch die gewaltigen Luftangriffe des Feindes wird man in Betracht gezogen haben ebenso wie die mögliche Landung von Truppen aus der Luft, die bereits in grosser Zahl ohne einen Schuss abgegeben zu haben, in weit ausgedehnten Minenfeldern zugrunde gegangen sind. Die ganze Invasionsschlacht wird, hierauf lassen die Vorbereitungen der Anglo-Amerikaner schliessen, von einer immer wiederholten Kette neuer Anlandungen bestehen und erst in einem weiter vorgeschrittenen Stadium der Kämpfe wird sich der eigentliche Schwerpunkt herausschälen. Was der Feind jedoch bisher unternommen hat, scheint bessere Chancen für den Verteidiger als für den Angreifer zu bieten.

Die Anglo-Amerikaner können jedoch im Verlaufe der Invasionsschlacht unternehmen was sie wollen, jede nur irgendwie erdenkbare Möglichkeit ist von der deutschen Truppenführung in allen Einzelheiten durchdacht worden und eine Fülle von Überraschungen steht den Invasoren bevor. Die wichtigste Waffe jedoch, die die deutschen Soldaten in dieser Entscheidungsschlacht um das europäische Gesamtschicksal mit hereinbringen ist das Bewusstsein ihrer Stärke und der Rechtlichkeit unserer Sache.

Berlin, 6. Juni

Der seit langem erwartete Angriff der Briten und Nordamerikaner gegen die nordfranzösische Küste hat in der letzten Nacht begonnen. Wenige Minuten nach Mitternacht setzte der Feind unter gleichzeitigen heftigen Bombenangriffen im Gebiet der Seine-Bucht starke Luftlandeverbände ab. Kurze Zeit später schoben sich, geschützt durch schwere und leichte Kriegsschiff-Einheiten, zahlreiche feindliche Landungsboote auch gegen andere Abschnitte der Küste vor. Die Abwehr liess sich an keiner Stelle überraschen. Sie nahm den Kampf sofort mit aller Energie auf. Die Luftlandetruppen wurden zum Teil schon beim Absprung erfasst und die feindlichen Schiffe bereits auf hoher See wirksam unter Feuer genommen. Viele Fallschirmeinheiten wurden aufgerieben oder gefangen, andere von hochgehenden Minen zerrissen. Trotz fortgesetzter heftiger Luftangriffe und schweren Beschusses durch die feindliche Schiffsartillerie griffen die Geschütze des Atlantikwalls ebenfalls sofort in den Kampf ein. Sie erzielten Treffer auf Schlachtschiffeinheiten und den sich einnebelnden Landungsbooten. Der Kampf gegen die Invasionstruppen ist in vollem Gange.

ALARM AM ATLANTIKWALL — PK-Aufn. Kriegsberichter Nieberle (Wb)

Der Angriff hat begonnen

Reichspressechef Dr. Dietrich zur Invasion

Berlin, 6. Juni

Reichspressechef Dr. Dietrich machte am Dienstagmorgen folgende Äusserung zum Beginn der Invasion:

„Heute früh sind unsere Gegner im Westen zu ihrem blutigen Opfergang, vor dem sie so lange sich gescheut haben, auf Befehl Moskaus angetreten. Der so oft angekündigte Angriff der westlichen Helfer des Bolschewismus auf die Freiheit Europas hat begonnen. Wir werden ihnen einen heissen Empfang bereiten. Deutschland ist sich der Bedeutung der Stunde bewusst. Es wird mit ganzer Kraft und mit leidenschaftlicher Entschlossenheit kämpfen, um Europa, seine Kultur und das Leben seiner Völker vor dem Ansturm der Barbarei zu bewahren."

An Frankreichs Nordküste

Stockholm, 6. Juni

Ein vom Hauptquartier des USA-Generals Eisenhower am Dienstag ausgegebenes Kommuniqué besagt:

„Unter dem Kommando von General Eisenhower haben Marinestreitkräfte mit Unterstützung starker Luftstreitkräfte mit der Landung alliierter Armeen an der Nordküste von Frankreich am Dienstagmorgen begonnen."

Scharfe Zensur

Briefe nach USA werden kontrolliert

Stockholm, 6. Juni

Briefe aus England werden in den USA genau kontrolliert und daher sehr lange zurückgehalten, bis sie den Adressaten ausgeliefert werden, so gab laut „News Chronicle" der Leiter der Zensur zu. Man müsse, so sagte er u. a., im Interesse der nationalen Sicherheit sehr vorsichtig sein und gehe im Einvernehmen mit der Armee und Marine vor. — Es handelt sich also um Briefe von USA-Soldaten und Matrosen aus England, die viele Dinge über die Zustände in England schreiben, die weder die Angehörigen noch die Zeitungen in den USA erfahren dürften.

Der Überfall der Aggressoren

Feindliche Angriffe bei Rom zusammengebrochen

Führerhauptquartier, 6. Juni

Das Oberkommando der Wehrmacht gibt bekannt:

In der vergangenen Nacht hat der Feind seinen seit langem vorbereiteten und von uns erwarteten Angriff auf Westeuropa begonnen. Eingeleitet durch schwere Luftangriffe auf unsere Küstenbefestigungen setzte er an mehreren Stellen der nordfranzösischen Küste zwischen le Havre und Cherbourg Luftlandetruppen ab und landete gleichzeitig, unterstützt durch starke Seestreitkräfte, auch von See her. In dem angegriffenen Küstenstreifen sind erbitterte Kämpfe im Gange.

In Italien führte der Gegner aus Rom mehrere vergebliche Vorstösse gegen unsere Sicherungen westlich und nördlich der Stadt. Östlich der Stadt brachen die mit zusammengefassten Kräften während des ganzen Tages geführten feindlichen Angriffe bei und westlich Tivoli nach erbittertem Ringen zusammen.

Jäger und Flakartillerie der Luftwaffe schossen über dem oberitalienischen Raum acht feindliche Flugzeuge ab.

Im Osten kämpften sich die deutsch-rumänischen Truppen, wirksam unterstützt durch starke deutsch-rumänische Fliegerverbände, nordwestlich Jassy gegen zähen feindlichen Widerstand in harten Kämpfen weiter vor und wiesen wiederholte Gegenangriffe der Bolschewisten ab. 39 feindliche Flugzeuge wurden in Luftkämpfen vernichtet.

Von der übrigen Ostfront wird nur örtliche Gefechtstätigkeit aus dem Kampfraum von Witebsk gemeldet.

In Kroatien haben Truppen des Heeres und der Waffen-SS unter dem Oberbefehl des Generalobersten Rendulic, unterstützt durch starke Kampf- und Schlachtfliegerverbände, das Zentrum der Bandentruppen Titos überfallen und nach tagelangen schweren Kämpfen zerschlagen. Der Feind verlor nach vorläufigen Meldungen 6240 Mann. Ausserdem wurden zahlreiche Waffen aller Art und viele Versorgungseinrichtungen erbeutet. In diesen Kämpfen haben sich die 7. SS-Gebirgsdivision „Prinz Eugen" unter Führung des SS-Oberführers Kumm und das SS-Fallschirmjägerbataillon 500 unter Führung des SS-Hauptsturmführers Rybka hervorragend bewährt.

Einige feindliche Flugzeuge warfen in der letzten Nacht Bomben auf Osnabrück. Zwei Flugzeuge wurden abgeschossen.

Vom Führer empfangen

Die Gesandten Kroatiens und Ungarns

Führerhauptquartier, 6. Juni

Der Führer empfing am Montag in Anwesenheit des Reichsministers des Auswärtigen von Ribbentrop den neuernannten Gesandten des unabhängigen Staates Kroatien in Berlin, Dr. Vladimir Kosak, zur Überreichung seines Beglaubigungsschreibens sowie des Abberuffungsschreibens seines Vorgängers.

Der Führer empfing weiterhin in Anwesenheit des Reichsministers des Auswärtigen von Ribbentrop den neuernannten königlich ungarischen Gesandten in Berlin, Dr. Alexander Hoffmann von Magysötetag, zur Überreichung seines Beglaubigungsschreibens sowie des Abberufungsschreibens seines Vorgängers.

Im Pazifik versenkt

Flugzeugträger, Kreuzer und Zerstörer

Tokio, 6. Juni

Aus dem Südwestpazifik wird gemeldet, dass die japanische Luftwaffe am 2. Juni feindliche Schiffsziele südlich der Insel Biak angriff. Ein feindlicher Kreuzer und ein Zerstörer wurden versenkt. Die japanischen Flugzeuge kehrten alle unversehrt zu ihrem Stützpunkt zurück.

Die USA-Marine gibt bekannt, dass der nordamerikanische Geleit-Flugzeugträger „Block Island" durch Feindeinwirkung im Atlantik im Mai versenkt wurde.

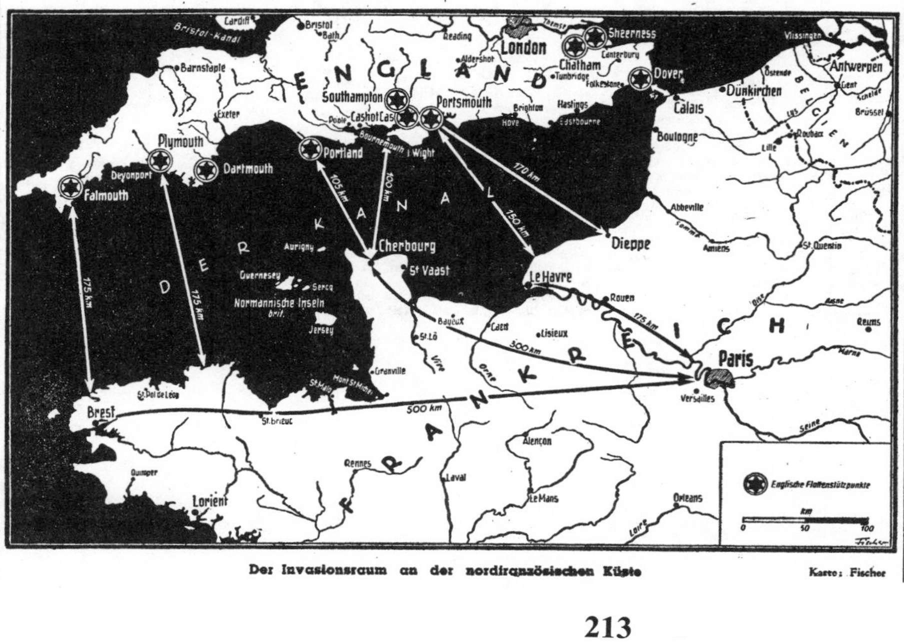

Der Invasionsraum an der nordfranzösischen Küste — Karte: Fischer

UM DIE ENTSCHEIDUNG

Der Kampf um die Festung Europa

DIE INVASION hat begonnen. In der Nacht zum 6. Juni sind die ersten Feindtruppen auf nordfranzösischem Boden gelandet. Engländer, Amerikaner und Kanadier haben die erste Bekanntschaft mit dem vielfältigen Verteidigungssystem des Atlantikwalls gemacht. Mit dem Überfall auf Europa ist in der vergangenen Nacht ein Verteidigungsapparat ausgelöst worden, der in den vorausgegangenen Monaten und Jahren für alle Eventualitäten längs der Atlantikküste aufgebaut worden ist. Es sind aber nicht nur die mit Waffen aller Art gespickten Wälle aus Eisen und Beton, nicht nur ein Aufgebot von besten Waffen und Munition, die den Aggressoren Widerpart zu bieten imstande sind, es ist in erster Linie der ausgeruhte und wohlausgerüstete deutsche Soldat, der endlich Gelegenheit hat, eine lang ausstehende Rechnung zu begleichen.

Das Risiko, um das sich Engländer wie Amerikaner so lange gedrückt haben, haben die Alliierten unter dem Zwang der Verhältnisse auf sich genommen. Sie haben damit bestätigt, dass die Entscheidung weder durch Luftterror noch durch Agitationsfeldzüge herbeizuführen ist. Nachdem sie bisher ihren Krieg nur mit Hilfsvölkern geführt haben, die sie bedenkenlos ihren imperialistischen Zielen geopfert haben, sind sie nun durch die Invasion gezwungen, ihre eigene Haut zu Markte zu tragen. Seit der Nacht zum 6. Juni wird der Krieg auch für sie jene Formen annehmen, die sie ihm in ihrem abgrundtiefen Hass und Vernichtungswillen gegeben haben. Der Irrsinn eines Roosevelts und Churchills, ohne Not einen Krieg zu provozieren und die Jugend ihrer Länder für Kapitalinteressen fern der ungefährdeten Heimat zu opfern, wird auf den Schlachtfeldern Nordfrankreichs offenbar. Dort erfüllt sich die bittere Voraussage, dass die Söhne Englands und Amerikas in fremder Erde für fremde Interessen untergepflügt werden. Mit der Landung in der Normandie haben sie den Verrat am europäischen Kontinent vervollständigt. Als Schleppenträger des Bolschewismus haben sie den von Moskau befohlenen Überfall auf Europa begonnen. Um das Bündnis mit Moskau zu halten, muss Grossbritannien jetzt im fünften Kriegsjahr genau das tun, was es bisher zu vermeiden gesucht hat. Es muss unter Einsatz seiner selbst auf dem Kontinent kämpfen. Der letzte seiner Bundesgenossen in Europa, die Sowjetunion, ist nicht bereit, dem Beispiel aller jener europäischen Völker zu folgen, die Grossbritannien den Gang auf das Schlachtfeld jahrelang abgenommen haben.

Aber auch die Amerikaner, die den grössten Teil der Invasionstruppen stellen, beabsichtigen nicht für England, sondern für ihre eigenen Interessen zu kämpfen. Was diese in Westeuropa zu suchen haben, weiss niemand. Die Amerikaner selbst messen dem Kriege in Ostasien, das heisst dem Krieg um die Reichtümer des Pazifik, grössere Bedeutung bei als dem Krieg um die Ruinen von Europa. Anders der Präsident der USA. Roosevelt brauchte den Krieg, um sich an der Macht zu halten. Er nahm ihn dort, wo er ihn am leichtesten bekommen konnte. Und dies war zunächst nicht Ostasien, sondern Europa. An der Herbeiführung der Invasion war Roosevelt ebensoviel gelegen wie Stalin. Es wird sich in den nächsten Wochen und Monaten erweisen, wieweit Roosevelts Wahlkampagne von den Ereignissen in Europa beeinflusst wird.

Aus der Phase der Vorbereitung ist die Invasion in das Stadium der Verwirklichung eingetreten. Damit hat fürs erste eine ungeheure Spannung eine Entlastung erfahren, und die weise Voraussicht der deutschen Führung ihre Bestätigung gefunden. Die Ereignisse der letzten vierundzwanzig Stunden beweisen, wie richtig Deutschland die Lage eingeschätzt hat und sich weder von Propagandamanövern noch durch Nebenkriegsschauplätze ablenken liess. Durch Monate und Jahre hindurch galt sein Hauptaugenmerk der allein entscheidenden Front im Westen. Es mag der deutschen Führung nicht immer leicht gefallen sein, gegenüber den vielseitigen Anforderungen aus dem Osten und Süden standhaft zu bleiben und ungeachtet zahlreicher Schwierigkeiten den Bestand für die entscheidende Stunde nicht anzutasten. Der bedrückende Talgang des letzten Jahres, die Zurücknahme der Front im Osten und im Süden und nicht zuletzt der Bombenkrieg über der Heimat, das alles erscheint seit gestern im Licht einer zwingenden Notwendigkeit. Der Führer hat in einer seiner letzten Reden betont, dass das Volk sich auf dem Schlachtfeld behaupte, das das letzte Bataillon einzusetzen vermag.

Mit der Landung der Anglo-Amerikaner hat die deutsche Führung das erreicht, was sie seit langer Zeit angestrebt hat. Deutschland hat die Operationsbasis, auf der die grösste militärische Entscheidung dieses Krieges herbeigeführt werden wird, selbst bestimmt und dort alles vorbereitet, wohin sie den Auftakt des Invasions-Unternehmens lenken konnte. Seit Wochen ist es der militärischen Führung klar gewesen, dass der Gegner diesem Raum seine besondere Aufmerksamkeit zuwandte. Das Moment der Überraschung, wie das Moment der Tarnung ist dadurch von vornherein ausgefallen. Man wird auf Grund der zahlreichen deutschen Veröffentlichungen der letzten Zeit wohl sagen dürfen, dass in diesen Räumen alles vorbereitet war, um dem Invasions-Abenteuer mit dem entsprechenden Nachdruck entgegenzutreten.

In diesen Stunden beginnt sich der Vorhang vor einem der dramatischsten Akte dieses an Überraschungen so rei-

First Photos of Yanks on Shores Of France

Only Los Angeles Newspaper With All Leading News Services—Associated Press, International News, United Press, Dow-Jones

NIGHT EDITION
HERALD-EXPRESS PHONE Richmond 4141 R

LOS ANGELES EVENING HERALD AND Express
AN INDEPENDENT NEWSPAPER
Registered United States Patent Office

HERALD-EXPRESS BUILDING 1243 Trenton St. Zone 15
The Evening Herald and Express Grows Just Like Los Angeles
HERALD-EXPRESS PHONE Richmond 4141

EXTRA

VOL. LXXIV | Two Sections Section A | FIVE CENTS | WEDNESDAY, JUNE 7, 1944 | *** | FIVE CENTS | NO. 63

ALLIES CLEAR BEACH; SKY TROOPS BATTLE

—Signal Corps Radio Photo from International News Sound Photo

This is the FIRST picture of the actual invasion of Europe. Under cover of naval shell fire, American infantrymen are shown wading through the surf to make the first landings on a French beach. At right is a United States transport from which the men disembarked. For additional action picture of the invasion see Page A-3.

Air Losses

Seventy Allied Planes Invasion Toll

By Associated Press

LONDON, June 7.—Allied airforces have lost 70 aircraft in this theater since the invasion started, today's announcements showed. Various announcements gave this breakdown:

Seventeen Allied fighters, 12 American C-47 troop carriers, 12 American CG-42 gliders, 13 British heavy bombers, six American Thunderbolt fighters, four American Havocs, two American Lightning fighters, two American medium bombers, one R. A. F. Beaufighter, one American heavy bomber.

Each C-47 is capable of carrying 24 fully-equipped soldiers together with pilot, co-pilot and navigator. CG-42 gliders can seat 15 men, but seldom are loaded that heavily.

Nazis Say Reserves In Action

By JOHN CAMSELL
International News Service Staff Correspondent

LONDON, June 7.—Field Marshal Karl Rudolph Gerd von Rundstedt, Adolf Hitler's personal choice to forestall or defeat Allied invasion of Europe, broke a spell of 24-hour silence today with a communique indicating a decisive phase of battle may have been reached.

The communique naturally was widely distributed by Nazi propaganda agencies and alleged the Allies had suffered reverses. But from the historical point of view it was of parallel interest and importance to the first German high command announcement of the last war and was published fully by all London newspapers.

The first official announcement from the Prussian militarist placed above Field Marshal Erwin Rommel in responsibiilty for opposing the Allied offensive, declared that Allied forces had come into contact with German "tactical reserves."

Only a short while before, Al-

(Continued on Page 5, Column 2)

Herald-Express Special Features

BULLETINS

Big Allied Fleet Reported Off Genoa, New Landing in Italy Predicted

By United Press

ZURICH, Switzerland, June 7.—Unconfirmed reports from German-occupied Milan said today that a large Allied fleet has been sighted off Genoa and a landing on the Ligurian coast of northwestern Italy is expected hourly.

Fires Hint Nazis May Be Preparing To Abandon Cherbourg Peninsula

By United Press

LONDON, June 7.—An airman reported today that "there were fires everywhere over the Cherbourg peninsula," indicating the Germans may have begun demolitions, possibly preparatory to withdrawal.

Allied Sky Troops Seize Sector On Normandy Peninsula, Say Nazis

By United Press

LONDON, June 7.—The German Transocean news agency said today that airborne Allied forces had occupied a circular area between Valognes and Carentan on the east side of the Normandy peninsula and opened a corridor to the coast.

Rommel in Command, Rushing 2 Armies to Meet Invaders

By United Press

ALLIED SUPREME HEADQUARTERS, LONDON, June 7.—Front dispatches reported shortly after 4 p. m. today that two German armies personally commanded by Marshal Erwin Rommel were racing toward the beachheads for a counterattack.

Berlin Estimates 2 to 5 Divisions Of Allies Landed During Night

By International News Service

LONDON, June 7.—A Berlin broadcast tonight quoted German estimated as saying that between two and five new Allied divisions were landed in France during last night.

NOTICE

The tremendous demand for The Herald-Express coupled with government restrictions on newsprint forces this newspaper to again omit a large amount of advertising. This newspaper feels that its first duty is to furnish the public with complete news and pictures of the great invasion to liberate Europe.

The omission of considerable amounts of advertising becomes necessary in order to get sufficient print paper to supply as nearly as possible the demand—a demand occasioned by the fact that The Herald and Express is the only Los Angeles newspaper having all four of the great wire services, and hence is in the most favorable position to supply all of the news of the great battles now in progress.

Weather

Those Gray Clouds to Give Way to Sun

Low clouds which hovered over Los Angeles this morning were scheduled to give way to fair weather late today and Thursday, the Weather Bureau reported.

The minimum temperature at dawn today was 58 degrees, rising to 62 shortly before noon.

The official forecast was:

"Fair this afternoon, tonight and Thursday, except night and morning low clouds along the coast and in coastal valleys; slightly cooler in coastal valleys this afternoon, otherwise little change in temperature."

Stocks Off Fractions

Dow-Jones 1 p. m. stock averages:
30 industrials 142.16, off .05.
20 railroads 39.36, off .44.
15 utilities 22.99, off .02.
65 stocks 50.59, off .15.

By Associated Press

NEW YORK, June 7.—Selective buying of lower-priced automotive and civilian manufacturing shares rolled the stock market forward again today, but for the most part the advance was in low gear.

A number of leading steel and oil issues managed to join the fractional rise, although investment and speculative interests alike concentrated chiefly on those equities expected to benefit from peace, such as the air lines.

Nazis Say Big Allied Fleet Off Le Havre

By International News Service

LONDON, June 7.—An Allied armada of more than 100 ships including battleships, cruisers, destroyers and landing craft is now off the French port of Le Havre, the Nazi agency DNB said today.

RECRUITING RECORD

KANSAS CITY, June 7.—(A.P.)—The Maritime Service recruiting office reported record-breaking volunteer enlistments on D-Day. More than 200 signed up.

By WES GALLAGHER
Associated Press Staff Correspondent

SUPREME ADVANCE COMMAND POST, Allied Expeditionary Force, June 7.—Allied troops have struck inland in France in heavy fighting, repulsing Nazi counterblows near Caen, 9 miles from the coast, after clearing the enemy from all their landing beaches and linking up some of the beachheads.

Reports from the Cherbourg Peninsula invasion front showed "decided improvement" at midday, and the Allies are making "considerable progress on the whole front" despite bad weather and stiffening resistance, a headquarters officer said.

Both sides dropped airborne troops into the flaming battlefront, with Allied parachutists and glider troops pouring down early today from a 50-mile-long reinforcing sky train.

Caen is at the base of the Cherbourg Peninsula, and southwest of Le Havre.

Headquarters said front reports showed improvement by midday after being "disappointing" early this morning.

Though the initial beachheads—which the Germans said extended over more than a 50-mile stretch—have been cleared and some linked with those nearby, a few may still be under German artillery fire.

Air headquarters declared the Allied air forces in mammoth support of the invasion thrust had flown more than 71,000 sorties between June 1 and last night.

The huge numbers of airborne Allied troops seized key positions and helped throw back Nazi tank-led counterblows. The Germans likewise rushed parachutists.

Various unconfirmed reports said penetrations had been made as deep as 12 miles at some places, but the fighting was so confused it was doubtful if any regular lines were established.

Berlin said Field Marshal Erwin Rommel was rushing up reserves of the German Seventh and Fifteenth Armies, with battles rapidly increasing to a grand scale.

For four months the Germans have been building an airborne army to fight the invasion, led by Lieut. Gen. Kurt Student, who engineered the landing in Crete. R. A. F. Mosquitos last night destroyed five Junkers-52 troop carriers.

Lieut. Gen. Omar Bradley is commanding U. S. ground

(Continued on Page 6, Column 1)

SEES CROSS-FIRE MOW DOWN YANKS

By JAMES C. M'GLINCY
United Press War Correspondent

LONDON, June 7.—Some of the first assault troops who stormed the French beaches were mowed down by German crossfire, but succeeding waves climbed over their bodies until a foothold was established, an eye-witness who returned from the beachhead reported today.

Bert Brandt, 28, an Acme news photographer, spent a half hour on the beach yesterday and several hours more cruising within gunshot of the landing scene.

"It was hotter than hell over there," Brandt said. "I was at Anzio, but Anzio was nothing like this."

He said the Germans laid down intensive fire on the beaches with well-emplaced machine guns. American casualties were spotty, heavy on some beaches and light on others.

On one beach, Brandt reported, the German machine gunners waited until the landing craft lowered their ramps and then poured deadly fire into the barges. The opposition met by the first wave delayed the landing of demolition parties scheduled to follow with heavy equipment.

The German defenses finally crumbled under the weight of attack and by the time Brandt left the beachhead at 3 p. m.

(Continued on Page 7, Cols. 3-4)

DEMOTE GENERAL FOR D-DAY TALK

By Associated Press

SUPREME HEADQUARTERS, ALLIED EXPEDITIONARY FORCE, June 7.—One of America's best known major generals was demoted to lieutenant colonel and sent home for indicating in advance the time of D-Day.

The supreme command allowed this information to be cabled abroad today after holding it up several weeks for security reasons.

Supreme headquarters would not permit the officer's name to be cabled. He was one of the commanders of the United States Airforce. An army man of long standing, he swiftly felt the supreme command axe after talking indiscreetly at a London cocktail party.

The conversation was said to have taken place almost two months ago when the invasion was expected almost daily. The general was reported to have said in the presence of several persons: "On my honor the invasion will take place before June 15."

His action was reported to security police by a woman guest, and General Eisenhower immediately ordered him reduced to the permanent rank of lieutenant colonel and sent home after an investigation.

THE GUINEA American

7 June 1944 Vol 2 No 60

LONDON: King Haakon of Norway from the Supreme Headquarters in London broadcast to his people a warning not to engage in premature demonstrations or uprisings. This was to organized and unorganized patriot groups.

INVASION

LONDON, 6 June--- In a message to the peoples of the occupied lands of Europe and in particular the people of France, General Eisenhower said, "keep at your jobs...be patient,prepare...your hour will come...those of you who belong to organized resistance movements will receive your orders...others can help by their passive resistance.

WINSTON CHURCHILL in an address to the House of Commons said that the operation has been successfully begun. He said that beach landings were still continuing and that paratroops have landed in the enemy's rear.

LONDON, 6 June---All troops participating in the invasion were read a message from General Eisenhower saying," The eyes of the world are upon you...you are embarking on a crusade... the task will not be easy...the enemy will fight savagely...The United Nations have inflicted great defeat on the German armies on other fronts...Let us all ask the blessing of Almighty God in this task

LONDON, 6 June---Number one communique from the Supreme Headquarters in London last night stated

"Allied naval forces, with the support of Allied Air forces, began landing Allied armies on the coast of northern France." General Eisenhower, the supreme commander issued an order of the day stating that"we will accept nothing less than full victory."

One of the earliest broadcasts said that American,British and Canadian troops landed on one of the heaviest fortified sections of France. Later newscasts said that the invasion coast extended from Le Havre at the mouth of the River Seine to the coast city of Cherbourg. Le Havre is the port city of Paris which is also on the River Seine. Cherbourg is due south of the town of Portsmouth in England.

The Allied Armies began the landings Tuesday morning. One of General Eisenhower's spokesmen in London said that the invasion was in the "naval stage" at present and that it was too early to make a statement on land action. However it was said that paratroops were being used. Berlin radio also confirmed this statement saying that the Allies were streaming ashore in the French Province of Normandy. An Allied spokesman said that there were some casualties on a naval vessel trans porting paratroops.

Very heavy naval bombardments are covering the Allied landings. Also gigantic waves of planes of the Allied Air Forces are supporting the landing troops. An Allied spokesman warned all civilians of northern France and people of other channel coast countries to move inland to a distance of 25 miles from the coast to avoid the heavy bombings which will be absolutely necessary in these reagions.

A late news flash stated that the invasion force of British, American and Canadian ground and paratroops was under the command of General Montgomery.

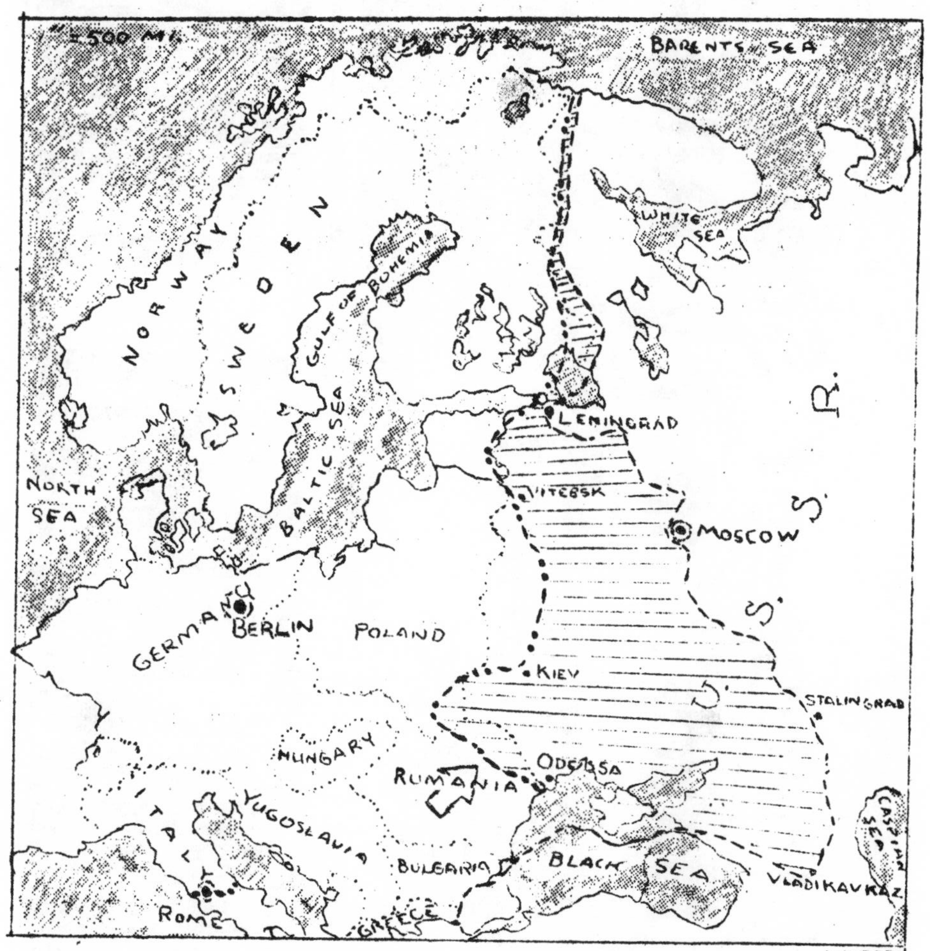

ONE UP— TWO TO GO.

PRESIDENT ROOSEVELT in a broadcast to the nation speaking of Allied success in Italy said,"It is significant that the troops who liberated Rome,the cradle of Christianity, are from many nations... French,English,Americans Canadians, Scotsmen,New Zealanders, Morrocans, Maiores, Punjabis, Gurkhas, Poles and Belgians" He also spoke of the millions of Italions who had migrated to this country and contributed so much to our culture. He said Rome was spared the ruin that Naples suffered because of the strategy of Allied generals which prevented the Nazis from remaining behind to sack the city. If they had done so they would have sacrificed their armies. The people of Rome were on the verge of starvation.

ITALY

NAPLES, 6 June---The occupation of Rome is complete according to reports received tonight. The bulk of the Allied troops have swept thru the city and are chasing the enemy to the north. Only a fifth of the city is reported to have been destroyed.

FLASH--- General Eisenhower spent most of Monday night visiting Para troops at airports in England as they boarded planes for France...

Over 1,200 enemy vehicles were destroyed on Sunday alone. Over 22, 000 captives were taken. Our losses were 20,000 killed in the Anzio drive according to Winston Churchill. The Nazis lost 25,000 dead

RUSSIA

MOSCOW, 6 June---A strong Nazi attack at Jassey in Rumanio has been repulsed by the Red army with heavy losses being inflicted on the enemy. The above map shows the line of Germany's furthest advance into the Soviet Union and the present Battle line.

FLASHES- Berlin radio says that Hitler will take personal command of Nazi defense forces... 640 naval guns hammered the invasion coast... Greatest mine sweeping operation in history was made... British radio says Allies are landing in Normandy... No serious Luftwaffe action... Dieppe taking heavy air smashes...De Gaulle is in London; he is expected to speak to the people of France........

New York World-Telegram

2nd NIGHT
Latest Wall Street Prices
Five Cents

Local Forecast: This afternoon and tonight clear, light winds. Tomorrow partly cloudy, continued warm.

SCRIPPS-HOWARD VOL. 76—NO. 290—IN TWO SECTIONS—SECTION ONE. NEW YORK, MONDAY, JUNE 12, 1944 Entered as second class matter Post Office, New York, N. Y.

Pyle Gives Vivid Closeup of Scene On Beachhead Hard-Won by Allies

By ERNIE PYLE,
World-Telegram War Correspondent.

NORMANDY BEACHHEAD (by Wireless).—Due to a last-minute alteration in the arrangements, I didn't arrive on the beachhead until the morning after D-Day, after our first wave of assault troops had hit the shore.

Ernie Plye.

By the time we got here the beaches had been taken and the fighting had moved a couple of miles inland. All that remained on the beach was some sniping and artillery fire and the occasional startling blast of a mine geysering brown sand into the air. That, plus a gigantic and pitiful litter of wreckage along miles of shoreline.

Submerged tanks and overturned boats and burned trucks and shell-shattered jeeps and sad little personal belongings were strewn all over these bitter sands. That, plus the bodies of soldiers lying in rows covered with blankets, the toes of their shoes sticking up in a line as though on drill. And other bodies, uncollected, still sprawling grotesquely in the sand or half-hidden by the high grass beyond the beach.

That, plus an intense, grim determination of work-weary men to get this chaotic beach organized and get all the vital supplies and the reinforcements moving more rapidly over it from the stacked-up ships standing in droves out to sea.

Victory a Miracle.

Now that it is over it seems to me a pure miracle that we ever took the beach at all. For some of our units it was easy, but in this special sector where I am now our troops faced such odds that our getting ashore was like my whipping Joe Louis down to a pulp.

In this column I want to tell you what the opening of the second front in this one sector entailed, so that you can know and appreciate and forever be humbly grateful to those, both dead and alive, who did it for you.

Ashore, facing us, were more enemy troops than we had in our assault waves. The advantages were all theirs, the disadvantages all ours. The Germans were dug into positions that they had been working on for months, although these were not yet all complete. A 100-foot bluff a couple of hundred yards back from the beach had great concrete gun emplacements built right into the hilltop. These opened to the sides instead of to the front, thus making it very hard for naval fire from the sea to reach them. They could shoot parallel with the beach and cover every foot of it for miles with artillery fire.

A Strong West Wall.

Then they had hidden machine-gun nests on the forward slopes, with crossfire taking in every inch of the beach. These nests were connected by networks of trenches, so that the German gunners could move about without exposing themselves.

Throughout the length of the beach, running zigzag a couple of hundred yards back from the shoreline, was an immense V-shaped ditch 15 feet deep. Nothing could cross it, not even men on foot, until fills had been made. And in other places at the far end of the beach, where the ground is flatter, they had great concrete walls. These were blasted by our naval gunfire or by explosives set by hand after we got ashore.

Our only exits from the beach were several swales or valleys, each about 100 yards wide. The Germans made the most of these funnel-like traps, sowing them with buried mines. They contained, also, barbed-wire entanglements with mines attached, hidden ditches and

(Continued on Page Two.)

CRACK CHERBOURG LINE

Nazis Abandon Carentan; Uprisings Spread; Reds Pour into Finland; Rout in Italy Grows

Finns Near Rout as Reds Race Through 25-Mile Gap In Mannerheim Line

By M. S. HANDLER,
United Press Staff Correspondent.

MOSCOW, June 12.—Karelian front dispatches said today that miles-long columns of Russian tanks, guns and troops were pouring through the broken Mannerheim Line above Leningrad in hot pursuit of Finnish forces retreating so fast they were unable to blow up roads and bridges.

"The turn of the Finnish satellites has come," the newspaper Pravda said of the Red Army offensive to knock Finland out of the war. "The Germans didn't help the Finns. The Germans aren't going to save the Finns. The same fate awaits Germany and her other satellites."

25-Mile Gap Opened.

Reports from the first front blasted open by the Red Army in its summer offensive indicated that the Finns manning the defenses across the Karelian Isthmus were beaten badly in the first few hours and now were in precipitate flight.

The initial impact of Gen. Govorov's assault crashed through the Mannerheim Line on a 25-mile front, and in 36 hours the Russians had advanced 15 miles within 48 miles of Viipuri, first big objective in the Soviet push which broke a lull of 31 months on the Finnish front.

(A Finnish communique reported intense fighting all day and night on the western part of the Karelian Isthmus. Tank-led Russian forces repeatedly attacked Finnish fortifications, it said, claiming that 18 Soviet tanks were knocked out.)

Soviet editorial comment and front dispatches made it evident

(Continued on Page Eight.)

Glides In, Kills 11, Flees Nazi Captors

By the Associated Press.

AT A NINTH AIR FORCE TROOP CARRIER BASE, June 12.—In a few hours of fast action Glider Pilot R. B. Fowler killed 11 Germans, was taken prisoner and escaped back to the American lines on a stolen Nazi motorcycle.

When the flight officer's glider crash-landed in Normandy on D-day Fowler killed nine Nazis with a hand grenade and his rifle. He was knocked unconscious then, and when he awoke he was a captive.

He was taken to regimental headquarters. A German colonel drove up and Fowler threw a hand grenade which the Nazis had overlooked in his pocket when they searched him. It killed the colonel and another soldier.

Fowler fled with the colonel's binoculars and carbine.

"All I'm waiting for now is the next tow job," he said.

Postwar Kitchens

If you have been visualizing miracles for your postwar kitchen you'll be interested in the first article of a new series, Your POSTWAR HOME in which Gertrude Bailey reveals what you actually will see and what you won't find in your peacetime kitchen. Start reading this timely series today on the WOMAN'S PAGE, 21.

Corporal's Girl Is Too Secretive

By the Associated Press.

CAMP PICKETT, Va., June 12.—Cpl. Lewis H. Applegarth, Cadiz, Ohio, thinks his feminine correspondent is taking too seriously the Army's admonition, Button Your Lip.

He received a letter saying simply: "I'll be in town for the week end." What's worrying the corporal is: (1) What week end? (2) What town? (3) Who's the girl?

World-Telegram Index

Sky Clear, Channel Smooth at Dover

By the Associated Press.

LONDON, June 12.—The sky over Dover Strait was blue and cloudless today. Visibility was good and the surface of the sea was barely ruffled by a light westerly wind.

The barometer rose steadily during the night after a drizzle of rain and there were indications that a period of fair weather might be expected. The temperature was in the 70s at 8 a. m.

Ration-Free Shoes On Sale July 10

By the Associated Press.

WASHINGTON, June 12.—Shoe purchasers will have a chance at about 7,000,000 pairs ration free from July 10 to July 29 during a national odd-lot sale, the OPA announced today. The shoes must cost at least 25 per cent less than their price on June 1, OPA declared.

This odd-lot sale will include footwear for men and women, boys sizes 1 to 6, but not children's, misses' and little boys' shoes which were included in the temporarily ration free shoes for three weeks in May.

Push High Above Rome Smashes 14th Army of Germany as Fighting Unit

By ROBERT V. VERMILLION,
United Press War Correspondent.

ALLIED HQ., NAPLES, June 12.—The triumphant Allied Fifth Army raced almost unopposed over the coastal and mountain highways 51 to 70 miles above Rome today and a headquarters spokesman announced that the German 14th Army ,which once numbered 150,000 veteran troops, "has ceased to exist" as a fighting force.

All semblance of organized resistance vanished in the path of the Fifth Army columns and official reports said the Nazi retreat had become a chaotic rout. Isolated bands of Germans were fleeing on foot and in horsedrawn farm carts, battling each other to the death for trucks and cars in a panicky race to escape.

Rear Guard Fails.

A few enemy rear guards, never more than one or two companies strong, attempted vainly to stem the Allied advance, but they were annihilated by Lt. Gen. Mark W. Clark's tank crews and riflemen.

Simultaneously, British Eighth Army columns drove the battered German 10th Army in headlong retreat on a broad front extending from the east bank of the Tiber 30 miles above Rome to the mouth of the Pescara River, on the Adriatic coast.

With their right flank exposed by the collapse of Nazi Gen. Eberhard von Mackensen's 14th Army, the 10th Army appeared to be pulling out at top speed to escape encirclement in the central and eastern Appenines.

Tanks Roll Ahead.

American tanks and infantry forces on the coastal flank of the advancing Fifth Army made the deepest penetration into the

(Continued on Page Twelve.)

Fifth War Loan Drive Opens

Millions of persons across the nation today prepared to back up the greatest battle for liberation in history with the greatest war financing effort in history.

The national quota of the Fifth War Loan, which starts officially today, is $16,000,000,000, of which New Yorkers will be called upon to subscribe more than a quarter—a minimum of $4,167,028,000 in War Bonds. The quota for the entire state is $4,801,000,000, nearly one-third of the national goal.

As in previous campaigns the individual purchaser must be the spearhead of the nation's financial attack. The city's quota calls for $227,526,600 worth of Series E bonds—those that start at $18.75 for a $25 bond.

Today has been officially designated Civilian D-Day in New York. Mayor La Guardia, War Finance Committee officials, war

(Continued on Page Six.)

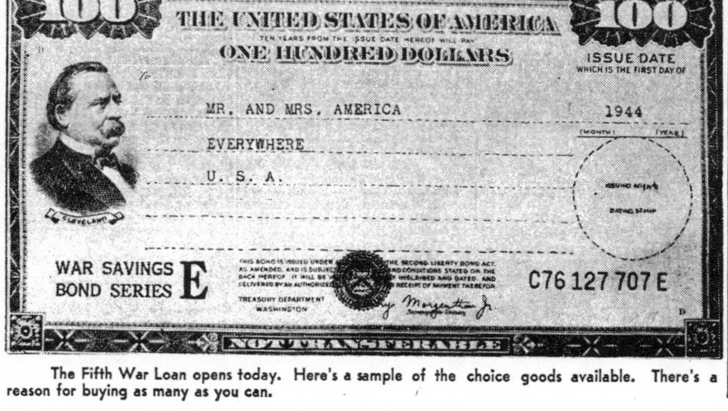

The Fifth War Loan opens today. Here's a sample of the choice goods available. There's a reason for buying as many as you can.

French Patriots Go Into Action

By JOHN A. PARRIS,
United Press Staff Correspondent.

LONDON, June 12.—Unprecedented uprisings were reported throughout France today in Spanish dispatches from the French frontier as German-controlled radio stations warned all patriots they would be shot and said that the big naval base of Toulon, on the southern coast had been bombarded by Allied naval vessels.

Travelers reaching the Spanish frontier said that approximately a half million French patriots were taking part in the uprisings, particularly in the Tarbes and Toulouse areas in southwestern France, and had engaged German troops and French militiamen in bloody fights.

[Earlier reports from Spain said French guerrillas had occupied Toulouse, Limoges and Tarbes, the Associated Press reported, but Frenchmen at the Spanish border said that Toulouse was so strongly garrisoned that it was unlikely that the French would challenge the Nazis there.]

Supplied by Parachute.

The patriots were said to be well armed, possibly with supplies and equipment parachuted by the Allies. Sabotage was widespread, it was said, with main roads and railroads blocked or torn up.

Reliable reports reaching Spain said all communication between Bordeaux and Paris had been interrupted, with confusion on the seriously damaged roads worse than during the time France fell.

Radio information obtained in

(Continued on Page Two.)

'Give 'Em Hell!' Says 7th to 8th

By the United Press.

PEARL HARBOR, June 12.—Members of the U. S. 7th Army Air Force sent this message to the British-based 8th Air Force, which is bombing Europe:

"Give 'em hell—We'll take care of Tokyo!"

The Weather

New York and Metropolitan Area: This afternoon partly cloudy, warmer, highest temperature 85 degrees, winds becoming moderate to fresh. Tonight partly cloudy, mild, lowest temperature 65 degrees.

New Jersey; This afternoon fair, moderate temperature.

TODAY'S READINGS.

	Temp.	Hum.		Temp.	Hum.
Midnight	71	..	5 a. m.	66	..
1 a. m.	69	..	6 a. m.	66	64
2 a. m.	68	..	7 a. m.	67	3
3 a. m.	67	..	8 a. m.	68	61
4 a. m.	66	..	9 a. m.	72	50
			10 a. m.	74	47

High and low a year ago, 75-66.

Americans Reach St. Lo's Outskirts, Berlin Reports; British 9 Miles East of Caen

By VIRGIL PINKLEY,
United Press War Correspondent.

SUPREME ALLIED HQ., LONDON, June 12.—The Germans announced the abandonment of Carentan, their main defense hinge between Caen and Cherbourg, today while American flanking columns to the north and south swept to within less than a dozen miles of Cherbourg itself and pushed into the Cerisy Forest on the approaches to St. Lo.

London newspapers quoted the German Transocean News Agency as saying that the Allies had reached the outskirts of St. Lo, transport center 15 miles south of Carentan.

[The Germans' Cherbourg peninsula line was cracking wide open at its center, the Associated Press said, and Nazi defenses also appeared in danger of giving way at Caen, the hinge of the line to the east. Field dispatches reported that Caen was virtually surrounded and already was being bypassed by flanking assaults. British forces have battled nine miles east of Caen in the threatened encirclement. This put the British near Troane.]

American troops, strongly supported by a naval bombardment from the sea, virtually had surrounded Carentan yesterday and last Allied reports had told of bitter hand-to-hand fighting in the outskirts with crack German forces who had rejected a surrender ultimatum.

The German Transocean Agency said the garrison evacuated Carentan "in order to continue the fight in terrain not so strongly opposed by naval artillery." Less than an hour later the German High Command confirmed the loss of Carentan in a communique which said the city was evacuated after heavy fighting. It added that Allied warships had opened a heavy bombardment on Nazi coastal defenses around St. Vaast la Hougue.

NEW LANDINGS REPORTED.

[Continuing a stream of reports of new Allied landings, Berlin's Transocean News Agency, according to the Associated Press, said seaborne forces had been put ashore at St. Vaast, which is near the top of the peninsula and 15 miles east of Cherbourg.] Transocean broadcast that fresh Allied airborne troops were landed south of Caen, but were destroyed except for "inconsiderable elements."

The fall of Carentan, flood control defense point 27 miles southeast of Cherbourg and a few miles inland from the west coast, was expected to pave the way for an American smash across the narrow waist of the Normandy Peninsula in an effort to cut the enemy's remaining north-south communications and isolate Cherbourg, railhead of a trunk railway to Paris and one of the best ports on the French coast.

Carentan is one of the principal junctions on the main Cherbourg-Paris railway and highway, but both previously had been cut to the northwest and to the east. From Carentan, the American probably will fan out toward the west coast junctions of La Haye De Puits, 13 miles to the west; Lessay, 14 miles to the southwest ,and Periers, 11 miles to the southwest.

TERRIFIC AERIAL COVER.

As the ground forces smashed ahead a fleet of possibly

(Continued on Page Two.)

Nazis Abandon Carentan as Cherbourg Line Begins to Crack

New Landings from the Sea Reported East of Key Port; Americans Drive on St. Lo

(Continued from Page One.)

1750 American heavy bombers and fighters struck the chain of German fighter bases behind the French coast, while more than 3000 other Allied warplanes swarmed over the Norman battlefields under rapidly clearing skies that promised the embattled doughboys their strongest aerial cover since D-Day.

The beachhead situation sector by sector:

South of Cherbourg—American troops fought their way into the outskirts of Montebourg, 14 miles southeast of Cherbourg, and also pushed around Montebourg to within 12 miles of Cherbourg.

Between Montebourg and Carentan—American forces forced the Merderet River a third of the way across the Cherbourg Peninsula after cutting both the Cherbourg-Jaris highway and railway. Vichy radio said the doughboys had pushed into Quineville on the east coast.

[The Associated Press put Lt. Gen. Omar N. Bradley's American doughboys halfway across the peninsula neck one a four-mile front between Qeureville and Montebourg and said they were smashing the last 12 miles to complete the cutoff of Cherbourg, whose docks and wharves would open to Allied forces their first great base on French soil.]

Southeast of Isigny—American troops advanced into the Cerisy forests on the approaches of St. Lo after a six-mile advance in 24 hours from Lisbon.

Tilly-sur-Seulles—British and Canadian troops held firm in the face of increasingly heavy German counterattacks designed to split the Allied beachhead.

Caen—Battle for Caen went into its sixth day of seesaw fighting, with British forces building up strength for an all-out assault on the town, southeastern anchor of the German line. [The Associated Press reported that the Berlin radio said major British forces were concentrating north of Caen and said the full force of the assault was expected to break upon the town during the day.]

25 Allied Divisions Seen.

German broadcasts estimated that the Allies have poured 20 seaborne and five airborne divisions—more than 350,000 troops—into their 50 to 60-mile beachhead along the north coast of Normandy. This equals "one-third of their invasion forces stationed in Britain," the Transocean agency said. ["The bulk of the huge forces of the 21st Amphibious Army group is still standing by to pounce on some important harbor," the German radio declared, according to the Associated press.]

The Germans were using 60-ton Tiger tanks in their attacks around a 15-mile arc before Tilly-sur-Seulles, 30 miles east southeast of Carentan, and a dispatch from the 21st Army group headquarters said it appeared to wedge through the beachhead to the sea.

Adm. Sir Bertram Ramsay, Allied naval commander, said on his return from the assault area that he was "very satisfied with the development and progress made."

"The invasion was made under the worst possible conditions," Adm. Ramsay said. "The weather was bad and it must have shaken up the troops long before they landed. Everything is going well, but we have many damaged landing craft lying on the beaches.

"What we need is a permanent bridge to the bridgehead. Once we get this everything may happen over on the other side."

Strong Aerial Support.

A note of "sober satisfaction" at current progress prevailed at supreme headquarters and Gen. Sir Bernard L. Montgomery, commander of the Allied ground forces in France, said his men "have achieved great success and have placed themselves in a good position from which to exploit this success."

Sunny skies over the Channel ushered in what was expected to be the biggest aerial assault in support of the ground forces since D-Day last Tuesday.

Striking furiously to deprive the hard pressed German coastal armies of their last vestiges of air support, almost 1000 American Flying Fortresses and Liberators ranged over a vast arc of northern France to bomb and burn "many" of the enemy's vital advanced air bases.

750 Fighters Strafe Nazis.

Up to 750 Thunderbolt, Lightning and Mustang fighters accompanied the giant raiders and swooped in low to dive-bomb and machine gun Nazi fighter nests.

Among the chief objectives blasted by the American heavies were major enemy airdromes within a 60-mile arc of the Channel coast.

Simultaneously other American heavy bombers raced in behind the coastal battle lines to send tons of blockbusters crashing down on bridges and road lines over which the Nazis were rushing supplies and reinforcements to the beachheads. [The Associated Press said Field Marshal Karl Gerd von Runstedt was rushing reserves up from as far back as Paris to meet the mounting menace of the Allied purge, but his new men and guns, and the roads over which they moved, were under bomb, cannon, rocket and machine-gun fire of an Allied air armada.]

Some Enemy Opposition.

Some enemy fighter opposition was encountered in the American sweeps and early reports indicated that the Luftwaffe, after a week of mysterious inactivity, might be ready to open its battle for the defense of Hitler's shaken West Wall.

A force of American Thunderbolts that streaked down on German troop columns behind the Norman coast at dawn today was jumped unexpectedly by about 50 Nazi fighters that gave the Americans their "roughest" battle since the invasion began.

While the American heavies were on the attack, swarms of medium and fighter bombers maintained a steady barrage of bombs and gunfire on the enemy's front line positions and communications, including an American Marauder raid on targets around the Vire River south of St. Lo.

By midday the Allied air forces had flown about 4000 sorties and that figure appeared certain to mount toward or beyond the 10,000 mark before nightfall, as the weather took a definite turn for the better.

As the tempo of the Allied air attack increased, Allied warships joined the bombardment of German guns and reinforcements. Among the warships were the U. S. battleships Navada and Texas, and the cruisers Tuscaloosa and Quincy.

The American 29th Division and other American forces surged into the Cerisy forests, only a few miles above St. Lo, strategic highway and railway junction 48 miles below Cherbourg and almost half-way across the Normandy peninsula, following a speedy six-mile advance from Lison, which fell only 24 hours earlier.

Fresh Troops Pour In—and There Is Need

Official U. S. Coast Guard Photo from Acme Newspictures.

On this Coast Guard-manned assault transport, troops wait for the arrival of a landing barge bringing wounded men. As the casualties are transferred to the larger ship, those now on board will take their places in the barge and go in to reinforce beachhead forces in France.

Photo by Bert Brand Acme Newspictures Radiotelephoto, via Army Radiotelephoto.

Friend and foe—the bodies of American and German soldiers lie still in death. It's France. They'll be buried when the battle, raging nearby, is over.

Pyle Gives Vivid Closeup Of Beachhead

(Continued from Page One.)

machine guns firing from the slopes.

This is what was on the shore. But our men had to go through a maze nearly as deadly as this before they even got ashore. Underwater obstacles were terrific. The Germans had whole fields of evil devices under the water to catch our boats. Even now, several days after the landing, we have cleared only channels through them and cannot yet approach the whole length of the beach with our ships. Even now some ship or boat hits one of these mines every day and is knocked out of commission.

The Germans had masses of those great six-pronged spiders, made of railroad iron and standing shoulder high, just beneath the surface of the water for our landing craft to run into. They also had huge logs buried in the sand, pointing upward and outward, their tops just below the water. Attached to these logs were mines.

In addition to these obstacles they had floating mines offshore, land mines buried in the sand of the beach, and more mines in checkerboard rows in the tall grass beyond the sand. And the enemy had four men on shore for every three men we had approaching the shore.

And yet we got on.

Wall Wouldn't Budge.

Beach landings are planned to a schedule that is set far ahead of time. They all have to be timed in order for everything to mesh and for the following waves of troops to be standing off the beach and ready to land at the right moment. As the landings are planned, some elements of the assault force are to break through quickly, push on inland, and attack the most obvious enemy strong points. It is usually the plan for units to be inland, attacking gun positions from behind, within a matter of minutes after the first men hit the beach.

I have always been amazed at the speed called for in these plans. You'll have schedules calling for engineers to land at H-hour plus two minutes, and service troops at H-hour plus 30 minutes, and even for press censors to land at H-hour plus 75 minutes. But in the attack on this special portion of the beach where I am—the worst we had, incidentally—the schedule didn't hold.

Our men simply could not get past the beach. They were pinned down right on the water's edge by an inhuman wall of fire from the bluff. Our first waves were on that beach for hours, instead of a few minutes, before they could begin working inland.

Navy Helped Spike Guns.

You can still see the foxholes they dug at the very edge of the water, in the sand and the small, jumbled rocks that form parts of the beach.

Medical corpsmen attended the wounded as best they could. Men were killed as they stepped out of landing craft. An officer whom I knew got a bullet through the head just as the door of his landing craft was let down. Some men were drowned.

The first crack in the beach defenses was finally accomplished by terrific and wonderful naval gunfire, which knocked out the big emplacements. They tell epic stories of destroyers that ran right up into shallow water and had it out point-blank with the big guns in those concrete emplacements ashore.

When the heavy fire stopped our men were organized by their officers and pushed on inland, circling machine-gun nests and taking them from the rear.

As one officer said, the only way to take a beach is to face it and keep going. It is costly at first, but it's the only way. If the men are pinned down on the beach, dug in, and out of action, they might as well not be there at all. They hold up the waves behind them, and nothing is being gained.

Odds with the Enemy.

Our men were pinned down for a while, but finally they stood up and went through, and so we took that beach and accomplished our landing. We did it with every advantage on the enemy's side and every disadvantage on ours. In the light on a couple of days of retrospection, we sit and talk and call it a miracle that our men ever got on at all or were able to stay on.

Before long it will be permitted to name the units that did it. Then you will know to whom this glory should go. They suffered casualties. And yet if you take the entire beachhead assault, including other units that had a much easier time, our total casualties in driving this wedge into the continent of Europe were remarkably low—only a fraction, in fact, of what our commanders had been prepared to accept.

And these units that were so battered and went through such hell are still, right at this moment, pushing on inland without rest, their spirits high, their egotism in victory almost reaching the smart-alecky stage.

Their tails are up. "We've done it again," they say. They figure that the rest of the army isn't needed at all. Which proves that, while their judgment in this regard is bad, they certainly have the spirit that wins battles and eventually wars.

Quake Shakes Coast

By the Associated Press.

LOS ANGELES, June 12.—A sharp earth shock, sufficient to awaken residents of nearby Pasadena and Laguna Beach, was reported at 3:45 a. m., Pacific war time, today. Police said windows and dishes rattled, but there were no immediate reports of damage.

Carentan Abandoned

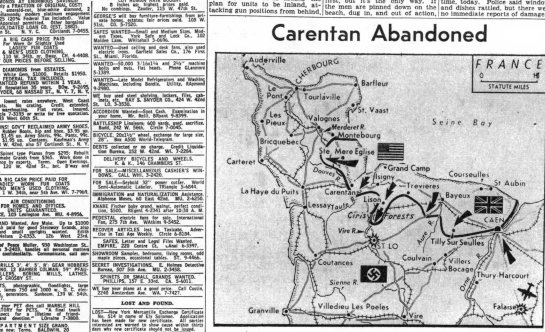

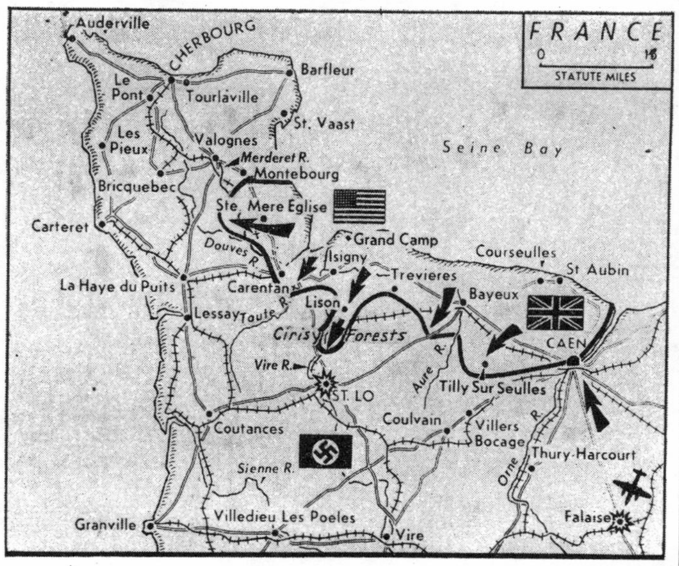

A. P. Map.

The Germans today admitted the evacuation of Carentan, main hinge between Caen and Cherbourg, while Nazi defenses appeared to be giving way at Caen itself, which was almost surrounded. Americans at the south swept into the Cerisy Forests on the approach to St. Lo. At the west invading forces were within 12 miles of Cherbourg and at the east British and Canadians fought against tank units in the Tilly-sur-Seulles area. Berlin's Transocean radio said seaborne forces had put ashore at St. Vaast, 15 miles east of Cherbourg.

'That From These Honored Dead—'

By JOHN A. MOROSO, 3rd,
Associated Press Staff Writer.

AN AMERICAN BEACHHEAD CEMETERY, France, June 9 (Delayed).—Stretched out with their pitiful personal belongings lying beside them on this bomb-blasted, shell-scorched bit of the Normandy beach lie the American dead—men and boys who paid the supreme price for wresting this strongly fortified position from the Nazis.

They lie here mutely waiting while troops dig long trenches for temporary mass burial. Nearby, also awaiting burial, are the bodies of 10 Germans and two Britons.

Negro troops digging these common graves labor silently, with an occasional awed glance at the stiff forms under the white covers.

This is America's first cemetery in France in this war.

It is not a pretentious place. A few days ago it was a German minefield separating the beach defenses from the rugged pill boxes and forts in a steep hill that rises a few hundred yards from the ugly, rock-strewn beaches.

The battle was so fierce that our grave registration officers—men who bury the dead and tell the folks at home about them—had to spend most of their time in foxholes. When the enemy retreated into the hills these officers gathered their weary men and began bringing bodies to this place—where the grass is turned black from the fury of high explosives.

Another cemetery is being prepared nearby because this hallowed ground is too small to care for the men who will not fight again.

Task Force Pounding Mariannas Again

By WILLIAM F. TYREE,

PEARL HARBOR, June 12.—A two-way aerial offensive on enemy bases protecting the Philippines appeared under way today following the second attack by a powerful U. S. Pacific fleet task force on the Marianas and the first land-based raid by Liberator bombers on Palau Island.

Virtually all types of combat ships, including battleships, were believed to have comprised the task force which battered the islands of Saipan, Tinian and Guam.

The assault came a day after Liberator bombers from the Southwest Pacific made their initial daylight raid on Palau, 560 miles east of the Philippines.

A brief communique by Adm. Nimitz described the task force as "powerful," indicating use of hundreds of carrier-based planes.

After the attack the fleet resumed radio silence. Task force operations usually are not disclosed until the fleet has returned to safe waters.

The last carrier-based attack on the Marianas was made Feb. 21.

In the raid on Palau Liberators caught the Japs by surprise, destroyed 22 parked enemy planes and returned without loss.

Other Liberators from Gen. MacArthur's command hit Truk for the fifth time this month. The Americans again met strong opposition by 30 fighters but dropped 60 tons of bombs. Three enemy planes were shot down or damaged. One Liberator was lost.

American Mitchells continued attacks on enemy shipping along the northwestern Dutch New Guinea coast, sinking a 1000-ton freighter, six coastal vessels and a barge off Manokwari, west of Biak Island.

Two goals to meet . . . on the WAR FRONT, the drive to Berlin. On the HOME FRONT, 16 billion dollars in WAR BONDS. Buy now . . . TODAY and every week . . . for the duration.

Shuttle Raiders Hit Foe in Balkans

By HARRISON SALISBURY,
United Press War Correspondent.

EASTERN COMMAND USSTAF, Russia, June 12.—A co-ordinated force, comprising more than 1000 American heavy bombers and fighters from Russian and Italian bases smashed four enemy air and communications centers in Romania and Yugoslavia yesterday in the path of an anticipated Red Army land drive into the Balkans.

With some of the planes using the new shuttle system between Italy and Russia, the American aerial forces battered the German communication points at Constanta, Romanian Black Sea port; Giurgui, south of Bucharest on the Bulgarian border; Focsani, 130 miles northwest of the Romanian capital, and the rail center of Smederovo, southeast of Belgrade, Yugoslavia.

One plane from the entire raiding force was lost and returning crew members reported they obtained excellent bombing results in the raid, carried out in excellent weather.

The shuttle mission was the third since American planes landed at Russian bases on June 2, personally led by Lt. Gen. Ira C. Eaker, commander of the Mediterranean Allied Air Forces who returned to Italy yesterday.

French Patriots Go Into Action

(Continued from Page One.)

Algiers from inside France said that Grenoble, near the Italian border, had been isolated for the last two days by French resistance forces, and a Zurich dispatch said the patriots were trying to storm the town.

As reports of similar uprisings in other areas, especially southern France, continued to come in from various sources, Vichy and Paris radios disclosed that German occupation authorities had taken over a vast area of central France, including the Vichy sector, and assumed executive power in the Departments of Allier, Cantal Hauteloire and Pu de Dome.

(Swiss and Swedish newspaper dispatches reported by the OWI said the Nazis had begun to execute hostages in reprisal for French patriot activity. Several hundred persons already were reported executed, and the OWI quoted the Swiss Courier de Geneve that 25 hostages had been "shot dead on the spot" at Annemasse alone.)

Swiss dispatches here also reported serious patriot attacks in the area near the Swiss frontier where the Germans established martial law in the railroad center of Bellegarde and carried out mass arrests in Lyon after ousting the police force and bringing in another from Loire.

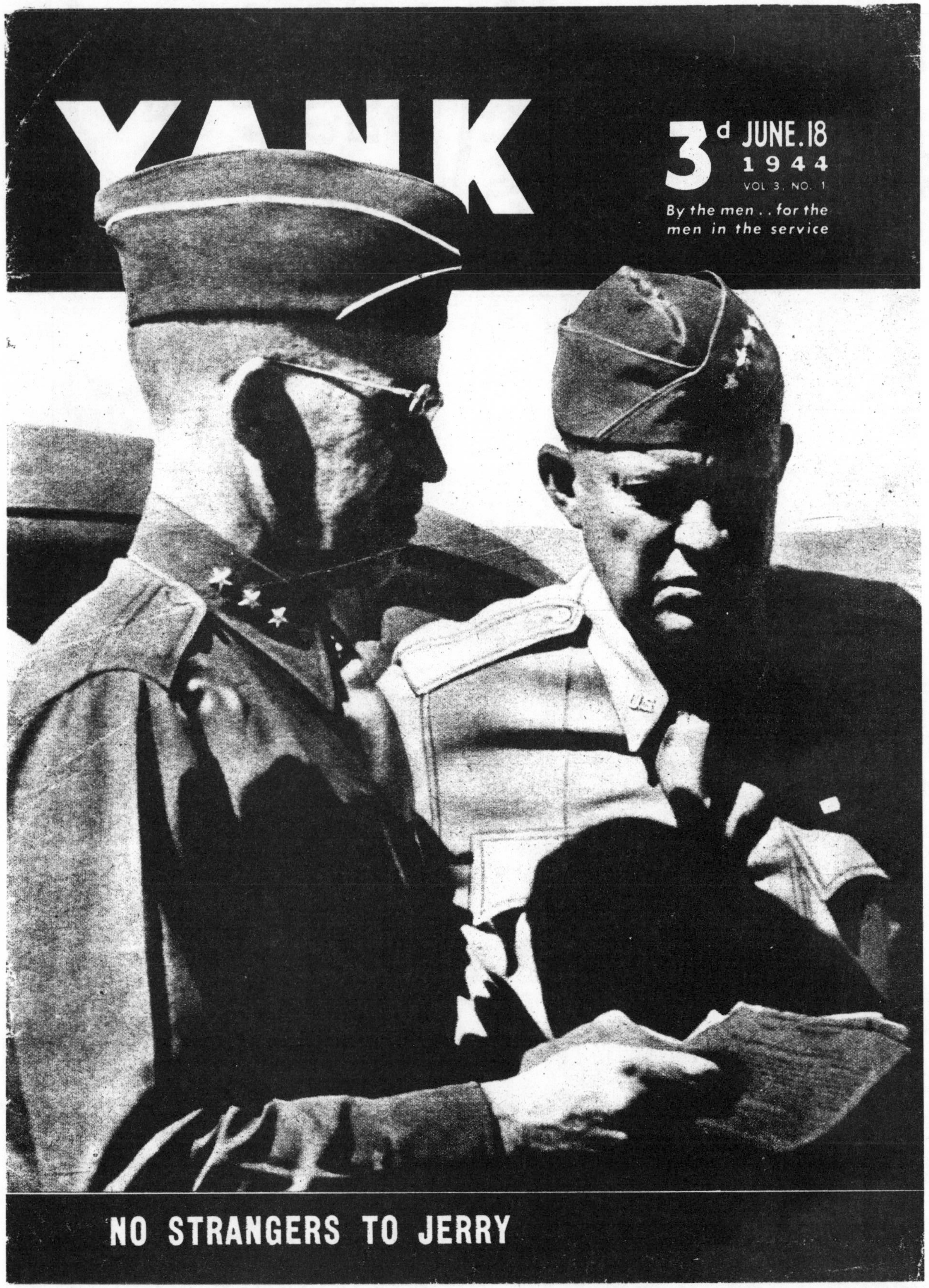

A YANK correspondent, who marched 500 miles through the jungle with this volunteer force, tells about our first infantry battle on the continent of Asia.

By Sgt. DAVE RICHARDSON
YANK Staff Correspondent

BEHIND JAPANESE LINES IN NORTHERN BURMA—The crackle of a couple of Nambu light machine guns and the whipsnap of Arisaka rifles stopped the single-file column of Merrill's Marauders and sent the men scrambling for cover on both sides of the narrow jungle trail.

They had trudged nearly 250 miles in the last four weeks. After marching up 116 miles of the Ledo Road, they had swung wide around the Jap positions that were holding up the Chinese drive in the Hukawng Valley of Northern Burma. They had followed narrow native paths and elephant trails through dense undergrowth and high elephant grass and across dozens of rivers and streams.

This was to be the first of their missions as a volunteer raiding outfit behind Jap lines—attacking the enemy rear supply base of Walawbum to force a Jap withdrawal 30 miles northward so the Chinese could push through. The Marauders, led by Brig. Gen. Frank D. Merrill, who had walked out of Burma with Stilwell two years before, were this afternoon only three miles from their goal.

The CO of the unit that had bumped into Jap resistance sent for 1st Lt. Logan E. Weston of Youngstown, Ohio. A slim, quiet poker-faced young officer, Weston edged his way through the brush to the CO's side.

"Weston," said the CO, "take your intelligence and reconnaissance platoon across the river and move south to a position near the riverbank that will cover us from the Walawbum area when we drive through this village of Lagang Ga on the east bank."

Lt. Weston, like most of the others in this Marauder unit, had fought Japs before. Quitting Transylvania Bible School in Freeport, Pa., midway through his study for the ministry, he had joined the Army. He went to the South Pacific as a squad leader in the 37th Division, he was graduated from OCS in the Fijis, and then he fought in New Georgia as a platoon leader in the 37th. That's where he picked up a nickname.

"Fightin' Preacher," his men called him. As one of his original platoon explained it, "Lt. Weston continued his Bible study in spare moments, but when we got into a scrap with the Japs he was one of the fightingest platoon leaders in the division."

In New Georgia the Fightin' Preacher had always made one point clear to his men: he did not like to kill. After each action he got his men aside and said, half-apologetically: "I'm sorry I had to kill those Japs, fellas, but today it was a case of either my getting them or their getting me."

Lt. Weston's tough, swaggering platoon was a marked contrast to its gentle, mild-mannered leader. Among his men were such veterans as Cpl. Werner Katz of New York, N. Y., who fought with the International Brigade in the Spanish Civil War and with the Americal Division on Guadalcanal. Katz, a burly first scout, became the first American infantryman to kill a Jap on the continent of Asia when the platoon had a fleeting brush with a Jap patrol the week before.

Then there was Pfc. Norman J. (Chief) Janis, a full-blooded Sioux Indian and former rodeo rider from Deadwood, S. Dak., who thought it was a bad day during the Buna battle in New Guinea if he had to use more than one bullet to kill a Jap. And Sgt. William L. Grimes of Lonaconing, Md., who won the Silver Star for knocking off 25 Japs at Guadalcanal. And a couple of dozen others who had battled Japs in the jungles and swamps of the South and Southwest Pacific. They had all volunteered for this "dangerous and hazardous" jungle-fighting mission.

THE Fightin' Preacher's men got to their feet and slung on their 60-pound horseshoe-type packs. They moved through the dark jungle undergrowth down to the muddy little river and crossed it Indian file, wading 40 feet to the

MORTAR CREW THAT COVERED ADVANCE: LT. WOOMER, PVT. ALDERMAN, SGT. KOPEC, PVT. McGOWAN.

HE DOESN'T LIKE TO KILL, BUT LT. LOGAN WESTON, THE "FIGHTIN' PREACHER," HAS KILLED PLENTY OF JAPS.

TWO DEAD JAPS, SLAIN BY ANOTHER PATROL, LINE MARAUDERS' PATH THROUGH THE 10-FOOT KUNAI GRASS.

Merrill's Marauders in Burma

other side through crotch-deep water. Then, rifles cradled in their arms, they climbed the bank.

They rustled their way through the brush alongside the riverbank all afternoon, cautiously covering a few hundred yards. Once or twice the scouts spotted Jap sentries and traded a few bullets with them, but the Japs got away. Just before dusk the platoon halted and dug in a perimeter of foxholes to spend the night. They could hear the main body of Marauders pushing through the Jap resistance across the river, using lots of tommy guns and BARs.

The men ate no supper; they had run out of K rations two days before. (While the Marauders were behind the Jap lines, they were supplied entirely by airdrop and there were never any drops when the men were sneaking close to their objectives, because this might reveal their position and strength.) There was nothing for the men to do but decide on the hours of perimeter guard and then curl up in blanket and poncho and go to sleep.

By dawn the next morning the Fightin' Preacher's platoon was on the move again. The scouts had located a bend in the river from which the platoon could command a wide field of fire to the south. From here they could cover the main Marauder unit as it pushed down the trail along the opposite bank.

The river bend was only 150 yards away from the night perimeter, and the platoon reached it in half an hour in the early-morning fog. They started to dig in at 0700 hours. Half an hour later Pvt. Pete Leitner, a scout from Okeechobee, Fla., was out in front of the perimeter collecting

THE stories and pictures on these pages are the first YANK has received from Sgt. Dave Richardson since he was swallowed up in the Burma jungles for more than three months.

Richardson's long hitch with the Marauder force, commanded by Brig. Gen. Frank D. Merrill, took him farther behind Japanese lines in Northern Burma than any other correspondent covering the theater.

A veteran of the New Guinea fighting, Richardson marched 500 miles with the Marauders and took part in all but one of their major actions. The accompanying account of the first battle between a U. S. Infantry platoon and a Jap force on the continent of Asia will be followed by other stories and pictures as they are received.

green branches to camouflage his foxhole when a Nambu light machine gun opened up.

Leitner was hit in the middle and crumpled to the ground, severely wounded. Before anyone could get his sights on the Jap machine gunner, he ran away through the brush. Sgt. Paul Mathis of Grey Eagle, Minn., platoon guide, and Lt. Weston went out and dragged Leitner back to the perimeter. The rest of the men in the platoon got down in their holes and braced themselves for a Jap attack.

They didn't have long to wait. Through the brush they spotted tan-uniformed Japs walking toward them at a crouch, some with twigs camouflaging their helmets. The platoon opened up. The Japs hit the ground and fanned out, crawling closer and shooting furiously. The Japs chattered among themselves; some seemed to be giving commands.

Then came the hollow snap of knee mortars being discharged behind the Japs. Seconds later the mortar shells exploded in the trees over the Fightin' Preacher's men. After that the mortars were fired in salvoes.

"Five Japs on the right flank!" somebody yelled. Sgt. John Gately of Woburn, Mass., spotted the first one and killed him. Pfc. Harold Hudson of Bristol, Conn., glimpsed the other four and mowed them all down, starting his tommy

Pfc. Norman Janis, Indian marksman who killed seven Japs, looks over Betsy, his M1.

Stubborn but sturdy mules carry machine guns, mortars and ammunition across river.

gun at the rear of the quartet and working forward.

The main Jap attack was coming in the center of the platoon's defense. A squad of Japs moved in closer, crawling, running a few steps, hitting the ground, creeping and shooting. Grimes, the Silver Star winner from Guadalcanal, now added to his record of 25 Japs by pumping bullets into each one who lifted his head. T-5 Raymond F. Harris of Pekin, Ill., sprayed the squad with his BAR as some of the Japs managed to creep within 30 feet of his position. One Jap shot at Harris just as he ducked his head to put a new magazine in his BAR. The bullet dented his helmet.

INSIDE the perimeter, Lt. Weston and his platoon sergeant, T/Sgt. Alfred M. Greer of Malden, Mass., got a message from Pfc. Benny Silverman of New York, N. Y., walkie-talkie radioman, that the main body of the Marauders had chased the remaining Japs from the opposite bank of the river and had taken up positions there.

"Fine," the Fightin' Preacher told Greer. "Let's get them to help us with their mortars." Acting as mortar observer, Greer got Silverman to radio back a rough estimate of Jap positions based on his grid map. Soon the crack of a mortar discharge answered from across the river. An 81-mm mortar shell burst with a hollow explosion behind the Japs. Greer gave Silverman new elevation and azimuth figures. Another mortar shell was lobbed over. It burst a little closer to the Japs but over to one side.

"Anybody got a compass with mils on it instead of degrees?" asked Greer. Near him Cpl. Joe Gomez, aid man from Gallup, N. Mex., had just finished pouring sulfa powder into Leitner's stomach wounds and giving him sulfa pills. He was working on Sgt. Lionel Parquette of Calumet, Mich., who was mortally wounded in the head. Gomez opened a pouch at his belt and handed his compass over to Greer. "We medics got everything," he grinned.

Greer told the mortars to lay in a smoke shell and he took an azimuth reading on it. Then he gave Silverman a new set of figures to radio the mortar crew.

Across the river, the mortar chief—1st Lt. William F. Woomer of State College, Pa., called "Woomer the Boomer" in New Guinea—shouted the figures to the mortar crew. Sgt. Edwin Kopec of Lowell, Mass.; Pvt. James McGowan of West Newton, Mass., and Pvt. Wise Alderman of Floyd, Va., set the figures on the scales and lobbed over another one. Theirs was the only mortar in position to fire across the river. Another mortar crew was changing its position to clear some trees with its trajectory.

Soon, with Greer's observation, the mortars were right on their target. Greer then varied the figures every few rounds to cover the Japs from flank to flank.

"Nice goin', boys," he yelled after a series of six bursts. "We just saw a couple of Japs blown out of their holes 40 yards from our point man." As fast as the mortarmen could rip open shell cases, they poured fire across the river.

The Japs kept coming. They edged into positions on three sides of the perimeter and were even trying to get between the river and the Fightin' Preacher's platoon. Their machine-gun and rifle fire increased in intensity and volume. Lt. Weston estimated that about a company of Japs was opposing him.

Then Silverman at the walkie-talkie got an order for the platoon to withdraw to the other side of the river. Its mission had been accomplished. There was no use staying to fight the Japs with such a small force when the main body of Marauders was moving south to make a direct attack on Walawbum.

Greer, Silverman and a couple of others made litters out of bamboo poles and buttoned-up fatigue jackets to carry the few wounded who could not walk. Then, under cover of Lt. Woomer's mortar fire, the platoon withdrew to the river and prepared to cross. The Japs followed, figuring on catching them in the riverbed.

Across the river four BARs opened up to cover the crossing. The bullets whined over the platoon's heads. Lt. Weston told Silverman to radio back that the Japs were on the flanks waiting to knock off some men crossing the river. Then two of the platoon peeled off their white undershirts and put one in a tree on each flank of the platoon to serve as firing guides for the BARs. Just before the crossing, Lt. Weston ordered the mortars to throw smoke shells to the rear and flanks of the withdrawing platoon to screen the move.

One by one, the men of the platoon splashed back across the river as BARs stuttered away and mortar bursts echoed down the riverbed. After Chief Janis, the Indian crack shot, had crossed, he turned to watch Pfc. John E. Clark of Windsor, Vt., and Katz, the International Brigade veteran, carry the wounded Leitner across on a litter. Out of the corner of his eye, Janis spotted a movement in the bushes on the bank. A Jap with a light machine gun had parted the bushes and was taking aim at the litter-bearers and their burden. Janis raised his M1 and fired two shots. The Jap squealed and slumped over his gun.

"I just wanted to make sure I got him," said Janis, explaining the extra shot. His score for the day was seven Japs.

MEANWHILE the BAR men covering the withdrawal were busy. Japs seemed to pop up all over the riverbank. Pvt. Bob Cole of Englewood, Calif., got six of them, and T-5 Clyde Shields of Egg Harbor, Wis., saw two roll down the bank in his sights.

At 0930 hours the last man withdrew. The sweating mortarmen were ripping open their 113th shell case when the cease-fire order came. Lt. Weston trudged wearily into the unit CP, head bent as he worked the bolt on his carbine.

One of his men watched him with obvious admiration. "You know," he said, "the Fightin' Preacher got at least two Japs before we withdrew. I thought he was going to apologize again. Instead, all he said was that he could have got another Jap if his bolt hadn't jammed."

First U. S. infantryman to kill a Jap in Asia is Cpl. Werner Katz, veteran of Guadalcanal.

Wet, weary and heavy-laden Marauders ford a Burma river on their end run around Japs.

COMPLETE Want Ads

THE CHICAGO DAILY NEWS

FINAL Edition

69TH YEAR—142. REG. U.S. PAT. OFF. COPYRIGHT, 1944 BY THE CHICAGO DAILY NEWS, INC. FRIDAY, JUNE 16, 1944—THIRTY-SIX PAGES. Telephone DEArborn 1111. FOUR CENTS

SECRET ROBOT BOMBS RAIN FIRE ON ENGLAND

Jap Steel Mills Ruined by B-29s

Yawata Plants Set on Fire on Kyushu Isle; Raid Stuns Tokyo.

Washington, June 16.—(AP)—Two mighty B-29's were lost in accidents but none through enemy action yesterday as America's new Super Fortresses turned Japanese industrial targets at Yawata on Kyushu Island into "glowing masses of wreckage."

The crew of one lost plane, however, is safe, the War Department reported.

The number of participating aircraft was not made known as first details emerged on the historic attack which marked the beginning of an entirely new chapter of aerial warfare with the greatest bombers ever built.

Sizable Task Force.

The text of the 20th Air Force communique:

"A sizable task force of B-29's from the 20th Bomber Command bombed industrial targets at Yawata on the Kyushu Island in the Japanese homeland on Thursday, June 15.

"Preliminary reports reveal that although enemy aircraft were encountered and anti-aircraft was moderate to intense, none of the planes was lost as a result of enemy action.

"Fliers who participated in the mission report the bombing was accurate and that large fires and explosions were observed.

From China Bases.

"The planes operated from bases in China which were completed recently. Two B-29's were lost as the result of accidents, one crew of which is safe. This communique is based on the preliminary incomplete reports from the combat zone."

The raid gave the Nipponese empire, in the words of an eyewitness "her answer to Dec. 7, 1941—Pearl Harbor.

Roy Porter, radio correspondent, first to report of 11 correspondents who accompanied the aerial dreadnoughts on their historic mission, said in a broadcast over the combined American networks from the Far East that "tons upon tons of bombs were dropped" on coke ovens and open-hearth furnaces of Japanese steel mills.

Japs Are Amazed.

The raid amazed the Japs, according to Porter, but flak defense went into prompt action.

"Japanese anti-aircraft fire poured into the sky," he said, "and shell fragments dug deeply into the super-bombers.

"But the engines kept turning, and nearly all the ships came home."

The returning ships, he added, showed "some bullet holes but very little material damage."

Mention 2 Other Cities.

Porter's only reference to a specific target was to name Yawata, but the Tokyo radio said Moji and Kokura also were hit. All three

(Continued on page 15, column 2.)

Mission Is No Adventure but Product of Cool, Scientific Planning.

BY A. T. STEELE.
SPECIAL RADIO
To The Chicago Daily News Foreign Service.
Copyright, 1944, The Chicago Daily News, Inc.

At a Super Fortress base in Western China, June 16.—There was a satisfied smile on the face of Brig.Gen. Kenneth D. Wolfe, commanding general of the 20th Air Force Bomber Command, as the last of the huge B-29's, which took off from here late yesterday to bomb Japan, returned through a drizzly dawn today—their mission accomplished.

It was the longest round-trip air raid in history, and the weight of bombs, while not comparable to that of big European raids, was sufficient to bring the Japanese to sudden realization that a new phase of the Pacific War had begun.

By hitting at the Imperial Iron & Steel Works at Yawata, Japan, Wolfe's very long-range strategic air force has struck at one of the nerve centers of Japan's most important basic industry. Situated at the westermost end of Japan's westermost island of Kyushu, Yawata is only a dozen miles southeast of the twin citits of Simonseki and Moji, which are the gateway to Japan from the Asiatic continent.

A Night Raid.

As this was a night raid, staged in utter blackness except for the glare of searchlights and blasts of bursting bombs, the material results can only be guessed at until fully checked.

The real significance of this long-distance attack is that it was accomplished with relatively light loss against relatively light opposition, and that it represents the beginning of the long-awaited and long-delayed strategic air war against the Japanese mainland.

While it may be some time befort these attacks reach the intensity and frequency of the Allied raids over Europe, the facility with which the mission was accomplished demonstrates that the Japs can never again rest easy behind their inner fortress.

Other Choice Targets.

There are many choice industrial targets within no greater range than Yawata from this China base, though our excruciating supply problem constitutes a difficulty.

The raid on Japan was the culmination of a gigantic preparatory job done in an astonishingly short time with the collaboration of the best minds in American aviation.

Realizing that only a year ago there was but one completed B-29 bomber in existence, it takes one's breath away to stand at this great new base and watch a whole procession of gleaming sky giants

(Continued on page 15, column 1.)

YANKS GAINING IN PUSH TO CUT CHERBOURG LINK

Supplies Pour In for New Phase in Battle for Normandy Cape.

BULLETIN.

London, June 16.—(UP)—American troops have advanced to within two and a half miles of St. Sauveur-Le Vicomte, German transport bottleneck south of Cherbourg, it was announced officially today.

BY HELEN KIRKPATRICK.
SPECIAL CABLE
To The Chicago Daily News Foreign Service.
Copyright, 1944, The Chicago Daily News, Inc.

Supreme Headquarters, Allied Expeditionary Force, June 16.—American forces under the command of Lt.Gen. Omar N. Bradley have advanced westward along the Pont L'Abbe sector of Cherbourg Peninsula, with a small gain toward La Haye, substantially increasing our chance to cut the peninsula.

Fighting in the Caen sector remains static and hard, with the possibility that both sides have dug in and are severely contesting every inch of ground.

In the Caumont-Tilly-Bocage triangle fighting has eased up slightly, suggesting that the armor here may have been drawn back slightly to regroup and re-engage.

More Supplies Pour In.

The buildup continues. This means that more men and materials are going into the now firmly held beachhead, with the probability, judging from previous operations of this kind, that units there, already engaged in fighting, are getting more transport and artillery.

It should be about time they were passing into the light stage, where vehicular support is substantially increased over that of the assault stage. It may be that they are already building up to the normal vehicular strength necessary for a real offensive.

In the northeast American sector we are on or approaching the Sinope River—probably on it in several places. The situation around Montebourg, 14 miles southeast of Cherbourg, remains obscure.

On the River Douve.

We are on the River Douve, at Pont L'Abbe, and at several other points, notably at Reingeville, though whether we have actually captured Reigneville is not certain. The Douve, which winds in a northwesterly direction west of Valgones, has flooded valleys west of Pont L'Abbe and west of the Cherbourg road.

North of Reigneville, however, the river presents no real obstacle to the advancing troops.

Air activity yesterday was on a considerably reduced scale, owing to the weather, the bulk of it being confined to the morning hours. Altogether, including last night's attacks on Boulogne by the Royal Air Force, there were 3,000 sorties flown. During daylight more than 200 separate missions pounded targets over the Seine River, where the Germans are undoubtedly trying to bring reinforcements into the battle area.

Attack Radio Station.

The 2d Tactical Air Force of the R.A.F. flew in close support of ground troops in the area east of Caen. Rocket typhoons attacked the radio station at Le Havre.

The R.A.F. last night at 10 and in daylight went for E-boats in Boulogne harbor. Photographs from their Wednesday night's raid on Le Havre show satisfac-

(Continued on page 15, column 3.)

HOW SECRET WEAPON MAY OPERATE—The sketch at top from Mechanix Illustrated Magazine shows the Nazi's secret weapon—radio-controlled, rocket-propelled glider bombs—as they are freed from a Nazi plane. The lower picture, smuggled out of Germany, shows the rocket gliders, with wings that fold back, as they were being tested before the war. A fleet of pilotless Nazi bombers last night attacked southern England. [Acme Telephoto from Mechanix Illustrated Magazine.] *(Buy War Bonds.)*

Nazis Unveil Mystery Craft

Pilotless Planes Zoom In and Explode; Skim Rooftops to Foil Ack-Ack.

London, June 16.—(UP)—A fantastic stream of pilotless Nazi bombers rained fire and explosives across southern England all last night and through the morning hours today, and the Berlin radio said the robot fleet had smashed at London itself in "the beginning of vengeance" for the Allied attacks on Germany.

Hitler finally had launched his boasted secret weapon against Britain and the mighty invasion arsenal piled up on the island, and British official sources made no effort to minimize the gravity of the attack.

All southern England was alerted, and Home Secretary Herbert Morrison confirmed the existence of the robot raiders and promised immedate counter-action, in a statement to Commons.

A German high command communique said south England and the London area were bombed last night with "new type explosives of very heavy caliber," and Berlin military commentators boasted that the mysterious raiders were "a new anti-invasion weapon of the greatest effect."

"The new weapon used against England is the beginning of vengeance" for the "barbaric" Allied bombing of the Nazi homeland, one enemy commentator said.

Reports from eyewitnesses who watched the pilotless parade swoosh across southern England during the night poured into London today, including one account that told of automatic machine guns raking the countryside.

Like String of Comets.

Flashing across the night skies like a string of fiery comets, the mysterious projectiles whizzed down on scores of unidentified districts in southern England, exploding into gigantic balls of fire.

Eyewitness accounts of the raid varied, but all reports indicated that the missiles were either

(The text of Home Secretary Morrison's address in which he described the new Nazi pilotless planes appears on page 6.)

rocket-bombs or radio-controlled planes crammed with high explosives set to go off within a matter of seconds after striking the ground.

Fly at Terrific Speed.

Observers said the projectiles came over at terrific speeds, singly or in groups of two or three, some soaring 3,000 feet or more in the air and others slamming over the rooftops in level flight.

R.A.F. night fighter pilots went up to challenge the robot raiders, diving recklessly through a terrific hail of flak thrown up by the British ground defenses in an effort to explode them in midair.

Many of the projectiles were believed to have been hit and eyewitnesses reported seeing tremendous explosions high overhead.

Many more fell with terrific impact on the countryside, and preliminary reports indicated that considerable damage and casualties resulted. Rescue squads still

(Continued on page 11, column 3.)

Robot Attack Fills the Bill As Nuisance

BY HELEN KIRKPATRICK.
SPECIAL CABLE
To The Chicago Daily News Foreign Service.
Copyright, 1944, The Chicago Daily News, Inc.

London, June 16.—Germany's new weapon—the pilotless, rocket-projected plane—made its first sustained appearance on the British stage last night and this morning.

A number of persons had a relatively sleepless night, but less because of the plane itself than because of the intense flak and the rockets sent hurtling to the sky to down it. Some of the new planes are believed to have been brought down, according to latest reports.

The Nazi reconnaissance planes were flying over early today, probably to see how the "new child" had been doing.

Undoubtedly, if the Germans had been allowed to proceed undisturbed to construct these pilotless planes and directing machinery on the French coast, the citizens of Britain might have been expected to spend many days and nights under a constant if merely annoying type of air attack.

But our constant raids on the Pas de Calais area in the months preceding our landings in France have seriously hampered German planes, and our strategic attacks on German aircraft production have reduced the threat of this new weapon to a point where it can now play only a sporadic nuisance role.

U.S. Advances in Marianas; 'Progress Good,' Says Nimitz

BY WILLIAM M'GAFFIN.
SPECIAL RADIO
To The Chicago Daily News Foreign Service.
Copyright, 1944, The Chicago Daily News, Inc.

With the U.S. Expeditionary Forces in the Pacific, June 16.—The island of Saipan, main Japanese stronghold in the Marianas, will be captured. Nobody with this vast naval, air and land armada doubts that. But its capture, initiated by American troops, who fought their way ashore Wednesday, is a tough assignment, albeit one which will prove well worth the effort.

Already the enemy is putting up a stiff fight, and further fierce, bloody combat is expected as wave after wave of our attackers storm the beaches.

This correspondent's next account will come from the island itself, as he is now about to go ashore.

The preparations for the attack, another forward step in the reconquest of the Pacific under command of Adm. Richmond Kelly Turner, the stern-faced commander of amphibious forces of our Pacific Fleet, have been in the making ever since the successful penetration of the Marshalls. All the lessons learned in our previous encounters with the Japanese are being put to good use, including effective advance shelling and bombing, which is expected to knock out a considerably larger proportion of Jap artillery than was possible at Tarawa, for example.

Spearheaded by Tanks.

The assault was spearheaded by amphibious tanks, later to be replaced by land tanks as they can be put ashore. The launching was under cover of a smoke screen, through which rolled our naval artillery and aerial barrage, with planes strafing the beachheads without a halt.

Every effort is being made to spare our men. There is no question of our naval and aerial supremacy. In the line of mechanized equipment the Japs may turn up a number of medium tanks with which we have had little experience as yet, and some amphibious tanks. They have two air strips, one at each end of the island, but we expect to knock out their air force on the ground early.

Adm. Turner, before embarkation, described the details of the campaign to correspondents. He

(Continued on page 13, column 2.)

WEATHER INDICATIONS

(U.S. Weather Bureau Forecast.)
June 16, 1944.

Chicago and vicinity — Partly cloudy and continued warm and humid today, tonight and tomorrow. Cooler near lake Saturday afternoon. Scattered thundershowers this afternoon and evening. Moderate winds. High today 90, low tonight 68, high Saturday 87.

Temperatures since 6 p.m. yesterday:

6 p.m.	90	7 a.m.	70
8 p.m.	85	8 a.m.	73
10 p.m.	79	9 a.m.	75
Midnight	67	10 a.m.	77
2 a.m.	68	11 a.m.	80
4 a.m.	67	12 noon	*82
6 a.m.	70		

*Unofficial.

Sunrise 5:15, sunset 8:28, sunrise tomorrow 5:15, moon rises at 3:23 a.m. tomorrow.

(Additional weather data on page 32.)

Oxie Gets Crick in Neck Watching a 4-Ring War

BY CLEM LANE.

"I do not wish to complain about the conduct of the war with a bond drive on but it is getting tougher and tougher on us civilians," Oxie O'Rourke, the tactful tactician, remarked today.

"It remind me of when I use to take the family to the circus. I would park my glims on what makes in the middle ring when the weaver would holler get a load of the horse being shot out of the cannon and I would swivel to the south ring only to nave Junior or Anastasia poke me in the ribs and scream Daddy, Daddy, look at the snake riding on the bicycle with no hands yet.

"Only a three-headed man can see all they is to see at a circus and this war is just like that only more so. How can a guy keep up with it? They is the Normandy front, the Italian front and the Russian front. And then on top of all them the Pacific front bust out in a blaze of glory and oversize pineapples for the Japanese.

"With them Capone bouquets bouncing off the mikado's front porch, the Japs will have to worry about saving more than their face, if you know what I mean, Mr. McGonigle."

"I do, said Torchnose.

"However," said Oxie, "them Japanese names is easier to pronounce, as all us radio commentators can tell you. They is many a sprained tonsil in the radio business since D-Day."

"Sound like a Caen game to me," said Torchie.

OWI Asiatic Agent Missing.

New York, June 16.—(AP)—Victor C. Rankin, 33, a field representative of the OWI in an Asiatic area, was reported missing by the War Department yesterday in a message to his wife here.

FIVE BOYS, 8-12, ADMIT SETTING N. SIDE FIRES

Five boys between the ages of 8 and 12 years, who have admitted starting at least seven fires on the Near North Side "for the fun of it," are being held today at the Juvenile Detention Home.

The boys told Chicago av. police they started the fires by throwing flaming torches, made of rags soaked in paint and wrapped around sticks, into the buildings. The $2,000 fire which turned more than 50 tenants out of a rooming house at 933 N. Wells st. June 5, was set by the gang, they confessed. Other blazes for which they were responsible, they admitted, were in buildings at 152-160 W. Walnut st., 938 N. Wells st., a drug store at Oak and Wells st, and the J. A. Sexton School at 160 Wendell st. None of those fires were serious.

Charges of arson will be brought against them June 23 in the Juvenile Court. The boys in custody are Robert, 9, and John McHugh, 12, of 218 W. Walton st.; Joseph McDonaugh, 8, of 930 N. Franklin st.; James Wilson, 12, of 938 N. Wells st.; Simon Callaway, 11, of 940 N. Wells st.

STORM BRINGS DRY AIR—BUT IT'S STILL HOT

It will be hot in Chicago today—Forecaster H. L. Jacobson mentioning temperatures around 90 degrees—but it will "feel cooler," he added, because of last night's strange storm.

Although thundershowers were a possibility late today, Jacobson admitted, there was little chance of a repeat performance of the storm which yesterday dropped the mercury 11 degrees in an hour, whipped a 41-mile-an-hour wind through the city, and left the air dry for today with a steady 20-mile wind.

There was one casualty in last night's big wind: Pleas Lend, 62, of 2320 S. State st., was injured by a window blown from a building at 301 E. 31st st.

A sign was blown from near the top of a two-story stone building at 200-209 N. La Salle st. and a large plate glass window on the first floor was broken.

Gusts of wind, some estimated at 60 to 85 miles an hour, lifted the roof off a two-flat building at 1036 N. Trumbull av. and ripped away the back porch. Otto Olson, 70, a retired policeman, and his wife, Amie, 65, an invalid, who reside there, were not injured, but rain brought discomfort to them and their daughter, Evelyn.

Other blasts of wind skyrocketed newspapers from Loop newsstands high into the air and whipped up the dirt on the streets into dust storms. At La Salle st. and Grand av. a two-ton truck was blown to the center of the street from its parking place.

IN THE DAILY NEWS TODAY

REVEILLE

THE SERVICES' NEWSPAPER

Founder-Editor - W. R. HIPWELL

PUBLISHED ALTERNATE MONDAYS 2D.

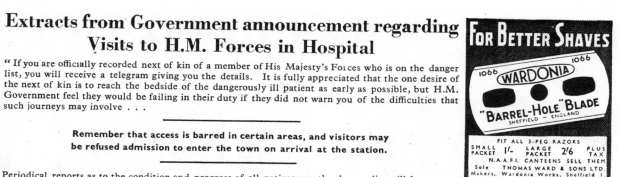

Extracts from Government announcement regarding Visits to H.M. Forces in Hospital

"If you are officially recorded next of kin of a member of His Majesty's Forces who is on the danger list, you will receive a telegram giving you the details. It is fully appreciated that the one desire of the next of kin is to reach the bedside of the dangerously ill patient as early as possible, but H.M. Government feel they would be failing in their duty if they did not warn you of the difficulties that such journeys may involve . . .

Remember that access is barred in certain areas, and visitors may be refused admission to enter the town on arrival at the station.

Periodical reports as to the condition and progress of all patients on the danger list will be sent to the next of kin."

"They also serve who only stand and wait"

THIS issue of "Reveille" is the first since the invasion was launched. It seems so long after the event that words of encouragement may fall somewhat flat, but I do want all of you to know that we of "Reveille" are with you in thought all the time, and wish you God Speed and a safe and speedy return.

I do not need to extol your merits—we all know what it means to you—but at this moment (and I know you will understand if I allow my sentiment to get the better of me) my thoughts turn to the mothers—YOUR mothers and your CHILDREN'S mothers; the steadfast courage and endurance of these women demand our utmost respect and admiration.

As a major in the R.A. (a hardened warrior who has seen service abroad before) on the eve of his embarkation for France last week said to me, "In the excitement of going over we hardly realise the danger, but it takes real courage for the missus to sit at home with the kids just waiting—waiting and hoping that all will be well. She can't leave them and pop over to the 'local' to drown her sorrows."

But YOU can help to allay her anxiety. Your letters are the one bright spot in her life. Your words of encouragement and cheer will help her through her vigil. She will be waiting to comfort you when you have "finished the job," but in the meantime, don't forget that every letter means a new lease of life to her, even if it's only to say that you are well. And remember that so far as "Reveille," YOUR newspaper, can help, it will. It will be little enough when compared with the part she is playing in this second war to end all wars. When it is over, we shall all go forward together—you fellows in the Forces, the women in your sister Services, the wives, mothers, and relatives of all who are serving—to make this a world worth living in, if not in our lifetime then in our children's.

W. R. Hipwell

"WHAT SORT OF PEOPLE DO THEY THINK WE ARE?"

THESE words, used by Prime Minister Churchill when speaking of Hitler and his gang of cut-throats, are echoed now by the relatives of the wounded men returning from France, who have read the Government announcement concerning visits to H.M. Forces in hospital, which was published in the National Press by the three Service Ministries, extracts of which are reproduced above.

As Minister of Defence, Premier Churchill is boss of the three Service Chiefs, but we cannot conceive that the announcement was issued with his consent or even with his knowledge, because he, of all people, will appreciate the tremendous sacrifices made by those taking part in the Second Front, and by their relatives who are anxiously waiting at home.

At this moment Churchill has the sympathy and loyalty of the entire nation, because we all, every one of us, appreciate the extreme anxiety that he must be experiencing just now, for his was the brain responsible for conceiving this vast campaign.

What Blimp thought up this one?

Some Blimp, then, is responsible for this warning to relatives not to visit their wounded menfolk in hospital. What sort of people do these Service chiefs think we are? We are not made of wood, but of flesh and blood.

One can visualise the feelings of frustration of these relatives and next of kin, who have stood by whilst their menfolk have gone to battle, being warned that they might not be given entrance to a banned area!

Their first instinct—and the authorities smugly state that they appreciate this fact—is to fly to the bedside of the wounded man, and no obstruction should be put in their way. We are all prepared to put up with inconveniences at a time like this, such as shortage of accommodation, and shortage of food, etc., but this is too much, especially when we consider that by the time this issue of REVEILLE is published other papers will be full of the stories of railway carriages jammed with racegoers en route to the present session of racing at Newmarket, to witness the running of those national institutions—the Derby and the Oaks.

"Reveille" trusts that some courageous M.P. will take heed of our exposure and pursue the right of the next of kin to visit their menfolk at a time when the loving sympathy of their relatives can often mean the difference between life and death.

N.B.—If banned areas are the real problem, 'Reveille' suggests the production of the official telegram to the next of kin should be sufficient to permit entry—or alternatively a police visa on the identity card.

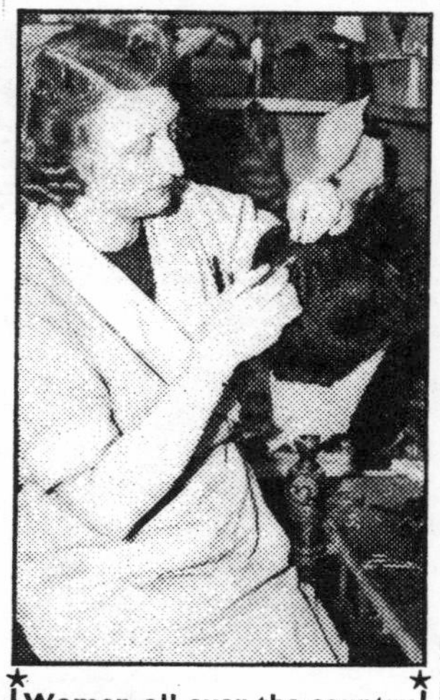

Women all over the country are sending their hair to be made into wigs for disabled Servicemen. Here is a girl engaged on the delicate operation of inserting hairs into the 'scalp.'

HOW TO BECOME AN M.P.

THE local military situation, distance, and transport facilities available may be the deciding factor in the success of a Serviceman who aspires to become an M.P.

This was emphasised by Sir James Grigg in the House of Commons recently, when he pointed out that a would-be Parliamentary candidate serving overseas could not be given short periods of leave to this country in order to attend Selection Committees, nor could any guarantee be given that he would be able to return in time for an election at short notice.

Here is the procedure to be followed by an aspirant to Parliamentary fame, as outlined by the War Secretary:—

An officer or soldier who wishes to stand for Parliament should inform his commanding officer in order that any application he may make for special facilities may be recognised.

Subject to the exigencies of the Service, he can be granted leave for the purpose of getting adopted as a prospective candidate or candidate, and is set free from his military duties for the whole period of the election.

"Old-school-tie" Peer rebuked

LORD BUCKMASTER was severely rebuked in the House of Lords recently when he contended that the boy from the elementary school had less courage and was less capable of enduring physical suffering than the boy who came from the public school.

Said Lord Latham:—

"When we are in the midst of this great, grim conflict, that statements of that kind should be made, which are entirely indefensible, seems to me offensive to the bulk of those who are serving in the Forces in the cause of liberty and freedom."

Cpl. Gordon—Official Reply

THE case of Cpl. Gordon, of the R.A.F., the airman with heart trouble who is kept on duties for which he has been certified unfit by two Harley-street specialists, came up for the attention of Air Secretary Sir Archibald Sinclair in the House of Commons last week.

Replying to Sir Ernest Graham Little (Ind., London University), who raised the matter following publicity in REVEILLE, Sir Archibald said:—

"The airman in question was admitted to hospital in March last for observation and treatment, and for a report by a Royal Air Force medical specialist. The latter recommended that the airman should be recategorised to Grade III and remustered to a sedentary occupation. This recommendation was endorsed by a medical board on March 13. The airman is at present employed on clerical duties in his present trade of station policeman pending remustering to a trade involving sedentary duties only."

Commenting on this, Cpl. Gordon said, "It is now four months since they first said they would remuster me. Meantime I am employed on clerical duties in the police office, but find things quite a strain, and do not feel at all better in health."

Tests for Civvy St.

SELECTION tests by psychiatrists, based on the tests given to recruits at the Army's primary training centres, may be applied to men and women leaving the Services after the war.

Because there are many of the Forces who will not want to go back to their old jobs, employers are considering the suggestion, made by Army psychiatrists, that Service men and women should be submitted to tests on demobilisation, to determine the type of occupation most suited to them.

By this means, it is claimed, ex-Service men and women will get into the right jobs, and square pegs in "civvy street" round holes will be avoided.

Paratroops' Pay

PARATROOPS and airborne troops who are wounded on active service will continue to receive their extra jumping allowance for 91 days.

If still incapacitated after that they must forgo the extra pay until able to return to their units.

Portal Home—'Worse and Worse'!

THE only answer to the almost universal criticism of the Portal House is a completely new plan.

This is the opinion of the Association of Building Technicians, who, while admitting that the amended plan has eliminated one of the major complaints—use of the kitchen as a passage—declare that resultant conditions are worse than before.

The living-room has now become a passage, while the extra door makes it impossible to sit in comfort round the fire.

Communication between the bedrooms and the bathroom is even more inconvenient.

An article on pre-fabricated houses appears on page 4.

Attention Mothers!

AND wives, sweethearts, and sisters, too!

Your man may be in France, but he'll still want to read his Reveille every fortnight.

The only way you can be sure he does so is by taking out a subscription on his behalf.

Full details appear on page 6.

NEXT ISSUE JULY 3, 1944

Final Markets THE CHICAGO DAILY NEWS FINAL Edition

69TH YEAR—147. REG. U.S. PAT. OFF. COPYRIGHT, 1944 BY THE CHICAGO DAILY NEWS, INC. THURSDAY, JUNE 22, 1944—THIRTY-EIGHT PAGES. Telephone DEArborn 1111. FOUR CENTS

ROUT JAPAN FLEET!

Carrier Planes Knock Out 14 Ships

One-Vote Deal On for Dewey

California and Illinois 'Dickering'; Bricker Won't Quit Race.

BY CHARLES N. WHEELER.

Gov. John W. Bricker of Ohio arrived today to rally his forces against the rising Dewey tide while the hotel lobbies were buzzing with reports that California and Illinois will unite to "cinch" the New Yorker's nomination for President on the first ballot.

Half an hour after Bricker, at a press conference, had declared he would not withdraw in the face of the Dewey strength, confirmation was forthcoming that Dewey is consulting by telephone with the members of the resolutions committee, presumably on the text of the postwar plank.

J. Russel Sprague, New York committeeman, told a press conference that Dewey's views on the platform were made available to the resolutions committee. Herbert Brownell Jr., Dewey's campaign manager in 1942, Sprague said, is the intermediary between the Albany switchboard and the platform builders at the Stevens Hotel.

Confident of Victory.

Dewey's report as chairman of the Mackinac subcommittee on government reorganization and domestic issues will be laid before the subcommittee of the resolutions committee tomorrow. Sprague said all arrangements, had been made for Dewey to appear before the convention, but not until "after his nomination."

"On what ballot?" was asked.

"I am not saying it will be the first ballot but I say he will be

(Continued on page 3, column 1.)

G.O.P. Leaders Striving for Harmony in Party's Foreign Plank.

BY BRUCE BIOSSAT.

Strong signs developed today that the Republican platform builders are striving earnestly to avoid party friction on the all-important foreign policy issue, but some quarters asserted it would be unwise to rule out the possibility of a fight along nationalist-internationalist lines.

The resolutions committee hoped to wind up public hearings on platform proposals by nightfall so it could hear reports tomorrow from the Mackinac conference subcommittees on foreign policy and various domestic topics.

Senator Arthur H. Vandenberg (Rep., Mich.), head of the subgroup on the foreign plank, is expected to arrive here by plane tonight and will present the proposal early tomorrow. Already endorsed by the six-man drafting body, it parallels the Mackinac charter, but is couched in more concise, direct terms.

Harmony in Sight.

With the subcommittee agreed and Gov. Thomas E. Dewey of New York said to be generally satisfied with the plank, chances appeared good that the oft-voiced objective of an entirely harmonious settlement of platform questions would be achieved.

It was understood, however, that some of the platform makers think the subcommittee has bent a bit too far backwards in seek-

(Continued on page 3, column 2.)

Woman Killed by Train At La Grange Crossing

An unidentified woman about 60 years old was struck and killed by a westbound Burlington train about 10:38 a.m. today at the Brainard av. crossing in La Grange. She weighed between 130 and 140 pounds, was five feet two inches tall, wore a dark blue jacket and blue house dress with white figures, and carried a coin purse. The body was removed to an undertaking parlor at 40 S. Ashland av.

WEATHER INDICATIONS

(U.S. Weather Bureau Forecast.)
June 22, 1944.

Chicago and vicinity—Mostly cloudy with an occasional thundershower tonight and Friday, continued warm and humid, moderate winds, low tonight 68, high Friday 85.

Temperatures since 6 p.m. yesterday:

6 p.m.	80	8 a.m.	75
8 p.m.	77	9 a.m.	75
10 p.m.	74	10 a.m.	75
Midnight	73	11 a.m.	74
2 a.m.	73	12 noon	75
4 a.m.	71	1 p.m.	78
6 a.m.	70	2 p.m.	82
7 a.m.	72		

Sunrise 5:15, sunset 8:20, sunrise tomorrow 5:16, moon sets at 9:25 a.m. tomorrow.

(Additional weather data on page 18.)

BASEBALL SCORES

NATIONAL LEAGUE

	1	2	3	4	5	6	7	8	9—R.	H.	E.
CINCIN'TI (1st game)	3	0	0	0	0	0					
PITTSBURGH	0	1	0	1	1	1					

Carter-Mueller, Cincinnati; Sewell-Davis, Pittsburgh.

	1	2	3
NEW YORK	1	0	0
BROOKLYN	3	4	

Fischer-Mancuso, New York; Wyatt-Owen, Brooklyn.

AMERICAN LEAGUE

	1	2	3	4	5	6	7	8
BOSTON (1st game)	0	0	0	1	0	0	0	3
PHILADELPHIA	0	0	0	1	0	2	0	1

Bowman-Partee, Boston; Black-Hayes, Philadelphia.

	1	2	3	4
WASHINGTON	0	0	0	0
NEW YORK	0	0	3	

Leonard-Ferrell, Washington; Zuber-Hemsley, New York.

	1	2
CLEVELAND	0	0
DETROIT	2	

Kennedy-McDonnell, Cleveland; Gentry-Richards, Detroit.

RACE RESULTS

AT AQUEDUCT, N. Y.

4—B. Bobby, 6.80, 2.90, 2.60; Histrionic, 2.70, 2.30; Powerhouse, 3.30.

AT SUFFOLK DOWNS, MASS.

2—Depi, 8.40, 4.00, 2.40; R. Descent, 4.60, 2.80; Grand Party, 2.40.
Daily double—Weapons Pride and Depi—paid 29.20.

AT CHARLES TOWN, W. VA.

3—D. Heights, 4.20, 2.80, 2.40; Heartburn, 3.80, 2.80; Big Moose, 3.20.
4—Dicky, 4.00, 3.40, 2.40; Gray Prince, 18.00, 6.40; Morocco D., 3.60.

IN THE DAILY NEWS TODAY

PLANES, CANNON POUND FOE FOR CHERBOURG FALL

Smoke and Flames Rage in Nazi Forts as Yanks Press Forward.

(BULLETINS.)

Supreme Headquarters, Allied Expeditionary Force, June 22.—(AP)—Allied planes and big guns today dealt Cherbourg a terrific pounding intended to crack the fortified city's last defenses. After a roaring 80-minute aerial barrage, the Germans were beset with an artillery attack that left smoke and flame sweeping their forts.

Supreme Headquarters, Allied Expeditionary Force, June 22.)—(UP)—"A few hundred yards from where I sit the Germans in their fortifications are being blown to pieces by one of the greatest combined air and artillery barrages in history," Henry T. Gorrell, United Press war correspondent, reported from near Cherbourg.

(Map on Page 2.)

BY ROBERT J. CASEY.

SPECIAL CABLE
To The Chicago Daily News Foreign Service.
Copyright, 1944, The Chicago Daily News, Inc.

London, June 22.—It began to look this morning like a cutthroat war on Cherbourg peninsula, with the fall of the port still probable in a matter of hours. It was officially stated that no surrender offer had been made to the Germans and that the defending army had made no attempt to evacuate.

Meanwhile, the Americans have moved forward steadily and in some places are three miles in advance of yesterday's line.

(The German communique today announced the death of Lt. Gen. Hellmich in the fighting on Cherbourg peninsula.)

Unfavorable weather still hampers operations somewhat, inasmuch as it has prevented air attack and has continued to interfere with the unloading of supplies on the beachhead. But this does not seem to have delayed the ground forces, which have taken high points above the city and are now in a position to start cracking down on the main zone of defenses.

Advance at 3 Points.

It seemed likely from unofficial reports that advance units of Lt. Gen. Omar N. Bradley's army are operating well ahead of the established line on both sides of the city, preparing the way for the nutcracker movement which, at this writing, seems unstoppable.

(Text of Allied communique No. 33, page 6.)

On the right flank of the attack Allied troops crossed the River Saihe and took the village of Le Theil. In the center they made substantial gains along Route Nationale 13, the Volognes-Cherbourg motor road, which seems likely to become the main axis of the advance. At the left of the sector they had come to within three miles of the sea above St. Croix-Hague.

(The Associated Press said the Americans have driven past St. Croix to within half a mile of Beaumont-Hague, west of Cherbourg, and have captured St. Pierre Eglise, the last road junction leading to the big port from Cape Barfleur, on the east side of the peninsula.)

On the south side of Cherbourg peninsula there was little activity, and elsewhere along the sprawling line at the south end of the beachhead the situation showed no change. In the neighborhood of Tilly, where the Germans made unsuccessful counter-attacks yesterday, an artillery battle was going on and patrol activities were reported between that point and the sea.

Despite the bad weather, Allied air forces carried out operations with considerable success. Fighter-bombers blasted railroads and bridges at Montdidier and Chauny in the region of Paris and at Evereux, Chartres, Coltainville, Cherisy and Conches.

An ammunition train was blown up by a plane attack north of Paris on the line to the battle area. **Six oil storage tanks were set afire at Niort.**

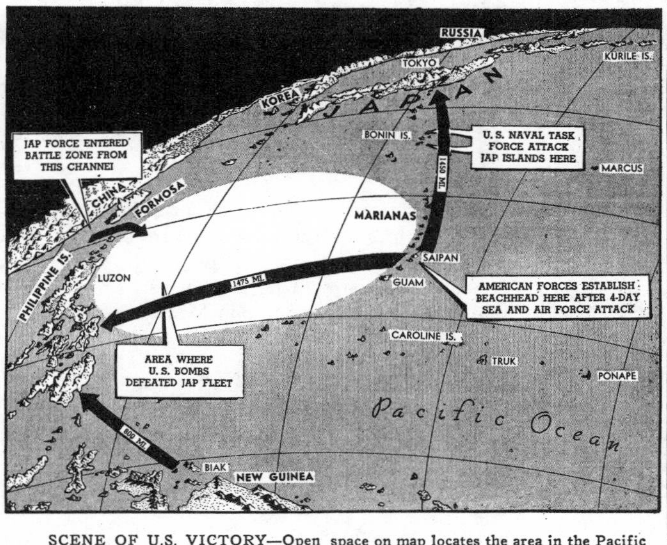

SCENE OF U.S. VICTORY—Open space on map locates the area in the Pacific between the Philippines and the Marianas, where Jap naval forces were smashed by U.S. Navy carrier-based planes. Black arrows (with mileage) show distances of possible future Allied drives. [By a staff artist.]

JAP SHIP FEELS MIGHT OF U.S. BOMBS—A Japanese battleship of the Kongo class (above) was damaged as 14 of the enemy's vessels were sunk or damaged in the action. [Associated Press Wirephoto.]

They'll Fight, Die for Less To Give the Strikers More

New York—The Associated Press has received the following communication by registered air mail, marked as coming from the U.S.S. Coos Bay, a seaplane tender, and stamped "Passed by Naval censor":

U.S.S. COOS BAY (AVP-25)
c/o Fleet Post Office
San Francisco, Calif.
10 June 1944

The Associated Press
Editorial Department
San Francisco, Calif.
Sirs:

We the crew of the U.S.S. Coos Bay, which consists mainly of survivors of other naval ships or veterans of major naval engagements, and who have all seen action not once but many times and who, while on this cruise, have not had a liberty for one full year, feel that we can do more than fight and even give our lives if necessary for our country. We are willing to help pay the wage increase from our meager pay that money-hungry strikers are demanding if they will just continue to produce the implements necessary so that we can end this war. We have seen war—and we hate it.

We have chosen you as our agent or go-between to represent us in our campaign to "buy off" the present strikers of the Wright Aircraft Corp. with the money we have collected from our small crew: a total of 41,200 pennies.

Please implore them to end their strike and accept our offer to help pay their wage increase which they feel is more important than our lives.

Ask them not to strike in the future but, instead, to let the men in the war zone know of their dissatisfaction and they will gladly chip in each month to save them from starvation so that they may continue to produce arms for us to defeat their enemy as well as ours, and so that we may come home soon to see the ones we love, our sons and daughters whom we have never seen and our wives and mothers who haunt us with memories day and night; also to see our country for which we are willing to die—yes—and to see you strikers; do you want to see us?

Out here we are close to our "foreign" enemies and can properly deal with them; our enemies at home we cannot reach. Therefore, in desperation, we can think "of nothing but to offer our money to 'buy' them back to work; this money having been earned honestly and in the belief that our efforts were the salvation and protection of those who are striking against us.

THE CREW OF THE U.S.S. COOS BAY.

P. S. If the Wright strike is over, just choose another. There are always plenty at hand.

LEADER DEFENDS UNION.

Navy Secretary Forrestal, when shown the contents of the letter today, said "no comment."

R. J. Thomas, national president of the U.A.W., issued the following statement at Washington;

"These men in the armed service have been propagandized. Our international office has done everything it possibly can and will continue to do more to stop all such strikes as the Wright strike. The people of Cincinnati at least know there was no wage issue involved. It was an anti-Negro issue. And they also know our international union demanded that these people go back to work."

"Our members returned to work on our demands, but about 600 nonunion people did not return to work and were disciplined by the management. Quite obviously we have no control over people who do not belong to our union. All the people in the armed services can rest assured that all the officers of the U.A.W. will do everything they possibly can to help those in the armed services to bring the war to a successful conclusion.

"Our organization did put up a fight for additional pay for the soldiers. We fought equally hard to get the G.I. bill through Congress, and we are also putting up a fight for jobs when our servicemen return."

VICTORY CALLED GREAT BUT NOT FATAL TO JAPS

Washington, June 22.—(AP)—Naval authorities estimated today that the victory over the Japanese fleet west of Saipan is a great but not a crippling blow to Japan's naval force.

The enemy fleet evidently was caught way off base. That was what started the engagement rather than any decision of the Tokyo admirals to steam out heroically to meet the challenge of U.S. sea-air might.

Units of the U.S. 5th Fleet sought to entrap the Japanese force by bold, deep strikes into enemy territory. They succeeded to the extent that American carrier planes reached and blasted the enemy's carrier force.

Many Ships Escape.

The distances American ships had to go in the mad chase were very great, however, and many of the Japanese ships are believed to have made good their escape so that the Japanese fleet remains as a factor to reckon with in the Western Pacific offensive.

These latest reports of the fighting strongly indicate that the Japanese fleet fulfilled the traditional role of an inferior sea force. It sought to defend its most important bases and interests and to harass the distant foe.

Didn't Step Out.

But it did not seek its own destruction against an overwhelm-

(Continued on page 6, column 2.)

Four Are Sunk, Nimitz Reveals

Other Enemy Vessels Left Burning; Three U.S. Craft Damaged.

U.S. Pacific Fleet Headquarters, Pearl Harbor, June 22.—(AP)—U.S. carrier planes sank one Japanese aircraft carrier and three tankers Monday in the war's third smashing blow on the Japanese fleet in a followup to Sunday's air battle off the Marianas in which 353 enemy planes were destroyed.

The combined blow was the third hardest blow at the Japanese Navy since Pearl Harbor.

Adm. Chester W. Nimitz, in an early-morning announcement today, said that possibly a fifth enemy vessel, a destroyer, was sunk in the Monday battle between the Marianas and the Philippine Islands.

Nine or 10 enemy vessels, in addition, were damaged.

Stunned by surprise, the enemy fleet offered no counter-attack and fled. There was no sign whatever that the two big fleets had joined surface battle.

The U.S. 5th Fleet suffered no ship losses. Only 49 of its planes were lost in the Monday air battle, which represented an attempt of Japanese carrier-based planes to break up the Saipan invasion. Saipan is the principal enemy stronghold in the Marianas and lies 1,500 miles from Japan and the Philippines.

Some of the American pilots downed may have been rescued, Nimitz said.

The action ended at nightfall with the Japanese fleeing and there was no indication that the battle had been resumed.

Adm. Nimitz also announced that 353 enemy planes were shot down in the Japanese futile attempt Sunday on Adm. Mitscher's force. This added 53 enemy craft to the previous estimate of 300 destroyed.

Two U.S. carriers and one battleship suffered "superficial damage" and 21 aircraft were lost in combat. A fleet spokesman said superficial damage means the ship's capacity for battle was not impaired, indicating these three probably participated in Monday's action.

The attack of the 5th Fleet under command of Adm. Raymond A. Spruance was such a complete surprise that the Japanese apparently made no counter-attack against any of our surface units.

Adm. Nimitz, who stayed at his headquarters past midnight receiving battle reports and still appeared bright-eyed despite his 60 years of age, said the Japanese force consisted of four or more battleships, five or six carriers, five fleet tankers and an unspecified number of cruisers and destroyers.

He listed these casualties inflicted on the enemy:

One carrier, believed to be the Zuikaku

(Continued on page 4, column 2.)

Der Rufer

FÜR DEN SS-TRUPPEN-ÜBUNGSPLATZ HEIDELAGER

Folge 49 | Herausgeber: Kdtr. des SS=Tr.=Ueb.=Pl. Heidelager | 8. Juli 1944

Entscheidung nur bei den Waffen

„Neues und Außergewöhnliches wird noch kommen" – Heuchlerische Plutokratenpolitik

Die Gewalt des Krieges überschattet alle politischen Vorgänge. An allen Fronten sind Schlachten großen Ausmaßes im Gange, so daß der eigentlichen Politik im Augenblick nur wenig Raum für ihre Wirksamkeit bleibt. Es ist immer betont worden, daß nur die Waffen über den Ausgang dieses Krieges entscheiden können. Im gegenwärtigen Zeitpunkt erkennt man die Bestätigung für diese Annahme.

Die Diskussion um Finnland ist in den letzten Tagen wieder in den Hintergrund getreten. Finnland hat sich, nachdem sich keine Möglichkeiten für einen annehmbaren Waffenstillstand mit der Sowjetunion ergeben haben, für die Fortführung des Kampfes an der Seite Deutschlands entschieden; es hat darüber hinaus seine Politik mit der des Deutschen Reiches in Übereinstimmung gebracht. So konnte es nicht ausbleiben, daß die Vereinigten Staaten die bisher immer noch aufrechterhaltenen diplomatischen Beziehungen mit Helsinki abbrachen. Ob diesem Schritt die Kriegserklärung folgen wird, muß abgewa[illegible]et werden, es sieht aber nicht so aus. [illegible] Haltung des Weißen Hauses gegen[illegible]land hat selbst in den USA manches [illegible]en ausgelöst. Ein großer Teil der [illegible]en Meinung erinnert sich noch zu ge[illegible]e Versprechungen, die Finnland im [illegible]939/40 von Washington gemacht [illegible] sowie an die damaligen Sympathien, als [illegible] jetzt eine völlige Umkehr erfolgen könnte. Die neutralen Staaten jedenfalls haben zur Kenntnis genommen, daß die USA dem finnischen Volk, das ebenso wie das amerikanische demokratisch gesinnt ist, in seiner schwersten Stunde nicht geholfen haben, sondern im Gegenteil die günstige Gelegenheit benutzten, um die immer lästiger werdende finnische Frage auf diese Art loszuwerden.

Der Führer hielt vor den Vertretern der deutschen Rüstung eine Ansprache; sie hat in England offensichtlich starken Eindruck gemacht, vor allem die Worte des Führers darüber, daß der deutsche Erfindergeist auch das nötige Gleichgewicht in diesem Kriege wiederherstellen und dem weiteren Verlauf des Krieges seine Prägung geben wird. Ganz allgemein, so berichtet jetzt ein schwedischer Korrespondent in einer ersten Meldung aus London, hat man diese Worte des Führers in Zusammenhang gebracht mit der „V 1". Die Quintessenz, die allgemein aus den Worten des Führers gezogen wird, ist die, daß „Neues und bestimmt Außergewöhnliches noch kommen wird".

Diese englische Reaktion, wie sie von einem schwedischen Korrespondenten beschrieben wird, muß als unmittelbare Folge des Einsatzes der „V 1" betrachtet werden. Es ist offensichtlich also vorbei mit den großspurigen Gesten und Worten, daß Deutschland nicht in der Lage sei, durch neue Waffen dem Krieg auch eine neue Wendung zu geben.

Die methodischen Vertuschungsversuche der britischen Regierung über die Wirkung der deutschen Vergeltungswaffe haben auch durch die Unterhaussitzung eine neue Beleuchtung erfahren. Allein die Tatsache, daß von den Abgeordneten aller Parteien die unverzügliche Ansetzung einer Geheimsitzung in dem britischen Parlament kategorisch verlangt wurde, beleuchtet die gegenwärtig in der britischen Öffentlichkeit herrschende Stimmung blitzartig. In der Berichterstattung aus London zeigt sich die Tendenz, die Beunruhigung der britischen Bevölkerung hauptsächlich darauf zu konzentrieren, daß es „an Informationen mangele". Es handelt sich hier um ein offensichtliches Ablenkungsmanöver gegenüber der Weltöffentlichkeit. Die Gründe liegen viel tiefer. Jedermann muß ja heute in England wissen, daß die Katastrophe, die Südengland betroffen hat, nichts anderes als eine unmitelbare Auswirkung des von Churchill erfundenen Terrorkrieges gegen die deutsche Zivilbevölkerung ist. Wenn heute nun Mister Churchill so energisch vor die Schranken gerufen worden ist, so geschieht das nicht etwa, damit er dort die Rolle eines väterlichen Ratgebers spiele, sondern in seiner Eigenschaft als Hauptverantwortlicher für den Luftterror. Dieser Umstand allein erklärt die Tatsache, daß sich Churchill so an den Ohren ziehen läßt, bevor er vor dem Parlament erscheint. Die beispiellos heftigen Szenen, die sich im Unterhaus abspielten, sind ein Beweis dafür, daß es sich hier nicht um die Befriedigung eines Informationsbedürfnisses handelt, sondern daß eine Grundwelle durch das britische Volk geht.

Eichenlaub für Rundstedt und Dollmann

Der Führer verlieh am 2. Juli das Eichenlaub zum Ritterkreuz des Eisernen Kreuzes als 518. Soldaten der deutschen Wehrmacht dem Oberbefehlshaber der VII. Armee, Generaloberst Friedrich Dollmann, nach dem Tode und als 519. Soldaten der deutschen Wehrmacht dem bisherigen Oberbefehlshaber West, Generalfeldmarschall von Rundstedt.

Neue Schwerterträger

Der Führer verlieh das Eichenlaub mit Schwertern zum Ritterkreuz des Eisernen Kreuzes an Oberstleutnant Josef Priller, Kommodore eines Jagdgeschwaders als 73., Major [illegible]drich Lang, Kommodore eines Schlachtgeschwaders als 74., und Oberleutnant Erich [illegible]ann in einem Jagdgeschwader als 75. Soldaten der Deutschen Wehrmacht.

Neuer Ritterkreuzträger der Waffen-SS

Der Führer verlieh das Ritterkreuz des Eisernen Kreuzes an SS-Obersturmführer Hans Eckert, Bataillonskommandeur in der SS-Panzerdivision „Das Reich".

Vorbereitung neuer Feindangriffe

Im Juni 312600 BRT versenkt und über 2000 Feindflugzeuge vernichtet

Der Erfolg der deutschen Abwehrkämpfe in der Normandie bei Caen wird von englischer Seite in der Form zugegeben, daß plötzlich von diesen bisher vielerörterten Kämpfen kaum noch die Rede ist. Tagelang war die englische Presse angefüllt mit Ankündigungen von großen Offensivplänen. Es wurde so hingestellt, als wenn Montgomery endgültig zu der „entscheidenden Operation" ausgeholt hätte. Tatsächlich war ihre Einleitung nicht nur [illegible] sondern auch bereits in den Morgenstunden des 4. Juli beiderseits der Straße Bayeux—Caen in Gang gesetzt. Der erhoffte Durchbruch ist aber nicht zustande gekommen, und Montgomery hat seine großangelegten Versuche mit sehr schweren Verlusten bezahlen müssen.

Jetzt versucht ihm der USA-General Bradley am Westflügel der Invasionsfront durch einen Vorstoß aus der Cherbourghalbinsel heraus Entlastung zu verschaffen. Aus den feindlichen Berichten geht dieser Charakter der amerikanischen Offensive, die sich vorläufig nur auf Gewinnung des Sockels der Halbinsel erstreckt, deutlich hervor.

Mit vermehrten Anstrengungen Montgomerys zur Wiederholung dieser Versuche ist binnen kurzem zu rechnen. Gegenwärtig aber hat er sich gezwungen gesehen, wie sogar englische Ankündigungen besagen, seine zum Teil abgekämpften und übermüdeten Streitkräfte umzugruppieren. Kein Wunder nach den bereits bisher erlittenen schweren Einbußen.

Schweres Vergeltungsfeuer liegt nun schon über drei Wochen auf London.

In Italien griff der Feind, von zahlreichen Panzern unterstützt, fast auf der gesamten Front an. Nach harten Kämpfen an der Ligurischen Küste, bei Volterre, nordwestlich Siena, im Raum von Arezzo, beiderseits Umbertide und an der Adria-Küste wurde der Gegner verlustreich abgewiesen.

Im Südabschnitt der Ostfront wurde die Stadt Kowel zur örtlichen Frontverkürzung planmäßig und ohne feindlichen Druck geräumt. Im Süden der Ostfront lebte am 5. Juli die Gefechtstätigkeit zwischen dem oberen Dnjestr und Kowel auf.

Im Mittelabschnitt wird an den Landengen zwischen den Sümpfen im Raum Baranowicze und Molodeczno weiterhin erbittert gekämpft. Nordwestlich des Narocz-Sees wurden sowjetische Angriffsspitzen aufgefangen, zwischen Dünaburg und Polozk zahlreiche Angriffe des Feindes abgewiesen. In einer Einbruchsstelle sind noch heftige Kämpfe im Gange.

In den schweren Abwehrkämpfen im Osten fanden die Kommandierenden Generäle, General der Artillerie Martinek und General der Flakartillerie Pfeiffer, sowie Generalleutnant Schünemann, an der Spitze ihrer Korps kämpfend, den Heldentod.

Nordamerikanische Bomber führten am 6. Juli einen Terrorangriff gegen Kiel. In der Nacht griff ein schwacher feindlicher Bomberverband den Raum von Wien an.

Im Kampf gegen die feindliche Invasionsflotte und den Nachschub über See versenkten Luftwaffe, Kriegsmarine, Heeres- und Marineküstenbatterien im Monat Juni einundfünfzig Fracht- und Transportschiffe mit 312600 BRT. Sechsundfünfzig weitere Schiffe mit 320000 BRT sowie zahlreiche kleinere Transportfahrzeuge und Landungsboote wurden zum Teil schwer beschädigt. An feindlichen Kriegsschiffen wurden zwei schwere und drei leichte Kreuzer, zweiundzwanzig Zerstörer, fünfzehn Schnellboote, ein Unterseeboot, Landungsboote und ein Bewacher versenkt. Mehrere Schlachtschiffe, darunter ein Schiff der „Nelson-Klasse", einundzwanzig Kreuzer, zweiundzwanzig Zerstörer, sechsundzwanzig Landungsspezialschiffe und zwölf Schnellboote wurden durch Bomber-, Torpedo- und Artillerietreffer schwer beschädigt. Mit der Vernichtung eines Teiles dieser Schiffe kann gerechnet werden. Die feindlichen Schiffsverluste erhöhen sich noch durch Minentreffer.

Die Anglo-Amerikaner verloren im Monat Juni bei ihren Unternehmungen im Westen, im Mittelmeerraum und über dem Reichsgebiet 2007 Flugzeuge.

Der Führer ehrt den Helden von Narvik

Der Führer bei der Kranzniederlegung am Sarge während des Staatsaktes, mit dem die deutsche Nation Abschied von Generaloberst Dietl nahm, der bei einem Flugzeugunfall ums Leben kam. (Siehe auch Seite 4.) Presse-Hoffmann

Auf dem Höhepunkt

Von *Hauptmann Werner Stephan*

Zweieinhalb Wochen nach dem Beginn der Invasion im Westen haben auch die Sowjets mit Großangriffen begonnen. Das ist gewiß keine Überraschung. Denn wenn sie ihre Bundesgenossen in England und US-Amerika durch immer neue Beschwörungen veranlaßt hatten, nun endlich nicht mehr nur an Behelfsfronten und noch dazu größtenteils mit fremden Hilfskräften zu kämpfen, sondern selbst an entscheidend wichtigen Stellen ihre Haut zu Markte zu tragen, so taten sie das natürlich nicht, um von nun ab lediglich als Zuschauer der Entwicklung der Dinge zuzusehen. Daß der neue Ansturm weitere schwere Opfer von den ausgebluteten bolschewistischen Armeen fordern wird, das ist den Machthabern im Kreml ebenso gleichgültig wie in den vergangenen drei Jahren des Krieges. Nachdem sichergestellt ist, daß sie sie nicht mehr allein zu bringen haben, sondern daß auch die Plutokratien beim Ansturm gegen die Befestigungswerke des Atlantikwalls Division auf Division einzusetzen gezwungen sind, traten sie 17 Tage nach den Anglo-Amerikanern auch ihrerseits wieder an. Dabei haben sie ihrer bisherigen Taktik entsprechend zunächst eine ganz breite Front gewählt, die von Nowoschow und Polozk im Norden über Witebsk und das Stromgebiet des Pripjet bis nach Tarnopol reicht. Sie haben an Panzern und Schlachtfliegern nicht gespart. Wo sie nun den Schwerpunkt ihres Angriffes zu wählen beabsichtigen, bleibt zunächst noch abzuwarten. Sie wollen erst einmal deutsche Kräfte binden und beschäftigen, tasten vielleicht auch zunächst ab, wo etwa das Terrain ihnen günstig sein könnte. Die deutsche Führung kennt dieses Verfahren, seit die Bolschewisten im Dezember 1941 zur ersten Winteroffensive antraten. Sie ist darauf vorbereitet und wird sich sicherlich an keiner Stelle verausgaben. Seit drei Monaten hatte sie Zeit, ihre Truppen neu zu gruppieren und auszurüsten. Ihre Verbindungslinien sind nicht den gleichen Beanspruchungen mehr ausgesetzt wie vor einem Jahre, als die Kämpfe bei Orel, Bjelgorod und Taganrog einsetzten. Sie weiß, was auf dem Spiel steht und ist auf schwere Kämpfe gerüstet.

Der Tag, der die ersten bolschewistischen Massenstürme dieses Sommers an der deutschen Ostfront sah, hatte im Westen die Amerikaner im Angriff auf die Festung Cherbourg gefunden. Nachdem es sich für den Feind als unmöglich erwiesen hatte aus dem gewonnenen Landekopf nach Osten, Süden und Südwesten vorzudringen, hatte er zunächst alle Kräfte auf die Gewinnung dieser Seefestung am Kanal geworfen, die mit dem französischen Festland nur durch den schmalen Hals der Halbinsel Cotentin verbunden ist. Die Engländer waren östlich der Orne und südlich Tilly, die Amerikaner bei St. Lô und Carentan völlig gescheitert. Beide Verbündeten konnten sich nicht weiter entwikkeln, als das Feuer ihrer Schiffsartillerie reichte. So hatten sie sich entschlossen, es trotz aller Verluste weiter so vollständig wie möglich zu nutzen und ihre Kräfte zunächst im nördlichsten Ausläufer des Festlandes, vor Cherbourg, zu konzentrieren. Der Hafen, um den sie sich bemühten, ist freilich kein Naturhafen wie etwa Brest oder Le Havre. Er verdankt seine Existenz Jahrzehnte langer mühseliger Arbeit, wobei die verschiedenen französischen Regierungen zu immer neuen Modernisierungen gezwungen waren. Er ist daher auch leichter als andere Häfen durch Zerstörungen verletzbar. Um ihn tobte ein schwerer Kampf. Die Gedanken aller Deutschen gingen in jenen Tagen zu den Männern, die in der Seefestung Cherbourg dem Ansturm des Feindes vom Lande, von der See und aus der Luft tapfer trotzten. Ihre Kameraden verstärkten inzwischen ihre Stellungen an dem südlichen Riegel, der die Halbinsel Cotentin in ostwestlicher Richtung absperrt. Bald wird es sich entscheiden, ob hier die große Schlacht geschlagen werden wird, die die Anglo-Amerikaner führen müssen, wenn sie aus der Enge des Küstenraumes in die Weite des Kontinents vorstoßen wollen, oder ob sie noch zu neuen Landungsversuchen an anderen Stellen gezwungen sein werden.

Die Operationen in rascherem Tempo vorwärtszutreiben, dazu sind insbesondere die Engländer genötigt, seit das deutsche Störungsfeuer auf London und Südostengland Tag für Tag und Nacht für Nacht sich fortsetzt. Über drei Wochen dauert es nun bereits so gut wie ohne Unterbrechung an. Ein neues, die Feinde schwer beunruhigendes Moment ist damit auf dem Höhepunkt des Krieges in die Operationen überraschend eingefügt worden. Alle Versuche, durch aktive Bekämpfung seiner Herr zu werden, sind fehlgeschlagen. Die Wiederholung der Terrorangriffe, etwa auf Berlin, können demgegenüber weder psychologisch [illegible]lich [illegible] den [illegible] für [illegible]

THE STARS AND STRIPES

MEDITERRANEAN

Vol. 1, No. 203, Monday, July 10, 1944 | ITALY EDITION | TWO LIRE

ALLIES TAKE CAEN, LA HAYE

Red Army Batters Into Wilno

Fall Of Lida Announced By Russians

MOSCOW, July 9 — Soviet troops today fought in the streets of Wilno (Vilna) after a lightning advance along a 50-mile front which carried tank-supported Red Army infantry spearheads across the rail network leading out of the city, threatening to isolate thousands of Germans who are contesting the Red Army advance in savage house-to-house fighting.

Russian armor and shock troops smashed into the former Lithuanian capital, with a pre-war population of almost a quarter of a million, shortly after Marshal Stalin in an order of the day announced the capture of Baranovichi, vital rail center on the main Moscow-Warsaw-Berlin trunk line, 115 miles south of Wilno.

An Order of the Day from Marshal Stalin tonight announced the capture of Lida, an important rail junction 90 miles west of Minsk and approximately halfway between Wilno and Baranovichi.

(A German News Agency report that five Soviet rifle divisions and an entire tank corps launched a new offensive against German positions in the Carpathians and east of Lwow was not confirmed.)

Baranovichi, where the Germans made their only determined stand since the fall of Minsk, controls the north-south railway from Wilno to Rovno and the line from Brest Litovsk, in addition to the Moscow - Warsaw - Berlin trunk route. The city's fall releases Marshal Konstantin Rokossovsky's

(Continued on page 4)

Troop Train Toll Mounts

JELLICO, Tenn., July 9—Two giant cranes swung cables into the boulder-strewn gorge of Clear River today, tugging at the last demolished troop car of the wrecked military train in which at least 25 persons died Thursday night. The Louisville and Nashville Railroad train was derailed seven miles south of Jellico.

Six additional bodies were recovered yesterday, raising the death toll of two crewmen and 17 soldiers previously listed. Ray Ellison, Jellico undertaker, said that the workers expected to bring out others when the remaining car was moved.

A spokesman for the Louisville and Nashville Railroad said it might take a few days before all the wreckage was cleared from the 50-foot defile, where the locomotive and four cars plunged after the derailment. A fifth car left the tracks but hung on the steep bank.

Rome Government

ROME, July 9 — The Italian government will return to its traditional seat at Rome next Saturday, Prime Minister Ivanoe Bonomi announced today. Simultaneously, the Allied Control Commission disclosed that its headquarters will move to Rome.

Slav Government Formed In London

LONDON, July 9 — A new "unity" government-in-exile for Yugoslavia has been formed in London under the premiership of Dr. Ivan Subasic, who recently visited Marshal Tito in liberated Yugoslav territory.

Two representatives of Marshal Tito's movement, Sreten Vukosavlyevich, a Serbian university professor who is one of the leaders of the Independent Democrats, and Drago Marusic, exgovernor of Slovenia, are included in the new cabinet.

B-29s Socked Five Targets

WASHINGTON, July 9 — Superfortresses returned to their China bases without the loss of a single plane when they celebrated the eighth anniversary of China's declaration of war upon Japan by blasting five objectives on Friday.

The B-29s blasted three Japanese targets and two in enemy-held territory in their raid. They hit Sasebo, Japan's "Norfolk," and the industrial centers of Yawata and Omura, all on Kyushu Island, southernmost link in the Japanese chain. Laoyatan, North China coastal port, and Hankow, the Yantze River harbor which serves as Japan's chief base in east China, also were blasted.

Meanwhile, U. S. forces slaughtered 1,500 out of 2,000 Japanese who launched a fanatic pre-dawn counter-attack on Saipan Island, Admiral Chester W. Nimitz' headquarters reported today.

The assault, which took place Thursday, carried the Japs to the outskirts of Tanapag before the Yanks smashed the desperate attackers. U. S. forces are now less than two miles from the northeast tip of Saipan.

At Southeast Asia headquarters

(Continued on page 4)

Fight Rages Below Foe's Gothic Line

Yanks Battling Leghorn Defense; Port In Flames

ADVANCED ALLIED HEADQUARTERS, July 9—The struggle for the approaches to the German's Gothic Line defenses of the Po Valley mounted in fury over the weekend as Allied troops drove slowly but steadily forward, today's communique revealed.

American troops of the 5th Army were drawing slowly closer to Leghorn, from which huge columns of smoke poured as German sappers put the torch to naval oil stores. Although apparently preparing for the loss of the city, German troops facing the Yanks a bare eight miles below Leghorn showed no signs of withdrawing.

U. S. tank and infantrymen on the Ligurian Sea flank yesterday pushed north of Rosignano and Castellina, which fell to the Yanks in bitter house-to-house fighting. U. S. troops above Castellina were meeting the enemy's 26th Panzer Grenadier Division, which had been shifted from the east. Enemy mortar and artillery fire was stepped up and heavy counterat-

(Continued on Page 4)

All Supplements Are Discontinued

The War Department has directed that publication of material provided The Stars and Stripes by Reader's Digest, Collier's and The Saturday Evening Post be discontinued immediately.

In line with the directive, no further supplements of the three magazines will appear.

Oops—Five More Generals Kayoed

MOSCOW, July 9—The Moscow radio last night announced the capture or surrender of five German generals: General Mueller Buelow, commander of the 246th Infantry; General Kraus, commander of the 78th Assault; Lt. Gen. Hoffmeister, commander of the 41st Tank Corps; Maj. Gen. Steinkeller, commander of the 60th German Motorized Division and Maj. Gen. Hirt, commander of the 381st Infantry Regiment.

The German News Agency meanwhile announced the "accidental" deaths of General Karl Eglseer, commander of a mountain army corps and General Emil von Wickede, an infantry commander.

15th Heavies Rock Ploesti

MAAF HEADQUARTERS, July 9 — The Concordia-Vega and Xenia refineries in Rumania's Ploesti oil fields today were hit by 15th USAAF heavy bombers which broke through strong flak and air resistance to strike another telling blow against the oil-starved enemy.

Liberators escorted by Mustangs scored direct hits on the Concordia-Vega works, which was the second largest in Rumania although its output has been cut down by previous Allied bombing attacks.

Formations of Flying Forts covered by P-38 Lightnings hit the Xenia oil refineries, which had been blasted last on June 6. Several of the enemy fighters which swarmed up to meet the attack were sent down in flames.

Mustang pilots who flew a sweep over the Ploesti region just after the bomber attacks reported three great columns of smoke rising from the refinery areas.

Anchor Point Of Nazi Line Is Captured

LONDON, July 9 — Twin Allied victories were scored today when British and Canadian troops of Lt. Gen. Miles C. Dempsey's 2nd Army captured Caen, right anchor of the German defense line in France, and Americans of Lt. Gen. Omar N. Bradley drove the enemy out of La Haye de Puits.

The American success at La Haye de Puits, on the northwestern and opposite end of the Normandy line, was made after a terrific struggle in which the Associated Press reported the Germans had made a "miniature Stalingrad" of the village. U. S. troops had to fight from house to house, each of which was leveled to rubbel as successive German strongpoints were reduced.

In the face of most stubborn resistance, General Montgomery's troops pressed in on Caen, with infantrymen making steady progress with heavy artillery and air support.

Northwest of the city, a strong arc of Allied troops was formed with the capture of several villages, incuding St. Contest, Epron and Hereuvile. On the northeast side, British and Canadian forces, in unceasing battle, reached the outskirts of the port and secured high ground only about a half mile from the center of Caen. On the eastern flank, British units advancing up the Orne River, by this morning had driven within 1,600 yards of the docks.

The smash into Caen was supported by intense artillery barrages and attacks by rocket-firing Typhoon fighter planes. Instead of using saturation barrages, the British and Canadian guns pulverized specific targets ahead of the infantry and tankmen. Between 40 to 50 German tanks appeared in small groups on the western side of Caen, but these were met by heavy AT and artillery fire and 18 to 20 of them were knocked out.

With Caen in Allied hands, Rommel's armor in the plain to the south of the city is open to

(Continued on Page 4)

Circus Officials Charged With Manslaughter

HARTFORD, Conn., July 9—There was hardly a church or a chapel in this sorrowing city today which had not scheduled final rites for one or more dead, while state and county municipal authorities opened an investigation into last Thursday's flaming circus tragedy which took at least 154 lives, the majority of them children.

Of those who died when the huge main tent of the Ringling Brothers, Barnum and Bailey Circus collapsed in flames, only 11 remained unidentified. In that group of unclaimed bodies were five children, four women and two men.

Five officials of the "world's greatest circus" were charged with manslaughter over the weekend after authorities had questioned hundreds of canvasmen, performers, roustabouts and members of the matinee audience of 10,000 who saw more than an acre of canvas dissolve into flame over their heads. Manslaughter charges were lodged against J. A. Haley, vice president of the circus; Edward Versteeg, chief electrician; David W. Blanchfield, chief wagon and tractor man; George W. Smith, general manager, and Leonard Aylesworth, boss canvas man.

CORONER IN CHARGE

An additional 15 executives were subpoenaed to a Tuesday inquest at which Coroner Frank E. Healy intends fixing the responsibility for the disaster. Under Connecticut law, the coroner has charge of the investigation of violent deaths in the pre-grand jury stage.

Mayor William H. Mortensen, who heads the committee of nine officials conducting a separate investigation, made two charges in his first public statement:

(1) The circus tent, the largest in the world, "had been sprayed with parafine, which had been melted in gasoline," (2) the steel runway used to bring the animals in and out of the big top "closed off an entire end of the oval, obstructing the exits." Approximately 60 bodies were found jammed against this runway, he said.

Authorities were concentrating on the spotlights perched high in the corners of the big tent which at the instant the fire broke out were illuminating the "Flying Wallendas, a high wire aerial act, in their white-hot glare.

Some witnesses said that the fire appeared directly above one of the spotlights.

At Hartford's hospitals, 25 of the many injured were reported still in a critical condition. Physicians are using penicillin to stem the mounting death toll, but it was feared that the final death list might be still higher.

(Stars and Stripes U. S. Bureau)

NEW YORK, July 9—The loss of life from fire in the main tent of Ringling Bros., Barnum and Bailey Circus in Hartford, Connecticut, was among the major fire tragedies in the United States, the Associated Press reported.

Chicago's Iroquois Theater fire of Dec. 30, 1903, when 602 persons met their death, was the nation's greatest catastrophe from fire.

Approximately 500 died in the San Francisco earthquake and fire of 1906 and 498 are known to have been killed in the fire at the Cocoanut Grove Night Club fire in Boston on Nov. 28, 1942.

Other major fires and their toll include: the Triangle Shirtwaist Company fire in New York City, March 25, 1911—145; the Crile Clinic Hospital fire in Cleveland, May 15, 1929—124; the Ohio State Penitentiary fire in Columbus on April 21, 1930—320; the Morro Castle fire off Ashbury Park, New Jersey, September 8, 1934—134; the New London, Texas, school explosion and fire of March 18, 1937—294.

Capture Caen, La Haye

WAR EXTRA

CHARACTER · QUALITY · AMERICA FIRST! · ENTERPRISE · ACCURACY

Los Angeles Examiner

AN AMERICAN PAPER FOR THE AMERICAN PEOPLE · THE GREAT NEWSPAPER OF THE GREAT SOUTHWEST

Reg. U.S. Pat. Off.

Examiner Telephone RIchmond 1212 · Examiner Building, 1111 S. Broadway

VOL. XLI—NO. 212 · LOS ANGELES, MONDAY, JULY 10, 1944 · PCC · Two Sections—Part I—FIVE CENTS

SAIPAN FALLS

YANKS CONQUER NIP ISLE AFTER 25-DAY BATTLE; 12,000 JAPS SLAIN BY U. S. FORCE

Get Bases to Bomb Japan, Philippines

By H. K. Reynolds
Staff Correspondent International News Service

WASHINGTON, July 9.—Saipan Island, only one thousand five hundred miles from Tokyo, was in American hands tonight after 25 days of the bloodiest fighting yet witnessed in the Pacific war.

The great victory, won by United States Marines and Army troops, was announced simultaneously in Washington and Pearl Harbor by Admiral Chester W. Nimitz in the following communique:

"Our forces have completed the conquest of Saipan.

"Organized resistance ended on the afternoon of July 8 (West Longitude date) and the elimination of scattered, disorganized remnants of the enemy force is proceeding rapidly."

Defense Cost Japs 10,000 Dead

Desperate defense of Saipan, which American forces invaded on June 14, cost the Japanese an estimated 10,000 to 12,000 troops killed, about 20 ships sunk or damaged and approximately 800 planes destroyed in combat.

American casualties at Saipan have been severe, but much less than those suffered by the Japanese, Navy officials said.

American units which bore the brunt of the gruelling ground fighting were the Second and Fourth Marine divisions, and the 27th Infantry division of the U. S. Army.

American Losses Also Heavy

For the first 14 days of the campaign, American casualties totalled 1474 killed, 7400 wounded and 878 missing. Further casualties have been incurred in the subsequent fighting, especially that of last Thursday when several thousand Japanese launched their final, suicidal attack.

Navy officials in Washington said that completion of the occupation of the island, key Japanese stronghold in the Marianas group, will enable United States sea and air forces to project their overwhelming might to the north, west and south to include the Japanese mainland, the Philippines and the greater part of the Dutch East Indies.

Saipan, with an area of 72 square miles, is relatively flat and ideal for air bases for U. S. Army B-29 Super Fortress bombers, expected to strike in increasing numbers against the Japanese homeland.

More than 1500 Japanese were killed in this single action, and American casualties also mounted as the enemy was thrown back to defeat.

Admiral Nimitz's communique

(Continued on Page 2, Column 8)

WOUNDED AT SAIPAN—American fighters wounded in fierce fighting for possession of Saipan Island receive emergency treatment at a first aid station on the beach before being transferred to Coast Guard manned assault transports anchored off shore.
—Associated Press wirephoto.

THE BOSS WATCHES—Vice Admiral Marc A. Mitscher watches strikes launched for Saipan from a vantage spot aboard a carrier during the battle of the Marianas.
—Associated Press wirephoto.

Allies Seize Nazi Anchors in Normandy

By Kingsbury Smith
Staff Correspondent International News Service

SUPREME HEADQUARTERS, ALLIED EXPEDITIONARY FORCE, July 9.—Forward-smashing Allied troops shattered the anchor points of the German battleline in Normandy today by occupying the nerve center of La Haye du Puits at the western edge and the fortified bastion of Caen near the eastern extremity.

La Haye du Puits fell to American troops driving headlong down the Cherbourg Peninsula, depriving the Nazis of a key communications center and concentration point from which possible large scale counterattacks could have been mounted.

Caen was occupied by battle-grimed British and Canadian forces under the over-all command of General Sir Bernard Law Montgomery little more than 24 hours after the start of their surprise offensive at dawn yesterday.

La Haye Under Yank Rule

La Haye was entered late last night by American troops attacking from the west and by 10 p. m. the town was completely under their control, official spokesmen revealed.

Caen, for which the Germans have waged a terrific defensive battle ever since the invasion got under way, was strongly defended to the last and was "considered heavily mined and booby trapped," spokesmen said.

German paratroops, acting as regular ground

Nazis Claim New Weapon

LONDON, July 9.—(AP)—The German radio reported today that an Allied battleship had been hit by bombs and beached off the Orne estuary in Normandy, while the German-controlled Paris radio asserted the Nazis had sunk 10 Allied ships in 10 minutes with a new secret weapon.

There was no confirmation of these reports or of a more modest claim by the German high command to have sunk an Allied cruiser and a destroyer with "weapons of the Germany navy."

A spokesman at supreme Allied headquarters said he had no knowledge of any new Nazi naval weapon.

The Paris radio said the beached battleship was the 22,189-ton Courbet, a 1913-model French vessel which has been in the fighting-French navy since the fall of France.

While German communiques repeatedly have claimed the sinking of various Allied naval vessels since the invasion began, it remained for the Paris radio commentator "Paquis" to make the most extravagant claims.

Commenting on "vengeance weapon No. 2," he said, "V-2 may be a magic torpedo which can sink 10 ships in as many

(Continued on Page 2, Column 6)

Nazis Flee in Disorder; Russ 92 Miles From East Prussia

MOSCOW, July 9.—(AP)—The German army fell back in disorder toward East Prussia and Poland today and the collapse of Hitler's front grew by the hour from the Soviet Baltic Republic of Lithuania—whose borders the Russians are well within—to the Pinsk bulge.

Red army men ,just as the Germans did in the fall of France, were knifing past large Nazi units leaving them behind to be cleaned up later.

Inside the Lithuanian border the Soviets were pushing through the streets of Wilno, the capital, and indications were that most of the city if not all of it would be in Russian hands by nightfall.

Northwest of Wilno Red Army units drove on toward Kaunas, the old Lithuanian capital, which is but 48 miles away from General Ivan D. Cherniakhovsky's tanks and cavalry.

92 MILES FROM BORDER

The Red Army today was only 92 miles from the borders of East Prussia.

The Russians have captured Lida, Premier Marshal Stalin announced from Moscow today in an order of the day.

Stalin's order was addressed to General Ivan D. Charniakhovsky, and declared the town was taken by tanks, cavalry and infantry.

As the Russians pushed on toward Brest Litovsk and Bialystok—the area of the Curzon Line which the Russians have proposed as the postwar Polish boundary—an observer in Pravda declared "the historical hour of liebration for the Poles approaches."

The Poles would be set free by the Red Army and the Polish Army in Soviet Russia, he asserted.

NEARING MAIN RAILWAY

Soviet units, as they cut across the Wilno-Daugavpils (Dvinsk) railway north of Wilno, are approaching the main German railway through the Baltics, the Berlin-Kaunas-Riga-Reval (Tallinn) Line.

Thus a slight 48 miles—the distance between Cherniakhovsky's

(Continued on Page 2, Cols. 3-4)

BARKLEY NOMINATES ROOSEVELT

THE WEATHER
Mostly cloudy, with moderate temperature this afternoon; showers and thunderstorms this evening and tonight.
Detailed Weather Report Page 19

Read The Baltimore News-Post for complete, accurate war coverage. It is the only Baltimore newspaper possessing the three great wire services—
ASSOCIATED PRESS
INTERNATIONAL NEWS SERVICE
UNITED PRESS

THE BALTIMORE NEWS-POST
AN INDEPENDENT NEWSPAPER
The Largest Evening Circulation in the Entire South

10

VOL. CXLV.—NO. 66 Entered as second-class matter at Baltimore Postoffice. THURSDAY EVENING, JULY 20, 1944 PRICE 3 CENTS

HITLER ESCAPES ASSASSIN
BURNED, BRUISED BY BOMB

Reds Take 2 Outposts Of Lwow

LONDON, July 20—(U. P.).—Premier Josef Stalin announced tonight that Red armies had advanced 31 miles on a 93-mile front in a new offensive in Lower Poland, and to the south had captured the big rail junctions of Rawa Ruska, 30 miles northwest of Lwow, and Wlodzimierz, 52 miles to the northeast.

Stalin issued two orders of the day in quick succession reporting the offensive aimed from the Kowel area toward Brest-Litovsk and later the fall to the First Ukrainian Army of Rawa Ruska and Wlodzimierz, major outposts of Lwow against which the Russians were closing.

STORM TWO JUNCTIONS

Marshal Ivan S. Konev's army stormed and captured the two rail junctions which Stalin described as "important strongholds of the German defenses in the Western Ukraine." Moscow regards that area of pre-war Poland as a part of the Ukraine.

The first order of the day said:

"Troops of the first White Russian front, having launched an offensive from the area of Kowel, broke through the heavily fortified German defenses and in three days of offensive battles advanced 31 miles, widening their breach to 93 miles."

LINKS BATTLE ZONES

Among the captured towns were Ratno, 46 miles southeast of Brest Litovsk, and Lyuboml, 30 miles west of Kowel.

The new drive linked Rokossovsky's battle zone with that of Marshal Ivan S. Konev, whose First Army of the Ukraine was pushing across the Bug river directly to the south and closing against Lwow.

At the other end of the front Berlin reported heavy fighting only eight miles from the frontier of East Prussia.

British Drive Beyond Caen Toward Paris

SUPREME H. Q., A. E. F., July 20 — (U. P.) .—The British Second Army, hammering out a steadily expanding Normandy break-through arc, drove through nine more towns today, stormed into the streets of Troarn and Bourguebus, and sent a spearhead down the Paris road to Vimont, eight miles southeast of Caen.

Many scores of Allied Sherman tanks were smashing through the network of German fortifications on the Caen plain in wild battles of armor against the Nazis who now had massed at least five and a half divisions in frantic effort to stem the march inland.

United Press Correspondent Richard D. McMillan reported that British and Canadian assault forces stormed six more villages in the area of the break-through. Whether they supplemented or duplicated the nine announced at Supreme Headquarters was not certain.

The German Transocean News Agency said American and Canadian Army forces under Lieut. Gen. George S. Patton had gone into action on the Normandy front. Gen. Dwight D. Eisenhower's headquarters had no comment.

CAPTURE MORE TOWNS

Inside the battle arc, lying an average of four miles from Caen—with advanced positions at Troarn, seven miles to the east, and Vimont, eight miles to the southeast—the British and Canadian troops captured Ifs, Cormelles, Bras, Hubert-Folie, Soliers, Four, Le Poirier, Cagny and Grentheville.

(BACKGROUND NOTE: The German DNB news agency asserted today that British and Canadian troops have opened a new offensive "from Colombelles, in the Touffreville and Sannerville area" of Western France. The enemy outlet said in their thrust the Allies took Emieville, Frenouville, Soliers and Bourguebus.)

A headquarters' spokesman said

Continued on Page 2, Column 7.

STADIUM LINE-UPS

Following are the line-ups for tonight's game at 8.30 P. M. between the Orioles and Newark Bears at Baltimore Stadium.

NEWARK	ORIOLES
6 Kuk, c.f.	7 Monaco, 2b.
16 Rhabe, r.f.	24 Tiedemann, ss.
23 Zimmerman, 1b.	23 Benjamin, lf.
5 Rabe, l.f.	18 Moss, cf.
9 Drescher, c.	9 Latshaw, 1b.
2 Buzas, 2b.	4 Mackiewicz, cf.
3 Portner, 3b.	35 Skaff, 3b.
4 Reynolds, s.s.	8 Lollar, c.
17 Holcombe, p.	25 Palica, p.
11 Hiller, p.	1 Brann, inf.
22 Bevans, p.	5 Riley, outf.
15 Maldovan, p.	6 Devlin, c.
21 Hiller, p.	29 Shaefer, outf.
14 Page, p.	x Imhoff, c.
10 Marleau, p.	x Holton, c.
18 Queen, p.	12 Van Slate, p.
8 Van Grofsky, c.	14 Rochevot, p.
7 Dwyer, o. f.	15 Lowry, p.
19 Flick, o. f.	20 Embree, p.
12 Crosby, inf.	21 Hooks, p.
1 Meyers, mgr.	26 West, p.
28 Kahn, c.	27 Burkart, p.
	28 Kleckley, p.
	18 Kleine, p.
	16 Pfiefer, inf.
	22 Thomas, mgr.

.Time of game, 8.30 P. M.

7 DIE OF POLIO

LOUISVILLE, Ky., July 20—(A. P.). — The State Board of Health reported today the seventh death this year in Kentucky from poliomyelitis and said the number of cases now totals 202.

Sen. Barkley Nominates Roosevelt

CHICAGO STADIUM, July 20 (A. P.).—The name of Franklin D. Roosevelt was placed in nomination for a fourth term today by Senator Alben W. Barkley of Kentucky and the Democratic National Convention moved toward speedy nomination and an acceptance speech by radio from the President tonight.

By WILLIAM K. HUTCHINSON
International News Service Staff Correspondent.

CHICAGO, July 20.—Vice-President Henry A. Wallace was within 48 votes of renomination in the Democratic National Convention this afternoon as chances of Senator Harry S. Truman winning were dimmed by action of Illinois in deciding to cast its 58 votes for its own Senator, Scott Lucas.

The Illinois caucus was accepted generally as indicating Mayor Edward J. Kelly of Chicago had given up hope of nominating Truman.

Wallace was out in front at 1.15 P. M. (C. W. T.) today with a total of 539 votes, according to an International News Service poll of delegations.

TRUMAN LAGS

Truman, the President's second personal choice as a running mate, lagged far behind with but 258½ votes. His chances were badly hit when Illinois failed to give him its 58 votes.

Senator Alben W. Barkley of Kentucky was in third place with but eighty-one votes. Fourteen other possibilities had scattered support.

If Truman fails of nomination it means this convention will have rejected both the President's first and second choices. Earlier the

Continued on Page 2, Column 1.

ADOLF HITLER
Fuehrer in Belligerent Mood.

Louis Bromfield Says:

Feudin' Enlivens Chicago Conclave

By LOUIS BROMFIELD
Author and Lecturer.
(Written Expressly for the Hearst Newspapers.)

CHICAGO, July 20.—Although outwardly all appears to be serene and under control, there is no such unity at the Democratic Convention as made the Republican gathering seem a dull affair.

Under cover there exists every sort of feud, division and even enmity between groups and even inside State delegations.

You have only to circulate through the corridors of hotels or drop into hotel bedrooms to find what is going on.

I have seen more out-and-out fights and more insults exchanged in a few hours than I heard during the whole Republican convention.

GREAT FEUD THERE

There is, of course, the great feud between the New Dealers and the Old Line Democrats, a fierce and bitter feud which flares up at the most unexpected moments.

And there is a feud that has developed at the last moment between the C. I. O. Political Action Committee and the organization bosses.

It has flared up suddenly when Philip Murray and Sidney Hillman showed their intention to dictate not only policies but who would be acceptable to them as Vice-Presidential candidate.

ARROGANCE IN TACTICS

There was clearly a kind of arrogance in their tactics which the political bosses found hard to swallow from these newcomers in the political game.

Far deeper and more profound is the resentment and hostility toward Murray and Hillman of scores of delegates from the Mississippi basin, the South, the Southwest and the Northwest.

These are the delegates from the small towns, the ranches, the farms, who, in one sense at least,

Continued on Page 2, Column 5.

Jackson Escorted By Gov. O'Conor

STADIUM CHICAGO, Ill., July 20.—Governor Herbert R. O'Conor of Maryland was named to the committee which escorted Senator Samuel D. Jackson of Indiana, the permanent chairman of the Democratic Convention, to the speakers' platform at the second day's session today.

Governor O'Conor got a big hand as he was presented to the audience in the vast hall and the organ and band played "Maryland, My Maryland."

The Governor's associates in the State delegation arose and raised the Maryland standard as O'Conor was presented.

West Coast Blast Death Toll At 322

PORT CHICAGO, Cal., July 20—(A. P.).—The death toll of the explosion of two ammunition-laden ships here Monday night stood at 322 today with a Navy announcement of 213 names of men known to be dead or missing.

Temperatures

Midnight, 68	9 A. M., 70
1 A. M., 69	10 A. M., 72
2 A. M., 70	11 A. M., 76
3 A. M., 69	12 Noon, 79
4 A. M., 70	1 P. M., 80
5 A. M., 70	2 P. M., 80
6 A. M., 70	3 P. M., 81
7 A. M., 69	4 P. M., 80
8 A. M., 70	5 P. M., 75

7 Generals Are Injured In Explosion

LONDON, July 20—(A. P.).—Adolf Hitler was slightly burned and bruised by a bomb in an attempt on his life today while he was surrounded by closest personal military advisers, an announcement from his headquarters said.

Seven generals and two admirals were injured by the blast, Berlin added.

(One broadcast attributed the blast to dyna-

NEW YORK, July 20—(A. P.).—The Berlin home radio said today "the would-be perpetrators of Hitler's assassination have escaped, but the police are on their trail," N. B. C. reported.

mite while another said "explosives" were used. An account recorded by N. B. C. said the unnamed perpetrators escaped, but that police were "on their trail.")

Closely controlled official announcements gave no inkling of the nature of the originators of the attempt, but London contacts with the German underground suggested that the sensational development was the result of serious feuds within the military hierarchy in Germany.

These sources said the attempt might have occurred at Breda, Holland, where Hitler was reported to have gone yesterday for a conference with Marshal Erwin Rommel, his commander in Normandy.

There was speculation that a general brawl may have resulted when Rommel demanded more divisions to prop his front and met with refusal.

SEES MUSSOLINI

Quick to stress the minor nature of the fifty-five-year-old dictator's injuries, the radio announcement said he conferred immediately afterward with Benito Mussolini and also received Reichsmarshal Hermann Goering, who was en route to the headquarters at the time of the atack.

By strange coincidence the attack took place only about 16 hours after Hideki Tojo, the third of the ill-starred Axis leaders who led their countries into war, had been shelved in Tokyo.

Among the seriously injured, Berlin said, was Lieutenant General Schmundt, chief of the German Army's personnel department and chief military aide de camp to Hitler for several years.

OTHERS INJURED

Two lieutenant colonels named Brandt and Borgmann and a "collaborator" named Berger also were listed as seriously injured.

Slightly injured were these:

Generals Jodl, Hitler's personal military aide; Karl Bodenschatz, aide to Hitler; Guenther Korten, chief of staff of the German Air

Continued on Page 2, Column 3.

Baltimoreans Sorry That Hitler's Safe

Prominent Baltimoreans gnashed their teeth in helpless rage today at an unkind fate that, apparently, had spared Herr Hitler when an assassin's bomb missed its target.

Their comment on the incident follows:

Mayor McKeldin:

"What I think about Skunk Hitler can't be printed. My best wish for him right now is that his injuries may take a decided turn for the worse."

G. H. Pouder, executive vice-president, Baltimore Association of Commerce:

"Hitler has bruised and burned the rest of the world. I certainly hope his injuries are nothing trivial."

City Solicitor Simon E. Sobeloff:

"Too bad it didn't succeed. Better luck next time."

State's Attorney J. Bernard Wells:

"It's a shame the assassin didn't take better aim. There ought to be a law in Germany to punish bad marksmanship."

Bernard J. Flynn, U. S. District Attorney:

"If Hitler were permanently out of the way I feel certain the war would be over a lot more quickly."

Col. Henry S. Barrett, State Commander, U. S. Citizens' Defense Corps:

"It's a damn pity they haven't assassinated him long ago."

VERY LATEST NEWS

(Race Results From Howard Sports Daily, Inc.)

RACING RESULTS

AT EMPIRE CITY

Seventh—Dit, $11.40. $4.00, $3.00; Boston Man, $3.20, $2.50; Eire, $3.40.

AT GARDEN STATE

Fifth—Adelphia, $3.30, $2.70, $2.50; Viva Teddy, $4.70, $3.30; Morning Choice, $5.50.

AT SUFFOLK DOWNS

Fifth—Due Sport, $22.80, $8.20, $3.20; Red Ted, $3.80, $2.60; City Bred, $2.40.

AT HAGERSTOWN

Third—Famas Time, $8.40, $3.90, $2.70; Semper Ego, $5.00, $4.10; Ler-Lin, $3.40.

Fourth — Worries, $16.40, $8.70, $5.60; Maroc, $3.90, $3.00; Myrtle M., $4.10.

AT ARLINGTON PARK

Second—Linger Along, $5.60, $3.40, $3.20; Stage Door, $6.00, $5.60; Big Bubble, $8.80.

Daily Double—Special Pet & Linger Along paid $165.00.

LATEST BASEBALL SCORES

(A) At Detroit—Detroit, 7; Wash., 5; end 8th.
(A) At Cleveland—Phila., 1; Cleve., 0; end 6½.
(A) At Chicago—Boston, 7; Chicago, 0; end 2½.
(N) At New York—St. Louis, 2; New York, 0; end 3d.

GARDEN STATE RESULTS

FIRST RACE—Five and one-half furlongs. Off 2.31½. Time, 1.06 2-5.

Leystan, 118 (J. Gilbert)	$67.20	$22.90	$13.20
Split The Wind, 118 (C. Kirk)		6.50	4.10
British Buddy, 118 (J. Breen)			5.10

Also Ran—Tellmenow, Sunredgra, Quatre Call, Royal Gem, Geronimo, Brookfield, Romanicus, Linza and War Archives.

SECOND—Five and one-half furlongs. Off 3.11½. Time, 1.06 3-5.

Lucky Aunt, 118 (L. Knapp)	$20.50	$11.40	8.10
In the Purple, 118 (A. Kirkland)		11.10	7.90
Bride's Biscuit, 113 (K. Scawthorn)			6.70

Also Ran—Beau's Nurse, Panacea, Guernsey Isle, bWar Hysteria, Ginokum, Four Queens, Center Stage, Santa Candida, bPolly Warden. bGlen Riddle Farms entry.

Daily Double—Leystan and Lucky Aunt paid $903.40

THIRD—Six furlongs (chute). Off at 3.41. Time, 1.12 1-5.

Pat O'See, 120 (J. Gilbert)	$11.90	$5.00	$4.40
dhFlying Tartar, 109 (R. Meade)		5.90	7.40
dhSir Echo, 114 (T. Luther)		3.10	3.60

Also Ran—Sunset Boy, Alatamo, Post War Style, High North, Miss Ada J., War Art, Dick Manners, Wise Decision, Nanny Bones. dhDead heat for place.

FOURTH—Six furlongs (chute). Off at 4.15½. Time, 1.11 2-5.

Hornbeam, 113 (N. Wall)	$41.90	$15.00	$9.20
Dawn Attack, 113 (L. Knapp)		4.00	3.20
Gallant Witch, 109 (W. Gerlock)			6.00

Also Ran—Picket Line, Wise Up, Fairy Trace, Dark Danger, Sir Counsellor, Blue Steel, Maecase, Gondalina and Boy Angler.

NEWS-POST

COMPLETE Want Ads

THE CHICAGO DAILY NEWS

FINAL Edition

69TH YEAR—170. REG. U.S. PAT. OFF. COPYRIGHT, 1944 BY THE CHICAGO DAILY NEWS, INC. THURSDAY, JULY 20, 1944—THIRTY PAGES. Telephone DEArborn 1111. ★ FOUR CENTS

TRY TO KILL HITLER!

Charges Fly as Chiefs Jockey for No. 2 Spot

Hannegan Is Accused of Bad Faith; Kelly Acts for Truman.

BY PAUL R. LEACH.

Chicago Stadium — The Democratic National Convention seethed today with intrigue and hotly worded charges, linked with political moves by big and little bosses, as the party leaders tried to bring about a finish tonight with a vice-presidential nomination following President Roosevelt's fourth-term nomination this afternoon.

Outstanding developments in a greatly confused convention picture were:

1.—Charges that National Chairman Robert E. Hannegan of Missouri is misusing a letter from President Roosevelt reported to be hand written, listing Truman and Douglas as presidential favorites next to Wallace. Senator Joseph F. Guffey of Pennsylvania, and Senator Claude Pepper, Wallace supporters, charged that Hannegan had been using only parts of the President's letter that indicated he wants Truman, concealing the Wallace first choice.

Charge Cheap Politics.

Hannegan was charged by Wallace supporters with playing cheap ward politics in the use of the supposed Roosevelt letter in behalf of his fellow Missourian, Truman.

At the Wallace headquarters in the Hotel Sherman it was expected that if the charges prove to be true, Hannegan's influence and that of the big-city machines in league with him will be damaged in the eyes of the delegates and will increase the prestige of Wallace.

2. Reports that Thomas G. Corcoran, former White House favorite, is using Secretary of the Interior Harold L. Ickes and Attorney General Francis Biddle in attempts to knock off both Vice-President Wallace and Senator Truman to bring about ultimate vice-presidential nomination of Supreme Court Justice William O. Douglas of Washington state.

3. Support for Senator Truman was increased following an Illinois delegation caucus at which Mayor Kelly of Chicago urged that all of the state's 58 votes go to Truman with the approval of the President.

Ickes in Action.

4. It was definitely stated that Ickes, following lengthy conferences with Wallace and Biddle, is trying to persuade the President to send a third letter to the convention saying that he wants Wallace renominated.

5. Southern delegations, which are opposed to Wallace, caucused inconclusively and tentatively brought out Senator John H. Bankhead of Alabama as a compromise candidate.

More political crossfire developed when Gov. Charles Edison of New Jersey came out for Wallace. Edison has been in a life and death struggle to drive Frank Hague, Jersey City mayor, out of state and national politics, and Edison saw his chance to get Hague off base in the Wallace scramble.

The Corcoran story centered upon the desire of "Tommy the Cork," according to well-informed sources close to the president, to get back in favor at the White House. Wallace or Truman as the vice-president, possibly succeeding to the presidency, would not help him. Corcoran is close to Douglas, and with the Westerner in the White House Corcoran would again be where he was in the early days of the New Deal.

Ickes and Biddle were said to be operating to suit Corcoran's purposes, whether they realized it or not. Ickes was reported today to have told Wallace that "your game is to get Truman smeared as a Tom Pendergast man and knock him off." At the same time the Southerners were being engineered away from Tru-

(Continued on page 4, column 1.)

IN THE DAILY NEWS TODAY

Oxie Hooting Who's Who in Second Race

BY CLEM LANE.

Chicago Stadium.—"Me and Henry Wallace is probably the only two people in Chicago which ain't sure who is gonna be the Democratic candidate for vice-president," Oxie O'Rourke, the bodacious balloteer, reported today.

"With Henry it is candidatitis, a kind of political d.t.'s which afflict candidates. With me it's just that my ears is bigger than my brains.

"Mr. Wallace enter the Stadium last night and the Democrats rise up and give him the big hello. I move his stock up 5 points until Mayor Kelly come in right in the middle of the demonstration and pass it up like it ain't any closer than Sioux City.

Some Basic Training.

"Then the convention open and the high command put the audience through basic training, to see if they could take it, in a series of exertises conduct by Chairman Hannegan and a lady from North Carolina.

"After these maneuvers they bust out the keynoter, Gov. Kerr of Oklahoma, who arouse great enthusiasm in the audience and confusion in me by placing in nomination, for vice-president, I think it was, the names of Winston Churchill, Uncle Joe Stalin and Generalissimo Chiang Kai-shek. It sound like Churchill is the fellow most likely to succeed.

He Forgot McCosmic.

"Them Democrats is smart people. Mr. Kerr give 'em a oral examination and mark 'em 100 per cent correct on the answers. The lesson ask should we fire them tired 60 years old — Nimitz, Halsey, MacArthur and Marshall? For some reason he do not include Col. McCosmic, who observe his 64th birthday a week from Sunday.

"The Democrats go into their dance when Gov. Kerr mention we are winning the war with these tired old gents and President Roosevelt, age 62. That is the signal for a rowdy demonstration which would of horrify the quiet and refine Republican convention I attend a while back."

No Texas Heart.

"Did everybody join in?" asked Mr. Torchnose McGonigle.

"No," said Oxie, "Texas went democratic and refuse to join. From the looks of the gent that froze to the Texas banner, they ain't no love and kisses for Mr. Roosevelt Deep in the Heart of Texas."

Gladys George Divorces Penn; Charges Cruelty

Long Beach, Calif., July 20.—(AP)—Actress Gladys George divorced her third husband, Leonard Penn, today on her testimony that the coastguardman and former actor struck her many times.

ACTRESS MOTHER — Ruth Hussey.

HOLLYWOOD, July 20.—(AP)—A 6-pound son, George Robert, was born yesterday to Ruth Hussey, film actress, and her husband, Lt. Robert Longenecker.

Democratic Convention Roars to Possible End Tonight

Convention Program

EVENING SESSION.
(Tentative.)

Call to order by Permanent Chairman Jackson, 8:15 p.m.

Invocation by the Rev. Joshua Oden, Irving Park Lutheran Church.

"The Star-Spangled Banner" by Danny O'Neill, U.S. Carrier Lexington, with Great Lakes Naval Training Station Choir directed by Lt.Cmdr. Steen.

Address by Mrs. Helen Gahagan Douglas.

Address by Quentin Reynolds, war correspondent.

Roll call for vice-presidential nominations.

The text, in part, of Gov. Kerr's keynote address is on page 10.

BY EDWIN A. LAHEY.

Chicago Stadium.—The national Democratic convention roared along in high gear today, in one long series of emotional spasms and with the possibility that it will complete all its business by tonight.

U.S. Senator Samuel D. Jackson of Indiana began the heavy business of the day with his address as permanent chairman, re-echoing the battle cry of defiance of all things Republican and confidence in Democratic victory that marked the keynote address of Gov. Robert S. Kerr of Oklahoma last night.

Before the charladies take over late tonight at the Chicago Stadium, the delegates will make great history; adopt a platform so remarkably cryptic as to be briefed by the almanac editors; nominate their vote-getting champion, Mr. Roosevelt, and possibly a running mate for him and feel their bunions reach the acute stage.

Warns of Overconfidence.

Senator Jackson, the opening spellbinder, told his fellow Democrats that they have a right to be confident of victory in November, considering the record of their leader, but he reminded them:

"Let us not be overconfident, for by that sin off-year elections have been lost. Because Democratic voters have considered victory won, they have neglected to do their full share. We shall leave this convention hall touched with the livid fire of conviction that we will win because we deserve to win.

"We shall not only insure against a disastrous overconfidence, but we shall make our victory so total that the hungry opposition will realize that their attempt to turn back the clock to the days of 'Privilege and Pillage' is absolutely vain, and will continue to be absolutely vain."

A Vigorous Battle.

As if all this stirring business were not enough for the Democratic convention, the fight for the vice-presidential nomination, of increasing importance in each succeeding Roosevelt term, for obvious actuarial reasons, rages in the outer chambers with a vigor that could not be more intense if the Democrats were out of office.

The burning question whether or not Vice-President Wallace shall be benched and sent back to the minors will not be resolved until the emotionalism of renominating the President subsides, perhaps sometime this evening.

The delegates were well prepared for their emotional binge

(Continued on page 4, column 4.)

ASSASSINS FAIL—Adolf Hitler, who escaped with light burns and bruises when assassins tried to kill him with a bomb. [Associated Press Wirephoto.]

PRO-U.S. CHIEFS MAY RULE JAPAN IN NEW CABINET

[By the United Press.]

Emperor Hirohito today commissioned Gen. Kuniaki Koiso and former Premier Adm. Mitsumasa Yonai, both known to be friendly toward the United States before Pearl Harbor, to form a new Japanese cabinet in succession to that of Gen. Hideki Tojo, which resigned en bloc after confessing it could not win the war.

Announcement by the official Japanese Domei news agency that two political "moderates" had been entrusted with the organization of a new government confirmed the report that the extremist military clique which put Tojo in power and engineered the sneak attack on Pearl Harbor had lost control of Japan.

The move was regarded as the first step toward an ultimate Japanese attempt to win a negotiated peace, though no immediate peace bid was expected.

A Temporary Setup?

Sources familiar with the Japanese political situation suggested the new cabinet would attempt to intensify the Japanese war effort, then give way to another government within the next few months as American successes in the Pacific mount. Only when a wholly civilian government comes into power, these sources believed, will Japan make a real effort to withdraw from the war.

Domei broadcasts heard by FCC monitors said that Koiso, governor-general of Japanese-occupied Korea, and Yonai, premier from January to July 1940, had been ordered by Hirohito to appear at an audience in the imperial palace at 5:10 p.m. Japanese time today to "form the succeeding cabinet in co-operation."

"They received the honor with great trepidation and departed

(Continued on page 12, column 2.)

WEATHER INDICATIONS

(U.S. Weather Bureau Forecast.)
July 20, 1944.

Chicago and vicinity: Fair and cool tonight and Friday, gentle to moderate winds. Low tonight 55, high Friday 80.

Temperatures since 6 p.m. yesterday:

6 p.m.	81	7 a.m.	61
8 p.m.	78	8 a.m.	63
10 p.m.	74	9 a.m.	64
Midnight	69	10 a.m.	66
2 a.m.	66	11 a.m.	67
4 a.m.	64	12 noon	*69
6 a.m.	61		

*Unofficial.

Sunrise 5:33, sunset 8:21, sunrise tomorrow 5:34, moon sets at 8:49 tonight.

7 Chicagoans Dead in Blast Of Navy Ships

Death and heroism were described today in Navy announcements received here as the fate of enlisted Navy men from the Chicago area in the explosion Monday night of two ammunition ships at Port Chicago, Calif.

Seven from this area were included in the list of 213 men already identified as dead or missing released last night by 12th Naval District officers as the death toll in the disaster mounted to 322.

Dead or Missing.

Listed as missing and presumably dead were:

Asare, Leslie K., son of Mrs. Alberta Asare, 3548 Wentworth av.

Bailey, William H., husband of Lizzie Bailey, 5032 Prairie av.

Carter, Robert A., brother of Mador Vallarta, 3839 Penn av., E. Chicago, Ind.

Evans, Ananias, husband of Lula Toy Evans, 2816 S. La Salle st.

Hannah, John W. Jr., brother of Gloria Hannah, 449 E. 46th st.

Miller, Ernest C., son of Mrs. Irene Miller, 1116 Wentworth av., Chicago Heights.

Sheckles, Joseph J., husband of Victoria Sheckles, 5948 St. Lawrence av.

Others on List.

In addition to the Navy list, casualties included 69 merchant sailors, 31 members of armed guard crews aboard the vessels, five coastguardmen and four civilians caught in the blast.

Four Negro enlisted men who fought flames around boxcars loaded with ammunition were praised by their commander for "coolness and bravery." Among them was William E. Anderson of Chicago.

Among the Chicago volunteers from Mare Island who were named by Capt. Merrill T. Kinne, commandant of the Port Chicago establishment, as having been observed in "courageous pursuit of their duty" were Richard E. Webb, Ivan A. Hoyle and Archie S. Covington.

Nine survivors of the E. A. Bryan Liberty Ship, one of the stricken craft, reported yesterday ready for new assignments. With Capt. John L. Hendrickson was Robert Lenz, 2208 Winona av.

Hangs 12 Hours in Tree In Tangled Parachute

Santa Rosa, Calif., July 20.—(AP)—Navy Lt. C. N. Seaver of Westmont, N. J., was rescued unhurt after dangling in a tree for 12 hours in his tangled parachute. He was pilot in one of the two planes that collided on a training flight.

B-29 WALKOUT HALTED, BUT 3 OTHERS GO ON

The first-shift force in the magnesium foundry at the Chicago Dodge plant, where engines for the B-29 superbombers are produced, reported for work today, ending the strike of 437 workers that started yesterday in protest against disciplinary measures taken against two employees.

The work stoppage was unauthorized by the union, the United Automobile Workers (C.I.O.), and union officials had urged the strikers to go back to work. They sat down on their jobs at 2:30 p.m., yesterday two hours before their shift ended.

No settlement however was reached in a series of work stoppages in three other Chicago area plants engaged in war production. Another walkout was reported in a Muskegon Heights (Mich.) plant, making a total of about 2,500 workers idle.

Navy Job Stalled.

Construction of naval landing craft was stopped last night at the Calumet Harbor yards of the Pullman-Standard Car Manufacturing Co. by a strike of about 500 night shift members of the United Steel Workers of America (C.I.O.). An additional 400 non-striking employees were made idle. Company and union spokesmen said the walkout was in protest against dismissal of an employee whom the company charged was found sleeping on the job. Day shift workers were said to be reporting for work as usual this morning.

Pullman officials made plans to close the company's Michigan City (Ind.) plant following yesterday's conference in which 150 riveters and roofers, who quit work last Friday, refused to return to their jobs. The strikers, company spokesmen said, have tied up the main assembly line.

1,200 Walk Out.

Production of gun mounts at the Norge division plant of Borg-Warner Corp. at Muskegon Heights stopped yesterday after 1,200 employees quit work in protesting discharge of a steward of Local 404, United Automobile Workers (A.F.of L.). George Murphy, union president, said the walkout at the plant, which is engaged about 90 per cent on war contracts, was not authorized.

Production of radio and radar parts at the Chicago Die Mould Manufacturing Co. was interfered with by a strike of 85 employees who are members of the U.A.W. Esper A. Peterson, company president, said the strike was called when he refused to discharge two girls who were circulating a petition in the plant protesting the union's methods.

EXTRA

Fuehrer Burned By Bomb Blast; Aides Injured

Official Announcement Lists Generals and Admirals Badly Hurt.

BULLETINS.

Supreme Headquarters Allied Expeditionary Force, July 20.— —An underground revolt in Belgium was reported tonight in a special communique from Gen. Eisenhower's headquarters.

London, July 20.—(UP)—Adolf Hitler suffered a "light brain concussion" in the attempt on his life.

London, July 20.—(AP)—The official German news agency DNB said today that a bomb attempt had been made on Hitler's life and that the German chancellor was "only slightly burned" and sustained some bruises.

Hitler was "not otherwise hurt and continued his routine work and received Mussolini," deposed Italian dictator who now heads a rump Republican Fascist government, the announcement said.

Reichsmarshal Hermann Goering at once went to Hitler upon learning of what had happened, the Berlin broadcast added.

The announcement listed as slightly injured the following generals: Alfred Jodl, Hitler's chief military adviser; Korten, Buhle, Bodenschatz, Heusinger and Scherff. Adms. Voss and Von Putkammer also were injured.

The DNB announcement said Lt.Gen. Schmundt, Lt.Col. Brandt and Lt.Col. Borgmann and collaborator Berger were "seriously injured."

Schmundt was chief military adjutant to Hitler in the days of Munich and had since remained close to the Fuehrer. He was at the Brenner Pass conference of Hitler and Benito Mussolini March 8, 1940, which preceded Italy's declaration of war upon the Allies.

The Berlin broadcasts did not immediately name the time or place of the bombing attempt. Hitler has been reported spending a great deal of his time on his eerie mountaintop at Berchtesgaden. The captured Gen. Hofmeister said it was there that Hitler recently held a confeence of 150 generals and admirals to outline his strategy. The Hofmeister statement, as published in Moscow, described Hitler then as of swollen face, of low and jumbled voice.

"The Fuehrer himself, besides light burns and bruises, sustained no injuries," the announcement from Berlin said. "He had immediately taken up his routine work afterwards and, as it had been planned, received the Duce [Mussolini] for a long discussion.

The text of the broadcast by DNB, official German news agency:

Dissension is Disclosed.

"A bomb attempt was made on the Fuehrer's life today. During the attempt, Lt.Gen. Schmundt and Lt.Col. Brandt and Lt.Col. Borg and Collaborator Berger, who were in Hitler's company, were injured seriously."

Only yesterday, the Russian press published a statement by the captured commander of the 41st German Army Tank Corps, Lt.Gen. Edmund Hofmeister, saying there was grave dissent in ranks of the German high command, with old generals dissatisfied with Hitler's strategy in refusing to retreat.

COMMUNICATIONS CLOSED AT REICH-SWEDISH LINE

Stockholm, July 20.—(UP)—Telephone and telegraph communications between Sweden and Germany were resumed at 7:30 a.m. (Swedish time) today following an unexplained interruption of 14 hours, which led to speculation in British newspaper circles regarding a possible internal upheaval in Germany.

The Daily Mail's Stockholm correspondent said that "fantastic reports are circulating in Sweden that Hitler is purging army and civilian personnel or making new efforts to bolster satellites."

Postal authorities in Stockholm and Berlin maintained their usual discretion concerning the reasons for the interruption, which was regarded as mysterious, since Berlin was not raided yesterday.

Russians Nearing Lwow; 8 Miles from E. Prussia

London, July 20.—(UP)—The Red Army hammered at the gates of East Prussia today, Berlin indicated in reporting heavy fighting only eight miles from the frontier, and far to the South the Russians drove within sight of the great fortress city of Lwow in Lower Poland.

Nazi broadcasts reported that Soviet assault forces had pushed to Augustow, 38 miles northwest of Grodno and on the border of the Suwalki triangle eight miles from the soil of Germany proper.

The Nazi report of violent fighting at Augustow, directly before lower East Prussia, was the first sign of a Soviet drive to the immediate environs of the German province.

The flat country between Augustow and the border offered no obstacle to the Russian advance, and all indications were that the Germans had abandoned hope of stemming the Soviets short of the frontier.

STREAM ACROSS BUG: ONTO PLAINS OF POLAND

Moscow, July 20.—(UP—Marshall Ivan S. Konev's tanks and infantry streamed across the Bug River on a widening front spread out across the central Polish plains below Warsaw today and split Germany's Eastern Front wide open in one of the important strategic victories of the war.

While Konev sent his vanguards deeper into undisputably Polish territory, his guns began shelling the fortress city of Lwow in support of ground forces already within eight and three-quarters miles northeast and 13 miles east of the stronghold.

Elsewhere along the 600-mile

(Continued on page 12, column 5.)

REPORT REVOLT IN NAZI ARMY

Stalked by The Gestapo
Dramatic Epic of Yankee with RCAF — Today's Chapter on Page 7.

5¢

NEW YORK Journal-American
AN AMERICAN PAPER FOR THE AMERICAN PEOPLE
Daily 5 Cents, Saturday 5 Cents in New York City; 10 Cents Elsewhere | SUNDAY, 10 Cents in New York City and 50-Mile Zone, 15 Cents Elsewhere
No. 20,645—DAILY FRIDAY, JULY 21, 1944 In Two Sections—Section One

7TH SPORTS WALL ST. SPECIAL

Yanks Land on Guam

Push Inland After 17-Day Air Attack

By JOSEPH A. BORS
International News Service Staff Correspondent.

WASHINGTON, July 21.—The Navy today announced that U. S. Marines and infantry assault forces have landed on Guam.

Under a heavy aerial and warship bombardment, waves of U. S. troops are pouring ashore and fighting their way inland in the long-awaited campaign to recapture the American island that fell to the Japs four days after the Pearl Harbor attack.

"The landings on Guam are continuing against moderate ground opposition," the communique said.

The invasion followed the most intensive bombardment in preparation for any amphibious operation in the Pacific. Today's was the 17th consecutive daily bombardment.

The steady, daily bombardment apparently knocked out many Japanese shore defenses and drove the enemy from the beaches.

Thus American fighting men returned to the Far Pacific outpost approximately two and a half years after the Japanese seized that territory with little opposition from a small Marine garrison.

Pacific Fleet headquarters said Marines and Army troops established beachheads on Guam yesterday (Pacific time) with the support of carrier aircraft and surface units of the mighty 5th Fleet.

FACE FIERCE FIGHTING.

Guam, 120 miles southwest of recently-captured Saipan, has nearly 225 square miles of tree-and-brush studded mountains and offers the Japanese a greater defense area with the prospect of more fighting as bitter as Saipan. The Yanks again face the task of

Continued on Page 2, Column 3.

Stocks Weaken On War News

The stock market interpreted the attempt on Hitler's life and the Tokyo cabinet changes as signs of early peace today. As a result, the opening was the weakest in months, with many speculators lightening acounts in order to meet any adjustments coming with the end of hostilities.

U. S. Steel fell $1 a share, with 3,500 shares being traded on the first deal. Bethlehem Steel lost 75 cents a share and Chrysler 50, all unusually large price changes for initial transactions.

Call Hitler HQ Blitz Scene

LONDON, July 21 (INS).—The Stockholm newspaper Aftontidningen reported without confirmation today that the alleged attempt on Hitler's life occurred during his usual afternoon conference at Berchtesgaden.

The attempt was made with a time-bomb, this report said.

Hitler was said to have escaped because he arrived at the meeting two minutes late and was standing in the doorway of the conference room when the explosion occurred.

THE WEATHER

Partly cloudy, moderate winds.
Sun rises 5:42 a. m.; sun sets, 8:22 p. m. High tide at Governors Island, 10:15 a .m. and 10:20 p. m.

HOURLY TEMPERATURES

4 a. m.	69	9 a. m.	69
5 a. m.	69	10 a. m.	70
6 a. m.	68	11 a. m.	70
7 a. m.	66	12 Noon	70
8 a. m.	67	1 p. m.	72

(Complete Weather Report on Page 5)

TODAY'S INDEX

The Journal-American has the largest circulation of any evening newspaper in New York City. 230

It is the only New York evening newspaper possessing the three great wire services—ASSOCIATED PRESS—INTERNATIONAL NEWS SERVICE—UNITED PRESS

—(PHONE YOUR NEWS TIPS TO CORTLANDT 7-1212)—

N.Y. State May Decide Race For 2d Place

By SANFORD E. STANTON

CHICAGO, July 21.—With its powerful block of 96 votes, New York today held the key to resolving the violent Vice-presidential contest that is splitting the Democratic National Convention.

Those 96 votes, or a preponderance of them, if thrown to Vice-President Wallace, will give him clear sailing for renomination—but James A. Farley, former Democratic National Chairman, today was resolutely battling that possibility.

Just before the convention met at 12:30 p. m. (New York Time), Wallace gained 23 votes from a caucus of Ohio delegates—but he still needed New York votes to win.

If given to Sen. Harry S. Truman of Missouri, his aspiration to be President Roosevelt's running mate may be clinched, in view of the newly published Presidential letter to Democratic National Chairman Robert E. Hannegan.

"Dear Bob: You have written me about Harry Truman and Bill Douglas, I should, of course, be very glad to run with either of them and believe that either

Continued on Page 5, Column 7.

Anti-Hitler Paraders Fired On in Budapest

ANKARA, July 21 (UP).—Many persons were killed and wounded when 60,000 demonstrators, parading Budapest on Sunday morning and shouting that "we don't want to fight for Hitler," were fired upon by Hungarian police and German soldiers, travellers arriving here from Europe reported today.

These sources reported that Cristof Kallay, son of the former Premier Nicolas Kallay, one of the ringleaders of the demonstration, was arrested while attempting to cross the Slovakian border.

Goering NOT There...Again!

Reichsmarshal Hermann Goering was the "big man who wasn't there" during three major occurrences in Hitler's career.

He hurried to Hitler's side after the abortive assassination attempt yesterday, even as he did following the bombing of the Munich beer hall Nov. 8, 1939.

Goering also was absent during the historic Reichstag fire in 1933, which facilitated Hitler's rise to power.

Russians Closing in On Lwow

MOSCOW, July 21 (UP).—Front dispatches today said Russian forces were closing against Lwow from three directions for the final assault on the Polish fortress city.

Far to the north, the Red Army was approaching the frontier of East Prussia.

Marshal Konev's 1st Ukrainian Army swept in over the north, east and south approaches of Lwow, already battered by a Soviet cannonade and by-passed on the north, and military quarters were confident of the early liberation of the biggest German base in lower Poland.

At the same time Russian Cossacks massed in the forests along the west bank of the Bug River north of Lwow for a speedy sweep across the Polish plains toward Warsaw, 94 miles away, and Germany beyond.

On the Baltic front, Gen. Cherniakovsky's 3rd White Russian Army was fighting for the junctions controlling the roads to East Prussia, and extending its gains

Continued on Page 2, Column 8.

Schmeling Believed Dead

LONDON, July 21 (INS).—A Reuters dispatch today from 1st U. S. Army Headquarters in Normandy said it was "rumored" a dead German soldier has been identified as Max Schmeling, former world heavyweight boxing champion.

The body was reported found in the vicinity of the battle-torn town of Pont Hebert during the drive toward St. Lo.

The dead German, identified as a member of a Nazi parachute regiment, was reported to have carried a passbook with the name Max Schmeling in it. But there was no definite confirmation it was the body of the prize fighter.

According to soldiers who found the body, the man had been dead for about two days.

Derailing Blocks Long Island Line

Eleven trains on the Montauk Division of the Long Island Railroad were delayed from 10 to 30 minutes today when an unoccupied passenger coach was derailed in the yards at Babylon at 5:37 a. m.

Normal traffic was resumed at 7 o'clock, although for an hour after that time trains on the Montauk Division arrived at Pennsylvania Station and the Atlantic ave. station, Brooklyn, from one to three minutes late.

WOV BROADWAY BARN DANCE—SATURDAY, 8:30 P. M. Palm Garden, 52 St., West of 8th Ave. Adm. 85c, Incl. Tax—Advt.

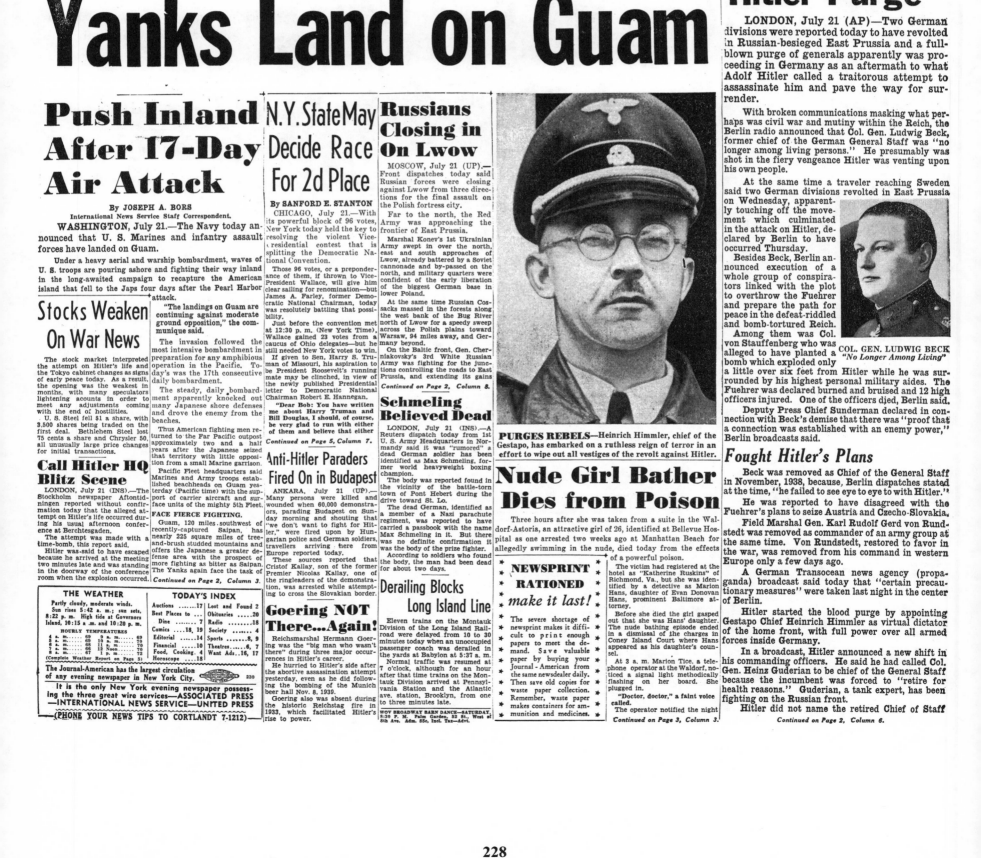

PURGES REBELS—Heinrich Himmler, chief of the Gestapo, has embarked on a ruthless reign of terror in an effort to wipe out all vestiges of the revolt against Hitler.

Nude Girl Bather Dies from Poison

Three hours after she was taken from a suite in the Waldorf-Astoria, an attractive girl of 26, identified at Bellevue Hospital as one arrested two weeks ago at Manhattan Beach for allegedly swimming in the nude, died today from the effects of a powerful poison.

The victim had registered at the hotel as "Katherine Ruskins" of Richmond, Va., but she was identified by a detective as Marion Hans, daughter of Evan Donovan Hans, prominent Baltimore attorney.

Before she died the girl gasped out that she was Hans' daughter. The nude bathing episode ended in a dismissal of the charges in Coney Island Court where Hans appeared as his daughter's counsel.

At 3 a. m. Marion Tice, a telephone operator at the Waldorf, noticed a signal light methodically flashing on her board. She plugged in.

"Doctor, doctor," a faint voice called.

The operator notified the night

Continued on Page 3, Column 3.

NEWSPRINT RATIONED
make it last!

The severe shortage of newsprint makes it difficult to print enough papers to meet the demand. Save valuable paper by buying your Journal-American from the same newsdealer daily. Then save old copies for waste paper collection. Remember, waste paper makes containers for ammunition and medicines.

Top Generals Executed in Hitler Purge

LONDON, July 21 (AP)—Two German divisions were reported today to have revolted in Russian-besieged East Prussia and a full-blown purge of generals apparently was proceeding in Germany as an aftermath to what Adolf Hitler called a traitorous attempt to assassinate him and pave the way for surrender.

With broken communications masking what perhaps was civil war and mutiny within the Reich, the Berlin radio announced that Col. Gen. Ludwig Beck, former chief of the German General Staff was "no longer among living persons." He presumably was shot in the fiery vengeance Hitler was venting upon his own people.

At the same time a traveler reaching Sweden said two German divisions revolted in East Prussia on Wednesday, apparently touching off the movement which culminated in the attack on Hitler, declared by Berlin to have occurred Thursday.

COL. GEN. LUDWIG BECK
"No Longer Among Living"

Besides Beck, Berlin announced execution of a whole group of conspirators linked with the plot to overthrow the Fuehrer and prepare the path for peace in the defeat-riddled and bomb-tortured Reich.

Among them was Col. von Stauffenberg who was alleged to have planted a bomb which exploded only a little over six feet from Hitler while he was surrounded by his highest personal military aides. The Fuehrer was declared burned and bruised and 12 high officers injured. One of the officers died, Berlin said.

Deputy Press Chief Sunderman declared in connection with Beck's demise that there was "proof that a connection was established with an enemy power," Berlin broadcasts said.

Fought Hitler's Plans

Beck was removed as Chief of the General Staff in November, 1938, because, Berlin dispatches stated at the time, "he failed to see eye to eye to with Hitler."

He was reported to have disagreed with the Fuehrer's plans to seize Austria and Czecho-Slovakia.

Field Marshal Gen. Karl Rudolf Gerd von Rundstedt was removed as commander of an army group at the same time. Von Rundstedt, restored to favor in the war, was removed from his command in western Europe only a few days ago.

A German Transocean news agency (propaganda) broadcast said today that "certain precautionary measures" were taken last night in the center of Berlin.

Hitler started the blood purge by appointing Gestapo Chief Heinrich Himmler as virtual dictator of the home front, with full power over all armed forces inside Germany.

In a broadcast, Hitler announced a new shift in his commanding officers. He said he had called Col. Gen. Heinz Guderian to be chief of the General Staff because the incumbent was forced to "retire for health reasons." Guderian, a tank expert, has been fighting on the Russian front.

Hitler did not name the retired Chief of Staff

Continued on Page 2, Column 6.

Sunday Graphic
No. 1,531 (C) SUNDAY, AUGUST 6, 1944 TWOPENCE

BIG GERMAN RETREAT

Enemy Falling Back Across Orne: Full Story On Back Page

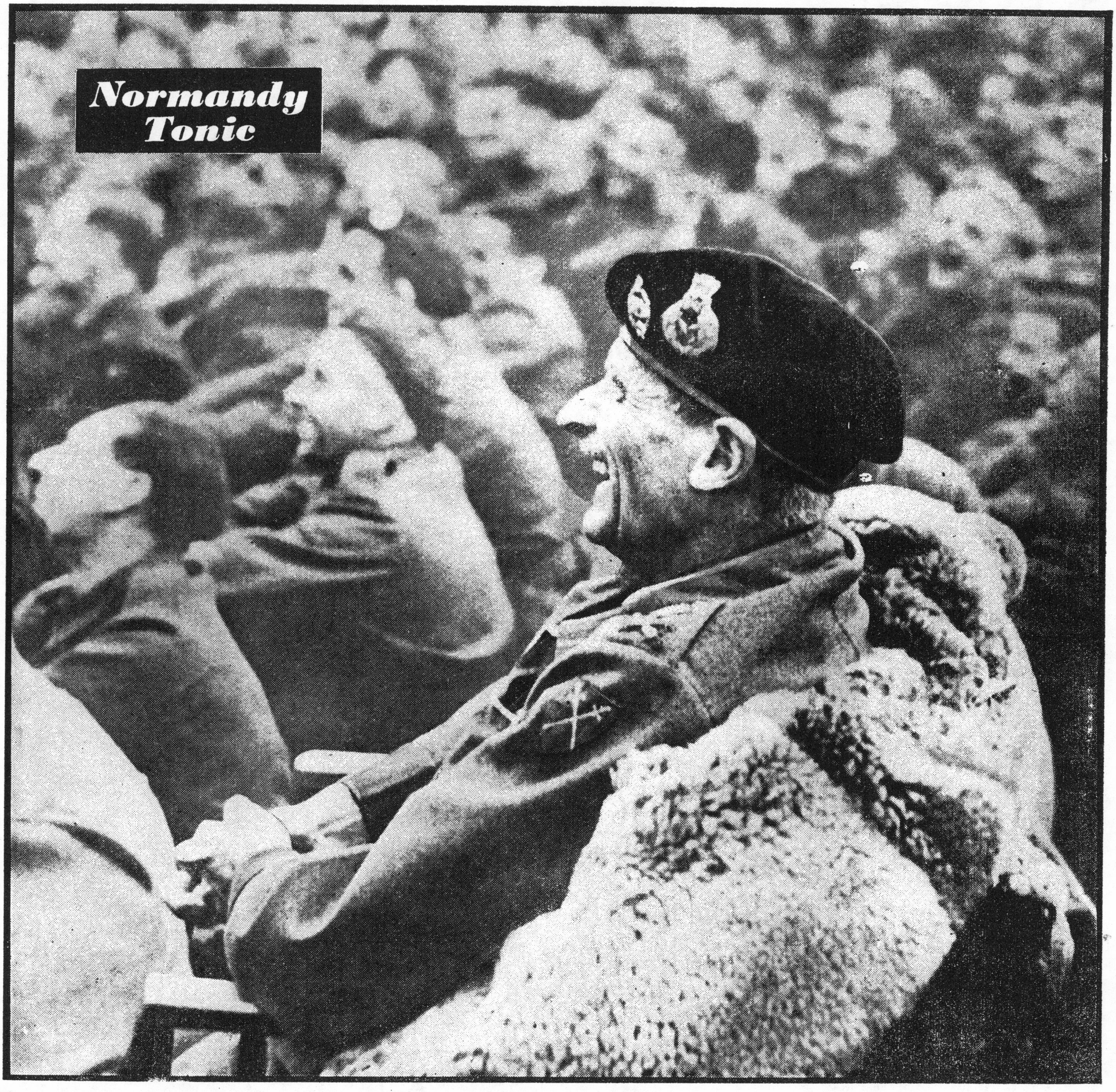

The campaign in Normandy is going well—in fact magnificently. This is reflected in General Montgomery's wholehearted laughter as he relaxes for a few moments with his men. George Formby, of ENSA, was responsible for the General's amusement.

FOUR PAGES OF LATEST NORMANDY PICTURES INSIDE

Sunday Pictorial

August 6, 1944
TWOPENCE
No. 1,534

BIG NEWS!

Russians Are Fighting On German Soil—Montgomery Bursts Through

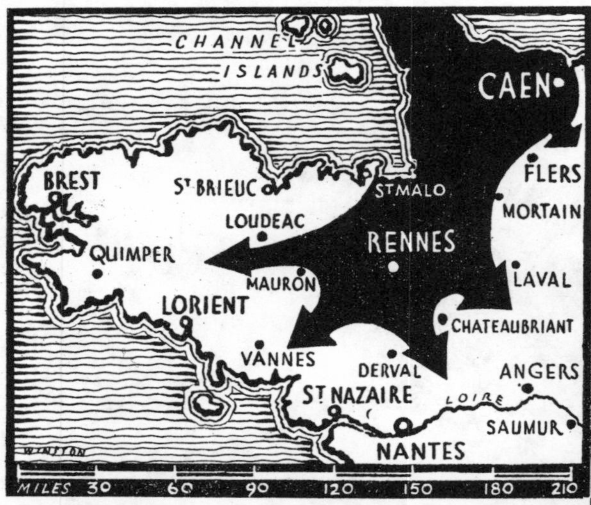

AS THE MAP SHOWS THE GERMANS FACE DISASTER

Fuller Says—

THIS MORNING WE BRING YOU NEWS OF TWO EVENTS THAT WILL RANK AMONG THE MOST IMPORTANT IN THE HISTORY OF THE WHOLE WAR. THEY MARK THE FINAL TURNING OF THE TIDE AFTER NEARLY FIVE YEARS OF WAR.

In the East the Russians have smashed across the frontier of East Prussia—and for the first time the Allies are fighting on German soil. The whole story is told on the back page.

In the West Montgomery has burst through the German defences. Our whole line is on the move, and the road into France becomes clear. And in Italy Florence has fallen.

The beachhead fight in Normandy has become the Battle of France.

Reeling under his two-fisted attack, the Germans, while attempting to hold a hinge in the Caen area, are swinging back their whole front with the evident intention of first trying to hold a line running from the Channel to somewhere on the Loire.

For the moment there is no settled front.

In the Caen sector, held by British and Canadian troops, our tanks are rolling eastward. The enemy in twenty - four hours have abandoned fifty square miles even in this vital area.

But even more spectacular is the way American tanks are sweeping through Brittany. The great peninsula, with its vitally important ports of Brest, Lorient and St. Nazaire—all U-boat bases—is already virtually cut off.

Pushing along the Channel coast the Americans are in St. Malo, though the town is not yet entirely captured. Fall of St. Malo means the cutting-off of the Channel Islands, which the Germans have heavily fortified to protect the ports that are now falling.

Berlin admits that the Americans have got six armoured and motorised divisions out into open country in Brittany and can give only the vaguest promises that much can be done to curb them.

Berlin also says that fifty-four Allied divisions are now in France. If this figure is correct it means we must have something like 650,000 men

"This settles the matter," commented Berlin. "Normandy is of decisive importance."

IT WILL NEED A MIRACLE TO SAVE ROMMEL NOW

The Germans in France are facing disaster, says Major-General J. F. C. Fuller, one of the world's leading tank experts and "Sunday Pictorial" Military Correspondent. Here, in his last night's commentary on the news, he explains that for Rommel to retrieve the position it is necessary for him to perform one of the most remarkable withdrawals in the whole history of war.

HISTORY I think will decide that the supreme event of the last few days is the collapse of the German front in Normandy. Because in strategic importance it exceeds all the great happenings in Eastern Europe—the assault on Warsaw, the occupation of the Gulf of Riga and the invasion of East Prussia. For tactically it has opened the long sought Second Front in the West.

Since the initial landing and until a few days ago, the Allied forces in Normandy occupied no more than a bridgehead. Now that bridgehead has vanished, and in its place we see a true base established from which operations are in full swing.

The Normandy door—the door to the whole of Western France—has been burst in at its lock—Avranches. Its centre, south of Gaumont, has been smashed, and what now remains of it is precariously swinging on its hinge—the Caen area.

Yet, even more important than this bursting, smashing and swinging, is that a gap has been created in the German strategic front in the West—a gap extending from the Gulf of St. Malo to the Mediterranean.

This is no exaggeration. For if, as has been proved, the Germans have not force enough to hold a front of a hundred miles, it certainly may be assumed that they have not force enough to hold one of greater length unless they can place between them and their enemy an obstacle of such strength that it will lend power to their waning numbers.

Only one such obstacle exists within reach. It is the river Seine—the magnet which all but certainly will draw them eastwards. And the more it does so, the wider grows the gap.

Can the Germans withdraw to it? Or can they be prevented from doing so? These, so it seems to me, are the two vital questions which must be answered by the Allied Command before they commit their forces to the next step.

As regards the first: Should Rommel, or whoever is now directing the German forces in Normandy, successfully carry out this retirement, then, indeed, it will be one of the most remarkable retreats in history.

Can this withdrawal be prevented? Here we touch on future operations and the answer must therefore be left to the future. Yet one thing may be mentioned. It is this:

Should the answer be that we can stop the retreat and do so, then the decisive moment in the Battle of France is approaching. Because the final overthrow of Rommel will follow, and that will knock the foundations from under the feet of every other German army corps, division and brigade now in France.

That is why I have stressed the importance of the winning of the strategic gap. For once Rommel and his army are annihilated that gap becomes France.

Begins Today

No woman in this war has had an adventure to equal that of Alice Leone Moats, young American authoress, noted for her daring and audacity. Unknown to anyone she made her way through Spain to the Pyrenees and then got the French to smuggle her to Paris.

For five weeks she moved among the Gestapo—to bring out an astonishing story of life under the German heel. She has written it all down and the "Sunday Pictorial" has secured the exclusive rights in Britain to tell it—the story of a girl the whole German Army could not stop. Miss Moats' narrative—

ON PAGE 4

AND CHEERS FOR THE BOYS DOING IT!

VICTORY EXTRA

BOSTON EVENING AMERICAN

FINAL

Entered as second class matter at Boston Postoffice

VOL. XLI—NO. 131 BOSTON, WEDNESDAY, AUGUST 23, 1944 28 PAGES PRICE 3 CENTS

PARIS FALLS

French Free Own Capital

NAZI SEINE DEFEAT NOW NEARING ROUT

STORY ON PAGE 2

Austen Lake Writes About N. E. Boys You Know

South End
West End
South Boston
West Roxbury
Brookline
Waltham
Medford
Woburn
Melrose
Lynn
Sharon
Taunton
Dorchester
Roxbury
Jamaica Plain
Cambridge
Somerville
Quincy

Russ Outline Peace Plan

WAR EXTRA

CHARACTER QUALITY · AMERICA FIRST! · ENTERPRISE ACCURACY

Los Angeles Examiner

AN AMERICAN PAPER FOR THE AMERICAN PEOPLE · THE GREAT NEWSPAPER OF THE GREAT SOUTHWEST

Reg. U.S. Pat. Off.
Examiner Telephone Richmond 1212 · Examiner Building, 1111 S. Broadway

VOL. XLI—NO. 256 · LOS ANGELES, WEDNESDAY, AUGUST 23, 1944 · PCC · Two Sections—Part I—FIVE CENTS

YANKS HEAD FOR REICH

Tanks 180 Miles From Germany

Allies Steel Arm Rings Marseille

RUSS PROPOSE 5 POINTS FOR KEEPING PEACE

Naval, Aerial Demonstrations Suggested in Severe Cases at Dumbarton Oaks Parley

By Leon Pearson
Staff Correspondent International News Service

WASHINGTON, Aug. 22.—Soviet Ambassador Andrei Gromyko today presented to the British and American delegates at the Dumbarton Oaks conference the official Soviet proposal for preserving peace after the war.

It included the following specific measures for "sobering an aggressor state":

1. To break off diplomatic relations.
2. To impose commercial and financial sanctions.
3. To cut off railway, telegraphic and aerial communications.
4. Complete blockade.
5. Naval and aerial demonstrations.

MEASURES TO BE APPLIED

These measures would be applied in the order above depending upon the seriousness of the threat to peace.

The last step would be taken in the most severe cases. Its application was described in the Soviet proposal as follows:

The new international organization would have under its control an international military corps to be used against agressors who have not been brought into line by more moderate measures.

The appearance of several hundred military aircraft, the Soviet proposal said, over the capital of a state which was preparing aggression could not but produce an appropriate impression. And if such a demonstration proved to be without results, it would be followed by the bombardment of definite military objectives of the aggressive state.

QUESTIONS ASKED

As Ambassador Gromyko read the Soviet proposal to the Dumbarton Oaks conference, he was interrupted from time to time by questions and requests for interpretation.

He preferred, however, to make note of the questions for discussion later. His presentation took the major part of the morning session. The afternoon was devoted to presentation of

(Continued on Page 6, Cols. 4-5)

SEEKS ANNULMENT—Mrs. Lawrienne Wilkinson, here holding her daughter, Pamela, yesterday sought an annulment of her marriage to Morrison J. Wilkinson Jr., former Army captain, who was court-martialed last June on attack and bigamy charges. (See Page 5.)
—Pacific Press photo.

A PLEASED PATTON—Pistol-packing Lieutenant General George S. Patton Jr. is a happy man in this picture, for the commander of the Third Army in France is fitting a new pistol into his holster—and to his collection.
—Associated Press wirephoto.

Two Russ Armies Gain in Ploesti Oilfield Drive

By Natalia Rene
Staff Correspondent International News Service

MOSCOW, Aug. 22.—Russia's Second and Third Ukrainian Armies, attacking in the new large-scale offensives on two broad fronts in Romania, slashed westward tonight in the direction of the vital Ploesti oil fields after overrunning more than 350 localities, including the communications centers of Iasi and Tighina, on the lower Dnester 70 miles from the Black Sea.

The new assaults aimed at knocking Romania out of the war following repeated warnings to break off with the Germans and cease hostilities were announced in separate orders of the day by Premier Marshal Joseph Stalin.

PIERCE NAZI LINES

The attack by the Second Ukrainian forces which resulted in occupation of Iasi was announced first. In this drive, in which Red army troops made a break 37 miles in depth and 74 miles wide in the German-Romanian positions, the Soviets fought their way into more than 200 inhabited places, including Targu-Rumos and Ungheni.

In the second simultaneous offensive the Red army troops of the Third Ukrainian front attacked south of Tighina (Bendr). In this drive the Russians advanced some 43½ miles across a front of more than 80 miles.

Infantry forces in both pushes

(Continued on Page 2, Column 4)

Dewey Plans Coast Visit

ALBANY, N. Y., Aug. 22.—(AP)—Governor Thomas E. Dewey will fill a speaking engagement in Oklahoma City on his way back from a campaign tour of the Pacific Coast, Senator E. H. Moore, Oklahoma Republican, announced after a conference with the G. O. P. presidential nominee today.

Moore said at a news conference that Dewey's visit had been set tentatively for September 25 but that details were to be completed by National Chairman Herbert Brownell Jr.

Moore and Representative Ross Rizley, Oklahoma Republican, conferred with Brownell in New York City yesterday before talking with Dewey here today.

Moore's disclosure that Dewey

(Continued on Page 7, Cols. 4-5)

German Secret Police Arrest Marshal Petain

GENEVA, Aug. 22.—(AP)—German secret police arrested Marshal Henri Philippe Petain, French "chief of state," at his residence and headquarters at the Hotel Du Parc in Vichy, advices from France said today.

The 88-year-old marshal, hero of Verdun in the First World War and head of the German-dominated Vichy government of France since 1940, was reported seized Sunday morning along with a number of associates.

MAY BE IN REICH

Others reported arrested were a General Bridoux, possibly the Vichy war secretary Lieutenant General Eugene Bridoux; an Admiral Blehaut; one Rochat, general secretary of the Ministry of Foreign Affairs, and Bernard Menetrel, private secretary to Petain.

The most reliable sources said that Petain refused a German request to go with Pierre Laval, chief of government, to the new provisional capital at Belfort, and that the old marshal was summarily arrested by force. Where he is was not known absolutely, although most guesses were that he is in Germany. Thus the old chief of state became officially what he has been in effect for a long time—a prisoner of the Nazis.

The Vichy regime is "finished," the Basel National Zeitung commented. The Swiss minister to Vichy is returning home and relations concerning France will henceforth be conducted through Berlin.

Reports from the French underground said that the Maquis were attacking Vichy at about the time of the seizures,

(Continued on Page 2, Column 7)

Paris Patriots Waging Fierce Street Battles

By Thomas C. Watson
Staff Correspondent International News Service

SUPREME HEADQUARTERS, ALLIED EXPEDITIONARY FORCE, Aug. 22.—A new American armored drive striking directly toward Germany's own borders captured the Loire River town of Sens, 57 miles southeast of embattled Paris and swept on tonight to within 180 miles of the nearest German frontier towns.

This dramatic news was flashed by I. N. S. War Correspondent Pierre J. Huss in a frontline bulletin. Meanwhile, other Yank forces struck northward from embattled Paris along both banks of the Seine to join Allied forces racing along the Channel coast at the river's mouth where a new trap is being forged around 100,000 more Nazis.

In a mighty 65-mile dash southeastward from the Paris area, the spectacular new drive on Lieutenant General Patton's U. S. Third Army forces dashed well beyond Sens—headed toward the Belfort Gap region adjacent to the German frontier town of Lorrach and the Swiss border city of Basle.

TREMENDOUS NUTCRACKER

Huss declared in his dispatch that the American "powerhouse" thrust now stands close enough to the German border to bear a definite military relation to the Russian offensives from the east—placing Germany in effect "within the jaws of a tremendous nutcracker."

(The Algiers radio declared that a "violent battle" is raging inside the eastern French city of Belfort itself, where French patriot forces were attacking the Nazi garrison inside the town.

(The strategic Belfort Gap area marks the region where the lower positions of the Maginot and Siegfried Lines are located and along which the Germans were reported to be preparing frantically for a "last stand" against an Allied invasion of the Reich from France.

(Pierre Laval and other French pro-Nazi puppet officials had taken refuge in Belfort during the last few days after fleeing from Vichy.)

FOE TAKEN BY SURPRISE

It was deemed possible that the new invasion forces in southern France which are making rapid advances northward may also strike toward the Belfort gap region to achieve a junction with the Patton army for a drive toward Berlin.

Huss reported in his frontline dispatch that the Yank cyclone capture of Sens, an ancient Roman town on the Yonne River

Toulon Navy Base Entirely Surrounded

By James L. Kilgallen
Staff Correspondent International News Service

ROME, Aug. 22.—Allied troops hammered tonight to within only three miles east of Marseille and looped a steel arm around the landward approaches to France's biggest seaport, while French assault forces sliced through Toulon's outlying streets after completely surrounding the naval base.

Marseille, second only to beleaguered Paris among French cities, was threatened imminently with encirclement by American forces that captured its inland communications gateway of Aix-en-Provence, 14 miles to the north, and then surged southwestward to approach the port's coastal escape route.

FOLLOW RIVER

At the same time, a powerful French armored column, after occupying Dandol to close a ring around Toulon to the west, thrust a swift spearhead farther west along the Riviera coastal route. A headquarters bulletin revealed officially tonight that this force had raced to within three miles east of Marseille, a one-day gain of more than five miles from the last announced position.

American columns, striking along the Durance River northwest of liberated Aix-en-Provence, came to within 27 miles east of vital Avignon, key to the heart of the rich Rhone Valley, on the heels of an enemy declared by the Allied invasion commander to be "perplexed and stunned" and "in full retreat."

Inside Toulon, 30 miles south-

(Continued on Page 2, Column 5)

Remember That Overseas WAC or WAVE With Xmas Ship Gifts *Details on Page 14*

RESTRICTED

24 Aug 1944

"THE SNIPER"

Published in FRANCE

PARIS-MARSEILLES FREED-RUMANIA JOINS ALLIES!

LONDON, 24 AUGUST:- ADOLPH HITLER'S FORTRESS EUROPE IS BEING REDUCED TO DEBRIS. IN A SENSATIONAL CHAIN OF EVENTS OVER A PERIOD OF 24 HOURS, PARIS AND MARSEILLES, THE NUMBER ONE AND TWO CITIES IN FRANCE, HAVE BEEN LIBERATED FROM THE TYRANICAL HOLD OF GERMANY, AND RUMANIA, GAS AND OIL DUMP FOR THE WEHRMACHT HAS SHAKEN OFF THE NAZI YOKE TO FIGHT ON THE SIDE OF THE ALLIES.

King Michael of Rumania, late last night, announced to the world that his country had capitulated and accepted the armistice terms offered by the Allies. The King further said that Rumania will now fight on the side of the Allies. What the immediate effect of Rumania's withdrawal from the House of Hitler will be is difficult to foretell. Whether Rumania actually will be able to turn her armies bodily against the German oppressor is a matter of conjecture inasmuch as the majority of Rumanian troops are doubtlessly commanded by German officers and non-commissioned officers. Within a week's time, however, it is extremely probable that the Rumanian combat ranks will be well advanced in liquidation proceedings of the German military leadership.

ACTION SIGN OF NAZI WEAKNESS

Within Rumania are the huge oil fields of Ploesti, which long have been a major source of fuel supply for the German war machine. Loss of these life lines at a time of desperate need is in itself a crushing blow to the disintegrating Nazi power.

Of tremendous significance is the Rumanian divorce from Germany. That the valuable Balkan state would dare thumb its political nose at the one time mighty master of Europe is alone a most prominent indication of Nazi collapse.

Together with Rumania, both Turkey and Bulgaria have abandoned Hitler's dream and the contagious fever of Balkan back-turning is sweeping through Hungary and Yugoslavia.

Uncle Adolph suddenly appears to have offensive breath and even his best friends won't tell him.

London, 24 Aug:- Rumanian and German troops are clashing at several points within the Rumanian borders. The action was believed to be centered around the Rumanian oil fields.

ALLIES HAIL LIBERATION OF CITIES

London, 24 August: Long hidden French flags blossomed from the thousands of windows yesterday in Paris and Marseilles as word was flashed to a waiting world that the two major cities of France had been liberated.

French patriots from within both cities coupled drastic measures with increasing Allied pressure to smash the German vise-like hold which has gripped France since the dark days of 1941.

The 2nd French Armored Division, part of the 3rd Army and coordinating force with the 90th Division in a recent operation, was reportedly now in the French capital aiding in the moping up efforts.

Marseilles was said to be the scene of wild jubilation unprecedented in French history. The National Athemn rang through the streets throughout the entire day. Troops were being royally entertained kissed, and bedecked with flowers in some parts of the city even while sporadic battle continued in other sectors of the metropolitan area.

Allied forces are now advancing on the third largest city in France, Lyons, and reportedly are making excellent progress. In Toulon, German troops are still holding out in defense of the city dock areas.

RESTRICTED

FEATURE PAGE

"TRAP FEVER" HITS BN.

WAR ROUND-UP.

SECRECY IS THE KEYNOTE OF ALL CURRENT ALLIED OPERATIONS. Rumania, in breaking with Germany, mentioned that peace terms offered by the Allies would be accepted. The fact that "terms" had even been offered was news to the world. In today's round-up of world wide fronts no mention was made by BBC of Russian progress in Poland or Rumania and yet it is assumed that the Soviet Army is moving steadily forward. For an entire week during the recent "trapping operations in the north, American correspondents were unable to tell a single word of the story. Hitler's board of strategy is forced to "sweat out" all movements of the phantom Allied armies...RELEASED FOR PUBLICATION, HOWEVER, IS WORD THAT ELEMENTS OF THE Third Army are now advancing on a 50 mile front between the outskirts of Paris and Sens, southeast of the capital..ONE AMERICAN ARMORED SPEARHEAD on the southern front has reached the town of Grenoble and is advancing northwest on Lyons, 50 miles away...NO CONFIRMATION has been forthcoming concerning reported landings of Allied troops in the Bordeaux area...ALLIED AIRCRAFT AND GROUND SUPPORT have sunk 500 German vehicles and 700 barges in the Seine during frantic Nazi retreat efforts...HUNGARY, COGNIZANT OF THE CRISIS IN the Balkans, is expected to be the next power to desert Hitler in his hour of need. Governmental officials are conferring regarding the action which must be taken within the next few days... IN RUMANIA TODAY A NEW DEMOCRATIC government has been formed under General Sanatescu. The new order does not include Marshal Antonescu...PRIME MINISTER WINSTON CHURCHILL YESTERDAY conferred with the Greek Prime Minister and have reached "complete agreement" regarding current affairs. No amplification as to the matters agreed upon was available.....YOU WITH YOUR WEAPON HAVE MADE TODAY'S GOOD NEWS POSSIBLE!

WHAT IS THIS - MANEUVERS?

Remember back in Texas and Louisiana when we used flags to stop attacks Well, believe it or not, the same tactics are still useful in France.

Friendly tanks, moving into position in a recent action, mistakenly opened fire on troops of the 357th Infantry.

Sensing the error, Sgt. James C. Little, of one of the units pinned down, managed to secure an orange flag from a nearby vehicle and with disregard for his own security, wigwagged the tanks into silence.

357TH INF BN. PLOTS OWN AMBUSH

"Trap Fever," the potent contagious bug that has been exploited so successfully in the Allied scheme of attack, showed up within the ranks of the 3rd Battalion, 357th Inf., in a recent operation and resulted in an ambush that kayoed 10 German vehicles, and ended the war for a large number of misguided Kraut.

The battalion, commanded by Major John H. Mason, and aptly called "Mason's Maulers" established a road block trap along a highway heavily used by German vehicles.

When the block was completed, the "Maulers" retired to cover alongside the highway and waited for Jerry to roll into the jaws.

PARADE BEGINS

Completely unaware of the presence of American forces, a German astride a motorcycle came sputtering down the road and was promptly dispatched into a convenient ditch by small arms fire.

A moment later two enemy trucks swept into view. A volley of shots by the "Maulers" convinced the Kraut personnel of the wisdom of immediate surrender.

All through the night German vehicles continued to roar into the unexpected block until the surrounding terrain looked like a scrap pile.

"Trap Fever" had again paid off.

15e Année. — N° 2.384 DEUX FRANCS Vendredi 25 août 1944

l'aube

Adresse provisoire : 10, faubourg Montmartre, Paris (9e) - Téléphone : Provence 98-74

Vive la France !
Vive de Gaulle !

PARIS EST DÉLIVRÉ

"LA RÉPUBLIQUE SERA PROCLAMÉE A L'HOTEL DE VILLE"

annonce le président du Conseil national de la Résistance

11 h. 15. — Place de l'Hôtel-de-Ville. Il pleut dru et l'espace est désert. Un groupe traverse en trottant, trempé, pressé; c'est M. Georges Bidault, président du Conseil national de la Résistance, qui vient, accompagné de ses collaborateurs, rendre visite aux défenseurs du cœur de Paris et aux nouveaux responsables de la vie de la cité.

On les attendait à 10 h. 30. Nous saurons bien vite que ce retard est dû à une bataille qui n'en finissait plus, sous les fenêtres mêmes du président. A l'entrée droite de l'Hôtel de Ville (on a délaissé pour encore un temps le cérémonial... et l'entrée principale) les membres du Comité parisien de la Libération accueillent le président. C'est le commandant Stéphane (que ses camarades appellent le « Dictateur de la Maison ») bras en écharpe, qui excuse d'abord l'absence de la plupart de ses hommes dispersés à la suite d'un engagement. Ainsi l'atmosphère de lutte, de bataille, de farouche volonté imprègne de suite ce qui eût été peut-être une « réception comme tant d'autres ».

Sont là : M. Flouret, préfet de la Seine, et son secrétaire général, M. Gazier ; M. Georges Marane, représentant M. Baudry, président du Comité parisien de Libération, qui n'a pu être présent ; M. Revel, membre du C.N.R. ; le commandant militaire Landry... et d'autres personnalités que nous nous excusons de ne pas nommer.

Au bas de l'escalier d'honneur, on présenta à M. Bidault les héros des jours douloureux et glorieux vécus depuis samedi.

Et c'est l'entrée dans le cabinet du préfet... Fenêtres ouvertes grandes, vitres percées de balles... Deux mausers, un lebel, une mitraillette allemande attendent leurs servants contre la fenêtre qui découvre la place.

Le président du C.N.R. prend place au bureau du préfet, face au portrait du général de Gaulle, qui orne la cheminée monumentale.

M. Georges Marane, au nom du C.P.L., adresse une fraternelle bienvenue à M. Georges Bidault et dit la fierté du peuple parisien d'avoir pris sa revanche sur l'ennemi, la fierté de retrouver sa liberté et sa grandeur.

Le président du C.N.R. se lève alors, remercie les membres du C.P.L.

— *Vous êtes ici, dit-il, dans la demeure traditionnelle des libertés de la capitale, au sein du donjon de la fierté française.*

Il souligne l'unanimité de tous dans le combat et adresse à tous le même salut, au nom de la Résistance, des morts, des blessés, de tous ceux qui se sont sacrifiés totalement.

— *Je voudrais qu'en un tel jour, nous saluions en commun ce pacte fraternel conclu sur les barricades. C'est la première fois depuis tant d'années que nous sommes tous d'accord pour la lutte et pour la victoire.*

C'est alors que M. Georges Bidault déclare :

— *Dans cette maison, dont vous avez bien voulu nous ouvrir les portes, nous reviendrons ;* nous y viendrons alors pour proclamer l'avènement de la République française.

En terminant, le président salue la femme de notre camarade Gildas, commandant des F.F.I. de Paris, arrêté par la Gestapo dans les dernières semaines qui ont précédé la libération. Il salue encore ceux qui ont pris l'Hôtel de Ville sans le secours ni l'aide d'uniformes étrangers, ni même amis.

Les applaudissements qui suivent traduisent mal l'émotion de tous, aux paroles simples et vibrantes de celui qui incarne la plus haute autorité de la Résistance.

Après avoir visité les postes de combat, le président se dirige vers la sortie, et nous avons la surprise d'y rencontrer trois « miliciennes » soigneusement rasées, que viennent d'amener quelques F.F.I.

Nous sortons donc, traversons le pont d'Arcole, et nous voici à l'entrée de la maternité de l'Hôtel-Dieu. Un maçon et un plombier reçoivent, tout héberlués, le président du Conseil national de la Résistance... Très vite, arrive M. le directeur Pernot, accompagné du professeur Ménard et des principaux collaborateurs. Nous apprenons que, depuis samedi, l'hôpital a enregistré 616 entrées, 173 hospitalisés allemands sont morts, ainsi que 75 Français. Alors, le président et le préfet suivent les docteurs et entrent dans chaque salle apporter quelques paroles de réconfort à ceux qui sont tombés pour la libération de notre pays.

Vers 13 heures, alors que notre groupe pénètre dans la salle des grands blessés, se déchaîne un ouragan de mitraille assourdissant, mais qui ne semble guère troubler les gens de l'Hôtel-Dieu.

Pendant de longues minutes, M. Bidault doit alterner ses paroles avec les coups de la bataille. C'est la Préfecture de police qui est assaillie une nouvelle fois.

Nous saurons à la sortie que la victoire est totale : six camions ennemis hors de combat, tous les Allemands prisonniers ou tués... Un camion flambe encore.

La visite est terminée. Georges Bidault, après avoir félicité et remercié docteurs, professeurs, chirurgiens, brancardiers, infirmières, au nom de la France, repart vers ses responsabilités de chef choisi par le peuple.

Union et courage

Voici le texte de l'allocution que Georges Bidault a prononcée hier, à 21 heures, à la radio. Il a été enregistré dans le quartier de la République, au milieu du fracas des armes automatiques et de la canonnade. Notre ami a dû, tellement la lutte était intense entre les patriotes et l'ennemi, s'interrompre plusieurs fois. C'est véritablement sur les barricades que Georges Bidault s'est adressé à la France et au monde.

PARIS s'est libéré — et s'est libéré lui-même — contre un ennemi en retraite et déjà en déroute, mais encore puissamment armé. Les Parisiens à l'exemple de tous les combattants qui, de la montagne à la forêt, ont délivré déjà de vastes parties du territoire national, se sont dressés dans un élan qui égala et dépassa par l'union, par la ferveur, par l'héroïsme, celui des plus grands jours du passé. Cinquante mois de honte et d'oppression sous le régime de la capitulation, de l'imposture et de la trahison sont aujourd'hui effacés et vengés. La France se retrouve plus grande au travers de l'épreuve; elle connait aujourd'hui ceux de ses fils sur lesquels elle peut compter, qui sont le nombre, qui sont l'élite, qui sont la nation.

Elle connait aussi le pouvoir de l'union et du courage. C'est par l'appel à l'union et au courage que le Conseil National de la Résistance, au nom duquel j'ai l'honneur et la fierté de m'adresser, par l'intermédiaire d'une radio affranchie, à la France et au monde, a pu dans la nuit de l'oppression dresser un peuple pour le combat, dans le moment même où des vieillards chamarés et d'abominables bandits s'efforçaient de prostituer toutes ses gloires.

La France est aujourd'hui, par le courage des combattants, qui ont su précéder l'arrivée de l'allié au lieu de l'attendre, à nouveau un pays d'hommes libres, un pays libre.

Grâce au général de Gaulle, qui le premier donna le signal du refus de capituler, et qui a incarné à tous les yeux l'indépendance et la tradition nationales, grâce aux combattants de la Résistance, grâce à nos martyrs sans nombre, morts silencieux sous les tortures, la liberté des citoyens, l'indépendance de la patrie, la fierté d'un grand peuple sont pour nous des patrimoines reconquis.

La lutte continue. Dans le quartier populaire d'où je vous parle le canon ennemi et le mousqueton français alternent presque sans interruption mais la confiance et l'enthousiasme ne sont pas du côté des gros calibres.

C'est aujourd'hui le combat. Nous associons d'un cœur reconnaissant à notre joie d'aujourd'hui nos alliés britanniques, soviétiques et américains qui, sur les champs de bataille de toutes les parties du monde, ont versé leur sang pour la cause qui nous est à jamais commune.

Bientôt les Alliés seront à Paris, accueillis par les Parisiens vainqueurs. Le général de Gaulle et le Gouvernement provisoire de la République Française seront reçus par le Conseil National de la Résistance et après tant de deuils et de douleurs nous reconstruirons dans la joie et dans la fierté un grand peuple, fort, indépendant et juste.

Georges BIDAULT.

LA MONNAIE FRANÇAISE CIRCULE LIBREMENT ET GARDE TOUTE SA VALEUR

Des informations très précises provenant des régions déjà libérées par les armées alliées permettent d'affirmer qu'aucune mesure n'a été prise par les autorités anglo-saxonnes pour affaiblir la valeur ou entraver la circulation de la monnaie française et notamment des billets de la Banque de France. Ceux-ci continuent à circuler « quelle que soit l'importance des coupures ».

Les billets spéciaux émis en quantités très limitées par les autorités militaires anglo-saxonnes sont échangés au pair, franc pour franc, contre les billets anciennement en circulation. Les bruits alarmistes répandus par Déat dans « L'Œuvre » et par Radio-Paris sont donc sans aucun fondement.

Déblocage de nouveaux points de textile

Le secrétaire général à la Production industrielle communique :

A partir de lundi prochain 28 août, 20 nouveaux points de textile seront débloqués. Ce sont les points 41 à 58 inclus de la carte A ancien modèle, papier rose.

La commission des Affaires étrangères de l'Assemblée consultative s'est réunie à Alger

Alger, 24 août. — La commission des Affaires étrangères de l'assemblée consultative a examiné, hier, la question du personnel diplomatique et consulaire. Après avoir étudié la réponse du commissariat aux Affaires étrangères, elle a décidé de reprendre certains des problèmes posés.

Les membres de la commission ont ensuite envisagé le développement de notre influence intellectuelle au Levant.

La déclaration sur les relations d'amitié entre la France et la Tchécoslovaquie, confirmant la dénonciation de l'accord de Munich, a été saluée avec enthousiasme. Par contre, la commission a manifesté son étonnement et ses profonds regrets de l'absence de la France aux négociations de Washington où sont discutées des questions de sécurité internationale auxquelles la France est personnellement intéressée.

Les forces françaises et alliées ont pénétré hier soir dans la capitale

Tandis que le gros des forces alliées bivouaque à proximité des portes d'Orléans et de Versailles, l'avant-garde de la 2e division blindée du général Leclerc a poussé jusqu'au cœur de Paris et est arrivée peu avant 21 heures 30 sur la place de l'Hôtel-de-Ville.

Des officiers gagnent immédiatement la Préfecture de la Seine où les attendent avec la joie et l'émotion que l'on devine les membres du C.N.R. et du Comité Parisien de Libération, des combattants des F.F.I. La nouvelle se répand immédiatement à travers la ville. Les cloches sonnent. Cependant en raison du danger que continue à faire peser la présence des tirailleurs allemands, les F.F.I. maintiennent la foule à distance.

Un détachement de troupes françaises se dirige ensuite vers la Préfecture de Police où, à 22 heures 15, M. Cérat reçoit le premier officier venu le saluer au nom du général Leclerc.

Les premiers éléments avaient pénétré dans la capitale par la porte d'Italie. Deux femmes, dont une Alsacienne en costume, étaient juchées sur le premier tank et agitaient des drapeaux tricolores. Sur tout le parcours, des acclamations frénétiques saluèrent les libérateurs français.

PARIS N'A JAMAIS CESSÉ D'ESPÉRER

Son attente était digne, mais toujours sa résistance s'affirmait, courageuse et intrépide.

Mais, l'heure venue, Paris, résolument, s'était engagé dans la bataille. Pendant quelques jours, nous avons vécu des heures telles que notre histoire n'en a pas connu de plus glorieuses.

Paris, sans nourriture, sans feu, sans armes, répondant à l'appel des chefs de la Résistance, s'engage farouchement dans la lutte. Il entend se libérer lui-même avant d'ouvrir ses portes aux armées victorieuses.

Nous ne les attendions pas encore puisque subsistaient quelques îlots de résistance.

Cependant, lorsque dans la nuit tombante, la nouvelle se répand, une vague d'enthousiasme déferle sur la capitale. Les églises de la ville ébranlent leurs gros bourdons que couvre le bruit des mitraillettes et des canons. Une foule délirante se répand dans toutes les rues, des groupes se forment parcourant les boulevards, drapeaux en tête, aux accents de La Marseillaise.

Paris a retrouvé sa fierté. Il a de nouveau salué son unité et resserré les liens de ses amitiés. Il peut, avec confiance, tourner ses regards sur l'avenir.

Francisque GAY.

La colonne franco-américaine signalée à Arpajon la veille a poursuivi, hier, sa marche victorieuse. Au début de l'après-midi elle avait atteint le Petit-Massy.

Un peu plus tard, du toit d'une maison de Cachan, à la hauteur de la dernière barricade occupée par les F.F.I., on pouvait voir brûler les maisons de Bourg-la-Reine. La bataille fait rage entre avant-gardes alliées et fantassins allemands. Aux alentours de la gare du métro et de la gendarmerie, les Allemands disposaient encore de quelques pièces antichars et de plusieurs chars. Les lueurs des coups au départ et les explosions des arrivées étaient nettement perçues.

L'ennemi se défend avec vigueur. Il essaie de regagner Paris par la route numéro 20, mais celle-ci est littéralement hérissée de barricades. Les boches devront, s'ils ne peuvent les entamer, fuir en passant par Fresnes — ironie du sort ... mais, là, des barricades les attendent encore et aussi des F.F.I. pas plus décidés à les laisser passer que ceux de Cachan-Bagneux.

Bientôt, des infiltrations américaines se produisent près de Bourg-la-Reine et le crépitement de la fusillade remplace le bruit du canon. Un coup de téléphone du chef de gare du Petit-Clamart signale l'occupation de la station par les Américains.

Du Petit-Clamart à la Vache-Noire

Puis, les premiers motocyclistes et blindés américains sont signalés à quelques kilomètres du carrefour de la Vache-Noire. Le canon gronde, à nouveau, très rapproché. Au début de l'après-midi, des engagements avaient eu lieu entre Allemands qui se repliaient et F.F.I. Ceux-ci ont fait des prisonniers et ont tué plusieurs ennemis. Partout, depuis la porte, la route d'Orléans est coupée de barrages construits avec des moyens improvisés par les patriotes, toutes les fenêtres sont ornées de drapeaux aux couleurs des Alliés.

Choisy-le-Roi est conquis

A 17 h. 50, on annonce à la préfecture de police que des combats de chars ont eu lieu entre la Croix-de-Berny et Bourg-la-Reine, par suite de l'avance des troupes du général Leclerc.

Les Allemands ont abandonné Choisy-le-Roi.

A Châtillon et Bagneux, ils tirent sur la population civile.

On a averti les habitants de Montrouge qu'ils devaient rester chez eux pour ne pas gêner l'avance des troupes françaises.

Les unités françaises du général Leclerc font leur entrée à Issy-les-Moulineaux

Les unités françaises de la division Leclerc viennent de faire leur entrée à Issy-les-Moulineaux, par l'avenue Bourgain, pavoisée aux couleurs françaises et alliées.

A Châtillon-sous-Bagneux

Les troupes américaines ont atteint Châtillon et l'on s'attend à les voir gagner la porte d'Orléans où l'enthousiasme est indescriptible.

Accueil délirant des Américains à Bagneux

A 19 h. 25, dans le tonnerre des canons, des chars américains bousculaient de Bourg-la-Reine les derniers éléments allemands qui partaient en désordre le long de la voie du métro.

Au P.C. du groupe des F.F.I. aux ordres du capitaine Cossard, des miliciens arrivaient.

Ils étaient quatre, dont trois sous-officiers. Le capitaine les interrogeait. Ils avaient fait « camarade » devant les patriotes armés de simples grenades et de pistolets automatiques.

A 19 h. 30, à quelques mètres du P.C., à travers les barricades et entre les groupes ennemis, le lieutenant Edgard J. Milton, de New York City, de l'armée des Etats-Unis, le Private Pete Meredit, accompagné du capitaine Girardin, chargé de mission par le Comité médical de la Résistance, arrivaient devant la mairie de Bagneux. Une foule en délire, le mot n'est pas trop fort, se rassemblait en quelques instants.

Le Jeep qui les avait amenés était couvert de fleurs et de drapeaux aux couleurs alliées.

Le premier soin du lieutenant Milton, qui a fait ses études à Janson et à Lakanal, a été de se mettre en rapport avec les services médicaux français pour s'enquérir des besoins de la population française en médicaments.

Une réception fut organisée sous les rafales de mitraillettes et tout près du canon chez M. Sergent, miroitier à Bagneux, en présence du nouveau maire et des principaux membres de la résistance.

LA RECEPTION A L'HOTEL DE VILLE DES SOLDATS FRANÇAIS

Dans la salle de la Préfecture de la Seine où se trouvaient réunis les membres du C.N.R. et du Comité Parisien de Libération, le capitaine Raymond Dionne a fait son entrée à 21 h. 28. C'est le premier officier français entré à l'Hôtel de Ville. Il fait partie d'un régiment d'infanterie coloniale, brigade Leclerc.

Georges Bidault l'accueille dans des termes émouvants. L'assistance tout entière chante « la Marseillaise.

Au moment où M. Bidault termine son allocution, des coups de mitrailleuse éclatent. Les lustres volent en éclats. Plusieurs personnes sont blessées.

Dehors, une violente bataille s'engage. La place de l'Hôtel-de-Ville est évacuée. Les chars français et allemands s'affrontent en une suprême rencontre.

A la Préfecture de police

C'est à 22 h. 15 que le premier soldat français a fait son entrée dans la Préfecture de police tenue depuis samedi dernier par les glorieuses forces françaises de l'intérieur. Il s'agit du soldat Pirlien, du 3e régiment de la 2e division blindée d'origine niçoise; Pirlien a fait toute la campagne d'Afrique. Peu après un officier, le capitaine Dionne, arrivait à son tour à la Préfecture.

Explosions de joie !

La nouvelle de l'arrivée à Paris des avant-gardes du général Leclerc se répand dans toute la ville. Le bourdon de Notre-Dame donne le signal et bientôt les cloches de toutes les églises sonnent.

Dans la cour de la Préfecture une vibrante « Marseillaise » s'élève. Le chant gagne bientôt les rues et les boulevards environnants.

On annonce que le général de Gaulle va faire son entrée à Paris.

Avant de quitter la Préfecture, le capitaine Dionne a déclaré qu'il allait regagner Bagneux pour chercher le président du Gouvernement provisoire de la République Française.

Nos premiers libérateurs

Voici les noms des premiers soldats qui accompagnaient le capitaine Dionne ; Grantaloupt Jean, de Saint-Etienne; Pottier, de Saint-Malo. Ces deux derniers de la 2e division blindée Leclerc.

Ils avaient tous un visage fatigué mais empreint de joie, d'émotion, d'enthousiasme.

Après la réception, le capitaine et ses soldats ont regagné leur char pour continuer la lutte.

La colonne est repartie vers le centre de Paris laissant trois chars pour la protection de l'Hôtel de Ville.

On a pu interviewer le lieutenant qui commande ces trois chars — c'est un séminariste qui est avec Leclerc depuis cinq ans — ce dernier dit que tout ce qui se passe cette nuit n'est rien car les 17.000 hommes de Leclerc seront là demain. Tous les éléments qui restent dans Paris ne résisteront plus dans quelques instants.

A Massy, ils ont rencontré un noyau de résistance qu'ils ont balayé rapidement.

La Nation française au peuple parisien

Dans la capitale libérée par l'insurrection nationale, les premières troupes françaises ont fait leur entrée — le jour pour lequel par dizaines de milliers les Français ont donné leur vie — ce jour de bataille et de victoire a lui clairement sur les barricades.

Nos soldats en uniforme et nos soldats sans uniforme ont opéré leur jonction au carrefour d'une ville tout entière debout malgré la mitraille.

Dans une même fierté, la France et Paris saluent et remercient les uns et les autres.

Cette victoire ne met pourtant pas encore un terme à la guerre.

Après tant d'années d'une trahison obstinée, il reste encore des positions où l'ennemi s'accroche, l'Allemagne hitlérienne n'est pas encore abattue.

Des terres françaises sont encore sous sa botte, pillées, souillées, ensanglantées. Aucune force ne doit se relâcher.

La guerre continue. Elle continue pour tous et partout. Elle continuera jusqu'à la victoire totale.

Aussi la France se présentera en grande puissance dans l'Assemblée des Peuples qui feront la paix.

Soyons dignes de nos morts.

Toute la France est aux côtés des Alliés pour les venger.

Le Conseil National de la Résistance.

Le Comité Parisien de Libération.

Le Commissaire d'Etat délégué du gouvernement provisoire de la République.

Se rangeant aux côtés des Alliés la Roumanie libère la Transylvanie et attaque la Hongrie

Londres, 24 août. — C'est par une proclamation adressée au peuple roumain que le roi Michel a annoncé la décision qu'il venait de prendre d'accepter les conditions d'armistice présentées par le gouvernement soviétique et de mettre fin aux hostilités avec les Etats-Unis et la Grande-Bretagne d'une part, et avec l'U.R.S.S. d'autre part.

Un gouvernement d'union nationale a été constitué et il a immédiatement manifesté son intention de prendre part à la lutte menée par les Nations unies.

Le roi a, d'autre part, annoncé que l'armée roumaine était entrée en territoire hongrois et avait libéré la Transylvanie.

Le maréchal Antonesco s'enfuit en Allemagne

Zurich, 24 août. — La radio suisse a annoncé aujourd'hui que le maréchal Antonesco s'est enfui en Allemagne.

Un nouveau gouvernement est constitué à Bucarest

Londres, 24 août. — La B.B.C. annonce qu'à la suite de la cessation de l'état de guerre entre la Roumanie d'une part, l'U.R.S.S., la Grande-Bretagne et les Etats-Unis d'autre part, un nouveau gouvernement national roumain a été formé à Bucarest par le roi Michel. Le nouveau président du conseil est le général Sanatescu. Parmi les principaux ministres on relève les noms de MM. Maniu et Bratiano.

A l'occasion de sa prise de pouvoir, le nouveau gouvernement a publié une déclaration par laquelle il s'engage à établir un régime démocratique garantissant la liberté à tous. Les camps de concentration ont été abolis et une amnistie a été accordée à tous les détenus politiques.

Cette déclaration fait suite à un message du roi Michel dénonçant l'alliance entre la Roumanie et l'Allemagne et assurant que la Roumanie libérerait la Transylvanie. Le message du roi se terminait par ces mots: « Aux côtés des Alliés et avec leur aide, je mobilise toutes les forces de la nation. Les gouvernements alliés, a précisé le souverain, ont garanti l'indépendance de la Roumanie ».

L'ex-roi Carol exprime sa joie

Mexico, 24 août. — Interrogé par un représentant de l'agence Reuter qui était venu le trouver dans sa maison des environs de Mexico, l'ancien roi Carol de Roumanie a exprimé dans ces termes sa satisfaction d'apprendre que son pays était sorti de la guerre : « J'espère voir se réaliser, le plus tôt possible, un de mes anciens vœux, celui de voir la Roumanie aux côtés des nations unies, non seulement sur le plan politique, mais aussi sur les champs de bataille. La reconquête de la Transylvanie aidera à la défaite de l'oppresseur qui, quatre années durant, avait tenu le peuple roumain en esclavage. »

Perdu !

SPORTING FINAL
★★★★★★
STOCK EXCHANGE CLOSING
AND BID AND ASKED PRICES

The Sun

Copyright, 1944, by The New York Sun, Inc.

SEVENTH SPORTS
Sport Results on Page 20
LATEST RACING RESULTS
This afternoon and tomorrow bright and sunny, moderately warm. Tonight clear and cool. Temperatures—Minimum, 55; Maximum, 74. Sun rises 6:15 A. M. Sun sets 7:40 P. M. (Detailed weather report on page 26.)

VOL. 111—NO. 301. Entered as Second Class Matter Post Office, New York, N. Y. NEW YORK, FRIDAY, AUGUST 25, 1944. FIVE CENTS EVERYWHERE

DE GAULLE IN PARIS; GERMAN COMMANDER SURRENDERS CAPITAL

SARATOGA RESULTS

Race Charts on Page 20. Other Results on Page 20.

	First.			Second		Third
First Race....	Pride of Hygro			Febridge		Tanrackin
Prices.....	$6.30	3.30	2.90	2.80	2.50	8.70
No scratches.						
Second Race..	All Bright			Respire		Scotch Irish
Prices....	$14.40	6.30	4.20	4.10	2.90	3.60
Scratched—Aunt Sis, More Wine.						
Daily Double Paid $76.40.						
Third Race...	Brown Plumage			Sea Frolic		Night Glow
Prices.....	$3.70	2.40	2.10	2.70	2.20	2.30
No scratches.						
Fourth Race..	Psychist			Miel		Sun Lady
Prices.....	$13.40	5.70	3.60	3.70	2.50	3.00
Scratched—La Grande, Turnplate.						
Fifth Race.....	Rouge Dragon			Knight's Quest		Redlands
Prices.....	$9.90	5.00	3.40	4.80	2.90	3.10
Scratched—Elkridge, Bridlespur, Bill Coffman.						
Sixth Race.....	Victim			Bardia		Sea Fare
Prices....	$14.60	7.00	5.60	*6.90	5.20	12.70
Scratched—Meneither, Sun Flame.						
Seventh Race..	Late City			Gig		Faiseur
Prices.....	$7.60	3.90	3.10	5.50	4.70	4.00
Scratched—Supper Dance.						

Germans Start Wild Retreat From Channel Coast Front

Canadian and American Troops Link Lines South of Seine as Von Kluge's Men Fall Back.

Supreme Headquarters, Allied Expeditionary Force, Aug. 25 (A. P.).—Field Marshal Gen. Guenther von Kluge was reported swinging his beaten German armies back to the line of the Somme and the Marne today in a headlong retreat which would abandon much of the channel coast and the vicinity of Paris.

The battle in the pocket below the Seine, swiftly whittled to an area of only twenty miles long and fifteen miles deep, appeared likely to be ended in another twenty-four hours as Americans, British, Canadians and Allied troops pressed in from all sides. The Canadians, advancing along the coast, captured Honfleur, five miles across the Seine bay from Le Havre.

According to a dispatch from a correspondent at the front with the Canadian First Army, Canadians late today established contact with American forces on the Seine River at Louviers south of Rouen.

A western Canada armored car regiment made the twenty-mile dash from Beaumont on the Risle

Continued on Page 6.

In The Sun Today

School News Appears in the Night Edition.

CANNES CAPTURED; AMERICAN TROOPS 10 MILES FROM NICE

French Maquis Reported to Have Entered City of Lyon.

Rome, Aug. 25 (A. P.).—American troops have captured Cannes in a lunge eastward from their Riviera beachhead in southern France, and have occupied Antibes, it was announced today. Antibes is ten miles southwest of Nice and twenty-four miles from the Italian frontier.

Other forces of Lieut.-Gen. Alexander M. Patch were close to Arles, at the mouth of the Rhone, and Parascon, a few miles to the north.

[Berlin radio declared German troops began withdrawing from southwestern France several days ago, and the German communique indicated the retreat extended over most of southern France.

[French headquarters said patriot troops had entered Lyon, 170 miles north of Marseille.]

On the western beachhead flank, the Allies opened great assaults to crush German pockets still holding out in Marseille.

The Americans who took Cannes also seized the nearby inland town of Grasse.

Another United States column,

Continued on Page 2.

Took Hour to Change Husbands.

Great Falls, Mont., Aug. 25 (A. P.).—At 3 P. M. Ruby Olsen was granted a divorce from Walter Olsen, and at 4 P. M. she married Joe Anderson with her ex-husband as best man.

First Eye witness Account of Fighting in Paris

[The following graphic account of the Allied entry into Paris by a veteran Associated Press correspondent is the first eyewitness dispatch to come out of the embattled capital of France. It was passed by field censorship and transmitted by regular press channels.]

By DON WHITEHEAD.

Paris, Aug. 25 (A. P.).—Street fighting raged through the heart of Paris today as American and French columns drove into the city from the south amid a tumultuous welcome from hundreds of thousands of Parisians.

The first French column to enter the city reached Luxemburg at 10:20 A. M. The Germans, the collaborationist militia and the French Gestapo organization opened fire with machine guns, rifles and pistols and the battle was on.

An American infantry column drove to Notre Dame at 11 A. M. in a spectacular ground attack to close in on strongholds still defended by the embattled Germans and the Vichy French militia.

[This dispatch was filed at 12:28 P. M., 6:28 A. M., Eastern wartime.]

The columns fought toward the center of the city where 5,000 French Forces of the Interior and city police have held out for the past week.

Machine guns and rifles cracked on all sides as the column I was with drove to within a block of the Luxembourg.

Joyous, happy throngs who greeted the entrance of the tanks and infantry with a thundering welcome fled to the safety of buildings and within a few mintues the streets that had been choked with humanity, laughing and crying over the liberation, were bare battlegrounds.

Where Nazis Hold Out.

As I write this story the Germans are still holding out in the area on both sides of the Seine halfway along the Champs-Elysees, Place de la Concorde, Quai d'Orsay, Tuileries, Gardens of the Louvre, the Madelaine, the Chamber of Deputies, the Senate and the Hotel Crillon.

French patriots have a grip on the Ile de la Cite, the Palais de Justice, the Prefecture of Police, the Prefecture of the Seine, most of the Mairies and the factory district.

But Frenchmen are fighting Frenchmen as well as Germans in liberating a city wild with happiness over the freedom which they waited for four years.

There was so much confusion and excitement over the entrance into the city that it is difficult to give a coherent account of the events that moved so swiftly, once the French armored column began rolling through the heavy morning fog that made vehicles look like prehistoric monsters appearing out of the swamps of creation.

But when the last enemy resistance crumbled at the gate to Paris then this heart of France went mad—wildly, violently mad with happiness.

All the emotions suppressed by four years of German domination surged through the people. The streets of the city as we entered were like a combined mardi gras, Fourth of July celebration, American Legion convention and New Year's Eve in Times Square all packed into one.

Our column began to roll at 7 A. M. from Longjumeau, six miles south of Paris. A French captain stopped all correspondents one mile from town and insisted he had orders that no one without a written permit could enter the city. He told three British correspondents they would be shot if they drove by without a pass.

An American colonel heard the story and said the captain was acting without proper authority. I drove to the blockade and suddenly my jeep lurched forward into the column (of troops). Unfortunately it was too late to turn back, so I kept going.

Two miles farther the column halted. Forward elements had run into a German strongpoint and mines on the road.

French Brig.-Gen. Jacques Leclerc and his staff went into conference. Tanks wheeled and started to outflank the position but after a while they returned because they ran into the route of an American infantry advance.

Strongpoint Knocked Out.

Then the column began to roll again. The strongpoint had been knocked out ahead of us. And at 9:57 A. M. my jeep rolled through the gates into Paris.

Never do I expect to see such scenes as I saw on the streets of Paris. There was only a narrow lane through which the armor could roll. Men and women cried with joy. They grabbed the arms and hands of soldiers and cheered until their voices were hoarse.

When the column stopped I was smothered, but pleasantly, with soft arms and lips giving not one kiss but the usual French double one. They hugged me and my jeep driver and pined French Tricolors on us, and left us exhausted, with our bosoms covered with emblems and ribbons.

Cries 'God Bless America.'

One old man came up, saluted, and said with tears in his eyes: "God bless America. You have saved France."

Men and women, old and young, and children stormed the jeep everytime the column stopped and they were wild with emotion.

Crowds were banked from the center of the streets to the sidewalks in a colorful, cheering throng which stretched for miles. There seemed to be no end and apparently every one in Paris except the Germans and collaborationists was standing there to cheer, shout, cry, and leave themselves exhausted with happiness.

Our column moved to a point one block from the Luxembourg. Then from all sides burst machine-gun fire. From housetops and windows guns rattled. Machine guns of tanks opened up in reply. We leaped from the jeep and took cover behind a tank.

Jerry Beatson of Rockford, Ill., was beside me and leveled his carbine at the top of the building. The gun cracked in my ear.

"There's one ——— up there," he cried, and kept firing at the rooftop.

Bullets rattled on the streets and glanced off with ugly whines.

The crowds, which a few minutes before lined the

Continued on Page 6.

ALLIES ADVANCE ON ITALIAN FRONT

Rome, Aug. 25 (A. P.).—Allied troops have made considerable advances in the upper Arno valley on the central sector of the Italian front and have occupied the villages of Castelnuovo, Fornich and La Montania, Allied headquarters announced today.

Just east of Florence, in the Pontassieve sector, Eighth Army forces have made good progress toward the Gothic Line and are firmly established on the western slopes of Monte Fecchieta.

In the Fifth Army sector west of Florence continued patrol activity was reported on both sides of the Arno.

Dave Boone Says:

Forty-seven American railroads and scores of railroad men and bankers are now sued by Attorney-General Biddle for something or other. If your name ain't on the list you can't be very prominent.

Well, the railroads should have expected it. They ought to know by this time that doing a difficult job as efficiently as they have been doing it can't be permitted to go unchallenged.

The war in the War Production Board is running the war in Europe a close second. Charles E. Wilson has surrendered unconditionally with a blast at Donald Nelson. Wilson says the hedgerow fighting in Washington is pretty tough, too.

Even with Mr. Nelson in China, Charlie wouldn't feel "liberated" completely, he replies.

I wish I could get straightened out on whether Paris has been liberated or not. The only consolation is that Hitler is probably more confused about it than anybody else.

3 GERMAN VESSELS SUNK OFF LE HAVRE

London, Aug. 25 (A. P.).—American and British light naval forces intercepting Nazi ships attempting to escape from Le Havre, at the mouth of the Seine, early today blew up an escort vessel, an armed trawler and an E-boat, and damaged at least five other enemy warships in a series of running battles.

Cow Has Twins 37 Days Apart.

Wabash Ind., Aug. 25 (A. P.).—Sharon Reed's Jersey cow calved in July. Thirty-seven days later she had another calf with identical markings.

YANKS AND FRENCH IN CENTER OF CITY

Nazis Give Up After Bitter Battle With Allies in Streets—Parisians Wildly Welcome Troops Entering to Rescue Them.

London, Aug. 25 (A. P.).—The Free French radio announced that Gen. Charles de Gaulle entered Paris at 7 P. M. (1 P. M., Eastern war time) today.

Radio Paris said that Gen. De Gaulle and Brig.-Gen. Leclerc, commander of the French forces which entered Paris met at the Montparnasse station this morning, according to a broadcast heard here by the NBC.

The German commander of Paris has surrendered to Gen. Leclerc and the commander of the French Forces of the Interior, the Paris radio reported today in a broadcast recorded by Columbia Broadcasting System.

Under terms of the surrender, German commanders were ordered to cease firing immediately and hoist the white flag.

"The weapons will be collected and the men gathered without weapons in a determined place, until new orders are given," the terms stipulated. "The weapons will be surrendered intact."

Other Surrender Terms.

Other terms of the surrender provided that all machinery for destroying buildings and vessels would be given up; that the Nazis would send to Gen. Leclerc an official accounting of the General Staff concerning the weapons and garrisons under German command; the conditions of evacuation of the personnel of the Wehrmacht will be regulated by Gen. Leclerc; soldiers who continue the fight because they were not informed of the surrender will be examined.

The Paris radio said this afternoon that "a few hours ago we had the moving experience of hearing Gen. de Gaulle tell us the German general who commands the region of Paris has just surrendered to Gen. Leclerc and to the commander of the F. F. I.

The broadcast, also recorded here by CBS, told of "a magnificent ceremony" as thousands acclaimed him as he, "in the name of France and with the unanimous support of Frenchmen, proclaimed his faith in the destiny of France."

NBC announced late today hearing a radio Paris broadcast which said that French Commander Leclerc and the German commander had just met in the Police Department Building and there proceeded to Montparnasse to sign the terms of the armistice.

Captured German officers were led from the Hotel de Ville today and police had to keep the crowd from lynching them, said radio Paris as heard by NBC.

Allies Seize Heart of City.

Supreme Headquarters, Allied Expeditionary Force, Aug. 25 (A. P.).—French and American forces seized the heart of Paris today just as it was falling from the failing grasp of patriots.

The first French column to enter the city reached the Luxembourg, near the center of the city, at 10:20 A. M. and engaged in a battle with the Germans and collaborationist militia.

In the fog of early morning, American infantry—the first of this second American Expeditionary Force within a generation to enter Paris—battled to Notre Dame, whose ancient bells a few hours before had welcomed the first French patrols to the city.

On all sides the liberating French and Americans were

Continued on Page 6.

ANCHOR TO THE TRUTH

THE CHICAGO SUN

FINAL

VOL. 3—No. 267 | REG. U.S. PAT. OFF. COPYRIGHT, 1944 BY THE CHICAGO SUN. | SATURDAY, AUGUST 26, 1944 | Tel. ANDover 4800 | THREE CENTS

First Story of Yanks in Paris: Cheers, Flags, Flowers, Bullets

Nelson May Leave WPB, F.D.R. Hints

Navy Officer Seen As Successor on Reconversion Job

By Ruth Moore.
Chicago Sun Washington Bureau.

Washington, Aug. 25.—Donald M. Nelson, chairman, may leave the War Production Board shortly after his return from China. His present job, plus the coming major task of putting industry back on a peacetime basis, may go to Lt. Cmdr. J. A. Krug, 36, who was appointed acting WPB chairman by President Roosevelt last night.

The President indicated that Nelson's future status was in doubt at his news conference today. Asked if Nelson would continue as chaiman of WPB, the President answered—in his own words—that's an iffy question, and I don't know. It's iffy to ask what's going to happen in the future, he added.

Rubber Chief Assails Nelson.

Bradley Dewey, who is leaving the post of rubber director Sept. 1, fired a broadside at Nelson today, charging that the WPB chairman was engaging in "typical Washington sniping" when he told the Senate committee investigating the war program that the rubber program "was completed, all but getting the tires."

Dewey told reporters for the three major press associations, whom he called into a press conference, that he never had said the rubber program was completed. He had only said that the synthetic rubber plants were turning out a surplus, and that the problem of making tires no longer required special powers.

Bradley Dewey.

When Nelson, questioned about Dewey's resignation, told the committee that to call the rubber program completed would be like "the Army saying that they are

See NELSON, Page 10, Col. 1.

Veteran Public Servant

LT.CMDR. J. A. KRUG, at 36, is a veteran public servant. Soon after his graduation from the University of Wisconsin in 1929 he went to the Wisconsin Public Service Commission.

In 1936 he transferred to the Federal Communications Commission and a year later to the Tennessee Valley Authority, where he was in charge of power operations. There he handled the negotiations with Wendell Willkie for TVA's purchase of Willkie's $80,000,000 Tennessee Electric Co.

By this time he had come to the attention of President Roosevelt, who sent him to Costa Rica on a utility mission and then brought him to the Office of Production Management to work on the expansion of aluminum facilities. He next moved into WPB, where he became program vice-chairman last February. On April 1, he entered the Navy.

Where It Is

The Weather

[SATURDAY, AUG. 26, 1944.]

Light to moderate rain today changing to thundershowers tonight. No decided change in temperature, fresh winds. High today, 70; low tonight, 67.

HOURLY TEMPERATURES.

5 a.m.....54	1 p.m.....73	9 p.m.....68
6 a.m.....55	2 p.m.....73	10 p.m.....68
7 a.m.....56	3 p.m.....74	11 p.m.....68
8 a.m.....59	4 p.m.....74	Midnight..68
9 a.m.....65	5 p.m.....74	1 a.m.....66
10 a.m.....71	6 p.m.....71	2 a.m.....64
11 a.m.....72	7 p.m.....69	3 a.m...*64
Noon......73	8 p.m.....68	4 a.m...*63

*Unofficial.

Pollen count for 24 hours ended 10 a. m. Friday: 9.

(Other Weather on Page 2.)

Police Dig For Bullets as Drake Clue

The new burst of activity aimed at solving the Drake Hotel slaying of Mrs. Frank Starr Williams through recovery of bullets buried near Bloomington, Ill., came to a brief recess last night.

Developments in the sensational case, brought back into the limelight by a Stateville convict's story that he might have given the murder weapon to a Chicago policeman 11 years ago, were:

1. **At 8:30 p.m. Chicago officers stopped digging in a field for bullets which the convict said might have come from the revolver that slew Mrs. Williams last Jan. 19.**

2. **Warden Joseph E. Ragen of Stateville denied a request that the convict, Walter Brown, serving a life term for murder, be brought to Bloomington to aid in locating the bullets. Ragen said Brown was too dangerous a character to be taken out of prison. It was decided to submit photographs of the field to Brown so that he could indicate the approximate location of the bullets with an X.**

3. **Policeman Adolph A. Valanis of the Warren Avenue Station, to whom Brown said he might have given the Drake death gun in 1933, after the bullets were fired into the field, was given a lie-detector test.**

4. **Police also went to Charleston, Ill., in a hunt for other bullets believed fired from the Iver-Johnson revolver Brown said he had 11 years ago.**

Mrs. Williams, wealthy wife of a former diplomat, was shot to death in her hotel room by a woman in a Persian lamb coat, according to Mrs. Williams' daughter, Mrs. Patricia Goodbody, only other person in the room.

Policeman's Sister Key Clerk.

Mrs. Ellen Bennett, oft-married sister of Valanis, was a key clerk at the Drake at the time of the slaying, and an Iver-Johnson revolver was found near the death scene.

Brown, who has twice been confined to the state hospital in Menard, before being returned to Stateville, is a lifelong friend of Valanis. They were reared as boys in the same orphanage.

According to the convict's story, he first acquired the gun from two friends, both of whom he described as holdup men, when he was running a roadhouse known as the Garden Club near Bloomington.

Fail to Find Bullets.

Testing the weapon, Brown declared, he went to the rear of a barn behind the club, which adjoins the Bloomington airport, and fired half a dozen shots into the ground.

In the hope that those bullets might be retrieved and by ballistics tests compared with the slug which killed Mrs. Williams, Charles M. Wilson of the police crime detection laboratory, and Sgts. John Mangin and Thomas

See MYSTERY, Page 18, Col. 3.

Miles to Berlin

By the United Press.

The road to Berlin:
311 miles from the Russian front.
490 miles from the northern French front (unconfirmed).
593 miles from the southern French front.
586 miles from the Italian front.

Yanks Reach Reims Area, London Hears

Foe Pushed Back Toward Rhine On 200-Mi. Front

[Map on Page 2.]

By Phil Ault.
United Press Staff Correspondent.

Allied Supreme Headquarters, London, Saturday, Aug. 26.—Allied troops, spurred on by news of the liberation of Paris, rolled the Germans back toward the Rhine River on a 200-mile front across France today. Unofficial reports said an American spearhead had crossed the Marne River and reached Reims, cathedral city 80 miles northeast of Paris and about 110 miles from the German border.

Allied headquarters sources also confirmed that American patrols had reached Troyes, some 130 miles west of the German frontier. While it appeared they had penetrated even further, any official confirmation of the Reims report was banned by the secrecy drawn over news of operations south and east of Paris.

Rouen's Fall Believed Near.

Some 200 miles to the northwest—beyond Paris, where Allied forces had rescued patriots in a battle against German resistance pockets in the streets — fleeing Germans still were scrambling across the lower reaches of the Seine under heavy air attack. Virtually all the territory below the Seine was in Allied hands.

The fall of Rouen, great communications center west of Le Havre, appeared imminent. The Germans, running for their lives, were in no position to defend it if the Allies chose to make a major attack northward in the direction of the Pas de Calais area and the rocket coast.

Tanks Destroyed.

Up to 6 p.m. U.S. 9th Air Force fighters and fighter bombers reportedly destroyed 54 German tanks and damaged 50 more, mostly along the south bank of the Seine from which the final remnants of the German 7th Army were fleeing. They also destroyed 158 motor vehicles.

Le Havre, across the broad mouth of the Seine from Allied troops and within easy artillery

See INVASION, Page 2, Col. 3.

Bartender Shot In N. Side Tavern

James J. Joseph, 32, of 4526 Sheridan rd., a bartender off duty, was shot in the abdomen at 10:20 o'clock last night by another customer in the Sheridan Tap, tavern at 4621 Sheridan rd. Town Hall police took a third customer, Arthur Fenton, 36, also of 4526 Sherdan rd., into custody. Fenton, a bartender at Washington Park Race Track, said the man who shot Joseph apparently did so accidentally as he displayed a revolver. Joseph was taken to Bridewell Hospital.

First Picture from Free Paris

Crowds of French patriots gather around one of the first Allied jeeps to enter the liberated city of Paris. Photo transmitted by radio from Cherbourg. Other pictures from Paris on back page.
ACME RADIOPHOTO FROM U.S. SIGNAL CORPS.

Soviet Drive in Romania Costs Germans 205,400

By Robert Musel.
United Press Staff Correspondent.

London, Saturday, Aug. 26.—Two Soviet armies, killing or capturing 205,400 enemy troops in a six-day Nazi Balkan catastrophe, pursued fleeing German forces 30 miles through chaotic Romania to within 108 miles of Bucharest yesterday and encircled another 12 Nazi divisions far behind the lines.

Sweeping forward with the aid of Romanian troops already reported clashing with the Nazis following Romania's declaration of war against her former ally, the 2d and 3d Ukrainian armies plunged to within 14 miles of Focsani, western bastion of the famed Galati Gap guarding the approaches to the Ploesti oilfields and the Romanian capital.

Drive to Danube River.

Soviet infantrymen, spearheaded by saber swinging Cossacks and giant tanks, swung deep into Romania, reached the Danube River and charged with ease through abandoned enemy defenses.

Plunging to with 32 miles of troops encircled 12 enemy divisions in Bessarabia. Already 13,000 of the surrounded enemy group have surrendered.

100,000 Killed in 5 Days.

The Soviet Information Bureau reported that in six days 100,000 enemy soldiers had been killed and 105,400 captured. Three Romanian generals were seized, including the commander of the 110th Romanian Division, Gen. Tenescu Trajan, and his staff.

At the same time, Russian Baltic troops, breaking some of the strongest German resistance of the summer offensive, captured the Estonian rail and university city of Tartu.

The 2d and 3d Ukrainian armies

See RUSSIA, Page 5, Col. 1.

THE WORLD AT WAR

[SATURDAY, AUG. 26, 1944.]

ROMANIA, first Balkan satellite to quit the Axis, declared war on Germany yesterday. Fighting between German and Romanian troops was reported throughout the country. Other Balkan states were reported shaking in their Nazi allegiance and there were indications the whole satellite structure might be near collapse.

* * *

THE Red Army was disclosed to have killed 100,000 German and Romanian soldiers and captured 105,400 in the six days of the Soviet offensive in Romania and Bessarabia. Yesterday the Russians advanced 30 miles toward Bucharest.

* * *

ALLIED troops rolled the Germans back toward the Rhine River on a 200-mile front, reaching Troyes, 130 miles west of the German border. Unofficial reports placed an American spearhead across the Marne River and at Reims, 110 miles from Germany.

* * *

IN SOUTHERN France, American spearheads advanced 10 miles and "closely approached" the lower Rhone River northwest of Marseille, thus cutting off a major German retreat road from southwestern France.

* * *

IN ITALY, 8th Army troops captured Mount Foresto in the area 30 miles west of Florence where German forces appeared to be falling back toward the Gothic Line.

* * *

SOME 3,000 Allied bombers and fighters continued the assault on oil and aircraft targets in northern Germany and Czechoslovakia.

'Doll Game' Ruled Gambling in Indiana

Continuing his crusading drive against gambling, Charles Gannon, Lake County (Ind.) prosecutor, clamped down last night on the "knock-down-the-baby-dolls; three-balls-for-a-dime" games at the county fair in Crown Point.

The fair's big midway was trown half into darkness when Gannon decided summarily that these games of chance came within the meaning of the state gambling laws.

The peep-shows were left to operate, however, when Gannon, after an inspection, ruled they were too tame to bother anyone.

Germans Flee Toward Lyon

By James E. Roper.
United Press Staff Correspondent.

Allied Headquarters, Rome, Aug. 25.—American spearheads, in a 10-mile thrust, reached the edge of the lower Rhone River at two points northwest of Marseille today. Other U. S. forces 125 miles to the east captured the Riviera resort towns of Cannes and Antibes.

The American drive into the eastern slopes of the Rhone valley near Arles and Tarascon slashed a major German road of retreat from southwestern France and cut off a coastal pocket extending eastward from the Rhone delta to Marseille.

Nazis Admit Retreat.

The Germans, by their own admission, were retreating up the Rhone toward Lyon, 150 miles north of Arles, presumably in an effort to reach safety before an American column last reported in Grenoble could cut off the northern end of the valley road.

[A French Forces of the Interior communique said the Maquis entered Lyon on Thursday, thus bottling up those Germans in the Rhone valley between Arles and Lyon.]

Headquarters announced 20,000 Germans had been taken prisoner in the 11 days that Lt.Gen. Alexander M. Patch's Franco-American 7th Army has been on the march across southern France. Hundreds more were being seized in the Mediterranean ports of Marseille and Toulon, where fighting still raged.

Marseille Mopup On.

A late bulletin said the French still were fighting the Nazis in the port area of Toulon and were mopping up the enemy in liberated Marseille. Front reports said the French had begun a final drive to crush the Germans still holding out in Forts St. Jean and St. Nic-

See FRANCE, Page 2, Col. 5.

Swiss Call Up Troops As 'Security Measure'

Zurich, Switzerland, Aug. 25.—(UP)—The Swiss Federal Council has ordered additional security measures taken and has called up more troops "in view of the situation," it was announced officially today. There was no immediate explanation as to just what circumstances prompted, the special Swiss precautions.

Kisses Shower On Americans

Gunfire Halts Celebration Only Momentarily in Capital

[Map on Page 3. First Radiophotos on Pages 1 and 18.]

By John Groth.
Artist-War Correspondent for Parade.
Special to The Chicago Sun.

Paris, Aug. 25.—Hundreds of thousands of people swarming through the streets, cheering, crying, laughing. Garlands of flowers everywhere. The tricolor, American, British and Russian flags. And over all of it the singing of snipers' bullets and the crumping of tanks firing.

That was the way Paris looked and sounded today when I went in with the French 2d Armored Corps as one of the first three American newsmen to enter the city.

With Gordon Gammack of the Des Moines Register and Tribune; Charles Haacker, photographer for Acme Newspictures, and Capt. Sacha Bollas of Los Angeles, I entered the city at 9:30 a.m. through the Porte d'Orleans.

Flowers, Confetti Fill the Air.

I found it a mad carnival of red, white and blue, the hysteria and wild emotion of seething people, the air filled with a rain of flowers and confetti, and beyond all this the sounds of fighting still going on, but still unable to dampen this great day of liberation.

On the road since dawn, we approached the city from the south, driving around pockets of German resistance and forced to retrace our steps to avoid mined roads, passing American armor, stopping, starting through the Orsay Longjumeaubourg-Reine and into the suburbs.

About four miles from the city itself, we were stopped by French soldiers with whom we had to argue to let us pass. We argued and succeeded because we were now far beyond more than 100 other correspondents we had seen delayed behind us.

French Provide an Escort.

After passing these guards, who in fact actually gave us a French lieutenant as an escort, we passed long columns of tanks and trucks loaded with Maquis, their rifles slung over their shoulders. On some of these trucks there were women in coveralls spotted among the Maquis and at the sides of the roads people were beginning to gather.

They were people in their Sunday best, they were children in baby carriages, they were invalids in wheel chairs, they were old French veterans in treasured parts of old uniforms. They were beginning to cheer wildly and wave and some of them ran after the steadily rumbling column and began to pelt the tanks and trucks with peonies, dahlias and roses.

Crowd Becomes Ocean of Faces.

As we bypassed the tanks and trucks and moved toward the head of the column, what had been a crowd now became an ocean—an ocean of tightly pressed faces, waving arms, more flags, more flowers, more faces—an ocean that broke all dams and flooded in around the vehicles when the column stopped as if to catch its breath before pushing on.

It was an ocean, too, of sound, of cries of "Merci, merci," of "Vive la France! Vive l'Amerique!"—sounds without any identity of sounds that came from women, children and men, but were no longer sounds but just a canopy of noise that surrounded and covered the column as it went on.

Girls Pulled Aboard Vehicles.

Through the Porte d'Orleans and up the boulevard of the same name, the column pushed. When it stopped or even slowed for a moment, girls dressed in red, white and blue, girls with flowers in their hair, all the girls you've ever seen, pressed around the vehicles. And when they reached up wildly to touch the men, there were many who were pulled up and drawn aboard, and in a moment these trucks and tanks became almost as floats in a Rose Bowl parade.

For on them now were these girls astride the turrets,

See PARIS, Page 3, Col. 1.

Pope and Churchill Confer in Vatican

Special to The Chicago Sun.

Vatican City, Aug. 25.—Pope Pius XII received Prime Minister Churchill on Wednesday and discussed with the premier "various essential questions relating to important problems of the present hour," it was announced in a special Vatican bulletin issued today.

[It was announced the Pope would make a world-wide radio broadcast on Sept. 1, and it was assumed much of his talk would hinge on topics discussed in his conference with Churchill.]

Churchill left Rome later the same day without any comment about the 45-minute conversation.

1,200 Miles in 10 Days

52 Shipwrecked Sailors Span Atlantic in Lifeboat

AN ALMOST unbelievable saga of the sea, the tale of how 52 men of the crew of a torpedoed American merchant ship rowed and sailed their lifeboat 1,200 miles across the Atlantic Ocean in 10 days—an average of 120 miles a day—was told here yesterday.

Coxswain James V. Spinelli, 19, son of Mrs. Jennie Spinelli of 709 S. Hermitage av., member of the Navy gun crew, said their trip began just off the coast of Africa and ended in the Barbados, in the British West Indies off the northeast coast of South America.

James V. Spinelli.

Spinelli said three torpedoes hit their merchant vessel and that they had just made the lifeboat and pulled away a few yards when the ship upended and sunk.

* * *

BECAUSE the wind was against them, they made for the west although the trip to Africa would have been only 300 miles, Spinelli related.

He said modern scientific equipment, the discipline of seafaring men and the fish they were able to catch kept them going, although it was so crowded no one could lie down.

Spinelli attended McKinley High School and worked for a biscuit company before joining the Navy in August, 1942.

PREIS fFr. 2.- · IM REICH 20 Pfg. · IN BELGIEN bFr. 2.

PARISER ZEITUNG

Postverlagsort Köln. — Verlag und Schriftleitung: Paris, 100, rue Réaumur. Tel.: Gut. 88-00, Tur. 54-40, Gut. 80-60 und 80-61 bis 66. Banken: Reichskreditkasse, Paris; Crédit Lyonnais, Agence H. Paris (2e). Nr. 43 523. — Postscheckkonto Paris Nr. 2655 94. — Im Reich: Postscheckkonto der Dresdner Bank, Berlin Nr. 800, mit Vermerk «Für Pariser Zeitung».

Nr. 219 / Jahrg. 4 / Sonnabend Sonntag, 26./27. August 1944

Die «Pariser Zeitung» erscheint täglich ausser Sonntags. Der Bezugspreis beträgt in Frankreich monatlich Frs. 45.—, im Vierteljahr Frs. 120.—. Bezugspreis im Reich RM 3.— zuzüglich Zustellgebühr. Bestellungen in Frankreich beim Verlag direkt. Zweigstelle: Paris (9me), 36, Boulevard des Italiens. Téléphone: Taitbout 44-90.

Sprecher der Nation

«In diesem Kampf um Sein oder Nichtsein geht es nicht um eine Staatsform, sondern um unser nationales Leben». Dieses aufrüttelnde Wort, das Reichsminister Dr. Goebbels in seiner Rede zum 10. Jahrestag der Machtübernahme am 30. Januar 1943 im Sportpalast dem deutschen Volk zurief, klingt heute wie eine eherne Glocke im Herzen jedes Deutschen. Dass nun gerade heute — zu einem Zeitpunkt, wo das deutsche Volk nach dem Erlass des Führers vom 25. Juli 1944 zum restlos totalisierten Krieg seine grösste Kraftleistung vollbringt — ein Buch von Reichsminister Dr. Goebbels mit dem mitreissenden Titel «Der steile Aufstieg» erscheint, bedeutet eine moralische Unterstützung des grossen Endkampfes, die ihre Wirkung nicht verfehlen kann. Den meisten ist es heute unmöglich, sich in der Zeit des vernichtenden Bombenterrors vielleicht eine eigene Sammlung der Reden und Artikel des Reichsministers anzulegen, anderseits aber besteht der Wunsch, nicht nur seine neuesten Artikel zu lesen, sondern auch immer wieder auf die vergangenen Worte, Gedankengänge und Probleme zurückgreifen zu können. Hier hilft das vorliegende Buch aus dem Franz Eher-Verlag, das die wichtigsten Reden und Leitartikel von Dr. Goebbels aus den Jahren 1942/43 auswählte, um damit gleichzeitig die innere Entwicklung darzustellen, die das deutsche Volk in diesen Jahren genommen hat. Wir befinden uns in einem gigantischen Kampf an den Fronten, wir stehen in der Riesenschlacht unserer Rüstungsproduktion, wir befinden uns aber ebensosehr in einem geistigen Kampf von beispiellosen Ausmassen. Für diesen geistigen Kampf bedeutet das neue Buch einen Rückhalt, der notwendig ist, um Überzeugung und Glauben zu festigen und zu stärken. Es gibt für diesen geistigen Kampf, der sich einmal gegen eine Zersetzung von aussen und innen richtet, und der anderseits den Ausdruck des Nationalsozialismus überhaupt darstellt, keinen besseren publizistischen Führer als Reichsminister Dr. Goebbels. Er kennt die Stärken und Schwächen des deutschen Volkes aus jahrzehntelanger Erfahrung. Ihm gelang es bei jeder Rede, sich immer wieder die Herzen seiner Zuhörer zu erobern. Vernichtende Ironie gegen die Feinde und überzeugende Offenheit vor dem Volke haben ihn zum Sprecher der Nation gemacht. Nie hat er auch nur eine Minute lang den Kontakt mit denen verloren, an dei er seine Worte richtete. Er kennt vor allen Dingen auch die Nöte seiner Volksgenossen, die er mit ihnen teilt. Diese Kenntnis, dieses Verbundensein versetzen ihn immer wieder in die Lage, mit sicherer und ruhiger Überlegenheit seine Hörer und Leser gleichsam an die Hand zu nehmen und sie über die schwierigen Wegstellen, besonders in den letzten fünf Jahren, zu führen.

Das offizielle Sprachrohr für die Thesen des Reichsministers ist die Wochenzeitung «Das Reich», die sich auf Grund dieser Leitartikel einen breiten Weg in alle Schichten des Volkes gebahnt hat. Das vorliegende Buch bringt daher neben den wichtigen Reden eine Auswahl der besten und packendsten Beiträge aus den Jahren 1942/43. Hier finden sich Schulbeispiele messerscharf geschliffener Ironie, aber auch schlichte, nach dem Herzen greifende Worte. Die Stärke jedes überragenden Publizisten liegt nicht darin, dass er durch geistreiche Worte in intellektuellen Kreisen lächelnden Beifall erntet, sondern dass er mit packenden klaren Sätzen das Herz des Volkes anspricht und überzeugt. Dass Dr. Goebbels dies erreicht hat, beweisen unzählige Zuschriften aus den Kreisen des Volkes und der Wehrmacht. Das Geheimnis seiner suggestiven Überzeugungskraft liegt in der «illusionslosen, nüchternen, niemals schönfärberischen und darum krisenfesten Betrachtungsweise», wie es M. A. von Schirrmeister in seinem Vorwort zu dem neuen Buch sagt. Das deutsche Volk befindet sich heute im totalen Krieg. Dr. Goebbels, der das nationalsozialistische Wort seit langen Jahren prägte, wurde vom Führer nun auch zum Organisator dieser gigantischen Kräftezusammenballung berufen. Er ist — und dies sagt eine neutrale Schweizer Stimme, — «der treibende Motor der totalen Kriegführung in Deutschland». Damit erhalten seine Artikel und Reden in dem vorliegenden Buch «Der steile Aufstieg» rückwirkend eine noch bedeutendere Stellung als bisher. Um diesen steilen Aufstieg zu meistern, um zu erkennen, was im Augenblick notwendig ist, um aus der Vergangenheit Lehre und Kraft für die Zukunft zu schöpfen, wurde dieses Buch dem deutschen Volke als helfender Freund und Kamerad zur Seite gestellt. B.

Wirrwarr unter den französischen Terroristen

Strassenkämpfe in Paris

Auch in Marseille und Toulon - Der Erfolg im Seinebogen

Berlin, 25. August.

Im harten Ringen im Invasionsraum lag der Schwerpunkt des feindlichen Druckes am Donnerstag westlich der unteren Seine und südlich von Paris. Im normannischen Raum ballte der Gegner seine Kräfte immer wieder gegen einzelne Punkte zusammen, um damit den Zusammenhalt der Abwehr zu zerreissen. So wurde am Mittwoch erbittert bei Pont L'Evêque, Lisieux, Orbec, Conches, Evreux und an der unteren Avre gekämpft. Der feindliche Plan aber, in die Südflanke der deutschen in der allgemeinen Linie Deauville-Lisieux-Obrec kämpfenden Truppen einzubrechen, misslang, wobei sich im Hin- und Herwogen der Schlacht die beiderseitigen Linien vielfach ineinander verschoben. An der Toucques und im Avre-Abschnitt gelang es dem Gegner, an einigen Stellen in unsere Sperrstellungen einzubrechen, doch wurden diese Einbrüche aufgefangen, durch Gegenstösse ausgeglichen oder durch die im Gang befindlichen Absetzbewegungen unwirksam gemacht.

Am feindlichen Seinebrückenkopf bei Mantes liegt im Südbogen der s-förmigen Seine-Schleife der verengte Brükkenkopf der Nordamerikaner, im Nordbogen versuchte der Feind seinen Raum durch Angriffe bei La Roche-Guyon zu vergrössern, erreichte aber keinen Erfolg. Während deutsche Schlachtflieger in Tiefangriffen mehrere Brücken zerstörten, überschritten die deutschen Truppen ihrerseits den Fluss und säuberten die nördliche Seine-Schleife im Nahkampf vom Feind.

Südlich Paris griffen die Nordamerikaner mit sehr starken Kräften unsere Riegel nördlich Rambouillet und Arpajumeau konnte der an zwei Stellen schwerpunktartig mit Infanterie, Panzern und Bombern angreifende Feind Einbrüche erzielen und durch eine hart westlich der Strasse Etampes-Paris geschlagene Lücke vereinzelte Panzer bis an den Stadtrand vorschieben. Erbitterte Kämpfe, in die auch französische Terroristen eingriffen, sind hier im Gange. In der Stadt selbst toben Kämpfe mit Terroristen, die sich im Louvre verschanzt haben. Hierbei handelt es sich vor allem um kommunistische Elemente, die das Leben der Pariser Einwohnerschaft gefährden. Andere französische Widerstandsgruppen suchen den Kommunisten die Herrschaft streitig zu machen, woraus zu sehen ist, dass unter den von den Angloamerikanern vorgeschickten Terroristen selbst keine Einigkeit besteht. Die Nordamerikaner überliessen am 24. August, den Stoss gegen den Stadtrand von Paris der gaullistischen 2. Panzerdivision. Die Division hatte aber sehr schwere Verluste une erreichte Bourg la Reine nur mit einigen wenigen Panzern, gegen die der Abwehrkampf weitergeht.

Oestlich Fontainebleau

Gleichzeitig griffen die Nordamerikaner, die am Vortage im Abschnitt Corbeil-Montereau die Seine erreicht hatten, aus dem Wald von Fontainebleau heraus an und überschritten die Seine mit starken Kräften. Sie wurden im Gegenangriff auf das Ufer zusammengedrängt. Durch die Gegenstösse des Vortages im Raum östlich Sens ist der Gegner so hart mitgenommen worden, dass er sich östlich der Yonne ruhig verhielt. Er versucht nun von Montargis aus in südöstlicher Richtung gegen die mittlere Yonne Panzeraufklärung vorzutreiben.

Im Seegebiet westlich der Cotentin-Haldbinsel und vor St. Malo entwickelten sich eine Reihe schwerer Feuergefechte. Ein aus Zerstörern und Schnellbooten bestehender britischer Verband stiess in der Nacht zum Donnerstag gegen Guernsey und Jersey vor, um unseren Schiffsverkehr zwischen diesen beiden Inseln zu stören und ein dort fahrendes Geleit aufzubringen. Bevor sich aber die feindlichen Kriegsschiffe unserem Geleit auf Schussentfernung nähern konnten, wurden sie von schweren Marinebatterien und von Heeresküstenbatterien unter Feuer genommen und zum Abdrehen gezwungen. Im Schutz des gutliegenden Artilleriefeuers liefen die Geleitschiffe planmässig und ohne Schäden in ihren Zielhafen ein.

Cezembres Heldenkampf

Die Marinebatterien auf der Ile de Cezembre bei St. Malo lag auch am Donnerstag wieder den ganzen Tag über unter schwerem Feuer der nordamerikanischen Artillerie. Nach fünfstündiger Beschiessung setzte vorübergehend das Artilleriefeuer aus und die Stützpunkte der Felseninsel wurden zunächst von Sturzkampffliegern und dann von Jagdbombern mit Bomben und Bordwaffen eine halbe Stunde lang ununterbrochen angegriffen. Sofort nach Beendigung der Luftangriffe setzte die Artillerie vom Fstland her die Beschiessung fort. Am 13. 8. gingen nicht weniger als sieben schwere Luftangriffe auf die kaum 600 Meter lange Insel nieder. Am 15. August schlugen 1100 Geschosse ringsum die Batterien ein, 12 Stunden später rissen die Granaten und Bomben während eines 10stündigen Feuerkampfes 2200 Trichter in das Batteriegelände, und dennoch brach das Feuer von Cezembre nicht ab. Seither liegt nahezu ohne Pause der feindliche Beschuss in wechselvoller Stärke auf diesem kleinen Inselstützpunkt. Im Raum von Toulon ist der Feind mit erdrückender Übermacht im Angriff. Nur unter hohen Verlusten konnte er dort einige Strassenzüge gewinnen und den Kampf bis zum Gefechtsstand des Seekommandanten vortragen; dort schlugen aber die Marineartilleristen die Angreifer in Nahkämpfen blutig ab, so dass der Hafen in ihrer Hand blieb. An der übrigen südfranzösischen Front drückten die Briten und Nordamerikaner weiter nach Nordwesten und Osten. Sie finden starke Unterstützung durch französische Freischärler, die in den Alpen zwischen Rhone und der französisch-italienischen Grenze die wenigen für Marschbewegungen geeigneten Strassen zu sperren versuchen, um unseren Truppen das Absetzen ins Rhonetal zu erschweren. Deshalb war für uns die Säuberung der Madalena-Passtrasse in den See-Alpen ganz besonders wichtig. Diese in Höhe bis zu 2000 Metern verlaufende Strasse ist das ganze Jahr über Schneefrei und eine der wesentlichen Verbindungen zwischen der Provence- und der Po-Ebene.

Dum-Dum-Munition

Von den Freischärlern wurde der Kampf nach Bandenart in hinterhältigster Weise geführt. Wie berechtigt das im Wehrmachtbericht in der letzten Zeit regelmässig gemeldete, harte Zuschlagen gegen diese Bandengruppen ist, beweist, dass dieser Tage bei einem Säuberungsunternehmen als Kampfmittel südfranzösischer Terroristen neben Sprengstoffen auch Dum-Dum-Munition gefunden wurde. Gewehrmunition mit Bleikern, deren Spitze abgekniffen war. Von solchen Maquis-Banden unterstützt, setzten die Briten und Nordamerikaner ihre Operationen gegen die untere Rhone fort. Hier und weiter nördlich sind an mehreren Stellen zwischen der Rhone und den westlichen Ausläufern der Alpen erbitterte Kämpfe im Gange.

Nördlich Marseille setzte der Gegner am Vortage Luftlandetruppen ab, die am Donnerstag zum Angriff auf die Stadt antraten. Erbitterte Kämpfe innerhalb des Stadtgebietes gegen vorgedrungene feindliche Panzer und Terroristen-Banden sind in vollem Gange. Unsere Batterien beschossen mit guter Wirkung die Anmarschstrassen des Feindes. Dadurch fühlbar entlastet, gelang es den Verteidigern trotz der Überzahl der Angreifer, die Strassen im Bereich der Marinestation in ihrer Hand zu behalten.

Verrat als Waffe

In zwei Jahren haben die Feinde Europas die Waffe des Verrates wiederholt mit wechselndem Erfolge gegen das Reich angewandt. Nicht mit Stalingrad begann die Serie schwerer Rückschläge, sondern mit dem Verrat einer französischen Führungsschicht in Nordafrika und Vichy. Der Attentismus nutzte schliesslich die deutsche Grosszügigkeit, wie sie sich in den Waffenstillstandsbedingungen niedergeschlagen hatte, zu einem flagranten Bruch dieses Frankreich noch einmal alle Möglichkeiten in einem neuen Europa eröffnenden Abkommens. Damit begann der Aufmarsch gegen die kontinentale Südfront, der das zweite verräterische Unternehmen einleitete. Der Akt schändlicher Untreue, begangen von einem italienischen König und seinem Marschall Badoglio fand sein Vorspiel in dem Weichen der italienischen Divisionen am Don auf einer viele Kilometer langen Front. Es war also nicht der mörderische Kampf um die Stadt Stalins an der Wolga allein gewesen, der die Reichsführung zu einer veränderten strategischen Konzeption gezwungen hatte. Hinzu kam noch die wachsende Invasionsbereitschaft starker Streitkräfte aller Waffenteile auf der englischen Insel. Was die Gegner durch den Treuebruch eines «unköniglichen Regimes nicht erreicht hatten, nämlich das Aufreissen der gesamten Südostflanke, sollte wenig später durch eine Wiederholung des italienischen Vorganges in Ungarn erzielt werden. Hier hatte der Ministerpräsident Kallay in Gemeinschaft mit dem Judentum die Hand zum Verrat geboten. Doch dieser Spuk verschwand infolge des deutschen Zugriffs in einer Nacht. Aber die Wortführer einer indirekten Strategie und billigen Kriegführung im Feindlager hielten sich bei dieser Enttäuschung nicht sehr lange auf. Sie suchten neue Ansatzpunkte für die Inszenierung eines hoch- und landesverräterischen Unternehmens und liessen dabei alle Minen des Nervenkrieges gegen Finnland, Bulgarien und Rumänien springen. Offensichtlich war also wieder der Balkan das Ziel ihrer Wünsche und das hatte seinen Grund.

Aus jener Zeit, in der noch der Weltmarktpreis einer liberalen Weltwirtschaft souverän den Lebensstandard des südosteuropäischen Bauerntums bestimmte, stammt die Verbreitung agrarkommunistischer Ideen im Balkanraum. Sie lebten in der kroatischen Bauernpartei Matscheks, in den landwirtschaftlichen Genossenschaften Bulgariens ebenso wie in der Gefolgschaft des rumänischen Parteiführers Maniu. Wenn sie auch der Zeit kapitalistischer Ausbeutung der agrarisch betonten Volkswirtschaften ihr Entstehen verdankten und durch die neuen europäischen Wirtschaftsverträge des Reiches, die den Bauern des Balkans im Festpreis und -absatz einen gesicherten und höheren Lebensstand gewährten, so waren diese Gedanken doch nie ganz verschwunden. Hier hat die bolschewistische Agitation den Hebel angesetzt. Aus diesen Quellen schöpften die Aktion des roten Bandenhäuptlings und «Marschalls» Tito und die kommunistischen Untergrundbewegungen im gesamten Donauraum. Seit je aber war der Balkan auch der Tummelplatz der widerstreitenden Interessen europäischer Grossmächte gewesen. Erst Deutschland hatte hier in Erfüllung seiner Führungsaufgabe viele Spannungen beseitigt, die einst von aussen in den Südostraum hineingetragen worden waren und ihn zum Pulverfass Europas erklärt hatten. In dem stillen und zähen politischen Kampf der feindlichen Bündnispartner unter sich bot er nun, solange noch ein Schlachtfeld, wie es den Angloamerikanern aussichtsreich erschien und erlaubt war, ihre Stimme gegen den bolschewistischen Bundesgenossen in diesem Bereich seiner Ambitionen zu erheben. Vor ihrer Kapitulation vor Moskau operierten so jene gegenüber Jugoslawien und Griechenland mit der britischen Garantie des Besitzstandes dieser beiden Länder, während die Sowiets den bulgarischen Kommunisten Mazedonien und Kroatien versprachen, wenn diese die Moskauer Pläne einer roten Balkanföderation und die Forderung auf Gewährung von Stützpunkten in Warna, Burgas, Kawalla und Dedeagatsch anerkannten. Die Angloamerikaner haben zwar auch noch nach ihrem politischen Abtritt, d. h. recht eigentlich nach den Diktaten Stalins in Teheran das balkanische Eisen versteckt im Feuer gelassen, aber ihre Rolle war doch ausgespielt. So verhandelten sie in Kairo noch mit dem rumänischen Prinzen Stirbey, der dem Königshause nahestand, und in Istanbul und in Ankara mit rumänischen Wirtschaftern, die sie zu bewegen versuchten, die Ueberschüsse der Ernte des Landes nicht an Deutschland, sondern an die Alliierten zu verkaufen, die das Getreide angeblich im Lande belassen wollten, bis es von der Mächtekoalition besetzt sei. Schon aber loderten immer häufiger kommunistische Brandherde auf und fungierte Benesch — nach Abschluss des Tschechenpaktes der besondere Vertraute Stalins — in seinen Briefen an Maniu als der Kommissionär Moskaus für Rumänien. Bald war deutlich, dass die bolschewistische Karte in dem unterirdischen Spiel auch hier gestochen hatte und die Angloamerikaner das Feld endgültig hatten räumen müssen. Dem trugen die Verräter um den König Rechnung. Wie der jüdischen Verschwörung in Ungarn das Handwerk gelegt worden ist, so wird auch jene Clique von reaktionären Hofschranzen und abgetakelten, mit der neuen Zeit auf Kriegsfuss stehenden Parteipolitikastern die Erfüllung ihrer traurigen Wünsche nicht finden, denn der Verrat frisst nun einmal die eigenen Kinder, wie es das italienische Beispiel am deutlichsten gezeigt hat.

Jede diese Verrätereien hat für Deutschland Belastungen mit sich gebracht, keine konnte jedoch die Abwehrfront zum Einsturz bringen. Dass daneben dem deutschen Volke ein im Bund mit dem Feind vorbereiteter innerer Verrat nicht erspart blieb, muss als Zeichen dafür angesehen werden, dass das Schicksal die härteste Probe wollte, bevor es die Entscheidung in diesem Ringen zuliess. Dass am 20. Juli nur ein kleiner, wenn auch an wichtigen Schaltstellen der Wehrmacht sitzender Kreis revoltierte, war für die hinter dem Verrat stehende feindliche Macht deshalb nur nützlich, weil sie im Falle des Gelingens jenes Anschlages mit der Beseitigung dieser Hasardeure wenig Mühe gehabt hätte.

Abwehrerfolg im Weichselbogen

301. Luftsieg von Oberleutnant Hartmann

Aus dem Führerhauptquartier, 25. August.

Das Oberkommando der Wehrmacht gibt bekannt:

Im Raum nordwestlich Paris folgte der Feind mit starken Kräften von Westen und Süden unseren Divisionen, die sich in Richtung auf den Unterlauf der Seine abgesetzt haben. Besonders heftig war der Druck südlich Elbeuf, wo im Verlauf des gestrigen Tages eine Frontlücke im Gegenangriff geschlossen wurde.

Westlich Paris trat der Feind, von zahlreichen Panzern unterstützt, zum Angriff an und drang bis an den westlichen Stadtrand vor. In den äusseren Stadtteilen sind heftige Strassenkämpfe entbrannt.

Versuche des Gegners, westlich Melun die Seine zu überschreiten, wurden im Gegenangriff zerschlagen. In einem Abschnitt halten sich noch feindliche Kräfte auf dem Ostufer des Flusses.

Im Raum von Toulon und Marseille wird weiter erbittert gekämpft. In einzelnen Stützpunkten verteidigen sich unsere Besatzungen, von Küstenartillerie wirksam unterstützt, und ermöglichen dadurch Absetzbewegungen aller übrigen Truppen in Richtung auf Lyon. Im Gebirgsgelände östlich der Rhône kämpfen unsere Flankensicherungen mit feindlichen schnellen Verbänden, die sich unseren Bewegungen im Rhône-Tal vorzulegen versuchen.

Vorpostenboote versenkten vor der Schelde-Mündung ein feindliches Schnellboot und schossen mehrere andere in Brand. Nach hartem Kampf ging dabei ein eigenes Boot verloren.

Im belgisch-französischen Raum wurden 202 Terroristen im Kampf niedergemacht.

Das Vergeltungsfeuer auf den Grossraum von London wurde bei Tag und Nacht in verstärktem Masse fortgesetzt.

Aus Italien werden ausser beiderseitiger Aufklärungstätigkeit keine besonderen Ergebnisse gemeldet.

Im Süden der Ostfront kämpfen sich unsere Truppen, nachdem Teile der rumänischen Verbände auf Aufforderung der königlichen Verschwörer-Clique den Widerstand gegen die Bolschewisten eingestellt haben, weiter auf Pruth und Sereth zurück. Zahlreiche feindliche Panzer wurden dabei vernichtet.

Zwischen den Karpathen und der Weichsel wurden starke örtliche Angriffe der Bolschewisten zerschlagen.

Im Weichselbrückenkopf nordwestlich Baranow haben unsere Infanterie- und Panzerdivisionen, von Fliegern und Flakartillerieverbänden wirksam unterstützt, feindliche Durchbruchsversuche nach Norden in harten Abwehrkämpfen und erfolgreichen Gegenangriffen vereitelt. Zwei Panzer- und zwei mech. Korps, sowie zwölf Schützen-Divisionen der Sowjets erlitten dabei schwerste Verluste. In der Zeit vom 11. bis 23. August wurden in diesen Kämpfen 434 feindliche Panzer und 634 Geschütze erbeutet oder vernichtet. Zwischen Bug und Narew wurde auch gestern der vom Feind erstrebte Durchbruch in erbitterten Ringen vereitelt. 39 feindliche Panzer wurden dabei abgeschossen.

Westlich Modohn scheiterten wiederholte feindliche Angriffe. Auch nordöstlich Walk blieben erneute Angriffe der Bolschewisten erfolglos. In mehrtägigen erbitterten Kämpfen wurde hier der Ansturm von zehn sowjetischen Schützendivisionen, die durch Panzer- und Granatwerferverbände verstärkt waren, abgeschlagen. Im Raum von Dorpat fingen deutsche und estnische Truppen starke feindliche Angriffe auf.

In Luftkämpfen und durch Flakartillerie verloren die Sowjets gestern 58 Flugzeuge. Hiervon schoss der mit dem Eichenlaub mit Schwertern zum Ritterkreuz des Eisernen Kreuzes ausgezeichnete Oberleutnant Hartmann, Staffelkapitän in einem Jagdgeschwader, allein elf Flugzeuge ab und errang damit seinen 301. Luftsieg.

Bei einem erneuten Luftangriff auf einen nordnorwegischen Marinestützpunkt wurden von Marineflakartillerie und Sicherungsfahrzeugen 20 britische Flugzeuge abgeschossen.

Bei einer Operation unserer Unterseeboote im Nordmeer wurden ausser dem am 23. August gemeldeten Kreuzer ein Hilfsflugzeugträger und vier Zerstörer versenkt. Ein weiteres Kriegsschiff wurde durch Torpedotreffer schwer beschädigt.

Nordamerikanische Bomber griffen mehrere Orte in Nord- und Mitteldeutschland sowie im Sudetenland und in Böhmen an. Hierbei wurden besonders die Städte Kiel und Pardubitz getroffen. Luftverteidigungskräfte brachten bei diesen Angriffen 48 feindliche Flugzeuge, darunter 43 viermotorige Bomber, zum Absturz.

Die Schlacht um die Seine

In den neuen Stellungen - Durchkreuzte Feindpläne

Berlin, 25. August.

Bezeichnend für den Zustand unserer normannischen Divisionen war es, dass sie sofort nach dem Durchbruch der feindlichen Umfassung wieder einsatzfähig waren, obwohl der Durchbruch nach Osten viele Stunden gedauert hatte und von unvorstellbar harten Kämpfen eingerahmt war. Weil es die seelische und militärische Verfassung der durchgebrochenen Divisionen erlaubt, sie sofort wieder einzusetzen, konnten vornehmlich westlich der unteren Seine neue Verteidigungsstellen aufgebaut werden. Diesen Riegel westlich der unteren Seine berennt der Feind mit allen Mitteln, weil er in ihm die geschickt angelegte Deckung eines Abmarsches nach Osten sieht, den er durch einen neuen Umfassungsansatz verhindern wollte. Es war eine amerikanische Kräftegruppe, die zu diesem Zweck aus dem Raume von Mantes nach Nordwesten eindrehte und die Seine herunterstossen wollte. Eine entsprechende feindliche Massnahme wie auf dem linken Ufer sollte auf dem rechten Ufer in Gang gebracht werden, nachdem rechtsseitiger Uferbesitz im Abschnitt Mantes erkämpft worden war.

Die Amerikaner wollten also sicher gehen, die einflussreichen Bewegungen der Umfassung selbst in die Hand nehmen und Briten und Kanadiern den frontalen Druck von Westen her überlassen, der, wie alle frontalen Angriffe, meist mit hohen Verlusten verbunden ist. Im Ringen um die untere Seine jagten die Amerikaner operativen Wunschbildern nach, obwohl ihnen die Schlacht von Falaise und Trun hätten sagen müssen, dass zwischen Wollen und Können ein weiter Weg liegt.

Alle operativen Gedanken des Feindes basierten auf dem Gelingen der amerikanischen Umfassungsmärsche. Wenn sich auch die feindlichen Angriffspitzen und die Südflanke unserer Abwehrlinie stark ineinanderschoben, so gelang es dem Gegner nicht, auf dem Westufer der Seine einzubrechen. Allerdings waren die Kämpfe von einer ausserordentlichen Erbitterung getragen. Jeder feindliche Angriff löste sofort einen deutschen Gegenangriff aus. Die feindliche Führung sah in einem Stoss auf das rechte Ufer der Seine stromabwärts einen besonderen Rückhalt ihrer Operationen. Sie hatte darum in den bei Mantes errichteten Brückenkopf verhältnismässig starke Kräfte gebracht. Der Feind wurde aber nordwestlich Mantes über die Seine zurückgeworfen.

Eine entsprechende Entwicklung hat dort stattgefunden, wo der Gegner danach trachtete, zwischen Fontainebleau und Troyes in jenes Geländequadrat hineinzustossen, das vom oberen Seinebogen und der Yonne gebildet wird. Auch hier traten dem Gegner, der die Yonne bereits überschritten hatte, aus den grossen Waldungen von Othe bewegliche deutsche Kampfgruppen entgegen, die den amerikanischen Panzern und motorisierten Teilen in die Flanke stiessen und sie zurückschlugen. Es ergibt sich durch diese Gefechte im allgemeinen Raum der Seine nicht nur ein Stillstand der feindlichen Vorwärts- und Umfassungsbewegung, sondern auch ein erster Rückschlag für den Gegner, der ihn grössere Verluste kostete — eine typische Erscheinung für Besitzwechselkämpfe um Flussufer — die er gerade in einem Augenblick schwer empfinden muss, wo er sich bemühte, an der vordersten Spitze seiner gepanzerten und beweglichen Marschkolonnen besonders stark zu sein.

Forsche Draufgänger

7 Mann gegen 2 Sowjet-Komp.

Führerhauptquartier, 25. August.

Bei Antaliepte griffen zwei sowjetische Kompanien einen Zug eines norddeutschen Grenadier-Regiments an. Auf engem Raum scharf zusammengefasst, brachen die Bolschewisten in die hier nur dünne Linie ein und stiessen gegen eine beherrschende Höhe vor. Der 21-jährige, in Lüffelberg bei Köln geborene Obergefreite Peter Felten, erkannte die drohende Gefahr. Der Kompanieführer war ausgefallen. Da sprang Felten mit einem Satz aus dem Deckungsloch und warf sich dem Feind entgegen. Sein schneidiges Verhalten riss sechs in der Nähe liegende Grenadiere mit.

Unter lautem «Hurra» brachen die sieben Mann in die zahlenmässig weit überlegenen Sowjets ein. Unter schweren, blutigen Verlusten wich der Feind auf seine Einbruchsstelle zurück.

V1-„Schlacht der Automaten"

Wellen fliegender Bomben über dem Kanal

Stockholm, 25. August.

Während der Nacht zum Freitag und am Donnerstag wurden wieder Wellen fliegender Bomben über dem Kanal abgefeuert. Die Angriffe erfolgten in grösserem Umfang als in der letzten Zeit. Rettungsmannschaften arbeiteten während der ganzen Nacht an den Schadensstellen. So meldete das Reuterbüro am Freitagfrüh.

Über die durchschlagende Wirkung der deutschen Vergeltungswaffe meldet Reuter aus Südengland: Zahlreiche Gebäude erlitten erheblichen Schaden. Zementblöcke wurden hochgehoben und 15 bis 20 Yards weit geschleudert.

Colin Bednall, der Luftfahrtkorrespondent der «Daily Mail» beschäftigt sich mit den bisherigen Gegenmassnahmen zur Bekämpfung des V 1-Feuers und teilt mit, dass General Sir Frederick Hill, der Oberbefehlshaber der britischen Flakbatterien, nunmehr seinen Stab an die Südküste verlegt habe, um besser die Bekämpfung der deutschen Ferngeschosse verfolgen zu können. Die Öffentlichkeit wisse noch immer nicht, dass die V 1-Schlacht in den letzten Wochen heisser entbrannte, eine Schlacht, die inzwischen zu einer «Schlacht der Automaten» geworden sei. Über dem Kanal lagernde Wolken liessen eine Verfolgung dieser Kämpfe mit dem blossen Auge nicht zu. Ohne technische Hilfe höre man nur ein donnerndes furchteinflössendes Getöse im Luftraum und sehe das V 1-Geschoss erst, wenn es abstürze. Aber man sehe nichts davon, wie die mit ungeheurer Geschwindigkeit anfliegenden V 1 bekämpft würden. Seit dem ersten V 1-Einsatz habe es keine wirkliche Pause in dem Beschuss Südenglands und Londons gegeben. Indessen sei eine Schlacht der Wissenschaftler entbrannt. General Pile habe die Hilfe führender amerikanischer und britischer Köpfe. Sachenverständige weilten in Scharen im Kampfgebiet, und Tag und Nacht würde die Abwehrtaktik und die Resultate geprüft.

Attlee nach Algier unterwegs

Bremsklotz für Sowjet-Mittelmeerraubpläne

Bern, 25. August.

In London fragt man sich nach dem Zweck der plötzlichen Reise des stellvertretenden Ministerpräsidenten Attlee nach Algier. Diese Reise erscheint um so verwunderlicher, als Churchill noch in Italien ist, das Kabinett in London infolgedessen ohne Führung bleibt. Ein weiterer Faktor, der zu eindringlichen Fragen führt, ist die Teilnahme Georges Hulls an dieser Fahrt. Hull ist der parlamentarische Unterstaatssekretär des Foreign Offibe, so dass seine Mitnahme darauf schliessen lässt, Attlee habe eine wichtige diplomatische Mission zu erfüllen.

Diese Vermutungen erhalten aus Algier selbst neue Nahrung. Am Sitz des gaullistischen Frankreich hält sich eine sowjetische Marinekommission auf, von der es heisst, sie wolle alle alliierten Stützpunkte im Mittelmeerraum besuchen.

Die sowjetische Kommission, die sich aus Kreml-Diplomaten zusammensetzt, hat nicht nur diese Aufgabe durchzuführen, vielmehr verlautet, dass die Sowjets ganz konkrete Forderungen vertreten: 1. suchen sie zu ermitteln, wo sich die italienischen Kriegsschiffe befinden, die ihnen auf Grund der Abmachungen mit Badoglio zustehen; 2. wollen sie durch die Inbesitznahme einiger Kriegsschiffe die Dardanellenfrage aktualisieren und von den Türken eine Zustimmung zur Durchfahrt der neuen sowjetischen Kriegsschiffe durch die Meerengen erzwingen. Mit diesem Schritt würde die Frage nach der zukünftigen Gewaltenteilung an den Dardanellen aufgerollt werden; 3. dient der Besuch der englischen und französischen Stützpunkte der Vorbereitung genauerer Wünsche, an welchen Plätzen die Sowjets künftig im Mittelmeer ihre eigenen militärischen Stationen einzurichten beabsichten.

Die Sowjets haben schon zu früheren Gelegenheiten kein Hehl daraus gemacht, dass sie sich insbesondere an den Küsten von Französisch-Nordafrika einzunisten gedenken. Ihre ursprüngliche erste Forderung lautete Bizerta. Wie jetzt aus Algier verlautet, scheinen sie neuerdings Algier vorzuziehen, da sie dort an den Juden und Kommunisten über den nötigen politischen Rückhalt verfügen.

Mr. Attlee, der offenbar als Aufpasser und Bremsklotz nach Algier entsandt ist, wird kein leichtes diplomatisches Feld vorfinden. Aber gerade darum wird man ihn geschickt haben. Er ist, falls er den Sowjets zu scharf entgegentreten sollte, am ehesten als politisch unverantwortlicher Vertreter des britischen Reiches abzuschütteln. Churchill hat ihn in allzu lebhaften Unterhaus-Debatten schon einige Male mit Erfolg als Prellbock benutzt, fühlt sich doch dieser Vertreter der englischen Arbeiterklasse geschmeichelt, wenn er von den Erzkonservativen zur hohen Politik zugelassen wird.

Reserven greifen ein

(SS-PK.-Aufnahme Kriegsberichter Truöl-Wb.)

Auf Schützenpanzerwagen aufgesessen fährt eine Aufklärungsabteilung an vorgehenden Grenadieren vorbei nach vorn

DAILY MIRROR, Friday, September 1, 1944.

Daily Mirror

SEPT 1

No. 12,701 ONE PENNY Registered at the G.P.O. as a Newspaper.

Lest we forget—the fifth anniversary

Today, September 1, five years ago, the war began.

Most people imagine that it started on September 3.

That is what the Germans hope people will go on thinking. For that was the day Britain and France went to war against Germany, and Germany will plead that she had to fight a defensive war against aggressor nations.

But on September 1 Germany attacked Poland. Germany was the aggressor. And that was the beginning of the war—September 1, 1939.

Monty, F.M.

THE War Office announces that General Montgomery is promoted as from today to the rank of Field-Marshal, supernumary to establishment.

"Field-Marshal Montgomery is 'supernumary to establishment' because by Royal Warrant we may only have eight Field-Marshals on full pay as such," a War Office spokesman told the "Daily Mirror."

"It will not mean any increase in pay for Field-Marshal Montgomery," he added. "A Field-Marshal gets the pay of the particular post he fills—thus Field-Marshal Montgomery will continue to get the pay of his job as Army Group Commander."

Field-Marshal Montgomery, who is fifty-six, is one of the few Generals who have been made Field-Marshal without having been Chief of the Imperial General Staff, the highest Army appointment.

Never put a foot wrong

LIEUTENANT-GENERAL NYE, Vice-Chief of the Imperial General Staff, speaking on the radio last night said:

"When a battle is won it all seems too simple. But for this battle there were three essentials:

First, thorough and imaginative staff work, and this we had started two years before D-Day;

SECONDLY—A HIGH STANDARD [illegible] SHIP. WE HAD IT AND OUR COMMANDER NEVER ONCE PUT A FOOT WRONG;

Thirdly—first-class fighting troops. We had them, and this country has never in its long history produced better."

WE STRIKE OUT AGAIN

BRITISH tanks and infantrymen are striking out from their newly won bridgehead across the Somme at Amiens, only sixty miles from Belgium, towards which the Germans are in headlong retreat.

Commanded by Lieutenant-General O'Connor, our troops thrust twenty-seven miles in twenty-four hours—sixty miles in two days—and seized three bridges at Amiens, which is firmly in our hands.

Amiens, the "Crewe" of North-East France, is the back door to the Pas de Calais, and its fall means that nearly 100 miles (one half) of the "rocket coast" has been cut off.

And there is now no major river line on which the Germans might hope to stand in their retreat to Belgium.

Last night the German High Command spokesman, Captain Sertorius, announced that the Germans had made a further withdrawal between the Channel coast and the River Oise, which flows parallel with the coast.

News of this, one of the most sensational developments of the invasion, came last night soon after General Eisenhower had been telling a London Press conference that the Allies were at least five days ahead of their plans.

For the last two days British forces which had fought their way across the Seine had been making a lightning drive towards the line of the Somme, where so many of their fathers

Continued on Back Page

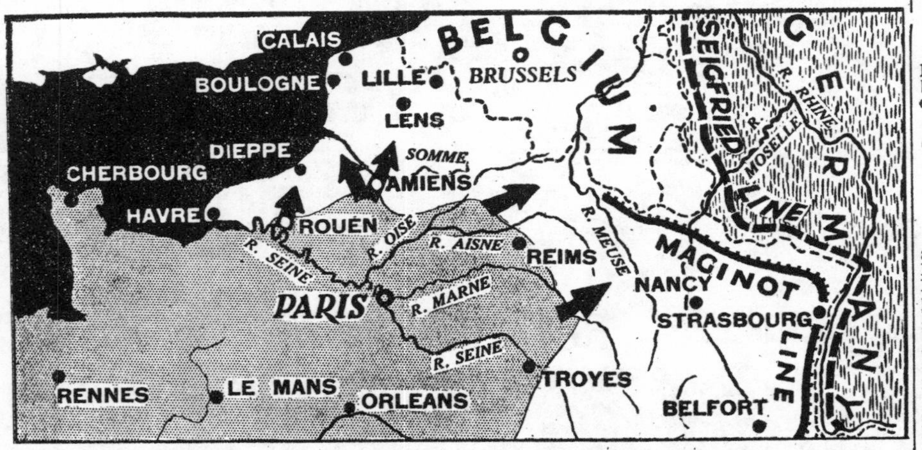

RED ARMY DRIVES INTO BUKAREST: BID TO QUELL OIL WELLS BLAZE

THE Russians have smashed their way into Bukarest, the Germans in the Ploesti area and to the south have been routed and the German threat to Bukarest from the north liquidated.

This was announced in a special Order by Stalin last night, and followed reports by Berlin of hard and fluctuating fighting between the great oil centre and the capital.

As the Red Army pressed on to Bukarest, fire-fighting squads with special equipment were subduing the blazing wells at Ploesti.

Soviet units entered the town through walls of flame. Not a single street remained untouched by the fire.

"Izvestia" says that the Russians arrived in the nick of time to help Rumanian troops to confine the fire. The entire population of Ploesti joined in the fight.

Berlin says the Russians have launched what amount to breakthrough attacks northeast of Warsaw.

'MILITARY GOVERNMENT OF GERMANY'

The U.S. State Department announced last night that Mr. Robert Murphy is coming to London as political adviser—presumably to General Eisenhower—with the rank of Ambassador, "as part of the machinery being established for the military government of Germany."

Mr. Murphy has been political adviser to General Wilson's Mediterranean Command.

British armies beat greatest Hun force ever

NEVER in the war on any front has the German army assembled so immense a force of armour as against the British Army since D-Day, said Lord Croft, Under-Secretary of State for War, speaking to his Home Guard battalion last night.

No other army has been confronted with such a density of defence during the war anywhere, he declared.

The British Armies held this great force and destroyed its fighting power on the vital keypoint of the whole campaign.

The whole available armour at Rommel's disposal was concentrated against the British half of the bridgehead, which he apparently regarded as the vital point for the defence of Paris and the Western Wall.

"The British Army, driving the great mass of the enemy east, has now crossed the Seine and STILL HAS MOST OF THE REMAINING GERMAN DIVISIONS FACING IT," said Lord Croft.

The British and Canadian armies, with their Allies' help, destroyed the last remaining first-class formations of the German Army.

"By sheer bloody fighting our armies held the German Army by the throat, and won so great a victory, killing or capturing 80,000 picked Germans in ten days in the pocket," concluded Lord Croft.

No extra beer yet for troops

TROOPS in France are unlikely to get a bigger beer ration yet.

There is no immediate likelihood of an increase, Mr. Claude Luke, chief P.R.O. for NAAFI, said at York yesterday, and he explained why.

The soldiers did not mind the price charged them, he said. What they wanted was more beer.

But there was no prospect of an increase in bottled beer exports. The ration—one reputed quart bottle a week—must remain until breweries in the bigger French towns fell into Allied hands.

[A reputed quart is a pint and a fifth, and the soldier gets a bottle for 1s. 5d. The beer is of a higher gravity than that sold at home, is specially brewed for export and is pasteurised.]

Conditions would not improve, said Mr. Luke, because staff to brew this special beer in this country was short. So were bottles.

"When we capture breweries in France we will import the ingredients and the beer will be brewed by French brewers under our control.

"We have already taken over one small town brewery in France."

NIGHT EDITION
★★★★★
MARKET OPENING
SCHOOL NEWS ON PAGES 20-21

The Sun

Copyright, 1944, by The New York Sun, Inc.

LATE NEWS
SCHOOLS — PICTURES

Today considerable cloudiness, continued warm; tonight cloudy with a few showers; tomorrow cloudy, cooler. Temperatures—Minimum, 72; Maximum, 74. Sun rises 6:22 A. M. Sun sets 7:29 P. M. (Detailed weather report on page 30.)

VOL. 112—NO. 1. Entered as Second Class Matter Post Office, New York, N. Y. NEW YORK, FRIDAY, SEPTEMBER 1, 1944. FIVE CENTS EVERYWHERE

VERDUN FALLS TO PATTON'S MEN

RUSSIANS HEAD FOR JUNCTURE WITH TITO'S MEN

Reds Have Reached Point Only 120 Miles From Yugoslav Border.

NAZIS TRY NEW DEFENSE LINE

Soviet Troops Make Another Attempt to Capture Warsaw—Some Forces 12 Miles Away.

Moscow, Sept. 1 (A. P.).—Red Army flying columns, skirting the southern shoulder of the Transylvanian Alps after marching triumphantly through Bucharest, headed today in the direction of Serbia's northeastern mountains, where Marshal Tito's Partisans are battling the common enemy.

A junction between Soviet and Yugoslav Partisan forces became a prospect of the near future as Gen. Rodion Y. Malinovsky's armored scouts approached within 120 miles of the Yugoslav-Romanian frontier.

The German command was reported trying to organize a new defense line along the Olt River, which runs within seventy-five miles of Serbian territory.

A vital north-south railway parallels the west bank of the Olt, connecting Sibiu—one of Transylvania's leading cities—with the Wallachian Danube port of Corabia, across the stream from Bulgaria.

Gen. Malinovsky threatened to cut this waterline at the southern entrance to Turnu Pass, whose possession would safeguard his right wing while he drove across the Danube plain to make contact with Tito.

The Soviet leader's forces, which paraded past the rubble of ...erman-bombed buildings in Bu...rest yesterday, drove rapidly ...ward along the Bucharest-...va railway.

Germans in Flight.

... dispatches said the Ger... were still in disorderly ... the Danube valley.

...rest's war-weary popu... ...w Gen. Malinovsky bare ...hanical power of his army. ...self-propelled guns, squat ...ickly armored tanks and a ...gly endless stream of mo... ...d infantry crossed the city ... end to end.

... Red Star correspondent,

Continued on Page 3.

In The Sun Today

School News Appears in the Night Edition.

AMERICANS NEARING TWO BORDERS

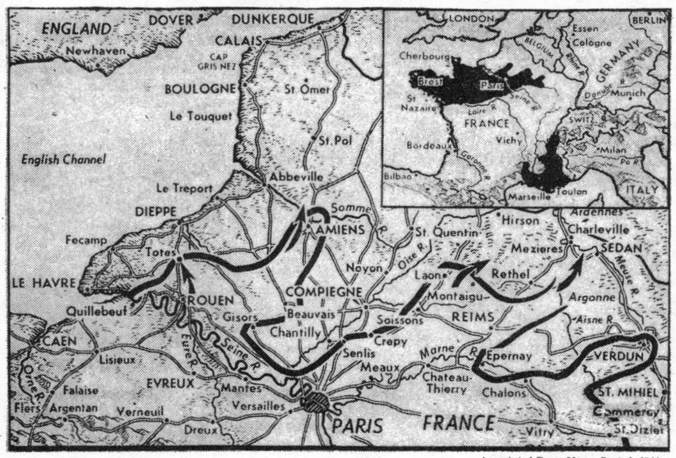

Associated Press Map. Sept. 1, 1944.

Speeding American armies are believed to have reached the Belgian frontier, while other Yank spearheads are said to be within twenty-five miles of Germany. The blackened area in the inset shows where the Allies have advanced.

Contrasts in Paris Life

Heinz Sees Thousands of People Standing in Food Lines All Day Long.

By W. C. HEINZ.
Special Radio to THE NEW YORK SUN.

Paris, Aug. 31 (Delayed).—When you ask the Army authorities about it here, they tell you that the food situation in Paris is well in hand. They tell you that the food situation here is far better than they thought it would be; that, in fact, even if no more food were able to be brought in, there is enough right here now to feed the population for ten more days. And a block away the people stand in line from morning to night.

When you ask the Army authorities about it here they tell you that France has always been self-supporting agriculturally, that in fact she actually is now. They tell you that it will not be necessary for the United States to feed France.

Of course, the Army authorities are right. When they speak of things like agricultural sufficiency and harvest they are absolutely right.

Grain Is in the Fields.

To see that the Army authorities are absolutely right, you have only to drive through France, through Normandy and through Brittany. The war has passed through these places indeed, and yet it has passed through quickly. In some fields the grain is golden and in others the cattle are grazing. On the trees th apples are reddening now. And around the corner the people are standing in line from morning to night.

And then, the Army authorities are right, too, when they remind you of what the Germans have been doing to France. They remind you of how the Germans have been milking France, and tell you that yesterday they found thousands of carcasses in refrigeration depots here awaiting shipment to Germany. They tell you that now these carcasses and all the others after them will no longer go to Germany but will go to France and that the situation is well in hand.

All that is true enough, you realize, but that is not what you see when you walk through the streets of Paris today. You see people standing in line from morning to night, and the military authorities say that they see this too, but that the people of England also stand in line. And besides, they are bringing in

Continued on Page 11.

1100 YANK FLYERS FREE IN BUCHAREST

Bucharest, Aug. 31 (Delayed) (A. P.).—Russian troops arriving in this Romanian capital today found 1,100 American airmen here — prisoners of war who had been liberated the day King Mihai proclaimed an armistice and who have since been given the run of the city.

The Americans had been confined in two camps — those who went down during the low level bombardment of Ploesti thirteen months ago being confined in a stockade near Brasov and the remainder in a camp at Bucharest.

Their treatment has been far from severe, the airmen themselves said, and the gates of both prisons were thrown open within a matter of minutes after Mihai issued his armistice proclamation.

The flyers were particularly elated over the German bombardment of the prison wing of the hospital where a number of Americans had been kept prior to August 24.

On that day they moved out and German prisoners were moved in. Only a few hours later Nazi dive-bombers came over, apparently singled out the building and plastered it with bombs.

Reno Divorces at Record High.

Reno, Nev., Sept. 1 (A. P.).—Reno divorce actions in August reached an all time high for any single month with 790 filed.

The figure broke a fourteen-year record of 710 suits filed in July, 1931.

Judy Barden Finds Still Gay Capital of France 'Does Something to You.'

By JUDY BARDEN.
Special Cable to THE NEW YORK SUN.

Paris, Aug. 31 (Delayed).—The first things that impress you about Paris are the perfumes and the women. They both grow lovelier and lovelier the deeper you get into the boulevards of Paris.

They both grow lovelier and lovelier the deeper you get into Paris.

The women's clothes get smarter and smarter until you hate your uniform, and long to put on eight-inch heels, short-pleated skirts and colorful georgette blouses.

Never have I seen such beautiful women. Never have I seen such gorgeous hair styles. They pile their hair as high on top as they can make it. Few of them have natural colored hair; it is all either jet black, very blond or bright red. Somehow, with their clothes and two-inch-long brightly colored earrings in Paris, this doesn't look out of place.

I came in last night by jeep and was mobbed. No film star ever had a better reception. I gave autographs of my name and paper, and I gave away all my cigarettes, soap and candy. Paris had not seen any of these things in a long time. Their gratitude and joy were overwhelming. Being the first American female they had seen, I was on show.

She Buys a Hat.

I had great difficulty getting to the hotel without being chaired.

That was yesterday. Today I walked the streets of Paris. I bought a hat and some perfume. You should see the hat. It is akin to a three-tiered wedding cake in black, with masses of georgette hangings down the

Continued on Page 11.

SPELLMAN IN LONDON

London, Sept. 1 (A. P.).—Archbishop Francis J. Spellman England today to visit United States military hospitals and Army airfields, and to confer with Catholic chaplains. He has been in Italy.

Yanks Speed for Reich and Belgian Borders; Battered Nazis Are Falling Back on Lyon

Some German Units Ordered to Get to Reich by Own Methods—Patch's Men Reported in Italy.

Rome, Sept. 1 (A. P.).—Sharp attacks by American tanks and infantry crumbled Nazi rearguard resistance in the upper Rhone Valley of southern France today and the Germans fled northwest at top speed with the pursuing Allies less than fifty miles from the great city of Lyon.

Valence, fifty-five miles below Lyon, fell at noon yesterday, Lieut.-Gen. Alexander M. Patch's headquarters said. Le Bourg du Pease, eleven miles to the northwest, capitulated earlier to Americans closing in from the east.

Apparently despairing of ever getting their Nineteenth Army out of southern France as an intact fighting unit, the Nazi command has ordered its units "to return to Germany by their own resources," an official report said. Such an order was given by artillery personnel in the Nimes area, prisoners related.

[The British radio said today that Swiss correspondents had reported that American troops after the capture of Nice crossed the Italian border and "effected a junction with Italian Patriots."

[The BBC-German language broadcast was recorded in New York by the Office of War Information.]

Nears Spanish Border.

From Narbonne a French flying column, in a sweep around Southern France's Mediterranean coast, was reported thrusting down to the Spanish border after shoving through Montpellier, Beziers and Narbonne—60 miles from the Spanish frontier—without meeting enemy resistance.

Other French units were well beyond Ales, thirty-eight miles west-northwest of Avignon.

The Seventh Army Command declared the situation remained unchanged on the Riviera, following American occupation of Nice.

In the Alpine regions along the French Italian frontier farther north, however, the Americans entered the village of Condamine. Chatelard, which the Germans had burned in reprisal for patriot activities.

From the devastated village the Americans pushed along mountain highways and paths and made contact with enemy outposts just northwest of nearby Lagache Pass on the Italian frontier, some fifty-five miles northwest of Nice.

Mopping Up Nazis.

On the west side of the Rhone French elements were mopping up scattered enemy pockets in Pont St. Esprit, Bourg St. Andeol, Vallon and Barjac. All of these towns were overrun or bypassed

Continued on Page 9.

TRAP FOILS ATTACK

Salt Lake City, Sept. 1 (A. P.).—Four-year-old Leonard Earl Radford has learned that the life of a Commando has its hardships.

While playing yesterday with two other boys, four and ten, he was ordered to advance across an open field. Leonard started bravely, but stepped into a booby trap, an eight-foot hole sixteen inches across, which had been camouflaged.

Firemen tunneled to the boy. One of them was injured when struck in the head with a pick, but at H hour plus 2:30 the boy was rescued and taken to a hospital.

He offered the firemen two pennies for their work.

SOUTH OF ENGLAND SHELLED BY HEAVY GUNS AT BOULOGNE

4-Hour Assault Described as Vicious—Berlin Talks of Mystery Weapon.

London, Sept. 1 (A. P.).—Heavy German coastal guns near Boulogne fired nearly 100 shells over a period of four hours early today in what Berlin described as a drum fire of the heaviest type against the English invasion port routes. Several British seacoast towns were reported heavily damaged and at least one man was killed.

Boulogne is on the channel, twenty-eight miles south of Dover and in the path of the swiftly advancing Allied armies in France. It appeared possible that the Germans with their communications shattered, were trying to unload as much ammunition as possible upon England before the Allies arrived.

English Channel reports were that a wide area was shelled and that the attack was vicious.

The Berlin radio attempted to make a mystery of the shelling with the assertion that "no explanation can be obtained from competent circles as to whether this drum fire constitutes measures against further invasion preparation or whether new, long-distant weapons have gone into action. "The British coastal batteries replied to the salvos which were of from five to eight shells each.

On the other hand, only a few robots were loosed against Britain during the night.

As usual some of the bombs

Continued on Page 9.

BURMA JAPS OUSTED

Kandy, Ceylon, Sept. 1 (A. P.).—Japanese troops were cleared today from the west bank of the Chindwin River north of Tonhe and enemy resistance collapsed on the Kabaw Valley track leading toward Thangdut.

A cleanup was progressing on the Tamu-Sittaung railway with the enemy ousted from another position. Tank-supported infantry engaged enemy rearguards thirty miles north of Tiddim, a southeast Asia command communique said.

London Hears Americans Are 25 Miles From German Border—Nazi Leader Calls Situation Hopeless for Present.

Supreme Headquarters, Allied Expeditionary Force, Sept. 1 (A. P.).—Mighty American assault forces drove down the final few miles toward the German frontier today after overwhelming the historic French fortress city of Verdun, less than fifty miles from the Reich.

Moving so swiftly that official information here lagged far behind developments, a mighty arc formed by the United States Third and First armies also swept to or across the border of Belgium in the vicinity of Sedan.

The NBC recorded a BBC broadcast today saying that reports from advanced correspondents in the Verdun sector place American forces only twenty-five miles from the German border.

[A dispatch from London quoted a German military spokesman today as describing the German situation in northern France as "hopeless for the time being." Speaking over the Berlin radio of two big Allied bulges in the Amiens and Meuse areas, the spokesman compared the plight of the Germans now with their "hopeless" situation four weeks ago which he said had been "mastered."]

Verdun fell yesterday to Lieut.-Gen. George S. Patton's Third Army troops, who advanced sixty-five miles from Reims in less than twenty-four hours. The swift stab directly through the Argonne forest, where American doughboys fought and died in 1918, carried across the Meuse River to the rear of the old Maginot Line.

Associated Press War Correspondent Edward D. Ball, writing from Verdun, said the Americans plunged on beyond the River Meuse in close pursuit of the Germans, who put up only a brief fight for the city.

Another column, advancing from St. Dizier, captured Commercy on the Meuse River, ten miles south of famed St. Mihiel and twenty-eight miles west of Nancy.

Front dispatches last night said that United States First Army Forces had penetrated Sedan, five miles from Belgium.

Everywhere the Germans were in full flight for the dubious safety of their homeland fort lines.

"The battle of France is all but over," wrote Associated Press War Correspondent William Smith White: "What is developing now is the beginning of the battle for Germany."

To the west along the coast of France, Field Marshal Sir Bernard L. Montgomery's Twenty-first Army group, now in high gear, rolled up the rocket bomb belt at a mile-an-hour rate and captured Gen. Eberbach—at breakfast—in a final ignominy to the broken German Seventh Army he commanded.

The escape gap for the guardians of the flying bomb sites in the Le Havre sector was narrowed to twenty miles by a British plunge to within twenty miles of Abbeville. Through this fun-

Continued on Page 9.

GERMANS ON MOVE IN SCANDINAVIA

National Broadcasting Company's reporter Bjorn Bjornson, speaking from Stockholm, said today that the Germans may evacuate Denmark and Norway without a fight. Already large troop movements are reported and German language papers such as the Neues Wiener Tagblatt are no more speaking of fortress Europe. "They have changed already to fortress Germany," the NBC reporter said.

Dave Boone Says:

A Russian newspaper correspondent says that Nazi agents continue to have things pretty much their own way around Turkey, despite the diplomatic break. Nazi consuls, generals and Gestapo agents enjoy their former liberties there, while the Turkish police help in the forcible ejection of anti-Nazis, he declares.

The Russians are pretty het up over it, and who wouldn't be?

I see where the Nazis have issued a statement that the R. A. F. began the air war on women and children. Everybody knew they'd get around to that. I expect Berlin to blame the long-suffering British civilians for causing all the trouble next.

September is here and it certainly sneaked up on us. Oysters are back in season but it is as hard as ever to get oyster crackers and cocktail sauce.

I wonder why neither candidate for the Presidency comes out for a good 50-cent oyster stew.

THE STARS AND STRIPES
MEDITERRANEAN
Vol. 1, No. 252, Tuesday, September 5, 1944 ITALY EDITION • TWO LIRE

Allied Armor Frees Brussels; Yanks, French Occupy Lyons

Belfort Pass To Germany Goal Of Foe

ADVANCED ALLIED FORCE HEADQUARTERS, Sept. 4 — American and French troops today were occupying Lyons, France's second most important communications center, from which the Germans had fled in an effort to reach the Belfort Pass to Germany before the American 7th Army blocks it.

According to this morning's official announcements, there was sharp fighting yesterday some 12 miles north of Bourg-en-Bresse, in and near the town of Montrevel. The Germans sent tanks against the Americans in hopes of keeping this one route clear for stragglers from southern pockets of resistance.

One such pocket was at Certine, six miles southeast of Bourg-en-Bresse. Another was at Ceyzeriat, in the same area, but in all cases the enemy positions appeared hopeless.

While the American forces were sweeping around the northwest of Lyons, the French troops dashed straight north up the Saone River valley and officially had entered Ville-France, 15 miles north of Lyons on the road to Macon. Operating in front of these forces, Allied airmen were bombing and strafing scattered groups of German 19th Army personnel wherever they spotted them.

The liberation of Lyons, whose peacetime population is about 570,000, also gave the Allied forces the use of a large airfield, just east of the city. It also gave the Allied engineers another big job, for few of the bridges across the Rhone and Saone Rivers, which divide the city, remained intact.

In addition to its importance as a communications center, Lyons is the heart of France's silk and rayon industries and has important machinery and chemical manufacturing plants.

Troops, Miles Apart, Win Town Of Pieve

ADVANCED ALLIED FORCE HEADQUARTERS, Sept. 4—The American and Canadian forces of the 5th and 8th Armies are operating more than 100 miles from each other, on a straight line across Italy, yet both liberated Pieve yesterday. It wasn't done with mirrors—there are two Pieves. One is on the eastern slopes of Mount Pisaro feature, near the west coast, the other is near the Adriatic, two miles south of Gradara. The only similarity is in the spelling of the names.

5th, 8th Advances Called Sensational

ADVANCED ALLIED FORCE HEADQUARTERS, Sept. 4—Allied troops today stormed through the broken Gothic Wall and up both coasts of Italy, driving the Germans into new dangers of annihilation by valiant Italian patriot forces menacing their Po valley retreat routes.

Official reports this morning placed Canadian and Polish troops within seven miles of Rimini, Adriatic gateway to the Po valley; revealed American spearheads to be six miles north of Pisa, and said other 5th Army troops had bypassed massive Mount Pisano and pushed to within seven miles of Pistoia, supposed to be an enemy stronghold.

The Adriatic drive, through a 20-mile hole in the Gothic Line, was nothing short of sensational. While Polish troops were mopping up Pesaro and cutting off Gradara, two Canadian columns skirted the Poles, crossed the Conca River on a three-mile front, then dashed eastward to the coast to isolate Cattolica.

Tanks and infantry moved with amazing speed across the Conca about 6,000 yards from its mouth,

(Continued on Page 8)

TROUBLE FOR JAPS

DAUNTLESS DIVE BOMBERS take off from their carrier on a mission in the Pacific. (OWI Photo)

Finnish Troops Ordered To Lay Down Weapons

LONDON, Sept. 4—Baron Karl Mannerheim, president of Finland and commander of its army, has ordered his forces to "cease firing" on the Russo-Finnish front as of 0800 hours this morning, and according to one report from Sweden, hostilities have ceased.

Comment in London, however, and lack of comment in Moscow, indicates that the situation is not entirely composed. There is evidence that the Allies, and the Russians in particular, are not pleased with Finland's declared intention to give the Nazis until September 15 to save some 160,000 troops now in Finland.

A detachment of German troops has already crossed the Finnish border into Norway, Reuter's Stockholm correspondent says.

Moscow and Helsinki agree in radio statements that Russia has insisted on two conditions prior to further discussions of an armistice: (1) a break with Germany, and (2) disarming or internment of any German troops remaining in Finland, the date being clear in the Finnish version and unclear in the Moscow version.

In repeating the official Finnish news agency announcement that Finland has already broken relations with Germany, Reuter's correspondent in Stockholm notes that the announcement does not say that "diplomatic relations" have been severed.

Reuter's diplomatic correspondent here, Randal Neale, characterizes the Finnish actions as "a case of cold calculation, not a change of heart." He adds that "in actual fact, there can be no doubt but that both conditions will be fulfilled and little doubt that the Germans will be only too glad to rescue their divisions in Finland from annihilation or internment."

King Sees Churchill

LONDON, Sept. 4—Prime Minister Winston Churchill was received in audience by King George yesterday, their first meeting since the Prime Minister's return from Italy Wednesday.

Nancy, Metz Said Taken By 3rd Units

BULLETIN

STOCKHOLM, Sept. 4—The U. S. 3rd Army has invaded German territory and captured Perl, just inside the German frontier near the junction of Germany, France and Luxembourg, dispatches received here today reported. An official of the Netherlands in London reported that the Allies had entered Holland. There was no confirmation of either report.

LONDON, Sept. 4—Allied armored columns racing northward from the French border have liberated the Belgian capital of Brussels and, according to one correspondent's report, were within 25 miles of the Dutch border at noon today.

The spectacular race by combined armor of the British 2nd and American 1st Armies threatened to cut off the German forces rushing out of the Pas de Calais area to the west, and was also close behind the Germans which pulled out of Brussels, apparently without a fight.

Southeast of Brussels, the Yank armor which broke across the border at Sedan yesterday was reported officially today to be "in the area of Charleroi." The Associated Press, however, reported the column had bypassed both Charleroi and Namur and was still going.

It was considered likely that the cloak of official secrecy which usually is thrown over such an extended thrust again was concealing

(Continued on Page 8)

Japanese Abandon Philippine Airfields

ALLIED HEADQUARTERS SOUTHWEST PACIFIC, Sept. 4—The Japanese air force has apparently been driven from the fields of southern Mindanao in the Philippines, General Douglas MacArthur announced today in a communique which revealed another heavy raid over the weekend on Davao, capital of the southernmost island.

It was the heaviest bombing strike against the Philippines since 1942," the report stated, with more than 100 tons of fragmentation bombs dropped. For the first time, Lightnings participated in a Philippine action, flying the greatest distance they have operated from a southwest Pacific base.

Meanwhile, a southwest Asia Command communique from Ceylon reported that "Tiddim road is now clear for 100 miles south of Imphal in India." It further stated that enemy rearguards are offering limited resistance to the advance.

Patriots Hurl Foe From Vienne

By Sgt. STANLEY M. SWINTON
(Stars and Stripes Staff Writer)

WITH THE MAQUIS IN VIENNE, Sept. 1 (Delayed)—This is No Man's Land on this mad front.

This morning the Maquis clamped irons upon the wrists of the last fanatical Nazis holding in a desperate rearguard action against the American forces driving on Lyons, the third city of France.

Today four American correspondents entered the rain-drenched city during the suspicious hours when the population still stared twice before cheering the American uniforms.

This story, written within an hour of the entrance into Vienne, has been interrupted by the parade of 15 collaborationists through the streets of this main way on the road to Lyons. One of them is a cross-eyed brunette, the rest men. Hard-eyed men, cradling machine pistols in their arms, guard them as they are marched through the hoots and jeers of the loyal Frenchmen toward the city courtroom.

American and French forces still have not thrown their power into the town as these words are written.

In Vienne, important source of woolens, between 100 and 200 Germans have been killed and 200 captured in the last week.

"There were two German generals here, yesterday. One of them, a corps commander," a huge FFI battler reported.

"On the road to Lyons there is not 100 yards without a wrecked German vehicle. The British and American air forces have done a magnificent job."

The town went mad at the arrival of the Americans. Women crowded around the jeep beside the demolition-torn bridge and asked if they might kiss the cheek of an American. Bottles of champagne and hoarded scotch were uncorked in wild celebration.

At the famed Chez Point Pyramid, where gourmets from all over the world flocked before the war, the host brought out plates of goose liver and rare wine for the first arrivals. Each must sign his name in the special guest book beside the autographs of the Duke and Duchess of Windsor, Josephine Baker, Charles Laughton, the traitor Doriot, Maurice Maeterlinck, and a host of other celebrities.

This city of Roman antiquity has paid dearly for its freedom. At Peaga de Rousaelon, nearby, the Patriots fought the enemy with pistols and captured 200 Germans.

(Continued on page 8)

Armed Forces Now Total 11,417,000

WASHINGTON, Sept. 4 — American armed forces are now estimated to be 11,417,000 strong and can be kept at full strength without changing present draft policies, it was reported yesterday by the Selective Service Committee.

At the same time, Congress was informed by an army officer that few Americans who are more than 26 years old will face a call up during the remainder of this year.

THE STARS AND STRIPES
MEDITERRANEAN

Vol. 1, No. 253, Wednesday, Sept. 6, 1944 ITALY EDITION TWO LIRE

Yanks In Germany

LIBERATION EXPRESS ROLLS ON

SPEARHEADED BY the 2nd British Army, Allied troops are reported to have swept on 30 miles north of liberated Antwerp and taken the Dutch town of Breda. The U. S. 1st Army, its progress veiled in official secrecy, was last reported driving on from Tournai, below Lille on the French-Belgium border. German troops in the white corner above Lille are said to be hopelessly trapped. A few hours after the map was drawn, Aachen, about 80 miles east of Brussels, was reported taken along with Saarbrucken, about 25 miles from Metz.

AP Says Aachen, Saarbrucken Won

LONDON, Sept. 5—American troops are fighting on German soil.

An Associated Press dispatch from the French frontier reported this afternoon that the Allies have captured Aachen and Saarbrucken, on both ends of the Siegfried line. The German News Agency reported that American troops had entered "southwest Germany's frontier region."

At the same time the AP reported that tanks of Lt. Gen. George S. Patton's 3rd Army had reached Strasbourg, capital of Alsace. Strasbourg is on the west bank of the Rhine and faces German territory.

The incredible onward sweep of the Allied forces deep into Nazi-held territory was so fast today that headquarters maps were changed hourly. Familiar place names of western Europe were captured by the score.

Louvain, Antwerp, Lille—all fell before the Allied steamroller. The Grand Duchy of Luxembourg was entered. A part of the Netherlands was taken, thus making another nation either liberated or on the point of being liberated.

Out of the thousands of reports came a picture of a German army beaten, disorganized, cut off from contact with the Reich and surrendering individually and collectively at every opportunity.

Frank Gillard, BBC reporter, said that despite "startlingly lengthened" Allied supply lines, the situation had been foreseen and that future supplies are assured. He said that so far the Allies in Belgium had encountered little flooded country.

Although there has been no official word for three days on American forces which broke into Belgium at Sedan, it was believed likely that they formed a line which cut off the German escape route east of Mons.

British troops driving in on the estimated 5,000 pocketed Germans at Le Havre were meeting considerable resistance and received no immediate reply to an ultimatum for surrender.

The Swedish radio said German administrative officers in Copenhagen were burning their official papers preparatory to pulling out of the Danish capital.

Ronald Clark, United Press correspondent who was one of the first to enter Brussels, described the entry as the most enthusiastically welcomed he had ever seen. Civilians waved flags and cheered as patriot forces took care of the Nazi rearguards left to cover the Germans' retreat. The British, he said, had no mopping up to do.

Rumors Begin

LONDON, Sept. 5—Reports were circulating today to the effect that Germany had capitulated. The exact origin of the rumor could not be traced, but it was repeated in Belgian broadcasts with strict reserve as to its accuracy.

Russians Declare War On Bulgaria

MOSCOW, Sept. 5—"A state of war" exists between the Soviet Union and Bulgaria, the Moscow radio announced tonight.

The Bulgarian minister, says the broadcast, has been informed that Russia regards this nation as an enemy not only of the United States and Great Britain, with whom Bulgaria has been at war for more than a year, but of the U. S. S. R., as well, with whom Bulgaria has hitherto been at peace.

The Russian government's declaration comes at a time when its troops are on—and possibly over—the Rumanian-Bulgarian frontier, and while a Bulgarian delegation waits in Cairo, Egypt, for the reply of Great Britain and the United States to its request of a week ago for an armistice.

Earlier today Tass, official Soviet news agency, had declared that the new Bulgarian cabinet, not yet a week old, must either cast its lot with the Allies by entering the war against Germany or stand responsible for the consequences.

With the statement came unconfirmed reports that the Red Army is establishing bridgeheads on the Bulgarian side of the Danube River.

Nazis In Italy Reeling

Allies Win Tank Battle

ADVANCED ALLIED FORCE HEADQUARTERS, Sept. 5—Bewildered German troops, kept off balance by vicious, well-screened Allied thrusts, reeled toward destruction in northern Italy today.

Their rear was exposed to increasing numbers of well-organized armed Italian Patriots, augmented by French Maquis pouring through the gaps in northwestern Italy.

The German flanks, particularly their vital eastern flank guarding the gateway to the Po Valley and to northeastern Italy, was duck soup for Allied naval guns. Their Gothic Line has proved as formidable as a Goebbels promise.

With the same ruthless fanaticism that has marked his tactics throughout the Italian campaign, Marshal Albert Kesselring has sent troops into suicide positions to screen withdrawals. He still was tardy in ordering withdrawals until such time as it was no longer possible to pull out in an orderly manner.

General Sir Harold L. Alexander used the same trick that worked in front of Cassino in preparation for the May offensive. With lightning speed and complete secrecy, General Sir Oliver Leese's 8th Army's 80,000 vehicles, 1,000 tanks and 1,000 guns, were moved across the Appenines from Florence to the Adriatic.

Kesselring, thinking he had only

(Continued on page 8)

7th Army Advances Far North Of Lyons

ADVANCED ALLIED FORCE HEADQUARTERS, Sept. 5—Nazi remnants, after looting Lyons and other French cities, today apparently had outdistanced American and French troops of Lt. Gen. Alexander M. Patch's 7th Army, forward elements of which were more than 75 miles north of Lyons.

The American troops, well beyond Montrevel where they suffered some losses in a stiff fight Sunday, met no serious opposition yesterday, it was stated officially. French regulars, speeding up Highway 6 through the Saone valley, were at the outskirts of Macon, 68 miles north of Lyons, without making contact.

The French columns were less than 75 miles from Dijon, junction of all important rail and highway lines between the Saone-Rhone area and Paris. Dijon is less than 50 miles from the area in which the U. S. 3rd Army was reported moving before operational security shrouded its positions.

The greatest impediments to the advancing forces from the south were bridge demolitions and ever-growing parades of prisoners. The French took some 2,400 in mopping up Ville Franche, to bring the 7th Army's total to more than 65,000 for the 21 days of the campaign.

140,000 Tons Dropped On Europe In August

LONDON, Sept. 5 — The RAF and the U. S. Strategic Air Force dropped a record of 140,000 tons of bombs on all enemy targets in August, the United Press reported.

Air Marshal Sir Arthur Coningham's 2nd Tactical Air Force reported scoring a record toll in August against enemy war materiel, destroying 10,500 German transports and 850 tanks.

Typhoons and Spitfires of the 2nd Tactical Air Force pounded enemy communications during the heavy fighting in Normandy.

Fighting Seemed Miles From Liberated Lyons

By Sgt. STAN SWINTON
(Stars and Stripes Staff Writer)

WITH THE AMERICAN FORCES IN LYONS, Sept. 3 (Delayed)—The kissingest, happiest musical comedy chapter in the war of southern France was today's liberation of Lyons.

Human road blocks of deliriously happy French women and cheering men turned the streets leading westward to the Rhone into a four-mile canyon of kisses. Dazed American doughboys, matinee idols for the day, were surrounded by surging mobs of pretty mademoiselles, mothers and white-haired grandmothers.

The snarl of snipers' rifles was forgotten as the populace pelted autos with flowers and scrambled for the privilege of touching the liberators.

It was still war, but it was fantastic war. The German garrison fled day before yesterday, abandoning the renegade Vichy militiamen who served them. Today FFI patrols roamed the streets seeking the trapped traitors, who sniped from buildings throughout the city.

There was unreality about the little organized fighting remaining. At the Cours Gambetta, close by the Rhone, T-Sgt. Robert W. Korthals, North Collins, N. Y., and the 35-man American patrol which en-

(Continued on Page 8)

DAILY MIRROR, Thursday, September 7, 1944.

Daily Mirror

SEPT 7

No. 12,706
ONE PENNY
Registered at the G.P.O. as a Newspaper.

BLACK-OUT OFF

From Sunday week, Sept. 17

FIRE GUARD

Ends Tuesday in most areas

HOME GUARD

No compulsion from Monday

C.D. CUTS

Workers switch to Forces or factories

BY BILL GREIG

HERE is the cheeriest home news Britain's long-suffering civilians have had since the war began five years ago.

The black-out is to end on September 17—a week on Sunday—when Double Summer Time ends. On that date street lamps will be lit once more and you will no longer have to obscure completely the lights from your windows—except in certain coast areas.

Peace-time curtains will do, unless they are very flimsy. The test will be: can objects in the room be seen from the outside?

But don't throw your black-out material away. If the sirens should sound you must be ready to black-out completely again.

Pre-war street lighting will be allowed in districts which have the "master-switch" system. Elsewhere, the lighting will be like that in side-streets before the war.

Fireguard duties will be abolished over a large part of Britain from Tuesday. Daylight guards are abolished everywhere, but in London and in parts of East and Southern England night guards will still be needed.

Over most of Britain whole-time Civil Defence workers are to be switched to the Army or essential work. Many part-timers will be released. For those who remain, maximum hours for duty and training will be cut to twelve a month.

Compulsory drills andtraining for Home Guards will end as from Monday next—including aid to Civil Defence. Home Guard duties still required will be left to volunteers. The H.G. call-up is suspended.

FULL DETAILS: BACK PAGE.

Canadians enter Calais in battle for the gunsites

CANADIAN troops were reported last night to have penetrated into Calais and to be less than a mile from Boulogne in the battle to free the south coast of England from the menace of the German cross-Channel guns.

The roar of the battle could be heard at Deal. At times big explosions shook English soil, and the German guns fired more salvos of hate across the Channel.

The south-east coast area had a shell warning from 1.50 p.m. to 3.40 p.m.

Meanwhile, British troops of the Canadian First Army were carrying out one of the toughest tasks since Caen.

After crossing the mouth of the River Seine in make-shift boats, they were faced with the job of cracking the "suicide" defence of the great port of Le Havre.

Among the British units are the Royal Scots Fusiliers, the Duke of Wellingtons and the King's Own Yorkshire Light Infantry.

They are going to serve another ultimatum on the hard-fighting German garrison, according to a Reuter message last night.

All through the Pas de Calais area organised Germans are resisting more strongly than they have done since the fight at the Seine. Most of the fighting is being done by three fresh coastal divisions.

Altogether about 50,000 Germans are pinned against the Channel coast and the North Sea.

Sixteen waves of Allied bombers attacked the port of Brest.

Here is a round-up of the scanty news from other fronts last night:—

EASTERN FRANCE.—A few hours after the Allied announcement that American patrols entered Germany for a few hours on September 3, Algiers radio said Allied troops had reached the outskirts of Strasbourg, on the Franco-German border.

CENTRAL FRANCE.—Swiss reports say that the Allies from the Riviera have linked up with the men from Normandy.

BELGIUM.—British troops have reached Ghent, inland port on the Scheldt. Another 10,000 prisoners have been taken in the American trap at Mons.

HOLLAND.—British were said to be "in sight of Rotterdam." Berlin denied that Breda or any other Dutch territory had been occupied.

Govt. plan for cradle-to-grave insurance

By Your Political Correspondent

THE Cabinet is to issue next week its own "Beveridge" scheme, the result of two years' struggle between Ministers of different views and parties.

I understand that it will create a new Ministry of Social Services, to administer a scheme expected to cost £500,000,000 a year at first and £700,000,000 in the years to come.

The main proposal is an all-in insurance scheme, to which everyone will have to contribute, covering them for

Unemployment and sickness.
Family allowances.
Maternity benefits.
Funeral assistance.

The family allowances, which will be paid without means test, will be 5s. a week for each child, as announced by Sir John Anderson more than a year ago.

Continued on Back Page

BBC instructs Nazi slaves

THE 10,000,000 foreign workers inside Germany were advised to leave the towns, hide, collect news and await the arrival of Allied armies by a staff officer of Allied H.Q. who broadcast in the B.B.C. European service last night.

His message was the second broadcast during the day to the workers inside Germany.

Watch the behaviour of the Germans, they were warned; be ready to give details about their crimes and render impossible the destruction of factories and plants, particularly of oil depots which may serve the Allies.

ONLY "IKE" CAN ACCEPT PEACE BID

By Your Diplomatic Correspondent

NO peace overtures from Germany have been made to any of the Allied Governments. Reports of mysterious visitors in London, Lisbon and elsewhere have no foundation in fact.

So far as is known, not one German of any standing has succeeded in leaving his country since the attack on Hitler.

We have, in fact, made it clear to the Germans that there is only one man with whom they can deal, and that is General Eisenhower.

He is empowered by all Allied Governments to accept unconditional surrender if offered by the German High Command.

He would, if necessary, deal with Kluge, his "opposite number" in the West, but only if assured that the surrender included also the armies fighting against Russia.

Meanwhile we are taking no risks of any of the Nazi leaders slipping through our hands.

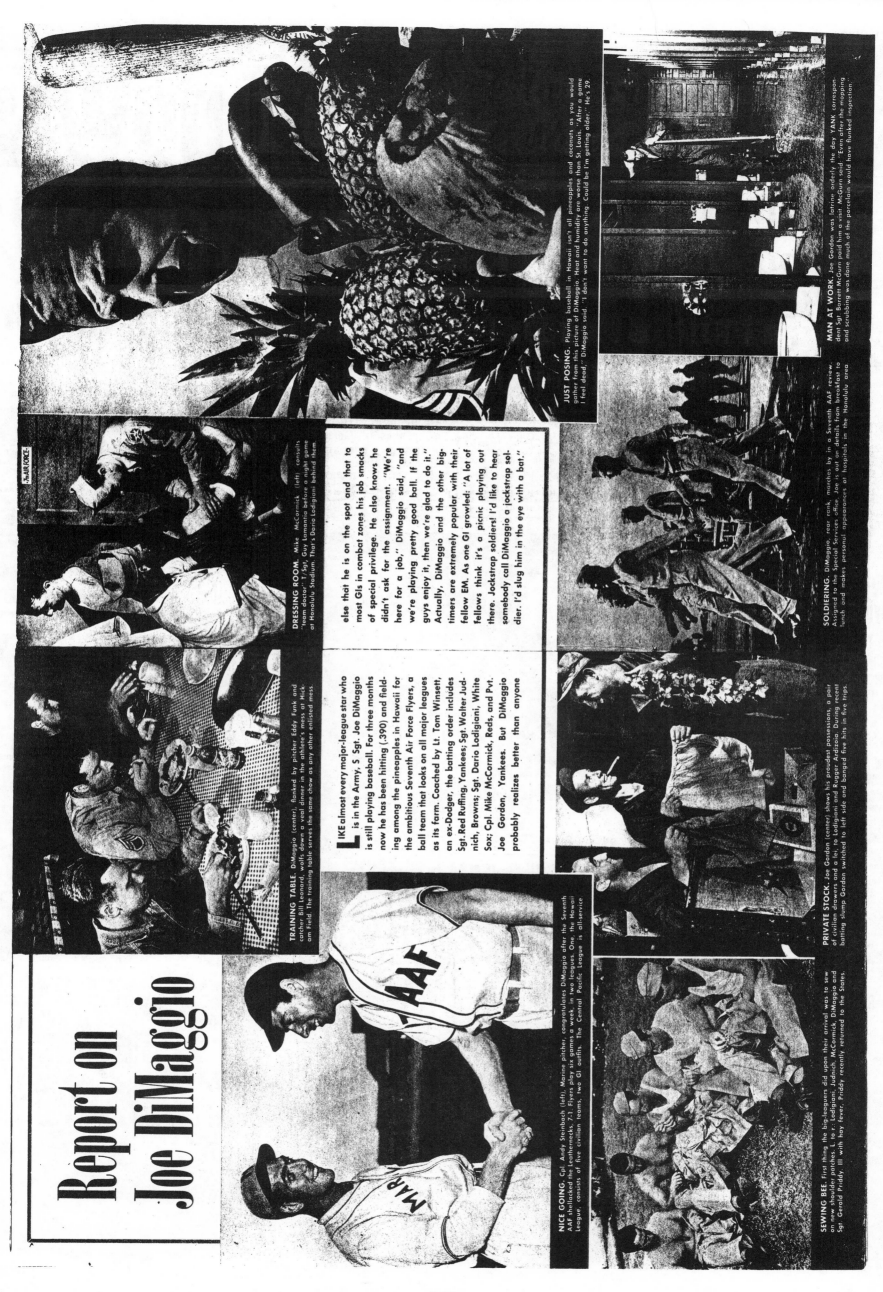

Report on Joe DiMaggio

TRAINING TABLE. DiMaggio (center), flanked by pitcher Eddy Funk and catcher Bill Leonard, wolfs down a veal dinner in the athlete's mess at Hickam Field. The training table serves the same chow as any other enlisted mess.

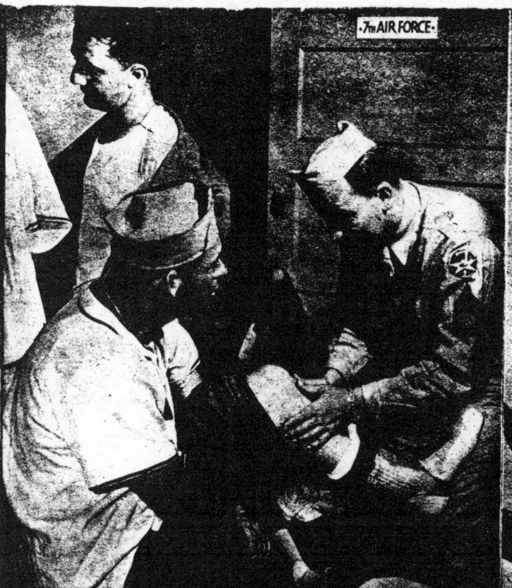

DRESSING ROOM. Mike McCormick (left) consults "team doctor" T/Sgt. Guy Lamantia before a night game at Honolulu Stadium. That's Dario Lodigiani behind them.

NICE GOING. Cpl. Andy Steinbach (left), Marine pitcher, congratulates DiMaggio after the Seventh AAF shellacked the Leathernecks, 7-1. Flyers play six games a week, in two leagues. One, the Hawaii League, consists of five civilian teams, two GI outfits. The Central Pacific League is all-service.

LIKE almost every major-league star who is in the Army, S Sgt. Joe DiMaggio is still playing baseball. For three months now he has been hitting (.390) and fielding among the pineapples in Hawaii for the ambitious Seventh Air Force Flyers, a ball team that looks on all major leagues as its farm. Coached by Lt. Tom Winsett, an ex-Dodger, the batting order includes Sgt. Red Ruffing, Yankees; Sgt. Walter Judnich, Browns; Sgt. Dario Lodigiani, White Sox; Cpl. Mike McCormick, Reds, and Pvt. Joe Gordon, Yankees. But DiMaggio probably realizes better than anyone else that he is on the spot and that to most GIs in combat zones his job smacks of special privilege. He also knows he didn't ask for the assignment. "We're here for a job," DiMaggio said, "and we're playing pretty good ball. If the guys enjoy it, then we're glad to do it." Actually, DiMaggio and the other big-timers are extremely popular with their fellow EM. As one GI growled: "A lot of fellows think it's a picnic playing out there. Jockstrap soldiers! I'd like to hear somebody call DiMaggio a jockstrap soldier. I'd slug him in the eye with a bat."

JUST POSING. Playing baseball in Hawaii isn't all pineapples and coconuts as you would gather from this picture of DiMaggio. Heat and humidity are worse than St. Louis. "After a game I feel dead," DiMaggio said. "I don't want to do anything. Could be I'm getting older." He's 29.

SEWING BEE. First thing the big-leaguers did upon their arrival was to sew on new shoulder patches. L. to r.: Lodigiani, Judnich, McCormick, DiMaggio and Sgt. Gerald Priddy. Ill with hay fever, Priddy recently returned to the States.

PRIVATE STOCK. Joe Gordon (center) shows his proudest possessions, a pair of civilian drawers and a lei, to Lodigiani and Rugger Ardizoia. During recent batting slump Gordon switched to left side and banged five hits in five trips.

SOLDIERING. DiMaggio, rear rank, marches by in a Seventh AAF review. Assigned to the Special Services office, Joe is out on details from breakfast to lunch and makes personal appearances at hospitals in the Honolulu area.

MAN AT WORK. Joe Gordon was latrine orderly the day YANK correspondent Sgt. Barrett McGurn paid him a visit. McGurn said: "Even after the mopping and scrubbing was done much of the porcelain would have flunked inspection."

DAILY MIRROR, Tuesday, September 12, 1944.

Daily Mirror

SEPT 12

No. 12,710 ONE PENNY

Registered at the G.P.O. as a Newspaper.

Luftwaffe came out of hiding and—

130 SHOT DOWN

Battle of Britain in reverse as armada fought across Reich

British in Holland after best 24 hours of Hun-killing

WHILE British troops of the First Canadian Army were attacking Le Havre with flame-throwing tanks last night, the Second British Army was nearing the end of its best 24 hours of Hun-killing yet.

Its tanks and infantry have entered the "inner porch" of the Dutch frontier and, in the words of an officer, "have got stuck into the Germans and fairly slaughtered them."

According to Brussels, British spearheads have crossed the border.

A forward H.Q. stated that more Germans had been killed and more of their equipment destroyed yesterday than in the 200-mile lightning dash to Brussels, says a Reuter correspondent.

It was not a day of sweeping advances through diluted and disorganised opposition.

It was a fight for a road junction, for a cluster of houses and finally for a bridge across the Escaut Canal, less than one and a half miles from Holland.

We attacked the crossroads with everything on hand, won it, and moved on through 200 German corpses. More than 500 prisoners were taken.

At 9 p.m. on Sunday the bridge across the canal was reported intact but strongly defended. We needed that bridge, and there was only one tactic—rush it.

A famous tank unit revved its engines and crashed through the German line.

Violent Fighting

By 11.10 the bridge was in our hands and held from the enemy, who were fighting violently.

A German battalion of 800 men were wiped out or taken prisoner in the same sector during the day's fighting.

"It was the hardest fighting since the Seine," said Captain Michael Constant, of Fontridge, Cobham, Surrey.

"We have slashed through thousands of Germans who will now try to get organised behind. We will have to do some mopping up now."

Three hundred miles away, under a clear sky, British troops were fighting grimly in the northern outskirts of the French port of Le Havre, garrisoned by 5,000 Germans ordered to fight to the last man.

Spearheaded by Churchill

Continued on Back Page

MONTY ORDERED A GENERAL TO BED

The British General leading the thrust into Holland is one of the few Generals Field-Marshal Montgomery ever ordered to rest for three days.

Monty was a little concerned about the health of his indefatigable lieutenant, who was with him in the desert, says a Reuter correspondent.

"You can't order a General to go to bed," said the C.-in-C. to the General's doctor. "But I can. You have got to get this man rested and better."

Only when the doctor, after three days, reported that the General was better did Monty release him for duty again.

THE Luftwaffe came out of hiding yesterday to attack in force a 1,000-bomber air armada striking at oil plants in Germany—and got one of the biggest daylight beatings it has ever had over the Reich.

THE 800 ESCORTING FIGHTERS SMACKED DOWN AT LEAST 130 GERMAN PLANES.

And this is not the final figure. The fighters' bag is expected to mount when all claims have been checked and totalled — AND THE BOMBERS' TOTAL HAS YET TO COME.

It was the Battle of Britain in reverse.

Some of the Luftwaffe formations were 100 strong, and the mighty aerial battle ranged all over Central Germany from Hanover to Leipzig.

The Thunderbolts, Lightnings and Mustangs screening the Forts and Liberators had the greatest day in their history.

Their bag of 130 is the biggest ever recorded by U.S. fighters over Germany.

It is not the biggest day's combined bag. The figure has been exceeded at least once before in a combined bomber and fighter score.

British fighters' biggest day's bag was 185 during the Battle of Britain.

Loss of 130 planes is a tremendous blow to the Luftwaffe on the eve of the Allied assault on the Siegfried Line.

Churchill arrives saying "Victories everywhere"

MR. CHURCHILL set the mood in which his conference is to be held with President Roosevelt at Quebec by exclaiming as he stepped from the train there yesterday: "Victories everywhere." He repeated the remark when he met Mr. Roosevelt.

The President's train from Washington and the special train that bore Mr. Churchill from Halifax, where he had disembarked, arrived almost simultaneously at Quebec, and Mr. Mackenzie King, Canada's Prime Minister, had to rush across the track to greet him.

Attired in his Trinity House uniform, smoking a cigar and carrying a silver-knobbed cane, Mr. Churchill strode round the station to where Mr. Roosevelt was seated in his car.

The two leaders greeted each other heartily, Mr. Roosevelt saying that Mr. Churchill had put on weight.

When Mrs. Churchill caught sight of Mrs. Roosevelt in a flame-coloured dress she exclaimed: "Oh, hello there," and they were soon busy chatting.

The informality was even carried so far that the President introduced Mr. Churchill to a Jewish photographer.

STALIN TOO BUSY

Stalin had to refuse an invitation to the conference between Mr. Churchill and President Roosevelt—owing to pressure of business on the Russian front.

In a message he sent to the two leaders at Quebec he said:

"At the present time, when the Soviet armies are fighting battles on such a broad front, I am deprived of the possibility of travelling from the Soviet Union and of leaving the direction of the Army for even the shortest period.

"All my colleagues agree that this is quite impossible."

NEW BUZZ-BOMB?

"We may hope V1 will return, in the old form or a new one."—*German radio commentator last night.*

CROSS-CHANNEL GUNS SEND OVER THIRD "HATE" IN 12 HOURS

SCORES of Allied bombers and fighters were crossing the Channel yesterday, while German long-range guns gave the south-east coast area its eighth shelling in fifty hours and the third in just over twelve hours.

The sudden crack of shells—four in ten minutes—sent people hurrying to shelter. The All Clear sounded after an hour and a half.

In daylight people on the south-east coast heard nothing of the gun battles around Boulogne, Calais and Dunkirk.

7 LB. OF DEATH IS MISSING

IN London this morning there may be children with "pills" that look like peppermints, but whih contain enough silver sodium cyanide to kill thousands of people.

The cyanide—7lb. of it in a yellow tin—was stolen from a workshop in Mildmay-avenue, Islington, N. One grain would prove fatal if eaten.

Last night the police were looking for the thieves, who are believed to be children.

Mr. Robert George Johnston, at whose premises the robbery was, told the *Daily Mirror*, "Nothing else was taken."

Russia 'cool' to Turkey

A diplomatic "coldness" has developed in the relations between Turkey and Russia.

The Turks claim to be extremely puzzled about the reason, and say that Moscow has made no demands on them that have not been met.

In neutral circles, however, it is said that Russia is extremely dissatisfied at the safety-first attitude of the Turks towards the war, and, despite the fact that she is an ally of Britain, is prepared to take drastic steps to secure her more active assistance.

Reports that Moscow contemplates breaking off diplomatic relations with Turkey could not be confirmed in London but the Turks are in a state of extreme anxiety.

20,000 of the right stuff

THE call of the sea, of travel, of adventure still finds a tremendous response in the heart of Britain's youth. Last week NAAFI advertised for a thousand boys between 16 and 17½ needed by Christmas for the Naval Canteen Service, the Navy's Naafi. THERE HAVE BEEN 20,000 APPLICATIONS FOR THE JOBS. An official told the "Daily Mirror" last night: "It is a great tribute to the sense of adventure of the young boy of today. The boys' work will be to help run canteens on board ships. They wear uniform, hold naval rank and have battle stations like ordinary members of the crew."

MARYLAND COAST IN PATH OF HURRICANE
LOWLAND RESIDENTS TOLD TO MOVE INLAND

THE WEATHER

Rain today, tonight and Friday. Increasing winds this afternoon, becoming of gale force tonight.

THE BALTIMORE NEWS-POST
AN INDEPENDENT NEWSPAPER
The Largest Evening Circulation in the Entire South

NIGHT
Wall St. Opening

VOL. CXLV.—NO. 113 Entered as second-class matter at Baltimore Postoffice. THURSDAY EVENING, SEPTEMBER 14, 1944 PRICE 3 CENTS

YANK 1ST ARMY TANKS, INFANTRY STREAM INTO REICH NEAR AACHEN

State Coast In Path Of Hurricane; Lowland Residents Told To Flee

As the outer fringes of a "killer" hurricane approached the Maryland coast today, residents of coastal lowlands were advised to move inland and the Red Cross prepared to mobilize, if necessary.

Winds at Ocean City, Md., reached 25-mile velocity and the tide was within 25 feet of the boardwalk. Residents and visitors were watching developments anxiously.

The edge of the hurricane was licking the North Carolina coast this morning, with estimated wind velocity of 140 miles an hour at the center and was expected to reach the Maryland area tomorrow afternoon.

MAY STRIKE TODAY

It was expected to strike the North Carolina mainland with full force today, possibly preceded by a tidal wave.

Winds at eBaufort, N. C., reached hurricane velocity of 75 miles an hour at about 8 A. M. (E. W. T.) and the sea pounded against the beaches in waves 40 feet high.

Beaufort and the town of Moorehead City, south of Beaufort, were isolated from the outside world as the storm slashed communication lines.

The communities have populations of about 2,000 each, but by dawn they were practically ghost towns, for their people had fled inland during the night.

WIDE DAMAGE FEARED

Emergency crews at Beaufort sent out word that a devastating tidal wave was a strong possibility.

Early stages of the storm were felt in the form of strong gusts of wind that snapped off and uprooted trees, but thus far there were no reported casualties.

Reports from various Eastern Shore points on the waterfront were that all boats were being held in harbors, storm and hurricane warnings were displayed and preparations were being made, if necessary, to evacuate residents of exposed beaches and low areas to inland points.

The Red Cross disaster control center at Alexandria, Va., said it had sent Paul Hyer, a field director, to take charge of the situation in Maryland's Eastern Shore, and that he was now in the vicinity of Cape Charles.

SEA 'VERY ROUGH'

At Ocean City the Coast Guard reported an east wind at about 25 miles an hour and increasing steadily. The sea was described as "very rough" and the tide last night came to within a few feet of the boardwalk.

Mayor Daniel Crimper, Jr., of Ocean City said:

"We have every hope that the storm will change direction. The last bad hurricane we had was about 10 years ago and many have passed here since. Almost invariably they have been slated to hit Ocean City and have moved out to sea instead.

"We are hoping that this one will, too. If not, we'll have to take it the best we can."

The Coast Guard at Cape Charles, situated on a small island about 25 miles from the town, reported that there was "every indication that the storm is going to hit right here."

40 PERSONS ON ISLE

There are 40 persons on the island, all military personnel. Cape Charles itself, a town of about 1,500, is on the bay side.

Continued on Page 2, Column 5.

Fleet Hammers Philippine Japs

By RICHARD V. HALLER

PEARL HARBOR, Sept. 14—(I. N. S.).—Powerful United States task forces, spearheaded by carrier-based aircraft, maintained relentless assaults against Jap strongpoints in the Philippines today in a mounting campaign to knock out principal enemy bases in advance of the promised invasion to reconquer the islands.

American naval forces operating in strength in conjunction with the aerial blows wrecked tremendous havoc on Jap positions and Nipponese shipping at points in the Philippines and in neighboring islands.

DESTROY 200 PLANES

Pacific Fleet Headquarters reported that in the latest action by its forces which have been cruising through waters of the Southern Philippines for the past week more than 200 Jap aircraft were destroyed.

The operations are continuing against "strong" opposition, headquarters said.

Cebu, Negros and Panay islands in the Central Philippines were targets in the latest revealed raid.

Continued on Page 2, Column 2.

Score Die In Train Wreck

TERRE HAUTE, Ind., Sept. 14 (A. P.).—At least 20 persons were killed and obtu 50 injured today in the collision of two Chicago and Eastern Illinois Railroad passenger trains near here. Virtually all of the dead and injured were soldiers.

The trains, one the crack Dixie Flyer, southbound and, the other a mail and express train, crashed head-on.

The engine, tender, two baggage cars and the first two of three Pullmans on the Dixie Flyer left the track and piled up along the roadway.

A major said all of the men were overseas Air Force veterans.

Saka New Turk Finance Minister

ANKARA, Sept. 14—(A. P.).—Hasan Saka, vice-jresident of the People's arty and former Finance Minister, assumed today the post of Foreign Minister, which Numan Menemencioglu resigned June 13 after a dispute resulting from armed German ships being permitted to pass through the Dardanelles.

Clear Copenhagen Hotels For Nazis

STOCKHOLM, Sept. 14—(A. P.).—The three largest hotels in Copenhagen were ordered cleared of civilians today presumably so high German officers could use them, the Danish press sermvice reported.

Nelson Confers With Gen. Chiang

CHUNGKING, Sept. 14—(A. P.).—Donald M. Nelson, War Production Board chairman, who is here on a mission for President Roosevelt, conferred today with Generalissim Chiang Kai-shek.

RETURNS TO HELSINKI

STOCKHOLM, Sept. 14 — (A. P.). — Prime Minister Hanntti Hackzell of Finland was reported en route today from Moscow to Helsinki for last minute conferences with his Government, possibly bringing with him Soviet peace terms for submission to the Finnish Parliament.

Scratches At Laurel

First Race — Sun Palo, Toilaway, Mid Knight, Blue Wise.
Second—Cast Out, Andy Mark, Unheard, Sister Talbot.
Fourth — Half Inch, Lupoba, Queen's Wreath.
Sixth—Rough Shower, Mister Chat, Patty Knot, Valdina Angel.
Seventh—Quent Reynolds, Grant Venture.
Eight—Sharp Reward, Carolina Bell, Frelan, Found Out.
Weather raining· track muddy.

Quebec Parley Agenda, Pacific War Blueprint Are Bared To Moscow

By ROBERT G. NIXON

QUEBEC, Sept. 14—(I. N. S.).—Soviet Russia's future role as an active partner in the global struggle against the Axis following the defeat of Germany became a matter of intense conjecture today in the light of revelations at the Quebec war strategy conference.

Soviet Marshal Joseph Stalin's refusal of an invitation to attend the present Pacific war strategy conference was announced officially three days ago.

It has now come to light, however, that the invitation sent by Washington and London to Moscow contained the complete agenda of the proposed talks as dealing with the drafting of a military blue print to crush Japan after Germany's fall.

CITES MILITARY SECURITY

Presidential Secretary Stephen T. Early announced in response to request by correspondents for the text of the invitation sent Stalin, that it could not be made public for reasons of military security because the invitation was woven into the fabric of an agenda setting forth the conference objectives.

Early also disclosed that had Stalin accepted, the meeting would have been held at a secret place elsewhere, presumably much nearer Russia. Mr. Roosevelt and Mr. Churchill decided upon Quebec as the most convenient location, Early continued, only after Stalin had declined to participate.

In the light of these developments, observers pointed out that to date there has been no indication from Russia that the Soviet Government will enter the struggle against Japan once victory in Europe is won.

STALIN SHUNS MEETING

Instead, Stalin has pointedly refused to attend a war strategy meeting with President Roosevelt and Mr. Churchill where the scope of discussions extended into spheres beyond the war in Europe itself.

Earlier in the war, when German armies were deep within Russia, it is conceded that an attack by Japan at the right moment on Russia in the Far East might have proved disastrous to the Soviet.

Throughout Stalin has main-

Continued on Page 2, Column 5.

More Authority Urged:

MacArthur Wins Praise Of Dewey

By LEO W. O'BRIEN

ABOARD DEWEY CAMPAIGN TRAIN EN ROUTE TO SHERIDAN, WYO., Sept. 14—(I. N. S.). Governor Dewey sped westward toward Wyoming and Montana today amid growing indications that in one of his West Coast speeches next week he will challenge the Roosevelt Administration on its handling of the war with Japan and events leading up to the Pearl Harbor attack.

The Republican Presidential nominee dropped a broad hint in that direction before leaving Valentine, Neb., last night when he accused the President of failing to make full use of the military talents of Gen. Douglas MacArthur and with neglecting to send the latter adequate supplies.

PRAISES MacARTHUR

"Now that General MacArthur no longer is a political threat to Mr. Roosevelt," he said it would seem appropriate that his many talents be given greater scope and recognition.

(BACKGROUND NOTE: It was indicated today that the Republicans will make a strong bid for the service vote. Governor Dewey, however, is not expected to visit any Army or Navy camp during his tour.)

Governor Dewey, who spent two days in Valentine, where he conferred with Republican leaders and cattle men from Nebraska and South Dakota, will conduct similar meetings at Sheridan, Wyo., today and Billings, Mont., tomorrow.

HAILED IN NEBRASKA

During a brief stop at Gordon, Neb., last night more than 3,000 persons jammed around the rear platform of the Dewey train to wave at the nominee. He did not make a speech but brought a laugh from the crowd when he remarked:

"You all look so healthy, I doubt if there is a New Dealer in the crowd."

Temperatures

12 Midn't, 70	6 A. M., 74
1 A. M., 70	7 A. M., 73
2 A. M., 71	8 A. M., 74
3 A. M., 72	9 A. M., 75
4 A. M., 74	10 A. M., 76
5 A. M., 74	11 A. M., 77

REAL LIFE ROLE—Michelle Morgan (above), French-born movie actress, became the mother of a son yesterday in Hollywood while William Marshall, also of the screen, paced the hospital corridor in typical expectant-father fashion. Their son will be named Michael William Marshall.

Report Riots In Berlin Streets

LONDON, Sept. 14—(A. P.).—The radio of the French forces of the interior at Lyon reported today that German S. S. (Elite Guard) troops had fired into a crowd of peace demonstrators in Berlin.

The broadcast did not indicate the source of the report and there was no information from other quarters concerning any such demonstration.

A similar report, however, was broadcast later by the French national radio at Lyon, the Ministry of Information said.

(The O. W. I. quoted the Lyon radio as saying that "riots are reported to have taken place in Berlin," and added:

("During one fight a small group of rebels routed an S. S. formation and went back into hiding before the arrival of police reinforcements.")

Report Germans Quitting Rhodes

ISTANBUL, Sept. 14—(A. P.). Reports reaching here today indicated the Germans were evacuating the island of Rhodes, largest in the Dodecanese. The Nazis were estimated at more than a division on the island.

Seek To Flank Nazi Defense Bastion From North In New Crossing

NEW YORK, Sept. 14—(I. N. S.).—Large units of the American First Army, including tanks and infantry, continue to stream across the German border south of Aachen today, according to a British broadcast recorded by C. B. S.

LONDON, Sept. 14—(A. P.).—Americans in the Metz area have begun an offensive with a terrific artillery bombardment, the German Transocean News Agency in a Berlin broadcast today.

LONDON, Sept. 14—(A. P.).—Gen. Dwight D. Eisenhower's Berlin-bound armies struck today into the 15-mile-wide appendix of the Netherlands in a thrust apparently intended to flank from the north the German border city of Aachen, already besieged from the south.

Supreme Headquarters said this new crossing of the Dutch frontier occurred near Maastricht, 15 miles north of Liege. It did not disclose the nationality of the attacking troops. The American First Army, however, has been operating in that sector.

There were no official progress reports on Lieut. Gen. Courtney H. Hodges' troops who, according to field dispatches last night, penetrated the outskirts of Aachen and captured the German village of Rotgen.

POSITIONS WIDENED

The daily communique, however, announced a widening of the Luxembourg positions from where the Americans first entered the Reich northwest of Trier.

The Algiers radio broadcast a report that Americans had entered Trier. This was not confirmed at Supreme Headquarters.

Resistance was said to be surprisingly weak near and south of Aachen, a northern keystone of the Siegfried Line. Field dispatches reported the Germans might be falling back for a major stand on the Rhine—some 40 miles to the east in this sector. This suggested that the Germans were making another trade of space for a time.

METZ UNDER FIRE

A Berlin broadcast this morning said a terrific aerial bombardment in the Metz area had touched off a new American offensive. There was no immediate official com-

Continued on Page 2, Column 1.

Reds Battling In Streets Of Praga

LONDON, Sept. 14—(A. P.).—The Berlin radio acknowledged today that Russian troops have penetrated Praga, Eastern suburb of Warsaw. In Transylvania the Germans evacuated the southern part of the Szekler gap to shorten their front against Russians and Romanians, it was announced.

By NATALIA RENE

MOSCOW, Sept. 14—(I. N. S.). Inflicting "enormous losses" upon the German defenders, the Soviet Army today held the strategic town of Lomza and hammered on toward East Prussia, while farther south other assault forces were battering down the defenses of Warsaw.

The Soviet communique also revealed that Russian troops have reached the Polish-Czechoslovakian border in a thrust from Krosno to Ciechania.

(A junction was effected at Negotin, near the eastern frontier of Yugoslavia, between the Red Army and Marshal Tito's Partisans, according to reports broadcast by the free Yugoslav radio.

(Another column of Soviet troops, the German radio stated, has spearheaded across the Rhodope mountains in the Bulgarian-Greek frontier and into Greece.)

The Russians, in Northern Transylvania, smashed ahead to a point near the Hungarian border, but the big news in Moscow was the seizure of Lomza.

NEWS-POST

DAILY MIRROR, Thursday, September 28, 1944.

Daily Mirror

SEPT 28

No. 12,724
ONE PENNY
Registered at the G.P.O. as a Newspaper.

NIGHT RETREAT ENDS HELL AT ARNHEM

THE EPIC STAND OF "THE FEW" AT ARNHEM IS OVER.

The remnants of the First British Airborne Division, which held out for more than 230 hours of hell, have been withdrawn by night to the south bank of the Lower Rhine, it was announced last night.

Thus the first Allied bid to win a crossing over the last big water barrier to the North German plain has failed.

But the "red devils" effort was not in vain. Without it the British Second Army could not have hoped to capture the even more vital Nijmegen bridge.

Last night there was an unconfirmed Allied report that at least 2,000 got back and that about 1,200 wounded were left behind in the care of British doctors, who chose to carry on in captivity.

An airborne division would normally be about 9,000 strong, and how many of them escaped from the pocket is not yet definitely known.

The Germans claimed to have captured 6,450, including 1,700 wounded. They gave the death roll as 1,500.

The failure of the Second Army relief column to reach the air troops on the north bank and the bad weather which made it impossible to drop adequate supplies were the chief reasons for the withdrawal.

British tanks pushing north of Nijmegen along raised roads were perfect targets for German guns, according to Richard McMillan, of British United Press.

They out-distanced the infantry and had to wait for them to clean up the German guns.

The cutting of the supply road and the delay in such equipment as assault boats reaching the river were other vital factors in this German local victory.

But the airborne stand prevented the Germans from flinging more powerful forces into the battle for the Waal bridge at Nijmegen.

The Waal is twice as wide as the Lower Rhine, and securing of a good crossing paves the way for a powerful build-up east of this great river barrier at the gateway to the Reich.

It was through a hurricane barrage of German gunfire that the Arnhem survivors were ferried over to our lines during Monday night.

"Let us get back again, give us a few tanks and we'll finish the job," they said.

"I was in Crete, and that was a piece of cake compared with Arnhem" one "Red Devil" officer, Captain Bethune Taylor, of Landsdowne-place, Cheltenham, said.

Worst ordeal throughout the nightmare siege were attacks by flame throwers, according to Lance-Corporal John Stillwell, of Ballance - road, Hackney Wick, who at one time was cut off after he went out with a patrol and wiped out an enemy machine-gun post.

"After lying up all night we got back to the fringe of the perimeter," he said, as wrapped in an Army blanket he sat exchanging jokes and quips with other survivors.

"I prayed to God I would live to see Hackney Wick again—and I never believed I should."

Last night the thrust by British and Belgian troops and tanks to the line of the Dutch Meuse continued favourably. The cross-Holland corridor has been widened.

The Germans at Calais have now been driven back into the town itself, where 1,500 tons of bombs were dropped upon them yesterday by the RAF.

Flat rate pay for men hurt at work

Compensation for men and women injured at work is to be dealt with under the Government's "Beveridge Plan" and not left to the employers, according to proposals made in a White Paper yesterday.

✦

There will, however, be no compensation based on loss of earnings and the highest-paid worker will get the same as the lowest paid. Rates range from 35s. a week to £3 a week pensions.

✦

Legal actions over ordinary compensation will no longer be necessary and all cases will be dealt with by local pensions officers and a tribunal.

(Full details on Page 2.)

INSIDE THE HELL

One of the first photographs of the British Airborne Division in action in the hell of the Arnhem pocket.

Taken under heavy enemy fire at the most critical period of the venture, it shows a paratrooper hitting back with a 3in. mortar.

They called the cheeky pull-out 'Operation Berlin'

FROM ALAN WOOD

WITH ARNHEM AIRBORNE FORCE, Tuesday (delayed).

THIS is the end. The most tragic and glorious battle of the war is over, and the survivors of this British airborne force can sleep soundly for the first time in eight days and nights.

Orders came to us yesterday to break out from our forest citadel west of Arnhem, cross the Rhine and join up with the Second Army on the south bank.

Our commander decided against a concerted assault on the Germans round us.

Instead, the plan was to split up into little groups, ten to twenty strong, setting out along different routes at two-minute intervals, which would simply walk through the German lines in the dark.

Cheeky patrols went out earlier tying bits of white parachute tape to trees to mark the way.

To hinder the Germans waking up to what was happening, Second Army guns laid down a battering box barrage all the afternoon.

The first party was to set off

Continued on Back Page

Allied sea and skytroops open Balkan invasion front

ALLIED forces have invaded the Balkans, landing along the coasts of Yugoslavia and Albania.

The landing on the mainland of Albania was announced from Allied H.Q. in Italy yesterday.

Seaborne and airborne troops of the land forces of the Adriatic, says another announcement, are now operating on a wide front in the Adriatic country, which includes both Albania and the islands off Yugoslavia.

The landing operations stretch northward from Albania along the whole Dalmatian (Yugoslav) coast, according to the German Overseas News Agency. Combined land and naval forces are taking part.

Islands Attacked

Strong Anglo-American naval and air forces attacked groups of islands off the Dalmatian coast yesterday morning, said the German Official News Agency.

It adds that they are meeting with violent German resistance and that the battle is still going on.

"For the past eleven days landing craft of the British Navy have been carrying Allied troops and partisans to the Balkans," said a radio reporter broadcasting from Italy yesterday.

"The announcement does not say at what point in Albania the landing was made, but obviously any thrust in that country threatens the German route of withdrawal northwards from Greece."

The Adriatic land forces were formed four months ago, and have since been giving the maximum amount of trouble to the German occupying forces, working in co-operation with the British Navy, the RAF, and Marshal Tito's forces.

"HOT GOSPELLER" AIMEE IS DEAD

Aimee McPherson, Los Angeles "hot gospeller," died suddenly in her hotel suite yesterday from a heart attack.

She founded the Angelus Temple and did a European tour with her evangelistic troupe.

SOME M.P.s SHOOK RAMSAY'S HAND

Captain Ramsay, released from internment, took his seat when the House of Commons met yesterday.

At question time he sat talking to Mr. Roston Duckworth and Admiral Beamish. Several members shook hands with him as they came in.

'PHONE TO MOSCOW

Direct radio telephone communication between Moscow and London was opened yesterday for the first time.

'HARD FIGHTING LIES AHEAD,' GEN TRUSCOTT

(Continued from Page One)
your weapons and your supplies over distances almost logistically unbelievable. You have, by your successes, not only contributed immeasurably to the advance of the northern Allied Forces by preventing the movement of reserves against them but have eliminated the German 19th Army as an effective fighting force. Your operations have been a most vital factor in clearing the enemy from almost all of France.

Your conduct here and your relationships with the people of France in the areas that you have liberated has been in accord with the highest standards of American military tradition. The fervent and wholehearted welcome which they have extended to you is testimonial of their gratitude and will remain, I am sure, a treasured memory in the minds of every member of this command. Your country has reason to be proud of your accomplishments and grateful for the services that you have rendered.

This campaign will stand as a monument to you Americans of the VI Corps—a tribute to your training, initiative, ingenuity, aggressiveness, boldness, determination, and fighting spirit and to the leadership of the officers and non-commissioned officers of all ranks. To every officer and to every man, I tender my sincere appreciation for your untiring efforts and my deep admiration for your accomplishments.

Our task is not yet done. Hard fighting lies ahead. A fanatical enemy, reorganized and reinforced, is at bay on his own doorstep. Rugged terrain confronts us. Rain, cold, and snow will soon increase the difficulties of operations and add to the hardships that you must sustain. But — surmounting every objective as you press on—you will destroy the enemy before you and, together with all the other forces at the command of the Allied Nations, will bring about his final defeat and unconditional surrender.

Veterans—men of the VI Corps — with respect and pride, your Commander salutes you.

L. K. TRUSCOTT, JR.
Lieutenant General, U. S. Army
Commanding

Here Is How It Was Done

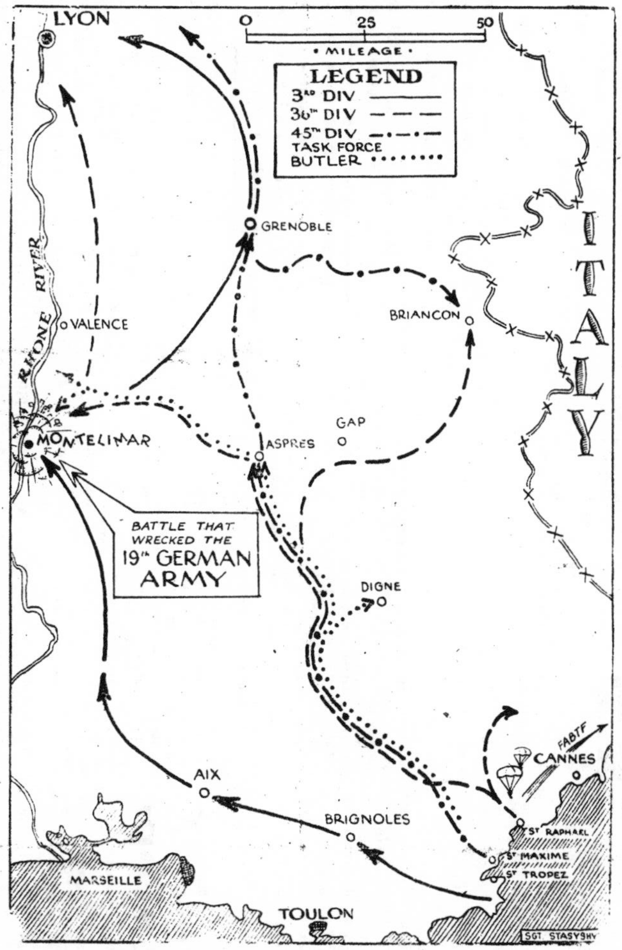

Forces that landed on the beaches August 15 streaked northward and in two weeks had defeated a great part of the opposing army and were knocking at the gates of Lyon, about 200 miles from their beachheads. The German attempt to escape was smashed at Montelimar. (APS)

UP AND OVER BEACH FOR ANZIO VETERANS

(Continued from Page One)
The 45th Division; "157th and 180th Infantry are in and in contact with enemy opposition." The radio cracked with static but over it the 36th Division reported that the 141st was in and advancing up the slopes and the 143rd was landing.

But later came the report from the 36th Division's 142nd Infantry, "Landing was held up by heavy artillery from hostile shore batteries." However, so complete was their plan that the commander immediately shifted from Red Beach to Yellow Beach and the operation went forward without a pause.

These battle hardened veterans operating behind the experienced, forceful, powerful and accurate navy and air corps knew how to dig krauts out of their pill-boxes and concrete fortifications. Everyone had his job to do, everyone did it.

All Ashore

Infantry had landed on the beaches running and were still running. Assault and maneuver overran the enemy and the army moved in as fast as the feet of the infantry could take them, as fast as the engineers could break the blocks for the tanks and other vehicles.

Engineers were clearing minefields, building roads, breaking road blocks. Signalmen were laying wire, constructing poles for larger wire. Medics were evacuating the few wounded and establishing hospital units—all on "D" Day.

French partisans appeared from everywhere with scores of German prisoners and evidence of scores of others already "taken care of." Our forces accounted for many more prisoners and German dead and wounded in the day's action.

French people, originally shocked by the impact of the mighty blow and not accustomed to freedom after their four years of oppression, became jubilant, throwing flowers, forcing kisses on soldiers, giving freely their precious wine. Their day of jubilation was at hand.

As "D" Day came to a close, the tenseness of the occasion gave way to a feeling of relief, we were ashore, and everyone realized that it was no longer "D" Day and that the battle—just begun was well on the way to another Allied victory.

SPANNED DOUBS RIVER IN TWENTY-TWO HOURS

Engineers of the 36th Division, when the Allied march reached the Doubs river, worked through the rain and dark night, to throw a bridge, 20 feet high, across the 150 feet of water. The job was done in 22 hours and the American armor moved on across the river.

Confronted by a demolished bridge and lack of materials, the Engineers scoured the area and built the bridge out of hand-sawn logs and planks, and whatever material they could find to substitute for the GI.

Onlookers, civilian and military, were amazed at the speed at which the engineers did the job.

FAMED CITADEL FELL TO THIRD DIVISION

High above the city of Besancon, in the path of the American advance, was an ancient fort. From its heights the entrenched Germans could fire down on the American troops approaching the city. All bridges but one approaching were blown. Hitler had ordered this city to be held until September 15 and the Germans rushed an entire new Division into that sector.

One battalion of Third Division troops crossed the one bridge over the Doubs, while two others were sent after the towering citadel guarding Besancon.

The old fort has never intended to withstand the shock of modern artillery. Troops crawling up the slopes got a 155 howitzer into position and pounded at the walls. The old walls held, but the German troops within couldn't. They filed out under a white flag.

Soldiers on leave now stroll around the parks, inspecting the scars of war.

Seven Men of Forty-Fifth Baptised in Southern France

Seven men in the 45th Division were the first men to be Baptized on the south-French beachhead when Captain Harvey F. Bett, Macon, Georgia, battalion chaplain immersed them in a small stream, at nine in the morning of the fourth day.

The men Baptized were William R. Tackaberry, Pfc. Robert J. Mole, Pvt. Delma Combs, Pvt. Harvey K. King, Pfc. Vernie B. Miller, Pfc. Troy F. Mandrell and Pfc. Robert I. Weyant.

NAZI COMMANDER FOUND SUICIDE AFTER BATTLE

One Nazi beat the rap on this front, according to a note found near the body. He was a colonel, a commander, and he wrote, "There is no chance. I can't admit defeat so I must leave."

Then he put a bullet through his own head.

GERMAN GENERAL SCHMIDT KILLED AT ROAD BLOCK

Major General Schmidt, much decorated German officer, was no different from legions of lesser Germans—he fell before the bullet of some Third Division soldier.

Riding in a sedan in convoy, the parade encountered a group of Third Divisioners preparing a road block. The Yanks opened up and while inspecting the debris later, the body of General Schmidt was found. A rifle bullet in the chest finished him.

BEACHHEAD NEWS
SOUVENIR EDITION
VOL. I, No. 100 Founded on the Anzio Beachhead Sunday, October 15, 1944

6th Corps Drives Through France

Veterans Hit Riviera Beaches

Mediterranean Vets Wade Ashore D-Day

August 15 was a tense day on the shores of Southern France. It was "D" Day. The veterans of Fedala and Oran, Licata and Gela, Salerno and Anzio were on the move again.

Months of study of maps and aerial photos; numerous landings on the shores by secret agents—previous to the final plans; weeks of practice by the infantry and engineers in overcoming obstacles similar to what they were to face on the landing; and weeks and weeks of calculation and coordination between the army, navy and air corps had preceeded the blow.

Parachutists had landed according to schedule and were clearing the landing grounds for the glider troops to follow them. Then came the long miles of planes and gliders in rows like traffic on a crowded city street, all onto their objective as pre-arranged.

On the Way

Now the stage was set. The actors were on the scene. During the early morning hours the navy had blasted at every target they had placed on their carefully planned charts. Planes of all sizes and description pattern bombed, dive bombed, and strafed pillboxes, roads, concrete fortifications and enemy gun positions.

The assault waves had headed for the beaches and had disappeared in the smoke and dust the bombardment had left. Then came that eternal wait for the first reports. The tenseness was to a point of breaking.

Commanders paced the decks of their flagships—waiting, watching, peering toward the beaches with high-powered field glasses. Had their plans been right? Was the landing going to be a success?

Then came the terse situation reports— from the 3rd Division, "7th and 15th Infantry have landed and are on their first objective — other elements landing."

(Continued on Page Four)

"The Yanks Are Coming"

The morning of August 15, 1944. Yanks leave an LCI, plunge into the water and wade to shore. Here a medic prepares to treat wounded. The MP is moving on to his post. (APS)

'You Did It', General Truscott Says in Tribute to Troops

TO THE OFFICERS AND MEN OF THE VI CORPS:

In the bright, prophetic sunlight of the early morning of the 15th of August, you men of the VI Corps—men of the 3d Division, the 36th Division, the 45th Division and of every reinforcing unit—veterans, all, of other amphibious operations—launched your memorable assault against the shores of Southern France. Supported by powerful air, airborne, and naval forces and assisted by long-oppressed and waiting French Allies, you destroyed the beach defenses of the 19th German Army and advanced inland to initial objectives with almost unprecedented speed.

The key ports of Toulon and Marseilles you soon isolated, thus facilitating their subsequent capture by our Allies. By your drive up the Durance River Valley, you trapped and annihilated a great portion of the fleeing 19th Army at the site of the now historic town of Montelimar. Without pause, you then turned to the northeast in a relentless pursuit of remnants, which you have continued almost to the German border. In thirty-eight days, you have traversed five hundred miles and have defeated a desperate enemy at every stand. You have forced a crossing of two major rivers. You have overcome every obstacle that a resourceful enemy could devise. You have, with even less than organic transport, managed to move yourselves,

(Continued on Page Four)

Up From the Sea To Threaten Reich

Story of Sixth Corps' Sweep Toward Germany

Following abruptly upon the fall of Rome in the Italian campaign the VI Corps was withdrawn from the lines and sent to the rear to prepare for the invasion of Southern France. For this new assault to be made upon the German continental bastion, the most veteran divisions in the Mediterreanean Theatre—the 3rd, the 36th and the 45th Divisons with the attendant number and variety of seasoned supporting units—were designated to comprise the VI Corps. The experience of North Africa, Sicily, Italy and Normandy were to be called upon in this great new operation in the western theatre.

Our Mission

Simultaneously with the fall of the City of Rome, the first Axis capital to be liberated, the landings in northern France had been launched. Operations were progressing satisfactorily but slowly. A strong threat from the south, one that would contain and divert much of the enemy strength in France, offered the best possibility of assisting the northern effort and of accelerating the progress of the forces engaged there. The attack by the Seventh Army with the Provisional Air-borne Division dropping just before H-hour and the VI Corps assault over the beach at H-hour, followed by the French Army was to constitute this threat.

Preparations

Personnel and equipment were gathered together, plans were formulated, intensive special training was engaged in by all units of the Corps, and everything was made ready. All of the multitude of meticulous details that characterize preparations for a distant large scale amphibious undertaking was perfected. All of the information which had been in progress of collection over a long period of time, regarding the strength and disposition of hostile forces, and of the conditions which might be expected to confront an at-

(Continued on Page Three)

FORMER WAAC STABBED TO DEATH HERE

THE WEATHER
Rain; moderate to strong winds tonight and Saturday.
Detailed Weather Report Page 36

Read The Baltimore News-Post for complete, accurate war coverage. It is the only Baltimore newspaper possessing the three great wire services—
ASSOCIATED PRESS
INTERNATIONAL NEWS SERVICE
UNITED PRESS

THE BALTIMORE NEWS-POST
AN INDEPENDENT NEWSPAPER
The Largest Evening Circulation in the Entire South

8

VOL. CXLV.—NO. 144 Entered as second-class matter at Baltimore Postoffice. FRIDAY EVENING, OCTOBER 20, 1944 PRICE 3 CENTS

600-SHIP ARMADA TOOK 250,000 TO PHILIPPINES

MacArthur In Islands Calls For Revolt

ADVANCED ALLIED H. Q., PHILIPPINES, Oct. 20—(U. P.).—General Douglas MacArthur and an army of at least 250,000 men stormed the Central Philippines from the greatest ocean-going invasion armada in history today, quickly seized control of the 75-mile east coast of strategic Leyte Island and were marching on Tacloban, its capital, 370 miles southeast of Manila. Returning with MacArthur to the Philippines was every living member of the ill-fated garrison who escaped with him from Corregidor two years and 10 months ago.

KEEPS HIS PROMISE—Leading the greatest ocean-going invasion army in the Pacific, Gen. Douglas MacArthur today had returned to the Philippines. He wears the Knight Grand Cross, bestowed on him by the King of England.

At least 600 ships formed the invasion force, the greatest armada ever gathered in the Pacific.

CALLS FOR REVOLT

In a broadcast to the people of the Philippines, General MacArthur called on them to revolt against their Japanese oppressors.

He said:

"Rally to me. Let the indomitable spirit of Corregidor and Bataan lead on. As the lines of battle roll forward to bring you within the zone of operation, rise and strike."

By nightfall more men were expected to be ashore on Leyte than the Allies landed in Normandy on D-Day. Fully a quarter of a million soldiers landed in France in the first 24 hours of the western front campaign.

SEIZE BEACHHEADS QUICKLY

Covered by the greatest naval and air bombardment of the Pacific war, jungle veterans of the American Sixth Army, under German-born Lieut. Gen. Walter Krueger, swarmed ashore from hundreds of assault craft and quickly seized beachheads against almost non-existent opposition and fanned out inland with tanks and mobile guns.

Three, and perhaps four, expanding beachheads were secured, front reports said. One column, advancing from San Ricardo, was nearing Tacloban, capital and principal city of Leyte, with a population of more than 30,000, only three miles to the north.

Early unconfirmed reports had said that Tacloban was captured; but, on the basis of later information, these appeared premature. The fate of Tacloban's big airfield, as well as other airfields just inland from the east coast, was not known.

Japanese opposition was reported developing in the Tacloban area and around Poanan, southernmost bridge-

WASHINGTON, Oct. 20—(A. P.).—President Roosevelt announced today that operations in the Philippines are proceeding on schedule with light losses and that the enemy was caught strategically off guard by the attack.

head, at mid-afternoon as the defenders, stunned and scattered by the devastating pre-invasion bombardment, began to rally their forces.

Enemy forces entrenched in the hills behind the coast were harrassing the invasion troops with mortar fire. Bloody fighting was believed in prospect when the doughboys reach the main defenses inland.

(A Domei transmission recorded by the FCC said Japanese forces "are at present engaged in strong counter-attacks against the enemy invaders" at Tacloban and in the Cabalian area at the southern end of Leyte.)

"Our ground troops are rapidly extending their positions, and supplies and heavy equipment already are flowing ashore in great volume," MacArthur said in a jubilant

Continued on Page 2, Column 1.

NEW YORK, Oct. 20—(I. N. S.).—Back upon the soil of his beloved Philippines, Gen. Douglas MacArthur today issued a stirring proclamation to the Filipino people pledging their complete liberation and destruction of the last vestigate of Japanese tyranny.

The proclamation, as broadcast from Leyte Island where the Stars and Stripes now fly and recorded by the OWI, said:

"This is the voice of freedom, General MacArthur speaking:

"Peoples of the Philippines: I have returned. By the grace of Almighty God our forces stand again on Philippine soil—soil consecrated in the blood of our two peoples.

"We have come, dedicated and committed, to the task of destroying every vestige of enemy control over your daily lives, and of restoring, upon a foundation of indestructible strength, the liberties of your people.

"At my side is your President, Sergio Osmena, worthy successor of that great patriot, Manuel Quezon, with members of his Cabinet. The seat of your Government is now therefore firmly re-established on Philippine soil.

"The hour of your redemption is here. Your patriots have demonstrated an unswerving and resolute devotion to the principles of freedom that challenges the best that is written on the pages of human history.

"I now call upon your supreme effort that the enemy may know from the temper of an aroused and outraged people within that he has a force there to contend with no less violent than is the force committed from without.

"Rally to me! Let the indomitable spirit of Bataan and Corregidor lead on!

"As the lines of battle roll forward to bring you within the zone of operations, rise and strike! Strike at every favorable opportunity. For your homes, and hearths, strike! For future generations of your sons and daughters, strike! In the name of your sacred dead, strike!

"Let no heart be faint. Let every arm be steeled. The guidance of Divine God points the way. Follow in His name to the Holy Grail of righteous victory!"

19 KILLED IN RIOT

ROME, Oct. 20—(A. P.).—Nineteen persons died as the result of a street battle yesterday in Palermo, Sicily, between a mob and Italian troops.

Ex-WAAC Is Stabbed To Death Here

An attractive brunette, Miss Evaline Acker, twenty-six, former member of the WAC, was stabbed to death at St. Paul and Read streets today, dying within an hour after she was taken to Mercy Hospital.

With almost her last breath, police said, the girl mentioned the first name of a man and said:

"I'm going to tell on you."

Her screams as she battled with her assailant in the middle of the street brought nearby residents to their windows, and at least two persons saw the slayer rush off into the darkness.

Both said he was dressed as a civilian.

MAN AT HOSPITAL

Shortly before the girl was brought to the hospital, a civilian, of somewhat similar description to the man seen struggling with the girl, rushed into the accident room and said:

"Send a doctor to St. Paul and Read street, quick! A girl has been badly hurt. I think she's dying."

Attendants told him doctors were not sent out on calls of that sort. The man hurried out. They heard an auto start up and speed away.

GIRL BROUGT IN

In a few minutes the girl was brought in by an ambulance crew.

She had been stabbed four times. There were three wounds in the left chest, one "probably puncturing the heart," one lower on the right side and her wrist bore a severe laceration, probably

Continued on Page 4, Column 1.

SLAIN — A twenty-six-year-old former WAAC, Miss Evaline Acker, was stabbed to death today at St. Paul and Read streets, only a few steps from her home in the 900 block St. Paul street.

(Other Pictures on Pages 3 and 4.)

Gale Slows Up, Moves North

WASHINGTON, Oct. 20—(U. P.).—The Weather Bureau reported at 8.30 A. M. today that the Atlantic hurricane, centered over the interior of South Carolina, continued to move slowly northward with diminishing intensity but that all danger of hurricane winds along the coast had passed.

The storm is located about 60 miles northwest of Charleston, the advisory said. It "continues to diminish in intensity" and has slowed down its forward speed.

Text of the 8.30 A. M. advisory:

"The hurricane is centered over the interior of South Carolina about 60 miles northwest of Charleston with central pressure about 29.94 inches. It has slowed down its forward speed but appears to be moving slowly northward.

WIND DANGER PASSED

"It continues to diminish in intensity and all danger of hurricane winds along the coast has passed, although strong onshore winds and gales of 35 to 50 miles an hour will continue today from about Wilmington, N. C., northward to Long Island and also over the interior of North Carolina and Virginia.

"Tides will be above normal but not dangerously high all along the coast from North Carolina to Delaware. General heavy rainfall will occur over all sections of the Carolinas and

Continued on Page 2, Column 7.

AachenFalls, Says Radio Report

NEW YORK, Oct. 20.—N. B. C. Reporter James Cassidy broadcast today that the city of Aachen has fallen.

SUPREME H. Q., A. E. F., PARIS, Oct. 20—(U. P.).—Both ends of Germany's western front swayed back today under Allied blows which laid open three passes leading through the Vosges to the Upper Rhine valley and split a Nazi pocket blocking the sea lanes to Antwerp.

LONDON, Oct. 20—(A. P.).—Canadian infantry and armor struck out in a new offensive through the mud and marshland north of Antwerp today to bolster the Allied powerhouse salient being built up in Holland against Adolf Hitler's northern defenses.

At the same time French infantry, fighting along the ridges of the Vosges at the southern end of the Allied line, outflanked the village of Ventron at the entrance to the 15-mile-long Bussang Pass, which opens out on the Rhine floor only seven miles from Mulhouse.

The Americans of the Seventh Army on the latter front also captured Bruyeres, 13 miles east of Epinal, in a further stab at two more passes leading through the Vosges to the Rhine flatlands around Colmar and Strasbourg.

STRUGGLE IN AACHEN

The First U. S. Army, holding more than half of Aachen, struggled slowly through mountains of debris in an effort to extinguish the last sparks of resistance in that Siegfried Line city.

The British Second Army, fighting to clear out the Germans

Continued on Page 2, Column 7.

Temperatures

12 Mid., 51	7 A. M., 50
1 A. M., 51	8 A. M., 50
2 A. M., 50	9 A. M., 50
3 A. M., 50	10 A. M., 51
4 A. M., 50	11 A. M., 51
5 A. M., 50	12 Noon, 52
6 A. M., 50	1 P. M., 52

Philippine Reaction:

'Great Stuff,' Say Yanks In Europe

By LOUIS AZRAEL
News-Post War Correspondent.

WITH U. S. FORCES IN GERMANY, Oct. 20.—Doughboys simply said "great stuff!" today as they learned about the American invasion of the Philippines—and went on with their work. There was no great elation visible.

This was partially due to the fact that the soldiers were confident this attack would come and are confident of its ultimate success.

They know enough about war, however, to realize that there will probably be setbacks, delays and bitter days for the men in the Pacific, just like there have been for themselves.

Furthermore, there is little time or mood for elation, even though these past few days have been the least active this front

Continued on Page 2, Column 3.

NEWS-POST

VERY LATEST NEWS

MARINE PLEADS INNOCENT IN GIRL'S SLAYING

WASHINGTON, Oct. 20—(A. P.).—Marine Pfc. Earl McFarland pleaded innocent today on first degree murder charges in the attack-slaying of Dorothy M. Berrum, eighteen-year-old Government clerk in East Potomac Park, October 5.

RIDICULED FAT GIRL STARVES SELF TO DEATH

ROCHESTER, N. Y., Oct. 20—(A. P.).—Self-induced starvation caused by playmates' gibes at her excessive weight, caused the death of a fourteen-year-old Rochester girl, Monroe County Coroner Richard A. Leonard said.

Man Spricht Deutsch
Eins, zwei, drei, vier, funf.
Ainss, tsvai, drai, feer, fewnf.
One, two, three, four, five.

THE STARS AND STRIPES

Daily Newspaper of U.S. Armed Forces in the European Theater of Operations

Ici On Parle Français
Je suis fatigué.
Juh swee fateeGAY.
I am tired.

Vol. 1—No. 94 | 1 Fr. | New York—PARIS—London | 1 Fr. | Saturday, Oct. 21, 1944

MacArthur Goes Back; Aachen Falls to 1st Army

Blast Nazis From Last City Fort

U.S. troops captured the first major German industrial center yesterday when Aachen, which the Nazis had chosen to defend literally stone by stone, fell to Lt. Gen. Courtney B. Hodges' First U.S. Army.

The fortified city proper was captured yesterday afternoon when the last German strongpoint was caved in by direct 135mm. rifle fire and defending Nazis were trapped underneath. Germans, however, continued fighting in the suburbs.

British Drive Slows

Coinciding with the opening of this gateway to the Rhine, the Canadians advanced five miles in a medium-scale attack launched yesterday morning 14 miles northeast of Antwerp. The assault, designed to ease pressure on the Beveland Causeway, was supported by tanks and planes.

South of Venraij, the British drive was slowed by stiffening German resistance and German artillery fire increased in tempo as the Nazis sought to regroup to halt further penetration of their Lowland defenses.

Unable to pry open the ring of steel Gen. Hodges threw around Aachen and snapped shut Monday night, the Germans sought frantically yesterday morning to drop supplies from planes to the trapped defenders. Five planes were shot down by U.S. gunners.

Germans Shell Dying City

Disregarding the lives of German civilians, German artillery shelled the dying city early in the morning as U.S. infantry flushed the Nazis defenders out of houses, buildings and heaps of rubble.

In the outskirts, it was estimated that 500 to 1,000 Germans were caught in a vice, between advancing U.S. infantrymen from the city proper and the ring of infantry around the embattled area.

Meanwhile, Third U.S. Army infantry, still four miles from Metz,

(Continued on Page 4)

Ninth Downs 18 Nazi Planes

Attacking enemy rail targets east of captured Aachen, Ninth Air Force fighter bombers, flying more than 550 sorties, yesterday encountered three Luftwaffe formations, destroying 18 enemy planes. Nine fighter bombers are reported missing.

Lightnings shot down 10 enemy aircraft over Cologne and two over Hamm, while P47s got six over Koblenz.

Fifteen Air Force Italy-based heavy bombers attacked the Rosenheim railway yards, located 35 miles southeast of Munich and oil-storage tanks at Regensburg, 60 miles north of Munich. Other targets attacked by 15th AF bombers were the Isotta-Fraschini tank component and motor plant and the Breda arms factory at Milan, Italy.

Corregidor Avengers Land

Reds Capture Belgrade, Drive to Budapest Area

Liberation of Belgrade, capital of Jugoslavia, was completed by Russian and partisan forces yesterday as the Red Army swept on across Hungary to what Brussels Radio called "the outskirts" of Budapest.

Meanwhile, Berlin made repeated announcements of a large-scale Soviet offensive into East Prussia along a front stretching from northern Poland to the southern coast of the Baltic Sea.

The liberation of Belgrade was announced by Marshal Stalin in an order of the day which also reported capture of Debreczen, in Hungary, for more than 10 days the scene of a mighty tank battle. Belgrade was freed by Marshal Feodor Tolbukhinx' Third Ukrainian Army and Tito's Jugoslav Army of National Liberation.

Though Moscow was still officially silent on activity in East Prussia, it is known that three Soviet armies are drawn up in a huge pincers around the historic land of the Junkers, extending from Poland north of Warsaw to the Baltic south of Memel.

Mutiny and civil strife inside Budapest appeared to be mounting yesterday. Hungarian soldiers were reported to have joined in street fighting against the Germans, while the Nazi Transocean News Agency announced special courts to handle "panic or disorder."

Write Your Own Caption

Yanks Pouring Into Philippines From 3 Beaches

Gen. Douglas MacArthur returned to the Philippines yesterday as a quarter of a million U.S. fighting men poured ashore virtually unopposed at three beachheads on Leyte Island, in the heart of the archipelago.

Smashing inland with tanks and mobile guns, veterans of Lt. Gen. Walter C. Kreuger's Sixth Army captured Leyte's capital city, Tacloban, and swept on toward the island's largest airfield three miles west.

The Americans, protected by a devastating naval artillery barrage, made simultaneous landings at three points along the island's eastern beaches, and until late in the day—when resistance began to stiffen—they were virtually unopposed.

It was a D-Day against Japan rivalling the D-Day against Germany. Approximately the same number of troops landed on Leyte as landed in Normandy on June 6

Gen. Douglas MacArthur
. . . . he kept his promise . . . .

—but there was no comparison in the cost.

President Roosevelt called the Philippine invasion "the greatest concentration of naval and air power ever concentrated in the Pacific."

President Sergio Osmena and his cabinet returned with MacArthur, and the Philippine government was re-established on its native soil. MacArthur broadcast a call to all

(Continued on Page 4)

Large Type Tells Nation Of Landings

NEW YORK, Oct. 20. — Newspapers all over the country again took out their biggest headline type today to tell the nation that "MacArthur Returns to the Philippines," but generally Main Street's reaction was calm.

Editorials lauded MacArthur for keeping his promise that "I shall return." The New York Times ran a three-column picture of MacArthur with the caption, "General MacArthur Fulfils a Gallant Vow," and in its editorial columns praised the captured defenders of the Philippines who are about to be freed after 2 1/2 years of captivity which "must seem like centuries in the stinking, pestilential Japanese prisons."

Congressmen hailed MacArthur as "miracle man" with "such tools as he had at his disposal."

Sen. Robert R. Reynolds (D.-N.C.) said, "When Gen. MacArthur said he would return to the Philippines, I was confident he would return, and return as a conqueror."

Lucky Life magazine appeared on newsstands this morning with a seven-page feature entitled "War Comes Back to the Philippines." The magazine went to press three days ago.

All Ships 'Salvaged,' Halsey 'Flees' Ahead

PEARL HARBOR, Oct. 20.—Adm. William F. Halsey, commander of the Third Fleet, must have had his tongue in his cheek when he sent re-assurances to Adm. Chester W. Nimitz which Nimitz described as "comforting."

The message said that Halsey "is now retiring toward the enemy following the salvage of all Third Fleet ships reported sunk by Tokyo radio."

7 ★★★★★★★ SPORTS
Wall Street Financial News

BROOKLYN EAGLE

WEATHER—Fair, cooler tonight; cloudy, warmer tomorrow.

103d Year. No. 291. DAILY & SUNDAY • (Copyright 1944 The Brooklyn Eagle, Inc.) • BROOKLYN, N. Y., MONDAY, OCTOBER 23, 1944 • Entered at the Brooklyn Post-office as 2d Class Mail Matter • 3 CENTS IN NEW YORK CITY ELSEWHERE 4 CENTS

LEYTE JAPS FLEE TO HILLS: EAST COAST BASTION FALLS

BALL BACKS ROOSEVELT ON PEACE POLICY

President Has Met Issue Squarely, G. O. P. Senator Declares

Washington, Oct. 23 (U.P.)—Senator Joseph H. Ball, (R., Minn.) said today that on the basis of President Roosevelt's stand on foreign policy "I shall vote for and support Mr. Roosevelt" in the Nov. 7 election.

Ball, a strong advocate of close international co-operation to maintain peace, had posed three questions concerning that issue and said the answers to them would determine whether he would vote for Mr. Roosevelt or for Governor Dewey.

"President Roosevelt in his Saturday night speech capped this record (American leadership in the war) of action by meeting squarely and unequivocably the two vital and controversial issues on which the isolationists kept us out of the League of Nations and will fight our entry into the United Nations security organization," Ball said in a prepared statement.

"He insisted that the United Nations organization be formed without delay, before hostilities cease, and that it be granted power to use military force against future aggressors without requiring individual approach of each member nation.

"Governor Dewey has opposed de-l-y but has not met squarely the second vital issue. He has spoken for a strong international security organization, but in each speech has so worded his commitment that both isolationists and internationalists could find comfort and support in what he said. A substantial part of his support is talking straight isolationist doctrine to the country."

Ball said Mr. Roosevelt "is in a position to receive a clear and tremendously forceful mandate on this great issue from the American people," but "Governor Dewey's mandate would be confused and weak and his leadership hampered by a serious division among his own supporters."

"On that basis I shall vote for and support President Roosevelt," Ball said.

Leyte Island Hero Offers Silver Star For Dog's Return

The love which Sgt. Michael Ryan, of 1998 New York Ave., the first man to plant the American flag on the beachhead during last week's invasion of Leyte Island in the Philippines, bears for his chow-and-coolie dog, Blinky, is so strong that he has instructed his wife, Frances, to give a highly coveted reward for the animal's return.

In a letter home he advises Mrs. Ryan to offer either the Silver Star, which General MacArthur awarded him for valorous conduct in rescuing under fire a wounded superior officer during the American attack on the Admiralty Islands or $100 in cash.

"Blinky and I were inseparable pals and his loss was the worst news I have received since I've been overseas," he told his wife. "Some of my fondest memories here in these jungles have been of that little dog. I have been looking forward to seeing him on my return home."

Firemen Battle Blaze In Church on 5th Ave.

A vigilant policeman and fast working firemen saved the 90-year-old Marble Collegiate Church at 5th Ave. and 29th St., Manhattan, from serious damage yesterday. Fire broke out in the wall of the organ loft above the 5th Ave. entrance and sfoke pouring from the loft was seen by a policeman, who turned in an alarm. The fire was extinguished before it had spiraled into the interior wooden framework of the 150-foot steeple, but a Tiffany stained glass window was ruined and hymnals and music scores were burned.

A number of service men and women who were guests at dinner served after the morning service were still in the building. At the evening service the pastor, the Rev. Dr. Norman Vincent Peale, called for special prayers of thanksgiving for the quick checking of the fire.

Favors Postal Pay Boost

Representative William B. Barry of Queens stated today he was "very strongly in favor of the House bill to raise the pay of postal employes by $400 a year."

Eagle Staff photo

ACCUSED AS A MATA HARI—Marie Koedel was seized today charged with spying on ships and cargo loadings on the Port of New York docks for the German government. Others, left to right, are Acting U. S. Attorney T. Vincent Quinn, Deputy U. S. Marshal George Reiss and Commissioner Epstein.

Pretty Ex-Boro Woman, Dad Held as Ship Spies

Charge Pair Sent Information on Loadings And Port Activity to Nazis Before the War

Exhibiting complete nonchalance, pretty Marie H. Koedel was arraigned before U. S. Commissioner Martin C. Epstein in the Brooklyn Federal Building today and held in $$25,000 bail on a charge of having conspired to violate the espionage law in obtaining and forwarding to German drops information concerning ships and their cargoes leaving the Port of New York between Oct. 1, 1939, and Oct. 25, 1941.

She was arrested today at her home, 542 W. 112th St., Manhattan, by FBI agents, at the same time that her father, Simon E. Koedel, was taken into custody by Government agents at Huntington, W. Va. The elder Koedel will be brought here for arraignment on a similar charge.

The woman gave her age as 26 and said she was an "operator" but did not specify in what field. She wore a gray corduroy modish styled coat, a black wool jumper dress, a white blouse, tan stockings and black oxfords.

There was a slight flush on her cheeks, under her thick, black wavy hair, as Acting U. S. Attorney T. Vincent Quinn asked Commissioner Epstein to fix the heavy bail, explaining that the Government regarded the case as one of importance which, had the offense occurred during wartime, could be punished with the death penalty. She now faces a maximum penalty of 20 years. She is about 5 feet 9 inches tall and weighs about 125 pounds.

According to Mr. Quinn, the girl was born in Brooklyn while her father, a native of Germany, has been a naturalized citizen for many years.

DE GAULLE REGIME IS RECOGNIZED BY THE ALLIES

Action Ends Long Controversy—Moscow Names Ambassador

Washington, Oct. 23 (U.P.)—The United States today recognized Gen. Charles de Gaulle's regime as the provisional government of the French Republic.

(London, Moscow and Ottawa announced similar action. Radio Moscow said Alexander Bogomoloff had been named Ambassador to Paris. Bogomoloff formerly was Soviet envoy to De Gaulle.)

The announcement by Acting Secretary of State Edward R. Stettinius Jr. brought to a close a long controversy over diplomatic recognition of De Gaulle's group as a provisional government.

Stettinius said in a statement that notice of recognition had been sent to the French Provisional Government and that Jefferson Caffery will, if agreeable to the provisional government, assume the duties of Ambassador to France.

"This action on the part of the United States Government is in harmony with its policy toward France as publicly enunciated from time to time by the President and the Secretary of State," Stettinius said.

After De Gaulle's visit to Washington last July, President Roosevelt announced the United States would recognize DeGaulle's group as "the French de facto authority." Since then De Gaulle and his associates have considered themselves as the provisional government and have urged the Allies grant them such recognition.

Most Criminals Shun Church, Report Shows

But Probation Figures Reveal 99.83 Percent Of Them Profess Faith in Some Religion

"Religion played but a minor part, apparently, in shaping the characters of our defendants."

With this statement Edmond FitzGerald's report to the county judges of Brooklyn summarizes religion in crime in Brooklyn. However, the figures he gives have great interest.

Mr. FitzGerald, who is chief probation officer of Brooklyn, has submitted an annual report on crime in Brooklyn that goes into the subject in a manner never attempted before. In yesterday's Brooklyn Eagle those portions of the report dealing with the work of the judges themselves was gone into extensively.

In treating with religious and neighborhood aspects of the report, the Brooklyn Eagle is guided by the important deductions that can be made from objective study, isolation of causes and eventually reduction of crime.

In the table giving the races and religions of persons convicted of crime in Brooklyn, a quick glance down the right-hand column of total percentages shows at once that the highest number of convicted criminals in 1943 were Protestants, with 47.82 percent. No attempt was

Continued on Page 2

KIDNAP SCARE ENDS WHEN BORO CHILD IS FOUND WITH RELATIVES

Joanne Dellanorte, 11, of 515 Bushwick Ave., who created a kidnap scare and caused a search of cellars and roofs in her neighborhood last night when she failed to return home after an afternoon's call, was discovered at 7:30 a.m. today sleeping at the home of an aunt, Mrs. Rachel Levy, 2060 66th Street.

The girl was last seen around her home at 1:30 p.m. Sunday when she left for a walk. When she had not returned home late last night her mother notified police and an emergency squad from the Greenpoint police station began a search.

This morning after telephoning friends and neighbors, the girl's mother, Mrs. Jean Dellanorte, called Mrs. Levy.

She was told Joanne appeared at the Levy home at 9:30 p.m. yesterday, saying she had been to a movie and was hungry. After feeding the child, Mrs. Levy put her to bed, believing Mrs. Dellanorte knew of the girl's whereabouts.

F. D. R. Carries 6th A. D.; Poll Rating Now 54.1%

By JOSEPH H. SCHMALACKER

President Roosevelt boosted his standing in the Brooklyn Eagle's Presidential straw poll today by carrying the 6th A. D., in the latest batch of the poll's returns.

The district, situated in the upper Williamsburg section and recently enlarged under the State Reapportionment Law to include the Lafayette-Washington Ave. area, went to the fourth term nominee by 60.15 percent to Governor Dewey's 39.85.

As a result, President Roosevelt climbs from 53.5 percent, his previous standing in the overall poll, to 54.1 percent with a corresponding loss to Governor Dewey from 46.5 percent to 45.9.

Mr. Roosevelt carried all but two of the seven localities of the 6th A. D., which the Eagle's straw poll

Continued on Page 2

Apartment Superintendent Found Beaten to Death

Ernest Gibson, 47, superintendent of 132 W. 117th St., Manhattan, was found dead in his bed today. Gibson's head had been bashed in, apparently with a piece of lead pipe found near by.

Ask French to Fight Japs

Paris, Oct. 23 (U.P.)—The War Ministry yesterday called on all reserve officers and noncommissioned soldiers to volunteer for service in the war against Japan after the defeat of Germany.

JAMAICA RESULTS

1—Plucky Grip 12.80-7.20-5.10, xTraceman 41.30-17.30, Circus Flag 13.00. x-Field. (Off 1:49)

Laurel Park Results

Kimberley, first; Brides Bisquit, second; Chance Ace, third.

British Clamp Assault Arc On Railway Hub in Holland

Smash 2 Miles To Peril Nazis' Front in Area

By J. EDWARD MURRAY

Supreme Headquarters, A. E. F., Paris, Oct. 23 (U.P.)—British armor and infantry plunged forward more than two miles against weakening resistance today to within three and one-half miles of Hertogenbosch, hub of the biggest transport network in south-central Holland.

Lt. Gen. Sir Miles C. Dempsey's 2d Army forces, advancing under cover of a 200-gun bombardment through the gray Autumn gloom, were clamping an assault arc on Hertogenbosch, the capture of which would imperil the stubborn Nazi stand in southwestern Holland.

The British push on Hertogenbosch gave powerful impetus to the Allied campaign to clear the Schelde estuary and open up the sea lanes to Antwerp. Canadian forces had captured Breskens and Draaibrug, main strongpoints on the south bank of the estuary, and all but one of the German batteries on the north shore had been smashed.

Three-Way Drive Gains

United Press correspondent Ronald Clark reported from the British front that a three-pronged drive on Hertogenbosch was gaining steadily in all sectors.

"There is little sign that the enemy has sufficient forces to do more than slow our advance," Clark reported. Thickly-sown land mines and the network of waterways lacing the damp ground appeared to be doing more than the German troops to slow the British.

The speedy tightening of the Canadian arc around the German pocket on the south bank raised hopes that the Allies soon may be able to force the Schelde and exploit their capture of Antwerp, probably the most important port yet seized for the reinforcement and supply of armies marching on Berlin.

Nazis Hurling Robots

The American 1st Army, rounding up enemy stragglers northeast of newly captured Aachen, reported the Germans had begun using robot bombs in quantity in the Aachen sector, for the first time on any fighting front, presumably in an attempt to throw any American prep-

Continued on Page 7

PUNCHES HEAD OFF HITLER—Pfc. Frank Thomas of 84-12 Penelope Ave., Forest Hills, thought he was much better looking than Adolf Hitler. To prove it, the Yank thrust his helmeted head through the appropriate part of an oil painting of the Fuehrer found in an abandoned Gestapo headquarters in Aachen, Germany.

Cop Pleads Guilty In Queens Robbery

Four men, including Patrolman George J. Lutzel, 40, of 115-31 197th St., St. Albans, Queens, attached to the E. 5th St. station, Manhattan, pleaded guilty today before Judge Peter T. Farrell in County Court, Long Island City, Queens, to a charge of second degree robbery in connection with the theft on the night of May 17, 1942, of a safe containing about $15,000 from the office of the United Parcel Service, Inc., at 132-05 Merrick Road, St. Albans.

The other men who pleaded guilty with the policeman were Walter F. Evans, 36, of 4 Frank St., Valley Stream; James J. Saccardo, 30, now serving a term of 25 to 48 years in State's Prison for a Brooklyn tavern robbery, and Thomas A. La Barca, 25, of 40-45 99th St., Corona, an Army Air Force private.

L. I. R. R. COMMUTERS DELAYED 8 TO 28 MIN.

Commuters on the Long Island Railroad were delayed in arriving at the Pennsylvania Station today when a "jumper" electrical connection went bad and stopped Train 89 after leaving Babylon at 6:29 a.m. After 28 minutes delay the train proceeded, running on express schedule from Wantagh to Springfield Gardens. Six following trains were from eight to 28 minutes late.

Soviet Press Again Quotes Iran Papers on Oil Issue

Moscow, Oct. 23 (U.P.)—The official Communist party newspaper Pravda today displayed prominently quotations from Teheran newspapers attacking the Iranian Government for its refusal to grant Russia oil concessions in Northern Iran.

It was the third time within a week that the Russian press printed selected comments from Iranian publications criticizing Premier Mahomed Saed's allegedly anti-Soviet policy toward the disputed oil concessions.

Reds Take Key Rail Hub In East Prussia Drive

Nazis Admit Loss of Goldap to Soviet Forces Pounding Toward Insterburg

By ROBERT MUSEL

London, Oct. 23 (U.P.)—The German high command today acknowledged the loss of the East Prussian rail and highway hub of Goldap to Russian forces pounding westward across German soil along three main railroads leading to Insterburg and the great supply fortress of Koenigsberg.

Nazi broadcasts indicated the Red Army had driven some 25 miles into East Prussia in a broadside campaign to open the way to Koenigsberg and was ripping up the Nazi defenses in a battle of mounting ferocity.

The reported fall of Goldap, key anchor of the German positions northeast of the historic Masurian Lakes, apparently cracked the strongest core of resistance below Insterburg, 30 miles to the northwest.

House-to-House Fighting

A Berlin communique said Goldap had been evacuted and other Nazi reports told of violent house-to-house fighting in the rail junction center. Its reported fall released the Russian besiegers to swing north toward Insterburg and Koenigsberg or south toward Lyck in a bid to collapse defenses of southeastern East Prussia.

Neither the Soviet press nor the official Russian communique had yet reported the offensive which German reports indicated had penetrated up to 20 miles inside the Reich proper.

But a dispatch from Henry Shapiro, United Press correspondent in Moscow, said battles "of far-reaching consequence" were being fought in East Prussia and that an announcement appeared imminent.

Three Drives Converging

The three drives into East Prussia were converging on Insterburg from the north, where the border city of Tilsit was under Red artil-

Continued on Page 7

C. I. O. Chief Takes Credit For Formation of P. A. C.

Pittsburgh, Oct. 23 (U.P.) — Philip Murray, chairman of the Congress of Industrial Organizations, in a speech defending the Political Action Committee, told a meeting of 2,000 P. A. C. workers meeting here yesterday, that he "assumed full responsibility" to the C. I. O. for the formation of the P. A. C. and said he recommended it to the C. I. O. before Sidney Hillman appeared on the scene.

91 Boro, L. I. Men Are Casualties

The War Department today made public the names of 84 Brooklyn, Queens and Long Island men killed in action in the Asiatic, Central Pacific and European areas. The Navy Department listed three local men dead and four wounded. Lists of local casualties are on Page 13.

Forest Hills Flier One of 83 Rescued From Jap Prison

Lt. Bert Schwarz, formerly of 96-11 65th Road, Forest Hills, was one of 83 American officers and men rescued from Japanese prison camps several weeks ago after a Jap transport was sunk off the Philippines by American arms, it was reported today.

Lt. Schwarz not only survived two and a half years' imprisonment but he escaped being machine-gunned when Japs opened fire on the prisoners struggling in the water after the transport was sunk. About 30 prisoners were killed in the water, General MacArthur announced.

Mr. and Mrs. Max Schwarz, the bomber pilot's parents, received their first reliable communication from him today when they got a seven-word cablegram saying that he was well and hoped to be home soon.

Autos Kill 2 in Boro Over the Weekend

Two Brooklyn pedestrians were killed by automobiles over the weekend. Mrs. Bella Kaufman, 52, of 599 Midwood St., was struck by a car which police said was driven by Joseph Greene of 130-33 Lefferts Boulevard, Richmond Hill. Thomas Olsen, 49, of 255 16th St., was killed by a hit-and-run driver for whom 5th Ave. station police have sent out a general alarm.

PALO SEIZED BY BATTALION OF AMERICANS

Capture of Hill 522 Silences Mortar Fire Against Invaders

By WILLIAM B. DICKINSON

General MacArthur's Headquarters, Leyte, Oct. 23 (U.P.)—American troops, slashing westward from their 20-mile beachhead on Leyte, today drove the Japanese toward the interior hills and jungles and consolidated a continuous coastal zone to a minimum depth of five miles all the way from Dulag north to Tacloban.

Capture of Palo, Leyte's second city, was accomplished Saturday in a whirlwind drive by less than a battalion of American infantrymen who drove forward so fast they didn't even take time out to send back a progress report.

Palo lies two and a half miles inland from the coast and about six miles south of San Ricardo. It is a city of 25,000 population and had been the last Japanese stronghold on the east coast road.

Capture Hill Height

In clearing out Palo the Americans also captured Hill 522, a commanding height at the northern end of the beachhead from which the Japanese had poured mortar fire at the invasion troops.

Hill 522, which dominates "Red Beach," where the northernmost landing was made on Leyte, was taken with little difficulty after cruisers and destroyers lying off shore plastered the Japanese batteries and navy dive bombers knocked out the Japanese emplacements.

Capture of Palo trapped a group of Japanese defense remnants between the town and the beachhead.

Japs in Pillboxes

The Japanese had built a series of pillboxes along the river which runs into Leyte Gulf at Palo. After the pillboxes had been worked over by artillery the infantry inched forward and finished off the Japanese.

Palo was taken by the elements of the 24th Division of the U. S. Army 10th Corps.

With the Japanese fleeing to the interior of the island, MacArthur said their plight would become "acute" due to lack of supplies.

Doughboys already had seized all but one point on the east coast road between Tacloban and Dulag, 20 miles to the south. Steadily expanding their positions everywhere, they enfiltrated and enveloped the Japanese lines in the same way the enemy had broken American resistance nearly three years ago.

Bombers Blast Path

Artillery, tanks and swarms of carried-based dive bombers blasted out a path of advance while flamethrowers firing into the embrasures cremated stubborn defenders of concrete pillboxes who resisted all other assault.

(A German DNB dispatch from

Continued on Page 7

Cleveland Fire Toll Might Reach 200

Cleveland, Oct. 23 (U.P.)—Coroner Samuel Gerber predicted today the death toll of Cleveland's worst fire might reach 2000 as firemen and volunteer workers resumed the task of searching the ruins for additional victims.

While 112 persons already were known to have been killed, Gerber pointed out that "at least 30 or 40" more bodies alone would be found in the wrecked buildings of the East Ohio Gas Company, where a storage tank explosion Friday set aflame a half-mile square area of the city's east side.

WHERE TO FIND IT

THE WEATHER

Sunny and warmer today; clear and not so cool tonight; Thursday fair with moderate temperature.

Detailed Weather Report Page 34

Read The Baltimore News-Post for complete, accurate war coverage. It is the only Baltimore newspaper possessing the three great wire services—

ASSOCIATED PRESS
INTERNATIONAL NEWS SERVICE
UNITED PRESS

THE BALTIMORE NEWS-POST

AN INDEPENDENT NEWSPAPER

The Largest Evening Circulation in the Entire South

EXTRA

10-Star Edition

VOL. CXLV.—NO. 148 | Entered as second-class matter at Baltimore Postoffice. | WEDNESDAY EVENING, OCTOBER 25, 1944 | PRICE 3 CENTS

JAP FLEET ROUTED ROOSEVELT ANNOUNCES

Receives Report From Admiral Halsey On Pacific Sea Battle

WASHINGTON, Oct. 25—(U. P.).—President Roosevelt today announced receipt of a dispatch from Admiral William F. Halsey, Jr., saying that "the Japanese navy in the Philippine area has been defeated, seriously damaged and routed by the United States Navy in that area."

WASHINGTON, Oct. 25—(U. P.)—Admiral Ernest J. King, commander-in-chief of the U. S. fleet, said today that practically the whole Japanese fleet is involved in the sea-air battle still raging in the Philippines area. He told newsmen at Secretary of Navy James Forrestal's weekly press conference that at least one of the three Japanese columns—the one in the Sibuyan sea—was so seriously damaged that it "turned back." He added, however, that "this doesn't mean it is going to stay turned back."

King said he could not give any information beyond that contained in Admiral

NEW YORK, Oct. 25—(I. N. S.).—Gen. Douglas MacArthur in a special statement broadcast from field press headquarters at Leyte said that the Japanese fleet has suffered the "most crushing defeat of the war." Reuter's reported the statement from London.

Chester W. Nimitz's early morning communique. The Admiral said:

"Presumably the Jap doesn't like the Leyte landings and is going to try to interfere with them."

King said that all the information he had to date was that only U. S. carrier aircraft were engaging the Japanese fleet. When it was pointed out that Nimitz's communique left this point in doubt, he insisted that that was all he could say.

Earlier, a Navy spokesman had said the language of Nimitz's communique could be interpreted as meaning a surface engagement was in progress.

BATTLE STILL RAGING

King said the battle was still going on. The first of the Japanese columns was picked up by American submarines in the vicinity of Palawan Island, in the West Central Philippines, he said, adding:

"The inference is they came from Singapore, although we don't have anything to support this."

King was asked:

"Would it be foolhardy for our forces to give chase to the Japanese fleet in the inland seas of the Philippines?"

He replied:

"If you get into hot pursuit you disregard a lot of factors that you would consider carefully in cold blood."

King conceded that such a chase would be hazardous because of the danger of mines, submarines and aircraft, not to mention the restrictions on movement.

"QUITE REMARKABLE"

He added that it was "quite remarkable" that the Japanese should have tried to move through the narrow waters of the central Philippines and that "we still can't fathom the reason" behind

Continued on Page 2, Column 3.

SCENE OF PHILIPPINES BATTLE—Numbers indicate Jap naval forces moving in on the Philippines to attack American forces which invaded Leyte. First enemy force appeared in Sibuyan sea, a second in Sulu sea and a third southeast of Formosa. Arrows indicate U. S. and Jap moves.

FRANCE, SPAIN AGREE

PARIS, Oct. 25—(A. P.).—France and Spain have agreed to re-establish normal diplomatic relations despite ideological differences between the De Gaulle and Franco regimes and tension over frontier incidents, well-informed diplomats said today.

SEEKS ANNULMENT

DENVER, Oct. 24—(A. P.).—Mrs. Francis Morris French, twenty-three, Chicago, who was arrested October 20 on a bigamy charge, has filed suit to annul her marriage to First Lieutenant David J. French, Army fighter pilot.

HULL'S CONDITION SAME

WASHINGTON, Oct 25—(A.P.). The State Department said today that Secretary Hull's condition remains unchanged at Bethesda (Md.) Naval Hospital.

VICTORIA'S DAUGHTER ILL

LONDON, Oct. 25—(I. N. S.).—Prince Beatrice, eighty-seven, only surviving child of Queen Victoria, was reported gravely ill today in a bulletin issued by her physicians.

VERY LATEST NEWS

(Race Results From Howard Sports Daily, Inc.)

AT LAUREL

Seventh — High Straight, $7.10, $4.00, $2.90; Dancing Archie, $4.90, $3.30; Kuota, $3.60.

Eighth—Sun Target, 1; Consignment, 2; Miss Kalola, 3.

AT EMPIRE CITY

Seventh — Sammy Angott, $7.60, $3.90, $3.00; Blue Whistler, $5.10, $3.40; Peace Fleet, $2.80.

AT ROCKINGHAM

Seventh—Aircraft, $7.40, $4.40, $2.60; Cab Sir, $7.60, $3.60; Plane Spotter, $3.40.

Eighth — Identic, $6.80, $3.20, $2.60; Gold Bill, $2.80, $2.40; Keene Advice, $3.20.

AT CHURCHILL DOWNS

Fifth—Civil Liberty, $3.80, $2.80, $2.80; Wise Paisano, $4.80, $4.00; Zig Zag, $9.80.

Sixth—Silvestra, won; Navy Cross, 2d; Zacapet, 3d.

AT SPORTSMAN'S PARK

Fifth—Bob's Dream, $19.40, $7.40, $5.40; Happy Pilot, $4.40, $3.00; Gold Regnant, $5.20.

U. S. SUPERFORTS BOMB OMURA

WASHINGTON, Oct. 25—(A. P.).—B-29 Superfortresses in medium force bombed the Japanese aircraft assembly and repair installations at Omura, on Kyushu Island, with "good" results today, the War Department reported. One of the big bombers failed to return.

British Trap Nazi Force In Holland

SUPREME H. Q., A. E. F., PARIS, Oct. 25—(U. P.).—Dutch front reports said the strategic transport center of Hertogenbosch fell today to British Second Army forces clamping some 50,000 Germans in a trap against the lower Maas river. The only possible escape routes from the Dutch pocket were three secondary bridges to the west, but they were described as incapable of handling heavy military traffic.

By KINGSBURY SMITH
International News Service Staff Correspondent.

SUPREME HEADQUARTERS, Allied Expeditionary Force, Oct. 25.—Gen. Dwight D. Eisenhower today wrote off the invaded Dutch communications center of Hertogenbosch as a base of any importance to the Germans and a rapid crumbling of all Nazi defenses in Western Holland seemed to be in progress.

A new British threat is developing westward from Best to the Nazi headquarters town of Tilburg, which the Germans were reported evacuating.

Hertogenbosch has been written off as an enemy supply center, headquarters said, as the railway lines connecting the town with the rest of Holland have been severed to the north and south.

In the Scheldt estuary area,

Continued on Page 2, Column 6.

Soviet Units Cross Into Norway

By NATALIA RENE

MOSCOW, Oct. 25—(I. N. S.). Victorious Russian forces slashed forward on widely separated sectors of the Eastern front today, invading Nazi-held Norway to seize the Arctic port of Kirkenes, clearing all Nazi resistance from Northern Transylvania and bleeding crack Wehrmacht divisions white in the bloody invasion of East Prussia.

Two special orders of the day from Marshal Joseph Stalin disclosed that Russian troops had scored two new triumphs.

AXIS CLEARED OUT

The first order, addressed to Marshal Rodion Y. Malinovsky, commander of the Second Ukrainian Army, revealed that Soviet capture of the Nazi strongholds of Satu Mare and Careii in Northern Transylvania had cleared that territory of Axis resistance.

A second order announced that Far Northern units of the Red Army had spearheaded across the Norwegian frontier to wrest the vital port of Kirkenes from Nazi hands.

REDS BLOCK RAIDS

As Marshal Stalin issued his special orders of the day on these victories Soviet legions smashing through German positions on the

Continued on Page 2, Column 8.

Jap Carrier, Two Cruisers Sunk In Fight

PEARL HARBOR, Oct. 25—(U. P.).—**The American Third Fleet has sunk at least one Japanese aircraft carrier, two cruisers and a destroyer and damaged a dozen other warships, including five or six battleships, in a showdown battle with three enemy naval forces for control of Philippine waters, it was revealed today. "General action is continuing," Admiral Chester W. Nimitz, commander of the Pacific fleet, announced in a communique disclosing that probably the greatest air-sea battle of the war had been joined southwest, northwest and north of invaded Leyte Island. Japanese shore-based aircraft, supporting enemy fleet units, sank the 10,000-ton American aircraft carrier Princeton, but her captain, 133 other officers and 1,227 enlisted men were rescued, Nimitz said. He listed no other American losses.**

Contact between the Third Fleet and two of the naval forces apparently was limited, at least initially, to aircraft, but the communique said the Third Force had been "brought to action" between the Philippines and Formosa.

NAVAL FORCES 25 MILES APART

In naval terminology, "brought to action" usually means an engagement between surface ships. Japanese propaganda broadcasts also said that the first large-scale battle between surface ships of the two fleets in two years was under way. Berlin said at one time the forces were within 25 miles or less of one another.

The communique said Admiral William F. Halsey's Third Fleet, at last bringing the Japanese fleet to battle,

Continued on Page 2, Column 1.

Daily Double (Sir Echo / Recce) Paid $12.90

LAUREL CHARTS

By Associated Press.

Weather clear. Track fast.

FIRST RACE—Purse $2,000. Claiming prices $2,500 to $2,250. For 3-year-olds and up. Six furlongs. Start good. Won easily, place driving. Went to post at 1.47. Off at 1.48. Winner b g 6, by Trace Call-Singing Heart by Strolling Player. Owner MRS. J. V. STEWART. Trainer J. V. STEWART. Value to winner $1,300, second $400, third $200, fourth $100. Time 1.15.

	Wt.	Post	St.	¼	½	Str.	Fin.	Jockeys	Odds
Sir Echo	113	7	1	5¹	3²	1ʰ	1¹½	A. Snelling	$1.55
Road Scraper	112	1	4	1³	1²	3¹½	2¹½	E. Skjeie	7.95
Fleetest	108	5	6	2¹	2½	2¹	3²	N. Jemas	74.15
Victory Blue	116	3	5	3ⁿ	4¹	4¹	4³	M. Bletzacker	2.45
Fairly Fly	115	12	9	7²	6¹	6¹	5½	C. Erickson	53.10
Attune	109	4	8	4½	5²	5½	6½	R. Meade	17.00
Chat Hopkins	110	2	7	6¹	7²	7²	7½	R. Arduini	34.75
Beneva	111	9	12	12	10³	8⁵	8⁴	A. Kirkland	7.00
Flying Kilts	117	8	2	8½	11⁴	11³	9¹	C. Kirk	129.85
Bell Soma	112	11	3	9¹	8²	10½	10²	D. Dodson	15.10
Discmont	114½	10	11	11⁸	9½	9½	11⁵	R. Wright	270.80
Huntlands	115	6	10	10½	12	12	12	J. McCoy	199.45

$2 Mutuels Paid—

Sir Echo	$5.10	$3.40	$3.00
Road Scraper		5.90	4.60
Fleetest			14.90

Sir Echo was well placed from start while racing on outside of leaders, responded when placed to drive and disposed of Road Scraper to win with speed in reserve. Road Scraper went to front early, drew out but could not resist winner while closing gamely. Fleetest was rushed to get closest to pace early and tired gradually in closing test. Victory Blue had no excuses. Fairly Fly raced wide and closed willingly. Attune had early speed and tired. Chat Hopkins was through early. Beneva was off slowly and had no chance. Bell Soma dropped out of it. Huntlands ran off three-quarters before start.

Handle, $64,261. Daily Double pool, $36,126.

Continued on Page 31, Column 4.

Temperatures

12 Mid., 55	9 A. M., 52
1 A. M., 54	10 A. M., 54
2 A. M., 53	11 A. M., 56
3 A. M., 52	12 Noon, 60
4 A. M., 51	1 P. M., 63
5 A. M., 50	2 P. M., 65
6 A. M., 49	3 P. M., 66
7 A. M., 48	4 P. M., 69
8 A. M., 49	5 P. M., 69

LINA MAY SEEK DIVORCE

HOLLYWOOD, Oct. 25—(I. N. S.).—Lina Basquette, screen actress and dancer, soon may seek a Mexican divorce from her flier-husband, Henry Mollison.

NEWS-POST

Dewey Flays New Deal:

Roosevelt Labor Policies Scored

(Text of Governor Thomas E. Dewey's speech in Minneapolis last night will be found on Page 9.)

By LEO W. O'BRIEN
International News Service Staff Correspondent.

MILWAUKEE, Wis., Oct. 25.—Gov. Thomas E. Dewey left Milwaukee today for a major night speech at Chicago after telling an open-air crowd of 8,000 persons that under the Roosevelt Administration "labor has been booted from pillar to post on every bit of business it has had with the Government."

The Republican Presidential nominee, greeted by crowds in excess of 26,000 during his three-hour stop in Milwaukee, declared that nothing will be so helpful in

Governor Thomas E. Dewey's speech in Chicago tonight will be broadcast at 10 o'clock by WCAO.

achieving an early victory in the war as to "stop the quarreling, fumbling, waste and confusion in Washington."

Summarizing the Democratic campaign to date, Governor Dewey

Continued on Page 2, Column 7.

Man Spricht Deutsch
Durchfahrt verboten.
Doorshfahrt ferboten.
No thoroughfare

THE STARS AND STRIPES
Daily Newspaper of U.S. Armed Forces in the European Theater of Operations

Ici On Parle Français
Quelle heure est-il?
Kel UR ay-t-EEL?
What time is it?

Vol. 1—No. 106 1 Fr. New York—PARIS—London 1 Fr. Saturday, Nov. 4, 1944

All Belgium Is Liberated

From German Cradle to German Grave

Hitler reaches cradlewards in a desperate attempt to defend Holy German Soil. Heiling youngsters, aged nine to 15, are receiving instructions from a German Army officer in the nomenclature and firing technique of a six-barreled Nebelwerfer.

On the other end of the faltering pendulum are the seamy-faced, tired oldsters. Preparing to fill the gaps in the Wehrmacht's lines as they already have on the Russian and Western fronts, men pressed into the German People's Army present a ragged platoon front.

First Army Edges on In Assault

Canadians completed the liberation of Belgium yesterday. They wiped out the last German resistance south of the Scheldt River at Zeebrugge. In Holland, north of the river approach to Antwerp, Canadian infantry and British Marines, who landed on Walcheren Island two days ago, captured Flushing and the commander of its German garrison.

In Germany, U.S. First Army patrols linked up beyond the village of Vossenack, southeast of Aachen, and dust which settled on the debris of wrecked houses and cratered streets in the village attested to the fierceness of the U.S. attack which had passed that way.

Heavy Nazi Opposition

Lt. Gen. Courtney H. Hodges' new assault, which began early Thursday and gained two miles, ran into heavy German opposition late yesterday. Front reports said the attack continued to progress, but no details of new gains were given.

It was disclosed at SHAEF, meanwhile, that First Army units are all the way through the steel and concrete crust of the Siegfried Line between Aachen and Geilenkirchen. A heavily fortified interior zone confronts Lt. Gen. Hodges' men, however, all the way to the Rhine.

New Bridgehead

In Western Holland, U.S. troops attacking in moonlight a few hours before yesterday's dawn threw another bridgehead over the River Mark from which they were thrown back two days ago. This time, they hung on in the face of savage attacks from 15th German Army rearguards.

Southward, in the Vosges foothills, Lt. Gen. Alexander Patch's U.S. Seventh Army captured the road junction of Baccarat, Associated Press said. Three villages north of it also were taken on the road to the Schirmeck Pass.

Chinese Take Jap Fort on Burma Road

Chinese troops yesterday captured the Burma Road town of Lungling, the last Japanese bastion remaining athwart the route of the new highway being pushed into China across northern Burma from Ledo in India.

At the same time Superfortresses from India made a heavy daylight attack on rail yards at the important Japanese supply base of Rangoon, in southern Burma, in support of the new Allied offensive in Burma. Washington announced that the B29s, on the comparatively short haul, carried "the largest individual bomb loads ever lifted in aerial warfare" but their weight was not disclosed.

The new Ledo road being built by U.S. engineers as the front progresses is designed to link up with the old Burma Road near Lungling, by-passing the southern portion of the old Burma Road from Lungling to Mandalay in Burmese territory now held by the enemy.

Drives on Leyte, Samar Near Goals

GEN. MacARTHUR'S HQ., Leyte, Nov. 3 (AP).—Gen. MacArthur's communiqué today announced that "the end of the Leyte-Samar campaign is in sight," and that Japanese casualties there now have risen to more than 30,000.

American forces made a junction in Cariaga, on the northwest coast, driving enemy remnants west and south toward Ormoc.

Pilot Gives Life to Avert Plane Dive on Boston

BOSTON, Nov. 3 (ANS).—Ensign J. J. Sheehy, of Far Rockaway, N.Y., chose to die rather than bail out of his plane over a densely populated section of Boston last night when motor trouble developed.

"I don't want to bail out—someone might be hurt if the plane crashes," he radioed the Squantum naval air station. The ship landed in flames on the bank of the Neponset River.

We Pass the Buck Slip

Want Combat? Fight Way Through GI Channels First

By Russell Jones
Stars and Stripes Staff Writer.

For the information of the 1,000-odd guys who have written asking for transfers from non-combat outfits to something more active, there isn't a thing we can do for you except pass on a little advice. And for the information of Pvt. E. Philip Malin, who started the whole thing by saying he was 1A in a 4F outfit and wanted combat, we are mad at you because Lou Rakin, who handles our B-Bag and Help Wanted departments, is so swamped with letters saying the same thing that he is going nuts.

As for Maj. Gen. C. H. Gerhardt, commander of the 29th Division, who fixed it so Malin was transferred to the 29th—well, we don't get mad at generals. Not in print, anyway.

But to get back to these guys who are itching for front-line duty: Reclassification and re-assignment authorities in the Adjutant General's section say that AR 615-200, as amended by Change 1, covers requests for transfers. This AR says SOS men will request through channels to their base section com-

(Continued on Page 4)

French Get U.S. Ships

The U.S. Navy has ceded 60 small vessels to the French Navy, it was announced in Paris yesterday. They included 11 patrol craft, 21 submarine chasers, 20 minesweepers and six tugs.

Reds in Sight Of Budapest

Powerful Soviet tank columns pushed within 20 miles of Budapest yesterday while a Cossack patrol charged to within sight of the city's spires.

Meanwhile panic mounted within the Hungarian capital, hundreds of merchants and wealthy industrialists fleeing before the Red Army's advance.

Budapest would be an attractive prize for the Red Army, providing an ideal supply and communications base for winter operations. There was no indication that the Germans planned to spare the city the ordeal of street-by-street resistance.

To the north, military operations were increasingly hampered by the early arrival of winter. There was heavy snow in East Prussia.

8th Bags 208 Nazi Planes In Record Day

Eighth Air Force heavy bombers and fighters destroyed 208 German aircraft Thursday in a record day's combat closing out a month of operations which heaped 43,000 tons of bombs on already battered Nazi targets.

Official figures, released yesterday, showed that the Eighth's Liberators and Fortresses flew 18,800 sorties over the Continent in October, and accompanying fighter planes another 13,500 sorties—a total 10,000 greater than the Eighth's entire first year of operations, August, 1942, to August, 1943. Bombers were unescorted all the way into Germany and back, however, in that first year.

October losses for the Eighth were 122 bombers and 69 fighters, with last Thursday's bitter battles over the oil refinery targets of Central Germany accounting for a combined fighter-and-bomber loss of 69. Luftwaffe jet-propelled fighters were beaten off in their second serious attack on American forces during the record battle which involved 2,000 U.S. and 400 to 500 German planes.

German fighter losses for the entire month were announced as 119 in air combat and 339 on the ground.

Attacking Siegfried Line areas for the second straight day, more than 150 Ninth Air Force Marauders and Havocs yesterday bombed five bridges without loss.

Ike Honors 4 Air Leaders

By Jules B. Grad
Stars and Stripes Staff Writer.

On a captured German airfield's runway near the twisted wreckage of Ju88s and ME109s, Gen. Eisenhower yesterday honored four Allied air leaders who made possible this symbol of crushing Luftwaffe defeat.

The supreme commander presented to Lt. Gen. Carl A. Spaatz, commanding the United States Strategic Air Forces in Europe, an oak leaf cluster to his Distinguished Service Medal.

The U.S. Legion of Merit's highest order—the degree of chief commander—was awarded to three of the RAF's air chief marshals: Sir Trafford Leigh-Mallory, Sir Arthur Harris and Sir Sholto Douglas.

Gen. Spaatz' mission was the strategic bombardment of German occupied Europe in an effort to soften up the continent for invasion. Harris directed the RAF's bombing contribution to the Allied aerial assault. Leigh-Mallory commanded the air component of the Allied Expeditionary Forces. Douglas headed all British and U.S. air forces in the Middle East.

The High Cost of Fraternizing

SHAEF, Nov. 3 (UP).—It costs an American soldier $25 to $65 if he so much as talks unnecessarily to a German civilian in the Reich.

Talking unnecessarily to Germans is fraternization and Gen. Eisenhower's non-fraternization dictum is now being so rigidly carried out that not the slightest unnecessary contact between Americans and Germans escapes the eyes of MPs. Offending soldiers are disciplined by fines.

The lengths to which the non-fraternization orders were being enforced were revealed here today by Lt. Col. C. P. Russell, of Carthage, Miss., executive officer of the 36th Armored Infantry Regiment of the Third Armored Division.

He said no effort was going to be spared to prevent relaxing soldiers from mingling with German civilians, who increasingly will include German agents hunting military information.

A soldier cannot buy beer outside the mess bar because the purchase assumes talking to a German bartender. Technically, he cannot even ask a German civilian on the street for directions or speak to German kids. He certainly cannot call at a German home socially nor have any contact of any kind with German girls.

The problem of billets has been solved by moving German families in with their neighbors so that soldiers are not billeted with German families.

Specific offenses for which fines have been levied were unavailable but a sergeant accompanying Russell said that GIs now refer jokingly to talking to a German civilian as "the $65 offense."

New York World-Telegram

SCRIPPS-HOWARD

Local Forecast—Today cloudy, occasional sprinkle. Tonight cloudy. Tomorrow cloudy and warmer.

VOL. 77—NO. 110—IN TWO SECTIONS—SECTION ONE. NEW YORK, WEDNESDAY, NOVEMBER 8, 1944 Entered as second-class matter Post Office, New York, N. Y.

ELECTION EXTRA
LATEST NEWS
Five Cents

ROOSEVELT WINS 4TH TERM

Democrats Stronger in Congress

CLOSE RACE IN JERSEY; FISH LOSES

Early Dewey Lead Finally Overcome

New Constitution Rejected; Smith Wins Senate Contest

BULLETIN.

Special to the World-Telegram.

NEWARK, Nov. 8.—Returns from 3353 of the state's 3647 districts today gave President Roosevelt an 18,767-vote lead over Gov. Thomas E. Dewey. The totals were 842,695 to 823,928.

By HERBERT KAMM,
World-Telegram Staff Writer.

NEWARK, Nov. 8.—Democratic Boss Frank Hague, gambling on the highest stakes since he seized power a quarter century ago, clinched his bitter battle against the new state constitution early today and also appeared to have prevented New Jersey's 16 Presidential electoral votes from landing in the Republican column for the first time since 1928.

New Jersey looked safe for Gov. Thomas E. Dewey until shortly before dawn. With 2458 of its 3657 districts reporting, the Republican nominee had 636,140 votes to 612,093 for President Roosevelt, and the general trend of the returns indicated the New York Governor would retain his margin.

GOP Lead Melts.

But then the Hague Hudson County organization uncorked its customary last-minute barrage of votes, and the latest figures gave Gov. Dewey a lead of less than 4000—654,260 to 650,661, with 2582 districts in.

The Hudson County figures, giving President Roosevelt 109,979 votes to Gov. Dewey's 71,814, were a far cry from the tremendous Democratic pluralities Mayor Hague is in the habit of producing. In 1940, for instance, President Roosevelt won New Jersey on the strength of a 101,000-vote advantage in Hudson.

But only 418 of the 658 districts in Hudson had completed their returns at a late hour this morning, and it was believed that Mr. Hague's final tally would compare more favorably with those of past years—perhaps sufficients to keep New Jersey in Democratic ranks nationally.

Smith Elected to Senate.

In the process of his all-out fight against the state Consti-

(Continued on Page Two.)

Results At a Glance

PRESIDENT.

POPULAR VOTE

(About 70 per cent of vote complete).

Roosevelt	17,262,463
Dewey	15,083,592
ELECTORAL vote	
Roosevelt	395
Dewey	136
UNITED STATES SENATOR	
Curran (R)	2,695,587
Wagner (D)	3,106,341

NEW JERSEY CONSTITUTION.

For	381,686
Against	480,503

NEW CONGRESS.

SENATE	
Democrats	50
Republicans	30
Progressives	1
Undecided	15
HOUSE	
Democrats	161
Republicans	62
Progressives	1
American Labor	1
Farmer Labor	0
Undecided	210

COURT OF APPEALS.

Van Voorhis	2,685,546
Dye	2,941,063

MUNICIPAL COURT

MANHATTAN

1st Dist.	
Friedman (Rep.)	15,543
Lupiano (Dem.)	16,417
Rothstein (ALP)	5,848
2nd Dist. (2 vacancies)	
Burnet (Rep.)	22,810
Wahl (Rep.)	22,913
Richman (Dem.)	13,931
Paura (Dem.)	13,577
Schachter (ALP)	2,665
Freedman (ALP)	2,689

BROOKLYN

1st Dist.	
Hays (Rep.)	30,002
Beckinella (Dem., ALP)	35,379

RICHMOND

1st Dist.	
Cosgrove (Rep.)	16,550
McKinney (Dem., ALP)	21,103
2nd Dist.	
La Rocca (Rep.)	16,457
Baker (Dem., ALP)	18,040

COUNTY JUDGE

KINGS COUNTY

Pinto (Rep., ALP)	540,251
Marasco (Dem., L.)	585,541

One Election Dist. missing.

Fish Loses to Bennet After 24-Year Tenure

Special to the World-Telegram.

NEWBURGH, Nov. 8.—Representative Hamilton Fish, pre-Pearl Harbor isolationist who had been repudiated by leaders of his own party, including Gov. Dewey, went down to defeat yesterday for re-election to a 13th term from New York's 29th Congressional District.

Augustus W. Bennett, four-party nominee who lost the Republican designation to Mr. Fish in the new district, comprising Rockland, Orange, Sullivan and Delaware counties, in the August primaries, appeared to have won election by a 5000-vote margin.

Conceding defeat in his headquarters in Newburgh, the tall, stern-faced Mr. Fish declared:

"I believe in the will of the majority, cast in the American way."

Bennett's Second Try.

Mr. Bennett, a lifelong Republican, was the nominee of the Democratic, American Labor, Liberal and Good Government parties. This was his second attempt to unseat Mr. Fish, who formerly represented the 26th (President Roosevelt's) District.

After the veteran Representative, who had served nearly a quarter-century in the lower

Continued on Page Twenty-three.

Dewey Victor At Birthplace

By the Associated Press.

OWOSSO, Mich., Nov. 8.—Complete returns from this central Michigan city in which Gov. Thomas E. Dewey was born gave him 3787 votes to 1947 for President Roosevelt. In 1940 the complete Owosso figures were Roosevelt 2178, Willkie 3040.

'Again, Again and Again,' Says Globe

By the Associated Press.

BOSTON, Nov. 8. — With a headline "Roosevelt Wins, Again, Again and Again," the Boston Globe said today that President Roosevelt would carry Massachusetts by an estimated 135,000 votes.

Roosevelt defeated Wendell Willkie four years ago by a little more than 136,000 votes.

Returns Followed Throughout Russia

By the United Press.

A network of loud speakers was set up in every city in Russia to carry the United States election returns, the American Broadcasting Station in Europe reported, quoting a Moscow correspondent.

Jersey Flier Killed

Special to the World-Telegram.

WASHINGTON, Nov. 8.—Lt. Clarence W. Slutter, 22, Dover, N. J., and his pilot, Lt. John C. Miller, were killed yesterday in a trainer plane crash near Camp Springs Air Base.

Plant Win E Award

Special to the World-Telegram.

LINDEN, N. J., Nov. 8.—The Navy E award was to be presented today to the Eastern Aircraft Division plant here by Vice Adm. Aubrey Fitch, deputy Chief of Naval Operations.

Senate Rule Clinched as Party Gains

Republicans Lose 14 Seats in House; Danaher Defeated

By the Associated Press.

WASHINGTON, Nov. 8. — Democrats today clinched a majority of the Senate and took stronger control of the House of Representatives as well.

The 79th Congress thus will keep its date with destiny next January predominantly Democratic. The President's intimates in the Senate can route important international commitments, perhaps even the final peace treaty, through the legislative machinery.

With election returns drifting in like a paper blizzard, the Democratic party cinched a mathematical majority of the treaty-making, appointment-confirming Senate long before dawn.

By 5 a. m. Democrats had won 14 House seats heretofore held by Republicans.

A fresh charge of Democratic power likewise gives the administration a stepped-up voltage in the other chamber.

The very first Senate turnover toppled John A. Danaher, Connecticut Republican whom Vice President-elect Harry S. Truman had termed an "isolationist." Republicans gained a seat when Iowa's Republican Gov. Bourke B. Hickenlooper took out Guy Gillette.

Hamilton Fish Defeated.

In the House, Hamilton Fish, Republican who long represented Franklin D. Roosevelt's New York home district but not his international policies, fell at last after 24 years in Congress.

Speaker Sam Rayburn of Texas scooted in without opposition, and Rep. Robert Ramspeck of Georgia, the Democratic whip, won handily. On the other hand, Rep. Playwright Clare Boothe Luce traded pointed glares with Mr. Roosevelt and bobbed up a winner in the Fourth Connecticut District.

The re-election of Senator Bob Wagner (D., N. Y.) made numerical Democratic superiority in the upcoming Senate a certainty. Before that the solid South had returned Senators George of Georgia, Overton of Louisiana and Hill of Alabama, and named Olin D. Johnston of South Carolina, Clyde R. Hoey of North Carolina and J. William Fulbright of Arkansas to other Democratic seats.

Senate Majority Leader Barkley of Kentucky zipped in as the Democratic current swept up through the border states. Millard Tydings of Maryland and Elmer Thomas of Oklahoma followed in shortly thereafter. Senators Hayden (D., Ariz.) and Thomas (D., Utah), two other administration first-stringers, also won.

It was Brien McMahon, Norwalk Democrat, who unseated young, erudite John Danaher, Republican wheelhorse.

Morse Elected in Congress.

The Republicans, meanwhile, were making the most of their demonstrated strength in the Midwest and New England to insure the safe return of Senators

Continued on Page Twenty-three.

Still the Champ

This extraordinarily fine likeness of President Roosevelt was made late last night as he spoke to throng gathered before the post office at Poughkeepsie, N. Y. Acme Newspictures.

Roosevelt, Jubilant, Retires at 3:50 A.M.

By MERRIMAN SMITH,
United Press Staff Writer.

HYDE PARK, Nov. 8.—President Roosevelt at 3:50 a. m., EWT, today shoved aside a litter of election charts, dull-pointed pencils and pieces of paper covered with figures and went to bed after going through a familiar experience—being elected President of the United States.

The President was tired, happy and confident. When Gov. Thomas E. Dewey, the Republican candidate, broadcast an admission of defeat about 3:16 a. m., the President sent Gov. Dewey this message:

"His Excellency, Thomas E. Dewey, Governor of New York, Roosevelt Hotel, N. Y.

"I thank you for your statement which I have heard over the air a few minutes ago."

"FRANKLIN D. ROOSEVELT."

Stephen T. Early, White House press secretary, told reporters, however, that the President had received no direct word of concession from Mr. Dewey beyond the broadcast.

Congratulates Truman.

Then the President wrote out some messages of thanks and congratulation for his running mate, Vice President-elect Harry S. Tru-

(Continued on Page Twenty-two.)

Electoral, Popular Vote Cut From 1940; Wagner In Easily; Nye and Danaher Beaten

By RAY GHENT,
World-Telegram Staff Writer.

President Roosevelt did it again for a fourth time, but not by either the electoral or the popular vote margin of 1940, incomplete national returns showed today. New York, however, he may carry by more than 250,000 or better than last time.

Latest returns, slowed up by heavy balloting generally and by the soldier vote count, showed the President ahead in 34 states with 407 electoral votes, while Gov. Dewey was leading in 15 with an electoral total of 124.

In addition to the 10 carried by the late Wendell Willkie in 1940, Mr. Dewey at last reports was leading in Ohio, Oregon, Wisconsin and Wyoming.

The popular vote was showing up closer than the 5,000,000 margin the President had over Mr. Willkie. The Associated Press reporting from 80,795 of the country's 130,810 voting precincts showed this vote to be 18,500,456 for Mr. Roosevelt and 16,240,576 for Mr. Dewey.

The Congressional side of the picture also was incomplete, but some Republican stalwarts went by the board, including Representative Hamilton Fish in this state and Sen. John A. Danaher in Connecticut, while at last reports Sen. Gerald T. Nye was trailing in North Dakota. All these had been labeled isolationist.

Wagner Wins Easily Over Curran.

Sen. Robert F. Wagner won handily over his GOP opponent, Secretary of State Thomas J. Curran, and Judge Marvin Dye of Rochester was victor in the Court of Appeals race against Judge John Van Voorhis, Republican.

New York City did handsomely by the President. The complete tabulation here showed he carried the city by 769,849, compared with 718,800 last time.

The vote here surpassed the fondest hopes of the Democrats. Another surprise was the total of 303,853 rolled up in the city by the newly born Liberal party for Mr. Roosevelt, while its foe, the left wing American Labor party, also outdid itself to return him a record 388,608. These two groups more than made up the margin needed by Mr. Roosevelt to carry the state.

The Roosevelt vote on three lines in the city totaled 2,039,932 to 1,270,083 for Mr. Dewey.

Manhattan gave the President an edge of 247,490, far more than had been expected by the most sanguine leaders, with the much hooted at Tammany turning in a chore for the head of the ticket. Mr. Roosevelt took this borough by 186,000 last time.

Brooklyn and Bronx Staunch.

Brooklyn also came through beyond expectations with a margin of 367,393 compared with 358,000 in 1940.

The Bronx did its share with a Roosevelt plurality of 235,362 as against 220,000 in 1940.

Anti-New Deal Queens did its best for Gov. Dewey, giving him a margin of 69,981 compared with its 35,000 for Mr. Willkie. Here for some reason Mr. Curran's hopes were dashed in the Senate race, for Queens gave him a lead of but 32,683.

Richmond did about as anticipated, giving Mr. Dewey a margin of 10,615, compared with 600 for Mr. Willkie last time.

Upstate Fails GOP.

Upstate Republican territory fell down badly as far as GOP hopes were concerned, and the Roosevelt sweep of upstate cities, including Syracuse which was in the Republican column in 1940, was seen as a result of CIO Political Action Committee activity. In Syracuse former Mayor Rolland B. Marvin, a GOP power in that territory, lost out in a race for the State enate.

The Roosevelt forces were carrying Albany County by a reduced majority, regarded as a consequence of Gov. Dewey's drive against the O'Connell machine, and also took Erie County by nearly 15,000 complete returns showed.

Banner Dewey counties were Nassau, which gave him a plural-

Continued on Page Twenty-three.

Result Makes Hillman No. 1 Labor Politician

By FRED W. PERKINS,
Scripps-Howard Staff Writer.

WASHINGTON, Nov. 8.—Up goes Sidney Hillman and down goes John L. Lewis in prestige as political labor leaders.

That is one apparent result of President Roosevelt's re-election, and in the future political structure of this country it may prove to be one of the most important.

Sidney Hillman.

If the final statistics prove what the incomplete returns indicate, Mr. Hillman will emerge triumphant over bitter campaign attacks to appear as the mobilizer of millions of labor votes that will be pointed to as Mr. Roosevelt's margin of victory.

There will be arguments that these votes, or most of them, would have gone to Mr. Roosevelt anyway, but the fact remains that the chairman of the CIO Political Action Committee was out in front of the labor drive for nearly a year.

PAC in for 4 Years.

There's no question now that the CIO Political Action Committee will continue, for four years at least, as a potent element in American politics, as will be made clear when exuberant leaders of the organization meet in Chicago Nov. 20 for the CIO national convention. Another result is that absorption of the CIO by the American Federation of Labor, which might have resulted eventually if the CIO had been on the losing end of this campaign, is now indefinitely deferred. The CIO, which has had many friends in government agencies in Washington, sometimes producing AFL charges of favoritism, will have more from now on.

This is the second major political blow suffered by Mr. Lewis of the United Mine Workers. Four years ago he came out 10 days before the election in favor of the late Wendell Willkie, but informed estimates were that not more than 10 per cent of the half-million

Continued on Page Twenty-three.

The War Today

Wednesday, November 8, 1944.

WESTERN FRONT—Americans and Germans throw infantry and tank reinforcements into mounting battle for Vossenack, 28 miles southwest of Cologne. In southwest Holland Allies tighten siege around last enemy pocket south of Holland deep in Moerdijk. (Page 5.)

PACIFIC—American carrier planes in new attack on Manila area raise toll to 30 Jap ships and 440 planes destroyed or damaged. Invasion forces join for final battle with Jap elements on Leyte, and Tokyo announces general who captured Bataan, Corregidor and Singapore had been placed in command of forces in Philippines. (Page 4.)

RUSSIA—Budapest radio reports Soviet troops, flanking Hungarian capital from South, land on island in Danube, four miles away. Berlin reports Red Army assault launched against 140-mile defensive line along Tisza River northeast of Budapest. (Page 6.)

World-Telegram Index

Mrs. Luce Claims A Close Victory

By the United Press.

GREENWICH, Conn., Nov. 8.—Claiming victory by a narrow margin in her campaign for re-election from Connecticut's Fourth Congressional district, Rep. Clare Boothe Luce said early today that "it was a very close fight, but we won."

Mrs. Luce's re-election was conceded shortly before 2 a. m. by Miss Margaret E. Connors, her Democratic opponent.

Mrs. Luce said that she "was never running against" Margaret Connors, her Democrat opponent.

"I ran against the whole New Deal up here and the PAC," she said.

With two towns in the district still to be heard from, Luce headquarters here estimated her victory by a margin of 400 votes.

Saying that she never was apprehensive about the outcome, Mrs. Luce added:

"I intend to serve the people who elected me as I have served them in the past."

Newspaper Lists Ballots for Mrs. Luce

By the Associated Press.

BRIDGEPORT, Conn., Nov. 8.—The Bridgeport Post-Telegram today claimed the re-election of Rep. Clare Boothe Luce (R), by 1655 votes over Miss Margaret E. Connors (D.) for Connecticut's fourth Congressional seat.

The newspaper said its returns were unofficial but complete. It gave Mrs. Luce, blonde playwright, serving her first term in the House, 101,636; Connors, 99,981.

Preis 20 Pfennig

JB

DONNERSTAG, 16. NOV. 1944
19. JAHRGANG :•. FOLGE 46

VERLAG FRANZ EHER NACHF.. GMBH.. MÜNCHEN 22.
Copr. Franz Eher Nachf., G. m. b. H., München 22.

Feldmarschall Rommel zum 15. November.

„Mag der einzelne auch fallen, der Sieg der Nation ist sicher." Dies Wort seines Generalfeldmarschalls Rommel beseelt das ganze deutsche Volk in seinem schweren Schicksalskampf bis zur Stunde des Sieges.

Zu unserem Bildbericht im Innern des Heftes „Das war unser Rommel" von Lw.-Kriegsberichter Karl-Heinz Lückel.

Entered as second-class matter April 15, 1931, at the post office at New Haven, Connecticut, under act of March 3, 1879

ILLUSTRATED CURRENT NEWS

Published Monday, Wednesday and Friday by Illustrated Current News, Inc., New Haven, Conn. Subscription Annually, $20.80

Nov. 20, 1944—No. 4872

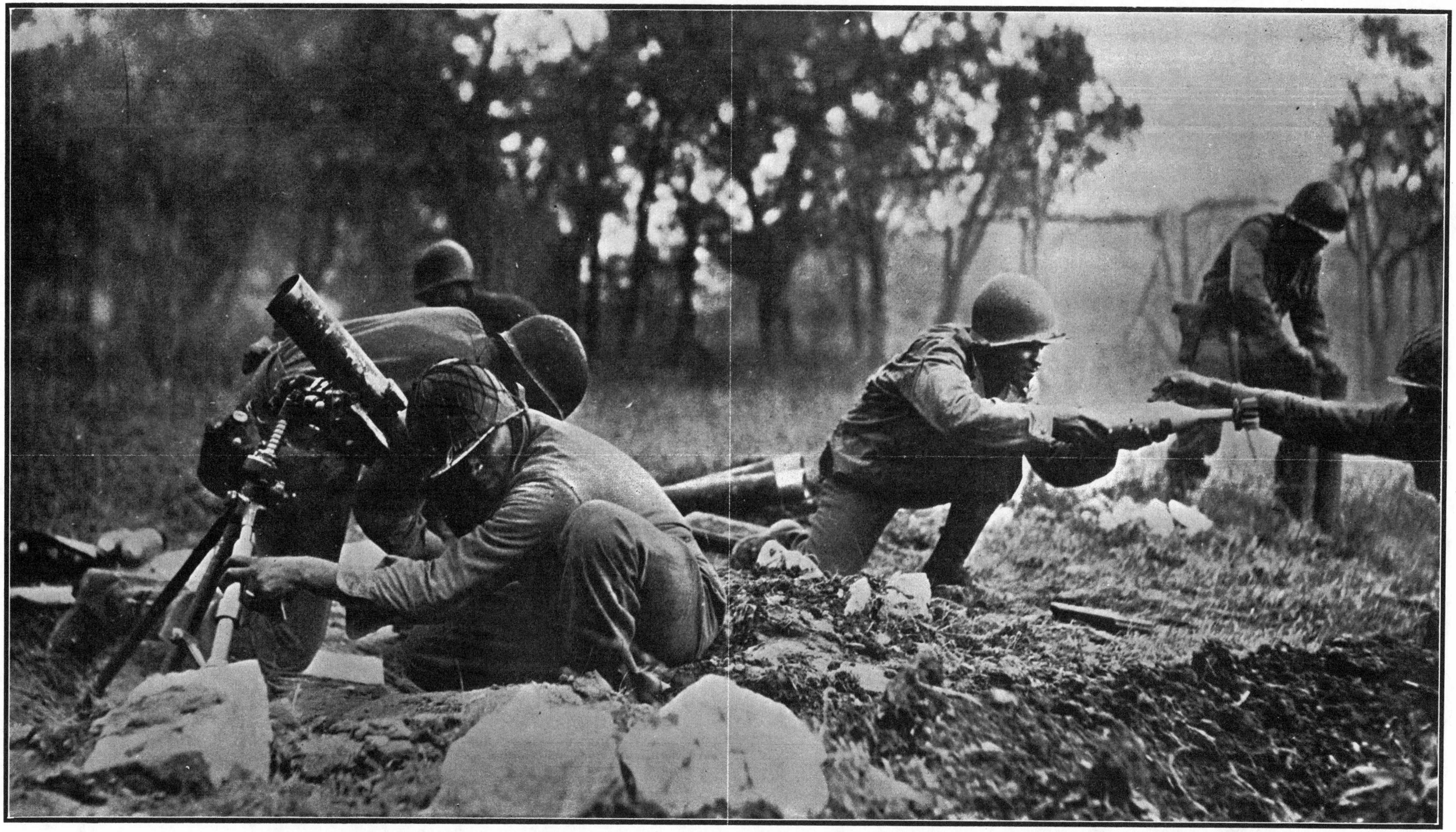

PASS THE AMMUNITION

Italy—Members of a Negro mortar company of the 92nd Division pass the ammunition and heave it over at the Germans in an almost endless stream near Massa, Italy. This company is credited with liquidating several machine gun nests. Company is commanded by Lt. Harry L. Cox, of San Mateo, Calif.

News Note: 6 Allied Armies Join In Great Offensive

THE STARS AND STRIPES
MEDITERRANEAN

Vol. 2, No. 15, Monday, November 27, 1944 ITALY EDITION TWO LIRE

Alexander New MTO Chief

Replaces Wilson, Who Goes To U. S.

Clark To Command New XV Army Group Comprising 5th And 8th Armies

LONDON, Nov. 26—Gen. Sir Harold R. L. G. Alexander, Commander in Chief of Allied Armies in Italy, has been named Supreme Allied Commander in the Mediterranean Theater with the rank of field marshal, it was announced here tonight by Prime Minister Winston Churchill.

Field Marshal Alexander will succeed General Sir Henry Maitland Wilson, who has been appointed head of the British Joint Staff Mission in Washington, succeeding the late Field Marshal Sir John Dill.

NEW CHIEF

MARSHAL ALEXANDER

General Wilson will also serve as Mr. Churchill's personal representative on military matters with President Roosevelt.

Lt. Gen. Mark W. Clark, commander of the Allied 5th Army in Italy and former deputy to Field Marshal Alexander, has been named Commander in Chief of the Allied XV (Fifteenth) Army Group, composed of the 5th and the 8th Armies, the announcement said.

No indication was given as to who will succeed General Clark as 5th Army Commander. Informed American observers here said that Maj. Gen. Geoffrey Keyes, commander of the II Corps, would be the likely choice.

The announcement by Mr Churchill said that the appointments of Field Marshal Alexander and General Clark were the result of an agreement between Mr. Churchill and President Roosevelt.

Dates of the actual transfer of command will be regulated, the announcement said, "in accordance with operational and other requirements."

The British War Office said that the promotion of Field Marshal Alexander was effective as from June 4, the date of the capture of Rome.

Field Marshal Alexander came to command of the Allied Armies in Italy after the conquest of Sicily and held the reputation in many quarters, according to Time magazine, as "being the ablest commander in Britain's service."

At Dunkirk he had taken command of the British Expeditionary Force when it was struggling for survival and he was the last man in his command to leave the

(Continued on Page 8)

Yanks Inch Onto Plain Of Cologne

British Reach Venlo As Maas Flood Stalls Drive

SHAEF, Nov. 26 — The American 9th and 1st Armies inched forward today in bitter fighting north and northeast of Aachen where stiff resistance was offered by the Germans in their effort to block the Allied drive onto the Cologne plain.

British 2nd Army troops, meanwhile, reached the outskirts of Venlo, the Dutch-German frontier town on the Maas River. German rearguards were protecting the city against a three-pronged British attack. South of Roermond on the Maas, other British troops were flooded out and were living on the housetops.

Frontline dispatches that Allied reconnaissance patrols had crossed the Rhine in the vicinity of Strasbourg into a battle of bridges as the Germans encircled each crossing of the Rhine with heavy machine guns and mortars.

Meanwhile, the trap around an estimated 50,000 German troops in Alsace tightened as Strasbourg was cleared and the French 1st Army pressed northward from Mulhouse. The threatened area is about 60 miles long and 35 miles wide and is bounded by the Rhine in the east, the Vosges in the west and the French and American troops in Strasbourg and the Mulhouse area.

With the fighting beyond Aachen growing in intensity, correspondents reported that it is in the Aachen-Geilenkirchen sector that Field Marshal Von Rundstedt has apparently decided he must make a determined defense of the industrial heart of Germany—the Ruhr. The Nazis were reported to have concentrated 12 divisions, half of them of the Panzer type, in the Geilenkirchen area alone.

American 9th Army troops were

(Continued on Page 8)

Troops 'From All Sources' Sought For Drive In China

CHUNGKING, Nov. 26 — Likelihood of extensive land operations against the Japanese in China, and of the drawing of troops for these operations "from all possible sources" is foreseen by Maj. Gen. Albert C. Wedemeyer, head of all American forces in China and Chief of Staff to Generalissimo Chiang Kai-shek.

General Wedemeyer said at a press conference here today that American armies will eventually be employed in China for a continental campaign aimed at driving out the Japs.

"Our future plans envisage the employment of all kinds of forces from all possible sources," he added, after a questioner had asked about the future role of U. S. Ground Forces in China.

"When the war in Europe ends," the General continued, "I want to be ready to tell General Marshall that 'we can use certain forces and supplies for a definite purpose.' You can be sure that such plans are being made."

He said damage done by B-29 raids on Japan is much greater than the enemy has acknowledged.

Bonomi Coalition Government Quits

ROME. Nov. 26—Italy's Prime Minister, Ivanoe Bonomi, and his cabinet resigned today.

Representatives of the six political parties which had originally formed the coalition government soon after the surrender of Italy to the Allies met today to discuss formation of a new cabinet.

The position of the cabinet has been unclear because it is not, like cabinets in many countries, responsible to any legislative body—nor, on the other hand, is the King of Italy accepted unanimously as the head of the nation in the British sense of the "the Crown."

The "Lieutenant of the Realm" is an office which to some extent exericses some functions of "the crown," but its role is by no means agreed.

In consequence of these unclarities of status, the cabinet has, strictly speaking, nobody to whom it can present a resignation.

But the tangle of legal questions is no more important than the reality. The cabinet is the only government Italy has, outside the controls of the Allies. The reality is that its "resignation"—even though addressed to no agreed authority—signals a genuine governmental crisis.

The resignations follow a critical period of several weeks. Four ministers—including Visconti Venosta, Undersecretary for Foreign Affairs, and Minister of Finance Soleri, had sought to resign last week, but were dissuaded temporarily.

The government announced its decision in the following communique:

"As a result of deliberations of the parties forming the coalition government and striving for a

(Continued on Page 8)

8th Army Launches Squeeze On Faenza

AFHQ, Nov. 26 — The big 8th Army squeeze on Faenza has begun.

In a broad outflanking move, British troops who reached the outskirts of the city on Friday swung around it from the east yesterday and reached the Lamone River on a wide front northeast of this important Forli-Bologna road junction.

One mile south of Faenza, British infantry, supported by tanks, forced a mile-wide bridgehead over the Marzeno River and are continuing their advance toward the Lamone against disorganized German resistance.

Panzer grenadiers of the 26th German Panzer Division, mauled

(Continued on Page 8)

Hull Quits Cabinet Post, Paper Reports

NEW YORK, Nov. 26 (ANS)—Secretary of State Cordell Hull submitted his resignation to President Roosevelt because of poor health, the United Press said today, quoting the New York Herald Tribune which stated that James F. Byrnes, Director of War Mobilization and Reconversion refused to confirm or deny the report of Mr. Hull's resignation.

Informed sources in Washington have said that President Roosevelt has assured Mr. Hull that the post of Secretary of State is his as long as he desires to hold it or for as long as his health permits.

Pre-election reports had men-

(Continued on Page 8)

General Pay Rise Denied By WLB To 'Little Steel'

WASHINGTON, Nov. 26 — The National War Labor Board last night announced its decision in the "Little Steel" case, which involved a dispute between 86 basic steel companies and about 400,000 employees represented by the United Steel Workers of America, (CIO).

Following are the highlights of a series of orders issued by the board concerning points at issue. The Board:

Granted wage increases of four cents per hour for night shift workers as added compensation for working undesirable shifts.

Declined to grant a general wage increase of 17 cents per hour sought by the union to offset a claimed rise in the cost of living, but said it would resume consideration of the demand for a general wage increase if there is any change in the national wage stabilization policy.

Approved a limited form of severance pay to be developed by collective bargaining, and stated that while it would not impose a guaranteed annual wage plan on the industry it would approve such plans worked out by collective bargaining.

Denied the demand of some companies that maintenance of membership provisions incorporated in existing contracts be eliminated.

Denied the unions demand for the elimination of geographical wage differentials.

SHAEF Clamps Down On Cigarette 'Deals'

WASHINGTON, Nov. 26 (ANS) —General Dwight D. Eisenhower had ordered court-martial for anyone charged with illegal sale of cigarettes, SHAEF disclosed Thursday. General Eisenhower promised combat troops five packs each week starting in the near future, with two packs weekly going to personnel in the rear areas.

A military spokesmen here ascribed the nationwide cigarette shortage as due in large part to several million cartons being bought on the domestic market for Christmas shipment to soldiers.

Judge Landis Dies At 78; Was Baseball Overlord

CHICAGO, Nov. 26 — Kenesaw Mountain Landis, high commissioner of organized baseball since 1920, died in his sleep today at 5:30 AM in St. Luke's Hospital. He had celebrated his 78th birthday last Sunday in the hospital, where he had been since Oct. 2, suffering from a cold and fatigue.

At first, his illness had been considered slight, but he suffered a setback last weekend which prompted his physician to issue a bulletin describing the aged jurist's condition as serious.

His wife, a patient in the same hospital with a broken wrist; his son, Col. Reed Gresham Landis, second-ranking American aviation ace of World War I, and his daughter and son-in-law, Mr. and Mrs. Richard W. Phillips, were at his bedside when he died.

According to his wishes, there will be no funeral services. The body will be cremated privately, and friends were asked to omit flowers.

Landis was sitting on the Federal bench in Illinois in 1920 when the scandal resulting from the 1919 World Series between the Chicago White Sox and the Cincinnati Reds was made public. The National and American Leagues were at each other's throats over matters of policy and Landis was called in to straighten things out.

He was given a contract as com-

(Continued on Page 8)

THE WEATHER

Partly cloudy with highest temperature about 42; cold tonight; light snow or rain tonight or Tuesday morning.

Read The Baltimore News-Post for complete, accurate war coverage. It is the only Baltimore newspaper possessing the three great wire services—
ASSOCIATED PRESS
INTERNATIONAL NEWS SERVICE
UNITED PRESS

THE BALTIMORE NEWS-POST
AN INDEPENDENT NEWSPAPER
The Largest Evening Circulation in the Entire South

NIGHT
Wall St. Opening

VOL. CXLVI.—NO. 37 Entered as second-class matter at Baltimore Postoffice. MONDAY EVENING, DECEMBER 18, 1944 PRICE 3 CENTS

NAZIS DRIVE YANKS BACK IN BELGIUM, LUXEMBOURG

Captured Americans Slaughtered By Germans

PARIS, Dec. 18--(A. P.).--Lieut. Gen. Courtney H. Hodges First Army fought today to blunt the greatest enemy blow struck against American troops in Europe. Throwing hundreds of carefully conserved planes, hundreds of tanks, many divisions and parachutists into a surprising winter counteroffensive, Field Marshal Karl Rudolf Gerd von Rundstedt had achieved a penetration of several miles in the American lines, re-invaded Belgium in the Monschau area 16 mies south of Aachen, and re-entered Luxembourg at two other points.

Today the Germans were pushing their advance along an 80-mile front from the Monschau area to the southern tip of the Luxembourg border with new and more violent attacks.

Allied military authorities directing the battle said it had been decided not to make public specific information now as to the exact places where the German columns were smashing through and how far they had advanced.

LONDON, Dec. 18—(A. P.).—The German High Command declared today that Nazi forces had overrun forward American positions "in the first onrush" of a broad offensive striking from southeast of Aachen to the northern border of Luxembourg.

NAZI COUNTER-ATTACKS—In what may prove to be the final Nazi effort to turn the tide of war, German troops in their first major counter-attack since Normandy are driving against the U. S. First and Ninth Army lines at seven points on the Western Front. Four Nazi penetrations have been made into Belgium and Luxembourg, near Malmady, Heckuscheid, Vianden and Echternach. U. S. forces (open arrow) smashed Nazi attack on Mariaweiler.

NAZIS GAIN SEVERAL MILES

But First Army headquarters dispatches said the Germans had gained several miles and American troops were locked in battle. The penetration apparently had been at leas four miles in one area 10 miles east of Malmedy, a Belgian town just north of the Luxembourg border.

This was a push by a strong German armored column supported overnight by artillery and bombing and strafing warplanes on a seven-mile front.

Several German armored divisions and infantry divisions were striking savagely and bending back the lines of the fiercely struggling doughboys.

Elsewhere along the 80-mile front the Germans were delivering stiff punches aimed at seeking soft spots, and there were indications the supreme German effort would mount in intensity before it subsided.

OTHER BLOWS SEEN

On many other Army fronts there were signs of impending German blows.

U. S. Third Army dispatches said the heaviest enemy rail movement ever seen behind the Third Army front had been observed yesterday.

Reports from the British Second Army front to the north and German fliers in the greatest strength since D-Day had appeared in the skies along the Achen sector, along with many reconnaissance aircraft over the British front.

A 10-mile long German column was blasted by Allied fighter bombers in the Neunkirchen area, 10 miles northeast of Saarbrucken.

In the Alsace plain German counterattacks rolled over three villages in the Colmar and Salestat areas.

But at General Eisenhower's

Continued on Page 2, Column 1.

Wilson Raps U. S. Policy On Poland

By DAVID SENTNER
News-Post Washington Bureau.

WASHINGTON, Dec. 18.—Congress will erupt this week over the deteriorating international diplomatic situation climaxed by Prime Minister Churchill's announcement of support for Soviet Russia's partitioning of Poland.

Information on the part American diplomacy in the hands of President Roosev 't has played—or failed to play—in the decision to handover one-third of Poland, in blatant violation of the principles of the Atlantic Charter, will be demanded in speeches being prepared for delivery before both chambers.

'SEEDS OF WORLD WAR III.'

Summing up the growing reaction of Congress to the boiling struggle between Communist Russia and Britain for spheres of influence in Europe, Representative Earl Wilson (Republican) of Indiana today asserted that recent European diplomatic events made it "clearer and clearer that we are sowing the seed for World War III."

He said:

"It appears that the principles laid down in the Atlantic Charter have been ignored, if not forgotten, by the three great Powers.

"Russia has forgotten it in her dealings with the Poles, the French, the Italians, the Bul-

Continued on Page 2, Column 8.

Japs Hint New Landings Due In Philippines

ALLIED HEADQUARTERS, PHILIPPINES, Dec. 18—(U. P.). The liberation of the Philippines gained momentum today, with American forces driving 12 miles inland on newly invaded Mindoro within 130 miles of Manila and splitting the Yamashita line on Leyte into three disorganized segments in a powerful offensive.

(Rodio Tokyo said an American fleet of "considerable strength" had been sighted in the Sulu sea south of Mindoro and speculated that another amphibious landing was in prospect, perhaps on Luzon, site of Manila and Gen. Douglas MacArthur's ultimate objective in the Philippines.)

REPAIR AIRFIELDS

American and Australian engineers on Mindoro alrady were rushing repairs to captured San Joe airfield and building new airstrips on what Gen. Douglis MacArthur called "excellent sites" to cover the next phase of the Philippines campaign.

Japanese resistance, both in the air and on the ground, continued negligible. Apparently paralyzed by the day and nig?ht raids on their Philippines airdromes by American carrier and land based planes, the Japanese were able to get few aircraft off the ground, and most of those were shot down.

TIGHTEN JAP TRAP

O Leyte, some 300 miles southeast of Mindoro, American forces brought the final annihilation of 20,000 to 25,000 Japanese trapped in the northwest corner of the island within sight of a series of surprise attacks from the south and east.

Triple B-29 Blow Rips Japs

WASHINGTON, Dec. 18—(U. P.).—Two fleets of Superfortresses hit Nagoya, Japan's biggest aircraft manufacturing center, and Hankow, one of her main supply bases in China, in twin raids yesterday, the War Department announced, and Tokyo said 70 of the B-29s returned for another attack on Nagoya today.

The raids on Nagoya were the second and, if confirmed by Washington, third in a week on Japan's third largest city, 165 miles west of Tokyo and home of the importtant Mitsubishi aircraft works and other high priority war factories.

FORCES OF 100 EACH

Approximately 100 B-29s from Saipan were believed to have participated in yesterday's attack hurling hundreds of tons of demolition and fire bombs on the teeming Honshu Island metropolis, while an equally large force from China hit Hankow.

Tokyo failed to confirm either of yesterday's attacks, but broadcast an imperial headquarters communique reporting that "some 70" of the big four-engined raiders raided the Nagoya area today, causing "slight damage."

At the same time, the comunique said, a "small number of planes" invaded the Kinki area, but "fled without dropping any bombs." The Kinki area includes Osaka, Japan's biggest industrial center, Nara, Wakayama, Gifu and Fukui, all in South Central Honshu.

PLANES OVER KYUSHU

Another Tokyo broadcast said Japanese planes and anti-aircraft units were giving a "hot reception" to several formations of B-29s over Kyushu, just southwest of Honshu, but it was possi-

Continued on Page 2, Column 3.

Temperatures

12 Mid't, 36	6 A. M., 34
1 A. M., 36	7 A. M., 34
2 A. M., 37	8 A. M., 35
3 A. M., 36	9 A. M., 36
4 A. M., 36	10 A. M., 37
5 A. M., 35	11 A. M., 39

Hero's Mother Aids Vets' Fund

By ALDINE R. BIRD

She'd give her right arm to talk to her boy at Christmas, but there's not a chance.

He made the supreme sacrifice on a small island in the Southwest Pacific and has been buried in a hero's grave over there.

His mother, back in Baltimore, has joined the growing legion of Gold Star Mothers, and now writes to the director of the Disabled Veterans' Fund of The Baltimore News-Post, as follows:

"I can no longer do anything for my son. All that I could do was to give him to his country. He did the rest.

"He's buried somewhere in the South Pacific.

"If I can make some lonesome, homesick boy in a hospital a little more cheerful at Christmas, it will make me feel I am at least doing my share."

ANOTHER 'HELLO MOM!'

She enclosed a check to pay for a long distance call so some wounded and helpless GI in a Government hospital near Baltimore can say "Hello, Mom" in a big way next week.

Through provisions of special telephone equipment being set up in six nearby hospitals, 5,100 men who nearly gave their lives that freedom might live on after them, will get the biggest Yule treat officials in those institutions say they could desire.

These calls will be made from bedsides as well as special tele-

Continued on Page 2, Column 6.

Nazis Slaughter Captive Yanks

AN AMERICAN FRONTIER CLEARING STATION, BELGIUM, Dec. 17—(Delayed)—(A. P.).—Weeping with rage, a handful of doughboy survivors described today how a German tank force ruthlessly poured machine gun fire into a group of about 150 Americans who had been disarmed and herded into a field in the opening hours of the present Nazi counteroffensive.

TANKS WRECK COLUMN

Said T-5 William B. Summers of Glenville, W. Va., who escaped by playing dead:

"We had to lie there and listen to German non-coms kill with pistols every one of our wounded men who groaned or tried to move."

The Americans were members of an artillery observation battalion ambushed and trapped at a road fork by a powerful German armored column of Tiger tanks, whose heavy guns quickly shot up the two dozen American trucks and lightly-armored vehicles.

Summers said:

"They had at least 15 to 20 tanks. They disarmed us and then searched us for wrist-

Continued on Page 2, Column 1.

Italian Hostages Hanged By Nazis

ROME, Dec. 18—(A. P.).—The Army newspaper "Stars and Stripes" today quoted a person who recently crossed the front line as saying the Germans hanged 35 Italian hostages in Bologna in reprisal for the blowing up of a Nazi ammunition truck.

RENEW V-BOMB ATTACK

LONDON, Dec. 18—(A. P.).—The Germans renewed their V-weapons attack on England last night. The British Ministry of Home Security said today that "damage and casualties were reported."

Scratches At Gulfstream

First Race—Inna Care, Light Sandwich, Bark, Epidown.
Second—Valdina Lord.
Fifth—Hayai Tinty.
Weather clear; track fast.

Retreat Is New Role For Yanks

By LEE CARSON

A FORWARD COMMAND POST, WITH THE U. S. FIRST ARMY SOUTH OF MONSCHAU, Dec. 18—(I. N. S.).—Retreat in the face of Germany's smashing counteroffensive on the Luembourg-Belgium frontier today is a new experience to the battle-tested doughboys of the American First Army.

There are no frightened faces among the Yank troops, no frantic milling about and very little confusion. Everyone is concentrating on one thing—and that is to ram this retreat back down the Nazi throates.

As this is being written, the Germans are roaring up nearby roads in their Tiger tanks, zooming down from the pink-streaked winter skies to shower our frontline positions with streams of hot lead, and tearing the world apart with their heavy artillery barrages.

MAJOR MOVES CALMLY

Major Edward R. Garton of Rhineland, N. J., second in command of a tank-destroyer outfit, is buckling on his sidearms. He is preparing to move forward with his men to contact the enemy.

A first-class armored clash, involving 29 Nazi tanks, is in prog-

Continued on Page 2, Column 7.

Yank Heavies Cross Channel To Blast Nazis

LONDON, Dec. 18—(A. P.).—Hundreds of U. S. Flying Fortresses and Liberators sped across the English Channel today to give Germany a daylight dose of the punishment poured on Munich, Ulm and Duisburg last night by 1,300 British heavy bombers.

The big R. A. F. planes dropped an estimated 7,000 tons of bombs on the three German cities, all key points in the Nazi railway network.

American Fighters with belly tanks of extra fuel ranged ahead of the American heavy bombers today to meet any challenge in the skies over Western Europe's flaming battle lines.

The triple blow last night—one of the first struck by R. A. F. heavy bombers in weeks—came in the wake of a day of bitter air combat between German and Allied fighters.

The Germans had 108 fighters and bombers blasted out of the air yesterday in air battles accompanying the enemy's ground attacks. Two R. A. F. fighters were lost, both due to flak, and 31 American pursuit craft were listed as missing.

From all sectors Allied fighter craft were summoned—even the R. A. F. Spitfires, Tempests and Typhoons from the Netherlands—as a sudden break in the weather exposed long columns of German tanks, trucks and troops moving slowly toward the battle raging in the American First Army lines.

AUTOGRAPH

PARIS, Dec. 18—(A. P.). A French civilian paid 63,000 francs ($1,260 at the current rate of exchange) for General Eisenhower's autograph yesterday at an auction in behalf of bombed-out residents of Normandy. Auction was held during a performance of the Folies Bergere.

NEWS-POST

THE WEATHER
Clear, cold, windy this afternoon. Clear, quite cold tonight and Wednesday.
Detailed Weather Report Page 19

THE BALTIMORE NEWS-POST
AN INDEPENDENT NEWSPAPER
The Largest Evening Circulation in the Entire South

10

VOL. CXLVI.—NO. 38 Entered as second-class matter at Baltimore Postoffice. TUESDAY EVENING, DECEMBER 19, 1944 PRICE 3 CENTS

NAZI COUNTERATTACK IN BELGIUM ROLLS ON

First Pictures From Scene Of Nazi Drive

NAZI PLANE COMES TO SMASHING END—Arms, legs and other crushed part of Nazi invaders lie where they crashed with a German transport plane that was brought to a smashing end by U. S. ack-ack in the Ninth Army area. At right is a "superman," a paratrooper, captured by the First Army when he jumped, at night, behind their lines. Louis Azrael, who is in the battle area told of seeing a crashed German transport plane surrounded by severed arms and legs in a dispatch in a late edition of the News-Post yesterday.

Yanks Begin Closing On Some Extended Columns, Clear One Village Of Foe

WITH AMERICAN FORCES IN GERMANY, Dec. 19—(I. N. S.)—American troops in a swift counter-attack today drove German forces from a part of one village taken by the Germans in their strong offensive thrust into Belgium. The situation remained serious, with the Americans striving desperately to seal off Nazi penetrations. The northern wing of the German push into Belgium has not yet been halted, but on the other flanks a sheath of American fire is laying waste to Nazi columns and is beginning to close in on them.

PARIS, Dec. 19—(A. P.).—Germany's all-out Christmas counter-offensive—shrouded in secrecy both by the Allies and the German high command—evidently hammered on tonight with the same fury that in three days had rolled the thinly-stretched American First Army back at least 20 miles into Belgium at one point.

A front dispatch from Associated Press Correspondent William F. Boni said Lieut. Gen. Courtney H. Hodges was throwing all available forces into the effort to stem the "most serious setback to American arms on this side of the world since Kasserine Pass in Tunisia."

AIR FORCES AID

Late today an emergency call brought a big force of U. S. Flying Fortresses and British Lancasters from British fields to spread 2,000 tons of fragmentation and high explosive bombs on rail and road junctions immediately behind the attacking Nazi forces.

They were forced to bomb through thick ground-clinging clouds and fog which shrouded the blazing 60-mile front and denied the hard-pressed doughboys the invaluable support of fighters and fighter-bombers.

'ATTACK CONTINUING'

As Field Marshal Karl Gerd von Rundstedt's battering ram smashed into the deeply-dented American line south of Aachen, Allied headquarters imparted only the terse information that "the attack is continuing." This curtain of silence appeared to indicate that the enemy's forward momentum had not been halted. The Germans still were packing the roads with equipment and men.

(BACKGROUND NOTE: The German High Command declared that Nazi tank forces "have broken through, smashed and dispersed units of the American First Army deep into the enemy rear." Like the Allies, however, the Germans dealt only in generalities.)

Up to tonight the only specific clue as to the extent of the German penetration was the report that British Typhoons had attacked a score of enemy armored vehicles "west of Stavelot," a town

Continued on Page 2, Column 1.

Gulfstream Race Results

FIRST RACE—Mile and one-sixte enth. Off at 1.42. Time, 1.47 1-5.

Razor Sharp, 117 (J. Higley)	$5.60	$4.20	$2.90
Swell Time, 105 (R. Meade)		10.50	4.90
Aldridge, 115 (D. Scocca)			3.40
Total mutuels			$31.50

Also Ran—Rosemere Rose, Epidown, Early 'N,' Smart, Shot One, Block Buster, Pomiva.

SECOND—Six furlongs (chute). Off at 2.12. Time, 1.13.

Manadroit, 117 (W. Rudert)	$23.20	$12.60	6.70
Stella's Sun, 117 (J. McCoy)		17.20	8.90
Easy Blend, 115 (S. Young)			5.80
Total mutuels			$74.40

Also Ran—Noslen, Jackina, Pi pt Lner, Davitt, Nibble, Lady Golden, Fairy Fly, Fortunatu s.

Daily Double—Razor Sharp and Manadroit paid $73.60

THIRD—Six furlongs (chute). Off 2.42½. Time 1.13 1-5.

Bob Mann, 118 (W. Gerlock)	$37.50	$15.90	$7.20
Valdina Math, 112 (S. Luce)		8.50	4.70
Wee Ossie, 117 (J. McCoy)			2.80
Total mutuels			$76.60

Also Ran—aHe Wineasy, aMibo b, Memphis Dave, Rotamal, Stork of Peace, Chance Fair. aGen ter and Rose entry.

Continued on Page 16, Column 5.

VERY LATEST NEWS

(Race Results From Howard Sports Daily, Inc.)

RACING RESULTS

AT CHARLES TOWN

Eighth—Maequel, $28.40, $8.80, $4.20; Cominch, $7.60, $7.20; Miss Gallant, $6.80.

ROOSEVELT TO STEER "LITTLE LEFT OF CENTER"

WASHINCON, Dec. 19—(A. P.).—President Roosevelt said today that he intends to keep on steering a course a little left of center during the war and afterward.

BELGIUM CUTS DOWN RAIL TRAVEL

BRUSSELS, Dec. 19—(U. P.).—Allied military authorities announced today that travel to and from Belgium would be limited strictly to business vitally affecting the war or the economic reconstruction of Belgium.

Roosevelt For Principles Of Charter

WASHINGTON, Dec. 19—(A. P.). — President Roosevelt declared today that the Atlantic Charter did not exist as a formal document signed by himself and Prime Minister Churchill, but that he still stood for its principles.

The Chief Executive told a news conference that the charter drafted in a conference at sea between himself and the British Prime Minister, existed as a series of memoranda, turned over to radio operators for transmission to Washington and London to be released to the press.

He asserted that it had been signed in substance, but not formally as a complete document.

At the same time, Mr. Roosevelt made it clear that he adhered firmly to the principles enunciated in the Charter as it has been promulgated.

BARKLEY BACK ON JOB

WASHINGTON, Dec. 19—(A. P.).—Majority Leader Barkley (Democrat) of Kentucky returned to the Senate today after several weeks in Bethesda (Md.) Naval Hospital for treatment of an infected eye.

BRITAIN-ETHIOPIA PACT

LONDON, Dec. 19—(A. P.).—An agreement between Great Britain and Ethiopia was signed today in Addis Ababa.

Senate Backs Grew For State Dept. Post

By WILLIAM S. NEAL

WASHINGTON, Dec. 19—(I. N. S.).—The Senate today confirmed President Roosevelt's nomination of former Ambassador Joseph C. Grew, a career diplomat for 40 years, to be undersecretary of state and then proceeded to vote on five assistant secretaries.

The action followed abandonment of a threatened filibuster by New Deal Senators, who had condemned the President's selection of the six men for the key State Department posts.

Grew was ambassador to Japan when the war began. He was undersecretary of state 20 years ago in the Coolidge Administration.

Just before the voting began on the State Department appointees, the Senate heard Sen. Robert M. La Follette (Progressive), of Wisconsin, charge that European developments indicate that the Atlantic Charter has become "a mere scrap of paper."

Temperatures

12 Midn't., 32	9 A. M., 25
1 A. M., 32	10 A. M., 26
2 A. M., 30	11 A. M., 27
3 A. M., 28	12 Noon, 28
4 A. M., 26	1 P. M., 29
5 A. M., 25	2 P. M., 30
6 A. M., 24	3 P. M., 31
7 A. M., 23	4 P. M., 32
8 A. M., 24	5 P. M., 31

Plane Saves Men Of Sinking Ship

WASHINGTON, Dec. 19—(U. P.).—A daring pilot in a flimsy float plane, and makeshift boat crews from a nearby vessel, saved nearly 80 per cent. of the crew of the burning and exploding naval oiler Mississinewa, sunk by recent enemy action in the Central Pacific, the Navy announced today.

The 23,000-ton craft, the 234th U. S. naval vessel lost in this war, carried a normal complement of about 250 men.

TOWS MEN TO SAFETY

The oiler skipper, Capt. Philip G. Beck of Brooklyn, N. Y., said the most ingenious rescue work was done by the pilot of the tiny scout observation float plane.

Beck said:

"The pilot of that plane had more nerve than I like to think of. He saw our plight and put his plane down on the water. Then he would taxi up to the rim of flames, throw out a thin line with a floater on it for the struggling men to grab onto, and then tow them to safety.

"He kept on going back, until he had rescued at least 20 men who otherwise probably would have burned to death. I wish I could find out who that pilot was—he just disappeared after his rescue work was done."

The nature of the enemy action was not announced.

SHIP BUILT HERE

The Mississinewa was built at the Bethlehem Shipbuilding Corporation's Sparrows Point (Md.) plant. It was commissioned last May 18.

Meanwhile boats from a nearby ship braved the scorching heat to pick up more survivors. Beck said the rescue boats were manned by men who just happened to be on deck, rather than by regular crews.

The first explosion ripped the ship's bow 17 minutes after reveille had been sounded. Seconds later the forward gas tanks blew up.

Greek Issue Debate Set In Commons

LONDON, Dec. 19—(A. P.).—The House of Commons will hold a special debate on Greece tomorrow, with Prime Minister Churchill expected to speak.

This was announced tonight several hours after Churchill had sidetracked a new effort in Commons to get his comments of the Greek situation. Churchill refused also to give a full-scale review of the war.

Cabinet ministers agreed to tomorrow's debate after a committee of the Labor party submitted a formal demand.

In Commons today Churchill was forced into a hot-tempered debate of British troops' intervention in Belgium.

B-29s Press 3-Way Blow At Japan

WASHINGTON, Dec. 19—(A. P.).—China-based Superfortresses today pounded an enemy aircraft plant at Omura on the Japanese home island of Kyushu and attacked targets at Shanghai and Nanking on the China coast.

A War Department communique said that results of the attack on the Omura aircraft plant could not be determined because of the heavy cloud cover. The B-29's bombed through an overcast with the use of precision instruments.

RAID SHANGHAI DOCKS

"Good to excellent" results were achieved in the raid on docks and engineering works at Shanghai and Nanking, however. Weather over the targets there was clear.

A medium force of the B-29s from the Twentieth Bomber Command, possibly comprising 40 planes, carried out the raids. Little opposition was encountered from enemy fighters, five of which were shot down by the B-29 crews. Three more enemy fighters were probably destroyed and nine damaged.

JAPS REPORT ATTACK

A Japanese Imperial communique reported that between 30 and 40 Superfortresses bombed Omura in the fifth reported attack on the city since last July.

The communique telling of the attacks followed shortly a report that serious damage had been inflicted on the Mitsubishi aircraft plant in yesterday's raid at Nagoya, Japan's third largest city.

Phone Employes Take Strike Vote

NEW YORK, Dec. 19—(I. N. S.).—More than 5,600 long-line telephone operators, telephone company administrative personnel and maintenance workers began taking a strike vote today. Under the provisions of the Smith-Connally Act, long-distance workers, if they decide to strike, must wait 60 days after notifying the WLB of the proposed walkout.

NEWS-POST

The Daily Sketch

NEWS AND PICTURES

No. 11,112 ★ THURSDAY, DECEMBER 28, 1944 ONE PENNY

HERE ARE THE **Headlines** For To-day Thursday, Dec. 28

WAR

WEST: Germans admit withdrawals in Luxemburg to Western Wall outposts. Rundstedt's position in bid to reach Meuse is regarded as critical by correspondents at Allied G.H.Q.

AIR: R.A.F. switch to attack new target, Rheydt, opposite British Second Army front.

ITALY: Allied bombers destroy Italy's biggest munition works (near Milan). On land: Eighth battle on; slight withdrawal by Fifth.—Back Page.

EAST: Russian tanks, driving for Vienna, battle 50 miles from Austrian border.

HOME

Call-up of the 250,000 extra men to be by three stages. No man more than 35 to go to the Army.—Page 3.

U.S. Housing Chief, Mr. Jacob Crane, offering aid to Britain in building new houses, says the whole world is facing a shortage of homes.—Page 3.

Free tuition and maintenance scheme for ex-Service men and women who want to be teachers is announced by Board of Education.

Mr. Lloyd George, Father of House of Commons, retiring from Parliament.

Germans send letters from British prisoners of war in V-bombs.

ABROAD

GREECE: Conference decides to set up a Regency till the nation votes on King George's return, says U.S. broadcast.

General Eisenhower switches Army leaders (names kept secret) to meet Rundstedt's drive. No question of looking for a scapegoat, says Paris report

If you cut this column out daily you can enclose it in a letter to anyone in the Services abroad. It gives a concise summary of the day's more important news.

BASTOGNE IS FREED

Luxemburg Troops Retire to West Wall—Berlin

Eisenhower Switches Army Commanders

Gen. Eisenhower

GENERAL EISENHOWER has made changes among his commanders at the front, says an Associated Press correspondent in Paris. The changes are based only on the necessities arising from the position following the enemy drive, adds the correspondent.

Under-estimation of the enemy's power, coupled with a failure to learn of or appreciate his mobile reserve, appeared last night to be the major factors for the German breakthrough. That seemed to place the responsibility well up into the staff level. However, Eisenhower has shown no tendency to hunt for a scapegoat.

The Washington correspondent of A.P. cabled last night that top assistants of General Eisenhower's command may be involved in a shake-up—particularly of the intelligence section.

Incomplete reports from the battle lines made evident to strategists in Washington that General Eisenhower has suffered heavy losses. It means, in the final analysis, that barring the hoped-for but unlikely break for the Allies, the fighting in Europe will go on far into next year, even into the winter.

GREAT BATTLES ON FLANKS

BASTOGNE, vital Belgian road and communications centre, where for more than a week encircled American battalions, supplied by "sky trains," have bitterly resisted the Germans, was reported last night to have been freed.

This news came from Luxemburg after a day in which even Germany admitted a number of Allied successes.

Berlin said that Rundstedt had withdrawn troops from some sectors of the Luxemburg front to the forefield of the Siegfried Line to "avoid unnecessary losses."

By the loss of Bastogne, the German supply tunnel through Belgium has been narrowed to less than 20 miles wide, and it is further threatened by a deep wedge driven into it by the Americans.

Berlin also admitted that on both flanks fierce tank battles had developed, and said that in the north Field-Marshal Montgomery had thrown one of his élite divisions into the battle zone east of the Luettich-Dinant line, as well as an American division transferred from Aix.

Great Air Blows

"The Allied aim is to crush our flank in the north with massed forces and a maximum of artillery near Grandmesnil, while on the southern flank a thrust near Vaux-les-Rosiers is designed to corner our divisions between the Salm and Ourthe rivers," said the German official agency.

Rundstedt's most dangerous thrust—that to the Meuse in the vicinity of Rochefort—has been halted, and we have recaptured Ciney and Celles, four miles from the river.

Late "flashes" from the Belgian front said that Allied air forces pounded the enemy ground forces and supply lines in great force yesterday.

As dusk was approaching the total sorties mounted to the 2,000 mark.

Rundstedt will stake all on his next blow.—By Leonard Mosley. See Page 8.

Reinforcements for United States troops fighting back against the German salient in Belgium are halted in this wintry valley, made more picturesque by its snow-covered trees and slopes.

GERMANS SENDING P.O.W. LETTERS IN V-BOMBS

'Daily Sketch' Correspondent

THE Germans are sending letters from British prisoner-of-war camps in V-bombs.

After a recent V-bomb attack on northern England a canister containing a leaflet marked "V.P.O.W. Post" and letters from prisoners of war were found.

The letters were in photostat and printed form. They were headed "Truth," and bore an illustration of a flash coming out of the mouth of a cannon

They contained such passages as, "Your son is in good health," "Your son is wounded."

Some of them carried what purported to be the signature of a medical officer of a British prisoner-of-war camp.

The leaflets contained propaganda and stated that Britain could not win the war because of the V-bomb.

They asked the finders to copy the letters and to forward them, saying: "The original letters are being sent through the Red Cross in the usual mail channel."

DEGRELLE SENTENCED

Leon Degrelle, Belgian Fascist leader, was sentenced to death in his absence yesterday by a Brussels war tribunal.

Berlin announced the fate of another quisling, M. Jean Bichelonne, successively Minister of Production and Transport and Minister of Labour in the former Vichy Government, has died in hospital near the German capital. He was regarded as Pétain's probable successor.

Greece: 'Regency Plan Accepted'

"GREEK political leaders and representatives of the Allies last night agreed to set up a Regency in Greece till the people vote whether they want the King back or not," says an American commentator, broadcasting from Athens. He adds:

"Mr. Churchill and Mr. Eden met war correspondents during the afternoon but what they said will not be released for some hours."

British paratroops were in action against the most violent ELAS defence of the Greek war as the delegates were collecting "at a secret meeting place" for the second time in 24 hours, cables Clare Hollingworth, DAILY SKETCH Correspondent in Athens.

Conference Breaks Up

Representatives of the Political Committee of EAM attended, as well as Svolos, ex-Minister of Finance, and more representatives of Papandreou's Government.

The conference began two hours late.

This second meeting was adjourned without agreement, after members of the Greek Populist Party had declared the ELAS terms to be unacceptable. The terms included:

Formation of a new Cabinet, with a President, agreed on by all.

Punishment of collaborators; purge of Government services, and dissolution of the gendarmerie.

A plebiscite to be held by the first Sunday in February and a General Election of the National Assembly by April.

Breach Of Faith

Feeling ran high at the previous day's session, which followed the Greeks' meeting with Mr. Churchill. Raised voices could be heard when ex-Dictator Plastiras criticised the guerilla forces

ELAS delegates refused the invitation of M. Papandreou to spend the night in the British zone.

"We are in a position to carry on the war for 40 years," boasted M. Saintos, Secretary of the Communist Party, after Mr. Churchill and the British delegates had left the conference.

The ELAS delegates at yesterday's conference were wearing British battle-dress and greatcoats, and they were accompanied by an A.D.C., armed with a tommy-gun, who remained outside the conference room.

Most serious incident of the day was a breach of faith by ELAS, who began shelling at 3.10 in the afternoon—ten minutes after the hour when we had promised to cease offensive air action against enemy gun emplacements

EIGHT FRENCH GESTAPO MEN EXECUTED

Eight of the nine French Gestapo men sentenced to death by the Paris court for dealings with the enemy were shot at the Fort Montronge, near Paris, yesterday The ninth will not be executed.

Pierre Bony, former police inspector of the Sûreté Générale (the French Scotland Yard), who played a prominent part in the Stavisky scandals inquiry, was among those executed.—Reuter.

TIMELY WORDS OF FAITH

To every thing there is a season, and a time to every purpose under the heaven.

Ecclesiastes: 3, 1.

'Thus Far, and No Farther..' New Saga of Yank Courage

By FRANK CONNIFF
International News Service Staff Correspondent.

WITH AMERICAN INFANTRY AT LA GLEIZE, Belgium, Dec. 29.—The shadow of every storied place in American history where our fighting men have drawn a line and said "thus far, and no farther" hovers today over this little town cradled on gently-flowing Belgian hills.

In that Valhalla where all good warriors go, the men of the Alamo, of Bunker Hill and Gettysburg must have prepared a special welcome for the gallant young initiates who joined their valiant fraternity during the past week.

They took their positions among the crooked contours of the Belgian hillside in an hour of utmost urgency. They were hopelessly outnumbered, and they knew it. The sacrifice they were to make would be unsung and unrecorded. They knew that, too.

But the kinship that links patriotism of the past with deeds of the present boasts a continuity that scoffs at the caprice of passing years, a pliant strength that no sophistication ever will really sever.

La Gleize today is ours again. In this pocket we ultimately destroyed tons of Nazi material and annihilated thousands of Hitler's best soldiers. The lightning rapier of Field Marshal von Rundstedt became a blunt and rusty sword as it probed for a soft spot that simply did not exist.

The men responsible died to do it. They were men who battled till the last breath, the last bullet, before the Nazi tide

Continued on Page 5, Column 3.

Japs Hint Invasion Of Luzon

5¢

NEW YORK Journal-American
AN AMERICAN PAPER FOR THE AMERICAN PEOPLE
Daily 5 Cents, Saturday 5 Cents in SUNDAY, 10 Cents in New York City
New York City; 10 Cents Elsewhere and 50-Mile Zone, 15 Cents Elsewhere
R
No. 20,803—DAILY FRIDAY, DECEMBER, 29, 1944 In Two Sections—Section One

LATEST NEWS
LATEST SCRATCHES

SMASH NAZI BULGE

1st and 3rd Closing Trap!

CIO Wire Men Vote to Join AFL In Red Protest

By HOWARD RUSHMORE

Former executive board members and chief stewards representing more than 3,000 members of the American Communications Association, CIO, voted late last night to join the AFL and repudiate the Communist leadership of the A. C. A.

This was announced by Charles A. Bardunias, former president of Local 40—the Western Union group of the A. C. A., who said that 40 leading members of the CIO union had unanimously approved the decision.

In addition to voting for the AFL affiliation the former CIO officers and representaives also passed a resolution condemning Communism as a threat to the entire American labor movement.

BARE RED RECRUITING.

Meanwhile it was learned that soon after the ACA had been set up to organize Western Union employes, its "labor" leaders launched a recruiting drive for the Communist Party.

These same leaders, openly supporting any and all Red issues, used their offices for Marxist political and propaganda purposes to the extent rank-and-file delegations pleaded with them to concentrate on trade unionism—but to no avail.

WHOLESALE RESIGNATIONS.

Henry Sierp, former general cihef steward of Local 40, ACA's largest group in the local communications field, made these charges today as wholesale resignations of Western Union workers from the

Continued on Page 5, Column 4.

City Meat Crisis Eased as Army Drops Its Cut

Fears by butchers that the meat crisis might persist despite the promised 12,000,000-pound influx to eight large wholesalers here within the next week were eased today with word that the Army will not cut into this 6,000-ton New York civilian bonanza.

Markets Commissioner Brundage disclosed that Army officials had given Mayor LaGuardia assurance to this effect.

80 % OF SHOPS OPEN.

With a Police Department check-up disclosing that nearly 80 per cent of 6,142 butcher shops tabulated were open for business, although many had empty refrigerators, officials of the New York City Retail Meat Dealers' Action Committee said the big supply expected from the West would be helpful if most of it actually reached the retailers.

Albert T. Wendel, chairman of the committee, pointed out that large amounts out of such shipments are often diverted to military or lend-lease needs.

Chill Greeting For New Year

An Icelandic atmosphere for the duration of waning 1944 seemed certain today. The Weather Bureau predicted more cold, snow and sleet.

Today's pre-dawn temperature was around 21, and the expected range for the day was between 20 and 28. The snow may begin tonight or tomorrow.

Avery to Stay On Job Until 'Thrown Out'

(Pictures on Page 5 and in Pictorial Review.)

CHICAGO, Dec. 29 (INS).—Chairman Sewell L. Avery grimly declared today he still was "head" of the Montgomery Ward & Co. mail order house in spite of the fact that its properties in Chicago and six other cities had been seized by the U. S. Army on Presidential orders.

He asserted he was determined to remain at the head of the vast institution, second largest of its kind in the world, until he was thrown out bodily, as he was last April when the Government seized the Chicago plants, or until he was removed by court order.

"NO LEGAL RIGHT."

"I intend to go to my office daily just as I always have in the past and I'll stay there unless I'm forcibly ejected as I was the last time," said the 70-year-old board chairman, with emphasis.

"I'm in charge of the place as before and the Army is in there without a court order. They have no legal right there and until such legal right is established, I'm in charge.

"They'll have to throw me out or fence me out."

A battery of Government lawyers, headed by Benedict Deinard, special assistant to Attorney General Francis Biddle, and Hugh B.

Continued on Page 5, Column 1.

THE WEATHER

Clear and cold.

Sun rises, 8:19 a. m.; sun sets, 5:37 p. m. High tide at Governors Island, 8:57 a. m. and 9:27 p. m.

HOURLY TEMPERATURES.

12 midnight	26	5 a. m.	21
1 a. m.	26	6 a. m.	21
2 a. m.	25	7 a. m.	21
3 a. m.	24	8 a. m.	20
4 a. m.	23	9 a. m.	20

Complete Weather Report on Page 8

TODAY'S INDEX

The Journal-American has the largest circulation of any evening newspaper in New York City
ALLIED PRINTING TRADES UNION LABEL COUNCIL NEW YORK 230

It is the only New York evening newspaper possessing the three great wire services—ASSOCIATED PRESS—INTERNATIONAL NEWS SERVICE—UNITED PRESS

—(PHONE YOUR NEWS TIPS TO CORTLANDT 7-1212)—

Death Valley Of Nazi Hopes

CHRISTMAS MESSAGE . . . Gen. Dwight Eisenhower gets into his jeep as he prepares to drive to meet representatives of all the Allied countries to deliver his Christmas message to the Allied forces. International News Photo.

NEAR CELLES, Belgium, Dec. 28 (delayed)(AP).—Everywhere over the abandoned front, which yesterday rocked with the crashing sounds of battle as an American armored outfit stopped von Rundstedt's drive three miles short of the Meuse River, lies a silence compounded of cold, fog and death.

It is a silence broken only by the chirp of quarreling snowbirds on a forlorn bough, the crunch of the feet of a few Doughboys walking stiffly across the glazed fields and the endless hum of trucks moving along slippery highways with food and bullets for a new front.

The evidence of recent battle, however, is plain to see—the bodies of hundreds of enemy dead and the wreckage of Nazi tanks, armord cars, trucks and field guns scattered over miles of field and woodland.

Sharing equally in the victory over the enemy striking force were American doughboys, tanks and artillery teamed in perfect coordination with Allied airpower.

"The airmen gave us wonderful support," said one American tank commander, who personally knocked out four tanks during the engagement. "Those planes helped us get 19 of our 63 enemy tanks. And some British Typhoons which pitched

Continued on Page 4, Column 8.

New Tax Plan Starts Jan. 1

WASHINGTON, Dec. 29 (UP).—New withholding tax schedules will be effective beginning Jan. 1, regardless of the pay period covered.

Some taxpayers will find more withheld, some less, and some will find no change. The full year tax bill will be the same as heretofore, but there will be less difference between what has been withheld and the amount finally determined as due, meaning fewer adjustments at the end of the tax year.

Tokyo Hints At Invasion Of Luzon

A Japanese communique said today that 30 American transports with an escort of 20 or more cruisers and destroyers were sailing westward through the Mindanao Sea in the Philippines, possibly to launch a new invasion in the archipelago.

The report followed recent Japanese speculation that Gen. MacArthur was about to begin amphibious landing operations against Luzon, site of the Philippine capital of Manila and ultimate American objective in the islands.

CLAIM 6 SINKINGS.

The Japanese communique, recorded by the United Press in New York, said Japanese planes had sunk six large American transports and heavily damaged two others in attacks yesterday.

Three transports were sunk Thursday morning and three others sunk and two damaged Thursday night, the communique said.

The enemy said the convoy entered the Mindanao Sea Wednesday night from the Surigao Straits, which lie between Leyte and Mindanao, the latter the southernmost of the Philippines.

The convoy reported by the Japanese appeared to be traveling the same route as that taken by amphibious forces which invaded Mindoro Dec. 16. Luzon lies across a nine-mile wide channel from the northeast coast of Mindoro.

It also was possible the convoy was bearing reinforcements and supplies for American forces on Mindoro.

British in Athens Attack Key Hill

ATHENS, Dec. 29 (INS).—Moving up behind an artillery barrage with 25-pounders and spearheaded by Sherman tanks, the British at dawn today attacked an insurgent Greek stronghold on Architos Hill, near the center of the capital.

For two hours the crump of shells and the chatter of tommy-guns did not cease.

A pall of smoke hovered over the whole southeastern suburban area of Athens.

Regiment In Pocket Wiped Out

(See sketch by Burris Jenkins, Jr., in Today's Pictorial Review.)

By THURSTON MACAULEY,
International News Service Staff Correspondent.

PARIS, Dec. 29.—The westernmost spearhead of German offensive forces in the Belgian-Luxembourg bulge was lopped off today by counter-attacking Allied troops. The Germans were forced into a general withdrawal on the southeastern flank of the salient.

Allied assault forces liquidated a regiment of Nazis who had been pocketed between Rochefort and Celles. The trapped Germans had been subjected to a fierce artillery pounding before ground forces closed in on the enemy units.

[*UP reported the Yank 1st and 3rd Armies were deep in the flanks of the German salient within 15 miles of a juncture that threatened to trap tens of thousands of crack Nazi troops in Adrennes forest.*]

Nazis Now on Defensive

Hard-hitting 3rd Army units forced the withdrawal of the Germans on the southeastern flank in the area of Echternach, near the Reich-Luxembourg frontier.

As the Germans pulled back generally in the Echternach sector, Lt. Gen. George S. Patton's troops moved up to the Sauer River as far as Rosport, four miles east of Echternach.

The northern flank of the German salient also underwent stern hammering, and an official headquarters spokesman said that the Nazis, who failed to make any appreciable gains anywhere in the past 48 hours, were being forced to fight defensively in most sectors.

Fleeing Nazis Swim Icy River

A front dispatch from Belgium said that the Germans were carrying out a disorganized withdrawal in the face of the 3rd Army drive, with Gen. Patton's troops hard on the heels of the enemy.

Fleeing Germans were reported trying to swim the icy Sauer River in their flight from the Americans, it was said.

While Gen. Patton compelled the Germans to

Continued on Page 2, Column 1.

Army To Draft All Fit Under 30

7TH SPORT .:. NIGHT FINAL WEATHER: FAIR Details on Page 13

THE CALL BULLETIN
SAN FRANCISCO — AN INDEPENDENT NEWSPAPER

CALL AND POST. VOL. 156. NO. 140
THE CALL-BULLETIN. VOL. 176. NO. 140
THURSDAY, JANUARY 11, 1945 5c DAILY

Stimson to Bare Allied Losses in Nazi Breakthrough

WASHINGTON, Jan. 11 (INS). Secretary of War Stimson today promised to make public casualty figures reflecting losses in the German breakthrough in Belgium and France at his news conference next Thursday.

The past week, which he said reflected casualties early in December, showed an increase of 7,999 from the previous report. They represent figures compiled through December 29 but, Stimson explained, they reflect actual casualties of a period of two or three weeks earlier.

Cumulative figures since the beginning of the war now are 106,952 killed, 333,849 wounded, 64,283 missing, 59,267 prisoners of war, making a total of 564,351.

The War Department totals added to the figures of the Navy, Marine Corps and Coast Guard, make a grand total of 646,370 casualties of all types.

Total naval casualties of today are 41,838, divided as follows: Dead 20,683, wounded 10,312, missing 8,307, prisoners 2,536.

Marine casualties total 39,328 as follows: Dead 10,186, wounded 26,292, missing 907, prisoners 1,943.

Coast Guard, total 862; dead 572, wounded 194, missing 97, prisoners none.

LUZON BATTLE ON

OCCUPATION NO ESCAPE, DECLARES STIMSON

WASHINGTON, Jan. 11 (INS). Secretary of War Henry L. Stimson declared today that increased draft needs of the Army will probably result in the induction of all able bodied men—even those in war industries, agriculture and government jobs below the age of 30.

Stimson told his news conference that an additional 700,000 war workers will be needed before July 1, 1945.

The secretary said that there is "no escape" from the induction of practically all able bodied men under 30 years of age, no matter what line of work they may be doing.

TO MEET NEEDS

These, he said, will be needed for the production of essential and critical war materials such as heavy guns and ammunition, truck tires and cotton duck, production of which has been lagging as well as for increased material needed to supply and equip French forces and to meet transportation needs and production for civilians.

At his news conference, Stimson denied that the Army is oversize, noting that there are 450,000 men who are injured or sick in Army hospitals who must be kept on a troop status until everything possible has been done for them.

He said that the effective size of the Army must be kept up to ceiling and that the necessity of maintaining a full force grows as the war gains in intensity.

UNDER LEAVE

He also cited the fact that 85,000 troops are being regularly relieved and cannot be counted as effective since they are on leave under the Army rotation plan.

Stimson backed up demands of the administration for an "effective" national selective service law, and asserted that increased Army draft calls—to 100,000 in March—have been forced by stepped-up requirements of the War Department.

(Details of Army-Navy needs, Page 5.)

Girl, 5, Kidnaped, Raped, Tortured

HOLLYWOOD, Jan. 11 (INS).—A sex fiend who kidnaped and tortured 5 year old Patricia Forrester was being sought throughout the state today following return of the little girl to her home in Hollywood.

The man, described as between 30 and 50 and of slender build, dragged the girl into his black sedan as she was playing in front of her home late yesterday.

Patricia told police that he drove to Highland Park and stopped near a lake, where he attacked her and burned the ends of her fingers with the cigar lighter attached to the car.

WIDE PROBE OF PRESTON UNDER WAY

SACRAMENTO, Jan. 11.—The Assembly today approved the O'Day-Haggerty resolution calling for a special committee to investigate the Preston School of Industry at Ione, 77 to 0. Members were Assemblymen O'Day (chairman), Haggerty, Collins, Call, Johnson, Dickey, Fourt and Middough.

SACRAMENTO, Jan. 11.—Conditions at Preston School of Industry have been under investigation for a year, since discovery that authorities there were using "strong-arm" squads of older boys admittedly "mature in crime" to discipline younger inmates, Governor Earl Warren revealed today.

At the same time Warren announced that O. H. Close, superintendent of the institution, has been suspended pending outcome of a sweeping inquiry into conditions at Preston resulting from charges inmates were subjected to cruel and inhumane treatment.

'WIPED OUT'

The governor made the disclosure at a press conference at which he added that such practices have been "practically wiped out" during the past few months.

The governor said that when Karl Holton, executive officer of the California Youth Authority, took office a year ago he found such practices had been "developed through the years."

Holton acted to correct the evils, Warren said, so that during the past month no such instances have been reported.

TO HIS ATTENTION

Warren said that conditions at Preston had been brought to his attention by The Call-Bulletin.

The governor said he "hesitated to criticize the courts for sending boys to Preston," and declared:

"The situation at Preston is

Continued on Page 2, Column 4

Allied Patrols Push 10 Miles; Take Laroche

PARIS, Jan. 11 (AP).—Allied troops captured strategic Laroche today and British patrols in a swift ten mile advance through the collapsing western end of the Belgian bulge reached the Champlon area, a mile east of the north-south road between Laroche and St. Hubert.

The road was cut without opposition.

The Germans quickened their skillful, orderly withdrawal in the deep snow as the American First and Third armies drove in from north and south and the British Second Army pursued through profuse minefields from the west.

PENETRATE FOREST

The main British force was four miles behind the patrols which penetrated the Champlon area, almost through the difficult Freyr Forest. The town is thirteen miles west of Houffalize, which the Germans may attempt to make the center of a new defense front shielding the eastern half of the bulge.

The cruelest enemy for both sides was the continuing blizzard, with temperatures 9 above zero Fahrenheit.

STRASBOURG THREATENED

With the bulge battle going well, the tenderest spot on the Allied side of the western front was Strasbourg. Germans threatened the Alsatian capital from positions 10 to 17 miles south and from nine miles north. Planes spotted 100 tanks below Strasbourg, evenly deployed on both sides of the Rhine, and claimed the destruction of nine and the damaging of 19.

The Germans did not appear to have exerted their full strength in that area, but neither the American Seventh Army on the north nor the French First Army on the south had yet shown sufficient strength to reduce the threat.

TEST NEW SECTOR

A short break in the clouds allowed a few Allied planes to get into the air above the Belgian bulge for a change. Two squadrons of fighterbombers raided two areas east of the key German base of St. Vith and pilots reported they exploded several stacks of ammunition, a train and ten railroads.

First Army patrols tested a new

Continued on Page 4, Column 2

3 Resign Over Big Gas Ration Stamp Looting

District OPA Director Robert B. Parks has accepted the resignations of the board chairman and two staff members of Ration Board No. 3 in the lake of last Sunday's burglary of 75,000 gallons worth of gasoline coupons and other ration stamps from the place, he announced today.

Parks said he accepted the resignation because he found, in the course of an investigation of the burglary, that carelessness on the part of board officials "was in part the cause" of the theft.

THE RULES

He said OPA regulations require that ration coupons should not be left in board offices overnight, but should be sent to a bank for safekeeping.

The officials who resigned were Fred A. Castle, board chairman; Mary Soyat, chief clerk, and Winifred Morris, custodian.

ONCE BEFORE

Parks said the place had been burglarized once before and the officials warned at that time.

Venereal Confab Called Here

Tavern owners and bartenders today were asked by military and city officials to aid in combating venereal disease in San Francisco by "cracking down" on women "bar contacts."

The appeal was made at a meeting in the Health building auditorium attended by approximately 200 tavern owners and bartenders and was called by John H. Wieder, representative of the State Board of Equalization.

Included among the speakers were Dr. J. C. Geiger, city health director; Major Edward Levin, representing the Army; Commander Benton Scott, representing the Navy; Deputy Chief of Police Michael Riordan and Richard A. Koch, chief of the venereal disease section of the city Health Department.

Ribbentrop Reported On Mission to Spain

LONDON, Jan. 11 (AP).—The Brussels radio, quoting Swedish newspapers, said today that Hitler has sent Foreign Minister Joachim von Ribbentrop to Madrid to [illegible]ck political stirrings that a[illegible] said to be endangering German influence in Spain.

SINGAPORE, TOKIO HIT BY B-29'S

WASHINGTON, Jan. 11 (AP). Super Fortresses blasted shipping installations at the Japanese naval base of Singapore today for the second time.

"Good results" were reported by the War Department.

The raid, apparently aimed at pinning down Japanese naval units at the big base while General MacArthur's troops are carrying out their invasion of the Philippines, was hammered home by upwards of forty B-29 bombers from India.

OFF GUARD

Roaring in during the early morning, the big bombers may have caught the enemy off guard since only "meagre and inaccurate" anti-aircraft fire was encountered.

Four enemy fighters that rose to meet the raiders were shot down by Super Fortress gunners.

None of the B-29's was lost to enemy action, the communique reported, without saying whether all had returned to their bases.

Singapore previously had been hit on November 5 by sixty B-29's from India.

2 B-29'S MISSING

The communique also disclosed that two B-29's are missing from the raid on Tokio Tuesday and are believed lost "as a result of enemy action." Additional reports on the raid showed that the Saipan based Super Fortresses destroyed fourteen Japanese planes.

Some damaged Japanese warships are believed to have scurried to Singapore for refitting after the naval battles in the Phillippine seas late in 1944.

Another Super Fortress raid on Tokio meantime was announced by the Japanese radio. The Japanese claimed without American confirmation that three B-29s from Saipan unloaded incendiaries yesterday. Likewise unsubstantiated was the Tokio claim that twenty-nine out of sixty of the big planes were shot down or damaged during the Tuesday strike against central Honshu.

Argentina Status Tops Foreign Ministers' Agenda

MEXICO CITY, Jan. 11 (AP).—An international conference of American foreign ministers will open here February 15 with the case of Argentina as an important part of its agenda, the Mexican foreign office announced last night. Argentina itself has not been invited.

Byrnes Refutes Move To Close Night Clubs

WASHINGTON, Jan. 11 (AP). War Mobilization Director James F. Byrnes reiterated today that he had given no consideration to the closing of night clubs.

Mrs. Bondshu Freed In Speeding Charge

Mrs. Vicki Bondshu, 27, 1516 Tyler street, Berkeley, wife of Neil Bondshu, widely known leader of a "name" dance band, who committed suicide last month, appeared in municipal court here today to answer a speeding charge.

Mrs. Bondshu explained to Judge Harry J. Neubarth she was arrested on the bay bridge December 21 while rushing to San Francisco upon receiving word of her estranged husband's disappearance. The citation listed her speed at 45 miles per hour.

Judge Neubarth dismissed the charge because, he said, of her state of mind and the nature of the emergency.

Yanks Drive Inland 20 Mi.

LONDON, Jan. 11 (AP).—An Australian radio broadcast recorded here today said the battle in the north Luzon plain already had started with a violent artillery engagement.

GENERAL MacARTHUR'S HEADQUARTERS, Luzon, Jan. 11 (AP).—Manila-bound American infantrymen stretched their beachhead over twenty-two miles of Lingayen Gulf and drove inland from four key towns today toward impending major battles with Japanese reinforcements struggling north over bomb cut roads.

Only damaging opposition came at sea, where night attacking Japanese planes and torpedo boats hit several ships in a convoy bringing up Fourteenth Corps reinforcements.

On land, the Yanks seized twenty towns and villages, captured Lingayen airfield and pushed their advanced spearheads to a little more than 100 miles north of Manila. (This represented an inland advance of about twenty miles from the original beachheads.) Nowhere was serious resistance reported.

(A London radio report recorded by the Blue Network said today that advanced American troops are less than 100 kilometers (62 miles) from Manila in their push southward on the Philippines island of Luzon. The London transmission said also that the average depth of the beachhead was about 35 kilometers, or some 20 miles—much deeper penetrations than officially reported.)

Thursday's communique announced the doughboys overran the towns of San Fabian, Lingayen, Mangaldan and Dagupan in the first 24 hours and pressed inland for an average advance of four miles. Patrols were well ahead of this average penetration.

A field dispatch from Fred Hampson, Associated Press war correspondent, disclosed units of the Fourteenth Army Corps pushing west along the coast from Lingayen, were within two miles of Port Sual. This broadened the base of the American drive to cover twenty-two miles of the southern Lingayen coastline.

The Seventh Fleet continued to pour troops, armament and supplies onto the beachhead, while General Tomoyuki Yamashita pulled his scattered Japanese divisions together.

A few bomb carrying Japanese swam or drifted among American vessels under cover of darkness in futile human-torpedo attacks on the crowded ships.

Associated Press Correspondent Al Dopking reported the Japanese approached American vessels "in slow boats, or swimming with their heads hidden under boxes, and pushing before them hand made torpedoes, tiny bombs and even hand grenades."

One hurled himself on the deck of a small craft and was blown to bits. Two others tried to blow up

Jap Air Might Hurled at Yank Fleet on Jan. 6

By CLARK LEE
Staff Correspondent International News

ABOARD ADMIRAL KINKAID'S FLAGSHIP, Lingayen Gulf, Jan. 11 (INS).—Vice Admiral Jesse Oldendorf told today how his heavy bombardment force withstood the weight of repeated heavy Jap air onslaughts throughout January 6, and then, to the Japs' astonishment, returned to Lingayen Gulf the following day to resume pounding of shore targets.

"The Japs threw everything at us when we first came in on the sixth," said the grizzled, tanned, smiling victor of the Surigao Straits battle during the epochal second naval battle of the Philippines.

"They never thought we would be able to take it," he said. "But the next day we were back and their air wasn't. My guess is that when they saw us pull out for the night they thought we were retreating and then drank so much sake they couldn't fly on the seventh."

Admiral William F. Halsey complained a few days ago about "anemic" Jap air resistance to his carrier strikes. But they were anything but anemic to Oldendorf's force.

"What happened," Oldendorf said, "was that 'Bull' (Admiral Halsey) chased their planes over to my side of the mountains."

The resulting attacks with more than 100 planes, usually in groups of four to six, were the roughest in Oldendorf's experi-

Continued on Page A, Column 3

3 Former Jap Premiers Confer With Present One

By Associated Press

Japanese government leaders past and present met today for three hours with Premier General Kuniaki Koiso.

The Tokio radio said the meeting included three former Japanese premiers—General Hideki Tojo, Baron Reijiro Wakatsuki and Koki Hirota; Admiral Baron Kantaro Suzuki, president of the privy council, and all ministers in Koiso's cabinet.

The broadcast, intercepted by the Federal Communications Commission, said the conference was for a "roundtable discussion of various subjects."

Clash at Fabian 'Bloodiest and Fiercest': Tokio

By Associated Press

Radio Tokio said today the "fiercest and bloodiest" battle is now raging along the Lingayen Gulf coast with San Fabian as the focal point.

The broadcast admitted Americans had infiltrated Japanese positions near San Fabian.

"About 4 p. m. Wednesday, led by tanks under cover of artillery fire, the Yanks began to advance eastward from San Fabian and about 40 minutes later part of the U. S. forces made a thrust into one corner of our positions," the broadcast said. "After a sanguinary melee, Japanese forces drove the enemy from these advanced positions."

HAND TO HAND CLASH

Thereafter, it said, the Americans opened "an intensive fire" and "resumed the attack and fierce hand to hand fighting ensued."

Conceding Yank air and surface action, Radio Tokio said:

"U. S. planes are tenaciously attempting to strafe our ammunition dumps and other installations and at nightfall U. S. warcraft in Lingayen Gulf threw up flare bombs while shelling our positions."

Japanese broadcasts declared American forces had attempted a new landing on Luzon yesterday at Labon, ten miles north of Fabian, but were beaten off.

VIOLENT FIGHTING

At the same time, Tokio said, Japanese ground forces were "engaging a considerable number of American tanks in violent fighting following the initial landing."

Previously the Japanese Domei agency admitted American invasion forces were "gradually increasing their reinforcements at San Fabian and Dagupan" and that a "considerable number of tanks have been landed at other beachheads."

BASTOGNE AREA RESISTANCE CRUMBLING

WITH U. S. THIRD ARMY, Jan. 11 (AP).—The Third Army attacked the pocket southeast of Bastogne from three sides today and in eleven hours wiped out half the area, and resistance in the remainder was collapsing rapidly. At the start the pocket was about five miles long and four wide.

AUSTRALIA JOINS IN PHILIPPINE CAMPAIGN

SYDNEY, Jan. 11 (AP).—War Minister Francis Forde said today Australian land, sea and air forces would be represented in wresting the Philippines from the Japanese.

BILL ASKS 'FAIR EMPLOYMENT' COMMITTEE

WASHINGTON, Jan. 11 (INS).—Representative Frank E. Hook (D., Mich.) introduced a bill in the House today to establish a permanent fair employment practice committee and asked that it get top priority as "win the war legislation."

1ST. HAVANA—Ladogan, won. 2.40, 2.20, 2.20; Scaggs, 2d, 2.20, 2.20; Pluto, 3d, 2.20. Time, 1:12.

Hint Spellman on Vital Peace Task

LONDON, Jan. 11 (AP).—The Morocco radio today broadcast unconfirmed Swiss reports that Archbishop Francis J. Spellman of New York had been entrusted by Pope Pius XII with an important mission in connection with future peace talks.

It gave no details, but said there was "great diplomatic activity in Rome."

A Rome dispatch last night said some Vatican circles believed there was a possibility Archbishop Spellman might become papal secretary of state, pro tempore, although a Vatican official had denied this.

Call-Bulletin Today

Special Features

("G" indicates Green Flash Section)

THE STARS AND STRIPES
MEDITERRANEAN

Vol. 2, No. 60, Thursday, January 18, 1945 ITALY EDITION ★ ★ TWO LIRE

RED ARMY TAKES WARSAW

Allies Storm West Front

Fierce Fight Rages North Of Aachen

Yanks Five Miles From St. Vith; 1st, 3rd Join

SHAEF, Jan. 17 — Allied forces all along the West Front were on the offensive today, rebounding in strength from the winter assault opened by Field Marshal Gerd von Rundstedt a month ago.

British 2nd Army forces advanced 1,000 yards against stiffening opposition in their assault yesterday in the southern hook of the Netherlands, 18 miles north of Aachen. The attack, which apparently surprised the Germans, appeared to have as its objective erasure of the German bulge between Geilenkirchen and Roermond.

In the Ardennes where the German salient now is no more than 15 miles deep, units of the American 3rd and 1st Armies met in occupied Houffalize and drove toward the German frontier. St. Vith, northern hinge of the flattened bulge, was under increasing pressure from the 1st Army which was within five miles of the strategic road center.

Far to the southeast, powerful 7th Army infantry and armored units opened an attack against the German bridgehead over the Rhine River eight miles north of Strasbourg. Front-line dispatches indicated that a gain of at least two miles had been made. The ground forces were preceded by swarms of Thunderbolts which divebombed and strafed German strongholds.

The 7th Army attack was heralded by a 300-gun barrage along a six-mile stretch of the river, and combat engineers, riding on tanks,

(Continued on page 8)

THEY WAIT for the next wave of enemy planes to come over, these men of a 5th Army AAA battalion. At this, as at other sectors of the Italian front, both the Yanks and the enemy are fighting heavy snows.

Says Right Here: Furloughs Upped

WASHINGTON, Jan. 17 (ANS) —All limitations on the number of soldiers who may receive 30-day furloughs have been removed by the War Department. As one result, the number of service men returning from war zones on leave probably will "increase markedly" in the next few months.

Gen. George C. Marshall, Chief of Staff, said that theater commanders now have the authority to return any men they can spare for one month plus travel time. The War Department is no longer directly involved in such decisions, he said.

Patrolling Is Brisk On 5th Army Front

ADVANCED AFHQ, Jan. 17—Patrolling was brisk on the 5th Army Front yesterday despite new snow and rain.

Yank patrols probed the enemy's forward positions and contacted German forces near Mt. Spaiduro, 10 miles southeast of Bologna, and at San Ansano in the central sector. Other clashes took place at Mt. Grande and at Recca Pitigliana, a town 25 miles southwest of Bologna off Highway 64.

In the same general area, near Bombiauon, Germans fired more than 200 rounds of mortar and artillery fire in two and one-half hours. A lone German plane dropped bombs in a left flank sector, but no damage was reported.

Eighth Army lines from the bulge below Imola eastward to the Comacchio lagoon were unchanged.

It was revealed that units of the 7th Armored Brigade took part in the recent action that swept the Germans from their bridgehead over the Senio River south of Cotignola, 11 miles due west of Ravenna.

'Big 3' Time And Place Set

WASHINGTON, Jan. 17 — President Roosevelt has announced definitely that the time and place has been fixed for the "Big Three" meeting and that he was about to go to join Prime Minister Churchill and Marshal Stalin, Associated Press reported today.

It was reported from London by United Press that most observers were inclined to believe the conference will open toward the end of this month. An advance party of high British government officials is standing by to depart on short notice, and will precede Churchill, who will remain in London a little while longer and then make a quick air trip to the scene of the meeting.

Most "well-informed" quarters in the British capital feel certain that the conference will take place in the middle east.

Participation of General Charles de Gaulle in the meeting of the big three is still subject to speculation.

The AP said that U. S. diplomatic quarters considered the French leader's inclusion as "virtually certain."

French officials here said they could not confirm reports that General de Gaulle had expressed a desire to attend the meeting, but they recalled his constant insistence that the future of Europe could not be settled without France.

State Department officials declined to comment on the report.

Diplomatic sources pointed out that General de Gaulle had won progressive acceptance of his provisional Government of the French Republic.

Moscow Radio has issued an "authorized denial" of an AP report that the Soviet Union had asked that General de Gaulle be invited on a promise that he would support Russian views on east European territorial adjustments.

100,000,000 Mines Left In French Soil

PARIS, Jan. 17 — One hundred million mines and booby traps still remain buried in French soil, the Paris Radio said today. A commentator announced that the labor of 20,000 men for 20 years would be required to clear the mines and booby traps and that the operation would cost 10,000 million francs

Cracow Is Freed, Says Lublin Radio

Russians Open Third Drive In Poland; Town 20 Miles From Reich Taken

MOSCOW, Jan. 17—Russian armies have opened a new offensive—the third in Poland—north of Warsaw, Marshal Stalin announced tonight. In the opening phase of the drive, they swept 25 miles forward on a 60-mile front and captured Ciechanow, 120 miles from Danzig.

Marshal Stalin also announced capture of Radomsko, only 20 miles from the German province of Silesia.

The Polish Provisional Government (Lublin) said Red Army troops had captured Cracow.

MOSCOW, Jan. 17—The Red Army today captured Warsaw, battered and ravaged capital of Poland.

Moscow's big guns fired a thunderous victory salute tonight to the men of Marshal Gregory Zhukov's Army who crowned the fourth day of their smashing offensive by wresting Warsaw from the grip of German oppression after five years.

Marshal Joseph Stalin's triumphant special Order of the Day, issued in mid-afternoon instead of in the evening as usual, hailed the liberation "of the capital of our Polish ally."

His announcement followed by less than five hours a victorious proclamation from Lublin, seat of the Polish Provisional Government. The Lublin Radio said: "Formations of the Russian Army and of the Polish Army have occupied Warsaw, capital of the Polish Republic."

The announcement was repeated three times, and then the Polish national anthem was played.

Warsaw A Devastated City

In Warsaw, the Red Army and the Polish contingent found a ruined capital. Its prewar population of 1,289,000 has been decimated by Nazi terror, starvation and the repeated armed defiance of the people against the Herrenvolk.

Warsaw was the first European capital to be captured by the Germans in this war, and to celebrate its recapture, Marshal Stalin ordered 24 salvos from 324 guns.

Warsaw was taken as a result of attacks from the north, south and west, Marshal Stalin said.

Zhukov's troops after breaking through south of the capital Sunday, wheeled to the right and outflanked Warsaw from the rear. Another large column breasted the Vistula River from the north and swung down on the city.

The speed of Zhukov's armor and infantry, supported by General Zigmund Pazlovski's 1st Polish Army, was so great that the Germans could not mount a defense. Apparently they left a skeleton garrison, pulling the main body of their troops back for a hasty retreat to the west. Zhukov's forces tonight were in close pursuit.

The German situation in southern Poland was equally grim, by their own admission. Marshal Ivan S. Koniev's Army which has covered almost 100 miles since its offensive began last Friday, was at the outskirts of the vital city of Czestochowa. His advance spearheads were about 15 miles from the borders of Germany's industrial Silesia.

Soviets 270 Miles From Berlin

On the outskirts of Czestochowa, the Red Army was 270 miles from Berlin, closest point to the German capital reached by any Allied army. In the west, Berlin was 310 miles from advance points held by the American 1st and 9th Armies.

Soviet dispatches pictured the offensive, according to Associated Press, as one of the largest, if not the largest, of this or any other war. They told of hordes of tanks and guns and thousands of soldiers mov- in what seemed endless waves across the windswept Polish countryside.

(Max Krull, German military commentator, said in a broadcast "nothing that has happened in the past five years of war can bear comparison with the masses of men and weapons the Russians have thrown into the winter offensive now raging between the Carpathians and the Baltic.")

A Moscow military spokesman, according to United Press, said that Zhukov, advancing in the general direction of Lodz, biggest industrial city in Poland, had poured terrific masses of tanks and artillery into his attack.

Last night's Soviet communique reported the capture of hundreds of towns and villages as the armies of Zhukov and Koniev poured through Poland.

Far to the south, the savage fighting that had highlighted Russian front news for weeks continued to rage in Budapest. Moscow announced last night that 120 more blocks of the Hungarian capital had been taken from the bitter-end defenders. A total of 3,160 prisoners was captured, bringing the bag for the fighting inside the city to 20,000.

THE STARS AND STRIPES
MEDITERRANEAN
Vol. 2, No. 82, Tuesday, February 13, 1945
ITALY EDITION * * TWO LIRE

Big Three Map Victory, Insist On Unconditional Surrender

Red Army Drives On Dresden

Koniev's Troops Capture Town Of Bunzlau

MOSCOW, Feb. 12—Flying armored columns of Marshal Koniev's 1st Ukrainian Army Group drove west and northwest today from their new 100-mile-long bridgehead on the west bank of the Oder. Marshal Koniev's men deepened their penetration of the Reich and were battling along the thickly-wooded area of the Bober River, 65 miles east of Dresden and 65 miles northwest of bypassed Breslau. Dresden, in the heart of the Reich, appeared to be the immediate objective.

In his second Order of the Day, Marshal Stalin tonight announced the capture of Bunzlau on the Bober River, approximately 75 miles from Dresden, confirming German reports that Marshal Koniev's men had broken into the town.

An earlier Order of the Day from Marshal Stalin announced the capture of Bielkso in southwestern Poland, 20 miles from the Czechoslovakian border. The city covers approaches to the Czechoslovakian industrial city of Moratska-Ostrava.

Front-line reports said today that Marshal Koniev's tanks had smashed through in many directions. The picture of inside Gernany tonight was that of the Wehrmacht trying to regroup in the face of disrupted communications over a wide area.

Soviet troops reported great German troop movements today. The roads near the forward zone were said to be crowded with German forces on the march.

Dispatches from the front also said that alarm was spreading to more and more German villages as

(Continued on Page 2)

Siegfried Line Stronghold Captured

21ST ARMY GROUP HQ., Feb. 12—The Canadian 1st Army has captured Cleve, northern bastion of the Siegfried Line, Reuter's reported tonight.

All organized fighting was said to have stopped in the town, and the last snipers were being mopped up. Hekkens, on the southern edge of the Reichwald Forest on the road from Cleve, also was reported occupied.

Allied troops, Reuter's added, also have taken Hau, fewer than two miles south of Cleve on the Cleve-Goch road.

Earlier in the day, United Press reported that advancing British and Canadian troops captured the Siegfried Line town of Gennep and that other forward elements had crossed the Spoy Canal which bisects Cleve.

The British had threatened to pass by the German stronghold of Gennep, on the Meuse River, and frightened the Germans into making a withdrawal from there.

Due east of the town forward elements forged a way across the little Niers River. In the center of the assault arc they pushed forward through the Reichswald forest.

More than 4,000 prisoners have been captured since the start of the offensive.

Today's battle was being fought under worsening weather conditions. Before the weather closed in, however, American, British and Canadian fighter bombers took a heavy toll of German rail movements east of the battlefield. It was the strongest attack in a week.

The grand total was 53 locomotives destroyed, 107 damaged, 99 railcars destroyed and 454 damaged.

A SHAEF announcement said that the 3rd Army today was fighting in the streets of the German road junction of Prum southeast of St. Vith. Front-line dispatches indicated that half of the town had been cleared.

Conference At Yalta Is Over

Occupation Of Reich Will Be Shared By 3 Powers

Unconditional surrender of Germany, as the only basis for the end of the war in Europe, was emphasized again last night in a communique issued at the end of an historic eight-day conference of the Big Three at Yalta in the Crimea, Russia.

President Franklin Roosevelt, Prime Minister Winston Churchill, and Marshal Joseph V. Stalin pledged the breakup of the Nazi political machines, confiscation of German military might, control of German industry, and punishment of war criminals.

They announced that a conference of the United Nations, to be sponsored by the Big Three in concert with France and China, would be held in San Francisco on April 25 to draft a charter for a postwar security organization based on the plans formulated at the Dumbarton Oaks conference.

Affirming that all traces of Nazism and Fascism must be erased from the countries of Europe, the Big Three emphasized that it is not their intention to destroy the people of Germany. They emphasized, however, that only when Nazism and militarism have been completely eliminated from the Reich will there be a hope for a decent life for the Germans and a place for them in the community of nations.

President Roosevelt, Prime Minister Churchill and Marshal Stalin affirmed the principles of the Atlantic Charter and enunciated a declaration for the liberated cou-

(Continued on Page 8)

Germans Aggressive On 5th Coast Sector

ADVANCED AFHQ, Feb. 12 — Enemy aggressiveness continued in the 5th Army coastal sector where repeated counterattacks were launched against Allied positions, but local operations in this area which have been in progress for the last few days have been concluded, today's communique announced.

Two German counterattacks near Mt. Casala, just east of Highway 1, were beaten off. West of the highway, Allied troops were forced to withdraw to stronger defensive positions south of Fiume La Foce in the face of heavy artillery and mortar fire.

In the Serchio River Valley, the enemy is making a determined effort to retain control of the Lama Di Sotto ridge. Between the valley and Highway 12, an American raiding party, operating deep in German territory, went out on a two-day patrol, raided enemy-held houses, destroyed several thousand rounds of small arms ammunition and other supplies and took a number of prisoners.

In the 8th Army coastal sector, a German patrol to the south bank of Fiumo Di Primaro River was repulsed.

To the west, along a bend in the river, Allied mortars shot up an enemy machinegun emplacement.

MacArthur Says Mop-Up In Manila Slow, Bloody

MANILA, Feb. 12—American troops are clearing persistent Japanese defenders from South Manila, in slow, bloody fighting, Gen. Douglas MacArthur's communique reported today.

The 1st Cavalry Division, making a second crossing of the winding Pasig River, pushed south toward Neilson Airfield. The crossing was made southeast of the main business district of Manila.

The 37th Division meeting fanatical resistance, continued its drive through the Ermita district, which is near the shore of Manila Bay.

South of this, two columns from the 11th Airborne Division pushed along the bay, through the Paranque and Baclaran districts, capturing 12 heavy machine gun emplacements and numerous pillboxes. Other men of this division were still probing near Nichols Field, where the Japs blew up two ammunition dumps.

Some of the Japanese defenders in South Manila were driven into the old Spanish walled city, where they were waging a battle to the death behind walls 30 feet thick.

(The Japanese News Agency said that Japanese sailors had been withdrawn from Cavite naval base on Manila and "other areas" and had taken up new positions south of the Pasig River and at Nichols Field. t was not disclosed whether the withdrawal signified complete abandonment of Cavite.)

IWO JIMA ENCORE

WASHINGTON, Feb. 12 — Super Fortresses from the Marianas today bombed military installations on Iwo Jima, principal Japanese air and naval base in the Bonin-Volcano group between the Marianas and Japan, the War Department announced.

Raids by lighter aircraft were reported on Formosa, where night patrol bombers started fires at an airdrome and destroyed a number of grounded planes. The raiders sank a cargo ship off the Pescadores Islands west of Formosa.

Conference Takes Name Of Crimea

LONDON, Feb. 12 — The second historic Roosevelt-Churchill-Stalin meeting will be known officially as the Crimea Conference. The first meeting of the Big Three in December, 1943, is called the Teheran Conference.

Marshal Stalin suggested the name for the meeting when he toasted the success of the talks.

Yalta, where the Big Three met, is a seaside resort town on the extreme southern coast of the Crimean Peninsula in Russia, approximately 50 miles east of the Russian naval base of Sevastopol.

Sabotage Urged In Reich

LONDON, Feb. 12—A statement from SHAEF last night called on German and foreign workers employed on the Reich's railways to begin widespread sabotage of Germany's rail transport system.

Shortening of the war and early success of the Allied military campaign can result from a coordinated campaign to disrupt the Reich's transport lines, the statement said.

It told the rail workers to absent themselves from work whenever possible, to prevent supplies and reinforcements from getting through to the front and to impede Nazi food distribution.

The statement to the foreign workers, which was similar to the one issued German rail employes, said in part:

"The time has come for you to absent yourselves whenever possible from work on the railways, and, if unable to do this, to ensure that the trains run slowly or break down, and to try to get the German railwaymen to do the same. Foreign workers on the railways, see to it that supplies and reinforcements do not reach the front, see to it that the railways do not transport food deeper into Germany.

"We ask you to show this great courage because it will play a decisive part in the coming military operations. Your own liberation and that of 12 million foreign workers in Germany and the lives of thousands of Allied soldiers depend on your actions."

Swiss Parley Set

LONDON, Feb. 12 (AP)—American and British representatives were received today by the president of Switzerland and, following the arrival of a French mission tomorrow, will open vital conferences dealing with Swiss trade during and after the war, the Swiss Radio said.

Text Of Communique

Following is the statement made by the President of the United States, the Prime Minister of Great Britain, and the Chairman of the Council of People's Commissar of the Union of Soviet Socialist Republics on the results of the Crimea conference:

We have considered and determined the military plans of the three Allied powers for the final defeat of the common enemy.

The military staffs of the three Allied powers have met in daily meetings throughout the conference. These meetings have been most satisfactory from every point of view and have resulted in closer coordination of the military effort of the three Allies than ever before. Fullest information has been interchanged.

Timing, scope and coordination of new and even more powerful blows to be launched by our armies and air forces into the heart of Germany from east, west, north and south have been fully agreed and planned in detail.

Our combined military plans will be made known only as we execute them, but we believe that the very close working partnership among the three staffs attained at this conference will result in the shortening of the war. Meetings of the three staffs will be continued in the future whenever the need arises.

Nazi Germany is doomed. The German people will only make the cost of these defeats heavier to themselves by attempting to continue hopeless resistance.

We have agreed on common policies and plans for enforcing unconditional surrender terms which we shall impose together on Nazi Germany after German resistance

(Continued on Page 8)

NIGHT EDITION
★★★★★
MARKET OPENING
SCHOOL NEWS ON PAGE 23

The Sun

Copyright, 1945, by The New York Sun, Inc.

LATE NEWS
SCHOOLS—PICTURES
Diminishing cloudiness and warmer this afternoon; tonight and tomorrow clear and colder.
Sun rises 7:50 A. M. Sun sets 6:31 P. M.
(Detailed weather report on page 38.)

VOL. 112—NO. 140. Entered as Second Class Matter Post Office, New York, N. Y. NEW YORK, FRIDAY, FEBRUARY 16, 1945. FIVE CENTS EVERYWHERE

1500 U. S. PLANES BATTER TOKYO FOR 9 HOURS

Russians Heading for Spree River

Konev's Armor Advancing on Two of the Strongpoints Southeast of Berlin—Sommerfeld Falls to Reds.

London, Feb. 16 (A. P.).—An armored mass of Marshal Konev's First Ukrainian Army bore down on Berlin's Spree River defenses from the southeast today, smashing toward Beeskow and Cottbus, thirty-one to fifty-two miles from the capital.

Soviet war correspondents indicated that the Neisse River defenses had been shattered after fierce battles in the areas of Forst and Guben, two towns on that river which joins the Oder south of Frankfurt.

They told of columns of tanks and cavalry rolling through shattered villages within sight of the Spree, and indicated that the main weight of Konev's First Ukrainian Army had been turned in the Berlin direction after forming a firm link with Marshal Zhukov's First White Russian Army for an assault on the German capital.

In a thirty-mile breakthrough Konev's troops yesterday toppled the Brandenburg province stronghold of Sommerfeld, sixty-seven miles from the, German capital.

His rapid thrust from the depths of Silesia already has destroyed the effectiveness of the Oder defenses where the Germans checked a direct march toward Berlin by Marshal Gregory K. Zhukov's First White Russian Army.

Building Up Strength.

With Zhukov steadily building up new strength for a large-scale crossing of the Oder, Konev now is in position to cut in behind the enemy's Fuerstenberg-Frankfurt-Kuestrin line. Whether the Germans could deploy their forces to

Continued on Page 17.

FIFTH WITHDRAWS AT MONTE CANALE

Rome, Feb. 16 (A. P.).—American Fifth Army troops in the Tyrrhenian coastal sector were disclosed by the Allied command today to have made further withdrawals following German infiltrations in positions at Monte Canala.

Headquarters of Lieut.-Gen. Mark W. Clark said enemy pressure on Monte Canala, four miles inland and the same distance southeast of Massa, "caused our troops to withdraw to the southern slopes of this feature.

"These are the positions held prior to the recent attack by our forces in the coastal sector," it was added.

This is the area in which the United States Ninety-second Division attacked last week, but subsequently was forced to retire.

Several enemy infiltration parties were engaged yesterday.

Canadians on Banks of Rhine Push 1 Mile Deeper Into Germany.

AMERICANS ALSO ADVANCE

But Floods, Fog and Mud Retard Allied Offensive on the Western Front.

Paris, Feb. 16 (A. P.).—The Canadian First Army, aiming for the heart of the indstrial Ruhr, thrust almost a mile deeper into the Lower Rhine Valley of northwest Germany today against a storm of heavy artillery and mortar fire and an ever increasing flood of enemy reserves.

The Canadians hold twenty miles of the south bank of the flooded Rhine from the Nijmegen sector to a point opposite Emmerich, but have so far made no threat to cross the wide waterway. They stormed and captured water-hemmed Huisberden, four miles east of Kleve and nineteen from the Ruhr gateway city of Wesel.

Scots, Britons and Welshmen under the Canadian Gen. Henry Crerar's command inched forward toward the defense keystones of Goch and Calcar at the center of the bulging twenty-mile front. One front-line dispatch said that the various British Empire forces spread out south of Moyland, indicating an advance into the area less than two miles from Calcar. The Scots swinging down the highway from Kleve moved to within 1,000 yards of Moyland, while other troops closed slowly toward Goch from three directions and were within easy artillery range. Goch

Continued on Page 20.

RAID ON TOKYO MAY FORCE JAP FLEET TO FIGHT

Washington Believes Attack Cannot Be Ignored by Enemy's Navy.

U. S. WARSHIPS ROAM AT WILL

Sea Routes of Nipponese Now Held Under Full Control of American Guns.

Special to THE NEW YORK SUN.
The New York Sun Bureau, Washington, Feb. 16.

The task force raid on Tokyo is being hailed by military observers here today as one of the most audacious moves yet taken by the United States in bringing the war home to the Japanese. It is also regarded as indicative of several things about the Pacific war which are sometimes forgotten.

For the raid to have taken place at all the task force, under Vice-Admiral Marc A. Mitscher, must have approached the Japanese home islands to within about three to five hundred miles. This indicates that the Japanese were either completely unaware of the movements of the American fleet in such close quarters or that the Nipponese knew what was going on and the Jap fleet choose not to take official notice of the facts.

Whatever the cause of the success of the movement, it is a certain indication that the South China Sea and the Pacific Ocean around the islands are no longer under the control of the Japanese as they were a few years ago.

For some time now, in fact since last October, when the Japanese fleet suffered a beating at the hands of American sailors and retreated, there has been little indication that the Japanese had any fleet at all. The only manifestations have been that such ships as they had were merchantmen and that they were steadily developing a downward movement at the insistence of American naval activities.

Fleet Not Destroyed.

But naval experts here have been wel laware that the last lefeat of the Japs, at Leyte Gulf a ndin the second battle of the Philippine Sea did not destroy the entire Japanese fleet. And they have been wondering just how muc hof skittering around the Americans would be able to get away with before the remains of the Nip navy came out of hiding. e

When the Navy Department announced several weeks ago that Admiral Mitscher had been having a bit of fun along the south-

Continued on Page 2.

Greatest Fleet Ever Assembled Stretches For 200 Miles Along Shores of Japan

COMMANDS TOKYO RAIDERS

Associated Press Photo.

Vice-Admiral Marc A. Mitscher.

Another Mighty American Task Force Shells Iwo Jima Island, but Enemy Navy Makes No Move for Defense.

United States Pacific Fleet Headquarters, Guam, Feb. 16 (A. P.).—Tokyo was raided by more than 1,500 American carrier planes today in an unprecedented attack which Japanese headquarters said lasted for more than nine hours while the greatest naval fleet ever assembled hunted for a fight within 300 miles of Japan's shores.

[The Tokyo radio warned today that "an enemy task force is still operating in our adjacent waters and there is held to be a strong possibility that the enemy will launch another raid on the Japanese mainland with carrier-borne planes tomorrow.]

Protecting Vice-Admiral Marc A. Mitscher's carrier forces, battleships, cruisers and destroyers of Admiral Raymond A. Spruance's Fifth Fleet spread out in a 200-mile column in Japanese waters, daring the enemy fleet to come out.

Seven hundred miles to the south another task force, which Tokyo said was comprised of more than thirty warships, including battleships and carriers, shelled Iwo Jima in co-ordination with land-based bombers which have been attacking the island outpost daily for more than two months.

A Japanese Imperial communique reported that "carrier-based planes of a powerful enemy task force which appeared in the seas adjacent to our shores" attacked airfields in and around Tokyo in successive waves from 7 A. M. to 4 P. M. today (Japanese time). The enemy Domei news agency added that heaviest blows were rained on bases from which interceptors take off against Superfortresses raiding the Nipponese capital.

Tokyo's seven millions, long familiar with Superfortress raids, had never seen anything like today's carrier attack. Something tremendous is unfolding.

The long-planned and extensive operations threatened the heart of the Japanese Empire with:

1. The probability of blockading it into a condition for eventual in vasion.

2. Continuous pounding to reduce its airplane factories to ruins.

Rocket and bomb-bearing Hellcats and Helldivers and Avenger torpedo planes, swinging over Tokyo's 214 square miles, tore into airfields and military defense zones and they tangled over the city with the Japanese air force in fierce sky fights.

Admiral Mitscher appeared bent on knocking out the bulk of Japan's home-based air force as his immediate objective. How well he can do that is suggested by the carrier air arm's achievements in January in destroying nearly 800 Nipponese aircraft in sweeps from Saigon, French Indo China, to Amoy, China. During 1944, carrier planes destroyed 6,650 enemy aircraft.

"This operation has long been planned and the opportunity to accomplish it fulfills the deeply cherished desire of every officer and man of the Pacific fleet," exultantly announced five-star Admiral Chester W. Nimitz at his new Guam headquarters, within 1,500 miles of Tokyo.

To Admiral Mitscher, whose carriers began the westward sweep in January, 1944, in the Marshalls, went the honor of completing the last mile of the 4,000 to Tokyo from Pearl Harbor ,where Japanese carriers opened the war December 7, 1941.

The close approach to Japan by the largest mass of American

Continued on Page 2.

NAVY FLYERS BLAST TOKYO

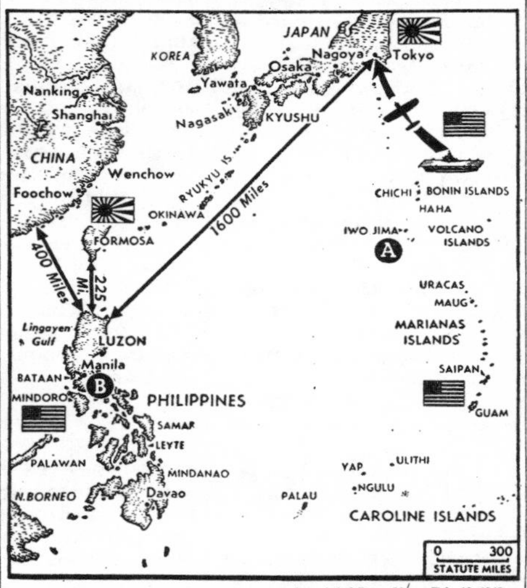

Associated Press Map. Feb. 16, 1945.

While carrier planes of a United States Navy task force attacked Tokyo, Admiral Chester W. Nimitz announced that Pacific fleet surface units bombarded Iwo Jima (A), in the Volcano Islands. On Luzon American ground forces were reported nearing victory in the offensive for Manila (B).

Smoke Kills One Fireman

Twenty-five Others Are Overcome Fighting Stubborn Woolworth Store Blaze.

One fireman lost his life and at least twenty-five others ·ere overcome by smoke early today while fighting a ur-alarm blaze in the F. W. Woolworth 5 and 10-cent ›re at 588-590 Ninth avenue, corner of 42d street.

'he fire started in the base- ıt of the two-story building, ı a thick pall of black smoke ring from the cellar made fire- ıting difficult. The second, d and fourth alarms were ›nded because of the number of firemen who were overcome by the fumes.

The dead fireman was James Ryan of Engine 1, at 165 West 29th street, whose body was found at the foot of a stairway leading to the basement after four pumpers had been pumping the water out of the cellar for an hour. Officials said that he apparently was overcome when a back draft developed, and his body subsequently was covered with water more than ten feet deep.

More than a score of firemen who were felled by the fumes were carried from the building by Capt. Patrick Green of Fire Rescue Squad 1 and his men. They were taken to the Hotel Holland at 351-359 West 42d street, where an emergency first aid station was manned by a small disaster unit from the Roosevelt Hospital, the Fire Department and the Police Department.

The last rites of the church were administered to the felled

Continued on Page 14.

n The Sun Today

"Pe
Y
wit
It's o
a curv
dull, gr
blue, an

Commons to Debate Crimea Parley

London, Feb. 16 (A. P.).—Arrangements are being made for a two-day war debate in Commons when Prime Minister Churchill reports on the Crimea conference.

LANDING REPORTED ON SCHOUWEN ISLE

London, Feb. 16 (A .P.).—The Berlin radio sai dtoday that the British attempted a landing on the Netherland island of Schouwen at the mouth of the Rhine north of the Beveland Islands on Wednesday night.

A transocean broadcast said the first wave of th eamphibious assault was thrown back under the heavy fire of German coastal batteries, and a second attempt was repelled with British units leaving behind their arms and ammunition.

Schouwen Isla nd is part of the Rhine estuary between the Costerschelde, a branc hof the sea, and Gravelingen Krammer Volkerak, one of the mouths of the Rhine. It is thirty-two miles northwest of Antwerp and twenty-four miles southwest of Rotterdam.

Transocean did not indicate whether the assault forces finally gained a foothold. The report of the attack had not been corroborated by Allied sources.

The reports served to recall, however, recent Allied naval statements disclosing that Allied forces are active along the Netherlands islands and pointing out that the European coast north of the Rhine affords the same opportunities for amphibious operations that were exploited in France.

MANDALAY BLASTED

Southeast Asia Command Headquarters, Kandy, Ceylon, Feb. 16 (A. P.).—Heavy bombers of the Eastern Air Command yesterday bombed Japanese supply dumps south of Mandalay and hammered road and rail communications feeding enemy forces on the Burma fronts, Allied headquarters announced today.

One plane was lost in the widespread operations, which included attacks on bridges on the Burma-Thailand and Bangkok-Chiengmai railways.

Headquarters reported continued mopping up operations on Ramree Island off the Burma west coast and in the Kangaw sector of western Burma, but otherwise gave little information on ground activity.

HITLER FLED REDS

London, Feb. 16 (A. P.).—The Moscow radio quoted a Soviet war correspondent today as saying Adolf Hitler had visited a German frontier town recently only two days before it was captured by the Red Army. The correspondent did not identify the town, but said Hitler had exhorted "young and old to take up arms."

Harold Browne Dies in Hotel Here

Harold Browne, 54 years old, of Rowayton, Conn., secretary and director of research for the National Industrial Conference Board, collapsed and died in his room at the Hotel Lexington last night. He had just returned from a meeting of the board. The police said that death was due to natural causes.

Dave Boone Says:

I figure plenty of folks hoping for a better world after the war are puzzled by that stand of 1,600 church leaders against the church having any say at the peace tables. It seems to me that's one place today where the church, regardless of creed, sect or denomination, should be.

If the good Lord can't count on help from the churches in getting into the peace meetings this time and making sure that the diplomats, world power politicians, professional blueprinters and international fixers don't get us into a deeper hole, there won't be much hope for the future.

Gosh, I'd like to see some Army and Navy chaplains—Catholic, Protestant and Jew—at the peace table. Any doughboy will tell you what these brave churchmen have meant to them in the toughest and darkest hours. They know a lot more about the horrors of war than most of the fellows who will have front seats when the peace is discussed.

They could help see that there isn't too much backsliding. And they would.

NIGHT EDITION
★★★★★
MARKET OPENING
SCHOOL NEWS ON PAGE 14

The Sun

Copyright, 1945, by The New York Sun, Inc.

LATE NEWS
SCHOOLS — PICTURES

Moderately cold this afternoon; tonight and tomorrow snow or rain; little change in temperature. Temperatures—Minimum, 27; Maximum, 32. Sun rises 7:43 A. M. Sun sets 6:37 P. M. (Detailed weather report on page 20.)

VOL. 112—NO. 144. Entered as Second Class Matter Post Office, New York, N. Y. NEW YORK, WEDNESDAY, FEBRUARY 21, 1945. FIVE CENTS EVERYWHERE

3500 U. S. MARINES CASUALTIES ON IWO

Thousands on Long Island Are Stranded by Rail Tie-up

Electrical Shoes Are Sheared Off 3 Trains, Delaying Passengers Over Two Hours —Some Walk Miles to Subway.

Thousands of commuters from the North Shore were left stranded at stations of the Long Island Railroad for a long period early this morning because the electrical contact shoes of three trains were sheared off by a fallen protection board at the Manhasset station.

When the trains finally got into Pennsylvania Station, one was two hours late, one an hour and thirty minutes late and the other was forty-five minutes behind time, causing many persons to reach their work in Manhattan behind schedule.

After the mishap, officials of the railroad discovered that a B. & O. boxcar on a freight train that has passed through Manhasset shortly before was slightly out of alignment and displaced a protection board at the station.

Train No. 411 left Port Washington at 6:30 A. M., arrived at Manhasset at 6:36 on schedule. When it reached Little Neck at 6:43, the train stopped and it was found its electrical contact shoes had been stripped off by the fallen protection board at Manhasset.

In the meantime, the train leaving Port Washington at 7:01 passed through the Manhasset station and sustained the same damage. A third train that left Port Washington at 7:16 A. M., had three of its contact shoes stripped off, but it was able to move on and push the two dead trains in front of it on into Man-

Continued on Page 2.

70 ARE RESCUED FROM FERRY BOAT

A minor rescue at sea was effected in the lower waters of the harbor today when a Coast Guard boat removed seventy passengers from the ferryboat Charles W. Galloway, which ran aground opposite Amboy Road at Tottenville, Staten Island.

The Galloway left Perth Amboy at 8:25 A. M. on one of its regular runs to Tottenville and in a manner not immediately explained the tide got the better of the ferryboat as it neared the Tottenville slip. Capt. Peterson, skipper of the boat, signaled for help and a Coast Guard boat arrived promptly to take aboard the passengers. The transfer was made quickly and without excitement and in a few minutes the passengers were landed at the Tottenville slip at Bentley avenue, and only a few minutes behind schedule.

The ferryboat appeared not to be damaged materially, but it will not be possible to move the vessel until the next high tide.

Chaplin Fights Deportation

Actor Declares Proposed Legislative Inquiry Is Political Persecution.

Hollywood, Feb. 21 (A. P.).—A proposed legislative investigation to determine whether Charles Chaplin should be deported as an undesirable alien has been attacked by the film comic as political persecution.

Senator Langer (R.-N. D.) introduced the legislation last Thursday, directing the Attorney-General to make an inquiry of the 55-year-old English-born actor-producer, recently made defendant in sensational moral and paternity charges. The bill was assigned to the Senate Immigration Committee.

In a statement to the press, Chaplin declared that political persecution of him had been going on for four years, "ever since I made an anti-Nazi picture, 'The Great Dictator,' in which I expressed liberal ideas."

"On account of this picture, I was called to Washington for questioning as a war monger by Senators Clark and Nye," the statement continued. "This investigation fell through after Pearl Harbor."

Blames Columnists.

"The persecution, however, increased after I dared to speak on behalf of Russia, urging the Allies to open a second front. For this I was bitterly attacked by reactionary columnists, using every device to discredit me with the public.

"I was called a communist and ingrate. I was accused of making money in this country without becoming a citizen. Never was it explained to the public that 65 per cent of my revenue comes from abroad and that the United States Government enjoys the full taxes on the 65 per cent as well as the 35 per cent I earn here.

"I believe that in a democracy I have the right to state that I am an internationalist, which ideas I expressed in 'The Great Dictator.'

Continued on Page 2.

In The Sun Today

School News Appears in the Night Edition.

Gas Responsible For Two Deaths

Russell Regensburger, 30 years old, of 119 Audubon avenue was found dead in the gas-filled kitchen of his apartment last night after making what police officials said appeared to be an unsuccessful attempt to hang himself. The police said that a shower curtain rod, ripped from the bathroom wall, indicated an attempt at hanging.

Helen Mulik, 27 years old, was found dead in bed in her apartment at 144 West 98th street late last night. Detectives said she was clad in a house dress and that three jets were open on a gas stove in an adjacent kitchen.

COMMONS CRIES 'POWER POLITICS' ON YALTA PACT

Churchill Reported Ready to Ask a Vote of Confidence.

DEFENDS ATLANTIC CHARTER

Prime Minister Tells House That It Is a Guide, Not a Rule.

London, Feb. 21 (A. P.).—A cry of "power politics" and a charge that the Atlantic Charter was violated in the Big Three's treatment of the Polish issue were raised in Commons today amid reports that Prime Minister Churchill would demand a confidence vote next week in connection with the Crimea Conference decisions.

Mr. Churchill told Commons that the Atlantic Charter "is a guide, not a rule." He made the statement in reply to a query from Maurice Petherick, a Conservative, on whether Article 2 of the charter applied to Poland, Latvia, Lithuania and Estonia. That article records the Powers as desiring to see no territorial changes that do not accord with the wishes of the people concerned. The Prime Minister is scheduled to give a first-hand report in Commons next week.

Douglas Lloyd Savory, Conservative party member, touched off a brief exchange on the Government's foreign policy when he asked Foreign Secretary Anthony Eden:

"In view of the fact that Eastern Galicia has never been in possession of Russia, what evidence does he (Churchill) have that inhabitants to the east of Poland's Curzon Line have any desire to be incorporated into Russia?"

Mr. Eden replied that the House knew the strength of the Ukrainian national movement "which has existed for many years in this territory," but added that the Government "could not be expected to have detailed, factual and up-to-date evidence on the question."

House Cheers Questioner.

Mr. Savory drew a burst of cheers as he snapped back with "Are you not bound by the Atlantic Charter to consider these

Continued on Page 2.

3-inch Live Shell Found in Street

A three-inch live shell, found lying in the street at Flushing and Franklin avenues, Brooklyn, late yesterday, was taken to the United States Disposal School on Whitehall street by Police and Fire Department officials. They said that the shell may have been accidentally dropped by a sailor or worker at the Brooklyn Navy Yard as it was found only a few blocks from the yard.

SCOTS CAPTURE GOCH IN DRIVE ON WEST FRONT

Patton's Armor Crosses Moselle in Gains Up to Five Miles.

11 REICH TOWNS ARE SEIZED

Many Prisoners Are Taken by American and Canadian Army Advances.

Paris, Feb. 21 (A. P.).—Scots of the Canadian Army captured the northern German fortress city of Goch today while in the center of the western front the American Third Army advanced up to five miles in a broad sweep in the Moselle Valley toward the Rhine, seizing eleven towns.

Lieut.-Gen. George S. Patton's tanks and infantry advanced through the Eifel Mountains on a fifty-mile front. Vanguards reached to within two miles of the heavily fortified road center of Saarburg, a key to German defenses along the Moselle.

In the north, the last enemy suicide squads were cleared from Goch, once a town of 13,500 and still the center of eight military highways. The Scots thrust on 600 yards southwestward. Goch is eight miles south of captured Kleve, terminal of the original Siegfried Line, and seventeen miles southeast of the Dutch city of Nijmegen, whence the Canadian offensive started. Beyond the town lies a small open plain in which no fixed German fortifications have been noted.

British Gain Momentum.

British Empire troops fighting with Gen. Henry Crerar's command gathered momentum and drove deeper into the center of German defenses in synchronized thrusts through Buchholt and Halverboom, villages near besieged Calcar. Scottish troops seized the Buchholt and pushed on toward the German stronghold of Uedem, only two and a half miles to the southeast.

On Gen. Patton's southern flank, the American Seventh Army pressed to within less than three miles of the ruined Saar district capital of Saarbruecken, plunged across the Saar River anew to capture the German village of Klein-Blittersdorf, and struck into the outskirts of Forbach, French rail center which almost joins Saarbruecken.

The British Second and Ameri-

Continued on Page 2.

Cigarette Thieves Sought by Police

Teletype and radio alarms were still out today for 70,000 cigarettes, the contents of 350 cartons stolen from a delivery truck which was driven off in the Bronx and later abandoned. The truck, found at 151st street and Walton avenue late last night, was stolen at 167th street and Walton avenue earlier in the evening.

Dave Boone Says:

Washington is controlling most everything, but it sure is surprising to wake up and find Federal control of sleep.

What I wonder is this: If a feller refuses to go to bed by midnight or so can he be taken over and operated by the Government?

That out-of-the-hotspots-by-midnight edict will probably bring more headaches than it will stop. I can see the return of the prohibition era speakeasy, night-club liquor served in teacups and the flask on every night-going hip.

However, there ain't much excuse for the all-night goings-on in New York or other places in time of two all-out wars.

If the theaters would raise the curtains at 8 o'clock instead of around nine the show would be over by ten instead of close to midnight. That would still leave the super-fun lovers a couple of hours at the night clubs and hotel floor shows.

Yanks Drive for Second Airfield on Isle; Others Storm Up Slope of Fortified Volcano

JAP PRISONERS WORK FOR U. S.

Associated Press Photo.

Under the watchful eyes of an American soldier, six Jap prisoners of war unload a cement truck on one of the Mariana Islands.

Americans Are Keeping Ahead of Schedule —Gains Average 500 to 1000 Yards —Jap Counter-blows Broken Up.

Pacific Fleet Headquarters, Guam, Feb. 21 (A. P.).—More than 3,500 Marines have been killed or wounded in the invasion of Iwo Jima, 750 south of Tokyo, Admiral Chester W. Nimitz announced today.

Fighting against terrific Jap defenses, but keeping well ahead of schedule, the tank-led Marines made a general advance toward the fighter strip in the center of the island, known as Motoyama Airfield No. 2.

The Fifth Marine Division advanced approximately 700 yards over mine-strewn rocky slopes, by-passing the southern end of the air strip on the west. The Fourth Division pushed directly toward the center of the field.

Along the entire line gains averaged 500 to 1,000 yards over wet, slippery ground which the Japs have criss-crossed with fortified defenses.

On the southern tip of the island other Marines drove more than 100 yards up the steep slopes of Mount Suribachi, volcanic fortress where pillboxes are spread at ten-foot intervals.

Every advance, Admiral Nimitz said, was made a yard at a time under a steady hail of Jap machine gun, rifle and rocket fire.

Of the 3,500 enlisted Marines and 150 officers killed or wounded by this merciless fire, 3,063 have been evacuated. An unannounced number of the total was listed as missing.

During the night the Marines broke up Jap attempts at infiltration and one small counter-attack with the aid of artillery and illuminating warships fired from the fleet standing offshore.

Pulverizing Fortifications.

Bombing, strafing and rocket-firing planes joined fleet naval guns, tanks and individual Marine units in slowly pulverizing the Jap defenses.

The Marines, fighting the toughest battle of their history, began the drive toward the fighter strip yesterday after conquering about a third of the island, including Iwo's bomber base, primary objective of the invasion.

The fighter field is 700 yards northeast of the three-way bomber field, which Marines captured Tuesday noon — twenty-seven hours after landing and thirty hours ahead of schedule.

Yanks Inching Ahead.

They inched forward 200 yards north of Motoyama Airfield No. 1, also known as Suribachi, before they had to dig in as enemy rockets and artillery shells poured down from heights.

Those Marines were on the north flank of a wedge which has been driven across the narrow south end of Iwo, giving the Americans a firm hold on one-third of the island, 750 miles south of Tokyo. The wedge links an east coast beachhead two and a half miles in width to holdings of 2,000 yards along the west shore.

On the south flank, at the island's tapering tip, 566-foot-high Mount Suribachi, a volcano, is sealed off by Marines meeting stiff opposition from Nipponese on its slopes. Its big guns, however, have been silenced during a six-day continuous bombardment by Rear Admiral W. H. P. Blandy's warships which already have fired more than 8,000 tons of shells on Iwo's defenses.

Rock Quarry Is Obstacle.

Up the east coast from Suribachi, Marines on the north flank had a tough job of ferreting Nipponese out of a rock quarry. The quarry is near the coast southeast of Motoyama Airfield No. 2 and is a position which must be cracked to facilitate getting at the bulk of the Nipponese garrison on the north part of the island.

Americans Hit Berchtesgaden In War's First Such Air Attack

Thunderbolts Swoop In Through Intensive Flak and Small Arms Fire to Pump Rockets Into Railway Yards.

Rome, Feb. 21 (A. P.).—United States Twelfth Air Force fighter-bombers made the war's first air attack yesterday on targets in and near Adolf Hitler's fortress town of Berchtesgaden, it was announced today. The American Thunderbolts swept in through intense flak and small arms fire, Allied air headquarters said, and pumped rockets into rail yards at low levels.

In attacks in the immediate vicinity of Hitler's mountain hideout, they knocked out a locomotive and eight rail cars. At other towns near Berchtesgaden, they set fire to two passenger trains, destroyed a troop train estimated to have 150 soldiers aboard, and destroyed or damaged nearly fifty rail cars, some loaded with tanks.

Only Part of Sorties.

The Americans, operating as a unit, were led by Major John L. Beck of Post Falls, Idaho. The Berchtesgaden operation formed only a part of the total of 2,400 sorties flown yesterday by Allied planes from Italy in what was called officially "an all-out effort against enemy communications" from northern Italy well into southern Germany.

Though this was the first announced air attack in the vicinity of the German dictator's mountain hideaway, Flying Fortress crews reported as long ago as last August that they had flown over the immediate region while bombing targets deeper inside Germany. Berchtesgaden lies in the southeastern tip of Germany, about seventy-five air-line miles southeast of Munich and the same distance from the Italian frontier.

An indication that the Nazi

Continued on Page 2.

REVEALS SNUB BY DE GAULLE

Jacksonville, Fla., Feb. 21 (A. P.).—Gen. Charles de Gaulle's refusal of an invitation to meet with President Roosevelt in Algiers recalled to Representative Price (D.-Fla.), the Congressman said last night, that the French General snubbed him and other members of Congress last October at an airfield near Paris.

"Of course we were a little excited and were desirous of meeting with the French General," Representative Price said. "Congressman Henry D. Larcade Jr., of Louisiana, who speaks French fluently, sent word to Gen. de Gaulle by a French soldier that he would like to meet him. Then we waited for an answer.

"De Gaulle, surrounded by his aids, without a smile on his face, approached within fifteen feet of where we were standing. He told an interpreter to inform us if we wanted to see him, we would have to make an appointment to see him at his Paris office—fifteen miles away."

Representative Price said that the Congressmen boarded a plane and did not try for a formal appointment.

TAXI-SHARING BILL BY-PASSES COUNCIL

Albany, Feb. 21 (A. P.).—New York city's taxicabs would be shared, but old-time chivalry would prevail for women and children, under a bill introduced today in the Legislature.

The measure, sponsored by Senator Moritt (D.-New York), would become State law for cities of more than 1,000,000 inhabitants until July 1, 1946. This eliminates the necessity of obtaining New York city council approval.

Mr. Moritt said that his measure would enable the public to get cabs and a slightly cheaper ride, and provided that unescorted women and children would not have to share cabs so that Mayor LaGuardia would have "no fears they would be harmed."

The driver would be responsible for loading his vehicle at the starting point and en route, provided that all passengers were traveling in the same direction. Each person sharing a cab would pay 10 cents less than the usual charge for his mileage.

Mr. Moritt maintained that his measure was a necessary war-time step, saying that taxis for lone passengers are practically unavailable while there is a shortage of fuel, tires and automobile parts.

OPA Inspector Charges Assault

It was only a 25-cent violation of the ceiling price, OPA Inspector Philip J. Fleischman complained to his superiors, but it so enraged the suspect that he attacked Mr. Fleischman with a claw hammer and tore up the summons as well.

The defendant, Dominick Racanelli, 45 years old, a coal and ice dealer, of 251 East 84th street, was to appear in Felony Court today on a charge of felonious assault. Mr. Fleischman was serving a summons based on a complaint that the fuel dealer had charged a quarter more than the 95-cent ceiling price for 100 pounds of coal.

The Sun will not be published Thursday, February 22, Washington's Birthday.

THE WEATHER

Clear, colder tonight. Saturday sunny, with little change in temperature.

Detailed Weather Report Page 34

Read The Baltimore News-Post for complete, accurate war coverage. It is the only Baltimore newspaper possessing the three great wire services—

ASSOCIATED PRESS
INTERNATIONAL NEWS SERVICE
UNITED PRESS

THE BALTIMORE NEWS-POST

AN INDEPENDENT NEWSPAPER

The Largest Evening Circulation in the Entire South

10

VOL. CXLVI.—NO. 91 | Entered as second-class matter at Baltimore Postoffice. | FRIDAY EVENING, FEBRUARY 23, 1945 | PRICE 3 CENTS

IWO PEAK CAPTURED

5,372 Casualties In Three Days

THIS IS BLOODY IWO. AMERICAN MARINES DIG INTO THE BLACK SAND AFTER TAKING AN "IMPREGNABLE FOXHOLE." THE DEATH TOLL IS RUNNING HIGH

Yanks Reported Opening 'Pay-Off' Cologne Battle

PARIS, Feb. 23—(U. P.).—Berlin reported that two and perhaps three Allied armies launched a grand-scale offensive before Cologne today, forced the Roer river line at six or more points on a 40-mile front and locked with the German Army in the pay-off battle of Western Europe.

Gen. Dwight D. Eisenhower's Headquarters claimed a blackout on all news of the great battle that the German High Command said was swaying back across the Rhineland, 20 miles or less from Cologne.

But accounts broadcast from Berlin said Allied tank and infantry divisions were streaming across the shattered Roer line behind an earth-shaking aerial and artillery barrage.

German troops, their defenses smashed by bombs and shells, were countering furiously all along the front. Berlin added its usual claim that all the bridgeheads had been "sealed off."

The American Ninth Army was out in front of the big push, striking on a 20-mile belt of the offensive line between Linnich and Dueren.

Units of the U. S. First Army

Continued on Page 2, Column 6.

VERY LATEST NEWS

REPORT BIG YANK DRIVE ON BERLIN LAUNCHED

NEW YORK, Feb. 23 — The National Broadcasting Company said it had learned this afternoon that American troops on the Western Front had jumped off in the first step of General Eisenhower's knockout drive toward Berlin. German announcements had said earlier the big drive was on.

5 OR 6 ALIVE IN AIRLINER CRASH, BELIEF

CEDAR SPRINGS, Va., Feb. 23—(A. P.).—Mrs. M. E. Meyers said today she had been informed by a man who visited the scene of a crashed New York-to-California American Air Lines plane that five or six of the 22 persons aboard were still alive.

Turkey Joins War On Japs And Nazis

LONDON, Feb. 23—(A. P.).—Ankara announced today the Turkish Assembly had voted unanimously to declare war on Germany and Japan as a result of a decision of the Big Three to qualify as "associated nations" all countries which take up arms against the Axis before March 1.

The disclosure that a declaration of war was the price of a seat at the San Francisco conference on world security in April was made by the Turkish Foreign Minister.

He told the Assembly that the British Ambassador on February 20 had handed the ministry a memorandum in which Turkey was invited to the San Francisco conference if the declaration of war was adopted.

The startling Turkish announcement pictured Russia in the front against Japan.

The announcement hinted that Russian armies might be thrown into the Pacific war as soon as Germany was crushed. It implied that the Soviet Union was aligned with Britain and the United States in the demand that neutral countries go to war with Japan as well as Germany.

The Big Three at their Yalta meeting held out the same price for a seat at San Francisco to Egypt, Iceland, Chile, Ecuador, Paraguay, Peru, Uruguay and Venezuela, the Ankara broadcast said.

Reds Capture Poznan, Take 23,000 Prisoners

LONDON, Feb. 23—(A. P.).—Marshal Stalin tonight announced the capture of Poznan, Poland's third largest city, after crushing a hold-out Nazi garrison which had blocked the main rail route from Warsaw to the Berlin front on the Oder.

Poznan, residence of early Polish kings, fell after a siege of 27 days. Stalin said 23,000 Germans of the hold-out garrison, including the commander, Major General Mattern, and his staff, were taken prisoners.

The city of 270,000 had been encircled since January 27 and was whittled down in ruins by a slow block-by-block fight which had pushed the Germans first into the northern edge and finally into a narrow citadel.

RAIL NETWORK

The fall of Poznan, 100 miles east of the Oder river and 137 miles west of Warsaw, opened to eventual Russian use a network of nine railways and six highways radiating from rear Russian bases to their Pomeranian, Oder and Silesian fronts.

Meanwhile, the Germans reported that the Russians, fighting within 32 miles of Danzig had broken into another encircled town, the Vistula fortress of Grudziadz.

Southeast of Berlin Marshal Ivan Konev directed a battle of mounting fury at the Neisse river fortresses of Guben and Forst and was reported reinforcing a toe-

Continued on Page 2, Column 3.

Sights Wreck Of Airliner With 22

BRISTOL, Va., Feb. 23—(A.P.). American Airlines officials at Tri-Cities Airport said an airplane pilot had spotted wreckage believed to be that of an overdue American Transcontinental Airliner, four miles southwest of Rural Retreat, Virginia.

Officials said the pilot reported the plane was "total wreckage," but had not burned. He said he flew over the wreckage at 100 feet but saw no signs of the 19 passengers and crew of three believed aboard the ship.

The pilot radioed back to the airport that the plane was down in "rough country." Rural Retreat lies some 34 miles north and east of here and is just off the main highway through the Valley of Virginia.

U. S. PACIFIC FLEET H. Q., GUAM, Feb. 23—(A. P.).—American Marines reached the summit of Mount Suribachi at the southern tip of Iwo Jima today and began a renewed drive on the central airfield after repulsing two Japanese counterattacks. The Stars and Stripes were raised over the volcanic Suribachi fortress 87 hours after the costly invasion began and marines began cleaning out Japanese still clinging to the crater with flame throwers.

Little progress was made elsewhere in the most costly fight in which the marines have ever been engaged—a fight that cost 5,372 American casualties, including 644 dead, in the first three days.

Japanese swimmers made a hopeless attempt to attack American forces on the Western side of the island from the rear last night. They were mopped up on the beaches this morning.

Surmounting of Suribachi was the brightest spot in the entire IWO campaign.

The leathernecks won command of the 564-foot height from which the Japanese had cast down a deadly mortar and artillery fire on other marines spread out over the south third of the embattled island. Its capture eliminated the threat to the rear of three devil-dog divisions attempting to drive north where the main strength of the enemy garrison is dug in.

Admiral Chester W. Nimitz condensed the drama into this special communique:

"The Twenty-eighth Regiment of the United States marines was observed raising the United States flag on the summit of Mt. Suribachi on Iwo Island at 10.35 A. M. today.

The extinct volcanic cone had been encircled by the Fourth Marine Regiment under Maj. Gen. Clifton B. Cates. Then for 28 hours the leathernecks clambered up the 45-degree cliffs despite grenades and demolition charges hurled down into their faces by the desperate defenders.

In his earlier communique Nimitz reported strong Japanese counterattacks on both flanks of the American force edging—only feet or yards at a time—toward the southern fringe of Iwo's central airfield.

The main airdrome to the south already is in American hands.

One of the counterthrusts apparently was repulsed, but there was no report on the other, on the American right flank. By official count, 644 U. S. marines were killed, 4,168 wounded and

Continued on Page 2, Column 1.

Tokyo Says:

SAN FRANCISCO, Feb. 23. (A. P.).—An unconfirmed radio Tokyo broadcast, picked up by the Blue network today, claimed that American marines on Iwo Jima have been driven back to the landing beachheads after being forced to abandon "one position after another by daring Japanese infiltration tactics."

Tokyo added bad weather and Japanese air attacks have prevented the Americans from landing additional men and supplies on the southern tip of the island.

$1,000,000 Supplies Lost In Italy Fire

ROME, Feb. 23—(A. P.).—More than $1,000,000 worth of uniforms and other post exchange supplies were destroyed by a fire which swept a U. S. quartermaster warehouse in Italy recently, Allied headquarters announced today.

Temperatures

12 Mid.,	53	9 A. M.,	42
1 A. M.,	53	10 A. M.,	44
2 A. M.,	52	11 A. M.,	46
3 A. M.,	50	12 noon,	47
4 A. M.,	47	1 P. M.,	48
5 A. M.,	45	2 P. M.,	48
6 A. M.,	42	3 P. M.,	49
7 A. M.,	41	4 P. M.,	53
8 A. M.,	42	5 P. M.,	52

NEWS-POST

FINAL ★★★★

SUNDAY NEWS

Copr 1945 by News Syndicate Co. Inc. NEW YORK'S PICTURE NEWSPAPER Trade Mark Reg. U. S. Pat. Off.

5 CENTS PAY NO MORE

Vol. 24. No. 43. New York, Sunday, February 25, 1945★ 72 Main + 8 Manhattan + 12 Comic + 20 Coloroto Pages

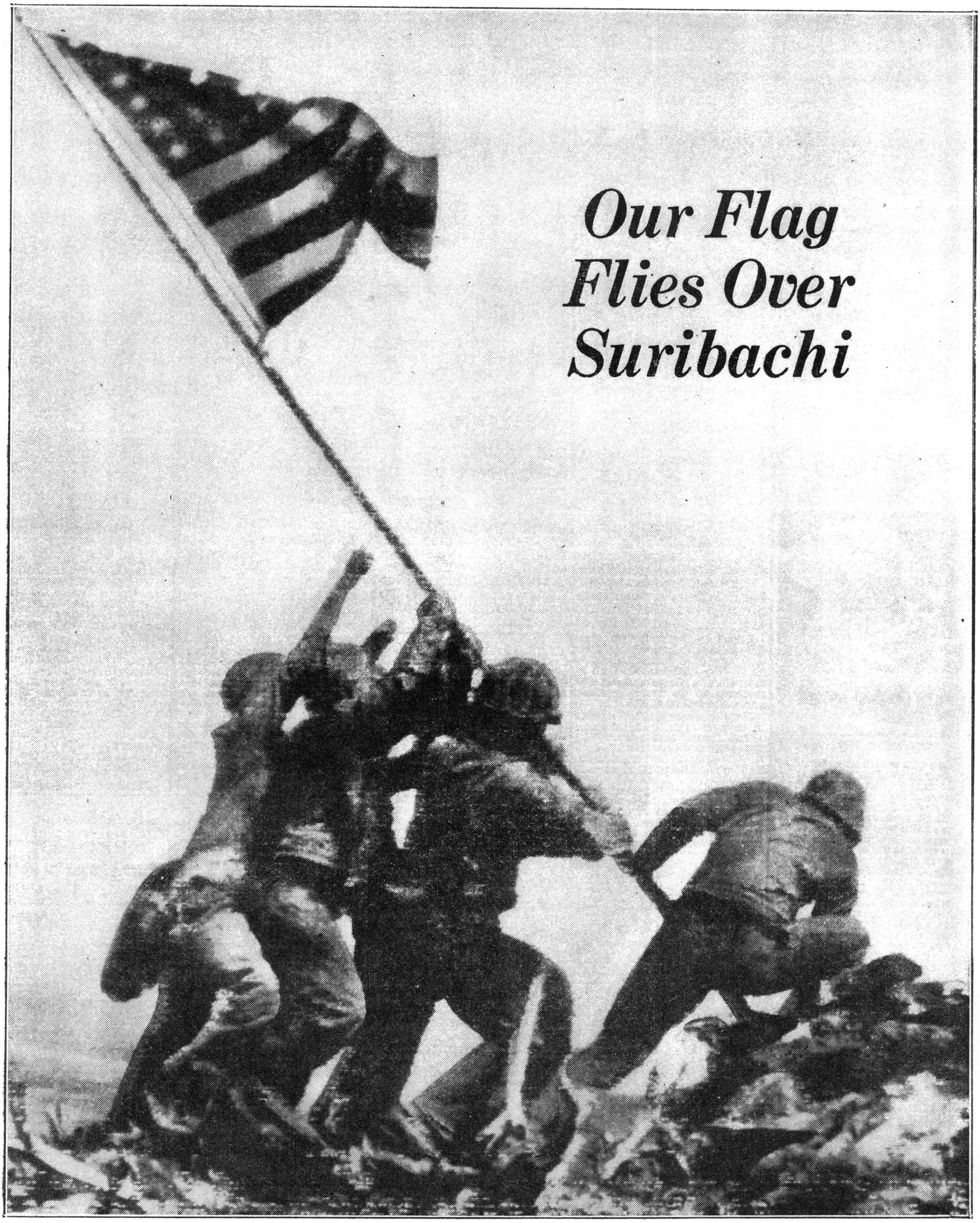

Our Flag Flies Over Suribachi

(Associated Press Wirefoto by Joe Rosenthal via U. S. Navy Radio from Guam)

The Spirit of '45—U. S. Marines of the 28th Regiment hoist Old Glory atop Mount Suribachi on Iwo.

Entered as second-class matter April 15, 1931, at the post office at New Haven, Connecticut, under act of March 3, 1879

ILLUSTRATED CURRENT NEWS

Published Monday, Wednesday and Friday by Illustrated Current News, Inc., New Haven, Conn.
Subscription Annually, $20.80

Feb. 21, 1945—No. 4912

1

2

3

4

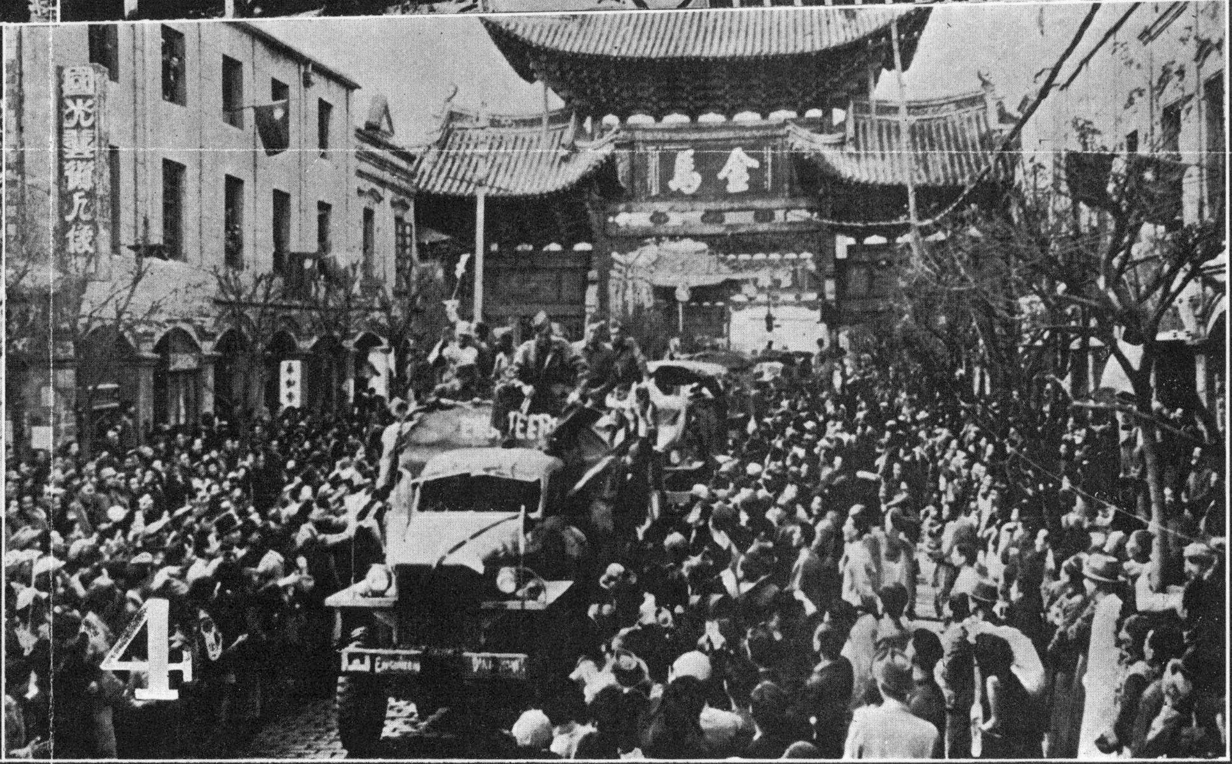

BURMA AND LEDO ROADS JOINED

Photos show climax of war's greatest engineering feat, when new Ledo Road was joined to Burma Road, making war supplies accessible to China. 1. American and Chinese troops cheer road's completion. 2. Road-marker, Yankee style. 3. Contrast in old and new transportation. 4. First truck convoy arrives in Kunming.

News Note: U. S. Troops Mopping Up Foe On Corregidor

Einzelpreis 15 Rpf.
zuzügl. ortsübl. Bestellgeld

Berlin, 1. März 1945
9. Folge 11. Jahrgang

Das Schwarze Korps

ZEITUNG DER SCHUTZSTAFFELN DER NSDAP
Organ der Reichsführung SS

Verlag: Franz Eher Nachf. GmbH., Zweigniederlassung Berlin, Berlin SW 68. Zimmerstraße 88. Fernruf: 11 00 22. Postscheckkonto: Berlin 4454. Anschrift der Schriftleitung: Berlin SW 68. Zimmerstr. 88-91. Anzeigenpreise laut aufl. Preisliste

Bezugspreise: Durch die Post 3,60 RM. halbjährlich zuzügl. Bestellgeld. In Groß-Berlin erfolgt Zustellung durch Austräger unserer Zweigstellen. Einzelne Nummern können bis auf weiteres nicht nachgeliefert werden

Soldaten Europas – verteidigt euch!

An der Schwelle der Entscheidung, ob Europa, Heimat der großen Träume und Gedanken, aus denen die Welt lebt, untergehen soll, rufen wir die Soldaten Europas auf: verteidigt euch! Laßt für eine Stunde des Nachdenkens nicht den Haß eure Gedanken regieren. Erhebt euch zu den einfachen und guten Wahrheiten, die ungetrübt durch Hetze und Verleumdung wieder den Sinn des europäischen Lebens erkennen lassen.

In schrecklichen Schaudern wälzt sich die dunkle Welle Asiens gegen unser Herz. Immer noch hält eine Front. Immer noch stehen, wie Jahr um Jahr zuvor, in den Gräben die altgewordenen Soldaten neben den jungen, deren Stirne noch den Hauch der Küsse tragen, mit denen ihre Mütter von ihnen Abschied nahmen. Immer noch heben sich unter den Stahlhelmen ihre fahlgewordenen Gesichter der dämonischen Flut entgegen. Immer noch bricht sich ihre Kraft an der unbeschreiblichen Treue der Deutschen, denen der Krieg alles genommen hat, was ein Leben schön und fruchtbar gestaltet, die hinter sich die rauchenden Trümmer ihrer Häuser, die von Bomben zerfetzten Kinder, die sterbenden Frauen wissen und dennoch über ihre Leiden hinweg immer wieder antreten, immer wieder die Arme zur Verteidigung ihres Vaterlandes heben.

Welchen Dank haben sie gehabt?

Sie haben als einzigstes die Liebe ihres Volkes immer um sich gewußt. Sie haben sich in ihren Träumen mit ihrem Volk vereint, das seine Hoffnungen in die Zukunft richtete, und an ein großes, freies Leben dachte, in dem die Wunden geheilt, die Tränen gestillt und die Erinnerungen an die Gefallenen über dem Leben der fernsten Kinder wie ein leises und ewiges Lied stand. In dem die Städte wieder erblühten und die Wege des Menschen frei waren von Sorge und Not. In dem jede Arbeit ihren gerechten Lohn fand. In dem der Herd des Menschen, um den sich die Familie versammelte, geschützt war. In dem über die Wiegen der Kleinsten nicht die Tränen der Angst fielen. In dem in die verlöschenden Augen der Alten der Widerschein des echten Friedens glänzte.

Sie hatten Träume und Gedanken, die weit in die Zukunft vorauseilten. Sie sahen ihr Leben in schöneren und helleren Farben. Sie waren bereit, was unter so schweren Opfern errungen, für alle Zeiten zu sichern. Sie gelobten, ein Volk zu werden, in dem nur große Maße und Gesetze die Handlungen des einzelnen führen sollten. Sie verschworen sich, für die Gerechtigkeit zu leben und die schamlosen Nutznießer ihrer Geduld, ihrer Treue, ihres Gehorsams unter sich auszumerzen, jene vor allem, die jemals den Namen einer großen und guten Sache in den Schmutz gezogen hatten, während sie, die Soldaten, die Sache mit ihren Leibern verteidigten.

Sie erkannten ihre Fehler und ihre bösen Leidenschaften. Aber in den furchtbaren Schlachten, die sie bestanden, prägten sie ein neues und wahrhaftes Bild ihres Volkes, Sie räumten die fremden Überlagerungen fort, sie sprengten die Verkrustungen der Klassen und Stände. Sie waren nicht länger mehr die Beute von Anschauungen und Formeln, aus denen die feindliche Welt sich ein Bild unseres Daseins gemacht hatte. In ihnen fand die Welt ein neues und wahrhaftes Bild unseres Volkes. Von hier aus erhob sich in freier Kraft eine neue Welt.

Erinnert euch, Soldaten Europas! Erinnert euch, daß der Ruhm dieser wundenbedeckten Männer und die großmütige Tapferkeit ihrer Frauen euer Herz mit der Ahnung eines unvergänglichen Wertes streifte. Erinnert euch der Stunde, in der ihr den Bannkreis jüdischen Hasses und jüdischer Angst einmal zerbrechen konntet, da euer Geist dem Geiste dieses Soldatentums nicht fern und fremd war. Erinnert euch der Zeit, wenn hinter den blutigen Nebeln dieses Krieges das Gesicht des deutschen Volkes sichtbar wurde und seine Frage vor euch hintrat, auf die ihr eine Antwort geben mußtet und auf die ihr keine fandet. Denn ihr hättet antworten müssen, wie euer Herz es euch eingab, und eine unverfälschte Stimme hätte euch gesagt: dieser Krieg ist die Entscheidung zwischen Gott und seinem Gegenspieler, dieser Krieg entscheidet darüber, ob der Welt erhalten bleiben soll, was Europa schön und begehrenswert, frei und glücklich gemacht hat. In diesem Krieg werden in den Gräben und auf den Schlachtfeldern nicht nur das Leben und der Besitz der Deutschen verteidigt, auch deckt keine der alten Erklärungen mehr den Krieg, der Europa zerfleischt, der seine Werke zerstört, seine Männer und Frauen vernichtet, seine Kinder verkrüppelt.

Erinnert euch, Franzosen! Ein Jahrtausend kriegerischer und geistiger Auseinandersetzungen hat zwischen unseren Völkern die Brücke nicht zerstört, auf der sich der Austausch unseres Wesens, unserer Gedanken und unserer Leidenschaften vollzieht.

Wir haben voreinander unsere Gegensätze nicht verschwiegen. Aber wir haben einander auch die Ehre gegeben, die dem Mut gebührt, die ein tapferes und kühnes Leben für sich fordern darf. Und in dem Gedächtnis unserer Völker leben die Namen der Männer und Frauen fort, die für die Ehre und den Ruhm, für die hohen sittlichen, schöpferischen Eigenschaften unserer Nationen ein kostbares Zeugnis abgelegt haben. In unseren Schulen, wo dem empfänglichen Sinn des Kindes die Beispiele großer menschlicher Kraft zu nacheifernder Anstrengung erklärt werden, waren Frankreichs große Männer und Frauen auch immer die Kronzeugen einer Gesinnung, die sich über den niedrigen Bereich des Hasses und der Verunglimpfung erhebt.

Hier wie dort durchbrach das Bewußtsein eines gemeinsamen europäischen Schicksals letztlich doch immer wieder die starren Wände, die in der Werdezeit unserer Nationen bei der Ausprägung unserer eigentümlichen nationalen Eigenschaften aufgerichtet wurden. Auch diese Wände waren Schicksal und Notwendigkeit, weil sonst die Gräber der Gefallenen und die Triumphpforten, die ihnen errichtet worden sind, sinnlos wären, weil sonst die Toten sich aus ihren Gräbern anklagend erheben würden, um zu erklären, daß sie nicht für eine Sinnlosigkeit und nicht für ein Mißverständnis gefallen sind. Wir haben kein Recht, über die Vergangenheit zu Gericht zu sitzen, aber wir haben die Pflicht, das Gemeinsame der ungeheuren Blutopfer zu suchen, und wir haben die Pflicht, zu fragen, welch letzter Sinn die Opfer heiligt, und welche Notwendigkeit für uns, die wir das Trennende nicht verewigen wollen, gesetzt ist.

Erinnert euch, daß das dramatische Gebet unserer Kirchen und Kathedralen das gleiche ist, hier wie dort. Erinnert euch, daß wir das Leben lieben und zu erfüllen trachten mit der gleichen Leidenschaft und mit der gleichen Sehnsucht nach seinem ewigen Sinn. Über uns sind die gleichen Sternbilder, und uns umweht der gleiche Wind, wir lieben unsere Erde, unsere Häuser, unsere Städte, unsere Straßen, unsere Wälder. Wir tragen Sorge um unsere Angehörigen, wir haben das gleiche Verlangen, glücklich zu sein, die unschuldigen Augen unserer Kinder zu sehen, den stillen Glanz auf der Stirne unserer Mütter, das Lächeln unserer erblühenden Frauen.

Wir wollen unseren Männern und unseren Frauen die Furcht des Lebens nehmen. Wir wollen ihr Herz aufschließen für die Tröstungen der Musik. Das Erhabene und das Heitere haben ihren Platz in Mitte. Freude bringt uns der Gesang der Vögel, und die zarte, doch mächtige Regung, mit der die Knospe sich atmend erschließt und zur vollen Blüte reift, läßt unser Herz erbeben über die Unschuld Gottes, die sich hier offenbart.

Das ist es, was aller Zerstörung standhielt und was in den Schauern der großen Vernichtungsschlachten bewahrt blieb als ein Zeugnis der letzten Gemeinschaft, die uns Europa heißt.

Dieses Europa aber, das allen Wert und alle Schönheit eines in tausend Jahren und mehr umkämpften Lebens in sich schließt, steht vor der Gefahr seiner Vernichtung. Unsere Männer, die Väter und Söhne sind wie ihr, Franzosen, halten die Schutzwälle vor den anbrandenden Sturmwellen aus der Tiefe Asiens besetzt. Damit verteidigen wir euer Glück, eure Sorglosigkeit, eure Ruhe. Eure Weinberge, eure Felder. Eure Frauen, eure Kinder. Noch einmal tritt die deutsche Kraft zu einer übermenschlichen Anstrengung an, aber es könnte der Augenblick kommen, in dem wir nicht mehr an euch und euer Glück denken können, in dem wir uns kämpfend nur noch um unsere eigenen Frauen und Kinder scharen und nur noch diese verteidigen, die unserem Leben am nächsten stehen.

Spanier! Im Escorial sind euch Schicksal, Ruhm und Größe eures Lebens aufbewahrt. Blickt zurück in die Vergangenheit, in der dieses Mahnmal des Todes den ritterlichen Geist Spaniens verteidigte. Erinnert euch der geheimen Bewegung, die dieses Zeichen der Erhabenheit unter euch schafft und in die armseligste Hütte des Bauern noch die Trauer, aber auch den Glanz des gemeinsamen Schicksals trägt.

Nicht nur die Könige ruhen dort; um sie sind versammelt die Geister der Nation, um sie ist vereint das Leben des Fischers, des Bauern, des Arbeiters, der je auf einem Schlachtfeld für die Größe Spaniens gefallen ist, auch wenn ihm niemals der Sinn dieses seines Sterbens bewußt geworden ist. Er fiel als Spanier; er war aufgerufen für einen Wert in dieser Welt, der nicht gemessen und nicht berechnet werden kann, um den aber das Trachten, die Leidenschaft und das Verlangen eines Mannes gehen, der nicht einen Begriff, sondern ein erlebtes Leben verteidigt und in das eingeschlossen ist, was ihm bisher das Leben lebenswert gemacht hat. Wollt ihr diese Werte, die über eure eigene Nation hinaus auch in das europäische Leben hineingewirkt haben, preisgeben, um nur noch die Sklaven der bolschewistischen Lebensmechanik zu sein?

Schweizer! Eure geschickten Hände, eure reinlichen Häuser, euer friedliches Leben, fern von allen großen Leidenschaften, die unser Volk um seines Lebens willen durchkämpfen muß, sind der Zerstörung überantwortet, wenn die bolschewistische Welle über euch kommt.

Italiener! Einstmals war Rom, als es das hellenische Erbe übernahm und zur Größe einer Weltmacht wuchs, ein Zentrum des Abendlandes und ein Feuer, das Europa erwärmte. Aus Schuld und Schicksal ist vieles gewachsen, was diesem Rom seine Herrschaft bestritt und seinen Glanz verdunkelte. Doch bleibt wie eine Sage von großen menschlichen Kräften das römische Ziel und wirkt in Europa hinein, wirkt mit vielen erlesenen Männern und Frauen, mit der Kraft seines fleißigen Bauern, der seinen Weinberg hütet und seinen Ölbaum pflanzt, wirkt mit der Kraft ruhmvoller Legionen, in denen die Söhne eures Landes sich versammeln, hungrig nach einem Zeichen der Erfüllung euser Träume, hungrig nach Raum und Leben, hungrig, das große Werk der Vergangenheit, das vor der Welt steht, wie ein Bild des erfüllten, gesättigten Lebens weiterzuführen. Bewahrt den Stolz, als Bürger Europas der Welt Unvergängliches geschenkt zu haben, erinnert euch daran, daß ein Bild oder ein Lied unvergänglicher ist als ein sowjeti-

Aufn.: SS-Kriegsberichter H. Ahrens

COLDER

Decidedly colder tonight; clearing. Rising temperatures Wednesday. High today, 34. Low tonight, 20. Sunrise, 7:18; sunset, 6:47.
(Chart on page 19.)

6 p.m. . . . 54	2 a.m. . . . 32	10 a.m. . . . 32	2 p.m. . . . 29
8 p.m. . . . 52	4 a.m. . . . 31	11 a.m. . . . 32	3 p.m. . . . 29
10 p.m. . . . 39	6 a.m. . . . 31	12 noon . . . 32	4 p.m. . . . 29
12 p.m. . . . 34	8 a.m. . . . 31	1 p.m. . . . 30	5 p.m. . . . 28

CHICAGO DAILY NEWS

RED STREAK

70TH YEAR—55. TUESDAY, MARCH 6, 1945—TWENTY-FOUR PAGES. Telephone DEArborn 1111. FOUR CENTS

COLOGNE IS OURS

Patton 25 Miles from Coblenz, Rhine

THREE-DAY DIET

Dr. Carlson Finds K-Rations Good--- If You're Hungry

Test for Army Proves Food Is Nutritious, but Lacks Taste

BY ADELE HOSKINS.

Dr. Anton J. Carlson, famed physiologist of the University of Chicago, has been on a K-ration diet—for three days.

He undertook the experiment at the invitation of the Army Quartermaster Corps.

During his career he has explored every kind of food, including dog, rattlesnake and toasted grasshoppers. He ate abalone 40 years ago when it was almost "untouchable" for white people. Today it is a delicacy.

K-rations are three waxed packages, about the size of crackerjack boxes, each containing a complete meal of meat or cheese product, coffee or fruit juice powder, candy bar, other energy foods and cigarettes. Designed to be eaten cold, they are issued to front line troops who are unable to reach regular Army kitchens for their meals.

* * *

FOR THE FOLKS back home Dr. Carlson's three-day preliminary study for the quartermaster corps has revealed:

1. K-rations supply all essential ingredients of a good diet for a long time (weeks) —

Dr. Anton J. Carlson.
[Daily News photo.]

even for young, vigorous, active individuals.

* * *

2. They are by necessity so concentrated that people used to ordinary home diets don't feel they fill the stomach sufficiently. Hence they say the ration is not "belly-filling." But veterans who lived on the rations for weeks said the stomach adjusts to concentrated food.

* * *

3. The great difficulty comes in connection with the sense of monotony. "As civilians, we are used to great variety," Dr. Carlson said. "Some people don't like cheese, but the cheese is probably the most delicious of the high-

(Continued on page 6, column 1.)

Ohio Flood Shuts War Factories

(Picture on back page.)

CINCINNATI—(AP)—The Ohio valley's first major wartime flood began to silence scores of munitions plants today as the river slowly swelled toward stages reached only twice before in history.

Transportation was crippled in sections, telephone service was jammed. In Cincinnati, for the first time in history, telephone subscribers were asked to cut their lines and take instruments with them if they had to evacuate their homes. Telephone company officials said instruments were virtually irreplaceable.

With the Ohio rising .2 feet an hour on the heels of a continuing rain three inches or more, federal, state, and city officials strained resources to meet calls for aid from residents of low-lying areas and from war plants in the bottoms areas.

* * *

THE MID-DAY stage was 64.9 feet, nearly 13 feet over flood stage. The Ohio threatened to reach at least 70 feet here, with comparable stages for many miles both up and downstream.

This compared with the record 79.99 stage of 1937 and 72 feet in 1913, the previc peak.

Backwaters of the Ohio and the Little Miami River ripped a 40-foot section from the Beechmont levee protecting Lunken Airport, isolating suburban Mount Washington except for a long detour and cutting all city gas service there. The airport already had been flooded.

* * *

CINCINNATI'S busy Mill Creek industrial area was protected from the Ohio by a barrier dam, but a flash flood in the Mill Creek head-

(Continued on page 6, column 2.)

'One Strong Heave Will Win the War'--Churchill

LONDON—(AP)—Prime Minister Churchill visited German soil overlooking the great Rhine barrier to Berlin last weekend and told front-line troops that "soon the enemy will be driven across the Rhine."

"Anyone can see that one strong heave will win the war," he declared.

The visit "touched off an atmosphere of great expectancy on the Western Front," said a dispatch by Roger D. Greene, Associated Press correspondent.

* * *

THE 70-YEAR-OLD British statesman fired an artillery shell directed to Hitler—the same Hitler who four years ago promised to visit Britain—and paid calls at the headquarters of Marshal Montgomery and Gen. Eisenhower.

Entering a gun-pit south of ruined Goch, Churchill wrote on a 240-mm. shell the words "To Hitler Personally." He chewed grimly on his cigar as he pulled the lanyard of the American-made gun, sending the missile screaming toward the Germans holding out on the Rhine banks.

* * *

CHURCHILL walked into the enemy country through the shattered Siegfried Line, once the symbol of Hitler's vaunted impregnability, and saw British laundry hanging there. German civilians gaped as they recognized the unmistakable figure.

Wildly cheering troops lined the road. Soldiers shouted "How're we doing?" and promised to "bring Hitler back alive."

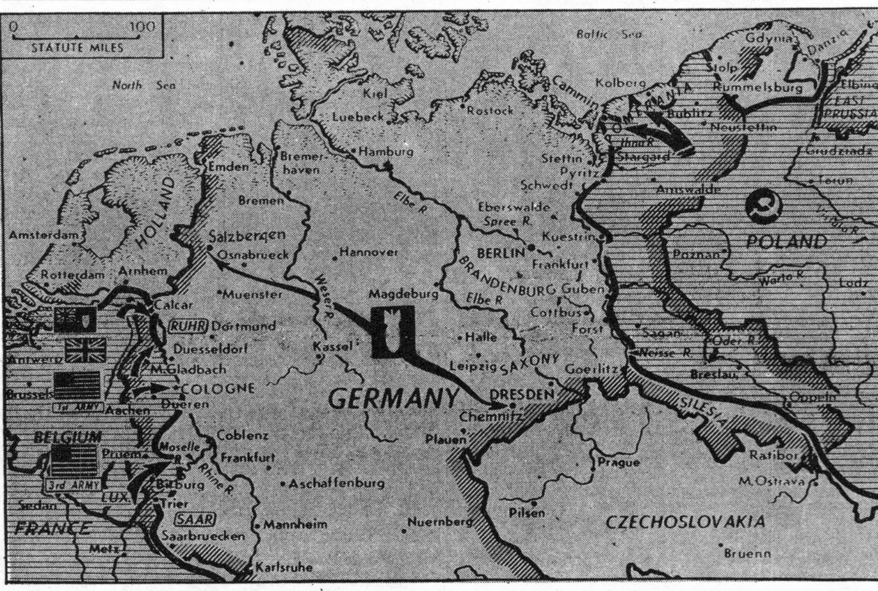

YANKS TAKE COLOGNE; RUSSIANS GAIN—As Cologne fell to American forces, Lt.Gen. Patton's 3d Army plunged eastward in the Moselle River area. North of Duesseldorf a fight was in progress for the last remaining crossing over the Rhine. On the Eastern Front the Russians took Cammin and other Baltic cities. Arrows show main drives from east and west. Cities hit by the continued air blitz are indicated by bomb symbol.
[Associated Press Wirephoto.]

Nazis Pull Out Toward South

3d Army Nearing Coblenz

PARIS — (UP) — Lt.Gen. Patton's 3d Army has broken through the German lines and driven eastward 32 miles since yesterday morning.

Patton's armor was across the Ues River and within 20-odd miles of Coblenz, which is at the confluence of the Mosle and Rhine rivers. The U.S. troops were still pressing eastward.

His break-through from the Kyll River line was as spectacular as the capture of Cologne by the 1st Army and recalled his historic race through France last August after the St. Lo smash. The drive was advancing almost a mile an hour.

* * *

THE BREAK-THROUGH was announced only after Patton's speeding forces had pushed from the Kyll River front east of Pruem to the area of Schonbach, 27 miles west of Coblenz at the confluence of the Rhine and Mosel rivers.

Maj.Gen. Hugh J. Gaffey's famous 4th Armored Division set the pace for the dash.

In the first hours of the push the 3d Army captured an estimated 1,500 prisoners, including a German corps commander, as well as at least a dozen German towns.

* * *

THE COMMANDER was identified as Maj.Gen. Graf Rothkirsch.

Brig.Gen. Holmes Daeger of Union City, N.J., led the attacking forces.

As the push developed, the

(Continued on page 4, column 5.)

U.S. Tanks Mop Up Remnants

COLOGNE — (AP) — The American 1st Army announced the capture of Cologne tonight as infantry an dtanks cleaned out the last vestiges of resistance within the shattered city on the Rhine.

The great industrial and communications center, largest German city yet to fall to the Allies, was conquered much more easily and speedily than had been anticipated.

The garrison, which elected not to stand and fight, fell back toward Bonn to the south through a narrowing corridor along the river.

* * *

COLOGNE'S capture was all more spectacular because it was accomplished by an army which only a few weeks ago was fighting for its life in the Belgian Bulge.

From the doorstep of defeat Lt. Gen. Hodges rallied his army for this steamrooler drive which began in the pre-dawn moonlight of Feb. 23 when his troops crossed the Roer River.

The 3d Armored Division and the 104th Infantry Division closed relentlessly on the last knot of resistance inside Cologne. The troops were amazed to see civilians amide the wreckage displaying friendliness and relief at their arrival.

* * *

THE FIGHTING was not the last stand, do-or-die defense that had been expected.

Cologne is no Aachen. It was not manned by a garrison prepared to fight house to house and street to street.

* * *

COLOGNE is an appalling mass of wreckage from the 42,000 tons of bombs dropped here by the R.A.F. and the U.S. Air Forces since May, 1942, when the R.A.F. made its first great raid on this industrial city.

Cologne is estimated to be 85 per cent in ruins with more than 95 per cent of the older part of the city a rubbleheap.

"Cologne looks like Stalingrad," said an R.A.F. officer. "There are some 2,000 acres of devastation in the city. Cologne's industry, like Detroit's, was spread through the city. The only way to atack the industry was to destroy the city."

Latest Bulletins

Freighter Explodes, Many Feared Dead

VANCOUVER, B.C. — (UP) — The 10,000-ton Park Steamships' freighter, Greenhill Park, exploded in the harbor here today and a heavy loss of life was feared. Between 25 and 30 men were believed to have been aboard the vessel when four blasts in the ammunition room blew the starboard side out and set it afire.

Senate Kills Manpower Jail, Fine Penalty

WASHINGTON—(AP)—The Senate struck from the Manpower Control Bill today a jail-and-fine penalty directed against employers wilfully violating employment ceilings set by the War Manpower Commission chairman. The vote was 44 to 35.

Latin Parley O.K.s Freedom of Press

MEXICO CITY—(UP)—A resolution providing for a guarantee of liberty of information in the Western Hemisphere was adopted today by the commission dealing with inter-American problems at this conference.

Navy Finds Phosphates in Captured Islands

WASHINGTON—(UP)—Substantial deposits of high-grade phosphates have been found in captured Japanese mandated islands, the Navy disclosed today.

Mosquitoes Bomb Nazis on Lower Rhine

LONDON—(UP)—R.A.F. Mosquito bombers escorted by Mustang fighters today attacked enemy troops, armor and transport at Wesel, on the lower Rhine, the Air Ministry officially announced.

13 Die, 60 Hurt as Plane Crashes

YORK, England—(UP)—Thirteen persons, including five soldiers, were killed and 60 persons were injured when a plane exploded and crashed in a suburb. Few of the 60 were hurt seriously.

Chicago Park Board Bill Voted Out

SPRINGFIELD, Ill.—The House judiciary committee, 12 to 4, voted out the Armstrong Bill to make the Chicago Park Board elective with recommendation that it do pass. (Earlier news, Page 6.)

Great Welcome Mapped For Death March Vets

SAN FRANCISCO—(UP)—A "large group" of Army officers and men liberated from the Jap prison camp at Cabanatuan in the Philippines is en route to San Francisco and will be given the most elaborate homecoming ever arranged for returning servicemen on the West Coast.

Announcement that the men, including veterans of Bataan and Corregidor and some survivors of the infamous "March of Death," were en route home was made by Maj.Gen. C. H. Kells, commanding general of the San Francisco port of embarkation.

They are part of the group of 510 prisoners liberated Jan. 31 by Gen. MacArthur's Rangers and Filipino guerrillas in a daring raid behind the Jap lines on Luzon.

* * *

THE TRANSPORT carrying the liberated men will be greeted outside the Golden Gate by the harbor boat Catalina, bearing a 75-foot sign painted in five-foot letters:

"Welcome Home."

Other harbor craft will escort the transport into San Francisco Bay.

Chicago-Bound Zephyr Derailed

The Chicago-bound Zephyr, streamliner of the Chicago, Burlington & Quincy Railroad, was derailed near South Omaha, Neb., early this morning.

Twelve cars left the tracks, a spokesman for the railroad said, but only one injury resulted. A porter was slightly hurt, it was said.

Mopsy Always Has A Word for It

Gladys Parker's sparkling cartoon character, "Mopsy," has a word for everything and she's good for a laugh any day. You'll find it on page 23.

Also on the inside:

THERE'S NO PITY NOW

Yanks Learned Their Lesson in Hate at Ardennes

BY ANN STRINGER.

NINTH U.S. ARMY HQTS.—(UP)—We were standing in the drive of a large German home which had been taken over for American officers.

A German woman, with her daughter and son about 8 and 5 years old, started walking toward the house, which had been their home.

The young officer with whom I had been talking walked over to them and shouted:

"Beat it! Go on, beat it! Get outta here!"

* * *

THE LITTLE boy was crying. The mother tried to explain something. The officer didn't listen. He kept repeating, "Beat it!"

Finally the littlt girl stalked past and took her doll buggy from the front steps and wheeled it to the muddy street. Her mother and brother followed.

The officer came back and apologized for the scene.

"A year ago," he said, "you wouldn't have seen a Yank doing something like that, would you? I wouldn't have permitted one of my men to do it.

* * *

"BUT AFTER you've seen what we've seen—if you'd been through Ardennes. . . .

"I hate 'em, I hate 'em. Every single one—the 'cits' (slang for 'civilians') just as much as the troops."

He spoke bitterly, gripping his fingers tight. Yet the scene had embarrassed him.

We were in one of the hottest battles since the opening of the Rhine offensive. German shells swished overhead and machine-gun bullets splattered only a block away.

* * *

ABOUT AN hour earlier, one of this officer's buddies had been shot in the stomach by a German sniper. He died before medics could reach him. Two days ago they had found another of his buddies lying in the middle of the road. There was a knife stab in his back. One in his neck and a third in his throat. He had been dead about six hours.

This young officer had been through all of the Battle of France. He had fought in the Ardennes break-through. He had changed a lot since he had left home.

"YOUR SWEETHEART IS WAITING"

"Why die? . . . it's easy to keep on living . . . Come on over"

Nazi leaflets with these and similar promptings — the pictures with the texts— the crude with the clever—will be published tomorrow. Watch for this sheaf of current Nazi tricks—sent back from the front by American fighting men—brought to you in

Tomorrow's DAILY NEWS

Ohio Flood Peril Grows

CHARACTER QUALITY · AMERICA FIRST! · ENTERPRISE ACCURACY

Los Angeles Examiner

AN AMERICAN PAPER FOR THE AMERICAN PEOPLE · THE GREAT NEWSPAPER OF THE GREAT SOUTHWEST

Reg. U.S. Pat. Off.

Examiner Telephone Richmond 1212

Examiner Building, 1111 S. Broadway

WAR EXTRA

VOL. XLII—NO. 87 LOS ANGELES, THURSDAY, MARCH 8, 1945 PCC Two Sections—Part I—FIVE CENTS

PATTON REACHES RHINE, 150-MI. LINE CRUMBLES

7 Red Armies in Berlin Push, Say Nazis

10,000 HOMES DESERTED IN OHIO FLOODS

Raging River Threatens 70-Ft. Water Wall at Cincinnati

International News Service

For the second time since the great 1913 flood, the raging Ohio River last night swept over the 62-foot floodwall at Portsmouth, Ohio, as Forecaster George Marth predicted a crest of from 64 to 65 feet there Thursday and a top of 70 feet at Cincinnati later.

The flood-swollen Ohio streamed across the Portsmouth floodwall in a block-long section, and, on the basis of Marth's prediction of a continued rise, was expected to pass over the big concrete and dirt levee at other points later.

Virtually all of Portsmouth's bottomlands have been cleared of civilians and the city's business district closed down.

The rampaging waters brought business activity throughout the Ohio Valley, and especially at Portsmouth, to a near standstill, sharply reduced vital war production, disrupted communications, train, airplane and bus schedules, and caused a decided curtailment in all other normal activities.

10,000 FAMILIES MOVE

Evacuations were mounting all along the Ohio, but were greatest at Portsmouth and in the Cincinnati-Newport, Ky., area. Approximately 10,000 families, or nearly one-half of Portsmouth's total population, have been or were to be moved from their homes today.

Similar situations existed in almost every community along the Ohio. At Pittsburgh, where the Allegheny and Monongahela Rivers join to form the Ohio, a 35-foot stage, 10 feet above flood level, was foreseen as a possibility. More conservative estimates on the Pittsburgh stage, however, were around 35 feet.

WAR PLANTS MENACED

Cincinnati's Mill Creek Basin, in which scores of war plants and packing houses are located, became the immediate concern of emergency crews following a break in the sandbagging atop the partially-completed Mill Creek barrier dam.

At Pittsburgh, U. S. Weatherman W. S. Brotzman increased his predicted flood crest for Pittsburgh from 33 to 33.5 feet be-

(Continued on Page 6, Column 2)

The Colors Over Corregidor

'Let No Enemy Haul Them Down'

OUT OF THE DUST OF 1942—To the top of the same parade ground staff from which the Japanese tore Old Glory and trampled it in the dust three years ago goes the American Flag. Saluting in the dramatic ceremonies are General Douglas MacArthur (circled) and members of the 503rd Parachute Infantry Regiment who recaptured the Rock. Said General MacArthur: "Have your troops hoist the Colors to its peak, and let no enemy ever haul them down!" —Associated Press wirephoto.

WORK OR JAIL PLAN REJECTED BY SENATE

Labor Draft Legislation Offered By Bailey Beaten 60 to 23

By Felix Cotten
Staff Correspondent International News Service

WASHINGTON, March 7.—Labor draft legislation was decisively beaten in the Senate today when the chamber slapped down by a vote of 60 to 23, a "work or jail" proposal offered by Senator Joseiah W. Bailey (Democrat), North Carolina.

The vote was interpreted as practically eliminating, so far as the Senate is concerned, the May-Bailey labor draft bill for men 18 to 45, and was the first test of how the Senate stands on an enforced labor-draft bill.

Bailey had offered the labor draft proposal as an amendment to a substitute bill introduced by Senator Chapman Revercomb (Republican), West Virginia. Revercomb proposed to apply the work or jail principle to "loafers," but Bailey sought to broaden it to include all men 18 to 45 not already engaged in essential war activity.

House passes bill inducting nurses into armed services. Page 6.

In the debate on the Bailey amendment, Senators indicated they regarded it as embodying the main elements of the May-Bailey Bill, which was passed by the House.

2 PROPOSALS LEFT

Senate rejection of the Bailey amendment left two main proposals before the Senate for action—the Revercomb substitute and the Kilgore-O'Mahoney manpower control bill.

In addition to forcing "loafers" to work, the Revercomb substitute would permit the War Manpower Commission to fix manpower ceilings for places of business subject to a provision that labor forces could not be cut more than 50 per cent.

It also would provide that persons discharged by application of ceilings could return to their old jobs if they could not find war work within 30 days.

The Kilgore-O'Mahoney bill would give legal backing to the War Manpower Commission. It

(Continued on Page 6, Column 2)

Reich Battered From 2 Sides

3rd Army Gains 10 More Miles

LONDON, March 7.—(AP)—Marshal G. K. Zhukov's First White Russian Army group began today the long-expected general frontal assault on Berlin from its Oder River bridgeheads 30 to 40 miles to the east, the Germans announced.

The attackers jumped off after a gigantic 24-hour artillery barrage and punched into the outer defenses of Kuestrin, which was under attack from north, east and south, Berlin's alarmed broadcasters said. They credited Zhukov with using seven armies, including two tank armies.

Moscow said nothing of any such developments, but Soviet silence is customary at the start of a major operation.

THREAT DESTROYED

Only yesterday the way was paved for an assault towards Berlin when Zhukov's right wing thrust to the Oder's Baltic Sea outlet and destroyed the threat of a German counterstroke on that flank. This success was vastly solidified today, Premier Stalin announcing capture of Stepenitz, Gollnow and Massow.

Stepenitz is a twin city on the east bank of the Oder where it flows into the Stettiner Haff (lagoon) 15 miles north of Stettin. Gollnow is 15 miles northeast of Stettin and Massow 20 miles east. Stettin, Berlin's Oder River outlet to the Baltic, thus was placed in increasingly grave danger and had lost much of its importance as an outer citadel for the capital.

Premier Stalin issued two other orders of the day, neither on the front east of Berlin. One announced that the Second White Russian Army had captured Starogard, 25 miles south of Danzig, and Mewe, 35 miles southeast; the other that the Second Ukraine Army had taken Banska-Stiavnica (Schemnitz) in Slovakia, 82 miles northeast of Bratislava.

KOLBERG ATTACKED

The Germans said the Russians had broken into the Baltic fortress of Kolberg and were hastening to end the entire Baltic campaign, but devoted most of their broadcasts to accounts of the offensives aimed at Berlin.

The Nazis said Zhukov was attacking repeatedly from bridge-

(Continued on Page 2, Cols. 2-3)

Light Enemy Resistance

WITH THE U. S. THIRD ARMY, March 7.—(AP)—The U. S. Fourth Armored Division reached the Rhine River today.

The Fourth Armored's sensational stab to the river was made against only light resistance. Hundreds of German prisoners surrendered as the tanks of Lieutenant General George S. Patton sped through town after town.

By James L. Kilgallen
Staff Correspondent International News Service

PARIS, March 7.—A 150-mile section of the German front west of the Rhine from south of American-occupied Cologne down to Bischweiler crumbled rapidly tonight as the U. S. Third Army hammered to within 12 miles of Coblenz and the American

NEW YORK, March 7.—(INS)—The clandestine radio Atlantic, heard by N. B. C., reported tonight that Allied armies are using a new weapon, described as an "electric grenade," with devastating effect.

First Army drove into the outskirts of Bonn.

Maintaining its sensational advances, the Third Army's Fourth Armored Division gained another 10 miles today and reached Polch, 12 miles west of Coblenz, where the middle Rhine receives the Moselle River, in a drive to within 21 miles of a junction with the

SHOWERS
ccasional showers tonight and Saturday. tonight, 50; high Saturday, 65. Sunrise, Sunset, 6:59. (Chart, page 14.)

CHICAGO DAILY NEWS

FIVE STAR FINAL Edition

TH YEAR—64. REG. U.S. PAT. OFF. COPYRIGHT, 1945 BY THE CHICAGO DAILY NEWS, INC. FRIDAY, MARCH 16, 1945—THIRTY-EIGHT PAGES. Telephone DEArborn 1111. FOUR CENTS

Price Is 19,938 Marine Casualties

BITTER IWO BATTLE WON

Ruhr Road Cut Twice

1st Army Plunges 2 Miles

Yanks Three Miles From Open Tank Country in Reich

PARIS — (AP) — The 1st Army cut the Ruhr-Frankfurt superhighway east of the Rhine in two places today and extended the Remagen bridgehead to at least 13 miles in length.

The Americans beat off a German tank attack in heavy fighting four miles northeast of Linz, in the area where the bridgehead is six and a half miles wide.

They fought into Koenigswinter in two-mile gains within three miles of open tank country leading to the great Ruhr basin.

"The Germans are building up for a major attack," Don Whitehead, Associated Press correspondent, reported from the bridgehead.

* * *

TO THE south, the famous 4th Armored Division broke loose again in a swift, unchecked 18-mile dash southeast of Coblenz. This 3d Army move was a supreme effort to trap Germans tarrying in outflanked sections of the Siegfried Line.

The 7th Army, still further south, rolled forward on a 50-mile front from Saarbruecken to the Rhine in an offensive against the Saarland co-ordinated with the 3d Army attack.

The Moselle was crossed anew by the 3d Army six miles southwest of Coblenz and at a point 18 south of Mayen. (BBC said the 3d Army had opened an assault on Coblenz.)

* * *

AERIAL REPORTS indicated the Germans already had started their flight to Frankfurt from the Saarland and Palatinate as the 3d and 7th armies tightened their coordinated squeeze.

The 7th Army was fighting at the edge of Saarbruecken and had outflanked and was north of the Maginot Line bastion

(Continued on page 4, column 1.)

More Manpower

LONDON—(AP)—The German radio, which previously estimated that 100,000 American troops have been poured into the Remagen bridgehead, declared today that four more divisions were being moved into the area, making it "the biggest single concentration of power on a narrow front ever seen in this war."

STALL AT CROSSING LIKELY

Bridgehead Tough to Exploit

BY B. J. McQUAID.
Daily News Foreign Service.

BAD GODESBERG, Germany—It begins to appear that we are content for the time being to maintain a limited foothold in the bridgehead area.

It is not clear, however, whether it is because of failure of our forces on the scene to exploit the Ludendorf Bridge seizure more quickly or because of the high command's unwillingness to abandon or adapt its overall plans for the Rhine crossing to fit the situation created by this "accidental development."

In what appears to be a decision not to commit the kind of major forces required to break through the stubborn ring of defenses Jerry has thrown around our perimeter, the high command is probably motivated by the belief that the job can be done more quickly and less expensively, in the long run, by a series of crossings in force at many points along the Rhine.

* * *

IT MUST BE conceded that the Remagen bridgehead is probably one of the worst crossing sites on the entire river.

After discouraging meager advances in the first few days of the operation, our men have advanced materially north and south in the last 48 hours, aided by weather which enabled our airmen to provide the maximum support.

Our troops, supprted by armor, have begun to come down off the heights into open country.

Even if we expand the bridgehead and drive north, we shall shortly come up against the necessity of another river crossing, this time the Sieg, which is a bigger river than the Roer and extends east from the Rhine, a little north of Bonn.

THE 'ROLLING 4TH' ROLLS AHEAD

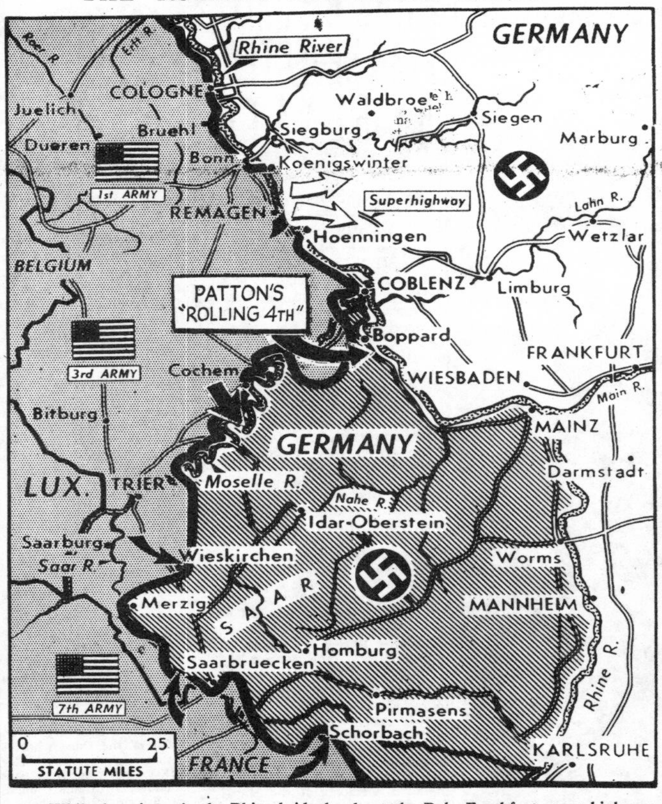

While Americans in the Rhine bridgehead cut the Ruhr-Frankfurt super highway in two places (open arrows) Patton's "Rolling 4th" Division cut a wide swath southeast of Coblenz and aimed toward the Rhine. The U.S. 7th Army is thrusting into the southern flank of the Saar Basin applying a nutcracker to German units remaining west of the Rhine.
[Associated Press Wirephoto.]

Russ Open 2 Offensives on Berlin Arc

BULLETIN.
LONDON—(AP)—A Berlin war correspondent said tonight that the Russians had broken into the "inner defense of Stettin."

LONDON—(UP) — Nazi radios said today that Red Armies had opened new offensives on :th wings of the Berlin front, in Silesia and before Stettin.

These attacks are to set the stage for the grand assault on the German capital.

Berlin broadcasts reported that Marshal Konev's 1st Ukrainian Army attacked on a broad arc south and southwest of Breslau and that Marshal Zhukov's 1st White Russian Army stormed the Nazi bridgehead across the lower Oder from Stettin.

* * *

DIRECTLY BEFORE Berlin, Soviet forces were reported pouring across the Oder into a growing bridgehead some 30 miles east of the capital for the final push forecast for some days by both Berlin and unofficial Moscow dispatches.

BALTIC CLAMP
[Associated Press Wirephoto.]

The battle of the Baltic Coast was drawing to a close, with Russian armies clamping a new assault arc on the East Prussian capital of Koenigsberg and storming the outposts of Danzig and Gdynia.

All signs from Berlin and Moscow indicated that Z:.ukov was about ready to order the advance against Berlin, whic hthe Soviets have predicted confidently will end with the Red banner flying over the heart of Nazidom.

Groom, 63, Takes A Bride of 18

Charles F. Asmus, 63, a secondhand goods dealer of 1732 Clybourn av., and Miss Lucille Brueckman, 18, of 205 Evergreen av., were married yesterday in the County Building by Judge William P. Boynton of Alton Municipal Court.

Jap Dead Placed at 21,000

4,189 Marines Killed In Costliest Invasion Of Pacific War

U.S. PACIFIC FLEET HEADQUARTERS, GUAM, Saturday, March 17.—(AP)— The Navy announced today that 4,189 American marines had been killed in the conquest of Iwo Jima, strategic Jap island within 750 miles of Tokyo, and that the battle for Iwo "has been won."

It added that 15,308 marines had been wounded and 441 are missing, making a total of 19,938 casualties sustained by three Marine divisions in seizing the island.

* * *

"A VERY considerable number" of the wounded already have returned to action, the press release said.

Iwo was invaded Feb. 19 by the 4th and 5th Marine Divisions, which were joined a few days later by the 3d Marine Division.

Adm. Nimitz said today that the bloody battle, costliest invasion in the Pacific war, had been won and asserted the marines fought "with certain knowledge of the cost of an objective which had to be taken."

* * *

ORGANIZED resistance on Iwo ceased at 6 p.m. last night when elements of the 3d and 5th Divisions broke through the enemy lines at Kitano Point at the northern tip of the island.

The casualties on Iwo, greatest of the Pacific war to date, topped those on Saipan of 16,525 in 24 days of organized resistance on that island in the Marianas, about 650 miles south of Iwo. The Iwo campaign lasted two days longer.

More than 21,000 Japs were killed or captured.

* * *

NIMITZ sent this message of congratulations to all forces of the Pacific Ocean areas:

"To Marines of the 5th Amphibious Corps and to all supporting forces I send my admiration and congratulations on an achievement that brings this war much closer to its inevitable end. In capturing Iwo which is as important as it was tough you have overcome the most difficult defenses that skill and ingenuity could construct on a small island that nature herself had already made strong for military defense."

"Your victory which was assured almost from the first landing will brighten the pages of American history. Today, your fellow countrymen humbly and proudly sing your praises."

* * *

IN A MESSAGE to Lt.Gen Holland M. Smith, commanding general of Marines in the Pacific, Lt. Gen. Robert C. Richardson, commanding general of Army forces in the Pacific Ocean areas, said:

"Warm congratulations for the magnificent fight which has been made by gallant marines in the capture of Iwo. It makes one proud to be an American, thinking what those brave men have done."

Army Seeking Cure For 'Desert Fever'

How military doctors are fighting a puzzling dust disease is told today by Paul R. Leach on page 15.

Also on the inside:

President Urges U.S. To Tighten Its Belt

Americans Must Eat Less So Others Will Not Starve

WASHINGTON—(AP) — President Roosevelt declared today that the American people have got to tighten their belts before the war is won.

Replying at a news conference to some criticism of the handling of food matters, Mr. Roosevelt said he thought the country would back up the idea of tightening our belts since it would mean keeping certain other people alive.

Holland, he said, is a case where need is urgent.

* * *

A COMMITTEE recently was created under War Mobilizer James F. Byrnes, representing various war agencies, to examine all the factors relating to exports, primarily of food stuffs.

Suppose, Mr. Roosevelt remarked in discussing the need for the committee, that there is a world shortage of sugar. Actually, there isn't, he said, but suppose we find that by cutting our consumption of sugar by 10 per cent we can keep people in some other country from starving. We are still going to live, he said.

The American people, he went on, are going to understand this, once it is explained to them. The whole thing is a matter of decency, he added.

He could not bring himself to think, the President said, that we are going to suffer very greatly in this country compared with others.

Japs Admit Raid Terror; Report Thousands Killed

By the United Press.

Thousands of persons were burned to death in the American B-29 raids on Tokyo, Nagoya and Osaka, the Japanese radio said today.

These reports came amid mounting clamor in the enemy capital for more adequate air relief measures.

The situation in Japan was reaching such serious proportions that the Jap propaganda outlets openly admitted damage caused by the increasing Superfortress attacks.

Tokyo's influential newspaper Asahi said the number of persons killed in the B-29 attacks could "never be called small."

Asahi's report, transmitted by Domei, said "incendiaries and bombs were poured like rain on the people's heads" at Tokyo and Nagoya when the Superfortresses struck at an altitude from 3,000 to 6,000 feet. "Whipped up by a strong wind, the flames and smoke swirled fiercely."

"Many townsmen have been bombed out from their homes. Thousands were severely injured and thousands were burned to death."

The report was attributed to a spokesman of the Jap imperial board of information, who, as usual, asserted that most of the victims were women and children. He also said that religious institutions, schools and hospitals were hit.

* * *

THE GRAVITY of the situation was emphasized by Domei which said that under an "extraordinary" arrangement, Premier Koiso would become a member of the Jap imperial headquarters.

The dispatch said the unprecedented action, fully sanctioned by Emperor Hirohito, was taken so that Koiso could participate in the direction of military operations. He will have a status equal to the army and navy chiefs of staff.

* * *

THE SOVIET Tass agency, in a radio dispatch, quoted its Tokyo correspondent as saying panic reigned in the enemy capital after the B-29 raid on Saturday. Even six days after the attack, Tass said thousands of refugees were crowding around the Tokyo railway stations trying to leave the capital.

Ride Victim Suspect in Vault Theft

Wencel Urban, gangster and safecracker indicted in the big Rumbold vault robbery, was taken for a death ride—the body found in a ditch near Kankakee was identified this afternoon as Urban's.

Urban, 49, a former member of the Egan's Rats gang of St. Louis, had made Chicago his headquarters in recent months and was accused in two other big safecracking jobs.

* * *

THE IDENTIFICATION was made at the Detective Bureau from a second set of fingerprints of the ride victim brought here from Kankakee by Sheriff Cecil Duguay.

The police laboratory here had just begun a study of the cloting, watc and eyeglasses of the dead man when the prints established the identity.

* * *

THE POLICE believe that Urban began operations in Chicago in 1943. On Dec. 23 that year he was captured with Timothy McCarthy at the Willett Teaming Co. 700 S. Desplaines st., after a gun battle with Capts. John P. Horan and Louis Capparelli. The pair had guns, nitroglycerine and other safecracking equipment.

However, Urban and McCarthy and a third man beat the case in court—contending they were "framed" by the police.

* * *

URBAN was also accused of the $1,177 robbery of the Olson Transportation Co., 222 S. Western av., March 6, 1944.

Urban was among a number of men indicted for the Rumbold vault robbery at 624 W. 119th st. last Jan. 20. The police did not disclose what evidence they had against Urban, but confessions of three men had been obtained.

U.S. Egg Shortage Growing

Spreading Black Market Already 'On the Gray Side'

BY GEORGE THIEM.
Staff Correspondent.

A nation-wide egg shortage and a developing black market appeared on the horizon today.

The growing food shortage showed up in depleted cold sto age warehouses which last ye were bulging.

There are plenty of eggs in Chicago and suburban food stores this week and there is no immediate danger of a famine. But the mand is heavy and the future o look uncertain. Prices are bu ing the ceiling.

* * *

FOOD STORE buyers said today it is getting increasingly hard to fil their orders and price ceiling evasion has begun.

For example, the wholesale ceiling on "current receipts," one buyer reported, is 32½ cents a dozen. But there are no current receipt eggs. You pay the 'standards" price of 34½ cents or go without.

This isn't exactly a black market but it's a little on the gray side.

* * *

THE NATIONAL egg shortage was highlighted by a War Food Administration report from Washington which disclosed these facts:

1. This week's government survey of 13 metropolitan markets showed egg supplies were not sufficient to meet demands.
2. The scarcity pushed prices to ceiling levels everywhere.
3. The meat scarcity has driven consumers to raid the egg counters.

Since Jan. 1 egg eating is at the rate of 400 per person a year, 50 more than last year and 100 eggs more than the prewar level.

* * *

EDWARD B. Heaton, secretary of the Institute of American Poultry Industries, explained why egg supplies are tighter.

"There were 42,720,000 fewer laying hens on farms Feb. 1 this year than 12 months ago," he said. "This is a 9 per cent reduction. People are eating more eggs and just now the demand by hatcheries is tremendous."

There is danger, Heaton added, that a developing shortage may reduce the baby chick hatch and bring on a scarcity of poultry meat later. The hatch is down 10 to 12 per cent since Jan. 1 compared to a year ago.

In Illinois, the January hatch was 30 per cent less than for the same month of 1944.

* * *

THE ARMED forces are scrambling for supplies and speculators are actively buying eggs to store against a predicted shortage when the spring egg flow tapers off.

At Chicago, the Quartermaster

(Continued on page 4, column 2.)

Easter Clothing Sales Highest Since '29

By the United Press.

The American woman's Easter costume is going to be the gayest and most colorful since the start of the war, and it certainly will be the most expensive since 1929, a survey revealed today.

Clothing sales in the nation's leading shopping centers have jumped from 20 to 46 per cent since the Easter buying rush began. Many department store managers predicted that sales would top the 1929 figure.

Women are buying the more frivolous items with emphasis on gay colors and femininity, clerks reported. Hats are more frivolous than they have been for several years and the supply is plentiful.

* * *

ALMOST all hats have veils and flowers, even the tailored ones, and the women don't question the cost.

One Chicago department store reported a scarcity of accessories, such as hose and gloves, at the present time.

Minneapolis and St. Paul showed the greatest increase in buying over last year. Sales in the Twin Cities were up 46 per cent.

* * *

FEDERAL Reserve statistics for the 9th district, which includes the north central Midwest, showed that Easter buying was up 28 per cent on the whole and buying was heavier than in any other section of the nation.

Washington reported sales up 25 to 30 per cent over last year and 40 per cent better than 1929. Tiny hats trimmed with ostrich feathers sold for $20 and up.

Throngs Hail Bataan Heroes

FINAL NIGHT EDITION WEATHER: RAIN Details on Page 6

THE CALL BULLETIN
SAN FRANCISCO — AN INDEPENDENT NEWSPAPER

CALL AND POST, VOL. 157, NO. 41
THE-CALL-BULLETIN, VOL. 177, NO. 41
TUESDAY, MARCH 20, 1945
5c DAILY

PATTON BAGS 50,000 IN BIG SAAR SMASH

British Recapture of Mandalay Reported

NEW YORK, March 20 (INS). B. B. C. reported today that Mandalay has been recaptured by British troops. The FFC heard the broadcast.

CALCUTTA, March 20 (AP).—British Thirty-sixth Division troops have occupied Mogok, world's ruby capital sixty-five miles northeast of Mandalay and an equal distance west of the Burma road city of Lashio, in the Allied drive to rid the area north of the Mandalay-Lashio road of the Japanese.

(A Reuters dispatch said Fort Dufferin, Japanese stronghold in the center of Mandalay, had been captured.)

American and British B-24 bombers of the strategic air force, flying almost 3,000 miles in one of the longest missions ever flown by Liberators, raided enemy communications on the Kra isthmus in Thailand, some 245 miles southwest of Bangkok, and results were said to be excellent.

The Inside on the Food Shortage

'44 Optimism Blamed For U. S. Crisis in 1945

(One of a Series)

By OVID A. MARTIN
Associated Press Farm Writer

WASHINGTON, March 20 (AP).—The United States faces a food situation which soon may put civilans on the slimmest diet of the war.

This is true despite the fact that we have had eight successive years of expanding and record breaking food production.

Why?

HOUSEWIVES PUZZLED

The question has been asked increasingly this month by housewives often unable to find butter, chicken, cheese, sugar and eggs.

Congress has heard demands for an investigation, with special attention to foodstuffs shipping to foreign lands.

Explanations are to be found largely in two facts:

1. The government released more food than it should have, judged by what we know now, to civilians in 1944.

2. In planning this year's production, officials operated on the belief that the war in Europe would end in 1944.

EXAMINE SITUATION

To understand how and why shortages have developed let's first examine the food situation in broad general terms.

After a slump during the early depression years, food production began to increase in 1937. It reached a peak in 1944. The increase was sharpest between 1941 and 1944. By the latter year, the output was 38 per cent above the 1935-39 average.

But in 1944, production of many commodities leveled off and

Continued on Page 4, Column 2

32 Lbs. Per Capita Cut in Meat Eating Slated for Civilians

WASHINGTON, March 20 (AP).—The annual per capita consumption of meats increased from an average of 125.6 pounds in the 1935-1939 period to 147 pounds in 1944, official estimates show.

The consumption rate for meats will be reduced to 115 pounds, during the April-June quarter of this year.

The per capita consumption of other major food items for the 1935-39 period and 1944, respectively, by pounds, included:

Eggs, 37.3 and 43.6; poultry (dressed weight), 20.5 and 26.1; fluid milk and cream, 340 and 421; cheese, 5.5 and 4.7; butter, 16.7 and 11.8; sugar, 96.5 and 88.4, and coffee, 14 and 16.

Lublin Poles Name U.S. Agent

WASHINGTON, March 20 (INS).—A propaganda battle over the Polish issue was in the making today as the Justice Department disclosed that the Polish provisional government)formerly the Lublin committee) has designated an agent to handle a press campaign in this country.

ADDRESS MOSCOW

The agent is Edward J. Falkowski, who has registered as the U. S. representative of "Polpress News," or the Polish press news agency. At the time of registration, Falkowski described it as "the semi-official news agency of the Polish Committee of National Liberation at Lublin, Poland, temporary office, Moscow, U.S.S.R."

At the same time, the Polish government in London is distributing propaganda in this country through its information center in New York.

LONDON, March 20 (AP). The United States and Britain were reported today to have launched a new effort to bring leaders of the Polish factions together with the hope of forming a representative government so that country can be represented at the San Francisco conference.

DISCUSSIONS SET

Tentative preparations already have been made for discussions in Moscow, but Washington and London are understood to be running into difficulties in negotiations with the Lublin administration.

Bay Girl Identity Case Probed

The theory that a 4 year old girl being held at the Martinez juvenile detention home might be Sylvia Sweet, child who mysteriously disappeared six months ago from a Reno dude ranch, was expressed today by Richmond police—but at the same time other authorities expressed doubt that she was the same youngster.

The girl, identified as Shirley Johnson, was taken to the home after Alvin Duncan, 32, of El Cerrito told police she had been left with him by a Mrs. Betty Johnson, with whom he said he had been living.

Richmond Policewoman Mary Peterson said Shirley matched the description of Sylvia issued by the Washoe County sheriff's office at the time of her disappearance.

However, Mrs. Frederica Edgar, chief Contra Costa County probation officer, said she did not believe Shirley was the missing youngster. The Sweet child, daughter of Mrs. Rosamond Sweet of Providence, R. I., wandered away from the dude ranch where her mother was staying while awaiting a divorce and was given up for dead after posses combed the surrounding area.

Reno authorities were en route to Martinez to see the child.

F. R. ASKS STUDY OF ANNUAL WAGE PLAN

WASHINGTON, March 20 (AP).—President Roosevelt today projected a study of the whole problem of an annual wage for America's workers. He directed a request to James F. Byrnes' Office of Mobilization and Reconversion, for such a study to be made by Byrnes' advisory board.

U. S. THIRD ARMY SWEEPS UP CITIES

WITH U. S. THIRD ARMY, March 20 (AP).—The Third Army today captured Worms, reached Mainz and entered and passed beyond Kaiserlautern.

RUSSIANS TAKE BASTION 4 MILES FROM STETTIN

LONDON, March 20 (AP).—Altdamm, a suburban bastion four miles east of Stettin, has fallen to the First White Russian Army, Marshal Stalin announced tonight.

'Dead' Hitler Foe in Peace Role

BERN, March 20 (AP).—The Swiss newspaper Die Tat, quoting "informed sources" in Berlin, said today that Dr. Karl Goerdeler, whom the Nazis had announced was killed for his role in the bomb attempt against Hitler last July, still was alive and was being held in reserve as a possible peace petitioner.

The newspaper said Hitler was planting peace rumors in last efforts to try to split the Allies but still wanted to continue fighting.

Swiss officials, commenting on rumors that Germans were seeking peace through Switzerland, declared that Nazi Foreign Minister Joachim Von Ribbentrop was not in this neutral country.

FETE 300 HEROES OF BATAAN

Thousands of San Franciscans crowded the sidewalks of Market street and leaned from office building windows today to roar their cheers and welcome for the second large group of liberated prisoners from the Philippines to arrive in San Francisco.

The men were the more than 300 liberated prisoners who arrived here last Friday aboard a huge transport, and for whom the city today extended its official welcome — the second time a group of liberated prisoners has been so honored.

PARADE THROUGH CITY

The men were taken from Letterman Hospital, where they have received new uniforms, medical checkups, decorations and campaign ribbons, in a special motor caravan that wound its way through the Marina and then on Market street to the City Hall.

As the men leaned out of the windows of the Army buses transporting them, San Franciscans waved and shouted their greetings to the soldiers, who were home at last after more than three years in Jap prison camps.

A special police motorcycle escort, sirens screaming, cleared the way for the caravan as grateful San Franciscans overflowed the sidewalks and crowded into the street.

CITY HALL RECEPTION

A reception arranged by a citizens' committee headed by Dr. Henry F. Grady, president of the San Francisco Chamber of Commerce, in accord with a suggestion of The Call-Bulletin, included ceremonies in the City Hall and a gala luncheon at the Hotel Mark Hopkins.

The caravan's route was from the Marina exit of the Presidio, over Marina boulevard to Cervantes boulevard, thence to Bay street, along Bay to the Embarcadero and to the Ferry building.

MAYOR'S GREETING

From the Ferry Building the caravan route was on Market street to Grove street, along Grove to Polk, thence to the front of the City Hall, where a special greeting from Mayor Roger D. Lapham awaited the liberated prisoners.

After the reception, the caravan of heroes was to proceed on Polk street to McAllister, thence to Van Ness avenue, and along Van Ness avenue and California street to the hotel, where a luncheon and entertainment program awaited them.

(Photos Page 1, Green Flash Section; story on Medal Awards, Page 2.)

Queen Wilhelmina Makes Triumphant Return Home

LONDON, March 20 (AP). — Queen Wilhemina, first of Europe's exiled monarchs to return home, has visited liberated areas of Holland and received a tremendous ovation from her people, it was learned today.

Call Marshall On Army Promotions

WASHINGTON, March 20 (INS).—The Senate military affairs committee in a turbulent session today decided to call General George C, Marshall, the Army's top ranking officer, before it to explain the Army policy on promotions.

Speedy approval of recent nominations of nine lieutenant generals to be full, four star generals was blocked as a result of the decision.

The committee was called into session by Senator Elbert Thomas (D., Utah), chairman, who sought action upon the nominations submitted March 13.

SAY TRADITION VIOLATED

Several members immediately began questioning War Department policy in the secret session, and demanded more information before voting on recommending confirmations.

Some members, it was learned, declared the present policy of promoting officers to such high positions as general during a war violates the tradition of the country of rewarding successful generals with high rank after a war has been fought.

Demand also was made for information as to why Lieutenant Generals Patton, Hodges, Simpson and Patch—leaders of American Armies now crushing the Germans—were passed over in promotion to four star generals.

ANGRY PROTESTS ON REDS

Recent disclosure of lifting the ban upon naming Communists as officers in positions of unusual secrecy in the Army brought angry protests from some members.

The charge was made, it was learned, that a high ranking general had failed to give the committee a true picture of the situation a year ago when the first order dealing with subversive records was issued. At that time, it was charged that papers showing subversive records were destroyed.

School Boy, 15, Dead In San Jose Mystery

SAN JOSE, March 20 (AP).—A 15 year old high school student who started out for a dance with a dollar in his pocket Saturday night and never got there, died last night of a fractured skull in County Hospital, and Sheriff William J. Emig was investigating the possibility he was murdered.

DIDN'T KEEP DATE

Jack King was found unconscious in a roadside ditch two blocks from his home at 10 a. m. Sunday. His mother, Eileen King, had kissed him goodby and tucked the dollar in his vest pocket at 7 p. m. Saturday as he left for a school dance two miles away.

Sheriff Emig has found no one who saw the boy in the interim. He didn't keep his date with the girl he was taking to the dance. He never came out of the coma to tell what happened.

The sheriff said robbery may have been a motive for murder. The dollar was gone. He said an examination of the body ruled out possibility the boy had been hit by a car.

ONE SLIGHT BRUISE

There were no bruises, except for a slight mark at the base of the skull at the point of fracture.

The clothing was not torn.

California His Home, Says Gen. MacArthur

SACRAMENTO, March 20 (INS).—California is home to General Douglas MacArthur.

So the heroic general declared today in a letter to the California Legislature in response to a resolution adopted in the Assembly January 26, commemorating the warrior's sixty-fifth birthday anniversary.

"I cannot tell you how deeply moved I was to receive a copy of the resolution passed by the Assembly on my birthday," said MacArthur's letter.

"I think of all days of a man's life, no matter however humble or however great he may be, that one holds for him the most poignant memories of his entire existence. It is redolent with reverent thoughts of mother, of father, and of home.

"My connection with California has been of such a nature that I can truly say that that great state falls within the third of these categories. To hear from home in such a way and on such a day fills me with a fullness of gratitude that comes to few men."

German General 'Sacked' In West Front Debacle

BAD KREUZNACH, Germany, March 20 (AP).—A captured German officer said today that Colonel General Johannes Blaskowitz had been sacked as commander of German army group G on the southern wing of the western front because of the German debacle, and that an S. S. general, Paul Hauser, was now in charge. Blaskowitz is now reported commanding an army in the north.

TASK FORCE BLASTS NIPS THIRD DAY

U. S. PACIFIC FLEET HEADQUARTERS, Guam, March 20 (AP). — Vice Admiral Marc A. Mitscher's mighty carrier force was reported bombing Japan today—a third straight day—defying the imperial fleet to come out for battle and giving the lie to enemy communique claims that seven of Mitscher's capital ships were sunk and one damaged.

Fleet Admiral Chester W. Nimitz announced briefly that carrier pilots moved northward Monday to loose bombs and rockets against shipbuilding Kobe and a major naval base, Kure, on the home island of Honshu. Sunday, carrier planes sent probably 2,500 tons of bombs winging down upon Kyushu and Shikoku, industrially-vital islands at the southern end of the empire.

ATTACKS CONTINUE

"Enemy attacks are still continuing," Tokio flashed in an English language broadcast to the United States today.

The announcer did not state whether the raid was on Honshu of whether the bombers had returned against Kyushu.

(The Tokio broadcast saying the U. S. attacks were still continuing was picked up in San Francisco by the NBC. Domei, Japanese news agency, made no mention of continuing raids in its broadcasts heard by the FCC, nor did the Nipponese imperial headquarters refer to them.)

TASK FORCE 58

Tokio identified the raiders as "the mainstay of task force fifty-eight"—the carrier force which leaped into fame last June by destroying 405 Japanese warplanes on one day; then sinking or damaging seventeen Japanese warships in a thrilling sea chase the next day.

The enemy radio said the force comprised five groups of ships, including fifteen carriers, and was about 300 miles south of Shikoku when first sighted Sunday. It added that Japanese fliers were continuing their attacks against the U. S. fleet.

NIPS ADMIT LOSSES

Japanese communiques claimed, without confirmation, that 183 carrier aircraft were shot down. Unofficial Tokio broadcasts admitted the loss of at least twenty Nipponese planes.

If Mitscher is continuing his attack, the total tonnage of incendiary and explosive bombs and rockets fired at the empire in three days would exceed 7,000 tons.

Soldier Doomed to Die 'Celebrates' His Birthday

LINCOLN, Neb., March 20 (INS).—Sergeant Joseph T. MacEvoy, Brooklyn, N. Y., soldier sentenced to die in the electric chair Friday for the rape-slaying of Anna Milroy, 16, of Sutton, Neb., "celebrated" his twenty-fifth birthday yesterday as he was transferred to death row to await execution.

Capital Of Panay Isle Tottering

(Map on Page A)

MANILA, Wednesday, March 21 (AP). — American infantrymen rapidly enveloped Iloilo, capital of Panay island, today and immediate capture of the important harbor city was expected as the Yanks capitalized on their virtually unopposed invasion of that central Philippines island.

Aerial immobilization of Formosa, Japanese bastion 225 miles north of Luzon, meanwhile reached an advanced stage, with American bombers often hitting lush targets without interference from enemy fighter planes.

Formosa, guarding the China coast and the southwest approach to Japan, has been hit almost daily for many weeks by American Liberators and fighters based on Luzon. It was estimated that the Japanese had at least 800 planes on Formosa when this neutralization campaign was launched.

GREETED BY GUERRILLAS

Americans of Major General Rapp Brush's Fortieth Infantry Division, originally of the California National Guard, but with a New York regiment added, who invaded Panay Sunday, were aided by guerrillas who already had cleared some sections of the island. Smiling, cheering Filipinos met the Yanks at the beaches as they landed with Naval and air support.

Hardly a man was lost in this twenty-fifth invasion of the liberation campaign, said Tuesday's headquarters communique. It contained the now familiar report that the landing achieved "complete tactical as well as strategic surprise."

Panay is important because of its position just south of the principal shipping lane through the central Philippines. Enemy planes based there could harass American vessels proceeding to and from Manila.

QUICKLY DRIVE INLAND

The landing was made on Panay's southeastern shore. The troops quickly drove inland to Cordova and eastward along the coast to Oton, midway between the beachhead and Iloilo.

Philippine based air forces also supported the various ground operations throughout the archipelago, maintained a tight blockade of the China coast and carried on their neutralization of Japanese airdromes and installations on Borneo.

Tokio 'Fire Alleys' Fail, Jap Commentator Admits

LONDON, March 20 (AP).—The Tokio radio said today that special "fire alleys" in Tokio and other Japanese cities had proved ineffective in halting the spread of conflagrations started by recent U. S. Super Fortress raids.

A Japanese commentator said the fire raid on Tokio on March 10 had left more people homeless than the heaviest raids on Germany.

U. S. TROOPS AT BONN AS FOE FLEES

WITH U. S. FIRST ARMY, March 20 (AP).—Lieutenant General Courtney H. Hodges' forces overran more than two score villages, smashed to the outskirts of Bonn on the Rhine's east bank and advanced to the south today to clamp an iron grip on a twenty-four mile stretch of the river.

PARIS, March 20 (AP).—German defenses collapsed in the Saar basin today while the rampaging American Seventh and Third armies raced toward an imminent junction near the Rhine.

Lieutenant General George S. Patton's Third Army flanked completely the Siegfried and alternate Hunsbrueck lines in the Saar and Palatinate and in sweeping gains moved within four miles of the second Palatinate city of Kaiserslautern, within nine miles of Mainz and twenty-three miles of the chemical center of Ludwigshafen.

POCKET EXTENDED

Lieutenant General Alexander M. Patch's Seventh Army was completely through a twelve mile stretch of the Siegfried line between Saarbruecken and Zweibruecken.

A pocket around Saarbruecken and the great steel mills of the Saarland was all but closed—if not already so, since reports were lagging hours behind developments.

In the Kaiserslautern area, the armies were only twenty miles apart and closing fast.

50,000 NAZI LOSSES

More than 50,000 of the originally estimated 80,000 Germans of the enemy's First and Seventh armies already were counted as casualties.

In seven blazing days, Patton's offensive has inflicted at least 45,000 casualties on the Germans in the Rhine-Moselle-Saar pocket, Correspondent E. D. Ball said in a dispatch from the front.

Ball messaged:

"With the Siegfried line flanked, the Third and Seventh Army should meet shortly somewhere near the Rhine."

BRIDGEHEAD WIDENED

The Germans said the First Army had launched a heavy attack in the southern end of the bridgehead east of the Rhine, penetrating seven miles into German lines beyond Hoenningen to reach the Rhine opposite Ander-

Call-Bulletin Today

Special Features

("G" indicates Green Flash Section)

'The Final Assault on Germany' Monty Calls It

6 ALLIED ARMIES ACROSS RHINE

WALL ST. STATE ST. COMPLETE
Boston Traveler
New England's Largest Evening Circulation
Associated Press and United Press Wire Services
SATURDAY, MARCH 24, 1945
EST. 1825—120th YEAR—NO. 221
10 PAGES 3 CENTS

See Map Page 2

Giant Sweep Into Heart of Reich Aided by Sky Army, Navy Units As Record Air Blows Stun Nazis

MONTGOMERY'S HEADQUARTERS, March 24 (AP)—Allied troops have entered Rees and Wesel on the northern front, captured the Nazi commander of Wesel, and killed a major-general in charge of flak forces in that area.

LONDON, March 24 (UP)—An unconfirmed Brussels radio broadcast said today that Allied ground troops were three miles beyond the Rhine on the 21st Army Group front.

By BOYD LEWIS

PARIS, MARCH 24 (UP)—Field Marshal Sir Bernard L. Montgomery sent four Allied armies — three on land, one in the air — across the Rhine on a broad front north of the Ruhr today on what he called "the final assault on Germany."

The American Ninth and British Second Armies spearheaded the ground assault on the Rhine with the Allied First Airborne Army's sky troops striking an undisclosed distance beyond the river.

TWO MILES BEYOND RHINE

The Canadian First Army also was disclosed to have joined the assault, and front reports said the Allied ground troops were at least two miles beyond the Rhine at some points.

Elsewhere also striking at the heart of Germany in the most gigantic offensive in history were the American First Army, commanded by Gen. Hodges, and the Yank Third Army, headed by Gen. Patton. Both armies earlier had bridged the Rhine.

OPPOSITION LIGHT

Clinton B. Conger, United Press war correspondent with the Ninth Army, said initial objectives were reached against surprisingly light opposition.

Official reports said the two ground armies were making "good" progress east of the river against the First German Paratroop Army — an enemy force numbering 15 to 20 divisions, or 150,000 to 200,000 men.

(Berlin's DNB news agency broadcast an urgent appeal to the German people to stand fast in the face of the Allied break-through and declared that "everything is at stake" in the battle of the Rhine.)

WIDESPREAD WRECKAGE

Ten thousand square miles of Germany's Ruhr Valley and Westphalian Plains, stretching back 150-odd miles beyond the Rhine, were littered with flaming wreckage from Allied air fleet raids.

Throughout the area thousands of American and British sky troops of the Allied First Army showered down behind the German rear defenders. Miles-long trains of gliders streamed across the Rhine all morning, landing infantrymen on enemy fields and scattering paratroopers across the countryside.

Veterans of the American Ninth and British Second armies crossed the Rhine in assault boats and U. S. Navy invasion craft from several solid bridgeheads in the 12-mile sector between Rees and Wefal. Wesel is 30 miles north of Duesseldorf and 14½ miles north of the Rhine-Ruhr confluence.

HIT BEHIND "MONTY" BARRAGE

The British started the attack in bright moonlight late Friday night, striking behind a "Monty" barrage.

GERMANY
(Continued on Page Two)

War Bulletins

MONTGOMERY'S HEADQUARTERS, March 24 (AP)—Pilots flying over Germany east of the Rhine and north of the Ruhr before dawn today reported seeing "whole towns and villages burning like torches."

EIGHTH AIR FORCE HEADQUARTERS, Britain, March 24 (UP)—Airmen returning from attacks near Wesel said today that a "colossal ground battle" was raging just east of the Rhine.

MONTGOMERY'S HEADQUARTERS, March 24 (AP)—Allied ground troops pushing across the Rhine established bridgeheads 2000 to 3000 yards deep by this afternoon. The great airborne landing has been completed.

(Continued on Page Two)

Red Cross Fund Lags; $700,000 Needed Here

Every resident of Greater Boston was urged in a joint appeal by Red Cross War Fund officials today to "assume individual responsibility for the success of the 1945 War Fund" which is more than $700,000 short of its goal of $4,192,600. The drive ends Monday night.

"I cannot emphasize too strongly

RED CROSS
(Continued on Last Page)

Flynn Has Second Audience with Pope

VATICAN CITY, March 24 (AP)—Pope Pius XII received Edward J. Flynn today for a second audience since the former Democratic National Committee chairman arrived in Italy. The audience, which lasted 15 minutes, was attended also by Myron Taylor, President Roosevelt's personal representative to the Vatican.

Taxi Driver Robbed Of $23 by Trio

Three taxi passengers turned out to be hold-up men after they stepped into the cab of William T. Norrish of Chauncy street, Watertown, early this morning at Brookline avenue and Jersey street, Back Bay, he reported to police. He lost $23.

Traveler Index

Reds' All-Out Berlin Push on, Germans Say

By DWIGHT L. PITKIN

LONDON, March 24 (AP)—The Germans said today that Marshal Gregory Zhukov had attacked "with strongest forces" from his Oder bridgeheads as part of a decisive drive on Berlin.

31 MILES FROM BERLIN

With perhaps 1,200,000 men massed along the Oder and ready to join in a multiple east-west Allied assault to crush the last breath out of the Reich, Zhukov threw six infantry divisions, waves of tanks and a tremendou artillery barrage into the new attack on both sides of Kuestrin and succeeded in reaching a point only 31 miles from the German capital, German broadcasts reported.

The German high command

RUSSIA
(Continued on Page Two)

German Armies Cracking; Nazis Retain Terror Grip

WASHINGTON, March 24 (AP)—The German army is expected by top Washington officials to begin disintegrating soon.

This is the basis for a widely held belief that the European war will be won in the next few weeks except for large scale mopping up operations.

There is hope but no real expectation that Germany will surrender. Despite multiplying peace-feeler

CAPITAL
(Continued on Page Three)

Yanks Batter Okinawa Isle for 2d Straight Day

By LEONARD MILLIMAN
(Associated Press War Editor)

American carrier planes raided strategic Okinawa island, between Japan and Formosa, today for the second successive day, Radio Tokyo reported a few hours after Admiral Chester W. Nimitz announced Task Force 58 shot down 81 attacking

PACIFIC
(Continued on Page Three)

Latest Nazi Propaganda Hokum an Artless Effort

By ANDREW TULLY
(Traveler Staff Correspondent)

WITH THIRD ARMY TROOPS IN THE RHINELAND, March 24—Notes from a correspondent's cuff. The latest German propaganda leaflet found on prisoners taken in the race to the Rhine is a post-card-size color job entitled, "Two ways of spending the war." At first glance it shows at the bottom only an American soldier dying on the battlefield but when held to the light it reveals on the top half a home fronter carousing with a scantily clad woman.

First Lt. Manuel Miller of 181 Bay State road, Boston, who showed me the card in Coblenz was unimpressed. "It's not even good art work," he said professionally. Lt.

TULLY
(Continued on Last Page)

Tommy's Forecast

In the Spring a turtle's fancy turns to love and things romancy. Turtle Tom, Traveler forecaster, meteorological weather master, predicts that winter is over the hurdles. Henceforth the weather'll be better for turtles. So tra-la-la-la and blah-blah-blah-blah, this is the season to sing: "O tweety-tweet-tweet, my sweety-sweet-sweet, hail to the twittering Spring." There they go dancing, hand in hand. Even the turties, ain't it grand?

Patton's Bold Stroke Saves Yank Lives

Widens His Hold Over the Rhine

By EDWARD D. BALL

WITH THE U. S. THIRD ARMY ACROSS THE RHINE, March 24 (AP)—The Third Army rapidly expanded today the Rhine bridgehead which it established yesterday after crossing the stream in one of the

PATTON
(Continued on Page Two)

Nazis to Fight on In Spite of All, Says Broadcast

LONDON, March 24 (AP)—A German broadcast declared today the German High Command "adopts the supreme principle of continuing the battle no matter under what conditions."

A Nazi military spokesman, after announcement of the Rhine crossing, asserted new German fronts

NAZIS
(Continued on Page Two)

Piercing of Rhine Line Dooms Huns, Says Churchill

LONDON, March 24 (AP)—The "decisive victory in Europe will be near" once the Rhine river line is pierced and the crust of German

CHURCHILL
(Continued on Page Three)

The Weather

U. S. OFFICIAL FORECAST
FAIR TONIGHT
Full Weather Report on Page Two
Sun rises 6:41; Sun sets 7
High tide 9:10 A. M., 9:48 P. M.
Light all Vehicles by 7:30 P. M.

Record Aerial Armada Storms Rhine Defenses

By HENRY B. JAMESON

LONDON, March 24 (AP)—More than 3500 Allied warplanes, the greatest armada ever to cross the English Channel at one time, swarmed over northwest Germany today in support of the Allied storming of the Rhine, as possibly 1500 transport planes and gliders showered a great army east of the river.

AIR RAIDS
(Continued on Page Three)

Light Opposition Amazes Eyewitness to Crossing

By ROBERT EUNSON

WITH THE U. S. NINTH ARMY EAST OF THE RHINE, March 24 (AP)—Lt.-Gen. William H. Simpson's victory-bound troops crossed the Rhine under fire in navy landing craft manned by sailors today and established a bridgehead on the east bank.

Riflemen from one of the war's most famous divisions, which beat the Germans first in the Normandy hedgerows and later chewed its way through the Siegfried Line, made the thrust under an ear-splitting bombardment.

The bombardment came from

CROSSING
(Continued on Last Page)

'9th Army's Navy' Drilled Months for Rhine Role

By CLINTON B. CONGER

ACROSS THE RHINE WITH AMERICAN NINTH ARMY, March 24 (UP)—The American Ninth Army stormed the Rhine en route to Berlin in the darkness early Saturday and achieved their initial objectives against surprisingly light opposition.

I came across the Rhine with our infantry and after two hours on the west bank of the great river not a single casualty had been erported by the group which I accompanied.

Opposition was so light that hopes

NINTH ARMY
(Continued on Page Two)

Monty's Message to Troops

LONDON, March 24 (AP)—Field Marshal Montgomery today addressed this message to all 21st Army Group troops:

"1. On the seventh of February, I told you we were going into the ring for the final and last round: there would be no time limit. We would continue fighting until our

MONTY
(Continued on Page Three)

Grapevine
26TH INFANTRY DIVISION
YD 26TH
1917★Ile de France★Lorraine★Aisne-Marne★St. Mihiel★Meuse-Argonne★Champagne-Marne★NORTHERN FRANCE [No2]★GERMANY [No1]★1945
Vol. II — No. 10 Somewhere in Germany Sunday, April 1, 1945

YD Whips Over Rhine, Rolls Far Into Germany

Go 50 Miles In 8 Hours - It's Spring

They advanced 50 miles in eight hours, and wouldn't have stopped then if the Rhine hadn't been smack in front of them.

In the advance, the 24 men of the 328th Infantry's I. and R. platoon captured ten towns, sent streams of prisoners back to the rear, and knocked out every road block in sight.

The platoon was divided into two groups, one under Lt. Eugene Grot of Irvington, N. J., and the other under T/Sgt. Herbert E. Walker of Springfield, Mass. Fighting with a TD Bn., the 26th Recon Troop and a tank outfit, they took off at 6:15 a. m., and reached the last town this side of the Rhine River early in the afternoon.

"We couldn't have advanced that fast without Hitler's help," Sgt. John G. McCullah, Beverly Hills, Cal., said. "He built those super-highways just for us to speed along, I guess."

Resistance was slight all the way. The platoon hit pockets of resistance, but finished them off without much trouble. At one spot, the Germans pushed a burning truck into the center of the road, but the tank outfit knocked

(Cont. on page 4)

Artilleryman Turns Dough

They may classify him an a Field Artilleryman, but infantrymen say 2d Lt. William A. Sicard is as much a doughfoot as any of them.

Sicard, 101st Field Artillery forward observer from East Providence R. I., and an infantry officer were driving along a road near the front lines when a group of Germans jumped in front of the vehicle and forced them to stop.

The infantry officer gulped, and stepped out of the vehicle, toward the Germans, yelling to them to surrender. But the Germans had other ideas, and aiming their weapons, advanced toward the car.

Lt. Sicard decided it was his turn to try something. He crept toward the right flank of the German patrol, and opened fire.

That settled the question. The Krauts — 13 of them in all — dropped their weapons and surrendered to the YD pair.

First At Rhine; Thinks It Stinks

Ever since hitting the ETO, Cpl. Thomas Devine's main ambition was to take a look at the Rhine. He'd read about it in geography books in high school, and had studied about it in his history classes.

As driver for Lt. Col. Noel Menard, CO of the 1st Bn., 328th Infantry, the Jamaica Plains, Mass., dough was the first enlisted man in the division to get a look at Germany's No. 1 river.

"After all that build-up, I was plenty disappointed," Devine said. "It wasn't much to see — just another river, and plenty dirty at that. It's something to build bridges over, that's all I'd rather look at the Charles any day. Preferably tomorrow."

Butter And Eggs Give Fritz Cramps

The Krauts wanted butter and eggs.

Doughs of the 101st Infantry's wire section figure that's what got the Germans in trouble.

The wire section went along with a platoon of 101st doughs who advanced 20 miles in front of the regiment to take a look at German positions. They had just driven into one town when the church bell started clanging away.

"We thought there was a reason," T/5 Walter Dorsey of Philadelphia, Pa., said. "And we were right. The Kraut civilians were trying to warn a German column on the outskirts of town that we were there."

The doughs dashed to the church and shooed away the bell ringer, before the chimes had clanged a dozen times. They could see the Jerry column on a road leading out of town, and waited to see if any German soldiers had heard the bell.

(Cont. on page 4)

Too Good For Hitler?

Signal Corps Photo by Sgt. Rothenberger

Sightseers of the 114th Medical Bn. take a gander at the memorial of Frederick Wilhelm IV, located on a mountain top above the Saar River. The medics give all such buildings careful consideration, because they figure Adolph will be needing a memorial, too — but quick.

YD Military Government Shepards Lost Flocks

Ten to 15 million Russians, Frenchmen, Poles and Slavs are on the march.

They're heading for their homelands after periods up to five years as slave laborers in Germany. It's the greatest mass movement in history, and one in which the YD plays a part through its military government section.

The division's military government unit has set up, so far, 10 centers for the displaced persons, where they are fed and housed until they can be returned to their own countries.

"We get food for them from German supply dumps," Lt. Col. Edward I. Condren, New York City, head of the section, said. "We do our best to feed all of the displaced persons — but we don't feed the German people. All we give the German people are orders."

When the YD liberated a group of Russian factory workers recently, the Russians decided to pay back the German factory manager for two years of cruel treatment which included, they said, the murder of two Russian girls. They picked up a tommy gun somewhere, and started looking for him.

"Affairs like that are one of our headaches," Sgt. Benjamin Miller, Brooklyn, N. Y., said. "The Russians were stopped that time, but I guess they had plenty of reasons for trying what they did."

The section, composed of five officers — all with field experience — and six enlisted men, sets up govern-

(Continued on Page 3)

104th Leads Jump Over Big Stream

Joining the greatest chase in history, the YD as part of the mighty Third Army crossed the Rhine early this week.

The 104th Infantry had the distinction of being the first unit in the division to cross the historic river when elements of it, attached to the 4th Armored Division, raced across the bridge built by U. S. Army engineers.

Moving 75 miles to the banks of the Rhine past thousands of stunned, awed and frightened German civilians, the 101st Infantry and 328th Infantry outposted the west bank of the Rhine within its zone of action in preparation for the division's movement across the bridge.

Once across, a combat team of the 328th Infantry was motorized and followed the 4th Armored to the suburbs of the devastated city of Hanau. After a day of bitter house-to-house fighting through bomb-torn streets, the city was completely cleared of the enemy.

In a 27-hour period, the regiment captured 1342 prisoners. Part of the haul included an entire railroad engineer battalion which surrendered intact along with five nurses, and two German equivalent of U. S. WACS. An engineer non-commissioned officers school capitulated after putting up a hard and stubborn fight. Casualties were extremely light.

While the 328th was taking care

(Cont. on page 4)

Don't Be Kind To Granny; May Be A Nazi Star

If you come across a Nazi General dressed as a broken down refugee or a grandmother, please tag him and forward him to either Lt. Guy Bateman, Cleveland, Ohio, Lt. Cloyde Brown, Boston, Mass. or the 101st infantry I & R Platoon. They need him to make the Heinie General Staff they picked up in the course of their travels across Krautland complete.

These cowboys in quarter tons zoomed into the town of Elmstein so fast that the Jerry G-2 was still in the bathtub soaping his back when They knocked on his door and informed him his combat days were over. The rest of the staff were caught eating the Jerry equivalent of Wheaties.

None of the German warriors expressed any regret at being retired from what remains of the Nazi war machine. They did express some regret that their commanding general wasn't with them. "He went off in the woods disguised as a refugee," the G-2 said with disgust.

The men of the 101st Infantry had more important work to do than go looking for a broken-down general.

Two MPs Follow Own Directions, Surprise Krauts as Well as Selves

Two division MPs decided to enter a town by-passed by the Berlin-bound YD, and ended up by capturing the town, 126 Kraut soldiers, six officers — including the garrison's commandant — and an arsenal of weapons. In the process, they also liberated 800 Russian prisoners of war.

Patrolling a German highway, Sgt. James F. Walsh, former cop from Northampton, Mass., and PFC. John Del Medico of Chicago, Ill., had just entered the outskirts of the by-passed village when they spotted three German soldiers lounging near the main street.

The two MPs banged away with a rifle and a pistol until the Krauts disappeared into a house. They were wondering what to do next when a Nazi major rushed into the street, almost falling over his own feet in his hurry. He yelled that he wanted to surrender.

"You'd better," Walsh said, waving his pistol.

Then Del Medico had an idea. "Where's the rest of your outfit?" he asked. "They'll want to surrender, too."

The major nodded, and led them up the street to the quarters of the town's garrison. He yelled, and the Germans started pouring out of the buildings. All heavily armed, they kept coming until they filled the entire street. Walsh counted them until he was dizzy, and figured they had corraled 126 soldiers and six officers.

Walsh waved his pistol and tried not to look scared. "You could have knocked me over with a pretzel," he said. "They could have made stiffs out of us on the spot."

The civilian population caught a view of the MPs, and displayed white flags from every window. At the same time, 80 Russian PWs — left unguarded at last — swarmed down on the two American liberators to show their gratitude.

When things had quieted down a bit, the major confessed he surrendered the garrison because communication with his CO on the other bank of the Rhine had been lost.

Walsh and Del Medico lined the Germans up, and marched them back to the nearest Army encampment where a PW cage was quickly improvised.

"And if all this wasn't enough," Walsh said, "just as we were leaving the PW enclosure, one last Kraut came running across the field. He was mad as all hell, because he thought he was being left out of the deal."

Flies Into Town To Catch Sleep

Sleep is a pretty powerful incentive, and Lt. Thomas Aylward will attest to that.

The Co. M. 328th Infantry platoon leader from Martha's Vineyard, Mass., was told that if he wanted a comfortable bed for the night, he'd have to take part of the German-held town that was situated a few miles ahead.

"That did it," Lt. Aylward said. "We flew into town, going at least 70 miles an hour. The Krauts tried to drop 88s on us, but we were too quick for them."

In fact, their speed was so terrific that it confused the Germans. The Co. M. vehicles zoomed into town so fast that the Germans took off for Berlin like rabbits, just to prove to the doughs that they could travel fast, too.

That was perfectly okay with Lt. Aylward. "We slept fine that night," he said. "Plenty fine."

Nazis Stiffen Resistance

Los Angeles Examiner

CHARACTER QUALITY AMERICA FIRST! ENTERPRISE ACCURACY

AN AMERICAN PAPER FOR THE AMERICAN PEOPLE — THE GREAT NEWSPAPER OF THE GREAT SOUTHWEST

Reg. U.S. Pat. Off.

Examiner Telephone RIchmond 1212 — Examiner Building, 1111 S. Broadway

WAR EXTRA

VOL. XLII—NO. 112 — LOS ANGELES, MONDAY, APRIL 2, 1945 — PCC — Two Sections—Part I—FIVE CENTS

YANKS ON OKINAWA:

100,000 INVADE JAP ISLE

Army, Marines Advancing Rapidly; Losses Light; Towns, Airports Fall

Yanks Close Trap on Nazis in Ruhr

Huge Force Cut Off at Lippstadt

PARIS, April 1.—(INS)—Between 25,000 and 35,000 German troops were declared officially, at Allied Headquarters tonight, to have been trapped in the Ruhr when that basin was surrounded by the junction of the American First and Ninth Armies near Lippstadt.

PARIS, April 1.—(AP)—American Armies closed a trap on the Ruhr and thousands of Germans today, and fought to within 165 miles of Berlin and 45 of Nuernberg. Two columns were within 100 miles of Czechoslovakia in sweeps across Germany.

The famed Second Armored Division of the U. S. Ninth Army and U. S. First Army elements met at 3:30 p. m. today at Lippstadt, 75 miles east of the Rhine and 18 west of Paderborn, thus sealing off the last escape route for perhaps 40,000 Germans in the rubbled Ruhr.

Vanguards of the U. S. Third Army made the closest approach to Berlin—165 miles—in advances southeast of Kassel, and their Seventh Army comrades farther south surged to the Main River only 45 miles from Nuernberg. Both the Third and Seventh Armies now were but 100 miles from Czecholovakia, and within 200 and 315 miles of junctions with Russians.

But the Germans were reacting with organized resistance for the first time since the Rhine breakthroughs, particularly in the Paderborn and Kassel areas. Allied planes reaped slaughter

(Continued on Page 4, Cols. 1-2)

'Big 5' Differ on Mandates

Parley Prior to S. F. Meet Suggested

WASHINGTON, April 1.—(AP)—The United States has suggested a "Big Five" meeting before the San Francisco United Nations conference, to work out an agreement on mandates.

The meeting, it was learned today, has been proposed for Washington about two weeks before the delegates sit down at San Francisco, April 25, to set up the international organization planned at Dumbarton Oaks.

The United States, Britain, Russia, France and China would take part.

DISAGREEMENT SEEN

This country advocates an international trusteeship system under which nations holding mandates over territories would be required to permit the development of self government leading toward independence.

But in sponsoring that idea the United States may find itself opposed by Britain and France, which have taken the position that mandates should be brought closer into their imperial systems.

Although the Russians have said little on the subject, it is believed they would tend to side with the Americans.

The Chinese position is yet un-

(Continued on Page 4, Column 4)

Jap Front Porch Hit by Yanks

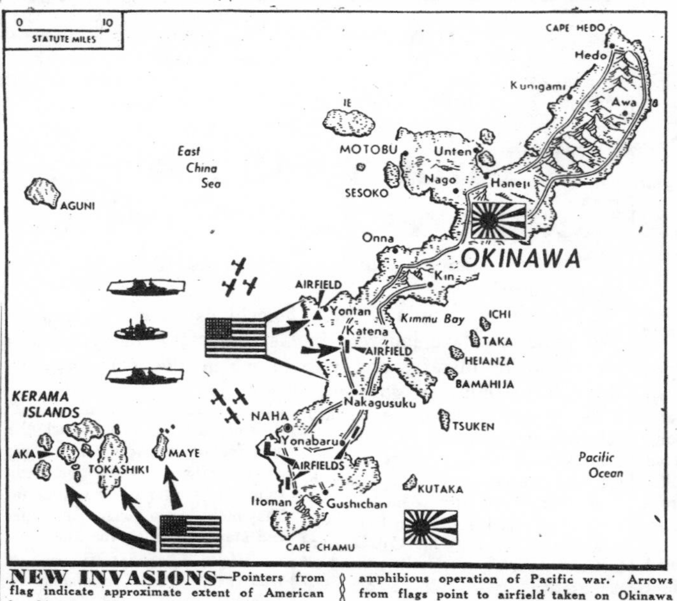

NEW INVASIONS—Pointers from flag indicate approximate extent of American beachhead on Okinawa, Japanese island in what Admiral Chester Nimitz described as largest amphibious operation of Pacific war. Arrows from flags point to airfield taken on Okinawa and to Kerama Islands taken five days ago. —Associated Press wirephoto.

Americans Drive 3 Mi. Against Weak Defense; Navy Planes Aid

GUAM, April 2 (Monday)—(AP)—Veteran infantrymen and Marines of the new 10th Army, numbering possibly 100,000 men, expanded their Okinawa Island beachhead to a depth of three miles at several points, still finding Japanese resistance light at dusk of the first day of their momentous Easter morning invasion.

Admiral Chester W. Nimitz reported in a communique today that "the landing beaches were made secure." Sporadic mortar and artillery fire fell on the beachhead during the day.

Nimitz Reports Losses

Nimitz in an earlier communique reported that "losses were light" in the initial landing on the islands in which more than 1400 ships were used.

The admiral also reported that two air ports were captured and a dozen towns taken in the first two and half hours of the invasion.

Heavy warships continued to shell enemy installations on the strategic island, just 325 miles south of the Japanese homeland.

Carrier planes from the mighty Fifth Fleet gave close support to the rapid ground advance.

British Pound Two Islands

British fleet units, now cooperating with the American Navy in attacks on the Ryukyus, heavily pounded two islands in the southern end of the chain on Saturday and Sunday. Fourteen Japanese planes were destroyed and six damaged by British aircraft.

Supported by the world's greatest sea force, which gave the island a 10-day air and fleet bombard-

IN COMMAND—Lieut. Gen. Simon Boli[illegible] Jr., comma[illegible] of Americ[illegible] Tenth [illegible]my, which in[illegible] —Associat[illegible]

New Manila Horror Bared

By Frank Robertson
Staff Correspondent International News Service

MANILA, April 1.—Documentary confirmation that the cold-blooded rape of Manila was directly ordered by the Tokyo high command was disclosed tonight in a bulky report which lists the bestial murder of thousands of civilian men, women and children during the Japanese defense of Manila.

Based on affidavits by competent ecclesiastical, civilian and military witnesses, the interrogation of war prisoners and captured documents, the 200-page report fully supports the sickening pictures of bayonetted babies, mothers with bayonet-slashed breasts and piles of bound and burned corpses. The macabre testimony of the enemy's coldly planned bestiality is "only a fragment of the mounting volume of available evidence," the document states.

It revealed that General Tomoyuki Yamashita flew to Tokyo on December 10 of last year to hear the city's death sentence. He returned on December 20 and left with Philippines puppet president Jose Laurel for Baguio the next day.

GUERRILLAS BURNED

Japanese diary entries record the awful crime ordered by Tokyo. A member of the Aktsuki force wrote:

"February 7: 150 guerrillas were disposed of tonight. I personally stabbed and killed 10. February 9: Burned guerrillas to death tonight."

The Japs regarded everyone as guerrillas, including children. A Kobayashi group order dated February 13 said:

"All people on the battlefield (meaning Manila city) will be put to death."

A battalion order of the same date stated:

"When Filipinos are to be killed, they must be gathered into one place and disposed of with consideratio[illegible] am-

(Co[illegible]nued on [illegible]n 4)

$500,000 Fire Damages Flag Plant, Lumber Yard

(Picture on Page 1, Part II)

Fire of undetermined origin destroyed the Menard and Tabery flag manufacturing plant, 3443 South Hill street, and Osts Lumber Yard, 3430 South Grand avenue, yesterday, causing an estimated damage of $500,000.

Fire fighters were called at 5 a. m. by a passer-by and battled the stubborn blaze for five hours before bringing it under control.

The fire, which started in the manufacturing plant, leaped to stacked lumber in the Osts yard and burne[illegible]ndred[illegible] sands of [illegible]eet [illegible]

Heat [illegible]

pany and forced firemen to turn a continuous stream of water on the walls of the Globe Lumber Company, across the street from the Menard and Tabery plant.

Damage to the flag plant was estimated at $350,000. Materials destroyed included a shipment of satin flags made specially for the San Francisco World Peace Conference. Fred L. Tabery, exalted ruler of the Elks, heads the manufacturing company, which also was engaged in making airplane parts

For your a[illegible] of the [illegible]mage

INS[illegible]ST IN WAR[illegible] AND HOLD

Plane in Sea Off S.F. Port

SAN FRANCISCO, April 1.—(AP)—A dramatic attempt at rescue of the crew and passengers of a Navy Transport plane was under way late today in the ocean off San Francisco Beach under the view of thousands of Easter holiday sightseers.

A Martin Mariner bound to Alameda from the United States Naval Air Station at Hawaii went into the ocean about two miles off shore at the foot of Taraval street.

The Twelfth Naval District said the plane's radio had reported no one had yet been injured and that the plane had hobbled in the last 200 miles on a single motor.

Attempts were being made to get the plane occupants aboard life rafts for transfer to the surface craft but high wind and waves were making rescue difficult.

55,000 at Forest Lawn Easter Sunrise Services

In a war-torn world, hope sprung anew yesterday in the hearts of hundreds of thousands gathered to celebrate Easter in the great outdoors or the churches of Southern California.

Forest Lawn, Hollywood Bowl and scores of other early-morning services greeted the dawn of the new day as it brought, in the story of the resurrection of Christ, new faith and new trust.

To many it was a joyous Easter, with the promise of peace in Europe. To others, with relatives in distant fighting lands, it was a day for solemn renewal of courage and devout prayer.

On the broad hilltop in Forest Lawn Memorial Park, a vast throng hailed the eternal triumph of faith.

There was a gray sky, but, as the 55,000 Easter morning worshippers knew that the sun was rising, so they knew that darker clouds would vanish and the dawn of peace would come.

For the great audience, and e[illegible] thousand[illegible] men and women to whom the war comes closely home, there was a word of deep meaning.

Through the Los Angeles Examiner, General Douglas MacArthur sent a message of profound sincerity and unshaken faith; the Easter message of a man who in dark hours pledged

Full page of Easter service picture on page 12, part I. Additional stories and pictures on pages 3 and 5.

that freedom would be restored to captive lands and peoples and whose promise is being kept by the strength of America. The Forest Lawn services were heard over a nationwide radio broadcast.

In rich, resonant voice, Vincent Price, noted actor, read MacArthur's words:

"Easter Sunday is a day of gratitude for His divine guid-

(Contin[illegible] on Page 3, Cols. 1-2)

Entire Nazi Gold Hoard Captured

WAR EXTRA

Only Los Angeles Newspaper With All Leading News Services—Associated Press, International News, United Press, Dow-Jones

THE SATURDAY PICTORIAL
ON ANGELES EVENING
HERALD AND Express
Registered United States Patent Office
The Evening Herald and Express Grows Just Like Los Angeles

NIGHT EDITION
COMPLETE N.Y. STOCKS R

VOL. LXXV Two Sections Section A SATURDAY, APRIL 7, 1945 G★ NO. 11

JAPAN'S BIGGEST BATTLESHIP SUNK

Yanks Grab Vast Treasure

By ROBERT RICHARDS
United Press War Correspondent

WITH THE NINETIETH INFANTRY DIVISION AT MERKERS, April 7.—American troops today captured what was believed to be the entire German gold reserve, possibly billions of dollars' worth of German and foreign currency, and a large store of Germany's most valuable art treasures hidden in a salt mine.

The treasure trove, evacuated from Berlin in the last six weeks, was found here in one of the largest salt mines in Europe, 90 miles west of Weimar.

German officials, captured at the trove, estimated there was 100 tons of gold in the mine. That would be $84,000,000 at the American rate of $35 a troy ounce.

TREASURE IN CURRENCIES

In addition, the Germans said, there was about $3,000,000,000 in paper reichsmarks, $2,000,000 in United States dollars, about $440,000 in English pounds, as well as 100,000,000 French francs, 4,000,000 in Norwegian crowns, and lesser amounts of other currency in the mine.

The art treasures include originals by Raphael, Rembrandt, Van Dyke, Durier, and Renoir. The Germans said there were 1000 cases of paintings and statues, 150 tapestries, thousands of engravings and 120 cases of the original Goethe collection from Weimar.

The gold was stored in a chamber 2100 feet below the ground. The doors of the gold vault had been jammed and it was impossible immediately to verify the story of the German officials.

However, with the American troops which found the trove I examined hundreds of priceless sculptures and paintings.

NO REASON TO DOUBT

Lieut. Col. William I. Russel, Chevy Chase, Md., military government officer of the Ninetieth, said there was no reason to doubt the story told by the Germans since they were under no pressure and had no point in telling a story which could quickly be proved or disproved.

The treasure was uncovered by accident.

Yesterday afternoon two German women who were on their way to find a midwife for a friend were stopped by two American military policemen.

As the M. P.s and the women walked past the mine, one of the

(Continued on Page 4, Column 2)

The Road to Berlin—

By Associated Press

Eastern front—32 miles (from Zellin).

Western front—130 miles (from Schlotheim area; German reports said 90 miles at Eisleben).

Italian front—544 miles (from Reno river).

Herald-Express Special Features

Push Past Bremen, Hanover

By Associated Press

WITH U. S. THIRD ARMY, April 7.—Smashing a heavy counterattack, the Sixth Armored and Sixty-fifth Infantry Division knocked out 40 German tanks northwest of Muehlhausen today.

By United Press

U. S. FIRST ARMY HEADQUARTERS, WESTERN FRONT, April 7.—Field Marshal Walter von Model, commander of the German army Group B, is believed to be among the German troops trapped in the Ruhr Basin, First Army headquarters said today.

By International News Service

WITH THE U. S. FIRST ARMY, April 7.—An American staff officer at Lieut. General Courtney H. Hodges' headquarters told correspondents today that "the Wehrmacht is falling apart." "We now are entering the stage of the great mopping-up," he added.

By United Press

PARIS, April 7.—Flying tank of the American Ninth and British Second Armies ripped 22 to 26 miles through disorganized opposition on the north German plain today in the twin breakthroughs that outflanked Bremen and Hanover and carried within 133 miles of Berlin.

The entire northern flank of the German battle screen covering the North Sea ports, the Danish peninsula and Berlin itself appeared to have broken wide open under the double-barrelled Allied assault.

The rigid military security blackout was thrown over the speeding armored forces of the British Second Army after a terse official announcement that their vanguards had reached an undisclosed point 150 miles beyond the Rhine.

Delayed front dispatches, admittedly lagging hours behind the battle, placed the British

(Continued on Page 4, Col. 2-3)

PRIDE OF THE NIP NAVY GOES DOWN

The Japanese battleship Yamato, 45,000 tons, the largest ship and pride of the Japanese navy, was one of the six enemy warships sunk by American forces in the giant battle 50 miles off Japan. The Yamato is shown as she was hit by bombs from Yank planes in the battle of the Philippines last October.

5 OTHER NIP WARSHIPS, 391 PLANES LOST

By Associated Press

GUAM, Sunday, April 8.—Six Japanese warships, including their largest remaining battleship—the 45,000-ton Yamato—and 391 enemy planes, were destroyed in a two-day battle between planes and surface units of the two fleets yesterday and today, only 50 miles from Japan, Adm. Chester W. Nimitz announced.

U. S. Navy carrier aircraft smashed probably the last strong Japanese naval force, as the Nipponese steamed out apparently in a "banzai" effort to turn the tide of war.

Fleet Admiral Chester W. Nimitz announced from his headquarters here that the battle was fought around noon Saturday, Japanese time (8 p. m. Friday, Pacific War Time).

The communique reported six Japanese warships, including the Yamato, and 391 enemy planes were destroyed in Friday and Saturday sea and air actions.

In Washington an official navy spokesman said "a good 25 per cent of the remaining Japanese major combat force" was lost or put out of action in the engagement.

United States Pacific Fleet losses were listed as three destroyers sunk, several other destroyers and smaller craft damaged and seven carrier planes destroyed.

The Japanese initiated the two days of desperate action in efforts to shatter the American amphibious force invading Okinawa Island, some 325 miles south of the Nippon homeland.

A large force of Japanese aircraft attacked the invasion ships and Okinawa shore positions Friday. The communique said the desperate Japanese airmen succeeded in sinking the three destroyers and damaging several other warships. United States fighter planes and gunners brought down 116

(Continued on Page 3, Column 1)

Germany
On Brink of Life or Death, Says Tokio

By International News Service

NEW YORK, April 7.—The German people are facing their greatest crisis since the outbreak of the war and are "standing on the brink of life or death," the Japanese Domei agency reported today in a dispatch credited to its Berlin correspondent.

The dispatch, broadcast from Tokio and recorded by the F. C. C., said that the powerful Allied offensives on the Western and Eastern Fronts had "greatly limited" the freedom of German forces. Domei also reported the organization of Nazi "Werewolves" dedicated to the killing of Germans collaborating with the Allies.

Calling attention to the fact that the German underground organization was "officially disowned," the Tokio spokesman said "there is little doubt" the Nazi guerrilla forces are directed by the government.

Furious Fighting In Vienna

By International News Service

LONDON, April 7.—Marshal Joseph Stalin is ready to strike at the Germans on the whole stretch of the Eastern Front from the Baltic to the Carpathians, Col. Alfred von Olberg, German Transocean News Agency military correspondent, said today.

By Associated Press

LONDON, April 7.—Russian troops have captured Moelding, southern suburb of Vienna, after bloody house-to-house fighting and the fiercest combat inside the Austrian capital is raging in the eastern quarter, where most of the city's utility plants are located, a German broadcast said tonight.

Soviet veterans of Stalingrad and Budapest had battered to within four miles of St. Stephan's Church in the center of Vienna. They were battling hastily reinforced Germans who resisted stubbornly.

The Germans also declared the Russians had speared 30 miles west of Vienna and reached S. Poelten on the road to Linz. The penetrating spearheads were wiped out, DNB added.

The broadcast said several Russian bridgeheads thrown over the Morava river east of Vienna had been smashed, and that the Soviets also were attempting to cross the Danube between Vienna and Hainburg, 25 miles to the east.

Moscow announced that the Germans not only were fighting for every factory and stone building, but also had thrown in a number of counter-attacks, which were repelled by Russian shock troops in bitter fighting.

The Yamato
Battleship Was Pride of Emperor's Navy

By Associated Press

GUAM, April 7.—The Japanese battleship Yamato was the pride of the Emperor's Navy and up until the time she was sunk 50 miles off Japan today, the most powerful ship left to Nippon's once proud fleet.

She was a 900-foot, 45,000-ton battleship carrying 16-inch guns and capable of a speed of 30 knots.

Eight torpedoes and eight heavy bombs sent her to the bottom of the East China Sea.

There had been two ships of that sizes in the Japanese Navy. Her sister ship, the Musashi, was sunk in the second battle of the Philippines last October.

Weather
Cooler, High Clouds, Is L. A. Forecast

Slightly cooler weather and some high cloudiness tomorrow is in store for Los Angeles and vicinity.

In its forecast, the weather bureau said:

"Generally sunny this afternoon and Sunday, but with some high cloudiness with local fog near coast Sunday morning. Somewhat cooler Sunday afternoon."

Minimum temperature today was 56, rising to 82.

SIR WM. H. HORWOOD DIES

ST. JOHN'S, Newfoundland, April 7.—(A.P.)—Sir William Henry Horwood, 82, chief justice of Newfoundland since 1902 and administrator in the governor's absence, died here today.

B-29s, Iwo Mustangs Hit Tokio

By Associated Press

GUAM, April 7.—A new phase in the aerial war against the Japanese homeland opened today as the war's greatest B-29 force attacked Tokio and Nagoya, protected for the first time by land-based fighter planes.

Two of the P-51 Mustang fighters from newly captured Iwo Jima were lost as they shepherded the more than 300 Superforts delivering demolition bombs on two large aircraft factories. The fighter pilots were credited with shooting down 21 enemy interceptors, probably downing six others and damaging 10.

A flight of 1500 miles was made by the Mustangs in the round trip from Iwo to Tokio.

Nip Claims
Tokio Says 21 U. S. Warships Smashed

By United Press

Tokio radio claimed 21 American warcraft have been sunk and damaged in waters off Okinawa Island from April 1 to April 6.

In a communique broadcast by Tokio radio and recorded by United Press at San Francisco the enemy claimed one cruiser, five cruisers or destroyers, two warships, one destroyer and two transports were sunk.

Damaged were one aircraft carrier, two cruisers or destroyers, two warships and five transports, Tokio said.

JAP PREMIER TELLS PEOPLE OF DESPAIR

By United Press

Premier Admiral Baron Kantaro Suzuki in a foreboding inaugural statement, today warned his people that the war situation "warrants not the least bit of optimism whatever for our nation's survival."

"The enemy has now firmly established themselves on our homeland," Suzuki said, referring to the American invasion of Japan's Okinawa prefecture less than 400 miles from Kyushu.

Following his investiture as premier, foreign minister and Greater East Asia minister, succeeding the discredited Kuniaki Koiso, Suzuki revealed himself to be thoroughuly pessimistic over Japan's chances of holding off the Pacific Allies.

"The present war, which is fought for the very existence of our empire, has come to the most important crucial stage, which warrants not the least bit of optimism whatever for our nation's survival. If the situation continues like this, the basis of our nation's existence might be threatened," Suzuki said.

"The resisting power to destroy the [illegible]ny and thereby protect our own fatherland can only be found in the sincerity shown to the throne by the entire nation. Now, Japanese, and only now is the time for the 100,000,000 people of Japan to rise as one to defend the honorable policy of our nation."

The statement was broadcast by Tokio radio and recorded by United Press, San Francisco.

Russian Press Scores Japan

By NATALIA RENE
International News Service Staff Correspondent

MOSCOW, April 7.—The official Russian newspaper Izvestia declared in an editorial today that abrogation of the Russo-Japanese neutrality pact was the result of Japan's policy of collaboration with Germany in "conducting a murderous war against the Soviet Union."

It was the first newspaper comment of any kind to be published since the first announcement of Russia's denunciation of the treaty.

On the other hand, all of Moscow has been buzzing with talk since the first announcement Thursday of the abrogation, and one thing seemed certain—the action had the approval of everybody from well-informed higher-ups to the citizen in the street. Public sentiment was never in favor of Japan.

Japan's activities in the past can not be easily forgotten.

Whatever doubt or speculation which existed in connection with the question of whether the abrogation was effective immediately or April, 1946, was cleared up by the Izvestia editorial, which explained the meaning of Article III of the agreement.

The editorial said that according to the original agreement the pact was valid for five years, but that it would have been considered automatically prolonged for another five years only on one condition: that either party did not announce one year before the pact's expiration date that it wished to abrogate the pact.

Since the Soviet Union did announce that it wanted no more of the agreement, the pact is now void.

News of the resignation of the Japanese government "for the purpose of giving way to a more powerful government in connection with the gravity of the situation" was unobtrusively published on the back page of Russian newspapers.

SUNRISE EDITION

PHILADELPHIA RECORD

NO. 27,702 · FRIDAY, APRIL 13, 1945 · THREE CENTS

ROOSEVELT IS DEAD

Editorial

HE DIED IN SERVICE

The only tribute to Franklin Delano Roosevelt we can put into words tonight is one we pay in common with millions more throughout the world.

President Roosevelt was our friend. We were proud of that.

Millions were proud to call him friend. That was the quality of his greatness. He was a friend of all mankind.

Now, at the floodtide of victory in Germany, even as our highest Army officers forecast the end of hostilities "in a few days," our President joins the Gold Star Honor Roll of American war casualties. He was just as much a war casualty as any GI Joe laid low by an enemy bullet.

Few of us have realized how hard Franklin Roosevelt drove himself, how he spared nothing, least of all his strength and devotion. Perhaps he knew it would be this way, that he decided all he had to give must be given before it was too late.

We may grieve that he has not lived to see completion of the Allied triumph which he planned so brilliantly and with such uncanny foresight. Yet before he passed on he could have no doubts that triumph was inevitable and imminent.

Posterity will think of us as "the Roosevelt generation." Often with envy. There never has been any doubt that his place in history was pre-eminent and secure.

History also will record that he was as great in peace as he was in war, a recognition already given him by the nation—through unprecedented election to four terms in the White House.

Yes, he was a valiant leader, loved by his people because he wholeheartedly loved them.

He is gone. And the only mitigation of the nation's sorrow is the realization that Providence gave him to America when America needed him most.

Tributes to Greatness Of Roosevelt Pour in From Nation and World

WASHINGTON, April 12 (U.P.)—The pulse of the world's greatest nation slowed tonight with the news of the death of its leader, but Americans nearing the hour of their greatest triumph pledged to support the man who succeeds him.

A sadness such as the United States probably never has felt before swept from one end of the country to the other as newspaper extras and radio broadcasts reported that President Roosevelt had passed away.

At first there was disbelief, even in the bold newspaper headlines, but gradually his death was accepted.

Leaders Voice Grief

From every corner of the nation, its leaders paused to express their grief and call for a united America pledged to stand behind the new President, Harry S. Truman.

Secretary of Commerce Henry A. Wallace was so moved by the death of the President that he had to be helped from the White House Cabinet room after watching Harry S. Truman take the oath of office. Wallace, vice president under Roosevelt during the third term, said later:

"Tonight we bow in prayer for that gallant world citizen who so unerringly acted to save democracy. Tomorrow, behind and with President Truman, we shall go forward into victory and peace."

Networks Cancal Programs

The nation's radio networks cancelled their regularly scheduled programs for the evening and offered special broadcasts and eulogies from key world leaders.

Eulogies came from all over the world for the man who had led the United States to the eve of victory in the world's greatest war.

Typical of comment on the President's death pouring in from all over the nation are the following:

Gen. George C. Marshall, Army Chief of Staff—"We have lost a great leader. His farseeing wisdom in military counsel has been a constant source of courage to all of us. No tribute from the Army could be so eloquent as the hourly record of the victories of the past few weeks."

Treasury Secretary Henry Morgenthau—"He, more than any one person, is responsible, in my opinion, for the successful conduct of this terrible war against the aggressor nations."

Interior Secretary Harold L. Ickes—"We have been fortunate, during the world crisis, to have given to civilization and the world the greatest leader in the history of our country."

Secretary of State Stettinius—"A great leader has passed on

Continued on Page 2, Column 3.

Pontiff Wires Message Of Regret to Mrs. F.D.R.

ROME, Friday, April 13 (AP)—Pope Pius XII received the news of President Roosevelt's death with visible sorrow early today and immediately telegraphed condolences to the President's family and the U. S. Government.

News of the President's sudden passing was communicated to the Pontiff in his private quarters by Monsignor Giovanni Battista Montini, acting for the Secretary of State, after the Pope already had retired for the night.

Italian Premier Ivanoe Bonomi, who was awakened after midnight to be given the news, expressed "profound sorrow" on behalf of the Italian people.

F.D.R.'s Death in Office Carries on Tradition

NEW YORK, April 12 (AP)—President Roosevelt's death today carried on an American tradition that Presidents elected at 20-year intervals die in office.

The list includes:

1840—William Henry Harrison.
1860—Abraham Lincoln.
1880—James A. Garfield.
1900—William McKinley.
1920—Warren G. Harding.
1940—Franklin D. Roosevelt.

YANKS POISED FOR DRIVE TO RUINED BERLIN

War Will End in Few Days, U. S. Staff Says

Read editorial, "No More Rivers to Cross on the Road to Berlin."

The U. S. 9th Army crossed the Elbe River and was poised for the final dash to Berlin as the 3d and 1st Armies closed in on Leipzig.

Organized warfare in Germany probably will end in a few days, high U. S. Army officers told the Senate Military Committee.

Nazi Propaganda Minister Goebbels declared that "the war cannot last much longer in my opinion."

By AUSTIN BEALMEAR

PARIS, April 12 (AP)—Tanks of the U. S. 9th Army swept across the Elbe River today on a six-mile front, 57 miles from Berlin. They awaited only orders from Lt. Gen. William H. Simpson to begin a dash on a wide open road that might put them by tomorrow into that capital of death and devastation.

Reich in Final Hours

A report attributed to French sources said Allied parachute troops were dropped at Brandenburg, 20 miles from greater Berlin, but this was without official confirmation.

Germany appeared in her final hours of organized resistance in the west as all Allied armies cut loose.

Three tank columns of the U. S. 3d Army, ripping beyond the heart of Germany in dashes up to 46 miles that overwhelmed Weimar—birthplace of the German republic—were 129 miles from the Russian lines, 40 miles from the Czech border and 109 miles from Berlin. The 9th Army was within 115 miles of the Russian lines.

With the U. S. 1st Army, which was thundering eastward at the rate of 30 to 40 miles a day, the 3d Army was closing on Leipzig, 75 miles southwest of Berlin and a communications city second only to the capital.

Nearing Leipzig

Advancing flank to flank, these two armies last were reported about 23 miles from Leipzig and a 1st Army field dispatch said the Yanks might be in the city by Friday.

(Other dispatches said German resistance in the Leipzig area

Continued on Page 19, Column 2.

. . . The Record Turns Its Rules . . .

A rule, in printers' language, is a strip of metal which prints a fine vertical line between columns of type in a newspaper. Hair-thin at the top, it is about 12 times as thick at the base. In 1799, the Ulster County (N. Y.) Gazette, in reporting the death of George Washington, turned its rules upside down to provide black mourning bands. Increasingly since then "turning the rules" has become a traditional newspaper method of mourning the passing of a President. Today on its front page The Record turns the rules.

THE NEXT EIGHT PAGES ARE DEVOTED TO THE PRESIDENT'S DEATH:

FRANKLIN DELANO ROOSEVELT, 1882—1945

'IT'S NOT TRUE,' THOUSANDS CRY AS NEWS SPREADS

City Stunned by Death of President; Men and Women Sob

By CHARLES FISHER

The news of the President's death spread through Philadelphia with fierce and terrible rapidity last night.

It struck at supper time on one of the finest spring evenings of the year.

It came at a time of high hope over approaching military victory.

It left the city—a city which quit its own political tradition in devotion to the Rooseveltian ideal—shaken with sorrow and dismay.

Here was a town which knew the President. It had turned out in unprecedented numbers to welcome him, had stood in the rain, grown chilled in open stadiums, waited in hot sunlight to salute him as he traveled its streets. He had evoked an affection be-

Continued on Page 8, Column 2.

The Weather

(By U. S. Weather Bureau)

Philadelphia and vicinity: Mostly cloudy and continued mild today; tomorrow, fair and slightly cooler.

Eastern Pennsylvania and New Jersey: Considerable cloudiness and continued mild today.

A Prayer

By Daniel A. Poling

God of our fathers and our God, walk with us in this dark hour that we be not afraid; comfort us that we be not in despair and lift our eyes to the torch that he bore.

We thank Thee for this man who in the generations ahead will be alive as Lincoln is alive, for he raised the standard in the earth to which the humble of all races repaired. We thank Thee for this great one who lived among us and who, as no other man, became man's hope for deliverance from the bondage of fear and for winning a just and enduring peace.

The world shall mourn him as no other yet has been mourned, but our sorrow is not without hope for Thou art still in Thy heaven and the spirit of Franklin Delano Roosevelt whom Thou hast taken unto Thyself will companion us as we finish the work we are in.

N. Y. EXCHANGE TO CLOSE

NEW YORK, April 12 (AP)—The New York Stock Exchange will be open tomorrow, but will close Saturday, the day of President Roosevelt's funeral.

TRUMAN PLEDGES SELF TO FOLLOW F. D. R. FOOTSTEPS

Sworn In as 32d President by Chief Justice in White House

By ROBERT ROTH
Record's Washington Bureau

WASHINGTON, April 12—Harry S. Truman became the 32d President of the United States at 7.09 P. M. today.

His first official act was to announce to the world his intention to fight the war, as his predecessor would have done, to victory.

Sworn in by Chief Justice Harlan F. Stone, he took office in a crisis that has but one parallel in American history, the accession of Andrew Johnson, of Tennessee, to the Presidency on the death of Abraham Lincoln, April 15, 1865.

At 5.15 P. M. today Truman received a telephone call from Stephen Early, veteran Roosevelt aide, asking him to "come quickly but quietly to the White House." He arrived there 10 min-

Continued on Page 3, Column 2.

DEMOCRATS POSTPONE JACKSON DAY DINNERS

WASHINGTON, April 12 (INS)—Democratic National Committee headquarters announced today that all scheduled Jackson Day dinners have been postponed indefinitely because of the death of President Roosevelt.

PRESIDENT DIES SUDDENLY AT WARM SPRINGS

Stricken While Posing for His Portrait in 'Little White House' Cottage; Two Doctors at Bedside

By THOMAS F. REYNOLDS
Copyright, 1945, Philadelphia Record-Chicago Sun

WASHINGTON, April 12—Franklin D. Roosevelt is dead.

Harry S. Truman, his third Vice President, was sworn in as his successor two and a half hours after Roosevelt died in the Little White House on the crest of Pine Mountain in Warm Springs, Ga.

Roosevelt's body will be returned to Washington aboard a special train leaving Warm Springs at 9 A. M. (E. W. T.) tomorrow. The funeral will be held in the historic White House East Room Saturday, afternoon. He will be buried Sunday in his native Hyde Park. The body will not lie in state.

Mrs. Roosevelt, stately and calm in her grief, flew tonight to Warm Springs, accompanied by Vice Adm. Ross T. McIntire, her husband's personal physician, and Stephen T. Early, his faithful secretary for the past 12 years.

Sudden and Painless End

Death came suddenly and painlessly to the President at 4.35 P. M. (EWT) from a brain hemorrhage on the eve of his greatest triumphs—triumphs of the American armed forces he created to defend his country and a triumph of his plan for a new organization to keep the peace of the world.

The news stunned Washington, the United States and the world. His passing signalized the end of an era—an era of great struggles at home to better the life of the common man and of titanic struggles abroad to defend the United States against its enemies and banish aggression from the world.

First Lady Notifies Four Sons

Roosevelt, who after 12 years and 38 days as President of the United States was perhaps the most powerful force in the world, died almost alone—attended only by two physicians.

His four sons are scattered around the world, in the fighting forces of their country.

His wife was in Washington attending the meeting of a wartime organization.

His only daughter was at the Naval Medical Center here at the beside of her sick son, Johnny, the President's grandchild.

Mrs. Roosevelt, once the first shock of the news had passed, cabled to her four sons—all on active service: "He did his job to the end as he would want you to do. Bless you all and all our love. Mother."

Death Came Without Warning

Death must have seemed to the President like a blinding flash. It struck him suddenly and without warning as he sat in a chair in the living room of the little frame house at the Infantile Paralysis Foundation where for the last 20 year he has fought his own personal battle with paralysis.

He was all right this morning. He was normal at lunch. After lunch he moved into the living room to sit for a portrait study that was in process. Approximately at 3 P. M. Providence decreed that his time was up.

He fainted without warning.

Doctors rushed to his bedside, immediately diagnozed his ailment as a cerebral hemorrhage.

At 4.35 P. M. he breathed his last.

He "slept away"—in the words of his faithful secretary,

Continued on Page 2, Column 6.

'I Am More Sorry for the World Than for Us,' Mrs. Roosevelt Says

WASHINGTON, April 12 (AP)—Mrs. Eleanor Roosevelt said, when informed of the death of the President:

"I am more sorry for the people of the country and the world than I am for us."

The First Lady received Vice President Truman in her second floor sitting room which adjoins the President's bedroom.

She told Truman "the President has just passed away."

"What can I do?" Truman said.

"Tell us what we can do," Mrs. Roosevelt replied. "Is there any way we can help you?"

WARM SPRINGS MIRROR

Local, State, and National News

"MORE THAN REFLECTS THE NEWS"

Entered as second-class mail at the P. O. Warm Springs, Georgia

VOLUME 16 NUMGER 16

WARM SPRINGS, MERIWETHER COUNTY, GEORGIA, FRIDAY, APRIL 20, 1945

ONE DOLLAR PER YEAR

PRESIDENT FRANKLIN DELANO ROOSEVELT DIED AT THE "LITTLE WHITE HOUSE" THURSDAY, APRIL 12

The people of Warm Springs and the nation were stunned when the word came late Thursday evening (April 12) that President Roosevelt had died suddenly at the Little White House, in Warm Springs, where he came two weeks previous, for rest.

President Roosevelt's last words were: "I have a terrific headache," spoken to Commander Harold Bruenn, naval physical. He then passed out without regaining consciousness.

President Roosevelt was 63, on January 30, and was serving his fourth term as President of the United States—longest ever held by any president.

Mayor Frank W. Allcorn had invited President Roosevelt to a barbecue at his Shaker Heights home overlooking Warm Springs at 4 p. m., and a number of newsmen and secret servicemen were there awaiting the President when the news came that he had died suddenly. The President was also planning to view a minstrel given by the patients following the barbecue.

Mrs. Roosevelt, who was in Washington, came by plane to Ft. Benning and rushed to Warm Springs from there by automobile.

On Friday morning a Guard of Honor from Ft. Benning lined the road from the Foundation entrance to the Southern Railway station as the funeral procession left from the White House. Approximately two regiments of troops were on hand as guard, and in the procession.

The funeral train pulled out silently at eleven o'clock Friday morning and arrived in Washington at 10 o'clock Saturday morning. The funeral was held there in the famous East Room of the White House at 4 p. m., with burial at his home in Hyde Park, N. Y., Sunday afternoon.

Lumber cut from Georgia pine and grown on the Warm Springs Foundation was used for making the bier on which rested the casket of President Roosevelt to Washington.

The sudden passing of President Roosevelt, at the very hour of victory in Europe, closed a great chapter in American history. He died, as he had lived, a good soldier for his country The effect of his death on the future of American life and especially politics, cannot be measured.

Roosevelt's Jefferson Talk Last Message To The American People

The last message of Franklin D. Roosevelt to the American people, written on the night before his passing, and intended for radiocasting to Jefferson Day dinners throughout the nation on Saturday night, is as follows:

Americans are gathered together this evening in communities all over the country to pay tribute to the living memory of Thomas Jefferson—one of the greatest of all democrats; and I want to make it clear that I am spelling that word "democrats" with a small "d."

I wish I had the power, just for this evening, to be present at all of these gatherings.

In this historic year, more than ever before, we do well to consider the character of Thomas Jefferson as an American citizen of the world.

As Minister to France, then as our third President, Jefferson was instrumental in the establishment of the United States as a vital factor in international affairs.

It was he who first sent our Navy into far-distant waters to defend our rights. And the promulgation of the Monroe Doctrine was the logical development of Jefferson's far-seeing foreign policy.

BATTLE FOR RIGHTS OF MAN

Today this nation, which Jefferson helped so greatly to build, is playing a tremendous part in the battle for the righs of man all over the world.

Today we are part of the vast Allied force— a force composed of flesh and blood and steel and spirit —which is today destroying the makers of war, the breeders of hate in Europe, and in Asia.

In Jefferson's time our Navy consisted of only a handful of frigates —but that tiny Navy taught nations across the Atlantic that piracy in the Mediterranean—acts of aggression against peaceful commerce and the enslavement of their crews—was one of those things which, among neighbors, simply was not done.

Today we ave learned in the agony of war that great power involves great responsibility. Today we can no more escape the consequence of German and Japanese aggression than could we avoid the consequences of attacks by the Barbary corsairs a century and a half before.

We, as Americans, do not choose to deny our responsibility.

Nor do we intend to abandon our determination that, within the lives of our children and our children's children, there will not be a third world war.

WE SEEK ENDURING PEACE

We seek peace—enduring peace. More than an end to war, we want an end to the beginnings of all wars—yes, an end to this brutal, inhuman, and thoroughly impractical method of settling the differences between governments.

The once powerful, malignant Nazi state is crumbling; the Japanese war lords are receiving in their own homeland, the retribution for which they asked when they attacked Pearl Harbor.

But the mere conquest of our enemies is not enough.

We must go on to do all in our power to conquer the doubts and the fears, the ignorance and the greed, which made this horror possible.

Thomas Jefferson, himself a distinguished scientist, once spoke of the "brotherly spirit of science, which unites into one family all its votaries of whatever grade and however widely dispersed throughout the different quarters of the globe."

Today, science has brought all the different quarters of the globe so close together that it is impossible to isolate them one from another.

Today we are faced with the preeminent fact that, if civilization is to survive, we must cultivate the science of human relationships—the ability of all peoples, of all kinds, to live together and work together, in the same world, at peace.

Let me assure you that my hand is the steadier for the work that is to be done, that I move more firmly into the task, knowing that you—millions and millions of you — are joined with me in the resolve to make this work endure.

The work, my friends, is peace, more than an end of this war—an end to the beginning of all wars, yes, an end, forever, to this impractical, unrealistic settlement of the differences between governments by the mass killing of peoples.

Today as we move against the terrible scourge of war—as we go forward toward the greatest contribution that any generation of human beings can make in this world—the contribution of lasting peace—I ask you to keep up your faith. I measure the sound, solid achievement that can be made at this time by the straight-edge of your own confidence and your resolve. And to you, and to all Americans who dedicate themselves with us to the making of an abiding peace, I say:

The only limit to our realization of tomorrow will be our doubts of today. Let us move foward with strong and active faith.

Warm Springs Mirror
Established 1930
Warm Springs, Georgia.

Published weekly by the West Georgia Press, 36 East Broad Street, Warm Springs, Ga.

Entered as second-class matter Nov. 14 1930, at Warm Springs, Georgia. under Act of March 3, 1879.

Advertising Rates on Request. Subscription Rates—One Dollar Per Year, in advance.

Card of Thanks, obituaries, notices are charged for at the rate of one cent a word, minimum charge $1.00, cash to accompany order for insertion.

Soups add to the heartiness of any meal. For a quick onion soup, saute onion in vitaminized margarine over a low flame. Then add to consomme or bouillon stock and simmer slowly for a few minutes. Serve with toast rounds in soup and parmesan cheese.

The Chief Lies Dead

The Chief lies dead.
No more we'll listen
To his friendly talks.
No more the hand that led us
Will lead on. He's gone.
The mighty weight of world affairs
That lay upon his shoulders
Became too much to bear
And in the calm of an April day
He lay them down.

And at Warm Springs.
What more restful place
Could he have chosen?
What more fitting place
Could he unbosm
All the thoughts of care and war
That were his Life?
He is at rest. At Warm Springs.
They will lift his banner there
Held aloft with fervent prayer.

We grieve.
But not with a grief that has
No recompense. Not with a grief
That seems to feel the way ahead
Is dark. He left us that great
Wealth of understanding
That will carry on and mark
A path to future way of Life.
He left us that great love
For his fellowman.

The Chief lies dead.
He's gone.
Sleep on, dear faithful one.
May no thought of struggle or of strife
Beset you. Yours has been a noble Life.
And in its going
It takes with it
That Faith, Hope and Love,
That cements you to the host
Of faithful followers you have left behind.

—Lillian Jackson Coleman
Alabama.
(Written Thursday night, 4-12-45)

State Parks To Be Improved By Department

The building of a State park on the coast of Georgia and improvement of several other parks of the state will feature an enlarged parks program which has been worked out in the Division of Conservation, it was announced by State Parks Director Ward Harrison.

Pine Mountain, Vogel and Magnolia Spings parks will feature the program to expand facilities. The coastal park will coast about sixty thousand dollars, of which $12,500 has just been approved by the State Budget Bureau to start construction. It will be located between Brunswick and Jacksonville. Included will be a dock for boating, clubhouse, cottages and picnic grounds.

At Pine Mountain Park, 24 more cottages will be provided.

WAR SOUVENIR TEA AT COMMUNITY BUILDING

One of the most unusual souvenir exhbits ever to be on display is being arranged for the War Souvenir Tea at the Community Building today (Friday.)

Souvenirs from many fighting fronts and a number of the foreign places our boys have visited, includes items of every description. Be sure and see them Friday afternoon, April 20, from 3 to 5:30. The tea is sponsored by the W. S. C. S. of the Methodist church. Proceeds go on building fund.

Franklin D. Roosevelt

National Shrine To President Roosevelt Proposed At Historic Warm Springs Site

Even before the passing of President Roosevelt Thursday, one of our local citizens had mentioned a shrine here to perpetuate the memory of the world's most famous humanitarian.

And now, P. T. McCutcheon Jr., clerk of Georgia's house of representatives, suggests that Governor Ellis Arnall lead a national drive to erect this memorial to "this greatest humanitarian, leader and president in American history" at Warm Springs.

Many letters and telegrams have been received by Governor Arnall and also by the mayor of Warm Springs, Frank W. Allcorn, offering sugestions and contributions.

There is no more logical place for the erection of this shrine to President Franklin Delano Roosevelt, than on the "Littl White House" premises where he has often came to rest, and where on April 12, 1945, he passed into history of the nation.

ANSWER TO LETTERS RECEIVED

During the past few days many letters have been received requesting copies of the current issue of this paper. We have been unable to answer, as so many have written.

Papers are being sent to all who wrote and we thank you!

THE PUBLISHERS

Memorial Services Held Saturday For Late President

Exactly at three p. m. CWT, the same time the services were being held in the Blue Room of the White House in Washington, the citizens of Warm Springs gathered in the Community Building here to pay tribute to its greatest "citizen."

To these people, Franklin Roosevelt was not just a President, but a sincere friend.

Even as the people entered the stone-built gathering place, their hearts were stirred by the inscription just above its entrance, "Dedicated to Mrs. Sara Delano Roosevelt,"—the President's mother.

After a short worship service conducted by the Rev. R. W. Greene Jr., many lingered in prayer and meditation—for this was to them something which touched their very utmost inner spirits.

And yet, as they thought of this man, who had been a regular visitor since 1924, they could no forget the characteristic smile, the carefree mood and friendly spirit which had always been exemplified in his associations with them.

F. W. Allcorn, mayor, told of the great interest which he showed in the people by saying: "The President spoke with me personally about the future of our town.'

Thus, in Warm Springs, there is a reverent feeling permeating the hearts of all its people. They shall always be proud of having been his friend, and know that in spirit he still lives—here and wherever he has been.

Memorial Exercises To Be Held Here April 26

Sponsored by the Warm Springs Woman's Club, the following Confederate Memorial Exercise will be given at the Community House on April 26, at eleven o'clock.

A cordial invitation is extended to everyone in Meriwether county, for a special tribute will be paid to the last member of the Meriwether Camp of Confederate veterans:

1. Call To Order.
2. Song "America"—By the school.
3. Invocation—Rev. W. G. Harry.
4. Reading, "Little Giffen of Tennessee—Mrs. J. O. Butts.
5. Reading, "A Georgia Volunteer"—Miss Mary Hardy.
6. Ode by Rev. W. G. Harry to the last member of the Meriwether Camp of Conferate Veterans, Franklin D. Roosevelt—Mrs. R. A. Sloan.
7. Song, "Tenting On The Old Campground—by the school.
8. Introduction of the speaker, Rev. R. W. Green Jr.
9. "Dixie"—Instumental.
10. Announcements.
11. Song—"Till We Meet Again."
12. Benediction, by Rev. L. P. Morris.

Neal Kitchens, Adjutant

Renew Drivers' Licenses April 23 To June 30

The period for renewing Georgia drivers licenses will begin Monday April 23, and end June 30, it has been announced by the Department of Public Safety.

The forms on which to apply for 1946 drivers' license may be obtained from any State Patrol Station, filling stations or other places convenient to the general public.

All applicants for renewal license are requested to be sure the form is completely filled out, that the renewal stub from the old license is attached and correct fee enclosed. Do not send personal checks, currency may be sent, at the risk of the sender.

In Church Circles

METHODIST CHURCH
Rev. R. W. Greene, Jr. Pastor
W. I. Nunn Supt. S. S.

Services will be held at the Methodist Church Sunday as follows:
Church School—10:00 A. M.
Morning Worship— 11 A. M.
Youth Fellowship—6:45 P. M.
Evening Worship—7:30.

The pastor will bring the message of the morning hour on the topic, "In His Steps We Follow." The service will be one of dedication to the principles of goodness as exemplified in the life of our past President. At 10:00 a. m., this message will be given at the Chapel on the Foundation, and at 11:00 in the local Methodist church.

At the evening service, the sermon will be entitled, "The Greatest Verse In The Bible." You are cordially invited to come and worship with us at each of these services.

ATROCITY VICTIMS

NAZI DEATH CAMP LEADER IN CHAINS BEFORE EXECUTION

TIME TO REMEMBER—Sitting dejectedly, legs in chains, is SS Storm Group Leader Josef Kramer. The brutal commander of the Belsen concentration camp—where 60,000 dead and starving men, women and children were found—reportedly has been tried and executed. Another Nazi eliminated!
—International News Soundphoto.

MASS BURIAL—When American troops captured Nordhausen and came upon 2500 dead political prisoners in a concentration camp, the military government officer ordered the burgomeister to round up 600 men to dig graves and bury the dead.
—Associated Press wirephoto.

SS WOMEN GUARDS—Reported to be as brutal and fanatic as the men, these women overseers were also captured by the British at Belsen concentration camp. Described as fat and well-fed, they were forced to help bury their tortured victims—men, women and children who numbered into the thousands. These are the type of women who sang and danced around burning prisoners.
—Associated Press wirephoto by radio from London.

HIS FREEDOM—Gasping in agony, this internee of the Belsen camp, 28 miles from Hannover, sits on a mound—too weak to walk on the day of liberation. The site of starving political prisoners was seized by the British forces. Most of the emaciated captives were unable to comprehend that they were free.
—Associated Press wirephoto by radio from London.

Vol. 5
No. 122
Saturday
April 28,
1945

THE JOURNAL

Greatest American Newspaper in Germany

Voice of the men of the 95th Division

REDS, YANKS LINK UP

Third Army Enters Austria; Seventh 25 Miles from Munich

One spearhead of Gen. Patton's Third Army has smashed across the Austrian frontier and is still moving forward several miles inside the border.

Other elements of the Third have captured the important rail center of Regensburg and have crossed the Danube in several more places.

Gen. Patch's Seventh Army is making remarkable progress in its drive on Munich, and at last reports were less than 25 mi. from the city. The Third, Seventh and French First Armies are all aiming their drives at Munich, third largest city in Germany.

French troops have cleared the last remaining German troops from the Maratime Alps in their drive into Bavaria.

Americans, Patriots Link Up

Reports from northern Italy state that elements of the Fifth Army and bands of Italian Patriots have joined hands in the coastal city of Genoa. These American troops aided in the liberation of the great city.

Milan and Turin have been cleared of all resistance. Patriots report that risings are going on all over northern Italy, and that many more cities up to the Brenner Pass have been cleared.

It is reported that the German troops who managed to get across the Adige River ahead of the Fifth and Eighth Armies are concentrating their troops for a stand north of the river. It is believed, however, that they will not have time to organize their forces, since the Allied Armies are already across the Adige.

Chairmanship To Rotate

The chairmanship of the San Francisco Conference is to rotate among the foreign ministers of America, Britain, Russia and China. The Ukraine and White Russia will be invited to join the new international body.

The Americans and Russian Armies linked up three days ago at the city of Torgau on the Elbe. Torgau lies 30 miles northeast of Leipzig.

The long-awaited meeting of the two armies took place only after months of bitter fighting all the way from Stalingrad on the east and from the coast of France on the west.

Statistics reveal that the Russians moved over 2,000 miles, the Americans almost 1,000.

Marshal Stalin, President Truman and Mr. Churchill have made statements welcoming the linkup and Marshal Stalin has issued an order of the day to the United States, British, and Russian Armies.

Near the linkup, Marshal Koniev's forces have captured the city of Wittenberg, only 18 miles from Dessau. Potsdam, 10 miles southwest of Berlin, has fallen to Marshal Zhukov's First White Russian Army.

In Berlin itself, the bitter fighting continues, with the Red Army slowly closing the death trap. Several more suburbs have fallen. The famous Templehof Airport was captured yesterday after a fierce battle.

The Red Army has fought its way to Rathenow, 40 miles west of the capital. Spandau, a city five miles northwest of Berlin, has also fallen.

Russian forces driving west near the Baltic Sea have pushed to a point 30 miles beyond Stettin.

Bremen Completely Cleared

The British Second Army has flushed out the last remaining German resistance in Bremen. The dock area, where enemy troops held out until last night, is still in good condition and can take care of Allied shipping. Only minor repairs are needed to put the great port back in good working order.

THE WEATHER

Rain and continued cool.

TEMPERATURES LAST TWENTY-FOUR HOURS

p.m.	53	3 a.m..	43	9 a.m..	47	3 p.m..	
10 p.m.	50	4 a.m..	42	10 a.m..	49	4 p.m.	
11 p.m.	49	5 a.m..	42	11 a.m..	51	5 p.m.	
Midnite	48	6 a.m..	41	12 Noon	54	6 p.m	
1 a.m..	46	7 a.m..	41	1 p.m..	55	7 p.m	
2 a.m..	44	8 a.m..	44	2 p.m..	57	8 p.m.	

To date you should not have used more than 97 per cent of your fuel oil allotment. Almanac on Page

Times Herald

EXTRA ★

LARGEST NET PAID CIRCULATION OF ANY WASHINGTON NEWSPAPER

VOL. VII, NO. 87 (Reg. U. S. Pat. Off.) Times-Herald Copyright, 1945 WASHINGTON, D. C. SATURDAY, APRIL 28, 1945 PRICE SINGLE COPY 5c

CITY HOME DELIVERY RATES	Daily	Sun.	Daily & Sun.
Weekly..............	$ .15	$ .10	$ .25
Monthly............	.65	.45	1.10

GERMANY SURRENDERS

LONDON, April 28.

Germany has surrendered unconditionally. All organized resistance to the allied armies has ceased. No further details are at present available. Further information in later editions.

The Tomahawk Strikes!

THE TOMAHAWK

The Paper For The Men Who Make The News

Vol. III, No. 6 — SOMEWHERE IN GERMANY, 29. April 1945 — Formerly THE WINDMILL

SS Officer Candidates Fail Tests Before Co. "G"

WITH AN INFANTRY DIVISION, GERMANY — A determined lot of SS troopers and students from a nearby Officer's Candidate School made for mean fighting when men from Company "G" attacked a road barrier along a range of hills during a night attack.

The Germans added punch to their stand by using tanks, anti—tanks guns and Panzerfausts, according to the company commander, Capt. John L. Faris, of Rockhill, S. C.

BACK TO THE WAR

It helped a lot when Pvt. Louis De Christopher, West Springfield, Mass., celebrated his return to the war from a furlough in the States by knocking out a German tank with a German bazooka.

The First Platoon, led by Lt. Thomas R. Giblin, of Carbondale, Penna., left 15 dead SS troopers around a roadblock that was defended stoutly with anti—tank guns, machine guns, and Panzerfausts.

About 100 prisoners were taken. In speaking to one of them S/Sgt Lawrence L. Mc Cracken, Bloomsburg, Penna., said off—hand., "Go and get your brother and bring him along, too."

The prisoner did.

Infantry CG Awards Silver, Bronze Stars

WITH THE 2ND TD GP., GERMANY – The commanding general of an infantry division presented seven Silver Stars and 19 Bronze Stars, including one Oak Leaf Cluster, to men and officers of the 823rd Tank Destroyer Battalion on April 24th.

The Silver Stars went to Capt. Ellis W. McInnis, Dallas, Texas; Sgt. Frank Krivosucky, Akron, Ohio; Sgt. Ray E. Dudley, Elko, Nev.; Sgt. William T. Stinnett, Antioc, Calif.; Pfc. Eslantislao C. Chavana, Corpus Christi, Texas; Pfc. Jesse F. Diaz, Orange, Calif., and Pfc. Doyle Mizell, Bogalusa, La.

Ist Lt. Clair F. Farley, Pittsburgh, Penna., received an Oak Leaf Cluster for his Bronze Star Medal.

Bronze Stars were presented to Capt. Lester J. Baranov, San Diego, Calif., Capt. George W. Sitz, Jr., Tracy City; Tenn.; Ist Lt. Joe H. Bruton, Abilene, Texas; Ist Sgt. Charlie B. Sandoval, Sante Fe, N. M.; T/Sgt. Benjamin O. Thompson, Fort Worth, Texas; S/Sgt. Henry H. Stein, Eureka, S. D.; T/Sgt. Albert A. Dill, Johnstown, Colo., T/Sgt. Patrick M. Warden, Clemmore, Ohio and T/3 Bennie P. Cucchiara; Independence, La.

T/4 Dale L. Eaton, Orange, Calif.; T/4 George W. Corf, Hawthorne, Calif.; T/4 Bernnon B. Flippo, West Columbia, Texas; T/4 Homer W. Kimpton, Gravity, Iowa; T/4 Simeon A. Roach, Washington, D. C.; Cpl. Lee Lopez, Jr.; Chino, Calif.; T/5 Rufus W. Hemphill, New Orleans, La.; T/5 Melvin C. Tingley, Toledo, Ohio, and Pfc. Houston A. Sandell, Natchitoches, La. also received Bronze Stars.

These awards bring the number of Silver Stars worn by the men of the 823rd to 26, while 93 now own Bronze Stars.

Town Finally Succumbs As All Ist Bn. Fights

WITH AN INFANTRY DIVISION, GERMANY — A town in the path of the First Battalion was so strongly defended that even those who do not usually fight as infantry grabbed rifles and got on the line to help crush the resistance.

Using Panzerfausts as artillery, and making the best of houses for machine gun positions, the Germans put up a good fight for the town whose crooked and narrow streets made the use of tanks impossible.

According to S/Sgt. Arthur Floyd, Norlina, N. C., cracking this town made the going easy on the rest of the drive.

While tank destroyers cleaned out the houses on the flanks, S/Sgt. Floyd picked off Germans from the battalion observation post as they ran from the houses attacked by the TDs.

KILLS 2 NAZIS

When the battalion S—2 was ambushed and wounded while reconnoitering a route for tanks to come up, Pfc. Nathan Kuperstein, Mauldin, Miss., stayed to give first aid, while Pfc. William Lord, Lebanon, Penna., killed two Germans in order to break out of the ambush for help.

Captain Allen S. Hubbard, Jr., Colebrook, Conn., rescued the wounded officer and his companion with a small task force which he had organized.

More than 600 prisoners were taken in the town after the Germans realized it was useless to fight on.

Ack-Ack Leads Armor On Newly Made Span

WITH THE 430TH AAA BATTALION, GERMANY — Dogging the heels of bridge-building engineers, this veteran unit came to a site where a bridge was to be built and deployed as protection.

The Infantrymen then arrived on the scene and crossed over in assault boats to mop up the East Bank. A few hours later, the last pontons and treads swung into position and the bridge was completed.

One platoon of the battery's guns commanded by Lt. Paul Cummins, Sarcoxie, Missouri, moved over immediately and within three minutes were in position, ready for any action that might come.

Then came the supreme thrill in the life of the Ack-Ack gunner; armor followed their spearhead across the bridge site.

743rd Tank Bn. Shermans Blast Nazis Since H-Hour

Lights Lure 4 Nazis To Paddle Over Rhine

WITH BATTERY "A", 226TH AAA (SL) BN., GERMANY — The big searchlights illuminating the night in forward areas can be seen for miles around. The Germans can see them, too, as it was proved to Sgt. Basil A. Thaxton, section chief from Charleston, W. Va., and his companion, T/4 Luther K. Trent, Sneedville, Tenn.

Just before the drive over the Rhine, the battery was in position south of Neuss. Four Germans approached the two sergeants and the crew on one of the lights and surrendered to them.

Explaining their surrender, the Jerries said they had seen the beam from their position across the river and made up their minds they wanted to give themselves up to ack-ack crews, since that was their job in the German Army.

"We left our area at 10:30, walked to the Rhine, found a small boat, paddled across the river, and followed your beam until we got here," they explained.

Recapture Half Track Taken Near Mortain

WITH THE 2ND TD GROUP, GERMANY — When the 823rd Tank Destroyer Battalion was slugging it out with Hitler's elite Panzers at Mortain, France, last summer, S/Sgt. William E. Higgins, Fillmore, Utah, platoon sergeant of the third platoon, Company "B", had his half-track overrun and captured by the Jerries.

Recently the platoon encountered the same unit in the battle toward the Rhine. The third platoon had just knocked out two enemy tanks and was drawing a bead on a half-track.

"Cease firing," yelled Sgt. Higgins, "That's my vehicle." Sure enough, shining bright on the bumper was the horse-head emblem the 823rd had painted on the track months ago and which the Nazis had neglected to remove.

It required a little extra care to get the vehicle back intact, but it was accomplished. Higgins commented, "The track is worn and has an extra thousand miles on her, but the maintenance isn't worth a damn. She'll still run good."

We have some extra copies of the blue, souvenier edition of THE TOMAHAWK, April 15th, if you want one to send home.

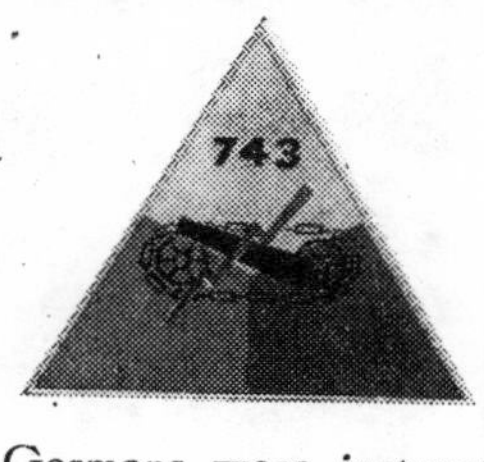

Germans were instructed not to take any prisoners wearing this patch of the "743rd Panzer Division."

Nazi Lt. Surrenders 45; No Longer Reason To Die

WITH AN INFANTRY DIVISION, GERMANY — Four American doughboys crouched on the west bank of a river and peered through the darkness. Against the light thrown by a blazing building the silhouettes of first one, then another and another German soldier appeared near the eastern approaches of the wrecked bridge.

This was what the doughboys were waiting for. Earlier in the day two German corporals with white flags had stumbled across the ruins of the bridge and asked surrender terms for their men. One went back at nightfall with this message, "If you aren't back within one hour, the artillery will fall thick and fast on your positions."

The Germans coming up to the bridge were well within the time limit. Several fell off the ruins of the bridge into the water, but swam to the western bank and were pulled out by the doughboys.

The count was 45 men and one officer, a lieutenant.

The men sent out by the Ist Battalion Headquarters to make the haul were Pfc. William P. Hoppe, Seattle, Wash.; Pfc. Ben B. Buten, Detroit, Mich., (interpreters.); Pfc. Mark Markuson, Omaha, Nebr., (driver) and Pfc. Henry Szpakowski, Jersey City. N. J.

The officer explained the surrender by showing a picture of his wife and saying, "There is no longer a good reason to die."

Meat On Hoof For Ex-PWs

WITH THE 110TH F. A. BATTALION, GERMANY — Pvt Michael Krayniak, Passaic, N. J., the Russian interpreter for his unit, recently found four liberated Russians who had been slave laborers for the Germans for many months.

The Russians had discovered a cow in a field and started out to alleviate the hunger brought on by two days of marching and a big backlog of days without food.

One man started to milk the cow, another was hacking away at the animal to kill her for steaks, and still another began to skin her. The fourth man got into the operation in holding the cow for the milking.

Thats the way the story came to us!

President Cites Tankers For 16 Hours on Beach; 13 DSC's Awarded

Twenty minutes before H Hour on June 6th, the first assault tanks of the 743rd Tank Battalion hit the beach with dough support from the Ist and 29th Infantry Divisions.

The moment climaxed two years of preparation for the medium tank battalion. They had trained to open the curtain on the greatest invasion in history at Fort Lewis, Wash., the California Desert and the beaches of England.

When their tanks rolled onto French sand, no troops ahead opened the way for them. They had to blast an exit from the tiny strip of beach into the hedgerow country beyond or die. Many never made it and were buried just over the first hill. Others did, and the beachhead was established. The 743rd won the Presidential Unit Citation ribbon and nine DSC's during the 16 hour's fighting.

A short article like this can't begin to give credit to a unit that has been in action since D Day. During campaigns in Normandy, Northern France, Belgium, Holland and Germany, the 743rd Tank Battalion has seen the bitterest fighting on the continent. Its real history rests in the men and their tanks. It will never be completely written.

Lt. Col. John S. Upham commanded the battalion when it landed. He was wounded on the beach and is now in a California hospital. The battalion's commanding officer is now Lt. Col. William D. Duncan, Sioux Falls, S. D.

The 743rd Tank Battalion was attached to the 30th Infantry Division on the 14th of June, and has been knocking out resistance for the XIX Corps ever since. The bag includes 70 tanks, 20 half tracks, 4 armored cars, 17 trucks, 9 artillery pieces, 47 anti-tank guns and two of the Luftwaffe destroyed, not to mention the equipment captured or destroyed which was not manned.

There has never been a time when the 743rd was not in combat or anticipating combat. They have fired

over a million rounds of light machine gun ammo and about 26,000 rounds of 75mm stuff from their Sherman tanks.

The award list is terrific. It includes 13 DSC's, 62 Silver Stars,

(Con't on next Page)

Rebuff Himmler Peace Envoy

Story on Page 3

2¢ Weather PARTLY CLOUDY (Details on Page 2) Daily Mirror 3c in Suburbs 5c Elsewhere in United States 2¢

Vol. 21. No. 266. C NEW YORK, MONDAY, APRIL 30, 1945 FINAL 6 A.M. ★★★★

MUSSOLINI EXECUTED WITH MISTRESS

Cries 'No! No!' at Firing Squad

7TH IN MUNICH; MILAN, VENICE, GENOA FALL

Stories on Pages 2 and 3

NUMERO SPECIALE • L. 10

CRIMEN

ANNO I - N. 8 • ROMA 4 MAGGIO 1945
SPEDIZIONE IN ABBONAMENTO POSTALE
ESCE IL VENERDÌ - QUATTRO PAGINE - L. 10
PREZZO DI VENDITA FUORI ROMA L. 11

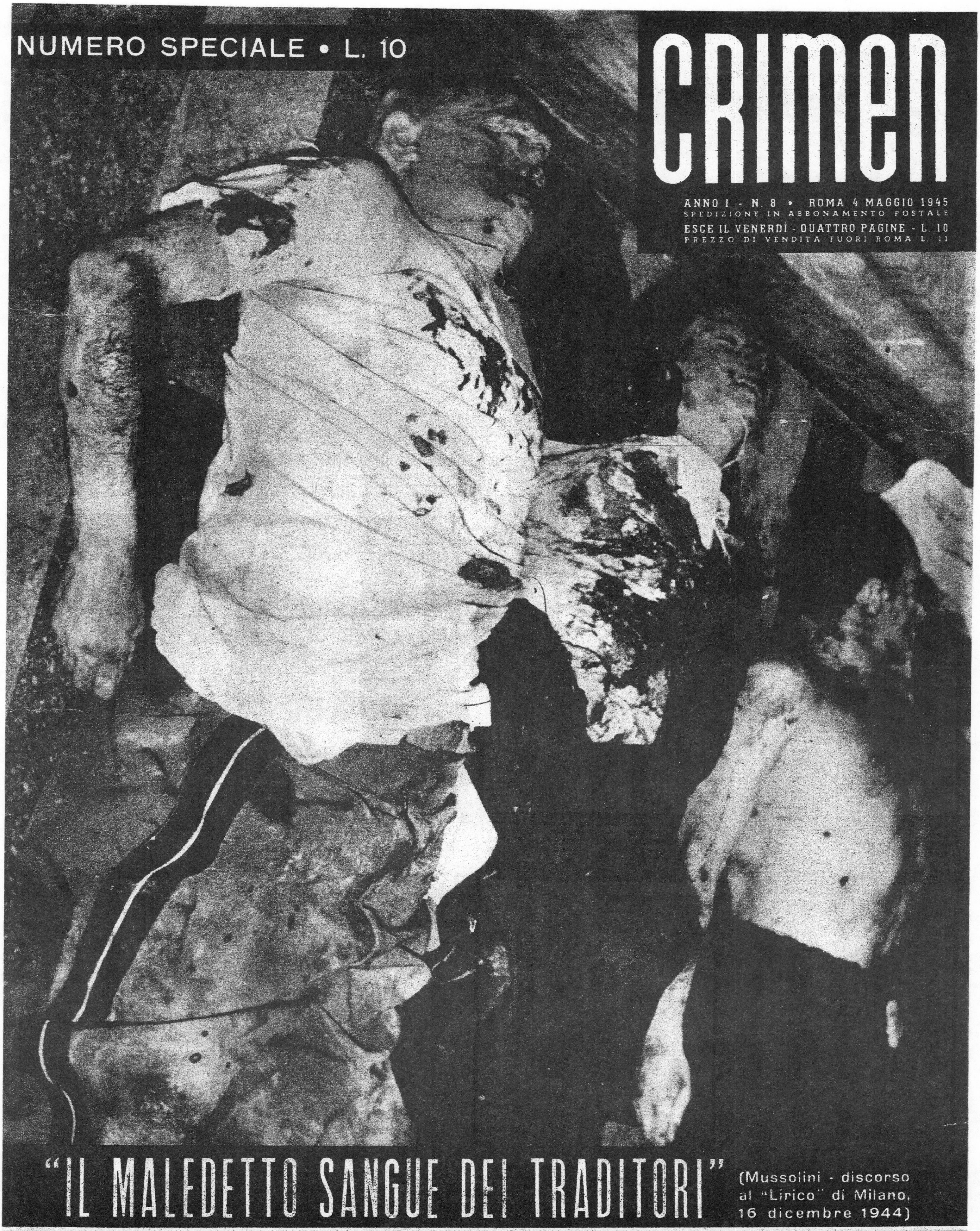

"IL MALEDETTO SANGUE DEI TRADITORI"

(Mussolini - discorso al "Lirico" di Milano, 16 dicembre 1944)

Mussolini, la Petacci, Starace, immobili e sinistri dinanzi al clamore delle folle milanesi. Tra poco i corpi saranno abbandonati alla terra in una tomba senza nome. Sopra di essa il popolo italiano ricostruirà con dolore tutto ciò che è stato distrutto da una guerra che fu subita come una vergogna

All They That Take the Sword Shall Perish With the Sword

—Matthew XXVI, 52

'FAREWELL! A LONG FAREWELL, TO ALL MY GREATNESS!' The end was in sight for Adolf Hitler as he strode reflectively in the ruins of a German town . . . a town that was to symbolize a destruction and disaster brought upon Germany by the mad aspirations of its Fuehrer. In the background, Hitler's henchmen followed, waiting for a sign. Shortly before this photo was taken, an attempt was made on Hitler's life. Maybe that, too, was giving Der Fuehrer food for thought.

EXTRA
LATE NEWS
Los Angeles Examiner
CHARACTER · QUALITY · AMERICA FIRST! · ENTERPRISE · ACCURACY
AN AMERICAN PAPER FOR THE AMERICAN PEOPLE · THE GREAT NEWSPAPER OF THE GREAT SOUTHWEST
Reg. U.S. Pat. Off.
Examiner Telephone Richmond 1212
Examiner Building, 1111 S. Broadway
VOL. XLII—NO. 142 · LOS ANGELES, WEDNESDAY, MAY 2, 1945 · PCC · Two Sections—Part I—FIVE CENTS

HITLER DEAD!

Nazis Say End Came in Berlin; Doenitz at Helm; To Carry On War

SMALL NATIONS ASSIGNED WIDE POWERS AT S.F.

Four Major Conference Groups Named for Postwar Policy

By Bob Considine
Staff Correspondent International News Service

SAN FRANCISCO, May 1.—The breath-taking job of trying to reshape the world was formally turned over today to little nations which have known intimately the horrors of war, privation, invasion and exploitation.

While the United States, Great Britain and the Soviet stepped modestly to one side, the steering committee of the United Nations' Conference put up the names of Belgium, South Africa, Norway and Venezuela as the four nations to head the most vital conference commissions.

Out of these commissions, and their subcommittees, which also will be studded with the voices of little nations, will come the historic new rules and regulations which seek to reform a world now rid of the tyranny symbolized by Mussolini and Hitler.

LUXEMBOURG GIVEN TASK

To ravaged little Luxembourg goes the task of making up the moral yardstick with which non-members of the United Nations will be measured before they can join this ever-growing family of nations. The appointments were:

Paul Henri Spaak of Belgium, president of the Commission on General Provisions which deals with purposes, principles, membership and secretariat.

Field Marshal General Jan Christian Smuts of South Africa, president of the commission on General Assembly, which deals with creation of that body and the trusteeship problem.

Trygve Lie of Norway, president of the Commission on Security Council, which deals with creation of that body and the broad problem of security.

Carraciilo Parra Perez of Venezuela, president of the Commission on Judicial Organization, which deals with creation of the new World Court.

GROUP CHAIRMEN NAMED

A host of small nations, including the newly admitted Ukraine, were given chairmanships of the

(Continued on Page 4, Cols. 2-3)

Mystery in His Demise

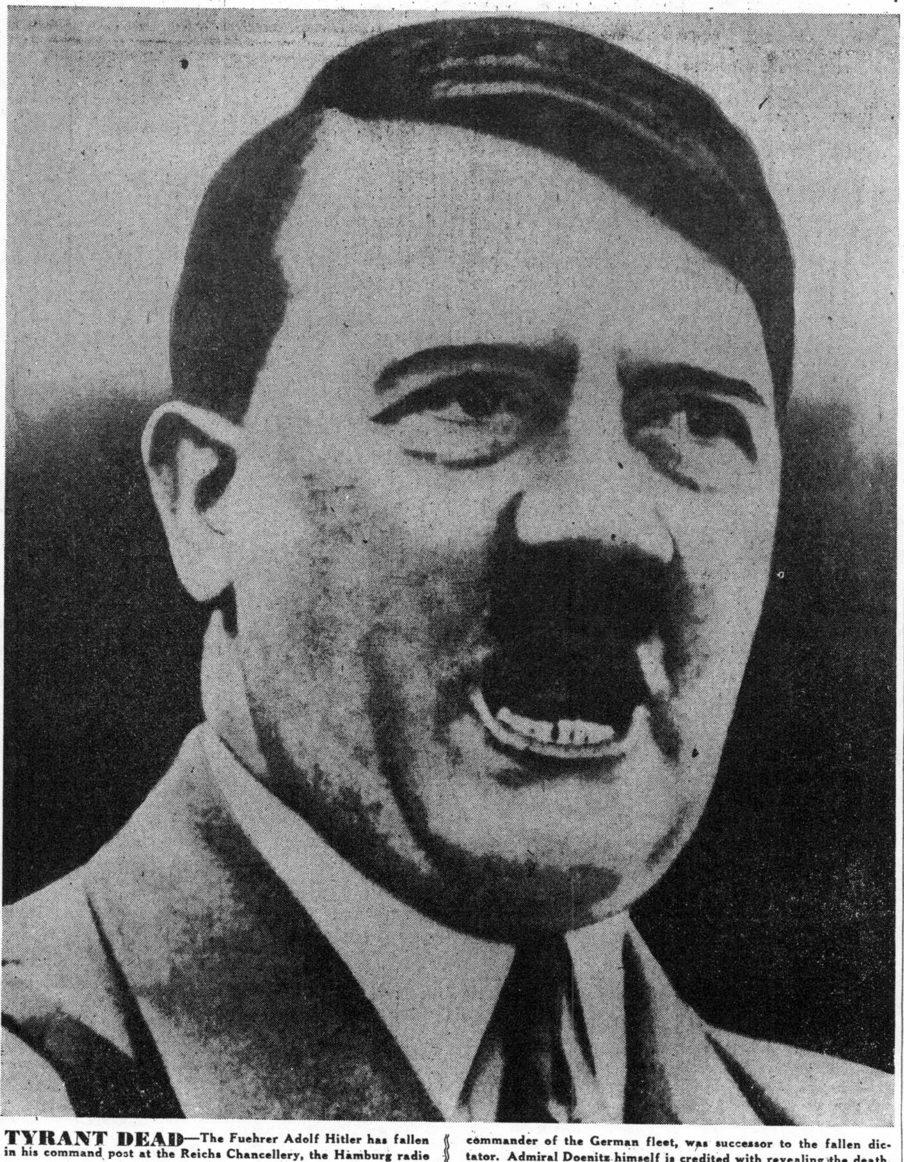

TYRANT DEAD—The Fuehrer Adolf Hitler has fallen in his command post at the Reichs Chancellery, the Hamburg radio announced yesterday. The broadcast said Admiral Karl Doenitz, commander of the German fleet, was successor to the fallen dictator. Admiral Doenitz himself is credited with revealing the death. The manner of Hitler's death was not explained by the new Fuehrer.

Radio Voice Urges People to Strike; Scouts Hero Label

LONDON, May 1.—(By Associated Press).—The Nazi radio at Hamburg said tonight that Adolf Hitler had died this afternoon at his command post in Berlin and had been succeeded by Admiral Karl Doenitz.

The broadcast, recorded by the Associated Press listening post in London, said:

"From the Fuehrer's headquarters it is reported that our Fuehrer, Adolf Hifler, has fallen this afternoon in his command post at the Reich's Chancellery, fighting up to his last breath against Bolshevism."

Doenitz, commander of the German navy, then was introduced by the announcer as 'our new Fuehrer," and declared that Hitler had died "a hero's death."

A ghost voice immediately interrupted, shouting, "This is a lie!"

(The British Broadcasting Company subsequently carried a report that Hifler actually had died of a stroke, rather than in battle against the Russians, N. B. C. in New York said.)

Doenitz said that Hitler personally had appointed him as successor yesterday (April 30).

The 53-year-year-old admiral vowed to continue the war "to save the German people from the advance of the Bolshevist enemy," while "against the English and Americans I have to continue the struggle as far and as long as they hinder me in the prosecution of the struggle against Bolshevism."

Hitler, who was 56 years old on April 20, was lauded by Doenitz as "one of the greatest heroes in German history.

Ghost Voice Breaks in on Talk

Here the ghost voice broke in:

"The greatest of all Fascists!"

"Filled with proud respect and mourning, we lower the banners before him," Doenitz continued.

"His death calls upon us to act," the ghost voice interrupted. "Strike now!"

Doenitz launched into a pep talk to the German people and troops, only to be interrupted again by

War at a Glance

Developments yesterday on the war fronts included the following:

Berlin—German resistance in German capital in final stages. Russians launch final attack on Nazis' Tiergarten fortress.

West Front—American Seventh Army drives within 15 miles of Brenner Pass.

Italy—U. S. troops push into Alps toward Brenner Pass; British drive on Trieste.

Pacific—Tank-paced infantry advance on Okinawa, close in on Firth airfield. Allied invasion of Borneo reported by Australia and Tokyo.

Hitler Is Dead

CAMERA TRACES TYRANT'S CAREER

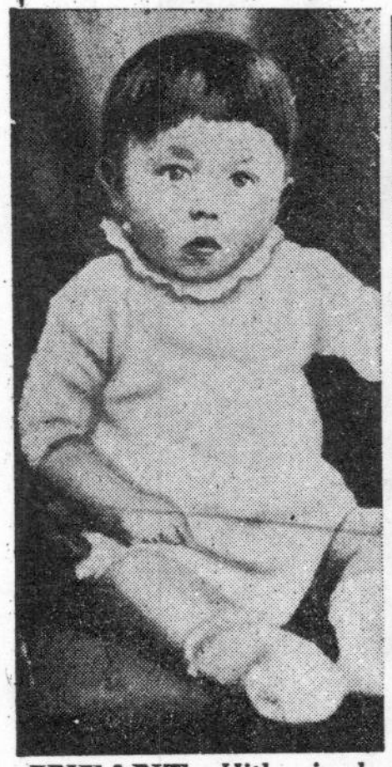

INFANT—Hitler is shown (left) as baby. When World War erupted, he volunteered in the army, was gassed, wounded, emerged a corporal (above right).
—International and Associated Press photos.

1923—A year after Armistice Hitler formed the Nazi Party, which earned the hatred and contempt of the world by its brutal persecution of the Jews. He is shown here in revolt of 1923.
—Picture from International News Photograph Service.

PRISON—Sedition charges followed his revolt. Hitler was sentenced to five years in Landsberg Fortress (above), where he wrote Mein Kampf.
—Picture from International News Photograph Service.

FREED—Paroled in 1925 after serving but 232 days, Hitler picked up where he had been cut off. He reorganized the Nazi Party and its brutality.

DER FUEHRER—Adolf Hitler, Austrian paperhanger whose stormy, war-wreathed career carried him to the dictatorship of Germany, is dead. Founder of the German National Socialist Party, he was born April 20, 1889, at Braunau, Austria. He was responsible for countless atrocities on Jews and war prisoners.

1933: Chancellor

IN POWER—Nazi Party grew rapidly under guidance of Hitler and associates. After several political setbacks he was named German Chancellor on January 30, 1933. He is shown with Von Hindenberg.

'Appeal to Reason'

WARNING—What Hitler termed *"a last appeal to reason"* was made to England in a Reichstag speech on July 19, 1940. *"A world empire would be destroyed,"* he boasted, if England opposed his conquest.

PAPERHANGER TO DICTATOR

MUNICH—The Munich Conference was called in 1938 after Hitler broke the Versailles Treaty. British Prime Minister Neville Chamberlain (right) went home with assurances there would be no war.
—Picture from International News Photograph Service.

BEER HALL—Shortly after this picture was taken on September 8, 1939, a time bomb in pillar behind Hitler destroyed Munich beer hall, Party shrine. Bomb killed several of the Nazi leaders.
—Picture from International News Photograph Service.

PARTNER—Premier Benito Mussolini of Italy was eager to accept partnership offered him by Hitler. Mussolini went down to defeat and public execution.
—Wide World photo

VICTOR—With stunning speed the Germans smashed through the Lowlands, overran France. In the same railway car which saw Germany's 1918 surrender, Fuehrer dictated a peace on June 22, 1940.
—Picture from International News Photograph Service.

ITALY NAZIS SURRENDER

THE WEATHER
Warmer tonight; intermittent rain tonight and Thursday.
Detailed Weather Report Page 23

Read The Baltimore News-Post for complete, accurate war coverage. It is the only Baltimore newspaper possessing the three great wire services—
ASSOCIATED PRESS
INTERNATIONAL NEWS SERVICE
UNITED PRESS

THE BALTIMORE NEWS-POST
AN INDEPENDENT NEWSPAPER
The Largest Evening Circulation in the Entire South

EXTRA
9-STAR WALL ST. CLOSE

VOL. CXLVI.—NO. 149 Entered as second-class matter at Baltimore Postoffice. WEDNESDAY EVENING, MAY 2, 1945 PRICE 3 CENTS

BERLIN FALLS

LONDON, May 2--(A. P.)--Premier Stalin announced tonight the fall of Berlin. The battle for the German capital began April 21. The announcement of the complete conquest of Berlin was made by the Moscow radio which declared that 70,000 Germans were captured in the cleanup of the city.

ROME, May 2---(A. P.).---All German land, sea and air forces in Italy and Southern and Western Austria --- estimated at nearly 1,000,000 troops---were surrendered unconditionally to the Allies today by their commander, with hostilities ordered to cease at 12 noon, G. M. T. (8 A. M., E. W. T.). The capitulation, signed in the presence of Allied officers, including Russians, ended more than one and a half years of the bloody Italian campaign and permits the Allies to advance unopposed to within 10 miles of Adolf Hitler's retreat at Berchtesgaden in Austria.

The surrender document was signed Sunday afternoon at Caserta by representatives of Col. Gen. Heinrich von Vietinghoff-Scheel, German commander in chief in the southwest, and of Obergruppenfuehrer Karl Wolff, supreme commander of the SS and police in Italy.

Field Marshal Sir Harold L. Alexander, supreme Allied commander in the Mediterranean, announced the mass surrender, and in an order of the day to his troops declared: "You have won a victory which has ended in the complete and utter rout of the German armed forces in the Mediterranean" and freed Italy.

The surrender exposed the flank of Col. Gen. Von Lehr, German commander in the Trieste area. British and Yugoslav troops already have linked at the head of the Adriatic northwest of Trieste.

At least 24 Allied divisions in Italy are freed for other duties.

Von Vietinghoff's command includes all Northern Italy to the Isonzo river in the northeast and the Austrian provinces of Vonarlberg, Tyrol, Salzburg and portions of Corinthia and Styria.

Surrendered troops include remnants of 22 German and six Italian Fascist divisions.

The following terms were imposed in the

Continued on Page 2, Column 3.

LONDON, May 2—(A. P.).—The Luxembourg radio said tonight that a German capitulation in Holland was imminent. The radio, which is Allied-controlled, said reports from the Canadian front indicated armistice negotiations had been in progress more than 24 hours.

WITH THE CANADIAN FIRST ARMY, HOLLAND, May 2—(A. P.).—A captured German officer asserted today that Grand Admiral Karl Doenitz had ordered German troops facing the western Allies to cease fighting and to withdraw to the east to oppose the Russians, a Canadian Army source said.

Truman Tells Japs, Germans To Surrender

WASHINGTON, May 2—(A. P.).—President Truman today announced the unconditional surrender of German forces in Italy and said:

"Only folly and chaos can now delay the general capitulation everywhere of the German armies."

In a statement announcing he had sent congratulatory messages to the Allied commanders, the President added:

"Let Japan as well as Germany understand the meaning of these events."

The text of the President's statement:

"The Allied armies in Italy have won the unconditional surrender of German forces on the first European soil to which from the west we carried our arms and our determination.

PART OF GENERAL TRIUMPH

"The collapse of military tyranny in Italy, however, is no victory in Italy alone, but a part of the general triumph we are expectantly awaiting on the whole Continent of Europe. Only folly and chaos can now delay the general capitulation of the everywhere defeated German armies.

"I have dispatched congratulatory messages to the Allied and American officers who led our forces to complete defeat of the Germans in Italy.

"They deserve our praise for the victory. We have the right to be proud of the success of our armies.

GIVES WARNING TO JAPAN

"Let Japan as well as Germany understand the meaning of these events.

"Unless they are lost in fanaticism and are determined upon suicide they must recognize the meaning of the increasingly swifter moving power now ready for the capitulation or the destruction of the so recently arrogant enemies of mankind."

Congratulatory messages were addressed to Gen. Mark W. Clark and British Field Marshal Sir Harold Alexander.

The White House made public the following message the President sent to General Clark:

"On the occasion of the final brilliant victory of the Allied armies in Italy in imposing unconditional surrender upon the enemy, I wish to convey to the American forces under your command, and to you personally, the appreciation and grati-

Continued on Page 2, Column 6.

VERY LATEST NEWS

LATEST BASEBALL SCORES

(N) At Philadelphia—New York, 0; Phila., 0; end 2d.
(N) At Pittsburgh—St. L., 4; Pitts., 1; end 8½, 1st gm.
(A) At New York—New York, 6; Philadelphia, 1; end 4½.
(N) At Brooklyn—Boston, 2; Brooklyn, 1; end 4½.
(A) At Boston—Washington, 0; Boston, 0; end 6th.
(A) At Detroit—Detroit, 2; Chicago, 1; end 3½.

LA CAVA SUES MARY PICKFORD FOR $1,653,750

HOLLYWOOD, May 2—(U.P.).—Mary Pickford, former silent screen star, today was sued for $1,653,750 by Director Gregory La Cava, who charged she backed out of an agreement to have him write, produce and direct the stage play, "One Touch of Venus," for the screen.

VICTOR AND VANQUISHED—Nearly one million Nazi troops became Allied prisoners today when Col. Gen. Heinrich von Vietinghoff-Scheel (left) surrendered his command in Italy and parts of Austria to the Allies. Gen. Mark W. Clark (right), chief of Allied ground forces opposing Germans in Italy, was congratulated by President Truman for his part in the victory.

Switzerland Closes Italian Frontier

BERN, May 2 — (A. P.).—All Swiss frontier exits to Italy have been closed until further notice, the Government announced today, thus suspending the return of fugitives who fled from Northern Italy before the advancing Allied armies. At the same time it was announced that telephone connections between Switzerland and Germany had been broken.

Eisenhower Knew Hitler Was Ill

PARIS, May 2—(A. P.).—General Eisenhower authorized a statement today that Heinrich Himmler had told Swedish Count Folke Bernadotte at a meeting at Luebeck April 24 that Germany was finished and "Hitler was so ill he might already be dead."

The Supreme Headquarters statement added that at the time, more than a week before Hitler's purported hero's death was announced by the Hamburg radio, Himmler had said Hitler "could not be expected to live more than two days longer."

German General Schillenberger who was present at the meeting said Hitler was suffering from a brain hemorrhage, the statement said.

SHAEF said:

"Admiral Doenitz's statement therefore that Hitler met a

Continued on Page 2, Column 1.

NEWS-POST

Temperatures

12 Midn't	48	8 A. M.,	47
1 A. M.,	48	9 A. M.,	50
2 A. M.,	47	10 A. M.,	52
3 A. M.,	47	11 A. M.,	55
4 A. M.,	46	12 Noon,	57
5 A. M.,	45	1 P. M.,	59
6 A. M.,	44	2 P. M.,	59
7 A. M.,	43	3 P. M.,	61

Reds Seize Rostock On Baltic

LONDON, May 2—(A. P.).—Rostock on the Baltic was captured today by the Red Army, Marshal Stalin announced today.

LONDON, May 2—(U. P.).—Marshal Stalin announced tonight that Red armies had captured more than 120,000 German prisoners in the liquidation of a pocket southeast of Berlin, created by the Soviet drive into the capital from the south.

Inside Berlin, Russian forces were storming the ramparts of the Reichschancellery, where the Nazis said Adolf Hitler died yesterday and where evidence of the accuracy of the report might be found.

The German High Command admitted that the handful of survivors in Berlin's garrison had been broken into isolated fragments in the Government district.

HEAVY RESISTANCE

United Press Correspondent Henry Shapiro reported from Moscow that the Soviet siege forces now were fighting for Ger-

Continued on Page 2, Column 4.

Bavarian Rulers In Yanks' Custody

WITH U. S. SEVENTH ARMY, GERMANY, May 2—(U. P.).—Troops of the Forty-fourth Division have taken into protective custody Prince Albert and Princess Marie of Bavaria and their retinue at their hunting lodge northeast of Fussen, it was revealed today.

Iwo Jima Worst Job, Says Writer

DAYTON, May 2—(U. P.).—Marine Lt. Jim Lucas, famed combat correspondent, who stormed five Pacific islands with the leathernecks, said today that the toughest assignment of all was Iwo Jima.

Report Laval, Deat Are In Barcelona

LONDON, May 2—(A. P.).—A Reuters dispatch said today the French collaborationists Pierre Laval, former French chief of government, and Marcel Deat had arrived in Barcelona by plane. Both have been in Germany.

IL POPOLO COMASCO

ORGANO DEL COMITATO DI LIBERAZIONE NAZIONALE DELLA PROVINCIA DI COMO

ANNO I - N. 4 | Como, 3 maggio 1945 | LIRE UNA

LA GUERRA IN ITALIA E' FINITA

Al lavoro

Il nuovo titolo del nostro giornale vuole significare la purificazione dei deviamenti dei traviamenti verificatisi durante la lunga vita del foglio che lo ha preceduto.

Vuol significare la creazione di un organo nuovo vitale, sano, che dal suo stesso titolo interpreti, difenda, quelli che sono gli interessi reali del popolo comasco.

La sua divisa politica sarà caratterizzata dal binomio che costituisce il denominatore comune a tutti i partiti a tutte le concezioni della vita pubblica locale: *democrazia* e *libertà*. E' con e per questa divisa sarà per essere non solo una palestra ove si saggiano e si temprano le opinioni, il pensiero, la interpretazione di interessi veramente generali, ma di queste opinioni, di questi pensieri, di queste interpretazioni diventerà laboratorio, centro di diffusione, mezzo di affinamento in virtù della elaborazione accorta, della discussione aperta, della critica sagace a cui parteciperanno, dovranno partecipare, quei cittadini che avranno qualche cosa da dire intorno ai grandi problemi che non tarderanno a sorgere in tutta la vita sociale, politica, amministrativa, sindacale, industriale, cooperativistica, culturale, assistenziale di questa fervida, alacre, seria, onesta terra comasca.

Democrazia è governo di popolo; è partecipazione del popolo al governo della cosa pubblica, partecipazione che non si esaurisce con un voto preferenziale dato periodicamente in sede di sezione elettorale, ma si completa con lo affiancamento degli uomini che sono avocati ai molteplici compiti; per dare ad essi una collaborazione efficace per rendere loro il compito meno difficile, per addestrarsi ai necessari avvicendamenti; onde non sia scarsità di uomini, onde la vita cittadina sia permeata di scienza e di coscienza per la soluzione dei più svariati problemi a soddisfazione, ripetiamo, degli interessi veramente generali.

Ma democrazia non si concepisce senza il suo attributo inscindibile, essa si aderge sovrana soltanto in virtù della libertà. Solo quando accettiamo la concezione democratica integrata con quella di libertà avremo la democrazia, con tutti gli effetti che si possono attendere da un reggimento volto al benessere di tutti, e cioè alla elevazione fisica e morale, spirituale e intellettiva, politica e sociale del popolo.

Naturalmente anche il concetto di libertà vuol essere affermato nella sua interezza: non basta che il giornalista possa dire la sua opinione dalla sua cattedra o quotidiana o periodica; non basta che l'operaio possa aderire al proprio sindacato, che il cittadino possa appartenere a una propria chiesa, ma deve essere consentito a tutti di manifestare apertamente il proprio pensiero, partecipare nominativamente alla agitazione di un determinato problema senza incorrere, anche se sostiene soluzioni diverse e antagoniste a chi gli da lavoro, a chi lo occupa, nella sanzione economica del suo avanzamento professionale.

Solo con la interpretazione integrale del concetto di libertà si può concepire una vera democrazia, assicurando alla vita pubblica del paese tutte le energie valide, tutte le forze operanti e facilitare il trapasso dalla vita individuale a quella meno angusta, più radiosa, soddisfacente a tutti gli interessi piccoli e grandi che è la vita collettiva!

* * *

Da questi concetti vogliamo derivare il programma del nostro giornale; la consuetudine di vita di questo nostro foglio quotidiano: esso ospiterà tutte le opinioni onestamente professate; polemizzerà con quelle che non fossero conformi al proprio pensiero, o a quello di altri cittadini che non consentissero nelle vedute precedentemente affermate, di guisa che ne sia per correggere le eventuali storture, le deviazioni, cui la vita pubblica locale dovesse subire, intervenendo con una critica spassionata, ardente, illuminata passibile di successive revisioni: aleggiando sempre la costante preoccupazione del bene comune a tutto il nostro paese, alla nostra plaga, alla nostra città.

I partiti avranno i loro organi; speriamo, auguriamo che ogni partito abbia la propria voce periodica, ma ciò non impedisce a questo nostro foglio di accogliere una vasta collaborazione intesa a perseguire i beni morali e materiali che aiutino il nostro popolo a salire, ad affermarsi, a contribuire sagacemente alla ricostruzione di questa, nostra Italia vittima del tradimento, della prepotenza di pochi, e, confessiamolo, della debolezza di molti!

La tremenda quasi trentennale iattura ci sia di scuola per l'avvenire!

Riprendiamo, ognuno di noi al proprio posto, il nostro lavoro, con ferma fede di lottare e di vincere contro un obbrobrioso passato, agitiamo i grandi problemi che mirano alla valorizzazione del lavoro; badiamo di legare questa nostra piccola unità provinciale agli organi che agiscono con la stessa fede al centro, onde non sfuggano al nostro controllo le soluzioni che ci riguardano direttamente perchè anche noi comaschi avremo sempre qualche cosa di interessante da dire nel gran concerto della rinascita italiana!

Se vogliamo reagire veramente a quello che fu il deprecato precedente periodo di storia italiana dobbiamo inaugurare un costume ben diverso e opposto; dobbiamo partecipare tutti alla vita pubblica: tutti dagli abitanti della plaga comense alla cittadinanza comasca: tutti dobbiamo seguire gli svolgimenti della cosa pubblica, dobbiamo controllare gli uomini preposti ad essa, dobbiamo fiancheggiare del nostro consenso, del nostro positivo apporto la Provincia, il Comune, la Camera di commercio, la Cattedra ambulante di agricoltura, la Camera del lavoro, la Cooperazione, la Municipalizzazione, gli istituti di assistenza gli organismi importantissimi votati all'arte, alla cultura.

Tutta questa vasta opera vorrà essere compiuta da nomi nuovi, non ancora alienati, onde debbono avere la strada appianata, l'appoggio incondizionato della cittadinanza per indurre alle soluzioni più sicure, non nel senso locale soltanto, ma in quello più generale degli interessi nazionali e sociali.

Pertanto il «Popolo Comasco» è qui: esso vuol essere qualcosa di più della eco di questo poderoso lavoro; esso, se tutti gli uomini di buona volontà sapranno avvalersi del suo mezzo, nel trinomio di democrazia, libertà, fratellanza, sarà organo efficace per le più alte realizzazioni!

G. BEDETTI

Altri criminali arrestati

La fucilazione del Conte di Toledo, di Borsani, di Colombo e della coppia Valenti-Ferida

MILANO, 2.

Celestino Cabrella, conte di Toledo, capo dell'Ufficio politico della «Muti» torturatore e seviziatore di tanti prigionieri politici, è stato fucilato in piazzale Cinque Giornate. Anche Carlo Borsani, ed il «colonnello» Colombo sono stati giustiziati. Giovanni Preziosi e la moglie si sono uccisi. Asvero Gravelli, ed E. Maria Gray sono in istato d'arresto. Si conferma la morte di don Calcagno.

Anche i torturatori della villetta di via Uccello, gli attori cinematografici Osvaldo Valenti e Luisa Ferida, sono stati giustiziati. L'esecuzione ha avuto luogo in via Poliziano, dove era stato massacrato il patriota Emilio Corassa.

Si è oggi costituito al C.L.N. il dott. Franco Fuscà, famigerato capo censura e stampa presso la ex-Prefettura fascista di Milano.

Sono stati pure arrestati l'ex-vice-comandante della legione autonoma «Muti» Spadoni, il generale Panzera ex-addetto al Ministero Interni del cessato regime, il comandante della legione di Polizia Carraro, il maggiore Barbieri e l'ex-prefetto Ercolani, presidente dell'Ente profughi.

A Inzago, dove avvenne la barbara esecuzione del prof. Di Vona, il distaccamento Volontari della Libertà «Matteotti» di Milano ha preduto alla cattura del famigerato Ermenegildo Biaggioni, di Carlo Ulmar, diplomatico e spia tedesca, nonchè di altri sette imputati.

Berlino completamente occupata dai russi

Il confine cecoslovacco varcato in altri punti - Gli alleati si avvicinano al Brennero - Quasi 3 milioni di prigionieri catturati sul fronte occidentale

LONDRA, 2

Un ordine del giorno del maresciallo Stalin annuncia: «Berlino è in mani sovietiche».

Un precedente ordine del giorno del maresciallo Stalin annunciava che la sacca tedesca a sud-est di Berlino era stata eliminata.

Truppe del I fronte della Russia Bianca hanno occupato altre importanti località. A sud di Berlino le truppe russe continuano a combattere per annientare le truppe tedesche ad est della città. Nella giornata del 30 aprile sono caduti 1400 soldati e ufficiali tedeschi.

Il supplemento del comunicato sovietico informa che durante la giornata di ieri a Berlino sono stati uccisi otto mila tedeschi. A sud est di Berlino gruppi nemici accerchiati continuano a combattere nel disperato tentativo di aprirsi un varco verso est.

Quattro mila tedeschi sono stati uccisi su questo fronte da una sola unità.

Nella Pomerania centrale continua l'avanzata. Le truppe del secondo fronte della Russia Bianca hanno liberato 23 località ed hanno catturato mille vagoni ferroviari e grande quantitativo di materiale vario. Le truppe alleate hanno varcato il confine cecoslovacco in altri punti.

Un comunicato ufficiale informa che la IX Armata si è congiunta con l'esercito russo ad occidente di Wittemberg.

«Mezzi corazzati alleati hanno fatto irruzione attraverso la testa di ponte dell'Elba ad est di Amburgo», annuncia il Comando supremo delle forze armate. Oltre l'Ihr è stata raggiunta Esel. L'autostrada Amburgo-Berlino è stata interrotta.

Nel settore meridionale i mezzi corazzati alleati avanzano incontrando poca resistenza. Monaco è stata completamente occupata. La frontiera austriaca è stata oltrepassata a 16 chilometri ad ovest di Innsbruck. Un'altra località è stata raggiunta. In Austria sono stati liberati numerosi prigionieri e alcuni alti funzionari civili e militari sia francesi che belgi. Tra questi vi sono sette generali francesi. Sono stati compiuti progressi anche verso sud e la frontiera italiana distava oggi ormai solo 56 chilometri.

Da statistiche pubblicate oggi dal Comando supremo delle forze alleate di spedizione risulta che gli alleati hanno catturato sul fronte occidentale, a partire dal 6 giugno 1944, 2.778.238 prigionieri tedeschi. Il giorno 30 aprile le forze alleate hanno catturato sul fronte occidentale 59.739 prigionieri.

Chiusura degli Istituti finanziari e dichiarazione di moratoria

Il gen. Alexander, Comandante in capo delle Armate alleate in Italia, ha emanato il seguente proclama:

Articolo I. — *Chiusura degli Istituti Finanziari.* — Sezione 1. - Chiusura di Istituti. — *Salvo quanto previsto nelle Sezioni 2 e 3 di cui appresso, ogni società, istituto, fondazione, ente o persona nel territorio del Governo Militare che tratti operazioni di accettazione e rimborso di depositi, di prestito, di compravendita di titoli, di cambiavalute, di custodia valori, di assicurazione, o qualsiasi altro genere di operazioni nel campo finanziario, deve immediatamente sospendere tali operazioni tutte o chiudere gli uffici, fatta eccezione di quanto altrimenti stabilito nel presente articolo. La ripresa di dette operazioni e la trattazione futura di affari finanziari saranno soggette, rispettivamente, a quei termini e condizioni ed a quelle restrizioni che il Capo Commissario o un ufficiale da lui autorizzato può di volta in volta prescrivere a mezzo di ordini. Tali ordini possono essere di carattere generico o specifico ed essere notificati con avviso pubblico od a mezzo di comunicazione scritta diretta alla società, istituto, fondazione, ente, o persona interessati.*

Sezione 2. - Istituti bancari. — *Gli Istituti Bancari sono autorizzati a compiere le seguenti operazioni: a) accettare versamenti dovuti agli stessi istituti bancari; b) consentire prelievi in contanti pel pagamento di imposte, tasse e contributi per assicurazione sociale; c) consentire prelievi in contanti, allorchè autorizzati dal rappresentante locale del Governo Militare Alleato; (1) a valere sui conti ufficiali intestati allo Stato, Provincie e Comuni; (3) sui conti intestati agli Istituti di Assicurazione e di Assistenza Sociale; (3) sui conti dei Consorzi; (4) sui conti di quegli uffici parastitali che fossero autorizzati dal Governo Militare Alleato. d) aprire conti ed intraprendere altrimenti nuove operazioni nei confronti delle persone e degli istituti di cui al precedente comma c).*

Sezione 3. - Società ed Istituti commerciali di assicurazione. — *Ogni società, compagnia mutua o di altro tipo, fondazione, ente o persona che tratti operazioni di assicurazione sulla vita o generale può continuare a ricevere e raccogliere quei premi ed altri pagamenti dovuti ed esigibili per effetto di assicurazione relativi ai rischi sulla vita o ai rischi generali, in Italia.*

Sezione 4. - Istituti di Assicurazione e di Assistenza Sociale. — *Ogni società, istituto, fondazione, ente o persona addetto all'amministrazione di un piano di Assicurazione Sociale o di Assistenza Sociale continuerà a ricevere e raccogliere tutti i contributi dovuti in base a tale piano e pagherà tutti i sussidi, le indennità ed ogni altra somma dovuti e liquidabili in base a tale piano, purchè questo fosse legalmente in vigore prima dell'8 settembre 1943. Fanno eccezione i pagamenti degli assegni famigliari e dei sussidi militari alle persone a carico di coloro che si trovano in Germania od in altro territorio nemico od occupato dal nemico e dei quali si sappia che collaborano col nemico.*

Articolo II. — *Moratoria.* - Sezione 1. - Obbligazioni colpite. — *Con il presente proclama viene dichiarata una moratoria nei confronti di tutti i debiti, rivendicazioni, depositi ed ogni altra obbligazione che richiedono pagamento in moneta. Il Capo Commissario od un ufficiale da lui autorizzato può con ordine generico o specifico sospendere o porre termine alla suddetta moratoria nei confronti di una qualunque obbligazione o tipo di obbligazione ovvero in una qualsiasi parte del territorio.*

Sezione 2. - Obbligazioni non colpite. — *La moratoria imposta con il presente proclama non si applica a: a) qualsiasi obbligazione colpita dalla detta moratoria allorchè l'importo totale dovuto e da liquidarsi per effetto di tale obbligazione non ecceda le lire 5.000, fatta eccezione delle obbligazioni derivanti da operazioni finanziarie secondo quanto specificato nell'Art. 1 del presente proclama; b) qualsiasi pagamento la cui effettuazione sia richiesta o consentita dalla Sezione 2, Sezione 3 e Sezione 4 dell'Art. 1 del presente proclama.*

Sezione 3. - Effetti della Moratoria. — *Durante il periodo della moratoria le obbligazioni colpite dal presente proclama sono sospese e prorogate per lo stesso periodo. Nessun diritto o potere deve in alcun momento essere esercitato nei confronti di tali obbligazioni unicamente per inadempimenti derivanti dal presente proclama. Salva la proroga accordata con il presente proclama, tali obbligazioni avranno tutta piena forza ed efficacia al termine di tale moratoria.*

La moratoria non si applica alle obbligazioni contratte in qualunque località nel Territorio Militare Alleato dopo la data di entrata in vigore del presente proclama nella località stessa.

La resa di tutte le forze nazi-fasciste che ancora resistevano in territorio italiano

Circa un milione di uomini ha lasciate le armi - I termini della resa - Un o.d.g. di Alexander - La firma dell'accordo nel palazzo reale di Caserta

MILANO, 2.

Le truppe tedesche al comando del generale Heinrich von Viettenghof si sono arrese incondizionatamente al Maresciallo Alexander, comandante supremo alleato del teatro di guerra nel Mediterraneo.

Il maresciallo Alexander ha diretto alle truppe tedesche che si trovano ancora in Italia la seguente comunicazione: «Il comandante in capo del gruppo d'armate sud-occidentale tedesche, colonnello generale Heinrich von Viettenghof, si è arreso con tutte le truppe tedesche e fasciste sotto i suoi ordini. Egli ha emesso ordini in questo senso, che devono essere ubbiditi immediatamente: «Dovete cessare il fuoco immediatamente e rimanere dove siete in attesa di ulteriori ordini».

L'invito di Graziani alle truppe ai suoi ordini

MILANO, 2.

Il maresciallo Rodolfo Graziani comandante generale delle forze armate italiane ha inviato un appello diretto alle truppe fasciste e tedesche sotto il suo comando, nel quale appello è detto che in questa battaglia finale della campagna d'Italia le truppe tutte si sono comportate con l'abituale disciplina e valore assoluto in condizioni inferiori rispetto al nemico. L'appello prosegue dicendo: «E' giunto il tempo in cui qualsiasi ulteriore resistenza sarebbe inutile, inumana e, per quanto riguarda me, criminale. Per alcuni giorni l'alleato comando germanico non ha diramato ordini».

A conclusione nell'appello è detto che Graziani il 29 aprile 1945 ha firmato una resa incondizionata e che questo ordine è stato portato a conoscenza delle truppe fasciste e tedesche a mezzo di volantini lanciati da aerei.

Le condizioni imposte

LONDRA, 2.

La zona sud-occidentale al comando del generale von Viettenghoff, comprende tutta l'Italia settentrionale fino all'Isonzo, le provincie austriache, del Farenborg, del Tirolo, di Salisburgo, e parte della Carinzia e della Stiria.

Si ritiene che le forze tedesche che si sono arrese, comprese le poche truppe che ancora resistevano a tergo delle linee, ammontano a circa un milione di uomini. Le unità arresesi comprendevano i resti di 22 divisioni tedesche e di 6 divisioni neofasciste.

Sono stati imposti i seguenti termini:

1. - *Resa a discrezione da parte del comandante in capo del fronte sud-occidentale tedesco di tutte le forze di terra, di mare e dell'aria che siano sotto il suo diretto comando o comunque da lui controllate, al comandante supremo delle forze alleate del teatro di operazioni del Mediterraneo.*

2. - *Cessazione di ogni atto di ostilità in terra, in mare e in aria da parte delle forze tedesche per le ore 14, ora italiana, del giorno 2 maggio 1945.*

3. - *Cessazione di ogni movimento logistico e immediato disarmo delle forze tedesche di terra, di mare e dell'aria.*

4. - *Obbligo da parte del comandante tedesco del fronte sud-occidentale di porre in esecuzione gli ulteriori ordini emessi dal comandante supremo delle forze alleate sul teatro di guerra del Mediterraneo.*

5. - *Ogni inadempienza agli ordini e mancata esecuzione di fatto dei medesimi darà luogo a quegli atti che ne conseguono legittimamente secondo le leggi e gli usi accettati di guerra.*

L'elogio ai soldati alleati

L'atto di resa porta poi la pattuizione che esso è indipendente da un più generale atto di resa che sarà imposto dalle nazioni unite o in loro nome.

Stasera il comandante in capo delle forze alleate del Mediterraneo, maresciallo Alexander, ha diramato ai soldati, ai marinai e agli aviatori al suo comando uno speciale ordine del giorno così concepito:

«Dopo questi due anni di duri e continui combattimenti vi ergete oggi a vincitori della campagna italiana. Avete conseguito una vittoria che si è conclusa nella rotta completa delle forze nemiche operanti nel teatro di guerra del Mediterraneo. Oggi i resti di quello che era un giorno un orgoglioso esercito hanno deposto le armi di fronte a voi; quasi un milione di uomini con armi e equipaggiamenti a voi si sono arresi.

Potete essere ben fieri di questa grande e vittoriosa campagna che sarà tramandata nella storia come una delle più importanti e delle meglio riuscite che mai siano state combattute. Nessun elogio è sufficiente per esaltare il trionfo che voi, soldati e marinai, aviatori e lavoratori delle forze unite in Italia avete conseguito. Vi sono grato e dichiaro che la mia ammirazione per voi non conosce confini. E' eguagliata soltanto dall'orgoglio che ho di essere il vostro comandante in capo».

Vivi applausi hanno salutato Churchill allorchè oggi alla Camera dei Comuni ha dato notizia della resa dei tedeschi in Italia. «*Ritengo fermamente* - ha dichiarato il primo ministro - *che tale resa costituisca un primato della guerra. Non potrà mancare di facilitare ancora più lo svolgersi di quegli eventi che noi tanto attendiamo*». Churchill ha rilevato che le forze alleate in Italia comprendono formazioni appartenenti a varie nazionalità, fra cui formazioni italiane.

Il presidente Truman ha inviato messaggi di congratulazione al maresciallo Alexander e al generale Clark in occasione della resa di tutte le forze armate tedesche che operano in Italia e in Austria. Nel messaggio indirizzato al maresciallo Alexander il presidente Truman così si esprime: «*Porto a voi, a mio nome e a nome del popolo degli Stati Uniti, le congratulazioni più sincere per il grande successo conseguito dall'esercito di terra, del mare e del cielo al vostro comando. La vittoria è frutto della costanza e della perseveranza delle truppe alleate, durante i molti mesi di una tre le più difficili campagne di questa guerra*».

Il corrispondente della «B. B. C.», che ha assistito insieme ad alcuni inviati alleati alla firma del documento di resa delle forze tedesche al Quartier generale del maresciallo Alexander nel palazzo reale di Caserta, così scrive:

Drammatica attesa

«Mancano pochi minuti alle due allorchè entrammo nello ufficio del capo di stato maggiore del maresciallo Alexander. La stanza era evidentemente predisposta per una riunione. Sul tavolo brillavano un massiccio calamaio di cristallo e una penna. Attorno numerosi candelabri, e la luce poneva in risalto numerose carte geografiche che tapezzavano le pareti. Di esse una carta dell'Italia settentrionale, una pianta topografica di Vienna e una carta d'Europa. In un angolo una macchina cinematografica da presa e un gruppo di fotografi ufficiali intenti a completare i preparativi.

Negli ultimi istanti di drammatica attesa ricordo di avere notato un ufficiale americano entrare nervosamente ed accertarsi che i calamai fossero pieni d'inchiostro.

Alle 2.5 esatte la porta di fronte a me si aprì ed entrarono 16 ufficiali superiori alleati condotti dal capo di stato maggiore del maresciallo Alexander, generale Morgan. Questi si portò ad un'estremità del tavolo e i rappresentanti britannici ed americani della marina, dell'esercito e dell'aviazione, si disposero ai suoi lati. Alla destra del generale Morgan, un generale russo e il suo aiutante da campo spiccavano con le loro caratteristiche uniformi; rappresentavano il governo sovietico presso la commissione alleata in Italia. In piedi, i muscoli della faccia tesi, in perfetto silenzio, i rappresentanti alleati attendevano.

Tre minuti dopo, alle 2 e 8 minuti, da una porta alla mia sinistra entrarono due ufficiali tedeschi: un tenente colonnello a nome del generale Viettenghoff, comandante in capo delle forze armate nella zona sud-occidentale, e un maggiore, a nome del generale Wolff, comandante delle SS. nelle zone retrostanti e plenipotenziario del nazionalsocialismo per tutta la zona, vale a dire l'Italia settentrionale e l'Austria occidentale.

Vestivano gli abiti civili. Entrarono, sbatterono i tacchi, fecero un inchino, quindi si misero rigidamente sull'attenti all'estremità opposta del tavolo.

Il generale Morgan fece un passo avanti e rivolse loro la parola: «Mi consta che siete pronti a firmare le condizioni di resa e che siete forniti dei necessari poteri. E' esatto? Il colonnello tedesco con un rapido inchino rispose «Ja». Il generale Morgan ripetè la domanda al maggiore delle S.S. che a sua volta rispose «Ja».

Come avvenne la firma

Dopo di che il capo di stato maggiore alleato proseguì: «Sono autorizzato a firmare l'accordo di resa a nome del comandante supremo, maresciallo Alexander. Esso avrà effetto a partire dal mezzogiorno, ora del meridiano di Greewinch, del 2 maggio. Vi prego di apporre le vostre firme. Quindi firmerò io».

Dopo un breve scambio di precisazioni sulle formalità della resa, i rappresentanti tedeschi, senza riuscire a nascondere il loro nervosismo, si sedettero e firmarono alla luce dei lampi di magnesio delle macchine fotografiche. Durante la cerimonia il gruppetto degli ufficiali alleati era in piedi. Gli uomini erano completamente impassibili.

Dopo la firma il colonnello tedesco si lasciò cadere la penna dalla mano. I documenti vennero quindi portati alla estremità opposta del tavolo, dove vennero firmati dal generale Morgan.

Esaurita quest'ultima formalità il generale si alzò e rivolgendosi ai rappresentanti tedeschi disse: «Di questo documento consegnerò a voi tre copie, una delle quali in tedesco. Le altre rimangono a me per il comandante supremo e i governi alleati».

Dopo una breve pausa aggiunse: «Vi ringrazio signori e vi prego di ritirarvi». Al che i due tedeschi si inchinarono seccamente, sbatterono i tacchi ancora una volta e uscirono lentamente. La cerimonia era durata 17 minuti.

Von Runstedt catturato

LONDRA, 2.

Si annuncia dal quartiere della 7.a armata che truppe americane hanno fatto prigioniero il maresciallo von Runsted già comandante supremo dell'esercito tedesco sul fronte occidentale. Il maresciallo von Runstedt è stato catturato in un ospedale, a 40 chilometri a sud di Monaco.

Inaudita vigliaccheria di soldati tedeschi

MILANO, 2

Il 26 corrente una colonna della Flac tedesca in ritirata, per coprirsi dai patrioti, si faceva precedere da un gruppo di donne e di bambini catturati durante la sua marcia.

Le macchine e i pezzi erano trainati da buoi, in mancanza di carburante. La colonna era circondata dalle truppe alleate presso Goito e catturata.

L'inumazione del cadavere di Mussolini

MILANO, 2.

I cadaveri, di Mussolini e degli altri fascisti giustiziati dai patrioti sono stati tratti stamane alla Camera Mortuaria Municipale di Milano per il riconoscimento.

Il cadavere di Mussolini è stato sepolto ieri sera senza cerimonie, insieme a quelli degli altri 177 fascisti giustiziati.

La morte di Hitler dovuta a emorragia cerebrale

BERNA, 2

Le radio del mondo intero hanno trasmesso e commentato la notizia della morte del cancelliere del Reich, Hitler, spentosi nel pomeriggio d'ieri a Berlino in circostanze non ancora note. Da fonte germanica si è dichiarato che Hitler è morto al suo posto di comando un giorno dopo avere nominato suo successore l'ammiraglio Doenitz.

L'annuncio della morte di Hitler è stato diramato dalla radio di Amburgo, al microfono della quale ha parlato immediatamente dopo l'ammiraglio Doenitz, successore del cancelliere, il quale ha dichiarato in particolare che assume la direzione del popolo germanico con il fermo proposito di continuare la lotta contro il bolscevismo fino a quando l'esercito e le famiglie tedesche dell'est potranno considerarsi al riparo dalla schiavitù e dalla distruzione. La Germania continuerà a combattere anche contro gli alleati occidentali perchè questi ostacolano la lotta dei germanici contro il bolscevismo».

Dopo l'annuncio della morte di Hitler nessuna nuova notizia è pervenuta circa la situazione interna tedesca. La notizia della morte è accolta con scetticismo a Londra, Washington e Mosca, dove la scomparsa del cancelliere in un momento tanto drammatico della guerra appare misteriosa e alquanto sospetta.

Il giornale svedese *Dagens Niheter* dedica alla morte di Hitler il suo articolo di fondo nel quale, sotto il titolo «Una buona notizia», è detto fra l'altro: «Uno spirito infernale è ripiombato donde era venuto. La maledizione di milioni di uomini lo accompagna».

L'*United Press* comunica che al Quartier Generale di Eisenhower è stato annunciato ufficialmente che il conte Bernadotte si è incontrato con Himmler a Lubecca e che Himmler e un altro generale tedesco hanno dichiarato che Hitler è stato colpito da emorraggia cerebrale e che forse non sarebbe sopravvissuto 48 ore. La dichiarazione di Eisenhower aggiunge che Himmler ha detto: «La Germania è finita». La dichiarazione afferma inoltre che l'asserzione di Doenitz, secondo cui Hitler sarebbe morto da eroe al suo posto di combattimento a Berlino, è in contraddizione con quanto hanno affermato Himmler e il generale tedesco. La dichiarazione osserva poi che il tentativo di Himmler di gettare la discordia tra i tre alleati non avrà alcun effetto.

Il corrispondente dell'*Associated Press* riferisce che la notizia della morte di Hitler si è diffusa ieri come un fulmine nelle praterie, in tutte le città, cittadine e villaggi della Germania. «Non sono state sparse lagrime» - dice il corrispondente. In obbedienza al coprifuoco ordinato dagli alleati, i tedeschi avrebbero dovuto dormire nelle loro case, ma il drammatico annuncio della morte del loro capo ha fermato tutti i civili alle porte e alle finestre delle proprie case, dove si sono svolte animate conversazioni».

Sulla morte di Hitler il corrispondente del *Times* scrive oggi: «Pochi uomini di tutta la storia e nessuno dei tempi moderni è stato la causa di così grandi sofferenze umane quanto Hitler, morto ieri a Berlino». Il *Daily Telegraph* scrive: «E' bene chiarire e ricordare che, comunque Hitler sia morto, non è stato l'amore per il popolo tedesco ad occupare gli ultimi giorni della sua vita, poichè in quei giorni l'ha portato a più completa rovina. E' probabile che la morte di Hitler servirà a togliere agli ultimi fanatici ogni velleità di continuare la lotta».

La radio di Amburgo ha annunciato che il nuovo cancelliere del Reich ha nominato ministro degli esteri il conte von Crosik.

La conferenza di San Francisco

Dichiarazioni del Maresciallo Smuts

LONDRA, 2.

«L'attuale conferenza può rappresentare una pietra miliare nelle relazioni internazionali e nelle collaborazioni delle nazioni verso la pace e la sicurezza mondiale»: così ha dichiarato il maresciallo Smuts nel corso dell'odierna seduta plenaria delle «nazioni unite», avanzando la proposta che nel preambolo della carta delle «nazioni unite» venga inserita una dichiarazione dei diritti umani e della fede comune che ha sostenuto i popoli alleati nella loro aspra e prolungata lotta per rivendicare questi diritti e questa fede».

Proseguendo, il maresciallo Smuts ha affermato che tale organizzazione mondiale deve tenere conto delle esperienze e delle lezioni della Società delle nazioni. Appare invece sempre più evidente che le misure conciliative non sono sufficienti, per cui le guerre devono essere prevenute a tutti i costi, e per tale scopo non bastano le mezze misure.

Concludendo, Smuts ha reso omaggio al defunto presidente Roosevelt e ha dichiarato: «In memoria sua e dei suoi servigi morali che questi ha reso al mondo, dobbiamo fare di questa conferenza un monumento degno del suo nome!».

Il comitato direttivo della conferenza di San Francisco ha affidato a quattro piccole nazioni la presidenza delle quattro commissioni principali, e cioè al Belgio la presidenza della commissione dei provvedimenti di carattere generale, al Sud-Africa della commissione per l'assemblea generale, alla Norvegia della commissione per il consiglio di sicurezza e al Venezuela della commissione per le procedure legali. Anche le presidenze dei comitati sono state attribuite a nazioni minori.

Il portavoce della delegazione sovietica alla conferenza di San Francisco ha dichiarato che i delegati dell'Ucraina e della Russia Bianca sono attesi per oggi.

I delegati arabi hanno dichiarato che la lega degli Stati arabi è in perfetto accordo con quanto previsto dalla proposta di Dombarton Oaks circa gli accordi regionali.

Il primo maggio celebrato nella Città del Vaticano

MILANO, 2.

Lo Stato della Città del Vaticano ha celebrato la giornata del primo maggio. Numerose persone sono intervenute alla messa dopo la quale padre Rolandi ha parlato sulla concezione cristiana del lavoro.

THE WEATHER
Occasional light showers and cooler tonight; Saturday partly cloudy, little warmer in afternoon.
Detailed Weather Report Page 29

Read The Baltimore News-Post for complete, accurate war coverage. It is the only Baltimore newspaper possessing the three great wire services—
ASSOCIATED PRESS
INTERNATIONAL NEWS SERVICE
UNITED PRESS

THE BALTIMORE NEWS-POST
AN INDEPENDENT NEWSPAPER
The Largest Evening Circulation in the Entire South

EXTRA
EIGHT STAR

VOL. CXLVI.—NO. 151 Entered as second-class matter at Baltimore Postoffice. FRIDAY EVENING, MAY 4, 1945 PRICE 3 CENTS

NAZIS SURRENDER IN N. W. GERMANY, HOLLAND DENMARK—EISENHOWER

Bulletin

PARIS, May 4--(A. P.).--General Eisenhower announced today that all enemy forces in Holland and Northwestern Germany and Denmark, including Helgoland and the Frisian Islands, have surrendered effective at 8 A. M. (2 A. M., Eastern war time) tomorrow.

Reds Mop Up Wehrmacht In Berlin

MOSCOW, May 4—(A. P.).—Unit after unit of the German Wehrmacht surrendered today along the still lengthy Russian front as weary Nazi troops anticipated a general capitulation, and dispatches from Berlin said the prisoner toll there stood at about 345,000 this morning, with hundreds of Germans giving up hourly.

Front dispatches said Nazi officers indicated they had "performed their duty" to Adolf Hitler and that their fates were now in their own hands.

From almost every sector of the front German regulars and Volksturmers, some sullen and arrogant, but most tired and depressed, were lined up for the long journey eastward.

CAN'T COUNT THEM

The Germans were being rounded up in such large numbers—sometimes in complete units—that it was difficult to get an accurate count, and it will probably be several days before complete figures will be issued for current captures.

In Berlin Russian forces were working day and night to restore the German capital's gas, water, light and communications systems to working order.

There was still no further word concerning Adolf Hitler, his Prop-

Continued on Page 2, Column 4.

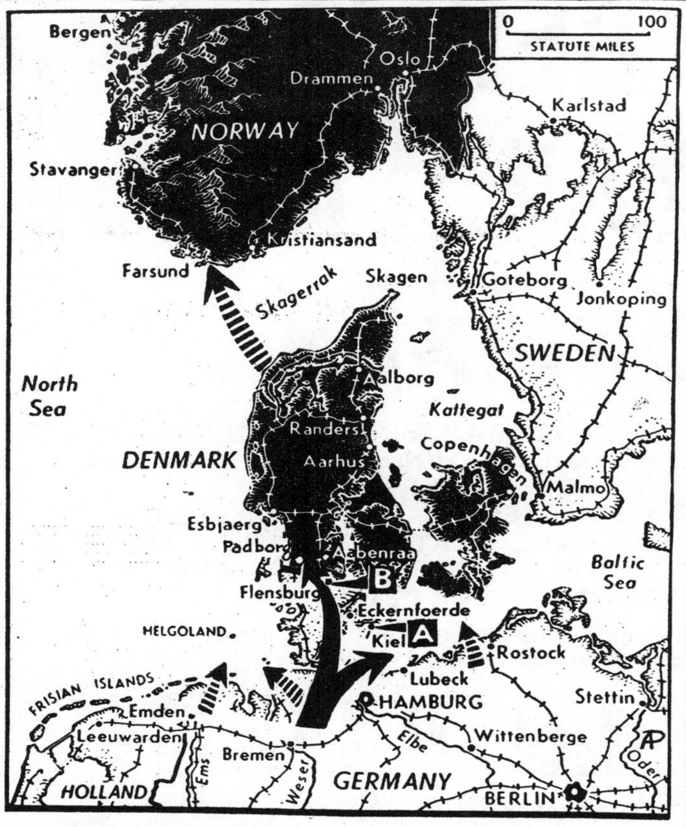

NAZIS FLEE BRITISH—The British Second Army, sweeping up northern remnants of German troops, smashed into Denmark today. Nazi radios said resistance in Denmark ended as Tommy units crossed the border and occupied Padborg (double arrow). At the same time declared two naval bases, Kiel (A) and Flensburg (B), open cities. Small broken arrows to sea show where fleeing Nazis were trapped by Allied planes in what was described as "Dunkerque in reverse." Large broken arrow indicates possible retreat route to occupied Norway. Black areas are German held.

Nazis In Denmark Out Of Control

PARIS, May 4—(U. P.).—Nazi spokesmen announced the end of German resistance in Holland today and negotiations for a general German surrender were reported under way in Denmark, where Marshal Sir Bernard L. Montgomery and the new Nazi Fuehrer, Admiral Karl Doenitz, were reported negotiating.

BRITISH SECOND ARMY ADVANCE H. Q., May 4—(U. P.).—The German Army facing the British—which includes the German High Command—is out of control.

The Germans are throwing away their arms by the hundreds of thousands. They are refusing to fight, trying to get home, or struggling to give themselves up as prisoners.

The highest German staff officers recognize the situation and admit it.

ADMIT FALL

The Germans admit the fall of Denmark. We are simply waiting for the final word which will confirm what the German leaders say.

With their army—or what is left of it—completely out of control, the German leaders cannot fight on if they want to. And they say so.

This is the last of resistance opposite the British Second Army. The war in Holland and Denmark also is near its close. (The German-controlled Oslo radio reported the cease-fire order had been

Continued on Page 2, Column 2.

Fifth, Seventh Armies Join In Brenner Pass

PARIS, May 4—(I. N. S.).—The Paris newspaper France Soir reported in a Stockholm dispatch today that the German high seas fleet, including the majority of its remaining submarines, has surrendered after indicating its positions to the British Admiralty.

PARIS, May 4—(A. P.).—The British drive toward Denmark halted abruptly today just short of the Kiel canal in Germany, possibly to await the surrender of Nazi troops garrisoned in that kingdom.

The American Seventh Army joined the Fifth Army 10 miles deep in Italy in the Brenner Pass after capturing Innsbruck and Salzburg. The American Third Army besieged Linz, invaded Bohemia, outflanked Pilsen and the Skoda works and neared a junction with the Russians west of Vienna, which would bisect the southern German pocket.

A wholly unconfirmed enemy broadcast said hostilities had ceased in Western Holland, where a truce was in effect allowing the Canadian First Army to feed Dutch civilians through German lines.

The Kiel canal is 38 miles south of the Danish peninsula. Earlier Swedish reports said that the British Second Army—which captured 500,000 of the routed enemy in the last two days—had invaded that kingdom. The Germans themselves proclaimed Kiel and Flensburg open cities and indicated their fall was near.

What Germans survived the catastrophe in the north were attempting a harried land and sea flight toward the uncertain refuge of Norway.

JOIN AT VIPITENO

The Seventh Army of Lt. Gen. Alexander M. Patch joined Lt. Gen. Lucian Truscott's victorious Fifth Army at Vipiteno in the Brenner Pass ten miles south of the snow-heaped Italian frontier.

The Seventh Army captured Innsbruck, capital of the Tyrol, and fourth largest city of Austria. The Cactus (One Hundred and Third) Division received a tumultuous ovation there last night before rolling on south through the Brenner Pass to join the Fifth Army in Italy.

Half a million Germans had surrendered in 48 hours to the British Second Army and at least three attached American divisions in the north.

The Germans who had not sur-

Continued on Page 2, Column 1.

HITLER'S BODY STILL MYSTERY

MOSCOW, May 4—(A. P.).—The Chancellery of the Third Reich in the Wilhelmstrasse has failed to yield the body of Hitler and now the building is burning, a Red Star dispatch from the German capital said today.

Nazi Radio Tells People Be Calm

LONDON, May 4—(A. P.).—An appeal to the German people to keep calm "in the last hours of the war" was broadcast today by the Wilhelmshaven radio, one of the last Continental transmitters still in Nazi hands.

Haw Haw Seized, British Speculate

LONDON, May 4—(U. P.).—Britain speculated today that William Joyce, the Lord Haw Haw of the German radio, may have been captured by the Allies.

Temperatures

12 Midn't	51	7 A. M.,	50
1 A. M.,	51	8 A. M.,	51
2 A. M.,	51	9 A. M.,	52
3 A. M.,	52	10 A. M.,	52
4 A. M.,	51	11 A. M.,	53
5 A. M.,	50	12 Noon,	54
6 A. M.,	49	1 P. M.,	55

VERY LATEST NEWS

NEPHEW OF LAST CZAR HELD BY YANKS

WITH U. S. THIRD ARMY IN AUSTRIA, May 4—(U. P.).—Prince Nikita of Russia, nephew of the last Czar, who has been racing westward from the Soviet advance, was held by the Eleventh Armored Division today as a "misplaced person."

TRUMAN GETS PLEDGE FROM U. S. BUSINESS

WASHINGTON, May 4—(I. N. S.).—President Truman received a pledge of complete cooperation today from the United States Chamber of Commerce and American business as a whole.

Bulletins

WITH U. S. SEVENTH ARMY, May 4—(I. N. S.). Nazi Field Marshal Karl Gerd Von Runstedt today blamed Germany's military defeat upon overwhelming Allied air power which paralyzed the Wehrmacht's mobility of transport and supplies.

STOCKHOLM, May 4—(A. P.).—Aftonbladet quoted reports from Sweden's west coast today that three or four German troop transports have been observed daily moving northward toward Norway from the direction of Denmark under guard of submarines. The transports were described as 10,000-ton craft, each capable of carrying from 7,000 to 8,000 men.

MALMO, Sweden, May 4—(U. P.).—Reports from Denmark said today that German troops in several barracks in Copenhagen mutinied yesterday, but were suppressed. Four hundred German sailors who mutinied at Aabenraa harbor were imprisoned, another report said.

'Big 3' Near Accord On Poland

By WILLIAM K. HUTCHINSON
International News Service Staff Correspondent.

SAN FRANCISCO, May 4.—Highest authoritative sources at the San Francisco conference are expressing new hopes today that the "Big Three" will announce a settlement of the Polish problem within 72 hours to make Poland the fiftieth United Nation.

The "Big Three" deliberations have entered their final phases. It is now or never.

All involved factions are aware that failure to solve this problem may endanger Allied plans for occupation of fallen Germany and

Continued on Page 2, Column 6.

NEWS-POST

Stampede To Surrender:

Nazis Swim, Use Rafts In Flight

LONDON, May 4—(A. P.).—German soldiers, surrendering to American and British forces by the thousand in a panicky effort to avoid falling into the hands of the Russians, have created a serious problem for Allied authorities charged with keeping them caged and fed.

Front dispatches said German officers and men were virtually racing each other to what they evidently consider the safety of American lines. London papers declared that the British and American armies already had taken so many German prisoners that Britain's facilities for feeding and housing them had become inadequate.

Associated Press War Correspondent Wes Gallagher reported from the Ninth Army front on Elbe river that the Germans were swarming across the stream, paddling in makeshift rafts or even swimming, in order to surrender. "And the doughboys," Gallagher wrote, "can't do anything but accept them."

The Daily Express said that more than 3,000,000 Germans had been taken prisoner since D-Day and that under the original agreement Britain must look after half of them, regardless of whether they were captured by British or American troops.

The paper said the British Government had asked the United States to take a large proportion of the captured Germans because all British prison camps are full and the food problem is acute.

Daily Mirror
MAY 5
Saturday, May 5, 1945
No. 12,909 ONE PENNY
Registered at G.P.O. as a Newspaper.

Fighting ends on British front

TRIUMPH DAY FOR MONTY'S MEN

Field - Marshal Montgomery, who, with his troops, has now reached Triumph Day. Yesterday a great German rival, the captured Field-Marshal Von Rundstedt, declared that Monty was Britain's greatest General. "He proved it in Libya, Tunisia, Sicily, Italy and again since D-Day," added Rundstedt.

ALL HUN FORCES SURRENDER IN N.W. GERMANY, HOLLAND AND DENMARK

AT 8 A.M. TODAY THE GERMAN FORCES THROUGHOUT NORTH-WEST GERMANY, IN HOLLAND AND IN DENMARK ARE LAYING DOWN THEIR ARMS.

IT IS TRIUMPH DAY FOR FIELD-MARSHAL MONTGOMERY AND HIS MEN. THEY HAVE BEATEN THE HUN TO HIS KNEES ALONG THE WHOLE OF THEIR FRONT, AND HAVE WRITTEN "FINIS" TO THE GERMAN REICH.

Today brings salvation to the starving millions of Holland, and joyous freedom to Denmark, crushed under the Nazi jack boot for five long years.

The surrender puts more than 200,000 German troops out of the war—about 110,000 in Denmark and about 100,000 strung out between Amsterdam and Wilhelmshaven.

Only two major centres of German resistance now remain—in Norway and the shattered redoubt in Austria and Czechoslovakia.

In addition, the Germans still hold pockets on the west coast of France, the Channel Islands, Dunkirk, some Polish coastal territory, strips of East Prussia and Latvia, and a few pockets in the south.

That is all that is left to the enemy.

The surrender includes Heligoland and the Frisian Islands.

It includes, too, all the naval ships in those areas.

It is an unconditional battlefield surrender involving all forces facing the 21st Army Group on their northern and western fronts.

Negotiations had been in progress between Montgomery and the German commander in Denmark since Thursday when the British

NO DOENITZ

Eleventh Armoured Division broke through the enemy's north and the Second Army took half a million prisoners.

The reports from Montgomery's headquarters reveal that Admiral Doenitz was not present for the negotiations which led up to the surrender.

But Admiral Von Friedeberg, Commander-in-Chief of the German Navy, who succeeded to that position when Doenitz became "Fuehrer" led the surrender party, together with his Chief of Staff, Rear Admiral Wagner, and General Dietel.

What has happened to Doenitz, Himmler, and members of the German General Staff who were known to be in the Northern German area is unrevealed.

Only one thing can be assumed—that they have not allowed themselves to be caught by the Russians.

Montgomery himself read out the terms of surrender to the German representatives.

The Germans signed in turn, and then Montgomery signed on behalf of General Eisenhower.

With only one big German city, Dresden, still remaining in their possession, and with shaky control over only 3,600 square miles of territory out of the total of 220,000 which comprises Germany, the remnants of the German Army elsewhere faces complete annihilation or surrender.

Fall of the German armies in the north leaves the British Second, Canadian First and the American First and Ninth Armies idle, to be hurled into an amphibious invasion of Norway or against the remains of the redoubt in Austria and Czechoslovakia.

The Czech Foreign Office two days ago reported an offer by a Nazi delegation to negotiate with Britain and the United States the with-

Continued on Back Page

7,000,000 are now saved from famine

SEVEN million people facing death from starvation will be saved in Holland by the German surrender.

Famine and flood following on the Nazi occupation had threatened the country with the greatest disaster of its history.

Callously the Germans disclaimed all responsibility for feeding or letting supplies reach the populace and the Nazis raided wholesale and retail stocks, removing everything.

So critical was the position that the RAF have been "bombing" starving Rotterdam with food, and crowds went frantic with joy as precious supplies were dropped by waves of Lancasters only a few days ago.

Flooding by the Germans put nearly a fifth of the total arable and pasture land under water and demolition had destroyed docks, flour mills and factories, adding to the plight of the tragic country.

Although Dutch physicians had warned the Germans that mass starvation was inevitable the Germans took no notice and in Rotterdam the deaths rose to forty a day.

Large supplies have been held in readiness for some weeks awaiting the liberation.

Quisling's call to "save" Norway

Fuglesang, Norwegian quisling chief, in a message over Oslo radio to all quisling party members, said:

"Today it is the foremost task of our party to maintain calm and order in our country and to prevent Norway from becoming a battlefield by all means. With this end in view we are prepared to collaborate with all forces willing to do so."

A fight to surrender

According to the German High Command communique, German forces are meeting severe opposition from the Russians in their efforts to get to the British lines and surrender.

"The body of our troops in the Mecklenburg area, and after heavy fighting, forced its way to the Western bank of the River Elbe, into the zone occupied by British and American troops and has there laid down arms," said yesterday's communique.

HER:
...oudy; scattered showers.
Complete weather conditions on Page 2.

The Montreal Daily Star.

FINAL

VOL. LXXVII, No. 107 — MONTREAL, SATURDAY, MAY 5, 1945 — SUN RISES 5.36; SETS 8.06 — PRICE THREE CENTS

GUNS STILLED IN NORTHWEST EUROPE; CANADIANS PLAN EARLY RETURN HOME

Red Armies Still Engaged

Surrender in Norway, Czechoslovakia Discussed

Bulletin

STOCKHOLM, May 5—(A.P.)—The German-controlled Scandinavian Telegraph Bureau reported from Oslo that the capitulation of German troops in Norway would be announced today.

Responsible Swedish political leaders also predicted a surrender in Norway.

LONDON, May 5—(C.P.)—The Flensburg (Germany) radio, quoting a German communique, said today British forces had occupied Kiel.

The broadcast said American troops had captured Linz, Austria.

The war in Northwest Germany, Holland and Denmark ended at 8 a.m. (2 a.m., E.D.T.), today with unconditional surrender of 500,000 Germans and cease-fire orders stilling the guns of battle, blood and death.

Coincident with this triumph, negotiations were reported well under way for capitulation of the last two major enemy strongholds—Norway and the Czechoslovak-Austrian pocket, which was still shrinking under blows of the Western and Eastern Allies.

Red Army forces liberated all of Slovakia yesterday and the German High Command said Soviet armor had launched a new drive west of Vienna, moving toward a junction with American troops which would cut off the Austrian redoubt from Czechoslovakia.

Russian troops smashed forward for 10-mile gains against bitter German resistance in the Czechoslovakian redoubt and staged a big tank battle near Olmuetz (Olomouc), Moravian war-production centre.

"Hostilites ceased at 0800 hours, British double summer time, today," on the 21st Army Group front, declared the 392nd communique from Allied Supreme Headquarters. "All German armed forces in Northwest Germany, Holland and Denmark, including the garrison on Heligoland and Frisian Islands, have surrendered unconditionally to Allied forces."

Reich Most Completely Shattered

The surrender—leaving the Third Reich one of the most completely shattered powers which ever lost a war—was negotiated by Field Marshal Montgomery, who flatly rejected a German offer to surrender also to him three German armies facing the Russians.

From 80,000 to 100,000 Germans surrendered in Holland—invaded by Hitler's legions on May 10, 1940, just five days short of five years ago—Ross Munro, Canadian Press correspondent reported.

Only two remote pockets—Norway and the Czech-Austrian sector—remained, and Daniel de Luce, Associated Press correspondent who has been in both Stockholm and Moscow recently, said negotiations were in progress for liquidation of these without a fight.

4,000,000 Germans Captured

The mass surrenders have boosted the total of German prisoners taken by the Western Allies to well above 4,000,000.

Only six per cent of the top-strength German Army, roughly 500,000 men, remained. The Wehrmacht, once the dread of all Europe, was reduced to garrisons of about 300,000 in Czechoslovakia and Austria with these surrendering at a rapid rate; 150,000 in isolated Norway and 50,000 in the French ports and Channel Islands.

The German homeland itself was completely overrun. Its cities lay in ruins. Its Fuehrer, who said he would shape the fate of Europe for a thousand years, was missing — perhaps dead by his own hand in the rubble of his capital.

Eleven months, almost to the day, from D-Day, Gen. Eisenhower declared that "on land and sea and in the air the Germans are thoroughly whipped. Their only recourse is to surrender."

With a swift series of dramatic developments, the war whirled into its final hours.

Eisenhower Announces Surrender

Gen. Eisenhower announced that Field Marshal Montgomery's 21st Army Group would accept surrender of all German forces in Holland, Northwest Germany, Denmark, Helgoland and the Frisian Islands.

Some 500,000 Germans were involved, and, with the capture of 500,000 on the British-Canadian front yesterday, 1,000,000 had given up, overshadowing even the mass capitulation in Austria and Italy.

The surrender order was signed by Montgomery and Admiral von Friedeberg, Commander-in-Chief of the German Navy, in a tent on Luneburg Heath, south of Hamburg.

The Supreme Commander announced that the last remnants of the German 9th and 12th Armies surrendered in the final pocket in Germany proper to a single division of the U.S. 9th Army.

The U.S. 7th Army captured 50,000 prisoners yesterday as it hacked Austria in two. Berchtesgaden, Hitler's vaunted fortress in the Bavarian Alps, was seized and cleared. Salzburg, bastion of the national redoubt, was in American hands, as was Innsbruck, key to Alps communications. The 7th drove

(Continued on Page 4, Col. 1)

The Situation "In an Eggshell"

FIELD MARSHAL MONTGOMERY'S HEADQUARTERS, May 5—(B.U.P.)—Field Marshal Sir Bernard L. Montgomery said today that over a million men were involved in the German surrender to his forces.

"It's a good egg," remarked Montgomery with a smile.

German Navy In Copenhagen Ignores Truce

Open Fire on Groups Of Danish Patriots

STOCKHOLM, May 5—(B.U.P.)—Copenhagen reports said German warships began a 25-minute shelling of the Oesterbro quarter of the Danish capital at 10 a.m. today, killing at least 10 persons.

City Areas Shelled

COPENHAGEN, May 5—(A.P.)—German warships in Copenhagen's harbor opened fire with machine-guns, anti-aircraft guns and cannon on several sectors of the city today and sporadic clashes broke out when Danish patriots sought to disarm the Nazis.

The German cruisers Prinz Eugen and Nuernberg resisted the patriots' efforts to disarm sailors aboard the ships, and many persons were killed or wounded.

At least 20 more persons were killed in the night throughout the city when the patriots entered German barracks to disarm the Germans, and in clashes with Danish Nazis in the streets.

German officials in the telephone and telegraph offices threatened to blow up the building this morning. But the idea was abandoned when Danish personnel walked out, disrupting service for a few hours.

On the whole the German troops appeared to have withdrawn to their barracks in accordance with the terms of capitulation yesterday to Field Marshal Montgomery, but the arrival of Allied troops was eagerly awaited as a quieting factor.

Werner Best, German Minister in Denmark, placed himself in the custody of the Danish Freedom Council.

Japs Interned

Members of the Japanese diplomatic staff from Berlin, who reached Copenhagen several days ago, were arrested by the patriots and interned.

The notorious Dagmarhus on Raadhuspladsen, German headquarters, was surrounded by armed Danish Freedom Fighters.

Six thousand members of the Danish police brigade, trained beforehand for the day of liberation in Sweden, arrived from Malmoe, Swedish port, early this morning. They were greeted by great crowds of Danes.

News of the surrender of German forces in Denmark to Field Marshal Montgomery was greeted with jubilation last night after five years under the German yoke.

King Christian X, the 74-year-old monarch who stiffly insisted upon Danish independence throughout the occupation, was reported to have designated former Premier Orla Buhl to organize a new government to lead Denmark into the United Nations family.

Mr. Buhl's new government may take office some time today.

When London broadcasts last night announced that at last Denmark was free, crowds swarmed into the streets happily.

Singing groups marched toward the Palace Square and would not disperse until a royal aide had come out and given them a word from the monarch.

Germans Think Hitler Died July 20

Few Cared During Last Days of Reich

Since last September Edward J. Beattie, British United Press war correspondent, has been inside Germany—a prisoner of war. He was captured last fall while going up to an advanced Allied combat position to cover a story. Yesterday he came out of Luckenwald prison camp. Today he is making a personal report to Gen. Dwight D. Eisenhower.

By Edward W. Beattie
British United Press War Correspondent

PARIS, May 5 — I do not know the answer to the mystery of Adolf Hitler, but I can tell you what a good proportion of the German people — from front-line troops to village housewives—think about it.

They think he has been dead since July 20, 1944.

They think the bomb plot against Hitler, hatched by German Army officers, succeeded. They think Heinrich Himmler and a small group of his henchmen seized control of Germany after July 20 and kept it in the war.

Few Germans believe the story their own propagandists put out—that Hitler died in battle as the Russians closed in against the heart of Berlin. The ones who do believe that are Nazi fanatics who also believe they can go underground and continue the fight against the Allies for years.

Didn't Care About Hitler

For the last few weeks no Germans with whom I talked cared where Hitler was. They didn't care whether he was dead or alive. The only thing they cared about was getting themselves into a position to surrender to the British or the Americans. At the Luckenwald camp, where I was a prisoner, the German guards talked frankly about what they intended to do when the Russians came storming up to the gates.

They said they intended to fire one token volley and then run. Actually, they didn't wait to do that. They fled before the Russians ever got there and turned the camp over to those of us who were prisoners.

The average German soldier seemed to have realized as early as last fall that he was fighting in a lost cause. I say that because there were two weeks after I was captured that I was forced to live in the battle field with a unit of the Germany Army.

Surrounded by Allies

We were surrounded by Allied troops southwest of Epinal on the western approaches to the Vosges. For transportation we had a strange convoy of French civilian automobiles and most of the daylight hours we were strafed by Allied planes. I jumped into ditches with my captors. I talked with staff officers, sergeants and privates. Sometimes they gave me sausages and cigarettes. One day I tried to buy a bottle of schnapps from a French distiller and offered him Allied occupation money in payment. He finally took it when some of my German captors told him:

"The Americans will be here in two days or so."

I knew then that the Germans knew they were licked.

My captors finally broke out of the Allied trap and then I was shuttled from place to place. In

(Continued on Page 5)

—Marconi Picturegram

MONTY IN FINAL STRIDES: Here Field Marshal Montgomery is seen as he crossed the Elbe River to greet paratroopers whose descent ahead of his army helped to cut off Huns in Denmark and Holland and hasten the surrender of more than a million men.

Aussies Make New Gains in Tarakan Drive

Japs Offering Bitter Resistance

MANILA, May 5—(A.P.)—Burrowing Japanese troops who survived a murderous artillery barrage held Australian veterans to moderate gains Thursday at Tarakan, Borneo oil centre. However, covered by guns of the U.S. 7th Fleet and by planes of the U.S. 13th Air Force and the Australian Air Force, Australian ground troops seized the military barracks in Tarakan city, headquarters here announced.

Field dispatches, however, said they were stopped when they tried to take a hill overlooking the town.

Spencer Davis, Associated Press correspondent on Tarakan, reported the Aussies broke into the western portion of the town after some of the most bitter fighting in the Southwest Pacific. They seized about 25 per cent of the rich oil wells in that vicinity.

Near Davao

The U.S. 24th Division, expecting a stiff fight as they advanced on Davao, major city on Mindanao in the Philippines reached the outskirts of the city and found indications that the main Japanese force had fled. As they entered the town, however, enemy snipers and suicide squads forced a house-to-house fight. The Americans passed through, to the northern outskirts. Allied Headquarters said the fighting was not severe.

On Luzon Island, American troops finished the mopping up of the Baguio area and liberated three small nearby towns.

Japanese hurled amphibious forces, the first major tank-led counter-assault of the Okinawa campaign, suicide boats, planes and pilot-guided flying bombs at American forces yesterday 325 miles south of Japan.

Every attack was broken up, but five light United States ships were sunk and others damaged.

Hundreds of the 4,000 attacking Japanese soldiers were slaughtered, 154 enemy planes shot down and 15 explosive-laden speed boats blown up.

Middle Course Backed By Canada at Parley

Ottawa Delegation Proposes Nine Amendments to Oaks Formula

By Gerald Waring
Special to The Star

SAN FRANCISCO, May 5—What must be termed a realistic approach to the problem of revamping the draft world security charter along lines more acceptable to the smaller nations characterizes Canada's proposals to amend the plan the Big Four drew up at Dumbarton Oaks eight months ago.

Canada has submitted nine proposed amendments. None of them could be considered very radical compared with suggestions being made by other countries at this United Nations Conference on International Organization. Rather, they tend to represent a middle of the road course, somewhere between the concessions most of the small powers would like to obtain from the Big Four or the Big Five, and what at this moment the great powers seem inclined to make.

Canada Wants Results

Canada wants results at San Francisco in the form of the most universally acceptable and the most workable charter for an organization to maintain international peace and security that can be formulated. And since that is her overall consideration, her attitude in submitting her nine proposed amendments is first, one of eagerness to co-operate, and second, one of willingness to compromise.

The small United Nations, which outnumber the great powers something like nine to one, want nothing that smacks of great power domination. Yet it is unthinkable that the great powers, which control a vast preponderance of the world's economic and military power and which in the last analysis must be the real keepers of the world peace, would submit to small power domination of the organization on the mere grounds of numerical superiority.

Only the great powers shared in the preparation of the Oakes Yalta draft charter, and reserved for themselves such authority in and control over the new League of Nations that the smaller countries felt not only slighted, but somewhat fearful of entering the or-

(Continued on Page 2)

Crerar Issues Victory Order

Hun Defeat Complete, Canadian Army Told

WITH THE 1st CANADIAN ARMY, May 5—(C.P. Cable)—Gen. Crerar, in a special message to his troops of the 1st Canadian Army early today said "a crushing and complete victory over the German Army has been secured."

Text of his message:

From Sicily to the river Senio, from the beaches of Dieppe to those of Normandy, and thence through Northern France, Belgium, Holland and Northwest Germany, the Canadians and their Allied comrades of this Army have carried out their responsibilities in the high traditions which they have inherited.

An official order that offensive operations of all troops of the 1st Canadian Army will cease forthwith and that all fire will cease from 0800 hours (2 a.m. E.D.T.) Saturday, May 5, has been issued.

A crushing and complete victory over the German Army has been secured.

In rejoicing at this supreme accomplishment, we shall remember friends who have paid the full price for the belief they also held that no sacrifice in the interests of the principles for which we fought could be too great.

Japs Pursued On Burma Coast

CALCUTTA, May 5 — (C. P.) — British 14th Army troops, after clearing Pegu, are pursuing fleeing Japanese forces eastward toward Moulmein, port city across the Gulf of Martaban from captured Rangoon, a Southeast Asia Command communique announced today.

The enemy was presumably retreating along the rail line that runs from Pegu, 50 miles north of Rangoon, to Moulmein.

Two Petain Aides Arrested in Germany

PARIS, May 5 — (A. P.) — Two former members of Marshal Petain's Vichy Government were located and arrested yesterday in a sector of Germany where French and American armies were fighting, l'Agence Francaise de Presse reported, naming them as George Bouthillier, former Finance Minister, and Gen. Auguste Laure, Petain's Secretary General.

Switzerland Bars Hungarian Ex-Premier

BERN, May 5 — (A. P.) —Switzerland has refused asylum to Dr. Laszlo de Bardossy, former Premier of Hungary, who had enforced severe anti-Semitic policies while he was in power in that country. The rejection was made by the Swiss Federal Council.

War's End To Speed Up Leaves

More to Get Furloughs To Dominion

By Ross Munro

WITH THE 1ST CANADIAN ARMY, May 5 — (C.P.) — The Canadian Army has fought its last battles in Europe. The end of the long road from the beaches of Sicily and Normandy came for Gen. Crerar's men at 8 a.m. today when between 80,000 and 100,000 Germans in Fortress Holland and about 30,000 in Northwest Germany surrendered.

It is not foreseen here that any Canadian forces will be employed in the elimination of remaining German pockets in operations — should they be necessary—in Norway, and already the Canadian command is shifting its attention from problems of war to those related to return to Canada and demobilization of its troops.

There may be an immediate increase in the number of those going home on rotation leave—preliminary to a mass exodus of Canadians from Europe to go home and leave the service. Acquisition of a fleet of Dakota air transports will speed this movement.

CLEAN-UP CHORES ALONE REMAIN

Before this can be brought about, however, there remain the final chores in the liberation of Holland and the cleaning out of the Emden-Wilhelmshaven pocket.

Gen. Crerar today told his men in a special message that they had won a "crushing and complete victory over the German Army."

Relief at the end of the gruelling campaigns which carried them through some of the toughest fighting in Western Europe—Caen, Ortona, Falaise, the Leopold Canal are a few of the battle-honors these troops bear—was mingled in the Canadian reaction with exhilaration.

The Netherlanders celebrated joyously in the streets of their towns last night — but, stolidly, ceased their dancing and retired at 10 p.m.—the habit-ingrained curfew hour the Germans had imposed.

Meanwhile the Canadians and Germans held their respective positions, and perhaps 36 hours remained before the 1st Canadian Corps would move into West Holland to take over the huge bag of prisoners.

Similarly, on the 2nd Corps front in Northwestern Germany, there may be a lapse of a day or more before the Canadians enter Emden and Wilhelmshaven.

Reason for the delay is that Canadian commanders have to obtain a mass of information from German officers regarding enemy minefields, road-blocks, obstacles, rations, gasoline and ammunition.

DETAILS COVERED BY SURRENDER

This is all being carried out under the surrender instrument signed by Field Marshal Montgomery and representatives of Grand Admiral Doenitz at the 21st Army Group commander's headquarters yesterday.

On the West Holland front, Maj.-Gen. Charles Foulkes of London, 1st Corps commander, met Col.-Gen. Blaskowitz' Chief of Staff to obtain this information this morning, and presumably a similar meeting took place on the 2nd Corps sector between the commander, Lieut.-Gen. G. G. Simonds of Kingston, and a German representative.

Until all this information is received from the enemy and the Canadians are satisfied it is correct, no Canadian Army troops will move. However probably by Sunday afternoon or night 1st corps troops will cross into the enemy area, with columns ad-

(Continued on Page 4, Col. 2)

'Monty' Foils Hun Plan to Flout Russians

By Charles Chamberlain

Attempt to Surrender Armies on Eastern Front Flatly Rejected

FIELD MARSHAL MONTGOMERY'S HEADQUARTERS, May 5 — (A.P.) — Field Marshal Montgomery rejected a Nazi offer to surrender to the Allies three German armies facing the Russians.

This was disclosed by the commander of the 21st Army Group himself as negotiations for the surrender of Northwest Germany, Holland and Denmark were completed yesterday.

Negotiations for the surrender of the Germans facing the Allies in the north had been under way for two days before the signing Montgomery revealed.

Gen. Guenther Blumentritt, commander of all German forces between the Baltic and the Weser River, sent a message to Montgomery May 2, offering to surrender the German 12th and 21st Armies and the 3rd Tank Army, which were facing the Russians. The Allied commanders reply was a flat: "No."

"Those armies are fighting the Russians," he said. If there is any surrondering to be done it should be to the Russians. I am not going to have any dealings on the eastern flank and the Russian front."

The unconditional surrender of the German armies on the British-Canadian front was consummated yesterday at 6:25 p.m. in a small tent near Montgomery's "House on Wheels," as a driving rain beat against the canvas. The Germans pledged to lay down their arms at 8 a.m. today (2 a.m., E.D.T.) All the armies opposing Montgomery except those in Norway were included in the surrender terms.

It took just two minutes for the immaculate German officers to affix their signatures. When it was all over Montgomery, clad in battle dress, his ribbons prominently displayed, stepped from the tent behind the sheepish Germans.

As he passed a group of correspondents, he winked at them.

"This is the moment," he muttered with a broad grin.

It was the moment that climaxed Montgomery's spectacular pursuit of the enemy across Africa and France and finally into the heart of the burning Reich itself.

The historic document was promulgated atop a wooded knoll overlooking Luneberg Health, a former training ground for a Nazi Panzer division. An ordinary mess table covered by a white cloth was the conference table and there Nazi Admiral von Friedeberg, successor to the new Fuehrer, Admiral Karl Doenitz, as commander of the German Navy, affixed his signature.

Others Sign

Gen. Kinsel, the Chief of Staff for Field Marshal Ernst von Busch; Rear Admiral Wagner an officer on Friedeberg's staff; a Maj. Friede, staff officer to Kinsel, and Col. Poleck, representing Nazi Field Marshal Wilhelm Keitel, chief of the German General Staff, also signed.

Text of Surrender

The text of the surrender terms as read by Field Marshal Montgomery:

The German Command agrees to the surrender of all German armed forces in Holland in northwest Germany including the Frisian Islands and Heligoland and all other islands in Schleswig-Holstein and in Denmark to the commander in chief, 21st Army Group, this to include all naval ships in these areas.

These forces to lay down their arms and to surrender unconditionally. All hostilities on land, on sea or in the air by German

(Continued on Page 4, Col..5)

Huns Thoroughly Whipped, Says Eisenhower Statement

PARIS, May 5—(AP) — Gen. Eisenhower issued a statement last night declaring: "On land and sea and in the air, the Germans are thoroughly whipped. Their only recourse is to surrender."

The Supreme Allied commander said:

"German forces on the Western front have disintegrated today. What is left of two German armies surrendered to a single American Division — the 102nd—commanded by Maj.-Gen. Frank A. Keating.

"In the north the remaining forces of Northwestern Germany, Holland, Denmark and the Frisian Islands surrendered to Field Marshal Montgomery.

"In the south Allied troops from Gen. Devers' command and from Italy have joined.

"On the Czech border a Panzer division gave up unconditionally to Gen. Bradley's forces.

"Any further losses which the Germans may incur on this front are due to their failure instantly to quit.

"They know they are beaten. Any further hesitation is due to their own stupidity or that of the German Government.

"On land and sea and in the air the Germans are thoroughly whipped. Their only recourse is to surrender."

Today's Features

The following features are all on page 22:

Other regular features are on the following pages:

V-E DAY THE MORNING CALL V-E DAY

VOL. CXXVI, NO. 110 Entered As 2nd Class Matter In P. O., Paterson, N. J., Act of Mar. 3, 1879 THE PATERSON MORNING CALL, TUESDAY, MAY 8, 1945 Daily Except Sunday 33 Church St., Paterson, N. J. * * * PRICE FOUR CENTS

EUROPEAN WAR IS OVER !

President To Proclaim Victory

Harry S. Truman

By W. H. MOBLEY

Washington, May 7 (AP) — President Truman made arrangements tonight to make a radio address at 9 A.M. (Eastern War Time tomorrow, presumably to proclaim the victory over Germany which is already known to be won.

A Big Three agreement put off the formal announcement of V-E Day until it can be proclaimed simultaneously by the major Allies–Britain, Russia and the United States.

While the capital greeted news of final Nazi surrender calmly as just another battle won — the biggest yet but not the last — the President stuck meticulously to the Big Three announcement agreement that it was never said in so many words that it is a V-E Day speech he will make.

Asked if that will be its nature, Jonathan Daniels, White House press secretary, told newsmen: "The statement speaks for itself."

He referred to a brief announcement given newsmen just after 6 o'clock this evening at the White House where many of them had been waiting all day for official announcement of the final victory

(Please Turn to Page 21—Col. 7)

Leader Of Victorious Armies

Dwight D. Eisenhower

By ALEX SINGLETON

London, May 7 (AP)--Germany surrendered unconditionally to the Allies today, completing the victory phase of the Second World War — the most devastating in history.

Prime Minister Churchill will proclaim the historic conquest at 9 A.M. (Eastern War Time) tomorrow from 10 Downing street and simultaneous announcements are expected from President Truman in Washington and Premier Marshal Stalin in Moscow.

Churchill then will report directly to Commons and ask for adjournment to Westminster Abbey for a service of thanksgiving.

The whereabouts of such war criminals as Himmler, Goering, even Hitler himself although he had been reported dead, were unknown or if they were known they had not been officially announced.

Germany's formal capitulation came at 2:41 A.M. (French Time) in the big Reims red schoolhouse, headquarters of General Eisenhower, supreme commander of the Allies in the West.

The crowning triumph came just five years, eight

(Please Turn to Page 28—Col. 5)

Daily Mirror
MAY 9
Wednesday, May 9, 1945
No. 12,912 ONE PENNY
Registered at G.P.O. as a Newspaper.

BRITAIN'S DAY OF REJOICING

In the centre of 50,000

Dense crowds in Whitehall, estimated by the police at 50,000—all cheering like mad—mobbed the Prime Minister when he emerged from Downing-street after his broadcast speech. With the broad grin of victory on his face—and a new cigar clamped between his teeth—Winston Churchill gave his famous V-sign.

Minute past midnight

THE final total surrender documents were signed by the Germans and the three Allies yesterday IN BERLIN. The Channel Isles were to be freed at once.

Hostilities in Europe ended officially at 12.1 a.m. today.

Sonder-Ausgabe

Die Mitteilungen

ALLIIERTES NACHRICHTENBLATT DER 21. HEERESGRUPPE FÜR DIE DEUTSCHE ZIVILBEVÖLKERUNG

Preis 20 Pf. (in Kriegsgebieten unentgeltlich). Mitwoch, den 9. Mai 1945 Nr. 9

DEUTSCHLAND KAPITULIERT

Feldmarschall Alexander

Marschall Koniew

Feldmarschall Montgomery

S. M. König Georg VI.

General Eisenhower

Marschall Zhukow

General Bradley

Die alliierten Befehlshaber, die den Krieg bis in das Herz Deutschlands verfolgt und die Wehrmacht zur bedingungslosen Uebergabe gezwungen haben.

Der Krieg in Europa endete um Mitternacht am 8. Mai

Der Dank des Königs von England

König Georg VI. hielt gestern abend eine Rundfunkansprache an das britische Weltreich. Er sagte:

„Wir danken heute dem allmächtigen Gott für diese große Erlösung. Ich spreche von der ältesten Hauptstadt des Weltreichs, die zwar vom Krieg schwer mitgenommen, aber nie auch nur einen Augenblick den Mut sinken ließ. Hier von London aus fordere ich Euch auf, dieser Danksagung mit mir beizuwohnen.

„Deutschland, der Feind, der ganz Europa in den Krieg trieb, ist endlich besiegt. Im Fernen Osten müssen wir noch mit Japan abrechnen, diesem entschlossenen und grausamen Feinde.

„Dieser Aufgabe werden wir uns mit der größten Entschlossenheit widmen und ihr alle unsere Mittel zuwenden.

„Laßt uns derer gedenken, die nicht mehr zurückkehren werden. Ihre Standhaftigkeit und ihr Mut in der Schlacht, ihre Opfer und nimmermüde Ausdauer einem erbarmungslosen Feinde gegenüber wird unvergessen bleiben.

„Laßt uns aller Männer aller Streitkräfte und aller Frauen, die diesen Streitkräften angeschlossen waren, gedenken, welche ihr Leben gegeben haben.

„Wir haben das Ende unserer Heimsuchungen erreicht, und die Toten sind nicht mehr bei uns, im Augenblick unserer Freude. Laßt uns daher mit aller Dankbarkeit die große Zahl der Lebenden ehren, die uns zum Siege geführt haben. Jedem nach seiner Leistung das ihm gebührende Lob zu zollen, ist mir unmöglich, da sich die Bemühungen aller im totalen Kriege zur selben Höhe und Hingabe an die gemeinsame Sache aufschwingen.

„Niemand weiß das besser als ich, und ich, Euer König, danke aus tiefstem Herzen denen, die zu Lande, zur See oder in der Luft gekämpft haben und danke nicht weniger den Zivilisten, die so schwere Lasten ertragen haben. Sie hielten unerschütterlich und ohne zu klagen stand. Mit diesen Erinnerungen vor unseren Augen laßt uns erwägen, was uns durch fast sechs Jahre von Leiden und Schrecken aufrecht erhielt. Es war das Bewußtsein, daß alles auf dem Spiele stand: unsere Freiheit, unsere Unabhängigkeit, ja unsere Existenz; aber auch das Bewußtsein, daß, während wir uns selbst verteidigten, wir auch die Freiheit der Welt verteidigten, daß unsere gute Sache nicht nur die dieses Staates oder des Weltreiches war, sondern die gute Sache jedes Landes, wo Freiheit hochgehalten und Gesetzlichkeit und Achtung der Persönlichkeit Hand in Hand gehen.

„In den dunkelsten Stunden waren wir uns bewußt, daß die versklavten und isolierten Völker Europas ihre Blicke auf uns richteten. Ihre Hoffnungen waren unsere Hoffnungen, ihre Zuversicht bestärkte uns in unserem Glauben. Wir wußten, daß mit unserem Nachgeben die letzten Schranken gegen eine die ganze Welt umfassende Tyrannei in Trümmern zusammengebrochen wäre.

„Aber wir gaben nicht nach. Wir hielten uns und einander die Treue. Wir hielten Treue und Einigkeit unseren großen Verbündeten gegenüber. Diese Treue und Einigkeit führten uns durch Gefahren, welche manchmal überwältigend erschienen, zum Siege.

„Durch Erfolg gestärkt wenden wir uns nun gegen unseren letzten noch verbleibenden Feind.

„Die Königin und ich sind uns der schweren Stunden wohl bewußt, die Ihr überall im Weltreich durchlebt habt. Wir sind stolz, manche dieser Sorgen mit Euch geteilt zu haben, und wir wissen auch, daß wir zusammen der Zukunft mit Entschlossenheit ins Auge sehen können.

„Unsere Bemühungen wären gescheitert und unsere Angehörigen würden ihr Leben umsonst geopfert haben, wenn der Sieg, für den sie starben, nicht zu einem dauernden Frieden führte, der auf Gerechtigkeit und gutem Willen beruht.

„Laßt uns daran an diesen Tagen der gerechten Vergeltung, des Triumphes und der stolzen Trauer denken, und dann als ein Volk wieder an die Arbeit gehen, fest entschlossen, nichts zu unternehmen, was derer unwürdig wäre, die für uns starben, und fest entschlossen, eine Welt zu bauen, wie sie von ihnenfür ihre und unsere Kinder erwünscht worden wäre.

„Unsere Ehre verpflichtet uns zu dieser Aufgabe. In der Stunde der Gefahr legten wir unsere gute Sache in Gottes Hand, die unsere Stärke und unser Schild war. In dieser Siegesstunde laßt uns dem Herrn für seine Gnade danken und wir vertrauen uns und unsere neuen Aufgaben der Führung derselben starken Hand an."

Der britische Premierminister spricht

Der britische Premierminister, Winston Churchill, sagte gestern in einer Rundfunkrede von London um 3 Uhr nachmittags:

„Gestern morgen um 2 Uhr 41 Minuten unterzeichnete General Jodl, Bevollmächtigter des Oberkommandos der Wehrmacht und des Großadmirals Dönitz, des gegenwärtigen Leiters des deutschen Reiches, im Hauptquartier General Eisenhowers die Urkunde der bedingungslosen Kapitulation aller deutschen Land-, See- und Luftstreitkräfte in Europa an die Alliierten Streitkräfte in Europa und gleichzeitig an das russische Oberkommando.

„General Bedell Smith, Stabschef der alliierten Streitkräfte in Europa und General Francois Savez, Vertreter der französischen Republik, unterzeichneten die Urkunde im Namen des Oberstkommandierenden der Alliierten Streitkräfte in Europa, und General Susloparoff zeichnete im Namen des Russischen Oberkommandos.

„Dieses Abkommen wird heute in Berlin ratifiziert und bestätigt werden. Luftmarschall Tedder, stellvertretender Oberstkommandierender der Alliierten Streitkräfte in Europa, General de Lattre de Tassigny werden im Namen General Eisenhowers, und General Zhukow im Namen des Russischen Oberkommandos unterzeichnen.

„Die Deutschen werden durch Feldmarschall Keitel, Chef des Oberkommandos der Wehrmacht, und Oberbefehlshaber der deutschen Flotte, Armee und Luftwaffe vertreten sein.

„Feindseligkeiten werden offiziell heute Nacht, den 8. Mai, um 12 Uhr 01 Minuten eingestellt werden. Aber um Menschenleben zu sparen, begann die Feuereinstellung gestern an allen Fronten, und unsere geliebten Kanal-Inseln werden heute auch befreit.

„An verschiedenen Stellen leisten die Deutschen den russischen Truppen noch Widerstand, aber sollte sich ihr Widerstand über heute Mitternacht hinaus fortsetzen, so machen sie sich natürlich des Schatzes der Kriegsgesetze verlustig und werden allerorten von alliierten Truppen angegriffen werden.

„Es ist nicht überraschend, daß bei so langenFronten u. bei der bestehenden Verwirrung des Feindes den Befehlen des deutschen Oberkommandos nicht in jedem Falle sofort Folge geleistet werden konnte. Auf Grund der besten uns zur Verfügung stehenden militärischen Informationen, sind wir der Ansicht, daß keine Ursache besteht, irgendeine der Tatsachen die General Eisenhower anläßlich der Unterzeichnung bekanntgegeben hat, der Nation vorzuenthalten; noch soll es uns daran hindern, den Sieg in Europa heute und morgen zu feiern.

„Heute werden wir vielleicht hauptsächlich an uns selbst denken. Morgen werden wir besondere Anerkennung unseren heroischen russischen Verbündeten zollen, deren Heldenmut im Felde so viel zum gemeinsamen Sieg beigetragen hat.

„Der Krieg gegen Deutschland ist daher beendigt. Nach jahrelangen, weitgehenden Vorbereitungen, überfiel Deutschland anfangs September 1939 Polen, und im Einklang mit unserer Polen gegebenen Garantie, erklärten Großbritannien und das britische Weltreich, gemeinsam mit der französischen Republik, auf Grund dieses schmählichen Angriffes den Krieg.

„Nachdem das tapfere Frankreich niedergeschlagen war, führten wir diesen Kampf, von dieser Insel und dem geeinigten Weltreich aus, alleinstehend, über ein Jahr fort, bis sich uns Sowjet-Rußland mit seiner militärischen Macht und Amerika mit seiner überwältigenden Kraft und seinen unbeschränkten Mitteln anschlossen. Schließlich war fast die ganze Welt gegen die Missetäter vereint.

„Aus allen Herzen auf dieser Insel und im britischen Weltreich strömt unsere Dankbarkeit unseren prächtigen Verbündeten entgegen.

„Wir dürfen uns wohl eine kurze Zeit der Freude gönnen, aber laßt uns auch nicht für einen Augenblick die Anstrengungen und die Bemühungen vergessen, die noch vor uns liegen. Japan, mit seinem Verrat und seiner schmählichen Habsucht, ist noch nicht unterjocht. Die Wunden, welche dieses Land Großbritannien und den Vereinigten Staaten zugefügt hat, und alle seine Grausamkeiten schreien nach gerechter Strafe und Vergeltung. Wir müssen nun unsere ganze Kraft und alle unsere Mittel der Vollendung unserer Aufgaben zu Hause und Uebersee widmen.

„Vorwärts Britannia. Es lebe die Freiheit. Gott schütze den König."

HORSE RACE BAN LIFTED

Pimlico Will Open Meet May 16

THE WEATHER
Clear and cold tonight. Thursday, sunny and warmer.
Detailed Weather Report Page 31

Read The Baltimore News-Post for complete, accurate war coverage. It is the only Baltimore newspaper possessing the three great wire services—
ASSOCIATED PRESS
INTERNATIONAL NEWS SERVICE
UNITED PRESS

THE BALTIMORE NEWS-POST
AN INDEPENDENT NEWSPAPER
The Largest Evening Circulation in the Entire South

7 HOME FINAL

VOL. CXLVII.—NO. 4 Entered as second-class matter at Baltimore Postoffice. WEDNESDAY EVENING, MAY 9, 1945 PRICE 3 CENTS

YANKS CAPTURE GOERING

Kesselring Also Taken By 7th Army

Racing Ban, Curfew Are Lifted

WASHINGTON, May 9—(A. P.)—Immediate lifting of the midnight entertainment . curfew and the ban on horse and dog racing was announced today.

Pimlico will open an 11-day meet May 16.
See Page 28.

By EARL MARCKRES
International News Service Staff Correspondent.

WASHINGTON, May 9.—America's homefront plans for a one-front war against Japan will be outlined today by War Mobilizer Fred M. Vinson who is expected to announce revocation of the racing ban and midnight curfew.

Vinson's review also will disclose plans for the retention of adequate man-power controls to maintain all-out war production for the Pacific conflict while speeding preparations for a 20 per cent increase in civilian output during the first quarter after V-E Day.

Belief that the curfew and racing ban would be lifted almost immediately followed the complete removal of the "brownout" order and came amid reports that racing would be resumed May 14. Racing was halted January 3.

MAN-POWER CONTROLS

Vinson is expected to take some action on the controversy between the War Production Board and War Manpower Commission over the relationships governing labor and materials controls after V-E Day.

In a heated letter to Vinson, WMC Chairman Paul V. McNutt proposed that "no substantial change should be made in the present programs for the allocation of man power."

The prospective labor situation for the six-month period after V-E Day, he said, will fluctuate drastically.

McNutt charged that WPB has continued its opposition to the

Continued on Page 2, Column 8.

MELLON LEAVES ARMY

PITTSBURGH, May 9—(U. P.). Col. Richard K. Mellon, former State draft director, has retired from the Army and after a vacation plans to resume as president of Mellon National Bank here, it was disclosed today.

Truman Signs Extension Of Draft

Draft calls in Maryland should be reduced from 20 to 25 per cent during the next few months because of Germany's capitulation, Col. Henry C. Stanwood, State Director of Selective Service, declared today. He said men being inducted after V-E Day will be used largely as replacements for service men the Army may discharge and for casualties. The State Director said the expectation of Germany's fall was not reflected in draft quotas for either May or June.

By ROBERT G. NIXON

WASHINGTON, May 9—(I. N. S.). — President Truman today signed the Selective Service Act extension, but he did so under protest, declaring that a section of the measure placed restrictions on the War and Navy Departments.

The Chief Executive expressed disapproval of the section of the measure forbidding the sending of eighteen - year - olds to fighting fronts until they have had six months of training.

PRESIDENT'S STATEMENT

In a statement the President made this explanation:

"I signed the legislation only because the immediate extension of the Selective Service Act is of compelling necessity in the continuance of military operations against Japan.

"I am reluctantly giving my approval of this legislation. I do not wish this approval to be interpreted as expressing my

Continued on Page 2, Column 6.

Yank Lines Slashed On Mindanao

MANILA, May 9—(A. P.).—Japanese troops, in their first show of strength on Mindanao since the April 17 invasion, penetrated American lines near captured Davao city and virtually isolated one Yank battalion, field dispatches reported today.

This battalion, which had seized the village of Mintal, two miles west of Davao city, was being reached by a few American reinforcements sent over a little-used trail, wrote Associated Press Correspondent Richard Bergholz.

SHELLS YANK POSITIONS

Japanese artillery shelled American positions at Libby Air Field, about one mile south of Mintal. The Yank hold on the airdrome was tenuous.

This was the first indication of a fight on Mindanao since Maj. Gen. Roscoe B. Woodruff's Twenty-fourth Division landed on Moro gulf and raced 140 miles overland to Davao City in 17 days. On Tarakan island, off Borneo, Australian and Dutch troops expanded their holdings north and east of Tarakan city and captured a hurriedly-evacuated Japanese headquarters.

37TH LINKED UP

MacArthur announced that Maj. Gen. Robert S. Beightler's fast-

Continued on Page 2, Column 7.

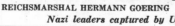

REICHSMARSHAL HERMANN GOERING MARSHAL ALBERT KESSELRING
Nazi leaders captured by U. S. Seventh Army troops.

No. 1 Nazi Chieftain Describes Escaping Hitler Death Sentence

PARIS, May 9—(U. P.).—Reichsmarshal Hermann Goering and Marshal Albert Kesselring, two of the leaders in the fallen Nazi hierarchy, are in the hands of the American Seventh Army, Supreme Headquarters announced today.

Goering said he was condemned to death by Adolf Hitler for suggesting on April 24 that he—Goering—take over the leadership of Germany.

(BACKGROUND NOTE: The Associated Press reported that Goering's wife and child were also taken into custody with him.

His arrested wife was the blond, blue-eyed former actress Emmy Sonnenmann, who, in earlier days, was Hitler's leading hostess.

Hitler's SS Elite Guardsmen arrested him, Goering said, but members of his own air force rescued him.

SUCCEEDED RUNDSTEDT

Kesselring had been commander in chief of Germany's western front since early March. He was believed to have taken over from Marshal Karl von Rundstedt—now also in Allied hands—after the Germans suffered a series of disastrous reverses in the west.

Gen. Jacob L. Devers' Sixth Army group headquarters relayed through SHAEF the announcement that Lt. Gen. Alexander M. Patch's Seventh Army had captured Goering and Kesselring.

The first reports of Goering's capture gave no details of his melodramatic report that Hitler condemned him and he was rescued by members of the Luftwaffe he commanded in its heyday.

The whereabouts of Goering had been one of the major mysteries of the collapse of the Nazi command in Germany. A few days before reporting that Adolf Hitler had been killed in battle, the German radio said Goering had been relieved of his air force command because of bad health.

Goering's was the first of Nazidom's "big three" names—Hitler, Goering and Goebbels—to be written off by the Germans in the closing phase of their resistance.

HITLER DEATH QUESTIONED

Confirmation of their report that Hitler was killed in Berlin still is lacking. Goebbels has been reported killed in Berlin, but no official Allied announcement has been made.

Goering's obesity and love of medals made him a favorite subject of caricaturists. He was an ace airman in the First World War and was credited with laying the foundation for and building up the German Air Force that was the scourge of Europe in the early years of World War II.

Japan Invasion Mapped--Nimitz

GUAM, May 9—(U. P.).—The joint chiefs of staff now are working on plans for an invasion of Japan, Admiral Chester W. Nimitz disclosed today.

With the war spotlight now focused on the Pacific theater, Nimitz also told a press conference the United States immediately will step up "very materially" its air bombardment of the enemy homeland.

He spoke as adverse weather slowed ground operations on Southern Okinawa, where five American divisions were hammering at the strongest Japanese defenses in the Pacific only a mile above Naha, capital of the island.

CURB NIP INFILTRATION

American battleships and cruisers knocked out enemy gun emplacements, artillery and mortars in a heavy bombardment. Illumination shells fired by the warships at night curbed Japanese infiltration of the American lines.

Navy patrol bombers sank 14,000 tons of shipping and damaged 3,500 in a series of attacks in Korean coastal waters Monday. A small freighter transport and a large fleet oiler were sunk.

Other patrol bombers sank two small cargo ships, a large fishing craft and a coastal cargo ship in the fourth straight day of raids off Southern Honshu yesterday. Four small cargo ships, four large fishing craft and a coastal vessel were damaged.

SAYS U. S. SHIP SUNK

(A Japanese Domei dispatch recorded by the FCC claimed that Japanese planes yesterday sank an American cruiser, heavily damaged a transport and damaged another cruiser or large destroyer off Okiwana.)

Asked if he thought the Japanese would capitulate before their homeland were invaded, Nimitz said:

"I don't know how much the Japs can take. If they can see the handwriting on the wall they can see what happened to Germany. We will plan the invasion of Japan and go ahead on the basis that the invasion will be necessary."

Latin-Americans Win Parley Fight

By WILLIAM K. HUTCHINSON
International News Service Staff Correspondent.

SAN FRANCISCO, May 9.—Latin-America won a momentous victory in the United Nations Conference today when the United States agreed to authorize the use of the Chapultepec security pact to suppress local aggression in the Western Hemisphere.

This means the nations of the Western Hemisphere can maintain peace among themselves without obtaining unanimous approval of the "Big Five" or of the World Security Council before acting.

It was a major upset to the original plans of the "Big Five."

The Latin-American victory will be incorporated in a formal addition to be offered later to the so-called Molotov amendment, which gives Russia similar authority to put down threats to peace in any enemy state of World War II, thus no member of the "Big Five"—neither the U. S., Britain, France, Russia nor China—can block use of the Chapultepec pact.

SEE NO OBJECTIONS

An American spokesman said neither Great Britain nor Russia

Continued on Page 2, Column 7.

Nazi Surrender Is Made Formal

LONDON, May 9—(A. P.)—A stern and coldly formal ceremony in Berlin, officially ratifying Germany's unconditional surrender, was described today by the Moscow radio.

The momentous document, the broadcast said, was signed in a gray house on the corner of Wiesenerstrasse and Rheinsteinstrasse by three top-ranking officers of the beaten enemy's land, sea and air forces.

Russian and Allied military chiefs watched as the papers were signed by Field Marshal Wilhelm Keitel as commander of the German Army; Admiral Gen. Von Friedeburg, Navy commander, and Col. Gen. Stumpf, a representative of the air force.

(BACKGROUND NOTE: The Japanese Government announced today the collapse of Germany "will not bring the slightest change" in Japan's determination to fight to the finish.)

Marshal Gregory K. Zhukov, commander of the victorious First White Russian Army, presided over the ceremony for the Soviet Union.

OTHER NOTABLES PRESENT

The Allied Supreme Command was represented by a delegation headed by Air Chief Marshal Sir Arthur Tedder, deputy to General Eisenhower. It included Gen. Carl Spaatz, commander of the U. S. strategic air forces in Europe, and Admiral Harold Burrough, commander of the Allied naval

Continued on Page 2, Column 1.

REDS ALONE AT PEACE

LONDON, May 9—(A. P.). Soviet Russia, with the signing of the capitulation agreement at Berlin last night became the only one of the Big Four Powers now at peace with the world. The United States, Britain, and China still faced the Japanese war in the Pacific.

Temperatures

12 Midn't	58	7 A. M.,	54
1 A. M.,	59	8 A. M.,	56
2 A. M.,	54	9 A. M.,	58
3 A. M.,	55	10 A. M.,	60
4 A. M.,	55	11 A. M.,	61
5 A. M.,	54	12 Noon,	63
6 A. M.,	53	1 P. M.,	65

German Fliers Smash Prague

LONDON, May 9—(U. P.).—Radio Prague said today German planes were bombing the capital and two other liberated Czechoslovak cities in open defiance of Germany's unconditional surrender.

The broadcast came only a few minutes after the same station reported that Russian troops had entered Prague and with Czechoslovak patriots fully cleared the city of German troops.

(BACKGROUND NOTE: British and American airmen who have escaped from prison camps in Czechoslovakia are being attacked by German troops, a Reuter report received in London said today.)

German planes began bombing Prague at 6.10 A. M. (E. W. T.), the broadcast said, and also had bombed Neuenburg, 25 miles east of Prague, and Melnik, 18 miles north. The broadcast urged inhabitants to take shelter.

REDS, YANKS LINKED

The last German ground resistance in Southern Europe had been virtually crushed. In addition to entering Prague the Russians linked up with the American Third Army south of the Danube in Austria.

In Northern Europe die-hard Nazis still held out on the Baltic

Continued on Page 2, Column 3.

NEWS-POST

Army Frees 2500 Saturday

'42 PRICES ON NEW GOODS, SAYS OPA

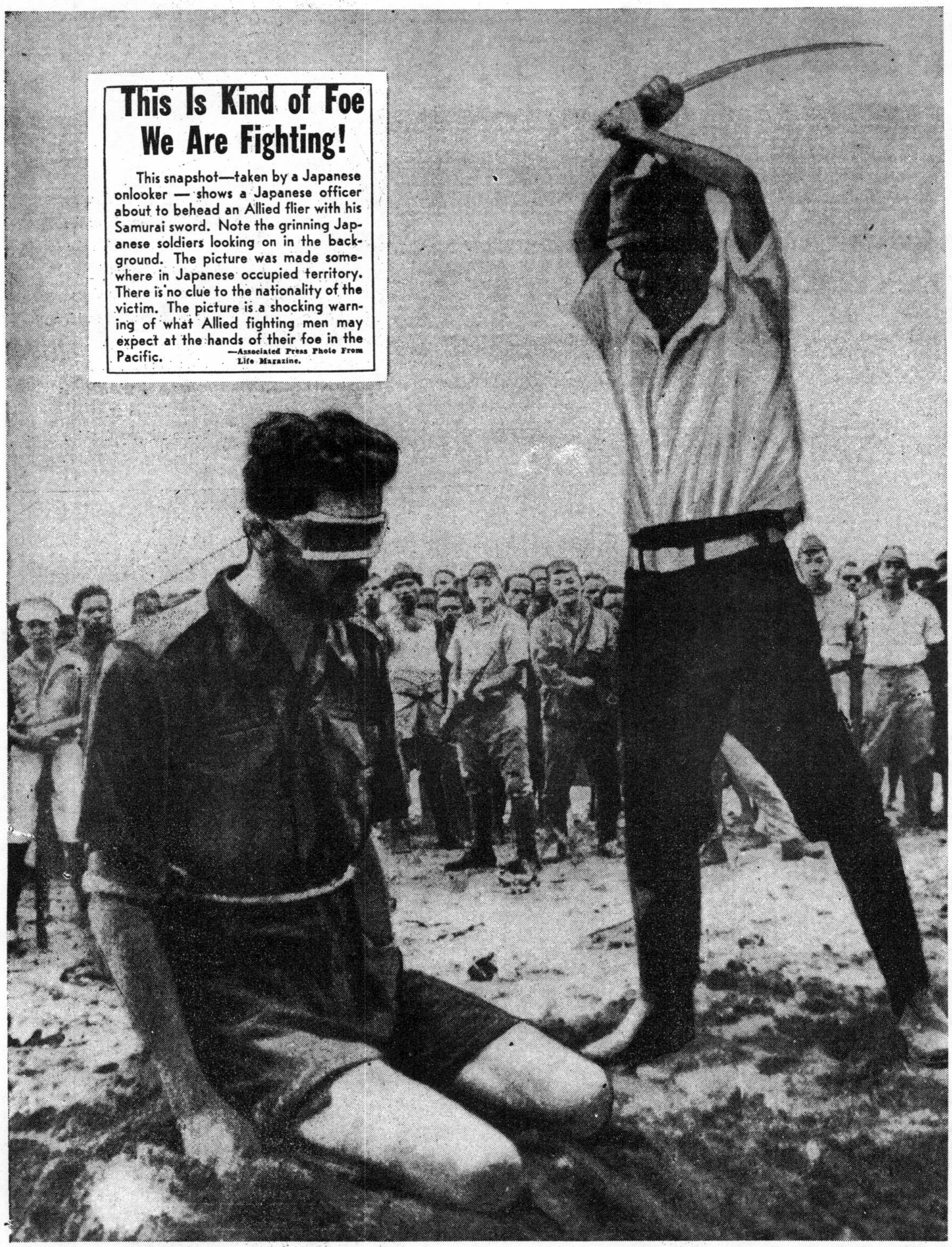

This Is Kind of Foe We Are Fighting!

This snapshot—taken by a Japanese onlooker — shows a Japanese officer about to behead an Allied flier with his Samurai sword. Note the grinning Japanese soldiers looking on in the background. The picture was made somewhere in Japanese occupied territory. There is no clue to the nationality of the victim. The picture is a shocking warning of what Allied fighting men may expect at the hands of their foe in the Pacific. —Associated Press Photo From Life Magazine.

FINAL NIGHT EDITION WEATHER: FAIR Details on Page 15

THE CALL BULLETIN
SAN FRANCISCO — AN INDEPENDENT NEWSPAPER

CALL AND POST, VOL. 157, NO. 86
THE CALL-BULLETIN, VOL. 177, NO. 86
FRIDAY, MAY 11, 1945
5c IN S. F. TRADING AREA: ELSEWHERE, 10c

B-29's Deal 3 Blows To Jap Home Isles

1942 CEILING OPA AIM ON NEW GOODS

WASHINGTON, May 11 (AP).—Price Administrator Chester Bowles today pledged 1942 retail prices for most reconversion commodities.

Outlining OPA's pricing policies for long scarce consumer goods, Bowles told a news conference:

"Everything we do in OPA must be directed toward making it possible for American enterprise and skills to produce a record volume of high quality goods at low prices and high wages.

"Nothing will more surely smother the fires of inflation than an avalanche of civilian goods and services."

Bowles said it is his belief that there will be few instances in which increases in retail prices above 1942 levels will be necessary, and in such instances the size of the increases "will be relatively small."

"We must keep prices from getting out of control," he continued, "and we must make certain that we avoid the kind of inflation and collapse that took place after the last war."

PRODUCTION COST FACTOR

Bowles acknowledged, however, that "important changes have taken place in the factors affecting production costs."

Declaring that in fixing price ceilings for these items it will be necessary to weigh increases in costs of raw materials and parts and in labor costs, he said:

"If substantial increases of this kind were to be disregarded, and reconverting manufacturers compelled to shoulder burdens they could not bear, the program for full employment and rapid reconversion would be hindered.

"Our job is to help this pro-

Continued on Page 4, Column 2

Shipping Hit Off Korea, Tokio Says

NEW YORK, May 11 (INS). The Tokio radio reported that nine torpedo planes had attacked Japanese ships off the southern coast of Korea at 10:40 a. m. today (Japanese time), flying "in single units or in units of several planes." "Our damages were negligible," the Japanese communique insisted.

GUAM, May 11 (AP).—Super Fortresses bombed Japan's homeland three times today, striking at three industrial centers and three airfields on Kyushu and Honshu Islands in a swift follow-up to yesterday's 400 plane B-29 raid.

In the heaviest attack 100 to 150 Super Fortresses attacked the big Kawanishi seaplane plant on Honshu, between Kobe and Osaka, as a smaller fleet blasted the Oita and Saiki air fields on Kyushu.

The latest attack was aimed at the important cities of Miyakanojo and Nittigahara, both on Kyushu, and at the Miyaksaki airfield.

WASHINGTON, May 11 (INS). General H. H. Arnold, chief of the Twentieth Air Force, disclosed for the first time today that B-29 Super Fortresses have been laying mines over almost the entire field of the Pacific war from Singapore to the Jap homeland.

STERN RULE OVER REICH REVEALED

By JOHN A. REICHMANN
Staff Correspondent International News

WASHINGTON, May 11 (INS). The United States today moved in on all phases of defeated Germany's domestic life with rigid control over its people aimed at exacting a just punishment and insuring their democratic rehabilitation.

General Dwight D. Eisenhower will be America's representative on the Allied Control Council of Germany.

Details of the control machinery set up by Secretary of War Henry L. Stimson with a staff collected secretly over many months was revealed at the War Department. It will govern every phase of German existence, from finance to the de-Nazification of schools and political activity.

STERN POLICY FIXED

The work of organization has been undertaken in collaboration with Great Britain, France and Russia under the Yalta "Big Three" declaration. It is aimed at imposing a "stern" military government.

The announcement did not reveal whether the commission would have its headquarters at Berlin, as the Yalta declaration provided, nor did it set forth the

DANISH EX-MINISTER FLIES TO COPENHAGEN

COPENHAGEN, May 11 (INS).—Henrik Kauffmann, former Danish minister to Washington, arrived here by air today to assume his post as a member of the new cabinet. Field Marshal Montgomery is scheduled to arrive by plane tomorrow.

VICHY JUSTICE MINISTER ARRESTED

LONDON, May 11 (INS).—The Paris radio reported tonight that Fernand Brinon, Vichy minister of justice, had been arrested in the French First Army area. x

NAZIS DROWN BERLINERS IN SUBWAYS

MOSCOW, May 11 (AP).—German SS troops turned tons of water into the Berlin subways when they learned of the German capitulation, the newspaper Trud said today. Hundreds of civilians as well as wounded soldiers were drowned.

UNCIO Acts to Keep Regional Pacts Alive

With the problem of keeping sound regional anti-aggressor agreements alive without weakening the authority of the big world peace-keeping organization being formed at the United Nations conference here the No. 1 unsolved problem, small countries took heart today in announcement that powers of the big nations will be modified.

British Foreign Secretary Anthony Eden disclosed that the Big Five nations had agreed to a proviso which would not permit a member of the proposed security council involved in a dispute to veto a recommendation made by another member.

Thus, a big nation could not quash complaints or demands for action made against it by small nation members of the councli.

This would apply to recommendations for military or peaceful action, it was explained.

At the same time the small and middle powers were cheered, too, by Eden's report that the general assembly—in which every member has a seat—would, under a Big Five agreement, be able to review any subject affecting a nation's welfare and security—including treaties.

Meanwhile, dire warning to the small-fry as well as the bigwigs of Nazidom came in disclosure that Judge Samuel I. Rosenman, President Truman's personal rep-

Continued on Page 6, Column 1

Racing Resumes, Bookies Wary

Like a cow just one fence away from a lush green lawn, San Francisco's veteran bookie operators today chewed their cuds of despair and grasped at the proverbial straw in the wind.

Racing resumes over the weekend on three or more important tracks and betting lettuce bulges from more pockets than ever before. But the local books are virtually stymied by the militant attitude of District Attorney Edmund ("Pat") Brown and the police department. Most books will remain closed in the face of

Continued on Page 13, Column 2

2,500 to Get Army Releases Tomorrow

WASHINGTON, May 11 (AP).—Approximately 2,500 soldiers will be released from the Army tomorrow under the point rating system announced by the War Department yesterday.

The discharges will take place at Army separation centers in various parts of the country, the department said.

The men, first to be released under the new discharge plan, will be drawn from soldiers with long overseas service returned to the United States for rest and recuperation under the rotation system in effect prior to the end of the war in Europe.

The separation center which will handle discharges of northern California of men is now operating at Camp Beale.

Soldiers who are residents of the United States will be given overseas credit toward discharge for any service outside the forty-eight states and the District of Columbia, while soldiers who are residents of territories and possessions will receive credit for all service outside the territory or

Continued on Page 4, Col. 4

Ex-Premier Leon Blum Arrives Back in Paris

PARIS, May 11 (INS). — Leon Blum, former French popular front leader, who was deported by the Germans, arrived in Paris today.

S. F. Man Will Captain 15,000-Ton Mercy Ship

NEW YORK, May 11 (INS).—The U. S. S. Benevolence, one of the six new 15,000-ton hospital ships being added to the Navy's fifteen-vessel mercy fleet, will be commissioned tomorrow at the Todd Shipbuilding Company yard in Brooklyn.

Her commander will be Captain C. G. Laws of San Francisco, whose last sea duty was as commanding officer of the U. S. S. Prometheus in the Pacific under Admiral Halsey's flag. He has five sons in the Navy.

Bombs Rained on Tainan Port, Jap Radio Says

NEW YORK, May 11 (INS).—Seventy bombers and more than forty fighters struck at the island bastion of Formosa by daylight today and concentrated the major weight of bombs on and around the port of Tainan, the Tokio domestic radio reported.

Call-Bulletin Today

Special Features

("G" indicates Green Flash Section)

HEART MOUNTAIN SENTINEL

Vol. IV No. 20 | Heart Mountain, Wyoming Saturday, May 12, 1945 | 2 Cents Within City 5 cents Elsewhere

Stan Hayami, '44 Grad, Falls in Italian Action; Pvt. Kawamoto Wounded

Pvt. Stanley K. Hayami, son of Mr. and Mrs. Frank N. Hayami, 8-2-B, last year graduate of Heart Mountain high school, was killed in action in Italy April 23, according to information received this week from the War department.

One other Heart Mountain youth, Pvt. Roy Kawamoto, son of James Kawamoto, 9-19-E, was reported slightly wounded in Italy the same day, it was announced here.

Both soldiers were inducted into the armed services in June, 1944.

The death of Private Hayami came as a double blow to the Hayami family since another son, Pfc. Frank Y. Hayami, was reported wounded in Italy on April 23.

At Heart Mountain high school Private Hayami was an outstanding student and served as art editor of Tempo, the 1944 yearbook. He was a talented artist and was largely responsible for the illustrations of the annual publication.

Before coming to Heart Mountain, Private Hayami attended Mark Keppel high school at San Gabriel, Calif., where his father was a prominent nurseryman at 617 East Valley boulevard.

Besides his mother and father and brother Frank, the soldier is survived by another brother, Walter, now attending school here, and a sister, Grace, formerly secretary in the community management division, now in Pasadena.

Private Kawamoto formerly lived on route three, 275 Los Gatos, Calif.

He attended Campbell high school and later San Jose state college.

Land Law May Be Invalid

WASHINGTON, D.C. — That two sections of Oregon's new Alien Land Law are "of very doubtful constitutionality" was the opinion expressed this week in an analysis of the law prepared by the WRA solicitor's office.

"The new Oregon law . . . does not change the . . . prohibitions of the alien land law of 1921, but merely provides a new penalty and sets up certain presumptions of evidence", Edwin E. Ferguson, solicitor, stated.

"If an alien evacuee wishes to return to Oregon as a farm laborer, or to live and work on or manage land owned by his children or other citizens, there is no reason why he should not do so," Ferguson said.

Evacuees should be able, Ferguson added, to furnish evidence that he has no interest in the land if he is called upon to do so by Oregon law enforcement officials.

The solicitor advises that such evidence may be in the form of powers of attorney or employment contracts making it clear that any compensation is for services rendered and that it is not dependent on the crops produced.

Devers Gives Cpl. Tsutsumi Bronze Medal

HEADQUARTERS 6TH ARMY GROUP—Gen. Jacob L. Devers, commanding general of the 6th army group this week announced the awarding of a Bronze Star medal to Cpl. Noboru Tsutsumi of Heart Mountain, Wyo. Besides Corporal Tsutsumi five other nisei soldiers from relocation centers were similarly honored.

Corporal Tsutsumi, formerly of White Salmon, Wash., entered the army in May, 1943 as a volunteer. His sister, Mrs. Tom Sagara, 21-4-EF, and an aunt, Mrs. S. Nakagawa, 23-6-B, lives at Heart Mountain, Wyo.

Following is Corporal Tsutsumi's citation: " . . . for heroic achievement in the vicinity of Il Terricio, Italy, on 6 July, 1944. When an enemy barrage severed the communication line leading to a forward element, Corporal Tsutsumi voluntarily repaired and restored its function. Subsequently, when communications again became disrupted, he proceeded into the impact area, made the necessary repairs, and remained in his hazardous position for the next hour in order to keep the communication line intact."

Following are the other citations: Tech. Sgt. Albert K. Nakama and Pfc. Ted T. Yamasaki, both of Hunt, Idaho. " . . . for heroic achievement on 14 Nov., 1944 in France. When their patrol leader was

(Continued on Page 5)

'Sole Son' Policy Goes Into Effect

WASHINGTON, D.C. — In a joint extension of their "sole surviving son" policy, the War and Navy departments have announced that they will place in non-hazardous duty other service members of families in which two or more persons have died in line of duty or are reported missing in action or prisoners of war.

War and Navy department officials estimate that the new policy will affect approximately 10,000 individuals in both services. They stated that no action to reassign surviving members will be taken unless requested by the serviceman involved or by a member of his immediate family.

Requests involving army personnel should be addressed to the Adjutant General, Washington, D. C. Cases which previously have been submitted and denied should be resubmitted for consideration under the new, broader policy, the joint statement advised.

One-Third of Residents Have Finished Program To Leave Center by June

During the four-month period ending April 30, one-third of Heart Mountain's population made plans for final relocation and with the closing of schools this month added impetus is expected among residents who plan to return to the American stream of life, Joe Carroll, relocation program officer, announced this week.

From the period of Jan. 2, through April 30, 1067 families with a total of 2402 members completed their final relocation plans through the assistance of the relocation division, Carroll said.

Of this number 531 families have already left the center, and it is expected that the balance will be gone by June 1.

Of the 1067 families, 673 made plans for outside of the evacuated areas; 190 were welfare cases, and the balance, 204 families made plans for the evacuated coast area.

As of Jan. 1, there were 3189 families in the center which means that the 1067 who have completed their plans represent one-third of the entire center population, Carroll declared.

"This is remarkable," Carroll said, "in that there was little planning during the months of January and February, as many of the evacuees held hopes that the center would remain open; but as they realized that WRA was definitely going to close the centers and they saw their neighbors making plans, they too started planning."

The volume of planning has increased to such a peak that on Monday of this week, final departure plans were made for 50 people, he added.

Carroll said that it is anticipated that even this high figure will be topped when schools close and other activities decline.

"As a matter of fact," Carroll declared, "this is already evidenced by the demand for reservations for the special railroad cars in June over the requests for May cars."

Special private railroad coaches to West coast points, according to Claud Gilmore, assistant relocation officer, are now scheduled to leave Heart Mountain on May 16, June 4 and June 18.

The special coaches, Gilmore emphasized, should not be confused with the special trains that evacuated the residents. Use of the coaches will be purely voluntarily and passengers will have the same privileges extended to all travelers.

Coaches leaving here will be spotted at the railroad station the night before leaving and will be loaded shortly after noon on the day of departure. Leaving here late in the afternoon the train will be moved to Frannie where it will become a part of the Northern Pacific.

The full schedule of travel will be published in Tuesday's bulletin.

Gilmore indicated that unless more persons going to Los Angeles sign up for the May 16th

(Continued to Page Six)

GI Fathers' Greetings Must Be Mailed May 15

With outgoing soldier mail volume now in excess of 40,000,000 individual pieces a week, the War Department today urged the wives and children of American soldiers serving overseas who are contemplating the sending of Father's Day greetings to get them into the mails between now and May 15 in order to assure delivery prior to Father's Day, June 17, 1945.

Bank Accounts Unblocked by US Treasury

WASHINGTON, D.C.—To aid WRA in its relocation and liquidation program, the Treasury department has informed the WRA that they will unblock all but a limited number of the accounts of evacuees on the army clear list.

Through the project director, forms to request unblocking orders will be forwarded to the Federal Reserve bank in San Francisco. The bank will determine whether the statements on the individual forms are correct. Individual unblocking orders will be mailed in care of the project director, and private banks will be notified.

Evacuees in these categories are ineligible to apply for unblocking orders through this special arrangement with treasury: (1) persons not on the army clear list, (2) those who have been issued specific blocking orders, (3) evacuees who have

(Continued on Page 6)

11 Will Report For Induction

The local selective service office has released the names of 11 Heart Mountain draftees, who have been ordered to report for army induction next week at Fort Logan, Colo. The inductees will leave from the Sentinel building at 8:30 a.m. Thursday.

With the departure of this group, the number of men called from the center since the reinstitution of selective service for nisei will total 297. The contingent will consist of the following:

Kaoru Egawa, formerly of Heart Mountain; Herbert June Fujii, 1-5-F; Sei Paul Horiuchi, 1-8-A; Katsumi Inouye, 14-9-F; Yoshiaki Ito, 25-13-C; Hiroshi B. Kumai, 30-10-B; Kawakami, 21-13-F; Masao Morimoto, 2-5-B; Frederic Saburo Morita, 7-11-E; Satoshi Oshinomi, 20-18-E, and Noriyuki Yonemura, 21-21-F.

New Measures Taken to Aid Resettlement

WASHINGTON, D.C.—Extraordinary measures to assist resettling evacuees in finding housing have been outlined by H. Rex Lee, relocation division chief, in instructions sent to all field relocation officers.

To further this effect, Lee said, a WRA staff member will be assigned in most large offices the specific responsibility of organizing community efforts toward providing housing for relocating evacuees.

Other principal steps to be taken include:

(1) Establishment of a clearing house for all available housing information, either as a part of the community activities program to assist resettlers or as a part of the relocation office;

(2) Improving provisions for temporary housing accommodations to take care of the resettler while he is finding permanent living quarters; and

(3) Closer examination of all phases of local public housing programs and of FHA privately financed building programs.

"Primary responsibility for finding housing for his family still rests with the resettler," Lee said. "However, WRA offices should spare no effort to better coordinate the efforts of all groups working on housing and to make much information available as possible to the home-hunting relocatee."

Relocation division instructions pointed out that "since vacancies in permanent housing do not remain so very long, it is essential that families desiring housing be on the spot to take advantage of any opportunities developed." For this reason district officers are urged to secure the establishment of one or more family hostels in communities where substantial numbers of evacuees are expected to relocate. Arrangements have been completed for limited loan of equipment for these hostels in some localities from WRA centers.

Three Local Men Accepted by Army

Of the 10 Heart Mountain registrants, who reported for pre-induction physical examinations on Feb. 16 at Fort Logan, Colo., three have been accepted by the army. They are Tomomi Matsushima, 12-20-B; Seichiro Sugiura, 14-20-AB, and Masami Terada, 1-22-A.

Senators Favor U. S. Control Of Strategic Islands

By DAVID SENTNER
Sunday American Washington Bureau.

WASHINGTON, May 19.—Unanimous approval of American postwar control of strategic Pacific islands was recorded today in the first 25 responses to a poll of the United States Senate being conducted by the Washington Bureau of the Hearst newspapers.

Furthermore, twenty-three of the twenty-five Senators replying to date to a written questionnaire, stated flatly that the United States should assume sovereign possession of such strategic bases captured from Japan.

Each member of the treaty-making upper chamber was asked the following questions:

1. Do you approve of postwar control by the United States of strategic Pacific islands captured from Japan?

2. Do you believe that the United States should assume sovereign possession of such strategic bases?

3. Do you believe that the United States should accept the trusteeship of such bases under jurisdiction of the proposed international security organization?

The two Senators who failed to join their colleagues in an affirmative answer to question number two mildly qualified their responses.

Senator John L. McClellan (Democrat) of Arkansas asserted the United States should obtain sovereign rights to "some" of these strategic bases. McClellan said:

"I prefer our taking absolute control over all that we regard as essential to our future

Turn to Page 4, Column 2.

THE WEATHER

Clear, cool, not so windy; sunny and warmer in afternoon.

CHARACTER QUALITY AMERICA FIRST! ENTERPRISE ACCURACY
Baltimore American
AN AMERICAN PAPER FOR THE AMERICAN PEOPLE
The Largest Sunday Circulation in the Entire South

Est. 1773 Vol. CCLXXII SUNDAY, MAY 20, 1945 Entered as second-class matter at Baltimore Postoffice Price 15 Cents

OKINAWA JAPS STALL 4 AMERICAN DIVISIONS

BALTIMORE, NATION FETE NEW CITIZENS

By ALDINE R. BIRD

Tens of thousands of Baltimoreans will join with millions of their countrymen throughout the nation today in a record-breaking celebration of "I Am An American" Day.

INTEREST AT PEAK.

At no time since the Hearst newspapers inaugurated the annual observance in 1939 has interest been so keen and so widespread, according to officials in charge of the programs.

In Baltimore, "I Am An American Day," proclaimed by Congress as a day of tribute to the new citizens of the nation, will be featured by one of the most colorful parades in history.

With 15 divisions marching behind their color standards, and including almost every drum and bugle corps and organized bands in the city, the mammoth procession will be reviewed by an estimated 200,000 persons.

20,000 TO MARCH.

The parade will form along South Broadway from Lombard street to the market and along intersecting streets, where about 20,000 marchers have been ordered to assemble at designated spots.

At 2 P. M., Commodore LeRoy Reinberg, commandant of the U. S. Coast Guard Yard, will give the order to march.

The celebrants will move along Lombard, Patterson Park avenue, Baltimore street and into the park where impressive ceremonies will follow.

At the athletic field in the park, Mayor McKeldin and Governor O'Conor will pay tribute to the new twenty-one-year-old citizens and others naturalized within the past year.

Cpl. John Evans, Baltimore barytone, will sing "I Am An American!" and other patriotic numbers, as well as lead the huge throng in singing the Star-Spangled Banner.

Gene Krupa, one of the world's

Turn to Page 2, Column 7

Route Of 'American Day' Parade

Here is the route of the "I Am An American" Day parade today:

Head of parade, Lombard and Broadway.

Route: East on Lombard to Patterson Park avenue, north to Baltimore, east to park entrance, thence to athletic field and past the reviewing platform where all units will assemble on the field.

Neighborhood service flags also will mass on the field for blessing and rededication ceremonies.

Citizenship tribute, main platform, 3.30 P. M.

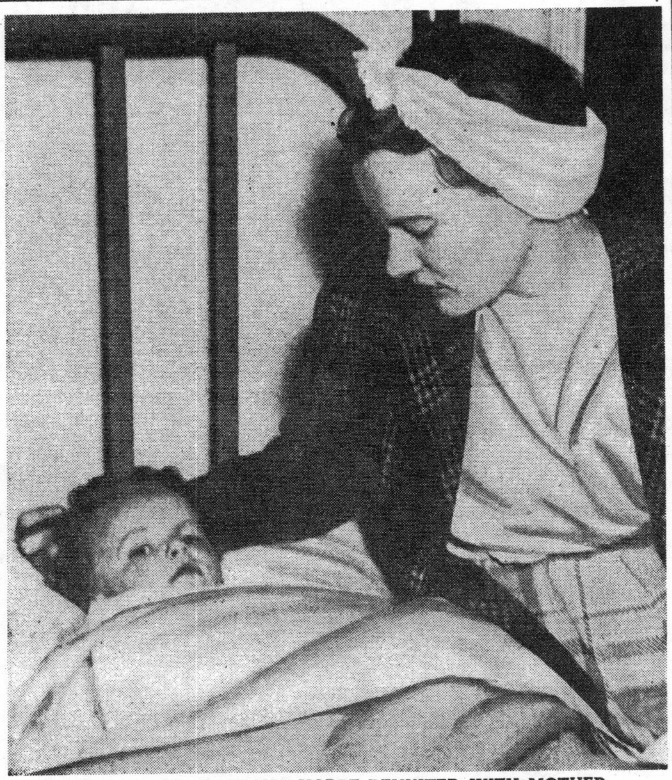

SAFE AT HOME—DIANA HOPPE REUNITED WITH MOTHER
Found after night in Joppa woods, child is put to bed.

Missing Child Safe Near Home, Guarded By Her Dog

After a search which lasted all Friday night and up through noon yesterday, three-year-old Diana Hoppe was found yesterday—found in a woods only 500 feet from the home of her grandparents, from which she had disappeared.

She is the daughter of Ensign and Mrs. Gordon Hoppe.

The blonde and blue-eyed child was discovered by three soldiers from Edgewood Arsenal, who formed one of the numerous posses which combed the country about Joppa, Harford county, where the child's grandparents, Mr. and Mrs. Joseph Hoppe, lived.

Standing guard over Diana, as she lay resting against a log, was one of her two pet dogs—a faithful sentinel.

The dogs, Kam and Butch, had disappeared with Diana on Friday as the child left the garden of the Hoppe's home after her grandmother had refused to give her a piece of cake.

Diana seemed exhausted and she was pinched and pale from exposure to the nipping night air. She had a few cuts and bruises. Otherwise, she seemed none the worse for her trying experience.

Ensign Hoppe, who has received two awards for outstanding performance, is on submarine duty in the South Pacific.

U.S., Norway, Danes Are Again In Touch

NEW YORK, May 19—(I. N. S.).—Telegraph and radio communications between the United States and Norway and Denmark have been resumed, RCA Communications, Inc., and Western Union announced today.

OPA To Permit Oil For Hot Water

WASHINGTON, May 19—(U. P.).—The Office of Price Administration said today fuel oil rations would be available this summer for all oil cooking stoves and hot-water heaters.

Herriot, Liberated, Flies To France

PARIS, May 19—(U. P.).—Former French Premier Edouard Herriot, who was liberated by the Russian Army from German imprisonment, arrived by plane from Tunis today at Marignane, near Marseilles.

Chaplin's Retrial Hearing Set May 25

HOLLYWOOD, May 19—(U. P.).—Superior Court hearing on Comedian Charlie Chaplin's motion for retrial of Joan Barry's charges that he fathered her baby daughter Carol Ann was set today for May 25.

5 PCT. DECLINE IN 1945 FOOD PRODUCTS SEEN

WASHINGTON, May 19 — (U. P.).—American farmers are expected to raise five per cent less food this year than they did last year, it was announced today as the Government began paying out a new $40,000,000 meat subsidy and a Congressional committee prepared to make recommendations to alleviate the sugar shortage.

The Agriculture Department said most of the expected five per cent drop from last year's record-breaking production would be caused by smaller slaughter of meat animals.

32 P. C. HIGHER.

The Department said this year's total farm output would be 32 per cent higher than prewar food production.

However, it pointed out, the per capita supply for U. S. civilians will drop 5 to 7 per cent from last year's figure.

This will bring civilian food

Turn to Page 2, Column 3

JAP SUICIDE 'AIR COFFIN' FAST ROCKET

By JOHN R. HENRY

GUAM, May 19—(I. N. S.). First description of Japan's new "Flying Coffin" in action was provided today by Lt. (j. g.) Andrew Chancellor, who said he was impressed by the blinding speed of a Baka-bomb which attempted to attack his destroyer off Okinawa.

Declaring the attack by the fantastic sky weapon—a winged rocket projectile flown by a human pilot on a one-way ride—occurred in less time than it takes to tell about it.

Chancellor said its destruction in the air was the result of "a lucky shot."

He explained:

"It came in at the height of a sustained battle with Japanese kamikaze (suicide) planes.

LIKE LIGHTNING.

"We had splashed two of the kamikaze boys, and we thought we had driven off a large twin-engine Jap plane flying with them. We were about to congratulate ourselves when that thing started at us like a streak of lightning."

The enemy bomber, Chancellor recalled, suddenly nosed up and turned away from ships his destroyer was screening. He said the plane flew as if it were trying to avoid fires from the destroyer.

"Then the bomber dropped what we first believed to be a belly tank, or maybe an ordinary bomb," he continued in describing how the object which turned out to be the human-guided rocket was launched from the mother plane at an altitude of about 600 feet.

GATHERED SPEED.

As it streaked toward the destroyer, the rocket propellant gathered tremendous momentum.

He added:

"The range-finder operator yelled that it was coming so fast he could not track it in, machine-gunners opened fire at it, and you could see their bullets bouncing off.

"Our five-inch mounts also were shooting—then there was a terrific explosion."

DIRECT HIT STOPPED IT.

The Baka bomb, which Chancellor described as a silvery, twin-tailed missile, disintegrated with its son of heaven some fifty feet off the side of the destroyer, its warhead tearing through the air across the ship's fantail.

The gleaming flying casket for the Jap aviator had sustained a direct hit from one of the destroyer's five inchers.

Chancellor estimated that the projectile was traveling at a speed of 420 knots when the sharp shooting destroyer's gunners obtained their "lucky shot."

LEGLESS AUTO DRIVER

EVERETT, Mass., May 19—(I. N. S.).—Richard Sinclair, twenty, became the first legless veteran of World War II to be given an automobile driver's license in Massachusetts.

BULLETIN

NEW YORK, May 19—(I. N. S.).—German civilians condemned to death, after approval by Gen. Dwight D. Eisenhower, will be shipped to German prisons where the execution by beheading will take place, B. B. C., heard by N. B. C., said today.

Von Wiegand Says:

Third World War Forecasts Loom

By KARL H. VON WIEGAND
Dean of American Foreign Correspondents.
(Written Expressly for the Hearst Newspapers.)

MADRID, May 19.—Political confusion, economic chaos, moral disintegration and hunger are growing apace in Europe with every passing day.

Nowhere yet is there any sign of genius or capacity for reorganization and reconstruction.

Instead, the public mind is being focused on the war crimes psychosis.

Behind the 7,000 "executions" of Italians in North Italy, which apparently is in a state of anarchy despite the presence of the American Fifth and British Eighth Armies, the 2,700 persons condemned to death and shot or hanged in Bulgaria; the 1,600 death sentences imposed in De Gaulle France, and the reportedly gradual extermination of the Magyar aristocracy, landowners and intelligentsia in Hungary, are the same sinister forces.

Paris announces officially that in France in the municipal elections just held, the Communists and Socialists won a majority in 458 municipalities, against the 279 previously held.

MODERATE PARTIES LOSE.

The moderate parties, who held 484 municipalities, dropped to 110, a loss of 374 cities, towns and villages.

This political barometric indication of coming storms is highly significant and not limited to France.

As Europe takes stock two weeks after the end of the war, it finds the general situation on the Continent growing worse.

With the common enemy, Germany, defeated and now the object of rival exploitation—and the German people a prize to be won for willing aid in the very possible future conflict—the spirit of the "grand alliance" of America,

Turn to Page 4, Column 1.

Matchless Gun Light Good As Six-Shooter Gas Thief

CHICAGO, May 19—(I. N. S.). A match apparently is as effective as a six-shooter in capturing a suspected gasoline thief.

Otto Makovicko testified yesterday that he saw Eugene J. Martin, eighteen, leaning over his automobile gas tank the other day and gave chase. The youth darted under a porch, when Makovicko lit a match to look for him, he said:

"For Pete's sake, put that thing out. I swallowed some of your gas and I spilled some on my clothes. Do you want me to blow up?"

The judge put the boy under court supervision until October.

'Bogey,' Miss Bacall On Way To Wedding

HOLLYWOOD, May 19—(I. N. S.).—Humphrey Bogart and Lauren Bacall were on their way East today on the Santa Fe Super-chief—object, matrimony. They will be married Monday at the Mansfield (Ohio) farm of author Louis Bromfield, long a friend of the screen's "tough guy." It will be Bogart's fourth marriage, Miss Bacall's first.

MOTHER CHOKES CHILD TO DEATH

BURLINGTON, Vt., May 19—(U. P.).—Mrs. Helen C. Hinchey, thirty-nine, wife of the State director of the Federal Housing Authority, strangled her baby daughter, attempted to strangle her infant son and then tried to drown herself in a bathtub today, police announced.

Frederick C. Hinchey made the discovery.

He told police that he had left home at about 8.30 A. M. and that at the time his wife appeared normal. Authorities said, however, that she had been suffering from despondency for perhaps a week.

In the house Hinchey and police found his children, Elizabeth, three, and John, five months, sprawled on a bed. His wife lay in the water-filled bathtub.

Elizabeth was dead, but the baby was revived.

State's Attorney Clark A. Gravel ordered the woman committed to the State (mental) Hospital at Waterbury.

TOKYO'S NEW 'GARDENS'

NEW YORK, May 19—(I. N. S.).—The Japanese Domei Agency reported today that "ravaged" areas of Tokyo are being converted into vegetable gardens.

LAND, SEA AIR FORCES IN BATTLE

GUAM, May 19—(U. P.). Japanese troops on Southern Okinawa battled four American divisions almost to a standstill today as the bloodiest campaign of the Pacific war went into its forty-ninth day on a note of rising fury.

Marines and Army troops were inside Naha, Shuri and Yonabaru, the three anchors of the Japanese line, but key hills dominating the cities were changing hands as many as four times in 24 hours in the swaying battle.

'JAPS CRACKING.'

There were some signs that the Japanese were cracking under the terrific American pressure and ceaseless land, sea and air bombardment.

However, commanders cautiously reserved final judgment. The battle was far from over.

A front dispatch said marines of the Sixth Division had penetrated as much as 500 yards into Naha, ruined capital of Okinawa and western anchor of the enemy line.

HAND-TO-HAND.

The First Marine Division finally won control of the northern slopes of Sugar Loaf hill northeast of Naha in bitter hand-to-hand fighting, but its crest was a no man's land.

Japanese still controlled the southern slopes of the hill, holding up virtually the entire western flank of the Okinawa front.

Marines have tried nine times unsuccessfully to dislodge them in the past week. The crest changed hands four times yesterday alone.

Complete conquest of the hill well might open up a corridor that would enable the Americans to envelop both Naha and Shuri.

A Pacific Fleet communique said Sugar Loaf Hill had been captured, but front dispatches indicated this was premature.

MARINES ADVANCE.

The Seventh Regiment of the First Marine Division advanced 250 yards and sent patrols into

Turn to Page 2, Column 1

Roosevelt Had Own Bomb Shelter

WASHINGTON, May 19—(I. N. S.).—Relaxation of censorship permits the disclousure today that a bomb shelter was built for late President Roosevelt and his family shortly after America's entry into the war. The shelter itself was a vault deep inside the Treasury Building, adjacent to the White House.

DIRECTORY

Australia Demands Execution Of Japan's Emperor Hirohito

AFTERNOON DAILY
(No Issue on Sunday)
Member: United Press

Guerrilla

"A FEARLESS PAPER FOR A FEARLESS PEOPLE"

Complete News of the Day
Clear, Concise, Consistent
Greater Than Ever

Vol. I — No. 24 | MANILA, FRIDAY, MAY 25, 1945 | TWENTY CENTAVOS A COPY

GESTAPO CHIEF HIMMLER KILLS SELF

Two Sides of the Question:

What Is G. O. 20?

CABILI BARES ATTEMPTS TO SABOTAGE P. I. ARMY RULING

ORDER BARRING "COLLABORATORS" FROM ARMY DEFINED BY HERNANDEZ

By UNITED PRESS

MANILA, May 24 (UP).—Secretary of National Defense Tomas L. Cabili told the United Press today there were evidence of "sabotage" in the enforcement of Philippine Army General Order No. 20, which defines the policy toward officers and men who served in any capacity under the Japanese or the puppet republic.

Commenting on a press report of a "rift" between him and Major-General Basilio J. Valdes, chief of staff of the Philippine Army, Cabili disclosed that he had written General Valdes asking him "if this is true."

Couched in characteristic Cabili language, the letter to the chief of staff challenged him to come out openly "if you have now changed your mind and do not agree in the enforcement of this order."

ORDER IS ORDER

Cabili, who has actually ordered recalled seven Philippine Army officers already en route to the United States for further studies on ground that they served under the Japanese, reiterated that he stands for strict enforcement of General Order No. 20, whose salient provision is as follows:

"By direction of the President and with the approval of the commanding general, USAFFE, the following policy has been established:

"No officer or enlisted man of the Philippine Army or the Philippine Constabulary, called into the service of the United States Forces in the Far East, will be retained in such service or on active duty in the Philippine Army who accepted appointment or performed service in a military or civil capacity in any activity controlled by the Japanese or by the so-called puppet 'Philippine Republic'."

"SUPERIOR ORDERS"

Charging laxity in the enforcement of the order, Cabili emphatically asserted that so far as he was concerned they were "superior orders" which must be carried out.

Cabili's utterances in this regard have drawn varied comment, including adverse criticism of his strong and at one time "unbecoming" language.

"Well," said Cabili, explaining his diction, "I did not go through a finishing school in Switzerland. I come from the wilds of Mindanao."

Tension in Cabili's department reached a high-water mark recently in the case of Brigadier-General Manuel A. Roxas, who was liberated by American forces recently near Baguio.

The loyalty status board, headquarters, Philippine Army, after considering General Roxas' case recommended that he be retained in the service. Cabili, however, has not approved the recommendation, which was forwarded to him by General Valdes.

NO CHOICE OF ACTION

The loyalty status board said "it is very evident that Brigadier-General Roxas is not adversely affected by General Order No. 20 in spite of his having accepted civil positions in the puppet 'Philippine republic' because he was never a free man, and had no choice of action."

The board had added:

"The fact that he 'was not given formal release papers' is an indication that he was still a prisoner of war during the whole time he was made to work for the puppet government, and as such had to do things imposed upon him. Even then, he succeeded in evading the discharge of his duties as member of the cabinet and did not receive any salary as chairman of the economic planning board and chairman of the Naric. The board had personal knowledge that Brigadier-General Roxas, as a member of the cabinet of the puppet president, Jose P. Laurel, had to go with the Japanese authorities to Baguio just before the arrival of the liberation forces in Manila. Hence he was a virtual prisoner of war up to the time he reached the American lines in the campaign for the liberation of Baguio.

BACKBONE OF RESISTANCE

In a memorandum to the national defense secretary, General Valdes indicated his approval of the decision of the loyalty board, said that General Roxas "was the backbone, in many instances, of the underground resistance

(Please turn to page 2)

These articles constitute my personal impressions of General Orders No. 20 and do not in any way represent official opinion of the Philippine Army. I present them to the people as a humble citizen of the Philippines.—AUTHOR

By JOSE M. HERNANDEZ

General Orders No. 20 was issued by the Chief of Staff of the Philippine Army by direction of the Secretary of National Defense.

The oft-repeated purpose of the order is to weed out collaborators from the Philippine Army.

General Orders No. 20 provides: that no officer or enlisted man who has served in a civilian or military capacity under the puppet Republic of the Philippines or Japanese agencies shall be retained in the service unless he resigned on or before 20 September, 1944, joined a guerrilla unit, and actively participated in guerrilla activities or in aiding the United States forces of liberation; that members of the chaplain and medical services who in the practise of their professions were engaged in humanitarian activities are exempted; that reserve officers who fall under . O. No. 20 shall be reverted to inactive status and regular officers shall be given the choice of a court-martial or resignation from the army.

LOYALTY BOARD FORMED

To carry out the provisions of this order a loyalty status board has been appointed to look over the affidavits and other processing papers submitted by officers and men who have reported for duty. Sufficient discretion is allowed the chief of staff in rendering decisions based on the findings of the board. At first the loyalty board was merely a classification body. Later it was given more discretion. But when it used its discretion as in the case of Brig. Gen. Roxas the secretary of national defense ruled that the members of the board should base their recommendations solely on the affidavits and processing papers, not on personal knowledge. As matters now stand the final decision on any case is in the hands of the secretary of national defense. In the hollow of one hand he holds the balance of life and death for about 90% of the Usaffe or roughly 30,000 Philippine Army officers and men and their 100,000 or more dependents.

ALSO COLLABORATORS?

Under General Orders No. 20, Brig. Gen. Manuel A. Roxas whose patriotism cannot be doubted even by the secretary of national defense is guilty of collaboration. Col. Mariano N. Castañeda who organized 14 regiments of guerrillas in Cavite is, likewise, a collaborator. Neither Roxas nor Castañeda resigned on or before 20 September, 1944. Thousands of others under similar circumstances are collaborators.

Under General Orders No. 20, hundreds of reserve officers have already been sent home without trial, and high ranking regular officers await court-martial charged with violation of Article of War No. 97.

(To be continued)

Americans Trap 30,000 Japs

YANKS GAIN 2,000 YARDS NEAR SHURI

East and West Pincers Steadily Moving To Seal Gap

FLANK PENETRATED

1,000 Japs Hurled Back In All-Day Counter-Attack

By FRANK TREMAINE
United Press War Correspondent

PEARL HARBOR, May 25—(UP)—American forces gained up to 2,000 yards in a new drive to encircle bitterly defended Shuri, in southern Okinawa, yesterday, front dispatches reported this morning.

The Marines in the west and the infantrymen in the east forged to close the new trap around the inland citadel and probably also the bulk of the island's 30,000 remaining Japanese troops.

One column went across the Asato River deep into the ruins of Naha, the Okinawan capital, and another knifed southeast toward the rear approaches of Shuri. Infantry units drove 2,000 yards into the Japanese flank from the captured east coast port of Yonabaru.

Three American divisions were virtually stalemated in the frontal assault on Shuri's powerful defenses. One division hurled back 1,000 counter-attacking Japanese after an all-day battle in which the enemy penetrated the American lines up to 600 yards. Some 150 Japanese were killed.

Naha may yet fall without a major battle, front dispatches indicated today. American patrols which pushed across the Asato from the Marines' bridghead found neither mines nor prepared positions. The possibility still remained, however, that the Japanese garrison may have gone underground and permitted the patrols to roam the streets unmolested in an effort to draw the main Leatherneck force into a trap.

Tokyo Admits Jap "Suicide" Airbases Destroyed By Yanks

180 Carrier-Planes Pound Airfields As Tokyo Blaze Rages

SINGAPORE RAIDED

Former British Fortress Blasted In First B-24 Raid

GUAM, May 25—(UP)—Tokyo Radio this morning reported that 180 American carrier planes attacked suicide airbases in southern Japan yesterday while miles of Tokyo's industrial waterfront still blazed from the record Superfortress raid.

The carrier planes began their attacks on the Kyushu airbases at 3 o'clock yesterday afternoon, Japan time, the broadcast said. Damage was said to be "relatively light."

An intercepted Domei report said that 23 American B-24 Liberators raided Japanese installations on Singapore yesterday. This was the first time that B-24's were reported over the former British fortress. The report did not give any clue about the base from which the Liberators staged the reported raid. Singapore is beyond the range of known Liberator bases.

The B-29 strike on Tokyo yesterday morning was the heaviest so far. More than 550 giant bombers took part, dropping 4,500 tons of incendiary bombs. Fires were visible 200 miles away at sea.

Radio Tokyo reported that the Shizuoka and Hamamatsu areas were also hit.

American bombs landed for the second time in Imperial Palace compounds and destroyed the imperial arbor, Radio Tokyo reported. A building housing fire fighting equipment in the Akasaka detached palace was also destroyed by fire.

Fires also were started in Yokohama, Kawasaki, Shizuoka and the southern district of the Saitama prefecture.

P. I. Freedom Before 1946 Sure-Osmeña

By RODOLFO L. NAZARENO
United Press Staff Correspondent

MANILA, May 24 (UP).—President Sergio Osmeña in a press conference today confirmed that Philippine independence could come before July 4, 1946, the date set by the Tydings-McDuffie law.

Mr. Osmeña said that President Truman, with whom he has conferred three times, assured him that the late President Roosevelt's policies concerning the Philippines, including the plan to advance the date of independence, will be carried out. He added that in this conection Mr. Truman appointed Senator Millard Tydings as his personal envoy to survey economic conditions in the Philippines.

In response to queries regarding future American military bases in the Philippines, the President said that he always had been in favor of those bases and he still is. He said that if it should be necessary to provide ground forces for those bases, the Philippines would do so. He added that he is even ready to go to the people if it should be necessary to do in connection with the establishment of those bases.

Asked whether he would convene the Philippine Congress, whose 100-day session period ends today, Mr. Osmeña said that in a week or so he would call a session of the lawmaking body. Congressmen have been meeting in caucuses, but thus far have not yet met in session. The senators likewise have not yet had a session.

Looking well and clear-complexioned although apparently a little tired, the President was in high spirits as he sat down in Malacañan's cabinet room after shaking hands with the crowds of newspa-

(Please turn to page 2)

Allies Expected To Answer Tito's Settlement Plan

ROME, May 25—(UP)—The Allies were expected to answer soon Marshal Joseph Tito's proposals for settling the Trieste problem.

One difficult point in Tito's proposal, according to reports today, was his suggestion to leave Yugoslav personnel in key posts in the disputed Italian province of Venezia Giulia.

Tito's latest note to the American and British governments is generally considered conciliatory but not entirely satisfactory, it is understood.

However, reliable sources said that the Yugoslav note virtually assured the peaceful settlement of the Trieste problem, which had been the major threat to peace in Europe since the surrender of Germany.

Churchill's Son Expected To Get Big Cabinet Job

By PHILIP AULT
United Press War Correspondent

LONDON, May 24 — (UP) — Prime Minister Winston Churchill sat up most of the night last night selecting his new cabinet, but political observers believed he would not make any sensational changes.

One appointment rumor in Whitehall circles is that Churchill would name his son, Major Randolph Churchill, to succeed Major Arthur Henderson as financial secretary to the War Office. Major Churchill returned from the Middle East last week.

The prime minister is also expected to name a number of young members of Parliament, who have not held office previously, to junior posts vacated by members of the dissenting Labor Party. The aim would be to give new blood to the cabinet.

At the same time, observers believed that Churchill would fill the top posts left open by the Labor Party's secession with tried, experienced administrators. His most difficult task will be to replace such able cabinet members as the First Lord of Admiralty Sir A. V. Alexander and Home Secretary Herbert Morrison, who directed Great Britain's defense against Nazi blitz.

Shell Explodes

Five Persons Killed, Eight Injured In Malate Blast

Five persons were instantly killed and eight others were seriously injured when three-year-old Antonia Lineses accidentally stepped on a big shell buried in the yard of her home at 1159 Int. 4 Agno, Malate, early Monday morning.

Those killed by the explosion were Antonia Lineses, Roberto San Antonio, Melquiades Picpic, Santos Picpic and Lucito Reyes, all residing at 1159 Int. Agno.

Those injured were Jesuita Ramilo, Virginia Ramilo, Angela Caballes, Salvadora Caballes, Teodoro Reyes, Norberto Pascual and Zenaida Sugitan, also residing at the same house.

JAP MIKADO BLAMED FOR PACIFIC WAR

Sino Spokesman Supports Demand For Hirohito's Execution

ATROCITIES CITED

U. S. Attitude Toward Prosecution Of Emperor Unknown

By EDWARD ROBERTS
United Press War Correspondent

LONDON, May 25—(UP)—Australia has formally demanded the indictment and execution of Emperor Hirohito, who as the head of the state, should be held responsible for Japan's "systematic barbarities," the United Press learned from reliable sources today.

An unofficial Chinese spokesman declared that China would support the demand before the United Nations War Crimes Commission. The spokesman claimed that Japanese atrocities committed in the Pacific war area were but a repetition of barbarous acts in China. In Nanking, he recalled, thousands were slaughtered and hundreds of women were violated when the Chinese capital fell in December, 1937.

The attitude of the United States toward the suggested prosecution of the Mikado as a war criminal has not been disclosed. Reports received here indicated that some State Department advisers believed that Hirohito should be spared and that the war responsibility should be placed solely upon Japanese military and economic leaders.

The reported Australian demand was said to have been attached to an authenticated report of Japanese atrocities in New Guinea which has just been submitted to the War Crimes Commission.

When the report first reached

(Please turn to page 2)

4 Stamp Agencies

The bureau of posts announced that for the benefit of people residing far from the Manila post office, four stamp agencies have been established at the drug stores located in the following places: corner of Antipolo and Rizal Avenue; corner of Bambang and Rizal Avenue; corner of Tabora and M. de los Santos; and at 554 Herbosa, Tondo.

NAZI LEADER DRINKS PHIAL OF CYANIDE

Hitler's No. 1 Hangman Ends It All In British Headquarters

ARREST DESCRIBED

Himmler Reveals Identity When Nabbed By Dempsey's Men

LONDON, May 24 (UP).—Heinrich Himmler committed suicide last night at the headquarters of the British Second Army, Radio Luxemburg reported today.

The broadcast referred to the report as an "official announcement."

By BRUCE MUNN
Special to the GUERRILLA

PARIS, May 24 (UP).—Gestapo Chief Heinrich Himmler is dead.

He committed suicide at the British Second Army Headquarters in Luneburg Wednesday night, it was officially announced tonight.

The man who assisted Adolf Hitler to rule the Third Reich and the occupied countries with terror swallowed the contents of a hidden phial of potassium cyanide.

Himmler had kept the phial in his mouth throughout the three days of his captivity, an Exchange-Telegraph dispatch from Luneburg said.

According to the dispatch, Himmler was wearing a pair of pearl colored horn-rimmed glasses and had shaved off his mustache when he was arrested. His body lay on the floor in the front parlor of the house and the mustache could again be seen on the cruel, thin upper lip.

He swallowed the poison while undergoing a medical examination designed to determine whether he was carrying poison. When the doctor told him to come under a light for an examination of his mouth, Him-

(Please turn to page 2)

Youth Kills Self

Despondent Soldier Commits Suicide At Hospital

Dr. D. Lacuna of the Psychopatic hospital in Mandaluyong reported to the police the suicide by hanging of Emilio Martin, 22 years, a soldier from Camp Murphy, who hanged himself at 5 p.m. on May 21.

Investigation disclosed that the victim was admitted into the hospital on May 19 for sanity test. When discovered, he was found hanging from an iron railing in an isolation room, using his fatigue uniform to end it all. The suicide was attributed to despondency over his condition.

Nueno Hits 'Compadre' System In City Gov't

Voicing the people's belief that "the resurrection of our democratic system of government, so dearly purchased at the supreme sacrifice of blood and treasure by both our victimized people and the unselfish, fearless and invincible American liberators would mean a better, more efficient and less self-seeking administration of public business," Jose Topacio Nueno, former city councilor, in a letter to Secretary of the Interior Tomas Confesor, declared that the people of Manila are beginning to "see the ominous writing in the wall of their exiled City Hall—red tape, nepotism, inefficiency, 'compadre' and 'kami-kami' system, discrimination, special favors for privileges, etc."

Nueno, who is now judge advocate of the Fil-American general headquarters staff, further stated that "the license racket" which re-

(Please turn to page 2)

Confesor To Address Pritil Mart Vendors

Secretary of the Interior Tomas Confesor will be the guest of honor and principal speaker on the celebration sponsored by Kalipunan ng Mga Nagtitinda sa Pamilihang Pritil on Sunday morning, May 27.

Under the guidance of President Saturnino de la Cruz, Miss Aurelia de Lara and Mr. Arturo Limson, treasurers, with the help of the market vendors, the affair promises to be a lively one.

N. ECIJA TO SELL 20,000 SACKS OF RICE TO ECA

Special to the GUERRILLA

CABANATUAN, May 25.—In accordance with an agreement entered into between Secretary of the Interior Tomas Confesor and Juan Feleo, representing the rice producers of Nueva Ecija, steps are being taken to gather 20,000 cavans of palay from 17 municipalities of the province to be sold to the Emergency Control administration at the controlled price of ₱3.00 per cavan.

The agreement provides that rice producers who sell palay to the ECA will be given an opportunity to buy prime commodities from the ECA at controlled prices, corresponding to the cost of palay sold to the government.

The palay will come from the following municipalities: Cabiao, San Isidro, San Antonio, Gapan, Jaen, San Leonardo, Peñaranda, Sta. Rosa, Cabanatuan, Aliaga, Zaragoza, Laur, Bongabon, Sto. Domingo, Licab, Quezon and Rizal.

Feleo will supervise the gathering of palay from the 17 towns. ECA trucks will haul the palay from these towns to its warehouses. It is stipulated in the agreement that Feleo will deliver to the ECA 20,000 cavans of palay before the end of this month.

P. I. Foreign Policy Ass'n Elects Heads

Dr. Bernabe Africa, Filipino political scientist, and Atty. Lorenzo Sumulong were last Wednesday reelected president and vice-president, respectively, of the Philippine Academy of Foreign Affairs (PAFA), formerly known as the Foreign Policy Association of the Philippines. The name was changed to avoid its being confused with the Foreign Policy Association in N. Y. City.

The other officers of the PAFA include Atty. Manuel Enverga, secretary; Atty. Enrique Palma, treasurer; Dr. Alberto Reyes, auditor; Dr. Andres V. Castillo, director of research; Dr. Victoriano Diamonon, director of legislation; Dr. Adeudato J. Agbayani, director of publications and public relations; Atty. Dominador M. Ambrosio and Prof. Jose Ma. Espino, directors-at-large.

Captain Carlos Lazo, press relation officer of a group of guerrilla forces, has been assigned to help gather reading materials for the PAFA reading room at the office of Atty. Enverga, second floor, State building, Rizal Avenue.

MAGALONA BILL WOULD GIVE BACK SALARIES TO GOV'T MEN

MANILA, May 23—(UP)—Representative Enrique Magalona of Occidental Negros has filled a bill providing for the payment of all salaries and wages of government officials and employees corresponding to the period of Japanese occupation.

The bill specifies that period as from January 1, 1942, when the Commonwealth government ceased to function in Manila, up to February 27, 1945, when it was reestablished following the arrival here of the American forces of liberation. Officials and employees of the University of the Philippines and of government-owned or government-controlled corporations are inclued in the provisions of the bill.

The measure specifically provides that officers and employees found guilty after due investigation of espionage or of an act constituting disloyalty to the Philippine government or to the United States at any time during the Japanese occupation or during the existence of the puppet republic shall not be entitled to any back pay.

"Equity and humanitarian considerations are the motives behind this measure," Magalona explained. "When the seat of our government was transferred to the United States, the commonwealth continued to function abroad, and it never ceased functioning also when the President evacuated Manila and stayed in Corregidor as well as during the Japanese occupation....

"Thus in law the Commonwealth government continued to exist here during all these three years of savage and cruel Japanese occupation . . . and the officers and employees who were virtually prisoners of the Japanese . . . did not lose their connection with the government of the Commonwealth. For this reason the back pay proposed is believed just and in order."

Tondo Man Injured

Agapito Cajele of Tondo was injured Sunday when he fished out of the sea a metal object, presumably a hand grenade, which a neighbor named Prasio threw into the water the day before. As Agapito was taking it apart, it exploded and injured his hands and face.

Marines Attack Naha Airfield

British Casualties In War 1,128,315

THE WEATHER
Sunny, warm this afternoon; fair, cooler, tonight; Wednesday cooler, showers in afternoon.

Read The Baltimore News-Post for complete, accurate war coverage. It is the only Baltimore newspaper possessing the three great wire services—
ASSOCIATED PRESS
INTERNATIONAL NEWS SERVICE
UNITED PRESS

THE BALTIMORE NEWS-POST
AN INDEPENDENT NEWSPAPER
The Largest Evening Circulation in the Entire South

NIGHT
Wall St. Opening

VOL. CXLVII.—NO. 21 Entered as second-class matter at Baltimore Postoffice. TUESDAY EVENING, MAY 29, 1945 PRICE 3 CENTS

YOKOHAMA BURNING AFTER BIG B-29 RAID

Egypt Backs Syria As 100 Die In Clash

LONDON, May 29—(I. N. S.).—Syria's determination to refuse to enter into any treaty with the French which would give them concessions in the Near East was voiced today by Acting Premier Kamil Mardam Bey. The statement came in the wake of a promise by Egyptian Prime Minister Nokrashy Pasha that Egypt would give its full support to Syria and Lebanon in their dispute with the French.

LONDON, May 29—(A. P.).—The tiny Middle-Eastern French mandates of Syria and Lebanon, backed by the Arab League, appeared today to be forcing a show-

BEYROUTH, May 29—(U. P.). One hundred Syrians have been killed and 300 wounded so far in widespread fighting with French forces in the Levant, Jemil Mardam, acting premier of Syria, reported today.

down which may cost France part of her empire.

Diplomatic observers in London, who are watching developments in the Levant with apprehension, expressed the view that France had only two alternatives—either she must stand by her demands and put down opposition by force if necessary or she must withdraw and accept inevitable loss of prestige as an imperial Power.

FIGHTING CONTINUES

Fighting already has broken out in Syria between French forces and natives protesting their presence. An Associated Press dispatch from Damascus said Syria's Acting Premier Jamil Mardam Bey had expressed fears that a "general clash" might be near as fighting spread to Homs, 120 miles north of the capital, after the French had moved reinforcements from there to quell an outbreak at Hama, 30 miles farther north.

SYRIAN AMBUSH

Syrians ambushed and captured three French armored cars, killing six crewmen and wounding three others.

French gendarmes were reported in control of the railroad station, with Syrian Bedouins moving in on the town from the desert to the east.

Marines Launch Big Battle For Naha Airdrome

By JOHN R. HENRY
International News Service Staff Correspondent.

GUAM, May 29.—Okinawa's largest air field was brought within the gunsights of American Marines today as the Leathernecks completed mopping up practically all of rubbled Naha and rolled to the edge of a narrow inlet separating them from Naha airdrome.

As elements of Maj. Gen. Lemuel Shepherd's Sixth Marine Division drew up on the northern bank of the 500-yard-wide inlet, only a mile of ground and Nip defenses were between them and the sprawling field. The 'drome is situated on the peninsula across the bay from Naha.

The marine guns already were able to play into the town of Kukibana, lying on the opposite shore, and the leathernecks can drop even mortar fire into the already heavily bomb-pocked airfield.

While these elements of the Sixth Division concentrated on this new target, others of Shepherd's troops hammered a wedge of envelopment deeper south of Naha in a continued effort to isolate Shuri. The latter bastion is already cut off from the east, north and west.

SHURI PERIL GROWS

Swinging couth and slightly to the southeast, these marines threatened Shuri from the rear, as did the Seventh Division standing two miles below that city. Patrols of veteran Seventh, meantime, pressed out into Chinen Peninsula, which forms the southern shoreline of Baten bay.

In this bay International News Service War Correspondent George McWilliams reported, reconnaissance troops captured 16 Japanese motor torpedo barges.

Other elements of the Seventh, however, were pressing toward the center of the island to cut off Shuri, the core of Japanese defenses, which already was under heavy fire from three sides. Shuri still held out desperately against the frontal thrusts of the First Marine Division, and of the Army's eSventy-seventh and Ninety-sixth Divisions.

Fleet Admiral Chester W. Nimitz said, though, that the U. S. Tenth Army marines and doughboys were making "substantial" progress. In the same communique, Nimitz revealed that Japanese airmen in attacks on

Continued on Page 2, Column 3.

MASS EVACUATION

GUAM, May 29—(A. P.). Eighteen hospital planes returned 576 wounded men from Okinawa to the Marianas today in the largest single air evacuation mission of the Pacific war.

Twelve of the planes were operated by the Naval Air Transport Service and six by the Army Air Transport Command.

4,800,000 Seen Out Of Jobs In Next 6 Months

WASHINGTON, May 29 — (A. P.).—War demands will turn loose 4,800,000 workers and fighters in the next six months, but fewer persons will be seeking jobs then than three months from now.

WPB Chairman J. A. Krug made these predictions today, estimating the decline in the number of war workers during June, July and August at 2,900,000.

Joblessness during that time, he said, will jump about 1,100,000 persons to around 1,900,000.

WORK FOR 700,000

Krug said about 700,000 of those to be released from war production in the next three months will continue or soon find employment in plants shifting to civilian production.

Others, he added, will be absorbed in civilian manufacturing, construction trades and services and other civilian occupations. Nevertheless, he figures there will be a net increase of 1,100,000 in unemployment.

AREAS LIMITED

As of May 12, Krug reported, the 1945 munitions program had been slashed by $7,000,000,000, leaving it at $55,000,000,000.

Krug predicted most of the unemployment would be concentrated in a limited number of areas "where it is not possible to match increases in civilian production against decreases in military production."

This is particularly true, he said, in some of the cuts in shipyards and aircraft plants.

TYDINGS IN MANILA—Senator Millard Tydings of Maryland (left) and Sergio Osmena (center), President of the Philippines, are greeted by Gen. Douglas MacArthur as they arrive at Nichols Field, Manila, to study Philippine rehabilitation problems. Associated Press Wirephoto.

Returning Pilots Report 'City A Blazing Inferno,' Smoke Rising 20,000 Ft.

By JULIAN HARTT
International News Service Staff Correspondent.

GUAM, May 29.—Yokohama was described today as a blazing inferno with smoke rising to more than 20,000 feet after upwards of 450 Superfortresses staged the first major sky assault against Japan's fifth largest city.

The Superforts, escorted by 150 Mustang fighters, ranged over the city for nearly two hours by daylight today, dropping 640,000 pounds of fire bombs from medium altitude.

Returning pilots said visibility was good and described flak fire as heavy "in spots." The American planes beat off what interceptor popposition the Japs had to offer. First Lt. Frank Klassen, Ford City, Pa., said:

"The southern part of the target area (probably the commercial core of Yokohama adjacent to principal piers) was burning like hell."

Sgt. Edward Bender, Newcastle, Pa., gunner aboard one of the Superforts, said:

"Smoke was higher than 20,000 feet. Their flak fire was moderate but not too accurate."

This was the first B-29 smash at Yokohama, lying just 20 miles south of Tokyo, which was still smouldering from two terrific Superfort raids last week.

DARING DAYLIGHT RAID

The strike against Yokohama's maze of vital warehouses, docks, canals and railroad systems was a daring daylight sweep of 72 square miles along the western shore of Tokyo bay. The only other daylight incendiary assault by the Superforts was against Nagoya.

It was the third time in six days that the sky giants have lashed with flaming destruction at the heart of Japan's war machine. The strikes against Tokyo last week were made on Thursday and Saturday—within a 48-hour period.

RAIDS STEPPED UP

Yokohama is Japan's most modern target yet him by Maj. Gen. Curtis LeMay's Twenty-first Bomber Command Superforts in the steadily rising crescendo of American aerial might.

The Marianas-based B-29s soared over three vital sectors of Yokohama in midmorning, raining their fire cargoes down on the city's great automotive industry to the north; docks, piers and warehouses of Yokohama harbor in the center, and the modern commercial and residential section to the southeast, where the popu-

Continued on Page 2, Column 1.

Million Inhabitants

GUAM, May 29—(U. P.). Yokohama has a population of 1,000,000, fifth largest city in Japan. It was one of Japan's principal naval bases and the main port for Tokyo and Northern Japan.

The city is packed with 72 square miles of shipyards, motor vehicle plants, steel plants and assorted aircraft, rubber, radio and petroleum works.

BULLETIN

Glenn L. Martin has withdrawn the offer of the Martin airport for purchase by the city gvernment, it was learned today.

Secretary Stettinius Says:

U. S. 'Stands Pat' On Veto Formula

By WILLIAM THEIS
International News Service Staff Correspondent.

SAN FRANCISCO, May 29.—The Big Five delegation chiefs were to meet today to clear their "stand-pat" interpretation of the Yalta veto formula for submission to the 49-nation world security conference.

Plans for the session of the major Power leaders, made in the wake of Secretary of State Edward R. Stettinius' foreign policy address, indicated word had been received from the other four home Governments.

Barring some last-minute change, formal announcement of the meeting will be made during the day to clear the decks for action on this one remaining issue before President Truman comes to San Francisco to close the historic charter conference.

REHEARSE SIGNING

Work of the conference was so far advanced that the delegations yesterday participated in a "re-

Continued on Page 2, Column 7.

Scratches At Delaware Park

Second Race—Silver Pennant, Calcutta, First Family, Traction. Pompa Negri.

Fourth—Brass King, Roman Matron.

Seventh—Brides Biscuit, Selectee.

Weather clear; track heavy.

Big Tax-Dodging Crackdown:

Baltimore Dealer Among Accused

WASHINGTON, May 29 — (U. P.).—Better get right with the tax collector.

Secretary of the Treasury Henry Morgenthau, Jr., is going to ask Congress to let him hire 10,000 extra agents to help him collect $1,000,000,000 in unpaid income taxes.

And he says it's Treasury policy to be lenient with persons making "voluntary disclosures" of income which they failed to mention in previous tax returns.

Morengthau is planning the biggest tax crackdown in U. S. history to catch up with the biggest wave of tax-dodging ever to sweep the country.

BALTIMORE DODGER

Citing two new examples of tax evasions, he told of meat dealers in the District of Columbia and Baltimore.

In the District of Columbia case, he said, a wholesale meat dealer sold about 250,000 pounds of beef and veal at six cents to eight cents a pound over ceiling prices in 1944. He owed the Treasury $400,000 more than he actually paid in income taxes.

In the Baltimore case, the dealer declared his 1944 income at $35,000. He likewise owed the Treasury $400,000, Morgenthau said. Most of the meat sold by the Baltimore dealer is said to have gone to the New York area. The dealer got 10 cents a pound over ceiling prices, according to Morgenthau.

He said at a press conference new disclosures prompted him to raise the order from the previously 5,000 figure. He said it would take 5,000 additional persons in

Continued on Page 2, Column 8.

Temperatures

12 mid'ht, 70	6 A. M., 64
1 A. M., 70	7 A. M., 65
2 A. M., 69	8 A. M., 67
3 A. M., 68	9 A. M., 68
4 A. M., 67	10 A. M., 70
5 A. M., 64	11 A. M., 72

Chinese Pushing On Suilu Base, Near Border

CHUNGKING, May 20—(U. P.) —Chinese vanguards are approaching Suilu, 48 miles southwest of the captured air base city of Nanning and only 50 miles from the French Indo-China border, a communique announced today.

CHUNGKING, May 28—(A. P.).—Unconfirmed reports said today the Japanese were withdrawing from the former American air base at Liuchow in Kwangsi Province as Chinese troops aimed a two-pronged attack at the railroad junction city.

Veteran Chinese troops pushed to the outskirts of Pinyang, 58 miles to the northeast and about 90 miles southwest of Liuchow.

PERILED FROM WEST

Liuchow also was threatened from the west. Chinese forces advanced from captured Hwaiyuan-

Continued on Page 2, Column 1.

British Casualties Total 1,128,315

LONDON, May 29—(A. P.).—Prime Minister Churchill announced today that the British Empire armed forces had suffered 1,128,315 casualties during the war, including 307,201 killed.

The reported death toll for the 66 months of the war was only a little more htan a third as large as that of the British Empire in the 52 months of the First World War.

In reporting to Commons Churchill said additional losses were inflicted upon the civilian population of Britain by enemy bombardment. He said civilian casualties totaled 60,585 killed, 86,175 seriously injured and upwards of 150,000 slightly injured.

LONDON, May 29—(U. P.).—Prime Minister Churchill indicated today that Great Britain had transferred some ships of the Royal Navy to Russia.

During the question hour Laborite Rhys Davies asked for information on the reported transfer of British ships to Russia. Churchill asked permission to put off the answer until next week, saying it would be too long.

NEWS-POST

SHOWERS

Light showers tonight; low 56. Occasional showers, thunderstorms and cooler Wednesday; high, 65. Sunrise, 5:19; sunset, 8:17.

(Chart on page 16.)

6 p.m. ... 63	2 a.m. ... 54	9 a.m. ... 64	1 p.m. ... 72
8 p.m. ... 61	4 a.m. ... 51	10 a.m. ... 65	2 p.m. ... 72
10 p.m. ... 58	6 a.m. ... 53	11 a.m. ... 67	3 p.m. ... 72
Midnight ... 56	8 a.m. ... 60	Noon ... 70	4 p.m. ... 74

CHICAGO DAILY NEWS

COMPLETE MARKETS
FIVE STAR FINAL Edition

70TH YEAR—127.

TUESDAY, MAY 29, 1945—TWENTY PAGES. Telephone DEArborn 1111. FOUR CENTS

Britain's No. 1 Traitor Wounded

CAPTURE LORD HAW HAW

Tokyo Raid Opens Saga of Adventure For Doolittle Vet

Jumps Onto Vesuvius, Lives In Cave, Wants to Fight Japs

BY WILLIAM H. STONEMAN.
Daily News Foreign Service.

150TH STATION HOSPITAL, LONDON—To an ordinary man it would appear that one adventure such as the first American raid on Tokyo in April, 1942, would just about exhaust one's capacity for "taking it."

To Lt.Col. Charles R. Greening, Tacoma, Wash., former group commander of the 17th Bomber Group of the 12th Air Force, the Tokyo raid was just a modest beginning.

He emerged from a German prison camp the other day after an additional series of wild and woolly adventures, including a parachute jump that almost landed him in the center of Vesuvius.

Other items in his saga included six months as a caveman with Italian and Yugoslav Partisans in the mountains of northeastern Italy and more than a year as a German prisoner.

* * *

TOGETHER with other heroes of our air forces, Col. Greening is now undergoing 16 days of enforced medical observation and fattening in this splendid American military hospital.

Greening started the war Dec. 9, 1941, when the three-man flight in which he was flying bagged the first Jap submarine collected by the Americans off the Pacific coast.

Then, four months later, he took part in the Tokyo carrier raid and managed to make it to China before running out of gas and bailing out.

With a party of 19 other Americans who had bailed out he trudged through the mountains until a plane picked them up 200 miles from Chungking.

* * *

GREENING headed for America in July, 1942, just in time to get in on the North African campaign. Flying B-26s, he and his squadron flew the South Atlantic and reached Marrakech just after our landing at Casablanca. Then they flew up to Tunisia for the tough winter campaign of 1942-1943.

Later he was in on the bombing of Pantellaria Island and the Sicilian campaign.

In July, 1943, flying his 27th mission in a 500-plane raid on Naples, Greening met his jinx.

Greenin-'s plane was the first to hit the target on that raid, and all the flak around Naples was concentrated on him. His controls were clipped before he dropped his bombs.

Finally the right engine was blown off. Everybody bailed out just as the plane blew up. The only ones to get down alive were the navigator and Greening, who landed halfway down the northern slope of Vesuvius, spraining both ankles and getting shot in the knee for good measure.

The next chapter came on Oct. 3, 1943, when the train in which he was traveling northward as a

(Continued on page 4, column 5.)

NOTICE.

There will be no issue of the Daily News tomorrow, Memorial Day.

Youth Missing In Attack Case

Deputy sheriffs set out with a bench warrant today to find Nick Malatesta, 18, when he failed to appear in Criminal Court.

Malatesta and two others are charged with criminal attack. They were accused by a Wac whom they lured into their car at a railroad station.

The others, Tony Giampa, 23, of 840 Lytle st., and Peter Otomanelli, 17, of 1357 Taylor st., pleaded not guilty before Chief Justice Harold G. Ward. It was found that Malatesta had been released in Boys Court on $7,000 bond. His arraignment was set for June 18 by Judge Ward today.

Ezra Pound Faces Trial as Traitor

WASHINGTON — (UP) — Attorney General Biddle disclosed today that Ezra Pound, American poet who became an evangelist for Fascism in Italy, will be returned to this country and tried for treason.

Pound and seven other Americans who espoused the Axis cause in Europe were indicted for treason several months ago. Pound thus far is the only one who has been captured, Biddle said.

The attorney general said the other seven also will be tried in this country after they are arrested.

Churchill Hints Early Big 3 Meet

LONDON—(UP)—Prime Minister Churchill said today he contemplates an early meeting with President Truman and Marshal Stalin. Churchill intimated last Saturday that a Big Three meeting might be held before Britain's general election, which is to be July 5.

Goebbels' Aid May Face Trial

Nazi Mouthpiece Makes False Move At Danish Border

LUENEBURG, Germany — (AP) — Scar-faced William Joyce, better known as Lord Haw Haw, Goebbels' anti-British mouthpiece, was shot in the thigh and captured at the Danish border near Flensburg yesterday, and his condition is reported critical.

A British soldier fired when Joyce made a threatening move with his hand in his pocket.

* * *

JOYCE IS BEING transferred to Lueneburg by ambulance, a senior intelligence officer with the British 2d Army said.

His wife also was captured.

An authoritative source said he probably would have to stand trial for treason in England.

Joyce, 39, is a native of New York, where he was born of Irish parents. An early British Fascist, his face was slashed by a razor 20 years ago during a fight with British Communists.

LORD HAW HAW.

His polished voice and precise English accent were attained at London University, where he was graduated with honors in 1927.

Throughout the war, he gave British and American radio audiences accounts of German air blows at London and other British cities and hailed every achievement of German arms.

* * *

EVEN WHILE he was boasting of the blitz, German bombers destroyed the London home of Lord Haw Haw's father, Michael Joyce, who died in February, 1941.

Haw Haw, far from undermining British morale, however, steeled the British and provided them with one of their few grim entertainments during the dark days of the war.

Lord Haw Haw's name appears on no announced list of war criminals. Any charge against him probably will come from the attorney general's office in Great Britain.

Joyce went to Germany on Aug. 25, 1939. Some reports said he took German citizenship, but this never was confirmed.

Hedy Lamarr Becomes Mother

HOLLYWOOD — (AP) — A girl, weighing 7½ pounds, was born today to Hedy Lamarr and her husband, John Loder, at Cedars of Lebanon Hospital. It is their first child.

Call 15-Year-Olds Into Russian Army

MOSCOW — (AP) — All Soviet youths of the eighth and ninth grades—between 15 and 16 years old—have been called for Army training scheduled to begin June 1, it was announced today.

Something for The Mystery Fans

"It's a Mystery to Me," a column by Craig Rice, giving the lowdown on the latest thriller-dillers, is a feature of Books and Authors, pages 11 and 12.

Also on the inside:

Late Sports

Baseball Scores

NATIONAL LEAGUE.

Brooklyn	105 110 0
Cubs	010 100 0

Chapman-Dantonio, Brooklyn; Stewart-Rice, Cubs.

New York	100 001 1
Pittsburgh	000 000 0

Feldman-Berres. New York; Roe-Lopez, Pittsburgh.

Philadelphia-St. Louis (night).

Only games scheduled.

AMERICAN LEAGUE.

White Sox	012 000 001—4	9	1
Boston	120 020 01*—6	13	1

Ross-Tresh, White Sox; Woods-Garbark, Boston.

St. Louis	000 000 00
New York	403 011 20

Kramer-Hayworth, St. Louis; Donald-Crompton, New York.

Cleveland	001 00
Philad'lphia	000 01

Reynolds-McDonnell, Cleveland; Flores-Hayes, Philadelphia.

Only games scheduled.

Race Results

LINCOLN FIELDS.
(At Hawthorne.)
Third Race.

1—Isaiah Girl	7.20	3.20	2.60
2—Billie's Choice		2.80	2.20
3—Mr. Jinx			2.60

Fourth Race.

1—Seaman's Pal
2—Spring-Quest
3—Judge Davey

AT CHURCHILL DOWNS.
Fourth Race.

1—Bail Bond	2.40	2.20	out
2—Quintero		2.20	out
3—Unconditional			out

AT NARRAGANSETT.
Fifth Race.

1—Jamoke	8.00	3.40	2.60
2—Cream		2.60	2.40
3—Gun Bearer			3.80

AT JAMAICA.
Sixth Race.

1—Equinox	29.80	11.90	6.60
2—Art of War		9.80	5.20
3—Gambling Andy			4.50

AT DELAAWRE PARK.
Third Race.

1—Billie F.	15.40	7.10	2.90
2—Proud Pappy		4.10	2.50
3—Abiel			2.30

EARLIER RACE RESULTS ON SPORTS PAGE.

Great Fires Sweep Yokohama After 450 B-29s Blast City

SPIES WORE U.S. UNIFORMS

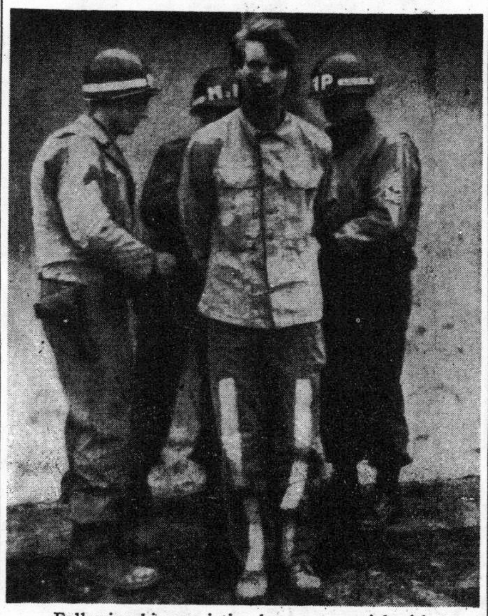

Following his conviction by court-martial with two other German spies captured wearing American uniforms and carrying radio equipment, a captured Nazi is tied to a stake by American military policemen for execution.

White targets are attached to the breasts of Corp. Wilhelm Schmidt, Officer Candidate Gunther Dilling and Sgt. Manfred Perness (right), who appears to be in an attitude of prayer.

The firing squad has responded to the signal. One of the executed spies is cut from the stake.
[Associated Press Wirephotos.]

Japs Get Warning On Yanks

Treat Captives Fairly, Nips Told; Ship Charge Denied

WASHINGTON—(UP)—The United States again has sternly warned the Jap government against mishandling American prisoners, the State Department revealed today.

The Japs hinted at a policy of reprisal against American prisoners and civilian internees because a U.S. submarine mistakingly sank a Jap supply ship that was traveling under an Allied grant of safe conduct.

* * *

THE UNITED STATES rejected a Jap protest about the sinking. However, the U.S. Navy has instituted court-martial proceedings against the commander of the submarine. The Jap vessel, believed to have been the supply ship Awa Maru, was sunk on April 1.

The United States, in a note sent on May 18, warned the enemy that "any retaliatory acts against Allied nationals will be a matter of the gravest concern to this government."

". . . Any persons issuing or executing orders in this connection will be severely dealt with at the appropriate time," the note said.

* * *

THE UNITED STATES "categorically denies" a Jap charge that the ship was "deliberately and willfully attacked and sunk."

At the same time, this government told the Japs that it "sincerely regrets" the incident and accompanying loss of life.

The Awa Maru, as explained in great detail in the Jap protest to the United States, was one of two Jap ships granted safe conduct by the Allies so it could carry relief supplies from Japan to prisoners in China and other Jap-held areas. The supplies had been sent to Russia by the United States.

Gas Blast Causes Bomb Scare

At first people in the vicinity of 1002 Montrose st. thought they were under bomb attack today—but then it developed that sewer gas had merely blown off a manhole cover.

Manuel Wasserman, who operates a drugstore at the Montrose address, told police the windows shook and a number of people were alarmed but no damage was done. He said a janitor had been repairing a basement coal chute with a blow torch, which ignited the sewer gas.

3,200 Tons Hit Big Jap Port

Smoke Rises 20,000 Feet From Shipyards, Factories

(Map on page 2.)

GUAM—(UP)—Yokohama, Japan's second port and fifth largest city, was "burning like all hell" today after more than 450 Superfortresses poured 3,200 tons of high explosives and incendiary bombs on the city in a daylight fire raid.

Returning B-29 crewmen said smoke rose as high as 20,000 feet over the blazing metropolis and also reported smoke over nearby smouldering Tokyo, target in two 500-plane assaults last week.

Shipyards, war plants, naval installations and block after block of business buildings and homes in Yokohama were reduced to charred wreckage as bombardiers laid their deadly cargoes in a pattern from the waterfront straight through the city.

(In Washington, the 20th Air Force reported "excellent results" on the raid. A communique said enemy aircraft opposition was weak and flak ranged from meager to intense. Two Superfortresses were lost in combat, the communique said.)

The assault was carried out from medium altitude with what pilots called "relative ease."

First Lt. Frank Klassen of Ford City, Pa., commander of the bomber "City of Oklahoma," declared Yokohama was "burning like all hell!

* * *

"**BLACK SMOKE,** such as would come from an oil storage tank, was billowing high into the sky. A strong wind seemed to be blowing on the ground."

Sgt. Edward F. Bender of New Castle, Pa., gunner on another plane, said: "Smoke was rising as high as 20,000 feet. Flak was only moderate but very accurate."

* * *

YOKOHAMA, a city of 1,000,000, was one of Japan's principal naval bases.

The big Marianas-based bombers struck from medium altitude at the 9 a.m. morning rush hour and, Tokyo accounts said, unloaded their cargoes of death and destruction in a steady rain for two and a half hours.

Mustang fighters from Iwo—estimated by Tokyo at 100 to 150 strong—ran interference for the Superfortresses and tangled with enemy fighters high over the port city. Tokyo said Jap anti-aircraft batteries also were in action.

* * *

A JAP COMMUNIQUE said 30 B-29s were shot down and 40 heavily damaged. It said the raid lasted an hour and a half with some bombs also falling on Tokyo and Kawasaki, midway between Tokyo and Yokohama.

"Considerable damage was caused in the city of Yokohama," the communique said.

Japs Strip Top Admiral Of 3 Jobs

SAN FRANCISCO—(UP)—Adm. Soemu Toyoda was removed from Japan's three top naval commands today in a general shakeup following the American successes on Okinawa and carrier-based raids on the Japanese homeland.

The Domei agency said the navy ministry announced that Toyoda had been relieved as commander in chief of the combined fleet, commander in chief of the newly established overall naval command and commander of the Naval Escorts Command.

All three posts were given to Vice-Adm. Jisaburo Ozawa, vice-chief of the naval general staff and president of the Naval Staff College, the announcement said.

Medal for Pyle?

WASHINGTON—(UP)—Senator Willis (Rep., Ind.) said today President Truman favors a special Congressional Medal for Ernie Pyle.

What? Where? Here Are Facts on Gen. Clark Greeting

WHAT — Reception for Gen. Mark Clark.

* * *

WHERE—Parade from airport through Loop to Congress st. plaza. Dinner at Palmer House.

* * *

WHEN—Tomorrow. Arrival at airport 1:30 p.m. Parade to Congress st., 2:45 p.m. Dinner at 7:30 p.m.

* * *

WHY—In keeping with Chicago's Memorial Day observance.

* * *

WHO—Gen. Mark Clark and 50 picked 5th Army heroes.

(Details on page 3.)

Such a Smell--Judge to Sniff Private Zoo

Mrs. Helen Conoccio, 40 and plump, doesn't like monkeys—especially when they live next door.

In Town Hall court today she held her stubby nose and told Judge Edward Luczak:

"All of us neighbors are against the smelling."

"That man"—and she pointed a finger at Edward E. Melind, 64, a meek businessman who lives at 2236 Melrose st. —"keeps eight monkeys in cages in his backyard." He was charged with disorderly conduct.

THE DEFENDANT, president of the H. L. Fisher Co., 4100 Ravenswood av., machinery jobbers, started to speak in defense of his pets.

"Why, they're as clean as ——"

At that point, Assistant City Attorney Chris Harvalis shouted, "How come you didn't bring one along."

Melind sputtered, and his lawyer, John Carey, took over. "That's ridiculous," he said. "As if a defendant in a disorderly conduct case has to bring anything into court except himself."

THE JUDGE admitted he had something there. "Guess you can't subpoena a monkey," he added.

So, the case was continued to June 8, Harvalis said he'd investigate to see if Melind is violating "some kind of a city ordinance by keeping monkeys," and—

Judge Luczak announced: "At 2 p.m., on June 7, I, personally, will go out to the Melind zoo and see what the conditions are. I not only will see—I will sniff the atmosphere."

Theater-Screen New Plays, Films, Concerts Discussed PAGES 4B, 5B

THE BOSTON HERALD

Mostly Cloudy
BOSTON AND VICINITY — Mostly cloudy, continued cool, occasional showers. Highest temperature 65. Tides—High: 5:21 A. M., 6:02 P. M. Low: 11:50 A. M., 12:16 P. M. Sunrise: 5:08. Sunset: 8:16. Full report Page 2.

VOL. CLXXXXVIII, NO. 154 (Copyright, 1945) Boston Herald-Traveler Corporation BOSTON, SUNDAY, JUNE 3, 1945—SIXTY PAGES With "THIS WEEK" Colorgravure Magazine TEN CENTS FIFTEEN CENTS Beyond THIRTY MILES of Boston

HALSEY BLASTS 'SUICIDE' BASES

Big Three Locked in Impasse Over Veto

SALEM BUS LINES TIED UP

Epic of Pilot, Shot Down Over Reich

How Yankee General Cowed Nazi Captors Climax of Heroic Story

By BILL CUNNINGHAM

The young Flying Fortress pilot had seen his mates of the Eighth Army Air Force write letters and leave them to be mailed in case they didn't return. "In Case I'm A Battle Casualty, Please Mail To . . .," they said. He'd never written any. They struck him as being bad psychology. Neither he nor any of the rest had any illusions about the job. This was before the days of full fighter protection, and they knew they rolled hot dice with death every time they roared out across that Channel over Germany.

Too, this raid didn't figure to be so tough. It was Bremen. The haul wasn't far. There was fighter protection part way. In fact there probably wasn't more than a half-hour without it. That wasn't the way it had been at Schweinfurt, Stuttgart and a dozen more. He'd flown them and had lived through the stiff slugs of flak and the slashing and hooking of the acrobatic German fighters. True he'd brought back a couple of planes pretty badly shot up, and once he's had dead and wounded aboard.

Close to His 25th Mission

But this was Bremen, just a little haul and a lot of help. It would be running him up close to his 25th mission. That would mean home. He went back and personally woke up his crew. The target had been assigned about midnight. Some pilots merely sent back word by somebody else, but this young fellow made a practice of personally awaking his own, of seeing how they felt, of seeing that they had all the information he had.

He did this, and then, for the first time, and for reasons he couldn't explain, Capt. Dexter Lishon, 23, pilot of the Eighth AAF B-17 Whale Tail 3rd, felt impelled to write his loved ones on the eve of the raid. Possibly it was premoni-

(Continued on Page Seventeen)

Law Found Helpless to Improve Tragic Lot of Chronic Drunkard

By JUDGE ELIJAH ADLOW

The best temperance lectures I ever heard were delivered by chronic alcoholics from the dock in my court. The presence of many horrible examples gave added weight to their arguments. If their pleas served to implore our charity, they also emphasized the tragic futility of the proceedings in which they were taking part. The all too frequent reappearance of these offenders in our courts completely discredits the present methods employed in handling alcoholics.

Some of these drunkards have a more extensive court experience than most of our flourishing lawyers. Experience has taught them much. They know how helpless the authorities are with respect to their problem. They know that if every drunkard insisted on his constitutional right to a trial by jury our entire

(Continued on Page Two, Section B)

Life on a Submarine the Life For Everett Hero of Deep Sea

By PAUL STEVENS

One of five survivors of the gallant crew of the submarine K-12 which went down with 47 hands has returned to his Everett home, delivered from death by a miracle, and carrying with him a knowledge of American heroism that will rank among the epics of undersea warfare when the history of this war is told.

He is Machinist's Mate First Class Harold K. Wilcox, 29. At his home, 105 Dartmouth street, Everett, he is reunited with his wife and two children he never expected to see again.

(Editor's Note: This story was written in October, 1943. The manuscript was sent to Washington, where Navy censors held it for reasons of security until last week. Wilcox, then, has

(Continued on Page Two, Section B)

TODAY'S FEATURES

Index to Classified Advertisements

LYNN SERVICE HALTED, BUT RESTARTED

Agreement to Defer Strike Pending Vote Of All Hands, Broken

Service on the Salem division of the Eastern Massachusetts Street Railway Company, which serves 50,000 passengers from 10 communities daily, was halted completely last night, when 150 division employes refused to abide by a strike-postponement agreement reached Friday between the company and spokesmen for all of the affected locals of the union.

Operations on the Lynn division, which resumed late yesterday after an unauthorized 13-hour strike, were disruped for several hours again last night when a delegation of 50 Salem strikers persuaded 45 out of the total of 65 Lynn division but drivers to leave their jobs. The Lynn drivers returned to work after being promised police protection.

FORCED BUS TO ROADSIDE

Mayor Arthur J. Frawley of Lynn offered the police protection after a group of men, riding in two cars, forced a Lynn bus to the side of the road on North Common street and ordered the driver to return to his garage.

Earlier, special details of police were sent to Central square, Lynn, as the Salem men urged Lynn drivers to strike in sympathy with them.

After a 14-hour meeting at the State House Friday it was agreed that the scheduled walkout by 1800 employes of the company, which serves a helf-million persons in 71 communities, would be deferred fro mmidnight Friday until all employes voted on contract proposals next Wednesday. The votes were scheduled to be counted Thursday.

However, employes on the Salem and Lynn divisions refused to report for work yesterday morning. Gov. Tobin, in a personal appeal to the 250 employes of the Lynn division, persuaded that group to return to work late yesterday afternoon.

The Salem group, however, remained adamant. Gov. Tobin talked on the telephone with John H. Cullen, president of the Salem local, and asked him to call a meeting and urge the men to return to work. Speakers at this meeting included James T. Moriarty, state commissioner of labor and industries, and Gen. Charles H. Cole, chairman of the state board of conciliation and arbitration.

VOTED TO REMAIN OUT

At the conclusion of the meeting, the employes voted "overwhelmingly," according to a union official, to remain on strike. Cullen said it was "the feeling of the men that

(Continued on Page Twenty-one)

(AP Wirephoto)

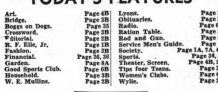

'BULL' HALSEY BACK ON JOB—Map shows high spots as Admiral Halsey returned to Third Fleet in Pacific. (1) On Okinawa Japs defenses crumble as foe reported new (Halsey) carrier attacks on Kyushu (2); Osaka (3) still burns from Friday's B-29 raid. Chinese troops (4) gained. On Luzon (5) Yanks reached Cagayan valley entrance, and (6) Americans made their sixth amphibious landing on Mindanao.

DeGaulle Charges British to Blame

Note on Levant In 'Wrong Spirit'

By HAROLD CALLENDER
[Boston Herald-N. Y. Times Wireless]

PARIS, June 2—In the most remarkable press conference of his career, displaying perfect aplomb and apparently complete self-assurance, Gen. Charles de Gaulle today placed the entire blame for the Levantine trouble upon the machinations of the British government and its agents.

He refused to admit that the present or past French governments or he himself had been guilty of any mistake and he "guaranteed" to the Allied correspondents that French people were united behind him in a determination to see that France's "interests and dignity are respected and, if necessary, to make them respected."

CITES "CEASE FIRE"

Gen. De Gaulle said today—in contrast with an earlier French official version—that the "cease fire" order to French troops had been given Wednesday—that is, the

(Continned on Page Eighteen)

OPA, Mayor Of Worcester In Car Row

Mayor William A. Bennett of Worcester has withdrawn all financial support of the Worcester War Price and Rationing Board because an application for a new automobile for his office was rejected by the regional Office of Price Administration, Boston OPA charged yesterday.

The chairman of the Worcester Ration Board, Michael J. Fitzgerald, said C. Vernon Inett, executive director of Worcester civilian defense, had written him as follows:

"This is to notify you that today, Friday, June 1, 1945, his Honor, Mayor William A. Bennett, has instructed me not to pay any more bills for the Ration Board, by the City of Worcester, on and after that date."

TWICE REJECTED

Last night, William E. Hale, assistant regional OPA administrator in charge of Massachusetts operations, assured residents of Worcester that "OPA would not let Mayor Bennett's action interfere with the service to them by the loctl Ration Board.

"Mayor Bennett's action," he said, "could result in hardship involving every citizen in Worcester. The rationing and price control

(Continued on Page Eight)

NEW LANDING ON MINDANAO

Sixth Seaborne Coup Perils Isolated Japs

MANILA, Sunday, June 3 (AP)—American forces made their sixth amphibious landing on Mindanao island Friday in a move designed to encircle and exterminate isolated Japanese garrisons.

The landing was made at Lauyon 75 miles south of Mindanao's capital city, Davao, and on the western shore of Davao gulf.

OPPOSITION LIGHT

Doughboys rushed ashore against light opposition, quickly secured their beachhead and moved inland in search of the enemy. The landing was made under cover of strong aerial and naval support.

The Japanese pulled back from the beach under shelling by a destroyer force commanded by Rear Adm. A. D. Struble.

Yanks found a destroyed Japanese radio station near Lauyon.

The maneuver was a shore-to-shore operation, shifting some American forces, probably from Maj. Gen. Roscoe B. Woodruff's 24th Infantry Division in the Davao sector.

It was not immediately indicated how many Japanese were in the Lauyon sector, an important area for that city guards the entrance to Davao gulf. Heavy guns set up along the coast of Lauyon or to the north could harass any shipping entering the gulf.

Japanese in the Lauyon area probably were cut off on southern Mindanao as Woodruff's outfit bisected the island in their recent sweep through the center to attack

(Continued on Page Twenty)

Huge Third Fleet Back as Okinawa Yanks Spur Drive

GUAM, Sunday, June 3 (AP)—Admiral William F. Halsey, just returned to action in the Pacific with his U. S. Third Fleet, sent carrier planes against potential suicide plane bases of the Japanese homeland on Kyushu island Saturday while the 10th Army tore into disintegrating enemy forces on Okinawa.

Today's fleet communique reported carrier planes of Halsey's fleet, operating under Vice Admiral John S. McCain, shot down two enemy planes, destroyed 11 on the grounds and damaged 23 more at Miyazaki, Kokubu, Tushira, Kagoshima and Chiran. Two enemy surface craft were destroyed off the coast.

Halsey was disclosed yesterday to have gone back into action against the Nipponese, boasting his fleet could move anywhere from the North to South Pole and even, if need be, into Tokyo bay.

Yanks Gain as Okinawa Rains Cease

In the Okinawa campaign, now in its closing phases, the 10th Army divisions ranged below the collapsed Naha-Yonabaru line Saturday for general gains up to 1000 yards. They were backed by tanks and heavy artillery, due to a cessation of rainy weather which has deluged Okinawa with 13 inches of rain in 10 days. Enemy resistance was moderate.

The Third Fleet's assault on enemy suicide plane bases came at a time when Tokyo radio was trumpeting that huge successes had been scored by such attacks on shipping at Okinawa and that the attacks would be stepped up. But Admiral Nimitz said today that enemy air action through Friday continued on a small scale as it had the past few days.

MARINES ADVANCE

Aground on Okinawa, in the west coast sector southeast of fallen Naha, the Marine First Division yesterday gained 1000 yards below Shuri and crossed the Naha-Yonabaru east-west highway.

Near the center, the 96th Infantry Division captured Chan village which is two miles below captured Shuri and pushed on below Chan toward Tera village. The Yanks seized high ground near Kamizato.

On the east coast side, the Seventh Infantry Division pushed southward in a move aimed at cutting off the Chinen peninsula and reopening the Nakagusuku harbor,

(Continued on Page Twenty)

Soviet Takes Strong Stand On Voting

By JAMES B. RESTON
[Boston Herald-N. Y. Times Dispatch]

SAN FRANCISCO, June 2—The United Nations Conference has reached a critical point. After agreeing on a wide range of amendments which liberalize the Dumbarton Oaks proposals, the "Big Five" were deeply divided tonight over a demand by Soviet Russia that the permanent members of the new league of nations' council have the right to veto discussion of international disputes.

It must be emphasized, despite the general opposition among the delegates to this new Soviet demand, that the area of agreement among the Big Five here is far greater than the area of disagreement, but this new dispute, like the Polish dispute, springs from different interpretations of the Yalta documents and for this reason it is both complicated and inflammable.

The disagreement developed last night in a meeting of the "Big Five" at American conference headquarters when the Russian ambassador, Andrei A. Gromyko, delivered a

(Continued on Page Six)

Pretty Danish Woman Editor Baffled Nazi Persecutors

By CATHERINE COYNE
[Boston Herald-N. Y. Times Wireless]

COPENHAGEN, June 2—Success of Denmark's destruction of the myth that good treatment could make a conquered people happy was in large measure due to the vigorous anti-German campaign waged by Frit Danmark, monthly underground newspaper edited by attractive Kate Fleron.

This 35-year-old journalist had been for 15 years an expert reporter on medical and social problems when the Germans, resenting her non-conformity, forced her discharge from the National Times shortly after the firing of Aage Schoch, liberal editor, who had the temerity in a carefully worded editorial to denounce the anti-comintern pact.

That was in 1942. Though she wanted, as did most patriotic Danes, to do something for democracy, she was unable to find her way immediately into the underground. She began writing the books for which she became famous during the occupation, books critical of the morals of Danish youth.

Another member of the National Times, Ole Kiilerich, with Prof. Modens Fog and Prof. Ole Chievitz of Finsan Institute for Radium, established Frit Danmark as an underground mimeographed paper. When Kiilerich was forced to flee from the Germans, he persuaded Miss Fleron to take his place as

(Continued on Page Sixteen)

Army Moved 4 Million Tons Of Cargo from Boston in 1944

By W. E. PLAYFAIR

The greatest troop movement the port of Boston has ever seen is now beginning.

The tide that set-in westward on the Atlantic after the German surrender will reach its flood in weeks, or even days, as America's armies and their equipment move towards home—or towards Tokyo.

Already, in this receding tide of war, more than 16,000 men have passed in-bound through the Boston Port of Embarkation — the wounded, the liberated prisoners-of-war, and the men who are being deployed to the Pacific or returned home for discharge. But these arrivals represent a mere trickle of the stream to come. This time the Yanks are coming, fast.

Within the next 10 months, the Army Transportation Corps, which moved the millions of men and the mountains of armament and supplies eastward to the European theatre, hopes to finish the reverse-process job through its four Atlantic-coast ports of embarkation. Boston, New York and Hampton Roads will bear the brunt of the troop movements. The Army hospital ships will continue to come in mainly through Charleston, S. C., but sick and wounded are being carried on transports through the other ports as well.

Ten months is the "target date" for completing the tremendous task of transporting more than 3,000,000 men across an ocean, while a desperate war is waged on the other side of the world. It is a target,

(Continued on Page Twenty-three)

Pope Flays Terror By Reds in Balkans

Upholds Right of Small Nations To Take Destiny in Own Hands

VATICAN CITY, June 2 (AP)—Pope Pius XII expressed the hope today that the German people, purged of Nazism, "can rise to new dignity and new life," but said that post-war Europe is menaced by a "tyranny no less despotic than those for whose overthrow men planned."

In a world broadcast on St. Eugene's day—his name day—the Pontiff reviewed the Vatican's pre-war German policy.

The Holy Father defended the rights of the small nations "to take their destinies in their own hands" and said the future "harmonious relations between men" were threatened by mobs of "dispossessed, disappointed and hopeless men who are going to swell the ranks of revolution in the pay of a tyranny no less despotic than those for whose overthrow men planned."

The Pope declared that the Vatican concluded the 1933 concordat with Germany "to set up a formidable barrier to the spread of ideas at once subversive and violent" and he asserted that Pius XI, his predecessor, denounced the Nazi regime in 1937 after the "solemn pact" had been deliberately violated by the Germans.

"The world," said the Pontiff, "was then still at peace: but what a peace and how very precarious!

"With a heart full of anguish, perplexed, praying, we bent over that peace like one that assists a dying man and fights obstinately to save him from death even when all hope is gone.

"The message which we than addressed to you reflected our sorrowful apprehension that the conflict which was ever growing more menacing would break out—a conflict whose extent and duration nobody could foresee. The subsequent march of events has not only justified all too clearly our saddest premonitions but has far surpassed them.

"Today, after six years, the fratricidal struggle has ended, at least in one section of this war-torn world. It is a peace—if you can call it such—as yet very fragile which cannot endure or be consolidated except by expending on it the most assiduous care; a peace whose maintenance imposes on the whole church, both pastor and faithful, grave and very delicate duties: patient prudence, courageous fidelity, the spirit of sacrifice!

(Continued on Page Thirty-two)

U. S. Food Situation Will Improve In Near Future, Truman Predicts

THE WEATHER
Clear and mild tonight; Friday fair, continued warm.
Detailed Weather Report Page 21

Read The Baltimore News-Post for complete, accurate war coverage. It is the only Baltimore newspaper possessing the three great wire services—
ASSOCIATED PRESS
INTERNATIONAL NEWS SERVICE
UNITED PRESS

THE BALTIMORE NEWS-POST
AN INDEPENDENT NEWSPAPER
The Largest Evening Circulation in the Entire South

WALL ST. CLOSE 9

VOL. CXLVII.—NO. 41 | Entered as second-class matter at Baltimore Postoffice. | THURSDAY EVENING, JUNE 21, 1945 | PRICE 3 CENTS

NIMITZ ANNOUNCES VICTORY ON OKINAWA

State Bond Sale Tops In U. S.

Maryland is over the top in the Seventh War Loan drive and stands first in oversubscriptions throughout the country with a total of $325,100,000, which is 141 per cent of the quota.

This announcement was made today by Charles S. Garland, State chairman of the War Finance Committee. The next nearest State, Mr. Garland said, is Montana, with 124 per cent. Missouri comes third with 114 per cent, North Carolina is next with 112 per cent and South Carolina is fifth with 101 per cent.

UNDER "E" BOND GOAL

Of the $325,100,000 record in sales set by Maryland, Mr. Garland said, after receiving reports from the Federal Reserve Bank in Richmond, Va., $113,500,000 represents sales to individualse, 77 per cent of the individual sales quota.

"E" bond sales, he stated, have reached $35,600,000, or 59 per cent of the "E" bond quota.

Mr. Garland said:

"We are gratified that we have made our over-all quota, but the big job, making the State's $60,000,000 E Bond quota is still ahead of us. That quota is the responsibility of all people who want to share in the victory over Japan."

SUB IS OPEN

Mr. Garland urged every Marylander to dig a little deeper into the pocket during the last remaining weeks of the drive and help Maryland achieve her E bond goal as she has already achieved her over-all goal.

The Nazi submarine U-505 will be on exhibit at Pier 4 Pratt street from noon through 8 P. M. today, but will leave Baltimore tomorrow morning. Purchasers of war bonds at the pier will be taken on a tour of the interior of the captured sub. Children purchasing a dollar's worth of war stamps will be entitled to admission to the sub.

Guests Must Pay Points At Resorts

WASHINGTON, June 21 — (A. P.).—Approximately 50 Washington restaurants have been accused of obtaining more than their lawful allotment of meat. The restaurants include many "name" eateries.

If you go to Ocean City this summer take your ration books with you.

Resort operators, including hotel owners, must collect one red stamp and one blue stamp each week and sugar stamps as they expire from the ration books of persons who spend seven consecutive days there and eat eight or more meals on the premises in that time.

Richard Wood, State OPA rationing official, disclosed today that the two-year-old regulation, which heretofore has been ignored more widely than it has been observed, is going to be enforced in Maryland and other States in this OPA region.

Maryland vacation resorts, including popular Ocean City, face food-ration cuts in the July-August and subsequent periods if they fail to collect ration stamps from summer boarders, Mr. Wood said.

Mr. Wood said the resort operators are being advised by letter that they must collect the required ration points from their summer guests. Local boards, he said, will be required to demand from resort operators enough food stamps to account for their May and June boarders.

OPA action against resort operators who have failed to collect food stamps from boarders or whose collections are far short is up to the local boards and may mean a reduction in the ration allowed for the camp or hotel, he added.

Temperatures

Midnight, 74	8 A. M., 75
1 A. M., 72	9 A. M., 78
2 A. M., 73	10 A. M., 81
3 A. M., 72	11 A. M., 84
4 A. M., 71	12 Noon, 86
5 A. M., 70	1 P. M., 87
6 A. M., 73	2 P. M., 88
7 A. M., 75	3 P. M., 88

Truman Sees More Food For U. S.

OLYMPIA, Wash., June 21—(U. P.).—President Truman today forecast a material improvement in the national food situation when the new Food Administrator takes over.

Mr. Truman made this forecast in a special news conference here in the office of Gov. Mon Walgren, his host during a vacation in the Northwest.

PRAISES CONGRESS

The President said he thought the food situation would straighten out automatically as soon as the new administrator—Representative Clinton Anderson (Democrat) of New Mexico, who becomes Administrator and Secretary of Agriculture—takes over his job.

Mr. Truman also praised Congress for its renewal of the Trade Agreements Act, saying this action "places the United States squarely behind the principles of international trade co-operation which must prevail in the interests of world peace and economic well being."

At the same time the President expressed gratification over the progress of the San Francisco United Nations conference, saying he was very happy that it had been a success.

He announced plans to make a brief stop Monday at Portland, Ore., en route to San Francisco.

PERMITS UTATION

He permitted direct quotation of his comment on Congressional action in renewing the Trade Agreements Act for three years:

"The action of the Senate in approving the legislation to renew and strengthen the Trade Agreements Act is indeed gratifying.

"The revitalization of this act places the United States squarely behind the principles of international trade co-operation which must prevail in the interests of world peace and economic well being.

"Trade co-operation, however, must go hand in hand with monetary and financial co-operation and I am confident that the Senate will also take favorable action on the Bretton Woods legislation."

WHISTLES GREET QUEEN MARY—Arriving in New York harbor with 14,526 Yanks aboard, the former luxurry liner Queen Mary today was accorded a noise welcome echoed by the uniformed thousands who packed her decks. Her passengers included Army and Navy veterans from Europe and released war prisoners. This air view taken from U. S. Coast Guard helicopter.

Bitter, Costly Conquest Ends As Japan Sets For Homeland Invasion

OLYMPIA, Wash., June 21—(A.P.).—President Truman promised today that the Japanese are in line for more of the same as a result of complete victory on Okinawa.

GUAM, June 21—(A. P.).—The end of the Okinawa campaign, after 82 days of savage fighting, was announced by Adm. Chester W. Nimitz today, giving American forces a strategic base only 325 miles from Japan.

Costliest of all the Central and Western Pacific campaigns, the Battle of Okinawa took a toll of 35,116 Americans killed and wounded up to four weeks ago, and cost the enemy more than 90,000 dead.

While the big guns of the fleet and the artillery battalions fell silent U. S. Tenth Army forces still hammered with tanks and flame throwers at two small pockets on the southern tip of the island, mopping up a handful of Japanese who refused to surrender.

Admr. Chester W. Nimitz, in a special communique, declared all organized resistance had been crushed.

PREDICTION FULFILLED

Victory was proclaimed only three days after Lt. Gen. Simon Bolivar Buckner, Jr., was killed by a Japanese shell burst as he watched the final, decisive assault.

It fulfilled Buckner's prediction, made a short time before he was struck down, it was unlikely the enemy could hold out more than a week longer.

Presumably one of the remaining pockets was near the southeast shore where the Japanese general commanding the garrison was holed up. The other probably is near the center of the front.

87,343 JAPS KILLED

The General's stand cost the Japanese 87,343 killed and 2,565 taken prisoner up until Tuesday, and the few soldiers still beside him were hungry, thirsty and short on ammunition.

U. S. Army and Navy casualties from March 18—when fleet units bombarded Japan's inland sea in preparation for the invasion—to May 24 were 9,602 killed and 25,514 wounded—but they do not include the last four violent weeks of the campaign.

INVADED EASTER

Largest Japanese island captured by Nimitz' forces, Okinawa was invaded Easter Sunday, April 1, with two strategic objectives.

First was the tightening of the blockade of Japan, The second

Continued on Page 2, Column 1.

6,356 More Casualties

WASHINGTON, June 21—(I. N. S.).—American casualties today reached a total of 1,023,453 dead, wounded, missing and prisoners of war.

This was an increase of 6,356 over last week's total for the Army, Navy, Marine Corps and Coast Guard.

Under Secretary of War Robert Patterson said the latest figures total 903,701, including 189,294 killed, 560,836 wounded, 39,956 missing and 113,615 prisoners.

NEWS-POST

VERY LATEST NEWS

(Race Results From Howard Sports Daily, Inc.)

AT BELMONT

Fifth — Surosa, $3.70, $3.40, $2.80; Turnplate, $5.50, $3.60; Mahmoudess, $3.00.

AT DELAWARE PARK

First—Jack Madigan, $10.00, $5.20, $3.80; Don't Delay, $6.80, $5.50; Stormy Bill, $5.20.

AT SUFFOLK DOWNS

Third—Banish Ruth, $5.40, $3.00, $2.40; Turkey Feather $3.00, $2.40; Light Tyrant, $2.80. T. M., $19.00.

AT CHARLES TOWN

Fifth—Strolling Lee, $36.00, $11.60, $5.60; Royal Step, $3.60, $3.00; Randle's Queen, $4.00.

AT HAWTHORNE

Second—Judge Davy, 1; Magna Ray, 2; Lord Caprice, 3.

LATEST BASEBALL SCORES

(N) At Philadelphia—Brooklyn, 1; Phila., 0; end 2d.
(N) At Chicago—Pittsburgh, 3; Chicago, 3; end 4½.
(A) At Boston—New York, 1; Boston, 1; end 4th.
(A) At Detroit—Detroit, 3; Cleveland, 0; end 4th.

CATE ACQUITTED IN JACOBS SLAYING

Lucius C. Cate, thirty-eight-year-old vending machine agent, charged with killing his lifelong friend, Frederick C. Jacobs, fifty, last April 30, was found not guilty today by a jury which deliberated one hour and seven minutes before delivering the verdict.

RACING RESULTS AT BELMONT PARK

FIRST RACE—Four and one-half furlongs (Widener course). Off 2.16. Time, .52 4-5.

Musical Comedy, 114 (E. Guerin)	$36.20	$13.10	$11.10
Ben Hur, 110 (L. Hansman)		4.80	4.00
Contortionist, 111 (W. Mehrtens)			12.60

Also Ran—Break It Up, Sason, Briggsy, Grand World, Menace, Good Pasture, My Julie and Sweet Tide.

SECOND—Six furlongs. Off at 1 51. Time, 1.14 1-5.

Johnstown Boy, 111 (F. McGowan)	$77.60	$25.40	$12.10
Gusher, 117 (R. Belanger)		9.50	5.40
Wise Bob, 115 (W. Cummings)			3.70

Also Ran—Tory Row, Reformatory, War Dressing, Thin Air, Picket Line, Puffed Up.

Daily D'ble--Musical C'm'dy, Johnstown Boy paid $596.40

THIRD—About one and one-half miles. Off 2.20½. Time, 2.47.

bMateson, 137 (W. Tyree)	$5.00	$3.10	$3.20
Fieldfare, 149 (S. Riles)		4.40	3.40
bRollo, 147 (J. S. Harrison)			3.20

Also Ran—Nordmeer, Sir Blue steel, aRice Cake, aSt. Patrick's Day, Army Power.

aJ. Stuart and T. T. Mott entry. bG. Brooke III entry.

FOURTH—Five furlongs (course). Off 3.01. Time, .59 1-5.

Darby Detroit, 111 (P. Roberts)	$35.60	$16.00	$7.70
Leeway, 109 (J. Onorato)		8.40	5.20
Admirals Call, 104 (W. D. Wright)			7.90

Also Ran—Menever, Grandpa Max, Ruling Time, Dual Purpose.

American League

At Boston— R. H. E.

New York 001 0
Boston . . . 000 1

Batteries—Dubiel and M. Garbark; Ferriss and Walters.

At Detroit— R. H. E.

Cleveland . 00
Detroit . . . 11

Batteries—Bagby and Hayes; Overmire and Swift.

Philadelphia at Washington — Night game.

Other clubs not scheduled.

National League

At Chicago— R. H. E

Pittsburgh 020
Chicago . . 201

Batteries—Roe and Salkeld; Wyse and Livingston.

At Philadelphia— R. H. E.

Brooklyn . 0
Phila. . . .

Batteries—Buker and Dantonio; Leon and Seminick.

Other clubs not scheduled.

International League

Jersey City at Rochester—Twilight-night double-header.
Newark at Montreal — Twilight-night double-header.
Baltimore at Buffalo—Night game.
Syracuse at Toronto—Night game.

Okinawa Conquest Longest, Costliest

GUAM, June 21—(A. P.).—The conquest of Okinawa was the longest and costliest of all the campaigns in the Central and Western Pacific.

With casualty figures still incomplete, the toll of enemy and American killed, captured and wounded all but equal the grand total of casualties in six major campaigns which led up to Okinawa.

The 82 days it took to break all organized resistance dwarfs the 26 days of Iwo Jima. The latter, however, is less than eight square miles in area, and Okinawa is roughly 485 square miles.

The figures for Okinawa, which include Japanese casualties through Tuesday and American casualties only to May 24, compared with those of six other campaigns, follow:

	Japanese		American	
	Killed	Captured	Killed	Wounded
Okinawa	87,343	2,565	9,602	25,514
Iwo Jima	23,244	1,038	4,630	15,308
Saipan	27,586	2,161	3,426	13,099
Guam	17,442	524	1,437	5,648
Palau	13,354	435	1,302	6,115
Tarawa	5,000	150	913	2,037
Tinian	6,939	523	314	1,515

Note: Figures for Americans killed includes missing.

General Marshall Says

YANKS TO INVADE JAPAN

Only Los Angeles Newspaper With All Leading News Services—Associated Press, International News, United Press, Dow-Jones

LOS ANGELES EVENING HERALD AND EXPRESS — AN INDEPENDENT NEWSPAPER

Registered United States Patent Office

NIGHT EDITION — COMPLETE N.Y. STOCKS

HERALD-EXPRESS BUILDING 1243 TRENTON ST. ZONE 15

The Evening Herald and Express Grows Just Like Los Angeles

HERALD-EXPRESS PHONE RICHMOND 4141

VOL. LXXV — Two Sections Section A — FRIDAY, JUNE 22, 1945 — **** — NO. 76

Hitler's Super-Aryan Baby Factory Found in Germany

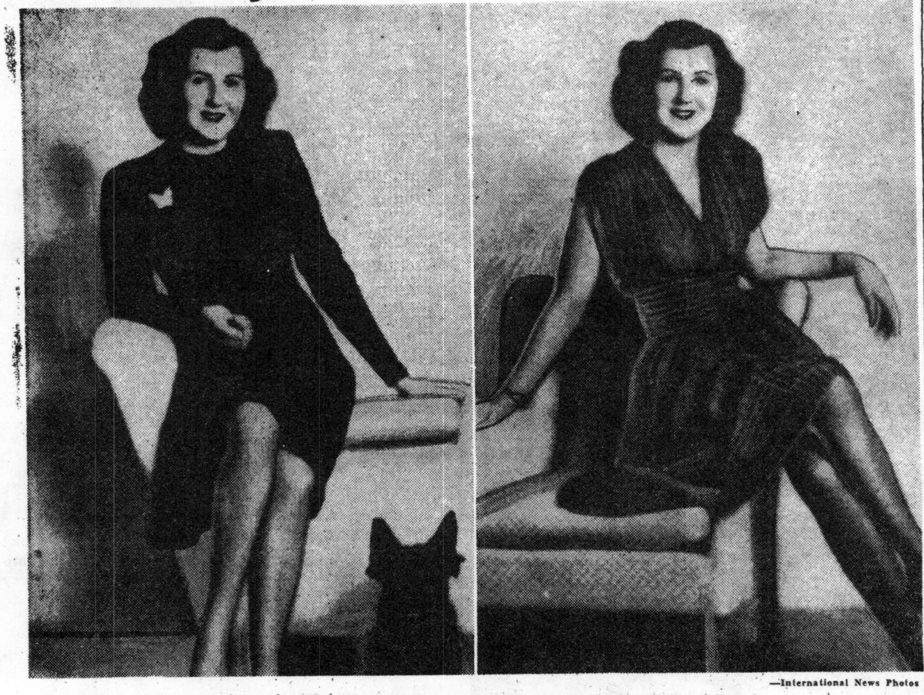

—International News Photos

RECENT PHOTOS OF EVA BRAUN—HITLER'S MISTRESS

These two photos show Eva Braun, longtime companion of Adolf Hitler, who was reported by some of Hitler's aides to have been married to the German dictator, and also to have been with him during the last hours he was known to be alive. The little black dog whose ears are visible in photo at left is Schnecki, a Scottie present from Hitler. Under Hitler's baby plan, Eva would become the mother of the super-super Nazi. The photos were obtained from Frau Gretel Fegelein, Eva's sister, who is the wife of an SS obergruppenfueher.

51 Young Nazis Still Left on Huge Estate

By United Press

HOHEHORST, Germany, June 22.—Fifty-one tow-headed, sturdy children gamboled today on the lawns of a magnificent estate near this picturesque village of North Germany.

They were the product of a dream by Adolf Hitler. He dreamed that if his S. S. generals and gauleiters were to mate with ideal "Aryan" womanhood, the result would be a race of born leaders destined to carry the Reich on to new and greater conquests.

Like the rest of Hitler's dreams, this one, too, lay shattered. But what to do with the offspring of Nazism's choicest blood lines remained to nag officials of the Bremen port command.

The Hohehorst setup was a maternity home. It was operated on a scale so lavish and yet so scientific that American investigators were deeply impressed.

When the Allies overran this area, they found 20 nurses and nurses' helpers caring for the children. That meant almost one expert attendant for each two children.

Every development of modern science that could be used in pediatrics was found in the huge mansion which had been converted into a maternity home. There were refrigerators for chilling food and special adjustable warmers for the sun-ray rooms.

Each mother had a large cross-ventilated room equipped with air conditioning. The diet was regulated carefully. But there was evidence that treatment of the mothers did not equal the care of the children, who in the eyes of the Nazi hierarchy were the really important inhabitants.

One of the United States investigators was Major Abraham Gelperin of Cincinnati. As far as he could make out, the highest ranking Nazis were permitted to send their mistresses or deliberately chosen mates to Hohehorst to have their children.

"It isn't likely that the SS generals or gauleiters who always had the pick of the loveliest and healthiest girls would waste any time on what they considered 'inferior' people," Gelperin said.

"I think it is safe to say that these upper crust Nazis sent to Hohehorst only their best mates. They could have had servant wenches or night club chorines, too, though they would never get into this exclusive establishment."

So sacrosanct was Hohehorst that admittance was by special pass only. And the passes were issued only by Nazi offices in Munich. They were hard to get.

American officials have records showing the mothers' names. But in place of the fathers' names are code letters, the key to which must be somewhere in the Nazi secret files.

Herald-Express Special Features

B-29s Hit 6 Japan Areas

By KENNETH M'CALEB

International News Service Staff Correspondent

GUAM, June 22.—The Japanese Navy's last home arsenal and five widely separated aircraft plants on Honshu were blasted in broad day light today with tons of high explosive bombs dropped by some 450 Superforts.

The six prime targets in the enemy homeland were selected for an abrupt switch in tactics from night fire-bomb raids against Japanese cities to daylight attacks at medium altitude without fighter escort.

Japanese communiques, reported by the Domei agency, claimed that a total of 26 Superforts were shot down or damaged and said that 410 B-29s carried out the strikes. There was no confirmation of the enemy report.

A large number of the Marianas-based B-29s on today's missions poured a heavy load of explosives on the Kure naval arsenal on southwestern Honshu.

Other targets for the American sky forts were two aircraft plants 20 miles north of Nagoya, two more in the Kobe area and another at Tamashima, 65 miles west of Himeji, raising to 16 the number of enemy homeland areas raided this week.

Sales Stall Top Stocks

By Associated Press

NEW YORK, June 22.—Assorted rails, steels, rubbers, amusements, utilities and specialties continued to push forward in today's stock market, many to highs for the past eight years, although light selling stalled many leaders.

Gains of fractions to a point or more predominated from the start. Dealings, fast for a while, inclined to taper as offerings appeared. Most advances were trimmed near the fourth hour.

Weather Balloon Causes L. A. Scare

A half-deflated Weather Bureau balloon used for recording weather data, created a community uproar today when it landed in the 3400 block on East Fourth street amid reports that it was a Jap balloon.

Frantic phone calls from excited residents sent police squad cars rushing to scene only to find the streets empty and residents peacefully going about their business.

The balloon was picked up by Frank Arbizu, 1703 Brooklyn avenue, and taken to the Hollenbeck Heights Police Station where it was turned over to authorities. A card attached to the balloon asked that it be turned in to its proper owners.

Natl. Debt Jumps Over 250 Billion

By Associated Press

WASHINGTON, June 22.—The national debt increased more than three billion dollars on June 20 and passed 250 billion on its way up—the biggest one-day jump since last December—the daily Treasury statement showed today.

U. S. Venereal Rate Soars in Europe

By Associated Press

LONDON, June 22.—The army newspaper Stars and Stripes said in a Paris dispatch yesterday that the venereal disease rate among U. S. Army ground forces in the European theater had increased more than 300 per cent between early April and the week ended May 25.

NEW SOVIET MINISTER

MOSCOW, June 22.—(A.P.)—The Presidium of the Supreme Soviet today appointed Ivan Kornilovich Zyabkin the Soviet minister to New Zealand.

Top Nazis Face Mass War Conspiracy Trial

Goering Heads List

By United Press

LONDON, June 22.—Supreme Court Justice Robert Jackson said today that he expects Hermann Goering, Joachim von Ribbentrop, Rudolf Hess and other major war criminals to be tried in a single group before a military tribunal late this summer.

Jackson, chief American prosecutor of war criminals, returned to London after a trip home for the closing sessions of the Supreme Court.

He emphasized he was not committing Britain, France or Russia to the plan of trying the accused persons in one group. This is an American plan, he said, to which the other nations have raised no objections so far.

He said the war criminals who are convicted will have no appeal except to history.

LIKE COURTMARTIAL

Jackson said the master trial would be conducted like a court-martial, which it in effect would be. Britain, Russia, France, and the United States would provide one or two judges each for the tribunal. No provisions have been made for smaller nations to be represented on the tribunal because of administrative complications.

The trial would start "at the earliest possible moment we can make a resanably complete case," Jackson said. He suggested late summer as a likely date. No site for the trial has been chosen.

He emphasized that the defendants will be permitted to choose their own countrymen as defense counsel and witnesses.

He outlined the proposal for the master trial in which Nazi leaders would be accused of conspiracy to conduct illegal war by illegal means.

The conviction of Nazi "X" for conduction of such a conspiracy with the SS, for instance, would establish the guilt of all SS men.

MEET PRESSURE PLEA

Jackson said, however, that individual S. S. men might plead their individual cases on such grounds as joining under pressure. But if they failed to convince the court of extenuating circumstances, they would be guilty and draw the blanket sentence established by the master tribunal.

Varying degrees of punishment might be established for lesser lights according to their policy of power and policy making, Jackson said.

He said such varied acts as unrestricted submarine warfare and atrocities all could be dealt with under the master plan. Asked what would be done with leaders who claimed exemption from the trial, he said the trial "is a privilege, not a right."

The trial was expected to be speedy, and completed before winter. The number of Nazis actually taken into court probably will be somewhere between 35 and 300, but probably no more than 100.

Maintain Peace by Being Ready for War, Patton's Reply to G. I. Letter

By Associated Press

HAMILTON, Mass., June 22.—Gen. George S. Patton jr. asserted today that he thought it was "stupid to run the risk of not being prepared for another war."

The commander of the Third Army, commenting on an imaginary letter from "one of the dead" in Stars and Stripes, United States Army newspaper, which criticized him for telling children of a Sunday school class that they would be the soldiers and nurses of the next war, declared:

"Having been through two world wars and having experienced the anguish of commanding men who were wounded or killed due to lack of training, I think that it is stupid to run the risk of not being adequately prepared for another war because you do not stop fires by abolishing the fire department.

"And you do not stop wars by being unprepared for them. The best way to maintain peace which naturally I want more than anyone else, having seen how bad war is, is to be ready for war."

"I don't want people to get the idea that I'm a war monger," Patton added. "I think it's terribly foolish not to be prepared and I think young people who may have to carry on in another war, should know that many men were wounded or killed, due to lack of preparedness, in this war."

Patton is spending a brief vacation at his summer home.

Siberia

Big Russ Army in War Maneuvers

By Associated Press

NEW YORK, June 22.—The Red Army command in Siberia is continuing the training of fighting reserves under battlefield conditions, the Moscow radio said today in a domestic broadcast reported by the F. C. C.

The broadcast quoted Lieut. Gen. Kurhanov, identified as commander of the Siberian military area, as expressing pride in the performance of "hundreds of thousands of Siberian soldiers" in the war against Germany, and adding that "the war in Europe is over but military and political schooling and the training of fighting reserves does not cease for a moment."

Weather

Timid Sun Tries to Chase Away Clouds

Sunshine, dim but enough to cast a slight shadow, peeked through drizzle-laden clouds lurking in the skies today, the second day of summer, but really clear weather does not appear in prospect before tomorrow afternoon.

The forecast for Los Angeles and vicinity:

"Fog and low clouds this afternoon, tonight and Saturday with scattered early morning drizzles with partial clearing afternoons. Continued cool today and slightly warmer Saturday."

Minimum temperature today was 57, rising to 68 degrees by noon, when the mercury was 4 degrees higher than yesterday's first summer day maximum of only 64.

Forecasting for five days, the bureau said that after tomorrow, the skies should be generally sunny with temperatures going up to normal.

Letter From G. I. On Patton Speech

By Associated Press

PARIS, June 22.—The United States Army newspaper Stars and Stripes published today an imaginary letter from "One of the dead" who served under General Patton's command, taking the general to task for telling children in a San Gabriel, Calif., Sunday school class they would be the soldiers and nurses of the next war.

The article, written by an army captain who signed only the initials J. C. B., begged General Patton to "just sort of hold your

(Continued on Page 8, Column 2)

Marshall Tells Plan Of Attack

By International News Service

WASHINGTON, June 22.—Gen George C. Marshall was revealed today to have informed Congress that Japan will be invaded after a shattering air offensive spearheaded by 1000-plane B-29 raids

This disclosure was made dur the new fiscal year beginning 285,951 war department bill for he new fiscal year beginning July 1, which was approved today by the House Appropriations Committee following lengthy executive sessions. It is fifteen billion dollars less than for 1945.

"There is little of military secrecy as to the general nature of our plans for the coming year," the army chief of staff told the committee.

PLANES TO PAVE WAY

"The offensives in the Pacific are to be intensified to the maximum degree possible. Air strikes of constantly increasing power will devastate the Japanese war-making facilities and defenses and pave the way for invasion."

Marshall, asserting that he is opposed to a blockade of Japan and a war of attrition, stated:

"Economy in lives and materiel, as well as the psychology of the American people, demand that we mount a swift, powerful offensive, forcing a victory at the earliest possible date."

"We plan to gain victory speedily," he continued, "by an overwhelming application of force—firepower and men; and, of course, planes and bombs mean firepower in the terms I am using."

CITES ATTRITION IDEA

"There is a theory among some nonmilitary people," interjected Representative Mahon, Democrat of Texas, a committee member, "that we should not use a large army to defeat Japan, but having won the necessary bases, we should perfect an airtight blockade of the Japanese islands, and just stick it out and win eventually a victory in a few years without the loss of life which would be entailed by landing on Japan and fighting it out with them

(Continued on Page 8, Column 6)

Nips Fear Kyushu Invasion

By ROBBIN COONS

Associated Press War Correspondent

GUAM, June 22.—American mop-up patrols began the grueling job today of annihilating Japanese sniper nests on Okinawa before the next big Allied invasion is staged from the newly won island base, 325 miles south of Japan.

Tokio radio reported Premier Kantaro Suzuki warned his cabinet an invasion of Japan was impending and said the people of Kyushu, home island nearest Okinawa, were prepared for an invasion, convinced "the enemy will certainly land" there.

Pacific fleet headquarters made no bones about the fact that Okinawa has become a forward staging base from which bomber and fighter planes can cover assault waves striking at Japan or China or both. An official memorandum from Adm. Chester W. Nimitz' headquarters said it is also an American naval anchorage, in the center of waters formerly patroled by the Mikado's imperial fleet.

American infantry stormed a giant coastal cave on Okinawa with flame throwers in an attempt to smoke out the enemy's commanding general. The Japanese general holed up in the cave near Mabuni on the southeast coast with a last handful of his men for a suicide stand. Seventh Division

(Continued on Page 8, Column 5)

DIARY: Family of Duce's Mistress Loved Graft, Scandal; Hitler's Leaders Called America a 'Big Bluff'

CLOUDY

Cloudy and warmer with showers tonight and tomorrow. Low tonight, 63. High tomorrow, 85. Sunrise, 5:30; sunset, 8.24.
(Chart on page 21.) (U.S. official weather report.)

6 p.m....75	2 a.m....60	8 a.m....63	Noon.....*74
8 p.m....72	4 a.m....58	9 a.m....66	*Unofficial.
10 p.m....64	6 a.m....57	10 a.m....71	
Midnight...62	7 a.m....60	11 a.m....72	

CHICAGO DAILY NEWS

FINAL Edition

70TH YEAR—167.

TUESDAY, JULY 17, 1945—TWENTY-SIX PAGES. Telephone DEArborn 1111. FOUR CENTS

TRUMAN, STALIN CONFER

Navy Thrusts to Tokyo Gates To Blitz Big Arms Factories

CIANO'S DIARY—NO. 25

Graft and Scandal Surround Family Of Duce's Mistress

It Becomes a 'National Problem'; U.S. a Bluff, Germans Agree

March 19-May 2, 1942.

As Italy blundered on toward ruin and collapse, the family of Mussolini's mistress, Claretta Petacci, emerged more and more as a sinister, selfish, thieving influence in the country's tottering society, it is plain from the diary of Mussolini's son-in-law and foreign minister, Count Ciano.

Even Mussolini's sister, the elderly Donna Edvige, became alarmed to the point where she determined to speak out to Il Duce. Ciano admitted to the privacy of his own records that the family had become a "national problem.'

International affairs continued to go badly. At Hitler's headquarters, Ciano heard it said repeatedly that "America is a big bluff." It was to him the whistling of small boys past the graveyard.

Ciano wrote:

MARCH 19—"Pavolini (minister of popular enlightenment) returns from a conversation with Goebbels (Nazi propaganda minister) and paints a dark picture of Germany's situation. He spoke of a crisis in the regime, and of 'walking on the edge of a razor.' . . . They no longer talk of beating Bolshevism. They will be satisfied if they reach the Caucasus.

"Pavolini related a funny story. When Goebbels sent Farinacci (Fascist secretary) a bust of Hitler, the bust was brought by the gauleiter of Essen, who pretends to speak Italian, but doesn't. In delivering it, he said: 'Your excellency, Minister Goebbels has entrusted me to bring you questa busta (this envelope, something empty without original ideas).' Goebbels is the first to laugh about it."

Nazis Planning For Defeat

MARCH 24—"I brought Il Duce a report by Luciolli on Germany. . . . He explains how politics was unable to assist the military conquest. They talked much about a New Order, but did nothing to bring it into being. The whole

Turn to page 7, column 1.

B-29 Blows Off Lid---Catches It

GUAM — (AP) — The B-29ers have brought back a souvenir from a town of the Jap homeland—inadvertently.

It's a large piece of tin roofing, snagged on the wing of a Superfort piloted by Capt. Samuel B. Hanford, Saybrook, Conn., over Sakai, a suburb of Osaka. The crew ripped it to bits to provide souvenirs for all.

The 20th Air Force explained the bomber entered the intensely hot updraft from the flaming target just in time to catch the soaring roofing on a wing.

'Live, Let Live,' Advice of Couple Wed 75 Years

HOPKINS, Mo.—(UP) — "Live and let live," is the advice the Edward G. Wolferses have to offer altar-bound couples.

The Wolferses might be considered connoisseurs of marital felicity—today they are celebrating three quarters of a century of married life.

Adding a hand to the celebration was just about every citizen of this little northwestern Missouri town, where Wolfers, as president of the local bank, for half a century ruled as the town's ranking business and civic leader. He is 96 and Mrs. Wolfers is 90.

Fatal Infection

DEVILS LAKE, N.D. — (UP) — Vera, a 45-year-old five-ton elephant owned by the Arthur Bros. Circus, died of an infected toe nail.

Get First Preview Of Fall Fashions

Virginia Leimert, Daily News staff writer, is reporting daily from New York on latest modes offered by stylists. On Page 13.

Also on the inside:

Miners May Get More Meat, Sugar

Increased meat and sugar rations for Illinois coal miners were predicted today as more men walked out in protest against light lunch boxes.

Carter Jenkins, OPA chief in the Springfield area, said he believed the WFA at Washington would step up the rations by Aug. 1 because of the "arduous nature" of mine work, United Press reported.

Union leaders estimated that 5,600 downstate miners are out and said others will stop work.

Calls for End Of OPA Offices

WASHINGTON —(AP)— Representative Jensen (Rep., Iowa) called on Price Administrator Bowles today to abolish all district and regional OPA offices "By so doing, you could eliminate all or most of the inefficient little czars who are today doing little but antagonizing and insulting good Americans," he said in a letter to Bowles.

Terrific Assault Goes On

2,000 U.S. Planes Roar Over Japan

GUAM, Wednesday—(UP)—U.S. warships moved almost to the gates of Tokyo last night with a thunderous bombardment of the factory city of Hitachi, only 75 miles north of the Jap capital, Fleet Adm. Nimitz announced.

The bombardment was continuing early today.

The battleship Iowa and other powerful dreadnoughts and warcraft of Adm. Halsey's rampaging 3d Fleet stood off Honshu Island—almost within sight of Tokyo's environs—and hurled tons of explosives into a group of important war-making plants.

This new shelling of Jap shoreline industrial installations was the third such daring foray against the enemy's homeland within four days.

* * *

THE BOMBARDMENT was preceded by a savage and apparently continuing air strike against the Tokyo area by a fast fleet of more than 1,500 carrier planes from a combined British and American armada. They were launched from a fleet of perhaps 150 men o' war.

Hitachi and adjoining Sukegawa are the center of the largest and most important complex of industrial targets north of Tokyo.

Industries there are jammed into a compact coastal area along the Fukushima-Mito highway in Tochigi prefecture. The cities face on the Sea of Kashima Nada, along a slightly curved coastline.

At that point Halsey's battleships were scarcely 30 or 40 miles from Tokyo Bay, separated only by the Boso peninsula

This was the first night sea bombardment of Jap homeland targets.

B-29s in three destructive raids previously destroyed 97.5

Turn to Page 4, Column 4.

Hunt Boy, 12, Seeking a Job

Mrs. Regina Greenberg of 3634 Roosevelt rd., believes her 12-year-old son, Alvin, is too young to seek his own living.

So she asked the Marquette police today to help find Alvin, who disappeared from home a week ago after saying he wanted to get a job. His father, Moe, is a railroad worker.

29 Rescued In Bus Fire

BECKET, Mass.—(AP)—A 15-year-old boy kicked out a window of a Chicago-bound bus early today when the emergency door apparently jammed and enabled 28 other passengers, trapped when flames enveloped the machine, to escape. **He was Earl Lepper of Walpole**, Mass. No injuries were reported.

FLEET POUNDS TOKYO MAINLAND

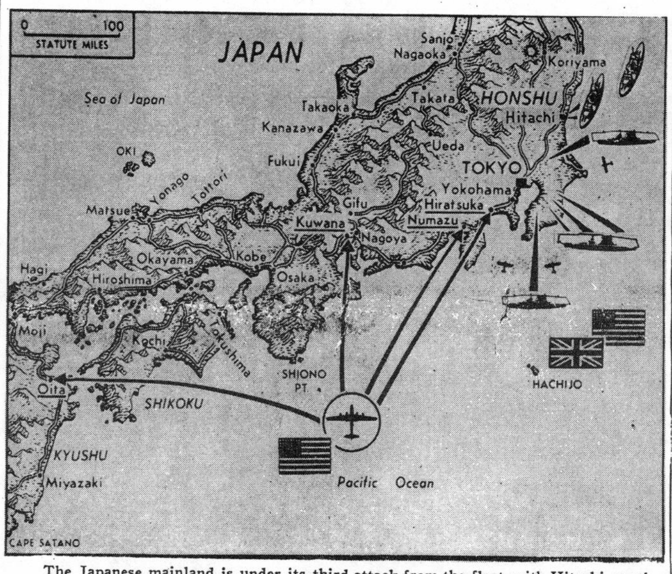

The Japanese mainland is under its third attack from the fleet, with Hitachi, north of Tokyo, being bombarded in the new action, which is reported to be continuing. Previously, a carrier force hurled 1,500 planes (ship, plane symbols) at the Tokyo area on the heels of a 500-plane B-29 fire raid (planes, arrows) on four Jap cities.
[Associated Press Wirephoto.]

200 Hurt In Blazing Lake Liner

SARNIA, Ont.—(AP)—The 360-foot Great Lakes passenger liner Hamonic, carrying 255 passengers, was destroyed by fire today with many persons injured and burned. A clerk at the Canada Steamship Lines said: "As far as we know no lives have been lost."

About 200 injured were in public and private hospitals.

* * *

THE CLERK, J. H. Aitchison, said it was believed all aboard scrambled to safety after fire that

broke out in the 1,000-foot long freight docks at Point Edward spread to the vessel. The docks were levelled.

American and Canadian fire fighters joined forces to combat the flames on the ship and ashore.

The Harmonic, one of the largest passenger ships on the lakes, had left Detroit last night on a cruise

Turn to Page 4, Column 7.

First European Vets Arrive in Philippines

BY JERRY THORP.

Daily News Foreign Service.

MANILA—The first American troops to be redtployed from the European theater to the Philippines since V-E Day landed here today, weeks after embarking at Leghorn, Italy.

All but five companies of the nearly 4,500 service troops, formerly of the 5th Army, were Negro troops, some of whom had been in Europe 28 months.

Four Army and Navy bands played lustily on the beach as the soldiers landed from L.C.M.'s, but otherwise there was little carnival atmosphere. The beach was soggy from rain, which drenched the heavily laden G.I.'s as they slogged through the mud to olive green boxcars on a railroad siding.

* * *

THE FIRST man ashore was Pvt. Joe Archilla, 26, of New York City.

Lt.Gen. W. D. Styer, commanding general of Army forces in the Western Pacific, briefly addressed some of the first men to come ashore.

"You are in on the last round of the fight," he said. "We welcome you not only for what you have already accomplished but because we need you. We will use your talents and services as determined by military necessity, but be assured that you will be given every consideration that good soldiers deserve.

* * *

ONE NEGRO soldier called out as he marched toward the boxcar: "Mr. Reporter, take a look at these." And he pointed sadly to six overseas stripes on the sleeve of his fatigue uniform, indicating 36 months of service outside of the United States.

Pvt. Whitfield Torbert, 6029 Champlain av., Chicago, volunteered: "I would just as soon be back home, but now that I'm here, **I guess it's all right."**

Capt. Neal Totzke, St. Joseph, Mich., formerly of 614 Forest av., Oak Park, observed that the mud, at least, was familiar. He had been in the Mediterranean area 14 months.

* * *

LT. EGAN DRIGGOTT, Chicago, led a detachment of medium automotive maintenance troops who had served 18 months in Tunisia and Italy.

The men were taken in three trains to a newly constructed camp seven miles from Manila. Later they will be divided into units.

Talks Open At Luncheon

President Host to Russ Chief Just Before First Big 3 Session

POTSDAM — (UP) — President Truman, Premier Stalin and their foreign ministers conferred for an hour today at the temporary White House preliminary to the formal opening of the Big Three conference immediately after lunch.

Stalin was Mr. Truman's luncheon guest after the introductory conference in the President's office on the second floor of his Potsdam villa.

An official announcement said Stalin, accompanied by his staff, arrived at Mr. Truman's villa at 11:50 a. m. The party was greeted on the steps of the villa by the President's military aide, Brig.Gen. Harry Vaughan, and naval aide, Capt. James K. Vardaman.

* * *

STALIN AND Foreign Commissar Molotov accompanied the aides to the office, where Mr. Truman and Secretary of State Byrnes were waiting.

The meeting cleared the way for the Big Three to get down to business. Prime Minister Churchill had called on the President for an informal talk yesterday while they were awaiting the delayed arrival of Stalin.

Mr. Truman sat at the head of the luncheon table. Stalin, wearing a fawn colored uniform and single star, was on the President's right. Next were the Soviet interpreter, V. N. Pavlov and Molotov.

* * *

BYRNES SAT to Mr. Truman's left, and next to him were the American interpreter, Charles E. Bohlen, and Adm. William F. Leahy, the President's personal adviser.

Mr. Truman wore a brown business suit.

On the luncheon menu were cream of spinach soup, fried liver and bacon smothered in onions, baked ham, potatoes, string beans, pumpernickel, jam, sliced fruit, cookies, mints, candy and cigars.

Information made available by the American section of the conference made no mention of alcoholic drinks.

An earlier announcement that the Big Three conference was opening directly after luncheon still stood. An official statement on it was expected late in the day.

* * *

DULL EXPLOSIONS of Allied demolition work in the ruins of Berlin were heard clearly in Potsdam as the conference shaped up. They were understood to have

Turn to Page 2, Column 3.

Russ Block Churchill's Honor Guard

Daily News Foreign Service.

BERLIN—Assistants to President Truman and Prime Minister Churchill at the Potsdam conference are learning that Russian soldiers carry out orders literally — without the slightest deviation.

This explains why a company of British grenadier guards, hand-picked as the Churchill guard of honor at the airport here, was stopped at the gate.

Russian soldiers had orders not to allow entrance after a given time but were told to permit a certain number of Allied soldiers to enter the field.

* * *

ONE UNIT arrived early, and when the lean, towering grenadier guards—every man at least 6 feet 2 inches tall—arrived in trucks, the Red Army soldiers blocked the way. They had their orders—and that was that.

The British commanding officer considered the situation and saw that he had time to get his men into position in case Churchill arrived ahead of schedule.

* * *

"ALL RIGHT, men," he told the soldiers standing in the trucks, "fix bayonets, off trucks, march!"

The guard company dismounted, formed up in a column of threes, fixed bayonets, upped arms and marched.

The Russians then withdrew, and the honor guard reached the position without further complications.

General Rescues Soldier and Girl On Hawaii Beach

HONOLULU — (AP) — Brig.Gen. Wayne C. Smith, chief of staff of the Central Pacific base command, rescued two persons from drowning at Waimanalo Beach yesterday.

Sgt. Fred Siceloff of Lexington, N.C., and Miss Kathryn Behrens of Chicago were floating on a raft offshore when Siceloff, a nonswimmer, tumbled into the water, dragging Miss Behrens with him.

Smith heard the couple's cries for help, plowed through the surf and loosened Siceloff's grip on the girl, then towed the soldier to safety.

Miss Behrens, a civilian secretary in the general's office, swam in.

British Probe Jap Positions

CALCUTTA — (UP) — British troops today probed Jap positions along the Pegu-Sittang canal near Myitkyo, 30 miles northeast of Pegu in eastern Burma, and moved against a fortified railway bridge at Nyaungkashe, the Southeast Asia command announced.

HE'S GOT THE BLUES

John Q. Public Loses His White Shirt

BY SUE MAHRER.

No longer can the well-dressed man yell blithely to his wife, "Honey, while you're downtown today, buy me a couple of white shirts."

A survey of 14 Loop men's shops and department stores uncovered just three toggeries with the popular long-sleeved, plain white broadcloth shirt in stock.

These three shops had white shirts, yes, but in a scattering of sizes. Only one store had the much desired size 15 neck and 33 sleeve length, and that was $5.

* * *

THERE WERE lots of gay sports shirts with open necks and short sleeves in bold plaids, gay checks, riotous stripes and clear, cool looking pastel shades.

Even some pin-striped dress shirts were to be had.

Salesmen in three of the Loop's largest department stores moaned, "We haven't had a white broadcloth shirt in months."

One offered a voile, "Very thin and airy," he said.

Another salesman fingered a slithery rayon and murmured, "Cool, very cool next to the skin."

STILL ANOTHER handsome haberdasher laughed mockingly.

"I could use 200 white shirts a day," he said. "What am I wearing? A plaid sports shirt."

Asked where all the shirts were, a salesman rejoined, "Ask Uncle Sam. He has the answer to that $64 question. We don't know when we will get any."

* * *

AND IF you have a teen-age daughter who goes in for Sloppy Joe styles, keep your shirts under lock and key.

She will covet them to wear with blue jeans. Or maybe she will take the tails, pull them to the front and knot them to make a bare midriff effect.

And that, along with the wear and tear of repeated laundering, hasn't helped the shirt situation for brother or dad.

ATOMIC BOMB HURLED AT JAPS

Goering's Wife Bares Attempt To Kill Hitler

Says Personal Physician Tried To Poison Fuehrer as Madman

(This is the first of three articles by Curt Riess, NEA foreign correspondent, based on exclusive interviews with Frau Emmy Goering, wife of the No. 2 Nazi leader.)

By CURT REISS

NEAR GERMAN-CZECHOSLOVAK BORDER, Aug. 6—Hermann Goering's wife, Frau Emmy Goering, told me that Adolf Hitler's personal physician sought on one occasion to poison the Fuehrer.

The exact time of this alleged incident she did not disclose, and there is a certain mystery inherent in the remainder of what she told me about it. She did give the reason. It was, according to Frau Goering, because the doctor realized that Hitler was mad.

Here is the story as she told it to me:

The Fuehrer had two physicians, Morell and Brandt.

FRAU GOERING

(Continued on Page Six)

Iwo-Based Planes Hammer Tokyo; Forts in New Raid

By WILLIAM F. TYREE

GUAM, Aug 6 (UP)—American fighter-bombers hit Tokyo and five surrounding prefectures today only a few hours after almost 600 Superfortresses set fire to five major targets along a 550-mile stretch of Japan in a pre-dawn assault.

CANADIAN ARRIVE

A Guam annoncement revealed that the vanguard of an expected 30,000 Canadian toops now has reached the Central Pacific. Canada also will place some of her crack air squadrons in the Pacific as well as at least 60 warships, including two aircraft carriers and two cruisers.

HIROSHIMA FIRED

A Tokyo broadcast said a few Superforts this morning dropped fire bombs and high explosives on Hiroshima, Honshu city of 350,000, northwest of Kure.

Radio Tokyo said 130 Iwo-based Mustangs swarmed over the Greater Tokyo area in two waves for an hour shortly before 9 A. M., bombing and strafing military and transport objectives. Urban areas of several cities also were said to have been attacked.

The first wave of 70 planes raided Saitama, Gumma and Tochigi prefectures, all north of Tokyo, the enemy broadcast said. The second wave, of 60 Mustangs, struck northern Tokyo itself and Chiba, Ibaraki and Tochigi prefectures, southeast, northeast and north of Tokyo.

The enemy claimed seven Mus-

PACIFIC

(Continued on Page Ten)

Briton Says Stalin, Allies Discussed War with Japs

By R. H. SHACKFORD

WASHINGTON, Aug. 6 (UP)—Official British and Chinese sources suggested strongly today that the Far Eastern war definitely was discussed in detail at Potsdam with Generalissimo Josef Stalin.

These sources stated almost unequivocally that Stalin participated in the talks which led to the British-American-Chinese ultima-

STALIN

(Continued on Page Twelve)

Yank Invaders of Nippon Face Human Bomb Peril

NEW YORK, Aug. 6 (UP)—Vice Admiral Mark Mitscher predicted today that thousands, perhaps millions, of Japanese will be ordered to lash themselves to explosives and blow themselves up in the path of American forces when they invade Japan.

The former commander of Task

SUICIDE

(Continued on Page Ten)

Suffolk Double

TRACK—FAST

1st—GRAND DAY

2d—RED AND BLACK

CHALK'S CHART AND CONSENSUS, PAGE 18

Boston Traveler AND ST. LOUIS POST DISPATCH

EXHIBIT OF GERMAN ATROCITY PICTURES LIFE SIZE

NOW SHOWING AT BOSTON PUBLIC LIBRARY THROUGH AUGUST 19

Weekdays: 11 A.M. to 9 P.M.
Sundays: 2 P.M. to 9 P.M.

ADMISSION FREE

The Weather

U. S. Official Forecast

RAIN TONIGHT

Full Weather Report on Page Two
Sun rises 5:41; Sun sets 7:58
High tide 10:48 A. M., 11:03 P. M.
Light all Vehicles by 8:28 P. M.

Atomic Bombs Developed at 3 Big Factories

WASHINGTON, Aug. 6 (AP)—The atomic bomb disclosed by President Truman today was developed at factories in Tennessee, Washington and New Mexico.

Mr. Truman in his announcement said that from 65,000 to 125,000 workers were employed on the project at Oak Ridge near Knoxville, Tenn., at Richland near Pasco, Wash., and at an unnamed installation near Santa Fe, N. M.

He said the work was so secret that most of the employes did not know the character of it.

Navy Bares Saga of The Hornet

(Photos, Page 15)

..WASHINGTON, Aug 6 (AP)—A mountainous wave lifted us and smacked down the 27,000-ton aircraft carrier Hornet so hard last June 5 that the forward corners of the flight deck folded down along the sides.

Thus nature, in the form of a 120-knot gale (138 miles an hour), achieved what the Japanese never were able to do in 14 months of hard-fought action—it damaged the big ship.

HORNET'S STORY BARED

The Navy told the Hornet's story today. It let the Japanese know

HORNET

(Continued on Page Ten)

Family Gets Bulk of Stone Estate, Art

The will of Mrs. Carrie M. Stone of Brookline and Marion, widow of Galen L. Stone, was filed in Dedham probate court today, disposing of a $4,000,000 estate and scores of famous paintings and quantities of priceless jewelry. Many bequests to

STONE

(Continued on Page Two)

Northeast Airlines Breaks Fare Records

Northeast Airlines broke passenger-carrying records during the weekend, it was announced today by President Paul F. Collins. NEA planes carried 850 persons Saturday, a new high for a single day, flew 891 yesterday, setting a new figure for the second day in succession.

Try Rose Hips For Vitamin C

CONCORD, N.H., Aug. 6 (AP)—Rose hips are good for housewives, husbands and children according to Miss Helen Hinman, nutrition consultant of the State Health Department.

"The wild rose," she said, "which grows so plentifully in New Hampshire is a splendid source of vitamin C if fruits or hips are used in September. It makes an excellent fruit juice, jam or marmalade if prepared after the hips or fruit have been touched by the frost. Six or eight rose hips supply an adults daily requirement of Vitamin C."

Secret Weapon Equals 20,000 Tons of TNT

Blast Force 2000 Times That of Any Other Bomb

WASHINGTON, Aug. 6 (AP) — Secretary Stimson predicted today that the atomic bomb will "prove a tremendous aid" in shortening the war with Japan.

WASHINGTON, Aug. 6 (AP) — The United States Army Air Force has released on the Japanese an atomic bomb containing more power than 20,000 tons of TNT.

2000 HEAVIER BLAST

It produces more than 2000 times the blast of the largest bomb ever used before.

The announcement of the development was made in a statement by President Truman released by the White House today.

The bomb was dropped 16 hours ago on Hiro Shima, an important Japanese army base.

The President said that the bomb has "added a new and revolutionary increase in destruction" on the Japanese.

Mr. Truman added:

"It is an atomic bomb. It is a harnessing of the basic power of the universe. The force from which the sun draws its power has been loosed against those who brought war to the Far East."

BOMB

(Continued on Page Ten)

Hiram Johnson, Calif., Dies at 78

WASHINGTON, Aug. 6 (UP)—U. S. Senator Hiram Warren Johnson (R., Calif.), one of the few survivors of the "little band of Willful men" who kept the United States out of the League of Nations in 1920, died today, a few weeks after he had reaffirmed his lifelong isolationism by opposing the United Nations Charter.

The California elder statesman, dean of Senate Republicans, died in his sleep in Bethesda, Md., Naval Hospital at 6:45 A. M., EWT. He would have celebrated his 79th birthday on Sept. 2.

JOHNSON, who had been in ill health for several years, took

JOHNSON

(Continued on Page Five)

Petain Saved Frenchmen From Slavery, Prince Says

By HERBERT J. KING

PARIS, Aug. 6 (UP)—Prince Xavier of Bourbon-Parma testified today that Marshal Henri Philippe Petain's orders caused the release of thousands of Frenchmen from concentration camps in Central France.

Prince Xavier, brother of Empress Zita of Austria and uncle of Archduke tto, was today's second witness at the treason trial of Petain, now in its third week. He returned recently from Dachau.

The prince said that if Petain had not signed the armistice with Germany in 1940, Frenchmen would have suffered the same fate as the Poles.

Xavier told the jury in the French high court hearing Petain's trial that the old marshal "wanted to wait until the Allies came, and then join in the attack against Germany."

Gen. Charles Lacaille, the first

PETAIN

(Continued on Page Six)

Co-operative Home Fills Wartime Need at Harvard

(Photos, Page 15)

BY RUTH MILLER

When housing authorities and Harvard University faculty wives suggested establishment of a co-operative house as a temporary home for the young wives of officers studying at Harvard for one to three months, there was a generous share of scoffing from some male "experts."

"What, put a half dozen women in a kitchen together and have peace—impossible," they contended.

CO-OPERATE

(Continued on Page Two)

WALL ST. STATE ST. FINAL
Boston Traveler
New England's Largest Evening Circulation
Complete Associated Press and United Press Wire Services
EST. 1825—121st YEAR—NO. 28—MON., AUG. 6, 1945 24 PAGES 3 CENTS

Murder Suspect Shouts Denial

Nashua Sailor, Held in Woman's Death, Home on Furlough 'To Blow off Steam'

By JAMES KELLEY

Lowell, Aug. 6—Slim, handsome and nonchalant, Alphee Desmarais of Nashua, N. H., Navy second-class cook accused of the murder of Mrs. Mary (George) Saunders in Dracut, lolled against the bars of his cell in the Lowell police station today to assert, in a shouted interview with a Traveler reporter outside a second barred door a half-dozen feet away, that he is innocent of the crime.

"The Man up Above (God) will take care of me," Desmarais declared. "He took care of me in the Pacific. If you're putting that in the paper you can say I trust Him."

CROWD ABOUT STATION

Meanwhile, a crowd of curious gathered outside the police station, some of them getting inside and craning their necks in an effort to see the man police charge was responsible for the death of Mrs. Sounders.

Desmarais declared he is a veteran of the battles of Sicily, Iwo Jima and Okinawa. And the star-studded battle ribbons on his dark blue jumper bore out his statement.

"I came home to let off a little steam," Desmarais said, relating his experiences in the Mediter-

INTERVIEW

(Continued on Page Twenty-one)

Franco Foe's Prison Break Excites Spain

Robles Escapes Jail in Portugal

LONDON, AUG. 6 (UP)—A Madrid dispatch to the Evening Standard said today that Gil Robles, exiled leader of Spain's Catholic and Monarchist parties, reportedly has escaped from a detention prison at Busaco in northern Portugal.

NEAR BORDER

"He is reported near the Spanish border beyond Oporto," he dispatch

SPAIN

(Continued on Page Two)

Taunton Area Hard Hit by Bus Strike

Deadlock Still Holds in Dispute

TAUNTON, Aug. 6—This city and surrounding communities felt the full impact of the three-day-old bus strike for the first time today as thousands of war plant workers and other commuters scrambled for alternate means of transportation.

The walkout of 48 drivers and 12

BUSFS

(Continued on Page Twenty-one)

More Low-Cost Garments Seen For Children

By EDITH GAYLORD

WASHINGTON, Aug. 6 (AP)—The children's low-cost clothing situation is looking up.

As Associated Press survey showed today that a greater number of essential garments should begin ap-

CLOTHING

(Continued on Page Twelve)

Navy Suspect Held in Lowell Without Bail

Placed with Victim At Dracut Resort

LOWELL, Aug. 6—Alphee Norman Dermarais, 22, Navy cook whose home is in Nashua, N. H., was held without bail in Lowell district court today for hearing Sept. 8 on a charge of murdering Mrs. Mary (Georye) Saunders of Manchester, N. H., and Lowell.

Judge Arthur L. Eno, in brief formal arraignment proceedings, ordered the plea of not guilty, mandatory in a murder case, entered for Desmarais.

Although crowds had gathered outside the Lowell police station where Desmarais was confined, only a small group of spectators was present in the courtroom.

BODY

(Continued on Page Twenty-one)

3 Troopships Bringing 119 N. E. Men Here

Total of 4135 Troops to Land

Three more shpis in the almost unbroken stream of troop transports bringing American fighting men home from Europe are due in Boston today with a passenger load of 4135, including 119 New Englanders.

Expected to dock at the Army Base at noon, with debarkation

TRANSPORT

(Continued on Page Nine)

War Cripple, Girl Deny They Plan to Be Married

(Photos Page 15)

NORTH WILBRAHAM, Aug. 6—"No romance," said Betty Koslovski at her home here today.

(And "No romance" said Pfc. James W. Wilson of Starke, Fla., at England General Hospital, Atlantic City, N. J.)

Betty was hurt and angry today, because weekend newspaper stories persisted in stating she and Wilson were in love and planned to marry.

Wilson is one of two Army men

ROMANCE

(Continued on Page Twenty-one)

Traveler Index

THE WEATHER

Sunny, cool today and tonight; Thursday sunny with moderate temperatures, low humidity, northerly winds.

Detailed Weather Report Page 26

Read The Baltimore News-Post for complete, accurate war coverage. It is the only Baltimore newspaper possessing the three great wire services—
ASSOCIATED PRESS
INTERNATIONAL NEWS SERVICE
UNITED PRESS

THE BALTIMORE NEWS-POST
AN INDEPENDENT NEWSPAPER

The Largest Evening Circulation in the Entire South

VOL. CXLVII.—NO. 81 Entered as second-class matter at Baltimore Postoffice. WEDNESDAY EVENING, AUGUST 8, 1945 PRICE 3 CENTS

EXTRA
NINE STAR

RUSS DECLARE WAR ON JAPAN

WASHINGTON, Aug.--(A. P.).--President Truman announced today that Russia has declared war on Japan. Mr. Truman made the momentous announcement to a hurriedly summoned newsconference. He said he had only a simple statement to make, but it was so important he could notdelay it.

B-29s Blast Four Jap Targets

GUAM, Aug. 8—(A. P.).—The growing fleet of Superfortresses struck for the third straight day today with multiple blows landing on the Japanese empire at Yawata, the Tokyo arsenal, the Nakajima aircraft factory, just outside Tokyo, and the chemical center of Fukuyama.

The B-29s hit with mounting fury as Admiral Halsey's mighty Third Fleet returned to Japanese waters for new attacks after riding out a typhoon—the only effective defense against its savage bombardment of the home islands.

HIT JAP "PITTSBURGH"

Beginning with a daylight raid on Yawata, the "Pittsburgh of Japan," four groups of Superfortresses cascaded destruction down on the home islands, the last raid striking Fukuyama just before midnight. Probably 400 B-29s, some with fighter escort, participated in the raids.

Fukuyama, 42 miles north of Kure on Honshu and one of the cities forewarned of its doom, was the target of 100 B-29s of Brig. Gen. Roger M. Ramey's Tinian-based Fifty-eighth wing.

The incendiaries hit a square mile industrial area containing among important industries the Imperial Dye Works, the Kawa-

Continued on Page 2, Column 7.

Blow Likely To Fall At Any Hour

WASHINGTON, Aug. 8—(A. P.).—President Truman, taking personal direction of the drive he believes will knock Japan out of the war, summoned Secretary of War Stimson today for a report on the atomic bombing of the enemy homeland. When the next bomb will be released was a military secret. But the Japanese continue to ignore the Potsdam ultimatum to surrender and it was reported the time was running short on another one of their cities fated to suffer the doom of Hiroshima. One of the President's first acts today was to set up a radio report to the nation for 10 P. M. (Eastern war time) tomorrow.

By JOHN A. REICHMANN

WASHINGTON, Aug. 8—(I. N. S.).—The Allied High Command today ordered fresh atomic bombing attacks on Japan.

The new devastating blows by the greatest weapon in history may come at any moment.

It is the consensus in Washington that the atomic bombings in themselves will serve as a new ultimatum to Japan to surrender unconditionally or be wiped off the face of the earth.

This development came as official reconnaissance photographs showed the first atomic bombing

Continued on Page 2, Column 6.

Temperatures

12 Midn't., 72	8 A. M., 68
1 A. M., 72	9 A. M., 70
2 A. M., 70	10 A. M., 72
3 A. M., 69	11 A. M., 74
4 A. M., 68	12 Noon, 76
5 A. M., 67	1 P. M., 77
6 A. M., 65	2 P. M., 78
7 A. M., 66	3 P. M., 79

PILOT DESCRIBES ATOMIC BOMB FLIGHT — Col. Paul W. Tibbits (standing), pilot of the B-29 which dropped the first atomic bomb on Hiroshima, Japan, relates his experience at U. S. Strategic Air Force Headquarters on Guam. Officers at the table (left to right) are: Brig. Gen. Thomas F. Farrell, Rear Admiral William R. Purnell, Gen. Carl Spaatz, strategic air force chief; Col. Tibbits, Maj. Gen. Curtis E. Le May. *(Story on Page 3.)*

Heat And Concussion From Single Missile Turns City's Heart To Dust

By KENNETH McCALEB

GUAM, Aug. 8—(I. N. S.).—One hundred and fifty thousand Japanese were estimated today to have been killed by the atomic bomb dropped Monday on Hiroshima. This estimate was made by scores of veteran airmen who viewed new reconnaissance photographs taken today by Okinawa-based planes which flew over the awesome scene of desolation and destruction.

Radio Tokyo virtually confirmed the staggering loss of life, declaring "practically all living things, human and animal, were literally seared to death" in the Southern Honshu city.

If the estimate of Lt. Col. Bob Herring, Breckenridge, Texas, and scores of his veteran airmen on Okinawa is right, then the lone atomic bomb wiped out in one blow more than the total number of Americans killed in the first World War, when 126,000 U. S. soldiers died in action.

The number of dead is equal to the population of cities like Albany, N. Y.; Sacramento, Cal., or Flint, Mich. The new reconnaissance photos failed to disclose a building or wall standing anywhere in the leveled city, which looked as if a million comets had dug up and disintegrated everything.

News of the terrifying destruction caused by the atomic bomb created the greatest furore among troops on Okinawa.

They foresaw the end of the war, believe that even the Japanese are unwilling to have their entire nation wiped out by the revolutionary bomb.

So widespread was the effect of the bombing that "those outdoors were burned to death, while those indoors were killed by the indescribable pressure and heat," Tokyo declared.

ONLY ONE BOMB

A single bomb, the most terrible weapon of destruction in mankind's history, transformed the heart of the city of 340,000 population into something that resembled cosmic dust.

In a momentous communique, Gen. Carl Spaatz, chief of the U. S. Army's strategic air forces, declared that four and one-tenth

Continued on Page 2, Column 1.

NEWS-POST

Convert Okinawa To Superfort Base

HEADQUARTERS EIGHTH A. A. F., OKINAWA, Aug. 8—(U. P.).—A flight of Superfortresses, forerunner of 1,000, have arrived here to nearly complete conversion of Okinawa into another gigantic B-29 base less than a third the distance from the Marianas to the Japanese homeland. This was announced today by Lt. Gen. James H. Doolittle, commander of the Eighth Air Force, whose first strikes against Japan he said will be made before the end of this month.

NO TRUMAN VACATION

WASHINGTON, Aug. 8—(A. P.).—President Truman has so much work ahead there is no immediate vacation in sight for him, Press Secretary Charles G. Ross said today.

Shangri-La Diary:

Glider Saves Trio In Valley

(Margaret Hastings concludes her "Shangri-La Diary" in the following chapter with a breathless description of the final rescue from the valley.)

"SHANGRI-LA DIARY"
CHAPTER 18—(Final Installment)
By CORPORAL MARGARET HASTINGS, WAC
(Written Exclusively for International News Special Service.)

OWEGO, N. Y., Aug. 8.—We should all have been as happy and content as kings in this lotus land.

Instead, we were wildly impatient to escape from paradise.

We spent a large part of our waking hours discussing just when and how we would be whisked out of the valley.

True, the glider strip was ready. We had expected to be rescued within 24 hours after reaching it. But day followed day and we seemed no closer to release from the "prison" of Shangri-La.

The Army plane came over

Continued on Page 8, Column 1.

Sign Key Plan For War Trials

LONDON, Aug. 8—(A. P.).—The key plan for the trials of Germany's major war criminals was signed today by the representatives of the United States, Britain, Russia and France. The document was signed as it was disclosed that top-ranking Nazis, held as prisoners of war at Mondorf, Luxembourg and elsewhere, would be moved soon to the Nuernberg jail, where they will lose their status as prisoners of war and be held as civil criminals.

SHIP AFIRE AT SEA

HALIFAX, N. S., Aug. 8—(I. N. S.).—The British freighter Argos Hill was reported today on fire at sea, about 200 miles off the Newfoundland coast. Three naval mine sweepers equipped with fire-fighting apparatus were rushed to the scene.

VERY LATEST NEWS

(Race Results From Howard Sports Daily, Inc.)

RACING RESULTS

AT BELMONT

Third—Ducker, $61.00, $19.80, $7.40; Fifty-Fifty, $4.60, $3.40; Meeting House, $4.10.

Fourth — Little Ann, $11.60, $7.30, $4.00; Forerunner, $31.40, $14.60; Cominta, $3.30.

AT GARDEN STATE

First — Knute, $11.00, $5.80, $4.60; Kapmec, $20.60, $11.70; No Quota, $4.60.

AT SUFFOLK DOWNS

First — Supai, $12.00, $5.80, $4.40; Marandy, $4.40, $3.40; Boonyard, $16.40.

Second—Pompous Fox, 1; Sals Sister, 2; Garden Pot, 3.

BELMONT PARK RESULTS

FIRST RACE—Six furlongs. Off 1.16½. Time, 1.25 2-5.

Portage Trail, 118 (Wright)	$4.90	$3.10	$2.50
Sunlette, 113 (Luce)		5.30	3.70
Global, 113 (McCreary)			11.70

Also Ran—Chance Grey, Mat akom, Grand Party, fLady Janice, aGusher, Purple Heart, fPhotoge nic, Gambling Andy, Rondo, aPicket Line, Flemingsburg.

aW. Bethel and Mrs. E. Can ning entry. f—Field.

SECOND—Five and a half furlo ngs (Widener course). Off at 151½. Time, 1.04 2-5.

Bridal Flower, 115 (H. Lind berg)	$14.00	$6.70	$5.70
Athenia, 115 (A. Kirkland)		4.10	3.50
Dutch Cut, 115 (J. Longden)			9.80

Also Ran—Sewed Up, fGoose F eather, Dorothy Brown, Wichuraiana, Hush Hush, Qona, Jingle Bells, Flying Level, Vigo, fFidgety Miss, fShes Home. fField.

Daily Double—Portage Trail and Bridal Flower, $51.30

Oak Ridge Attacks Japanese

STAY ON THE JOB

OAK RIDGE JOURNAL

U. S. POSTAGE
SEC. 562, P. L. & R.
PAID
Oak Ridge, Tenn.
Permit No. 1

Vol. 3—No. 4 | OAK RIDGE, TENNESSEE | Thursday, August 9, 1945

Workers Thrill As Atomic Bomb Secret Breaks; Press And Radio Stories Describe 'Fantastically Powerful' Weapon; Expected To Save Many Lives

Teamwork Responsible, Nichols Says

Teamwork was the outstanding factor in the accomplishments of CEW, Col. Kenneth D. Nichols stated at a press conference this week. The scientists started their their work first, but the laborers who worked on the roads and the thousands of workers who cooperated so amazingly deserve much credit.

Organization was the keynote in accomplishing the job quickly and safely, and the results of the CEW Safety program alone are outstanding. The 1944 employe injury rates of the plants were less than half the average rates of all U. S. manufacturing plants.

Explaining the progress of fundamental research in physics and chemistry prior to the war indicated that utilization of atomic power might have been feasible in fifteen to twenty years, Col. Nichols declared that the combined efforts of the many different people and organizations connected with the project has compressed the time to three years, an accomplishment which will endure as a monument to the ingenuity and vision and determination of all those, from scientists to laborers, who have had a part in the work.

"These people and organizations — scientific, engineering, contracting, manufacturing, procuring and others—working in harmony among themselves, and with government agencies, deserve credit for the successful accomplishment of an almost impossible vast and complicated task," Col. Nichols declared.

In addition, he pointed out that the district staff of specially selected officers, WACs, enlisted men and civilians deserve a large measure of credit for the success of the Army's part in the project. Paying tribute to the work they have done, Col. Nichols declared that, "Each assistant has spent long hours of work each day and collectively have made it possible for the Manhattan District to control the large volume of research, construction and production necessary to complete the project."

Workers React To Biggest News Story Of Year

When the story of Oak Ridge was told Monday, an Oak Ridge Journal reporter stopped people on the street and asked them their reactions. Here are some of the answers:

Mrs. Susie Richards, a TEC employe, said, "Something turned over inside me when I heard the news. I had no idea what I was

Continued on Page 7

To Contractors, Workers, And Residents Of Oak Ridge:

CONGRATULATIONS to all workers at the Clinton Engineer Works and to the people of Oak Ridge! You have done the impossible.

I am sure that you shared with me the thrill which came with President Truman's announcement that the results of our hard work and American "stick-to-it-iveness" have been delivered to the Japs with a world-shaking crash —the thrill that comes with the knowledge of a tough job well done.

This project has been, from the start, a cooperative enterprise, based on mutual faith—faith of the scientist that engineers could translate his discoveries—yes, and his world stirring dreams—into practical process designs; faith of the engineer that material and construction men could turn those designs into bricks and mortar and process equipment: faith of the Army that all contractors would have the vision, courage, and drive to do the seemingly impossible; faith of the operating contractors that local nontechnical workers could be trained to perform new and strange tasks so exacting that they would normally be entrusted only to skilled scientific experimenters; faith of the construction workers and operators that their supervisors knew their business; and faith of all groups—management and employees—scientific and service—that somehow ways and means would be found to house, feed, and transport them. This faith has now been justified by the successful use of your product against the Japs.

The success of the project was made possible only because everyone did his or her part and "stayed on the job," from the Nobel Prize winners whose scientific theories and experiments mushroomed into huge production plants to the sweating construction worker and the cafeteria girl with her tray of dishes. The same spirit is necessary to continue an uninterrupted supply to the fighting man at the front. More and more production is needed and can be realized only by even greater efforts to get maximum output from our plants. Let's not give the Jap a chance to catch his breath between blows.

You now surely realize the wisdom of our security program which was effective only because of your faithful cooperation. No known case sabotage has been committed to slow our work or to endanger your lives. This is a real tribute to all of you.

The complete surprise to the enemy with all the military advantage that attended such unheard-of destruction has made our weapon much more effective. This tremendous weapon must be kept "our weapon" alone, so that the peace of the world can be reestablished and preserved. This can be done only by even greater security precautions with respect to vital information. Do not reveal to anyone information not contained in the official releases. The security policy for information that has not been officially released has not been changed.

A grateful nation's thanks are due all of you for a magnificent performance and history will record the full significance of your fabulous achievement in unlocking the stupendous energy of the atom. May it be used not only as an effective war weapon but in the future may it play a major part in humanity's service.

K. D. NICHOLS,
Colonel, Corps of Engineers,
District Engineer.

First Man-Made Atomic Explosion In New Mexico Desert Heralds Man's Arrival At 'Atomic Age'

(Official Release)

Mankind's successful transition to a new age, the Atomic Age, was ushered in July 16, 1945, before the eyes of a tense group of renowned scientists and military men gathered in the desertlands of New Mexico to witness the first end results of their $2,000,000,000 effort. Here in a remote

Continued on Page 2

Bomb Has More Power Than 20,000 Tons Of TNT; Pride Is Reaction Of Workers

The most exciting day in the era of secrecy and suspense which has governed the life of Oak Ridge residents occurred Monday with President Truman's announcement that an "atomic bomb" had been used against the Japanese, and the subsequent stories in the press and on the radio describing the part of the CEW in the production of the fantastically powerful weapon.

The reaction of Oak Ridge residents and workers on the whole was a feeling of pride that they had a part to play in this vital development, and a thrilling satisfaction in knowing that their efforts had been so effective, as the story of the efficacy of the bomb was told.

Stating that the bomb had more power than 20,000 tons of TNT, the President described it as "harnessing of the basic power of the universe. The force from which the sun draws its power has been loosed against those who brought war to the Far East."

Secretary of War Stimson's statement followed the President's disclosure of the use of the atomic bomb, giving facts concerning the production center here; at Richland, near Pasco, Washington; and near Santa Fe, New Mexico.

"We have spent two billion dollars on the biggest gamble in history—and won," the President declared. The "battle of laboratories" held "fateful risks" for the United States, "and we now have won the battle of the laboratories as we have won the other battles," he said.

Look Inside . . .

MAJ. GEN. LESLIE R. GROVES—
Officer in charge of this government's Atomic Bomb project. See story on Page 5. (For a picture and story on Col. Kenneth D. Nichols, District Engineer of the Manhattan Engineer District, see Page 2.)

One Result . . .

One result of the week's big news story is that the Oak Ridge Journal appears today without the words "Not to be mailed or taken from the area," for the first time in its history.

MORE READERS
Than All Other
County Publications
Combined

CHEROKEE DAILY TIMES

ASSOCIATED PRESS
LEASED WIRE SERVICE

UNIVERSAL IN THE CHEROKEE TRADE TERRITORY

Consolidation of Cherokee Evening Times, established 1870, and Cherokee Chief, established as The Democrat, 1886.

THE TIMES, NOW IN ITS
SEVENTY-FIFTH YEAR

IF YOU DID NOT
Receive Your Paper
CALL 64
For Special Delivery
Service

EVERY EVENING EXCEPT SUNDAY | OFFICIAL COUNTY AND CITY DAILY | CHEROKEE, IOWA, THURSDAY, AUGUST 9, 1945 | OVER 16,000 DAILY READERS | VOLUME 17, No. 294

SECOND ATOMIC BOMBING HITS NAGASAKI

Sgt. Archer Hero Of Philippine Battle

Wounded Three Times, Cherokean Returns To Fight

One Of Three Americans In Two-Hour Fray

WITH THE U. S. SIXTH DIVISION, LUZON, PHILIPPINES (AP)—Three Americans, two of them Iowans, dominated a two-hour battle across scarred Ifugao Ridge during an early morning Japanese counter attack, according to officers.

The Iowans were Sgt. James L. Archer, jr., of Cherokee, a husky farmer turned rough and tough fighting man, and Pfc. Algert L. Barnes of Beloit, who was described as always a devil in the field and at least an imp when it came to obeying rear base regulations.

"Archer before this event, already was legendary," Russell Brines, Associated Press reporter wrote. "The type of man who sniffs out action an courts it. He has been wounded three times, but no one can keep him from volunteering for a new assignment that promises excitement. On Biak island, recovering from his third wound, he disappeared from the hospital. He was found later with a forward patrol."

During the battle, officers said, the three acting individually, stood up from their foxholes amid the noise of the fighting and raced across the ridge to rally wavering Filipino lines. They turned on the Japanese with crackling automatic fire. They were everywhere, encouraging and fighting hard.

The third member of the trio was Sgt. John Fann of Knoxville, Tenn.

Cherokee Bean Pickers Total 10 Tons Of Beans

Seven Cherokee young people had perfect attendance during the bean picking program which began July 19, Otto Huebner, farm labor assistant, announced Thursday.

These youngsters were Gloria Hahn, Shirley Hansen, Joan Parrott, LaVonne and Delores Pettengill, Eddie Sexton, and Gerald McKenzie.

Eleven actual days were spent in picking, averaging 5½ hours a day. There were 79 different pickers from Cherokee and 23 from Aurelia. The group went to Storm Lake every morning where the beans were picked for the cannery.

Average daily attendance was 32.7, Huebner stated. Total pounds of beans picked by the Cherokee crew was 26,085 and the Aurelia total was 7,655 pounds.

Three from Cherokee and one from Aurelia picked 1000 or more pounds during the actual picking time. They were Mary Bush, Lola Hansen, Joan Parrott, Cherokee, and John Wilson from Aurelia.

Mary Bush, with a total of 203 pounds, picked the most of anyone during any one day.

"Each picker may have the satisfaction of knowing that every bean that he picked goes to our fighting men," Huebner said. "These beans are slated for the army."

Pvt. Leo Mahoney In Hawaii Broadcast

Pvt. Leo V. Mahoney, son of Mr. and Mrs. W. J. Mahoney, whose wife and daughter reside at 257 East Maple street, Cherokee, was heard in a radio broadcast from an army hospital in the Hawaiian islands Wednesday night, being one of those interviewed on a program presented by the army. Pvt. Mahoney, who distinguished himself in service in the Okinawa campaign, was wounded during an attempt to capture Conical Hill and has since been hospitalized, suffering from concussion of the chest and injury to the shoulder. He is the holder of the Purple Heart decoration, the Asiatic-Pacific ribbon with one battle star and the combat infantry badge.

In the radio interview Pvt. Mahoney said he was "feeling pretty good" and was looking anxiously forward to returning home.

Cpl. Headley, Cherokee Soldier, Shown At Air Field In Bombay, India

Cpl. Donald B. Headley, son of Mr. and Mrs. Charles B. Headley of Cherokee who is serving with the American air forces in Bombay, in northeast India, is shown here atop his plane, a P-38, preparing to take off from a field in India. Cpl. Headley is a member of air engineering squadron 383 of the air service group and has been in India since December, 1944.

Russia's War Declaration Gives Her A Seat At The Pacific Peace Table

By JACK BELL

WASHINGTON (AP) — Russia has gained a seat at the Pacific peace table, and her presence there may have far-reaching diplomatic and territorial implications.

By her declaration of war against Japan, the Soviet union became a partner with the United States, Great Britain and China in settlements that will determine, among other things, which strategic islands American forces are to hold after the fighting ends.

The disposition of these islands, such as Iwo Jima and Okinawa, went unmentioned in the master plan for dismembering Japan agreed upon at Cairo in November, 1943, by President Roosevelt, Prime Minister Churchill and Generalissimo Chiang Kai-Shek.

The assumption in diplomatic quarters here is that when the Soviets finally agreed to enter the conflict against Japan, they automatically accept the terms of the Cairo agreement, in which they did not participate.

This belief is strengthened by authentic disclosures that at Yalta in February Generalissimo Stalin told Mr. Roosevelt and Churchill, both Cairo signers, that he would enter the Pacific war. But he did not then set a specific date.

At Cairo the three powers then fighting the Japanese renounced all territorial expansion for themselves.

They agreed that Japan would be stripped of all Pacific islands she had seized or occupied since the beginning of World War I in 1941.

They said territories she had stolen, such as Manchuria, Formosa and the Pescadores, would be restored to China. The three powers also agreed that "in due

CONTINUED ON PAGE TWO

Pied Piper Parade Features Annual Play Day Aug. 31

Many Prizes Offered For Day's Special Events

Friday, August 31, is very definitely the day for Cherokee's annual pre-school celebration. The feature of this is the great Pied Piper Parade, according to chairman, Jay Yaggy of the Retail Trade committee. This date is the first day of the County 4-H Show and will be an outstanding event for the boys and girls of country and city alike.

The Pied Piper parade will form at 1:00 o'clock and march at 1:30. This parade affords an opportunity for every boy and girl, either singly or in groups, to enter the parade and to show the things in which they are interested either in action or through their own building efforts.

At the present time the parade as organized will be an shown below:

Division I.
Class I Doll buggies and dolls.
Class 2 Costumes.
Class 3 Impersonations.
Class 4 Our Armed Forces.
Class 5 Groups-This class is especially for schools, Sunday Schools, 4-H clubs, garden club, Scouts, or others active group organizations.

Division II
Class 6 Bicycles.
Class 7 Mobiles.
Class 8 Contraptions.
Class 9 Pushmobiles.

Division III
Class 10 Dogs.
Class 11 Pet stock.
Class 12 Clowns.
Class 14 Ponies and Horses.

Cash prizes are offered to every boy and girl who enters and marches in the parade properly outfitted to qualify for one of the classes.

Following the parade a street program of twelve events will be

CONTINUED ON PAGE TWO

Propaganda Leaflets Dropped On Japan

MANILA (AP)—The first mission of the far eastern air force in support of their new Soviet allies in the war with Japan was carried out this morning when millions of leaflets printed in Japanese were showered on the Japanese population only a few hours after war was declared.

The leaflets, printed in advance, were designed to explode a psychological bomb on the war weary enemy civilians.

Brig. Gen. Bonner F. Feller, psychological warfare officer, admitted the advance preparation was a gamble that the Soviet union would come into the war,

Mueller Brothers Home On Leave

The Mueller brothers, Emil and LeRoy, sons of Mr. and Mrs. Otto Mueller, 695 N. Roosevelt, are both home for 30 days.

Emil, SM 1/c, has been in service for three years and four months, having been at sea for two years. He has seen duty in the south Pacific, where he was assigned to a commercial ship. He will report back to San Francisco at the end of his leave.

T/5 LeRoy has been in service for 30 months, serving overseas for six months. He has been in the European theater in the 20th armored division of the Seventh army. LeRoy will report to Jefferson Barracks for reassignment.

4-H Girls Sponsor Larrabee Style Show

The Spring Cedar Peppy Pals 4-H club will hold their local Achievement show at the Methodist church basement in Larrabee Tuesday evening, August 14. The program and style show will begin at 8:30 p. m. Girls will exhibit articles of clothing which they have made during the year.

Dates For Plowing Match And 4-H Club Shows Postponed

Events Will Be Aug. 30 to Sept. 1 In Cherokee

Dates for the 34th annual Pilot Rock Plowing match have been changed from August 16, 17, 18 to August 30, 31, and Sept. 1, the committee in charge decided at a meeting Wednesday evening.

The change was made because of the delay in threshing it was announced. Farm boys and girls are too busy now to participate fully in the show events.

Entry day for 4-H members will be the afternoon of Thursday, August 30, it was stated. These who have entries in the Marcus colt show will make their entries in the Cherokee show late that afternoon, and others may enter their exhibits at any time.

Girl's 4-H achievement day events will be as scheduled on August 31 and judging for both boys' and girls' events will be on that day. The boys' 4-H livestock sale will be on September 1.

The garden shows will be the afternoon of the 31, it was stated.

Pilot Rock Grounds May Become State Park

Pilot Rock and the grounds surrounding it, one of the historical spots in northwest Iowa, may become a state park. H. W. Freed, landscape architect with the Iowa State Conservation commission, was here Wednesday and in company with N. L. Stiles, who has been actively interested in the project for a number of years, visited the Pilot Rock project and inspected its historical setting and the possibilities for future development.

Mr. Freed's report will be filed with the Conservation commission, which has had the project under consideration for some time. Favorable action by the commission is expected.

European Vet To Hot Springs

Veteran of 11 months in the European theater, three months as a German prisoner, Pvt. Paul C. Nielson has reported to the army ground and service forces redistribution station, Hot Springs, Ark., for reassignment.

V.F.W. To Open New Club Rooms

The V.F.W., in a meeting Wednesday night, completed arrangements for the renting of the second floor of the Rapson Motor Company to be used for club rooms, C. H. Smith, chairman of the committee in charge of the transaction, stated Thursday.

The rooms will be suited to the needs of the club as soon as possible, it was stated, and if possible, the group plans to hold their next meeting on Friday, August 17, in the new building.

Russell R. Smith, E 2/c, who just returned from Guam, was obligated in the local membership.

Band Concert At Tomahawk Field

The band concert, which was flooded out of Wescott Park last Sunday, will be given at Tomahawk Athletic field at 7:30 p. m. August 12, Norman Meyer, director, announced. The program will be the same as that planned for a week ago, it was stated.

The Weather

Cherokee Temperatures Wednesday

Maximum—78 (for 24 hours preceding 7 a. m.)
Minimum—61 (for 12 hours preceding 7 a. m.)

Considerable cloudiness with occasional local showers tonight and Friday. Warmer tonight and in extreme west portion Friday.

MAJOR BONG KILLED IN CRASH

Here is the wreckage of a jet-propelled P-80 plane which crashed at Burbank, Calif., killing Maj. Richard I. Bong, America's ace fighter pilot in the south Pacific area before he was returned to the United States and reassigned to test flying duty. Witnesses said the plane exploded with a terrific roar and disintegrated. (AP Wirephoto)

Chicken Dinner, Dance Feature Maryhill Picnic

Annual Affair Will Be Held Tuesday, Aug. 21

Fried chicken, a bowery dance, and many concessions will be among the main attractions for the annual Maryhill picnic which will be held Tuesday, Aug. 21.

This event is one of the big attractions for people in this and neighboring communities, great crowds coming each year for the chicken supper and carnival entertainment.

The bowery dance will be staged on a 36 by 84 foot floor with Elwyn Thomas' six piece orchestra furnishing the music.

Committees have been appointed as follows:

Publicity — John Glassmaker, Bert Heinen, Maydar Lux.

Bingo—Lawrence Kohns, Lloyd Lux.

Chuckluck—Lester Rupp, Aloys George.

Sandwiches—Mrs. William Bush, Mrs. John Umhoeser, Mrs. J. Kohns.

Ice cream and pie—Mr. and Mrs. Andy Reinert, Mr. and Mrs. Tony George.

Blanket wheel—Carl Rupp, Ray Glassmaker.

Pop stand—Lester Bush, Mike Pitts.

Dance floor—George Rassel, Ed Wiemold, Wilmer Rupp, Lloyd Rupp, Ed Corzilius, Leland Bush, Wilmer Bush.

Cash wheel—E. J. Baum, Ed Lunders.

Bingo—children—Paul Kohns, John Davis.

Police—Louise Bauers, Charles Reynolds, Joe Baum, Joe Pitts, Albert Rupp, Ed Stoos, John Specht, Ray Henke.

Penny pitch—Joe George, Bob Heinen, Darrell Zimmer, Dick Rupp.

Ladies stand—social union officers.

Building—Joe Henke.

Demonstration On Terrace Building

Terrace construction with a disk tiller will be demonstrated on August 22, at the P. M. Peterson farm. This farm is located 5½ miles south of Cherokee on Highway No. 59.

The John Deere Company is furnishing the tractor and disk tiller and will demonstrate a simple and efficient method of terrace construction.

The demonstration is aimed to show that terracing is one of the most effective practices which aid in minimizing soil and water losses by decreasing erosion and making slopes shorter; this means a reduction in the speed of runoff water and its silt carrying capacity.

It will further tend to prove that terracing is an excellent means of making "running water walk". However, it must be remembered that terracing is a supporting practice and will not eliminate the need for a good crop rotation and good soil management practices.

Japan's Day Rapidly Draws To A Close With Russian Attack And New Bomb

By DEWITT MACKENZIE
AP Foreign Affairs Analyst

Japan's day is rapidly drawing to a close.

Russia's entry into the war, coming on top of the advent of the atomic bomb with its awful powers of annihilation, place Nippon in a position where she must surrender quickly or suffer destruction. The oriental mind is inscrutable to the western world, but even so one would expect the Japanese war-lords to surrender forthwith if they possess even a modicum of sense.

Moscow's declaration of war represents a masterly psychological coup. First came the atomic bomb on Hiroshima, destroying that great city and, as the Japs themselves say, killing every living thing. There followed the Soviet blockbuster in the form of war which today is tearing into both sides of Japan's Manchurian stronghold. And finally, we have today's successful atomic bomb attack against the great port of Nagasaki.

There's nothing for Japan to do but surrender—or commit national hara-kiri. Now that we have the facts before us, it is clear that these events are the result of careful and astute planning over a considerable period. The Big Three apparently put the finishing touches on it at Potsdam. No wonder President Truman was anxious to hurry back home and cancelled plans for a European visit.

Of course Japan was well on the road to defeat before the atomic bomb was brought into ac-

CONTINUED ON BACK PAGE

Iowa B-29 Veterans Complete Missions

TINIAN (AP)—Three Iowans, Superfortress veterans, have completed their tour of B-29 combat missions and are eligible for return to the United States. Formerly stationed in the India-China theater, they pioneered B-29 operations from there before being transferred to Tinian.

The Iowans are Lt. Donald W. Barton, Harlan; Lt. Charles E. Mc Dermott, Holstein, and S/Sgt. Hugh C. Polson, Council Bluffs.

Lt. McGaffin Is En Route Home

Lt. Vernon Dale McGaffin, who has been with the American air forces in Europe and most recently has been based near Paris, is enroute back to the United States according to a cablegram received by his wife, Mrs. Margaret McGaffin, who resides on North Euclid avenue, Cherokee. Lt. McGaffin, son of Mr. and Mrs. F. J. McGaffin, who saw service over Germany, is expected to arrive in Cherokee shortly. He announced that he would wire home immediately on arrival in the United States.

PROMOTION RECEIVED

Henry Merle, son of Mr. and Mrs. C. H. Merle, was promoted from seaman first class to machinest's mate third class, his parents have learned. Merle is serving in the Philippines.

Lester Zugg, 48, Found Dead This Morning In Cherokee

Coroner States Death Caused By Heart Attack

Lester Joel [illegible] was found dead at 9:00 a. m. Thursday by Mrs. Josephine Abbott in the room off from her photo studio, Archie Nelson, county attorney, stated. She immediately summoned Albert Hurd, whose office is nearby, and Dr. P. B. Cleaves. Dr. J. E. Bunker, county coroner and Sheriff Don Phipps also were notified.

Dr. Bunker issued a statement that the death was caused from a heart attack. Mrs. Abbott stated that she and Zugg had attended the Alta fair Wednesday evening and when they arrived in Cherokee he complained of feeling ill, Sheriff Phipps reported.

Zugg had operated a steak shop at Webster City and later worked at Hun's Night Club in Storm Lake. More recently he had been employed at Casey's Inn in Cherokee.

No inquest will be held, the county attorney stated. Funeral arrangements have not been made as yet. Boothby Funeral home is in charge.

Lt. Charles Coon Home For Furlough

Lt. Charles C. Coon, son of Mr. and Mrs. C. R. Coon, arrived home Thursday morning to spend a 10 day furlough with his parents before reporting to Camp Roberts, Calif.

Lt. Coon just completed his officers training course at Fort Benning, Ga., where he has been stationed for the past 4 months. He received his commission August 7. He was in service for a year.

Coon flew to Chicago and came home from there on the Hawkeye. He will report at his new camp on August 21.

MacArthur Predicts Pincer Movement

MANILA (AP)—General MacArthur said today he was "delighted at the Russian declaration of war against Japan."

"This will make possible a great pincher movement which cannot fail to end in the destruction of the enemy," he said. "In Europe, Russia was on the eastern front and the Allies on the west. Now the Allies are on the East and Russia on the west—but the result will be the same."

Hartley To Hold Achievement Day

Hartley, IA. The O'Brien county 4-H achievement day show and club congress will be held at Hartley on Monday and Tuesday, August, 20 and 21. The county girls' clubs have chosen their demonstration teams that will appear at the show.

Mighty Atom Dropped On Important Seaport

Round-The-Clock Bombings Continue Against Enemy

GUAM (AP)—The world's most destructive force—the atomic bomb—was used for the second time against Japan today, striking the important Kyushu island city of Nagasaki with observed "good results."

More than one bomb may have been dropped in this second attack and it might have been of a different size than the first one which destroyed 60 per cent of Hiroshima. The carefully worded communique said only that the second use of the atomic bomb had occurred, leaving to speculation all other details.

The bomb was dropped at noon, Japanese time—about nine hours after Tokyo radio reported Red army troops supported Russia's declaration of war on Japan by attacking enemy forces in eastern Manchukuo both by land and by air, and while four other Japanese cities still burned from round-the-clock B-29 incendiary and demolition attacks.

The Japanese had had time to study the devastation wrought at Hiroshima, where they reported "practically every living thing" was destroyed as the world's first mighty atom wrecked 60 per cent of that city of 343,000 Monday.

Nagasaki, western Kyushu seaport and railroad terminal with an estimated 255,000 population in its 12 square miles, was a far more important military target.

General Spaatz' U. S. army strategic air force headquarters said Nagasaki, with its houses jampacked probably was even more vulnerable to an atom bombing. The wordi[illegible] of [illegible] first official announcement [illegible] not preclude the possibility that more than one bomb was dropped, speaking of "the second use of the atomic bomb".

Crewmen who dropped the mighty atom on Nagasaki immediately flashed "good results" via radio to Spaatz' headquarters. The general said no further details would be available until the mis-

CONTINUED ON PAGE TWO

President Due To Settle Quarrel Between OPA - WPB

WASHINGTON (AP)—The war production board and the OPA are split wide apart on an issue embracing fundamental price and reconversion policy.

Likely to be referred to President Truman for settlement, what was once just a disagreement now has boiled to an angry quarrel over this basic point:

May WPB remove or ease controls on materials no longer scarce if OPA feels such controls must be retained to help hold down the cost of living.

While this issue arose in connection with a specific WPB proposal to ease restrictions on clothing production, OPA has taken the position that overall price and reconversion policy is involved.

OPA officials believe materials controls should be kept firmly in place in any case where living costs might rise if they were removed.

WPB, on the other hand, is committed to a policy of eliminating controls as soon as the supply of material warrants it.

This difference has the two agencies at loggerheads with representatives of each predicting the quarrel eventually will have to be resolved by Mr. Truman.

Wheat Embargo Lifted At Omaha

OMAHA (AP)—A six day embargo on the shipment of wheat into the Omaha-Council Bluffs, Ia., market was lifted at mid-night last night.

Imposed last Friday by the interstate commerce commission because of the large volume of military traffic through Omaha, the embargo enabled grain men to clear the Omaha yards of wheat cars, which last week tied up terminal and switching facilities.

Lifting of the embargo will make it unnecessary to impose a permit system which had been set for inauguration this week.

Nippon Times

No. 16,669 (THE 20th YEAR of SHOWA) TOKYO, SUNDAY, AUGUST 12, 1945 第三種郵便物認可 昭和十五年十二月二十七日 Price 35 Sen

U.S. PRESIDENT'S SPEECH BARES USE OF NEW BOMB

Truman Threatens Its Further Use If Japan Does Not Surrender

President Harry Truman in his nation wide radio broadcast on Thursday night, August 9, declared that the "Japanese have seen what our atomic bomb can do—if Japan does not surrender, bombs will have to be dropped on Japanese cities," according to a Domei report from Lisbon quoting a Washington dispatch.

In his speech lasting 30-minutes, the President disclosed that the Soviet Union agreed to enter the war in the Pacific before she had been informed of the new weapon. He added that the military arrangements made at Berlin were of course secret. "One of those secrets was revealed when the Soviet Union declared war on Japan," he said.

Wants no Territory

The President then declared that though the "United States wants no territory or profit or selfish advantage out of this war, we are going to maintain the military bases necessary for the complete protection of our interests. Bases which our military experts deem to be essential for our protection, and which are not now in our possession, we will acquire. We will acquire them by arrangements consistent with the United Nations Charter."

Declaring that there were "no secret agreements or commitments" at Berlin—apart from current military arrangements—there was one strictly military matter uppermost in the minds of the American delegates, the President declared. "It was winnnig the war against Japan. On our program, that was the most important item," he said.

"Our first non-military agreement in Berlin," Truman revealed, "was the establishment of the council of Foreign Ministers. One of the first tasks of the Council is to draft proposed treaties of peace with former en... ...tries—Italy, Rumania, Bulgaria, Hungary and Finland."

The President also revealed that the conference of Berlin laid down the specific political and economic principles under which Germany will be governed by the occupying powers. "They are intended to eliminate Nazism, armaments, war industries, the German General Staff and all its military tradition. German industry is to be decentralized in order to do away with the concentration of economic power in cartels and monopolies," he declared.

President Truman emphasized that German economic power to make war is to be eliminated. Chief emphasis is to be on agriculture and peaceful industries, he said.

Reparations in Assets

Concerning reparations, the President declared "we do not intend again to make the mistake of exacting reparations in money and then lending Germany the money with which to pay. Reparations this time are to be paid in physical assets from those resources of Germany which are not required for her peacetime subsistence."

The President explained that the the idea of atempting to fix a dollar value on the property to be removed from Germany was dropped and instead decided to divide the property by percentages. Russia and Poland are to get approximately half of the total, he said, and the remainder should be divided among all the other nations entitled to reparations.

The President disclosed that the United States proposed at Berlin that there be "free and unrestricted navigation of inland waterways" of Europe such as the Danube, the Black Sea straits, the Rhine, the Kiel Canal, and all the inland waterways of Europe which border on two or more states.

However, the proposal was not decided upon at the conference and was referred to the Council of Ministers, he said.

Stressing the point that victory can be lost after you have won it, the President explained that the people of western Europe "lack clothes and fuel and tools and shelter and raw materials. They lack the means to restore their cities and factories. As the winter comes on, the distress will increase."

The President appealed for urgent aid. "Unless we do what we can to help, we may have lost next winter, what we won at such a terrible cost last spring. Desperate men are liable to destroy the structure of their society to find in the wreckage some substitute for hope. If we let Europe go cold and hungry, we may lose some of the foundations of order on which the hope for world-wide peace must rest."

Envoy Oshima, Others Reach Pennsylvania; Given No Paper, Radio

Ambassador Hiroshi Oshima, former Japanese envoy to Germany, and the embassy staff members and others numbering 126 reached Bedford Springs, Pennsylvania, on August 8, according to an announcement of the U.S. State Department, Washington dispatch of August 9 relayed to Domei from Lisbon. The party is being detained in a large hotel with 325 rooms under special contract with the American Government but access to newspapers or the radio has been banned and the ambassador and others are doing their own cooking in the hotel.

BANK OFFICIAL SOUGHT DEATH AS MAN ON FRONT

Funeral Held for Vice Governor Of Bank of Japan Killed In Air Raid

The funeral of Tsuneji Taniguchi, Vice Governor of the Bank of Japan, who was killed in an air raid on May 25, was held at the Bank of Japan shortly after 11 a.m. on August 10.

At the funeral Viscount Keizo Shibusawa, Governor of the Bank of Japan, in an address referred to a letter left by Mr. Taniguchi which brought tears to those present. He said:

"Mr. Taniguchi was prepared to die for the country at any moment like a man at the front. Long before he was killed in the raid, he had put his personal matters in the hands of friends, so that he might meet death bravely at any moment."

Mr. Shibusawa read the letter, which was addressed to him. In part it follows:

"I thank your for your kindness to me since I was appointed Vice Governor. Please tell the officials of the Bank that I have a profound sense of gratitude for the way in which they have made themselves helpful to me during my term of office. I have a wish that you will look after my affairs when I am no more."

Viscount Shibusawa added that Mr. Taniguchi, once Finance Minister, remembered himself to his former superiors and colleagues in the Finance Ministry.

Mr. Taniguchi, Viscount Shibusawa went on, asked him to see that when he was no more he would see that the tiding would be broken to his aged mother, living at Saga, Kyoto.

Viscount Shibusawa commented to say that few were so stone-hearted as not to be moved by his affection for his mother.

The letter, dated April 28, a month before his death, Viscount Shibusawa disclosed, ended with a request that his body be exposed to the view of as few persons as possible.

Viscount Shibusawa commented that Mr. Taniguchi had a great longing to live and die in the way of the officers and men at the front.

RAILWAY MEN HONORED

Prompt Action on Burning Train Kept Damage Down to Minimum

In recognition of the unbending sense of duty and superb fighting spirit demonstrated by Arihisa Nakatogawa 35, Sukezo Iwamoto 42, Minoru Shimoda 28, and Kaneshige Suzuki 20, of Yamakita Station on the Gotemba line, in minimizing damage on a freight train when it was attacked by enemy aircraft on August 7, prizes will be awarded by the concerned Minister.

On August 7, when enemy P-51's raided the Kanto District, one of the raiders machinegunned Freight Train No 862 which was parked in the precincts of Yamakita Station. The fifth car from the front, packed with explosives, was hit by some enemy shells and the explosives began to detonate one after another. The engineer and the assistant engineer were seriously wounded.

Just then the aforementioned four employes of Yamakita Station jumped into the engine car. Mr. Nakatogawa manuevered the burning train into a nearby woods and ordered Mr. Suzuki to detach all the cars behind the first six from the others. Furthermore Mr. Nakatogawa managed to maneuver the exploding train into a forest and there, after detaching the burning car from the others, he safely brought the remaining cars to Matsuda Station. Ten minutes later, the fifth car, which was the one packed with explosives, was completely blasted.

Thanks to the quick action of the four men, only slight damage was done to a part of the railway line and no casualties were caused. Not only that, but all the cars, which were loaded to capacity, except the fifth, were saved from damage.

AUSTRALIA IS WORRIED BY RUSSIAN WAR ENTRY

Country Will Have to Adjust Policies in Light of New Development

Russia's intervention in the Pacific war poses grave questions for Australia, wrote the Yorkshire Post on Friday adding that the Soviet Union will henceforth play as commanding a role in East Asia as in Europe and that the Commonwealth will have to adjust its policy accordingly, it is disclosed in a dispatch reaching Lisbon.

Whether the Australians like it or not, it said, their destiny lies in the Pacific and their hopes for survival depend on their relations with countries differing from them in speech, religion, philosophy and aspiration.

The Sydney Daily Telegraph, meanwhile, summed up the position baldly by saying "We have to think afresh many ideas about ourselves—our remoteness from the dangerous and foolishly restless world; our security inside the empire, our racial superiority, and our God-given right to remain unchallenged beneficiaries of the continent.

"These problems are now right upon us," the paper stated, "as the Pacific war enters its last phase and one of the world's strongest power announces her interest in all the things that intimately interest us."

Economist Raps Settlement

The leading political and financial journal, Economist, on Friday condemned the general settlement agreed at Potsdam as a "Hitlerian peace" and charged that the economic control system as laid by the Potsdam declaration is "impossible," according to a London dispatch reaching Lisbon.

Observing that "Russia's determination to loot may not be unconnected with her failure to obtain reconstruction credits in the west," the Economist urged that every possible means be taken to get the Russians' changed attitude and went so far as to suggest that the western Allies should disclaim responsibility for what happens in the Russian zone.

"We can follow our own convictions in the west," the journal wrote, "where what is left of Germany can be given prospect in fullness of time of achieving liberty, equality and prosperity within western Europe that is conscious of its political and economic unity."

The journal added, "The system of economic control on a scale envisaged by the Potsdam declaration is probably impossible under any conditions. It is certainly impossible as part of the treaty which public opinion in the western world will find increasingly hard to defend.

"The joining of bad territorial and bad economic settlement," it added, "to a cumbrous system of Allied occupation seems precisely designed to create in a few years' time revulsion of feeding in the west compared with which the revulsion against Versailles will be as nothing."

FRENCH ZONE IS DECIDED

Already Established in Reinickendorf Borough in Berlin

The Allied Commander in Berlin announced on Thursday night that the French would occupy their section of Berlin at noon August 12, according to a Domei dispatch from Lisbon quoting a Berlin report.

The report said that the French occupation zone was not defined in the communique, but that the French zone will be carved from the United States and British areas. The French are reported to be already established in Reinickendorf borough.

Soviets Ask UNRRA Aid

The Soviet Government, which has been eager to get supplies from the UNRRA, made a formal request on August 10 to the association for materials amounting in value to $700,000,000, according to a Domei Lisbon dispatch based on a London report.

U.S. Casualties Mount

The United States war casualties since the outbreak of the war rose to a total of 1,067,179—922,139 suffered by the army and 145,040 by the navy, it was announced on Thursday, according to a Washington dispatch reaching Lisbon.

His Imperial Highness the Crown Prince In Best of Health, Making Good Progress

His Imperial Highness the Crown Prince will shortly be graduated from the Primary Department of the Peers' School. His Imperial Highness attained his 13th year this summer.

His Imperial Highness is enjoying the best of health and observes strict discipline. His Imperial Highness, together with his classmates, daily undergoes severe training and school lessons. His Imperial Highness enjoys trips to mountains and seas like any of his classmates.

His Imperial Highness rises at six o'clock in the morning and has never neglected his daily service, as well as physical exercise, including fencing with his tutors. From seven in the morning to four in the afternoon, His Imperial Highness undergoes school lessons, physical exercises and training just like other students. His Imperial Highness even takes part in the cleaning of the school rooms, and partakes of the simplest kind of morning meal consisting of one bowl of rice, soup and a dish of pickles. His Imperial Highness' lunch and dinner are also as simple as the ordinary people's ration meals, with dishes of fish being served only occasionally. His Imperial Highness dines in the same dining room with other pupils.

His Imperial Highness the Crown Prince has made a remarkable improvement in horse and bicycle riding in recent months, and is showing profound concern in current affairs.

Baron Hozumi's Statement

Baron Dr. Shigeto Hozumi, who was recently appointed Grand Steward to the Crown Prince Tutors' Office and concurrently Grand Chamberlain to the Crown Prince, made the following statement to the press on his appointment:

"It is with awe and trepidation that I have accepted my new post. I know very little about the affairs of the Imperial Court, but I have had the good fortune of being acquainted with the Minister as well as Vice-Minister of the Imperial Household Department from whom I shall learn about the customs and other affairs of the Imperial Court. His Imperial Highness the Crown Prince is in the best of health, has been showing great intelligence, and will shortly be graduated from the Primary Department of the Peers' School. In consultation with the other officials concerned I desire to execute my duties as far as possible in order to bring about the perfection of His Imperial Highness' education and training."

FARMERS ARE EXHORTED TO INCREASE PRODUCTION

Sengoku of Agricultural Body Stresses Their Duty to State and People

Dr. Kotaro Sengoku, President of the Wartime Farm Corporation, issued the following statement on August 10, exhorting the farmers to increase production.

"By a sudden change in the war situation, the Empire is now facing a serious crisis. I firmly believe that the Government will adopt the best policy for dealing with the crisis for the good of the State and the people. Farmers should maintain an immovable structure and devote themselves to the full prosecution of their tasks, watching calmly the development of the situation.

"Whatever the future situation may be, it is absolutely essential that farmers should endeavor to increase food production for the sake of the State and the people. Farmers are requested to exert their utmost efforts for the achievement of their important mission.

"The responsibility imposed upon agricultural organs, farmers and rural communities is increasing in importance. Prefectural agricultural associations should concentrate the total power of the farmers in the districts under their control and devise measures for taking united action whatever situation we may face in the future."

"THREAT TO PEACE"

Outlawing of New Bomb Suggested By Daily Herald

The suggestion to outlaw the use of "the new-type bomb" employed by the United States was contained in the Friday editorial of the London Daily Herald, official organ of the British Labor Party, it is disclosed in a London dispatch reaching Stockholm.

Describing the bomb as a "threat to peace" the editorial suggested a gathering of the powers to consider it. Opposing the proposal that the secret of the new weapon should remain an Anglo-American monopoly the paper charged that this would start an armament race far more sinister than any known hitherto.

"Secrecy and suspicion would cast poisonous light upon all international relationships," the paper declared. "Economic monopoly in the use of the energy of the new weapon would be just as dangerous to peace as military monopoly."

The Daily Herald, therefore, urged a drastic revision of the existing arrangements for establishing world authority and "agreement not to manufacture such weapons at all and to concentrate solely on developing the discovery for peaceful purposes."

U.S.-Canada Talks

The United States Commerce Department has announced that America is negotiating with Britain and Canada for conclusion of new trade agreements, says a Domei Lisbon dispatch of August 10 quoting a Washington report. The Commerce Department announce[illegible] that America is going [illegible] tiations for revision [illegible] agreements with Ind[illegible] and [illegible]w Zealand.

WAR MINISTER EXHORTS ARMY IN STIRRING CALL

Press Forward to Smash Enemy With Spirit of Nanko, Tokimune, Declares Message

War Minister Korechika Anami addressed himself to all officers and men of the Imperial Army on August 10, urging them to realize the spirit of Nanko and Tokimune and press on vigorously with the work of beating and crushing the enemy.

His statement to the Army follows:

"I declare to all officers and men of the army!

"The Soviet Union, directing its armed might in the wrong direction, has invaded Japan. It is quite clear that it aims at invading Greater East Asia although it endeavors to justify its action. Things having come to such a pass, I have nothing more to say in the subject. All that remains to be done by us is to carry through to its end the holy war for the protection of the Land of Gods.

"We are determined to fight resolutely although that may involve our nibbling grass, eating earth, and sleeping in the fields. It is our belief that there is life in death. This is the spirit of Great Nanko who talked of being reborn seven times in order to serve the country or the vigorous fighting spirit of Tokimune who warned against entertaining delusions and talked of pressing on vigorously with the work of crushing the ugly enemy.

"All officers and men of the entire army without exception should realize the spirit of Nanko, the vigorous fighting spirit of Tokimune, and press forward actively with the beating and crushing of the haughty enemy."

STETTINIUS GIVEN POST

Named Delegate on United Nations Body With Rank of Ambassador

President Truman on Thursday announced that former U.S. Secretary of State Edward Stettinius has been appointed as the United States representative on the Preparatory Commission of the United Nations organization with the rank of ambassador, it is disclosed in a Washington dispatch reaching Lisbon. He has already been designated as the American delegate to the World Security Council.

The Preparatory Commission, the report said, will function during the period in which the United Nations organization is being ratified. The White House added that it is unlikely that Stettinius will attend the initial routine meeting of the commission's Executice Committee which will be held on August 16 at London.

Girl Fighting Corps Set

An all-girls special fighting corps has been organized at the Kitakata Station on the Banetsu West Line. The 50 members, armed with pickaxes are just now solidifying the ground under the rail ties. They say that if the enemy should come out with tactics disrupting traffic service, they will defend the railway ne... without depending on the aid ...thers.

CRUEL HAVOC WROUGHT BY NEW-TYPE BOMB TOLD

Only 3 Buildings Left in Affected Area of Hiroshima; Rescue Work Pushed

The cruel havoc wrought by the new type bomb used by the enemy against Hiroshima is so horrible that it is utterly beyond description. All the buildings within the affected area were totally destroyed and many innocent women and children, killed, writes a Yomiuri-Hochi correspondent who visited Hiroshima following the raid. The gist of the correspondent's report is as follows:

"Upon entering the suburbs of Hiroshima city, I found that all the windows of houses had been blown out and the tiles were covered with dust. The trunks of burnt trees were scorched black.

"Only three buildings, including the Police Station remain in the city. Making the Police Station their headquarters Governor Kono and other officials of Hiroshima Prefecture are pushing rescue work. It is very touching to see them working hard without sleep in spite of the fact that they have lost their families. I was also impressed by the complete composure of those citizens who were assisting in the rescue work."

An eye witness story of the explosion of the new bomb, as told by an old woman, Ai Kono, 61, who resides in the city, was reported by the same reporter as follows:

"I looked skyward as I heard the droning of an airplane and saw a black spot floating. At this instant, the spot shed blue and red lights like lightning. No sooner I had become dizzy, than a scorching heat struck my body."

Dangers to Humanity

With the revelation of the gross fiendishness of the enemy's new type bomb, Europe has been swept by a wave of terror. The enemy, after prolonged experiments on the new bomb finally put it to use with full knowledge of its huge destructive power. According to a London dispatch of the Exchange News Agency of July 20, the following statement was made in the House of Lords when the subject of long-distance weapons came up for discussion.

"The German V-1 bomb had a speed of 560 kilometers, but its explosive content never exceeded one ton. In contrast to this, British scientists have succeeded in inventing an explosive with considerable destructive power, but of comparatively little weight, making possible the wholesale destruction of large cities by long-distance weapons.

"There is only one measure to be taken against the dangers consequent to the use of such weapons, and that is to organize an international body which will have full control over the use of such arms. In the absence of any international regulation, England, in cooperation with the United States, must solve the problem of the long-distance weapon and maintain its authoritative position in this field. The leading authority on long-distance weapons, Lord Dunley himself is reported to have said that warfare conducted with such a weapon not only destroys humanity but leads to the destruction of the whole world.

"However, future wars will be conducted along vastly different lines. British scientists are fully confident that the long-distance weapon will in a few years' time be so perfected that its accuracy can be guaranteed. The prophecy that a time will come when far distant cities may be destroyed by long distance weapons is therefore not wholly erroneous. Through this new tendency in coming wars, Britain has lost its geographical advantage, endangering her position. It cannot be said that the British fleet at the present time can fully ward off this danger, and unless some international organ which will actually give protection is set up, Britain must not spare any efforts in this direction."

The long distance weapon hinted at by Lord Dunley is the inhuman atomic bomb.

Red Cross Delegate Here

Dr. Marcel Junot, Chief Delegate in Japan of the International Red Cross Committee, accompanied by Mrs. Margrit Strar, Technical Adviser, arrived at his post on August 9. Dr. Junot is a surgeon from Geneva. He was active during the Ethiopian war and the Spanish civil war. When the present war broke out Dr. Junot represented the International Red Cross in Germany, Britain, France, Denmark Greek, Italy and Poland.

Regular Cabinet Meet Is Convened on Friday; All Ministers Attend

The regular Cabinet meeting was held at the Prime Minister's official residence at 2 p.m. on Friday and was attended by all Cabinet members from Prime Minister Admiral Baron Kantaro Suzuki downward. Agriculture and Forestry Minister Tadaatsu Ishiguro submitted a report on the supply of fresh vegetables. Then, Hisatsune Sakomizu, Chief Secretary, made a report on the National Volunteer Corps. The meeting adjourned at 4:30 p.m.

CARRIER PLANES CONTINUE RAIDS ON KANTO SECTOR

1,000 Aircraft From Task Force Off Tohoku Area Took Part In Friday's Raid

Following the morning raid by 180 deck planes on Kanto on Friday, about 35 more planes from an enemy task force appeared over Chiba from Katsuura around 1 p.m. the same afternoon. For one hour and a half they raided airfields and military facilities.

40 other carrier planes in the Tohoku Army District operated for half an hour from noon in north Niigata and strafed army establishments, factories and shipping.

One B-29, coming in from Cape Omae at about 11:35 a.m. reconnoitered over Mount Fuji and Otsuki.

The Tohoku Army District Headquarters issued the following communique at 3 p.m. on August 10:

The enemy task force which approached the Tohoku District on Thursday mainly attacked the Pacific coast area and Yamagata Prefecture in several waves from 1 p.m. on Friday with an aggregate total of some 1,000 carrier aircraft. The enemy raiders mainly attacked air fields, munitions factories and land and sea communication routes. Damage on our side was slight.

Up to 1 p.m. Friday, the war results obtained on August 9 and 10 include 11 planes downed and for others damaged the following day.

Shortly after midnight on Friday Japanese Air Units spotted an enemy task force whose main strength was composed of four aircraft carriers at about 140 or 150 nautical miles east of Kinkazan. Special attack units immediately opened an attack on the task force, damaging and setting ablaze one large warcraft while reports are to hand that several planes made ramming attacks, inflicting a considerable blow on the enemy.

However the task force thereafter withdrew for a time but again made an appearance in the waters near the mainland. The strength of this task force is believed to be generally the same as the one which was active on July 10.

At about 9 p.m. Thursday the first wave of about 50 Soviet planes attacked a fleet of Japanese vessels off Yuki Bay east of North Chosen. The second wave of approximately 30 craft began its attack about 10 p.m. but Japanese convoys with A. A. guns downed 14 of the raiding planes. No losses were suffered by the Japanese.

Some 210 enemy planes made up of 45 B-24's, 40 B-25's and other small planes from the Okinawa base invaded the Kyushu region on Friday morning and operated all over Kyushu. The enemy planes subjected Kumatoro and Oita to an incendiary attack. The enemy planes also strafed facilities in the airfields and ships at sea and fled at about 2 p.m.

The Japanese AA Units shot down three B-25's, three small type planes and damaged four B-25's.

NAGASAKI HIT BY NEW BOMB

Damage Comparatively Slight, Western Army Announces

The Western Army District Headquarters issued the following communique at 2.45 p.m. on August 9:

"1. Two large-sized enemy planes penetrated the city of Nagasaki at about 11 a.m. on August 9 and dropped what looks like a new type bomb on the city.

"2. The damage caused by the bomb is now being investigated but the damage is comparatively slight."

U.S. Cabinet Meeting

The U.S. Cabinet will convene in an emergency meeting on the night of August 10, according to a Washington dispatch reaching Domei through Lisbon the same day.

VARIOUS INVASION MOVES MADE BY SOVIET TROOPS

Activities Seen on Borders of Manchoukuo, Outer Mongolia, Chosen, Karafuto

The Soviet forces have been reinforced in the eastern and western sectors of the Manchoukuo-Soviet border. On the afternoon of August 9 they crossed the border near Chiko, about 100 kilometers southeast of Heiho, on the northern border. In the Outer Mongolian sector they crossed the border at Solun and in North Chosen they crossed the Tumen River, invading Chosen from the area near Keiko. On August 9, bombing attacks were made by Soviet planes on Hsinking, Ssupingkai and North Chosen.

Invade Karafuto

Crossing the border from about 2 p.m. on Thursday, a small number of Soviet soldiers invaded number of Soviet soldiers invaded the vicinity of Buika in Karafuto, at the same time firing a few shots on the southwestern side of Buika and the western area of [illegible]. It was announced at 7 p.m. [illegible] day by the North Army [illegible] Headquarters.

Kwantung Under Martial [illegible]

The Ryojun-Dairen Defense Headquarters proclaimed martial law for Kwantung Province at 2 p.m. on Friday in view of the war situation, according to a Domei dispatch from Dairen.

Soviet Force Weak

The Chosen Army District Headquarters issued the following communique at 6 p.m. on August 10:

"The Soviet force which crossed the northern frontier of Chosen is very weak. The number of Soviet planes is very small and their activities are restricted to north of Seishin.

"In self-defense, the Japanese Army has intercepted the Soviet force both in the [illegible] and [illegible]

ENEMY ATTACKS REPULSED

[illegible]anese Continue to Check Invaders on Balik Papan

Domei

SOUTHERN BASE, August 10.—In the Balik Papan area the war situation on the two days of August 6 and 7 stood as follows:

Under cover of trench mortars, a small number of enemy soldiers in the Samarinda sector made several attacks but were repulsed. The enemy first line at present extends from Samarinda to a point 18 kilometers from this place.

The enemy again attempted an attack at about 11:30 a.m. on August 7 to be driven back toward evening by the Japanese Forces. In the Sangasanga Oilfield area, one small enemy unit with trench mortars and protected by B-25's failed in their attempt to pierce the Japanese positions.

Shock attack units were also active during this time, causing turmoil among the enemy troops. On these two days about 150 enemy soldiers were killed or wounded while a fire which broke out in the Second Airfield was still raging.

VETERAN JOURNALIST DIES

Shimpei Toko Killed in Plane Accident; Was Java Shimbun Head

Shimpei Toko, President of the Java Shimbun and concurrently President of the Press Association in Java, who was in the service of the Army, died at his post on July 13 in an airplane accident, it is reported by a Domei dispatch from Djakarta. He was 64 years of age. His remains were cremated on the spot and the ashes brought back to Djakarta on July 13. On July 27, funeral services were solemnized at the city's Special Funeral Hall.

The late Mr. Toko hailed from Kumamoto Prefecture. Graduating from Tokyo Higher Normal School in 1919, he became a staff member of the Osaka Asahi Shimbun in the following year. Later in 1925, he was promoted to the post of Assistant Managing Editor of the same newspaper company and three years later he became Managing Editor. In 1942, he was dispatched to Java to head the Java Shimbun and concurrently assumed the post of the President of the Java Press Association.

Succeeding the late Mr. Toko, Toyohiko Masuda, Assistant Managing Editor of the Java Shimbun, has assumed the post of the President of the same newspaper and concurrently the post of President of the Java Press Association.

EXTRA! Victory EXTRA!

IT DID HAPPEN!

Seattle, Wash.—(U.P.)—Thieves aren't satisfied with stealing just automobiles these days. A suburban bus disappeared from its parking stall one morning. Police later found it abandoned outside the city limits.

Waterloo Daily Courier

FIRST WITH THE NEWS

Fair and cooler.

Complete weather forecast, page 2.

ESTABLISHED 1854

WATERLOO, IOWA, TUESDAY, AUGUST 14, 1945

PEACE!

WAR ENDS; JAPANESE ACCEPT ALLIED TERMS ON EMPEROR

You Can't Read This, But It's the Way the Japanese Said—

"Unconditional Surrender"

無條件降服

Waterloo Starts Celebration as Word of Nip Decision Is Flashed to Battle-Weary World

SURRENDER ANNOUNCED AT 6 P. M. AUG. 14, 1945

Other important dates in World War II:

Sept. 1, 1939—Germany invades Poland.
May 10, 1940—Hitler invades Low Countries, France.
June 20, 1940—France signs armistice.
June 22, 1941—Germany invades Russia.
Dec. 7, 1941—Japs attack Pearl Harbor.
June 5, 1942—Jap fleet smashed at Midway.
Nov. 8, 1942—Landing in north Africa.
July 9, 1943—Allies invade Sicily.
Sept. 3, 1943—Italian surrender signed, Italy invaded.
June 6, 1944—Invasion at Normandy.
Oct. 20, 1944—U. S. returns to Philippines.
May 8, 1945—Germany surrenders.

Truman Flashes Victory Smile

President Harry S. Truman demonstrates his victory smile for the photographer. Millions of Americans and Allied peoples all over the world showed similar joy when the news of Japanese capitulation was flashed around the globe. After nearly six years of the most gigantic war in history, the avenging armies of the Allies had defeated the last of the Axis powers. Pearl Harbor, at long last, had been remembered. Now, in every land and every home, one word expressed the thoughts of all: PEACE!

ANNOUNCEMENT MADE BY PRESIDENT TRUMAN TO CHEERING NEWSMEN

Washington, D. C.--(UP) -- President Truman announced tonight that the Japanese government has accepted the surrender terms without qualification.

He made the announcement at a press conference.

He read a statement which said:

"I deem this reply a full acceptance of the Potsdam declaration which specified the unconditional surrender of Japan. In the reply there is no qualification."

The president also revealed that he had named Gen. Douglas MacArthur the supreme commander to receive the Japanese surrender.

TRUMAN

Allied Terms To Japan

WASHINGTON, Aug. 15 — These were the terms Japan was asked to accept :—

1) The Japanese Emperor and Government are to subject their authority to that of the Allied Supreme Commander. (Gen. Douglas MacArthur has been unofficially tipped for the post).

2) The Japanese Emperor is to order the surrender of Japanese troops in all theatres.

3) The Japanese Government is to transport prisoners and civilian internees to places of safety immediately.

4) The Japanese people are to be free to decide their ultimate form of Government.

5) Allied troops are to remain in Japan for a specified period.

(Continued on page 2)

WEDEMEYER

Extra THE CHINA LANTERN Extra

VOL. 4, NO. 12, AUGUST 15, 1945 PRECENSORED FOR MAILING FOR U.S. ARMED FORCES

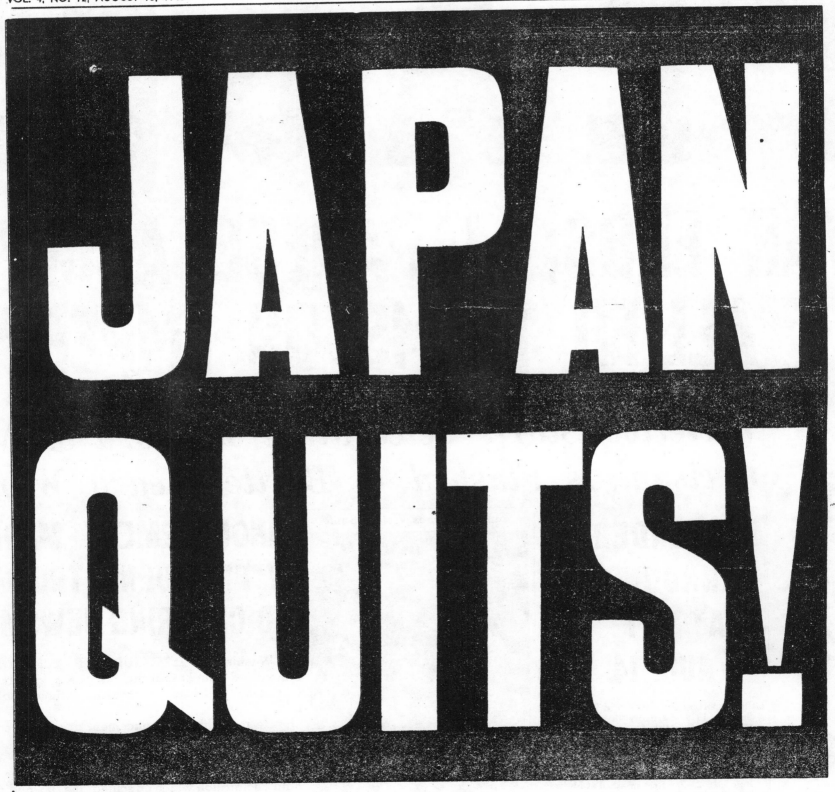

JAPAN QUITS!

WASHINGTON, Aug. 15 (ANS) — Japan has officially accepted the Allied terms for unconditional surrender without qualification, Pres. Truman announced last night.

Terms of the treaty provide that the authority of the Emperor shall be subject to the Supreme Commander of the Allied Powers, with the Emperor issuing such orders as the Supreme Commander requires.

TODAY IS THURSDAY 16 AUGUST

DAILY PACIFICAN

The Army Newspaper in the Western Pacific

MORNING EDITION

Vol. I No 64

Thursday, 16 August 1945

MacARTHUR COMMANDS JAPAN SEND EMISSARIES TO MANILA FOR ALLIED SURRENDER TERMS

By Staff Correspondent

MANILA—In a radio message addressed to Japan last night General of the Army MacArthur commanded the Japanese Government to send "competent representatives" to Manila with power to receive the terms of surrender in the name of the Emperor and the Imperial General Headquarters.

The Allied Supreme Commander for the Allied Powers ordered the Japanese to send an accredited envoy accompanied by "competent representatives" of the Japanese army, navy and air forces. The air forces advisor must be familiar with airdromes in the Tokyo area.

General MacArthur's message said: "The envoy will report to the Supreme Commander for the Allied Powers upon arrival a document authenticated by the emperor of Japan empowering him to receive the requirements of the Supreme Commander of the Allied Powers."

The Japanese were instructed to send the emissary to Manila in an unarmed plane of the Zero type model 22 L2 D3.

MacArthur ordered the Japanese to travel to an airdrome on the island of Ie Shima from which point they will be transported to Manila in a U. S. aircraft. The emissary will be returned to Japan in the same manner.

The Japanese plane will be painted white and will bear green crosses on the sides of the fuselage and the top and bottom of each wing easily recognizable at 500 yards. The plane will be capable of inflight voice communications in English of 6970 kilocycles.

Weather permitting the surrender party will leave from Sata Misaki on the southern tip of Kyushu between 8 a.m. and 11 a.m. Friday and fly to the U. S. airdrome on Ie Shima off Okinawa.

The Japanese were told the route and altitude of the flight and the estimated time of arrival at Ie Shima should be broadcast six hours in advance in English on a frequency of 16125 kilocycles. General MacArthur said acknowledgement by radio from Manila of receipt of such broadcasts is required prior to the take-off of the plane.

The code designation "Bataan" will be employed in communications regarding the flight.

MacArthur commanded the Japanese plane to approach Ie Shima on a course of 180 degrees and circle the landing field at 1,000 feet or below the cloud layer until joined by an escort of U. S. P-38s which will lead it to a landing. The escort may join the airplane prior to arrival at Ie Shima, the Supreme Commander declared.

MacArthur's Message to Tokyo

Following message was sent in the clear yesterday by General of the Army Douglas MacArthur as Supreme Commander for the Allied Powers to the Japanese Emperor, the Japanese Imperial Government and the Japanese Imperial General Headquarters.

"I have been designated as the Supreme Commander for the Allied Powers—United States, Republic of China, United Kingdom and USSR—and have been empowered to arrange directly with the Japanese authorities for the cessation of hostilities at the earliest practicable date.

"It is desired that a radio station in the Tokyo area be officially designated for use in handling communications between this headquarters and your headquarters. Your reply to this message should give call signs, frequencies and station designated.

"It is desired that the radio communications with my headquarters in Manila be handled in English text.

"Pending designation by you of a station in the Tokyo area for use above indicated, station JNR on frequency 16125 kilocycles will be used for the purpose.

Upon receipt of this message, acknowledge."

Japanese Face Defeat With Sobs

LONDON, (UP) — The anguish with which the Japanese people received the fact of their defeat was revealed in a Domei account intercepted by the BBC monitors in London.

Domei was quoted as saying: "How shall 100 million people, filled with trepidation reply to the emperor? His Majesty's subjects are moved to tears by His Majesty's boundless and infinite solicitude, for on Aug. 14th, 1945, the Imperial decision was granted.

"The Palace Grounds are quiet beneath dark clouds. Honored with the Imperial edict in the sublime palace grounds, a crowd of loyal people are bowed to the very ground in front of 'Nijubashi,' as their tears flow unchecked.

"How can the people raise their heads? With cries of 'Forgive us, oh Emperor, our efforts were not enough,' their heads bow lower and lower as their tears flow unchecked..."

Jurors Sentence Petain to Death In Treason Trial

PARIS, (UP) — Henri Philippe Petain, 89-year-old Marshal of France and head of the vanished Vichy regime, was sentenced to death shortly after the conclusion of his treason trial at the high court of justice yesterday.

The verdict was given by a jury composed of members of the resistance movement and members of the Chamber of Deputies who did not collaborate with the Germans during the occupation.

Petain is the twelfth marshal of France to be sentenced to death in French history since 1440. The eleventh was Marshal Achille Bazaine, whose sentence, in 1873, was later commuted to life imprisonment.

Thousands of Japanese Lose Lives Because of Delay in the Surrender

(*by Associated Press*)

Thousands of Japanese paid with their lives for the delay in acceptance of the Potsdam surrender terms.

Guam reported more than 1,000 planes of the U. S. Army Strategic Air Forces, including 800 Superfortresses, smashed at Japan with approximately 6,000 tons of demolition and incendiary bombs during the 24 hours preceding the transmission of Japan's capitulation.

Flying in probably record numbers the B-29s dropped their farewell loads on Japan, including the Hikari naval arsenal and Osaka army arsenal Tuesday and early Wednesday. Nearly 200 fighters from Iwo Jima escorted the big bombers.

Soviet troops in Manchuria had taken 5,000 Japanese prisoners in the first four days of the battle.

Nippon Times

No. 16,673 (THE 20th YEAR of SHOWA) TOKYO, THURSDAY, AUGUST 16, 1945 第三種郵便物認可 昭和十五年十二月二十七日 Price 35 Sen

TRUMAN ISSUES DETAILS REGARDING ATOMIC BOMB

Revealed 16 Hours After Attack On Hiroshima—Attlee Tells Britain's Role

Sixteen hours after the first atomic bomb was dropped on the populous city of Hiroshima, President Truman revealed for the first time the existence of the atomic bomb and declared that the new weapon was more powerful, than 20,000 tons of TNT. The President revealed that the research work had been carried out through Anglo-American cooperation first in Britain then later in the United States and that the whole process was veiled in strict secrecy.

The President also revealed that the new atomic bomb carried more than "2,000,000 times the blast power of the British 'Grand Slam' which is the largest bomb ever yet used in the history of warfare."

Declaring that it had been the accepted belief of scientists that it was theoretically possible to release atomic energy but that no one knew any practical method of doing it, Truman declared that by 1942 he had known that the Germans were working feverishly to find a way to add atomic energy to the other engines of war, but they failed.

Carried Out in U.S.

The President declared that since America held a large number of scientists of distinction and tremendous industrial and financial resources necessary for the project, and since laboratory work and production plants would be out of reach of enemy bombing contrary to Britain who was exposed to constant air attack and was still threatened with the possibility of invasion, Churchill and President Roosevelt agreed that it was more advisable to carry on the project in the United States.

"We now have two great plants and many lesser works diverted to the production of atomic power," Truman revealed. "Employment during the peak of construction numbered 125 000 men and over 85,000 individuals are even now engaged in operating the plants."

Referring to the secrecy adopted during the project, the President disclosed that few workers have worked for two and a half years, but few knew what they have been producing. "They see great quantities of material going in and they see nothing coming out of these plants for the physical size of the explosive charge is exceedingly small."

The President declared that $2,000,000,000 had been spent on the "greatest scientific gamble in history."

Britain's Role Revealed

Prime Minister Attlee in a statement from 10 Downing Street on the night of August 6 said "The problem of release of energy by atomic fission have been solved and an atomic bomb has been dropped on Japan by the United States Army Air force.

Declaring that President Truman and War Secretary Stimson had described the nature and vast implications of this new discovery, Attlee gave the account of the part Britain played.

By the year 1939, he stated, it had become widely recognized among the scientists of many nations that the release of energy by atomic fission was a possibility, but that the problems which remained to be solved before that possibility could be turned into practical achievement were manifold and immense. Nevertheless, potentialities of the project were so great that Britain thought it right that research should be carried out.

By the summer of 1941, Attlee declared. it was reported that there was a reasonable chance that the atomic bomb could be produced before the end of the war and at the end of August, 1941, Lord Cherwell had reported substantial progress. General responsibility for the scientific research carried on under various technical committees lay with the then Lord President of the Council, Sir John Anderson.

Project Is Coordinated

On October 11, 1941, President Roosevelt suggested that any extended efforts be coordinated and accordingly all British and American efforts were joined and a number of British scientists concerned proceeded to the United States.

Attlee declared that complete secrecy guarded all these activities, but it was decided that Great Britain was within easy range of the German bombers and the risk of raiders from the sea or air could not be ignored. The United States had been free from these dangers and the decision was taken to build full-scale production plants in America.

The main practical effort and virtually the whole of its prodigious cost now fell upon the United States authorities who were assisted by a number of British scientists.

Attlee disclosed that every effort was made by the British intelligence service and by the air force to locate in Germany anything resembling the project bring created in the United States.

In conclusion Prime Minister Attlee declared. "We must indeed pray that these awful agencies will be made to conduce to peace among nations and that instead of wreaking measureless havoc upon the entire globe they may become a perennial fountain of world prosperity."

Gen. Anami Kills Self To Atone for Failure, War Ministry Bares

War Minister General Korechika Anami killed himself at his official residence Tuesday evening to express his sincere regret to His Majesty the Emperor for not having been able to fulfil his duty in assisting His Imperial Majesty, it was anounced by the War Ministry on Wednesday.

POLITICAL BODY STRESSES NATION'S RECONSTRUCTION

Exhorts People to Face Coming Trials With New Hope And Courage

In a public statement, the Dai Nippon Seijikai urged the people to bear the great trials lying ahead and strive for the peaceful reconstruction of the Empire. The statement follows:

"Receiving the Imperial Rescript, we are overwhelmed with great sorrow, and we do not know what to do. The brave and patriotic war efforts made by our officers and men that had even made the Gods weep, and also the efforts of the people behind the guns have not been effective.

"The responsibility of the people of the Empire to the Imperial Family and to the Imperial Forefathers surely deserves thousands of deaths. But the Imperial Rescript has already been issued, and the course of the Empire is fixed. For the people there is no way but to stop fighting under the Imperial Decision, and devote themselves solely to the task of postwar reconstruction. There is no need to say that the future road of the Empire will be thorny, but the prosperity of the Imperial Family and the life of the Japanese race are both eternal.

"The people should renew their spirit, reveal in culture and industry the strength they had shown in the war, and thus contribute to world progress with the morality and culture of the Empire. Though the situation has come to such a pass, to end the war with this reserve strength still left must be regarded as the gift of numerous brave officers and men who offered their lives to the Throne and Empire under the August virtue of His Majesty the Emperor.

"We pledge ourselves that together with the people, we will bear the great trial that the Gods have imposed on us, and proceed bravely for the peaceful reconstruction of the Empire with new hope and courage."

JAPANESE IN MOSCOW SAFE

Embassy Staff Members Staying at Envoy Sato's Residence

Staff members of the Japanese Embassy in Moscow and newspaper correspondents are staying temporarily at the official residence of Naotake Sato, Japanese Ambassador to the Soviet Union, and the Embassy building, it is reported by a Domei dispatch from Stockholm dated August 13, quoting a Moscow report.

However, freedom of action is allowed to all of them, and they are free to purchase foodstuffs as formerly. The use of telephones is also allowed, but radio sets and arms have been confiscated.

DeGaulle to Visit U.S.

President Truman announced on August 13 that French President General Charles de Gaulle is scheduled to arrive at Washington on August 22, according to a Lisbon dispatch to Domei quoting a Washington report.

Truman, Wei Confer

President Truman conferred with Chungking Ambassador to Washington Wei Tao-ming on August 13, it is reported from Lisbon to Domei, quoting a Washington dispatch.

NOTES SENT BY JAPAN, ALLIES' REPLY REVEALED

Final Japanese Communication Accepting Potsdam Declaration Dispatched August 14

The Japanese Government on August 10 informed the United States, Britain, Soviet Union and China that it was prepared to accept the Potsdam Declaration under the understanding that the declaration "does not comprise any demand which prejudices the prerogatives of His Majesty as a sovereign ruler."

The answer by the four nations was received on August 13 whereupon the Japanese Government studied the answer with extreme care. The Imperial Decision was sought and on August 14 a note was sent that it would be completely accepted.

The texts of the notes exchanged between the Japanese Government and the United States, Britain, Soviet Union and China follow:

Note of the Japanese Government regarding their acceptance of the provisions of the Potsdam declaration.

In obedience to the gracious command of His Majesty the Emperor who, ever anxious to enhance the cause of world peace, desires earnestly to bring about an early termination of hostilities with a view to saving mankind from the calamities to be imposed upon them by further continuation of the war, the Japanese Government asked several weeks ago the Soviet Government with which neutral relations then prevailed, to render good offices in restoring peace vis-a-vis the enemy Powers. Unfortunately, these efforts in the interest of peace having failed, the Japapnese Government, in conformity with the August Wish of His Majesty to restore the general peace and desiring to put an end to the untold sufferings entailed by war as quickly as possible, have decided upon the following:

The Japanese Government are ready to accept the terms enumerated in the Joint Declaration which was issued at Potsdam on July 26, 1945 by the heads of the Governments of the United States, Great Britain and China, and later subscribed to by the Soviet Government, with the understanding that the said declaration does not comprise any demand which prejudices the prerogatives of His Majesty as a sovereign ruler.

The Japanese Government hope sincerely that this understanding is warranted and desire keenly that an explicit indication to that effect will be speedily forthcoming.

August 10th, the 20th year of Showa.

Answer of the United States Government to the Japanese Government on behalf of the Governments of the United States, the United Kingdom, the Union of Soviet Socialist Republics and China dated August 11, 1945.

With regard to the Japanese Government's message accepting the terms of the Potsdam Proclamation but containing the statement with the understanding that said declaration does not comprise any demand which prejudices the prerogatives of His Majesty as a sovereign ruler, our position is as follows:

From the moment of surrender, the authority of the Emperor and the Japanese Government to rule the state shall be subject to the Supreme Commander of the Allied Powers, who will take such steps as he deems proper to effectuate the surrender terms.

The Emperor will be required to authorize and ensure the signature by the Government of Japan and the Japanese Imperial General Headquarters of the surrender terms necessary to carry out the provisions of the Potsdam Declaration and shall issue his commands to all the Japanese military, naval and air authorities and to all the forces under their control wherever located to cease active operations, and to surrender their arms and to issue such other orders as the Supreme Commander may require to give effect to the surrender terms.

Immediately upon the surrender, the Japanese Government shall transport prisoners of war and civilian internees to places of safety as directed where they can quickly be placed aboard Allied transports.

The ultimate form of government of Japan shall, in accordance with the Potsdam Declaration, be established by the freely expressed will of the Japanese people.

The armed forces of the Allied Powers will remain in Japan until the purposes set forth in the Potsdam Declaration are achieved.

Communication of the Japanese Government of August 14, 1945 addressed to the Governments of the United States, Great Britain, the Soviet Union and China.

With reference to the Japanese Government's Note of August 10 regarding their acceptance of the provisions of the Potsdam Declaration and the reply of the Governments of the United States, Great Britain the Soviet Union and China sent by American Secretary of State Byrnes under the date of August 11, the Japanese Government have the honor to communicate to the Governments of the four Powers as follows:

1. His Majesty the Emperor has issued an Imperial Rescript regarding Japan's acceptance of the provisions of the Potsdam Declaration.

2. His Majesty the Emperor is prepared to authorize and ensure the signature by His Government and the Imperial General Headquarters of the necessary terms for carrying out the provisions of the Potsdam Declaration. His Majesty is also prepared to issue his commands to all the military, naval, and air authorities of Japan and all the forces under their control wherever located to cease active operations, to surrender arms, and to issue such other orders as may be required by the Supreme Commander of the Allied forces for the execution of the above-mentioned terms.

Benevolent Words of Imperial Solicitude Bring Tears to Leaders at Epochal Meet

With the appearance of the cruel new weapon, the atomic bomb, the united efforts of the Japanese people for the prosecution of the war have been nullified. The powerful destructive power of the atomic bombs which were dropped on the city of Hiroshima on August 6 and on Nagasaki city on August 9, brought about a basic change in the process of the war. All the officers and men at the front and the people on the home front who are imbued with the fierce fighting spirit of the Special Attack Units had to change their ways of fighting, as a result of the use of this super-explosive. All the Japanese cities faced a grave situation of being reduced to ashes and many more harmless Japanese people exposed to the menace of being wantonly killed by the new bombs. It was at this critical moment that His Majesty the Emperor was benevolent enough to have caused His Government to adopt necessary measures to stop the war.

Since August 9, a series of meetings by the Supreme War Conference and extraordinary Cabinet sessions had been held daily for the purpose of devising necessary measures to protect the fundamental political set-up of Japan and to preserve the integrity and honor of the Japanese nation. The wholehearted efforts of Prime Minister Admiral Baron Kantaro Suzuki and all Cabinet members under him as well as other high Government and military officers had been concentrated on the measures.

A very important and historic conference was held in the Imperial Palace at 11 a.m. on August 14 in the August presence of His Majesty the Emperor. All the Cabinet Ministers and other key persons were present. Attended by His Chief Aide-de-Camp, General Shigeru Hasunuma, His Imperial Majesty made His appearance. In addition to the Cabinet Ministers, four other high Cabinet officials, namely, the Chief Secretary of the Cabinet, the Director-General of the Legislative Bureau, the President of the Board of Information, and the Director-General of the Coordinated Planning Board, were also there. Lieutenant-General Masao Yoshizumi, Director of the Military Affairs Bureau of the War Ministry and Vice Admiral Zenshiro Hoshina, Director of the Naval Affairs Bureau of the Navy Ministry, also were present as Government officials.

The Privy Council was represented by Baron Kiichiro Hiranuma, President of the Council.

The Military Command was represented by General Yoshijiro Umezu, Chief of the Army General Staff, and Admiral Soemu Toyoda, Chief of the Naval General Staff.

When all these officers took their seats, the Conference began. Opinions were expressed by them as to the decision of the final attitude of Japan concerning the reply sent by the Allied Nations. It is with awe and trepidation to say that His Imperial Majesty calmly listened to the opinions expressed by His officers out of their truest sincerity of loyalty and mind to save the Empire.

It is reported that His Imperial Majesty was gracious enough to say the following at the Conference:

"As a result of carefully pondering over the general trends of the world as well as Japan's situation, We should like to carry on the policy as has been already fixed, by enduring the unendurable and suffering what is insufferable to atone Ourselves before the hallowed spirits of Our Imperial Ancestors and to save the millions of Our subjects. You may have opinions of your own, but the answer of the Allied Nations, We believe, recognizes the sovereignty of the Emperor and you all should understand this as We believe. Whatever may happen to Us, We cannot stand to see the nation suffer from further hardships."

All those in attendance, upon hearing these benevolent Imperial Words, burst into tears in spite of the August presence. This historic Conference came to an end at noon. Prime Minister Suzuki and all other Cabinet Ministers retired to the Prime Minister's official residence, where they further met together three times, and went through the necessary procedures for making known to the entire nation the policy adopted by the Government.

KILLED IN HIROSHIMA RAID

4 Prominent Government Officials Die in August 6 Bombing

Isei Otsuka. Governor-General of the Chugoku Regional Administrative District, was killed on August 6 in the enemy atomic bomb raid on Hiroshima. He was 61 years of age.

Mr. Otsuka hailed from Kumamoto Prefecture, and upon graduating from the Political Science Department of Tokyo Imperial University in 1909, became chief secretary of the Metropolitan Police Board. During his career he was chief of the prefectural police in Tokushima, Miyagi and Kanagawa Prefectures and later secretary of the Home Ministry.

In the same air raid, Kunio Kawamoto, chief secretary of the Chugoku Government-General, Mayor Senkichi Awaya of Hiroshima and Tadashi Yoshida, Director of the Communications Bureau in Hiroshima were also killed, it was announced on August 12 by the prefectural authorities. Takero Akiyoshi, Chief of the Internal Affairs Section of the Hiroshima Prefectural Government is still missing, it is further reveale

REALIZE AUGUST WISHES, HOME MINISTER URGES

Issues Statement on Imperial Rescript; Asks for Peace, Order, Unity

Urging the whole people to live up to the August Wishes of His Majesty the Emperor, by maintaining peace, order, and unity, and by devoting themselves to the reconstruction of national power, Home Minister Motoki Abe issued the following statement in connection with the proclamation of the Imperial Rescript:

"The Imperial Rescript was proclaimed today. I have no words with which to beg forgiveness of His Majesty the Emperor, and I am sorry for the whole people who have so far exerted their strenuous efforts.

"The Gracious Wishes of His Imperial Majesty to safeguard and maintain the structure of the Imperial State and the deep benevolence shown for His subjects fill us with trepidation. We must devote ourselves by offering both our spirit and body to the quick reconstruction of national power, by maintaining order and unity, thereby living up to the August Wishes of His Majesty the Emperor. Should the unity of the people be relaxed and peace and order disturbed at this moment, a serious and irrecoverable situation would be brought about.

"We may face in the future hardships and difficulties which we cannot foresee at present. I earnestly hope that the people, by keeping on intimate terms with one another, by observing morality, by enduring privation and hardships, by helping one another, and by maintaining unity with the Government, will be enabled to pass through the present difficulties.

"I firmly believe in the loyalty and strength of the Yamato race—qualities which have been cultivated during the last 3,000 years. Whatever difficulties we may encounter, we, the entire nation as one body, determine to march courageously toward the construction of our future by promoting the strength of our race, thereby safeguarding and maintaining the eternal prosperity of the Imperial Throne."

Saga Police Chief Killed

Sadakuni Okuma, Chief of the Saga Prefectural Police Department, was killed during the enemy air raid on Saga City on August 12, while he was engaged in traffic control.

CONFERENCES LEADING TO PEACE DESCRIBED

Various Meetings Held Here From August 9 to 14 When Decision Was Made

The following describes what took place at the Supreme War Conferences, Extraordinary Cabinet Meetings and other important conferences during the period from August 9 to 14, resulting finally in the establishment of world peace:

August 9:

In the face of a new situation arising out of the employment by the American air force of the atomic bombs against Japan and the Soviet Union's participation in the war against Japan, a Supreme War Conference was held in the Imperial Palace from 10:30 a.m. till 1:30 p.m. The conference was resumed at 2:30 p.m. and lasted till 5:30 p.m. This was followed by an Extraordinary Cabinet Meeting which was convoked at the official residence of the Prime Minister at 6:30 and lasted till 10:10 p.m. At the meeting Prime Minister Admiral Baron Kantaro Suzuki listened to the views of the Cabinet Ministers.

As a result of these meetings, a Conference in the Imperial Presence was held in the Imperial Palace at 11:55 p.m. lasting till 3 a.m. on the following day. This conference was attended by Baron Kiichiro Hiranuma, President of the Privy Council, General Yoshijiro Umezu, Chief of the Army General Staff, Admiral Soemu Toyoda, Chief of the Navy General Staff, Prime Minister Admiral Baron Kantaro Suzuki, War Minister General Korechika, Anami, Navy Minister Admiral Mitsumasa Yonai and Foreign Minister Shigenori Togo.

At this council the decision was reached to accept the Potsdam Declaration.

Another Extraordinary Cabinet Meeting was opened at the official residence of the Prime Minister at 3:10 a.m. until 4 a.m.

August 10:

A conference of senior statesmen was opened at the official residence of the Prime Minister at 1 p.m. till 2:50 p.m. An extraordinary Cabinet meeting was held at 2 p.m. till 4.30 p.m. in which the Cabinet Ministers examined the manner in which the decision would be made public.

August 11:

At 7 a.m. the notification was made through the Swiss Government of the acceptance of the Potsdam Declaration. The President of the Board of Information issued a statement. War Minister General Anami issued a proclamation to the Army.

August 12: On the basis of a telegram from the enemy side, Prime Minister Suzuki proceeded to the Imperial Palace at 2:05 p.m. and stayed there till 2:44 p.m. An extraordinary Cabinet meeting was opened at 3 p.m. till 5:30 p.m. at the official residence of the Prime Minister. At the meeting the Cabinet Ministers exchanged their views frankly and thoroughly on the telegram from the enemy side.

On the other hand, a conference of the Imperial Princes was held in the Imperial Palace at 3 p.m. till 5 p.m.

Those who proceeded to the Imperial Palace in succession included General Umezu, Chief of the General Staff, who proceeded to the Imperial Palace at 8:20 a.m. Admiral Toyoda, Chief of the Navy General Staff, at 9:04 a.m. Foreign Minister Togo at 11 a.m. Baron Kiichiro Hiranuma, President of the Privy Council, at 1:47 p.m. and Prime Minister Suzuki at 2:05 p.m.

August 13:

Receiving the formal reply of the Allied nations at 8 a.m, the conference of the Prime Minister, War Minister, Navy Minister, the Chief of the Army General Staff and the Chief of the Navy General Staff, or the six persons who compose the Supreme War Council, was held at the Prime Minister's official residence from 8:50 a.m. to 9:10 a.m. In the meanwhile, the Chief of the Army General Staff and the Chief of the Navy General Staff proceeded to the Imperial Palace, during the recess of the conference. The conference was then reopened at 10:30 a.m. and continued until 3 p.m. The fundamental question of safeguarding the fundamental character of the Empire was discussed. Then the Cabinet meeting was held at the Prime Minister's official residence from 4 to 7 p.m. and further continued the deliberation on the question of safeguarding the fundamental character of the Empire, but the Cabinet did not come to a complete agreement.

August 14:

Prime Minister Suzuki proceeded to the Imperial Palace twice, from 8 to 8:55 a.m. and from 9:40 to 10 a.m. and received the Imperial Wish to call suddenly a conference in the presence of His Majesty the Emperor. On the other hand, at 10 a.m was held in the Imperial Palace a conference of Field Marshals and Fleet Admirals. From 10:45 a.m. to noon, there was held a conference in the presence of His Majesty the Emperor which had no precedent in history. His Majesty the Emperor attended the conference accompanied by Chief Aide-de-Camp General Shigeru Hasunuma. President Hiranuma of the Privy Council, Prime Minister Suzuki, all State Ministers, the Chief Secretary of the Cabinet, General Umezu of the Army General Staff and Admiral Toyoda of the Navy General Staff attended the conference. Receiving the Imperial Decision all those attending the conference retired from the Imperial Palace greatly impressed.

Then the Cabinet Council was held three times, from 1 to 3:20 p.m., from 7:20 to 8:30 p.m and from 9 to 11 p.m. In the meanwhile, the Prime Minister proceeded to the Imperial Palace at 8:30 p.m. and completed all necessary procedure. Thus the Imperial Rescript was promulgated on August 14.

Cabinet Will Establish Commission for Study Of Postwar Problems

The setting up of a commission to deliberate on matters relating to postwar problems was decided at the Cabinet meeting on Tuesday. The new body is to effect liaison among the Ministries and make investigations on matters pertaining to the rehabilitation of the country, production increase of foodstuffs, expansion of transportation capacity and anti-inflation measures. Meanwhile, an extraordinary Cabinet meeting is scheduled to be held daily at 1 p.m. as from Wednesday to deliberate on postwar problems.

GOVERNMENT WILL NOT DECLARE MORATORIUM

Every Effort to Be Bent for the Stabilization of the People's Livelihood

The assurance that no moratorium will be declared by any bank within the Empire on account of the latest emergency situation was made on August 15 by Finance Minister Toyosaku Hirose.

The Finance Minister stressed for future economic measures (1) the maintenance of the economic order, (2) the stabilization of the people's livelihood, and (3) early economic rehabilitation. The Finance Minister's press interview was worthy of note in that it clarified various concrete measures pertaining to the stabilization of the people's livelihood, the rehabilitation of the life of the war sufferers, the shift of industries and the prevention of inflation.

The Finance Minister said:

"The Empire has come face to face with the most difficult situation since the founding of its history. The way to cope with the future of our economy is to maintain its order throughout, seek to stabilize the people's livelihood and realize an early economic recovery. As regards the currency and financing measures necessary for these purposes, the Government is determined to make all available endeavors

"1. Concerning bank deposits, the Government will assure their safety and absolutely will not take such a measure as a moratorium.

"2. As regards the funds needed for the production increase of foodstuffs, the guarantee and stabilization of the people's livelihood and the recovery of the life of the war sufferers, positive efforts will be made for their accommodation.

"3. Funds necessary to shift the major industries will be securely accommodated. At the same time, proper adjustment will be made of the claims and obligations.

"4. For the purpose of maintaining the credit of currency, strong measures will be taken concerning the prevention of inflation, and efforts will be made for its full enforcement.

"I sincerely hope that you people of this country will look the present situation in the face, have full understanding for the various measures of the State, exercise patience and caution and maintain calm and composure and thus cope with the present difficult situation."

U.S., Britain Receive Reply

President Truman issued the following statement at 7 p.m. on August 14, according to a Domei Lisbon dispatch quoting a Washington report: "I received this afternoon the reply of the Japanese Government to the note sent to the Japanese Government by the Secretary of State on August 11."

British Prime Minister Clement Attlee in his broadcast made at midnight on August 14 announced that the British Government had received the reply of the Japanese Government on the termination of the war, an urgent Domei dispatch from Lisbon dated August 15 reported.

CABINET'S PROCLAMATION ISSUED TO ENTIRE NATION

Prime Minister Exhorts Direction of All Efforts to Defend National Structure

In a Cabinet Proclamation issued on Tuesday, Prime Minister Admiral Baron Kantaro Suzuki called upon the Japanese people to concentrate all their efforts to overcome the difficulties to come following termination of the war and thus to give their all for the defense of the national structure.

In the proclamation, the Prime Minister said:

"Today we have been graciously granted an Imperial Rescript. The Empire has taken part in the War of Greater East Asia for almost four years and now has had to bring it to a close by an emergency measure by His Imperial Majesty. For the subjects of His Imperial Majesty, the awe and trepidation are indeed inexpressible. Looking backward, it is remembered that the officers and men who have fallen buried far from home [illegible] foreign zones since the outbrea[illegible] war have been innumerab[illegible] the damage to the hom[illegible] sacrifices of the in[illegible] These things cau[illegible] profound emotions. But there was no way to realize the aims of the war and the trend of the war was not favorable. The way of the war underwent a fundamental change by the use of the new bomb which possessed a destructive power hitherto unprecedented in scientific annals. This was followed by the declaration of war by the Soviet Union on August 9 against the Empire. And the Empire was met with an unprecedented crisis. Graciously and benevolently wishing the peace of the world and the welfare of His subjects H[illegible] Majesty issued an Imp[illegible] The Imperial Decis[illegible] made. The way f[illegible] take is in its [illegible]

"It goes [illegible] this th[illegible] com[illegible] the p[illegible] great[illegible] difficulties. [illegible]pire must open the nation's destiny in the future by making these difficulties bear fruit. Holding back all my tears, I ask my compatriots to bear these difficulties.

"The people must be concerned now with the defense of the national structure. There must be no internal strife over already past facts to allow others to take advantage and there must be nothing done lightly in the heat of emotion to cause the world to lose trust in the country. All must muster their efforts for the protection and assistance of the bereaved families of the war dead, officers and men and civilians.

"The Government will, together with the people, in unquestioning compliance with the Imperial Wishes, fight all hardships and always conform with the Imperial Will, absolutely to recover the national prestige and answer the will of our ancestors.

"I would also like to say a word about the duties of officials in dealing with this crisis. His Imperial Majesty has graciously declared that He knows full well the sadness of His people. The officials, as H[illegible] Imperial Majesty's agents, must carry out this Imperial Will of benevolence and become the spearheads for arousing a firm spirit of recovery.

August 14, 1945

Baron Kantaro Suzuki,
Prime Minister"

AIR RAIDS CONTINUE

250 Deck Planes Attack Kanto Area Early Wednesday

Some 250 deck planes in three waves came attacking the Kanto zone from the Boso region on Wednesday for approximately two hours from about 5.30 a.m. and strafed chiefly airfields and part of the city districts, the Eastern Army District Headquarters and the Yokosuka Naval Station Headquarters jointly anounced at 11 a.m. the same day.

The communique also said that following the attack of these deck planes a small number of carrier-borne plane attacked the Chiba and Ibaraki districts.

War results known by 11 a.m. include nine planes shot down and two others damaged.

Nippon Times

No. 16,678 (THE 20th YEAR of SHOWA) TOKYO, TUESDAY, AUGUST 21, 1945 Price 35 Sen

IMPERIAL ARMED FORCES ORDERED TO CEASE FIGHT

Display True Essence of Soldierly Spirit, War and Navy Offices Exhort

By the Imperial decision on armistice His Majesty the Emperor has shown the way the people are to follow and at the same time through the Imperial Rescript given to the soldiers His Imperial Majesty has directed them to endure the unendurable in order to solidify permanently the foundation of the State.

In accordance with the Imperial decision the Chief of the General Staff and the Chief of the Naval General Staff ordered the entire Imperial Japanese Forces to suspend hostilities. At the same time the War Office and the Navy Office notified all the Navy and Army Forces over the radio the following matters that should be attended to following conclusion of an armistice agreement:

"The Imperial Command on armistice has already been given and concrete matters we should observe will be made known one after another in the near future. We have received the Imperial Command with a determination by overcoming our intense grief. We should conduct ourselves with care with a view to crowning the united Imperial Forces with the last honor. A thousand emotions will crowd our minds as we see before our eyes the concrete matters which we must observe after the armistice.

"His Imperial Majesty fully aware of the feeling of the warriors has commanded that we 'endure the unendurable' for the sake of the whole of the Empire. The entire armed force should now thoroughly realize the feeling of those units who had to withdraw full of emotions by suppressing their individual feelings from Guadalcanal island leaving behind them the corpses of their comrades with whom they had pledged to die together.

"As to the measures to be taken following the conclusion of an armistice regarding arms, ammunition, munition articles and personnel, concrete orders shall be issued. In that event, every soldier is requested to conduct himself strictly in accordonce with orders and stipulations true to the spirit of the Imperial Forces.

"Should any soldier resort to a reckless action caused by his own judgment or in disregard of clear stipulations such action will result not only in multiplying the hardships of 100,000,000 people but disobeying the Imperial Command.

"It is more difficult for soldiers to defend than to attack. It is much more difficult for them to conduct themselves in time of adversity than a favorable situation. We are now facing the very situation in which we should display the essence of the spirit of soldiers as directed by the August Wishes of His Majesty the Emperor."

COMMENTS ON ATOMIC BOMB

N.Y. Herald Tribune Questions Retaining by U.S. of New Weapon

The New York Herald Tribune in a comment on Friday questioned whether it was wise for the secret of the atomic bomb to be retained by the United States and urged the "nationalization" of the new weapon, according to a Domei dispatch from Lisbon.

"It is true that there are grave differences between Russian, British and American viewpoints as to the policy in Europe," the paper said. "It is also true that the atomic bomb has introduced a new instrument of policy into the world." "But," the paper stressed, "it is a far too explosive weapon to be applied to the international scene."

The Herald Tribune declared that the "object of all reasonable men must be not to play with the exclusive exercise of power, but to aim at genuine internationalization of both constructive policies and destructive forces out of which the new international society is to be shaped."

Light Control Lifted Throughout Country From August 20 Noon

Beginning noon on Monday the precautionary light control was removed all over the country by the order issued by the Air Defense Headquarters of the Home Ministry on the basis of Article 4 of the Light Control Regulations. By this step all outside lights and the lights in the buildings above three stories may be put on without any restrictions.

His Imperial Majesty Asks Government To Brighten Up the People's Daily Life

The gracious solicitude of His Majesty the Emperor for brightening up the people's daily life was revealed by Prime Minister H.I.H. General Prince Naruhiko Higashikuni at the Cabinet Council held Sunday afternoon.

When the extraordinary Cabinet Council was opened at 2 p.m. Sunday afternoon, the Prime Minister announced that, in being received in audience by His Majesty the Emperor the same day, His Imperial Majesty gave the following most gracious words.

"Brighten up the people's life after the conclusion of the war. For instance immediately lift the light control and brighten up the streets; hurry the re-establishment of amusement facilities, and speedily abolish mail censorship."

The Cabinet decided immediately to observe the spirit of the gracious Imperial wish and hurriedly put into effect various measures for brightening up the people's daily life. The Council then approved the appointment of the new Home Vice-Minister and was closed at 4 p.m.

INSTRUCTIONS ARE ISSUED TO INDUSTRIAL WORKERS

Welfare Ministry Asks Obedience to August Wishes, Maintenance of Calm

In consideration of the uneasiness, about their future livelihood. of some of the industrial workers who have been hitherto engaged in the production of war arms, the Welfare Ministry last week issued the following statement earnestly advising the workers to keep calm until practical measures to cope with the present situation were announced

"Upon receiving the Imperial Rescript to end the war, we cannot but express our sincere regret that we were not able to serve His Majesty the Emperor as we had wanted to and at the same time pledge that we are resolved to forge straight ahead for the reconstruction of the country, enduring whatever difficulties may be ahead of us.

"We express our sincere sympathy to some millions of workers who have hitherto devoted themselves to the production of war arms. The Government authorities are determined to enforce proper measures to cope with the present situation, in accordance with the Imperial Wishes and in consideration of the worries of those workers.

"Should any one resort to thoughtless action, he must be accused of not living up to the August Wishes.

"Pending the enforcement of adequate measures by the authorities concerned and the workers' livelihood is established afresh. the workers are requested to observe discipline under the guidance of factory owners or managers and thus to faithfully maintain their dignity as industrial workers."

Restriction on Social Life

As a result of the acceptance of the Potsdam Declaration the social life of the Japanese people will be subjected to restrictions and no easy idea as to the future livelihood of the Japanese people can be entertained, warned the Yomiuri-Hochi in an article which runs as follows:

After the conclusion of an armistice the occupation forces of the Allied Armies will advance into Japan and will enforce military administration. Although it is not clear at present as to the strength of the occupation forces it is regarded that the armed strength of the occupation forces will be around XX thousand. The occupation forces will be stationed in designated areas and will attend to the task for the fulfillment of the articles of the Potsdam Declaration.

The territory of Japan as announced by the Potsdam Declaration will be divided into the occupied zone under the military administration and the unoccupied zone. It goes without saying that the offering of living quarters and foodstuffs to the occupation army will seriously affect the livelihood of the people both at present and in the future.

The control of transportation organs such as railway, motor cars and others and the censorship of communication will be enforced. By the disarmament of the whole armed force the army fleets, aircraft and munitions industry will cease to exist. A big change will occur in the society as a result of the demobilization and dissolution of all munitions companies. It must be expected that this state of affairs will last semi-permanently.

Currency inflation is now presenting a serious problem and as a basic measure for coping with this situation it is considered essential that necessary articles of the people should be marked in large numbers. Reparations imposed on Japan must be paid in kind and this will conflict with the basic contermeasure or the preventing of vicious inflation. Because of this situation the question of currency inflation will inevitably assume serious proportions.

In addition to the question of reparations in kind. there is a big question of payment in goods and that of specie for the military scripe issued in the southern areas which were under the Japanese occupation and for the notes of the Central Reserve Bank of China and the Federal Reserve Bank of China in Central China and North China, and for the notes of the Bank of Manchoukuo in Manchoukuo and those of the Bank of Chosen and the Bank of Taiwan in Chosen and Taiwan respectively. It must be expected that this question will seriously affect the economic life of the Japanese people.

CHIANG WILL TRANSFER HIS CAPITAL TO NANKING

Move Will Be Compieted by October 10; N. China Political Body to Carry On

According to a Reuter dispatch from Chungking dated August 19, a Domei dispatch from Lisbon dated August 19 reported.

According to the information from well-informed quarters some 20,000 to 30,000 Chinese communist troops are making preparations for a forestalling attack on Wuhu in preparation for penetrating Nanking. However, the Chinese communist troops are poorly armed and the Chungking authorities are not attaching much importance to the development of the situation.

Authoritative Chungking Government quarters assert that the transfer of the capital to Nanking is expected to be completed by October 10, the Double Tenth Festival, according to a Chungking report relayed to Domei from Lisbon on August 17.

Meanwhile, 60 bankers are expected to be dispatched to Shanghai soon to prepare for the installation of banks in Shanghai, Nanking and Hankow, Chungking Government authorities announced on August 17.

Dissolution Postponed

With the dissolution of the National Government, the North China Political Affairs Commission met to discuss future steps. As a result, it was decided that in consideration of the commission being a regional organ, it would not be immediately dissolved but would remain for the present to wind up various matters and apply itself to securing the livelihood of the people, according to a Domei dispatch from Peking on August 18.

Tani Exhorts Chinese

Masayuki Tani, Japanese Ambassador to China, took the occasion of the dissolution of the National Government at Nanking to appeal to the leaders of the Government and to all thinking people in China to revert to the way of the sage which has been observed in East Asia from generation to generation for untold ages, according to a Domei Nanking dispatch of August 17. Ambassador Tani said:

I find deep feelings crowding my mind after reading the declaration of the National Government stating its intention to dissolve. It is more than two years since I assumed office. The interval has been a period during which I have come into close touch with the various leaders of the National Government, and I am persuaded that I am a Japanese knowing their purposes better than any other.

As a result of the change which has come about in the general situation, I find these people confronted with entirely new conditions. But their endeavors in the past, I am convinced, have not been without purpose.

Like us, they have during the past four-odd years worked laboriously in order to maintain the general situation in East Asia. Upon looking back, I find my sympathy going out unendingly to them. The situation has changed and they have to make a fresh start.

I have no doubt that all in China will try to profit by what they have done in the past, lay plans for the future, and working in close unity, start on the way toward a rehabilitated and a reconstructed China.

There is a Chinese saying about behaving like a sage even in a dispute. There is the way of the sage to be followed by men even when they are engaged in a struggle. The moment the fight is over the parties concerned should return to relations as between sages. This is applicable not only to disputes within China but also to ones between Japan and China.

The present is the time for us to recollect the fact that we were born in the Orient and try to go back to the way based on morality. I have a conviction that the thinking people of China will share my views and acquit themselves according to these lights in the new situation in which they find themselves. From the depths of my heart I extend my best wishes for the health of the leaders of the National Government.

LIEUT. GENERAL OBATA IS GIVEN CABINET POST

Named Minister Without Portfolio; Furui Is Vice-Chief Of Home Affairs

Lieutenant General Toshishiro Obata, on Sunday was appointed Minister without Portfolio, the Board of Information announced at 5 p.m. the same day.

Lieutenant General Obata, 65, hails from Kochi Prefecture. In 1932 he served as a departmental chief in the General Staff, and in 1935 was appointed President of the Military Staff College. In the following year he was placed on the reserve list. He is a noted military strategist and was asked to enter the Cabinet because his ability is needed in handling various postwar issues.

Furui Home Vice-Minister

Yoshisane Furui, Governor of Aichi Prefecture, was appointed Vice-Minister of Home Affairs on Sunday. Together with his appointment, those of Masazane Hashimoto, Governor of Ibaraki Prefecture, and Nobuya Ban, former Chief of the Metropolitan Police Board, as Director of the Peace Bureau of the Home Office and Chief of the Metropolitan Police Board, respectively, were announced.

Mr. Furui, 43, comes from Tottori Prefecture. Upon graduation from Tokyo Imperial University in 1925, he entered the Home Office. In July, 1943, he was appointed Governor of Ibaraki Prefecture. At that time he was reputed as the youngest Governor.

In April, this year, simultaneous with the resignation of the Koiso Cabinet, Mr. Furui resigned as Governor of Ibaraki Prefecture but in June he was appointed Governor of Aichi Prefecture.

GREEK CABINET FORMED

Appointees for Five New Posts Bared by Premier Voulgaris

Greek Premier Admiral Petros Voulgaris on August 17 completed the formation of the new Greek Cabinet which has been functioning with some posts unfilled since August 11, according to a Domei report. According to the announcement the Premier has taken the portfolio of Minister of Interior.

Other new appointments were John Politis, Foreign Affairs; Bail Dyriacopoulos, Justice; Colonel Mahas, Transport; Admiral Christos Louis, Posts and Telegraphs; and Vasil Dendramis, Undersecretary of the Press Ministry.

Must Make Decisions

The new Greek Government has two main decisions to make; namely, to appoint a delegation to attend the Conference of Foreign Ministers to be held in London next month and the question of fixing a date for the elections, according to a London report of August 19 received in Stockholm.

Technically, elections should be possible by the middle of October although in three districts of northern Greece things have been too unsettled for election preparations so far. There is also the issue where displaced people should vote. However, the Greek Government's chief difficulty is to find a date which all parties will accept as fair.

Resignations Are Accepted

The White House announced on Friday that the resignations offered by Archibald MacLeish and J. C. Holmes, Assistant Secretaries of State, had been accepted, according to a Washington report reaching Lisbon. Their successors hav'ly Mabeen selected yet, the report said.

DE GAULLE VISITING U.S. FOR TALKS WITH TRUMAN

French Head Expected to Explain France's Future Ties With Reich, Indo-China

The United States State Department announced on August 18 that President Charles De Gaulle of the Provisional Government of France is expected to arrive in Washington on August 22 and meet President Harry Truman in conference, according to a Washington dispatch to Lisbon on August 18, quoted by Domei.

Reuter Scribe Comments

Commenting on General De Gaulle's coming visit to President Truman, Reuter's press correspondent, Harold King, states that the meeting is regarded as the first opportunity for the head of the French Government to discuss directly with one of France's major allies the vital problems connected with the peace settlement. It is hoped that the Washington talks will be followed by similar talks in other Allied capitals.

A French spokesman has indicated that among the questions on which General DeGaulle will explain the French viewpoint are the future relations of France with Germany, Indo-China, French interests generally in the Pacific, and aid to French economy.

No reply has been received from Washington or London to the French request to take part in the Japanese armistice. The correspondent states, that unofficial talks in Paris that the Allies must be unwilling to return Indo-China to France, is not shared by the French Government.

As for Germany, France is particularly interested in the Ruhr and its outlying districts. These areas together with Alsace Lorrain form an economic and industrial bloc from the French point of view that are divided between the French and the British as far as the zones of occupation in Germany are concerned. The basic French idea is that the highly industrial western part of Germany, including the Ruhr, must be withdrawn from political control of any central German Government and must permanently be administered by an international body representing the Western Allies.

REVOLT IN BUENOS AIRES

Danger of Heavy Fighting Averted As Police Overpower Nationalists

Pressmen in Buenos Aires had a grandstand view of the battle for the Buenos Aires Building on Thursday night in which 26 Argentine nationalists had barricaded themselves, according to a Buenos Aires report reaching Lisbon.

Over 20 shots were fired, the report said, and later there was danger of heavy fighting. Finally, the police reinforcement arrived armed with submachine guns calling on the nationalists to come out of the building with their hands up. Twenty-six men came out shouting "Long live nationalism."

The building is in the street where many newspapers and news agencies have offices.

Barrio Chosen President

Diege Martinez Barrio, Speaker of the Spanish Cortes during the Republican regime, on Friday, was elected provisional President of the Spanish Republican Government by more than 100 deputies meeting in Mexico City, according to a Domei dispatch from Lisbon quoting a Mexico City report. Barrio took oath of office and President Avila Camacho of Mexico granted an extraterritorial status to the City Hall where the ceremony took place so the acts by the Cortes will have legality, the report said.

5 Bulgarian Ministers Quit

Five Ministers in the Bulgarian Government resigned on Friday as a protest against holding elections on August 26, a Reuters report from Sofia reaching Stockholm said. The Ministers handed in their resignation after Premier Kimtan Georgeiv announced that the national elections would be held as scheduled on August 26. Four Ministers who held the portfolios of Agriculture, Finance, Railways and Social Policy had sought the postponement of the elections, the report said.

Thai Cabinet Resigns

The Khuang Aphaiwong Cabinet of Thailand tendered its resignation en bloc at 3 p.m. August 17 to Prince Pridi Phanamyong, member of the Council of Regency, according to a Domei dispatch from Bangkok on August 18.

Ired by Use of Atomic Bomb, London Vicar Disobeys King's Order to Hold Special Rites

The Vicar of St. Albans Church in London refused to open his church for Thanksgiving Services, which the King ordered to be held all over England, according to the London correspondent of the Aftonbladet in his report dated August 16, says a Stockholm report.

The reason for this is that the Vicar does not wish his Church to be used for any Thanksgiving of "Manslaughters" of Hiroshima and Nagasaki. The Vicar of St. Albans is far from being the only person with these views.

London papers are full of letters from readers who express their indignation over the use of the atomic bomb and who cite the Vatican's attitude toward this weapon.

Several Labor members of Parliament have also categorically condemned the atomic bomb. If it continues like this, there will be a storm of opinions against the atomic bomb, although it was this weapon which shortened the war.

BRITISH BARE INTENTION TO REOCCUPY HONGKONG

London Spokesman Affirms Claim—Struggle Seen With China for Crown Colony

A British Foreign Office Spokesman said the colony of Hongkong is a part of the British Empire and that Britain intends to occupy it just as any other part, according to a London dispatch relayed from Stockholm. However, according to the Associated Press, this British spokesman said the British are not racing with the Chinese to see who gets there first. Hongkong is a British Crown Colony and has been British-held for 100 years. The future of Hongkong is said to be under official discussion. This British spokesman said that he could not confirm that China had told Britain she intended to occupy this great base.

Struggle Seen Looming

Indications are that there will be quite a struggle over the question of occupation of Hongkong between the Chinese and British, according to reports reaching Lisbon. A London datelined report said that the British Foreign Office has affirmed its claim on Hongkong and declared "we intend to occupy it—we will not race the Chinese to it.

A UP report from China claimed that the Chinese want Hongkong and many are determined to raise a row that would be heard in every United Nations capital if the British retain it as almost certainly they will For many Chinese, the report said, a Hongkong in British hands would be a bitter and shameful reminder of China's submission to extraterritoriality.

On the other hand, the report continued, the British contend with legalistic accuracy that the colony has no connection with extraterritoriality and had been part of the empire for 103 years.

Well-informed, high-placed Chinese said, "We will be shocked if Britain insists on retaining Hongkong after the war. We believe the pressure of opinion of other nations can be brought to bear to make the British return Hongkong to China."

Paradoxically, Chinese diplomatic circles in London on Sunday night categorically denied American reports of the race between the Chinese and British forces to reach Hongkong first and declared "China has no such intention to seize any Allied territory whether Hongkong or any other."

These circles stated that it is the "established policy of China to seek settlement of any and all questions affecting her interests only by amicable negotiations and agreement. Sino-British relations have been and remain most friendly."

INDUSTRIAL RECONVERSION MAPPED OUT BY AMERICA

The United States Government on Friday mapped out plans for a swift industrial reconversion and took a number of steps to "cheer" the country which was staggered by official forecasts of 5,000,000 people being unemployed within six months and 9,000,000 within a year, it is disclosed in a Washington dispatch reaching Lisbon on August 17.

According to the report the main emphasis was on President Truman's proposal for the legislation which would enable the government to establish a yearly program of "full employment" even if the government must provide the work.

The report expected that the elimination of 400 wartime controls on materials will aid the industry's reconversion to peacetime economy. These are to be announced at the weekend and reportedly will speed up raw materials to starved peacetime factories.

President Truman on Thursday relaxed the "wage freeze" policy to permit wage boosts providing there was no increase in prices. He has also asked labor to renew wartime "no strike" pledge which was repudiated after the end of the war by the important CIO.

Metals Control Abolished

The U.S. War Production Board on Friday night abolished virtually all its control over three basic metals used by the war industry—steel, copper and aluminum—thus making their use available for manufacture of civilian products, according to a Domei report from Lisbon quoting a Washington message.

GREW IS [illegible]TED TO GET VITAL P[illegible]ITION IN JAPAN

Former Am[illegible]sador to Tokyo Expected [illegible] Control Administra[illegible] Here

An International News Service dispatch from Washington reported that [illegible]eph C. Grew, who has resigned the post of Undersecretary of State, is expected to be given an important post regarding the administrative control of Japan, a Domei dispatch as relayed from Stockholm on August 18 reported.

Grew as Adviser

The resignation of Joseph C. Grew, U.S. Undersecretary of State and former Ambassador to Tokyo, immediately brought the speculation that he would be appointed political adviser to General Douglas MacArthur in connection with ruling Japan, according to an August [illegible] Lisbon dispatch quoting a Washington report.

Mr. Grew stated in his letter of resignation that he was lea[illegible] after many years in the foreign service and that this was the proper time to lay down the responsibility of public affairs.

Mr. Grew's name has been prominently mentioned for appointment as adviser to General MacArthur and his resignation from the State Department would pave the way for his taking up duties again in the Orient.

Meanwhile, another report said that President Truman announced the resignation of Mr. Grew and the promotion of Assistant Secretary of State, Dean Acheson, to his post.

Mr. Acheson will handle State Department relations with Congress and will serve as Acting Secretary of State during the absence of Secretary of State James Byrnes who is expected to leave Washington shortly for the meeting of the Foreign Ministers of the United States, Britain, the Soviet Union, China and France.

U.S. CASUALTIES MOUNT

Washington Reveals Army and Navy Losses Reach 1,070,000

The United States Government announced on August 17 that the total casualty list of the United States army and navy in the present war reached 1,070.000, including 252,146 dead, according to a Domei report from Lisbon, quoting a Washington dispatch.

It said that the army suffered 199,183 dead 570,997 wounded; 118,302 taken prisoners; 33 653 missing or a total of 922,135, while the navy includinf Marines and Coast Defense Guards disclosed dead, 52,963; wounded, 80,171; taken prisoners, 3,694; missing 10,553 or a total of 147,381.

The total dead reaching 252,146 shows an increase of 2,534 compared with last week's announcement.

In the above casualties are not included the 1,196 crew members of the heavy cruiser Indianapolis which was sunk recently by the Japanese in the Philippine waters, and several thousands who were killed or wounded in the recent battles in the Pacific area.

ARMISTICE OBSERVED BY SOVIETS AND JAPANESE

Negotiations Being Conducted Successfully on Spot By Both Missions

Negotiations are being successfully conducted right on the spot between the Japanese and the Soviet military missions which arrived at Hsinking, Mukden and Kungchuling, respectively on August 19, it is reported by a Domei dispatch from Hsinking dated August 20. In the meantime, armistice is being observed by the Soviet troops and the Japanese Forces on the front.

Chinese Mission Arrives

A cable from Manila reported that the Chinese delegates to the armistice talks headed by General Hsu Yung-chang arrived in Manila by air from Chungking on August 18. The party included besides General Hsu one army and navy officer respectively and 12 American, Australian and Chinese ne[illegible] Domei dispatch from [illegible] August 18 reported.

British Obje[illegible]

Britain will disp[illegible] force to Jap[illegible] and sailors [illegible] the B[illegible] release [illegible] Reuter [illegible]d. According [illegible] Domei [illegible] Lisbon.

Australia Seek Bigger Role

Demanding [illegible]reater part in the forthcoming [illegible] conference Au[illegible] [illegible]inister Josph [illegible] [illegible] following state[illegible] according to [illegible] country [illegible] war efforts. The Australian Government notified the British Government that the former was ready to dispatch its Army, Navy and Air forces to participate in the operations against the Japanese mainland. Thus, the Australian forces consisting of some warships, two brigades and two air companies have been included in the British Pacific Fleet. Not only that, Australia promised to share responsibilities with Britain in the Southeast Pacific area by suggesting to look after Borneo and other territories now occupied by the Japanese Forces. With a view to participating in the reoccupation of Singapore and Malay, Australia will dispatch its representatives to witness the surrender of Malay."

Dutch Troops for E. Indies

The Dutch Government has decided to dispatch a part of the army in Holland to the Netherlands East Indies in September and October. It is further reported that the Dutch Government plans to send an additional 25,000 men next year. The Dutch Expeditionary Force is now being trained in England, a Do[illegible] dispatch from Lisbon dated Au[illegible] 18 reported, quoting a Hagu[illegible] patch.

Norwegians to Take Over

The Norwegian Government [illegible] take over the civil administra[illegible] of Norway on September [illegible]; it was announced on Saturday by the Luxembourg radio according to a [illegible] report from Stockholm. No[illegible] since liberation from the Ge[illegible] had been administered by the Al[illegible] military government.

Pearl Harbor Facts Demanded by Walsh In Note to [illegible]

In a note sent to Navy Secretary Forrestal, Chairman David Walsh of the Senate Navy Committee, demanded the public announcement of the true facts concerning the Pearl Harbor attack, according to a Washington report, says a Domei report from Lisbon. With the conclusion of the war, any excuse for keeping the Pearl Harbor incident a secret is gone, and the Navy Department should immediately release all documents and results of investigation concerning the Pearl Harbor attack he said. Congress will also ask for clarification of the responsibility for the attack. He also asked that Navy authorities submit to the Navy Committee all documents respecting the Pearl Harbor case.

Entered as second-class matter April 15, 1931, at the post office at New Haven, Connecticut, under act of March 3, 1879

Published Monday, Wednesday and Friday by Illustrated Current News, Inc., New Haven, Conn. Subscription Annually, $20.80

Sept. 5, 1945—No. 4996

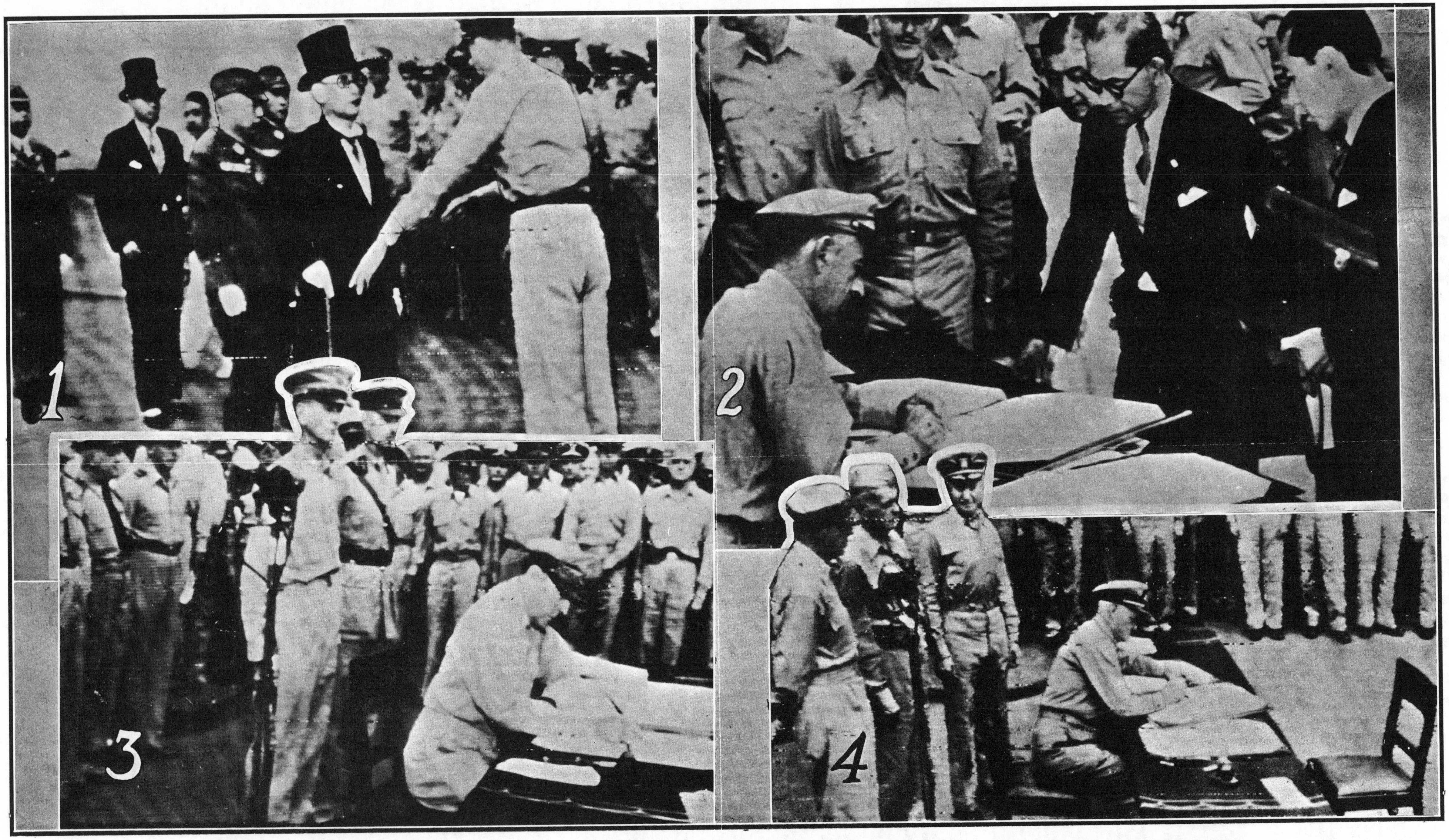

JAPS SIGN SURRENDER PAPERS

Radiophotos from the USS MISSOURI in Tokyo Bay record the historic scene as the beaten Japs make surrender official and peace comes to the world. 1. Silk-hatted Nip government and military leaders arriving aboard ship. 2. Japs watch closely as Lt. Gen. Sutherland corrects surrender document. 3. Lt. Gen. Wainwright, left, and Lt. Gen. Percival (British) stand back of General MacArthur as he signs for the United Nations. 4. Admiral Nimitz signs for U. S. as (left to right) Gen. MacArthur, Admiral Halsey and R. Admiral Sherman look on.

News Note: Yanks Move To Occupy 2nd Jap Island By Sea and Air

重 慶 *The* 新 聞

Chungking Reporter

..I. II. No. 27. CHUNGKING, CHINA 總中華郵政登記認為第一類新聞紙類東川郵政管理局執照第九五六號 SEPTEMBER 6, 1945 $30 PER COPY

..esident Urges To Set Up Unified, Democratic China Based On San Min Chu I

..esident Chiang Kai-shek ..ered his VJ-Day message to .. nation in a broadcast over ..A Monday afternoon.

..irst, the fundamental object ..r National Revolution and .. of Resistance," the Pre.. ..t stated, "is not only the ..t of the enemy, but also .. establishment of a new .. a based on the Three ..le's Principles."

.. the second point that the ..eralissimo emphasized in .. message is the prompt in.. ..ration of constitutional de.. ..acy. The highest ideal of .. National Revolution, he .. is the participation ..ll the people in national ..ics, and the most important ..are for the realization of ..deal is to return the power ..overnment to the people. ..tional unity is the third .. the President asserted .. absolute requirement of ..dern state. He said that .. a united nation can reap .. the fruits of victory.

.. conclusion, the Gen.. ..simo said that these three ..s are "the least that we ..d accomplish at present." ..must in a spirit of self.. ..ce make China an equal ..r in the family of free ..odern nations, and satisfy ..opes of our foreign well-..s, he added.

..phasizing that our people, ..g gone through tremen.. ..us hardships, should be .. ample opportunity to .. and recuperate, President ..g Pointed out that farmers .. been the main source of ..manpower and workers the ..stay of our war and peace .. production, then he declar.. .. the government's decree ..uncing one year's sus.. ..ion of conscription and .. tax collection.

..e sincere support of the ..le as a whole and leaders of ..arks of life to the govern.. .. was urged by the President .. early convocation of the ..nal Assembly and attain.. ..of democracy.

"Only a united nation," the President reasserted, "can accomplish the task of national reconstruction, and contribute to international peace and world prosperity. The important condition for national unity is the nationalization of all armed forces in the country."

The President also declared that responsible offices and local governments will be charged with the task of formulating plans to reduce land rent in accordance with the general principle of "a reduction by 25 per cent" and taking into consideration the local conditions.

He assured the nation the government's intention of abolishing wartime press censorship and facilitating political assembly and orgainzation. He said, "Only thus can we tread the path of democracy traversed by the United States and Great Britain and establish a model democratic state in the Far East."

Referring again to the nationalization of armed forces, the Generalissimo pointed out that the Kuomintang branch headquarters, had been entirely abolished as the first step towards the accomplishment.

..ks Held Between ..sident And Mao

..sident Chiang Kai-shek ..ao Tse-tung, Communist .. had met on several occas.. ..d on two occasions they ..gthy and comprehensive ..r. K. C. Wu, Minister of ..nation, told the foreign ..spondents at a press con.. ..ce yesterday.

..gotiations between the ..nment and the Communists ..arious subjects are still ..on, Dr. Wu said.

JAPANESE SURRENDER CEREMONY IN NANKING POSTPONED TO SEP. 9.

T. V. Soong To Visit England And France

Dr. T. V. Soong, president of the Executive Yuan, is expected to visit London and Paris next week at the invitation of both the British and French Governments.

After the conclusion of the Sino-Soviet negotiations in Moscow, Dr. Soong flew to the United States where he had several conferences with President Harry S. Truman and Secretary of State James Byrnes. Matters resulted from the relinquishment of the American Lend-Lease Act, were particularly stressed in their talks.

In a trip to Canada last Friday the President met W.L. Mackenzie, Canadian Prime Minister, and other members of the Canadian Government with whom discussions on matters of mutual interest is said to be made.

As some urgent home affairs waiting him to deal with, Dr. Soong may return to China in a few weeks, it is learned.

Wartime Press Censorship To Be Abolished, Says Wu

Abolition of wartime censorship has been decided by the government and it will be carried out as soon as possible, Dr. K. C. Wu, newly appointed Information Minister, declared at the foreign press conference yesterday afternoon.

Dr. Wu expressed his desire to supply the foreign correspondents with frank, candid and truthful information. He would, he said, let them form their own judgment, by simply giving them facts, bare and naked, without color and bias.

He pointed out that some criticisms on China have been due to wrong interpretation of facts during the past few years. China was criticized for being unwilling to fight, he said, but now it may be revealed that many attempts made by Japan for conditional peace had been rejected by the Chinese government. All peace rumors were certainly groundless, he added.

As China has been criticized for being not liberal nor democratic due to rigid censorship, Dr. Wu made some explanations. He said that every country invoked it when the war was on, and it was all the more necessary for a country not quite well-organized as China to have stringent censorship in time of emergency. He further pointed out that China has not developed a balanced and detailed law of libel and slander.

The Minister said that some fair-minded foreign friends who have been in China for twenty or thirty years, must have seen the difference between the times of warlords and the times of progress. No one can doubt the presence of the liberal and democratic tendency in China, he added.

Though presiding at the conference for the time, Dr. Wu has been one of the government spokesmen for three years, He asked the foreign correspondent to treat him as friend instead of a government spokesman. "Consult me personally, if you have anything in doubt," he said, and then told them his telephone numbers at a request.

Japs To Submit In Various Areas; MacArthur Moving Hqs. To Tokyo

The signing of the Japanese surrender in the China Theater which was originally scheduled to take place in nanking on September 6 has been postponed to September 9, it was announced by the Chinese Headquarters in a communique today.

Representatives from the United States, the United Kingdom, the Soviet Union France, the Netherlands, Australia and Canada, are welcomed by the Chinese government to take part in the ceremony.

In a memorandum to Lieut.-Gen. Yasutsuka Okamura, Commander of the Japanese Army in Central China, General Ho made specifications regarding the surrender of Japanese troops in various areas in the China Theater.

Owing to weather condition the movement of the troops of the New Sixth Army, under the command of Lieut. Gen. Liao Yao-siang, to Nanking by air, which was scheduled to take place Tuesday, was postponed till yesterday morning.

Over 2,000 Chinese airborne troops arrived in Shanghai yesterday morning. The advance headquarters of the Third War Area was established Tuesday in Shanghai under the command of General Chang Hsueh-chung, Vice-Commander of the Third War Area.

About forty officers and men of the Chinese Air Force, headed by Colonel Chang Tingmeng, arrived in Peiping in two Douglas planes 1 A.M. Tuesday, according to a Tokyo newscast. The planes landed at Nanyuan airprome and more Chinese airdorne troops were expected to reach Peiping soon, it was reported in the broadcast.

Maj.-Gen. Pai Yu-sheng, commanding general of Service of Supply of the Chinese Army, arrived in Kaiyuan by plane Monday to visit Commander Lu Han, of the First Area Forces to talk on matters concerning the surrender of Japanese troops in French Indo-China.

Troops under the command of General Ku Chu tung entered Kinhwa, important town on the Chekiang-Kiangsi railway, Monday. General Ku had sent General Han Teh-chin, Deputy Commander of the Third War Area, to Hangchow to set up advance headquarters. General Han's party is now moving toward Hangchow from Fuyang, south of Hangchow.

Packing, important town in western Hunan, was recovered by the Chinese troops under the command of General Wang Yao-wu, Commander of the Fourth Area, Forces, Sunday.

Our troops under the command of General Hsueh Yueh, Commander-in-Chief of the Ninth War Area, entered the city of Leiyang last Saturday. Those under the command of General Yen Hsi-shan, Commander-in-Chief of the Second War Area, entered the city of Tatung the same day.

Loyang, the important city in Honan, on the south bank of the Yellow River, was reoccupied by the troops commanded by General Hu Tsung-nan, Commander-in-Chief of the First War Area, on Aug. 26.

The Japanese Diet convened its 88th special session Tuesday afternoon following a joint session that morning when Emperor Hirohito read a rescript commanding the Japanese people to work towards surmounting the hardships and trials attending the end of the war, labor towards establishing a peaceful state and win the confidence of the world.

(Continued on Page 8)

Weather To Turn Cold Beginning Sept. Here

The Central Observatory predicted that September will be a rainy month in Szechuan. Weather will turn cold after the middle of the month.

It is also expected that the Chungking-Chengtu area is to be frequented by night rains.

According to the Chinese calender, it has already been in autumn. Hot weather, however, is bothering residents here.

National Assembly May Meet Nov. 12

The government has not contemplated the postponement of the convocation of the National Assembly, as it is the wish of the government and the people to establish a constitutional government at the earliest possible date, Dr. P. H. Chang, government spokesman and counsellor of the Executive Yuan, told the foreign press conference yesterday.

As to where the convocation will take place, Dr. Chang said that it depends on facilities of transportation. Most probably it will be held in Chungking, he added.

ZEITUNG
DER DEUTSCHEN
KRIEGSGEFANGENEN
IN USA

Edited and Prepared
for German Prisoners of War
by German Prisoners of War

DER Ruf

Erscheint halbmonatlich * Herausgeber: Die deutschen Kriegsgefangenen in USA * Anschrift: "To the Editor of DER RUF" G.P.O. Box 20 New York, N. Y. * Verantwortlich fur den Gesamtinhalt: Arbeitsgemeinschaft DER RUF Gesamtinhalt durch die Zensur genehmigt

* Nur in den Kantinen aller deutschen Kriegsgefangenen-Lager in den Vereinigten Staaten von Amerika zu haben.

1. SEPTEMBER 1945 PREIS 5c Nr. 12

Aus dem Inhalt

POTSDAM: EINE ETAPPE

Deutschland nach der Konferenz

Die entscheidendste Bedeutung der Konferenz von Potsdam liegt in der Tatsache, dass die drei Grossmächte den so überaus schwierigen Prozess des gegenseitigen Augleichens an die völlig veränderten Verhältnisse der Nachkriegswelt erfolgreich begonnen haben. Wieder wurde ihr Wunsch, sich auf jeden Fall untereinander zu verständigen, offenbar. Für Deutschland brachte das Ergebnis der Konferenz eine Art Vorfrieden. Es schuf den Rahmen, in dem das deutsche Volk für die nächste Zeit zu leben hat. Eine Reihe anderer sehr dringlicher Fragen — Österreich, Balkan, Türkei, Ferner Osten — blieben in Potsdam vorläufig noch offen. Aber man kann nach den sonstigen Ergebnissen der Konferenz hoffen, dass alle noch schwebenden Probleme in derselben ausgleichenden Art zwischen den Grossmächten gelöst werden. Die Welt hat unter diesen Umständen vielleicht eine längere Friedensperiode vor sich, als manche Skeptiker heute noch erwarten.

Die Entscheidung, die die Konferenz über Deutschland getroffen hat, wird von zwei Merkmalen bestimmt. Das eine ist der Gedanke der vollen Verantwortlichkeit des deutschen Volkes für diesen Krieg. Dabei gelten die direkten Strafbestimmungen nur für die eigentlichen Kriegsverbrecher. In diese Gruppe fallen auch alle, die auf wirtschaftlichem Gebiet mitgeholfen haben, den Krieg und andere kriminelle Taten vorzubereiten. Die Bestimmungen, in denen festgelegt ist, wann Personen zu internieren oder aus ihrem Amt zu entlassen sind, heben dagegen mehr die Gefahr hervor, die die Betreffenden in der Zukunft für die Besatzungsbehörden bilden würden.

Das andere Merkmal ist der Wunsch nach absoluter Sicherheit vor irgendwelchen Gefahren, die in Zukunft noch von Deutschland ausgehen könnten. Die beschlossenen Massnahmen wie territoriale Veränderungen, Auflösung aller militärischen Verbände, wesentliche Beschränkungen des deutschen Industriepotentials, scharfe langjährige Kontrolle aller Lebenszweige, schaffen in Mitteleuropa von nun an einen machtpolitisch neutralen Streifen zwischen West und Ost. Ganz gleich zu welcher Seite das deutsche Volk einmal selbst hinstreben möchte, es würde für keinen Teil mehr einen nennenswerten Gewinn bedeuten und in keiner Weise in der Lage sein, im Gleichgewicht der Mächte das sogenannte Zünglein an der Waage zu bilden.

Dem Wunsch nach Sicherheit und Neutralisierung wurden in Potsdam alle anderen Punkte untergeordnet. Die Grossmächte verzichteten lieber auf ein Höchstmass an Reparation und — wenigstens vorläufig — auf ein Deutschland, das in der Nachkriegswirtschaft einen nennenswerten Handelspartner bilden könnte. Wieviel an industrieller Produktionskapazität Deutschland noch besitzen wird, nachdem die Kriegsindustrie zerstört worden ist, lässt sich im Augenblick noch nicht übersehen. Jedenfalls dürfte Deutschland, wie die New York Times bemerkte, in Zukunft kaum mehr als eine industrielle Macht dritten Ranges sein.

Die Aufgabe für das deutsche Volk, in dem heutigen Rahmen zu existieren, ist nicht leicht. Das verbleibende Gebiet beträgt etwa 390 000 qkm mit einer Friedensbevölkerung von 62 Millionen. Die Kriegsverluste dieser Bevölkerung dürften durch etwa 12 Millionen Deutsche, die aus den Ostgebieten, der Tschechoslowakei und Ungarn umgesiedelt werden, mehr als wettgemacht sein. Die Ergebnisse von Potsdam lassen aber andererseits erkennen, dass die Grossmächte weder wirtschaftliches Chaos, noch soziale oder politische Unrast in Deutschland wünschen. Alle Reparations- und Kontrollmassnahmen erfolgen daher unter der ausdrücklich festgelegten Voraussetzung, dass Deutschland ein gewisser Lebensstandard erhalten bleibt. Wenn daher die Anlaufschwierigkeiten der neuen Friedenswirtschaft überwunden sind, ist zu hoffen, dass zunächst wenigstens ein Existenzminimum für jeden Deutschen gesichert werden kann. Darüber hinaus wird es vielleicht im Laufe der Zeit auch wieder möglich sein, wenn sich das Niveau der anderen europäischen Länder hebt, für das deutsche Volk angemessene Lebensbedingungen zu erreichen. Die Aufgabe wird durch die Tatsache erleichtert, dass Deutschland während der Besatzungszeit wirtschaftlich als Einheit behandelt werden soll.

Politisch wird Deutschland allerdings dezentralisiert werden. Die Konferenz legte den Nachdruck auf die Glieder des früheren Reiches und befürwortete das Heranziehen der Deutschen zu einer zunächst regionalen Selbstverwaltung. Das Recht, wieder Parteien zu bilden, und die gewährte Pressefreiheit sind in diesem Zusammenhang besonders wichtig. Sie ermöglichen es, das politische Leben im Sinne einer demokratischen Erneuerung wieder aufzubauen.

Noch ist allerdings keine zentrale Regierung geschaffen worden. Deutschland ist daher vorläufig eher als ein durch eine Wirtschaftsunion verknüpfter Staatenbund denn als ein einheitliches Reich anzusehen.

So zeigen die Ergebnisse von Potsdam, dass trotz aller grundsätzlichen Entscheidungen, die bereits getroffen wurden, andererseits wichtige Dinge, wie die staatsrechtliche Neugestaltung und der genaue Umfang der Deutschland gestatteten Friedenswirtschaft offen bleiben. Potsdam ist deshalb nur eine Etappe auf dem Wege zu einer friedlichen Neugestaltung Europas in der Welt. Sie wird im letzten Sinne und auf einer letzten Stufe erreicht sein, wenn nach der Friedenskonferenz Deutschland wieder, wie es der Absicht der Grossmächte entspricht, in die Gemeinschaft der Völker aufgenommen worden ist.

Doppelter Todesstoss gegen Japan

Die Sowjet-Union hat Japan den Krieg erklärt.

Komissar Molotov veröffentlichte folgende Erklärung im Namen des russischen auswärtigen Amtes:

„Getreu ihrer Aufgabe den Alliierten gegenüber hat die Sowjet-Union den Alliierten Vorschlag angenommen und sich der Erklärung der Alliierten Mächte vom 26. Juli angeschlossen."—

Es ist klar dass, obschon gewisse Differenzen zwischen den alliierten Mächten bestehen mögen, diese Differenzen sich in keiner Weise in der internationalen Zusammenarbeit schädlich bemerkbar machen werden.—

Die amerikanische Atombombe.

Zwei Tage vor der russischen Kriegserklärung hat ein amerikanisches Bombenflugzeug die erste Atombombe, das bisher wirkungsvollste Zerstörungsmittel, auf die japanische Stadt Hiroshima abgeworfen. Diese eine Bombe entspricht der Vernichtungskraft von 20 000 t TNT-Sprengstoff: einer Bombenlast von 2000 Superfortresses.

Eine umwälzende Entdeckung macht somit „ungeahnte Kräfte" durch die Zertrümmerung von Atomen frei. Deutsche Wissenschaftler, die aus dem Deutschland Hitlers ausgestossen wurden, waren an der Entwicklung der Atombombe beteiligt. Die Vernichtungskraft der Atombomben wird zweifellos eine beschleunigende Wirkung auf den Krieg im Fernen Osten haben, wenn, wie Präsident Truman ankündigte, Atombombe auf Japan herabregnen sollten.

Jetzt scheint das „Atom-Zeitalter" anzubrechen, denn es bestehen Absichten, die neuen Entdeckungen auch für den Frieden auszunutzen. Kriegsminister Stimson stellte in Aussicht, dass die ursprünglichen Kraftquellen Kohle, Ol und Wasser durch Atomenergien ersetzt werden können. Wenn diese neuen Energien nur für den Frieden frei werden könnten, dürften sie ihre bedrückende Unheimlichkeit verlieren.

Parteien

Rückblick und Ausblick

HWE Der Medizinmann von Berchtesgaden pflegte seine Anpreisungen des von ihm heraufbeschworenen „tausendjährigen "Reichs mit höhnischer Verdammung der „vierzehn Jahre der Schmach und des Parteigezänks" zu begleiten. Die Verunglimpfung des Parteienstaates fand in den Jahren der Verwirrung oft williges Gehör. Da die letzten Jahre der Republik für weite Kreise Arbeitslosigkeit und Enttäuschung bedeuteten und oftmals die Wahlkämpfe der Parteien oder ihre lärmenden Auseinandersetzungen in den Volksvertretungen im Vordergrund des politischen Interesses gestanden hatten, wurden Parteiwesen und wirtschaftliches Chaos, Parlament und unüberwindbare Zwietracht der Nation miteinander identifiziert.

Oft wurden hier Symptome und Ursachen verwechselt. Unzulänglichkeiten der deutschen Parteien in der Weimarer Republik, Fehlentwicklung in Führung und Organisation waren Ausfluss der allgemeinen Geschichte des deutschen Volkes und bedeuten nicht Verurteilung des politischen Parteiwesens überhaupt. Die von Bismarck bewusst herbeigeführte Unfertigkeit der parlamentarischen Zustände, die Deutschland im ersten Weltkrieg zum Fluch geworden ist, hatte die Parteien für fast fünfzig Jahre zur Ohnmacht in allen entscheidenden politischen Angelegenheiten verdammt. Keine der Parteien, auch die sogenannten Regierungsparteien nicht, hatt je die Möglichkeit besessen, aktiv an Regierungsgeschäften teilzunehmen, bedeutungsvolle politische Entscheidungen vorzubereiten, die Durchführung der Wünsche des Parlaments wirksam zu überwachen oder gar die Führer der Nation zu bestimmen. Mit der Legende von der politischen Interesselosigkeit des deutschen Volkes stimmt es schlecht zusammen, dass bei den Reichstagswahlen im kaiserlichen Deutschland die Wahlbeteiligung stärker war als die in irgend einem demokratisch regierten Land. Und in der letzten Wahl vor dem Ausbruch des Weltkrieges stimmten rund zwei Drittel der Wähler für Parteien, die sich ausdrücklich gegen die Pläne imperialistischer Aussenpolitik erklärt hatten. Aber da es den Parteien und ihren Abgeordneten wegen der verfassungsrechtlichen Gestaltung des Reichs an wirklicher Macht fehlte, da sie darauf angewiesen waren eine rein negative Politik zu treiben, konnten Wahlzettel nichts an den bestehenden Zuständen ändern. An der Macht und dem eitlen Unfehlbarkeitsglauben der Beamtenherrschaft brachen sich Reformwünsche und politische Willensbildung der Parteien.

Mit dem Zusammenbruch des Kaiserreichs wurden die Parteien buchstäblich von einer Woche zur anderen zu den verantwortlichen Trägern politischen Lebens. Es fehlte nicht an Programmen. Gerade weil die deutschen Parteien von wirklicher Machtausübung ferngehalten worden waren, hatten sie sich als Weltanschauungsparteien entwickelt; die Ämterpatronage, eine wichtige Funktion der politischen Parteien im demokratischen Staatswesen, hatte bis zur Ausrufung der Republik kaum eine Rolle gespielt.

Woran es den Parteien fehlte, waren praktische politische Erfahrung und — im engen Zusammenhang damit — demokratische Führerpersönlichkeiten.

Die sozialdemokratische Partei war seit ihrer Gründung durch ständige Drangsalierungen im Hass gegen den bestehenden Staat gross geworden; von jeglicher Verantwortung in politischen oder auch nur Selbstverwaltungsangelegenheiten war sie ferngehalten worden. Nun musste sie binnen kurzem nicht nur rund 900 Abgeordnete und Stadträte stellen, sondern auch tausende

Entered as second-class matter April 15, 1931, at the post office at New Haven, Connecticut, under act of March 3, 1879

ILLUSTRATED CURRENT NEWS

Published Monday, Wednesday and Friday by Illustrated Current News, Inc., New Haven, Conn. Subscription Annually, $20.80

Sept. 7, 1945—No. 4997

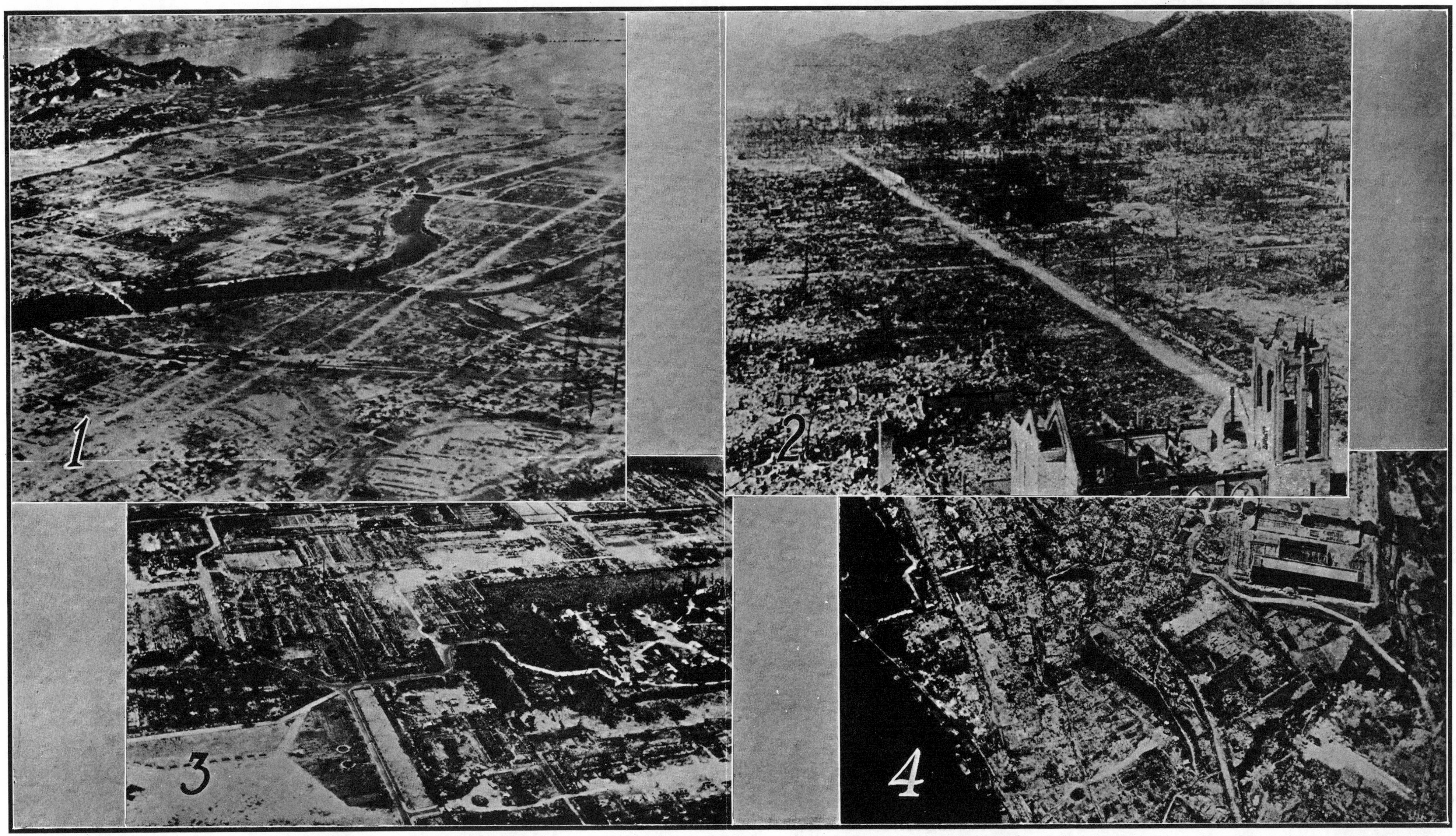

WHAT ATOMIC BOMBS DID TO HIROSHIMA AND NAGASAKI

1. Once a thriving city the size of Denver, Hiroshima was blown off the map by the first atomic bomb. 2. Another view. Ruins of church in foreground. Latest reports gave 53,000 Japs dead, 30,000 missing, 13,960 wounded, 45,000 injured. 3. Another view of the wreckage. 4. Nagasaki, devastated by the second atomic bomb, as it looks today.

News Note: Mac Orders 2 Jap Armies Disarmed

TOJO SHOOTS SELF TO EVADE ARREST

Kept Alive by U. S. Plasma

By CLARK LEE, International News Service Staff Correspondent

TOKYO, Sept 11.--Jap war lord Gen. Hideki Tojo, who was Premier at the time of the sneak attack on Pearl Harbor, attempted suicide at 4:21 p. m. (3:21 a. m. E. W. T.), today by shooting himself in the chest with an army pistol. Hours later the man who would have destroyed the United States was given a chance to live through American blood plasma flowing now in his veins.

Tojo shot himself in his home about 20 miles from Tokyo as U. S. Army men came to arrest him on the orders of Gen. MacArthur.

He was rushed to the U. S. 1st Cavalry Division Hospital in Meiji Park at 7:10 p. m. (6:10 a. m. EWT).

Late tonight he was taken to the U. S. Army Hospital at Yokohama.

At the hospital, Tojo was given better than an even chance of recovery, but he was hopeful that he would still cheat Allied justice.

Waving away attendants, the war leader said:

Don't make any trouble about me; I'm going to die anyway."

Lt. Gen. Eichelberger, U. S. 8th Army commander, was in the operating room, according to a MBS report, and to him Tojo said:

"Co-operate to make a better Japan."

Eichelberger made no reply.

Condition Declared Serious

Capt. James B. Johnson, Jr., 35, of Newark, O., the attending physician, said after administration of the plasma that the former Premier's condition is serious but added that he is suffering from "a common type of wound from which many persons have recovered."

Tojo is 62.

A note, which he managed to dictate after the shooting, said:

"The war in the Greater East Asia region started right. That's my conviction. But we lost. It is proper that Americans took over the person responsible for this war. But I do not want to stand before a jury or Allied commission.

"While I believe Japan was right I believe, too, that America thinks she was right. The righteousness or fairness of that will be decided by an impartial cool observer, a third person or party.

"I feel great regret for the people of Japan and for the people belonging to East Asia.

"As for me I would have tried to commit suicide by hara kiri but sometimes it isn't so successful so I decided to use a pistol.

"I wanted to shoot through my heart to make my suicide sure. I'm very sorry I missed my aim.

"I hope the nation of Japan foresees the future and follows the right path with unshaken heart. First and last I pray for the prosperity of the Japanese Empire and here is my banzai to the Emperor."

The note came as a surprise as in many high quarters Tojo was thought ready to stand up before an Allied court.

The war lord, who only yesterday told this re-

Continued on Page 2, Column 1.

5¢ Journal NEW YORK American

AN AMERICAN PAPER FOR THE AMERICAN PEOPLE

Daily 5 Cents, Saturday 5 Cents in New York City; 10 Cents Elsewhere | SUNDAY, 10 Cents in New York City and 50 Mile Zone. 15 Cents Elsewhere

No. 21,053—DAILY—TUESDAY, SEPTEMBER 11, 1945

In Two Sections —Section One

7TH SPORTS RACING ☆☆☆☆☆☆☆ SPORTS COMPLETE

Confesses War Blame After 'Banzai'

ATTEMPTS SUICIDE . . . Former Jap premier Hideki Tojo shot himself today when American military police appeared at his home to arrest him on orders from Gen. MacArthur. Tojo, who directed the sneak attack on Pearl Harbor that plunged this country into war, was said to be in a serious condition. International News Photo.

By KENNETH McCALEB
International News Service Staff Correspondent

TAMAGAWA, Sept. 11.—Former Premier Tojo attempted to commit suicide late today (3:21 a. m. EWT) but several hours after he fired a bullet into his chest he was still alive.

At 7 p. m. (6 a. m. EWT) I watched Tojo's labored breathing.

But it was evident that he was resting easier than he was a few hours before when Clark Lee, of International News Service; Harry Brundidge, of Cosmopolitan Magazine, and I rushed to his side after hearing the shot which he fired from his Army pistol.

This turn for the better in Tojo's condition won't make him happy.

As we stood beside his crumpled body, he repeated over and over again:

"I am now happy to die. Banzai."

But his son and daughter, who were in the house at the time of the suicide attempt, wept bitterly.

Tojo's wife was not in the house when the shot was fired.

When an American doctor and

Continued on Page 2, Column 6,

Plenty of Meat But the City's Point Hungry

There is no shortage of meat in New York today. On the contrary meat is, literally, going begging.

Porterhouse steaks . . . sirloins . . . rib roasts . . . large, succulent hams dangle in market windows . . . And chickens, both milk fed and fancy spring keep them company.

A New York Journal-American reporter, who made a mouth-watering tour up 9th ave., from 34th st. to 42d st., vowed he could have loaded a large truck with these viands inside half an hour, if he had been in possession of a truck —and sufficient red points.

And there's the rub—points. Housewives, who have long been jerry-building their menus, can have meat on the table today—if they have points.

With the same situation obtaining in other parts of the city where meat markets are in-

Continued on Page 4, Column 5.

Points Taken Off Cheese

WASHINGTON, Sept. 11 (INS). —OPA Administrator Bowles announced today that the point value of all varities of cheese will be removed, effective at midnight tonight.

Haw Haw on Trial Monday

LONDON, Sept. 11 (AP).—The trial of William Joyce, 39, American-born Nazi radio propagandist known as Lord Haw Haw, on a charge of treason has been set for next Monday.

Husband Grilled On Pushing Wife To Subway Death

A wife's fatal injuries under an IRT subway train resulted today in questioning of her husband, Louis Meltzer, 35, of 732 E. 47th st., Brooklyn, to determine whether he had pushed her to the tracks.

His wife, Sally, 33, died shortly after 3 p. m. in New York Hospital, several hours after two cars of a southbound local passed over her at the Lexington ave. and 68th st. station.

Meltzer at first was removed to Bellevue Hospital psychopathic ward, but after his wife's death, was taken to the E. 67th st. police station for questioning by an Assistant District Attorney.

The tragedy had its inception this morning, when Mrs. Meltzer, her daughter, Natalie, 3, and her sister, Mrs. Sarah Stricoff, accompanied Meltzer to New York Hospital, seeking a mental examination for him.

Doctors held, however, that he was not in their jurisdiction and suggested they go to Long Island College Hospital.

The four were on their way back to Brooklyn when the mishap occurred, in the child's presence. Meltzer a moment later fell unconscious and was taken to Bellevue.

It was on statements of Mrs. Stricoff that detectives launched an inquiry to determine whether Meltzer, despondent since sustaining financial loss in his taxicab business, had pushed his wife to the tracks.

Okay Permanent Rank

WASHINGTON, Sept. 11 (AP). —A bill granting permanent rank to the nation's wartime Generals of the Army and Fleet Admirals won unanimous approval today of the Senate Military Committee.

Hero Vet Fights To Stay in School

(Photo in today's Picture Section.)

SUCCASUNNA, N. J., Sept. 11.—Jimmy Hornberger Jr. wet the tip of his pencil, knuckled a fist into his forehead and began wrestling with a problem in compound interest today in the eighth grade of Roxbury Township's grammar school.

A duplicate of the scene could probably be found in thousands of schoolhouses across the nation, but Jimmy's case was different. He is 24 and a veteran of Pearl Harbor and a half dozen campaigns in the Pacific.

And now Jimmy is fighting another campaign. His Succasunna neighbors don't want him in school. They feel he has no place in a classroom with 12 and 13-year-olds. They think the kids will find Jimmy's war exploits too big a diversion to find time for their own books.

But Jimmy thinks differently and he is determined to fight it through to the finish just as he fought through the Fijis, the Wallace Islands, New Hebrides, Tulagi until a tropical fever downed him and sent him home.

WANTS TO GET AHEAD.

Jimmy wants to get ahead and "I can't get anywhere in radar or radio until I complete high school."

"Besides," Jimmy said, "the GI Bill of Rights is behind me. These kids are O. K. It's their parents—and they don't know

Continued on Page 3, Column 4.

Start Roundup Of Jap War Criminals

By FRANK ROBERTSON
International News Service Staff Correspondent

TOKYO, Sept. 11.—Gen. MacArthur's Headquarters launched a widespread roundup tonight of top war criminals on the heels of former Jap Premier Gen. Tojo's attempt at suicide to avoid arrest by American authorities.

MacArthur ordered 39 persons arrested immediately as the Jap government moved to intervene in Tojo's case because of the "seriousness of his condition."

Listed as No. 1 on the war criminal roster issued by MacArthur was Shigenori Togo, foreign minister in Gen. Tojo's "Pearl Harbor" cabinet.

Nine fellow ministers of Togo were also included in the list.

One American and two Australian names were among those accused of perpetrating atrocities from the Philippines to prisoner of war camps in Japan.

WAKE COLLABORATOR.

The lone American was identified only as "Streeter," a civilian construction worker on Wake Island who wrote scripts and participated in Tokyo radio propaganda activities.

The Australians sought by MacArthur are Maj. Charles H. Cousens, formerly of Sydney and a member of the Aussie army, along with John Holland, also known as David Lester.

Holland was said to have broadcast propaganda over the Jap-trolled Radio Shanghai while the former army officer spoke over Radio Tokyo with Streeter.

HOMMA ON LIST.

Also included in the list is Lt. Gen. Masaharu Homma, the man held responsible for the Bataan death march who truculently accepted Lt. Gen. Wainwright's surrender on Corregidor in 1942.

The hunt for Jap war criminals began after MacArthur ordered dissolution of the Jap imperial general staff, effective Thursday, and applied rigid military censorship to Jap press and radio outlets.

Four hundred Allied officers were engaged in the job of compiling evidence against Jap prison camp guards as the hunt for top war criminals got under way.

THE WEATHER

Clear, cooler tonight and tomorrow.

Sun rises, 6:32 a. m.; sun sets, 7:13 p. m. High tide at Governors Island, 12:31 p. m.

HOURLY TEMPERATURES.

7 a. m.	73	12 Noon	79
8 a. m.	73	1 p. m.	73
9 a. m.	73	2 p. m.	70
10 a. m.	75	3 p. m.	72
11 a. m.	77	4 p. m.	73

(Complete Weather Report on Page 10)

TODAY'S INDEX

The Journal-American has the largest circulation of any evening newspaper in New York City. 230

It is the only New York evening newspaper possessing the three great wire services—ASSOCIATED PRESS —INTERNATIONAL NEWS SERVICE—UNITED PRESS

(PHONE YOUR NEWS TIPS TO CORTLANDT 7-1212)

National Herald

自由西報

VOL 23 No. 7222 Registered at the Chinese P.O. for Transmission With Special Mark in China 内政部證記新聞紙警字第九九五九八號 中華郵政特准掛號立券報紙 CHUNGKING MONDAY Sept. 17, 1945 中華民國三十四年九月十七日 星期一 $100 a copy

26 ON JAP WAR CRIMINAL LIST ACCOUNTED FOR

24 Have Surrendered Or About To Surrender: Two Have Committed Suicide

Shigehori Togo Gives Himself Up

All Members Of Tojo Cabinet Turned Over By Jap Gov't To U.S. Army

TOKYO, Sept. 15 (Central-USIS)--Out of 47 persons named by General Douglas MacArthur as war criminals, 26 thus far have been accounted for, according to a United Press survey today. Twenty-four have surrendered or are about to surrender and two have committed suicide.

Among those who gave themselves up were Shigenori, Togo, Foreign Minister in the Tojo Cabinet at the time of the Pearl Harbor attack, who has been placed in house arrest in Tokyo, and Jose P. Laurel, President of the puppet Philippine Government during the Japanese occupation. Laurel, his son and Benigno Aquino, President of the Philippine puppet assembly, were arrested at a resort town near Osaka.

Lt..Generals Masaharu Homma and Shigenori Kuroda, who were successive commanders of Japanese troops in the Philippines, walked into Kanagawa Prefectural Police Station this afternoon to give themselves up, after driving there from Tokyo.

General Homma denied that he was responsible for the infamous "death march" on Bataan but said he was ready to "take full responsibility for any acts of my subordinates."

General Kuroda, 58-year old officer who spent 36 years in the Japanese Army, said, "We lost the war. There must have been some mistake."

At least 14 other persons, according to the United Press, surrendered during the morning to the Eighth Army. These included four members of Tojo's Cabinet.

The Eighth Army also received word that Colonel Hashimoto and Vice-Admiral Hoda were ready to surrender. Colonel Hashimoto is said to have been one of the seven leaders of the notorious and terroristic Black Dragon Society and Hoda was formerly Chief of Naval Aviation Headquarters.

Togo, one of the most important men on General MacArthur's "wanted" list, directed peace negotiations with the United States while Japan prepared for the sneak attack on Pearl Harbor. He declined to be interviewed by correspondents, saying he was "too tired".

Press dispatches indicated a nation-wide manhunt may be instituted by General MacAr-

(Continued on Page 4)

Wavell Arrives In New Delhi

NEW DELHI, Sept. 16 (Central): Lord Wavell, India's Viceroy, arrived here from Karachi at one p.m. today.

It is learned that he would meet with the Executive Council presently to report it the discussions he had in London on the problem of solving the Ind'an deadlock. No statement is expected from Viceroy Wavell for several days.

BRUTAL TREATMENT OF WAINWRIGHT AND OTHERS BY JAPS DESCRIBED

NEW YORK, Sept. 14 (Central-USIS): The brutal treatment of General Jonathan M. Wainwright and other Bataan survivors imprisoned with him by the Japanese was revealed at a press conference here attended by the general and his staff yesterday. An account of the conference in today's New York Herald Tribune said:

"In view of General Wainwright's own retience, staff officers declined to answer questions about statements that their chief had been beaten but Colonel John R. Pugh, his aide, said the American captives in their final camp in Sian, Manchuria, had to hunt down rats for food and cultivate pigweed for salad.

"Implications were clear that General Wainwright had not been spared even physical beating for Colonel Pugh observed at one point that 'many people were beaten because they could not hear or see well', and Brig.-General Lewis C. Beebe, General Wainwright's Chief of Staff, said that 'rank or station had nothing to do with treatment.'

"Describing the chronology of his captivity, General Wainwright said that 'it would be less embarrassing if there were no questions. During the siege of Corregidor, on account of the bursting of heavy shells, my hearing was seriously damaged. One ear gave out and the other is not much use. It would be rather embarrassing to try to answer questions.'

"He told of his first incarceration in Manila, when he was not accorded the prisoner of war status, and traced it through stays at Tarlae on Luzon, two camps in Formosa and his transfer to Sian last October. The Japanese had 'put a lid on news,' he said, and he got no letters, so he foresaw a much longer war than was thought."

Officers revealed that General Wainwright and members of his staff "were stripped and forced to stand under the blazing August sun while the Japanese searched for contraband," the Tribune said.

After the general had left the conference, the paper continued, "members of his staff described their imprisonment in much more detail. While neither General Beebe, Colonel Pugh nor Lt.-Colonel Thomas Dooley was beaten, they saidl they had seen many physica, assaults on prisoners.

Sinkiang P.P.C. concludes First General Session

TIHUA, Sept. 15 (Central): The Sinkiang Provisional People's Political Council concluded its first general session yesterday after a series of meetings lasting 14 days.

In addition to adopting 253 resolutions, the Council also decided to send a mission to Chungking to pay respects to President Chiang Kai-shek on behalf of the 4,000,000 people in Sinkiang.

Dr. Soong Leaves Washington For London By Plane

Chinese Premier To Visit Paris On Way Back To Chungking

WASHINGTON, September 15 (Central)--Dr. T.V. Soong, President of the Executive Yuan of the Chinese Government, today left here for London by plane.

LONDON, Sept. 15 (Central)--Dr. T.V. Soong, President of the Executive Yuan of the Chinese Government, is expected to arrive here tomorrow and his visit will be brief, probably only two or three days, according to information from the British Foreign Office today.

Meanwhile, it is learned that Dr. Soong will visit Paris on his way back to Chungking. It is understood that the French Government's invitation to Dr. Soong to Paris was extended while Dr. Soong was attending the San Francisco Conference.

175,000 More U.S. Troops On Way To Japan

TOKYO, Sept. 15 (Central-USIS): General Douglas MacArthur's headquarters announced today that additional American divisions--approximately 175,000 men -- will land in Japan this month and during October.

The United Press carried an estimate of 100,000 U.S. troops now in Japan.

World Police Force Program Mapped Out By War Department

Proposing Far-Reaching Integration Of Allied Forces In Asia, Europe

NEW YORK, Sept. 13 (Central) The War Department has drafted a program for a world police force to maintain the common peace in Europe and Asia, according to Mr. Roscoe Drummond, Christian Science Monitor's Washington correspondent.

Mr. Drummond said that the program constitutes the most specific detailed exposition of the American military policy in the postwar world. He said that the program proposed the far-reaching integration of the Allied forces both in Asia and Europe.

He said that the program has the following features:

Firstly, that all forces be placed under the direction of the combined Chiefs of Staff; secondly, that the combined Chiefs of Staff maintain their headquarters in Central Europe, either at Prague or Vienna or at another place near Bohemia; thirdly, that the combined Chiefs of Staff arrange with Czechoslovakia for stationing an European contingent of the United Nations Army in Bohemia; fourthly, that the combined Chiefs of Staff should work out plans for the United Nations air and naval forces besides the United Nations Army with the British Fleet constituting the initial United Nations' Atlantic Fleet; fifthly,

(Continued on Page 4)

British-American Trade Confab In Preliminary Stage

No Change Reported In Widely Different British, American Methods Of Approach

NEW YORK, Sept. 14 (Central)-- The Anglo-American Financial Trade Conference is still in the preliminary stage with Lord Keynes and British Ambassador to the United States Halifax continuing the presentation of the British case today before the American delegates.

After the British have completed presenting the reasons why the British need American financial aid, the Conference will enter the second phase when the American attitude will be stated and various expedients are considered.

Meanwhile, official circles generally agreed on the objective of helping Britain, the crux of the issue is how American aid can be provided on mutually satisfactory terms. Up to now there has been no reported change in the widely different British and American methods of approach.

American economic observers pointed out that three practical difficulties must be solved before American assistance to Britain is possible: firstly, how can the United States refuse the requests of Russia, China, France and other United Nations for similar aid once the United States grants Britain economic help; secondly, how much additional credit can the United States afford to give now that the American internal war debt approximates $300,000,000,000; and thirdly, would it be politically expedient for President Truman's administration to continue overburdening American taxpayers and extending foreign credits in the face of the American people's clamor for lower taxes and the lifting of wartime restrictions. All this will be weighed by Congress when the final formula is arrived at in the British-American negotiations.

However, enlightened self-interest will characterize the Anglo-American talks which might last for weeks before a satisfactory compromise is reached.

JAP NAVY SAYS 2,500 SUICIDE CRAFT READY AGAINST INVASION

TOKYO, Sept. 15 (Central-UP)--The Japanese Navy said that more than 2,500 suicide craft were ready to defend the Japanese homeland from invasion and that 1,499 speed-boats, loaded with explosive designed to be rammed against troop-loaded transports and other surface vessels, awaited the attackers and in addition 273 midget submarines and 2[illegible] human-piloted torpedoes were available.

The Navy said that the outer ring of defense was provided by 91 suicide boats stationed in Chichijima and Haha jima, 1[illegible] in the Chusantao Islands, [illegible] in Formosa and 200 in the Miyako Islands and that the work on five carriers under construction was halted last April 1 and under construction when the war ended were three destroyers, 15 escort carriers and 77 other vessels.

The Navy said that nearly one half of Japan's merchant tonnage was "not in active service" at the end of the war and that it had a total of 760 merchant vessels of over 100 tons each, totalling 1,277,000 tons but 154 ships totalling 452,000 tons were out of service. Only 515 wooden vessels were in active service in the entire Japanese East Asia Empire although the Navy said that it had on hand 914 steamers and 1,066 wooden vessels.

Disarming Of Jap Troops In S'hai To Be Completed Today; Chinese Take Over Jap Navy

Japs At Kiukiang Surrendering Arms To Chinese; Ku Chu-Tung Gives Orders To Jap Surrender Envoys, Chinese Gendarmes Arrive In Hankow

SHANGHAI, Sept. 16 (Central): The disarming of Japanese troops in Shanghai is expected to be completed tomorrow, it was learned from Chinese military sources.

All the heavy Japanese arms in the Shanghai area were turned over to the Chinese military authorities late last night while the surrender of enemy arms in surburban areas is expected to be completed tomorrow.

Japanese troops is Yangtzepoo, Chapei and Hongkew have been disarmed by one of the regiments of the 121st Division of the 94th Army which is garrisoning the aforesaid areas.

Two other regiments of the same division have been assigned garrison duties inside the city.

SHANGHAI, September 16 (Central)--The Chinese Navy Headquarters was set up at the Yangtze Wharf, the former site of the Japanese Naval Headquarters after Admiral Chen Shao-kwan's return to Shanghai from Nanking today.

The taking-over of the Japanese Navy is being carried out without a hitch. The Japanese Marine Corps Headquarters, the 2nd Navy observatory, Headquarters of the Air Force of the Japanese Navy and the Office of the Japanese Naval Court Martial were taken over today. Large quantities of the enemy's heavy and light arms and ammunition were also turned over to the Chinese Navy.

On Sept. 17, other Japanese Navy equipment in Pootung will be taken over.

NANCHANG, Sept. 16 (Central) -- General Hsueh Yueh, Commander of the 9th War Area, has sent General Sun Tu, a Group Army Commander, to Kiukiang to supervise the disarming of the Japanese troops there who are handing over their arms as directed by General Hsueh after signing the Japanese surrender.

Governor Tsao Hao-sen of Kiangsi dispatched Mr. Kang Ching-lien to accompany Government troops to Kiukiang.

HANGCHOW, September 15 (Central) -- General Ku Chu-tung, Commander of the Third War Zone, summoned the representative of the Commanding General of the Japanese 13th Army, and other Japanese Army commanders this morning in his headquarters.

After examining the credentials of the Japanese envoy, General Ku handed to him his first and second orders regarding surrender arrangements.

HANKOW, Sept. 15 (Central) -- Two battalions of gendarmes of Regiment No 11 arrived here today to keep peace and order in Hankow.

NANKING, Sept. 15 (Central): General Ho Ying-chin, Commander-in-Chief of the Chinese Army Heardquarters, has appointed Major-General Lin Hsi-chun Commander of the Gendarmerie Headquarters here.

The Gendarmerie Headquarters will be established and start to function shortly.

Work Of Council Of Foreign Ministers To Be Speeded Up

Deliberations On Italian Peace Settlement Already Started

LONDON, Sept. 15 (Central) --With the preliminary stages of the discussion over, it can now be confidently expected that the work of the Council of Foreign Ministers will be considerably speeded up during the next few days on the first item on the agenda, namely, the peace settlement with Italy.

The release of an official communique to the effect that the Council yesterday already started deliberations on the Italian peace settlement was highly welcomed in all quarters as signifying solid harmony within the Council.

A number of rumors has been circulating privately in London during the past few days, hinting about a preliminary hitch regarding priority topics to be discussed and whether the Italian Government should be invited to express views on the question of a Italian peace treaty.

Last night's definitive communique indicates that the Council is now well on its way towards the thrashing out of the various aspects of the Italian question.

Great significance is being

(Continued on Page 4)

Mexican Embassy Here Celebrates Independence Day

In celebration of Mexico's 135th Independence Day, a tea-dance was given by the Mexican Embassy for Chinese Government officials and foreign diplomatic representatives at Chialing House yesterday afternoon.

Among those present at the party were Mr. Yu Yu-jen, President of the Control Yuan, Dr. Sun Fo, President of the Legislative Yuan, General Wu Te-chen, Secretary-General of the Executive Committee of the Kuomintang, General Chen Cheng, Minister of War, Mr. Walter S. Robertson, representing the American Ambassador, Sir Horace Seymour, British Ambassador, M.L.M. Miklashevsky, representing the Russian Ambassador, General Zinovi Pechkoff, French Ambassador, Major-General Victor Odlum, Canadian Ambassador, Mr. A. H.J. Lovink, the Netherlands Ambassador, Mr. Jacques Delvaux de Fenffe, Belgian Ambassador, Mr. Joaquim Eulalio, Brazilian Ambassador, Mr. Sven Allard, Swedish Minister, Mr. Keith Officer, Australian Charge d'Affaires, Mr. Nesdet Ozmen, Turkish Charge d'Affaires, and M. Asghar Parsa, Iranian Charge d'Affaires.

More Jap Occupied Towns Recovered By Chinese Troops

A special release from the National Military Council today reads:

General Sun Wei-ju's troops commanded by General Ho Chi-li entered Siokan (west of the Peiping-Hankow Railway) in Central Hupeh on Sept. 14.

Troops under the command of General Hu Lien reached Siangyan and Yoyang in northern Hunan on Sept. 14.

Troops under the command of General Chen Ting-hsun entered Lanfeng in eastern Honan on Sept. 14.

General Hsu Ching-tang was appointed by General Yu Han-mou as Chief of the echelon headquarters. General Hsu and his staff left Kityang on Sept. 13 and set up his headquarters at Swatow in eastern Kwangtung.

Troops under the command of General Yu Han-mou recovered Lukfung on Sept. 6.

Commerce, Industry Council Is Sending Mission To China

To Confer With Chinese On Early Resumption Of Sino-American Trade

NEW YORK, Sept. 15 (Central) -- The China-American Council of Commerce and Industry is sending a trade-industrial mission to survey China's economic conditions, to confer with Chinese officials, industrialists and financiers on the early resumption of Chinese-American trade, a on its way to encourage American business taking an active role in China's industrial development of projects.

The Council was formed in February of last year to aid China's postwar development and strengthen the future two-way international trade.

According to the announcement, plans for the purchase of $2,000,000,000 worth of American equipment and supplies in the next few years and the postwar rehabilitation and reconstruction have been worked out closely with the American agencies responsible in China trade.

At the same time, it was announced that William Clayton, Assistant Secretary of State in charge of economic affairs, has endorsed the objectives of the Council for promoting friendly relations between Chinese and American businessmen and establishing mutually profitable Chinese-American postwar trade.

However, the Council cautioned that great many questions need clarification before opportunities can be realised.

Mr. Clayton said that an immediate step should be taken to study Chinese economy and the potentialities of China's industrial development and foreign trade in view of the destruction and occupation by the Japanese during the war.

He said that a comphrehensive survey of the frank discus-

(Continued on Page 4)

TIGER RAG

Vol. II No. 47 BENGAL AIR DEPOT NOVEMBER 17th, 1945

CHEER UP ALL YOU PANTING PILGRIMS

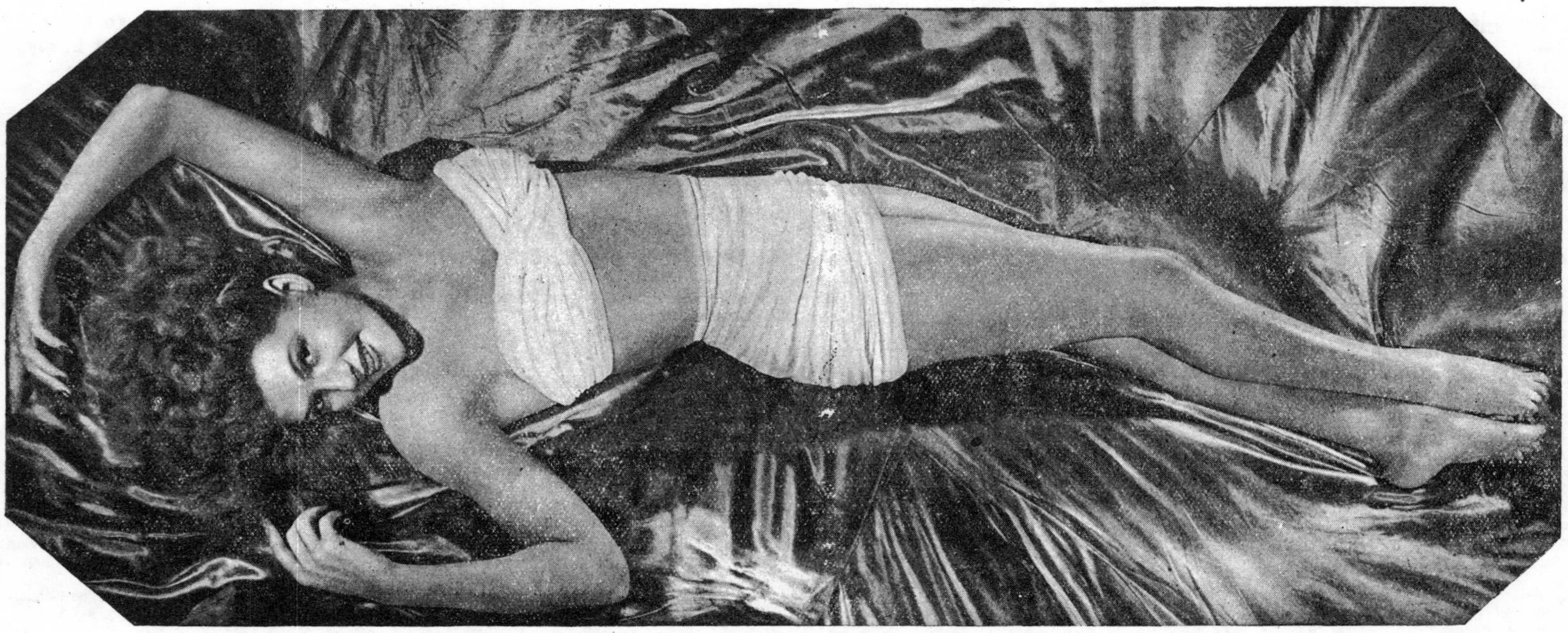

MEET YOUR THANKSGIVING HEADLINER

How To Remain Confused—Tho' Married

The ancient fallacy that women can't keep a secret was shattered this week, at least as far as Major James S (Dusty) Rhoades, Depot Control Officer, is concerned. For Major Rhoades, after a recent happening, is firmly entrenched behind the conviction that women can not only keep a secret, but depending upon the circumstances, can bury it deeper than a fox terrier hiding a prize bone.

It seems that Major Rhoades received a letter from his wife. Also about the same time he received a company newspaper, dated long before his wife's letter, from a strip mill he was previously associated with in Pittsburgh.

While scanning through the paper Major Rhoades ran across an item mentioning that his wife had just won a Church Pool lottery to the tune of one grand; a thousand frogskins to you! His wife made no mention of this wealth windfall in her letter. . . and Major Rhoades is wondering. Who wouldn't?

"She probably banked it." Major Rhoades said glumly," half to my son and half to her. My cut on the deal will probably be what the dog saw as he approached the fence. . . knotting!"

Harmonics For The Homesick

1st Lt "Bud" Widom, Special Services maestro, abetted by electricians T/3 David E Johnson and T/4 James Hensley, 893rd Signal Co, as well as personnel from the telephone office, have all combined their respective talents to furnish spiritual manna—music—for the masses. And under their guidance Depot personnel will be well saturated with the same, every day, and oftener than like crazy as long as recordings and the newly erected amplifying system which girdles the Post holds out.

Amplifiers have now been installed at Rajah's Rest, Air Corps Supply the Post Theater, and stop the water tower in back of the PX. All of which spells music from opera to corn throughout the noon hours.

Primarily a request program, all anyone need do to bless their ears with their favorite tune is phone Ext 72 or submit a slip to Special Service requesting their favorite lyric. Mimeograph slips for their preferred selection are available at yonder PX basha.

The musical program now inaugurated melodizes from 12 to 1 with a brief break from 1230 to 1245 to highlight the daily news. These melodic moments are marshalled for your enjoyment, men, while you loll fatigued on that bunk counting your points. So get those requests in. Anything goes; from "The Prisoner's Song" to "I Never Had A Chance."

FREE PENCIL PORTRAITS FOR PERSONNEL

The newest addition to the Rajah's Rest staff is Cpl Alan R Trego of Pasedena, California. Procured and assigned to the club under the auspices of Laura "Pete" Peterson head of morale and "a good time was had by all" department, Cpl Trego will lend his talent as an artist and painter of portraits.

His duties will be drawing portraits and sketches of fellows at the club, and designing and painting the multitude of posters that advertise the club's activities.

SPECIAL THANKSGIVING SERVICES TO BE OBSERVED

A special Thanksgiving service will be held at the Post Chapel, Thursday, November 22nd, at 9 am by Chaplain William C Hart. The Depot Choir Quartet will be on hand to render a Thanksgiving anthem.

Thanksgiving Mass will be held the same day at 7 am by Chaplain T F Brosman.

The Jewish Thanksgiving service will be observed Wednesday evening at 1830 hours by Chaplain Abraham Simon at the Post Chapel.

A cordial invitation is extended to all to attend the services.

PLEASURE VEHICLES OBTAINABLE FOR FOOT-WEARY GIS

Limited recreational transportation for small groups of enlisted men is now available according to the latest Depot Regulation pertaining to Travel and Transportation.

The transportation will be available nights after 1730, all day Sunday and official holidays, and after 1230 on Wednesday. The transportation's use will be limited to the areas and time limits specified on the Class "A" pass.

Vehicles will be driven only by a qualified driver and must be full. that is, a minimum of four persons in a jeep, six in a weapons carrier or command car, and thirteen in a 6x6 truck.

The enlisted man in charge must be of the first four grades, and must make the original request for the transportation in letter form through his orderly room. Unit commanders should have the letter indorsed and at Headquarters before noon on the day the vehicle is desired. The exception is that if the vehicle is desired for use on Sunday, holidays, or Wednesday afternoon, the request must reach headquarters by noon the previous day.

The letter requesting recreational transportation must state the reason for the request, give the number of persons to be transported (civilian or military, male or female), inclusive hours of use, and other information such as route, etc.

Truant Truckers Face Traffic School

A Traffic Control School for traffic violators was inaugurated at the Depot, Monday, November 12th.

The school will consist of a series of four-week courses in various subjects pertaining to operation and maintenance of military vehicles. Allied subjects such as Convoying and Bivouacing, Loading and Load Limits, Depot Traffic Regulations, and Handling of Explosives and Inflamable Liquids, will be included in the course.

When the four-week course is completed a new one will be started. A new schedule will be issued every four weeks and will include the names of instructors and supervisors.

Any officer or enlisted man adjudged by the Legal Officer as having committed a traffic violation after 8 November 1945, will be required to attend school six nights a week for four weeks.

TIMELY TIP FOR ALL TERPSICHOREANS

The ARC '60' Club anounced this week through Special Service news sources that a new Saturday night feature will go into operation on the 24th of this month.

A night club sort of entertainment will be the vehicle that will carry the evenings festivities. The charge will be 5 rupees per couple for an evening of dining, dancing, and Stateside entertainment.

The 40th Special Service Company will provide an orchestra and a weekly floor show. Food will be served in the manner of a smorgasbord.

Reservations for the opening night can be made directly at the Club or by telephoning Miss Pam Atkinson at Park 784. They must be made before the 22nd of November.

In connection with the opening of the night club feature, the 60 Club announces a contest for the best name of the night club. The winner will receive 25 rupees and the club will be officially christened with the winning name on opening night. All suggestions must be submitted to the Program Director at Club 60 by November 20th.

BIG EYE TO BE COMPLETED

Washington—Construction of the World's largest telescope—the 200-incher atop Mt. Palomar in California—is being resumed after a wartime layoff. The Carnegie Institution of Washington, which cooperated with the California Institute of Technology in designing the telescope, says the finishing work will take two years.

"BEER MUGGS"

The *Tiger Rag*, in connection with Special Service and the PX, herewith presents a new feature "Beer Muggs." The two lucky gents sporting the bullseye above have just won a free case of beer whether they're aware of the fact or not. All they have to do to claim this free case of suds is skip over to the *Rag's* office personally and identify their mug with the picture.

This impromptu photographic feature will be a weekly event in your publication henceforth. Various spot photos will be taken wherever a crowd is available. Two lucky men hitting the bullseye will each receive a free case of beer merely by establishing identification.

To eliminate possible thoughts of favoritism the contest is conducted by giving each man in the picture a number. Two numbers are drawn with the fortunate two "bullseyed." That's all there is to it!

So watch for "Beer Muggs." Your picture might appear in next week's issue. And beer, bub, is wonderful......especially when secured a la gratis, no strings, for free!

WEEKEND EDITION - - *News Views* - - *Colored Comics* - - *This Week Magazine*

CLEARING

Cloudy, light showers, clearing this afternoon. Fair Sunday. Low tonight 45. High Sunday 62. Sunrise: 6:53; sunset, 6:25.
(Chart on Page 12.) (U.S. Weather Report.)

6 p.m. . . . 63	2 a.m. . . . 59	8 a.m. . . . 58	Noon *66
8 p.m. . . . 61	4 a.m. . . . 59	9 a.m. . . . 59	
10 p.m. . . . 60	6 a.m. . . . 58	10 a.m. . . . 64	*Unofficial.
Midnight. . . 59	7 a.m. . . . 58	11 a.m. . . . 66	

CHICAGO DAILY NEWS

FM ☆FINAL

70TH YEAR—236. REG. U.S. PAT. OFF. COPYRIGHT, 1945 BY THE CHICAGO DAILY NEWS, INC. SATURDAY, OCTOBER 6, 1945—SIXTEEN PAGES. Telephone DEArborn 1111. FIVE CENTS

'BELSEN BEAST' ADMITS CRIMES

Storm Gates Early for Series Here

Cubs Seek Third Win With Prim

Top Tigers 2-1; Face Trout Today

BY JOHN P. CARMICHAEL.

The World Series didn't come home to Wrigley Field a minute too soon for Chicago. Fans by the thousands stormed the gates as early as 8 o'clock today, overflowing the bleachers, snapping up standing-room and filtering more slowly into the reserved sectors.

Queues of impatient customers extended for blocks around the home of the Cubs, hopeful of finding some vantage point inside at $3.30 per vantage. Flags and bunting, missing from Briggs Stadium in Detroit, fluttered from the ramparts where Ray Prim, Cub southpaw, was to face "Dizzy" Trout, the Tigers' right-handed fast ball pitcher this afternoon. With a seating capacity for series play of more than 41,000, Wrigley Field may be taxed with 44,000 fans for this inaugural.

* * *

THE WEATHERMAN had forecast showers today but by noon the skies still were dry and so was the field, although gray clouds floated across Chicagoland and there was enough of a nip in the air to eliminate the "white-shirt" complex from the bleachers which annoys Cub hitters. In that respect, at least, the type of day was made to order for, after all, this can be an important event in local history. This is the sixth team the Cubs have entered in series competition since 1910 but it's the first that ever went into the fourth game out in front.

In 1918, for instance, the Red Sox held a one-game margin going into No. 4. In 1929 Connie Mack's Athletics had whipped the Cubs two straight before losing the third battle. In '35 an earlier edition of Detroit champs had won two of the first three games and in '32 and '38 the Yankees smothered the Cubs in four consecutive starts.

So the Cubs have made statistical progress at least after all these years. Two more triumphs will give them their first title in 37 years.

* * *

THANKS to the superlative pitching of Claude Passeau, who wrote series history against the gray gloom of Briggs Stadium in Detroit yesterday, the Cubs have saddled the Tigers with the pressure of coming from behind.

This is the most prolific Cub team to carry the National banner

Turn to Page 10, Column 3.

McNutt O.K.d

WASHINGTON — (AP) — Paul McNutt, high commissioner to the Philippines, is to be admitted to the Supreme Court bar Monday.

Mrs. O'Leary's Cow—Her Place in Art

When we celebrate the great Chicago Fire of '71 next week perhaps we should have a parade. At all events the old time fire departments had the parade wagons, and they also had paintings that would grace the Art Institute. Read Don Russell's nostalgic article on page 4.

Also on the inside:

Hotels Saved For 3d Fleet

SAN FRANCISCO—(AP)—Twenty-five major San Francisco hotels are refusing reservations from Oct. 13-28 to handle a part of 100,000 Navy men, liberated prisoners and their relatives expected here during the triumphal visit of elements of Adm. Halsey's 3d Fleet.

The admiral, aboard the battleship South Dakota, will lead three other battle wagons, two carriers, two cruisers, destroyers and submarines through the Golden Gate on Oct. 15.

Oil Tieup Believed Near End

Resumption of work Monday in the Calumet oil refining area was expected as a result of today's voting by 6,000 strikers on whether to end their work stoppage.

The strikers, members of Local 210, United Oil Workers' International Union (C.I.O.), received the "request" from O. A. Knight, union president, to terminate the strike during a meeting in their union hall at Hammond last night.

They decided to do their balloting during another meeting later today.

* * *

UNION OFFICIALS were reluctant to say flatly that the men would go back to work.

However, strikers in other parts of the country already have abandoned their walkout. Union heads pointed out that Local 210 gave a vote of confidence Wednesday to Knight.

* * *

KNIGHT late yesterday from Washington wired strikers to go back to work, following the Navy's seizure of struck plants.

Knight said the union's executive council had decided the workers must not strike against the Navy but that the union still considered itself as striking against the companies.

Pickets were withdrawn from the seven struck plants of the Calumet area.

* * *

THE NAVY seizure order directs the workers to return pending negotiation, under the conditions which prevailed before the strike.

This means 52 hours pay for 48 hours work.

The union has demanded that much pay for 40 hours—equiva-

Turn to Page 3, Column 1.

Hurry or Miss Air 'Boat,' Chicago Told

Chicago's future as a center of world air travel is being endangered by the delay in finding adequate airport facilities, the Chicago Association of Commerce warned.

Directors of the association adopted a resolution urging that Mayor Kelly's recently appointed airport site selection committee "speed its deliberations."

* * *

IN CONJUNCTION with the resolution, Frank S. Whiting, chairman of the association's aviation committee, issued a report in which he warned that airline companies may be forced to alter their operations unless port facilities are provided soon in Chicago.

"Other cities," he said, "are far beyond Chicago in their airport development and preparation."

Truman Names Another Aid

WASHINGTON — (AP) — Richmond B. Keech, corporation counsel for the District of Columbia since 1940, was appointed by President Truman yesterday as one of his administrative assistants.

SERIES FANS LINE UP FOR BLOCKS

The lineup of series-hungry fans seeking bleacher seats at Wrigley Field stretched for more than a block and looped back to the entrance this forenoon. [Daily News photo.]

Truman Off On 6-State, 5-Day Trip

WASHINGTON—(AP)—President Truman left today on a five-day, six-state trip.

His first stop was Berryville, Va., where he was best man at the wedding of Bennett Champ Clark and Violet Heming, British actress. Clark is a former U.S. senator from Missouri and now is a U.S. appellate judge.

* * *

BEFORE leaving Washington Mr. Truman added Reelfoot Lake, west Tennessee's favorite rendezvous for fishermen, to his itinerary. The Chief Executive started his journey by automobile but later will use a plane.

Besides his official party, the President was accompanied by Mrs. Truman and his daughter Margaret. The latter planned to return to Washington from Berryville later in the day.

Others with Mr. Truman included John W. Snyder, reconversion director, and Brig.Gen. Vaughan, presidential military aide.

* * *

AFTER the Clark wedding, the President was to motor to Martinsburg, W.Va., to board his plane, The Sacred Cow.

He was scheduled to arrive in Blytheville, Ark., late this afternoon and then to drive to Caruthersville, Mo., to attend the annual American Legion fair tomorrow—an event he has not missed in 12 years.

* * *

ON MONDAY he will go by automobile to Reelfoot Lake, a reservoir basin of the Mississippi River formed by an earthquake in 1811. He will spend two nights at a private fishing lodge.

* * *

THE PRESIDENT will be up bright and early Wednesday for the drive to Gilbertsville, Ky., for a forenoon speech dedicating T.V.A.'s big dam there. He is expected to outline administration plans for a postwar flood control and public power development.

He will return to Washington early Wednesday night.

Falls One Floor, 24 Floors Up

NEW YORK— (UP) —Roy Murray escaped death when his safety belt broke as he was washing a 24th floor window, because he landed on a 5-foot ledge on the 23d floor.

He suffered a concussion and possible internal injuries.

TROUBLE IN THE HOLY LAND

Report Troops in Action After Palestine Fighting

JERUSALEM—(UP)—British troops were reported to have gone into action on the northern frontier of Palestine today when fighting broke out between border police and Jewish "immigrant smugglers."

First reports from the scene said the disorders began when frontier police arrested a large group of Jewish immigrants trying to enter the Holy Land illegally.

Local Jews came to the rescue of the immigrants. They attacked the police station and seized from 50 to 70 of the prisoners.

* * *

BRITISH troops were rushed to the scene, but there was no immediate indication whether fighting was continuing.

The incident occurred near the border village of Kefr Galadi.

News of the outbreak coincided with an announcement by the Syrian government that motorized detachments had been sent to the Syrian-Palestine border to prevent illegal Jewish immigrants—many of them reported carrying arms—from crossing into Palestine.

* * *

OBSERVERS feared the incident might have serious repercussions throughout the Holy Land.

Zionist groups planned a nationwide anti-British demonstration Monday in protest against restrictions on Jewish immigration.

(A review of U.S. policy in the Palestine dispute is on page 2.)

'Miracle' Woman Waits New Vision

UPPER SANDUSKY, Ohio — (UP) — Minabelle Cross, 39, a former schoolteacher, waited today for another divine visitation to dictate her life's work.

Miss Cross, dark-eyed, 5-foot-7-inch brunette, last Saturday left the bed where she had lain helpless for 16 years when, she said, a "white robed figure of God" appeared and told her to arise and walk because there was work for her to do.

Heart Victim

Alexander A. Kosel, 53, of 7743 Kingston av., assistant superintendent of the south station of the Peoples Gas, Light & Coke Co. for the last 17 years, died of a heart attack suffered in front of 7625 Kingston av.

Catch That Pass! The Pigskin's a Loaded Grenade

Football is a doubly dangerous game when you play it the way they do in the 2000 block of Roscoe st.

Andy Kopera, 4517 N. Ashland av., a truck driver, paused yesterday to watch a gang of 8-year-olds playing football in the alley at the rear of 2049 Roscoe st. Curiosity prompted him to take a closer look at the boys' "pigskin."

It was a loaded hand grenade.

Kopera broke up the game and took the grenade to the police. It was sent to Fort Sheridan bomb disposal unit.

Nature Defeats Scientific Yegg

PORTLAND, Ore. — (AP) — A burglar, more scientific than domestic, didn't make any progress in a Portland home.

Clem Johnson awoke and found his bed sprinkled with chloroform, a precautionary measure taken by the scientific prowler.

However, the intruder forgot to treat the baby's bed and the yowling child scared him away.

Jap Pacifist New Premier

Baron Shidehara Appointed To Form New Government

TOKYO—(UP)—Baron Kijuro Shidehara, who quit the foreign ministry 14 years ago in protest against Jap aggression, was appointed premier today to form a new peace government.

Emperor Hirohito named the 73-year-old Shidehara, a former ambassador to Washington, to succeed resigned Premier Prince Naruhiko Higashi-Kuni during a 15-minute audience shortly after midnight.

Shidehara conferred immediately afterward with his protege, Shigeru Yoshida, foreign minister in the resigned Higashi-Kuni government. Yoshida is sure to reassume the post of foreign minister in the new cabinet.

* * *

YOSHIDA, a liberal who was jailed earlier this year for participating in a Jap peace plot, had been urged to take the premiership but refused in favor of Shidehara.

It was understood the aging baron also was reluctant to head the government in the face of increasingly drastic occupation directives from Gen. MacArthur designed to wipe out Jap militarism.

Gen. MacArthur today abolished military press censorship, effective immediately. Censorship of the Jap press and radio will continue, however.

Resignation of the Nigashi-Kuni government yesterday was attributed to its failure—either through refusal or inability—to enforce these directives.

MacArthur already may have approved the choice of Shidehara. Yoshida conferred for an hour yesterday with Lt.Gen. Richard K. Sutherland, MacArthur's chief of staff, and was reported to have suggested several candidates for the premiership for approval.

* * *

SHIDEHARA was foreign minister in five Jap cabinets between 1924 and 1931, when he resigned in protest against the Jap army's seizure of Manchuria. He had not participated in politics since.

He entered the Jap diplomatic service in 1899, served as consul in London later that year and became councilor of the Jap. embassy in Washington in 1912.

He returned to London as councilor in 1914 and the following year was made vice-minister of foreign affairs. Appointed ambassador to the United States in 1919, he remained in Washington for three years.

Shidehara went to the Imperial Palace in response to a summons from the Emperor shortly after

Turn to Page 3, Column 3.

Bar Relatives On Gripsholm Pier

Relatives of the 1.300 civilian repatriates from Europe and the Near East coming home on the Gripsholm will not be permitted on the pier when the ship docks Tuesday in Jersey City, N.J.

Messages and money can be delivered through Red Cross representatives by using the following address: Name, Gripsholm Repatriate, c/o Home Service, New York Chapter, American Red Cross, 315 Lexington av., New York 16, N.Y

Fancy Meeting You Here, Mac

TOKYO —(AP)— Japan's new premier, Baron Shidehara, related to newsmen today how he had attended a social function in the United States many years ago and was told by his host:

"I want you to meet a promising young officer in the U.S. Army who is very unpopular here."

He enjoyed meeting the young officer, Shidehara added. The officer was Douglas MacArthur.

Shidehara Pledges to Co-operate

TOKYO —(UP)— Baron Kijuro Shidehara, Japan's new premier-designate, pledged unstinted co-operation with Allied military authorities in an interview with the United Press today.

Shidehara sketched a program of work, sobriety, and patience which he hoped would surmount Japan's difficulties and re-establish this country in the international family of nations.

"Naturally I would not appoint anybody to the cabinet who might be designated by Allied headquarters as suspected of responsibility for the war or classed as a war criminal," he said.

"I do not know but that I may be under suspicion myself," he continued.

* * *

WHILE IT obviously was too early to foresee the exact lines of Shidehara's policy, it seemed likely that in view of his record he would adopt the following course:

ONE. A strong effort to democratize all phases of Jap life as speedily as possible with a view to obtaining the end of Allied military control at the earliest possible date.

TWO. An early effort to improve relations with China, in view of his lifelong belief that Japan and China must co-operate in the interests of both nations.

THREE. The most complete possible co-operation with Gen. MacArthur and the Allies, not only because this was the only practical course to follow, but also because Shidehara gave every evidence of believing that the future of Japan lies in following the paths of the Western democracies.

Used Gas To Kill Prisoners

Places Blame On Himmler

LUENEBURG, Germany—(UP) — Josef Kramer, the "Beast of Belsen," admitted in an affidavit read at his trial today that gas chambers were used to slaughter inmates of Nazi internment camps.

Orders for the executions—including those of whole groups of women—came direct from Gestapo Chief Heinrich Himmler in Berlin, Kramer's affidavit said. It contradicted an earlier affidavit in which he had denied all knowledge of the gas chambers.

* * *

AN AFFIDAVIT by Elizabeth Volkenrath, 26, another of the 45 men and women SS guards on trial for their lives for atrocities in the Belsen and Oswiecim internment camps, charged that Himmler had visited Oswiecim and "saw for himself what happened."

Himmler committed suicide after he had been taken into custody by British occupation forces near Hamburg.

Both affidavits were read to the British military court by the prosecutor, Col. T. M. Backhouse, as he closed his case against the 45 guards.

The defense will open Monday and Kramer may take the stand himself. Defense testimony is expected to take three weeks.

Though admitting he knew of the gas chambers, Kramer still denied in his latest affidavit that he had anything to do with the operation of them.

* * *

WHILE attached to another concentration camp in Alsace, he said, he received orders from one Grupenfuehrer Glucks and signed by Himmler ordering the execution of a number of women in gas chambers. The bodies were ordered sent to Strasbourg, Kramer said.

Kramer said a professor gave instructions on the use of an ordinary room and chemicals for the executions.

He saw his first specially-constructed gas chamber at Oswiecim, where he was put in command of one section of the camp, he said.

The Oswiecim chamber was used on written orders of the camp commander, a man named Hoess, he said.

Kramer said that if he had been in Hoess' position, he, too, would have carried out the execution orders since any refusal would have meant his arrest.

As for the infamous Belsen camp which he later commanded, Kramer said that he "did everything I could to remedy conditions."

* * *

HE SAID he did not think his SS staff would mistreat anybody because he had issued specific orders against ill treatment of prisoners. Shooting began at Belsen only when Hungarian troops took over in the last few days before the arrival of British forces, he said.

Volkenrath, in her affidavit, also tried to shift the blame for excesses at Oswiecim to Hoess.

"I always was very strict, but I never murdered anyone," she said.

Plane Overdue

LONDON — (AP) — The Daily Sketch announced today that a plane carrying Bryan Reynolds, 37, the paper's Pacific war correspondent, was two days overdue.

WEIGHTY PROBLEM

Only Their Ties Fit Now, Veterans Find

BY NORINE FOLEY.

Army life has so transformed the contours of G.I. Joe that not one serviceman in 100 can wear the clothes he left behind.

This is the consensus among State st. merchants who are working feverishly to satisfy the plea of discharged vets for "anything I can get to fit—gotta be out of this uniform in 48 hours."

* * *

STAFF SGT. Earl J. Goetz, 28, of 8220 Rhodes av., is typical.

"I didn't know I was a growing boy when I joined the Army," he said, "but Uncle Sam stretched my height two inches up to 5 feet 11½. I also gained 20 pounds.

"The moths can have my old clothes."

Goetz wanted a "blue pin-striped suit, single-breasted, like we used to see in Esquire and dreamed about owning during those 28 months in the Aleutians."

* * *

GOETZ' SALESMAN agreed that many of his customers have stretched one to three inches.

"We're all out of suits for tall men," he said. "Nothing left but 'stylish stouts.' "

When a serviceman has a choice of apparel, his taste leans to the conservative, said the buyer for a clothing house.

"Occasionally one will go hog-wild and bedeck himself in all the colors of the rainbow," he said, "but the majority have quiet tastes."

* * *

JULIUS GOODMAN, discharged sailor of 1812 W. Washington blvd., bought a blue suit!

"I didn't plan it that way, he said, "but made the mistake of buying shirts, ties and socks to harmonize with some old blue suits.

Then I found the weight I had acquired through regular meals and lots of sleep knocked the dickens out of my wardrobe."

British Clocks

LONDON—(AP)—Great Britain will abolish summer time at 3 a.m. tomorrow, turning clocks back an hour to Greenwich time.

2¢ Weather FAIR, COOL. Details on Page 2

Daily Mirror

3c In Suburbs
5c Elsewhere
2¢

Vol. 23. No. 86. NEW YORK, TUESDAY, OCTOBER 1, 1946 R FINAL 6 A.M.★★★★

GOERING TO DIE!

Hess, Ribbentrop, Rosenberg, Keitel Also Guilty, Schacht Is Acquitted

By JOSEPH GRIGG

NUERNBERG, Tuesday, Oct. 1 (UP).—Hermann Goering, second only to Adolf Hitler in the Nazi regime, was found guilty on all counts today at the last session of the four-power war crimes tribunal and it was expected that he and at least 17 of his arch-conspirators would be hanged or shot for their crimes.

Rudolf Hess was found guilty on two counts of the indictment and Joachim von Ribbentrop guilty on all four counts.

Hjalmar Schacht, the Nazi's financial wizard, was acquitted.

Field Marshal Wilhelm Keitel, chief of the German High Command, was found guilty on all four counts.

Ernst Kaltenbrunner, head of the Nazi secret police under the late Heinrich Himmler, was found guilty on two counts.

Alfred Rosenberg, the philosopher of National Socialism, was found guilty on all four counts.

Julius Streicher, notorious Jaw-baiter, was found guilty of count four and innocent on count one.

Fritz von Papen, ace Nazi diplomat, was acquitted.

Admiral Erich Raeder and Karl Doenitz of the German Navy were found guilty of counts two and three and innocent of the first count.

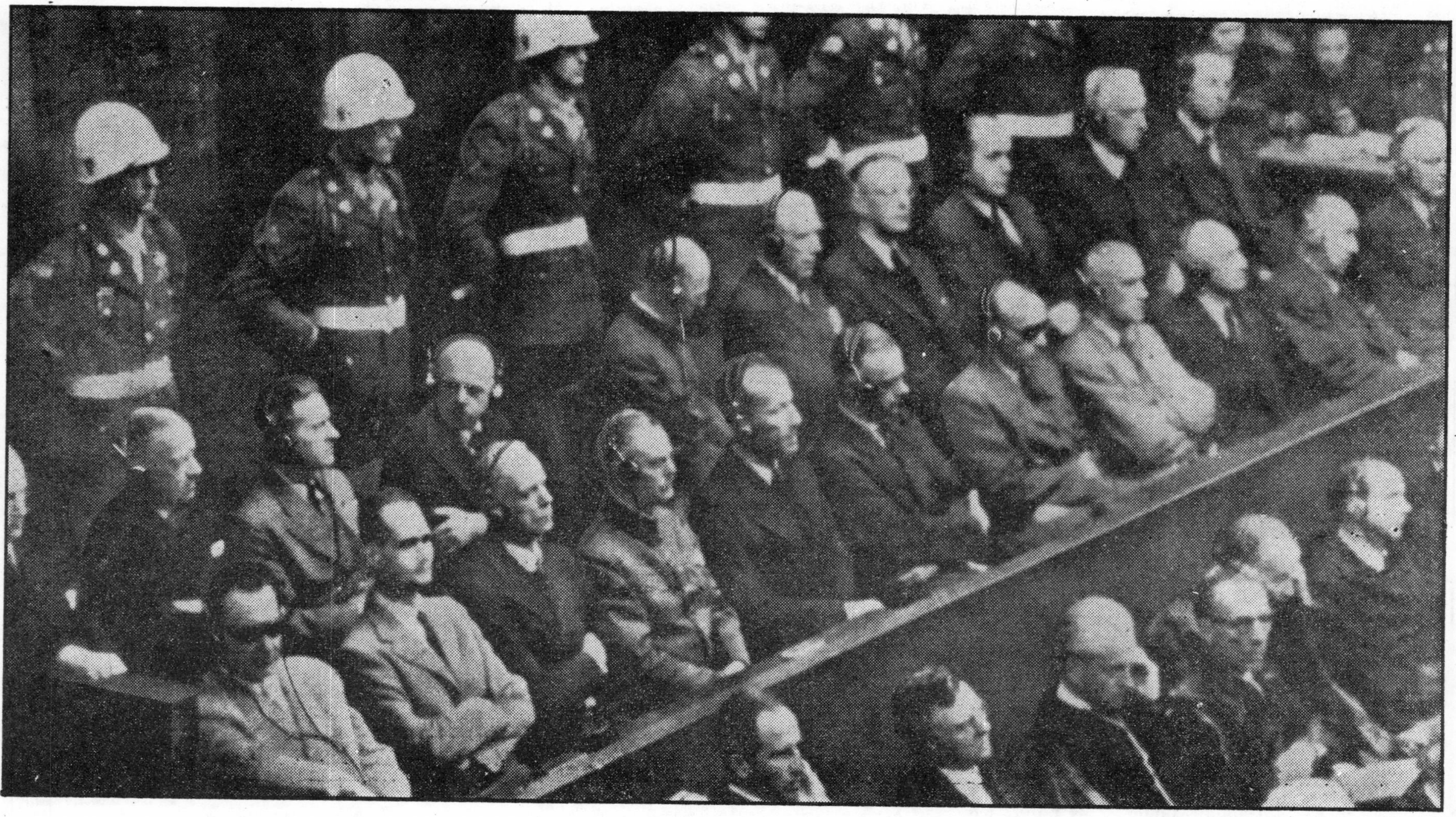

(International RADIOphoto)

Front row, left to right: Goering, Hess, von Ribbentrop, Keitel, Kaltenbrunner, Rosenberg, Frank, Frick, Streicher, Funk and Schacht. Rear row: Doenitz, Raeder, von Schirach, Sauckel, Jodl, von Papen, Seyss-Inquart, Speer, von Neurath and Fritsche.

WORLD'S VERDICT: GUILTY The 21 ex-leaders of Nazi Germany, shown in prisoners' box and wearing earphones, hear themselves doomed by the International Military Tribunal at Nuernberg for war crimes. Sentence will be pronounced today. All are due for gallows or jail. *(Other Photos on Page 3)*